An Encyclopedia of Religion

An Encyclopedia of Religion

Edited By

VERGILIUS FERM

Compton Professor and Head of the Department of Philosophy in The College of Wooster

THE PHILOSOPHICAL LIBRARY

NEW YORK

15 EAST 40TH STREET, NEW YORK, N. Y.

LITHOGRAPHED IN THE UNITED STATES OF AMERICA

EDITOR'S PREFACE

When, more than three years ago, it was suggested that I undertake the editorship of an *Encyclopedia of Religion,* I had no idea of the immensity of the task or of the complications involved in its execution. The idea, however, seemed good to me, especially in view of the fact that there was no desk-size ready reference work in this vast field, authoritative and up-to-date, to which one could conveniently turn. Dean Shailer Mathews' and Dr. Gerald Birney Smith's *Dictionary of Religion and Ethics,* published nearly a quarter of a century ago, many of us have found valuable and useful; but the time did seem right for a new work, with more recent scholarly information and one which, perhaps, would carry articles of wider scope and treatment, more recent bibliographies and, perhaps, more representative of conflicting schools of thought.

It was clear, at the outset, that the services of a large number of specialists must be sought and their counsel enlisted, if such a work was to measure up to satisfying requirements.

The first task was to draw up a prospectus to make clear the nature of the volume sought and, on this basis, to engage the interest of others. Among the items contained in this prospectus were the following: 1) a concise definition to be given terms of importance and topics of primary significance in the field to be treated with more fullness; 2) the size of the volume to be limited to that of a handy desk-reference; 3) the topics to include the widest ranges of the field: the theologies of the major religions, denominations and cults with special attention to Biblical literature and Christian theology, ecclesiastical history and polity, the usual divisions of cultural and academic interests as these relate to religion, viz., philosophy, psychology, ethics, sociology, history, comparative religion, art and architecture, musicology and liturgy, important controversial disputes, missionary enterprises, religious education, and the like, together with the masters and leaders of classical religious thought; 4) the composition to be guided by three ideals of writing: authority, simplicity and succinctness; 5) the treatment of subject matter to be historical and descriptive rather than apologetic; 6) variant meanings and usages of terms to be given wherever necessary, together with etymologies of the more technical terms; 7) articles to carry an appended bibliography carefully selected by the expert in the subject with year dates of publications; 8) the identification of each contribution to be designated by authors' initials; 9) suggestions of whatever sort to be solicited from specialists both as to the selection of topics and the names of fellow-scholars as contributors; and 10) the encyclopedia to be constructed in a manner which would be most useful to both scholars and students and, at the same time, intelligible to cultured laymen. To this was added a pledge by the editor to work out somewhat generously a system of cross-references to facilitate the reader's search for specific information and to lead him on to related topics which appear in the work. (The editor alone is responsible for the insertion of these references.)

The correspondence involved in the undertaking has proved to be of such proportions as to make the size of this volume small by comparison. It has, however, been a most rewarding experience. The editor has been privileged to sit at a kind of switchboard and to bring into contact with one another scores of minds and the results of disciplined scholarship. What otherwise might have been an altogether wearisome burden has been turned to an almost exciting experience by the warm response which was so widely and generously given to this undertaking by those who have shared in it. One conviction has emerged: in the commonwealth of scholarship there is a spirit which unites rather than divides and it is in this altogether too esoteric company that one sees the concrete expression of that ideal of unity-in-diversity which ought increasingly to undergird all validly religious thinking and practice.

In this volume, there is a truly cooperative effort on the part of men and women of the widest ranges of background, of interests and even commitments. Here the conservative student in the calm irenic spirit of mind exhibits himself, his cause and his exposition alongside the liberal who matches that spirit; here meet Protestant and Roman Catholic men of learning together with scholarly representatives of the various households of Jewish thought and practice; here meet disciplined expositors of the many denominations to summarize the story of their churches and to present their doctrines; here meet historians, students of Biblical criticism, sociologists, psychologists, philosophers, theologians, and an array of other specialists.

Naturally, in such a wide domain as the field of religion, many limitations had to be set. For example, it seemed best, in drawing the circle of exclusion, to pass by the names of strictly contemporary religious thinkers, making exceptions only in certain cases and particularly in the names of foreign scholars.

This prefatory word should include some further summary statements of editorial policy:

As a general rule, the place of publication of books appearing in the bibliographies is given only for foreign books. In the absence of such designation, it may be assumed that the publication has appeared in this country. It has seemed advisable to print foreign words in transliteration for the purposes of this volume.

After some correspondence with the contributors concerned, it was agreed, in principle, to omit diacritical markings except in relatively few cases since there is a considerable lack of agreement among scholars as to their use and since, in most cases, the terms are recognizable without such markings. Furthermore, inasmuch as many of the terms defined are of foreign derivation and since, due to the different systems of transliteration in use among scholars, there exist in common usage variant spellings of certain terms, it seemed best to list a given word in its proper alphabetical order according to each of the various spellings with a cross-reference to its place of definition. Professors Charles S. Braden and Wing-tsit Chan, who have defined the large list of Hindu and Chinese-Buddhist terms, respectively, have agreed to this procedure. That diacritical marks, however, do occur here and there in this publication, in spite of this general principle, due chiefly to their persisting appearance in submitted manuscripts and the lack of editorial vigilance, need not be cause of concern.

The star (*) and double stars (**), it will be clear to the reader, are employed as symbols of cross-reference (taking the place of *q.v.* and *qq.v.* which are usually found in many corresponding works of reference). The double star, of course, indicates that more than one stated term is discussed elsewhere in the volume. In highly exceptional cases, the star appears either as reference to a footnote of an article or for a purpose which is clearly indicated.

The articles bearing the initials of contributors of the Roman Catholic church carry the *imprimatur* of their religious superiors.

It needs to be emphasized that a work of such a nature and scope could never have been carried out without the direct help and sympathetic collaboration of many scholars. In every sense of the word, this is a cooperative enterprise. The editor expresses his warm appreciation to the one hundred and ninety colleagues who have so generously shared in its publication. Many of them have contributed more than a score of articles and given themselves generously in correspondence. To Professor Edgar Sheffield Brightman, I owe a word of special thanks for his counsel in editorial matters, as well as for his encouraging help in the more difficult days of preparation. To Dr. Dagobert D. Runes, president of the Philosophical Library of New York, I am greatly indebted. Without his unfailing support, encouragement and patience, particularly in these difficult days, this work would not have seen the light of day. I remember with gratefulness the help given me by a certain group of my students of the Philosophy Department at The College of Wooster, whose names are known among ourselves, and who, I am sure, share my joy in the completion of a task involving so many details of execution.

Vergilius Ferm

The College of Wooster
Wooster, Ohio

KEY TO CONTRIBUTORS' INITIALS

A.C.	Allen Cabaniss
A.C.K.	Albert C. Knudson
A.C.M.	Arthur Cushman McGiffert
A.E.H.	A. Eustace Haydon
A.E.W.	Arthur Evans Wood
A.H.S.	Abba Hillel Silver
A.K.R.	Andrew K. Rule
A.P.W.	Allen P. Wikgren
A.S.	Anne Seesholtz
A.T.B.	Anton T. Boisen
B.C.	Boaz Cohen
B.E.M.	Benjamin Elijah Mays
B.R.	Bertin Roll
B.S.	Brice Schratz
B.S.E.	Burton Scott Easton
B.Z.B.	Ben Zion Bokser
C.E.S.	Charles Edward Smith
C.H.	Charles Hartshorne
C.H.M.	Conrad Henry Moehlman
C.J.B.	Conrad J. Bergendoff
C.P.S.	Clarence Prouty Shedd
C.R.	Christopher Rengers
C.R.S.	Clarence R. Skinner
C.S.B.	Charles S. Braden
C.S.E.	Clayton S. Ellsworth
C.T.C.	Clarence Tucker Craig
C.V.	Cyril Vollert
C.W.L.	Charles W. Lowry
D.C.H.	D. C. Holtom
D.C.O'G.	Daniel C. O'Grady
D.D.W.	Daniel Day Williams
D.F.E.	Donald Fossett Ebright
D.S.M.	David S. Muzzey
D.S.P.	D. de Sola Pool
D.U.	Dominic Unger
D.V.S.	Douglas V. Steere
E.A.R.	Edward A. Ryan
E.B.	Ephraim Bennett
E.C.C.	Ernest Cadman Colwell
E.C.K.	Elmer C. Kiessling
E.C.R.	Edith C. Rodgers
Edn.H.	Edna Heidbreder
E.D.S.	Edwin Diller Starbuck
E.D.Sn.	Edward Douglas Snyder
E.E.E.	Earle Edward Eubank
E.F.S.	Ernest Findlay Scott
E.G.H.	Eric G. Hawkinson
E.G.K.	Emil G. Kraeling
E.H.	Edward Heimann
E.H.B.	Edward Hall Broadhead
E.J.G.	Edgar J. Goodspeed
E.M.N.	Eva May Newnan
E.M.W.	Earl M. Wilbur
E.P.B.	Edwin P. Booth
E.R.H.	Edward Rochie Hardy
E.R.M.	Ernest R. Mowrer
E.S.B.	Edgar Sheffield Brightman
E.T.C.	Elmer T. Clark
E.T.R.	Edward T. Ramsdell
E.W.K.	Ethyn W. Kirby
F.A.L.	Felix A. Levy
F.C.G.	Frederick Clifton Grant
F.C.S.	Francis Carr Stifler
F.E.	Fred Eastman
F.G.E.	Francis Gerald Ensley
F.J.B.	Frank J. Bruno
F.L.P.	Fred L. Parrish
F.R.W.	F. R. Webber
F.T.P.	Frederick T. Persons
F.W.B.	Francis William Buckler
F.W.N.	Fred W. Neal
G.E.W.	G. Ernest Wright
G.E.Z.	George Elias Zachariades
G.G.A.	Gaius Glenn Atkins
G.M.	Gardner Murphy
G.P.A.	Gaylord P. Albaugh
G.R.C.	Gerald R. Cragg
G.S.S.	George S. Stevenson
H.C.	Howard Comfort
H.E.J.	Howard E. Jensen
H.G.R.	Henry G. Russell
H.H.	Herman Hausheer
H.Hfk.	Hanna Hafkesbrink
H.H.N.	Harold H. Nelson
H.K.	Herman Kieval
H.N.W.	Henry Nelson Wieman
H.R.M.	Harriet R. Mowrer
H.R.N.	H. Richard Niebuhr
H.R.W.	Harold R. Willoughby
H.W.J.	Hjalmar W. Johnson
J.A.C.	James A. Corbett
J.A.M.	John A. Mackay
J.B.C.	Joseph B. Code
J.C.M.	John Courtney Murray
J.E.N.	Jannette E. Newhall
J.F.T.	Joseph F. Thorning
J.J.F.	John J. FitzGerald
J.L.	John Line
J.L.C.	John L. Cheek
J.M.	Julian Morgenstern
J.M.M.G.	Joseph M. M. Gray
J.P.H.	J. Philip Hyatt
J.S.B.	Julius Seelye Bixler
J.T.M.	John Thomas McNeill
J.W.B.	John Wright Buckham
K.E.G.	Katharine E. Gilbert
K.H.C.	Kenneth H. Cousland
L.A.W.	Luther Allan Weigle
L.F.	Louis Finkelstein
L.H.DeW.	L. Harold DeWolf
L.J.S.	Lewis J. Sherrill
L.L.	Louis Lipsky
L.R.W.	Leo R. Ward
L.W.C.	Lowell W. Coolidge

M.G.R.	Millard George Roberts
M.H.	Moses Hadas
M.L.C.	Maynard L. Cassady
M.M.K.	M. M. Knappen
M.R.	Martin Rist
M.Reu.	Michael Reu
M.Rh.	Max Rheinstein
M.S.	Matthew Spinka
M.S.E.	Morton Scott Enslin
M.Sp.	Martin Sprengling
M.S.S.	Mary S. Sims
N.G.	Nelson Glueck
O.A.P.	Otto A. Piper
O.A.W.	Oscar A. Winfield
P.A.B.	Peter A. Bertocci
P.E.J.	Paul E. Johnson
P.G.M.	Paul G. Morrison
P.H.V.	Paul H. Vieth
P.R.H.	Paul R. Helsel
P.S.M.	Philip S. Moore
P.V.N.	Percy V. Norwood
Q.B.	Quirinus Breen
R.B.B.	Richard B. Brandt
R.B.Y.S.	R. B. Y. Scott
R.C.P.	Ray C. Petry
R.D.	Richard Davidson
R.E.E.H.	R. E. E. Harkness
R.E.W.	Roland Emerson Wolfe
R.H.B.	Roland H. Bainton
R.H.N.	Robert Hastings Nichols
R.H.P.	Robert H. Pfeiffer
R.K.	Richard Kroner
R.M.H.	Raphael M. Huber
R.M.J.	Rufus M. Jones
R.W.A.	R. W. Albright
R.W.F.	Robert Worth Frank
S.A.B.	S. A. Burgess
S.C.	Simon Conrad
S.C.T.	Stephen C. Tornay
S.E.	Sherwood Eddy
S.E.M.	Sidney E. Mead
S.G.	Simon Greenberg
S.H.B.	Sheldon H. Blank
S.J.C.	Shirley Jackson Case
S.L.T.	Samuel L. Terrien
S.M.G.	Samuel MacLean Gilmour
S.R.	Samuel Rosenblatt
S.S.	Shalom Spiegel
S.S.C.	Samuel S. Cohon
T.A.K.	T(aito) Almar Kantonen
T.E.D.	Thomas E. Drake
T.F.H.	Theodore F. Herman
T.J.	Thorkild Jacobsen
T.J.B.	Thomas J. Bigham
T.P.C.	Tom Peete Cross
T.T.M.	Thomas T. McAvoy
U.L.	Umphrey Lee
V.F.	Vergilius Ferm
V.F.H.	Vincent F. Hopper
V.J.B.	Vernon J. Bourke
W.B.C.	Warren B. Catlin
W.E.G.	Winfred Ernest Garrison
W.E.R.	Walter Edwin Roush
W.G.H.	William Glen Harris
W.H.	Werner Hannin
W.K.W.	William Kelley Wright
W.M.B.	William M. Beahm
W.M.H.	Walter M. Horton
W.N.P.	W. Norman Pittenger
W.N.S.	W. N. Schwarze
W.P.	Wilhelm Pauck
W.S.H.	Winthrop S. Hudson
W.S.R.	W. Stanley Rycroft
W.T.C.	Wing-tsit Chan
W.W.C.	William W. Comfort
W.W.R.	William Walker Rockwell
W.W.S.	William W. Sweet

ENCYCLOPEDIA OF RELIGION CONTRIBUTING EDITORS

ALBAUGH, GAYLORD P., B.D.
Lecturer in Church History, School of Theology, McMaster University, Hamilton, Ontario, Canada.

ALBRIGHT, R. W., B.D., M.A., Th.D.
Professor of Church History, The Evangelical School of Theology, Reading, Pa.; also Professor of Church History in Temple University, Philadelphia, Pa.

ATKINS, GAIUS GLENN, LL.B., Litt.D., D.D., L.H.D.
Formerly, Hoyt Professor of Homiletics and Sociology, Auburn Theological Seminary; Professor Emeritus. North Marshfield, Mass.

BAINTON, ROLAND H., B.D., Ph.D.
Titus Street Professor of Ecclesiastical History, The Divinity School, Yale University, New Haven, Conn.

BEAHM, WILLIAM M., Ph.D., D.D.
Professor of Christian Theology and Missions, Bethany Biblical Seminary, Chicago, Ill.

BENNETT, EPHRAIM, B.A.
Rabbi at Beth El Synagogue, Cedarhurst, Long Island, N. Y.

BERGENDOFF, CONRAD J., M.A., B.D., Ph.D., Th.D.
President of Augustana College and Theological Seminary, Rock Island, Ill.

BERTOCCI, PETER A., M.A., Ph.D.
Assistant Professor of Philosophy and Psychology, Bates College, Lewiston, Maine.

BIGHAM, THOMAS J. Jr., S.T.B.
Fellow and Tutor of the General Theological Seminary of the Episcopal Church, New York City.

BIXLER, JULIUS SEELYE, M.A., Ph.D., D.D.
Recently, Bussey Professor of Theology, Harvard University; now President of Colby College, Waterville, Maine.

BLANK, SHELDON H., Ph.D.
Professor in the Hebrew Union College, Cincinnati, Ohio.

BOISEN, ANTON T., M.F., M.A., D.D.
Chaplain in the Elgin State Hospital, Elgin, Ill.

BOKSER, BEN ZION, M.A., Ph.D.
Rabbi at the Forest Hills Jewish Center, Forest Hills, New York and Lecturer at the Institute of Religious Studies at the Jewish Theological Seminary.

BOOTH, EDWIN PRINCE, S.T.B., Ph.D., D.D.
Formerly, Professor of Historical Theology and now Professor of New Testament, Boston University School of Theology, Boston, Mass.

BOURKE, VERNON J., M.A., Ph.D.
Associate Professor of Philosophy, St. Louis University, St. Louis, Mo.

BRADEN, CHARLES S., B.D., Ph.D.
Professor and Chairman of the Department of History and Literature of Religions, Northwestern University, Evanston, Ill.

BRANDT, RICHARD B., Ph.D.
Assistant Professor of Philosophy, Swarthmore College, Swarthmore, Pa.

BREEN, QUIRINUS, Ph.D.
Assistant Professor of History in the University of Oregon, Eugene, Oregon.

BRIGHTMAN, EDGAR SHEFFIELD, M.A., S.T.B., Ph.D., Litt.D., LL.D.
Borden Parker Bowne Professor of Philosophy in The Graduate School, Boston University, Boston, Mass.

BROADHEAD, EDWARD HALL, M.A., M.Mus.
Organist and Instructor in Music in Duke University, Durham, N. C.

BRUNO, FRANK J., S.T.B.
Professor of Applied Sociology and Chairman of the Department of Social Work, Washington University, St. Louis, Mo.

BUCKHAM, JOHN WRIGHT, D.D.
Professor Emeritus of Christian Theology, Pacific School of Religion, Berkeley, Cal.

BUCKLER, FRANCIS WILLIAM, M.A., S.T.D.

Michigan Professor of Church History, The Graduate School of Theology, Oberlin College, Oberlin, Ohio.

BURGESS, S.A., B.A., LL.B.

Formerly President of Graceland College, Lamoni, Iowa; Church Historian, Reorganized Church of Jesus Christ of Latter Day Saints.

CABANISS, ALLEN, B.D., Ph.D.

Minister, Presbyterian Church, Columbia, Miss.; Historian, Grand Lodge of Mississippi, F. and A. M.

CASE, SHIRLEY JACKSON, M.A., B.D., Ph.D., D.D., D.C.L.

Dean of the Florida School of Religion, Lakeland, Fla.; Dean Emeritus, The Divinity School, The University of Chicago.

CASSADY, MAYNARD L., Th.B., M.A., Ph.D.

Principal Civilian Mobilization Adviser, Office of Civilian Defense, Washington, D. C. and recently Chairman, Department of Religion, University of Rochester, Rochester, N. Y.

CATLIN, WARREN B., Ph.D.

Fayerweather Professor of Economics and Sociology and Chairman of the Department, Bowdoin College, Brunswick, Maine.

CHAN WING-TSIT, M.A., Ph.D.

Professor of Chinese Culture, Dartmouth College, Hanover, N. H.; Formerly, Professor of Chinese Philosophy and Institutions, Oriental Institute, University of Hawaii, Honolulu, T. H.

CHEEK, JOHN L., M.A., B.D., Ph.D.

Minister in the Brookfield Methodist Church, Brookfield, Ill.

CLARK, ELMER T., M.A., B.D., S.T.D., LL.D., Litt.D.

Editorial Secretary of the Board of Missions and Church Extension of the Methodist Church; Editor of the *World Outlook*, New York City.

CODE, JOSEPH B., S.T.D., Sc.Hist.D.

Director of the Inter-American Institute, Kansas City, Mo.

COHEN, BOAZ, Ph.D.

Associate Professor of Rabbinics and Assistant Librarian in the Jewish Theological Seminary of America, New York City; Chairman of the Committee on Jewish Law of the Rabbinical Assembly.

COHON, SAMUEL S., D.D.

Professor of Jewish Theology, Hebrew Union College, Cincinnati, Ohio.

COLWELL, ERNEST CADMAN, B.D., Ph.D.

Professor of New Testament Literature, Chairman of the Department of Early Christian Literature, Dean of the Divinity School and Dean of the Faculties, The University of Chicago, Chicago, Ill.

COMFORT, HOWARD, M.A., Ph.D.

Associate Professor of Ancient Languages, Haverford College, Haverford, Pa.

COMFORT, WILLIAM W., M.A., Ph.D., Litt.D., LL.D.

President Emeritus of Haverford College, Haverford, Pa.

CONRAD, SIMON.

Capuchin College, Washington, D. C.

COOLIDGE, LOWELL W., M.A., Ph.D.

Assistant Professor of English, The College of Wooster, Wooster, Ohio.

CORBETT, JAMES A., Arch.Pal., Ecole Nationale des Chartres, Paris.

Notre Dame University, Notre Dame, Ind.

COUSLAND, KENNETH H., M.A., B.D., D.D.

Professor of Church History in Emmanuel Theological College, Victoria University, Toronto, Canada.

CRAGG, GERALD R., M.A.

Professor of Systematic Theology and Lecturer in Christian Ethics, United Theological College, Montreal, Canada.

CRAIG, CLARENCE TUCKER, Ph.D., S.T.B., D.D.

Morgan Professor of New Testament Language and Literature in The Graduate School of Theology, Oberlin College, Oberlin, Ohio.

CROSS, TOM PEETE, Ph.D., Litt.D.

Professor of English and Comparative Literature, The University of Chicago, Chicago, Ill.

DAVIDSON, RICHARD, M.A., Ph.D., D.D.

Late Principal and Professor of Old Testament in Emmanuel College, Toronto, Canada.

DeWOLF, L. HAROLD, S.T.B., Ph.D.

Professor of Philosophy, Boston University, Boston, Mass.

DRAKE, THOMAS E., Ph.D.

Assistant Professor of History and Curator of the Quaker Collection at Haverford College, Haverford, Pa.

EASTMAN, FRED, Litt.D.

Professor of Biography, Literature and Drama in The Chicago Theological Seminary, Chicago, Ill.

EASTON, BURTON SCOTT, Ph.D., B.D., Th.D., D.D.

Professor of the Literature and Interpretation of the New Testament, General Theological Seminary of the Episcopal Church, New York City.

EBRIGHT, DONALD FOSSETT, B.D., M.A., Ph.D.

Fellow, The Divinity School, The University of Chicago, Chicago, Ill.

EDDY, SHERWOOD, M.A., LL.D.

Author, Lecturer and World Traveler, New York City.

ELLSWORTH, CLAYTON S., Ph.D.

Assistant Professor of History, The College of Wooster, Wooster, Ohio.

ENSLEY, FRANCIS GERALD, S.T.B., Ph.D.

Instructor in Homiletics and Professor-elect of Systematic Theology in Boston University School of Theology, Boston, Mass.

ENSLIN, MORTON SCOTT, B.D., Th.D.

Professor of New Testament Literature and Exegesis in Crozer Theological Seminary, Chester, Pa.; Lecturer on Patristics, University of Pennsylvania; Editor, *Crozer Quarterly*.

EUBANK, EARLE EDWARD, M.A., Ph.D.

Professor and Head of the Department of Sociology, University of Cincinnati, Cincinnati, Ohio.

FERM, VERGILIUS, B.D., M.A., Ph.D.

Compton Professor and Head of the Department of Philosophy, The College of Wooster, Wooster, Ohio.

FINKELSTEIN, LOUIS, Ph.D.

President and Solomon Schechter Professor of Theology in the Jewish Theological Seminary of America, New York City.

FITZGERALD, JOHN J., Ph.D.

Assistant Professor of Philosophy, The University of Notre Dame, Notre Dame, Ind.

FRANK, ROBERT WORTH, M.A., B.D., D.D., Ph.D.

Professor of Philosophy of Religion and Ethics in the Presbyterian Theological Seminary, Chicago, Ill.

GARRISON, WINFRED ERNEST, B.D., Ph.D., Litt.D.

Professor of Church History, Disciples' Divinity House and The University of Chicago; Literary Editor, *The Christian Century*.

GILBERT, MRS. KATHARINE E., M.A., Ph.D.

Chairman, Department of Aesthetics, Art and Music, Duke University, Durham, N. C.

GILMOUR, SAMUEL MACLEAN, B.D., Ph.D.

Professor of New Testament Literature and Exegesis in Queen's Theological College, Kingston, Ontario, Canada.

GLUECK, NELSON, B.H., Ph.D., LL.D.

Professor of Bible and Biblical Archaeology in Hebrew Union College, Cincinnati, Ohio.

GOODSPEED, EDGAR J., B.D., Ph.D., D.D., L.H.D., Doc.Litt.

Distinguished Service Professor Emeritus of Biblical and Patristic Greek, The University of Chicago, Chicago, Ill.

GRANT, FREDERICK CLIFTON, B.D., S.T.M., Th.D., D.S. Litt., D.D.

Edward Robinson Professor of Biblical Theology, Union Theological Seminary, New York City.

GRAY, JOSEPH M.M., B.D., D.D., Litt.D., S.T.D.

Formerly, President of American University, Washington, D. C.; now Minister of the Bexley Methodist Church, Columbus, Ohio.

GREENBERG, SIMON, Ph.D.

Rabbi, Har Zion Temple, Philadelphia, Pa.; Associate Professor in the Jewish Theological Seminary of America.

HADAS, MOSES, M.A., Ph.D.

Assistant Professor of Greek and Latin in Columbia University, New York City.

HAFKESBRINK, HANNA, Ph.D.

Professor of German and Chairman of the German Department, Connecticut College, New London, Conn.

HANNIN, WERNER.

Capuchin College, Washington, D. C.

HARDY, Jr., EDWARD ROCHIE, S.T.M., Ph.D.

Instructor in the Department of Hebrew; Fellow and Tutor, in the Departments of New Testament, Ecclesiastical History, Theology and Liturgics in the General Theological Seminary of the Episcopal Church, New York City.

HARKNESS, R. E. E., M.A., B.D., Ph.D.

Professor of the History of Christianity, Crozer Theological Seminary, Chester, Pa.; President of the American Baptist Historical Society.

HARRIS, WILLIAM GLENN, M.A., M. Th., Ph.D.

Minister in the First Presbyterian Church, Birmingham, Mich.

HARTSHORNE, CHARLES, M.A., Ph.D.

Associate Professor of Philosophy, The University of Chicago, Chicago, Ill.

HAUSHEER, HERMAN, B.D., M.A., Ph.D.

Late Retired Professor, Lamoni, Iowa.

HAWKINSON, ERIC G., Ph.B., M.A.

Instructor in Church History and Homiletics in the Seminary of the Evangelical Mission Covenant of America, North Park College, Chicago, Ill.

HAYDON, A. EUSTACE, B.D., M.A., Ph.D.

Professor of the History of Religions; Chairman of the Department of Comparative Religion, The University of Chicago, Chicago, Ill.

HEIDBREDER, EDNA, M.A., Ph.D.

Professor of Psychology and Chairman of the Department of Psychology, Wellesley College, Wellesley, Mass.

HEIMANN, EDWARD, Ph.D.

Professor in the Graduate School of the New School for Social Research, New York City.

HELSEL, PAUL R., M.A., B.D., Ph.D.

Associate Professor of Philosophy in The University of Southern California, Los Angeles, Cal.

HERMAN, THEODORE F., D.D., LL.D.

President and Professor of Systematic Theology in the Seminary of the Evangelical and Reformed Church, Lancaster, Pa.

HOPPER, VINCENT F., M.A., Ph.D.

Associate Professor of Literature, New York University, New York City.

HOLTOM, DANIEL CLARENCE, B.D., Ph.D., D.D.

Recently, Professor in the Theology Department, Aoyama Gakuin, Tokyo and Dean of the Theology Department, Kanto Gakuin, Yokohama; now in residence at San Gabriel, Cal.

HORTON, WALTER M., Ph.D., S.T.M.

Fairchild Professor of Theology, Graduate School of Theology, Oberlin College, Oberlin, Ohio.

HUBER, Very Rev., RAPHAEL M., O.F. M.Conv., S.T.D., S.T.M.

Associate Professor of Church History, Catholic University, Washington, D. C.

HUDSON, WINTHROP S., B.D., Ph.D.

Formerly, Instructor in the History of Christianity, Colgate - Rochester Divinity School, Rochester, N. Y.; now Assistant Professor of History of Christianity in the British Isles, Federated Theological Faculty, University of Chicago.

HYATT, J. PHILIP, M.A., B.D., Ph.D.

Associate Professor of Old Testament Language and Literature in the Vanderbilt University School of Religion, Nashville, Tenn.

JACOBSEN, THORKILD, M.A., Ph.D., Dr. Phil.

Research Associate in the Oriental Institute, The University of Chicago, Chicago, Ill.

JENSEN, HOWARD E., M.A., B.D., Ph.D.

Professor of Sociology and Chairman of the Department of Sociology and Anthropology in Duke University, Durham, N. C.

JOHNSON, HJALMAR W., B.D., Ph.D.

Professor of Philosophy, Augustana Theological Seminary, Rock Island, Ill.

JOHNSON, PAUL E., M.A., S.T.B., Ph.D., D.D.

Professor of the Psychology and History of Religion in Boston University School of Theology, Boston, Mass.

JONES, RUFUS M., M.A., LL.D., D.D., Litt.D., D.Th., S.T.D.

Emeritus Professor of Philosophy, Haverford College, Haverford, Pa.

KANTONEN, T(aito) ALMAR, S.T.B., M.A., Ph.D., D.D.

Professor of Systematic Theology in the Hamma Divinity School, Wittenberg College, Springfield, Ohio.

KIESSLING, ELMER C., Ph.D.

Professor of English at Northwestern College, Watertown, Wis.

KIEVAL, HERMAN, B.A.

Rabbi at Beth Judah Synagogue, Ventnor, N. J.

KIRBY, MRS. ETHYN W., Ph.D.

Formerly, Assistant Professor of History in Wells College; now in residence, Providence, R. I.

KNAPPEN, M.M., Ph.D.

Professor and Head of the Department of History and Political Science, Michigan State College, East Lansing, Mich.

KNUDSON, ALBERT C., Ph.D., Theol.D., D.D., LL.D.

Dean Emeritus, Boston University School of Theology, Boston, Mass.

KRAELING, EMIL G., Ph.D.

Formerly, Assistant Professor in the Department of Old Testament in Union Theological Seminary, New York City.

KRONER, RICHARD, Ph.D.

Professor of Philosophy in McGill University, Montreal, Canada; visiting Lecturer in the Union Theological Seminary, New York City.

LEE, UMPHREY, M.A., D.D., Ph.D., LL. D., Litt.D.

President of Southern Methodist University, Dallas, Texas.

LEVY, FELIX A., Ph.D., D.D.

Ex-President of Central Conference of American Rabbis; Rabbi in Emanuel Congregation, Chicago, Ill.

LINE, JOHN, M.A., S.T.D., D.D.

Professor of Philosophy of Religion and Systematic Theology, Emmanuel College, Toronto, Canada.

LIPSKY, LOUIS.

Vice-president of the Zionist Organization of America; American member of the Executive of the Jewish Agency for Palestine; formerly, Editor of *The New Palestine*.

LOWRY, Jr., CHARLES W., M.A., B.D., D.Phil.

Professor of Systematic Divinity, The Virginia Theological Seminary, Alexandria, Virginia.

MACKAY, JOHN A., M.A., B.D., D.D., Litt.D., LL.D.

Professor of Ecumenics and President of Princeton Theological Seminary, Princeton, N. J.

MAYS, BENJAMIN ELIJAH, M.A., Ph.D.

Formerly, Dean of the School of Religion at Howard University, Washington, D. C.; now President of Morehouse College, Atlanta, Ga.

McAVOY, THOMAS T., Ph.D.

Archivist of the University of Notre Dame Archives (formerly the Catholic Archives of America); Head of the Department of History, Notre Dame University, Notre Dame, Ind.

McGIFFERT, Jr., ARTHUR CUSHMAN, B.D., M.A., D.D.

President of the Pacific School of Religion, Berkeley, Cal.

McNEILL, JOHN THOMAS, M.A., B.D., Ph.D., D.D.

Formerly, Professor of the History of European Christianity, The University of Chicago, Chicago, Ill.; now Auburn Professor of Church History, Union Theological Seminary, New York City.

MEAD, SIDNEY E., M.A., Ph.D.

Gerald Birney Smith Instructor in Divinity, The Divinity School, The University of Chicago, Chicago, Ill.

MOEHLMAN, CONRAD HENRY, B.D., M.A., Ph.D., D.D.

James B. Colgate Professor of the History of Christianity, The Colgate-Rochester Divinity School, Rochester, N. Y.

MOORE, PHILIP S., Ph.D., Arch. Pal. Ecole Nationale des Chartres, Paris.

Associate Professor of Mediaeval Studies, The University of Notre Dame, Notre Dame, Ind.; Editor of *Publications in Mediaeval Studies*.

MORGENSTERN, JULIAN, Ph.D., D.H. L., L.H.D.

President of the Hebrew Union College, Cincinnati, Ohio.

MORRISON, PAUL G., M.A., Ph.D.

Curator, Rare Book Room, The University of Chicago Libraries, Chicago, Ill.

MOWRER, ERNEST R., Ph.D.

Professor of Sociology, Northwestern University, Evanston, Ill.

MOWRER, HARRIET R., M.A.
Consultant in Marital Adjustment in Chicago and Evanston, Ill.; formerly, Domestic Discord Consultant for the Jewish Social Service Bureau of Chicago; Lecturer in Sociology in Northwestern University, Evanston, Ill.

MURPHY, GARDNER, Ph.D.
Chairman of the Department of Psychology in The College of the City of New York, New York City.

MURRAY, JOHN COURTNEY, S.J., M.A., S.T.D.
Professor of Theology, Woodstock College, Woodstock, Md. and Editor of *Theological Studies.*

MUZZEY, DAVID S., B.D., Ph.D.
Literary Editor of *The Standard;* Graduate Professor of American History, Columbia University, New York City; Director, The Society for Ethical Culture in the City of New York.

NEAL, FRED W., B.D., Ph.D.
Fellow in the Divinity School of the University of Chicago, Chicago, Ill.

NELSON, HAROLD H., Ph.D.
Acting Director of the Oriental Institute of the University of Chicago, Chicago, Ill.; Field Director of the Epigraphic and Architectural Survey of the Oriental Institute, Luxor, Egypt.

NEWHALL, JANNETTE E., M.A., Ph.D.
Assistant Librarian of the Andover-Harvard Theological Library in Harvard University, Cambridge, Mass.

NEWNAN, EVA MAY, M.A., Ph.D.
Assistant Professor of Classical Languages and Head of the Department of Greek, The College of Wooster, Wooster, Ohio.

NICHOLS, ROBERT HASTINGS, Ph.D., D.D.
Professor of Church History in Auburn Theological Seminary and Auburn Professor of Church History in Union Theological Seminary, New York City; Member of the Faculty of Political Science in Columbia University; Stated Clerk of the Synod of New York of the Presbyterian Church in the U.S.A.

NIEBUHR, H. RICHARD, M.A., B.D., Ph.D., D.D.
Professor of Christian Ethics in the Divinity School, Yale University, New Haven, Conn.

NORWOOD, PERCY V., M.A., B.D., Ph.D.
Professor of Ecclesiastical History and Liturgics in Seabury-Western Theological Seminary, Evanston, Ill.

O'GRADY, DANIEL C., Ph.D.
Professor of Philosophy, The University of Notre Dame, Notre Dame, Ind.

PARRISH, FRED L., M.A., B.D., Ph.D.
Professor and Head of the Department of History and Government, Kansas State College, Manhattan, Kansas.

PAUCK, WILHELM, L.S.T., D.Th.
Professor of Historical Theology in The Chicago Theological Seminary and in the Divinity School of the University of Chicago, Chicago, Ill.

PERSONS, FREDERICK T., M.A.
Librarian, Congregational Library, Boston, Mass.

PETRY, RAY C., Ph.D.
Associate Professor of Church History in the Divinity School of Duke University, Durham, N. C.

PFEIFFER, ROBERT H., S.T.B., M.A., Ph.D., S.T.M.
Lecturer in Semitic Languages and Curator of the Semitic Museum, Harvard University, Cambridge, Mass.; Chairman of the Department of Semitic Languages, Harvard University; Editor of the *Journal of Biblical Literature.*

PIPER, OTTO A., Th.D., D.D.
Professor of New Testament Literature and Exegesis in Princeton Theological Seminary, Princeton, N. J.

PITTENGER, W. NORMAN, S.T.M.
Tutor and Fellow in the General Theological Seminary of the Episcopal Church, New York City.

POOL, D. de SOLA.
Rabbi of the Spanish and Portuguese Synagogue, Shearith Israel, New York City.

RAMSDELL, EDWARD T., M.A., S.T.B., Ph.D.
Professor of Theology and Philosophy of Religion in Vanderbilt University, School of Religion, Nashville, Tenn.

RENGERS, CHRISTOPHER.
Capuchin College, Washington, D. C.

REU, MICHAEL, Th.D., Litt.D.
Late Dean of the Graduate School and Professor of Theology in the Wartburg Seminary, Dubuque, Iowa.

RHEINSTEIN, MAX, Dr.utr. iur. (Munich)
Max Pam Associate Professor of Comparative Law, The University of Chicago Law School, Chicago, Ill.

RIST, MARTIN, B.D., Th.D., Ph.D.
Professor of New Testament Literature and Interpretation in The Iliff School of Theology, Denver, Col.

ROBERTS, MILLARD GEORGE, B.D.
Fellow in American Church History, The Divinity School, The University of Chicago, Chicago, Ill.

ROCKWELL, WILLIAM WALKER, S.T.B., S.T.L., M.A., Ph.D., D. Theol.
Librarian Emeritus, Union Theological Seminary, New York City.

RODGERS, EDITH C., Ph.D.
New York City.

ROLL, BERTIN.
Capuchin College, Washington, D. C.

ROSENBLATT, SAMUEL.
Rabbi of the Beth Tfiloh Congregation, Baltimore, Md.

ROUSH, WALTER EDWIN, B.D., M.A., D.D., Ph.D.
Professor of Old Testament Language and Interpretation in The Bonebrake Theological Seminary, Dayton, Ohio.

RULE, ANDREW K., Ph.D.
Professor of Church History and Apologetics in the Louisville Presbyterian Theological Seminary, Louisville, Ky.

RUSSELL, HENRY G., M.A., Ph.D.
Instructor in Biblical Literature, Bowdoin College, Brunswick, Maine.

RYAN, EDWARD A., S.J., Docteur en Sciences Historiques.
Professor of Church History, Woodstock College, Woodstock, Md.

RYCROFT, W. STANLEY, Ph.D.
Secretary of the Committee on Cooperation in Latin America, New York City.

SCHRATZ, BRICE.
Capuchin College, Washington, D. C.

SCHWARZE, W.N., Ph.D., D.D.
President Emeritus of the Moravian College and Theological Seminary; Archivist of the Northern Province, Moravian Church in America; Bethlehem, Pa.

SCOTT, ERNEST FINDLAY, M.A., D.D.
Emeritus Professor of New Testament Criticism, Union Theological Seminary, New York City.

SCOTT, R.B.Y., B.D., M.A., Ph.D.
Professor of Old Testament Literature and Exegesis in the United Theological College, Montreal, Canada.

SEESHOLTZ, ANNE, M.A., Ph.D.
Sometime Fellow in Theology at Marburg, Germany; on Peace Mission to the Orient for the International Fellowship of Reconciliation; Member of the Faculty of the National Lutheran Board for Deaconess Work, Baltimore, Md.

SHEDD, CLARENCE PROUTY, M.A., B.D., Ph.D.
Stephen Merrell Clement Professor of Christian Methods and Director of Studies on Religion in Higher Education, The Divinity School, Yale University, New Haven, Conn.

SHERRILL, LEWIS J., B.D., Ph.D.
Dean and Mary Hamilton Duncan Professor of Religious Education in the Louisville Presbyterian Theological Seminary, Louisville, Ky.

SILVER, ABBA HILLEL, D.D., Litt.D., D.H.L.
Rabbi of the Temple, Cleveland, Ohio.

SIMS, MARY S., Ph.D.
Executive of the Committee for National Interpretation and Support of the National Board of the Young Womens Christian Associations of the United States, New York City.

SKINNER, CLARENCE R., M.A., D.D.
Professor of Applied Christianity and Dean in Tufts College School of Religion and Crane Theological School, Tufts College, Mass.

SMITH, CHARLES EDWARD, M.A., Ph.D.
Professor of History in the College of Arts and Sciences, Louisiana State University, University, La.

SNYDER, EDWARD DOUGLAS, M.A., Ph.D.

Professor of English, Haverford College, Haverford, Pa.

SPIEGEL, SHALOM, Ph.D.

Professor of Hebrew Language and Literature in the Jewish Institute of Religion, New York City.

SPINKA, MATTHEW, Ph.D.

Waldo Professor of Medieval, Reformation and Modern Church History, The Hartford Theological Seminary, Hartford, Conn.

SPRENGLING, MARTIN, Ph.D.

Professor of Arabic, The Department of Oriental Languages and Literatures in the University of Chicago, Chicago, Ill.

STARBUCK, EDWIN DILLER, M.A., Ph.D.

Formerly, Professor of Philosophy and Director of Character Research and now Professor of Psychology, The University of Southern California, Los Angeles, Cal.

STEERE, DOUGLAS V., M.A., Ph.D.

Professor of Philosophy, Haverford College, Haverford, Pa.

STEVENSON, GEORGE S., M.D.

Medical Director, The National Committee for Mental Hygiene, New York City.

STIFLER, FRANCIS CARR, M.A., D.D.

Editorial and Recording Secretary, American Bible Society, New York City.

SWEET, WILLIAM W., B.D., M.A., Th.M., Ph.D., D.D., Litt.D.

Professor of the History of American Christianity, The University of Chicago, Chicago, Ill.

TERRIEN, SAMUEL L., S.T.M., Th.D.

Instructor in Hebrew and the Old Testament, Union Theological Seminary, New York City.

THORNING, JOSEPH F., M.A., Ph.D., S.T.D.

Professor of Ethics and Sociology in Mount St. Mary's Seminary and College, Emmitsburg, Md.

TORNAY, STEPHEN C., S.T.D., M.A., Ph.D.

Instructor in Philosophy and the Classics, University of Utah, Salt Lake City, Utah.

UNGER, DOMINIC, O.F.M. Cap.

Professor of Sacred Scripture and Liturgy, Capuchin College, Washington, D. C.

VIETH, PAUL H., B.D., Ph.D.

Horace Bushnell Professor of Christian Nurture in the Divinity School, Yale University, New Haven, Conn.

VOLLERT, CYRIL, Ph.D., S.T.D.

Dean of St. Mary's College, St. Marys, Kansas, the School of Divinity of St. Louis University.

WARD, LEO R., Ph.D.

Associate Professor of Philosophy, The University of Notre Dame, Notre Dame, Ind.

WEBBER, F. R.

Editor, *Lutheran Church Art,* New York City.

WEIGLE, LUTHER ALLAN, M.A., Ph.D., D.D., Litt.D., S.T.D., LL.D., J.U.D.

Dean of the Divinity School and Sterling Professor of Religious Education, Yale University, New Haven, Conn.; recently, President of the Federal Council of the Churches of Christ in America.

WIEMAN, HENRY HUDSON, Ph.D., Litt.D., D.D.

Professor of Philosophy of Religion, The Divinity School, The University of Chicago, Chicago, Ill.

WIKGREN, ALLEN P., M.A., Ph.D.

Assistant Professor of New Testament Language in the Divinity School of the University of Chicago, Chicago, Ill.

WILBUR, EARL M., M.A., S.T.B., D.D.

Emeritus Professor of Practical Theology and formerly President of Pacific Unitarian School for the Ministry, Berkeley, Cal.

WILLIAMS, DANIEL DAY, B.D., M.A., Ph.D.

Assistant Professor of Theology in The Chicago Theological Seminary, Chicago, Ill.

WILLOUGHBY, HAROLD R., M.A., B.D., Ph.D., D.D.

Associate Professor of New Testament in the University of Chicago, Chicago, Ill.

WINFIELD, OSCAR A., B.D., M.A., Ph.D.

Formerly, Acting President of Gustavus Adolphus College; Professor of Philosophy, St. Peter, Minn.

WOLFE, ROLLAND EMERSON, B.D., S.T.M., Ph.D.

Assistant Professor of Old Testament in Tufts College and Crane Theological School, Tufts College, Mass.

WOOD, ARTHUR EVANS, S.T.B., B.D., Ph.D.

Professor of Sociology in the University of Michigan, Ann Arbor, Mich.

WRIGHT, G. ERNEST, B.D., Ph.D.

Assistant Professor of Old Testament, Presbyterian Theological Seminary, Chicago, Ill.; Editor of *The Biblical Archaeologist.*

WRIGHT, WILLIAM KELLEY, Ph.D.

Professor of Philosophy, Dartmouth College, Hanover, N. H.

ZACHARIADES, GEORGE ELIAS, Ph.D.

Professor of History and Greek in the Greek Theological Seminary, Pomfret Center, Conn.

A

Aaronites: See blessing, priestly.

Ab, ninth of: (Hebrew form, *Tisha b'Ab*) Jewish fast day commemorating the fall of Jerusalem and the destruction of the Temple by the Romans in 70 C.E. In addition to fasting, tradition also enjoins the abstention from all diverting activities. At the divine services, all synagogue ornaments are removed and the liturgy includes various dirges and the reading of the Biblical book of Lamentations. See Jewish religious festivals. B.Z.B.

Abailard, Peter: Peter Abailard has been best known for his romance with Heloise. But he was one of the greatest intellectualists of the entire Middle Ages. Born at Palais or Le Pallet, Brittany, in 1079, he early became a wanderer in search of knowledge. His wanderings brought him to Paris sometime before 1108, where he became the pupil of the dialectician and "exaggerated realist" William of Champeaux*. Before this he had probably studied under the nominalist Roscelinus and under the famous teachers of the School of Chartres**. He opposed William's position on 'universals', and drove him from the cathedral school in 1108. He also opposed the nominalism of Roscelinus. But always the dialectician, his own solution to the philosophical problem of universals* is unsatisfactory and not too clear. It is not far removed from the nominalism* he opposed. Around 1115 he decided to study theology under Anselm of Laon. After a short training, he began to teach and write. His first theological work was condemned at Soissons in 1121, and his later works at Sens in 1141. For his *Sic et non,* he was accused of trying to undermine the patristic authority, but this charge was false. He is important as dialectician who was dissatisfied with 'positive' theology and who wanted reason to play its part in the solution of theological problems. Being neither philosopher nor theologian, he sometimes failed to recognize the limits of reason. He died in 1142, leaving behind him the following writings: *Logica 'Ingredientibus'*, and other dialectical works: *Theologia 'Summi Boni'* (*Tract. de unitate et trinitate divina*); *Theologia christiana; Theologia 'scholarium'* (*Introd. ad theologiam*); *Comm. in epistolam ad Romanos; Sic et non; Historia calamitatum.* See atonement in Christianity; Scholasticism; William of St. Thierry. P.S.M.

S. M. Deutsch, *Peter Abälard* (Leipzig, 1883); E. Kaiser, *Pierre Abelard* (Fribourg, 1901); J. Reiners, *Der Nominalismus in der Frühscholastik* (Aachen, 1910); C. F. M. De Remusat, *Abélard, sa vie, sa philosophie et sa théologie.* 2 vols. (Paris, 1845); F. J. Picavet, "Abélard et Alexandre de Halès, créateurs de la méthode scholastique" *Sciences Religieuses,* Vols. V, VI (Paris, 1894, 1895); J. G. Sikes, *Peter Abaelard* (Cambridge, 1932). H.H.

abbess: The superior of a monastery of twelve or more nuns*. Although she does not have the jurisdiction belonging to abbots, she uses the crosier* as a symbol of her rank, and wears a ring. The title is in use among the Benedictines, Poor Clares and others. See abbey. J.B.C.

abbey: A monastery canonically erected and independent, housing at least twelve members. The buildings are constructed around the quadrangle, and consist chiefly of the church, cloister, guest-house, infirmary, refectory, chapter-house, and almonry. Carthusian* abbeys are constructed differently from those of other Orders in that three sides of a quadrangle are made up of small three room cottages occupied by individual monks. The buildings used in common enclose the fourth side. If the abbey is occupied by monks it is ruled by an abbot (Aramaic, *abba,* father). This title was given by St. Benedict* to the superior of a monastery of a settled location. The office is elective, made by secret ballot of the professed members, and for life. The authority of an abbot in his monastery is paternal and quasi episcopal. Jurisdiction differs. Ordinarily it extends only to members of the Order, sometimes it goes beyond the limit of the abbey over clergy and laity in a territory which may be an integral part of a bishop's diocese or which is no part of any diocese. In this latter case they are called abbots *nullius.* After election abbots receive the blessing of a bishop, and are invested with the mitre, crosier, ring, pectoral cross, and other insignia of their office. J.B.C.

Abbott, Lyman: See New theology, the.

abbreviations of names of Catholic Religious Orders: See Catholic Religious Orders.

Abhidharmakosa: See Buddhist Terminology.

abhiseka: A late Vedic rite of annointing or sprinkling of emperors, kings or even lesser state officials on the occasion of their accession to power or of some signal achievement. The term is also used by Buddhists for their tenth stage of perfection, and more popularly for the ceremonial bathing in sacred waters as widely practiced in Hinduism. C.S.B.

abjuration: (Lat. *ab.* from, *jurare,* to swear) In R.C. Church law, the formal renunciation of apostasy, heresy, or schism.** L.R.W.

abnormal psychology: That branch of psychology which deals with the disorders of the personality and with related processes such as dreams, hypnosis, telepathy* etc. As distinct from clinical psychology* it is theoretically rather than practically oriented and it makes little use of standardized tests. It is the non-medical equivalent of "psychopathology." See parapsychology.

W. McDougall, *Abnormal Psychology* (1926); J. J. B. Morgan, *Psychology of Abnormal People* (1928); Morton Prince, *The Dissociation of a Personality* (1906). A.T.B.

Abraham, Testament of: Jewish apocryphal book telling of Abraham's death and ascension to heaven. Probably written in Hebrew in the second century by a Jew or a Jewish Christian. B.Z.B.

absolute: (Lat., *absolutum,* past participle of *absolvere,* set free, complete or finish) 1) Whatever is self-sufficient, unconditional, independent, not relative. 2) The all-inclusive, all-comprehending totality of the real; e.g., Hegel's Absolute. 3) The First Cause, the World Ground (Lotze, Bowne), self-existent "infinite energy producing and sustaining the world" (Knudson); this is the theistic Absolute. Cf. God as Personal. E.S.B.

absolution: (*absolvere,* free from) The power and act of the Church that is expression of reconciliation with the visible Church as a sign and means of reconciliation with God, which frees a penitent sinner from his sin and from external disciplines due to his sin. For Protestant theology, following Luther and Calvin, absolution is identical with the saving power of the declaration of the Gospel. For Catholic theology, Roman, Eastern, and Anglican, absolution includes this (e.g., the declarative and precatory forms in the public services) but is specifically the act of the priest in Confession* remitting post-baptismal sin (for which the formulae of absolution before the 11th century were precatory but now in the West are indicative). The concept of absolution is dependent upon the concept of sin as offending both God and man, particularly fellow Christians, and upon the concept of the Church as a society that is channel of grace. Absolution is contrasted with forgiveness,* which is God's action, as the action of the Church congruent with the action of God. See Confessor; initiation rites; penance; retention of sins. T.J.B.

abstinence: Abstaining from indulgences in certain pleasures as a discipline of the soul, usually from marriage, certain foods, and wine. Extreme observance may take the form of asceticism—withdrawal from the World. R.E.E.H.

abstinence, total: See temperance movement.

Abu Hanifa: (d. 767 A.D.) Persian Moslem. Founder of one of the four orthodox (Sunnite*) schools of jurisprudence; regarded by the orthodox followers as an infallible interpreter of the Koran and Sunna** (manners and customs of the people), and one whose interpretations are representative of the consensus of Islam*. When compared with Arabic schools of interpretation he, a Persian, depended less upon tradition and more upon his independent personal judgment in cases at law in which the Koran is not explicit, even to setting aside the written authority of the Koran and Sunna in those cases in which he thought such action necessary to secure justice.

D. B. Macdonald, *Development of Muslim Theology, Jurisprudence and Constitutional Theory* (London, 1903); I. Goldziher, *Mohammed and Islam* (1917). F.L.P.

Acacius of Caesaraea: (d. 366) The pupil, successor (340), and biographer of Eusebius, and after the death of Eusebius of Nicomedia (342), the leader of the Arian* party at court; bitter opponent of Cyril of Jerusalem*; nominated (acc. Jerome) Felix (antipope of Rome, 358). F.W.B.

accident: (Lat. *ad,* toward, and *cadere,* to fall; *accidere,* to happen) In philosophy, that which does not exist in or of itself but in another; e.g. quality, size. L.R.W.

accidie; acidie: (Lat. *acedia*) A state of mind characterised by indifference or even repugnance felt toward religious exercises, a repugnance not of conviction, but resembling ennui. It was reckoned as one of the seven deadly sins.* P.G.M.

Acoemetae: (Gr. sleepless) A monastic* sect founded in the early fifth century. Divided into choirs, the monks kept up a continuous round of prayer. Best known foundation: the Studium at Constantinople. S.M.G.

acolyte: (Gr. *akolouthos,* attendant or follower) A cleric not yet in major orders, with such functions as preparing wine and water for Mass, and assisting the ministers at Mass, tasks now usually done by altar boys, sometimes called acolytes. L.R.W.

acosmism: (Gr. *a,* priv.; *kosmos,* world) Doctrine that the universe is unreal. E.g., Shankara and F. H. Bradley** saw nothing as real save the ineffable super-cosmic One, of which all in space, time, and finite experience is mere maya* or appearance. C.H.

act psychology: See psychology, schools of.

Act of Six Articles: This act, pushed through parliament in 1539 by Henry VIII*, was called "the whip with six strings" by the Protestants. It reaffirmed transubstantiation, auricular confession, communion in one kind, and clerical celibacy**, and provided the death penalty for the denial of these doctrines. W.S.H.

Acta Apostolicae Sedis: See Pius X, Pope.

Acta Martyrum: Accounts of the trials of early Christian martyrs which were circulated among Christians of the early centuries as tracts for their edification.

O. v. Gebhardt *Acta martyrum selecta* (Berlin, 1903). S.M.G.

Acta Sanctorum: A collection of abstracts of court proceedings against early Christians (*acta*) together with brief accounts of the death of the martyrs (*passiones*), published in sixty-nine volumes by the Jesuit fathers (Bollandus, etc.) at Antwerp during the years 1643-1910. Also in a Brussels edition, 1845-1926. S.M.G.

action sermon: In Scottish Presbyterianism, a sermon preceding the Lord's Supper. The expression comes from *actio gratiarum*, the offering of thanks. Once familiar, it is now mostly obsolete. R.H.N.

Acts of the Apostles: The second volume of Luke's book on Christian beginnings, which carries the story on from the descent of the spirit to Paul's arrival in Rome and two years' stay there. Luke* owed his knowledge of Paul's labors and journeys probably to Paul himself, with whom he travelled from Assos to Jerusalem, and after two years in and about Caesarea, from that place to Rome. His information about the early church in Jerusalem and Palestine, the bulk of chapters 1-12, he might easily have obtained in the course of the two years he spent in and about Caesarea, waiting for Paul's release. Acts tells the story of the Christian movement, groping its way out of Jerusalem and Judaism into widening circles—proselytes, Samaritans, Greeks, and then being carried out into western provinces, crossing from Asia into Europe, until Paul finds it already planted at Rome. The swiftly moving narrative carries the reader from one dramatic scene to another, through the splendid cities of the Graeco-Roman world—Jerusalem, Antioch, Athens, Corinth, Ephesus, Rome. Social, humanitarian, and historical interests mark this as they do the earlier gospel volume. Numerous common traits bind the two volumes together; and many things point to a date long after Paul's time: his death assumed in the farewell at Miletus, the hero stature he has attained, the degree of church organization reflected, the dawn of Christian liturgy, the emergence of the sects. The use of written sources in the Acts must be given up; the so-called "We-sections" once ascribed to somebody's travel diary, are now seen to indicate in an unobtrusive way the writer's presence with Paul's party. Probable date (with Luke) 90 A.D.

Henry J. Cadbury, *The Making of Luke-Acts* (1927); F. J. Foakes-Jackson and K. Lake, *The Beginnings of Christianity:* Part I, *The Acts of the Apostles,* V vols. (1920-1933); E. J. Goodspeed, *New Solutions of New Testament Problems,* chapter vi: "The Origin of Acts." (1927); A. C. McGiffert, *A History of Christianity in the Apostolic Age* (Revised ed., 1906). E.J.G.

Acts of Paul, of John, of Peter: See pseudepigrapha, N.T.; apocrypha in the N.T. church.

Acts of Pilate: See Pilate, Acts of; Nicodemus, Gospel of.

Acts of Thomas: See Thomas, St.

Adad (or Ramman): Babylonian-Assyrian god of wind, storms, lightning, rain, and thunder. He is both beneficient (through rain) and destructive (in Assyria he is also a god of battles). In Syria he is also called Hadad or Hadar, and corresponds to Teshub. See Mesopotamian religions. R.H.P.

Adalbert, Archbishop of Hamburg and Bremen: (ca. 1000-1072) Through the favor of the emperor, Henry III, he became archbishop of Hamburg and Bremen, 1045, with jurisdiction over the churches of Scandinavia to which he appointed numerous bishops. He is blamed for exercising an injurious influence upon young Henry IV.

J. Beinlich, *Die Persönlichkeit Adalberts von Bremen* (Breslau, 1918). J.T.M.

Adalbert, Saint, of Prague: (956(?)-997) (Czech name, Wojtech) Educated at Libice and Magdeburg, he became bishop of Prague, 982. Favored Roman against Slavonic liturgy. After years of retirement at Rome he labored in Bohemia, Hungary and Poland, and in Prussia where he was slain by a heathen priest. While in Hungary (994) he baptized Vayik, i.e. Stephen, the royal saint of Hungary.

H. G. Voigt, *Adalbert von Prag* (Berlin, 1898). J.T.M.

Adam: The first man and the father of the human race, the name being Biblically derived from the Hebrew "adamah," earth, the ultimate substance from which man as a bodily creature is constituted. As the primal source of all human life, Adam symbolizes in Jewish tradition the basic unity and equality of all mankind. Jewish theology treated Adam's fall as a parable of the imperfections which inhere in all human life, but not as their cause. Man is also endowed with an original impulse to virtue; and each person suffers death for his own sins. See fall of man; original sin; pre-Adamite. B.Z.B.

Adamites: An obscure sect, originating in North Africa in the second and third centuries, mentioned by Epiphanius and Augustine and perhaps referred to by Clement of Alexandria. They called their church *Paradise,* condemned marriage as not observed by Adam, and practiced nudism in common worship. Also a similar sect in Bohemia in the 15th century. S.M.G.

Adamnan: (624?-704) Irish monastic leader, ninth abbot of Iona (679-), author of the *Life of St. Columba* and apparently of the important legal document *Cain Adamnain.* J.T.M.

Adams Foundation, The: Established in 1928 by Mrs. Anna B. Adams at the First Methodist Church, Bloomington, Indiana. The capital sum is

$50,000. Its purpose is to bring outstanding speakers to discuss various phases of religion and to aid rural churches. Lecturers have included Drs. E. J. Goodspeed, E. S. Brightman, Bishop Oxnam and H. H. Crane. (Data furnished by the Minister of the Church.) V.F.

Adapa: Babylonian hero, created by Ea* to tend his temple at Eridu and endowed with wisdom. When he broke the wings of the south wind and was summoned before Anu,* in obedience to Ea's advice he unwittingly refused the food of immortality. R.H.P.

Adelard of Bath: An Englishman by birth who flourished in the early part of the twelfth century and taught in Paris and Laon. During his voyages in Italy, Sicily, Greece and in Mohammedan Spain, he acquired a great storehouse of knowledge. He distinguished himself not only in philosophy and theology, but in astronomy, the natural sciences, in geometry and even in animal psychology. His best known work is *Quaestiones naturales*. He is the first to use Aristotle's argument from motion to prove the existence of God. S.C.T.

Adelophagi: (Gr. *adelos*, secretly; *phago*, to eat) A sect of the late 4th century which maintained, in supposed imitation of the prophets, that a Christian ought to eat in secret. S.M.G.

adiaphora: (Pl. of Gr. *adiaphoron*, indifferent) An ancient Greek term, used especially among the Stoics, indicating things regarded as morally neutral or indifferent, i.e. neither good nor bad. Used by some as a theological term in early Protestant thought to designate things regarded as scripturally neutral, i.e. neither required nor forbidden by God (e.g. certain rites or ceremonies, holy days, images, etc.), hence to be used, or not, according to individual or ecclesiastical preference. E.T.R.

adiaphoristic controversy: A seventeenth century debate arising out of the Augsburg Interim* (provisional scheme of compromise between the religious parties, pending a general council). Though neither Catholics nor Protestants were satisfied, Melanchthon* accepted the Interim as regards things indifferent (adiaphora), such as jurisdiction of bishops, observance of certain rites. As a practical issue the question was settled by the terms of the peace of Augsburg,* but the discussion of adiaphora continued for some time in the Lutheran Church. In 1681, a second adiaphoristic controversy arose between the Lutherans and pietists, regarding the lawfulness of amusements. See Leipzig, Interim of. G.R.C.

Aditi: An abstract goddess of Vedic Hinduism, mother of the Adityas.* The name signifies "boundlessness." (Rv. I, 89, 10 says: "Aditi is the sky; Aditi is the air; Aditi is the mother, father and son; Aditi is all the gods and the five tribes; Aditi is whatever has been born; Aditi is whatever shall be born.") She is sometimes identified with the sky, again with the earth and at other times is hailed as a cow. C.S.B.

Adityas: A group of Vedic gods given variously as six, eight and in later times, twelve, all sons of Aditi.* Varuna is the most important, the others being little more than his personified attributes. The list includes Varuna, Mitra, Aryaman, Bhaga, Daksa and Amsa. Others added sometimes are Dhatar, Indra, Vivasvant, Martanda, Surya and Vishnu. The twelve Adityas of later Vedic times seems to correspond with the number of months. C.S.B.

adjuration: (Lat. *ad*, to or toward, *jurare*, to swear) Appeal to do or not to do, for fear of punishment. L.R.W.

Adler, Alfred: (1870-1937) Terming his branch of psychotherapy "Individual Psychology," he decried, in contrast to his master Freud,* the importance of sex. He made considerable contributions to science before his separation from Freud. He urged a simpler answer to the vexing problem of the cause of neurosis. His name is most frequently associated with the problem of personal inadequacy that has received a great deal of attention in the psychiatric and child psychology literature. He has added largely to the clarity of the role which inferiority feelings play in human beings. In 1917 he attempted a systematic interpretation of behavior based on the motivating force of a "will to power," i.e., an urge toward completeness and normalcy in physical development and in achievement. Later, in 1928, he recognized that insistence on the etiological importance of physical inferiority is limiting. He now attributed the child's feeling of inferiority not only to physical abnormalities when compared to parents, but also to his uncertainty or lack of independence, his feeling of subordination to parents or older siblings, or similar psychosocial factors. He accounted for conduct, character, and neurosis as so many varieties of "masculine protest," the wish to deny weakness or inadequacy. It is absurd to define all emotional reactions by his central formula. He ignored the fact that passive desires are just as common as aggressive ones; that neurosis does not predominate among the victims of actual inferiority, among the cripples or the feebleminded; that repression and the unconscious are significant. His psychotherapy stressed not drives or causes, but present purposes and goals. Concerning himself largely with the direction in which the individual is moving, his method is preferred to the therapeutics of Freud and Jung because theirs are too delicate and too involved to be entrusted to anyone but a highly trained professional psychiatrist. Adler's method became more widely known and accepted because his ideas were easily understood, and his treatment required much less time than did the orthodox method. Adler is not so much criticized for the falsity of his views as for their superficiality. Despite this justified criticism, his system will go down in history as a lasting contribution to the effort of man to understand himself. In 1920 he established his first clinics for the training of teachers in the treatment of maladjusted pupils. He brought to contemporary expression many of the truths which a long line of distinguished students of human life—Macchiavelli, Schopenhauer, Nietzsche—have offered. The central assumptions he made regarding human nature represent an important contribution to the understanding of people. His chief insights, such as the centrality of the "will to prestige," the importance of "social interest for health," and his "geometry of love" are valid insights into the working of the mind. See psychology, schools of.

His chief works: *A Study of Organ Inferiority and its Psychical Compensation* (1917); *Neurotic Constitution* (1917); *The Practice and Theory of Individual Psychology* (1924); *Understanding Human Nature* (1927); *The Education of Children* (1930); *What Life Should Mean to You* (1931); *Social Interest* (1939). H.H.

Adler, Felix: See Ethical Culture Societies.

Admadiya: A recent Moslem sect founded at Qadian, India, by Mirza Ghulam Admad, who in 1879 offered himself as the promised *Mahdi* and Messiah in the likeness of Jesus. He re-interpreted the *jihad** (holy war) as a striving after righteousness. Extensive missionary activity is carried on by devoted followers in Asia and Africa, Europe and America with considerable success. See Mahdi. P.E.J.

administrative law: See law.

admonition: (Lat. *admonitio,* a warning to) a) Paternal: a secret remonstrance by a prelate to a suspected cleric; and if this is disregarded, b) Canonical: a legal summons to trial. L.R.W.

adolescence in religion: (Lat. *adolescentia,* fr. *adolescere,* to grow up) Period of development between childhood and maturity (roughly from the early teens to the early twenties), marked by profound physiological and psychological changes. With the maturing of sexual functions, the boy becomes newly self-conscious as a developing man, the girl as a developing woman. A period of awakening and self-discovery; of awareness of physical growth, of emerging intellectual powers and creative interests; of lively imagination; of developing insight into differences in moral quality; of responsiveness to higher values; of susceptibility to ideals and of capacity for strong loyalties. Commonly a period of conflict 1) between the maturing sex drive and acknowledged ideals and 2) between the assertiveness of the developing ego and conventional ideas and attitudes. Self-discovery brings a new sense of independence with inevitable criticisms of adult patterns and mores and of inherited beliefs. Such criticism and doubt are often simply a vehicle of youthful expression. Religiously the period is important as a time of dedication (variously recognized in the organized religions of the world and even in primitive forms), when the religious nurture of childhood must issue in personal commitment if significant religious maturity is to follow. See conversion.

F. D. Brooks, *The Psychology of Adolescence* (1929); E. S. Conklin, *Principles of Adolescent Psychology* (1935); K. C. Garrison, *Psychology of Adolescence* (1934). E.T.R.

Adonis: See Mystery Religions.

adoptianism: The theory that Jesus was in nature a man who became the Son of God by adoption—current in 2d and 3d centuries. Prominent in the Spain of the 8th century, its Christological doctrine, in stressing the complete reality of the man Jesus, argued that the son of man at his conception was spiritually, not substantially or physically, accepted by the will of the son of God. Thus the personal identity between the son of man and the son of God is preserved.

A. Harnack, *Lehrbuch der Dogmengeschichte,* vol. III (Freiburg im Breisgau, 1890); A. Hauck, *Kirchengeschichte Deutschlands,* vol. II (Leipzig, 1887); J. Bach, *Dogmengeschichte des Mittelalters vom christologischen Standpunkt* (Vienna, 1873-1875). H.H.

adoration: Primarily this term suggests the objective worship of God in his holiness and majesty, but it has become the name of an extraliturgical service, and a devotional practice, common in the western Catholic Church for many centuries. The service is the worship of Jesus present in the sacramental elements, reserved in a tabernacle or aumbry on or near the altar; such a service includes psalms, a collect and other material, a rite devised by S. Thomas Aquinas often being used. The devotional practice is the reverencing by the people of Jesus present in the sacrament, often exposed upon the altar, but more frequently in the tabernacle. See forty hours' devotion. W.N.P.

Adrian IV, Pope: (1154-1159) Adrian IV, the only pope of English birth (Nicholas Breakspear) experiencing parental cruelty at St. Alban's in England and monastic insubordination at St. Rufus in France, which occasioned his removal as abbot, was sent in 1152 on a delicate and important mission as Papal Legate* to Scandinavia. While here he raised Trondjem, in whose church he found the relics of St. Olaf, to the independent archepiscopal see of Norway, reformed abuses and aided in ameliorating civil institutions of the country. As pope, Adrian is famous for his vigorous stand against the encroachments of the Normans in Sicily, the Republican brigandry in Rome (Arnold of Brescia*) and the imperial pretensions of Frederick I (Barbaross: 1152-1190) in Germany. The latter's refusal, on the occasion of his visit to Rome to be crowned emperor, to hold at Sutri, June 9, 1195, the stirrup for the pope—an old medieval custom of courtesy—was a significant prognostication of the controversies that were to ensue due to the hitherto too loosely defined legal status and relation between pope and emperor in the Leonine-Carolingian Church-State (*Kirchenstaat*). Matters came to a head in the acrimonious controversy at the Diet of Besancon (1157) and in the declaration of the Bolognese jurists at the convocation at Roncaglia, 1158, concerning the imperial prerogatives. But Adrian was equally adamant in his stand concerning the position of the medieval pope, for, since the emperor held his title as emperor from the pope the emperor was both *spiritually,* as a son of the "Father of all Christianity," and temporally, as dependent on the pope for his superiority over the other European Christian princes, inferior to him. The controversy dragged over into the pontificate of Adrian's successor, Alexander III.*

For sources, including Boso's *Life of Adrian IV* cf. Watterich, *Vitae Pont. Roman* (saec. IX-XIII, Leipzig, 1862), vol. II, 323-374; included also in Migne, PL, vol. 188, pp. 1351-1360. For John of Salisbury's Life of Adrian cf. PL, vol. 199. Regarding the disputed donation of Ireland by Adrian, in virtue of the Bull "*Laudabiliter*" to King John II of England, at the request of John of Salisbury, cf. *Cath. Encyc.* I 158. R.M.H.

adultery: See infidelity.

advaita: A Hindu philosophic term meaning non-dualism. In the Vedanta it is the denial of the dualism of self and the world, spirit and matter. There is only one reality, Brahman. C.S.B.

Advent: 1) The birth of Jesus Christ or more properly the coming of the Son of God in human form, the Incarnation through the Virgin birth. 2) Refers to the Second Coming of Christ; at times, under stress of hardship, deprivation and suffering, the exact time of his coming has been proclaimed. 3) The special observance by R.C. and Lutheran churches of four Sundays (E. C. six) preceding Christmas as a preparation for the Feast of the Nativity. Began middle of sixth century from which time Advent also marks the beginning of the Church Year. See Church Year Cycle. R.E.E.H.

Advent Christian Church: See Adventists.

Adventist sects: There are six adventist sects: Advent Christian Church; Seventh Day Adventists; Church of God (Adventist); Life and Advent Union; Church of God (Oregon, Ill.); Primitive Advent Christian Church. These have about 2,500 churches and 165,000 members. These sects, however, contain but a fraction of the believers in adventism. The Mormons, nearly all pentecostal sects*, and many other conservative bodies teach the doctrine. Cf. communistic settlements, religious. E.T.C.

Adventists: Religious sects springing from the "Advent movement," which originated with the teachings of William Miller (1782-1849). Members of the movement believe in the personal and premillenial second advent of Christ, and the renewal of the Earth as an abode for the redeemed after a physical resurrection of the dead.

William Miller,* the originator, took the prophetic and apocalyptic passages in the Bible literally and by calculations based on the Book of Daniel, concluded the second advent would occur between 1843 and 1844. Lecturing first in Dresden, N. Y. in 1831, Miller soon succeeded in converting great numbers throughout New England to his belief. The danger of an approaching doom filled many with fear, and led sometimes to such excesses as sale of property, and the donning of robes to await the end. Thousands read of the impending end of all things in the *Midnight Cry*, *Signs of the Times*, and *Trumpet of Alarm*—periodicals of the movement.

With the dying down of the first excitement a nucleus of believers met in Albany, N. Y. to assert their continuing loyalty to the cause and there formed an organization. Their principal tenets were annihilation of the wicked, and sleep of the soul from the hour of death to the Day of Judgment. The newly created heavens and earth would be inhabited only by "the people of the saints of the most high." The only millenium was the thousand years intervening between the resurrection of God's chosen at Christ's return, and the raising of all others a thousand years later. There was no promise of this world's conversion; Satan would continue on earth with the good until the end. For the purposes of publishing and fellowship, members organized as the "American Millenial Association"; the organization, however, did not outlive its original members.

Many groups have withdrawn from the first body on doctrinal grounds. Jonathan Cummings, holding that immortality was a gift of Christ to a few chosen at the resurrection, organized one group called the "Advent Christian Church" at Worcester, Mass. in 1861 which in 1926 listed 29,430 members, with 444 churches valued at $11,069,449. In 1844 James Bates and James White, because of scriptural precept, began observing the seventh day rather than the first, and held completely to the Bible as their rule of faith and practice. At a conference held in Battle Creek, Michigan, in 1860, the "Seventh Day Adventist Denomination" was formed. This group, holding to scripture as law, baptism only by immersion, expulsion for the use of tobacco or intoxicants, and an unrevealed, but imminent date of the Advent, grew rapidly. In 1926 it listed 261,834 members, 5,862 churches, and over $48,000,000 in property. The "Church of God, Adventist" originated in Michigan under the leadership of Elder Cranmer, in protest against the claimed divine inspiration of one of the founders. This branch lists 1,550 members in 58 churches in 1926. Still another group, the "Life and Advent Union," was founded by Adventists in New York in 1863, under the leadership of John T. Walsh, who held there would be no resurrection of the wicked. Only 7 churches and 535 members were listed for this group in 1926. Finally, the "Churches of God in Jesus Christ," holding to all general adventist doctrines, are an organization of independent congregations formed at Philadelphia in November, 1888. It lists 86 churches and 3,528 members.

C. E. Sears, *Days of Delusion* (1924); A. C. Johnson, *Advent Christian History* (1918); W. Miller, *Evidence from the Scriptures and History of the Second Coming of Christ* (1838); Census of Religious Bodies, *Adventist Bodies, Condensed Report, 1926* (1928). M.G.R.-W.W.S.

advocatus dei: (Lat. *advocatus*, the called or summoned and *Deus*, God) The one officially promoting a case of beatification or canonization.** L.R.W.

advocatus diaboli: (Lat. *advocatus*, the called or summoned and *diabolus*, the devil) A person, also called *Promotor Fidei*, appointed to prepare in writing all possible grounds for not beatifying or canonizing one proposed for such honor. See beatification; canonization. L.R.W.

advowson: (*advocatio*) In English law, the right of a patron* to presentation*; but when the bishop himself is the patron this right is known as collation. Till 1898 advowsons might also be donative, in which case the patron's rights were practically unrestricted. The Crown is patron paramount and presents where other patrons fail. Where the right belongs to a Roman Catholic it is exer-cised by Oxford or Cambridge University. Q.B.

Aelfric: (ca. 955-1020) Anglo-Saxon abbot and author. Compiled a grammar (hence his cognomen "Grammaticus"). Translated parts of OT. Wrote several widely used books of homilies, most famous being "The Lives of the Saints." Influenced the development of English prose. E.C.K.

aeon, eon: (Gr. *aion*, age) 1) An age,* or the whole duration, of the world; eternity. 2) In Platonic philosophy, the Eternal Being whose counterpart in the world of sense is Time (Timaeus 37D). 3) In earlier Gnosticism,* the Absolute Being, or, in later Gnosticism, successive emanations* from the Supreme Deity, which form the Pleroma ,the world of light or higher reality, divided by a gulf from the darkness of phenomenal being. This doctrine almost certainly derives from Mithraism.* E.M.N.

aesthetics: Aesthetics, as the philosophy of art, shows 1) how the common liking of sensuous appearances may grow into instructed liking through knowledge and training. The datum for study is the immediate concrete situation with the human being and his sentiments, approvals, and aversions on one side, and a phenomenon with a colored or sounding surface, form, and intention on the other, with, finally, a relationship of agreement or disagreement between the two. This indissoluble unity of human aesthetic experience remains throughout the aesthetician's control. But he examines the development of value* and meaning in it by analyzing it into parts, and establishing the conditions under which the parts, and the whole, gradually become richer and more harmonious. Pleasant feeling rises to connoisseurship by long acquaintance with and study of the best that man has produced throughout time in the arts. The aesthetician therefore studies the psychological and social conditions of taste in various periods: e.g., the infusion of religious conviction into the taste of St. Augustine and Ruskin, of acquaintance with Japanese prints into that of Whistler, of predilection for scientific clarity into that of Descartes and Fechner.** Light is thrown on the directions of taste not only by the general climate of interest in any period or particular individual, but also by physical and psychological researches: e.g. by Helmholtz's work on the "partials" or "overtones" of a given sound and Scripture's on voice production.

The initial liking and disliking become finally transparent structures with bonds of necessary relaiton, and thus judgments with authority in their own sphere, analogous to the judgments of the physicist or chemist on the constitution of the physical world.

2) But the philosopher of art notes not only the conditions of change from bare and brute liking to instructed taste, but also the tendency of authoritative preference in the arts to become active *forming* instead of passive *receiving*. Learning about art rises toward the doing of artistic deeds. Liking takes on more and more the quality of the creative imagination, so that there is truth in the paradox that a good critic or connoisseur is a second creator. But if aesthetic liking grows into imaginative making, an understanding of creation in the arts is a presupposition of the understanding of taste. Samuel Alexander's researches on the relation of artistic creation to the constructive instinct and to cosmic creation as also Coleridge's and Croce's** definitions of art as lyrical making, tend to recast, in the aesthetician's theory, that original datum of the aesthetic situation that was composed of liking, a phenomenon, and proportion. It ceases to be possible for the philosopher to study the end-product of artistic activity without reference to the activity and inspiration of its producer.

Two inadequate views of aesthetics have been common: 1) that it has to do with the immediate appreciation of sensuous values and relations, apart from historical and scientific knowledge; 2) that it treats generalized meanings: the various definitions of critical terms used in connection with the arts, in abstraction from a delighted sense of the body of art facts relevant to the definitions. *Mutatis Mutandis,* Kant's* pronouncement on abstract empiricism and abstract rationalism applies here: appreciation without knowledge is empty; definition without feeling is dead.

The method of aesthetics is neither a serial consideration of definitions, conceptions, problems, or topics, nor a summary of impressionistic reactions to beauties, but a dialectical development of the full meaning of art's meaning and place in human experience. See fine arts.

Students of Aesthetics often best support their theories by critical works in the arts, as for example: Lascelles Abercrombie, *The Theory of Poetry* (1926); Carroll C. Pratt, *The Meaning of Music* (1931); Erwin Panofsky, *Studies in Iconology* (1939); but in Aesthetics proper, DeWitt H. Parker, *Principles of Aesthetics* (1920); Louis Flaccus, *The Spirit and Substance of Art* (1941); Max Schoen, *Art and Beauty* (1932); Theodore M. Greene, *The Arts and the Art of Criticism* (1940); John Dewey, *Art as Experience* (1934); are useful compendia. Samuel Alexander, *Beauty and Other Forms of Value* (1933); R. G. Collingwood, *The Principles of Art* (1938) are more original essays in the field. K.E.G.

aetiology: See etiology.

affinity, marital impediment of: See marital impediments.

African Methodist Episcopal Church, the: See negro church, the.

African Methodist Episcopal Zion Church, the: See negro church, the.

African Orthodox Church: A colored religious sect founded and headed by George Alexander McGuire, who holds the title of Metropolitan and Primate. McGuire was a priest in the Protestant

Episcopal Church, but founded his own denomination when he obtained what he and others regarded as valid orders in apostolic succession* from Joseph Rene Vilatte, who was ordained by Archbishop Alvarey of Ceylon, by permission of the Patriarch of Antioch, Syrian Jacobite Church, to be archbishop of the American Old Catholic Church. McGuire in turn ordained a bishop, who seceded from him and started a rival church in Brooklyn. The African Orthodox Church claims 13 congregations with nearly two thousand members. E.T.C.

affusion: Baptism in the Christian churches has been single and trine, in running and still water and from or in fonts, into or upon the name of Jesus and the Trinity and in three forms: immersion, or dipping; pouring, or affusion, or infusion; and sprinkling, or aspersion. C.H.M.

agape: (Gr. love) Among the Christians of the early centuries the Agape was a common religious meal of fellowship (love-feast*) of uncertain origin. Although at first it was probably a separate rite (possibly a Christian adaptation of similar meals which were quite prevalent in the Mediterranean world), it was frequently associated with the sacrament of the Eucharist, and at times (cf. Ignatius of Antioch) it was assimilated to it. However, from the second century on it was increasingly detached from the sacrament, and in contrast to it was normally celebrated in the evening, and seldom on Sunday. A real meal, not symbolic like the Eucharist,* it was held in private homes or in churches, with a bishop, presbyter, or deacon presiding. According to Hippolytus, the host provided the meal, invited the guests (among them the poor and needy), and expected the guests in return to pray for him. From Tertullian we learn that the meal was preceded by and concluded with prayer. Also, after eating, each one present sang a hymn or psalm, and possibly "prophesied." The function of the Agape was to promote Christian fellowship (love) among those participating, and to unite them in closer relationship with Christ, who was considered to be the unseen head of the table. In this respect it was functionally related to the Eucharist. Increasingly the meal became a charity supper, or else a memorial to the departed, and by the eighth century had practically disappeared. In modern times the Love-Feast, in one form or another, was revived by the Moravians, Mennonites, Dunkards,** and other sects, and also was used by the Methodists. See sacramental meal. Also see Lundensian theology. M.R.

agapetae: (Gr. *agapetai*, beloved) 1) In the 1st century, virgins consecrated to God by a vow of chastity, but so closely associated with laymen that abuses occurred which the Council of Ancyra (314) condemned. 2) Branch of the Gnostics* (395). J.B.C.

Agatha, St.: A Sicilian noblewoman, put to death during the Decian persecution at Catania in A.D. 251 because of her Christian beliefs by Quintianus the Consular of Sicily. S.M.G.

age: According to Jewish time reckoning. Till thirteen years of age and a day a boy is regarded as a minor (*Katan*) and legally incompetent. Thereafter, provided he shows certain signs of physical maturity, he reaches his legal majority. In the case of a girl, minority ceases at the age of 12 years and a day, but her full legal competency begins 6 months after that. *Mishnah Abot* 5:21 which lists the various ages of man, makes 18 the proper age for marriage. The Biblical conception of the span of life is expressed in Ps. XC, 10: "The days of our years are three score and ten . . . and if by reason of strength they be fourscore years . . ." Similarly in the Talmud,* "If one dies at 80, one has reached old age" (*Baba Batra* 75 a). B.Z.B.

age, canonical: The age at which by canon law* the Church permits the faithful to receive the Sacraments, e.g., or requires them to fast. L.R.W.

ages: See aeon; culture epochs; cycles of time; golden age.

Agnes, St.: Roman virgin martyr of the persecution of Diocletian, venerated as a model of purity and patron of young girls. E.R.H.

Agni: The Vedic god of fire, whether the hearth fire, lightning or the sun. He was the priest god since it was through fire that the offerings were transmitted to the gods. He also had definite ethical functions as forgiver and punisher of sin. See Fire Gods. C.S.B.

Agnoetae: (Gr. not omniscient) In the 4th century, a sect which denied that God remembered the past without reflection or knew the future with any certainty. Sometimes called Theophronians, from their leader Theophronius of Cappadocia. In the 6th century, a sect of the Monophysites* which asserted that in some respects the human soul of Christ was not all-knowing. Sometimes called Themistians, after the deacon Themistius who first adopted the view. S.M.G.

agnosticism: (Gr. *a-*, not, and *gignoskein*, to know) The belief that certain knowledge has not been attained, either in some particular field (usually the religious), or in any and all fields of supposed knowledge. Agnosticism often shades into skepticism,* but the agnostic leaves open the possibility of future knowledge, while the skeptic (except for the methodological type) denies any such possibility. The term "agnostic" was first used by T. Huxley in 1869 (OED); he based it on Acts 17:23. E.S.B.

agnus dei: (Lat., Lamb of God) 1) The figure of a lamb, symbolizing Jesus (John 1, 29) as the sacrificial victim for the world's sins. 2) The liturgical invocation, "O Lamb of God, that takest away the sins of the world, have mercy upon us," used in the Mass* or service of Holy Communion. P.V.N.

Agobard: (769-840) Scholar, saint. Archbishop of Lyons, 816. He opposed 'weathermaking," judicial ordeals, Jews, allegorization of worship; assisted the revolt against Charlemagne's successor, Louis.

agrapha: "Things unwritten"; the technical term for sayings of Jesus not recorded in the Gospels. Several of them are found elsewhere in the NT (e.g. Ac. 20:35. 1 Thess. 4:15); others in the Apocryphal Gospels; most of them in the early Fathers. Recent discoveries, chiefly in Egypt, have brought to light a number of sayings ascribed to Jesus, and two leaves of papyrus, found at Oxyrhyncus, were evidently part of a considerable collection of such sayings. The existing agrapha may be reckoned at several hundreds, but very few, perhaps not so many as twenty, have any real claim to authenticity.

A. Resch, *Agrapha* (1897; 1906); M. James, *The Apocryphal N. T.* (1924); B. Pick, *Paralipomena* (1908). E.F.S.

Agricola, Johannes: (1494-1566) German Reformer, was involved in bitter controversy with Luther over antinomianism.* He was later influential and active at the court of Brandenburg. G.R.C.

ahimsa: Variously translated as harmlessness, non-injury, non-killing. A Hindu doctrine expressive of the oneness and sacredness of all life, human and sub-human, it is held with various degrees of strictness by different Indian religious groups. It is observed more rigorously in Buddhism than Hinduism generally, but most strictly of all by the Jains.* Mr. Gandhi's technique of non-violent non-cooperation is a political adaptation of the principle. C.S.B.

Ahriman (Angra Mainyu): Personified principle of evil and opposed to Ormazd. See Persia, religions of; Zoroastrianism. V.F.

Ahura Mazda: See Ormazd.

Ajivikas: A humanistic sect of Hinduism founded by Gosala Mankhali-putta in the sixth century B.C. Closely similar to Jainism, but differing chiefly in their rigorous doctrine of determinism; and in certain moral practices. C.S.B.

Akbar: (1542-1605) Third of the Moghul Emperors of India, 1556-1605. A Moslem by birth and training he was remarkably tolerant for his age. In his Hall of Worship he presided over religious discussions participated in by Hindus, Moslems, Christians, Atheists, Jews, Parsis and others. He founded a new eclectic religion which he called "The Divine Faith." C.S.B.

Akiba: (c. 50-c. 135) One of the greatest of the Palestinian Tannaim* or early teachers of the Law.* The first 40 years of his life Akiba spent in complete ignorance; however, at the urging of his wife, Rachel, he devoted himself to the study of the Law and, after 12 years, was recognized as a master. He systematized the accepted Halakah* (religious practice) of his day and propounded new hermeneutic principles which greatly expanded the scope of the Halakah and facilitated its development. Akiba's genius also made itself felt in philosophy, in Haggadah* and in contemporary political events. He, more than anyone else, merits the title "father of Rabbinic Judaism." See rabbinism. E.B.-L.F.

Akron theatre plan: See church building.

alb: A long tunic, often worn under other vestments*; in the East of any color, in the West usually and in modern times invariably white. hence the name (Lat. *alba*). E.R.H.

Albert of Brandenburg: (1490-1545) Elector and archbishop of Mainz. Against the abuses of an indulgence granted him by Leo X,* Luther made his famous protest. Albert was one of the more liberal Catholic princes during the Reformation struggles and a patron of art and learning. G.R.C.

Albert, the Great (Albert of Bollstädt): See Albertus Magnus.

Albert of Prussia: (1490-1568) Grand master of the Teutonic Order. He accepted the Reformed faith, and transformed Prussia into an hereditary duchy. As first duke he influenced the fortunes of Reformation in eastern Europe. G.R.C.

Albertus Magnus: Albert was born at Lauingen, Suabia, in 1206, the eldest son of the Count of Bollstädt. He attended the University of Padua, and from there entered the Dominican Order* in 1223. After teaching in several German cities, he came to Paris in 1245, where he remained for three years and received his doctorate in theology. His next twelve years were filled with teaching and administrative duties. In 1260 he was named bishop of Ratisbon. He continued active until his memory failed in 1278. Death followed two years later in 1280. Pius XI named him Doctor and extended his feast to the universal Church. One of the greatest minds of the thirteenth century, Albert's writings cover a great scope. His interest and achievements in the experimental sciences were phenomenal for his time. He is also justly famous as the man who recognized the genius of the young Thomas Aquinas.*

T. M. Schwertner, *St. Albert the Great* (1932); J. Sighart, *Albert the Great* (tr. from the French by T. A. Dixon, London, 1876). P.S.M.

Albigenses: A body of heretics in S. France, named after the town Albi, in 11th-13th centuries, a branch of the Cathari.* Their external anti-clerical criticism was the main cause of their persecution. The ecclesiastical authorities discovered, however, that they held Manichaean* doctrines and followed Manichaean practices. For long this was regarded as an invention of the Church of Rome, but the work of A. V. Williams Jackson and F. C. Burkitt in recent years has established the truth of this "charge." The result is a mystical asceticism, based on the concept of the evil of matter and of light as the only good. The best summary of their doctrine of salvation is the 18th century hymn "Eternal Light, Eternal Light." F.W.B.

Albo, Joseph: (1380-1444) Largely rehashing the problems which occupied Maimonides,* Gersonides and Crescas, he was a popularizer rather than an original follower of his teacher Crescas. For Albo the defense against Christian polemicists became an even more outspoken issue. He formulated an orthodox Jewish theology, the *Book of Principles* (Heb. *Sefer Ha-Ikkarim*). Living in an age of religious disputations and forced conversions, he defended Judaism against Christianity, showing his people that Judaism is the true religion. The establishment of essential dogmas was his central theme. He contends that divine religion is based upon three general principles: existence of God, revelation, reward and punishment after death. Then there are special or derived principles peculiar to a particular religion, following from the initial general principles. He refutes Christian principles against Judaism as errors in fact, not as errors in approach.

S. Back, *Joseph Albos Bedeutung in der Geschichte der jüdischen Religionsphilosophie* (Breslau, 1869); Husik, I., *Sefer Ha-Ikkarim.* 5 vols. Critically edited on the basis of Hebrew manuscripts and old editions and provided with a translation and notes. (1929-1930); I. Husik, "Joseph Albo, the last of the Jewish Mediaeval Philosophers," in *Proceedings of the American Academy for Jewish Research* (1930); A. Tänzer, *Die Religionsphilosophie Joseph Albos nach seinem Werke Ikkarrim systematisch dargestellt und erläutert* (Frank a. M., 1896). H.H.

Albright, Jacob: See Evangelical Church, the.

Alcuin: (735-804) Born England. Greatest scholar of his age. Master Charlemagne's Court school, superintended his educational program. Opposed adoptionism.* Revised the Vulgate. Sought conversion of Invaders by evangelization, not force. See scholasticism. R.E.E.H.

Alden-Tuthill Lectureship, The: To provide each year a series of lectures at the Chicago Theological Seminary upon the subject of religion on some frontier of modern life. Founded, 1925. Among the distinguished lecturers have been Dr. Richard C. Cabot, the Honorable Henry A. Wallace, Professor William E. Hocking, Dr. Arthur E. Morgan, Dean Willard L. Sperry, Professor John C. Bennett, and Professor Halford E. Luccock. F.E.

Aldhelm, Saint: (ca. 640-749) Anglo-Saxon abbot, bishop and scholar. Introduced Benedictine rule and extended influence of Roman Christianity in southern England. Wrote flowery prose and poetry. Most famous work: 101 riddles in Latin hexameters. E.C.K.

Alexander, St., Bishop of Alexandria: (A.D. c. 273-326) The ecclesiastical superior of Arius* and initiator from the orthodox standpoint of the Arian Controversy; the patron and episcopal predecessor also of Athanasius.* Theologically Alexander seems to have belonged to the anti-"scientific" school of Christian thought that had arisen in Alexandria early in the fourth century and that may have been rooted in earlier developments. While not uninfluenced by one side of Origen's* thought (cf. Athanasius) and not accustomed to express itself precisely in the terms of the Nicene theology, its position is esentially that of the Creed of A.D. 325. Indeed the ultimate debt of the Nicene* position to Alexander is very great.

Harnack (*History of Dogma,* vol. IV) gives the best account of Alexander's doctrinal standpoint. See also J. H. Newman, *The Arians of the Fourth Century* (1833). Alexander's "Epistles on the Arian Heresy" are printed in English in *The Ante-Nicene Fathers,* vol. VI. Cf. Bibliography given under the article "Arianism." C.W.L.

Alexander of Hales: (died ca. 1245) Through his powerful incomplete *Summa universae theologicae,* he is the founder of scholasticism in the strict sense. It is a large handbook of speculative theology, dialectically elaborated. His theory of principles elaborates the thoughts of Augustine, Anselm and Hugo of St. Victor in accordance with Aristotelian categories. Scholasticism owes to him the perfection of a teaching method in philosophy and theology, namely the triple division of a question into the *pro,* the *contra,* and the *resolutio;* and the application of dialectic to dogma. His view on religious knowledge became normative for the entire older school of Franciscans.

J. A. Endres, "Des Alexander von Hales Leben und psychologische Lehre," *Philosophisches Jahrbuch* (Fulda, 1888); F. J. Picavet, "Abélard et Alexandre de Halès, créateurs de la méthode scholastique," *Sciences Religieuses,* vols. V, VI (Paris, 1894, 1895). H.H.

Alexander III, Pope: (1159-1181) Born of a famous Sienese family, Orlando Bardinelli distinguished himself as a canonist (Commentary on the *Decretum Gratiani,* cf. "Decretals") at Bologna. In 1150 he was called to Rome by Pope Eugene III where he was successively created Cardinal Deacon, Cardinal Priest and Papal Chamberlain. As trusted adviser of Adrian IV* he was regarded as the soul of the independent party of cardinals who sought to escape the German yoke by allying the Church with the Normans of Naples. For openly asserting before Frederick Barbarossa at the Diet of Besancon (1157) that the imperial dignity was a papal *Beneficium* (in the general sense of favor, not feudal sense of fief) he incurred the wrath of the German princes and would have fallen on the spot under the battleaxe of his life-long foe, Otto of Wittelsbach, had Frederick not intervened. Despite the emperor's influence over the cardinals, exercised especially by the afore-said Otto of Wittelsbach and Rainald von Dassel, Cardinal Orlando received 19 out of a possible 22 votes for the papacy and took the name of Alexander III. Cardinal Ottavian, although receiving only the remaining three votes, was crowned as Anti-Pope,* Victor IV (1159-1164). Alexander responded to the packed Assembly at Pavia, that was to decide between the two contenders for the tiara, by promptly excommunicating from Anagni the emperor, Feb. 11, 1160 and by releasing the latter's subjects from their oath of allegiance. From now on the pope allied himself with the Lombard League (cf. "Guelfs and Ghibellines") which erected in his honor the city of Alessandria. The ensuing schism, far more disastrous to the empire than to the papacy, despite the creation of three additional anti-popes: Paschal III (1164-1168); Callixtus III (1168-1179) and Innocent III (1179-

1180), lasted seventeen years and ended only after the Battle of Legnano, 1176 and the unconditional surrender of the haughty Barbarossa, in Venice, 1177. That the pope on this occasion placed his foot on the emperor's neck is a childish legend.

While an exile in France (1162-1165) Alexander came in direct contact with Henry II of England, at that time the most powerful monarch of the West. The pope was notably drawn into the controversy between the king and Thomas of Becket* regarding the rights of the Church of England and lived to see Henry penitentially praying for pardon at the tomb of the martyred Archbishop of Canterbury. Alexander III's crowning triumph for the Church was the celebration of the Third Lateran Council (cf. "Lateran Councils") in 1179, attended by 300 bishops, in which the famous decree was enacted reserving henceforth the election of a pope exclusively to a two-thirds majority vote of the cardinals. The pope died shortly thereafter, Aug. 30, 1181. Alexander III was a learned canonist, not inferior to Boniface VIII (cf. "*Unam Sanctam*") or Innocent III*; a diplomatic strategist and an energetic defender of the liberties of the Church.

His letters were published by Jaffé, in *Regesta Roman. Pontif.*, nos. 10584-14424 and by Löwenfeld, *Epistolae Pontif. Roman. ineditae* (Leipzig, 1885). Other sources; *Liber Pontificalis* (edit. Duchense) II, 394-446. cf. *ib.* Preface, p. XLII-XLIII and Hefele, *Conciliengeschichte*, 2, V, 520-720. R.M.H.

Alexander, Samuel: (1859-1938) Developed the famous distinction between deity and God. Deity is the fact that just beyond any level of evolution a new emergent level is to arise. God is the universe conceived as possessing deity. He regards human consciousness as being in a sense deity, and holds at the same time that the human spirit is deity, not for man, but for the lower level, body. The human soul is deity for the body. In the next stage of cosmic evolution some unimaginable, yet inevitable superman is deity for man. God is not identical with human aspiration, but is an objective character of nature as a whole. God is objectively real.

Space, Time, and Deity. 2 vols. (London, 1920). H.H.

Alexandrian Library: The most famous of ancient libraries, founded by Ptolemy I, in connection with the Museum, a group of scholars supported by the state. It was greatly enlarged by his son Philadelphus, and his librarian Demetrius of Phalerum, who proposed to assemble in it copies of all the books in the world. He told the king he already had 200,000 rolls, and hoped soon to have 500,000. Seneca says 400,000 books were burned during Caesar's campaign at Alexandria, but the Library was reestablished, and Aulus Gellius, in the second century after Christ, says it contained 700,000 books. It was for this library, according to Jewish tradition, (Letter of Aristeas) that the Septuagint version* of the Jewish scriptures (probably meaning the Law of Moses, Gen.-Deut.) was made. The smaller library, in the Serapeum, was probably destroyed by the Patriarch Theophilus, about A.D. 390, along with the Serapeum, though others (following Abu'l Faraj—Barhebraeus—14th century) say it survived until A.D. 641, when the Caliph Omar had the books burned to heat the baths of Alexandria. On the whole, the fate of the Alexandrian libraries remains obscure. The Great Library was headed by a succession of distinguished scholars. E.J.G.

Alexandrian (Coptic) rite: The complexus of liturgical and disciplinary laws and customs originally used in the patriarchate of Alexandria. Variants of this rite are followed by the Monophysite Copts (1,120,000 in Egypt; 2,700,000 in Ethiopia) and by Catholic Egyptians and Ethiopians (59,000). The Orthodox Coptic Melchites* follow since the 13th century the Byzantine rite.* E.A.R.

Alexandrian school: The provisions made at Alexandria for the training of the catechumens* led to the development of a Christian university there under the inspiring succession of Pantaenus (died 202), Clement (died 220), and Origen** (died 254). Its chief characteristics were an allegorical method of Scriptural interpretation, and a speculative type of theology under the influence of Greek philosophy and especially of Philo.* The influence of this spirit was widespread in the East, and the term Alexandrian School is commonly used to designate those who reevaled this spirit, whether they were actually Alexandrians or not. See allegorical interpretation. A.K.R.

Alexians: The name given to the Alexian Brothers. At Mechlin, in Brabant, in the 15th century during the "Black Death," a number of laymen, taking no vows or rule of life, united under a certain Tobias to care for the sick. Later this group chose as a patron St. Alexius, who had served in the hospitals in Syria for many years, and they called themselves the Alexian Brothers. The order spread rapidly through Germany, Brabant, Flanders, and other countries. At present they have several hospitals in the United States, as well as others in England and Belgium. T.T.M.

Alfarabi: (died 950) One of the famous Arabs who attempted to harmonize Hellenistic philosophy and Mohammedan* mysticism. He recognized the need of logic for islamitic speculation, at the same time he found great support in Neo-Platonism* for his Sufi* mysticism. Alfarabi anticipated many of the doctrines of Avicenna and Averroes.** His interpretation of the human soul as an activation of the light emanating from a cosmic intellect, clearly antedates Averroes' doctrine of the mind. Alfarabi's logical treatises, his commentaries and his *De Ortu Scientiarum* were greatly used in the Middle Ages. S.C.T.

Alfred the Great: (849-899) King of the West Saxons (871-), warrior and Christian scholar. Alfred is culturally important for his translations of Orosius, Boethius, Bede, Gregory the Great, etc., and for his promotion of education. J.T.M.

Algazali; Al-Ghazzali: (1059-1111)The greatest theologian of Islam.* Professor at the Nizamite Academy at Baghdad four years, he abandoned his career for a pilgrimage in search of certainty. Widely learned in the knowledge of his age, his work has been compared with that of St. Augustine in Christianity. His chief work *Ihya Ulum ad-Din* (The resuscitation of the sciences of religion).

D. B. Macdonald, *Muslim Theology* (1903).

P.G.M.

Al-Kindi or Alchindus: (d. 870) Arabian astrologer and physician at the court of Al-Mamoon, Caliph of Bagdad. He considered science, mathematics and logic as the proper approach to philosophy, and made Aristotle accessible to his followers. In his own theology he was a Neoplatonist.*

P.E.J.

Allah: (Contraction of Arabic *al-ilah*, meaning the god, or the worshipped) The proper name for God in Islam. The term seems to have been used by Arabians in ancient times as a supreme god, and since the reforms of Mohammed as the only God. The first article in the Moslem creed declares, "There is no God but Allah." It is also used as the name for God by Arabic-speaking persons of other faiths, as Syrian Christians. See Mohammedanism. P.E.J.

allegorical interpretation: When a book, or collection of books, from the past is regarded as an inspired, authoritative standard of religious belief and conduct, it becomes necessary to reinterpret it to fit later beliefs and practices, disregarding its literal or plain meaning. Many ingenious methods of reinterpretation are resorted to, among them the allegorical by which a hidden, symbolic, metaphorical, "spiritual" meaning is discovered beneath the literal. Thus the later Greeks rationalized, thereby retaining, the Homeric myths (likewise the myth of Isis and Osiris) by finding in them a veiled but highly significant religious, philosophical, and ethical teaching through allegorization. Similarly, the Jews of Palestine, in accommodating the inspired words of Scripture to later times, adopted various types of interpretation, including the allegorical. Allegorical exegesis, however, was much more widely applied by the Hellenistic Jews, among them Philo* of Alexandria, confronted as they were by the necessity of reconciling their inherited faith with the Hellenistic thought which they had appropriated. The first Christians accepted the Jewish Scripture as binding and authoritative, but made it so by allegorizing it, finding underneath the literal meaning veiled prophecies concerning Christ and the new dispensation. Still later Christians, such as Justin, Clement, and Origen,** by using the Philonic method of exegesis, accommodated the O.T. to the developing theology, which was increasingly Hellenistic in character. In time parts of the N.T. were allegorized, with Augustine,* for example, reading the entire scheme of salvation into the parable of the Good Samaritan. Allegorical exegesis of the Bible dominated the succeeding centuries, and is widely used even today; but needless to say is rejected by modern biblical scholarship. See Alexandrian school; anagogical interpretation; exegesis; literal interpretation; types.

The following monographs, though somewhat old, have not been superseded: F. W. Farrar, *History of Interpretation* (1886); G. H. Gilbert, *Interpretation of the Bible: A Short History* (1908). M.R.

allegory: (Gr. *allegoria*) Literally a description of one thing under the image of another. Although in popular usage often confused with parable,* the two are essentially dissimilar. The parable sets one thing against another, the allegory substitutes one thing for another. A properly constructed parable must be true to life, must picture people acting as people really act, and normally seeks to make but one point clear. For the allegory no such requirement exists. Justice may be depicted with veiled eyes though she holds in her hands scales which she must read. Every detail of an allegory (unlike a parable) is added, not because it is needed for the story, but to mean something, to represent something else which the teller wishes to represent. Thus frequently the allegory (unlike the parable) is of great length. This form of figurative speech is ancient and has been popular in the literatures of most nations. Examples from antiquity are provided in the allegory of the Vine (Ps. 80), the Door (John 10), and the so-called Similitudes in the Shepherd of Hermas. Among the most elaborate and sustained examples are Spenser's *Faerie Queene* and Bunyan's *Pilgrim's Progress*.

By *allegorical interpretation* is meant the attempts by later readers to treat as allegory what was not originally so intended. This type of pseudo-exposition has been common among all peoples of all ages. Familiar examples may be seen in the transmutation of some of the more robust stories from Homer into philosophical principles and in the Jewish and Christian treatment of the Song of Songs. Other examples of this universal tendency may be seen in the writings of Philo Judæus and in the Epistle of Barnabas. See exegesis; interpretation; types.

B. T. D. Smith, *The Parables of the Synoptic Gospels* (1937). M.S.E.

alleluia: A responsorial chant used in the mass* every Sunday except during Lent. The word Alleluia occurs in neumatic style with an elaborate melisma on the last vowel. See plainsong; psalmody. E.H.B.

Alliance of Reformed Churches: "The Alliance of the Reformed Churches Throughout the World Holding the Presbyterian System," i.e. Reformed* or Calvinistic churches of Presbyterian polity, was formed in London in 1875. It held "the First Presbyterian General Council" in Edinburgh in 1877. Its general councils are quadrennial. It is divided into Sections pertaining to hemispheres, Eastern and Western. The Sections hold annual meetings. The councils and meetings are for conference and have no ecclesiastical authority.

R.H.N.

All Saints' Day: November 1, each year, is observed in the Roman, Anglican and various other Christian groups as a day upon which saints, not otherwise mentioned by name in the calendar, and those whose names are not known in the Church

Militant, are commemorated. In recent years, Protestant denominations have also observed the day. W.N.P.

All Souls' Day: A day set apart each year in the Roman, Anglican and other non-Protestant Christian groups for the commemoration of "holy souls" who have departed this life, and are in the intermediate state awaiting their final end. The day is observed with solemn services, usually including requiem masses. November 2 is normally the date, in the calendars of churches of western Christendom. See necrology; requiem. W.N.P.

alms and almsgiving: See charity and almsgiving.

Alogi: A name given in contempt to those who rejected the Logos doctrine of the Fourth Gospel. They flourished towards the end of the 2nd century, and their leader seems to have been one Gaius, against whom Hippolytus wrote a book which is now lost. The word "alogos" has the double meaning of "opposed to the Logos" and "devoid of reason."

E. J. Goodspeed, *Early Christian Literature* (1942). E.F.S.

alphabetic writing: System of writing invented in the second millenium B. C. (?) by the Semites or the Egyptians, which greatly improved upon the ideographic and syllabic writings by discriminating between consonantal and vocalic sounds. The Ugaritic* alphabet represents a North-Syrian attempt, of cuneiform* appearance, which was later abandoned. The Old Hebrew Alphabet, which is probably derived in part from the script of the Serabit-el-Khadim inscriptions (Sinai), is related to the Phoenician and most of the modern Alphabets. Square Hebrew, in which the Massoretic text* of the OT is written, is an Aramaic transformation of the Old Hebrew Alphabet. See moabite stone; Siloam inscription; and Lachish Ostraca.

H. Bauer, *Der Ursprung des Alphabets* (1937); J. W. Flight, "The Present State of Studies in the History of Writing in the Near East," in *The Haverford Symposium on Archeology and the Bible*, edited by E. Grant (1938) pp. 111-135. S.L.T.

altar: A place for communicating with a god or the dead by means of sacrifice* or offerings. In early religions, when man found supernatural potencies in many phases of the natural environment offerings were sometimes presented on the ground, on mountain tops, thrown into water or attached to trees wherever these powers were manifest, with no artificial preparation of a sacred place. The constructed altar was a later development. The earliest forms were simple—a natural rock, the ground strewn with a special grass, a mound of earth or a heap of stones. Among the Semites* the altar was a place of slaughter. A natural rock with channels for carrying off the blood, a mound of earth or of unhewn stones surrounded by a trench preceded the elevated cut-stone structure with a wide platform. The presence of the deity was marked by a standing stone smeared with the offering. The fire altar, the altar of incense came later when gifts to the god were burned. The bronze altars of Solomon's* temple may show Phoenician influence. The Indo-European altar was a ritually-prepared sacred place strewn with grass. In India, the importance of the sacrifice and the ingenuity of the priests produced elaborate structures embodying symbolism in their form and manner of building. In China the local altars from earliest times have been mounds of earth. In the state cult, however, the mound was replaced by imposing marble altars in the annual sacrifices to Heaven and Earth. The altar of Heaven was circular with three terraces, the altar of Earth square with two terraces. Since the early gods of the religions were nature powers, the altars were originally in the open air. They range in form from the simple rock or mound to the magnificent sculptured altars of Greece, China's dignified altar of Heaven and the Brahmanic fire altar which took a year to build. Wherever the deity was enshrined in a temple, the altar took the form of a table. Sacrifice by slaughter and burning yielded to more subtile, symbolic forms of communion. The altar of the eucharist, the "Lord's Table"* of the Christian church retains the sacrificial idea in refined form. See blood; dancing; sanctuary; temples. A.E.H.

altar bread: Bread specially prepared for the Eucharist, whether unleavened (West and Armenian Church) or leavened (East); in Anglicanism the use of unleavened altar bread was among the customs revived in the 19th century. Wafer is a purely popular term for the Western form of unleavened altar bread. See ritualism. E.R.H.

altar-fellowship: A term popular among the Lutherans in referring to participation in the Eucharist as signifying unity of faith, mixed altar-fellowship being synonymous with "open communion" and unmixed altar-fellowship with "close communion."* See Galesburg Rule. T.A.K.

Althaus, Paul: (1888-) He first taught in Rostock. Now he is at the University of Erlangen. A leader of confessional Lutheranism, he has been laboring in giving its theological heritage a new form. As a systematic theologian, he has reinforced the theological consciousness of the study of the NT; the use of the religious-historical material in hermeneutic investigations. With Heim,* he regards the rearrangement of apologetic principles and analyses indispensable. He is the leading theologian of the group *theologia militans*, a group which showed for some time noticeable resistance to Nazi ideology. In contrast to Barth* he upholds the traditional concept of general revelation. He has important ideas about the dialectical tension between creation and sin, eternity and history. His views on the doctrine of the divine orders renders the prospect of a Christian social ethic more adequately possible. His greatest contribution is to eschatology in which field he wrote the most important work of our time.

Die Prinzipien der deutschen reformerten Scholastik (Leipzig, 1914); *Das Erlebnis der Kirche* (Leipzig, 1919, 2 ed., Leipzig, 1924); *Religöser Sozialismus* (Gütersloh, 1921); *Die letzten Dinge* (Gütersloh,

1922, 4 ed., Gütersloh, 1933); *Staatsgedanke und Reich Gottes* (Erlangen, 1923, 4 ed., Erlangen, 1931); *Die Krise der Ethik* (Berlin, 1926); *Die Weltreligionen und das Christentum* (München, 1928); *Grundriss der Dogmatik* (Erlangen, 1929); *Christentum und Kultur* (Leipzig, 1929); *Theologische Aufsätze* (Gütersloh, 1929); "Die Theologie" in K. Schweitzer *Das religiöse Deutschland der Gegenwart* (Berlin, 1930); *Grundriss der Ethik* (Erlangen, 1931); *Unsterblichkeit und ewiges Leben bei Luther* (Leipzig, 1931); *Theologie der Ordnungen* (Gütersloh, 1934); *Politisches Christentum* (Leipzig, 1935); A. Beyer, *Offenbarung und Geschichte* (Schwerin, 1932); K. E. Olimart, *Der Begriffe der Schöpfungsordnung in der Ev. Theologie der Gegenwart* (Essen, 1933). H.H.

Amana Community, the: Located in Iowa County, Iowa, originally composed of pietistic Germans, dates from 1714 when Eberhard Ludwig Gruber, a Lutheran clergyman and Johann Friedrich Rock, rebelling against the formalism of German Lutheranism, withdrew from the Church and formed what they called the Community of True Inspiration. Persecution drove them to America (1842) where they purchased land in Erie County, New York, established several villages, built numerous industries and cultivated the soil on a large scale. Their way of life was completely communistic and they prospered. The rapid growth of the City of Buffalo, threatening their isolation led them to remove to Iowa in 1854. Here they established seven villages, instituted manufacturing enterprises, and placed under cultivation many thousands of acres in one of the garden spots of Iowa. In 1832, by unanimous vote of the members of the community their communistic organization gave way to a Joint Stock Company and religion and business were completely separated. This was made necessary not only because of changing economic and social conditions surrounding them, but also because of the waning of the old religious idealism and the gradual departure from the spiritual enthusiasm of their fathers. See communistic settlements, religious.

Bertha M. H. Shambaugh, *Amana, The Community of True Inspiration* (1908); and *Amana that Was and Amana That Is* (1932). W.W.S.

Amarites, the: See communistic settlements, religious.

Amarna: See Tell-el-Amarna Tablets.

Amaterasu-Omikami: (Lit. "Heaven-shining Great August Deity") The primitive Japanese sun goddess. Worshipped now as the head of the imperial line and the founder of the state. D.C.H.

ambo: (Gr., *ambon,* a platform) A pulpit, reached by steps, from which the liturgical lections were sung in the ancient basilica churches. Frequently there were two, on the south for the Epistle, on the north for the Gospel. P.V.N.

Ambrose of Milan (340-397) One of the notable of the exegetes, hymn-writers and orators of the early Christian Church. Forming the bridge which led from Cyprian* to St. Augustine,* Ambrose, the bishop of Milan, was energetically engaged in the expansion and defense of inherited Christian doctrines. Noticeable intimations and beginnings of Augustine's theology are found in his views: that faith rests upon biblical authorities, that the authoritatively transmitted truth can be to some degree rationally explained; of the relation between *auctoritas* and *ratio;* the receding of the legalistic view of religion, of *lex* and *merita;* on the expansion of Adam's sin and guilt in the race by physical propagation; on the effects of Christ's work; an emphasis on the *iustificatio sola fide;* on baptism, repentance and the church. His writings and those of his contemporaries disclose also the growing invasion of the influence of the Epistle to the Romans into occidental thought. See Gregorian chant; hymns.

Th. Förster, *Ambrosius* (Halle, 1884); J. Tixeront, *Histoires des dogmes,* vol. 2 (Paris, 1906-1912). H.H.

Ambrosian chant: A form of chant* characteristic of the Milanese rite, the origin of which is traditionally ascribed to St. Ambrose* P.V.N.

Ambrosians: The name given to an order founded under the patronage of St. Ambrose* by Alexander Givelli, Antonio Petrasancta, and Albert Besazzi near Milan. In 1375 Gregory XI gave them the rule of St. Augustine modified by certain special constitutions. The new order took the name of *Fratres Sancti Ambrosii ad Nemus.* They followed the Ambrosian rite in liturgy and their duties included preaching and apostolic labors. In 1441 Eugenius IV merged all Ambrosian monasteries whose sole bond of union hitherto had been their unity of custom. In 1579 St. Charles Borromeo reformed the discipline of the order; in 1589 Sixtus V united the Brothers of St. Barnabas to the Congregation of St. Ambrose. Finally, in 1650, under Innocent X the order was dissolved. T.T.M.

Ambrosians: 16th century Anabaptist* sect which claimed immediate communication with God through the Holy Ghost. They denied the necessity of ministers, and Ambrose claimed revelations higher in authority than those of Scripture. G.R.C.

Ambrosiaster: (4th cent.) (Pseudo-Ambrose). A name given to the unknown author of a brief but important commentary on the Epistles of St. Paul, written at Rome sometime during the years 366-384. In the Middle Ages this was commonly ascribed to St. Ambrose. S.M.G.

amen: (So be it; So it is; Verily) Hebrew word of uncertain origin. In the OT the term is used responsively to give solemn ratification to a doxology,* to a curse or oath; or to some statement that has been made. In the synagogue* (but apparently not in the temple) it was repeated responsively by the congregation after doxologies and following each verse of the priestly benediction. It was not recited after prayers, either public or private, unless these ended with doxologies. Apart from the synagogue usage, individuals were enjoined to repeat it after every doxology, as, for example, those uttered before and after meals. In addition, it might be a responsive ratification of any blessing, expressed desire, wish, curse, or oath. Not unnaturally, it tended to acquire a mystical, almost magical significance. Like the Jews, the Christians from an early time came to use amen liturgically as a response to doxologies, prayers, and hymns (which usually concluded with doxologies). However ,it was not at first repeated after creeds and other liturgical formulae. Further, it was recited responsively after the consecration of the eucharist, upon receiving communion, and following baptisms and exorcisms.* In general, as among the Jews, it indicated solemn assent or ratification. Also, it came to be widely used in private prayers, in anathemas, and in gnostic or magic formulae. In Rev. 3:14 amen is a proper name for the heavenly Christ; similarly, among certain gnostics known to Hippolytus it is the name of an angel. In the synoptic gospels certain teachings of Jesus are introduced with amen (verily), apparently for the purpose of emphasis. This may well have been a characteristic of Jesus' speech, but the authenticity of the duplication of the amen as reported in John is questionable. M.R.

Amenemope: See Proverbs.

American Baptist Association: A group of conservative Baptist churches found almost, but not quite, exclusively in the South. They are the survivors of the so-called "Land Mark" Baptists, and claim direct descent from Christ and the apostles, hence "they are the divine custodians of the truth" and "they only have the divine right of carrying out the commands of Jesus as stated in the great commission, and of executing the laws of the kingdom, and of administering the ordinances of the Gospel." In theology these churches are severely fundamentalist. Headquarters are at Texarkana, Ark.-Tex. There are 1,064 churches with 115,000 members, nearly all in the rural areas. E.T.C.

American Lutheran Church: See Lutheran Church in America.

American Lutheran Conference: See Lutheran Church in America.

American Lutheranism: See Lutheran Church in America.

American Lutheranism: A name given to a movement within the American Lutheran Church led by S. S. Schmucker* beginning in the 1840's, aiming to preserve a highly moderate confessional type of Lutheranism which had become native to America (typified earlier by the body of Lutherans known as the General Synod) as over against a rising tide of conservative and strictly confessional type of Lutheranism. Those holding to the large body of confessional books of the church as normative were given the name of "Old Lutherans." The controversy which raged reflected the European conflict among Lutherans, between the "Symbolists" and "Anti-Symbolists," following the Prussian Plan of Union of Lutheran and Reformed churches of 1817. It also reflected the growing denominational consciousness and rivalry throughout Protestant America of the period. Hosts of conservative German Lutheran immigrants crowded the American Lutheran scene with a flood tide in the thirties, forties and fifties. Schmucker, the American liberal, saw the impending confessional shadow and began his campaign to save his church from falling into traditional forms and provincial isolation. The controversy reached its climax with the anonymous publication of the *Definite Synodical Platform* in 1855: a work circulated among district synods aimed at uniting American Lutherans on the common confessional ground of a more simple "American Recension of the Augsburg Confession." This pamphlet, a desperate effort on the part of S.S.S. to stem the conservative tide was not only unsuccessful but it tragically hastened the day of the loss of his leadership and it broke ties of friendship. American Lutheranism never rallied from that day to this. See Kurtz, Benjamin; Sprecher, S.

The whole story is written up in *The Crisis in American Lutheran Theology* (1927), Vergilius Ferm. V.F.

American Sunday School Union: See Sunday School movement in the United States.

American theology, early: The theology of the American colonists was naturally that of the European groups from which they sprang. Anglicans professed the Thirty-nine Articles;* Lutherans brought to America the faith set forth in the Augsburg Confession,* and Reformed that of the Heidelberg Catechism;* Congregationalists and Presbyterians adopted the Westminster Confession.*

The Puritans* of New England were the first to develop an American literature in theology. Much of their writing in the seventeenth century had to do with the problems of church polity and discipline, incident to their separation from the Church of England,* their development of "the Congregational way," and their attempt to maintain a theocracy.* After 1662, these problems were increasingly centered about the Half-way Covenant,* with Increase Mather (1639-1723), of Boston and Solomon Stoddard** (1643-1729), of Northampton the principal exponents of opposite ways of dealing with those who could give no convincing public evidence of regeneration. Yet from the first the ministers of New England were busied with theology, in the strict sense of the term, as the systematic, methodical exposition of the revelation of God.

The New England Puritans were Calvinists,* not because they attributed any external authority to John Calvin,* but because they found his doctrines to agree with their own study of the Word of God. They stated the truths of the Word in terms that were characteristic of the Federal theology,* with its emphasis upon God's covenant, and its distinction between the covenant of nature or of works and the covenant of grace. This particular way of formulating Christian theology was comparatively new, its principal English founders having been William Perkins (1558-1602), John Preston (1587-1628), and William Ames (1576-1633). The works of these men were much read in New England, and Ames' *Medulla Theologiae* (1623), or its English translation, *The Marrow of Sacred Divinity* (1643), was widely used as a theological textbook; as were also John Wollebius' *The Abridgement of Christian Divinity,* Zacharias Ursinus' *The Summe of Christian Religion,* and Petro van Mastricht's *Theoretico-Practica Theologia.* Among books written in New England may be cited: Peter Bulkeley (1582-1659), *The Gospel Covenant* (1646); John Cotton (1585-1652), *The Covenant of God's Free Grace* (1645), and others; Thomas Hooker (1586-1647) *The Faithful Covenanter* (1644); Thomas Shepard (1605-1649), *The Sincere Convert* (1640); Thomas Cobbett (1608-1685), *A Just Vindication of the Covenant* (1648).

A comprehensive work was the lectures on theology by Samuel Willard (1640-1707), president of Harvard College, published by two of his students under the title, *A Compleat Body of Divinity* (1726). A theological best-seller, though hardly a weighty contribution to the subject, was the poem by Michael Wigglesworth (1631-1705), *The Day of Doom,* first published in 1662, going through many editions, and reprinted in New York as late as 1867.

The principle of religious liberty was expounded and defended by Roger Williams* (1603-1683), and John Clarke (1609-1676), the founders of the Baptist* churches in America. The democratic genius inherent in Congregationalism* was brought to clear expression in the books by John Wise (1652-1725), entitled *The Churches Quarrel Espoused* (1710), and *A Vindication of the Government of New England Churches* (1717). He asserted boldly that "Democracy* is Christ's government in church and State"; that "Power is originally in the people"; and that "By a natural right all men are born free." In 1772, nearly fifty years after his death, his works were reprinted, and two editions were required to meet the demand of a people about to declare their political independence upon the basis of principles such as he had expounded.

A recent study of the sermons preached on the annual election day in each of the New England colonies ,published under the title, *The New England Clergy and the American Revolution,* shows that for more than one hundred and forty years the ministers of New England had been preaching doctrines with respect to the Sovereignty of God, the moral constitution which He ordained for the universe, the natural rights of man, and the nature and function of government, which are substantially the same as the principles underlying the Declaration of Independence.

It is often assumed that when the founding fathers of this nation spoke of the laws of nature and of natural rights** they meant something atheistic and in opposition to revealed religion. But that was not so. Nothing is more constant in these seventeenth and eighteenth century sermons than their assumption that the laws of nature belong to God, and that there can be no contradiction between God's will as revealed in nature and His will as revealed in the Scriptures.

From the point of view of the sciences the first of the "self-evident truths" stated in our Declaration of Independence is not evident. It is simply not true that all men are created equal. But from the point of view of the law and love of God it is true; and that is the point of view that the authors of the Declaration took. They assumed the equality of men in the light of "the laws of nature and of nature's God." A theological premise underlies and is distinctly avowed in the Declaration of Independence.

The Great Awakening* of the fourth and fifth decades of the 18th century, with its insistence upon religious conversion and its conception of the church as a spiritual institution, emphasized the difference between church and state, and contributed greatly, though indirectly, to the movements which led to their eventual separation, and to the adoption in the American constitutions of the principle of religious freedom. The theologian of the Great Awakening was Jonathan Edwards* (1703-1758), the burden of whose preaching was the absolute sovereignty and holiness of God, the sinfulness and complete dependence of man, the necessity of a changed heart and life, and the power of God's grace to bestow this gift. He preached the gospel of divine immanence and divine initiative. He saw that all things have their being in God; and that a god who is less than the source and power of all being, is but a half-god. This greatest of all truths of religion was bound up, for him, with two other ideas: the denial of the freedom of the human will, and the doctrine of particular election,* that God has arbitrarily and irrevocably chosen some for salvation and some for damnation. Edwards had one of the most powerful minds that America has brought forth, and remains its greatest theologian. His theology has philosophical grounding, depth, and poise; and his treatise on *The Freedom of the Will* has been said to be "the one large contribution which America has made to the deeper philosophic thought of the world."

The Great Awakening was opposed by Charles Chauncy (1705-1787), chiefly upon the ground of its emotional excesses; and he was followed by others who called in question the basic tenets of Calvinism. Among them were Lemuel Briant (1722-1754), and Jonathan Mayhew (1720-1766); and in time this movement culminated, under the leadership of William Ellery Channing* (1780-1842), in the Unitarian* schism of the Congregational churches, and the organization of the American Unitarian Association.

Meanwhile two parties had developed among the ministers of New England who remained on Calvinistic ground, holding positions that were termed orthodox, evangelical, and trinitarian. One of these parties stemmed directly from Jonathan Edwards, and sought to carry his theology to its full logical conclusions and consequences. The outstanding theologians in this party were Joseph Bellamy (1719-1790), and Samuel Hopkins (1721-1803), both pupils of Edwards; and Nathanael Emmons** (1745-1767). They developed what was variously known as the "New Divinity," "Consistent Calvinism,"* "Strict Calvinism," or the "Hopkinsian theology."

In opposition to what were regarded as the innovations of these followers of Edwards, was the party which came to be known as "Old Calvinists."* Leaders among them in the theological war of pamphlets and books were Jedidiah Mills (1727-1776), Moses Hemmenway (1735-1811), William Hart (1713-1784), and Moses Mather (1719-1806).

From 1797 on, New England experienced what has been called its "Second Great Awakening." This was part of a nation-wide revival of evangelical religion in which practically all denominations shared.

Except on the frontier, this movement differed from the earlier Great Awakening in its relative quiet and lack of extravagances, in the fact that it was not attributable to a few outstanding leaders such as Edwards and Whitefield had been, and in the breadth and permanence of its results. It checked the spread of infidelity, and resulted in a remarkable increase in the membership of the churches. It was responsible for the beginnings of home-missionary effort and of the foreign-missionary enterprise. It led to the founding of Christian colleges and academies and to the establishment of theological seminaries for the training of ministers. It stimulated the organization of philanthropic societies and gave impulse to the beginnings of religious journalism.* In short ,the Second Great Awakening set the general pattern which American Protestantism* has followed to this day.

With the dawning of the Nineteenth century, the differences between "Hopkinsians" and "Old Calvinists" tended to be reconciled, and the parties disappeared. This was partly because they shared alike in the Second Awakening and the activities it stimulated, and partly because they were drawn together in a common resistance to Unitarianism. In 1808 men of both parties united in the founding of Andover Theological Seminary. The theology of Timothy Dwight (1752-1817), president of Yale College, and of Nathaniel W. Taylor** (1786-1858), first professor of theology in the Yale Divinity School, was practical-minded, preachable, and directed toward the conversion of the sinner. Taylor, in particular, made such "improvements" upon Calvinism that his opponents charged that he had improved it away and substituted for it a new doctrine of the freedom of the will; and suspicion of the "New Haven theology"* had something to do with the division of the Presbyterian Church into Old School and New School** assemblies in 1837. Finally, Horace Bushnell* (1802-1876), a pupil of Taylor who refused to be bound by his mathematically logical methods, "challenged men to a new habit of thought." His work marked the passing of the older New England theology* and the opening of a new period in liberal, evangelical thought concerning the great truths of the Christian faith.

Except in New England, there was little or no cultivation of theology in colonial America. Samuel Johnson (1696-1772), first president of King's College, now Columbia University, wrote on philosophy rather than on theology; and the first of the Episcopal ministers, perhaps, who could be recorded as a theologian was Bishop John Henry Hobart (1775-1830), of New York. Among Presbyterians may be named John Witherspoon (1722-1794), president of the College of New Jersey at Princeton, signer of the Declaration of Independence; and Archibald Alexander (1772-1851), and Charles Hodge* (1797-1878), professors in the Princeton Theological Seminary. Henry M. Muhlenberg* (1711-1787), was a pietist and a great practical leader of the Lutheran churches rather than a theologian. Samuel S. Schmucker* (1799-1873), founder of the Lutheran institutions at Gettysburg, devoted his life to the teaching of theology and the education of ministers. He sought to adapt Lutheranism to the needs of America as he saw them; he published plans and proposals looking toward the ultimate unity of the Protestant churches; and he was one of the first advocates of the movement which culminated in the formation in 1846 of the Evangelical Alliance. With the great influx of German immigration in the middle of the century, however, a reaction set in toward a more strict, conservative adherence to the traditional positions of the Lutheran Church. See New England theology; New Haven theology.

The best accounts of early New England theology are in Perry Miller: *Orthodoxy in Massachusetts* (1933), and *The New England Mind* (1939). The 18th century developments are described in Frank H. Foster: *A Genetic History of the New England Theology* (1907), and George N. Boardman, *A History of New England Theology* (1899). See also Alice M. Baldwin, *The New England Clergy and The American Revolution* (1928).

Recent biographies of *Jonathan Edwards* (1940) by Ola Winslow, *Timothy Dwight* (1942) by Charles E. Cuningham and *Nathaniel W. Taylor* (1942) by Sidney E. Mead are well done and helpful.

Vergilius Ferm: *The Crisis in American Lutheran Theology* (1927) is the best account of the earlier period of Lutheran theology in America. L.A.W.

American Tract Society: See religious tract movement.

Americanism: The term applied by Pope Leo XIII in his apostolic letter, *Testem Benevolentiae* of January 22, 1899, to those methods of apologetics which stressed natural virtues to the neglect of dogmatic teachings and to those notions of spiritual direction which insisted on individual inspiration and the active virtues in preference to external guidance and the passive virtues. Although the letter of condemnation was addressed to Cardinal James Gibbons and the American hierarchy, Cardinal Gibbons in his reply stated that no American bishop, priest or layman properly instructed in his faith had ever held the condemned doctrines. In the background of the condemnation was the attempt of certain European liberals to advocate for general adaptation in Europe, especially in France, the American relation between Church and State. Against this tendency certain theologians pictured these "Americanist" heretical tendencies which they claimed they found in certain American religious activities and in the biography of Father Isaac Hecker* written by Father Walter Elliott and adapted by Father Felix Klein in the French. Pope Leo in his condemnation of the heresy did not say that it existed in America. Furthermore, he specifically excluded from the condemnation American political institutions and those national characteristics common to the American people as a nation. T.T.M.

Amesha Spentas: Attendants of Ormazd,* high god in the Zoroastrian religion. Personifications of the character of Ormazd: good thought; perfect righteousness; desired kingdom; holy harmony; saving health; and immortality. See s.v. virgin birth. See Persia, religions of; Zoroastrianism. V.F.

Amiatinus, Codex: The leading manuscript of the Latin Vulgate version, written in England about the beginning of the eighth century, and carried to Italy in 716 and presented to the Pope. It was used in the preparation of the Sixtine edition of the Vulgate,* 1585-1590, and is now in the Laurentian Library in Florence. See manuscripts of the bible. E.J.G.

amice: (Lat. *amictus,* clothing) A separate collar worn with the alb.* E.R.H.

Amish, the: See Mennonites.

Amita: See Buddhist Terminology.

Amon: Wicked king who ruled Judah 641-639 B.C. In one of the most degenerate periods of Judean life, he perpetuated, until assassinated, the paganisms of his father Manasseh. See Manasseh and Zephaniah. R.E.W.

amora: (from the Hebrew and Aramaic, *Amar,* to "say" or "speak") Official title for a teacher or lecturer who expounded the Mishnah* in use from the time of the death of Judah I (219) to the completion of the Babylonian Talmud (500). B.Z.B.

Amorites: See Canaanites.

Amos: Earliest OT prophetic book, containing poems recited by this Judean shepherd of Tekoa while visiting northern Israel about 750 B.C., possibly one long address delivered at Bethel (Morgenstern), but probably excerpts from at least twelve poetic sermons uttered in Samaria, Gilgal, Bethel, etc. In a peak of prosperity, social degeneracy had weakened the moral life until Amos feared Israel would be destroyed by foreign aggressors. He sacrificed his vocation to warn his sister-nation, hoping to save her from impending doom by reforming her life. After intensive ministry of a few months, he probably was executed following a clash with Priest Amaziah of Bethel. His revolutionary ideas were 1) that Yahweh* was a god of justice, 2) that the deity expected people to be just with each other, and 3) that worship was a mockery unless accompanied by ethical living. Although still a henotheist,* strictly speaking, Amos ridiculed Israel's belief that she was Yahweh's chosen people and paved the way for internationalism and monotheism.* He was a literary master, founder of the line of eight century prophets, and pioneer in the social gospel.

See *The Prophets and their Times* (1941), by J. M. P. Smith and W. A. Irwin, pp. 55-69 and *Amos Studies* (1941), by J. Morgenstern. R.E.W.

amphictyony: (Gr. *amphiktyonia,* from *amphiktiones,* dwellers round about) A religious association of Greeks worshipping at the same shrine. The most important was that of Delphi, which maintained the temple of Apollo at Delphi and that of Demeter at Thermopylae. In legend it was founded by Amphictyon, son of Deucalion and brother of Hellen, ancestor of the Greeks. E.M.N.

ampullae: (Lat. *ampullae,* bottles) Jars or bottles in early times for holy oils, or in mediaeval times the jars in which pilgrims sometimes carried oil from shrines. L.R.W.

amulets: See charms and amulets.

Amyraldians: See Cameron, John.

Anabaptists: A name of abuse frequently used in the Reformation period. Properly and often loosely applied to any who questioned the validity of infant baptism. Anabaptism emerged at the end of 1521 when three "prophets" (of whom Muenzer was the most prominent) came to Wittenberg from Zwickau. They attacked the limited scope of Luther's reformation, especially in relation to baptism. Their activities resulted in widespread confusion, and they gained—quite unjustly—the reputation of being wholly opposed to learning. On Luther's return to Wittenberg, his previous attitude of caution gave way to sharp opposition. The Anabaptists were ejected first from Wittenberg and then from other towns, but spread widely over the country-side. During this period, Muenzer* preached with increasing emphasis the revolutionary elements, both religious and political, in his creed, and this phase of the movement reached a crisis in the Peasants' War.* Under Muenzer's leadership, a revolt originally directed against feudal oppression, became an attempt forcibly to erect his ideal Christian community of equality of status and community of goods. The rising was crushed and Muenzer was executed, but the movement immediately sprang up elsewhere. At Münster, the Anabaptists seized control of the town, and attempted to establish their holy state. Under John of Leiden, the movement ran rapidly to excesses. The apocalyptic element came strongly to the fore. Wild visions were the justification of wild measures, such as polygamy. The excesses of the Münster experiment made the word Anabaptist a term held in widespread horror, and explain its convenience as a means of discrediting religious adversaries. This tendency in part explains the difficulty of tracing the exact course of the movement after the overthrow of the Münster theocracy. There is no doubt of the courage of the Anabaptists under persecution, but it is equally true that many suffered as Anabaptists who really did not merit the name. This was especially true of the early Baptists.

Though the Anabaptists are usually regarded as the extreme wing of the Reformation, it is likely that they were as often indebted to earlier sects and movements. In addition to their views on the nature of baptism, the Anabaptists seem to have shared certain other convictions. For example, we often find them holding to a Marcionite* view of the manner of the Incarnation. They repudiated oaths* and believed that Christians should not have recourse to law courts. True Christians were not to bear arms or forcibly resist evil men. They were to obey the authorities, but Government belonged to the province of the world, and so Christians should not hold office. The Anabaptists held strict views as to the exclusion of unworthy members from the Christian society. Some indeed believed that those who are truly baptised cannot sin.

It is important to notice that the early Anabaptists were convinced that religious reform must have social consequences. At this point they were clearly in advance of many of the reformers, who were often markedly conservative in political and economic matters. Anabaptism appealed most strongly to the people in the humbler strata of society, and failed to win the support of princes and prosperous townsmen.

It is also necessary to note the existence of moderate Anabaptists in Switzerland, centering chiefly in Zürich. See Ambrosians; Denck; Hofmann, M.; Hübmaier.

R. Heath, *Anabaptism from its rise at Zwickau to 1536* (London, 1897). G.R.C.

Anacletus: See Peter, St. First Bishop of Rome. Clement, St., Pope.

anagogical interpretation: (Gr. *anagogo*, to lead upwards) The discovery of hidden spiritual truth in the literal text of Scripture. A type of allegorical interpretation*. See exegesis. S.M.G.

Anahita: ("the unspotted") Ancient Persian goddess of a river (Yasht 5), who became the goddess of fertility, love, and childbirth. R.H.P.

analogy: (Gr. *ana*, according to; *logos*, ratio, proportion) A similitude in relationship. Thus, to say that God is to his creatures as a father to his children is to describe him by analogy, or proportionally; and similarly, when it is said that God is the poet of the world (Whitehead), or that the world is a divine poem (Peirce). Other theological analogies are: ruler of the universe, heavenly king, "light whose smile kindles the universe" (Shelley), soul of the universe "whose body nature is and God the soul" (Pope). Even such terms as "creator" or "maker of all things" or "first cause" are analogical; for they mean that as the artist to the statue, or as the farmer to his crops, or any agent to the results of his activity, so (with whatever qualifications or differences) is God to things other than God. The earliest known monotheism, the sunworship of Ikhnaton*, seems to have been an implicit analogy: as are the sun's light and warmth to the growth and happiness of living things on earth (assuming that the sun is a conscious being aware of what it does), so is God to men and all beings. Since the natures of things are essentially relational, except perhaps for such simple qualities of feeling as redness or sweetness (Peirce*), there is probably no sharp line between analogical and non-analogical similarity. Hence when it is said (as by Thomas Aquinas) that qualities cannot be ascribed to God and the creatures in the same sense but only analogically, it may be asked if this is not usually the case when properties are ascribed to diverse things. Is not all similarity "with a difference" and in relation to something? Men and dogs are fathers, not in the same sense but analogically. The "kindness" of a wife and a business partner are not wholly the same. The problem is always to define the exact scope and limits and relational reference to each resemblance. But whatever the qualifications, some abstract feature or *ratio* in common is implied, and this common feature must not be denied if anything is to be left of the analogy. If God is Father, he must not at the same time be in every specifiable respect other than fatherly, on pretext that similarity to a father in such respects would be "anthropomorphic".

The theological use of analogy is exposed to failure in three ways: through vagueness, through inappropriateness, and through self-contradiction. The last arises through the effort to avoid the first two. For example, there are many sorts of fathers, and no one would think that there was any complete proportion between the relations, child-father and creature-creator. Hence the fatherhood of God, if not further explained, has at best only vague meaning. But by thinking of a quite definite sort of human father, say the best one knows or can imagine, it is possible to give definite meaning to "heavenly father." However, this definiteness may be at the expense of the mode of superhuman excellence or perfection which also one wishes to ascribe to God. Thus an inconsistency or vacillation arises, by which one avoids a too vague analogy only by falling into an objectionably anthropomorphic one, and then, when the anthropomorphism* is noted, takes refuge again in the vagueness. The intellectual integrity of theology stands or falls with the finding or failure to find a remedy for this too long customary but scandalous procedure. The proposition that God knows and loves the creatures and has purposes for them can be given definite meaning; but if at the same time it be insisted that God is totally immutable and unaffected by anything temporal or contingent, and thus is exactly as he would be did the creatures not exist at all, then what is left of the definiteness? One who purposes something is one whose anticipatory plan precedes the something in time; with God, it has been usual to say, there is no such precedence, since he possesses the fulfillment of his plan from all eternity. One might go on with other features of the theological analogy, as traditionally treated, and show that all are similarly nullified. As Kant* showed, all our meanings involve space and time, and if God (as Kant believed, though here without proof) is simply nonspatial and non-temporal, then he is for us unknowable, even by analogy. Scholars are beginning to recognize that there is a way of avoiding this result, namely to admit that in some analogous if not univocal sense God is temporal and spatial (and dependent and complex) as well as conscious and good and purposive and powerful. Not that God is mutable or extended or dependent in just the way and degree we are, any more than he is good or powerful in just the way we are, but always with a difference or in some proportional way. It is illogical to admit subtle analogical meanings for the one set of concepts while insisting upon a crude univocalness—and therefore a denial of their applicability to God—for the other set. If God has a body, it will not be as a fragment of reality surrounded by an external environment; but all the universe of things other than God will be this body. A partial, localized being (see Omnipresence) will have a partial, localized body; the inclusive, cosmic being will have an inclusive, nonlocalized body. Moreover, the integrity of the universe must be supposed adequate to the divine perfection; for instance, the cosmic organism is to be conceived as the sole that is indissoluble, all dissolution being rearrangement of parts or creation of new parts within the cosmos, which throughout retains its essential unity.

The above does not mean that God must be admitted in all respects mutable, extended, or dependent. Even man has an aspect ("the soul") which is relatively or imperfectly fixed, inextended, independent of contingencies; analogously, in God there may be a perfectly fixed, non-spatial, and independent or necessary aspect, his "essence", whose logical status may and must, in consistency, be supposed different from that of his accidents. (See Transcendence.)

The three key analogies are perhaps the social analogy (prominent in the idea of the divine fatherhood), that God is to us as a superior and benevolent human being is to other human beings; the mind-body analogy, that God is the soul of the universe as a man is the soul of so much of nature as is included within his skin; and the artist analogy, that God creatively produces and shapes the universe. Each analogy has its defects. Thus father and child are mutually external, and conceivably may cease to have anything to do with each other or to know of each other's doings; the mind seems to have a non-social relation to the body, a relation of use or exploitation rather than a social relation of mutual sympathy and understanding; and the artist analogy involves both the externality of the first analogy—the artist and his product (once created) being separable and potentially independent of each other—and involves also the non-sociality of the second analogy. A perfect or the most perfect possible analogy must somehow combine the merits and avoid the defects of these analogies. This can be done by supposing a relationship as intimate and constant as that between mind and body, as sympathetic as that between the ideal father and his child, and as active as that between artist and his materials. Thus God must be the world-soul, but in such fashion that he loves each creature as a cell within his own body, and that he molds the life of the entire organism consciously with regard to its inner health and value. It may be maintained that the mind-body relation in some degree has these characters even in us. For, while we do not think lovingly of individual cells within our bodies, it may be that we do feel something of their feelings sympathetically, so that, for example, our suffering is our confused sense of pains endured by groups of our bodily cells at the time, and our acts of volition do mold the lives of cells, even though without our clear awareness of these cells as individuals. In God the "cells" become all individuals within the world-body, and instead of feeling mere masses of cells he has clear sympathetic awareness of individuals composing these masses. See God as personal; omnipresence; panentheism; perfect; Whitehead.

"Analogy" in J. Hasting's *Encyclopedia of Religion and Ethics* (1908-27); "Analogy" in D. Runes, *Dictionary of Philosophy* (1942). C.H.

analytic psychology: See psychology, schools of.

anaphora: (Gr., offering up. Lat., *oblatio*) The consecratory eucharistic prayer of the Eastern liturgies, corresponding to the Preface and Canon of the Roman Mass*. The earliest extant example is in the *Apostolic Tradition* of Hippolytus*, c. 220. P.V.N.

anarchism: (Greek, *an* without, *arche*, government) A social theory which regards the state as the source of our major social and moral ills, and which seeks to establish justice and equality among men by abolishing political government, and by substituting for it an entirely spontaneous cooperation of free individuals, organized into purely voluntary territorial and functional groups for the purpose of producing and distributing the goods and services essential to the satisfaction of the physical, intellectual, esthetic, and emotional needs and aspirations of human beings. It holds that human nature is essentially good, and that social order can best be maintained, not by an external and invasive authority, but by the ever changing equilibrium of social forces and influences, none of which would have the unfair and artificial advantage of state support.

Although anarchistic ideas were expressed among the Greeks by Aristippus, (ca. 435-356 B. C.) and more fully by Zeno (ca. 342-270 B. C.), the latter in phrases similar to those now in use, the political and economic concepts of anarchism were first formulated by William Godwin in his *Enquiry Concerning Political Justice*, (2 vols. 1793) and the term was first employed to describe the theory of a stateless society by Pierre Joseph Proudhon in his *Qu 'est-ce que la proprieté?* in 1840.

Anarchism is a varied and protean movement, but at least four types of theory can be distinguished within it: 1) *Individualistic anarchism* or *Proudhonian Mutuellisme*, which accepts private property freed from all state-created restraints and privileges; 2) *Communistic anarchism*, which repudiates the coercive collectivism of Marxian socialism* in favor of the common possession of the means of production by the free agreement and cooperation of voluntary groups; 3) *Christian anarchism* of Tolstoy* and his disciples, who derive anarchistic doctrines deductively from the teachings of Christ, and 4) *Terroristic anarchism*, which follows Max Stirner (Johann Kaspar Schmidt) in advocating assassination and other individual acts of terrorism as means of promoting their doctrines by "the propoganda of the deed." See communistic settlements, secular.

Eunice Minette Schuster, "Native American Anarchism", in *Smith College Studies in History*, Vol. XVII, Nos. 1-4 (1931-32); Bertrand Russell, *Proposed Roads to Freedom* (London, 1919); Paul H. Douglas, "Proletarian Political Theory" in C. E. Merriam and H. E. Barnes, (eds.) *A History of Political Theories, Recent Times* (1924), pp. 178-269; Paul Elzbacher, *Anarchism*, translated by Stephen T. Byington (1908).

H.E.J.

anathema: Literally, "something set up",—as a votive offering, or as an object polluted or accursed. In this latter sense it is used by Paul (Gal. 1:8, 9. 1 Cor. 12:3, 16:22) of one who is utterly rejected by God and man. It became the term regularly employed in the act of excommunication*.

E.F.S.

Anaxagoras: (c. 500-430 B.C.) Anaxagoras of Clazomenae, Asia Minor, a supposed disciple of Anaximenes, author of *peri phuseos,* is credited with having first diverted argumentation (or philosophy) from Ionia to Athens where he exerted a powerful influence upon Pericles and his age. Plato and Aristotle mention "disciples" and "followers" of Anaxagoras, possibly Archelaus and Euripides among others. In Athens, Anaxagoras was called *Nous.* He anticipated Socrates* in free thought. He declared that the sun was not a god but a moulten mass of fire. For such heresy, Josephus states he was sentenced to death. (Diels, 46A 19). In any event he was banished and, depressed by disgrace, ended his life in Lampsacus on the Hellespont.

Anaxagoras was first to introduce *nous** (mind) as a principle of cosmic interpretation. Of him Aristotle said "When one man said, then, that reason (mind) was present—as in animals, so throughout nature—as the cause of order and of all arrangement, he seemed like a sober man in contrast with the random talk of his predecessors." Anaxagoras made no attempt to account for the origin of "matter." He believed in a primeval, chaotic, corporeal mixture of everything—*migma.* So-called primary determinations were thought present, but so-called secondary qualities were contingent upon the principle of order and developed concomitantly with the progress of cosmic formation. To this chaotic mass *nous* imparted the initial impulse of motion. Opinion divides as to whether Anaxagoras conceived of *nous* as effecting a single impact and then withdrawing, or whether he thought *nous* was progressively present wherever matter was and administered, continually and efficiently, superintendency of arrangement of cosmic order. (Diels, 46 B, 12, 13 and 9, 12).

Besides attempting to account for inorganic and organic objects, Anaxagoras computed the size of the sun, (Plutarch, *Lysander* XII, 2) first determined the phases of the moon, (Hippolytus, *Philosophumena ou Ref. de Toutes les Heresies* I, 8, 10) explained the origin of the winds, cause of thunder and earthquakes, (Diogenus Laertius, II, 9) the shape and support of the earth, (Hippolytus I, 8, 2) the falling of meteors, (Plutarch, 12) and the production of life and its development into species (Diogenes Laertius, II, 10).

Probably most notable were characteristics which he ascribed to *nous. Nous* was simple, unmixed and alone, a spiritual essence whose activity affected material elements, without partaking of the nature of matter. It was infinite, knew all things, was self-ruled, its activity originated motion, differentiated and selected, was teleological, and betrayed further and crucial characteristics of person in its capacity of time-transcendence: "Whatever things were to be, and whatever things were that are not now, and whatever things shall be, all these *nous* arranged in order." (Diels, I, 8, 2).

H. Diels, *Die Fragmente der Vorsokratiker* (Berlin, 1922); Max Heinze, *Uber der Nous des Anaxagoras,* Reports of the Deliberation of the Royal Scientific Saxony Society, Vol. 41 (Leipzig, 1890).

P.R.H.

ancestor worship: A complex phenomenon, beginning, in rudimentary forms, in primitive religion* and developing through later stages; growing out of beliefs that the spirits* of the dead linger about their earthly habitations; have continued needs for food, drink, etc.; are motivated like living persons; have ways of avenging their neglect; and have powers of protecting and blessing those responsible for their care. The motives of ancestor worship, therefore, although involved and not always the same, are chiefly: 1) the desire to tend the dead (not always, however, leading to worship); 2) fear of ghostly visitations and of their avenging acts (leading as often to magic as to worship); 3) desire for the protection and blessing which the departed spirits can give; and 4) the feeling that reverence is due them. Services to, and veneration* of, the dead become worship only in so far as these practices and attitudes involve some sense of real dependence upon the ancestral spirits and the consequent desire to placate and honor them. Such observances are primarily family responsibilities, becoming general only in the case of tribal or national heroes and leaders and only then involving (and not always) actual deification. Special shrines, appropriate rites, and appointed times for the ceremonies commonly characterize ancestor worship. In our century, the practice is common, though not universal, among the primitive peoples of the world;, among the Chinese masses (where it is integral to the family system and the primary virtue of filial peity); and in Japan, where it is important not only for family life but for the whole imperial system, having, therefore, strong political as well as religious bearings. See Chinese religions; hero worship.

E.T.R.

anchoret or anchorite: (Gr. *anachoretes,* a recluse, retired man) Applied to an extreme type of Christian ascetics, appearing first in the third century, who sought spiritual perfection by withdrawing from the community, often exposing themselves to hardships such as inadequate clothing or shelter, wearing coarse cloths and sometimes chains. Some even spent years on top of pillars; among these the most famous was St. Simon Stylites. See asceticism; hermit; recluse. Cf. cenobite.

R.B.B.

Andover Controversy, The: A somewhat vague designation of a vigorous expression of conflicting theological opinions regarding the state of heathen, to whom the Christian gospel had never been preached, after death. Robert A. Hume and one other candidate for appointment to foreign missionary work under the American Board of Commissioners for Foreign Missions held the opinion of some professors in Andover Theological Seminary, that there was, for such heathen, a "second probation after death."

For this the officials of the Board refused to commission them. The liberal constituency of the Board denied the right of the "Prudential Committee"—the executive agents of the Board—thus to determine the theological standards of the Congregational Churches. A vigorous conflict of personalities and opinions was initiated which was in action from 1886-1893. The retirement of conservative leaders and a more irenic temper finally ended the controversy and missionaries on the field, under the administration of the American Board, were assured the same freedom of thought as the ministers of the Congregational churches generally. The problems of Christian theology in the 19th century also engaged the interest of the Andover men. See Smyth, E. C.

H. K. Rowe, *History of Andover Theological Seminary*, (1933); *The Andover case . . .* (1887). *Andover defense; defense of Prof. Smyth; arguments of Prof. Theodore W. Dwight, Prof. S. G. Baldwin, Hon. C. T. Russell and ex-Governor Gaston* (1887).

Andover heresy . . . Prof. Smyth; argument together with the statements of Profs. Tucker, Harris, Hincks and Churchill (1887).

Andover Theol. Seminary, arguments on behalf of the complainants in the matter of the complaints against Egbert C. Smyth. Dates and data, (1926).

G.G.A.

Andover theology: See Progressive Orthodoxy.

Andreae, Laurentius: (c. 1470-1552) Andreae had studied in Germany, been on church missions to Rome, before he, as archdeacon in Strengnäs diocese, became chancellor of Gustavus Vasa, and the king's influential counsellor in making the royal power independent of Pope in the Church and superior to nobility in government. Andreae had a part in translation of the Swedish Bible, otherwise his efforts were in the realm of the state, where until 1531 he was a dominant figure. C.J.B.

Andrew of Crete: (d. 720 or 740) A Byzantine theologian, a zealous iconodule, and hymn writer, metropolitan of Gortyna in Crete. Although not a great hymn writer himself, he inspired a considerable number of gifted Greek writers to compose hymns. Andrew is credited with the invention of a number of canons; many of his works have not yet been published. M.S.

Angelico, Fra: (1387-1455) Religious artist. Born Guido di Pietro, and in religion known as Giovanni da Fiesole. Because of the spiritual quality of his art he earned for himself the title of "Angelico", and because of the holiness of his life and his beatification he is called "Il Beato". His finest work is in the chapel of Nicholas V in the Vatican. J.B.C.

angels: Angels belong to the class of beings generally known as demons. They are living creatures of the spirit world, intermediate between gods and men, who may be either hostile or friendly toward humanity. Angelology had been specially developed in Persian religion from which it passed over into Judaism and then into Christianity. In those religions that stressed the personality of the deity angels served as agents for expressing and revealing the mighty will of God. Judaism had a hierarchy of angels at whose head stood seven (or four) archangels who with their myriads of subordinates discharged varied functions. They were servants and messengers of God; their original demonic nature was revealed in their connection with natural phenomena like wind and lightning; they mediated divine revelation to men and interceded for them before God; and they served as protectors for both individuals and communities. The early Christians believed that a supporting host of angels would accompany the triumphant Messiah's return (Mark 8:38, 13:24), even as his birth had been announced by an angelic choir (Luke 2:13f.). Also angels were a kind of spiritual double for men (Matt. 18:10; Acts 12:15). The worship of angels occurred in early Christianity, although it was frowned upon in some quarters (Col. 2:18; Rev. 19:10; 22:8f.). But in the second century Justin Martyr* said that Christians paid reverence to the army of good angels. After the fourth century the cult of angels became more general, the archangel Michael being especially honored. Angels figured conspicuously in medieval Christian art, but their worship was discredited by the Protestant leaders and the Enlightenment relegated them to the domain of poetic fancy. Cf. Cherub, Cherubim; Mohammedanism; spirits.

W. Lueken, *Michael* (1898), W. Bousset, *Die Religion des Judentums* (1906), pp. 368-381, F. Andres, *Die Engellehren der griechischen Apologeten* (1914).

S.J.C.

angelus: (Lat., angel or messenger)

1) A prayer said three times a day in honor of the Incarnation; essentially three *Aves*, to which were later added three scriptural verses and a concluding prayer.

2) The bell rung for the prayer. L.R.W.

anger of God: See wrath of God.

Anglican Evangelicals: See Evangelicals, Anglican.

Anglicanism or Anglican Church: See Church of England.

Anglo-Catholics: The term "Anglo-Catholic" first appears in the 17th century as a description of the position of the Church of England*. The tradition of the Caroline divines was continued by the isolated High Churchmen of the 18th century; in America they were influential in the northern colonies, and after the Revolution became one of the major influences in the Episcopal Church. The Reform movement threatened the traditional position of the English Church and led churchmen to look for firmer foundations. John Keble's* protesting sermon on "National Apostasy" (July 14, 1833) is counted as the beginning of the Oxford Movement* soon carried further in the series of *Tracts for the Times.* The tractarians* preached an objective, authoritative, ethical, sacramental religion; J. H. Newman's* *Via Media* (more correctly *Lectures on the Prophetical Office of the Church,* 1837) defined their claim to Catholic authority as against both Protestantism and Rome. The controversy raised by Newman's Tract XC culminated in his defection to Roman Catholicism in 1845. This ended the Oxford Movement as such, but only spread Anglo-Catholicism; in its practical expression the sobriety of the Tractarians was succeeded by the more popular appeal of ritualism*, while until his death in 1882 the learned orthodoxy of Pusey* dominated its theology.

In 1889 *Lux Mundi* (edited by Charles Gore) began a movement toward Liberal Catholicism, and brought into the Anglo-Catholic tradition the social Catholicism of F. D. Maurice*. Even the more conservative theologians, such as the American F. J. Hall and Bishop Weston of Zanzibar, were not unaffected by these tendencies; but most Anglo-Catholics stopped short of the Cambridge School of the 1900's, with its pragmatic and modernist sympathies. Recent tendencies are various. Beginning in 1920 the Anglo-Catholic Congresses brought together the academic and parochial wings of the movement. *Essays Catholic and Critical* (1926) is one specimen of a considerable theological activity. Recent Anglican Prayer Book revisions show much Anglo-Catholic influence; the Church Union Summer School of Sociology at Oxford is a center of discussion of social theory and practice. The Oxford Movement Centenary of 1933 gave occasion for a review of tractarian principles, which are still central in Anglo-Catholicism; their expression is diversely worked out not only by clerics, but by lay writers of such diverse appeal as Evelyn Underhill, T. S. Eliot, Dorothy Sayers, and Henry A. Wallace. See Christian Social Union.

R. W. Church, *The Oxford Movement* (the classic account) (1891); W. L. Knox and A. R. Vidler, *The Development of Modern Catholicism* (1933); *Report of the Oxford Movement Centenary Congress* (1933). E.R.H.

Anglo-Saxons and the Introduction to Christianity: When the Teutonic tribes invaded Britain south of the Rivers Forth and Clyde (5th century), they established a number of independent kingdoms which were christianized one by one. The first was Kent by St. Augustine* who set up the see of Canterbury in 597. The Celtic inhabitants of Britain pushed back into Wales and Cornwall, later engaged in a series of controversies with the newly converted Anglo-Saxon Christians. One subject of discussion was the time of the observance of Easter*, but both Roman and Celtic were loyal in spirit to Rome. The second kingdom to be converted was Essex, with London as the see in 604. The others in the following order: Northumbria (York, 625); East Anglia (Dunwich, 630); Mercia (Lichfield, 656); Wessex (Winchester, 669), and lastly Sussex (Selsey, 708). In addition to St. Augustine, sent directly to England by Pope St. Gregory the Great*, the following took part in the evangelization of the Anglo-Saxons: St. Aidan, a monk of Iona, Scotland; Sts. Cedd and Chad; St. Cuthbert and St. Wilfrid*. Latin was used in the liturgy and in the canonical hours, and the ritual was very much like that of southern Italy due undoubtedly to the traditions of Monte Casino brought into England by the Benedictines. Devotion to the Blessed Virgin was deep and widespread. There were certain interesting innovations, but none of a doctrinal character.

John Lingard, *History of Antiquities of the Anglo-Saxon Church* (London, 1845). J.B.C.

Angra Mainyu (Ahriman): See Persia, religions of; Zoroastrianism.

animals, worship of: A vast array of living forms of air and earth and sea have claimed the awed respect of man. The thought forms of prehistoric man were so different from ours that it is difficult for us to understand the reasons for his attitudes toward the animals. Certainly he felt himself more akin to them than does modern man. Yet they had qualities that set them apart. Some were dangerous, some had great strength, some were mysterious, some cunning, some were available for food*. The efforts of early man to make alliance with some animal forms and to protect himself from others may account for much of what is called animal worship. The need for food, coupled with an early apprehension regarding blood and killing gave rise to some cults. The desire to preserve the food supply accounts for others. When grain became a staple food, various animals were identified with the fertility of the earth. The snake, associated with underground waters, was revered as the source of vegetation, fertility in field and home, wealth and healing. Some cults arose from the belief that the souls of the dead reappeared in animal form. Because of appropriate qualities, animals were sometimes associated with the various nature gods as their companions, temporary embodiments or symbols. The so-called animal gods may be a variation of this practice. The animal as the sign of the district became identified with the god, and the divine symbol retained both the animal and human form. Alliance of a tribe or an individual, for various reasons, with an animal species resulted in the many forms of totemism*. A.E.H.

animatism: See primitive religion.

animism: See primitive religion; spirits.

annates: A tax on ecclesiastical appointments consisting of the first fruits, or first year's revenue of a benefice. During the late middle ages, it was payable to the papal treasury. In England after 1531, it was payable to the crown. W.S.H.

annihilationism: The doctrine that the death of the wicked involves the extinction of their being. One form of annihilationism teaches that this extinction is the final result of the gradually disintegrating effect of sin on the being of the evil doer. Other annihilationists teach that after death the wicked will suffer punishment in proportion to the evil deeds committed during their earthly lives, but that this future punishment* will be followed by complete cessation of being. See future life.
H.W.J.

Annunciation: 1) The announcement by the Angel Gabriel to the Virgin Mary* that she should give birth to Jesus (Luke 1:26-38). 2) The festival of the church, March 25, celebrating this event.
R.E.E.H.

Annunciation, Orders of: Include under this appellation all of the orders founded under the patronage of the Annunciation of the Blessed Virgin Mary*. There are in the history of religious orders six of this type 1) A military order, the Order of the Annunziata, founded under Amadeus VIII, duke of Savoy in the 15th century. 2) The Annunciades, a penitential order, founded by St. Jeanne de Valois, daughter of Louis XI of France in 1501. It continued until the French Revolution at which time it was suppressed. 3) The Celestial Annunciades, a religious order of women founded by Bl. Maria Vittoria Fornari at Genoa in 1604. 4) The Annunciates of Lombardy, known also as the Sisters of St. Ambrose; they were organized in 1408 at Pavia by young women of Venice and Pavia under the direction of Father Beccaria, O.S.B., for the cure of the sick. 5) The Archconfraternity of the Annunciation was established in 1460 in Rome to provide dowries for poor girls who were to be married. 6) The Annunziata is a name sometimes given to the Servites* since their chief monastery at Florence is dedicated to the Annunciation.
T.T.M.

anointing: (The English word is derived from *in* and *ungere*, "to smear"). The ritual application of oil* was employed among many religions and peoples for the elimination of disease or demons and for the introduction of divine power. Boys and girls have often been anointed as a preliminary to the ceremonies of puberty. In ancient Israel, sacrifices were anointed (Ex. 30.26); oil was used in the consecration of priests (Lev. 8:12) and in the anointing of kings (I Sam. 10.1); the latter was an infrequent custom among other peoples. Hence the future king was the "messiah"* or anointed one. In the NT, sick are anointed (Mk. 6.13; Jas. 5.14). This led to the Roman Catholic sacrament of extreme unction* and the Orthodox anointing of the sick. See chrism.
C.T.C.

An-omoi-ans: The extreme Arian* party in the last stages of the struggle opposing not only *homoousion* but also *homoiousion* and *homoion*** as descriptions of the relation of the Son to the Father. This extreme position holds that the Son is not only of a different essence from the Father but also stresses their unlikeness. See Eunomianism.
F.W.B.

Anselm, St. of Canterbury: (1033-1109) He was the first in scholasticism* to make respected speculation in the grand style. Like earlier theologians, he collected sentences from Augustine's works; but, as no one before him, he lived himself into Augustine's spirit. He energetically re-introduced the spirit of Augustine into theology. Opposed to an unfruitful use of dialectics, his thought was determined by an apologetic interest against it. His interest in philosophy was purely religious. He showed little interest in the technical problems of contemporary philosophy. His moderate realism lent wings to his speculation. It was not his method to hold together the separate theses by a net of dialectical wires, but upon the basis of inner experience to reproduce speculatively the inherited Augustinian ideas: *auctoritas, ratio,* free will and grace. He concurs with Augustine that Christianity agrees with universal rational knowledge, that from the standpoint of Platonic idealism Christianity is the highest truth. In his *Cur Deus Homo?*, he subjected, for the first time to a scientific examination, the view that the forgiveness of sin was made possible by the death of Christ. He created the doctrine of atonement. The great merit of his theory of satisfaction was to have posed the question of the possibility of the forgiveness of sin, to have worked it out by remarkable dialectical ability, and to have understood it as the objective basis of the existence of the church. In the *Proslogium*, and above all, in the *Monologium* he expounded his famous ontological argument for the existence of God*. See atonement in Christianity; feudalism; satisfaction.

B. Funke, *Grundlagen und Voraussetzungen der Satisfaktions-lehre des heiligen Anselm* (Munster, 1903); M. Grabmann, *Geschichte der scholastischen Methode*, Vol. I (Freiburg im Breisgau, 1909); F. R. Hasse, *Anselm* (Leipzig, 1843-52).
H.H.

Ansgar: (801-865) "Apostle of the North". Saintly, visionary monk of Corbie in Picardie and the daughter monastery, Corvey, established 822, in Westphalia. Missionary to Denmark 826-828, to Sweden ca. 829-831. Returned to become Archbishop of Hamburg, the new Missionary See, 831. Later Archbishop of Hamburg-Bremen. Inspired a missionary succession. Visited Sweden again ca. 852. Returned to stabilize his See, the only institutional continuum of his troubled life and work.
E.G.H.

antediluvians: The men who lived before the Flood*, listed in Sumerian* inscriptions, in Berossos*, and in Gen. 4 and 5.
R.H.P.

Ante-Nicene Fathers: The term "Fathers" is used to designate the early writers of the Church, the line ending, for the Western Church, with Gregory the Great*. Strictly used, the term indicates their orthodoxy, approbation by the Church, and sanctity of life, as well as their antiquity; but it is also used somewhat more loosely to include men whose orthodoxy has later been challenged.

The Ante-Nicene Fathers were those whose activity antedated the Council of Nicaea* in A.D. 325, including the Apostolic Fathers*, the second century Apologists*, and later writers like Irenaeus and Hippolytus, Tertullian and Cyprian, Clement of Alexandria and Origen**. A.K.R.

anthem: (Gr. *antiphona,* through the Saxon, *antefn*) A form of sacred choral music with non-liturgical words, used in the Anglican and related Protestant services. Originally synonymous with antiphon*. The English anthem in the Elizabethan and early Stuart periods took the place of the motet* in the Latin service and differed from it only in the use of English instead of Latin. William Byrd and Orlando Gibbons were significant composers in this period. In the restoration period John Blow and Henry Purcell changed the form, added length, used solo voices interspersed with mixed choruses and introduced string orchestral interludes. In the 18th century Greene and Boyce followed the style of Purcell changing the string sections to organ. The outstanding composer of the 19th century was Samuel Sebastian Wesley who first used an independently conceived organ accompaniment to the choruses instead of the traditional duplication of voice parts.

E. Dickinson, *Music in the History of the Western Church,* (1931); N. B. Foster, *Anthems and Anthem Composers* (1901). E.H.B.

anthesteria: (Gr. *anthestēria,* from *ánthos,* flower) The Feast of Flowers, a three days' festival of Dionysus at Athens in the month Anthestērion, (Feb.-Mar.), in which the slaves participated. E.M.N.

Anthony, Saint: (251-c. 356) Abbot, founder of Christian monasticism*, b. Coma, Egypt, died Mt. Colzin, near the Red Sea. At the age of twenty he gave away his inheritance to the poor and for twenty years lived in solitude in the mountains. At the end of this time he organized the monastic life for the crowds who had come to him. He visited Alexandria in 311 to support the Christians in persecution, and again in 350 to preach against the Arians. His feast is celebrated on Jan. 17, and his relics repose in a church near Vienne. He is the patron of Hospitallers*, butchers, basketmakers, grave-diggers, domestic animals, etc. He is invoked against skin-diseases, epilepsy and pestilence. See Anthony, St., Orders of. J.B.C.

Anthony, St. Orders of: Include under this name all the orders founded under the patronage of St. Anthony* the Hermit, or professing to follow his rule. Of these orders there are five: 1) The Disciples of St. Anthony (Antonians) were the men drawn to his hermitage in the Thebaid by the fame of his holiness; this group formed the first religious community of Christendom. 2) Antonines or Hospital Brothers of St. Anthony were a congregation founded by a certain Gaston of Dauphne and his son c. 1095. Their first house and hospital were built near the church of St. Anthony at Saint-Didier de la Mathe. The order continued until the French Revolution. 3) Antonians was the name given to a group of orthodox Armenians founded during the 17th century at the time of the persecution of Catholic Armenians. The founder was a certain Abram Atar Poresigh. 4) A Congregation of St. Anthony was founded in Flanders in 1615 under the rule of St. Augustine. 5) The Chaldean Antonians of the Congregation of Sain-Hormisdas was founded in Mesopotamia by Gabriel Dambo in 1809. T.T.M.

anthropology: 1) A branch of systematic theology which deals with the doctrines of man's origin, primitive condition, probation and apostasy, original sin, actual transgressions, and free agency.

2) The general science of man, comprising two major divisions: *physical anthropology* which treats of what man was and is as an animal, and *cultural anthropology,* which treats of what he has discovered and invented, learned and communicated, as a social being.

The word seems to have been coined by Aristotle in his *Ethics,* where he uses it in a non-complimentary sense, to describe negatively the lofty-minded man who, he says is *ouk anthropologos,* not a gossip nor a talker about himself. It was first employed in English in an anonymous book, *Anthropologie Abstracted; or, the Idea of Humane Nature Reflected in Briefe Philosophical and anatomical collections,* published in 1655. But not until after the appearance of the *British Encyclopedia* of 1822 did the term acquire its present inclusive scientific meaning.

Physical anthropology is a branch of natural science, and is in turn composed of several subsidiary disciplines. (a) *Anthropogeny* treats of the origin of man and his ancestors, including the geological evidence to determine the time and physical conditions of their appearance, the biological evidence to discover their living companions, both plant and animal, and the anatomical evidence to demonstrate their similarities to and their differences from present living races. It is therefore largely dependent upon general palaeontology. (b) *Somatology* studies the physical characteristics of the various races and sub-races. Since these can be accurately compared only when reduced to quantitive terms, it has developed the technique of *anthropometry,* or the measurement of the physical dimensions and proportions that characterize races. Because of the great emphasis formerly laid upon the characteristics of the skull as criteria of race, somatology has stimulated the intensive study of *craniology,* and because in the case of fossil races only the bones or bony fragments have survived the ravages of time, somatology also depends for its knowledge of prehistoric races largely on *osteology,* which treats of the development, structure, articulation, etc., of the parts of the skeleton. (c) The geographical distribution of races and the influence of environment upon physique, a branch of *anthropogeography,* has long claimed the attention of physical anthropologists. (d) *Racial psychology* has made little progress, owing to the subtle nature of such racial differences in structure of the central nervous system as may exist, and to the impossibility of measuring their functions directly apart from the effects of training and experience. (e) Renewed interest in the problems of *racial physiology and bio-chemistry* has resulted from recent advances in those fields, while Dr. Edward Loth's attempted study of (f) the *comparative anatomy and morphology of the soft tissues* in 1931 yielded limited results because few if any accurate dissections have been done on some of the races of man.

Cultural anthropology is a branch of the historical and social sciences, and has also given rise to many specialities. Of these (a) *linguistics,* or the comparative study of language, is basic, since language is the chief means through which culture is symbolized and communicated. (b) *Technology* is the comparative study of the material inventions and cultural equipment of races and peoples, the origins, development, and geographical distribution of their arts and industries. (c) *Prehistorical archaeology* is "technology in the past tense;" it studies the earliest remains of man's handiwork, and permits inferences as to the extent, distribution, and development of early industries, and the sequences and duration of prehistoric periods. It reveals, however, only partial knowledge, since man's early handiwork in wood, bone, and other perishable materials has rarely been preserved, and the techniques and skills employed in supplying wants are often left to conjecture. (d) *Social anthropology* is the comparative study of custom and tradition, social organization and institutions, including marriage and the family, economics, education, moral ideas and codes, government and law, folk-lore, magical and religious beliefs and practices, etc. Social anthropology has been distinguished from sociology in its development in that the former has been chiefly concerned with peoples who do not possess a written history. This is due to the fact that when social anthropology became conscious of itself as a science, other specialized disciplines were already engaged in the study of peoples of advanced culture, and the period of exploration had brought the European and American powers into close contact with alien races and customs. Anthropologists found a fresh field for scientific investigation in this enormous mass of new material and in the practical problems which arise when peoples of very different cultural backgrounds become socially interdependent. Both social anthropology merges into sociology insofar as R. R. Marett's caution, that "anthropology must not be allowed to sink to mere barbarology" is heeded.

As a comparatively new science, anthropology has been divided into antagonistic schools, of which the more important are the evolutionists, the diffusionists, the functionalists, and the American historical school. (a) The early *evolutionists,* such as Herbert Spencer and E. B. Tylor in England and Daniel Brinton in the United States, believed that the psychic unity of mankind impelled societies independently to invent the same ideas, institutions, and appliances in similar circumstances, regardless of historical contacts, and that all cultures and all elements of culture must pass through the same stages in the same order. The evolutionists were right in assuming that all races everywhere possess the capacity to invent the basic elements of civilization, and they had correctly observed the progress of knowledge, the increasing complexity of cultural forms, and their better adaptation as means to ends through the elimination of antiquated elements. But they erred in assuming that by the study of examples collected at random they could reconstruct a universal evolutionary scheme according to which every past and existing culture could be given its place in a single ascending line. Furthermore, the evolutionists never really understood Darwin, for his theory suggests neither independent origins, nor parallelism, nor unilinear evolution. He did not assert that each species had arisen again and again from humbler prototypes, nor that the various species had passed through identical stages of development. (b) The *diffusionist, or European historical school,* led by Fritz Graebner and Wm. Schmidt in Germany and by G. Elliott Smith and W. J. Perry in England, minimizes the possibilities of multiple inventions, denies the existence of necessary evolutionary sequences, and emphasizes the role played by borrowing from a few centers of cultural origin. The theory reaches its extreme form in W. J. Perry, whose hypothesis of a pan-Egyptian origin of all cultures is contradicted by an abundance of well-authenticated archaeological and historical data. (c) The *functional school,* led by Bronislaw Malinowski, turns aside from historical reconstructions and theories of origin of disparate elements of culture and devotes intensive study to specific cultures as integrated wholes with a view to "establishing the relationships between the various elements" and disclosing "the part played by any one factor of a culture within the general scheme." (4) The *American historical school,* under the leadership of the late Professor Franz Boas, has been less speculative and more thoroughly inductive in its methods. Its objective, as stated by Professor Boas, is to understand culture as a whole through "the reconomstruction of human history" and "the determination of types of historical sequences [and] the dynamics of change." It has tended to integrate the psychological approach of the older evolutionists with the diffusionist's caution against *a priori* schemes of cultural development and the functionalist's appreciation of the interplay of factors that constitute a particular society. Only thus, as T. K. Penniman has observed, can the anthropologist really "study Man, and not merely develop his own notions." See evolution; folklore.

Alfred C. Haddon, *History of Anthropology* (London, 1919); Robert H. Lowie, *The History of Ethnological Theory,* (1938); T. K. Penniman, *A Hundred Years of Anthropology,* (1936); Ralph Linton, *The Study of Man,* (1936). H.E.J.

anthropology, theological: The doctrine of man (from Greek *anthropos* and *logos*). What distinguishes the theological doctrine from philosophical and psychological views of man, is its having regard solely to man as he is known in his relation to God. Man was created by God to share God's purposes and enjoy followship with Him. He was endued with powers of mind and spirit appropriate to this. He has, however (historically and each of us in himself), chosen perversely his own way (the Fall*); and while theologies differ as to the effect of this apostasy on man's proper being (Is the divine image in him erased, defaced or only obscured?), all agree that by it man's rank before God is that of sinner, and evil and disorder are brought into his world. Nor is there recovery either for his world or himself in his own resource; but only in the fact that He who created man to such high estate and destiny has, now that these are forfeit through man's disobedience, employed His power a second time to retrieve and restore. Divine grace* and salvation* are the complement of the Christian doctrine of man.

H. W. Robinson, *The Christian Doctrine of Man* (3rd ed. 1926); E. Brunner, *Man in Revolt* (1939); Oxford Conference (1937) series on Church, Community and State, II: *The Christian Understanding of Man* (1938); R. Niebuhr, *The Nature and Destiny of Man*, I (1941); II (1943). J.L.

anthropomorphism: (Gr. *anthropos*, man; *morphe*, form) Ascription of human traits to things other than man. Term often used to discredit any analogy, however remote, between man and the non-human. Yet the alternatives to a legitimate, limited analogy between human and non-human are an illegitimate, inaccurate analogy, or an unintelligible dualism. The purely "unknowable" is, as Peirce* said, the sole (and illusory) escape from the task of finding a reasonable anthropomorphism. See analogy; anthropopathism; God as Personal. C.H.

anthropopathism: (Gr. *anthropos*, man; *pathein*, suffer) Ascription of human feelings to the non-human. Ruskin's "pathetic fallacy" disparaged the process as applied to inanimate nature. Ruskin condemned the attribution, not of all mental states to nature, but only of specifically man-like states. So, to ascribe feeling to God is not necessarily to ascribe human feeling to Him. See anthropomorphism; God as Personal. C.H.

anti-Benevolent Society agitation in the U. S.: See anti-missionary movement in the U. S.

anti-Bible Society agitation in the U. S.: See anti-missionary movement in the U. S.

antichrist: Literally, one who opposes or denies Christ. More specifically, a great antagonist who is expected to fill the world with wickedness but who will be defeated by Christ at his second coming. The earliest occurrence of the word is in the NT (I John 2:18, 22; 3:7; 4:3; II John 7). The origin of the belief (as distinct from the title) may be seen in the Iranian conflict between Ahriman and Ahura Mazda*. From Persia this view of strife between the supreme powers of good and of evil made its way into Jewish thought and eventually into Christianity. In subsequent Christian thinking Antichrist has been identified with the Roman empire or emperors (especially Nero), with Mohammed, and not infrequently with the Roman popes (*e.g.*, by Wycliffe and Luther).

W. Bousset, *Kyrios Christos*, (2nd. ed., 1921). M.S.E.

antilegomena: (Gr. *anti*, against; *lego*, to say, speak) A term anciently used of literary works whose genuineness was questionable, and applied by Origen, Eusebius and others to the group of NT books whose place in the canon was disputed in their day. With some justification from Eusebius it has in modern times been loosely used (*e.g.*, Preuschen, *Antilegomena*, 1901) as practically equivalent to apocrypha*. See Canon. A.P.W.

anti-missionary movement in the United States: Commonly considered to have originated as a frontier offshoot of Baptist life and to have since remained peculiarly associated with the history of that denomination. Recent findings, however, indicate that this movement has been of broader scope than suspected. In origin it does not now appear to have been solely a frontier phenomenon, nor does the Baptist denomination appear to be the only one to have experienced its inroads.

About the year 1820 there arose almost simultaneously at home bases and on the frontier a mighty gust of anti-missionary activity to which at least nine distinct religious groups are known to have contributed momentum. Of these groups only the factions led by John Taylor, Daniel Parker and Alexander Campbell* can be said to have taken root immediately in Baptist soil. The remaining groups in probable order of the strength of their opposition voices were the unaffiliated "Free Thinkers", the Universalists, the Christian Connection (both New England and Western divisions), the "Reformed" Methodists, the Hicksite Quakers and the Unitarians.

A search for the reasons occasioning this unsuspectingly widespread opposition to missionary endeavor reveals a basic cause buttressed substantially by a number of subsidiary considerations peculiar to one or more of the specific groups involved.

The basic cause was a deep-running fear of the consequences of the early eighteenth century tendency toward centralization of religious authority. In light of the age, the fear is quite understandable.

From 1796 to 1830 "national" organization for "benevolent" purposes came to be an American religious epidemic. One after another the evangelical denominations effected the organization of "national" Missionary, Bible, Sunday School, Tract and Educational societies for the propagation of their distinctive beliefs both at home and abroad. Then in turn each denomination took upon itself the task of establishing a theological seminary where young men might be trained under benevolent auspices to be sent forth as salaried missionaries to remote areas. Finally came the startling innovation of "national" benevolent societies which waived denominational doctrines to secure united religious action—notably the "American" Bible, Peace, Sunday School, Tract, Colonization, Seamen's, Temperance and Prison Reform societies. To minority groups within denominations as well as to minor denominations this ever-increasing tendency to "national" organization and concentration of financial resources in the hands of a few society executives loomed as a great danger to religious liberty. A single denomination or group of denominations might conceivably become so powerful as to effect a practical union of Church and State despite constitutional guarantees to the contrary. It was imperative therefore that *all* benevolent societies organized on a "national" basis be vigorously opposed. Whether or not the society carried the word "missionary" in its title was immaterial. All national benevolent societies stood as possible missionary vehicles for the union of church and state and needed to be opposed as such.

Serving as subsidiary props to support this basic fear of centralization of religious authority were anti-missionary arguments that may be classified in one of three categories: 1. Scriptural, 2. Doctrinal, 3. Cultural. The argument that benevolent societies were "human" institutions contrary to Scripture was the special weapon of Campbell and Parker, but used freely by all the anti-missionary groups excepting the Unitarians and "Free Thinkers". The doctrinal argument is not so easily explained. On the one hand, the hyper-Calvinism of the Baptist reactionaries tended naturally to belittle the "human" efforts of benevolent societies to meddle with the divine plan. On the other hand, liberally inclined theological groups like the "Reformed" Methodists, the Hicksite Quakers, the Unitarians and the Universalists felt in variant degree the necessity of sanctioning anti-missionism as a means of resisting powerful orthodox combines. Holding a middle position, the Christian Connection remained true to its basic doctrine that all names should be cast aside but that of "Christian" by opposing the sectarian character of most benevolent societies, yet could not bring itself to support undenominational benevolent effort for fear that it would lead to orthodox ascendancy. As for the cultural roots of the movement, they were both intellectual and crude. To the Harvard trained Unitarian, the sophistically inclined Universalist and the outspoken "Free-Thinker" the missionary movement as conducted was an unnecessary waste of excitement, money and life. Especially was this true with respect for foreign missions, inasmuch as it was claimed that no thinking person could credit a loving God with condemning to perdition an ignorant heathen who had not yet heard of Christ. The conversion of the heathen could wait until such time as the cause of liberal theology had been won at home. To the rugged frontiersman who was one of the chief objects of the missionary enterprise, evangelical benevolent efforts were even more incomprehensible. Dapper young missionaries educated in the eastern "priest factories" were being sent to convert him as if he hadn't had any religion up to now. Moreover, they were being paid to do it. They were working for money instead of for God. The old semi-literate farmer-preacher with his "call to preach" for nothing was much preferred.

About 1840 the basic fear of a denominational or orthodox combine that might achieve practical union of Church and State began to abate. With its diminishment anti-missionary propaganda naturally began to lose its force. By degrees active opposition to benevolent enterprise came to be confined chiefly to the "Primitive" and "Two-Seed-in-theSpirit (Parkerite)**" Baptists who concentrated in the south central states. The story of the exact nature of the recession of the opposition spirit in other-than-Baptist groups awaits further research.

The early twentieth century has added two new types of anti-missionism. Russellism, due to Pastor Russell's anti-ecclesiastical zeal, has offered some support. Fundamentalism, quite irrespective of denominational lines, has contributed its heated charges of heterodoxy against forward-looking missionaries, liberal members of theological faculties and pioneering personnel in other benevolently sponsored projects.

Today, however, anti-missionary agitation is once more reverting to its perennial Primitive Baptist base in the South where some 100,000 supporters, one third of whom are Negro, still rally.

The Baptist phases are treated at length in B. H. Carroll, *The Genesis of American Anti-Missionism* (1902) and W. W. Sweet, *Religion on the American Frontier: the Baptists* (1931), Chap. IV. Book material on 18th century activity within other groups is not available, but 18th century periodicals provide ample data. For the Christian view see *Gospel Luminary* (Rochester and New York City, 1825-33, and *Christian Messenger* (Georgetown, Ky., 1826-45). For "Free-Thinker" argument see *Reformer* (Phila., 1820-35), *Plain Truth* (Canandaigua, N. Y., 1822-1824: Rochester, N. Y., 1828-29), *Correspondent* (N. Y. 1827-1829), *Priestcraft Exposed* (Lockport, N. Y., 1828-29) and *Priestcraft Unmasked* (N. Y. and Phila., 1830). For Hicksite Quakers see *Berean* (Wilmington, Del., 1824-28). For Reformed Methodists see *Telescope* (N. Y., 1822-24), *Friendly Visitor* (N. Y., 1825), *Cry From the North* (Boston, 1827), *Cry From the Four Winds* (Boston, 1827-28) and even some issues of the *Christian Adovcate* (N. Y., 1826 through 1840). For Unitarian view see *Christian Examiner*, Boston, Vol. I no. 3 (June 1824) pp. 182-196. For Universalists see *Trumpet* (Boston, 1828-64), *Sentinel and Star in the West* (Cincinnati, O., 1829-36) and almost any Universalist periodical 1828ff. G. P. Albaugh, *An Annotated Bibliography of Religious Periodicals and Newspapers in What is Now the United States*, 1730-1830 (1943) expands this list considerably and gives library locations. For Russellite view see C. W. Ferguson, *Confusion of Tongues* (1929), Chap. IV, especially pp. 79,80. For Fundamentalism see S. G. Cole, *History of Fundamentalism*, Index under "Missions", "Theological education", etc. G.P.A.

anti-national religious organization agitation in the U. S.: See anti-missionary movement in the U. S.

antinomianism: A term used to indicate types of ethical thought in which hostility to the law of Moses has led to a tendency to immoral teaching or practice. There are traces of this kind of thought in the NT, where it represented a phase of Paul's struggle to clarify the relations of the Gospel and the Law. There is a strain of antinomianism in the Gnostics*, and certain other groups —the Marcions and the Manicheans**, for example—rejected the Mosaic law, though without using this as an excuse for immorality. Throughout the Middle Ages there were various heretical groups which preached antinomianism, and some went so far as to claim that even harlotry was not sinful to the spiritual man. Antinomianism was prominent in the discussions of the sixteenth and seventeenth centuries. In England the Famillists gained a foothold, and during the Civil War all such groups increased considerably. The best known sect—and one regarded at the time with most horror—was the Ranters*. They believed that nothing is sin except what a man believes to be so. There was also a Baptist antinomianism of a different order which sprang from hyper-Calvinism. Antinomian controversies raged furiously throughout the sixteenth and seventeenth centuries. The best known was in Germany, and involved Luther, Melanchthon and Agricola**. It was ended by the Formula of Concord* (1577). Antinomian controversy also flourished in England and even more so in New England. See Adamites. G.R.C.

antinomy: (Gr. *anti,* against, and *nomos,* law) A pair of contradictory propositions each of which can be shown to follow necessarily from a common premise. The presence of antinomy proves either that the common premise is false or that reason is inherently self-contradictory. Kant* drew the former conclusion in his dialectic, and denied that the empirical world is "a given whole," since from that premise there followed with equal necessity the assertion and the denial of the infinite divisibility, etc., of space and time. See N. K. Smith, Commentary on *Kant's Critique of Pure Reason* (1918). See antinomianism. E.S.B.

Antioch (in Pisidia): A city in Phrygia on the main road connecting Syria with western Anatolia (the *Sebaste*), founded by Seleucus Nicator ca. 280 B.C. In the 1st century A.D. it was thoroughly Hellenized, with a large Jewish population, and had become the center of Roman civil and military administration in South Galatia. Two visits of St. Paul to the city are referred to in Acts 13:14 and 14:21, and two others possibly implied in 14:6 and 18:23. S.M.G.

Antioch (in Syria): A city on the Orontes river, about twenty miles from the Mediterranean. Founded ca. 300 B.C. by Seleucus Nicator. In 64 B.C. made the capital of the Roman Province of Syria. Some unnamed Christians fled to Antioch from Jerusalem following Stephen's martyrdom and founded a new church which included among its members Greeks as well as Jews (Acts 11:19 ff.). It was at Antioch that the term "Christian" was first given to converts to the new faith (Acts 11:26). It was Paul's point of departure on his first missionary journey (Acts 13:4). S.M.G.

Antioch, Synod of: There were two synods held at Antioch in 340 A.D. in connection with the Arian* controversy. The first was held by the Semi-Arians* or Eusebians, at which Athanasius suffered one of his many depositions. The second synod, in an effort to conciliate the West which was strongly Nicean, drew up four creeds one after the other which were as Nicean as possible without actually using the term *homo-ousios** (the same substance), to which the Semi-Arians objected as much as the Arians did. A.K.R.

Antiochene (Syrian) Rite: The complexus of liturgical and disciplinary laws and customs originally used in the patriarchate of Antioch. This rite in variants is followed by the Syrian Jacobites*, who are divided into a Monophysite Church with 80,000 members, and a Catholic Church with 71,000 members. A group of Malabar Christians (250,000) also follows the Antiochene rite. In 1930 five thousand of these in Malankara were united with Rome. The Syrian Melchites, both Orthodox and Catholic, follow since the thirteenth century the Byzantine rite*. E.A.R.

Antiochian School: Not a school in the sense of a teaching institution with buildings and a regular succession of teachers and students; but rather a certain type of theological attitude, begun possibly by Lucian* of Antioch, and associated with Antioch until, after the condemnation of Nestorius* in A.D. 433, its centre was transferred to Nisibis and Edessa*. In conscious opposition to the allegorical method of Scripture interpretation associated with the School of Alexandria,* and sometimes through bitter controversy with it and its adherents, the school of Antioch practiced the sounder grammatico-historical method. (See Biblical criticism.) But this basic method that was common to all the adherents, could be associated with such widely different kinds of spirit as the pre-Arian point of view of Lucian and the rationalism of Theodore*, on the one hand, and the basic orthodoxy of Chrysostom and Theodoret** on the other. A.K.R.

Antiochus Epiphanes, crisis under: Seleucid king (175-163 B.C.), who attempted to "coordinate" the Jews in his Hellenization program. Forbade Jewish worship and religious customs under penalty of death and defiled temple at Jerusalem with an idol 167 B.C. His oppression reflected in Dan. 7:8, 25, 8:11-14, 24-26, 9:27, 11:31-36. The temple was purified and rededicated Dec. 165 B.C., (an event commemorated in the Hanukka* festival). See Judas Maccabeus; Maccabees, Books of. E.G.K.

antiphon: (Gr., responsive sound) 1) A phrase from Scripture sung before and after the canticles and psalms in the Divine Office*, giving the "color" of the festival or season. 2) A psalm sung antiphonally by the two sides of the choir. See anthem. P.V.N.

Antiphonary: (Lat., *antiphonarium, liber antiphonarius*) The liturgical book containing the chants sung by cantors and choir in the Divine Office (Breviary)**. P.V.N.

anti-pope: An anti-pope is a false claimant to the Holy See* in opposition to a canonically elected or universally recognized Roman Pontiff or Bishop of Rome. Such pretenders, subsidized by schismatical factions in the Church, German Emperors, or rebellious cardinals, appear in various periods of the Church's history. According to Hergenroether there were twenty-nine such anti-popes, beginning with Novatian*, 251 A.D. and ending with Felix

V. (Amadeus of Savoy: 1439-49). At times, as e.g., during the Great Western Schism* (1378-1417), there were as many as three contemporary claimants to the Holy See. Due to the confusion of the times; to the subjective uncertainty of even well-meaning cardinals, bishops, generals of Religious Orders, kings and even saints; and to the loyal adherence of the greater part of the Church to any given claimant, Alexander V, (1409-10), elected at the Council of Pisa and John XXIII (1410-14) are not considered anti-popes whereas due to restricted nationalistic adherence of their subjects and open rebellion from the very start, Clement VII (Robert of Geneva: 1373-94) and Benedict XIII (Peter de Luna: 1394-1414) are characterized as such. Cf. article Alexander III, Pope; Pope.

Cath. Encyc. I, 582; *The New Cath. Dict.* (London, 1929), 52-53. R.M.H.

anti-saloon league: See temperance movement.

anti-semitism: A popular name for the prejudice against Jews to which various social pressures have contributed. In each period of history, however, this prejudice has found distinct outlets. In ancient times, the Jews like the Christians, were charged with disloyalty to the Roman Empire for refusal to conform to the emperor cult as idolatrous. In the Middle Ages, Jews were condemned for persisting as a religious minority. In modern times anti-semitism has been fostered by various fascist states which have found Jewish universalism inconsistent with their own tribal nationalism. Anti-semitism has been condemned by the leading ecclesiastical representatives of both Catholicism and Protestantism, as is well summarized in Jacques Maritain's *A Christian Looks at the Jewish Question,* (1939) (Catholic); and *Protestants Answer Anti-Semitism,* edited by Beatrice Jenney, (1941). See ghetto. B.Z.B.

Antisthenes: (ca. 444-368 B.C.) See Cynics.

anti-Sunday School movement in the U. S.: See anti-missionary movement in the U. S.

anti-theological education agitation in the U. S.: See anti-missionary movement in the U. S.

anti-Tract movement in the U. S.: See anti-missionary movement in the U. S.

anti-Trinitarianism: See Unitarianism.

Anu: Sumerian god of the sky, head of the pantheon; in Babylonia he was worshiped at Uruk (Erech), in Assyria at Ashshur*. See Mesopotamian Religions. R.H.P.

Anubis: See Hermes; Egypt, Religions of.

Anunnaki: See Igigi.

Apis: Egyptian bull-god; a black bull with distinctive white markings whose worship was linked with various gods. At Memphis, Egypt, the bull (Apis) was regarded as the body of the god Ptah; when the bull-god died it was buried with elaborate ceremonies. Embalmed bodies of bulls discovered in the Apis cemetery belonged to the period from the Late Empire until the Ptolemies. See Egypt, religions of. F.L.P.

Apocalypse of Moses: See Jubilees, Book of.

apocalypticism, apocalyptic literature: (Gr. *apokaluptein,* to uncover or disclose) A type of thought which flourished in late Judaism and early Christianity, producing a distinctive kind of literature (165 B.C.-120 A.D.). The purpose of these writings was to nerve the faithful to stand firm against the cruel fate they were enduring, with confidence that speedily the tables would be turned and evil would be destroyed. Underlying these writings was the view (not native to Judaism) that the present evil age, under the dominion of the archfiend, would come to a dramatic close. The world would literally come to an end, would be consumed with fire to purify it from evil. The righteous would rise to take their place in a new and purified world. The present evils (the worship of God prohibited by a foreign tyrant, or Israel oppressed by Rome, or Christians persecuted by nonbelievers) were in large part due to the machinations of evil spirits who had unleashed their forces in a final clash with the forces of good.

The best-known apocalypses are the canonical Daniel and Revelation, but many others of similar nature were produced, among which are Ethiopian Enoch, Slavonic Enoch (*Secrets of Enoch*), Syriac Baruch, IV Ezra, *Apocalypse of Peter, Ascension of Isaiah.* In addition are several semiapocalypses, such as the *Assumption of Moses, Book of Jubilees,* and *Shepherd of Hermas.* Mark 13 has not infrequently been regarded as an earlier apocalypse recast as a prophetic word of Jesus.

Regularly these writings purport to have been written by the great men of the past—Ezra, Moses, Abraham, Noah, Adam—who had had revealed to them in visions by angels appointed for this purpose what was to come to pass, but who had kept the matters secret, to be revealed just before the end. Frequently under the transparent fiction of fearful beasts and the lush angelology the actual circumstances which convinced the anonymous writer that the bell was about to strike can be detected. The essential difference between these writings and those of the prophets, with which they have often been compared and contrasted, is that the prophets raised their voices in protest in times of prosperity, to rebuke and to warn; the apocalyptists, on the contrary, wrote in times of distress to nerve the faithful to stand firm—the darkest moment always presages the dawn.

The origin of this type of thought is probably to be found in Persian dualism—the twelve-thousand year struggle between Ahriman and his demonic hosts and Ormuzd and his angels. While certain elements of this thinking (notably the notion of resurrection and future life) came to be appropriated by normative Judaism and was read back into its scriptures, apocalypticism and its writings never became central or even prominent in orthodox Jewish thought; they were, in fact, totally ignored by the rabbinic writers. For Christians it was quite different. From the first the early disciples saw in Jesus the supernatural son of man* mentioned in Daniel, and expected his imminent return on the clouds of heaven (see Millenarianism). The Christians eagerly appropriated them and recast the material to form new ones of their own. Cf. Final Judgment.

R. H. Charles, *The Apocrypha and Pseudepigrapha of the Old Testament*, 2 vols. (1913).
M. S. Enslin, *Christian Beginnings* (1938), pp. 351-372. M.S.E.

apocatastasis: The word means literally "re-establishment", and was used in Stoic* philosophy to express the belief that all things, after a cycle of ages, would return to their original condition. This idea has commended itself to various thinkers (e.g., Nietzsche), and has been defended on mathematical grounds. Luke employs the term in Ac. 3:21 to convey to his Greek readers the conception of the Kingdom of God. In its verbal form it also occurs in Mt. 17:11 where it applies to the restoration of true religion before the advent of the Messiah.

W. L. Davidson, *The Stoic Creed* (1907). E.F.S.

apocrypha, early Christian use of: In NT times the canon of scripture was still, to some extent, fluid, and many books not definitely included in the OT were regarded as in some sense biblical. The NT attitude to them seems to be indicated in the difficult passage 2 Tim. 3:15, 16, where it is said that Timothy from his childhood had known "sacred literature", i.e., books dealing with religious themes. Every such writing, it is added, is inspired by God, and is helpful to the Christian teacher, forming a kind of supplement to scripture proper. A number of passages can be collected from the NT in which reference is made to books now reckoned apocryphal. The familiar verses Matt. 11:28-30 are reminiscent of the closing words of Ecclesiasticus*. Luke quotes expressly (11:49) from some lost apocryphal book, described as "the wisdom of God". Paul frequently echoes the apocrypha, and most notably the Wisdom of Solomon*, from which the argument in the first two chapters of Romans is largely borrowed. The author of Heb. takes one of his examples of faith from the 2nd book of Maccabees*. The Jewish Apocalypses (see Apocalyptic Literature) formed a group by themselves. Although not scriptural they claimed to preserve visions granted to holy men, and could thus be regarded as in some sense of divine origin. The author of Revel. makes free use of ancient apocalypses, and references to them can be traced throughout the NT. See Old Testament.

References are minutely noted in R. H. Charles *Apocrypha and Pseudepigrapha of the Old Testament* (1912). E.F.S.

apocrypha in the New Testament church: The books included in our NT were only a selection from a considerable literature which was current in the church of the first two centuries. Before the canon was finally determined a number of those early writings found a place in it, along with those which we still read. Some of them came to be rejected for no other reason than that they were obviously inferior, both in literary and religious value, to our present Gospels and Epistles. Although they were dropped from the NT they are still preserved in the collection of the Apostolic Fathers (e.g., I Clement, Shepherd of Hermas, Epistle of Barnabas). Others are known as Apocrypha, with the suggestion that they never had any valid title to acceptance. For the most part these apocryphal books were deliberate fabrications. It was a common practice, especially among the Gnostics, to propagate heretical doctrine by means of writings composed in the name of revered Apostles. In the more ignorant communities these forgeries were sometimes used without suspicion in the church service. Other spurious books were written with no theological motive but merely in imitation of the genuine NT writings. All the different types of NT literature were thus imitated. There still survives an Epistle purporting to be Paul's lost letter to the Laodiceans. We possess in whole or in part a number of Gospels (e.g., the Gospel of the Hebrews, the Gospel of Peter, the Gospel of the Infancy). The book of Acts afforded the model for numerous works which might be described as historical romances (The Acts of Paul and Thecla, the Acts of John, the Acts of Thomas*). The book of Revelation gave rise to a whole series of similar books, of which the earliest and most notable is the so-called Apocalypse of Peter . It has often been regretted that so many of the apocryphal writings exist only in fragments, or have left nothing but the record of their names. From what we possess, however, it does not appear that they were of much value. It is evident, for instance, that the authors of the non-canonical Gospels had no information about the life of Jesus apart from that given them in the NT records. Everything they add is derived from their own fancy or their peculiar doctrines. See pseudepigrapha, N.T.

M. James, *The Apocryphal New Testament* (1924);
B. Pick, *Paralipomena* (1908) E.F.S.

apocrypha, Old Testament: (Gr. neuter pl. of adjective *apokryphos*, hidden, secret). Writings of scriptural form or content, but excluded from the canon*, designated in Hebrew *sepharim hizonim*, "outside books", and *siphre minim*, "heretical books" (Sanh. X, 1). The term first bore a laudatory meaning of esoteric writings withheld from the uninitiated because of their sacred and mysterious nature (4 Ezra 14. 44-47; cf. Dan. 12. 4, 9). Owing to its application to writings of sectarians, like the Gnostics*, it acquired (since the second century) a disparaging sense of non-canonical, untrustworthy, spurious, and even false and heretical. It came to denote especially works of doubtful origin or authorship, pseudepigraphs.

Specifically the Apocrypha of the OT contains fourteen books commonly found in the Greek Bible (the Septuagint*) and the Latin Vulgate* in excess over the Hebrew Bible. They are (in the order in which they appear in the Authorized and in the Revised Versions): 1) 1 Esdras; 2) 2 Esdras (same as 4 Ezra**); 3) Tobit*; 5) Additions to Esther*; 6) Wisdom of Solomon*; 7) Ecclesiasticus* or Wisdom of Jesus the Son of Sirach; 8) Baruch*, with the Epistle of Jeremiah; 9) Song of the Three Children*; 10) History of Susannah*; 11) Bel and the Dragon*; 12) Prayer of Manasses*; 13) 1 Maccabees; 14) 2 Maccabees**.

Excepting 1 and 2 Esdras and the Prayer of Manasses, these books form part of the Catholic canon. At the Council of Trent* (1546) their canonicity was formally reaffirmed. The Protestants, on the other hand, following Jerome*, exclude them from sacred Scriptures. Accordingly they initiated the usage of Apocrypha for a collection of books appended to the OT and (up to 1827) generally added to every English Bible*. While some Reformed Churches banished the Apocrypha from public worship, the Church of England* prescribes its reading in public services "for example of life and instruction of manners".

Catholics class these books as "deuterocanonical" and reserve the name Apocrypha for other quasi-scriptural books in excess over those of the Vulgate to which Protestants give the name Pseudepigrapha. The difference in nomenclature is purely arbitrary. The term Apocrypha may be well applied to the whole body of non-canonical literature of the Jews produced in the last centuries B.C. and the first century C.E. in Palestine and in Egypt, mostly in Hebrew and Aramaic and some in Greek.

The books of the Apocrypha proper may be classified as: 1) Historical, including histories, historical tales, legends, supplements and embellishments of the OT; 2) Didactic or Sapiential; and 3) Apocalyptic. The last type predominates in the Pseudepigrapha. The entire material is of greatest value for the Jewish religious development between the Old and the New Testaments.

See apocalyptic literature; canon; Judith; pseudepigrapha.

R. H. Charles, *The Apocrypha and Pseudepigrapha of the O. T. in English* (Standard work), (Oxford, 1913); M. R. James, *Lost Apocrypha of the O. T.* (1920); E. Schuerer, *History of the Jewish People* (1909), Vol. 3.

S.S.C.

Apollinarianism: A name given to the theological system of Apollinaris of Laodicea*. Apollinaris held that Christ had a human body and a human soul but no human mind or spirit. In Him this was replaced by the divine *Logos,* the source of Christ's self-consciousness. Apollinaris attracted a considerable following in spite of the fact that his ideas were anathematized by synods of the church, but soon after his death the sect became extinct. See Christology. S.M.G.

Apollinaris of Laodicea: (died A.D. 390) Bishop of Laodicea in Syria in the late 4th century. In his early days an opponent of Arianism*. Collaborated with Apollinaris the Elder in the reproduction of the Scriptures on classical models to compensate Christians for the edict of the emperor Julian denying them the right to teach the classics. Author of a theological system condemned as heretical by several synods, and in particular by that of Constantinople in 381. S.M.G.

apologetics, Christian: The science of the defence of Christian truth. In contrast to polemics*, Apologetics deals with points of view so fundamental to the Christian faith that argument with professing Christians is not anticipated, and only the attacks of non-Christians are envisaged. Negatively, an effort is made to anticipate the points of possible attack, and to defend them by evidence and sound reasoning. Positively, a Christian view of God and the World is elaborated, aiming to make it so adequate and winsome as to obviate attack before it even gets started. A.K.R.

apologists, early Christian: Early Christianity was soon subjected not only to physical violence but to severe criticism from Jewish and pagan opponents, and as it gradually came to feel its individual character as a new faith, it began to defend itself against these attacks. The earliest writing of exactly this kind of which we know was *The Preaching of Peter,* written early in the second century, and now lost except for a few fragments. It attacked both Greek and Jewish ways of worship, and described the Christians as "a third race". A second apology was that of Quadratus*, written in Athens in A.D. 125 or 129, to be presented to Hadrian, in order to obtain more lenient treatment for the Christians, but only a single sentence of it is preserved. A few years later, probably between A.D. 138 and 147, another Athenian, Aristides, addressed a defense of the new faith to the emperor Antoninus, but this too has disappeared, except for a Syriac translation and a free recast of the Greek in the mediaeval romance of Barlaam and Joasaph. It attacks Chaldean, Greek, Egyptian and Jewish forms of worship, in contrast with Christian worship and morals.

The dialogue was seized upon for purposes of Christian apologetic about A.D. 140 by Aristo of Pella, in Perea, and while his book has disappeared, Origen says it showed how the Jewish prophecies of Christ applied to Jesus. Both apology and dialogue were made use of by Justin* a few years later (150-165) for the purposes of Christian apologetic. See Minucius Felix, Marcus. E.J.G.

Apology of the Augsburg Confession: See Augsburg Confession.

apostasy: (Gr. *apo,* from, and *stasis,* standing) An interior or an exterior lapsing from the Faith, in a conscious and formal way or only in a material sense, after having received faith and baptism. The external, formal apostate is excommunicated*. See heresy; reprobation. L.R.W.

apostles: A word which is used in the N.T. with a variety of meanings: 1) The immediate disciples of Jesus. 2) The personal witnesses of the

Resurrection. 3) Men endowed in a special degree with the power of the Spirit. 4) Christian missionaries generally. The word apostle means literally "one sent out", and was used of the officials who left Jerusalem year by year to collect the temple-tax from Jews of the Dispersion. According to one view the church adopted the name from this Jewish custom, and applied it to emissaries formally appointed. But the suggestion is always present, in NT usage, that the "sending out" was the act of God or Christ, and that the church, at its public meeting, merely accepted, on the impulse of the Spirit, a choice already made. The significance of the word is important since the opposition to Paul was grounded on the charge that he was not a true Apostle. His enemies apparently held that no one was entitled to this name unless he had personally known Jesus, and Paul replies that he had seen him in his glorified body on the way to Damascus. (1 Cor. 9:1, Gal. 1:15, 16). He also points to the success of his work and his manifest possession of the Spirit as proof of a real apostleship. At a later time the name became little more than a conventional one. All who had been duly ordained to missionary work became by that act apostles. E.F.S.

Apostles' Creed: Not of Jerusalem or apostolic origin, arose through natural expansion of a trinitarian formula because of the inner needs of the churches and not in opposition to Marcion*. Its earliest Roman form: I believe in God, Father Almighty and in Christ Jesus, his Son our Lord, and in holy spirit, holy church, and resurrection of the flesh. In the fourth century, the myth of composition by the twelve apostles appears. It disappeared at Rome for centuries but was preserved, expanded, and returned to Rome by the Franks. Its text was never fixed by council and assumed its present form in the sixteenth century. There is no agreement regarding its interpretation. See creeds of Christendom; old Roman Symbol.

Burn, A. E., *The Apostles' Creed* (1928); Holl, Karl, *Gesammelte Aufsaetze*, II, 115-128 (1928); Lietzmann, Hans, *Geschichte der alten Kirche*, II (1936); Moehlman, C. H., *Protestantism's Challenge* (1939) and *Journal of Religion*, 1933, 301-19.

C.H.M.

Apostolic age and Apostolic Fathers: The term "Apostolic Age" is a vague and somewhat misleading one. Properly it should denote the period during which personal disciples of Jesus were still alive; but there is no means of determining when the last of them died. Moreover the church had entered on a new age when some of its original members must have been living. Paul died about 62 A.D., and with him the primitive period may be said to close. In modern usage the term "Apostolic Age" covers the whole century during which the NT books were written, although the later part of this century is described as "sub-apostolic". When the meaning of the word is thus extended a group of writers may be justly designated by the name commonly given to them of "Apostolic Fathers." Some of their works date from a time anterior to the later NT books, and are thus of the highest value for the light they throw on early Christian thought and practice. Several of them (e.g. Papias) are only known from quotations in the History of Eusebius. The works which survive are the Epistle of Clement, a homily known as the Second Epistle of Clement, the Epistle of Barnabas, the seven Epistles of Ignatius, the Didachê, the Shepherd of Hermas, the Epistle to Diognetus. The earliest of these writings is the First Epistle of Clement, dating from the end of the first century. The longest is the Shepherd of Hermas, an allegory in the form of visions, which illustrates some features of the popular Christianity of its day. The most important is the collection of letters by Ignatius, bishop of Antioch, written on his way to martyrdom at Rome. The Didachê (Teaching of the Twelve Apostles) was only discovered near the end of last century, and is a brief manual of early church order. See Patristics.

A. C. McGiffert, *The Apostolic Age* (1897); G. Weiss, *Urchristentum* (Eng. tr. 1938); J. B. Lightfoot, *The Apostolic Fathers* (1890). E.F.S.

Apostolic Canons: A collection of 85 rules for the direction of clerical life, forming the last chapter of the 8th book of the *Apostolic Constitutions**. Only the first 50 of these were recognized as valid by the Western Church. The Council of Trullo (692) repudiated the *Apostolic Constitutions* but gave its formal approval to the *Apostolic Canons*.

S.M.G.

Apostolic Christian Church: A sect of 57 churches and 5,800 members made up of German and Swiss churches established by Benedict Weyeneth about the middle of the nineteenth century. It is a holiness evangelistic association. See Evangelistic Associations; holiness churches.

E.T.C.

Apostolic Christian Church (Nazarene): A sect of 31 churches and 1,600 members said to have been brought to this country from Hungary and to represent the doctrines of the Swiss preacher Froelich. It is a pacifist group. See Evangelistic Associations; holiness churches.

E.T.C.

Apostolic Church Directory: A collection of 35 articles of moral and ecclesiastical instruction, made in the early 4th century and credited to the Apostles. Often called *Apostolic Church Ordinances*. S.M.G.

Apostolic Constitutions: A recension in eight books of the *Didascalia*, the *Didache**, and other early Christian writings, published late in the 4th century as a manual of Church discipline, worship and doctrine, and purporting to be the instructions of the Apostles as compiled by Clement* of Rome.

S.M.G.

apostolic delegate: See legates and nuncios, papal.

Apostolic Faith Mission: A pentecostal sect* originating in 1900 at Topeka, Kansas, and under the leadership of Miss Minnie Hanson and Mrs.

M. White. It denies being a denomination, and stresses sanctification, feet washing, spirit guidance, and healing; it treats sick persons by sending blessed handkerchiefs through the mails. It has 17 churches and 2,300 members. See Evangelistic Associations; holiness churches. E.T.C.

Apostolic Fathers: See Apostolic age.

Apostolic Methodist Church: See holiness churches.

Apostolic Overcoming Holy Church of God: A colored pentecostal sect founded in 1916 by W. T. Phillips, a former Methodist preacher, who became the bishop of his new group. The headquarters are at Mobile, Ala. See pentecostal sects. E.T.C.

apostolic see: (Gr. one sent, apostle, and Lat. *sedes,* seat) The see or diocese of the Pope; also called the Holy See*. L.R.W.

apostolic succession: The continuity of the Christian ministry is expressed by traditional Catholic groups in their doctrine of the apostolic succession, which in Roman theology tends to be understood as the historical sequence of the three orders of sub-deacon, deacon and priest (in the two grades of priest and ordaining priest or bishop); in Anglican theology as bishop, priest and deacon; and similarly in the Eastern Orthodox Church. Particular stress is laid upon the function of the bishop, especially in the Anglican and Orthodox communions. Among Protestant groups, Presbyterians have a theory of apostolic succession which locates it in the presbyterate functioning as a whole, or in an episcopal capacity. The entire conception of apostolic succession is defended, by all groups maintaining it, as a means of securing the purity and continuous character of Christian faith, and its preservation through the ages by a body especially designated for the purpose, namely the ministry as "from above" rather than evolved from congregations. This continuity is traced back to Christ and his apostles. See clergy. Cf. Consolamentum. W.N.P.

apotheosis: (Gr. *apothéosis,* from *apó,* quite; *theós,* god) 1. The act of transforming into a god, deification*. E.g., the apotheosis of Roman emperors at death, by state decree. (See emperor worship.) 2. The ascription of divine power to a human being; glorification. E.M.N.

apotropaism: The magic art of averting or overcoming evil influences and ill luck by resort to supposedly effective ritual acts, incantations, or other magic formulae; protective or defensive magic. R.E.W

a priori: See epistemology.

apse: (Gr. *apsis,* vault or arch) A semi-cylindrical projection, roofed with a half dome. It was derived from Roman precedent and was a constant feature of the early Christian basilicas* and the various schools of the Romanesque. It developed into the Gothic *chevet.* F.T.P.

Aquinas, St. Thomas: (1224?-1274) Theologian, philosopher and Dominican monk. Born in Italy the son of the Count of Aquin and the Countess of Theatre. As a child he was educated by the Benedictines* at Monte Cassino and in Naples; at twenty he joined the Dominicans*, and for many years studied at Paris and at Cologne under St. Albert the Great. At the age of 32 he obtained at Paris permission to teach, and from that time was a professor there and at the Papal Curia in Rome and at Naples. His writings are voluminous, but the chief ones are these, done mainly in the order given: A Commentary on Peter Lombard's *Sententiae,* the *Summa Contra Gentiles,* Commentaries on Aristotle's works, the *Summa Theologica,* and the *Questiones Disputatae* which are thorough discussions on Truth, on the Power of God, and on Evil.

He is at first influenced most by St. Augustine* and his theology and to some extent his philosophy are always indebted to this source. But his later works show him more and more, especially in psychology and epistemology, under the influence of Aristotle whom he calls the Philosopher. Among his characteristic teachings are the following. Things have determinate natures; human intellect can abstract these, and thus "know" things, but all our knowing is dependent on sensory images and on the body. God is knowable, not intuitively nor by way of St. Anselm's ontological argument, but a posteriori and naturally from things. Nature and its way must always be defended; e.g., though supernatural charity comes from God, we may not say with Peter Lombard* that it is the Holy Ghost dwelling in the soul. Aristotle is wrong in holding that the world-movement must be eternal, but philosophy cannot prove that it is temporal. Philosophy is based on natural data, theology on supernatural data; hence each has its own being. Man is a person and as such has rights beyond the temporal and political and is like God, and yet he is limited and dependent. See reason in religion. Scholasticism; soul; *Summa Theologica;* Thomism; universals, battle over. Cf. William de la Mare.

Martin Grabmann, *Thomas Aquinas,* His Personality and Thought. (Tr. 1928).
Jacques Maritain, *St. Thomas Aquinas,* Angel of the Schools. (Tr. London, 1933).
Martin D'Arcy, *Thomas Aquinas.* (London, 1930).
L.R.W.

Aralu: Abode of the dead in Babylonian mythology; the underworld, a vast dark and gloomy subterranean cave entered through a hole in the earth guarded by seven doors; all persons went there at death and none ever returned; they led a semi-conscious existence and lived on dust; they could give oracles to people on earth, hence the alternate name Shualu (signifying "to ask") which appears as Sheol* in the OT; referred to also under the names Ekur, Kigallu, and many epithets and metaphors. R.E.W.

Aramaic Language: Ancient tongue in which some parts of the O.T. were written (Jer. x, 11; Ezra iv, 8—vi, 18; vii, 12—26; Dan. ii, 4b—vii, 28). Jesus Christ spoke an Aramaic dialect.

Belongs to the North-Western branch of the Semitic family. See H. H. Rowley, *The Aramaic of the Old Testament* (1929). S.L.T.

Arameans: Ancient people kindred to the Hebrews, who occupied mainly the region of Syria. Often mentioned in the OT. See E. G. Kraeling, *Aram and Israel* (1918). S.L.T.

Aranyakas: Literally "forest treaties." That part of Hindu sacred literature which lies between the Brahmanas and the Upanishads. Either composed by or designed for those in the third of the four *ashrama*, the forest dwellers. See sacred literature, Hindu. C.S.B.

arcani disciplina: (Lat., discipline of the secret) A modern expression describing a practice which prevailed in the Church in the early centuries of debarring all but baptized believers from the celebration of the Eucharist. S.M.G.

archaeological periods: (Near East) A. Paleolithic (Old Stone Age)

1. Early Paleolithic

Surface finds have been found in Palestine and highland regions of Western Asia, while in Egypt Chellean and Acheulian flint tools have been found in geological formations, especially on the terraces of the Nile. There are no certain human remains earlier than this period in the Near East. Though dating is, of course, uncertain, this age is probably to be placed in the Pleistocene (geologic) Age, perhaps as early as the second or first interglacial period in Europe (over 200,000 yrs. ago at the least). A most important series of cave deposits in Palestine began at the end of the period (middle or late Acheulian), in the first phase of the third glacial age.

2. Middle Paleolithic

Age of Neanderthal man (Mousterian Period in Europe), the first distinguishable race, dwelling in Europe and Western Asia more than 50,000 to 100,000 years ago, in all probability. The first complete skeletons have been found in Palestine (12 in number) in caves of the Mt. Carmel range, though these specimens appear to be mixed with characteristics of *homo sapiens*. Neanderthal hunters had begun to inter their dead in such a way as to indicate a belief in an after life—the first trace of religious belief discernible.

3. Late Paleolithic

First appearance of *homo sapiens* in Europe (Cro-Magnon man), and the great development of cave painting in southwestern Europe. There was a great advance in the arts and crafts. Bodies were often buried with ornaments, and the first stone, bone, and ivory statuettes of nude women appear. The figurines and cave paintings probably indicate advanced religious or magical speculation, the nature of which is difficult to determine.

B. Mesolithic (Middle Stone Age)

Better represented in Palestinian caves (the Natufian culture) than anywhere else in the world. The culture was flourishing about 12,000 years ago, coming to an end before 6000 B.C. at the latest. Palestinian man of this age was small in stature (5 ft. to 5 ft. 4 in. high), and probably represents the earliest appearance of an historical race. He had learned to grow cereals (probably millet or wheat), domesticate animals, make stone basins, mortars, and simple stone constructions; and he was a firm believer in an after life.

C. Neolithic (Late Stone Age, cir. 7000-4500 B.C.)

In Europe this age is represented by the introduction of agriculture, the domestication of animals (both introduced into the Near East in the preceding period), the invention of pottery, and polished stone implements. In the Near East pottery was invented, and the first villages or experiments in community life appear. At Jericho the first sizeable building has been found, and from figurines discovered within and without may perhaps be interpreted as a temple. There are indications of a rather developed religious cult (including phallic models), and plastic statues in triads (father, mother, child) were found. Though the evidence is difficult to interpret, it has been suggested that the mythology and cultic symbolism associated with the gods of fertility must have been developed in this age. It is also probable that this is the age when megalithic burial monuments, such as dolmens and cromlechs, were built, not only in Europe but also in the Near East, though we are to reckon with a cultural lag in the case of the European Neolithic.

D. Chalcolithic ("Copper-Stone" Age, cir. 4500-3000 B.C.)

Transition period of great prosperity in the Near East, when copper first came into use, beautiful painted pottery developed in the Fertile Crescent, the first great public buildings built, writing developed (cir. 3500 B.C.), and agriculture and religion flourished. Temples became institutions of great power and influence. Abstractions, such as "soul", "divine", "mankind", "holiness", "goodness", "purity", and 'truth" were conceived. Basic cereals, fruit, and vegetables were grown.

E. The Bronze Age

1. The Early Bronze Age (cir. 3000-2000 B.C.)

A term in popular archaeological use, though bronze seems not yet to have been known. It is the age when the first organized states appear in Egypt and Mesopotamia, and can be said to mark the beginning of the historical period. Monumental architecture (including the Egyptian pyramids), statuary, and inscriptions occur, and mental activity was turned into a wide range of channels, including the production of great epics, such as the Sumerian creation and flood stories, and the first sign of a developing conscience in the realm of social idealism.

2. The Middle and Late Bronze Ages (cir. 2000-1500, and 1500-1200 B.C.)

Period of great international and intellectual activity, the rise and fall of the Egyptian, Babylonian, Hyksos, Hittite, and Mitannian (Horite) empires, the appearance of the first monotheism (14th cent., in Egypt), and the emergence of the Israelite people as a group, organized under a religious bond, in the highlands of Palestine.

F. The Iron Age

1. The First Iron Age (also called "Iron I" or "Early Iron Age", cir. 1200-900 B. C.)

Period of international turmoil, marked by the irruption of the "Sea-Peoples", including the Philistines, into Palestine and Syria, the introduction of iron into common use, and the greatest expansion of the Israelites as a nation under David and Solomon.

2. The Second Iron Age ("Iron II" or "Middle Iron", cir. 900-600 B.C.)

Period of the Divided Monarchy and prophetic reformation in Israel, of the great Phoenician commercial expansion (from whom the Greeks borrowed the alphabet), and of the rise and fall of the Assyrian empire.

3. The Third Iron Age ("Persian" or "Middle Iron", cir. 600-300 B.C.)

Period of the Neo-Babylonian and Persian empires, and of the Exile and Restoration of the Jews.

Subsequent periods need only be listed, since the outline of their history is fairly well known.

G. The Hellenistic-Roman Period (cir. 300 B.C.-300 A.D.)

H. The Byzantine Period (cir. 300-640 A.D.)

I. The Arab Period (cir. 640—)

W. F. Albright, *From the Stone Age to Christianity,* (1940) ; V. Gordon Childe, *New Light on the Most Ancient East,* (London, 1935) ; C. F. C. Hawkes, *The Prehistoric Foundations of Europe to the Mycenaean Age,* (London, 1939) ; *The Cambridge Ancient History,* Vols. I-XII (1923-1939).

See Biblical archaeology. G.E.W.

archaeology: A term made up of two Greek words, *archaios,* "ancient", and *logos,* "discourse". It means, therefore, the systematic study of antiquities; a science which begins its study when man first appears on earth in the closing epoch of geology. It is concerned with those remains of past civilizations which have been excavated, in the widest sense with both epigraphic and anepigraphic discoveries. See anthropology. G.E.W.

archbishop: See bishop.

archdeacon: See clergy.

archimandrite: See clergy.

architecture: See art, ecclesiastical, Christian; cathedral; church building; temples.

archives, ecclesiastical: The word archive, originally signifying a building where records were kept, came to be applied to the records. Ecclesiastical archives comprise all records, documents, historical materials, histories which a church organization preserves. R.H.N.

Arianism: The heresy especially associated with the name of Arius*, but continuing as a powerful force within the Church for two generations after its condemnation at Nicea (A.D. 325). From this date until 344 the Arian party, led by Eusebius of Nicomedia*, fellow-pupil with Arius of Lucian*, remained under cover, but attempted by court intrigue and slanderous attacks to eliminate the leaders of the Nicene party. From 344 to 361, as a result of the favor of Constantius, the second son of Constantine and an Arian, Arian views were given comparatively free play. It is during this period that three distinct schools of Arianism arose: the strict Arians or Anomoians*, the Semi-Arians or Homoiousion party, and the Homoians. The first group asserted the unlikeness of Christ to the Father; the second affirmed the famous "of like being (or substance)"; the third stood on the intermediate platform of "like the Father". After 361, the lead being given at a Synod of Alexandria held early in 362 and presided over by Athanasius*, the Semi-Arians and Nicenes gradually drew together and the way was prepared ecclesiastically for the condemnation of Arianism along with Apollinarianism* at Constantinople in 381—the Synod later to be known as the Second Ecumenical Council. Imperial convictions and policy, however, had a part in the termination of the Controversy, as they had had in its continuation. The subsequent history of Arianism is largely confined to its impressive missionary career among the Germanic tribes. In this connection the name of Ulfilas* (A.D. 311-383), "apostle to the Goths" and translator of the Scriptures into Gothic, is the most notable.

The Writings of Athanasius, Basil of Caesarea, Gregory of Nyssa, and Gregory Nazianzus; The Church Histories of Eusebius, Socrates, Sozomen, and Theodoret—also of Philostorgius (fragments preserved by Photius) ; J. H Newman, *The Arians of the Fourth Century* (1833) ; H. M. Gwatkin, *Studies of Arianism* (1882) and *Arian Controversy* (1889) ; F. J. Foakes-Jackson, "Arianism" in *Ency. Rel. and Ethics;* the standard histories of Christian Doctrine. C.W.L.

Aristippus: (ca. 435-366 B.C.) See Cyrenaics.

Aristotle (384-322 B.C.) and Aristotelianism: A great biologist, moralist, logician, and metaphysician, who came closer than any other thinker to imprisoning mankind within the confines of his system. According to this system, the world is a many of substances. A substance is something which corresponds to the subject of a proposition and can never properly be treated as a predicate. A predicate is in a substance, but a substance is in itself. [Is it not also in the world?] Substance has two aspects, matter and form—plus "privation," or the absence of this or that particular form. There can be no matter without form (except as a mere idea in the mind) and no form without matter (except in the case of God, an exception which threatens the consistency of the system). The matter is that by which the same substance can have, now one form, now another, and by which several substances can have the same form. Matter is potentiality as contrasted to actuality; for its nature is to be capable of forms beyond those which it actually has. On the other hand, forms are actual or nothing; for—in contrast to Plato's system (as Aristotle interprets it) —there is no such thing as a mere form unembodied in matter (except for God, who perhaps in a sense is embodied in the world, a doubtful point in the system, however you take it), so that the only real forms are those which have their matter, whereas there may be matter which is lacking nearly all its possible forms. Yet Aristotle says that the generic form is matter to the species, the relatively universal potential to the relatively particular. Nor is this the only indication that "matter" and potentiality are not really equivalent. For the non-material side or form of a man, for example, his soul, is said to be his actuality, although it seems clear that the unrealized potentialities of the soul surpass those of the physical as such. The doctrine seems to be that it is the physical stuff which in the case of man takes on soul or becomes actually conscious, sentient, etc. But (in modern scientific terms) do electrons, say, think human thoughts? They become associated with such thoughts in some way, and must previously have had the capacity for such association, but they never had nor can have the capacity to think, which the soul has. The final expression of the idea that the superior or spiritual is the actual as such, in contrast to the potential as such, is in the idea of God as pure actuality or pure form, without potency or becoming. God has no matter or particularity in Him, but only pure form, taken as pure spirituality, and hence he knows nothing but this very spirituality (all his thinking is of thinking itself). Were he to know mere material things, this would introduce potency and inferiority into the content of his immediate intuitions, and so contradict his perfection. It is a momentous paradox, to use no stronger word, that Medieval thinkers (with the honorable exception of Levi ben Gerson*) attempted to combine the doctrine of God as pure actuality with the doctrine that God knows contingent particulars, as existent. To put such entities, as existents, with their matter, into the content of divine knowledge seems utterly contrary to the Aristotelian principles proclaimed by those who indulged in the procedure. (See Omniscience, Perfection.) And the evidence of experience is that each level of being has potencies which are just as expressive of its superiority to lower levels as are its actualities. A man *can* think and experience many things he does not actually think, and these things an atom or an ant *could* not think. Similarly the highest being, or God, must be capable of thoughts and experiences he does not actually enjoy and of which no lesser being is even capable. In no other way can the reality of possibilities and of time for God be maintained, and, since Omniscience measures reality, to deny potency to God is to deny that potency (and particularity) exists. Here Aristotelianism and, by the usual interpretations, Platonism* also, misled theology for over two millenia.

Aristotelian ethics has played a similarly dubious rôle in historical theology. The Aristotelian view of substance as what belongs to itself not to another thing is suitable to an ethics (or pseudo-ethics) of self-interest, not to an ethics which makes love the absolute divine principle of all things. Substances are precisely not "members one of another." For a strict Aristotelian, a cell is not a real individual in the individual human being, nor an atom in the cell, and Aristotle scarcely dreamt of either cells or atoms as they are now known to exist. His is the physics and biology of the naked eye, unaided by any lucky guess as to what more powerful instruments would reveal (partly because Aristotle detected certain philosophical errors in Greek atomic theory, and was too busy refuting these to explore more philosophical versions). Plato, on the contrary, thought of the world as an organism, as nearly as possible ideally perfect, of which all lesser organisms are members, and so by implication, through their interdependence in one organism, also members one of another. Yet Plato also kept slipping into a self-interest ethics, and never fully developed the doctrine of reality as composed of organisms organic to one another.

The theory of separate substances not organic to one another results in a dilemma which sums up much of the difficulty in later philosophy. Either the totality of the real is not a substance, or else this totality is the only substance—on the assumption that a substance can have no other substances as its parts. (Aristotle expressly denies that an organism has real parts.) If we take the first horn of the dilemma, the universe as not a substance, we have, among other difficulties, that the most stable of all orders, the cosmic order, belongs to a whole which has no substantial unity at all. If we take the other horn, and suppose the whole to have substantial unity, then all other apparent substances must be held unreal; for the world substance by hypothesis has no substantial parts. Thus assuming Aristotelianism, we have either a world-whole without parts (Spinozism*) or a world of parts without real wholeness (the doctrine of Hume*). In more theological terms: if God is not the substance of which others are members (and thereby members of each other) then besides God we have the totality of the creatures forming, with God, the super-totality, God and the creatures, and either this super-totality is more than God, greater than the greatest being, or else the creatures, being neither in God nor additional to him, are just nothing. The violence of medieval attacks upon "pantheism"* are to be explained partly by the inability of Aristotelianism to construe God either as including the world or as not including it.

The theological employment of Aristotle's concept of God as "unmoved mover" overlooked the possibility that the unchanging might be an abstract aspect of a being which concretely or as a whole changes. (See transcendence, time.) It was argued that what moves tends toward an end and if the end is reached motion ceases, while if the end is not reached there is imperfection. This overlooked the inexhaustibility of possible values, their absolute infinity as possible, and their necessary finitude as actual (since possible values are partly incompossible, cannot all be realized together—Berdyaev and Whitehead).

Aristotle's works cannot be dated. Among them are: Organon (the Treatises on Logic); Physics; The Soul; Metaphysics; Nicomachean Ethics; Politics; Poetics. These and others are conveniently available, with an introduction, in *The Basic Works of Aristotle* (1941), ed. by Richard McKeon. See eudemonism; hylomorphism; mean, Aristotelian; metaphysics; soul.

C.H.

Arius: (A.D. 256-336) Presbyter of Alexandria and most prominent exponent of the heresy known as Arianism. Arius was a pupil of Lucian* of Antioch, a disciple of Paul of Samosata*, who had however combined the monarchian* and adoptianist standpoint of the latter with the Logos Christology of Origen*. This is the starting point for understanding the thought of Arius. One of his motives was monarchian; with this was combined the Greek idea of the utter transcendence and inaccessibility of God. The Logos, as for Origen, is the medium of the Father's creation, but for Arius He is entirely a creature, produced out of nothing as the beginning of the creation, endowed with free will, and made the recipient of the Divine Grace. Following the Gospel according to St. John, Arius taught that this Logos became flesh in Christ, but denied that the latter possessed a human soul.

The Arian Controversy began in A.D. 318, when Arius openly opposed his Bishop Alexander* on the eternity of the Son. Against this Arius insisted that the Father must be older than the Son, and that "there was when the Son was not." After his excommunication by Alexander, Arius found many allies, and "in a short time the whole Eastern Church became a metaphysical battle-field." The climax of the controversy was the Council of Nicea called in 325 by the Emperor Constantine*. Here Arius' views were condemned, and the famous anti-Arian Creed of Nicea was promulgated. Its most important phrase, "of one being (or substance) with the Father", survives in the Creed commonly called the Nicene and used in many of the Liturgies of Christendom. See Arianism for the further development of this heresy and for a bibliography. C.W.L.

ark: The sacred ark, conceived to be the palladium of Yahweh*, appears to have been the chief cult object of the Ephraemitic sanctuary of Shiloh. It was borne by the priests in military expeditions as visible symbol of Yahweh's presence. (Num. 10. 35-36; cf. Ps. 68.1). Captured by the Philistines* in the second battle of Eben-ezer, it brought disaster upon the people of Ashdod and Gath, who returned it in desperation to the Israelites (1 Sam. 4-6). It remained at Kiriath-jearim until David* installed it in the new sanctuary at Jerusalem*. Subsequently it was transferred to Solomon's* temple and deposited within the *debir* or the Holy of Holies*. (2 Sam. 6; 1 Kings 8.1-11) In the light of advancing ideas of God, the ark was now reinterpreted to function as the receptacle of the tables of the Law* and was referred to as "the ark of the covenant of God". What happened to the ark later on is not known. Tradition reports that there was no ark in the Second Temple (Menahot 27b). The Priestly Code* traces the ark to Moses*, who constructed it at God's behest and set it within the Tabernacle* to shelter the Decalogue* and to serve as the throne of God, upon which He sat between the cherubim*. (Ex. 25. 10-22; 37. 1-9).

In the synagogue* the ark is built or placed in the eastern wall as the container of the scrolls of the Law. High in front of it hangs the perpetual light; above its door there is generally a representation of the Decalogue; and a curtain is placed behind or in front of the door. The ark thus symbolizes the Holy of Holies of the Temple*. See propitiation. S.S.C.

Arles, Synod of: The first general council of the Western Church, which met in Arles in southeastern France in A.D. 314. Called by the emperor Constantine* to settle points at issue between Donatists* and Catholics in North Africa, which had been left unsettled by the Synod of Rome in 313. Attended by representatives of bishoprics in western Europe (including Britain) and North Africa. 22 canons condemned the Donatists and their main contentions and dealt with matters of ecclesiastical discipline that had emerged since the persecution under Diocletian. S.M.G.

Armenian Church: See Eastern Orthodox Churches.

Armenian version: See versions of the Bible, ancient.

Arminian theology: Arminian theology places its chief emphasis upon man's freedom of choice. It arose in the Reformed Church of the Netherlands as a protest against the extreme form of Calvinism which prevailed at the beginning of the 17th century. It takes its name from James (Jacobus) Arminius (1560-1609), a mild-mannered professor of the University of Leyden.

The protest of Arminius and his followers was against the dogmas of unconditional election and irresistible grace.

Their opponents held that God elects certain persons for salvation while others are denied that privilege. Furthermore, because God wills it so, it is just. Arminius held that, "He cannot will to do . . . that which He cannot do of right. For His will is restricted by justice." Arminius held that divine foreknowledge enables God to foresee the purely contingent. That is to say that God knows in advance that a man will sin by free choice but that God does not will nor predestine the man to do so. Arminius held, further, that man's freedom stands in contrast to compulsion, to necessity, and to spontaneity. Even in the desire for happiness, which is spontaneous, man is not free. Freedom exists only where there is the power of alternate choice. Man faces alternate choice and is actually free.

The opponents held that the grace of God, which is made available for the elect, cannot be resisted. The Arminians held that grace is not irresistible, but that those who "are ready for the conflict, and desire His (Christ's) help, and are not inactive" will be kept from falling.

The influence of Arminian theology spread widely when it was adopted by the Methodist and related movements in the 18th century. Its viewpoint has promoted a spirit of tolerance. It has led to an emphasis upon human duties rather than speculative theology. See Dort, Synod of; Five Points of Arminianism; Remonstrants, the.

G. L. Curtiss, *Arminianism in History* (1894);

James Arminius, *The Works Of*, translated from the Latin by James Nichols (1853); Selected list of Writings of Arminius: *The Priesthood of Christ* (1603); *The Object of Theology* (1603); *The Author and the End of Theology* (1603); *The Certainty of Sacred Theology* (1603); *On Reconciling Religious Dissensions Among Christians* (1606); *A Declaration of Sentiments* (1608); *A Dissertation on the True and Genuine Sense of the Seventh Chapter of the Epistle to the Romans* (1599); *A Letter on the Sin Against the Holy Ghost* (1599); *Analysis of the Ninth Chapter of the Epistle to the Romans* (1593).

W.E.R.

Arnold, Gottfried: (1666-1714) Serving as professor of secular history for only one year in Giessen, he held pastorates in Werben and Perleburg. He was endowed with a poetic gift and translated the works of several religious mystics. He also wrote several spiritualistic works. His church history was the first one written in German. He was an exponent of a pneumatic or spiritualistic interpretation of the history of the Christian church. The work was a ruthless break-through of traditional ecclesiastical tendencies. It was a passionate sermon of repentance to corrupted Christianity, whether Catholic or Protestant. The central coherent idea of the work was the idea of the gradual process of corruption of the historical church.

Unparteiische Kirchen und Ketzerhistorie von Anfang des Neuen Testamentes bis auf Jahr Christi 1688, 2 vols. (Frankfurt, 1699-1700).

H.H.

Arnold, Matthew: (1822-1888) English educator, poet, and critic. Although actively engaged for thirty-five years as an inspector of schools, he lectured and wrote extensively on a wide range of subjects. His poetry, issued mostly between 1849 and 1867, is sombre and often skeptical in tone, reflecting what he termed "the main movement of mind" of the age. In his subsequent prose writings, however, he undertook to resolve his doubts. His principal excursions into the fields of social and religious criticism are *Culture and Anarchy* (1869), *St. Paul and Protestantism* (1870), *Literature and Dogma* (1873), *God and the Bible* (1875); all are marked by a strong ethical emphasis deriving from Stoic as well as Christian sources.

The Macmillan edition of the *Works* (15 vols., 1903) is the most nearly complete. Outstanding among recent studies is *The Poetry of Matthew Arnold: a Commentary,* by C. B. Tinker and H. F. Lowry (1940).

L.W.C.

ars moriendi: Counsel for the dying; especially a written guide to the priest in his ministry to the dying. Many *artes moriendi* appeared in the late middle ages. (A. Hardeland, *Geschichte der speciellen Seelsorge*, Berlin, 1897-8.)

J.T.M.

art: See dancing; hymns; idols and images; poetry.

art, ecclesiastical Christian: The earliest Christian art of which we have any examples are the crude drawings in the Roman catacombs*. The earliest church buildings are the Roman basilicas* whose apses* and adjacent walls are decorated with mosaics. This form of church persisted in Italy till well into the Middle Ages, and the campanile* appears with the basilica and is used with all the other Italian styles. After Constantinople became the capital of the empire the Byzantine style had a glorious reign in that city. It was developed from oriental and Roman precedents and was characterized by the use of the barrel vault, the apse and the dome on pendentives, and its interiors were profusely decorated with a veneer of colored marbles and gorgeous mosaics. Sancta Sophia at Constantinople (532-562) and St. Mark's at Venice (c. 1100) are outstanding remaining examples.

The Romanesque style began in Lombard territory in northern Italy and is characterized by cross vaults supported by independent ribs and a crude but vigorous sculpture decoration. St. Ambrogio at Milan c. 1075 is generally considered the initial monument of the style. The Tuscan Romanesque of central Italy of which Pisa (1063-1118) is a notable example, is characterized by abundant external arcading and veneer of colored marbles but without any attempt at vaulted interiors. The Romanesque of southern France is of especial importance and has a school of sculpture showing in the south, strong Roman influence, but is more crude but vigorous farther north. A Romanesque school flourished in the Rhine valley and some other parts of Germany in the eleventh and twelfth centuries, showing strong Lombard influence, of which the great churches of Mainz, Speyer and Worms are representative examples.

The Gothic developed from the Romanesque in the Isle de France in the twelfth and thirteenth centuries and became the most noteworthy school of art in all Christian history. The profuse sculpture of its churches ranks with that of Greece of the fifth century B.C., and its stained glass has no equal in all art. The Gothic movement spread into all European countries. Spain has splendid churches in the Gothic and Romanesque styles. In England the Gothic developed from the Norman Romanesque in the thirteenth century and is second only to that of France. Its iconography*, while not so profuse, is in its best examples, of a choice and striking character. Its cathedrals, parish and abbey churches and university buildings rank high among the buildings of the world, with much stained glass that is unexcelled.

The architectural Renaissance began with Brunelleschi's dome in Florence in 1420. In the first century of the movement it was a revival of all the preceding styles of European architecture except that of Greece. But it soon became a revival of the Roman classical and in this form it spread to the various European countries. The best example of this latter phase is the work of Palladio (1518-1580) and in its Palladian form it came to England, and was the chief influence in the work of Sir Christopher Wren (1632-1723). Wren's modified Palladian is the style seen in the London churches and the school is known as the Georgian.

The first churches in the American colonies of the seventeenth century, in Virginia, Pennsylvania, New Amsterdam, etc., were in the debased Gothic of the times, but the Georgian prevailed in the Anglican churches and so continued through the eighteenth century. The non-Anglican churches, however, especially in New England, were the plain meeting houses of English nonconformist precedent. It was not till after the Revolution that the American Georgian began to appear in other than Episcopal churches, and the white New England churches with their storied steeples are splendid examples of this movement continued at its best till about 1820.

The Georgian period was followed by the Greek, Gothic and Romanesque revivals till about the time of the Civil War when the so-called "dark ages" of American architecture began, which lasted well through the nineteenth century.

Since about 1900 there has been a remarkable awakening to the ecclesiastical proprieties in this country. The last vestiges of the "meeting house" ideal are rapidly disappearing. The "auditorium" is giving place to the more seemly house of worship. The hitherto unfinished "pulpit end" of the church has in numerous instances been completed with the appropriate chancel in which the altar is again taking its proper place. Under the leadership of brilliant artists like the late Ralph Adams Cram, fine Gothic churches with appropriate stained glass and abundant symbolism have been built, and the other historic styles have many fine examples in the towns and cities of this country. See church building.

D. M. Robb & J. J. Garrison, *Art in the Western World* (1935); H. Gardner, *Art through the Ages* (1936); S. Reinach *Apollo* (1910); F. Kimball & G. H. Edgell, *A History of Architecture* (1918); E. H. Short, *The House of God* (1926); R. Sturgis, *Dictionary of Architecture and Building* (1901-1902).

F.T.P.

art in the Enlightenment: See Enlightenment, the.

art, philosophy of: See aesthetics.

Articles of Religion (Methodist): These articles were included in the Sunday Service for the Methodists of North America, prepared by John Wesley in 1784, for the newly formed Methodist Episcopal Church. Originally they consisted of twenty-four articles, based upon the thirty-nine articles of the Church of England. Later the American Methodists added an article *Of Rulers of the United States of America.* Broadly speaking the Methodist articles differ from the thirty-nine of the Episcopal Church in that all references to Calvinism are excinded. W.W.S.

arts, fine: See fine arts.

Arval Brothers: Fratres Arvali, a college of priests in the religion of ancient Rome. Perhaps of Etruscan origin. The archaic "Song of the Arval Brethren" indicates an agricultural function, a charm for the protection of the crops and for successful harvests.

W. W. Fowler *Roman Festivals* (1899).

P.G.M.

Arya Samaj: A modern reform movement in Hinduism founded by Dyananda Sarasvati in 1875. Although undoubtedly an indirect result of the Christian invasion of India it is notably hostile to Christianity and has sought the re-conversion to Hinduism of Indians who have become Christian. It represents a back-to-the-Vedas* movement, the founder having discovered in the ancient scriptures many of the values which modern India* has come to appreciate. He even finds monotheism there, since the multiple so-called Vedic gods are discovered to be but variant names for the one true God. The movement is strictly non-idolatrous in its worship, but it retains the characteristic Hindu beliefs in Karma and transmigration** which the founder thought were taught in the Vedas. Salvation is thought of as emancipation from rebirth.

Dyananda was nationalistic to a high degree and his movement has been part cause, part effect of the modern rise of nationalism in India. It has become quite the most aggressive branch of Hinduism*.

The Arya Samaj has about a half-million followers at present, nearly a hundred times the membership of the Brahma-Samaj* from which Dyananda borrowed a number of the principal features of his society. But its influence on Indian life has not been in proportion to its relative superiority in numbers. C.S.B.

Aryan religion: The religion of the ancient Aryans, the ancestors of the Iranians and Vedic Indians. The Aryans are a group which separated from the pro-ethnic Indo-Europeans about 2000 B.C. or soon after, and settled in Iran and in India. (See India, Religions of). Their religion, consequently, is a development of the Indo-European religion. The latter recognized, aside from tribal deities, cosmic divine beings: the supreme god was Dyeus (Greek, Zeus; Latin, Jupiter), the shining god of the sky, the giver of rain and fertility, the vanquisher of his foes through his lightning bolt. He is the father (not the creator) of gods and men and, unless identified with a local god, has no national limitations. His counterpart and consort is Mother Earth. Other gods of light (*deivo*, cf. Latin, *deus* [god]) are the Sun (*svarya*), the Moon (*mas*), and the Dawn (cf. Greek *eôs*). Fire worship was also common, as well as the local worship of minor deities in trees, stones, springs, and rivers. The gods fight unceasingly against the demons of darkness; these have sometimes stolen a divine treasure which must be recovered.

Culturally more advanced than the Indo-Europeans, the Aryans progressed religiously, without however loosing that sense of universality and fellowship with nature which are characteristic of the former. Dyeus was gradually displaced by Indra*, a younger and more heroic god of storms and lightning who killed the dragon Vrtra, but the sun and moon gods persisted sporadically among them. By the side of Indra we now find the heroic Trita, as also the Nasatyas (Asvins) in their war chariot. The real contribution of the Aryans was the development of deities regulating human society (Iranian *Ahura*, Indian *Asura**), by the side of these gods of nature (*deivo*): eventually the Asuras (except Varuna*) became demons in India, while the Daevas, through Zoroaster, became demons in

Iran. The gods of justice and right are: Mitra (Iranian, Mithra; meaning "compact"), the defender of the sanctity of contracts between individuals and of treaties between nations; and Varuna, the defender of the sanctity of oaths (identified with Ahura-Mazda* by Zoroaster). Mithra may have been a solar deity, Varuna the god of the ocean encircling the earth (in India he became a sea god). The Aryans achieved some notion of the cosmic order, the uniform law of nature, *arta* (Indian, *rta;* Avestan, *asha*), dominating over gods and men and unsuccessfully disregarded by demons, who consequently are but illusions (*druh;* Iranian, *druj*). To obtain the blessings of the gods, men must fulfil the requirement of "good thoughts, good works, good deeds"—originally a ritual precept, gradually moralized in Zoroastrianism and Buddhism. The preparation of the sacred drink (Vedic, Soma*; Avestan, Haoma*)—later a god,—the sacrificial worship, and the liturgies belonging to it (particularly the magical spells, *mantra**) are the monopoly of the priests, who attained consequently a high social position. Two classes among them are known: the "lighters of fire" (Indian, *atharvan;* Iranian, *athravan*), and the "callers" (Indian, *hotar;* Iranian, *zaotar*) who invoke the gods through ritual formulae and also through improvised hymns (Iranian, *gatha**). Before Zoroaster and Buddha*, the priests were responsible for religious progress among the Aryans.

O. Schrader, in J. Hastings, *Encyclopaedia of Religion and Ethics,* vol. II (1908) pp. 11-57 (chiefly on Indo-European religion); E. Meyer, *Geschichte des Altertums* (3rd ed., 1913), 1:2, pp 914-931.

R.H.P.

ascension: The rising of Christ in his resurrected body from earth into heaven (Acts 1:9).

Beliefs in similar experiences on the part of holy men do not involve the fact of the resurrection.

R.E.E.H.

Ascension Day: See Church Year Cycle.

asceticism, in Judaism and early Christianity: (Gr. *askein,* to practice, train, exercise) The view that through moderation or renunciation of those things commonly considered pleasant one reaches a higher spiritual state. Asceticism was alien to the genius of Judaism, and not unnaturally so, since asceticism is peculiarly individualistic and dualistic: the longing to rid one's soul of the defiling corruption of the body. The Rechabites and Nazarites** of the O.T. were not properly ascetics but reactionaries, men out of step with the times, who sought to reënact the good old days. The prohibition against wine by the Rechabites was thus not on ascetic grounds—still less on moral grounds—but was a protest against the settled life of Israel subsequent to the occupation of Canaan. Vineyards were the sign and product of a type of life impossible for nomads. Ascetic groups such as Essenes and Therapeutæ** were present in later Judaism, but were far departures from its genius and apparently exerted little influence upon the rank and file.

Some branches of Christianity eventually took on an ascetic nature, as an acquired characteristic. It is not to be seen in the earliest days, although not infrequently it has been mistakenly read into Paul's cautious words regarding marriage. In I Cor. 7:36 ff. there is probably to be seen an indication of the so-called spiritual marriages (*virgines subintroductae*), which later caused a great moral problem for the church. Col. 2: 20 ff. suggests that early in the first century ascetic notes were being stressed—from the outside—and were being as heatedly opposed. As the years wore on, they became increasingly prominent, leading to a disparagement of marriage and a temporary unwholesome exaltation of the type of life characterized by the so-called pillar saints. In many circles of Christians there is still to be discerned the nervous suspicion that anything pleasant and natural to man is under the wrathful ban of God and will have to be atoned for at the bar of judgment.

See anchoret; communistic settlements, religious; hermit; recluse.

O. Zöckler, *Askese und Mönchtum* (1897); E. Fehrle, *Die kultische Keuschheit des Altertums* (1910); J. Main, *Religious Chastity* (1913); C. H. Moore, "Ascetic Tendencies of the Greek and Roman" in *Harvard Essays on Classical Subjects* (1912), pp. 97-140; M. S. Enslin, *Christian Beginnings* (1938), pp. 120-126.

M.S.E.

Asgard: Home of the Norse gods, where Odin's seat was. In it lived the twelve gods and twenty-four goddesses, and in it was the hall of the chosen slain, Valhalla, surrounded by the forest of trees whose leaves were all of red gold. F.G.M.

Ashkenazim: The biblical Ashkenaz (Gen. 10.3) was identified in medieval Hebrew with Germany, and the name Ashkenazim came to designate the Jews of Germany and their descendants in northern, central and eastern Europe, Great Britain, and the Americas. They constitute more than ninety per cent of all Jews. S.S.C.

Ashshur: Assyrian national god; the lord of the Assyrians, without connection with natural phenomena, active in war, represented shooting the bow inside of a winged disk. R.H.P.

Ashtart: See Mother Goddesses; cf. Ashtoreth.

Ashtoreth: (Possibly a distortion of Ashtart*, on the analogy of *Bosheth,* shame; Gr. Astarte) Supreme goddess of Canaan and female counterpart of Baal (cf. Baalism), known in Babylonia as Ishtar* and in S. Arabia as Athtar (masc.). Ever-virginal, she was also the fruitful mother and creatress of life. The Philistines* seem to have emphasized her warlike character (I Sam. 31.10). The numerous Ashtaroth represent various forms under which she was worshipped in different places (Judges 10.6; cf. I Kings 11.33; 23.13). Her name was given to the city of Og, king of Bashan (Deuter 1.4.). See Mother Goddesses. S.S.C.

Ash Wednesday: The first day of Lent in the West, since it was prolonged by four days (early Middle Ages) to make a 40-day fast; the name came from the imposition of ashes on penitents, later on the congregation generally. See Shrovetide. R.R.M.

Asmoneans: See Hasmoneans.

asperges: A ceremony preceding high mass, during which the celebrant of the mass, with assisting ministers, goes in procession through the congregation, sprinkling the members with water, and reciting meanwhile appropriate words from the Psalter and elsewhere. The purpose of the ceremony is to symbolize the purity of heart which should mark those who participate in the holy mysteries of the Church. W.N.P.

Assam: A British Indian Province, north of Bengal and bordering on Burma. The prevailing religion of Assam is Hinduism*, in the form of Shaktism and Vishnuism**. About a third of the population is Moslem. In recent times Christianity has made notable gains among the people. C.S.B.

Assemblies of God, General Council: The largest of the pentecostal sects, having headquarters at Springfield, Mo. The group has about 2,600 churches and 148,000 members. See pentecostal sects. E.T.C.

Assize of Clarendon: An edict of Henry II in 1166 which was of major importance in English constitutional development. It allowed the king's justices to invade private jurisdictions and regulated the rights of possession. See Constitutions of Clarendon. T.J.B.

Associate Reformed Church: See s.v. Reformed Presbyterian Church in N. A.; United Presbyterian Church of N. A.

associationism: See psychology, schools of.

assumption: (Lat. *assumptio, domitionis;* Gr. *koimeois, analepsis*) The doctrine that the Virgin Mary* was at her death assumed into heaven by her Son. Record of the belief, which is held both in East and West, is first found in 4th century writers, notably S. Epiphanius*, who thought the history obscure. The belief became widely popular, partly because of the absence of any relics but largely because of increased Mariolatry*. Theologians generally construe the event as an anticipation of the General Resurrection, Roman Catholics following the argument *potuit, decit, fecit,* and holding the doctrine a pious opinion that no one is permitted to doubt, as Benedict XIV* declared. Devotion centers not in the event but in the subsequent status of St. Mary as first among the saints already with the Lord. T.J.B.

Assumption, Augustinians of the: A Roman Catholic missionary order established in 1843 at Nîmes, to combat irreligion in Europe and schism in the East. Suppressed in 1900 on suspicion of royalist intrigue, it continues work in the Near East. T.J.B.

Assumption, Feast of the: August 15th. A commemoration which had spread from Jerusalem to Rome, Gaul, and Egypt by the 6th century. A holy day of obligation in most countries in the Roman Catholic Church, it is kept as a principal feast by the Orthodox and is in some Anglican books. T.J.B.

Assumption of Moses, the: A fragment of a larger Apocalyptic* work now lost. Its form is that of an address delivered by Moses*to Joshua before his death. It was originally written either in Hebrew or Aramaic and it was composed during the first decade after the death of Herod or about 6 C.E.

See pseudepigrapha. B.Z.B.

assurance (of salvation, God's favor): There is a plain doctrine of assurance in the N.T. The purpose of the Gospel is the salvation* of men through their reconciliation to God; the subjects ᶜ this salvation know themselves such. Attestation is twofold (Wesley*: direct and indirect witness of the Spirit): the witness within, to divine sonship (Rom. 8:16); the witness without, of its power and fruits ('We know . . .' I John 3:14).

In the Church, assurance has reflected the conception of faith*. Scholasticism, e.g., made faith decisive in salvation, but it was faith (belief) in the creeds and the teaching of the Church. This meant continual dependence on the Church and lacked definitiveness for full divine confidence at any given moment. The Reformers saw faith as directly Godward and the work of God; hence sure as is God. Assurance a part of faith (Augsburg Confession, IV); for Calvin faith includes *certitudo salutis.* But he allows that contrary elements within may dull this certitude; generally as Reformation progressed, teaching concerning assurance became less insistent (Westminster Confession, XVIII: 'believers *may* be certainly assured . . . this assurance not of the essence of faith'). In Pietism and Methodism**, a revival of the doctrine occurs; faith again in the divine Spirit would could not fail. For Wesley, assurance every believer's clear privilege; common testimony was to certainty of acceptance with God.

Christian assurance does not beget complacency or exclude perseverance*. It is the nerve of the latter; knowledge that God has begun His work earnest of its completion. For comparison of assurance as spiritual convincement and certainty as mode of knowledge, see certainty.

D. M. Baillie, *Faith in God and its Christian Consummation* (1927); W. A. Brown, *Pathways to Certainty* (1930). J.L.

Assyria and Babylonia, religions of: See Mesopotamian religions.

Astruc, Jean: (1684-1766) French specialist in inoculations, skin, and venereal diseases; physician to Louis XV; while doing research on the medical laws in the Bible, he discovered the significance of the names Elohim and Yahweh in differentiating biblical sources; published *Conjectures on the Original Memoirs . . .*, thus laying the basis for the documentary concept of biblical origins. R.E.W.

Asura: An epithet applied to the Vedic gods, to emphasize their mysterious nature and power. Literally it means mysterious lord. In later Vedic literature the Asuras became demons, evil beings opposed to the good gods. See Aryan religion. C.S.B.

Asvins: Twin Vedic deities closely related to Ushas*, goddess of dawn as brothers or husbands. They are represented sometimes as divine physicians who cure the diseased and are closely connected with love marriage and offspring. C.S.B.

asylum: a) An institution for the care of some class of destitute or afflicted persons, such as the poor or insane. This use of the term is somewhat outmoded in modern times, such institutions being designated by the words *hospital** or *infirmary.* b) A place where in ancient Hebrew or classical times persons guilty of unintentional homicide might take refuge, being immune there from blood vengeance* on the part of some member of the victim's family. Hence, the phrase, "right of asylum". Among the early Hebrews six places were designated as Cities of Refuge which had their counterpart among the Greeks and Romans. Temples, altars and other sacred places have also been regarded as sanctuaries for certain classes of criminals from which they could not be taken without sacrilege. In medieval times Christian churches often served the same purpose. c) In international law an area of a country within which citizens of other nationalities exercise exterritorial rights. A.E.W.

Atargatis or Derceto: The Syrian Goddess of whom Lucian wrote his *de Dea Syria.* Perhaps only a Syrian form of the general Semitic goddess Ishtar* Cf. "Atargatis" by Lewis Paton, *ERE,* II, 164 ff. Cf. Mother-goddesses. P.G.M.

Athanasian Creed: (Often called from its opening words, the *Quicunque* Vult*) One of the three so-called Ecumenical Creeds, the other two being the Apostles' and the Nicene. As in the two latter cases, its name is strictly speaking inaccurate, although in relation to the origin and import of the Creed not unjustified. Further, like the Apostles' Creed*, the Athanasian is Western rather than genuinely Ecumenical, although it is included as an Appendix in the Hour Offices of the Eastern Orthodox Church. The "Athanasium" originated almost certainly in Southern Gaul as a commentary on, or an exposition of, the *fides Athanasii* or Nicene Creed. It seems fairly certain also that it was post-Augustinian and reflected the desire to state the doctrine of the Trinity* in the terms of the Augustinian paradoxes, although Waterland's celebrated argument in favor of its origin in "Apollinarian times" (by this phrase he meant pre-Nestorian) has never lacked supporters.

Whether the Athanasian Creed was also conceived of from the first as a rule of faith, is unclear. At any rate it was from an early time in high favor among the Monasteries as a suitable subject for meditation and memorization. With the revival of Church music under Charlemagne*, it came into use as a canticle and was placed in the office of Prime*. In the first Prayer Book of Edward VI (1549) it was directed that the Athanasian Creed should be "sung or said" after the Benedictus at the greater Feasts. In the Fifth English Prayer Book (1662), which is still the only official Book of Common Prayer* in the Church of England, it was directed that this confession should "be sung or said at Morning Prayer, instead of the Apostles' Creed" on thirteen Feasts (including all the major Festivals). The American Prayer Book (distinct from the English since 1789) never included the Athanasian Creed. See creeds of Christendom.

D. Waterland, *A Critical History of the Athanasian Creed* (1723; ed. J. R. King, Oxford, 1870); A. E. Burn, *Introduction to the Creeds* (1899); E. C. S. Gibson, *The Three Creeds* (1908); J. H. Colligan, *The Arian Movement in England* (Manchester, 1913). See also art. "Creeds (Ecumenical)" in *Ency. Rel. and Ethics,* and Harnack, *History of Dogma,* Vol. IV, pp. 134-7; Vol. V, pp. 303-4. C.W.L.

Athanasius, St., Bishop of Alexandria: (A.D. 293? 296?-373) The great defender of the Nicene faith against prolonged attacks by numerous and powerful Arians*. His life is an incomparable epic of heroism, fortitude, and faith. To him more than to any other single individual is due the triumph of the Nicene position as opposed to a doctrine now universally acknowledged to have represented the reduction of Christianity to a thinly disguised paganism. As a theologian Athanasius won his spurs before the outbreak of the Arian Controversy. In his *Contra Gentiles* and *De Incarnatione*—really a single apologetico-dogmatic treatise in two parts—we have a work by a comparative youth which represents the high-water mark of Ante-Nicene theology in its central line of development. At Nicea Athanasius undoubtedly supported Alexander*, but the decisive terms came from the West. As Bishop of Alexandria from 326 on, Athanasius planted himself steadfastly on the Nicene Creed and increasingly made his own its terminology. He maintained, for example, the synonymity of *ousia* and *hypostasis***, but with an attitude at once Christian and statesmanlike he conceded to the Semi-Arians* in 362 the right to say three hypostases, provided that they accepted the single *ousia.* (See art. "Arianism"). Behind all his doctrinal writings, polemical and otherwise, is the central conviction that "God Himself has entered into humanity." From this angle Harnack is right in asserting that the point of view of Athanasius underwent no development. Loofs, however, is correct in holding that Athanasius' way of expressing his views underwent considerable development, and that contact with the West was not without influence in this respect. See Cenobite; creeds of Christendom.

Among the important writings of Athanasius, in addition to the two already cited, are: *Orationes contra Arianos IV, Apologia contra Arianos, De Decretis, De Synodis, Ad Afros.*

For a translation of these and other basic works see *The Nicene and Post-Nicene Fathers,* Second Series, Vol. IV. The Introduction to this volume by A. Robertson is memorable. For the whole corpus of Athanasius' writings in the original, see J. P. Migne, *Patrologia Graeca.* Among modern monographs Loofs' "Athanasius" in *Realencyklopädie für Protestantische Theologie und Kirche* (3rd ed.), is indispensable. See also bibliography under "Arianism". C.W.L.

Atharva-Veda: The latest of the four Vedas, the Veda of popular religion. Contains many magic charms and incantations along with hymns and prayers similar to those in the Rig Veda. While collected later than the Rig-Veda it represents a much more primitive stage of religion. C.S.B.

atheism: (Gr. *a-*, not, and *theos,* god) 1) The denial that there is any god*, no matter in what sense "god" be defined. 2) The denial that there exists a being corresponding to some particular definition of god; frequently, but unfortunately, used to denote the denial of God as personal (the denial of theism), or, more particularly, of a personal God as defined in a particular (e.g., trinitarian, Catholic, or Calvinistic) creed. See theism. E.S.B.

Athenagoras: A Christian philosopher and apologist in Athens in the late 2nd century. Author of the *Legatio pro Christianis* (Appeal on Behalf of Christians) and of *De resurrectione* (On the Resurrection of the Dead). S.M.G.

Athos, Mount (or the Holy Mountain) The largest historic center of Eastern Orthodox monasticism. It is a peninsula jutting into the Aegian Sea from the main Peninsula of Chalcidice. It was reorganized as a monastic center in the tenth century by St. Athanasius the Athonite. At present the monastic republic consists of twenty establishments, of which eleven are cenobitic* (where the brethren share all things in common) and nine are idiorrhythmic (where the monks receive remuneration for their work). Of these twenty monasteries, seventeen are Greek, one is Bulgarian, one Serbian, and one Russian. According to the strict rule, no woman is permitted on the territory of the peninsula. M.S.

atman: A term of uncertain origin which in its oldest usage meant "breath" but came to signify "the self", and, in the Upanishads, the universal self, ultimate reality being represented as Brahman-Atman. It was through knowledge of the identity of the individual self with Brahman-Atman that *moksha** was attained in one of the philosophic schools of Hinduism. C.S.B.

atman: (Indian) In early Vedic times: wind, breath, nature of a thing. Late Brahmanas and after: mind or consciousness of man, or soul of man; also, cosmic mind, cosmic consciousness, world soul: a unit in the cosmic aggregate of souls (*purusha*)*. F.L.P.

atonement in Christianity: The theme of all Christian doctrines of the atonement is the sentence: Christ died for our sins. From the very beginning of the church, the cross* of Christ was understood as a vicarious suffering. According to the records of the gospels, Jesus himself seems to have interpreted in such a way the death on the cross which he anticipated with certainty. His reinterpretation of the Messiah*-idea in terms of the Isaianic conception of the suffering servant and the manner in which he instituted the Last Supper clearly indicate this probability. After the crucifixion, His followers were persuaded by their experiences of His resurrection that His death was not only a triumph rather than a defeat but also a sacrifice by which all sacrifices to God were ended. This conviction was to them all the more marvelous because they were sure that God had sent in Jesus His Son. Thus Paul could declare that in Jesus (and when he thought of Jesus he thought of Him as crucified!) God had reconciled the world unto Himself. He believed that, by the grace of God, Christ had bought men free from the slavery to the dominions and powers, particularly of the law, sin, and death.

Whatever the theories behind these interpretations, the religious truth inherent in them was proved by the impression of the person of Jesus upon His believers.

As the church developed its liturgy, theology and ethics, these ideas of the NT constituted the core around which all later interpretations of the meaning of Christ's vicarious suffering grew. Among the doctrines of the atonement that were formulated in the course of time the following are outstanding:

1) *The Ransom-theory.* The theologians of the ancient church interpreted the death of Christ as a ransom paid to the devil. Irenaeus, Origen, Athanasius, Augustine** were the chief expositors of this doctrine. The presupposition of their teaching was that Jesus Christ was the divine Logos Incarnate (this holds true also for all later theories). In rather crude ways they explained that Jesus Christ by permitting Himself to become the victim of death and the devil, had destroyed their power not only by offering them the price of His life in place of that of mankind, but also by proving in His resurrection, His supremacy over them. This teaching has long been recognized as theologically quite dubious, especially on account of the fact that it appears to imply that the devil is a power that can or must be bought off even by God, but it is nevertheless significant, because it carries within it the assertion of the belief in the victory of life over death and of good over evil, accomplished in the death and resurrection of Christ.

2) *The Anselmic (or objective) theory of the atonement.* The ransom theory dominated Christian thinking until the time of Anselm* of Canterbury. In his book *Cur Deus Homo?*, Anselm showed the inadequacies of the traditional theory and advanced a new one in its stead. Reflecting the spirit that dominated the church's practice of penance and possibly the spirit of feudalism, he argued that the death of Christ, the God-man, must be understood as a reparation or "satisfaction"* paid to God for the sins of mankind by which his honor is offended. This violation being infinite in character demands a retribution infinite in value. In Jesus God became man in order to make this payment possible in His voluntary vicarious death on the cross which infinite in character constitutes a superabundant "satisfaction" for human sin.

Even in Anselm's day, this doctrine was criticized not only for the arbitrary overemphasis upon the death of Christ which excludes a soteriological consideration of the whole life and person of Jesus, but also for the view of the nature of God which it implies, namely that God should demand the death of a wholly and supremely innocent person in order that His honor and justice be upheld. However, in spite of these weaknesses, Anselm's theory has determined and reflected Christian piety throughout the ages insofar as it was believed to articulate the religious experience of the weight of human sin in the presence of the cross of Jesus (Anselm himself wrote, pointing to the crucified one: *Nondum considerasti quantum ponderis sit peccatum?*). Moreover, his insistence upon the idea that God demands an absolute recognition of His justice while He forgives the sins of man, was rightly understood as an expression of the fundamental Christian conception of God as Holy Father.

3) *The Abailardian (or subjective) doctrine of the atonement.* Abailard* advanced an interpretation of the death of Christ in which the weaknesses of the Anselmic teaching were avoided. According to his view, the contemplation of the cross so moves the believer, that he will recognize in it the transforming power of God's sacrificial love and thus be led to repent of his sins, devoting himself henceforth to a life of sacrificial love.

The doctrine found much favor among the medieval scholastics. It was significant, however, that it was combined by them, especially by Thomas Aquinas*, with that of Anselm, because the teaching of the latter preserved the objective centrality of the cross in the Christian faith in a way which Abailard's theory rendered impossible.

Hence, it remained customary to interpret the death of Christ as a "satisfaction". This holds true generally also for Protestant theology, although the reformers and the humanist theologians introduced either modifications or criticisms of it. Under the leadership of Luther, the Reformers taught to understand the suffering of Christ as the divine punishment for the sins of the world. With this emphasis, which Anselm had intentionally avoided, they combined a renewal of the ransom theory, particularly those aspects of it which signified Christ's victory over hell, death and the devil.

The humanists, particularly the Socinians*, rejected the entire complex of ideas which explained the cross as a satisfaction. They pointed out that the conception of law underlying it rendered the Christian gospel of divine forgiveness and love invalid. In the course of time, the attitude of mind reflected in this criticism became quite general. Arminians, Rationalists, and modern liberal theologians thus contributed to the downfall of the traditional theories. Only Abailard's doctrine was occasionally restated in modern forms.

Recently, the idea that the cross of Christ is to be understood as a suffering of God began to find some favor among theologians. In a way, this idea is implied in all traditional atonement theories. However, the conception of God as immutable, which early became an essential part of Christian thinking, always caused the church to assert the divine impassibility. Hence it was never possible to speak of the suffering of God, not even with respect to Christ. Indeed, the Christological dogma made it possible to state (as it was universally the case) that Christ suffered insofar as He was human but not insofar as He was divine. The recent suggestion that the passion of Christ must be viewed as the suffering of God therefore requires a new Christological statement.

See holocaust; propitiation; reconciliation; sacrifice; salvation; satisfaction.

Gustav Aulen, *Christus Victor* (1931); Hastings Rashdall, *The Idea of Atonement in Christian Theology* (1919). W.P.

Atonement, Day of: (Heb., *Yom Kippur*) The holiest day in the Jewish year observed as a fast from the evening of the ninth of Tishri to that of the tenth, essentially expiatory and characterized as "a sabbath* of solemn rest" and a holy convocation, upon which all manner of work is forbidden under the threat of excision. (Lev. 23. 27-32). The ceremonial of the day at the Temple* centered in the person of the High Priest* and in his atoning sacrifices and confessions, (Lev. 16. Cf. Mishnah* Yoma) Following the fall of the Temple, a liturgy of prayer replaced the priestly ceremonial, stressing confession of sin, repentance, and whole-hearted reconciliation with God. Cf. Kol Nidre.

See **Jewish religious festivals.** S.S.C.

atrium: (Lat., reception room or entrance-hall of a house) In early Church architecture, an open court situated between the vestibule and the main body of the church, with a well or fountain in the center where worshipers could wash their hands before entering. Sometimes used as a burying ground. S.M.G.

Attis: See Cybele-Attis.

attributes of God: (Lat. *ad-tribuere,* to assign) An attribute, in metaphysics and theology, is that quality of an entity which expresses its essential nature and is therefore indispensable or necessary to its given being. Contrasting with the impermanence of modes or accidents, attributes become the *summa genera* whereby modes are understood and have their being in substance (*cf.* Spinoza).

The exact relation of attributes to God has been disputed. Some, like St. Augustine and Schleiermacher, suggest that they have no distinct being in God's nature (omniscience *is* omnipotence), while others think they are expressive of the divine nature in itself apart from the human viewpoint. "The attributes have no existence apart from the being of God, and the being of God has no reality apart from its attributes." (See A. C. Knudson, *Doctrine of God,* 1930.)

The classification of attributes is somewhat arbitrary, but unity, spirituality, eternity, omnipotence, ubiquity, immutability, and absoluteness have been orthodox *meta-physical* attributes, while wisdom,goodness, holiness, and beauty composed the *ethical.* See analogy; God. See under specific attributes. P.A.B.

attrition: In medieval theology, that sorrow for sin which (in distinction from contrition*, is incomplete or motivated by fear of penalty rather than by love to God. The Council of Trent (XIV, iv) regards attrition as sufficient for justification when followed by penance. The doctrine was opposed by Protestant and Jansenist theologians. See penance. J.T.M.

Auburn Affirmation: "An Affirmation Designed to Safeguard the Unity and Liberty of the Presbyterian Church in the United States of America" was issued in May, 1924, over the signatures of about 1300 ministers. These men were resisting the efforts of fundamentalists* to dominate or divide the church. In this document they affirmed their adherence to evangelical Christianity. The General Assembly of 1923 having attempted, by promulgating the "Five Points" of fundamentalism, to define the doctrine of the church in this sense, the signers maintained that under the constitution of the church its doctrine could be defined only with the concurrence of the presbyteries. While asserting biblical revelation, they rejected biblical inerrancy, a cardinal point of fundamentalism. The public taking of this position by so many ministers, many of them influential, accomplished the object which they sought, so that the Affirmation was a decisive event in the church's history. It acquired the name "Auburn" because it was distributed from Auburn, New York.

R.H.N.

Auburn Declaration: This name was attached to the doctrinal statement of the Auburn Convention of August, 1837 of the New School Presbyterians (see New School and Old School Presbyterians). The General Assembly of 1837 had asserted the prevalence of sixteen "doctrinal errors". The Auburn Convention repudiated these virtual accusations and adopted sixteen corresponding propositions. Dealing with salvation and the doctrine of man, these formulated Calvinistic doctrine as influenced by the New England theology*. The "Auburn Declaration" came to be regarded as an authoritative expression of New School teaching. Its approval by the Old School General Assembly of 1868 prepared for the reunion of the two Schools in 1869.

P. Schaff, *Creeds of Christendom,* III (1874) ; *Minutes of the Auburn Convention* (Auburn, 1837).

R.H.N.

auditor: (Lat. one who hears) In canon law*, the person appointed by the bishop to summon witnesses and get all matters ready for a trial.

L.R.W.

Aufklärung: See Enlightenment, the.

Augsburg Confession: The principal creed of Lutheranism and both historically and doctrinally the most important statement of the faith of the Reformation*. Written by Melanchthon* on the basis of the earlier Articles of Marburg, Schwabach, and Torgau,** it was presented to the Emperor Charles V at the Diet of Augsburg on June 25, 1530. Bearing the approval of Luther*, who had added, however, that he himself "could not tread so gently and softly", the creed had been signed by the Protestant potentates. It contains two main divisions: 1) Articles 1-21, concise doctrinal statements on God, original sin, Christ, justification, the ministry of the Word, the new obedience, the Church, the means of grace, the sacraments, confession and repentance, ecclesiastical government, ceremonies, civil government, Christ's return to judgment, free will, the cause of sin, good works, and the invocation of saints; 2) Articles 22-28, a lengthier practical and polemical exposition of the ecclesiastical abuses repudiated. After the Catholic reply, *Confutatio Pontificia,* had been read August 3, Melanchthon prepared the *Apology* of the Confession in sharp polemical tone and published both the Confession and its Apology in 1531. Already in this *editio princeps* the author changed slightly the original document of 1530, and in the succeeding editions of 1533 and 1540 he introduced further changes. The 1540 edition, known as the Variata, differed considerably from the original, especially on the Lord's Supper, and became the basis for the controversy between the Melanchthonians (Philippists, Crypto-Calvinists**) and the rigid Lutherans. The compilers of the Book of Concord (1580) sought to return to the original text handed in at the Diet (the unaltered Augustana or Invariata) but by mistake printed from a poor copy, so that their German text differs from the original at nearly 500 places. Their Latin text, that of Melanchthon's *editio princeps,* is sounder. Both the German and the Latin texts of the Book of Concord* are authoritative. The unaltered Augsburg Confession is generally accepted by Lutherans* as their doctrinal standard. It is the foundation of Lutheran confessional literature and the source of many other confessions, e.g., the Anglican 39 Articles*. See Confessions, Formal of the Christian Church. T.A.K.

Augsburg, Interim of: See Interim.

Augsburg, Religious Peace of: The settlement of the Protestant-Catholic controversy reached at the Diet of Augsburg, Germany, in 1555, whereby all adherents of the Augsburg Confession*, regardless of edition, were acknowledged as Protestants and given legal status and religious freedom. The religion of the ruler was to be the religion of the subjects, dissenters being given the right to emigrate. Ostensibly a victory for the Protestants, the Peace contained an "ecclesiastical reservation" of the forfeiture of the estates of Catholic princes who became Protestant, thus keeping a large part of the land permanently Catholic despite the Protestants' numerical majority. T.A.K.

Augustana: (Lat. "pertaining to Augustus") The Latin name of the Augsburg Confession*. Since the German city of Augsburg, where this basic Protestant confession was presented, derived its name from the Roman emperor Augustus, the confession soon came to be known as the Augustana.

T.A.K.

Augustana Synod: See Lutheran Church in America; Hasselquist, T. N.; Lindberg, C. E.; Olsson, O.

Augustine and Augustinianism: A descendant of the Punic people, Aurelius Augustinus' life and career coincided with the disintegration of the Western Empire of Rome. Born November 13, 354 A.D. in Tagaste, North Africa, he practiced the profession of *rhetor* at Carthage, Rome, and Milan. At the latter place where he experienced a spiritual catastrophe in 386, he was baptised with his son by St. Ambrose during Easter, 387. He became Bishop of Hippo in 395, and died as the Vandals surged around the wall of his episcopal town in August 430 A.D. Coming under the influence of Cicero in his youth, he adhered for nine years to Manicheanism* and favored for a short period the scepticism of the New Academy. He experienced in Neo-Platonism a culmination of his intellectual and religious quest, and concurrently, by the authority of the Catholic church, his moral conversion.

Uniting occidental Christianity with antiquity Augustine conserved and ennobled both. He gave them a fixed relation to the highest problems of the future and made the church the shepherdess of antique culture for the future. With her Augustinian heritage the church was able to realize the new tasks which the Middle Ages posed. His richly endowed, dynamic diversity of personality stamped him as the first modern man and as the last great man of antiquity, making him the creator of the culture and religion of the Middle Ages. His spirit presented the church with eagle wings with which to rise above states and peoples; he gave direction to the aspirations of the mystics; he posed the problems of scholastic science, and the opponents of scholasticism refreshed their spirit in him; he sketched the general directions of the tendency of the church towards world rule; and he lent the critics of the realized world rule of the church their sharpest weapons. Not only the pious, but also the children of the world received stimulation from him. Not only the princes of the church, but also the secular rulers went to school to him. As a priestly king he has been the silent pope of the occident, whose spirit really ruled the church. He was not a man of will, nor a critic, like St. Paul and Luther. The pleasure of destroying he lacked entirely. He was not by nature a reformer. He was of an eminently conservative nature, yet capable of assimilating everything that science and religion offered him. His doctrine is at one and the same time very orthodox and very liberal, very traditional and very personal. He was not only the master of science, but also the doctor of Christian piety. A remarkable power of observing nature, reality, and above all the recesses of the human soul; a lively, restless urge for knowledge and an instinctive sense for religion united in him, furthering and stimulating one another. He seized things and thoughts in their depths, unconsciously extracting from them the good and durable elements and fusing them with his own into a unity. Hence the elements of tradition did not overawe him as is usually the case with predominantly receptive natures. The world historical power of Christianity, which he immediately sensed, gave him both the inner freedom toward tradition and made him into its faithful protector. He was at one and the same time conservative in the highest sense and a man of progress. All temporal problems became for him questions of life and eternity. His description of nature, of history, of man, of anything had always a decisively personal color. His own conversion-experience was always in the background, serving as the point of departure for all his theorizing. The doctrines in which the inspiration of Augustine prevails cannot be reduced to synthetic expositions. Augustinianism is the seeing in the saint's mature ideas of sin, predestinarian grace, original sin, predestination, free-will and church a technically closed and finished unitary structure, ignoring its many knots, gaps and flaws. Rigid Augustinians have ceased to be aware of the many changes in the saint's theology. Augustine was natively incapable of organizing his thoughts into a closed system. He developed a comprehensive philosophy of the church and a new sacramental doctrine in opposition to Donatism*. A potent religious and ethical idealism is joined with church political tendencies in his hierarchical conception of the church. In contrast to Pelagius' rationalistic view of sin and grace*, he worked out an essentially voluntaristic doctrine of sin and grace. See allegorical interpretation; justification; libertarianism; original sin; predestination; philosophy of history; time; trinity. Cf. Cassian.

The Library of Congress lists about 200 entries in various languages for studies of St. Augustine, of which at least 120 are recent publications. E. Chapman, *St. Augustine's Philosophy of Beauty* (1939); M. C. D'Arcy, *Monument to Saint Augustine;* essays on some aspects of his thought, written in commemoration of his 15th centenary (1930); E. Gilson, *L' introduction a l'étude de saint Augustin* (1929); H. Hausheer, *The Genius and the Influence of St. Augustine* (Doctoral dissertation State University of Iowa, 1922); H. Lesaar, *Saint Augustine*, tr. by T. P. Arkell (1931); J. Mausbach, *Die Ethik des heiligen Augustinus*. 2 vol. (1909); H. Pope, *St. Augustine of Hippo* (1930); W. P. Tolley, *The Idea of God in the Philosophy of St. Augustine* (1930). H.H.

Augustine, Saint, of Canterbury: (died 604) Apostle of the Anglo-Saxons. Sent to England by Gregory I* at the head of a mission of 40 Benedictines, Augustine arrived in Kent 597, converted the king, Ethelbert, founded the see of Canterbury and became its first archbishop. See Anglo-Saxons and the Introduction to Christianity. E.C.K.

Augustinians, or the Hermits of St. Augustine: All the monastic* groups following the Rule of St. Augustine, in imitation of the religious clerical body formed by St. Augustine* of Hippo. A chief center for them in the U. S. is at Villanova, Pa. See Black Fathers and Black Sisters; Mendicant Orders. L.R.W.

Aulén, Gustav Emanuel Hildebrand: (1879-) Swedish theologian, professor at University of Lund, and since 1933 bishop of Strengnäs. In the field of dogmatics and history of doctrine, Aulén has emphasized connection between Reformation and early fathers. He has been active in church music studies, and been editor of leading Swedish theological periodical, *Svensk Theologisk Kvartalskrift.* See Lundensian theology. C.J.B.

auricular confession: Private religious consultation with a clerical or lay adviser was common in the early church, though the formal disciplinary confession (*exomologesis*) was public. Secret confession of sins to a priest is normally indicated in the penitential books of the Celtic churches. An annual confession under seal of secrecy was made obligatory for all by the Fourth Lateran Council, 1215. See: Penance. J.T.M.

austerites: Severe self-discipline of the body, even to the infliction of cruel torture, for the sake of the soul's welfare and spiritual purity. R.E.E.H.

authority: The word authority connotes a special character or power; a person, e.g., having authority may mean: something inhering in him establishes a presumption of the validity of his word, or will for others; or his position enables him to impose or enforce his will.

Religion may claim authority in latter sense; a Church, Christian or other, may hold itself to be the one duly instituted medium of truth from God to men; it has divine mandatory authority in the sphere of men. Such concept of the Church is "authoritarian"; against it is belief in the direct testimony and diffused activity of the Spirit; whence the distinction: "Religions of Authority and Religion of the Spirit" (Sabatier); which loses its force with a more dynamic conception of religious authority.

Such as lies in what the people discerned in Jesus; He taught as having authority (*exousia*), not as the scribes (Mk. 1:22). The comparison well illustrates types of authority; the scribes "taught from authorities, balancing one traditional opinion with another; Jesus spoke with authority . . . confidence and power were felt in His words" (H. G. Wood). Like to His own was the authority Jesus commended and gave; its sanctions the divine power received and felt by men (Lk. 9:1, 2; Math. 7: 15-20; 11: 2-6). Paul's authority of the same order; his Apostleship from God (1 Cor. 1: 1), but those who know its virtue are its seal (9: 2). In all this, authority and operation of the Spirit are closely akin; not alternate as above.

This is far from meaning that Christian truth is chiefly of subjective attestation; it is *offered* as truth, as well as proved so by hearing. Hence for most Christians, institutions whence they learn truth have authority; all acknowledge in some way, e.g., the authority of Scripture. Mystics may seek a goal where Deity is so immediate that aids are superseded; yet Scripture and other guides have pointed the ascent (cf. Baron von Hügel* on George Fox and Inner Light in *Essays and Addresses,* II). Some have held Scripture to contain exact verbal transcript of divine thoughts; its writers amanuenses of the Spirit. But this dictation theory of verbal inspiration is not as native to Christianity as to certain other faiths anent their Sacred Writings; for Christians, Scripture enshrines the constituent Facts, the Rock whence Christianity was hewn. It is replete with the truth and power of that which it enshrines; which the Spirit attests to the reader, making it saving truth for him. This is the authority of Scripture: in it here and now God's Word is heard.

Christians own the authority of the Church, the corporate witness through the years; but variously, from the doctrine of the infallible Church, necessary to certify Scripture amid discordant interpretation, to liberal appraisals of group and historic consensus. Defenders of the ecclesiastical view hold the Church's fixing Canon of Scripture a testament to its authority. But the Church versus Bible issue is now revealing itself as fruitless. The Church did not create the Bible, nor the Bible the Church; both come from one source, Jesus Christ and those who first experienced His saving work. This discloses the real locus of Christian authority. To the Church (Math. 18: 17, 18) or the ministers (16: 18, 19), authority is delegated to administer its life; but Christ's first commission to His followers was of service rather than authority (Headlam: cf. Mk. 10: 42-45; Lk. 22: 25, 26).

This realizability of the authority of the Church, as of the Scriptures above, in the believer's or the believing community's life, gives hints as to the mode in which experience is the vehicle of authority. Christianity is no religious psychologism, its truth derivable from or compounded of psychic states. Yet its being *in se* is manifest in the decisiveness of its intrusion into man's spirit; experience bears authority as it authentically betrays this action of what is not of itself. Transcendence of experience differentiates (Christian) religious authority from rational and political concepts. Rational authority rests on *a priori* principles, noncontradiction, etc., that are immediately self-attesting; hence the acceptability of structures coherently grounded on them. The authority of a political system consists in its being the best available for the order and advancement of the group it rules and serves. But Christian truth has its foundation in the Word that, so far from having its norms in human conditions, is primordially determinative, as it is to be redemptive, of them; its Authority is of the same rank as its Source and End. See sacred literatures; traditionalism.

J. H. Leckie, *Authority in Religion* (1909); C. H. Dodd, *The Authority of the Bible* (1928); R. H. Strachan, *The Authority of Christian Experience* (1929); Tambaram (Madras) Series, I, *The Authority of the Faith* (1939), International Missionary Council.
J.L.

Authorized version: See Bible, English.

autocephali: (Gr., independent) A term which described certain bishops* in early Christian times who were independent of their immediate metropolitans* and subject only to higher authority. S.M.G.

auto-da-fé: (Port., act of faith) Term applied to the public ceremony accompanying the official final sentence of the Inquisition*. The ceremony, especially during the 16th century in Spain, consisted of a procession to the place of condemnation for heresy, a sermon at the place, a reconciliation or a condemnation, and finally the turning over to the civil power those still found guilty of heresy*. J.B.C.

autonomy: (Gr., *autos*, self, and *nomos*, law) Self-imposed law. In Kant*, a principle of rational will; an autonomous obligation is one that is imposed by the will on itself, yet is at the same time rationally universal. According to Kant, only autonomous acts are morally good. See heteronomy. E.S.B.

auxiliary bishop: A bishop without jurisdiction who acts as assistant to another; the office, frowned on in the early Church, has become regular in modern times. E.R.H.

Avalokiteśvara: See Buddhist Terminology.

Avataṅsaka: See Buddhist Terminology.

avatar: The Hindu term for divine incarnation. Thus Vishnu has manifested himself according to tradition in nine great avatars, and one is yet to come. "When righteousness declines, when wickedness is strong, I rise . . . take visible shape and move a man with men" . . . declares Krishna in the Bhagavad Gita*. C.S.B.

Avellana: See Decretals.

Ave Maria: The Hail Mary*, or Angelic Greeting. A salutation to Saint Mary (St. Luke 1:28 & 42) used from c. 513 to which a precatory sentence was added in the late Middle Ages, it has long been a popular devotion along with *Credo* and *Pater Noster**, and is the repeated prayer of the Rosary and of the Angelus**. T.J.B.

Avera Bible Lectureship: Established in 1897 by Mrs. W. H. Avera at Duke University, Durham, N. C., with a capital sum of $2,500 and given at intervals of two years. The lectures deal with Biblical literature. Among those who have appeared on this foundation: H. S. Coffin; Bishops W. W. Duncan; G. Campbell Morgan; D. G. Lyon; W. F. Tillet.

(Data furnished by the office of the Dean of the Divinity School.) V.F.

Averrhoes or Averroes: (1126-1198) (Averroists) Famous Arabian philosopher and physician born at Cordova, appointed judge at Seville and Cordova. His writings were numerous including works on astronomy, law, logic, medicine, philosophy and theology. He was devoted to Aristotle and for his great commentary on Aristotle was known and admired by Christian and Jewish scholars as "The Commentator". He denied freedom and immortality, teaching that God eternally produces intelligences by a process of emanation. P.E.J.

Avesta: The sacred book of the Zoroastrians* (Parsis in India and Gabars in Persia), also called Zend ("tradition or commentary")—Avesta (presumably, "knowledge"). The original Avesta (according to tradition) comprised all knowledge and was destroyed for the most part by Alexander. Out of its remnants, a work in 21 volumes (or *nasks*) was prepared in the 3rd cent. A.D., but only one nask (Vendidad) survives complete; the *Dinkard* (in Pehlevi) gives a list of the others. After the 9th century, only the parts dealing with the worship were taken to India and are extant in five parts: Yasna (including the Gathas*), Vispered, Vendidad, Yashts, and Khorda Avesta. See Persia, Religions of.

English translation of the Avesta by J. Darmesteter and L. H. Mills in *Sacred Books of the East*, 1880-87, vols. 4, 23, 31. R.H.P.

Avicebron: (1021-1058) Jewish philosopher and poet of Spain, Solomon ben Judah ibn Gabirol. His chief works are *Meqôr Khayyim* (The fountain of life) and *Mibkhar ha-Peninim* (The choice of pearls). Influenced by Arabic Neoplatonism, his independent thought foreshadowed Spinoza. But like Philo, Jesus and Paul, his work had more influence among Gentiles than among Jews. Also written up under Ibn-Gabriol, Solomon Ben Judah. P.G.M.

Avicenna or Ibn-Sina: (980-1037) Most influential of Arabian physicians. Born in a village of Bukhara he mastered Moslem theology and Greek science by the age of sixteen. To him are ascribed about 100 treatises of which his five-volume Canon of *Medicine* became standard for centuries. Other writings on logic and metaphysics were also widely read. See Michael Scot. P.E.J.

Avignon: A city in France, is famous in history chiefly as the residence of the Popes from 1305 to 1378. The period is often called the Captivity of the Popes in reference to the period of captivity of the Jews in the Old Testament. The popes who reigned during this time were all Frenchmen. They were: Clement V (1305-1394); John XXII (1314-1334); Benedict XII (1334-1342); Clement VI (1342-1352); Innocent VI (1352-1362); Urban V (1362-1370); and Gregory XI* (1370-1378). T.T.M.

Awakening, the Great: The name usually given the intercolonial revivals which swept the American Colonies from 1725 to the opening of the War for Independence. Beginning in the Middle Colonies under the preaching of the pietistic Dutch Reformed minister at New Brunswick, New Jersey, it spread rapidly among the Scotch-Irish Presbyterians where it ran its course under the zealous leadership of a group of young evangelists who had received their training at William Tennent's "Log College". The New England phase was largely Congregational and began in Jonathan Edwards'* Church at Northampton, Massachusetts in 1734, exercising its chief influence in Central and Western Massachusetts and in Connecticut.

The three southern phases of the Awakening came last. The first was the Presbyterian, centering in Hanover County, Virginia. Beginning as a lay movement it took on a Presbyterian complexion with the coming of Presbyterian evangelists from the Middle Colonies, chief among whom was Samuel Davies. The Southern Awakening's second phase was begun by Baptist farmer preachers from Connecticut, formerly Congregationalists, who came, with their families, to Virginia and then to Sandy Creek, North Carolina in 1755. They introduced a new technique in evangelizing communities hitherto untouched by religious influence, thereby setting the pattern for the great western revivals of a generation later. The coming of the Methodists to the colonies was the last phase of the Colonial Awakenings. They had their largest successes in Maryland and Virginia where they were aided by the evangelical Anglican clergyman of Bath Parish in Virginia, Devereux Jarratt. Though representing several distinct phases, the Great Awakening was in a real sense a single movement, in which the emphasis was everywhere upon inner, personal religion. George Whitefield*, who made seven journeys to America between 1738 and 1770, cooperated with all the several phases of the revival and was one of its principal unifying influences. See American theology, early; Dwight, Timothy; New Lights; New Side Presbyterians; Old Side Presbyterians.

Joseph Tracey, *The History of the Revival of Religion in the Time of Edwards and Whitefield* (1842); C. H. Maxon, *The Great Awakening in the Middle Colonies* (1916); W. M. Gewehr, *The Great Awakening in Virginia* (1930); W. W. Sweet, *Religion in Colonial America* (1942). W.W.S.

axiology: (Gr. *axios*, valuable, and *logos*, theory) A comprehensive theory of value, correlating and interpreting the results of psychological, logical, aesthetic, religious, epistemological, and metaphysical investigations. Term first used by P. Lapie (1902) and popularized by E. von Hartmann (1908). See value and the bibliography there given. E.S.B.

axiom: (Gr. *axioun*, think worthy; from *agein*, lead, weigh) A proposition taken as self-evident or beyond question, at least for a given inquiry. Present-day philosophy is reluctant to admit the absolute self-evidence of any proposition, partly because it has been found possible to dispense with one of the axioms of Euclid. Some hold that self-evident means not absolutely, but intrinsically, evident, evident from the mere meaning of the terms involved, whether this intrinsic evidence be conclusion or not. Peirce*, in his "Critical Commonsensism," posited indubitable beliefs, but held that they are vague, and that when put into sharply definite language they become open to doubt. For example, "nature is not without order," when given the more specific rendering, "nature is wholly orderly." C.H.

Ayer Lectureship, The Francis Wayland: Founded in 1928 by Mr. and Mrs. Wilfred Fry of Camden, New Jersey, in memory of Mrs. Fry's father, Francis Wayland Ayer. Shortly after the establishment of the Lectureship, the Rochester Theological Seminary and the Colgate Theological Seminary became the Colgate-Rochester Divinity School under whose auspices the Ayer Lectures are now given. Under the terms of the Foundation the lectures fall within the broad field of the history and interpretation of the Christian Message. Four lectures are given each year and are subsequently published in expanded form. Dean W. L. Sperry of Harvard inaugurated the series in 1928 speaking upon *Signs of These Times*. C.H.M.

B

ba: 1) In Egyptian religion, the soul, which could return to the body so long as its body had not been destroyed. 2) The name of the sacred goat worshipped at Mendes, in Egypt. See Egypt, religions of. P.G.M.

Baader, Franz v.: (1765-1841) A practicing physician, he was honorary professor at the university of Munich. Due to his aphoristic style, his excessive use of phantasy, the wealth of analogies and etymologies, his thought is unduly vague. Greatly indebted to Jacob Boehme, he combines the latter's mystical thought with elements of Schelling and Fichte**. Human knowledge is co-knowing of the divine. Man is neither practically nor theoretically spontaneously active, but only receptively. Further knowledge is possible on the basis of the nature of man. Baader adheres to Catholic doctrine in the Anselmian sense. He accuses the founders of Protestantism to have upheld the principle of revolution instead the principle of reform.

Sämmtliche Werke, 16 vols. (Leipzig, 1851-60); J. Hamburger, *Die Cardinalpunkte der baadischen Philosophie* (Stuttgart, 1855); J. Claasen, *F. v. Baaders Leben und Theosophische Weltanschauung als Inbegriff christlicher Philosophie,* 2 vols. (Stuttgart (1886-87); H. Reichel, *Die Societätsphilosophie F. v. Baaders* (Tübingen, 1901). H.H.

Baalism: Designation of a nature religion, the main emphasis of which is on fertility. Fertility religion assumed various forms in the Near East, but was most highly developed in Canaanite (Phoenician*) religion, and played a major role in the OT by way of stimulus for syncretism and prophetic reaction. From various sources, including especially the OT, the Ras Shamra* tablets from North Syria, and Philo Byblius, the basic concepts are clear. El was the father of the gods (though he played little part in the affairs of men), and Asherah was the mother-goddess. Chief among their progeny was the familiar god who controlled the weather and vegetation, known as Baal, "Lord" (apparently a grandson). His consort was the goddess of fertility, Astarte (OT Ashtaroth [see Ashtoreth] though at Ras Shamra another goddess, Anat, was consort), and his greatest enemy was Mot, "Death."

To understand the story it is necessary to understand the climate of Syria and Palestine. In March-April the rains cease, and do not begin again until October-November. During the dry season, therefore, there is little vegetation which can grow, whereas in the spring as a result of the winter rains the whole country is covered temporarily with verdure. The Canaanite personified the forces responsible for this climatic cycle. The reason the rains stopped and the vegetation dried up was that the god of weather and vegetation, Baal, had been killed in a fierce struggle with Mot, "Death." The rains returned in the fall because friends, especially the Sun (Shapsh or Shemesh) and Fertility (Astarte), brought Baal back to life. The earth flowered in the spring because of the copulation of Baal and Astarte. (See nature worship.)

Due to geographic and climatic influences on the struggle for survival the major emphasis of the religion was thus on fertility. Worship and the various festivals were licentious, appealing to man's baser instincts, and fostering in a prominent role both male and female prostitution.

This religion had a great influence upon Israel in various ways, until the religion of the majority of the common people, especially in North Israel, became highly syncretistic. This occasioned the strong prophetic reaction and the posing of the question by Elijah and his successors as to whether Yahweh or Baal was to be Israel's God. Coupled with this was the denunciation of the symbols and acts of Canaanite religion, including Asherah (whose symbol was the sacred tree, grove, or post), pillar (perhaps the symbol of Baal, though this is not certain), and the *terāphîm* (images, including the fertility-goddess figurines which were so very numerous in popular religion).

Probably due to this prophetic reaction to Baalism also is the rare use in the OT of the term "father" as applied to Yahweh, and "son of God" as applied to man. The OT has no word for "goddess", and the terminology of its religion centers around the conception of Yahweh as the ruling Lord or King. The righteous Ruler gives his commands, statutes, or ordinances to man by means of his messengers (lawgivers and prophets). Man is His servant, and owes his Lord absolute obedience. Thus religion in the OT is expressed by the word "to serve," and it is "the fear of the Lord" which is the beginning of wisdom. This careful avoidance of sexual terminology was undoubtedly due to reaction to surrounding polytheistic and fertility religions.

W. F. Albright, *From the Stone Age to Christianity* (1940), pp. 175-179 and references there citied; Millar Burrows, *What Mean These Stones?* (1941), especially Chap. V; W. C. Graham and H. G. May, *Culture and Conscience* (1936), pp. 119 ff.; Z. S. Harris, "Ras Shamra: Canaanite Civilization and Language," *Smithsonian Report*, (Washington U. S. Government Printing Office) 1937, pp. 479-502; C. F. A. Schaeffer, *The Cuneiform Texts of Ras Shamra-Ugarit* (1939). G.E.W.

Babel era: See Sunday School movement in the United States.

Babism: See Bahaism.

Babylonian Captivity, The: The Babylonian Captivity refers to the period in Jewish history beginning with the year 597 B.C.E., when the first large group of Judeans, together with their king Jehoiachin or Jeconiah, were deported by Nebuchadnezzar to Babylonia, and ending in the year 538 B.C.E., when Cyrus, the conqueror of Babylonia, issued a rescript granting the Jews the right to return to Jerusalem and rebuild the Temple*. During this period several other deportations took place, among them the deportation following the destruction of the Temple in 587 B.C.E. The sources differ as to the number of Jews who were carried off to Babylonia (cf. II Kings 24:14, 16; Jeremiah 52:28-30), however, it is safe to assume that at least 20,000 were deported.

The condition of the Jews who settled in Babylonia was comparatively favorable. The soil was much more fertile than that of Judea and easily supported many Jewish farmers. Some Jews even rose to positions of wealth. So comfortable was the lot of the Jews that many refused to take advantage of the proclamation of Cyrus, but contented themselves instead with giving financial aid to those who were returning to Jerusalem.

Approximately 42,000 Jews returned to Judea in 538 B.C.E. Those who remained in Babylonia formed the nucleus of the community that, centuries later, was to become the center of Jewish learning and culture. E.B.—L.F.

Babylonian Religion: See Mesopotamian Religions.

Bach, Johann Sebastian: See cantata; chorale; fugue; hymns; mass; passion music.

backsliding: A term used to characterize the conduct of those who, having once made a credible profession of the Christian faith, seem no longer to be living in the faith. Whether this means that they have actually fallen from grace, are no longer children of God, and would finally perish if they died in this condition, or that they are still children of God but disobedient is a question that divides Arminians and Calvinists**. See apostasy; conversion. A.K.R.

Backus, Isaac: (1724-1806) Congregationalist, Separatist, Baptist minister and historian. 1771, agent of Baptists with government. 1774, before Continental Congress, champion religious liberty. Travelled 68,600 miles. C.H.M.

Bacon, Benjamin Wisner: (1860-1932) Biblical scholar. Was a Congregational pastor until his appointment to Yale in 1897, where he was Professor of New Testament Criticism and Exegesis until his retirement in 1927. A leader in his field of study, he contributed a number of important books and articles. Among these are the following studies: *The Fourth Gospel in Research and Debate* (1909); *Is Mark a Roman Gospel?* (1919); *The Gospel of Mark: Its Composition and Date* (1925); *Studies in Matthew* (1930); *The Genesis of Genesis* (1891); *The Gospel of the Hellenists* (published posthumously in 1933). M.R.

Bade, William Frederic: (1871-1936) Biblical scholar, naturalist, archeologist. Professor of Hebrew and OT Literature Moravian College 1898-1902, OT Literature and Semitic Languages, Pacific School of Religion 1902-1936. Bade conducted archeological expeditions to Palestine (discovering Mizpah, Tel en Nasbeh) the results of which are described in a forthcoming volume edited by Prof. C. C. McCown.

Author: *The Old Testament in the Light of Today* (1915); *Life and Letters of John Muir;* papers and articles on biblical themes, nature study and archeology. J.W.B.

baetyl: A sacred stone, often a meteorite, before which worship was offered to some superhuman power. P.G.M.

Bahaism: A modern religious sect founded in Persia by Moslem leaders in the 19th century. At first it was called *Babism* for the leader who in 1843 claimed to be the predicted prophet and assumed the name of Bab-ed-Din (forerunner of the cause). Another leader in 1862 announced himself as the manifestation of God foretold by the Bab, and took the name of Baha Ullah (author of the cause). Bahaists believe in the unity of all religions, world peace, universal education, and equality of men and women. See eclecticism; Mohammedanism. P.E.J.

Bahya Ben Joseph: Judge at the Rabbinical court and philosopher, who lived in, the first half of the 11th century at Saragossa, Spain. He wrote the "Guide to the Duties of the Heart" in Arabic in 1040, which was the first systematic presentation of Jewish ethics. B.Z.B.

Baius (or Du Bay) Michael: (1513-1589) Author of the theological system which denies the gratuity of original justice, affirms an intrinsic corruption of human nature through original sin, and rejects the notion of inherent, physical grace in justification. Seventy-nine Baianist propositions were condemned by an *ex cathedra* pronouncement of Pope Pius V*. Baius himself abjured his errors and died a Catholic. C.V.

Balder: Son of Odin & Frigga, god of peace. He was slain by Hoder with a javelin of mistletoe, unintentionally, but as Hoder was an unwilling tool of Loki, the blame for Balder's death rightly belongs to the latter. P.G.M.

baldichinum: (It. *Baldocco,* Baghdad) A cover or canopy built over the altar, originally to protect it from dust; it is supported by columns or suspended by chains. L.R.W.

Balkan Churches: See Eastern Orthodox Churches.

Ballou, Hosea: The most important theologian of modern Universalism*. Born, Richmond, N. H., April 30, 1771. Died June 7, 1852. Son of Baptist minister. Very poor family. No formal schooling. Rebelled against Calvinism. Excommunicated. Became itinerant preacher. Tireless controversialist. Became settled minister in Mass., Vt., N. H., and finally in Boston, Mass. Denied the Trinity, thus being the first systematic Unitarian* in the U. S. Declared God's nature is love. Man saved from sin; not eternal punishment. Voluminous writer. Major work: *A Treatise on the Atonement* (1805).

Thomas Whittemore, *Life of Hosea Ballou* (1854); Maturin Ballou, *Biography of Hosea Ballou* (1852); Oscar F. Safford, *Hosea Ballou* (1889). C.R.S.

Ballou, Hosea (2nd): Born Oct. 18, 1796, died May 27, 1861. Educator, scholar and clergyman. Assisted in editing early Universalist* magazines. Author of *Ancient History of Universalism.* Became the first President of Tufts College, 1854-61. Member Board of Overseers of Harvard College 1843-58.

Hosea Starr Ballou, *Hosea Ballou, 2nd, D. D.* (1896). C.R.S.

Baltimore, Councils of: This is the name usually given to the national councils of the Roman Catholic Church in the U. S., held with the approval of the Pope and under the presidency of the Archbishop of Baltimore, either as Archbishop in the provincial Councils of 1829, 1833, 1837, 1840, 1843, 1846, 1849, or as Apostolic Delegate in the Plenary (or National) Councils of 1852, 1866 and 1884. The Provincial Councils consisted of the bishops of the Province of Baltimore, except that of 1849 at which the Archbishop and Bishops of the province of St. Louis were in attendance. The Plenary Councils were attended by all the bishops of the country. Their decrees, as approved by the Holy See, were obligatory for the whole Catholic body of the country. Cf. Commandments of the church.

Peter Guilday, *A History of the Councils of Baltimore 1791-1884,* (1932). T.T.M.

bambino: (It. child) A wax or other figure of Jesus as child in the manger or crib; this figure is exposed for honor from Christmas to the Epiphany; e.g., at the church Ara Coeli in Rome little boys and girls take their turns in a pulpit during that season in reciting brief eulogies in honor of the Christ Child. L.R.W.

bamot: See high place.

ban: 1) An official ecclesiastical excommunication* or denunciation. 2) A fine imposed by ecclesiastical authority for sacrilege or other crimes. 3) In German history, the ban was a formal edict of interdiction*. The expression "ban of the empire", under which a prince was placed, refers to his divestiture of all honors and privileges, and the prohibition of all association with him. Entire towns or communities might be placed under the ban, and hence deprived of their rights and privileges. C.V.

banns: (A. S., *bannan,* to summon) A public announcement, verbal or published, of a proposed marriage by a church. Required in R. C. it is observed by custom in certain evangelical churches. R.E.E.H.

baptism, Christian: Christian baptism is of uncertain origin. That Jesus, and possibly his first disciples, had been baptized by John seems likely, but in the teaching and practice of Jesus himself baptism is never made a condition of discipleship. Not until after his death when his followers carried their missionary labors beyond Palestine did baptism clearly emerge as Christianity's distinctive initiatory rite. It was the converts to be gathered from among "the gentiles" (*ta ethne*) whose baptism was enjoined in the so-called Great Commission (Matt. 28:19). Possibly the baptism of Jewish proselytes furnished the model followed by the early Christian missionaries on gentile soil, and the act may originally have implied repentance and a purificatory consecration to the new way of life. But as early as the time of Paul a more distinctly sacramental significance was attached to baptism. It was the act that symbolized, if indeed it did not effect, the union of the believer with Christ. The act itself was so efficacious that no importance attached to any official ministrant. Even Paul had not figured conspicuously as a baptizer at Corinth, yet he assumed that everyone in the church had been baptized and thus had become united as one body to Christ (I Cor. 1:13f.). At first the rite seems to have been performed simply in the name of Christ, but before the close of the first century the trinitarian formula had come into use, as attested in Matt. 28:19. At first immersion was the common practice but as the movement spread to territory where the needed water was not available it was deemed sufficient to pour water on the head or moisten it with the finger tips. In the early days of the missionary activity the candidates for baptism were adult converts, but when sacramental efficacy began to be connected with the act it came to be performed for the benefit of children and even for the deceased (I Cor. 15:29). During the second century both the form and the significance of the baptismal rite were more specifically defined. The description by Justin Martyr* mentions a preliminary period of fasting followed by the act of baptismal regeneration issuing in an illumination of the understanding. The practice in North Africa in the time of Tertullian* was even more formal. First came a period of fasting and confession, then the candidate publicly renounced the devil and perhaps professed his acceptance of some doctrinal formula, an invocation was pronounced over the water to render it an effective sanctifying agency, the candidate was immersed three times in the name of each person of the trinity, on his coming out of the water unction was administered, this was followed by the laying on of hands, and the performance closed with a ceremonial tasting of milk and honey. The influence of contemporary gentile rites of purification and initiation is here clearly apparent.

From the second century on the intrinsic value of the baptismal act was uniformly recognized. It was to be performed only once, since it meant forgiveness of sins and regeneration. Post-baptismal forgiveness was questionable, consequently baptism was sometimes long postponed. Another problem was raised by the conversion of heretics who had been baptized by irregular ministers, but finally the rite was held to be valid irrespective of the person by whom it was administered. Still later the Donatists* raised a similar issue but the Catholic church maintained the inherent validity of the rite. The power of God operated in the sacrament quite apart from any human instrument. This interpretation prevailed until the time of the Protestant reformation. The early reformers, while not minimizing the importance of baptism, listed it as only one of the means of grace. Different Protestant bodies also varied the manner of performance and differed in the meaning they attached to the ritual act. See sacraments. Cf. Anabaptists; infant salvation; confirmation; laying on of hands; milk and honey.

W. Brandt, *Die jüdischen Baptismen* (1910); W. Heitmüller, *Taufe und Abendmahl im Urchristentum* (1911); F. Gavin, *The Jewish Antecedents of the Christian Sacraments* (1928). S.J.C.

baptism, lay: See lay baptism.

baptism, non-Christian rites: The efficacy of water as a cleansing fluid led to its ceremonial use as a means of removing the contagion acquired by contact with dangerous potencies (blood, death, things tabued), and then by extension, the contagion of moral failure or sin. Baptismal rites fall into three classes—infant baptism, usually associated with name-giving, adolescent baptism as part of the ceremony of tribal initiation*, and baptism as a mode of admission to the privileges of a religion. The baptismal fluid, usually water, may be variously applied—by immersion, washing, pouring or threefold immersion (Tibetan Buddhism). Because of their peculiar virtues, wine, oil, honey, blood, and cow's urine are sometimes used. The officiant is usually a priest but the father or the headman of the village often performs this priestly function for a child. The baptism removes from the infant the impurities of birth and protects it from lurking unseen dangers. The name-giving ceremony, which has generally been merged with baptism, recognises the child as a legitimate member of the family and puts him under the protection of clansmen, ancestors and the family and tribal gods.

Baptism at puberty marks the end of childhood and the assumption of adult rights and responsibilities. Initiation is a second birth and the "twice-born" youth often receives a new name.

The mystery religions* (Eleusinian, Orphic, Mithraic, Egyptian, Syrian) required baptism for the washing away of moral evil as a preparation for the rites of communion with the deity whose mastery of death assured immortality to the initiates. These baptisms sometimes symbolized dying to the old life and rising again to the new. The same idea underlies the baptism by immersion which was part of the initiation of proselytes to Judaism. A.E.H.

baptism for the dead: Some Christians at Corinth about the middle of the 1st century are reported by St. Paul (I Cor. 15:29) to have been baptized on behalf of friends or relatives who had died before being admitted by that rite into the Church. The practice persisted among Marcionites and Montanists** in the 2nd century, and survives today among Mormons. S.M.G.

baptismal regeneration: See regeneration.

baptismal vow: A profession of intention to live according to the Christian faith and a renunciation of evil made by a candidate for baptism before the administration of the rite. Customary in the Church as early as the time of Justin Martyr*. S.M.G.

Baptist Brethren, German: See Dunkers.

Baptist Churches: See: American Baptist Association; Christian Unity Baptist Association; Duck River Baptists; Free Will Baptists; General Association of Regular Baptist Churches in the U. S. A.; General Baptists; General Six-Principle Baptists; Hard Shell Baptists; Independent Baptist Church of America; National Baptist Convention; National Baptist Ev. Life and Soul Saving Assembly of the U. S. A.; Primitive Baptists; Regular Baptists; Separate Baptists; Seventh Day Baptists; Seventh Day Baptists (German); Two-Seed-in-the-Spirit Predestinarian Baptists; United American Free Will Baptist Church (Colored); United Baptists.

Baptist Churches, negro: See negro church.

Baptist Young People's Union: See Young People's Societies, Christian.

baptistery: Among Roman Catholics, it is usually that portion of a church which contains the font and is reserved for the act of baptism, though occasionally it is a separate building devoted to a like purpose. Among Baptists, it is a large tank located at the front of the church and used for baptism by immersion. W.S.H.

Baptists: Baptist mythology traces continuity from John and Jordan by churches, makes immersion and complete separation of church and state original issues, includes John Milton and Roger Williams* among the Baptists, lets John

Locke acclaim them pioneers of separation of church and state, asserts that John Gano immersed George Washington at Valley Forge. Historically speaking, Baptists originated in the early seventeenth century within English Congregationalism as affusionists* and the separation of church and state issue first appears among American Baptists toward the end of the eighteenth century. The first Baptist confession of faith to prescribe immersion was published in London in 1644 by Particular, or Calvinistic Baptists. No English General, or Arminian Baptist confession of faith prior to 1660 even refers to immersion. As a minority group, early English Baptists naturally desired religious liberty for themselves but as premillenarian* enthusiasts were contemplating the establishment of a Mosaic commonwealth rather than a democracy.

The Arminian* English Baptists began within migratory Congregationalists in the Netherlands, 1609, when John Smyth poured some water upon himself. From Congregationalism* they took over the two principles of the autonomy of the local church and fellowship with other churches. Smyth's attempt to affiliate with the Dutch Mennonites* led to schism and the dissenting contingent returned to England in 1612 to continue the practice of affusion of believing adults until the Restoration. Their principal emphasis was that membership in a Christian church is voluntary, local, and limited to such as had personally experienced salvation and publicly professed faith in Jesus as Lord. A second type of English Baptists known as Particular, or Calvinistic Baptists issued from a series of schisms within the Jacobs-Lathrop Congregational Church in London. This group introduced immersion early in 1642.

American Baptists did not come in a body from England but coalesced as a non-immersionist group in Providence, 1639, and as an immersionist body in Newport, R. I., 1644. Of the former Roger Williams was a member for only a few weeks when he separated. Their numbers, growth, and cultural level prior to the Great Awakening* were low. Fifty years later they reported a membership of over 65,000 of which more than fifty-five percent was in the Southern states with Virginia numerically sixth but relatively first. In 1790 out of 1132 Baptist ministers only 23 had earned academic degrees while in 1819 there were only "three liberally educated Baptist ministers west of the Hudson". But this humble body had been very influential in promoting the adoption of the First Amendment to the Constitution of the United States.

The Baptists of Germany date from 1834 and the convictions of Johann Oncken. This kind of Baptist promoted the beginnings of Baptists in Denmark, Holland, Sweden, Austria-Hungary, Poland and points beyond. For all these Baptists the issue of complete separation of church and state has never existed.

The acceptance of immersion by the Congregational missionaries Adoniram Judson and Luther Rice while on their way to India led to the organization of the Baptist Foreign Missionary Society in 1814. A decade later the Baptists founded a publication society to conduct propaganda through tracts, hymn books, periodicals, handbooks, Bibles, and Sunday School literature, naming it American Baptist Publication Society in 1840. The needs of the shifting American frontier called the American Baptist Home Mission Society into life in 1832.

There is no Baptist church. There are only Baptist churches. The local church legally is sovereign and may alter its conditions of membership or ordain any candidate for the ministry by majority vote. The usual spiritual officers are ministers, deacons, and deaconesses. For missionary and educational endeavor and to provide orderly procedure, Baptist churches have grouped themselves into associations, state conventions, and national conventions. In the north something like organizational chaos prevailed until the formation of the Northern Baptist Convention, 1907, which affirms the independence of the local church but practices a very considerable control. There are no binding general Baptist creeds or confessions of faith. Theoretically a Baptist creed is always subject to revision by appeal to the Bible. Innumerable local and sectional binding confessions and covenants exist, the Philadelphia confession being practically the Westminster. Baptists are biblical literalists with no generally recognized interpretation of the Bible. The resulting confusion signifies debate and progress. Former simplicity in worship is rapidly disappearing and some Baptist churches are architecturally monuments of medieval Gothic with lighted altars and pre-Christian symbolism. The Lord's Supper is rapidly losing its commemorative significance and is becoming a genuine sacrament. Close communion* still prevails in the Bible Belt. Numerous Baptist churches no longer insist upon immersion as prerequisite to membership and many more welcome all evangelical Christians to some type of restricted membership.

As early as 1653, the General Six Principle Baptists arose through insistence upon Hebrews 6:1, 2 as binding. In 1671, the Seventh Day Baptists refused to accept the new First Day Sabbath of the Westminster Confession of Faith*. Conflict over the Negro slavery issue ended in the organization of the Southern Baptist Convention, 1845. More than a decade earlier the Disciples* broke with the Baptists principally over the interpretation of the significance of immersion. At present there are at least eighteen minor Baptist groups from Duck River to Two-Seed-in-the-Spirit-Predestinarian*, from Separate to United Baptists. A total catalogue of fundamentals would indicate emphasis upon absolute predestination, limited atonement, natural inability, irresistible grace, perseverance of the saints, conditional predestination, universal atonement, saving faith, resistible grace, uncertainty of perseverance, full verbal inspiration, premillennialism, laying on of hands, observance of the seventh day, foot washing, the celebration of the Lord's Supper in the evening, anointing the sick with oil, close communion, the seed of God and the seed of the serpent, opposition to a paid ministry and to the education of ministers, and opposition to missionary organizations, secret societies, Sunday Schools, and church organs**. Evidently the causes of separation are three-fold: 1. Divergence of opinion over the five points of Calvinism* and the five points of Arminianism*; 2. Literalism*; 3. Adiaphora*. Of these the first and third are disappearing, but literalism survives. Indeed, literalism has come to its own again in Fundamentalism*, which has been the leading issue among Baptists during the last quarter century.

Baptist religious statistics are not reliable. According to the census of Religious Bodies, United States, 1936, the largest American Baptist group is Negro with 46 percent of the total; next, the Southern Baptists, about one-third; then, the Northern Baptists, about one-sixth, with the eighteen minor groups constituting one-twentieth of the Baptist population. The Southern Baptists are 87 percent rural, the Negro Baptists two-thirds, and the Northern Baptist almost 60 percent. The value of church edifices in 1936 was estimated at about 390 millions. Out of a reported membership of over eight millions, Baptists send less than 14,000 of their children to parochial schools. When Brown University, the University of Rochester, and the University of Chicago are classified as Baptist schools, an imposing educational front is presented.

Champlin Burrage, *Early English Dissenters* (1912); A. H. Newman, *History of Baptist Churches in the United States* (1915); J. H. Shakespeare, *Baptist and Congregational Pioneers* (1906); H. C. Vedder, "Baptists" in *Americana;* W. T. Whitley, *History of British Baptists* (1923). C.H.M.

baraita: An Aramaic term referring to tannaite* traditions not incorporated in the Mishnah*. Its relation to the Mishnah is similar to that of the Apocrypha* to the canonical Biblical writings. B.Z.B.

Barat, St. Madeleine Sophie: (1779-1865) French nun, foundress and first superior-general (1806-1865) of the Society of the Sacred Heart, which under her direction spread through the world. Of unusual energy and extraordinary mental gifts, she was noted for her wisdom in government, her charity and humility. E.A.R.

Barclay, Robert: (1648-1690) Of Ury, Scotland, having received a Calvinistic education at Paris, Barclay was "convinced" of Quakerism* in 1666 and from 1670 was the leading Quaker systematic theologian. His outstanding work is the *Apology* (Latin ed., 1676; English, 1678, frequently reprinted) expounding Quakerism, tinged with Calvinism, in accepted theological idion in partial reply to the Westminster Confession and Shorter Catechism. His scholarship and original contributions attracted widespread attention, and Quakers still consider him a weighty authority. See Society of Friends.

Collected *Works, Truth Triumphant,* etc. (1692); M. C. Cadbury, *Robert Barclay, His Life and Work* (1912). H.C.

bard: A professional singer among the Celtic peoples. Somewhat more elevated in rank than a minstrel or troubador, the bard's songs dealt with heroes, genealogies and religion. P.G.M.

Bardesanes: (154-222) (Syr., *bar,* son; Daisan, the river on which Edessa was situated) Born in Edessa in Syria, where he became a pioneer teacher of Christianity. Founder of Christian Syriac literature and writer of many hymns in Syriac. Praised by Eusebius but condemned by Ephraem and other Syrian fathers of the 4th century. Tried to relieve God of responsibility for evil by asserting that He was organizer but not creator of the world, and accused of gnostic* tendencies. S.M.G.

Bar Kokhba: (Aramaic, "son of the star") Leader of a Jewish revolt (132-135) against Hadrian. Name originally Bar Kozeba was changed to Bar Kokhba on his assumption of command. His generalship prolonged a brave but futile fight against Rome. He died in the Battle of Bethar 135, otherwise little is known about him. N.G.

Barlaam and Josaphat: Popular Middle Ages romance based on the legend of Buddha*. Josaphat was the son of a 4th-century king in India who persecuted the Christians. After keeping his son in seclusion in order to prevent his conversion to Christianity, the king himself was converted by Barlaam, a hermit. Josaphat later succeeded his father on the throne, then resigned and joined Barlaam in the desert. There are many versions of this legend. J.B.C.

bar mitzvah: (Heb. *bar,* son; *mitzvah,* duty or command) Term applied to 1) a Jewish boy on attaining his thirteenth year, the age of religious duty and responsibility; 2) the solemnization of the event by calling up the boy, on the following Sabbath, as one of the seven men to read the weekly portion of the Law, or, as the eighth man, to read the Haphtarah (prophetic lesson). Occasionally the boy delivers a religious address. The event is celebrated by the family. Henceforth the boy is included among the ten males required for public worship, and wears phylacteries during week day morning prayers. Cf. initiation rites. S.S.C.

Barnabas: Barnabas ("son of prophetic speech") was the name given to Joseph, a Cypriote Levite (Acts 4:36). An association with Paul in Antioch (Acts 11:22-26) and missionary work (Acts 13-14) was dissolved by dissension (Acts 15:36-40; Gal. 2:13). Further mention in I Cor. 9:6; Col. 4:10. B.S.E.

Barnabas, Epistle of: A short writing which probably originated in Alexandria about 130. Owing to its early date and the tradition which linked it with Barnabas, it was at one time included in the NT. It is anti-Jewish in sentiment, and allegorises the OT in a manner that sometimes suggests the Epistle to the Hebrews*. See canons of various churches.

J. B. Lightfoot, *The Apostolic Fathers* (1890); E. J. Goodspeed, *Early Christian Literature* (1942). E.F.S.

Barnabites: The popular name given to the Congregation of Clerks Regular of St. Paul which was founded in 1530 by St. Anthony Mary Zaccaria. Its purpose is to preach, catechize, give missions, etc., seasoning all of its works with special references to the epistles of St. Paul. The members take the usual three vows of religion plus an additional one whereby they vow not to seek or accept any ecclesiastical dignity unless ordered to accept it by the Holy See. There are no houses of this order in the United States. T.T.M.

Barnes, Albert: (1798-1870) American Presbyterian minister who supported the new school of theological thought represented by Nathaniel W. Taylor* differing from strict Calvinism and out of harmony with the Westminster Confession. Barnes became the storm-center in the Presbyterian church, his sermon "The Way of Salvation" being made the basis of a heresy trial. V.F.

Baronius, Caesar: (1538-1607) The ecclesiastical historian, was born at Sora and educated at Veroli and Naples. He joined the Oratory at Rome in 1557 under St. Philip Neri, whom he later succeeded as superior in 1593. In 1596 he was raised to the rank of cardinal and then made Vatican librarian. Twice the papacy was almost bestowed upon him, but both times he was defeated because of the hostility of the Spanish delegation whose rancor sprang from Baronius's support of the papacy against the claims of the Spanish crown. He is best known for his great historical works, *Annales Ecclesiastici,* which were undertaken as a refutation to the Magdeburg *Centuries.* Between 1588 and 1607 twelve folio volumes of this work appeared. Baronius's *Annales,* although marred by errors in Greek history caused by his having to use second hand sources, was one of the first attempts to write history from a purely objective viewpoint. T.T.M.

Barrows, John Henry: (1847-1902) Congregational clergyman was born near Medina, Mich., and was a son of Rev. John Manning and Bertina Anthony Barrows. He graduated at Olivet College and studied theology at Yale, Union and Andover seminaries. On May 6, 1875 he married Sarah Eleanor Mole. After brief pastorates at Springfield, Ill. and Lawrence, Mass. he had a distinguished ministry at the First Presbyterian Church in Chicago from 1881 to 1896. He organized the World's Parliament of Religions at the World's Columbian Exposition in Chicago in 1893, much of the success of which was due to him. He greatly stimulated the public interest in the ethnic religions, was Haskell lecturer at the University of Chicago in 1895 and Barrows lecturer in India and Japan the following year. He was President of Oberlin College from 1898 till his death, and greatly promoted the interests of that institution. His published works include: *The World's Parliament of Religions* (1893); *Henry Ward Beecher, the Shakespeare of the American Pulpit* (1893); *Christianity the World Religion* (1897); *A World Pilgrimage* (1897); *Spiritual Forces in American History* (1899); *The Christian Conquest of Asia* (1899).

Dictionary of Am. Biog., v. 1, p. 651; *Congreg. Yr. Bk.,* 1903, p. 14. F.T.P.

Barrows Lectures, The: A foundation established in 1894 by Mrs. Caroline E. Haskell at the University of Chicago, these lectures deal with the subject of Christianity and are given by leading scholars of Europe, Asia and America "as a new golden bond between the East and the West." The seven lecturers have been: J. H. Barrows, A. M. Fairbairn, C. C. Hall, C. R. Henderson, C. W. Gilkey, F. J. McConnell and Shailer Mathews. The endowment is $17,498.00. (Information from the offices of the Dean of the Divinity school and the secretary of the University.) V.F.

barsom: A bunch of twigs (Avestan, *baresman*), cut from the trees with appropriate rites and litanies and presented in the temples; only the priests could carry it during prayers or magical ceremonies. Modern Parsis* have substituted metal rods. R.H.P.

Barth, Karl: Reformed theologian born 1886 in Basel, Switzerland; 1911 pastor in Safenwyl; 1921 professor of Reformed Theology in Goettingen; 1925 professor in Muenster-in-Westphalia; 1930 in Bonn. 1935 exiled by the Nazis; since 1935 professor in Basel.

The prophetic vigor and the earnestness of his *Roemerbrief* (1919) caused a great and deepgoing stir in the religious and theological life of Germany, which soon spread to the other countries of the Continent. He became almost immediately the head of a new theological movement. He had been under the influences of neo-Kantianism, Kierkegaard** and the religious socialism of Ragaz and Kutter. In the first phase of his public activity he uttered a condemning protest against the self-complacency of theology and church, confronting them with the Word of God as the manifestation of the "Wholly Different One", by means of which everything man-made was questioned (Theology of Crisis). In this protest Barth was seconded by kindred spirits, especially Fr.Gogarten, Emil Brunner and Eduard Thurneysen**. The group published the magazine *Zwischen den Zeiten.* Barth himself regarded this first phase of his theology as a corrective of every type of theology, reminding them of the fact that all our statements concerning God are but stammering attempts to give expression to the unspeakable (Dialectical Theology). (See Dialectic). The second phase, beginning about 1925, is characterized by the growing influence that Calvin and orthodox Calvinism had upon Barth's thinking. Barth developed a highly elaborate theological system, established upon the formula *Deus dixit.* Therein he opposes natural by scriptural theology, but at the same time insists upon the cogency and absolute authority of rational conclusions drawn from Scripture.

Theological divergencies led to breaks with both Gogarten and Brunner**. In the German

Church conflict Barth, originally reluctant, later took an active part, until the Gestapo barred him and his books from Germany. Although he has numerous disciples all over the world the several and deepgoing changes in his theological outlook were not favorable to the formation of a Barthian school in theology; but the profundity of his spiritual insights and the energy of his thinking have made it imperative for every theologian to take issues with Barth. In recent years Barth became particularly influential in Continental church life and politics through a series of pamphlets, published under the title *Theologische Existenz heute* (1933-1938), which was continued from Switzerland by a new series entitled *Theologische Studien.* Cf. Dostoievski.

Works:

All the important books of Barth have been translated into English.

The Word of God and the Word of Man (1928); *Come Holy Spirit. Sermons* (1933); *The Epistle to the Romans* (London, 1933); *The Resurrection of the Dead* (1 Corinth ns 15) (London, 1933); *Credo. A presentation of the chief problems of dogmatics with reference to the Apostles' Creed* (London, 1936); *Church Dogmatics* (Edinburgh, 1936-), (So far, two volumes have been published.) *God in Action, Theological Addresses* (1936); *The Holy Ghost and the Christian Life* (London, 1938); *The Knowledge of God and the Service of God according to the Teaching of the Reformation.* Gifford Lectures 1937/38 (London, 1938); *The Church and the Political Problem of Our Day* (1939); *This Christian Cause. A letter to Great Britain from Switzerland* (1942).

Books on Barth and Dialectical Theology.

Emil Brunner, *The Theology of Crisis* (1929); Torsten Bohlin, *Glaube und Offenbarung. Eine kritische Studie zur dialektischen Theologie* (Berlin 1928); John McKonnachie, *The Significance of Karl Barth* (London, 1931); Wilhelm Pauck, *Karl Barth, prophet of a new Christianity* (1931); Otto A. Piper, *Recent Developments in German Protestantism* (London, 1934); C. G. Berkouwer, *Karl Barth* (Kampen, Holland, 1936); F. Kent, *Karl Barth and his teaching* (London, 1937); P. H. Monsma, *Karl Barth's Idea of Revelation* (1937); W. M. Horton, *Contemporary Continental Theology* (1938). O.A.P.

Bartholomew: Bartholomew was one of the Twelve in the Synoptists and Acts but nothing else is known about him; identification with Nathanael in John 1:45 ff is only conjectural. B.S.E.

Bartholomew, Massacre of St.: The name given to the great massacre of Huguenots* in France which began on St. Bartholomew's Day, August 24, 1572. It influenced the trend of Protestant thought and tactics throughout Europe. See Wars of religion. W.S.H.

Bartolus of Sassoferrato: (1314-1347) Greatest jurist among the post-glossators, whose aim was application of the principles of Roman jurisprudence to the political actualities of the time, particularly Italy. A doctor of law at twenty, he taught at Pisa (1339-43) and Perugia (1343-57). His influence on jurisprudence* which was strong for two and a half centuries after his death rests partly on the comprehensiveness of his work and particularly on his sense of realities. So while he does not dispute in theory the ultimate supremacy of the Church over the Empire, actually he holds them to be equal; while he holds that the Empire is universal yet each civitas is *sibi princeps.* Great was the authority of his defense of the principle *Rex in regno suo est imperator regni sui.*

C. N. S. Woolf, *Bartolus of Sassoferrato, his Position in the History of Medieval Political Thought,* (Cambridge, 1913); Ephraim Emerton, *Humanism and Tyranny, Studies in the Italian Trecento* (1925), (contains translations of Bartolus's *De Tyrannia* and *De Guelphis et Gebellinis.* O.B.

Baruch: The companion and amanuensis of Jeremiah* (Jer. 36. 4-32). *Baruch* is likewise the title of four different, non-canonical, Jewish books, of varying character, all ascribed to or centering about the figure of the historical Baruch. These writings date in all likelihood from the first and second centuries A.D.

See apocrypha, Old Testament; pseudepigrapha. J.M.

Bascom, John: (1827-1911) A. B. Williams College, 1849, Andover Seminary 1855; pres. Univ. of Wisconsin 1874-1887; prof. political science, Williams College 1891-1901.

Author of volumes on political science, aesthetics, psychology, ethics and theology, including the following: *Philosophy of Religion* (1876); *Natural Theology* (1880); *The New Theology* (1891); *Evolution and Religion* (1897); *God and His Goodness* (1901). J.W.B.

Basel, Council of: (1431-48) Was summoned by Pope Martin V in order to deal, among other matters, with the Hussite schism, for the Crusades conducted against the Bohemians for the purpose of subjugating them had failed. The Council regarded itself as possessing an authority superior to that of the pope (as the Council of Constance, 1414-18 had declared), although Martin's successor, Eugenius IV, never acknowledged the claim. In the matter of the Hussites*, they were granted certain of their demands—among them the use of the cup in the Eucharist, although this was never approved by the Pope, and later was withdrawn by Pope Pius II. On these terms, the Calixtine party among the Hussites was received into communion with the Church. Eugenius was able to reassert the claim to papal superiority over a general council when in 1437 he ordered the Council of Basel to reconvene at Ferrara. Most of the fathers obeyed, although the recalcitrants remained at Basel, and in their protest against Eugenius' claims deposed him in 1439 and elected a new pope, Felix V. In 1448 the rump of the Council moved to Lausanne, but after the abdication of Felix V gave their adherence to the successor of Eugenius, Pope Nicholas V. Thus the schism was healed, but at the cost of the abandonment of the conciliar theory. See compacts or compactata; Ferrara-Florence, Council of. M.S.

Basil, the Great: (ca. 330-379) As churchman, theologian and representative of the monastic ideal, he gave normative suggestions to the articulation of Greek orthodoxy. In particular he rejoiced in extensive physico-theological discussions. But he also exhibited a strong urge to transcend everything hylic, to ascend to God, and to live only in Him. See Basilians; Cappadocians, the three; Cenobite.

K. Holl, *Amphilochius von Ikonium in seinem Verhältnis zu den drei grossen Kappadociern* (Tübingen & Leipzig, 1904). H.H.

Basilians: The monks of the Eastern Orthodox churches* who follow the Rule of St. Basil the Great*, the archbishop of Caesarea of Cappadocia (329-379). He had founded a monastery on his own ancestral estates, and c. 356 drew up a Rule for the members of the community basing it upon the Rules he had studied on his visit to Egypt and other countries. This became the basis of most of the subsequent Rules of various monastic reformers of the Eastern churches. The chief revision was made by St. Theodore of Studion* (d. 829), and it is in this form that it enjoys the widest use at present. There has never developed the multiplicity of various monastic orders in the East as has been the case in the West. Since all the hierarchs of the Eastern churches are chosen from among the monks, monasticism has exerted an influence upon the East which is even greater than that in the West. But the Basilian Order is not restricted to the Eastern communions, for there exists a small number of Latin Basilian monasteries as well.

Ernest F. Morison, *St. Basil and his Rule* (London, 1912); W. K. L. Clarke, *St. Basil the Great* (Cambridge, 1913). M.S.

basilica: (Gr. *basilikos,* royal) A building for public assemblies, law courts, etc. In Roman times they were also used for markets. They were great halls with nave and aisles separated by columnar arcades and usually having apses* at one or both ends. The early Christian churches are supposed to be modelled after them. *Basilica* is still the regular Latin word for a church. F.T.P.

Basilides: Taught at Alexandria during the reign of Hadrian. A leading exponent of Gnosticism* in a Christian version. Held that the Creator of this world was the God of the Jews, an inhabitant of the lowest heaven. Jesus came to end Jehovah's sovereignty. Jesus was only human in appearance. Simon of Cyrene suffered in His stead on the Cross. S.M.G.

basin: Sprinkling bowl used in a sacrificial service in the Jerusalem Temple, and made of copper, brass, silver, or gold. B.Z.B.

Battle-Axe experiment: A shock-producing perfectionist* adventure fathered by one of America's oddest nineteenth century religious figures—Theophilus Ransom Gates (Born 1787 at Hartland, Conn.: died 1846 in environs of Philadelphia).

Full understanding of the experiment requires mention of three basic factors that combined to make Theophilus an extreme religionist. First was his inherent disposition. Probably inheriting in degree his father's tendency toward "seasons of derangement", he early experienced strange apparitions which left him deeply fearful for the present state of his soul. Second was his reforming zeal. Convinced that his unhappy state of mind was due to the inability of existing religious establishments to satisfy human needs, he refused attachment to any and set out as a wanderer in search of greater truth. Ideas crystallized by a call to preach which came in 1810, he settled in Philadelphia to lash existing religious practices with tongue and pen. The latter proved to be his most effective weapon. From 1810 to 1818 he published at least a dozen pamphlets, most apocalyptic in tone, reflecting vaguely an interest in a new life of holiness, purity and perfect love. Then from 1820-1835 he conducted with remarkable success the monthly *Reformer* in which he criticized mercilessly all digressions from "primative" or "pure" Christianity, particularly priestcraft, benevolent organizations and sectarianism. A supplementary periodical attempt, the bimonthly *Christian* (Phila., 1830-31) of similar design but more radical in expression was less successful, ending quickly in merger with *Reformer,* which union brought almost as quick demise to the latter publication heretofore so well patronized. Reforming zeal thus frustrated by the loss of the most effective medium of spreading his ideas, the third and decisive factor in Theophilus's life began to exert its influence. Somehow, exact date uncertain, he was drawn into marriage. The match was exceedingly unfortunate. Home life came to be a "dog-cat" relationship of the most miserable sort with wife constantly insinuating insanity of husband. Dual strain of calumny at home and in relationships at large drove neurotic tendency to an extreme. Fiery reformer turned radical perfectionist.

Already under the influence of "Free-Love" ideas akin to those of John Noyes, Theophilus now strode forth to proclaim a millenium based thereupon. In 1837 through three numbers of an inflammatory periodical sheet entitled *Battle-Axe and Weapons of War* (terminology from Jeremiah) he outlined his new "Order of God". Unhappy marriages were to be dissolved. Binding rules respecting relationships between sexes no longer existed. Free choice was to prevail in selection of mate and in the matter of having offspring; care to be exercised always that the "principle of holiness", not the "beast principle" motivated action. In fact, freedom was proclaimed in every area. There was to be no Sabbath, no sacrament, no preaching, no restricting custom of any kind to inhibit the growth of the perfect spirit in the individual. Thus the perfect society on earth was to be established.

Strange things began to happen in the environs of Philadelphia. A number of men unhappy in their present state unceremoniously approached women of their choice announcing they had been directed by God to present themselves as soulmates, receiving favorable response. Some women approached men in like manner with like results. Sometimes one or both parties were already married, but this was immaterial to the "Battle-Axer". Not welcome in the city proper, devotees to this new order gathered some thirty-five miles outside in "Free-Love Valley", forming there a little colony. Probably never more than several dozen in number at any one time, their lot was nevertheless one of constant persecution. Growing fondness for nudity and development of weird religious rite in no way eased their plight.

By this time the experiment had transgressed the bounds Theophilus had set for it. He chose to fade into the background. Hannah Williamson, his most fervent disciple, became active leader of the group. It now quickly became clear that the persistence of the adventure was due chiefly to the personality of its founder. Devoid of his present leadership, the movement within a generation dwindled into legend, as did so many religious schemes of the restless thirties and forties.

The only general treatise to date is C. C. Seller's admirable booklet *Theophilus, The Battle Axe: A History of the Lives and Adventures of Theophilus Ransom Gates and the Battle Axes.* A list of known "Battle-Axers" and a Bibliography of Gates' works are appended. Original source material dealing with Gates's pre-Battle-Axe thought and experience is fairly plentiful. The volume *The Life and Writings of Theophilus R. Gates* (Sec. ed. with Additions, Phila., 1818) is a collection of the known pamphlets published by him, except *Truth: or the Religious Sentiments of Theophilus Gates* (Poughkeepsie, 1811) and *A Measuring Reed* (Phila., 1815) which can be consulted separately. The three periodicals mentioned *supra* are indispensable for data 1820-1837. Thenceforth reversion to Sellers, who does not give specific documentation, is necessary. Most likely sources of additional information are periodicals and newspapers in environs of Philadelphia 1837ff and the writings and journalistic publications of John Noyes who constantly took issue with Gates whom he considered a plagiarist.

G.P.A.

Bauer, Bruno: (1809-1882) Hegelian, was the most radical of the NT critics of his age; attributing no historic value to the documents and treating Christianity as an amalgam of the teachings of Seneca, Philo and Josephus**. None the less, certain of his conclusions regarding the relation of Christianity to Hellenism* have stimulated later research.

B.S.E.

Baur, Ferdinand Christian: See Tübingen School. Also see Lives of Jesus.

Bautain, Louis, Abbé: (1796-1867) A Catholic philosopher, was reconverted to the Church in 1821, after some years of philosophical skepticism. He continued after his conversion to accept Kant's objections to all rational theistic arguments but taught that God may be known through *faith,* through *feeling* and through direct mystical *insight.* This "fideistic" theory of religious knowledge was officially condemned in 1840, and Bautain signed a formula of recantation. See fideism.

W.M.H.

Baxter, Richard: (1615-1691) Born in Kidderminster, Gloucester, he began his career as an obscure lecturer, without a university degree, but during the Puritan Revolution he became a power in Puritan* affairs and a prolific and widely read writer. At the Restoration he took an active part in the Savoy* Conference, although he displayed a less cooperative attitude than Thomas Manton or Edward Reynolds; and while he accepted a chaplaincy from Charles II, he later rejected the bishopric of Hereford. In 1662 he became a nonconformist*. He was a leader in dissenting affairs and strove constantly to secure a comprehension of the Presbyterian group in the Anglican church. See Puritan Ethics.

His best known writings are: *The Saint's Everlasting Rest* (London, 1650); *A Christian Directory* (London, 1673); and his autobiography, *Reliquiae Baxterianae* (London, 1696). His *Practical Works* have appeared in two editions, 23 vols. (London, 1830); 4 vols (London, 1868). See F. J. Powicke, *The Life of the Reverend Richard Baxter* 2 vols. (London, 1924-27).

E.W.K.

Bayle, Pierre: (1647-1706) Eminent tolerationist in the France of Louis XIV. Since 1681 he resided mainly in the Netherlands. Brought up a Protestant, he was for a few months a Catholic, then returned to Protestantism, but was strongly influenced by Descartes*. A pioneer in popularizing literature through an international review, he is best known for his *Dictionnaire historique et critique* (1695-1702; 1740; English translations available), which was an important source of the French encyclopaedists and philosophes, and is largely useful still today. See reason in religion.

K. Martin, *French Liberal Thought in the Eighteenth Century: A Study of Political Ideas from Bayle to Condorcet* (London, 1929); H. Robinson, *Bayle the Sceptic* (1931).

Q.B.

beadle: 1) An usher attendant upon ecclesiastical or academic dignitaries, bearing the mace. 2) A parish officer appointed to keep order in church.

P.V.N.

beast: This is the usual English translation of the Greek *thērion* in Revelation* 13 and 17. The original means a wild and robbing animal. John's portrayal was based on the fourth beast in Daniel* 7.4 which its author certainly intended to refer to the Seleucid Empire. Already in the rabbinic* exegesis, however, it was interpreted as Rome. An originally mythological concept was given historical application in Jewish-Christian apocalyptic*. In Revelation 13 the Beast is an agent of the Dragon* and hence antichrist* in contrast to the Christ of God. In contrast to the lamb who is slain, (5.6) the Beast has a death wound which was healed (13.3). This was influenced from the Nero legend according to which the Emperor was not dead, but would return from the East, or later from the dead. The number 666 (13.18) is most plausibly interpreted as Caesar Nero, though it may simply be a falling short three times of the perfect number 7. The Greek letters for Jesus added up to 888, one more than the perfect number. In Revelation 17 the seven heads of the Beast are interpreted as Emperors indicating that the end was near for they lived under the sixth.

C.T.C.

beatification: (Lat. *beatus,* blessed and *facere,* to make, do) The formal papal declaration that a deceased person, because of holiness of life, or heroic death, deserves to be called "blessed"; that is, to be regarded as enjoying Heaven. See advocatus dei; advocatus diaboli; canonization. L.R.W.

beatific vision: The supreme reward of the righteous, consisting of the unimpeded sight of God in heaven. So taught by both Jews (2 Esd 7:98) and Christians (1 Cor. 13:12; Rev. 22:4). B.S.E.

beatitude: The name given to each of the nine sayings of Jesus in Mt. 5:3-11 or the four in Lk. 6:20-23, all of which begin with "Blessed are." They set forth the supreme ideal of character and are often used as the most succinct summary of Jesus' teaching. See blessedness. B.S.E.

Bec: A famous monastic center of learning for Normandy and England, founded c. 1034 near Rouen. Immortalized by the incumbency of its great teacher-administrators, Lanfranc and Anselm**, it was also distinguished by a roster of students later influential as theologians, legists, and archbishops. R.C.P.

Beck, Johann Tobias: (1804-1874) Protestant theologian. Born Balingen, Wurtemberg, 1836, professor of N.T. Basel; 1842, professor inTübingen. Principal modern representative of Biblical realism. Equally fruitful in exegetical and theological works. The idea of the Holy Spirit as agent of creative life from above is central in his theology. He saw the Spirit's work both in the history of the chosen people, interpreted as the growth of a supernatural organism, and in the making of the Bible. Faithfulness to the Bible text in connection with his organistic view of church history enabled him equally successfully to oppose the selfcomplacency and the static views of 19th century orthodoxy and the moralism as well as the unhistorical speculations of theological liberalism. Through his followers, especially Ad. Schlatter and his disciples, Beck still exercises a profound influence upon Continental theology. Principal works:

Die christliche Lehrwissenschaft nach den biblischen Urkunden (Stuttgart, 1841, 2nd ed. 1875); *Umriss der biblischen Seelenkunde* (Stuttgart, 1843 3rd ed. 1871); *Vorlesungen über christliche Ethik* (Gütersloh, 3 v. 1882-1883); *Vorlesungen über christliche Glaubenslehre* (Gütersloh, 1886); *Pastoral Theology of the New Testament* (Edinburgh, 1885); Art. Beck, J. T., in Schaff-Herzog's *Encyclopaedia,* v. II p. 20 f. O.A.P.

Becket, Thomas: (1118-70) Saint. Archbishop of Canterbury and Chancellor of England. He was born in London and died in Canterbury. The favorite of Henry II and a man distinguished as a soldier and as a statesman he was appointed by the king as Archbishop of Canterbury, while still a deacon. He was ordained a priest the day before his consecration. His loyalty to the Church and his opposition to the encroachments of the State in Church affairs merited for him the anger of the king. He was obliged to take refuge in France. A reconciliation was finally effected, and he returned to England, only to face new difficulties with the king. Becket was murdered in his cathedral of Canterbury by four retainers of Henry. He was canonized within three years after his death. His burial place was one of the great pilgrimage shrines until it was violated by Henry VIII*. His feast is celebrated on Dec. 29. See Constitutions of Clarendon. J.B.C.

Bede (Baeda), the Venerable: (673-735) English monk and scholar, author of *An Ecclesiastical History of the English People* (c. 731). At the monastery of Jarrow, where he spent the greater part of his life, he was highly esteemed both for piety and learning, his fame extending to the Continent. His miscellaneous writings, about forty in number, are overshadowed by the *History,* which remains an important source book for the early English Church. L.W.C.

Bedlam: (contraction of Bethlehem) Famous hospital in London founded in 1247, for the Order of Our Lady of Bethlehem, as a general hospital for the poor. It became an insane asylum in 1405. After several changes of location it was finally removed to the present site in St. George's Fields, Southwark. It was managed in its Catholic days by religious who made every effort to cure their patients, but later it became the symbol of every abuse. In the 18th century its inmates were exhibited to visitors for an admission fee. Today it is known for its humane and successful treatment of the insane. J.B.C.

Beecher, Henry Ward: (1813-1887) Congregational clergyman, was born in Litchfield, Conn. and was a son of Rev. Lyman* and Roxana Foote Beecher. He graduated from Amherst in 1834 and studied theology at Lane Seminary, Cincinnati, Ohio. For two years he was pastor of a small church at Lawrenceburg, Ind. and for eight years more of the Second Presbyterian Church in Indianapolis. In 1847 he was settled over the Plymouth Church (Congregational) in Brooklyn, N. Y. where he remained for the rest of his life.

Beecher is commonly rated as one of the most brilliant and influential preachers of modern times. He was a leader in the anti-slavery movement and other reforms and was a strong supporter of the Union whose cause he aided by a speaking tour in England in 1863. He supported Andrew Johnson and was violently opposed by the radical Republicans.

In 1874 occurred the famous trial in which charges of adultery were brought against him by Theodore Tilton, which ended in the disagreement of the jury. Later he was tried by an ecclesiastical council and acquitted.

He was a constant contributor to the press, edited the N. Y. *Independent,* 1861-1864 and the *Christian Union,* 1870-1881. Among his numerous books are: *Lectures to Young Men* (1850); *Star Papers* (1855); *Life Thoughts* (1858); *Royal Truths* (1864); *Norwood* (1864); *Life of Christ,*

v. 1, (1871); *Sermons on Evolution and Religion* (1885).

In his latter years he became an advocate of the doctrines on evolution and theological modernism. He was a strong supporter of Grover Cleveland and probably contributed substantially to his election to the presidency in 1884.

On Aug. 3, 1837 he married Eunice White Bullard of West Sutton, Mass, and their family consisted of ten children. See New Theology, the.

Dictionary of Am. Biog. v. 2, p. 129; *Congreg. Yr. Bk.* 1888, p. 19; L. Abbott, *Henry Ward Beecher* (1903); L. B. Stowe, *Saints, Sinners and Beechers* (1934); P. Hibben, *Henry Ward Beecher, An American Portrait* (1927). F.T.P.

Beecher, Lyman: (Oct. 12, 1775-Jan. 10, 1863) Congregational and Presbyterian clergyman, revivalist, educator, entered Yale College in 1793 and was greatly influenced by Timothy Dwight* who became its president in 1795. In 1799 he was ordained over the Presbyterian Church at East Hampton, L. I. Becoming widely known through the publication of his sermon on dueling, in 1810 he moved to the Congregational Church at Litchfield, Conn. As "Pope" Dwight's lieutenant and "field marshall" of Connecticut Congregationalism*, he organized that group to fight disestablishment, which, however, was accomplished in spite of his efforts in 1818. He then led the Connecticut orthodox to oppose the Unitarians and was effective in checking the spread of Unitarianism* in New England. A close friend of Nathaniel W. Taylor*, he collaborated with the Yale group in the development of the New Haven theology*—an evangelical Calvinism modified to meet the aspersions of infidels and Unitarians. In 1826 Beecher went to the newly formed Hanover Street Church in Boston, where his fiery anti-Catholic preaching was at least indirectly responsible for the mob sacking of the Ursuline convent in Charlestown in 1831. In 1832, sensing the great importance of the west, he went to Cincinnati to become president of Lane Seminary and minister of the Second Presbyterian Church. There followed a hectic period, during which most of the Lane student body was lost to Oberlin when the administration tried to suppress the discussion of abolitionism on the part of the students led by Theodore Dwight Weld, and Beecher was dragged through several trials on charges of heresy brought by Old School Presbyterians*. In 1850 he resigned his work in Cincinnati, and spent the remaining years of his life in the home of his famous son, Henry Ward Beecher*, in Brooklyn.

Lyman Beecher, *Autobiography . . .*, ed. Charles Beecher, 2 vols. (1866); F. B. Dexter, *Biographical Sketches of the Graduates of Yale College,* V (1911); C. C. Stowe, "Sketches and Recollections of Dr. Lyman Beecher," *Congregational Quarterly,* VI (1864); Constance M. Rourke, *Trumpets of Jubilee* (1927); S. E. Mead, *Nathaniel W. Taylor* (1942). S.E.M.

Beecher Lectures, Lyman: A lectureship at the Yale University Divinity School, established May 2, 1872, in memory of the Reverend Lyman Beecher, B.A. 1797. The lectures are on preaching and the work of the Christian ministry, and have been delivered in all but four years since the date of the foundation. Among the courses have been those by Henry Ward Beecher, 1872-73-74; Phillips Brooks, 1877; A. M. Fairbairn, The Place of Christ in Modern Theology, 1892; Sir George Adam Smith, Modern Criticism and the Preaching of the Old Testament, 1899; George A. Gordon, Ultimate Conceptions of Faith, 1903; Charles Sylvester Horne, The Romance of Preaching, 1914; Harry Emerson Fosdick, The Modern Use of the Bible, 1924; George A. Buttrick, Jesus Came Preaching, 1931; Ernest F. Tittle, Jesus After Nineteen Centuries, 1932; Albert E. Day, Jesus and Human Personality, 1934; Charles C. Morrison, What is Christianity, 1939. L.A.W.

Beelzebub: A NT name for the chief of the devils* (Matt. 10.25; 2: 24, 27; Mark 3.22; Luke 11: 15, 18, 19); therefore a synonym of Satan*; transmitted in Sept. as Beelzebul, but in Vul. as Beelzebub. In the O.T. Beelzebub (Baal Zebub) occurs only once (2 Ki. 1.2), as the name of the god of the Philistine city of Ekron. Baal Zebub probably means "lord of flies." J.M.

Beghards: Male counterpart of Beguines*. Earliest Flemish groups were weavers. Many members and groups became tertiaries of the mendicant orders. Others became associated with French wanderers who begged, so they were known as beggars. Condemned as heretics, they were persecuted and did not survive the 14th century. A.S.

Beguines: Name given to women of semi religious sisterhoods living in large or small enclosures, called *beguinages.* They engaged in weaving, lace making, care of sick with emphasis on devotional life; they took vows, not perpetual, of poverty, chastity and obedience; as a rule not mendicants, they controlled their own property. They often sought instruction as well as the protection of the mendicant friars. Founded c. 1170 by Lambert la Bégue, priest of Liege, the movement spread in western Europe with aid of clergy and rulers, for ex. King Louis IX, France. One of the largest groups included 18 houses with 700 members. Beguines were variously regarded by popes, prominent clergy and scholars either as heretics to be severely punished, or as worthy religious persons. To this day, the *beguinage* at Bruges is well known A.S.

behaviorism: See psychology, schools of.

Behistun (or Bisutun): Village at the foot of a steep rock in the center of the Zagros range in Persia. The name was originally Bagistana ("place of the gods"). High upon the rock, Darius I (521-485) engraved a long inscription (in Old Persian, Babylonian, and Elamitic), describing how through the help of Ahura Mazda* he defeated Gaumata and nine rebel chiefs. A bas-relief above the inscriptions represents Darius and the captive rebels. R.H.P.

Beissel, Conrad: See Ephrata Society. Also see communistic settlements, religious.

Bel: See Baalism.

Bel and the Dragon: One of the three additions to the canonical Book of Daniel* found in the LXX*, comprising two tales further illustrating the cleverness and miraculous successes of Daniel, written in imitation of the stories in Dan. 1-6. Dates from c. 100 B.C. See apocrypha, Old Testament. R.B.Y.S.

Belgic Confession: A Reformed creed of thirty-seven articles, prepared in 1561 by Guido de Bres; in amended form, adopted by various synods from 1566 to 1581, and finally by the great Synod of Dort*, 1619. It is a recognized symbol of the Reformed Churches of Holland and Belgium, and of the Reformed (Dutch) Church in America. See Confessions, Formal.

P. Schaff, *Creeds of Christendom* (1919), I pp. 502-508; III, pp. 383-436. A.K.R.

Belial, Beliar: 1) In most of the O.T. *belial* is a Hebrew common noun meaning baseness, i.e., "man of baseness," "daughter of baseness," etc., covering a variety of types such as worthlessness, falsehood, wickedness, depravity, etc. 2) A new usage seems started in Nahum 1:15 (H. 2:1) where belial may be Belial, a personalized designation of the Assyrian conqueror. 3) In the N.T. it appears as Beliar, a proper noun, apparently referring to the prince of the devils and therefore a variant to the name Beelzebub. 4) In pseudepigrapha* it is a name applied to Satan*, the Anti-Christ*, or an emissary of Rome. 5) Milton adds to the figure by describing him as the lewdest of the spirits that fell from Heaven. R.E.W.

Bellamy, Joseph: (1719-1790) Pupil and popular interpreter of Jonathan Edwards*. Famous for such paradoxes as the following:—"*God does as he would be done by*, when he punishes sinners to all eternity." "*The more unable to love God we are, the more we are to blame.*" Introduced the Grotian theory of the Atonement (See Grotius) into New England theology. Chief works: *True Religion Delineated* and *The Wisdom of God in the Permission of Sin.* See New England theology. W.M.H.

Bellarmine, St. Robert: (1542-1621) Italian Jesuit, Archbishop of Capua and Cardinal. His *De controversiis christianae fidei* was the best Catholic discussion of the early Protestant position. Giving evidence of an understanding of Christian antiquity rare for the period and based on an exact knowledge of traditional theology and of the teachings of the adversaries, it won for its author an European reputation. E.A.R.

bells: See carillon; peal ringing.

Belot, Gustave: (1859-1930) Firmly convinced of the impossibility of *a priori* speculation and the uselessness of metaphysics to establish a positive morality or a moral technique, he opposed the science of morals. He cited the example of Socrates, Jesus, socialism and Tolstoy as having gone contrary to all the morals of their epoch. He saw many similarities between the operations of morality and those of scientific techniques. Genuine morality he felt was a matter of growth.

L'idée et la methode de la philosophie scientifique chez A. Comte (Paris, 1902); *Etudes sur la philosophie morale au XIX siècle* (Paris, 1904); *Etudes de morale positive* (Paris, 1907). H.H.

Beltane: (Irish, *bealtaine*) The spring festival, celebrated on May Day, in Celtic lands in pre-Christian times. It was one of the four major festivals of the year, with Samhain, Imbolc and Lugnasad. The May pole dance is a survival of its lost ceremonies. P.G.M.

Bender, Wilhelm: (1845-1901) He taught at the University of Bonn. He completed the anthropological twist of Ritschlianism*, which pushed God and His revelation to a secondary position, by coming an exponent of the illusionistic critique of religion.

Das Wesen der Religion (Bonn, 1886). H.H.

Benedict of Aniane: (751-821) Called Witiza until he left soldiering for monastic life, was born at Maguelone of Visigothic race. He founded the monastery of Aniane (779), compiled monastic rules, and, having removed to the vicinity of Aachen, became general supervisor of the Frankish monasteries (817). W. Williams, *Monastic Studies*, (Manchester, 1938). J.T.M.

Benedict XIV, Pope: (1740-58) Prospero Lorenzo Lambertini, born at Bologna, March 31, 1675 was created cardinal in 1726 (announced in 1728), named Bishop of Ancona 1727, and Archbishop of his native city in 1731. He ranks among the most learned of the popes and enjoyed the reputation of being an exceptionally gifted canonist even before his elevation to the papacy, Aug. 17, 1740. Without compromising principles, he met as far as possible the impirially inclined statesmen of his day with moderation and tactful concessions. Of all the popes, due to his good humor and understanding nature he probably had the most friends and the least openly-avowed enemies. For which reason also he was able to settle differences between the Church and various countries, e.g., in Portugal (cf. "Innocent X") in Naples (1741), in Sardinia, Spain (Concordat of 1753), and Austria. The same good feeling prevailed in his dealings with Protestant and Mohammedan princes. He recognized the title, King of Prussia, assumed by the Elector of Brandenburg in 1701. He referred to the Sultan as the "Good Turk". Voltaire dedicated to him his work on "Mohammed". Benedict brought back into communion with Rome two Eastern Churches, the Greek Melchites* of Antioch and the Maronites*. He renewed, however, the prohibition of Clement XI against Freemasonry (Mar. 18, 1751 and condemned the system of Christian "accommodation" to heathen rites, employed mostly by the Jesuits in India and China (Molabar Rites). (See Chinese Religions). Benedict merited well also for the interior life of the Church. He practically suppressed usury in his day (Encyclical *Vix pervenit,* 1745). He promoted the Liberal Arts. Through the help of the learned Evodius Assemani he compiled a catalog of books in the Vatican Library; founded four Academies (cf. "Pontifical College") or literary associations for the deeper study of 1) Roman and Christian Antiquities; 2) the History of the Church and Councils; 3) the study of Canon Law and 4) Sacred Liturgy; and enriched the collections of Museums in Rome and Bologna. He founded chairs for chemistry and mathematics in the Roman University, known as the *Sapienza,* and many others for painting, sculpture, etc., at other schools and colleges. Even though he had never become pope, his name would remain immortal in ecclesiastical circles in virtue of his famous works on the "Beatification and Canonization of Saints"; on the "Sacrifice of the Mass"; the "Feastdays of Christ and of the Blessed Virgin Mary", etc. His *"De Synodo Dioecesana"* is classical. His literary works were collected and published at his wish by Emmanuel de Azevedo, S. J. (Rome, 1747 ff.) in 12 vols.; republ. at Prato, 1839-46 in 17 volumes. His letters were published by F. X. Kraus[2] in 1888. Additional works were published in 1904 by Heiner, and by R. de Martinis (Naples, 1888 ff.) His *"Institutiones Ecclesiasticae",* a collection of 107 documents on matters pertaining to pastoral, dogmatical and moral Theology were translated into Latin by P. Ildephonsus a S. Carlo.

Guarnacci, *Vitae et Res Gestae Roman. Pontif. et Card. a Clemente X usque ad Clementem XI* (Rome, 1857); for biographies cf. L. Pastor's *History of the Popes* in either the original German or Italian; (German ed., 1931; Italian, Rome Desclee, 1933) the English transl. has not as yet appeared; also L. Ranke-E. Foster, *The History of the Popes,* 3 vols. (London, Bohn, 1853) Vol. II, 433 ff; *Cath. Encyc.* II 432-36 where a complete enumeration and good evaluation of his various literary works may be found.

R.M.H.

Benedict XV, Pope: (1914-22) Born of an old (XIII century) noble family (della Chiesa), Nov. 21, 1854, the future Pope counted on his mother's side (Migliorati) as one of his predecessors in the Chair of Peter, Innocent VII. Giacomo Paolo Giovanni B. della Chiesa received his doctorate in Laws at the University of Genoa; studied (since 1875) Theology at the Gregorian University, Rome; was ordained priest in 1878; became an alumnus of the Academy for Noble Ecclesiastical Students in 1879 and in 1882 an Assistant in the Office of the Secretary of State. In 1883 he accompanied as personal secretary the famius nuncio (Cf. "Papal Legates") Rampolla, to Madrid. When Rampolla was recalled to Rome as Secretary of State by Leo XIII*, della Chiesa followed him. He remained in the Secretariate of State even after Pius X* had chosen the youthful Merry del Val to take Rampolla's place. Although his appointment as the new nuncio to Madrid was generally expected, Pius X preferred to give him the archbishopric of Bologna (1907) as successor to Cardinal Svampa. It was only in the Consistory of May 25, 1914 that Pius elevated him to the cardinalitial dignity. Due undoubtedly to his training under the diplomatic Rampolla, (a prominent candidate for the papacy after the death of Leo, XIII) della Chiesa was elected pope (1914). Benedict XV's pontificate falls during the First World War (1914-18). Impartial and disinterested but with a heart filled alike with anguish and charity towards all, Benedict strove by every means conceivable—allocutions, addresses, encyclicals, protests, prayers, peace-feelers, etc., to induce the warring nations to foster thoughts of peace and reconciliation, or at least to avoid as far as possible, all inhuman methods of warfare. Famous are his "Appeal to the Nations" of Aug. 1, 1917 and his "Fourteen Points of Peace" which bear a marked resemblance to those later adopted and proposed by President Woodrow Wilson. Although his offer of intermediation was not accepted and a place at the peace table of Versailles was denied him (due to the secret machinations of Italy, Russia and England) the prestige of the Vatican grew among the nations, especially when Benedict's fatherly solicitude (*"cor paternum"*) became manifest to the world through his donations to the peoples of all countries (especially to Russia and the Orient) thus helping them to bind up the wounds of war; through his program for the exchange of incapacitated prisoners of war and the Vatican exchange of mail to missing loved ones—soldiers and relatives. Even during, and after the treaty of Versailles, Benedict warned that a change of sentiment in men's hearts was more important than a mere cessation of hostilities, because hatred conceived in injustice, said he, only generates new wars. (How true his teachings in the face of World War II now raging!). After the war was over, Benedict had the pleasure of seeing the official number of national representatives at the Vatican raised from 14 to 25, including England, France and Holland. Even between the Quirinal and the Vatican, due to the help Italy found in religion during the post-war embroglios, a closer rapprochment was clearly discernable. Among the more important inner activities of Benedict's pontificate must be mentioned the promulgation of the new Code of Canon Law* (begun under Pius X*) as of Pentecost, 1918; the encyclical for the XV century commemoration of the death of St. Jerome, the great biblical scholar (1920); the encyclical *"Maximum illud"* (1929) regulating anew the affairs of foreign missions which had been victimized by the World War (28 new Vicariates and Prefectures having been erected); the creation of the new Roman Curial Congregation for Seminaries and University Studies (1915); the new Oriental Congregation, of which the pope, as of the Holy Office and the Consistorial, remained Prefect (1917); and finally the institution of the Oriental Institute in the interest of theological unity and ecclesiastical union. Benedict XV will go down into history as the "Apostle of Peace during World War I". He lies buried in the crypt of St. Peter's, Rome, in a bronze tomb donated by his devoted people of Bologna, whereas a plaque describing his efforts for peace in a war-torn world surmounts his statue (in a kneeling posture) in the left aisle of the Basilica.

The official Acts of the Pontificate of Ben. XV will be found in the *Acta Apostolicae Sedis* (Rome, 1914-22). Biographies and studies by: A. Brennan (London, 1917); Francis Vistalli (Rome, 1928); cf. Seppelt-Löffler, *Papstgeschichte* (Munich, 1933) pp. 499-518; Engl. trans. by Frommelt (1932 of an earlier edition); pp. 521-541; G. Quirico, *Cor Paternum* illustr. (Rome, 1919); Anoys., *Papst, Kurie und Weltkrieg* von einem Deutschen 2 (Berlin, 1921); G. Goyau, *Papauté et chretienité sous Bénédict XV* (Paris, 1922); *Cath. Encyc.* Suppl. of 1922 p. 95; Premoli, O., *Storia Eccles. Contemporanea: 1900-1925* (Torino-Rome, 1925) p. 38-61 (also transl. into Engl.). R.M.H.

Benedict, St. of Monte Cassino: (of Nursia) (c. 480-543) Founder of the celebrated monastery at Monte Cassino, and author of the *Rule* of 529, he was to become known in later centuries as the legislator-in-chief of western monasticism*. Learning from his own costly experience of monastic rigors, he gave to the brethren of his religious house a simple guide, gathered from the best in the past, to the truly moderate way of renunciation through the dedicated common life. He capitalized the Roman genius for organization in thought and action to lay the basis for a program of service to God through Divine Worship, manual labor, and disciplined reading. From this humble beginning was to issue, later, the far-flung and socially reconstructive order of the Benedictines*. See Cenobite; itinerarium.

H. B. Workman, *The Evolution of the Monastic Ideal* (London, 1927). R.C.P.

Benedictines: The oldest religious order in the Occident, founded by St. Benedict of Nursia* in the sixth century and living according to the rule of life drawn up by him. By their vow of stability, these monks are attached for life to one monastery, so that each new foundation becomes a permanent center of religious activity and generally civilizing influence. This feature of the Benedictine life was of paramount importance especially during the early Middle Ages, and enabled the Order to preserve and extend western civilization during the centuries following the collapse of the Roman Empire, when all Europe was in turmoil. The Benedictines have ever been champions of religion, scholarship, and the cultivation of the arts. Cf. Olivetans. See Black monks; communistic settlements, religious; monasticism.

D. Knowles, *The Monastic Order in England* (1940). C.V.

benediction: A blessing* of persons or things to dedicate them. For persons, an intercession for God's blessing that to Protestant thought has subjective effect on them, to Catholic thought also has objective effect. Blessing things to Protestant thought is by metonomy, to Catholic thought objectively effective in regard to their use. See laying on of hands. T.J.B.

Benediction of the Blessed Sacrament: (Fr.: *Salut;* Ger.: *Segen*) A devotion before the Sacrament*, dating from the 14th century, of hymns and prayers composed by St. Thomas Aquinas, concluded by a Benediction with the Sacrament. T.J.B.

benedictus: (Latin) Part of the mass*, following immediately after the sanctus* and considered with that section. E.H.B.

benefice: An ecclesiastical office to which property or the revenue of property is annexed. The right of presentation to a benefice belongs to a patron, a person or corporation. The patron may present a clergyman to the ecclesiastical authority to be admitted to the benefice, if found qualified. Descending from conditions under the feudal system, the practice now prevails only where this once existed. Cf. regale. R.H.N.

benefit of clergy: Signifies the exemption of clerical persons from jurisdiction of the secular courts. Practiced already to a limited extent in the Fourth Century, it reached a full development in the 12th and 13th centuries. The growth of clerical courts was due to belief in the separate character of the clergy, to generally better procedure in the clerical courts than in the secular, and to a prevailing desire of many to stand trial in them because of milder punishments. Those classed as clerics came to comprise not only priests and monks, but all who were connected in any way with churches, universities (e.g., students), in fact, all who could read. Theoretically the cases under clerical jurisdiction were those touching religion and morals only, but it was often successfully argued that these involved probating, breach of contract, etc. Benefit of clergy had a specially interesting history in England (see, particularly, Thomas A. Becket) till its abolition in 1827. The United States abolished it in 1789-90. See immunity; Canon Law; ecclesiastical courts.

Encyclopedia of the Social Sciences (1937), Vol. II, 511-513, has a good bibliography. Q.B.

benevolence, disinterested: In New England theology*, the doctrine that true virtue is of the affections or passions and is to be defined as the unselfish love for intelligent being in general. Each particular being is to be loved according to its place in the scale of being. Hence love for God, the greatest being, is the supreme virtue. Sin is love for self to the exclusion of other beings.

Jonathan Edwards* (*Nature of True Virtue*) defined "being in general" as a certain quality of being, or the essence common to all being, insight into which is given to the regenerate alone. Samuel Hopkins* gave a more practical twist to the doctrine by defining it as "all being," or the simple summation of all individual beings. Hence the regenerate make their state manifest by their love for all beings. In this form the doctrine provided the motivation for a great deal of consecrated devotion to the great missionary and philanthropic crusades of the early nineteenth century.

Joseph G. Haroutunian, "Jonathan Edwards," *Journal of Religion,* XI (1931); *Piety Versus Moralism* (1932); C. H. Faust & Thomas H. Johnson, *Jonathan*

Edwards in American Writers Series (1935); Gilbert H. Barnes, *The Anti-Slavery Impulse 1830 - 1844* (1933); Oliver W. Elsbree, *Rise of the Missionary Spirit in America 1790-1815* (1928). S.E.M.

Benevolent Societies: See anti-Benevolent Society agitation in the U. S.

Bengel, Johann Albrecht: (1687-1752) Protestant theologian: Born Winnenden, Wurtemberg. Active as minister, teacher and administrator in the Lutheran Church of Wurtemberg. Father of Swabian Pietism. Most influential as N.T. scholar. He was the first to arrange the N.T. manuscripts in families. His brief exposition of the N.T. (*Gnomon Novi Testamenti*, 1742) is remarkable for the author's thorough knowledge of the N.T. Greek idiom no less than for his terse and profound remarks on the spiritual implications of the text. The book has had great influence on N.T. exposition to the present day. Wesley was considerably indebted to it. Bengel's eschatology paved the way to a new Biblical interpretation of history (Heilsgeschichte)*. Through his prediction of the Parousia for 1837 Bengel became the father of modern premillennianism*. An English translation of his Exposition of the Apocalypse, in which he developed his eschatological ideas, appeared as early as 1757.

Works:

Ordo Temporum (1741). *Apparatus Criticus ad Novum Testamentum* (2nd ed. Tübingen 1763). *Gnomon Novi Testamenti* (1742 Engl. tr. 4 v. Edinburgh 1859).

On Bengel:

Eb. Nestle, *Bengel als Gelehrter* (1893); Friedrich Nolte, *Joh. Albrecht Bengel* (Gütersloh, 1913); Art. Bengel in Schaff-Herzog's *Encyclopaedia*, v. II p. 52 ff. Albrecht Ritschl, *Geshichte des Pietismus*, v. III (Bonn, 1886). O.A.P.

Bentham, Jeremy: (1748-1832) British writer on jurisprudence, ethics, economics, logic, and other subjects. His agitation did much to simplify laws and court procedure in England and other countries. His version of Utilitarianism* affirms a "hedonistic calculus" by which the relative worth of different pleasures can be measured quantitatively. Starting from psychological hedonism* as a fact, he believes that the four external sanctions (physical, political, moral, and religious) produce actions in accordance with his maxims of "the greatest good of the greatest number" and "each to count for one, and none for more than one". He championed *laissez faire* individualism in economics. His best known work is *The Principles of Morals and Legislation* (1789). See deontology. W.K.W.

Berdyaev, Nikolai Alexandrovitch: (1874-) Threatened with expulsion from the Russian Orthodox Church in 1917, he became professor of philosophy at the University of Moscow. Expelled from the Soviet Union, he established in Berlin his Academy of Religious Philosophy. Later he moved his institute to Paris. He is the leading lay-theologian of the Russian Orthodox Church who has once been a revisionist Marxian. He is practically and theoretically active in the development of the ethical and social side of the orthodox faith. His works reveal penetrating criticisms of extreme rationalism and rationalistic liberalism. He is a trenchant critic of Communism, Thomistic scholasticism, atheistic humanism, democracy and capitalism. His thought resembles that of the Christian Gnostics. He favors the negative theology of the extreme mystics. His religious philosophy owes a great deal to German idealism and mysticism. His eschatological philosophy of history reminds one of Spengler. In his view, Christianity did not inaugurate a social millenium, but it introduced a potent tension in the historic process. It above all prepared the way for modern science and technology. Critical of the doctrine of progress, he visioned the rise of Fascism and Nazism.

Russian Works: *Subjectivism and Individualism in Social Philosophy* (St. Petersburg, 1901); "The Ethical Problem in the Light of the Philosophic Idealism" in *Problems of Idealism* (Moscow, 1902); *Sub Specie Aeternitatis* (St. Petersburg, 1907); *The New Religious Conscience and Society* (St. Petersburg, 1907); *The Philosophy of Liberty* (Paris, 1911); *Aleksiei Stepanovitch Khomiakov* (Moscow, 1912); *The Meaning of Creation* (Moscow, 1916); *The Fate of Russia* (Moscow, 1918); *The Philosophy of Inequality* (Berlin, 1923); *The New Middle Ages* (Berlin, 1924); *The Philosophy of the Free Spirit* (Paris, 1929). English translations: *Christianity and Class War* (1933); *The Bourgeois Mind* (1934); *The End of Our Time* (1935); *The Fate of Man in the Modern World* (London, 1935); *Dostoievsky* (1936); *The Meaning of History* (1936); *Freedom and the Spirit* (1937); *The Destiny of Man* (1937); *Solitude and Society* (1937); *The Origin of Russian Communism* (1937); *Spirit and Reality* (1939); *Konstantin Leont'ev* (London, 1940). H.H.

Berengar of Tours: (999-1086) An acute mind, but not a great character. On behalf of a rationalistic, yet profoundly personal and spiritual doctrine of the eucharist, he opened a ruinous fight against authority in the name of science. Cf. impanation; Lanfranc.

Grabmann, M. *Geschichte der scholastischen Methode*, vol. 1 (Freiburg im Breisgau, 1909); Schnitzer, J., *Berengar von Tours* (Stuttgart, 1892). H.H.

Bergson, Henri: (1859-1941) Brilliant French Jew, one of the most notable and influential philosophers of contemporary time. He did not clearly declare the religious implications of his philosophy until the appearance of his last work. He arrived at a modified, non-scholastic theistic position, moving away from the absolute, static perfection of scholastic theology toward a God who is manifest in concrete events and in the intimate history of living individuals and organisms. He plainly rejected the absolute deity of Aristotle for a dynamic personal God of love, the *a priori* method for an empirical approach. Bergson was a temporalist theist, conceiving of God not as complete but as growing in knowledge, goodness, spiritual power and social awareness. As the self-identity of process, God is that which alters and in altering remains himself. Being the subject of change, he endures and escapes the ravages of time. The vital impetus is God operative in evolution and present in all life and reaching a higher level of attainment of his purposes in man. The reality of time, the waste in the onward movement of the vital impetus, the importance of freedom, novelty and struggle, connect God with the thought of a limited, but ever creative, cosmic force.

Social processes, customs, mores and taboos, strengthened by religious beliefs and practices, in preventing man from using his newly acquired intellectual power or reason for individual ends detrimental to society, are the first, conservative influence of the two sources of morality and religion. Later on in social evolution the weight of customs is liable to hold mankind back, both by its inertia and rigor, by lack of deep inward emotion and aspiration, threatening freedom and making progress impossible. This is averted by a second, higher and intuitive source of morality and religion. Despite theological differences found among the great mystics, all basically agree in testifying that they have come into contact with a deeper spiritual reality than the majority of men. While only a few are capable of such profound inward experience, most individuals have felt something sufficiently approximating it and react sympathetically to the testimony of these souls. They follow to some extent their leadership. Bergson believed religion and morality can further spiritual, social, political and economic progress. Regarding human personal immortality as probable, he hoped psychic research would ultimately demonstrate it scientifically. See time.

Chief works: *An Introduction to Metaphysics* (1912); *Time and Free Will* (London, 1913); *Matter and Memory* (London, 1913); *Creative Evolution* (1913); *The Two Sources of Morality and Religion* (1935). H.H.

Berkeley, George: (1685-1753) Irish Bishop, founder of subjective idealism (also set forth, perhaps independently, by Jonathan Edwards*). All thought depends upon concrete data, which are essentially "ideas" (also "notions", see below), entities given only as data-for-subjects. Data as they would be if not given at all, data as not ideas, are incapable of being given, hence also of being thought. "Matter", taken as independent of mind, is self-contradictory, since its properties are all ideas. We know ourselves as subjects by a special form of givenness yielding a "notion" rather than an idea (for it is active, not passive); and somehow we know from the pattern of our own data that there are other human subjects. Physical reality or nature is the fixed and shareable order of data. Ideas that are merely ours are under control of our wills, whereas what we perceive physically is forced upon us all according to a common system. The only force we know from the given is will. The only adequate will-cause of the orderly constraint we feel in perception is God. Thus all data are signs in a single vast language by which God communicates to us. See idealism, metaphysical.

G. Berkeley, *Treatise on the Principles of Human Knowledge* (1710); *Three Dialogues Between Hylas and Philonous* (1713); *Siris* (1744). Also J. Wild, *George Berkeley* (1936). C.H.

Bernard of Clairvaux: Bernard was born at Fontaines-les-Dijon (Côte-d'Or) in 1090. He fled the world and entered Citeaux in 1112. Three years later he founded the Abbey of Clairvaux. From his solitude Bernard went forth to become the most powerful churchman of twelfth century Europe. Counsellor and critic of popes and kings, builder of monasteries, preacher of crusades and indefatigable pursuer of all whose orthodoxy was suspected, he yet found time for considerable writing—sermons, letters, and theological treatises. He was chiefly responsible for the condemnation of Abailard's* works at Sens in 1141. Arnold of Brescia and Gilbert Porrée** knew the power of his pursuit. But it is unjust to accuse him of anti-intellectualism, though he feared the philosophical treatment of theological problems. His own theology was essentially mystical. Death came to him in 1153. See Knights Templar. P.S.M.

A. Neander, *Der heilige Bernhard und sein Zeitalter* (Gotha, 1889-1890); J. Ries, *Das geistliche Leben in seinen Entwicklungs stufen nach Bernhard* (Freiburg im Breisgau, 1906); A. Steiger, *Der heilige Bernard* (Brünn, 1908); E. Vacandard, *Vie de S. Bernard*, 2 vols. (Paris, 1895). H.H.

Bernard of Cluny: (of Morlaix) A Benedictine poet of the early 12th century; author of the poem, *On the Contempt of this World*, satirizing the life and notables of his period. His work is dedicated to Peter the Venerable, Abbot of Cluny. He may have influenced Dante's *Divina Commedia.* Numerous hymns and possibly a treatise on the Trinity were written by him. V.J.B.

Bernard of Tours: (B. Silvestris) A 12th century scholar, possibly of the school of Chartres author of the *De mundi universitate*, in alternate prose and verse. Gilson has shown that, contrary to the view of older histories, Bernard is interested in Christian theology, particularly in the interpretation of *Genesis*, but that he belongs to the tradition of Christian Platonists who tried to supplement the Christian account of creation with the doctrine of the *Timaeus.*

See E. Gilson, "La cosmogonie de B. Silvestris," *Arch. d'hist. doct. et lit. du moyen age*, III (1928), 5-24. V.J.B.

Bernardine, St. of Siena: See Observants.

Berthold of Regensburg: (c. 1220-1272) Popular Franciscan* preacher whose deep missionary interest is reflected in his wide-ranging travels, his scriptural basis, and his powerful ethical appeal. His sermons were enlivened by all the fellow-feeling with simple men, the graphic challenge to spiritual inwardness, and the techniques of vital appeal, which make real preaching truly great at all times. R.C.P.

Bes: An Egyptian god of pleasure, able to counteract witchcraft*. His prominence in the Saite period was doubtless instrumental in the adoption of his image as an amulet by the Gnostics. P.G.M.

Besht: See Chasidism.

Bessarion: (1403-1472) Bessarion was born in Trapezous, Pontus. In his twenties he became a monk. He distinguished himself for his learning, deep insight, and his great intellect. He studied in Constantinople and Sparta under the famous Greek philosopher Gemistos. Later he became priest, bishop and Archbishop of Trapezous when he won great fame as a teacher and preacher of the Social Gospel of Christian Love. He was appointed as a representative of the Greek Church for the proposed Union of the Churches (1436) in the Conference of Pherraro, Italy. After the Fall of Constantinople the Catholic Church gave him the title of Cardinal, for his good services.

As a Cardinal of the Catholic Church in Rome he tried many times to organize a crusade against the Turks but failed. He wrote many theological, philosophical and philological books, the collection of his MSS was one of the best in his period. Bessarion still remains one of the great figures in the proposed Union of the Churches, but he failed in his attempts on account of his changed religious attitudes. G.E.Z.

bestiaries: (Lat., *bestia,* wild beast) Books of prose or poetry giving illustrations or descriptions of animals, fabled and real. Popular in the Middle Ages, they contributed to the animal decoration of Romanesque and Gothic** sculptural ornamentation, where animals assumed a symbolical importance. J.B.C.

bet hamidrash: Literally in Hebrew a house of study or a place where students gather to listen to the midrash*, the exposition of Scripture. It is frequently referred to the Synagogue* as well, since synagogues always housed study groups in Bible and various Rabbinic studies. B.Z.B.

Bet Hillel and Bet Shammai: Two schools, composed of the disciples of Hillel* and Shammai respectively, which flourished during the 1st century C. E. They reflect in the hundreds of legal questions disputed by them, the spirit of their founders. On the whole, the Hillelites were lenient in their interpretation of the Law* while the Shammaites were uncompromisingly severe. At first the legal decisions of Bet Shammai seem to have prevailed. However, about the year 100 it was decided that in all legal disputes between these two schools, the opinions of Bet Hillel should be followed. E.B.—L.F.

Beth, Karl: (1872-) He is professor at the University of Vienna. He has investigated a great number of religious phenomena and principles in the light of contemporary philosophy, psychology and sociology. In his writings on miracles he adopts Reinhold Seeberg's* teachings that "Christ is so great the miracle becomes small in comparison with him". Defining religion as the natural "metabiontic determinant in human life", he made use of the various types of modern *Ganzheitspsychologie,* of psychoanalysis, of existential philosophy for the analyses of religious problems. He rejects Freud's* criticism of religion as well as Karl Barth's* dialectical theology, Wilhelm Hauer's, H. Mandel's* and Emmanuel Hirsch's secularisation of Christendom.

Die Grundanschauungen Schleiermachers in seinem ersten Entwurf der philosophischen Sittenlehre (Berlin, 1898); *Die orientalische Christenheit der Mittelmeerländer* (Berlin, 1902); *Das Wesen des Christentums und die moderne historische Denkweise* (Leipzig, 1904); *Die Moderne und die Prinzipien der Theologie* (Berlin, 1907); *The Miracles of Jesus* (1907); *Das Wunder. Prinzipielle Eröterung des Problems* (Gross Lichterfelde-Berlin, 1908); *Urmensch, Welt und Religion* (Gross Lichterfelde-Berlin, 1909); *Hat Jesus gelebt? Eine Kritik der Drew'schen Christusmythe* (Berlin, 1910); *Die Entwicklung des Christentums zur Universalreligion* (Leipzig, 1910); *Religion und Magie bei den Naturvölkern* (Leipzig-Berlin, 1914); *Gesunddenken und Gesundbeten. Eine Beurteilung des Scientismus* (Wien, 1918;) *Einfuehrung in die vergleichende Religionsgeschichte* (Leipzig, 1920); *Religion und Magie. Ein religionsge-schichtlicher Beitrag zur psychologischen Grundlegeung der religiösen Prinzipienlehre* (Leipzig-Berlin, 1927); *Frömmigkeit der Mystik und des Glaubens* (Leipzig-Berlin, 1927); *Die Krise des Protestantismus* (Berlin, 1932). H.H.

Bethlehem: Also called Bethlehem-Ephrathah, town of Judah, five miles South of Jerusalem, famous for the grave of Rachel shown on the road nearby (Gen. xxxv, 19; xlviii, 7) and more especially as the birth-place of David (I Sam. xvi, 1-18) and of the Messiah (Mic. v, 2), prophecy fulfilled for the Christians by the birth of Jesus-Christ (Mt. ii, 6; cf. Jn. vii, 42). See F. M. Abel, *Géographie de la Palestine,* vol. ii, (1938), pp. 276-277. S.L.T.

Bethlehemites: 1) A military Order dedicated to Our Lady of Bethlehem which came to Bohemia in 1217 from Palestine. 2) An Order of knights dedicated to Our Lady of Bethlehem founded by Pope Pius II in 1453 to defend the island of Lemnos. 3) An Order of Hospitallers* founded in 1650 in Guatemala. At the time of their suppression by the government in 1820, they had 33 houses of monks and one of nuns in Central and South America. J.B.C.

Beyschlag, Willibald: (1823-1900) Beyschlag was a leader in the "mediating theology," combatting both rigid orthodoxy and the radicalism of Strauss* and others; and working passionately for church unity. His best known works are his *Life of Christ* (1885 and later) and *New Testament Theology* (1891 and later). B.S.E.

Beza, Theodore: (1519-1605) A friend and biographer of Calvin, his successor at the head of the government in Geneva, who published anonymously the pamphlet *Du Droit des Magistrats sur leur Sujets* (1574). The stress of circumstances drove Beza, as it had driven Knox, to reverse not only Calvin's teaching, but his own previous conviction in favor of passive obedience. He clearly, yet reluctantly, urged the right of inferior magistrates, though not of private citizens, to resist a tyrant, particularly in defense of true religion. See Gallican Confession; hymns.

J. W. Allen, *A History of Political Thought in the Sixteenth Century* (London, 1928); J. N. Figgis, *Studies of Political Thought from Gerson to Grotius.* 2 ed. (Cambridge, 1923); R. Treumann, *Die Monarchomachen* (Leipzig, 1895). H.H.

Bhagavad Gita: India's most popular and best loved book of devotion. Although actually it is only one section of the great epic, the Mahabharata*, which is not "sruti"* or the completely inspired word of God, it is rated as "sruti" by some modern Hindus.

It is in form a dialogue between the warrior Arjuna and his charioteer the god Krishna in disguise. In the course of the 18 chapters it sets forth not one but many view points in religion. It is probably its eclectic character which gives it its almost universal appeal.

While expounding the way of knowledge and the way of works, its preeminent emphasis is on the way of faith or devotion (Bhakti) as the way of salvation which is open to all. "Be sure that none can perish, trusting me . . . though he be born from the very womb of sin, woman or man, sprung of the Vaisya caste or lowly disregarded Sudra". It is dated variously by competent scholars from 200 B.C. to 200 A.D. It has been more often translated into English than any other Hindu sacred writing.

For a list of translations see R. E. Hume *Treasure House of the World's Religions* (1935), pp. 424-428. See Hinduism. C.S.B.

bhakti-marga: The way of devotion, love, faith. One of the three recognized ways of attaining *moksha* or salvation in Hinduism. It finds its noblest expression, perhaps, in the Bhagavad-Gita*, where Krishna promises salvation to all of whatever class who come to him. *Bhaktas*, i.e., those who follow the way of faith or devotion, are found in great numbers in both the Vishnu and Shiva sects of Hinduism. There is a great wealth of devotional literature expressive of this way of approach to deity.

See *Psalms of the Marathi Saints,* translated by Nicol, MacNicol, Association Press, Calcutta. Also *Temple Bells,* edited by Appasamy. See salvation, Hindu. C.S.B.

Bible: See Biblion, Biblia; canon; canons of various churches; Old Testament; New Testament.

Bible, the: The word is derived from *biblia,* the plural of the Greek noun *biblion**, meaning book. That in turn was derived from the word for Egyptian papyrus*, the writing material on which books were written. The word was mistaken by Latin readers for the feminine singular. Hence we have a singular noun for what is really a library of 66 books. 39 books comprise the Old Testament*. This name arose through the wrong translation of the Greek *diathēke;* though that noun could be used as a "last will and testament", its biblical meaning is normally that of a sovereign dispensation by God. These Hebrew scriptures were read by the early Christians in the Greek translation or Septuagint*, and gradually 27 of their own writings were put beside them as the New Testament*.

The Jews divided their scripture into three sections, the Law, Prophets and Writings. The English Bible, however, follows the Septuagint in a rearrangement of the last two groups of books. The English New Testament follows the order of the Latin Vulgate*—gospels, Acts of the Apostles, Pauline Epistles, General Epistles, Revelation.

From the beginning of the Christian church, the Bible was given a high place of authority*. The Jews had believed that the Pentateuch* was divinely dictated to Moses*. The verbal inspiration of scripture was assumed in such passages as II Tim. 3.16 and II Pet. 1.19-21. Still, no biblical writer claims infallibility for himself. A high conception of inspiration was maintained by the early Fathers from Justin Martyr on, but authority was also ascribed to tradition.

In the Middle Ages, the Bible was authoritative in theory. In practice, however, the Church stood between the individual Christian and the Bible. The Reformers took a quite free attitude toward the letter of the Bible, not hesitating to criticize the limits of the canon*, and laying greater emphasis on content than on form. But the seventeenth century was a period of rigid definition and violent controversy. In conflict with Jesuits and Socinians, Protestant orthodoxy came to identify inspiration with infallibility.

With the rise of criticism under the stimulus of Rationalism in the latter half of the eighteenth century, that became increasingly impossible. Textual criticism had shown the uncertainty of many readings; deviating accounts of the same event were pointed out; the uncertainty of interpretation of many passages contributed to render any claim of infallibility incredible (See Biblical criticism.)

Still, there remains today division in interpretation. There are fundamentalists* who hold that at least the original manuscripts* were literally dictated by the Holy Spirit. There are many conservatives who insist that since the Bible contains the revelation of God, only in the light of this assumption and under the guidance of the Holy Spirit can its pages be understood. On the other hand, there are devoted students of the Bible who approach it as a selection from the extant literature of the Hebrews and early Christians which must be investigated by trained scholars as any other literature from the ancient world. Judgments of value must come *after* its impartial study. Only then is anyone in a position to affirm its authority, inspiration or revelation**. This is not on the basis of any pre-conceived theory, but from its discovered worth. See versions; Word of God. C.T.C.

Bible Belt: American colloquialism for the more orthodox and fundamentalist South United States. C.H.M.

Bible, Books of, in chronological order: See Books of the Old Testament, the, in chronological order; Books of the New Testament, dates of the.

Bible, chapters and verses: See chapters and verses.

Bible Churchman's Missionary Society, the: See Evangelicals.

Bible communism: See Oneida community, the.

Bible, English: The first translation of the complete Bible into English was the work of the reformer John Wyclif* and his assistants. It exists in two forms: the early version, completed about 1382, by Wyclif and Hereford; and the revision by John Purvey, assigned to the year 1388. The great defect of this translation was that it was made from a translation—the Latin Vulgate*—rather than from the original languages, Hebrew and Greek. Following the Latin order, it included the books of the Apocrypha* scattered in Septuagint* fashion among the O.T. writings. Its circulation was in manuscript form, and it did not have much control on the subsequent history of the English Bible. Nevertheless, its long use by the Lollard* preachers made it a factor in preparing Englishmen for the Reformation.

Nearly a century and a half after Wyclif's time, important sections of the Bible were first translated into vernacular English from the original languages. William Tyndale's* New Testament of 1525, and his Pentateuch of 1530, were rendered in vigorous "plowboy" English from Greek and Hebrew texts. Both of them were incorporated into Myles Coverdale's* editorial cento of 1535, which was the very *editio princeps* of the printed English Bible. The Psalter of this first printing, as later re-edited by Coverdale himself, became the liturgical Psalter of the Book of Common Prayer.* As such it is still constantly and extensively used in public worship after four full centuries.

The salutary Tyndale increment in the English Bible was increased when his rendering of the historical books, from Joshua through Chronicles, was made a part of the "Thomas Matthew" Bible two years later. This version was further revised by Coverdale himself when he produced the Great Bible of 1539, the first English version to be definitely authorized for use in public worship. Unfortunately the Great Bible completely overshadowed the synchronous revision by Richard Taverner; for his editorial work was quite meritorious, especially in the Greek section.

From the very earliest printing of the Bible in English, the books of the Apocrypha were grouped together between the two Testaments, following the precedent established by Martin Luther*. Thus segregated, it was all the easier for Puritans* much later to accomplish the ultimate ostracism of the Apocrypha from Protestant printings of the Bible.

Partizan versions: Puritan, Anglican, and Catholic next made their appearance in sequence. Protestant exiles in Geneva, during the Marian period, produced the Puritan Geneva Bible* of 1560. In the latter part of the O.T. this version was more faithful to the Hebrew text than its predecessors had been. It had useful characteristics: convenient size, clear type, verse divisions*, and explanatory notes. Its long-extended popularity with Puritans and Pilgrims was intelligible and creditable.

Already in the middle sixties the early popularity of the Geneva Bible forced Archbishop Parker to organize a hasty episcopal revision of the Great Bible. The result was a magnificent piece of folio printing, the second authorized English Bible "appoynted to bee read in the Churches." For four decades the Bishops' Bible of 1568 continued in that favored position.

In the mid-Elizabethan era Catholic exiles at Rheims did for their co-religionists what Protestant exiles at Geneva had earlier accomplished. They backed the production of an English version from the Vulgate text. The methodical translator was Gregory Martin. He worked at the rate of exactly two chapters per day. A highly Latinized translation was approved. Only the Rheims New Testament was published at once in 1582. For sheer lack of funds the appearance of the Douay Old Testament was deferred until 1609. (See Douai Bible.)The Rheims work should be remembered as having had a modicum of influence on the King James version of 1611.

King James I of Great Britain (VI of Scotland) was deservedly the eponym of the third authorized English Bible. When at the Hampton Court Conference of 1604 the leader of the Puritans proposed a retranslation of the Bible, the king at once made the proposal effective by naming a translation committee composed of "the best learned in both the Universities." The outcome was not a retranslation, but a moderate revision of the Bishops' Bible. Even so, it epitomized the very best English efforts at Bible revision and translation to date. Moreover it was a convenient and noble summary of almost a full century of development in English language and literary style.

Also it signalized the beginning of a new era as well. Immediately it succeeded the Bishops' Bible in church use. Ultimately it displaced the Geneva Bible, even, in home use. After three centuries and a third, it is still popularly the dominant and most revered version of the English Bible.

From 1615 to 1769 there were repeated revisions of the King James version. These were mainly in the direction of modernizing the spellings and contemporizing the usages. Bishop Lloyd, and Drs. T. Paris and B. Blayney, were among the conscientious editors of such recognized revisions. Thus the Authorized Version itself did not remain static. Even today the process of silent modernization continues—though in very great moderation.

A nearly forgotten section in the history of the English Bible is the story of the distinctive private translations that appeared with fair frequency during the centuries from the seventeenth to the nineteenth inclusive. William Whiston, successor of Sir Isaac Newton at Cambridge; John Wesley, instigator of the Methodists; Archbishop Newcome, Anglican primate of Ireland; Charles Thomson, secretary of the Continental Congress; and Noah Webster, author of the Dictionary, were all reasonably proud of what they accomplished in Bible revision, or even translation.

These same centuries also saw the dramatic recovery of crucially important Biblical manuscripts*. This series of events began with the presentation of Codex Alexandrinus* by the ecumenical patriarch, Cyril Lucar, to the king of England, not long after the publication of the King James Bible. It culminated in the discovery of Codex Sinaiticus* by Tischendorf in the middle decades of the 19th century.

The effect of such discoveries in stimulating textual studies and developing the techniques of criticism was extremely invigorating. In the field of Bible translation they led to an overwhelming demand for a comprehensive revision of the Authorized Version which should make full use of the better Biblical texts now available. The Revised Versions of 1881 and 1901 were the English and American answers to this sound demand. See Bible, modern translations.

Samuel Bagster, *The English Hexapla* (London, 1846); Charles C. Butterworth, *The Literary Lineage of the King James Bible, 1340-1611* (1941); Edgar J. Goodspeed, *The Making of the English New Testament* (1925); Richard Lovett, *The English Bible in the John Rylands Library, 1525-1640* (Manchester, 1899); Ira M. Price, *The Ancestry of Our English Bible* (9th ed., 1934); Harold R. Willoughby, *The Coverdale Psalter and the Quatrocentenary of the Printed English Bible* (1935). H.R.W.

Bible, Lost Books of: See Lost Books of the Bible.

Bible, manuscripts of: See manuscripts of the Bible.

Bible, modern translations of the: Modern speech translation of the Bible commonly refers to editions of Scripture in more or less colloquial English which have appeared since the English Revision of 1881-85, and largely since 1900. The emphasis on "modern speech" is relative, since every period has shown a desire for contemporary English translation. Rodolphus Dickinson expressed an attitude typical of his time when in his N.T. published at Boston in 1833, he stated his purpose to conform the Scriptures to the "revolution in the English language" since the days of King James. Also typical was his use of Griesbach as a critical text of his day. Rather unusual by contrast was the fact that his English, while faulty, showed considerable freedom from the language of the Authorized Version of 1611. Most translators after expounding the need for fresh translation, and emending the text, were content simply to revise the King James edition. By the close of the century, however, the general trend took a more liberal text for granted, and began to produce a simple, modern style of everyday English which the common man could easily read and understand.

Several purposes have served to motivate modern biblical translators: 1) As indicated, a primary aim has been to modernize the English of the Authorized Version. "Carriage" (Acts 21:15) no longer means "baggage" as it did in 1611. "By and by" and "presently" no longer signify "at once." Archaic pronoun and other stylistic forms, and the old verse paragraphing, hinder the reader's understanding. The modern papyri* discoveries in Egypt show the N.T. largely to have been written in the colloquial Greek of every-day speech, and there is no reason why we should not continue to translate the Bible for each generation into appropriate, but colloquial English.

2) The text of fresh translation must be adjusted to the continual progress made from new manuscript discoveries, and constantly improved methods and results.

3) In the Authorized Version, the O.T. was more inaccurately rendered than the Greek of the N.T. because Hebrew and Aramaic were then more imperfectly understood. In each of these languages there has been a tremendous advance since that date in the understanding of word meanings and principles of grammar and syntax. Much light has come in recent years from inscriptions, the papyri in Egypt, and other documents. Montgomery was able to give an unusually vivid translation of Hebrews 11:1 because the word translated "substance" in the Authorized Version was found in the papyri to be used of a "title-deed"to property.

4) Translation is necessarily interpretation; when for example the text offers several possible meanings, the translator must choose one. New translations must attempt to embody the best possible understanding and interpretation of the biblical writings themselves.

The English Revised Version offered no radical change, yet it marked the first more general departure from a rigid acceptance of the King James. It began formally in 1870 with action taken by the Upper House of the Southern Convocation. The actual work of revision, in which eventually sixty-five English scholars took part, was started the same year, with one company working on the Old, and one company on the N.T. Rules adopted required them to make as few alterations and to keep the Authorized Version language as far as possible; to go at least twice through the Bible; to make or retain no textual change on the second or final revision except by a vote of two-thirds of those present; to revise chapter and page headings, punctuations and paragraphing; and so far as possible to use the same English word for a given word in the text. Some three years later Old and N.T. companies were organized in America with the cooperation of Philip Schaff, to make suggestions on the English Revision, a number of which were adopted. The N.T. was published in 1881, the O.T. four years later. The new revision evoked great enthusiasm, and sharp criticism. The N.T. text on the whole was much improved; the O.T. followed the Massoretic text with a few exceptions.

The American companies were more ready to introduce changes in text and style; and were also conscious of differences between the respective English of England and America. Bound by a pledge to wait at least fourteen years, they published in 1901 their own revision, which became known as the American Standard Edition.

By this time, actual modern speech translations had begun to appear in numbers. Probably the two most widely accepted modern speech translations in English today are the Smith-Goodspeed

American Translation, and Moffatt's New Translation. Both are largely in ordinary English; Moffatt gives us more of British flavor, the Smith-Goodspeed Bible, American. Goodspeed's N.T., published in 1923, used the Westcott and Hort text, and a free, pleasing colloquial American style. Smith and associated scholars issued their O.T. in 1927, a little more conservative in English style, with some textual emendation. Both testaments were issued together in 1931, later re-edited, and the Apocrypha still later added by Professor Goodspeed to form the Complete Bible. Moffatt for his N.T. used Von Soden's text, and fortunately with considerable freedom. He also exercised greater freedom in arrangement of passages, and in emendation of the Hebrew.

Two N.T. translations which did much to popularize modern speech editions, and which still are widely used, are the Twentieth Century New Testament (1899-1900), and Weymouth's New Testament in Modern Speech, produced in 1903 or two years after Moffatt's Historical New Testament. Despite his title, Weymouth was more greatly influenced by King James style. Ferrar Fenton's Bible of 1900 performed a similar service of popularization, but did not stand up equally well under critical use. F. S. Ballentine's translation of the Gospels in 1897 and the Modern American Bible (1899-1901) which contained more of the N.T., were commendable though not widely known. Others worthy of particular mention are Wm. G. Ballantine's Riverside New Testament of 1923, based on Nestle's text, with a somewhat more conservative style; Helen B. Montgomery's Centenary Translation of the New Testament (1924), more popular today; and the New Testament in Basic English, which appeared in 1941. An excellent Jewish edition of the Holy Scriptures was published in 1917 as a revision by a company of Jewish scholars under the leadership of Max Margolis. Baer's Hebrew text was used with slight variations. Father Spencer produced his Gospels in 1898 and went on to translate the remainder of the N.T. It was edited and published in 1937, twenty-four years after his death, as a modern translation for popular use by Catholics. Many commendable and attractive features are vitiated by a poor text. These are only a few of the surprisingly large number of private English translations which have been made in the modern period.

As this is written, a new revision of the American Standard Version is nearing completion. Thomas Nelson and Sons assigned ownership of the copyright in 1929 to the International Council of Religious Education. A beginning was made in revision under Luther Weigle of Yale as chairman. The movement was halted by lack of funds, but was resumed in 1937. Some sixteen American scholars are now engaged in the task. The N.T. committee has virtually finished. The text, though composite, will be a more critical one, and the English style more modern.

Ira M. Price, *The Ancestry of Our English Bible*, 9th ed., Rev. (1934), pp. 283-322; John V. Madison, "English Versions of the New Testament; A Bibliographical list", *Jr. of Biblical Lit.*, XLIV (1925), pp. 261-288; Edgar J. Goodspeed, *The Making of the English New Testament* (1925), pp. 62-124; Max L. Margolis, *The Story of Bible Translations*, Jewish Publication Society of America (1917), pp. 79-106; John L. Cheek, *The Translation of the Greek New Testament in America* (Unpublished dissertation at the University of Chicago, 1938); T. W. Chambers, *A Companion to the Revised Old Testament* (1885); Philip Schaff, *A Companion to the Greek New Testament and English Version* 4th ed. (1894).

J.L.C.

Bible School: See Sunday School movement in the United States.

Bible Societies: There are four great parent Bible Societies of the world, the British and Foreign Bible Society, the American Bible Society, the National Bible Society of Scotland and the Netherlands Bible Society. They all came into being in the early years of the 19th Century as a part of the modern movement for World Missions. There are also many other smaller national societies.

In policy and practise the great Bible Societies are all essentially the same—being instituted to encourage the wider circulation of the Scriptures without note or comment and without purpose of profit. They are essentially missionary institutions, concerned principally with the supplying of the Scriptures to those who but for them would not be able to secure the Bible.

The work of a Bible Society so conceived, naturally falls into three principal categories, aiding translators, publishing and distributing.

Due mostly to the encouragement given by the Bible Societies to missionaries confronted with the necessity of translating the Scriptures, some part of the Bible has, since 1800, passed into over 900 languages of which 184 now have the whole Bible. Counting those translations made before 1800 the total number of languages now possessing some part of the Bible is 1058.

The four great Bible Societies publish and distribute annually about 17,000,000 volumes of Scripture throughout the world; an additional 8,000,000 being distributed by other organizations. The manufacturing of these books is done in hundreds of languages and in about forty different cities scattered throughout the world. In so-called "missionary" lands the distribution is carried on principally by colporteurs and missionaries, many of whom take the books into the uncultivated areas where regular missionaries have never been established. In the United States, the American Bible Society operates through its various District Offices and its special Agency among the Colored People. It maintains five depositories from which the books are circulated. The concern of the Society in the homeland is that the Scriptures shall reach the poor, the needy, the unevangelized, those in penitentiaries and almshouses. Thousands of bulky volumes in embossed systems and talking book records are also distributed for the blind. In times of war the Bible Societies supply the armed forces with appropriately bound pocket testaments, free, through the chaplains. In the present war the American Bible Society has furnished through its office in Geneva, Switzerland, about half a million Bibles, Testaments and Portions in over 25 different languages to prisoners of war in Germany and elsewhere.

With the rapid rise of literacy which is destined to follow the war, the demand for the Bible in so-called non-Christian lands and the dearth of the supply available in Europe will call for a prompt and extensive expansion of the production and operation of the Bible Societies. See Wilberforce, W. Cf. anti-Bible Society agitation in the U. S.

The Book of A Thousand Tongues (1938), edited by Eric M. North. Annual Reports of the American Bible Society and the British and Foreign Bible Society. F.C.S.

Bibles, polyglot: See polyglot Bibles.

Biblia pauperum: Pictured representations of scenes from the N.T. accompanied by those from the O.T. which were typologically associated with them. Circulated especially in the fifteenth century. J.T.M.

Biblical archaeology: Biblical archaeology is concerned with the recovery of the cultural (including material and religious) life of those ancients who produced or influenced the Bible. Since the Bible is a portion of the literature of Israelite, Jewish, and Christian people, obviously its concepts, allusions, modes of thought, and history cannot be well understood without constant reference to the culture of the age which produced it.

Before the last century the history and life of the ancient Near East were but dimly known from classical sources, which often gave an entirely erroneous or distorted picture. From that background the Bible projected like a mysterious fossil, with little contemporary witness to its meaning or authenticity. The most fantastic canons of interpretation were often employed, and, lacking pertinent data, dogma was usually the final arbiter of what the Bible said and what it meant to life.

Today our perspective is vastly enriched with the recovery of the material and epigraphic remains of ancient civilizations. Egyptians, Canaanites (Phoenicians), and Philistines; Hittites, Horites, and Amorites; Babylonians, Assyrians, and Persians; Aramaeans, Nabataeans, and Arabians are only a few of the many ancient peoples who played a part in biblical history, remains of whom have been recovered. In addition, excavations in Palestine especially have illuminated the history of Israel from the Conquest through the Roman period, providing a background and a check for the biblical accounts and concepts.

Archaeology as a discipline employing the scientific method has had a history which may be divided into four main periods. 1) Before 1800, a period largely notable for the reports of travellers and the awakening of interest in the subject. 2) 1800-1890, the period of the decipherment of Egyptian and Accadian (cuneiform) in particular, the development of lexicography and grammar, the first great excavations in the palaces of Assyria, the first scientific exploration of Palestine by the American scholar, Edward Robinson (the first great biblical archaeologist), and the first excavations in various countries, including Asia Minor (Troy), Palestine, and Egypt. Excavations were little more than treasure hunts, and biblical archaeology largely apologetic. 3) 1890-1915, a period when scientific methods of excavation were developed (especially by Reisner and Fisher at Samaria), and the key to chronology, the study of pottery, was discovered (by Sir Flinders Petrie, 1890). 4) 1920-1940, the period of greatest development of methodology and of most intensive exploration, excavations, and interpretation. Up to this time most archaeological work had been dominated by a biblical interest, largely apologetic. A more general cultural interest is now dominating the field, and biblical archaeology among its leading adherents has liberated itself from a narrow view of its purpose and function.

A few observations may now be noted as to the precise effect which the new information has had upon our view of the Bible.

1. The discoveries have demonstrated that far more trust in the substantial reliability of the narratives is now in order, and that lateness of written record does not necessarily mean complete unreliability. There are countless illustrations of this fact, though perhaps one of the most noteworthy is the recovery of the Patriarchal period. Our written sources for this period are 9th to 5th century in date, and the stories have generally been thought to reflect the age in which they were written, rather than the age which they purport to describe. Naturally, archaeology cannot prove the actual existence of the characters in question, and it has shown that details like camels, Philistines, and some of the Egyptian names in the Joseph story are later additions. Yet apart from such details the color and background of the stories can be shown from a large amount of evidence to fit perfectly in the age which is supposed to be described (cir. 2000-1700 B.C.), but imperfectly in any subsequent period.

This example is a good illustration of the use of archaeology in biblical study. Its aim is neither to "prove" or "disprove", but to find truth. In so doing, however, much is found to confirm, some not to confirm. Most of the discoveries do neither, but fill in the background which is needed for the understanding of the meaning and context. From the above it is also evident that questions concerning the validity of religious concepts and the actual existence of such historical characters as Isaiah and Jesus cannot often be expected to find either confirmation or denial from archaeological sources, for archaeology has its limitations. It is only an aid to history, not history itself. It has demonstrated, however, that a more conservative treatment of the sources is in order. There are still those who believe, for example, that it is impossible to write a history of Jesus, since the sources reflect to a greater or lesser degree the beliefs of the Early Church. It is improbable that archaeology will ever solve this problem directly; but those scholars who study the results of archaeology on oral tradition in the O.T. cannot fail to come to the conclusion that the hypercriticism of *Formgeschichte* has often been carried too far.

2. The discovery of the literature of surrounding peoples and of more ancient texts and versions (especially the papyri) of the Bible has furthered the work of textual criticism immeasurably. Corrections of texts and the knowledge of the meaning of obscure words has advanced so far as to render all lexicons, especially those of the O.T., out of date. The work of classifying MSS and versions into families and sub-families is proceeding, and a more accurate methodology has been developed for determining correct readings. It is interesting to note that the evidence for the text of the N.T. is much greater than for any other book from antiquity, and some of the papyri date not more than one hundred fifty years after the writing of the original MSS. Recent discoveries, by and large, have supported the text of our best Greek versions, and few new readings of much significance have been discovered. In the O.T. the discoveries have been of great lexicographical value, but it has become evident that for the most part the texts have been transmitted with remarkable fidelity, and our knowledge of the teaching of the great biblical figures has been little increased or altered.

3. The classic reconstruction of O.T. history and religion is that of the Graf-Wellhausen school, which in turn was based on a Hegelian scheme of progression: pre-prophetic, prophetic, and legal; or (animistic) polytheistic, henotheistic, monotheistic. While there can be little doubt about the *general* nature and date of the documents of the Hexateuch (J,E,D,P), they must now be considered as mainly editions, employing far older material; and the evolutionary scheme, supposedly derived from them, is now known to be far too simple. For example, ancient religion by the time of the Patriarchs was far advanced beyond an animistic stage, though survivals of animism are common throughout the Bible. In fact, archaeology through its demonstration of the antiquity of "high gods" reveals that the whole question of a simple animism is open to some suspicion.

4. The sources and nature of Biblical borrowing from other cultures and syncretism are increasingly clear. Close study of this subject reveals, however, that the most important thing here to be noted is the remarkable transformation through which all that was borrowed underwent. The Israelite-Jewish people, though always relatively poor and contributing nothing to the material progress of mankind, nevertheless had a genius possessed by no other ancient people—a genius of which their religious leaders were fully and justifiably conscious. Today, as a result of a century of archaeological work, we are in possession of a vast literature from the ancient east. Taken as a whole, however, the Bible unquestionably represents the cream of this literature. In histrionic presentation, character delineation, and especially in religious insight into the nature of God and man, the Bible stands without peer in the ancient world; and, when confronted with it amid the ruins of other civilizations, the honest archaeologist can only stand amazed.

5. Archaeological search into man's origin in the "cradle of civilization" now enables us also to view the Bible with a new temporal perspective. When the Israelite nation was founded, over 200,000 years at the least had elapsed since man began to make artifacts. This does not merely mean that a large amount of new data has been furnished for a study of the origin of religion. Rather, since only 2000 years have passed since the close of the Canon, the place of the Bible in human history is clearer, and on *a priori* grounds it can no longer be claimed that the Bible is merely an ancient literature of no relevance to modern man. This, of course, is not to be taken as support for obscurantist views of Scripture. In fact, one view which archaeology has definitely disproved is that of verbal inspiration. In addition, it is quite evident to any reader that there is much that is temporal and relevant to its time alone. But archaeology has furnished a wealth of new data by which the changeless can be separated from the changing, the timeless from the temporal.

Much remains to be done, not only in further discovery, but in interpretation. Biblical lexicography is in need, as is also the study of religious concepts. Pioneer work has been accomplished, but we have only begun to understand these concepts in the wider setting now provided. See archaeological periods.

Archaeology has been much misused by well-meaning authors in their search for "confirmation" of Scripture. In addition, progress has been so rapid within the last two decades that the results have been difficult to assimilate. Consequently, practically all of the handbooks now available are out of date or untrustworthy or both. The greatest work to appear recently, one which attempts to view biblical history in the new perspective, is that of W. F. Albright, *From the Old Stone Age to Christianity,* (1940). Next should be placed the volume by Millar Burrows, *What Mean These Stones?* (1941). These works contain references to all the pertinent source material.

Attention should be called also to the small quarterly journal, *The Biblical Archaeologist* (New Haven, American Schools of Oriental Research), designed to keep those who are not specialists informed. Among the older handbooks, G. A. Barton, *Archaeology and the Bible* (Philadelphia, American Sunday School Union, 7th edition, 1937), though out of date, is still the best. The best handbooks in other languages are: A. G. Barrois, *Manuel d'archéologie biblique* (Paris, 1939); K. Galling, *Biblisches Reallexikon* (Tübingen, 1937); and C. Watzinger, *Denkmäler Palästinas,* I—II (Leipzig, 1933 and 1935).

G.E.W.

Biblical Commission, the: See Commission, the Biblical.

Biblical criticism: Biblical criticism denotes the application of sound historical methodology to the individual books of the Bible to establish their reliability and credibility as historical sources and to determine what meaning they had for their authors and first readers. This scholarly investigation of the Bible is a complex operation consisting of a number of mutually related disciplines which may be briefly summarized.

In view of the many errors, both deliberate and unintentional, which have corrupted the text of each book of the Bible, it is necessary to detect and correct these corruptions so as to restore as nearly as possible the actual wording of the original autograph or manuscript of the author. This specialized branch of study, termed textual or lower criticism, is prerequisite to the literary-historical study of the Bible, frequently but unfortunately referred to as higher criticism.

A second prerequisite is the intensive application of linguistic studies to the books of the Bible, with attention to every nuance of vocabulary and subtlety of expression, so that these books, written in ancient languages, may be adequately understood and properly translated.

With these basic requirements satisfied, the student should next localize a given book, determining the author, if possible, and all that can be learned about him (for his name alone is of little significance); the place and date of writing; the public to whom it is addressed; and the cause, purpose, or occasion of composition. Without this definite localization, no writing from the past can be adequately interpreted. Closely related to localization is the problem of genuineness, whether a work is pseudepigraphic*, or whether in the course of tradition it has been given a false ascription.

Further, in connection with the study of a number of Biblical books the problem of source analysis arises, since some may be based upon sources, both oral and written, which should be identified and localized if possible. Also, since certain books have been subjected to later redaction*, the work of the redactor must be taken into account.

The literary style of an author, together with his characteristic vocabulary and manner of expression, deserves consideration. Further, literary criticism classifies a given book, or its component parts, according to type or form, whether prose, poetry, liturgy, homily, legend, myth, oracle, apocalypse, drama, parable, allegory, chronicle, letter, and so on, for this has a direct bearing on purpose and meaning.

In addition, it is most important to consider a writing comparatively, with reference to its historical, social, cultural, political, economic, intellectual, and religious background, as this may be determined by a thoroughgoing study of all the available collateral evidence, literary, archaeological, epigraphic, geographical, numismatic, and the like. Only by such a social-historical or environmental integration can the original meaning and significance of a work for its own times be discovered.

Biblical criticism is complicated by the fact that unlike most other historical sources the books of the Bible have been considered canonical, that is, are the divine word of God revealed to mankind through inspiration. However, a critical study of the historical process by which these books became canonical should provide a corrective, if one is needed. See exegesis; manuscripts of the Bible.

E. Bernheim, *Lehrbuch der historischen Methode* (1894); C. V. Langlois, and C. Seignobos, *Introduction to the Study of History* (tr. from the French, 1898); R. L. Marshall, *The Historical Criticism of Documents* (1920); A. T. Olmstead, "History, Ancient World and the Bible: Problems of Attitude and Method," *Journal of Near Eastern Studies* II (1943), 1-34; G. H. Gilbert, *Interpretation of the Bible: A Short History* (1908); K. Fullerton, *Prophecy and Authority: A study in the History and interpretation of Scripture* (1919); E. C. Colwell, *The Study of the Bible* (1937).

M.R.

Biblical criticism, sketch of history of: With the exception of the short-lived Antiochean* grammatico-historical school, the Bible has not been studied in a critical manner until relatively recent times. Down through the centuries most Bible study has been conditioned by dogmatic presuppositions and pragmatic considerations, and characterized by allegorical interpretation*and other fanciful methods of exegesis*. With the rise of humanism attention was directed to the Hebrew O.T. and the Greek N.T., and editions of both were printed. Furthermore, scholars began to study the Hebrew and Greek languages, and before long translations were made from the "original" tongues into modern European languages. Along with these developments it was noted that the text of both the O. and N. Testaments had been corrupted in the course of centuries of manuscript transmission. This occasioned textual or lower criticism, particularly of the N.T. where the manuscript evidence was richer and more varied, which in time resulted in the publication of critical texts. Interest was also aroused in the manner in which the various books of the Bible came to be regarded as scripture, and histories of the canon of both O. and N. Testament were produced.

As early as the Reformation freedom in studying the Bible without dogmatic presuppositions was advocated, but actually in practice the bonds of dogmatism were but gradually loosened. However, attention was increasingly directed toward such problems as literary type, authorship, date, and possible sources. In the O.T. the poetic sections were identified and studied as poetry, and still later the significance of other types, such as legends, sagas, and myths was noted. The literary types of the N.T. were also given consideration, with special emphasis being placed at the present time upon the "forms" which the gospel tradition assumed. The traditional authorship of numerous books in the Bible, such as the Pentateuch, Daniel, various Psalms, the Pastoral Epistles, Hebrews, and the Gospel according to John** was seriously questioned, and along with this line of inquiry many of the books were redated. In the application of source analysis the composite nature of books like Genesis and Isaiah was demonstrated, and in the N.T. attention was called to the synoptic* problem. More recently attempts to reconstruct the "gospel" before the gospels have been made.

The rise of science, with the discovery of natural laws, led to scepticism concerning the miraculous elements in the Bible. This at first resulted in the rationalization of miracles* and other supernatural evidences, but more lately these have been interpreted against the background of the supernaturalism that prevailed when the various books of the Bible were written. Darwin's theory of evolution*, which appeared in print in 1859, was soon reflected in Biblical studies, and scholars began to write about the evolution of Hebrew religion, of Hebrew literature, of early Christianity. Likewise, the discovery of the Assyrian Flood-tablets by George Adam Smith in 1872 gave impetus to the study of the O.T., of Hebrew religion and history, in the light of the literature, religion, and history of the neighbors of the Hebrews. Similarly, the N.T., the early church, and Jesus and Paul have been studied against their historical and religious background. In this connection special emphasis has been placed upon Talmudic* writings, apocalypses, and Philo**, and upon the evidences for Graeco-Roman religions. Furthermore, the arbitrary distinction between canonical and uncanonical has been overcome, with the result that uncanonical Christian writings more or less contemporaneous with the books of the N.T. have been studied alongside of the canonical works. In addition, the knowledge gained from the investigation of primitive cultures and religions is being utilized in the study of the more primitive areas of the O.T. Similarly, modern psychology is being reflected in psychological studies of the prophets and of Jesus and Paul which have been made.

To summarize, Biblical criticism has been influenced by the discoveries, theories, and methods which have first appeared in other fields of investigation. The Bible is now considered to be a human record, not a record of revelation, and is being studied by the best methods of historical criticism applied to all the available sources of information. This is far removed from the traditional methods of Biblical study. Two final observations should be made: first, the study of the Bible has lagged behind secular studies of a similar nature, and second, the study of the N.T., regarded as the more sacred part of the Bible, has lagged behind that of the Old. See Biblical criticism.

G. H. Gilbert, *Interpretation of the Bible* (1908); K. Fullerton, *Prophecy and Authority: A Study in the History of the Doctrine and Interpretation of Scripture* (1919); A. S. Peake, *The Nature of Scripture* (1922); G. B. Smith, editor, *A Guide to the Study of the Christian Religion* (1916), chapters ii-v.

M.R.

Biblical drama: See religious drama.

Biblical exegesis: See exegesis.

Biblical history in Christian instruction: It took nearly 1800 years before instruction in biblical history received that measure of attention which it deserves. Instruction in the catechism in this or that form dominated. And yet, there was no period in the church without some instruction in biblical history. In the early church the *Endeixis* of Irenaeus contained a good deal of it. The *Chronica* of Sulpicius Severus, the *Libri Evangeliorum* of Juvencus, the *Carmen paschale* of Sedulius—none of them a biblical history in the present understanding of this term—served as means of making the people, especially the catechumens, acquainted with much of the pertaining material. Augustine in *De catechizandis rudibus* demanded that the lecture preparatory for the catechumenate* should include a historical survey of the kingdom of God from creation to the present time. Chrysostom advised the Christian father to tell the principal facts of biblical history to his children, laid down fundamental principles for such narration and showed by examples how they are to be applied. During the Middle Ages Theodul's *Ecloga*, the *Heliand* and *Krist*, the *Scholastica Historia* of Peter Comestor in its Latin form and many translations served as means to make acquaintance with biblical history; their use, however, was limited to the Latin schools and the educated home. What the children and the common people learned of biblical history was offered to them by the many *Passionalia*, the *Biblia Pauperum** (O.T. and N. T. pictures placed side by side with brief explanations), the *Speculum Humanae Salvationis* (a biblical picturebook), the mural and window paintings in the church, the observance of the church year and the various *postillae*, i.e., sections from the O.T. and N.T. for the Sundays and some week days, containing sometimes up to 500 biblical sections. Description of this material is given in M. Reu, *Luther's German Bible* (1934). But there was no regular instruction in biblical history.

Luther's *Passionale* of 1529 can be called the first biblical history for the Christian home. It was a collection of 49 biblical pictures with explanatory texts in the words of Scripture and arranged in historical sequence with special emphasis upon the passion and resurrection story. In 1555 followed Hartmann Beier's *History Bible*, likewise designed for the Christian home, but very extensive. In the Latin schools were used *Dialogi Sacri* by Castellio, the *Historia Sacra* by Fabricius, and the pericopes of the church year. So the common assumption that the 16th century had no instruction in biblical history at all is no longer tenable. (Cf. M. Reu, *Quellen zur Geschichte des kirchlichen Unterrichts* (1906), vol. II.) In 1656 Justus Gesenius published "Bible stories of the Old and New Testaments chronologically arranged for the benefit of the young and unlearned, divided into two parts each with 54 lessons." Ernest the Pious of Gotha introduced biblical history into his Christian public schools (1662). "Twice 52 Stories from the Old and New Testaments" by Johann Huebner appeared in 1714 and helped very much to make biblical history a regular branch of study in the common schools. With the awakening of the Christian life after 1830 the understanding for the historical foundation of Christianity increased and helped to open the eyes for the importance of instruction in biblical history so that it obtained afterwards a larger place in the school curricula than instruction in catechism, resulting even in a complete exclusion of the catechism. This much is true, we should start with biblical history, should later deduce the principal truths of the catechism from the bible stories and finally use the catechism as the concluding unifying material. Isaac Watts gave us in 1732 with his *Scripture*

History the first bible history in English, used in England and America. Later the Sunday school movement helped to obtain for biblical history a regular place in religious instruction, in the Lutheran Church often supplemented by a course in regular biblical history.

Concerning the method of instruction see M. Reu, *Catechetics* (1927), pp. 285-308. See also A. Schmieding, *Teaching the Bible Story* (1935); Th. Heckel, *How to teach Evangelical Christianity* (1935), tr. by N. E. Richardson and H. J. Stratemeier. M. REU

Biblical Introduction: This title is still retained for that branch of theological study which deals with literary and historical criticism. It was the ancient custom to prefix to each biblical writing a brief note concerning the author, the place of origin, the destination. These and similar data were formerly taken over from vague tradition or from mere conjecture. They are now found to involve elaborate enquiry, and to have the most important bearings on the nature and value of the books themselves. Thus an "Introduction" to the prophecies of Isaiah or the Fourth Gospel, once confined to one or two sentences, may run to a large volume, or a whole library of volumes. E.F.S.

Biblical theology: Until near the close of the 18th century it was taken for granted that the creeds approved by the church were in full correspondence with the Bible teaching, or differed from it only in so far as the scriptural ideas were elucidated and harmonised. With the progress of criticism it became apparent that later theologies were largely based on philosophical ideas which were foreign to the biblical writers. The effort was made to construct a theology which should be wholly derived from the Bible teaching. This effort was doomed to failure, for reasons which have become ever more cogent as the true nature of the Bible has been more clearly understood. 1) The Old and New Testaments are separate, and represent two religions, differing in some of their essential principles. 2) The O.T. covers a period of a thousand years, during which all religious ideas underwent profound changes. 3) The N.T. likewise is found to offer a number of different interpretations of the Christian message, and they cannot be simply fused together and considered as a whole. The term "Biblical Theology" has therefore been largely abandoned, not only because it is inaccurate but because it rests on a false conception of the Bible. The book is read as if it were all of one piece, the manifesto of a single religious system, while it stands for a wide variety of religious thinking. This is one of the secrets of its greatness. It makes room for many different attitudes, all of them true and legitimate, in man's relation to God.

Not only has biblical thought ceased to be viewed as a whole but its frontiers are no longer sharply defined. We are now aware that Hebrew religion was exposed to Babylonian and Persian influences, that early Christianity borrowed largely from the cults and philosophies of the Hellenistic world. We know, too, that in the period between the Testaments there had been a great development in Judaism, and that Rabbinical and apocalyptic ideas must be studied along with those of the canonical writings. For that part, the canon itself was fixed in a more or less arbitrary fashion, and for theological purposes the Bible must include the apocrypha and those early Christian books which belong to the same general period as the N.T. The idea of a biblical theology has still, however a real value, all the more so as the field which it once covered has been so much divided. In the effort to distinguish between the separate types of thought there is always a danger of forgetting that there is an underlying continuity, and in some respects an identity. Certain broad conceptions, religious, ethical, philosophical, run through the whole Bible. While allowing for all the diversities which appear in the biblical writings it is necessary to remember that they are inter-related, and belong to a single movement. From this point of view the idea of a biblical theology is still a valid and helpful one.

E.F.S.

Biblicism and Bibliolatry: Biblicism denotes adherence to the strict letter of the Bible; in its most extreme form called "Bibliolatry" ("Bible worship"). B.S.E.

Biblion, Biblia: From *Biblos*, "papyrus"*. Biblion is a length of papyrus suitable for a Greek roll or scroll, some eight or nine yards long, a convenient length of practical use, and capable of accommodating the Gospel of Matthew, or of Luke, or the Acts. It came to mean a book, always in the roll form. The plural, Biblia, "the papyrus rolls," came to be used of the Christian sacred books of the O.T. and N.T., and passing into Latin as a feminine singular became our word Bible*. E.J.G.

bidding prayer: In Anglican service books, a series of requests for intercessions with the response of the Lord's prayer. Derived from Gallican* sources, it was the chief vernacular worship in pre-Reformation England. T.J.B.

Biddle, John: (1615-1662) "The father of the English Unitarians," b. Gloucestershire; educated at Magdalen Hall, Oxford; Master of Crypt School, Gloucester; d. London. Profoundly versed in the Bible he became convinced that the common doctrine of the Trinity accords with neither Scripture nor reason. Charged with heresy he published in defence four small tracts, which created a profound sensation and called forth several extensive refutations in both England and Holland. Prosecuted for heresy he spent the greater part of the last seventeen years of his life in intermittent imprisonment, but whenever at liberty held religious meetings for his followers in London, the earliest Unitarian congregation in England. Did not deny the Trinity, but aimed to purify the doctrine of unscriptural corruptions that seemed to him to approach tritheism. A man of exalted personal character and devout piety. His congregation did not survive him, but his influence was continued by his writings, republished by the Anglican philanthropist, Thomas Firmin, which did much to stimulate the Trinitarian Controversy of the two following generations and thus pave the way for Unitarianism*.

See Joshua Toulmin, *Life of Biddle* (1789); Robert Wallace, *Antitrinitarian Biography* (1850), iii, 173-206. E.M.W.

Biedermann, Alois Emmanuel: (1819-1885) Was for many years professor of theology at the University of Zürich, Switzerland. Infinity and spirituality are central to the idea of God. Together they form the concept of the absolute spirit, to which the term personality is not applicable. The ground of the world is as goallessly eternal as it is spacelessly ideal. Religion is not completely merged with the religious idea.

Die freie Theologie oder Philosophie und Christentum in Streit und Frieden (Tübingen, 1845); *Christliche Dogmatik,* 2 ed. 2 vols. (Zürich, 1884-85); Th. Moosherr, *A. E. Biedermann nach seiner allgemeinen Philosophischen Stellung* (Berlin, 1893); O. Pfister, *Die Genesis der Religions philosophie A. E. Biedermanns untersucht nach Seiten ihres psychologischen Aufbaues* (Zürich, 1898); A. Fleisch, *Die erkenntnistheoretischen und metaphysischen Grundlagen der dogmatischen Systeme von. A. E. Biedermann und R. A. Lipsius* (Zürich, 1902). H.H.

Biel, Gabriel: (d. 1495) Professor at Tuebingen. Occamist nominalist. Wrote commentary on *Sentences* of Lombard, also treatise on money. Luther was introduced to theology through his writings. E.C.K.

bigamy: (Lat. *bis,* twice; and Gr. *gamos,* marriage) a) In criminal law the act of contracting marriage while married; b) in church law, a word for a valid marriage after the death of the first spouse. L.R.W.

Billing, Einar Magnus: (1871-1939) Billing exercised a deep influence as teacher of theology at Upsala, 1900-1920. Opposing current trends he interpreted Christianity as a dramatic force in history, in conflict with evil, expressing itself in Church as a present struggle. Bishop of Västeras, 1920, he won new freedom for church by obtaining freedom to leave for those not interested. He contributed much to the religious education program of Sweden. C.J.B.

bilocation: (Lat., *bis,* twice, and *locatio,* place) The doctrine that although a corporeal being can be in only one place at a time, a spiritual being may conceivably be in some way in many places at once, and Christ in the Eucharist, though under the form of bread, is really and substantially present in every consecrated host. Alleged cases of bilocation on the part of saints are regarded by St. Thomas, Vasquez and others as explicable as phantasmal replication. L.R.W.

bilocation: (Lat. *bi,* twice, doubly, and *locus,* place) In psychic research and in thaumaturgy, the phenomenon wherein a body occupies or seems to be present in two (bilocation) or more (multilocation) places simultaneously. Theologians and philosophers endeavor to explain or at least describe the reports of hagiographers by distinguishing real presences from apparitions and also by differentiating definitive, circumscriptive and mixed replications. It should be noted that there are various modes of presence, ubication, location or occupation of a place and that the latter is a derivative or secondary effect of quantity whose primary or essential effect is the possession (not the extension or distribution) of integral parts. D.C.O'G.

Bimeler (Baümeler), Joseph Michael: Leader of Zoar settlement. See communistic settlements, religious.

bination: (Lat., *binarius, bini,* two by two, two at a time) Offering Mass twice by one person on the same day. At least as early as St. Augustine's time (d. 430) Mass was offered daily, and later two or three times daily; later it was restricted to once a day; priests now may say two Masses on Sundays or holydays if otherwise many would have to miss Mass. L.R.W.

Biran, Maine de: (1766-1824) Recognized as the most important French psychologist of the nineteenth century and as the profoundest French thinker before Comte*, he was the patron saint of French spiritualism which roughly corresponds to our idealism. Reaching independently views on the unconscious mental processes, he held the immediate consciousness of our own self-activity as the foundation of knowledge. For him religion is primarily feeling rather than faith. In later years the unsettled question for him was how it is possible to distinguish between that which springs out of the soul's own soil and that which is due to the influence of divine powers.

Oeuvres philosophiques (Paris, 1841); G. Barbillion, *De l'idee de Dieu dans la philosophie de Maine de Biran* (Grenoble, 1927); V. Delbos, *Maine de Biran et son oeuvre philosophique* (Paris, 1931); G. LeRoy, *L'expérience de l'effort et de la grace chez Maine de Biran* (Paris, 1937); E. Naville, *Maine de Biran, sa vie et ses pensées* (Paris, 1857); *Oeuvres inédites de M. Biran* (Paris, 1859); E. Rostan, *La religion de Maine de Biran* (Paris, 1890). H.H.

biretta: (It., originally a cloak and hood) A clergyman's headdress worn during parts of certain ceremonies; at first it was a skull cap, then a soft cap, now a square cap with three or four ridges. L.R.W.

Birgitta, Saint: (1303-1373) Also called St. Bridget. Born in Uppland, Sweden, of noble family, and married to one of king's councillors, Birgitta moved in highest circles, applying sternly her interpretation of God's will for church and kingdom. After her husband's death in 1344, she thought of herself as Bride of Christ, receiving from Christ and the Virgin revelations, which, after her removal to Rome in 1349, concerned the reformation of the Church and the return of the Popes from Avignon. Partial fulfilment of her long efforts to establish a new order came in 1370—Vadstena, Sweden, became the center, with many daughter institutions in Europe. Following a pilgrimage to Jerusalem, she died in Rome in

1373. She was canonized in 1391. Her visions were not so much of a mystic nature as of direct ethical commands for reformation of abuses in church and state. Her writings were published in Latin, in Lübeck, in 1492. See Brigittines. C.J.B.

bishop: "Bishop" is derived from the Greek *episkopos* ("over-seer"), a wholly non-technical word applicable to anyone holding any authority over others. In I Pet. 2:25 it is a divine title. In Phil. 1:1 it groups together the ruling authorities of a Christian community; in Acts 20:28 (compare v. 17) and Tit. 1:7 (compare v. 5) "bishop" is a precise synonym of "elder" and the same must be true of I Tim. 3:2 likewise. But beginning with the Ignatian* epistles (not yet in Clement) the word assumes a highly technical sense and describes the single "monarchical" head of a local church; an office (without the title) that may have N.T. antecedents in that held by the addressees of the Pastoral Epistles* and seized by Diotrephes in 3 John. During the second century this form of church organization made wide progress, except perhaps in Egypt; Irenaeus* (III, iii) maintains that the bishops are in a very real sense successors of the apostles, both in teaching and ruling authority, while Hippolytus* (*Apostolic Tradition* 9:8) asserts that they alone have the power of ordination.

In the first centuries each locality had its own bishop, so that in most places the office was little more than that of a congregation's pastor. But in the larger cities the bishops presided over many congregations and they gradually extended this rule over surrounding communities, whose own bishops disappeared; in this way the office was changed from a local into a territorial ("diocesan") dignity. And higher degrees within the episcopate were created, the bishops of the more important places becoming "archbishops," "metropolitans" or "patriarchs," with unique and universal claims made by the bishop of Rome.

Catholic theology holds that bishops are necessary for the very existence of the Christian church; in them exclusively are vested ruling authority, teaching authority and ordaining authority. But only the third of these functions is wholly inseparable from the office; in the Irish medieval church, for instance, it was the sole prerogative allowed the bishops, who in other regards were subject to abbots. And in the modern Anglo-Catholic* revival the ruling and teaching authority of bishops is often lightly regarded. In any case ruling authority is everywhere controlled by church law, while teaching authority obviously depends on individual capacity; only the collective teaching authority of the episcopate as a whole is regarded as infallible.

A subsidiary prerogative of bishops is confirmation*. But in the Eastern churches the right to confirm is regularly delegated by the episcopate to the lower clergy and a similar delegation is occasionally, although much more rarely, granted in the Roman communion; never, however, in the Anglican communion.

In various Protestant denominations, apart from Anglicanism, the episcopate has been retained (as by certain Lutheran bodies) or revived (as by the Methodists). But these bishops have only certain restricted ruling authority; exclusive power to ordain is attributed to them, if at all, only in very small and uninfluential sects. See autocephali; clergy; Evodius; patriarch. B.S.E.

Bishop Hill colony: See communistic settlements, religious.

Bishops' Bible: See Bible, English.

bismillah: An Arabic term meaning in the name of God. "In the name of Allah", is a common exclamation among Mohammedans. P.E.J.

Black Book, the: See Devil Worshipers.

Black Fast, the: A name given to an austerity practiced until the tenth century during Lent and just preceding ordination. On such fast days the quantity and quality of the food was limited as on other fast days; but in addition the time wherein such food might be eaten was designated as only in the evening. Only one meal was allowed at which flesh meat, eggs, butter, cheese, milk, and wine were forbidden. In the tenth century the custom of taking this one meal at three in the afternoon arose; in the fourteenth century the time was advanced to noon. Gradually the black fast disappeared as the practice arose of taking a small breakfast and an evening collation on fast days. See Feasts and Fasts, R. C. T.T.M.

Black Fathers and Black Sisters, the: The name popularly applied to the religious, male and female, who follow the "Rule of St. Augustine." They are properly called the Canons and Canonnesses Regular of St. Augustine. The congregations following this rule came into being in and after the eleventh century. See Augustinians. T.T.M.

Black Friars, the: The name commonly applied to the Dominican* friars in England because of the black cloak (*cappa*) and hood which they wear when outside the monastery. The cloak and hood are not worn as much in the United States as in countries where the garb is worn publicly. T.T.M.

Black monks, the: The name popularly applied to the Benedictine* monks because of their entirely black habit. T.T.M.

Black Rubric: While Edward's Second Prayer Book was in the process of preparation in 1552, a controversy developed over the practice of kneeling at the communion. It was asserted that the posture suggested an idolatrous attitude toward the elements. At the insistence of John Knox, though kneeling was still prescribed, an explanatory declaration was inserted. This statement, that the act did not imply any belief in the doctrine of transubstantiation, was later called the "Black Rubric" by High Churchmen. W.S.H.

Blavatsky, Madame: See theosophy.

blessedness: The state of being blessed, of enjoying happiness or favor, especially divine favor. In the last sense used in the AV of Rom 4:6, 9 (RV "blessing"); almost in the sense of "self esteem" in the AV of Gal 4:15 (RV "gratulation"). See happiness. B.S.E.

blessing and cursing: A blessing or a curse is a wish in words winged with the energy of emotion. Belief in the efficacy of the spoken words probably came from the feeling of satisfaction following emotional release. The effectiveness of a blessing or curse varied with the status of the individual uttering it. The words of a religious official, a patriarch, a parent or a dying man had more power than those of an ordinary person. Aryan and Semite alike dreaded especially the curse of those individuals who had no other redress—beggars, women, slaves and the oppressed poor. Gestures which express anger or affection became formalized accompaniments of cursing and blessing. Pointing directed the energy to its object. Blessing or cursing was usually a private affair but both were used as public rituals in higher religions. The protection of property by a curse applied to landmarks or tombs was an extension of the original usage. An oath* was often worded in the form of a curse to take effect upon the speaker if he failed to fulfill certain conditions. When a blessing or a curse was routed through a god it became a prayer. A qualified person could destroy the effect of a curse by a blessing or a counter-curse. A god might turn an undeserved curse into a blessing. See laying on of hands. A.E.H.

blessing, priestly: The blessing of the people by the Aaronites (the priests who were the descendents of Aaron), prescribed in Numbers 6:22-27, was an important part of the Temple service in Jerusalem and is still included in many synagogue* rituals. The priests were required to discard their footwear and wash their hands before facing the congregation to chant the blessing with upraised hands. Some synagogues no longer have a descendent of the Aaronites recite this blessing, but it is frequently used by the minister as a benediction following a religious service. B.Z.B.

bliss: (A.S. *blis*) Unmixed happiness and joy; more particularly the supreme happiness and joy of heaven. See blessedness. B.S.E.

Blondus, Flavius: (Flavio Biondo, 1392-1463) Humanist historian and archeologist, secretary to four popes. His posthumously published works on ancient Rome and Italy and on the medieval era make him one of the chief founders of modern historiography. J.T.M.

blood: In the early stages of all cultures blood has been treated with awed circumspection. It had a mysterious potency which could be dangerous unless properly handled. Warriors after battle and women after menstruation or childbirth carried a contagion and required ceremonial cleansing. The Semites* identified the blood with the life, forbad the eating of it, and carefully channelled the blood of sacrifice* on the sacred altar*, deposited it in a holy place, covered it with earth, or applied it to a stone representing the god. In this way the mysterious danger was controlled. Other peoples drained the blood into a trench or strangled the sacrificial animal to avoid the spilling of blood. On the other hand, blood could be efficacious for good. It was a powerful protective agent when sprinkled on doorposts or other objects. It could carry strength and healing. Youthful blood was used to give renewal of life to the aged. Blood poured into the grave served to revive the shades of the Grecian dead who were pictured as hungry for blood. The blood bath was a cure for epilepsy. Blood was an effective means of purification* from all forms of contagion, physical or moral. The blood baptism of the mysteries illustrates this use in a highly developed form.

The qualities of one person could be transferred to another who drank or was sprinkled with his blood. Reconciliation after a quarrel or a pledge of loyalty was sometimes sealed by the drinking of blood. On all the continents, when the idea of blood relationship was established, an outsider could be admitted to kinship in a clan by the exchange of blood with one of its members. A solemn covenant* was made binding in the same manner. See law. A.E.H.

blood revenge: The duty of a kinsman to kill the killer of his kin. By this method, tribal societies enforced a rough justice by exacting a life for a life according to strict rules of justice. Responsibility fell first upon the next of kin, then on the family, then on the tribe. The Hebrews provided cities of refuge to protect the accidental killer from death. See lex talionis. A.E.H.

Blumhardts, the: Christoph Blumhardt (1805-1880), the father, growing out of Swabian pietistic circles, was first a teacher at the Basel Missions School. Later as pastor of a rural community in Southern Germany, he came face to face with the depths of demonic powers, in the victorious struggle of which he was instrumental in leading a spiritual awakening that reminded one of a return of the world of the New Testament.

Christoph Blumhardt (1842-1919), the son, left the pastorate of the official state church, threw off all pietistic theological mannerisms and placed himself boldly into the affairs of the contemporary world. He saw in the secular movements the workings of the living God, pregnant fermentations in creating a new world. He particularly discerned in the early social movement his hope of a redeemed material and human world. He joined Social Democracy not as a party member, but as a free Christian, and sat for a time in the diet as its representative. He served socialistic ideas at a time when it took courage to declare oneself for social democracy.

Until twenty years ago only a small circle of

men had heard of the two Blumhardts, of the spiritual events that transpired at Möttlingen and at Bad Boll, the places of their struggles and victories. Men and women of high and low stations in life received there new depths of meaning, felt the victorious testimony of the reality of Jesus, a wonderful commentary to the Gospels. Since the days of the prophets and apostles few individuals spoke as luminously, freely and potently out of God's word.

Fr. Zündel, *Johann Christoph Blumhardt*, 9th ed. (Giessen and Basel, 1922); L. Ragaz, *Der Kampf um das Reich Gottes in Blumhardt, Vater und Sohn und weiter* (Erlenbach, Switzerland, 1922); E. Jäckh, *Blumhardt Vater und Sohn und ihre Botschaft.* 2 ed. (Berlin, 1925). H.H.

B'nai B'rith: See student religious organizations.

Boccaccio, Giovanni: (1313-1375) Italian poet and novelist who shares with Petrarch* the honor of being the earliest humanist. Although he was a life-long student and admirer of Dante*, and wrote many poems clearly showing the influence of his master, he is best known for his *Decameron.* The work has merited for him the title of creator of the novel as an art-form and of Italian prose. Boccaccio later deplored the licentiousness of certain pasasges in his writings. See Renaissance. C.V.

Bodelschwing, Friedrich von: (1831-1910) Son of an old Prussian family, skilled in finances and religiously charitable, Bodelschwing became a theologian of childlike faith, a pastor of wide compassion who chose to live amidst the poor. He was a military chaplain from 1866-1870. From 1872 to the close of his life, he organized and administered "a colony of mercy", Bethel in Bielefeld, Westphalia. Here for more than seventy years, thousands of afflicted persons mostly epileptics have lived in family groups. All their needs such as food, clothing, shelter, medicine, books, are met by each working as he is able. Nearby are a labor colony for unemployed, a farm colony, hostels for migrant laborers,—these became models for similar groups throughout Germany. The headworkers are given training in Bethel in two schools for deacons and deaconesses*. The beautiful cruciform church in the woods is the center or heart of the activities of this large commonwealth of sufferers. A.S.

G. v. Bodelschwing, *Friedrich von Bodelschwingh* (Berlin, 1922). H.H.

Bodhidharma: See Buddhist Terminology.

Boehm, Martin: (1725-1812) Expelled from the Mennonites because of his evangelistic zeal and enthusiasm, became co-founder with Otterbein* of the Church of the United Brethren in Christ*. Bishop, 1800-1812. W.E.R.

Boehme, Jacob: (1575-1624) A German Protestant mystic, a Görlitz shoemaker by trade, and the composer of an obscure religious and philosophical system whose influence is still operative in Germany, England, and the United States through his effect upon such religious movements as German pietism* and English Quakerism* and through his influence upon such men as William Law* and William Blake in England and on Hegel, Schelling, Baader, and Schopenhauer in Germany. Boehme's suggestive doctrine of the play of contraries within the will at the heart of all creation furnishes a Christian theosophy which has still to be fathomed. His writings are obscured by terminology and analogies that borrow heavily from the alchemist literature of his time.

The Signature of All Things (London, 1912); *Six Theosophic Points* (London, 1919); *The Way to Christ* (London, 1911); Howard Brinton, *The Mystic Will* (1930); Alexandre Kayre, *La Philosophie de Jacob Boehme* (Paris, 1929). D.V.S.

Boethius: Anicius Manlius Severinus Boethius was born of patrician family around the year 480. He received the best education possible in the Rome of his day. He early rose to political eminence, and in 510 he became consul. Twelve years later his two sons were raised to the consular dignity, and on him was conferred the title, *Magister Officiorum.* But his fortune was soon to change. Charged with treasonable relations with the Byzantine Court, he lost the friendship of Theodoric and was exiled to Pavia. After lingering some months there in prison he was cruelly put to death in 524/25. Boethius knew Greek, and his early ambition was to make the works of Plato and Aristotle accessible to his Latin contemporaries. In this he was little successful, but in compensation he wrote several original works in the arts, in philosophy, and in theology. He was especially influential in mediaeval music, while his translations of the *On Interpretation* and the *Categories* were the only logical works of Aristotle known to the West until the twelfth century. His great philosophical work is the *On the Consolation of Philosophy,* written while he languished at Pavia. Boethius was a Christian and the theological works attributed to him are now known to be authentic. P.S.M.

M. Grabmann, *Geschichte der scholastischen Methode* 2 vols. (Freiburg im Breisgau, 1909, 1911); F. Überweg, *Geschichte der Philosophie,* vol. II (Berlin, 1905). H.H.

Bohemian (or Czech) Brethren: In this organization the native Czech Reform found its best expression. Its spiritual father is Peter of Chelcice (c. 1390-c. 1460), who appeared on the religious scene in 1420. His first treatise, *The Spiritual Struggle,* 1421, demands clerical poverty, repudiation of war, of political power, of human laws, and of the papacy. His most important work, *The Net of Faith,* repudiates all connection between the spiritual and secular powers, and affirms that the church must completely separate itself from the state.

These notions were accepted by a group of pious folk under the leadership of a poor noble, Gregory, a nephew of the Utraquist Archbishop, John of Rokycany. The group withdrew in 1458 to a village of Kunwald in eastern Bohemia in order to live according to their strict principles. But King George of Podebrady disliked to tolerate any religious groups beyond those acknowledged by law; hence the small brotherhood suffered repeated and cruel persecution. Finally, they were driven, contrary to their original intention, to separate themselves from both the Utraquists and the Catholics by setting up their own church organization. This occurred in 1467. They repudiated the doctrine of the apostolic succession*, and chose three priests one of whom, Matthew, became the head of the church, an office later called episcopal.

The Unity repudiated all participation in the political life and held world-renouncing views in general. But in 1490 a liberal party broke down the old barriers, and since then the group attracted to itself some of the best elements in the nation. Nevertheless, it remained outside the law, and suffered periodic persecution. The most severe occurred in 1547, when King Ferdinand I proscribed all adherents from the country. They found refuge mainly in Poland. Since then, the center of gravity was shifted to Moravia.

But their fortunes improved when in 1575 they were recognized by Emperor Maximillian II as a legal communion, since they adhered to the *Confessio Bohemica* put forth by the Lutheranized Czech Utraquists. They were likewise included in the religious liberties granted in 1609 by Emperor Rudolph II in his "Letter of Majesty." However, all Czech Protestants, including the Czech and Moravian Brethren, lost their right to exist in the territories of the Bohemian Crown after the Battle of White Mountain (1620). Their last bishop, John Amos Comenius* (1592-1670), was the world-famed "father of modern educational theory and practice."

The organization was renewed when a small group of the Brethren from Moravia settled on the estates of Count Nicholas von Zinzendorf* at Herrnhut in Saxony. This reorganized Unity of Brethren (1722) known under the title of the Moravian Church*, exists to this day.

J. Th. Müller, *Geschichte der böhmischen Brüder* (3 vols. Herrnhut, 1922-31); J. Goll, *Chelcicky a Jednota v. XV stoleti* (Praha, 1916); E. de Schweinitz, *The History of the Church known as the Unitas Fratrum* (Bethlehem, 1885). M.S.

Bohlen Lectures, The: Established in 1875 by Mr. John Bohlen of Philadelphia with a capital sum of $10,000 at the Philadelphia Divinity School and, with frequent exceptions, given annually. "The subject of such lectures shall be such as is within the terms set forth in the will of the Rev. John Bampton for the delivery of what are known as the 'Bampton Lectures' at Oxford, or any other subject distinctively connected with or relating to the Christian religion." A few of the lecturers: Fleming James, "The Personalities of the Psalter"; George A. Barton, "Formative Ideas and Influences of the Apostolic Age"; Walter Lowrie, "Theology of Crisis".

(Data furnished by the chairman of the lectureship committee.) V.F.

Böhmer, Heinrich: (1869-1927) As professor in Bonn, Marburg and Leipzig, he was one of several theological minds who added to the understanding of the Reformation. His observations about the Christianization of Germany were later tested by a new generation of investigators.

Luther im Lichte der neueren Forschung (Leipzig, 1905, 5 ed. 1918); *Der junge Luther* (Leipzig, 1925). H.H.

Bois, Henri: (1862-) Dean of the Theological Faculty at Montaban, France. He defends a personalistic theism, (See Personalism) aiming to satisfy to the full the religious need and describing a God endowed not unlike man with sentiments, passions and will. Pantheistic and agnostic philosophies, in particular, stress the negation of all personal relations with the deity. The appearance of Jesus Christ marks the culmination of a progressive evolution of piety towards a most exalted conception of divinity. Bois attributes the extreme reserve of a great many religious thinkers regarding the possibility of a divine personality to the eternal temptation of pantheism and monism. He is convinced that Renouvier's* neo-critical personalism alone develops the true solution of the problem of God.

"L'eternité de Dieu", *Revue de théologique et des questions religieuses.* vol. VI. (Montaban, 1898); *La personne et l'oeuvre de Jésus Christ.* (Paris, 1907). H.H.

Bollandists: Society of Belgian Jesuits, initiators of the systematic criticism of historical source-material in their *Acta Sanctorum* (1634-1794; 1837-). They take their name from Jean Bolland (1596-1665), one of their first directors. The work was begun by Heribert Rosweyde. Arranged according to feast days of the saints and beginning with January 1st, the collection has reached November 10th in 64 volumes. See hagiography. E.A.R.

Bonald, Louis Gabriel Ambroise, Vicomte de: (1754-1840) Along with Joseph de Maistre* Bonald was the founder of the "traditionalist" movement in French Catholic thought. All error, both in politics and in religion, is traceable to deviation from an original "primitive revelation", to which the fundamental unity of all languages bears witness, but of which the Catholic Church is now the supreme repository. Principal works: *Théorie du pouvoir politique et religieux* (3 vols., 1796), *Legislation primitive* (1802), *Recherches philosophiques* (2 vols., 1818). W.M.H.

Bonar, Horatius: (1808-1889) Best known for his hymns, this Scotch Presbyterian minister wrote "I heard the Voice of Jesus say", "What a Friend we have in Jesus" and many others familiar to users of Protestant hymn-books. V.F.

Bonaventura, St.: (1221-1274) Of irenic and mediating nature, he was always ready to recognize the truth elements of rejected opinions, to reconcile different views, or to refrain from final decision. His favorite authority was St. Augustine*, in whom he saw the synthesis between Plato and Aristotle. In his religious, as well as in his general epistemology, he subscribes to the theory of illumination. A mystical-contemplative theology of experience unites itself as with Augustine, Anselm and Hugo of St. Victor**, with a rigorous voluntarism. An ecclesiastical positivism combines with an authoritative faith, a strict orthodoxy, a ready adaptibility to the reality of actual church life, and a lively ethical and mystical interest. See scholasticism.

E. Gilson, *La philosophie de S. Bonaventura* (Paris, 1924); E. Lutz, *Die Psychologie Bonaventuras* (Münster, 1909). H.H.

Boniface VIII: (Pope, 1294-1303) Sought to reestablish the supremacy of Papacy as asserted by Innocent III*. His chief conflict was with Philip the Fair of France who at War with England, taxed his clergy and refused to make peace at the Pope's command. Boniface issued the bull "Unam Sanctam"* purporting to prove absolute papal dominion. Agents of Philip took him prisoner and shortly thereafter he died. See Clericis Laicos; Doctor of the Church. R.E.E.H.

Boniface, Saint: Martyr. (675-755) Apostle of Germany, he was born in Devonshire, England, and died at Dokkum, Netherlands. He was educated in Exeter, joined the Benedictines and was ordained a priest in 705. In 719 he was sent by Pope Gregory II to preach to the Germans east of the Rhine. In 722 he was consecrated a bishop by Gregory who gave him the name of Boniface, perhaps the latinized form for Wilfrid, his original name. He dealt a final blow to heathenism in Germany by destroying the sacred oak of Thor, at Geismar. In 732, Gregory III made him an archbishop. He founded bishoprics, reformed the whole Frankish Church, held Councils, and in 748 was made archbishop of Mainz which see he resigned in 754 to evangelize the people of Friesland. He was slain by pagan savages and today is buried in the cathedral at Fulda. His feast is celebrated on June 5. Having unified the Church in Germany, he is not only its apostle but its patron. J.B.C.

Bonosians: Followers of Bishop Bonosus of Sardica (4th-5th cent.), condemned for denying the perpetual virginity of Mary. Survived in Spain and Gaul till the seventh century. M.S.

Book of Changes, The: See I Ching.

Book of Common Prayer: The Anglican book of public worship and administration of the sacraments and other rites. Its primary sources were the medieval Latin service books used in England prior to the Reformation—Missal, Breviary**, Manual, Pontifical. The skill with which these were simplified, combined, reformed, and rendered into the language of the people, reveals the genius of Archb'p. Cranmer*. The first P.B. of Edward VI (1549) clung closely to tradition; the second Edwardine Book (1552) reflects a decided swing toward the Reformed churches, as the influence of Geneva replaced that of the Lutheran reformers. Subsequent revisions (1559, 1604, 1662) have taken their starting point from the P.B. of 1552. The present official P.B. of the Church of England* is that of 1662, Parliament having refused its assent to alternatives adopted by the Church Assembly in 1927-28.

The Episcopal Church in America adopted its first P.B. in 1789 and has twice revised it. The present American Book dates from 1928. Other constituent churches of the Anglican communion have undertaken liturgical revisions in the interest of enrichment, flexibility, and adaptation to modern life. The general trend is toward the recovery of much of the liturgical tradition that was sacrificed in the P.B. of 1552. See Bible, English; catechism; Sarum use.

F. Procter and W. H. Frere, *New History of the Book of Common Prayer* (London, 1905); L. Pullan, *History of the Book of Common Prayer* (London, 1900); W. K. Clarke and C. Harris, editors, *Liturgy and Worship* 1932). P.V.N.

Book of Concord: The collected confessional documents of Lutheranism*, consisting of the three ecumenical creeds, Augsburg Confession*, Apology of the Augsburg Confession, Schmalkald Articles*, Luther's Small and Large Catechisms, and Formula of Concord*. Published by joint agreement of the Lutheran potentates of Germany in 1580 to commemorate the fiftieth anniversary of the Augsburg Confession and to put an end to internal doctrinal controversies, the Book of Concord has been accepted as authoritative by the majority of Lutherans throughout the world. Large bodies of Lutherans, however, e.g., the state churches of Sweden and Norway, have never formally subscribed to the whole Book of Concord. See Confessions, Formal of the Christian Church. T.A.K.

Book of the Dead: One among the sacred books of the religion of ancient Egypt consisting of magic, ritual and myth. See Egypt, religions of; sacred literatures. V.F.

Book of Homilies: See homily.

Books of the New Testament, dates of the: The determination of the dates of the various books of the N.T. is beset with difficulties and uncertainties. In the first place, none of these works is explicitly and definitely dated by its author. Nor does any writing contain unmistakable references by which it might be accurately dated. Further, it is highly probable that most of the authors are unknown to us, save for Paul, for apart from his letters the books in the New Testament are almost without exception either anonymous, or, what is worse, pseudonymous. Finally, the external attestation to their authorship and date is meager and as a rule unreliable. Despite all this, approximate dates which have been generally if not universally accepted have been assigned to the books of the N.T. through the application of historical criticism to all the available data.

It is generally admitted that the genuine letters of Paul (I Thessalonians, Galatians, I-II Corinthians, Romans, Colossians, Philemon, and Philippians) are the earliest writings in the N.T. However, there is no certainty concerning their exact date or chronological sequence. I Thessalonians, usually considered the first of Paul's extant letters, is dated as early as the summer of A.D. 50 through the correlation of a Delphic inscription, which gives the time of the proconsulship of Gallio in Greece, with the relevant data in Acts 16-18. The so-called imprisonment epistles (Colossians, Philemon, and Philippians) are the latest if they were actually written during Paul's imprisonment in Rome during the early part of the sixth decade. However, if, as many think, they were composed during a previous imprisonment in Caesarea or Ephesus they must be given an earlier date. (For a recent reconstruction of the sequence of Paul's letters see Riddle, *Paul, Man of Conflict*, 1940, pp. 201-211).

The authenticity of II Thessalonians has long been questioned. It was probably composed in the name of Paul a generation or two after the apostle's death to account for the delay in the promised coming of Christ. According to most authorities Ephesians is also pseudonymous. An increasing number are receptive to Goodspeed's suggestion that it was written as an introductory or covering letter for the corpus of Paul's letters which was collected and published in Ephesus towards the end of the century. (Cf. Goodspeed, *The Meaning of Ephesians*, 1933).

While the gospels contain material that is earlier than the letters of Paul, the oldest written gospel, Mark, which is used as a major source by the other three, is no earlier than the siege of Jerusalem (A.D. 66-70) to which it refers, and may be a decade or so later. The two-volume work Luke-Acts is now seen to be an apology for Christianity written in a time of increasing tension between the Roman Empire and the Church. If it is dependent upon certain passages in Josephus' *Antiquities* its *terminus a quo* is A.D. 93-94. This agrees with other data pointing to the close of the reign of Domitian (d. A.D. 96), but a later period is by no means precluded. Matthew, which reflects a developed, ecclesiastical interest, is probably no earlier than Luke-Acts. John, using Luke and possibly Matthew in addition to Mark as sources, was probably composed in the first part of the second century. Its Hellenized Christology, refutation of heresies, and apologetic motif (on this point see Colwell, *John Defends the Gospel*, 1936) tend to corroborate this conclusion. In connection with the gospels it should be borne in mind that they are anonymous; the authors, and dates, traditionally assigned to them stem from the piety and credulity of the latter half of the second century.

I Peter, Hebrews, and Revelation obviously come from periods of persecution. I Peter, dependent as it is upon the letters of Paul, is not by Peter. Rather, it dates from the reign of Domitian, or, as some assert, from that of Trajan (d. A.D. 117). The later date is supported by data in the correspondence between Pliny and Trajan relative to the status of the Christians in Bithynia. (Cf. Case, "Peter, the Epistles of," *Dictionary of the Apostolic Church*). Hebrews, of unknown authorship, may be from the time of Domitian. The use of Hebrews by I Clement, usually assigned to this period, tends to confirm this opinion. (Cf. Riddle, "Hebrews, I Clement, and the Persecution of Domitian," *Journal of Biblical Literature* XLIII, 1924). Revelation is also ascribed to the reign of Domitian, in whose reign Christians were persecuted for their refusal to worship him as a divinity, but a Trajanic date is not impossible.

I John, which is anonymous, together with II and III John, attributed to an otherwise unknown presbyter, may be contemporaneous with the gospel. They seem to be directed against schisms and heresies similar to those combatted by Ignatius (who died as a martyr in the reign of Trajan). The authority claimed by the writers closely resembles that claimed by the bishop of Antioch.

Very few today argue for the Pauline authorship of I-II Timothy and Titus. Quite obviously the Pastorals were written in the name of Paul, not by him, to counteract heresies, including that of Marcion (all but mentioned by name in I Timothy 6:20), which flourished in the middle of the second century. (Cf. Rist, "Pseudepigraphic Refutations of Marcionism," *Journal of Religion*, XXII, 1942). Likewise Jude and II Peter, which uses Jude as a source, are pseudepigraphs like the Pastorals, composed in this same period to refute similar heresies in the name of the apostles. In verse 17 the writer of Jude inadvertently refers to the apostolic age as being long past, while II Peter warns against certain heretics, apparently Marcionites, who are twisting Paul's letters to their own destruction (3:16). James, largely didactic in content, is difficult to date. However its language and style definitely preclude the authorship traditionally assigned to it. As with other works mentioned above, its pseudonymous character, its late appearance in the writings of the church fathers, and its tardy acceptance in the canon indicate a second century date. See under specific books; NT., literature.

Limitations of space have prevented the presentation of the evidence for the conclusions which have been given in this summary treatment. For further information see the standard commentaries and the following introductions: J. Moffatt: *Introduction to the Literature of the New Testament*, 3rd ed. (1918); A. Jülicher: *Einleitung in das Neue Testament*, 7th ed. rev. by E. Fascher (1931); P. Feine: *Einleitung in das Neue Testament*, 8th ed. rev. by J. Behm (1936); M. S. Enslin: *Christian Beginnings* (1938); E. J. Goodspeed: *An Introduction to the New Testament* (1938); E. F. Scott: *The Literature of the New Testament* (1932); D. W. Riddle *Early Christian Life as Reflected in its Literature* (1936); M. Dibelius: *Geschichte der urchristlichen Literatur* (1926), Eng. tr., *A Fresh Approach to the New Testament and Early Christian Literature* (1936).

M.R.

Books of the Old Testament, the, in chronological order: Genesis (1200-450); Exodus (1200-450); Judges (1150-550); I-II Samuel (1000-500); Numbers (850-400); Joshua (850-350); Kings (850-350); Amos (750); Hosea (745-735); Isaiah 1-39 (740-700; 550-250); Micah (702; 500-250); Deuteronomy (630); Jeremiah (626-586); Zephaniah (625; 600-300);

Nahum (614; 300); Habakkuk (600); Job (600); Proverbs (600-200); Ezekiel (593-571); Lamentations (570-450); Leviticus (560-450); Isaiah 40-66 (546-400); Haggai (520); Zechariah 1-8 (520-518); Psalms (500-100); Obadiah (470); Malachi (460); Nehemiah (432); Ruth (400); Joel (350); Jonah (350-300); Zechariah 9-14 (300-200); Song of Songs (250); I-II Chronicles (250); Ezra (250); Daniel (164); Ecclesiastes (160); Esther (125).

Note.—All dates are of course B.C. The books earlier than 300 contain additions made later than the dates given, which in most cases are of necessity approximate. When a book contains writings of various dates, the period covered by the most important of them is indicated. The Apocrypha*date from 180 (when Ecclesiasticus was written) to the beginning of our era. R.H.P.

Booth, Ballington: See Volunteers of America.

Booth, William: See Salvation Army.

Bornhausen, Karl: (1882-) He taught first in Breslau. Now he is professor in Frankfurt a. M. A pupil of Herrmann and Troeltsch**, he aimed at a Jesus-centered Christianity, free from historical ballast, and in intimate union with the deepest roots of classical idealism.

Religion in Amerika (Giessen, 1914); *Pascal* (Basel, 1920); *Vom christlichen Sinn des Deutschen Idealismus* (Gotha, 1924); *Der christliche Aktivismus Nordamerikas in der Gegenwart* (Giessen, 1925); *Der Erlöser* (Leipzig, 1927); *Die Offenbarung* (Leipzig, 1928); *Schöpfung* (Leipzig, 1930). H.H.

Bornholmians: (from the Danish island, Bornholm) Influenced by the revivalist movement of the mid-nineteenth century in Sweden, under Hedberg and Rosenius*, followers of these men on the island of Bornholm around 1860 joined a group headed by a Bornholm preacher, P. L. Trandberg. Emphasis was on the free gift of grace independent of man's condition. Trandberg broke with state church but he gradually lost leadership Other lay preachers carried Rosenian doctrines into Denmark and Slesvig, and the name Bornholmians also used indiscriminately of revival followers. The movement gradually tended to merge with the Danish Inner Mission. C.J.B.

Bossuet, Jacques Bénigne: (1627-1704) Bishop, orator, controversialist, ascetic writer, and philosopher of history; born in Dijon, educated there by Jesuits, ordained a priest in 1652, and after seven years went to Paris and gave his whole time to preaching; in bitter controversy against Fénelon on Quietism**. L.R.W.

Bouglé, Celestin Charles Alfred: (1870-1940) Rejecting the economic, familial and racial theories as unsatisfactory in explaining the origin of the Hindu caste system, he attempted to correlate religion with a political and social system. He maintained also that a moral code can never become pure and wholly responsive to the needs of a changing society unless it grows dissociated from the special sanctions of religion.

C. C. A. Bouglé, *Essai sur le régime des castes* (Paris, 1908); *The Evolution of Values* (1926). H.H.

Bourdaloue, Louis: (1632-1704) French Jesuit and pulpit orator. His influence was due to his saintly character and to the simplicity and coherence of his sermons, which appealed to all classes. E.A.R.

bourgeoisie: A name for the middle class, originally expressing the superior or patronizing but not wholly unkind attitude of a feudal aristocracy toward the supposedly somewhat vulgar manners and pursuits of shopkeepers and business people generally. It was appropriated by the Marxian socialists** or communists to designate the employing group to which they attribute certain crafty, calculating and oppressive tactics. In this sense it carries considerable bitterness of feeling and revolutionary intentions. The term is not frequently heard in America, perhaps because of its foreign sound and because in the absence of a feudal heritage it has less significance. Americans pride themselves upon their social capillarity and still dislike class distinctions. But some accounts of the ruthlessness and buccaneering methods of our captains of industry and of the materialism and cultural deficiencies of "Main Street" suggest the same critical attitude. Cf. capitalism; proletariat.

H. W. Laidler, *A History of Socialist Thought* (1927), ch. xiv and pp. 484 ff.; W. Sombart *Quintessence of Capitalism,* trans. (1915); Cf. Charles and Mary Beard, *The Rise of American Civilization* (1927), vol. ii, ch. xx and xxv. W.B.C.

Bourignon, Mme. Antoinette: (1616-1680) French mystic of the school of Quietism.* V.F.

Bousset, Johann Franz Wilhelm: (1865-1920) He taught at the universities of Göttingen and Giessen. With Hermann Gunkel* he was a leader of the religious-historical theological group of scholars. With brilliant investigations he shed light upon the whole N.T. and the early centuries of the history of the Christian church.

Jesu Predigt im Gegensatz zum Judentum (Göttingen, 1892); *Der Antichrist in der Überlieferung des Judentums, des Neuen Testaments und der alten Kirche* (Göttingen, 1895); *Kommentar zur johannischen Apokalypse* (Göttingen, 1896, 2 ed., Göttingen, 1906); *Die Religion des Judentums im neutestamentlichen Zeitalter* (Berlin, 1903, 3 ed., by H. Gressmann, Tubingen, 1926); *Kyrios Christos. Geschichte des Christenglaubens von den Anfängen des Christentums bis auf Irenäus* (Göttingen, 1913, 2 ed. by G. Kruger und R. Bultmann, Göttingen, 1921, 4 ed., Göttingen, 1935); *Das Wesen der Religion* (Halle, 1903, 4 ed., Tübingen, 1920); *Jesus* (Halle, 1904, 4 ed., Tübingen, 1927). H.H.

Boutroux, Emile: (1845-1921) Was the eminent teacher of the history of philosophy at the *Ecole Normale Superieure* and at the *Sorbonne.* His works have proved a potent stimulus to the movement which aims at a criticism of exact science. They were a continuation of that spiritual metaphysical philosophy whose pioneers were Biran*, Ravaisson and Lachelier**. For him the basic reality is freedom. There are stages of freedom in nature. Whatever happens, happens freely, and is the expression of an eternally creative activity, of cosmic consciousness and cosmic reason. The laws of nature have no absolute existence, no iron necessity. Religion being the soul of Boutroux's philosophy, he lays stress upon the free creative power of the deity as immanent God. God is the perfect being of supreme goodness and beauty. Religion must show man that the supreme ideal is for him to realize in his own nature the idea of God. Religion, not being a matter of blind faith, it must necessarily be intellectually satisfying.

De la contingence des lois de la nature (Paris, 1874); *Pascal* (Manchester, Eng., 1902); *Science and religion in contemporary philosophy* (London, 1909); *Historical studies in philosophy* (London, 1912); *Education and ethics* (London, 1913); *Natural law in science and philosophy* (London, 1914); *Morale et religion* (Paris, 1925); Schyns, M., *La philosophie d'Emile Boutroux* (Paris, 1924). H.H.

Bouvier, Ami Auguste Oscar: (1826-1893) A Genevese theologian for whom the personality of God is a great hypothesis and which it is necessary to verify by speculation. Whenever he speaks the language of piety his explanations of God are personal. When he speaks the language of philosophical speculation his explanations of God are impersonal. In the description of the divine attributes he frequently slips into an immanentism in which the spirit of the world, of man and of God are identical. Bouvier is opposed to the traditional formulas of the doctrine of trinity. He conceives the trinity as consisting of three successive states, levels, or phases of the divine life: an expression of an evolution of God. God is an absolute personality. The personal state precedes the impersonal state in the divine order. Jesus is a relative personality, the exclusive subject of the religious realm. The Holy Spirit is impersonal. He constantly speaks of divine paternity both in terms of philosophical speculation and also of the Christian who knows, having experienced the religious realities of his profound intuitions.

Dogmatique chrétienne (Paris, 1903). H.H.

Bovet, Pierre: (1878-) He is co-founder with E. Claparede of the *Institute de Jean Jacques Rousseau* in Geneva, Switzerland. He interprets moral, social and religious forms of life as a sublimation of the fighting and sexual instincts. Moreover, the religious sentiment is an alteration of filial love, the projection upon divinity of the attributes that children confer upon those whom they cherish.

Le dieu de Platon (Geneve et Paris, 1908); *Fighting Instinct* (London, 1923); *The child's religion; a study of the development of the religious sentiment* (1928). H.H.

Bovon, Jules: (1852-1904) A native of Vaud, French Switzerland, he was professor of theology at the University of Lausanne.

God as an infinite personality is infinite in respect to the physical phenomena, and personal from the point of view of spiritual life. The divine personality is obtained by analogy with an incomplete description of human personality. As Heavenly Father God is personal, and as principle of the universe He is infinite. Bovon distinguishes two kinds of divine attributes. The metaphysical attributes picture God as infinite, beyond all our efforts to comprehend him. The personal attributes picture God as resembling us.

Dogmatique chrétienne (Lausanne, 1895). H.H.

Bowne, Borden Parker: (1847-1910) Born at Leonardville, New Jersey. After graduation from New York University in 1871, he pursued further studies in Paris, Halle, and Göttingen. Martin (of New York), Ulrici and Lotze were his chief teachers. His first book, *The Philosophy of Herbert Spencer* (1874), a penetrating critique, was published while Bowne was still a student at Halle. In 1875 he was on the editorial staff of the *Independent.* In 1876 he was called to Boston University, where he remained as professor of philosophy, and from 1888 on, as Dean of the Graduate School, until his death. He developed an independent form of Lotzean idealism, which he called Kantianized Berkeleianism, transcendental empiricism, and personalism*. He trained many teachers of philosophy and theology, and exerted a liberalizing influence on religious thought and philosophy of science.

See F. J. McConnell, *Borden Parker Bowne* (1929).
His chief works are *The Principles of Ethics* (1892), *The Theory of Thought and Knowledge* (1897), *Metaphysics* (2nd ed., 1898), *Theism* (1902), *Personalism* (1908), *Studies in Christianity* (1909), and *Kant and Spencer* (posthumous, 1912). E.S.B.

Boyle, Robert: (1627-1691) Regarding atomism as an instrument of method, not as a philosophical theory of the universe, Boyle held that the facts of human reason and intelligence, of order, beauty and adaptation in the universe at large, point to an intelligent creator and designer, who initiated motion. He was eager that others might undertake the work of science in the worshipful spirit of religion.

T. Birch, *The Works of the Honourable Robert Boyle.* 6 vols. (London, 1672); J. Meier, *Robert Boyles Naturphilosophie* (München, 1907); S. Mendelsohn, *Robert Boyle als Naturphilosoph* (Würzburg, 1902); L. T. More, *Life and Works of Robert Boyle* (1942). H.H.

Bradley, Francis Herbert: (1846-1924) Prevented by ill-health from assuming the duties of an academic career, Bradley spent the greater part of his life in seclusion as a research fellow of Merton College at Oxford, England. As an acute dialectician and objective idealist he waged war on contemporary naturalism and the British empirical and utilitarian tradition. As he had the wit to see that the Absolute cannot serve as an object of religious worship, God cannot be the all-inclusive absolute. God must be finite. As such He is not the whole; but He is limited by that in the Absolute which is external to God. Although religion needs the peace that only an Absolute can give; yet the only God religion can have is heroic, finite and unsatisfying. See neo-Hegelianism.

Appearance and Reality (London, 1914); *Essays on Truth and Reality* (Oxford, 1914); C. A. Campbell, *Scepticism and construction; Bradley's sceptical principle as the basis of constructive philosophy* (London, 1931); H. Rashdall, *The Metaphysic of F. H. Brad-*

ley (London, 1912); R. G. Ross, *Scepticism and dogma; a study in the philosophy of F. H. Bradley* (1940); T. K. Segerstedt, *Value and reality in Bradley's philosophy* (Lund, 1934). H.H.

Bradwardine, Thomas: (ca. 1300-1349) English mathematician, theologian and prelate. By a conversion experience he became a high predestinarian. His *De Causa Dei contra Pelagium* influenced Wyclif and many others. He died of plague immediately after his appointment as archbishop of Canterbury. J.T.M.

Brahmā: A personal creator god, one of the great Hindu trimurti, Brahmā, Vishnu and Shiva. He is of comparatively little importance as a cult figure. It is said that there is but one temple to him in all India. The neuter Brahman, on the other hand, of which he is the personalized form, plays a major role in philosophic Hinduism*. C.S.B.

Brāhman: Signifying only prayer or the prayer spell in the Rig-Veda, the term came to represent the power behind that spell and finally in the Upanishads it came to stand for the ultimate world-ground or reality. Brāhman is absolute, impersonal, and ultimately indescribable, "neti, neti", "not that, not that," as one of the Upanishads declares. Identified with Atman in the Brahman-Atman equation, Brahman-Atman became the monistic, or as some scholars prefer, the pantheistic world soul which informs Hinduism as a whole, and particularly its more intellectual expressions. All the gods, Brahmā the creator, Vishnu, Shiva, Krishna and even the lesser deities of popular religion may be assimilated to Brāhman as personal manifestations of a reality which is itself impersonal or super-personal.

Brāhman is also the name of the highest caste in India. (Spelled also as caste designation Brāhmin.)

See atman, also Hinduism—gods. P. Deussen, *Philosophy of the Upanishads* (1906); S. Radhakrishnan, *Indian Philosophy*, Vol. I., (1923); S. Dasgupta, *History of Indian Philosophy*, (1922, 1932, 1940). C.S.B.

Brāhmanas: Hindu priestly writings attached to the Vedas* and produced probably sometime between 800 and 600 B.C. which reflect the increasing complexity of the Vedic ritual. They contain directions for the sacrifices and purport to explain the significance of the ritual. Infinitely detailed and repetitious, they are dull and uninteresting in the extreme, yet they also contain not a little mythological lore and theological speculation. They represent a transition stage between Vedic religion and the rise of philosophic Hinduism*. C.S.B.

Brahmanaspati: Literally Lord of prayer. An abstract Vedic deity closely related both to Indra and Agni*; the apotheosis of the mysterious power that is in Brāhman*, or the prayer spell. C.S.B.

Brahmanism: See Hinduism.

Brahma Samaj: A modern eclectic reform movement in Hinduism founded by Ram Mohan Roy* in 1828, called first *Brahma Sabha*, but soon afterward changed to the *Brahma Samaj*. The founder, a wealthy Indian who had been one of the earliest students of comparative religions, was much influenced by Islam toward a monotheistic view of God, and by Christianity in its Unitarian form. Associated with him was Dwarka Nath Tagore, grandfather of the poet Rabindra Nath Tagore, while the poet's father Debendra Nath Tagore was one of its most distinguished leaders. Another prominent figure of the movement was Keshub Chunder Sen who, more deeply influenced by Christianity than the rest, formed in 1881 the Church of the New Dispensation, one of the several sects into which the society has divided. The chief emphasis of the Samaj as a whole has been on the non-idolatrous worship of but one god, the practice of congregational worship, and the furtherance of moral reform largely in accord with Christian ethics, of which it has been one of the most influential exponents in modern India. Never a numerous body, it has nevertheless, because of the quality of its membership, exercised a profound influence on Indian religion and life. According to the last census (1931) there were 5,378 members of the Society, a substantial decline from the 1921 census report of 6,388.

Related movements which were either sects of, or outgrowths of the Brahma Samaj are the Prarthana Samaj (literally prayer society) with headquarters in Bombay, the Adi Brahma Samaj, or the original Brahma Samaj, the Brahma Samaj of India (Bharatvarshiya Brahma Samaj), The New Dispensation Church, or Nava Vidhan, and the Sadharan Brahma Samaj.

Manilal C. Parekh, *The Brahma Samaj, A Short History*, Rajkot, Kathiawad, India (1929); J. N. Farquhar, *Modern Religious Movements in India* (1918). C.S.B.

Breeches Bible: The popular name given to the Geneva Bible* because of the fact that in Genesis 3:7 it says that Adam and Eve "Made themselves breeches." W.S.H.

Brentano, Franz: (1838-1917) Taught at Würzburg and Vienna, for a time (1862-66) member of a Dominican convent, later a leader of the liberal party in the Church, he finally (1873) resigned his priesthood. His first published work was on Aristotle. He became a founder of the "act" psychology which, opposed to the "content" psychology of Wundt, described all mental life as activity, experience as a way of acting rather than a body of content. A psychical act implies an object since it always points at one or "intends" it. To love is to love an object, to judge is to judge concerning an object. It is the task of psychology to discover what this pointing at objects or "intending" them means. Brentano is noted for his personal courage and honesty as well as his psychological insight. He had a great influence on his two most famous pupils, Stumpf and Husserl, and, through the latter, on the phenomenologists, especially Scheler and Hartmann. See psychology, schools of.

Chief Works: *Vom Dasein Gottes* (1868); *Psychologie vom empirischen Standpunkt* (1874); *Vom Ursprung sittlicher Erkenntnis* (1884); *Über die Zukunft der Philosophie* (1893); *Von der Klassifikation der psychischen Phänomene* (1911). J.S.B.

Brethren Church ("Progressive"): See Dunkers.

Brethren, Church of the ("Conservative"): See Dunkers.

Brethren of the Common Life: A modified monastic order without vows which was founded during the fourteenth century by Gerard Groote* and Florentius Radewijns. It consisted of both Brotherhoods and Sisterhoods and it included both lay and clerical members. The principal aim was to secure a revival of practical personal religion and its members were deeply devoted to the cause of education. See Albert Hyma, *The Christian Renaissance* (1924). See Imitation of Christ.
W.S.H.

Brethren in Christ: See River Brethren.

Brethren, German Baptist: See Dunkers.

Brethren, United: See United Brethren.

Bretschneider, Karl Gottlieb: (1776-1848) He was general church superintendent in Gotha. Many-sidedly productive, he wrote a systematic survey on the dogmatics of German Protestantism which is today still indispensable. Notwithstanding the all-determining concept of revelation, he never transcended the orthodox intellectualism of the Enlightenment.

Handbuch der Dogmatik der evangelisch-lutherischen Kirche, 2 vols. (Leipzig, 1814, 4 ed., Leipzig, 1838); *Systematische Entwickelung aller in der Dogmatik vorkommenden Begriffe nach den symbolischen Schriften der evangelisch-lutherischen und reformierten Kirche und den wichtigsten dogmatischen Lehrbüchern ihrer Theologen* (Leipzig, 1804, 4 ed., Leipzig, 1841).
H.H.

Breviary: (Lat., *breviarium,* abridgement or compendium) The book containing the psalms, hymns, lections, prayers, etc., of the Divine Office*, according to the Roman rite. Usually printed in four volumes for the four seasons of the year. Prior to the 12th and 13th centuries the material now included in the Breviary was contained in several books arranged for the various persons participating in the Choir Office. See Hours.
P.V.N.

Brewster, William: (c. 1560-1644, known as "Elder Brewster") Was the leader of the Pilgrims who came over in the Mayflower in 1620. He was born at Scrooby in Nottinghamshire and studied for a time at Cambridge. About 1587 he settled in Scrooby Manor House where he held the position of "post" entertaining travellers, attending to the mails, etc. It was in this house that the Separatists* held their services. Brewster removed to Holland in 1608 and engaged in the publication of puritan* literature. In 1619 he secured a patent from the Virginia Company for a tract of land in America. He was the leader and Ruling Elder of the Plymouth Colony till his death and was their Teacher and Preacher till 1629; but owing to his lack of ordination did not administer the sacrament of the Lord's Supper. His *Memoirs of Elder Brewster* are a valuable source. See Congregationalism.

Dictionary of Am. Biography v. 3, p 29; Schaff-Herzog, *Encyclopedia of Religious Knowledge,* v. 2, p 264.
F.T.P.

Bridel, Philippe: (1852-) Professor of theology at the University of Lausanne, Switzerland. The theses of his thought are: The notion of a personal God represents above all a reaction against the spiritual dangers of pantheism. The human terms as applied to God are inadequate and relative. Divine paternity is in fact the essential character of God, the attribute by which we are able to learn something of His nature. Rather than philosophy, so attractive to the magic of present-day gnosticism, Bridel prefers the revelation of the Heavenly Father in Jesus Christ.

L'humanité et son chef, essais d'apologétique et de morale chrétiennes (Lausanne, 1925); Clerc, C., *Portrait de Philippe Bridel* (Lausanne, 1938).
H.H.

Bridget, Saint: See Birgitta, Saint.

Bridget, Saint: (452-523) A daughter of a prince of Ulster, Ireland. She spent her life in seclusion, in a cell on a site believed to be the modern Kildare. Her remains finally placed beside bodies of St. Patrick and St. Columba. In England and Scotland her legends are associated with the name of St. Bride. Her feast day is February 1.
C.J.B.

Bridgewater Treatises: Eight treatises "on the power, wisdom, and goodness of God, as manifested in the Creation," published in the years 1833-36 with funds provided by the will of the eighth earl of Bridgewater.
W.S.H.

brief: (Latin, *breve,* short) A bull is a papal or royal document addressed to some group, the bull or *bulla* being its leaden seal; the Brief is a simpler and less formal letter. See bulls, papal.
L.R.W.

Briggs, Charles Augustus: (1841-1913) Semitics scholar and author of numerous monographs and books upon the Old Testament. Founder and American editor of *International Theological Library* and *International Critical Commentary.* Defender of the theory of the Virgin Birth of Jesus. Professor at the Union Theological Seminary, New York City, 1874-1913. Tried for heresy by the General Assembly of the Presbyterian Church, 1892, and suspended from the Presbyterian ministry, he was ordained by the Protestant Episcopal Church, 1898. See A. C. McGiffert and H. P. Smith.
C.H.M.

Brigittines: Nuns of the Order of St. Savior, founded by St. Bridget* of Sweden in 1344. The Order is contemplative, and observes strict enclosure. The nuns devote themselves to prayer for the souls in Purgatory*, and engage in literary work of a religious and devotional nature.
C.V.

Brihaspati: Literally "lord of speech". One of the abstract deities which appear in late Vedic* literature. Closely related to Agni*.
C.S.B.

Brinsers: See River Brethren.

British Council of Churches: Formed in 1942, this federation unites the major church bodies of Great Britain and Ireland (except Roman Catholic) for conference and cooperation. E.R.H.

British Moralists: British Moralists of the 18th century, mark an important step in the history of Ethics*. They confined themselves almost entirely to empirical and rational methods, and thereby made ethics an autonomous discipline, no longer subordinate to revealed religion and theology. These latter they did not usually attack. Important names are: Anthony Ashley Cooper, third Earl of Shaftesbury (usually known as Shaftesbury) 1671-1713; Francis Hutcheson, 1694-1746; Joseph Butler, 1692-1752; William Paley, 1743-1805; Richard Price, 1723-1791; William Wollaston, 1659-1724; David Hume, 1711-1776; Adam Smith, 1723-1790.

Cf. *British Moralists,* edited by L. A. Selby-Bigge, 2 vols. (1897). W.K.W.

Broad Churchmen: The term was first used about 1850 to describe those Anglicans for whom comprehensiveness was the outstanding characteristic of the Church of England*. It is a simplification of the 18th century term Latitudinarian*, and the tradition goes back to the desire of the Cambridge Platonists* and others to get away from the harshness of 17th century controversies. Erasmus' stay in England enables Broad Churchmen to claim a pre-Reformation precedent as well. For some Latitudinarians liberal principles were a cloak for indifference, often combined with an unedifying struggle for preferment. Others did good service in defending the main principles of theism and Christian ethics, though less interested in positive theology; most of them desired the Church to be as broadly national as possible, paying little attention to its specific traditions. Thomas Arnold (1795-1842), headmaster of Rugby, brought a zeal for personal righteousness into liberal churchmanship as well as into English education. The Broad Churchmen of the 1850's were largely pupils or admirers of Arnold; the movement rose to prominence in the Church when A. P. Stanley became Dean of Westminster (1864-1881) and A. C. Tait Archbishop of Canterbury (1868-1881). Such men added to the tolerant Broad Church spirit something of the Catholic sense of the historic and corporate and the Evangelical emphasis on personal religion. Broad Churchmanship was attacked in the condemnation of *Essays and Reviews* by Convocation, but won a victory in the relaxation of the subscription required of the clergy in 1865. An analogous movement in America was in origin largely a reaction against Evangelical Calvinism (Latitudinarianism had influenced the Proposed American Prayer Book of 1785, but did not survive); the preaching of Phillips Brooks (died 1893) gave it great influence in the Episcopal Church. In England Broad Churchmanship was further advanced by the Biblical and historical scholars of the Cambridge School (Lightfoot, Westcott, and Hort). Since about 1900 it has been in part replaced by a definite Modernism, in part fused with the comprehensive central churchmanship of modern Anglicanism.

N. Sykes, *Church and State in England in the XVIII Century* (1934); L. E. Binns, *Religion in the Victorian Era* (1936). E.R.H.

Broadus, John A.: (1827-1895) Baptist minister, New Testament scholar, president Louisville Theological Seminary, delivered Lyman Beecher Lectures at Yale. C.H.M.

Brook Farm (Mass.) community: See communistic settlements, secular; social gospel.

Brooke, Stopford Augustus: (1832-1916) Writer and preacher, born in County Donegal, Ireland, priest of the Church of England and a chaplain to the Queen; left the Church of England in 1880 and became an independent churchman of Unitarian sympathies. Author of books and plays, including a collection of Irish poetry with introduction. W.N.P.

Brorson, Hans Adolf: (1694-1764) Brorson, one of Denmark's three great hymnodists (see Kingo, Grundtvig). Ordained 1722, he served as parish priest and after 1741 as bishop. Especially successful as writer of Christmas hymns, all his verse is marked by pietistic sincerity and simple beauty, as well as unusual singability. C.J.B.

Bross Foundation, The: Established by William Bross in 1879 at the Lake Forest College, Lake Forest, Illinois, this memorial lectureship was founded "to call out the best efforts of the highest talent and the ripest scholarship of the world" and to reward more generously those who make significant contributions to Christian thought. The donor's plan was to produce a continuing series of books by means of competitions and by publication of lectures at Lake Forest. Since its inception the Foundation has presented eleven series of lectures ranging over a wide variety of subjects. The capital sum of $40,000 was completed in 1890. Among the distinctive volumes associated with the name of this Foundation are:

J. A. Thomson, *The Bible of Nature* (1907); Josiah Royce, *Sources of Religious Insight* (1911); D. C. Macintosh, *The Reasonableness of Christianity* (1925); and H. F. Rall, *Christianity* (1941). (Data from the Office of the Acting President of Lake Forest College.) V.F.

Brothers of Christ: See Christadelphians.

Brothers of the Common Life: See Brethren of the Common Life.

Browne, Robert (1550-1633) and Brownism: Brown was born at Tolethorpe near Stamford, England, and was educated at Corpus Christi College, Cambridge. He gathered a dissenting congregation at Norwich and for his denunciation of Episcopacy was imprisoned in 1581 and escaped to Middleburg in Holland the following year. Here he produced his famous *Reformation without Tarrying for Any* and his *Free Christians* in which he set forth his theory of Congregational Independency. (See Independency) He recanted his Separatist* views, was ordained to the Anglican priesthood in 1591 and was rector of Ashchurch-cum-Thorpe for the remaining forty-two years of his life. His changed views were set forth in his *Reproof of Certain Schismatical Persons and their Doctrine concerning the Teaching and Hearing of the Word of God,* (1587-1588).

Brown considered a church to be a body of believers united by a voluntary covenant, choosing its own officers and owning allegiance to Christ only. Each church is absolutely independent in government, discipline and the choice of its officers. This system is strongly opposed to the union of church and state and contains in germ at least, the Congregational principle of fellowship. See Congregationalism.

W. Walker, *A History of the Congregational Churches in the U. S.* (1894); G. G. Atkins & F. L. Fagley, *History of American Congregationalism* (1942) Schaff - Herzog, *Encyclopedia of Religious Knowledge,* v. 2, p. 279. F.T.P.

Browne, Sir Thomas: (1605-1682) English prose writer. By profession a physician, Browne brought to his meditations on religion an innate mysticism qualified by the eclecticism of studies at Oxford, Montpellier, Padua, and Leyden. His most notable work, *Religio Medici* (1643), is at once a confession of faith and a collection of curiously compounded opinions. Among his other writings are *Pseudodoxia Epidemica* (1646), better known as *Vulgar Errors,* and *Urn Burial* (1658). L.W.C.

brownie: See fairy.

Browning, Robert: (1812-1899) English poet and dramatist. Religious in training (English Dissent) and conviction, Robert Browning became one of the most discerning and vital modern interpreters of Christianity through the medium of poetry. In "Cleon," "Imperante Augusto," and "A Strange Epistle" he made vivid and real the Jesus of history; while in "Christmas Eve," "Easter Day" and "A Death in the Desert" he gave a lucid and profound interpretation of the spiritual meaning of incarnation and revelation.

The reality and power of a future life received fresh and impressive affirmation in "Saul," "Evelyn Hope" and "Prospice," and the too far obsolescent doctrine of providence* gained a unique and suggestive revalescence in "Ferishtah's Fancies." Browning was one of the first to grasp the spiritual meaning in evolution, and in "Paracelsus" and other poems he gave to the law of development a strikingly humanistic and Christian construction.

Browning is *par excellence* the poet of the development of the soul—which appeared to him to be the one thing of supreme interest. In "Rabbi Ben Ezra," "The Ring and the Book," "One Word More," the dramas, Bishop Blougram and many other poems, his portraiture of character is remarkable for sympathetic understanding and deft delineation.

His Christian optimism and confidence in spiritual values as expressed in "Pippa Passes," "Abt Vogler," "The Grammarian's Funeral," "Love Among the Ruins," "Childe Roland to the Dark Tower Came" are ardent and appealing and should prove greatly enheartening in rebuilding a shattered civilization. J.W.B.

Bruederhof (Huterite) communities: See communistic settlements, religious; Mennonites.

Brunner, Emil: Protestant theologian. Born 1889, Winterthur, Switzerland. Since 1924 professor of Systematic Theology in Zurich, Switzerland. 1938-39 guest professor, Princeton Theological Seminary, Princeton, N. J. The clearest and most systematic thinker of the school of Dialectical Theology. (See Dialectic.) Opposed to Schleiermacher and 'Erlebnis' theology as much as to theological intellectualism his theology places the person of Jesus Christ into its center and interprets his work in classical terms. But theology to Brunner is subservient to living religion. He simplifies orthodoxy by eliminating all topics that in his view have no bearing on spiritual life (Virgin Birth, most of the N.T. miracle tales). Moreover, unlike his more aggressive friends he shows a tendency to conciliate theology and the modern mind. His system of ethics is an interesting combination of Kant's criticism with the realism of the Bible and modern Lutheranism. He is an independent supporter of the Oxford Group Movement*. See Barth, Karl.

Works: *Die Mystik und das Wort* (Tübingen, 1924, 2nd ed. 1928); (Criticism of Schleiermacher); *Der Mittler* (Tübingen, 1927), Engl. tr. *The Mediator: A study of the central doctrine of the Christian faith* (London, 1934); *Religions philosophie evangelischer Theologie* (München, 1927), Engl. tr. *The Philosophy of Religion from the Standpoint of Protestant Theology* (London, 1937); *The Theology of Crisis* (1929); *The Word and the World* (London, 1931); *Das Gebot und die Ordnungen* (Tübingen, 1932), Engl. tr. *The Divine Imperative: A study in Christian ethics* (1937); *Natur und Gnade. Zum Gespräch mit Karl Barth* (Tübingen, 1934, 2nd ed. 1935); *Our Faith* (1936); *God and Man: Four essays on the nature of personality* (London, 1936); *The Church and the Oxford Group* (1937); *Der Mensch im Widerspruch* (1937), Engl. tr. *Man in Revolt: A Christian Anthropology* (1939); *Wahrheit als Begegnung* (Berlin, 1938); *Offenbarung und Vernunft. Die Lehre von der christlichen Glaubenserkenntnis* (Zürich, 1942). O.A.P.

Bruno, Giordano: (1548-1600) Neapolitan insurgent who began his career a Dominican, was forced by his ardent and imaginative nature, by his adherence to Copernican theory, and by his anti-Aristotelianism, into constant friction with the Church. He was finally burned at the stake, convinced that the Church should not dictate truth.

Essentially an inconsistent rationalist, Bruno changed from pantheism to a deterministic system in which graded animate monads were given some independence from the "informing" Source. The transcendent God is known by faith, but the immanent is reflected in myriad animate unities which constitute reality. Bruno especially influenced Spinoza, Leibniz, Descartes, and Schelling.

Della Causa (1584); *Del Infinito* (1584); *Spaccio della Bestia Trionfante* (1584). P.A.B.

Brunschvicg, Léon: (1869-) He is the leading champion of the French school of critical idealism.

Reality is for him a part of the mind's inner development, a plastic product of the spirit. To know is to impose on objectivity the forms of subjectivity. Man's true progress is towards the form of inwardness. Science in adding nothing to naive experience, transforms it. Philosophy in adding nothing to the increase of human knowledge only reflects about it. Brunschvicg develops a rational humanism, stressing the immanent conception of God. He rejects an anthropomorphism which projects the human soul into things and God Himself.

La modalité du judgement (Paris, 1894); *Les étapes de la philosophie mathématique* (Paris, 1912); *L'idéalisme contemporain* (Paris, 1905); *Nature et liberté* (Paris, 1921); *L'expérience humaine et la causalité physique* (Paris, 1923); *Le progrés de la conscience dans la philosophie occidentale* (Paris, 1927).

Spinoza 2 ed. (Paris, 1906); *Oeuvres de Blaise Pascal* 11 vols. (Paris, 1903-1914); *Spinoza et ses contemporains* 3 ed. (Paris, 1923); *Le génie de Pascal* (Paris, 1924); *Pascal* (Paris, 1932); "De la vraie et de la fausse conversions", *Revue de Metaphysique et de Morale* (Paris, 1930, 1931, 1932); *De la Connaisance de soi* (Paris, 1931).

Pierre Boutroux et Félix Gazier were coeditors with Brunschvicg of the *Oeuvres de Blaise Pascal*.

H.H.

Bucer, Martin: (1491-1551) Protestant Reformer. While minister at Strasbourg he earnestly sought for a formula to reconcile Protestant views of the Lord's Supper. He became a professor at Cambridge, and was influential in English theological life. See Tetrapolitan Confession.

G.R.C.

Buchanan, George: (1506-1582) The Scottish poet and scholar who in his revolutionary *De jure regni apud Scotos* (1579) placed central stress upon the right to resist. Outspoken in justifying tyrannicide*, he argued that power is derived from the community and must therefore be exercised in accordance with the law of the community.

J. W. Allen, *A History of Political Thought in the Sixteenth Century* (London, 1928); J. N. Figgis, "Political Thought in the Sixteenth Century" *Cambridge Modern History*, vol. III (1904).

H.H.

Buchmanism: See Oxford Group.

Budde, Karl: (1850-1935) Professor of O.T. for thirty-five years at Marburg; scholar, commentator, Orientalist, theologian, and prolific writer; one of the great masters of biblical studies. R.E.W.

Buddha, Gotama: See Buddhist Terminology.

Buddhahood: See Buddhist Terminology.

Buddha-Mind School: See Meditation School.

W.T.C.

Buddhism: See Buddhist Terminology.

BUDDHIST TERMINOLOGY:

Abhidharmakośa School: *Idem*: Kośa School*.

Amita: (Skr. immeasurable, Chin. A-mi-t'o, Jap. Amida) According to the smaller *Sukhāvatī-vyūha Sutra,* Amita is so named because "His light is boundless, penetrating without impediment the ten quarters," and because "His life and the life of his people is boundless in countless length of time." Thus he is Amitābha, the Buddha of Infinite Light (space), and also Amitāyus, the Buddha of Infinite Life (time), corresponding respectively to the Law-body and the Enjoyment-body of the Buddha, and representing Buddha's Perfect Enlightenment and ideal Buddahood. In the Mystical School, he is also the King of Sweet Dew (Amṛta), the Transformation-body.

Buddhist scriptures call this most popular deity by many names. The larger *Sukhāvatī-vyūha* gives thirteen. Various schools interpret him differently. In the T'ien-t'ai and Mystical Schools**, he is one of the five Wisdom-Buddhas. As such, he is the Buddha of the West in the Mystical School, called Amitāyus in the Realm of "Matrix Repository" and Amitābha in the Realm of "Diamond Element," thus in a sense identical with the Great Sun Buddha in the center. In other schools, he is considered the ninth son of Mahābhijñā Jñanabhidhu, the Great Buddha of Supreme Penetration and Wisdom. Avalokiteśvara is often regarded as one of his incarnations. He appears in various combinations in the Buddhist Triad*, usually in the center, with Avalokiteśvara, the embodiment of mercy, on the left, and Mahasthamprata, the embodiment of wisdom, on the right. He is usually in the standing position, on the lotus throne, with long ears symbolizing wisdom, a white curl on the forehead indicating his manifest teaching, and a long arm to guide and welcome people. In the group of five, Kshitigarbha and Nāgārjuna are added.

Specifically Amita is the object of devotion in the Pure Land School*, who, as the Lord of the Western Quarters, welcomes all faithful to the Pure Land (*Sukhāvatī*) where they will eventually become Buddhas. When he was a bodhisattva he made forty-eight vows, promising not to attain Buddhahood until all people are saved. His Pure Land, fully described in the *Sukhāvatī* texts, is to many devout Buddhists the final abode of life, although strictly speaking it is but a stage towards Nirvāṇa.

arahaṁ (Pāli), arhat (Skr.), lohan (Chin.), arakan (Jap.): One "who has removed worldly attachments," or "who is worthy to receive alms." The Worthy One or saint of Hīnayāna, who has attained self-salvation instead of universal salvation sought by the bodhisativa* of Mahāyāna. There are two, three, six, seven, and nine kinds of arhat, according to various ways of moral and religious endeavour, and there are groups of sixteen, eighteen, and 500 supposedly appointed by the Buddha to save the world. To attain arhatship, a follower goes through the Four Paths and enjoys the Four Fruits: 1) Entering the Stream (*sotāpanna*). He is free from the first three of the Ten Fetters, namely, the delusion of self, doubt, and the belief in the efficacy of ceremonials, and has joined the movement of the holy ones, never to be born in the Realms of Hells, Animals, and "Hungry ghosts." 2) The Once-Returner (*sakadāgāmin*). He is rid of two additional Fetters of the delusion of the sense and ill-will, and will return to be born on earth only once more. 3) The Non-Returner (*anāgāmin*). He is free from the Fetters of attachment to life on earth (Realm of Form) and the desire for future life (Formless Realm), and will never be born again in any realm of desires. 4) The arhat. He is free from the last three Fetters of pride, self-righteousness, and ignorance, and will never suffer rebirth. See vehicles.

Asaṅga: (c. 410-500?) Founder of the Buddhist Idealistic School* in India. See Vasubandhu.

Aśoka: Indian king who united India and reigned c. 240 B.C. Converted to Buddhism, he spread Buddhism over India, made it known from the borders of China to Macedonia and Egypt, took many religious tours himself throughout India, probably sent his son to promulgate Buddhism in Ceylon, and erected many Rock-Edicts to teach Buddhist morality. He was chiefly interested in morality. Because of this he retained his respect for non-Buddhist religions.

Aśvaghosha: (c. 100 A.D.) a) A learned Brahmin converted to Buddhism, the author of *Buddha-carita,* Eng. tr. by S. Beal, *The Fo-Sho-Hing-Tsan-King, a Life of Buddha* (1879), *Mahāyāna-śraddhotpada,* Eng. tr. by D. T. Suzuki, *Aśvoghosha's Discourses or the Awakening of Faith in the Mahāyāna* (1900); and by T. Richard & Yang Wen-hwui, *The Awakening of Faith in the Mahāyāna Doctrine* (1894), and other works. He accepted the doctrines of ālaya-consciousness and thusness*, and laid the foundation of Mahāyāna. His authorship of the *Mahayana-sraddhotpāda* is not accepted by some scholars. b) Names of several other Indian teachers.

Avalokiteśvara: (Skr.) The most widely revered bodhisattva* in the Far East, especially in the T'ien-t'ai, Mystical, and Meditation (Zen)** Schools. He is the embodiment of mercy and compassion. He goes through much suffering, assumes various forms of a Buddha, an arhat, and even an animal, and goes everywhere, including heavens and hells, to save all beings who hear his name or bear it in mind, to free them from pain and evil passions, to bestow on them offsprings and other blessings, and to lead them to the Pure Land of Amita*. According to the 25th chapter of the *Lotus Sūtra* (Chin. trans. 406 A.D.) which is entirely devoted to him, he appears in thirty-three transformations to suit his audience in teaching the Doctrine.

"Avalokiteśvara," taken as *avalokita-īśvara,* means either "the Lord of *avalokita* (to look at)" or "the Lord who is *avalokita,*" and is generally interpreted as the Lord Who Is Seen, but may denote the Lord of What We See (the present world) or the Lord Who Looks. Hsüan-tsang (596-664) correctly understood its meaning when he translated it as Kuan-tzŭ-tsai (see-self-exist). The earlier translation as Kwan-yin (Chin.) or Kwannon (Jap.) meaning "seeing the sound," from *avalokitaśvara,* is definitely wrong.

Avalokiteśvara was worshipped in India from the third to the twelfth century, became popular in China in the eighth. In Tibet, the Dalai Lāma is believed to be his incarnation. As he possesses many aspects of Hindu gods, especially Śiva, he is probably a development of Indian *bhakti* (devotion). Efforts have been made, however, to connect him with Sumana of Ceylon, Istar of Babylon, Apollo Patareus of Asia Minor, Sun worship, and many others. Certainly, he attained eminence when Buddha worship was extended to bodhisattva worship. Significantly he is the attendant of Amita.

The feminine form of Avalokiteśvara (Goddess of Mercy) is peculiar to China and Japan, and did not appear in China until the eleventh century. In China he became identified with Miao-shan, who, according to the vulgar story invented by an ignorant monk in the Yüan dynasty (1280-1368), was a young (*miao*) and virtuous (*shan*) girl who vowed to serve the Buddha, fled to a nunnery when her father forced her to marry, was killed in a temple which was burned by her father's agents, became an immortal. Her father was made blind as a punishment for his evil deeds. She plucked her own eyes to restore the sight of her father. Because of this, she became the Goddess of Mercy.

Avalokiteśvara is also confused with the Goddess of the Sea. P'ut'o has been regarded as the port where she landed from India or as the birth place of Miao-shan, evidently a confusion of Potaraka in Northern India, the mythic residing place of Avalokiteśvara.

No educated Buddhist takes these stories seriously. In Buddhism, Avalokiteśvara appears in 6, 8, 33, and 37 forms, the most standard representation in temples, especially in those of the Mystical School, being the Six Transformations. These are: 1) the Holy Avalokiteśvara (Jap. Sho Kwannon), the embodiment of Great Kindness and savior of the Realm of "Hungry Ghosts," the original and the most Buddhist of all, generally in feminine form, with Amita's image on the head; 2) the Thousand-armed Avalokiteśvara, the embodiment of Great Mercy and savior of the Realm of Hells, the thousand hands symbolizing universality, each of which having an eye and some implement to see and save all; 3) the Horse-headed Avalokiteśvara, the embodiment of Courage and savior of the Realm of Animals; 4) the Eleven-faced Avalokiteśvara, the embodiment of Universal Illumination and savior of the Realm of *Asuras;* 5) Chandī, in feminine form, the embodiment of Heroism and savior of the Realm of Men; and 6) Avalokiteśvara with a Wishing Wheel, embodiment of Far-reaching Penetration and saviour of the Realm of Heavenly Beings. Other popular representations are the white robed Kwan-yin, the Kwan-yin Crossing the Sea, the Willow-leafed Kwan-yin, the Fish-basket Kwan-yin, the Child-bestowing Kwan-yin, and the Bamboo Kwan-yin.

Buddhist Terminology

Avalokiteśvara usually holds a lotus, symbol of the life-giving principle, a dish or vase to collect morning dew symbolic of life and purity, a willow branch to sprinkle the dew over all, the *Lotus Sūtra,* or a roll of prayer. He occupies an important place in the Buddhist Triad*. Special days of worship are the 19th day of the second, sixth and ninth months. See Lāmaism.

Avatansaka: (Skr. "Wreath" School) See Hua-yen School.

Bodhidharma: (d. between 534 & 537) A native of South India (of Persia according to the *Loyang Chia-lan Chi*), the 28th patriarch of the Meditation School in India, who arrived in Nan Yüeh (present Canton area), China, in the Liu Sung period, 420-479 A.D. (instead of 520 as generally believed), and became the First Chinese Patriarch. In answer to the Chinese Emperor, he said that the pious deeds of the Emperor "have no merit," that the "Noble Truths have no nobility," and that he "did not know the one who was facing the Emperor." He advocated the doctrine that Buddha-mind or Buddha-nature is pure unity, devoid of all specific character, and identical with the True State, Thusness, or Nirvāṇa*. His way of meditation involved 1) "direct intuition" of truth, an intuition as direct as "facing the wall," and 2) religious conduct. According to tradition, he went to the Wu-t'ai ("five terraces") Mountain where for nine years he "faced a wall" and meditated. Finally he gave a robe and a bowl as the sign of transmission to Hui-k'o and recommended the *Laṅkāvatāra Sūtra* (the four-part version) as the essence of Buddhist teaching. See Meditation School.

bodhisattva: (Skr. being of enlightenment, Pāli bodhisatta, Chin. *p'u sa,* Jap. *bosatsu*) A Buddha-to-be, a "being of enlightenment" who has attained the *pāramitās* or perfections, has gone through the ten stages* and is therefore qualified to enter nirvāna* and become a Buddha* but prefers to remain a bodhisattva in order to work for the salvation of all beings. He takes many vows, among which are these famous ten: 1-6) To abstain from violating the discipline, from being haughty, from anger, from envy, from jealousy, and from attachment to material things; 7) to practice the four acceptances, charity, loving words, benefiting deeds, and working together in order to help others, and to abide in non-attachment; 8) to free all beings from sufferings; 9) to protest against the violation of discipline; and 10) to keep the true law. He is distinguished by the tremendous amount of suffering and toil which he goes through, and by his great compassion and heroism in working for the salvation of all people. Because of these he is revered, and even worshiped in temples. He is the ideal of Mahāyāna in contrast to the arhat (See araham) of Hīnayāna who works for his own salvation. Popular bodhisattvas are Avalokiteśvara, Mañjuśri, Samantabhadra, and Mahāsthāma. In China and Japan the term is also applied to non-Buddhist deities. See incarnations.

Bön: Indigenous, pre-Buddhist, animistic, devil-dancing, and Shamanist religion of Tibet, a debased form of Tantrism, with two sects, Black and White, strong in Northeastern Tibet. It has been to a great extent assimilated into un-reformed Lāmaism*. See Ling Chos.

Buddha, Gotama: It is difficult to distinguish facts from fiction about a man who was one of the greatest ever to have lived on this earth and who has influenced the life and thought of more than half the human race. Because of the nobility of his character, the vastness of his vision, the depth of his compassion, and the profundity of his teachings, idealization of his life was inevitable. Imaginative tales and outright myths crept into the most primitive account of him. Even the recognized facts of this account are not entirely reliable, for the Pāli Canon in which this account is contained was 200 years later than the events it described, and it represents only one of the several schools that sprang up in the meantime. Some scholars, like Przuluski, even reject the account as primitive.

But no scholar except Senart and one or two others would discard the Pāli record entirely. Even Kern, who regarded the story of the Buddha as a sun-myth, did not rule out the historicity of the hero. It is safe to go at least as far as Mrs. Rhys Davids and accept the essential parts of the Pāli document. We are reasonably sure that the Buddha was born of the warrior caste, son of Suddhodana ("having pure rice"), a rājā, or chief, of the Śakya tribe whose principal town was Kapilavastu, about 100 miles north of Benares in North India. Whether he was born when his mother (called Māyā?) was on a journey is not certain. He was called Siddhattha (Skr. Siddhārtha, "he who has accomplished his aim"), Sākyamuni ("sage of the Śākya tribe"), and Gotama (Skr. Gautama) which was his family name, and later honored as the Buddha (see Buddhahood) or the Enlightened One, Bhagavat or the Lord, and Tathāgata or He Who Has Thus Come or He Who Has Thus Gone. His mother died when he was young, but not seven days after his birth, as ordinarily believed, and he was raised by his aunt Pajāpatī. Presumably, at nineteen he married his cousin Yasodharā. They had a son, Rāhula.

In his youth, he was seriously thinking over the problems and meanings of life. He decided to seek the counsel of the wandering wise men who moved over all India at the time. According to Mrs. Davids, he had no idea of forsaking his home, but intended to return after he had gone as far as Vesāli. Tradition has dramatized this episode as the "great renunciation," and says that he, at the age of twenty-nine, first saw the sights of sickness, old age, and death, then resolved to sacrifice his home together with all its comforts and luxuries, and finally took a last glimpse of his young son in the arms of his sleeping mother and fled in the darkness of the night.

He met Alāra Kālama in Rajagaha (in Vesāli, Mrs. Davids said), who recommended to him the dualistic philosophy of Sānkhya, and later Uddaka Rāmaputta, who urged asceticism. Not satisfied with these ways of life, he decided to become a Wanderer himself and kept on searching, striving, and meditating. In time his five companions scattered (or deserted him). After six years of continuous and strenuous effort, he finally found the true Path. Tradition has also turned this "Great Enlightenment" into a romance, saying that the first philosopher taught the Buddha the doctrine of nothingness and the second taught him the doctrine of neither consciousness nor non-consciousness, that he attained nirvāṇa*, i.e., Enlightenment, under a *bo* tree or tree of Wisdom, at sunset, after conquering the temptation of Māra, and that afterwards he fasted for seven times seven days.

Desirous of sharing the newly discovered Truth with others, especially his five former companions, he went to the Deer Park near Benares and preached his first "sermon" in which he neatly stated his fundamental principles (see Buddhism). These were accepted by the five ascetics, and in three months, some fifty more people followed him. Twelve years after he left home, his father sent for him. He met his father outside the city, in accordance with a Wanderer's etiquette, but went begging inside the city the next day, met his parents, wife, and son, who later adopted his Way of a mendicant's life. For forty-five years he worked hard to spread his doctrine, travelling up and down the Valley of the Ganges. In the twentieth year his cousin Ānanda joined him and eventually became his most favored pupil. Altogether there were 1,000 or 1,200 disciples. They lived as mendicants, gradually forming an Order with established rules governing their activities. Women were admitted to the Order though not from the beginning. During all these years, the Buddha always paid close attention to the layman, for, as Mrs. Davids emphasized, his mission was not to tell people to renounce the world, but to live in the world as a great brotherhood according to the Eightfold Noble Path (see Buddhism).

Scholars do not agree on the dates of the Buddha. His birthday is variously given at 568 B.C. (T. W. Rhys Davids), 563 B.C. (E. J. Thomas), 566 B.C. (Takakusu), etc. The date of his death is variously given as 483 B.C. (the Theravāda School), 477 B.C. (Cunningham, Max Müller, Bühler), 483 B.C. (Geiger), 486 B.C. (Takakusu), c. 480 B.C. (Oldenburg), 386 B.C. (Ui), etc. Records of the Theravāda School give 534 B.C. as the year of the Buddha's departure from home, and 528 B.C. as the year of his Enlightenment.

Most scholars, however, agree that the Buddha died at the age of eighty, after eating some pork when he was a guest of Chunda the smith. To these facts, tradition has added that he prophesied his own Nirvāṇa, that he entered into four trances, and that he died between two *sāla* trees outside of Kusinārā (identified with Kasia in the Gorakhpur District, North India).

As he arrived at Nirvāṇa, he said, "Now then, monks, I address you: subject to decay are all compound things. Strive with earnestness." Or, according to Mrs. Davids, "The Way in the worlds:—that is my message to you! Make it known! Let it never be forgotten! The Way in the worlds . . . ." See miracles in non Christian religions.

H. Oldenberg, *Buddha, His Life, His Doctrine, His Order* (1881), tr. by W. Hoey (1882); E. J. Thomas, *The Life of Buddha as Legend and History* (1927); C. A. F. Rhys Davids, *Gotama the Man* (1928).

Buddhaghosa: Born in central India, he went to Ceylon in "about 430 A.D.," translated many Buddhist works from Sinhalese into Pāli, wrote *Visuddhi-magga*, Eng. tr. by P. M. Tin, *The Path of Purity* (1923-1931) and other works, and became a great systematizer of early Buddhism. Almost all the Pāli commentaries existent are ascribed to him.

Buddhahood: The term "buddha" (from *budh*) is interpreted in the two senses of awareness and awakening, the former denoting perfect wisdom and the latter denoting self-awakening, awakening others, and the perfect unity of awakening and ultimate truth. Thus a Buddha is an Enlightened One, who possesses Supreme, Correct, Universal, and Perfect Wisdom (*anuttara-samyak-sambodhi*). He has the Ten Powers, including those of omniscience and abiding release in this life. He has the thirty-two characteristic marks of the Great Man, such as hands reaching below the knees, golden-color body, a ten-foot halo around him, a white *ūrṇā* or curl between the eyebrows symbolizing wisdom, etc., as we see in Buddha images. He has 108 names, including the Ten Titles of Tathāgāta, Arhat, The World-Honored One, etc. He is supramundane, omnipotent, and "immensely benevolent" and "immensely merciful."

The Buddha appears from time to time as the need arises. The *Dialogues* of Gotama Buddha* mentioned six Past Buddhas; other parts of the Pāli Canon add twenty-eight more. Gotama himself prophesied a Future Buddha, Maitreya*. Hīnayāna admits only one Buddha at a time. Mahāyāna, on the other hand, accepts a multitude of contemporaneous Buddhas each with a world of his own. They exist as one or all of from one to ten "bodies," the most common being one of the Three Bodies or *trikāya**, under the different names of Śākyamuni, Amitābha, Maitreya, Locana, Vairocana, etc. They are, however, but various aspects of the same Eternal, Supreme, Primal Buddha (Ādi-Buddha), who appears in numerous transformations to preach the Law which is his "mother," and to save all beings who are his "sons." To most Mahāyāna schools, all beings possess the same nature and essence as the Buddha and therefore everyone except the *icchantika* in some cases—can become Buddha, and so do right in this world. Some schools make him identical with the universe, thusness* or the True State.

Buddhism: I. *Teachings of Gotama Buddha.* Buddhism, the system of Gotama Buddha, arose as a protest against the animistic superstition, the Upanishadic* pantheism, the ethics of asceticism and hedonism, the philosophies of eternalism and annihilationism, and above all, the *sat-cit-ānanda,* or Being-Knowledge-Joy ideal of Brahmanism* in India in the sixth century B.C. In opposition to these, the Buddha* taught the Four Noble Truths.

The first of the Noble Truths (*ārya-satyāni*) is the Truth of Suffering. Existence is pain, according to the Buddha, because it is irrevocably bound to *sansāra* or the cycle of births and deaths. Such an idea was not peculiar to the Buddha; it was also the conviction of the Sāṅkhya and Yoga Schools**. Mrs. Rhys Davids maintained that the Buddha never taught the doctrine of suffering (*dukkha*); instead, he taught happiness (*sukha*). There is no doubt that the Buddha taught the way to bliss, and bliss is to be attained by the removal of suffering.

The second Noble Truth is the Truth of the Cause of Suffering. This cause is craving, which is in turn due to ignorance, as explained by the twelvefold Chain of Causation (*pratiya-samutpāda*): Ignorance is the cause of the aggregates; the aggregates are the causes of consciousness; consciousness is the cause of name and form or body and mind; name and form are the causes of the six sense-organs; the six sense-organs are the causes of contact; contact is the cause of sensation; sensation is the cause of craving; craving is the cause of grasping; grasping is the cause of coming into existence; coming into existence is the cause of birth; and birth is the cause of old age and death. This chain bears a striking resemblance to the Sāṅkhya categories, but it may (said Keith) or may not (said Thomas) have been borrowed from Sāṅkhya. At any rate, the Buddha was not interested in the deduction of categories; he was wholly concerned with the practical problem of removing the cause of suffering. To this end he put forth the doctrines of Impermanence (Pāli *anicca,* Skr. *anitya*) and Non-ego (Pāli *anatta,* Skr. *anātman*), in direct contrast with the Brahman ideals of Being (*sat*) and Self (*ātman*). The Buddha declared that things, as compounds, are always in the processes of Production, Stagnation, Deterioration, and Extinction, and are therefore impermanent. Neither is the self permanent, because it is but an aggregate (*skandha*) of elements. This does not mean, as Mrs. Davids has emphatically pointed out, the denial of the empirical self, but a refutation of the permanent, abiding personal identity. These doctrines suggest no nihilism; they were intended to reveal the true nature of existence, which to the Buddha was dynamic Becoming instead of static Being or Non-being.

The third Noble Truth is the Truth of the Cessation of Suffering. When suffering is destroyed, nirvāṅa*, negatively the extinction of passions and positively the state of bliss, is attained. One then becomes an arhat or the Worthy One, either in this life or after death.

The fourth Noble Truth is the Truth of the Way (*mārga*) to remove Suffering. This involves a comprehensive system of moral cultivation, but the fundamental way is the Noble Eightfold Path (*ārya-mārga*): right views (of the Four Noble Truths), right intention (to renounce sensual pleasure, to bear no malice, to do no harm, etc.), right speech, right action (such as love, joy, abstinence from immorality), right livelihood, right effort (to avoid evil state and produce good state of mind through the practice of Morality, Meditation, and Wisdom), right mindfulness (to be alert with regard to sensations, ideas, etc.), and right concentration. These form the standard of our threefold karma (action-energy) or conduct, speech, and thought. In reduced form, the Eightfold Path becomes the Threefold Learning (*śikshā*), i.e., Discipline or Morality, Meditation, and Wisdom. Morality (*śīla*) demands right volition, right mental states, and a highly developed moral consciousness (see Disciplinary School). Meditation (*samādhi*) as in all Indian systems, means concentration. That is to say that through the meditation on the forty objects such as the ten universals, the ten impurities, the four sublime states, etc., and through the experience of the four trances, one can attain both "calmness" and "insight." This is Wisdom (*prajñā*), the insight into the Supreme Truth.

The most important element of these teachings is the Middle Path (*madhyamā-pratipad*) between the extremes of passions and asceticism, the Way to realize the Four Noble Truths which the Buddha elucidated in his first sermon at Benares. Throughout the entire history of Buddhism, the Middle Path has remained the central concept, although its interpretation varies with different schools. To the Buddha, it was a *way* of life, a sensible, moderate, comprehensive, and practical system of ethics. He called the Truths "noble" (*ārya*) because he regarded nobility as a moral, and not a racial (Aryan), quality. His Order was established on moral principles, a Brotherhood without distinction of castes. Karma*, which to the Brahmins was hardly more than a mechanical, superstitious, fatalistic operation of retribution, was transformed by the Buddha to mean moral energy with which a man may exercise his free will, break the Chain of Causation, chart the course of his future, and produce the meritorious fruits of his own conduct. The Buddha was primarily concerned with a good life. This spirit is characteristic of all his *Dialogues.* He urged the removal of the Ten Fetters, the Four Intoxications (bodily passions, becoming, delusions, and ignorance), the Five Hindrances (hankering after worldly advantages, the corruptions arising out of the wish to injure, torpor of mind, fretfulness and worry, and wavering of mind), etc. He taught the novice the Ten Precepts (abstinence from taking life, from theft, from impurity or sensuality, from lying and harsh speech and foolish talk, from intoxication, from irregular eating, from dancing and similar entertainments, from garlands and ornaments, from high and broad couches, and from accepting gifts of gold and silver) as the minimum requirements of a mendicant's moral life. For a fuller life, whether for the monk or layman, he taught virtue, kindness, love, compassion, non-injury in the broadest sense of the term, liberality, moderation, temperance, consideracy, the Golden Rule, the mutual duty of human relationships, etc. A good life and a moral life was the goal of his preaching. He shunned metaphysical speculation and condemned ritualistic practices as non-conducive to wholesome living. His system was neither religion nor philosophy.

II. *Religious and Philosophical Development.* Nevertheless, the potentiality of his Way was too great to remain purely an ethical system. It was inevitable that his followers attempted to place it on a philosophical foundation and to give it the emotional content centralizing on their teacher. Consequently, even before the death of the Buddha, signs of both religious and philosophical developments were already evident. Whether or not we accept the legend that his disciples made an image of him for the purpose of offering veneration during his absence, we cannot doubt the fact that they regarded him as supernatural, called him the Bhagavat (the Lord), Tathāgata (One Who Has Thus Come), etc., and believed in his omniscience. Their reverence for his relics was definitely religious. By the first century A.D., the original, simple cult of the worship of relics had developed to be a cult of image worship. Before this, a series of Councils* had already formulated the Doctrine, regulated the discipline, and fixed the Scripture (see Canon, Buddhist). The missionary efforts of King Aśoka, c. 240 B.C. had spread Buddhism from the Ganges Valley over all India and Ceylon. As the religion developed, it took over the rituals and deities of Hinduism*, and, in the fifth century A.D., adopted the magic and spells of Tantrism*. Two hundred years later, its rapid decline began. By the time of the Mohammedan invasion in the twelfth century, it practically ceased to be a religion of any potency. Today there are only 233,000 uninfluential Buddhists in India. (See India, Religions of.)

While Buddhism developed along religious lines, its philosophy also gradually unfolded. The tendency to grow along diverse directions was apparent in the First Council right after the Buddha's death. At the Second Council (c. 383 B.C.), the liberal Mahāsaṅghikas or the "Great Community" broke away from the conservative Theravādas (Sthaviravādas) or Elders. In time each of the two branches split further into more schools, so that by 200 B.C. there were eighteen or twenty including the two mother schools. The Southern or Pāli tradition and the Northern or Sanskrit tradition differ in the number and names of these schools and the reasons for their division.

The most orthodox, the most powerful, and the most lasting school was the realistic Sarvāstivāda*, which regarded all dharmas (elements) as real but the self as unreal.

In the first century A.D., a new movement, which can be traced to the progressive Mahāsaṅghikas, got under way. It was given impetus by Aśvaghosha*, c. 100 A.D. who laid the foundation with his doctrine of ālaya-consciousness and thusness*. This movement was later labeled Mahāyāna, or the Great Vehicle (see vehicles), in contradistinction to Hīnayāna, or the Small Vehicle, the name given to the eighteen earlier schools. In the second century, the Mādhyamika School of Nāgārjuna*, c. 100-200 A.D., came into prominence with the interpretation of the Middle Path as the Ultimate Void which is "devoid" of all specific characters (see Middle Doctrine School). Four hundred years later, another great system appeared, namely, the Yogācāra School* of Asaṅga (c. 410-500?) and his brother Vasubandhu* (c. 420-500?), which regarded the Middle Path as Thusness or the Absolute, and considered consciousness alone as real (see Idealistic School). Thus, according to Stcherbatsky, there were three successive movements of Buddhism in the first 1,500 years of its history—Hīnayāna pluralistic realism (the denial of the self) from 500 B.C. to the beginning of the Christian era, Mahāyāna Negativism (the denial of all elements) of the Mādhyamika School from the first to the fifth century, and Mahāyāna Idealism (the denial of the external world) of the Yogācāra School from 500 to 1000 A.D. Hīnayāna and Mahāyana co-existed until the former declined in the fifth century. Mādhyamika and Yogācāra, the two wings of Mahayana, rivaled each other for a long time but eventually both disappeared from India.

This decline was inevitable. Buddhism was too deeply confounded with Hinduism and Tantrism. Its central emphasis on the Order deprived it of the popular support of the mass. Its philosophical progress had reached the point where new soil was necessary for further growth. Long before this, Buddhism had begun to shift to China. The final collapse in India made the transplantation complete.

III. *Buddhism in China.* Just when Buddhism first reached China is uncertain, but undoubtedly years, perhaps centuries, before 67 A.D., the traditional date of introduction, it had penetrated China. Records show that Buddhist sūtras existed in China in the reign of Ai-ti (6-1 B.C.). At any rate, by the first century A.D., Buddhism had already spread from the Loyang area to South and East China. It existed as a system of worship, charms and spells, and similar practices, side by side with the Taoist* religion.

Soon great masters successively arrived from India; important scriptures were gradually translated; and Chinese talents quickly exhibited themselves. Disciplinary rules, the practice of meditation, and the philosophy of the Void as embodied in the *Prajñaparāmitā* literature were popular, especially with the Taoists who cherished Lao Tsŭ's ideal of Non-being. Then one doctrine after another was introduced by such great Buddhists as Kumārajīva*, 344-413 A.D., and Hsüantsang*, 596-664, until there were ten schools. These were: Kośa, Satyasiddhi, Vinaya, Mādhyamika, Yogācara, Meditation School, Mystical School, Hua-yen, T'ien-t'ai, and Pure Land**. The history and doctrines of these schools are briefly outlined elsewhere in this volume. Suffice it here to note three significant points about them, namely, the development of Mahāyāna in China, the Chinese transformation of Buddhism, and its changes in Japan.

IV. *Growth of Mahāyāna in China.* Although among the ten schools, three—Abhidharmakośa, Satyasiddhi, and Vinaya—were Hīnayāna, the story of Chinese Buddhism has been essentially that of Mahāyāna. The three Hīnayana schools neither lasted long nor underwent any development. Mādhyamika, on the other hand, was elaborated and completed by Chi-tsang*, 549-623, and Yogācāra by Hsüan-tsang and his pupil K'uei-chi, 632-682. Although the Meditation and Mystical doctrines were essentially Indian in spirit, they were largely systematized in China by Bodhidharma* (d. between 534 & 537) and Subhakarasimha, etc., respectively. Hua-yen, T'ien-t'ai, and Pure Land were purely Chinese products.

Along with these developments, new doctrines were promulgated. The distinctive features of Mahāyāna—idealism, negativism, thusness, void*, ālaya-consciousness*, Twofold Truth, Three Vehicles, paramitās, Transcendental Wisdom, fourfold nirvāṇa*, the universality of Buddha-nature, salvation for all, salvation by faith, vows, abrupt enlightenment, the transfer of merits, expediency (*upayā*), mass for the dead (*ullambana*), the emphasis on positive ethical ideals such as compassion, charity, benefiting others, loving words, effort, tolerance (see bodhisattva; stages), the absolute prohibition of meat-eating, etc.,—either originated or were perfected on Chinese soil. Even the Buddha and bodhisattva** doctrines, which germinated in Hīnayāna, so vastly expanded in Mahāyāna and developed so many new aspects such as paradise, *trikāya*, triad, and *triratna***, that they can no longer be considered Hinayanistic. From these it is clear that the difference between Hīnayāna and Mahāyana is not limited to the distinction that Hīnayāna, or Pāli Buddhism, is the Small Vehicle because it entertains the ideals of arhatship and salvation for the self, and that Mahāyāna, or Sanskrit Buddhism, is the Great Vehicle because it seeks the goal of bodhisattvahood and salvation for all. Many doctrinal and practical variations separate the two Vehicles. Even the directions of their geographical expansion have been different. Hīnayāna went southward to Ceylon, Indo-China, Siam, and Java, where it flourishes today, whereas Mahāyāna went eastward to China, Korea, and thence to Japan, and northward to Tibet and Mongolia (see Lāmaism).

V. *Chinese transformation of Buddhism.* As to the Chinese transformation of Buddhism, it is sufficient to say that in its Mahāyāna development, Buddhism almost completely changed its complexion in China, becoming less Indian and more Chinese. The development of the ten schools shows the Chinese character even more clearly. None of the realistic Kośa (Chü-shê) which held that "all exists," the nihilistic Satyasiddhi (Chêng-shih) which insisted that "both the dharmas and the self are unreal," or the formalistic Vinaya (Lü) had a long history in China. Also, neither the idealistic Yogācāra (Fa-hsiang) which reduced everything to "consciousness only" nor the negativistic Mādhyamika (San-lun) which regarded reality as "Void" flourished in China for long. Even the esoteric Mystical (Chên-yen) and the intuitional Meditation (Ch'an) Schools, which were formed and developed in China, did not last. They were either too extreme or too mystical for the Chinese. From the earliest days of Buddhism in China to the present, the Chinese have clung to the more practical and more moderate aspects of the system. As early as the fourth century A.D., before any Buddhist school became a concerted movement in China, Tao-an promoted, and Hui-yüan* 334-416, completed the T'ien-t'ai system and its doctrines of the identity of the One and the Many, the harmony of phenomenon and noumenon, the universality of Buddha-nature, and salvation for all. In the fifth century Tao-shêng founded the Pure Land (Ch'ing-t'u) movement on the simple idea of salvation by faith. These movements were supported by the philosophy of the Hua-yen School based on the theory of "universal causation of the Elements of the Principle" and the ideal of "grand harmony without obstacle" or All-in-One and One-in-All. Today the T'ien-t'ai and the Pure Land Schools are still the strongest in China, the two combining to a great extent into one movement. Of the 738,000 monks and nuns, 267,000 temples, some 3,000,000 "home disciples," and an unknown number of Buddha-worshipers in China proper today, it is safe to say that a great majority belong to these two Schools. (See Chinese Religions.)

VI. *Buddhism in Japan.* All the ten schools were introduced into Japan. Due to the efforts of Prince Shotoku (573-621) and such Great Masters as Kobo Daishi, 774-835 and Dengyo Daishi (767-822), Buddhism prospered. In Japan the Pure Land School developed into four sects, Jodo, Shin, Yūzunembutsu, and Ji, and Tendai** (T'ien-t'ai) gave rise to the Nichiren School*. Among the specially Japanese features of Buddhism, we may mention its identification with the national life, especially in the case of the extremely nationalistic Nichiren, its mysticism as indicated by the popularity of the Mystical (Shingon) and Meditation (Zen) Schools (which have almost entirely disappeared from China), its modern reforms including the sanction of marriage for priests in most schools, and its vitality in general. Truly Japan is the land of Buddhism, where there are 42,249,229 adherents, 71,326 temples and 7,753 churches, where most Buddhist schools still flourish, where Buddhist literature has been best preserved, where Buddhist study is most active, and where many world-renowned scholars have emerged. See cosmogonies; cycles of time; Japanese Religions; sacred literatures; temples, Far Eastern; transmigration.

E. J. Thomas, *Early Buddhist Scriptures* (1935); Aśvaghosha. *The Awakening of Faith in the Mahayana* (1900), tr. by D. T. Suzuki; *Saddharmapundarika, or the Lotus of the True Law* (1884), tr. by H. Kern; Th. Stcherbatsky, *The Central Conception of Buddhism and the Meaning of the Word "Dharma"* (1923); E. J. Thomas, *The History of*

Buddhist Thought (1933); D. T. Suzuki, *Studies in the Lankavatara Sutra* (1930); C. Eliot, *Hinduism and Buddhism*, 3 vols. (1921); J. B. Pratt, *The Pilgrimage of Buddhism and a Buddhist Pilgrimage* (1928); B. L. Suzuki, *Mahayana Buddhism* (1938).

Canon, Buddhist: The Buddhist Canon, called *Tripiṭaka* (Skr.) or *Tipiṭaka* (Pāli), literally "three baskets (*piṭaka*), contains 1) *sūtras* (Pāli *sutta*) or the discourses of the Buddha, 2) *vinaya* (Pāli & Skr.) or rules, and 3) *śāstras* (*Abhidharma*) or treatises. The Pāli version is accepted by Hīnāyāna. The Sanskrit version, which differs considerably from the Pāli *Tipitaka*, is followed by Mahāyāna and has been rendered into Chinese, Tibetan, Mongolian, and Manchurian. Of all the editions, from the first Chinese edition of 968 A.D. on, the most complete one is the *Taishō Shinshu Daizokyo*, or the Taisho edition of the *Tripitaka* in Chinese, ed. by J. Takakusu, K. Watanabe, & G. Ono, containing 13,520 *chüans* or parts in 100 volumes of 1,000 pages each (Tokyo, 1924). The Tibetan Canon (*Kanjur* or *Ka-gyur*) comprises the *Tripiṭaka* and some Tantric works in seven parts totaling 108 volumes, and is supplemented by a collection of commentaries called *Tanjur* (or *Tan-gyur*), in 225 volumes, altogether making 5102 *chüans*. This Tibetan version was rendered into Mongolian, and its *Kanjur* portion was translated into Manchurian. Only a very small portion of either the Pāli *Tipiṭaka* or the Sanskrit *Tripiṭaka* has been translated into Western languages. See Councils, Buddhist.

Councils, Buddhist: The First Council, of 500 monks, was held in Rājagaha immediately after the death of the Buddha (c. 483 B.C.) and lasted for seven months. Presided over by the disciple Mahākassapa (Mahākaśyapa), the Council heard Ānanda recite the *Dhamma* (doctrines) and Upāli the *Vinaya* (rules), made a collection of scriptures, and fixed the number of Buddha's discourses. The Second Council of 700 was held 100 years later (c. 383 B.C.) at Vesāli to uphold the original discipline and condemn the ten illegal practices which had spread among the Vesāli monks. This Council lasted for eighteen months. Simultaneously a liberal group of 10,000, called the Mahāsaṅghikas, held a rival council outside the city in opposition to the orthodox Elders or Theravādas. The third Council, participated by 1,000, took place during King Aśoka's reign (c. 240 B.C.) at Pātaliputta and lasted for nine months. At this Council, the *Abhidhamma* literature (collection of treatises) was added to the *Dhamma* and *Vinaya*, completing the "three baskets" of the Canon, or *Tripiṭaka*. Thus the Canon was fixed, though not written down until later.

All schools accept the first two Councils. Although the third is not mentioned in Pāli works or in the works of the Sarvastivādins, most scholars do not doubt it. Details about the three Councils, however, greatly differ among the various records, which were not written until several centuries later. The tradition of Northern Buddhism adds a Fourth Council in Kashmīr in c. 70 A.D., at which time the Mahāyāna doctrine was promulgated and commentaries on the three divisions of the Canon were compiled, using Sanskrit for the first time instead of Pāli. See Buddhism.

Chi-tsang: (549-623) Great patriarch and systematizer of the Middle Doctrine School* of Buddhism, honored as the Great Master of Chia-hsiang, and author of many important works, including the standard commentaries of the three *Treatises* of the School.

Disciplinary School: (Pāli & Skr. Vinaya; Chin. Lü; Jap. Ritsu) The school is called Disciplinary because it is based on the *Vinaya* section of the Canon (see Canon, Buddhist), the Four-Division School because it follows particularly the *Rules in Four Divisions*, and the Nan-shan or South Mountain School because it was elaborated and completed in China by Tao-hsüan, 596-667 A.D., in that mountain.

Vinaya aims at the discipline of action, speech, and thought. It includes "prohibitive precepts," 250 for monks and 348 for nuns, and "precepts for performance" or rules governing ordination, convocations, etc. There are four aspects of discipline: first, the "rules of discipline" laid down by the Buddha, secondly the "substance of discipline" or the moral consciousness aroused by taking vows in ordination, which is ever active in dictating meritorious deeds, thirdly the "action of discipline" expressed in action, speech, and thought, and fourthly the "character of discipline" which should be so good as to be exemplary. The earlier Four-Division tradition, following the "void of dharma-nature" doctrine that neither dharmas (elements) nor the ego are existent, conceived the substance of discipline as neither the material element nor mind, while the South Mountain School, following the Idealistic doctrine that consciousness alone is real, interpreted it as seeds in the ālaya-consciousness.

The School belongs to the Hīnayāna* and hardly exists in China as an independent sect. It has 23 temples and 58,000 adherents in Japan where it is called Shin Ritsu (New Disciplinary School) since it was reformed by Eison, 1201-1290, who put it on the basis of "self-vow discipline," i.e., a vow taken privately instead of at ordination is valid.

Forty-two Chapter Sūtra: Subject of intensive research by both Chinese and Occidental scholars in recent years, the *Sūtra*, according to latest findings, is not a translation of any Sanskrit text but a translation of selected fragments of various Hīnayāna* scriptures. It was first quoted in 166 A.D. There were two Chinese translations, one made in the Han dynasty (206 B.C.-220 A.D.), which was lost after the Liu Sung period (420-479), the other by Chih-ch'ien of the Wu era (222-280 A.D.). This latter translation has gone through many editions, each time undergoing some changes and accumulating Mahāyāna ideas and Taoist** concepts. The edition containing a commentary by Emperor Chên-tsung (998-1022) is the oldest, probably going back to the Southern and Northern Dynasties (420-589). The popularly accepted edition is much later, and has evidently been greatly altered by Buddhists of the Meditation School*. Eng. tr. by S. Beal, "Sūtra of Forty-two Sections," in his *Catena of Buddhist Scriptures from the Chinese* (1871); and by D. T. Suzuki, "The Sūtra of Forty-two Chapters," in Soyen Shaku's *Sermons of a Buddhist Abbot* (1906).

Hinayāna: See Buddhism.

Hsüan-tsang: (596-664) Founder of the Idealistic School* of Buddhism in China and the most important figure in the Mahāyāna* development in the Far East. Ordained at thirteen, Hsüan-tsang early became familiar with Buddhist philosophy. He traveled extensively to study under many masters, but was not satisfied with their explanation and the translations they used. In 629, accompanied by a small group, he secretly set out on a long, hazardous trip to India against governmental order. He overcame many insuperable hardships on his way, and finally arrived at the homeland of Buddhism. He studied under, and deliberated with, all great Indian philosophers of the time in practically all the great Indian universities. Thus he not only acquired a firsthand knowledge of Indian philosophies and religions, both Buddhist and non-Buddhist, but also became the most important historian of the thought and conditions of India in the seventh century. He visited Ceylon and returned to China by way of Persia in 646 after seventeen years of study and travel, bringing with him seven images of the Buddha and 657 Buddhist works, mostly new to China. His return was the occasion of a warm Imperial welcome and marked a new epoch of Buddhist history. Upon Imperial command, he resided, taught, and worked in the Tz'ŭ-ên Monastery. Here he introduced many new trends of Buddhist thought, translated 75 basic Buddhist texts totaling 1,335 chapters, which have been accepted as standard, and produced many outstanding Buddhist scholars. See Buddhism.

Hua-yen School: (Skr. Avataṅsaka, Chin. Hua-yen, Jap. Kegon, all meaning "Wreath" or "Flowery Splendor") This Mahāyāna* school, as far as we know, never existed in India. Its name is derived from the title of its chief scripture, the *Avataṅsaka Sūtra.* One chapter of the *Sūtra* was translated separately as the *Gandāvyūha* and another as the *Daśa-bhumika.* With the translation of the latter in 512 A.D., the Ti-lun or Dasabhumi School came into being in China. This was replaced by Hua-yen which was nominally founded by Tu-shun (557-640). The real founder of Hua-yen, however, was its patriarch Fa-tsang (643-712), the Great Master Hsien-shou, who completed the system and after whom the School is also called the Hsien-shou School.

The main tenet of the Avataṅsaka doctrine is the Universal Causation by the *Dharma-dhātu.* Literally the Realm of the Law, *Dharmadhātu* means on the one hand Ultimate Truth, i.e., the Realm of Principle, and on the other the universe itself, i.e., the Realm of All Elements. Universal Causation is the mutual causation of all dharmas (elements) which are inter-related, inter-dependent, and inter-originating. The universe is conceived to be fourfold: the World of Facts, the World of Principle, the World of Principle Realized in Facts, and the World of the Harmony of these Facts. This harmony is achieved through "inter-identification" and "inter-penetration" of all facts and principles, resulting in the Universe of One-Truth.

To explain the possibility of such world of Harmony, the School advances the "Ten Profound Propositions": 1) All things are co-existent, corresponding to one another. 2) The intension and extension of one thing involve those of others without any obstacle. 3) The One and the Many are mutually inclusive. 4) All things are identical with one another. 5) The hidden and the manifested mutually perfect each other. 6) All minute and abstruse things penetrate one another. 7) All things reflect one another. 8) Truth is manifested in facts and facts are the source of Enlightenment. 9) The past, present, and future are inter-penetrating. 10) All things are manifestations and transformations of the Mind.

The Ten Profound Propositions are based on the Doctrine of the Sixfold Character of Dharmas to the effect that each dharma has the six characteristics of Universality, Speciality, Similarity, Diversity, Integration, and Differentiation. These characteristics make possible the universal inter-relations as well as the individuality of all things, thus making them both One and Many, and resulting in a world of "Perfect Harmony without Obstacle." Such world of Harmony is called the Realm of the Lotus-store or the World Illumined by the Buddha of Perfect Enlightenment, in which all beings will be carried to Buddhahood through the One vehicle*.

The Hua-yen doctrine was brought to Japan by Shinsho (Shên-hsiang) in 736. The School has now 35 temples and 23,000 adherents in Japan but very few in China.

Hui-yüan: (334-416 A.D.) Established the White Lotus Society in the Lu Mountain, advocated the doctrine that nirvāṅa* and the nature of dharmas (elements) are unchangeable, taught "thinking of Buddha" which involves meditation as well as repetition of Buddha's name, wrote "Monks Need Have No Respect For Kings" in which he stressed the indestructibility of the spirit and the transcending character of the Ultimate which is above life and death, and being and non-being, and founded the Pure Land School* on pietism originally advocated by his teacher Tao-an.

Idealistic School, Buddhist: One of the two wings of Mahāyāna Buddhism* in India, the Yogācāra (Self-concentration) School was founded by Asaṅga (c. 410-500 A.D.?), author of the *Yogācāra-bhūmi Śastra* and the verses of both the *Mahāyāna-samparigrapha* and the *Madhyanta-vi-*

bhaṅga. The Yogācāra doctrine was elaborated by his brother Vasubandhu* who wrote the *Viṁśātikā*, Eng. tr. by C. H. Hamilton, *Wei Shih Er Shih Lun* (1938), the *Triṁśikā*, Fr. tr. by S. Lévi, *Matériaux pour l'etude du système vijñaptimātra* (1932), and the commentaries on both the *Mahāyāna-saṁparigrapha*, partial Fr. tr. by E. Lamotte, *La somme du Grand Véhicule* (1907; 1911) and the *Madhyānta-vibhaṅga*, Ch. I tr. by Stcherbatsky, *Discourse on the Doctrine of the Middle and the Extreme* (1937). With the translation of the *Mahāyāna-saṁparigrapha* by Paramārtha (499-569), the Shê-lun (Saṁparigrapha) School came into existence. Eventually it was absorbed by the Fa-hsiang (Dharma-Character, Jap. Hosso) School founded by Hsüan-tsang* (596-664). Hsüan-tsang visited India, examined all Buddhist philosophies, returned to summarize, select, and translate the important works of ten great idealists, especially Dharmapāla (439-507), in his *Ch'êng Wei-shih Lun*, Fr. tr. by L. de La Vallée Poussin, *Vijñapti-mātrāta-siddhi, le siddhie de Hiuentsang* (1928-1929), in which he developed and completed the Yogācāra system in China. His pupil K'uei-chi (Ki) (632-682), profound author of standard treatises, carried the idealistic doctrine to new heights. As the basis of these Chinese works, the Idealistic School in China and Japan follows six Sanskrit sūtras, of which the *Sandhi-nirmacana Sutra*, Fr. tr. by E. Lamotte, *Explication du mystère* (1936) is the fundamental, and eleven Indian treatises, of which the *Yogācāra-bhūmi* is regarded as primary. The important tenets of the major works of the School, however, are contained in Hsüan-tsang's *Ch'êng Wei-shih Lun* (Completion Mere-Ideation Treatise), which gave rise to another Chinese name Wei-shih (Skr. Vijñānavāda, Jap. Yuishiki). In English, Fa-hsiang or Wei-shih is often called the Mere-Ideation or Consciousness-only School.

The School reduces existence to 100 dharmas (elements) in five divisions, somewhat similar to those of the Kośa School*. Instead of regarding the mind as one dharma, however, the School analyzes it into eight consciousnesses (*vijñāna*), namely, the five sense-consciousnesses, the sixth consciousness (*Mano-vijñāna*) or the sense-center which forms conceptions, the seventh consciousness or the mind-consciousness (*Manas*) which wills and reasons on a self-centered basis, and the eighth consciousness which is called the *ālaya-vijñāna* (*citta*) or "store-consciousness." The last consciousness is so-called because it stores the "seeds" or effects of good and evil deeds which exist from time immemorial and become the energy to produce manifestations.

The ideation-store consciousness is the "first transformation" of ideation, forever in the state of instantaneous change, the seeds perpetually influencing or "perfuming" external manifestations and manifestations perpetually "perfuming" seeds. These three elements—seeds, manifestations, and perfuming—keep on evolving and influencing one another eternally, acting at the same time as cause and effect. The mind-consciousness is the "second transformation," which depends on the ideation-store consciousness but in turn conditions it. Its nature and characteristics consist of intellection, and it is always accompanied by the evils of self-interest. The first six consciousnesses are the "third transformation," which consist of the discrimination of the objective world. Thus the self and all the dharmas are instantaneously issued from the ālaya-consciousness and restored to it at once, thereby constituting our life and the world.

Each of the consciousnesses has four "functional aspects," the objective aspect, the subjective aspect, the self-witnessing aspect in which the mind sees and acknowledges its subjectivity, and the rewitnessing aspect in which the mind witnesses itself once more. The objective aspect originates from the subjective aspect, which alone is the fundamental function of consciousness. In other words, all dharmas of the objective world are products of ideation.

With regard to the nature of dharmas, the School classifies them into three species. Those of the "character of sole imagination" have only "false existence." Those of the "character of dependence" have "temporary existence," as things produced by causal combination enjoy neither self-nature nor permanent reality. Only those of the "character of ultimate reality" have "true existence." This ultimate nature is thusness*, the true noumenon transcending all specific characters. It is the Middle Path which rises above both Reality and the Void. It is Nirvāṇa.

In order to reach this state, spiritual development through the ten stages (see stages) and the attainment of the Ten *Pāramitās* are prerequisite. These will lead to Perfect Wisdom, or the Four-fold Wisdom of the Buddha. In other words, the first five consciousnesses will become the "wisdom of action," the sixth consciousness will become the "wisdom of insight," the mind consciousness will become the "wisdom of equanimity", and the ālaya consciousness will become the "wisdom of magnificent mirror."

Not all people can reach Nirvāṇa, however. Of the Five Species of men, the three species corresponding to the three vehicles* and the "indeterminate species" can attain Nirvāṇa, while those having passions but no Buddha-nature, called *icchantika*, are beyond salvation.

The Fa-hsiang School in China began to decline in the eighth century and disappeared several hundred years afterwards. Recently Buddhist scholars have made an attempt to revive the idealistic philosophy. The Fa-hsiang Doctrine was taken into Japan by Dosho (628-700), a Japanese priest who studied under Hsüan-tsang. Today it is a very small institution, having only 42 Hosso temples and 19,000 adherents. See nirvāṇa.

A. B. Keith, *Buddhist Philosophy in India and Ceylon* (1923); E. J. Thomas, *The History of Buddhist Thought* (1933).

Ji(Shu): (Jap. Time Sect) A branch of the Pure Land School* of Buddhism in Japan, founded by Ippen in 1276 on the doctrine that reciting the hymns of Zendo (d. 681, Chin. Shan-tao) six times a day will lead to the Western Heaven.

karma, karman: (Skr.) Action, action-influence, deed. It is the dynamic manifestation of mental and physical energy in deeds, speech, or thought, inevitably producing the good, evil, or neutral effect, either immediately or in the future, according as the action is good, evil, or indifferent. The effect itself becomes the cause of further effect, making the self, in the case of an individual, a process of unceasing transformation from one life to another in the wheel* of transmigration*, and the world, in the case of the universe, a process of perpetual becoming. Thus karma is 1) action-energy, past or present, latent or manifest, actual or potential; 2) a self-operating law of causality and retribution; 3) the entity of the individual or the universe carried along in the series of the Wheel of Life (*saṁsāra**).

Kobo Daishi: (Jap. The Great Master Kobo, 774-835) Was in China from 805 to 806 as pupil of Hui-kuo, returned to Japan to found the Shingon School (see Mystical School, Buddhist) in the East Temple (Toji). He was the foremost Japanese calligrapher, originator of popular education, and possibly the inventor of the Japanese alphabet (in the form of the "Iroha" poem).

Kosa (Abhidharmakosa) School: (Chin. Chü-shê, Jap. Kusha) Buddhist Hīnayāna Realism, an outgrowth of the Sautrāntika branch of Sarvāstivāda (All-Exists School). Named after Vasubandhu's *Abhidharma-kośa Śāstra* ("The Store of the Higher Dharma or Law"), the Realistic School in China followed Hsüan-tsang's* translation (651-654) and replaced the Pi-t'an School which had promulgated the Sarvāstivāda* doctrine. The Kośa teaching was first brought to Japan by Chitsū and Chitatsu in 658 and again by Gembo in 735. In neither China nor Japan did it exist for more than a few centuries.

The chief tenets of Kośa are summed up in two propositions: "The reality of the three periods of time and the entity of all dharmas or elements" and "The unreality of the self and the reality of all dharmas." These dharmas are reduced to 75 and classified under two categories, the Created and the Non-created. The Non-created Dharmas or elements of negative becoming form one group and include the three dharmas of Space, "Extinction through Intellectual Power," and "Extinction without a Productive Cause." The Created Dharmas fall into four groups: 1) Form (*rūpa*, material elements)—the five sense-organs, the five sense-objects, and "form-with-no-manifestation" (11 dharmas); 2) Mind (*citta*); 3) Concomitant Mental Functions—46 dharmas in six subdivisions; and 4) Elements which are Neither Substantial Forms Nor Mental Functions—14 dharmas.

All Created Elements co-exist in the actual world, and they exist only momentarily. They, the mind included, are regarded as objects, since the School is concerned with objects only and does not recognize any subject. To the Buddhist realists, the self is nothing but the fivefold Aggregate of Form, Sensation, Conception, Volition, and Consciousness. As such it has no reality.

To explain the momentariness of dharmas, Kośa offers the theory of Six Causes. These are: 1) the Active Cause or the effective factor in the production of a dharma, 2) the Co-existent Cause such as the Four Great Elements (Earth, Water, Wind, Fire) always working together, 3) the Similar-species Cause or a cause helping other causes of its kind, 4) the Concomitant Cause like associated causes of mind and mental conditions, 5) the Universally Prevalent Cause or human ignorance, and 6) the Cause Ripening in a Different Life or the cause that produces the effect. In addition to these, there are the Four Conditions or Secondary Causes, namely, the Cause Condition or the chief cause, the Continuous Condition which immediately follows a preceding condition, the Objective Condition which has an object or environment as a concurring cause, and the Upheaving Condition which brings all the abiding causes to a culmination. Since these Causes and Conditions are always operating and producing new situations, a dharma remains in a state only for one single moment. The actual world is real and it is real as a dynamic becoming.

Kwan-yin: (Chin.) *Idem*: Avalokiteśvara*.

Kumārajīva: (343 or 344-413 A.D.) An Indian born in Kucha, founder of the Middle Doctrine School* in China, who arrived in 401 A.D. and translated some 300 stitched volumes of important Buddhist texts into Chinese, including the basic *Treatises* of his School, the fundamental *Satyasiddhi Śāstra* of the Satyasiddhi School*, and the widely followed *Lotus Sūtra** of the T'ien-t'ai School*. While he translated, he elucidated the various doctrines of the texts to the 500 or 800 who assisted him, and to the thousands of scholars who gathered around him from all parts of China. Aside from rejecting realism and firmly establishing the negativism of the Three Treatises in China, he made clear for the first time there the Buddhist doctrine of the unreality of the self and put the doctrine of the Ultimate void* on a firm foundation. His pupils, the most brilliant scholars of the time, started several Buddhist currents: the Three-treatise Negativism by Sêng-chao, the Nirvāṇa doctrine by Tao-shêng*, and Satyasiddhi Nihilism by Sêng-tao and Sêng-sung. Among his pupils were the "Four Sages," the "Eight Eminent Ones," and the "Ten Wise Men."

Lāmaism: A popular term for Tibetan Buddhism, an appellation not used by the 'Buddhists themselves. Mahāyāna Buddhism in the form of Yogācāra idealism was first introduced into Tibet about 650 A.D. by King Srong-btsan Gam-po through the influence of his two Buddhist wives. It was firmly established under King Khri-srong De-btsan who invited Padma Sambhava (or Padmākara) from Northwestern India in 747. He came from a center of Mantrayāna, or ritualistic, mystic, Tantric, and esoteric Buddhism. He gained popular support by subduing native heathen chiefs with the aid of spells and charms and by incorporating into Buddhism a great deal of the indigenous animistic, phallic, neocromantic, devil-dancing, and demon-worshiping Bön* religion. In philosophy, he replaced Yogācāra idealism with Mādhyamika* Negativism. Systematic translation of the Canon (see Canon, Buddhist) was carried out with remarkable accuracy. A system of patriarchal succession was inaugurated, calling the high priests "lāma" (*bla-ma*) or "elders."

In the tenth century, following the chaos created by persecution, Lāmaism gained temporal power and purged itself of Bön corruptions. The religious reform was carried out by the Indian monk Atīśa who arrived in 1038, continued the translation of the Canon, and established the Kā-dam-pa (Order of the Unity of Discipline) which later split into several sects. Priests were allowed to marry, and the system of transmission of headship from father to son was started. Kā-dam exerted tremendous political influence, and in the thirteenth century finally achieved political supremacy through alliance with Kubhlai Khān, then emperor of China, who made Lāmaism the state religion of his empire.

In time the religion became highly corrupted, involving outright adultery in the name of "mysterious, blissful, meditative calmness" and "perfect harmony without obstacle." Radical reform was inevitable. This was accomplished by Tsong-kha-pa (c. 1356) of Northeastern Tibet, who founded the reformed sect of Ge-lug-pa, "the virtuous sect," which later split into several sub-sects. In place of the old red attire, sect members wore yellow hats and robes, which practice gave rise to the name Yellow Hats. Celibacy was enforced, fortnightly recitations of rules were resumed, religious assemblies and retreats were held. Ceremonies, fasts, confessions, the use of bells, rosaries, and holy water, the worship of saints, the division into dioceses, the concentration of power in the central authority, etc., bear striking similarity to Catholicism. However, there is no evidence of borrowing, though influence from Nestorianism in China cannot be ruled out. The reform was distinguished by the adoption of the yellow attire, the reaffirmation of karma or retribution, and the practice of celibacy. Philosophically, Tsong-kha-pa continued the compromise of Mādhyamika Negativism and esoteric Mantrayāna.

In the fifteenth century, the church was divided under two Grand Lāmas, the origin of the division having been attributed by native historians to Tsong-kha-pa's son, his two pupils, or his elder contemporary. The Dalai Lāma (Gyal-wa-rin-po-ch'e, vast as the "ocean") is the temporal ruler residing in Potala at Lhāsa, regarded as the incarnation of Avalokiteśvara*. The Panchen Lāma (panchen-rin-po-ch'e, "great jewel pandit"), or Tashi Lāma after his residence at Tashi, is the spiritual head with divine power and infallible authority over doctrinal matters, and is regarded as the incarnation of Amitābha (see Amita). A new lāma is selected by discovering the infant born at approximately the same time the previous lāma died, of whom the infant is supposed to be his incarnation.

Tibetan Buddhism, whether in its original or reconstructed form, is based on Vairocana as the Law-body (see trikaya) of the Buddha, Amitābha as the Supreme Being, and Avalokiteśvara as the chief bodhisattva*. It is a mystical system of "secrets," with the "seeing of self-nature and the mind of supreme wisdom" as the cause of the religious life, and the salvation of all beings as the result. In practice it emphasizes the "fourfold teaching," including 1) confession, 2) worship of images, 3) recitation of the six-syllabled magic formula *om manipadme hūm* which constitutes the "true words" that bring about the perfect communion between the Buddha or the bodhisattva and the aspirant, and 4) discipline. These are supported by a wealth of magic verses, rituals, charms, and other esoteric practices, and the extensive use of the praying wheel.

Yellow Hat Lāmaism is prevalent in Tibet, Sinkiang, Mongolia, Manchuria, the Western border of China, and parts of Siberia and European Caucasus, with a total of some 1,000,000 priests and followers in Tibet alone. Red Hat Lāmaism exists in Mongolia and Kokonor. See Buddhism; death and burial practices.

C. Bell, *The Religion of Tibet* (1931); J. E. Ellam, *The Religion of Tibet* (1927); L. A. Waddell, *The Buddhism of Tibet* (1895); F. D. Lessing, *Jung Ho Kung* (1942).

Lotus Sūtra: (Skr. *Saddharma-puṇḍarīka,* true-doctrine lotus) The most popular Buddhist scriptures in the Far East, containing the tenets of the Mahāyāna schools of T'ien-t'ai and Nichiren**, which regard the sūtra as the king of all sūtras and the embodiment of the Ultimate Doctrine. It teaches salvation for all creatures, reducing the Three Vehicles* to One Vehicle, on the principle of "One is all and All is One." We know nothing of its authorship or its place of origin, but its first translation into Chinese is dated c. 255 A.D. Of the three existent Chinese translations, that by Kumārajīva* in 406 A.D. is universally used in China and Japan, along with important commentaries by Chih-k'ai. Eng. tr., H. Kern, *The Saddharma-puṇḍarīka, or the Lotus of the True Law* (1884); W. E. Soothill, (abridged), *The Lotus of the Wonderful Law* (1930).

Mādhyamaka: See Middle Doctrine School.

Mahāvairocana: (Skr. The Great Sun Buddha) The Buddha of the Mystical School* "who illumines the whole world as the sun does." The universe is his Law-body (see trikaya), forever preaching his truth, and all phenomena are his manifestations. The "Realm of Matrix Repository" is his Law-body of Principle, while the "Realm of Diamond Element" is his Law-body of Wisdom, both being aspects of the same Law-body. These two Realms are pictorially represented in "Circles" (*maṇḍala*). In the *maṇḍala* of the Repository Realm, Mahāvairocana has the "sign of meditation," whereas in the *maṇḍala* of the Diamond Realm where he is the first of the Five Wisdom-Buddhas, he has the "sign of wisdom-fist." In both *maṇḍalas* he sits in the center, surrounded by Buddhas and bodhisattvas, all of whom are his manifestations.

He has many transformations, but the Mystical School is emphatic in denying the identity of Mahāvairocana and Sākyamuni (see Buddha), insisting that the three bodies of each are different. The Law-body of the former is the reality of the Six Great Elements, whereas that of the latter is an abstract principle. See Vairocana.

Mahāyāna: See Buddhism.

Maitreya (Skr.), Metteya (Pāli): (Chin. Mi-lê; Jap. Miroku) a) A bodhisattva* who was the direct or indirect teacher of Asaṅga, (c. 410-500 A.D.?). b) The Future Buddha prophesied by Gotama Buddha, who is to come after 5,670,000,-000 years to spread the Doctrine and to save all beings. His name means benevolence, and another name, Ajita, means invincibility. Definitely a mythological figure, he is said by tradition to have been born in South India, and is often confused with Asaṅga's teacher. In Buddhist temples, he is represented in the hall of the Four Heavenly Guardians as the Future Buddha, fat and laughing, facing outward and welcoming all worshipers, one hand holding a flower or rosary, each bead of which represents 1,000 years he spent in doing merciful deeds during previous existence, and the other hand holding a mystic bag containing future happiness for all. See Buddha; Buddhahood; incarnations.

Mañjusri: a) (Skr., Chin. Wên-shu, Jap. Monju) A bodhisattva*, symbolic of Wisdom, is usually placed on the left of Śākyamuni in temples, while Samantabhadra, representing Compassion, is on his right. There are six interpretations of the name, but the most generally accepted is "wonderful and auspicious." His standard representation includes five curls to his hair, representing the fivefold Wisdom of the Buddha; a sword in his hand, suggesting the penetrative quality of Wisdom; and a lion, indicating the power of Wisdom. Sometimes he rides on a peacock and holds a sūtra instead. He is regarded as the parent of many Buddhas, the ninth predecessor of Śākyamuni, the head of the bodhisattvas, the chief disciple of the Buddha, the son of the Buddha, etc. His most famous center is the Wu-t'ai ("five terraces") Mountain in Shansi, China, the Mecca of many Buddhists. b) A Tantric god.

Meditation School: (Skr. *Dhyāna,* Chin. *Ch'an,* Jap. *Zen*) Buddhist meditation has been specially developed in the Ch'an School in China, better known to the West by its Japanese equivalent *Zen.* The doctrine of Zen is "not founded on words or scriptures," but is "a special transmission outside of the Sacred Teaching," a "transmission from mind to mind." Based on the theories of the "universality of Buddha-nature" and the possibility of "becoming a Buddha in this very body," Zen teaches "directly pointing to the human mind and to become a Buddha by seeing one's nature." Nature denotes the "Store of the All-seeing True Law and the Profound Mind of nirvāna,"* i.e., the Buddha-mind in its highest attributes and true essence. The Buddha-mind knows no distinction of manifestation and silence, mind and its objects, enlightenment and ignorance, or Buddha and sentient beings. It is identical with the "Highest Vehicle," the "Supreme Truth," the "True State," and the "Universal Realm of the One-Truth" of other schools. When this Buddha-mind is penetrated, Buddhahood* is attained.

Interpretations of the Buddha-mind among Zen Masters vary, but in general it is conceived as the void* which is "neither holy nor unholy, neither cause nor effect, neither good nor evil, neither form nor characteristic, neither the root nor the attachment of feelings, and neither the Buddha nor sentient beings." The world of multiplicity, with all its specific characters and distinctions, is the result of our ignorance and attachment, and as such is but a dream. Consequently, to penetrate the Buddha-mind some Masters urged "wu-nien" or absence of thought in the sense that the mind is not in any way to be attached to or influenced by objects. Others advocated "wang ch'ing" or "ignoring our feelings." Still others, contending that the phenomenal world was after all the manifestation of the Buddha-mind and therefore even ignorance involved Buddha-nature, recommended "jên hsin," i.e., letting the mind take its own course.

The fundamental method of attaining Buddhahood, however, is meditation, which the School distinguishes into Tathāgata Meditation and Patriarchal Meditation. The former, the Buddha's way of meditating as set forth in the *Laṅkāvatāra Sūtra,* presupposes keen deliberation and a clear understanding of the identity of the Buddha and the originally undefiled mind, whereas the latter, the way of meditation as taught by the Patriarch Bodhidharma*, requires no intellectual effort in bringing about the intuition of the Buddha-mind. Although one can meditate in any position, the regular way is meditation while sitting cross-legged (Jap. *zazen*). Enlightenment (Jap. *satori*), or the culmination of meditation, may be either gradual or abrupt. It may come before, after, or simultaneously with the cultivation of the religious life. The major tradition, however, is that of "abrupt enlightenment preceding gradual cultivation," on the theory that cultivation must be gradual and guided by the perfect understanding of Truth.

To sharpen the imagination and to sensitize the consciousness so that the Buddha-mind can be more readily intuited, different sects of the School developed different "styles." These include "questions and answers" (Jap. *mondo*) and also "public problems" (Jap. *koan*), which are strange and non-logical and are intended to quicken intuition. The Linchi (Jap. Rinzai) Sect employs the "lightning" method, which involves scolding and beating as a way of awakening consciousness, while the Ts'ao-tung (Jap. Soto) Sect prefers careful instruction and gentle guidance.

Zen attributes the mystical beginning of the School to the Buddha* himself, who, so the Zen story goes, one day in the Spirit Vulture Peak imparted to his disciple Mahākāśyapa (Pali, Mahakassapa) the Doctrine of the Buddha-mind by merely plucking a flower without a word. Consequently the School is also called the Buddha-Mind School. It was formally established in China by Bodhidharma in the Liu Sung period, 420-479 A.D., (and not in 520 as generally believed), when the meditation doctrine had been widely accepted and practiced ever since it was first advocated by An Shih-kao (c. 150 A.D.), and when the novel doctrine of "Abrupt Enlightenment" had been advanced by Tao-shêng* and had anticipated a heated controversy among Chinese Buddhists. Bodhidharma passed on to Hui-k'o (Jap. Eka), thus starting the "patriarch transmission." This transmission terminated with the sixth patriarch Hui-nêng (638-713) and was replaced by "special transmissions," namely, the Northern School of Gradual Enlightenment and the Southern School of Abrupt Enlightenment. The Northern School, founded by Shên-hsiu (605-706), soon disappeared, but the Southern School, founded by Hui-nêng, developed into seven sects. Since the eleventh century, however, only the Lin-chi and the Ts'ao-tung Sects have continued in China. In Japan, Zen was introduced several times from the seventh to the ninth century. Eisai founded the Rinzai Sect in Japan in 1191, and Dogen founded the Soto Sect in 1227. The former promulgated Zen as the "protection of the nation," while the latter advocated the restoration of power to the Throne, thus linking Zen with the Japanese national life. The Fuke Sect, founded by Kakushin in 1255, eventually became a community of *ronins* ("lordless warriors") and was abolished in 1868. The Japanese Obaku Sect, founded by Ingen in 1654, has 587 temples and 120,000 adherents, while Soto has 14,257 and 6,848,000 and Rinzai has 5,979 and 2,530,000 respectively. See Buddhism.

D. T. Suzuki, *An Introduction to Zen Buddhism* (1934); *Essays in Zen Buddhism*, First Series (1927), Second Series (1933), Third Series (1934), Fourth Series (1938); *Studies in the Lankavatara Sutra* (1930).

Middle Doctrine School: The Mādhyamaka (Skr. Middle Doctrine) School of Nāgārjuna (c. 100-200 A.D.), one of the two wings of Mahāyāna Buddhism* in India, was introduced into China by Kumārajīva* (d. 413 A.D.) who translated Nāgārjuna's three *Treatises* into Chinese, namely, the *Mādhyamika Śāstra*, Ger. tr. by Walleser, *Die Mittlere Lerhe* (1912), partial Eng. tr. by Stcherbatsky, *The Conception of Buddhist Nirvāṇa* (1927), the *Dvādasa Śastra* ("Twelve Gates"), and the *Śata Śāstra*, tr. by G. Tucci, in *Pre-Dinnāga Buddhist Texts on Logic from Chinese Sources* (1930). Consequently the School is also called Three-Treatise (Chin. San-lun, Jap. Sanron) School.

The doctrines of the School, transmitted through Sêng-chao (383-414 A.D.) were so greatly elaborated and systematized by Chi-tsang (549-623) that beginning from him the School was known as the New San-lun. It rapidly declined after the eighth century and soon disappeared. Introduced into Japan by Ekwan in 625, it never existed there as an independent sect.

This School has been variously characterized as Nihilism, Relativity (by Stcherbatsky), and Negativism. Its ideal is the Absolute or Ultimate Void. From the standpoint of "common truth," dharmas (elements) may be said to be real. From the standpoint of the "higher truth," however, they are merely relative since they are produced through causation. They are phenomenally real, but have no independent reality or self-nature. Reality is therefore the total absence of specific character. It is the "Middle Path of Eightfold Negation" which recognizes "no production, no extinction, no annihilation, no permanence, no unity, no diversity, no coming, and no departure." That production, extinction, etc., are unreal can be proved by the use of the "Four Points of Argument," i.e., by refuting an idea as *ens*, as *non-ens*, as *either ens or non-ens*, and as *neither ens nor non-ens*.

The belief of being or non-being is an extreme which must be replaced by a "middle" which affirms both being and non-being. But this "middle" is merely a "relative middle," itself an extreme, and must be rejected in favor of a "middle devoid of extremes." The result of this dialectic method is the Absolute Middle which is the "Middle Path of the Eightfold Negation."

The "True State of the Middle Path" is the total negation of self-nature and all specific characters. It is the "inexplicable in speech and inconceivable in thought." It is nirvāṇa*. It is the Ultimate Void.

Void* as interpreted by this School is negatively non-entity but positively Reality "devoid" of specific nature, which means "absence of nature" (*svabhāva-abhāva*) or Dharma-nature (*Dharma-svabhāva*). The Void is first of all the Void in the sense of "antithesis of being," secondly the Void "devoid of specific character," and thirdly the "Void in the Highest Sense," the highest synthesis of all oppositions. In short, it is the Absolute Middle, the Ultimate Void. See śūnya.

Mystical School, Buddhist: The School, a branch of Mahāyāna*, considers the universe itself to be the Great Sun Buddha (Mahāvairocana*, who has the two aspects of Principle, which corresponds to the "Realm of Matrix Repository (*Garbhakośa-dhātu*)," and Wisdom, which corresponds to the "Realm of Diamond Element (*Vajra-dhātu*)." "Diamond Element" means hardness and utility, suggesting that the ever-present Secret Truth cannot be destroyed and that the power of Wisdom removes every obstacle on the way to Enlightenment. This Realm is Buddha's Law-body (see trikaya), of Wisdom, the realm of clear discrimination, of mental dharmas (elements), of the vertical cross-section of the universe, of Effect, of Great Enlightenment, and of the Buddha. "Matrix Repository" means to hold and to cover, i.e., to keep things within the original body of being, like keeping a child in the mother's womb. This Realm is Buddha's Law-body of Principle, the realm of absolute equality, of the dharmas, of form, of the horizontal cross-section of the universe, of Cause, of Great Compassion, and of sentient beings. But the two

Realms constitute one universe; they are but two aspects of the same Law-body. "They are two and yet not two."

The nature of the universe consists of the Six Great Elements, namely, Earth, Water, Fire, Air, Space, and Consciousness, which are called the "Six Great Originations." They are mutually dependent and penetrating, so that none can exist without the others, as, for example, no Buddha exists outside of sentient beings and no sentient being exists outside of Buddha. This is the principle of the "Harmony of the Six Elements Without Obstacle."

The character of the universe is described in terms of the "Four Circles (*mandala*)," meaning the fourfold perfection of the character, form, name, and function of things. Each of these in any or all levels of existence involves all of them in all levels of existence.

The activity of the universe consists of the "Three Mysteries," i.e., the Mysteries of Action, Speech, and Thought. All phenomena are the action, speech, and thought of the Great Sun Buddha. For human beings, the "Three Mysteries" are "finger-intertwining" and other activities of the body, "mystical verse" and other "true words," and yoga concentration. This threefold ritual is considered the only effectual means of communion with the Buddha, and it is from the second "Mystery" that the School gets its names True-Word (Chin. Chên-yen, Jap. Shingon) and Mantra (Secret, Chin. Mi Tsung). Concentration leads to identification with the Buddha, resulting in "Buddha-in-me and I-in-Buddha." This takes place in the present world, as one can "become the Great Sun Buddha right in this body." Because of these mystical tendencies, the School has always regarded itself as esoteric and others as exoteric.

The Mystical Doctrine was transmitted in China by three Indian teachers, Subhakarasiṁha (637-735) who came to China in 716 and translated the basic scripture of the School, the *Mahāvairocana Sūtra;* Vajrabodhi (663-723) who arrived in 720 and translated the *Vajra-śekhara Sūtra;* and Amoghavajra (705-774) who came with his teacher Vajrabodhi and translated the *Tattva-saṅgraha Sūtra.* The School rapidly declined after the ninth century. Today only certain of its rituals are practiced in Lāmaism*.

In Japan, on the other hand, the School (Shingon) is the second largest Buddhist sect, having 11,947 temples and 9,117,000 adherents with the Koya Mountain as the center. The doctrine was brought from China by several Great Masters, among whom was Kobo Daishi (Kūkai, 774-835) who organized and systematized the School, becoming its founder. This is the mystical doctrine handed down by him in the East Temple (Toji), called Tomitsu, as distinguished from Taimitsu*. See trikāya.

Nāgārjuna: (c. 100-200 A.D.) A native of South India, pupil of Aśvaghosha's follower Kapimala, and teacher of Āryadeva (Deva). He wrote many important Buddhist treatises, and founded one of the two major Mahāyāna movements, namely, the Middle Doctrine School*. The Mystical School* is also traced to him.

Nichiren: (Jap. Sun Lotus) The Nichiren School, an offshoot of the Tendai School* of Mahāyāna Buddhism, is indigenous to Japan and is distinguished by its fighting attitude and nationalistic spirit. It is based on Kumārajīva's Chinese version of the *Lotus Sūtra,* but more significantly on the personality of its founder Nichiren (1222-1282). Son of a fisherman, Nichiren determined to revive the Tendai doctrine, viciously attacked other schools, saying that "the Jodo School is hell, Zen is devil, Shingon will cause national collapse, and Ritsu is an enemy of the country." He wanted the government to suppress these sects by force. Eventually his militant attitude led first to his exile and later to his death sentence, which he managed to escape. He identified his religion with the destiny of his nation, and called himself "the pillar, the eye, and the vessel" of Japan.

While Nichiren aimed at the revival of Tendai, he differed from the Tendai of Dengyo Daishi in his interpretation of the *Lotus.* He regarded all other Buddhist scriptures and the first fourteen chapters of the *Lotus* as the "trace doctrines of the Trace Buddha," i.e., doctrines of the incarnate Buddha, and asserted that the last fourteen chapters contained the "essential original doctrine of the Original Buddha." In these latter chapters the Buddha speaks of his own personality, saying that his historical existence was but a manifestation of his original person which is his Law-body (see trikaya). As the School purports to promulgate the original doctrine of the Original Buddha contained in the *Lotus,* it also calls itself the Hommon-Hokke (Original *Lotus*) School.

Furthermore, Tendai considered thought as important, in which all the "three thousand worlds" are imminent. Nichiren, on the other hand, contended that all worlds centered around the personality of the Buddha. He went back to the original Tendai doctrine of the identity of principle and fact, and emphasized not only right thought, but also right practice, which would lead to "Buddhahood in this very body."

There are at present eight branches in Japan, with 5,031 temples and 7,376,000 adherents. The Nichiren School proper and the Kempon-Hokke (Elucidating the Original *Lotus*) branch are the most influential. See Buddhism.

M. Anesaki, *Nichiren, the Buddhist Prophet* (1916).

nirvana (Skr.), nibbāna (Pāli): A term of various interpretations according to different possible stems. Nirvāṇa in general means "blown out" as of a lamp, i.e., one having attained enlightenment through extinguishing all of his desires. The Chinese translate it as "emancipation," "tranquil extinction," "non-production" of the cause of life and death, "non-creation" of the conditions of karma, "bliss," and more generally "extinction and ferrying across," i.e., extinguishing the cause and effect of reincarnation and crossing the sea of *saṅsāra* or the cycle of birth and rebirths.

Buddhist Terminology

Although the Buddha was silent on the subject, nirvāṅa has become the goal of all arhats, bodhisattvas*, and the followers of the Buddha. Hinayanists confine it to monks, conceiving it as extinction of evil passions and false views and as freedom from *saṅsāra.* This does not mean annihilation of individual existence as often supposed, but the cessation of rebirth, the extinction of passions, and the replacement of suffering by bliss.

There are two kinds of nirvāṅa, both leading to arhatship. One is the "Nirvāṇa with Remainder," or nirvāṇa with the material and immaterial conditions of being (*upādhi*) remaining, with the cause, but not all the effects, of reincarnation destroyed. The other is "Nirvāṇa without Remainder," or total extinction of conditions of life, with both the cause and effect of reincarnation destroyed. The former is attainable during life; the latter occurs at death. The *Vijñaptimātratā-siddhi* of the Idealists School distinguished four kinds of Nirvāṇa: 1) the "Nirvāṇa of originally Pure Self-nature" equivalent to the Law-body or the reality underlying existence that is present in all human beings; 2) & 3) as above; and 4) "Nirvāṇa without Abode" or thusness*.

While Hīnayāna regards Nirvāṇa and *saṅsara* as incompatible, Mahāyāna regards them as identical just as the ocean and the waves are inseparable. The nirvāṇa of Hīnayāna means non-being, transcendence of the human cycle of life and death, emancipation, and the three conditions of permanence, bliss, and purity. Nirvāṇa in Mahāyāna, on the other hand, is above being and non-being, transcends all cycles of life and death, involves the Law-body and Supreme Wisdom in addition to emancipation, and denotes personality as well as the three conditions mentioned above. The emphasis on the fourfold meaning of permanency, bliss, self, and purity gives the nirvāṇa of Mahāyāna a positive character. These are to be interpreted as transcendental qualities of the Buddha, who as the Tathāgata in nirvāṇa, is entirely free from desires, abides eternally, is above life and death as well as subjectivity and objectivity. Nirvāṇa is after all transcendental. It is neither existent, nor non-existent, nor either existent and non-existent, nor non-existent and not non-existent. It is the Law-body, thusness, the void, the True State, attainable in this world, by achieving Supreme Wisdom and "seeing into the abode of Reality as it is." It is attainable by all people, even the *icchantika* (i.e., devoid of Buddha-nature).

L. de La Vallée Poussin, *The Way to Nirvana* (1917); Th. Stcherbatsky, *The Conception of Buddhist Nirvana* (1927).

Obaku Shu: A branch of the Meditation School* of Buddhism in Japan.

Pure Land School: (Chin. Ching-t'u, Jap. Jodo) Buddhist Mahāyāna pietism, most popular school in China and Japan. Founded in China by Hui-yüan, 334-416 A.D., and in Japan by Honen, 1173-1212, the School aims at birth in the Pure Land (Skr. *Sukhāvatī*), the Land of Bliss, the Western Heaven of Amita*. Following the teachings of its three scriptures, the larger and the smaller *Sukhāvatī-vyūha Sutras* and the *Amitāyur-dhyāna Sutra* (all translated in the *Sacred Books of the East,* XLIX), the School teaches absolute faith in Amita and salvation through "Other's Power" as the "Easy Way" or the "Pure Land Path," instead of salvation through "One's Own Power" as taught by other schools, which is the "Difficult Way" or the "Holy Path." Reliance on Amita is expressed in the daily repetition of "Namo Amitābha" *nembutsu*, and in the recitation of the 48 vows of the Buddha described in the larger *Sukhāvatī*, especially the three fundamental ones, namely, the eighteenth which promises birth in the Pure Land to the faithful, the nineteenth which promises a personal welcome by Amita to all good people at their death, and the twentieth which assures birth in the Pure Land as the result of the repetition of Buddha's name. In the Pure Land, attainment of nirvāṇa* is sure and easy. Though least philosophical of all Buddhist schools, the Pure Land doctrines of salvation by faith and salvation for all are based on the Infinity of the Buddha, the presence of Buddha-nature in all creatures, and the idea of One-in-all and All-in-one. Minor differences exist in the four Japanese sects of Jodo (8,245 temples & 3,646,000 adherents), Shin (19,815 & 13,327,000), Yūzunembutsu (357 & 153,000), and Ji (494 & 350,000).

Rinzai Shu: A branch of the Meditation School* of Buddhism in Japan.

Sarvāstivāda (Skr.), Sabbatthivada (Pali): The "All-Exists" School, also called Hetuvāda and Vibhajyavāda. Realism in Hīnayāna Buddhism, a branch of Therāvada (see Councils, Buddhist), which regarded all dharmas (elements) and the three times (past, present, and future) as real. It flourished in Northern India, especially in Kāshmīr and Gandhāra, in the fifth century B.C. and ultimately divided into some seven schools, among which was Sautrāntika*, forerunner of Kośa*.

Satyasiddhi School: (Skr. completion of truth, Chin. Ch'êng-shis, Jap. Jojitsu) Buddhist Nihilism. Based on the *Satyasiddhi Śāstra* by Harivarman (c. 250-350 A.D.) of Central India, the School purported to "complete" the Four Noble Truths (see Buddhism) by showing that not only dharmas (elements), of which the School recognized 84, but also the ego are non-existent. This Twofold void* is established on the doctrine of Twofold Truth to the effect that from the standpoint of Worldly Truth, the ego and the elements are real as "temporary names," temporary because 1) they are produced by causes, 2) they are transitory, and 3) they are dependent on other factors; whereas from the standpoint of the Supreme Truth, Nirvāṇa* alone is real. Nirvāṇa is conceived as the Ultimate Void and the total "annihilation" of the "consciousness of temporary names," the "consciousness of the elements," and even the "consciousness of the Void itself."

Whether there was ever a Satyasiddhi School in India is not known. Its doctrine was introduced into China when the *Śāstra* was translated into Chinese by Kumārajīva* in 411 A.D., becoming one of the earliest Buddhist schools of thought in China, and exceedingly popular in the fifth and sixth centuries. At first it was regarded as Mahayanistic, but Tao-hsüan (596-667) finally traced it to the Indian Sautrāntika School of Hīnayāna. Since the ninth century, it was absorbed by the Middle Doctrine School*. It always existed as a branch of that School in Japan where it was introduced by the Korean priest Ekwan in 625 A.D. Today it is no longer an active sect in either country.

Sautrāntika: (Skr. "Sūtra" School) Early Buddhist school which regarded the sūtras or dialogues of the Buddha as the only authority, in opposition to both the Abhidharmikas who relied on the *Abhidhamma* literature three or five hundred years after the Buddha*, and the Vaibhāṣikas who relied on its commentaries. See Canon, Buddhist.

Shin (Shu): (Jap. True Sect) Most popular Buddhist sect in Japan, founded by Shinran (1173-1262), a branch of the Japanese Pure Land School*. It differs from the orthodox Pure Land in that it takes only the eighteenth vow of the larger *Sukhāvatī-vyūha Sutra* to be necessary, teaches absolute reliance on Amitābha (Buddha of Infinite Light), instead of one's own act, considers the repetition of "Namo Amitābha" merely as thanksgiving instead of a necessity for salvation, and allows priests to live an ordinary life including marriage and eating meat.

Soto Shu: (Jap.) A branch of the Meditation School* of Buddhism in Japan.

stages, ten: (Skr. *daśa-bhūmi*) Stages of a bodhisattva's* spiritual development towards Buddhahood*. The Hīnayāna* schools of Mahāsaṅghika and Theravāda and the Mahāyana* schools of Mysticism (see Mystical School, Buddhist) and Idealism (see above) have their own Ten Stages. There are also Ten Stages for each of the Mahāyāna Vehicles* as well as the Ten Stages common to the Three Vehicles. The most widely accepted set in Mahāyāna, however, is that for the bodhisattva, set forth in the *Daśa-bhūmi Śastra* of the Hua-yen School*. It includes: 1) The Stage of Joy, in which the bodhisattva develops his holy nature, removes wrong views, and realizes the principle of the Twofold Void; 2) The Stage of Purity, in which he attains the Perfection of Morality; 3) The Stage of Illumination, in which he attains the Perfection of Patience or Humility and also the deepest introspective insight; 4) The Stage of Flaming Wisdom, in which he achieves the Perfection of Energy; 5) The Stage of Utmost Invincibility, in which he achieves the Perfection of Meditation and realizes the harmony of the Worldly Truth and the Supreme Truth; 6) The Stage of Presence, in which he achieves the Perfection of Wisdom, thereby eliminating the discrimination of purity and impurity; 7) The Stage of Far-going, in which he attains the Perfection of Expediency by going afar to save all beings; 8) The Stage of Immovability, in which he attains the Perfection of Vow and realizes the principle that all specific characters of dharmas (elements) are unreal; 9) The Stage of Good Wisdom, in which the bodhisattva achieves the Perfection of Effort, attains the Ten Holy Powers, and preaches to both the redeemable and the unredeemable; and 10) The Stage of the Cloud of the Law, in which he completes the *pāramitā* of Perfect Knowledge and preaches the Law to save all creatures, like the cloud drops rain over all.

śūnya, śūnyatā: (Skr.) Empty, emptiness; Void. The doctrine of Void is especially promulgated by the two Buddhist "Void" Schools, Satyasiddhi* Nihilism of Hīnayāna*, which affirms the Twofold Void of the self and dharmas (elements), and Mādhyamaka* Negativism of Mahāyāna*, which asserts the Ultimate Void which has no specific character. The doctrine, however, is common to all Mahāyāna schools, which have analyzed the Void under as many as eighteen categories. It has been variously interpreted as Nihilism, Negativism, and Absolutism. In the *Treatises* by Nāgārjuna*, who first formulated the doctrine, causal relations and the entities they produce are dialectically negated, leaving the Void above all specific characters and partial or temporary existence. In the *Prajña-pāramitā* literature, especially in the *Vajracchedika* (*Diamond Sūtra*; several Eng. trs., including one by Max Müller, "Sūtra of Transcendental Wisdom," in the *Sacred Books of the East*, XLIX, 1894), the Tathāgata is emphatically stated to "have no marks" or characteristics, which are illusory and have no independent reality. Ultimate Reality, whether called the Tathāgata, the True State, thusness, nirvāṇa**, the Middle Path, or the Void, is above all specific qualities, including the quality of being Void itself. Thus the Void essentially involves the negation of names, characters, self-nature, and independent reality for things, which are accepted as phenomenally and temporarily real but not ultimately real. To the Hua-yen* and T'ien-t'ai Schools*, however, Temporariness and Void are identical.

D. T. Suzuki insists that the Void not only has the negative aspect of unreality, but also the positive aspect of Suchness or Thusness (*tathatā*) or the Absolute. Th. Stcherbatsky interprets the Void as Relativity, in the sense that a thing can be identified only by relating it to the Absolute. J. Takakusu prefers the Chinese word *k'ung* which connotes all the necessary phases of meaning: first, Void in the sense of antithesis of being; second, the state of being "devoid" of specific character; third, Void in the highest sense, or Transcendental Void, i.e., all oppositions synthesized (as in Hua-yen and T'ien-t'ai); and fourth, the Absolute Void or the Unconditioned.

As Absolute, the Void cannot be expressed in words or apprehended by "common knowledge," but can only be described by "Neti! Neti!" (not so, not so) and attained by direct intuition.

Taimitsu: (Jap. Tendai Mysticism) There are two doctrines of Buddhist Mysticism in Japan. One was handed down by Kobo Daishi (774-835) in Toji (East Temple), called Tomitsu or Eastern Mysticism. The other was handed down by Jikaku Daishi (794-864) of the Tendai School, called Taimitsu or Tendai Mysticism. The former considers the Great Sun Buddha* to be different from Śākyamuni, while the latter regards them as identical. The former relies on the teaching of the *Great Sun Sūtra* which teaches that there are two aspects of the universe (see Mystical School, Buddhist), whereas the latter follows the *Lotus Sūtra** which insists on the One-True. Hence the different sects of Ryobu (Double Aspect) Shinto and Ichijitsu (One-True) Shinto* based on the two doctrines respectively.

Tao-shêng: (d. 434 A.D.) A pupil of Kumārajīva*. He exerted tremendous influence on Chinese Buddhist thought along four lines: 1) He violently opposed the "icchantika" doctrine of the six-chapter *Nirvāṇa Sūtra* to the effect that this class of people can never become Buddha. He maintained that Buddha-nature is all-pervading and therefore even the *icchantika* can attain Buddahood*. His novel idea so shocked and enraged his fellow Buddhists that he was excommunicated in 428 or 429. Later his theory was upheld by the *Mahāparinirvāna Sūtra* subsequently introduced, and became the foundation of the Mahāyāna* doctrine of "salvation for all" promulgated in the T'ien-t'ai, Pure Land, and Meditation Schools**. 2) He completed the "abrupt enlightenment" doctrine which became exceedingly strong in the T'ang dynasty (618-907), especially in the Meditation School. He argued that Truth, being a unity, must be intuited all at once. 3) He maintained that nirvāṇa* is above the distinction of life and death—it is the True State or the Law-body (see trikaya) of the Buddha, which has no specific character. Holding such distinctions as purity and impurity, or cause and effect, to be unreal, he declared that "the Buddha has no Pure Land," and that "goodness should not be rewarded." 4) He denied that Buddha-nature was identical with the soul, thus overthrowing the traditional interpretation ever since the Han dynasty (206 B.C.-220 A.D.).

Tendai School: (Jap.) *Idem*: T'ien-t'ai School.*

thusness, suchness: (Skr. *bhūtatathatā, tathatā*, Chin. *chên ju*, Jap. *shinnyo*) a) The state of nature, which is 1) real in the sense of transcending appearance and specific characters, and 2) eternal. Thusness is neither produced nor annihilated, neither one nor differentiated, neither being nor non-being nor both or either. It is the Absolute, identical with Self-nature, Buddha-nature, the Law-body (see trikaya), the Tathāgata, the Void*, *dharma-dhātu*, Dharma-nature, the True State, and nirvāṇa*. b) Truth in the Buddhistic sense.

T'ien-t'ai School: (Chin.) The T'ien-t'ai doctrine centers around the principle of the Perfectly Harmonious Threefold Truth, i.e., the truth of the void*, the truth of Temporariness, and the truth of the Mean. All things are Void because they depend on causes and therefore have no independent reality, but because they are produced they enjoy temporary existence. Being both Void and Temporary is the nature of dharmas (elements), and as such is the Mean. Thus the Void, Temporariness, and the Mean involve one another—they are both three and one.

From the standpoint of Temporariness, the phenomenal world consists of ten Realms, those of the Buddhas, Would-be-Buddhas, Buddhas-for-Themselves, Direct Disciples of the Buddha, heavenly beings, spirits, human beings, departed beings, beasts, and depraved men. Each Realm has the characteristics of all ten Realms, thus giving the total of 100 Realms. Each of these in turn are characterized by ten features in the sense that all their dharmas are "thus-characterized, thus-natured, thus-substantiated, thus-caused, thus-forced, thus-activated, thus-conditioned, thus-remunerated, and thus-completed-from-beginning-to-end." Again, each of these one thousand Realms consists of the three divisions of living beings, of space, and of the aggregates which constitute being, thus making a total of 3,000 Realms.

But the Realm of Temporariness or the phenomenal world is at the same time the Realm of the Void, the noumenon, and also the Realm of the Mean which is both phenomenon and noumenon. These Realms are so interwoven, so inter-penetrating, and so inter-related that they may be considered to be "immanent in a single instant of consciousness." This does not mean that they are produced by the thought of man or the Buddha, although the T'ien-t'ai doctrine does have definite connection with the Idealistic theory. It rather means that in every thought-moment all the possible worlds are involved.

The Realms exist by virtue of their own dharma-nature; they are "immanent in principle". As they come into being through causes and conditions, they are also "immanent in fact." "Immanence in principle" and "immanence in fact," however, are identical. The dharmas of beings, the dharmas of the Buddhas, and the dharmas of consciousness are in the final analysis the same. Cause and effect are but two aspects of the same process, and the material element and mind are fundamentally one. This One-is-All and All-is-One philosophy is crystallized in the saying that "Every color or fragrance is none other than the Middle Path." In other words, every dharma is the embodiment of the real essence of the True State, which is also called Absolute Reality, Ultimate void, thusness, or nirvāṇa*.

As everything involves everything else, it follows that even the nature of Buddha is not free from evil, and the nature of the depraved man is also good. "Buddha-nature is everywhere over the world." This being the case, all beings are qualified to become Buddha. The School therefore strongly insists on the doctrine of "salvation for all," and completely rejects the "icchantika" (i.e., devoid of Buddha-nature) theory. Only one vehicle*, the Buddha Vehicle, is recognized instead of three.

The T'ien-t'ai School has developed a special formula of meditation called "calmness and insight." Calmness, literally "at rest," connotes putting the wrong mind at rest by realizing that dharmas are neither produced nor annihilated, and insight means the intuition of both the Void and the Temporariness of Reality.

This Mahāyāna School*, also called the Lotus School, was founded in China by Chih-k'ai, the Great Master of T'ien-t'ai (Chih-i, 531-597) in the T'ien-t'ai ("heavenly terrace") Mountain on the authority of the *Lotus Sūtra**. The doctrine is traced to Hui-wên (d. 577) who was inspired by the *Mādhyamika Śāstra* and the *Mahaprajñapāramita Sūtra.* At present T'ien-t'ai is very popular in China, and is to a large extent combined with the Pure Land Sect*. In Japan where it was founded in 804 by Dengyo Daishi (Saicho, 767-822), the School (Tendai) has three branches (Sammon, Jimon, and Shinsei) with 4,438 temples and 2,141,000 followers. See trikāya; Triad.

Triad, Buddhist: The Buddhist Triad has different meaning from the Christian trinity. It means: a) the Triple Body or *trikāya**; b) the Three Precious Ones or *Triratna**; and c) the Three Honored Ones, groups like 1) Mañjuśri* representing Wisdom, Śākyamuni, and Samantabhadra representing the Principle (called the Three Holy Ones of the Hua-yen School*; 2) Mahāsthāma(prata), the embodiment of Wisdom, Amitābha, and Avalokiteśvara* the embodiment of Compassion (T'ien-t'ai School*); 3) Bhaishajvaguru as the Lord of the Lost Paradise, Śākyamuni as the Lord of the present world, (often with minor figures of Ānanda and Mahākassapa on his sides), and Amitābha as the Lord of the Future Paradise (Meditation School*); 4) Samantabhadra, Avalokiteśvara, and Mahāsthāmaprata; 5) Manjusri, Avalokitesvara and Vajrapani, embodiment of power.

trikāya: (Skr. triple body) A Mahāyāna* doctrine arising about the second century and crystalizing in the fifth century A.D., the *trikāya* idea has not only theological, but also ontological and cosmological meanings. The Buddha is conceived to have three bodies: 1) *Dharma-kāya* or the Law-body, interpreted by Hīnayāna* as the soul of the Buddha, but by Mahāyāna as reality as such, identical with suchness, Tathāgata, the void*, the Middle Path, the Absolute. It is the embodiment of Law both transcending and immanent in all phenomena. It is the same for all Buddhas. The Mystical School* alone treats the Law-body as personal. 2) *Sambhogakāya,* the Enjoyment-body, Reward-body, or Body of Bliss. Not mentioned in the Hīnayāna Canon, this is the embodiment of Wisdom, the Buddha who enjoys and makes others enjoy the fruits of his saving efforts as a bodhisattva*, the Buddha forever preaching to the bodhisattvas, the Tathāgata personified, the chief object of worship. 3) *Nirmāṇa-kāya* or Transformation-body. This is the embodiment of Compassion. In general this means the historical Buddha Śākyamuni. Since the transformation of the Tathāgata is not limited to Śākyamuni, however, *Nirmāṇa-kāya* Buddhas are to be found everywhere and at all times. The Three Bodies are really not separate Bodies, but three aspects of the same Buddha, one involving the other two. There are also further divisions into four, five, six, and ten Bodies. See nirvana; thusness; Triad, Buddhist; Triratna.

Triratna: (Skr. three treasures) The Three Precious Ones: Buddha, Dharma (Doctrine), and Saṅgha (Order). They are understood in various ways: 1) The *trikāya** as represented in temples, generally Amitābha, Vairocana*, and Locana respectively. 2) These three treasures embodied in every Buddha and every member of the Order. 3) These three treasures embodied in thusness*. 4) *Dharma-kāya,* the One Vehicle Doctrine, and bodhisattvas of the One Vehicle (T'ien-t'ai School*). 5) The *Trikāya,* the Three Vehicle Doctrine, and followers of the Three Vehicles*. 6) The *Trikāya,* the six pāramitas, and the saints of the Ten Stages (see stages, ten). 7) The Transformation Buddha, the Four Noble Truths and the Twelvefold Chain of Causation, and the Four Effects of Enlightenment. 8) Buddha image, Scripture, and the shaved hair of monks and nuns. The last three groups are common to Hīnayāna*. See Triad, Buddhist.

Vairocana: (Skr.) a) The true Buddha-body, i.e., Godhead. Interpretations vary: 1) Meaning "omnipresent" and "purity" respectively, Vairocana and Locana are Law-body and Enjoyment-body in the *trikāya**, corresponding to the Principle or Law and Wisdom. (T'ien-t'ai & Idealistic Schools**.) 2) Vairocana and Locana are identical, the two names being the same and meaning "light illumining everywhere." They are the Enjoyment-body of the Buddha. (Hua-yen School*) 3) Vairocana, interpreted as "The Great Sun" and "universal illumination," is Mahāvairocana*. (Mystical School*) b) In *Triratna**, he represents the Doctrine, while Locana symbolizes the Order. The former has hands folded over the breast while the latter has the right hand resting in his lap. See Buddha.

Vasubandhu: (c. 420-500 A.D.) (Takakusu), or d. 350 A.D. (Péri) A native of North India, and younger brother of Asaṅga who converted him from Hīnayāna to Mahāyana**. He was the author of the fundamental treatises of the Hinayanistic Kośa* and the Mahayanistic Idealistic Schools*, and some fifteen other works representative of various phases of Buddhist philosophy. As such he was not only the central figure of both Buddhist Realism and Idealism but also a great philosopher of Buddhism in general.

vehicles: (Skr. *yāna,* originally meaning "career," extended to connote a vehicle that carries living beings across the sea of life and death to nirvāṇa*). There are divisions from One Vehicle to Five Vehicles. Among the most important are: 1) The Three Vehicles (*Triyāna*) of Mahāyāna: a) Śravaka or "hearer," i.e., the direct disciples of the Buddha or obedient followers. This is also called Hīnayāna or Small Vehicle, as the aim is for the individual to become an arhat (see araham) through the realization of the Four Noble Truths. b) *Pratyeka-buddha* or "Buddha for oneself" through the realization of the Twelve-fold Chain of Causation. This is also called Mādhyamayāna or Middle Vehicle. c) Bodhisattva* or Future Buddha who leads all beings to salvation. This is also called Mahāyāna or Great Vehicle. 2) The One Vehicle (*Ekayāna*) or Mahāyāna, as advocated in the Hua-yen and T'ien-t'ai Schools**. These Schools consider the various Vehicles as merely "expedient" ways, and the One Vehicle, i.e., the Buddha Vehicle (*Buddhayāna*) as set forth in the *Lotus Sūtra**, as the inclusive, final, and "true" Vehicle which carries all beings to nirvāṇa.

Vinaya School: See Disciplinary School.

void: See sūnya; Middle Doctrine School.

Yogācāra: (Skr.) See Idealistic School, Buddhist.

Yūzūnembutsu Shu: (Jap. All-Permeating-Faith-in-Amita Sect) A branch of the Pure Land School* of Buddhism in Japan, founded by Ryonin (1071-1132), with the doctrine that merits of faith are transferable to others, based on the teaching of faith of the Pure Land School, the One-and-All idea of the *Avataṅsaka* Sūtra,* and the salvation-for-all idea of the *Lotus Sūtra**.

Zen: (Jap.) See Meditation School. W.T.C.

Bugenhagen, Johann: (1485-1558) German Protestant Reformer. A distinguished scholar and close friend of Luther, he was chiefly remembered as an able organizer of the Reformation in Northern Germany and Denmark. G.R.C.

Bulgaria, Church of: See Eastern Orthodox Churches.

bull, papal: The name given to the official letters published by the Sovereign Pontiff in the most solemn form. Written in the most solemn style, they begin with the words "Episcopus Servus Servorum Dei" and contain usually decrees about doctrinal matters, decrees of canonization, decrees on matters of ecclesiastical discipline, proclamations of jubilees, the promulgation of general indulgences, the concession of the pallium, and other matters of general importance. The name is derived from the Latin word *bulla* which signified a small circular ball of metal which has been used with varying imitations for centuries for sealing the more important papal documents. The oldest known usage dates back to the seventh century; and these early seals were made of lead. Until the time of Pope Leo XIII bulls were sealed with lead and briefs with red wax seals stamped with "the Fisherman's ring." But Pope Leo XIII* changed the usage and limited the use of lead seals to such documents as the erection, suppression or provision of bishoprics. These lead seals now have on one side the images of SS. Peter and Paul and on the other the name of the reigning pontiff. Since that time the other bulls are sealed with red wax seals bearing the images of SS. Peter and Paul and around them the name of the reigning pontiff. Classed frequently with bulls are papal briefs. Briefs*, the name of which comes from the Latin word *breve* signifying short, came into use during the Middle Ages and were used indifferently for titles, judicial acts, and similar documents of all kinds formally drawn up. This word *brief* with time lost its original meaning and it has come to mean lesser kinds of papal documents bearing the papal seal and dealing with dispensations of all kinds, with the permission to keep the Blessed Sacrament, to give Holy Communion, etc. Briefs have their importance from the matter with which they deal, as bulls have their greater importance because of the weightier matters with which they are concerned. Outside of these distinctions the main difference between brief and bull are matters of usage and of form. Briefs usually begin with the name of the pope, such as "Benedictus papa XV" and end with the words "sub annulo piscatoris." In addition to these ordinary bulls there exist "demi-bulls" (*Bullae Demidiatae*), which are solemn formal papal documents issued by a newly elected pope between the time of his election and coronation; the seal bears on one side the heads of the apostles Peter and Paul, but the other side is blank. "Little bulls" were papal documents in which smaller leaden seals were attached to the parchment. This custom held during the Middle Ages; and so-called "little bulls" should be distinguished from briefs. "Bulls of gold" were seals in which gold replaced the lead; these, however, were used only on exceptional occasions such as when addressing rulers, etc. Bulls and briefs are distinct from a *motu proprio** and rescripts*. A *motu proprio* is a papal letter without the seal and usually drawn up on the initiative of the pope himself and signed by him personally. It usually deals with matters of lesser importance. A rescript is a document answering a question or petition to the Pope or one of the sacred congregations and usually affects only the persons or person to whom it is addressed. See encyclicals. T.T.M.

Bullaria: See Decretals.

Bullinger, Heinrich: (1504-1575) Swiss Reformer. After experience as a teacher and pastor, he succeeded Zwingli* as chief pastor of Zurich in 1531. He was an able writer and forceful thinker, but in a controversial age he showed himself able to understand others and anxious to find grounds of agreement with them. His controversial works show dignity and restraint. Responsible for the Helvetic Confession* (1566); influential in English religious life. See Zürich, Concensus of. G.R.C.

bull-roarer: A piece of wood, tied to the end of a string, which makes a roaring sound when it is whirled about. It was used by Australian aborigines in religious ceremonies. See Spencer & Gillen. P.G.M.

Bultmann, Rudolf: (1884-) He first taught in Breslau and Giessen. Now he is professor in Marburg. He is a working member of the dialectical* theologians, one of the most radical groups that has prophetic significance in our day. Bultmann has also been active in the historical and form-historical study of the gospels. See Form Criticism.

Die Geschichte der Synoptischen Tradition (Göttingen, 1921); *Der Begriff der Offenbarung im Neuen Testament* (Tübingen, 1929); *Die Erforschung der synoptischen Evangelien,* 2 ed., (Giessen, 1930); *Glauben und Verstehen* (Tübingen, 1933); *Jesus and the Word* (1934). H.H.

Bunyan, John: (1628-1688) English preacher and prose writer, remembered chiefly as the author of *Pilgrim's Progress* (Part I, 1678; Part II, 1684). Despite poverty, lack of formal education, and a twelve year imprisonment resulting from his activities as leader of a Nonconformist congregation at Bedford, he produced nearly sixty books and tracts on religious subjects. Aside from his masterpiece, which has had a circulation second only to the Bible, his most important works are *Grace Abounding to the Chief of Sinners* (1666), *The Life and Death of Mr. Badman* (1680), and *The Holy War* (1682). L.W.C.

Burchard of Worms: (ca. 965-1025) Bishop of Worms (1000-). Canonist and ecclesiastic. Rescued the see of Worms from disorder. Author of the *Decretum* in twenty books (Migne, *P. L.* CXL), probably the most important collection of disciplinary canons before the work of Gratian. J.T.M.

Buréau Paul: (1865-1921) Vigorously rejecting sociolatry and sociocracy, his moral and sociological works were an expression of the religious revival in Catholicism.

La crise morale des temps nouveaux (Paris, 1907); *L'indiscipline de moeurs* (Paris, 1920); *Introduction a la methode sociologique* (Paris, 1923). H.H.

burial practice, Roman Catholic: The practice includes the bringing of the body to the church, divine services in the church, and interment of the body in consecrated ground. The liturgical service expresses sorrow over the bereavement, a plea for God's mercy toward the departed soul, and a buoyant confidence in the promised resurrection. The service for baptized infants is entirely joyous, since they are assured of heaven. As Catholic burial is a privilege of union with the Church, it is not granted to unbaptized persons, to baptized non-Catholics (unless either of these had expressed a desire to become Catholics), or to nominal Catholics who died as unrepentant public sinners. C.V.

burial practices: See death and burial practices.

Buridan, John (Jean): A scholastic philosopher, born circa 1288 in Béthune, France. Studied at the Univ. of Paris under William of Occam*, the Nominalist, among whose followers he is numbered as one of the more famous dialecticians. He maintained, despite ecclesiastical condemnation, that the will and the intellect are basically the same, and that human freedom consists in the power of choosing between two or more desirable alternatives: hence, the will is "determined" by the strongest motive. Attributed to him, but with probable falsity, is the famous dilemma of "Buridan's Ass", which would starve because of its inability to choose between two loads of hay, equal as to quantity and quality and equi-distant. In his *Compendium Logicae* he developed at length the art of finding the middle term of a demonstration, which eventually came to be called the "Bridge of Asses", i.e., the bridge by which stupid scholars were enabled to pass from the minor or major, to the middle, term of a syllogism. His alleged rectorship of the Univ. of Paris and his connection with the founding of the Univ. of Vienna are both considered hypothetical. J.F.T.

Burke, Edmund: (1729-1797) An Irish born leader of the most enlightened group of the Whigs, combining in his politico-philosophical outlook conservatism and liberalism. Reverential in attitude toward the state, he practically united politics with religion. He believed good citizenship to be inseparable from religious piety, defending the establishment of the Anglican church as a consecration of the nation. He looked upon the social structure, its history, its institutions, it many duties and loyalties with a reverence akin to religious awe. As every individual has his place in the state, continuing order of his nation, so every nation has its place in a world-wide civilization unfolding in accord with "a divine tactic".

L. Stephen, *English Thought in the Eighteenth Century,* 2nd ed. 2 vols. (London, 1881); J. MacCunn, *The Political Philosophy of Burke* (London, 1913); H. J. Laski, *Political Thought in England from Locke to Bentham* (London, 1920); A. Cobban, *Edmund Burke and the Revolt against the Eighteenth Century* (London, 1929); F. J. C. Hearnshaw, *The Social and Political Ideas of some Representative Thinkers of the Revolutionary Age* (London, 1931). H.H.

burnt-offering (O.T.): An animal sacrifice wholly consumed on the altar, as distinguished from cereal offerings and from animal sacrifices of which only the blood and fat were put on the altar, while the flesh was (cooked and) eaten by priests and worshippers. See holocaust; sacrifice, Hebrew and Jewish. R.B.Y.S.

Burton, E. D.: (1856-1925) Baptist educator. Author: *Syntax of the Moods and Tenses in the New Testament Greek* (1893). Editor *Biblical World* and *American Journal of Theology.* At University of Chicago, 1892-1925 (President 1923-25). C.H.M.

Bushido: (Lit. "The Way of the Knight") The code of the Japanese warrior, compiled on a basis of Confucian ethics and Zen discipline. D.C.H.

Bushnell, Horace: (1802-1876) American preacher and theologian, graduate of Yale College and Divinity School, pastor of North Church in Hartford. His work marks the passing of the "New England theology."* He helped to emancipate the churches, says his biographer, Dr. Munger: "first, from a revivalism that ignored the law of Christian growth; second, from a conception of the Trinity bordering on tritheism; third, from a view of miracles that implied a suspension of natural law; and fourth, from a theory of the atonement that . . . failed to declare the law of human life." In *Christian Nurture* (1846, rewritten 1861) he sharply criticised the prevalent individualism, the reliance upon revivals, and insistence upon a dated, emotional experience of conversion; and set forth what he called the true principle of Christian education: "That the child is to grow up a Christian, and never know himself as being otherwise." He dealt with the doctrine of the Trinity in *God in Christ* (1849) and *Christ in Theology* (1851), and prefaced the former volume by a remarkable *Dissertation on Language as Related to Thought and Spirit.* He published *Nature and the Supernatural* in 1858, and two works on the atonement, *Vicarious Sacrifice* (1865) and *Forgiveness and Law* (1874). Bushnell "challenged men to a new habit of thought." He turned away from the formal and precise definitions, mathematically-minded demonstrations, and the sterile formulae of the old New England theology, and sought to interpret life itself as lived in the power of the Spirit of God. For him, theology had its starting-point in experience, its basis in moral right, and its center in Christ. There is something intuitive, given, mystical in all true religion; and it is the business of theology to see and interpret this. Christian doctrine, he said, should be "formulated Christian experience." He was one of the greatest preachers of his century, and his published sermons will long continue to be read. See Christian Nurture; American theology, early; New England theology; New theology.

Life and Letters of Horace Bushnell (1880); T. T. Munger, *Horace Bushnell* (1899). L.A.W.

Butler, Joseph: (1692-1752) An Anglican theologian and moralist. He was born of Presbyterian parentage, but chose to prepare himself for service in the Established Church. He wrote *Fifteen Sermons,* when he was preacher at Rolls Chapel, and the *Analogy* (1736) while he was Clerk of the Closet for Queen Caroline. (See Deism.) He became bishop of Durham and some say he declined to become Archbishop of Canterbury. Butler believed that there is a sound way of life which has a rational foundation in nature, that the mandates of natural law harmonize with Revelation, and both unite to impose an inescapable moral responsibility. Nature holds all phenomena in causal connection, and relates them to the purpose of organic unity. The order and beauty of lifeless things disclose an intelligence creating and manipulating all objects with some conscious design in view. See teleology.

W.G.H.

Byzantine Church: See Eastern Orthodox Churches.

Byzantine Empire: Comprised the Eastern portion of the Roman Empire after its final division into two parts by Emp. Theodosius in 395. In theory, the two portions, the Western, or Latin, and the Eastern, Byzantine, were one. But for a variety of reasons, the separation of the two was inevitable, and politically this was signified by the assumption, on the part of Charlemagne (800), of the title of the Emperor of the Holy Roman Empire. Religiously, they were separated in 1054 by the Great Schism*. The Byzantine Empire long continued to be the dominant economic and cultural unit in Europe. But the Arab conquests (7th cent.) and later the Crusades (11th to 13th centuries) and finally the Turkish conquests (11th to the 15th centuries) brought about its ultimate downfall. Its last stronghold, Constantinople was taken by Sultan Mohammed II in 1453.

A. A. Vasiliev, *History of the Byzantine Empire,* 2 vols. (1928-29); R. Byron, *The Byzantine Achievement, A. D. 330-1453* (London, 1929); C. Diehl, *History of the Byzantine Empire* (1925). M.S.

Byzantine Rite: Originally the liturgical forms of the Patriarchate of Constantinople, which by the end of the thirteenth century were extended to the other three ancient Eastern patriarchates of Alexandria, Antioch, and Jerusalem. It is now used by the entire Eastern Orthodox Church* including some Uniate churches*. No one liturgical language is exclusively in use. The liturgy in ordinary use is that of St. Chrysostom*. See liturgy.

M.S.

Byzantine Style: See art, ecclesiastical, Christian.

Byzantium: The city founded c. 658 B.C. by a colony of Megarians led by Byzas, after whom the settlement was named. Emperor Constantine chose it, in 325, as the new capital of the Roman Empire and rebuilt it to suit the new purpose. The new city of Constantinople was dedicated in May 11, 330 A.D. M.S.

C

Cabala: See Kabbalah.

Cabet, Etienne: See communistic settlements, secular.

Caesarius of Arles: (c. 470-542) Devout Gallican monk, preacher, and monastic legislator. In addition to long service in monasteries of Lerins and Arles, he was, from 502 to his death, bishop in the latter city. He left a *Rule* for monks and another for nuns. In these, as in his whole career, there was a truly remarkable emphasis upon renunciatory discipline, prayer, and the primacy of God's Word. R.C.P.

Caesarius of Heisterbach: (d. c. 1240) Loyal Cistercian* monk most famous for his attempt to eradicate social and economic corruptions of his order and for that invaluable commentary on medieval life and religion, *The Dialogue on Miracles.* See the translation by H. v. E. Scott and C. C. Swinton Bland, 2 vols. (London, 1929). R.C.P.

caesaropapism: Supremacy of state over church (as in the Byzantine Empire, and in Russia till 1917), is generally considered to be the converse of ecclesiastical hegemony over states (as of Innocent III*). By definition, thus, the relation of church and state* in England and Protestant Germany (16th century *seq.*) has been that of caesaropapism. The term may be misleading, for the issue is rather one of freedom for both church and state in their respective spheres. Churches have been relatively free or unfree in Roman Catholic and in Protestant states. See Erastianism.

For fruitful discussion, cf. J. N. Figgis, "Political Thought in the Sixteenth Century", *Cambridge Modern History,* Vol. III. ch. XXII, and bibliography. Q.B.

Caird, Edward: (1835-1908) A Scottish philosopher and theologian; brother of John Caird*. He was professor of moral philosophy at Glasgow (1866-93) and Master of Balliol College Oxford (1893-1906), following Jowett. His personal influence upon his students was exceptional. He was interested in social reforms, in the education of workingmen, and in the extension of university education to women. He is known as one of the founders of neo-Hegelianism* in England and as an outstanding critic and interpreter of Kant from the Hegelian point of view. His chief works are: *A Critical Account of the Philosophy of Kant* (1877), *The Social Philosophy and Religion of Comte* (1885), *The Evolution of Religion,* Gifford Lectures at St. Andrews (pub. 1893), and *The Evolution of Theology in the Greek Philosophers,* Gifford Lectures at Glasgow (pub. 1904). J.E.N.

Caird, John: (1820-1898) A Scottish clergyman; brother of Edward Caird*. He became Principal of the University of Glasgow in 1873. In *An Introduction to the Philosophy of Religion* (1880) he expounded his neo-Hegelianism*. He delivered two series of Gifford Lectures at Glasgow on *The Fundamental Ideas of Christianity* (pub. 1899). He was also the author of an excellent little work on *Spinoza* (1888). J.E.N.

calendar, church: See church year; church year cycle; festivals and holy days, Christian.

calendar, Julian and Gregorian: See Gregorian calendar.

calendar, Moslem: See hegira.

caliph or khalif: (Fr. *calife,* Arabic *Khalifa,* successor) The title of Mohammed's successors in temporal and spiritual power. The first four caliphs (A.D. 632-661) Aleu Bekr, Omar, Othman and Ali were generally recognized as true successors, as all were closely associated with the Prophet. Later the caliphate became a prize for ambitious rivals and led to factional strife. See Mohammedanism. P.E.J.

Calixtines: See Hussitism.

Calixtus, Georg: (1586-1656) Lutheran theologian, notable for his attempts to reconcile Christendom by removing all unimportant differences. His attempts at reconciliation between different bodies made him suspect by all, and gave rise to the Syncretistic* controversy. G.R.C.

Calixtus II, Pope: See Worms, Concordat of.

call: See vocation.

Calvary: (Lat. *calvaria,* a translation of the Gr. *kranion,* in turn a translation of the Aramaic *golgotha,* "skull") The name given to the place of the Crucifixion in the AV of Lk 23:33, taken from the Latin Vulgate. The other Gospels have the Aramaic form. The word is usually explained as "skull shaped knoll," but this explanation is not certain. B.S.E.

Calvary Pentecostal Church: See pentecostal sects.

Calvin, John: (1509-1564) Born at Noyon, Picardy; educated for the Church, and then the legal profession; but had begun a literary career and published his commentary on Seneca's *de Clementia* when he experienced his "sudden conversion", 1532. A fugitive for his new faith in France and the Rhine cities until Farel* persuaded him to settle in Geneva, 1536, and guide the Reformation that had already begun there, he yet managed to publish *The Sleep of the Soul* (Orleans, 1534), and the first edition of *The Institutes* (Basel, 1536). Banished, with Farel and Courauld, from Geneva in 1538, he settled in Strassburg, working as professor, pastor, author and delegate to the various Colloquys, until, in 1541, at the repeated urging of the Genevan Councils, he returned to Geneva, remaining till his death in 1564. There, in addition to advising the Councils on the organization and discipline of the whole life of the town, he guided the Church and many of the Churches throughout Protestantism, and published controversial tracts, and commentaries on most of the books of Scripture. See Calvinism; catechism; catechumenate.

P. Schaff, *History of the Christian Church* (1923), Vol. VII, pp. 223ff.; B. B. Warfield, *Calvin and Calvinism* (1931). A.K.R.

Calvinism: That system of theology and of Church organization and practice which grew out of the work of John Calvin*. Theologically it is marked by the acceptance of the supreme role of Scripture in revelation, the interpretation of the same being under the guidance of the Holy Spirit. It affirms a lesser degree of revelation in both nature and reason. From Scripture it deduces the doctrine of the total sovereignty of God, its basic doctrine. With these presuppositions the system evolves logically: To do God's will is man's first duty; in Adam this was possible; in the Fall this power was destroyed; all are rightfully damned; God in Christ redeems whom He wills, i.e., the elect; these live by faith in union with Christ; they find themselves able to do God's will in the world; His purpose moves through history to its destined end. A solid basis for ethics is established in the concept that the ability to live the Christian Law is evidence of probable election. The Church, the sacraments, (Baptism and The Lord's Supper), and the Civil Government are divine institutions. Abuse of the system is frequently by means of over-emphasis upon a single unit, but the whole is powerful and effective. Historically it worked itself out in the Church-State of Geneva, the Huguenots of France, the Reformed Churches of the Rhineland, the Presbyterians of Scotland, the Puritans of England and New England, and other groups. See five points of Calvinism; libertarianism; New England theology; predestination; Reformed Churches; reprobation.

John Calvin, *The Institutes of the Christian Religion;* Thomas Lindsay, *A History of the Reformation in Lands beyond Germany* (1917); Williston Walker, *A History of the Christian Church* (1918). E.P.B.

Calvinistic Methodists: At first a number of entirely independent revivalistic movements originating about 1735 in South Wales and in England, similar to those which soon sprang up under the Wesleys* in being popular in appeal, and connected with the Church of England, but differing in being Calvinistic. An early tendency to form a loose organization under Whitefield's* leadership ended about 1748. After 1790 the movement received a fresh impulse, and began to organize—a process which came to fruition when the first General Assembly of the Welsh* Calvinistic Methodists was held in 1864. They are often called Presbyterians, and a branch established in American united with the Presbyterian Church, U. S. A. in 1920. See Huntingdon's Connexion. A.K.R.

Calvinists, consistent: See Calvinists, old; means.

Calvinists, old or moderate: In New England, the theological party that took the midde position between the liberals of eastern Massachusetts who rejected basic tenets of Calvinism*, and the Consistent Calvinists or Hopkinsians* who, with inexorable logic, pushed the doctrines of Calvinism to their harshest forms. All shades of Calvinists emphasized the sovereignty of God, but in opposition to the Consistent Calvinists, the moderates held that it was preserved in "appointed means" (see "Means"). The party emerged after the great colonial revivals in defense of the moderate position against "consistent Calvinism", especially that of the Hopkinsians. Always the majority party, its basic principles prevailed in the evangelical Calvinism (New Haven Theology*,) developed after the Revolution. See New England theology.

G. L. Walker, *Some Aspects of the Religious Life of New England* (1897); Joseph Haroutunian, *Piety Versus Moralism* (1932); F. H. Foster, *Genetic History of the New England Theology* (1907); S. E. Mead, *Nathaniel William Taylor* (1942). S.E.M.

Camaldolese (Camaldolites, Camaldulians, Camaldulensians): A Roman Catholic order of hermits and cenobites*, founded by St. Romuald at the beginning of the 11th century. The original hermitage was at Camaldoli (*Campus Maldoli*) in Tuscany. After the death of the founder, some houses became cenobitic. Pope Alexander II first recognized the Order in 1072. The original austere rule, maintained by oral tradition, has been modified in cenobitic establishments to an approximation of the Benedictine* regulations. The habit is white; outdoors the Camaldolese are distinguished by very full, long white cloaks. A few Italian convents of nuns follow the same rule. Not devoted to preaching or teaching, the Order has not profoundly influenced Catholic theology. V.J.B.

Cambridge Arminians: See Latitudinarians.

Cambridge Platform, The: The New England model of church government adopted by a Synod in 1648 and, guardedly, approved by the Massachusetts General Court in October, 1651 and recommended to the churches. It remained the standard of Congregationalism* in Massachusetts throughout the colonial period, and in Connecticut until the Saybrook Platform* was adopted in 1708.

Pointed inquiries about the New England way from ministers in the mother country, the troubles with Roger Williams and Anne Hutchinson**, the appearance of Baptist views, the assertion of strong Presbyterian sentiments in the colony, and other factors all combined to make the leaders in the Bay Colony recognize the necessity to define their position. Hence at the instigation of a group of ministers the Court called a synod to do so. The Platform adopted in August, 1648 was written by Richard Mather, modified in synod, and provided with a preface by John Cotton. It approves "for the substance thereof" the doctrinal parts of the Westminster Confession, and, on the assumption that "the partes of Church-Government are all of them exactly described in the word of God," it attempts to define the Scripture pattern of the Church. Carefully deliberated, the Platform's seventeen chapters are a summary of the best thought of the New Englanders on Congregationalism, after almost twenty years experience in its practical administration. As Williston Walker says, it states clearly the "abiding principles of Congregationalism. The covenant as the basis of the local church, the autonomy of each congregation, coupled with its dependence on other churches for fellowship and counsel, the representative character of the ministry, above all the absence of all final authority in doctrine or polity save the Word of God, are the essential features."

W. Walker, *History of the Congregational Churches in the United States* (1899); *Creeds and Platforms of Congregationalism* (1893). S.E.M.

Cambridge Platonists: A group of ethical scholars led by Cudworth* with headquarters in Cambridge. The movement was designed to promote the traditional philosophy of the Humanistic era. It was born out of antagonism against Hobbes who advocated a mechanical theory of ethics. The Cambridge Platonists sought to refute this theory with renewed emphasis on teleology. Henry More (1614-1687), John Norris (1628-1677), Samuel Clarke (1675-1729), William Wollaston (1659-1724), Richard Price (1723-1791), Richard Cumberland (1632-1718), were members of this group. See Platonism. W.G.H.

Cameron, John: (1579-1623) Born in Glasgow, where he received his early education, and where he later served for less than a year as Principal of the University. Most of his life, however, was spent in the service of the French Protestant Church, as professor of divinity at Saumur and at Montauban. He was basically a Calvinist, but approached the Arminian position on the doctrine of grace, thus becoming the founder of a party within the French Protestant Church, often called Amyraldians. A.K.R.

Cameronians: The most resolute and irreconcilable of the Scotch Presbyterians who, refusing to accede to the effort of Charles II to establish his supremacy in the Scottish Church*, were ousted in 1622. Neither the bitter persecutions of Charles, nor the indulgence of James II, nor even the restoration of full Presbyterianism under William of Orange, could win them all. They continued as a separate Church, usually called the Reformed Presbyterians, until most of them united with the Free Church* in 1876. See Covenanters. A.K.R.

Camisards (Barbets, Assemblers, Children of God): Protestant peasants of Cévennes who, under the leadership of Jean Cavalier, teen-aged son of a baker, fought Roman Catholics because of the revocation of the Edict of Nantes*, from 1702 to 1705 and after. Described in Clement XI's* bull as the "ancient Albigenses*," they did spring from the same soil as did those medieval heretics. The movement was fanatical, accompanied by ecstatic prophecies, prodigies, voices, preternatural lights in the sky, and was stirred by the publication of Pierre Jurieu's *L'accomplissement des prophéties* (1689). The excesses were deplored by the other French Huguenots*. A.C.

campanile: (Lat. *campana,* a bell) An Italian bell tower usually detached from the rest of the building. Sometimes used in the case of other towers. F.T.P.

Campbell, Alexander: (1788-1866) Leader in a reformatory movement which, designed to promote the unity of Christians by restoring primitive Christianity and especially the primitive conditions of Christian fellowship, issued in a separate religious body, the Disciples of Christ*. Born in County Antrim, Ireland, son of Thomas Campbell, he spent a year in Glasgow University and came in 1809 to America whither his father had preceded him. He settled in what is now the panhandle of West Virginia and took up the work which Thomas Campbell had already initiated. He was ordained, preached widely, founded and edited two monthly magazines, the *Christian Baptist* (1823-30) and the *Millennial Harbinger* (1830 until his death in 1866), was a member of the Virginia Constitutional Convention of 1829, founded Bethany College, of which he was president for twenty years, engaged in five great debates which were subsequently published, and all the while conducted a large and profitable farm which was the source of a considerable fortune.

Robert Richardson, *Memoirs of A. Campbell* (1868); Benjamin Lyon Smith *Alexander Campbell* (1930). W.E.G.

Campbell, John McLeod: (1800-1872) Best known for his work on *The Nature of the Atonement* (1856) in which he held that Christ had effected the requisite repentance on behalf of humanity and fulfilled the conditions of forgiveness. Christ's sufferings were not penal (as held by his contemporaries). His theory paved the way to an ethical and away from the legal interpretation of the doctrine of the atonement. In 1830 his views were pronounced heretical by the Presbyterian General Assembly but he continued his theological studies and a career in an undenominational church. V.F.

Campbell, R. J.: See New theology, the.

Campbell, Thomas: (1763-1854) An Irish Seceder Presbyterian minister, of Scottish descent, who came to America in 1807, became dissatisfied with the doctrines and practices of his church and, for the promotion of Christian union, organized the Christian Association of Washington, Pa., and wrote "A Declaration and Address" which embodied the principles upon which his son Alexander* built the movement which became the Disciples of Christ*.

W. H. Hanna, *Thomas Campbell* (1935); R. Richardson, *Memoirs of Alexander Campbell* (1868).

W.E.G.

Campbellites: A term sometimes applied to Disciples of Christ* a) whimsically, by themselves; b) ignorantly, by the non-church public; c) viciously, as well as ignorantly, by the less enlightened members of the less enlightened sects. Obsolescent, with the general advance of religious intelligence and interdenominational courtesy.

W.E.G.

Canaanite religion: See Baalism.

Canaanites: Ancient people of Palestine, kindred to the Phoenicians* and to the Hebrews, often mentioned in the O.T. Also called Amorites.

See W. F. Albright, "The Present State of Syro-Palestinian Archeology", in *The Haverford Symposium on Archeology and the Bible* (1938), edited by E. Grant, pp. 1-46. See Tell-el-Amarna Tablets.

S.L.T.

Canada, the United Church of: See United Church of Canada, the.

Candlemas: The feast of the presentation of Christ in the temple (St. Luke 2:22), known in the West as the Purification of the Blessed Virgin Mary* and in the East as the Meeting with Simeon and Anna. Celebrated since Justinian on February 2nd, this date in Rome coincided with the penitential processions* derived from the pagan Amburbale in which the officiants carried lights. That custom and the reference in Simeon's song have made this the day for the blessing of candles for the year and a procession with candles, whence the name. T.J.B.

Canisius, St. Peter: (1521-1597) Dutch Jesuit, leader of Counter-Reformation in Germany. The friend of bishops and princes, he was influential in revitalizing German Catholic universities, and founded a dozen Jesuit institutions which remained for centuries centers of culture. In addition he was an indefatigable preacher and writer. His catechism became standard in Catholic Germany.

E.A.R.

cannibalism: Eating by man of human flesh. The practice seems to have been universal in the early stages of culture. Hunger was the primary motive. The first limitation came when the tribal law "do not kill kinsmen" was extended to "do not eat them". Yet the desire to keep the powers of a person of outstanding qualities in the clan often led to the eating of his body. Enemies were eaten as a pleasant way of treating them with anger and contempt. Members of the tribe who had broken the group code sometimes suffered the same fate. The desirable qualities of an enemy might be acquired by eating a part of his body. When a man was sacrificed as the embodiment of a god he was eaten in a kind of communion. Sorcerers sometimes qualified for office by eating putrid human flesh. Holy men might show their contempt for the world in the same way.

A.E.H.

canon: In music, a polyphonic* composition in which a melody repeats itself at a definite interval of pitch and of time. A common example is a canon at the interval of an octave and the distance of one measure. E.H.B.

canon: (Gr. *kanon,* "rule" "standard") Usually an ecclesiastical law pertaining to doctrine or, more generally, discipline; the codified laws of the Roman Catholic, Anglican and possibly other communions are "canons" or "canon laws." In liturgics* a part of the service especially in accord with rule; among Roman Catholics the part of the Mass* following the Sanctus* and concluding before the Lord's Prayer (or after the priest's communion); in the Orthodox church "canons" are certain canticles or litanies**. In a quite different sense (from the Lat. *canonicus*) certain clergymen are "canons"; originally because their names were entered on the "canon" or list of a large church. The title is now reserved for members of a cathedral staff or of certain religious orders. B.S.E.

Canon, Buddhist: See Buddhist Terminology.

canon, Old and New Testament: The list of books accepted as scripture by the Christian church, usually reckoned by Protestants at 39 in the O.T. and 27 in the N.T. While Jewish piety pushed back the beginning of its scripture to Moses himself, it probably began with the finding of Deuteronomy in the temple in the course of Josiah's reformation in B.C. 621. It was accepted as the text book of the reformation and became the literary nucleus of the Jewish Law, Gen.-Deut., which reached its full development early in the fourth century before Christ. It was regarded as the full expression of the will of God.

The Prophets, Former and Latter, came to be recognized as authoritative between B.C. 250 and 175. The Former Prophets were the books of Joshua, Judges, Samuel, and Kings; the Latter were Isaiah, Jeremiah, Ezekiel and the Twelve Minor prophets, grouped as one, since by reason of their brevity they made a roll shorter than either Isaiah or Jeremiah. By B.C. 175 other books were coming to be accepted by the Jews as scripture. Sirach speaks of the "rest of the books," and by the latter part of the first century Luke could speak of the Law, the prophets and the Psalms, as making up the Jewish scriptures. It was not until the end of that century however that the Hebrew canon reached completion, the third section of it consisting of the Psalms, Proverbs, Job and the Five Rolls,—Song of Songs, Ruth, Lamentations, Ecclesiastes and Esther, each of which was read at one of the five feasts, from Passover to Purim; and finally of Daniel, Ezra-Nehemiah, and Chronicles. This made a total, as the Jews counted, of twenty-four sacred books in their scriptures. Song of Songs and Ecclesiastes remained longest in doubt, and even after the Synod of Jamnia, in A.D. 90, some rabbis would not accept Esther as scripture.

The early church very soon adopted the Jewish scriptures, but in the Greek version, which included a number of other books, Judith, Tobit, the Wisdom of Solomon, the Wisdom of Sirach (Ecclesiasticus), I Esdras, I, II, III and IV Maccabees, Baruch, an expanded form of Esther, and the additions to Daniel—Susanna, the Song of the Three Children, and Bel and the Dragon. There were other additions too, in some lists and manuscripts: the Psalms of Solomon, the Prayer of Manasseh, the Book of Enoch, etc. Melito of Sardis pointed out the narrower proportions of the Hebrew canon, and Jerome was aware of them and designated the Greek additions to it "Apocrypha," not by way of condemnation, but simply as secret or hidden books, perhaps overlooked by the Jewish canonists. He admitted them to the Latin vulgate version, and through it they passed more or less completely into the German Catholic Bible and Wyclif's and Purvey's English version, 1382-88.

But when Luther had completed his translation of the Hebrew O.T., there remained a dozen pieces familiar from the Vulgate and the Old German versions which had to be dealt with, and these Luther and the Zwingli Bible of 1530 treated separately, as the Apocrypha. The first printed English Bibles followed this procedure—Coverdale, Rogers, Taverner, Great, Geneva, Bishops', King James. But by 1599 the Puritans began to omit them from some printings of the Geneva, and in 1629 copies of King James began to appear without them. The Bible Societies, both British and American, since 1827 have declined to use their funds to print them, and one seldom sees a hand copy of King James that contains them. The English revisers (1895) gave them very slight attention, and the American (1900) none at all. They have great value however as giving us the Jewish religious background of N.T. times. The standard list in complete English Bibles is I and II Esdras, Tobit, Judith, Additions to Esther, Wisdom, Ecclesiasticus, Baruch, Song of the Three Children, Susanna, Bel and the Dragon, Prayer of Manasseh, I and II Maccabees.

Christianity began as a religion not of the letter but of the spirit, and inherited a rich religious literature; moreover its keen apocalyptic expectations were unfavorable to literary composition. And yet it found its way in no long time to a scripture of its own, in addition to its great inheritance. The first unconscious step in that direction was the collection of the Letters of Paul, not long after A.D. 90. Of this we may be sure, since the early gospels and the Acts are so clearly unacquainted with them, while almost every Christian work written after that time shows their influence. They were collected not as scripture, but purely for their obvious religious usefulness. The collection of the four gospels, some twenty-five years later, was a second step toward a Christian scripture, though it was not so intended. It was probably meant to further the influence of the new Gospel of John. Marcion's* movement toward uniting and organizing the churches involved the rejection of the O.T. and putting in its place a Christian scripture consisting of the Gospel of Luke and ten letters of Paul. These were to be read in church instead of the Law and the Prophets. Christians of the more standard type preferred to retain the O.T., and to put with it the Four Gospels; this is the stage reflected in Justin Martyr, A.D. 150-160.

That was the blooming time of the sects, as Harnack put it, and when Marcionism and Gnosticism were followed by Montanism with its extravagant prophetic claims, the non-schismatic churches united under Roman leadership, into a standard, general, "Catholic" church, with a creed denying the chief heresies of the time (substantially what we know as the Apostles' Creed*), a three-fold ministry (bishop-elders-deacons), and a N.T. scripture, to stand beside, not in place of, the Old.

This consisted of the two great collections of the four gospels and the Pauline letters; the latter had already begun to be read in some churches, as the Acts of the Martyrs of Scilli shows; they were now supplemented by the Pastoral Letters (to Timothy and Titus), which disowned the main positions of Marcionism, and provide rules for church officers and organization. These two collections were united by the book of Acts which related them to each other and showed the apostolic foundation of the church. And with Acts stood a small group of minor letters bearing the names of apostles, I Peter, I John, Jude. There were also a few apocalypses,—the Revelations of John and of Peter, and the Shepherd of Hermas. These books (no one seems to have accepted more than twenty-two of them) were to be read in church along with the Greek O.T., and resorted to as authorities in doctrinal controversies.

This was the situation about A.D. 180, at least in the west, where Irenaeus at Lyons, and Tertullian at Carthage in the following decades reflect it, and expressly acknowledge the leadership of the Roman church in their course. This was a N.T. of twenty-two books. But Christian leaders of Egypt were not satisfied with so small a N.T. Clement of Alexandria around the end of the second century added Hebrews to the Pauline letters, and the letters of Barnabas and of Clement of Rome to the general or Catholic Letters. He accepted the Preaching of Peter (now lost) without question, so that he had a N.T. of at least thirty books, and perhaps more, for some which he quotes as scripture are now nowhere to be found. Origen, in the first half of the third century living first at Alexandria and then at Caesarea, had twenty-nine books in his N.T.,—our twenty-seven and Barnabas and the Shepherd. Syria on the other hand held to twenty-two books, accepting only three Catholic letters and no apocalypse.

In general however, the east accepted Hebrews, while the west did not; Hilary (367) was the first western father to accept it, and Jerome a few years later declared the custom of the Latins did not receive it, but nevertheless included it in his Vulgate version. The west had no doubts about Revelation, which the east was divided upon, after Dionysius of Alexandria about the middle of the third century had shown the difficulty of assigning it and the Gospel of John to the same author.

The canon of Eusebius was substantially ours (A.D. 326) but there was no little difference of opinion in the fourth and early fifth centuries. But the voice of Athanasius in his Easter letter of A.D. 367 went far to settle the matter, in favor of the N.T. of twenty-seven books which we know. That was also the list of the Latin Vulgate a generation later. The Greek N.T. was seldom gathered into one manuscript volume, but better book-making in the west made it possible to put the Latin N.T. into one small leaf-book, and that physical presentation of the N.T. went far to clinch its victory, which was completed by the printed forms of the Greek and the new translations from 1516 onward. In general, the growth of the N.T. was not the work of councils, but a response to the practical needs of the churches. See under specific books mentioned. See Apocrypha, Old Testament; O.T. Lit.; N.T. Lit.

B. F. Westcott, *A General Survey of the History of the Canon of the New Testament* (London, 7th ed., 1896); J. Leipoldt, *Geschichte des Neutestamentlichen Kanons* (2 vols. Leipsic, 1908); A. Souter, *The Text and Canon of the New Testament* (1913); A. Harnack, *The Origin of the New Testament* (1925); E. J. Goodspeed, *The Formation of the New Testament* (1926).

E.J.G.

canon and canoness: (Gr. *canon,* rule) Canons are men half way (a *quid medium* as Erasmus said), between monks and the secular clergy; their work is neither that of the monastic life nor that of the parish priest, but simply the celebration of the sacred mysteries. They claim to have originated with St. Augustine. Since the eighth century, the title canoness is given to women professing a common life though not following the rule of St. Augustine; their work is contemplation, or nursing the sick, or educating children.

L.R.W.

Canon Law: The law of the Catholic, especially the Roman-Catholic Church, law being understood in the sense of a system of norms of conduct emanating from an authority claiming unquestioning obedience, and sought to be formulated with precision. Such a system of law became necessary as soon as the Church aspired at being an ecumenical organization and as such the sole and institutionalized dispenser of divine grace and teacher of the word.

Canon law is a species of the wider concept of ecclesiastical law which signifies either any type of law autonomously developed for its own regulation by a church or a law imposed upon a church by the state. In a different and narrower sense the term canon law is occasionally used in the Roman-Catholic Church as signifying the rules contained in the *Corpus Juris Canonici* or now in the *Codex Juris Canonici* as distinguished from Church Law expressed in such other sources as non-codified papal decretals and *leges,* church regulations emanating from bishops and other subordinate authorities, concordates concluded between the Church and state governments and uncodified general or particular Church customary law.

The essential bases of the Canon Law are thought to consist of divine law, i.e., of norms directly established for His Church and directly revealed by God Himself and therefore of immutable character. This character is ascribed especially to the rules establishing the Pope's infallibility and plenitude of jurisdiction, the juristic personality of the Church and the Holy See, and the *hierarchia ordinis* as well as *jurisdictionis;* also the rules concerning the nature of the sacraments, among them those establishing the indissolubility of marriage and prohibiting mixed marriages involving *periculum perversionis* for the Catholic part or the offspring. The bulk of rules established upon the basis of the divine law is recognized as man-made and therefore changeable *ius positivum.*

The unwieldy mass of papal decretals and conciliar canons that had accumulated in the course of the centuries and had been sought to be assembled in such collections as the *Dionysio-Hadriana* (6th century), the *Hispana* (8th century) and the *Pseudo-Isidoriana,* (a successful forgery of the 9th century) were finally and systematically digested around 1140 in the *Concordantia discordantium canonum* of Gratian of Bologna. Subsequently recognized as authoritative this epochal work became the first part of the *Corpus Juris Canonici,* the monumental counterpart to the Emperor Justinian's *Corpus Juris Civilis* (533-565). The legislative efforts of three-and-a half centuries were expended on the canonical law book which, in addition to Gratian's* work commonly called the *Decretum,* consists of the following parts: *Liber Extra,* issued in 1234 by Gregory IX, the *Liber Sextus* of Boniface VIII (1298), the *Clementinae,* originally published by Clement V in 1313 and revised by John XXII in 1317, and, finally, the originally private collection of the *Extravagantes Ioannis XXII* and the *Extravagantes communes* which contain decretals down to the end of the pontificate of Sixtus IV in 1484. The whole work was officially published as *editio Romana* in 1582 by Gregory XIII. The accumulation of such new materials as later papal *constitutiones, leges,* and *rescripta,* decrees and instructions of the Sacred Congregations, offices and tribunals of the Holy See and the canons and decrees of the Council of Trent (1545-1563) and the Vatican Council (1869-1870) made a new codification desirable. This work was begun under Piux X and completed under Benedict XV, by whom it was promulgated under the date of Pentecost 1917. The new *Codex Juris Canonici* is substantially the work of Cardinal P. Gasparri. Profiting from the techniques developed in the elaboration of such temporal codifications as the Code Napoleon of 1804, the German Civil Code of 1896 and the Swiss Code of 1907, the new Codex shows a much higher technical perfection than the bulky old *Corpus Juris Canonici.* The entire mass of materials has been condensed into 2414 canones, which are expressed in monumental Latin and distributed among the following five Books: *Normae generales, De personis, De rebus, De processibus, De delictis et poenis.*

New laws of the Church which, according to the express Papal pronouncement of the *Motuproprio "Cum iuris canonici"* of 1917 are to be issued but sparingly, are ordinarily promulgated in the *Acta Apostolicae Sedis,* the official gazette of the Church.

Today the Canon law contents itself with covering the constitution of the Church, its organization and administration, the discipline of the clergy, the religious orders and the Catholic, i.e., on general principle, still the entire Christian, laity, and the administration of the sacraments, among them marriage, and of the sacramentals. Topics of mere doctrine or liturgy do not fall within the scope of the law. In the days of the Church's aspiration at world domination the scope of the canon law was considerably wider. Claiming not only criminal and civil jurisdiction over the clergy and church property but also an extensive jurisdiction over the laity in criminal and civil matters touching sin the Church became involved in a century-long struggle with the temporal powers. Being successful in this struggle for long periods the Church found occasion to elaborate rules on such topics as contracts, civil and criminal procedure, wills and administration of decedent estates. For these topics the Church, elaborating and modernizing traditions of Roman law, developed rules and techniques which were far in advance of contemporary temporal law and became exemplary for the temporal lawyers. See decretals; ecclesiastical courts; jurisprudence; law.

A. Cicognani, *Canon Law* (1934); S. Woywood, *Practical Commentary on the Code of Canon Law,* 5th ed., 3 vols. (1939); C. A. Bachofen, *Commentary on the New Code of Canon Law,* 6th ed., 8 vols. (1937); H. A. Ayrinhac, *Marriage Legislation in the New Code of Canon Law* (1918); U. Stutz, *Der Geist des Codex iuris Canonici* (1918); *The Jurist,* publ. by the School of Canon Law of the Catholic Univ. of America (1941 et sq); F. W. Maitland, *Roman Canon Law in the Church of England* (1898); Carl Zollmann, *American Church Law* (1933); H. D. Hazeltine, "Canon Law" vol. 3, *Enc. Soc. Sc.* p. 179. M.Rh.

canon law of Islam: See figh. Cf. Sunna.

canonical hours: See divine office. E.R.H.

canonization: (from the Gr., *kanon,* rule) Official proclamation on the part of the Pope that some person is to be venerated everywhere as a saint. The papal statement is made only after beatification*, or the decree permitting the person to be honored in a limited area, and after at least two miracles through the blessed one's intercession are authenticated. See saints, veneration. L.R.W.

canons, Anglican: The revision of canon law* ordered in 1534 was never completed (though a draft *Reformatio legum ecclesiasticarum* was published in 1571, and so technically mediaeval canons are in force in England unless revised. But in 1604 the English Convocations adopted a code of canons embracing the most practically needed parts of mediaeval and later ecclesiastical legislation; this has been slightly amended since 1865, but more affected by a legal decision of 1736 which denied the power of Convocation to bind the laity. Outside England the Anglican Churches have, as voluntary societies, their own codes, though the mediaeval and 1604 canons may be appealed to as precedents. The American Canons, first issued in 1789, have been frequently amended since. E.R.H.

Canons, Collections of Apostolic: (Gr. *kanon,* rule) An ancient collection of decrees for the government of the Church. L.R.W.

canons of various churches: The Bible of Jesus was the Hebrew O.T.* which when closed in the second century of the Christian era contained thirty-nine books according to the Christian enumeration but twenty-four as the Jews counted. The Bible of Paul* and the early Gentile* Christians was the Greek translation of the Hebrew O.T. still expanding and containing additional books, now known as Apocrypha*. Catholicism followed the Alexandrian* tradition; Protestantism returned to the shorter Bible of Palestine.

The Council of Trent*, 1546, included Wisdom of Solomon, Ecclesiasticus, Tobit, Judith, I, II. Maccabees plus Additions to Daniel, Rest of Esther, Baruch with the Epistle of Jeremiah in its list and published III Ezra, IV Ezra and the Prayer of Manasses** in an appendix to the N.T. The Vatican Council* devoted an anathema to anyone either failing to acknowledge the list of Trent or denying their inspiration. After earlier hesitation the Greek Church, Synod of Jerusalem 1672, granted canonical standing to Wisdom of Solomon, Ecclesiasticus, Tobit and Judith. Codex Vaticanus* interweaves these four books with the other 39 books of the Palestinian list. Codex Alexandrinus* does the same for the additions to Jeremiah, Daniel and Esther, Tobit, Judith and I—IV Maccabees. Wyclif* similarly lists III Ezra, Tobit, Judith, Wisdom of Solomon, Ecclesiasticus, Baruch. Some of the "Pseudepigrapha"* of the O.T. were accepted in the separate churches, especially the Ethiopic church. The question is further complicated because the N.T. itself not only quotes from the Apocrypha but from Jewish apocalypses* (I Cor. 2:9, Jude 9, 14 ff) as well.

Regarding the limits of the N.T., Catholicism and Protestantism are in general agreement but the Provincial Churches often dissent.

The seven Catholic epistles and Revelation** waited long for admission to the canon of both Eastern and Western Catholicism, and the old questions were debated anew in the sixteenth century. Revelation is not read in worship in the Eastern Church. The Nestorian and Syrian Churches** have not received II, III John, II Peter, Jude and Revelation but the latter uses III Corinthians, Testament of the Lord, six books of Clement, etc. The Ethiopian Church has 46 books in the O.T. and 35 in the N.T. The Armenian Church*, 1276, added 5 books of Clement*, Ananias of Damascus, book of James, 2 books of the Canons of the Apostles, 3 sermons of Justus, 4 books of Dionysius the Areopagite*, and 5 books of the Preaching of Peter*. Codex Sinaiticus* contains the Epistle of Barnabas and the Shepherd of Hermas** and Codex Alexandrinus, I, II Clement. The Coptic Church* did not read Revelation but was fond of the Apostolic Fathers*, apocryphal gospels and acts, homilies of the Greek fathers, etc. See apocrypha in the N. T. church.

J. A. Bewer, *The Literature of the O. T. in its Historical setting* (1922); R. H. Charles, *The Apocrypha and the Pseudepigrapha, of O. T.* (1913); O. Eisfeldt, *Einleitung in das A. T.* (1934); E. J. Goodspeed, *An Introduction to the N. T.* (1937); C. R. Gregory, *Canon and Text of N. T.* (1907); W. O. E. Oesterley, *An Intro. to the Books of the Apocrypha* (1934).

C.H.M.

cantata: The 17th century cantata, given definitive form by Carissimi, consisted in a series of arias for one or two solo voices accompanied by harpsichord and a few other instruments such as violoncello, lute, or oboe. Other composers who followed this practice were Alessandro and Domenico Scarlatti and Handel.

The church cantata of the 18th century reached its culmination in the 295 cantatas of Bach. In about 40 cases Bach used only solo voices but employed an orchestral accompaniment. In the majority of cases the works open with a large chorus, continue with a series of recitatives and arias, and conclude with a simple chorale in which the congregation took part.

The modern cantata makes greater use of the chorus and may be either sacred, like a small oratorio*, or secular, a lyric drama or story not intended to be acted.

E.H.B.

canticle of the Blessed Virgin: (Lat., *canticum*, song) The magnificat* found in St. Luke, I, 46-55; sung or recited every day at Vespers. L.R.W.

canticles: Hymns of praise from Biblical texts other than the Psalms which are sung in the Roman liturgy. Among the most familiar are the *Nunc dimittis* (Luke 2:29); the *Benedicite omnia opera* (Daniel 3:57); the *Magnificat* (Luke 1:46); and the *Benedictus Dominus Deus Israel* (Luke 1:68).

E.H.B.

cantionale: (Lat. *cantus*, song) A collection of church music for complete liturgical worship, including appropriate material for the pastor, the choir, and the congregation. Originating in the Lutheran Reformation, the classical cantionales were compiled during the sixteenth and seventeenth centuries. Outstanding among them are those of Spangenberg (1545) and Lossius (1561) and the Kralitz Cantionale of the Bohemian Brethren (1576). The Mecklenburg Cantionale (four volumes, 1868-1887) is the most complete modern work. In a looser connotation the term has been used as a synonym for hymn book. T.A.K.

cantor: (A word taken from the Assyrian *Hazzan*, overseer) Originally "the servant" of the synagogue. He is a synagogue official who leads the congregation in prayer. N.G.

capitalism: The system of production and exchange which has prevailed in Great Britain since the Industrial Revolution of the eighteenth century, and which has since been adopted in turn by and among most advanced industrial countries. The term evidently originated as an epithet with the socialist critics of the system, but for lack of a better descriptive word has now become largely innocuous and is used quite generally by economists. Different writers, however, have emphasized different features. Werner Sombart, whose *Der Moderne Kapitalismus* (1902, 1928) is the most comprehensive analysis, assigns a major role to the business organizer and his consuming zeal for profit. Karl Marx was chiefly struck with the trend toward concentration and its disastrous effects upon the workingman. Eugen v. Böhm-Bawerk (*Positive Theory of Capital*, trans. London, 1891) thought he had found the secret of capitalistic efficiency in the time factor or roundaboutness characteristic of the system. John A. Hobson (*The Evolution of Modern Capitalism*, London, 1895, 1901) deliberately selects machinery and its effects upon economic and social life as the salient point. Others stress the price economy and the expansion of the market. Certainly capital itself, although it furnishes the stem word for "capitalism", need no longer be regarded as a mark of identification since in Russia we now see it used in large masses and highly technical forms under communistic control.

The fundamental assumption of capitalism, as we know it, is that private property in the means of production and private enterprise, operating under competitive conditions and with a minimum of governmental interference, will redound to the best economic interests of a people—the fullest and most rapid development of natural resources, the most rapid advancement in technology and the practical arts, the maximum production of commodities suited to the needs of all classes of consumers at the most reasonable prices, fair payment and abundant opportunity for advancement to wage-earners, and the achievement of high rank as a world power. The motives behind business activity are admittedly self-centered, but it is held by the defenders of the capitalistic system that the public is none the less well served, and that the consumer and the workingman are adequately protected by competition and the alternatives open to them.

High capitalism, as Sombart uses the term, is usually dated in Great Britain from about 1760; in our North Atlantic States from the first quarter of the nineteenth century; in France from about 1830, although France has never committed itself fully to the system; in Germany after 1850 and mainly since 1870; in our southern states since the last quarter of the nineteenth century; and in Japan within the present century. The conditions and the course of evolution have been strikingly similar in all areas. Four factors, in addition to such stimulus as governments may have given, have been at work and each of them has been partly cause and partly effect: 1) The growth of population, particularly where swarming or migration was not easy, has from the first been a reason for the more intensive use of resources and the development of new methods of production. It creates a demand for more goods and furnishes the labor supply to carry out larger enterprises. But the most rapid increase in population in England and in other capitalist countries has come since rather than before the factory system. 2) The growth of commerce, drawing raw materials and foodstuffs from all over the world and distributing the products of industry to every nook and corner, has been a much more potent influence. It made mass production possible and brought about a higher standard of living. 3) Invention and the progress of technology, while they had to wait upon the advancement of science, were largely the outcome of this growing market. They made it possible to harness great natural forces—water-power, heat, electricity—which had hitherto lain dormant and useless. 4) The accumulation of capital to finance the system was made possible by the profits of trade and the establishment of some degree of law and order. Once started, capitalism has largely financed itself from its own earnings.

Present-day democracies are by no means so confident as were the *laissez faire* economists of the last century that the blessings of capitalism will be automatically bestowed upon an expectant and gullible world. Where consumer and producer are so widely separated there are too many chances for what Professor E. A. Ross calls "smokeless sin". We are not sure but that monopoly is as natural, at least in some industries, as is competition. Labor, especially, cannot take it for granted that "the Universe is friendly", and must stand up for its rights. Hence the rise of consumer movements, the labor movement, and the demand for regulation, even for government ownership in some fields.

See bourgeoise; labor movements; proletariat. Cf. Puritan ethics.

W. Sombart and J. A. Hobson, as above; F. L. Nussbaum, *A History of the Economic Institutions of Modern Europe* (1933); W. Cunningham, *Growth of English Industry and Commerce* (Cambridge, 1912), vol. iii.

W.B.C.

capitularies: Royal edicts issued by Merovingian and Carolingian kings dealing with matters of legislation and administration. So called because divided into chapters (capitula). Were codified in collections of ecclesiastical and secular capitularies.

K.H.C.

Cappadocians, the three: The "three lights of Cappadocia" (inland province in Asia Minor) were Basil the Great, his brother Gregory of Nyssa and Gregory of Nazianzen**. As their major contribution to the solution of the Trinitarian problem was practically identical, they are treated as one.

In working out a new theory of Trinity*, the Cappadocians took their point of departure from the three divine hypostases* which they tried to bring under the concept of the one divine being or nature. The former have concrete separate existence, and the latter is the common substance. Each concrete existence of the three divine hypostases has certain distinctive characteristics. As the characteristics refer to the descent of the hypostases from one another, they at the same time reciprocally unite the hypostases. The individual existence of the hypostases rests thus upon the peculiarity of their reciprocal relation. The Father, the Son and the Spirit are in relation to one another like principle, realization, and completion.

The Cappadocians labored with great energy for the unabridged divinity of Christ and of the Spirit. They had a lively interest in the absolute deity of these as in them the absolute really became operative, intelligible and tangible. The Cappadocians determined the difference of the divine hypostases out of their inner divine origin, and not out of their different operations. The three persons of the deity have not only the identical energy, but also have equality of dignity and nature. The Cappadocian conception of the Triune Deity preserves both the hypostatic distinction and the substantial unity. They were radical in their new theory of the absolute unity of God. God is eternal nature, who as Father through the Son and in Spirit is unitarily operative. The Cappadocians brought to a close the Trinitarian problem. Although they fully assured the reality of the three divine hypostases, they had difficulty to prove their unity. In helplessly vacillating between unity and triad, Arian* polemics accused them of the tritheistic heresy. As creators of Greek orthodoxy they interpreted Athanasius* in the spirit of a modified Origen*.

F. Diekamp, *Die Trinitätslehre des hl. Gregor von Nyssa* (Münster, 1896); J. Hergenröther, *Die Lehre von der göttlichen Dreieinigkeit nach dem hl. Gregor von Nazianz* (Ratisbon, 1850); F. Nager, *Die Trinitätslehre des hl. Basilius des Grossen* (Paderborn, 1912).

H.H.

captivity of the popes: See Avignon.

Capuchins: This autonomous branch of the Roman Catholic mendicant Order of Franciscans (Friars Minor*) dates from the reform of 1525 in Italy. Friar Matteo di Bassi, founder of the reformed group, aimed at a return to the original high-minded spirituality and austere rule of St. Francis of Assisi*. The long, pointed hood (*capuche*), similar to that worn by St. Francis, was adopted as a symbol of this reform and was the source of the name, Capuchin. The habit is brown and coarse-textured. Theologically, the Capuchins generally prefer the thought of St. Bonaventura* to that of the other great Franciscan theologian, Duns Scotus*. Their missionary activities have taken them all over the world; the early spread of Christianity in the Americas owes much to their labors. V.J.B.

cardinal: An ecclesiastical title and office. The cardinal, originally the title of great clergymen in important cities such as Constantinople, ranks before all other prelates. The chief functions of cardinals are to elect the Pope, to advise and assist him in governing the church, and to vote at oecumenical councils. See clergy; College of Cardinals. L.R.W.

cardinal virtue: (Lat. *cardo,* hinge; Lat. *virtus,* strength, excellence, virtue) The four chief virtues on which all other moral virtues are said to hinge. The four are justice, temperance, fortitude and prudence, a division found in Greek philosophy; the custom of calling them cardinal goes back at least to St. Ambrose. L.R.W.

Carew Lectureship: Presented annually at Hartford Theological Seminary, Hartford, Conn., and established in 1873 by Joseph and Eliza B. Carew. Its capital sum is $5,000. A special lectureship "for the benefit of the students and public." V.F.

Carey, William: (1761-1834) An English Baptist minister who was largely responsible for the formation in 1792 of the earliest English foreign missionary society. He was the first missionary sent out by the society, arriving in India in 1794 and remaining there until his death. While in India he distinguished himself in the field of linguistics. W.S.H.

carillon: (car-re-yoñ) A carillon is a progression of true bells, ascending chromatically through at least two octaves, and containing not less than 23 bells. A carillon differs from a chime of bells, in that it contains five chromatic notes in each octave, although in large carillons, the lowest C# is sometimes omitted. A carillon differs from a ringing peal in that its bells are always "hung dead", that is, bolted firmly to a framework of steel beams, and played from rows of hand levers; while in a ringing peal, the bells are swung until mouth upward, by means of a rope, wheel, headstock, stay and slider.

The smallest possible carillon contains 23 bells, while the largest may contain as many as six octaves, or 72 bells including the chromatic notes. There are some fifty carillons in America, the largest of which is in New York. The bourdon bell of this carillon is ten feet in diameter and weighs 20½ tons. The smallest bell of many carillons is but six inches in diameter, and weighs about eleven pounds.

A carillon is played manually, from a keyboard containing two rows of levers, spaced about 1¾ inches on centers, and an additional row of foot levers corresponding to the pedal board of a church organ. This clavier is connected to the bells by means of a delicately adjusted series of steel wires, treated so as to resist corrosion, roller boards, springs and balanced clappers. The bell hangs stationary, while the clapper is drawn quickly against the sound-bow of the bell, traveling but an inch or two.

Most American carillons are to be found in church and college towers, with a few in civic centers. Almost all of them were built either by Gillett & Johnston, of Croydon, England, or by John Taylor & Sons, of Loughborough, Leics., England. Interest in the carillon is due largely to the labors of the Hon. William Gorham Rice, of Albany, and his books and magazine articles on the subject.

The carillon's home was in Belgium, Holland and French Flanders, where almost every village had its fine carillon, and where carillon recitals attracted widespread interest. The most famous of these is the carillon of 43 bells in the great tower of St. Rombaut, in Malines, whose carillonneur for forty years or more was the late Jef Denyn.

Almost any music that can be played on a church organ may be played on a carillon, in three-part or four-part harmony. There is a famous school of carillon playing at Malines, Belgium, where many of America's best known carillonneurs have been trained. See peal ringing. F.R.W.

Carlstadt, Andreas Rudolf Bodenstein: (1480-1541) Notable as one of the pioneers of the Protestant Reformation. He held an important position at Wittenberg, and on some important points anticipated Luther's development. He had the courage of his convictions, but lacked balance of mind and steady common sense, and some of his efforts at applying reformed principles, at Wittenberg and elsewhere, nearly led to chaos. In his earlier years he was inclined to be an extremist, and the animosity he aroused repeatedly led to exile and much suffering. G.R.C.

Carlyle, Thomas: (1795-1881) British man of letters. Born at Ecclefechan, Scotland, and educated at the University of Edinburgh, he underwent in youth an intense spiritual struggle, of which *Sartor Resartus* (1833-34) is in part the record. After 1834 he lived in London. Although much of his energy was expended on such historical and biographical works as *The French Revolution* (1837) and *Frederick the Great* (1858-65), he became most widely known for his essays in political and social criticism. *Chartism* (1839), *Heroes, Hero-Worship and the Heroic in History* (1841), *Past and Present* (1843), and *Latter-Day Pamphlets* (1850) were influential. *Sartor Resartus,* however, is the most fully representative of his genius.

Among many editions of Carlyle's *Works,* perhaps the best is by H. D. Traill (31 vols., 1897-1901). The standard biography is by J. A. Froude (1884). L.W.C.

Carmelites: (Order of Our Lady of Mount Carmel) A Roman Catholic mendicant order* founded about the middle of the 12th century, in the Holy Land. Albert, Patriarch of Jerusalem formulated the original rule in 1210. Carmelite historians have endeavored to trace the antecedents of the Order to Pre-Christian, Jewish brotherhoods. First recognized by the Church, in 1274, on the recommendation of the second Council of Lyons, the Carmelites adopted their characteristic white wool mantle in 1287, hence the English name: "Whitefriars." There are two divisions of the Order: 1) *Calced,* the older and less rigorous branch; 2) *Discalced,* now more numerous, dating from the reforms of St. Teresa* of Avila, c. 1560. Theologically, the Carmelites have been noted for their opposition to Wycliffism and their rather close adherence to pure Thomism**. See John of the Cross. V.J.B.

Carneades: (c. 215-125 B.C.) Gr. philosopher, founder of the Third Academy, the outstanding sceptic* of ancient times (Zeller) and the first to bring out the difficulties in the idea of God (when defined as living and rational but also absolute and immutable). Held that logic must take account of free will and the probable indeterminateness of the future: thus "*x* will occur" may be neither true nor false, since there may at present exist no cause to make it so. Really, "*x* will occur" and "*x* will not occur" are both false if the truth is, *x* may-or-may-not occur. As Levi ben Gerson* insisted, where there is no determinate reality, all determinate assertions are false. (See foreknowledge, divine.) No writings survive.

See E. Zeller, *Philosophie der Griechen,* III.I, pp. 514ff. (1909). C.H.

Caro, Joseph: (1488-1575) Born in Spain, died in Safed, Palestine. Known chiefly as the author of the *Shulhan Aruk,* which since the seventeenth century, became the standard authority for Jewish law, ritual and observance. Caro was also a mystic as may be inferred from the diary compiled by him which deals with the discussion he had with his heavenly mentor.

Louis Ginzberg, *Jewish Encyclopedia* Vol. III (1903), pp. 583-588; Boaz Cohen, *The Shulhan Aruk as Guide for Religious Practice Today* (1941). B.C.

Caroline Books: Document issued towards end of 8th century under name of Charlemagne attacking the authority and findings of 2nd Council of Nicaea (787) and vigorously opposing image* worship. K.H.C.

carols: See hymns.

Cartesianism: The philosophical position of R. Descartes* and his followers has many points of contact with theology. In methodology, the mathematical rationalism and use of an initial doubt paved the way for free-thinking, religious rationalism and a critical approach to dogma. The psychological dualism of mind and body, coupled with a mechanical interpretation of physiology, placed greater emphasis on the intentional nature of sin. The cosmic dualism of nature and supernature, of the two types of finite substance (mind and matter) as contrasted with the Infinite Substance (God) made the rôle of Divine Grace obscure. A tendency (eventually explicit in the Occasionalists*: Malebranche, 1638-1715, and Geulincx, 1625-1669) to minimize the work of secondary, natural causes and to expand the function of primary (Divine) causality is evident. The dynamic theory of substance leads to a less-realistic explanation of Eucharistic transsubstantion* than that of Thomism. Demonstrations of the existence of God resemble the *a priori* argument of St. Anselm*, or start with facts of consciousness rather than with an *a posteriori* knowledge of the physical world. The Will of God is the ultimate reason, or ground, for the truth and goodness of reality, somewhat after the fashion of Ockham's* voluntarism. The influence of Descartes on orthodox Catholic theology is largely negative. Later Ontologism may owe something to him. The theological views of Leibniz and Spinoza** are influenced by Cartesianism.

E. Gilson, *La doctrine cartésienne de la liberté et la théologie* (Paris, 1913); H. Gouhier, *La pensée religieuse de Descartes* (Paris, 1924). V.J.B.

Carthage, Synods of: Ancient greatness of Carthage gave city a prestige which made it the main centre of the North African church*. Frequent meetings of the bishops and clergy were held there from c. 220 until fall of Carthage to Vandals (439), and again from recovery by Byzantine Empire until Moslem invasion in 7th century. These dealt with questions of baptism by heretics, readmission of the lapsed and heresy. A somewhat independent attitude was taken towards Rome. Among the most influential figures were Cyprian and Augustine**. The most important decisions were those taken in opposition to the Donatists and Pelagians**. K.H.C.

Carthusians: A Roman Catholic Order of monks founded by St. Bruno in 1084. The original establishment was at Chartreuse in the diocese of Grenoble (*Cartusia* in late Latin, corrupted as *Charterhouse** in England). The Carthusians live as solitary hermits, only coming together for certain religious ceremonies. The habit is white. In spite of a regimen which is not calculated to produce scholars, the Carthusians have had several noted theologians, of whom Dionysius Rickel (1402-1471) is best known. His works constitute a veritable encyclopedia of previous Scholastic thought. Popularly, the Order is known for the manufacture of chartreuse, a fine liqueur, revenues from which are devoted to charitable purposes. V.J.B.

Cartwright, Peter: (1785-1872) Colorful Methodist frontier preacher and enthusiastic evangelist ("the jerks"). Presiding elder over four decades. A member of Illinois legislature for two terms. In 1846, defeated for Congress by Lincoln. Author of anti-Calvinist letter to the devil. C.H.M.

Cartwright, Thomas: (1535-1603) Leader of the Elizabethan Puritan party and opponent of Whitgift.

See A. F. S. Pearson, *Thomas Cartwright and Elizabeth Puritanism* (1925). W.S.H.

Cassian, John: (ca. 360- ca. 435) A monk of Southern Gaul who introduced rules of Eastern monasticism* into the West and who led a memoral protest against the fatalism of Augustine's doctrine of predestination*. See seven deadly sins. S.M.G.

Cassiodorus, Magnus Aurelius: (c. 480-575) Scholar, churchman, and administrator who, upon the completion of his service as minister of state to Theodoric the Ostrogoth in 540, retired to his own monastic foundation of Vivarium in Southern Italy. Here he continued his versatile, scholarly pursuits, inaugurated the work of the monastic scriptorium, facilitated the acquisition of a remarkable library, and, in general, provided monasticism* with a challenge to learning and cultural preservation hitherto lacking. He was the author of such works as *The Chronicle, The Tripartite History, Letters and State Papers, The Institutions,* and *The Gothic History.* The last is now preserved only in Jordane's vastly inferior work by the same title. R.C.P.

caste: A social system best represented by India. It is believed that caste was a color line imposed by the conquering Aryans on the darker Dravidians, as the Sanskrit varna (caste) means color. The Aryans* composed the priestly and the warrior caste, while the lower ones were formed by the native populations. P.G.M.

casuistry: (Lat. *casus,* case) 1) The application of ethical principles to specific cases. 2) Quibbling, rationalization, sophistry or an attempt to justify what does not merit justification; this meaning is often associated with methods used by Jesuits. See equivocation. E.S.B.

catacombs: Catacombs is a term applied to the ancient underground burial chambers that are especially numerous in the vicinity of Rome. The vast majority of these cemeteries belonged to the Christians who constructed them during the second, third and fourth centuries. At present some thirty-five of these ancient burying grounds have been discovered. Each consists of a complicated network of subterranean passages from three to four feet wide and six or more feet high, with excavations in the walls for several tiers of bodies each carefully sealed in with cemented slabs or tiles. These corridors occupy two or more levels, sometimes even seven, and their total length has been estimated at several hundred miles. The once common notion that the catacombs were originally designed as hiding places for the early Christians in time of persecution is no longer tenable. Rather, they were publically recognized cemeteries used by the Christians who, due to their belief in physical resurrection, were unwilling to adopt the current Roman practice of cremation. See art, ecclesiastical, Christian; crypt.

W. Lowrie, *Monuments of the Early Church* (1901); O. Beyer, *Die Katakombenwelt* (1927). S.J.C.

catechesis: (Gr. *ēchein* to sound, ring, peal, *kata* downwards, *katēchein tina* to reach one by sound from above, as from the platform of the speaker or the desk of the teacher, impart knowledge by oral transmission) In the general sense of imparting oral information the verb *katēchein* is used by Luke 1:4, Acts 18:25; 21:21. Paul uses it in the more definite sense of giving oral instruction in religion. Rom. 2:18; I Cor. 14:19; Gal. 6:60. So the noun catechesis became the technical term for instruction and training preparatory for baptism, and still later for all religious instruction and training preparatory for the reception into the full membership of the church in whatever form it is given. Sometimes it denotes every individual lecture or lesson in religious education, e.g., the 18 catecheses of Cyril of Jerusalem, or 96 catecheses (or catechisations) on Luther's Catechism. M.REU.

catechetics: Abbreviation for *katchetikē techne,* the art of imparting knowledge in oral form, especially religious knowledge preparatory for full membership in the Christian church. So catechetics is what we call theory and practise of religious education*. It treats the historical development of religious education, its subject (the pupil and his inner life), the aim, the material, the method and the close of religious education.

M. Reu, *Catechetics or Theory and Practise of Religious Education* (rev. ed. 1927). M.REU.

catechism: Catechism means originally the action of oral instruction in religion, later, the book which contains the rudiments of religious instruction in whatever form they are given, whether in thetical form or in the form of questions and answers. To limit the term to the latter form is based on the wrong derivation from *echo,* the echo; nevertheless the majority of the catechisms are written in that form. Catechisms are as old as the catechumenate*. The first six chapters of the Didache* containing the way of life and death have been rightly called a catechism of the post-apostolic age. The *epideixis* of Irenaeus offering much Biblical History besides its creedal statements, Tertullian's explanation of the Lord's Prayer, the *Testimonia* of Cyprian, mostly a collection of Scripture passages for the catechumens, the *catecheses* of Cyril of Jerusalem, sermonic material for the competentes, the illustration added to Augustine's *De Catechizandis Rudibus,* Augustine's and others' explanation of the Creed for the *competentes,* all these can be called catechisms of the Ancient Church. Writings which have been called catechisms have come down to us from the time of Charlemagne. We mention only two of the most important ones: the so-called Weissenburg Catechism of 789, containing the following five parts: 1. The Lord's Prayer in German with a brief explanation based on Tertullian and Cyprian, 2. an enumeration of mortal sins according to Gal. 5:19-21, 3. the Apostolic Creed in German and Latin, 4, the Athanasian Creed in German and Latin, 5. the *Gloria in Excelsis* in German and Latin; and the *Disputatio puerorum per interrogationes et responsiones,* which is an explanation of the Creed and the Lord's Prayer in question and answer form, used for centuries and attributed to Alcuin. A number of catechetical writings from Thomas Aquinas down to Gerson mentioned in Reu's *Catechetics* pp. 71 and 75, belong to the second half of the Middle Ages. We name only three intended especially for the instruction of the children primarily in the home: *ABC des simples gens,* by John Gerson (about 1420); *Tafel des christlichen Lebens,* by an unknown author of the latter part of the 15th century; the *Cathechyzon,* 1510, by John Colet of London. Besides these we should not forget to mention Wiclif's *Poor caitiff,* tracts on the Creed, Decalogue and Lord's Prayer for the home; the first Hussite Catechism (between 1420 and 1436); the Catechism of the Moravian Brethren (before 1502) and *Las interrogacions menors* for the Waldenses in Bohemia.

A new period in the history of the Catechism began with Luther's emphasis on the religious education of the Church's youth. Cohrs describes about thirty catechetical writings for the home, the school and the church that appeared between 1520 and 1529. Near the end of 1528 and early in 1529 Luther published the first three parts of his later so-called *Small Catechism* in the form of sheets or tablets that could be fastened to the walls of the home, the church and the school. These tablets were followed in May by the first Wittenberg book edition of the whole *Small Catechism.* The Large Catechism based on his three series of sermons on catechetical material delivered in the fall of 1528 was published in April. It was intended primarily for the pastors and the adult congregation. The Small Catechism was written *pro pueris et familia* and consisted primarily in an explanation of the Ten Commandments, the Apostolic Creed, the Lord's Prayer, the Sacraments of Baptism and the Lord's Supper; there were, however, also sections on confession and daily prayers and a Table of Duties (consisting in Scripture passages concerning the various "holy orders and estates" of life in which the Christian has to prove his Evangelical morality). The new feature in Luther's Small Catechism was not its question and answer form—this was applied already by Alcuin and others during the Middle Ages; nor the assemblage of the Ten Commandments, the Creed, the Lord's Prayer and the other material for the religious instruction of the youth—we find these parts used for the same purpose before Luther's time; nor the fact that he added an explanation of these texts—even in the Middle Ages we find similar attempts; but entirely new and surpassing all the labors of the Early Church as well as the Middle Ages was the deep Evangelical interpretation of this material, an interpretation that centers in the article of justification. Because of its elimination of the polemical element, its limitation to what is necessary for salvation, its emphasis on evangelical life, its religious warmth and its simple diction, it is unsurpassed. This feature, the name of the author and a few other facts explain the triumphant march of this catechism through the countries of Europe, and why it is still today the basis of religious instruction in the Lutheran churches and missionfields in all the world. Compare Reu, *Quellen zur Geschichte der Kirchlichen Unterichts,* (Gütersloh, 1904-1935), and Reu, *Dr. M. Luther's Small Catechism. A History of its Origin, its Distribution and its Use* (1929).

Heidelberg, Zuerich and Geneva were not less active in this field than Wittenberg. The Heidelberg Catechism* appeared in 1563. Originally intended for the Palatinate alone and written by its theologians, Ursinus and Olevianus, it later became the official catechism of all the Reformed churches in Germany, Poland, Hungary, Transylvania and especially in the Netherlands, and is still today being used either as a textbook for religion or at least recognized as confessional writing. It has found its way into Reformed churches even beyond Europe (e.g., United States of America). Although rather dogmatical, it is justly renowned for the answer to its first question and its whole structure treating 1. of man's misery, 2. of man's redemption, 3. of man's gratitude—a structure borrowed from an earlier Lutheran catechism. Of Leo Jud's two catechisms the shorter one (1535) became Zuerich's official catechism; although still rather extensive, it is permeated by a sound evangelical spirit and written in simple popular diction. Calvin wrote two catechisms in French, 1537 and 1541. The Latin translation of this latter catechism by Calvin himself in 1545 as well as other translations were used in many churches; the English translation became through the "Book of Discipline" of 1560, the official textbook for the church of Scotland. It is less polemical than the catechism of 1537 and barely touches the question of eternal predestination, while the one of 1537 had a special section on this doctrine with emphasis on the *gemina praedestinatio.* It falls into four parts: 1. The Creed, 2. The Obedience towards the Law of God, 3. The Prayer, 4. The Word of God and the Sacraments. It is surprising how near it tries to come to the Lutheran doctrine of the Sacraments. In England Marshall's *Goodly Primer* in its second edition (1535) contained, besides much other material, Luther's *Short Form* of 1520, this forerunner of his *Small Catechism,* and in 1548 Cranmer translated Luther's Small Catechism together with its excellent explanation as it is found in the Nuernberg *Sermons for Children* of 1533 and published it under the title: *A Short Instruction into the Christian Religion for the Syngular Commoditie and Profite of Children and Young People.* But ultimately it was not Luther's catechism which came into general use, but the *"Instruction to be Learned of Every Child"* of 1549, somewhat changed in 1552 and supplemented by questions concerning the Sacraments added in 1604. Although very brief and in the form of 1549 containing only the text of the Creed, the Decalogue and the Lord's Prayer with a very short explanation, its characteristic mark is that it starts with a statement concerning sponsorship and thus views the entire contents from the standpoint of Confirmation where the children themselves confess and promise what was confessed and promised by the sponsors in their stead. This catechism is still a part of the Book of Common Prayer* and is official in all Episcopal churches in the world. When in the Westminster Assembly of Divines (1643-49) the opposition to the episcopal system of the Church of England was victorious, there were adopted besides the Westminster Confession, also two catechisms, the Larger and the Shorter Westminster Catechism. They exerted very little influence, however in the Church of England because Charles II in 1660 restored episcopacy with the Thirty-nine Articles and the Book of Common Prayer (including the catechism of 1549). But they were adopted by the Church of Scotland* and the Shorter Catechism is recognized as confessional writing in the Presbyterian churches of the world still today, although no longer in general use as a textbook in religious education and practically given up entirely by the liberal wing of this church. The Shorter Catechism has often been regarded as the ripest fruit of Puritan experience and theology. Ph. Schaff: "It exceeds all other catechisms by the terse brevity and precision of the questions and answers, and differs from most by the following peculiarities: 1. It embodies the question in the answer, so as to make this a complete statement; 2. It substitutes a new and logical order of topics for the old historic order of the Apostolic Creed; 3. It deals in dogmas rather than facts and addresses the intellect rather than the heart; 4. It puts the questions in an impersonal form, instead of addressing the learner directly; 5. To this may be added the theological and metaphysical character of the answers."

In 1693 the General Assembly of the Particular Baptists in London requested Wm. Collins to draw up a catechism "containing the substance of the Christian religion for the instruction of children and servants." It has been reproduced in *Confessions of Faith and other Documents* by E. B. Underhill (London, 1854). In the United States among Baptists the catechisms of A. C. Dayton and J. A. Broadus have been widely used in the last century. These are the principal catechisms of historical Protestantism. The scope of this Dictionary does not permit mentioning all the other Protestant catechisms used in the various denominations; still less does it permit a history of all those many catechetical writings based on the catechisms mentioned. Their number is legion. Reu in his *Quellen* filled not less than nine large volumes and yet told only the story of catechetical literature and instruction in Germany from 1530 to 1600.

A word, however, must be added concerning the catechisms in the *Roman Catholic Church.* The educational efforts of the churches of the reformation induced the Roman Church to make some earnest endeavors of her own toward providing more general and thorough instruction for the young. A considerable number of catechisms appeared in the sixteenth century, especially after the Jesuits* (1540) began to devote themselves to this work. Canisius, the father confessor of Emperor Ferdinand I, deserves special mention. In 1556 he issued a small catechism (i.e., a synopsis of his *Summa Doctrinae Christianae*) under the title, *Summa Doctrinae Christianae per quaestiones tradita et ad captum rudiorum accommadata.* This catechism was soon also issued in German and translated into many other languages. For more than two centuries this book was the chief catechism of the Roman Church.

In 1559 Canisius wrote a catechism for higher schools of learning which despite its bulky size bore the title, *Parvus Catechismus Catholicorum*, and which became the standard exposition of the smaller *Summa.* Even the *Catechismus Romanus* (also called *Catechismus Tridentinus*) though composed by the order of the Council of Trent and intended to be a manual for priests, or the textbooks consequently based on this catechism and designated for exclusive use (1598) did not succeed in dethroning the textbooks of Canisius. In its German form his catechism was republished even in 1810 in Philadelphia and was widely used in this country. In 1847 Jos. Deharbe published *Katholischer Katechismus oder Lehrbegriff,* based on the *Catechismus Romanus.* It was translated into many modern languages and up to the present time has been the most widely used catechism of the Roman Church. In the Orthodox Church of Russia there appeared in 1721 a rather rudimentary catechism. During the whole 19th century and later a more extensive book was used which divided the material into three parts: Faith (Nicaenum, Sacraments), Hope (Lord's Prayer, Beatitudes), Love (Ten Commandments). See catechumenate.

M. Reu, *Catechetics* (rev. ed. 1927); Ferd. Cohrs, *Katechismen, und Katechismus Unterícht, Real encyclopadie,* vol. X, (Leipzig, 1901), Compare also the article on Catechisms in Schaff,Herzog, Vol. Ii, pp. 442-449; Fr. Procter and W. H. Frere, *New History of the Book of Common Prayer* (London, 1905); W. Carruthers, *The Shorter Catechism of the Westminster Divines,* with Historical Account and Bibliography (London, 1897); Ph. Schaff, *The Creeds of Christendom,* 3 vols. (New York, 1877); Ferd Cohrs, *Die evangelischen Katechismusversuche vor Luther's Enchiridion* (Berlin, 1900-1907); M. Reu *Quellen zur Geshichte des kirchlichen Unterichts im evangelischen Deutschland zwischen 1530 und 1600* (Guetersloh, 1904-1935); A. Lang, *Der Heidelberger Katechismus und vier verwandte Katechismen* (Leipzig, 1907); Fr. H. Thalhofer, *Entwicklung des katolichen Katechismus in Deutschland von Canisius bis Deharbe* (Freiburg, 1898); T. B. Scannell, "Doctrine Christian", *The Catholic Encyclopedia,* vol. V, pp. 75-88, (1913).

M.REU.

catechism: See Sunday School movement in the United States.

catechumen: The term means literally "one who is taught by word of mouth", and was applied to a convert who received instruction with a view to baptism. It happened constantly that men and women were emotionally stirred by the preaching of missionaries without any clear idea of the truths involved in it. Before they could be received as Christians it was necessary that some definite knowledge should be imparted to them. Paul refers to "him who occupies the place of the unlearned" (I Cor. 14:16), and seems to imply that particular seats were assigned in the weekly meeting to those who were still in process of instruction. This is known to have been the practice at a later time. We learn from the book of Acts that Aquila and Priscilla gave private teaching "in the way of God" (Ac. 18: 26). Luke dedicates his Gospel to Theophilus, and speaks of him as a "catechumen", to whom he wishes to impart fuller and more accurate knowledge. From the notice in Luke it seems evident that the instruction was largely concerned with the historical facts on which Christianity was founded. It also dealt with matters of doctrine, as may be gathered from the account of Aquila and Priscilla. With the spread of heresy in the second century the need for grounding all converts in sound doctrine became ever more urgent, and the chief emphasis in the Pastoral Epistles is on this requirement. The catechumens, properly speaking, were Christians not yet baptised, who had to be trained in the elements of the faith, but the term could be so extended as to include mature and gifted converts, who were preparing to be teachers. Paul speaks of a higher wisdom which he communicated to a select group at Corinth (I Cor. 2:6ff.). The Ep. to Heb. seems to be addressed to a similar group at Rome. At Alexandria there grew up a regular "catechetical school",—what would now be called a theological college,—which played an all-important part in the development of doctrine. Among its teachers were Clement and Origen**.

L. Duchesne, *Early History of the Church* (1924); R. B. Tollinton, *Clement of Alexandria* (1914); C. Bigg, *Christian Platonism of Alexandria* (1886).

E.F.S.

catechumenate: This term denotes that institution by which the church, in agreement with Matt. 28:18-20 and John 21:15-17, prepares the catechumens, that is, those who are instructed in religion, for full membership in her midst, either adults coming from the outside or children born and baptised in her midst. In this wide sense the history of the catechumenate is identical with the history of religious education*.

The catechumenate in the *Early Church* primarily dealt with adults coming from the synagogue or from paganism. Jews or proselytes, since they were well acquainted with the O.T. were admitted to baptism and membership when they accepted Christ as the promised Messiah (Acts 2:37-39; 8:26-28), and even the preparation of the Gentiles was very brief (Acts 16:25-33). Later, when persecution set in and relapses occurred, the preparatory instruction and training became more extensive in time and more thorough in character. The Didache (Chap. 1-6), Justin Martyr (*First Apology*), Irenaeus (*Epideixis*), Tertullian (*Lectures for Catechumens*), Hippolytus (*Canones*), Cyprian (*Testimonia*), Origen (*Contra Celsum*), and Lucian Martyr (*Didascalia*) testify to this greater emphasis on religious training in the various parts of the church during the second and third centuries. We find the catechumenate in its perfected form between 325 and 450 (so-called *Apostolic Constitutions*). The applicant for church membership was oriented in a general way by a special lecture concerning the history and nature of the church (Augustine's *De Catechizandis Rudibus*) and then enrolled as a catechumen. As such he was permitted and expected to be present at the first part of the regular Sunday worship (not at the *missa fidelium*), and to read the Bible and other religious books. After two years or more (some postponed it until their old age or approaching death) these catechumens entered the class of *Competentes* or catechumens in the narrow sense. Here during several, often seven, weeks of ascetic, educational and liturgical training they were prepared for baptism. The educational training consisted usually in lectures on the Apostolic Creed and the significance of baptism (Cyril's *Catecheses;* Augustine's *De Symbolo ad Catechumenos*). This training culminated usually at Easter with Baptism and their first participation in the Lord's Supper. During the week following Easter they were expected to hear lectures explaining the Lord's Prayer and the liturgical forms of baptism and the Lord's Supper. On the first Sunday after Easter (*Quasimodogeniti*) they put off their white baptismal robe. The catechumenate had come to an end; they had entered full membership in the church. After 450 this catechumenate decayed rapidly. It was shortened in point of time and the religious instruction was so completely overshadowed by liturgical elements that often not more remained than the memorization of some creedal forms and prayers. The Early Church did not possess nor create a special agency for the religious education of those born in the church and baptized in infancy or childhood. The Christian home was entrusted with this task. In sermons and tracts the parents were repeatedly admonished to fulfill this obligation, and a man like Chrysostom showed them by way of example when and how they should carry it out. Some Fathers of the Early Church even advised the parents to have their children educated in convents.

During the Middle Ages the missionaries among the heathen followed the suggestions of Augustine in his *De Catechizandis Rudibus*, but too often they were satisfied with the mere memorization of the Creed and the Lord's Prayer and the subjection under the rules of the church. At home infant baptism had become the universal rule. Charlemagne, following the example of the Early Church, held the parents and sponsors responsible for teaching the baptized children the Creed and the Lord's Prayer, and in connection with the Confessional the church could control how far this duty was fulfilled. In the parish school, still more in the cathedral and convent schools, established by Charlemagne, the texts of the Lord's Prayer and the Creed were explained at least to those children who were fortunate enough to attend these schools; some psalms and hymns were memorized and now and then the pericopes prescribed for the Sundays of the church year were read. At that time the first catechisms, often bilingual (German or French or English and Latin), appeared and were used. In the following centuries many of these institutions decayed, but were revived in the thirteenth century. Helps for the domestic catechumenate appeared, a few even designed for children, as well as helps for the priests enabling them to supplement in the Confessional the meager domestic instruction. Many cities established Latin schools or at least schools for reading and writing the mother tongue, where training in participation in the religious life was given. In some places even Biblical history found its place in the curriculum. Compare M. Reu, *Luther's German Bible* (1934). However, as far as the common people were concerned their religious knowledge did not as a rule advance further than a mechanical memorizing of the Ten Commandments (more generally used since the 14th century), the Creed, the Lord's Prayer, the Ave Maria, the catalogue of the so-called deadly sins and a few prayers (morning, evening and table prayers), and very often not even this minimum was accomplished, especially in the country where the rule to read these parts Sunday for Sunday before the assembled congregation was often not observed. There was, indeed, room for reformation. Wiclif (*Poor caitiff*), Hus, the Moravian Brethren and the Waldenses did much for their circles, but the real reformation was brought about by Luther.

Luther's great merit in the field of religious education does not primarily consist in the establishment of new institutions and agencies, but in this, that he revived institutions formerly created, made them universal in the whole Evangelical Church and filled them with new evangelical life. Under his guidance it became a general rule that the Ten Commandments, Creed, Lord's Prayer and the words of the institution of Baptism and the Lord's Supper were recited every Sunday; that these texts were explained in short sermons four times during the year, and in more extensive sermons in the matin or vesper services; that no one was admitted to the Lord's Supper without knowledge concerning its significance and examination of his proper preparation; that the sexton drilled that part of the catechism with the children of the parish every Saturday and taught them to sing the hymns of the church and to read; that often on Sunday afternoon instead of the vesper sermon, exercises in the catechism were held, that the children were examined by the pastor in the catechism before they were admitted to the Lord's Supper for the first time; that the vernacular schools in the towns not only opened and closed with a short religious service, but taught besides reading and writing also the catechism and the hymns of the church; that the Latin schools in the cities increased greatly in number, and were transformed from primarily humanistic schools into real Christian schools in which the Gospel permeated the entire curriculum; that Luther's most excellent Small Catechism was used in the home, the school and the church, whereby streams of sound Evangelical knowledge and divine blessing found their way into the whole church. From Wittenberg and Germany these forms of religious education spread into all the other Lutheran countries. Moreover also Bucer at Strassburg, Leo Jud at Zuerich and Calvin at Geneva were very active in this direction and laid the foundation for similar forms of instruction in the various parts of the Reformed church on the continent and in England. At times even their followers surpassed the Lutherans in their zeal for thorough religious education.

In Germany the Thirty Years' War destroyed what had been built up so carefully by Luther and the sixteenth century. And yet in the midst of its terrors Duke Ernest the Pious of Gotha in Thuringia (1601-1675) moved by such eminent pedagogues as Ratichius and Comenius and by the lamentable condition of his subjects, not only revived the former institutions, but established in all towns and villages of his duchy Christian public schools which had to be attended by all boys and girls from five to twelve years of age. He is the real founder, not of our religiously neutral, but of the *Christian* public school. The Bible, Catechism and Biblical History were the foundation stones of this school; besides these, the three R's and even rudiments of geography and natural science were taught. Through August Hermann Francke (1663-1729) and the teachers prepared at his Teacher's Seminary at Halle, this type of Christian Public School remained during the entire parts of Germany and the continent. When in 1763 its principal features had been incorporated in the Prussian School Regulations it had conquered nearly all of Germany and had found its way into all those parts of the continent where the state-church system obtained. At the same time a movement set in, influenced by Rousseau and started by Basedow, to loosen the bond between the church and the school by seeking to free it from the church's authority. While the Christian Public School remained during the entire 19th century bringing forth some splendid fruits, the opposition movement became stronger and stronger and in wide circles created a situation which made it possible for Hitler to sever completely the bond between school and church and thus make an end to the Christian or Confessional Public School, leaving it to the church to find new ways for the religious education of her youth.

In the Reformed churches of Hungary, Transsylvania, in the Palatinate, and in the Netherlands the Heidelberg Catechism of 1563 was the basis of religious instruction. Since 1585 it was divided into 52 lessons, one for every Sunday. In the German speaking sections of Switzerland Leo Jud and Bullinger's catechetical works were of influence; in Geneva and in the Reformed church in France Calvin's catechism of 1545 became the basis. In England after Lutheran beginnings (Marshall's *Goodly Primer* of 1535; Cranmer's *Catechism* of 1548 being a translation of Luther's Catechism and the Nuernberg Sermons for Children of 1533) the state-church introduced, 1549 the "Instruction to be Learned of Every Child" printed in the Book of Common Prayer and enlarged by the section on the sacraments in 1604, which is still today to be recited at the time of confirmation. The "Book of Discipline" edited by Knox in 1560 for Scotland followed the Geneva pattern of instruction and introduced his catechism of 1545. In 1548 the Presbyterian church of England adopted the "Shorter Westminster Catechism" which is still today the official text for religious instruction in England, Scotland and all true Presbyterian churches in the (English speaking) world, although in practical use it has often been replaced by others. Space does not permit a detailed account of the religious education of all the other Evangelical churches of Great Britain. During the last century a good deal of religious instruction was given by the modern Sunday school system, which was in many cases the only agency for religious education.

In America it was primarily the home where religious instruction was given, usually on the basis of those catechisms that had been brought along from Europe or on the basis of John Cotton's "Milk for Babes" (1646) which together with the "Shorter Westminster Catechism", made a part of the "New England Primer" (about 1690) and Isaac Watts' "Divine Songs", his two "Plain and Easy Catechisms" (1730) and his "Scripture History" (1732). This instruction in the home was often supplemented by instruction given in the church. Thus the Pilgrim Church at Plymouth resolved in 1680, "that the deacons of the church be requested to assist the minister in teaching the children during the intermission of the Sabbath" (i.e., between the forenoon and the afternoon services). Where the state established schools (as in Massachusetts, 1647) the principal texts were religious books (comp. the New England Primer). The same holds true for many "neighborhood schools" in Pennsylvania, and especially for the regular church schools of the various Christian denominations. The church, as was so often the case in Europe, was the leader in education, and in Pennsylvania she provided nearly all the elementary education available down to 1834. The Sunday School movement was transplanted from England to America in 1791 and changed from an elementary school for neglected children to a religious school for all children and adults. And when the ever improving secular school had in many places crowded the religious day school out of existence, the Sunday school became the only religious school. In many denominations it was and is, however, supplemented by special classes of preparation for Confirmation or—where there is no Confirmation—for admission to full membership in the church,—this is what we might call the present day catechumenate. In the Lutheran church this confirmation* instruction is given with special care, often extending for two years and supplemented by the Vacation Bible School and Saturday School. In some parts of the Lutheran church the Parochial* or Christian Day School is still fostered with excellent care and great sacrifices. It is the glory of the Lutheran Synod of Missouri* extending over all the United States and beyond to have established and to have kept in force a system of parochial schools which in all secular branches stands on the same level with our best Public Schools and at the same time does not only have special hours for strictly religious education but allows the Christian spirit to permeate also all other instruction and the whole school life. See Biblical history in Christian instruction; catechism; Pantaenus; Sunday School movement in the U. S.

M. Reu, *Catechetics,* or *Theory and Practice of Religious Education* (rev. ed. 1927) (Here extensive bibliographies); S. Ch. Parker, *A Textbook in the History of Modern Elementary Education* (1912); C. L. Maurer, *Early Lutheran Education in Pennsylvania* (1932); F. G. Livingood, *Eighteenth-century Reformed Church-schools* (Harvard thesis, 1930); W. H. Beck, *Lutheran Elementary Schools in the United States* (1939); H. Shelton Smith, *Faith and Nurture* (1941).

M.REU.

categorical imperative: According to Kant,* the ultimate moral obligation that applies *a priori* to every one under all circumstances. He states it in three different formulations: 1) act according to that maxim which you could wish to be a universal law of nature upon which every one should act at all times; 2) always treat humanity in yourself and others as an end and never as merely means; 3) act always as if you were a member of a merely possible kingdom of ends. The three formulations Kant thought identical in import and application. W.K.W.

category: (Gr. *kategoria,* originally an accusation, derivatively, predication) 1) Fundamental mode of predication*; irreducible type of grammatical relation expressed in language (so Aristotle). 2) Fundamental mode of being, as substance, quantity, quality, relation, place, time, position, state, action, or affection (Aristotle, *Categoriae*, 4). 3) A principle essential to the very being of a given universe of discourse. E.g., the categories of Kant's *Critique of Pure Reason* are the principles essential to the realm of experience defined by Newton's physics, while the categorical imperative* is essential to the universe of moral experience. Hegel's categories are the principles essential to the being of the all-inclusive universe of discourse (the Absolute). Thus we may also speak of categories of logic, ethics, physics, religion, etc. 4) Popularly, used as equivalent to class or general idea (so Royce in Baldwin). E.S.B.

catena: (Lat., a chain) A collection of excerpts from early ecclesiastical writers, strong together to exhibit a connected interpretation of some Scriptural passage. S.M.G.

Cathari: (Also known as Albigenses*) A medieval, puritannical and heretical movement ruthlessly exterminated. A repristination of Manichaeism* and Gnostic christology*, maintaining to be the only true church of a holy hierarchy and efficacious sacraments.

J. J. v. Döllinger, *Beiträge zur Sektengeschichte des Mittelalters,* Vol. II (München, 1890); Ch. Schmidt, *Histoire et doctrine de la secte des Cathares ou Albigeois* (Paris, 1849); J. L. v. Mosheim, *Versuch einer unparteiischen und gründlichen Ketzergeschichte* (Helmstedt, 1746).

H.H.

cathedra: (Gr. a chair) The official seat or throne of the bishop in a church. See chair of St. Peter; ex cathedra. F.T.P.

cathedral: (Gr. *cathedra*, a chair) The church in which is set up the bishop's throne. The principal church of a diocese. See duomo. F.T.P.

A cathedral is the chief church of a diocese, and connected with it are a bishop, a dean and chapter, and various other dignitaries. The term must not be applied loosely to a large parish church.

The best known cathedral church in America is St. John the Divine, New York. This church, 601 feet in length, was begun in 1892, and is still unfinished. The chancel, choir, nave, baptistery and seven apsidal chapels are practically complete and in use. The two transepts and the great central tower are yet to be built, while the two western towers rise to but one-half their final height. The cathedral has cost $20,000,000 to date, and to complete it will cost $10,000,000 more. When complete, it will be the third largest cathedral in the world. St. Peter's at Rome has an area of 227,069 square feet, Seville Cathedral 128,570, while St. John the Divine has an area of 109,082 square feet. In exterior length it will stand second, for St. Peter's exceeds it by 109 feet.

Washington Cathedral, begun in 1907, is but partially completed. It will be 500 feet in length and its area will be 63,500 square feet. In size it will compare favorably with Reims, which has an area of 65,000 square feet; York, with an area of 63,800 square feet and Canterbury, with an area of 57,200 square feet.

There are a number of other cathedrals in America, and while each is a true cathedral, with its bishop, dean and other cathedral clergy, yet the buildings themselves, in size and arrangement, frequently are but large parish churches serving the purpose of a cathedral. See norman. F.R.W.

Catherine of Alexandria, Saint: A virgin and martyr whose feast is celebrated on November 25. Scarcely a single alleged fact concerning her withstands critical scrutiny. She is venerated as the patron saint of philosophers. According to unsubstantiated tradition she defeated fifty philosophers in public debate at Alexandria. Legend states that at her martyrdom the spiked wheel on which she was to be mangled broke into pieces at her touch, and that then she was beheaded, sometime toward the beginning of the fourth century. C.V.

Catherine de' Medici: (1519-1589) Queen of France, and regent during the period of the religious wars. Devoid of moral sense, she used the contending religious forces as counter-poise to each other—a policy which led to constant trouble. She was ready to use assassination or even massacre as political weapons—as in the massacre of St. Bartholomew*. See wars of religion. G.R.C.

Catherine of Siena, Saint: (1347-1380) Of humble birth and little education, Catherine through her radiant faith and many works of mercy, became a political leader admonishing leaders in church and state, a travelling emissary between local governments and popes; had many disciples and achieved sainthood. Canonized 1461. Learned disciples edited her writings, of which more than three hundred letters are of historical, literary value.

Dialogue of the Seraphic Virgin, Trans. by Algar Thorold (London, 1896); *S. Catherine of Siena as seen in her letters*, trans. by Vida D. Scudder (London 1906). A.S.

catholic: A term used to describe the universal character of Christian beliefs, worship, and of the Church. Derived from *kath holou*, its original meaning is "integral" (cf. *The Church of God*, 1934 ed., by E. L. Mascall); later it came to imply "the great Church" as against schismatic or heretical bodies. The word is often employed to distinguish Roman, or Roman, Anglican and Greek, Churches, from the Protestant denominations dating from the Reformation. W.N.P.

Catholic: See Roman Catholic.

Catholic Apostolic Church (Irvingites): A religious organization in part growing out of the prophetic preaching of Edward Irving*, the noted Scotch divine (1792-1834). Irving had taught that the gifts Christ bestowed on the Apostolic Church, such as prophecy, miracles, healing, and speaking in diverse tongues, were meant for all who in later times should have the living faith. After his death in 1834, some of his followers, feeling personally called as "prophets", established a church in London with a full hierarchy of apostles, prophets, evangelists, and pastors. The church was from the beginning ritualistic, making use of vestments, candles, holy oils, and chrism in its services.

Begun in America through immigration of members, the church has two divisions: the Catholic Apostolic Church and the New Apostolic Church, the latter differing in the number of "apostles" each church may have. The last census reports available listed 25 churches and 4,000 members for both bodies in the United States. See pentecostal sects.

Mrs. M. Oliphant Wilson, *Life of Edward Irving* (London, 1862); W. Wilks, *Edward Irving* (London, 1854); S. T. Coleridge, *Notes on English Divines* (London, 1853); E. Miller, *History and Doctrine of Irvingism* (London, 1878). M.G.R.—W.W.S.

Catholic charities: See social work of the churches.

Catholic Church, Liberal: See Liberal Catholic Church.

Catholic Clubs, College: See student religious organizations.

Catholic Directory: See Directory, Catholic.

Catholic emancipation act, the: Or the Catholic Relief Act, was an act of the British Parliament in 1829 by which the laws imposing certain civil disabilities upon Roman Catholics in England were repealed. Henceforth, Catholics (with the exception of clerics) were allowed to hold civil and military offices and to sit in Parliament. This measure had special reference to Ireland. The emancipation was forced by the repeated election of Daniel O'Connell (1775-1847), thereafter called the Liberator, to Parliament from Ireland. The repeal of the disabilities was necessary before he could take his seat in Parliament. T.T.M.

Catholic Epistles: The title given to the group James, I-II Peter, I-III John and Jude**, because most of them are not addressed to a single church but have a more "catholic" or general destination. See canons of various churches. B.S.E.

Catholic Journalism: Dates practically from the invention of printing in western Europe. The types of Catholic periodical literature are so varied that there are no set categories in which they may be classified. Most represent only the opinion of that Catholic institution or group which publishes them. The *Acta Apostolicae Sedis**, which is issued monthly from the Vatican Press, is the chief authentic publication. It contains the official letters of the Holy Father and the decrees of the various congregations and other public documents. Its predecessor, before the reorganization of the Papal Curia under Piux X, was the *Acta Sanctae Sedis.* Of general interest to the Church throughout the world are monthly and quarterly periodicals, such as *Biblica,* which contain authoritative commentaries on Catholic doctrine and decrees. Most of these are published in Rome but some come from papal universities. Next in authenticity are the publications of Catholic universities and research bodies, although the authority of these publications is that solely of the contributors. Each country and nearly every language has its own Catholic press. The publications of these presses include quarterlies, monthlies, weeklies and, in countries having compact Catholic populations, dailies. The nearest to an authoritative Catholic daily is the *Osservatore Romano,* published in Vatican City, but even that does not have the authority of the *Acta Apostolicae Sedis,* although its editorials are usually in close sympathy with Papal opinions. In the United States there is no Catholic daily. Most of the dioceses have diocesan weeklies which are edited under the supervision of the bishop. Some of the editors are laymen and are usually allowed considerable latitude in expression of opinion on contemporary events. The nearest to an official publication for the hierarchy is *Catholic Action* published under the direction of the National Catholic Welfare Conference which chronicles chiefly the activities of the Conference and the pastorals of the hierarchy. The other publications of national interest are sponsored by Catholic universities, or religious communities and have only the authority of their editors and contributors. The *Commonweal* is published weekly by a group of Catholic laymen. The best known Catholic weeklies are *America* and the *Ave Maria;* and generally read Catholic monthlies are the *Sign* and the *Catholic World.*

A. W. Baumgartner, *Catholic Journalism: A Study of its development in the U. S. 1789-1920;* Paul J. Foik, *Pioneer Catholic Journalism in the United States* (1930). T.T.M.

Catholic parochial schools: See parochial schools, Catholic.

Catholic Reformation, The: The Catholic Reformation was the answer of the Papacy to the challenge of the Lutheran revolt against Rome at the beginning of the XVI century. Clement VII (1523-34), although as resolute against the Emperor as towards the King of England, fearing a renewal of the conciliar theory of the superiority of General Councils over the Primacy, refused indeed to convene a General Council as planned by his predecessor, Hadrian VI (1522-23), but Paul III (1534-49), who might rightly be looked upon as the transition between the Renaissance-and Reformation popes, finally convoked the Council of Trent* "ad reformationem cleri et populi christiani". From the V to the XXV (or final) session, a section "de reformatione" ran concurrently with the section "de fide". Every phase of Catholic doctrine attacked by the reformers was re-defined, especially the whole system of justification, involving original sin, grace, redemption, the Sacraments, the Sacrifice of the Mass, Purgatory, etc. Similarly, every violation of discipline that had served as a motive for the repudiation of continued catholic unity under the papacy was denounced; reform measures enacted and their observance ordained under pain of severe ecclesiastical censures. Two of the cardinals who presided over the plenary sessions (del Monte and Cervini) became popes: Julius III (1550-55) and Marcellus II (1555); a third, Reginald Pope, became under Queen Mary Tudor, the Catholic, (the last) Cardinal Legate to England, where he labored for Catholic Restoration. Pius IV dealt a blow to unworthy nepotism in the execution of two men appointed by his personally holy, strict and stern, but at times imprudent predecessor, Paul IV (1555-59). Pius IV (1559-65) solemnly closed the Council of Trent with the institution of the "Sacred Congregation of the Council" to enforce and interpret authentically the Council's decrees. He also published a new "Index of Forbidden Books". The statutes of the Council were put into effect by such reforming popes as St. Pius V (1566-72: reform of the Roman Missal and Breviary; introduction of the Tridentine Catechism); Gregory XIII (1572-85: reform of the Julian Calendar; Roman Theological Colleges); and Sixtus V (1585-90: re-organization of the Roman Curia; repression of banditry); by such saintly archbishops and bishops as St. Charles Borromeo of Milan (d. 1584) and St. Francis de Sales of Geneva (d. 1622); by the founders and members of such newly founded Religious Orders and Congregations as the Jesuits, the Capuchins, the Theatines, the Somaschi, the Oratorians, and, among the Communities of Women, the Ursulines, the Daughters of Charity and the Vistandines. Through these popes, bishops and religious men and women reform among the clergy and religious of both sexes was accentuated (celibacy; cloister; preaching; religious instruction; canonical visitations of dioceses; episcopal and pastoral residence; diocesan and provincial synods, etc.); Catholic education fostered (institution of Diocesan and Regional Seminaries; academies for girls; colleges and High Schools for boys); deep-rooted piety nurtured (Marian Sodalities; parochial charitable societies, etc.); foreign missionary activities multiplied (institution of the "Propagation of the Faith" by Gregory XV (1621-23); and frequent reception of the Sacraments, despite the restraints of the Jansenists, fostered. The Inquisition, too, did much in these years to keep Italy and Spain, and her dependencies, within the fold of Rome. Although Leo X (1513-21) had excommunicated Luther, and Pius V, Elizabeth, Clement VIII (1592-1605), despite the Edict of Nantes, was willing, after a protracted delay, to receive back into communion with Rome, Henry IV. Innocent X (1644-55) however, notwithstanding the machinations of Richelieu and Mazarin, could not be induced to accept the terms of the Treaty of Westphalia (1648) regulating the aftermath of the Thirty Years War.

For the best critical *Lives of the Popes* of the Reformation and Post-Reformation period cf. Pastor either in the original German or in any of the authentic translations e.g., English, French, Italian or Spanish and the literature therein quoted.

The best critical edition of the Acts (Decrees, Canons, Letters, Treatises, etc.), of the *Council of Trent* is undoubtedly that of the Görres-Gesellschaft (1901 ff.); a handy and complete edition of the decrees and canons is that of the S. Cong. of the Propagation (Rome, 1882). An English trans. of both the Acts of the Council and of the *Catechism of the C. of T.* was publ. by Rev. J. Waterworth.

For the history of the C. of T. cf. Sforza Pallavicini (Ital. ed., Rome 1656-57; *ib.* 1883 (edit. Zaccaria); Latin trans. by Giattino (Antwerp, 1670); Paolo Sarpi (London, 1619); Mendham, *Memoirs of the C. of T.* (London, 1834; Suppl. 1883).

For documents of the C. of T. cf. Le Plat, *Monumentorum ad historiam C. T. spectantium amplissima collectio*, 7 vols. (Louvain, 1781-87); Druffel-Brandi, *Monumenta Tridentina* I-V (Mainz, 1844-99); cf. also Parsons, *Studies in Church History* Vol. III, 511 ff. (New York, 1907); Fr. Cuthbert, O. S. F. C., *The Capuchins: A Contribution to the History of the Counter-Reformation* 2 vols. (London, 1928); Tacchi-Venturi, *Storia della Compagnia di Gesu in Italia* (Rome and Milan, 1901 ff.); Thos. J. Campbell, *The Jesuits* 2 vols. (New York, 1921); *Cath. Encyc.* IV 426:XV 30-35; *Dict. de la Théol. Cath.* under "Council de Trent" and all kings, popes, cardinals and bishops prominent in the Cath. Reformation as indicated in this present article.

R.M.H.

Catholic religious orders. Abbreviations of names of: S.J. for Society of Jesus or member of the Jesuits; O.P. for Order of Preachers or member of the Dominicans; O.S.B. for Order of St. Benedict, or member of the Benedictines; O.S.A. for Order of St. Augustine or member of the Augustinians; O.M. Cap. for member of the Capuchins; O.F.M. for Friars Minor or Franciscans; C.M. for Congregation of the Mission; C.S.C. for Congregation of Holy Cross.

For other abbreviations consult: *The Catholic Encyclopedia* (1907), Vol. I, pp. 27-28; *The National Catholic Almanac* (1942), pp. 271-273; *The Official Catholic Directory, 1942* (1942), p. 917.

L.R.W.

Catholic Societies: Those pious associations, distinct from religious organizations properly speaking, erected by the Church for the promotion of a more perfect Christian life in its members, to encourage works of piety or charity, or to promote public worship. The proper erection of such societies belongs to the pope and to the bishop of the diocese, with the exception of those for the erection of which special powers have been given to others by Apostolic privilege. However, even in the last mentioned case, the written consent of the bishop of the place is required for the valid foundation of a society, unless the contrary is explicitly stated in the concession. Every association must have its own statutes which are to be examined and approved by the Apostolic See* or the bishop of the diocese, and every association is subject to the authority of the ordinary who has the right and duty to watch over them. These associations properly established may possess and administer temporalities under the direction of the Ordinary. For the enjoyment of the rights, privileges, indulgences and other spiritual privileges of the association it is necessary and suffices that the members be validly received in it according to the proper statutes of the organization and not legitimately expelled from it. The Code of Canon Law* recognizes three kinds of pious associations in the Church: 1) secular third orders*, 2) confraternities* and 3) pious unions. Secular tertiaries are those who live in the world under the direction of an Order, and endeavor to attain Christian perfection according to the spirit of that Order in a manner compatible with secular life, and according to rules which have been approved by the Holy See. The best known tertiaries* are Tertiaries of St. Francis, of the Order of St. Dominic and of the Carmelites, and the Oblates of St. Benedict**. Associations of the faithful founded to further works of piety or charity are known as pious organizations or pious unions; if they constitute an organic body they are called sodalities*. Sodalities that have for their object the enhancement of public worship are called confraternities. The title or name of a confraternity or pious union must be taken from the attributes of God, or the mysteries of the Christian religion, or the feasts of Our Lord or the Blessed Virgin Mary, or from the saints or from the specific work of piety carried on by the organization. Confraternities may be established only by a formal decree of erection; but for pious unions the approbation of the local bishop suffices and enables them to gain spiritual favors, especially indulgences, although it does not constitute them moral persons. It is the duty of the diocesan bishops to see that the Confraternities of the Blessed Sacrament and of Christian Doctrine be established in every parish, and once erected these confraternities are by law aggregated to the same Archconfraternities erected in Rome by the Cardinal Vicar. Sodalities or confraternities that are empowered by law to affiliate to themselves other associations of the same nature are termed archconfraternities, or archsodalities, or pious unions, congregations or societies of primary rank. No pious association can validly affiliate itself to other pious associations without an Apostolic indult*. In the order of precedence the Code lists these lay organizations as follows: 1) Third orders; 2) Archconfraternities; 3) Confraternities; 4) Primary pious unions; 5) Other pious unions. In the United States there are established all forms of these lay associations under their respective rules. See Confraternities; Sodalities.

T.T.M.

Catholicism in China: See Chinese religions.

Catholicism in India: See India, religions of; India, Missions to.

Catholicos: The title of Nestorian and Armenian patriarchs. It originated in Persia during the reign of King Yazdegerd I (399-420), who approved the organization of an autonomous Persian Christian Church, and elevated the metropolitan of the capital, Seleucia-Ctesiphon, to the rank of primate with the title of Catholicos.

Aubrey R. Vine, *The Nestorian Churches* (London, 1937). M.S.

Catholics, Old: See Old Catholics.

cause: (Lat. *causa*) Something whose existence is a precondition of the existence of something else; a *sine qua non* or "necessary condition" of an existent. "The" cause of anything is sometimes defined as its necessary and sufficient condition. Taken absolutely, this definition implies determinism, for it means that the cause suffices to ensure the effect and thus uniquely determines it. The definition also implies that there is no ultimate distinction between possible and actual existence; for if the necessary and sufficient condition be lacking the effect is impossible, and if it be present the effect is inevitable and its non-occurrence impossible. Thus necessary occurrence and necessary non-occurrence are alone permitted. A definition which admits a distinction between necessary and merely possible existence and does not exclude determinism is as follows: the cause of a thing is the necessary and sufficient condition of the possible existence of the thing. As for its actual existence, perhaps that involves no further condition, but is a sheer contingency or creative addition to possibility, something that may or may not occur, and the knowledge of whose occurrence or non-occurrence is to be had (even by Omniscience*) only by "waiting to see." Thus the effect would require and imply the cause, but the cause would not absolutely require or imply the effect. An intermediate or in one sense deterministic, in one sense indeterministic, conception is that the cause is sufficient condition, not indeed of the existence of any one determinate or individual effect, but of "some one or other" of a class or kind of possible effects. Thus the cause would guarantee that *some* effect or other of a certain general sort would follow, but not just which one of the possible variations of the sort it would be. Current physics seems to conceive such a limited guarantee to obtain in both directions between cause and effect, so that neither cause nor effect is uniquely and determinately inferrable from the other, but only statistically and probably. The class of the effect is given if the cause is given, and vice versa; and it is assumed that there must be some real member of the class. However, our sense that the past is determinate, in contrast to the future, which is a matter of option between still open alternatives, seems to imply that—whatever it may suit the technical convenience of physics to suppose—the past, the cause, is unique or determinate when the present, the effect, takes place; and thus that the effect requires the cause individually, while the cause requires the effect only generically or approximately, leaving some free or creative option, however slight.

The deterministic version of cause when applied to theology makes the creator require his creation as definitely as the creation requires the creator. Given God, the world must be; just as, given the world, God must be. Each is necessary to the other. Since there are no degrees of necessity, the least creature, being indispensable, would be as important as God.

The purely indeterministic view would mean that, given God, there need be no world at all. From God's existence nothing would follow at all as to the world. God might have perfect self-knowledge, and yet know nothing of the world (except as a mere possibility of existence) since as existent the world would not be involved in his own being. (The failure to see or admit this is common in the tradition, though the usual view of God as totally "independent" in every way is precisely the pure indeterministic view of causality in its theological application.)

The intermediate or qualifiedly indeterministic view of God as cause is that His existence makes it inevitable that there be some world or other, but not just the world which in fact exists. Thus God's independence is of the particular world, not of world-as-such. (Even of the particular world, he is independent only in his essence, not in his total being, which must contain just the actual world, if he is to know this world and love it. —See omniscience; panentheism; perfection; transcendence). The intermediate view makes it possible to exempt God from responsibility for the details of the world and its evils, and yet to regard him as "the" cause of the world. His existence makes it inevitable that there be some world but only possible that there be just this world.

Causes are often divided into *efficient* and *final*, and Aristotle* spoke also of *formal* and *material* causes. All of them are conditions of their effects. A statue would not exist had the plan in the mind of the artist not existed, or had there been no material from which to make it. But a final cause is somewhat indeterministic in a special way, in that the same desired outcome may be reached by more than one route. The final cause is indeterministic also in that success is not guaranteed, since the material may not prove altogether pliable. But further, a final cause does not even intend to fully determine its effect. To know exactly what one desires would be to have it, since knowledge of value is possession in the most literal sense. One would never go to the theater if he knew precisely and vividly what was to occur there, for then he would be enjoying the play already. And the artist sees his form with full precision and detail only when his work is finished. Theologians have striven to avoid applying this principle to God, or have simply overlooked the problem; but it seems doubtful if it means anything to speak of divine purposes in regard to the world if God enjoys its values in advance or in eternity*. Even if it be said that his purposes are purely disinterested or altruistic, this only evades the issue, not only because we have no meaning for altruism other than a taking pleasure in promoting the pleasures of others, or an interest in satisfying their interests, but because it cannot be a good that the interests of the creatures should be satisfied when, should the creatures not exist at all, all possible values would exist anyway in God. It is superfluous to promote the welfare of superfluous beings, whether from a disinterested or from an egoistic standpoint, since even a disinterested survey must perceive the futility of trying to add values to existence as including absolute value eternally. As Bergson, Peirce, Whitehead**, and others have been reminding us, the only conceivable purpose of creation is to achieve new values, and if really new they must be new for omniscience*, the measure of reality. God requires that there be a world, if the value of His life is to be enriched. And a God whose life cannot be enriched must either achieve all possible value eternally—which is a contradiction, since there are incompossible values—or he must be eternally limited to some arbitrary quantum or degree of value less than is possible, in which case he is in no significant sense perfect. Thus a God simply independent of the world is unintelligible in terms of final causation. But a God dependent absolutely upon just this world which exists, rather than simply upon world as such, is equally unintelligible, for the idea implies an enrichment every detail of which is involved in the being to be enriched, and this is a contradiction. Thus the intermediate or qualifiedly indeterministic view of the cause-effect relation is no less applicable to the divine as final than as efficient cause.

David of Dinant* identified God and "matter" or potentiality, thus making God the universal material cause. Aquinas* called this view crazy; but it is so only if Thomism is assumed as the norm of sanity. The ultimate potency which is molded into actual form is the uniquely flexible, uniquely modifiable life of deity. For consider, whatever may become real, if and as real it will be known by omniscience and loved by the perfect love. But knowledge and the known, loving and the loved, must in some way correspond to each other, and God must therefore be ready to correspond to whatever can occur, and this potential correspondence is part of the potential being of the things. To make a creature, *X*, is for God to make Himself to know and care for *X* as an actuality, for were *X* not actual, God would not know and love it as actual. (See Gerson, Levi ben.) Thus, in creating, God creates states of himself, and thus treats his being as matter to be given form.

Cause, First or Prime: The cause which is first in a logical sense, supreme or universal among causes, the one which is required for any and all effects. To affirm it does not involve denying the infinity of past causes. It is enough that the supreme cause be supposed to have sustained the series of secondary causes through its perhaps infinite past. The supreme cause is thus not necessarily first temporally except that it must be the only cause that has operated at all past times, however remote. It is thus temporally earlier than each and every but not perhaps than all secondary causes (if these be infinite in number). Nor does the argument for a first cause depend for any of its force upon an assumed or demonstrated finitude of the series of second causes. The argument is as follows. Ordinary causes are always logically arbitrary or contingent in their very existence. If there is nothing but the sum of such contingent causes, then that anything at all exists is sheer accident. Yet this cannot be, for "it might be that nothing exists" is an absurdity, since there would "be" at least the fact of the non-being of everything. Though all details of being are contingent (and, as Peirce showed, a non-contingent detail would be a contradiction in terms), it cannot be contingent that there are details of being, some details or other. But what is the being which must receive some details or other, what is the ground of alternatives such that not all of them can be unrealized? The being which will be there no matter what else is there is the universal being, the first cause. The ground of alternatives which makes it impossible that none be realized is not itself a member of an alternative, but rather the being to whose existence there can be no alternative, the necessary or self-existent being which requires that there shall be some non-necessary actualities or other. Thus the first cause is not in every sense independent of other causes, but rather in its essence it depends upon (in the sense of necessitating or omnipotently requiring) the class of contingent beings as such, while in its accidents the necessary being (necessary only in essence and as to having some accidents or other) depends upon just which contingent beings in fact exist.

The traditional procedure of inferring a necessary being from contingent beings held to be in no way involved in the necessary being which was supposed to explain them was self-contradictory and a chief cause of scepticism and atheism. The absurdity of denying a first cause lies precisely in the implication that contingent predicates inhere only in contingent subjects, that accidents happen only to the accidental. The absurdity is avoided only by regarding accidents as contingent phases of the life of a Being as in essential reality not accidental but the necessary recipient of all accidents, the non-alternative medium of all open alternatives. To make the contingent being merely contingent, and the necessary being merely necessary, is to evade the essential question: how are they together one reality? "The contingent-

and-the-necessary" must form some sort of whole (all reality, all that is what it is whether human beings know what it is or not) and this whole cannot be exclusively contingent or exclusively necessary. Nor can it be less than God, the supreme cause but, for that very reason, also the supreme effect; the one being who (in his essence) has always been and always will be involved in all causation, and equally the one being who (in his accidents) always has been and always will be enriched by every effect, garnered without loss in his loving omniscience. See concursus; fatalism; fate; Hume, David; omnipotence; pantheism; transcendence.

A. N. Whitehead, *Process and Reality* (1929), especially the last chapter. C.H.

Cavasilas, Nickalaos: (d. 1371) Greek Archbishop in the city of Salonica. He was educated in Italy and became famous for his mystic and philosophical ideas and thoughts. He is considered one of the greatest representatives of the Greek Church in mysticism. He played also an important role in politics of the Byzantine Empire.

He wrote many books of mystical value, as *The Union of Man with Jesus Christ* which will be obtained through the Sacraments of Baptism, Extreme Unction, and Holy Communion.

He was an opponent of the Roman Catholic Church, and against the proposed Union of the Greek and Catholic Churches. G.E.Z.

Cecilia, Saint: Roman virgin and martyr, whose feast is celebrated on November 22. A great deal of legend has grown up about her, but little can be established with certainty. Not even the century in which she was martyred is known. The connection of this saint with music probably arises from a misinterpretation of the first antiphon of Lauds on her feast day. C.V.

celibacy: See communistic settlements, religious; marriage.

celibacy: (Christian) (Lat. *caelebs*, unmarried) The obligation imposed since the time of Gregory the Great (d. 604) on clerics in major orders to observe chastity under vow; hence the forbidding of marriage, or, if the person is married, the use of marriage. L.R.W.

Celsus: Opponent of Christianity, its "first great polemical adversary", whose anti-Christian treatise, *True Discourse*, written about A.D. 177, was answered by Origen* in his lengthy work *Contra-Celsum.* It is from Origen alone that we have any knowledge of Celsus, but he tells us nothing of the latter's personal history. In the *Contra Celsum*, however, we have copious quotations from Celsus, which bring out clearly the line of his argumentation against Christianity.

Origen, *Contra Celsum;* F. C. Baur, *Christendom and the Christian Church in the First Three Centuries* (1853); Theodor Keim, *Celsus's Wahres Wort* (1873); E. De Faye, *Origene, Sa Vie, Son Oeuvre, Sa Pensée.*, Vol. II (1927). C.W.L.

cemetery: (Gr. *koimeterion*, "sleeping chamber") A place of burial. Christian care for the dead and faith in a resurrection gave a religious value to cemeteries from a very early date (see catacombs). Burial normally took place in consecrated ground adjoining a church (the "church yard"), from which unbelievers, excommunicate persons and suicides were excluded. See crypt; death and burial practices. B.S.E.

Cenobite: (Gr. *koinos*, common; *bios*, life) Monks who live in community as distinguished from hermit* or anchorite* who lived solitary or eremitical lives. The cenobitical type of monasticism was instituted in the East by St. Pachomius* about 318, but was greatly modified by St. Basil. It was introduced into the West by St. Athanasius* in 340. The founder of Western monasticism* is St. Benedict*. J.B.C.

censer: Another term to describe the thurible, or receptacle used for incense* in the services of the Church. Sometimes the term is also employed for the person using the thurible. W.N.P.

censorship of books: (Lat. *censor*, man who takes census) Supervision of the press, by Church or State or army, etc., to prevent misuse of it. The Catholic Church, e.g., takes it as her work to preserve and propagate Christ's teachings, and thus she concludes that no Catholic may publicly contradict those teachings; since 1571 she has a special body of censors called the Congregation of the Index, and a book disallowed by this body is "on the Index." See Gregory XIII, Pope. Also see Office, Sacred Congregation of the Holy. L.R.W.

censure: (Lat. *censura*) A term taken from Roman law and meaning an ecclesiastical penalty depriving of particular goods such as the use of the Sacraments; imposed on a baptized person who has committed a serious external fault and is obstinate about it. L.R.W.

census, religious: See federal census of religious bodies.

Cerberus: In Greek mythology, the three-headed dog guarding the entrance to Hades*. In Hesiod he is described as having fifty heads. P.G.M.

Cerinthus: The earliest Gnostic* teacher of whom anything definite is known. He was active about the year 100 A.D., in the region of Ephesus, and according to tradition was an adversary of St. John. It is possible that the heresy denounced in the 1st Ep. of John was that of Cerinthus. Nothing of his writing has survived, and the accounts of him in the early Fathers are vague and conflicting.

L. Duchesne, *Early History of the Church* (1924). E.F.S.

certainty, religious: The special mode of religious knowledge. Religion has been wont to claim knowledge beyond the scope of rational search or proof. Gnostics* (Christian and non-Christian) professed *gnosis* higher than discursive thought; mystics* an immediacy in apprehending God distinct from the conclusions of ratiocination. More widely in the Church faith, again in priority to reason, has been the pathway to certitude: *credo ut intelligam.* The special religious knowledge is conceived as exceeding other knowledge both in substance and in the certainty with which it is held. The N.T. views some claims to higher knowledge as spurious (I Tim. 6:20); yet its own truth too is above human wisdom (1 Cor. 1: 17-25). It is revealed not to the wise, but to the trustful and receptive (Math. 11:25; 1 Cor. 2:9-11); the very heart of Christianity is so given (Math. 16: 16, 17; 1 Cor. 12:3). Apostolic witness is not to the fruits of inquiry but to what, divinely vouchsafed, is directly perceived (John 1: 14-18; 1 John 1: 1-5). By the saving intent of the truth (John 17:3), certainty as to it is akin to assurance* as *spiritual* realization of divine gifts.

D. C. Macintosh, *The Problem of Religious Knowledge* (1940); W. A. Brown, *Pathways to Certainty* (1930); J. Baillie, *Our Knowledge of God* (1939); W. W. Bryden, *The Christian's Knowledge of God* (Toronto, 1940). J.L.

Cerularius, Michael: (1043-58) Patriarch of Constantinople. Repudiated the claims of Pope Leo IX* to the universal headship of Christendom. He based his contention on the ancient view that each patriarchate was supreme within its own territory. The papal legates sent to Constantinople found him adamant in his refusal and excommunicated him and his adherents on July 16, 1054. This inaugurated the "Great Schism"* between the Western and Eastern churches which persists to this day.

B. J. Kidd, *The Churches of Eastern Christendom* (London, 1927).

J. M. Hussey, *Church and Learning in the Byzantine Empire, 867-1185* (Oxford, 1937). M.S.

chair of St. Peter: The expression has a threefold meaning: 1) the actual episcopal chair or throne used by the Prince of the Apostles, firstly, the one at Antioch, the other at Rome, symbolizing his episcopal office in both cities; 2) the feast-days established by the Church to commemorate Peter's episcopacy in both places; and 3) the symbolical or dogmatical meaning of the expression "*ex cathedra*"*.

1) In exactly what places St. Peter* first lived at Rome (certainly in no one place uninterruptedly from 42-67 A.D.) or where the first Bishop of Rome had his episcopal headquarters (to use an expression of today) cannot be ascertained with certainty. Many pre-Constinian places contend for the honor: *Santa Pudenziana, Santa Priscilla, Santa Prisca,* etc. That St. Peter as first Bishop of Rome, like other early bishops of other sees, has an episcopal chair is attested by catecumbal representations; by allusions to his *cathedra,* either real or symbolical, in the early Fathers, e.g., Irenaeus, Cyprian, Jerome**, etc.; by such historians as Eusebius* and Orosius, and by an unbroken tradition. Parts of that original episcopal chair or *sedes gestatoria* (apparently of pagan origin, used perhaps by some pre-Christian teacher or judge and donated by friends to St. Peter) was in later centuries (IX) elaborated with gold, ivory and costly decorations. Throughout the Middle Ages it was venerated by pious pilgrims who came to old St. Peter's to do homage to the Prince of the Apostles buried there beneath the High Altar. By order of Pope Alexander VII (1655-67) it was enclosed in a gigantic casing of bronze, designed by Bernini, and now occupies the principal place of honor above the apsidal altar of the present St. Peter's Basilica, known as the "Altar of the Chair". 2) The Feast of the Chair of St. Peter at Antioch is celebrated in the Roman Liturgy on February 22; that at Rome, on January 18th. Both feast days, however, are of Roman origin. 3) The Greek word for chair *kathedra* has long become symbolical of doctrine and power: divine, royal, juridical; professional, ecclesiastical: hence, the word "cathedral", the bishop's church containing his "cathedra", chair or throne; also the expression to speak "*ex cathĕdra*", when applied to the Bishop of Rome, i.e., to speak authoritatively and pronounce definitely some article of faith "as pastor and teacher of all Christians". (Constitution: *Pastor Aeternus,* Vatican Council.)

Litt. *Cath. Encyc.* III, 551-4; P. J. Chandlery, *Pilgrim Walks in Rome* (London, 1927) pp. 102-7; *Lexikon f. Theol. u. Kirche,* VIII, 478, 559-560; Orazio Marucchi, *The Evidence of the Catacombs* (London, 1929), pp. 94-109; Anton de Waal, *Roma Sacra* (Munich, n.d. 1905?), I chap. R.M.H.

Chalcedon, Council of (451): The Fourth Oecumenical Council, summoned to reverse the findings of the Latrocinium (Ephesus, 449*) on the heresy of Eutyches* of Constantinople, supported by Dioscorus of Alexandria that the Person of the Son had only one nature, the divine, hence the name of the heresy—Monophysitism*. The formula was based on the Tome of Leo I*, which was satisfactory only because it stated the problem without facing the issues. The findings of Ephesus (431)* against Nestorius* were confirmed and Constantinople was assigned seniority next to Rome—over Alexandria (contra. Nic. c. vi). Leo refused to accept this canon. See Christology; Dyophysites. F.W.B.

Chaldean (Persian) Rite: The complexus of liturgical and disciplinary laws and customs used in the Nestorian Churches. Variants of this rite are followed by the Nestorians* in Mesopotamia and Persia with 80,000 members and by the Mellusians in India with 15,000. Catholics of the patriarchate of Babylon of the Chaldees with 70,000 members and of Malabar with 532,000 also follow variants of this rite. E.A.R.

chalice: (Lat., *calix,* cup) The vessel used in the Eucharist to contain the wine to be consecrated. Usually of precious metal. See paten. P.V.N.

Chalmers, Thomas: (1780-1847) Distinguished Scottish preacher, theologian, ecclesiastical statesman, educator, reformer and mathematician. Under his leadership the Free Church of Scotland* was founded in protest to patronage and political meddling. He refuted Hume's objection to miracles and issued a notable Calvinistic work *Institutes of Theology.* V.F.

Châlon sur-Saone, councils of: Held in 603, 649, 813, 1062, 1129. That of 649 reaffirmed the formulae of Nicea and Chalcedon. Important is that of 813 which adopted sixty-six canons on the discipline of clergy and laity, teaching, preaching, ordination, confession and penance, prayers for the dead, pilgrimages, etc. J.T.M.

chance: See fortune; tychism.

chancel: (Lat. *cancelli,* lattices or screens with which it was formerly enclosed) The portion of the church eastward of the nave* set apart for the clergy, choir and altar. The easternmost part which contains the altar* is called the sanctuary*, while the western portion is the choir*. F.T.P.

chancel plays: See religious drama.

Chancellor's Lectureship: Founded in 1893 at Queen's University, Kingston, Canada, with a capital gift of $8,000 by Sir Sandford Fleming, then Chancellor of the University, to provide each year a course of four lectures to members of the Queen's Theological Alumni Association, the lectures to deal in the main with the philosophical basis of religion. The Lectureship was held for ten years from the time of its founding by Prof. John Watson of Queen's. In recent years James Moffatt, E. F. Scott, John Bennett, Reinhold Niebuhr, Nathaniel Micklem and President J. S. Thomson of the University of Saskatchewan have been among the lecturers. S.M.G.

Chancery, Apostolic: (Lat. *cancellans,* chancellor) The papal office issuing such important documents as those appointing bishops and those erecting new dioceses. L.R.W.

change: See time.

changeless, the: See eternal.

changeling: In Celtic folklore the "little people" or fairies* often stole a human infant and left a changeling in his cradle. The changeling, about the size of the baby, generally had a wizened face, and did not grow normally. P.G.M.

Changes, The Book of: See I Ching.

Channing, William Ellery: (1780-1842) American preacher and theologian. Launched the Unitarian controversy with his Baltimore sermon (1819) on "Unitarian Christianity," where Christ is described as "one mind, one being, and a being distinct from the one God." See liberal theol.; Unitarianism. W.M.H.

chant: (Lat., *cantus,* song) An ancient form of simple ecclesiastical music used in singing the psalms and canticles. The chant normally used in the Latin Church is called Gregorian*, from Pope Gregory the Great*, to whom it is traditionally ascribed. Plainsong*. The so-called Anglican chant is somewhat more elaborate and metrical. P.V.N.

chapel: (Lat. *capella,* a cloak. Term first applied to depository of St. Martin's cloak.) A small church, or a subordinate building attached to a church and containing an altar; or a place of dissenting worship; or, the place of worship of a private residence, school or college or other institution. F.T.P.

chaplain: (Late Lat., *capellanus,* fr. *cappa,* cape) A priest serving an institutional chapel, or appointed to the army or navy. The term was apparently first applied to the priest-custodian of the cape (*cappella*) of St. Martin of Tours. P.V.N.

chaplet: (O. Fr. *chapelet,* dim fr. *chapel,* hat, garland) The "rosary"*: a form of meditative-oral prayer made up of fifteen decades or tens of *Aves* with a *Pater* between each two; also called the beads, esp. when abbreviated to five decades. L.R.W.

chapters and verses of the Bible: In most books of scripture a natural division is traceable. Luke, for instance, intends the book of Acts to fall into seven parts, and marks the end of each of them by a formula indicating a further stage in the expansion of the church. Before the time of Christ the Law had been divided into sections for reading in the synagogue, each of them bearing a special name, e.g., "The Bush" (Mk. 12:26). This system was extended to the whole of the O.T., and the "Parashas" are still marked in the Hebrew Bible. It was not till the 13th century that Stephen Langton*, Archbishop of Canterbury (the framer of Magna Charta) introduced the present chapter divisions into the Vulgate. Verses were much later, and were first marked off by the printer Stephanus in his edition of the Greek N.T. in 1551. Shortly afterwards, in the Antwerp Polyglot* of 1569-72 the system of numbered verses was applied to the whole Bible. See verse division of the Bible. E.F.S.

character education: See Sunday School movement in the United States.

character, indelible: According to traditional Catholic theology, held by Roman, Anglican and Eastern Orthodox, the orders of those ordained to the sacred ministry are "indelibly" (that is, irreplaceably and without possible loss) conferred. Hence, they possess a "character" (a stamp or mark upon them by reason of ordination) which cannot be removed or suffer defection, although the exercise of such orders may be abrogated by ecclesiastical authority. W.N.P.

charismata: The word means literally "things freely given", and is applied in the N.T. to the new gifts or energies which were bestowed on Christians by the Spirit. In I Cor. 12:4-11 Paul enumerates a large number of these "spiritual gifts", pointing out that they were highly diverse in character. Many of them we would now regard as merely the natural aptitudes which could be employed in Christian service, but for Paul, and the early church generally, they were conferred by a special grace. It was believed that since a man's whole being is transformed by the Spirit he not only receives new endowments, but those which he has already become different. The term "charismata" was used chiefly of the strange phenomena which accompanied Christian worship, and especially of the speaking with tongues*. These gifts were plainly extraordinary, and therefore appealed to the common mind as direct manifestations of a new divine power. Paul makes his protest against this view, and maintains that the Spirit is most truly present in activities which may impress no one as abnormal. Love, he declares, is the very highest "charisma". See holiness churches; pentecostal sects. E.F.S.

Charity, Brother of: A Roman Catholic religious congregation founded in Belgium by Father P. J. Triest in the 19th century. The purpose of the group is to care for the sick, aged, orphans and other needy people. Many distinct groups of religious women are known as Sisters of Charity*. V.J.B.

Charity, Sisters of: See Sisters of Charity.

charity and almsgiving (Christian): While the forms and motives of primitive Christian charity had their sources in Egyptian and Semitic cultures, their practice apparently was more extensive than in any other contemporary group. Its structure was the "enclesia," or mutual benefit society, whose services were available at times to other than members. Probably, in these early days Christians established hostels for reception of strangers, which became the typical institutions of the middle ages, ministering primarily to the sick and aged. This spread over all Europe and religious orders sprang up to man them, such as the famous Hospitallers* of Malta. It was not much before the 18th century, with its scientific advances in the treatment of disease, that hospitals were defined for the treatment of the sick, exclusively. However, this is only a general statement, with notable exceptions such as the colony for insane and feebleminded at Gheel, Belgium, which had offered a remarkable service under the egis of the church during the whole medieval period to the present.

With the growth of metropolitan centers of population and accumulation of surplus wealth, medical institutions came into the front rank of private benevolence. St. Bartholemew and St. Thomas in London antedate the reign of Henry VIII; the first hospital in this country was the one founded in Philadelphia by Benjamin Franklin in 1751. Public hospitals grew out of the workhouse, as Bellevue in New York City, that was originally a function of the "Public Workhouse and House of Correction" established in 1736. In contemporary times general hospitals may be private, such as Presbyterian in New York City, municipal, such as Cook County in Chicago, or under denominational auspices, of which almost every considerable community has examples. The Federal government has hospitals for veterans, for acute or chronic patients as well as for mental diseases. Generally, hospitals for the insane are under State auspices, although a few municipalities have them, such as St. Louis and New York City, and there are some private mental hospitals, such as Bloomingdale in New York City (1791).

Provision for dependents was widely furnished by the church which accumulated large sums of money for this purpose. At times, this was distributed indifferently and there were many protests against either the method of distribution or the dishonesty of its almoners. But there was a vast amount of intelligent and courageous service that is less known: such as provision for lepers, rescue stations on dangerous highways, such as over the Alps, services to seamen in port and when shipwrecked, ransom of captives of pirates who infected the Mediterranean, provision for unmarried mothers and their children, as well as development of means of foster care for dependent children.

As the Middle Ages passed into the modern era with its rapidly growing urban centers, monastic and ordinary religious provisions for the care of dependents proved inadequate and various experiments in organization of charitable effort were undertaken in the cities of western Europe and Great Britain. In territories in which the Catholic Church successfully resisted the Protestant movement, they in effect resulted in a merging of ecclesiastical resources with municipal supervision. In Protestant countries they resulted in creating secular organizations in connection with existing ecclesiastical bodies, such as the programs established in Germany by Luther and in Zurich by Zwingli; or in outright municipal and state administration of public assistance as in the English Poor Law of a century later (1601).

On the Continent, administration of assistance rarely came wholly under public service, as the resources of volunteers, such as in the Elberfeld scheme, were widely used. In England, where it was entirely handled as a public function, assistance had a troubled existence, although never entirely suppressed. By 1834, a strong reaction against all such aid had placed severe restrictions upon its practice which did not lift until under the influence of a more liberal theory of economics than laissez faire and of a socialistic philosophy public assistance and its more acceptable substitute, social insurance now cover almost all contingencies of economic need.

The story in the United States follows closely that of England, except that the last, and more generous, stage is not so well established.

In the private field, the two pioneers of the 19th century were Thomas Chalmers of Glasgow and Frederick Ozanam of Paris, who introduced methods of individualization, investigation, record keeping and supervision in the 1830's which finally flowered in the charity organization movement (London, 1869; Buffalo, 1877), which is generally considered the starting point for contemporary methods of treating dependency. It advocated coordination of all charitable effort, the definition of the method used in treatment, called social case work, the criteria and educational preparation of personnel for what has come to be looked upon as a profession. This has involved an evaluation of the sciences contributing to an understanding of human behavior, the establishment of schools in connection with universities, and the production of professional literature.

The story of treatment of the delinquent is less extensive. Following the custom of classical temples, churches were used as sanctuaries, and such function jealously protected. However, most delinquents until the rise of contemporary nationalism were political, and the first prisons used largely for debtors, witnesses and persons awaiting execution. Crimes in the modern sense were either very severely dealt with—exile, slavery or death, or left to be avenged or compensated for between the injured and injuring parties.

With the 19th century various schools of thought, the classical, established by Beccasia (1769) and the scientific, initiated by Lombroso (1872), Ferre (1881) and Garofalo (1885) arose and a more careful study of the criminal as a person began to be made. On the continent it is confined in general to extensive psychological studies of the convict, although in Germany of the era of the Republic (1920-1933) some interesting experiments in individualization of treatment were inaugurated. In the United States certain reforms in procedure and treatment were introduced and have taken firm root, such as the Juvenile and to a less extent the Family Court (or Court of Domestic Relations) the indeterminate sentence, probation and parole, changing prisons from places of punishment to schools for the reeducation of the inmate, and the slow—very slow—education of public opinion in a realistic understanding of the problem of delinquency*. See asylum; charity organization; orphanages; social work of the churches.

G. Uhlhorn, *Die Christliche Liebesthätikeit* (Stuttgard, 1890) ; A. Emminghaus, *Der Armenwesen und die Armengesetzgebung in Europäischen Staaten* (1870) ; Charles S. Loch, *Three Thousand Years of Social Service* (London, 1910, new ed., 1938) ; Charles D. Watson, *The History of the Charity Organization Movement in the United States* (1922) ; Stuart A. Queen, *Social Work in the Light of History* (1922). F.J.B.

charity and almsgiving (non-Christian): As long as society remained one of primary contacts, familial aid among kinsmen and mutual aid between members of a community were the only resources for the necessitous. When—or where—this stability and simplicity of society evolved into mobile and complex groups, two distinct attitudes developed toward those in need. Among the Greeks and Romans charity toward the needy was lightly regarded. The culturally approved qualities of mercy, generosity and unselfishness were those exercised toward one's own class or peers. In ancient Greece, citizens of a state voted themselves certain remuneration as payments for services in the public assembly. Later, as citizens became more necessitous, Pericles instituted vast public works, such as the buildings and sculpters that adorned the Acropolis, the constitution of the roadway between Athens and the Pireaus as means of relief, or work relief as we should say. In both Greece and Rome, citizens as early as the fifth and third century B.C., respectively were sold grain at greatly reduced prices, and later it was distributed freely. In Rome, families acquired the right to receive the beneficence of the State, and handed it down to their children. In addition, Rome instituted extensive colonization schemes, partly as a device to keep down the number of workless citizens in the urban centers.

Charity, in its modern sense, was not highly regarded. Slaves* were sufficiently valuable to be cared for in self interest of their owner. Strangers, if known, were afforded hospitality ordinarily. But the sentiments and practices termed charitable in modern usage were reserved for a sort of glorified mutual aid, reciprocal services between equals in times of need: ransom from captivity; attention when ill; financial aid to one temporarily distressed.

While in Rome the State limited its gratuities to its citizens to certain allowances of food (and perhaps amusements) these gratuities were heavily reinforced by the aristocracy who in courting public favor gave lavishly in a wide variety of ways.

In Egypt and the Orient generally, on the other hand, charity was the practice of religious virtue on the part of the wealthy, especially the rulers, toward the economically exploited, and on the theoretical basis of winning divine approval and favor in the future life. It seems as if its distinctive characteristic consisted in its being considered a means of securing rewards in the future life. The needy claimed it on precisely the same ground; but also looked to divine protection that would compensate them in the next life for what they suffered here.

This idea in other Eastern religions merged into the belief of poverty as a virtue in itself, possibly because of its inescapable exploitation. Such an idea reached its fullest development in Persia and especially India, where poverty and sanctity became almost synonymous, but its influence was strong in primitive and medieval Christianity.

Chinese and Japanese philanthropy was until modern period wholly a matter of familial services. Because of the large groups composing these oriental families, they were able to care for their members who were economically imperilled. In modern times both nations adopted modern systems of public welfare, but because of national poverty and war, it has not been actually put in operation in either country.

Second International Conference of Social Work (Baden, 1933) ; *Report of the Third International Conference of Social Work* (London, 1938) ; Yu-Yue Tsu, *The Spirit of Chinese Philanthropy* (1912) ; Hendrick Bolkestein, *Wohltätigkeit und Armenpflege im vorchristlichen Altertum* (Utrecht, 1939). F.J.B.

charity organization: Charity Organization is a term given to a movement originating in London in 1869; transplanted to the United States in 1877 (Buffalo), and variously named here, such as Associated Charities (Boston, 1882), Society for Organizing Charity (Philadelphia, 1878) and, when combined with earlier agencies, as Federated Charities (Baltimore) or United Charities (Chicago). The movement spread over all of the English speaking world, with similar agencies in some of the larger cities of China and India. It made no lodgement on the Continent where social and cultural conditions had already created different methods of dealing with poverty.

Its founders reacting against the chaotic condition of relief in the older cities proposed plans for the correlation of the activities of agencies giving relief, and the improvement of methods of studying the problems of poverty in the individual and in the community. In its growth, it developed the use of the case committee, by which coordination and improvement of methods, the districting of cities to keep administration and beneficiaries more closely together and, in the United States especially, the promotion of other specialized services in child welfare, medical and psychiatric social services, probation and social work in the public schools. In some communities, especially the younger ones in which there had not been strong relief-giving agencies, they became the leading private agency for the care of the dependent.

Out of the charity organization movement several independent agencies gradually emerged. To mention just a few, the Social Service Exchange, a clearing house for all case working agencies, and the Council of Social Agencies, which took over the "organizing" function of the earlier societies. Many reform movements, such as Anti-Tuberculosis, Tenement House Reform, Control of Small Loan practices, laws governing family relations such as child labor, divorce, desertion and non-support owe their main or sole promotion to such societies. In its later phases of growth, these societies have contributed either initially or in common with others to the definition and development of the two characteristic features of contemporary social work, the definition, method and content of social case work, and the criteria of professional personnel.

Charles S. Loch, *Charity Organization* (London, 1892); Edward T. Devine, *The Principles of Relief* (1904); Richard C. Cabot, *Social Service and the Art of Healing* (1909); Frank D. Watson, *History of the Charity Organization Movement in the United States* (1922). F.J.B.

Charles V: (1500-1558) Charles V of the House of Habsburg, was from early young manhood Holy Roman Emperor and King of Spain. The greatest ruler of his House, he was nevertheless unable to solve the problems of those difficult times, but his wise moderation in dealing with the Protestants and his energy against the Turks made this convinced Catholic an important defender of the religious unity of Europe. Cf. Reformation; Spires, Diets of; Worms, Diet of.

E.A.R.

charms and amulets: In origin a charm was an emotion-charged wish expressed in words. In world-wide usage it is any combination of words filled with a mysterious potency and effective in fulfilling desires. An amulet is a material object efficacious in securing benefits for its possessor. A written charm and an object charmed are amulets. The distinction between charm and amulet is often forgotten and the material object is commonly called a charm. The amulet is worn on the person. Since its essential function is to fulfil wishes, it is expected to give wealth, strength, good-fortune, success in love, victory in war, to protect from dangers, to cure disease, to injure an enemy, to be a shield against demons, ghosts, and the envious, evil eye. See fetishism; magic; phylacteries; relics. A.E.H.

Charterhouse: The famous pre-Reformation monastery of the Carthusians* in London. The name was an English corruption of *Chartreuse.* In 1611 one of England's great public schools was founded on the site of the former charterhouse monastery. Today it is located at Godalming, Surrey. J.B.C.

chartism: A movement named from a Parliamentary petition called the "Peoples' Charter" drawn up in 1836, demanding manhood suffrage, annual parliaments, vote by ballot, abolition of property qualification and payment of members in the House of Commons, and equal electoral districts. The petition was overwhelmingly defeated at the time, but all the suggestions, except annual meetings of the Parliament, have been adopted subsequently.

It was the first proletarian protest of the Industrial Revolution. The Reform Act of 1832 was largely a middle class victory. The Poor Law of 1834 bore heavily upon the artisans, miners and unskilled laborers of England. The Chartist movement, making radical demands and proposing a general strike on two occasions, 1839 and 1842, was not immediately successful, and some of its leaders were deported, yet it furnished the beginnings of the progressive and radical organizations which so strongly influence development of England political action during the last half of the XIX Century; Socialism and the Labor Unions.

E. D. Jones, *Chartism*—a chapter in English Industrial History. Transactions of the Wisconsin Society of Sciences, Arts and Letters (1900); Frank R. Rosenblatt, *The Chartist Movement in its Social and Economic Aspects* (1916). F.J.B.

Chartres, the school of: Famous school in France founded at the end of the tenth century by Fulbert*, bishop of Chartres from 1006-1028. Leaders of the School were Bernard of Chartres (died between 1124-1130) and his younger brother Thierry* of Chartres (died around 1150) further Bernard Silvestris, chancellor at Chartres (around 1156), William of Conches*. (1080-1145) Walter of Mortagne*, Bishop of Laon (died 1174) and Gilbert de la Porrée*, Bishop of Poitiers and chancellor at Chartres (1076-1154).

In theology the School followed Boetius, in philosophy Plato and his doctrines in the *Timaeus.* Although considered second only in importance, the logical treatises of Aristotle, too, were cultivated. The School of Chartres distinguished itself with its love of the natural sciences also. The works of Hippocrates, Galen and even the medical treatises of the Arabs found a home within its walls. A characteristic feature of the School was a genuine love of classical antiquity and a study of the humanistic books of the past.

S.C.T.

Charvakas: A thoroughly materialistic school of Indian philosophers who regard the soul or self as a mere function of the body which completely ceases to exist when at death the body dissolves. An abundant life of the senses is the highest good. See Lokayata. C.S.B.

chasidim: (Heb. *Chasid*—pious) The party of the pious, the devout champions of the Law* and the up-holders of the traditional faith, who flourished in Palestine during the second and third centuries B.C. From their circle came the most determined opposition to the worldly and assimilationist Hellenisers among the people. They were the backbone of the Maccabean revolt and the forerunners of the Pharisees**. A.H.S.

Chasidism: A significant and extensive mystic movement which rapidly spread among the Jews of Poland in the second half of the 18th century. It came in the wake of earlier mystic messianic movements and the social and economic collapse of the Jewish communities of Eastern Europe following the Cossack uprisings in the middle of the 17th century. The Chasidic movement spread very rapidly, and by the middle of the 19th century, it embraced nearly one-half of the Jews of Eastern Europe. The movement stressed the values of piety, spiritual exaltation and the joy of complete surrender to God as a counter-poise to rigid religious formalism, rabbinic intellectualism, and the spiritual depression of the times. "Pure faith without any sophistries" was the key-note. The essence of Judaism was the love of God and the way to God was open to the poor and ignorant man whose prayer is sincere and whose faith is boundless as to the scholar who is steeped in Talmudic* lore or to the ascetic who denies himself the innocent enjoyments of life. The theologic emphasis was upon the omnipresence of God, man's ready communion with Him, and the power of fervid and ecstatic prayer.

The movement, steeped in religious emotionalism, came into violent conflict with official orthodox Rabbinism centered in Lithuania, seat of great Rabbinic academies, and its followers were frequently persecuted and excommunicated by their opponents who came to be known as "Mitnagdim". The Chasidim came to have their own separate synagogues and special prayer books and their own communal organization within the larger Jewish community. For a time Chasidim and Mitnagdim would not intermarry.

The founder of this movement was a man of humble origin, Israel ben Eliezer (d. 1760) who, because of his reputation as a healer and a miracle-worker, was known as Baal Shem Tov (Besht—the Master of the Good Name). The movement was always centered in the personality of a Tzadik (The righteous one, also called Rebbi) who was the supreme guide of his disciples and their mediator before God. These Tzadikim came to exercise enormous influence over their followers, some of them establishing hereditary dynasties, holding "court" and accumulating great wealth. The movement began to decline sharply towards the middle of the 19th century as a result of its own inner stagnation and the spread of modernism and secularism among the Jewish masses.

Among the more prominent leaders of the movement were Rabbi Baer of Meseritz (d. 1772) the successor to Besht, Rabbi Jacob Joseph of Polonnoye (d. 1782) first literary figure in Chasidism, Rabbi Nahum Tchernobyl (d. 1797), Rabbi Levi Isaac of Berdychev (1740-1809), Rabbi Shneur Zalman of Liady (1746-1819), the philosopher and "rationalist" of the movement and founder of the "Habad" branch of it, and Rabbi Nachman of Bratzlav (1770-1811). See Lurianic Kabbalah.

S. Schechter, *Studies in Judaism* (First Series), (1896); Jacob S. Minkin, *The Romance of Hassidism* (1935); Louis I. Newman and Samuel Spitz, *Hasidic Anthology* (1934); Martin Buber, *Jewish Mysticism* (1931); S. A. Horodezky, *Leaders of Hassidism* (1928). A.H.S.

Cheese Sunday: See church year cycle.

Cheltenham (Mo.) community: See communistic settlements, secular.

Chemnitz, Martin: (1522-1586) German Lutheran dogmatician, "prince of the theologians of the Augsburg Confession" (Quenstedt). Learned in mathematics and astrology as well as theology, Chemnitz brought into the doctrinal controversies of his day vast knowledge coupled with clear thought and discriminating judgment. As superintendent of Brunswick he was the leader of the Lutheran Church of Lower Saxony and influential in unifying the Lutherans of Saxony and Swabia on the basis of the *Formula of Concord**, of which he was one of the principal authors. His *Loci Theologici*, published posthumously in 1591, is a commentary on the *Loci Communes** of Melanchthon whose respectful disciple Chemnitz remained in spite of his own firmer orthodoxy. Against the Crypto-Calvinists* he wrote *De Vera Praesentia* (1560) defending the strict Lutheran view of the Eucharist* including the emphasis on ubiquity*. Against Socinianism* he wrote *De Duabus Naturis in Christo* (1570). His greatest work is the four-volume *Examen Concilii Tridentini* (1565-1573), an incisive analysis of the Roman Catholic position adopted at Trent and an able defense of Protestantism. See communicatio idiomatum. T.A.K.

Chemosh: National deity of the Moabites*, as proved by the O.T. and archaeological monuments (Moabite Stone*). He on occasion was appeased by human sacrifice (2 Ki 3:27). Solomon* is reported to have built a sanctuary to Chemosh in Jerusalem, which was maintained until the reform of Josiah (*ibid*, 23:13). H.K.—L.F.

cherub, cherubim: (Heb. *Kerub*, pl. *Kerubim*) Winged celestial beings, part human and part animal, who served as the chariot of the Almighty and as guardian angels*. Figures of Cherubim decorated the doors and walls of the Temple of Solomon**. Two Cherubim made of olive wood, and covered with gold, were set up in the inner Sanctuary of the Temple, their over-arching wings touching each other in the middle of the chamber beneath which rested the Ark*. The Ark itself had two Cherubim of gold set up, facing each other, at the two ends of the Ark-cover (Kaporet), their wings spread out on high, screen-it. It was here, between these two Cherubim, that the deity revealed Himself and communicated His commands. (Ex. 25.17-22; Num. 7.89). Yahweh is therefore referred to in the Bible as "He Who is enthroned upon the Cherubim". (I Sam. 4.4; II Sam. 6.2; IIK. 19.15; Ps. 80.2; 99.1). There were no Cherubim in the Second Temple.

In the vision of Ezekiel (Chap. 1 and 10) the Divine Throne rested upon the wings of four Cherubim, each of which had the form of a man with four faces—that of a man, a lion, an ox and an eagle, and each one possessed of four wings, under which were the hands of a man. The soles of their feet were calves' soles. Each Cherub had a wheel at its side which moved as the Cherub moved, and both Cherub and wheel were full of eyes. These Cherubim served as the Divine chariot.

Cherubim were the guardian spirits not only of the Sanctuary and the Ark, but also of the Tree of Life after the Fall. (Gen. 3.24).

In the angelic hierarchy which was developed in later times, the Cherubim came to be variously placed in the scale, but their function remained primarily that of guardian angels. Such subsidiary deities of composite forms acting as winged guardians, one finds in Babylonian, Assyrian, Hittite and Egyptian mythology, and representations of them are to be seen on monuments and sculpture.

It has been suggested that the Cherubim were the personifications of clouds, wind or storm.

A.H.S.

Chesterton, Gilbert Keith: (1874-1936) English journalist and author, whose brilliant essays, *Heretics* (1905), *Orthodoxy* (1909), and other volumes interpreted Christianity from a mystical Catholic viewpoint strikingly transcending yet intimately related to contemporary thought.

J.W.B.

chiasmus: A sentence in which one set of words is repeated in inverted form, so that the two clauses are crossed as in the letter Chi (X).

E.F.S.

Chicago School of theology: Under the leadership of such men as Shailer Mathews*, John Merlin Powys Smith, and Shirley Jackson Case, the Divinity School of the University of Chicago developed in the early part of the century a theological method which drew heavily upon the insights of the social sciences then coming into academic prominence. At that time the University of Chicago itself was fast on the way to establishing the leading department of sociology in the country, and numbered among its philosophers George Herbert Mead.

The gist of this Chicago theological method is the interpretation of Christian writings, historical events, thought, and service in the light of their social environment. Christian loyalty, it is held, has had perforce to express itself in contemporary culture patterns such as empire, feudalism, national sovereignty, democracy, and law. To understand the Christian religion of the past as well as to express it in the present require an understanding of the social milieu and the changing intellectual climates past and present. Social experience is to be explored as a key to the interpretation of all phases of the Christian movement. Metaphysical and systematic theology thus become subordinate to functional and cultural theology. Theology in fact does not create Christian loyalty. Loyalty rather begets successive theologies to fit the changing times. Consequently no theological formula can ever be considered final or as conveying absolute truth. Cf. Foster, G. B.

Shirley Jackson Case, *The Social Origens of Christianity* (1923); Shailer Mathews, *The Atonement and Social Process* (1930); J. M. P. Smith, *The Prophets and Their Times* (1925); *The Journal of Religion* issued by the Divinity Faculty and Conference of the University of Chicago.

A.C.M.

child marriage: The marriage* of persons who have not yet reached maturity. Generally, the term is applied to any marriage in which either the wife is under 18 years of age or the husband has not yet reached his twenty-first birthday, these being the most common ages at which persons can marry without parental consent and prevailing in three-fourths of the jurisdictions in the United States. Fifteen jurisdictions, however, prescribe the same minimum age for both males and females; eleven requiring both to be not less than 21, one setting 20 as the minimum, and three permitting marriage at 18. Nevertheless, in more than a half dozen jurisdictions marriage may be consummated by parental consent at 14 for males and 12 for females. While these states are exceptional, the standard generally prevailing is 18 for males and 16 for females.

Among preliterate peoples, marriage is almost invariably permitted after puberty. In this preliterate peoples have not differed from many historical peoples. Talmudic* law fixed the legal age for contracting marriage at puberty. The prevailing marriageable age for girls in Europe during the Renaissance was twelve years. Furthermore, marriages were often celebrated among Europeans until well into the 17th century between persons who had not yet achieved puberty, as was also true in India until very recent times, but under these circumstances the marriage generally remained a fiction until puberty or beyond.

E.R.M.

children: See family; juvenile delinquency; juvenile protection.

Children of the Light: See Society of Friends.

chiliasm: (*chiliad-* a thousand) Doctrine of Christ's return to reign a thousand years on earth. See millenarianism.

R.E.E.H.

China: See Chinese religions; Chinese Terminology.

China Inland mission: Founded by J. Hudson Taylor who went to China in 1853. It now has over 1000 missionaries there. Vocational and spiritual preparation, careful training in languages are required. No direct appeal is made for funds and no fixed salary is guaranteed. Missionaries are stationed in inland provincial capitals to extend the gospel through the interior. P.E.J.

Chinese religions: See Chinese Terminology.

CHINESE TERMINOLOGY (not including Buddhism):

Chang (Tao) Ling: Historical founder of the Taoist religion, who was born between 147 and 167 A.D. By his Taoistic writings and magic healing, he attracted many followers to the Dragon and Tiger Mountain (Lung Hu Shan) where he lived. These followers were required to contribute five bushels of rice each, from which the movement was called "the Way (Tao) of Five Bushels of Rice" and "Rice Bandits." He was called the Heavenly Teacher (*T'ien Shih*) and the religion he organized was called the "Way of the Heavenly Teacher."

The movement was continued by his son Hêng and grandson Lu. The latter led a revolt in northwestern China for thirty years, supported by charity, magic, and superstitious beliefs. Thus from early days, the movement was both political and religious. After his surrender, the political feature disappeared but the religious aspect continues to this day under the name of Taoism*.

Chinese religions: Confucianism, Buddhism and Taoism** are usually considered the religions of China. This description, whether in the qualitative or quantitative sense, is correct only to a limited extent. In the first place, there are more religions in China than these three. Secondly, Confucianism can hardly be called a religion (see Confucianism). Thirdly, Chinese religions are so interfused that it is difficult to draw a line between them. Running through them is the ancient and popular religion of the masses, which may be called the Religion of the People.

Outside of the professional Buddhists and Taoists, the people at large do not distinguish themselves as Confucianists or Buddhists or Taoists. They follow a general religion, which antedates, combines, and overshadows all the so-called "three religions." This general cult is characterized by several prominent features:

1) *Animism and polytheism.* From time immemorial, the Chinese have worshiped four classes of spirits. The first class, called *Shên**, includes the spirits of Heaven. Of these, Shang-ti* is the highest, the sun, the moon, and the stars second, and wind, rain, etc., third. The second class includes the *ch'i* or spirits of Earth, notably Shê Chi* or Gods of the Ground and the Grain, the five Holy Mountains led by T'ai Shan or the Holy Mountain of the East, other mountains, rivers, and valleys. The third class, called *kuei**, includes the spirits of human beings, especially ancestors. The fourth class refers to the *kuai* or spirits of animate and inanimate objects. This ancient classification is no longer followed, nor is the order of seniority still in effect. Because different localities have worshiped different gods at different times according to their need, some gods have disappeared while others have emerged. Those that have survived as the fittest are Shang-ti, Shê Chi, T'ai Shan, the God of Land, the City God, the Dragon God, the God of Wealth, the God of Medicine, the Kitchen God, Kuei-hsing, Kuan Ti*, Yo Fei*, the Fu Lu Shou, the gods of various clans and professions, etc.

2) *Worship of Shang-ti**. Although Shang-ti is one of the many heavenly spirits, he is really a category by himself, for he is identical with Heaven (see T'ien) and is comparable to Amita* in Buddhism or God in Christianity. He is purposive, personal, and perfect. Until 1912, it was the supreme duty of the emperor to make sacrifice to him in behalf of the people.

3) *Ancestor worship.* "As the foundation of things is Heaven, so the foundation of man is the ancestors." With this conviction, the Chinese have worshiped their ancestors with a seriousness equal to their worship of Heaven. As we learn from the inscriptions on oracle bones of the Shang period (1765-1122?), ancestor worship was highly developed at that time. It is an extension of filial piety and should not be compared with the worship of other spirits. The ancient practice of impersonating (*shih*) the deceased usually by his grandson, the subsequent custom of offering before tablets, the building of ancestral temples, the elaborate system of burial and mourning, the extensive practice of visiting graves, etc., are but expressions of continued respect for parents, without any sense of fear or gain. To the Chinese, "Worship is to fulfill human relations." Ancestors are believed to be still alive as spirits (see hun), with human qualities and human needs. Consequently, the Chinese insist that in sacrifice there must be the feeling that ancestors "are really there." Food is offered them, and, beginning with the T'ang dynasty (618-907), paper money is burned as a gift to them. Other necessary things in the sacrifice are candles and incense. The former grew out of the ancient custom of worship before dawn while the latter was borrowed from Buddhism.

4) *Worship of Confucius.* As ancestor worship is the extension of filial piety, so the worship of Confucius is the extension of respect for a teacher. The Chinese worship Confucius, Lao Tzŭ**, and Sakyamuni (see Buddha, Buddhist Terminology) as the Three Sages in certain temples. But the worship of Confucius alone is national, for every county throughout the empire was required to have, and most of them still have, a *K'ung miao* (Confucian temple), a *wên miao* (temple of culture), or a *hsüeh kung* (temple of learning).

State worship of Confucius began with the offerings by the founder of the Han dynasty before Confucius' tomb in 195 B.C. It developed when Wu-ti established in 136 B.C. the Confucian College of Doctors, consisting of five faculties corresponding to the Five Classics (see Confucianism) and adopted these Classics in 125 B.C. as basis of civil service examination. These gestures were political. Later on, however, when P'ing-ti conferred the posthumous title of "Duke" on Confucius in 1 A.D.; when sacrifices in his honor were decreed in all schools in larger cities in 59; when the Five Classics were engraved on stone slabs by Imperial order and placed in the Temple of Confucius at the capital, Ch'angan, in 175 A.D.; when a Temple of Confucius was erected in his birthplace in 442; when his lineal male descendant was made hereditary Duke; when images or portraits of him were ordered set in place in schools throughout the empire in 637; when he was honored as "The Foremost Teacher" in 666, as "King" in 739, and as "Perfect Sage" in 1013; and when the same sacrifice was made to him as to Shang-ti in 1906, the honor was conferred out of genuine respect. The Chinese people, from the emperor down, regarded Confucius as the example of man and worshiped him as an ideal instead of a power over the fortunes of human existence. State and school worship of Confucius was terminated in 1912. In 1934, however, the government decided that the birthday of Confucius, August 27th, be observed as a national holiday, decreed that a high government official participate in the worship of Confucius at his native place, Ch'üfu, and appointed his 77th direct descendant as "Sacrificial official for the Grand Perfection, Ultimate Sage, and Foremost Teacher."

5) *State Cult.* In a sense the worship of Confucius was a state cult, as state worship was accorded Confucius ever since the Han dynasty, except in the T'ang (618-907) and Yüan (1280-1368) dynasties when Taoism and Lamaism, respectively, were more popular with the rulers. The term state cult, in the case of China, however, meant nothing more than official sanction of and participation in the worship of Heaven, ancestors, Confucius, etc. It was different from the state cult of Imperial Rome or Japan. Theoretically the emperor was the Son of Heaven and the head priest of the people. But this did not imply the theory of divine right or governmental control of religions or exclusion of other cults. The emperor's part in the worship of Heaven and Confucius was purely ceremonial. Government regulations of religions were political rather than religious. It is true that each dynasty fixed its own order of worship. The Ch'ing dynasty (1644-1911), for example, paid grand sacrifices to Heaven and Earth, the Gods of the Ground and the Grain, the past Emperors, and Confucius; paid secondary sacrifices to the spirits of Heaven, famous rulers of antiquity, great Con fucianists, and outstanding historical persons; and paid ordinary sacrifices to other deities. This classification, however, had little meaning to the people at large. It is also true that in all state capitals, the emperor himself was worshiped in the Wan-shou-Kung (Temple of Long Life). But there was no idea of the divinity of the emperor as in Japan, the worship being merely an expression of hope for the sovereign's longevity. Since the founding of the Republic in 1912, the state is no longer officially connected with any religion.

6) *Superstitions.* Aside from these various phases of worship, there is in the Religion of the People a strong element of superstition called *shu shu**, or divination and witchcraft. It is based on the belief that the Great Ultimate (*T'ai Chi**), yin yang* or the negative and positive cosmic forces, the Five Elements (*wu hsing**), and the Eight Trigrams (*pa kua**) could be so coordinated and controlled as to bring about good fortune. The search for long life and blessings was very extensive in ancient times, first promoted by the priest-magicians (*fang shih**) and later crystalized in the Huang Lao* movement. From then on, astrology, almanacs, dream interpretation, *fêng shui**, witchcraft, phrenology, palmistry, *ouija* to recall the soul, and fortune-telling in all forms have played an important part in the religious life of the illiterate and ignorant. The educated Chinese, however, have stood aloof from these.

7) *Ethics.* In the Religion of the People, generally speaking, worship is dominated by gratitude and superstition is dominated by fear. In each case, the underlying motive is ethical. Not only is worship an extension of filial piety and respect, most of the historical figures idolized are worshiped as embodiments of moral ideals such as loyalty, courage, justice, righteousness, etc. Religion, to a large extent, means to the Chinese sanction of ethics.

Ethical ideals cherished in this Religion are predominantly Confucian. However, the most important principle that underlies this Religion is the law of retribution to which both Taoism and Buddhism have contributed. This law is expressed in the Chinese proverb "If we plant melons, we reap melons; if we plant beans, we reap beans;" in the Confucian saying that "Good deeds bring good fortune and evil deeds bring ill fortune;" in the Taoist teaching of response and retribution; and in the Buddhist doctrine of cause and effect and transmigration. To the Chinese mass, the deities are essentially guardians of this law. They believe that their supreme duty is to observe the law by promoting the good and avoiding evil.

8) *General characteristics.* From the foregoing summary, it will be seen that the Religion of the Chinese People is basically practical, moral, and humanistic. It is the this-worldly interest that has kept it from developing a system of theology or a system of heaven and hell. The belief in the law of retribution has avoided the sense of sin and the idea of chance. It has helped the Chinese to keep their optimism in life and maintain a calm attitude towards misfortune. It has emphasized moral responsibility of the individual, resulting in the absence of any machinery for conversion or missionary work. The performance of rituals is more ethical and social than religious in the strict sense. While there is a great deal of formalism, conventionalism, superstitions, and waste (such as the great amount of

cultivable land used for graves), the basic assumptions and the general outlook of the Religion are rational. It is this rationalistic character that has prevented mysticism and fanaticism. The amount of myths is surprisingly small. Immortality is explained on a rationalistic basis (see hun). It is also due to this rationalistic attitude that the Chinese have become remarkably tolerant in religious matters. There have been few religious persecutions in Chinese history. While the persecutions of Buddhism in 446, 574, 845, and 955 were severe, they were for social and political rather than religious reasons.

The most outstanding characteristic of Chinese religion is its eclecticism. The Chinese, even when they attend Buddhist and Taoist temples, worship Buddhist and Taoist deities as members of a general pantheon. For example, they regard the Dipper God, a typical Taoist deity, as a god of the common people. It is extremely important to keep this eclectic character in mind even when Confucianism, Buddhism, or Taoism is considered separately. These systems are described under separate headings (see Confucianism; Buddhism; Taoism; Temples, Far Eastern). What follows is a summary of the religions of the minority.

1. *Mohammedanism.* Mohammedanism was introduced into China in 628 A.D. according to Mohammedan records, but in 651 according to recent Chinese research. It came both by sea and by land, from the Arabian Sea to the coastal provinces of Kwangtung, Fukien, and Chekiang, and from Persia to Sinkiang, Shênsi, Kansu, and Yunnan. Moslems believe that Mohammed's maternal uncle, whose Chinese name was Wan Ko-ssŭ, first brought the religion to Canton where his tomb still lies outside of the city. Whether this is true, the Huai Shêng Mosque in Canton is definitely the first mosque in China.

The religion is called by Chinese Moslems Ch'ing-chên Chiao, or the Religion of Purity and Truth, and by others T'ien-fang Chiao, or the Religion from the Heavenly Direction (Arabia), and Hui Hui Chiao. The latter is probably a transliteration of Uighur in Eastern Turkestan through which the religion came.

There are two types of Mohammedans in China. Those in Sinkiang and Chinghai retain their own languages and customs, and are called Turban Mohammedans (*ch'an hui*). Those in other parts of China are largely descendants of Moslem traders and Arabian soldiers who were sent to China to quell a rebellion in 755 at the emperor's request. Aside from adhering strictly to their religion in the Arabian fashion and refusing to eat pork or to worship idols and ancestors, they have been fairly thoroughly assimilated by the Chinese, keeping aloof, however, from opium and alcohol. They have adopted Chinese names such as Ma, Mo, Mu, Ha, Hê, and Ho, which sound like abbreviations of the name Mohammed. They have intermarried with the Chinese. They have attended Confucian schools, held Confucian degrees, accepted Confucian teachings and the Neo-Confucian philosophy of Reason and the Vital Force (*ch'i*), and approved the worship of Heaven as identical with Allah. They have served in the government, and have contributed to Chinese medicine and the calendar. They speak the Chinese language and follow Chinese customs. Although few Chinese have become Mohammedans and few Mohammedans have followed Chinese religions, the two groups have lived in an atmosphere of amity and tolerance. Mohammedan revolts during the Manchu dynasty (1644-1911) were entirely political. In profession, Moslems are horse traders, caravan merchants, cow slaughterers, and keepers of baths and inns. Unfortunately, few can read the Koran; fewer can understand Arabic. The Koran was not translated into Chinese until some seventy years ago. Today only five of the original twenty parts are existent, and these five were not published until 1927. There are in China 48,104,241 Mohammedan followers and 42,371 mosques, largely in Sinkiang, Chinghai, Manchuria, Kansu, Yunnan, Shênsi, Hopei, and Honan. A number of outstanding generals and government leaders are Mohammedans. Missions and students to Arabia and Egypt have aroused interest in the Mohammedan religion.

2. *Christianity*: (a) *Nestorianism**. The first Christian movement in China was Nestorianism. Some scholars claim that Christians came to China as early as the first century. However, there is no evidence to prove such a contention. The earliest record of Christianity in China is the Nestorian Tablet which was erected in Ch'angan (Sian) in 781 and discovered in 1625. According to this Tablet, the faith was introduced into China by A-lo-pên, whose identity is still disputed, and who arrived in the capital Ch'angan in 635 and received Imperial welcome. According to Saeki, Nestorianism was a form of "Oriental Christianity developed outside the sphere of the Graeco-Roman civilization." The religion known as Ching Chiao, or the Religion of Brilliance, enjoyed popularity until the persecution of 845. The persecution was primarily directed against Buddhism but it almost extinguished Nestorianism. Only slight traces of it could be found ever since.

(b) *Catholicism.* Catholicism reached China in the Yüan dynasty (1280-1368) with the arrival of such Franciscan fathers as Jean de Plan-Carpin and Guillaume de Ruysbroeck. Twenty churches were established, including the most famous one in Cambulic (Peiping), built in 1299, and other important ones in Yangchow, Hangchow, Ch'üanchow, and Canton.

Not much progress was made, however, until the Jesuits came in the Ming dynasty (1368-1644). The first to arrive was St. Francis Xavier who reached Kwangtung in 1552 and died in the same year. In 1580 Michael Ruggieri (d. 1607) and Matteo Ricci* (1552-1610) arrived in Macao. They were followed by J. Adam Scholl (1591-1666), Ferdinand Verbriest (1623-1688), etc. These Jesuit fathers enjoyed court favor, converted a number of high officials to their faith (including Prime Minister Hsü Kuang-ch'i, 1562-1633, with whom Matteo Ricci translated Euclid's *Geometry*), served the Chinese government as astronomers, and contributed a great deal by introducing Western science (mathematics, astronomy, the manufacture of guns and explosives, etc.), and translating Western classics.

By the end of the seventeenth century, they had about 200,000 followers. They promoted Confucianism and approved the worship of Heaven and ancestors. Early in the eighteenth century, the Dominicans and Franciscans objected to this Confucian tendency of the Jesuits. A bitter quarrel followed, resulting in the intervention of both the Chinese Emperor and the French King and finally the suppression of Catholicism which almost ended the movement.

However, various branches of Catholicism continued to be active in different parts of China. Progress was slow but steady. Today there are 3,262,678 Chinese Catholics. They operate 438 orphanages, 315 hospitals, 20,520 schools, including three institutions of higher learning, a number of museums, libraries, and research institutions of high standard. In 1922, the first apostolic delegate to China was appointed by Pope Pius XI, thus putting the religion on a firm basis. Foreign priests number 2,980, while Chinese priests total 2,073, including a number of bishops.

(c) *Protestantism.* Protestantism started in China with the arrival of Robert Morrison in Canton in 1807. Within 135 years, its membership has grown to about 1,000,000 (Christian community members), or about 500,000 (communicants). In 1934, there were 17 British societies, 64 American and Canadian societies, 23 European societies, 2 Australian, and 1 international. In 1935, there were 6,150 missionaries, representing 93 denominations and subdivisions.

These figures are not as impressive as those of Mohammedanism and Catholicism, but what the religion has done is of tremendous importance. It has contributed substantially to education, medicine, and philanthropy. In 1937 it operated 271 hospitals (18,266 beds) and branches. Most of the best hospitals in China are Christian, and in many interior areas, only Christian medical service is available. The many lower schools with about 150,000 pupils, the 249 secondary schools with 47,940 students, and the fifteen colleges and universities with 7,098 students (all 1937 figures) have won the respect of the Chinese. The Red Cross, the Y.M.C.A., the Y.W.C.A., etc., are nation-wide movements with extensive support of non-Christians. In social reform, Christianity has taken part in the fight against footbinding, opium-smoking, child marriage, blind marriage, nepotism, and the like. It pioneered the successful fight for the freedom of widows to remarry, for the right of young men and young women to choose their own life-mates and professions, for the independence of women, and for the opportunity for women to receive education. Both education for women and coeducation started in missionary schools. Christianity has helped to introduce and promote Western science, modern knowledge, and physical education. It has assisted Chinese political revolutions and reforms. Most important of all, it has a share in training Chinese leadership, having molded the character of such great men as Sun Yat-sen, Chiang Kai-shek, and other national leaders.

From the point of view of its contribution, then, Protestantism has been successful. It could have been more successful if it had adopted a more sympathetic approach, if it had worked more vigorously among the educated class, if it had spread out all over China instead of largely centering around the coastal cities, if missionaries had mixed with the Chinese more and adopted some of their good customs, if the religion had been entirely free from Western imperialism by refusing the protection of unequal treaties, if both missionaries and Chinese Christians had a more understanding attitude towards Chinese culture, if they had appreciated Chinese virtues just as deeply as they hated Chinese vices, if missionary schools had not ignored Chinese studies as they did, if the Church had achieved more unity, and if it had not over-emphasized theology to which the Chinese are by nature indifferent. In the last twenty years, Christian leaders have been quick to grasp opportunities for advancement. The United Church of Christ in China was founded in 1927. Through emphasis on Chinese culture and keen appreciation of the Chinese philosophy of life, Christianity is rapidly winning the favor of Chinese intellectuals and the Chinese government. Chinese leadership within the Church is growing. Missionaries remaining in the war zones to carry on their service during this war have gained the admiration of the entire people.

3. *Other Foreign Religions*: (a) *Judaism.* Judaism has been known to exist in China for many centuries. According to records, a group of Jews came to China in the twelfth century and built a synagogue in K'aifêng in 1163. They might have come as early as the first century to escape the persecution in Babylon in 34 A.D. or for trade. Originally there were seventy families. By 1866, only seven were left, numbering about 300 people. The number has, of course, grown since then. Their traditional center has been K'aifêng in Honan, but many of them live now in Ningpo, Hangchow, and Shanghai. Because they called their synagogue by the same name as a Mohammedan mosque (Ch'ing Chên Temple), they have been regarded as a branch of Islam and called Ch'ing Hui Hui, or Blue Mohammedans. They pick out the sinew of the flesh they eat, and for this reason their religion is called Ts'iao Chin Chiao (Sinew Picking Sect). Only a very small number in K'aifêng still cling to this ancient faith. Their synagogue has been replaced by an Episcopal church. They neither observe sabbath nor practice circumcision. They have been largely assimilated by the Chinese.

(b) *Manicheism**. In 694 a religion called Ch'ih-ts'ai Shih-mo Chiao (the Religion of Vegetarianism and Demonism) came to China, settled in Chekiang and adjacent provinces. It was also called Mo-ni Chiao and Ming Chiao (the Religion of Light) and was identified as Manicheism. Persecuted in 823, 825, and 915, it almost entirely disappeared, but managed to survive. It participated in uprisings, mixed with Taoism and Buddhism, prospered in the Southern Sung dynasty (1127-1279), confounded with secret societies, shifted to Fukien province after Yuan (1280-1368). Towards the end of Ming (1368-1644) a Manichean temple still existed there.

(c) *Zoroastrianism**. Between 516 and 519 some Zoroastrians brought their religion into China. During the T'ang period, temples were built in the capitals and important cities by imperial command, evidently to attract the peoples of Central Asia. No Chinese was allowed to follow the religion. It declined after the persecution of 845, leaving only a slight trace in the Five dynasties (907-960). There has been no mention of it in Chinese literature since the Southern Sung dynasty (1127-1279).

(d) *Others.* Modern religious movements like Theosophy, Bahai, Christian Science, Japanese Tenri and Dairei, etc., have found their way to China. But they are represented only by a very small group in one or two localities and have not made any imprint on Chinese religious life.

4. *Secret Societies*: The religious picture of China is incomplete without a word about secret societies, although these societies have been more political than religious. The best known one was the T'ai P'ing Rebellion led by Hung Hsiu-ch'üan (1806-1865). He became the patriarch of The Society of Shang-ti (God), organized by Chu Chiu-ch'ao, ostensibly for the promulgation of religion but really for revolution against the Manchus. After a vision and after reading a book given him by a Christian missionary, Hung enlarged his organization, called Jehovah his Heavenly Father and Jesus his Heavenly Brother, and extended his religion to Kwangsi. In 1848 he started the revolution from there, established the T'ai P'ing T'ien Kuo (the Heavenly Kingdom of Great Peace) in 1850, and proclaimed himself the Heavenly King. He captured Nanking in 1853, disciplined his army with religion, prohibited alcohol-drinking, foot-binding, and queue-wearing. Because of internal disorder, religious fanaticism, extreme destructiveness, and strong opposition from the Christians as well as the public in general, the Heavenly Kingdom crumbled in 1865 after a brief existence of fifteen years.

The oldest secret society that has some religious character is the White Lotus Society (Pai-lien). It was organized by Han Shantung's grandfather in the beginning of Yüan (1280-1368) with the intention to restore the Sung dynasty. It worships both Buddhist and Taoist deities, although it stresses the repetition of Buddha's name. The Boxers were one of its branches. Today it flourishes in North China.

The Tsai Li Chiao, also called Li Chiao and Li Mên (all meaning Rationalistic Religion), dates back to the seventeenth century. It is similar to the White Lotus Society, so much so that it is often considered a branch of it. Its chief emphasis, however, lies in abstinence from smoking, snuffing, and drinking. It is chiefly found in North China.

The Triad Society (San Tien Hui or San Ho Hui), organized in 1674 for political purposes, follows a number of Buddhist and Taoist practices and worships Emperor T'ai-tsung (939-997). It has participated in several revolutions, including the one started by Sun Yat-sen. Its stronghold is South China.

Besides these, there are the Wu Shan Shê, or the Society for the Intuition of the Good, founded in 1915 in Szechuan by T'ang Huan-chang to synthesize Confucianism, Buddhism, Taoism, Catholicism, Protestantism, and Mohammedanism; and the Tung Shan Shê, or the Society for Common Good, founded in 1922 by Chiang Ch'ao-tsung and others for the purposes of worshiping Śākyamuni, Confucius, and Lao Tzŭ, and cultivating the spirit by means of meditation. Both societies have spread to North and Central China. The former is patronized by the lower classes of society, while the latter includes mostly the educated. Other small, local, or temporary societies are too numerous to mention. See sacred literatures; Temples, Far Eastern.

J. J. M. de Groot, *The Religious System of China, Its Ancient Forms, Evolution, History, and Present Aspect* (1892-1910); de Groot, *The Religion of the Chinese* (1910); W. E. Soothill, *The Three Religions of China* (1919); Henri Doré, *Researches into Chinese Superstitions* (1914); J. K. Shryock, *The Temples of Anking and Their Cults* (1929).

ch'ing ming: (Chin. clear & bright) The festival of the third moon of the old Chinese lunar calendar, which falls on April 5th or 6th. On this day the Chinese visit graves and enjoy the clear and bright atmosphere of Spring.

Chuang Tzŭ: See Taoism.

Chu Hsi: See Confucianism.

Confucius: (K'ung Ch'iu, K'ung Chung-ni, K'ung Fu-tzŭ or Grand Master K'ung, 551-479 B.C.) Confucius was born in a poor family in the state of Lu (in present Shangtung), a descendant of the people of Sung. His father died soon after his birth. When he grew up, he was put in charge of a granary, then cattle and sheep, and then public works in his native state. Later he became Grand Secretary of Justice and then Chief Minister. He regained some territory lost to a neighboring state purely by arguments based on morality. He executed a minister who created disorder, and brought peace to the land to the extent that "things lost on the highways were not stolen." He resigned when the attention of the ruler of his state was completely attracted by a group of dancing girls sent by a jealous neighboring country.

In 496 B.C., he began fourteen years of travel from state to state, offering his service to the rulers. He was politely consulted by them, but no one would put his moral doctrines into practice. He was even sent away from Ch'i, threatened in Sung, driven out of Sung and Wei, and surrounded between Ch'ên and Ts'ai. When in difficulty, he exclaimed, "Heaven has endowed me with a moral destiny. What can Huan Tuei (who threatened him) do to me?" Eventually he retired to Lu to study, teach, and write.

He lived in a time when the moral and cultural traditions of Chou were in rapid decline. Attempting to uphold the Chou culture, he taught poetry, history, ceremonies, and music to 3,000 pupils. He became the first Chinese educator to offer education to any who cared to come, with or without tuition. He taught culture, human conduct, being one's true self, and honesty in social relationships. Most probably, he wrote the chronicles called *Ch'un Ch'iu* (*Spring and Autumn Annals*). His tacit judgments on social and political events were such that "unruly ministers and villainous sons were afraid" to repeat their evil deeds.

He severely disciplined himself and practiced what he taught. He loved poetry, ceremonies, and music. He was serious, honest, polite, filially pious towards his mother, stern towards his son, and friendly towards his pupils. His most reliable teachings are found in the *Lun Yü* (*Analects*), aphorisms recorded by his followers. His teachings (see Confucianism) have dominated Chinese life and thought for some two thousand years. Both he and his pupils have become objects of worship (see Chinese religions).

See Bibliography under Confucianism.

Confucianism: Confucianism is called in Chinese *Ju Chia* (the School of the Learned) and *Ju Chiao* (the Teaching of the Learned). It is a vital movement that has dominated Chinese culture for two thousand years, and those of Korea and Japan for almost as long. It is based on, and developed out of, the teachings of one man, Confucius*.

Confucius (551-479 B.C.) advocated true manhood (*jên*) as the highest good, the superior man (*chün tzŭ*) as the ideal being, and cultivation of life (*hsiu shên*) as the supreme duty of man. Consequently he emphasized moral perfection (*chih shan*) for the individual and moral and social order (*li*) for society. These are to be attained by the practice of "chung," or being true to the principles of one's nature, and "shu," the application of those principles in relation to others. *Chung* and *shu* form the "one thread that runs through" the entire Confucian teaching. The total objective is *chung yung*, the Golden Mean or Central Harmony, that is, "the central basis of our moral being and harmony with the universe." To this end, knowledge must be directed, names rectified, and social relationships harmonized. The whole program involves the investigation of things, the extension of knowledge, sincerity of the will, rectification of the heart, cultivation of the personal life, regulation of family life, national order, and finally, world peace.

Mencius (371-289 B.C.) carried this moralism and humanism further. He held that we not only should be good, but must be good, since human nature is originally good. True manhood (*jên*) and righteousness (*i*) are considered man's "mind" and "path," respectively. A man must "develop his nature to the fullest" and "exercise his mind to the limit." Government must be established on the basis of benevolence as against profit and force. Hsün Tzŭ (c. 335-c. 288 B.C.), believing human nature to be evil, stressed moral discipline and education, especially through the rectification of names, music, and the rules of propriety (*li*). In the book *Chung Yung*, the doctrine of central harmony is further developed. Our central self or moral being is conceived to be the central basis of existence, and harmony or moral order is the universal law of the world.

In the second century B.C., Confucianism became merged with the Yin Yang* philosophy. As advocated by Tung Chung-shu (177-104 B.C.), man and nature have direct correspondence. As the cosmic order results from the harmony of yin and yang or the negative and positive universal principles in nature, so the moral order results from the harmony of yang and yin in man, such as husband and wife, human nature and passions, and love and hate. The Five Agents (see wu hsing), through which yin and yang operate, have direct correspondence not only with the five directions, the five metals, etc., in nature, but also with the Five Constant Virtues, the five senses, etc., in man. Thus human affairs and natural events were explained in terms of a neat macrocosm-microcosm relationship, and Tung became the master of the "science of catastrophies and anomalies." At the same time, there was a movement called *ch'an wei*, or "prophetic writings and apocryphal complements" to the Confucian Classics. These writings treated natural phenomena as causes or effects of human conduct. It was not until Liu Hsin (d. 23 B.C.), who insisted that "the Six Classics were history" and not prophetic literature, that the Confucian and the Yin Yang movements were separated.

The Six Classics referred to were the *Shih Ching*, *Shu Ching*, *I Ching*, *Ch'un Ch'iu*, *Li Chi*, and *Yo Ching*. The *Yo Ching* or *The Classic of Music* was lost early in the Han dynasty. The other five were made, in 136 B.C., the literature of the five faculties of the Imperial Confucian College of Doctors, and in 125 B.C., the basis of civil service examination, thus establishing the supremacy of Confucianism.

The *Shih Ching* or *The Book of Poetry* (Eng. tr. by Arthur Waley, *The Book of Songs*, 1937) is a collection of ancient songs which were popular at the time of Confucius. While the Sage evidently was fond of them, especially as records of sentiments and customs, he did not select and edit them as tradition has claimed. The *Shu Ching* or *The Book of History* (Eng. tr. by James Legge, *The Shoo King*, 1882) is a collection of ancient historical documents. There are two texts. The text in the "modern script" is, to a large extent, authentic but that in the "ancient script" is definitely a forgery. Whether Confucius edited this Classic is doubtful. The *I Ching* or *The Book of Changes* (Eng. tr. by James Legge, *The Yi King*, 1882) is a collection of propositions and explanations used in divination written by various authors of different periods up to as late

Chinese Terminology

as the third century B.C. The traditional theory that King Wên (1184-1135 B.C.?) wrote the propositions and Confucius wrote the appendices is unacceptable, although the book certainly contains a good portion written by Confucianists. It is an important book because it contains ancient philosophy and principles of government. The *Ch'un Ch'iu* or *The Spring and Autumn Annals* (Eng. tr. by James Legge, *Ch'un Ch'iu,* 1879) is a history of Confucius' native state Lu, probably written by Confucius on the basis of previous records. The *Li Chi* or *The Book of Rites* is a collection of Confucian treatises of the third century B.C. on ancient ethics, government, and customs. All these Five Classics have suffered corruption and interpolation. From the second century B.C. to 1905, they were the foundation of Chinese education and, therefore, Chinese life and thought.

To these Five Classics, the Neo-Confucianists of the Sung dynasty (960-1279) added the Four Books which had been of even greater importance. These are the *Ta Hsüeh, Chung Yung, Lun Yü,* and *Mêng Tzŭ* (Eng. tr. by James Legge, *The Four Books,* 1871, 1932), basic texts of Chinese schools until 1905. Both the *Ta Hsüeh* (*The Great Learning*, Eng. tr. by Lin Yutang in his *The Wisdom of Confucius,* 1938) and the *Chung Yung* (*Golden Mean* or *Central Harmony,* Eng. tr. by Ku Hung-ming, *The Conduct of Life,* 1906, revised by Lin Yutang in *The Wisdom of Confucius,* 1938) are sections of the *Li Chi,* singled out by Neo-Confucianists. The *Ta Hsüeh* is attributed to Tzŭ Ssu, grandson of Confucius, and the *Chung Yung* to a Confucian pupil. Most of these two books represents original teachings of Confucius. The *Lun Yü* or the *Analects* (see Confucius) was probably compiled by followers of Confucius between the fifth and fourth century B.C. and contains authentic sayings of Confucius and his immediate pupils. All these books have been corrupted to some extent. *Mêng Tzŭ* or *The Works of Mencius* is the most original of all.

The Sung Confucianists not only elevated these Confucian writings to great eminence, but they also carried Confucian philosophy to new heights, producing the system of *Li Hsüeh,* or Rational Philosophy, usually called Neo-Confucianism in the West. This Rational Philosophy developed in three phases, namely, the Reason School in the Sung period (960-1279), the Mind School in the Ming period (1388-1644), and the Empirical School in the Ch'ing period (1644-1911). The central idea of the movement is focused on the Great Ultimate (*T'ai Chi*) and Reason (*li*). The Great Ultimate moves and generates the active principle, yang, when its activity reaches its limit, and engenders the passive principle, yin, when it becomes tranquil. The eternal oscillation of yin and yang gives rise to the material universe through their Five Agents of Water, Fire, Wood, Metal, and Earth. Thus reality is a progressively evolved and a well-coordinated system.

This dynamic and orderly character of the universe is due to Reason and the Vital Force (*ch'i*). As the Ch'êng brothers (Ming-tao, 1032-1086, & I-ch'üan, 1033-1077) said, "All things have the same Reason in them." Thus, Reason combines the Many into One, while the Vital Force differentiates the One into the Many, each with its own "determinate nature." The two principles, however, are not to be sharply contrasted, for neither is independent of the other. Reason operates through, and is embodied in, the Vital Force. It is this cooperative functioning of theirs that makes the universe a cosmos, a harmonious system of order and sequence. "Centrality is the order of the universe and harmony is its unalterable law." As such the cosmos is a moral order. This is the main reason why the greatest of the Neo-Confucianists, Chu Hsi (1130-1200), said that "the Great Ultimate is nothing but the Reason of ultimate goodness."

Furthermore, the universe is a social order, and nothing can stand by itself. At the same time, everything has its opposite. "No two of the productions of creation are alike," and the Taoist doctrine of equality of things must be rejected. In the eternal sequence of appearance and disappearance every creation is new, and the Buddhist doctrine of transmigration must be rejected.

In order to appreciate fully the meaning of the universe, man must comprehend Reason. This can be done by "investigating things to the utmost," that is, by "investigating the Reason of things to the utmost." When sufficient effort is made, and understanding naturally comes, one's nature will be realized and his destiny will be fulfilled, since "the exhaustive investigation of Reason, the full realization of one's nature, and the fulfillment of destiny are simultaneous." When one understands Reason, he will find that "All people are brothers and sisters, and all things are my companions," because all men have the same Reason in them. Consequently one should not entertain any distinction between things and the ego. This is the foundation of the Neo-Confucian ethics of *jên,* true manhood, benevolence or love. Both the understanding of Reason and the practice of *jên* require sincerity (*ch'êng*) and seriousness (*ching*) which, to the Neo-Confucianists, almost assumed religious significance. As a matter of fact, these have a certain correspondence with the Buddhist *dhyāna* and *prajña,* or meditation and insight. Gradually the Neo-Confucian movement became an inward movement, the mind assuming more and more importance.

When it came to the Ming period, especially in Wang Yang-ming (1473-1529), Reason became identified with Mind. Mencius' doctrine of native knowledge was revived and made the basis of his theory of the identity of knowledge and conduct and the sacred duty of man to "fully exercise his mind" and to "manifest his illustrious virtues."

Wang Yang-ming considered desire as an obstacle to the mind. The Neo-Confucianists of the Ch'ing period, especially Tai Tung-yüan (1723-1777), however, argued that since desire is part of our nature, it has its rightful place, just as the Vital Force has its rightful place beside Reason.

As a matter of fact, Reason can only be discovered in daily events and experience, or in short, in the Vital Force itself.

Throughout the development of Confucianism, the basic concept *jên* has remained the center of Confucian ethics. It is the general virtue, the principle "by which a man is to be a man," which may be rendered as the Good or True Manhood. Fundamentally it means the development of one's nature to the fullest extent and the application of that principle in relation to others, that is, to treat others as oneself or to put oneself in the position of others. Specifically, it means the Three Universal Virtues of wisdom, benevolence, and courage, the Five Constant Virtues of benevolence, righteousness, propriety, wisdom, and good faith, and the eight ideals of filial piety, respect, loyalty, good faith, propriety, righteousness, integrity, and the sense of shame.

In a rationalistic and humanistic system such as Confucianism, its religious position is difficult to define. On the one hand, the Confucian outlook of the universe is obviously naturalistic. On the other hand, the universe is conceived as a moral order to which man's destiny is closely tied. This ambiguity has led many to consider Confucianism as a religion and others to regard it as a nonreligious ethical system. Many have viewed Confucius as a promoter, or even a founder, of a religion, while others have described him as an agnostic. Confucius was neither. In ancient China, Lao Tzŭ*, the atheist, represented the left wing in the matter of religion, and Mo Tzŭ*, the vigorous promoter of the ancient faith, represented the right wing. Confucius followed the middle course, with tendency towards the right. The fact was that Confucius was primarily interested in life. Consequently he "did not talk about spirits," but said that "if we cannot serve man, how can we serve spirits?" and would not discuss death. However, life to him contained religious elements. Consequently he prayed, worshipped Heaven (see T'ien) as his predecessors did, promoted the ancient practice of ancestor worship, and knew and obeyed the decrees of Heaven. To him and to his followers, the religious life and the moral life could not be sharply distinguished. Confucian humanism does not and has not precluded religion. As a matter of fact, all Confucianists agree that the "ancient sages founded teaching (*chiao*) on the way of gods." Confucianism, as *Ju Chiao*, or Teaching of the Learned, is both ethical and religious.

Of course, if religion is interpreted as an organized system, then Confucianism is definitely not a religion. It has no priesthood, no church, no Bible, no creed, no conversion, and no fixed system of gods. It has no interest in either theology or mythology. Even Confucian ceremonies are more social than religious. It is true that Confucius has been made an object of worship (see Chinese religions), but he was not deified as Lao Tzŭ and Sākyamuni (see Buddha, Buddhist Terminology) were. The Confucianists, and the Chinese in general, worship Confucius as the ideal man, the "Grand Perfection, Ultimate Sage," rather than as a ruler of any Heaven, such as Lao Chün or the Buddha. The last of the great Confucianists, K'ang Yu-wei (1858-1927), believing that Western powers became strong because they had organized religions, made repeated attempts to establish Confucianism as a formal and official cult. But he met with no success.

On the surface, it would seem that Confucianists have not been interested in religion. It is true that they have remained aloof from superstitions and idol worship, leaving these to ignorant people. It is also true that they have not shown any high degree of piety. Nevertheless, the worship of Heaven and ancestors has been so strongly promoted by Confucianists that it has been considered characteristically Confucian. Although Confucianists vary a great deal in their philosophy of human nature, their general conclusion is that human nature is good. To them this good nature comes from Heaven, whose outstanding quality is *jên* or love, as evidenced by the unceasing production of things. The Confucianists not only believe in Destiny, but believe to such extent as to be fatalistic.

By virtue of this attitude towards Heaven, ancestors, human nature, the universe, and Destiny, Confucianism, while not a religion in the strict sense, is religious. This religious character is not found in any fanaticism, external observance, formal organization, or irrational beliefs. It is found in the whole Confucian philosophy of life. See cosmogonies; death and burial practices; Japanese Religions; Temples, Far Eastern.

Fung Yu-lan, *A History of Chinese Philosophy*, Pt. I, tr. by D. Bodde (1937); Lin Yutang, tr. *The Wisdom of Confucius* (1938); H. A. Giles, *Confucianism and Its Rivals* (1915); J. P. Bruce, *Chu Hsi and His Masters* (1923); F. G. Henke, tr. *The Philosophy of Wang Yang-ming* (1916).

fang shih: (Chin.) "Man with formulae," or priests and magicians who flourished in the Ch'in and Han dynasties (249 B.C.-220 A.D.) and who offered divination, magic, herbs, charms, alchemy, breath technique, and other crafts (*fang shu*) and superstitions in terms of Yin Yang and Taoist philosophies as means to immortality, inward power, restored youth, and superhuman ability.

fêng shui: (Chin. wind & water) This was originally a system of geomancy to determine the position and direction of graves, based on the belief that through the control of wind and water, the vital force (*ch'i*) of the deceased would not be dissipated by them. The system, which involves the doctrines of yin yang* and the Five Elements (see wu hsing), has been generally applied to determine the location of all types of buildings.

fu lu shou: (Chin.) These are the "Three Plenties" of 1) blessing or happiness, 2) official emolument and the honor it brings, and 3) longevity. They are also called the Three Stars, as each of them is believed to be dependent on a star-god. They are represented by either the three Chinese characters, or by the bat (*fu*) symbolizing happiness, the deer (*lu*) symbolizing honor, and the peach symbolizing longevity, or by a smiling figure with or without children around him, representing happiness, an official representing honor, and an old man representing long life. These representations are used as charms, as objects of worship, or simply as felicitation.

fung shui: (Chin.) See fêng shui.

hsien: (Chin. immortal) The belief in immortals was very strong in the Ch'in and Han periods (249 B.C.-220 A.D.) and was later strengthened by Taoism. The *Yün-chi Ch'i-ch'ien* of Taoism enumerates nine classes of immortals. Of the many immortals who inhabit the Realm of Great Purity (see San-ch'ing) and who move in this world in various forms to promote good and suppress evil, the *pa hsien*, or the eight immortals, are the most famous. They are Li T'ieh-kuai who is always depicted as a beggar with his crutch and gourd full of magic medicine, Chung-li Ch'üan who has a bearded face and carries a fan or a peach, Lan Ts'ai-ho who is represented as a young man or young woman carrying a basket of fruit or playing a flute, Chang Kuo (Lao) who is depicted as riding on a white mule or carrying a phoenix feather or a peach of immortality or a bamboo tube, Ho Hsien-ku who is a beautiful maiden holding a magical lotus-blossom or playing a musical instrument, Lü Tung-pin who carries a magic sword or a fly-whisk, Han Hsiang Tsŭ with a basket of peaches or holding a bouquet of flowers, and Ts'ao Kuo-chiu carrying a pair of castanets.

The grouping of immortals in sets of a certain number was not common until the first century A.D., after the introduction of Buddhism*. The term "pa hsien" was first mentioned in the *Li Hui Lun* by Mou Young of the first century A.D. Later works referred to groups of other numbers; of these the groups of eight and nine were the most popular. After the T'ang dynasty (618-907 A.D.), however, the group of eight became the most favored one, for reasons as yet unknown. By the end of the Sung dynasty (960-1279), the "eight immortals" had already appeared on the Chinese stage. To this day, the "eight immortals," either singly or in groups have been popular subjects of representation in art, on the stage, and in a thousand other ways.

Though the number eight became established, the members of the "eight immortals" changed from time to time. The earliest set known to us was the "Eight Lords of Prince Liu An," who, according to the general belief of the Six Dynasties (222-589 A.D.), were old men who visited the Taoistically inclined Prince, regained their youth and became immortals. The present group cannot be much earlier than the Yüan dynasty (1280-1368), since no mention of them can be found in literature earlier than this period. From the thirteenth century on, however, this group came to be accepted. Were they copied from the "Eight Lords of Prince Liu An"? Were they parallels of the "Eight Officials" of the Wu-t'ai Mountain of the Chin dynasty (265-290 A.D.) as some historians maintained? Or were they the legendary version of the "Eight Lords" of scholarship of the Sung dynasty (960-1279), as suggested by Chu Hsi? Writing in the sixteenth century, an outstanding authority on the "eight immortals," Wang Shih-chêng, confessed that it was impossible to know the origin of the present group.

The existing group is evidently the survival of the fittest. The general opinion is that the Chinese are satisfied with them because they represent all kinds of people—old, young, male, female, civil, military, rich, poor, afflicted, cultured, historical persons and fictitious figures, and people of early, middle, and later historical periods. It may, however, have been due to the fact that they offered the greatest variety of individuality, and individuality was highly important in literature, art, and drama in which they were often depicted. It may also have been due to the growth of landscape painting in the tenth century which suspended for several hundred years the tradition of Buddhist and Taoist figure painting and discouraged new grouping of immortals for art, thus allowing the present group to set a strong hold in the thirteenth century. It may even have been due to the Taoist universal imitation of Buddhism, resulting in a set group of Taoist immortals to parallel or to compete with set groups of Buddhist arhats. By the fourteenth century, the artistic and religious significance of the "eight immortals" was overshadowed by the utilitarian, for in the art and drama of this period, they were usually associated with birthday felicitations. This is the reason why today they are symbolic of happiness in general and of longevity in particular.

Hsüan-wu: (Chin. dark & strong) Name of the Taoist Dipper god, also called Hsüan-t'ien Shang-ti (the Lord on High in the Dark Heaven) and T'ai I (the Great Unit). It is often symbolized by the tortoise and the snake, by virtue of their position in the north which is dark, and their strength. A shrine for this deity is usually found in the back of a Chinese village. As the Lord on High in the Dark Heaven, the deity enjoyed immense popularity during the Han dynasty (206 B.C.-220 A.D.) and is today equally prominent as Wên-ch'ang*.

Huang Lao: The religious movement flourishing from the first century B.C. to the fourth century A.D. under the names of Huang-ti, or the mythological Yellow Emperor (-2599? B.C.) and Lao Tzŭ (570 B.C. or the fourth century B.C.). It involved divination, alchemy, and the belief in immortals. It provided Taoism* with some of its basic features. Ethically, the Huang Lao movement emphasized simplicity, transcendental bliss, *wu wei** (non-artificiality), inner peace, and the nourishing of one's original nature.

hun: (Chin.) The active, positive, or heavenly (yang) part of the soul, as contrasted with the passive, negative, or earthly (yin) part of the soul called *p'o*. (See Yin yang). Hun is the soul of man's vital force (*ch'i*) which is expressed in man's intelligence and power of breathing, whereas *p'o* is the spirit of man's physical nature which is expressed in bodily movements. In heavenly spirits, *hun* predominates, whereas in earthly spirits, *p'o* predominates. When *hun* is separated from *p'o* in man or things, change ensues.

I Ching: (Chin. The Book of Changes) See Confucianism.

immortals, Taoist: See hsien.

Ko Hung: A Taoist philosopher. See Taoism.

Kuan Ti, Kuan Kung: (Chin.) Kuan Yü (d. 219 A.D.) was minister and sworn brother of Liu Pei, king of Shu, who fought desperately to restore the Han dynasty. Kuan Yü's absolute loyalty to Han and to his master and his unparallel righteousness and chivalry towards his opponents have been a great inspiration to the Chinese. He has been honored as Kuan Shêng Ti Chün, or the Sage, Lord, and Master Kuan. He is worshipped by all Chinese as the God of Loyalty and Righteousness (but not as God of War), and as the Military Sage, somewhat corresponding to the civil sage Confucius. Until 1912, he was object of state worship in the *wu miao* or Temple of Strength, which is limited to him and Yo Fei*, while the Temple of Culture or *wên miao* is limited to Confucius. Also called Kuan Kung, or Duke Kuan, Kuan Ti is the most popular masculine deity in China.

Kuei, Kwei: (Chin.) See Shên.

K'un: (Chin.) Earth, symbolized by ☷ in the Eight Trigrams (pa kua*); the trigram of the negative or female cosmic principle, yin, opposite of ch'ien.

Lao-tse: *Idem* Lao Tzŭ*.

Lao Tzŭ: Whether Lao Tzŭ was the founder of Taoism*; whether he was the same as Li Erh and Li An; whether he lived before or after Confucius; and whether the *Tao Tê Ching* (Eng. trans.: *The Canon of Reason and Virtue,* 1913, 1927, by P. Carus; *The Way and Its Power,* 1935, by A. Waley, etc.), contains his teachings are controversial matters. According to the *Shih Chi* (Historical Records), he was a native of Ch'u (in present Honan) and a custodian of documents whom Confucius* went to consult on rituals. Thus he might have been a priest-teacher who, by advocating the doctrine of "inaction," attempted to preserve the declining culture of his people, the suppressed people of Yin, while Confucius worked hard to promote the culture of the ruling people of Chou. Although many modern scholars accept the eighteenth century theory that Lao Tzŭ lived in the fourth century B.C., the matter cannot be considered settled.

As the ancient *fang shih** or priest-magicians movement became popular in the Ch'in and Han dynasties (249 B.C.-200 A.D.), Lao Tzŭ became a popular object of worship (see Huang Lao). When this movement was incorporated into Chang Ling's "Way of Five Bushels of Rice" in the first century A.D., Lao Tzŭ was considered the founder of the religion which assumed the name Taoism. Later Taoist tradition made him the historical member of the Taoist Triad (see San-ch'ing), under the name of Lao Chün, or Lord Lao. The Buddha was regarded as his incarnation. In 666 A.D., he was honored by Imperial order as the Most High Emperor of Mystic Origin (T'ai-shang Hsüan-yüan Huang-ti). Again in 1013, he was honored as the Most High Lord Lao (T'ai-shang Lao-chün). Today he is worshiped either as a member of the Triad or separately.

Lieh Tzŭ: See Taoism.

Mencius: See Confucianism.

Mohism: See Mo Tzŭ.

Mo Tzŭ: (Mo Ti, between 500 & 396 B.C.) Founder of Mohism and author of *Mo Tzŭ* (Eng. tr. by Y. P. Mei, *The Ethical and Political Works of Motse,* 1929), he advocated: 1) "benefit" (*li*), or the promotion of general welfare and removal of evil, through the increase of population and wealth, the elevation of conduct, the regulation of benevolence and righteousness towards this practical objective, the elimination of war, and the suppression of wasteful musical events and elaborate funerals; 2) "universal love" based on the will of Heaven; 3) "agreement with the superiors;" 4) a method of reasoning which involves a "foundation," a "survey," and "application;" and 5) the belief in Heaven and the spirits both as a religious sanction of governmental measures and as an effective way of promoting peace and welfare. Compared with Confucius and Lao Tzŭ** he was the strongest defender and promoter of the ancient faith. His followers, Mo Chê, or Neo-Mohists, probably developed into a religious order involving asceticism and a system of "elders."

pa kua: (Chin.) a) The Eight Trigrams or Elements (☰ Heaven, ☷ Earth, ☳ Thunder, ☶ Mountain, ☲ Fire, ☵ Water, ☱ Water in motion, ☴ Wind and Wood), by which all existence and transformations are explained, analyzed, and predicted. A *kua* is a combination of trigrams and represents a *hsiang*, a phenomenon, an image, or an idea. For example, the trigram of water over the trigram of fire means triumph, good fortune, etc. The system is used both in Chinese cosmology and system of change (*i*) as well as in divination. b) A figure consisting of the eight trigrams is used by the Chinese as charm, as object of worship, and as art mortif. See T'ai Chi.

Pao-p'o Tzŭ: *Idem* Ko Hung*.

San-ch'ing: (Chin. three purities) a) The Three Purities in Taoism, namely, Essence (*ching*), Vital Force (*ch'i*), and the Spirit (*shên*). b) The Three Pure Ones of Taoism. The first is Wu-hsing T'ien-chün or the Heavenly Honored

One Without Form, also called T'ien-pao Chün or the Lord of the Jewel of Heaven. He lives in the Realm of Jade Purity which is populated by holy men (*shêng jên*). The second is Wu-shih T'ien-chün or the Heavenly Honored One Without Origin, also called Ling-pao Chün or the Lord of the Jewel of Intelligence. He lives in the Realm of Superior Purity which is populated by pure men (*chên jên*). The third is Fan-hsing T'ien-chün or the Heavenly Honored One of Brahma Form, also called Shên-pao Chün or the Lord of the Jewel of Spirit. He lives in the Realm of Great Purity which is populated by immortals (hsien*).

This Taoist Triad is definitely a feeble imitation of the Buddhist *Trikāya* (see Buddhist Terminology). The first One is Yüan-shih T'ien-chün*; the second, Tao Chün or the Lord of Tao; and the third, the historical Lao Tzŭ, also called Lao Chün. Sometimes the Jade Emperor (see Yü-huang) is mentioned as the first member. However, neither the relationship between Yüan-shih T'ien-chün and Yü-huang nor the relationship between the first and second members of the Triad is clearly defined.

Shang-ti: (Chin. the Lord on High) a) Identical with Ti or the Lord. b) The Lord of Heaven (see T'ien). c) Title of the highest Taoist deity (see Yüan-shih T'ien-chün). d) Chinese name for the Christian God. e) "The Superior Lord," referring to sovereigns of antiquity. See Chinese religions.

Shê Chi: (Chin.) The Chinese Gods of the Ground and the Grain. In ancient times the emperor, the feudal lords, and the people all had their own Shê Chi, but it was the duty of the feudal lords to make offerings to Shê Chi as thanksgiving for the blessings of territory and food. Today Shê Chi is usually worshiped in an open altar beside a tree at the head of a village.

Shên: (Chin.) *Shên* and *kuei* are usually mentioned together. Etymologically *shên* consists of the radical *shih,* which means indication from above (sun, moon, and star), and the stem which gives it the pronunciation *shên,* and which means extension, that is, bringing about the myriad things. *Kuei,* on the other hand, means to return. The following are the common interpretations of *shên* and *kuei*: a) Shên, heavenly spirits; *kuei,* spirits of deceased human beings. (Ancient Chinese religion) b) "*Shên* is spiritual power which is unfathomable," or "what is unfathomable in the movement of yin and yang or passive and active universal principles." "*Shên* refers to the mystery of the myriad things," that is, "the unity of things." (*I Ching,* third century B.C.) c) *Kuei* and *shên* are respectively yin and yang*. "The concentration of the vital force (*ch'i*) of yang to produce things is an extension of *shên,* whereas the dissipation of the drifting *hun** and the diminishing *p'o* or positive and negative aspects of the soul, resulting in a change, is the *kuei* that is returning (to the elements). (Ancient & medieval Chinese philosophy & religion) d) "*Shên* to man is like water to ice." (Wang Ch'ung, 27-c. 100 A.D.) e) "*Kuei* and *shên* are the native and good ability of the two vital principles of yin and yang," in the sense that "coldness is an example of *kuei* while hotness is an example of *shên.*" "To come into being from non-being is the nature of *shên;* to change from being to non-being is the nature of *kuei.* (Chang Hêng-ch'ü, 1021-1077) f) "*Kuei* and *shên* are the traces of creation," or "the operation of the universe." (Ch'êng I-ch'üan, 1033-1107) g) "*Kuei* and *shên* are the increase and decrease of the two universal forces of yin and yang." "From the standpoint of the two forces or principles, then *shên* is the efficacy of yang and *kuei* is the efficacy of yin. From the standpoint of the one universal force (*ch'i*), then what has become and extended is *shên* and what has departed and returned (to its origin) is *kuei.*" "The vital force of Heaven is unceasingly producing things; that is *shên.* . . . The vital force of human beings returns to the elements (at death); that is *kuei.*" (Chu Hsi, 1130-1200).

The above interpretations are summed up by Chang Shih: "Generally speaking, what has become but is unfathomable is *shên,* and what has gone is *kuei.* Specifically, the vital force of Heaven, Earth, mountain, river, wind, snow, etc., is *shên,* whereas what is worshiped in an ancestral hall or temple is *kuei.* With reference to man and things, what has concentrated and come into being is *shên,* whereas what has dissipated and passed away is *kuei.* With reference to a person, the vital force of *hun* (the positive aspect of the soul) is *shên,* whereas the vital force of *p'o* (the negative aspect of the soul) is *kuei.*"

The word *shên* is also used in philosophy and religion to mean god-like power, spiritual power, creative power, mystery, a divine man, god-like man, holiness beyond our knowledge, vital force, the mind, energy; and in aesthetics, rhythmic vitality, expression, wonderful quality, style full of spirit or vivacity.

Shih Ching: (Chin. the Book of Poetry) See Confucianism.

Shu Ching: (Chin. the Book of History) See Confucianism.

shu shu: (Chin.) Divination and magic in ancient China, including astrology, almanacs, the art of coordinating human affairs by the active and passive principles of the universe (yin yang*) and the Five Elements (*wu hsing**), fortune telling by the use of the stalks of the divination plant and the tortoise shell, and miscellaneous methods such as dream interpretation, the regulation of forms and shapes of buildings, etc.

T'ai I: (Chin. the Great Unit) a) The Great Unit before Heaven and Earth, identical with T'ai Chi*). b) The Lord of Heaven. c) A star god in the East, a minister of the Lord of Heaven in charge of sixteen other star gods. d) The Great Unit, a Taoist deity variously identified with Hsüan-wu*, the highest of the heavenly spirits, the first of the nine constellations, etc. e) A branch of Taoism*, founded by Hsiao Pao-chên between 1138 and 1140 to promote the practice of charms and magic in an attempt to realize the Great Unit and the Three Origins (Heaven, Earth, and Man) of existence.

T'ai Chi (Chin.) a) The Great Ultimate or Terminus, which, in the beginning of time, "engenders the Two Primary Modes (*i*), which in turn engender the Four Secondary Modes or Forms (*hsiang*), which in their turn give rise to the Eight Elements (*pa kua**) and the Eight Elements determine all good and evil and the great complexity of life." (Ancient Chinese philosophy). b) The Great Ultimate which comes from, but is originally one with, the Non-Ultimate. Its movement and tranquillity engender the active principle, yang, and the passive principle, yin, respectively (the Two Primary Modes), the transformation and the union of which give rise to the Five Agents (*wu hsing*) of Water, Fire, Wood, Metal, and Earth, and thereby the determinate things. (Chou Lien-hsi, 1017-1073). c) The Great Ultimate which is One and unmoved, and which, when moved, becomes the Omnipotent Creative Principle (*shên**) which engenders Number, then Form, and finally corporeality. Being such, the Great Ultimate is identical with the Mind; it is identical with the Moral Law (*tao*). (Shao K'ang-chieh, 1011-1077). d) The Great Ultimate which is identical with the One (*I*), or the Grand Harmony (*T'ai Ho*). (Chang Hêng-ch'ü, 1020-1077). e) The Great Ultimate which is identical with the Reason (*li*) of the universe, of the two (yin yang*) vital forces (*ch'i*), and of the Five Elements (*wu hsing*). It is the Reason of ultimate goodness. "Collectively there is only one Great Ultimate, but there is a Great Ultimate in each thing." (Chu Hsi, 1130-1200).

Taoism: The term "Tao Chia" (the Taoist School) did not appear until the *Shih Chi* (Historical Records) of 97 B.C. But the movement which later assumed that name had been going on for centuries. Whether Lao Tzŭ* was the founder of the movement is disputed. At any rate, the School opposed nature to man, glorifying Tao or the Way, spontaneity (*tzŭ jan*), "inaction" (*wu wei*) in the sense of non-artificiality or following nature, simplicity, "emptiness," tranquillity and enlightenment. These were all dedicated to the search for "long life and lasting vision" (in the case of Lao Tzŭ), for "preserving life and keeping the essence of our being intact" (in the case of Yang Chu, c. 440-360 B.C.), and for "companionship with nature," "transcendental bliss," "peace of mind," naturalness "like a new born calf," "equality of things and opinions," and "spontaneous and unceasing transformation" (in the case of Chuang Tzŭ, between 399 & 295 B.C.). As the *Shih Chi* recorded it, the Taoist School "urged men to unity of spirit, teaching that all activities should be in harmony with the unseen (Tao), with abundant liberality towards all things in nature. As to method, they accepted the orderly sequence of nature from the Yin Yang* School, selected the good points of Confucianists and Mohists** and combined with these the important points of the Logicians and Legalists. In accordance with the changes of the seasons, they responded to the development of natural objects."

While this philosophy of life was developing, another movement was under way, namely, the search for immortality, inward power, and superhuman ability through divination and magic (see shu shu). This movement, in progress from time immemorial, was vigorously promoted by priest-magicians (*fang shih**). By the first century B.C., it had already become a concerted movement called Huang Lao*, or the Yellow Emperor and Lao Tzŭ, and enjoyed Imperial patronage as well as tremendous popular following.

As the *fang shih* movement grew in popularity, religious and political reformers competed to incorporate it into their own schemes. In this, Chang Ling* of the second century A.D., the historical founder of the Taoist religion, was most successful. He made use of Lao Tzŭ not only because the Huang Lao cult was powerful, but also because Lao Tzŭ's *Tao Tê Ching* (see Lao Tzŭ) contained enough vague phrases such as "the Spirit of the Valley," "the divine man," "the mysterious female," the harmonious "infant," the "One," "long life," etc., which could be so interpreted as to give his movement a mysterious and magic character. His movement, styled the Way (Tao) of Five Bushels of Rice, grew in strength. He became the Heavenly Teacher with headquarters in the Dragon and Tiger Mountain in Kiangsi. His direct descendants continued to spread the religion and held the hereditary title of the Heavenly Teacher (the Pope of Taoism) until 1927 when the Chinese Government abolished the papacy.

In the third century A.D., a Taoist philosopher, Wei Po-yang, carried the Taoist religion to new heights. In his *Ts'an T'ung Ch'i* (inter-penetration unified and harmonized), he attempted to combine the Taoist philosophy and that of the *fang shih* with those of the *I Ching* (*The Book of Changes*) and the Yin Yang School*, and to unify and harmonize them. The ultimate goal of the book was to prolong life through the practice of alchemy whereby, it was believed, the yin and yang or negative and positive cosmic forces could be harmonized and the vital force (*ch'i*) of the universe could be concentrated on the individual's body. The book became the basis of the *Lung Hu Ching* (the Dragon and Tiger Classic) of unknown date, *Huang T'ing Ching* (the Yellow or Internal and Realm or External Classic) of the late third century A.D., and the *Yin Fu Ching* (the Secret Accord Classic) by Li Ch'üan of the eighth century, all of which have become Bibles of Taoism. The latter Classic, often attributed to the legendary Yellow Emperor, teaches the way to attain unity and immortality for the individual and wealth and power for the state.

Soon after Wei Po-yang, another Taoist philosopher arose, namely, Ko Hung (c. 268-c. 334), also called Pao-p'o Tzŭ, or the "philosopher who embraces Simplicity." His book *Pao-p'o Tzŭ* is a mixture of Taoist philosophy and Confucian ethics. Its emphasis on alchemy, especially internal alchemy (*Nei tan*), raised the practice of breath control, thought control, taking medicine, eating charms, etc., to a position of prominence in the Taoist religion.

These two philosophers provided Taoism with a firm theoretical ground and an elaborate system of practice. The time was ripe for a finishing touch of the cult. This was accomplished in the fifth century by K'ou Ch'ien-chih (414 A.D.). He regulated the ceremonies and codes of the cult, fixed the names of its deities, and formulated its theology. Through his influence Taoism was made the state religion in 440 A.D. while Buddhism was persecuted.

State patronage of Taoism was repeated in 574 and 891. Imperial favor reached its height during the T'ang dynasty. Because both the founder of the dynasty and Lao Tzŭ were of the same surname Li, Lao Tzŭ was honored by Imperial order as T'ai-shang Hsüan-yüan Huang-ti (the Most High Emperor of Mystic Origin) in 666, ranking above Confucius and the Buddha. Princes and dukes and those below them were required to study the *Tao Tê Ching*, and Taoist temples were ordered established throughout the empire. In 742, Lao Tzŭ's four great pupils were conferred posthumous titles by Imperial order. Chuang Tzŭ (between 399 & 295 B.C.) was honored as the Pure Man of Mount Nanhua (Nanhua Chên Jên) and his book (*Chuang Tzŭ*, Eng. tr. by H. A. Giles, 2nd ed. 1926, & Fung Yulan, 1931) was canonized as the *Pure Classic of Nanhua* (*Nanhua Chên Ching*). Lieh Tzŭ, contemporary of Chuang Tzŭ, and the book *Lieh Tzŭ* of third century A. D. (Eng. tr. by L. Giles, *Taoist Teachings from the Book of Lieh Tzŭ*, 1912) were honored as the Pure Man and Pure Classic of Simplicity and Emptiness, (Ch'ung Hsü). Wên Tzŭ (fifth century B.C.?) and the book *Wên Tzŭ* attributed to him were honored as the Pure Man and Pure Classic of Penetration of Mystery (T'ung Hsüan). Kêng-sang Tzŭ, contemporary of Chuang Tzŭ, and the book bearing his name were honored as the Pure Man and Pure Classic of the Spirit of the Grotto (Tung Ling). In the following dynasties, however, although Taoism always enjoyed Imperial respect, it never again existed as a state cult, but as a religion of the mass, especially the illiterate and the superstitious.

As a religion of the mass, Taoism, also called Hsüan Chiao, or Religion of Mystery, is distinguished by several prominent features:

1) First of all, it has one of the most thickly populated pantheons in the world. Aside from creating many deities of its own, such as the Jade Emperor (see Yü-huang), the Three Pure Ones (see San-ch'ing), the Three Rulers (San-kuan), the Dipper God (see Hsüan-wu), the Great Unit (see T'ai I), the Liu-chia, the Liu-ting, God of Literature (see Wên-ch'ang), Progenitor Lü (Lü Tsu), the many immortals, the 28 stars, etc., it has adopted most of the traditional deities and even some Buddhist gods, especially Kwan-yin. Traditional deities like the City God (Ch'êng-huang), the God of Land *Hou-t'u*), Kuan Ti*, the Gods of Wealth, Medicine, Kitchen, Doors, etc., became so prominent in Taoism as to appear almost exclusively Taoist. It has a god for almost everything, including the whole and parts of the body. It worships the spirits of animate and inanimate objects as well as ancestors and famous historical persons. It worships a great number of stars. To these it has added ten great "Heavenly Grottoes," 36 subsidiary "Heavenly Grottoes," and 72 "Blessed Places" where Taoist True Men and immortals rule and await people to seek the Way (Tao). Imitating the Buddhists, the Taoists have their own 33 heavens which they have increased to 81.

2) The objective of Taoist worship is twofold, to seek blessings and long life. To this end, Taoism has developed the most elaborate system of alchemy (see wai tan) (nei tan) in the world. Many Taoists take alchemy more seriously than anything else. By means of alchemy, they hope to realize the Three Original Principles of Taoism, namely, Essence, Vital Force, and Spirit (San Yüan).

3) Taoism is a rich reservoir of superstitions. It has capitalized the traditional *fêng shui** and the Buddhist patterned heavens and hells. In addition, it has incorporated and elaborated divination, *na chia*, fortune telling, witchcraft, astrology, communication with the dead, and many others.

4) In organization and literature, the Taoist religion is a wholesale imitation of Buddhism. Its system of clergy is similar to that of the Buddhists in election, classification, ordination, and transmission. The priests, called *Tao shih*, are of two types. There are the "home *Tao shihs*" who stay with their family, either wearing the Taoist robe or not, and there are the regular *Tao shihs* who renounce their homes, adopt vegetarianism, and live in monasteries. Both are required to fast on occasions, to recite the holy writings, and to perform in ceremonies. They differ from Buddhist monks in retaining their lay surnames and keeping their hair. Today there are far fewer *Tao shihs* than Buddhist monks, and there are no Taoist nuns. Taoist temples, called *kuan* (literally *see*, that is, to see deities and immortals), and *kung* or palaces as the large ones are called, are also modeled after Buddhist temples. Equally Buddhistic are Taoist ceremonies and music. The Taoist Canon, too, is also an imitation of the Buddhist *Tripiṭaka*. However, the Taoist Canon (*Tao Tsang**) is more eclectic in that it contains Confucian and other non-Taoist works.

5) Although Taoism concerns itself a great deal with spirits and immortals of the other world, it is its ethical teaching that has kept it alive. To most followers, the religion is essentially a sanction of ethics. In addition to the Five Precepts (not to kill, not to drink alcohol,

not to lie, not to steal, and not to commit adultery) borrowed from Buddhism, Taoism advocates the Ten Virtues, namely, filial piety, loyalty to the emperor and teacher, kindness towards all creatures, patience, remonstration of evil deeds, self-sacrifice to help the poor, setting living creatures free and planting trees, digging wells and building roads, teaching the unenlightened and promoting welfare, and studying the holy writings and offering to the gods. These and other precepts, together with a well worked out merit system, present a moral code that contains the best elements of Confucianism and Buddhism as well as Taoism. The two most popular Taoist books, the *T'ai-shang Kan-ying P'ien* by Li Ch'ang-ling, d. 1008 (Eng. tr. by D. T. Suzuki & Paul Carus, *Treatise by the Exalted One on Response and Retribution*, 1906) and the *Yin-chih Wên* (Eng. tr. by Suzuki & Carus, *The Tract of the Quiet Way*, 1906) by an unknown author and attributed to the deity Wên-ch'ang*, both teach the Confucian virtues of filial piety, loyalty, benevolence, and righteousness, the Buddhist doctrines of *karma* and transmigration, and the Taoist ethics of patience, simplicity, contentment, and harmony. These two books, with retribution as their keynote, have been most influential among the lower strata of Chinese society.

6) Taoism has been thickly mixed with eclectic sects and secret societies (see Chinese religions). However, it has traditional sects of its own. The division into sects took place in the Sung dynasty (960-1279). In the Yüan period (1280-1368), there were four sects, the Chên Ta Tao Chiao, the T'ai I Chiao, the Cheng I Chiao, and the Ch'üan Chên Chiao. At present only the latter two are existent. The Chêng I Chiao, or the True Unity Sect, is the southern school prevalent south of the Yangtze River. It is traced to Chang Ling and is, therefore, orthodox, but it was actually founded by Liu Hai-ch'an of the tenth century. It emphasizes man's nature, that is, man's spirit or true self, and relies on charms and magic formulae to preserve man's original nature. As such it is the "self-power" sect of Taoism (see Pure Land School). It is idealistic and informal. Its followers are all "home *Tao shihs*." On the other hand, the Ch'üan Chên Chiao, or the Preserve-Purity Sect, is the northern school with Peiping as its center. It is traced to Lü Tungpin (Lü Tsu) but was actually founded by Wangchê of the tenth century. It emphasizes man's life, that is, man's vital force (*ch'i*), and depends on medicine and diet to prolong life. As such it is the "other-power" sect of Taoism. It is materialistic and formal. Its followers are regular *Tao shihs*. See sacred literatures; Temples, Far Eastern. See Bibliography at the end of article "Chinese religions."

Tao Tsang: (Chin. the Taoist Canon) The origin of the Taoist Canon, which was certainly an imitation of the Buddhist *Tripitaka* (see Canon, Buddhist Terminology), is unknown. According to the *Yün-chi Ch'i-ch'ien*, it had increased from 3,744 parts (*chuan*) in the eighth century to 4,565 parts in the 1019 collection. Many of these volumes were lost after the destruction in 1281. The existing edition was made in 1446 and supplemented in 1607. It contains 5,200 parts, including a number of non-Taoist works. This edition was reproduced in 1120 volumes by the Commercial Press in 1925.

Ti: (Chin.) a) The Supreme Lord (see T'ien) b) The world-honored deities (such as those of the four directions and the Five Elements). c) Mythological sovereigns whose virtues approximate those of Heaven and Earth.

T'ien: (Chin. heaven) a) Physical heaven. b) The Supreme Lord who is purposive and personal, identical with Ti (Lord), Shang-ti*, Huang-t'ien (Almighty Heaven), and Huang-t'ien Shang-ti. (Ancient Chinese philosophy and religion, especially Confucius and Mo Tzŭ**. After Confucius, T'ien and Ti* were distinguished, the former referring to the Lord in the sense of omnipresence and all-inclusiveness and the latter referring to the Lord as the directing and governing power. c) The course and operation of Destiny beyond human control. d) The creative process, which involves yin and yang*, or the negative and positive universal principles. (*I Ching*, third century B.C., and Neo-Confucianism**. e) The principle of excellence or perfection. f) Nature. "Heaven follows the standard of Tao; Tao follows the standard of Nature." (Lao Tzŭ*) "Heaven and Earth follow the course of constancy," to be contrasted with man. (Chuang Tzŭ, between 399 & 295 B.C.) "The course of Heaven is constant." (Hsün Tzŭ, c. 335-286 B.C.) "From the Great Vacuity we have the name Heaven." "The concentration and the dissipation of the vital force of Heaven and Earth are many and various, but its principle or Reason is never wrong." "Heaven is that according to which the Great Ultimate (see T'ai Chi) and the Two Primary Modes (yin & yang) attain their nature and unity." (Chang Hêng-ch'ü, 1021-1077) "There is no Heaven outside of Nature." "Heaven and Earth are merely the greatest of existence; since they exist, they have a limit." "Heaven involves yin and yang." (Shao K'ang-chich, 1011-1077) "Heaven and Earth are merely products of the vital force (*ch'i*) of yin and yang." "Heaven is nothing but the vital force," that is, "the pure aspect of the material principle." (Chu Hsi, 1130-1200) g) Reason (*li*). "Heaven is the universal Reason." (Ch'êng I-ch'üan, 1033-1107, & Ch'êng Ming-tao, 1032-1086) "Heaven and Earth unconsciously produce and transform things." (Ch'êng I-ch'üan) "Heaven and Earth are what is metaphysical." "As there is Reason, there are Heaven and Earth." (Chu Hsi) To Chu Hsi, as to most Neo-Confucianists, Heaven is moral, for "*Jên* or love is the character of Heaven," because "Heaven is constantly producing things." h) Heaven as against hell. Orthodox Chinese religion has none, Buddhism has 33, and Taoism 33 and even 81 such heavens.

wai tan: (Chin.) External alchemy, as a means of nourishing life, attaining Tao, and immortality. It includes transmutation of mercury into gold (also called *chin tan*), medicine, charms, magic, attempts at disappearance and change of bodily form. Both internal alchemy (*nei tan*) and external alchemy have been practiced in Taoism*.

Wang Yang-ming: See Confucianism.

Wên-ch'ang: (Chin. literary glory) a) A star worshiped from ancient times. b) The Taoist God of Literature. He was originally a historical person by the name of Chang Ya-tzŭ whose heroism and death in fighting for the Chin dynasty (265-420 A.D.) inspired people to erect temples and worship him. In 1314 he was conferred the title Tzŭ-t'ung Ti-chün, meaning the Lord Master of his native district Tzŭ T'ung. As Taoists believed that he assisted the Lord of Heaven in administering affairs of literature and officialdom, they regarded him as the God of Literature and Arts and worshiped him in schools until recently. He is often erroneously confused with the Wênchang star. K'uei-hsing is the associate god of literature.

wu hsing: (Chin.) a) The Five Agents, Elements, or Powers of Water, Fire, Wood, Metal and Earth, the interaction of which gives rise to the multiplicity of things, and which have their correspondence in the five senses, tastes, colors, tones, the five virtues, the five atmospheric conditions, the five ancient emperors, etc. Also called *wu tê*. (The Yin Yang School in the third & fourth centuries B.C. & the Han dynasty, especially Pan Ku, 32-92 A.D., & Tung Chung-shu, 177-104 B.C.). b) The Five Agents which are the five vital forces (*ch'i*), engendered by the transformation of yang, the active cosmic principle, and its union with yin, the passive cosmic principle, each with its specific nature. When the being of the Great Ultimate (*T'ai Chi*) and the essence of yin and yang* come into mysterious union, determinate being ensues, with the heavenly principle, yang, constituting the male element and the earthly principle, yin, constituting the female element, giving rise to the myriad things. (Chou Lien-hsi, 1017-1072). c) In the Taoist religion, especially in its geomancy, the Five Elements are the agents of the spirits.

wu wei: (Chin.) Literally "not to make" and also "not to act," the term fundamentally means non-artificiality, non-assertion, following nature, and secondarily means inaction, inactivity and passivity. According to Taoism*, artificiality must not replace spontaneity, and the state of nature must not be interfered with by human efforts or superficial morality and wisdom. "Tao undertakes no activity," or "Tao acts without assertion," and "yet there is nothing left undone," said Lao Tzŭ*.

Yi Ching: (Chin. the Book of Changes) See Confucianism.

Yin yang: (Chin.) a) Passive and active principles, respectively, of the universe, or the female, negative force and the male, positive force, always contrasting but complementary. Yang and yin are expressed in heaven and earth, man and woman, father and son, shine and rain, hardness and softness, good and evil, white and black, upper and lower, great and small, odd number and even number, joy and sorrow, reward and punishment, agreement and opposition, life and death, advance and retreat, love and hate, and all conceivable objects, qualities, situations, and relationships. b) The Two Modes (*i*—— and—— in trigram, or *kua*, symbols) of the Great Ultimate (T'ai Chi*), from the interplay of which all things are engendered. c) A system constituted by the Five Agents or Elements (wu hsing*), of Water, Fire, Wood, Metal, and Earth, which in turn constitute the Great Ultimate. (Chou Lien-hsi, 1017-1073). d) The two forces of *ch'i*, or the vital force which is the material principle of the universe. (Neo-Confucianism) e) Name of a school (400-200 B.C.) headed by Tsou Yen, which advocated that all events are manifestations of the passive or female force and the active or male force of the universe, and which was closely associated with popular geomancy, astrology, etc. See cosmogonies.

Yo Fei: (Chin.) Embodiment of patriotism and loyalty, Yo Fei (1103-1141) is worshiped by the Chinese as a military sage, sharing the honor of state worship in the Temple of Strength (*wu miao*) with Kuan Ti*. As a general of the Sung dynasty, he devoted himself to the suppression of insurrections and resistance against Tartar invasion. He would have saved the empire if the prime minister Ch'in Kuei had not surrendered to the Tartars and taken Yo Fei's life by treachery. On his back were found written the words "Loyalty to do utmost." Today outside Yo Fei temples is often found a kneeling image of Ch'in Kuei as a monument of shame.

Yü-huang: (Chin.) The Jade Emperor or Pearly Emperor of Taoism. First mentioned by Han Yü (768-824), the deity, symbolic of "jade" or Absolute Purity, was probably a creation of the Southern and Northern Dynasties (420-589) when the name Yüan-shih T'ien chün* appeared. They have been identified by some people. However, their relationship is not at all clear. As a result of the efforts of Emperor Chên-tsung (998-1022), Yü-huang emerged as the leading god in the Taoist Pantheon. Popular legends trace him to various historical persons. At any rate, he corresponds to, but is more humanized than, the traditional and Confucian Shang-ti* and the Buddhist Amita*.

Yüan-shih T'ien-chün: (Chin. the Heavenly Honored One of Origin and Beginning) The highest deity of Taoism*. Also called Yüan-shih T'ien-wang (the Heavenly King of Origin and Beginning), he is the first member of the Taoist Triad (see San-ch'ing). According to Taoism, he was the essence of existence, the operation of the Force of the One Origin, existing before Heaven and Earth became cosmos and yin and yang* (negative and positive universal principles) became a system. Later, when Heaven and Earth were formed, the Ta-yüan Yü-nu (the Jade Lady of Great Origin) came into existence. By uniting with her, the Heavenly Honored One gave rise, in successive order, to the Emperor of Heaven, the Emperor of Earth, and the Emperor of Man. From these came the ancestors of the Chinese. In Taoist temples, sometimes the Yüan-shih T'ien-chün and sometimes Yü-huang* is worshiped as the highest deity. Some people regard them as identical. However, their relationship is not at all clear.

See Buddhist Terminology. W.T.C.

chivalry: (Fr., *chevalerie,* horsemanship, knighthood) The aggregate of all which guided the Medieval gentleman's conduct both in peace and war. Historically chivalry may be traced to the general conditions existing after the death of Charlemagne. When a military aristocracy took over the task of saving the Christian West from utter ruin, it was necessary for the Church to moderate the actions of the soldier-knights. The Church taught ideals of conduct which gave to medieval manhood its reputation for valor and honor, and especially its reverence for women. Later when knighthood withdrew from the influence of the Church, chivalry degenerated into gallantry. See crusades. J.B.C.

choir: (Lat., *chorus*) 1) The body of trained singers who render the liturgical choral music of the Eucharist or the Divine Office**. 2) That part of the church building, generally west of the high altar, where the singers have their stalls. See chancel. P.V.N.

chorale: A hymn-tune the style of which was introduced by the Lutheran reformers. The text was always in German rather than in Latin; the whole congregation sang. The tunes were selected from the best of the Gregorian* tunes, from secular tunes, or from the original works of Lutheran composers, notably Johann Walther. The original purpose was to give the congregation a greater share in the service than had been the Roman Catholic tradition. The tunes were very metrical, much more harmonic than contemporary compositions, yet more contrapuntal than modern hymns. The chief melody was long kept in the tenor part. The chorale has been used as a basis for later works by such outstanding composers as Bach, who made many organ settings called chorale-preludes, and Felix Mendelssohn, who used familiar chorales in his organ sonatas, cantatas*, and oratorios*. Modern organ compositions employing chorales or hymn-tunes form a valuable part of organ literature which is most suitable to use in the Protestant church services.

W. Douglas, *Church Music in History and Practice* (1937); J. Julian, *Dictionary of Hymnology* (1915). E.H.B.

chrism: (Gr. *chrisma,* anointing*) An oil*, compounded of olive oil and balsam, blest by the bishop and used in certain ceremonies, such as baptism and confirmation. L.R.W.

chrismon: A monogram made up of the first two Greek letters in CHRISTOS, "Christ." Also called "Chi Rho," the names of these letters. B.S.E.

Christ: See Jesus Christ.

Christ, the living: Christ now living and working in the world is not Jesus, and not even Jesus Christ* when Christ is a title applied to Jesus solely in his bodily existence. Neither is the living Christ merely the influence of Jesus' life on subsequent generations, nor the ideals that men have followed in the name of Jesus Christ. Rather the living Christ is a reality which works in the world today, having come into history after the crucifixion. This reality was brought into the world by the Cross and its effective context. The effective context of the Cross was the heritage of the Hebrew prophets, plus other historical and psychological conditions prevailing at the time of the crucifixion, plus the life and teachings of Jesus which preceded the Cross and made it significant, plus the disciples whose lives were deeply shaped by all this. From the Cross in this context comes forth the living Christ that works continuously in the world unto this day, through whom sin is forgiven, who is the mediator and means of grace and the savior of the world.

The grace of God through the living Christ stands in contrast to the work of God under the law. The law is any established order with its regulations and ideals, its sentiments and habits. When God's creativity works under the law it makes us appreciatively aware of one another's interests in so far as we learn to love and cherish the goods and obey the standards of the accepted way of life. However, when we live under the sovereignty of the law God's creativity cannot make us actively and appreciatively aware of the interests of people who live by different standards from our own. These others may belong to some different race, class or culture, or they may be persons so unique in individuality or in depth that our standards cannot reach them. So, when we live under the sovereignty of the law, a barrier intervenes between us and all "outsiders."

The Cross, in the context which we have noted, shattered the sovereignty of the law. Jesus cried at last, My God, My God, why hast thou forsaken me. It became manifest to him in the last expiring agonies of the Cross that God would not intervene and save the world by way of the Jews. To the disciples also it became apparent that the hope and promise of the law were not to be fulfilled by way of a Messiah who would rule the world under the law of Israel.

This realization did not come to the disciples full-bodied and suddenly. It grew upon them after the crucifixion. Furthermore, it did not grow upon them primarily as theory or idea. It grew upon them as a way of living. They found themselves living with more freedom and fullness of growing community with many sorts of people and with many unique personalities which the standards of the law would not have permitted when it was sovereign over their lives. They found themselves living in his way first of all because of what they had gotten from Jesus during his life, and, secondly, because the Cross had shattered the hope which made the law supreme. This hope continued with them for a time as a theory and an idea, but its power to shape and control their living became less and less. That fulness and freedom of the creativity of God that Jesus had initiated among them could not be bound by the law although it was so bound during the life of Jesus. It could not be bound by their own ideas and hopes and fears. It could not even be bound by the purposes and aspirations of Jesus himself. The creativity of God working through Christ crucified broke the confines of the law by way of the Cross and released the grace of God to work beyond the law. This released and magnified power of the creativity of God in history, community and personality is the living Christ.

The living Christ can work in the world in this manner only through those who accept his sovereignty over their lives beyond the sovereignty of the law. The law, meaning some accepted order of life, must always stand. But in Christ it is servant, not master. When the living Christ rules our lives, the standards which we obey and the goods which we seek and cherish are held subject to the unbounded creativity of God. This unbounded creativity broke free of the law by way of the Cross. It lives among us through those who accept the sovereignty of Christ over their lives. The living Christ is this sovereignty of unbounded creativity whereby community may deepen and widen without limit.

This creativity beyond the law is the grace of God through Christ whereby our sins are forgiven. To sin is to have any interest which makes us resistant to the creativity of God, which means resistant to any extension of our appreciative awareness of the interests of others. We are never free of sin, but when our ultimate commitment is to the creativity of God beyond the law, then the set of standards by which we live cannot longer estrange us incurably from others who live by different standards. We are always estranged but in Christ the fear, hate, suspicion, prejudice, indifference which we feel toward people with standards opposed to ours can be overcome by the work of God. When the law is supreme, God cannot overcome this estrangement, because our devotion to the law intervenes. This is corrected when the creativity of God in Christ is the ultimate source of control.

Sin continues even when we give ourselves to Christ, but when the living Christ controls us our sin in the form of pride, hate, fate, prejudice, indifference to others is forgiven in the sense that it no longer blocks the work of God in our lives. It is no longer deadly. The death involved in unforgiven sin is any final limit put upon the work of God in our lives. Forgiveness of sin is removal of any such finality and this is accomplished by the living Christ.

The living Christ in the world today carrying the grace of God beyond the law is that creativity whereby we may become appreciatively aware of one another's interests, no matter how unique the individual personality may be, nor how diverse the race and culture of the people with whom we deal, nor how otherwise inadequate our standards may be to compass the diversity of interests which we encounter. Our standards make us sinners, not because standards necessarily are evil, but because we follow them in such a way as to put limits upon that creativity of God which works to make us vitally participant in one another's interests. The living Christ is the creativity of God released into history under such conditions that the grace of God can overcome these limits when we accept Christ as sovereign over the law. H.N.W.

Christ myth: A theory popular in Germany from about 1910. It represents Jesus as either an astral deity who has come to earth, suffered, died, and risen again, or as the projection of the repressed social, economic and political aspirations of the lower classes in the Roman Empire.

See S. J. Case, *The Historicity of Jesus* (1912); F. C. Conybeare, *The Historical Christ* (1914); M. Goguel, *Jesus the Nazarene—Myth or History?* (1926). F.C.G.

Christ's Sanctified Holy Church Colored: A Negro holiness (second blessing) sect organized in 1904 at West Lake, La. There are 31 churches (16 in Louisiana and 9 in Texas) and 665 members. See pentecostal sects. E.T.C.

Christadelphians (Brothers of Christ): A religious sect founded by John Thomas (1805-1871), an English physician who settled in Brooklyn, N. Y., in 1832. He first joined the Disciples of Christ, but repudiating that faith because of its stand on baptism and its type of organization, he founded his own church in 1848.

This group, premillenial in belief, called for a restoration of primitive Christianity, and held that the Holy Spirit was not a person, but an outreaching of God's power in man. It looked toward a world-wide theocracy centering at Jerusalem. Last published statistics give the group 134 societies and 3,352 members in 24 states; the church has no ministers. A periodical, the *Christadelphian Advocate*, is published.

R. Roberts, *Dr. Thomas, his Life and Work* (London, 1884); F. J. Powicke, art. Hasting's *Encyclopedia of Rel. & Eth.; The Christadelphian Advocate* (Des Moines, Iowa). M.G.R.—W.W.S.

christening: (Anglo-Saxon fr. Gr.) The act of receiving into the church of Christ by baptism*; making a Christian; baptizing. Or, in churches where baptism is at the time of conversion, a service of dedication of infants. T.J.B.

Christian art: See art, ecclesiastical, Christian.

Christian Biography, Lectureship in: Established in 1928 by Dr. and Mrs. E. S. Tipple at Drew Theological Seminary, Madison, New Jersey. The capital sum is $25,000. The purpose of the lectureship is to provide an annual series of lectures on the life and thought of Christian leaders. The following have served on this lectureship: F. L. Wiseman; W. W. Sweet; Bishop H. Welch; E. H. Griggs; D. Malone; Bishop F. J. McConnell.

(Data furnished by the Office of the President of the University.) V.F.

Christian Brothers: The name by which the Brothers of Christian Schools are commonly known. This order, founded by St. John Baptist de La Salle* in 1684, arose as a congregation of laymen bound by the three simple vows, and dedicated to the education of the poor. Its training college for teachers at Rheims (1685) was the first such institute for primary teachers. It is found in many dioceses of the United States. The Irish Christian Brothers is a separate but similar institute founded in Dublin by Edward Ignatius Rice in 1802. This latter order also has schools in the United States. T.T.M.

Christian Church: As the name of a denomination, designates the union of three groups which repudiated sectarian names: a movement led by James O'Kelley, Methodist, in North Carolina, 1794; one by Abner Jones and Elias Smith, Baptists, in New England, 1801; one by Barton W. Stone and others, Presbyterians, in Kentucky, 1803. Mutual acquaintance led to union in 1820. Many of the churches and their leaders, including Stone, united with the Disciples of Christ* in 1832. The successors of the remainder merged with the Congregationalists in 1930 to form the "Congregational and Christian Churches." Local congregations of Disciples of Christ are often known as Christian churches, but that body as a whole is not properly called "the Christian Church." See Christian Union.

C. C. Ware, *Barton Warren Stone* (1932).

W.E.G.

Christian Congregation: A holiness sect, exclusive in nature, organized at Kokomo, Ind., in 1899. It has dwindled to one church with 57 members. See Evangelistic Associations; holiness churches. E.T.C.

Christian, early, use of Apocrypha: See Apocrypha, early Christian use of.

Christian, early, use of Old Testament: See Old Testament, early Christian use of.

Christian Endeavor Society: See Young People's Societies, Christian.

Christian ethics: See ethics, Christian.

Christian Knowledge, Society for Promoting (S.P.C.K.): Founded for the promotion of education and religion in 1698, now mainly active as an Anglican publishing house. E.R.H.

Christian and Missionary Alliance: A conservative evangelistic and missionary group founded by A. B. Simpson in 1881. It has missions in many countries and carries on widespread evangelistic work in the United States. There are 444 churches with 32,000 members. See holiness churches. E.T.C.

Christian missions: See Chinese religions; India, missions to; Japan, Christianity in; missionary movements.

Christian Nation Church: A conservative religious sect in Ohio, having five churches and slightly more than one hundred members. The movement originated in 1892 and took the form of an organized sect in 1895. The purpose was to carry on an intensive evangelistic work and to teach a stricter manner of living than that prevalent among other Christians.

The practices and teachings of the sect are largely negative in nature, stressing opposition to prevalent doctrines and practices. It opposes the wearing of ornaments, membership in organizations other than the church, divorce and remarriage, marriage with an unconverted person, desecration of the Sabbath, entertainments in churches, artificial steps for limiting the size of families, charging admission to places of worship, idleness, the use of tobacco, jesting, singing of secular songs, and similar practices. On the positive side the group teaches entire sanctification, divine healing, and the second coming of Christ. See holiness churches. E.T.C.

Christian Nurture: The idea expounded by Horace Bushnell* in his book with that title (1847), that the child in the Christian home "ought to *grow up as a Christian*, and not to be trained up for future conversion." This book represented Bushnell's reaction against the extreme position of the revivalistic Calvinists who developed the New Haven theology*, who, losing sight of the historic doctrine of children in the covenant, seemed to imply that the child must be permitted to become "ripe enough in sin to have a conscious battle with it" before he could become a Christian. Bushnell's view met considerable opposition at first, but gradually prevailed. He called the attention of the churches to the necessity for training the young, he expounded a clear doctrine of Christian growth, and he suggested methods for religious training. He is rightly known as the father of the religious education movement.

Besides Bushnell's own works, see the article on Bushnell by C. A. Dinsmore in the *Dictionary of American Biography*; Lewis B. Schenck, *The Presbyterian Doctrine of Children in the Covenant* (1940).

S.E.M.

Christian Reformed Church: (Gereformeerd Kerk) See Kuyper, A.

Christian Science: Christian Science in its current use designates a denomination which has since 1875 come to share the religious field with the historic Christian denominations. It is centrally organized and directed but it functions denominationally in local churches with their own buildings, leaders and "readers", stated times and forms of worship. It is, therefore, descriptively accurate to entitle the entire movement as The Christian Science Church and its local groups as Christian Science churches, although the "Mother Church" in Boston occupies a unique position. Specifically it was in its origin a variant of American Protestantism though it has since extended internationally.

Christian Science, thus inadequately summarized, was definitely initiated by a leader finally known as Mary Baker Eddy and was the issue of a long and complicated series of events, experiences, relationships and even philosophies which it is extremely difficult to follow, disentangle and appraise. It began as a faith healing cult for which Phineas Quimby of Maine supplied a theory. He finally identified his system with the teachings of Jesus and seems beyond any question to have called it "Christian Science". Authoritative Christian Science literature does not acknowledge this but it is documented by the *Quimby Manuscripts.*

Mrs. Eddy after her second marriage went to Quimby for treatment. It was a turning point in her life and she became in her turn a teacher and healer. She secured a following and in Lynn, Massachusetts (in 1875) organized a society known as the Christian Scientists. The first edition of *Science and Health,* the authoritative work for the movement, was published in 1875. Mrs. Eddy says in the preface to the 1909 edition of *Science and Health* that she began "Christian Science mind healing" about the year 1867 and copy-righted her first pamphlet in Christian Science in 1870, but it did not appear in print until 1876 though copies had been in "friendly circulation." The work itself seems to have been a final redaction of "copious notes of Scriptural exposition." It has since gone through many editions and suffered editorial changes.

Basically, the supporting philosophy of Christian Science is simple. It is a pure idealism. "Nothing is real and eternal; nothing is spirit—but God and His ideal; evil has no reality." All this is developed in *Science and Health* at length with scriptural support ingeniously argued. Since God is good, He cannot have created nor be responsible for all the shadowed side of life. Man is "God's spiritual idea" and belongs by right to an order in which there is neither sickness, sin, sorrow or death. Such things are errors of his mortal mind. They have no reality for him save as he admits them. Deny them and they cease to exist. There are, therefore, two fundamentally opposed systems of belief, the true and the false. Man is entangled in a false system of belief whose sources Mrs. Eddy does not convincingly trace. He may escape that entanglement with all its consequences by affirming the other system and demonstrating his affirmation by faith, self-discipline and practice.

Centrally, in practice, Christian Science has been and is the application of its philosophy and theology to bodily healing, but there are marginal demonstrations in comfort, prosperity and general well-being. It has made a religion of healing and a healing of religion. It has had, therefore, a peculiar power of appeal and an ample field in which to operate. In its first rapid period of extension it drew markedly from the older Christian communities and disturbed their leaders. The result amongst other things was a highly controversial literature which begins to be dated. The movement has always been most adroitly led and its department of public relations—so to speak—extremely effective. Its idealistic philosophy has naturally led to an idealization of the movement in general and Mrs. Eddy, in particular but its official historians. The complexity of the elements involved makes an analysis of it unusually difficult. Its theology substantially modifies the inherited theologies while continuing much of their terminology.

As a religion it is strongest in teaching that God should have meaning for the whole of life and resolving—in its own way—the inherited difficulty of adjusting Divine power and goodness with what theologians have called the problem of evil. The result has been a definite type of religious devotion, effective with neurotic and self-centered personalities. As a system of mental or faith healing it is a strongly drawn system of psycho-therapy. Its cures operate in regions responsive to suggestion, and it is usually held that only functional disorders are thus responsive. But under any opinion of the medical faculties, this leaves a large field open to Christian Science practitioners.

One may say, therefore, that Christian Science is a philosophy, a semi-theology, a system of Biblicism and a psycho-therapy effectively organized, amply financed and aptly propagated. Its followers have an unusually strong group consciousness. Statistics are not available and the movement has been somewhat regional, but all large cities have, however, strong Christian Science churches and it is representatively disseminated through the United States. See New Thought Movement.

Borden P. Bowne, *Philosophy of Christian Science* (1908); Mary Baker Eddy, *Science and Health with a Key to the Scriptures* (1934. Trustees under the will of M. B. Eddy); E. Mary Ramsay, *Christian Science and its Discoverer* (Christian Science Pub. Soc. 1935); James M. Campbell, *What Christian Science Means and What We can Learn from It* (1920); M. B. G. Eddy, *Miscellaneous Writings, 1883-1896* (1924, Trustees); Sibyl Wilbur, *The Life of Mary Baker Eddy* (1907); Edwin Franden Dakin, *Mrs. Eddy; the Biography of a Virginal Mind* (1929); G. G. Atkins, *Modern Religious Cults and Movements* (1922). G.G.A.

Christian Social Union: A league founded in 1889 by Bishop Wescott, Scott Holland, and Charles Gore (that year editor of *Lux Mundi*) to arouse the social conscience of members of the Church of England*, especially those at once devout and well-to-do. From 1900 on it had some 6000 members, mostly Anglo-Catholics*, until 1914 by which time it had largely spent its force. Its greatest influence was among the ordinands at Oxford and Cambridge and in urban parishes. It inspired similar interests among some Nonconformists and Roman Catholics, and collaborated with them in the movement of the Conference on Politics, Economics and Citizenship (Copec) after the first World War (1920, 1924) and provided the background for the English interest in the Life and Work movement and the Malvern Conference. Cf. social gospel. T.J.B.

Christian socialism: See social gospel.

Christian Union: A sect (or the general designation covering two sects) which grew out of a merger of several independent religious movements in 1864. Followers of James O'Kelley, Barton W. Stone, J. V. B. Flack, and other independents were involved and the movement drew heavily on the Methodists. (See Christian Church.) There are no distinctive doctrines apart from the general evangelical position. This sect has 93 churches and 6,000 members.

An offshoot of Christian Union is the Church (or Churches) of Christ in Christian Union of Ohio. The breach occurred in 1909 over holiness. The Churches of Christ in Christian Union are fundamentalist, stressing entire sanctification as a "second work of grace," divine healing, and the second coming of Christ. There are 86 churches with 3,500 members. E.T.C.

Christian Unity Baptist Association: A group of 7 small Baptist churches (180 members) in North Carolina, Tennessee, and Virginia, which formed a distinct organization as a result of a resolution in a Regular Baptist* association to drop all churches practicing "open communion." They practice feet washing but otherwise do not depart widely from ordinary Baptist positions. E.T.C.

Christianity*: Christianity may be tentatively defined[1] as a spirit-filled[2] life of faith and love embodied in a/the religion 1) of revelation and 2) of redemption 3) experiential in nature 4) eternal in value-content 5) historical in structure, person and event 6) intuitional in its access to reality 7) interpreted by a theology Christo-centric in method, Theo-centric in incentive and objective and anthropo-centric in direction 8) incorporated in a community of fellowship (the Church) with its Lord[3] 9) implemented by a free personal-social ethic, grounded in the Divine Will and 10) having as its goal a universal moral-spiritual Social Order—The Realm (or Kingdom) of God.[4]

The component parts of the definition may be more fully outlined as follows:

1. Christianity is distinctly revelatory—convinced that God reveals Himself and His purposes progressively (Divine impartation prompting human discovery) in Nature, in the Reason and Conscience of Man, in History, and culminatingly in Jesus Christ (as summarized in the prologue of the Fourth Gospel and in the Epistle to the Romans)—the vehicle of revelation being *the Word* (Logos) incarnate in Christ and articulate in the inspired writings of the Bible.

2. Organically, Christianity is a religion of regeneration and *redemption*, coming to man as sinful with the forgiving and renewing grace of God[5] to save and empower him both individually and socially with the spirit of a new life in Christ.

3. Psychologically, Christianity is *experiential*, having its roots in *racial religious experience*—which may be defined as the sense of the sacred (numinous)[6]—purified and transformed by the Divine Spirit and made potent and creative in life and thought through the exercise of *faith*, i.e., the free energizing of the individual self and the group in appropriating spiritual life and truth.[7] In Christian experience *emotion* blends with *cognition* and *volition* to produce an inner harmony and well-being described as "the abundant life,[8] and "life and peace."

4. Ontologically, Christianity consists of *eternal values* of intrinsic, self-evidencing validity and worth, embracing the true and the beautiful and consummated in the Good. These values being essentially personal subsist and are unified for the Christian mind in the Self-existent Eternal Being, who is the One Good,[9] whose existence is known by his *Presence*,[10] confirmed by knowledge of "His works and ways".[11]

5. Having as its purpose to realize eternal realities and values in *time*, Christianity is structurally, concretely and developmentally *historical*. Springing from a Hebraic-Judaic root which itself sprang from Semitic religion, as that in turn from primitive religion, Christianity is indigenously related to all religions, and may be regarded as indebted to all[12] and as fulfilling whatever of truth and virtue (while rejecting what is false) is in all. Entering into the cultural environment of the Graeco-Roman world, Christianity creatively appropriated Hellenistic as well as Hebrew-Judaic thought forms, the synthesis of which proved singularly adaptable and fruitful for the purpose.

As concretely historic, Christianity centers in a supremely endowed, self-disciplined,[13] self-realized, redemptive person, who appeared at a pregnant moment in the historic process (called by Paul "the fullness of time"), fulfilled a unique mission and founded the Kingdom of God.*[14] His spiritual portrait, life, death and resurrection, as drawn in the N.T., are accepted by the Christian Faith as authentic, trustworthily portrayed by the hand of love. Him Christianity has taken as its Lord and Master, one who has not only given to it its distinctive precepts and ideals but who was, and is, himself the Faith personalized and, as the risen and living Christ, is still ever more widely exercising his redemptive mission.

The historic character of Christianity does not preclude symbol, drama and myth but rather justifies and enhances these —*symbol* being essential to the expression of religion, both in interpretation (language) and in art, *drama* offering an incalculable aid in heightening the impression and effect of history (Christianity is the most dramatic of all religions) and *myth*, including legend and tradition (provided neither is a substitute for history but only an acolyte), lending to historic deeds and persons color, vividness, and significance such as history could not otherwise convey.

6. While Christianity is primarily an experience, a life, it is also a *knowing* and as such relies upon a form of knowledge implicitly yet intelligently *intuitional*—not less so in that its nomenclature is concrete, empirical and personal rather than abstract and speculative. While depending cognitively upon intuition the philosophy of Christianity is catholic, comprehensive and hospitable and may be said to embrace the affirmative truths and values, not only of intuitionism, valuism and personalism, but of mysticism, idealism,

realism, empiricism and pragmatism. In other words, Christianity is philosophically at once convinced and reasonable, distinctive and inclusive, intuitive and interpretive.

Logically, Christianity is markedly *dialectical*, setting dipolar truths over against each other and resolving the dichotomy by a dialectic which is *decisional* (either-or) in respect to contraries and moral alternatives and *synthetic* (both-and) in uniting mutually fulfilling opposites. This gives birth to paradox[15]—an expressional product of dialectic which, uniting wholeness of view with discrimination, is peculiarly germane to the Christian mind.

7. As revelatory, experiential and intuitional, engaged in incorporating eternal values in human life, projected as it is in time and in history, Christianity requires and creates a creedal, didactic, doctrinal *instrument of interpretation*, or *ideology*, consisting of a mystical-rational, intuitional-systematic *theology*, the leading conceptions of which may be defined somewhat as follows; with the understanding that all Christian doctrines—as contrasted with *dogmas* which are valid *semper ubique et ab omnibus* (and which Christianity has also)—are in need of continual renewal and reinterpretation.

The Christian conception of God is that of Love,[16] borne to man in the benignant arms of the reassuring (analogical) symbol of *Spiritual* (Heavenly) *Father*,[17] as it is witnessed (seen) in living reality in the sonship of Jesus[18] and felt in the moving impulsions of the Holy Spirit.

Although sufficient for faith, Divine Fatherhood has been given metaphysical formulation by Theology under the further symbol of *Triunity* in the doctrine of the *Trinity** which, appearing first in worship and afterward taking conceptual form stands for the completeness of God and the union in Him of transcendence and immanence, power and love, revelation and redemption.

Interpreting all things in relation to God, Christian theology is thus Christo-centric in approach, Theo-centric as its object and its teleology.

Divine Fatherhood, enlarged in depth and range, involves and interprets the doctrine of Creation (*creativity*) long regarded as mechanical but coming to be understood, in the light of advancing knowledge, as developmental, progressive and cooperative, God as "Creator of creators"[19] giving to creation itself, and chiefly to man, a vital part, through inceptive and increasing freedom, in the universal creative, harmonizing and perfecting process which moves toward universal reconciliation and the fulfillment of the highest possible good for all.[20]

Jesus Christ for Christian theology is the beloved Son of God, the incarnate Logos, the archetypal and ideal man (Paul), Savior and Lord, uniting the Jesus of History and the Christ of Faith, who by dying upon the cross in vicarious suffering on behalf of man implemented timeless reconciliation in time and by his resurrection from the dead brought life and immortality to light. In this historic-symbolic moving drama Christianity unites experience and event, factuality and personality, deed and idea, symbolism and history, begetting an assurance of spiritual verity as not otherwise available for faith.

Man, as viewed by Christian theology, is "made in the image of God" and as such is rational, moral and free. Having by abuse of freedom become sinful, he is, by virtue of the same freedom, and by the *grace of* God, redeemable and *immortable*.[21] Through the freedom of Faith, Christianity conceives humanity's immortable nature as "an inner man" perpetually renewed, and thus transmuted into a "spiritual (resurrection) body" which serves the surviving spirit as an instrument to express personality and commune with others in a Larger Life beyond death.[22]

Evil, in the light of Christianity, is a multiform demoralizing, corrupting force, arising, wilfully, "from within out of the heart of man"[23] and becoming a sinister organized destructive power which assumes the guise of a personality (Satan) but will be overcome by the greater power of good.[24]

8. As a religion of love Christianity unites its members to their Lord and to one another in a *beloved community*[25] in which is cherished the highest possible human fellowship and which by its self-sacrifice and radiant spirit (by no means wholly lost)—especially manifest on the mission field—unfailingly wins adherents to the Christian "Way." This unity being spiritual and affectional is potentially strong enough, as a sacrament and a covenant, to bring together Christians of varied types of belief and worship and unite people of all races and nations and social stations in one world-embracing body, a consummation long delayed by needless misunderstandings and divisions but now moving forward with accelerated speed, fostered by the alienations and enmities of a war-torn world.

9. Being an active, redemptive, constructive Faith, Christianity implements its mission by a vital, free, *individual-social ethic* which moulds personality and society toward the fulfillment of the highest attainable ideal. As such the Christian *ethos* expands in adjustment to changing social, economic and political patterns, although less by external influences than by the propulsion of its own autonomous character and power of adaptation and application.

10. The goal of the Christian ethic, as of Christianity itself, is *the Kingdom of God*, anticipated by Hebrew prophecy and announced by Jesus as already present and exercising its healing and life-giving benefits through himself but also *to come* far more fully in the future in two contrasted but mutually fulfilling ways, one *biological* (the parable of the mustard seed) and the other *apocalyptic*, overcoming, through conflict and upheaval, the Kingdom of Evil.[26]

Christianity commits to the Church the chief agency in bringing in the Kingdom, itself also, as "the body of Christ," an integral part of the Kingdom entrusted with the conduct of worship, the task of religious instruction, the regeneration of individuals, of society and the world-wide extension of the Evangel.

The Kingdom, or Reign, of God which thus animates the vision and enlists the devotion of Christians is a universal, all-inclusive reign of "righteousness and peace and joy in the Holy Spirit,"[27] a brotherhood of men of all nations and races that is to conserve all the highest values garnered from the age-long growth of good and adventure of man,[28] a Kingdom advancing through growth and struggle toward realization in the present world, yet is already established and can be consummated only in the eternal world, the prayer for which is:

"Thy Kingdom come, on earth, as it is in heaven!"

Confronting as it does today, with a fresh sense of responsibility, the indispensable and urgent need of *religion* in the task of world reconstruction, Christianity is coming to realize, with new enlargement of vision and consciousness of dedication, its own undeveloped resources as the Faith above all others of inherent developmental potency, uniting in an unexampled degree doctrine and deed, *eidos* and *ethos*, (e.g., the unrealized ethical implications of the Fatherhood of God), with power to meet, on the one hand, the pressing intellectual problems aroused by the new knowledge of man and the cosmos and on the other the overwhelming demands of racial, economic and political world reorganization. Possessing as has been proven by nearly twenty centuries of trial, invincible motive, insight and faith in God and man, it may be predicted without hesitation that Christianity is on the eve of a new era of inner renewal and resolution and outer achievement in its God-given task.

* It need hardly be pointed out that this definition makes no pretension to be other than the endeavor of a single limited individual mind to summarize the conception of Christianity garnered after extended study and reflection. Had there been ampler space for the purpose the definition might well have been made much more elastic and have included variant interpretations of subjects upon which there is room for wide differences of viewpoint.

1 The attempt to form a definition of Christianity reveals as nothing else could its *indefinable* wealth, resourcefulness and comprehensiveness as a religion, making it incomparably universal in character and value.

2 Rom. 8. The scripture references throughout are used as indices or illustrations of meaning, not as proof-texts.

3 John 15.

4 "On earth as it is in heaven."

5 Eph. 2:8.

6 Rudolf Otto.

7 Matt. 17:20; Heb. 11:1.

8 John 10:10, Rom. 8:6.

9 Matt. 19:17.

10 Acts 17:23-28.

11 Rom. 1:20.

12 Rom. 1:14.

13 "Though he was Son, yet learned he discipline through what he suffered and being made perfect he became the author of Eternal perfecting (Salvation) to all who give him their heart's heed" Heb. 5:9.

14 Ritschl.

15 E.g., "He that saveth his life shall lose it."

16 I John 4:8.

17 The Lord's Prayer.

18 "He that hath seen me hath seen the Father."

19 Bergson, *The Two Sources of Morals and Religion*, p. 243.

20 Col. 1:20. "By him to reconcile all things unto Himself." Acts 3:21. The period of the great Restoration (Moffatt). Eph. 1:10 "That in the coming of the fullness of times he might gather together in one all things in Christ".

21 Having the capacity for immortality.

22 I Cor. 15:35—49; 2 Cor. 4:16.

23 Mark 7:20—23.

24 Luke 10:18; Rom. 16:20.

25 John 13: 34-35.

26 This dual character of "the Second Coming", though essential to its nature, has been seriously missed by theology as well as in popular misunderstanding.

27 Rom. 14:17.

28 Parable of the Harvest (Wheat and Tares) Matt. 13:24-30.

Bibliography: The bibliography of Christianity is too extensive and varied for specific citation. Embracing as it does the N.T., the chief writings of Patristic literature, the great works of Medieval and of Protestant theology, the classics of Christian Mysticism and the books representing such resuscitations of life and thought as Wesleyanism, Puritanism, the Oxford Movement, Ritschlianism, Christian Romanticism, Pietism, Liberalism, Unitarianism and "the New Theology" and such contemporary movements as Social Christianity, the New Scholasticism, Barthianism, Reconstructed Liberalism, Personalism and Christian Realism; also the histories of the Church, of Christian Doctrine and Missions, and the productions of Christian Art and Literature, Poetry and Science (in so far as these have been animated by Christianity) it is unnecessary to do more than direct attention to this affluent output of virile literature to indicate the wealth of cultural and spiritual fruitage that Christianity has evoked. J.W.B.

Christianity in China: See Chinese religions.

Christianity and the mystery religions: See mystery religions.

Christmas (origin and customs): The celebration of the anniversary of the birth of Christ now observed on December 25. There is uncertainty as to when or why this date was chosen. There is no data in the N.T. by which it may be definitely determined.

There seems to have been no interest in the birthday until the time of Hippolytus, Bishop of Rome, in the first half of the 3rd century. He first chose January 2; others proposed May 20, April 18 or 19, March 25 or 28. For some time January 6 had been observed as Christ's spiritual birthday or date of his baptism and there is evidence that it was also celebrated by some as the day of his natural birth.

Two main reasons are generally accepted in explanation of the decision favoring December 25.

1. The "Plan of the Ages." By complicated and fantastic calculations the creation of the world was estimated as beginning March 25, so Christ, the Paschal Lamb, the new Creation, had his conception on March 25 and his birth therefore December 25.

2. The New Testament. By other unsubstantiated reasoning from the Gospel stories the conception of John the Baptist is placed in September and so Christ's in March and thus his nativity in December.

Obviously, the choice of these dates was influenced by pagan observances, though to what extent may not be determined. The date of the conception, March 25, is related to the sun as is also that of the nativity. There had long been the Spring festivals joyously celebrating the rebirth of nature as there had been the Saturnalia (December 17-24) and Brumalia (December 25) rejoicing in the end of the winter solstice and the "birthday of the unconquered Sun." As the Day of the Sun became the Lord's Day (Sunday) so, other pagan days and festive occasions were conquered by Christ and became Christian holy days.

According to authentic records no church festival was held in celebration of Christ's birth until the first half of the 4th Century. Only slowly was December 25 adopted in the East where January 6 was observed in honor of both the physical and spiritual births. This date was celebrated by Jerusalem until 549 and has been by the Armenian Christians to the present.

Few of the customs connected with the celebration of Christmas are actually church festivals—that is, have been consecrated by the church or come within the church year. Perhaps the only one is The Cradle of Christ an observance of Christmas Eve which has its origin in the story of the Magi bringing their gifts to the infant Christ. Doubtless this is a reflection of the more ancient Adonis cult, the "adoration in the Cave."

The fact that these customs are popular again help to explain the choice of December 25. They were not imposed by the church but were born of elemental human qualities. Ancient practices and festivals growing out of man's reaction to the seasons, the strange and striking moods and changes of nature, were continued by the Christians with a new significance attached. Man remains a creature of nature though a Christian.

Rejoicing at the end of the winter solstice, the darkness of the shortest day of the year turning again to the lengthening light—the Romans celebrated this "Birthday of the Unconquered Sun" in the madness of the Saturnalia by the lifting of almost all restraints, the closing of schools, restriction of punishment, freedom of slaves, merrymaking, gaming and feasting, the exchange of gifts especially tapers and dolls for children.

The same natural phenomena were observed by more northern people in the Yule* feast, song festivals and ceremonies symbolizing protection from demons and evil Spirits and assurances of abundant harvests in the new year. The fir tree is in all probability a later German adoption, its history going back no further than the 17th Century. The mistletoe is of Celtic origin and is of modern adaptation to the Christmas customs. Each of these symbolizes light in the darkness, life in the midst of death.

The Christmas Tree, so universally celebrated now in connection with the Sunday School, is the happy home and family festival transferred to the Church and thus given more hallowed and religious connotation. Cf. Sol Invictus. See church year; church year cycle.

Lilly Frazer, *Leaves from the Golden Bough* (1924); Randolph E. Haugan, editor, *Christmas;* Jocelyn Rhys, *Shaken Creeds*, Appendix I, p. 227 (1922). R.E.E.H.

Christology: Schleiermacher* defined Christianity as "a monotheistic religion of a teleological kind in which everything is related to Christ, the Redeemer". The meaning of this definition in the context of his theology can here be ignored, but what is to be emphasized is that he believed it impossible to conceive the Christian religion apart from the centrality of Christ. Indeed, the Christian religion cannot be theologically understood except by a rigorous Christocentrism. Christology is the name for the theological interpretation of the meaning of the belief in Christ; it is the doctrine of the person and work of Christ.

While it cannot be said that Christology as a developed doctrine can be found in the N.T., it must be acknowledged that the books of the N.T. are full of Christological notions. The names of dignity with which Jesus* is endowed (Son of Man; Son of God**; Christ; Lord; Saviour; Lamb of God; etc.), reflect interpretations of His life and work in terms of theological ideas. To what extent Jesus Himself made them possible by His own sense of messianic* mission, we can no longer definitely establish. But it is clear that soon after His crucifixion, which His disciples in the resurrection experiences came to understand not as a defeat but as a marvellous confirmation of His messianic mission, His person and life were explained in terms of certain passages of the O.T., particularly the so-called messianic prophecies and the Isaianic passage of the suffering servant.

The apostle Paul* who by the vision accompanying his conversion was persuaded that the crucified Jesus was indeed the Christ, developed a first Christology. He viewed Christ as a pre-existent divine being who as the servant of divine grace and love had humbled himself by becoming a man, in order to save men from the dominion of the "powers" of law, sin, and death, and who having broken them by his obedience unto the death of the cross, was raised up to sit at the right hand of God, the Father, from whence he would come again to judge the world. Thus Christ was seen as the center of a divine drama of salvation. In it his incarnation and his resurrection were the most important factors.

This Pauline view which was incorporated in modified and extended forms in the teachings of the late N.T. books, especially in the gospel according to John, was less representative of the doctrine that prevailed among the early Christians than of their worship and common life. The "Lord" Christ Jesus was the center of their cultus and the fountain of their new life. They worshipped in his "name" and as "new creatures" they believed to be "in Christ".

The Christological notions of the N.T. reflect the concern to understand the meaning and character of Jesus in terms of Jewish and Hellenistic ideas. (In this connection it is important to see how these ideas, e.g., the title "Lord", gained a new significance when they were connected with Christ and the Christian faith.) They served as the basis of all later Christological work throughout the history of the church, proving to be an almost inexhaustible source of a great variety of doctrines.

The most significant post-Biblical Christological development was begun when the so-called Apologists, of whom Justin Martyr* was most representative, introduced the so-called Logos Christology. Adopting the mode of thought which the Jewish philosopher Philo*, a contemporary of Paul, had employed, when he used the Platonic-Stoic idea of the Logos (the divine principle of creation and rational world order), they declared Jesus to be the incarnation of the Logos. Thereby they endeavored to maintain the monotheistic character of the Christian religion, on which the Christians had insisted from the beginning, at the same time explaining the worship of Christ as a divine agent of revelation and salvation. Their accomplishment was historically most important insofar as by their identification of Jesus Christ with the Logos* they could claim that in the Christian religion the Jewish hope for the Messiah and the Greek-Hellenistic yearning for the disclosure of divine, ultimate truth had been fulfilled. Understanding the divine revelation in Christ as the climax of Jewish religion and Greek philosophy, they could explain the uniqueness of the Christian religion in distinction from Judaism and Hellenism by pointing to the Incarnate "Word" (Logos). But the price they and their theological successors had to pay for this achievement was high. For the Logos-Christology explained the meaning of Jesus' person and work primarily in metaphysical and cosmological terms (which, by the way, have proved unacceptable to us moderns). Thus the historical figure which is in the center of the N.T. message was lost sight of. Christological speculation turned almost immediately to the problem of how the relation of the Logos with God must be understood. Another question, namely that of the character of Jesus' person and life waited to be raised.

The first problem was solved in the course of the Arian* controversy (318-381), the setting of which had been prepared by the work of the great theologians of the third century, particularly Origen*. The trinitarian dogma declared by the Council of Nicaea (325) and confirmed by the Council of Constantinople (381) taught the *homoousia** (consubstantiality, sameness of being) of the Father and the Logos. (See Constantinople, Councils of.)

When the Nicaean theologians defined the nature of Christ as "God from God", "begotten not made", they were concerned to safeguard a certain interpretation of the salvation through Christ as it had been first introduced by Irenaeus. When he taught that in Christ "God became man that man might become God", he regarded the Incarnation as the ground of the hope of immortality (for in it eternity had entered time) and the Resurrection as the ground of the ultimate victory of good over evil (for by it death and sin, the "wages of death") had been defeated. By the Arian metaphysical teaching that the Son had a beginning, (that "there was a time when he was not") the truly divine character of this salvation was denied. Hence the Nicaeans under the leadership of Athanasius fought for the dogma of the divinity of the Son (Logos) with the conviction that in it the very essence of the Christian faith was expressed. It must be noted, however, that in attributing divinity to Jesus Christ, they proceeded on the basis of the question what he must have been in view of their doctrine of salvation and not what the gospels described him as having been.

The same abstract and artificial approach which, by the way, has been characteristic of most Christological thinking, was also that of the controversy which followed almost immediately upon that initiated by Arius and was essentially concluded by the work of the Council of Chalcedon* (451). The problem which demanded solution was the following: If the Logos has to be regarded as "consubstantial" with the Father, what kind of a person was Jesus in whom the divine Logos became incarnate? Since Tertullian it had been customary to describe the character of Jesus Christ as "one person in two natures" (human and divine). In the light of the Nicaean teaching there arose the possibility of three Christological heresies: Nestorianism*, which stressed the difference between Christ's human and divine natures in such a way that it became impossible to conceive him as one person; Monophysitism*, which so emphasized the divine nature of Christ as the essential aspect of his being that his human nature was virtually denied; and Apollinarianism*, which defined the person of Christ in such a way that he could be regarded as neither human nor divine. The Christological dogma of Chalcedon excluded all these heresies by defining the person of Christ as one person with two natures, so unified that they must be regarded as neither mixed with one another nor as separated from one another. The artificiality of this definition is obvious, yet it saved the Christian faith from serious Christological aberrations. It preserved the fundamental Christian conviction that God had acted in the man Jesus.

For centuries, it remained henceforth a basic Christological tenet that Christ was both man and God (Origen had coined the phrase *theanthropos*, God-man). Thus the Greek dogma came to dominate all Christological thought. To be sure, the medieval scholastics (in this respect following Augustine) were not much interested in metaphysical Christological speculations. Hence they took the ancient teaching on the person of Christ for granted and paid particular attention to the work of Christ. It became their special concern to understand his passion and death. The Crucifix thus became *the* symbol of medieval western Christianity. Anselm* of Canterbury saw the death of Christ as the only sufficient reparation (satisfaction) paid to God for human sin. Abailard* interpreted it as that disclosure of divine love which will decisively turn man to the love of God. Bernard of Clairvaux* made it the object of a mystical contemplation by which man might become one with God. Thomas Aquinas blended all these notions into one.

This preoccupation with the question what Christ had done for man, particularly by his death, led to a concern for the Christ of the N.T., which the ancient theologians had avoided. Thus medieval Christianity developed the ideal of the "imitation of Christ" (Damiani, Norbert of Xanten, Francis of Assisi, Thomas a Kempis). The gospel picture of Christ once more asserted itself. One began to write books entitled "The Life of Christ" (Ludolf of Saxony). Nevertheless, the dogma of the two natures remained in the foreground.

This fact was left unchanged also in the times of the Renaissance and the Reformation. To be sure, Erasmus placed the teachings of Christ (*philosophia Christi*) in the center of his moralistic and enlightened interpretation of Christianity. And Luther professed to be not primarily concerned for the metaphysical aspects of the Christological dogma, emphasizing instead the soteriological character of Christ as "the mirror of the fatherly heart of God." Actually, the main implications of the old dogma remained in force. In Luther's fully developed Christology they became apparent in his teaching on the atonement* of Christ's death as a penalty for human sin (a teaching which the Reformers adopted) and in his doctrine on the ubiquity* of Christ, which he put forth in connection with his doctrine of the Lord's Supper (a doctrine the Christological implications of which particularly the Calvinists vigorously denied).

Orthodox Protestantism retained the old dogma intact, extending it merely in furtherance of partisan interests. The rational criticism to which it was subjected by the Humanists, Spiritualists, Anti-Trinitarians (particularly Socinians*) and Arminians never led to a construction of new Christological doctrines.

In the teachings of the philosophers and theologians of the Enlightenment* the doctrine of the two natures of Christ finally lost its validity. Their vigorous anti-supernaturalism and Rationalism permitted them to see in Jesus only the supreme moral teacher. They were unable to comprehend the centrality of Christ in the Christian faith.

A reconstruction of a fully Christian doctrine of Christ was begun by Schleiermacher* who in separating himself both from Orthodoxy and Rationalism taught to regard Christ as the Redeemer, insofar as he communicates to believers the perfectness of his own God-consciousness, and as the Founder of the Christian Church, insofar as he determines its common life by the impulses that proceed from his perfection. Ritschl*, depending on Schleiermacher, believed it possible to combine with these teachings the Christocentrism of the Lutheran Reformation. Rigorously excluding the old dogma from consideration, he insisted that the historical Jesus, the founder of the Christian movement, must be seen as the revealer of God, particularly insofar as in his life he perfectly fulfilled his vocation of disclosing the divine plan of the Kingdom of God.

When Ritschl became the head of the theological "school" that bears his name, the modern investigation in the life of Jesus had already begun. His own teachings greatly encouraged the interest in the historical Jesus. Neglected, almost forgotten for centuries, the historical figure of the man of Nazareth came to dominate the life of liberal Protestantism. Theologically, the old Christology was relegated to the past in which it had developed; religiously, it continued to lend power to the meaning which one claimed to derive from the "Jesus of history." Today, the church is in need of a new Christology. See communicatio idiomatum; creeds of Christendom; Cyril of Alexandria; Dyophysites; Eutyches; Jesus, our knowledge of; kenosis; monotheletism; Nihilianism; perichoresis; Virgin Mary.

H. R. Mackintosh, *The Doctrine of the Person of Jesus Christ* (1912). W.P.

Christotokos: See Nestorianism; Virgin Mary.

Chronicles, I and II: Historical books of the O.T., contained in the third and latest division of the Hebrew canon, the "Writings" or Hagiographa*. They were originally one volume, and cover Hebrew history from Adam to Cyrus (538 B.C.). with special attention devoted to David* and the subsequent kings of Judah. The work is obviously a revision of earlier, canonical books of the O.T., especially I, II Samuel and I, II Kings**, in accordance with the interests and ideas of the author. He shows particular interest in the Temple*, its cult and clergy (especially the Levites); in racial purity (see the elaborate genealogies); and in the dogma of divine retribution. Jewish tradition attributes the work to Ezra*, but modern scholarship usually assigns it to a writer of a later period, in the first half of the third century B.C., who also wrote Ezra-Nehemiah*. If Ezra lived in the first half of the fourth century, it is not impossible that he was actually the author. The principal source used was the earlier historical books, Genesis-Kings, but it is possible that other authentic sources were utilized. It is seldom, however, that the Chronicler gives accurate additional information concerning history, and his work is chiefly of value for study of the ideas and institutions of the author's period. The Books of Chronicles are supplemental to, and in the spirit of, the Priestly writings (see P), but represent a somewhat later stage in ecclesiastical development.

See E. L. Curtis and A. A. Madsen, *The Books of Chronicles* (International Critical Commentary) (1910); W. F. Albright, "The Date and Personality of the Chronicler", *Journal of Biblical Literature* XL (1921), pp. 104-124. J.P.H.

chronological order of Biblical Books: See Books of the Old Testament, the, in chronological order; Books of the New Testament, dates of the.

Chrysoloras, Manuel: (c. 1355-1415) Of noble Byzantine family, was sent to Italy by Greek Emperor to beg aid against Turks, settled in Florence on invitation of the city, and became first important teacher of Greek in Italy. Died en route to Council of Constance. W.E.G.

Chrysostom, John: (347-407) John of Antioch, the "Chrysostom" being a title, meaning "Golden-mouthed", bestowed because of his matchless pulpit eloquence. Born in Antioch in 347, given an excellent education by his saintly mother Anthusa. Became an advocate in Antioch, but later, after three years of instruction by Bishop Meletius in Antioch, was baptized. He avoided election as bishop in 370, and, after the death of his mother who had opposed his desire, he went into monastic retirement. Returning to Antioch in 380, he was appointed Deacon in 380 and Presbyter in 386. Then in 387 he was made Patriarch of Constantinople. There a friendly act involved him in the Origenistic controversies*, which provided an occasion for his banishment owing to the hostility of the Empress whose loose life he had rebuked. He died in exile in 407. He wrote commentaries, expository homilies, apologetic treatises, and a work on the Priesthood in which he commended virginity and asceticism. He is the only member of the Antiochan school* whose orthodoxy has never been challenged. A.K.R.

Chuang Tzŭ: See Chinese Terminology.

Chubb, Thomas: Dee Deism.

Chu Hsi: See Chinese Terminology.

church: See ecclesia; sect; temples.

Church and State: See caesaropapism; Concordat; Papal States; legates and nuncios, papal; Westphalian treaties.

church architecture: See art, ecclesiastical, Christian; church building.

Church Army: A Church of England organization, founded in 1882 by Prebendary J. C. Carlile, which carries on work similar to that of the Salvation Army. An American branch was established after the first world war, with a training school for men and women in New York City. W.N.P.

church building: In the earliest days of Christianity, Christian worship was conducted in private homes. While it may be true that the basilicae* of the Mediterranean countries influenced to some extent the plan and the structural system of the earliest Christian churches, yet modern investigation would seem to prove that too much has been taken for granted in this respect.

Perhaps the oldest Christian place of worship known today is the ancient church at Glastonbury, in Somersetshire. Local tradition asserts that it was built by Joseph of Arimathea, who is believed by some to have introduced Christianity into Britain in 63 A.D. Extensive excavations were carried out by Frederick Bligh Bond, Esq., and others, and brought to light evidences that a Christian place of worship stood on the site in earliest times. The present building, a roofless structure of sturdy stone construction, is certainly not the original building, but it is probably a heavy veneer of stone that may have been built to protect one or more earlier structures. The original church, according to tradition, was of wattle and daub construction, rectangular on plan, and of simplest construction.

America was colonized by northern Europeans, and it is but natural that they brought to this country the traditions of northern lands, rather than the planning and methods of construction of the southern and eastern countries. The American colonists were not wealthy, and there was no attempt to introduce the large, imposing type of church buildings that are characteristic of France, Spain and Italy, nor the massive Romanesque that prevails so largely in Germany.

Partly because so many of the early settlers in America were Englishmen, and partly because the majority of English churches were of the small, simple parish-church type, English types of architecture prevailed in America from the start. There were a few attempts at a very simple type of Gothic*, but the style more typical of Colonial days was the Georgian. London had burned in 1666, and many of its city churches had been rebuilt by Sir Christopher Wren, in a style somewhat new to England. Their plan was often a simple rectangle, rather wide and short, with a comparatively shallow chancel. These buildings were simple, but Sir Christopher saved them from mediocrity by constructing towers and spires of considerable richness and of great originality.

The simplicity and ease of construction of these churches appealed to the austere American Puritan mind. Wren's Georgian style was further simplified, and our own Colonial churches were the result. Many of these still exist. Among them are North Church, Old South Church, Park Street Church, the Roxbury Meeting House, the Dorchester Church, all in Boston, and the First Church in West Roxbury, the last no longer standing. Close by are the two churches in Dedham, and churches in Wayland, Lancaster and many other communities. Providence has an especially fine example, and at East Lyme is a restoration of another good Colonial example. Almost every New England village has one or more examples, and good Colonial is found here and there along the coast, as far as Charlestown, S. C.

Colonial did not influence the Middle West to any extent until recent years. The prevailing style there was a type of building incorrectly called Victorian Gothic. These churches were rectangular on plan, with a thin tower and spire on the main axis. The chancel degenerated into a shallow recess, and in the worst examples, was occupied by the organ and the singers. About the year 1867, the so-called Akron theatre-plan was introduced, and gained much popularity throughout the Central States. A decade or so later, H. H. Richardson and his followers introduced a modified form of Romanesque, but its vogue was of short duration.

In 1892, a firm of young architects known at first as Cram, Wentworth and Goodhue, and later as Cram, Goodhue and Ferguson, built All Saint's Episcopal Church, Peabody Square, Boston. This was the beginning of the remarkable Gothic revival that was destined to hold sway in America for half a century. This famous firm of architects built churches in almost every important city in America, and these range all the way from small chapels seating but a hundred people to the vast fabric of the Cathedral of St. John the Divine, New York.

An attempt had been made in England to revive the Gothic style, which had been a dead style for four centuries. Eminent architects, such as the Pugins, the Scotts, Bentley, Bodley & Garner, Paley & Austin, Stokes, Butterfield, Sedding, Comper, Tapper and others had done much brilliant work, but it was in America, and at the hands of Ralph Adams Cram, Bertram G. Goodhue and a number of men either trained or influenced by them, that the most remarkable age of church building since the Middle Ages, came into being. It lasted from about 1892 to 1930, when the financial depression and other causes caused a swift decline.

Not only in church building, but in all the associated arts, was there a most remarkable awakening. Connick, Burnham, d'Ascenzo, Lakeman, Reynolds, Francis & Rohnstock and a number of others produced stained glass of a quality fully equal to anything done abroad. Skinner, Austin, Casavant and others built organs of finest quality, exceeding even their eminent predecessors, the two Roosevelts, Hutchings, Johnson and Hook & Hastings. John Kirchmayer's wood carving became known throughout the world, while Irving & Casson, William F. Ross and others did work of exceptional merit. In ecclesiastical metal work were such men as Krasser, Koralewski and Yellen, whose work was the rival of that of Mediaeval Hildesheim. Sculptors, workers in mosaics, in church embroidery, in encaustic tiles for church floors, and to a lesser extent in mural decoration, transformed many of our American churches into places of great richness. It was only in bell founding and in the construction of carillons* that the English and continental product was superior to that of America.

Partly due to the industrial depression of 1930-1940, and partly because so many of these famous and gifted architects and craftsmen died within a short period of time, enthusiasm waned, and by the time of the Second World War, comparatively few churches of merit were being built. There was no longer the demand for careful planning, sturdy honesty of construction and perfection of craftsmanship.

Efforts have been made from time to time to adapt the so-called Modern style to church building, but without conspicuous success. A few good Modern churches have appeared in the Scandinavian countries and in Finland. Those of Germany and France are unquestionably ugly. A few rather good examples are to be found in England, such as St. Saviour's Eltham, Hanwell St. Thomas's, the new parish church at Hook and the proposed Guildford Cathedral. The vast cathedral at Liverpool, not yet completed, is Gothic but with decided Modern influence. In America and Canada a very few Modern churches have appeared, but thus far they have not attracted wide attention. See art, ecclesiastical, Christian; bells; cathedral; norman; temples. F.R.W.

Church Congress: Annual meetings of members of the Anglican Communion in England and in America, at which problems facing the Church are discussed and differing points of view presented. In England, a semi-official committee supervises the plans for the meetings; in America, an organization entitled The Church Congress sponsors the conferences. The American group has a working committee with headquarters in New York; the committee publishes booklets and syllabi for study. W.N.P.

church government. See clergy; polity. Also see under various churches.

Church Missionary Society, the: See Evangelicals.

church, the institutional: See institutional church, the.

church, the, in historic Christianity, conceptions of: The term church is used to designate a group of more or less closely related phenomena and values, all related to the continuation in human history of the work and influence of Jesus Christ. Questions about the "true" meaning of the word, about the essence of the church and about the "true" church are fundamentally moral questions relating to the comparative worth of various human actions. The meaning of the term varies between two poles but in every case some reference to both is involved; the first of these is the idea of a special community of men constituted by Jesus Christ or by God through Christ; the second is the idea of an institution which carries on or witnesses to the work of Christ among the "natural" communities of mankind. Each idea is subject to a variety of interpretations; hence three main sets of problems have been discussed in theology with reference to the church: the nature and function of the community, the nature and functions of the institution, the relations of institution to community.

In the sub-apostolic period the church was thought of primarily as a chosen people of God, a new race elected to take the place of the previously chosen, now rejected, Israel; it was on the one hand the special recipient of divine favors, on the other hand the special instrument of the divine will. Membership in the community was the result of regeneration rather than of natural birth; the law of the people was the new law revealed by Jesus Christ; it was not a geographically localized society but scattered throughout the world. While this idea of the church as a new and universal people remains a constant theme in the thought of later periods it is made the leading theme by medieval sects, in part by the monastic orders and, in the Reformation period, by the Anabaptist* groups and their successors. It is of great importance also as one motif in the major reform movements from Wyclif* onward. The problems and conflicts which marked the development of the Jewish doctrine of the chosen people reappear, though with significant differences, in the history of the idea in Christendom. The most important of these center around the following points: the degree of separateness of the new community from other societies with which it is intermingled spatially, culturally and economically; the relation of the new law to common human mores, and the rigorousness with which the former is to be interpreted and applied; the relative importance of the letter of traditional law and of individual inspiration; the extent to which suffering or rulership represents the function of the people in the divine economy; the mode of government of the community; the question of membership, to what extent it is dependent on personal decision, on divine action, on social or spiritual inheritance; the relation of definite and definable local or provincial societies to the vaguely definable general community of all Christians.

The idea of the church as institution, while represented in the early recognition of the apostolate and never wholly absent from Christian thought, tends to take some precedence over the idea of the church as community with the increasing Christianization of the Roman empire, the development of an official clergy and the episcopate, of the rites and the sacramental system. It is in part the consequence of the growing maturity of the Christian movement, in part the result of the accommodation of Christianity to prevailing social and religious practices. Cyprian* (d. 258) brought such ideas of the church into systematic form. For him the church was primarily an institution of salvation, centering in the bishops, the successors of the apostles and *dispensatores dei.* For medieval Roman Catholicism* "church" means fundamentally the hierarchical institution, which mediates grace through the sacraments*, brings offerings for the people and also governs as representative of God. In general, the major Protestant movement, as represented by Luther and Calvin, did not so much break with the institutional conception of the church as it challenged the priestly conception of its function. The proper work of the church, in the conviction of the Reformers, was the preaching of the gospel to which the administration of the sacraments was subordinate. Calvin and Calvinism* united with this a large interest in the governing function, as indicated in the fact that *discipline* was regarded in this branch of the Reformation as one of the marks of the church alongside of the preaching of the gospel and the proper administration of the sacraments. In the period of Protestant scholasticism the prevailing conception of the church was that of a school which taught right doctrine, a notion which was confused with the idea of the preaching of the gospel; but with the evangelical revival in the 18th and 19th centuries the original Reformation emphasis was reestablished, so far as the conception of the institutional function was concerned.

Despite variations of emphasis on community or institution both elements have needed to be considered in all thought about historic Christianity and a major question at all times has been the question of the relation of the two aspects. For Roman Catholicism the institution of the priesthood, culminating in the papacy*, is the representative and the visible embodiment of the new community; no one is a true member of the community who is not loyal to the institution. Lutheran and Calvinist Protestantism regard the community as an object of faith rather than of experience while the "visible church", or the institution of preaching and discipline is an instrument which God uses, though not necessarily so, for the creation of the invisible community; on the other hand, the presence of the institution may be regarded by faith as an indication of the presence of the community. Sectarian Christianity, which became profoundly influential throughout Protestantism in the evangelical revival, subordinated the institutional to the communal conception and sought the establishment of visible societies of Christians to which it applied the term church, without showing much interest in the problems of the relation of such societies to historic and universal movements or communities.

A. Harnack, *Mission and Expansion of Christianity in the First Three Centuries,* 2 vols. (1908), 2nd ed.; F. Loofs, *Symbolik*; C. Gore, editor, *The Church and the Ministry* (1919); Hort, *The Christian Ecclesia.*

H.R.N.

church, the primitive Christian: Jesus was not, in the literal sense, Founder of the church, for what he looked for was the Kingdom, when men would spontaneously obey the will of God, and no formal organization would be necessary. The references to the church in Matthew's Gospel can be proved, on critical grounds, to be doubtful. At the same time the church was the inevitable outcome of the work of Jesus. He gathered around him a body of disciples which could not but expand and take on it the form of a regular community. Above all, he proclaimed the Kingdom of God, and his followers were those who broke with the present world and threw in their lot with the new order which was at hand. This, in its origin and all through its history, has been the formative idea of the church. It is the society of those who are seeking in this world to order their lives by the principles of a higher world, in which the will of God is the sole law.

The church had therefore no definite beginning. After Jesus' death his disciples continued to live as they had done in his company, and as their numbers grew they were obliged to introduce some kind of order, which became ever more elaborate. Before they knew, the church as an institution had become an accomplished fact. It regarded itself as the new Israel, and its very name "Ecclesia" is one of the names applied in the O.T. to the assembly of Israel. The view has commonly been held that the church in its origin was nothing but an imitation or counterpart of the Jewish theocracy, but it was something radically new. Its members were Jews and naturally fell back on the models offered them in Judaism, which was the only religion known to them. This, however, only affected the outward structure of the new community, which arose directly out of the message of Jesus.

The primitive church was the same in its essential character as the later one, which aimed at reproducing it on a larger scale; but it had several peculiarities which give it a place apart. 1) Its mood was one of intense ardour and confidence. Inspired by the Resurrection visions the disciples were now certain that Jesus was the Messiah, that he had ascended to heaven, that he had sent down the Spirit to help them. They believed that at any hour he would return in glory to bring in the Kingdom of God. This mood of exaltation gave a special character to the church worship. While modelled on that of the synagogue it allowed room for ecstatic manifestations, above all for the "speaking with tongues", in which prayer was made by means of an inarticulate language, supposed to be that of the Spirit. 2) The church embraced the whole life of its members, and took the form of a communistic society. This was no doubt due in some measure to the belief that the world was near its end and that private possessions had now lost their value. But it must also be explained from the effort to follow out literally the teaching of Jesus, who had declared that his disciples must surrender everything before they could enter the Kingdom. 3) There was nothing in the nature of an official ministry. A precedence was allowed to the immediate disciples of Jesus, and especially to Peter; and their counsels were generally followed. But in theory all believers were on the same footing. They all took an active part in the church worship, and no important step was taken except through the common meeting. It was assumed that the church was controlled solely by the Spirit, which was present in all its members and might express its will through any of them.

A society of this kind could only maintain itself for a short time, when it was small in numbers, and confined in one place, and animated by a tense enthusiasm which was bound, in natural course, to die down. In its primitive form the church may be said to have continued for about twelve years,—up to the time of the persecution by Herod Agrippa (A.D. 42). The disciples were then expelled from Jerusalem, and when they returned shortly afterwards they appear as an organized society, governed by a board of elders under the presidency of James. Before this time a new turn had been given to the whole Christian movement by the rise of the Gentile mission. The Gentile churches took the mother community for their example but inevitably made many changes in its theory and practice. Yet in substance the ideas of the primitive church were those which determined the whole future of Christianity. It has always been recognized that we must go back to them in order to understand the nature and purpose of the church.

E. F. Scott, *The Nature of the Early Church* (1941); O. Linton, *Das Problem der Urkirche* (1932).

E.F.S.

churchwarden (Anglican): A layman appointed to assist the rector or vicar in administering the temporal affairs of the parish. Normally two in number, of whom one may be named by the rector, the other chosen by the parishioners.

P.V.N.

church year: The early Christians carried over from Judaism the idea of a weekly holy day—the observance of Sunday* as a day of worship soon replacing the legal observance of the Sabbath*. They also continued the Passover*, now become the feast of the Resurrection. In the 2nd century the Quartodeciman* controversy revolved around the observance of Easter* on the 14th Nisan or the Sunday following. A short strict fast before Easter grew into the varied observance of Lent, while the 50 days between Easter and Pentecost* were treated as festal. From at least about 150, martyrs were remembered on the anniversaries of their deaths. Thus in ante-Nicene times the framework of the church year with the two cycles *de tempore* and *de sanctis* was already established. In the 4th century two feasts of the Manifestation of Christ, December 25 and January 6, were introduced; except in the Armenian Church, which observes only January 6, they are combined by devoting December 25 (Christmas) to the Birth and January 6 (Epiphany*) to other Manifestations. Further development is a fixing of details—the ordering of the cycle of Sundays and the increase of saints' days. In the Greek Church all Sundays depend on Easter or Pentecost, but in Western calendars some weeks before Christmas and after Epiphany are attached to those feasts. In the Greek calendar every day, in the Roman almost every day now has a saint or saints (others besides martyrs having been added since the 4th century, St. Mary and virgins since the 5th); but in observance Sundays take precedence over minor saints' days. At the Reformation Lutherans and Anglicans retained the temporal and part of the sanctoral cycle. The Reformed Churches sometimes rejected all except Sunday (to which, by a revival of a mediaeval tendency, English-speaking Puritans applied the sabbatarian laws), but observance of at least the major festivals is now almost universal. See festivals and holy days, Christian.

J. Dowden, *The Church Year and Kalendar* (1910); K. A. Kellner, *Heortology* (1908).

E.R.H.

church year cycle: The main points of the usual Western Church Year are the feasts of Christmas* and Easter*, each preceded by a penitential and followed by a festal season. Advent* (Latin *adventus*, coming, *i.e.*, of Christ) begins on the fourth Sunday before Christmas; the festal season continues through the Epiphany and its octave**. Lent* covers six Sundays and 40 weekdays before Easter; since the early Middle Ages the three preceding Sundays have been called Quinquagesima and, by extension, Sexagesima and Septuagesima (by inclusive reckoning, Quinquagesima is 50 days before Easter, Sexagesima 57, Septuagesima 64; hence the first name is correct, the second approximately so, the last not even that—but the influence of the series was strengthened by a symbolic parallel between the penitential season and the 70 years of the Babylonian Captivity). The last two weeks of Lent are Passiontide, further distinguished as Passion Week and Holy Week*. Ascension Day is the 40th day after Easter (Acts 1:3), Pentecost or Whitsunday** the seventh Sunday (Lev. 23:15, Acts 2:1). Its octave completes the paschal season. The variations in the date of Easter are adjusted by longer or shorter series of common Sundays, numbered after Epiphany (1-6) and after Pentecost (23-28)—in some mediaeval and in modern Lutheran and Anglican uses these last are numbered after Trinity (22-27), from the Feast of Trinity*, observed since the 13th century on the Sunday after Whitsunday. The Greek calendar is similar, except that Christmas does not affect the cycle and Sundays are numbered after Pentecost until pre-Lent; the pre-Lenten Sundays are named from the Gospel read (as Prodigal Son Sunday) or the gradual beginning of the fast (as Cheese Sunday, in the last week in which cheese may be eaten). Saints' Days and Holy Days are fixed by the civil calendar; in case of conflict minor Holy Days yield to common Sundays and all to the major festivals*. See bibliography under church year. E.R.H.

Church, the Brethren ("progressive"): See Dunkers.

Church of the Brethren ("conservative"): See Dunkers.

Church of Christ (Holiness) U. S. A.: A sect of colored holiness believers organized in 1894 by C. P. Jones, a Baptist preacher at Selma, Alabama. It claims 106 churches and 7,400 members. See pentecostal sects. E.T.C.

Church of Daniel's Band: A holiness sect organized in imitation of the early Methodist class meeting at Marine City, Mich., in 1893. It has 5 churches and 120 members. See Evangelistic Associations; holiness churches. E.T.C.

Church of England: 1) History. Romano-British Christianity, probably dating to the 2nd century, was weak even in the 4th, though it survived in Wales and planted the Celtic Churches of Ireland, Scotland, and Brittany, later of great importance. The conversion of the English began with Augustine's mission to Canterbury, 597. The English Churches, of Roman, Celtic, and other foundations, were united and organized under Archbishop Theodore of Tarsus, 668-690*. Foreign contacts were less after period of organization until the Norman conquest, 1066. Thereafter the two provinces of Canterbury and York functioned as a normal part of the Western Church—in practical matters Pope, King, and local bodies struggled for control. "The Church of England shall be free" in Magna Charta, 1215, referred mainly to capitular election of Bishops, gradually lost, however, to royal influence and papal "provisions;" the latter were forbidden by Statutes of Provisors and Praemunire (1351-1394), but common by royal permission, the Pope usually providing the King's candidates.

Henry VIII's policies forced repudiation of papal authority by clergy and Parliament, 1531-1534—Bishop Fisher, Thomas More, and some others died for refusing Oath of Supremacy. Under Edward VI (1547-1553) there was a rapid movement towards Protestantism, under Mary (1553-8) a short-lived Counter-Reformation. After Elizabeth's accession the "Elizabethan Settlement"* refused both extremes; Henry's claims were moderated, but Roman Catholics were subject to much persecution, and against Puritans* (at this time mainly Presbyterian) the Church remained Episcopal in government, liturgical in worship, non-Calvinist in theology. After the Puritan triumph under the Commonwealth the Church was restored with the King, but ceased to be inclusively national with expulsion of the Nonconformists, 1662 (recognized by Toleration Act, 1689). Eighteenth century inertia was broken by the Methodist revival, but the Methodist Societies separated after John Wesley's death, 1791. Evangelicals* since about 1760 and Anglo-Catholics* since 1833 have brought new life to the Church, which retains contact with the intellectual and civic life of the nation. In spite of occasional tension, disestablishment in England (widely discussed after Reform Bill of 1832) seems remote, though effected in Ireland (Church of Ireland nominally united with English, 1800, disestablished, 1869) and Wales (1920).

2) Organization and Status. The Anglican Communion includes, besides the above, the Episcopal Church of Scotland (separate from Church of Scotland since 1689), Anglican Churches in U. S. A., Canada, West Indies, South Africa, Australia, New Zealand, India, China, and Japan, and various missionary dioceses. Its organ is the informal Lambeth Conference of Bishops, meeting normally every ten years (since 1867). Except in England it is self-governing on the basis of a constitutional episcopate, with Synods of clergy and laity. The constitutional position in England is obscure; the "establishment" consists of legal and personal restrictions on the one hand (the most conspicuous being the obligation of chapters by a law of 1534 to elect the royal nominee), and rights to ancient endowments and a vague but probably useful national position on the other. The Convocations of Bishops and clergy of the two provinces have since 1532 required royal assent to canons; a legal decision of 1736 denied them the right to bind the laity. Since 1919 they have formed with a House of Laity the National Assembly, which may propose ecclesiastical measures for parliamentary confirmation; few have been rejected, but among them an important one, the Prayer Book Revision, 1927-8 (See Book of Common Prayer), after much controversy and discussion (and in fact by Nonconformist and Northern Irish votes). At present there are 43 dioceses in England, and c. 20,000 clergy; active membership is reflected by Easter communicants, usually about 2,800,000—adherents are probably several times as numerous, and in the rest of the Communion at least as many again.

3) Theology. From about 675-775 England was a center of ecclesiastical learning, its chief lights being Aldhelm of Sherborne, the Venerable Bede, historian and commentator, and Alcuin, through whom England contributed to Carolingian scholarship. King Alfred (870-901) did much to revive learning, especially by translations, after Danish invasions; vernacular homilies and other

works were produced to the end of the Anglo-Saxon period. Lanfranc and Anselm of Canterbury were among the theologians brought to England by the Normans; the Universities of Oxford (c. 1167) and Cambridge (1209) were among the first north of the Alps. Fourteenth century Nominalism at Oxford produced the anti-ecclesiastical views of William of Ockham and John Wycliffe (condemned 1382). Wycliffe influenced John Hus** to an extent yet undetermined; in England his ideas, repressed by Church and State, lived on in the Lollards and appear in the Erastian strain in Anglicanism and in the Congregational tendency of English Protestantism. In the early 16th century learning revived with a group of Catholic humanists and reformers, of whom Dean Colet and Thomas More were the most conspicuous.

After the Reformation, Anglican theology, when it clarifies itself as neither Roman Catholic nor Calvinist, strives to continue the long tradition of English Catholic scholarship. Archbishop Parker (1559-1575) published Anglo-Saxon homilies, while the "judicious Hooker" (died 1600) in his *Laws of Ecclesiastical Polity* defended the Elizabethan settlement. His love of the Fathers and devotion to the Incarnation as the central dogma have remained typical of Anglican theological writing. Even more than by theologians, however, the Anglican temper was formed by the Book of Common Prayer—Cranmer's great work of 1549, considerably revised in 1552, and gradually restored and amplified in later revisions. Its services combine Reformation loyalty to the Bible with Catholic love for the Church and its ancient ways of worship. In the 17th century Hooker's work was continued by the Caroline Divines, while the Cambridge Platonists were the beginning of the Broad Church* school. The Deist controversy of the 18th century produced a solid school of apologists; Bishop Butler's *Analogy of Religion . . . to the Constitution and Course of Nature* has been widely influential. The Oxford Movement (1833-1845) led to a revival and extension of the Catholic tradition in Anglican thought; the Broad Church group became more articulate (*Essays and Reviews*, 1862), and Christian Socialism found an early champion in F. D. Maurice (1805-1872). In 1889 *Lux Mundi*, edited by Charles Gore, later Bishop, was an Anglo-Catholic effort to come to terms with the principle of development; some ten years later Liberal influence found expression in the Modern Churchmen's Union. Among the tendencies of our day may be mentioned an increased interest in social theory and practice, in which the school of Maurice has broadened out to influence almost the whole Church, a renewed study of Moral Theology (Bishop Kirk), a Christian approach to the organic philosophy of science (A. E. Taylor, Archbishop Temple), and such diverse trends as neo-Thomist philosophy, pacifist ethics, and the liturgical movement*. The specific corruption of Anglicanism is a disposition to excessive contentment and calm. But today its practical activities are numerous and its intellectual life vigorous. There is much interest in the pressing problems of church unity and world organization. And in the person of William Temple it has for the first time since Anselm a primate who is the ablest philosopher of the Church of England as well as an energetic promoter of its practical mission.

G. K. A. Bell, *A Brief Sketch of the Church of England* (1929); Y. Brilioth, *The Anglican Revival, Studies in the Oxford Movement* (1925); S. C. Carpenter, *Church and People, 1789-1889* (1933); F. J. Foakes-Jackson, *Anglican Church Principles* (1924); *The Lambeth Conference* (1930); More and Cross, *Anglicanism* (1935); Stephens and Hunt, ed., *A History of the English Church*, 10 vols. (1899-1910).

E.R.H.

Church of the Full Gospel, the, Inc.: A religious sect of four churches and 300 members, organized by R. H. Askew at Goldsboro, North Carolina, in 1935. It is a conservative group teaching sanctification, the second coming of Christ, eternal punishment, and the baptism of the Holy Spirit. Foot washing is practiced. See holiness churches. E.T.C.

Church of Georgia: See Eastern Orthodox Churches.

Church of God: A pentecostal sect with headquarters at Cleveland, Tenn. It was first organized as "Christian Union" in 1886, reorganized as the "Holiness Church" in 1902, and took its present name in 1907. It claims to be in accord with Methodist theology, but stresses "second blessing" holiness, speaking in unknown tongues, immersion, and feet washing. It has 1,081 churches and 45,000 members. See pentecostal sects. E.T.C.

Church of God, Adventist: See Adventists.

Church of God (Anderson, Ind.): A holiness sect (distinguished from others having the same name by including the address of its headquarters) originating as a branch of the Winebrenner evangelistic movement. It stresses sanctification but repudiates speaking in unknown tongues. It has 1,032 churches and 57,000 members. See holiness churches. E.T.C.

Church of God (Apostolic): A holiness sect organized at Danville, Ky., in 1897 by Thos. J. Cox under the name of "Christian Faith Band Church." The present name was assumed in 1919. Feet washing and immersion are practiced. See Evangelistic Associations; holiness churches.

E.T.C.

Church of God (Oregon, Ill): See Adventist sects.

Church of God (Salem, West Virginia): A sabbatarian and adventist* sect which branched off from the main trunk of Millerite adventism (see Adventist Sects) in 1861 when the main body adopted the name "Seventh Day Adventist Denomination," and also because of disbelief in the inspiration of the adventist prophetess, Mrs. E. G. White. It is fundamentalist and stresses literal interpretation of the Bible. Its officers are twelve apostles, seventy elders, and seven stewards. It now claims that its real headquarters is Jerusalem. There are 39 churches and 1,150 members. E.T.C.

Church of God and Saints of Christ: A Negro sect founded in 1896 by William S. Crowdy, a railway cook, in response to a vision. Its doctrines include a belief that the Negroes are descendants of the "lost tribes of Israel," hence circumcision, the Passover rites, and other Jewish customs must be observed along with Christian ceremonials. The sect has a communistic* colony at Belleville, Va. E.T.C.

Church of God as Organized By Christ: A small sect originating in a schism among the Mennonite* Brethren in Christ led by P. J. Kaufman in 1886. The cause of the schism was a general dissatisfaction with all other churches. It is an "anti-sect," marked by its oppositions rather than affirmations. It opposes "second work holyites" or sanctification, other sects, union meetings, tobacco, lodges, war, suits at law, Sunday schools, revivals, talking in unknown tongues, shouting, theatres, jewelry, fine clothing, creeds, and "a hireling ministry." It claims to be the "true church." It has 13 congregations (but only 3 buildings) and 360 members. See Evangelistic Associations; holiness churches. E.T.C.

Church of God in Christ: A Negro sect founded by C. H. Mason, a Baptist preacher, in 1897. It is pentecostal in nature, emphasizing the "gift of tongues" and divine healing. It has 772 churches and 31,000 members in 36 states. See pentecostal sects. E.T.C.

Church of Ireland: See Ireland, Church of.

Church of Jesus Christ, the: See Latter Day Saints.

Church of the Nazarene: The largest of the holiness denominations, the outgrowth of the National Holiness Movement following the War Between the States. It has 2,197 churches and 136,000 members. It is represented in all the States.

The Church of the Nazarene represents the merger of a large number of holiness sects and associations. Over the years it has had several names. In 1890 several New England churches organized the Central Evangelical Holiness Association; in 1895 other churches organized the Association of Pentecostal Churches of America in New York; in 1896 these united under the latter name. The First Church of the Nazarene was formed at Los Angeles in 1895, and in 1907 the Nazarenes united with the Pentecostal Association, taking the name of Pentecostal Church of the Nazarene. Other holiness bodies joined from time to time: New Testament Church of Christ, Independent Holiness Church (united in 1904 and called the Holiness Church of Christ) and the Pentecostal Alliance (or Mission). In 1919 the word "Pentecostal" was dropped and the sect became The Church of the Nazarene. See holiness churches.

Chapman, *A History of the Church of the Nazarene;* Jernigan, *Pioneer Days of the Holiness Movement in the Southwest;* E. T. Clark, *Small Sects in America* (1937). E.T.C.

Church of Revelation, the: A religious sect founded by Janet Stine Lewis at Long Beach, California, in 1930. The only distinctive principle is the practice of metaphysical and magnetic healing. Ministers are unsalaried. There are three churches and about 350 members. E.T.C.

Church of Scotland: See Scotland, Church of.

church school: See Sunday School movement in the United States.

Church Student movements: See student religious organizations.

Churches of Christ: a) Many of the older New England churches, antedating serious competition of other denominations with the Congregational standing order, are called Churches of Christ, e.g., "The United Church of Christ in New Haven." b) Local congregations of Disciples of Christ are often called Churches of Christ. c) The only group which has no other name, and the one to which it refers in government statistics, is the body of churches which separated from the Disciples of Christ*. They are strict constructionists in "restoring primitive Christianity," to the extent that they repudiate missionary societies and the use of the organ in public worship, both of which are deemed unscriptural. Some also disallow Sunday schools and the use of individual communion cups. Their extreme congregational independency does not admit any general organization, and their statistics are therefore uncertain, but they probably number about 500,000, with their greatest strength in the South, especially in Texas. Their separate existence was first recognized in the religious census of 1906. W.E.G.

Churches of Christ in Christian Union. See Christian Union.

Churches of God, Holiness: A Negro holiness sect organized by K. H. Burrus at Atlanta, Ga., in 1916. It teaches divine healing and entire sanctification. There are 35 churches and 5,800 members. See pentecostal sects. E.T.C.

Churches of God in Jesus Christ: See Adventists.

Churches of God in North America: A conservative sect which originated in the revivals of John Winebrenner, a preacher of the German Reformed Church*. He left that denomination (under charges growing out of his preaching of experience) about 1825 and organized a "Church of God," later called the "General Eldership of the Church of God." In 1896 the name became General Eldership of the Churches of God in North America. These churches oppose "sectarianism" and insist that "Bible things should be known by Bible names, and a Bible name should not be given to anything not mentioned in the Bible."

Immersion and feet washing are practiced. The sect operates Findlay College at Findlay, Ohio, and has a publishing house at Harrisburg, Pa. There are 352 churches and 30,000 members. E.T.C.

Churches of the Living God: Two Negro sects growing out of a group organized by William Christian at Wrightsville, Ark., in 1889 under the name of "Church of the Living God, Christian Workers for Friendship." In 1925 E. J. Cain led off a group which took the name "Church of the Living God, the Pillar and Ground of Truth." Mrs. Ethel L. Christian is now "Chiefess" of the body operating under the original name. She lives at Memphis, Tenn., and claims doctrines given to her by direct revelation which are not communicated to "gentiles." Among these is the revelation that Jesus Christ and King David were Negroes. The "Christian Workers for Fellowship" branch has 96 churches and 4,500 members. "The Pillar and Ground of Truth" has 119 churches and 4,800 members. See pentecostal sects. E.T.C.

Churches of the New Jerusalem: See New Jerusalem, Church of the.

churches, social work of: See social gospel; social work of the churches.

ciborium: (From Gr. *kiborion,* cup) 1) A chalice-like covered vessel from which the consecrated eucharistic bread is communicated and in which it is reserved upon the altar. 2) A canopy supported on pillars and covering the altar. P.V.N.

circumambulation: Ceremonial walking around an object or person. It is usually done three times, keeping the right side toward the object encircled. The practice is almost universal. Whatever may have been the origin of the custom, the many peoples have used it for many purposes—to show respect, to give protection, to consecrate a building site, to secure good fortune, to identify oneself with or acquire the sanctity of a sacred object or holy person. Walking in the reverse direction shows disrespect and has evil effects. See death and burial practices; magic circle. A.E.H.

circumcision: Circumcision, or amputation of the male prepuce, is one of the oldest as well as one of the most wide-spread customs. It is or was practised (although with many variations as to the method of circumcision, age at the time of circumcision, who may perform the rite, etc.), among the Jews, Mohammedans, Egyptians, Polynesians, the Indian tribes of the New World and many of the primitive tribes of Africa and Australia. In fact it is estimated that 1/7 of the male population of the world is circumcised.

Many theories are advanced to explain the origin and purpose of this custom; such as a) for hygienic reasons, b) as a mark of tribal affiliation, c) as a preparation for sexual life, d) as an initiatory test of courage before acceptance into the tribe, e) as a means of sanctifying the generative faculties, f) as a sacrifice redeeming the male from the god who gave him life.

For the Jews circumcision is one of the most important of the 613 commandments. It was interpreted as a sign of the covenant between God and Israel and, therefore, indispensable as a mark of affiliation with the latter. (cf. Gen. 17:10-14; Ex. 12:44-49).

In the Talmud*, many prescriptions are laid down regulating the act of circumcision. It may be performed even on the Sabbath, if that is the eighth day after birth. It consists of a) *milah,* the amputation of the prepuce, b) *periah,* the baring of the glans, and c) *metzitzah,* staunching the flow of blood. Appropriate benedictions are recited before and after the circumcision and the child is given a name at this time. The circumcision ceremony is usually followed by a festive meal, at which a special Grace is recited in which reference is made to this event. See feasting; Jewish Christianity; Mohammedanism.

E.B.—L.F.

Circumcision, Feast of the: January 1. Circumcision was a sign of the covenant between God and the Jewish nation. The feast commemorates Christ's reverence for the Law in undergoing this rite eight days after His birth. The feast was also observed as an occasion of reparation for the immoral pagan excesses connected with the worship of Janus on this day. See New Year's celebrations.

Cf. Addis and Arnold, *A Catholic Dictionary,* p. 185. S.C.

Cistercian Order, the: A rigid revival of the Benedictine* rule, substituting manual labour for learning. It was founded by Robert de Thierry, Abbot of Citeaux (Lat. *Cistercium*) whence the order derived its name. Its main point lay in the insistence on simplicity in its churches, houses and dress. Their habit was a white gown and hood over a black cassock. A black cloak was worn outside the precincts of the monastery. Their best known members were Stephen Harding, the third Abbot and St. Bernard*. The order spread rapidly as far as Russia in the East, Jerusalem, to England where the shrines of Fountaines and Rivaulx Abbeys testify to the wealth the Order acquired. In Henry VIII's* reign, 75 houses and 26 nunneries of the Order were suppressed in England alone. Cf. Caesarius of Heisterbach.

F.W.B.

city missions: The agencies and work by which the church ministers to the spiritual and material needs of the poor and under-privileged in the cities of Christian lands. It includes housing, clothing, feeding, reforming, teaching, providing occupation and recreation, preaching, counseling and social case work. P.E.J.

Civa: See Shiva.

civil law: See law.

clairvoyance: See occultism; parapsychology; psychical research, societies for.

Clark Foundation, the: The Clark Foundation, in the amount of $10,000, established by the late Mr. Arthur O. Clark at Pomona College, Claremont, California, makes it possible for the college to offer each year a lecture or course of lectures in the general field of religion. A.C.M.

Clarke, James Freeman: (1810-1888) Unitarian minister. Born, Hanover, N. H.; d. Boston, Mass.; Harvard College, 1829; Divinity School, 1833. Minister, Louisville, Ky., 1833-40; Church of the Disciples, Boston, 1841-88; Professor at Harvard Divinity School, 1867-71. Established his Boston church as perfectly free in faith and customs, less bound by traditions than the older ones, and made it a vital force in all religious, moral, social and political reforms. Apart from his work as pastor, he was long a leading spirit in the organized work of his denomination, active in public education, social betterment, anti-slavery, civil-service reform, equal suffrage, temperance. Irenic and of wide religious sympathies he published *Orthodoxy: its Truths and Errors* (1866); *Ten Great Religions* (1871); *Common-sense in Religion* (1874); *Vexed Questions in Theology* (1885); etc.

See *Autobiography* (1891), ed. E. E. Hale.

E.M.W.

Clarke, William Newton: (1841-1912) Baptist minister and theologian; graduated, Madison (now Colgate) University, 1861, Colgate Theological Seminary, 1863, held important pastorates in Newton, Mass., Montreal, and in Hamilton, N. Y.; taught N.T. Interpretation in Toronto Baptist College; became professor of Christian Theology, Ethics and Apologetics, Colgate University in 1890. Here he taught with marked ability until his death.

Author: *An Outline of Christian Theology* (1898); *The Christian Doctrine of God* (1909); *Can I Believe in God the Father* (1899), *Sixty Years with the Bible* (1909); *The Ethics of Jesus* (1911). A biography was published in 1916. Dr. Clarke's *An Outline of Christian Theology*, notable for its clarity, experiential quality and irenic spirit, at once met with approval and became one of the most acceptable and constructive texts in Systematic Theology.

J.W.B.

Class, Gustav: (1836-1908) He taught philosophy at Erlangen. Not unlike R. Eucken*, he was influenced by Fichte and Steffensen. He had the courage of continuing a metaphysic of the spirit, in which he assigned to religion a universal significance.

Untersuchungen zur Phänomenologie und Ontologie des menschlichen Geistes (Leipzig, 1896); *Die Realität der Gottesidee* (München, 1904). H.H.

class struggle: See socialism.

classics of Confucianism: See Confucianism.

classification of religions: The divisions, classes, and subclasses, etc., into which the religions of history differentiate; a grouping of the historical religions into kinds, requisite to the scientific study of religion.

Classifications have heretofore uniformly failed in that they have impaired the wholeness or integrity of religious cults and systems of the past. Such classifications used criteria which emphasized the qualitative, at the expense of the quantitative, aspect of a religion. They failed to show with clearness what it was in religious history that definitely marked off a "religion" as a historical whole; and what it was that determined the historical unity and the individuality of a single religion within the entire field. They failed to make a thorough use of the basic religious concepts found imbedded in, and giving character to, the actual historical religions.

Examples of types of classifiers will illustrate. A) Hegel* tried to classify historical phenomena in religion with a concept not found in the historical religions themselves. Quite significantly, he did pay his respects to genuine basic concepts of the religious factor in historical religions of Hebrews and Greeks[1], concepts actually possessing control over religious patterns; however he failed to use them in their historical character, and restricted their use to the service of his speculative concept of the *Absolute*. This so altered the historical meaning they actually carried in their service as concepts, that all attempts of Hegelians to perfect Hegel's classification, without having to alter his criterion, were bound to fail. B) Maurice Vernes, typical of another large group of classifiers, failed in that he made use of culture, a non-religious concept, for a criterion.[2] Concepts such as race, culture, language, geography, etc., are ineffectual as criteria for grouping religions of history for scientific study of religion. C) Goblet D'Alviella[3] is an example of a large group of classifiers which used *entity* concepts. He sought to arrange religions in a series according to groups of religious entities, from nature worship and worship of the dead to monotheism.

The problem of classification approached a solution satisfactory for scientific study when, for a criterion, consistent use was made of the concept of the religious factor, which is found imbedded in each and every religion of history. Once the evolution of the meaning in the concepts of the religious factor in the historical materials, was uncovered, there was found a skeletal frame or pattern of the religions in the entire field of history. Materials of a new classification were revealed; they were the characteristics of the religions themselves, were genetic in nature, and had their limitations both in place and time. Historical religions were observable as wholes, and required definitions that depended upon the range of the basic concept involved. And that basic concept was the concept of the religious factor.

Briefly, the classification indicated the following: The entire field of religions is seen to break into two great divisions: *two-factor religion*, and *one-factor religion***. The one-factor religion is differentiated into five subdivisions which for convenience and identification are: *ruah* religion, *nous* religion, *mainyu* religion, *brahman* religion, and *ch'i* religion; each of these five are further differentiated into religious systems which serve about 90% of the peoples of the world today: conceptually, from the standpoint of structure and function, they all have class relationships. In the two-factor religion, there are differentiations which break as wholes, and are conveniently identified by the manner of life of the human societies represented: whether hunter religion, herder religion, religion of hoe-culture peoples, or religion of field-culture or urban culture peoples. Each such class has its member representatives, which are religions of single societies . . . If, therefore differentiation of historical religion is followed beyond the divisions, representing the religious factor on a man-nature basis, it reaches next to the classes representing the religious factor on a region-culture basis; beyond that it reaches to the subclasses, representing the religious factor on an integrating functioning religious society basis . . . If followed to its end the differentiation reaches the individual religious member of human society.[4]

[1] G. W. F. Hegel, *Philosophy of History,* tr. by J. Sibree (1901), pp. 53-60.
[2] Maurice Vernes, *L'Histoire des Religions* (Paris, 1887), pp. 67-94.
[3] Goblet D'Alviella, *The Origin and Growth of the Conception of God* (London, 1897), sec. ed., pp. xii-xv.
[4] For fuller consideration of the whole question of classification, see Fred L. Parrish, *The Classification of Religions* (1941). F.L.P.

classis: In some Reformed polities, e.g., that of the Reformed Church in America*, a judicatory corresponding to the presbytery*, i.e., a body of the ministers of a region and elders representing the churches, having authority over churches and ministers under the superior judicatories. R.H.N.

Claudius of Turin: (d. *ca.* 827) Bishop. A Spaniard (tainted by the Adoptionism of Felix of Urgel?*), he was favored by the Carolingian court because of Biblical scholarship, having compiled several commentaries (Genesis through Kings, Matthew, Pauline epistles). Opposing cult of pictures, crosses, saints, he engaged in controversy with Jonas of Orléans and the Irish Dungal. A.C.

Claver, St. Peter: (1580-1654) Spanish Jesuit, for thirty-five years the volunteer servant and spiritual father of the African negroes who were brought to Cartagena, Colombia, to be sold as slaves. E.A.R.

Cleanthes: (ca. 304-233 B.C.) A leader of the Athenian school of Stoics* following Zeno of Citium*. Author of a "Hymn to Zeus" (tr. in Bakewell, *Source Book of Ancient Philosophy*). J.E.N.

clearstory: See nave.

Clement of Alexandria: (A.D. c. 150 - c. 213) Christian Platonist, Logos theologian *par excellence,* teacher of Origen*, by general consent one of the most attractive figures in Christian history. Clement like his great pupil sets out from the Creed and appeals steadfastly to Scripture. He is important as a witness to the virtual completion of the N.T. Canon. The center, however, of Clement's Christianity is neither the Father in Heaven nor the Son made man to be the Redeemer of the world. It is the ever-active Logos, the guide, guardian, champion, and educator of humanity. This Logos is related to the One or highest God as mind to its unknown foundation; through it the Absolute enters into relations, the many are derived from the one. Bigg credits Clement with being the real founder of Neo-Platonism* (*Christian Platonists,* p. 64). See Pantaenus.

The principal works of Clement are the *Protrepticus* or "Exhortation", which has been called an evangelistic tract; the *Paedagogus,* which is concerned with the training of the Christian convert; and the *Stromateis* or "Carpet-bags", which is the most theological of the trilogy and expounds a Christian *gnosis.* Notable also is the one homily of Clement extant, *Quis Dives Salvetur.*

J. P. Migne, ed *Patrologia Graeca* (cf. the critical ed. of Stählin in the *Griechischen Christlichen Schriftsteller* series); *Ante-Nicene Fathers,* II; C. Bigg, *Chr. Platonists of Alex.* (1886); E. de Faye, *Clément d'Alexandrie* (1898); R. B. Tollinton, *Clement of Alexandria* (2 vols. 1914); standard histories of doctrine. C.W.L.

Clement, St., Pope of Rome (ca. 92-101) and Clementine Epistles: Pope St. Clement was after Linus and Cletus (Anacletus) the third successor of St. Peter as Bishop of Rome. Since Origen's* time he has been identified with the Clement mentioned by St. Paul in Phil. 4, 3. Whether he was a Jewish- (Lightfoot, Nestle) or heathen-(Funk) convert to Christianity is disputed. According to Tertullian (*De Praesc.* 32) he was consecrated a bishop by St. Peter himself. Despite the silence of Ireneus, Eusebius and Jerome, he was honored as a martyr and a crypt was erected to his memory during the reign of Constantine*. Whether he is to be identified with or is distinct from the martyred Consul (A.D. 95) T. Flavius Clemens, is still a subject of controversy. The *Martyrium Clementis* (IV century cf. Migne, PG II 617) is certainly legendary and based on unhistorical documents. According to a well-founded tradition, the Apostle of the Slavs, St. Cyril, found the relics of the saint in the Crimea during the IX century and brought them to Rome, depositing them in the present Basilica of St. Clement (now in charge of the Irish Dominicans) where they are still honored. Feast Day in the Roman Liturgy: Nov. 23; in the Greek and Syrian: Nov. 24; in the Russian Church, Nov. 24. St. Clement is looked upon as the first of the "Apostolic Fathers"* and is usually depicted with an anchor, because allegedly drowned for the Faith.

Clementine Writings.

Of the many writings ascribed to St. Clement only his first Epistle to the Corinthians is considered authentic. According to Ireneus*, who styles it "most important" and Eusebius* who calls it "magnificent", this letter of Clement was read publicly in the assemblies of the early Christians and given the same prominence as the Sacred Scriptures themselves. The purpose of the Epistle was to quell disturbances and misunderstandings between the clerics and laics at Corinth. (cf. I Cor. 1, 10-16). The first part of the Epistle

(Ch. 1-36) has preserved to posterity precious descriptions of Ancient Christian life, practices and doctrines; the second part (Ch. 27-61) enters specifically into the causes of the controversies at Corinth and exhorts the faithful to penance and submission to the presbyters. Important for the historian is the reference to the martyrdom of St. Peter at Rome; his primacy (cf. "Pope" and "Peter, St., First Bishop of Rome") also over the Church at Corinth; and the journey of St. Paul to Spain.

The *"Second Epistle of St. Clement to the Corinthians"*, a homily of general content, although delivered at Rome or Corinth as early as ca. 150, is not authentic but rather the composition of another. Hilgenfeld and Harnack would adscribe it to Pope Soter. Other unauthentic writings are: Two Epistles *"Ad Virgines"* (i.e., to the unmarried), perhaps of the III century; the *Pseudo-Clementine Homilies;* the *Apostolic Constitutions* and the so-called *Clementine Liturgy,* contained therein is a Jacobite (Syrian Monophysite) Liturgy; the *Clementine Canons* and five letters placed at the beginning of the Pseudo-Isidoran Decretals*. See canons of various churches.

For the Epistle of St. Clement to the Corinthians cf. Migne, *PG* (Paris, 1857-66), Vol. II; P. Young (Junius, Giunio) (Oxford, 1633); 2nd ed., *ib.* (1637), "editio princeps"; J. B. Cotelier, *Patres Aevi Apostolici* (Paris, 1672); Engl. tr. in Roberts-Donaldson, *Ante-Nicene Fathers* (1911-19); cf. Otto Bardenhewer, *Geschichte der Altchristlichen Literature* I, 116-31 (Freiburg, 1913-24)²; *Id. Patrologie* (Freiburg, 1894); Adolf von Harnack, *Geschichte der Altchristlichen Literatur bis Eusebius,* Vol. I (Leipzig, 1893-1904); Gustav Krüger, *History of Early Christian Literature in the First Three Centuries* (1897); J. B. Lightfoot, *Clement of Rome* 2 vols. (London, 1890)—highly praised; *Id. The Apostolic Fathers* (London, 1890), Vol. II, Part 1, 271-316; Joseph Tixeront, *Handbook of Patrology* 2 (1923); Gebhard Harnack, *Texte und Untersuchungen zur Geschichte der altchristlichen Literatur* (Leipzig, (1883-1913); *Cath. Encyc.* IV, 12-17. R.M.H.

Clement, XI, Pope: See Camisards; Unigenitus.

Clement XIV, Pope: (1769-74) Giovanni Lorenzo (his name as a Franciscan-Conventual) Ganganelli was born October 31, 1705 at Sant' Arcangelo, near Rimini, the son of a physician. In 1723 he entered the Order Friars Minor* Conventual; became in 1746 Consultor of the Holy Office, and in 1759 cardinal. A learned theologian, he was mild and lovable, holy and free from Nepotism. It is untrue that he promised the Bourbon princes—unduly active through their ambassadors at the Holy See in the stormy conclave that preceded his election—that if elected pope he would suppress the Jesuits*; at most he recognized the possibility of such a papal action. Following the example of Benedict XIV* he was lenient and perhaps too conciliatory towards the secular courts of the "ultra-enlightened" age of the late XVIII century, with which, as expressed in his first Encyclical, he wished to be at peace so as the more easily to combat irreligion. He dispensed with the annual reading of the "Holy Thursday Bull" (*In Coena Domini*) regarding papal censures for certain violations by secular princes. His relations with England were friendly. He officially received with royal honors the King's brother at the Vatican in 1772, while refusing the same honors to the pretender. His friendly gesture prepared the way eventually for Catholic Emancipation in England. His nuncio (cf. "Papal Legates") was favorably received at the English Court. In the East, the Nestorian Patriarch Mar Simeon and six of his Suffragens, were received into union with Rome. His conciliatory spirit enabled him to renew diplomatic relations with Portugal, broken off since 1760, and to bridge over difficulties with Parma. But no concessions would satisfy the Bourbons in their demands for the suppression of the Jesuits. If Clement finally did yield it must be remembered: 1) that the trouble did not begin under his pontificate; it was inherited as an unwelcome child from his predecessors, especially Benedict XIV and Clement XIII. (cf. *Cath. Encyc.* IV, 32-34 and II, 434-5); 2) that the Jesuits had already been civilly expelled from Spain, France, Sicily, Parma and Portugal *before* Clement XIV became pope; 3) that Clement resisted to the bitter end and only gradually put his decision into effect by suppressing their colleges in the Papal States and prohibiting the reception of novices; 4) that the Brief *"Dominus et Redemptor"* of July 21, 1773 was merely a disciplinary measure, as used repeatedly by other popes in similar circumstances; and 5) that the Brief waives entirely the truthfulness or untruthfulness of the accusations of the Bourbons against the Jesuits and merely intends to meet a temporary emergency—to "save the body as it were through the amputation of an otherwise important limb". Clement XIV personally had the highest regard for the Jesuits, by whom as a youth at Rimini he had been educated. He suppressed the Jesuits not because they were Jesuits, but in spite of it. The return of Avignon and Benevento by France and the Kingdom of Naples was hardly a consolation for the sorely tried pope. The good work done by the Jesuits suffered as a result of the suppression primarily in the American colonies that had been under Bourbon crowns. During his short pontificate Clement sought to better the deplorable financial conditions of the Papal States*; to encourage commerce and industry; and to subsidize arts and sciences. He began the valuable Pio-Clementine Museum of the Vatican. It is untrue that he was poisoned by a Jesuit or that his mind was affected before death.

The Bulls and Discourses of Clement XIV were published in Italian at Florence in 1845; his (Latin) letters and briefs by A. Theiner, 2 vols. at Paris, 1852. His best sympathetic and apologetical life is by the same A. Theiner, *Geschichte des Pontifikates Clem. XIV,* 2 vols. (Paris, 1853). Other biographies and studies by: F. X. Ravignan (Paris, 1854); J. Crétineu-Joly, *Clem. XIV et les jésuits* 3 (Paris, 1848). Pastor's story of Clement XIV was left unfinished, due to death, and was published posthumously, with additional chapters by others. It forms volume XVI, parts 2 and 3 of the original German edition. It is rather "un-Pastorian" in its harsh criticism of a pope and provoked unfavorable comment. The Italian translation by P. Cenci appeared at Rome (Desclée, 1933), Vol. XVI, part 2. The English trans. has not as yet appeared. *Cath. Encyc.* IV, 34-38. R.M.H.

clergy: (Gr., *kleros,* a lot—Acts 1:17—, hence late Lat. *clericus*) The origin of the ministry of the Church is shrouded in historical confusion out of which has emerged the opportunity to create systems of traditions of artificial clarity in order to justify some or other form of authority. In the NT there is little or nothing to distinguish definitely any cadre of *offices* from a series of functions necessary for the maintenance and expansion of the Church, the Apostles alone excepted. There is nothing to indicate that the seventy had any permanent basis or that the "seven deacons*" were anything more than lay officers appointed to administer to the relief of the poor and to relieve the apostles of secular duties. The *presbyteroi* are the senior members of the church, whether in age or standing is not clear even from I *Ep. Clem.;* the oversight of the Church is also initially rather a function than an "office", and is (as late as the Canons of Hippolytus) apparently confined to an individual church, as the equivalent of *pastor* (*poimēn*). After the Gnostic and Montanist crisis, however, another factor comes into prominence: the concept of orthodoxy resting in the tradition handed down from bishop to bishop and ultimately derived in direct succession from the Apostles. The appeal to episcopal or apostolic succession* is used in this sense by Irenaeus* in reply to the Gnostic successions. The transformation of the episcopate* to its later form of the monarchical episcopate with its seat (see) in a city is difficult to account for historically. As early as Ignatius*, the bishop* is the symbol of the presence of Christ at the eucharist, but this is not incompatible with either the *presbyteros* or *poimēn* in his duty of supervision over the individual church. It is suggested that the cause lies elsewhere. In pre-Christian times the word *episcopos* is applied to a variety of duties: the inspector (*episcopos*) of cavalry, and the supervisor (*episcopos*) of a *deme* or racial unit within a city or its *territorium.* Where there were several *presbyteroi,* one was the president of their *collegium,* and he appears to have performed the *function* of episcopate. The combination of these two functions, together with membership of the city council which advised or was responsible to the governor, would account for the elements of permanent tenure and civil power which becomes one of the characteristic features of the episcopate, even before 313. The ecclesiastical factor is found in the Cyprianic* conception of the *ecclesia* as limited to the clergy, the laity being in a subject status, and the crystallization of the doctrine of Apostolic Succession as a principle of continuing authority and Divine Right. (In Persia, there is a parallel development after 499, and there the *Catholikos* has the status of an ecclesiastical *wazir* or minister of state.)See Nestorianism. The process is completed by the increase of civil privilege and duties under Constantine I and Theodosius I and, in the West by the Valentinian Decree of 445, by which "the primacy of the Apostolic See is assured by the merit of St. Peter, prince of the episcopate, by the rank of the City of Rome and also by the authority of the Sacred Synod." In Pseudo-Isidore's Decretals (c. 850 A.D.), the Cyprianic concept is defined in terms of the Holy Roman Empire that "the humblest priest is superior to the mightiest emperor" and the Pope is the supreme judge of Christendom.

The system that emerged conformed to the Roman Imperial system. The usual term for a bishop was *Papa* (pope*); this was more commonly used of a Patriarch (bishop of an Apostolic See), before its use was confined to the Bishop of Rome. In Rome, the chief clergy of the City came to be called *Cardinales*—of three ranks: bishops, priests, and deacons. A Papal Domestic chaplain now receives the title *monsignor*. Outside Rome, an Archbishop receives the jurisdiction of a province; the bishop, of a diocese, the presbyter or priest (*sacerdos*) of a parish or other charge. The bishop's secular officer is the Archdeacon, originally the chief of the deacons. In addition there were the ranks of lector (reader), sub-deacon and other lay offices. In the Greek Orthodox Church and its kindred, the names are generally the same in Greek form, though the Archimandrite (Abbot or chief of abbots) plays a more markedly ecclesiastical *rôle* than his Western counterpart. In Persia, the title Pope is supplanted by *Catholicos* or *Mar Catholicos.*

Since the Reformation, the Western systems have generally assumed a simpler form. The Churches of England and Sweden have retained the ranks of Archbishop, Bishop, Priest and Deacon (the threefold ministry). The Scottish (Presbyterian) and Reformed (Calvinist) have retained the word Presbyter for the full minister or pastor; the Lutheran Churches, Congregational, Baptist and their derivatives, pastor; the English Methodists: superintendents, minister; in the U.S.A., bishops are added over the superintendents. The main effect of the Reformation was to revive lay selection and the authority of the congregation and so to avoid the creation of hierarchies. See benefit of clergy; priest; regular clergy; secular clergy.

The most complete survey of the question is in A. C. Headlam and others, (ed. R. Dunckerley), *The Ministry and the Sacraments* (1937); T. M. Lindsay, *The Church and the Ministry* (n.d.); B. H. Streeter, *The Primitive Church* (London, 1927); for legal status and liabilities, J. M. Dale, *Clergyman's Legal Handbook* (London, 1898), ed. by J. S. Risley. F.W.B.

Clericis Laicos: The Bull of Pope Boniface VIII* (1296) occasioned by the protests of French and English clergy against the taxes levied upon them by their respective monarchs then planning military campaigns. Boniface countered such extraordinary taxation with the threat of excommunication. R.C.P.

clerks, regular: Religious institutes of men, e.g., the Jesuits, if combining the works of secular priests and the solemn vows of monks. L.R.W.

clinical psychology: That branch of psychology which is concerned with the diagnosis and treatment of persons who require assistance with their social and psychological problems. From abnormal psychology* it is differentiated chiefly by its practical orientation.

This field is relatively undeveloped. At present the clinical psychologist's function is chiefly that of diagnosis and he places his reliance upon various standardized tests. On the basis of averages obtained from the study of a large number of persons he seeks to rate the individual. Actual therapy is left to the physician, the social worker and the teacher.

The intelligence tests, which figure so prominently in the repertoire of the clinical psychologist, found their first important use in the identification and grading of feeble-minded children. Their use has been extended to identify superior children and to distinguish special aptitudes and personality traits. They are thus used in child guidance, in vocational guidance, in industrial psychology and in personnel work in colleges and elsewhere. Among the names most closely associated with their development that of A. Binet (1857-1911) deserves special mention. See psychologists, English school of.

L. M. Terman, *The Measurement of Intelligence* (1916); F. L. Wells, *Mental Tests in Clinical Practice* (1927); C. M. Louttit, *Clinical Psychology* (1936). A.T.B.

cloister: (Lat., *claustra,* bar, bolt, bounds) a) An open court surrounded by an arcaded walk found in connection with monastic establishments and sometimes with cathedrals*. Intended mainly for a retired walk for monks and clergy. b) A monastery. F.T.P.

closed communion: A term employed by religious bodies to describe the practice of admitting to the Holy Communion only those who are regularly enrolled members, and in good standing, in their respective denominations. The Roman Church, on the one hand, and the Baptists traditionally, on the other, represent the two extremes which hold to this practice. See altar fellowship. W.N.P.

Clotho, Lachesis, Atropas: See fate.

Clovis: (c. 466-511) Real founder of Frankish kingdom. Adopted Christianity in orthodox form for himself and his people. Extended kingdom at expense of heretical (Arian) neighbours. Laid foundation of strong new state important in making of Europe. In it the Teutonic and Roman civilizations became blended. K.H.C.

Cluniacs: Members of the Order of Congregation of Cluny. Founded in 910, the Congregation, in the person of the Abbot Berno and his immediate successors, sought a reformation of monastic life through a more disciplined reapplication of the Benedictine* rule. The early emphasis upon personal poverty, labor, and rigid discipline declined apace as the mother foundation arrogated to itself the feudal control of numerous subject houses. Mother and daughter establishments at their peak of worldliness evinced striking examples of architectural brilliance, literary studies, and cultic magnificence, Drawn increasingly into the stream of papal politics, the wealthy order rapidly lost its pristine, reforming character and gave rise to the sad spectacle of privilege and decay.

See L. M. Smith, *The Early History of the Monastery of Cluny* (Oxford, 1920). R.C.P.

Cluny: A Benedictine monastery founded at Cluny in France early in the tenth century, and famous as the home or school of many distinguished mediaeval men, e.g., Gregory VII*, also called Hildebrand. L.R.W.

Cocceius, Johannes: (1603-1669) Eminent theologian. Professor in Franeker and Leyden (Holland). A Bible-centered theology. Most complete exposition of the Federal Theology* with its stress on Covenant of Grace. Was a modification of rigid Calvinism. Conflict of his followers with Voetian party. K.H.C.

codex: A leaf book, as distinguished from a roll or scroll. The codex was a Roman invention, suggested by the cluster of two or three hinged tablets surfaced with wax on which Romans jotted down their memoranda. Early in the second century Christian publishers began to employ papyrus codices in their work, perhaps as being more convenient to use and more capacious than rolls, as in the codex both sides of the material was written on. See manuscripts of the Bible. E.J.G.

Codex Alexandrinus: Fifth century manuscript of the Greek Bible, almost complete; the N.T. in what Hort called a fundamentally "Syrian" text in the gospels, though not elsewhere. It was given to the King of England in 1628 by Cyril Lucar, Patriarch of Constantinople, who had probably brought it from Alexandria. It is now in the British Museum. See canons of various churches; manuscripts of the Bible. E.J.G.

Codex Amiatinus: See Amiatinus, Codex.

Codex Bezae: A sixth (or even fifth) century manuscript* of the four gospels (Matthew-John-Luke-Mark) and the Acts, in Greek and Latin, the Greek on the left hand page, the Latin (in the Old Latin version) on the right. It was given to Théodore de Beze (or Beza) the great Greek scholar of the French Reformation, after the sack of Lyons in 1562, and in 1581 was given by him to the University of Cambridge, which still has it. It has many interpolations and curious readings, and is the leading document of what is called the "Western" text. E.J.G.

Codex Curetonian Syriac: See versions of the Bible, ancient.

Codex Ephraemi: A fifth century manuscript* of the Greek Bible, from which the writing was effaced in the twelfth, to make room for some works of Ephrem the Syrian, in a Greek version. While only 64 leaves of the O.T. remain, from the poetical and Wisdom books, more than half of the N.T. (145 leaves out of 238) survives. It was brought to France by Catherine de Medici in the sixteenth century and is in the Bibliothéque Nationale, in Paris. Its text though very uneven is often excellent. The decipherment of this palimpsest was the first notable work of Tischendorf who published its text in 1843-45. It ought now to be studied with the aid of ultra-violet or infrared light, so effective in work on palimpsests. E.J.G.

Codex Juris Canonici: See Canon Law; decretals.

Codex Sinaiticus: A fourth century manuscript* of the Greek Bible, found by Tischendorf in the convent of St. Catherine on Mt. Sinai, in part, in 1849, but the bulk of it in 1859, when he secured it for the Czar of Russia. It preserves about one-third of the O.T. but the N.T. is complete, and is accompanied by the Epistle of Barnabas and about one-fourth of the Shepherd of Hermas**. It was purchased in 1933 for the British Museum, where it now is. In text it is second only to the Codex Vaticanus*, with which it often agrees. See canons of various churches. E.J.G.

Codex Vaticanus: A fourth century Greek manuscript* of the Old and New Testaments, which has been in the Vatican Library at least since 1481. It has lost some portions: it now begins at Gen. 46:28, lacks part of the Psalms, and breaks off at Hebrews 9:14. But its text is in general so good that it is recognized as our most valuable manuscript of the N.T. and indeed of the Greek Bible. See canons of various churches. E.J.G.

Coetus: See Reformed Church in the U. S.

Cohen, Hermann: (1842-1918) The idea of God occupies the central position in his philosophy of critical idealism. The idea contains the connotation of a basic harmony between the structure of the universe and the aspiration of mankind. Cohen's introduction of the idea of God into his philosophy is an attempt to satisfy the longing of men to believe that the ethical ideal is real in a more solid sense than that of an aesthetic ideal.

God as an idea is neither alive nor a person. He can be discovered by the processes of reason itself. Religion, properly so-called, arises with the emergence of the ethical consciousness. The "function" of God is not to provide prosperity, or even happiness, but to aid the efforts of men to discriminate between right and wrong. The idea of God assures the continued existence of nature for the ethical work of man.

Religion is wholly the result of the fiat of man. It is a stratagem of the spirit, a psychological instrument employed by man for the sake of improving his character. Man does the work of redemption. God is the sign, or the name signifying the attainment of a victory over sin. Religion alone is capable of producing the ideal of individuality. The conception of sin is in principle applicable to an individual only, not to a social group. The cultivation of intellectual faculties is a religious duty. The religious philosophy of Cohen has idealistic, positivistic and humanistic elements derived from his intuition concerning the objective validity of ethical experience. See Neo-Kantianism.

Religion und Sittlichkeit (Berlin, 1907); *Der Begriff der Religion im System der Philosophie* (Giessen, 1915); *Die Religion der Vernunft* (Leipzig, 1919); J. Hessen, *Die Religionsphilosophie des Neukantianismus* (Freiburg, 1924). H.H.

Cole Lectureship: A lectureship at Vanderbilt University founded by Colonel E. W. Cole of Nashville, Tennessee. His object was "to establish a foundation for a perpetual lectureship in connection with the School of Religion of the University to be restricted in scope to a defence and advocacy of the Christian religion." The lectures are delivered annually in the spring. The original donation was $5,000, but this has been increased to $12,000 by a subsequent donation by Mrs. Cole, by the sale of published volumes, and in other ways. Among the lecturers have been: F. J. McConnell, Robert E. Speer, Charles E. Jefferson, L. H. Hough, H. E. Fosdick, S. P. Cadman, H. S. Coffin, Shailer Mathews, Rufus M. Jones, G. A. Buttrick, E. S. Brightman, and F. C. Grant. J.P.H.

Coleridge, Samuel Taylor: (1772-1834) English poet, critic, and philosopher. Following a studious career at Christ's Hospital and Cambridge, an association with Wordsworth* resulting in the *Lyrical Ballads* (1798), and a visit to Germany whence he drew much of his subsequent inspiration, Coleridge drifted into a period of narcotic ineffectiveness from which he emerged during his last years to do some brilliant but fragmentary writing and to exert a strong contemporary influence through his lectures and conversations. Of his critical and philosophical works the most important are *Biographia Literaria* (1817) and *Aids to Reflection* (1825); *Table Talk* (1835); *Confessions of an Enquiring Spirit* (1840), and other collections appeared posthumously. Perhaps the greatest of his contributions to English thought was the currency which he gave to German idealism. See Marsh, James; New theology.

There is no complete edition of Coleridge's prose. The *Complete Poetical Works* have been critically edited by E. H. Coleridge (1912) and the *Biographia Literaria* by J. Shawcross (1907). An excellent selection from the whole range of his writings is to be found in Stephen Potter's *Coleridge: Select Poetry and Prose* (1933). Of recent biographies the best is by E. K. Chambers (1938), although that by J. D. Campbell (1894) has long been regarded as standard. See also J. H. Muirhead's *Coleridge as Philosopher* (1930). L.W.C.

Colet, John: (1467-1519) English Reformer, studied in Italy. Emancipated by the Renaissance he returned to England; appointed Dean of St. Paul's he rejected the allegorical method, winning appreciation by his fresh historical interpretation of scripture. R.E.E.H.

collation: See advowson.

collect: A short, terse prayer of the Western rites, so called as either a) "collecting" or summing up the devotions of the people, or b) the prayer *ad collectam*, when the people were assembled to go in procession to the church appointed for the public (stational) Mass of the day. In the Roman Missal* the collect preceding the Epistle is called *Oratio*. P.V.N.

college apostolic: (Lat., *collegium,* a group or body) The apostles as one body with St. Peter* at their head. L.R.W.

College of Cardinals: The body of ecclesiastics nearest to the Roman Pontiff in dignity. Since the time of Sixtus V* (1586) the College of Cardinals numbers seventy members, of whom six are to be Cardinal Bishops, fifty Cardinal Priests, and fourteen Cardinal Deacons. However, the places are practically never all occupied. The cardinals*, while in no sense members of a parliament, constitute a sort of advisory council, with the duty of assisting the Holy Father in the government of the Church. They have the sole right of administering ecclesiastical affairs during a vacancy of the Holy See, and of electing the new Pope.* C.V.

college, pontifical: See pontifical college.

colloquy: In the original constitution of the French Reformed Church the colloquy corresponded to the presbytery* and the classis*. In a reorganization in 1852 "consistories"* replaced the *colloques*. R.H.N.

Colored Cumberland Presbyterian Church: See Cumberland Presbyterian Church.

Colored Methodist Episcopal Church, the: See negro church, the.

Colossians, Epistle to: An epistle written by Paul to a church a hundred miles inland from Ephesus, which he had never himself visited. Through his disciple Epaphroditus, who had founded it, he had learned of a heresy which was now threatening its existence, and wrote from Rome (or according to a recent theory, from Ephesus) to refute the false teaching. The nature of the Colossian heresy is doubtful. It was evidently some primitive form of Gnosticism, but was peculiar in its inclusion of Jewish customs and beliefs. Its central motive appears to have been that while Christ reconciled us to God we have still to reckon with the material forces, presided over by angelic beings. Worship has therefore to be rendered to the angels, and since they rule in the material sphere this worship must be material, concerned with objects and rites and places and cabalistic signs. Paul answers the heretical teachers by insisting on the all-sufficiency of Christ, who gathers up in himself the power which controls all others. The epistle contains some of Paul's profoundest thinking, but is often difficult, owing largely to his ironical use of the heretical jargon, which is now unintelligible. The date of Colossians is 60 or 61 A.D.

J. B. Lightfoot, *Commentary on Colossians* (1876); E. F. Scott, *The Literature of the New Testament* (1932). E.F.S.

Colportage: See religious tract movement.

Columbanus, Saint: (543-615) Abbot of Luxeuil and Bobbio, was born in West Leinster, Ireland, and in about 583 with twelve companions set out for Burgundy. Invited by king Gontram he erected a monastery at Annegray, and established others at Luxeuil and Fontaines. For these monasteries he wrote a rule, embodying the customs of the Celtic monasteries. After twenty years in Burgundy he was attacked by the jealous Frankish bishops and the dissolute king Thierry II who banished him from Burgundy. After much wandering, he settled at Bobbio, between Milan and Genoa, where he founded his famous monastery and where his relics rest. He wrote a rule which was approved but which was superseded by the rule of St. Benedict. His feast is celebrated on November 21. See monasticism. J.B.C.

Colver Lectures, the Nathaniel: Established in 1915 by Mr. and Mrs. Jesse L. Rosenberger in honor of Nathaniel Colver, first theological professor in the old University of Chicago. Endowment $3,500. (Data from the office of the secretary of the University of Chicago.) V.F.

Comenius, John Amos: (1592-1670) Born in southern Moravia, at Nivnice, he was educated in the school of the Unity of Brethren and later at Herborn in Nassau and the University of Heidelberg. Driven out of his parish at Fulnek early during the Thirty Years' War, he found refuge, along with many of his people, at Leszno, in Poland. It was here that in 1631 he published his *Janua linguarum reserata* which established his fame as an educational reformer. Later he was given the task of reforming the school system of Sweden, and subsequently of Hungary. In the course of this activity he worked out an educational system which entitles him to the title of "the father of modern educational theory and practice." The pedagogical works are published in his *Opera didactica omnia* (1657).

But his influence was much wider. In the ecclesiastical field, he became an important member of that small group of men who worked for the union of Christendom. His ecumenical proposals and practical schemes entitle him to be regarded as a prophet of modern ecumenicity*.

And finally, he advocated an integrated, unified "pansophic" view of culture, a philosophico-scientific point of view. It was for the purpose of founding a "pansophic" college that he spent a winter in London, and only the outbreak of the Civil War in England prevented the carrying out of the project. However, he continued to elaborate the scheme for the rest of his life. His pansophic proposal is best presented in his *Via lucis* written during the stay in London.

He died at Amsterdam in 1670.

See Bohemian (or Czech) Brethren; Moravian Church, the.

Matthew Spinka, translator, Comenius' *The Labyrinth of the World* (1942); Matthew Spinka, *John Amos Comenius* (1943); E. T. Campagnac, translator. Comenius' *The Way of Light* (Liverpool, 1938). M.S.

commandments: See decalogue.

Commandments of the Church: In general, any laws issued by the Church and binding all the faithful; in the U. S., six particular regulations of the R. C. prescribed by the third plenary council of Baltimore* (1886), regarding attendance at Mass, frequenting confession and Holy Communion, keeping fasts and abstinence, supporting pastors, and the degree of kinship allowed for marriage. L.R.W.

commercial theory: See redemption.

Commission, the Biblical: The *Commissio Pontificia de re biblica,* established October 30, 1902 by Leo XIII*, and consisting of a committee of cardinals (5) and a number of consultors, whose work is to secure the observance of proper interpretation and defence of the Sacred Scriptures according to the prescriptions of the Encyclical "Providentissimus Deus." This committee is constituted on the lines of other pontifical commissions and its duties are: to protect and defend the integrity of the Catholic faith in Biblical matters; to further the progress in the exposition of Sacred Scripture by taking notice of all recent discoveries and discussions; to decide controversies on grave questions that may arise among scholars; to see that the Vatican library is properly stocked with codices and other necessary books for Biblical study and research; and to publish studies on Scripture. Pius X*, on February 24, 1904, granted the committee the right to confer upon those who have passed the necessary examinations the degrees of Licentiate or Doctor of Sacred Scripture. T.T.M.

commissions, ecclesiastical: See ecclesiastical commissions.

common grace: (*gratia communis*) A term used in Reformed* theology. It is sharply distinguished from special grace which pertains only to eternal salvation. Common grace, which pertains only to terrestrial things, affirms: 1) That God as Creator loves all things as creatures, even sinful men who may be predestined* to damnation. 2) That irrespective of their eternal destiny man as man can have a sense of right (not eternal righteousness), beauty, and truth, but that he does not have such sense by virtue of being a creature merely, but by virtue of divine favor. It tends to mitigate God's hate of the unsaved, which they merit by sin, but it does not remove the hate. 3) That believers may share in the terrestrial concerns of unbelievers, because as creatures they also are recipients of common grace. The theory of common grace is Calvin's* adaptation of an idea which had already been elaborated by Melanchthon*. This idea was that while human culture has nothing to do with salvation (cf. Luther's "justification by faith *alone* and *not* by works"), the believer must concern himself with it because God wills it. It is related to the two-fold truth theory* in philosophy. The theory of common grace has been of great importance in promoting liberal culture in Reformed circles.

Reformed thinkers have sometimes reacted variously to the theory: Some have doubted that God would love men without intending to save them, and therefore two extremes have been adopted: the one denies the existence of a common grace; the other tends to make common grace coincide with saving grace, leading to universalism*. Again, some consider that this theory really reduces human culture to a plane of relative unimportance, which in turn has resulted in diverging views: some hold that this is as it should be; others tend towards cultural secularization. It has been difficult to hold common and saving grace in balance. There is on this subject an enormous literature, particularly in The Netherlands and among American Calvinists. See also Abraham Kuyper, Herman Bavinck, Benjamin B. Warfield. See grace.

common law: See law.

common law marriage: See marriage.

communicatio idiomatum: (Lat. communication of properties or attributes) A Christological* doctrine seeking to explain the relation of the divine and human natures in Christ, developed by Luther* and his followers on the basis of the Formula of Chalcedon*. This doctrine, designed to safeguard the unity of Christ's person while distinguishing between His two natures, is germinally present in the concept of *perichoresis** (interpenetration) of the ancient Church. The controversy over the real presence* of Christ in the Lord's Supper was the occasion for its further development in the sixteenth century. Over against Zwingli*, Luther insisted: "the divine nature gives the human its property, and the humanity also the divine nature". Since the divine nature may thus endow the human nature with omnipresence, the bodily presence of Christ in the Lord's Supper becomes possible. The doctrine was systematically formulated by Chemnitz* in *De duabus naturis in Christo* (1571) and confessionally stated in Art. VIII of the Formula of Concord*. T.A.K.

The transposition of names, a term in Christology which paradoxically affirms the conjunction of the two natures in the one Person of Christ by designating the Person according to a name appropriate only to one nature and predicating an attribute of the other nature. E.g., God was asleep in the back of the boat, the Creator was crucified, the Master stilled the waves, the Carpenter of Nazareth created the universe. T.J.B.

communion: An antiphonal chant* sung during the partaking of the elements of the eucharist. See plainsong; psalmody. E.H.B.

communion, holy: See Lord's supper.

communion of saints: The term is variously explained. It originally was a mystic communion with the perfect and the just in heaven. The existing church owes its endurance to the saints. For Augustine* the communion of saints is the communion of the good and pious. They love God and one another. They pray for the church. Everyone in this communion has inwardly a part in the spiritual estate of the others. The saints alone are the inheritors of the future kingdom of God. The communion of saints does not originate and exist through the visible church, though it is in the visible church. The communion of saints is passed on in the church. For some medieval theologians the term is applied to the participants in the grace-offering sacraments. Others apply it to the members of the triumphant church. For still others it is sharing the spiritual properties acquired by the saints. Lastly, for others, it is the communion of the pious of all times and places. See intercession.

J. P. Kirsch *Die Lehre von der Gemeinschaft der Heiligen* (Mainz, 1900). H.H.

communism: See labor movements; Marx; socialism.

communistic settlements, religious: A large number of religious sectarian groups within the Hebrew-Christian tradition have from time to time attempted to organize their life on a collectivistic basis. Most frequently they have stressed community of property in consumption of goods, but occasionally production also has been organized along communistic lines. Sexual relations, however, have usually been regulated in harmony with traditional moral and religious concepts. Some of them have been celibate, either confining their membership to one sex, or segregating the sexes within the community; some have merely regarded celibacy as the preferred estate; while among others individualistic family life has been accepted as divinely established. Only one, the Oneida Community* in New York, founded by the New England Perfectionists* under the leadership of John Humphrey Noyes, is known to have extended communism to all personal relations, including marriage and family life. Most of these communities have been short lived, and have left few traces or none. Others have exerted considerable influence upon religious history, only a few of which can be noted here.

Early Hebrew-Christian Communities. Complete communism in consumption goods first appeared among the Hebrews in the largely celibate communities of the Essenes* in the second century, B.C. It was also characteristic of the early church in Jerusalem, but soon disappeared as a central tendency in the development of Christian belief and practice, only to reappear sporadically in reformist groups as Christianity ceased to be mainly a Jewish sect and became a competing faith in the lands of classical paganism.

Such revivals of Christian communism have had a common basis in the ascetic* traditions within Judaism, in Old and New Testament views as to the "deceitfulness of riches," in the Manichaean doctrine of the corruption of private possessions, and in the attempt to apply literally the teachings of the Sermon on the Mount. The Benedictines* of the sixth century were the first monastic order to reintroduce communism into orthodox Catholic circles, while the most extensive development of collectivistic and cooperative practices under Catholic auspices was undertaken by the Jesuits in Paraguay, who between 1602 and their expulsion by Spain in 1767 gathered over 100,000 Indian converts into about 30 agricultural communities, with trade on a barter basis among families holding individual allotments, and with common "fields of God" tilled and operated collectively for the benefit of the needy.

Early Modern Sectarian Communities. Communistic modes of life appeared with increasing frequency with the rise of the numerous heretical sects during and following the thirteenth century, and especially during the period of the Reformation. Among the more important of these were the Waldenses, the Albigenses, the Cathari**, the Apostolican Sect of Alanzo in Italy and France, the Beghards of France and Germany, the English Lollards** of Norfolk, the Bruges Weaving Friars, the Dutch Fraternity of the Common Life, the Bohemian Taborites, the Moravian Brethren, and others. But the establishment of collectivistic communities in the midst of hostile institutions in a well settled society proved difficult at best, until the settlement of America offered a new hope of success and a new opportunity for expansion in a new land favorable to new ideas. During the eighteenth, and more especially during the nineteenth century, the English colonies, and later the United States, became the haven of communistic sects suffering from persecution and threatened with annihilation in Europe.

The Labadists in Maryland.* The first to come were the Dutch disciples of Jean de Labadie (1610-1674), a former French Jesuit who later preached the perfectibility of man, and found in arrogance and cupidity the chief deterrents to man's living as Christ had lived. Fleeing from the persecution of Cardinal Mazarin in France, Labadie finally settled at Weiward in Holland, from whence the Labadists set forth to the spiritual conquest of the world. After an abortive attempt to establish a colony in Surinam, two leading members of the Weiward community, Jaspar Danckaerts and Peter Sluyter, were sent to New York in 1679 on a similar mission. Driven out by the persecutions of the Catholic governor, Andros, and the Dutch clergy, they finally settled near the present site of Elkton, Md., on a 3,750 acre tract donated to them by Augustine Hermann from his vast estate of Bohemia Manor in 1683. Their colony was communistic in both production and consumption, but their attitude toward sex was pathologic, culminating in extreme self-torture to destroy carnal appetite. The sexes lived and ate in separate quarters, and performed different functions, but they shared the same rights and duties. The colony was successful economically, but only at the sacrifice of its religious principles on the part of their leader, Peter Sluyter. At first passionately opposed to both tobacco culture and slavery, Sluyter persuaded them that in order to survive, they must accept both. Sluyter increasingly subordinated the common good to the profit motive and finally in 1698 he persuaded the colonists to return to private ownership. In the division which followed he retained the best lands for himself, and died a rich man in 1722. The community had completely disappeared by 1727.

This first communistic experiment in America contained about a hundred members, men, women, and children, at the height of its development.

German Separatist Communities. German Lutheranism was especially prolific in the production of communistic sects. Earliest among these were the followers of the ex-Lutheran pastor, Johann Jacob Zimmermann, who sought for his followers retreat from "the Babylon of Europe" in the wilderness of the New World. But Zimmermann died at Rotterdam the day before embarkation and Johann Kelpius (1673-1708), a young Rosicrucian intellectual and eccentric who came successively under the influence of Jacob Boehme*, the mystic, Jacob Spener*, founder of the Pietists, and Jane Leade, of the English Philadelphists, assumed the leadership of the enterprise. They established their colony on the Wissahickon, near the present site of Fairmount Park, Philadelphia in 1694. Hermit Spring and Hermit Lane, in Fairmount Park, still commemorate their occupancy of this tract. They referred to themselves as the "colony of the Contented of the God-loving Soul," but were known by others as the *"Society of the Woman in the Wilderness,"* owing to their aspiration to become the Beloved of the woman described in Rev. 12:1ff as advancing from the wilderness, leaning on the arm of her Beloved, to deliver the true Church. They were millenialists and celibates who believed that the return of Christ would occur in the immediate future. They accordingly regarded the world as ephemeral and adopted a cenobitic pattern of life. Under the inspiration of Kelpius none were more ready to endure hardship and danger to aid the ill and needy, but after his death from tuberculosis at thirty-five, they withdrew more and more into their solitary cells. A few recanted, married, and joined various churches, but the leading spirits continued in their way of life until death put an end to their enterprise.

The fame of Kelpius spread throughout Europe, and in 1720 a group of German believers under Johann Conrad Beissel (1690-1768) arrived only to find the colony in decay. After a sojourn among the Dunkards at Conestoga, they established a colony at Ephrata (see Ephrata Society), between Reading and Lancaster, Pa., in 1732. Like the Labadist and Kelpian groups, they were millenialists and celibates. The colony was divided into three groups, the Solitary Brethren (unmarried men), the Order of Spiritual Virgins (devoted to virginity) and married couples who, on joining the community, were pledged to continence. Beissel himself cared little for material prosperity, although for a time, under the leadership of the three Eckerlin brothers, Ephrata became a flourishing and diversified industrial establishment, and even marriage became an issue. But the Eckerlins were expelled in 1745, and the community again assumed its former austerity. Ephrata has often been referred to as the most long-lived communistic settlement in history; but it never comprised more than 300 members, and its distinctive characteristics passed with the generation of the founders. It still exists for students and tourists, but little of the original spirit remains. During its first decades, however, it sent forth many disciples who attempted to found branches elsewhere, of which the best known were those established in South Carolina by an English convert, Israel Seymour, and at Snow Hill, Franklin Co., Pa. by an American, Peter Lehman.

Ephrata was followed by two other German Separatist groups of importance, the *Rappites or Harmonists,* and the *Separatist Society of Zoar.* George Rapp (1757-1847) was the son of a Wurtemberg farmer and grape owner, an ardent student of the Bible and of the works of Arndt, Boehme, Spener, and Swedenborg*. He began preaching in his house and soon gathered about him a group of Separatists numbering about 200 families. His preaching was a variety of Lutheran pietism heavily laden with mysticism and milenialism. After years of persecution, Rapp, his son John, and a few friends emigrated to America in 1803. They purchased 3000 acres of improved land in Butler County, Pa., and sent for their followers who arrived during 1804 and 1805. One ship load settled in Lycoming Co. under the leadership of Haller. The majority organized the *Harmony Society* with a written constitution on Feb. 15, 1805, which provided for a communistic theocracy with Rapp as actual dictator. Rapp then developed the strange doctrine that Adam had contained within himself both sexes, that as a result of sin the sexes had been made separate, uncreative within themselves as individuals, and that through consecration men and women could recapture their lost powers and be able, each within himself, to bear children. Celibacy, which was adopted in 1807, was thus a temporary expediency necessary to regain man's lost creativity.

Owing largely to Rapp's extraordinary energy, intelligence, and moral power, the colony was successful economically in spite of two expensive relocations, two serious defections, and various lawsuits by apostates who sought to acquire their individual shares of the community property. The rival communities of dissidents failed, and though they depleted the treasury and reduced the membership, especially that led by the bogus Count de Leon who settled at Phillipsburg in 1832, they removed the discordant elements and prepared the way for greater peace within the society. The lawsuits, beginning as early as 1821 and carried through the higher courts, were decided in favor of the society and rendered great services to communistic settlements in general by establishing the legality of their compacts and the inviolability of the communal property against claims of members for wages and for reimbursement for their original contributions. Even the relocations marked stages of material advancement. Because their property was becoming too small for their members, because it was not situated on a navigable waterway, but more especially because it was not suitable for their favorite European employment, viticulture, they sold their holdings in 1814 for $100,000 and purchased nearly 25,000 acres on the lower Wabash River in Indiana. Here they built a new Harmony and prospered as never before. Within ten years they had added more than

14,000 acres to their holdings, expanded their industries, extended their commerce, and increased their membership to over 1000 souls. But the site proved malarial and their neighbors hostile. In 1824 they sold their properties to Robert Owen for $182,000 and purchased a 3000 acre tract on the Ohio River 18 miles below Pittsburgh. Here they built *Economy,* their third settlement, in 1825. The society grew wealthy through manufacturing and its progressive use of labor saving machinery. It became famous for its wines, whiskeys, woolens, and other products. But after the death of Rapp, his successors, through unwise charities, unsound investments, and lax bookkeeping, accounting, and inventory methods, brought it into serious financial straits. In 1892 a new Senior Trustee, John Samuel Duss, employed a firm of accountants who disclosed an indebtedness of nearly $1,500,000. For years Duss struggled to liquidate the debts and to provide for its aging membership with some success, but the rule of celibacy and the lack of fresh converts resulted in dwindling numbers, and the society disbanded in 1906.

Rapp confined his attention to religious affairs and accepted communism as a way to realize spiritual values, without contradicting or conflicting with the civil authorities. Others of the Separatists of Wurtemberg, Baden, and Bavaria were of a different mind. They condemned civil as well as religious authorities, opposed taxation and military service, and insisted upon the supremacy of the individual. In 1817 a group of about 300 under the leadership of the woman mystic, Barbara Grubermann, decided to emigrate to America. Their leader died before they left Germany, but on the voyage one of their number, Joseph Michael Bimeler (or Baümeler) (1778-1853), doctored the sick, encouraged the depressed, imparted secular and religious instruction, and by sheer force of intelligence and character became the indispensable leader of the group. On a 5500 acre tract in Tuscarawas Co., Ohio, they established their settlement which they called *Zoar,* after Lot's city of refuge on the shore of the Dead Sea. Their intense individualism was at first not compatible with communistic principles, but after two years they decided, against Bimeler's judgment, that to succeed they must have community of goods. Drastic measures were necessary at first. In order to pay for their land they agreed that no one was to marry and that husbands were to live apart from their wives. But they never believed in celibacy as more than an expedient, and when their debt was cleared, they reintroduced marriage, Bimeler himself being among the first to take a wife. Their society was incorporated in 1832. Unlike the Rappites, their government was thoroughly democratic. It consisted of a board of three directors, each elected for a term of three years, assisted by a council of five, elected for one year. The highest administrative officer was an agent-general. Bimeler himself served in this capacity. He was a practical as well as a spiritual genius. He established a brewery, two flour mills, woolen and linen factories, and an iron foundry. At one time the membership reached five hundred, and the communal property was worth over a million dollars. Bimeler was greatly reverenced and after his death no general agent was appointed, nor did a religious leader emerge. The functions of the former devolved upon the cashier or one of the directors, while in place of the latter, one of Bimeler's "Discourses" was read each week. These "Discourses" which the members regarded as inspired, had been delivered extempore, and covered topics ranging from abstract theology through practical morality to sanitation and hygiene, for Bimeler was also physician to the colony. One of the younger members had taken notes for the benefit of his deaf father. After Bimeler's death these notes were collected and published in three volumes. But deprived of the statesmanship and driving force of their leader, the group stagnated, and finally disbanded on March 10, 1898.

Like the Zoarites, the *Amarites* were not interested in communism before their arrival in America. The wealthier members had assisted the less fortunate, and established woolen mills and knitting works for their employment. They were a group of German pietists* who traced their origin to the seventeenth century, to the teachings of Rosamunde Juliana, a lady of noble rank, and Dr. Johann Wilhelm Peterson, a learned professor at Luneberg, whose followers regarded them as "Inspired Instruments," but the real foundations of the movement were laid by the ex-Lutherans, the Rev. Eberhand Ludwig Gruber and Johann Friederich Rock, in Hesse in 1714. The group became known as the *"Society of the True Inspiration."* After 1817 the mantle of inspiration fell upon Christian Metz (1794-1867) and Barbara Heinnemann. In 1842 Metz and two companions were sent to America to select a location. They purchased 5000 acres of the Seneca Indian Reservation near Buffalo, N. Y. for $50,000 which they subsequently increased to 9000 acres. Their original plan was to hold only their lands and houses in common, and each member's contribution to the purchase price was to be secured by a proportionate share of the real estate and to bear a reasonable rate of interest. But the plan proved to be impracticable, and absolute communism became the rule of the society. Their group was organized as the *Ebenezer Society,* and within four years about 800 persons had arrived from Germany. Some Canadians also joined the movement, and established a branch society at Kenneberg, 45 miles northwest of Buffalo, and another 12 miles north of Buffalo, known as *Canada Ebenezer.* By 1854 the society had outgrown its property. Adjacent land was held at too high a price, and the rapidly growing city of Buffalo interferred with the secluded life desired by the colonists. They finally secured 26,000 acres of land in central Iowa where they established their village of Amana* in 1855, followed by six other villages before 1862. In 1859 the community was incorporated as the *Amana Society.* Their life was plain and austere. No adornment was permitted in dress, in architecture, or in household furnishings. Hymnology was encouraged, but musical instruments were prohibited. Though marriage was permitted, it was not extolled, and the sexes were segregated at meals, at church, and at work. Diversified industries were introduced, especially those concerned with the manufacture of woolens. At one time, the society had nearly 2000 members, and has perhaps seventy-five percent as many at present. In recent decades it has been losing its communistic features, and has been assuming a semi-capitalistic character. In 1932 it was reorganized as a joint stock company in which the stockholders are both owners and employees. The old austerity had passed; the women are assuming positions of leadership; the people now own their own homes, but what goods they wish, and pay their own bills. The economic and social life is no longer dictated by the religious authorities. They have adopted many progressive social measures, such as free medical services and methods of dealing with poverty and other social ills.

The communities at *Bethel, Mo.,* and *Aurora, Ore.,* although composed largely of German immigrants, were of distinctively American origin. Their founder, Dr. Wilhelm Keil, was a milliner and merchant tailor of Nordhausen, Prussia, who became successively amateur actor, mystic, hypnotist, and medical charlatan. He came to America in 1835, and after spending some time in New York, opened a drug store at Pittsburgh. Influenced by Paracelsus and Cagliostro, he plunged into the study of medicine, botany, and physics in search of the "Universal-medizin" which was to be the elixir of the ages. He practiced hypnotism and mental healing, sold his elixir in infinitesimal quantities at high prices, and soon became popular among the simple-minded German masses as "Der Hexendocktor." In 1838 he was converted to Methodism, and burned his "medical" prescriptions with appropriate awe-conspiring ceremonies. But he soon revolted against Methodism, declared he would bear no other name than Christian and accept no other creed but the Bible. He began to preach, and gathered about him a number of German emigrants to whom he claimed to be one of the two witnesses mentioned in Rev. 11:3. He was later joined by the disillusioned Rappites who had followed de Leon, and began to plan a communistic society somewhat like Rapp's, but without the rule of celibacy. In 1844 they settled at Bethel, Shelby Co., 48 miles from Hannibal, Mo. Here they prospered, and within a decade had established a distillery, a grist-mill, a saw-mill, a cording and woolen mill, and all the mechanical trades needed by the farmers in their neighborhood. With their increasing wealth, Dr. Keil longed for a broader field, and imagined that he might establish a larger community on the Pacific Coast. In 1855 he set out with a group of followers, and, after a futile attempt to settle at Willapa, Ore., moved to a happier location 29 miles south of Portland, which they named Aurora, after Keil's favorite daughter. Here again a self-sustaining economy was established on a barter basis. No money was used within the community. Their beliefs were simple and elastic in all matters excepting their devotion to the communistic ideal. There were no restrictions of diet or dress, few regulations of conduct, and no creed save "love to one another." Government, they believed, should be parental, as is the government of God, and Keil's rule was regal, though mild and just. His indicated wish had the force of law in both communities, and when in his later years he inclined increasingly toward celibacy, few members had the courage to marry. Bethel attained a population of 400, and Aurora over 1000. But they were held together by the will of a forceful leader, and when he died, they disintegrated, and the colonies disbanded in 1880-81.

Bishop Hill Colony. Scandinavian Lutheranism also produced its communistic sects. These arose out of the activities of the Devotionalists, or Readers (*Läsare*), who sought to lead the State Church back to the zeal, simplicity, and faith of the early Christians. Among the leaders of this movement in Helsingland, Sweden, was Eric Janson, who settled with a party of Swedes at *Bishop Hill, Ill.,* so called after his birthplace in Sweden. Few communistic groups suffered such hardships in their earlier years. One ship was lost at sea, two were shipwrecked with but few survivors, and only one reached New York. After they arrived they lived in dug-outs and sod houses, subsisted on pork and corn, and suffered from malaria and cholera, 114 dying within two weeks. In 1848 two hundred left the colony because they could not accept Janson's extravagant religious claim that he was the actual reincarnation of Christ. Their agriculture and industries flourished, and at the time of Janson's assassination at a court trial brought by a disaffected follower, John Root, in 1850, they numbered 1000 persons. Janson's death was a severe blow to the believers, who fully expected their leader to rise, like Christ, on the third day. When this hope failed, they chose Jonas Olson as their leader. He was less of a mystic and more of a business man than Janson, and the colony became comparatively wealthy, realizing in 1854 over $35,000 on their crop of broom corn alone. But Janson made two mistakes. He attempted to introduce celibacy, and he permitted a speculator, Olaf Janson, not a relative of the founder, to secure financial control and invest the funds of the community in unsound business enterprises. The former alienated the young people, and the latter reduced the colony to penury in the panic of 1857. From this it never recovered, and was finally liquidated in 1862.

Shaker Communities. These sectarians are officially known as the "United Society of Believers in Christ's Second Coming." They believed that their founder, Mother Ann Lee (1736-1784) was this second appearance of Christ. The sect originated among the English Quakers who had been influenced by the exiled French Camisards*. In obedience to a vision of Mother Ann, the first group arrived in New York in 1774, and two years later established their first settlement at Niskayuna, now Watervleit, N. Y. From here they conducted evangelistic tours through the adjacent New England states until the death of Mother Ann. They established their first completed community at Mt. Lebanon, N. Y., in 1787. Within the next seven years eleven communities had been established in New York and New England, and before 1825 seven more had been founded in Ohio, Kentucky, and Indiana. Finally, an outpost was established as far away as Florida. They were strictly celibate, but there was no discriminating of race or sex, the communities freely admitting Negroes and Jews, and the women bearing an equal share in the ministry with the men. Each community was governed by two Elders and two Elderesses who had charge of spiritual affairs, and two Deacons and two Deaconesses subordinate to them who supervised temporal matters. There were also several ministries, each consisting of two brothers and two sisters who had charge of two or more societies, the Ministry of Mt. Lebanon being known as the Head of Influence, and recognized as the central executive of all the societies. As successful communists, excellent farmers, and skilled mechanics, they exercised considerable influence in nineteenth century America. They numbered about 6000 in 1840, but now have less than 100 members in five surviving communities.

The *Bruederhof or Huterite Communities* were founded by the followers of Jacob Huter, an early sixteenth century Mennonite* reformer who added communism, abstinence from profit, usury, and from all forms of political life to the pacificism and quietism of their co-religionists. They are the oldest communistic society in the world. The group consists largely of Germans who sought refuge from military service in Southern Russia, from whence they migrated to South Dakota. Thirty-five or forty families settled at Wolf Creek and Bon Homme in 1874. A third community of some seventeen families settled at Elm Spring in 1877. The last contingent arrived from Russia in 1879. Fourteen other colonies were offshoots of these three. Since they were farmers, they settled in compact groups in the open country, sometimes as many as a dozen families under one roof. Some of the Huterites settled on private farms, but within the Bruederhof everything is run on a strictly communistic basis. The government is theocratic and patriarchal, and is administered by a teacher, a preacher, and a Wirt, or business manager, who appoints assistants and apportions the work to individual members. These three, together with the elders, form a ruling hierarchy who are elected for life by the male members over twenty-one years of age. Their entire number, including those on private farms, was about 2000 in 1917, but as a result of persecution during the war, all but five of the colonies moved to Canada. The present Huterite population is composed of the descendants of the original families who endured persecution in South Germany, Moravia, and the Tyrol in the sixteenth and seventeenth centuries. Few new converts have been added since that time.

Another large Russian communistic religious sect, the *Doukhobors,* settled in Canada in 1897. (See Russian sectarianism.)

Mormon Communism. America has also produced its own native varieties of religious communism. The most important of these was the *United Order of Enoch,* established by the Mormon prophet, Joseph Smith*, who received a revelation to the faithful to "consecrate all thy properties, that which thou hast, unto me, with a covenant and deed which can not be broken." In return each man was to receive a "stewardship" for which he must render an annual accounting. The Order was first set up in Thompson Co., Ohio, and in Jackson Co., Mo., but the Mormons were driven out before they had a chance to work out its details. Several communities in Utah were later organized on the principles of the United Order, especially at Orderville in southern Utah, where there was no private property except clothes. But the experiment was abandoned after ten years' trial in 1884, and the property distributed to the members.

Lesser American Religious Communities. Among the native American communities built up about the idea of Christ's second Advent (see adventist sects) were those founded by Jemimah Wilkinson at Jerusalem, N. Y. (ca. 1789-1820), by Peter Armstrong at Celesta, Pa., (ca. 1861-1866) and by Frederich T. Howland at Adonai-Shomo, Petersham, Mass. (ca. 1864-1896). The total number of lesser communities of American origin is unknown, but there were probably about 100 of them in all. Among them were the Spiritualist *Brotherhood of the New Life,* at Portland, N. Y. (ca. 1867-1880), the *Woman's Commonwealth* of Belton, Texas, and Washington, D. C. and the *Lord's Farm* near Westwood, N. J. Various cultist groups have also attempted to establish communities. Among these were *Shalam, or the Children's Land* near Dona, N. Mex. (1884-1901), the Universal Brotherhood and Theosophical* Society at Point Loma, Calif. (ca. 1900), the *Koreshans* in Chicago and at Estero, Fla. (ca. 1902), the *Dowieites* at Zion City, Ill. (1893-) the *House of David* at Benton Harbor, Mich., (1903-) and Father Divine's* *Heavens* in New York and his *Promised Land* up the Hudson, opposite Hyde Park. See Church of God and Saints of Christ.

V. F. Calverton, *Where Angels Dared to Tread* (1941); W. A. Hinds, *American Communities* (2nd rev. ed., 1908); J. H. Noyes, *History of American Socialisms* (1870); Chas. Nordhoff, *The Communistic Societies of the United States* (1875). H.E.J.

communistic settlements, secular: With the development of utopian socialism* under the leadership of Claude-Henri, Comte de Saint Simon* (1760-1825), Charles Fourier (1772-1837), and Etienne Cabet (1788-1856) in France, and Robert Owen (1771-1858) in England, a number of attempts were made in America to establish communistic settlements on a purely secular basis. The earliest of these was made by Owen, who purchased the former Rappite (See communistic settlements, religious) site on the lower Wabash River in Indiana, which he rechristened *New Harmony,* and began colonization in the spring of 1825. Its purpose was to free man from what Owen declared to be "a trinity of the most monstrous evils, . . . private or individual property, absurd and irrational systems of religion, and marriage founded upon individual property, combined with some of these irrational systems of religion." Owen himself joined the colony on Jan. 18, 1826, accompanied by a brilliant galaxy of scientists and scholars. But the greater part of the settlers were, as Owen's son later described them, "a heterogeneous collection of radicals, enthusiastic devotees of principle, honest latitudinarians and lazy theorists, with a sprinkling of unprincipled sharpers thrown in," and in spite of adequate financial resources the community had but a brief history. Seven constitutions were adopted in less than 18 months, and after each new revision, groups would secede and form a new community, of which there was at one time ten in existence. The enterprise was finally abandoned in June, 1827.

Owen was the inspiration of at least nine other communistic colonies. Of these the more important were at *Yellow Springs, Ohio,* by Daniel Roe (1824) and at *Nashoba, Tenn.,* by Frances Wright (1825-28). They were all ephemeral, lasting from a few months to a maximum of three years.

A group of quasi-secular communities were founded in Massachusetts during the decade of 1840-49. They were an outgrowth of the "theological thaw" which resulted in the breakup of New England orthodoxy and the rise of Unitarianism, Universalism, and the transcendental philosophy, which, as O. B. Frothingham says "was satisfied with nothing so long as it did not correspond to the ideal in the enlightened soul; and in the soul recognized the power to make all things new." The earliest and most enduring of these was Adin Ballou's *Hopedale* (1840-56) in the town of Milford; the most bizarre was the vegetarian community of *Fruitlands* (1843-44) founded by Bronson Alcott in the town of Harvard; and the most famous was *Brook Farm* (1841-47) at West Roxbury. Although led by clergymen and religiously motivated, they resembled the secular communities in social organization rather than the other religious communities, and they were less concerned with restoring the literal pattern of the N.T. Church. They are chiefly significant as preparing the intellectual climate for the reception of the Fourieristic phase of communistic settlement. They were more congenial to the American mind than the stark agnosticism of the Owenites. They attracted the attention of the best known intellectuals of the time, including Emerson, Channing, Hawthorne, Lowell, Whittier, Charles A. Dana, Theodore Parker, Orestes Brownson, and others. Many of them visited or resided in the settlements, especially at Brook Farm, and aroused widespread interest in their activities by sermons, lectures, and publications. As Emerson* wrote to Carlyle, "We are all a little wild here with numberless projects of social reform; not a reading man but has a draft of a new community in his waistcoat pocket."

Public interest was thus prepared for the reception of the teachings of Charles Fourier, introduced into America by his disciple, Arthur Brisbane (1809-90). Brisbane's writings were enthusiastically received by the transcendentalists, and he had the good fortune to convert the dean of American editors, Horace Greeley, who engaged him to conduct a daily column in the New York *Tribune* on the theories and practice of *Fourierism.* The central idea of this system was a scheme of social organization which would necessarily result in social harmony through the spontaneous formation of social groups of sympathetic individuals. People were to be assembled into "phalanxes" of about 1800 persons, composed of "groups" of from 24 to 32, and "series" of from seven to nine, composed of individuals attracted to each other by one of the four affective "passions," friendship, love, ambition, and familism. They were to occupy a "phalanstery," a beautiful and spacious building like a modern apartment hotel, located in the midst of a self-sustaining agricultural tract. The surplus remaining after providing for the common support of all were to be divided into 12 shares, 5 of which were to go to labor, 4 to capital, and 3 to talent. Fourier shared Owen's anti-religious bias, the chief difference of his scheme from that of his British contemporary being his retention, at least temporarily, of private property and inheritance. Although only two Fourieristic phalanxes were attempted in France, over 40 were undertaken in the United States, chiefly in New York, Pennsylvania, Ohio, and Wisconsin. The first of these was the short-lived *Sylvania Phalanx* (1843-44) in Pike Co., Pa., and the most important, the *North American Phalanx* near Red Bank, N. J. (1843-55). Noyes calls this "the test-experiment on which Fourierism practically staked its all in this country." It was the longest lived and most successful of them all, but internal dissensions and a disastrous fire brought it to an end, and Fourierism in America passed into history.

Brook Farm was reorganized as a Fourieristic phalanx in 1844 under the influence of Brisbane and Greeley. It undertook the construction of a phalanstery which was destroyed by fire in 1846 as the members were preparing to celebrate its completion. The financial resources of the community were exhausted in this enterprise, and it was dissolved the following year.

Of all the secular communistic colonies in America, the Icarian settlements had the longest history. They were based on the teachings of Etienne Cabet (1788-1856) as developed in his social romance, *Voyage en Icarie* (1840), a work inspired by reading Sir Thomas More's *Utopia* while Cabet was a political refugee in England. In contrast to Fourierism, which was based on agriculture and the handicrafts, *Icaria* was to be a highly mechanized society. Cabet differed from both Owen and Fourier in the role assigned to religion in social life and in his emphasis on strict monogamy. Monogamous marriage was obligatory and binding, and in his *La vrai christianisme* he interpreted Christ's mission as the establishment of social equality.

Cabet's views were for a time immensely popular, and he numbered his adherents by the thousand. He sincerely believed that a state similar to Icaria was an immediate possibility, and that it could be realized within fifty years. Failing to secure the support of the government of France for a colony in his native land, he sent a detachment of his followers to establish a community in northeastern Texas in 1848. But their numbers were quickly reduced by hardship, disease, and desertion, and the remnants made their way back to New Orleans where they were joined by fresh recruits, including Cabet himself, early in the following year. The site recently abandoned by the Mormons at Nauvoo, Ill., was then secured, and about 280 Icarians followed their leader thither in 1849. Here for a time they prospered, but dissensions centering chiefly in the somewhat arbitrary government of Cabet culminated in the expulsion of the leader in 1856. With about 180 of the faithful minority, Cabet retired to St. Louis, where he died on Nov. 8, 1856, a broken and disappointed man. His personal adherents established a new colony at *Cheltenham*, Mo., in 1858, which continued for six years.

Factional strife between the older and younger generations persisted at Nauvoo after Cabet's withdrawal. Weakened and impoverished by repeated secessions, they placed their property in the hands of receivers to satisfy their creditors and by 1860 the entire group had removed to *Corning, Iowa.* Further conflict resulted in two other settlements in the same vicinity, the last of which came to an end in 1895. A third group migrated to Cloverdale, California, in 1881, where they founded a new colony, *Icaria Speranza,* which was dissolved in 1887.

The anarchistic villages founded by Josiah Warren, *Equity, Ohio* (1830-32), *Utopia, Ohio,* (1847-51) and *Modern Times* on Long Island (1851-60) present an interesting reaction to Owenism. Disillusioned with communism as a result of his experiences at New Harmony, he resolved to found groups based on "the sovereignty of the individual," in which money and outside capital were to be dispensed with, and goods exchanged on the basis of the labor-time expended in their production. The colony founded at *Skaneateles, N. Y.* by John A. Collins, a former associate of Garrison in the abolition cause who later fell under the influence of Fourierism, was anarchistic in its system of social control. It was, however, also Owenite in its anti-religion and communistic in its property arrangements. See communistic settlements, religious; social gospel.

M. Hillquit, *History of Socialism in the United States* (1906). H.E.J.

commutation of penance: The alteration of a prescribed penance,* usually by shortening the period and intensifying the discipline, but often with liberal relaxation. See composition. J.T.M.

compacts or compactata: These were the agreements concluded between the Council of Basle* (chiefly through its representative, legate Palomar) and the Hussite* parties of Bohemia. The negotiations, lasting four years, were concluded on July 5, 1436, at Jihlava. Since the Hussite armies had been defeated in the disastrous battle of Lipany in 1434, the Council was able to dictate largely its own terms. Accordingly, although the Czech Hussites were allowed to administer the eucharistic elements of bread and wine, their other demands were not granted. In return, the Council revoked the former condemnations of the Hussites—or Calixtines as they were called—and restored them as faithful sons into the bosom of the Church. Thus the Hussite struggle with the church was terminated. M.S.

comparative religion: Whenever religions have met historically comparison has inevitably resulted. The basic motive has generaly been an apologetic one, to exhibit the superiority of one over the other. But in the nineteenth century there began to emerge what its exponents called the Science of Comparative Religion, or recognized as one phase of a more inclusive Science of Religion which began with the history of religion, moved through the classification and comparison of religions to the philosophy of religion. Its claim in itself to being a science rests upon the fact that the method used is the scientific method in so far as that is applicable in the field of human thought and human relations. Theoretically it approaches the field with no presuppositions, it seeks all the facts that are discoverable through the researches of the philologist, anthropologists, archaeologists, psychologists, sociologists, historians, and others who seek to understand the development of man and his culture. It assembles the facts, relates them, classifies them, and finally attempts some generalizations as to the origin, the nature and development of religion. That workers in this field succeed perfectly in eliminating personal bias can scarcely be maintained, any more than it can in any of the social sciences, but great gains have been made, and in true scientific spirit conclusions and generalizations are held subject to revision as new data may require.

The hopes held out for the field by such writers as L. K. Jordan early in the century have scarcely been realized. It may not be without significance that the Encyclopedia Brittanica, while it carries articles on Comparative Anatomy, Psychology, Philology etc. has no article on Comparative Religion. Terminology in the field is notoriously lacking in uniformity and much of the work in the comparative field is now carried on in departments of religion, history of religion, and even philosophy of religion in the universities of the world. See gods.

H. Pinard de la Boullaye, *L'Etude Comparee des Religions.* 2 vols. 3rd Edition (Paris, 1929). Vol I; J. Reville, *Les phases successives de L'histoire des religions* (Paris, 1900); L. H. Jordan, *Comparative Religion; Its Genesis and Growth* (Edinburgh, 1905); *Comparative Religion, Its Adjuncts and Allies* (London, 1915). C.S.B.

comparative symbolics: See Konfessions Kunde.

compline: (Lat. *completorium*) The late evening hour of the Divine Office*, so called because it completes the day's round of prayer. E.R.H.

Complutensian polyglot: See polyglot Bibles.

composition: In medieval customary law, payment made to the injured or to the relatives of the murdered by the offender in crimes of violence. In penance*, payments in lieu of penitential austerities.

J. T. McNeill and H. M. Gamer, *Medieval Handbooks of Penance* (1938). J.T.M.

compurgation: In primitive and medieval law, acceptance of the oaths of a prescribed number of witnesses (e.g., twenty-four) chosen by the accused, as proof of the latter's innocence. The system encouraged perjury. J.T.M.

Comte, Auguste: (1798-1857) French philosopher, founder of positivism and of the science of sociology.* His system, which was influenced by Saint-Simon (with whom he for a while collaborated, then quarreled), was not unlike Kantian phenomenalism.* It excludes metaphysics and is based on scientifically verifiable (positive) knowledge. Social and individual culture exemplifies the "law of the three stages" (discovered by Comte in 1822, but, as Boas notes, anticipated by Turgot in 1750). These stages are: the theological (personal gods); the metaphysical (impersonal forces), and the positive (laws derived from observation and experiment). In the positive stage, the six pure sciences are developed: mathematics, astronomy, physics, chemistry, biology (which includes psychology), and sociology. After 1845, his mystical friendship with Clotilde de Vaux led him to an interest in religion, and he founded "the religion of humanity," with humanity itself as the Supreme Being and object of worship, great figures of culture as its saints, every day in the year a saint's day, woman the object of worship in the home, and himself as chief priest. He attempted to found a church with but meager success. Modern religious humanism* owes much to Comte. Comte coined the terms positivism and altruism. See positivism.

His chief works are: *Cours de philosophie positive* (1830-1842), 6 vols.; *Catéchisme positiviste* (1852); and *Système de politique positive* (1851-1854), 4 vols.

See John Stuart Mill, *Auguste Comte and Positivism* (1865); H. Spencer, *Reasons for Dissenting from the Philosophy of M. Comte* (1884). E.S.B.

conceptualism: (Lat. *concipere, cept,* concept from *capere,* take) The theory in logic and epistemology which attempts to solve the medieval problem of universals* by holding that concepts, universals or abstract ideas, exist as such only in the mind devoid of any basis in reality or objective counterpart. However these concepts are more than mere words of empty sounds (cf. nominalism). This view has been attributed to Abailard* and (?) to Ockham*. Like nominalism, this view is opposed to and by the ultra-realism of Eriugena, William of Champeaux** *et al.* Cf. Scotism; terminism; etc. D.C.O'G.

conciliarism: The doctrine of the authority of representative church councils as over against that of the monarchical papacy. The doctrine became explicit in works by John of Paris (1302) and Marsiglio of Padua (1324) and was revived by Henry of Langenstein, John Gerson, Pierre d'Ailly** and numerous others after the beginning of the papal schism (1378). The councils of Pisa, Constance, Basel and Ferrara-Florence gave expression to the conciliar theory. This is summed up in the decree *Sacrosancta* of Constance*, 1415, which states that the council represents the catholic church militant and that all, including the pope, are bound to obey it in matters of faith and of the unity and reformation of the church. Conciliarism aimed at a representative system of church government. Protestant church polities in general may be called conciliar. The Gallican church in a nationalistic spirit reaffirmed the decrees of Constance in 1682.

G. J. Jordan, *The Inner History of the Great Schism* (London, 1930). J.T.M.

conclave: (Lat. *cum,* with, and *clavis,* key) The enclosure of the cardinals while electing a pope, an enclosure ordered in 1274 by Pope Gregory X and in some measure ever since practiced. See scrutiny. L.R.W.

Concord, Book of: See Book of Concord.

concordances: Alphabetical tables of words used in works of literature, with references for finding them. There were mediaeval concordances of the Latin Vulgate,* and a concordance of the Hebrew Bible was produced in the second quarter of the fifteenth century. A much improved edition of it was published by Buxtorf in 1632. The standard modern one is that of Mandelkern (Leipzig, 1896, Berlin, 1925). Of the Septuagint* the best concordance is that of Hatch and Redpath (Oxford, 1897-1900); of the Greek N. T., that of Moulton and Geden (1897). Cruden's useful concordance of the King James Version appeared in 1737, but for the student the best modern ones are Young's *Analytical Concordance* (Edinburgh, 1879), and James Strong's *Exhaustive Concordance of the Bible,* including the Revised Version (1894, 1923). E.J.G.

concordat: A concordat (*concordia, capitula concordata, pax, conventio, pactum, pactio*) is an agreement made between the highest officials of Church and State concerning the mutual relations they propose to observe permanently in any given country concerning either all matters, or only in certain eventualities, that might otherwise cause friction, and as agreed upon. Concordats generally refer to matters of a mixed nature, e.g. diocesan or religious organizations, appointments to important ecclesiastical positions (pastors, canons, bishops, etc.), matrimonial contracts and celebrations; schools and educational matters; financial assistance on the part of the State, etc. Cs. vary according to the origin of their legal obligatory force. At times this may be a law previously agreed upon and enacted by both Church and State as separate bodies, e.g. the Concordat of Worms;* or it might be a Papal Bull, accepted by the head of a government and then ratified by its regular legal channels (XIX cent. concordats); or finally, it might be a convention mutually agreed upon, properly phrased (usually both in Latin and in the language of the country concerned); then ratified by the corresponding heads—pope and king— or if with a Republic frequently also by Parliament or Chamber of Deputies, etc. Cs. are usually signed, for the pope, by the Cardinal Secretary of State; for the government, by an ambassador to the Holy See. A *Modus Vivendi* is differentiated from a C. in as much as it is not as yet a permanent, but only a tentative agreement, subject later either to ratification, alteration or annulment. (Pius XI agreed on such a *Modus Vivendi* with Czecho-Slovakia). Concordats, being bilateral, are considered sacred pledges and may not be rescinded, altered or abolished without the consent of the other party. It is evident that the Church does not consider herself in conscience or honor bound to respect agreements wrung from her by force.

There are predominantly three theories to explain the legal nature or binding force of Cs.: a) the Legalists Theory, which considering the State the supreme society, holds that it can only obligate, not agree with, any inferior body, such (as they hold) the Church; b) the Compact Theory, that makes the contract a bilateral contract; and c) the Privilege Theory, which holds that Cs. are obligatory only on the part of the State because of the privileges conceded by the Church. The last-named is often considered the more plausible theory. In reality, however, the papacy has traditionally always remained faithful to her part of an agreement and for that reason has not failed to protest, at times most emphatically, against infractions or violations on the part of the State, e.g., Pius X* (Encyclical: *Vehementer*, Feb. 11, 1906) regarding the persecution of the Church and Religious Orders in France; and Pius XI* (Encyc. *Mit brennerder Sorge*, May 14, 1937) regarding Nazi Germany. Famous historical Cs. are the: Concordat of Worms, 1122 between Callixtus II and Henry V of Germany ending the Investiture* Troubles; the C. of Constance*, Martin V and Spain, France, Germany and England; the French C. of 1516 between Leo X and Francis I of France, and of 1801, between Pius VII* and Napoleon I; and finally, the Lateran Treaty and Concordat of 1929 between Pius XI* and Italy, ending the so-called Roman Question. Papal Cs. are made only between the popes and such countries as have diplomatic (ambassadorial or ministerial) relations with the Holy See. In recent years (since 1926) in Germany, as in many other predominantly Protestant, Evangelical and non-Catholic countries, Cs. have frequently been signed between the corresponding governments and the responsible heads or controlling bodies of such (Evangelical, etc.) Churches.

Lexikon f. Theologie u. Kirche, VI, 134-8; *Cath. Encyc.* IV, 196-203; A. Mercati, *Raccolta di Concordati* (1098-1914) (Rome, 1919); *Dict. de la Théol. Cath.* III, 727-44. R.M.H.

Concordat of Worms: See Worms, Concordat of.

concupiscence: (*con*—intensitive, and *cupio*, desire) In Augustinian theology* the technical term, from Tertullian through the Vulgate's translation of *epithumia*, for the excessive desire both general and sexual that characterizes fallen man. St. Thomas held original sin* to be formally privation of original righteousness, and materially to be concupiscence. See sin. T.J.B.

concursus: (Lat. *con*, and *currere*, to run along with) That aspect of Divine Providence whereby God co-operates with the operations of created, or secondary, causes.* It is frequently divided into (i) *moral concursus*, which is the divine co-operation with the natural and supernatural actions of rational beings, and (ii) *physical concursus*, which is God's co-operation in all the actions of secondary causes in created nature. There has been much discussion as to the manner in which divine concursus works, especially in regard to the question of the pre-determination of the moral and religious acts of man. The problem is related on the one hand to the freedom of moral creatures and the relative autonomy of contingent physical agents, and on the other hand to the omnipotence and foreknowledge** of God, in particular to the extent and efficacy of the creative decree. An additional difficulty is presented by the fact of morally evil actions, in which God concurs without giving approval to their evil aspects. V.J.B.

condignity: (Lat. *con*, and *dignus*, worthy) A moral relationship in which the subject of a right is regarded as being of comparative equality with the term of the right. In its perfect form, condignity applies to the situation of commutative justice. Condign merit is that moral exigency devolving upon another person to reward or punish a subject in accordance with the exercise of his right. Contrasted with congruity*. V.J.B.

conditional immortality: See immortality, conditional.

conductus: A polyphonic*, unaccompanied, choral composition based upon an original Latin text, not employing a Gregorian chant* as its foundation. The rhythm was similar in all parts and words were often sung in only one part. Its popularity in the 12th and 13th centuries centered in Paris where Pérotin was a prominent composer. Due to greater interest in the polytextual motet* the conductus fell into disuse by the 14th century.

H. E. Wooldridge, *Oxford History of Music*, Vol. I (1901); L. Ellinwood, "The Conductus," *Musical Quarterly* (April, 1941). E.H.B.

confession: The acknowledgment of sins to a priest as the representative of God and the Church, for the purpose of obtaining absolution* and counsel. In Catholic theology and devotion Confession has develped from a means of removing excommunication, as Penance* was in the patristic period, to a means of progress in devotion in the medieval and modern period. The changes are 1) private instead of public penances (public confession itself had changed to private confession with public penance by the beginning of the patristic period); 2) lenient and precatory instead of severe and penal penances; 3) frequent and regular use for all sins instead of use only for great sins; and 4) administration by a priest instead of by a bishop.

Confession has become in modern Catholicism the chief means and center of moral and pastoral work. The Roman Catholic Church* makes confession before communion at least once a year (the Easter duty) obligatory. The Orthodox Church (See Orthodox Churches) expects confession annually, the Anglican Church (See Church of England) as often as the penitent needs it. Of the penitent is required a) contrition, b) confession, c) satisfaction, which mean a) self-examination, sorrow, purpose of amendment, b) honest and full confession, and c) fulfillment of the assigned penance. The priest decides upon the fulfillment of these requirements and gives or refuses absolution. He is described as fulfilling the spiritual offices of judge, father, physician, and teacher. Among Protestants recent revivals of confession involve the last three of these offices, here in accord with Zwingli* who regarded as valid only the office of teacher, the direction of souls, but with more attention to the work of physician in accordance with modern psychological counseling.

P. Batiffol, *Etudes d'histoire et de theologie positive* (Paris, 1902--06); C. E. Schieler and H. J. Heuser, *Theory and Practice of the Confessional* (1905); K. E. Kirk, *Vision of God* (London, 1932); *Some Principles of Moral Theology* (London, 1934).

T.J.B.

confession, seal of: See seal of confession.

confessional: A stall, or prayer desk and chair where confessions are heard, usually in this country an enclosed structure where the priest sits into which the penitent speaks through an aperture. Sometimes, by metonymy, the whole discipline of penance. See confession; penance; penitential (manual). T.J.B.

confessionalism, Lutheran: See neo-Lutheranism; Missouri Lutherans.

confessions of faith: See symbolics.

Confessions, Formal, of the Christian Church: For Eastern* Catholicism the deposit of faith is not only in the Nicene Creed but also in the findings of the Councils of Ephesus (431), Chalcedon (451), Constantinople (553), Constantinople (680) and Nicaea (787).

Of the twenty articles in the Confession of Gennadius (1453) the last seven were added later, the dialogue with the Turk is entirely unauthentic, and what remains is not standard because the definition of the trinity has been weakened.

The four answers of Jeremiah II,* Patriarch of Constantinople, to the Tuebingen Lutheran theologians (1574-81) criticizing the Augsburg Confession* are considered a symbol.

The Confession of Metrophanes Critopulus (1625) composed for the Helmstaedt theologians, published 1661, recognizes only baptism, penance, and the eucharist as necessary mysteries and contained a polemic against Roman Catholicism but not against Protestantism and excludes the apocrypha from the canon. Formal ecclesiastical sanction is lacking.

Of the eighteen paragraphs in the Confession of Cyril Lucar (1629, 1631, 1633) ten are tinged with Calvinism,* gained from reading and correspondence and not sojourn in Calvinistic countries. Chapter II accepts the Bible as superior in authority to the church. Cyril reduces the seven sacraments to two and substitutes the real but spiritual presence for transubstantiation.* The doctrine of purgatory* has also disappeared and justification by faith is approved. This Patriarch of Constantinople was five times deposed, five times reinstated and at last strangled to death (1638). Against this confession, Peter Mogilas, Metropolitan of Kiev and father of Russian theology in 1638 composed a confession (1642, approved; 1667, published) which was made a canonical confession and doctrinal standard of the Russian Church in 1839.

The orthodox ecclesiastical rejection of Cyril Lucar's confession came in 1672 at the synod of Jerusalem and in consequence of charges of secret sympathy of the Eastern church with Calvinism. This synod was the most important in modern times for the Eastern church. Dositheus, Patriarch of Jerusalem, was fanatically orthodox and the eighteen articles of his confession plus the closing four questions and answers place his church unequivocally on the side of Rome and in opposition to Calvinism.

Roman Catholicism in addition to approving the "ecumenical creeds" accepts the findings of its own councils and the declarations of its popes. The Council of Trent* (1543-63) sought the authorization of Pope Pius IV. The oath of obedience to the pope had held for archbishops since the thirteenth century, for bishops since the fifteenth and was now extended to canons. The pope reserved the exclusive right of interpreting the proceedings of Trent even as he confirmed the decrees of the 255 fathers on the Nicene Creed, the Scriptures, original sin, justification, the various sacraments and purgatory. The Profession of the Tridentine* Faith (Creed of Pius IV, 1564) is binding upon all priests and public teachers. It consists of the western form of the Nicene Creed of 381, a summary of the conclusions of Trent, additional articles and solemn pledges of allegiance to the faith and to the pope. The Roman Catechism, 1566, deals with Apostles' Creed, the seven sacraments, the decalogue and the Lord's Prayer.

The papal definition of the immaculate conception* of the Virgin Mary*, 1854, and of papal infallibility*, 1870, round out the formulation of the Roman creed. The former reads "the 'Blessed Virgin Mary in the first instant of her conception was by a singular grace and privilege of Almighty God, in view of the merits of Christ Jesus the Savior of mankind, preserved free from all stain of original sin . . ."; the latter, "the Roman pontiff when he speaks *ex cathedra,* that is, when in discharge of the office of pastor and doctor of all Christians, by virtue of his supreme Apostolic authority, he defines a doctrine regarding faith or morals to be held by the universal Church . . . is possessed of that infallibility with which the divine Redeemer willed that his Church should be endowed for defining doctrine regarding faith or morals; and that therefore such definitions of the Roman Pontiff are irreformable of themselves and not from the consent of the Church."

The Book of Concord* (1580) of the Evangelical Lutheran Church contained nine symbols:

The Apostles' Creed, the Nicene Creed (with filioque*), the Athanasian Creed, the Augsburg Confession**, the Apology of the Confession, the Articles of Schmalkald*, the two catechisms of Luther and the Formula of Concord. In Editions printed in Saxony since 1700 the Visitation Articles of 1592 appear.

By 1530, Lutheranism was defined. The doctrinal conflicts after the death of Luther were synthesized in the Formula of Concord* which signified a return to the theology of Luther from the mediating tendencies of Melanchthon*. The late sixteenth century formulation held generally until Pietism and the Enlightenment** won out at the German universities in the early eighteenth century. This victory was a defeat for old Lutheranism. Toward the end of the Napoleonic epoch a new Lutheranism emerges, demanded by and corresponding to the new German nationalism. The doctrinal parallelogram consists of a christocentric emphasis after the Pauline pattern, a feeling of solidarity with the confessional inheritance, a reawakening of the sacramental motives, and the significance of the church-concept. Literalism and biblicism yield to spiritual connections between the Bible and the Reformation. Since 1919 and particularly since 1933, the Lutheranism of Germany has been faced by a political and syncretistic religious challenge whose outcome cannot be predicted.

The central core of Lutheranism is justification* *sola fide* which immediately called in question the penitential* system of medieval Catholicism, eliminated the sacrifice of Christ in the mass*, demanded the priesthood of every believer and secularized piety and asceticism. Where this fundamental was not in question, Lutheranism remained conservative in worship, organization, and practice. The secularization of ethics prevented theocratic adventures. Provincial churches retarded the rapid development of a sense of solidarity changing with the appearance of a national state and consciousness.

The refusal of Luther at Marburg, 1529, to recognize the Swiss and South Germans as of the same faith was the birthday of the Reformed* faith. Inability to agree upon the interpretation of the eucharist was the parting of the way between Lutherans and the Reformed faith. For Calvinism* the authority of the Bible is the norm of faith and practice. Here a confession of faith is an attempt to summarize the Bible. The "ecumenical creeds" were accepted because felt to be in agreement with the Bible. Christology was not the point of departure. The foci of the Reformed ellipse were predestination and the Bible. Everything and everyone are predetermined yet man falls voluntarily and God is not the originator of sin. Through sin man is incapable of any good act and salvation is wholly of God. Faith itself is the gift of God. Good works can only be the fruitage of faith and never merit. Only the predestined belong to the church. *Finitum non capax infiniti!*

There are over thirty Reformed confessions of faith ranging from the Sixty-seven articles of Zwingli*, 1523, to the Westminster Confession* of Faith, 1647, and thereafter. The Heidelberg Catechism* became very popular. The Westminster Confession, a development of the Irish Articles*, 1615, is the basis both of the Savoy Declaration*, 1658, and the Philadelphia Confession, 1688 and its English Baptist ancestor, the Assembly or Second London Confession, 1677. It was immediately adopted by the Scottish Kirk and parliament. Thus it is the standard for Presbyterians, Baptists, Congregationalists** and many bodies deriving from them. It is the culmination and end of creative reformed Protestant thought.

The Thirty-nine Articles*, whose theology is that of the Augsburg Confession, with many subsequent changes, derive from the forty-two Edwardine articles and the thirteen articles of 1538. Anti-Roman Catholic sentiments appear in some ten articles, for example, "as the church of Jerusalem, Alexandria, and Antioch, have erred; so also the Church of Rome hath erred, not only in their living and manner of ceremonies, but also in matters of faith." The twenty-one homilies, Article XXXV, could not be approved by any Catholic censor of books as good selections for perusal by the faithful. "The Prayer Book and the Thirty-nine Articles are not vital parts of the Episcopal church but the two creeds are." "The theology of the Thirty-nine Articles is the theology of the Confession of Augsburg."

The confessions of faith of the democratically organized European Protestants begin when the Anabaptists* whose modern descendants are the Mennonites* drew up their first confession in 1527. It dealt with baptism, excommunication, breaking of bread, avoidance of abominable pastors in the church, sword and swearing. The Mennonite confession of about 1580 consists of forty articles and was necessitated by the disagreement and dissension that involved discipline and the understanding of Jesus. It has many biblical prooftexts for every clause in each article. It rejects infant baptism, the oath, the sword, war but acknowledges "just and moderate power."

In the democratic Protestant bodies creeds are little more than local as far as their binding nature is concerned since the covenant supersedes them. For Congregationalists and Baptists the general theology of the Westminster Confession holds. Even platforms and declarations vanish among the Friends* although the Apology of Robert Barclay is valued by the more orthodox Friends. At present fundamentalist groups among the Baptists are insisting upon binding ministers and teachers by subscription to creeds.

After the adoption of the United States Constitution and the Bill of Rights, it was necessary for some denominations to revise their confessions of faith. Chapters XX, XXIII, and XXXI of the Westminster Confession and Question 109 of the Larger Catechism required attention as did the Royal Declaration and especially Article XXXVII of the Thirty-nine Articles. The Formula of Concord was revised in the anathema section. The Methodist Articles of Religion, 1784, made changes in their Article XXIII. In 1784 the

Roman Catholic Church in the United States took action to meet the requirement of the United States forbidding "its Catholic subjects to have foreign vicars-apostolic as their superiors". The American environment has deeply modified interpretations of the inherited faith. Unitarianism* declares its faith to be the fatherhood of God, the brotherhood of man, the leadership of Jesus, salvation by character, progress of man onward and upward forever, while Universalism* asserts the universal fatherhood of God, the spiritual authority and leadership of his Son, the trustworthiness of the Bible as containing a revelation of God, the certainty of just retribution for sin, and the final harmony of all souls with God.

For the confessions of faith of the hundreds of American cults and sects, the last United States Census of Religious Bodies (1936) should be consulted which is easily the best source book on contemporary religion in the United States. See creeds of Christendom. See also Belgic Confession; Cambridge Platform; Dordrecht Confession; Forty-two Articles; Gallican Confessions; Helvetic Confessions; Scots Confession; Syllabus of Errors, Papal; Tetrapolitan Confession; Thirteen Articles; Torgau Articles.

Census Religious Bodies, U. S. (1936); W. A. Curtis, "Confessions" in *Hastings E. R. E.,* 3, 831-901; C. Hardwick, *History of the Articles* (1884); W. J. McGlothlin, *Baptist Confessions of Faith* (1911); J. T. Mueller, *Die sym. Bücher der evang. luth. Kirche* (1869); P. Schaff, *Creeds of Christendom,* 3 vol. (1876). C.H.M.

confessor: (Lat. *cum,* with, and *fiteor,* to witness) a) A priest juridically hearing confessions and giving absolution*; b) a person who "has given heroic testimony" to the Christian faith. L.R.W.

confirmation: The completion of Baptism* by the laying on of hands* or unction* (or both), thus bestowing full initiation* into Christian discipleship with its gift of the Holy Spirit—so understood in the early and mediaeval Church on the basis of Acts 8:14-17, 19:1-7, and references to imposition of hands or anointing*. From at least the second century the normal minister was the Bishop*. From about the fourth, unction was considered the essential sign; in the Eastern Church the close connection with Baptism was retained, leading to administration by presbyters (using chrism* consecrated by the Bishop—in modern times usually by Patriarchs)—in the West episcopal administration was adhered to, leading to delay in most cases for some years. The Council of Trent* recommended the age of seven, allowing for some instruction before confirmation. The Bishop is the proper minister, though delegation to priests is possible. Anglicanism retained the rite, with laying on of hands as the sign (though chrism has been revived in some quarters, beginning with 18th century Non-Jurors*); postponement to adolescence became common and the candidate's "confirming" of baptismal vows often received more attention than the Bishop's confirming of the candidate. In recent years there has been some return to a younger age. In Lutheranism confirmation was continued as the conclusion of catechetical instruction and admission to communion, with the pastor's blessing—as such it has spread in some other Protestant circles (in combination with or as an alternative to the Evangelical practice of "joining the church" after conscious conversion*). Confirmation, however understood, completes Christian initiation and so normally precedes First Communion—although in current Roman Catholic practice the order is often reversed. Strength for Christian discipleship is the gift prayed for. Where the outward sign is held to convey the gift confirmation is commonly called a Sacrament, as in Roman Catholic and Orthodox teaching, and often in Anglican except where the name is strictly limited to the two Sacraments "generally necessary for salvation". See catechumenate; laying on of hands; initiation rites; sacraments.

W. K. L. Clarke and others, *Confirmation or the Laying on of Hands* (1926), 2 vols. Matthias Laros, tr. G. Sayer, *Confirmation in the Modern World* (1938). E.R.H.

confiteor: (Lat., I confess) The form of general confession preparatory to the Roman Mass. A similar form is used also in prime and compline**. P.V.N.

Confraternities: Pious unions requiring a formal decree of erection, founded for the increase and spread of some act of public worship. The best known confraternities in this country are those of the Blessed Sacrament and of Christian Doctrine, a branch of which are required in each parish. Archconfraternities are those confraternities having the right to affiliate other confraternities or sodalities, and to communicate to them their privileges. See Catholic Societies. T.T.M.

Confucius: See Chinese Terminology.

Confucianism: See Chinese Terminology.

congregation: Etymologically, an assembly of persons. The word is used mostly in religious connections. It signifies 1) a gathering at a particular time for worship; 2) an organized local group meeting regularly for worship and other religious purposes; in this sense the congregation is the basis of congregational polity; 3) in Roman Catholic usage, a branch of a monastic order or an association or an administrative body, e.g., the Congregation of the Propaganda*. R.H.N.

Congregation of the Index: See censorship of books.

Congregational Holiness Church: A pentecostal sect having 56 churches and 2,100 members in the Carolinas, Georgia, Alabama, and Florida. It was organized in 1921 in a secession from the Pentecostal Holiness Church. Its main principles are sanctification, divine healing, speaking in unknown tongues, feet washing, and the second coming of Christ. See pentecostal sects. E.T.C.

congregational independency: See independency.

Congregational Methodist Church: See holiness churches.

Congregationalism: In its current uses designates an American protestant denomination, or a fellowship of "free-churches" in Great Britain. One may, therefore, accurately speak or write of the Congregational denomination. Baptists, Unitarians, Disciples** and other smaller American denominations are congregational in their church polity, but are not so designated denominationally. American Congregationalism cannot be understood apart from its history. It is English in its origin and can be loosely dated as a movement from about 1550.

Its history can be generalized under four phases. The first was entirely an aspect of the English Reformation. Certain Anglican clergymen of a radical temper refused to accept the Elizabethan settlement of the confused religious situation, withdrew from the Church thus established and refused to conform to the authority and procedures of the Anglican Church. They gathered and led fluid groups of humble people and sought to constitute independent churches after what they believed to be New Testament models. Such inchoate churches later chose their own ministers and administered their own affairs. They were in substance Congregational though not so named. These non-conforming* groups were bitterly persecuted and the most steadfast were driven into exile in Holland.

This connecting group between the English and American phase of Congregationalism maintained themselves in Leyden, Holland for about twelve years under the capable leadership of John Robinson, pastor, and William Brewster**. They then migrated to New England and founded the Plymouth Bay Colony. They were purely independent in polity. Massachusetts Bay was settled by Puritan* migrants whose leaders formed a Presbyterian polity, though with qualifications. Their lonely situation, and possibly the influence of Samuel Fuller of Plymouth, led them to organize their first church at Salem, Massachusetts on a congregational basis—though that use of the word is anticipatory.

The second phase of American Congregational history was marked by a struggle between the Presbyterian bias of many Massachusetts Bay leaders and a more democratic form of church government. The result was a compromise called, in contrast with the then dominant English Presbyterian* puritanism "The New England Way," or else the "Congregational Way" which seems the first use of the word in its present connotation. The local church maintained its independence and administered its internal affairs by congregational decision but was subject in the ordination and installation of its pastors and teachers to the advice and approval of its neighboring churches. Also and naturally, theirs was a growing community of action.

In the third phase of its history Congregationalism, as thus established, maintained a priority in the New England colonies—and later in the New England states—and may be accurately defined as the religious aspect of their social, political, economic and cultural life. During this period which lasted until the beginning of the Nineteenth Century, Congregationalism may be called the most geographically and culturally unified religious fellowship in America.

In its fourth phase Congregationalism for many reasons, among which must certainly be noted an attempt at a most intimate cooperation with New York and New Jersey Presbyterianism, failed to maintain this priority in the rapid and always widening growth of the Interior and Western States. Its polity made any central control and direction difficult. Toward the middle of the 19th century this weakness was so strongly felt that movements toward a national organization were initiated which, being consistently pursued, have resulted in an increasingly unified control of all shared enterprises, though individual churches still maintain their congregational status.

Theologically, American Congregationalism inherited and continued Calvinism*. The Westminister confession* was accepted as a doctrinal basis and later the Savoy declaration* which was extremely Calvinistic. The system was debated, defended, expounded and improved by a distinguished succession of theologians beginning with Jonathan Edwards* and ending with Professor E. A. Park*. Their systems were known as a New England rather than a Congregational theology, though they were all Congregationalists. They debated the questions with which all Calvinistic theology has concerned itself; freedom, moral responsibility, the sovereignty of God, the scheme of salvation, etc. They mitigated somewhat the severities of the system as their succession lengthened.

There were, however, both restraining and liberating forces in Congregational polity, which saved the churches from rigid subscription to a denominational creed and defended enquiring minds from heresy trials. Behind these defences a liberalizing movement was begun, principally by Horace Bushnell*, and continued by Congregational preachers, scholars and teachers. For perhaps forty years preceding the first world war the Congregational mind strongly influenced the religious transition which eventuated in America in 19th century religious liberalism.

Congregationalism took an acknowledged leadership in the promotion of Foreign missions and in the founding of early American universities and colleges. Its historic dominance in New England has been affected by economic changes and a great infiltration of non-Protestant population elements. Its churches are now generally distributed across the continent but, save through its concern for Negro education, it has found no field in the Southern states. Some years ago it achieved a really organic union with the Christian denomination*.

There were in 1940 6,006 Congregational Christian churches in the United States with 1,058,807 members. These churches gave $2,023,350.00 to benevolent and missionary causes. Their expenditures for their own maintenance were $14,

966,108.00. See American theology, early; Cambridge Platform; New England theology; Saybrook Platform.

Henry M. Dexter, *The Congregationalism of the last 300 years, as seen by its literature* (1880): Williston Walker, *A History of the Congregational Churches in the U. S.* (1899); Albert E. Dunning, *Congregationalists in America* (1894); Leonard Woolsey Bacon, *The Congregationalists* (1904); G. G. Atkins and F. L. Fagley, *History of American Congregationalism* (1942). G.G.A.

congresses: Assemblies promoting the spiritual, social and intellectual welfare of Catholics. Congresses are religious, educational, political, social, sociological; regional, diocesan, national and international. The first noted Congress convened at Mainz, Germany in 1848. B.R.

congruism: (Lat. *congruitas,* fitness) The theological reference is to fitness to receive grace*. Not merit versus grace in salvation itself, but man can so live to deserve grace. Scotists* held this; Thomists*: man can do this only by God's aid. Anglican Thirty-nine Articles*, XIII, denies Scotist position. J.L.

congruity: (Lat. *congruus,* suitable) A moral relationship in which the subject of a right is not regarded as the equal, but as the inferior or superior, of the one who is the term of the right. Such a situation is found in distributive justice, where the receiver of a benefit is not duty-bound to make an equal return as he would be under commutative justice. Thus, congruous merit is rewarded on the basis of a ratio of subject to term which is other than that of equality. See **condignity.** V.J.B.

Conrad of Gelnhausen: (1320-1390) Theologian, professor at the University of Paris, later Chancellor of the University of Heidelberg. His *Epistola Concordiae* advocating the conciliar method for ending the great western schism influenced the thinking of later conciliar* theologians, notably Henry of Langenstein and Jean Gerson**. F.W.N.

Consalvi, Ercole: (1757-1824) Cardinal, Secretary of State under Pope Pius VII*. He patronized the fine arts, science and literature. The Concordat* between the Papacy and Napoleon was largely due to his statesmanship. C.V.

consanguinity, marital impediment of: Consanguinity, or relationship by blood within prohibited degress, is a marital impediment* that prevents the conclusion of a valid marriage or enforces dissolution of a *de facto* union the parties to which are so related.

The canon law is based upon the Roman law (*Cod. Just,* V, iv, 18-19; *Cod. Theo.,* III, xii, 1-3), scriptural passages especially Lev. XVIII, 7-14, and the interpretations of these passages by St. Ambrose and St. Augustine. From the 6th to 13th centuries many conciliar canons and papal decretals forbade marriages of persons related within the seventh degree, but the rigor of this prohibition was relaxed by the Fourth Lateran Council (1215) which stipulated the fourth degree as the limit.

After much controversy among the canonists, the decision of Alexander II (1061-1073) was accepted. He held that the degree was the number of generations between the parties and a common ancestor, excluding that ancestor. (Migne, *Patrologiae,* CXLVI, 1379-81). Gregory IX (1227-41) decreed that when the parties to a marriage were related to a common ancestor in different degrees the longer line was to be the determining factor in calculation of the degree for canonical purposes. (Decretals, IV, xiv, 9).

P. E. Corbett, *The Roman Law of Marriage* (Oxford, 1930); H. Feije, *De impedimentis et dispensationibus matrimonialibus* (Louvain, 1885); C. E. Smith, *Papal Enforcement of Some Medieval Marriage Laws* (1940). C.E.S.

conscience: The term originally denoted simple consciousness without ethical bearing. As a kind of consciousness it exists at all levels: perceptual, classificatory and creative. In Neo-Platonism self-consciousness obtained an ethico-religious color. With the rise of Christianity conscience is described as an independent source of moral insight. In the Middle Ages *synderesis* came to be connected with conscience. The former is the permanent inborn disposition of the mind to think general rules of moral conduct from which the individual can reason in directing his moral activities. Very common in the thirteenth century, the term was interpreted either as a disposition of the will or of the intellect. The scholastics clearly distinguished between synderesis and conscience, the latter being practical reason endowed with special principles, enabling the individual to act morally. It was in the beginning of the modern period that conscience, in contrast to consciousness, came to stand for a specialization of mental function distinguishing between right and wrong. With the rise of modern speculation conscience became an inner, primeval faculty. Theological tradition explained conscience as the voice of God in our souls, a divinely implanted conviction of right and wrong. The corruption of the will by sin causes uncertainty in its voice. This doctrine in its many forms characterizes especially the religious thought of Western civilization, attesting to the growing importance of morality in religious experience. Where the theologian, unable to derive conscience from any human source, calls it a divine endowment, the intuitionist says it is underived, an innate endowment. Some intuitionists have regarded it as a direct perceptual capacity; others have stressed its emotional quality; a feeling of approval or disapproval; still others have explained it as the direct and authoritative guidance of our moral life. All these doctrines affirm the direct certainty of conscience and assume an evident finality in the moral direction of our lives. Empirically, conscience is simply the inference from our past experience as guidance for the future. Its sanctions are relative to specific experiences and situations. Its authority is ever subject to revision and recall. It is the voice of man's fuller self, the man that he may yet be. Intense devotion to duty when allied to bigotry, obscurantism, if sanctified by the halo of religion may lead to unspeakable evil (Torquemada's consignment of the heretics to the flames). Conscience is not infallible. Hence it needs to be trained, kept enlightened, learning to be conscientious about itself, and self-critical of its judgment. Being unyielding and imperative in principle, despotic and ruthless in execution, it can result in tragedy. A too self-confident conscience is a moral peril. It becomes stunted unless it transcends itself. It must face the reality of its own possible shortcomings.

Sociological naturalists maintain that conscience is the result of the pressure of society upon the individual, an echo, the reality of which are the folkways. Their theories do not do justice to the type of behavior in which men defy their group. The individual character of conscience does preclude determination of most moral judgments by the opinions of the group. Neither the social character of most moral judgments nor the pressure of society upon the individual explain the nature of conscience. Historically related to both the rational and impulsive elements in human nature, it is as unique as the capacity for conceptual knowledge. Like the latter it may be strengthened, enlarged by discipline, or it may deteriorate from lack of use. It is more potent when it supports one impulse against another than when it sets itself against the total force of the individual's desires. It operates more effectively when it consolidates and stabilizes socially valuable impulses. Although the development of reason increases the opportunities for exercising conscience, it is very dubious if the growth of reason strengthens the force of conscience as much as is claimed. Religion is much more potent in this task. Although we need books that nourish conscience, it is even more essential that we have books that facilitate an understanding of the nature of conscience and of its role in society, books that reduce the claims of conscience to proportions that bear sustained scrutiny, that reward sincere devotion and that can withstand criticism.

L. F. Anderson, *Die Seele und das Gewissen* (Leipzig, 1929); J. H. Breasted, *The Dawn of Conscience* (1933); M. St. Gillet, *L'education de la conscience* (Paris, 1913); C. T. Gorham, *Why we do right: a rational view of conscience* (London, 1924); V. Jankelevitch, *La mauvaise conscience* (Paris, 1933); H. Jeffs, *Concerning conscience, studies in practical ethics* (London, 1912); K. E. Kirk, *Conscience and its problems; an introduction to casuistry* (London, 1927); T. V. Smith, *Beyond Conscience* (1934); P. Sollier, *Morale et moralite; essay sur l'intuition morale* (Paris, 1912); H. G. Stoker, *Das Gewissen, Erscheinungsformen und Theorien* (Bonn, 1925).

H.H.

consensus gentium: See epistemology; immortality, arguments for and against.

consensus patrum: (Lat. consent of the Fathers) In matters of faith or morals, when the Fathers of the Church teach with moral unanimity a doctrine to be of faith, that doctrine is of faith. In the same way, what they unanimously condemn as heretical, is heretical. Further, the logical conclusions which they unanimously draw from articles of faith provide us with theological arguments that are certain. In philosophical or scientific matters, the authority of the Fathers is only as strong as their arguments. C.V.

conservation of value: The phrase was coined by Harald Höffding* (*Philosophy of Religion*, tr., 1906) to express the "characteristic axiom of religion" parallel to the scientific axiom of the conservation of energy. Contemporary as well as ancient religious thought confirms Höffding's claim that the innermost tendency of all religious experience is the minimum faith and demand, not simply that there will always be value*, but that there will be the "continuous conservation of value throughout all transformations" (*Ibid.*, p. 11). Implicit in this faith, as Höffding, W. R. Sorley*, and E. S. Brightman, among others, have noted, is the realization that values cannot be conserved without being increased continuously.

Thus to be completely accurate the phrase should read: faith in the continuous realization of the *highest* values beyond the limitations of human experience and history. As Höffding says, "the faith does not presuppose that there must always be a certain amount of actual value in existence, but only that there must always be the same possibility for the coming into being of value." (*Ibid.*, p. 222).

The particular theoretical foundation of this faith varies with the metaphysical account of value. W. R. Sorley, for example, maintains that the faith presupposes rather than indicates the objective validity of a realm of values, since there is not enough empirical evidence for such preservation. For some thinkers God is the impersonal, objective system of values, while for others the highest values are ideals in God's consciousness.

W. R. Sorley, *Moral Values and the Idea of God* (1930); E. S. Brightman, *Philosophy of Religion* (1940).

P.A.B.

conservative Judaism: See Judaism, conservative.

consilia evangelica (evangelical counsels): They comprise poverty, celibacy and obedience, the following of which leads to a higher perfection. Individuals intent upon striving toward perfection take them as norm for their conduct. They are accepted by voluntary solemn promise. Their positive aim is the furtherance of love. They are instruments of perfection. H.H.

consistent Calvinists: See Calvinists, consistent.

consistory: Generically, an assembly of ecclesiastical office-bearers for transacting business. In Roman Catholic usage a consistory is a meeting of cardinals, the Pope** presiding; such now are merely formal. In some Reformed polities, e.g., the Reformed Church in America, the consistory, composed of the pastor of a church and the elders and deacons, has authority over the congregation, corresponding to the session*. The system of government originally established in the Lutheran churches of the German states was called consistorial, the consistories, district and general, being administrative bodies of clerical and lay membership appointed by the civil authority. These succeeded to the medieval consistorial courts through which the bishops administered their dioceses. In later Lutheranism the consistorial system has been much modified. In the Church of England consistory courts in dioceses remain. R.H.N.

consolamentum: The Catharist rite of spiritual baptism whereby the spirit of consolation was administered to an individual for the forgiveness of his sins and the liberation of his soul from the kingdom of fleshly evil to that of spiritual good. Imparted by the laying on of hands* by one who already possessed it, and further signified by placing John's gospel on the recipient's head, the consolation conferred true apostolical succession* upon the candidate, thus rendering him a member of the "perfect". Necessary to salvation, it was rarely administered to "believers" until the moment of death. R.C.P.

consolation: 1) Alleviation of sorrow; the soothing of disappointment or sadness. The word occurs frequently in ascetical and devotional literature, to denote the happiness that succeeds periods of spiritual depression or aridity in prayer.

2) Evening meal of monks. An evening repast given to monks by way of addition to their ordinary supper or *collatio,* as a sort of compensation on occasions of extraordinarily prolonged prayer or work; also, more generous and tasty portions of food or wine served on great feasts. C.V.

Constance, Council of: (Nov. 5, 1414-April 22, 1418). The high-water mark of the Conciliar Era, this council, which ended the Great Schism*, was called by John XXIII under the aegis of Sigismund. There were three objectives: *unity* in the headship of the church, for there were three popes John XXIII (Council of Pisa), Gregory XII (Rome), Benedict XIII (Avignon); *reform* in respect to clerical abuses (there was a general demand for reform of the church in head and members, and some even urged abolition of the cardinalate); and *heresy* (Wycliffism, Hussism). The order in which these three issues were to be taken up was long and hotly debated.

By July of 1417 the three popes had been disposed of, by deposition with papal ratification (John XXIII), by resignation (Gregory XII), and deposition without papal ratification (Benedict XIII). Nov. 11, 1417 Cardinal Otto Colonna was elected, who took the name of Martin V.

With respect to heresy the council brought to trial John Hus* who was executed in 1415, despite imperial safe-conduct. In 1417 Jerome of Prague* was executed. Wyclifite errors were anathematized.

As to reform there was sharp difference of opinion, mainly on the question of whether the pope (or pope-in-council) or whether the council (with the pope as executive officer) is the true agent of reform. This was expressed learnedly but with moderation by Gerson* in his sermon, March 23, 1415. In its decree *Haec sancta* of April 6, 1415 (Fifth Session) the Council laid down the principle that its authority is from Christ and that even the pope had to submit to its decrees. In its decree *Frequens* of October 9, 1417 (Thirty-ninth Session) the principle of conciliar* periodicity was adopted; the next councils would meet after five years, then after seven years, and thereafter decennially. Councils might, in case of schism, meet without formal convocation. A commission appointed by the nations was to work with the pope to bring about desired reforms in the whole ecclesiastical system. To the college of cardinals were to be joined six from each four nations so that in papal elections the whole church might be represented.

Martin V accepted the decrees generally but with the important reservations based on the inviolability of papal supremacy.

See Nicholas de Clémanges, Pierre D'Ailly, ecumenical councils (bibliography).

M. Creighton: *A History of the Papacy from the Great Schism to the Sack of Rome* (London, 1905-07), Bk. II "The Council of Constance" in vol. i, 299-vol. ii, 128. L. Pastor, *The History of the Popes, from the Close of the Middle Ages* (London, 1923), vol. i, 193-207.

C. Mirbst, *Quellen* (Tübingen, 1934), pp. 227-231, 242 f.

M. Spinka, *John Hus and the Czech Reform,* (1941). Ch. III 'The Trial". Q.B.

Constantine the Great, Emperor: (272 or 274-337 A.D.) Son of Constantius Chlorus who was successively Caesar and Augustus over the prefecture of Gaul, a competent soldier and constructive ruler. His mother was Helena, whose relationship to Constantius is debated. From 292 to 305 Constantine was at the court of Diocletian, ostensibly for education but really as a hostage. After Diocletian's abdication in 305 he fled the imperial (Galerius') court to join his father who had become Augustus. Upon the latter's death in 306 Constantine was designated Augustus (by the paternal testament and army). He gained popularity in Gaul, especially with the Christians for his mild treatment of them. In 311 he "delivered" Rome from Maxentius in the Battle of the Milvian Bridge. On the way to Rome he had seen his vision of the cross and the words "In hoc signo vinces." In 313, together with Licinius, he issued the celebrated Edict of Toleration. Constantine now controlled the prefectures of Gaul and Italy; a defeat of Licinius, partly because of the latter's persecution of Christians, ended in Constantine's final defeat of him in 324 and in his issuance of a decree of universal toleration. In 325 he convened and took part in the Council of Nicea*. In 326, on charges by Fausta his wife he put to death his son Crispus, and soon after, perhaps, ordered her to be executed. In 330 he dedicated the city of Constantinople (whose building had perhaps been planned already in 324) on the site of Byzantium. His last years were spent in wars and ecclesiastical affairs. He was baptized on his death-bed. Constantine was the subject of several legends, e.g., Donation of Constantine* . See Arles, Synod of; Donatism; Lactantius.

A Select Library of the Nicene and Post-Nicene Fathers (New York, 1925), vol. i contains translations of important sources: Eusebius' *Ecclesiastical History*, (translated and edited by A. C. McGiffert); Eusebius' *Life of Constantine* and *Oration in Praise of Constantine*, together with *Oration of Constantine* (translated and edited by E. C. Richardson). C. B. Coleman, *Constantine the Great and Christianity*, and M. A. Huthmann, *The Establishment of Christianity and the Proscription of Paganism* (vol. lx of *Studies in Hist., Econ., and Public Law*, edited by the Faculty of Political Science of Columbia University, 1914). Q.B.

Constantinople, Councils of: There were three general councils which met at Constantinople, namely, the Second (381), the Fifth (553), and the Sixth (680-81).

The Council of 381 was called by Theodosius the Great (379-95), and its chief claim to fame is that it terminated the struggle over the Nicene Creed* by the approval of a version of it which is in substantial agreement with that adopted at Nicaea (325). The chief difference between the two versions is that the clause of the Nicene Creed regarding the Holy Spirit was expanded to read "who proceedeth from the Father." This later gave rise to the age-long controversy between the East and the West when the latter church added to this clause the famous "Filioque"* phrase. The Council also prescribed "that the bishop of Constantinople should have the next prerogative of honor after the bishop of Rome, because that city was New Rome." (Socrates, *E. H.*, vii, 8).

The Council of 553 was called by Emperor Justinian (527-565), and was predominantly Eastern in attendance. The Emperor dominated the proceedings, and succeeded in securing legislation concerning the so-called Three Chapters Controversy*, condemning Theodore of Mopsuestia*, Theodoret of Cyrus, and Bishop Ibas* of Edessa. Since this was interpreted as an action implying a criticism of the Council of Chalcedon*, Pope Vigilius (who had been kept practically a prisoner in Constantinople since 547) at first refused his consent to the decree, but fearing to be exiled, yielded at last in 554.

The Council of 680 convened by Emperor Constantine IV Pogonatus (668-685), dealt with the mooted question of Monotheletism* (one-will theory) which, by asserting that the two natures in Jesus Christ possessed only one common will or energy, practically conceded the substance of the Monophysite* doctrine that He possessed only one nature—the divine. Even Pope Honorius of Rome had adopted this heresy. The Council of 680 condemned the one-will theory, and specifically anathematized Pope Honorius. Thus it completed the doctrinal formula regarding the two natures in Jesus Christ which had been centuries in evolving: it asserted that there were two natures, two wills, in one person in Jesus Christ.

Since neither the Fifth nor the Sixth General Council had passed any canons, a supplementary Council was held at Constantinople (in Trullo) in 691, which rectified the omission. It is usually known as the Quinisext Council. See ecumenical councils.

Adolf von Harnack, *History of Dogma*, 7 vols. (1895-1900); A. C. McGiffert, *A History of Christian Thought*, 2 vols. (1933). M.S.

Constantinopolitan Creed, The: Often called the Nicene-Constantinopolitan Creed. The Council of Chalcedon*, 451, ascribed it (but perhaps mistakenly) to the Council of Constantinople, 381. It differs from the Nicene Creed*, 325, in its elaboration of the statement about the Holy Ghost; to the Nicene "and in the Holy Ghost" it added "the Lord and Giver of Life; who proceedeth from the Father; who with the Father and the Son together is worshipped and glorified; who spake by the prophets." It also adds statements about the church, baptism, and the resurrection. There is a striking similarity between this creed and the formula of Epiphanius*, 374. See creeds of Christendom.

P. Schaff, *The Creeds of Christendom* (1919 ed.), Vol. II, pp. 31-61. Q.B.

constitutional law: See law.

Constitutions of Clarendon: (1164) Provisions framed by Henry II's advisers at Clarendon and agreed to by Thomas Becket but later repudiated by him. They assert the king's jurisdiction over ecclesiastics in questions of advowsons*, crimes of clerics, their absence from the realm, trials of laymen in church courts, excommunication of tenants-in-chief, appeals, and elections of bishops and abbots.

E. P. Cheney, *Readings in English History* (2 ed., 1922). J.T.M.

constitutions, papal: Important papal laws or grants used for dogmatic or disciplinary pronouncements. Since 1911 Constitutions have been used for erecting or dividing dioceses. Constitutions now have the old Bull* form. B.R.

consubstantiation: A term often used to designate the Lutheran view of the Lord's Supper* but rejected by most modern Lutheran theologians because of its ambiguity. If it is used, as by Luther, to mean the real presence* of Christ together with the earthly elements, it is correct. But historically "consubstantial", the Latin translation of the Greek "homo-ousios", was used in the ancient Christological* controversies to mean "of the same substance". When applied to the bread and the body of Christ in the Lord's Supper, it connotes "the kneading up of both substances as it were into one lump" (Hooker's *Eccl. Polity*). Such a *tertium quid* the Lutherans deny, as well as the implication that the body and blood of Christ are present and received in the same way as the bread and wine. See Lutheran Doctrine of the Lord's Supper. Cf. impanation. T.A.K.

content psychology: See psychology, schools of.

continence: The state of restraining oneself from using his sex faculty; the virtue of chastity; one of the fruits of the Holy Ghost. S.C.

contingent: (Lat. *con-tingere*, to touch together or on all sides, to happen)
The contingent is that which can be or not be,

that of which the essence does not include existence. Opposed to necessary being*. See cause.

L.R.W.

contrition: The state of sorrow for sin, coupled with the intention to abstain from such sin in the future. Such contrition is held by Catholic theologians to be necessary if forgiveness of sin is to be attained. Contrition is to be distinguished from attrition*, which means a state of sorrow approximating emotional disturbance, because of sin; the latter is not necessary in order to obtain forgiveness. Cf. retention of sins. W.N.P.

contumacy: Contempt of a court order. In ecclesiastical law the word is especially applied to failure of an accused person, after citation, to answer a charge in court. Contumacy usually results in summary judgment. R.H.N.

conventicle: Etymologically, a meeting or assembly. In church history the word signifies a religious assembly not sanctioned by civil law, e.g., meetings of Protestant dissenters in England when such were illegal and the gatherings of the Covenanters*. The word also meant a meeting-house where illegal worship took place. R.H.N.

Conventicle Act: This was an act passed in 1664 making it an offense for more than four persons of sixteen years of age and up to attend services "in other manner than is allowed by the liturgy." The act was followed by severe persecutions until in 1672 the king granted nonconformists licensed places of meeting for services and for preaching if not derogatory to the Established Church. The act was repealed in 1812.

V.F.

conventions: See culture.

convents: (Lat. *conventus,* an assembly) There are two distinct technical meanings of this term in the history of monasticism*. First, a religious community of either sex considered in its corporate capacity. The word was first used in this sense about the fourth century, when the hermit monks of the East began to group themselves about a common superior. In Western monasticism, where the eremetical form was practically non-existent, the term *conventus* was used from the beginning to describe communities of monks or nuns under a superior. Secondly, the word signifies the building in which a religious community of either sex resides. Today the popular signification of the term connotes a residence of religious women.

Convent life varies according to the specific object for which a particular convent was established. In general, the contemplative life, wherein women dedicate themselves to prayer, seclusion, and mortification, was the idea of the older religious orders. The more modern congregations concern themselves to a greater degree with the active work of conducting schools, hospitals, orphanages, homes for the aged or defectives, and other charitable institutions. Labor of some useful kind is a characteristic of all convent life. As in early times convents played an important part in the spread of Christian civilization, so today they are key organizations in the work of the Catholic Church.

A. Ross, *Religious Orders of Women* (1916).

C.V.

Conventuals: One autonomous branch of the Roman Catholic mendicant Order of Friars Minor*. The name, Conventual, has been used since 1431 to designate the Friars following a less rigorous rule, but this group was not recognized until 1517. Three Popes have been elected from the Order of Conventuals. The term, Conventual, has also been used to designate groups following a rule less strict than the original (particularly in regard to the corporate possession of property) in several other religious Orders. V.J.B.

conversion: The term conversion, as applied to religions, means fundamentally a rather definite and somewhat sudden change in the dominant beliefs, or attitudes, or sympathies, or allegiances or aspirations of an individual. The word probably cannot be rightly defined, for each case of conversion seems, in most respects, to be unique,—just as are poems or plots of plays, or scientific discoveries, or peculiarities of "personality," or sunsets. If one should collect and study hundreds of confessions of conversion as has the writer of these lines, he would be inclined to say "each is an original."

One can at least designate certain types, or shall we say species within the genus, of these picturesque,—often altogether dramatic,—experiences. The classification that follows, used for descriptive purposes, cannot be exhaustive,—only suggestive and provocative.

1. The drama of conversion is apt to center in *the birth of a new and higher selfhood.* The organism, from the day of its inception, is basically and fundamentally integrative. Like magic it heals wounds, assimilates difficulties, and accepts challenges. (W. B. Cannon, *Wisdom of the Body,* also *Bodily Changes*). The storm and stress of youth is the testing ground for the birth of the new selfhood. "The thing we long for that we are for one transcendent moment." "Seek and ye shall find." These pregnant sayings are good biology and good psychology. New energies are set free. Fresh coordination of "higher" impulses do occur.

Despite a considerable number of "backslidings"* (five or six per cent) and recurrences of struggles with old attitudes and habits (about one-third of the entire number), it appears, from an intimate study of many hundreds of confessions, that something of permanent value is carried over into later years. (Starbuck, *Psychology of Religion* (1899), Ch. 28).

2. Conversion is, rather fundamentally, a *blossoming,* or *fruition, of the basic biological and psychological urges and drives.* A reach, a quest for novelty, characterizes most living creatures, including children and youth. The finer impulses seek an outlet. They ripen into dreams, then into longings. The bud does burst. The vision clears,

—sometimes slowly and almost imperceptibly, sometimes "like flashes struck from midnight."

Several statistical inquiries indicate definitely the age-coincidence of conversions and accessions to puberty. For the most adequate, also most challenging critique of this notion, consult Elmer T. Clark's *The Psychology of Religious Awakening* (1929). (G. A. Coe, *The Spiritual Life;* Starbuck, *The Psychology of Religion*).

Hence a victory for the Freudians*, and also for G. Stanley Hall (*Adolescence*) who are convinced that religion is a "sublimation" of sex, or in its refined forms, the "libido."

Is not this event, however, a sublimation also of self regard, (the seeking of personal salvation); of fear, (of final destruction); of gregariousness, (fellowship of the saints); of self-expression, (missionary zeal); of appreciation, (the beauty of holiness); and perhaps a dozen or score of other fundamental "instincts" or propensities, which in their blending or fusion constitute the kingdom of righteousness in the heart. The sweet singer of Israel, realizing the majesty and glory of the heavens and of the universe, exclaims "The Law of the Lord is perfect converting (or restoring) the soul."

Due, doubtless, to faulty education and training, the child is caught quite too completely in a bristling world of things and chores, of specificities of activities and informations, and of superimposed attempts at logical thinking. In adolescence* with new contacts and ripening biological functions which throw new energizing fluids into the life stream the real self may be born or reborn sometimes with dramatic intensity. Viewed in this perspective, conversion may well mean a regeneration*, a rebirth, a transformation from childhood to maturity, from indifference to vitalized social contacts, from fact-mindedness to appreciation of meanings and values, from thoughts *about* life and the universe to participation soulfully in the drama of living.

3. Conversion often signifies the *resolution of a conflict.* It may center in the battle between sensuous enjoyments and cultivated tastes, between sin and righteousness, or in the struggle between a God and a satanic force. With St. Augustine* and many of the great souls this battle assumes the majesty of a seemingly life-and-death struggle. David himself knew the terror of the conflict. "Wash me from mine iniquity." "In sin did my mother conceive me." "Create in me a clean heart. Then will I teach transgressors the way and sinners shall be converted unto thee."

4. Conversion often involves *a Copernican revolution of values from egocentricism to a response to a universe of spiritual and cosmic Reals.* That which lies behind and within this transforming experience has been called by many names: "The Father" (Jesus), "Dear City of God" (Marcus Aurelius), "The Over-Soul" (Emerson), "Jehovah" (Moses), "The All-pervading Beauty" (Plato). Those persons who have made this revolution from earthiness to spirituality have sometimes been designated, in a phrasing borrowed from the Hindu traditions, "twice born souls." (William James, *Varieties of Religious Experience* (1902), pp. 166, 363, 488).

5. The term conversion often signifies *the definite acceptance "unto salvation" of a creed or doctrine or fellowship.* This revolution of values is usually done under the stress of personal appeals, or waves and tides of social pressures. Ideas or vital experiences are impelling. If shared they become irresistible. Propagandism and proselytism among humans run deep racially and rise high in their intensity. Greek philosophy early became evangelical. So it was in India. In about the fifth century B.C. likewise, Buddhism struck deep roots in the cultural soil of that country and spread dramatically across eastern Asia and westward as well. Christianity from its inception was dynamically evangelical. The familiar Bible story of Paul and Barnabas converting individuals and entire communities during their successful journey, is illustrative of the way the mind behaves religiously. Perhaps à lively percentage of wars on the planet have been fundamentally religious conflicts.

6. There are negative or "counter-conversions" that take one away from an already accepted fellowship or doctrine and into a riper or more adequate one. These are usually accompanied by similar strains and agonizings and then final satisfactions as were originally experienced by the devotee. (James, *The Varieties of Religious Experience,* pp. 175 ff.) (Starbuck, *Psychology of Religion,* p. 137 ff.) Of this number, some move out into bleaker mental weather and build for themselves islands of rest and satisfaction not poorly symbolized by the remark "He believes in no-God and worships It." See James' *Varieties of Religious Experience* for a description of Ratisbonne and other striking instances of a serene and satisfying counter-conversion.

7. There are *ethical conversions.* It would be unfair to omit those who profess and advocate an "ethical conversion." As Felix Adler, founder of the Ethical Culture Society*, indicates,—a person may be a Christian for many years and yet not be recognized as one until he has become regenerated. We find in the Stoic sage, the Christian and the Hindu the same notion of a second birth which will make it seem as if he had really become a new man and leading an entirely new life . . . We too must become regenerate, be born into the new spirit so that morality will never again seem cold and bare to us but that the divine element which is in it will become uppermost in consciousness. (*The Standard,* February, 1943, pp. 134 and 135).

8. Conversion as the state of being *thrice*-born. Just as the youth in his teens and twenties may outgrow the mere sensory delights of childhood and ripen into an appreciation of life's purposes, programs and meanings, so the mature man or woman too much entangled with and enslaved by domestic duties, civic responsibilities, economic problems and social distractions,—even religious observances whose spirit has begun to ossify,—may inwardly rebel and seek afresh the things of "the spirit." In the late middle years the

physical and mental powers pass their peak of efficiency. The dynamic of living is deep seated in every organism. Defeat and death come hard. The deeper-higher selfhood cries out for deliverance. The Universe's answer to men and women of spiritual fortitude is a second rebirth of power and insight. This phenomenon is so truly indigenous to human experience that it has repeated itself in cults and personal lives in most of the cultures of the world. The Buddha* (5th century B.C.) after much wrestling of the spirit during his maturer years won the victory and could say "Hell is destroyed in me. . . . I am converted. I am no longer liable to be reborn in a state of suffering and I am assured of final salvation." Seneca*, although involved in the furies of the world statesmanship of the first century A.D. affirmed "I regard myself not so much as a reformed but as a transfigured man."

9. Conversion in terms of "Other-Worldliness." In many ways the most radical revolution of religious values is that in which one renounces altogether this ordinary world of drabness, worry, and distraction and in his maturer years, if not earlier, flees from it, in fact as well as in fancy, and escapes into his own sphere of meditation, or into a cave, or a convent, or a monastery. To solitude and self-denial as marks of "godliness" are often added the soul-discipline of bodily torture. A quite adequate account of the asceticisms and monasticisms** of the world as they spread through nearly all the civilizations is found in Hastings *Encyclopedia of Religion and Ethics*, Vol. I, pp. 63 to 110. They flourished and spread until the Renaissance. From that time onward they have tended to decrease.

10. Conversion and *whole-mindedness*. Conversions are likely to occur under emotional stresses and strains and are in danger of emphasizing a partial view of life and religion. William MacDougall has pointed out the pathological character of the "sin complex." (*Social Psychology*, p. 68). Dr. H. I. Schou "views with some skepticism all sudden conversions occurring after long periods of depression." (*Religion and Morbid Mental States*). George A. Coe has established through hypnotic suggestion a definite correlation between radical conversion and hallucinations and motor automatisms. (*The Spiritual Life*, p. 120). Consult for further data E. T. Clark *The Psychology of Religious Awakening*, Ch. VII).

In the thoughtful, even "scientific," interpretations of the facts of conversion that have flourished for just about a half century, scholars representing the recognized religious orders have participated as warmly and helpfully as have those of more distinctly academic interests. There would seem to be a high degree of agreement that conversion marks certain types of release in the minds and hearts of men and women, of the progressive truth, beauty and righteousness that will bless and "regenerate" and "redeem" humanity. Conversion, then, would seem to be the act of taking a *positive*, not a negative or indifferent, attitude towards the vital things of human life and destiny. See psychology of religion; salvation.

E. T. Clark, *The Psychology of Religious Awakening* (1929); George A. Coe, *Psychology of Religion* (1916), (University of Chicago publications in religious education. Handbooks of ethics and religion) and *The Spiritual Life* (1900); Edmund S. Conklin, *The Psychology of Religious Adjustment* (1929); George B. Cutten, *Psychological Phenomena of Christianity* (1909); G. Stanley Hall, *Adolescence* (1904); William James, *Varieties of Religious Experience* (1911); Charles C. Josey, *Psychology of Religion* (1927); J. H. Leuba, *The Psychology of Religious Mysticism* (1925); J. B. Pratt, *The Religious Consciousness* (1920) and *The Psychology of Religious Belief* (1907); Edwin D. Starbuck, *The Psychology of Religion* (1899); K. R. Stolz, *Psychology of Religious Living* (1937); G. M. Stratton, *Psychology of the Religious Life* (1911); W. B. Thomas, *Psychology of Conversion* (1935); Robert H. Thouless, *An Introduction to the Psychology of Religion* (1923); A. C. Underwood, *Conversion, Christian and Non-Christian.*

Encyclopedia Articles: *Encyclopedia Britannica*—13th Edition, Vol. VII pp. 46 ff; *Catholic Encyclopedia*—Vol. IV pp. 347-348; Hastings' *Encyclopedia of Religion and Ethics*—Vol. IV pp. 104-110; *Jewish Encyclopedia*—Vol. IV pp. 249 ff; *New Schaff-Herzog Encyclopedia of Religious Knowledge* Vol. III pp. 261 ff.

E.D.S.

conviction of sin: Conviction of sin* is not the ordinary natural feeling that we are not perfect, that we err or make mistakes. It is a definite evangelical experience connected with sin as that in our life which is contrary to God. It is the realization by the individual of the chasm that divides him from God, that lies between his inner state and the holy demands of God. Thus it comes through the vision of God (Isa. 6:1-5), or by the presence and action of the Holy Spirit* (John 16: 7 ff). It includes remorse and despair of oneself, and is preparatory to repentance toward God and to salvation as the gift and work of God. Much is heard today of social conviction of sin, the sin of the community against its members. This touches a phase of the moral life; but it is at the depth of evangelical conviction only as individuals feel responsibility even for this sin and are moved to repent. See repentance.

H. R. Mackintosh, *The Christian Apprehension of God* (1929), (Student Christian Movement); R. S. Moxon, *The Doctrine of Sin* (1922).

J.L.

cooperation: The literal and general meaning is a working together. In a more special sense, cooperation began in a successful way among the now famous Rochdale Pioneers in England in 1844, though remarkable abortive attempts at cooperation were made in the late eighteenth century in southern England. In its narrowest meaning, it is a getting together or a pooling of economic interests: in matters of lending and borrowing, or of buying, or of processing and shipping. A whole community or that part of it with interests in common joins hands, to see to the quality of its own production and also to control markets and to get fair prices for products; thus middlemen tend to disappear; besides, people own their own stores and service stations, and set up their own clinics and employ nurses and doctors. In these ways, cooperation seems to many persons to be essentially economic. But it is not exclusively economic, since it engages other human needs and capacities, such as the moral, political, educational and religious; and some authorities think it to belong primarily to adult education. See labor movements.

G. Richardson *ABC of Cooperatives* (1940); F. Hall and W. P. Watkins, *Co-operation*. A survey of the history, principles and organization of the movement in Great Britain and Ireland (Manchester, Eng., 1937); J. P. Warbasse, *Cooperative Democracy*, 3rd ed. (1936). L.R.W.

cope: An ecclesiastical vestment, worn by bishops, etc., and also by priests for certain ceremonial purposes, as, e.g., processions, etc. An adaptation of the ancient *cappa*, but usually ornamented richly. W.N.P.

Copernican astronomy: Copernicus (Polish astronomer, 1473-1543) pointed out the superior mathematical coherence of the view that the earth moves around the sun, and is thus not the motionless center of things it was held to be in Ptolemaic astronomy*. The sun, however, in the new astronomy assumed the role from which the earth was displaced. (Newton later denied centrality even to the solar system.) That the earth moves had been suggested long before, as early as 250 B.C., and that mathematical elegance and unity are to be looked for in nature was taught by Italian neo-Platonists who influenced Copernicus, and by the ancient Pythagoreans*. Copernicus, Kepler, Galileo, and Newton** effected the shift from a teleological to a mathematical way of interrogating nature. Or at least, the *telos* or end that is made primary by these men is no longer human welfare, but the abstract and universal end of mathematical rationality—the glory of God as cosmic mathematician, rather than as cosmic ally and judge of humanity.

N. Copernicus, *De revolutionibus orbium coelestium* (Ed. of 1873), Ger. trans. by Menzzer (1879). L. Prowe, *Nicolaus Coppernicus* (1883-84). C.H.

Coptic Church: The native Egyptian church derives from the ecclesiastical-political rivalry between Alexandria and Constantinople* rather than from the christological* controversy over monophysitism*. It was Egyptian nationalism represented by natives and monks against Byzantine* imperialism. When the Council of Chalcedon (451) decided against Eutyches, the nationalist Copts lined up against the Byzantine Melchites making the provincial Coptic Church a reality. Since 1882, western missionaries have had access to Egypt and the Coptic Church at present constitutes about one-twelfth of the population and has a patriarch, metropolitans and bishops with interests also in Jerusalem and Jaffa as well as at Khartoum. See canons of various churches. C.H.M.

Coptic versions: See versions of the Bible, ancient.

Cord, confraternities of the: Four societies authorized by the R. C. Church to honor: 1) Our Lady of Consolation, founded by Saint Monica; 2) St. Francis of Assisi; 3) St. Joseph, commemorating a miraculous cure; 4) St. Thomas Aquinas, to secure chastity. C.V.

Corinthian style: See temples, Greek and Roman.

Corinthians, First and Second Letters to the: While Paul was at Ephesus, on the third missionary journey, he was in occasional communication with Corinth, across the Aegean. His first recorded letter to them, mentioned in I Cor. 5:9, may be preserved in part in II Cor. 6:14-7:1. Visitors from Corinth brought him disturbing news of factions and immoralities in the Corinthian church, and soon after a letter of questions on practical matters was brought him from Corinth (I Cor. 7:1). He dealt with the report he had received and with these questions in our I Corinthians. Of especial importance are his discussion of how rights should sometimes be waived, ch. 9, and his account of the place of love in Christian living, ch. 13, and of the Christian hope of immortality, ch. 15. The Corinthians were more incensed than pleased with this great letter, however, and he wrote a third, anguished letter, written with many tears and regretted after it was sent, probably preserved in II Cor., 10-13, which enables us to look into the very heart of Paul. This was carried to Corinth by Titus, and Paul waited anxiously for his return. He concluded his work at Ephesus, and went to Troas, where he hoped to find Titus. But he was not there, so Paul went on to Macedonia. There he found Titus, with good news from the Corinthians; they had seen their mistake and were once more loyal and devoted to Paul. Paul writes a fourth letter, our II Cor. 1-9, setting forth the motives and methods of his ministry, 2:12-6:10, in a milder, more conciliatory strain. Chs. 8, 9 deal with the collection he was making for the poor Jewish Christians of Jerusalem. The whole Corinthian correspondence falls in the years 54-56.

Literature: H. Lietzmann, *Handbuch zum Neuen Testament: An die Korinther, I-II* (2d ed., 1923); A. Robertson and A. Plummer, *First Epistle of St. Paul to the Corinthians* (2d ed., 1916); A. Plummer, *Second Epistle of St. Paul to the Corinthians* (1915). E.J.G.

Corning (Iowa) community: See communistic settlements, secular.

corporal: The cloth, usually linen, on which the eucharistic vessels rest (and in the Roman ceremonial the Host* itself until just before Communion); originally covering the whole altar, but now not much over 1 ft. square; the name is from *corpus*, body, because the Body of Christ rests on it. E.R.H.

corporate personality: Expression designating the unity of the social group (family, clan, tribe or nation) which binds its members together by fictitious or actual blood-tie. Implies also a realistic solidarity with the past and future generations, the social group being an organic body in space as well as in time. Notion of considerable importance for the correct understanding of the O.T. doctrines of Covenant, Sin, Atonement, Vicarious Suffering, Sheol, Individualism, and even of the N.T. conceptions of Church, Communion of Saints, etc.

See J. Pedersen, *Israel, Its Life and Culture* (1926), pp. 263 ff., 474 ff., etc.; H. Wheeler Robinson, "The Hebrew Conception of Corporate Personality," in *Werden und Wesen des Alten Testaments* (1936), edited by P. Volz, F. Stummer and J. Hempel, pp. 49-62. S.L.T.

Corporation Act of 1661: This act excluded Dissenters* from membership in municipal and similar corporations in England; it gradually fell into desuetude after 1718, but was not formally repealed until 1828. E.R.H.

Corpus Christi: (Lat., Body of Christ) The Thursday after Trinity Sunday, a feast instituted in 1264 through the efforts of St. Juliana of Cornillon (Belgium), to honor the Real Presence* of Jesus Christ in the Eucharist. C.V.

Corpus Doctrinae: (Lat. body of doctrine) A term applied to collections of confessional writings in force in various Lutheran state churches in Germany before the Book of Concord* in 1580 brought about a uniform confessional basis. Among the most authoritative was the *Corpus Doctrinae Prutenicum* (1567) drawn up by Chemnitz* and Mörlin for the Church of Prussia. T.A.K.

Corpus Juris Canonici: See Canon Law; decretals.

cosmic egg: See cosmogonies.

cosmogonies: The earliest theories regarding the origin of the wold were suggested by man's own creative activity. It is not surprising, therefore, that a single culture may have several creation* stories. In these speculations a god is usually the actor. He weaves the world on a loom (Egypt, India; the Babylonian Ea wove reeds together over the primeval waters, covered them with earth as the dwelling place for the gods); he molds the earth as a potter (Egypt), or if the earth is already in existence molds man from clay (American Indian, Hebrew); he creates the universe by sacrifice (India); he builds the world as a master artificer (Egypt, India); he speaks the earth into existence by the magic word (Egypt, Israel, India, Babylonia). The sexual union of the parent gods, Heaven and Earth, was a common motif. It occurs in Japan, Egypt, Greece, India, China and America. The emergence of life from an egg suggested the idea of a cosmic egg floating on the waste of waters from which comes the creator (India, Egypt, Greece, Polynesia).

All of these early creators worked with pre-existent materials. There was no thought of creation out of nothing. The belief was almost universal that before the beginning of creation there was nothing but a vast expanse of waters shrouded in darkness. Greek thought placed before the origin of man's world a variety of existences material and abstract—ocean, chaos, aether, night, time, earth and heaven from whose union the gods were born. The Egyptian schools made several geneological arrangements of ocean, earth, heaven, sun and air. The creation of the ordered world and man came later. In the Hebrew creation stories Yahweh* found the pre-existing barren earth and ordered it, or subdued chaos and the dark deep, putting the waters above the firmament and spreading the earth over the lower waters. Then he created the sun, moon and stars, the creatures of the sea, the earth and man. Christianity inherited the Hebrew cosmogony. In the Middle Ages the creation of the world out of nothing became a dogma for Judaism, Christianity and Islam.

Philosophic thought in Greece and India played with the idea of a single basic principle underlying the evolution of the universe—water, air, fire, the four elements, *nous**, breath, desire. In most cultures one of the gods was credited with the work of creation. At least ten gods claimed the honor in India and the choice was not finally made among them before philosophy and the idea of a cyclic universe made creator gods meaningless. Zoroastrianism divided the creative work, Ormazd* producing all good things and Ahriman the evil.

When philosophy makes the choice of a beginningless universe rather than a beginningless god the forms of the existing world are the result of a cyclic movement of eternal change. (See cycles of time.) In the Sankhya* system of India the attraction of Purusha, the infinite number of eternal souls upon Prakriti, eternal matter, produces the world. Classical Confucianism* posits at the beginning the Great Unity. This one unfolds into the Yang and Yin*, then the five dynamic elements and through their infinite combinations produces material things, plants, animals and man. In Hinduism and Buddhism** vast cycles of beginning and destruction of the universe covering incalculable time spans take place within the eternal absolute. Buddhist cosmography provides heavens, worlds and hells for all types of existences from beings of bodiless, pure thought to the demons and the damned. A total system may include a thousand million universes. See evolution. A.E.H.

cosmological argument: See cause; God. Cf. teleological argument.

Coulanges de, Fustel: (1830-1889) Being one of the most prominent French historians of the ancient world and of medieval history, he attempted to show that ideas—in particular religious ideas—generally are the causes of social changes and the primary factor of social phenomena. He showed that wherever new religions arise, introducing new ideas, they radically modified society.

Fustel de Coulanges, *The Ancient City* (1900). H.H.

council: See synod.

Councils, Buddhist: See Buddhist Terminology.

councils, ecumenical: See ecumenical councils.

Councils, Lateran: See Lateran Councils.

counseling, personal: See clinical psychology; psycho therapy; cure of souls.

counter conversion: See conversion.

Counter-Reformation: See Catholic Reformation, the.

covenant: (O.T. *berith;* N.T. *diatheke*) One of the fundamental words in biblical religion; a formula, originating as the legal basis of society, used to describe the special relationship between God and people.

A. O.T. Conception

A discussion may be divided into two parts: the covenant 1) as the basis of community and 2) as theological terminology.

1. In early Israelite society as in all nomadic or semi-nomadic society covenants between men and between groups were the legal arrangements which made peaceful community relations possible. In the O.T. the expression most frequently used is: X cut a covenant with Y. Other verbs are occasionally employed, but "cut" is the most common, and probably refers to sacrificial rites which originally initiated the agreement. Two familiar illustrations of O.T. covenants are those made between David and Jonathan (I Sam. 18:3, 20:8, and 23:18) and between Jacob and Laban (Gen. 31: 44-55). In the latter the rite consisted of the setting up of a pillar (E source), or heap of stones (J source), vows, sacrificial offering, and community meal. It is important to notice that the deity (or deities? Cf. vs. 53) of the respective groups was made a party to the agreement and would see that it was kept (n.b. the Mizpah Benediction). Thus the covenant was absolutely binding and could never be safely broken. Righteousness in the O.T.,* therefore, is primarily the maintenance of the covenant, while sin was its trangression, a breach of an agreement.

2. With this background the theological significance of the word is clear. The sources agree that in the period of the Wandering, Conquest, and Settlement that which held the various groups of the people of Israel together was a religious bond or covenant (cf. Exod. 24 and Josh. 24), made of their own free will with Yahweh. God chose Israel to be His people, and Israel chose Him to be her God. Israel was thus conscious of a special contractual relationship existing between her and God, a relationship carrying with it certain obligations, the keeping of which meant life or death, blessing or curse (Dt. 30:15 ff.; see further: lovingkindness).

Later writers, especially Hosea, Jeremiah, Ezekiel, and the authors of Deuteronomy and the Priestly Writings, made frequent use of this conception. Israel, it was claimed, had broken the covenant (Hos. 6:7, 8:1; Jer. 11: 1 ff., 34:18). An explanation was accordingly provided for the problem of suffering, though to some it was not entirely adequate, since it raised the problem of theodicy (cf. Hab. and Job). A fundamental difference of opinion between religious leaders in the O.T. was in regard to the precise obligations which the covenant with God entailed. While the priestly group emphasized the external prescriptions of the law, in particular the ritualistic law, the greatest of the prophets were more concerned with deeper ethical and religious issues, a point of view which found one of its highest expressions in the prediction of a new covenant, not like that made on Sinai which had been broken by Israel, but one which was to be written on the hearts of men (Jer. 31:31 ff.). See blood; circumcision; corporate personality.

B. N.T. Conception

The Greek word *diatheke* was most commonly employed in Hellenistic Greek for "will," "testament," but in the LXX and N.T. it is also used to designate the O.T. idea of covenant. The most frequent use of the latter in the N.T. is in the Pauline writings and in the Epistle to the Hebrews, where the contrast is made between the Old Covenant of law and the New Covenant in Christ. The O.T. conception, expressing the comprehension of the divine election and the binding relationship of the elect to God, is not developed in the N.T. The idea of covenant there is used rather to clarify the difference between Christianity and Judaism (cf. Luke 22:20; I Cor. 11:25; Gal. 3:15 ff.; Heb. 8 ff.).

G. Kittel, ed., *Theologisches Wörterbuch zum Neuen Testament,* Zweiter Band (Stuttgart, 1935), pp. 105-137. This is a careful study of the word in both the O.T. and N.T. with full bibliographical reference. See also J. Pedersen, *Israel* (1926), pp. 279 ff., 363 ff., 414 ff.; and L. Köhler, *Theologie des Alten Testaments* (Tübingen, 1936), pp. 43-58.

G.E.W.

covenant (or federal) theology: This arose late in the 16th century, apparently independently, among the Reformed of western Germany, English Puritans and Scottish theologians. These Calvinists, hesitating over the representation of God involved in the foreordination of individuals before time, devised a historical conception of His dealings with man, in the form of two covenants, of works and of grace, all on a Scriptural basis. Under the former God offered to man eternal life on condition of obedience; this covenant being broken in Adam, God altered His plan by establishing the covenant of grace, under which He gave salvation through faith. This doctrine strengthened its hold in the early 17th century among English Puritans and in Scotland, and therefore has large place in the Westminster Confession*. Various formulations of the covenant of grace appeared; in the West. Conf. it is said to be "administered" in three periods: before the Mosaic law, under the law through the sacrifices and the prophets, finally fully in the gospel. In the 17th century this theology was elaborated by Dutch Calvinists, chiefly Cocceius* and Witsius and by the Swiss Turretin. The covenant formed the thought of New England Puritanism, not only in theology but also in matters ecclesiastical, social and political. As a definite scheme the covenant theology has lost most of its once wide vogue and strong influence, but it has left permanent deposits in conceptions of God's gracious purpose and human obligation to Him, and records in hymns and prayers still used. See feudalism.

J. Ball, *A Treatise of the Covenant of Grace* (London, 1645); T. Boston, *The Marrow of Modern Divinity,* in *Whole Works,* VII (Aberdeen, 1850); J. Cotton, *A Treatise of the Covenant of Grace* 1645); W. Hastie, *Theology of the Reformed Church* (Edinburgh, 1904); P. Miller, *The New England Mind* (1939), pp. 365-462 and bibliographical appendix.

R.H.N.

Covenant Church of America, Evangelical Mission, the: See Evangelical Mission Covenant Church of America.

Covenanter Churches: See Reformed Presbyterian Church in N. A.

Covenanters: The name comes from the Scottish National Covenant of 1638, which bound the signers to keep the Church of Scotland* as it was fashioned at the Reformation, i.e., Presbyterian. At the Restoration episcopacy was re-established in the church and the royal supremacy over it asserted, and ministers not episcopally instituted were deprived. A large part of the people in the name of the Covenant refused to attend the parish churches and heard the deprived ministers preach outdoors. The government of Charles II enforcing church attendance by soldiery who committed cruelties, the "Covenanters" raised organized rebellion, holding armed conventicles for preaching. After their defeat at Bothwell Bridge in 1679 some compromised with the government, but others, the Covenanters *par excellence,* maintained implacable resistance. They were savagely persecuted by the government under Charles II and James II, especially in the Killing Times of 1684-88. At the Revolution of 1689 Presbyterianism was restored in the Church of Scotland. But the extreme Covenanters were dissatisfied with some features of this settlement and held aloof from the church. At length in 1743 this party organized the Reformed Presbytery, out of which in 1863 came the Reformed Presbyterian Church* of Scotland. See Cameronians. See League and Covenant, the Solemn. R.H.N.

Coverdale, Myles: (1488-1568) Translator of the first complete Bible to be printed in English (1535) and editor of the Great Bible (1539), the first of the English "authorized" versions. Spent much of his time on the Continent to escape persecution for heresy. Bishop of Exeter in 1551 but deprived of his See on the accession of Queen Mary. See Bible, English; hymns. S.M.G.

cowl: A hood, usually attached to a mantle, and worn by Benedictines, Cistercians**, and all the old monastic orders. Its ancient use by monks is attested by Sozomen and Palladius. C.V.

Cowper, William: See hymns.

Cranmer, Thomas: (1489-1586) Archbishop of Canterbury. Cranmer advanced at a step to a position of national importance in connection with the first divorce of Henry VIII*. In recognition of his work, he was elevated to the see of Canterbury. Cranmer's most important work was in directing the course of the English Reformation, particularly in two respects—promoting the circulation of the Bible in the vernacular, and in readjusting the creed and liturgy of the Church. The second of these constituted Cranmer's chief work during the latter part of his life. He was martyred under Mary. See Book of Common Prayer; catechism; catechumenate. G.R.C.

Crashaw, Richard: (1613-1649) English poet. Educated at Cambridge, where he was for a time fellow of Peterhouse, Crashaw became a Roman Catholic during his last years and took refuge on the Continent. His principal work, *Steps to the Temple* (1646), written while he was still nominally an Anglican, is marked by a devotional ecstasy almost unique in English literature. L.W.C.

craze: See culture.

creation: (Lat. *creare,* to produce) Historically creation first referred to the act whereby the underived self-existent God brought into being what had no form of independent existence hitherto. This Christian notion contrasted radically with the Greek concept of "creation" as an "informing" or reshaping of a pre-existent entity. So strong was the Christian, theistic belief in an absolute, transcendent God who worked under no external limitations, that creation was said to be absolute or *ex nihilo.* This original meaning of the term excludes any emanation or diffusion theory of the origin of things, though it does not exclude the continued immanence of God in creative entities by successive acts of creation (see St. Augustine, St. Bonaventure, Descartes, Malebranche).

Difficulties in the *ex nihilo* doctrine, and consideration of the exact relation between an eternal God and a temporal world, led modern thinking to emphasize the dependence of the world on an immanent though unaffected God, sometimes without specific adherence to an *ex nihilo* doctrine and sometimes with complete denial of God's transcendence (cf. Spinoza's *Deus sive Nature*). In recent thinking (J. Ward, A. N. Whitehead, C. Hartshorne), the attempt is made to escape pantheism, and yet hold that the emergence of novelty in the world is essential to God's development, and not completely pre-ordained. See analogy; cause; cosmogonies; cycles of time; infinite; time; Ussher, James.

H. Bergson, *Creative Evolution* (Eng. tr., 1911); A. N. Whitehead, *Process and Reality* (1929). P.A.B.

creationism: The theory, approved by the Roman Church, that God is the immediate creator of every new-born human soul at the moment of conception. The soul is not the product of physical or parental generation (as the traducianists* held), or of divine emanation. P.A.B.

credo: (Lat.) The third section of the ordinary of the mass*. The Nicene Creed is the creed of the mass. The profession of faith, I believe in one God. E.H.B.

credulity, primitive: See suggestion.

Creed of Toledo: See Toledo, Creed of.

creeds: See symbolics.

creeds of Christendom: The Christian creeds and confessions of faith may be classified as ecumenical, Eastern Catholic, Western Catholic,

Provincial Church, confessional Protestant, democratic declarations, and American Protestant, sect and cult. The three creeds which formerly were regarded as ecumenical are the Apostles' Creed*, the Nicene Creed and the Athanasian Creed* (the particular confessional statements of the various Catholic and Protestant bodies are discussed under Confessions, Formal of the Christian Church).

The Apostles' Creed has been very popular in both the Catholic and Protestant churches. The apostles were not concerned with its composition and its romantic history has only recently been recovered. It did not result from the conflict with Gnosticism and Marcionism** but was in process of formation from the early days of Christianity. Simple confessions to Jesus, two member confessions to God and Christ and three member confessions to God, Christ and the Holy Spirit are embedded in the N.T. The early Roman form of the Apostles' Creed (see Old Roman Symbol) consisted of "I believe in God the Father Almighty and in Christ Jesus his Son, our Lord, and in holy Spirit, holy Church and resurrection of the flesh." The final form of the Apostles' Creed was reached in Gaul whence it returned to Rome in the eighth century. The traditional text can hardly be traced beyond the sixth century and the word "body" of the eleventh affirmation dates from A.D. 1543.

The complete history of the Nicene Creed is very much in question. The Lambeth conference of A.D. 1888 raised the question of the desirability of the revision of the English version. The debate over its text was very violent between A.D. 325 and 381 resulting in a considerable expansion, in changes in meanings of words, and finally in the formation of the various provincial churches (Persian, Nestorian, Jacobite, Coptic, Ethiopian, Armenian). In 325, *homoousios** denoted communion and equality and identity of being between Father and Son; in 381, only the two former. During the bitter controversy, A.D. 325-381, Athanasius* the chief defender of the orthodox view was sent into exile four times and accused of the use of black magic and of murder as well. When the Roman church in the eleventh century finally added the notorious *filioque** to the third article, making the procession of the Holy Spirit* from the Father *and the Son,* the permanent schism* between the Roman church and the Greek church came on.

That the Athanasian Creed, or *Symbolum Quicunque* should still be considered ecumenical is strange indeed. In the Latin it consists of 44 short theses. Its origin is unknown although contemporary criticism assigns it to the sixth century. Athanasius of course did not compose it. Only in the late seventh century is it assigned to Athanasius. It may have been a consensus of sermonic materials or the work of a single theologian in Gaul or Spain. It was first used in worship in the time of Charlemagne and only in the thirteenth century regarded as equal to the Apostles' Creed and the Nicene Creed.

Anglicanism has given it liturgical value but the American Protestant Episcopal Church omits it in Article VIII and in worship. It was never adopted in the Eastern Church* and hence no authorized Greek text exists. By substitution of a trinity of the one Divine person for a trinity of persons this creed would have been acceptable to Swedenborg.

The essence of the Athanasian Creed is: "And the Catholic Faith is this: That we worship one God in Trinity and Trinity in Unity; neither confounding the persons: nor dividing the Substance . . . that our Lord Jesus Christ, the Son of God, is God and Man . . . at whose coming all men shall rise again with their bodies; and shall give account for their own works."

In Catholicism, the Bible and tradition are fundamental for truth and faith. Hence its creeds are absolute and infallible in authority. Eastern Catholicism claims infallibility for seven "ecumenical" councils* from I Nicene Council (325) to the II Nicene Council (787). Western Catholicism extends the claim to the Council of Trent and the Vatican Council** and pronouncements of the popes when intended as official decisions on matters of faith and morals.

For orthodox Protestantism*, the Bible* is the only infallible rule of Christian faith and practice and hence the authority of confessions of faith is relative, subordinate, limited. The confession is not a rule of faith but of doctrine and its sanction ecclesiastical. For other types of Protestantism, the confession is only *credo* (a personal profession) and never *credendum* (a necessary and imposed creed). The idea of the covenant prevails among various democratic Protestant bodies.

Historically considered, creeds are convenient summaries arising out of definite religious situations, designed to meet urgent contemporary needs, and serving as tests of orthodoxy. Therefore they are inadequate in new crises and unable to secure uniformity of belief. No confession of faith has ever been composed that has done justice to the faith and experience of its subscribers. They overemphasize some values and overlook others and cannot anticipate future issues. None of the creeds answers our questions regarding disarmament, race prejudice, pacifism. They do not detect error and make Christianity an intellectual affair, sometimes producing religious astigmatism and dishonesty. Ecumenicity applies at the very best merely to approval and never to content of any creed. See Christology; Constantinopolitan Creed; Trinity.

W. A. Curtis, "Confessions" in *Hastings' Encyclopedia R. E.* 3, 831-901; A. von Harnack, *History of Dogma,* 7 vol. (1894-1899); K. Holl, *Gesammelte Aufsaetze,* II, 115-128; H. Lietzmann, *Geschichte der Alten Kirche* (1936), vol. 2; C. H. Moehlman, *Protestantism's Challenge* (1939); P. Schaff, *The Creeds of Christendom,* 3 vol. (1876).

C.H.M.

cremation: See death and burial practices.

Cremer, Hermann: (1834-1903) He was professor in Greifswald. A personally influential Lutheran pioneer of biblical theology. Interpreting forensically and very energetically the Pauline doctrines of sin, justification and judgment on the basis of conscience, he fought the speculative doctrine of God in favor of a biblical doctrine.

Lehre von den Eigenschaften Gottes (Gotha, 1897); *Das Wesen des Christentums* (Gütersloh, 1902).

H.H.

crescent: (from Lat., *crescens,* present participle of *crescere,* to grow) An emblem representing a half-moon with horns turned up. The crescent and star were ancient Byzantine symbols of Constantinople assumed as the standard of the Ottoman Turks upon their capture of the city. The Order of the Crescent was founded by Selim II in 1799 to confer knighthood upon Christians for service to the Turkish state. It is now extinct. Metaphorically, it may refer to Islam*. P.E.J.

crime and criminal law: See guilt; juvenile delinquency; law; penology; prison reform.

crisis theology: See Barth, Karl; Gogarten, F.; Thurneysen, E.

Critical Realism: See epistemology.

criticism: See Biblical criticism.

cromlech: A circle of huge stones, standing upright, as at Stonehenge on Salisbury Plain. Sometimes the cromlech surrounded a tomb, sometimes a stone altar. P.G.M.

Cromwell, Oliver: (1599-1658) Born in Huntingdon, Cromwell was educated in the grammar school under the Puritan Thomas Beard and in Sidney Sussex College, Cambridge. As a member of the Parliament of 1628 and of the Short and the Long Parliaments (1640-1649) he displayed an unrelenting hostility to bishops and Puritan* sympathies which led him to become an Independent. A military leader of marked ability, he organized the army which defeated Charles I and the Scots. Having become Protector (1653-1658) through its support, he granted toleration to all except Roman Catholics, Anglicans, and the extremist sects, and attempted to establish a national church, Calvinistic in dogma, which should embrace Presbyterians, Independents, and Baptists.

Wilbur Cortez Abbot, *A Bibliography of Oliver Cromwell* (1929); *id., The Writings and Speeches of Oliver Cromwell* (1937-), which when completed (the third, and last, volume is now being written), will be the definitive biography of Cromwell. E.W.K.

crosier, crozier: A bishop's pastoral staff in the form of a shepherd's crook, symbolizing episcopal jurisdiction and pastoral office. P.V.N.

cross: In the N.T. the Cross is often used as a synonym of the death of Jesus. Paul declares that his Gospel is that of the Cross, i.e., it centers on the fact that Christ secured man's redemption by his death. The Cross is thus identified with the "blood of Christ" though, properly speaking, in crucifixion* there was no shedding of blood. It is the fact of a violent death, not the manner of it, which is uppermost in the minds of the N.T. writers. Often, however, a special significance is attached to the mode of death, and all the ideas connected with crucifixion are woven into the Christian message. It was tormenting, and the followers of Christ are to bear pain without shrinking. It was long drawn out, and they are to suffer patiently. It was ignominious, and they must brave ridicule and abasement. A symbolic value is found even in the details of this manner of death, e.g., crucifixion took place outside of the city gate; it involved a lifting up; the Law had pronounced a curse on those who suffered it; the offence they expiated was placarded above their heads (cf. Col. 2:14). Again and again in the N.T. the Cross is brought into sharp contrast with the exaltation of Christ. By humbling himself to the uttermost he attained to the sovereign glory (Phil. 2:8, 9. Heb. 12:2. Rev. 5:9-14). Much of this reflection on the mere circumstances of Jesus' death may appear morbid or fantastic, but it must be remembered that in N.T. times crucifixion was a familiar spectacle, with many degrading associations. Christian teaching had to take account of these, and change the impression they had left on men's minds. Perhaps it was the chief triumph of Christianity that it transformed the Cross into the symbol of all that is grandest and most sacred. See atonement in Christianity; propitiation; stations of the Cross.

F. C. Porter, *The Mind of Christ in Paul* (1934) G. B. Stevens, *The Pauline Theology* (1892); W. Morgan, *Religion and Theology of Paul* (1917).

E.F.S.

Crozer Lectureship Fund, The Samuel A.: A lectureship established at Crozer Theological Seminary, Chester, Penn., by Mr. Samuel A. Crozer in 1880. A gift of $10,000 provided that the topics of these lectures be profitable for Christian ministers and students and may be given by laymen as well as ministers from any evangelical denomination or country. The course continued annually until 1926 and since that date no course of lectures has been given by any one man. Lectures are now provided by outstanding men during the school year. The first lecture was given by the President of McGill University, Canada, in a large auditorium in Philadelphia, the Pennsylvania railroad providing students of the school with free transportation. (Data from the office of the President of the Seminary.) V.F.

crucifix: (Old Fr. or late Lat., *crucifixus,* from *crux,* cross; *figere,* to fix or fasten) A representation of Christ on the cross; loosely, a cross* used as a Christian symbol. The cross has always been a sacred Christian sign. The Crucifix came into general use after the sixth century. At first, Christ was usually represented as robed. Oriental artists began to depict the crucifixion realistically during the sixth century, probably as a reaction to the Monophysite* contention at the time. In the west the realistic presentation became normal from the ninth century on. See symbols, particular Christian. C.V.

crucifixion: This mode of execution was adopted by Rome from Carthage, and was notoriously the most dreadful of all tortures. It was devised to rack every part of the body, and to protract the suffering over a period of many hours, and sometimes of several days. See cross. E.F.S.

Crusades: (From Med. Lat., *cruciata,* marked with the Cross, through Sp. *cruzada* and Fr. *croisade*) Originally a series of wars for the recovery of the Holy Places of Christendom, particularly Bethlehem and Jerusalem; subsequently, any war against heretic or infidel sponsored as such by the Bishop of Rome.

Causes: With the decline of the Abbāsid Caliphate of Baghdad, the Seljuk Turks conquered Armenia, routed the Byzantines at Manzikert (1071), subdued Asia Minor, established their capital at Nicaea and, marching on Palestine, they proceeded to take Jerusalem (1076), where their atrocious cruelties to Christian pilgrims caused the greatest indignation and horror. It is important to notice that they were as much enemies to the Caliphate as to Christendom. A period of intense propaganda followed in the West, particularly under Peter the Hermit* (1093), leading to the decision to send an army of warriors bearing the Cross at the Council of Clermont 1095, proclaimed by Pope Urban II. The date fixed was August 15th, 1096. The desire of the Western Church to assist the Holy land was not unmixed with practical motives—the desire to provide the lawless feudal barons of the West with a more remote outlet for their fighting energy. The promise of plenary absolution, great wealth if they survived and a direct path to heaven if they perished ensured the initial success of the movement.

The principal Crusades are: *The First Crusade* (1096), in which no king took part. It captured Antioch (1098) and Jerusalem (1099), where they set up the Latin Kingdom (1099-1143). *The Second Crusade* (1147-1149) as a result of the fall of Edessa 1144, led to the preaching of Pope Eugenius III and St. Bernard who persuaded the Emperor Conrad III and Louis VII of France to lead it. It was a failure. *The Third Crusade* (1189-1192) was summoned by Pope Gregory VIII on account of the capture of Jerusalem (1187) by Saladin, the leader of united Muslim forces. The Emperor Frederick Barbarossa, Philip Augustus of France, Richard I of England and William of Sicily all took the Cross. Frederick was drowned in 1190. Acre fell after "prodigies of valour" in 1191; Saladin promised the return of the True Cross and an indemnity. Quarrels between the leaders and the consequent failure to capture Jerusalem and when peace was concluded with Saladin (1192) rights of pilgrimage and trade were all that was accomplished. *The Fourth Crusade* (1202-1204) owing to the treachery of the Genoese resulted in the capture of Constantinople (July 1203 and April 1204), which yielded a booty of over $7,500,000 for the Latins. The Latin Empire was established (1205-1261) and the Byzantine power was broken on the eve of the rise of the Ottoman Turks. There followed *The Children's Crusade* (1212), *The Fifth Crusade* (1216-17), which was a complete failure; *Frederick II's Crusade* (1228-1229), which is not recognized as Frederick was under the ban of excommunication. Frederick II concluded a treaty with El Kamil of Egypt (February 1229) and crowned himself as King of Jerusalem (March 1229), as the local clergy refused to cooperate. Had the ecclesiastical authorities cooperated, his success would have been greater. Smaller crusading parties continued to go, e.g., Theobald, King of Navarre (1239-40), Richard of Cornwall and Simon de Montfort (1240). *The Sixth Crusade* (1248-1254) was led by St. Louis (King Louis IX of France), who after a series of defeats was taken prisoner at Damietta (1249) by Turan Shah, who was murdered the following year (1250). A fifteen year truce was arranged with his successor Musa of Egypt. Louis returned to France in 1254. He pressed the pope to be reconciled with Frederick II. In 1270 he undertook his second crusade, with Prince Edward (Edward I) of England but died of plague at Carthage 1270. Edward left Palestine in 1271 and reached England 1274. This is the last of the genuine crusades. The Crusade of Pius II, the author of the Bull *Execrabilis* (1460), assembled at Ancona and the death of the Pope (1464) marks the end of the movement.

It is impossible to notice more than a few of the results: the rise of the towns, the *rôle* of chivalry*, the decay of serfdom, the development of national monarchies, the rise of romantic literature, heresy, the widening of interest and trade, banking and shipping. The main result was the final separation of Christendom and Islam on terms of bitter enmity. The second result was the increased power of the Papacy ("the Crusades were the foreign policy of the Papacy"), partly from the initial prestige, partly by way of diversion of attention from papal policy and partly through the extension of legatine power. In the end, the policy of Crusades was either abandoned owing to royal demands for a General Council, or was diverted to the suppression of dissent and movements for reform. It may be mentioned that General Allenby's march on Jerusalem (1917) was not a Crusade, and that Muslim troops who participated were so assured. See military religious orders.

T. A. Archer and C. L. Kingsford, *The Crusades* (*Story of Nations*) (1900); E. Barker, *The Crusades* (*World Manuals*) (Oxford, 1925); *Camb. Med. Hist.*, esp. vol. IV; L. Halphen, *L'Essor de l'Europe* (*XI-XIII*) (Paris, 1932). F.W.B.

Crusius, Martin, The Philhellene: (1526-1607) Humanist and Professor of classical languages in the University of Tübingen, Germany. He promoted the idea for the Union of the Greek Orthodox and the Lutheran Churches and worked with all his zeal for it. He also cultivated the friendship of many important laymen and clergymen in Greece. He introduced the study of the Modern Greek language in Germany. He was the first real philhellene in the 16th century. He also wrote important books for the study of Modern Greece as *Turcograecia* (Basileae, 1584) and *Germanograecia* (Basileae, 1585). His books are of great value today. G.E.Z.

crux ansata: The cross with a handle, or ankh, carried in the hand of gods and goddesses in Egyptian inscriptions. Presumed to be a symbol of life, or indicating that existence is a quality of the person who holds it. P.G.M.

crypt: (Lat., *crypta*, a concealed, subterranean vault) Early Christian subterranean burial place or catacomb*. Later, an excavation under a church used for burial purposes. Often just "Lower Church" or "Subterranean Chapel." S.M.G.

Crypto-Calvinism: (Gr. *kryptos*, hidden) An opprobrious term applied during the doctrinal controversies of the latter half of the sixteenth century by the strict adherents of Luther's theology to Lutherans suspected of secret preference of Calvin's* views on Christology* and the Lord's Supper*. The Wittenberg theologians Major, Eber, and Crell, and the physician Caspar Peucer, Melanchthon's son-in-law, were the leading Crypto-Calvinists, while Matthias Flacius* was their principal opponent. See Augsburg Confession. T.A.K.

Cuchulainn: (Pronounced coohoolin) The champion of the king of Ulster, in Irish mythology. He killed the hound of Culann, and in atonement acted as Culann's hound, guarding his castle as a watch-dog does, for a period. He finally perished in battle, overcome by Druidic spells. At his death his wife, Eimer, died of a broken heart. P.G.M.

Cudworth, Ralph: (1617-1688)The most prominent of the Cambridge Platonists*. He believed qualities to be absolute and eternal no matter how they may be labeled. (The squareness of a square could be called circular, but the label would make no change in the eternal quality either of squareness or circularity). Whatever exists, exists by nature, and not by will. His work was designed to refute Hobbes and is based largely on teleology. Author of *The True Intellectual System of the Universe; A Treatise On Immutable Morality.* W.G.H.

cujus regio, illius religio: See Westphalian treaties.

cultural anthropology: See anthropology.

culture: An anthropological term defined by E. B. Tylor as "that complex whole which includes knowledge, belief, art, morals, law, custom, and any other capabilities and habits acquired by man as a member of society." It comprises the totality of human invention and achievement, including all the principles, agencies, and techniques of control which man has acquired over physical nature and human behavior, and all the personal and social experience he has externally accumulated, stored, interchanged, and transmitted by means of tools and symbols.

Physically, culture consists of artifacts, the material inventions and objects made and used by man as a social being, including all man-made modifications of nature, both animate and inanimate. Socio-psychologically, it consists of (a) customs, or socially acquired behavior patterns, folkways, mores, and all overt usages and modes of action habitual to the group; (b) traditions, or all verbally transmitted systems of thought, beliefs, moral codes, philosophy, science, religion, and the like, considered as objectively distinguished from their creators, and stored externally in oral and written language; and (c) group feelings, or sentiments, attitudes, predispositions, and mental sets habitual to the group and basic to its thought and behavior. Culture also includes combinations of traditions, customs, feelings, and artifacts such as institutions, technologies, and occupational and professional skills. Since the material aspects of culture are the products of man's mental life, some anthropologists now refer to them as cultural equipment, reserving the term culture for the subjective aspects of man's group life. The totality of culture and cultural equipment conceived of as handed down from the past is sometimes referred to metaphorically as the *social heritage* or *group inheritance.*

Custom or *usage* is the totality of the acquired ways of acting which are habitual to a group. They are distinguished from inherited or biological determined behavior patterns or instincts on the one hand, and the purely personal idiosyncracies of individual habit on the other. Thus, the biologically determined behavior of eating is inherited, but the custom of eating with oriental chopsticks or occidental cutlery is learned. Habit and custom are for the most part correlative terms. Habit is used to designate a learned behavior pattern if it is thought of as residing in the individual, custom, if it is conceived of as having its locus in the group. The customs of the group are the source of most of the habits of the individual, but the latter, if they diverge from the group patterns, may become customs if they correspond to a group need and the individual is able to impress them on his fellows. Although historically custom had its origin in individual habit which became diffused throughout society by the interaction of individuals, in any given group custom as a factor in forming individual habit so overwhelmingly predominates over individual habit as a factor in creating custom that the sociological aspects of the process take precedence over the psychological aspects. Many customs become so stereotyped and mechanical through repetition that they are performed unreflectively, involving little conscious awareness or deliberate personal judgment. To these W. G. Sumner has applied the term *folkways.* Other customs are conceived of as normative. They are believed essential to the group welfare, and the individual is coerced to conform to them by the disfavor of his associates if he fails to respect them. To designate such usages Sumner revived the old Latin term *mores.* The foregoing distinctions are universally recognized by anthropologists and sociologists, but there is wide difference in terminology, some designating the folkways and mores as here defined by the terms, usages and customs respectively, while others limit the term usage to the field of language. Linguistic peculiarities which have not become established as usage constitute *slang.* If customs are thought of as prescribed rules of conduct apart from legal, moral, or religious sanctions, they are referred to as *conventions, manners,* or *etiquette;* if such sanctions are added they become respectively *law, mores, ritual* or *ceremony.* A custom of short duration is referred to as a *fashion;* if it is still more ephemeral it is a *fad, craze,* or *vogue.*

Tradition is the total body of accepted group beliefs. It is the subjective or ideational side of social behavior, as custom is its objective or behavioristic side. It provides the historical background and rationalization of custom. Tradition may be either *oral* or *written. Legends* are traditions of slow growth embodying popular feeling and consisting of admixtures of fact and fancy which are presented as historical. *Myths* are legends which lack the nucleus of fact. Some authorities would limit tradition to beliefs which lack a competent rational or factual basis, and hence would exclude such transmitted systems of thought as philosophy, and especially science and mathematics. But it may be observed that discoveries in these fields, once made, establish themselves as traditions and are dislodged with difficulty by new discoveries not in accord with the accepted beliefs.

Culture also patterns the affective life of man. *Sentiments, attitudes,* and the like are ways of feeling which differentiate groups, and which are acquired by the individual as a result of his social experiences.

Finally, *institutions* are vast complexes of social behavior integrating elements of custom, tradition, sentiment, and material equipment in the furtherance of basic life interests, such as the domestic, the economic, the political, the esthetic, the recreational, and the like. A family, a school, a church, a state, or any other institution, consists of such an integration of cultural features. *Technologies* and professional and occupational *skills* are also composed of such combinations. Medicine, the ministry, or any skilled occupation or profession, requires the mastery of the accepted body of knowledge, the assimilation of the customs and sentiments of the group, and the skilled manipulation of the cultural equipment which provides its tools and physical instrumentalities. In a word, culture, which was invented to facilitate the process of human living together, has become increasingly its dominating factor. See environment; folklore; law.

E. E. Eubank, *The Concepts of Sociology* (1932); E. S. Bogardus, *Contemporary Sociology* (1931).

H.E.J.

culture epochs: 1) *In anthropology**, the stages in the evolution of culture through which it was formerly believed all peoples had passed. The theory has a long history, but its modern development is largely due to Lewis H. Morgan who, in his *Ancient Society* (1877), revived the eighteenth century classif. into savagery, barbarianism, and civilization, and attempted to give it greater precision by sub-dividing each of the first two epochs into lower middle, and higher stages and by specifying the cultural characteristics of each stage. Alexander Sutherland, in his *Origin and Growth of the Moral Instinct* (1898) similarly subdivided civilization, and added a fourth status which he called "Cultured," in which he also distinguished three stages.

Modern anthropologists have objected to this classification because the popular connotations of the terms employed imply characterizations of peoples not justified by the facts, and because the earlier theory that they represent necessary historical stages which *every people* has had to traverse in consequence of an inherent natural law of cultural evolution has been rendered untenable by the progress of anthropological research. The course of cultural evolution is not unitary or unilinear. It presents many alternatives of development, and the different races and peoples diverged early, rapidly, and in many different directions. Nevertheless, as C. A. Ellwood has pointed out in his *Cultural Evolution* (1927), since cultural development is the process whereby man has *learned* control of physical nature and human behavior, its evolution *in the history of mankind as a whole* must necessarily conform psychologically to stages in a learning process, however much the history of any given people may have deviated in historical details owing to varied conditions both internal and external to the group, including its isolation from or contact with more advanced peoples. Thus, the late L. T. Hobhouse and his collaborators, in their *Material Culture and Social Institutions of the Simpler Peoples* (1930), classified the races studied into Lower and Higher Hunters and Lower, Middle, and Higher Agriculturalists, adding Lower and Higher Pastoralists as alternative developments to Agriculture, and concluded that these stages represent "an order corresponding to the degree of control over nature and mastery of material conditions manifested in each."

2) *In educational theory,* the cultural epochs theory involved the idea that the development of each child recapitulates* the stages in the development through which the race or people to which he belongs has passed, and that this parallelism provides the guiding principle for the sequence of topics of instruction in the educational curriculum. But with the passing of the view that there is just one inherent natural line of concrete development for every culture, this theory has collapsed, due to the loss of its former supposed scientific basis.

H.E.J.

Cumberland Presbyterian Church: In the need for ministers caused by the revivals in Kentucky and Tennessee about 1800 the Presbytery of Cumberland of the Presbyterian Church in the U. S. A. gave standing as licentiates to several young men who were not college graduates, as required by the church, and who also subscribed to the church's Confession of Faith partially, dissenting from its predestinarian* statements. On appeal by a minority of the presbytery the Synod of Kentucky disciplined the licentiates and the majority. The

General Assembly at length in 1809 upheld the Synod. Thereupon in 1810 an independent Presbytery of Cumberland was formed. By 1813 this had become a synod, and in this year the constitution of the Cumberland Presbyterian Church was adopted, including a confession omitting predestinarianism. As the United States expanded this church, zealously evangelistic and liberal, grew rapidly in the south and southwest. By 1890 it had about 180,000 communicants. In 1903 a revision of the Confession of Faith by the Presbyterian Church* in the U. S. A. opened the way for a reunion between it and the Cumberland Church, which was accomplished in 1906. A minority dissented and continued the Cumberland Presbyterian Church, which in 1943 had about 72,500 communicants. There is also a Colored Cumberland Presbyterian Church. R.H.N.

cuneiform: ("wedge-shaped", Lat., *cuneus*) The term refers to wedge-shaped signs made on wet clay, a method of writing invented by the Sumerians in Mesopotamia during the 4th and 3rd millennia B.C. It was employed for the writing of many different languages of antiquity during the 2nd and 1st millennia, finally displaced entirely by the Egyptian pen, ink, and paper (papyrus) shortly before the Christian era. G.E.W.

curate: (Lat., *curatus*) Priest responsible for "cure of souls"—in France parish priest is *curé;* in England he is rector or vicar, curate commonly means (assistant) curate. E.R.H.

cure of souls: A term used in Roman and Anglican communions to describe the pastoral work of the priest, to whom at ordination is committed the "cure of souls" in whatever parish he may serve. Normally included in this commission are administration of sacraments, visitations, supervision of parochial matters, etc. A similar idea is found in Lutheran circles in Germany, where the pastor is spiritual father of his flock, with *seelsorge.* See counseling, personal. W.N.P.

Curia Romana: The body of sacred congregations to whom the Pope* delegates part of his jurisdiction to be used by them in the government of the universal Church. At present the Curia consists of twelve Congregations, three Tribunals and five Offices. B.R.

curriculum of religious education: See Sunday School movement in the United States.

cursing: See blessing and cursing.

cursives: Manuscripts written in running, or small-letter hands, such as were anciently used for personal and business purposes, and later from the tenth century on came to prevail in literary manuscripts or as we would say, books. See manuscripts of the Bible. E.J.G.

custom: See culture; folklore; law.

Cybele-Attis Cult: See Mother Goddesses; mystery religions.

cycles of time: The regular rhythm of death and rebirth of the seasons probably suggested the idea of a cyclic movement of decay, destruction and renewal of the world as a whole. Usually the perfect age is placed at the beginning of the cycle and is followed by periods of progressive deterioration. The selection of fire, flood and wind as the universal agents of destruction at the end came from sad experience with nature's forces. The Aztecs added famine to the other three destroyers. The last night of every fifty-second year was for them the critical moment—the beginning of doom or the renewal of life. Hesiod set the pattern for Greek thought with his four ages—golden, silver, brazen and iron—each later era worse than the one before. The idea of cyclic renewal was established by Plato's time. Measurement of the time span of a cycle he borrowed from Babylonia. It was the period required for the sun and all the planets in conjunction at the beginning to return to the same position at the end. Zoroastrianism* divided the duration of the world into four ages of three thousand years each but had no theory of eternal recurrence. The four ages of the Hindu* cycle lasted twelve thousand divine years, equal to 4,320,000 human years. In a beginningless and endless universe this time seemed too modest. Later thinkers multiplied it by a thousand and to the cyclic period added a night of equal length before a new cycle began. The Buddhist* cycle begins with the age of destruction and moves through four vast periods to the age of perfection and then back again to the evil age. Each of these eras is of immense length. Texts and countries vary in their calculation of the time, but whether we accept the number of year as 1 followed by 52 ciphers or 1 followed by 168 ciphers it is still a long time. These great periods constantly recur to end in cosmic cataclysms of fire or water or wind followed by renewal. The Jain cycle begins with an ideal age four hundred trillion oceans of years in length, declines through six ages of decreasing length and returns through six ages to the starting point. See church year cycle; cosmogonies; creation; philosophy of history. A.E.H.

Cynics: A Greek school of ethics founded by Antisthenes (disciple of Socrates) and named for the gymnasium (Cynosarges) where he lectured. Antisthenes (fl. 400 B.C.) taught that the good life should be sought for its own sake, and should be restricted to essentials. The good man is independent of externals (such as family, wealth, happiness), keeping his desires under the strict control of reason. Later Cynics regarded all pleasure as evil, including even mental pleasures like the study of philosophy. Some Cynics, like Diogenes, rebelled against social courtesies and even against law. Stoicism* was a less severe and more humanitarian outgrowth of Cynicism. J.E.N.

Cyprian of Carthage: (ca. 200-258) The greatest church-man of the third century. Born in Carthage of a noble and wealthy heathen family. About 245 A.D. he was converted to an ascetic type of Christian life. Became Bishop of Carthage, and thus head of the North African clergy, two years later. Martyred under Valerian, September 14, 258 A.D. Contributed to the theory and practice of ecclesiastical administration and discipline rather than to theology.

Cyprian went further than Ignatius* of Antioch in developing a "high" doctrine of the Church, for he insisted that there is no salvation beyond the bounds of the visible Church, and that the Church is in the bishop. He also contributed to the doctrine of works of super-erogation*, which later played a large part in the Romish penitential system. See clergy. A.K.R.

Cyrenaics: A Greek school of ethics founded by Aristippus (a disciple of Socrates) of Cyrene, hence the name. The good life, they held, was that which contained the most pleasure and the least pain. The satisfaction of physical desires brings more intense pleasure and is regarded as higher than mental satisfactions. But the wise man must exercise prudence, not from moral scruples but in order to avoid pain. The theory was known as hedonism*. J.E.N.

Cyril of Alexandria: (376-444) An acute theologian, but violent controversialist, who became Patriarch of Alexandria about 412 A.D. He administered this high office in a high-handed and not disinterested manner. His Alexandrian rivalry with the Antiochians* led him to active opposition to Chrysostom*. After 428 he became the most influential, but an unprincipled, champion of Christological* orthodoxy against the Nestorians*. He was a zealous advocate of veneration of the Virgin Mary*. A.K.R.

Cyril of Jerusalem: (ca. 315-386) Became Bishop of Jerusalem about A.D. 350. From 357 to 381 he suffered much as a champion of the Nicene faith against the Arians*, though he found it possible to be friendly with Semi-Arian* bishops. He made contributions to the doctrine of the sacraments and to the liturgy of the church. A.K.R.

Czech Church Reform: See Hus; Hussitism; Bohemian Brethren. See also Eastern Orthodox Churches; Milic.

D

D: Symbol used for the author(s) of the Book of Deuteronomy* and for a school of historians or editors of the century following publication of Deuteronomy (621 B.C.) who employed the same vocabulary and style as that book, and were imbued with similar religious viewpoints. These editors were responsible for editions of Joshua, Judges, I, II Kings, Jeremiah**, and possibly other books.

See R. H. Pfeiffer, *Introduction to the Old Testament* (1941) pp. 284f., 304ff., 332ff., 365ff., 377ff., 410 ff.; J. P. Hyatt, "Jeremiah and Deuteronomy," *Journal of Near Eastern Studies* I (1942), pp. 156-173. J.P.H.

Dagan: An early god of Babylonia, associated with Anu* and Ninib (Ninurta*). He was identified with Bel*, and by many authorities with Dagon*. P.G.M.

Dagda: (*dago, devos*: good god) An old Irish god who ruled the Tuatha de Danaan after their defeat by the Milesians. He was the father of Oengus, and possibly a god of fertility. See *Revue Celtique*, v. 4, 12 and 16. P.G.M.

Dagon: A god of the Philistines*, mentioned in the Bible, and supposed by some scholars to have been adopted by the invading Philistines from the aborigines of Palestine. Apparently a god of agriculture.

A. T. Clay, *Amurru* (1909), p. 146; *ERE*, v. 4, p. 326. P.G.M.

D'Ailly, Pierre: (1350-1420) Bishop of Cambrai and Puy, Cardinal, Chancellor of the University of Paris where he was the teacher of Jean Gerson*, conciliarist. Ardent worker for the unification of the church during the great western schism, he is most distinguished for his leadership in the Council of Constance*. See conciliarism. F.W.N.

daimon: (Greek) Before 600 B.C. a) In Homer: A common name used for the gods; personalized powers derived from non-human objects and forces. b) Hesiod imagined a Golden Age in the remote past when the *psyche* after death became a *daimon*, but such, he held, was not true in the later Silver Age and Bronze Age; 'power' worshiped independently of the cult of the 'dead'.

After 600 B.C., Pythagoras held diamones to be the same as the psyches of men. Heraclitus identified 'character' in man with the daimon. For Plato the daimon is a tutelary divinity, the *nous* in every man. Similarly, the daimon, to the Stoic philosopher Marcus Aurelius, is every man's understanding and reason: 'Let the daimon in thee be the guardian.' See nous; psyche; Socrates. F.L.P.

dakhma: "A tower of silence", constructed for the disposal of the dead in Zoroastrianism. The bodies are laid upon stone slabs, naked, to be devoured by vultures.

D. Menant, *Les Parsis* (Paris, 1898) gives illustrations and floor-plans. P.G.M.

Dale, Robert William: (1829-1895) English Congregationalist, was born in Bermondsey. He was educated at Spring Hill College, Birmingham and in 1853 became connected with Carr's Lane Chapel of which he was sole pastor from 1858 till his death. Dale was a public spirited citizen of Birmingham and did much to promote education and religious freedom. He was a strong denominational leader, wrote a *Manual of Congregational Principles* and was president of the Congregational Union of England and Wales before he was forty. He presided at the first International Congregational Council in London in 1891. He was a strong advocate of ministerial education and it was largely through his influence that Spring Hill College was moved to Oxford and became Mansfield College. He was the first Englishman to give the Beecher Lectures at Yale.

He edited the *Eclectic Review* and the *Congregationalist* for eight years, and contributed largely to *Quarterly Review*, the *Nineteenth Century*, *Contemporary Review*, *Good Words*, and the *Sunday School Magazine*. His *Lectures on the Atonement* are a permanent contribution to theological literature. Among his many other notable works are a *History of English Congregationalism*, (edited by his son in 1897) and several volumes of homiletical and expository work.

Eng. Congreg. Yr. Bk. (1896), p. 208. F.T.P.

dalmatic: An embroidered over-tunic, worn as a mark of honor—first ecclesiastical use by deacons at Rome, later extended (in West) to other deacons, and Bishops. Cf. tunic. E.R.H.

dancing: Emotional expression by patterned, rhythmic movements of the body.

The two principal sources of dancing are religion and romantic love. In most savage communities dancing comprises a considerable part of traditional religious observance. The periodic ceremonial Indian dances in the southwestern United States are well-known examples. They are also typical of both the dancing and the religion of rude cultures, in being closely associated with the seasons and the food supply. In many tribes dancing has also an important role in courtship, often bearing marked resemblance to the strutting and pompously formal self-display of certain birds and animals. Sometimes, on the other hand, it seems to be primarily a means of auto-intoxication for strenuous activity, as, e.g., in the war dance. Again, it may be thought a method of working magic*, as when the women of a tribe dance continuously while the men are away in battle. In such use it obviously serves also to release excess nervous strain.

The Greeks were the first to develop the dance as a value in itself, for the sheer beauty of line and movement, without regard to the occasion. They may therefore be said to have originated the dance as a form of art. It was sensualized and degraded by the Romans, however, until only harlots were dancers. The Christian Church revived the dance in pantomines and ballets before the altar in the Middle Ages. At the same time it continued as an independent art in Spain. The first theatrical ballet was composed by Cardinal Riario (*c.* 1500).

In modern times the dance has been in a perpetual conflict among forces appearing within the activity itself. Among the degrading trends are the tendencies to gorgeous display, mere motor skill, and sensuality. In the middle of the eighteenth century, in France the ballet had sunk to the level of a bold advertisement of prostitutes under royal command. The damage to morals and health inflicted by much social dancing in American public halls and other poorly supervised places, especially when accompanied by alcoholism, is well-known. On the other hand, there has occurred, since 1900, a new revival of the dance as a fine art, and since 1918 this movement has made rapid strides.

Both the recreational and artistic values of dancing at its best are undeniable. As a manifestation of religious and ethical feeling, too, the dance may be remarkably effective, because of the complete personal commitment involved in this form of expression. Lucy Lampkin stresses this value in her book, *The Dance in Art* (1935), the motto of which is the call of Edwin Markham, "Come, let us live the poetry we sing." But the fact that the human body is itself the artistic medium in the dance, the very fact which makes possible some of its finest symbolism of self-purification and consecration, constitutes also an ever-present threat of abuse and degradation, as its history shows. For this reason, and through the influence of Puritanism* and other ascetic movements, many religious groups have been led to oppose dancing in every form, and others to tolerate it only under watchful suspicion.

See La Meri, *Dance as an Art-Form* (1935); W. O. E. Oesterley, *The Sacred Dance* (1923).

L.H.DeW.

Daniel: Hebrew book with large Aramaic enclave 2:4b-7:28. The latter is presumably somewhat older "eastern" material hurriedly adapted to new use in Palestine by revisions in chapters 2 and 7 and Hebrew introduction 1:1-2:4a and additional visions, ch. 8f., in the crisis under Antiochus Epiphanes (175-163 B.C.)* The book, as a whole, is composed of two parts: 1-6 the story; 7-12 the visions of Daniel. Historical errors (Belshazzar not last king of Babylon; Darius not first ruler after fall of Babylon) make sixth century origin of stories impossible. Dating of present book can be determined from visions, especially "prophetic" survey of history of Greek kingdoms in chapter 11, which becomes more detailed as the author's own time is reached and only becomes genuinely predictive in 11:40f. Of particular importance because of its influence on Jesus and the primitive church is the vision of chapter 7, with its figure of the "one like a Son of Man*." The book's acceptance of the doctrine of the resurrection of the dead (12:2-3), and the later Jewish angelology is also noteworthy. Daniel is the only Jewish apocalypse* to get into the Palestinian Canon. Great influences, both good and bad, have gone forth from it. On the credit side stand the book's philosophy of history and the strength and courage it gave to men; on the debit side there is the prominence given apocalyptic calculation and the first use of devices for reinterpreting or revising figures that prove disappointing (chapter 9). Identification of the fourth empire of chapters 2 and 7 with Rome rather than Greece (so already the Jews of the time of Christ) is totally untenable. Cf. Susannah, History of. See beast.

See R. H. Pfeiffer, *Introduction to the Old Testament* (1941); J. A. Bewer, *Literature of the Old Testament* (rev. ed., 1933).

E.G.K.

Dante, Alighieri: (1265-1321) Italian poet, author of the *Divine Comedy*. He was born in Florence of a Guelph family; in early youth came under the transforming influence of Beatrice (Portinari?), the "glorious lady of his mind"; was exiled in 1302 after a brief but turbulent political career; wandered throughout most of Italy, finally settling at Ravenna, where he died. The *Divina Commedia,* begun about 1300 and finished shortly before his death, is an allegorical epic, recounting the poet's journey through Hell, Purgatory, and Heaven under the guidance of Virgil and at last of Beatrice. Replete with symbolism and allusion, it is generally regarded as the supreme poetic embodiment of medieval thought. Besides the *Commedia,* Dante wrote in Italian the *Vita Nuova,* containing the story of his love for Beatrice; an unfinished philosophical discourse, the *Convivio;* and a number of lyrical poems. In Latin he wrote a political treatise, *De Monarchia;* a treatise on philology, *De Vulgari Eloquentia;* and several epistles and eclogues.

For the English reader the most satisfactory editions are those in The Temple Classics, containing parallel texts and translations together with brief commentaries. Among the more notable verse translations of the *Commedia* are Cary's (1812), Longfellow's (1867), and J. B. Fletcher's (1931). Paget Toynbee's *Concise Dante Dictionary* (1904) is a valuable handbook.

L.W.C.

Danu: Old Irish goddess of knowledge and culture. Often identified with Brigit*. Much of her cult and ritual passed over to St. Brigit. She was a daughter of Dagda*. P.G.M.

Darwin, Charles: (1809-1882) Having studied medicine and theology without feeling attracted by either, Darwin, in the interest of natural science, joined the Beagle in its voyage around the world (1831-1836). The observations gained therefrom formed the first foundation of his famous biological theory.

As an inquirer he was distinguished by his open and childlike mind. He guessed at an all-pervading interconnection, contending that definite and constant laws prevail throughout nature. He was a good observer by reason of his ability in speculation and in making hypotheses about what he perceived as new in nature. He had a remarkable capacity for grasping objections and keeping them in sight. He admitted that his evolutionary theory did not admit of any direct proof. He regarded the proof of his theory as centering in the intelligible thread of reason by which it connected a vast number of facts. He introduced the habit of dispensing with theological causes. In inquiry it was a victory for the principle of natural causation, the principle of which he brilliantly verified. The significance of his method and its results extended far beyond his special field of interest. His works exercised a significant influence on our entire conception of the world, above all upon the historical sciences, including politics and morals. In fact, his method affected every department of thought. He initiated a great revolution in biological views, adumbrations of which he gladly acknowledged. His merit does not consist in his having been the first to conceive the idea of evolution, nor in the causes of transmutation, but in the application and verification of these in the world of facts. His discovery of natural selection shows a painstaking checking up of preconceived ideas by accurately determined facts and a readiness to discard hypotheses that did not square with such facts. He did not regard his theory as a dogma but as a tool to set on foot further inquiries. He neither offered a rounded philosophical system as Herbert Spencer* and Ernst Haeckel claimed, nor a generalized theory of evolution to break down the line between the non-living and the living, the mental and non-mental. His general theory is that organic forms are the result of a long process of development from the most insignificant beginnings under the continual influence of the environment. He opposed to the dogma of the immutability of species the facts of their variability. According to Darwin man is the descendant of a favored variety of apes. According to Genesis our species sprang from a clod of earth, a much more humble origin than the origin from apes (not monkeys as popularly assumed). The real greatness of man suffered in his view no diminution because man developed out of lower forms. He opposed the theological and romantic view of men as fallen angels. He held the realistic view that man developed from an animal into a spiritual and moral being. Neither psychologically nor physically did he allow any but quantitative differences between man and beast. Darwin's scientific materialism is characterized by its mechanical explanation of the world, its absolute negation of final causes, and its denial of design.

His evolutionary hypothesis was at first bitterly opposed by many, if not all, theologians. In time an ever increasing number of them embraced it. Not a few of them justified it speculatively, though Darwin would not have accepted their views of adjusting his theory with their theology. Objections of an ethical and religious nature were brought against his theory by theologians and radical thinkers. Darwin himself proposed to reconcile evolution with traditional ethics through the concept of adaptation. He never could bring himself to regard natural selection as a means in the hands of Providence. First a theist and later an agnostic, he lost his religion when he assumed that religion depended upon a definite scientific view. Those who see in Darwinism the final destruction of religion fail to realize that religion does not rest upon a hypothesis concerning the origin of living beings any more than that it rests upon an Aristotelian-Ptolemaic cosmology. Organized religion undermines its own existence by affiliating itself with and demanding of its members a blind subscription to any scientific system. Living religion has no biology and cosmology. It does not rest upon unexplainable natural events, but upon the experience of the heart. See evolution.

Origin of Species (1859); *Variation of Animals and Plants under Domestication* (1868); *Descent of Man* (1871); *Expression of the Emotions in Men and Animals* (1872); S. P. Cadman, *Charles Darwin and other English thinkers, with reference to their religious and ethical value* (1911); L. Husley, *Charles Darwin* (1927); G. Jaeger, *Die Darwin'sche Theorie und ihre Stellung zur Moral und Religion* (Stuttgart, 1869); B. Stölzle, *Charles Darwin's Stellung zum Gottesglauben* (Leipzig, 1922). H.H.

Dasyus: The name applied by the Aryan invaders to the dark skinned aboriginal inhabitants of the Punjab. The word may originally have meant enemy. It may also refer to demons or supernatural enemies. C.S.B.

datum: (Lat. *datum*, that which has been given; pl. *data*) In logic, epistemology, psychology, or any inductive science, *datum* generally refers to that which is used as a basis for knowledge. In epistemology it refers specifically to the object of consciousness given to, rather than created or supplied by, the mind. See religious datum.

P.A.B.

Daub, Karl: (1752-1836) Professor of theology at the University of Heidelberg. At first he held to the critical standpoint of Kant*. Later he approximated the mystical theosophical elements and the doctrine of identity of Schelling*. As a decisive adherent of Hegel*, he finally attempted to reinterpret the Protestant dogmas in terms of Hegelian ideas.

Judas Ischariot, oder das Böse im Verhältnis zum Guten (Heidelberg, 1816); *Die dogmatische Theologie jetziger Zeit, oder der Selbstsucht in der Wissenschaft des Glaubens und seiner Artikel* (Heidelberg, 1833); *Philosophische und theologische Vorlesungen* 7 vols. (Berlin, 1838-1844); W. Herrmann, *Die speculative Theologie in ihrer Entwickelung durch Daub* (Hamburg u. Gotha, 1847). H.H.

David: King of Judah and Israel (c. 1016-976 B.C.) mentioned in the books of Samuel and the first book of Kings**. Many-sided personality, warrior, politician, and poet, he rallied all the Israelite tribes around the new capital city of Jerusalem.

F. James, *Personalities of the Old Testament* (1942). S.L.T.

David of Dinant: A man of whom we only know that he came from Belgium and lived for a while in the papal curia of Innocent the third. He is the most outspoken of all medieval pantheists*. He identifies the first substance of everything with God who is the underlying stuff for both corporeal and spiritual reality. This materialistic pantheism summed up in his *Quaternuli,* was condemned by the church at the Council of Paris in 1210. See cause. S.C.T.

David, House of: See communistic settlements, religious.

Davidson, Andrew Bruce: (1831-1902) Professor of Oriental Languages at New College, Edinburgh (1870-1900). His unfinished commentary on Job (begun 1862) was the first really scientific commentary on the O.T. in English. He was a member of the O.T. Revision Committee. He was the author of many commentaries, particularly on books of the O.T., "Theology of the O.T." in the *International Theological Library,* and the article "God" in Hastings' *Bible Dictionary.*

He also wrote two volumes of sermons, *The Called of God* and *Waiting Upon God.*

H.K.—L.F.

Day of Atonement: See Atonement, Day of.

Day of Yahweh: 1) Day popularly anticipated (between time of Solomon and Amos) when Jahweh would bring unprecedented prosperity, intervene to eliminate foreign enemies, and reestablish his nation on a glorious scale even surpassing Solomon's time. 2) Amos and his successors reversed this. Yahweh would come, but to punish his sinful nation by immediate military conquest. 3) In post-exilic times the "Day of Yahweh" concept was eschatologized and referred to the Judgment Day. An editor from this school inserted excerpts here and there throughout the prophetic writings, giving their already fulfilled predictions new validity for "the Great Day." See Amos; Joel; Post-exilic; Solomon; Zephaniah. R.E.W.

deacon: In the N.T. a ministerial order generally associated with assisting the bishops (see Phil. 1:1; I Tim. 3: 1-13); perhaps, though not definitely, established by the apostles to relieve them of such external duties as administering the charities of the early church (see Acts 6:2-6). Later it was the next to the highest of the *seven* Roman Catholic orders, preparatory to that of the priesthood. A deacon is one of the two necessary assistants at a High Mass. In Anglicanism* the diaconate is the lowest of the *three* orders and primarily the normal ordination required before that of priest. Similarly in Methodism* it is the lower of the *two* orders of ministry, a stage in the advancement to the eldership. Among European Lutherans it is not a separate order but the function of a parish minister's fully ordained assistant. In Reformed* churches the deacon is an ordained layman entrusted with the care of the physical and material properties of the church and with the customary administration of its charitable activities. Thus in Catholicism, Anglicanism, and Methodism the deacon is a minister of a lower degree preparing to become a member of a higher order. In European Lutheranism the diaconate as a clerical order is lost and refers merely to a subordinate function or duty performed by a fully ordained minister. In Reformed Protestantism and American Lutheranism it is a lay order separate and distinct from both the lay eldership and the ministry and is not a necessary qualification for either of them. See clergy. A.C.

deaconess: In the N.T. the term which means servant or minister was given to men, especially to those officially appointed to care for the needy women and children of the congregations (Acts, VI). Women helped voluntarily in church work, such as Phoebe, whom St. Paul names as deaconess in commending her to the church in Rome. (Rom. XVI). Pliny of Bithynia (c. 110 A.D.) records the torturing of two deaconesses by civil authorities in order to secure information about prevalent Christian practices. In "The Apostolic Constitutions" (current during the first five centuries of the church's history) the work of deaconesses is prescribed. Chrysostum* (d. 407) when Bishop of Constantinople had as assistants in his parish forty deaconesses and eighty deacons. During the next thousand years, deaconesses were replaced by the cloistered nuns and deacons had become an order of the clergy. Within the R.C. Church St. Vincent de Paul* (1576-1660) formed an association of women, not cloistered, who ministered to the poor and sick, and became known as "Sisters of Charity"*. In the nineteenth century, deaconesses appear locally in the Reformed churches, e.g., among the Mennonites in Holland. In Kaiserswerth, Germany in 1836, Pastor Theodor Fliedner* established the first institution for the special training of church women for works of mercy to be done in the spirit of Christ. With this parent institution, by 1940, 50,000 Lutheran deaconesses in Germany, Holland, Scandinavia, Switzerland, U. S. A., were affiliated. There are at least three other German church institutions for training deaconesses. Similarly other communions such as the Anglican, Ev. Methodists, Presbyterian have educated deaconesses at work in local parishes and in benevolent institutions caring for the sick and needy. The program of work varies with community needs. See Löhe, W.

A.S.

dead, the, prayers for: See office of the dead; prayers for the dead. Also: baptism for the dead; death and burial practices.

Deae Matres: Goddesses of the Celtic & Germanic peoples in Roman times, about whom little is certainly known, although much has been written. The standard work on the subject is still Max Ihm's *Der Mütter-oder Matronenkultus und seine Denkmäler,* Bonner Jahrbücher 83 (1887) pp. 1-200.

P.G.M.

dean: (Lat., *decanus,* the head of a group of ten) The presiding dignitary of a cathedral or collegiate chapter (Dean and canons). By extension, the head of an academic faculty.

Rural Dean: A priest, usually appointed by the bishop, having general supervision over a group of parishes constituting a deanery. P.V.N.

death and burial practices: Man has always been a protestant against death. Even high cultures have refused to recognize its universal rule and projected the hope of an immortal life free from all future assaults of death. Confucianism alone has accepted a "good death" as the normal term of a life fully lived. In the early world death seemed unaccountable. Primitive thinkers could not believe that sickness and death were intended to have a place in the human scene. They explained that it must have come as a result of a mistake or failure of one of the lower animals or the disobedience, or curiosity or carelessness of the first human pair. Usually the woman was blamed. Some stories attribute man's loss of immortality to the anger or enmity of a god. Whatever the theory regarding the origin of death, rarely was the death of the individual taken as natural. Some deaths were clearly the work of nature gods acting in storm or lightning or torrent. Death by violence might result from the superior magic of an enemy, the malignancy of an unhappy ghost or a hostile spirit. Death by disease was commonly credited to sorcery. Masters of magical techniques, of powerful curses and spells, with or without the help of malicious spirits, were believed to be effective dealers in death.

The many modes of treatment of the dying and the dead are the result of the accretion of ages and combine ideas drawn from earlier and later levels of culture. Some practices arose from a primitive fear of contact with the defilement and danger of death—carrying the dying out of the house, lifting him from the bed to die in contact with the earth or in a prepared grave; abandonment of the dying, destruction of the hut in which he died, or removal of the settlement from the death scene; preparation of the dead for burial by medicine men* or professional corpse handlers immune to the death danger; and the universal rites of protection and purification*. Some practices depend upon the idea of a separable soul*—calling to the spirit to come back immediately after death, instructing the dead man regarding his changed condition and separation from his former habitat, safeguarding the living from the death demon or from the dead if he should become an angry and malignant ghost*. When the dead man dwelt where his body was placed he was fed there, consulted, advised as to happenings in the family. The later idea of a special abode for souls in a realm of the fathers, a heaven or paradise gave rise to ceremonies to secure safe passage. Extreme unction* in Christianity, recitation of the *Patet* and *Ashem-vohu* by the Parsis are such rites for the dying. In Tibet a lama draws the soul out of the body immediately after death and shows it the way to the Western Paradise. Teachers of the dead instruct the Moslem in his tomb how to reply to the two examining angels. Because customs are retained after the ideas underlying them are outgrown, death and burial practices are often complex and confusing but the rites clearly combine three purposes—to protect the survivors from the dangerous contact with death, to initiate the dead man into his new status of separation from the living and to give him safe conduct to his new abode.

Immediately after death most peoples wash the corpse, close his eyes and change his clothes. Sometimes the hair and nails are cut and the feet tied. Weeping is not universal. In some cases it is expected; there may even be hired mourners. In old Japan the relatives wept while friends caroused. Hinduism and Zoroastrianism forbad tears because they hurt the dead or made his passage to the afterlife difficult. It was bad form to weep for a Moslem saint or for an old man in China. Food for the dead was sometimes provided; more frequently the mourners ate a meal in the presence of the corpse setting aside a portion for him. In many lands friends watch the body while it is waiting for burial. This wake* is often the occasion for feasting and eulogizing of the dead man. The watchers are supposed to protect his body and soul from demon assault. In Buddhist countries the priests recite the sacred texts in relays, day and night, during this period. Death also demands a change of garb and appearance for the mourners, usually a reversal of the ordinary mode. Black and white garments are most common. Moslem women wear blue. Sometimes all customary work must be stopped, care of the body neglected for a time, and no jewelry or adornments worn. It may be that this altered appearance, like the wreath or branch placed outside the death house, was once intended to give warning of the presence of the pollution of death.

The funeral may follow within a few hours after death or may be delayed several months. Primitive precautions to guard against the return of the soul still linger in some lands, for example, taking the body out through a window or a hole broken in the wall, going to the grave and returning by circuitous routes, crossing water, turning the body around several times on the way. The funeral procession is often elaborate. In cultures thousands of years old it may combine primitive with more sophisticated usages or forms contributed by the successive religions that have shaped the lives of the people. The funeral may include images, animals, musicians or noisemakers to clear the path of evil influences, specially selected wailers, public recognition of the virtues of the dead man, provisions for his future well-being, carrying or recitation from a sacred book, rites to safeguard the mourners. Circumambulation* of the corpse, of the church, of the grave, of the funeral pyre is practically universal.

Many modes of disposal of the dead are used. Priestly preference may give one form dominance in an area but uniformity is rare. The monetary, moral, social or ecclesiastical status of the dead man may decide the mode. Eating the corpse was an approved practice in some tribes. Exposure in trees, on platforms or on the ground was common. In ancient Iran the dead were given to the dogs and birds. The modern Parsis retain this practice by exposing the bodies to vultures on the towers of silence. In one form of disposal in Tibet the flesh is cut from the bones and fed to dogs and birds. The bones are then buried or crushed, mixed with meal and given to the animals. A more careless variant of this form is throwing the body into water or jungle or desert places. There is a ceremonial mode of burial in water when the body is placed in canoe or ship, escorted to the deep and the vessel sunk or set on fire. Cave burial has been practiced since prehistoric times. Commonest of all forms in past ages and generally preferred in modern cultures are burial in the earth and cremation. The Egyptian theory of the afterlife required the preservation of the body which led to the construction of magnificent tombs for the aristocrats. In Tibet the bodies of grand lamas are embalmed and kept on display for worship as deities.

Generally slaves and common people received less ceremonial treatment than priests, kings and nobles. Children dying before initiation* were disposed of with little ceremony. The unbaptized in Christian Europe were denied church burial and a place in holy ground. The unmarried, barren women and women dying in childbirth who might become vengeful ghosts were often buried with rites to counteract the danger. Criminals, suicides, lepers and those who met accidental death were in many lands refused burial rites, thrown away or buried with protective ceremony.

The body may be buried in a crouching or sitting posture, or lying extended on the side or back, with or without a coffin. The orientation of the fâce is fixed by tribal or religious tradition. The East is the favorite direction, but some peoples turn the dead toward the sunset, the South, the North, the old home of the clan, the birthplace of the dead man or the holy city of his faith. In ancient times it was customary to put into the grave food and drink, tools, weapons, personal belongings, clothes, money and mementos of his friends. An important man might take with him in death his wives, companions, servants, his favorite horse and dogs. This waste of human life and property was overcome later by the substitution of effigies of persons and symbolic forms of material goods.

A feast usually followed the funeral at the tomb, or at the home or both and was often repeated at stated times afterward until the dead man was settled in his new abode. Thereafter he shared in anniversary feasts or in the general ceremony in which all souls were fed. In some lands, however, the feeding of the dead was a fixed ritual of the family cult. The annual and anniversary feasts tended to become memorial occasions.

Before taking up the regular routine of living, purification was necessary for all closely in contact with the dead. If the impurity remained, as some thought, from one to thirty days, the usual work, attire or toilet could not be resumed during that time. Individuals and the home, sometimes the village had to be cleansed of pollution. The individual was purified by passing through fire or smoke, touching fire or water, sprinkling with water or cow's urine or by taking a bath. Fumigation or sprinkling with cleansing fluids made the death room safe again. There were also formal ceremonies to separate the dead from the living and restore the normal rhythm of life. The mourning period varies widely from a few days to three years. See burial practice, R. C.

"Death and Disposal of the Dead" *Encyclopaedia of Religion and Ethics,* ed. by J. Hastings, IV, 411-511; "Burial of the Dead" and "Death" *A Dictionary of Islam* (1885) by T. P. Hughes, pp. 44-47, 79-81; *U. S. Bureau of American Ethnology, Annual Report* . . . nos. 1, 5, 26; L. A. Waddell, *Buddhism of Tibet* (1895); J. J. Modi, "On the Funeral Ceremonies of the Parsees, their Origin and Explanation", *Journal of the Asiatic Society of Bombay,* v. 2 (1892); R. P. Bender, "Beliefs, Rites and Customs of the Jews Connected with Death, Burial and Mourning" *Jewish Quarterly Review* (1894), ff. J. A. Dubois, *Hindu Manners, Customs and Ceremonies* (Eng. trans. 1897). A.E.H.

decalogue: (Gr., *deka,* ten; *logos,* word, matter) The "Ten Commandments" held to be the foundation of Christian morality, and said to have been given to Moses* by God at Mount Sinai, written on table(t)s of stone: Exod. 31:18; 34:1. (See Tables of the Law) Found in their most familiar form in Exod. 20:2-17 and (with a different reason given for the 4th Cdt.) in Deut. 5:6-21. A different version specifically designated (Exod. 34:28) as "the ten words (Eng., commandments)" but dealing only with festivals and offerings appears in Exod. 34:10-26; it is said to be what was written on the second pair of stone tablets after Moses had broken the first, which contained the "ten words" of Exod. 20:2 ff. No explanation is given of the inconsistency, which is doubtless due to the unresolved claim of each version to priority. Still other by-forms of the Decalogue appear in Deut. 27 and in Levit. 19.

The several forms of the Decalogue apparently were "threshold liturgies' whereby worshippers at different sanctuaries and in different periods acknowledged the essential requirements of Yahweh* worship (cf. Psalms 15; 24:3-6; 118:20; and the place of the Ten Commandments in the Anglican office of Holy Communion). The reason for the number "ten" is mnemonic. The variety witnesses to this usage as characteristic from the earliest times but makes the ascription of any single form of Moses precarious. The Decalogue of Exod. 20—Deut. 5 was evidently in familiar use both in Israel and in Judah in the time of the classical prophets (Jer. 7:9; Hos. 4:2), and is commonly held to embody their teaching. Since, however, the prophets* represented a renewal of the prophetism of Moses there is no sufficient reason to deny the possibility that this Decalogue, in the terse original form preserved by the 6th, 7th and 8th commandments or "words", may be Mosaic in origin. See Torah. R.B.Y.S.

Decius: (201-251) Roman Emperor 249-251; soldier and administrator. Adherent of ancient faith. For reasons of state began systematic persecution to exterminate the Christians. K.H.C.

decrees, Divine: See Divine decrees.

decretals: (*epistolae decretales*) Papal decrees collected and inserted in medieval law books as well for the student of Canon Law* as for the faithful and clergy who are bound to observe them, but in particular for ecclesiastical superiors and judges who are to regulate their actions and judgments according to their tenor. The name "Decretal" appears for the first time in the Roman Synod of 496. In general a Decretal like a Constitution (cf. under "Encyclical") is some universal law in contradistinction to a "Rescript"* intended for an individual or for some particular case. If, however, a Rescript is later made the norm for all similar cases, it assumes the nature of a D. The oldest known and preserved D. is that of Pope Siricius, 385, sent to Bishop Himerius of Tarragona concerning clerical celibacy. One of the earliest collections of D. is the "*Avellana*", which contains besides papal also imperial decrees. We distinguish between authentic and false D. e.g., the Pseudo Isidoran, a collection originating most probably in France, not in Rome, during the IX century and intended to curb the growing power of the Metropolitans, Provincial Synods and State interference by emphasizing episcopal jurisdiction and centralization in the papacy to which the "causae majores" were to be referred. D. are distinguished from the decrees of General Councils*, which are usually termed "Canones". After Gratian's* time however, the term D. was used to designate any collection of Church Laws (Decrees or Decretals of Gratian). Among such important medieval collections were the "*Compilationes antiquae*", the "*Corpus Juris Canonici*" (comprising the D. collected by Raymond of Penafort by order of Gregory IX*, the "Liber Sextus" (D. of Boniface VIII*) and the "Clementinae" (D. of Clement V), as also the unofficial "Extravagantes (X.=Extra decretum Gratiani vagantes) Communes"; the Extrav. of John XXII and finally the "Liber Septimus" (D. of Clement VIII). More recent collections of papal legislations are known as "Bullaria". All the provisions of the medieval D., as embodied in the venerable old *Corpus Juris Canonici,* the last redaction of which by Jean Chappius gave way to the new *Codex Juris Canonici,* begun by Pius X* and promulgated as of May 19, 1918 by Benedict XV*. The old D. still retain historical, and many of them, as in so far as they are embodied in the new Code, even legal value. (Cf. *Codicis Juris Canonici Fontes EMI. Petri Card. Gasparri Editi* (Rome: Typ. Polylgl. Vat., 1923. ff.)

Litt. *Dict. Théol. Cath.* IV, 206-22; *Cath. Encyc.* IV, 670-73. R.M.H.

dedication: 1) consecrating an object to a god, saint or sacred use; 2) name of the being to whom a church is dedicated; 3) anniversary of the dedication, often degraded by excesses. W.W.R.

Dedication, feast of: See Jewish religious festivals.

Defender of the Faith: (*Fidei Defensor*) A title bestowed on Henry VIII* by Leo X* on 11th October 1532 in recognition of a work on the seven sacraments against Luther. It was Henry's desire to have a papal title like Rex Christianissimus (France) and Rex Catholicus (Spain). F.W.B.

Definite Synodical Platform controversy: See American Lutheranism; Schmucker, S.S.

deicide: The killing of a totem animal or of a priest-king in primitive religions, either real or symbolic. Discussed at length in J. G. Frazer, *The Golden Bough* (1890). See also Gerald Heard, *The Substance of Religion* (1931) and *The Ascent of Humanity* (1929). P.G.M.

deification: (or, from the Greek, *apotheosis*) The ceremony or social process of some kind which raises man to divinity. It was known among the Greeks after scepticism and Euhemerism had narrowed the gap between human and divine. Imperial Rome by degrees adopted deification, at first for deceased emperors, then for the living ones. Alexander the Great obtained his first apotheosis* at the oracle of Amon in Egypt. See hero worship. P.G.M.

deism: (Lat. *deus* god) An important rationalistic movement in England arising in the seventeenth century and continuing through the eighteenth. Deism asserted belief in one God, creator of the universe, but regarded him as detached from the world and making no revelation. The light of nature (*lumen naturae*) *i.e.,* reason, was man's only reliance. Thus while there was a wide diversity in the opinions of the several deists, they were at one in their opposition to revealed religion in general and to Christianity in particular. The Old and New Testament alike aroused their attack as a collection of unauthentic and fabulous books. Among the more extreme deists were Thomas Morgan (*The Moral Philosopher,* 1737), Thomas Chubb (*Discourse concerning Reason,* 1731; *True Gospel of Jesus Christ,* 1739; *Posthumous Works,* 1748), and Thomas Woolston (*Six Discourses on the Miracles of our Saviour,* 1727-1729). Lord Herbert of Cherbury (1583-1648), usually styled "the Father of Deism," had been far more guarded in his strictures, being content to commend natural religion, free from the errors and corruptions incident to transmission, which was not to be accepted on the basis of authority but because it was demanded by reason itself. He thus studiously sought to avoid denying the validity of Christianity or of revealed religion in general. His successors were less restrained. The two writings which are perhaps to be accounted the most influential were John Toland's* *Christianity not Mysterious* (1696) and Matthew Tindal's *Christianity as Old as the Creation; or the Gospel a Republication of the Religion of Nature,* (1730). This latter work, which went through four editions in as many years, was the most complete and balanced statement of the position of deism and is commonly called the "deist's Bible." As such, it aroused the especial attention of Bishop Butler.*

None of these men was a scholar of the first order; many of their utterances seem by present standards sheer bombast and schoolboy criticism. Nevertheless the movement is not to be easily dismissed as simply a vagary. Rather it was the natural expression of suspicions, which, though crude, grew into the critical sciences, and an indication of a wholesome unwillingness to allow a few doors to remain locked, even though they bore the sacrosanct seal of ecclesiastical sanction. Thus its championship of freedom for inquiry and its desire to reach solid foundations make it one of the real milestones in the history of theological thought. See Enlightenment, the; theism; Theophilanthropy, Society of.

Leslie Stephen, *History of English Thought in the Eighteenth Century,* Vol. I (2nd ed. 1903); and John Hunt, *Religious Thought in England* (rev. ed. 1896).

M.S.E.

Deissmann, Adolf: (1866-) New Testament scholar of Heidelberg and Berlin. His observation that N.T. Greek was the Greek of the papyrus documents of every day life (*Bibelstudien,* 1895, 1897) led to the modern speech movement in N.T. translation. Drew attention to the distinction between private personal letters such as Paul's, in the N.T., and more formal epistles, such as Hebrews, written in imitation of them. Especially active in bringing the papyri and the inscriptions to bear upon the N.T. (*Licht vom Osten,* 1908) and in presenting a vivid biography of Paul (1910). E.J.G.

delinquency, juvenile: See juvenile delinquency.

Delitzsch, Franz Julius: (1813-1890) German Christian Hebraist (of Jewish parentage) and Lutheran theologian. Professor of Theology at the University of Leipzig. He was a champion of the scientific but reverent study of the O.T. He was a great student of Hebrew literature, not only Biblical and Rabbinic, but also medieval.

He wrote many commentaries on the O.T., works on Hebrew poetry, and on Lutheranism, and translated the N.T. into Hebrew. He was the father of Friedrich Delitzsch, the famous Assyriologist. H.K.—L.F.

Delphos: A king of Delphi mentioned by Aeschylos in his Eumenides. P.G.M.

deluge: The legend of a disastrous flood which destroyed all but a few of the inhabitants of the earth is found in the religious traditions of almost all peoples. That there was a universal deluge, the evidence of science denies. That there were devastating local floods which brought death to most of the people in ancient river-valley or island civilizations is probable. Fire and hurricane are credited with the destruction of the world in some cultures. Water was not the only destroyer but more usual and more wide-spread and therefore more far-famed in story. These deluge legends were magnified by time and molded by theology. There are also signs of borrowing and of mutual influence. The biblical story is a variant of the Babylonian, refined and adapted to fit the theological and moral ideas of Israel. Native myths in modern times have been colored by missionary teaching. In Babylon and Greece the divine decision to destroy all mankind was thwarted by friendly deities who warned their favorites. In the biblical version Yahweh both willed the flood and gave advance warning to Noah. In Iran the high god instructed Yima to build a walled enclosure to save the good people. In these cases the original stories have been shaped to moral ends. In India the flood was not the result of a divine decree but one of the series of cosmic cataclysms which periodically destroy the world. According to one version of the legend, Vishnu* took the form of a great fish to save Manu who had befriended him. The Chinese flood was clearly a local affair. See Gilgamesh epic. A.E.H.

Demeter: See Mother Goddesses; mystery religions.

demiurge: An old Greek term for a craftsman, literally a "worker for the people." In Platonic* philosophy it was applied to the creator of the world, and in that sense it was used by the Gnostics* to designate the inferior deity who had created the evil world of matter, in contrast with the supremely good god of the purely spiritual world whom Jesus had come to reveal. S.J.C.

democracy: In 1639, the people of Connecticut resolved to "associate and conjoin ourselves to be as one Public State or Commonwealth; and do, for ourselves and our successors and such as shall be adjoined to us at any time hereafter, enter into combination and confederation together, to maintain and preserve the liberty and purity of the gospel of our Lord Jesus Christ which we now profess, as also the discipline of the churches, which according to the truth of the said gospel is now practiced among us; as also in our civil affairs to be guided and governed according to such laws, rules, orders and decrees as shall be made, ordered and decreed . . ." Democracy is evidently a two-fold compact, of individuals forming a body politic and of this body with government. It is the sovereignty of the people and the political equality of all citizens. It is representative government. Its roots are in the Graeco-Roman civilization and the Judeo-Christian religion. The former transmitted the particularly Stoic ideas of purpose, providence, forethought, progress, and natural law; the latter, the Bible, the decalogue, and intangible values such as God, evermore one and the same, dependable and good; obedience to God's law the supreme duty of man; the dignity of man and all men brothers; justice tempered by kindness and goodwill; ability patiently to endure with faith in the ultimate triumph of the truth, and the sense of destiny.

The Reformation* by emancipating the state from control by the church and exalting the significance of the individual through making him a child of God, dependent upon his own conscience and finally responsible to a sovereign God, provided the religious basis for the compact theory of government. If men belong to God and therefore can only grant and not assign to their rulers use of a sovereignty inherent in themselves, political freedom is on its way. Thus, John Locke* insisted that government exists for man and should have only "the authority which reasonable men living together in a community . . . might be disposed to submit to willingly." Puritanism* interpreting freedom as an inherent right of the individual made the First Amendment to the Constitution of the United States with its "Congress shall make no law respecting an establishment of religion, or prohibiting the free exercise thereof" inevitable. Rousseau* basing sovereignty of the people upon the higher right of the community arranges for a state-religion in his *Social Contract.* The Anglo-American way discriminating between political and individual rights uses the former to protect the latter.

Democracy, then, is unity amid difference, faith in the higher law and the worth of the individual, a government in which the people as a whole participate and share responsibility. It is the recognition of freedom of conscience and the classification of the churches as corporations. It is representative government, an enlightened electorate, the acceptance of the verdict of the majority, and progress by growth. It is education for life. See American theology, early.

Bibliography: W. A. Dunning, *A History of Political Theories,* 3 vols. (1902-1920); E. B. Greene, *Religion and the State* (1941); Gilbert Murray, *The Stoic Philosophy* (1915); C. E. Stevens, *Sources of the Constitution of the United States* (1894); C. G. Haines, *Revival of Natural Law Concepts* (1930); C. H. Moehlman, *American Constitutions and Religion* (1938).

C.H.M.

demonic: (Gr. *daimon*: spirit working unconsciously in nature and man) D. is the power applied to devilish purposes, especially the perversion of merely human and selfish concerns into supposed divine and holy commandments or institutions. R.K.

demons and demonology: Universally accepted notions particularly at early cultural levels. In general demons are superhuman beings who lack the dignity of gods but who may be either benevolent or malevolent in their dealings with men. In Hebrew and Christian thinking it became customary to regard all demons as evil, in contrast with God, Christ and the angels* of heaven. Demons were the angels of the Devil active in implementing his will and breeding trouble for man. The early Christians took very seriously the widespread belief of the time in the menace of demon possession. Since both mental and bodily ill health was thought to be caused by the indwelling of a demon, cures were to be effected by expelling the evil spirit. This could be accomplished by summoning to the aid of the sick person a more powerful good spirit before whom the evil spirit would flee. Thus Jesus commanded the demons and they obeyed him (Mark 1:27) because as supernatural beings they recognized in him a unique divine presence bent on destroying them and their works. The disciples of Jesus also cast out demons by pronouncing his powerful name in the presence of persons possessed (Acts 16:18; Mark 9:38; Luke 10:17). Belief in the activity of demons was especially widespread among gentiles where Christianity at first won many disciples and naturally the early church gave serious attention to the practice of exorcism*. Paul might proclaim the nothingness of the idol, but the demon behind the idol was a reality to be feared and shunned, and only when one was fortified by the indwelling presence of Christ could the demons be rendered harmless. By the third century the church had a class of officials who were professional exorcists charged with the task of driving away the demons. See devil; incubi and succubi; jinn; malleus maleficarum; spirits.

H. Duhm, *Die bösen Geister im Alten Testament* (1904); M. Dibelius, *Die Geisterwelt im Glauben des Paulus* (1909); J. Tamborino, *De antiquorum daemonismo* (1909); E. H. Zaugg, *A Genetic Study of Spirit-Phenomena in the New Testament* (1917).

S.J.C.

Denck, Hans: (c. 1495-1527) Turbulent figure in the Reformation period. Rector of a school at Basel, then at Nuremberg; ejected for preaching Anabaptist* views. Similarly expelled from other German cities. Died at Basel. G.R.C.

Denis, Saint: Martyr, patron saint* of France and first bishop of Paris. Started work in Gaul c. 250. For a time was mistakenly identified with Dionysius the Areopagite*. K.H.C.

Denny, James: (1856-1917) A prominent N.T. scholar and theologian of the United Free Church, Scotland. Born in Paisley; educated there and in Glasgow; was pastor in Broughty Ferry, 1886 to 1897, and then became Professor of N.T. in the U. F. College, Glasgow. Author of *Studies in Theology* (1894), *The Death of Christ* (1902), *Jesus and the Gospel* (1909), *Christian Doctrine of Reconciliation* (1918); and others. A.K.R.

De Nobili, Robert: (1577-1656) Italian Jesuit, original and successful missionary in Madura, India. The first European to master Indian literature, he is noted for his defense of Indian social usages. E.A.R.

deontology: Science of moral obligation or duty. The term was used by Bentham* as a title for an ethical treatise. It is sometimes used to distinguish a theory which emphasizes obligation or duty as opposed to what is required by the agent's own interest or self-realization, or even as opposed to a purely utilitarian ethic. R.B.B.

deposition: Judicial deprivation of clerical office, variously performed according to the disciplines of different churches. Sometimes a deposed cleric returns to lay status, sometimes excommunication follows deposition. R.H.N.

depravity: The absence of original righteousness involving an innate moral corruption and tendency to evil* inherited by man from Adam as the result of Adam's fall into sin* and exposing man in his sinful condition to the wrath of God*.

Total Depravity: The doctrine that man whose entire being is infected by his sinful inheritance from Adam is of himself totally incapable of making any availing effort toward salvation* and must therefore be regenerated* by the Spirit of God who takes the initiative in man's redemption. Many theologians, while claiming to affirm the doctrine of total depravity, admit the presence in man of qualities or traits which are commendable as judged by human standards, but maintain nevertheless that the controlling disposition of man being destitute of love to God is self-centered, possessed of a latent or active hostility to God, and subject therefore to an increasing progression in depravity unless saved from that condition by the grace* of God. See original sin. H.W.J.

dervish: From the Persian word for mendicant, although most dervishes are actually from the laboring class. Refers to members of Islamic ascetic orders, closely related to and intellectually derivative from the Sufi* sects, first appearing in the 12th and 13th centuries, although religious exercises going beyond ordinary rituals date back as far as the time of Mohammed himself. They are peculiar chiefly because of the form of their devotional exercises, which includes the repetition of religious formulae. This may be done silently, but the better known orders engage in chants, accompanied by a precisely defined sequence of bodily motions, which usually become more violent and rapid as the exercise proceeds, often ending in some kind of trance or ecstasy. Some orders conclude their exercise with forms of self-laceration. See faker.

L. M. Garnett, *Mysticism and Magic in Turkey* (1912); J. P. Brown, *The Dervishes* (1868).

R.B.B.

Descartes, René: (1596-1650) French philosopher and mathematician. Born at La Haye, he was first educated at the Jesuit College of La Flèche and later studied at the U. of Poitiers. From 1617 to 1621, he served in the armies of Maurice of Nassau and of the Duke of Bavaria. The rest of his life was spent in travel and private studies; he lived in Holland from 1629 to 1649 and died at the court of Queen Christina of Sweden. Though apparently a devout Roman Catholic throughout his life, Descartes' views on many topics were far removed from Thomism*. Cartesianism has, in fact, many affinities with Augustinianism. His interest in the use of mathematical method in philosophy, his application of mathematics to physics and music, his method of doubt, his opposition to the authority of Aristotle—these are characteristic of his rationalism and entitle him to be called one of the "Fathers" of modern thought. Chief works: *Discours de la méthode, Meditationes de prima philosophia, Le monde,* and *Traité des passions de l'âme.* See Cartesianism; Enlightenment, the.

Oeuvres complètes, ed. Adam et Tannery, 13 vol. (Paris, 1896-1911); Haldane, *Descartes, his Life and Times* (Lond. 1905). V.J.B.

descent into hades: (*descensus ad inferos*) Legends and myths of the visits of mortals and deities to the lower world, the abode of the dead, are quite common in the religions of the world. These descents are reported not only among primitive peoples, but are also related in basic myths of the Babylonians, Egyptians, Greeks, and Romans. To a more limited extent similar visits are also found in Jewish sources, but with less significance attached to them. The motives for these descents are varied: to satisfy curiosity; to obtain some boon or gift; to rescue relatives and friends; to warn the living upon return to earth; and to conciliate or control the spirits or deities of the nether regions. At times the descent motif is connected with religious rites, such as the initiations of the Hellenistic mysteries. The earliest Christians, Paul among them, believed that the spirit of Jesus was in Sheol* or Hades* in the period between his death and resurrection* (however, cf. Lk. 23:43 for a different view). Before long Christians were teaching in addition that Jesus had preached to the dead while in hades, saving some (the O.T. patriarchs, as a rule), and that he had also overcome the power of Satan* and Death during his stay there. Further, the motif was associated with baptism, the Christian counterpart of the mystery initiations. The belief, in one form or another, became increasingly common in the early centuries, and at length was generally accepted by the church, being written into the Apostles' and Athanasian creeds. In the Middle Ages it became a popular theme in miracle plays*, art, and literature. During the Reformation period it was quite generally included in confessions and other statements of belief. In more recent times the *Descensus* has been a subject for controversy. However it is still accepted, but with varying interpretations, by the greater part of Christianity, both Catholic and Protestant, although an increasing number of the evangelical denominations have rejected it. M.R.

design argument: See Butler, Joseph; God; Paley; teleology.

determinism: See cause; fatalism; fate; libertarianism and necessitarianism; predestination.

Deutero-Isaiah: See Isaiah.

Deuteronomic School of Historians: See D.

Deuteronomy: The last book of the Pentateuch* purporting to be in the main final discourses delivered by Moses* in Moab, giving to the Israelites the laws they would need in Canaan; it contains also the Song of Moses (ch. 32), the Blessing of Moses (ch. 33), and an account of his death and burial (ch. 34). Jewish and Christian tradition ascribe the work to Moses himself, but the Talmud (*Baba Bathra* 14b) excepts the last eight verses, ascribing them to Joshua. Modern critical scholarship is almost unanimous in maintaining that the original nucleus of Deuteronomy (probably the bulk of chapters 5-26, 28) constituted the basis of the reforms of Josiah in 621 B.C. as described in II Kings 22-23, the book having been written sometime earlier.* This theory was adumbrated by Jerome and formulated by DeWette in 1805; recent attempts to prove that Deuteronomy was much earlier than Josiah (Welch, Oestreicher *et al.*) or of exilic or later date (Hölscher, Kennett *et al.*) have not found wide acceptance. The Book of Deuteronomy is a harmonization of priestly and prophetic ideals of religion, seeking to establish on the one hand exclusive and pure worship of Yahweh in a single sanctuary, and on the other hand a high social morality based on prophetic teachings. In its conception of Yahweh as a God of love and justice and its lofty humanitarianism, it is one of the finest books in the Old Testament and represents a pivotal point in Hebrew religious history. See D.

See S. R. Driver, *Deuteronomy* (International Critical Comm. 3rd ed., 1902); Bewer, Paton and Dahl, "The Problem of Deuteronomy: a Symposium," *Journal of Biblical Literature* XLVII (1928) pp. 305-379. J.P.H.

Deva: The Devas in ancient Aryan religion were the "bright heavenly ones", sons of the sky father Dyaus. The term becomes the general designation for God in Hinduism*. In Zoroastrianism* it is applied to the evil spirits which are opposed to Ahura Mazda*. It is the Sanscrit word from the Indo-European root from which come also the Latin *deus,* Greek *theos,* as well as devil. C.S.B.

devil: The chief of evil demons*. In later Jewish and early Christian usage he was identified with Satan*. He was the source of all evil and was bent upon enslaving mankind. It was he who tempted Jesus at the beginning of his public ministry; he was at the head of the demonic powers in conflict with Jesus; he was the "prince of the power of the air" (Eph. 2:2) to whom Paul would hand over the Corinthian offender for discipline in the flesh (I Cor. 5:5); and he was the author of the bloody persecution feared by the author of the Book of Revelation*. In the subsequent history of the church he continued to figure conspicuously in Christian speculation even though his power was thought to have been undermined by Christ. But in spite of this reverse the Devil was always close at hand to tempt and destroy the faithful whenever he might catch them off their guard. As the responsibility for evil in recent times has been saddled more definitely upon man himself, modern theological thought has become somewhat dubious about the actual personality of the Devil. See spirits.

W. Fischer, *Die Geschichte des Teufels* (1906). S.J.C.

devil worshippers: The Yezidi religious community numbering about 20,000 and living in Kurdistan (East of Mosul) and elsewhere (near Aleppo, Diarbekr, Bitlis). Yezidi (from the modern Persian *ized,* angel or deity), means "Worshiper of God." They call themselves Dasin or Dasni (from the name of a Nestorian diocese) and for the most part speak Kurdish. They isolate themselves strictly from the rest of mankind (issued from Adam and Eve), regarding themselves as descendants of Adam alone. Their religion is a mixture of pagan, Zoroastrian, Manichaean, Jewish, Nestorian, and Muslim** elements. Their two sacred books are "The Book of Revelation" and "The Black Book." The supreme, transcendent God is passive, leaving the preservation of the world to seven angels of whom the most important is Malak Ta'us (peacock angel), who fell but repented (his tears extinguished the fires of hell) and is worshipped because he is good and active (his name "Satan" must not be uttered); he manifests himself in Shaikh 'Adi (d. 1161), who through transmigration has become divine.

Th. Menzel in *The Encyclopaedia of Islam* (1934) vol. IV, pp. 1163-70. R.H.P.

devotions and devotional literature: See Baxter, Richard; Bunyan, John; Dionysius the Areopagite; Forty Hours' Devotion; Francis de Sales; Gerhard; Groote; hymns, Hebrew and Jewish; Imitation of Christ; liturgics; liturgies; mysticism; Pascal; pietism; poetry and theology; Psalms; spiritual direction; spiritual life, the; stations of the cross; Taylor, Jeremy; Theologia Germanica; worship.

De Wette, Wilhelm Martin Leberecht: (1780-1849) Professor in Heidelberg, Berlin and Basel, Switzerland. Creative in all fields of theology, his works attained an extraordinary influence. As he grew older his thought assumed a dogmatically more conservative tenor. He discussed with uncommon clarity the great questions that moved the theology of his day: the relation of religion to the general intellectual life, the relation of Christianity to history, of theology to the general science of religion. By connecting Fries's* philosophy of religion with the strict historical-critical study of the sources and a warm personal Christianity, he procured a theological structure that was independent of the speculative, rationalistic theology and of Schleiermacher's theology. His theology, remained, in decisive points, enchanted by the natural religion of German idealism. His estimate of Jesus Christ showed an unclarified interlacing of revelation and the apotheosis of the humanistic ideal of mankind. He did not succeed in showing the relation of feeling and foreboding to the theocentric, to the objective question of truth.

Lehrbuch der christlichen Dogmatik, in ihrer historischen Entwicklung dargestellt, 2 vols. (Berlin, 1813-1816); *Über Religion und Theologie* (Berlin, 1815); *Theodor oder des Zweiflers Weihe, Bildungsgeschichte eines evangelischen Geistlichen,* 2 vols. (Berlin, 1822; 2 ed., Berlin, 1828). H.H.

dharma: A Hindu word of many meanings, law, justice, sometimes religion. The Laws of Manu*, is a *Dharmasastra.* Popularly used to designate the customs, usages, practices of any caste or group.

In Buddhism it is one of the three jewels, "the law", in which the monks take refuge. C.S.B.

dhyāna: Meditation. A very important practice in Hinduism and Buddhism**, requiring freedom from the distractions of the work-a-day world and concentration upon a single idea. Sometimes synonomous with yoga*. C.S.B.

dialectic: (Lat. fr. Gk., *dialektike,* art of debate; *dia,* through, *legomai,* converse). The art of discussion (Aristotle) or of logical controversy. Concern with the Ideas (Plato). The self-development of the Idea (Hegel). This term is ambiguous or at least analogical, signifying among other things, logic, discursive thought, problematic knowledge (opinion), criticism of ideas, history of ideas, etc. See Zeno of Elea. D.C.O'G.

dialectic: (Gr. *dialegesthai: to converse*) I. The term is best known today as characterizing the theory of Karl Marx* and his followers, commonly called "dialectical (or historical) materialism". But this is only one of a multitude of meanings connected with the term d. and not the most important nor the original one. D. signifies a certain mode or method of thought and at the same time the nature of things known by means of this method. The meaning of the term d. is thus at once logical (or epistemological) and ontological (or metaphysical). This coincidence is based upon the cardinal supposition that things happen in accordance with a principle (or principles). D. relies ultimately on the metaphysical conviction (or dogma) that thought and reality, essence and existence are in perfect agreement with each other, and that it is therefore possible to give a satisfactory account of the necessity of all changes be it in nature or in history. Marx e.g., believed in the possibility of expounding and even foreknowing and forestalling the course of social and political life.

II. D. issues from the fact that thought always moves from one point to another point, from one concept to another concept, be it from the subject to the predicate in a proposition, or from the principle of a theory to its conclusions, or from the conditions to the consequences, or from the cause to the effect, or howsoever. It maintains furthermore that reality is modelled after this precept, that the real also is divided into opposite elements, links, poles, stages and so on. There is always, according to the principle of d., action and reaction in the world as there is always thesis and antithesis in the movement of thought, for at bottom both the world and our theories originate from the same source and belong to one and the same Universe. Indeed, they themselves (world and theories) represent only one of the opposite sides that can be distinguished by thought, which also exist as poles in the Universe.

III. The underlying assumption of all d. systems and theories is that an identical reality exists divided against itself into opposite sides or aspects or parts, and that these parts integrate each other and form together the whole. This identical root of all appearances can be conceived by dialectical means either as the radical unity of the opposites existing before all actual differentiation, or as the final synthesis emerging out of the strife between the opposites, or as the one and the other at the same time. The latter possibility, of course, is the most comprehensive form of metaphysical d. It was developed by the system of Hegel*, from whom Marx borrowed the method of his own theory.

IV. The first dialectician in the history of European thought was the Ionian thinker Heraclitus*, who declared it a law of nature to be determined by opposite poles, such as day and night, winter and summer, black and white, moist and dry and so forth. He asserted that there is a conflict between those extremes the result of which is a certain balance or harmony in the Universe. "War is father and king of all", he says; "everything is generated by strife". A twofold movement in the world, an upward and a downward path characterize the opposite directions in which all things continually change. Nothing stands ever still, everything flows. Heraclitus not only described thus the cosmic flux, he believed also that a cosmic law, a universal "logos", rules over the flux and directs it so that no chance, but an eternal necessity regulates all movement.

The d. of Heraclitus had an enormous influence upon almost all systems of European thought. It is onesided to characterize his d. as materialistic, but it is also onesided to call it spiritualistic, since this opposition, like many other ones later connected with d., was not yet developed in the philosophy of the first dialectician. Following Heraclitus, it should be noted, stood Plato* as one of the greatest dialecticians of all times, if not the greatest. He was the first to coin the term and to apply it to his method of exhibiting and discussing problems by way of a conversation depicted in his dialogues (the name of which is derived from the same word as d.). The specific type of dialectical metaphysics as propounded by Plato is commonly called idealism* because of the central position of the Ideals in it. But many different shades of Platonic d. have been propagated in the course of the history of Platonism which is almost the course of European philosophy itself.

V. The term d. has been used also by an important theological school in recent days, although it has not its original and proper meaning in this theological d. founded by Karl Barth*. He asserts that a certain d. is the main feature of the Christian conception of man and history. A d. opposition is the fundamental principle of Christian faith: the opposition between God and man.

Other oppositions like that of heaven and earth, the Infinite and the finite, the Eternal and the temporal, the Holy and the profane, the Creator and the creature and so on are derived from the fundamental principle. But whereas d. in the original sense and in all philosophical systems means that the oppositions are to be conceived and unified by logical means and by means of reality as well, the dialectical theology on the contrary maintains that they cannot be treated in such a way, but that they are revealed by God, and that God alone can overcome the gulf between them. See socialism.

For further references see books on the history of philosophy, especially those on Plato and Platonism; also books on Marx and Marxism; on Barth and Barthianism (often partial and onesided). R.K.

dialectic materialism: See dialectic.

diaphony: See organum.

Diasia: The festival of Zeus Meilichos (the Propitious). Mommsen places it in the month Anthesterion (Feb.-Mar.). See his *Feste der Stadt Athen* (Leipzig, 1906). P.G.M.

diaspora: (Gr., dispersion) Name given to Jewish communities scattered outside of Palestine, especially after the Babylonian Exile, 597 and 586 B.C. (II Kgs. xxiv, 12-16, etc.).

See Elephantine Papyri; Babylonian Captivity, the; Judaism.

A. Causse, *Les Dispersés d'Israel, les Origines de la Diaspora et son rôle dans la formation du Judaisme* (1929); W. O. E. Oesterley and Th. H. Robinson, *History of Israel,* vol. ii (1932). S.L.T.

Diatessaron: A harmony* of the 4 gospels, combining their accounts into a single narrative, especially that compiled by Tatian* in 2nd century. Popular in Syrian church*. See versions of the Bible, ancient. K.H.C.

Dibelius, Martin: (1884-) He first lectured at the University of Berlin. Now he is at the University of Heidelberg. He also lectured at Yale. The most positive and perhaps the most permanent results of his labors are his emphasis on preaching as a formative factor in early tradition, his claim that the Passion narrative was from the beginning a continuous story, and his identification and discussion of certain narratives in the Gospels to which he gives the name *paradigms.* He plays a prominent part in the progressive and comprehensive development of Gunkel's* form-historical program of the N.T. sources. Not only is he one of several N.T. scholars who makes earnest with eschatology, but he also is with M. Kaehler*, K. L. Schmidt, Rudolf Bultmann* and Karl Holl*, one of those who has done most to destroy the usually liberal conception of Jesus, Paul and Luther. His work and theirs was carried on by the most approved modern methods that undermines modernistic illusions. See Form Criticism.

Die Geisterwelt im Glauben des Paulus (Göttingen, 1909); *Die urchristliche Überlieferung von Johannes dem Taeufer* (Göttingen, 1911); *Die Formgeschichte des Evangeliums* (Tübingen, 1919, 2 ed., Tübingen, 1933); *Geschichtliche und übergeschichtliche Religion im Christentum* (Göttingen, 1925, 2 ed., Göttingen, 1929); *Geschichte der urchristlichen Literatur* (Berlin & Leipzig, 1926); *Evangelium und Welt* (Göttingen, 1929); *From Tradition to Gospel* (1934); *Botschaft von Jesus Christus* (Tübingen, 1935); *A fresh approach to the New Testament and early Christian literature* (1936).

An authoritative criticism of Form Criticism is found in E. Fascher, *Die form-geschichtliche Methode* (Giessen, 1924). H.H.

dichotomy: See soul.

Dictatus Papae: Dictatus Papae, also called Dictatus Hildebrandini, has been until lately believed to be a statement of Gregory VII's* regarding papal rights and prerogatives. It is now known that the statement is not Gregory's composition but the compilation of his followers drawn up around 1085, several years after Pope Gregory's death. The dictate of the Pope is a collection of twenty-seven theses and is a powerful document expressing Gregory's views in matters of Church and State. S.C.T.

Didache, The: The Teaching of the Apostles, or The Teaching of the Lord through the Twelve Apostles, a short manual of church life and morals, written probably about A.D. 150. The first part of it gives a series of terse prohibitions and warnings embodying a somewhat legalistic code of conduct. (The substance of this appears also in the Letter of Barnabas*, ch. 18-20, and seems to have come from an earlier form of the Didache, now extant only in Latin.) This is enriched with material taken from the Gospel of Matthew. The second part consists of directions as to baptism, fasts, prayer, and the Lord's Supper. Forgotten for a thousand years, it was discovered in 1873, and published in 1883. See Apostolic Constitutions; catechism. E.J.G.

Dies Irae: (Lat., Day of wrath) A Latin hymn attributed to the thirteenth century Franciscan, Thomas of Celano, and used as the sequence in requiem* masses. P.V.N.

Diet of Worms: See Worms, Diet of.

Dietrich of Niem: (ca. 1343-1418) German conciliarist. After many years of service as a papal secretary he broke with Gregory XII (1408), and supported the council of Pisa. John XXIII's maladministration led him to thorough conciliarism*. His numerous writings include *De modis uniendi et reformandi ecclesiam* (1410).

H. Heimpel, *Dietrich v. Niem,* (Münster, 1932). J.T.M.

diffusionist school, the: See anthropology.

Diggers, the: A group of revolutionists appearing in 17th century Cromwellian England, insignificant in numbers, who called themselves the True Levellers. (See Levellers). They conceived the political revolution as an opportunity to bring about economic equality. They were the beginning of utopian communism regarding political reform as superficial unless it could redress the inequalities of the economic system. They drew their numbers from the ranks of the propertyless. They were the first English appearance of a proletarian philosophy.

L. H. Berens, *The Digger Movement in the Days of the Commonwealth* (London, 1906); Ed. Bernstein, *Cromwell and Communism* (London, 1930).

H.H.

Dillmann, Christian Friedrich August: (1823-1894) German Lutheran O.T. scholar, professor at Kiel, Giessen, and Berlin, distinguished for research in Ethiopic language and literature and Jewish apocalyptic. T.A.K.

Dilthey, William: (1833-1911) Rebelling against scientific positivism and naturalism and influenced by Hegel, Dilthey turned to the stream of history as experienced, first, in one's self, and then in the phenomena of culture, for an understanding of both philosophy and the world. His *Einleitung in die Geisteswissenschaften* (1883) directed attention to the *Geisteswissenschaften* or "sciences of spiritual things" which had their own methods and were independent of the natural sciences. One must *erleben* the life within and then *verstehen* the cultural evidences in society. Dilthey's influence grew rapidly after his death. It is especially noteworthy in Heidegger, Spranger, and Spengler**.

Other works: *Das Erlebnis und die Dichtung* (1905); *Das Wesen der Philosophie* (1907); *Gesammelte Schriften,* 9 vols. (1913-34). See psychology, schools of. J.S.B.

Dinsmore, Charles Allen: (1860-1941) Minister, theologian, and educator. After thirty-two years in the pastorate of Congregational churches, he joined the faculty of the Yale University Divinity School in 1920, as lecturer on the spiritual content of literature. Unsurpassed among American scholars in the interpretation of Dante, concerning whose work he published three volumes, he wrote also upon the English Bible, the great poets as guides to the meaning of life, and the problems of religious faith. His most widely read book, *Atonement in Literature and Life* (1906), has won a permanent place in the literature of theology. L.A.W.

diocese: (Gr. *dioikesis,* a governor's jurisdiction or district) Originally used to describe the Greek provinces of the Roman Empire, and, apparently, followed by the church to describe the Episcopal areas of jurisdiction. In the West, the *Diocese* is the unit of a bishop's jurisdiction, at one time larger than the present dioceses, which are the result of subdivision. F.W.B.

Diocletian: Roman Emperor (284-305). Reorganized and divided administration of empire for sake of efficiency. Feared strength of Christian church. Instituted the last great persecution. Cf. Elvira, Synod of. K.H.C.

Diognetus, Epistle to: A highly rhetorical apologetic fragment, dating probably from the third century. It is ostensibly addressed to Diognetus, perhaps meaning the tutor of Marcus Aurelius*, and pictures the Christians as being to the world what the soul is to the body. The closing chapters 11, 12, are from a homily by some other hand. See patristics. E.J.G.

Dionysiac Mysteries: See mystery religions.

Dionysius of Alexandria: (d. A.D. 265) "Great bishop of Alexandria" (Eusebius), "teacher of the Catholic Church" (Athanasius), and eminent pupil of Origen*. Dionysius undertook the task of refuting the Atomic Materialists, but is notable in the History of Doctrine as having opposed both Chiliasm and Sabellianism**, and as himself having been taken to task by his "namesake" and colleague, Dionysius of Rome*, for unsound doctrine (pluralism verging on tritheism). For an account of this controversy, labelled by Harnack a "prelude to the Arian* conflict", see the latter's *History of Dogma* and other standard works of the same subject.

For a radical interpretation of the differences between the Dionysii, see F. R. Green in *Essays on the Trinity and the Incarnation* (1928), ed. A. E. J. Rawlinson, pp. 254-7. See also Athanasius, *De Sententia Dionysii,* and *Ante-Nicene Fathers,* Vol. VI.

C.W.L.

Dionysius the Areopagite: An unknown writer, claiming to be the judge whom Paul converted on the Aereopagus (Acts XVII, 34) and by legend the first bishop of Athens and a martyr in Paris where he was believed to be the first bearer of the Christian evangel, he commended his mystical writings to the Christian world and for a period of a thousand years from 500 A.D.-1500 A.D. was a principal influence on Christian theology. His works, *On the Celestial Hierarchy, On the Ecclesiastical Hierarchy, On the Divine Names, On Mystical Theology,* together with ten letters are now generally agreed to date from the end of the fifth century, to be heavily infused with Neo-Platonism* derived especially from Proclus, and to be the work of a devout Neo-Platonist Christian. It is almost impossible to overestimate the influence of these writings as a bridge over which Neo-Platonism traveled in order to fuse with the Christian thought and the devotional practice of the Middle Ages. See canons of various churches; Denis, St.

Works, tr. by J. Parker (London, 1897-99); *Divine Names and Mystical Theology,* tr. by C. E. Rolt (London, 1920). D.V.S.

Dionysius of Rome: (d. A.D. 269) Bishop of Rome, eminent promoter of the authority of this See in matters of the Faith, and opponent of the extreme "Origenistic" doctrines of Dionysius of Alexandria*. The extant fragments of the Roman Dionysius—preserved by Athanasius*—have been printed in English in the *Ante-Nicene Fathers,* Vol. VII. Their title and the Editors' comments on Dionysius must be viewed with caution. See Dionysius of Alexandria. C.W.L.

diplomatics, papal: The two main documents issued by the Papacy are the Bull*, (from *bulla,* the globular leaden seal) and the less formal Brief, sealed with red wax by "the fisherman's ring." Bulls are registered and indexed under the opening words, e.g., *Inter cetera* (1492) and *Regnans in Excelsis* (1570). F.W.B.

diptychs: A term used to describe the lists of persons, dead and living, for whom prayers were to be offered in the eucharistic services of the primitive Church. The diptychs are still retained in some liturgies, as, e.g., the Latin canon of the mass, which has a number of names mentioned at each offering of the sacrifice. W.N.P.

Directory, Catholic: A large, paper-bound volume of nearly one thousand pages, published annually by P. J. Kenedy and Sons of New York. The Directory presents the names, location, and other statistical data about the Catholic Hierarchy, its secular and regular priests, its brothers, nuns, dioceses, parishes and manifold institutions. Topographically arranged, the book follows four main divisions: 1) Vatican City; 2) The United States; 3) Canada and New Foundland; 4) Ireland, England, Scotland, Wales, Mexico and Cuba. C.V.

dirge (O.T.): Lament for the dead, of which two fine examples are ascribed to David (2 Sam. 1:19-27; 3:33-34). Used figuratively in psalms lamenting desolation of Jerusalem (Bk. of Lam.), and by prophets in announcing coming downfall of their own people (Amos 5:2), or (ironically) that of foreign oppressors (Isa. 14:4-21). As a literary form it is characterized by exclamatory "how!", by contrast of past and present states of the lamented one, and by a limping (3:2) metre. R.B.Y.S.

discant: (*discantus*, or descant) 1) The simultaneous and harmonious sounding of two or more melodies in metrical rhythm. The addition of meter to "new organum"*. Described first by Franco of Cologne in *Ars Cantus Mensurabilis*, discant originated in the 12th century.

2) The second counterpoint added to the plainsong* was called the discant. Derived from this idea, a discant came to refer to any melody added to a given melody. It was often improvised. E.H.B.

discernment of spirits: 1) Recognition of authenticity of ecstatic utterance (as in primitive church). 2) Recognition of source of moral and spiritual impulses (as in rules given by St. Ignatius). See spirits. K.H.C.

Disciples of Christ: The largest religious body of purely American origin, having (1942) 1,664,943 members, 8,002 churches and 7,693 ministers in the United States and Canada, and a world membership of 1,826,434. In 1942 they expended $13,480,374 for local church maintenance and gave $2,023,614 for missions and benevolences.

Thomas Campbell* gave the initial impulse and his son Alexander* was the leader of the movement when it gained, or had forced upon it, a separate identity, and for many years after. Thomas Campbell was an Irish Seceder Presbyterian minister who migrated to America in 1807, was soon disciplined by the synod of his church for divergence from its practices and doctrinal standards, specifically for admitting persons of other communions to the Lord's supper and for holding that a qualified layman (e.g., a ruling elder) might conduct a religious service when no minister was available. Back of this lay a zeal for the reunion of the divided church and a belief that the ground of its divisions was the use of creedal and theological terms of fellowship instead of the simple requirements practiced by the apostolic churches as recorded in the N.T. Upon these, he believed, there was general agreement among all Christians. Divisions had occurred because more had been required than the Apostles required, so that faith was buried under a mass of theological opinions codified into creeds. The remedy, obviously, was to discard creeds and their contents as tests of fellowship and to do and say what the Apostles said and did in regard to terms of communion and the structure and practices of the church. This was called "restoring primitive Christianity."

While still a Seceder Presbyterian, Thomas Campbell gathered about him a group, most but not all of whom were Presbyterians, whom he organized into "The Christian Association of Washington (Pa.)" for which he wrote a "Declaration and Address" (1809) as a statement of principles and purposes. The Disciples of Christ count this as their beginning and therefore celebrated their centennial in 1909. The Christian Association soon became the Brush Run Church. One of its first acts was to license Alexander Campbell to preach. He had recently arrived from Ireland by way of Glasgow, where he had spent a year in the University. In seeking the Apostolic way, the group came to the belief that only the immersion of believers was Apostolic baptism. Agreement with the Baptists* on this point led the Brush Run Church to join the Redstone Baptist Association. From 1813 to 1830 the "reformers" were Baptists, but Baptists with the distinctive views indicated above. Through A. Campbell's magazine, the *Christian Baptist* (1823-30), his debates with the Presbyterians, Walker and McCalla, and his preaching tours, these views obtained a wide acceptance among Baptists. Separation from the Baptists was precipitated by Walter Scott who, as evangelist for the Baptist Mahoning Association in eastern Ohio, developed a simple and preachable formula of conversion which combined Campbell's Lockian conception of faith as the belief of testimony (an act of which the natural man is fully capable with no special act of enabling grace), repentance as sorrow for sins and amendment of life, and baptism as the final requirement upon which the promise of remission of the penitent believer's sins is conditioned. This was in sharp contrast with the theory that the penitent and "mourning" sinner must await some definite action upon him by the Holy Spirit, and must have an inner experience of this action and of his acceptance with God before he could have saving faith. The new slogan was, "In conversion, the Holy Spirit acts only through the Word." The resulting evangelistic technique was highly effective. The dissolution of the Mahoning Association (1830) led to the dissolution of several other

Baptist associations which had been permeated by these views, the exclusion of the "reformers" from still other associations and churches, and the beginning of their separate existence as Disciples of Christ. Their local churches were generally called "Christian Churches" or "Churches of Christ."

Meanwhile a similar body known as "the Christian Church"* had been formed by the coalescence of three movements of independent origin but similar principles. The first of these was started by James O'Kelly, Methodist, in North Carolina; the second, by Elias Smith and Abner Jones, Baptists, in New England; the third, by Barton W. Stone and four associates, Presbyterians, in Kentucky. A considerable part of this group, especially the part most directly influenced by Stone in Kentucky and southern Ohio, united (1832) with the movement led by the Campbells and Scott. To this combined nucleus of independent "Disciples" and "Christians" were soon added thousands of converts. The appeal of the new rational evangelism was effective both with dissatisfied members of other denominations and with unbelievers who had hitherto resisted the mourner's bench type of revivalism that was current on the frontier. Proselytism was practiced without restraint or apology, but the evidence indicates that the gains were far more from the "world" than from the "sects."

As members and churches multiplied, the need of organization was felt. The first national convention met at Cincinnati in 1849 and formed the American Christian Missionary Society, which did both home and foreign missionary work—but not much of either, for the first foreign missions (to Jerusalem and Liberia) were failures, and by far the greater part of the expansion in America was due to the work of individuals, local churches and migrant Disciples who were moving westward with the tide that followed the frontier. The Disciples went through the Civil War without division, but later a conservative group gradually withdrew because of a conviction that missionary societies and instrumental music in public worship were alike "unscriptural." These anti-society separatists (known as "Churches of Christ" in the federal census since 1906) were not anti-missionary and had no theological affinity with the "anti-means"* Baptists. An awakening of missionary zeal among the Disciples led to the formation of the Christian Woman's Board of Missions (1874), the Foreign Christian Missionary Society (1875) and, soon after societies for church extension, benevolence, ministerial relief, and education. In 1920 these societies were merged to form the United Christian Missionary Society, with headquarters first at St. Louis, later at Indianapolis, Ind.

The earliest colleges were Bacon (1836), later merged with Transylvania at Lexington, Ky., and Bethany (1841), at Bethany, W. Va., of which A. Campbell was founder and for twenty years president. Many other colleges were founded—more, in fact, than could be supported, for scores of them died young. There are now listed, as cooperating with the Board of Higher Education, 13 colleges and universities, eight foundations at state universities, one independent divinity school, and the Disciples Divinity House of the University of Chicago.

Disciples of Christ have taken an active part in all interdenominational movements for Christian cooperation or union, from the International Sunday School Association and Christian Endeavor to the Federal Council of Churches of Christ in America and the nascent World Council of Churches.

Errett Gates, *The Disciples of Christ* (1905); E. Gates, *The Early Relation and Separation of Baptists and Disciples* (1904); W. T. Moore, *A Comprehensive History of the Disciples* (1909); W. W. Jennings, *A Short History of the Disciples* (1929); W. E. Garrison, *Religion Follows the Frontier, A History of the Disciples of Christ* (1931). W.E.G.

disinterested benevolence: See benevolence, disinterested.

Dispater: Father Dis, a god of the underworld, synonymous with Hades or Pluto. Current in Rome after 249 B.C. P.G.M.

dispensationalism: An interpretation of God's work in history which finds its classical expression in the Scofield Bible. The root idea is that God has tried various expedients that have not succeeded, each one having been completely abandoned before its successor has been tried, so that the divine prescriptions for one "dispensation" have no force in the next. A.K.R.

Dissenter: A term used after 1662 to replace Puritan* which had gained ill-repute in many quarters during the Protectorate. The term included all Protestant groups dissenting from the Anglican church, yet it was not quite the equivalent of Puritan which covered the non-conformist Episcopalians who did not break away from the church. In modern usage the term is frequently utilized in a much broader sense; e.g., Champlain Burrage in his *Early English Dissenters* (1912). See Corporation Act of 1661; nonconformity; Separatist. W.S.H.

divination: Practises aiming at gaining knowledge of future or otherwise unknown events. In the O.T., diviners are listed among influential men, together with judges, prophets and elders (Is. iii, 2). Divination by *Urim* and *Thummim** (perhaps some sort of sacred dice) was widely practised in early times (I Sam. xiv, 41, reading of LXX; I Sam. xxviii, 6; Deut. xxxiii, 8); divination by necromancy* or evocation of ghosts was already prohibited by Saul in the eleventh century B.C. (I Sam. xxviii, 3). Diviners of all kinds (Heb. *qosemim*) together with necromancers, sorcerers, interpreters of dreams and of clouds, were censured by the great prophets (Mic. iii, 6-7; Is. ii, 6, read *miqqesem* instead of *miqqedhem;* Is. viii, 19; Jer. xxvii, 9; Deut. xviii, 10, 14; II Kgs. xxi, 6; cf. Lev. xix, 26, 31; xx, 6, 27; etc.). See Etruscan religion; gambling; hepatoscopy; medicine men; omen; shu shu s.v. Chinese T'm.; sooth saying. Also see magic.

A. Guillaume, *Prophecy and Divination among the Hebrews and the Semites* (1938). S.L.T.

divine decrees: The decretive will of God is distinguished, as relating to what He proposes to effect or to permit in time, from the preceptive will which relates to what His creatures ought, or ought not, to do. Thus the divine decrees are the distinguishable acts of His will which together constitute His purpose, and which, as realized by Him in time, constitute history in the widest sense, but especially involving the eternal destiny of men and of angels. See election; predestination.

A.K.R.

divine law: See ius divinum; law.

divine liturgy: See liturgy.

divine office: (Lat. *officium*, duty) The daily services of prayer, so called as constituting (with the Eucharist) the Church's duty of praise to God. From the ancient Vigil observed before Sunday (Acts 20:7) and on other occasions were derived Matins and Lauds, and Vespers** in the evening. Private prayers at the 3rd, 6th, and 9th hours came in the fourth century to be observed in common by monks, and Prime and Compline** were soon added; some monastic uses had an even more extensive series of hours of prayer. In the Greek Church since the 8th century rhythmical hymns have become prominent in the Office; in the West it still consists mainly of Scriptural elements—Psalms, canticles, and lessons. As time went on the feasts of saints multiplied, and by the 15th century the offices were complex and monotonous; in the 13th century they had been abridged into one volume (hence called Breviarium), and in practice were often said in two or three groups. The Roman Breviary has been several times reformed, most recently in 1911, to restore the ancient use of the whole Psalter; its recitation is binding on all in Holy Orders. In England two daily offices were formed out of the Breviary* in 1549, and have since remained the staple of Anglican non-eucharistic worship. See notes on individual services. See liturgy.

P. Batiffol, *History of the Roman Breviary* (3d ed., 1912); W. C. Bishop, *The Mozarabic and Ambrosian Rites* (1924); E. C. Ratcliff, "The Choir Offices," in W. K. L. Clarke, *Liturgy and Worship* (1932).

E.R.H.

divine right: A modern theory of kingship, chiefly associated with the Stuart monarchs in seventeenth century England, which held that kingship is a personal and hereditary right of divine institution. It should be distinguished from the ancient doctrine of the divinity of the ruler and from the medieval notion of the divine authority of the king's office. Under this theory, as expounded by James I and later Stuart adherents, the king possesses a personal right to rule by virtue of his birth and the divine authority inheres in his person and not in his office. See kings, divine right of.

J. N. Figgis. *The Divine Right of Kings* (1896).

W.S.H.

Divine Science Church: An "egocentric" sect based on divine healing, founded at San Francisco in 1885 by Mrs. Malinda E. Cramer who believed she had been healed after an illness. It has an involved teaching similar to that of Christian Science* and reports 18 churches and 4,000 members.

E.T.C.

divorce: The legal dissolution of the union between husband and wife. May be of two types: absolute divorce, *a vinculo matrimonii*, which provides complete and final dissolution of the marriage* with freedom to marry again; legal separation or partial divorce, *a mensa et thoro* (separation from bed and board) which provides for establishment of separate residences without freedom to marry again.

Almost all peoples have recognized divorce yet the conditions under which it is granted have varied widely and continue to do so. The oldest divorce regulations are to be found in the Assyrian code of Hammurabi*, about 2300 to 2500 B.C., which provided that man might divorce his wife at will without stating a reason. Among preliterates, one finds peoples such as the Veddas of Ceylon who do not permit divorce, others not only recognizing it but making the procedure quite simple. Thus a Zuni wife who no longer wishes to keep her husband makes known her decision by placing his personal belongings at the entrance of the house and upon seeing these, he returns to his parent's home. In the United States the first divorce was granted in Massachusetts in 1639.

The divorce rate varies widely from country to country and state to state within a country, the United States probably having the highest divorce rate among those countries having a modern culture. In the United States one finds not a single divorce in South Carolina for the year 1932 while in Nevada a high rate of 428.9 per 10,000 population. The explanation of this wide variation in the divorce rate lies in the lack of uniformity of divorce legislation. South Carolina has no law under which divorce may be granted while Nevada because of its liberal residence requirement encourages persons from other states having strict legislation to go to Nevada for divorces. Likewise there is found considerable variation in rate between rural and urban areas, the rural rate in 1932, the latest available, being approximately one-third the urban rate. Thus the divorce rate reflects the process of urbanization in modern society.

Among the more general legal grounds for divorce are: desertion, cruelty, drunkenness, adultery, and neglect to provide, these varying from state. Thus whereas New York State recognizes only one cause for divorce, adultery, several states recognize ten or more separate causes. The divorce rate in the United States, seven times as great in 1937 as in 1870, reflects the process of social change in our society. The divorce rate is often assumed to be an index of family instability but is in fact highly unreliable since it is no measure of the large number of cases of domestic discord which never reach the divorce court as well as the cases of desertion and non-support which although known to the special courts are not there for divorce action. Neither do the grounds upon which the divorce is granted reflect the causes of family instability since they are only legal straight-jackets into which the real causes must fit in order that the decree may be obtained. See family; infidelity.

Ernest W. Burgess and Leonard S. Cottrell, *Predicting Success or Failure in Marriage* (1939) ; Alfred Cahen, *Statistical Analysis of American Divorce* (1932) ; Mabel A. Elliott, "The Nature and Extent of Divorce," in Becker, Howard and Hill, Reuben (ed) *Marriage and the Family* (1942) ; J. P. Lichtenberger, *Divorce: A Social Interpretation* (1931) ; Ernest R. Mowrer, *Family Disorganization* (rev. ed., 1939) ; E. R. Mowrer, *Disorganization: Personal and Social* (1942) ; E. R. Mowrer and Harriet R. Mowrer, *Domestic Discord* (1928) ; Harriet R. Mowrer, *Personality Adjustment and Domestic Discord* (1935) ; Lewis N. Terman and Associates, *Psychological Factors in Marital Happiness* (1938). H.R.M.

docetism: The doctrine that Christ was too divine to suffer agony and death, and that he only *seemed* (Greek, *dokeo*) to do so. Some color was found for it in the cry upon the cross, "My God, my God, why have you forsaken me?" (Ps. 22:1) the Hebrew of which might be rendered "My Power," as in Aquila's version. This position was supported in the Gospel of Peter, A.D. 120-140, which translates the cry in this way, and in the Acts of John, A.D. 170-180, which describes Jesus as appearing to John on the Mount of Olives while his body was apparently being crucified across the valley. Docetism is opposed in the Gospel of John, which insists upon the reality of Jesus' death, 19:33-35, and in the Letters of Ignatius, A.D. 110-117, who declares that Christ's sufferings were real, not merely semblance, and that the Docetists themselves are but semblance. The Docetists had much in common with Gnosticism*, but eventually became a distinct sect. E.J.G.

Doctor of the Church: Official title given to one who has distinguished himself by holiness and learning. The title must be conferred by the Pope or a General Council. The eminent learning of the person enables him to be followed as a safe guide in theology, as a doctor of the Church as well as a doctor in the Church. Pope Boniface VIII* was the first to confer the title in 1295. At present there are 28 doctors of the Church.

Also a title bestowed on learned theologians in the Middle Ages. Thomas Aquinas is known as the Angelic Doctor; Duns Scotus as the Subtle Doctor.

Cf. *The New Catholic Dictionary* (Vatican Edition) ; *National Catholic Almanac* (1941), p. 109. S.C.

Dods, Marcus: (1834-1909) Scottish minister, Professor of N.T. at New College, Edinburgh from 1889, and Principal from 1907. Author of commentaries on *Genesis* and *I Cor.* in the Expositor's Bible and on *John* and *Hebrews* in the Expositor's Greek Testament. S.M.G.

dogma: (Gr. *dogma*) Decrees or edicts: used in the N.T. of government decrees (Lk. 2:1; Acts 17:7) and of ordinances of Jewish law (Eph. 2:15; Col. 2:14). Used of Church promulgation once only in N.T. (decrees of Council of Jerusalem: Acts 16:4). Dogma may mean any fixed belief; as when the mechanistic view of nature is spoken of as a dogma of the 18th century physics. But more properly it is Church belief; not essays in doctrine by individual theologians, but doctrine formulated in Creeds and Articles for acceptance by the Christian Community. Individuals may receive and explicate dogma (e.g., Barth, *Church Dogmatic*). Dogma is the body of truth in which people who grow up within the Church are instructed; for Roman Catholics it is the authoritative law of the Church and acceptance of it is necessary; for Protestants too it bears the Church's authority as being vital or even essential to Christian faith and life.

N. Micklem, *What is the Faith? I. The Nature of Dogma; II. The Content of Dogma* (1936) ; O. C. Quick, *Doctrines of the Creed* (1938). J.L.

dogmatic theology: "Dogmatics is the presentation of dogmas* in a coherent system" (Haering, *The Christian Faith*); the attempt to construct a 'Science of Christian Faith' by orderly explication of its intellectual content and meaning. The substance of dogmatic theology is revealed truth; but the discipline is continuous of giving this truth arrangement and form suited to the comprehension of each succeeding age. See systematic theology.

T. Haering, *The Christian Faith: A System of Dogmatics*, tr. Dickie and Ferries (1913). J.L.

dogmatism: (Gr. *dogma,* opinion or belief) 1) Belief in propositions supposed to embody revealed truth or required articles of faith. "Dogmatism is necessary to religion (*Catholic Encyclopedia*). 2) Any system of philosophy "which assumes a certain set of principles as its starting point" (Stetson in Baldwin). Particularly, since Kant, belief in metaphysical propositions without preliminary epistemological criticism of the nature and limits of knowledge; Wolff is a typical dogmatist in this sense. 3) Positiveness in the assertion of opinions (Webster). 4) Belief in any propositions for which there is insufficient evidence. 5) Fixed, arrogant, or arbitrary belief, accompanied by unwillingness to examine its grounds or to modify it for any reason; the National Socialist world view seems to be dogmatic in this sense. E.S.B.

Döllinger, Johann Joseph Ignaz von: (1799-1890) Theologian and church historian, he was ordained a priest in 1822 and since 1826 taught theology, later church history, at Munich. He was early connected with Lamennais* the Liberal Catholic, and corresponded with the English Tractarians. Döllinger was the leading German savant to oppose the R. C. definition of the dogmas of the Immaculate Conception* (1854) and of the Papal Infallibility* (1870). Upon refusing to submit he was excommunicated. Fellow-dissentients organized the Old Catholic Church*, ordination being provided by Dutch Jansenist bishops. He promoted efforts towards union of Old Catholic, Greek, and Anglican churches. Among the eminent men who had been his pupils was Lord Acton. Notable works of Döllinger are *The Reformation*, 3 vols. (1846-48), *Past and Present of Catholic Theology* (1863).

J. Friedrich, *Ignaz von Döllinger, Sein Leben auf Grund seines Schriftlichen Nachlasses* (Munich, 1899-1901), is by a contemporary; *Catholic Encyclopedia*, "Döllinger"; C. Mirbt, *Quellen . . . .* (1934 ed., Tübingen), p. 572 f. Q.B.

dolmen: A Celtic name, probably meaning stone table, given to a structure of two or more upright monoliths supporting a flat roof-stone. Since bones are sometimes found beneath the table, a dolmen is commonly regarded as a tomb. It might have been a primitive temple. P.G.M.

Dominic, St.: Founder of the Order of Preachers (O. P.), and with St. Francis* of Assisi a leader in the medieval reform of Christian living. He was born at Calaroga in Castile *ca.* 1170, and died in 1221 in Bologna. A tireless apostle and incessant traveler, he prayed constantly, preached with great success up and down Europe, practiced extraordinary penance, and down to the present time exerts influence for good through his spiritual sons and daughters, the members of the three divisions of the Dominican Order*. C.V.

dominical letter: An old-time chronological device for finding the day of the week for any given date. L.R.W.

dominicale: (Lat., from *dominus,* lord) A veil worn by women when approaching the Communion table. According to the Council of Auxerre (585 or 587) it is explained as a cloth with which women were to cover their hands when receiving the Eucharist. But the *Penitentiale* of Theodosius refers to the *dominicale* as the prescribed head-covering of women. Accordingly, *dominicale* has the sense of both a head-dress and a napkin. It may well be that the same veil served both purposes: placed upon the head, the hanging ends could be grasped by one or both hands, and thus the Eucharist could be placed in the latter. C.V.

Dominican Order: The Order of Preachers, an order of mendicant friars, founded by St. Dominic* early in the 13th century, to assist in the reform of Christian life. The main purpose of the Dominicans has always been preaching the Word of God, which work they have accomplished effectively down to the present time. They have manifested great ability as controversialists, scholars, experts in social studies, and the standard they have maintained in ecclesiastical studies is exceptionally high. St. Thomas Aquinas*, known universally as the "Angelic Doctor", is the greatest glory of the Dominican Order. See Black Friars; magister sacri Palatii; Lacordaire; mendicant orders.

D. A. Mortier, P. Conway, B. Jarret, *The Lives of the Brethren of the Order of Preachers* (1924). C.V.

dominicum: (A substantive formed from the Lat. *dominus,* lord; hence "The Lord's House") The term designating the buildings in which Christians celebrated their liturgical functions during the periods of the early persecutions. They were houses like ordinary residences of the time, but somewhat larger and more ornate. The term *dominicum* was still in use in the fourth century. C.V.

Domitian: Roman Emperor, 81-96. Undertook reforms in administration, morals and religion. First emperor to assume divine honours in lifetime. Took measures against Christians in Rome. K.H.C.

Donation of Constantine: A document in which the Emperor Constantine* is represented as conferring sovereignty over the western portion of the empire to Pope Sylvester I. It was generally accepted as authentic and was utilized as the basis for the papal claim to temporal supremacy until 1440 when Lorenzo Valla thoroughly demonstrated its spuriousness. W.S.H.

Donatism: A schismatic sect of the ancient Christian church, which arose from personal and local controversies in the Carthagenian church over the requested surrender of sacred writings during the Diocletian persecution. Initiated at first within a local church, a number of factors contributed to its rise: the pride of martyrs, the revitalized piety caused by the pressure of persecution, the conception of the holiness of the church, archaic religious reminiscences, the pressure suffered from magistrates, the alliance of the Catholic church with the state and miserable social conditions. It had not even a nominal membership outside of North Africa. Its membership grew particularly among the lower social classes. Socialistic ideas, extreme separatistic and exclusive tendencies, blind fanaticism resorting to destructive violence, characterized its members. The movement was declared heretical in 405 A.D. Being essentially a conservative movement, largely rooted in Cyprian's* ideas, it underwent various schisms. It advocated an episcopal basis of the church, demanding of its bishops that they be holy men, and contending that only under this condition were the sacraments effective. At the Synod of Arles* (314 A.D.) it was decided that the validity of ordination and baptism was not dependent upon the merit of the administrator. See intention, sacramental.

F. Ribbeck, *Donatus und Augustinus* 2 vols. (Elberfeld, 1858); D. Völter, *Der Ursprung des Donatismus* (Freiberg im Breisgau, 1883). H.H.

Donne, John: (1572-1631) English poet and churchman. In early life a Roman Catholic, Donne took Anglican orders in 1615, having long before that date essayed the roles of soldier, minor diplomat, and man of the world as well as having explored the learning of Oxford, Cambridge, and Lincoln's Inn. From 1621 until his death, he was Dean of St. Paul's, London, considered by many the most eloquent preacher of the 17th century. The extraordinary range of his experience, both secular and religious, found full expression in his poetry, the first collection of which appeared in 1633. His *Divine Poems,* although not numerous, are among his most important, setting the pattern for Herbert, Crashaw**, and others of the so-called metaphysical school. As a prose writer he is at his best in his *Ser-*

mons, of which three folios were published between 1640 and 1669. *Devotions upon Emergent Occasions* (1624) is also memorable.

H. J. C. Grierson's edition of the *Poetical Works* (2 vols., 1912) is standard, as is the *Life and Letters of John Donne* by Edmund Gosse, 2 vols. (1899). There is an excellent volume of selections from the *Sermons,* edited by L. P. Smith (1919).

L.W.C.

Dordrecht Confession of Faith (Dutch Mennonite): Though considering the making of theological distinctions inimical to the life of the spirit the Mennonites adopted a Confession of Faith at a Conference held in Dordrecht, in Holland, April 21, 1632. It consists of eighteen articles heavily weighted with Scriptural proof texts. The distinctive articles are: XI, *The Washing of the Saints Feet;* XIV, *Defense by Force;* XV, *The Swearing of Oaths;* XVII, *The Shunning of Those Who are Expelled.* See Confessions, Formal.

W.W.S.

Doric style: See temples, Greek and Roman.

Dorner, August Johannes: (1846-1920) A son of the mediating theologian of the same name, he was professor in Königsberg. He continued liberal theology most strictly. As he considered metaphysics a meeting of philosophy and religion, the proofs of God, above all the ontological one again played an important role.

Grundriss der Dogmengeschichte (Berlin, 1899); *Enzyklopädie der Theologie* (Berlin, 1901); *Religionsphilosophie* (Berlin, 1903); *Enzyklopädie der Philosophie* (Berlin, 1910); *Metaphysik des Christentums* (Stuttgart, 1913).

H.H.

Dorner, Isaac August: (1809-1884) An eminent German Lutheran theologian; taught in the Universities of Tübingen, Kiel, Königsberg, Bonn, Göttingen and Berlin (1862-1884).

His great work was, *The History of the Development of the Doctrine of the Person of Christ* (1835-1839), (enlarged ed. 1845-1856). He also published the valuable *History of Protestant Theology* (1867, English tr., 1871) and *Christliche Glaubenslehre* (1879-1881).

Dorner was widely esteemed for his Christian character as well as for his teaching and his creative work in theology. He was active also in the service of the Church and a leader in the cause of Christian unity, in the interest of which he visited America in 1873 as a delegate to the Sixth Conference of the Evangelical Alliance.

J.W.B.

Dort, Synod of: The Synod of Dort (Nov. 13, 1618—May 9, 1619) was called by the States-General of Holland to pass upon the Arminian* controversy. It was intended to be a general council of the Calvinistic churches. Representatives from England, the Palatinate, Hesse, Switzerland and Bremen were present but these were very few compared with the large number from Holland itself. The Arminians were Republicans. The Calvinists of Holland supported the efforts of Prince Maurice, the Stadholder, to centralize authority in himself. Maurice and his followers were in control. By unanimous vote, the five articles of the Remonstrance* were condemned and the Arminian ministers were deposed. See Belgic Confession; five points of Arminianism; five points of Calvinism.

W.E.R.

Dositheus, Patriarch: See Jerusalem, Synod of.

Dostoievski, Fyodor Mikhaylovich: (1821-81) Russian writer, born in Moscow on October 30, 1821. In 1841 he graduated from the School of Military Engineers in Petersburg, but he abandoned his military career to devote himself to literature. His first novel *Poor Folk* (1845), written under the influence of Gogol, won him early fame as a writer. In 1849 D. became involved in the trial of the Petrashevski circle, a group of young radicals advocating social reform. He was sentenced to penal servitude in Siberia. During years of extreme physical suffering he underwent a profound spiritual transformation. Through his discovery of the spiritual depth of Russian folk religion, D. became an opponent of the materialistic atheism and nihilism of modern European civilization. After his release from prison, D. wrote *The House of Death* (1861), containing the memoirs of his Siberian captivity, and a novel *Humiliated and Insulted* (1862). Financial reverses following the failure of two magazines he had founded after his return to Petersburg, forced D. to go abroad to escape his creditors. These years represent a time of tremendous literary production. In 1869 he wrote *Memoirs from Underground, Crime and Punishment, The Gambler, The Idiot;* in 1870 *The Eternal Husband;* in 1871 *The Devils.* In 1871 D. returned to Petersburg. He reached the climax of his literary career with the publication of his novel *The Brothers Karamazov* (1880) and his famous address at the unveiling of the Pushkin memorial in Moscow. He died on January 28, 1881.

D. has exerted a strong influence not only upon modern European literature, but also upon contemporary theology. Particularly the Swiss theologian Karl Barth* found in D.'s profound analysis of man an interpretation of human existence which supported his own attack against the anthropology of modern humanistic idealism. D.'s sympathetic portrayal of the downtrodden and the humiliated furnished the modern background for Barth's reformulation of the original Christian understanding of sin and grace.

H.Hfk.

Douai Bible: The Bible translated into English at Douai in Flanders by Gregory Martin and other Englishmen in the 17th century, and revised by Bishop Challoner in the 18th century. The translation of the N.T. was completed at Rheims. This is the Bible used in English by Roman Catholics. See Bible, English.

L.R.W.

double predestination: The belief that God in His inscrutable wisdom issued before all worlds a twofold decree, whereby He chose some for life everlasting (election), while condemning others to eternal death (reprobation). The milder doctrine, single predestination*, is that God by His sovereign will purposed positively only the decree of election*, taking merely negative action with regard to the remaining men and angels, simply passing them by (preterition), leaving them to suffer the just consequence of their sin. Cf. Gottschalk. A.C.

double standard of morals: This term is used to refer to the widespread social practice of permitting greater freedom in sexual conduct to men than to women. Generally this has taken the form of permitting illicit sexual experiences upon the part of men until marriage while requiring that women remain virgins. Not infrequently this tolerant attitude toward sexual irregularity upon the part of the male has been extended beyond marriage although no such freedom was accorded the female. The existence of this double standard of sexual conduct has led the femininists to take one of two positions: 1) the standard of sexual conduct imposed upon women should also be enforced upon men, or 2) women should be allowed the same liberties as are men. E.R.M.

double truth: See twofold-truth theory.

Doukhobors: See communistic settlements, religious; Russian sectarianism.

Dowieites: See communistic settlements, religious.

doxology: A formal ascription of praise to God. Traditionally used by Jews and Christians at the conclusion of public prayer. Bishop Ken's stanza "Praise God from whom all blessings flow" has become a popular form among English speaking congregations. See gloria in excelsis; gloria patri; Te Deum. Also see amen; kaddish; trisagion. V.F.

dragon: The common designation for the mythological serpent that appears in various early cultures. The Hebrew tradition made it the source of evil in the world, and Christianity carried forward the same idea. In the Book of Revelation* the dragon is "the old serpent," the Devil and Satan (12:9)**. As a menace to mankind dragons were especially feared during the middle ages, and popular saints or heroes were reputed to have slain these mythological monsters. See beast. S.J.C.

drama, religious: See religious drama.

Dravidian: A rather loose term generally used to designate that portion of the Indian population which is neither Aryan, Scythian or Mongoloid, or still more loosely as the indigenous inhabitants of India before the coming of the Aryans. Their religion corresponds well to the cultural level at which they are found today. Much of it has been taken over into Hinduism*. Indeed Hinduism at its lower levels is in great part ancient Dravidian religion. It is animistic to a considerable degree. Its deities are many, most of them animal or nature objects or powers, and many are malevolent. One of the most common is the Small-pox deity, known under many names. Most of them are quite local. Unlike Hinduism proper, the worship does not require Brahmin priests but is carried on by functionaries which resemble the medicine men or shamans* in other cultures. There are many religious festivals, and they have to do largely with the food supply, such as hunting festivals, and planting and harvest feasts, though many are designed to control the malevolent spirits.

Their faith and practise have been well described in Henry W. Whitehead, *Village Gods of Southern India* (1916, Second Ed., 1921), and W. T. Elmore, *Dravidian Gods in Modern Hinduism* (1915). C.S.B.

Driesch, Hans Adolf: (1867-1940) He worked experimentally at the zoological station in Naples, Italy. In 1907-8 he was Gifford lecturer at the University of Aberdeen and taught successively at the universities of Heidelberg, Cologne and Leipzig. He also was guest professor at the University of Peking. He was the most eminent representative of the neo-vitalistic movement which began in Germany with Eduard Johannes Reinke. Epistemologically, he was intimate with neo-realism and phenomenology. He recognized the special significance of parapsychological* phenomena for the future of metaphysics.

God, the superpersonal entelechy, expresses itself for Driesch developmentally in the ethical consciousness of human history. God is the apex of the teleological structure of the world. He is the reality who is the metaphysical basis of the development of the super-personal life. He is conceivably and factually unconditional, conditioning everything. As an empirical rationalist, Driesch rejected atheism. He reached the conclusion that genuine pantheism (in Bergson's formula *Dieu se fait* in freedom, in timeless development); emanatory theism (the same God passes completely through stages of development, He is the existing stage of reality and is able to attain other levels); and creative theism (God creates the world next to Himself and endures from eternity to eternity as complete totality)—are irresoluble theological questions. Sceptically and cautiously, yet solemnly, Driesch proceeded toward transcendent human interests. Regarding death as the door to the highest metaphysics, he gave the problem of death a central place in his doctrine of reality. His view of reality ended in a supernaturalistic philosophy of redemption according to which salvation consists in a change of our metaphysical reality. Death is conceived as a change to a new form of knowing and experience. Freedom being a part of the question of God, immorality. His view of reality ended in a superworks distinguish themselves by their most rigorous matter-of-factness.

The Science and Philosophy of the Organism (London, 1908); *Ordnungslehre. Ein System des nichtmetaphysischen Teiles der Philosophie* (Jena, 1912, 2 ed., Jena, 1923); *The Problem of Individuality* (London, 1914); *The History and Theory of Vitalism* (London, 1914); *Wirklichkeitslehre* (Leipzig, 1917, 2 ed. ,Leipzig, 1922, 3 ed., Leipzig, 1930); *Das Problem der Freiheit* (Berlin, 1917, 2 ed., Darmstadt, 1920); *Wissen und Denken. Ein Prolegomenon zu aller Philosophie* (Leipzig, 1919); *Die Probleme der Naturphilosophie im Rahmen eines Systems* (Berlin, 1922); *Relativitätstheorie und Philosophie* (Karlsruhe, 1924); *Grund probleme der Psychologie. Ihre Krise in der Gegenwart* (2 ed., Leipzig, 1926); *The Possibility of Metaphysic* (London, 1926); *Die sittliche Tat* (Leipzig, 1927); *Mind and Body. A Criticism of Psychophysical Parallelism* (London, 1927); O. Heinichen, *Drieschs Philosophie* (Leipzig, 1924); A. Gehlen, *Zur Theorie der Seztzung und das setzungshafte Wissen bei Driesch* (Leipzig, 1927); *Festschrift Hans Driesch zum sechzigsten Geburtstag,* vol. I, ed. by E. Becher et al; vol. II, ed. by P. Biro et al(Leipzig, 1927); H. Burchard, *Der Entelechiebegriff bei Aristotles und Driesch* (Münster i. W., 1928); *Der Mensch und die Welt* (Leipzig, 1928); E. Heuss, *Rationale Biologie une ihre Kritik (eine Auseinandersetzung mit dem Vitalismus H. Drieschs)* (Leipzig, 1938). H.H.

druids: Priests of the early Celts, given much publicity by Julius Caesar in his commentaries. They figure as weavers of spells in Irish folk-lore, and Welsh writers have woven a magnificent legend of philosophy and wisdom about them. Their rite of cutting mistletoe with golden sickles is fairly well authenticated.

J. Williams, *Barddas* (Llandovery, 1862). P.G.M.

Drummond, Henry: (1851-1897) Born in Stirling, Scotland August 17, 1851. Drummond was educated at Edinburgh University, studied for the ministry in Free Church College, and was made Lecturer on Natural Science in the same in 1877. He was associated for two years (1874-1875) with D. L. Moody* in evangelism in Britain and America. In 1880 he published *Tropical Africa,* in 1883 *Natural Law in the Spiritual World,* which won wide approval but was criticized for confusing analogy and identity, and in 1894 *The Ascent of Man* (Lowell Lectures) depicting the struggle for the life of others in the animal world. Drummond was peculiarly adept in presenting the Christian life in its intellectual and spiritual appeal to students. His address "The Greatest Thing in the World" became widely known and valued.

Cf. George Adam Smith, *Life of Henry Drummond* (1899); also *The Ideal Life* (1897). J.W.B.

Druses: A religious sect named for one of the founders, Darasi, who in the 11th century claimed al-Hakim, Caliph of Egypt (996-1021) to be the incarnation of God. He fled to the mountains of Lebanon and taught the people there, who have maintained religious and political independence for nearly nine centuries. Their faith mingles the teachings of the Mosaic law, the Christian Gospels, the Koran and the Sufi** allegories. They believe in one God, (calling themselves Unitarians), transmigration of souls, constant progress, and final perfection. The territory of Jebel Druse was created in 1925 when Syria was divided under French mandate into four territories. Their population is numbered at 86,000. They have created an extensive theological literature. P.E.J.

dryad: In Greek mythology, a tree nymph* or spirit of a tree, inhabiting it and appearing occasionally to men as a beautiful maiden. She perished when her tree was cut down or died. P.G.M.

dualism, epistemological: See epistemolcgy.

dualism, metaphysical: See ontology.

Duck River Baptists: A group of conservative Baptist churches, all in the South, usually grouped as "Duck River and Kindred Associations of Baptists," and sometimes called the "Baptist Church of Christ." They drew apart from other Baptists and joined separate associations in early discussions over Calvinism and missionary work. They are mildly Calvinistic and believe in the "perseverance of the saints." They practice immersion and feet washing and oppose a salaried ministry. While they have no missionary work they do not class themselves among the antimissionary groups. These churches differ little from the United and Regular Baptists**. There are 91 churches claiming nearly 8,000 members, nearly all being in the hill country of Tennessee and Alabama. E.T.C.

Dudleian Lectureship: Founded in 1751 by the will of Paul Dudley of the class of 1690 at Harvard it provides for "an Anniversary Sermon or Lecture to be held or preached at the said Colledge once every year successively." Three subjects specified by the testator are now treated in rotation: 1) natural religion, 2) revealed religion, 3) the validity of non-episcopal ordination. Recent appointees to the lectureship have included: J. B. Pratt, L. P. Jacks, James Moffatt, D. C. Macintosh. The lecturer for 1942 is Reinhold Niebuhr. J.S.B.

Duhm, Bernhard: (1847-1928) He taught at the universities of Göttingen and Basel. He wrote significant commentaries on Isaiah, the Psalms and Jeremiah. Unlike Wellhausen* who sought to determine the historical place of prophetism, Duhm was essentially interested in opening up the understanding of the content of the prophetic message.

Theologie der Propheten (Bonn, 1875); *Israels Propheten* (Tübingen, 1916). H.H.

Dukhobortsy: See Russian sectarianism.

dulia: See Mary, cult of; saints, veneration. Cf. latria.

Dunant, Jean Henri: See Red Cross.

Dunkards: See Dunkers.

Dunkers (also Dunkards or Tunkers): A popular name for the German Baptist Brethren, from the German *tunken,* to dip. In 1708 at Schwarzenau, Germany, Alexander Mack* led eight persons in founding a religious fellowship which held the N.T. as their only creed and agreed to accept new light as it came to them. They practised adult baptism by trine immersion*; held love-feasts* including feet-washing, kiss of charity*, meal called Lord's Supper, and the communion; anointed the sick for healing; emphasized simplicity in living; opposed legal oaths, lawsuits, and military service; urged non-resistance to evil and non-coercion in religion.

In 1719-29 they settled in Pennsylvania which remains their strongest center, although they have members in nearly every state. Colonial activities included the press of Christopher Sower* and his famous German Bible published in 1743. They were mostly farmers until 1850 after which they revived their publishing, established colleges and theological schools, and sent missionaries to India, China, South America and Africa. With many urban settlements they remain predominantly rural. They continue their historic peace position by maintaining, with the Mennonites and Friends**, Civilian Public Service Camps for conscientious objectors.

Beside deacons and ministers, they have ordained elders who preside over local congregations and larger church bodies. The traditional free ministry is slowly shifting to paid pastors. In polity they are congregational but since 1742 their Annual Meeting, composed of a Standing Committee of elders and a general delegate body from the congregations, has made decisions which are considered binding on the whole church.

After the schism of 1728 led by Conrad Beissel of the Ephrata Society*, various offshoots have appeared, but the main present groups stem from the 1881-82 division, viz: The Old German Baptist Brethren ("Old Order"), numbering in 1936 3,589, who publish *The Vindicator* at Brookville, Ohio; The Brethren Church ("Progressive") numbering in 1936 30,636 (now two groups), who publish *The Brethren Evangelist* at Ashland, Ohio; and The Church of the Brethren ("Conservative"), numbering in 1941 178,271, who publish *The Gospel Messenger* at their headquarters in Elgin, Illinois. Cf. River Brethren.

Martin G. Brumbaugh, *A History of the German Baptist Brethren in Europe and America* (1899); Henry R. Holsinger, *A History of the Tunkers and the Brethren Churches* (1901); Otho Winger, *History and Doctrines of the Church of the Brethren* (1919).

W.M.B.

Dunkmann, Karl: (1868-) He was professor in Greifswald. Now in retirement he writes mostly on sociological questions. As a dogmatic theologian and religious philosopher he belongs to the modern positive group.

Geschichte des Christentums als Religion der Versöhnung und Erlösung (Leipzig, 1907); *Der historische Jesus, der mythologische Jesus und Jesus der Christus* (Leipzig, 1913); *Metaphysik der Geschichte* (Leipzig, 1914); *Die theologische Prinzipienlehre Schleiermachers* (Gütersloh, 1916); *Religionsphilosophie* (Gütersloh, 1917); *Der christliche Gottesglaube* (Gütersloh, 1918).

H.H.

Duns Scotus, John: (ca. 1266/1274-1308) His astute, virtuose handling of the scholastic method was normative for the dissolution of scholastic theories. As a realist, maintaining both the reality of universals and individuality (haeccity) in things, he held that a complete certainty of the reality of a thing can only be attained by sensory experience. He considered individuality to be the real purpose of nature. The doctrine of the primacy of the will was also central to his thought. In view of the fact that an absolutely certain knowledge of the existence of God, of the immortality of the soul, of the resurrection is unattainable by scientific means, that the objects of faith are never logically necessary and certain of proof, his evident scepticism and emphasis on the relative character of religious knowledge made him a pioneer of nominalistic criticism. He radically distinguished between theology and metaphysics. He developed a definitive ecclesiastical positivism, he studied the idea of predestination, and his Christology exhibited more understanding for the human life of Jesus than the rest of the great scholastics. Accused of formalism by his successors, he also taught them to apply dialectics without consideration for the deepest religious mysteries. He doubted the agreement of dogma and philosophy; whereas the incomprehensible and irrational was truth for him by virtue of the authority of the church. See scholasticism.

P. Minges, "Ist Duns Scotus Indeterminist?" (*Beiträge z. Geschichte d. Philosophie d. Mittelalters*) (Münster, 1905); other studies of Minges on Duns Scotus in the *Philosophisches Jahrbuch* (Fulda, 1906, 1907); P. Minges, *Das Verhältnis zwischen Glauben und Wissen, Theologie und Philosophie nach Duns Scotus* (Münster, 1908); P. Minges, *Der angebliche excessive Realismus des Duns Scotus* (Münster, 1908); E. Pluzanski, *Essai sur la philosophie de Duns Scotus* (Paris, 1887); R. Seeberg, *Die Theologie des Johannes Duns Scotus* (Leipzig, 1900); K. Werner, *Johannes Duns Scotus* (Vienna, 1881).

H.H.

Dunstan, Saint: (ca. 924-988) Abbot of Glastonbury; archbishop of Canterbury. As primate he brought about a thorough reform of the church and was virtually leader of the Anglo-Saxon government under several kings, notably Edgar.

E.C.K.

duomo: (Lat. *domus*, a house) The common Italian term for a cathedral*.

F.T.P.

Durandus of St. Pourcain: (1270-75 - 1334) A substantial, independent thinker, the *doctor resolutissimus* of his age who preferred reason to authority. Although a Dominican, he stood in strong opposition to Saint Thomas Aquinas* (1225-6-1274) for which he was repeatedly censored. His views are Platonic-Augustinian, untainted by Nominalism*. As Bishop of Meaux he concurred to the condemnation of William of Ockham* (circa, 1300-1349).

S.C.T.

Dürkheim, Emile: (1858-1917) According to Dürkheim, the essence of religion is to maintain the distinction between profane and sacred things, manifested in innumerable forms and exhibited in ceremonies, the purpose of which are to purify man from sin, make a profane individual a participant of the sacred, or give an added portion of it. It is his theory that the source of religion is society itself, that religious conceptions are nothing but symbols of the characteristics of society, that the sacred, or God, is but a personified society, that the social function of religion consists in the creation, expansion, reinforcement and maintenance of social solidarity. The essence of religion is eternal; only its concrete forms change. See primitive religion.

E. Dürkheim, *The Elementary Forms of Religion* (London, 1915).

H.H.

Dutch Radicals: A term applied to an extreme school of critics of the history and literature of early Christianity. In their view none of the writings of the N.T. are earlier than the second century. In contradistinction to the Tübingen scholars* they regard history as a gradual and slow evolution. Among representatives holding this general point of view may be mentioned Pierson, Loman, van Manen, and van den Bergh van Eysinga. The most convenient treatment in English is to be found in the volume of the last named scholar, *Radical Views about the New Testament* (1912). M.S.E.

Dwight, Timothy: (May 14, 1752 - Jan. 11, 1817) Congregational clergyman, theologian, revivalist, educator, graduated from Yale College in 1769, was Principal of the Hopkins Grammar School to 1771, and tutor at Yale until 1777 when he resigned to become a chaplain in the Colonial forces. In 1779 he left the chaplaincy to care for his widowed mother and family at Northampton, Mass., and in November, 1783 was ordained over the church at Greenfield Hill, Conn. There he conducted a "school for both sexes," wrote some of his well known poems, and became a leader among the clergy. Upon the death of Ezra Stiles in 1795, Dwight was elected President of Yale College, in which position, and as professor of theology, he served until his death. Dwight was a great teacher and a forward-looking educator who gave Yale its first appearance of a modern university. Tremendously concerned over the encroachments of "French infidelity" and the decline of Christianity in America, he shaped his theology (*Theology: Explained and Defended*, 5 vols., 1818) to meet the challenge, and under his powerful preaching a revival was started that grew into what is now known as the Second Great Awakening. Dwight was the theological teacher of Lyman Beecher, Nathaniel W. Taylor** and those who later shaped the New Haven Theology*. He taught them to go back to the Old Calvinism* of pre-Revolutionary days for their basic tenets, and their views were built upon that foundation. See American theology, early.

Charles E. Cuningham, *Timothy Dwight* (1942); *Memoir*, vol. I of his *Theology;* Charles R. Keller, *The Second Great Awakening in Connecticut* (1942); S. E. Mead, *Nathaniel William Taylor* (1942). S.E.M.

Dwinell, Israel Edson: (1820-1890) Theologian and Professor of Homiletics, Pacific School of Religion, 1884-1890. Author: "Christianity a Religion of Expectancy," "The Mind Back of Consciousness" (articles). Associate Editor; *Bibliotheca Sacra.*

See also Memoir (1892) by Henry Jewett; *Religious Progress on the Pacific Coast.* J.W.B.

Dyananda Sarasvati: See Arya Samaj.

Dyaus: The ancient Aryan sky god, already clearly past the zenith of his development by the time the Vedic hymns were composed. Corresponds with the Greek Zeus, Roman Jupiter, and Teutonic Ziu or Tiu. C.S.B.

dynamics: Change of intensity of tone denoted by such terms as crescendo, diminuendo, sforzando. E.H.B.

dynamism: See ontology.

dynamistic monarchianism: See monarchianism.

Dyophysites: (Gr., *dyo*, two; *physis*, nature) Those in the 5th century who held the doctrine of the coexistence in Christ of two natures, the human and the divine, defined in the Chalcedonian formula (451) as without "confusion, change, division or separation." Opposite of Monophysites*. See Chalcedon, Council of; Christology. S.M.G.

dyotheletism: The Christological doctrine that Christ the god-man had two wills (human and divine) corresponding to the two natures. Orthodox theologians, in particular, taught the doctrine. There also were monotheletes* who adhered to the two-nature Christology adopted by the Council Chalcedon*.

H. v. Schubert, *Geschichte der christlichen Kirche im Frühmittelalter* (Tübingen, 1921). H.H.

E

E: Symbol used for one of the component narratives of certain O.T. books, derived from the initial letter of the divine name Elohim which it employs before the revelation of Jahveh to Moses. It is found in Genesis-Judges, and possibly also in I, II Samuel*. E was written in the northern kingdom, Ephraim, probably in the eighth century B.C. The existence of E as a separate narrative has recently been contested by some scholars (Volz, Rudolph), who assign certain parts of the supposed E document to other documents (J, D, P)** and consider other parts as editorial matter. See Hexateuch.

See E. S. Brightman, *The Sources of the Hexateuch* (1918), W. Rudolph, *"Der Elohist" von Exodus bis Josua* (Beiheft z. Zeitschrift für die alttestamentliche Wissenschaft, 69) (1938). J.P.H.

Ea: (Sumerian *Enki*, "lord of the deep") Babylonian-Assyrian god of the waters and of wisdom, master of crafts and learning, particularly of magical arts; the creation of the world, originally his work, was later attributed to his son Marduk*; his chief temple was at Eridu on the Persian Gulf. See Mesopotamian religions. R.H.P.

Earl Lectureship, The E. T.: Established by Edwin T. Earl at Pacific School of Religion in Berkeley, California, in 1901, by a capital gift of $50,000. The purpose of the foundation is to aid in securing at the University of California, as the center of secular learning for California, the adequate presentation of Christian truth, by bringing to Berkeley, California, year by year, eminent Christian scholars to lecture upon themes calculated to illustrate and disseminate Christian thought, and minister to Christian life; thus serving the purpose of a high evangelism.

At least one course of lectures shall be given each year. From the beginning occasional courses and lectures have also been presented yearly.

Among the Earl Lecturers have been Lyman Abbott, Henry Van Dyke, William Jewett Tucker, Francis Greenwood Peabody, James Bryce, George Adam Smith, Walter Rauschenbusch, Theodore Roosevelt, Arthur Cushman McGiffert, William Howard Taft, James Henry Breasted, T. R. Glover, Arthur Holly Compton, Henry Agard Wallace, Reinhold Niebuhr, and Carl J. Hambro. A.C.M.

early American theology: See American theology, early.

Easter: At the end of the second century, the celebration of Easter as the feast of the resurrection of Christ was general among the Christians. In all probability, its origins lie in the very beginnings of the Christian church.

The date of Easter remained uncertain for a long time. This was due to the fact that the ancient Christians celebrated both the death and the resurrection of Jesus at the time of the Jewish Passover*, which fell on the 14th day of the month Nisan. The early Jewish Christian congregations seem to have observed Easter together with the Passover. The gentile Christians rejected the Jewish custom. But they could not agree on the date on which they should celebrate Easter nor could they establish uniformity in the manner of the celebration. The Christians of Asia Minor, depending upon an old tradition, possibly determined by the gospel according to John, held that Jesus died on the day of the Passover (the 14th of Nisan) and they celebrated the death and resurrection of Jesus on that day of the year. The Western Christians, however, had developed the practice of celebrating the Resurrection on a special feast day, which they observed on the Sunday following the 15th of Nisan, on which day of the year they believed (in dependence upon the Synoptic gospels) Jesus to have been crucified. Thus they differed from the Eastern Christians not only in the manner but also the date of the Easter celebration. The Roman Bishop Victor (189-199) attempted to unify the practice and arbitrarily excommunicated the Easterners who refused to follow the Western example. The issue was definitely settled only by the Council of Nicaea (325) which decreed that Easter as the feast of the Resurrection should be celebrated on the first Sunday following upon the Spring equinox. The old Passover tradition was preserved in the celebration of Holy Week in which the whole passion of Christ from the entrance into Jerusalem to the Resurrection was celebrated.

Today, Easter is observed among us on the first Sunday following the first full moon after the Spring equinox.

Pagan practices were introduced into the Christian observance of Easter at an early age on account of the fact that the feast coincided with the beginning of Spring (the word Easter is derived from the name of *Eastre*, the Spring-goddess; the French word *Pâques* (Italian: *Pasqua*) comes from the Greek *pascha*, the Passover!). At that season of the year, the New Year and the Creation of the World were celebrated in ancient times by an exchange of gifts (Easter-eggs) and by generous hospitality to friends, to the poor, etc. See church year; church year cycle; Quartodecimans.

W.P.

Eastern Orthodox Churches: Originally comprising the Eastern patriarchates* of Constantinople, Alexandria, Antioch, and Jerusalem, the number of the churches included in this confederation has been gradually increased by missionary work of the Byzantine* church and its daughter churches, and other causes.

The patriarchate of Constantinople, after the Arabs had conquered Syria, Palestine, and Egypt, in course of time practically absorbed the formerly autocephalous ancient patriarchates of the lost territories, although in theory they always remained separate. The Russian Church proclaimed its independence from Constantinople in 1448, just prior to the downfall of the Byzantine Empire*. But the Byzantine church survived the fall, and the patriarch of Constantinople was granted, by Sultan Mohammed II, the office of the ethnarch, i.e., the civil government over the Greeks within the Turkish Empire. This important prerogative finally gave the patriarch jurisdiction over all the Orthodox within the borders of the Turkish Empire, irrespective of their nationality.

During the nineteenth century, by a series of revolts against the political dominance of Turkey, a number of Balkan nations secured their political independence, which was followed by an ecclesiastical autocephaly. Thus arose the churches of Greece, Serbia, Roumania, and Bulgaria (where the religious independence preceded the political).

Before the World War, there were fifteen Orthodox bodies in existence. But the war made great changes in the political configuration of Eastern Europe, which resulted in a similar change in the ecclesiastical realm; the number of churches increased to twenty-one. Of these, the Greek group of churches consists of the greatly enfeebled and reduced Patriarchate of Constantinople, which barely survived the exodus of the Greeks from the Turkish Republic (with the exception of Constantinople and its environs) consequent upon the forcible exchange of population in 1923. The Church of the Republic of Greece, however, was the beneficiary of this exchange. The Orthodox Church of Cyprus, whose autocephaly dates back to 431, with the Church of the Dodecanese Islands (in the possession of the Italians), complete this group.

The so-called Melkite churches (predominantly Syrian or Arab) comprise the numerically weak patriarchates of Alexandria, Jerusalem, and Antioch.

The third group, consisting of the Russian group of churches, is numerically by far the largest and prior to the World War was without doubt the most important. In the first place, the Russian Orthodox Church at present consists of two groups: the Patriarchal, under the leadership of the patriarchal *locum tenens*, Metropolitan Sergius, and the Synodical, which resulted from the union of a number of smaller bodies which had revolted from the jurisdiction of Patriarch Tikkon.' Under the Soviet régime, all church membership was greatly reduced, although there exist no reliable statistical data. Closely connected with the fate of the Russian Church is that of the Church of Georgia. Since 1801 it had been a part of the Russian Church, and suffers at present the same treatment as the latter. The other succession Orthodox churches, organized in countries formerly belonging (in part or wholly) to Russia, are the churches of Finland, Estonia, Lithuania, and Poland. Their status, in consequence of the situation arising out of the present war, is uncertain.

The Balkan group of churches, in consequence of the collapse of the Russian leadership, has become the most important, although the present war makes any definite judgment of the future impossible. The largest of the Balkan unit is the Rumanian Church, which after the World War more than doubled its territory, and consequently assumed the patriarchal rank. The Serbian Orthodox Church likewise was greatly expanded by the unification of six formerly independent units. The new church then assumed its former rank of patriarchate. Another, although relatively insignificant member of this group, is the Church of Albania. The Church of Bulgaria, although formally at schism with the Greek churches, is recognized by all the others as a rightful member of the Orthodox family.

Finally, a mention must be made of the small Czechoslovak, and the Japanese Orthodox churches.

The future of all Orthodox communions will undoubtedly be greatly affected by the outcome of the present war, so that all statements made about them are subject to that consideration.

Besides these Orthodox churches, the Eastern Christendom comprises a number of separated churches, such as the monophysite* groups of the Syrian National, the Coptic, and the Abyssinian; the Nestorian* Assyrian church; and the Armenian (Gregorian) church which is pre-Chalcedonian in its creedal statement. (See Gregory the Illuminator.)

The Orthodox churches form a loose confederation, bound together not by any centralized authority, but only by loyalty to a common faith. The ecumenical patriarch of Constantinople enjoys no special prerogative of jurisdiction, but only of honor. Each autocephalous church is self-governing and independent of all others.

As for the doctrinal basis, there is no generally acknowledged creed, such as the Tridentine* in the Roman Catholic Church. Instead, the doctrinal decisions of the Seven Ecumenical Councils* are held as dogmatically binding. The rest of the theological tenets although as a matter of fact traditionally fairly uniform, need not necessarily be so. Each autocephalous church has the authority to define the non-dogmatic teaching for itself. In the Russian church, since the middle of the nineteenth century, there has occured a remarkable theological revival, lay in character, which promises to produce an integration of the Eastern Orthodox theology with the modern culture. The leaders of the movement—men like Vladimir Solovev and Nicholas Berdyaev—are recognized as outstanding religious philosophers not only among the Eastern Orthodox theological thinkers, but among Christian leaders in general. See Basilians; canons of various churches; Confessions, Formal of the Christian Church; exarch; Holy Synod; Jeremiah II; liturgy; proto-pope; Uniate Churches.

B. J. Kidd, *The Churches of Eastern Christendom* (London, n.d.); Hugh Y. Reyburn, *The Story of the Russian Church* (London, 1924); Matthew Spinka, *The Church and the Russian Revolution* (1927); Matthew Spinka, *Christianity Confronts Communism* (N. Y. and London, 1936, 1937); Matthew Spinka, "Post War Eastern Orthodox Churches," in *Church History*, IV (1935), pp. 108-122; Sergius Bulgakov, *The Orthodox Church* (n.d.). M.S.

eating the god: See theophagy.

Ebenezer Society: See communistic settlements, religious.

Ebionism: (*Ebionim*, the Hebrew word for "the poor") Probably it was an early designation for the Jewish Christians* at Jerusalem. Later it was applied to the Jewish Christian sect communities. The name first appears in Irenaeus* (ca. 185) *adv. haer.* I, 26, 2. Apparently they held to the Torah*, rejected Paul, and denied the virgin birth, though Origen says this was not true of all. Their gospel was either a version of Matthew or the Gospel to the Hebrews. C.T.C.

Ecce Homo: (Lat. of Joh. 19:5, Behold, the Man) The title of many paintings of the suffering Christ. A book on the teaching of Jesus by Sir John Seeley, published in 1880 and often reprinted. S.M.G.

ecclesia: The N. T. denotes the local and universal fellowship of the Christians with the word, *ekklēsia*. The Latin Christians took it over in its original Greek form (*ecclesia*). The word means a "specially called assembly of people". It received a religious meaning when the translators of the Septuagint* adopted it in order to render the Hebrew words referring to Israel as the people of God and the people before God (the "true Israel") into the Greek. When the Christian community applied this name to itself, it therefore appropriated for itself the claim of being the "true Israel", "God's holy nation", the messianic fellowship.

The English translation of *ecclesia* is "church", a word which like its equivalents *Kirche, Kirk, Kerk*, etc., is probably derived from the word *Kuriakon* (—"that which belongs to the Lord"), used in late ancient or early medieval times to denote Christian properties (buildings, cemeteries, etc.). W.P.

Ecclesiastes: Book representative of "pessimistic" type of Oriental wisdom literature*. The title replaces the name Solomon with "The Preacher" (Greek, *Ecclesiastes;* Hebrew, *Koheleth*). Solomon* was evidently regarded as a great "convener of assemblies" (Koheleth, cf. Hebrew, *Kahal*, "assembly"), which he then supposedly addressed in words of wisdom. While Egyptian and Babylonian parallels show that pessimistic books were possible at Solomon's time, traces of late origin are abundant in this particular work. It is to be dated in the 3rd century B.C. and reflects the inroads made by Greek civilization. The book contains a loosely knit collection of materials. It is difficult to separate some of the entities or find any progress of thought. 9:17-10:20 could stand in "Proverbs"*. Other sections show the speaker reflecting on his own experience or admonishing another person. The basic philosophy that all is vanity (1:2) and that a young man should enjoy his youth (11:9-12:8) is subject to some qualifications. The book was already toned down in certain places by ancient editors (cf. 2:26, 3:17, etc.). The concluding additions, in particular, express both a criticism of the original book (12:12) and a new and forced interpretation of its substance (v. 13, 14). Its canonicity was still disputed in the Jewish schools at the time of Christ.

Cf. R. H. Pfeiffer, *Introduction to the Old Testament* (1941); J. A. Bewer, *Literature of the Old Testament*, (rev. ed., 1933). E.G.K.

ecclesiastical art, Christian: See art, Christian, ecclesiastical.

ecclesiastical commissions: Bodies of ecclesiastics juridically established to whom are committed certain specified functions or charges. The chief types of commissions are: (a) Pontifical: These commissions consist of a group of cardinals appointed by the pope for some particular function such as the revision of the Vulgate*, the interpretation of the canon law*, etc. (b) Prelatitial: These are commissions of Roman prelates, secretaries, consultors, etc.; they may be presided over by a cardinal. The commission for Sacred Archeology is an example of this type. (c) Diocesan: These commissions are four in number and exist in each diocese: 1) The commission for seminaries; 2) The commission of examiners of clergy which is to aid in control of all competition for vacant parochial benefices; 3) The commission on sacred music; 4) The vigilance commission for the suppression of modernism*. The pontifical documents creating these commissions, the legislation pertaining to Roman congregations, or common ecclesiastical law* limit the scope of the authority of each of these commissions. T.T.M.

ecclesiastical courts: Church courts, especially the courts of the Roman-Catholic Church, the Eastern Church and the Church of England. With varying success the medieval Church claimed for its courts an extensive jurisdiction far beyond the internal regulation of its organization and administration. (See art. Canon Law). While jurisdiction over such topics as heresy, marriage or, in some countries, testaments, was willingly conceded to the Church by the temporal authorities, the assumption of ecclesiastical jurisdiction over contracts provoked the jealousy of the lay courts and the Church's claims of exclusive jurisdiction over the clergy and over Church property resulted in violent clashes with the temporal rulers, for instance the fateful conflicts between Henry II and Thomas Becket or between the Emperor Henry IV and Pope Gregory VII*. After the Reformation the English ecclesiastical courts continued to play an important role as instruments of the policy of the Tudor and early Stuart kings to establish and maintain the union of the state and the established church under the common supremacy of the king. The Court of High Commission, the leading ecclesiastical court, exercised an extensive jurisdiction over the orthodoxy and morals of both clergy and laity and became one of the principal targets of the Puritan Revolution, by which it was abolished in 1641. However, the courts of the Church of England retained jurisdiction not only over matters of church discipline and organization but also over tithes, church dues and dilapidations and, until 1857, over certain matrimonial causes and testamentary matters, a jurisdiction which was continuously narrowed not only by legislation but also by the jealousy of the common law lawyers. Such jurisdiction as is still left in the courts of the Church of England is now exercised mainly by the Archbishop of Canterbury's Court of Arches, the Consistory Courts of the dioceses, and the Judicial Committee of the Privy Council.

In some Roman-Catholic, Orthodox and Oriental countries ecclesiastical courts still exercise a more or less extensive jurisdiction over matters other than affairs of internal church organization. In Palestine, Egypt, Syria and French North Africa Christian, Mohammedan and Jewish spiritual courts are recognized as competent to deal with matters of personal status, family and inheritance of their native members and with rights in church property including real estate. In parts of the Balkans, Spain, Portugal, Peru and the formerly Russian parts of Poland matrimonial causes are still handled by spiritual courts. In Italy matrimonial causes of Roman-Catholics were handed back by the Fascist state to the Church by the Concordate of 1929. The corresponding concession of the Austrian Concordate of 1933 was undone shortly after Austria's annexation to the German Reich.

In the United States and other countries with disestablished or unestablished churches ecclesiastical courts can no longer exercise compulsory jurisdiction. Insofar as the faithful voluntarily submit to its jurisdiction the position of an ecclesiastical court is analogous to that of a commercial arbitrator voluntarily chosen by the parties.

For the internal organization of the Church and for the matrimonial causes of the faithful, the ecclesiastical courts of the Roman-Catholic Church still play an important role. The ordinary court for each diocese is that of the bishop who exercises his judicial function through a legally trained mandatory, the *officialis*. Appeals may be taken from the diocesan court to that of the archbishop or, if the case arose in the first instance, in the diocesan court of an archbishop, to the court of a designated bishop of the province. The supreme court of the Church is the *Sacra Romana Rota* at the Holy See, whose decision may in certain exceptional cases be subject to cassation by the *Signatura Apostolica*. The *Rota* consists of 10-12 judges who must be priests learned in the canon law. Its decisions are currently published since 1912 under the title of *Sanctae Romanae Rotae Decisiones*. See benefit of clergy; immunity.

F. W. Maitland, *Constitutional History of England* (1908); W. S. Holdsworth, *History of English Law*, vol. 1, 3d ed. (1922); H. W. Cripps, *Law Relating to the Church and Clergy*, 7th ed. (1921); H. D. Hazeltine, Ecclesiastical Courts, vol. 5, *Enc. Soc. Sci.*, p. 307; see, furthermore, the literature referred to *sub voce* Canon Law. M.Rh.

ecclesiastical Latin: The official, international, language of the Roman Catholic hierarchy. Differentiated in function from, though not rendered inferior to, the classical Latin, it has been especially adapted, through the centuries, to the administrative, literary, and liturgical needs of the Roman Church*.

See "Latin" in *A Catholic Dictionary* (1941), edited by Donald Attwater. R.C.P.

ecclesiastical law: See Canon Law.

Ecclesiasticus: See Jesus, the Son of Sirach.

Eck, Johann Maier: (1486-1543) Catholic theologian of Germany and foremost champion of the Papacy against Luther and Zwingli**. A skilful debater, Eck is best remembered for the public disputation in Leipzig in 1519, in which he succeeded in drawing from Luther the assertion that the general councils of the Church are subject to error. Luther's breach with Rome thus became irreparable, and in 1520 Eck obtained the famous papal bull *Exsurge Domini* condemning Luther. As professor and vice-chancellor of the University of Ingolstadt for three decades, Eck exerted tremendous influence. His *Enchiridion adversus Lutherum* ran through 46 editions between 1525 and 1576. T.A.K.

Ecke, Gustav (1855-1920) A pupil of M. Kaehler, he taught in Königsberg and Bonn. He tried to understand Ritschlianism in the positive-ecclesiastical sense, to work out its truths and to come to an agreement with them.

Die evangelischen Landeskirchen Deutschlands im 19 Jahrhundert (Berlin 1905); *Die theologische Schule Albrecht Ritschls und die evangelische Kirche der Gegenwart*, 2 vols. (Berlin, 1897-1904); *Unverrückbare Grenzsteine* (Berlin, 1905, 5 ed., 1911). H.H.

Eckhart, Johannes Meister, O. P.: (c. 1260-1327) Born in Thuringia; *Magister* Sacred Theology, Paris 1302; distinguished as administrator and teacher in Dominican Order, and as theologian, writer in Latin, as preacher of great vitality and clarity in German; best known as "father of German mysticism" and a religious genius. He strove to explain the mysteries of the Godhead and the relation between Creator and individual man in realistic terms; he ably defended himself against charges of heresy. Cf. Suso; Tauler.

Meister Eckehart. Edited by Franz Pfeiffer, 4th ed. (Leipzig, 1924), trans. by C. de B. Evans (London, 1924). A.S.

eclecticism: Eclecticism in religious philosophy may be defined as an endeavor to form a competent pattern of religious thought by means of the principle of *selection.* Irenic in spirit, open-minded (although not always without bias) eclecticism promotes intellectual breadth and tolerance and catholicity of spirit. It lacks organic and structural character, experiential valuational vigor and recognition of the principle of historic inception and development. There has been a tendency in the direction of eclecticism in left-wing liberalism and in that type of philosophy of religion which aims at a survey rather than a system of religious truth.

Most of the current religio-philosophical cults in America are eclectic in principle, with a strong preference for Oriental and mystical elements, together with emphasis upon the optimistic and health-giving aspects of religion. They have arisen largely because of the neglect of principles inherent in Christianity relating to metaphysical and mystical truths and to physical well-being.

Among eclectic movements Bahaism* represents a more synthetic type, imposing teachings selected from various faiths, especially Christianity, upon a historic and personal Persian basis and adopting the principle of revelation through incarnation, although substituting successive incarnations for the single, unitary incarnation of Christianity. Christian Science*, being Christian and a church instead of a cult, is eclectic only in its eclection of certain Christian doctrines above others and its unbalanced metaphysical optimism and health-seeking emphasis. J.W.B.

economics: See sociology.

ecstasy: A trance-like state of emotional rapture and mental exaltation in which the subject is so transported by emotion or so engrossed in some object of contemplation as to be extremely if not completely insensible to normal external stimuli. It is the culminating point of the intuitive and affective experience of religious mystics and is often called the "unitive" stage (as distinguished from the "purgative" and "illuminative" stages which precede it) of the mystic way of life because of the subject's claim that he enjoys union with the divine. The state is marked by narrowness and unity of consciousness, exclusion of the world of sense, passivity, intensity of joyous emotion, visions, and the claim of an immediate experience of the divine which has noetic value and yet is ineffable. Plotinus* held that in ecstasy union with God and perfect knowledge of divine truth were realized. Ecstasy among primitive peoples is induced by drugs, fasting, flagellation and dancing and is interpreted as spirit possession. Among civilized peoples it is induced by definite mystic practices which involve bodily disciplines, prolonged contemplation and persistent auto-suggestion. The experience yields different types of exaltation and different kinds of satisfaction such as sensuous, intellectual, aesthetic and religious. It is generally agreed that some temperaments are more susceptible to the experience than others.

For variant interpretations see W. E. Hocking, *The Meaning of God in Human Experience* (1912); J. B. Pratt, *The Religious Consciousness* (1920); J. H. Leuba, *The Psychology of Religious Mysticism* (1929); E. Underhill, *Mysticism* (1930); H. N. and R. W. Wieman, *Normative Psychology of Religion* (1935). R.W.F.

ecumenical councils: Lists vary according to conceptions of the nature of an ecumenical council. Two rival ideas prevail: One is that such a body should be composed of members representing all parts of Christendom, and that it is responsible to the represented churches or constituencies. The other holds that such a body is essentially head-and-members (pope-in-council) and only indirectly responsible to the churches; its primary function is the faithful interpretation of the traditional faith; and no conciliar deliverance is valid if the head disapproves. Universally acknowledged are the following:

Nicea I, 325 A.D., to which largely may be attributed the Nicene Creed, occasioned by the Arian controversy.

Constantinople I, 381, elaborated the Nicene Creed so as to define more explicitly the deity of the Holy Ghost.

Ephesus, 431, defined the personal unity of Christ, and the Virgin as Theotókos, as against Nestorius.

Chalcedon, 451, defined Christ's two natures.

Constantinople II, 553, reaffirmed the first four councils and condemned errors of Origen and others.

Constantinople III, 680-681, defined two wills in Christ, as against Monotheletism.

Nicea II, 787, regulated veneration of images.

Constantinople IV, 869, dealt with the Photian Schism. This council, in which East and West were undoubtedly represented, is not everywhere received as ecumenical.

(Protestants do not generally consider as ecumenical the councils since Chalcedon; they also hold that all councils, even Nicea I, may err, and that only the Scriptures cannot err.)

In addition, the following are held to be ecumenical by the Roman Catholic Church*, on the principle of pope-in-council:

Lateran I,* 1123.
Lateran II, 1139.
Lateran III, 1179.
Lateran IV, 1215.
Lyons I, 1245.
Lyons II, 1274.
Vienne, 1311-1313.
Constance, 1414-1418, in part.
Basle-Ferrara-Florence, 1431-1439, in part.
Lateran V, 1512-1517.
Trent, 1545-1563.
Vatican, 1870, adjourned and unfinished.

G. D. Mansi, *Sacrorum conciliorum . . . collectio,* 31 vols. (Venice, 1769-98) (the most generally available body of documents); C. J. von Hefele, *Con-*

ciliengeschichte (1873-80); A. Hahn, *Bibliothek der Symbolen und Glaubensregeln der alten Kirche* (3rd ed., 1897); H. R. Percival, *The Seven Ecumenical Councils of the Undivided Church*, vol. XIV of *Select Library of Nicene and Post-Nicene Fathers* (1900); P. Schaff, *The Creeds of Christendom* (1919); *Catholic Encyclopedia*, "Councils, General." Q.B.

ecumenical creeds: See s. v. Athanasian Creed; creeds of Christendom.

ecumenics: A word coined from the Greek *ta oikoumenika*, "the things relating to the *oikoumenē* (i.e., inhabited earth)". Upon the analogy of the application of the term *oikoumenē* to the Greek, and later to the Roman, world, Ecumenics is used to designate everything pertaining to the Christian Church in its ecumenical aspect, that is, as coextensive with the inhabited globe. In Princeton Theological Seminary, where the term was first used in 1937 in the "Chair of Ecumenics", which took the place of the "Chair of Missions", Ecumenics means: the science of the Church as the world Christian community, its nature, function, relations, and strategy. Thus, as sociology is the science of society in general, so Ecumenics is the science of the world Christian community. J.A.M.

Eddas: Derivation uncertain. The heroic literature of the Norse folk, written in Old Icelandic. The Elder or Sæmund's *Edda* was completed in the twelfth century, while the younger *Edda*, or Snorri Sturluson's (1179-1241) runs over into the thirteenth. The Eddas are the chief source of our knowledge of Norse mythology. P.G.M.

Eddy, Mary Baker: See Christian Science.

Edersheim, Alfred: (1825-1889) English pastor, scholar, translator and author, sometime Lecturer on the Septuagint at Oxford. Best known for his *Life and Times of Jesus the Messiah* (1st ed., 1883), widely used in the late 19th and early 20th centuries as an authoritative text on the life and teaching of Jesus against the background of late Judaism. S.M.G.

Edessa: The Gr. name of an ancient city in North-Western Mesopotamia (the modern Urfa). Capital of a semi-independent Syrian Kingdom which served as a buffer-state between Rome and Parthia from 132 B.C. until it was made a Roman Province in A.D. 244. Important as the earliest center of Syriac speaking Christianity and of Syriac Christian literature. The Syriac version of Tatian's *Diatessaron** (Gospel harmony) was the popular form in which the Gospels were read from ca. 170 A.D. until the *Peshitta**, a final revision of Old Syriac translations of the Gospels, displaced it early in the 5th century. See Antiochean School; Syrian churches. S.M.G.

Edict of Milan: Document issued jointly by Constantine and Licinius in 313 granting toleration to the Christians and restoring church property. Marks end of the policy of persecution. K.H.C.

Edict of Nantes: See Nantes, Edict of.

Edict of Worms: See Worms, Edict of.

Edomites: The people inhabiting Edom, the high table-land lying southeast of Palestine proper, between the southern portion of the Dead Sea and the Arabah on the west and the Arabian Desert on the east. The Edomites were a Semitic people, closely related to the Israelites. Biblical tradition represents them as descendants of Esau, the brother of Jacob. They settled in Edom in the thirteenth century B.C. and retained control of that country for almost a thousand years, until finally displaced by the Nabataeans. They subsisted largely as caravaneers, carrying on the traffic in spices and other precious commodities between Arabia and Damascus. They were conquered by David at about 1000 B.C. and remained tributary to Judah for approximately two hundred and fifty years. Early in the fifth century B.C. through political circumstance they became the arch-enemy of the little Jewish people, and for their ruthlessness in the ensuing war were scathingly denounced in various biblical writings of this period. J.M.

Edwards, Jonathan: (Oct. 5, 1703-Mar. 22, 1758) Congregational minister, theologian and philosopher, was the fifth child and only son of eleven children born to the Rev. Timothy (1669-1758) and Esther Stoddard Edwards of East Windsor, Conn. He graduated from Yale College in 1720. In Feb. 1727 he was ordained colleague pastor with his grandfather, Solomon Stoddard of Northampton, Mass., and after Stoddard's death in Feb. 1729, Edwards remained as pastor until he was dismissed in June, 1750. In Aug. 1751 he went to the Stockbridge Indian mission, where most of his great theological treatises were written or completed. In Feb. 1758 he became president of the College of New Jersey (Princeton), and died the following month. In July 1727 he married Sarah Pierpont of New Haven. Twelve children were born, best known of whom is the second son, Jonathan Edwards the younger (1745-1801).

Although Edwards early rebelled against the Calvinistic doctrines of the day, his own most vivid personal religious experience left him "fully satisfied, as to this sovereignty of God" which thereafter appeared to him a doctrine "exceeding pleasant, bright, and sweet." This "delightful conviction" formed the basis of his preaching that brought the revival to his Northampton congregation in 1734, and is the breath of life that he breathed into Calvinism*, warming and personalizing it.

Edwards, in his writings, wrestled with both the practical and speculative problems of his day. His works may conveniently be dealt with under four heads: 1) those written to defend the revivals in New England as truly a work of God, 2) those written against the Half-Way Covenant* plan and demanding a purified church of regenerate members only, 3) those written to champion Calvinism against the encroachments of Arminianism* (notably the treatise on the Will), and 4) those in which he laid the foundations for a modified system of Calvinistic divinity that was developed by his followers, especially by Joseph Bellamy, Samuel Hopkins, and Nathaniel Emmons**. See

American theology, early; benevolence, disinterested; Hopkinsianism; New England theology; New Haven theology; Taylorism. See also s. v. Berkeley, George.

Sereno E. Dwight, *Life and Works of President Edwards,* 10 vols., (1829); A. V. G. Allen, *Jonathan Edwards* (1889); Ola E. Winslow, *Jonathan Edwards,* 1703-1758 (1940); A. C. McGiffert, *Jonathan Edwards* (1932); H. B. Parkes, *Jonathan Edwards, the fiery Puritan* (1930); Thomas H. Johnson, *The Printed Writings of Jonathan Edwards, A Bibliography* (1940); Clarence H. Faust & Thomas H. Johnson, *Jonathan Edwards,* in the *American Writers Series* of the American Book Company (1935).—S.E.M.

efficient cause: See cause.

Egypt, religions of: The ancient Egyptian religion (c. 3000 B.C.-200 A.D.), Christianity, and Islam* (after 642). Before Menes united Egypt under his rule, the country had been divided first into independent districts (not to be identified with the 20 nomes of Lower Egypt and the 22 of Upper Egypt), then into two kingdoms (Upper and Lower Egypt). Each district or city had originally its patron god, retaining it in some cases through three millennia. The most important of these early local gods are the following: Anubis (See Hermes) of Cynopolis, jackal-headed god of the dead; Atum of Heliopolis, later identified with the sun-god Re* and regarded as the evening sun; Bastet, the cat-goddess of Bubastis; Hathor*, the cow-goddess of Denderah and Aphroditopolis; Horus, the solar falcon-god of Behdet (Hermopolis parva) and Edfu, who became the royal god of Egypt; Khnum, the ram-headed god of Elephantine and the cataract region; Khonsu, the moon-god of Thebes; Min, the ithyphallic god of Coptos and Akhmim, later a vegetation god; Montu, the hawk-headed war god of Hermonthis and the Theban nome, supplanted by Amon (whose sacred animal was the ram) in the 11th dynasty; Neith, the goddess of Sais and Esna; Nekhbet, the volture-goddess of El-Kab; Ptah, bull-god of Memphis, patron of artists; Sebek, the crocodile god of the Fayum and of Kom Ombo; Thot*, ibis-headed god of Hermupolis, inventor of writing, patron of learning, whose sacred animal was the baboon. In addition to deities with animal heads, the Egyptian worshiped actual living animals: Apis*, a black bull with white spots, at Memphis; Mnevis, a light colored bull, at Heliopolis; and others. Besides the local deities, gods of nature with a wider jurisdiction were recognized by the whole nation in early times (Re, the sun; Hapi, the Nile; Nun, the ocean; etc.). Some of them were joined together at Heliopolis, under the local god Atum, into an ennead: first Atum; then the couple Show (the air) and Tefnut (the dew); then the couple Geb (the earth) and Nut (the sky); then the two couples Osiris and Isis, Seth and Nephtys.

Moreover, the theologians of Heliopolis during the 5th dynasty (2560-2420 B.C.) played a leading rôle in the development of the Egyptian religion by identifying their local god, Atum, with the sun-god Re thus giving rise to a national religion. Already in prehistoric times Seth of Ombos had become the god of Upper Egypt and Horus of Behdet of Lower Egypt; apparently in another period the volture-goddess Nekhbet of El-Kab and the uraeus or cobra goddess Buto of Buto became the tutelary deities of Upper and Lower Egypt, respectively. Then Horus was identified with Atum-Re-Harakhte of Heliopolis and became the royal god of Upper and Lower Egypt, the patron of the Pharaohs ("the sons of Re"). This tendency persisted, and many local gods, like Sebek and Amon, became solar gods like Re and one with him; the hegemony of Thebes in the 18th dynasty made of Amon-Re the supreme god. But Amenophis IV (Ikhnaton) (1375-1358), in open opposition to Amon and his clergy, attempted to give to the solar theology of Heliopolis the character of a religion for the masses: he chose the visible manifestation of Atum-Re-Harakhte, the solar disk surrounded by rays ending in human hands (Aton) as the sole god, creator of all animate beings and inanimate things; but this religious reformation ended soon after his death, and Amon triumphed again under his second successor, Tut-ankh-Amen. Other gods had greater attraction for the masses. They expected help in their daily problems from minor gods such as agricultural deities (Sekhet, the goddess of the cultivated land; Nepri, the god of grain; Rennut, the goddess of harvest), the goddesses of childbirth (Heket, Meskhenet, and the seven Hathors who, like the fairies, fixed the destiny at birth), the monstrous Toeris (with feet of a lion, arms and breasts of a woman, belly of a hippopotamus, and head of a crocodile) helpful in childbirth and against evil spirits, the ridiculous malformed dwarf Bes (with the tail of a leopard) who protected child-bearing women and concerned himself with music, dancing, and the toilette of ladies. Some Syrian deities also achieved popularity: Baal, Resheph, Qedesh, Anath, and Astarte. Serapis, the Hades of Sinope on the Black Sea, was introduced into Egypt after Ptolemy I (305-283) had seen him in a dream; his name was at once explained as Osiris-Apis and, being identified by the masses with Osiris*, his cult and that of his consort Isis flourished throughout the Hellenistic and Roman worlds. While the solar theology of Heliopolis tended to create an official national religion without stirring the masses profoundly, in early times the myth of Osiris, which arose among the common people, was incorporated into the official religion and the Osiris cult became eventually so dominant that early Greek visitors, like Herodotus (II:42), received the impression that Osiris and Isis were the only national deities of Egypt. This popularity was due to the happy immortality which Osiris was thought to assure to his worshipers. The Egyptians believed that at death the *ba* (soul) and the *ka* (a ghostly double or a guardian spirit) could live on if the body be preserved (hence the practice of mummifying the corpse) and the necessary shelter (tombs) and food (funerary offerings) be provided. A happier immortality was offered to the Pharaohs in the Pyramid Texts of the 5th dynasty: the deceased king could ascend to the sky and sail over it in the ship of the sun-god Re; or he could be restored to life like Osiris. According to the myth, Osiris (originally a vegetation god) was killed by his brother Seth (Greek: Typhon), restored to life by his wife Isis, and avenged by his son Horus; he then became the king of the dead, absorbing the earlier gods of the Underworld: Khentamentiu (the dog-headed god of Abydos), Ptah-Sokar of Memphis, and Geb. Many scattered temples housed parts of his body, but Abydos (where his head was buried and his tomb was shown) became the center of his worship. Led by the jackal-headed Anubis, the soul of the deceased appeared before the tribunal of Osiris; in the presence of 42 terrible judges of the dead, the soul denied having committed 42 sins (ch. 125 of the *Book of the Dead**, from the New Kingdom); Anubis and Thoth weighed its heart on the balance; if justified, the soul enjoyed a happy immortality with Osiris. The official worship in the great temples consisted in the personal service of the god, primarily dressing and feeding him, performed by the clergy. The layman did not have any part in the worship, but on certain festivals he could see the statue of the god (hidden by a veil) carried in procession. With the coming of Christianity in the 2nd century this ancient religion lost its hold on the people, and it ceased to be practiced in 391, when Theodosius I closed the great ancient temples of Egypt. See death and burial practices; mystery religions.

G. Steindorff, *The Religion of the Ancient Egyptians* (1903-4); A. Erman, *A Handbook of Egyptian Religion* (London, 1907); *Die Religion der Aegypter* (Berlin and Leipzig, 1934); J. H. Breasted, *Development of Religion and Thought in Ancient Egypt* (1912); *The Dawn of Conscience* (1933); A. W. Shorter, *An Introduction to Egyptian Religion* (London, 1931); S. A. B. Mercer, *Horus: Royal God of Egypt* (1942). R.H.P.

Egyptian temples: See temples, Egyptian.

eigenkirche: In early medieval Germanic law lay lords who at their own expense had built churches were held to have rights of appointing clerical incumbents as well as rights over the physical properties. By the 9th century both the state (cf. *Capitulare ecclesiasticum* of Louis the Pious, 819) and the church (cf. *Defense of Eigenkirche* by Hincmar of Rheims, c. 860, in *Collectio de ecclesiis et capellis*) were hedging these boundless rights of possession. Appointment became presentation*. See also patron.

Meyers Lexikon (Leipzig, 1925), "Eigenkirche," vol. III, 1272; C. Mirbt, *Quellen*, pp. 122-128, gives valuable material from Louis the Pious' "Capitulary" and Hincmar's "Defense." Q.B.

eisegesis: The opposite of exegesis*; interpreting a Biblical passage so as to express one's own ideas. B.S.E.

El: See Baalism; Phoenicians.

elder: Generically, a word referring to the leaders of a group or community, by senior age or character. The NT records "elders" in Christian organization, the word being a translation of Greek *presbuteroi*, plural of *presbuteros*, transliterated "presbyter."* The word has come down in many Christian churches. In Reformed polity it refers commonly to "ruling elders," chosen by and out of congregations for spiritual oversight and possessing in general church affairs authority equal to that of ministers. The latter are sometimes denominated "teaching elders." In Methodist polity "elder" is the ecclesiastical title of ministers, and they are called elders in some other churches. R.H.N.

Eleatics: Eleaticism developed from one of the two philosophic principles of the Milesian school: all things come from one cosmic substance. Its reputed founder was Xenophanes,* its real founder was Parmenides.* It built its structure of thought upon what is now called the principle of rational consistency, whose first specification is due largely to Parmenides, the Eleatic: how can the existent, non-exist and the non-existent, exist? Accordingly reason had no answer, therefore the Eleatics denied change and its corollary, motion. See Zeno of Elea. P.R.H.

election: See American theology, early; double predestination; Edwards, Jonathan; predestination; reprobation.

election, canonical: Designates a person to an ecclesiastical office. In a loose sense it includes presentation,* collation* and nomination;* but more precisely it is appointment by an electoral college, e.g., cardinals* for a pope,* cathedral chapter for a bishop, etc. Q.B.

elements: 1) The simplest constituents of the object under investigation; what cannot be further divided. 2) In theology, the bread and wine used in Holy Communion. J.E.N.

Elephantine Papyri: Documents written in Aramaic, discovered at Elephantine, Egypt, in 1901. They offer valuable information on the social and religious aspects of the early Jewish Diaspora. See A. Cowley, *Aramaic Papyri of the Fifth Century B.C.* (1923); A. Vincent, *La Religion des Judéo-Araméens d'Eléphantine* (1937). S.L.T.

Eleusinian rites: See mystery religions.

elevation of the host: The ceremonial action, dating from the early Middle Ages, of lifting up the sacred Host* for the adoration of the faithful immediately after its consecration, which, in Catholic belief, transubstantiates the bread into the Body of Christ. The action is now, from the ceremonial aspect, a climax of the Mass,* accompanied by bells, torches, and incense, and momentarily interrupts the sacrificial action to make this solemn act of adoration of the Real Presence* of Christ in the Eucharist. Cf. Corpus Christi. C.V.

elf: In Norse mythology, diminutive beings who live in hills and woods, like the Celtic fairies,* who are sometimes friendly, sometimes malicious, to men. P.G.M.

Elijah: Prophet of Yahweh, living in the ninth century B.C. (I Kgs.* xvii-xix; xxi; II Kgs. i-ii). A religious and political influence, he precipitated the fall of the house of Ahab and repared indirectly the prophetic movement of Amos and Hosea.** See F. James, *Personalities of the Old Testament* (1942) pp. 166-186. S.L.T.

Elipandus: Adoptionist archbishop of Toledo, opposing Islam and Nestorianism, distinguished God's natural Son, the divine Jesus, from God's adoptive Son, the human Jesus, a heresy condemned by Hadrian I, 785. A.C.

Elizabeth, St.: (1207-1231) Daughter of an Hungarian king and wife of a Thuringian prince, Elizabeth, in the midst of her obligations to husband and children, gave herself to a career of charitable works. Her early spiritual development was fostered by Franciscan* advisors, and upon her husband's death she sought a more markedly ascetic vocation. Prevailed upon to forego convent life, she distinguished herself by a social ministry as a Franciscan Tertiary. She was canonized by Gregory IX* in 1235. R.C.P.

Elizabethan Settlement: The term used to describe the English church as established at the beginning of Elizabeth's reign by the Acts of Supremacy and Uniformity. W.S.H.

Elkesaites: Followers of Elkesai, the reputed recipient through angels of a revelation teaching the forgiveness of all sins however great to those who would accept a certain form of baptism and believe the doctrines set forth in his book, which was brought to Rome early in the third century, and called forth the vigorous opposition of Hippolytus.* They seem to have formed a school, of wide influence, which was active later in Babylonia and existed in Arabia as late as the tenth century. E.J.G.

Elohim: Hebrew word for deity; a plural form which usually should be translated "gods" (in contrast with individual deities such as Yahweh, Dagon, Bel, etc.) in documents written before the exile. During this period the singular form became so obsolete that when monotheism came in the plural elohim was retained but understood in singular sense of "God." Usually, Hebrew writers speak of gods (elohim) and Yahweh (their god) before the exile but God (elohim) thereafter. See exile; henotheism; monotheism. R.E.W.

Elvira, Synod of: A synod attended by nineteen bishops and twenty-six presbyters, at Elvira (possibly on the site of modern Granada) in Spain, in A.D. 306 the year following the cessation of the Diocletian* persecution in that area. Its leading spirit was the famous Bishop Hosius* of Cordova. Its canons were severe in condemning heathen immoralities, especially those of the numerous Jews, and in favoring strict ecclesiastical discipline. A.K.R.

Ely Lectureship: The Elias P.: Established in 1865 by Zebulon Stiles Ely with a capital sum of $10,000 and given at least once in two or three years at the Union Theological Seminary, New York City. The course is given with the purpose of establishing the proposition that "Christianity is a religion from God" and that "it is the perfect and final form of religion for man." Topics range from the nature and need of revelation to the philosophy of religion "in its relation to the Christian system." Among the lecturers, the following have served: James McCosh, H. P. Smith, J. Moffatt, E. F. Scott, G. H. Palmer, John Baillie, B. H. Branscomb.

(Data furnished by the Office of the Registrar of Union Theological Seminary, N. Y.) V.F.

Elysium: The paradise of Homer and Hesiod, "the Elysian plain where life is easiest for men. No snow is there, nor yet great storm, nor any rain; but always ocean sendeth forth the breeze of the shrill West to blow cool on men." Odyssey 4:563 (Butcher and Lang). Later poets placed it in the underworld. F.G.M.

Ema, Emma-O: (Jap) See Yama.

emanation: The doctrine that all existing things have issued from the supreme, absolute Reality or Being. Gnosticism,* an early Christian heresy, taught that Christ was such an emanation. See Neo Platonism. R.E.E.H.

Ember Weeks and Days: Periods of fasting at the four seasons (Lat. *quatuor tempora*), observed on the Wednesday, Friday, and Saturday following December 13, the 1st Sunday in Lent, Pentecost, and September 14; the custom, of Roman origin, spread through the West with the Roman rite; the Ember Weeks are traditional times of ordination, marked in the Anglican Prayer Books (since 1662) by special prayers. E.R.H.

Emerson, Ralph Waldo: (1803-1882) American philosopher and man of letters. Educated at Harvard for the Unitarian ministry, he resigned his pulpit in 1832 because of his indifference to the sacraments, settled in Concord, Massachusetts, after a brief sojourn in Europe, and thereafter devoted himself to writing and lecturing. His first book, *Nature* (1836), contained the essence of his ideas, which were given fuller development in *The American Scholar* (1837), the so-called *Divinity School Address* (1838), two famous series of *Essays* (1841, 1844), and numerous other publications, including two collections of poems. The chief exponent of New England Transcendentalism,* Emerson exerted a strong influence on subsequent liberal thought in England as well as in America. See communistic settlements, secular.

The Complete Works of Ralph Waldo Emerson (12 vols., 1903-04) are supplemented by his *Journals* (10 vols., 1909-14) and *Letters* (ed. R. L. Rusk, 6 vols., 1939). Among notable biographies are those by O. W. Holmes (1884), J. E. Cabot (1887), and O. W. Firkins (1915). F. I. Carpenter's *Ralph Waldo Emerson* gives the best brief introduction. L.W.C.

Emmons, Nathaniel: (1745-1840) American theologian, follower of Samuel Hopkins.* Attempted to reconcile human activity and responsibility with the utter dependence of each human "exercise," virtuous or vicious, upon the omnipotent First Cause. See Edwards, Jonathan; New England theology. W.M.H.

emperor worship: Among the Romans perpetuated an ancient custom derived from the east where worship of rulers had been in vogue for many centuries. The kings of Egypt, Babylonia and Persia were thought to be semi-divine beings, and the ideal king of the Jews was to be an individual especially anointed by God and thus a superman. Among the Greeks heroes were half divine and were elevated to full divinity after their departure from the earth. Both the Greek and the Oriental heritages combined to accredit Alexander the Great as an incarnate deity. Alexander's successors in Syria perpetuated the idea that the ruler was "God manifest" and Antiochus IV tried to impose worship of himself upon even the Jews in Palestine. When Octavius (Augustus) brought an end to the civil war following the assassination of Julius Caesar certain communities in the east requested the privilege of building temples in honor of Augustus and celebrating religious festivities in recognition of the divine gift of peace that had been bestowed upon mankind when Augustus had been born to be the world's savior. At Rome the republican spirit was still too strong to deify outright a living monarch, but the senate voted divine honors to the deceased Julius Caesar and in the provinces Augustus was worshiped during his lifetime. Later emperors, such as Caligula and Domitian, urged worship of themselves upon their subjects. Thus the demand to acknowledge the lordship of Caesar and offer incense before his image became a typical form of oath of allegiance to the state. Jews, being recognized as an established social group that refused to take this oath, were excused, but Christians lacked this social prestige and for two centuries were subject to intermittent persecution for their refusal to say "Caesar is lord." See hero worship; kings, divine right of; Roman religions.

E. Beurlier, *Essai sur le culte rendu aux empereurs romains* (1890); S. J. Case, *Evolution of Early Christianity* (1914), pp. 195-238; L. M. Sweet, *Roman Emperor Worship* (1919); Lily R. Taylor, *The Divinity of the Roman Emperor* (1931).

S.J.C.

empirical psychology: See psychology, schools of.

empirical theology: A theology may be called "empirical" in the broad sense if a) its fundamental conceptions are drawn from experience, and if b) its basic propositions are accepted because they seem required by experience, perhaps as generalizations from it or as hypotheses which make it intelligible; or at least if the theology approximates to these two features. As such, it is contrasted with theologies which draw upon alleged revelations, use concepts not drawn from experience and hence regarded as innate and *a priori*, dispense with reasoned proofs altogether, or rely upon *a priori* principles and metaphysical reasoning (such as epistemological arguments, or proofs that space and time are self-contradictory). Theologies which are empirical in this broad sense may be grouped in several classes. First, some (F. R. Tennant*) are empirical in the sense that they support their doctrines by reference to observable facts drawn from all kinds of fields (including natural science); in this sense a use of the teleological argument* could be said to make a theology to some degree "empirical." Second, some writers (Sorley*), regarding moral experience as the reveleation of an objective realm of values, would make this "experience" either the central theological fact, or at least one of the central data on which a theology may be constructed. Third, some writers emphasize the specifically religious "experience" (e.g., D. C. Macintosh, R. Otto*) as the largely sufficient basis of theology, and it is writers of this persuasion whose doctrines have been especially identified as "empirical theology," and whose work would generally be referred to by this name. It should be noted that the term "experience" has been used in many differing senses, and consequently some writers of these second and third groups seem to include within the denotation of "experience" not merely data which are "immediately given" in the way in which, say, an after-image is given, but also entities allegedly revealed by "intuition" or "insight"; and on this account their right to call themselves "empiricists" would be strongly contested by many philosophers. Members of this third and more specifically "empirical" type of theology (the origination of which should probably be credited to Schleiermacher*) have in common a general opposition to traditional doctrines about Christ, the church, sacraments, etc., which they desire to transform into statements about religious experience, so that they can be verified by ordinary scientific methods. A significant difference of opinion among these writers, which affects their attitude to scientific method in theology, concerns the essential nature of religion, especially whether in religious experience generally (and particularly in mystical experience) there is a peculiarly religious cognition, and whether, if so, it is the grasp of an unique datum* (e.g., of the numinous*), or rather the synthetic grasp of a whole of experience somewhat along the line of Bergson's* conceptions. An interesting method of some of them is to define "God" so that there is no doubt of his existence (e.g. as the reality to which we must adjust ourselves in order to achieve the greatest goods), and then to rely on religious experience (in this case, experimental adjustments, and observation of results) for ascertaining further the nature of "God" and the laws governing his behavior, especially in relation to human beings. The conception of God arrived at in this way may eventually approximate the traditional theist idea, but it is common for most of these theologians to admit that this purely "scientific" method has so far taken theology little, if at all, beyond naturalism, and on this account to admit that if the concept of God is to be of religious value the purely "scientific" method must be supplemented and more personal characteristics ascribed to the divine being on more speculative, or even pragmatic, grounds. It would be widely recognized that the carefully "empirical" writers, who eschew "intuition," are apt to have very great difficulty in justifying any "transcendent" divine being, and hence in distinguishing theology as a science from psychology or sociology. There is no sharp line dividing these writers from professed humanists, who assert that the methods of empirical science cannot reach any conclusions significantly similar to traditional beliefs about God.

Discussions of branches of this movement, both pro and con, will be found among the following treatises:

John Baillie, *The Interpretation of Religion* (1926) and *Our Knowledge of God* (1939); P. A. Bertocci, *The Empirical Argument for God* (1938); C. A. Bennett, *A Philosophical Study of Mysticism* (1923); E. A. Burtt, *Types of Religious Philosophy* (1939); W. M. Horton, *Realistic Theology* (1934), and article in *Religious Realism* (1931), D. C. Macintosh, editor; R. M. Jones, *The Testimony of the Soul* (1936); E. W. Lyman, *The Meaning and Truth of Religion* (1933); D. C. Macintosh, *Theology as an Empirical Science* (1927), and *The Problem of Religious Knowledge* (1940); essays for D. C. Macintosh, *The Nature of Religious Experience* (1937); A. C. McGiffert, *The Rise of Modern Religious Ideas* (1915); John Oman, *The Natural and the Supernatural* (1931); F. D. E. Schleiermacher, *The Christian Faith* (English translation, 1928); F. R. Tennant, *Philosophical Theology* (1929-30); H. N. Wieman, *The Wrestle of Religion with Truth* (1927).
R.B.B.

empiricism: See epistemology.

Ems, Congress of: Protest meeting (1786) of certain German archbishops against interference of Curia* through papal nuncios.* Ems agreement stated their position and suggested reforms but no concessions were secured. K.H.C.

Encratities: "The Self-disciplined". Name given to certain 2nd century Christians regarded as heretics. Really represents an attitude rather than a sect. Was early expression of ascetic tendencies.
K.H.C.

encyclicals: An encyclical (*Litterae Encyclicales*, from the Gr. *engkuklios*, in a circle, hence the German *Rundschreiben*) signifies any communication sent to many people, specifically however, a letter formerly sent by a bishop to his flock (now more commonly known as a "pastoral" letter) but especially by the pope to several dioceses, as e.g. of a Province, or to the whole world in matters of grave importance. Encyclicals are usually dictated by some grave and timely necessity e.g. those of Leo XIII* on the Labor Question (*Rerum Novarum*) and of Pius XI* on Atheistic Communism (*Divini Redemptoris*) and on the Persecution of the Church in Germany (*Mit brennender Sorge*); by anniversaries of important historical events or personages e.g. the one of Pius XI on the 1500th anniversary of the Council of Ephesus* (431-1931) and on the 700th anniversary of the death of St. Francis* (1226-1926); or by the desire to promote some special devotion e.g. Leo XIII on the Rosary, on the Christian Family to be modelled on the Holy Family etc. Some of the encyclicals of Pius XI were awaited with keen interest throughout the world. His *Casti Connubii* (on marital relations and birth control, Dec. 31, 1930) is said to have been one of the longest single trans-Atlantic communications sent to any newspaper in the U. S. A. Encyclicals differ from Papal Constitutions or Bulls* in as far as they are instructions rather than dogmatical definitions. Similarly, they differ from decrees* which enjoin some command or prohibition; and from a Rescript,* which is personal or local in nature, unless later universally extended to the whole Church. Encyclicals are written originally in Latin and then translated into the various living languages of the world. Like Papal Bulls they are quoted by their initial words. They are considered officially promulgated when they appear in the *Acta Apostolicae Sedis.** Many have appeared singly in English, published e.g. by the *America Press*, by the *Paulist Press* (both of N. Y. C.) or by the NCWC of Washington, D. C. R.M.H.

Encyclopedists: A group of French scholars of the Enlightenment* who collaborated in the preparation of the 35 volume *Encyclopédie, ou Dictionnaire raisonné des sciences, des arts et des métiers par une Société de Gens de Lettres* (ed. by Diderot and others, 1751-1780). Diderot was responsible for the first 17 volumes. D'Alembert was his chief collaborator but other famous contributors were Montesquieu, Voltaire, Turgot, Holbach, Grimm, and Rousseau. Diderot tried to combine a twofold purpose: first, to give an inventory of all human knowledge and, secondly, to expose prejudices, which meant the undermining of much of contemporary Christianity, in the interests of "natural morality." The articles on religion vary widely as the two interests are fulfilled. Many of the articles are orthodox (as on the Trinity) but patently insincere. Naturally such a work was unpopular with the Church and it was violently attacked by Jesuits and Jansenists** alike. The first two volumes were suppressed for a time and the editors were repeatedly threatened with imprisonment. A full account of their difficulties can be found in the *Encyclopedia Britannica* article on "Encyclopedia." For an analysis of the religious aspects of the *Encyclopédie* see J. E. Barker, *Diderot's Treatment of the Christian Religion in the Encyclopédie* (1941). J.E.N.

endogamy: A social practice in which marriage* is restricted to members of one's own group. A common practice in stratified societies, particularly among the ruling and aristocratic classes. Thus in modern Europe marriage in the royal families has been restricted to royalty, and the aristocracy has maintained its "purity" by inbreeding. Taboos against intermarriage between religious and racial groups in America are also expressions of endogamy. Compare with exogamy. E.R.M.

Engi Shiki: "The Ceremonies of Engi." So-called because of compilation in the Engi Era (901-922 A.D.) of Japanese history. The actual date of publication is probably 927 A.D. A collection of fifty books relating to ancient court life and Shinto shrines and ceremonies. D.C.H.

England, Church of: See Church of England. See also Free Church of England.

England, Lutheranism in: Toward the end of the 17th century, many people from Lutheran countries migrated to England. In the year 1694 a congregation was established in London, which became known as St. Mary's Evang. Lutheran Church of the Unaltered Augsburg Confession.* Queen Anne (r. 1702-1714) married a Lutheran, and this fact gave prestige to the Lutherans of the city.

King George I, (r. 1714-1727), was a nominal Lutheran. He was a German by birth and training, and throughout his reign German was the spoken language of the immediate family of the King. He brought two German Lutheran court chaplains to London, and St. Mary's congregation seems to have worshiped in a building adjoining the Savoy palace. A parochial school was maintained, and its sessions were held within the palace grounds.

Lutherans grew numerically, with an influx of people from the European continent. Other Lutherans from the Scandinavian countries settled in the English cities bordering on the North sea. Other congregations were organized in London, York, Sunderland and elsewhere.

Later, St. Mary's church was moved to Cleveland street, near Fitzroy square, where it exists to this day, although in later years it became affiliated with German State Church tendencies. Another congregation exists in the Dalston section of London, and adheres to the Hamburg Confession. Lutherans in the past have maintained a hospital and an orphanage in London. In 1866 a considerable number of deaconesses were brought over from the Rauhe Haus, and found fields of labor in London, in Sunderland and even in Ireland. A large hospital was founded in Tottenham by a wealthy Lutheran, and its staff was made up of German deaconesses.

Some fifty years ago a group of young men withdrew from St. Mary's Lutheran church and founded Immanuel in Kentish Town and Holy Trinity in Tottenham, and these two congregations united with the American Missouri Synod. They are the only two congregations in England with a direct connection with the American bodies.

The Swedish Lutheran church in Paddington occupies a beautiful modern stone church building. All told, there are less than twenty Lutheran congregations in London. Scattered congregations may be found throughout England, and one or two in northern Ireland. A number of Lutheran families throughout England, and in Scotland, are visited from time to time by the Missouri Synod* pastors from London, and occasional services conducted.

In 1935 an energetic lay missionary, Mr. J. H. Pedlar, went to Cornwall, and has met with considerable success in establishing a number of preaching stations. F.R.W.

English Bible, the: See Bible, English.

English school of psychologists: See psychologists, English school of.

Enlightenment, the: The name of the movement which characterizes the general atmosphere of the 18th century. Its origin is to be sought in the mental coming of age and spiritual emancipation of man in the Renaissance* era, which with its naturalistic and individualistic tendencies evoke in the minds of people a proud consciousness of the autonomy of reason. As a historic phenomenon, the Enlightenment movement represents the effort of applying the rule of reason to actual life. Western mankind was to be raised to the height of an intellectual civilization by the "Aufklärung," i.e., illumination of every phase of life with the dominant principle of rationality.

This movement of general enlightenment penetrated every domain of life: religion, literature, the arts, philosophy, the sciences and political establishments, revealing itself in a variety of forms in the various parts of Europe. Beginning from the Netherlands and England, the Enlightenment reached its climax in France, the waves breaking in Germany and in the rest of Europe up to the Volga river.

Enlightened religion in the several forms of Deism* was conceived as a set of rational propositions, indispensable for life. From Herbert of Cherbury (1581-1648), whose *De veritate* (1627) pronounces the autonomy of reason in religion to John Locke's* (1632-1704) *The Reasonableness of Christianity* (1695) and John Toland's* (1670-1722) *Christianity not Mysterious* (1696), up to Matthew Tindal's (1656-1733) *The Deists' Bible*, the same idea of a purely natural religion is expressed.

The enlightenment in literature is represented by the classical spirit which pervaded most of the literary products of the period and can be admired in the superb achievements of the great trio Pierre Corneille (1606-1684), Jean Racine (1639-1699) and Jean Baptiste Molière (1622-1673). Nature controlled by reason, is the keynote of their productions. Perhaps the most typical representatives of this enlightened literature were the Frenchmen: Montesquieu (1689-1755) with his *L'esprit des lois* (1748), Diderot (1713-1784) whose *Encyclopedie* (1751-1780) is the summary of the results of the Enlightenment through reason and Voltaire* (1694-1778), the torchbearer of the light of intellect.

The Enlightenment in art may be traced by a dominance of the "Apollonian element" of clarity, formal discipline and impersonal restraint in the artistic creations of the era. The light of controlling rationality and objective formality characterizes the symmetrical dignity of the palace at Versailles; the stateliness and sobriety of the Dutch Rembrandt (1606-1669) and the Flemish Rubens (1577-1640); the classicist externality of France's landscapist Wattean (1684-1721); the surface glory of the paintings of England's Gainsborough (1727-1788) and Turner (1775-1851); and the sublime transparency of Germany's enlightened musician Bach (1685-1750) and his school. Typical for the application of a reasoned-out-art-autocracy is the rigid intellectuality of the

French Academy of Sculpture and Painting, founded in 1648.

Philosophical Enlightenment may be seen in the monumental achievements of Descartes'* (1596-1650) "I think, therefore, I am" methodology; in Spinoza's* (1622-1677) world, reduced to a geometrical scheme; in Leibniz's* (1646-1716) monads which unfold toward higher and higher degrees of clarification.

For the scientific Enlightenment Newton's* (1642-1727) *Principia Mathematica* (1687) is usually pointed out as the crowning accomplishment of a world-view, conceived in terms of intelligibility.

Enlightened economics found its expression in the rationally controlled and centrally regimented system of mercantilism, while Enlightened politics can be followed up in the ideal of the "Enlightened Despot," such as Frederick II, the Great of Prussia (1740-1786), Joseph II of Austria (1780-1790), and Catherine II of Russia (1762-1796), whose aim was to rule by the light of right reason.

The Enlightenment movement declined, as many movements decline, by an overemphasis of its own principle. See Encyclopedists. S.C.T.

Enlil: See Mesopotamian religions.

Enoch: The seventh of the ten ante-diluvian patriarchs of Gen. 5. The biblical record tells that he lived three hundred and sixty-five years; "and Enoch walked with God; and he was not, for God had taken him." This biblical record has furnished the motif for two Jewish, post-biblical, non-canonical, apocalyptic books. Both books recount the journeyings of Enoch, under divine guidance, through the entire earth and through the seven heavens, and the divine revelation to him of all the mysteries of heaven and earth, that he, in turn, might reveal them to mankind. The older and larger book, usually designated as I Enoch, was of composite authorship, written in Palestine, probably in Aramaic, between the third and first centuries B.C., and is preserved complete only in an Ethiopic translation, though some fragments of the ancient Greek translation likewise exist. II Enoch was probably written in Egypt, in Greek, during the first half-century A.D. It has survived only in a Slavonic translation. See parable; pseudepigrapha. J.M.

ens: The present participle of the verb *esse,* to be, usually translated as "being." In philosophical terminology it is used as a noun. As such, the term has the most abstract signification conceivable. It is predicated about anything that exists or may exist, actual or possible things, without implying any reference to their existence or non-existence. Ens, then, or entity, simply means a something which is not entirely nothing. In that sense it may be predicated about the infinite and the finite, the substance and the accidence and about any other thing which is not pure nothing. S.C.T.

Enthusiasts: See Eu-chites.

environment: The natural and social conditions under which mankind, or groups of men, have developed. a) Natural conditions refer to geographic and meteorological factors, such as location, climate, rainfall, soil fertility, food, minerals and other resources, altitude, temperature, humidity, mountain barriers, access to the sea and other water ways, land contours, and other aspects of the physical environment. Such conditions have profound influence on areas of settlement, physical types of men, distribution of races, migrations, diet, health, and other human affairs. Moreover, certain mental habits and the outlook of men, their religion and social organization, may reflect influences from their natural environment. It is obvious that the very survival of man depends upon such products of the natural environment as food, water and the means of shelter.

b) Assuming that physical survival is assured, the major concerns of men are with their social environment, which consists of institutions or groups such as the family, state and community; regulatory techniques as may be found in traditions, folkways, customs of laws**; forms of association, and all the other elements of social structure. These comprise the superorganic or cultural environment. Within such a framework the hebavior of men and their social interaction are controlled. They constitute the sociological aspect of environment, but are subject to profound changes from age to age. See culture; heredity.

K. Young, *Source Book for Sociology* (1935).

A.E.W.

Ephesians, Epistle to: The words "in Ephesus" (1:1) are wanting in the best MSS, and Paul can hardly have written a letter so impersonal to a church with which he was so intimately associated. According to one conjecture it is the letter to Laodicea referred to in Col. 4:16; others would regard it, perhaps rightly, as a circular letter, in which a blank was left for the name of each particular church. The authenticity of the letter has sometimes been doubted, chiefly because it follows so closely the lines of Colossians, but this argument is inconclusive, and in view of its intrinsic excellence and its profound understanding of Pauline thought it may safely be attributed to Paul. Its theme throughout is the Church, regarded as the Body of Christ. This idea is developed in a mystical sense. Christ has re-incarnated himself in the church, so as to fulfil God's hidden purpose of reconciling all things. In the whole creation some cleavage has taken place, which has introduced conflict everywhere. In Christ "all things have been gathered together into one" (1:11) and through the church, in which old divisions have been broken down, he carries out his work of harmony, which will finally include the universe. If the Epistle was written by Paul, during his Roman imprisonment, it may be assigned to 60 or 61 A.D.

J. A. Robinson, *St. Paul's Epistle to the Ephesians* (1904); E. F. Scott, *The Literature of the New Testament* (1932).

E.F.S.

Ephesus, Council of: Third Ecumenical, A.D. 431. Condemned Nestorius.* Composed of opposing groups of Alexandrians and Antiochans** which met separately. Larger Alexandrian group under Cyril* was later officially recognized after reconciliation effected. K.H.C.

Ephesus, Robber Synod of: A.D. 449. Phase of Eutychian controversy. Bishop Dioscurus of Alexandria secured temporary restoration of Eutyches* and condemnation of Antiochans. Denounced by Leo I of Rome as "Synod of Robbers." K.H.C.

ephod: Part of the sacerdotal costume among the Israelites, and/or instrument of divination* (Jud. viii, 24-27; xvii-xviii; II Sam. vi, 14, 16, 20-22; etc.) See W. R. Arnold, *Ephod and Ark*, (1917). S.L.T.

Ephrata Society: A celibate and communistic religious movement founded at Ephrata, Pennsylvania in 1732 by Johann Conrad Beissel. He was originally closely associated with the Dunker* movement and drew many followers from them. The community included solitary Brethren, Sisters, and married couples who gave themselves to religious exercises, farming, and trades. They were also noted for their music and their publication of religious literature. They kept the seventh day as the Sabbath and after 1814 were known as the Seventh Day Baptists.*

The Society flourished well past the founder's death in 1768 and the original cloister buildings still stand as a monument. The membership, however, is limited to a few small communities in the counties of Bedford, Franklin, Lancaster, and Somerset, Pennsylvania. See communistic settlements, religious. W.M.B.

epiclesis: The invocation* of the Holy Spirit which follows the words of institution in the office of the eucharist of the Eastern Orthodox churches. It is believed by the members of these communions that the miraculous change in the elements of bread and wine into the body and blood of Jesus Christ occurs at this moment of the service, rather than during the recitation of the words of institution, as the Roman Catholics believe. However, most orthodox theologians consider both the words of institution and the epiclesis as essential.

F. E. Brightman, ed., *Liturgies Eastern and Western* (Oxford, 1896). M.S.

Epictetus: (ca. 50-120) Stoic philosopher and slave of Epaphroditus in Rome. He was later freed and taught philosophy, first in Rome and, after banishment by the Emperor Domitian, in Nicopolis in Epirus. He held that happiness* depends upon the will and therefore is within the grasp of everyone who can control his will. Externals are unimportant. His ethical theory is essentially religious, resting on belief in a rational God who controls the universe and cares for men. Since all men are children of God, they should love one another. His *Discourses* were reported by his pupil, Flavius Arrianus, and are available in many translations (cf. Everyman's Library and Loeb Classical Library). See fate. J.E.N.

Epicureanism: A system of ethics developed by Epicurus*. Like the Cyrenaics* he regarded happiness* as the *summum bonum**, but, unlike them, he stressed the lasting pleasures of the mind rather than present satisfaction of physical appetites. He adopted Democritean atomism because it abolished for him all superstitious fears of death and future punishment. Death is not an evil since the dead have no feelings and, for the living, death does not yet exist. The gods have no interest in human affairs. Therefore we need not fear the future and may concentrate on present happiness.

Epicurus taught the value of the simple life with few desires. Prudence was for him a cardinal virtue. He gave high place to friendship but was indifferent to political affairs. His views were expounded by Lucretius* and later by Gassendi*. J.E.N.

Epicurus: (ca. 342-270 B.C.) A Greek philosopher, founder of the school of ethics which bears his name. He wrote several works, but only a few letters have been preserved. J.E.N.

epigraphic: An archaeological term referring to written inscriptions of all types, as distinct from material or unwritten remains discovered in excavations. G.E.W.

Epiphanius: (c. 315-403) A fourth century bishop of Constantia (Salamis), capital of Cyprus (elected in 367), celebrated for his violent opposition to every form of heresy, particularly to what he regarded as the dangerous teachings of Origen*. His chief work, the *Panarion*, a treatise describing and refuting some eighty heresies, survives, as also his treatise on Christian doctrine, the *Ancoratus*. See Migne, *Patr. Graec.*, 41-43. See lapidaries. E.T.R.

Epiphany: (Gr., *epiphaneia*, manifestation) The festival (Jan. 6) commemorating the manifestation of Christ as God Incarnate. In the East it was the original feast of the Nativity (as it still is with the Armenians) and now commemorates primarily Christ's baptism. In the Western Church it is associated with the visit of the Magi. See church year cycle. P.V.N.

episcopacy: Government of the church by bishops, as the chief of the three orders of bishop, priest and deacon**. See clergy. T.J.B.

Episcopal Church: See Church of England.

epistemology: (Gr., *episteme*: knowledge; *logos*: study of) The problem of knowledge. The following are definitions of various positions taken as to a theory of knowledge:

The doctrine that knowledge comes by way of experience is known as *empiricism*. *Realism* in epistemology is the doctrine which asserts that there is a world-out-there independent and prior to our knowledge of it which we somehow grasp in the knowledge relation. Generally it is assumed that the world-out-there is other-than-mind in character. When an idealist (metaphysical idealist) claims to be a realist he redefines the term to mean a world-out-there independent of an individual's mind although of the same character as mind. *Representative realism* holds that ideas in the mind represent the objective reality. *Epistemological dualism* is the doctrine that the object and the idea of it are two separate elements. *Subjective idealism, psychological idealism**, *subjectivism* are names for the position that the only world we know is that of our idea. (See idealism, epistemological.) Such a doctrine leads to the position known as *solipsism*: only the ideas within myself constitute the extent of knowledge and the range of reality. *Mentalism* is the term sometimes given to subjective idealism. *Objective idealism* affirms the objective reality of idea. *Sansationalistic empiricism* is the view that experience as presented by the senses is the datum of knowledge. *Common sense realism* is the term attributed to the so-called Scottish School which built its epistemological theory upon the view held by the man in the street, viz., a world-out- there independent of mind but somehow known by mind. *Rationalism* in epistemology is the view that knowledge comes by way of reason. *Phenomenalism* (the Kantian view) is the position arrived at in view of the claim that knowledge is limited to the world of appearance as distinguished from a world-in-itself (the noumenal world). Such a view is sometimes referred to as *agnostic realism. Epistemological monism* is the view that the real object of knowledge and the knowledge of it are one in the knowledge-relation. *Naive realism* is the view of the man on the street who holds uncritically a real world and our knowledge of it as dependable. *Critical realism* in the general sense is an inclusive term referring to any realistic position defended by some critical view; as such critical realism is opposed to naive realism. *"Critical Realists"*, however, are those who have set up a special school so named by their published manifesto *Essays in Critical Realism* (1920). This school, in general, holds that the object is given to the subject through media; the object is not directly presented in the knowledge-relation. Critical realists differ among themselves in their exposition of this medium. The following were members of this school: D. Drake; A. O. Lovejoy; J. B. Pratt; A. K. Rogers; G. Santayana; R. W. Sellars; C. A. Strong.

New Realists is the name given to those epistemologists who rebelled against metaphysical idealism. Their position is: knowledge comes by way of a direct (monistic) contact with the object in the knowledge-relation. There are no media, no representations. The external world is literally given to the knower. There is a direct disclosure. Two schools of New Realists are: the English (G. F. Stout; G. E. Moore; B. Russell; S. Alexander; T. P. Nunn; A. Wolf) and the American (F. J. E. Woodbridge; G. S. Fullerton; E. B. McGilvary and the six men who joined in a published manifesto *The New Realism* (1912): E. B. Holt; W. T. Marvin; W. P. Montague; R. B. Perry; W. B. Pitkin; E. G. Spaulding). According to the New Realists, mind is not a unique stuff or soul standing over against the objective physical world; the mind is a part of that objective world (hence, *panobjectivism*). The English group of New Realists affirm that the mind is a kind of awareness or diaphaneity through which the objective world is directly disclosed. The mind is a relation of awareness within the world. The American group tended to make mind less "mental" and leaned towards calling it a behavior-activity of the organism or a relation among relations. If the external world is physical the view then developed into a materialism, e.g., Woodbridge; Montague; however, if the world is neutral the view developed into a neutralism, e.g., Holt and Russell. In other words, many of the extreme New Realists (the American variety) developed an outspoken materialisic ontology and their psychology into behaviorism. In a word, whereas idealists stressed the world in terms of mind, the New Realists stressed the mind in terms of the world.

Critical monism, the view developed by D. C. Macintosh, is a form of critical realism, asserting that knowledge of the external reality is a two-way affair: monistic in that the world is actually disclosed to the mind in terms of the primary qualities (number, rest, motion, figure, solidity, extension); critical in that the mind furnishes the secondary qualities (color, taste, sound, smell).

Intuitionism is the view which claims that knowledge is immediate. The immediacy may be rationalistic, e.g., *a priori* innate ideas (the older intuitionists); or it may be "pure perceptions" as distinguished from concepts (e.g., Bergson); or it may be that of "feeling" (Hocking) or primitive animal awareness; or it may be empirical in the sense of a perception in a complex of sensation (Macintosh). *Pragmatic realism* is the view (held by J. Dewey) that knowledge is not affair of a spectator-mind looking out at the world but an instrument of adjustment; reason and experience are but two names of a process by which the organism gets on in a world; the organism being a part of that world. Realism thus stresses the objective world; and pragmatism points to biological adaptation.

For a discussion of the development of epistemological theories as applied to religious epistemology, see D. C. Macintosh, *The Problem of Religious Knowledge* (1940). For a thorough discussion of the general field of the problem of knowledge see: D. C. Macintosh, *The Problem of Knowledge* (1915); W. P. Montague, *The Ways of Knowing* (1925). For an introductory survey of epistemology see V. Ferm, *First Adventures in Philosophy* (1936), Chaps. XX-XXII. V.F.

epochs: See ages; culture epochs.

Epworth League: See Young People's Societies, Christian.

equalitarianism: A term likely to be applied either approvingly or disparagingly to any view proposing equality for all individuals in some important respect not customary at the time: e.g., equal civil and political rights and abolition of the privileges of the aristocracy during the French Revolution; at present, equal economic and educational opportunities for all, or complete social equality among persons of all races and religions. W.K.W.

equiprobabilism: The theory that in debatable moral questions one may adopt either of two courses of action, if the arguments for both are equally probable. It represents the mid point between probabilism* and probabiliorism (that the more probable course is to be chosen). The theory was developed by St. Alphonsus Liguori* who had previously defended both the other views. J.E.N.

Equity (Ohio): See communistic settlements, secular.

equivocation: (Lat. *aequa,* equal, and *vox,* voice or word) The use of one word with two or more meanings; fallacies (and puns) arise from it. "Things are said to be named 'equivocally' when, though they have a common name, the definition corresponding with the name differs for each" (Aristotle, *Categoriae,* 1). Equivocation is sometimes used in casuistry*, theoretically differentiated from lying. E.S.B.

Erasmus: (1466-1536) Dutch scholar and man of letters, occupied a unique position in the learned world of the early sixteenth century. For the famous Froben press of Basel he edited a notable series of the Fathers, and in his prefaces revealed a gift of appealing to his readers' interests and showing the relevance of ancient works to current needs. His edition of the Greek N. T. exposed the inadequacy of the Vulgate*, and opened the way for a critical study of the text. His own writings were very popular. In the religious struggles of the day he occupied a neutral position which exposed him to the hostility of both sides. The explanation lies not in timidity but in a certain quality of mind to which partisanship is an impossibility. See Renaissance. G.R.C.

Erastianism: The theory concerning the relations of church and state developed by Thomas Lüber (1524-1583), known as Erastus. Opposing Genevan claims that excommunication belonged to the church, Erastus taught that in a Christian state the magistrates possessed the disciplinary power, and he attacked the infallibility of the church. His views were developed by John Selden and other Erastians in the 1640's to combat the militant presbyterianism of the Westminster Assembly*, and reached their most extreme expression in Thomas Hobbes'* *Leviathan* (1651). See caesaropapism.

J. N. Figgis, "Erastus and Erastianism," in *The Divine Right of Kings,* 2d. ed. (Cambridge, 1914); E. W. Whitney, "Erastianism and Divine Right," *Huntington Library Quarterly,* II, 373-398. E.W.K.

Eriugena, John Scotus: (ca. 800-ca. 880) An Irish scholar and philosopher with a command of Greek who appeared in France some time before 847 A.D., became a favorite of Charles the Bold, headed the Palace School, and translated the Pseudo-Dionysian works from Greek into Latin making their mystical doctrine available for the centuries that followed. In theological controversy with Gottschalk* over the doctrine of Predestination, Eriugena produced a very free mystical optimism declaring God's all-loving nature to be incompatible with any evil in His dealings with men. His greatest philosophical work is his *On the Division of Nature* in which his mystical interpretation of the ever hidden yet eternally self-revealing creator God is set forth in a highly original and suggestive manner. See reason in religion; scholasticism; William of Malmesbury.

Huber, *Johannes Scotus Eriugena* (Munich, 1861); Henry Betts, *Johannes Scotus Eriugena* (Cambridge, Eng. 1925); Thomas Whittaker, *Apollonius of Tyana and other Essays* (London, 1905). D.V.S.

Erlangen School: A theological school of thought, starting from the pupils of John Christian Konrad Hofman* (1810-1877), whose work on the unity of the bible and antagonism to the doctrine of vicarious atonement coincided with the rise of the opposition to the *Origin of Species.* Of these pupils the most outstanding was Franz Herman Reinhold von Frank* (1827-1894) who changed 'the mode of teaching the old truth,' admitted the doctrine of Evolution by extending it to 'the humanity of God as the order of salvation.' He was known as "the theologian of the School." See neo Lutheranism; Thomasius. F.W.B.

Ernest, the Pious, of Gotha: See catechumenate.

Erskine, Ebenezer: (1680-1754) A minister of the Church of Scotland*, first at Portmoak and then at Stirling. Being suspended from the ministry on account of his opposition to the state connection, he and three others organized a separate church court, called the Associate Presbytery, in 1733. The Established Church made this break official in 1740. When, in 1747, the Associate Presbytery split into Burghers and Anti-Burghers, Erskine adhered to the former body. He continued to preach in Stirling until his death. A.K.R.

Erskine, Thomas: (1788-1870) A Scottish writer who, on inheriting the family estate of Linlathen in 1816, retired from the practice of law in Edinburgh, and devoted the rest of his life to the propagation, by tongue and pen, of his peculiar theological views. Determined in all his thinking by his flattering view of the value and dignity of man, he was an early advocate of the characteristic humanistic theology of the nineteenth century, and a close friend of such men as F. D. Maurice, Edward Irving, and Thomas Carlyle.

A.K.R.

eschatology: (Gr., *eschatos* furthest, last; *logy*) Literally the doctrine of the last things, derived from such phrases in the N.T. as "it shall come to pass in the last days" (Acts 2:17). The term, arising from the early Christian confidence that the end of the present age was at hand and that Christ would soon appear to set up the Final Judgment*, has come to include all that seems to be taught in the Bible about the fate of the individual, the nation, and the world in general.

In early Hebrew thinking there was, properly speaking, no doctrine of the hereafter, at least for the individual. At death the "breath of life," i.e., the animating principle (*ruach*) left the flesh (*basar*), and the individual (*nephesh*) ceased to exist. "There is no work, nor device, nor knowledge, nor wisdom in sheol*, whither thou goest" (Eccl. 9:10) reveals the early orthodox view of the hereafter, as is evident from the almost fanatic desire for a son and the institution of levirate marriage*. To the gloomy haunt of sheol all must go—good and bad alike. From it there is no return. There is hope for a tree that "if it be cut down it will sprout again," but "man dieth, and is laid low; yea, man giveth up the ghost, and where is he?" (Job 14: 7 ff.). Attempts to read back into early Hebrew thinking later notions of a resurrection—even worse, the Greek idea of immortality—are quite unjustified by the evidence.

Such hopes for the future as there were were in terms of the nation. Israel's history, a little state constantly worsted by her more powerful neighbors, was hardly commensurate with her growing confidence that the supreme God of the whole world was actually King in a peculiar sense of Israel alone. The years had told a sad story of internal discord, a divided kingdom, the successive collapse of the north and south before the inroads of the invaders. Could this be Israel's fate? There seemed but one answer. Eventually the scales of the balance would right themselves. A good time was coming. God had promised it; he could not forswear himself. The days of David and Solomon—seen in a romantic and unhistoric haze by the abject nation—would return. Purged of her sins, freed from oppression, Israel would enjoy an era of peace and blessing, with her God recognized and worshipped by all.

In the centuries subsequent to the exile Judaism underwent many changes and accumulated much that was alien to her inheritance. The notion of life after death, of a cataclysmic dissolution of the present world and the birth of a new one, the garish display and eschatological nightmares of the apocalyptic literature* peopled by angels and hideous beasts—all these came into the picture, due in no small part apparently to the influence of Persian dualism upon Jewish thinking. A new emphasis on the importance of the individual emerges, and with it a belief in future life for the individual in terms of a resurrection of the body at the time of a great final judgment. This distinctly non-Hebraic view eventually became a part of orthodox Jewish belief and was read back into the scriptures, as is evidenced by Josephus, the N.T., and the rabbinical writings.

Early Christianity was the heir of these views and developed them. From the start it was confidently expected that the kingdom of God, which had apparently bulked large in the teaching of Jesus, was speedily to appear, and that Jesus himself would return spectacularly on the clouds of heaven to preside at the Final Judgment. Gradually this passionately held belief passed from the forefront of Christian thinking; a long delay must be expected, but eventually it would come (see millenarianism). As Christianity spread out into the Mediterranean world of thought other and drastic modifications of the views of the future resulted, for here too there had been far-reaching changes. A clear-cut notion of the dual nature of man—an imperishable soul tenanting a mortal body from which it received welcome release at death—had resulted in the hellenistic world in a wide (but by no means universally held) belief in the immortality of this all-important soul—the real man. In addition, the earlier view that at death good and bad alike passed to a dreary and drab ghostlike existence on the asphodel plains (cf. the Hebrew Sheol) had yielded to the view that the soul, as the thinking and willing part of the man, would receive in the hereafter rewards or punishments appropriate to the kind of life lived.

Christian thinking has attempted to combine these originally contradictory views of the resurrection* of the body and immortality* of the soul, a great Final Judgment at the end of this age and the immediate rewards and punishments to each individual at death. See also apocalypticism, Messianic hope; Mohammedanism; soul.

G. F. Moore, *Judaism*, 3 vols. (1927 and 1930); W. Bousset, *Die Religion des Judentums im späthellenistischen Zeitalter* (3rd ed., 1926). M.S.E.

Esdras, Books of: Esdras is the Greek and Latin rendering of the name of the biblical hero, Ezra*. Various books, popularly attributed to Ezra, are known as the Books of Esdras. There is some confusion in their enumeration. Both Septuagint and Vulgate designate the biblical books of Ezra and Nehemiah as I and II Esdras. Two other non-canonical works, included in the Vulgate, are called III and IV Esdras. Not infrequently, however, they are spoken of as I and II Esdras, while the two biblical books are referred to by their customary titles, Ezra and Nehemiah. Occasionally the last two chapters of IV Esdras, really a separate work, are designated as V Esdras. III Esdras is a pseudo-historical work, which recounts freely certain portions of the narrative of the biblical books, Ezra, Nehemiah and Chronicles, with some legendary material added. It seems to have been written in the second century B.C. and probably in Greek. IV Esdras is an important apocalyptic* work, of composite authorship, written in Hebrew during the first century A.D., but preserved only in translation in various ancient languages. See apocrypha, Old Testament; pseudepigrapha.

R. H. Charles, *The Apocrypha and Pseudepigrapha of the Old Testament* (Oxford, 1913), I, 1-58; II, 542-624; W. O. E. Oesterley, *II Esdras (The Ezra Apocalypse)* (London, 1933). J.M.

essence: (Late Lat., *essentia**, from *esse*, to be) That by which a thing is what it is, as distinguished from the thing's existence; that by which a thing is constituted in a definite species. In God essence and existence are necessarily identical; but in all other things they are in some fashion distinct. "I can understand what a man is, and still not know whether he actually exists", as St. Thomas states in his *De ente et essentia*, chap. 5. C.V.

Essenes: A Jewish sect* which flourished in Palestine during the second Jewish Commonwealth. Its members lived in monastic communities from which women were excluded and they generally limited their occupations to handicrafts. The origin of the name remains obscure. Some have traced it to the Syriac term for pious, while others have derived it from the Aramaic *asya*, physician, because the Essenes served as popular healers. See asceticism; communistic settlements, religious. B.Z.B.

essentia: (Lat., *esse*, to be, for Gr., *ousia*) That which makes a thing what it is as opposed to accidents or properties and attributes. It is used also in contradistinction to existence or that by which a thing is. *Essentia* or essence is roughly equivalent to substance, nature, quiddity and is virtually the same as the popular terms constitution, stuff, composition. D.C.O'G.

Established, or State Churches: These churches enjoy legal privileges and endowments not accorded to other ecclesiastical bodies. In spite of the legalization of Nonconformist churches, the Church of England*, for example, continues to be the national church. Until 1834 the ministers of the Congregational churches in Massachusetts were paid from town taxes. The rights and actual procedures of established churches vary greatly so that each particular case must be considered on the basis of both law and fact. W.W.R.

Esther: A book of the O.T., placed at the end of the historical books in the English Bible (following the Septuagint and Vulgate**), but in the Hebrew canon included in the third and latest division, the "Writings" or Hagiographa*. It is one of the five *Megilloth** ("Scrolls") which are read at certain Jewish festivals, Esther being used at the Feast of Purim*. The book relates the story of how the Jewess Esther was elevated to be queen of Ahasuerus (apparently Xerxes I) and thus saved her people from the destruction which had been planned by Haman, and tells of the institution of the Feast of Purim in commemoration of that deliverance. While the author shows some accurate knowledge of Persian architecture and customs, and Ahasuerus is a fairly authentic figure, the story as a whole is not history, but fiction. It was probably written in the second century B.C. to inspire nationalistic patriotism and to afford a quasi-historical occasion for the Feast of Purim (the actual origin of which is unknown). The Septuagint contains 107 additional verses not found in the Hebrew text, which have been relegated to the Apocrypha. Their purpose was to supply the religious element which is conspicuously absent in the Hebrew version. See apocrypha, O.T.

See M. Haller and K. Galling, *Die fünf Megilloth* (*Handbuch z. Alten Testament*, 1940). J.P.H.

Esther, fast of: See Jewish religious festivals.

eternal: (Lat., *aeternus* for *aeviternus*, akin to Gr. *aion*, lifetime, age) Existing or obtaining primordially and forever, without beginning or ending in time. It is often taken as synonym for changeless, but this usage is questionable, for it tends to obscure the fact that "ever-existing" and "never-changing" are logically quite independent ideas. For, on the one hand, the unchanging need not exist forever. Thus, according to Bergson, Whitehead, and other philosophers and theologians, every event, or portion of process, once it has come to be, is changelessly itself (see time). It is immortal, not eternal; temporally without ending, but not without beginning. Further, some thinkers believe that abstract qualities can be created at a given moment in time, and yet remain ever after fixed and self-identical. On the other hand, what exists forever might change, provided it never began and never ceased to change, and provided the change was in its accidents, never in its individual essence. (The denial that these conditions can be met is too controversial to be put into the definition of so commonly used a term as eternal.) Thus the unchanging may or may not exist forever, and the ever-existent may or may not be unchanging. The ever-existent which is ever-changing may be called "everlasting." Since it embraces both self-identity and self-difference, both permanence and change, whereas the other form of eternity* abstracts from self-difference or change, it is difficult—in spite of tradition—not to see in it the concrete and ultimate form of eternity, of which the unchanging form is an abstract aspect and not the whole.

See omniscience; perfection; transcendence. dence.

E. S. Brightman, "A temporalist view of God," *Jour. of Relig.* (1932), 12, 545-55; A. E. Garvie, *The Christian Faith* (1937), p. 105. C.H.

eternal law: See law.

eternally begotten: The words have reference to the doctrine of Origen* (185-254) who taught that the Logos as Son proceeds from God the Father not by way of division but spiritually by an eternal generation. The Logos as Son, Eternally Begotten of the will of the Father, is a numerically distinct subsistence or hypostasis but in substance or nature He is essentially one with the Father though subordinate to the Father. See Trinity. H.W.J.

eternity: The state of being eternal*. Has been conceived in three ways. 1) The absence of time and change: timelessness, immutability (the view of Aquinas and many others). 2) The inclusion, in one unique, determinate state or "single now", of all time taken as a fixed total of events (Royce*, *et. al.*). The totality of mutations is thus taken as immutable. However, it is doubtful if they could really be mutations, since every item, in its place in the whole, simply is what it is, and no item changes. Such a view "spatializes time" (Bergson*) or contradicts the distinctive character of time as the dimension of creation, not of mere being. 3) The inclusion in a protean, partially indeterminate, state of all time taken as a growing totality of events, each of which is first indeterminate (within limits), and then determinate; or is first future and incomplete in its reality, and then present and complete. Each event as it becomes complete or present is an addition to the previous totality of complete events. Thus eternity as 3) is the summation of all actual or elapsed events in an ever-growing present, to whose increase there is neither beginning nor end. The content of such a present, so far as acquired, is henceforth immutable; the only mutation being the acquisition of new content, or the change from the potential and indefinite to the actual and definite. Thus 3) combines elements of 1) and 2), and in addition is able to account for time as real change within the eternal being; whereas 1) leaves the relations of time and eternity unintelligible, being able to construe time-and-eternity neither as a temporal nor as an eternal whole; and 2) puts time within eternity only through denial of its temporality.

See foreknowledge; omniscience; time; Whitehead. C.H.

ether: (Lat., *aether;* Gr., *aither*, upper air, sky) In physics, the all-pervasive "fluid" formerly assumed as medium of impalpable radiations, e.g., light, magnetism. Today one admits that no fluid nor other palpable body gives much idea of the property of space (or of reality in space) whereby wave-phenomena are transmitted through otherwise vacuous regions. C.H.

Ethical Culture Societies: The Ethical Culture movement was inaugurated by Professor Felix Adler (1851-1933) in New York City, on May 15, 1876. Adler had come to this country as a child of four from the Rhineland, and after taking his degree at Columbia College became instructor in oriental languages and literature at Cornell University. He had been trained to succeed his father as rabbi of the Temple Emanuel in New York, but he revolted against the theology and ceremonialism of the Hebrew religion and founded, with the support of a few sympathizers who left the synagogue with him, a society pledged "to assert the supreme importance of the ethical factor in all relations of life, personal, social, national and international, apart from any theological or metaphysical considerations." The New York Society for Ethical Culture grew steadily until it reached its present membership of 1150 persons. Meanwhile similar societies were formed in Chicago (1882) by William M. Salter, in Philadelphia (1885) by S. Burns Weston, in St. Louis (1886) by Walter L. Sheldon, in Brooklyn (1906) by Leslie Sprague, and in Westchester County (1927) by David S. Muzzey. These six societies, with a membership of about 2500, are affiliated in the American Ethical Union (1889), which publishes as its organ *The Standard,* now in its thirtieth year. Societies were also established in England, France, Germany, Austria and Japan; but it is only in England that the movement has survived the onslaught of nazi and fascist tyranny.

Besides the proclamation of a purely ethical religion from their Sunday morning platforms, the societies have engaged in a variety of educational, philanthropic, and social reform activities. The Ethical Culture Schools, founded in New York as a Workingman's School at the beginning of the movement and in Brooklyn in 1923, have introduced the systematic teaching of ethics in all the grades and have stressed the democratic idea by the inclusion of rich and poor, Negro and white, in their enrollment, by a system of scholarships. The New York society introduced the free kindergarten and district nursing; and the societies generally have been active in such reform projects as settlements, child labor, adult education, tenement house reform, improvement in the condition of the Negroes, and, since the outbreak of the war in Europe, aid to the refugees from nazi persecution in getting acclimated to their new homes in America and learning our language and the principles of our democratic "way of life."

Though the Ethical Societies have a membership so small that they are not listed in most of the tabulations of American religious bodies, and though they are not recognized, as are Catholics, Protestants and Jews, as a "religious" sect by the registrants of the Selective Service, yet their influence has been a decided factor in the liberalizing of orthodox churches, and their educational contributions have been acknowledged by the schools and colleges of the country. Their "leaders" perform the usual functions of ordained ministers in conducting marriage and funeral services. Their property, insofar as it is devoted to religious and educational uses, is exempt from taxation.

Membership in the societies is open to all persons who accept the single doctrine of the ethical aim as the supreme aim of life, without regard to their individual opinions on such questions as the existence of God or the immortality of the soul. Theists, deists, and atheists (if there be any) are equally welcome. Men and women have come to the societies from the church, the synagogue, and the great mass of the "unchurched." Members and leaders are alike free to entertain and to express whatever theological or philosophical convictions they may have, the only bond of union being a common devotion to "the increasing knowledge, love, and practice of the right." The public "services" are extremely simple, consisting of music, inspirational readings, and the ethical address, or "sermon." Some of the societies have introduced congregational singing and responsive readings; but there has generally been a reluctance to "copy" the service of the churches. There is no oral prayer; but, again, in some of the societies a brief period of "meditation" has been adopted.

On Professor Adler's death in 1933, the senior leadership of the New York society passed to his colleague for 40 years, Dr. John L. Elliott; and on the latter's death in 1942, the board of (five) surviving leaders shared the work without the appointment by the trustees of a "senior leader." Meanwhile the founders of the other societies had passed away, to be succeeded eventually by the present leaders: Horace J. Bridges in Chicago, W. Edwin Collier in Philadelphia, J. Hutton Hynd in St. Louis, and Henry Neumann in Brooklyn.

Felix Adler, *An Ethical Philosophy of Life* (1918) and *The Reconstruction of the Spiritual Ideal* (1923); William M. Salter, *Ethical Religion* (1889); Horace J. Bridges, *The Ethical Movement* (1911); Alfred Martin, *The Distinctive Features of the Ethical Movement* (1926); Percival Chubb, *On the Religious Frontier* (1931); Henry Neumann, *Education for Moral Growth* (1923). D.S.M.

ethics: (Gr., *ta ethika,* customs) Moral philosophy, the scientific or philosophical investigation of moral judgments which pronounce conduct "good", "bad", "right", "wrong", what "ought" or "ought not" to be done. All men make moral judgments of some kind. Primitive peoples base moral judgments upon customs deemed obligatory, sometimes attributed to ancestral or divine origin, but rarely explained rationally. In the early civilizations of Egypt, China, India, Persia, and Israel, morality became sufficiently reflective for sages to enunciate precepts and proverbs. However, Socrates* was probably the first philosopher to criticize moral judgments constructively and prepare the way for the rise of systematic ethics. Among his pupils, Plato* advanced the best system of moral philosophy. While Plato, in the *Republic* and elsewhere, affirmed that ethics has an ultimate metaphysical foundation in the Idea of the Good, he conceives ethics largely in terms of citizenship in a free state in which every individual performs his proper functions guided by the virtues of wisdom, courage, temperance, and justice. Aristotle*, who dictated the first treatise devoted exclusively to systematic ethics, gives a longer list of *moral* virtues, each of which is a golden mean between vices: e.g., courage lies between cowardice and foolhardiness. A moral virtue is an acquired habit, which should be intelligently cultivated. Ethics is organically related to Politics, and the moral virtues to citizenship. Higher than moral virtues and civic life, however, are the dianoetic virtues, chiefly rational insight and understanding, the only activities in which the gods conceivably engage.

With the downfall of the Greek free city states after the Macedonian conquest, later moral philosophers were forced to think of man less as a citizen than as an individual. Epicurus* and his followers counselled the wise men to seek a life of simple but refined pleasures for himself and his friends, avoiding entanglement in public affairs. Zeno and the other early Stoics* advocated a life of strict virtue and the cultivation of calm apathy, undisturbed by internal emotions and external calamities. Later Stoics, especially in Roman times, like Epictetus and Marcus Aurelius Antoninus**, were less rigid and more humane: all men are by nature equal, sparks of the divine fire, children of God and brothers, citizens in an ideal state; class distinctions are artificial and irrational. Ancient Skeptics, in view of the uncertainty of all supposed knowledge, advocated a life in which one should not commit oneself in any avoidable manner. Plotinus and other neo-Platonists** found the highest good in mystical absorption in the One, of the Absolute.

Gleams of systematic ethical insight can be found occasionally in the writings of the later ancient church fathers like St. Augustine of events, and finding its criteria and motivation in Hippo*; while the great scholastics of the thirteenth century, notably St. Thomas Aquinas*, incorporated the best of ancient systematic ethics in Christian teaching, and themselves made valuable contributions to ethical theory. However they subordinated ethics to moral theology. Attempts were made by Bruno in the sixteenth century and by Hobbes and Spinoza** in the seventeenth, to emancipate ethics from theology, and general recognition of ethics as an independent discipline was finally won in the eighteenth century by the third earl of Shaftesbury, Francis Hutcheson, and other British moralists*. Most but not all of these moralists tended to be empiricists, basing morality upon the observation of psychological processes like natural affections, a moral sense, the desire for pleasure, conscience, immediate intuitions, the association of ideas, and sympathy.

Kant, dissatisfied with British empiricism, thought that ethics must be based on principles as certain and universal in application as mathematics. These he believed that he found in his formulations of the categorical imperative*. Hegel* distrusted subjective intuitions and sought an objective foundation in social institutions,—the family, civil society, the state. Subsequent German moral philosophers have been likely to find a point of departure in either Kant or Hegel, much as they have diverged from them in the elaboration of their own systems. British moral philosophers in the nineteenth century included supporters of Utilitarianism*, Intuitionism*, and neo-Hegelianism,—see Green, T. H.—which last maintained a non-hedonistic moral ideal, known eternally by the Absolute and gradually realized in human moral progress. French moral philosophers of the last hundred years have often favored positivism: e.g., Auguste Comte*, and in different ways, J. M. Guyau, Durkheim*, Levy-Bruhl, G. Belot, and A. Bayet. They reject supernatural and metaphysical sanctions and approach ethics largely from a sociological standpoint.

British moral philosophers of the twentieth century sometimes have mediated between Idealism and Utilitarianism (e.g., Hastings Rashdall*), or reduced ethics to a few unanalyzable intuitions supplemented by empirical generalizations—G. E. Moore in *Principia Ethica* (1903), and in a quite different manner Sir W. David Ross in *Foundations of Ethics* (1939)—. Edward Westermarck in England and Finland, and with reservations John Dewey in the United States have supported ethical relativism*. A recent movement, represented in the United States by W. M. Urban, R. B. Perry, *et al.*, seeks to incorporate ethics within systematic treatments of values* in general (axiology). The contemporary German moral philosopher who is now attracting most attention in the United States is Nikolai Hartmann* whose humanistic system is a synthesis of elements derived from Kant, Plato, Aristotle, recent German value theories, and other sources.

This article has discussed *systematic* ethics, the attempt to evaluate moral judgments and incorporate them into systems. Other fields of ethics to which (the present writer thinks, unfortunately) less attention is now given than a generation ago are: Comparative Ethics, critical investigations of moral judgments in different stages of social evolution; Psychological Ethics, study of mental processes in order to ascertain their function in human conduct; Political and Social Ethics, applications of the conclusions of systematic ethics to contemporary public problems. Work in these last three subjects, so far as i is continued, seems to be passing from philsophy departments to the social sciences. See eudaemonism; happiness; haustafel; mean, Aristotelian; Puritan ethics; seven virtues; social ethics; summum bonum.

J. Dewey and J. H. Tufts, *Ethics* (1908, rev. ed., 1932); H. Rashdall, *Theory of Good and Evil*, 2 vols. (1907); N. Hartmann, *Ethics*, 3 vols. (1925, Eng. Trans., 1932). W.K.W.

ethics, Confucian: See Confucianism.

ethics, Christian: The term is employed to designate: 1) the conduct of Christians; 2) statements of principles or rules which are recommended as norms of such conduct; 3) the critical effort, carried on in the Christian community, to discover, systematize and apply moral principles of greatest generality and certainty and to use such principles for the sake of gaining greater consistency and precision in conduct. While descriptions of Christian behavior and injunctions to it abound in Christian literature and while ethics in the third, critical, sense has been a part of theology from the beginning, the separate study of Christian moral principles is the relatively late development of the modern period, despite some earlier instances such as Abailard's* *Scito te ipsum.* Such separation, save as it is a limited device used for educational purposes, rests largely on the assumption that moral principles are both more general and more certain than those of religious faith—an assumption which is widely challenged in the twentieth century not only by theology but also by critical secular ethics. Insofar as it is recognized that moral principles in general and those of Christians in particular are dependent upon a pre-ethical acceptance of a final good or goods Christian ethics is seen to be inseparable from theology as secular ethics is understood to be dependent on a "science of values". From this point of view Christian ethics may be defined as that part of Christian theology which deals with the principles of human response to divine action in creation, revelation and redemption. The types, schools and problems of such ethics are not independently analyzable but must be understood with reference to the fundamental theological orientation.

Insofar as the critical study of the Christian moral life can be abstracted from the study of Christian faith it appears that the main problems and schools of Christian ethics parallel those of philosophical ethics in the West. The problem of method (whether ultimate principles are to be sought by means of analysis of value—or of duty-consciousness) has led to the development of both teleological and deontological types of Christian ethics, though the influence of the Hebraic tradition and especially the Christian conception of God makes a deontological element inevitable in even the most pronouncedly teleological theories. In Christian teleology the questions at issue are those of the relative importance of the objective end (e.g., the glory of God) and the subjective end (e.g., the happiness or perfection of man), and of the individual or social character of the latter (theological utilitarianism, the social gospel**). The deontological method is used in a positivistic manner by those who regard revelation as disclosure of specific demands and as taking the place of reason. Such moralists regard right Christian conduct as consisting of obedience to the specific injunctions of Scriptures as a whole or in part (the Ten Commandments, the words of Jesus, the Sermon on the Mount). More formal schools reduce the revealed principles to two—love of God and of neighbor—or to one—obedience to the will of God or the law of love. The differences between all schools of thought are modified by common reference to God as both the good and the source of right and to Jesus Christ as the exemplary righteous man. The problem of the knowledge of good and evil, or of right and wrong, has led to the development of more rationalistic schools for whom revelation is fundamentally republication of rational principles, of intuitionist or spiritualist schools, and of positivistic as well as critical revelationism. See revelation; social ethics.

K. E. Kirk, *The Vision of God. The Christian Doctrine of the Summum Bonum* (London, 1931); C. E. Luthardt, *History of Christian Ethics* (Edinburgh, 1889); E. Troeltsch, *The Social Teachings of the Christian Churches* transl. by Olive Wyon, 2 vols. (London, 1932); E. Brünner, *The Divine Imperative* (London, 1937); E. Gilson, *Moral Values and the Moral Life. The System of Thomas Aquinas* (1931). H.R.N.

ethics, social: See social ethics.

ethnarch: See Eastern Orthodox Churches.

ethnology: (Gr., *ethnos,* race; *logos,* science) A science that treats of the classification of mankind into races, their origin, distribution, relations, and peculiarities. F.L.P.

etiology, aetiology: (Gr., *aitia,* cause) Theory of causes. C.H.

etiquette: See culture.

Etruscan religion: The Etruscans remain largely enigmatic, as does their religion. Archaeology* and Latin literature supply most of our information. Themselves influenced by the Greeks, the Etruscans helped to transform the Roman animistic religion into an anthropomorphic one, especially during their domination of Rome, introducing their triad, Jupiter, Minerva, and Juno, along with other divinities. Their religion was one of fear, which they likewise transmitted to the Romans, emphasizing meticulous attention to detail in the performance of religious ritual. We know most about two aspects of Etruscan religion, 1) the art of divination*, and 2) their beliefs in the after-life and the rites attached to them. Liver divination is undoubtedly Oriental, reflecting possibly the Lydian origin of the Etruscans who practised it in Italy. They adopted the Orphic-Pythagorean belief in rewards and punishments in the after-life, as shown in tomb paintings from the fourth century B.C. The torturing Devils in Dante's Inferno seem reminiscent of Etruscan tomb paintings at Corneto. Rescue from the torments in the after-life could be effected only by postmortem sacrifices performed by priests. Cf. the Masses for the Dead of the Roman Catholic Church. See prayers for the dead.

Robert Seymour Conway, *Ancient Italy and Modern Religion* (Cambridge, 1933); Friedrich Poulsen, *Etruscan Tomb Paintings* (Oxford, 1922); David Randall-MacIver, *The Etruscans* (Oxford, 1927). E.M.N.

eucharist: This is properly the Greek word for "thanksgiving". In the N.T. it is used of prayer in general, which springs out of a sense of thankfulness to God. It is applied more specially to thanks offered before or after a meal. Hence it became the regular term for the Lord's Supper*, at which Christ distributed the elements "when he had given thanks". See agape; arcani disciplina; sacraments. E.F.S.

eucharistic liturgy: See liturgy; missa.

eucharistic sacrifice: See mass, Roman Catholic.

Eucken, Rudolf: (1846-1926) Professor of philosophy at Jena, winner of the Nobel prize for literature in 1908. Eucken was a prolific writer on philosophical subjects but is known more for his personal influence as a teacher than for the originality of his thought. His philosophy was an "activism" which accepted Kant's moral rigorism while rejecting his skepticism and consistently emphasized both the reality of spiritual values and the need of realizing them practically in human life. His thought affected the early work of Max Scheler*. His influence continues in the "Euckenbund" and the periodical *Die Tatwelt* (Jena). See Fichte.

Main Works in English: *The Problem of Human Life* (1909); *The Life of the Spirit* (1909). See W. R. Boyce Gibson: *Rudolf Eucken's Philosophy of Life* (1907). J.S.B.

Eu-chites or Euchetes: 1) Also known as *Messalians* (praying people). Acc. Epiphanius date from reign of Constantius (337-361) a mystical cult in Syria and Mesopotamia, with strange exorcist practices. Their mystical technique similar to Muslim mystical practices. Male and female votaries. Attacked by Flavian of Antioch and at a Council of Side. Called *Enthusiasts* by Theodoret*.

2) A recrudescence of the earlier form with Manichaean elements in the 10th and 11th centuries. F.W.B.

eudaemonism: (From Gr. *eudaimonia,* happiness, well-being) The theory, first propounded by Aristotle*, that the aim of the good life is happiness* or well-being. For Aristotle happiness is the life of highest excellence. The term is often confused with hedonism* by later writers. J.E.N.

Eunomianism: Sect holding Anomoean* (extreme Arian) views, named after Eunomius, Bishop of Cyzicus, who established a separate organization at Constantinople. Did not long survive his death (c. 393). K.H.C.

eunuch: A male who has been castrated. In the religious practice of various Semitic peoples, close neighbors of the Israelites, eunuchs played a peculiar role as devotees of the mother-goddess*. Chiefly for this reason, no doubt, they were formally disqualified from membership in the Jewish community and participation in Judaism (Deut. 23.2). However, an anonymous prophet, at about 500 B.C., took up the cudgels for them in this respect (Isa. 56. 3-7), but apparently to no avail. See Skoptsy. J.M.

Eusebius of Caesarea: (A.D. c. 263-c. 340) Premier church historian, eminent scholar and Christian apologist, influential ecclesiastical statesman—Bishop of Caesarea, "head of Judea", for a quarter of a century. The character of Eusebius has puzzled modern historians and remains a matter of dispute. The same is true of his precise doctrinal standpoint. What is certain is that he was a second generation Origenist, that he was a staunch adherent of the philosophical Logos-theology, that he was sympathetic with Arius in the latter's dispute with the Bishop of Alexandria, and that he was embarrassed by the final recension of his Caesarean creed adopted at Nicea. Later also Eusebius sided actively with the Arian* faction against Eustathius, Athanasius*, and Marcellus*: "his acts", wrote Neuman, "are his confession."

The great work of Eusebius' life was the preparation of the *Ecclesiastical History*, published in 324 or 325. When all criticisms are registered, it remains true that Eusebius after St. Luke is the pioneer in this field. Of the other volumes published by Eusebius, which according to Jerome were "innumerable", the most important among those extant are the *Chronicle, Preparatio evangelica, Demonstratio evangelica, Contra Marcellum, De theologia ecclesiastica,* and Commentaries on the Psalms and Isaiah.

J. P. Migne, ed. *Patrologia Graeco* (161 vols.); *Nicene and Post-Nicene Fathers,* 2nd Series, I; Stein, *Eusebius Bischof von Caesarea* (Würzburg, 1859); arts. *Dict. Chr. Biog.* and *Ency. Brit.* (11th ed.); standard histories of doctrine and of Christian literature. C.W.L.

Eusebius, bp. of Nicomedia: (d. A.D. 342?) Leader of the Arianizing party from 325 (Nicea) till his death. A "fellow-disciple" with Arius of Lucian of Antioch, Eusebius never deviated from radically Arian views*. He was, however, more of a politician than a theologian. He signed the Creed of 325 against his convictions and thereafter gained an influential position in the royal household. He is believed to have been the baptizer of the emperor Constantine as the latter was dying. C.W.L.

Eutyches: Archimandrite* of a monastery outside Constantinople in the first half of the fifth century, was a devoted disciple of Cyril of Alexandria*. He interpreted the teaching regarding the natures of Christ in such a manner as to deny the two natures in Jesus Christ—the human and divine—affirming that after the incarnation He possessed only the divine nature. At a council held by Flavian, Patriarch of Constantinople, Eutyches' teaching was condemned, and he himself deposed and excommunicated. But this sentence was interpreted by Dioscurus, Patriarch of Alexandria and successor of Cyril, to impugn the orthodoxy of the latter. The controversy which ensued led to the calling of the Second Council of Ephesus (449) at which Dioscurus by sheer physical violence annulled the excommunication of Eutyches (Pope Leo called it the Robber Council and refused to recognize it as legal—See Ephesus, Robber Synod of). In turn this led to the calling of the Council of Chalcedon* (451) which decided the controversial question by ruling that Jesus Christ possessed two natures in one person, and condemning both Eutyches and Nestorius alike, while approving Cyril of Alexandria. Dioscurus was deposed, but his Egyptian church rallied about him and repudiated the Chalcedonian decision. Thus the Egyptian church, along with the Ethiopian, adopted monophysitism* (the doctrine of one nature in Christ, the divine) as its creed, and drifted into a permanent schism with the Orthodox (i.e., the Chalcedonian, Imperial) church. In this they were followed by the patriarchates of Jerusalem and Antioch. The Arab Mohammedan conquests of Syria, Palestine, and Egypt made the monophysite schism permanent. See Christology.

J. B. Kidd, *The Churches of Eastern Christendom* (London, n.d.); Arthur A. Luce, *Monophysitism, past and present* (London, 1920). M.S.

evangelical: (Derived from the Greek word *euaggelion* meaning "gospel" or "good news") That which pertains to the gospel* is evangelical. Since the Reformation considered itself a return to the Bible, the word came to be used in Germany and Switzerland as a contrast to Roman Catholic. In England it is roughly synonymous to "low church". It is currently used for those expressions of Christianity which stress the need for atonement for sin and the rebirth of the individual. C.T.C.

Evangelical Church, the: The Evangelical Church was begun in Pennsylvania in 1800 by Jacob Albright (1759-1808) (then Albrecht), a son of German immigrant parents and a member of the Lutheran Church who was religiously reborn under the preaching of pietistic Reformed ministers and joined the Methodist Church. Sensing a real need for evangelical preaching among his fellow German-Americans, Albrecht left the Methodist Church, which offered little to the Germans, organized his three classes in 1800 in eastern Pennsylvania and by the time of his death in 1808 had won several hundred followers and had begun a Discipline—a Book of Rules and Order—which was completed by Rev. George Miller (1774-1816) and published in 1809 in Reading, Pa. John Dreisbach (1789-1871) was the first presiding elder and founded Evangelical Press at New Berlin, Pa. in 1817.

The Evangelical Church spread westward, catering almost exclusively to German speaking people for fifty years, and now has expanded to the Pacific. In 1850 a mission was begun in Germany in 1875 in Japan, and in 1900 in China. Other missions are located in Africa, among the mountaineers of Kentucky and among the Italians in Wisconsin. Three colleges and two theological seminaries* are maintained in the United States.

A division in the Church in 1891-4 led to the beginning of the United Evangelical Church which reunited in 1922 to form the present body of about 250,000 members in the United States and Canada and about 30,000 on the mission fields. Negotiations have been practically completed for the merging of the Evangelical Church and the Church of the United Brethren in Christ* (a similar contemporary group of Reformed and Mennonite background, William Otterbein and Martin Boehm** founders in 1800) which may occur by 1946. Both groups are Arminian* in theology and have a modified episcopal form of government. See Ev. Congregational Church.

R. W. Albright, *A History of the Evangelical Church* (1942). R.W.A.

Evangelical and Reformed Church, the: See s. v. Reformed Church in the U. S.

Evangelical Congregational Church: A sect (formerly a part of the United Evangelical

Church) tracing back to the evangelistic work of Jacob Albright* in Pennsylvania, a Methodist preacher who evangelized among the Germans and became the founder of the Evangelical Association. The United Evangelical Church branched off in 1894. A reunion was effected in 1922, but the East Pennsylvania Conference remained apart and became the Evangelical Congregational Church. It is a Methodistic body with no distinctive doctrines or principles.

E.T.C.

Evangelical Mission Covenant Church of America, The: An immigrant population in America deeply influenced by the revivals in Sweden and conditions in the churches of the Swedish Mission Covenant organized in 1878 would naturally seek to found a similar church in America. After unsatisfactory affiliations, representatives from Swedish Mission Churches met in Chicago in 1885 and organized the Swedish Evangelical Mission Covenant of America. In the rapid process of assimilation, the name has been changed to the Evangelical Mission Covenant Church of America. The *Year Book* of 1941 reports 453 affiliated churches comprising a membership of 46,617 in 30 states and Canada.

In church polity the Covenant seeks to combine Congregational and Presbyterian principles. The local church has complete freedom. This freedom, however, is voluntarily cooperative in the 13 Conference Meetings and the Annual Conference to which the churches send delegates whose decisions control matters such as license and ordination, the missionary enterprise in Alaska, China, and Africa, and the larger policies of Covenant institutions.

Two schools are maintained by the Covenant: North Park College and Theological Seminary in Chicago, and Minnehaha Academy in Minneapolis. In addition, the Covenant and its Conferences operate two hospitals, eight homes for the aged, two orphanages, and two sailor's homes.

Theologically the denomination has its deepest roots in the Lutheran tradition. But inasmuch as there is deliberately no specific creed, and educationally the historical approach to theology is encouraged, a considerable variety of conservative theological opinion exists. Clergy and people unanimously approve the general theological principles as formulated by the president of the Covenant, Theodore W. Anderson, in *Covenant Memories,* 1935: the supremacy of the bible; the necessity of spiritual life; belief in the unity of all true Christians; the autonomy of the local church; and, the urgency of the missionary task.

Headquarters: 1005 Belmont Avenue, Chicago, Illinois. See Waldenstrom, Paul Peter.

The Covenant Weekly; David Nyvall, *The Swedish Covenanters* (1930); George M. Stephenson, *The Religious Aspects of Swedish Immigration* (1932); Leland H. Carlson, *A History of North Park College* (1941).

E.G.H.

Evangelical Union: This organization was founded in 1843 by James Morison who with three other ministers had been expelled from the Evangelical Synod of Scotland because of their dissent from its Calvinistic doctrines. They founded an independent denomination with each church complete in itself. They founded a theological academy with Morison at its head and established an annual Conference. Their energetic measures gathered a considerable membership and their periodicals had a wide circulation. They became pioneers in the temperance movement in Scotland and no liquor dealer was allowed in their membership. In 1896 they were merged with the Congregational Union of Scotland.

Schaff-Herzog, *Encyclopedia of Religious Knowledge,* v. 4, p. 224.

F.T.P.

evangelicalism and evangelical revival: The term "evangelical" refers to the Evangel or Gospel and has a long history. In the Synodical Letter of A.D. 382, sent by the Eastern Bishops to those assembled at Rome, which contains the first full-fledged theological statement of the doctrine of the Trinity*, the "evangelical faith" is spoken of as that for which persecutions have been endured and as having been "ratified by the 318 fathers at Nicea." In Eastern Orthodox and Roman Catholic tradition "Evangelical" commonly refers to the imitation of Christ according to the counsels of perfection set forth in of Europe "evangelical" is a usual designation for the Churches of the Reformation. In English the Gospels. In Germany and adjacent sections however the term "evangelical" refers to the position and emphasis of the movement known as the Evangelical Revival, which began in the third decade of the eighteenth century and had a continuous history for over a century. The precursors of Evangelicalism were Moravianism, Pietism, and Cocceianism* or Federalism (in Holland); in theology it represented a return to the doctrines of the Reformation; in ethics and conception of the Christian life it was largely influenced by the High Anglican ascetic William Law.

The founders of Evangelicalism were Charles and John Wesley and George Whitefield. The movement arose within the Church of England, its first phase being the "Holy Club" started by Charles Wesley at Oxford and presided over by John Wesley upon his return from Epworth to Oxford in 1729. Methodism as a term of designation dates from this phase, though the theology of the first Oxford Movement was Anglican of the right-wing High Church variety and its devotional and liturgical practices were those of the primitive Church. The Evangelical element was the serious and strenuous imitation of the life of Jesus Christ as urged with brilliant persistence and stirring effect by William Law. It was only after John Wesley's experience of disillusionment and failure as a Missionary and Parish Priest in Georgia, and after his return to England in 1738, that Evangelicalism emerged as at once a saving doctrine of Justification* by faith alone and a consciously felt experience of God's saving power. The media here were the writings of Luther and the example and personal direction of the Moravians*. Whitefield's partly independent experience of the New Birth and discovery of power in preaching deserve mention as a distinct factor in the total complex of the Revival. Likewise his Calvinism exerted a strong influence upon the so-called Anglican Evangelicals*. The doctrine of the Wesleys in contrast remained definitely Arminian*. This divergence in theology together with the foundation and remarkable growth of the "United Societies", which were patterned on the old Religious Societies of the Church of England but were organized and governed largely by John Wesley himself, was a potent factor in the independent establishment eventually of Methodism. Equally important, though by no means the sole element making for separation, was the latitudinarian apathy of the English Bishops.

The Evangelical Revival was eminently a preaching revival. This preaching, which was primarily of the Gospel of God's saving grace and power against a background of His judgment upon all sin and unrighteousness, was of three kinds: Parochial, Field, and Society. Parochial preaching met opposition but continued and developed into what may be called Anglican Evangelicalism. Whitefield was the pioneer and great exemplar of field preaching, in which however the Wesleys early joined him. It was in the meetings of the Religious Societies, a well established institution of the Church of England of which Samuel Wesley of Epworth had been a patron and advocate, that the marked conversion phenomena of the Revival were first manifest. The Revival spread rapidly, meeting an astonishing response in the hearts and lives of the masses of the British people, and is commonly credited by historians as having averted a counterpart of the French Revolution. For its sociological results see evangelicals, Anglican. See also Law, William; Methodism; Wesley, Charles and John; Whitefield, George; Zinzendorf, Nicolaus. Cf. Pietism; Pietistic sects in America.

George R. Balleine, *History of the Evangelical Party in the Church of England* (1908); Leonard Elliott-Binns, *Evangelical Movement in the English Church* (1928); W. E. H. Lecky, *History of England in the Eighteenth Century* (1882-91); John H. Overton, *Evangelical Revival in the Eighteenth Century* (1886); James Stephen, *Essays in Ecclesiastical Biography* (1849); Leslie Stephen, *History of English Religious Thought in the Eighteenth Century* (2 vols., 1876). C.W.L.

evangelicals, Anglican: The English use of the word for those who preach the gospel of personal conversion as the heart of religion dates from c. 1750. Modern English-speaking Evangelicalism in general derives from the religious revival of that period. In England Evangelicals were distinguished from Methodists* by their loyalty to the parochial system of the Church; most of them in the early period were Calvinist in theology. After 1790 they acquired more cohesion around two centers—Clapham near London, where a group of active laymen lived, and Cambridge University, where Charles Simeon (died 1836) was their leader. The chief writings of the Evangelicals were sermons, commentaries, devotional works, and hymns; their chief practical achievements were in the field of missions (the Church Missionary Society, founded 1799, soon became and has remained the largest Anglican Society) and reforms related to personal morality—Wilberforce leading the antislavery movement and Shaftesbury that for factory reform. After 1840 the Evangelicals were for a while largely absorbed in controversies—against ritualism*, evolution, and higher criticism; but from about 1880 their traditional interest in missions and personal religion again became central. In the present century there has been a Liberal Evangelical movement, endeavoring to combine the religious emphasis of evangelicalism with freedom of thought and dignity in worship. In reaction the strict conservatives, finding the standards of the C. M. S. lax, organized in the early 1920's the Bible Churchmen's Missionary Society, based on the inerrancy of Scripture as a fundamental of the faith. But this group, though well supported, is only a fragment of the Evangelicals, whose chief influence is probably in the emphasis on personal devotion and conduct common to all forms of English religion. See Church of England.

L. E. Binns, *The Evangelical Movement in the English Church* (1928); C. Smyth, *Simeon and Church Order* (1940). E.R.H.

Evangelistic Associations: A group of sects so classified by the census because, while virtually denominations, "they are dominated by the evangelistic conception rather than by doctrinal or ecclesiastical distinctions." Some object to the designation of denomination. Many have holiness leanings and are Methodist in character. See under the headings: Apostolic Christian Church; Apostolic Christian Church (Nazarean); Apostolic Faith Mission; Christian Congregation; Church of Daniel's Band; Church of God (Apostolic); Church of God as Organized by Christ; Hepzibah Faith Missionary Association; Metropolitan Church Association; Missionary Bands of the World; Pillar of Fire. See holiness churches. E.T.C.

evangelization propaganda: See religious tract movement in the U. S.

evensong: An English name for vespers,* the sixth of the seven canonical hours, applied since the Reformation to the Anglican office of Evening Prayer which is derived from vespers and compline*. See divine office; matins. T.J.B.

Everyman: See religious drama.

evil: (A.S. *yfel;* Ger., *übel*) Antithesis of good or value*; disvalue; whatever is harmful, painful, or undesirable, or disapproved; what is contrary to any purpose (dysteleological) or ideal, especially to the moral or to the religious. Moral evil is called wrong and religious evil, sin*.

I. *Types of evil.* Evil is chiefly a relative

term, its meaning being dependent on the kind of good which it negates or excludes. We must, however, distinguish between *instrumental* and *intrinsic* evil (see Value); there are states of pain and misery which are evil in and of themselves, whether they hinder or promote the good. Evils are usually, but oversimply, classified as moral (voluntary) and natural (independent of human volition). More concretely, we may list: 1) evil will (wrong, sin); 2) intellectual evil (ignorance, error); 3) aesthetic evil (ugliness); 4) religious evil (irreverence, blasphemy); 5) maladjustment (psychological, biological, social); 6) incompetence; 7) surd evil (evil of any sort in which there is no principle of improvement; its only function is to be endured, rejected, conquered, or passed by).

II. *Problem of evil.* Problems arise from the presence of contradictions or incoherencies in experience. Good and evil seem to be contradictory. The problem is: How can we think the real in such a way as to account for its seemingly contradictory manifestations of good and evil? James's question, "Doth a fountain send forth at the same place sweet water and bitter?" may be asked of the universe. The need for a coherent explanation of good and evil exists for every thinker, whether he be theistic or not.

III. *Theodicy.* (Gr., *theos,* God; *dikē,* justice) This is the attempt to "justify the ways of God to man," that is, to solve the problem of evil in the light of faith in the love and justice of God. The problem of evil is obviously more acute for theism* than for any other type of philosophy or theology; if it cannot be solved, theism must be abandoned, retained by faith in hope of a future, as yet unattainable, solution, or held as a truth above reason (or a *credo quia absurdum*).

IV. *The apparent insolubility of the problem.* Many hold that the origin and explanation of evils are a mystery hidden in the divine counsels and impossible for man to solve. They point to the climactic words of Job, "I am vile . . . I will lay my hand upon my mouth . . . I abhor myself and repent," overlooking Jehovah's endorsement of Job's arguments against the 'comforters', "Ye have not spoken of me the thing that is right, as my servant Job hath." The tendency to treat the problem as insoluble arises from agnosticism, from humility (the fallacious belief that reason is essentially proud), from the belief that a practical solution suffices (oppose evil!), and from the variety of proposed solutions. Yet the same arguments which declare this problem insoluble would readily lead to atheism*. Most thinkers are challenged by difficulties, rather than being led to abandon search for truth. Those realists and naturalists who hold that the universe is indifferent to good and evil (neutral), offer their neutralism as evidence that the problem is artificial; but their neutralism leaves wide areas of experience (values) irrelevant to reality.

V. *Proposed solutions.* 1) Moral evil (sin) is explained by human freedom; this is accepted by most theists as a reasonable explanation, thus leaving natural (nonmoral, nonvoluntary) evil as the seat of the chief problem. 2) All natural evils are a product of freedom. Macintosh, on a panpsychistic basis, has suggested that natural evil is explicable as due to the free choices of the monads constituting nature; but it must be pointed out that the effects of these free choices on man is most unjust, and that God is responsible for creating beings capable of producing such evils. 3) Nonmoral evils are a deserved punishment for Adam's (or man's) sin. This (still popular) theory of Genesis and of Theosophists is rejected by Job and by Jesus (Jn. 9:3), and is refuted by the obvious lack of correlation between sin and suffering. 4) Nonmoral evils are disciplinary. Their purpose is to refine, to develop strength, to teach man energy and dependence on God. This is logically and morally conceivable (if the use of nonmoral evil as a means to moral good is justifiable); but the frequent failure of evil to effect discipline and its maladaptation to that end raise questions. 5) Evil is incomplete good. This theory, often advanced in absolute idealism*, has much basis in experience. Part of a painting, or a character, may be offensive, whereas the whole is good. Yet from incompleteness alone the goodness of the complete cannot be inferred; some apparent goods are parts of an evil whole. The view proposed may be granted only partial validity. 6) Evil is said to be needed as a contrast to good. Variety is itself good. This aesthetic principle is destructive when applied to moral values. It is not necessary to sin in order to enjoy virtue any more than it is necessary to eat a rotten apple in order to enjoy a ripe one. Further, there is more evil than is needed for effective contrast. 7) What is evil for man may be good for other beings in the universe. This argument is a sound rebuke to human pride and to undue anthropocentrism; but it does not explain why God has to give man earthquakes, alcohol, insanity, and cancer in order to benefit superhuman or subhuman beings. Why could not our good also be their good? 8) All evils serve an unknown good. This is conceivable; but how do we know that the unknown is good? Does the unknown good make the known evils less evil for man? 9) Evil is illusory. This view is held by some Buddhists, Hindus, Christian Scientists**, and others. Evil is "maya," "error of mortal mind." However, the illusion somehow exists, and belief that the illusion is evil is itself an unexplained evil. 10) Nonmoral evils are a result of factors in the universe which limit God's power. For a discussion of this solution, which is the most popular explanation of surd evil today (other than the traditional views mentioned in 3), 4), and 8), see finite God. See also Hume; wrath of God.

F. C. S. Schiller, *Riddles of the Sphinx* (1891, 1910); J. Royce, *Studies of Good and Evil* 1898); F. R. Tennant, *The Origin and Propagation of Sin* (1902); O. Lempp, *Das Problem der Theodizee* (1910); W. D. Niven, art. "Good and Evil" in ERE, VI (1914); E. S. Brightman, *The Finding of God* (1931); W. Monod, *Le probleme du Bien* (3 vols., 1934); N. Berdyaev, *Spirit and Reality* (tr., 1939); Vergilius Ferm, *First Chapters in Religious Philosophy* (1937), section "Evil and Theodicy," pp. 145-174. E.S.B.

evil spirits, warding off of: See exorcism; spirits.

Evodius or Euodios: The predecessor of Ignatius* in the episcopal chair of Antioch. He is referred to by Eusebius in his *Ecclesiastical History* as the first bishop of the city. If St. Peter be regarded as the first bishop of Antioch, Evodius would then be the second. As such he was among the earliest monarchical bishops* anywhere. M.S.

evolution: A term which denotes a process of orderly change from a simple toward a more complex state. In accurate usage it is restricted to processes which exhibit the characteristics of organic unity and growth. The three areas in which the concept is used are as follows: 1) In biology it refers primarily to the transformation of one species into another. It may also be used to designate the process of growth within a species or within a biological individual. 2) In sociology and anthropology** the term denotes the modification of human institutions and ideas when this process is considered as taking place according to a law which involves orderly change from simplicity to complexity; 3) in metaphysics the term is applied to the cosmic process in those philosophies which regard the universe itself as exhibiting a pattern of growth.

Biologists are practically unanimously agreed as to the fact of evolution in the course of life on this earth. The unsolved problems, from the standpoint of scientific theory, are related to the question of what factors and forces are to be regarded as operative in evolution. Various theories still are held on this point. 1) Following Charles Darwin* one school holds that the central factor in evolution is the natural selection of variations which aid in the struggle for survival. Modern Darwinians have developed this conception through the further analysis of the types of modifications which tend to be selected. In this connection new knowledge concerning mutations, modifications in the hereditary factors, is of prime importance. 2) Another school, following J. B. Lamarck, holds that modifications which occur during the life of an organism may be transmitted to its descendents. Neo-Lamarckians have attempted to show that the activities of the organism modify its structure; and that such modifications can be inherited. Others in this school have held that a psychic factor must be operative in inheritance; and have thus explained the inheritance of acquired characteristics. Evidence adequate to support the Lamarckian hypothesis has yet to be produced in the opinion of many competent biologists. 3) The theory of orthogenesis presupposes a developmental principle or factor at work within the biological species itself which brings about the evolutionary changes. The work of contemporary biology is laying stress upon detailed research and experiment in the many aspects of life including those studied in morphology, heredity, and ecology.

The conception of evolution has been applied to the development of human institutions by a school of cultural anthropologists who presuppose a fundamental unity in human nature and interpret the process of human culture as a gradual progress toward more complex and higher forms. This pattern is used to interpret also the development of particular elements in culture*, such as religion. Contemporary anthropology is less willing to generalize any one pattern of the history of human culture, and is inclined to reject the uniformitarian and deterministic assumptions which the older view involved. The social Darwinists should be noted as having tried to apply to human culture the biological laws which Darwin formulated as explaining the process of evolution. Thus Bagehot, Gumplowicz, and others interpreted human institutions in terms of the struggle of groups for survival.

Most modern philosophies have attempted to incorporate the notion of evolution into metaphysics. One influential school of "emergent evolutionists" has interpreted the cosmic process in terms of the emergence of new and unique orders of being out of previously existing orders. See cosmogonies.

On the theory of evolution see Bavink, *The Natural Sciences* (Eng. tr. of the 4th ed., 1932), Parts 3 and 4; Joseph Needham, article "Evolution" in the *Encyclopedia of the Social Sciences* (1930); Julian Huxley, *Evolution, the Modern Synthesis* (1943). For criticism of Darwinism see S. Butler, *Unconscious Memory* (3rd ed., 1920). For the theory of emergent evolution see C. Lloyd Morgan, *Life, Mind, and Spirit* (1926); and S. Alexander, *Space, Time and Deity* (London, 1920). For general criticism of the doctrine of evolution see L. T. More, *The Dogma of Evolution* (Princeton, 1925). For discussion of the evolutionary concept in anthropology see Alexander Goldenweiser, *Anthropology* (1937), chapters 30 and 31. For a general survey, see "The Idea of Evolution," Chap. XV in V. Ferm, *First Adventures in Philosophy* (1936). D.D.W.

evolution, the controversy over: The theory of biological evolution, which was given its first adequate scientific defense by Charles Darwin* and Alfred Russell Wallace, precipitated a controversy in religious thought which involved questions concerning the nature of the Christian revelation and the re-statement of the Christian world view. Specifically, the theory of the evolution of species challenged the accepted religious doctrine of special creation*, which was claimed to be founded on the Scriptures. Thus the problem was posed of how the scriptural record is to be understood in relation to scientific knowledge. Further, the Darwinian theory that natural selection is the operative factor in evolution raised metaphysical issues concerning the ultimate cause or causes in the universe and forced a reconsideration of the traditional arguments for the existence of God, particularly the argument from design.

For a period of about fifteen years after the publication of *On the Origin of Species* in 1859, the reception accorded the new theory by theologians varied from cautious acceptance on the part of a few to a wider-spread rejection and denunciation. In the early 1870's the controversy became sharpened and a division developed in Protestant thought between those who denounced Darwinism as atheism and those who took biological evolution as an established fact and who were beginning to revise theological conceptions in order to incorporate the new knowledge. Many cultural factors contributed to the varieties of reaction. A militant fundamentalist* movement holding to a world view based upon a literal interpretation of the Scripture over against all scientific theories emerged from the reaction against Darwinism. On the other side theologians like George Harris and Lyman Abbott, and religious philosophers like John Fiske* interpreted evolution as God's method of creation. These thinkers also accepted the theory of historical development as the basis for interpreting revelation in the Scriptures and for understanding the history of the Christian movement and its thought.

The Roman Catholic Church avoided in large part an open rupture over evolution, though it had its own modernist* movement to contend with. The church kept itself from any open break either with science or with its own teaching by refraining from pronouncing for or against the theory, by holding to the church's right to interpret the Scriptures, and by holding to its own doctrine regarding the nature of man. A Catholic biologist, St. George Jackson Mivart, defended the theory of biological evolution in his *Genesis of Species* (1871). Catholic apologists now hold that the church can accept any scientifically established theory of biological development, always with the provision that the church's teaching concerning the supernatural and special creation of the human soul is not denied.

For the evolutionary controversy in America see B. J. Lowenberg, "Evolution in New England, 1859-1873," *The New England Quarterly,* Vol. VIII, 1935, No. 2; F. H. Foster, *The Modern Movement in American Theology* (1939). On the Roman Catholic reaction see W. M. Agar, *Catholicism and the Progress of Science* (1940); Henri de Dordolot, *Darwinism and Catholic Thought* (1923). D.D.W.

Ewald, Georg Heinrich August von: (1803-1875) German Orientalist, Hebraist, biblical critic and historian; popularizer of the Development Hypothesis of O.T. growth; writer of the first great modern introduction to the O.T. R.E.W.

exaltation of Christ: The glorification of Christ in His Transfiguration, Resurrection, and Ascension**, whereby He manifested His divinity, as opposed to His humiliation* at the instant of the Incarnation*, in which He concealed His divinity by assuming a human nature, and His obedience unto death for our salvation. The doctrine is strikingly outlined by St. Paul in Phil. 2:5-11. C.V.

exarch: An ecclesiastical title in use among the Eastern Orthodox communions, which corresponds in general to the Western terms of apostolic vicar or primate. Originally it designated the office of a metropolitan* of such important sees which were more than metropolitanates but yet failed to attain the rank of patriarchates*. In the usage of the Bulgarian Orthodox Church, the exarch has jurisdiction over the Bulgarians outside the boundaries of the tsardom. The primate of Georgia also bears the title of exarch. M.S.

ex cathedra: (Lat. "from the chair") A technical term employed by the Roman Catholic Church in connection with the infallibility* of the Pope*. According to the Vatican Council*, the Roman Pontiff is by divine assistance infallible when he teaches *ex cathedra,* that is, "when in the discharge of his office as pastor and teacher of all Christians, by virtue of his supreme apostolic authority, he defines a doctrine regarding faith or morals, to be held by the universal Church." See chair of St. Peter. C.V.

excommunication: Partial or total exclusion, whether temporary or permanent, from a religious body. Such exclusion involves a privation of civil rights wherever participation in the religious fellowship is prerequisite to the exercise of the privileges of citizenship.

Among the Biblical passages which are cited in support of a doctrinal basis for excommunication are the following: Ezra 10:8; Matt. 16:19, 18:15-18; Rom. 16:17; 1 Cor. 5:3-5, 11, 13; Eph. 5:11; 2 Thess. 3:6, 14; 1 Tim. 1:20, 5:20-21; Tit. 3:10; 2 Jn. 10, 11.

Excommunicates are grouped by the R. C. Church as *vitandi* and *tolerati.* The former group consists of those whom the Holy See has expressly excommunicated by name as persons to be specially shunned in religious matters and so far as possible in secular matters. Other excommunicates are *tolerati.*

Some groups of Protestantism place all responsibility for final disciplinary action in the assembled Church body; others delegate the responsibility for such action and the revision of membership roles to a Church council or committee. See apostasy; ban; sin. H.W.J.

exegesis: "Exegesis" is the transliteration of the Gr., *exegesis,* which could mean "narrative," "translation" or "interpretation." It is in the last sense that the noun is used in theology; "exegesis" is "interpretation," more particularly and usually "interpretation of Scripture." In technical parlance the word describes the actual interpretation of a concrete passage, while the general principles of Biblical interpretation are classed together as "hermeneutics"*.

In the O.T. period the official interpreters of the Law (see law, Hebrew) were the priests (Hag. 2:10-13), who in the "intermediate" and N.T. periods were succeeded by the scribes*; especially the scribes belonging to the Pharisaic* party, who alone continued after A.D. 70. Their hermeneutic principle maintained that the Law, being divine, foresaw all possible problems and so by fresh interpretation could be indefinitely expanded; the theory that produced the overwhelming luxurience of Talmudic* Judaism. And this method was aided by allegory*, Greek in origin but adopted by the Jews before the Christian era, which sought for a "spiritual" sense underlying Scripture; Philo of Alexandria* exhibits the lengths to which allegory could be carried. The first Christian exegesis followed the contemporary precedents unquestioningly (1 Cor. 9:9-10; Gal. 4:21-31, etc.), and allegory in the second century reached fantastic heights, controlled only by insistence that "orthodox" theology must not be violated. The immense authority of Origen* virtually canonized the allegorical method, despite protests from the Antiochean school* and elsewhere, and its more extreme votaries disregarded the "literal" sense altogether. More usually, however, the literal sense* was supplemented by the "higher" senses, which in the scholastic age were usually fixed as three: "allegorical" (doctrinal or devotional), "moral" and "anagogical"* (describing the future life). With the Reformation the idea of a multiple sense of Scripture was less regarded but Protestants and Catholics alike continued to demand correspondence with accepted doctrinal formularies from exegetes. A true historical exegesis was not possible until the growth of a true historical consciousness in theology generally and in its major development belongs to the nineteenth century.

In contemporary Biblical study attempts to erect hermeneutics into a formal discipline have been largely abandoned. Correct exegesis is the final aim of all historical Biblical endeavor and to it all other fields of Biblical research contribute: textual criticism, to determine the precise wording of the passage to be interpreted; lexicography*, to assure correct translation of the words employed; Hebrew or Hellenistic Greek grammar, to determine the relation of these words to one another; historical criticism, to establish the authorship and historical setting of the passage; together with all possible further aids gained from archaeology*, historical geography, contemporary history, form criticism*, etc. Conversely a better exegetical alternative may react on the contributing fields to decide between textual, lexical, grammatical, historical and other possibilities. So a subjective element is always present. Biblical exegesis demands from its practitioners not only sound historical knowledge but fine religious and literary sensitivity as well; really eminent exegetes are as rare as really eminent figures in any other form of human endeavor.

Competence, however, can be attained by capable and sincere students who are adequately equipped in the contributing fields. The sole question to be answered is, "How did the writer expect his first readers to understand his words?" The simplest answer is usually therefore the best. And, generally speaking, this answer is to be deduced solely from the passage itself. Harmonizing with other Biblical passages is to be avoided unless from the same author, and even in this case harmonizing must be used very cautiously. And the utility of an interpretation for modern doctrinal, ethical and devotional purposes must never weigh with exegetes, who are concerned only with what the words meant when written, not with what we should like to have them mean today. See Biblical criticism; interpretation; senses of Scripture; types. B.S.E.

exegetical preaching: Preaching based on sound exegesis* of a Biblical text or (more usually) passage, in which the historical sense is explained before a modern application is sought. B.S.E.

exemplum: An anecdote, drawn from history, legend, or fictitious natural history, to enforce moral lesson of medieval sermon. Collections of exempla for preachers were common. E.C.K.

exile: See Judaism; pre-exile; post-exilic.

existentia: (Lat. *ex*, out of, and *stare*, to stand) That by which a thing is or is constituted in the order of actuality. L.R.W.

existentialism: Psychology: see psychology, schools of. Phil. and Theol.: see Kierkegaard, S., Barth, K.; Heidegger, M.; Jaspers, K.

ex nihilo: See cosmogonies; creation.

Exodus: The second book of the O.T., containing the account of the oppression of the Israelites in Egypt and their exodus from that land and journey to Mt. Sinai under the leadership of Moses (chapters 1-18); and the account of various events at Mt. Sinai, including the making of the covenant and the promulgation of certain laws (chapters 19-40). Although Moses* is traditionally considered as the author, it is a composite work by J E and P**. Chapters 25-31, 35-40 are exclusively P material; the rest of the book is a combination of the three sources. Exodus is of special interest for its record of the revelation of Yahweh to Moses (ch. 3 JE, 6:2-13 P), and of the giving of the Ten Commandments. The ethical decalogue* is found in chapter 20, usually attributed to E, but a "ritual decalogue" was discovered by Goethe in chapter 34, and many scholars have maintained that this was the original Mosaic decalogue. This is improbable, since the prescriptions of this chapter are applicable almost exclusively to a settled agrarian society; if Moses did not give the familiar Ten Commandments of chapter 20 (in a shorter form, with restricted application), we do not know what laws he gave. The date of the exodus has been the subject of extensive debate. No theory has been advanced which fits all the archaeological and Biblical data, but a date in the thirteenth century B.C. seems most satisfactory in view of the archaeological evidence.

A. H. McNeile, *The Book of Exodus* (Westminster Comm., 1908); G. E. Wright, "Epic of Conquest," *The Biblical Archaeologist,* Vol. III, No. 3, Sept. 1940.

J.P.H.

exogamy: A social practice in which marriage* between members of one's own group is prohibited. In the definition of what constitutes one's own group customs vary widely. Universally, however, marriage is prohibited between parent and child, brother and sister. Cousin marriage is also widely prohibited. The group within which marriage is tabooed is most commonly that defined by common descent, but among many preliterate peoples there are many variations in which persons biologically unrelated are forbidden to marry and in other instances certain biologically related persons are eligible as marriage partners. Compare with endogamy. E.R.M.

ex opere operato: A term used to indicate the R. C. teaching that the objectively administered N.T. sacraments do not depend for their primary effect upon subjective factors whether in minister or recipient, but are effectual of themselves conferring grace* "from the work wrought" (ex opere operato) providing that the recipient place no obstacle in the way. See opus operatum; sacraments. H.W.J.

exorcism: (Gr. *exorkizo,* to bind with an oath, to adjure, to exorcise) Exorcism expressly denotes the expulsion of malevolent spirits* or demons* from possessed persons (or from objects and places) by the utterance of an adjuration (or exorcism) in which the aid of more powerful spirits or deities, usually invoked by name, is sought. A possessed person exorcised in this way is presumedly freed from sickness, sin, uncleanness, death, or some other evil caused by the presence of these malevolent spirits. Various formulas, singly and in combination, with and without the invocation of the "name," came into use, among them entreaties; prayers; threats; maledictions; commands; quotations from sacred writings; and magical words of all kinds. Also, through further extension of its meaning, exorcism comprises any overt act or combination of acts, performed with or without a spoken formula, by which evil spirits are expelled. These include such techniques as flagellation; the application of various substances; the production of hideous sounds and foul odors, the offering of sacrifices; the making of some sign or gesture; and the use of charms, amulets, and phylacteries. Exorcism also came to refer to those preventive techniques performed to repel or ward off evil spirits. Almost universally practiced in primitive religions*, with the medicine man, shaman, or priest** as the exorcist, exorcism has likewise had an important place in higher religions, including Christianity. In order to demonstrate the power of Jesus over Satan the Synoptic Gospels depict him as exorcising demons, but through his own supernatural authority rather than by the invocation of God's name and help. Christians, in both early and later periods, exorcised in the name of Jesus, less frequently in the name of God, claiming that the invocation of these holy names made their exorcism religious rather than magical. The rise of a minor order of exorcists in the church testifies to the wide currency of Christian exorcism. The present Catholic practice of pre-baptismal exorcism, together with the exorcism of demoniacs and of objects like oil, water, and salt, originated in early times. Today, however, the priest alone is permitted to exorcise. The power attributed to the "name" of Jesus survives in the customary conclusion to Christian prayers in which his name is invoked. See laying on of hands; magic.

W. Heitmüller, *Im Namen Jesu* (1903); T. K. Oesterreich, *Possession: Demoniacal and Other* (tr. fr. the German, 1930). M.R.

experimental psychology: See psychology, schools of.

expiation: See holocaust; propitiation; sacrifice.

explicit faith: The standard demanded of the higher clergy in the Middle Ages, requiring the intelligent acceptance of the doctrines of the Church, and involving therefore a clear apprehension of the details of those doctrines; opp. to implicit faith*. H.W.J.

exposition: The explanatory or interpretative presentation of the content, purpose or significance of a writing or discourse, or other subject matter. H.W.J.

expository preaching: That type of preaching which, utilizing the results of exegetical* and historical study of the subject matter though not unnecessarily exhibiting the terms or procedure of such prerequisite analysis in the sermon, attempts to expound and apply in a connected and systematic manner the main ideas or teachings contained in an extended passage, chapter, or book of the Bible; usually, though not always, distinguished from that type of homiletic* discourse in which a brief text is used as the basis or unifying idea of the sermon*. H.W.J.

exsultet: In the Roman rite, the deacon's *praeconium* at the lighting of the paschal candle, on Holy Saturday, named from the opening words, *Exsultet jam Angelica turba.* E.R.H.

extreme unction: A sacrament of the Roman Catholic and Eastern Orthodox church of anointing* the dying. The R. C. rite to be valid must be performed by a properly ordained priest using oil* consecrated to this purpose only. Eyes, ears, nostrils, lips, hands and feet are anointed; in each case the formula is repeated: "Through this holy unction, and His own most tender Mercy, may the Lord pardon thee whatever offences thou hast committed by sight (or hearing, etc.)." The rite differs somewhat in the Eastern Church. See sacraments. R.E.E.H.

Ezekiel: Book of a priest who was among those deported with Jehoiachim (II Kings 24:15) in 598 B.C., and was called to be a prophet in the fifth year after that event (1:2). The last date of a prophecy is the twenty-seventh year (29:17), 571 B.C. The book consists of three parts: 1-24—prophecies against "Israel" (Judah) and Jerusalem; 25-32—prophecies against foreign nations (secondarily placed in the present position—prophecies 24:26-27 are continued in 33:21-22); 34-48—salutary prophecies for the Israel of the Future (40-48 the vision of the new temple, city and Holy Land forming a distinct unit within the section). The book has been a storm center of criticism in late years. Radical solutions such as Torrey's (a third century B.C. pseudepigraph!) have added to the confusion. The moderate critical position which seems best is the following. The "authentic" pieces giving experiences or utterances of the prophet are all dated except 12:1-10, where the date may have been lost (through transposition?), and are arranged in chronological order (now slightly disturbed, cp. 29:19, a later date than 40:1). But each date applies only to the first unit following it; other distinct pieces subjoined to dated units are suspect of having been placed there redactionally, and their authenticity must be judged separately. That the book has been much expanded by other hands, notably also in chapters 40-48, is certain. But even a critically "reduced" book will show that Ezekiel was a man of great originality of thought and character. His influence on the subsequent religious and theological development was large. He has been called the John Calvin of the O.T. Cf. Gog and Magog.

R. H. Pfeiffer, *Introduction to the Old Testament* (1941); J. A. Bewer, *Literature of the Old Testament* (rev. ed., 1933). E.G.K.

Ezra: According to the record in Scripture, Ezra was the leader of a caravan which returned from Babylonia to the Holy Land in the reign of Artaxerxes, King of Persia (Ezra 7.1). (It is usually assumed that this Artaxerxes is the first king of that name, and the date of Ezra's arrival in Palestine is thus fixed at 458 B.C. It has, however, been suggested that the Artaxerxes referred to is the second, and that the date of Ezra's arrival should be fixed at 397 B.C.). The authenticity of Ezra's memoirs, now included in the Book which bears his name, is being defended with increasing vigor by Bible students; and the tendency to declare his whole existence mythological is definitely weakening under the pressure of new studies in the Biblical text and more precise information regarding Persian life. Ezra's fame, so far as Judaism is concerned, rests only secondarily on the main incident recorded in his memoirs—his forcible separation of the Judaite from the heathen wives whom many of them had married. Tradition attributes to him the repromulgation of the Pentateuch* as the accepted and binding discipline of Law for all Israel. In this sense, Ezra is held to have completed the work initiated by Moses*, a millenium before him. It seems certain that Ezra was an important factor in the establishment of the synagogue* worship, the custom of reading the Law as part of this service, and the ultimate substitution of the student of the Law for the Prophet as the moral guide of the people. In this sense, undoubtedly, Ezra was the founder of Rabbinic legalism.

W. F. Albright, *From the Stone Age to Christianity* (1940), pp. 248ff.; L. Finkelstein, *The Pharisees, The Sociological Background of their Faith* (1938), pp. 557ff.; R. Kittel, *Geschichte des Volkes Israel* (4th and 5th eds., 1921-22), III, 2, pp. 575ff.; Albert T. Olmstead, *History of Palestine and Syria* (1931), pp. 583ff.; Robert H. Pfeiffer, *Introduction to the Old Testament* (1941), pp. 813 ff.; Hans H. Schaeder, *Esra der Schreiber* (1930). L.F.

Ezra: A historical book of the OT, which is contained in the third division of the Hebrew canon, the "Writings" or Hagiographa*. In Hebrew this book originally formed a single work with the Book of Nehemiah*, and the two books together recount the history of the return of the exiles from Babylonia in 538 B.C. and the subsequent rebuilding of the temple in Jerusalem (Ezra 1-6), and of the work of Ezra (Ezra 7-10; cf. Nehemiah 7:73b-10:39) and Nehemiah (Nehemiah 1-13). The chronology of the two books as they now stand is confused, and there must be displacements in the arrangement of material. The Book of Ezra is unusual in that two sections, 4:8-6:18 and 7:12-26, are in the Aramaic language. It is certain that the author of these books also wrote I, II Chronicles* because of the close similarities in diction, religious viewpoints, and historical methods. Jewish tradition attributes the Book of Ezra to Ezra*; if he was not actually the author, his Memoirs formed one of the author's sources. Another source was certain Aramaic documents, consisting chiefly of official papers of Persian kings. The authenticity of the latter has been widely questioned. Ezra himself has been considered by some modern scholars as a purely imaginary figure (Torrey, Hölscher), but such skepticism is unwarranted. He is an authentic figure in the Persian era, standing for racial purity, promulgation of the Law, and strict ritualism; it is probable, however, that his importance has been exaggerated by tradition. His activity is to be dated in the first half of the fourth century, following Nehemiah, both upon internal evidence of the Biblical record and the evidence of the Elephantine papyri*. See Esdras, Books of; L.

Batten, *The Books of Ezra and Nehemiah* (International Critical Commentary), (1931; C. C. Torrey, *Ezra Studies* (1910). J.P.H.

F

Faber, Jacobus: (c. 1455-c. 1536) French humanist and reformer (Calvinist). His work in Biblical studies was notable, and he produced the French version of the N.T. which underlies all subsequent translations. G.R.C.

faculty psychology: See psychology, schools of.

fad: See culture.

fairy: When one religion triumphs over another the gods of the vanquished faith may be identified with those of the victorious one, or rejected as demons. The Celtic religion evaded both prongs of this fork, and by shrinkage of the old gods made fairies, brownies, or "little people" of them. Thus they are still here, still helpful, although sometimes mischievous, and always shrink from holy water and the sign of the cross. See elf. P.G.M.

faith: Faith is the giving of oneself to be controlled and remade by what commands trust and devotion. What thus commands trust and devotion may be only a belief. On the other hand, it may be an operative reality so insistently present in all experience that we cannot seriously and practically doubt it no matter what logical devices for creating doubt may be invented. Examples of such insistent and inescapable realities are one's own self, other selves and the acquisition of thoughts, feelings and interests through communicative interaction with others. Any alleged instance of these realities may be doubted, but the practical coercions of everyday life make it impossible to doubt seriously that there are such realities.

The giving of oneself to be controlled and remade by a reality most surely known is an act of faith just as genuine as the giving of oneself to something not so surely known. The act of faith often occurs when there is little evidence or none to support it, but that is blind or ignorant faith and is not necessary to faith as such. Faith may be the surest knowledge. Such knowledge by itself alone is not faith but it becomes faith when one acts upon it in the manner of self-giving described above.

When the object of faith is a belief and not an actual reality most surely known by all inquiry, one does not want to be troubled by questions concerning the truth of his belief. In such case one guards it against all inquiries which might demand some revision or discarding of it. This protection of the belief against inquiry is accomplished by holding it to be supernaturally sanctioned. On this account it is alleged to be given by revelation or by indubitable intuition or by mystical experience or in some other way is set beyond the bounds of human inquiry and testing. He who raises a question concerning its truth is treating it as though it were a way of getting knowledge. But for him who treats it as object of faith it is not a way of getting knowledge. It is a way of sustaining his sense of worthfulness in living and he clings to it in faith for that reason.

It is true that some modernists are committed in faith to certain beliefs and at the same time hold these beliefs subject to criticism and every form of intellectual inquiry which is pertinent. But when they do this they weaken faith in two ways. They weaken it as a belief because no faith can be strong under such conditions. They weaken it as commitment to actual reality because they do not give themselves in faith to something most surely known.

If the reality to which one gives himself in faith is physiologically and psychologically inescapable, one does not need to cling to any belief. However vaguely apprehended, one cannot doubt it. So one can criticize and cast out every belief he likes. The reality will not let him go and he knows that it will not, no matter how much he may cultivate his doubts. This something-or-other most important for all human living does not continue to be a mere vague something-or-other. It is this only in the beginning when it originates faith. It becomes more or less clarified into definite forms of knowledge as faith drives continuously to further inquiry into its nature.

Thus neither knowledge nor belief is the source of genuine faith. The knowledge which one gets is a consequence of the faith. The source of faith is in the human body. The body so reacts that one is coerced to be aware that one is sustained and that something-or-other is most important. Beliefs of the mind may distort, suppress, conceal or confuse this apprehension that emerges from the body. They may also clarify and inform this bodily apprehension with true knowledge. But beliefs of the mind cannot do this latter if they are themselves made the objects of faith. They can clarify and inform the faith only when used as means of reaching out after whatever may be most important however vaguely at first it may be sensed. Such a faith magnifies intelligent understanding. It also opens the way to all the supreme fulfilments of life. See reason in religion. H.N.W.

faith, explicit and implicit: See explicit faith; implicit faith.

faith healing: See psychotherapy.

faith, Pauline: See Paul, the Apostle; righteousness, N.T. conception of.

faith, saving: See saving faith.

faker or faqir: (Arabic, poor) A Moslem monk. In general any ascetic holy man who becomes a wandering beggar or miracle-worker. The term *dervish** is synonymous with *fakir* for Moslem monks who usually belonged to a religious order, but now often go about as independent mendicants. P.E.J.

fakih: (Arabian, *faqih,* meaning one learned in the law) A title given in Africa to schoolmasters. P.E.J.

Falashas: A tribe of dark-skinned Jews living in Ethiopia for many centuries. Their origin is unknown, but they claim ancient descent. They call themselves "Beta-Israel" (House of Israel) but the natives call them Falashas, or "exiles", "immigrants".

Although diverging from standard Jewish practice at many points, they hold steadfast by Judaism of Mosaic type, based on an Ethiopic version of the Pentateuch*, but considerably modified by their complete ignorance of Hebrew. They are strict monotheists and lead a highly moral life.

Living completely apart from the natives, they will not allow anyone outside their group into their hut-like homes or their synagogues (*mesgid*). They strictly observe laws of ritual purity and therefore establish themselves near running water.

Their leaders are divided into *menokassie* (Nazarites), *kahens* (priests), and *dabteras* (learned men), who are all non-professionals. H.K.—L.F.

fall of man: Mythical story of Mesopotamian origin, adapted by the Israelites in the O.T. (Gen. iii), describing the temptation and transgression of the first man and woman, and their subsequent expulsion from the garden of Eden. The biblical narrative aims at explaining three aspects of the human lot: universal death, toil for man, travail for woman and her subjection to him. It implies also that human beings have acquired the faculty of discernment by an act of disobedience, but does not teach the doctrine of original sin* (IV Ezra iii, 7-8; Rom. v, 12; etc.). Cf. Gnosticism; golden age; progress.

See N. P. Williams, *The Ideas of the Fall and of Original Sin* (1927); P. Humbert, *Etudes sur le récit du Paradis et de la Chute dans la Genèse* (1940). S.L.T.

False Decretals, The: (commonly the Forged Decretals) A collection of documents of Canon Law* under the name of Isidore Mercator (or Peccator) emanating from Rheims before the middle of the ninth century c. 849-50 (Fournier). The collection is based on earlier collections of Isidore of Seville* and the Dionysia-Hadriana together with the record contained in Cassiodorus*, *Historia Tripartita.* The forgeries occur where decretals issued or presumed to have been issued had been lost, therefore the Pope Damasus writes in ninth century Latin! The underlying scheme is an attempt to deliver the Church from the menace of feudal disorder and violence, hence the author exalts the authority of the humblest priest over the greatest Emperor, giving his excommunication the full authority of the Church; a scheme of ecclesiastical reform is introduced; the authority of the bishop is maintained against the Metropolitans; they provide for an impartial tribunal and consequently for the development of Papal jurisdiction. Their authority was questioned by Hincmar of Rheims* in a letter to Nicholas I (858-867); the question whether Nicholas I* used them or not is still regarded as open; their authority was not effectively challenged until the Renaissance. They are ultimately the basis alike of Gregorianism, Ultramontanism and Laudian Anglicanism. See decretals. F.W.B.

family, the: A group of persons united by common descent or by marriage* and practicing a common economy. The term is generally used to cover a number of different types of groupings. Thus a family may consist of a husband and wife with or without children; one parent with children if the other has deserted, died, or been divorced; brothers and sisters who live together after the deaths of their parents; the unmarried couple with or without children whose relationship constitutes a common-law marriage. Historically and among primitive peoples the family often comprised the larger unit of persons related by common ancestry, but in modern society we picture the typical family as a more or less stable relationship of husband and wife with or without children.

The origin of the family is unknown. There is every reason to believe that it is very old since in every record of early man there is evidence of family life. It is found in every known society both civilized and preliterate. Writings attempting to determine the prehistoric development of the family have been largely speculative and contradictory. Primarily these writers have dealt with the form of the family, especially as to whether the earliest relationship between men and women was promiscuous, or if not promiscuous, whether the first form was that of a patriarchate or a matriarchate**. The family probably arose in response to the universal need in all societies for satisfying certain functions. While the basis for family life is undoubtedly sexual, these needs may be satisfied promiscuously, so this explanation alone cannot be accepted as the all important reason for the continuance of a permanent union. The dependence of the child upon the mother for satisfaction of its organic needs was probably another important factor in the development of a family organization. As the family developed, it undoubtedly took on numerous other functions consistent with its particular economy and cultural contacts.

It has been customary to speak of the historic functions of the family as economic, educational, religious, recreational, protective, and affectional. Of these, only the affectional survives in the modern family except in the most limited degree, the others having been taken over by communal agencies. Thus industry is no longer found in the home; the educational responsibility for the child after six or even earlier has been transferred to the school; recreation has for the most part been commercialized; and the church and Sunday school have largely taken over the religious function. Many writers have taken this loss of the functions of the family as the cause of its increasing instability. In so doing they have lost sight of the increased importance and nature of the affectional function. As modern life has grown more complex, social relations less primary, social distance greater, reactions more stereotyped and conventional, the individual has turned more and more to affectional satisfactions expressed through intimacies and demonstrations of affection, sympathy, sharing of aspirations, common goals, etc., whose locale is the family. The focusing of attention upon this one function, so intimate and emotional in character and thus naturally fraught with possibilities of conflict, has placed such a premium upon its attainment as to cause the success or failure of family life to be measured in these terms alone. Thus as modern life has inevitably made greater demands upon the individual, he in turn has placed greater strain upon the family relationship, in other words upon that continuous process of affectional adjustment and readjustment which marriage entails.

Another function of the family is often neglected, that of personality development. The family may be spoken of as the cradle of personality in that it is the first group which the child enters and it is here that his personality is molded through interaction with family members, the whole constituting a unity of interacting personalities. The family, adaptable institution as it is, has kept abreast of social change. It is upon this adaptability in fact and the shifting emphasis of its functions in terms of the cultural setting that its continued existence depends.

See divorce; infidelity; motherhood; widows, treatment of; woman, religious and ethical status of.

Ray E. Baber, *Marriage and the Family* (1939); Ruth S. Cavan, *The Family* (1942); J. K. Folsom, *The Family and Democratic Society* (1943); Ernest R. Mowrer, *The Family* (1932); Harriet R. Mowrer, "Marriage Conflict" in Becker, Howard, and Hill, Reuben (ed), *Marriage and the Family* (1942); Harriet R. Mowrer, *Personality Adjustment and Domestic Discord* (1935); M. F. Nimkoff, *The Family* (1934); E. B. Reuter and J. R. Runner, *The Family* (1931); Edward Westermarck, *History of Human Marriage* (London, 1921). H.R.M.

fana: The final state of ecstasy as understood by Sufi* mystics. Lammens translates it as "the passing away of human personality" although not, of course the cessation of the individual's life.

Henri Lammens, *Islam, Beliefs and Institutions* (London, 1929). P.G.M.

fanaticism: (Lat., *fanaticus*, divinely inspired, mad, fr. *fanum*, temple) Such excessive and irrational zeal as to impair self-criticism and destroy moral perspective. While arduous support of any cause, especially of reform, may incur thoughtless charges of fanaticism, the word is now properly used only of extreme preoccupation with one narrow system of beliefs with consequent unreasonable and injurious neglect of other ideas and values. L.H.DEW.

fanon: (Gr., *phano*, a cloth) An ornamental shoulder-piece used by the Pope, the present collar-like form of which derives from the Middle Ages. Earlier the term was applied to various other cloths used in worship, such as the priest's maniple, the handkerchief used by the faithful in presenting their bread-offerings, the amice, the subdeacon's shoulder-veil, and even the flaps of a bishop's mitre. C.V.

Far Eastern temples: See temples, Far Eastern.

Farel, G.: (1489-1565) Protestant reformer, born and educated in France; a bold and successful preacher of the reformed faith at Basel, Neuchatel and other Swiss towns; also at Strasbourg and Metz. While at Geneva, he was responsible for the beginning of Calvin's ministry in that city. See Calvin, John; Neuchâtel. G.R.C.

Farrar, Frederic William: (1831-1903) Anglican divine, Canon of Westminster and Dean of Canterbury. Born in India, he studied at Cambridge and was a schoolmaster at Harrow and Marlborough before going to Westminster Abbey. He is known especially for his writings on Biblical times, including works on the early churches, a life of Christ, and a study of the Bible. He was a central churchman, with wide interests. W.N.P.

fashion: See culture.

fasting: The bodily and mental experiences of early man during times of lack of food may account for the practice of fasting as a religious technique. Prolonged hunger gives rise to visions. The fast was used for this purpose by the American Indian in acquiring his private totem,* by shamans in making contact with spirits, by those who consulted the Greek oracles. The suffering involved in fasting made it a fitting way of expressing penitence, seeking forgiveness or making atonement. The fast was practically universal as one phase of the ceremony of mourning. It was widely used as a preparation for participation in such ceremonials as firstfruits, baptism, initiation and communion.** Where the flesh and the desires of the flesh were considered obstacles to the release of the soul from bondage, fasting was an essential of religious discipline. It was also a means of acquiring supernatural power. It gave added efficacy to a rite, and sometimes was combined with other austerities to command or control the gods. The amount of fasting required in the great religions varies widely. Judaism, Christianity and Islam have fixed fast days. Islam adds the annual fast of Ramadan,* which requires abstention from food during the daylight hours for a month. The fast has been most extensively used in India. Zoroastrianism forbad fasting.

A.E.H.

fatalism: Fatalism, differs from fate*, in that the former provides for the inevitableness of events, causes or no causes, while the latter sees events determined within relation of cause and effect. In this sense, Fatalism is more nearly akin to the indeterminism of fortune.* Accordingly, fatalism is spoken of commonly as blind. It is recognized, of course, that there are those who relate fatalism to the consequences of fate and thereby subject it to the nature of circumstances or causes.

Fatalism is a *Weltanschauungen* whose logical issue is pessimism as is illustrated by the cyclical view of history. See kismet. Cf. determinism; predestination.

P.R.H.

fate: (Greek and Roman) Fate is the belief that events constitute a chain of causes* and effects within determinism. It differs from Fortune* in that the latter falls outside of determinism, and from Fatalism* which necessitates unconditionally the event. The conception of Moira is basic to that of fate. The notion of Moira is analogous to real estate allotments whose boundaries must not be transgressed. That is to each individual is assigned a sphere or a becomingness which he is obliged to acknowledge and observe. This applies, likewise, to all living objects including the gods. Phaeton transgressed his proper bounds and paid the consequences. Heraclitus* thought that if the sun over-stepped his bounds, the Errynes (Fates) would bring him back again.

During Homer's time the gods did the work of fate but with Hesiod, three individual characters emerged as spinsters with appropriate names. "Clotho the youngest, spun the thread of life . . . Lachesis the second, twisted it . . . and Atropas the third sister, armed with a huge pair of shears, remorselessly cut short the thread of life." (H. A. Guerber, *Myths of Greece and Rome,* p. 165).

Although recognized by thinkers prior to the time of the Stoics, such as Heraclitus and Plato, belief in fate came into its own with Epictetus and the Stoics** who held that the will of God is inescapable whether one wishes it or not. In the situation it is the task of the individual to chasten himself into the conviction that somehow it will minister to his good.

P.R.H.

Father Divine's Peace Mission: A Negro religious sect led by M. J. Devine, or Divine, formerly in the Harlem section of New York but later removed to Philadelphia. This cult leader achieved great notoriety because of the emotional excesses attending his meetings, alleged healings and other miracles, his unexplained possession of large sums of money, his valuable properties, called "heavens," "kingdoms," and "promised land," and the claims of divinity made by or for him. He was frequently before the courts on various charges but refused to divulge the source of his wealth. "I have money without limit," he said, "because my money comes from God."

It seems that "Father Divine" is really George Baker, who was born of Gullah slave parents near Savannah, Ga. In Georgia he was once sentenced to the chain gang and later tried for insanity because of his messianic claims and disorders incident thereto. He achieved fame in Sayville, Long Island, about 1920 and became a "lion" in Harlem about 1930. He gave elaborate banquets to his followers, who greeted each other with the salutation "Peace," and claimed millions of adherents. Meetings in the "peace missions" were characterized by emotional excesses of various kinds, and his halls were bedecked with signs bearing "Father Divine is God," "Father Divine, God Almighty," "Father Divine is the Messiah," "Father Divine is the King of Kings and Lord of Lords," and similar sentiments. In court he refused either to deny or affirm that he was God. See communistic settlements, religious.

E. T. Clark, *The Small Sects in America* (1937); Hoshar, *God in a Rolls Royce* (1936); Parker, *The Incredible Messiah* (1937). The Peace Mission publishes two papers in New York: *The World Herald* and *The Spoken Word.*

E.T.C.

fatherhood: State of being a male parent. More significantly, the character and social role of such a parent. In nearly all primitive and savage societies known, and in most civilized communities, fathers have been dominant in family life and fatherhood regarded with high respect or even with religious awe. Some anthropologists, as J. J. Bachofen, L. H. Morgan, and R. S. Briffault, believe that the few matriarchates* which now exist are vestiges of the once prevailing form of family. But, as E. Westermarck has argued (though with exaggerated emphasis), there is more evidence against this theory than in favor of it.

Jesus' description of God's relation to human beings as one of Fatherhood emphasizes 1) His creatorship to which men owe their very being, 2) our likeness to Him as persons, 3) His authority (for the father's authority was absolute in both Hebrew and Roman families of Jesus' time), and 4) His love. This description, so important to theology, also bears witness, as do many other evidences, to the kindness and devotion with which the typical Jewish father, in the first century, exercised his patriarchal* power and responsibility. See analogy.

L.H.DeW.

Fathers: See Ante-Nicene Fathers; Apologists; Apostolic Fathers.

Fatiha or Fatihah: (Arabian *fatihah,* that which opens) The short opening *sura* (chapter) of the Koran,* used by Moslems in prayer many times a day, and to whom it means as much as the Lord's Prayer does to Christians. P.E.J.

fatwa or futwa: A Hindu and Moslem legal term, meaning a formal legal opinion given by a canon lawyer. Hence, a judicial sentence. P.E.J.

fauns: (Lat., *faunus,* from *faveo,* to favor, protect) Playful rustic divinities, like the Greek satyrs, deriving their name and characteristics from the old Latin god, Faunus, bestower of fruitfulness and foresight, who was himself identified with Pan of the Greeks; hence his horns and his goat's feet. E.M.N.

Feast of Fools, Feast of Asses: A burlesque of the ritual by the lower clergy (hence sometimes called "Feast of the Subdeacons"), celebrated late in December or at the beginning of January from the 12th century to the opening of the 16th, in France and less commonly in England and other countries. Features of the celebration often included the election of a boy bishop and the entrance of an ass into the church. It was condemned by moralizing preachers such as Gerson and Huss. See New Year's celebrations.

E. K. Chambers, *The Medieval Stage,* 2 vols. (Oxford, 1903). J.T.M.

Feast of Tabernacles: See Tabernacles, Feast of.

feasting: Feasts usually occur at the important transition times in the life of the individual, the turning points of the year, anniversaries of happy occasions in the history of a religion and events in the lives of the gods. In the first class are marriage feasts, the feast to celebrate pregnancy, the feasts at birth and naming. Where circumcision* was practiced, a feast was part of the ceremony. When childhood was outgrown, admission to adult privileges and responsibilities through initiation was celebrated by feasting. At the end was the funeral feast, followed by commemorative feasts at stated times afterwards. The seasonal feasts varied with the peoples. Usually they centered around the food* supply, but some religions included not only the turning of the seasons but also changes of the moon as times for festivals. On many occasions of animal sacrifice* to the gods the flesh made a feast for the people. The feasts which are peculiar to a particular religion usually celebrate events in the lives of its gods, saviors or saints. See death and burial practices; harvest festivals. A.E.H.

feasts and fasts, Jewish: See Jewish religious festivals.

feasts and fasts of the Roman Catholic Church: Feasts are days designated by ecclesiastical authority for giving special honor to God, to Christ in His sacred humanity, to the Virgin Mary, the angels, saints, and holy things. Feasts vary greatly in liturgical significance. Of prime importance because of their influence on Catholic life are the holydays of obligation, that is, days on which the faithful are obliged to assist at Mass* and to abstain from servile works. The days of obligation include all Sundays, and some other feasts the number of which varies in different countries. In the United States six special feasts are observed as days of obligation: three in honor of the Savior (Christmas, the Circumcision, Ascension Thursday), two in honor of the Virgin Mary (the Assumption, August 15, and the Immaculate Conception, December 8), and one in honor of the saints (All Saints', November 1).

Fasts are days of special penance.* The ecclesiastical fast consists essentially in the taking of only one full meal a day, either at noon or in the evening. Meat may be eaten at the full meal unless the day is also one of abstinence. Two very light meals are also allowed, the quantity and quality of which are defined by approved local usage. The times of fast are Lent, the Ember Days, and the vigils of Christmas, Pentecost, the Assumption, and All Saints'. The Ember Days, vigils, and some of the days of Lent are also days of abstinence. See Black Fast, the; festivals and holy days, Christian.

H. A. Ayrinhac, *Administrative Legislation in the New Code of Canon Law* (1930). C.V.

Febronianism: From the pseudonym Febronius used by N. von Hontheim, Auxiliary Bishop of Trier (1701-1790), in *De statu ecclesiae,* 1763; a German Gallicanism, declaring papal primacy limited by General Councils in doctrine, national churches in discipline; basis of anti-papal policy of German Archbishops and Emperor Joseph II. E.R.H.

februa: See s. v. Lupercalia.

Fechner, Gustav Theodor: (1801-1887) As a pantheistic panpsychist he advanced a doctrine of psycho-physical parallelism for which he had some impressive experimental evidence. As founder of psycho-physics or experimental psychology, he held that there is a definite mathematically determined quantitative relation between the mental and the material. Conceiving the universe as an organism imbued with a consciousness of itself, and being the body of God, for him God's perfection does not consist in a static completeness, but in unlimited progress. Plants, animals, planets, stars, and the cosmos as a hierarchy of souls are unified within the soul of God.

Zendavesta (Leipzig, 1851); *"Uber die Seelenfrage* (Leipzig, 1861); *Die drei Motive und Gründe des Glaubens* (Leipzig, 1863); *The Little Book of Life After Death* (1912); E. Dennert, *Fechner als Naturphilosoph und Christ; ein Beitrag zur Kritik des Pantheismus* (Gütersloh, 1902); W. James, *The doctrine of the earth-soul and of beings intermediate between man and God; an account of the philosophy of G. T. Fechner* (1909); C. Lülmann, *Monismus und Christentum by G. Th. Fechner* (Berlin, 1917); F. A. E. Meyer, *Philosophische Metaphysik und christlicher Glaube bei Gustav Theodor Fechner* (Göttingen, 1937). H.H.

federal census of religious bodies: The Seventh Federal Census, taken in 1850, was the first to publish religious statistics. Prior to that time religious groups objected to any federal action on the ground that a census of church membership might lead to governmental control of church members. Indeed, some church organizations did not believe that it was right for anyone to count their flocks, citing the pestilences and death which had come to seventy thousand men because David ill-advisedly had taken the census of the Israelites. Secular objection to a federal census of churches was raised as late as 1850 by the state rights school.

The federal government began cautiously in 1850 with figures on the number of churches, church accommodations, that is seating capacity, and the value of church property. These items were repeated in 1860. In 1870 a distinction was made between church edifices and church organizations. Ten years later elaborate attempts were made to broaden the scope of the religious census. Much material was collected, and partially compiled; but, for reasons which cannot now be determined, the material was not published. No more government figures were published until 1906 when *Religious Bodies* appeared, to be repeated each successive decade. The figures of 1906 included information on the date of establishment of local church organizations, debts, the language in which the services were conducted, and, most important of all, data on the history, polity, missionary and educational work of each denomination. In 1926 urban and rural churches were separately tabulated. In 1850 special marshalls were employed by the government to collect the figures. This method was then abandoned in favor of correspondence.

These religious statistics are not perfect. Yet historians have not fully utilized, and church leaders have not fully realized the significance of the extensive facts collected by the federal government.

The introduction to each special census report contains pertinent historical data. Part one of *Religious Bodies: 1906* (1910) has the best historical summary.

C.S.E.

Federal Council of The Churches of Christ in America: An official federation of the national bodies of the churches, designed "to manifest the essential oneness of the Christian churches of America in Jesus Christ as their divine Lord and Saviour," and organized in 1908 "for the prosecution of work that can be better done in union than in separation." Most of the major Protestant bodies and one of the Eastern Catholic group are constituent members of the Council, having 140,000 local congregations with a combined membership of well over 25,000,000. The Council meets biennially. Between meetings its business is carried on by the Executive Committee, of about one hundred representatives of the constituent bodies.

Among the objects of the Federal Council are "to encourage devotional fellowship and mutual counsel concerning the spiritual life and religious activities of the churches" and "to secure a larger combined influence for the churches of Christ in all matters affecting the moral and social condition of the people, so as to promote the application of the law of Christ in every relation of human life." It is specifically provided in the constitution that "This Federal Council shall have no authority over the constituent bodies adhering to it. . . . It has no authority to draw up a common creed or form of government or of worship, or in any way to limit the full autonomy of the Christian bodies adhering to it."

In addition to the Field Department, which encourages the formation of local and state councils of churches, and promotes the entire cooperative program on the field, the Council works through the Departments of Evangelism, International Justice and Good-will, the Church and Social Service, Race Relations, Research and Education, Relations with Churches Abroad, and National Religious Radio, together with various commissions dealing with specific fields of interest and activity. The General Commission on Army and Navy Chaplains is intimately related to the Federal Council; and the Council is partly or wholly responsible also for the work of the Christian Commission for Camp and Defense Communities, the Commission on Aliens and Prisoners of War, the Committee on the Conscientious Objector, the Committee on Foreign Relief Appeals in the Churches, and the Commission to Study the Bases of a Just and Durable Peace. A monthly magazine is published, called the *Federal Council Bulletin;* and a weekly Information Service furnishes accurate reports on contemporary public issues of interest to the churches. The officers for 1940-1942 are Dean Luther A. Weigle, President; Dr. Albert E. Day, Vice-President; Dr. Samuel McCrea Cavert, General Secretary. Cf. Interchurch World Movement of North America; social work of the churches.

L.A.W.

federal theology: See covenant theology.

federated churches: This expression describes a development in church organization since about 1910 in hundreds of smaller American communities where over-churching has become a problem. Two or more churches of different Protestant denominations combine for worship and work, under one minister, preserving their own organizations, memberships and denominational connections. The churches do not really federate; "associated churches" would be more accurate. Sometimes an additional undenominational church, called "the federated church," springs up alongside the others. Methods of organization and work on this basis vary widely, as do the results. In some cases federation has led to union; in others it has long continued satisfactorily; in others it has been abandoned.

R.H.N.

feet washing: A term which refers to the incident in Jn. 13:1-17. Washing of the feet was an incident always offered to a guest at an ancient feast, and a menial was set apart for this service. Jesus himself performed it for his disciples before the Last Supper. From his example the custom passed into the early church, and is mentioned in 1 Tim. 5:10 as one which fell to the charge of pious women. Religious kings in the Middle Ages (e.g. St. Louis) washed the feet of the poor at stated seasons, and the ritual is still observed by dignitaries in the Catholic church. See Dunkers; holiness churches; Mennonites; River Brethren, washing (ritual, in O.T.). E.F.S.

Feinn Cycle: Legends of the old Irish heroes, Finn mac Cool, Fergus, Ossian and others. Also known as Fenian cycle. P.G.M.

Felix of Urgel: (Spain; d. 818) Bishop. With Elipandus,* the chief theologian of Spanish Adoptionism. His teachings, answered by Alcuin,* were condemned by synods of Ratisbon (792), Frankfort (794), Aix-la-Chapelle (799). Deposed, he was given into custody of Leidrad, bishop of Lyons, dying seemingly penitent and orthodox. Agobard* later discovered tract showing his recantation was superficial. A.C.

Fénelon: (Francois de Salignac de la Mothe) (1651-1715) Archbishop of Cambrai, perceptor of the Duc de Bourgoyne for whose instruction he wrote *Télémaque*, one of the most read French books. Adopted the Quietist* ideas of Mme. Guyon* for which he was condemned at Rome. Author of a treatise *De l'éducation des filles* and other religious works. W.W.C.

fêng shui: See Chinese Terminology.

fenrir or fenrisulf: A wolfish monster, offspring of Loki.* One of the enemies of the gods, who is to swallow Odin* himself at the last day, only to have his jaws torn apart by Odin's son Vidar. He is also fated to swallow the sun. Saemund's *Edda.* P.G.M.

Ferrara-Florence, Council of: When the Council of Basel* (1431) proved intractable, owing to the feud which broke out between the adherents of the conciliar* theory and of papal supremacy, Pope Eugenius IV transferred his faction to Ferrara, where it held sessions from September 1437 to January 1439. The chief subject of discussion, and the main reason why this Council finally won out over the rump Council at Basel, were the negotiations with the Byzantine Emperor John VIII, which promised to result in the reunion of the Eastern and Western churches. However, during the Ferrara sessions, no agreement was reached. It was not until the Council was once more transferred, this time to Florence, that the Western Church scored a victory over the Eastern, insofar that the "Filioque"* clause of the Nicene Creed was admitted by the Easterns, but in the sense that the "Holy Spirit proceedeth from the Father through the Son," not "and the Son." This and other concessions were virtually forced, for the Greeks came primarily to seek military aid against the Turks; consequently, the Council was in a position to dictate its terms. Finally, the negotiations resulted in the "Act of Union" proclaimed on July 6, 1439. This in theory terminated the Great Schism* which had lasted since 1054. Nevertheless, the Byzantines* in large numbers refused to acknowledge the decree, and after the capture of Constantinople (May 29, 1453), it lapsed. In Russia, the decree was never accepted.

K. J. Hefele, *A History of the Christian Councils*, 5 vols. (Edinburgh, 1871-96). M.S.

fertility cult: See Baalism.

festival of orthodoxy, the: See images.

festivals, harvest: See harvest festivals.

festivals and holy days, Christian: On the theory that every day ought to be a feast day for Christians, the Primitive Church recognized no festivals. Need for times of common devotion and the desirability of giving new significance to days and seasons long associated with Jewish or pagan tradition finally overcame the opposition to such observance and led to the establishment of special Christian solemnities. This movement, however, was of such slow growth that Easter and Pentecost** constituted, with Sunday,* the only universal festivals of the Church until the addition of Christmas and Epiphany** in the fourth century. After the triumph of Christianity, when these days had gained in sanctity and importance through legislation prescribing their observance, festivals increased more rapidly. Feasts in commemoration of the Virgin, the Apostles, and such events as the Circumcision, the Ascension,** and the Invention of the Cross were introduced from the fifth to the ninth centuries. Wider celebration of local festivals honoring martyrs, confessors, and lesser saints* followed. By the time of the issuance of Gratian's* *Decretum* (ca. 1150?) no fewer than thirty-six holy days, besides Sundays, were tabulated by the Church for general observance. Further expansion of the ecclesiastical calendar the popes sought to control by reserving to themselves the right of canonization, and urging that the episcopal power to institute new festivals be exercised only in favor of saints recognized by the Apostolic See. Still the list of feast days grew substantially from the middle of the twelfth century to the Reformation. Since the Church stipulated that all compulsory holy days be observed with attendance at mass and abstinence from unnecessary servile work, many communities were bidden to keep virtually two Sundays in the week.

To practical reformers the celebration of holy days in such numbers seemed ill-suited to a people who lived by manual labor. As early as 1274 Humbert de Romans had therefore suggested to the Council of Lyons* that permission to work after mass be granted on all but the greater holy days. Although frequent complaints about the misuse of holiday leisure lent weight to this proposal, it met with little approval. The argument was gradually strengthened, however, by the feeling of men like Wyclif* that multiplication lessened the value of these days and fostered indifference to them. Such a point of view gained ground slowly until the opening decades of the fifteenth century, when the movement acquired impetus through the advocacy of Jean Gerson,

Pierre d'Ailly,** Francesco Zabarella, and Nicolas de Clémanges.* The efforts of these reformers are reflected in a recommendation to the Council of Constance* for the abrogation of lesser feast days. Inasmuch as no action was taken here, or at the Council of Basel,* the matter did not become an issue again until Luther* made his appeal to the Nobility of the German Nation (1520). As a practical measure he then proposed the abolition of all holy days except Sunday, although New Year's, Ascension Day, and Pentecost were included in a later memorandum (1528). If additional festivals were observed, he suggested the transference of their celebration to Sunday. Other reform churches followed a similar, or even more rigorous, policy.

After severance of its ties with Rome, the English Church retained in its calendar few major holidays with special services, but kept a larger number of minor ones, without provision for their observance. In Catholic countries a comparable step was not taken until 1642, when, under Urban VIII, holy days of obligation were reduced to thirty-six, in addition to Sunday. In subsequent years the list of feasts for the universal church has been further curtailed, and certain countries have been made exempt from celebrating all of these. In the United States, for example, only the Feasts of New Year's, the Ascension, the Assumption of the Virgin, All Saints', the Immaculate Conception, and Christmas require observance. Since the middle of the last century, however, Protestant churches have shown a tendency to appoint new festivals such at Missionary Day, Children's Day, and the Feast of the Dead, and to celebrate with services national memorial days like Thanksgiving and Armistice Day. See church year; church year cycle; feasts and fasts of the Roman Catholic Church; New Year's celebrations; wake.

Nicolas de Clémanges, "De novis celebritatibus non instituendis", *Opera omnia,* edited by J. M. Lydius (1613); L. M. Duchesne, *Les origines du culte chrétien* (1898), 2nd ed.; Walker Gwynne, *The Christian Year* (1915); K. A. H. Kellner, *Heortology* (trans. from the German, 1908); E. C. Rodgers, *Discussion of Holidays in the Later Middle Ages* (1940); Hutton Webster, *Rest Days* (1916).

E.C.R.

festivals, Jewish religious: See Jewish religious festivals.

fetishism: The use of a material object, which is the temporary or permanent abode of a soul or spirit as a means of acquiring values. The term, fetish, has largely lost its usefulness in the religious sciences because of the variety of meanings which have crept into it since the close of the 18th century. August Comte* extended its meaning to include nature worship, but it is now generally agreed that nature powers are not fetishes. The term has been used as practically synonymous with idol and amulet. As distinct from a fetish an idol is a material symbol or representation of a god. An amulet is a material object effective through its own mysterious potency and not because of the power of an indwelling spirit. Like the amulet, a fetish may be any material thing. It is selected because of its origin, as the tooth or claw of an animal, or a human skull; because of its unusual character, or because of some experience of the possessor with it. A priest or shaman may persuade a spirit to take up its abode in the object. The fetish may be specialized to provide one specific value: more often it has a general usefulness in giving protection, preventing or healing disease, assuring success, fulfilling the desire for children or for more material things. If it fails it is discarded. When a fetish belongs to a village or a tribe and acquires a social cult, the embodied spirit is close to the status of a god. See charms and amulets; idols and images; magic; spirits.

A.E.H.

feudalism: The state of society in Europe from the ninth to the fifteenth century, in which the decisive political power rested with a landed aristocracy (barons) and among these a measure of security was attained by an intricate series of contracts of suzerainty and vassalage. As the possessor of property the medieval church became deeply entangled in the feudal nexus (See: eigenkirche; advowson; patronage.) The theological and ecclesiastical thought of the period in some degree reflects the feudal social pattern and its presuppositions. Hildebrand's claims of papal authority, and the papal policy of securing oaths of fealty from secular rulers, accord with the feudal conception of lordship. But papal claims went beyond the bounds of contract and mounted to absolutism. Anselm's doctrine of atonement seems to assume a concept of God as resembling a feudal suzerain, offense against whom has the degree of gravity which corresponds to his dignity or rank. Feudal notions of contract lie behind the typical seventeenth century political doctrines, and may have affected the rise of the "covenant theology" in the Reformed Church.

J. Calmette, *La société feodale,* 2nd ed. (1927); O. Gierke, *Political Theories of the Middle Ages,* (transl. F. W. Maitland, 1900).

J.T.M.

Feuerbach, Ludwig Andreas: (1804-1872) Belongs to the so-called "left wing" of the old Hegelian school. He taught that religion is the mirror of man's own nature and ideals only, that God and the gods are nothing but products of a merely human imagination. He criticized severely Hegel's* speculative metaphysic for having completely oppressed the element of sensation, and he finally propagated sensualism and materialism. Cf. Ullmann, Karl.

Grundsätze der Philosophie der Zukunft (1843); *Wesen des Christentums* (1841); *Wesen der Religion* (1845); K. Grün, *Ludwig Feuerbach* (Leipzig, 1874); K. Löwith, *Von Hegel bis Nietzsche* (1941).

R.K.

Fichte, Immanuel Hermann: (1797-1879) Son of J. G. Fichte,* Immanuel H. Fichte, was in succession professor of philosophy at the universities of Bonn and Tübingen. He demanded a return of philosophy to the principle of personality. God must no longer be conceived as the universal but as the personal. In his ethical theism he strongly emphasized the social question. He was the editor of the *Zeitschrift für Philosophie und Speculative Theologie.*

Die Idee der Persönlichkeit und der individuellen Fortdauer. 2 ed. (Leipzig, 1855); *Speculative Theologie* (Heidelberg, 1846-47); *System der Ethik* (Leipzig, 1850-53); *Die Seelenfortdauer und die Weltstellung des Menschen, eine anthropologische Untersuchung und ein Beitrag zur Religionsphilosophie, wie zu einer Philosophie der Geschichte* (Leipzig, 1867); *Die theistische Weltansicht und ihre Berechtigung* (Leipzig, 1873). H.H.

Fichte, Johann Gottlieb: (1762-1814) Holding professorships at the University of Jena and at the newly established University of Berlin, he worked for the restoration of the German nation. No philosopher has ever made a patriotic appeal upon a higher moral plane.

Intent upon upholding the reality of religious and spiritual aspects of human life, Fichte asserts the independence, inwardness and validity of spiritual life. All religious symbols being merely makeshifts are nevertheless valuable in proportion as they make clear and living the thought of an ethical world order. In the consciousness of our empirical ego resides the more comprehensive infinite principle, the pure ego, the higher moral world order. Not being finished and in continuous development, the realization of the moral world order is the true goal of man. Fichte's religion in his earlier works, consisting in the belief in a moral world order, is a religion of cheerful right-doing. In his later works he stressed the life that stirs and wells up within the individual. In curious contrast to the earlier stress he laid on individuality, he now contends that personality is only a means, a tool to work for the highest good. Being but of a vanishing importance, the individual annuls himself, not by mystical brooding, but in active service. The vocation of individuals and nations is union with God in perfect love. The individual can gain a consciousness of this union in the present life. Both Rudolf Eucken* and Hugo Münsterberg, the late technical pilosophers, owed much to Fichte.

Fichte's Popular Works, tr. by W. Smith (London, 1889); L. Albers, *Der Gottesbegriff bei Fichte* (Breslau, 1915); Fr. Gogarten, *Fichte als religöser Denker* (Jena, 1914); E. Hirsch, *Christentum und Geschichte in Fichtes Philosophie* (Tübingen, 1920); *Fichtes Religionsphilosophie im Rahmen der philosophischen Gesamtentwicklung Fichtes* (Göttingen, 1914); J. v. Hofe, *J. G. Fichtes religöse Mystik nach ihren Ursprüngen untersucht* (Bern, 1904); J. A. Leighton, *Typical modern conceptions of God; or, The absolute of German romantic idealism and of English evolutionary agnosticism, with a constructive essay* (1901); Fr. Zimmer, *Johann Gottlieb Fichtes Religionsphilosophie nach den Grundzügen ihrer Entwicklung dargestellt* (Berlin, 1878). H.H.

Ficino, Marsilio: (1433-1499) Central figure in Renaissance Florentine Academy. As a promising and winsome young scholar he became a member of the household of Cosimo de' Medici, who chose him to head the Platonic cult inspired by Gemisthus Pletho* a few years earlier. Translated Plato, Plotinus and Dionysius the Areopagite into Latin, and sought to make Platonism an introduction for cultured minds to Christian faith.

Marsilii Ficini Opera (Basel, 1576). W.E.G.

fideism: Fideism has two distinct meanings in French religious thought. 1) In Catholic thought, it refers to the teaching of the Abbé Bautain* that "faith precedes reason" in the knowledge of God, and "reason alone" is metaphysically incompetent. Bautain was required to sign a formula declaring that "Reasoning can prove with certitude the existence of God and the infinity of His perfections." 2) In Protestant thought, it refers to the teachings of Ménegoz* that man is saved "by faith, independently of beliefs." Both types of fideism show the influence of Kant's* critical philosophy.

On Fideism in the Catholic sense, see bibliography in the *Catholic Encyclopaedia,* art. "Fideism"; W. M. Horton, doctoral dissertation *The Philosophy of the Abbé Bautin.* On the "Symbolo-Fideism" of Sabatier and Ménégoz see the article "Symbolo-Fideism" in *H. E. R. E.*; W. M. Horton, "The Theology of Eugène Ménégoz", *Journal of Religion* (March, 1926). W.M.H.

Fifth Monarchy Men: A radical politico-religious group in England in the 1650's. In its opinion the unsettled conditions following the Civil War and the execution of Charles I indicated that the time was ripe for establishing the Fifth Monarchy foretold in Biblical prophesy. Its schemes failed, but as late as 1662 it was a threat to political stability.

Louise F. Brown, *The Political Activities of the Baptists and Fifth Monarchy Men in England during the Interregnum* (1912). E.W.K.

figurine: A small carved or molded figure of a human being, animal, or bird. G.E.W.

Filelfo, Francesco: (1398-1481) Most famous of migrant Renaissance scholars, by turns at Padua (where he was professor at 18), Naples, Venice, Constantinople, Florence, Milan. A racketeer of humanism who successfully employed his powers of satire for blackmail and distributed panegyrics for profit. But his comprehensive knowledge of Greek literature was probably unexcelled in his time.

J. A. Symonds: *Revival of Learning* (1877), pp. 268-288. W.E.G.

filioque: A Western addition to the Creed, defining the procession* of the Holy Spirit as "from the Father *and the Son,*" partly as an emphasis on the renunciation of Arianism* (e.g. by the Goths). The doctrine was defined in the East (C. Nicaea, 787) as "from the Father *through* the Son;" in the West (C. Frankfort 794) the "Filioque clause" was adopted under the influence of Charles the Great. It became one of the main causes of separation between the Eastern and Western Churches. See creeds of Christendom; interpolation; Trinity. See also Constantinople, Councils of; Ferrara-Florence, Council of. F.W.B.

final cause: See cause; finalism; teleology.

finalism: (Lat., *finis,* end) The belief that the universe is striving for ends, or for one supreme end. Bergson* thinks of finalism as restricted to preconceived and fixed ends, rather than including developing or creative ends; most philosophers and theologians use the term in the more inclusive sense. Syn., teleology.* E.S.B.

final (or last) judgment: The assize to be presided over by God or Christ, at which time all men, living and dead, will be judged. Well before the beginning of the Christian era this belief is found in Judaism, although it is not improbable than the basic notion of one final judgment at the end of the age (instead of periodic judgments at times of historic crisis) and of all men (not Israel's enemies only) is Persian, not Jewish in origin. This view, with many shades and modifications, is prominent in the apocalyptic writings* and was eagerly taken over and developed by Christians who asserted that their crucified Christ would be the presiding judge. The final separation of good and bad is the theme of two of the gospel parables—Wheat and Tares, Dragnet. The canonical book of Revelation* (19:11-21:8) provides the classical (if garish) picture of the scene as adopted and adapted by Christians. It has been a favorite theme for artists and preachers alike and is probably still accepted by many Christians today. See also apocalypticism (with appended bibliographies); eschatology; millenarianism. M.S.E.

final perseverance: A doctrine, characteristic of Calvinism,* that regenerated souls, in spite of their sins, would continue, not through their own merit or in their own strength, but through the grace* of God, as children of His household, until the end. The doctrine is based mainly on such Scripture passages as 2 Tim. I. 12. See five points of Calvinism; perseverance of the saints. A.K.R.

fine arts: Such human activity as converts feeling into forms possessing a high degree of intrinsic value. The class normally includes music, poetry, painting, sculpture, architecture; also with more restriction, the dance, theatre, and various forms of literature other than poetry. The fine arts are distinguished by emphasis rather than by a sharp line from the practical, minor, or industrial arts, such as agriculture, pottery-making, or medicine, which latter alter man or his environment for the convenience of common life. The distinguishing marks of the fine or beautiful arts have been variously named. The most often given is: the tendency to produce pleasure or delight in the fit audience; but the sublimation of passion or skill into contemplation, the expression of emotion, the achievement of emotive language, and perfection of workmanship have also been given. For bibliography, see Aesthetics, the delimitation of the fine arts being normally considered one problem in any general treatise in the field. K.E.G.

finite: See infinite.

finite God: A God* whose power is limited by realities which he did not create. These realities may be external to God (dualism) or may be internal to him (personalism). Antonyms to finite: absolute, absolutely omnipotent, infinite in power. A God whose will is limited by the free acts of persons whom he has created is not finite in the sense defined. Believers in a finite God have usually held that God is infinite in goodness and in knowledge (at least, that he knows all that is knowable), and that his power is adequate for man's needs. The belief has usually arisen from the problem of evil.*

All primitive Gods were finite. Polytheistic deities were limited by each other as well as by the primeval chaos.* Zoroastrianism,* with its conflict between Ahura Mazda and Ahriman, is the source of one type of finitism. Plato (see Platonism) was the first to develop a philosophic theory of God as finite; his Artisan God confronted a rational Pattern and an Irrational Receptacle (see the *Timaeus*) which were external conditions of God's activity. Epicurus (341-270) forced the dilemma that God is either able or unable, willing or unwilling, to do away with evils. The gods of Epicurus were finite and neutral toward man, neither omnipotent nor benevolent. Marcion,* the Gnostic, represented the Heavenly Father as perfectly good, but limited by evil matter ruled by the devil, and by the cruel Creator God of the OT. Mani* (215-276), an eclectic, developed Zoroastrian finitism into Manichaean theories; Mani, in turn, influenced Pierre Bayle (1647-1706). Meanwhile mystics, like J. Boehme (1575-1624), recognized a real struggle within God. The Philo of Hume's* *Dialogues Concerning Natural Religion* (1779) discussed, not too seriously, the idea of a finite deity. Kant* in the *Critique of Pure Reason* (1781) admits that the teleological argument proves "at most" a limited world-architect, but does not carry the idea further. The Hegelian dialectic (see Hegelianism), although leading to an Absolute, points to antitheses, negativities, conflicts within God. Schelling* spoke of *die göttliche Unvernunft* and *der göttliche Unwille* (that in God which is not reason or will).

The rise of naturalism in the 19th cent. led Mill in his posthumous *Three Essays on Religion* (1874) to declare for a finite God who "was obliged to adapt himself to conditions independent of his will." In 1891, F. C. S. Schiller stated that a finite God "may be proved," and in 1907 William James's *Pragmatism* advocated a God who is *primus inter pares.* J. M. E. McTaggart in *Some Dogmas of Religion* (1906) and *The Nature of Existence* (1927) held that a finite God is preferable to an infinite one; but he denies any Creator God, on the ground that creation presupposes the reality of time, which he rejects. H. Rashdall, a personalist, from 1910 on favored a finite God; L. P. Jacks takes a similar view. In 1917 H. G. Wells popularized the idea of a finite God in *God the Invisible King,* a curious and fantastic notion of a youthful God, recently born, but nobly developing. H. Bergson in *Two Sources of Morality and Religion* (Eng. tr., 1935), on empirical grounds, denied that God is the creator of suffering and drew the inference that he is not omnipotent.

Recent American philosophy and theology have witnessed a marked increase of belief in the finiteness of God. J. E. Boodin has been advocating it since 1916. A. N. Whitehead's modern Platonism in *Process and Reality* (1929) has exercised a strong influence in favor of a finite God. H. N. Wieman has developed an impersonal naturalistic finitism, while C. Hartshorne has moved toward a panpsychistic theism (a finite-infinite God), both inspired by Whitehead. Meanwhile a finite God has been advocated independently by H. B. Alexander (1929), W. P. Montague in *Belief Unbound* (1930), E. S. Brightman (1930 on), especially in *A Philosophy of Religion* (1940), by W. T. Stace in *The Nature of the World* (1940), and by D. H. Parker in *Experience and Substance* (1941).

The chief sources of modern belief in a finite God have been awareness of the suffering and waste of the struggles for survival (prehuman as well as human), a keen sense of the problem of suffering on account of wars and economic depressions, the development of modern physics (quanta, indeterminacy), heightened religious sensitivity to the goodness of God, and increased confidence in empirical as distinguished from *a priori* methods.

Among contemporaries who accept a finite God differences center about one problem: Is the Given (that which limits God's power) something external to God or something within his own eternal experience? Many naturalists (for whom the problem of the will of God does not exist), realists, and dualists (whether Platonists or creationists) find the Given external to God; for example, P. E. More, H. N. Wieman, W. K. Wright, R. Demos, G. Harkness, and many others. Among those who find the Given (or some limitation) within God are E. S. Brightman (reason and brute facts like sensation and suffering constitute a rational and a nonrational Given within the unity of the divine personality), N. Berdyaev, P. Tillich, R. L. Calhoun ("rigidities" within God), John Bennett, C. Hartshorne (*Vision of God*, 1941), and P. A. Bertocci.

The idea appears in the poetry of Rainer Maria Rilke, as well as in the more popular verse of Studdert-Kennedy and Edwin Markham, and in the dramatic form of *The Green Pastures*.

See evil; infinite; value. Cf. Renouvier.

In addition to the bibliography cited in the article, see: V. Ferm, *First Chapters in Religious Philosophy* (1937), and, for the best critique of the idea of a finite God, A. C. Knudson, *The Doctrine of Redemption* (1933); R. B. Baker, *The Concept of a Limited God* (1934), is informing but not objective. Methodologically illuminating is P. A. Bertocci, *The Empirical Argument for God in Late British Thought* (1938). E.S.B.

Finney, Charles Grandison: (1792-1875) American evangelist and theologian, noted for his adoption of dramatic revival methods, such as the "anxious bench." These methods logically expressed his faith in the capacity of man's will to respond to God's just moral demands when clearly and decisively confronted with these demands. See Oberlin theology. W.M.H.

Finnian: (Findian and various spellings) of Clonard (d. ca. 550). Irish monastic founder, called "Tutor of the Saints of Ireland." Finnian of Moville was a younger contemporary: the *Penitential of Finnian* has been ascribed to the latter, but is more probably the work of the Clonard saint.

J. F. Kenney, *Sources for the Early History of Ireland. I. Ecclesiastical* (1929). J.T.M.

Fioretti: (Ital., "Little Flowers"; full title, *Fioretti di S. Francesco d'Assisi*) A collection of popular legends concerning St. Francis* and his early companions, which exemplify the Saint's childlike faith and his sense of the supernatural. The collection consists of fifty-three chapters, written about 1328, and four appendices, added later. There are several English translations. C.V.

fiqh: The authoritative theology and law of Islam. This canon law was developed by four orthodox schools: 1) the Hanbolite of Arabia, 2) the Hanifite of central Asia, 3) the Malikite of upper Egypt and north Africa, 4) the Shafiite of lower Egypt, India, Malay and Syria. P.E.J.

Fire Baptized Holiness Church of God of the Americas: A Negro pentecostal sect, found mainly in South Carolina but having congregations in several other states. It was organized by W. E. Fuller in 1898 at Anderson, S. C. The sect holds the customary doctrines of the pentecostal groups, stressing speaking in unknown tongues, feet washing, and divine healings. In its statement of doctrine to the U. S. Census it claims to uphold "the premillennial second coming of Christ" but opposes "false and unscriptural adventism." It has 59 churches and 2,000 members. See pentecostal sects. E.T.C.

fire gods: Agni and Atar: Agni* divinized fire in the Vedas* and in later Hinduism,* was the son of the earth, the bond between superhuman powers, the mediator between gods and men, the protector and purifier. In Zoroastrianism,* Atar,* the sacred fire, was not as fully personified as Agni, but as son of Ahura Mazda* he fought against the powers of evil, particularly the dragon Azhi. R.H.P.

firmament: (Lat., *firmamentum*, from *firmare*—to strengthen) The arch or hollow vault of the heavens, in ancient astronomy regarded as a fixed sphere which contained the stars. Sometimes used for heaven, the abode of God. J.E.N.

first cause: Metaphysicians generally feel the necessity of assuming a First cause, either as axiom or postulate. The evolutionary type of thought process, for example, has strengthened the tendency. It is claimed by some that the nature of thought requires a *pou sto*, a place to stand, as a condition of its activity. Also, that in selecting the character of a First cause, sufficient characteristics and qualities should be ascribed to it to provide adequate implementation of inference that may be desired later at any level of interpretation. That is to say that the potentiality of First cause should be adequate for the demands of actuality. See cause. P.R.H.

First Day Sabbath: See Sunday.

first fruits: The first fruits ceremonies probably originated as a tribal method of protecting the food* supply until it was mature and ready for general use. The firstfruits were usually offered to the gods most concerned with the production of the crops or to the priests of the gods. When ancestors were credited with control over the food supply they received the firstfruits. Where fish or animals were the main source of food, the first of the catch and the firstlings of the flock were ceremonially treated as firstfruits. The practice spread sometimes to include the human first born. Crops were usually released for use by a ceremonial eating by king or priest or chief or by a general feast. The shrines of Greece and the priests of Israel drew their revenues from the firstfruits. See harvest festivals; human sacrifice; tabu. A.E.H.

fish as symbol: The Greek word was *Ichthus* which is composed of the first letters of the words, *Jesous Christos Theou Huios Soter,* "Jesus Christ, God's Son, Savior." But this was probably a later explanation, and the origin is to be sought in other connections. The fish lives in water, as the Christian lives by his baptism. The fish in the story of the miraculous feeding made it a symbol of the Christ on whom they fed. There were many fish gods in antiquity. The Christian use of the acrostic may be traced to the second century. C.T.C.

Fiske, John: (1842-1901) An American historian noted also for his writings attempting to show that evolutionary theory is compatible with religious faith. He was graduated at Harvard College 1863 and at Harvard Law School 1865. Lecturer on Philosophy and History and thereafter assistant librarian at Harvard. Lectured at Washington University (St. Louis), University College London, and at the Royal Institution. According to Fiske, the events of the evolutionary process are the results of the immanent causality of the living God, "the infinite and eternal Power that is manifested in every pulsation of the universe." Since the evolutionary process has progressively tended toward the highest ethical and spiritual qualities of man, we recognize the essential kinship of the human soul with God and we affirm as a reasonable faith the "quasi-personal" and moral character of God the immanently operating Cause. The revelation of such immanent teleology* involving the "essential kinship" of the human soul with the "Quasi-Human God" suggests moreover that man is destined for personal immortality.* See immanence.

Among Fiske's main works are the following: *Outlines of Cosmic Philosophy* (1874); *The Unseen World* (1876); *Darwinism and other Essays* (1879); *The Destiny of Man* (1884); *The Idea of God* (1885); *Through Nature to God* (1899); *Life Everlasting* (1901). H.W.J.

Fitch, Eleazer Thompson: (1791-1871) Congregational clergyman and Yale professor, graduated from Yale College in 1810 and entered Andover Theological Seminary in 1812. Graduated after the regular three year course, he remained as assistant to the Professor of Homiletics, meanwhile helping Jeremiah Evarts to edit the *Panoplist,* the periodical established by the Orthodox to oppose the Boston liberals. In July, 1817, Fitch was called to Yale to succeed Timothy Dwight* as the Livingston Professor of Divinity in the College. In this position his chief duty was to supply the College pulpit, and to instruct undergraduates in Natural Theology and the Evidences of Christianity. Long concerned for the advanced training of theological students at Yale, he gave freely of his time and money and was an important factor in the foundation of the Divinity School in 1822. In that school he served as Acting Professor of Sacred Literature (1822-1824), and as Lecturer in Homiletics for almost forty years (1824-1861).

It was Fitch and his colleagues at Yale who shaped the New Haven theology*. His influence in the movement was considerable, and has probably been underestimated because he was outshown by his more colorful companions. His *Two Discourses on the Nature of Sin* (1826), were the outstanding pronouncement of the Yale group on that subject, and Taylor's* *Concio ad Clerum* of September, 1828, which has received the center of attention because it precipitated the controversy with the conservatives, has rightfully been called a re-statement of Fitch's position.

Franklin B. Dexter, *Biographical Sketches of the Graduates of Yale College,* VI (1912), 316-321; S. E. Mead, *Nathaniel William Taylor* (1942). S.E.M.

five-mile-act: The Act of Uniformity of 1662 led to the dismissal of about two thousand of the clergy from the Church of England. They and numerous schoolmasters were leaders of the Dissenters.* Restrictions were added: In 1664 the Conventicle* Act and in 1665 the Five Mile Act by which Non-Anglican ministers and schoolmasters were forbidden to come within five miles of a corporate borough or city. This intolerance was a considerable factor in giving a sort of united front to Dissenters till the Toleration Act* (1689). Q.B.

five points of Arminianism: In 1610, the Arminians addressed to the government of Holland a protest in five articles (The Remonstrance) against the five points of Calvinism*. Prepared by Uytenbogaert and signed by forty-five ministers (The Remonstrants*), the Remonstrance emphasized the following:

1) Election and condemnation, conditioned upon the faith or unbelief of men.

2) Atonement for all but only believers enjoy its benefits.

3) Man, unaided by the Holy Spirit, unable to come to God.

4) Grace not irresistible.

5) Doctrine of the perseverance of the converted open to inquiry. See Arminian theology; Dort, Synod of. W.E.R.

five points of Calvinism: The five points emphasized by the Calvinists in their discussions with Arminius came to be known as the Five Points of Calvinism. They are:

1) Unconditional election.
2) Atonement limited to the elect.
3) Depravity, total as to ability and merit.
4) Irresistible grace.
5) Perseverance** of the saints. See Arminian theology; Calvinism; Dort, Synod of; Remonstrants, the. W.E.R.

flabellum: (Lat., a fan) A fan used in Catholic worship. Originally designed for the practical purpose of warding of insects from the offerings at the Eucharistic Sacrifice, it was used in the East as early as the fifth century. It soon lost its primitive purpose, and was transformed into a metallic ornament, decorated usually with six-winged cherubim.* Never of very wide use in the West, it was principally a processional ornament. In solemn papal functions of a non-liturgical character, large, ostrich-feather fans accompany the papal entry. C.V.

Flacius, Matthias: (1520-1575) Lutheran Reformer, much involved in the religious controversies of his day. Disagreement with other reformers led to recurrent expulsion, but in spite of adverse conditions his extensive literary output was significant in exposing bad history and bad exegesis. G.R.C.

Flagellants: (Lat., *flagellum,* a scourge) Religious enthusiasts giving rise, sporadically, throughout thirteenth-century Europe in particular, to self-administered floggings, *en masse,* as penance for sin. Their processions, relatively moderate and often spiritually effective at first, took on chiliastic abandon and anti-hierarchical extremes that elicited mounting ecclesiastical disapproval and persecution. R.C.P.

Fletcher, John William: (1729-1785) Vicar of Madeley, Yorkshire, public supporter of the Wesleyan Revival, defender of Arminianism,* called by John Wesley the holiest man he had ever met, or expected to meet, "this side eternity." F.G.E.

Fliedner, Theodor: (1800-1864) He was the founder of the feminine diaconate. He first started a prison society which aimed to take care of dismissed inmates of penitentiaries. This became the seed for the origin of Fliedner's Kaiserswerth institution. He founded the house of the deaconnesses* in 1836. The institutions of Kaiserswerth embraced practically all the branches of feminine evangelical welfare.

G. Fliedner, *Theodor Fliedner,* 3 vols. (Kaiserswerth, 1892); Th. Schäfer, *Die weibliche Diakonie in ihrem ganzen Umfang,* 3 ed. vol. I (Potsdam, 1911), 2 ed. vols. II and III (Potsdam, 1892). H.H.

flood: See deluge.

Florence, Council of: See Basel, Council of; Ferrara—Florence, Council of.

Florilegia: Collections of choice passages from some author or literature. These florilegia or anthologies (for the Latin word is an exact translation of the Greek) were frequently made in early Christian times, when books in their completeness were difficult to procure. The best known example is the collection of extracts from Origen* by Basil and Gregory Nazianzen.

J. A. Robinson, *Philocalia* (1893). E.F.S.

Flournoy, Théodore: (1854-1920) Professor of experimental psychology at the university of Geneva; a pioneer in religious psychology. Many of his articles in this field appeared in the *Archives de Psychologie* between 1901 and 1915, which he founded with E. Claparède.

Etudes sur un cas de somnambulisme avec glossolalie (Geneve, 1900); *La philosophie de William James* (Sainte-Blaise, 1911); *Le génie religieux* (Sainte-Blaise, 1911); *Métaphysique et psychologie,* 2 ed. (Geneve, 1919). H.H.

Flowers Lectureship, the John McTyeire: Established in 1921 with a capital sum of $5,000. by Mr. B. N. Duke at Duke University, Durham, N. C. Primarily intended for the promotion of lectures on Far Eastern subjects although not limited to this field. The lectures are given at varying intervals. Among the lecturers: Dr. Paul S. Reinsch; Dr. W. W. Keen; Prof. J. T. Shotwell. (Data furnished by the office of the Dean of the Divinity School.) V.F.

Flügel, Otto: (1842-1921) As pastor in Wansleben, Germany, he was one of the most active of Herbartians* of his day. God is finite and differs in degrees from every individual. He is not strictly omnipotent as He is outside the world and as He depends upon the externally given reals. He is not eternal as the content of his spirit is due to His relation to the world. Only the moral attributes are unconditionally expressing Him. Christian revelation fills out the gaps of knowledge.

Der Materialismus vom Standpunkt der atomistisch-mechanischen Naturforschung beleuchtet (Leipzig, 1865); *Das Wunder und die Erkennbarkeit Gottes* (Leipzig, 1869); *Die Speculative Theologie der Gegenwart kritisch beleuchtet* (Cöthen, 1881); *Zur Philosophie des Christenthums* (Langensalza, 1900). H.H.

folklore: Folklore is the science of tradition. It deals with superstitions, practices, tales and songs that are the property of the unlearned and are transmitted by word of mouth as contrasted with manuscripts or printed books. The study of folklore, like anthropology and archaeology**, has as its purpose the reconstruction of the mental and spiritual history of mankind. It is based on the fact that in civilized as well as in savage communities there exist customs, beliefs, and memories that are relics of an ancient and often unrecorded past. It recognizes the truth that no superstition is completely without foundation and that, however, unscientific or otherwise insufficient may be the data on which superstitions are based, the superstitions themselves may be utilized in such a way as to cultivate greater tolerance and mutual understanding among the various races and communities of the earth and to minimize the conflict between classes and masses.

The data of folklore are found not only in customs current among the uneducated but also in fairy tales, ballads, and much else that has made its way into written history and into sophisticated literature. When history asserts that the site of a certain city was indicated by the movements of a supernaturally endowed animal, or when a literary work such as *Hamlet* has as a hero a noble youth disinherited by a wicked kinsman who has murdered his father and married his mother, we are dealing with themes that have their roots deep in the lore of the folk. Folklore is also connected with the history of religion in that it includes numerous saints' legends,* and many myths and practices belonging to the "elder faiths" of mankind but no longer accepted by the great organized religions. The Bible contains many allusions to folk customs and rituals, such as the distinction between clean and unclean. To the domain of folklore also belong many tales and traditions having to do with magic* and witchcraft*. Numerous popular superstitions are included in folk medicine and in peasant lore regarding crops, the seasons, and the weather. Folk tradition also explains most of the popular cures for warts, omens drawn from the howling of dogs and from black cats, and the belief that the planting of certain crops should be regulated by the changes in the moon. Folklore also embraces various types of animal stories, beliefs regarding lucky and unlucky numbers, popular proverbs, rhymes and riddles, including those current among children, and many short narratives, designed to inculcate some simple practical lesson, as in certain versions of *Cupid and Psyche* and *Blue Beard*. Especially instructive for the student of folklore are aetiological myths and *pourquoi stories*—tales told to explain why, for example, a certain cliff is called "Lover's Leap", why the robin has a red breast, or why the Pleiades consist of seven stars. Indeed, there is scarcely an observation or experience possible to simple folk from the cradle to the grave which does not furnish beliefs that belong to folklore.

The scientific study of folklore began during the late 18th century as a result of the Romantic Movement, and since that period numerous hypotheses have been proposed in explanation of the phenomena involved. Many scholars, beginning with Jacob Grimm, have sought to explain folk-tales and ballads as merely broken-down myths of the ancient Aryans, but their conclusions have gradually lost favor. Other investigators, known as the Anthropological School and best represented by Sir James G. Frazer's *The Golden Bough*, believe that many tales and superstitions now regarded as silly or incomprehensible originated in remote times in social groups where they had a very definite and understandable meaning. Another group have devoted their attention particularly to traditions which, though widely separated in place, bear a close resemblance in form or content. An illustration is furnished by the numerous stories of grateful, helpful animals of which versions exist or are known to have existed in India, in Europe, and in Africa. Opinion seems to be divided as to whether similar folk-tales arise independently under similar social conditions in different places (polygensis) or whether the parallels observed are due to transmission from one place to another. A certain amount of progress toward a solution of the problem has been achieved by the Folklore Fellows, an international organization composed of scholars who, by analyzing as many variants as possible of a given popular tale or superstition, attempt to reconstruct the archetype and to establish its approximate place and date of origin. In general, however, the folklorist must content himself for the present with collecting materials in the hope that when larger numbers of examples are available in recorded form, they may serve as the basis of more convincing theories.

Alexander H. Kroppe, *The Science of Folk-Lore* (1930); E. Hoffmann-Krayer, ed., *Volkskundliche Bibliographie* (1917-, Berlin and Leipzig, 1919-); Stith Thompson, *Motif-Index of Folk-Literature* (1932-36) (F F Communications), 6 vols. T.P.C.

folkways: See culture.

fomorians: Powers of darkness, in Celtic legend, overcome by the children of Danu, Tuatha De Danann; usually represented as misshapen giants. They came from under the sea. P.G.M.

Fondren Lectureship: Established in 1919 at Southern Methodist University, Dallas, Texas, by Mr. and Mrs. W. W. Fondren, from whom a gift of $10,000 was received. Its purpose is to provide each year at the University a series of lectures on Christian Missions or the Christian Faith. Among the lecturers have been R. E. Speer, J. M. Moore, J. Moffatt, F. J. McConnell, C. R. Brown, A. C. Knudson, E. H. Hughes, Edwin Lewis, A. E. Day. A.C.K.

font: (Lat., *fons*, fountain) The vessel for the baptismal water. In the early church a tank; later a bowl mounted on a pedestal, often elaborately decorated. B.S.E.

food: Food has always been a primary value for man. In early cultures, the necessity of securing, protecting and guaranteeing the food supply gave rise to a very large proportion of the religious ceremonies. Practical and ceremonial techniques were always combined, the ceremonial expressing the emotional tension centered in the hunger drive. In addition to these fundamental techniques for securing food a bewildering number of rules were made to control its use or misuse and to forbid the eating of certain forms. Where the supply was precarious, restrictions were placed upon the young or upon women; groups abstained from eating their totem* animal and performed the ritual to multiply it for the use of others; a closed season was often established to protect food sources growing scarce; the law of first-fruits* guarded the crop until it matured. Some tribes refused to eat certain animals for fear of acquiring their qualities. Groups on all the continents, for different reasons, avoid the eating of pork. Jewish law forbad the eating of certain animals, the blood and intestinal fat of food animals, and all animals torn by beasts or dying a natural death. The development of the rule of non-injury in India restricted the killing of animals for food. Owing to the sanctity of the cow after the Vedic period, beef was especially banned although the Laws of Manu* permit the eating of it under certain conditions. Food was generally offered to the dead and to the gods. In some cases these ceremonial offerings developed into communion meals. See animals, worship of; cannibalism; feasting; kosher; milk and honey; nature worship; sacramental meal; tabu. A.E.H.

Fools, Feast of: See Feast of Fools.

foreknowledge, Divine: Traditionally, God's view of events, to us future, from His supertemporal standpoint. According to Thomism,* God knows our future acts, even though they are free, because he knows events, not through their conditions in earlier events, but directly, in themselves. He is as the center of a circle, equally near to every point of time. This assumes that events to us future are yet in themselves real and determinate, or that time is analogous to a circle and not to an endless line whose points are added to it from moment to moment and form no completed sum. Scotists* reject the Thomistic view, but hold that God knows the future because its determining conditions are in his will; but thereby human freedom is contradicted. Ockham* held that the philosophically reasonable view is that the future, being more or less indeterminate or free, cannot be known determinately, even by God; but revelation, he thought, forces us to renounce this view. Yet the Socinians* and others later adopted it as precisely the one supported by Scriptural religion. Many philosophers and theologians now hold that only past events—inclusive of the present—are fully real or determinate, so that for God to "know" "all" events as determinate would be for him to know some of them falsely or as they are not. Future events being indeterminate, not merely in relation to earlier events, but intrinsically, it follows that perfect knowledge grasps the past inclusive of the present as determinate, but the future only with such determinacy as it really has—this depending upon the not unlimited extent to which past conditions already determine it. Any determination beyond that can exist and be known as existent only, it is held, when the future comes into full being as a present, new in itself and for all true knowledge. Time is not a complete whole, to be viewed in one complete vision, but a whole ever-to-be-increased-somehow-or-other, that is, in a way not determined either in advance or eternally. ("What will be will be" begs the question of whether time consists wholly of will-be's and will-not-be's, rather than, in part at least, of may-or-may-not-be's reducible to determinate being only by their creation as present events. If time be such, then omniscience* is only possible as itself temporal—as knowing new facts when there are new facts to know, but always knowing all the facts there are at the time. See eternity; perfect; predestination; reprobation; time.

See G. T. Fechner, *Zendavesta* Ch. 11, (1851); O. Pfleiderer, *Grundriss der Christlichen Glaubens- und Sittenlehre* (1888); A. E. Garvie, *The Christian Faith* (1937). C.H.

foreordination: The doctrine that the nature of God, who is perfect in wisdom and knowledge, and whose Holy Love is the sovereign power of all being, necessarily involves the existence of His eternal and determining purposes with reference to all events, including the volitions of men. The particular theological interest in this doctrine has been concerned with the relationship of the divine teleology to human freedom, responsibility and assurance in the matter of salvation. See predestination. H.W.J.

forged decretals: See false decretals.

forgeries: A number of writings have appeared in medieval and modern times based wholly or in part on biblical or apocryphal literature, or suggested by sources and incidents recorded in the Bible (*e.g.*, the Book of Jashar or "the Upright"), which have been fraudulently represented and published as ancient and authoritative documents. The nature of these publications makes it often difficult to trace their origins and editions. For accounts including these data as well as descriptions of contents one may consult encyclopedias of Religion and Bible and E. J. Goodspeed, *Strange New Gospels* (1931), and *New Chapters in New Testament Study* (1937), chap. VIII. The following are some of the better known of such spurious documents: The Confession of Pontius Pilate, The Aquarian Gospel, A Correct Transcript of Pilate's Court (known also under various other titles, especially the Archko Volume), the Unknown Life of Jesus Christ or Life of St. Issa, Best of the Sons of Men, The Letter of Benan, The Letter of Jesus Christ or Letter from Heaven, The Twenty-ninth Chapter of Acts, The Gospel of Josephus or Concerning the Life of Jesus of Nazareth, The Book of Jashar (various forms), The Crucifixion, by an Eyewitness. For other lesser works see Goodspeed, *op. cit.* See also Lost Books of the Bible. A.P.W.

forgiveness: The Christian religion is supremely distinguished from other religions by placing the divine forgiveness of sins in the center of the relation between man and God. To be sure, all religions that know of a relation with a personal deity teach the forgiveness of sins. But it is the special character of the Christian gospel that it proclaims on the authority of the life and teaching and death and resurrection of Jesus Christ, that it is the nature of God to be a forgiving, merciful Father. The source of the Christian life is therefore the forgiveness of sins as it is assured by Christ. Because this is so, the Christian ethic is pre-eminently a religious one. For the Christian is taught to acknowledge himself a sinner in the presence of the merciful God and, having been released from his sin through forgiveness and responding with gratitude to the divine gift, to be an agent of forgiving love in the relations with his fellow men.

Christian theology has expounded the gospel of forgiveness by devoting special attention to the meaning of the work of Christ as the author and perfecter of the faith in this gospel (see Jesus Christ; Christology; atonement; justification) and by explaining how forgiveness is related to justice, namely by superseding it without destroying its validity (see justice, and gospel). See absolution; pardon; penance; redemption; retention of sins; satisfaction; sin. W.P.

form: (Lat., *forma,* form; Gr., *eidos,* shape, form) In Aristotle and the Scholastics, the intrinsic determinant of existence in any being; in material beings, form is what actualizes, specifies and makes determinate. In Kant, the form of knowledge is one of the *a priori* molds, such as time or space, causality or relation, into which our experiences fit. See Aristotle and Aristotelianism; Kant. L.R.W.

formal cause: See cause.

formalism: The attachment of great significance to the scrupulous observance of external rules in morality or religion, with a view of thereby earning the rewards which are believed to follow from such a course of action. The critics charge formalism with jeopardizing the autonomy of the human spirit by failing to give proper recognition to the essentially inward character of the moral and spiritual realities which are the sources and the controlling factors in the outward expression and the external embodiment of the genuinely moral and religious life. H.W.J.

form criticism, or Formgeschichte: A method of research which has grown up in Germany since 1919 when Martin Dibelius* published *Die Formgeschichte des Evangeliums* (Eng. tr., *From Tradition to Gospel,* 1935). The method had been anticipated in a number of earlier works, e.g. those by Johannes Weiss* and, especially with reference to the OT, by Hermann Gunkel.* Form criticism is really an attempt to recover the units of oral tradition which were in circulation before the gospels were written; a better name for it would be 'Tradition Criticism.'

As practiced by Dibelius, Rudolf Bultmann,* and other leaders of the school, the first step is to classify the material in the gospels. Dibelius' scheme is the following: The Old Stories (including the Passion Narrative), Parables, Sayings, The Great Miracle Tales, Legends. It is of course recognized that later editorial settings (or 'frames': *Rahmen*), interpretations, revisions, and constructions must be removed. Some critics undertake to distinguish Hellenistic from earlier Jewish-Christian material; no doubt there are traces of Hellenistic influence in the method of telling or in the interpretation given to some of the stories in the gospels; but it does not necessarily follow that 'Hellenistic' material is necessarily 'later' than Jewish-Christian—the Hellenistic movement began very early in the history of the church. One point is of special interest: the form of the oldest stories is much simpler than that of 'the great miracle tales,' which upon other grounds probably were later in date of formulation. Another important feature is the recognition of the poetic structure in practically all Jesus' sayings. Like many other wisdom teachers, he was a poet.

Form criticism stresses the dependence of the tradition upon the community which handed it down. Some critics go the length of assuming that the community *produced* most of the tradition; the majority, led by Dibelius, assume that the community *preserved* the tradition, emphasizing and interpreting and of course first of all selecting those traditions which best met current needs and problems. In other words, the gospel tradition was a community tradition, from the start, and was not the private possession of individuals. Perhaps the chief value of form criticism is its emphasis upon the fact that the gospel tradition was handed down within the group, the church. The significance of this for the earliest interpretation of the tradition and also for the growth of doctrine is clear.

See Dibelius, as above, also *The Message of Jesus Christ* (1939), *Gospel Criticism and Christology* (1935); R. Bultmann, *Die Geschichte der synoptischen Tradition,* 2nd edition (1931); R. H. Lightfoot, *History and Interpretation in the Gospels* (1935); V. Taylor, *The Formation of the Gospel Tradition* (1933); B. S. Easton, *The Gospel Before the Gospels* (1928); F. C. Grant, *Form Criticism, a New Method of New Testament Research* (1934) (incl. tr. of *The Study of the Synoptic Gospels,* by R. Bultmann, and *Primitive Christianity in the Light of Gospel Research,* by K. Kundsin); Dibelius' *Message* contains his reconstruction of the Oral Pericopes which underlie the gospels. F.C.G.

Former Prophets, The: See Old Testament; Canon, Old and New Testament.

Formula of Concord: The latest of the Lutheran confessional writings, this document was issued in 1577 by the Lutheran Church of Germany and later incorporated in the Book of Concord.* It is a deliberate effort to arrive at a final solution of the doctrinal conflicts raging since Luther's death between the rigid adherents of Luther (Gnesio-Lutherans) and the more liberal followers of Melanchthon (Philippists**). The Formula, based upon a critical use of documents evolved in previous efforts at unity (Swabian Concord, Formula of Maulbronn, Book of Torgau), was the work of mediating theologians, chief of whom were Jacob Andrea and Martin Chemnitz.* It has two parts, a brief Epitome, written by Andrea, and a larger "Solid Repetition and Declaration" of joint origin. In its twelve articles on the mooted questions of original sin, free will, justification, good works, law and gospel, eucharist, Christology, descent into hell, adiaphora, predestination, and sects, the Formula steers a careful middle course between the extremists of both sides, but succeeds in reaffirming the basic teaching of the Augsburg Confession.* Submitted to Lutheran princes and city councils for official adoption, it met with only limited success. It became, however, a permanently significant statement of the consensus of Lutheran belief, the basis of Lutheran orthodoxy, and the means by which Lutheranism* has maintained its independence from Calvinism.* See antinomianism; Confessions, Formal of the Christian Church; perichoresis. T.A.K.

Fortunatus, Venantius: See hymns.

fortune in the Greek and Roman religions: Tyche (Gr. *Tychē,* from *tynchāno,* to happen), Fortune or Chance, never became fully personified in Greek religious thought nor a subject of mythology, but her importance grew as the authority of the old gods declined. Fortuna (Lat. *Fortūna,* from *fero,* to bear), an ancient Italian oracular divinity, Destiny, worshiped at Praeneste as Primigenia, first-born daughter of Jove. She is represented with cornucopia and ship's rudder. As pure chance, the goddess is known as Fors Fortuna. Cf. fatalism; fate. E.M.N.

forty hours' devotion: Also called Forty Hours' Adoration, Forty Hours' Prayer. Consists of forty continuous hours of prayer in presence of the Blessed Sacrament publicly and solemnly exposed, in order to adore and praise and thank Christ in the Eucharist for the benefits granted to mankind, and to petition Him especially for public needs, in particular for peace. In places where it is too inconvenient to have the adoration continue during the night, the exposition may be interrupted for the night. It is continued for forty hours because of the supposed forty hours that Christ was in the tomb.

The devotion is accompanied by special services. It opens with a public votive Mass* of the Blessed Sacrament, followed by a procession of the Blessed Sacrament and the chanting of the Litany of All Saints. It closes on the third day with the public votive Mass of the Blessed Sacrament, the chanting of the Litany of All Saints, and the procession of the Blessed Sacrament. On the second day a public votive Mass for some necessity, usually peace, is celebrated. At least twenty candles burn continuously on the altar where exposition takes place, and it is adorned with many flowers. The faithful who make a visit to a church where Forty Hours is in progress and fulfill the other conditions required may gain a plenary indulgence each day during the Forty Hours; and since the decree of Pope Pius X* in 1914, these indulgences can be gained even when the Forty Hours is interrupted for the night. Since the promulgation of the Code of Canon Law in 1918 Forty Hours Devotion is obligatory in all churches where the Blessed Sacrament is habitually reserved, unless it is too inconvenient or impossible.

History:

The origin of Forty Hours' Devotion lies hidden in obscurity. Some historians think that the Barnabites, St. Anthony Mary Zaccaria and Father Bonus of Cremona began it about 1527-1529. Others think the honor goes to the Capuchin Father, Joseph of Fermo who about 1534 organized forty continuous hours of prayer to be held successively in all the churches of Milan so that Milan would not be without Forty Hours' Prayer throughout the year, in order to counteract the forces that were threatening the peace of the Church at that time. During this Forty Hours the Blessed Sacrament was on the altar but not necessarily exposed to the view of the faithful. Shortly after St. Philip Neri and the Jesuit Fathers introduced Forty Hours into Rome. It was approved by Pope Paul III in 1539.

In 1592 Clement VIII issued the apostolic constitution *Graves et diuturnae* by which he prescribed the Forty Hours' Devotion for Rome. In 1606 Paul V confirmed the decree of Clement VIII and established it in perpetuity for Rome. It seems that he ordered the public votive Masses to be said during Forty Hours. Succeeding Popes issued various regulations governing the Forty Hours' Devotion. These were collected under Clement XI in 1705 and are known as the Clementine Instructions. In 1730 Clement XII made a few slight changes and promulgated these instructions anew for Rome. They are still the law for Rome and have been the guide for Forty Hours elsewhere.

When Forty Hours Devotion was introduced into the United States is not clear. It seems that it was introduced as a form of diocesan devotion by the saintly Bishop Neumann in the diocese of Philadelphia in 1853, although it was practiced in individual churches prior to that. The Plenary Council of Baltimore of 1866 formally enjoined Forty Hours upon all the dioceses of the United States. D.U.

Forty-Two Articles: Articles of faith framed largely by Cranmer, issued (without formal authorization) for the Church of England in 1553; later served as basis of the Thirty-Nine Articles*. See Thirteen Articles. E.R.H.

fossarians: (Lat., *fossor,* a digger) Christian grave-diggers who, in the Church of the second or third century, came to have a specialized, professional status. Probably at one time counted among the minor clergy, they were remunerated from voluntary offerings, out of the common treasury, or through economic immunities. By the fifth century their abuse of far-reaching corporate rights led to their dissolution as a group. R.C.P.

Foster, Frank Hugh: (1861-1935) Graduate Harvard Univ. 1873, Andover 1877. Professor of Systematic Theology, Pacific Theological Seminary, 1892-1902; Philosophy and History, Olivet College, 1907-1916. In his earlier teaching an exponent and defender of New England Calvinistic orthodoxy, he later announced its collapse and became its leading historian.

Author: *Grotius' Defence* (1889) a translation with notes; *Fundamental Ideas of the Roman Catholic Church* (1899); *Christian Life and Theology* (1900); *A Genetic History of the New England Theology* (1907); *The Modern Movement in American Theology* (1939), lectures published by Dr. J. G. Green. J.W.B.

Foster, George Burman: (1858-1918) Theologian and philosopher. Noted as a great teacher and as a champion of freedom in religious thinking. Educated at Shelton College, U. of W. Va., Rochester Theol. Sem., Univs. Göttingen and Berlin. Ordained Baptist ministry, 1878. Pastor of the First Baptist Church, Saratoga Springs, N. Y. 1887-1891. Prof.. of Phil., McMaster Univ. 1892-1895. At the Univ. of Chicago as asso. prof. (1895-1897) and prof. (1897-1905) in the Department of Systematic Theology, and as prof. of the Philosophy of Religion in the Department of Comparative Religion (1905-1918). Among Foster's most influential writings are the following: *The Finality of the Christian Religion* (1906); *The Function of Religion in Man's Struggle for Existence* (1909). Foster also made contributions which include: a) a sermon on *The Function of Death in Human Experience in Univ. of Chicago Sermons* (1915), ed. by T. G. Soares; b) a chapter on "The Contribution of Critical Scholarship to Ministerial Efficiency" in *A Guide to the Study of the Christian Religion* (1916), ed. by Gerald Birney Smith; numerous articles in *The Biblical World, The American Journal of Theology, Journal of Religion,* and other publications. Most important among the writings published posthumously are: a) a volume embodying Foster's lectures on the dogmatics and ethics of the Christian religion, ed. by Douglas Clyde Macintosh under the title *Christianity in Its Modern Expression* (1921); b) Foster's lectures on Nietzsche, ed. Curtis W. Reese, and published in a volume entitled *Friedrich Nietzsche* (1931).

Foster was profoundly concerned with the problem of the objective validity of religious faith and especially with the problem of the ontological reference of the God-idea. The history of Foster's religious thinking is the record of his pilgrimage from theistic supernaturalism to Ritschlianism* and thence under the increasing influence of the functional interpretation of religion to an emotional naturalism which retained a deep devotion and loyalty to human values. Acceptance of the conclusion that Foster at the end had intellectually abandoned theism and had adopted a humanistic naturalism has been rendered difficult for some of his interpreters because of the fact that Foster continued to utilize *emotionally* the God-idea which *intellectually* he declared to be without objective, ontological validity. Foster's thought has exercised a great influence upon the rise and development of "religious humanism"* in America.

"The Religious Thought of George B. Foster" by H. W. Johnson. (An unpublished dissertation dep. in the Yale Library.) H.W.J.

foundling asylums: Homes where infants or children, deserted by their parents are cared for and educated. Many such homes are supported by private charities. St. Vincent de Paul* was the illustrious apostle of the movement.

Cf. *The National Catholic Almanac* (1941), p. 279. S.C.

Fourier, Charles: (Fourierism) See communistic settlements, secular.

Four Square Gospel Church: See International Church of the Foursquare Gospel.

Fourth Gospel, the: See Gospel and the Gospels; John, Gospel of.

Fox, George: (1624-1691) Founder of the Society of Friends* (Quakers*) Fox was of devout middle-class Lancashire parentage. In 1643 he turned against the shallow insincerities of accepted religious and social practice; 1646, received his great mystical "opening"; 1647, having composed his views, he commenced active preaching; was frequently persecuted for blasphemy, disturbing the peace, etc. and imprisoned eight times; 1669, married Margaret Fell of Swarthmore Hall; 1671-1673, led a mission to Barbados, Jamaica and North America; 1677, 1684, led missions to Holland and Germany. Fox's mysticism was indirectly, but strongly, influenced by the Familists and Boehmists. Though meagrely educated he was an effective and indefatigable evangelist, traveller, pamphleteer and correspondent in "publishing Truth," and possessed an intuitive genius for democratic organization. All histories and expositions of Quakerism include detailed discussions of Fox. See Society of Friends.

George Fox, *Journal* (two vols., 1901), frequently published; Rufus M. Jones, *George Fox, Seeker and Friend* (1930); Rachel H. King, *George Fox and the Inner Light* (1940); R. M. Jones, *Story of George Fox* (1919); Rachel Knight, *Founder of Quakerism* (1922); T. E. Harvey and others, *New Appreciation of George Fox* (1925); A. N. Brayshaw, *Personality of George Fox* (1918); Thomas Hodgkin, *George Fox* (1896). H.C.

Foxe, John: (1516-1587) The English martyrologist and Marian exile. While on the continent he wrote his most famous work *Actes and Monuments of these latter and perillous Dayes,* which is more commonly known as the *Book of Martyrs*.. W.S.H.

Francis of Assisi, Saint: (1182-1226) The spiritual founder of the Friars Minor*. His conversion from worldly acquisitiveness to the imitation of Christ's voluntary poverty elicited a small following. He presented them for papal approval as Christ's chosen few, peculiarly destined as men of His church for world service through gospel renunciation. Their subsequent transformation into an order at the hands of the hierarchy weakened neither his loyalty to the church nor his example of service, through liberating poverty, to all human need. Popularly revered as a saint at his death, he was canonized two years later. See Fioretti; Franciscans; Gregory IX; hymns.

L. Salvatorelli, *The Life of St. Francis of Assisi* (1928); R. C. Petry, *Francis of Assisi, Apostle of Poverty* (1941). R.C.P.

Francis (Francois) de Sales, Saint: (1567-1622) Bishop of Geneva, director of souls, and co-founder of the Congregation of the Visitation, who was also the author of the devotional classic *Introduction to the Devout Life* and of a work of high importance in ascetical theology, *The Treatise on the Love of God.* See Visitation, Order of the. D.V.S.

Franciscans: Francis' brethren whose tentative papal authorization to follow him in renunciation soon led to their institution as an order. Their early years were characterized by rigid poverty of possessions, individual and collective, and the limited use of material goods. They labored diligently for their livelihood but received no money. They begged alms for soul discipline and as a further means of suport. Humblest services rendered rich and poor, leper and outcast, town and country made theirs an unprecedented social ministry. Freedom from worldly cares obligated them to preach peace and repentance as the preparation for the imminent coming of God's kingdom. Even in Francis'* lifetime they experienced a growing tension between the demands of poverty idealism and the exigencies of practical life. Contending parties, whose divergent poverty observance sadly rent the order, were given belated papal recognition. Today, the Frairs Minor,* now a united order (The First), comprise "three distinct and independent branches." They are the Frairs Minor, the Friars Minor Conventual, and the Friars Minor Capuchin, with some 34,500 professed members in all. With nuns of the Second Order, the Poor Clares, and the Tertiaries, regular and secular, they continue their ministry to church and society. See mendicant orders; Visitation; William de la Mare.

See P. Gratien, *Histoire de la fondation & de l'évolution de l'ordre des frères mineurs au xiii siècle* (Paris, 1928); V. D. Scudder, *The Franciscan Adventure* (1931). R.C.P.

Franck, Sebastian: (1499-1542) German freethinker of the Reformation. First a Catholic priest, later a Lutheran, Franck emerged as a self-appointed champion of heretics, fighting single-handed every form of ecclesiastical authority and every theology claiming to possess the only true faith. Luther called him "the Devil's mouth." Expelled from Strassburg and from Ulm, he set up his printing-press in Basel. A fearless critic and social reformer, Franck expounded a humanistic mystical syncretism including non-Christian sources and anticipating modern liberalism. His chief work is *Chronica* (1531). T.A.K.

Francke, August Hermann: (1663-1727) German Pietist leader and founder of the orphanage and schools at Halle bearing his name. Simultaneously pastor, professor, and pioneer in social service, Francke combined evangelistic fervor with Biblical scholarship and executive skill. He exerted wide influence in vitalizing devotional life, introducing the Bible-centered principle into education, and stimulating charitable and missionary activities. See catechumenate; pietism. T.A.K.

Frank, Franz Reinhold v.: (1827-1894) He was professor at Erlangen—one of the most noted confessional Lutheran theologians. His comprehensive exhibition of the entire systematic theology was supported by his sharp analysis of Ritschl*. He examined in detail the entire Lutheran dogmatic theology from the point of view of the pietistic tenet of rebirth. His reconstruction of orthodoxy was externally nourished by speculative idealism. See Erlangen School; neo-Lutheranism.

Die Theologie der Konkordienformel, 4 vols. (Erlangen u. Leipzig, 1858); *System der christlichen Gewissheit*, 2 ed., 2 vols. (Erlangen u. Leipzig, 1881-1884); *System der christlichen Wahrheit*, 3 ed., 2 vols. (Erlangen u. Leipzig, 1894); *System der christlichen Sittlichkeit*, 2 vols. (Erlangen u. Leipzig, 1884-1887); *Geschichte der neueren Theologie, insbesondere der systematischen seit Schleiermacher*, rev. ed., by R. Grützmacher (Leipzig, 1908). H.H.

Franzelin, John Baptist: (1816-1886) Austrian Jesuit and Cardinal. Professor at Rome and influential in the Vatican Council, he was one of the leading Roman Catholic theologians of his century. E.A.R.

fravashi: The eternal part of the righteous individual, his guardian angel, fighting in the ranks of the angels which protect the pious Zoroastrian*; first mentioned in the Avesta* in the "Yasna of the seven chapters" (Yasna*, chs. 35-42); later in Yashts* 13 and 61. R.H.P.

Frazer, James George: (1854-1941) He was an eminent investigator of primitive society and human beliefs. He reached the conclusions that beliefs are efficient factors of human behavior and social control, that the role of superstitions has been rather beneficial, that superstition has among certain peoples and at certain times strengthened the respect for government—especially monarchical government—for private property, for marriage, and contributed to a stricter observance of the rules of sexual morality, and for human life. His theory has been corroborated and supported by many field studies. See primitive religion.

J. G. Frazer, *Psyche's Task: A Discourse concerning the Influence of Superstition on the Growth of Institutions* (London, 1909). H.H.

Free Christian Zion Church of Christ: A Negro religious sect founded by E. D. Brown at Redemption, Arkansas, in 1905 in a controversy over church finances. It claims to be in general accord with the Methodist Church in theology and organization. There are nine churches in Arkansas and Texas, with a total membership of 1,850. E.T.C.

Free Church of England: The name often given to the religious bodies in England which are separated from the Established Church (the Anglican Communion). The Roman Church, and certain Unitarian bodies, are excepted. In recent years, the Free Church (which includes Wesleyans, Congregationalists, Baptists, etc.) has established a Free Church Council, to coordinate their relations and present a common front. W.N.P.

Free Church of Scotland: In the Church of Scotland* long before 1843 there was protest against the legal system under which lay patrons chose parish ministers. Court decisions strengthening lay patronage so subjected the church to the state that in this year 474 ministers out of 1203 and a larger proportion of congregations formed the Free Church of Scotland. This name stood for both a national church and the church's spiritual freedom. Property worth over half a million dollars was surrendered. Preparatory work led by Thomas Chalmers* gave the church at the outset effective support of its ministry and adequate buildings. All the foreign missionaries of the Church of Scotland joined it. A strong theological school, New College, was immediately established in Edinburgh, and others were added in Glasgow and Aberdeen. Throughout its life the Free Church was one of the most important of Protestant churches, eminent for preaching, missions and service to Scotland. Its distinguished theological scholarship becoming decidedly progressive in the late nineteenth century, was widely influential. In 1892 it liberalized its interpretation of the Westminster Confession*. In 1900 with the United Presbyterian Church* it formed the United Free Church of Scotland*, having then 293,396 members. A small dissenting body continues the Free Church. See Cameronians; Guthrie, Thomas; Rainy, Robert. Cf. Moderates, The.

J. R. Fleming, *The Church in Scotland, 1843-1929*, 2 vols. (Edinburgh, 1927, 1932); P. Bayne, *Free Church of Scotland* (2nd ed. 1894). R.H.N.

Free-Lovism: (Gates style) See Battle-Axe experiment.

freedom: See cause; religious liberty.

Freemasonry: A world-wide philosophical fraternal institution, whose origins are lost in the immemorial past, but whose present organization dates from 1717, the establishment of the premier Grand Lodge of England. It is a speculative art, teaching morality and basic religion by means of symbols, particularly those derived from the builders' craft. As an oath-bound body, it is secret only as regards its modes of recognition, ritualistic practices, and certain legendary dramatic presentations. Because of its democratic qualities and supra-national character, it is feared by spiritual and political tyrants, and many attempts have been made to suppress it, notably papal action beginning in 1738 and the present Nazi government of Germany.

Freemasonry is non-sectarian and proposes to be "the center of union, and the means of conciliating true friendship among persons that must have remained at a perpetual distance." However, there are certain religious professions required: first, belief in God, the Great Architect of the Universe; and, second, belief in the immortality of the soul. Much of the occult lore of the Middle Ages (alchemy, the Kabalah, Templary, *etc.*) has left its imprint upon the Order, especially in the higher degrees.

The fraternity differs in organization, and to a certain extent in ritual, from country to country. In the United States, after the first three degrees (the Blue Lodge), there are two divisions: the so-called Scottish and the American (commonly called the York) rites, culminating respectively in the 32nd and Knight Templar degrees. Some of the eminent American Masons have been George Washington, Benjamin Franklin, and Albert Pike.

R. F. Gould, *History of Freemasonry* (1885); R. F. Gould, *Concise History of Freemasonry* (1903); A. G. Mackey, *Encyclopedia of Freemasonry* (Clegg-Hughan revision, 1924); J. F. Newton, *The Builders* (1914); Albert Pike, *Morals and Dogma* (reprinted 1930). A.C.

Free Methodist Church: See holiness churches.

Free Spirit, Brothers and Sisters of the: Lay religious groups of western Europe in the middle ages whose main interests were personal piety and freedom from clerical authority. In practice, some were ascetic and others, quite the reverse. Unpopular generally and persecuted as heretics through the fourteenth century. A.S.

free-will: See libertarianism.

Free Will Baptists: A group of Baptist churches which accept the Arminian or free will theology as opposed to Calvinism or predestination. They are among the oldest sects in the country, the movement having come from Wales about 1701. There are 920 churches and more than 76,000 members. E.T.C.

Freud, Sigmund: (1856-1939) He maintained that love of the ideal is a sublimation of sexual love. In contrast, classical tradition has maintained that sexual love is subservient to the love of the ideal. The basic paradox of his metapsychology consists in the fact that psychoanalysis as a cathartic method of mental healing involves a philosophy in which reason and the urge of life are primary; whereas, actually Freud's irrational monism and theory of repressive instincts, lead to a philosophy of death.

Notwithstanding his leaving a healing art loosely connected with a body of speculations which require radical transformation before it meets with ease the standards of science, the concept of the unconscious, the creation of the analytic technique of free association, and the development of a specific form of doctor-patient relationship, were his greatest contributions to psychiatry and therapeutic psychology. Greater emphasis upon the etiological and perpetuating role of anxiety, greater stress upon intra-social rather than intra-psychic phenomena, and greater interest in the transference of and in the immediate present than in the past are the significant new trends in psychoanalytic therapy.

In his application of psychoanalysis to the study of religion Freud has been much less convincing than elsewhere. In *Civilization and its Discontents,* he discussed the conscious feeling that one is immortal. He argued that it is not a rational proof of theological premises, for the subjective experience of immortality is a regression to an infantile mode of thought. Almost two decades ago he staggered the religious world in *The Future of an Illusion* with the charge that religion "is a universal, obsessional neurosis of mankind," by means of which individuals are able to nurse themselves into an unhealthy state of immaturity. He contended that religion is an illusion due to be destroyed when mankind has overcome its infantile prejudice. God, in short, is nothing but a creation of man. Religion is a technique by means of which the person who is afraid of life tries to find a haven of false security. He reduced the idea of God to a rationalization of the father ideal and the infantile wish for protection from the terrors of nature. He departed from his life-long analysis of unconscious motivations and attacked theology. He ignored the religious needs of men, and attacked the logic of theology which justifies these needs by arguing that science, the supremacy of intellect, can take its place. In his last work (*Moses and Monotheism*) he attempted to write a biography of the founder of the Hebrew nation, largely used as an occasion to work out and expand his well-known theory of religion. It was an ambitious construction resting on an extremely slight and tenuous foundation of historical data. Wishful speculation loomed large.

In attacking religion unsparingly in his works, he was least astute here, and his polemics did him no credit. His discussion of religion showed a misunderstanding of what religion is, and he fell into a morass of inconsistencies. Notwithstanding Freud's eminent failure to understand the religious needs of men, he has done mankind a real service in ruthlessly exposing the unhealthy kind of religion, in distinguishing sane religion from neurotic religion. As a person grows healthy and independent, he abandons the ways of using religion as a crutch. Freud regarded religion as mainly associated with human weakness. He was attacking the abuse rather than the use of religion. He never concerned himself with healthy religion. In fact, he did not know what normal, sane religion is. See psychology, schools of.

His main works: *The Future of an Illusion* (1928); *Civilization and its Discontents* (1930); *New Introductory Lectures on Psychoanalysis* (1933); *Gesammelte Schriften* (Leipzig, Vienna, Zürich, 1934); *A General Introduction to Psychoanalysis* (1935); *The Problem of Anxiety* (1936); *The Basic Writings of Sigmund Freud* (1938); *Moses and Monotheism* (1939). H.H.

Freudian psychology: See psychology, schools of.

friar: (Lat., *frater;* Fr., *frère*) The somewhat obsolete English name for any member of any of the four original, mendicant Orders (Franciscans, Dominicans, Carmelites and Augustinians) in the Roman Catholic Church. To be distinguished from *monk,* in that the friar is a minister of the gospel, engaged in pastoral work and teaching, whereas the monk is a cloistered religious, only working in public under unusual conditions. It should be noted that, though mendicants, the Jesuits are not friars but regular clerics. For specific details see the four Orders named above. V.J.B.

Friars Minor: (Franciscans) A Roman Catholic mendicant Order founded by St. Francis* of Assisi, 1207-1209. The original rule was very strict, stressing extreme poverty. As a result of later reforms, three branches with autonomous heads developed: Conventuals, Observants and Capuchins*. At first gray, the habit was changed to brown. Early in the 13th century the Franciscans took up university teaching and produced some of the most influential Catholic philosophers and theologians: Alexander of Hales, St. Bonaventura, Matthew of Aquasparta, Duns Scotus, and William of Occam. Their theology is traditionally Augustinian, modified by Aristotelianism in the late 13th century. The Order is also noted for its widespread missionary activity. See Franciscans. V.J.B

friendly societies: The device by which persons pool their resources to meet contingencies of illness, death or other emergencies is widespread and very old. The Tong societies among the Chinese in our country fulfil such a function. In the later colonial days almost all national groups formed their societies for mutual aid. Although all associations of private citizens were forbidden in the Roman Empire, an exception was made in favor of "enclesia," mutual aid societies formed of persons belonging to specific nationalities living in Rome and other cities of the empire for the care of their poor, sick, for burial and other contingencies. However, the early medieval religious guilds, and later the trade guilds were the predecessors of contemporary friendly societies of England, which arose almost immediately after the confiscation of the property of the guilds by Henry the VIII in the 16th century.

The modern friendly society, strictly speaking, is an English institution, which may have a social function such as the Independent Order of Odd Fellows, or be a trade union. Gradually, after many experiments and failures, the funds entrusted to such societies have come under some sort of governmental supervision, to insure their solvency and therefore their service to its members.

When social insurance was introduced into England the government placed some of the administrative responsibility for sickness insurance with the friendly societies, as for example that of supplying hospitalization, when indicated. It was anticipated with the coming of social insurance the usefulness of the friendly society would lessen; but their growth since 1911 has belied that fear. The movement is essentially the expression of the intent of its members to maintain their own economic self-sufficiency rather than to rely on the state.

W. T. Pratt, *The Law of Friendly Societies—with Acts* (London, 1909); J. F. Wilkinson, *The Friendly Society Movement, Its Origin, Rise and Growth* (London, 1891). F.J.B.

Friends of God: An informal fellowship of German mystics, in large part laymen, during the fourteenth century centering around John Tauler* and Heinrich Suso*.

A. G. Seesholtz, *Friends of God* (1934). W.S.H.

Friends, Society of (Quakers): See Society of Friends (Quakers).

Fries, Jakob Friedrich: (1773-1843) German philosopher. Professor of Philosophy in Jena, 1800-1805 and again 1816-1843; 1806-1816 in Heidelberg. Transformed Kant's philosophy by means of a combination of Platonic and Romanticist views. Over against Kant's metaphysical agnosticism he held that the human mind was capable of directly apprehending the transcendental reality of the ideas by means of "Ahnung," i.e., the highest development of the faculty of 'feeling.' This view enabled him to interpret religion in a way similar to that of Schleiermacher's*—with whom he shared the Moravian upbringing and the indebtedness to Fichte*—as direct contact with the ideal reality. At the beginning of the twentieth century Fries' philosophy was revived in Goettingen by the Neo-Friesian School (Leon. Nelson, Wilh. Bousset, Rudolf Otto**).

Wissen, Glaube, Ahndung (1805), new edition by L. Nelson (1905); *Neue Kritik der Vernunft* (1807); *Fries' Biography* by E. Th. Henke (1867); see also: Th. Elsenhans, *Fries und Kant,* 2 vols. (1906); Rudolf Otto, *Kantisch-Friessche Religionsphilosophie,* 2nd ed. (1921); Ueberweg's *Geschichte der Philosophie,* 12th ed. (1923), vol. IV p. 147 ff. O.A.P.

Frigg or Frigga: Daughter of Fiörgyn and wife of Odin*. She was the mother of Thor, Balder and other gods. Variously regarded as goddess of the earth and air. The constellation Orion was her spinning-wheel. As patroness of conjugal love, she was especially worshipped by married couples. P.G.M.

Frohschammer, Jakob: (1821-1893) Ordained as Catholic priest, he was professor of philosophy at the university of Münich. Many of his earlier writings were placed on the Index. He fought with conviction, decisiveness and self-sacrifice for the independence of philosophy from Catholic theology. He explained the world in terms of the principle of imagination. Imagination is the most fitting medium to represent the existence of the nature of an absolute divine being, avoiding pantheism and affirming the personal relation of the creator to the world. The world is conceived as derived from the imagination of God.

Das Christenthum und die moderne Naturwissenschaft (Wien und Leipzig, 1868); *Das Recht der eigenen Uberzeugung* (Leipzig, 1869); *Das neue Wissen und der neue Glaube* (Leipzig, 1873); *Die Phantasie als Grundprincip des Weltprocesses* (München, 1877); *Uber das Mysterium Magnum des Daseins* (Leipzig, 1891); A. Altensperger, *J. Froshammers Philosophische System im Grundriss* (Zweibrücken, 1899). H.H.

Frommel, Gaston: (1862-1906) Swiss theologian, followed Vinet* in his approach to religious belief through the moral conscience, but stressed the element of binding obligation in conscience rather than the element of freedom. Criticised the subjectivism and relativism of the Paris theologians. See Sabatier; Ménégoz. W.M.H.

Fruitlands (Mass.) community: See communistic settlements, secular.

fugue: (Lat., *fuga,* flight) A polyphonic* form of composition used chiefly in instrumental music but often employed in choral* music as in Bach's *B Minor Mass.* The fugue originated in the vocal motet* and in the instrumental ricercare both of which consisted of an orderly exposition of material without any development which characterizes a fugue.

J. S. Bach, *The Art of Fugue;* D. F. Tovey, *Companion to "The Art of Fugue"* (1931). E.H.B.

Fulbert of Chartres: (960-1028) A pupil of the famous Gerbert of Aurillac*, he became the founder in 990 of the celebrated school of Chartres*. By nature an obedient follower of the Church Fathers, yet he sets limits to the human intellect in its flight toward the mysteries of God which, in his view, no erudite speculation but only a humble faith can comprehend. He died as bishop of Chartres. S.C.T.

functional school: See anthropology.

functionalism: (functional psychology) See psychology, schools of.

fundamentalism: Was a Post-World War theological and religious reaction which received its name from a series of little books entitled *The Fundamentals: A Testimony of the Truth* (12 vols., 1910-1912) which were published and circulated widely, with money furnished by two wealthy laymen. The doctrines listed as fundamental were: the Virgin birth of Christ; the physical resurrection; the inerrancy of the Scriptures in every detail; the substitutionary theory of the atonement, and finally the imminent, physical second coming of Christ. Those who supported these views did not hesitate to denounce those who denied them as "no Christian" with the result that all the larger evangelical churches in America were soon in the midst of a bitter controversy. The movement was organized to resist what they considered dangerous tendencies, especially in many well-known Theological Seminaries, to use scientific methods in dealing with the Scriptures.

The Baptists and Presbyterians were the denominations most affected by the controversy, though among the Methodists and Disciples the issues were sharply drawn. The Baptists not having any general church courts in which heretics might be brought to book the fundamentalist leaders were driven to the expedient of denouncing the *Modernists* in their public pronouncements in their pulpits and National Conventions. Several new fundamentalist Baptist Theological seminaries were established to counteract the influence of the liberal institutions. Among the Presbyterians there was a schism led by Professor John Gresham Machen* of the Princeton Theological Seminary. A new Theological Seminary was formed in Philadelphia which took the name of Westminster, and a new fundamentalist church emerged which has taken the name Bible Presbyterian Church.

Among the loosely organized Disciples body the issues involved were argued back and forth in the columns of their individually controlled church papers; the *Christian Century* supporting the liberal view, and the *Christian Standard* upholding the so-called fundamentals. Among

Methodists the conservatives attempted to set up rigid doctrinal standards to which ministers were to subscribe, which was out of harmony with Methodist history and tradition. Cf. Auburn Affirmation; evolution, controversy over.

S. G. Cole, *The History of Fundamentalism* (1931). w.w.s.

funeral customs: See death and burial practices.

fung shui: See Chinese Terminology.

future life, conceptions of: See annihilationism; final judgment; immortality, kinds of; immortality, conditional; resurrection; rewards and punishments; transmigration.

future punishment: See final judgment; rewards and punishments.

G

Gabars or Ghebers: The popular name for Zoroastrians* residing in Persia in contrast to those known in India as Parsis. With Moslem conquest those who remained unconverted to Islam were persecuted. A small group of Gabars, perhaps 10,000 survive today. See kafir. P.E.J.

Gabirol, Solomon Ibn: (1021-1058/1070) Known to scholastics as Avencebrol, Avicembron and Avicebron*, Gabirol is the first Spanish-Jewish poet-philosopher of distinction. He produced such a colorless philosophical work (*Fons Vitae*) that he was taken for a Muslim and a Christian until the discovery of Falakera's epitome by S. Munk in the last century. While his influence on subsequent Jewish life and thought was slight, he is regarded as the fountainhead of classical Jewish mysticism and of much medieval Christian mysticism. He was a monistic Neo-Platonist. He assigns to matter, the metaphysical stuff, the supreme position. Matter is the underlying substance for all being from the highest to the lowest, with the exception of God. He rejects the Neo-Platonic teachings regarding an impersonal and necessary cosmic process, and stresses the will of God. God is known only through his will, his effects in the world. As a mystic he even goes out of the way to find a physiological correlate to human virtues and vices. He also wrote Judaistic, intellectually inferior but popular ethical writings, in which he conspicuously avoided theological positions. .

N. Bialik, and I. H. Ravnitzky, *Shire* (Poems). 7 vols. (Tel-Aviv, 1927-32) ; I. Husik, *A History of Medieval Jewish Philosophy* (1941) ; J. Guttmann, *Die Philosophie des Salomon ibn Gabirol* (Gottingen, 1889) ; D. Kaufmann, *Studien über Salomon ibn Gabirol* (Budapest, 1899) ; S. Munk, *Mélanges de Philosophie Juive et Arabe* (Paris, 1859). H.H.

Gad: One of the twelve sons of Jacob, and so one of the twelve tribes of Israel. Also, as the name means "luck, fortune," a goddess. See Isaiah 65:11 (R.V.). P.G.M.

Galatians, Letters to the: Returning to Antioch after the second missionary journey Paul learned that teachers of a Judaizing form of Christianity had appeared in Galatia and persuaded the Galatian Christians to accept a legalistic variation of Christianity which he considered fatal to the great experience of faith. Writing in the name of the whole local brotherhood—the great missionary church of Antioch—he denounced the new teaching in the most vehement manner, asserted his apostolic commission as directly and divinely given, showed the hollowness of the Judaizers position, from various angles, and asserted the sufficiency of the attitude of faith, in the Christian experience; legalistic observances could add nothing to it, in fact they could only impair and nullify it. Galatians is a great assertion of Christian freedom; this freedom has its dangers, but it is nevertheless absolutely essential to the exercise of faith. Galatians was written from Antioch, about A.D. 52 or 53. The Galatian churches were probably those of Derbe, Lystra, Iconium and Pisidian Antioch, not of north Galatia, as some have argued.

E. D. Burton, *The Epistle to the Galatians* (1920) ; J. B. Lightfoot, *St. Paul's Epistle to the Galatians* (10th ed., 1890). E.J.G.

Galen (Galenus), Claudius: (2nd century) A cultured physician of Pergamum and later family physician to Marcus Aurelius* in Rome. An eclectic Aristotelian, he wrote voluminously on medicine, anatomy, and philosophy. J.E.N.

Galesburg Rule: A declaration concerning pulpit and altar fellowship with other denominations, adopted by the General Council, a body of conservative American Lutherans*, at Galesburg, Illinois, in 1875. The Rule, worded by Dr. C. P. Krauth*, is: "Lutheran pulpits are for Lutheran ministers only; Lutheran altars are for Lutheran communicants only." T.A.K.

Galilei, Galileo: (1564-1641) As his thought moved in dynamic terms, he inverted Aristotelian metaphysics. Instead of stressing the principle of final causality, he regards God as the first efficient cause or creator of the atoms.

Dialogues and Mathematical Demonstrations concerning Two New Sciences (1914) ; J. J. Fahie, *Galileo, his Life and Work* (1903) ; F. Wieser, *Galilei als Philosoph* (Basel, 1919) ; Z. Harsanyi, *The Star Gazer* (1939). H.H.

Gallican Confession: Also called "Confession of Rochelle," was drafted by Calvin*, enlarged and adopted by the Synod at Paris, in 1559, as a confession of faith and an order of discipline. Afterwards it was repeatedly revised under the direction of Beza, and finally ratified at the Seventh National Synod at La Rochelle, in 1571, in the presence of the Queen of Navarre and her son (Henry IV). The Gallican Confession, the work mainly of Calvin himself, and of his friend and successor, Beza*, in 40 articles contains a concise and faithful summary of the doctrines and discipline of John Calvin. It was superseded by "The Declaration of Faith of the Reformed Church in France," 1872.

Philip Schaff, *The Creeds of Christendom* (1877), vol. 1.

T.F.H.

Gallican liturgies: The ancient rites of the non-Roman Western Church, many features of which were adopted in the Roman rite when it superseded them in the early Middle Ages. See liturgy.

E.R.H.

Gallicanism: The name of two overlapping movements in the French Church—political, defending royal and lay rights as against Pope and clergy, and ecclesiastical, maintaining the autonomy of the French Church and the subordination of Popes to General Councils; both were united under Louis XIV in the Gallican Articles of 1682; thereafter Gallicanism declined gradually, although as late as 1869-1870 there was some French opposition to the doctrine of papal infallibility. See Loyson; Old Catholics; ultramontanism.

L. Pullan, *Religion Since the Reformation* (1923).

E.R.H.

Gamaliel I: Gamaliel I, also known as Gamaliel the Elder or Hazaken, a grandson of Hillel*, was one of the most prominent and respected teachers of the Law* of his day (30-60 C.E.) and occupied a leading position in the Sanhedrin*, the highest court at Jerusalem. In fact according to one tradition, he may have been the *Nasi** or head of the Sanhedrin.

There are not many laws or opinions in the Talmud* attributed to Gamaliel. However, a study of those that are recorded in his name show that he was keenly aware of the needs of his day and did not hesitate to act boldly to meet them. One of the principles which guided him in many of his enactments was that law must lead to the "improvement of the world" (*mippne tikkun Ha'olam*) and promote the common good.

Gamaliel is mentioned in Acts 5:34ff. as the Pharisee* who favored leniency at the trial of the disciples, arguing that "if this work be of men, it will be overthrown; but if it is of God ye will not be able to overthrow them." Gamaliel is also mentioned in Acts 22:3 where Paul* states that he was "brought up at the feet of Gamaliel."

E.B.-L.F.

gambling: The staking of money or other valuable or important considerations on a future event, chance, or contingency, which is unknown or uncertain to the participants. The essential element in gambling is *wagering*, or the act of staking or hazarding *per se*. In *gaming*, the future event is the outcome of a game of chance, or mixed chance and skill. Insofar as the outcome can be predicted by knowledge of the strength, skill, *et cetera*, of the contestants, the element of pure chance is usually increased by odds in favor of, or by handicaps against, the probable winner. Gaming is closely related to divination*, through which primitive man sought to forecast future events; in fact, the instruments devised for the one purpose were frequently employed for the other. Gambling, however, is more inclusive than gaming, since wagers may be laid on any uncertain social or physical contingency, such as the outcome of an election or the amount of precipitation during a given month or season. The *lottery* is a form of gambling in which prizes are distributed by lot or chance among persons who have paid for the chance to win.

Gambling is distinguished from legitimate forms of commercial speculation and insurance in that the latter perform useful social services by stabilizing the market and by shifting the incidence of loss or gain due to economic changes which would take place in any event, whereas the former increases instability, creates risks which serve no corresponding economic needs, and adds losses to some and equivalent gains to others which would not occur in the absence of the gambling transaction itself. On the other hand, speculative transactions become both socially and ethically a form of gambling when the intention of the parties is that no deliveries of commodities or securities shall be ever made, and that the whole price shall never be paid, but that the difference in value shall be ascertained at some future date and the excess or difference shall be paid directly from one party to the other.

John Ashton, *History of Gambling in England* (London, 1898); B. Seebohm Rowntree, *Betting and Gambling* (1905); Ernest D. MacDougall, *Speculation and Gambling* (1936).

H.E.J.

gaming: See gambling.

Gandharva: In the Vedas the term is usually singular. An obscure but very old figure, he is said to be the measurer of space and is related to the sun, and also with Soma. In the Avesta *Gandarewa* is a dragon like monster. Some scholars regard the Gandharvas as spirits of the wind. They are in later times represented as divine musicians in Indra's heaven. The Sanskrit word for music is *Gandharva.* They possess mysterious power over women. They are beloved of the Apsarases or heavenly nymphs of Indra's heaven.

C.S.B.

Gandhi, Mohandas Karamchand: Indian National leader, born Oct. 2, 1869, in Porbandar, India. Studied law in London; began practices in Bombay; in 1893 went to South Africa on legal business; soon, however, renounced wealth and position to lead the South African Indians in their struggle for greater justice, developing the doctrine of non-violence and truth-force into a powerful political and economic instrument. Returning to India in 1914, Gandhi was loyal to the British Government during the First World War with the expectation that India would receive self-government within the Empire. After the Amritsar Rebellion and the Rowlatt Enactments, he declared April 6, 1919 a day of National Humiliation and exhorted the people to a program of passive resistance, implemented by economic and political boycott and the development of home industries. In Dec. 1921, he became the recognized leader of the Indian National Congress, with comlete national independence as the avowed goal. Popularly Gandhi was titled Mahatma* (Great Soul). Though a devoted Hindu, he has found support for his doctrine of non-violence in the Sermon on the Mount and has commonly used the NT along with the Bhaghavad Gita* for spiritual guidance. He has been consistently sympathetic with the demand of the Hindu Untouchables for abolition of the caste system and has sought politically to unite Hindus and Moslems. In this latter effort he has been unsuccessful, with the Moslem Party finally demanding "Pakistan", a separate independent Moslem state. Gandhi has repeatedly used the hunger strike and the fast unto death as spiritual instruments to protest against British policy and to unify his people. In the crisis of 1942, with Japan threatening India, Gandhi was still sufficiently powerful to lead in a program of civil disobedience against British rule, resulting in his internment, in Aug., 1942, in the palace at Poona.

M. K. Gandhi, *Young India* (1927); C. F. Andrews, ed., *Mahatma Gandhi, His Own Story* (1930), and *Mahatma Gandhi at Work* (1931); Jashwant Rao Chitambar, *Mahatma Gandhi, His Life, Work and Influence* (1933). E.T.R.

Ganesha: The elephant headed son of Shiva, a popular divinity of Shivite Hinduism. He is the god of good luck, prosperity and of wisdom, and the remover of obstacles. He is usually represented as very fat and riding on the back of a rat. C.S.B.

Gano, John: (1727-1804) Baptist clergyman. Chaplain Continental Army. Prayed in Washington's headquarters at cessation of hostilities. Did not immerse Washington at Valley Forge. C..H.M.

Gansfort, John Wesel: (Doctor contradictionum), 1420-1489, educated by and ever a close associate of the Brethren of the Common Life.* Generally claimed by Protestants as a precursor of Luther*; but while they thought alike on many points, Wesel stressed "faith in love" to Luther's "faith alone," and, like Erasmus* later, he was irenical. Q.B.

Garizim: Sacred mountain of the Samaritans, near Shechem, Palestine (Deut. xi, 20; xxvii, 12; Jos. viii, 33). See F. M. Abel, *Géographie de la Palestine,* vol. i (1933), pp. 360-369. S.L.T.

Garman, Charles Edward: (1850-1907) A graduate of Amherst College in 1876 and Yale Divinity School 1879. Garman was called to Amherst to teach Philosophy in 1880 and thereafter occupied the chair of Mental and Moral Philosophy until his death. His teaching of philosophy was original in method and exceptionally stimulating to religious and theistic thought.

Cf. The memorial volume, *Letters, Lectures and Addresses of Charles Edward Garman* (1909). J.W.B.

Gass, Friedrich Wilhelm Joachim Heinrich: (1813-1889) He taught at the universities of Breslau, Greifswald, Giessen and Heidelberg. As a church historian he knew himself above all as a pupil of Schleiermacher*.

Geschichte der protestantischen Dogmatik in ihrem Zusammenhang mit der Theologie überhaupt, 4 vols. (Berlin, 1854-67); *Geschichte der christlichen Ethik,* 3 vols. (Berlin, 1881-87). H.H.

Gassendi, Pierre (1592-1655) French philosopher and mathematician; professor of theology and philosophy at Aix and later of mathematics at the Collège Royal in Paris. He was a leading opponent of Descartes* and revived interest in the materialism of Epicurus and Lucretius**. His chief works are *De Vita et Moribus Epicuri* (1647); *Philosophiae Epicuri Syntagma* (1649); and *Syntagma Philosophicum* (1658).

See G. S. Brett, *The Philosophy of Gassendi* (1908). J.E.N.

Gates, Theophilus: (1787-1846) See Battle-Axe experiment.

Gathas: The oldest part of the Avesta* (Yasna, chs. 28-34, 43-51, 53), consisting of 17 hymns arranged into 5 gathas according to meter; they preserve in its most authentic form the teaching of Zoroaster (for which see, Persia, religions of). R.H.P.

Gaunilo: (unknown—around 1083) The Count of Montigny, later a monk in the monastery Mar-Moutier, near Tours, who made himself famous with his *Liber pro insipiente,* "Book in behalf of the Fool". (Who said in his heart: there is no God.) In this treatise, Gaunilo subjected Saint Anselm's* (1033-1109) ontological argument* for the existence of God to a pungent criticism to which the ages could not add very much. S.C.T.

gayatri: A famous prayer repeated daily by all orthodox Hindus, taken from the Rig Veda (Book 3, lxii, 10) "Let us meditate on the adorable splendor of Savitar; may he enlighten our minds." It is also the name of one of the meters employed in the Vedic hymns. C.S.B.

Gehenna: (Gr., *Geenna,* from Heb., *Ge Hinnom*) The valley of Hinnom, near Jerusalem where early Israelites sacrificed children to Moloch*; afterward regarded a place of abomination and refuse, where fires continually burned to prevent pestilence. In the N.T. it refers to hell, and in general use indicates a torture chamber or place of suffering. See heaven and hell. P.E.J.

Geiler, John of Kaisersberg: (1445-1510) Popular preacher at Strassburg Cathedral. His sermons abound in practical illustrations, racy language, satire, humor. He strove to reform outward manners and morals. E.C.K.

Geisteswissenschaften: "Sciences of the mind" as opposed to the natural sciences. Term originating in the philosophy of Hegel* who distinguishes logic, philosophy of nature and philosophy of mind as the three main parts of his system. Wilhelm Dilthey* used the term G. in his *Einleitung in die G.* (introduction into the sciences of the mind). W. Windelband and H. Rickert defined G. as those sciences which deal with history and culture. R.K.

Gemara: The term *Gemara* is the Aramaic word for "learning", and as technically used is applied to the discussions of the Rabbinic scholars on the Mishna*, the code of Jewish law, formulated by the famous Rabbi Judah I the Patriarch and his colleagues, early in the third century. This Code became a text book in the Palestinian and Babylonian academies, where oral discussions of it, and comments on it, were crystallized into memorized books. These have come down to us in the form of the Palestinian Talmud* and the Babylonian Talmud. The former originated in the academies of the Holy Land, in the third and fourth centuries; the latter in those of Babylonia in the third, fourth and fifth centuries. The Talmud includes both the Mishna and the comments; the term Gemara is used exclusively for the comments. Cf. amora. L.F.

Gematria: See Kabbalah.

General Assembly: The phrase is scriptural (Heb. 12:23). In church history and now it is used principally as the title of the supreme judicatories of Presbyterian churches*, e.g., those of Scotland and the United States. The general assembly has authority executive, legislative except as limited by the need of the concurrence of presbyteries, and judicial. In other Reformed churches of Presbyterian polity the General Synod is equivalent. R.H.N.

General Association of Regular Baptist Churches in the U. S. A.: A group of Baptist churches in the North which united in "an endeavor to get back to the old-fashioned ideals, policies, and practices of Baptists as they used to be." It claims to be a "fellowship" as distinguished from a "convention," and that its churches are not "members," since "a Baptist church cannot be a member of anything outside itself." Its theological position is fundamentalist. There are 84 churches and 22,000 members. E.T.C.

General Baptists: A sect of Arminian or free-will Baptists in the United States. They differ little from other "free-will" or "general" Baptists**, but are organized in a separate denomination. They claim 422 churches and 36,000 members. E.T.C.

General Conference Mennonites: See Mennonites.

general councils: See councils.

General Six-Principle Baptists: A sect of Arminian Baptists emphasizing the "six principles" of Heb. 6:1, 2: repentance, faith, baptism, laying on of hands, resurrection of the dead, and eternal judgment. The sect claims to be the original Baptist church in America, founded by Roger Williams. It now has only 4 congregations and fewer than 300 members. See Baptists. E.T.C.

Genesis: The first book of the O.T., being an account of the creation of the world and the primeval history of mankind (chapters 1-11) and the history of the patriarchs (chapters 12-50). Moses* is considered to be the author by Jewish, Christian and Islamic tradition, but the book is the product of a long process of writing and editing by J, E and P**, reaching its final form *cir.* 400 B.C. Some scholars have claimed for the book other sources, such as S*, an Edomitic* document (R. H. Pfeiffer) and L*, a primitive lay source (Otto Eissfeldt). In its present form Genesis shows a greater unity of conception and purpose than most of the other composite books of the Hexateuch*. The first eleven chapters contain profound religious myths which resemble those of other civilizations of the ancient Near East; the story of the flood*, for example, so closely resembles the account of the flood in the Gilgamesh Epic* as to suggest direct or ultimate dependence upon it. The remainder of Genesis consists of legends concerning the patriarchs, the ancestral fathers of the Hebrew nation. Recent archaeological discoveries, especially at Nuzi in northern Mesopotamia, tend to authenticate the general background of these legends, but their historicity in detail cannot be affirmed.

S. R. Driver, *The Book of Genesis* (Westminster Comm., 2nd ed. 1904); R. H. Pfeiffer, *Introduction to the Old Testament* (1941). J.P.H.

Genesis, the Little: See Jubilees, Book of.

Geneva Bible: Sometimes known as the Puritan Bible or "Breeches" Bible*. It was the work of a group of Marian exiles at Geneva, and was distinguished by the copious use of marginal notes for the interpretation of passages. The first edition was printed in 1560. Even after the publication of the King James Version in 1611, this Geneva version remained for many years the most popular English Bible. See Bible, English. W.S.H.

Genevieve, St.: (c. 422-512) Saint, patroness of Paris. Woman of deep piety and monastic zeal to whom powers of prophesying were attributed. Her shrine attained great popularity. K.H.C.

gentile: The rendering in English of a Gr. word used in the Septuagint* to mean "non-Jew," "foreigner," or "heathen," and occurring in the

N.T. also in that sense. "Gentile Christianity" describes the Church which drew its members from among non-Jews. According to Acts 11:20 f., non-Jews (as distinguished from Jewish proselytes) were first admitted to the Church at Antioch*. Paul soon came to be recognized as the "apostle to the Gentiles," and before the writing of the *Epistle to the Romans* Gentile Christianity had come greatly to outnumber Jewish Christianity*. S.M.G.

Gentili, Alberico: (1552-1608) An Italian Protestant who fled to England, becoming Regius Professor of Civil Law at Oxford. The greater part of *De Jure Belli Libri Tres* (1598) is devoted to an analysis of the rules that ought to govern the conduct of war. He advocated for Europe an international government with decisions made by the majority of states.

T. A. Walker, *History of the Law of Nations*, vol. I. (Cambridge, 1899). H.H.

genuflexion: (Lat., *genu-flexio*, bow the knee) A ceremonial posture adopted in the Catholic Church at certain points, as, e.g., before the Blessed Sacrament, at the *incarnatus* in the Creed, etc. See kneeling at communion. W.N.P.

Georgian style: See art, ecclesiastical, Christian; church building.

Gerbert of Aurillac: (Pope Sylvester II, 999-1003) Born in Auvergne, he acquired not only the training of his native land, with the Benedictines* of Aurillac, but also the culture of Spain, in which country he studied mathematics, astronomy and music with the bishop of Vich. Subsequent to a sojourn in Rome, he became a student at Rheims where he distinguished himself as teacher of philosophy, dialectic, and mathematics, and as head of the episcopal school. He later appeared in public disputation at Ravenna before Otto II who bestowed upon him the abbacy of Bobbio. For a short time, and not very happily, abbot of this famous monastery, he returned to Rheims where he was to become archbishop. In 999, Otto III secured the papacy for his old tutor who took the name of Sylvester II. R.C.P.

Gerhard, Johann: (1582-1637) German Lutheran dogmatician and foremost exponent of Lutheran orthodoxy. Professor at Jena for two decades, Gerhard was at once a highly respected teacher, an ecclesiastical leader, and a counselor of princes. But his fame rests on his doctrinal works, chiefly his *Loci Theologici* (1610-1622) in nine huge volumes and the four-volume *Confessio Catholica* (1634-1637). His devotional book *Meditationes Sacrae* (1606) has been translated into most European languages and is still widely used. An irenic and constructive theologian, Gerhard interprets Lutheranism in terms of evangelical catholicity. In massive learning, comprehensive scope, accuracy of detail, and logical precision Gerhard is a Lutheran counterpart of Aquinas. His contemporaries regarded him as the greatest of living theologians. T.A.K.

Gerhardt, Paul: See hymns.

Gerlach, Stephen (1546-1612) Champlain for the German Embassy in Constantinople. He studied in the University of Tübingen, Württ. As pastor in the East, he cultivated the friendship of literary men and his diary is a valuable source of information about Greece, Turkey, Palestine and Egypt. He studied many literary and social problems of the enslaved Greek nation and brought back to Germany valuable manuscripts and the much needed information about the Near East. The reward for his work in Greece was his appointment as Professor of Theology in the University of Tübingen. G.E.Z.

German Baptist Brethren: See Dunkers.

German Reformed Church, the: See Reformed Church in the U. S. See Churches of God in North America.

German separatist communities: See communistic settlements, religious.

Gerson, Jean Charlier de: (1363-1429) The most influential French ecclesiastic of the later 14th and early 15th centuries, Chancellor of the University of Paris for thirty-four years, theologian, preacher, conciliarist. His administrative reforms raised the standards of instruction at the University of Paris. As a churchman and preacher he strove for the reform of the church and sought to increase the piety of its members. His clear espousal of the conciliarist cause is notably expressed in his tracts, *De Unitate Ecclesiastica* and *De Auferibilitate Papae Ab Ecclesia*, and exemplified by his dynamic leadership at the Council of Constance*. In philosophy he held a modified nominalist position. In theology he was a mystic. See conciliarism. F.W.N.

Gerson, Levi ben (Gersonides): (1288-1340) Jewish theologian and astronomer. A bold, rigorous thinker, unflinchingly Aristotelian* in theology. God does not know matter or particularity; not that His knowledge is imperfect, but that the formal, rational order of things alone is worth knowing or fully real. Also, man's will being free, and acts he might, in future, perform or not perform being thus indeterminate, the divine or true knowledge, which sees things as they are, will see these acts only *as* indeterminate or possible. (See foreknowledge, divine; and Carneades.) This second argument implies that past and present events, being determinately particular, must by divine knowledge be known as such, but G. overlooks this because (equally with Maimonides*, the chief object of his polemic) he believes God to be immutable and devoid of contingency, whereas, he argues, only what is in some way contingent and changing can know the contingent and changing. The premise is that an object of knowledge "substantializes" the knowing (were the object not actual, the knowing of it as actual would be potential only). This Maimonides had conceded of human knowing, and he had conceded further that if the contingent objects of God's knowing are similarly required for the actuality of his knowledge of them (as actual), then part of God's actuality must be contingent. M. avoided this conclusion by denying any and all analogy between humanly conceivable and divine "knowledge" (or other attributes). G. points to the theological havoc wrought by this denial, and proposes instead the denial that God knows contingent objects, except in their non-contingent, providential, immaterial elements or aspects. This denial, held to be none, of omniscience is a heroic effort to save the purely absolutistic conception of God (see cause; perfect; omnipotent; personal, God as) while avoiding the paradox of a knowing which is necessary through and through although what it knows exists to be known (as existent) only contingently. It did not occur to G.—or to other medieval thinkers—that if God's knowing is really analogous—with whatever sublime differences—to man's, it may, like man's, though in radically superior fashion, involve elements of contingency and change. See time, L. Gerson, *The Wars of God* (in Hebrew; Ger. trans. by B. Kellermann, 1916). See I. Husik, *A History of Jewish Philosophy* (1916). C.H.

I. Weil, *Philosophie religieuse de Levi ben Gerson* (Paris, 1868); M. Joel, *Beiträge zur Geschichte der Philosophie* (Breslau, 1876); I. Husik, "Studies in Gersonides," *Jewish Quarterly*. vol. III. (1917-18); J. Guttmann, *Die Philosophie des Judentums* (München, 1933); J. Karo, *Kritische Untersuchungen zu Levi ben Gersons Widerlegung des Aristotelischen Zeitbegriffes* (Leipzig, 1935). H.H.

Gesenius, Friedrich Heinrich Wilhelm: 1786-1842) German Orientalist and Biblical critic, born at Nordhausen, Hanover. He was professor of theology (after 1810) in the University of Halle, where he became the most popular teacher in Germany in his field and a pioneer in establishing the scientific study of Semitic languages (especially Hebrew) and of the O.T. His Hebrew grammar and lexicon have gone through many editions and have been widely translated. J.P.H.

Gess, Wolfgang Friedrich: (1819-1891) He first taught at the Basel Mission House; then at the universities of Göttingen and Breslau. Embracing kenotic* christology, he gave it especially pronounced biblical traits.

Christi Person und Werk nach Christi Selbstzeugniss und den Zeugnissen der Apostel, 3 vols. (Basel, 1870-87). H.H.

gestalt psychology: See psychology, schools of.

Geulincx, Arnold: (1624-1669) Dutch theologian in Löwen (Louvain) who later became a Calvinist and died as professor at the University of Leiden. He owes his fame to his doctrine of Occasionalism* according to which we are only onlookers not actors of our lives. The body is only an instrument; neutral reflexes and the inner will are only *occasiones, causae occasionales* for God who as a *vera causa* performs all our actions. His most important book *Tractatus Ethicus primus* appeared in 1665. S.C.T.

Ghazzali, Al-: See Algazali.

ghetto: Originally the word, ghetto, was used to designate the separate section of the city in which Jews resided following the diaspora* whether from choice or compulsion. More recently it has been applied to the immigrant community in America in which any group differing in language, race, religion, or general culture has for a time been segregated. Segregation of the Jew first took place in response to common needs and mutual desires; later from compulsion. The compulsory ghetto restricted the movements of the Jew, his economic opportunities, and in general isolated him from the remainder of the population. Commonly the compulsory ghetto was enclosed by walls within which all Jews were compelled to remain under penalty except for restricted hours when they were permitted access to the surrounding community for business purposes. Such ghettos had gradually disappeared until revived by the Nazi regime in Germany.

The voluntary ghetto, whether of Jews or non-Jews, reached its zenith in the United States at about the time of World War I where it provided a transition from the Old World to the New for the large influx of immigrants. As the immigrant has been assimilated, with the restrictions upon immigration through quotas the areas of first settlement have tended to disappear except for the segregated colonies of Negroes who because of race prejudice are confined to restricted areas in American cities in much the same fashion as was the Jew in historical Europe. See anti-semitism. E.R.M.

Ghibellines and Guelfs: Both terms are medieval and signify two different trends of thought, parties or affiliations in the former Holy Roman German Empire*, the one emphasizing the spiritual, the other the temporal power. The Ghibellines favored primarily the German emperors in their relations to the Papacy; the Guelfs favored the popes. Historically, the terminology of the two factions can be traced as far back as 1215, when the nobility of Florence was divided, the one faction favoring the exploits of the Emperor (Frederick II) into Italy, the other, in union with the people of Tuscany and Lombardy, opposing them. Later, the terms were used to differentiate, especially in the larger cities and communes, the feudal nobles (Ghibellines) and the plebeans or peoples' party (Guelfs) whom the popes always favored in their struggles for independence and freedom. Pavia and Siena, e.g., were Ghibelline; Milan and Florence, Guelf. Although Pope Benedict XII, in 1334, had forbidden under ecclesiastical censure use of the terms, the nomenclature temporarily remained at least as catch words of two different political trends and traditional animosities, until the advent of Charles V into Italy (1529) who established a new relation between Pope and Emperor. That the terms were in usage also in Germany (Waiblingen and Welfen) as early as the XII century is held by many authors, as representing the rivalry between the House of Welf (the Dukes of Bavaria) and the House of the

Hohenstaufen (the Duke of Suabia), the former being the Guelfs, the latter, the Ghibellines. The terms served in Germany also to differentiate the followers of Emperor Frederick I (Barbarossa) and those of Pope Alexander III* in the Lombardic struggles for supremacy. In Germany the terms disappear in the XIV century.

Paulet, *Guelfs et Gibelines,* 2 vols. (Paris, 1922); *Lex. f. Theol. u. Kirche,* IV, 486; *Cath. Encyc.* VII, 56-58. R.M.H.

ghost: See death and burial practices; primitive religion; spirits.

Gideons, The: An interdenominational laymen's association organized in 1899 by John H. Nicholson, Samuel E. Hill and William J. Knights at the Janesville, Wis., Y. M. C. A. Its program includes a ministry of evangelism and the purchase and distribution of Bibles placed in hotels, hospitals, penitentiaries and since 1937 in public schools.

The International headquarters are located in Chicago, Ill. V.F.

Gilbert de la Porree: (1076-1154) Besides being the greatest logician of the twelfth century, he also represents the culmination of moderate realism, a middle ground between Plato and Aristotle. He held that the persons of the trinity owed their existence, their unity, to divine subsistence.

A. Berthaud, *Gilbert de la Porrée et sa philosophie* (Poitiers, 1892). H.H.

Gildas: (ca. 493-ca. 570) British monk, author of *The Fall of Britain,* a gloomy description of Christian Britain (Wales) during and after the Anglo-Saxon invasion of the island.

H. Williams, *Gildas.* (Cymmrodorion Record Series III, 1899.) J.T.M.

Gilgamesh epic: The principal work of ancient Assyro-Babylonian literature which has survived. It recounts the heroic exploits and wanderings of Gilgamesh, who had apparently been originally an historical ruler of Uruk but became a mythical figure, and his friend, Engidu, half-man and half-bull. It contains the Babylonian Flood* Story, which is told to Gilgamesh by his ancestor Utnapishtum, to whom he had gone seeking the secret of immortality. The best preserved version of this epic is from the Assyrian library of Ashurbanipal, but the Babylonian version was probably composed about 2000 B.C. and was based in part upon Sumerian legends of the third millennium B.C. A translation into English free verse has been published by William Ellery Leonard: *Gilgamesh, Epic of Old Babylonia,* (1934). J.P.H.

Gioberti, Vincenzo: (1801-1852) At first devoted himself to a clerical career, later he was professor at the university of Turin, Italy. He was imprisoned and exiled for trying morally and politically to regenerate the Italians. He tried to reconcile the papacy with political liberalism. He developed a Platonic ontology, reminding one of Malebranche and Spinoza**.

Teoria del sovranaturale (Brussels, 1838); *Del primato morale e civile degli Italiana* (Brussels, 1843); *Discorso preliminare sulla teoria del sovranaturale* (Paris, 1850); *Della riforma cattolica della chiesa* (Torino, 1856); *Della filosofia della rivelazione* (Torino, 1856); B. Spaventa, *La filosofia di Gioberti* (Napoli, 1863); L. Ferri, *Essai sur l'histoire de la philosophie en Italie au XIX siecle* (Paris, 1869); K. Werner, *Die italienische Philosophie des neunzehnten Jahrhunderts.* 5 vols. (Wien, 1884-86). H.H.

Girgensohn, Karl: (1875-1925) German Protestant theologian. He was born in Oesel, Latvia. From 1903-1907 he was privatdozent in Dorpat, from 1907-1918 professor of Systematic Theology, Dorpat; from 1919-1922 at Greifswald, and from 1922-25 in Leipzig.

He was a representative of conservative Lutheran theology and was a prolific writer. Especially was he influential through his psychology of religion, in which he attempted to apply experimental methods to the study of the Christian faith.

Principal works: *Die Religion, ihre psychischen Formen und ihre Zentralidee* (1903); *Seele und Leib* (1908); *Der seelische Aufbau des religiösen Erlebens. Eine religions-psychologische Untersuchung auf experimenteller Grundlage* (1921); Autobiography in *Die Religionswissenschaft in Selbstdarstellungen,* vol. 2 (1926). O.A.P.

given, the: 1) Reality*, or the universe, regarded as independent of man's thought. 2) The total field of experience as it is at any particular time, or at all times (so D. C. Williams). 3) The sensory content or data with which thought deals; also any aesthetic, moral, religious or other experiences regarded as subject matter for interpretation by thought. 4) That in a personal consciousness (especially in God's) which is not created or produced by the choice or will of the person (so Brightman). See finite God. E.S.B.

Gladden, Washington: (1836-1918) A. B. Williams College 1859; engaged in hospital work with the U. S. Army 1863; pastor Congregational Church, North Adams, Mass. 1866-1871; North Church, Springfield, Mass. 1875-1882; First Congregational Church, Columbus, Ohio, 1882-1918. He was on the editorial staff of *The Independent* 1871-1874.

Author: *Being a Christian* (1876); *How Much is Left of the Old Doctrines* (1899); *Present Day Theology* (1913); *Ruling Ideas of the Present Age* (1895); *Social Salvation* (1902); *Ultima Veritas* (poems) (1912); *Recollections* (1909) (an autobiography); etc.,—some forty volumes in all.

Dr. Gladden was an energetic and fearless leader in liberating and socializing American theology and in vitalizing church and civic life.

His familiar hymn "O Master, let me walk with Thee" (1880) serves to keep living the spirit of his "lowly" but wide and forward-looking service. See New theology, the. J.W.B.

Glassites: A small Scottish sect so-named from its founder, John Glas (1695-1773); also known as Sandemanians from his son-in-law, Robert Sandeman (1718-1771), who modified the teaching of the sect. It repudiated the State connection as antichristian; sought to conduct its affairs after the pattern of primitive Christianity; and was extremely strict and exclusive in matters of conduct. A.K.R.

Glogau, Gustav: (1844-1895) Was professor of philosophy at the university of Kiel, Germany. Only psychology can show how the spiritual forces—ethical, social, artistic and religious—emerge in actual history. At the apex of all philosophy is the existence of God. God is because I am. Derived from God is the world of ideas. These exert a "solicitation", whereby the finite spirits inwardly develop. Glogau combats an intellectualism that exalts logical activity for its own sake. His thought approximates theosophy or mysticism.

Ein Beitrag zur Religionsphilosophie (Kiel, 1891); *Gustav Glogaus Vorlesungen ueber Religionsphilosophie*, ed. by H. Claasen (Kiel, 1898); J. Andrich, *Glogaus Theorie ueber die Entwicklungsstufen des Geistes* (Erlangen, 1913). H.H.

gloria: (Latin) The second section of the ordinary of the mass, used regularly except during Advent, Lent, and at funerals. A song of joy originating at the Christmas festival. E.H.B.

gloria in excelsis: The ancient Angelic Hymn (cf. Luke 2, 14). It is of Greek origin, and in the Eastern Church is used at Matins (*Orthros*). In the Roman Mass it is used (but not in penitential seasons) after the *Kyrie**. In the Anglican Communion service it is a post-communion hymn of thanksgiving. P.V.N.

gloria patri: A brief ascription of praise to the three persons of the Trinity*, used in the Western Church at the end of the psalms and canticles of the divine office* and in several other contexts. P.V.N.

glory, Old Testament conception of: A theological *terminus technicus* used most frequently to translate the Hebrew word *kābôd*. 1) Its primary meaning in secular usage was "to be heavy." A man's "Glory" was that about him which was weighty, important, the place of honor which his material possessions gave him, or whatever was imposing about him (cf. Gen. 31:1; 45:13; Psa. 49:17). 2) When applied to God, it refers to the imposing nature of His appearance. It is impossible for man to see God, but man does see God's "glory", a shining envelope surrounding His being. Thus we hear of the pillar of cloud and of fire in the wilderness, of the cloud at the dedication of Solomon's Temple and in the visions of Isaiah (chap. 6:4) and Ezekiel (chap. 1: 26ff.). 3) The term seems to have been further developed as the inclusive name for the self-revelation of God, whether in nature or in history (cf. Isa. 6:3; 60:1-3; Psa. 19:1). 4) Man, on his part, should "give glory to God": that is, recognize the weight and claims of God's revelation and regulate his life accordingly (Isa. 42:12; Psa. 29:1, etc.). G.E.W.

glosses: (from *glossa* meaning "tongue", or a word needing explanation) Hence it came to be used of the additional comments added in the margin or between the lines which later copyists incorporated into the text. From that it has come to mean any sentences or phrases not belonging to the original writing. C.T.C.

gnomic couplet: A maxim or proverb epitomizing some point of moral wisdom based on experience, cast in the characteristic parallelism of Hebrew verse; e.g., Proverbs 10:1. R.B.Y.S.

Gnosticism: Decades of modern research into the origin of Gnosticism have issued in a vast accumulation of materials for analysis, comparison, and synthesis and in the setting aside of earlier explanations but not in any final solution of the intricate problems presented. The early church fathers called gnosticism, Greek wisdom; Harnack* termed Christian gnosticism, the "acute Hellenization of Christianity"; Gnosticism is now regarded as "pre-Christian oriental mysticism." The emphasis has shifted from interpreting it as philosophy and speculation to appreciating it as mysticism and primitive religious elements with Anz tracing its beginnings to the Babylonian religion; Friedlaender observing pre-Christian Jewish tints; Reitzenstein looking first to Egypt and then to Iran for its origin; Troje turning to India, Bousset to Babylonia and Iran and Eisler to the Orphic cults as sources. The total trend, designated Gnosticism, has become a syncretistic whirlpool with one eddy the orientalization of the Graeco-Roman civilization and the other the hellenization of the Orient.

The particular relation between Christianity and gnosticism has been defined as derivation of the former from the latter, as non-existent, and as the impact of the syncretism caused by the amalgamation of orientalism with Graeco-Roman culture upon Christianity. Christian gnosticism was the attempt to separate Christianity from its past by fusion with its environment.

Gnosticism was always a plan of salvation, a cosmic or supercosmic drama accompanied by a corresponding historical drama, outlining the story of the world from its creation to its redemption to its destruction; depicting the story of Man from his origin to the last man; narrating the story of the heaven-sent redeemer who recapitulated in his own life the drama of the cosmos; portraying the story of the individual man who likewise completed the cycle of suffering, dying, and rising again.

Gnosticism formerly understood as dualistic has become both dualistic and monistic, with a high God and a demiurge*; a cosmic fall* and an historic fall; a pleroma and an hysterema; spirit opposed to matter; good and evil desire; Man of Paradise and man of history. But it also had a synthesis, *coincidentia oppositorum*, the good God responsible for the demiurge and his evil world, the restoration of the original situation whence the next stage of movement proceeded. Light associated with darkness but returned to light. Spirit and soul were finally separated from the evil body. Elements of the pleroma that sank to the hysterema finally returned to the realm of perfection, immateriality, and the absolute.

The ethic of gnosticism was cooperation with the world process and therefore both ascetic and libertine. Without esoteric, revealed knowledge and magical practices and sacraments the way of salvation could not be known. Earthly men were of three kinds: hylics, psychics, pneumatics with the psychics redeemed by faith and the pneumatics by gnosis.

Christian gnosticism tended toward repudiation of the O.T. and made Jesus an appearance and his death only apparent. The high aeon* entered the body of Jesus at baptism and deserted it before the death upon the cross. It discriminated between creator-god and the Father of Jesus. The gnostic god was a philosophical abstraction with mystical trimmings and redemption a divine comedy. In gnosticism the same god could not be both creator and judge and redeemer. If gnosticism had triumphed, Christianity would have become just another Graeco-Roman mystery cult. See Agapetae; Basilides; mystery religions; Ophites; salvation; Valentinus.

S. Angus, *The Mystery Religions and Christianity* (1925); W. Bousset, *Hauptprobleme der Gnosis* (1907); S. J. Case, *The Evolution of Early Christianity* (1914); R. Eisler, *Orphisch-dionysische Mysteriengedanken in der Christlichen Antike* (1925); John Knox, *Marcion and the New Testament* (1942); N. Leisegang, *Die Gnosis* (1924); R. Reitzenstein, *Poimandres* (1904); *Das iranische Erloesungsmysterium* (1921); *Die hellenistischen Mysterien—religionen* (1927); P. Wendland, *Die hellenistische—roemische Kultur* (1912), 163 ff.

C.H.M.

goblin: (Perhaps from med. Lat. from Greek *kobaloi*, spirits invoked by rogues) A mischievous, repulsive demon.

F.L.P.

God: There are numerous theories as to the origin of the belief in God or gods. Some of these theories have had an anti-religious motive. They have sought to discredit theistic faith by ascribing its origin to fear, to the objectification of desire, to perverted sexuality, to priest and state craft, to social injustice, to dreams and trances, or to some other unworthy or untrustworthy aspect of human life or experience. The sufficient response to all such theories is that the validity of a belief or institution is not dependent on its historical genesis but on its present rationality and worth. Astronomy, chemistry and manual labor are not discredited by their historical connection with astrology, alchemy and slavery. And the same holds true of religion, in so far as it emerged out of earlier superstitious beliefs of one kind or another.

On the other hand, the belief in God cannot be validated by tracing its origin back to a primitive revelation, as some religious apologists have done. For aside from the impossibility of scientifically establishing such a theory, a divine revelation cannot be recognized as such without an antecedent belief in God. So setting aside the idea of a miraculous revelation some philosophical theologians have argued that theistic belief is rooted in a native human religious capacity which is as fundamental, as independent, and as trustworthy as is the theoretical, the moral, and the aesthetic reason. This is the theory to which the epistemology of Kant and Schleiermacher naturally leads.

In the evolution of the biblical idea of God there were two developments of special significance. One was the moralizing and the universalizing of Jehovah, by the great Hebrew prophets: Amos, Hosea, Isaiah, Jeremiah, Ezekiel, and Deutero-Isaiah. This spiritual achievement under the extremely adverse political conditions that then prevailed is without parallel in the religious history of mankind. It constituted one of the great epochs of the human spirit. The other development was the fulfilment or culmination of the prophetic movement in the life and death of Christ. In the teaching of Jesus and Paul the God of Israel became not only a righteous and universal Deity in a more absolute sense than heretofore, he became a suffering God, a God of sacrificial love. This ideal through its embodiment in the person of Christ gave rise to the doctrine of the Trinity, with which we are not here concerned.

The prophetic-Christian conception of God was predominantly practical rather than theoretical in its source. But it became gradually fused with congenial theistic elements in Greek philosophy, and out of this fusion arose the rationalized Christian doctrine of God. This doctrine in its main outlines has persisted in the church down to the present. It is monotheistic. It represents God as a unitary, personal Being, as immutable, as omnipotent, as omnipresent, as omniscient, as eternal, as the Creator and Preserver of the world, as a morally perfect Being, as a righteous and loving Father.

The existence of such a Deity was assumed in primitive Christianity. There was no need of proving it. But in the Graeco-Roman world the situation was different. There skepticism was common, and the church soon found it necessary to provide an apologetic for its faith. In the subsequent history of the theistic argument three periods may be distinguished. The first extended to 1200 A.D., the second from 1200 to 1800, and the third from 1800 to the present. During the first period the "ontological" argument was dominant, during the second the "cosmological" and "teleological" arguments, and since 1800, the "moral" argument.

The ontological argument received its classical formulation from Anselm* (d. 1109) but its underlying principle or principles go back to Plato. According to Platonic or Neoplatonic realism the more universal an idea is, the greater is its reality, the greater its causal efficiency, and the greater its worth. The supreme universal is, therefore, the supreme cause, the supreme good, the supreme truth, the supreme reality. The very idea of a supreme or perfect Being thus implies his existence. For if he did not exist, he would not be supreme or perfect. Existence is implicit in the idea of perfection. But from the modern individualistic standpoint this "conceptual" argument, as it may be called, has no cogency. Between idea and reality there is a gulf which no logic can bridge.

The cosmological and teleological* arguments came into ascendancy with the revival of Aristotelianism in the thirteenth century. These arguments reason from the existence of the world to the existence of God as its cause, and hence may together be called the "causal" argument. According to Kant, the cosmological argument rests on "indefinite experience only", and, according to Thomas Aquinas, consists in reasoning from motion to a Prime Mover, from efficient or secondary causes to a First Cause, and from contingent existence to a necessary Being. The teleological or "physico-theological" argument, on the other hand, takes its start, according to Kant, "from definite experience, and the special constitution of the sense world thus revealed to us". By Aquinas it is called the "argument from the governance of the world." More commonly it is known as the "design" argument. These two arguments are in principle valid, if the validity of the category of cause is admitted. But God as mere Creator falls far short of the full Christian idea of deity.

The moral or "valuational" argument was Kant's substitute for the preceding theoretical arguments. It is based on the demands of the moral nature. Conscience assumes that the moral ideals are realizable. But they can be realized only if there is a supreme moral will. Morality thus leads inevitably to religion. God is a postulate of the moral law. This line of thought, supplemented by Schleiermacher's and Lotze's conception of the objectivity of religious as well as moral values, makes provision for the God of Christian experience, as the purely theoretical arguments did not.

The history of Christian thought with respect to God reveals on the whole remarkable continuity. But there have been several important developments or changes of emphasis, such as 1) the change from a universalistic to an individualistic conception of the divine nature or essence, 2) a change from a more or less dualistic to an immanental view of God's relation to the world, 3) a tendency toward an idealistic as distinguished from the earlier realistic conception of nature, 4) a stress on the orderliness of the divine will as opposed to the earlier emphasis on its arbitrary character, 5) an emphasis on the "passibility" of God as distinguished from the earlier emphasis on his "impassibility", and 6) the grounding of theistic belief in the practical rather than the theoretical reason. See analogy; attributes of God; cause; creation; finite God; first cause; foreknowledge; God as personal; eternal; eternity; immanence; infinite; omnipotence; omnipresence; omniscience; panentheism; pantheism; perfect; super-personal; theism; theodicy; time; transcendence; trinity.

B. P. Bowne, *Theism* (1902); A. E. Taylor, Art. "Theism," in Hastings' *Enc. Rel. Eth.* (1917-22); A. S. Pringle-Pattison, *The Idea of God* (1917); W. R. Sorley, *Moral Values and the Idea of God* (1919); F. R. Tennant, *Philosophical Theology*, Vol. II (1930); A. C. Knudson, *The Doctrine of God* (1930), and *The Philosophy of Personalism* (1927).

A.C.K

God, as personal: Persons as we know them are social, that is, they enjoy personal relations. A "personal God" suggests one who can respond to prayer. But we may distinguish two forms of response, local and cosmic. God, if a cosmic being, can "answer" one man's prayer only as he simultaneously and without foolish bias takes account of other men's prayers and of all cosmic needs. God may nonetheless respond to the universe with full regard to the individuals which actually compose it, and in this sense may enjoy personal relations (See omnipotence and perfection.)

Since a person is a conscious individual, an impersonal deity must lack either consciousness or individuality (or both). Both have been often denied to God, and for the same reason: that they imply limitations. To be conscious of something is to be subject confronted by object, determined by it, and with it constituting a whole greater than either subject or object alone. Again, to be an individual is to be one member of a class or species rather than another, is to be this while failing to be that, for example, here and now in space and time rather than there and then. Men are individuated from one another, it is argued, by their defects and inabilities; but the being with all power and value must be being and value as such, "pure" being, rather than this or that being or personality in particular. It is also often said that God is not conscious or individual because he is super-conscious, super-personal*. It may be doubted, however, if "super" has here any meaning; since value is an affair of valuation and enjoyment, and superior value can only be superior satisfaction for some valuer, and a "super-personal valuer" seems only verbally distinguished from a superior type of person.

The limitations inherent in "personality" are of two kinds, only one of which need apply to a personal God. 1) Men are individuated partly by their localization in space-time, by the fact that they are parts of a larger whole, able to deal effectively with but a small portion of this whole. But suppose a being able to deal effectively with all portions of reality and in this sense non-localized. (See omnipresence.) 2) Such a being would still have a kind of limitation, in that it would deal with reality as it is and not as it might be. Even the whole of actual reality is limited, by comparison with the logically possible; and the being who, in non-localized or universally efficacious fashion, deals with all actual things as actual, can yet deal with possible things only as possible, until they too have been actualized (and not all of them can be at once—see perfection), and so he must lack whatever value would be found in dealing with these possible things as actual, should they become actual. Our human individuality is that of parts of the cosmos; the divine individuality may be that of the cosmos itself as integrated into a single self-identical life. (See panentheism.) If the parts of the universe have individuality, the whole cannot be mere being in general. However, it may be asked if the whole has sufficient unity to be personal; for the individual is contrasted not only to the general but to the ununified or unintegrated. The universe has integrity at least in the sense that it is the only whole whose literal dissolution seems unthinkable. The pervasive laws of nature also suggest cosmic unity. If in us a precarious and imperfect integration of activities, easily disrupted, has for its internal reality a fitful and imperfect individual awareness, the seemingly inviolable integration of all cosmic activities into the grand pattern studied by science (a pattern which, as Fechner likes to insist, is omnipresent and unfailing) may mean a perfect consciousness. Thus, on the one hand, one may argue from the cosmic body to the cosmic all-ordering mind. On the other, we have no analogy* by which to conceive God as an individual mind or person unless we impute to him a body adequate to his cosmic functions. What but the cosmos itself could be such a body? True, the cosmic body has defects, since its parts have defects. However, the perfection of an integrated whole is in principle of a different order from the sum of the values of its parts. God cannot, in every sense, escape limitation and yet have a cosmic body (or a cosmic mind, in any sense that is humanly conceivable, even dimly); but he may very well escape our forms of (localizing) limitations, and thus may enjoy a unique kind of perfection*, though not in every sense an absolute one. And though the cosmic body must inevitably bring tragedy into the life of God—for there is discord in the life of that body—this fact, so far from contradicting the religious perfection of God, may be its very expression. For it means that our tragedies are not matters of mere indifference to the perfectly loving being, nor yet matters of pure (and ethically monstrous) bliss, but of sympathetic sorrow tinging the divine blessedness, though not overcoming it. (For this reason Whitehead* speaks of the "heroic" character of God, and says that to impute mere happiness to him is a profanation.)

The purely absolute* and wholly unlimited God of the main philosophical and theological tradition is scarcely to be termed personal, if words are to retain any meaning. The positing of the "persons" of the Trinity*, even when combined with the doctrine of the Incarnation of one of the persons, seems not to remove the basic contradiction between individuality and the sheer absence of limitation. Since philosophy is now inclined to doubt the consistency of the traditional absolutism, regardless of whether or not this absolutism be combined with a personal view of God, and since the limitations inherent in personality as such are no more than are implied by the concept of the universe as an integral whole, the supposition that a more philosophical view of God is attained by sacrificing his personality is seen to have been an error. C.H.

God, modern conceptions of: Great diversity and much controversy are found in theology today between those who hold different ideas of God. Some of the major points at issue will be noted. Then the criteria will be listed whereby one distinguishes from other realities that reality of God which is working upon us.

The relation of God to the world is one point in dispute. Some hold that God stands in utter opposition to the world (absolutely other). Differing from this extreme transcendence are views representing all degrees of immanence and transcendence of the deity. Extreme immanence is pantheism which declares that the world is the body of God and that there is no divine being apart from this world taken in its organic totality. In between are they who think that God is an operative reality in the world but is neither outside it nor inclusive of it.

The nature of God's perfection is also an issue. Some say that God is absolutely perfect in every respect. All that has been, will be and now is, are equally present to God, controlled by God, enjoyed by God. No improvement, addition, loss or change of any sort can apply to divine reality. Contrasting to God thus absolute in every respect are other ideas interpreting him as absolute in some respects only. God may be conscious of all that is and has been but cannot be conscious of the future because the future in concrete fullness of existence is not. Hence the future can be known, controlled and enjoyed only in respect to abstract possibilities having varying degrees of probability.

The categories of consciousness, intelligence and purpose as applied to God are in question. Some say that the total cosmos is the mind of God and is completely conscious. At the other extreme are they who insist that consciousness applies only to sentient organisms as found in man and the lower animals but does not apply to God because God does not have nerves and muscles and glands. God has powers so vastly different and greater than ours, they say, that it is foolish to apply our little characteristics of consciousness, intelligence and purpose to God. God operates on too vast a scale and too intimately with each one of us to be limited by such animal-bound functions as these.

Ideas differ in respect to personality in God. Some say that personality is the ultimate metaphysical reality upon which matter and all else depend continuously for existence and that God is the one supreme personality. Others declare that an analysis of personality and the necessary conditions of its existence reveal that God cannot be a personality because the necessary conditions on a cosmic scale are lacking. In any case, say these interpreters, personality is too limiting and restrictive. The powers of God must necessarily burst the bounds of personality.

Differences also appear regarding the creativity of God. Some say that God creates everything from nothing. Others think that God creates the present state of the world out of some prior state and that prior states run back endlessly so that there was never a beginning. Still others hold that the creativity of God is only one reality at work in the world, that it must work against the resistance of manifold forms of inertia and aberration found in certain states of inanimate matter, biological organism, human personality, closed community and historic tradition. On this view, God continuously creates the order of value in the world but not these resistances to his creation.

The data and criteria by which God may be known are in dispute. Some assert that we know God in a way peculiar to inter-personal knowledge and that revelation is identical with the way in which any person makes himself known to another. However there is no agreement on the way one person knows the mind of another, so this analogy does not solve the problem. It is claimed by some that we know God as a theory or rational hypothesis derived by inference from experience of what is not God, this experience being either our own consciousness or the processes of nature. Others insist that no true knowledge of God is had at all unless we have direct experience of the divine reality working upon us. If we have any real knowledge of God it can only be by distinguishing from other realities the actual operations of God working upon us directly to create us, to correct us, and to destroy evil and create good.

Such are some of the main points in dispute. We pass now to the criteria by which to distinguish the working reality of God from all other realities which are immediately experienced by us. We believe most Christian theologians would accept the fourteen criteria here listed. These do not, however, yield any knowledge of God when treated merely as a theory or rational hypothesis tested indirectly by observations on other realities than that of God immediately experienced in creative action upon us. Each of the fourteen applies to what is immediately and continuously experienced in the way of divine reality. The last seven are most emphasized in Christianity.

1) The creativity of God as distinguishable from all that is done by human beings must be something done to us, not by us, although men may provide some of the conditions required for its working. 2) It must be creative of the human mind and personality. 3) When given dominant control it must continuously sustain the human mind and personality in what is called "mental health." 4) It must save human life from all the major ills to the degree that it is given full control by way of man's self-commitment to it. 5) It must create human community and history and keep these in growing abundance of good just so far as obstructions to its working are removed. 6) It must be the creative source of all the highest intrinsic human good. 7) It must create the world relative to our minds in the sense that it can make the world anew when men give to it supreme control over the individual, social and historical developments of human existence. 8) It must answer prayer. (See prayer.) 9) For the Christian it must have been released into history with augmented power and scope by the Cross of Christ. 10) It must be what we sin against and also the forgiver of sin through Christ. (See Living Christ for 9 and 10). 11) It must have a *unity* peculiar to itself, incomparable and incommensurable with everything else, and in that sense absolute and perfect. 12) It must have *power* likewise incomparable and incommensurable with any other. 13) It must have a *goodness* not greatest in terms of human goodness but a goodness incommensurable and incomparable to any other because its goodness is that of being the creative source of all good. 14) It must have the quality of *holiness* by reason of having such *unity*, *power*, and *goodness* incomparable and incommensurable with any other.

Chas. Hartshorne, *Man's Vision of God* (1941); A. N. Whitehead, *Process and Reality* (1929); E. S. Brightman, *The Problem of God* (1930); W. E. Hocking, *The Meaning of God in Human Experience* (1912); Otto, Macintosh, Wieman, *Is There a God?* (1932); William Temple, *Nature, Man and God* (1935).

H.N.W.

God, wrath of and love of: See wrath of God.

Godet, Frederic: (1812-1900) Swiss Protestant theologian. He was born at Neuchâtel, now Switzerland but until 1848 Prussian Crown land. From 1833-1844 he was teacher of the prince Frederik of Prussia, later Emperor Frederik III, whose intimate friend he remained to the latter's end. Pastor in Neuchâtel, 1850-1873, he became professor of N.T. exegesis in the University of Neuchâtel. Conservative in his political and theological views he supported the formation of the Independent Church of the Canton of Neuchâtel*, and he taught from 1873-1887 in the Free Faculty of Theology. His insistence on Biblically inspired doctrine and religion made him one of the outstanding leaders of conservative Protestantism. His commentaries, which were translated into German and English, are written in fluent and dignified language and bear witness to the author's vast learning and his keen critical judgment. His aim was throughout to develop the theological significance of the text. Biography by his son Philippe Ernest Godet (1913). Principal works:

Commentaire sur l'evangile de St. Jean, 3 vols. (1863-1865, 3rd ed. 1881-1885, Engl. tr. 1885-1886); *St. Luc* (1871, 3rd ed. 1888, Engl. tr. of the 2nd ed. 1881); *L'épitre aux Romains* (1880, Engl. tr. 1888); *Premiere épitre aux Corinthiens* (1887, Engl. tr. 1893).

O.A.P.

godfather, godmother: The man and woman who act as sponsors for a child in the ceremony of baptism. The godparents contract a spiritual guardianship over the baptized with the obligation to instruct the person and see to it that he is faithful to his baptismal vows.

S.C.

Godfrey of Fontaines: Scholastic theologian and philosopher, Bishop of Tournai. He was born *ca.* 1260, died *ca.* 1320. His fourteen *Quodlibeta* defend and develop Thomistic ideas, although he differed from Aquinas* in making substantial form the principle of individuation.

C.V.

Gods: Most of the early gods had their origin in man's emotional response to beneficent phases of the natural world—the dawn light which banished the cold and dangers of the darkness, the warming, stimulating sun, the storm rain which brought refreshment to pasture lands and crops after drought, the cooling winds, the fresh, life-giving waters, the fertile, food-producing earth. Other lesser gods emerged from emotional attitudes toward parts of the family dwelling—the hearth fire, the door, the food stores, the land. All of these deities were visible and tangible realities, friendly and helpful to man in his struggle for the goods of life. He talked to them and by his language gave them human qualities and personality. They would never have weathered the centuries of culture history, however, if they had remained simply phases of the friendly environment. Their chance for limitless growth came when they were blended with the idea of spirit* and became spiritual beings dwelling in the unseen behind and beyond their material manifestations. No longer fettered to tangible reality, with a reputation already established as bountiful givers of the goods of life, they were free to grow into cosmic beings capable of fulfilling all human desires and guaranteeing the highest human hopes. The mystery of the unknown surrounding man's limited realm of mastery added to their grandeur.

Many thousands of such gods began the pilgrimage through time with the various peoples of the earth. Only a few have survived as great gods. Others have clung to existence in the retinue of the high gods or as manifestations of them. Some of the little gods have lived, in spite of the blighting light of philosophic thought, because they were useful to the lowly folk. But vast multitudes of the early deities have fallen by the wayside unable to endure the winds of change. Ancestral gods, culture heroes, bound to a particular race or local habitation could never break their human bonds and become cosmic figures. They have rarely been able to survive the convulsions of changing cultures.

Each of the great gods has his own distinctive character acquired through the centuries by his relationship to the social and intellectual history of his people. The gods grow, change and die as they respond or fail to respond to human needs. The powers of the gods are enlarged to meet the growing desires and hopes of men. Sometimes they assume new duties when a culture moves to a new level, or in the interaction of cultures take on the functions of gods they have displaced. A tribal god* may grow into a national or imperial god following the political triumphs of his people. The gods grow in moral character with each advance in the social ideal since no god can live and be less moral than his worshippers. Sometimes the problem of evil has forced an omnipotent god to become finite, sacrificing his power to save his goodness. Often gods die when they lose their land and people by conquest, but the commonest cause of death is their failure in usefulness. Useless gods move slowly into neglect and oblivion. The greatest challenge that has confronted the gods was when they fell into the hands of the philosophers in quest of a metaphysical ultimate. Then they were often reduced to ineffable abstractions useless for the needs of religion.

The gods of the world and the ages may be classified in a few types: 1. The nature powers. Almost all of the early gods and the great gods of history in their beginnings belong to this class. They were Dawn, Sun, Moon, Storm, Rain, Thunder and Lightning, Wind, Earth and Heaven. The overarching Heaven, source of the lesser sky and air gods, as the embodiment of cosmic order often rose to the supreme rank over the nature gods. Frequently Father Heaven and Mother Earth were the parents of the other deities. (See nature worship.) 2. The family gods—Door, Well, Storehouse and especially the Hearth Fire. 3. Potencies like the Roman Numina, formed on the model of the nature gods but without personality. To this class belong also the abstract deities, qualities and virtues deified—Peace, Purity, Righteousness, Love. 4. Human gods, men who had served the people in memorable ways were often deified after death—first ancestors, culture heroes, kings, sages, great warriors and masters of healing and the arts. (See ancestor worship; emperor worship; hero worship.) 5. Fertility gods, the Mother Goddesses* and their sons or consorts. Originally they were the earth and the grain-source of the food supply. Refined by thought in later culture they became the gods of the Mysteries*. The central figure was a dying and rising savior who gave immortality to those who were initiated into the church and shared the mystic communion meal of bread and wine. (See fertility cult.) 6. Creator gods. They are the result of speculation on origins. Usually the most important of the existing gods is chosen for this rôle. Sometimes there is confusion and several gods in a single culture are credited with the work of creation or a new god may be invented, such as the Hindu deity, Viśvekarman, the "All-Maker". In the Orient, when philosophers adopted the idea of a beginningless and endless universe creator gods were no longer needed. 7. The supreme personal gods—Yahweh of Israel, the God of Christianity, Allah of Islam, Ahura Mazda of Zoroastrianism and Amaterasu-Omikami** of Japan. Although the life stories of these gods are very different they are invested with all the attributes of solitary, supreme rulers of the world and of human destiny. Ahura Mazda* has one distinction. He is a finite god* of infinite wisdom and goodness at war with Angra Mainyu, co-eternal with him and the creator of all the evil of the world. 8. The impersonal gods. In some cultures thousands of years ago thought pushed beyond the personal gods to an impersonal unity either spiritual or material—a Cosmic Order, Fate, Logos, First Cause or Absolute**. Examples of these philosophic ultimates are Brāhman or Paramātman of Hinduism, the Dharmakāya of Buddhism, the Stoic Logos, T'ien, Tao or T'ai Chi of China, Zervan Akarana of

Iran. These divine beings are usually tolerant of the popular gods of religion who may be considered as manifestations of them or as broken lights of their unknowable reality. Buddhism provided innumerable personal Buddhas and Bodhisattvas and human incarnations to make the Dharmakāya serviceable for religion. The high god of Hinduism was also incarnated many times for the salvation of men at periods of crisis in remote and modern ages, and the personal gods of the sectarian religions are all one with it. Impersonal Absolutes are never jealous gods. See religions mentioned.

A. E. Haydon, *Biography of the Gods* (1941); M. Jastrow, *Aspects of Religious Belief and Practice in Babylonia and Assyria* (1911); J. H. Breasted, *Development of Religion and Thought in Ancient Egypt* (1912); M. P. Nilsson, *Minoan-Mycenaean Religion* (1927); W. W. Fowler, *Roman Ideas of Deity* (1914); H. S. Nyberg, "Die Religionen des Alten Iran" German trans. H. H. Schaeder, *Mitteilungen der vorderasiatisch-aegyptischen Gesellschaft* (1938); M. N. Dhalla, *History of Zoroastrianism* (1938); H. D. Griswold, *The Religion of the Rigveda* (1923); J. E. Carpenter, *Theism in Medieval India* (1921); E. J. Thomas, *The History of Buddhist Thought* (1933); H. G. Creel, *The Birth of China* (1936); Fung Y-lan, *A History of Chinese Philosophy*, trans. D. Bodde (1937); D. C. Holtom, *The National Faith of Japan* (1937); T. J. Meek, *Hebrew Origins* (1936); M. M. Kaplan, *The Meaning of God in Modern Jewish Religion* (1937); D. B. Macdonald, "Allah" *Encyclopaedia of Islam*, v. 1. A.E.H.

Gods, Sumerian: See Mesopotamian religions.

Goethe, Johann Wolfgang von: (1749-1832) German poet, dramatist and thinker. Well nigh universal in the scope and power of his genius, Goethe was deeply engaged with the profoundest problems of human experience and destiny, moral, metaphysical and theological and made a rich contribution to them all.

In his study of the human soul, its temptations and achievements, he may be called the poet of *salvation by aspiration.* This appears at the close of his great drama *Faust,* whose composition was the work of his whole life-time. When Faust, after being led by Mephistopheles into various iniquities comes at length to the hour unto which he cries: "Oh stay, thou art so fair"—in contemplating the future fruits of his labor in reclaiming a tract of waste land which is to become the scene of human happiness and well-being—instead of being borne away to hell by triumphant devils, he is rescued by angels singing:

The noble spirit now is free
And saved from evil scheming.
Whoe'er aspires unendingly
Is not beyond redeeming.

That aspiration toward the highest, and salvation thereby, is not, however, man's act alone but is concurrently the work of Eternal Grace in him suggested (together with the most striking use of *symbolism* in literature) in the closing words of the mystic chorus:

All that is transient
Is symbol, not soul;
All insufficiency
Moves toward the Whole.
The end, long despaired of,
Yet shall be won.
Love ever graciously
Leadeth us on.

Goethe's theory of the nature of evil appears in the answer of Mephistopheles to the question of Faust: What art thou, then?

Part of that Power not understood
Which always wills the Bad.
And always works the Good.

In *Götz von Berlichingen* (1773), *Iphigenia in Tauris* (1787), *Egmont* (1788), *Hermann und Dorothea* (1798), *West-ostliches Divan* (1819) and other noble dramas and lovely lyrics—as also in other of his writings and in his conversations with Eckermann, Goethe offers a profound interpretation of both Romanticism and Classicism in the light of Christianity. J.W.B.

Gog and Magog: Enigmatic names occurring in Ezekiel's* apocalyptic vision of the final assault of the fierce armed hordes of the North on the land of Israel prior to the inauguration of God's sovereignty (Ezek. 38-39). While Josephus* identifies them with the Scythians (Ant. 1. 6, 1), the Sibylline Oracles III, 319 locates them in Ethiopia. In Rabbinic* literature they figure as the rebel peoples who rise up against God and His annointed (Midr. Psalms, ed. Buber, 2.2; Ber. 7b. Cf. Revel. 20.8). S.S.C.

Gogarten, Friedrich: (Born 1887, Dortmund) Protestant theologian. 1927 privatdozent Jena, 1930 Professor of Systematic Theology in Breslau, 1935 in Gottingen. In opposition to the historism of his teacher Troeltsch*, but in the traditions of German idealism he aspired after a system of "glaeubiges Denken" (reasoning born out of faith). This led him temporarily to the Biblicism of Kierkegaard and Luther and to a relentless criticism of liberal and idealistic Protestantism (so-called Theology of Crisis). For a number of years he regarded himself as a theological ally of Karl Barth* and he defended the position of Dialectical Theology* with great vigor and lucidity. But following Grisebach and Buber he abandoned his supernaturalism. He came later under the spell of conservative political thinkers and finally espoused the religious philosophy of National Socialism. He became one of the theological representatives of the "German Christians", who teach that the actual revelation of God takes place in national history.

Principal works:

Die religioese Entscheidung (1921, 2nd ed. 1924); *Von Glauben und Offenbarung* (1923); *Ich glaube an den dreieinigen Gott* (1926); *Politische Ethik* (1932); *Gericht oder Skepsis: eine Streitschrift gegen Karl Barth* (1937); *Weltanschauung und Glaube* (1937); *Das Bekenntnis der Kirche* (1939).

O.A.P.

gohei: (Lit. "Great Offering.") A Shinto purification device, usually made of paper strips and strings of hemp fastened to a wooden handle, in shape suggesting a duster. D.C.H.

Goldberg Memorial Foundation, The Jeannette Miriam: Established in 1938 by co-workers and friends of Jeanette Miriam Goldberg, Jewish social worker and educator and Executive Secretary of the Jewish Chautauqua Society (1906-1935). The interest from the funds of this Foundation is used to maintain annual series of lectures exchanged between the Hebrew Union College, of Cincinnati, Ohio, and various Christian theological seminaries, by members of their respective faculties, on phases of Judaism and Christianity respectfully, an appreciation of which, it is felt, is desirable for their students. To date such lecture relationships have been maintained by the Hebrew Union College with Union Theological Seminary, Yale University Divinity School and Duke University Divinity School. The Trustees of the Foundation are Rev. Dr. Louis Wolsey and Mr. Arthur P. Fleisher, both of Philadelphia. J.M.

golden age, the: The conception of a golden age in the past is well-nigh universal. Its most explicit formulation possibly is by Hesiod, who outlined four: golden, silver, brass and iron. This characteristic of increasing degeneracy is also common. It is illustrated in the Hebrew-Christian tradition by the idea of the Fall*. See cycles of time; Messiah; millenarianism; progress.

Hasting's *Encyclopaedia of Religion and Ethics* I, 183-210. P.R.H.

golden mean: See s. v. mean, Aristotelian.

golden rose: A rose-shaped ornament of pure gold, blessed by the Pope on Laetare Sunday* (the Fourth Sunday of Lent), and conferred from time to time on eminent Catholics as a token of the Pope's esteem. C.V.

Golgotha: See Calvary.

Good Friday: The name traditionally given in the Catholic communions to the Friday before Easter, upon which (traditionally) Jesus was crucified. The origin of the name is shrouded in obscurity, but it presumably emphasizes the value to men of that which was accomplished at the Crucifixion. W.N.P.

Goodrich, Chauncey Allen: (Oct. 23, 1790-Feb. 25, 1860) Congregational clergyman; educator, lexicographer, graduated from Yale College in 1810, was rector of the Hopkins Grammar School to 1812, and tutor at Yale, 1812-1814. In July, 1816 he was ordained over the church in Middletown, Conn. In 1817 he became professor of rhetoric at Yale, and in 1838 was transferred to the newly created Professorship of preaching and pastoral work, which position he retained until his death. Goodrich worked for many years on Webster's dictionary, editing an abridgement in 1829 and, with colleagues, a thorough revision in 1847. He studied theology with Timothy Dwight* while a tutor at Yale, and throughout his life was a close friend and associate of Dwight's other pupils who formed the New Haven theology*. He did a great deal to further the establishment of the Yale Divinity School in 1822, and to get N. W. Taylor* as the Professor of theology around whom the school was built. In 1828 when Bennet Tyler* and the conservatives attacked the New Haven liberals, Goodrich bought the *Christian Spectator* and issued it as a quarterly in defense of the New Haven views until 1836. S.E.M.

Gordon, George Angier: (1853-1929) Born in Insch, Scotland, January 2, 1853, George Gordon sailed (steerage) for America in 1871, engaged in manual toil in Boston until a discerning minister persuaded him to go to Bangor Theological Seminary to study for the ministry. Completing his course there, he entered Harvard University, graduating with honors in philosophy in 1881.

After serving the Congregational Church in Greenwich, Conn. for three years he was installed pastor of the Old South Church in Boston in 1887 and entered upon a notable pastorate which continued over forty years. He served also at different times as college preacher and pastor at Harvard and Yale Universities. As preacher, pastor and author he exercised a wide influence and next to Bushnell* became the leading advocate of the New Theology* in America. Dr. Gordon was an ardent student of Plato and Aristotle, an earnest Trinitarian, a severe critic of Calvinism (but with a high regard for the New England Theology*) and an undiscouraged upholder of "the Larger Hope."

Chief among his books are *The Christ of Today* (1895); *Ultimate Conceptions of Faith* (1903); *Religion and Miracle* (1909); *Aspects of the Infinite Mystery* (1916); *Immortality and the New Theodicy* (1897), the first Ingersoll Lecture. In 1925 he published *My Education and Religion,* an outstanding religious autobiography. See also J. W. Buckham, *Progressive Religious Thought in America* (1919). J.W.B.

Gore, Charles: See Anglo-Catholics; Christian Social Union.

Gorgons: (Gr., *Gorgones,* from *gorgos,* grim, fierce) Three hideous sisters, with serpent-entwined locks and glaring eyes that turned to stone anything that met their gaze. Hence the Gorgon's head in armorial devices. Medusa, the one mortal sister, was slain by Perseus and from her blood sprang the winged horse, Pegasus. E.M.N.

Gosala: A contemporary of Mahavira in the 6th century B.C. and founder of the Ajivikas. C.S.B.

gospel: See evangelical; social gospel.

gospel and the gospels: The word for gospel (Gr. *euaggelion,* Lat. *evangelium*) meant originally a reward paid the bringer of good news; then it came to mean the good news itself. In the N.T. and in other early Christian literature, it means the message of salvation through Christ, preached by the apostles and evangelists of the early church. Even when the term is found upon the lips of Jesus himself (as in Mark 1:14) it bears this meaning.

Even after written accounts of the life and teaching of Jesus began to appear, the term gospel still meant the Christian message of salvation; hence the titles of the gospels in our N.T.: "The Gospel, *according to* Matthew, Mark," etc. It was not until some time in the first half of the second century that the term gospel came to be applied to the individual books. The formation of the four-gospel canon about (or soon after) 150 A.D. naturally contributed toward this result, though at the same time it retained the older emphasis upon the unity of "the gospel".

The gospels are not biographies either in the modern or in the ancient classical sense. They are written with another purpose than to give a complete account of Jesus' life and teaching. That purpose may be apologetic (John 20:31, Luke 1:4) or didactic (as in the case of Matthew, which is arranged for use in teaching); or the purpose may be to encourage a church faced with persecution and the prospect of martyrdom (as in Mark, the earliest gospel).

Back of all the gospels is the oral tradition out of which they grew. This tradition was naturally not uniform, although it had probably become more or less stereotyped before being written down. There were no doubt written sources which antedated the gospels, some even earlier than the Gospel of Mark (see articles "Synoptic Gospels" and "Form Criticism"). This material, much of it already in fixed form, and some of it probably already in writing, was translated into Greek. The process of fixation of form continued even after translation into Greek —some of the narratives seem to have acquired their present form in a Hellenistic milieu rather than in a Semitic. Moreover, the authors (or compilers) of the gospels contributed much in the way of editorial setting and arrangement (rather than in the positive revision or reconstruction of contents).

The result was not books intended for publication and reading by the general public; the gospels were 'community books' intended for use within the Christian community, whose sacred tradition they now enshrined. They were 'traditional books'; hence their impersonality and anonymity.

The same holds true of the Gospel of John, as of the synoptics. It is probable that the author has made use of earlier sources, in some respects parallel to the synoptic traditions and in one or two cases overlapping those traditions. But the author has gone much farther than the compilers of the synoptic gospels have gone, in revising, reorganizing, supplementing, and reinterpreting his material. The purpose of the author is to prove that Jesus was the Son of God, and at the same time to place upon his lips, as the authoritative 'Word' of God, the Christological doctrine of the church in the author's own time. That is, he aims to set forth the meaning Christ has come to have for the church, dramatically stating these doctrines as teachings of Christ himself.

It is a question whether or not the author of John knew the synoptic gospels*. A good case can be made out for the view that he was correcting the synoptics; perhaps an even better case can be made out for the view that he was using a tradition somewhat similar to the synoptic, but was reinterpreting it. The difficulty in the way of the view that he was correcting the synoptics arises from the large number of obvious points, in need of correction from his point of view, which he ignores. (See P. Gardner-Smith, *St. John and the Synoptic Gospels*, 1938). See evangelical; logos; Matthew; Mark; Luke; John.

See books cited following article "Synoptic Gospels." Commentaries: Matthew, A. H. McNeile, 1915; B. T. D. Smith, 1927. Mark, A. E. J. Rawlinson, 1925; B. H. Branscomb, 1937. Luke, B. S. Easton, 1926; J. M. Creed, 1930; H. K. Luce, 1933. John, G. H. C. MacGregor, 1930; see also R. H. Strachan, *The Fourth Evangelist*, 1925, new ed., revised, 1941 (*The Fourth Gospel, its Significance and Environment*); E. F. Scott, *The Fourth Gospel, Its Purpose and Theology*, 1908. Theology: E. W. Parsons, *The Religion of the New Testament*; E. Hoskyns and F. N. Davey, *The Fourth Gospel*, 1940.

F.C.G.

gothic style: Gothic is a method of construction that developed in northern France and in the English midlands during the 13th and 14th centuries. Popularly it is supposed to be nothing more than the use of pointed arches and deeply coved mouldings, but these things are but accidents that accompanied revolutionary ideas in methods of construction.

During the previous Romanesque period, wall-bearing construction was the rule. Churches were relatively narrow, and their roofs rested upon solid walls, which were necessarily of great thickness so as to resist the thrust of the roof. Where clerestories existed, these were carried on piers of great bulk, set close together.

Since many churches were damaged by fire, builders strove to throw a vault of stone over chancel, nave, transepts and side aisles. Cérisy-la-Forêt, Jumièges and St. Georges de Boscherville, all in France, show indications of this transition. The aisles and triforia of Jumièges are vaulted, and this as early as the end of the 11th century. In the Abbaye aux Hommes, in Caen, we find a crude sexpartite vault, of 12th century date. St. Nicholas, Caen, has a ribless vault over the choir. Boscherville is also vaulted, the present work of 13th century date.

As the skill of the builders developed, they found it possible to support their heavy stone vaults on lofty shafts of stone, rather than upon continuous stone walls of great thickness. Where the weight and thrust of the stone vault was carried formerly by stone walls of enormous thickness, it became possible now to carry the vaulting on stone columns, comparatively slender in cross-section, and to reduce the thickness of the side walls considerably by using buttresses and flying buttresses. Thus thrust was met by thrust, and the weight of the heavy vaulting carried downward and grounded, by means of a system of buttresses and flying buttresses, the latter spanning the side aisles. The dead loads of the Romanesque era were supplanted by a system of live loads and balanced thrusts. Walls were made thinner, resulting in an economy of material. Windows, which had been very small in Romanesque days, now could be made large, because the vault was supported by isolated columns, and not by the wall proper.

The pointed arch is but a by-product of this highly articulated system of engineering. Where it was necessary to vault spans of unequal width, it was found possible to keep the crown ribs of the vaults on the same level by using pointed arches. A round arch of a given width can rise but one-half its span above the springing line, but a pointed arch may be made higher or lower at will.

Ornament is but a minor detail of Gothic. Its most important feature is found in its live loads and balanced thrusts. It is a form of highly developed engineering. Early Gothic work is rather simple in design, but in the later periods it became the custom to fill the large windows with carved stone tracery of rich and intricate design. Vertical columns, plain during the Romanesque period, became increasingly rich in the Gothic era, with deep coves cut into the stonework. There were ornately carved capitals, richly moulded bases and elaborate string courses. On the outside of the building, row upon row of prophets, apostles and martyrs, carved in stone, occupied niches with richly carved canopies. Stained glass of dazzling color filled the great windows. See art, ecclesiastical, Christian; church building.

For those who would trace the story of this development of the Gothic style, see R. A. Cram's *The Substance of Gothic* (1927). F.R.W.

Gottschalk: (805-868?) Hapless Saxon monk of tragic proportion, he became gloomily predestinarian*. His book condemned, he was imprisoned, impenitently Augustinian. His poetry expressed his resigned spirit. See double predestination. See Eriugena, John Scotus. A.C.

Gottschick, Johann: (1847-1907) He taught practical theology in Giessen and Tübingen. He was with Ferdinand Kattenbusch* one who most faithfully guarded the inheritance of A. Ritschl*.

Luthers Anschauungen vom christlichen Gottesdienst und seine tatsächliche Reform desselben (Freiburg, 1887); *Die Kirchlichkeit der sogenannten kirchlichen Theologie geprüft* (Freiburg, 1890); *Ethik* (Tübingen, 1907); *Homiletik und Katechetik* (Tübingen, 1907); *Luthers Theologie* (Tübingen, 1914). H.H.

Gourd, Jean Jacques: (1850-1909) Of French origin, he was professor of philosophy at the University of Geneva. Religion was for him an assemblage of incoördinables, which results from the opposition of scientific, moral, aesthetic and social laws. Religion, he thought, seeks to comprehend the neglected aspects of the manifoldness of the concrete. He viewed Christianity as the best conformation of the theology of incoördinables.

Philosophie de la religion (Paris, 1912). H.H.

governmental theory: See Grotius; redemption; satisfaction.

grace: (Gr., *karis*) The word has the simple general meaning of favor shown or received, and the disposition to show favor, hence liberality, agreeableness (Lk. 1: 30; 2: 40, 52; 6: 32, 33, 34; Acts 2: 47). Its special Biblical and theological use is of the divine favor to sinful men. When men were without strength or even will to save themselves, God's unrestrained kindness interposed and salvation* is now freely offered to them through the crucified and risen Christ (Rom. 3: 24; 5: 1-10). It is not of merit or in any sense earned; the sole condition in the recipient is faith (see saving faith), and it too is of God (Eph. 2: 7-9). Grace is further the divine help continually afforded by which men are kept and sustained, and enabled to do what is otherwise beyond their power (2 Cor. 12: 9).

Grace is a concept of the universal Church, prominent in its theology, Catholic and Protestant, and in its epochal figures, Paul, Augustine, Luther, Wesley, et al. Augustine*, on this theme as on others, is the source of variant traditions. Grace is the love of God shed abroad in our hearts by the Holy Spirit*; it is moral enablement, the remedy for man's moral inability. But it is also nutriment for the spiritual life conveyed to the individual from without through material channels. This notion paved the way for the Catholic theory of sacramental Grace which still separates Catholic and Protestant teaching. For both, salvation is the gift of God (emphasized for Catholics in the doctrine *ex opere operato**); but Catholics regard the sacramental* system as the divinely appointed medium for the communication of it. Protestants stress the personal relation: God imparts His grace when men personally surrender to Him in hope and trust.

Differences have arisen in theology over the precise proportions of divine-human participation in the work of grace. Does man of himself desire grace, or does the presence of desire mean that grace is already given? Augustine held the latter, contending against Pelagius* that God bestows will as well as the grace that is willed (*velle* as well as *esse* and *posse*). This is prevenient grace (*gratia praeveniens*); although all grace is prevenient as being of God's initiative who knows and anticipates man's every need before man himself awakes to it. Grace is sufficient, some maintain efficacious: i.e., by divine power the will is not only enabled, but effectually impelled, savingly to believe. God's initial grace is a specific act; but it continues in the Christian life as concurrent Grace (*gratia cooperans*). Controversy has been keen over the relation of Grace to man's free choice . Does man voluntarily align himself with Grace (synergism*)? Is grace effectual, in those in whom God exerts it, to the degree of being irresistible? This question has sundered Evangelicals (Calvinists and Arminians**); those who hold grace to be irresistible adduce predestination* to explain apparent resistance (in the unsaved).

Catholics, Protestants, Evangelicals of all schools, proclaim the Gospel of grace; yet theologies that make grace the sole instrument of salvation (*sola gratia*) and lay no store by works, ritual or ethical (as means; they are essential as fruits) are known as the Doctrines of Grace. Grace is the symbol of God's otherness and transcendence in its relation to the immanent forces of history; it is God's Love poured forth and in its present action for the redemption* of the world. See common grace; congruism; infusion of grace; forgiveness; justification; opus operatum; perseverance of the saints; redemption; regeneration; terminism.

J. W. Oman, *Grace and Personality* (1925); J. Moffatt, *Grace in the New Testament* (1931); L. Hodgson, *The Grace of God in Faith and Philosophy* (1936). J.L.

grace, Old Testament conception of: The words "grace" and "gracious" are used most often to translate the Hebrew verb *hānān* and its derivatives. 1) The secular usage of the verb and the noun *hēn* has no religious significance and refers to physical excellence and beauty, to elegance of speech, to a favorable or well-disposed attitude toward another, etc. (cf. Prov. 1:9; 31:10; Ruth 2:10; Psa. 45:2). 2) In religious usage only the verb and the derived adjective *hannûn* are employed. The fundamental sense of the verb is to bestow a kindness which could not have been claimed. The derived adjective refers to the unmerited kindness thus bestowed. The action is always from a superior to an inferior, the former the bestower and the latter the recipient. While much of the religious terminology of the Old Testament is borrowed from covenantal and legal practice (man or God must or will act in a certain way because of a contractual agreement—see covenant, righteousness, justice), there is also present the belief that God will do more for man than the latter deserves. This is best expressed in the stereotyped sentence: "God is gracious and merciful, slow to anger, and plenteous in *hésed*" (for the last word, see lovingkindness). This first appears in the 9th-8th century (Exod. 34:6-7), but is more common in post-Exilic literature (2 Chron. 30:9; Neh. 9:17, 31; Joel 2:13; Psa. 86:15; etc.). G.E.W.

Gracian, Balthasar: (1601-1658) Spanish Jesuit and philosopher of baroque pessimism. A thinker and satirist he influenced Schopenhauer and Nietzsche**. E.A.R.

Graded Sunday School Lessons: See Sunday School movement in the United States.

gradual: (From Lat., *gradus,* step) Originally a psalm sung from the steps of the ambo*, but now shortened to two verses with *alleluia.* It is used in the Mass* between Epistle and Gospel and is the most elaborate of the liturgical chants. The term is loosely applied to any musical interlude between the eucharistic lections. See plainsong; psalmody. P.V.N.

Gradual Psalms: The Songs of Ascent or of Degrees. Psalms 120-34. Sometimes called the Pilgrim Psalms, on the supposition that they were sung on pilgrimages to the Temple at Jerusalem. P.V.N.

Graduale: The liturgical book containing the chants sung in the Latin Mass. P.V.N.

Grail, Holy, the: See Holy Grail.

Granth: The sacred book of the Sikhs*. Consists largely of the poems of Nanak the founder, but also writings of Kabir and the Gurus who succeeded Nanak as leaders of the faith. The 10th Guru refused to appoint a successor to himself declaring that henceforth the Granth should be the Guru. And so it has been. In the course of time the Granth itself became an object of worship.

Translated by Ernest Trumpp (London, 1877). See also M. A. McAuliffee, *The Sikh Religion* (Oxford, 1909). C.S.B.

gratia creata: (grace or favor given or performed) It is the effect of *gratia increata,* the divine act in the soul. H.H.

gratia gratis data: (grace or favor given freely or willingly) By itself grace is in general freely given. *Gratia gratis data* is the stirring of the soul beyond its purely natural stirring. It designates the charismatic* gifts capable of preparing others to receive grace. It is the influence of God preceding the infusion of real grace, the *gratia gratum faciens.* It induces the individual to the right use of the sacramentally infused grace. It is the work of divine grace through the word. H.H.

gratia gratum faciens: (grace or favor which binds one or which makes one grateful) It is the real grace in contrast to the *gratia gratis data.* It is something created in man whereby he becomes pleasing to God and whereby he is accepted by God. It is the grace communicated by God through the sacraments. It is the Divinely created new quality or habituality in man which restores the *donum superadditum* man originally possessed at creation, but lost through sin. H.H.

gratia increata: (grace or favor not given or performed) The term designates the divine love and its work. H.H.

Gratian: The *Decretum* (ca. 1150?) of Gratian is an ordered arrangement and completion of the collections of the eleventh century later developed and much commented upon by the successors of Gratian. Gratian did for Canon Law* what Peter Lombard* accomplished for theology "two eggs from the same nest" as the *Decretum* and Peter Lombard's *Quattuor Libri Sententiarum* are called. See decretals; festivals and holy days, Christian. S.C.T.

Gratry, Alphonse: (1805-1872) French Catholic theologian best known as opponent of the dogma of papal infallibility* which however he accepted after its promulgation at the Vatican Council*. Also known for his remarkable philosophical work, *De la Connaissance de Dieu* (1855), for his critique of Renan's* *Life of Jesus* (1864), and for his charming *Souvenirs de ma Jeunesse* (posthumous). W.M.H.

graves: See death and burial practices.

Great Awakening, the: See Awakening, the Great.

Great Bible: See Bible, English; Coverdale.

Great Schism, the: See Cerularius, M; schism.

Great Synagogue, the: The Great Synagogue*, also known as the Great Assembly, refers to the group of scholars who met from time to time, beginning during the days of Ezra* and continuing for two centuries after him, to interpret existing laws and to enact new ordinances. The exact nature of this group, their number and internal organization are somewhat obscure. Later generations, however, ascribed many important institutions to this body, from which we may infer that it was very active and was regarded as authoritative. E.B.—L.F.

Great Vehicle: See Buddhism; Vehicles.

Greek culture, ancient: See Hellenism.

Greek Orthodox Churches: See Eastern Orthodox Churches.

Greek religion: The religion of the Hellenic peoples from about 1500 B.C. to about 500 A.D. The Achaean religion of about 1000 B.C., classically depicted in the *Iliad* and in the *Odyssey* (redacted out of traditional ballads by "Homer," who according to Herodotus lived about 850 B.C.), although never practiced anywhere as such, is ostensibly the religion of the Greek aristocracy far from the shrines of its homeland; it combines the deities and rites of many local cults. It derives primarily from the religion of the Minoans in Crete (about 2000-1400 B.C.), adopted in part by the Mycenaean princes of Greece (about 1600-1200); from the religion of the Greek invaders coming from the North; and that of the primitive Aegeans (called "Pelasgians" by the Greek), whose bronze age civilization (about 2500-1100 B.C.) is called "Helladic" by modern archaeologists. It seems fairly certain that Rhea and Artemis are Minoan; Athena is Mycenaean; Zeus (the Indo-Europeans *Dyeus*, the god of the sky) and Hestia are Greek; Hermes*, Demeter, and Kore (Persephone) are Aegean. Other deities came from Cyprus (Aphrodite, originally identical with the Western-Asiatic Ishtar or Astarte), Anatolia (Apollo and Hephaistos), and Thrace (Dionysos, ignored by Homer, and Ares). Whether Poseidon is Greek or Helladic remains uncertain; Hera is Ionian. The Homeric religion is anything but primitive: the deities are no longer forces of nature or its moving spirits, and the primitive rites connected with magic, tabu, and the cult of the dead (which persisted, as we know from Pausanias, in remote rural districts) lost their superstitious meanings. The Homeric deities are glorified human beings, immortal—even though subject to wounds and pain (*Iliad* V:334-362), driven by human moods and passions, plotting against one another, and taking sides in human conflicts. Their mansions are on Mount Olympos (*Odyssey* VI:41-46). Men attribute their misfortunes (*Odyssey* I:188-189) and even their evil impulses (*Iliad* XIX: 85-89) to Zeus or to Fate (*Moira*), but Zeus protests that human misfortunes result from human folly (*Odyssey* I:32-34; contrast *Iliad* XXIV: 525-533). The gods are entreated by sinners through sacrifices (cf. *Iliad* I: 458-468), vows, libations, the sweet savor of burnt offerings, and particularly prayers (*Iliad* IX: 499-512); they make known their wishes through diviners, priests, and interpreters of dreams (*Iliad* I:62-63).

The influence of Homer was decisive, although Herodotus (II:53) exaggerates in attributing to Hesiod and Homer the genealogy, the titles, the prerogatives and functions, and the appearance of the Greek gods. By the side of local cults, Homer created a common religion of all the Greeks, the worship of the Olympian gods headed by Zeus; he gave to the deities clear-cut personalities, as also human figures and countenances so well delineated that later painters and sculptors could reproduce them unhesitatingly (Phidias, according to Valerius Maximus III:vii, 4, confessed that his statue of the Olympian Zeus was inspired by *Iliad* I:528-530). But other religious movements arose and grew from the seventh to the fourth centuries. While the Delphic oracle of Apollo and the great Hellenic games stressed the Pan-Hellenic aspects of religion, and the veneration of heroes conversely emphasized its parochialism, corrosive influences were attacking the Homeric religion. The orgiastic rites in honor of Dionysios, the Eleusinian mysteries of Demeter, and particularly Orphism brought to the individual the assurance of salvation and eternal bliss through mystical communion with the deity. Homeric anthropomorphism was attacked (Xenophanes) or spiritualized through allegory (Stoicism), while poets (Pindar, Aeschylus, Sophocles, and Euripides) and philosophers (the Eleatics, the Sophists, Socrates, Plato, and Aristotle) in various ways gave to religion the noblest ethical and philosophical significance. Both in its primitive popular aspects and in its Platonic sublimation, the Greek religion has had a lasting influence on Christianity. See mystery religions; temples, Greek and Roman.

O. Gruppe, *Griechische Mythologie und Religionsgeschichte* (I. Müller's *Handbuch*, V, 2, 1902-1906); L. R. Farnell, *Cults of Greek States*, 5 vols. (1896-1909); *The Higher Aspects of Greek Religion* (1912); G. Murray, *Four Stages of Greek Religion* (1912); E. Rhode, *Psyche*, 7th-8th ed. (1921); Jane E. Harrison, *Prolegomena to the Study of Greek Religion* 3rd ed. (1922); A. B. Cook, *Zeus*, 3 vols. (1914-40); M. P. Nilsson, *Greek Popular Religion* (1940).
R.H.P.

Greek religious drama: See religious drama.

Green Lectureship, The Stephen: Established c. 1920 at Andover Newton Theological School, Newton Centre, Mass., by Mrs. Natalia L. Greene and sons with the purpose of securing "from time to time the services of scholars prepared to deliver lectures on important subjects related to

Christianity in recent history." Its capital sum is $10,000. Lectures are presented at irregular intervals. Among those appearing on this foundation have been Dr. W. L. Sperry and Bishop F. J. McConnell.

(Data from the Office of the President of the Theological School.) V.F.

Green, Thomas Hill: (1836-1882) British neo-Hegelian* philosopher, who contended that since man has self consciousness he cannot merely be a product of material forces. The moral ideal, eternally known to God, is gradually realized in human moral progress. Men are advancing in personal character and appreciation of a larger common good. Green successfully opposed skepticism and naturalism, reconciled religion with science for the time being, and advocated social reforms. His chief works, published after his early death, are *Prolegomena to Ethics* (1883) and *Principles of Political Obligation* (published separately, 1901). W.K.W.

Gregorian calendar, the: To rectify an error in the computation of time according to the Julian Calendar (established in 47 B.C. by Julius Caesar), Pope Gregory XIII (1572-85)* edited in the year 1581 a Papal Bull *"Inter gravissimas"* in virtue of which ten days (Oct. 5-14) of the year 1582 were to be eliminated from the calendar. Accordingly October 4, 1582 was followed immediately by Oct. 15. The cause of the discrepancy lay in the fact that in the Julian Calendar the year was set at exactly 365¼ days with a leap year every fourth year. The 24th day of February was celebrated twice each leap year, hence the Roman expressions *"bis-sextilis"* or "bis sexto Kalendas Martias". Moderns simplified matters by adding a 29th day to February. As the actual time required for the revolution of the earth around the sun is not 365¼ days or 365 da. and 6 hrs., but rather 365 da. 5 hrs. 49′ and 46″, the calendar was running ahead of the earth each year 11′ and 14″. By January 1, 1582 astronomers calculated the discrepancy amounted to ten full days. The Julian leap year every four years was retained by Gregory XIII, but to make up for future (after 1582) discrepancies, only those century years equally divisible by 400 were to be retained as leap years, thus e.g., the years 1600, 2000 etc., whereas others e.g., 1700, 1800, 1900 were to be rejected. The calendar as thus amended is good for another 10,000 yrs. The Gregorian Calendar was introduced only gradually into Protestant countries. England and her colonies adopted it in 1752. George Washington was thus born on Feb. 11, 1732 as correctly recorded at his homestead in Mount Vernon, Va. because at that time the Colonies were still using the old style of calculation. After the new calendar went into effect, his birthday was made to conform to the Gregorian calendar and thus placed at February 22, because by 1752 there was a discrepancy of 11 days. All modern countries have now adopted *civilly* the "new style" of the Gregorian calendar; some Orthodox and Greek Schismatic Churches still retain *ecclesiastically* and *liturgically* speaking, the "old style" in the celebration of their feasts, especially Christmas, Epiphany and Easter. A similar distinction applies to Orthodox Jews in the celebration of their Easter and New Year, because calculated on another system of lunar or Jewish years.

Litt. cf. *The Columbia Ency.* (1935), 275-6; P. W. Wilson, *The Romance of the Calendar* (1937). R.M.H.

Gregorian chant: The plainsong* chants of the Roman Catholic church. A monodic, solo or unison, unaccompanied, rhythmic but unmetrical chant*. Gregorian music consists of a great collection of more than 600 compositions on Biblical texts, begun by St. Ambrose*, bishop of Milan in the fourth century and Pope Gregory I* in the late sixth century. Aside from its use in its own right, Gregorian chant served as the basis for all polyphonic* composition through the 12th century and for many later works both polyphonic and harmonic.

The early manner of performance of Gregorian music was revived in the late 19th century by Dom Mocquereau at the Benedictine Abbey of Solesmes in France. In 1904 Pope Piux X* ordered a return to the use of Gregorian chant throughout the Roman Catholic church, without, however, excluding good music of other styles. See modes.

Dom A. Mocquereau, *Paléographie musicale,* 16 vols. (1889-1931). E.H.B.

Gregorian tones: Formulas for the recitation of the verses of the Psalms between the antiphons. Sung in a type of speech-song. There was a Psalm-tone for each of the eight medieval modes and one irregular one with two reciting notes called Tonus peregrinus. E.H.B.

Gregory the Great, Gregory, I: (540-604) Called the "father of mediaeval papacy." His theology is Augustinian only in its formulas. Although a breath of Augustine's spirit is in his writings, the less valid traditional elements—miracles, hierarchical and priestly practices, emphases on merit, reward, fear and hope,—predominate. Ugly superstitions, mythological reflections about angels and demons pervade his works. He is consciously orthodox in Trinitarian doctrine and Christology and in agreement with the Councils of the Church. He rightly designated his writings as bran in comparison with the wheat of Augustine. Although almost all of his ideas have their roots in Augustine, yet almost none of them are genuinely Augustinian. The fear of uncertainty that aspires to attain security through the institutions of the church, dominates his whole thought. He became Bishop of Rome in 590, advancing papal power in the realm of politics; organized missionary efforts and interested himself in liturgy and music. See celibacy; chant; Gregorian chant; schola cantorum; seven deadly sins.

Ed. Clausier, *St. Gregoire* (Paris, 1886-1891); F. H. Dudden, *Gregory the Great, his place in the history of thought,* 2 vols. (1905); G. J. Th. Lau, *Gregor I der Grosse* (Leipzig, 1845). H.H.

Gregory the Illuminator: (c. 257-333) Builder of the Christian church in Armenia. Through his efforts Christianity replaced paganism as the religion of the country. Brought Armenian church* into touch with Christendom. K.H.C.

Gregory of Nazianzus (ca. 329-390) A great theologian of the Eastern Church. A friend of Basil the Great* with profound religious perception he coined in his brilliant, but overloaded rhetoric, the leading formulas for his time. With Basil he conceived of religion as a life of the spirit in which reason first visions the eternal beauty of God in his works in order to advance later to the blessed height of the contemplation of the unveiled God. See Cappadocians, the Three.

K. Holl, *Amphilochius von Ikonium in seinem Verhältnis zu den drei grossen Kappadociern* (Tübingen & Leipzig, 1904); C. Ullmann, *Gregorius von Nazianz, der Theologe.* 2nd ed. (Gotha, 1867). H.H.

Gregory of Nyssa: (ca. 332-398) Eminent Greek theologian, bishop of Nyssa. In quiet serious mental work he turned back far more pronouncedly than his two colleagues (the Cappadocians) to Origen*. He was a splendid expert of scientific psychology, fond of describing the ascent of the soul to God. He concurred with the typically Greek view that God, or the good, attracts man. The will is not thereby moved, but the intellect and a certain aesthetic perception. The feeling to be one with God is blessedness. See Cappadocians, the three.

K. Holl, *Amphilochius von Ikonium in seinem Verhältnis zu den drei grossen Kappadociern* (Tübingen & Leipzig, 1904); H. Koch, "Das mystische Schauen bei dem heiligen Gregor von Nyssa" in *Theologische Quartalschrift.* vol. 80 (Tübingen, 1898). H.H.

Gregory, VII., St., Pope: (1073-85) Pope St. Gregory VII, the "Monk Hildebrand" (b. between 1020-25), is rightly looked upon by Church historians as the turning point from the so-called "Dark Ages" of the papacy to the brighter future of Medievalism. He was not, however, the first of his century either to see or inculcate the need of ecclesiastical reform. His contemporaries, St. Peter Damien* (d. 1072), Cardinal Humbert of Lorraine (d. 1061), St. Hugh, Abbot of Clugny (d. 1109) and his predecessors in the Chair of Peter, from St. Leo IX (1049-54)* to Alexander II (1059-61) were, like him, intent on reform and on formulating a program that was indeed to find its culminating peak in Gregory, but its final victory only some 40 years later in the Concordat of Worms* in 1122, between Emperor Henry V (1106-25) and Pope Callixtus II (1119-24) ratified the following year by the First Lateran Council (1123)*. Gregory's main attacks were directed against concubinage of the clergy, simony in the procuring of ecclesiastical benefices, and investiture by secular princes. (See investiture conflict). The chief offenders among the latter was Emperor Henry IV of Germany (1056-1106), although the evil had been prevalent in the Church for centuries. To obtain his end, Gregory was finally forced to excommunicate the Emperor, thereby releasing the German princes and people from their oath of fealty. They were on the verge of electing a successor at Augsburg, Feb., 1077, when Henry voluntarily appeared (midwinter, Jan. 1077) in penitential garb at Canossa, the palace of the Countess Mathilda, whose guest the pope had been on his way towards Germany, and sought the pope's absolution, which was granted him. Ungrateful for his rehabilitation Henry continued to violate the Church's canons and to persecute by military arms the very pope who had saved for him the imperial crown. Gregory died in exile, at Salerno, May 25, 1085. He did not seek to dominate secular princes, as is frequently, but falsely asserted; rather, he sought to free the Church from their unwarranted usurpation, internecine strife and interference in matters ecclesiastical and primarily spiritual. He is considered to have been one of the greatest of the Roman Pontiffs and one of the most remarkable of men of all times. He was beatified by Gregory XIII in 1584* and canonized in 1728 by Benedict XIII. Feast: May 25. See Dictatus Papas.

Monumenta Germaniae Historica (MGH) referring to Henry IV and Henry V; L. Duchesne, edit. *Liber Pontificalis* II 282-9; Migne PL Vols. 143-148; Eric Caspar, edit. *Gregorii Registrum* (Berlin, 1920-23); Hefele-Knöffler, *Conciliengeschichte* Vols. V-VI (Freiburg in Br., 1886-90); Mansi, *Sacrorum Conciliorum nova et amplissima collectio* (Florence and Venice, 1759-98) Vol. XX 60-391; A. Fliche, *Les Prégoriens* (Paris, 1916); *Id., La Réforme Gregorienne* (Louvain, 1924); *Id.* Saint Grégoire VII in the series *Les Saints* (1920); J. Gay, *Les papes au XI siècle* (Paris, 1926); W. Schneider, *Papst Gregor VII und das Kirchengut* (Greifwald, 1919); Alex. C. Flick, *Rise of the Medieval Church* (1909); Dr. J. P. Whitney and L. N. Brooks in *Cambridge Medieval History,* Vol. V. For a good bibliographical survey cf. *Cath. Hist. Rev.* XVII No. 3 (Oct. 1931) 257-67 by Thomas Oestreich. R.M.H.

Gregory IX: (1227-41) Born at Anagni, 1170, Count Ugolino of Segni, studied at Paris and Bologna; became under his uncle Innocent III papal chamberlain; in 1198 Cardinal Deacon and in 1206 Cardinal Bishop of Ostia. As Papal Legate* he showed great political skill as well in Germany (selection of a new emperor) as in Italy. Although before his election as pope a friend of Emperor Frederick II, he came into open conflict with him during the very first year of his pontificate due to the fact that the emperor had striven to extend his farflung empire also over the Church's domains (cf. "Papal States") and furthermore had continually delayed his solemnly pledged crusade against the Saracens. When on an occasion of an epidemic Frederick relinquished the idea entirely, he was immediately excommunicated by the pope. During the absence of Frederick in the Orient, who, although still under ecclesiastical ban, had finally consented to take up the crusade, papal troops stormed Apulia, but were soon routed by the returning emperor. When at the Peace Treaty of Ceperano, Aug. 28, 1230, prepared by the initiatives taken at San Germano, Frederick made wide and important concessions, the ban was lifted. Peace lasted for nine years. The conflicting political viewpoints of pope and emperor occasioned a new rupture, this time regarding Lombardy. Frederick was again excommunicated, March 20, 1239. The issues were fought bitterly on both sides with arms and manifestoes. The pope even went so far as to counsel and encourage through Albert of Behaim, the Archdeacon of Passau, the election of an anti-king. In retaliation Frederick hindered the convening of a General Council that had been set for Easter, 1241, in Rome. He stood with an army before the gates of the Eternal City as Gregory died. Despite passionate energy and lack of deeper consideration for others, both as Cardinal Ugolino and as Pope, Gregory IX showed a friendly and fatherly interest in the Poverello of Assisi, Francis of Assisi*. As Cardinal Protector of the Order Friars Minor* he not only advised Francis in all of his actions pertaining to the Roman Curia and the expansion of the Franciscan* Order, but likewise exercised a wide influence on the development of the Third Order*. The pope also favored the Dominicans* and confided to them almost exclusively the charge of watching over the purity of the Faith, especially through the Inquisition*, which up to that time had been in charge of the Episcopal Curias. (Centralized in 1232). He permitted the free study of the expurgated editions of the works of Aristotle and through Raymond of Penaforte published the famous collection of Decretals*, which henceforth were to be the official juridical codex of the Roman Church. The pope did much to retain the Latin Empire in Constantinople.

Potthast, *Regest. Pont.* I, 680-940; II, 2009-2110; *Mon. Germ. Epist. Saec. XIII*, I (1883); L. Auvray, *Registres de Greg. IX* (Paris, 1890-1918). Biographies by Balan (Modena, 1872-73) and Joseph Felton (Freiburg in Br., 1886); H. Mann, *The Lives of the Popes in the Middle Ages*, Vol. XIII (London, 1925).

R.M.H.

Gregory XI: (1370-78) Born in 1329 in the Diocese of Limoges, Pierre de Beaufort (the last French pope), was created cardinal at the age of 19 by his uncle Clement VI. He was a good canonist, pious and morally above reproach. As pope he condemned 18 theses of Wiclif*. Due to the presence and influence of the hated French officials throughout the Papal States* a national rebellion, instigated and led by Florence, spread throughout the papal domains. Florence was placed under ecclesiastical interdict and, through the aid of Breton hirelings under the Cardinal Legate* Robert of Geneva (later the Anti-Pope Clement VII), the insurrection was squelched. On the insistent pleas of St. Catherine of Siena*, Gregory finally decided to return to Rome and thus end the 70 yrs. "Babylonian Exile" at Avignon.

Baluzi, *Vitae paparum Avenionensium* ed. G. Mollat, Vol. I (Paris, 1916) 415-67; J. P. Kirsch, *Die Rückkehr der Päpste Urban V und Gregor XI nach Rom 3* (1898); G. Mollat, *Les papes d'Avignon 3* (Paris, 1921); L. Pastor, *History of the Popes* Vol. I and II (1923).

R.M.H.

Gregory XIII, Pope: (1572-85) Born of a distinguished Italian family, Jan. 1, 1502, Ugo Boncampagni studied law in his youth and later became professor of the same subject in his home city. In 1565 he was created cardinal and sent to Spain as Papal Legate*. Elected pope on May 13, 1572 through the influence of Cardinal Granville, Gregory XIII strove to imitate his saintly predecessor, Pius V* in his own personal life and to continue the Catholic Reformation* inaugurated by him in accordance with the decrees of the Council of Trent*, in which, despite the opposition of France, he was successful. He reorganized the Congregation of the Index* referring to forbidding books, etc. In behalf of Germany he created a special cardinalitial Congregation as also two nunciatures (cf. "Papal Legates") one for Upper, the other for Northern Germany. To further the interest of union with the Church he despatched Possivino to Sweden and to Russia, where he was able to influence King John III to return to Rome. His endeavors for a new crusade against the Turks failed. In other matters however, especially in educational, legal and missionary affairs he was highly successful. In 1582 he reformed the Julian, and introduced the Gregorian Calendar*; ordered a new edition of the *Corpus Juris Canonici**; and encouraged the reform of ecclesiastical music. But, next to the revision of the calendar, his name will be best remembered for his interest in, and subsidizing of foreign missions (India and Japan); for the erection of 23 new seminaries, placed in charge of the Jesuits*; for the founding of the English, Hungarian, Greek, Armenian and Maronite colleges in Rome; for the endowments of the German College and of the Roman College (*Sapienza*) of which he is called the second founder. Although entirely innocent of the Massacre of St. Bartholomew*, despite the *Te Deum* at St. Peter's chanted for the safety of the King of France, he is accused of having encouraged the Irish in their rebellion against Elizabeth. As a result of his extensive educational endowments and building expenses incurred in enlarging and beautifying Rome (Quirinal, Gregorian Chapel in St. Peter's Basilica, etc.) the papal treasury was depleted, causing dissatisfaction and inviting banditry. It was only under his successor, Sixtus V* that both evils were remedied.

Bullarium Diplomatum et Privilegiorum Summ. Roman. Pont. Taurinensis editio, Vol. VI (Torino, 1860), vol. VII and VIII (Naples, 1882); Pagi, *Breviarium gestorum Pontif. Roman.* (Antwerp, 1873), VI, 718-863; L. Pastor, *History of the Popes*, Vol. XIX-XX (1930).

R.M.H.

Gregory of Rimini: (unknown—1358) A member and later general of the Augustinian Order*. He taught at Bologna, Padua, Perugia and at Paris. At this latter place he embraced the nominalism of Ockham* (around 1300-1349) of which he became a leading representative ("antesignanus"). Author of a book "On Usury". (Armini, 1622). S.C.T.

Gregory, Thaumaturgus: (d. c. 270) Energetic bishop of Neocaesarea in Pontus. Man of piety, learning and missionary zeal. A leading theological writer and follower of Origen*. Called "The Wonder Worker." K.H.C.

Gregory, St. of Tours: (538-594) Bishop of important see in Frankish kingdom. Historian of the Franks. Main historical value of his *Historia Francorum* lies in section dealing with contemporary events. K.H.C.

Grenfell, Sir Wilfred T.: (1865-1940) English medical missionary, born at Parkgate, Cheshire, educated at Marlborough and Oxford, receiving the M.D. degree. After studying at the London Hospital he joined the Mission for Deep Sea Fishermen for three years as medical missionary. In 1892 he started his mission in Labrador, building hospitals, establishing homes, schools and industrial enterprises. His lectures and writings aroused interest in England, Canada and America, which created an organization known as the International Grenfell Association. P.E.J.

Groningen school, the: A group of Dutch liberal theologians who gathered around P. Hofstede de Groot, L. G. Pareau, van Oordt, W. Muurling, and others. They developed their views for many decades in the meetings of a little group of professors and pastors from the University of Groningen. As a mediating theology, influenced by Schleiermacher, Lessing, Herder and the Dutch philosopher W. van Heusde, its rationalism was frankly heterodox, but thoroughly supernaturalistic. As a group they made themselves free from the older supernaturalism. They were humanistic and synergistic. They viewed the whole history of the world as an education of mankind by God in the good, the true and the beautiful. They regarded education as the chief task of the church. They were less intellectualistic than the supernaturalists. They did not regard doctrine as the most important. Their great merit was that their theology centered in the personality, work and example of Christ. They honored the historical Jesus as divine personality; but they refused to recognize Him as a God, and rejected the *satisfactio vicaria.* Christ was for them as for Arius a created heavenly being and the Holy Spirit was not a person. They taught preexistence, but not the logos doctrine. They denied the doctrine of the Trinity. They declared Christianity to be the true and the most excellent stage of human religion, but they regarded Christianity not as the exclusively true religion. They rejected the dogmas of regeneration and atonement. They denied the total sinfulness of man and the existence of demons. They taught that the education of God terminated with a restoration of all things; that the O.T. was ultimately surpassed, that Paul had effected a transformation of the pure gospel of Jesus Christ. They acknowledged the validity of miracles for which reason they combatted modernism. They declared themselves decisively against restriction on liberty and doctrine, and against the obligation of the teachers of the church to agree with the confessional standards. Until 1880 they exerted a great influence in church administration. Though their present number is small, yet their theological influence is proportionately large. At present closer to the orthodox attitude, they are still opponents of confessional church politics.

P. Hofstede de Groot, *De Groninger Godgeleerden in hun Eigenasrdigheid* (Groningen, 1855); J. Herderschee, *De modern-godsdienstige Richting in Nederland* (Amsterdam, 1904); W. F. K. Klinkenberg, *De Evangelische Richting* (Baarn, 1907); J. Lindeboom, *Het bijbelsch Humanisme in Nederland* (Leiden, 1913); K. H. Roessingh, *De moderne Theologie in Nederland; hare Voorbereiding en eerste Periode* (Groningen, 1914). H.H.

Groote, Gerard: (Gerardus Magnus, 1340-1380) Born in Derventer near Utrecht, educated in Paris, Aachen, Cologne and Prague. Distinguished professor of theology and philosophy in Cologne and holding important church positions, Groote at thirty, left honors and wealth to follow in the footsteps of Jesus Christ. He spent three years of study and in ascetic practices in the Carthusian* monastery of which an old college friend was the prior. He visited also the renowned Flemish mystic Jan van Ruysbroeck* whom he resembles in his well balanced life and in practical service to his fellowmen. Groote became an itinerant preacher to whom thousands listened. He founded the Brotherhood of the Common Life* whose main work was educating youth. Their free schools were scattered throughout the Rhine valley. The Brothers and Sisters of the Common Life in their services suggest the work done by modern social service organizations.

Groote kept a diary of his own religious experiences and when restrained from preaching by offended contemporary clergy, he retired to write. By his preaching, teaching and writing he became known as the father of the religious movement, *Devotio Moderna* or the New Devotion whose members schooled themselves by daily practice of Christ's teachings. In 1921 in Lübeck, a Netherlandish ms. of sixty chapters on "Admonitions concerning Interior Things" was discovered among manuscripts belonging to the Sisters of the Common Life. This discovery establishes Groote as the author of the greater part of "The Imitation of Christ"*, usually attributed to Thomas a Kempis who without doubt edited the devotional book. Thomas a Kempis as member of the Windesheim congregation founded by Florentius Radewyns a follower of Gerard Groote was also biographer of Groote. See *The Following of Christ,* (1941, tr. into English from the Netherlands text), Joseph Malaise, S. J. A.S.

Grosseteste, Robert: (1175-1253) An outstanding scholar, teacher, and churchman whose influence was deeply felt by such leaders as Roger Bacon and John Wyclif**. A lecturer and chancellor at Oxford, he served for years as secular master of the Franciscan school there. His scholarly interests and patronage fostered achievements in the learned tongues, the physical sciences, theology, and philosophy. As bishop of Lincoln, he stressed a disciplined Christian life among clergy and laity alike. He consistently emphasized the Scriptures, preaching, and the dignity of the pastoral function. In his later years, he championed the freedom of the English church against papal and royal encroachments.

F. S. Stevenson, *Robert Grosseteste, Bishop of Lincoln* (London, 1899); L. Thorndike, *A History of Magic and Experimental Science*, Vol. II (1923), pp. 436-453. R.C.P.

Grotius, Hugo: (1583-1645) Dutch jurist. He provided through his *De Jure Belli et Pacis* (1625, rev ed. 1631) a standard for the conduct of war in terms of social and mundane objectives. Whereas the Catholic writers had approached the problem of war primarily as moral philosophers, Grotius looked at the matter as a lawyer and one with experience in statesmanship. His importance lay in the philosophical principles upon which he sought to found the relations between sovereign states. He is also known for his "governmental theory" of atonement, i.e., the death of Christ satisfying as a penal example God and the sovereignty of law. See satisfaction.

J. N. Figgis, *Studies of Political Thought from Gerson to Grotius*. 2 ed. (Cambridge, 1923); F. J. C. Hearnshaw, *The Social and Political Ideas of some Great Thinkers of the Sixteenth and Seventeenth Centuries* (London, 1926); H. Vreeland, *Hugo Grotius* (1917). H.H.

Grundtvig, Nicolai Frederick Severin: (1783-1872) Intensely patriotic, Grundtvig gave new interpretation of old Norse mythology, labored for greater freedom in Church and Society, founded Danish Folk High School. The Apostles' Creed summarized, to him, the Gospel, and through it the Church was in fellowship with the Living Christ, who is described in Scriptures and meets the Church in the sacraments. He wrote over 1,000 hymns, a large number originals. A parish priest most of his life, Grundtvig was Denmark's greatest personality of the 19th century, and has deeply affected the life both of Church and Society in Denmark.

C.J.B.

Grützmacher, Richard Heinrich: (1876-) He was professor of theology in Greifswald, Rostock and Erlangen. Attaching himself to the program of modern positive theology of R. Seeberg*, he gave a tri-theistic turn to the dogma of the Trinity*. He stressed the modern for apologetic purposes; but soon returned to a more strict conservatism. He sees in every neo-Protestantism a revival of old errors. See neo-Lutheranism.

Studien zur systematischen Theologie (Leipzig, 1905); *Modernpositive Vorträge* (Leipzig, 1906); *Nietzsche und wir Christen* (Gross-Lichterfelde, Berlin, 1911); *Textbuch zur systematischen Theologie* (Leipzig u. Erlangen, 1919); *Alt und Neu Protestantismus* (Erlangen, 1920); *Spenglers "welthistorische Perspektiven"* (Leipzig, 1923). H.H.

guardian spirit: See primitive religion.

Guelfs: See Ghibellines and Guelfs.

guidance: See Oxford Group; providence.

guilt: The state of a moral agent who has disobeyed a law and thereby made himself liable to the penalty of such violation. The term *guilt*, recognizing the interdependence of all men in all phases of life, emphasizes the consequent responsibility and culpability which society bears to a greater or lesser degree for conditions in the social order which are harmful to the highest well-being of man. In the effort to determine the degree of guilt for the violation of human law by any individual there is often in legal practice a recognition not only of the overt and forbidden act whose performance regardless of intention may constitute legal guilt, but also of the antecedent presence or absence of criminal, i.e., guilty, intent on the part of the person committing the violation. This innocent or guilty intent may in human legal procedure have important bearing on the verdict with reference to guilt.

The term *guilt* as used in theology has reference to sinful man's condition of deserving the condemnation of God. This condition of man is represented in the Scriptures as an objectively existing fact whether accompanied or unaccompanied by subjective feelings such as sorrow, shame, or any other emotion. The objective fact of guilt involved in sin* is affirmed to be a universal fact "for all have sinned, and fall short of the glory of God" (Rom. 3:22-23). While affirming the universality of human fellowship in sin, involving guilt, the Scriptures do recognize various degrees of guilt; cf. Mt. 11:24, 12:31-32; Lk. 12:47-48; Jn. 19:11; Rom. 2:6; Heb. 2:2-3, 10:28-29.

The doctrine of original sin*, affirming the solidarity of the human race in Adam*, declares that his transgression involved all men in the condition (including the guilt) of an innate moral corruption and a consequent tendency to evil. From that condition, which is in itself sinful and deserving of God's condemnation, as well as from the fact involving the guilt of actual sin, man can be saved only by Divine grace*. See forgiveness; imputation. H.W.J.

guna: According to Sankhya* philosophy, *prakriti** or primitive matter is composed of three *gunas*, or substances, or qualities according to some translators. These are *sattva*, *rajas* and *tamas*, terms which do not admit of exact translation though etymologically their meaning is goodness, passion, and darkness. In Sankhya thought as long as primitive matter is completely quiescent, the gunas are in equilibrium. When the equilibrium is disturbed by souls the gunas become active, each seeking ascendancy. The nature of all things is determined by the degree to which one or the other of the constituent gunas predominates. Thus *sattva* is uppermost in the world of divinity, *rajas* in the world of man and *tamas* in the world of the lower orders of life and in matter. C.S.B.

Gunkel, Hermann: (1862-1932) He taught in Giessen and Halle. In studying Israelitic history of literature, he developed new ways of religious historical study. He sought with fine feeling for the means to open the original documents of religion historically. Supported by a strongly aesthetic ability, he evolved the form-historical method. He also worked out the various species of religious speech and writing. See Bousset, J. F. W.; form criticism.

Die Wirkung des heiligen Geistes nach den populären Anschauungen der apostolischen Zeit und nach der Lehre des Paulus. 3 ed. (Göttingen, 1909); *Zum religionsgeschichtlichen Verständnis des Neuen Testamentes.* 2 ed. (Tübingen, 1910); *Schöpfung und Chaos in Urzeit und Endzeit.* 2 ed. (Göttingen, 1921); *Die Propheten* (Göttingen, 1917); *Das Märchen im Alten Testament* (Tübingen, 1917); *Einleitung in die Psalmen* (Göttingen, 1928-33).

H.H.

Gunnerus, John Ernst: (1718-1733) Professor of theology in Denmark, 1754, and bishop of Trondheim after 1758. Author of *Flora Norvegica,* Gunnerus was the cultural leader in Norway, and instrumental in the founding of the Scientific Society, 1770. C.J.B.

Günther, Anton: (1785-1863) A secular priest, some of whose theological and psychological views were condemned by the church authorities at Rome. He sought to surmount the pantheism of Schelling and Hegel** by a dualism and theism similar to Cartesianism. The *cogito ergo sum* is not an immediate intuition for him, but an ontological, metaphysical and rational inference. A large literature in defense and in opposition to his views arose.

Gesammelte Schriften. 4 vols. (Wien, 1881); L. Kastner, *Die philosophischen Systeme A. Günthers und Martin Deutingers* (Regensburg, 1873); J. Flegel, *Günthers Dualismus von Geist und Natur* (Breslau, 1880); M. Klein, *Die Genesis der Kategorien im Processe des Selbstbewusstwerdens* (Breslau, 1881).

H.H.

Gurney, Joseph John: (1788-1847) and Gurneyites. English Quaker minister and philanthropist. Wealthy, well-connected, and well-educated, he embraced the evangelical theology of his time, tempering it in practice by seeking the guidance of the Spirit through silent worship. His influence in the United States was even greater than in England, and a large number of American evangelical Friends* are sometimes called "Gurneyites." See his *Observations; Essays; Memoirs.*

T.E.D.

guru: Teacher or spiritual guide in Hinduism*. In some cases he is regarded as an incarnation of deity and salvation is alone possible through the guru. In the Sikh faith* the successive heads of the movement were known as gurus until the tenth who decreed that henceforth the Granth* the sacred book should be their guru. C.S.B.

Guthrie, Thomas: (1803-1873) Eloquent Scotch clergyman, best known for his opposition to patronage*, in the course of which he became one of the leaders in the Disruption of 1843 and in the resulting organization of the Free Church*. His sensitive social consciousness led him to champion such causes as the organization of the Y.M.C.A. in Glasgow (1842), the "Ragged School" movement (1847), and the temperance movement. See *Autobiography of Thomas Guthrie,* etc., (London, 1874-5). 2 vols.

A.K.R.

Guyau, Jean-Marie: (1854-1888) A profoundly original French thinker whose thought was a reaction against the evolutionism of Herbert Spencer*. His conception of life was largely a moral and aesthetic vitalism. In the field of religion he aimed at a singular synthesis of scientific positivism and spiritualist metaphysics. The negation of every dogma, traditional and supernatural authority, miracle, myth and rite was central in his conception of irreligion. It was not antireligious, but rather a-religious in the sense of being opposed to every current and actual religion. Convinced that all attempts at the establishment of a new religion had failed, he looked towards a purified religion, a religion of the harmony of individual and social ideals.

Esquisse d'une morale sans obligation ni sanction (Paris, 1885); *L'irréligion de l'avenir* (Paris, 1887).

H.H.

Guyon, Madame: (1648-1717) Centre of the Quietist* movement in France. The resemblance of her theological doctrines to those of her contemporary, the Spaniard Molinos*, aroused the suspicion of the French clergy. Fénelon*, however, espoused her cause, but like her was compelled to submit to Rome and renounce her doctrine of possible perfection in mystic union with God. A prolific author.

Works in 40 vols. (1790). Principal titles: *Le Moyen court et tres facile de faire oraison,* and *Les Torrents spirituels.* W.W.C.

H

Habakkuk: A two chapter poem on the fall of Babylon, with minor interpolations in chs. 1-2. Chapter 3 consists wholly of later appended psalm materials. Although usually dated 612-586 B.C., it appears more likely Habakkuk was an exile, writing his poem between 455 and 445 B.C. as it began to appear that Persia might be able to conquer Babylonia. After reviewing the past depradations of Babylon, he asked God how soon the overthrow would be, receiving assurance it would be sure and soon. The poem ends with woes upon Babylon. The distinctive prophetic ethics, religion, and reforming genius is absent. Like Nahum*, Habakkuk was more distinctly a poet. His was an outburst of indignation against Babylonia, who had brought the Judeans into bondage.

See *The Prophets and the Rise of Judaism* by A. Lods (1937), pp. 232-36. R.E.W.

habdalah: (From the Hebrew, distinction) A religious ceremony performed in home and synagogue at the close of the Sabbath and festivals, thanking God for distinguishing with unique holiness certain occasions over the routine days of the year. Blessings over wine, the lighting of a candle and the smelling of spices, constitute the ritual. B.Z.B.

habit: An acquired bodily or mental function which, through repetition, becomes a relatively stable pattern of action characterized by efficiency and facility in performance and a readiness to respond to the appropriate stimulus. Habits are not to be thought of as merely passive structures but rather as dynamic drives to certain modes of activity. They are formed through involuntary learning, as in the conditioning of native responses, or through deliberate attention and voluntary repetition, as in learning to use a typewriter. With repetition they tend to become more and more automatic and to operate with less and less conscious attention. They are of signal importance in all learning and character formation, the latter being defined by some educators as the sum and coordination of the individual's habits. They are conservative in nature and in the form of custom, which is collective habit, offer the greatest resistance to change. R.W.F.

Hachiman: The name under which the spirit of the Japanese emperor Ojin (traditional dates, 201-312 A.D.) is worshiped as the god of war. D.C.H.

Hadad: See Adad.

Haddon-Colt Foundation for the Supernatural, The: Established in 1938 by Mrs. Charles K. Haddon and Mrs. Don S. Colt at Drew Theological Seminary, Madison, New Jersey. The capital sum is $1,000. This annual lecture deals positively and affirmatively with some phase of the general problem of the relations of the natural and the supernatural. Drs. H. P. Sloan, J. M. M. Gray and J. A. Mackay have served on this foundation.

(Data furnished by the Office of the President of the University.) V.F.

hades: The realm of the dead; their abode in the underworld; so called after the Greek name of its mythical ruler. It is used in the N.T. for the Hebrew *Sheol,* a vast, dark region in the depths of the earth, not a place of punishment, but yet one of comfortless gloom. See descent into hades; sheol. E.J.G.

Hadith or hadis: (Arabic term for tradition) The body of traditions from the time of Mohammed and his associates constitutes the basis of *sunna** (norm), the standard of Moslem orthodoxy. P.E.J.

hadj or hajj: (Also Hagge) Arabic term used by Moslems to indicate a pilgrimage to Mecca*. A pilgrim is called *hadji.* P.E.J.

haecceitas: Scotist term meaning "thisness", coined by John Duns Scotus* (1270-1308) to indicate the principle of individuation*. Man becomes an individual by the addition to his generic and specific nature of an individual differentia, "Socratitas" or "haecceitas", which is the ultimate ground of his individuality. S.C.T.

haftarah: (From the Hebrew "conclusion") The prophetic selection concluding the Scripture lesson which is read in the synagogue at each Sabbath and festival service. B.Z.B.

haggada: (Also Agada or Aggadah) A general Hebrew term for utterance, and applied specifically to the non-legal portion of Rabbinic literature. It is also the title of the text recited at the festive meal (Seder*) on the first two nights of Passover*. B.Z.B.

Haggai: First post-exilic prophetic book, with record of four addresses to the returned exiles at Jerusalem between August and December in 520 B.C. The eighteen year old community had become discouraged by crop failures, drought, and hostility of neighbors until they were ready to return to Babylon. Haggai reprimanded them for leaving the temple unbuilt. After they started a small structure, Haggai spoke again, calling the people to build even more gloriously than Solomon*. He also planned to restore the monarchy with Zerubbabel as king. Very different from reforming pre-exilic prophets, Haggai was more priestly, stressing temple worship and ritual as the key to prosperity. See *The Prophets and Their Times* by J. M. P. Smith and W. A. Irwin (1941), pp. 241-48. R.E.W.

hagiographa: (Gr., *hagios,* sacred; *grapho,* I write) The "sacred writings", an alternative designation of Christian origin for the books of the third division of the Heb. canon of scripture, viz., all books other than those of "the Law" and "the Prophets". This is known to Jews as "the Writings" (Kethubim). R.B.Y.S.

hagiography: (Gr., *hagios,* holy, and *graphein,* to write) That part of learning which has as object the saints, their lives, and the honor shown to them; as practical, it is, e.g., the list of martyrs drawn up, in early times, with the end of celebrating their anniversaries; but it is also critical or scientific as dealing with the documents or alleged documents on saints' lives. The Bollandists* are best known as hagiographers. L.R.W.

hail Mary: The prayer in honor of the Blessed Virgin Mary composed of the angel's salutation at the Annunciation*, and Elizabeth's greeting at the Visitation. The Church added the conclusion to the prayer. See Ave Maria. S.C.

hair, religious significance of: Hair is given a religious significance in all religions. Particularly, attention is shown its style, its length, its symbolic character as a link with the owner. Among primitive peoples, there was a style for festivals, for mourning, for weddings, for leaders, and medicine men, for persons in disgrace. (See Frazer, *Golden Bough,* vol. 3, pp. 264-7.) Long hair meant strength, integrity. Samson's hair was source of his power (Judges 16:17); Nazarites let their hair grow while under a vow (Judges 13:5) and Israelites extolled long hair in contrast to the clipped heads of their enemies (Lev. 19:27, Jer. 49:32). Shaving the head meant humiliation, punishment or penance. Semites generally forbade shaving. In later times, Hebrew men cut their hair but regarded women's long hair as her glory. (I Cor. 11:15). Christian monastic orders practiced use of the tonsure*. Hindu ascetics and hermits set high store by hair arrangement (or disarrangement). The symbol of penitence in the O.T. is "sackcloth and ashes." Vedic students were directed specifically how to wear their hair. The hair was sometimes cut and given in sacrifice, as a symbol of a sacrifice of his own body to God. In Greece, hair was offered to the gods by youths at the initiation rites. Religions have taken advantage of the fact that the state of the hair can reveal a person's inner state; his character and position; his order or rank. M.L.C.

halakah: (A derivative from the Hebrew, *holek,* to go) Used as general name for authoritative law, which is a way of life. Refers also to those parts of Rabbinic literature which deal with any phase of Jewish law. Cf. Akiba. B.Z.B.

Hale Lectures, The: Established in 1901 by Bishop Charles R. Hale of Cairo, Illinois at Seabury-Western Theological Seminary, Evanston, Illinois. The capital sum is $50,000. The object of the lectures is "the Glory of God, and the Good of His Church." They are given about once in every three years. Lecturers and subjects include: the Rev. Fleming James, "Personalities of the Old Testament"; the Rev. Winfred Douglas, "The Praise of God, or Church Music in History and Practice."

(Data furnished by the Office of the President of the Seminary.) V.F.

Halevi, Jehuda ben Samuel: (1085-1140) Practicing physician in Toledo, Spain, and the most gifted Hebrew poet and philosopher of his day. His religious poetry was dominated by a great longing for the restoration of the Holy Land and some of it was incorporated into the liturgy of the synagogue. In the *Kuzari,* a philosophical work in Arabic, he offered a philosophic defense of the Jewish religion. Toward the end of his career, he made a trip to Palestine, where he died. B.Z.B.

half-way covenant, the: Origin of the phrase uncertain. It was a procedure by which the children of parents who attended and supported the New England churches, but had not met the severe experimental tests then demanded for full church membership, could be baptized. About the third generation after the settlement of the colonies there was an increasing number of such parents and church leaders had no choice but to leave their children unbaptized, lower their own demanding standards for full church communion or compromise.

Many churches and ministers, therefore, decided to accept for baptism the children of parents whose lives were not "scandalous", on condition that the parents would publically covenant to attend and support the church, though not, by virtue of such a covenant, being permitted to share the Lord's Supper or vote in church meetings. (Actually the terms of such a "Half-Way Covenant" were, in many instances, more demanding than most churches now require for full membership.) There was no general agreement about this arrangement and it engendered heated disputations. Its inception may be dated from 1657-1662. After the period of the great revivals it faded as a subject of controversy out of the New England picture. Cf. S. Stoddard.

The "Half-Way Covenant" has occasioned a most considerable literature. Williston Walker's *Creeds and Platforms of Congregationalism*, (1893) is authoritative. See also his *History of the Congregationalists* (1916), pp. 156, 158, 160, 170-182, 220, 262, 283, 287, 366. G.G.A.

Hallaj or al-Hallaj: A Moslem mystic who was put to death in 922 A.D. for crying out in Bagdad, "I am Reality", i.e., the sole reality God. He taught that man is essentially divine, created by God in his own image. God incarnates himself not only in Adam and Jesus, but in every man. His self-deification was repudiated by other *Sufis**. P.E.J.

Hallel: (Heb., praise) Designation of Psalms 113-118; included in the Jewish liturgy for New Moon and the festivals of Tabernacles, Chanukah, Pentecost, and in the Passover service. N.G.

hallelujah: (Heb., *hillel*, he praises; *Jah*, form of Yahweh-Jehovah used in compound words) Literally, Praise ye Yahweh. A liturgical phrase originating in Jewish temple worship, where it invited a response of people and/or choir in a shout of praise (cf. Psalm 135). In its Gr. form *alleluia** it is a familiar feature of Christian praise from the earliest times, cf. Rev. 19:1-6. R.B.Y.S.

hamadryads: (Teut.) Tree-people, forest-people, spirit-folk; derived from potencies of trees and other plants, live in the woods; may be either friendly or hostile to human beings; when combined with souls of the dead the wood-spirits develop into tutelary spirits. F.L.P.

Hamann, Joh. Georg: (1730-1788) German Protestant thinker. ("Magus des Nordens"). He was born in Königsberg, Prussia and died in Münster-in-Westphalia. His religious realism played an important role in the making of German classicism and idealism. Herder, Jacobi*, Goethe and Hegel** were deeply indebted to him, notwithstanding the unsystematic character of his thought and the obscurity of his language. He emphasized the wholeness of life over against the abstractions and artificial divisions of purely rational philosophy. The ultimate root of all reality is to be found in God, who tends to reveal himself in nature, language, history and social institutions, so that the same structural elements can be found in all of these departments.

Works:

Hamann's Schriften, herausg. von Roth und Wiesner, 9 vols. (1821-1843); Another edition by C. H. Gildemeister (1851-1873) and by Petri (1872-1873). See also: R. Unger, *Hamann und die Aufklärung*, 2 vols. (1911, 2nd ed. 1925); F. Blanke, *Hamann als Theologe* (1928). O.A.P.

Hamilton, Sir William: (1788-1856) Scottish philosopher, professor at Edinburgh, 1836-1856. He is well known for his theory of consciousness. He held that all knowledge is relative and limited to finite human experience and that the Infinite cannot be known (agnosticism), but can be experienced through the moral certainty of faith. He was influential in England and America. His most important writings were articles in the *Edinburgh Review* and the posthumous *Lectures on Metaphysics and Logic* (1859).

See J. S. Mill, *An Examination of Sir William Hamilton's Philosophy* (1865); J. Veitch, *Memoir of Sir William Hamilton* (1869). J.E.N.

Hammurabi, Code of: An ancient Babylonian legal code containing 282 laws purportedly given by the Babylonian god of justice, Shamash, to King Hammurabi for the rule of his people. There is evidence that it is based upon a much more ancient collection of laws, revised and expanded by order of Hammurabi variously dated by scholars from c. 2100 B.C. to 1800 B.C. The code written in cuneiform characters on a stone pillar was unearthed by French excavators at ancient Susa in 1901-02. The broken pieces were put together and lodged in the Louvre, Paris.

See R. F. Harper, *The Code of Hammurabi* (1904). C.S.B.

Hampton Court Conference: A conference held at Hampton Court in January 1604 between James I and the Puritan leaders. By it the Puritans hoped to secure reforms in the church, but their hopes were not fulfilled. It was the occasion of James' succinct judgment on ecclesiastical polity: "No bishop, no king." W.S.H.

Hanbal: Ibn Hanbal (d. 855) was the founder of one of the four orthodox schools of Moslem law, which formerly prevailed in Mesopotamia and Syria, but has gradually yielded to the Hanifite school. P.E.J.

Handel, Georg Friedrich: (1685-1759) See oratorio; passion music.

hands, laying on of: See laying on of hands.

Hanifa: See Abu Hanifa.

Hanukkah: (From the Heb., dedication) The eight day Jewish festival commemorating the rededication of the Jerusalem Temple to the faith of Israel in 165 B.C.E., after the Maccabees had defeated the armies of the Syrian Greeks in a war for religious liberation. See Antiochus Epiphanes; Judas Maccabeus. B.Z.B.

haoma: In Mazdaism and Parsism**, a sacramental drink, prepared by priests, and obtained by mixing juice from a plant, haoma, with milk and water; the sacrament, used in religious services, typifies the drink of immortality which is yet to come to the faithful. See Aryan religion. F.L.P.

Hapi: See Apis.

happiness: The state of satisfaction which is experienced in the pursuit but more obviously in the attainment of that which is regarded as desirable or good. The efforts to indicate the essence of such good fortune or happiness have led to divergent interpretations. In the intellectualism of Plato* the supreme good for man is represented as wisdom which involves, to whatever varying degrees may be possible, the cognition of and the participation in that type of being which is constituted by the genuinely real though abstract, general, timeless "ideas" or forms, i.e., essences or universals, which as instances of the Good, Plato's designation for reality at its highest and best, are themselves ideal, i.e., changeless and perfect in their eternal nature, perfection being the principle of reality and of knowledge. The supreme realities are the ideas and not God who makes the world to the pattern of the ideas. God is good but not *the* good which is the source of the pattern. Nevertheless Plato (in the *Theaetetus* 176) regards the ascent of man to the Ideal Good as being in some not explicitly defined way related to the necessary condition that man "become like God, as far as this is possible; and to become like him, is to become holy, just, and wise. . . . And he of us who is the most righteous is most like him. . . . To know this is true wisdom and virtue, and ignorance of this is manifest folly and vice." In the practical intellectualism of Aristotle*, happiness is constituted by living in obedience to the intellect; it is the fulfillment of man's distinctive intellectual function as a rational being. While committed theoretically to the annihilation of emotion, Stoicism* professed to find satisfaction by living in conformity to nature. By some ancient and modern Hedonists*, happiness as the dominant motivating principle of conduct and the realization of that happiness are regarded as relevant to the mundane present only. In the qualitative Utilitarianism* of John Stuart Mill*, happiness has reference to the "higher" pleasures, the welfare of all men being the standard of right conduct. Although verbally rejecting enlightened eudaemonism* as a moral end and defending a stern legalism from which utilitarian considerations are allegedly excluded and morality for its own sake affirmed, even so rigorous a moralist as Kant* could not actually escape the conviction that virtue and happiness do belong together, a synthesis which led to the postulates of immortality and the existence of God. Opposed to the recognition of happiness as the highest goal of human striving are the various doctrines of Pessimism* maintaining the inevitability of unhappiness for man. In contrast to such reasoned despair are the systems of Optimism*, which in their extreme versions attempt to supply warrant for happiness by declaring that the actual order of existence is, indeed, the best possible world. Advancing beyond the conception of outward prosperity or any other favorable external conditions as essential signs of divine blessing and necessary conditions of happiness, though not denying the legitimacy of mundane requirements (Mt. 6: 32-33), the Christian doctrine affirms that Blessedness* (the term used by many as the synonym for N.T. happiness; cf. Mt. 5:2 ff) is spiritual and inward, a present quality of being arising from the personal relationship of faith in and love for God through Jesus Christ. Even those sufferings which may have to be endured in and because of that relationship (Mt. 5:10-12) are compelled to contribute to the blessedness of the believer (I Pet. 4:12-14) for whom the indwelling Christ is the hope of glory (Col. 1:27). The blessedness of eternal life which is in part realized even in this world as a gift of God accompanying the faith which works through love is also other-worldly in character since it will have its perfect fruition in the life to come. (Jn. 17:22-24; I Jn. 3:1-2). See Epictetus; Epicureanism; ethics; Platonism; summum bonum; value. H.W.J.

harakiri: (Lit., "belly-cutting") A vulgar name applied to Japanese suicide by disembowelment. A more dignified expression for the same thing is *seppuku*. D.C.H.

Hard Shell Baptists: A name formerly applied to Baptist churches which opposed missionary societies, Sunday schools, salaried ministers, instrumental music, and similar "innovations" which they alleged were not mentioned in the Bible. They are now for the most part found in the Primitive Baptist* and the Two-Seed-in-the-Spirit Predestinarian Baptist* sects. E.T.C.

Häring, Theodor: (1848-1928) He taught at the universities of Zürich, Switzerland, Göttingen and Tübingen. Descending from a mild Swabian pietism, he gave the ideas of Ritschl* a softer tone. He stressed the revelation of God in the historical person of Jesus the continued influence of the risen Lord in the community and in the acts of His divine calling the special significance of His passion and death. Häring became the mediator between Ritschlianism and conservative biblicism. By his understanding for those who thought differently, he contributed to a mitigation of theological antitheses.

Über das Bleibende im Glauben an Christus (Stuttgart, 1880); *Zur Ritschls Versöhnungslehre* (Stuttgart, 1888); *Dogmatik* (Stuttgart, 1906, 2 ed., Calw, 1912); *Christian Faith: A Systematics* (London, 1913). H.H.

Häring, Theodor Lorenz: (1884-) Son of the theologian Theodor Häring*, he is professor of philosophy at the University of Tubingen. He not only has been creative in the psychology of valuation and in epsitemology, he also has labored in the fields of the philosophy of history and science. But he is best known by his work on Hegel*. He presents the most detailed analysis of Hegel's early theological and philosophical writings which exist so far. He visions a Christian, theistic and dynamic metaphysics.

Die Materialisierung des Geistes (Tübingen, 1919); *Die Struktur der Weltgeschichte* (Tübingen, 1921); *Philosophie der Naturwissenschaft* (München, 1923); *Über Individualität in Natur und Geisteswelt* (*Wissenschaft und Hypothese.* Bd. XXX), (Leipzig and Berlin, 1926); *Hegel, sein Wollen und sein Werk.* vol. I. (Leipzig und Berlin, 1929), vol. II (Leipzig und Berlin, 1938); *Die philosophischen Grundlagen der heutigen Universitätsbildung* (Tübingen, 1933); *Die Entstehungsgeschichte der Phänomenologie des Geistes* (Tübingen, 1934); *Naturphilosophie in der Gegenwart* (Tübingen, 1934). H.H.

Harmonists: (Rappites) See communistic settlements.

harmony: 1) The science which treats of chords, their construction and their relationships in progression to each other. Its musical structure is vertical and implies a basis of tonality* Homophony contrasted with polyphony*.

2) A group of tones sounding simultaneously, a chord. E.H.B.

harmony of the gospels: A harmony of the gospels is an arrangement of their contents which places parallel passages in parallel columns. The purpose of the older harmonies was to weave together all data for the life and teaching of Jesus, found in all four gospels; the purpose of present-day harmonies is to present the material for a comparison of the gospels in the interest of showing their mutual relationship, use of sources, and editorial revision of one by another (e.g., Mark as revised by Matthew and Luke). Accordingly, present-day harmonies usually do not include the Fourth Gospel. Cf. Diatessaron.

See Synoptic Gospels; E. D. Burton and E. J. Goodspeed, *A Harmony of the Synoptic Gospels* (1917, Greek text, 1920); A. Huck, *A Synopsis of the First Three Gospels* (9th edition by H. Lietzmann and F. L. Cross, 1936—Greek with German and English headings); A. Wright, *A Synopsis of the Gospels in Greek* with . . . Notes, 3rd edition, 1906. F.C.G.

Harms, Claus: (1778-1855) Vigorous champion of Neo-Lutheranism* and author of the celebrated Ninety-five Theses (1817)* condemning rationalism and unbelief and denouncing the Prussian Plan of Union of Lutheran and Reformed Churches and calling for a steadfast loyalty to the Lutheran standards and to confessionalism.

See V. Ferm, *The Crisis in American Lutheran Theology* (1927), Ch. IV. V.F.

Harnack, Adolf von: (1851-1930) Professor at various German Universities including Berlin (1888-1921). President of the *Kaiser Wilhelm Gesellschaft zur Förderung der Wissenschaften* and Librarian of *Preussische Staats-bibliothek*. A founder of *Evangelical-Social Congress,* president 1903-1912. His students established *Die Christliche Welt,* suppressed under Hitler. Teacher of Karl Barth* whom he later opposed. Author of hundreds of monographs and books. Greatest German church historian of his day. His *History of Dogma* (3 vol.) appeared in six editions (1889-1922). His work on the *Apostles' creed* in 27 editions. His *Das Wesen des Christentums* (What is Christianity), 1900, in 15 translations and over 71,000 printings. Greatest single work probably, *Marcion,* 1921, second ed., 1924. Cf. Sohm, R. C.H.M.

Harnack, Theodosius: (1817-1889) Father of Adolf Harnack*, he was a Baltic orthodox Lutheran. He was professor of practical theology and university preacher at Dorpat (now Tartu, Estonia). He fought romantic hierarchism and pietistic collegialism. He sharply distinguished between the essential and the empirical church. He also was one of the main representatives of the study of practical theology between Schleiermacher and Ritschl**.

Luthers Theologie (Erlangen, 1862-86); *Die Kirche, ihr Amt, ihr Regiment* (Erlangen, 1862); *Praktische Theologie* (Erlangen, 1877-78), 2 vols. H.H.

Harper, W. R.: (1856-1906) Baptist educator. At 14, B.A., at 19, Ph.D. Popularized the study of Hebrew. Professor Semitic languages at Yale, 1886-91. First president of the University of Chicago. Chautauqua lecturer. Established four quarter university plan making Summer Quarter of rich variety, and Junior Senior College and Graduate School system. Promoted scheme of credit for courses by correspondence. Founded various scholarly journals. Valiantly defended historical approach to the Bible. C.H.M.

harpies: (Gr., *Harpuiai,* from *harpazo,* to snatch) Weird creatures of Greek mythology, represented as 1) stormwinds that can blow a mortal away, or 2) birds of prey with faces of women. Since popular fancy pictured the soul as a bird with woman's face and credited the souls of the dead with carrying off the souls of the living, this ghost of the dead may be the prototype of the mythological figure of the harpy. E.M.N.

Harris, Samuel: (1814-1899) Graduated, Bowdoin College, 1833, Andover, 1838. Professor of Systematic Theology, Bangor Theological Seminary, 1855-1867; President, Bowdoin College, 1867-1871; Dwight Professor of Systematic Theology, Yale Divinity School, 1871-1899.

Author: *The Philosophical Basis of Theism* (1883); *The Self-Revelation of God* (1886); *God, the Creator and Lord of All* (1896). In these volumes Harris constructed an intuitional theism based philosophically upon Kant (whose theistic antinomies he regarded as bi-polar) of exceptional insight, breadth and strength.

Cf. "American Theists," *Harvard Theological Review,* Vol. XIV, July, 1921. J.W.B.

Hartmann, Edward von: (1842-1906) His philosophy is the outgrowth of the misery resulting from the dying materialism and positivism of the natural sciences, the consequent spread of indifference and scepticism, and from the results of applied science and the achievement of technology following the Franco-Prussian war of 1870. Hartmann vindicated the ideal against materialism by partially satisfying the metaphysical needs of his contemporaries, and emancipated philosophy from the extraneous literary, scientific and even university influences.

Taking up a military career, he was forced to relinquish it due to a disorder in his knee. He refused a professorship on account of health and the limitation of freedom. At the age of 27 he published his three volume *Philosophy of the Unconscious* (1869), a comprehensive work the discussion of which stimulated a large literature. Historians of philosophy have judged and evaluated the work on the basis of the first edition, ignoring the later additions and changes Hartmann made. He published during his life some 453 writings.

His books on religion were addressed to those who have been emancipated by the critical study of positive Christian dogma. Polemical towards existing religious views throughout his life, he expressed his religious opinions without reserve. He considered Christianity bankrupt in the means of satisfying the religious needs of the present which he thought was the most irreligious period of history. He thought the essence of Christianity was exhausted in the Middle Ages. In his time it ceased to be Lutheran, Augustinian and even Pauline. He wrote a severe criticism of the speculative Protestantism of a Biedermann, Pfleiderer and Lipsius**. In his criticism of both the O. and the N.Ts. he blindly accepted the assertions of the most radical critics. He condemned the belief in a personal God as he thought there could be nothing divine that was not impersonal and unconscious. He denied the need of any mediator. Every man is his own savior if he was saved. He called the worship of Jesus a form of heathenism, the Jesus of evangelical faith a fetish. He pilloried the idea of the God-man, holding that humanity itself was divine. He repudiated all the historical elements of Christianity or any need of them. He thought Christian morality puerile because based on rewards, happiness and heteronomous virtues. He flouted the assumption that the end of religion is to bring happiness now and hereafter as akin to a sensuous heaven or work for a pay day. He denounced the concept of personal immortality. Church authority was for him the most insidious and dangerous of all for both mental and moral culture. He anticipated the gradual disappearance of the church. He opposed the ethic of Jesus because of its transcendent eudaemonism. He was sincere in contending that the modern spirit, with its culture, has so far outgrown historical Christianity that it no longer had anything to offer in the solution of the religious question. He developed a philosophical religion which is only for the educated world. He strove to surmount abstract monism and theism, replacing these by a concrete monism.

He also sketched the general outlines of an ideal and future religion in which the little that was left vital in mummified Christianity becomes synthesized with all pantheistic and monistic tendencies. The new religion is to be a new dispensation of and a new synthesis between the pessimistic negative religion of India and the optimistic affirmative religion of Persia. If in urging these negations with vehemence, he seemed to hate theology and the church, it was because of his great love for what he deemed the ideal religion. He was convinced of the indispensability of religion for the development of mankind and for the maintenance and advance of culture. He urged that the church was only half-hearted and shallow-in-thought in its faith. He found his *point d'appui* in the Persian conception of the necessary war between light and dark, or the rational idea and blind instinct and irrational will.

Hartmann's ethical and religious writings are much less abstract than his other works. Pessimism becomes a weaker factor in them. He held to the prepotence of pain over pleasure in the interests of morality and piety. Not eudaemonological pessimism, but evolutionary optimism, aggressive participation in the processes of culture was his creed. He demanded no flight from reality, or renunciation but self-immolating sacrifice and work for God's sake. He turned from passive quietism to the eternal yea of Zarathustra. Hartmann's God is the blind, but impelling power that utters itself in and through the entire process of cosmic evolution, which makes for righteousness, which animates all his work and of all soldiers of the spirit, and is revealed in the lives of all the great light-bringers in history.

Die Selbstzersetzung des Christenthums und die Religion der Zukunft (Berlin, 1874); *Die Krise des Christenthums in der modernen Theologie* (Leipzig, 1888); *Das religiöse Bewusstsein,* 2nd ed. (Berlin, 1888); *Das Christenthum des Neuen Testamentes* (Berlin, 1905); *Die Religion des Geistes,* 3rd ed. (Berlin, 1907); *Grundriss der Religionsphilosophie* (Berlin, 1909); L. Braun, *Die Persönlichkeit Gottes; eine Auseinandersetzung zwischen E. v. Hartmanns Philosophie des Unbewussten und dem kritischen Theismus,* 2 vols. (Heidelberg, 1929-31); F. W. Brepohl, *E. v. Hartmann und das Erlösungsproblem* (Berlin, 1910); C. Neumann, *E. v. Hartmanns Erlösungslehre* (Breslau, 1910); F. J. Rintelen, *Pessimistische Religionsphilosophie der Gegenwart* (München, 1924); J. P. Steffes, *E. v. Hartmanns Religionsphilosophie des Unbewussten* (Mergentheim, 1921).

H.H.

Hartmann, Nicolai: (1883-) Known chiefly for the contributions to a theory of objective values made in his monumental *Ethik* (1926), (Eng. tr. in 3 vols. by Stanton Coit, 1932). With Scheler, Hartmann applies the phenomenological method to experiences of value and with him comes to the conclusion that values are independent, possessing a hierarchy of their own, and that consciousness does not create but must take account of them. Unlike Scheler* he believes that if a God exists it is wholly impersonal.

Other works: *Grundzüge einer Metaphysik der Erkenntnis* (1921); *Das Problem des geistigen Seins* (1933); *Zur Grundlegung der Ontologie* (1935).

J.S.B.

harvest festivals: The harvest festival harks back to primeval ideas regarding the annual death of vegetation, when the Earth Mother or her child withdrew into the underworld and fertility and growth were suspended on the earth. The grain died at the harvest. In Europe great importance attached to the cutting of the last sheaf because it was supposed to embody the life of the grain. It was called "mother", "maiden", "old woman", "great mother", sometimes made into a doll dressed in woman's clothes and carried home in joyous procession. The reaper of the last sheaf acquired its mysterious potency and was given a place of honor with it at the harvest supper. The fertility of the new crop was bound up with this sheaf. It was sometimes sprinkled with water, thrown into a river or mixed with the seed grain. The idea of the mother of the maize or of the rice appears also in Asia. In Judaism the primitive practices associated with the death of vegetation dropped out of the official ceremony and the harvest festivals became simply times of rejoicing. In general the harvest feast* completed what the firstfruits* ceremony began. It combined a solemn communion of eating with or in the presence of the corn spirit, rejoicing over the completion of the harvest, and anxiety regarding future fertility. The socially approved licence which accompanied some harvest ceremonies may be bound up with this fertility motif.

A.E.H.

Hase, Karl August von: (1800-1890) German theologian. He was born at Steinbach (Saxony); in 1823 he became privatdozent at Tübingen, 1828 at Leipzig, and from 1830-1883 he was professor of Church History in Jena. Hase is one of the outstanding men in German theology of the 19th century, remarkable for his comprehensive culture, the universality of his interests and his lofty idealism. Notwithstanding his vast erudition his academic and literary interest was in the sympathetic understanding and artistic presentation of the subject rather than in detailed research.

Influenced by Schelling, Schleiermacher** and German romanticism Hase occupied a mediating position between rationalistic liberalism and orthodoxy. His theology was a re-interpretation of 17th century Lutheran orthodoxy through German idealism. More than any of his contemporaries he laid great emphasis on the aesthetic element in religion. In the political and ecclesiastical fight against Roman Catholic ultramontanism* he became soon one of the protagonists, a role for which he was qualified by regular journeys to Italy and contacts with many of the leading men in Rome. Politically he was an active fighter (he was for this reason imprisoned from 1824-1825). He helped much to develop the idealistic type of religion among the educated class in Germany. In Church History he excelled in biographic studies. A prolific writer, his *Works* in twelve volumes (1890-1893) incorporate only one-half of his literary production.

Principal works: *Evangelisch-protestantische Dogmatik* (1826, 5th ed. 1860); *Hutterus Redivivus* (1829, many editions); *Leben Jesu* (1829, 5th ed. 1865); *Kirchengeschichte* (1834, 12th ed. 1899); *Handbuch der praktischen Polemik gegen die römisch-katholische Kirche* (1862, many editions); *Gnosis, oder protestantisch-evangelische Glaubenslehre für die Gebildeten in der Gemeinde wissenschaftlich dargestellt,* 3 vols. (1827-1829, new rev. ed. 1869-1870); *Ideale und Irrtümer* (autobiography) (1871).

See also: "Hase" in A. Hauck's *Realenzykl* (3rd ed. vol. VII, pp. 453-461) by his disciple, Gustav Krüger; Fr. H. R. v. Frank, *Geschichte der protestantischen Theologie* (1894), pp. 141 ff.

O.A.P.

Hasideans: The Hasideans (Heb., *Hasidim* "saints") Jews, organized during the fourth or third century B.C. for the purpose of promoting the observance of Jewish ritual and the study of the Law. It is clear from the subsequent history, that their society was the group out of which developed the Society of the Pharisees*, concerning which we are much better informed. The Hasideans are probably referred to in some of the Psalms, e.g., Ps. 149.5: "Let the Hasidim be joyful in glory . . . the high praises of God are in their mouth, and a two-edged sword in their hand." If the Psalmist was referring to the Hasideans in this passage, the incident he has in mind is undoubtedly the Maccabean war against the Syrian king, Antiochus IV. There are more explicit references to the Hasideans in the Books of Maccabees. Thus I Macc. 2.41 records that Hasideans, "mighty men in Israel . . . such as were devoted to the Law", joined the Maccabean opposition to Antiochus. In I Macc. chap. 7, they are described as welcoming a compromise peace with the Syrians. The relationship between this group and the Essenes* has been much discussed, but has not yet been clarified.

L.F.

Hasidism: (Hebrew, pietism, from *hasid,* pious) Mystical movement in modern Judaism, founded by the practical cabbalist Israel Baal Shem Tob (abbreviated *Besht,* the Kind Master of the Name, 1700-1760) shortly before the middle of the 18th century. This simple man of the people, famed as a miracle worker and healer, was a true saint and mystic. Through his own revivalist ardor and through the learning and organizing skill of his disciples, Rabbi Jacob Joseph Cohen of Polonnoye and Rabbi Dov Baer the Maggid (preacher) of Meseritz (1710-1772), the movement attracted a large following from among the untutored Jewish elements of the Polish Ukraine as well as a considerable number of scholarly men. Some of the more gifted of their disciples established dynasties, perpetuating their leadership of bodies of Hasidism by transmission from father to son.

The movement touched off the creative spiritual impulse of the Jewish people, rousing the masses to spiritual ardor and producing many luminous personalities. The foremost thinker of the movement was Rabbi Shneur Zalman of Liadi (1747-1812), who formulated a system of rational theology known as *Habad* (abbreviated from Hochma—wisdom, Bina—understanding, and Daas—knowledge). Among its popular saints are R. Levi Isaac of Berditchev, R. Elimelech of Lizianka, R. Jacob Isaac the "Seer" of Lublin, and R. Nahman of Bratzlav.

Thoroughly orthodox in character, Hasidism adheres strictly to every cardinal doctrine and practice of traditional Judaism. Yet it transformed everything by its emphasis on Divine immanence, on constant communion with God in thought and in prayer, on faith in the inspiration and wonder-working powers of the leaders (Zaddikim), and on ecstatic joy and fervor in worship. In Hasidism mysticism appears no longer as an esoteric doctrine and a system of asceticism, but as the vital singing faith of the people. It appealed not by apocalyptic visions of speedy Messianic deliverance, but by lifting the gloom from the depressed and impoverished masses, by easing their pain and suffering, and by quickening the despondent with renewed hope. It preached contentment, meakness and modesty, without suppressing the natural impulses of the heart.

The adoration of the leaders as intermediaries between God and ordinary men and as the sources of both earthly and spiritual blessings, and the stress on salvation by faith rather than by works and by study of Torah*, endangered the foundations of rabbinical Judaism. The overenthusiastic cheerfulness of the devotees of Hasidism —induced sometimes by spirituous liquors—jarred on the sensibilities of the puritanic rabbis of the old order, and led to bitter conflicts and to persecution. The growing influence of the Zaddikim, the establishment of separate prayer-houses, the new method of worship and adoption of the ritual of the Palestinian Cabbalists (*Nusah Ari*), and the slight variation in the mode of killing animals for food virtually separated the Hasidim from the rest of Jewry as a distinct sect. For a time intermarriage between them and their opponents (*Mithnaggedim*) was prohibited.

Despite the opposition, Hasidism made great progress, and, during the first half of the 19th cent., won over nearly half of all the Jews of the world. A more formidable danger menaced the movement with the rise of the *Haskalah* (Enlightenment), which sought to spread Western culture among the Jews of Russia, Poland, Galicia, etc. In the changed intellectual atmosphere of the second half of the 19th cent. the power of Hasidism waned. The credulity and superstition of the ignorant people and the craftiness of some of the Zaddikim drew the fire of the apostles of the Enlightenment. Still Hasidism continued as a living force in Russia to the Bolshevist revolution, and in Poland, Hungary and Rumania to the Second World War. In attenuated form it continues in Palestine, America, and other lands to which it was transplanted by the Hasidim. The positive spiritual values of the movement, its glowing faith and optimism, its exuberant folklore and folksong have enriched every phase of Jewish life and culture. They have fertilized the creations of musicians like Ravel and Ernst Bloch and of poets, novelists and dramatists like Judah Leib Peretz, S. Ansky, Sholom Ash and S. Agnen, and have fascinated students like S. Schechter, A. Horodetzki, Simon Dubnow, and Martin Buber.

M. Buber, *Die Chassidischen Buecher* (1928); S. Dubnow, *Toldot Hahasidut* (1932); S. A. Horodetzki, *Leaders of Hasidism* (1928); *idem. Hahasidut Vehahasidim.* 4 Vols. (1922-28); A. Kahana, *Sefer Hahasidut* (1922); A. Z. Idelson, *Jewish Music* (1929); *idem, Thesaurus of Hebrew and Oriental Melodies,* Vol. X: *Songs of the Chassidim* (1932); Jacob S. Minkin, *The Romance of Hassidism* (1934); L. Newman and S. Spitz, *Hasidic Anthology* (1934); G. Sholem, *Major Trends in Jewish Mysticism* (1941). S.S.C.

Haskell Lectures, The Charles E.: Established in 1894 by Mrs. Caroline E. Haskell these lectures are given at the University of Chicago on the subject of comparative religion. Among the twenty lecturers who have appeared on this foundation are: J. H. Barrows, G. F. Moore, M. Jastrow, Jr., F. Cumont, M. Anesaki, S. Radhakrishnan, Hu Shih, D. C. Holtom. Endowment, $20,724.00.

(Data from the offices of the Dean of the Divinity School and the secretary of the University.) V.F.

Haskell Lectureship, The: This lectureship was established in 1905 by Mrs. Caroline E. Haskell of Michigan City, Ind., at the Graduate School of Theology, Oberlin, Ohio. The capital sum is $20,000. It is given in a series of six lectures annually and deals with the relationship of Christianity to the East. Among the distinguished lecturers the following have served: G. F. Moore; W. M. Ramsay; F. A. Loofs; M. Jastrow; H. Rashdall; E. F. Scott; C. C. Torrey; K. Lake; H. R. Mackintosh; J. H. Breasted; W. E. Hocking; R. M. Jones; R. Otto; T. R. Glover; B. H. Streeter; A. Deissmann; J. B. Pratt; J. Morgenstern; M. Sprengling; and F. C. Grant.

(Data from the office of the Dean of the Graduate School.) V.F.

Hasmoneans: (also Asmoneans) The dynasty commencing with Simon, brother of Judas Maccabeus*, deliverer of the Jewish people from the oppressive Syrian yoke, who became king of the Jews in 142 B.C., and ending with Antigonus, executed by Mark Antony in 37 B.C. These successive rulers combined in their persons the offices of king and high-priest. Herod the Great, an Idumean, became king after Antigonus, and strengthened his claim to the throne by marrying Mariamne, the last Hasmonean princess. J.M.

Hasselquist, Tufve Nilsson: (1816-1891) Born in Sweden, studied at Lund, and ordained as pastor 1839, Hasselquist emigrated in 1852 to America. He was a pioneer among the Swedish immigrants, among whom he became the spiritual leader for a generation. Pastor at Galesburg, Illinois, he was active in the organization of the Augustana Synod in 1860, and became president of Augustana College and Theological Seminary in 1863. Through his founding of the Swedish press in America (1855) his influence extended wherever Swedish settlers made their homes. C.J.B.

Hatch, Edwin: (1835-1889) English theologian, noted especially for his work in the history of the early Christian Church. Two of his most important works are *The Organization of the Early Christian Churches,* (Bampton Lectures, 1880; published, 1881), and *The Influence of Greek Ideas and Usages upon the Christian Church* (Hibbert Lectures, 1888; published posthumously, 1890). Hatch maintained that Greek thought bequeathed a disastrous legacy to the Christian Church by deflecting it from an original vital moral simplicity to a body of orthodox metaphysics, thus giving dogma preeminence over conduct. H.W.J.

Hathor: (Egyptian) Cow goddess of ancient Upper Egypt; cow goddess of the sky of which the sun is born; sky imagined as an immense cow whose legs were established at the four corners of the earth, and who is upheld by other gods. See Egypt, religions of. F.L.P.

Hauck, Albert: (1845-1918) German Protestant theologian. He was born in Wassertrüdingen

(Middle Frankonia). From 1878-1889 he was professor of Church History in Erlangen and from 1889-1918 in Leipzig. He laid the foundations for a systematic exploration of the sources of German Church History in the Middle Ages. He was a master in the interpretation of the legal and political tendencies that framed the history of that age. He was co-editor, with J. J. Herzog, of the last volumes of the second edition of the *Protestantische Realenzyklopädie* (RE) and sole editor of the third edition of that work. (1896-1913).

Principal works: *Kirchengeschichte Deutschlands,* 5 vols. (unfinished) (1892-1920); 3rd and 4th ed. vol. I (1904), vol. III (1906); *Die Entstehung der bischöflichen Fürstenmacht* (1891); *Deutschland und England in ihrer kirchlichen Beziehung* (1917); Biography by H. Boehmer, in *Beiträge zur sächsischen Kirchengeschichte,* v. 33 (1919). O.A.P.

Hauge, Hans Nielsen: (1771-1824) A Norwegian lay preacher, who proclaimed a living Christianity as against formal Rationalism and superficial Pietism, Hauge was persecuted under Conventical laws, but by writing and followers roused the whole people to more sincere spiritual life. Hauge also contributed to social regeneration of Norway by new, scientific interest in agriculture and industry. C.J.B.

Hausrath, Adolf: (1837-1909) As professor in Heidelberg, he furthered above all by his critical work and descriptive art interest in the apostle Paul and in the relation of growing Christianity with the existing world.

Der Apostle Paulus (Heidelberg, 1865); *Neutestamentliche Zeitgeschichte,* 4 vols. 3 ed. (Heidelberg, 1879); *Jesus und der neutestamentliche Schriftsteller,* 2 vols. (Berlin, 1908). H.H.

haustafel: Literally house-table, but more freely, code of domestic morality. According to Weidinger, *Die Haustafeln* (1928), there existed in the ancient world, side by side with the code of public morality, a private, unwritten code of domestic morality which at times found written expression. To this code he gave the name *Haustafel,* a designation now generally accepted. A *haustafel* usually begins with a statement of the individual's duties to the gods and to his country, and continues with the mutual obligations and duties of husbands and wives, parents and children, masters and slaves, and friends to each other. More or less complete examples of this moral pattern may be found in Hellenistic writers like Epictetus, Seneca, Diogenes Laertius, Philo, and Pseudo-Phocylides. It is also present, with Christian adaptations, in the following early Christian writings: Colossians 3:18-4:1; Ephesians 5:20-6:9 (probably derived from the Colossian example); I Peter 2:13-3:9; Titus 2:1-10; I Clement 21:6-9; Barnabas 19:5-8; Polycarp 4:1-6:3; Ignatius to Polycarp 5:1-2. The identification of the *haustafel* throws some light on the origins of Christian morality. M.R.

Hazen Foundation, The Edward W.: With an initial endowment given to the Foundation by Edward W. Hazen of Haddam, Conn., in 1925, this foundation was incorporated the same year and has since Mr. Hazen's death received supplementary endowment funds from his estate. In the Articles of Association the purpose is stated: "to promote the public welfare either by supporting existing agencies or through independent activities . . . such agencies or activities to be exclusively religious, charitable, scientific, literary, or educational in character." The specific field of this Foundation has focused in later years upon "young people and . . . activities designated to promote a sound character", particularly college students. Total appropriations from 1925 to 1939 have amounted to $763,534.68. The field of religious and character development in higher education has come to occupy a dominant place in the Foundation's program with emphasis upon aiding and promoting the professional growth of leaders. Conferences are held in regional areas bringing together an invited group of college teachers and administrators, university pastors and secretaries to study questions relating to college young people. Theological discussion groups have been sponsored among younger thinkers and a series of published pamphlets and books on religion have received grants. Headquarters, Haddam, Conn. V.F.

Heads of Agreement: (1691) A union document of Congregationalist and Presbyterian leaders in England. Cooperation in the ordination of ministers followed, but the union was impermanent.

W. Walker, *Creeds and Platforms of Congregationalism* (1893). J.T.M.

heart: The heart was universally recognised in ancient cultures as the seat of emotion. It was sometimes thought to be the center of life or the dwelling place of the soul. When the personality functioned through several souls, the heart-soul was one of them. Plato placed the mortal soul in the heart as the ruler of emotion and intelligence. In the Greek myth of the eating of Dionysus Zagreus by the Titans, his heart was rescued, brought to Zeus and reborn through Semele. In primitive and some higher cultures the heart was the mainspring of courage. The heart of a brave man, or of a ferocious animal was eaten to acquire courage and strength. In ancient Mexico and in some other cultures it was the part of the victim offered to the gods. It had a prominent place among the amulets used for protection, especially against witches and the evil eye. See charms and amulets. A.E.H.

heathen: The nations outside the Jewish people and hence not entitled to share in the promises of salvation and blessing in which the Jews believed. See pagan. E.J.G.

heaven and hell: Heaven is the biblical term for the expanse which seemed to the ancients to cover the earth as a domed vault in which the heavenly bodies seemed to be placed. Generally a plurality of heavens was accepted, either three or seven. In the second place, it was looked on as the dwelling place of the Deity and therefore could be used in metonomy for God. (Lk. 15.18) since his name was too holy to pronounce. In later Christian theology heaven was looked upon as the celestial abode of the redeemed dead. That is really not witnessed in the N.T.; in Revelation* the martyrs are temporarily in heaven but they are soon to reign with Christ on earth. (Rev. 7:9 ff., 20:4). But it is inhabited by various angels*, some of whom were hostile to God. (Rev. 12:7 ff.) Hence, heaven had to be redeemed in the eschatological* reconstitution. With the giving up of the primitive hope, heaven was looked upon as the permanent abode of the redeemed.

Hell is the word used to translate several different biblical terms. It is used for *sheol** in the O.T. That was the abode of all the dead according to the early Jewish view, but in Enoch* 22 there is already a division of Sheol. Again, hell is used in the Authorized version for the Greek word *Hades**; (Lk. 16.23). Tartarus, the heathen term for the place of punishment of the incurably corrupt lies behind II Pet. 2:4. Most frequently, hell is used for *Gehenna**, (Mk. 10.43, etc.) which took its name from the valley of Hinnom outside Jerusalem. It came to be the designation for the place of future punishment. Other terms for ultimate punishment in the N.T. are unquenchable fire, outer darkness, second death, lake of fire, and wrath to come. See rewards and punishments. C.T.C.

Heber, Reginald: (1783-1826) English poet and bishop of Calcutta, India. He is best known as a hymn-writer, his works including "Holy, Holy, Holy", "From Greenland's Icy Mountains" and "Brightest and Best of the Sons of the Morning." See hymns. W.N.P.

Hebrew language: Ancient tongue in which most of the O.T. was written. Transformed and used in the Rabbinic Literature, today revived by the Zionists*. Belongs to the North-Western branch of the Semitic family. Characterized by its consonantal stability, the triliterality of its radicals, its wide use of prefixes and suffixes, of nominal construct states, the flexibility of its verbal voice-system and the simplicity of its syntax. Offers concise and forceful means of expression, especially for epic and lyric poetry.

See Th. H. Robinson, *The Genius of Hebrew Grammar* (1928); H. Bauer and P. Leander, *Hebräische Grammatik* (1933). See alphabetic writing. S.L.T.

Hebrew temples: See temples, Hebrew.

Hebrew theology and religion: See Israel, religion and theology; Judaism.

Hebrews, Epistle to: This writing has come down without any note of authorship, and has been variously assigned to Paul, Barnabas, Luke, Apollos, Aquila and Priscilla. Its title, likewise, is due to later guesswork, and in view of its classical style, its philosophical assumptions, its disregard of Jewish legalism, it cannot have been intended for some reactionary group of Hebrew Christians. A number of indications, and particularly the closing salutation "Those of Italy salute you", suggest that it was written for the Roman church by one of its teachers who for the time being was in a foreign city. It is not properly a letter but an eloquent discourse, to which a few personal greetings are appended. Its purpose is to demonstrate to a group of Christians, now growing indifferent, that Christianity is the final and perfect religion. Christ is the "great High-Priest", who has brought to reality all that was merely foreshadowed in previous forms of worship. While he works with the apocalyptic conception of a temple in heaven the writer thinks, like Plato and Philo, of an ideal world, over against the visible one, which is apprehended by faith. Although it lacks the purely religious insight of Paul and John, Hebrews is one of the noblest and most impressive of the N.T. books. The date of Hebrews is about 85 A.D.

A. B. Davidson, *The Epistle to the Hebrews* (1882); J. Moffatt, *The Epistle to the Hebrews* (ICC, 1924); E. F. Scott, *The Literature of the New Testament* (1932). E.F.S.

Hebron: Ancient city of Southern Palestine, 19 miles South of Jerusalem, formerly called Kiriath-Arba (Jud. i, 10-15); first capital of David (II Sam. ii, 4, etc.). See F. M. Abel, *Géographie de la Palestine,* vol. ii (1938), pp. 345-347. S.L.T.

Hecker, Isaac Thomas: See Americanism; Paulists, the.

hedonism: (Gr., *hedone,* pleasure) General name for psychological and ethical theories making pleasure the aim of conduct. *Psychological* hedonism maintains that every person in fact always does act from a desire for pleasure. *Ethical* hedonism may be egoistic or universalistic: if *egoistic,* it affirms that every person ought always to act in the way that will bring most pleasure to himself in the long run; even on this view Hobbes* believed that the Golden Rule is valid. *Universalistic* ethical hedonism is another name for Utilitarianism*. See Cyrenaics; eudaemonism; happiness; s. v. Kant. W.K.W.

Hefele, Karl Joseph von: (1809-93) Historian, Bishop of Rottenburg, b. Unterkocen, Württemberg; d. Rottenburg. Following Möhler he taught church history at Tübingen (1836-69), introduced a course on Christian archaeology and opposed Illuminism. At the decisive session of the Vatican Council regarding papal infallibility Hefele voted "non placet"* but acquiesced when the dogma was defined. His standard work is a history of the Councils in seven volumes. B.R.

Hegel, Georg Wilhelm Friedrich: (1770-1831) An absolute idealist, most influential German philosopher of the first quarter of the nineteenth century, originator of "philosophy of religion" under that name. He was born in 1770 in Stuttgart, Swabia. He studied at the University of Tübingen (1788-1793), where Hölderlin and Schelling were his friends. He taught philosophy in Jena (1801), where he collaborated with Schelling, and wrote his first masterpiece, *Die Phänomenologie des Geistes* (1807). After some experience as newspaper editor (Bamberg, 1807-1808) and as director of a gymnasium (Nurnberg, 1808-1816), he returned to a university professorship, at Heidelberg (1816-1818). Meanwhile he had written his *Wissenschaft der Logik* (1812, 1816) and his system in outline, the *Encyclopädie der philosophischen Wissenchaften* (1817). In 1818 he accepted a call to the chair of philosophy in Berlin, where he became virtual "dictator" of German philosophy, growing somewhat more conservative in the process. His popularity was irksome to his rival, Schopenhauer*, whose pessimism contrasted with Hegel's idealistic optimism. In 1821 he published his *Grundlinien der Rechts-Philosophie,* and, from 1827 on, contributed to the *Jahrbücher für wissenschaftliche Kritik.* In 1830 he served as Rector of the University, and died the following year.

After his death, his works and lectures were published by a group of his students, "friends of the immortalized one." Among the most influential of his writings are the lectures thus published posthumously on the basis of students' notes. These are: *Vorlesungen über die Geschichte der Philosophie; Vorlesungen über die Philosophie der Religion; Vorlesungen über die Philosophie der Weltgeschichte;* and *Vorlesungen über die Aesthetik.* All are available in English translations.

See Hegelianism.

See R. Haym, *Hegel und seine Zeit* (1857); E. Caird, *Hegel* (1883); and T. L. Häring*, *Hegel, sein Wollen und sein Werk* (2 vols., 1929, 1938). Hegel's works are in process of republication in a critical edition by Lasson and Hoffmeister (pub. in *Phil. Bib.* by Meiner); Glockner has reprinted the old text complete in the *Jubiläumsausgabe* (1928-1939), to which he adds *Hegel* (2 vols.) and an invaluable *Hegel-Lexikon* (4 vols.).

E.S.B.

Hegelianism: The philosophy of Hegel* and his school; absolute idealism*, with special emphasis on interpretation of history, society, the state, art, and religion.

I. The principles of Hegelianism.

1) "The true is the whole;" that is, for an adequate understanding of any particular experience a grasp of its relations to experience as a whole is needed. Hence the emphasis on history, development, and correlation of sense data with value experience.

2) Experience is the source of all knowledge. Logic, natural science, art, religion, and philosophy are various levels of interpretation of experience (the *Phänomenologie des Geistes* is the basis and pre-supposition of all Hegel's thought). Haering calls Hegel "the empiricist of consciousness."

3) "The actual is the rational;" that is, the surface appearances of consciousness require reformulation by coherent thought. Not the uncriticized surface, but rationally critical thought about experience, yields an adequate account of actuality. Hence Hegel opposes Schleiermacher's emphasis on feeling. (See reason in religion).

4) The method of philosophy is dialectic*, which originally meant the process of question and answer in truth-seeking (Zeno of Elea, Socrates, Plato). Hegel assumed that all thought is a description of the real (the Absolute*). He took dialectic to mean the movement of thought which drives it on from any point of view which it assumes (thesis) to an opposed point of view (antithesis), so that the relation between the two generates a new insight or aspect of reality (synthesis). Thus, logic starts with the most necessary and abstract category, *being* (thesis); but to assert pure being drives one to admit that one has really said *nothing* (antithesis); yet the change from being to nothing is a *becoming* (synthesis). Logic as a whole deals with Being (*Sein,* immediate experience, potentiality), Essence (*Wesen,* external relations, actuality), and Notion (*Begriff,* internal relations, the movement from potentiality to completed actuality). Philosophy as a whole, starting from the *Phänomenologie,* becomes a dialectical movement from Logic ("the system of pure reason," "the representation of God as he is in his eternal essence before the creation of nature or any finite spirit"), to Philosophy of Nature (the "other" which experience reveals to thought—"a living whole," of dialectical stages, the mechanical, the physical, and the organic); but the relations of Logic and Nature compel dialectical thought to find its synthesis in Philosophy of Mind ("the concretest, highest, most difficult knowledge;" its stages are subjective or individual, objective or social, and absolute; in the Absolute, the highest truth is grasped through art, religion, and philosophy). Technically, dialectic is the opposition of thesis and antithesis; movement to the synthesis is "speculation" (*Encyclopädie,* secs. 79-82).

5) The principle of negativity is the source of dialectical movement. Negativity means that we can understand any *A,* not by declaring (with Aristotle) that *A* is not *non-A,* but by examining the relations between *A* and *non-A.* The mind is "a system of movements" (*Phänomenologie,* Lasson, 239); negativity is the principle that one must interpret what is present by reference to what is absent, or omitted, or overlooked, or not yet developed. "Each one of us is what some other moment of his life reflectively finds him to be" (Royce); reference to the life of God as "the play of love with itself" is trivial if "the seriousness, the pain, the patience and labor of the negative are lacking" (*Phänomenologie,* 20). No finite being or stage of dialectic can fully overcome negativity; only the whole can be adequate truth.

6) The Absolute Idea or Absolute Spirit is the all-inclusive and completely coherent eternal consciousness of which every stage of dialectic is a partial description. Hegel rejects Spinoza's pantheism, on the ground that his Substance is not Subject (personality). Hegel's Absolute, which he discusses far less than his followers and his critics, is not "the night in which all cows are black" (Hegel's description of Schelling's Abso-

lute) nor a "block universe" (W. James's view of Hegel's Absolute), but "the eternal and fully realized Idea, which is eternally active, and eternally produces and enjoys itself as Absolute Spirit" (*Encyclopädie,* sec. 577).

7) Hegel's philosophy is evolutionary; not in the Darwinian, but in the cosmic and metaphysical sense. The universe is a constant movement, in which the syntheses suggest "creative evolution." No stage of evolution is final. Philosophy can only interpret the stages that have been traversed, but cannot predict the future.

8) Hegel's philosophy of religion (the first systematic account under that name), like his pure philosophy, has for its content "God and God alone as the truth." Religion is man's experience of relation to the Infinite "in feeling, intuition, and divination, in pictures, and in devotion," rather than in the intellectually adequate form of philosophical truth. "Religion is the Divine Spirit's self-knowledge, by mediation of the finite spirit." In it "all riddles of the world are solved," in an experience of freedom and blessedness. The history of religions is the evolution of spirit in its dialectical apprehension of the divine, from nature religions, through religions of spiritual individuality, to the Absolute Religion, which is Christianity, with its dialectic of Father (thesis), Son (antithesis), and Spirit (synthesis). See Trinity.

II. Hegelian Schools.

Hegelianism in Germany illustrated the dialectic by dividing into a *right wing* (orthodox, supernaturalistic, represented by Gabler, Hinrichs, and Göschel, whom Hegel once endorsed); a *left wing* (radical, heterodox, tending toward more or less impersonal pantheism, as D. F. Strauss—*Leben Jesu,* 1835—and Bruno Bauer, of the Tübingen School* of N.T. criticism, or toward materialism, as L. Feuerbach and Karl Marx**, founder of modern socialism); and a *center* (avoiding both extremes and developing Hegel's own thought, as Hegel's biographer, Rosenkranz, the historian of philosophy, Erdmann, the Old Testament critic, Vatke, and the group who edited Hegel's works). Hegel exerted a wide influence in Great Britain (Stirling, T. H. Green, E. and J. Caird**, Bradley, Bosanquet) and America (the St. Louis School, Royce, Creighton, Calkins). Anglo-American Hegelianism was predominantly personalistic absolutism (Green, the Cairds, A. E. Taylor, Royce, Calkins); but Bradley inclined to a superpersonal Absolute and Bosanquet (and Creighton) to a more impersonal view.

III. Hegel's Influence.

No philosopher has influenced nineteenth and twentieth century thought more extensively than Hegel. 1) He changed history of philosophy from a chronicle of individual opinions to a living, logical development, each stage of which is necessary to the truth; Erdmann and Windelband in Germany and Croce in Italy have carried on this insight. 2) Hegel was the first to grasp world history as an organic evolution of all nations. 3) His lectures on the fine arts have enabled aestheticians to understand better the contributions of each stage in the history of art, as well as the inter-relations of the arts. 4) His emphasis on rational development guided W. T. Harris as United States Commissioner of Education (1889-1906), as well as inspiring John Dewey in his democratic revolt against Harris's methods, and Gentile in his organization of education in Fascist Italy. 5) In social philosophy, Hegel's influence has been both conservative (his historical emphasis) and revolutionary (the advance of dialectic). His philosophy of right rests on an organic theory of the state, and as such has influenced both Fascist and National Socialist theories, as well as Communism (through both Marx and Lenin). 6) His theory of the state led to a glorification of war as a noble sacrifice of the individual for the social whole. 7) His interest in economic institutions contributed to Marxist socialism. 8) Hegel's philosophy of religion, with its recognition of the value of every stage of development in all religions, prepared the way for modern Biblical criticism (F. C. Baur was influenced by Hegel in founding the Tübingen School), history of religions, comparative religions, and anthropology. He was one of the chief founders of "modernism" and liberalism in Christian thought, although entirely opposed to anti-metaphysical humanism. He sounded the evolutionary keynote of modern times. Hegel has been called "ein alles Umfassender," in contrast to Kant, who is "ein alles Zermalmender." See metaphysics; neo-Hegelianism.

See, besides the standard histories of philosophy: A. Seth, *Hegelianism and Personality* (1887); B. Croce, *What is Living and What is Dead of the Philosophy of Hegel* (Ital., 1907; Eng., 1915); McTaggart, *Studies in Hegelian Cosmology* (1918), 2nd ed.; Reyburn, *The Ethical Theory of Hegel* (1921); W. T. Stace, *The Philosophy of Hegel* (1924); N. Hartmann, *Die Philosophie des deutschen Idealismus: Hegel* (1929); Moog, *Hegel und die hegelsche Schule* (1930); W. Schultz, *Die Grundprinzipien der Religionsphilosophie Hegels und der Theologie Schleiermachers* (1937); Marcuse, *Reason and Revolution* (1941).

E.S.B.

Hegesippus: The author of a book entitled *Memoirs* which was written about 180 A.D., and was probably the earliest Christian history after the Acts of the Apostles. This work is now lost, but fragments of it are preserved by Eusebius, and contain some of the most valuable notices we now possess concerning men and events in the early church.

E. J. Goodspeed, *Early Christian Literature* (1942).

E.F.S.

hegira: (Arabic, *hijrah,* flight) The flight of Mohammed from Mecca* to Medina* in A.D. 622. After his death the Moslem calendar was dated from this event July 6, 622 A.D., and history is dated A.H. (year of *hegira*). P.E.J.

Heidegger, Martin (1889-) Professor of philosophy at Freiburg since 1928, Heidegger has become well known for his fresh attack on traditional problems. Influenced by Aristotle, the scholastics, Kant, Kierkegaard**, and Husserl's phenomenological* method he has tried to meet the problems of ontology through an analysis of man's moral and emotional situation. The

Greeks, he believes, were right in their sense for the philosophical importance of ontology, wrong in their stress on the perceptible object and the spoken proposition with its copula "is". Subject and predicate exist only in the larger subject-object situation where the object reveals itself directly and in its relations of "withness" (*Seinbei*). Confronting his world, man finds ties binding him to objects, companions, life, also to his essential possibilities, to matters of concern (*Sorge*) and to death. To understand these one should understand Time. See Jaspers, Karl.

Chief Works: *Sein und Zeit* (1927); *Kant und das Problem der Metaphysik; Vom Wesen des Grundes* (1929). J.S.B.

Heidelberg Catechism: A Reformed (Calvinistic) Catechism* drawn up by two Heidelberg professors, Ursinus* and Olevianus, in 1562 A.D., at the instance of the Elector of the Palatinate, Frederick III, "The Pious" (1559-1576). It was intended for use in the schools, as part of the effort being successfully made by the Elector to swing his territories from Lutheranism to the Reformed faith and practice. It is irenic in spirit, except in its references to the Catholic mass*; and has been widely accepted by the Reformed churches* within and outside of Germany. See *In Commemoration of the Three Hundredth Anniversary of the Heidelberg Catechism,* published by the German Reformed Church in the U. S. of North America (1863). A.K.R.

Heilsgeschichte: (history of salvation) A Protestant interpretation of history that in the 18th century superseded both the Augustinian and early Protestant views. The purpose of history is believed to be the formation of God's chosen people in a process of gradual growth, the Holy Spirit being the agent of this development. Progressive revelation of the saving truth is one aspect of his work. Jesus Christ is the center of the whole process; the establishment of his Kingdom through a fight with the powers of evil is his aim. J. A. Bengel* created this view. He modified the mechanical dispensationalism* of Coccejus and Vitringa by applying to history the idea of organic growth and forestalled naturalistic misinterpretations of this view by confining the specific agency of the Holy Spirit to the chosen people. This view lived on in North German Pietism (Collenbusch, Hasenkamp, Gottfried Menken), in 'Swabian Pietism' (Oetinger, J. T. Beck, Carl Aug. Auberlen) and in the School of Erlangen (Joh. Chr. K. von Hofmann*). It is widely accepted by Continental theologians.

Gustav Weth, *Die Heilsgeschichte. Ihr universeller und individueller Sinn in der offenbarungsgeschichtlichen Theologie des 19. Jahrh.* (München, 1931); Albrecht Ritschl, *Geschichte des Pietismus.* v. III (Bonn, 1886); Gottlob Schrenk, *Gottesreich und Bund im älteren Protestantismus, vornehmlich bei Johannes Coccejus. Zugleich ein Beitrag zur Geschichte des Pietismus und der heilsgeschichtlichen Theologie* (Gütersloh, 1923); Gustav Krüger's *Handbuch der Kirchengeschichte,* v. IV: *Die Neuzeit,* by H. Stephan and H. Leube (2nd ed. Tühingen, 1931); Otto A. Piper, *God in History* (1939). See also the articles on the above mentioned theologians in Schaff-Herzog's *Encyclopaedia.* O.A.P.

Heim, Karl: (1874-) He first taught in Münster, then in Tübingen. Rooted in Swabian pietism, he combines an uncompromising faith in Christ with a bold world and life-embracing, epistemologically oriented, reflection. He shares the new Protestant orthodoxy with Barth, Brunner and Aulén**. He revives the old idea of Satan. He is an evangelicalistically minded philosopher. He defends a realistic eschatology against the Platonizing eschatology of Barth's earlier writings. His theocentric theology emphasizes afresh divine transcendence, and demands a new understanding of all fundamental philosophical assumptions. He is in intimate touch with the various contemporary philosophical currents. He keenly experiences the distress resulting from a sceptically developed criticism and relativism. He not only seeks the destruction of the current world views dominating the age, but he also gives faith a more vital concreteness. His theology is an impressive attempt to make the power of intensive faith also externally fertile.

Das Weltbild der Zukunft (Berlin, 1904); *Das Gewissheitsproblem in der systematischen Theologie bis zu Schleiermacher* (Leipzig, 1911); *Leitfaden der Dogmatik* (Halle, 1912, 3 ed., Leipzig, 1923); *Glaubensgewissheit* (Leipzig, 1916, 3 ed., Leipzig, 1923); *Die Weltanschauung der Bibel* (Leipzig, 1920, 5 ed., Leipzig, 1928); *Das Wesen des evangelischen Christentums* (Leipzig, 1925, 4 ed., Leipzig, 1929); *The New Divine Order* (London, 1930); *The Church of Christ and the Problems of the Day* (1935); *God Transcendent* (1935); *Der evangelische Glaube und das Denken der Gegenwart*: vol. I: *Glaube und Denken* (Berlin, 1931, 4 ed., Berlin, 1938); vol. II: *Die Herrschaft des Christus,* (3 ed., Berlin, 1937); vol. III: *Jesus der Weltvollender* (Berlin, 1937). H.H.

Heimdallr, Heimdall: (Teut.) Norse-Icelandic watchman-god. In the saga he is stationed by the gods at the foot of the rainbow bridge linking heaven and earth, over which gods pass to descend to judge people in the underworld; stationed at the foot of the bridge, with his dog, Garm, he prevents any of the earth-born giants (gods) from scaling the heights of heaven and entering Asgard*, the home of the gods. He sees as well by night as by day, and can hear the wool growing on the backs of sheep; his great strength is derived from the earth and the sea. F.L.P.

Heinrici, Karl Friedrich Georg: (1844-1915) He was professor in Marburg and Leipzig. Critical of naturalistic evolutionism and radical relativism, he was greatly interested in the Hellenistic influences in primitive Christianity.

Die Sendschreiben des Apostels Paulus an die Korinther, 2 vols. (Berlin, 1880-87); *D. A. Twesten nach Tagebüchern und Briefen* (Marburg, 1889); *Theologische Enzyklopädie* (Freiburg, 1893); *Beiträge zur Geschichte und Erklärung des Neuen Testamentes,* 4 vols. (Leipzig, 1894-1908); *Die Bergpredigt* (Leipzig, 1905); *Der literarische Charakter der neutestamentlichen Schriften* (Leipzig, 1906); *Hellenismus und Christentum* (Berlin, 1910); *Die Hermesmystik und das Neue Testament* (Leipzig, 1918). H.H.

hell: See heaven and hell; Gehenna; sheol.

Hellenism: A term used to describe ancient

Greek culture. After the time of Alexander the Great the Greek speech and manner of thinking pervaded the lands around the eastern end of the Mediterranean Sea and thus there arose a cultural development termed Hellenistic in contrast with the original Hellenic civilization of Greece itself. In English the noun "Hellenism" may refer to either of these phases of Greek culture, but it is the Hellenistic rather than the Hellenic that is of greatest significance for Judasim in the Dispersion and for early Christianity on gentile soil. See Judaism, Hellenistic. S.J.C.

Helvetic Confessions: The name of two documents which set forth the common faith of the Swiss Protestant Churches. The first (1536) proved both too short and too Lutheran in tone for it to be very popular, and it was displaced by a document written by Bullinger* (1562 & 1564) for his own use. This was adopted throughout Switzerland, and also in Scotland, Hungary, France, and Poland. It is one of the most widely recognized confessions of the Reformed Church*. G.R.C.

Hengstenberg, Ernst Wilhelm: (1802-1869) German Lutheran theologian, professor in Berlin for four decades, founder and editor of an influential journal, *Evangelische Kirchenzeitung.* He published numerous commentaries on the Bible and a three-volume *Christology of the Old Testament* (1829-1835). Hengstenberg was one of the principal leaders of orthodox Lutheranism in its struggle against rationalism. See neo-Lutheranism. T.A.K.

Henke, Heinrich Philipp Konrad: (1752-1809) He was director of the theological seminary in Helmstedt. He was a convinced adherent of rationalism. As a deist he did not differentiate between the history of the church and the history of dogma. He hoped to emancipate the Christian doctrine from the superstitions of christlatry, bibliolatry and onomatolatry. Not only did he not realize the scope of his method, but he also failed to see the possibilities of a profounder idea of revelation.

Lineamenta institutionum fidei Christianae historico-criticarum (Helmstedt, 1793); *Allgemeine Geschichte der christlichen Kirche,* 6 vols., (4 ed., Braunschweig, 1799-1804). H.H.

henotheism: Intermediate stage between polytheism and monotheism; worship of one god by an individual, clan, or nation to the exclusion of others; term applies when worshiper has achieved this measure of unity but is not sufficiently philosophically advanced to deny the existence of other gods; stage of Israelite belief in God from Moses to the exile. See Amos; exile; monotheism. R.E.W.

henoticon: (Gr., union) A law promulgated by the Emperor Zeno in 482 in an unsuccessful effort to conciliate Monophysites* and Catholics. Based on the formula of Nicaea rather than Chalcedon. S.M.G.

Henry IV: (1553-1610) King of France. Wide experience of the internal wars of France convinced him of the need of religious accommodation and a strong centralized power. His conversion to Catholicism (in conjunction with the Edict of Nantes*) provided the one; his firm administration the other. See Wars of religion. G.R.C.

Henry IV of Germany: See Gregory VII, St., Pope.

Henry VIII: (1491-1547) King of England. His personal affairs became intimately involved in political and religious matters, but his divorce was the pretext, not the cause of the Reformation in England. He abolished the papal jurisdiction in England, and reduced clerical privilege and property. He proclaimed the royal supremacy even in the church, but in his break with Rome he found a basis of strong national support. He was an able if often unscrupulous ruler, with great practical gifts and unusual political perception. See Defender of the Faith; Six Articles; Supremacy, Acts of; Ten Articles. G.R.C.

Henry of Ghent: (?-1293) Scholastic philosopher and theologian. He ranks a close second to his eminent contemporaries, Sts. Thomas and Bonaventure, and Duns Scotus**. His greatest works are the *Quodlibeta,* and his incomplete *Summa Theologica.* W.H.

Henry of Langenstein: (c. 1340-1397) Professor at the University of Paris, Rector of the University of Vienna, theologian, whose *Epistola Concilii Pacis* (1381) was an influential document calling for conciliar reform and union of the church. See conciliarism. F.W.N.

Henry of Lausanne: (d. c. 1145) Fiery itinerant preacher and ascetic, he was influential especially in Provence, probably in company with Peter de Bruys*. Calumniated by such men as Peter the Venerable and Bernard of Clairvaux*, he died soon after one of his numerous arrests by ecclesiastical authorities for alleged attacks on the faith of the church. R.C.P.

heortology: (Gr., *heorté,* feast) The study of sacred calendars, especially the church year*. E.R.H.

hepatoscopy: "Liver observance." A form of divination practiced among Babylonians, Hittites, Etruscans, and others; the divination* is based upon the primitive assumption that the seat of life is in the liver, and that the structure of the world and the fortune of the individual may be traced on the liver of a sheep. The priest-diviner puts questions to a god, then sacrifices the sheep, and secures answers through the examination of the markings on the liver and interpreting what he finds as favorable or unfavorable in terms of power to the individual involved in the questions. F.L.P.

Hepzibah Faith Missionary Association: A holiness sect having 20 churches and about 700 members, nearly all in the west north central states. It was organized at Glenwood, Iowa, in 1892 by uniting some scattered independent churches. It has no distinctive tenets or practices but follows the general pattern of sects which seek holiness or sanctification through emotional reactions. See Evangelistic Associations; holiness churches. E.T.C.

Hera: (Gr., *Hērā*) Queen of the gods, sister and wife of Zeus*, with whom she was worshiped on the mountain tops. Mother of Ares, she was honored with games of war; women paid tribute to her as goddess of marriage. Her temples at Olympia, Argos, and Samos are renowned. E.M.N.

Heraclitus: (fl. 504-501 B.C.) Called "the obscure;" a Greek philosopher living in Ephesus. One of the most brilliant of the pre-Socratics. Held that all things change; nothing is permanent except the law (*logos**) of change. The world process of many cycles is compared to fire. "All things flow; we cannot step twice into the same river." "War is the father of all." *Logos* doctrines of N.T. and Stoics* were influenced by him. Hegel admired him. See dialectic.

See Diels, *Fragmente der Vorsokratiker;* Burnet, *Early Greek Philosophy.* E.S.B.

herbaries: (herbals) Books on the medicinal and magical virtues of plants. The early medieval *Herbarium* attributed to Apuleius had a wide vogue. O. Cocayne, *Leechdoms, Wortcunning and Starcraft of Early England* (1864), Vol. I. J.T.M.

Herbart, Johann Friedrich: (1776-1841) Professor at Königsberg and Göttingen and exponent of an analytic metaphysical realism. His theory that the aim of education is the development of good will, tested in his pedagogical seminary and model school in Königsberg, exerted considerable influence on American education. He wrote little on the philosophy of religion but believed in God and regarded religion as a practical support for moral education. His view of God was deistic, resting on a teleological and aesthetic view of nature. Several of his disciples attempted to construct a philosophy of religion on Herbartian principles, notably M. W. Drobisch, A. Schwarze, L. Strümpell, and G. F. Taute.

See his *Werke* (ed. Hartenstein, 1850-52) and especially his *Aphorismen zur Metaphysik und Religionslehre* (*Werke,* IV, 591-622). J.E.N.

Herbartianism: See Herbart, J. F.; psychology, schools of. See also O. Pfleiderer, *Philosophy of Religion* (1887, tr. by Menzies) Vol. II, pp. 214-228. J.E.N.

Herbert, George: (1593-1633) English clergyman and poet, remembered chiefly for a collection of devotional verse, *The Temple* (1633). Notable also is his brief prose volume of pastoral instruction, *A Priest to the Temple* (1652), which, like the poems, reveals a sober but gracious piety and a staunch adherence to Anglican tradition. L.W.C.

Herbert of Cherbury, Lord: See deism; Enlightenment, the.

Hercules: (Lat., *Herculēs,* from Gr., *Herakles*) The Roman counterpart of the Greek Heracles, who early in his wanderings came to Rome. As god of victory and traders, he had an ancient altar in the Forum Boarium (Cattle Market). The lion-skin and club were his symbols; his tree the poplar. E.M.N.

heredity: a) Refers in biology to the transmission of characteristics to offspring in accordance with the constitution of the germ plasm of parents. In man both physical and mental traits are so transmitted. The former would include race, color, sex, height, longevity, color and texture of hair, color of eyes, some diseases, physical type, in short, all the basic traits of the physical constitution. Mental characteristics as determined by heredity include mental ability, aptitudes, temperament, certain sensory characteristics, proneness to some mental disorders, and other tendencies or qualities of mind. From all this we may say that each individual is born with an original nature which is determined by that of his immediate and more remote progenitors. However, it is necessary to add that whatever one's original nature it is affected or modified in important ways by life experience in the environment under which it develops. See original nature.

b) The term has also sociological significance that antedates our modern knowledge of biology. That is, one comes into the world not only with a biological inheritance, as discussed, but also with a social heredity that consists of elements, such as language, social position, traditions, laws, customs, folkways, economic techniques, diet, social organization, and so on for all the superorganic aspects of the life of man. All these are in the nature of a group possession, the vehicle for the transmission of which is communication, chiefly language. Human behavior is a resultant of the interaction between one's physical and social heredity. See culture; environment.

H. S. Jennings, *The Biological Basis of Human Nature* (1930). A.E.W.

heresimach: (Gr., *haeresis,* heresy *machesthae* to fight with or against) An active opponent and critic of heresy and heretics; a heresy hunter. See also heresiologist. M.S.E.

heresiologist: (Gr., *haeresis* heresy *logy*) Literally, a student or chronicler of heresies (heresiographer), but commonly employed of one who wrote against them (cf. heresimach). Among the leading heresiologists of early Christianity may be mentioned Irenæus, Tertullian, Hippolytus, Dionysius of Alexandria, and Epiphanius**. M.S.E.

heresy: A term signifying any doctrine or belief which, though held by a professed adherent, is in opposition to the recognized and generally accepted standards of truth which are authoritatively defined and enforced by the established institution, party, or system concerned.

According to the R.C. point of view, it is a heresy for anyone professing the Christian faith to reject deliberately and pertinaciously by formal denial or by doubt the dogma established by the authority of the Catholic Church. In addition to the *formal heresy* of the deliberate rejection of the Church's teaching, the R.C. Church distinguishes *material heresy*, that is error which though heretical is the result of ignorance and not of deliberate choice.

The term heresy should be distinguished from *schism**, which signifies a separation from the unity of the Church; and from *apostasy** which signifies the abandonment of the faith.

Protestantism, generally speaking, recognizes the Holy Scriptures as the standard of truth authoritative for faith and practice. The term heresy is applied by a Protestant Body to any doctrine or belief professing to be Christian which is declared to be at variance with the teachings of the Holy Scriptures as interpreted by that Church Body, whether set forth in established creeds or in less formal theological standardizations. See sect. H.W.J.

heresy, Roman Catholic view: According to Roman Catholic terminology, heresy consists in denying any dogma, that is, any truth clearly revealed in Sacred Scripture or Tradition. A truth of this kind need not necessary be explicitly defined by the Church. It suffices that the truth be evident from Revelation. To be a true heretic, one must be baptized; his error must be voluntary; and his denial must be characterized by obstinacy. Cf. auto-da-fé. W.H.

Hermann, Rudolf: (1887-) He is professor of systematic theology at the Ernst Moritz Arndt University in Greifswald, and occasionally acts as its Director. Although soteriology received from many sides new impulsions, he revived older soteriological acquisitions. He manifests strong religious-philosophical interests and has done considerable research on Luther. He associated himself with the group Theologia militans that has shown for some time noticeable resistance to Nazi ideology.

Christentum und Geschichte bei Wilhelm Herrmann. Mit besonderer Berücksichtigung der erkenntnistheoretischen Seite des Problems (Lucka, 1913); *Der Begriff der religiös-sittlichen Anlage in der Apologetik Kählers* (Gütersloh, 1917); *Zur Frage des religionspsychologischen Experiments; erweitert aus Anlass der Religionspsychologie Girgensohns* (Gütersloh, 1922); *Luthers These "Gerecht und Sünder zugleich" eine systematische Untersuchung* (Gütersloh, 1930); *Luthers Theologische Grundanliegen* (Greifswald, 1933); *Die Bedeutung der Kirche bei Schleiermacher* (Greifswald, 1934); *Theologische Anliegen zur Kirchenfrage* (Greifswald, 1937); *Deutung und Umdeutung der Schrift* (Leipzig, 1937).

H.H.

Hermas, Shepherd of: The longest of the writings which are included in the collection of the Apostolic Fathers*. According to an ancient testimony it was written about 140 A.D., but it is probably of still earlier date. The author is Hermas, a Roman Christian who describes in three sections (Visions, Mandates, Similitudes) the message brought to him by Christ under the guise of a Shepherd. The principal object of the work, which is of no great literary or religious value, is to ensure a second repentance for sins committed after baptism.

J. B. Lightfoot, *Apostolic Fathers* (1890); E. J. Goodspeed, *Early Christian Literature* (1942).

E.F.S.

hermeneutics: The science of the laws and principles of interpretation and explanation. In theology it is applied to the study of the general principles whereby the meaning of the Scriptures is to be ascertained. It precedes exegesis* which is the actual interpretation of particular passages. It requires a knowledge of the original languages of the Bible and includes discussion of the qualifications of an interpreter and the methods and history of interpretation. A.K.R.

Hermes: (possibly from Greek *herma,* a cairn or stone-pile, or upright stone from which the later Herm figure was derived)

1) Early Greek: God of herds, guardian of paths or trails, and of guides to travellers; swift messenger of the gods; inventor of the lyre and shepherd's pipe. Later, a conductor of the dead to the underworld; he carries a caduceus or ancient herald's wand, and is pictured in the cults wearing winged sandals, and occasionally wings on his cap; patron of heralds, of traders, of orators, of market places, and of thieves; a god of healing and a 'quieter of pestilence'. Finally, with the attainment of the assumption by Greeks of the unity of nature, Hermes, as with Pindar*, changes to a divinity of righteousness and truth; and fades into the jurisdiction and power of a greater cosmic deity.

2) In Egypt: Hermes and Hermanubis. In Egypt the power of the Greek god is more apparent than real. To the Greek mind in Egypt, the Egyptian god Hermanubis (a name compounded of Horus* and Anubis, two Egyptian gods), a messenger of the gods guiding the dead before Osiris*, suggested an identification with their Hermes, Psychopompos, in a similar role. Out of this identification of function a type arose which represented Hermanubis as a Greek god, crowned with a modius, and carrying a caduceus and palm branch, etc. But this Hermanubis fails to gain the worship of Anubis who was worshiped with Isis and Osiris at Rome.

Hermes was also identified with other Egyptian gods, the chief, perhaps, being Thoth*, the god of learning. (See below, 3). Due no doubt to this linkage the name Hermes became attached to special writings of a magical character which developed in the Roman period. Hermes was linked also with local Egyptian gods, and connected with various animals, plants, sun, moon, etc., probably because of the tie with the powerful Egyptian gods Anubis and Thoth. See Egypt, religions of.

3) In Egypt: In the Roman imperial period, Hermes appears as a god of revelation for man's regeneration; worshiped at Hermopolis; father of Thoth, Egyptian god of wisdom; revealer of divine wisdom by which man may become a new man, a son of God. See Mercury.

These and other doctrines are derived from one Hermes, a descendant of the god Hermes and are found in *Hermes Trismegistus,* a philosophical and religious literature of the third or early fourth centuries A.D., which embodied a conglomerate of ideas of various religious philosophies of the age, mostly Greek in origin, and strongly Platonic, with a dash of loyalty to the religion of ancient Egypt which was in a state of decay. The point of view is pro-Egyptian. The doctrines show little resemblance to Christianity. F.L.P.

hermit: (Gr., *eremos* desert) Used in a general sense, as synonymous with anchorite*, to describe a solitary without official order or rule, devoting himself to God's service. In its technical usage the term denotes membership in a regulated eremitical association. Anchorites and hermits, who gave to Christian monasticism* its early character, did not cease to function upon the introduction of the cenobitic* forms. R.C.P.

Hermits of St. Augustine: See Augustinians.

Hernnhut: See Zinzendorf; Moravian Church.

hero worship: Reverence or devotion offered to men who have become divine or semi-divine because of their qualities, rank or the services rendered to their peoples. Culture heroes who taught men agriculture, building, weaving, healing or other arts of civilized living are revered in almost every land. Some heroes were founders of states or religions or families. The first ancestor of a clan and the prophet of a successful gospel very frequently reached divine status. The ancestors of the ruling dynasty in China shared honors with Heaven. Many of the popular gods were men appointed after death to divine office in their districts. In Egypt dead kings were worshiped because of their royal rank. The emperor of Japan receives devotion as the lineal descendent of the Sun Goddess. The epic heroes of northern Europe, Greece, and India are revered because of personal achievements as mighty warriors, men of wisdom, great saints or ascetics. Some of India's heroes are worshiped as incarnations of the high god. The warrior dead of Japan are enshrined with divine honors. In ancient Greece the cult of heroes had a prominent place. The heroes were expected, in return for sacrifices, to give guidance, healing, fertility and help in war. See ancestor worship; emperor worship.

A.E.H.

Herodotus: See philosophy of history.

Herrites: See Mennonites.

Herrmann, Wilhelm Johann Georg: (1846-1922) As professor at the University of Marburg, he emphasized a close affiliation between ethics and religion. He was the first theologian to openly ally himself with A. Ritschl*. He regarded the introduction of metaphysics into theology and vital religion as detrimental. He was suspicious of the encroachment of philosophy and of the influence of mysticism upon vital religion and theology. For him ethico-religious experience was the basis of religion. He introduced the distinction between faith-ground and faith-content, and tried to base the theology of faith upon the inner life of Jesus. He considered the moral principle as altogether the product of ethical personality. To attain an ethical personality was to get away from one's self and work for the well-being of man in general. He sought to give content to the formal, empty categorical imperative of Kant. Religion had for him its own distinctive way of arriving at its assurance of God and of framing a comprehensive view of the world.

Die Religion im Verhältnis zum Welterkennen und zur Sittlichkeit (Halle, 1879); *Der Begriff der Offenbarung* (Freiburg, 1887); *Die Gewissheit des Glaubens und die Freiheit der Theologie* (2 ed., Freiburg, 1889); *Ethik* (Tübingen und Leipzig, 1901, 2 ed., Tübingen und Leipzig, 1909); *The Communion of the Christian with God* (London, 1895); *Faith and Morals* (1904); *Die Wirklichkeit Gottes* (Tübingen, 1914); *Systematic Theology* (London, 1927); E. Troeltsch, *Gesammelte Schriften,* vol. II (Tübingen, 1913); W. Schültz, *Das Grundgefüge der Herrmanschen Theologie, ihre Entwicklung und ihre geschichtliche Wurzeln* (Berlin, 1926); M. Redeker, *Wilhelm Herrmann im Kampf gegen die positivistische Lebensanschauung* (Gotha, 1928). H.H.

Hestia: (Gr., *Hestia,* hearth) Sister of Zeus*, virgin goddess of the hearth, both of the home and of the city. With libations to her, sacrifices began and ended. Each colony took sacred fire from the city's hearth to its new home. Cf. Vesta of the Romans. E.M.N.

heterodoxy: (Gr., *heteros,* other; *doxa,* opinion) Contrary to or differing from a standard (Bible, creed, or conciliar decree) acknowledged as orthodox*; usually denotes a departure not serious enough to be punished as heresy*. F.G.E.

heteronomy: (Gr., *heteros,* other, and *nomos,* law) Law imposed by another. Used by Kant* in his ethics to mean any principle determining moral action which does not arise from the rational will of the agent. Thus, conduct is heteronomous when it arises from emotion, desire, pleasure, affection, or the will of another. See autonomy. E.S.B.

Hewett Lectureship, The: Established in 1923 by Waterman T. Hewett with a capital sum of $10,000 and given at the Union Theological Seminary, New York, the Episcopal Theological School, Cambridge, Mass., and the Andover-Newton Theological School, Newton Center, Mass. The lectures are given annually, biennially or triennially on the subjects dealing with "the truths of Christianity as shown in revelation, reason and in history", on the value and authority of Scriptures, on the church and missions, or on fresh discoveries in archaeology relating to "Christian truths." Lecturers: Canon B. H. Streeter, A. D. Lindsay, C. H. Dodd and Richard Kroner.

(Data furnished by the Office of the Registrar, Union Theological Seminary.) V.F.

Hexapla: See Origen; polyglot Bibles; versions of the Bible, ancient.

Hexateuch: Literally, "six books" The term employed by biblical scholars to designate the first six books of the Bible. It contrasts with the term, "Pentateuch,"* "five books." This latter term reflects the popular belief, based upon the biblical record itself, that the first five books of the Bible, Genesis, Exodus, Leviticus, Numbers and Deuteronomy,** were all written by Moses,* under divine inspiration, constitute therefore a distinct literary unit, and possess a unique authority as the divinely revealed law of God. This belief, that these so-called "five books of Moses" or "Torah,"* to use the traditional Hebrew term, are the record of God's law, revealed to Israel, give to these five books an additional unity, that of content.

Already in the seventeenth century, however, scholars began to perceive serious internal contradictions and duplications within the Pentateuch, in both its narrative and legal sections. Steadily the conclusion became firmly established that the Pentateuch could not possibly be the writing of one man or of one single age, but was a composite literary work, the product of numerous writers and of a long period of time, worked together, more or less skillfully, into a seeming literary unit by various editors or redactors. Beginning in the second quarter of the nineteenth century, and with the task still far from completed, biblical scholars have painstakingly unravelled the various strands of narrative and legislation and determined with relative accuracy the broad content and approximate date of each literary strand or "document," as generally called.

They distinguish in the main four major documents, the Jahwist Code (J*), coming from the Southern Kingdom and dated to 900-500 B.C., the Elohist Code (E*), composed in the Northern Kingdom at about 850-700 B.C., the Deuteronomic Code (D*), 621-350 B.C., and the Priestly Code (P*), 450-250 B.C. None of these major documents is itself a literary unit. On the one hand, they have incorporated into themselves a number of smaller codes, such as the Kenite Code (K) in J, the Book of the Covenant (C) in E, and the Holiness Code (H) in P; and, on the other hand, they consist themselves of various internal strands. Actually, therefore, each of these four major documents represents a school of theological thought and literary composition extending over several centuries.

Very quickly after this scientific analytic process began, it became apparent that at least three of these four major documents, viz. J, D and P, and perhaps E also, continued into the sixth book of the Bible, the Book of Joshua,* and that therefore, not the first five, but the first six books of the Bible constituted the true, literary unit, as it was fashioned by its successive editors. It is this literary unit, viz., the Pentateuch plus Joshua, which the term, "Hexateuch," describes. In these six books there is a definite unity of thought as well as of composition, for together they record the traditional history of the birth of the Israelite people, its migration to and settlement in Egypt, its deliverance from Egyptian bondage through divine aid and in accordance with divine promise, its journey through the desert under divine guidance, and its final settlement in Palestine. Without the record of the fulfillment of God's promise in the Book of Joshua, the history would be incomplete.

Obviously the Hexateuch was the original literary unit. Probably not until some time in the fourth century B.C. was the Book of Joshua separated from the first five books and relegated to a subordinate position. This was done largely because of theological and ritualistic considerations, primarily to emphasize the significance of the Torah, the divinely revealed law, in the life, belief and practice of the Jewish people. The Pentateuch is therefore actually a later and historically less real literary unit than the Hexateuch.

J. E .Carpenter and G. Harford, *The Composition of the Hexateuch* (London, 1902) ; J. A. Bewer, *The Literature of the Old Testament* (1933) ; R. H. Pfeiffer, *Introduction to the Old Testament* (1941).

J.M.

Hicksites: See Society of Friends; anti-missionary movement in the U. S.

hierarchy: (Gr., *hieros,* sacred; *archein,* to rule) Divine government, or usually holy orders. The function of representing God to man and man to God within any social group requires some recognized order. The simplest form of this, the religious function of the *pater familias,* was in ethnic religions copied in the state, but a priesthood* separate from government became necessary to maintain and guard developing bodies of knowledge about theology and cultus and to insure training for right performances of function. The organization of different cults and the interrelationship of them in polytheism (e.g., Amon in Egypt and Assur in Assyria) and political alliances of countries with hereditary priesthoods (e.g., in Israel, Syria, and Egypt) brought about increased gradations of function. Succession within a hierarchy may be by inheritance (e.g., the Aaronic priesthood in Israel, and the Aztecan kings), by caste (e.g., the Brahmims), or by consecration and ordination (e.g., the rabbinate in post-Exilic Judaism, and the Christian ministry. The word hierarchy first appears with the Pseudo-Dionisius who compares the nine orders of angelic beings with three groups of three each of Christian people, of whom two were laity and one that of the three holy orders of bishop, priest and deacon**. See clergy. T.J.B.

hieroglyphic writing: System of writing used by the ancient Egyptians, mainly ideographic, which later gave way to the Hieratic and to the Demotic systems. Deciphered by Champollion in 1822 with the help of the trilingual inscription of the Rosetta Stone. S.L.T.

Hieronymites: A name best known in connection with a monastic* order which in the fifteenth and sixteenth centuries possessed some of the most famous monasteries in Spain (e.g., the Escurial). Though marked by great austcrity, and given largely to study and the active ministry, they gained great influence at court. G.R.C.

high altar: The principal altar in a church as distinguished from the lesser or side altars. P.V.N.

high church: A term applied under Queen Anne to strong supporters of the Church of England in politics, later to Anglicans who held a high view of the church and its sacraments. See Anglo-Catholics. E.R.H.

high mass: See mass.

high place: (Semitic places of worship) "High place" is the translation of the Hebrew word *bamah* which signifies both "elevation" and "sanctuary," in accordance with the Semitic* and particularly Canaanitic* custom of establishing sanctuaries at high points. The connection of divinity with mountains is found in all parts of the Near East, especially in Syria and Asia Minor. Not all *bamot,* however, were on hills, e.g. that of Gezar. They were sometimes in valleys, open-air shrines marked by *mazzebot* (stone pillars) and *asherah* (sacred wooden post), lavers, images of the gods and other cultic objects. In such cases the word *bamah* seems to refer to the elevated structure of the shrine itself, and this may well be the original meaning of the word.

These *bamot* were not exclusively Canaanitic. YHWH, God of Israel, also had His legitimate *bamot.* The corrupt influences of foreign idolatry, however, rendered the continued existence of *bamot* in Israel and Judea a distinct danger to the holiness of YHWH and to national survival, and the prophets denounced them in the strongest terms. Several attempts were made, as a result, by Judean kings to root out the *bamot,* the most famous under Josiah (2 Ki 22:3, 2 Chron. 34:3). H.K.-L.F.

high-priest: The highest ecclesiastical official in the Jewish priestly organization in biblical literature. Biblical tradition represented him as being a descendant of Aaron; this is, however historically untrue. Actually all passages in the Bible which refer to the high-priest date from the last quarter of the fifth century B.C. or even later. The office itself was instituted only in 411 B.C. The high-priest was the chief ecclesiastical ministrant in the Temple at Jerusalem at the most important religious festivals and functions in the Jewish calendar, and especially in the momentous ceremonies of the annual Day of Atonement. He likewise presided over the Sanhedrin. The office came to an end with the destruction of the Temple by the Romans in 70 A.D. See priesthood, Hebraic and Jewish; Urim and Thummim. J.M.

higher criticism: See Biblical criticism.

Hilary of Poitiers, St.: (ca. 300-367) Bishop of Poitiers ca. 350 A.D. A protagonist of orthodoxy against Arianism.* Exiled by Constantine to the East, where he attempted to bring about a reconciliation between semi-Arians* and Catholics. Restored to his See in 364. S.M.G.

Hildebrand: See Gregory VII., St. Pope.

Hillel: Hillel I, also known as Hillel the Elder (Ha-Zaken), was the most prominent Jewish teacher of the first century (30 B.C.E.-10 C.E.), the founder of an influential school which bears his name (Beth Hillel*), and the ancestor of the patriarchs, the leaders of Palestinian Jewry during the first four centuries of the common era. A Babylonian by birth and, according to tradition, of Davidic stock, Hillel migrated (in early manhood) to Palestine to sit at the feet of the great masters of Biblical interpretation and exposition, Shemaiah and Abtalion. Despite great poverty and hardship (cf. Yoma 35b), Hillel pursued his studies with rare diligence and zeal, and rapidly became one of the keenest masters of the Bible. Such was his fame that when the Bene Bathyra, the heads of the college, resigned, Hillel was appointed to succeed them and became the recognized authority among the scholars of the Law.* Later generations are indebted to him for the formulation of seven rules for the systematic exposition of the Bible. These rules became basic for later Rabbinic* reasoning.

Hillel is revered not only for his profound scholarship but also for his inspiring saintliness. Humbleness and love for his fellowmen are the keystones of his character. All the legends which later generations wove about him as well as the sayings ascribed to him reveal these two characteristic traits. Perhaps the best appreciation of his character can be gained from the story of the heathen who came to Hillel and asked for a very concise statement of the essence of Judaism. Hillel replied, "What is hateful to thee, do not unto thy fellowman; this is the whole Law; the rest is mere commentary." (Shab. 31a). E.B.-L.F.

Hillel Foundation, the: See student religious organizations.

hillul hashem: See kiddush hashem.

Hinayana: See Buddhist Terminology.

Hincmar of Rheims: (c. 806-882) Archbishop of Rheims, personal councilor to the West-Frankish kings, annalist, most powerful Gallican ecclesiastic of his time. His high conception of his office as Metropolitan led to an inevitable and losing struggle with Pope Nicholas I* which brought into prominence for the first time the Pseudo-Isidorian decretals.* F.W.N.

HINDU TERMINOLOGY: See abhiseka, Aditi, Adityas, advaita, Agni, ahimsa, Ajivikas, Akbar, Aranyakas, Arya Samaj, Assam, Asura, Asvins, Atharva Veda, atman, avatar.

Bhagavad Gita, bhakti-marga, Brahma, Brahma Samaj, Brahman, Brahmanas, Brahmanaspati (Brihaspati), Brahmanism—see Hinduism.

Charvakas.

Dasyus (Dasus), Deva, dharma, dhyana, Dravidians, Dyaus.

Gandharvas, Ganesha, gayatri, Gosala, Granth, guna, guru.

Hinduism, Hiranyagarbha.

India, religions of; Indra, Ishvara.

Jagganath, Jainism, jnana-marga.

Kali, kalpa, karma-marga, Keshub Chunder Sen, Krishna, kshatriya.

Lakshmi, linga, Lingayats, Lokayata.

Mahabharata, Mahadeva, Mahavira, mahatma, mantras, manu, Maruts, maya, Meru, Mohenjo-daro, moksha, mukti.

Nanak, Narayana.

om.

Parjanya, Parvati, Pitris, Prajapati, prakriti, prapatti-marga, pretas, prithivi, puja, Puranas, purohita, purusha, Pusan (Pushan).

rakshas, Ram Mohan Roy, Rama, Ramakrishna, Ramananda, Ramanuja, Ramayana, Rig Veda, rishi, rita, Rudra.

sacred thread, sadhana, Saivism, (Shivism, Shivaism), sakti, see shakti, samadhi, Sama-Veda, Samhita, samsara, Sankhya, Sankhya-Yoga, sannyasi, sati, see suttee; Sarasvati, Savitri, shakti, (Shaktism, Saktism), Shankara, Shiva (Civa), shraddha, Sikh, smriti, Soma, Sraddhas, see Shraddhas, sruti, see shruti, sudra, Surya, sutras, suttee, swastika.

Tantras, tapas, Temples, Indian, Thags, Trimurti.

Uma, Upanishads, Ushas.

Vac, Vaicesika, Vaiseshika, see Hinduism; Vaisnavism, see Vishnuism; vaisyas, Varuna, Vasudeva, Vayu (Vata), Vedanta, Vedas, Vedic religion, see Hinduism; Vishnu, Vishnuism, Vivekananda.

Yajur-Veda, Yama, yantras, Yima, Yoga Philosophy, see Yoga, Hinduism; Yoga, yogi.

Hindu triad: See s. v. Vishnu.

Hinduism: A broad term used by modern historians of religion to designate the traditional religion of India, past and present. Its various stages of development historically are as follows: 1) Vedic Hinduism; 2) Brahmanic Hinduism; 3) Philosophic Hinduism; 4) Devotional or Sectarian Hinduism; and 5) Reformed Hinduism, to which might also be added Heretical Hinduism to include the Buddhist and Jain movements which arose in the 6th century B.C.

I. Vedic Hinduism. Before the Aryan invasion of India there was, of course, a native religion which may be characterized as Dravidian* or pr - Aryan Hinduism, a great deal of which survives in the popular Hinduism of the present time. That there was a flourishing and highly developed cult in the Indus valley as long ago as 3,000 B.C. is now well established by archeological discoveries of the past two decades. That some of the major conceptions and practices, and probably also, divine figures of post-Vedic Hinduism were known in that remote period is also fairly clear. (See Mohenjo-daro).

Whatever the original native religion, it was pretty well displaced for a number of centuries by the vigorous Aryan invaders who came into India at some unknown period, probably going back of 1,500 B.C. (See Aryans.) The Vedic religion was a relatively optimistic, life-loving, on the whole this- worldly faith, though not without a conception of the afterlife. The prayers and hymns found in the Vedas, which are the source books of that period of Hinduism, reflect the wants and needs of the people as being an abundant food supply in the form of cattle and dairy products mainly, large families, success in war (they were still an invasion force) and length of life. The gods were on the whole nature forces such as Varuna, sky; Indra, storm, fertility, war; Agni, fire; Soma, the intoxicant which was a constant element in sacrifice and the elixir of immortality. Then there was also wind, Vayu; Ushas, dawn; and many others. Of sun gods there were many. The cult was originally a family affair, becoming increasingly complex with an elaborate priesthood, an involved ritual, and a numerous collection of hymns, prayers, and incantations embodying the essential desires and needs of the people. The four Veda and the Atharva-veda,** are the literature of the period and have come to be regarded as the basic scriptures of all Hinduism.

II. Brahmanic Hinduism is that transitional stage of Hinduism represented in the literature known as the Brahmanas and represents the decadence of ancient Vedic Hinduism into an infinitely tiresome and costly ceremonialism which by its over-emphasis on the magic power of the cult reduced the very gods to the position of relative impotence in that the power of the spell or charm came to exceed that of the gods themselves, and so led to their ultimate discrediting. During this period there began to emerge the ideas of Karma and transmigration which were to become the most characteristic features of later Hinduism. Also there is the beginning of some philosophic speculation as to man's origin and destiny. Caste became a fixed institution during this period and was to be henceforth the framework of Indian society.

III. At a period not far from that in which Greece began to speculate about the nature of the world and man, men began in India likewise to reflect concerning the origins of man and his world, the nature of the reality behind the universe and how man might attain to salvation. The record of this reflection is preserved in the Upanishads,* the great basic philosophical texts of Hinduism from which all subsequent Indian philosophical speculation takes its start. By this time the idea of Karma, the law of the dead, or the law of sowing and reaping, and the idea of reincarnation, a series of lives in which each successive life is determined by the Karma of previous existences, were well established and the deep desire of man had become that of escape from the round of rebirth. As to the nature of reality, philosophical Hinduism, arrived at the idea of Brahman, the neuter world soul, a monistic world view, or, according to many authorities, a pantheistic conclusion, and salvation came to be thought of as possible, not through the practise of sacrifice, however expensive and complicated, but by the way of knowledge. The nature of the knowledge required was conceived of differently by later schools of interpretation, whether that of knowledge of the identity of the self with the self of the universe, or the knowledge of the total unreality of all existence including that of man himself and the universe, that is, that all is illusion; or whether as in one school, the knowledge of the eternal separateness of spirit and matter. But all held that it was knowledge alone that could avail for escape or moksha.* The method of attaining knowledge varies likewise, but the general method of Yoga* that is a process of highly disciplined meditation under physical conditions the most favorable possible, was the almost universal method. Vedic Hinduism disappeared, likewise Brahmanic, but Philosophic Hinduism interpreted variously by different philosophical schools such as that of Shankara and Ramanuja, continues still and has cast somewhat of a philosophical film even over some of the cruder forms of sectarian Hinduism. Perhaps the best known modern school is the Vedanta*.

IV. As a natural reaction on the one hand to the decadence of Bhramanic Hinduism and the highly speculative and somewhat intangible thought of Philosophical Hinduism which served mainly the intelligentsia of India, there arose two highly divergent tendencies. One took the form of atheism, at least so far as any dependence on the aid of the gods was concerned. Out of this general tendency came, in the 6th century B.C., Buddhism* and Jainism.* Both came to be regarded as distinct religions and will be so discussed in this volume. Some authorities still treat them merely as heretical sects of Hinduism.

V. There is evidence that as the ancient Vedic deities declined in power two great personal deities began to emerge. One of these, Vishnu, was a minor Sun deity in the Vedas. Gradually he became almost a monotheistic figure to whom the devotion of great bodies of Indians was attracted. Here was a great personal, powerful deity in whom one could trust, who was not limited as were the Vedic deities by the power and magic of ceremony, nor so vague and impersonal as the philosopher's deity, Brahman. When, possibly due to the influence of philosophic Hinduism, he became assimilated to the impersonal Brahman, there arose the belief that Vishnu had manifested himself in concrete form through a series of incarnations, ten in number traditionally, which reached their climax in Rama and Krishna.* These deities with their consorts are the major objects of worship of the Vishnu sects of Hinduism and are widely spread throughout India. Here the way of salvation is not through sacrifice nor through knowledge, but through loving faith, and devotion to the great god or his incarnation, in other words salvation by faith (bhakti).* There had now come to be also an elaborate system of hells and heavens into and out of which the soul might be born in its endless cycle of births. To the philosopher this salvation seemed inadequate, one from which the soul must again come to rebirth until through knowledge it achieved complete emancipation. To the humble devotee (bhakta), however, it seemed enough that through the gracious help of Krishna or Rama he should attain to eternal communion with god.

Shiva, the other great personal deity which emerged was probably only the resurgence of a great deity who had been eclipsed by the coming of the Aryans. To be sure, he is linked with Rudra of Vedic times and bears somewhat the destructive character of that god of storm but the main lineaments of Shiva are probably drawn from the pre-Aryan faith. Certainly there are numerous traces of the Linga which is the phallic symbol of Shiva in the ancient ruins of the buried cities of the Indus. Shiva and his consorts who are numerous and of varied character are widely worshipped, he being represented usually as the generative force of the universe, symbolized either by the bull, Nanda, or by the Linga. Kali* is perhaps the most widely worshipped of his consorts. Here likewise salvation is largely of a devotional type rather than that of knowledge or through the performance of ceremonials or austerities. There are many sub-sects both of Vishnuism and of Shivism. The literature of these sects is the Puranas. The Bhagavad-Gita is the great devotional classic of Krishna worship but has a universal quality about it which makes it usable among the people of many sects.

VI. Reform Movements in Hinduism. The great Aryan invasion produced Vedic Hinduism; The Moslem invasion about 1,000 A.D. brought Hinduism and Islam into intimate contact; the resulting syncretism produced a movement at the end of the 15th century known as the Sikh movement. It was founded by Nanak* at about the time of the European Reformation. From Islam it took three things, its monotheism, somewhat modified to be sure in the course of time, second, its non-idolatrous worship, and third, its militance. It early became a theocracy and controlled Northwest India. It is largely limited to that area still. Its sacred book is the Granth.* It is regarded now as a separate religion by many historians.

The invasion of the west beginning in the 16th century brought Christianity and Western culture into contact with Indian culture. This resulted eventually in a number of reform movements such as the Brahma-Samaj* founded in 1828, the Arya-Samaj* founded in 1875, the Rama-Krishna movement, Servants of India, etc. All of these borrowed heavily from Christianity but retained significant features of Hinduism and are active forces in India today.

Is there anything common to Hinduism as thus far described? Not much, yet some things. For instance, the respect for the Vedas is almost universal though repudiated in some modern movements; the principle of Karma and reincarnation runs through all save Vedic Hinduism; the principle of caste is the social framework through which most of them operate and for which most of them find religious authority; a strange mystic strain pervades most of Hinduism and a respect for the sanyasi* or holy man is almost universal. The principle of non-injury of Ahimsa, while not universal is widely held though with varying degrees of strictness. It may be that Professor Das was right when he characterized Hinduism as only an anthropological process. It is broad; it is tolerant; it has an absorbtive quality which enables it to assimilate almost anything with which it comes in contact. When it was officially asked for census purposes, "What constitutes a Hindu?", the only answer that one writer could find as satisfactory was this, "Any one who says he is a Hindu, is one." See cycles of time; sacred literatures; salvation; transmigration.

Vedic Hinduism

H. D. Griswold, *The Religion of the Rig-Veda* (1923); Maurice Bloomfield, *The Religion of the Rig-Veda* (1908).

Philosophic Hinduism

Robert E. Hume, *The Thirteen Principal Upanishads* (1931); S. Das Gupta, *History of Indian Philosophy*, 3 Vols. (Cambridge, 1922, 1932 and 1941); S. Radhakrishnan, *Indian Philosophy*, 2 Vols. (London, 1923, 27).

Modern Hinduism

J. N. Farquhar, *Modern Religious Movements in India* (1918); H. D. Griswold, *Insights into Modern Hinduism* (1934); S. Radhakrishnan, *The Hindu View of Life* (London, 1927).

General

S. Das Gupta, *Hindu Mysticism* (1927); J. B. Pratt, *India and Its Faiths* (1915); Nichol McNicol, *Living Religions of India* (London, 1935); M. Monier-Williams, *Brahmanism and Hinduism* (London, 1887); Mrs. Sinclair Stevenson, *Rites of the Twice-born* (1920). C.S.B.

Hippolytus: (ca. 160-235) A learned Roman Christian, who wrote many important works. From 217-235 he headed a local schism but was nevertheless canonized after martyrdom. B.S.E.

Hiranyagarbha: (Lit. Golden Germ) The cosmic intelligence or soul, "related to the universe in the same way as the individual soul is related to its body." (S. Radhakrishnan, *Indian Philosophy*, I, 1923) In Rig Veda X, 121 it is said, "In the beginning arose Hiranyagarbha, the earth's begetter, who created heaven." However, in Svetāsvatara Upanishad the golden germ is said to have been created by Rudra. C.S.B.

historical criticism: See Biblical criticism; exegesis.

historical materialism: See Marx, Karl.

history, philosophy of: See philosophy of history.

History of Susannah: See Susannah, History of.

Hittites: Name of an ancient people living in Asia Minor, mentioned in the OT. Some of their archives were discovered on thousands of clay tablets at Boghar-Keui, Turkey, in 1906-1910.

See A. Goetze, *Hethiter, Churriter und Assyrer* (1936); "The Present State of Anatolian and Hittite Studies," in *The Haverford Symposium on Archeology and the Bible* (1938), ed. by E. Grant, pp. 136-157; G. Furlani, *La Religione degli Hittiti* (1936); *Saggi sulla civilta degli Hittiti* (1939). S.L.T.

Hobbes, Thomas: (1588-1679) A mechanistic materialist who defended the cynical view that the whole of human life is "one continuous exercise in self-love." Ascribing the origin of religion to the primeval fear of the unknown, he, like Epicur and Lucretius, derived religion from terror and superstition. His uncomon hatred of theology is connected with the ecclesiastical pretensions of the papacy. Blindness and thoughtlessness of faith have been in no system so expressly stated. He distinguished the essential and the non-essential elements of religion, and explained away obvious contradictions between Scripture and faith. Religion is not philosophy, but law. It demands not discussion, but obedience. The state decides all religious questions. By removing immortality to the general resurrection at the Last Day, he, like Milton and Priestley, combined materialism with faith. Hobbes is proof of the fact that materialism and atheism are not identical, even if related conceptions. He was a devoted partisan of the Episcopal High Church. A great deal of unnecessary effort has been spent on his theology. He seemed to conceive of God as a part of the universe—controlling, universally spread, uniform, and by its motion determining mechanically the motion of the whole. Cf. Erastianism.

F. Brandt, *Thomas Hobbes' Mechanical Conception of Nature* (London, 1928); George E. G. Catlin, *Thomas Hobbes as Philosopher, Publicist, and Man of Letters* (Oxford, 1922); J. Laird, *Hobbes* (London, 1934); Z. Lubienski, *Die Grundlagen des ethisch-politischen Systems von Hobbes* (Münich, 1932); L. Strauss, *The Political Philosophy of Hobbes* (Oxford, 1936). H.H.

hobgoblin: (*hob*, elf or fairy*; *goblin*, an ugly sprite* having malicious or mischievous intentions) A bogy; a fancied object of fear. F.L.P.

hocket: (Fr. *hocquet*; Lat. *hoquetus*) Literally meaning hiccough, the proper Latin term is truncatio. A medieval device in which rests were frequently interspersed between notes of the melody, causing a chopping up of words and syllables without regard for meaning. Also a sudden cessation of one singer, whose expected note is sung by another voice. As an ornament to church music this technique was heartily disliked by such ecclesiastics as Pope John XXII. E.H.B.

Hodge, Charles: (1797-1878) Eminent American theologian, the chief figure in the group of theologians known as the Princeton School, and best known by his three volume *Systematic Theology* (1872-73). From 1822 to 1878, with the exception of three years' special study in Germany, Dr. Hodge was a professor in Princeton Theological Seminary. In 1825 he founded *The Biblical Repertory*, a theological journal subsequently called *The Princeton Review* which, under his editorship, became the most influential American religious journal of the nineteenth century. Besides his *Systematic Theology* and innumerable articles in *The Princeton Review*, Hodge's principal works are: *Commentary on the Epistle to the Romans* (1835); *Constitutional History of the Presbyterian Church in the United States of America* (1839-40); *Commentary on the Epistle to the Ephesians* (1856); *Discussions in Church Polity* (1878). Charles Hodge has been the most internationally known and influential Calvinist theologian in the United States since the days of Jonathan Edwards. J.A.M.

Höffding, Harald: (1843-1931) Danish philosopher and professor in Copenhagen. His early thought was influenced by Kierkegaard.* He was anti-metaphysical and tended toward positivism,* but with a deep concern for ethical and religious values. He finds the essence of religion in the axiom of the "conservation of value"* but denies immortality. His view of God is impersonal.

His chief works are: *Etik* (1887, not tr.) ; *History of Modern Philosophy* (1895, Eng., 1900) ; *Problems of Philosophy* (1902, Eng., 1905) ; and *Philosophy of Religion* (1901, Eng., 1906).

See J. de la Harpe, *La religion comme conservation de la valeur dans ses rapports avec philosophie generale de Harald Höffding* (1920). J.E.N.

Hofmann, Johann Chr. von: (1810-1877) Protestant theologian and church leader. Born in Nuremberg, Germany, he became in 1838 privatdozent in Erlangen, in 1842 professor, Rostock, and from 1845-1877 at Erlangen, principal representative of Lutheran biblicism as opposed to the confessionalism of Stahl and Hengstenberg.* Deeply influenced by the historians Raumer and Ranke he interpreted Biblical religion as divine history (Heilsgeschichte*), the main characteristic of which is the correlation between prophecy and fulfilment. Unlike the older school he taught to find prophecy primarily in historical events, and only secondarily in the interpretative words of the prophets. Thus the unity of the Bible rests upon its historical substance rather than upon the inspiration of its writers. Every stage of Biblical history points beyond itself to the subsequent stage of the purpose of God and ultimately to its fulfilment in Jesus Christ's first and second coming.

Hofmann was equally remarkable as exegete and as theological thinker. In his systematic presentation of the Christian truth he started from the experience of regeneration. But whereas Schleiermacher,* by whose theological approach he was influenced, interpreted experience subjectively, i.e. as having the evidence of its truth in itself, Hofmann interpreted it historically, i.e. as deriving its certitude from its historical causes, namely the history of the Church and the history of the Old and New Covenants. Head of the Erlangen School.* See neo-Lutheranism.

Principal works:

Weissagung und Erfüllung (1841-1844); *Der Schriftbeweis* (1852-1856, 2nd ed. 1857-1860) ; *Die Heilige Schrift zusammenhängend untersucht* (1862-1877, incomplete).

After his death his disciple Volk published: *Die Biblische Geschichte des Neuen Testamentes* (1883) ; *Biblische Theologie des Neuen Testamentes* (1886) ; Biographies: R. Wapler, *Das Leben J. Chr. K. von Hofmanns* (1914) ; see also article "*Hofmann*" by A. Hauck in Herzog's *Realenzyklop.* 3rd. ed., vol. VIII, pp. 234-241. On his theology see: Joh. Hausleiten, *Grundlinien der Theologie von Hofmanns in seiner eigenen Darstellung* (1910). O.A.P.

Hofmann, Melchior: (c. 1498-c. 1544) Anabaptist*, was an indefatigable lay preacher in many centres of northern Europe. Though at first on friendly terms with Luther, his leanings to Anabaptism caused a breach between them. He also differed from Luther on sacramental doctrine. His anabaptist tendencies led to his expulsion from one city after another. G.R.C.

Holbach, Paul Henri Dietrich, Baron d': (1723-1789) He developed in his System of Nature a systematic materialistic metaphysics according to which the universe is neither governed by God nor chance, but by immutable and necessary laws. He combatted the idea of God in every possible form, even pursuing deistic and pantheistic ideas of deity, which made him violent enemies even among freethinkers. Contending that cunning priests are the real makers of God, he held religion to be the chief source of all human corruption.

M. P. Cushing, *Baron d'Holbach; a study of eighteenth century radicalism in France* (1914) ; F. A. Lange, *History of Materialism* (1925) ; G. V. Plekhanov, *Essays in the history of materialism* (London, 1934) ; W. H. Wickwar, *Baron d'Holbach; a prelude to the French revolution* (London, 1935). H.H.

holiness: See sanctity.

holiness: A term of universal use and importance in religion. It has a variety of meanings but everywhere refers to an essential feature of the divine and distinguishes the sacred from the profane. Its main primitive denotation was an extraordinary and inscrutable power connected with certain objects, beings, events or actions by virtue of which they were set apart from common contact and use, invested with tabus, treated with special precaution and reserved for religious regard and use. At this level its meaning is quasi-material, non-ethical, super-natural power of great value and great danger for men.

In the course of moral and religious development, traceable eminently in the Bible, the term has gradually acquired another principal and more familiar meaning, namely, ethical purity and moral perfection of character. It has never become an exclusively ethical term, however, but remains an essentially religious word denoting that perfect and loving rightcousness which characterizes God's nature and power. Such holiness is His crowning attribute. In so far as the term is applicable to men it refers to that moral likeness to God which is the fruit of His grace bringing them into perfect moral sonship and obedience to Him. R.W.F.

Holiness Church: A "second blessing" holiness sect organized by three Methodist preachers in California in 1896. It professes to adhere strictly to the standards and practices of early Methodism. It stresses sanctification, the second advent, and divine healing, and opposes tobacco, lodges and jewelry. Ministers are unsalaried and for the most part support themselves by working at other tasks. There are 15 churches having 400 members. See holiness churches; pentecostal churches. E.T.C.

holiness churches: A group of perfectionist* sects* which stress Christian perfection, perfect love, or holiness as a "second blessing" or work of grace instantaneously accomplished subsequent to justification. The group has a left-wing or extreme branch consisting of sects which insist on various *charismata** or spiritual gifts, usually the gift of speaking in unknown tongues,* as the sign and seal of holiness. These are customarily known as Pentecostal churches.

Although perfectionism has been present in the Church for many centuries, the modern holiness movement in the United States may be said to stem directly from John Wesley* and early Methodism.* Wesley taught Christian perfection, though with some reservations and inconsistencies, and emotional excesses resembling the typical *charismata* featured some of his meetings. Early American Methodism was known for its teaching of holiness and its first general conference stated one of its objects to be "to spread scriptural holiness over these lands." In the background of all this, of course, was the previous pietism* and the general perfectionist theology.

Most of the holiness groups in the United States have the Methodist background; many represent direct offshoots of the Methodist body and some definitely lay claim to Wesleyan traditions. The lessening of the emphasis upon holiness as Methodism increased in size, wealth, social prestige, and administrative machinery created a dissatisfaction which gave rise to the National Holiness Movement soon after the War Between the States; beginning with meetings of small holiness groups within the Methodist and other denominations, and the promoting larger holiness conventions and camp meetings in various parts of the country, this movement eventually resulted in the creation of several independent holiness denominations.

There have been various splits and unions within the general group, and certain bodies which originally stressed "second blessing" holiness have laid less stress on the doctrine as they increased in size and influence. Indeed, the whole modern history of the movement tends to show that holiness as a vital element decreases as the group grows in numbers and wealth and the need for an elaborate administrative organization appears. Most of the sects which sloughed off from the main Methodist bodies not only adopted holiness but also eliminated the episcopacy and other administrative offices.

Making allowances for this constantly shifting emphasis upon the doctrines of holiness and the fact that very many small sects are actually holiness in character even though they do not clearly state the tenet in their creeds, and excluding the extreme Pentecostal sects,* it may be said that the leading holiness groups in the United States at the present time are as follows:

Group	*Churches*	*Members*
Christian and Missionary Alliance*	444	32,000
Church of God (Anderson, Indiana)*	1032	57,000
Church of the Nazarene*	2197	136,000
Apostolic Christian Church*	57	5,800
Apostolic Christian Church (Nazarean)*	31	1,600
Apostolic Faith Mission*	17	2,300
Christian Congregation*	1	57
Church of Daniel's Band*	5	120
Church of God (Apostolic)*	13	300
Church of God as Organized by Christ*	13	360
Hepzibah Faith Missionary Association*	20	700
Metropolitan Church Association*	14	1,000
Missionary Church Association*	47	3,600
Missionary Bands of the World*	6	200
Pillar of Fire*	46	4,000
Holiness Church*	15	400
Wesleyan Methodist Connection	565	22,000
Primitive Methodist* Church in the U.S.A.	91	12,000
Congregational Methodist Church	121	8,000
Free Methodist Church	1,084	37,000
New Congregational Methodist Church	25	1,500
Holiness Methodist Church	3	200
Reformed Methodist Church	9	300
Apostolic Methodist Church	2	30
Reformed New Congregational Methodist Church	8	300
Christian Nation Church*	5	100
Church of the Full Gospel, Inc.*	4	300
Kodesh Church of Immanuel*	9	560

E. T. Clark, *The Small Sects in America* (1937); Chapman, *A History of the Church of the Nazarene;* Flew, *The Idea of Perfection;* Lee, *The Historical Background of Early Methodist Enthusiasm;* McDaniel, *Origin and Early History of the Congregational Methodist Church;* Nagler, *Pietism and Methodism;* Pardington, *Twenty-five Wonderful Years;* Warfield, *Studies in Perfectionism,* 2 vols.; White, *Looking Back from Beulah;* Yahn, *History of the Churches of God in North America.* E.T.C.

Holiness Code: Name of a section of the book of Leviticus* (xvii-xxvi, perhaps also Ex. xxxi, 13-14a; Lev. xi, 43-45; Num. xv, 37-41) made of a collection of laws called P 1 or H, inspired by the school of Ezekiel, and warning against moral transgressions, ritual corruptions and pagan influences. Was later incorporated in the Priestly Code.* See R. Pfeiffer, *Introduction to the Old Testament* (1941), pp. 239-250. See Hexateuch. S.L.T.

holiness, Divine: See s. v. wrath of God.

Holiness Methodist Church: See holiness churches.

Holl, Karl: (1866-1926) German Protestant theologian. He was born in Tübingen, Würtemberg. From 1901-1906 he was professor of Church history in Tübingen and from 1906-1926 (together with Harnack) professor of Church History in Berlin.

His principal fields of research were the Ancient Church and the Reformation period. His publication of Epiphanius* (2 vols. 1915, 1922) in the Berlin edition of the Greek Fathers is a model of accuracy and learning. His interpretation of Luther—an attempt to understand the reformer out of the inner logic of his theology and experience—made a deep impression upon Continental Protestantism and helped to usher in the Luther Renaissance. Holl was the teacher of a considerable number of New Testament and Church History students. See neo-Lutheranism. Principal works:

Die Sacra Parallela des Johannes Damascenus (1897); *Enthusiasmus und Bussgewalt beim griechischen Mönchtum* (1898); *Gesammelte Aufsatze,* 3 vols. (1922-1928 Volume I, dealing with Luther). O.A.P.

Holman Lectureship: In connection with the endowment effort of 1865 for the Gettysburg Lutheran Seminary, the Rev. Samuel A. Holman, then a young pastor in Altoona, Pa., gave $2,000, the annual income from which was used to secure a lecture each year on one of the 21 doctrinal articles of the Augsburg Confession. Beginning with Dr. J. A. Brown on Article I in 1866, there has been a continuous succession of these annual lectures by prominent professors and pastors. They have led to a more thorough study and exposition of the mother symbol of Protestantism and were no small factor in the doctrinal development of the General Synod of the Lutheran Church in America. All were printed in the *Evangelical Review* and the *Lutheran Quarterly*. The first series of 21 lectures were published in 1888. The names of the annual lecturers down to the present appear in A. R. Wentz, *History of the Gettysburg Seminary* (1926), pp. 298-299. (Data from the office of the President of the Gettysburg Lutheran Theological Seminary.) V.F.

holocaust: Completely burnt offering*. LXX's* rendering of Hebrew *olah* literally "that which is brought up" to the Deity. A synonym is *kalil,* signifying complete burning, not only of the holy inwards and fat, but of the carcass as well. The *olah* was the atonement sacrifice par excellence; other expiatory* sacrifices* atoned for particular transgressions. At first both a private as well as a public offering, it later became, in the form of the daily "tamid," the great national sacrifice of all Israel, prototype of the daily Jewish prayer services of today. H.K.-L.F.

Hölscher, Gustav: (1877-) He has been teaching at the universities of Halle, Giessen, Marburg and Bonn. Now is at the University of Heidelberg. As an individualist, influenced by the psychologist W. Wundt,* he dared to initiate independent beginnings in the field of the study of the OT.

Der Sadduzaeismus (Leipzig, 1906); *Die Propheten* (Leipzig, 1914); *Hesekiel. Der Dichter und das Buch* (Giessen, 1924); *Das Buch Hiob* (Tübingen, 1937); *Die Hohenpriesterliste bei Josephus und die evangelische Chronologie* (Heidelberg, 1940). H.H.

Holtzmann, Heinrich: (1832-1910) He was professor in Heidelberg and Strasburg. In spite of his critical scientific attitude, he won considerable influence. By his comprehensive works he became more just to the NT writings than was the construction of F. C. Baur.* See Lives of Jesus.

Die synoptischen Evangelien (Tübingen u. Leipzig, 1863); *Lehrbuch der historisch-kritischen Einleitung in das Neue Testament* (Freiburg, 1885); *Lehrbuch der neutestamentlichen Theologie.* 2 vols. (Tübingen, 1896). H.H.

Holy Alliance, The: Was organized after the Congress of Vienna (1815) by Alexander I of Russia together with Francis I of Austria and Frederick William III of Prussia. Its purpose was to base the relations between their States on the religion of Christianity whose precepts were to have a direct bearing on the councils of Princes. The rulers were pledged to mutual assistance; their relation to their subjects was to be that of fathers to families; their subjects were to consider themselves as members of one and the same Christian nation. Other powers which avowed these principles were asked to join. Most of the European sovereigns did so, notable exceptions being Great Britain, the Pope, and the Sultan. The Holy Alliance with its vague paternalistic idealism has often mistakenly been identified with the Quadruple Alliance. Too, it has had a bad reputation as suppressor of liberty, as in the crushing of the Hungarian Revolution (1849). But to the 19th Century Tsars it continued to express their mystic faith in the potency of rule by divine right for effecting the highest ends; thus it is said to have inspired Nicholas II to take measures resulting in the first international peace conference at The Hague, 1899.

Cambridge Modern History, Vol. X, ch. I. H.O

holy days, Jewish: See Jewish religious festivals; Sabbath.

holy days and festivals, Christian: See church year; church year cycle; feasts and fasts of the Roman Catholic Church; festivals and holy days, Christian; Sabbath, Christian.

holy family: The family of Joseph, Mary and Jesus. Often the title of paintings. In Roman Catholic circles regarded as a model for Christian households and an object of veneration. S.M.G.

Holy Grail, the: A medieval legend* of pagan and of Christian apocryphal origins, it varied widely in the telling. (On the word "Grail" see *Joseph of Arimathea . . .,* edited by W. W. Skeat, London, 1871, pp. xxxvi-xli.) In the main there are two kinds of legends. One has interest centered on the Grail as such and is associated with the Cup of the Eucharist, Joseph of Arimathea, etc. The other is concerned with the quest, the most celebrated searchers being Perceval (Parzifal) and Galahad, knights of Arthur's Round Table. The great stories on the quest theme were written within the last quarter of the 12th and the middle of the 13th centuries, the most notable being Chrétien de Troyes' *Perceval le Gallois* or *Le Conte del Graal,* and Wolfram von Eschenbach's *Parzifal.* Perceval, who was to have been the next Lord of the Grail, had been shown the Grail; but he failed to ask about its significance, and therefore it was lost to him. In Wolfram this failure is attributed to ignorance (like that of Oedipus), and his lordship of the Grail is rewon by becoming wise. Wolfram's treatment is a moving one and deeply spiritual.

Sir Thomas Malory, *Morte d'Arthur* (Fifteenth Century), Books XIII-XVII contain the most popular tradition of the quest. (Many editions.) R. Jaffray, *King Arthur and the Holy Grail* (1928). Q.B.

Holy of Holies: (*Kodesh Ha Kodashim*) The most sacred chamber of the Tabernacle and then Temple**, where the high priest performed the Day of Atonement* ritual. The Ark* of a Covenant was kept there. The exact measurements of the Holy of Holies in the Temple of Solomon are described in I Kings vi. B.Z.B.

holy orders: See apostolic succession; bishop; canon law; cardinal; clergy; deacon; deaconess; orders; ordination; pope; priest; sacraments; vicar.

holy place: A site held sacred because of its religious associations. The principal holy place in Judaism is the site on which formerly was the Temple* in Jerusalem, with the portion of wall which still survives and which is known as the "wailing wall". It is a popular place for Jewish pilgrims who wail there for the tragedies of the Jewish dispersion. See blood. B.Z.B.

Holy Rollers: See pentecostal sects.

Holy Roman empire, the: This institution roots in the Christianization of the Roman Empire, when (at least by 395 A.D.) to be Christian was to be Roman, and *vice versa.* Throughout the 4th to the 8th centuries a cleavage between East and West took place, brought about by growth of imperial autocracy (cf. Diocletian, Constantine, Constantinople), barbarian invasions, conversion of the barbarian nations to Catholic Christianity, and the power of the Roman Church (which increased in the West, decreased in the East). What came to be thought of as the Holy Roman empire was distinctly a Western phenomenon: it was (theoretically) co-extensive with the Latin Church, its rulers were of "barbarian" stock. Its appelation of "Roman" was intended to be more than nominal; for the barbarian peoples had long admired the Roman Empire, they desired to be its heirs and to preserve its institutions, in consequence of which it is not surprising that the emperors of the H. R. empire considered themselves in line of succession to the Roman emperors.

In the first phase of its history the empire takes the part of protector and extender of the Latin Church. It began with the conversion of the Franks (496) and their conquests. In the 8th century the Saracen and Lombard perils drew the papacy into closer association with the Krankish State, an important result being the creation of the title of ruler by divine right. (Cf. Charles Martel, Pepin the Short, Donation of Pepin, St. Boniface.) In 800 A.D. Charlemagne was crowned Emperor by Leo III, with which act the formal history of the Empire may be said to have begun.

Its second phase is characterized by the breakup of the Frankish State and the shift of the Empire to Germany (Henry the Fowler, 918-936, Otto I, 936-973), the imperial concern about church reform (Henry II, 1002-24, Henry III, 1039-56), and the struggle of emperors and popes for supremacy (Henry IV, 1056-1106, Frederick Barbarossa, 1152-89, Frederick II, 1212-50; cf. also Gregory VII, Alexander III, Innocent III, Gregory IX; Dictatus Papae, Concordat of Worms). In this struggle the popes generally prevailed, while the Empire declined. Important factors were: German ducal competition for the crown, want of a single imperial capitol, the impossible ideal of including Italy in the Empire, the ambition of some emperors to establish a national church, and the extraordinary prestige of the papacy (cf. *translatio imperii,* Doctrine of the Two Swords). Meanwhile, in this period the empire claimed supremacy over Germany, and, in varying degrees, over Hungary, Poland, Denmark, France, Scandinavia, Spain, England, Ireland, Italy (save Venice), Cyprus, Armenia. The revived study of Roman law dates from this period (University of Bologna). The third phase may be dated from the Interregnum (1254-1273) to the fall of the empire in 1806. It had now become more or less exclusively a German state, and eighteen of its twenty-seven emperors were Hapsburgs. While its medieval glory was passing the imperial ideal had memorable champions (cf. Dante's *De Monarchia,* William Ockham, Marsilius of Padua). Charles V, 1519-56, united the imperial crown with that of a national state (Spain), which led to protracted wars, particularly with France. Throughout the 16th century Reformation the empire defended Catholic orthodoxy as the religion of all Europe, its principle being challenged by the Protestant *cuius regio, huius religio.* A serious blow was dealt the Empire in the Peace of Westphalia*, 1648, which was drafted bv nation states only. In 1806 Napoleon brought about the Emperor's abdication, maintaining that the Empire had by "translation" gone to him as the Charlemagne of the West. See Ghibelline and Guelf.

J. Bryce, *The Holy Roman Empire* (1909 ed.); *Cambridge Medieval History; Cambridge Modern History;* C. H. McIlwain, *The Growth of Political Thought in the West, from the Greeks to the End of the Middle Ages* (London, 1932); C. C. Eckhardt, *The Papacy in World Affairs* (1937).

Q.B.

holy see: See see; pope.

holy sepulchre: The body of Jesus, after his death on Calvary, was conveyed to a rock-hewn tomb, evidently very close at hand, which was offered by Joseph of Arimathea. Christian tradition or conjecture has identified this tomb with a cave now enclosed by the church of the Holy Sepulchre, but the true position of Calvary, and therefore of the adjoining tomb, has not yet been ascertained. E.F.S.

Holy Spirit: The roots of this conception are to be found in primitive religion. (Cf. Spenta Mainyu) It was observed that men at times become different from themselves, for instance in madness or high enthusiasm, and this was explained by the presence in the world of a mysterious power, which may chance to enter the man and make him its instrument. In the O.T. this power is called the *ruah* or *breath,* and to it are attributed the strength of Samson, the genius of Bezaleel, the insanity of Saul. In a later age it was peculiarly associated with the frenzy in which a prophet uttered divine oracles, and from the physical state of the prophet it was transferred to his exalted mood, and hence to all divine impulse and knowledge and action. An age was anticipated when God would "pour out his Spirit on all flesh" (Joel, 2:28) and not merely on his chosen prophets. It was believed in the early church that this promised age had now opened, and the strange phenomena on the day of Pentecost were supposed to mark the coming of the Spirit. In the Synoptic teaching of Jesus himself the conception of the Spirit has little or no place. Perhaps the only reference which can be deemed authentic is that which deals with blasphemy against the holy Spirit, and Jesus here is only meeting the charge of his enemies who said that he was possessed of an evil spirit. It was the departure of Jesus which brought the idea of the Spirit to the fore-front. He had himself ascended, but for the brief interval that would elapse before his return he had sent the Spirit to take his place. At first it was regarded simply as a miracle-working power, and this is the conception which dominates the book of Acts. Paul invested it with a new significance. He thought of it not as coming at rare intervals in sudden gusts but as the abiding principle of the Christian life. He connected it with moral and not merely with abnormal activities, and made love the chief manifestation of the Spirit. With Paul it became in a full sense the alter ego of Christ, so that he can say (2 Cor. 3:17) "the Lord is the Spirit". This idea is further developed in the Fourth Gospel, although the work of the Spirit is there confined almost exclusively to revelation. In the N.T. there is no direct suggestion of a doctrine of the Trinity. The Spirit is conceived as an impersonal power by which God effects His will through Christ. At the same time Paul invariably thinks of God and Christ and the Spirit together, most notably in the Benedictions; and to this extent the later doctrine, which grew up in the course of the second century, had its origin in the N.T. See conviction of sin; grace; procession of the Holy Spirit; regeneration; sanctification; seven gifts of the Holy Spirit; Trinity.

E. F. Scott, *The Spirit in the New Testament* (1927); H. J. Holtzmann, *New Testament Theologie* (1897; 1911); H. Weinel, *New Ttestament Theologie* (1911).

E.F.S.

Holy Synod: In Russia the institution of the Holy Governing Synod was created by Tsar Peter the Great in 1721, as a substitute for the patriarchate*. It became one of the departments of the centralized government through which the Tsar could exercise his control over the church in matters not affecting the Orthodox faith. Its members were appointed by the Tsar, and took the same oath as the Senators. In his "Spiritual Rules," Peter prescribed in detail the duties of the members of the Holy Synod and the entire hierarchy. It was presided over by a layman, the ober-procurator, who represented the Tsar, and was responsible to him. In course of time, he became the most powerful figure, for the ecclesiastical policy was largely determined by him. It was through the instrumentality of the Holy Synod that the State exercised control over the church, and made it subservient to its political aims. For that reason, when after the downfall of tsarism in the Spring of 1917, the provisional government called a Church Council for the reorganization of the ecclesiastical structure, this body abolished the Holy Governing Synod, and restored the patriarchate. Nevertheless, the patriarch was not granted autocratic powers in the administration of the church, but shared this function with the Holy Synod and the Supreme Ecclesiastical Council. The membership of the former consisted of twelve bishops, and its functions had to do mostly with matters of the inner life of the church—doctrine, liturgy, religious education, discipline, and missionary and publication work. The Supreme Ecclesiastical Council was of mixed membership—hierarchical, priestly, and lay. Its duties were of economic and financial nature.

A similar organization obtains in other Orthodox national or autocephalous churches: thus, for instance, the Ecumenical Patriarchate (of Constantinople) was organized on this basis in accordance with the Constitution of 1862. The patriarchal administration of spiritual matters was shared with the Holy Synod, composed of twelve metropolitans; alone, the patriarch could not take any decision apart from this organ of supreme administration, and himself was subject to it. Accordingly, properly speaking, it was the Holy Synod which was made the governing body rather than the patriarch. The National Mixed Council, composed of four clerics and eight laymen, was charged with the administration of schools, hospitals, and other benevolent institutions, as well as the finances of the church and other secular business.

The organization of the administration of other Orthodox communions, such as the churches of Roumania, Yugoslavia, Bulgaria, and others, follows essentially the same principle, and need not therefore be described in detail. See Eastern Orthodox Churches.

Matthew Spinka, *The Church and the Russian Revolution* (1927); Paul Milinkov, *Outlines of Russian Culture,* ed. by Michael-Karpovich (1942), I.

M.S.

Holy Thursday: Common name for Maundy Thursday*, but in older English usage (so in Book of Common Prayer since 1662) Ascension Day. E.R.H.

holy water: Ordinary water* which has been sanctified by the blessing of the Church. Salt is added to ordinary water to signify that this water is now preserved from corruption. It is used extensively in ceremonies of blessing. W.H.

Holy Week: The week before Easter, beginning with Palm Sunday. Observed with traditional ceremonies in Catholic churches, and including especially Maundy Thursday (when the institution of the Lord's Supper is commemorated), Good Friday (when the Passion and Death of Christ are remembered), and Holy Saturday (when baptisms traditionally take place). See church year cycle. W.N.P.

home missions: The work of the church devoted to minority and immigrant peoples within the home land. Ministry to the under-privileged in cities and rural districts, including every form of Christian and humanitarian service the church is able to offer. The purpose is identical with but in geographical contrast to foreign missions. Cf. city missions; inner mission. P.E.J.

homiletics: That branch of theology which deals with the art and science of preaching*. The word itself is a transliteration of a Greek word meaning "to be in company with." Its secondary meaning was "easy and companionable conversation." The early conversations of Christian teachers with Christian groups about the Old and New Testaments thus came to be called, from a related Greek word, "homiletics", probably in 3rd Century Alexandria. The art of public speech had been highly cultivated within Greece and Rome and the Christian preacher inherited the tradition. Some training in the art of preaching has, therefore, always distinguished theological education, though the prominence given it has naturally varied with the importance attached to the sermon itself.

Homiletics so defined has created a vast literature on the preparation and delivery of sermons, to which English speaking non-liturgical Protestantism, with its emphasis upon preaching, has made distinguished contributions. Particularized homiletic instruction, with professional instructors, is more stressed in Scotch and American theological post-graduate schools than in the English Univerities. A representative course in homiletics would include instruction in the principles of effective public address, the examination of standard sermon types, some history of preaching and studies of representative preachers, training in voice and gesture, the proper development of texts and topics, "practice preaching", followed by criticism and such marginal procedure as the instructor considers helpful, since the field is both spacious and elastic. The larger theological schools have often more than one specialist in homiletics in their faculties. See rhetorici.

Charles R. Brown, *The Art of Preaching* (1922); Raymond Calkins, *The Eloquence of Christian Experience* (1927). G.G.A.

homiliarium: Any medieval book of homilies, or sermons, compiled either for the benefit of parish preachers and congregations or for reading in the choir offices of the clergy. E.C.K.

homily: (fr. Gr. *homilia,* converse, discourse; fr. *homilos,* crowd, assembly) A term in use from the early Christian Church to designate an informal discourse on some doctrinal subject, scriptural passage, Christian virtue or vice, or ecclesiastical observance. Contrasted with the sermon* which developed as a more formal type of preaching*. Homilies written by celebrated preachers came to be widely used by the clergy of the medieval Church for reading to their local congregations. In the Church of England, the *Book of Homilies*, constituting such a collection of discourses, was royally authorized (First Book publ. in 1547; Second Book in 1563) and appointed to be read in the churches for the purposes of offsetting false doctrine and moving the people to the true worship and service of God. E.T.R.

homoios: A Greek word meaning "like", or "similar." It was the watchword of the group among the fourth-century Semi-Arians* who opposed the use of the Nicene formula, *homoousios**, to describe the relation of Father and Son. They objected that *ousia** is an unscriptural term and affirmed that the Son is "like" the Father, without specifying their actual metaphysical relationship. F.G.E.

homoi ousios: A Greek term meaning "of like (or "similar") essence (or "substance")." It was the watchword of the mediating party in the Arian* controversy to express the relation of the Son to the Father: of like, but not of the same, essence. Opposed to *homo ousios**, the orthodox formula. F.G.E.

homo ousios: A Greek word meaning "consubstantial," "of the same essence," or "substance." It represents the formula championed by Athanasius* (293-373) and adopted by the Nicene Council (325) to express the relation of the Father and the Son. They are in substance one, numerically identical, indivisible, in contrast to the Arian* view which subordinated the Son to the Father. See an-omoians; creeds of Christendom. F.G.E.

honesty: A general term for a virtue stressed in all ethics. It denotes the disposition and practice of fair, truthful and straight-forward dealing with others and with oneself. It signifies, in particular, special regard for the rights and property of others, respect for the principles of conduct of others, fidelity in keeping one's agreements, and freedom from all fraud and imposture. R.W.F.

honor: The term may refer to 1) the high regard and esteem paid to a person of worth, achievement or position; 2) the symbols of distinction (e.g., titles) granted as a mark of such esteem; and 3) the inner consciousness of worth and delicate sense of rights and obligations felt by such a person. The last is the ethical use of the term and it is usually associated with the "code of honor" binding upon a member of the aristocracy or of a special group with peculiar duties and privileges. In Christian ethics the honor of a Christian emanates from God, the final moral Judge who is "the reader of all hearts." R.W.F.

hope: The attitude of looking forward to a future good or to the fulfilment of a cherished desire. Pagan thought stressed its illusory character. It is the dominant note of the Bible, however, and one of St. Paul's triumvirate of graces (I Cor. 13:13) which became the three theological

virtues of Christian ethics. In Christianity it is an expectation of spiritual blessings based upon faith in the love of God as revealed in Christ. As a Christian grace it begets a joyous temper, patience and perseverance amid trials, and a confident, optimistic outlook upon life and the future.
R.W.F.

Hooker, Richard: (1554?-1600) English theologian, author of the treatise *Of the Laws of Ecclesiastical Polity* (1594-97). A man of wide learning and a master of English prose, Hooker formulated the classic defence of the Church of England as a *via media* between the extremes of Rome and Geneva. In an age of petty controversy, his work is remarkable for its philosophic breadth and tolerant spirit. L.W.C.

Hopedale (Mass.) community: See communistic settlements, secular.

Hopkins, Samuel: (1721-1803) American theologian, pupil and follower of Jonathan Edwards*, whose teachings he expounded in a complete *System of Doctrines* (1793). Most characteristic teaching: definition of true holiness as "disinterested benevolence*." Self-love was to Hopkins the root of all sin, and no man was saved unless so completely devoid of self-love that he would be willing, if necessary, to be "damned for the glory of God." *Inquiry into the Nature of True Holiness* (1773). See Hopkinsianism; New England theology. W.M.H.

Hopkinsianism: A name given to the systematic formulation of Jonathan Edwards* theology by Samuel Hopkins*. The creed of Andover Seminary, designed to guard it against Unitarian heresy, was very largely a Hopkinsian creed, though containing some concessions to Old Calvinism*. Cf. Calvinism, consistent; means.
W.M.H.

horae: See hours.

hormic psychology: See psychology, schools of.

Hormisdas, Pope: (514-523) Of a wealthy family in Latium, he had been married, and his son was a later pope (Silverius, 536-7). He was a deacon under Pope Symmachus (498-514) whom he succeeded. As pope he first healed the schism of Laurentius (anti-pope). Till 519 he was mostly occupied with the schism begun by patriarch Acacius* of Constantinople; out of the negotiations came the Formula Hormisdae (frequently cited at the Vatican Council). At his direction Dionysius Exiguus brought out a translation of the canons of the Greek Church. The pope also issued a new edition of the Gelasian Canon. See also henoticon; Justinian.

Catholic Encyclopedia, "Hormisdas." C. Mirbt, *Quellen z. Gesch. d. Papsttums u. d. Röm. Katholizismus* (Tübingen, 1934), O. 89. Q.B.

horns: Horns are primarily a symbol of power. The bull with its ferocious strength furnished the symbol. As sign of their power, many deities of the Middle East wore horns. For the same reason, horns decorate the head dress of kings, priests, and warriors. The bull was also associated with the divine powers of fertility. As a result, horns symbolized prosperity and plenty. The primary meaning is illustrated in the use of horns for the protection of houses, persons and graves. The secondary meaning appears in the cornucopia. The blowing of a horn was effective against demons, sickness and other evils.
A.E.H.

horoscope: (Gr. *hora,* time; *skopos,* observer) Observation of the sky or planets at a certain moment, especially at a person's birth; a scheme showing an aspect of the heavens at a particular moment; from an aspect of the heavens at the moment of a person's birth, the astrologer professes to forecast the events of a person's life; an example of such as aspect is the use of a sign of the zodiac which rises above the horizon at the moment of an individual's birth; the zodiac is a schematic arrangement of the circuit of the heavens into twelve segments, each segment with its sign or star-pattern. Interpretations of the aspect presented follow the customary and fixed rules established by the pseudoscience of astrology. F.L.P.

Horus: (Egyptian) In the Early Kingdom, sky or sun god of the rulers of lower Egypt, or delta region; the falcon god; later, in the myth of Osiris*, Horus is the son who overthrows Set*, the brother of Osiris. See Egypt, religions of.
F.L.P.

hosanna: (Gr. form of Heb. *hosha'-na,* O Save) A liturgical cry of entreaty (cf. Psalm 118:25) used in Mark 11:9, 10 and parallel passages apparently as an ejaculation of praise, a meaning acquired through association with other praise cries. R.B.Y.S.

Hosea: A combination of two originally separate collections, the Parables of Hosea (chs. 1-3) and the Prophecies of Hosea (chs. 4-14). The book contains about fifteen prophetic poems delivered by Hosea, a farmer, on marketing trips to nearby cities Jezreel and Samaria. His oracles are dated 743-735 B.C., reflecting steps in national disintegration. With the prosperity of 750 B.C. (see Amos) giving way to civil war and Assyria organizing westward campaigns, Hosea tried to save his nation. Primarily a political prophet, he worked for national unity, opposed foreign alliances, and demanded just public administration. He reaffirmed the religious contributions of Amos, advancing beyond the justice idea to conceiving Yahweh as a god of longsuffering love. He saved Israelite religion from absorption into Baalism* with its sexual worship. His call was intimately connected with his marriage. Domestic tragedy caused by his wife's subsequent unfaithfulness gave him insight into the feelings of Yahweh toward the faithless nation. Last prophet of north Israel, Hosea was noted for popularizing the parable, using figures of speech, and coming closer than other O.T. writers to Jesus' conception of God.

See J. M. P. Smith and W. A. Irwin, *The Prophets and their Times* (1941), pp. 69-84; E. Hamilton, *The Prophets of Israel* (1936), pp. 76-85.

R.E.W.

Hoshana Rabba: (Heb. "save, we beseech Thee") Name of the 7th day of Tabernacles, derived from the chant of Psalm 118:25 during the procession around the altar on each day of the feast, with citrons, palm branches, myrtles and willow branches (Lev. 23: 40-41; 2 Macc. 10:7; cf. John 12:13). The last day, which was marked by seven circuits, acquired the name "Great Hosanna". It formed the climax of the water drawing festivities preceding the beginning of the winter or rainy season. Part of its ceremonies consisted in beating small bunches of willow sprigs on the ground at the side of the altar. Hence the day was also known as "the day of beating the willow" (or "palm tufts"). The Cabbalists (see Kabbalah) invested it with mystic significance as the time when God's decrees regarding each person, sealed on the Day of Atonement*, take effect. See Tabernacles or Feast of Booths. S.S.C.

Hosius: Bishop of Cordova in Spain ca. 295 and a champion of orthodoxy against Arianism* in the early 4th century. An adviser to the emperor Constantine when dealing with the Donatists*. Presided at the Council of Nicaea. A friend of Athanasius. In 351, under pressure, he signed an Arian declaration. See Elvira, Synod of; Sylvester I. S.M.G.

hospice (5th cent. and St. Bernard) Building set aside for use of travellers, the sick and unfortunate. Developed from hospitality early practised by monastics of the East and carried on in West by Benedictine and Columban** (Celtic) monks. Hospice of the Great St. Bernard, founded by Bernard of Menthon in eleventh century is famous for rescues made in Alpine passes.

K.H.C.

hospitality: See charity and almsgiving.

hospitallers: Used in a general sense to designate those whose religious vocation involved the care, in hospitals, of the aged, the homeless, orphans, and the sick. Among those dedicated to such service were numerous orders and congregations, some of them for women. In the crusading* period, hospitalizing services came to be closely associated with the functions of such military orders as the Templars, Teutonic Knights, and the Knights Hospitallers of St. John. In this connection see Military Religious Orders. See Anthony, St.; Bethlehemites; charity and almsgiving (Christian); Knights Templar.

R.C.P.

hospitals: See charity and almsgiving (Christian).

host: (Lat., *hostia,* victim) The unleavened eucharistic bread used in the Western Church, which is held to become by consecration the body of Christ offered in the sacrifice of the Mass*. See corporal; elevation of the host; monstrance; pyx.

P.V.N.

Hotman, Francois: (1524-1590) Best known Huguenot* writer on constitutional theory. He attacked papal pretensions, and urged a formal declaration of independence from Rome by France. His large tract, entitled *Franco-Gallia* (1573) was called out by the Massacre of St. Bartholomew*. His argument for the view that the French king was elective and his power limited by the States General depended upon the principle of medieval constitutionalism, that political institutions derive their right from immemorial practices inherent in the community itself.

J. W. Allen, *A History of Political Thought in the Sixteenth Century* (London, 1928); E. Armstrong, "The Political Theory of the Huguenots" *English Historical Review,* vol. IV (London, 1889); E. Barker, "A Huguenot Theory of Politics," *Church, State and Study* (London, 1930).

H.H.

hours: (*horae.* The canonical hours) The system of prayer at stated times during the day and night, arising in part out of the primitive vigil (Vespers, Matins, Lauds)**, partly out of times of private devotion (Terce, Sext, None—the Little Hours)**, and in part out of monastic life (Prime, Compline)**. These eight hours together constitute the Divine Office*, canonically binding upon all clergy and Religious in the Roman Communion (with slight exceptions). The core of the Office is the Psalter. See Breviary; Psalmody. P.V.N.

House of God, the Holy Church of the Living God, The Pillar and Ground of the Truth, House of Prayer for all People: A Negro religious sect founded by R. A. R. Johnson in Washington, D. C., in 1913. It is based on twenty-four principles which Bishop Johnson claims were revealed to him by God. These principles contain the ordinary theology of the fundamentalist type. Women are recognized as evangelists and foot washing is practiced. Headquarters are at Beaufort, South Carolina. There are four churches and 200 members. E.T.C.

House of the Lord: A religious sect founded by W. H. Johnson in Detroit, Michigan, in 1925. It now has four churches and 300 members. Its members are not allowed to engage in any occupation involving tobacco, whiskey, nor may they be "bell hops", play cards, go pleasure riding ,or attend motion picture or other theaters, ball games, dances or horse races. Modest apparel is insisted upon. Christian perfection is taught in the literal sense and the baptism of the Holy Spirit accompanied by speaking in unknown tongues is sought. However, no person can be sanctified if he owns property of any kind. There is opposition to taking oaths, joining secret fraternities, and carrying life insurance. See pentecostal sects.

E.T.C.

House of Prayer: A Negro pentecostal sect founded by one "Bishop Grace," who is regarded as a sort of messiah by his followers. Among its practices are divine healing, speaking in unknown tongues, trances, and other extreme emotional excesses. See pentecostal sects. E.T.C.

Houtin, Albert: (1867-1926) Participant in the Catholic Modernist* movement; later (after leaving the priesthood) its most complete historian. *Histoire du modernisme catholique,* (1912); Autobiography, *Mon expérience* (1926). W.M.H.

Howison, George Holmes: (1834-1916) Born in Montgomery Co., Maryland, the son of parents who freed their slaves and removed to Marietta, Ohio, George Howison graduated from Marietta College in 1852, and from Lane Theological Seminary in 1855. After teaching school in Salem, Mass. and elsewhere he became instructor in mathematics in Washington University, St. Louis, where he joined the Kant club studying Hegel and Kant. Removing to Boston he lectured in the Harvard Divinity School, the Concord School of Philosophy and was professor of the Philosophy of science and logic in the Massachusetts Institute of Technology (1871-79). In 1883 he was lecturer on philosophy in Michigan University and was called in 1884 to the chair of philosophy (afterward the Mills Chair) in the University of California. Here he became "one of the most successful and inspiring teachers of philosophy that America has produced." (*Cambridge History of American Literature.*)

Author: *A Treatise on Analytic Geometry* (1869); *Limits of Evolution and Other Essays in Philosophy* (1901, 2nd ed., 1905); *The Conception of God* (joint author, 1907); also reviews and addresses.

Howison's philosophy, which he termed *Personal Idealism,* is an original, theistic Personalism*, defining God as Perfect Person, Final Cause, and Center of the Republic of persons and emphasizing "the freedom and dignity of the soul."

J. W. Buckham and G. M. Stratton, *George Holmes Howison, Philosopher and Teacher* (containing a biographical sketch, The Limits of Evolution and other principal writings) (1933); "The Personal Idealism of George Holmes Howison" by C. M. Bakewell, *Philosophical Review,* Vol. XLIX, Nov., 1940; "The Contribution of Professor Howison to Christian Thought" by J. W. Buckham, *The Harvard Theological Review,* Vol. IX, July, 1916.

J.W.B.

Hoyt Memorial Foundation, The: A fund established in 1925, in honor of Dr. Arthur S. Hoyt, for thirty years professor of homiletics at Auburn Seminary (Auburn, N. Y.), by the alumni of the Seminary. The income from this fund, now amounting to $10,000. is to provide for ministers-in-residence, missionary and other speakers during the seminary year.

(Data furnished by W. S. Davison, Executive Director of Auburn Theological Seminary.) V.F.

Hsüan-tsang: See Buddhist Terminology.

Hübmaier, Balthasar: (1480-1528) Scholarly leader of the German Anabaptists*. Having been professor in the University of Ingolstadt and influential preacher in Waldshut, under the influence of the Swiss reformers he broke off with Rome. In 1525 he became an Anabaptist and fled to Zürich. There, with Zwingli's* connivance, he was imprisoned and tortured. Going to Moravia, he was arrested two years later, taken to Vienna, and burned at the stake. Singularly free from mystical elements, Hübmaier was a cogent interpreter of Scripture. His death was due directly to his refusal to recant the view that the Eucharist and adult baptism are the only two sacraments. T.A.K.

Hügel, Baron Friedrich, von: (1852-1925) A Roman Catholic interpreter of religion whose writings and personal influence, especially in England where he resided during his adult life, were greater outside his own communion than within it. His *Mystical Element of Religion* (2 volumes, 1908; 2nd edition, 1923) is one of the greatest studies of the phenomena of mystical religion of all times. The emphasis upon the transcendent reality of God increases steadily in the books that follow: *Eternal Life* (1912); *Essays and Addresses in the Philosophy of Religion* (1st Series 1921; 2nd Series 1926); *Selected Letters* (1927); and *The Reality of God* (1931).

M. Nédoncelle, *Baron Friedrich von Hügel.*

D.V.S.

Hugo (or Hugh) of St. Victor: (1096-1141) Writer of the first dogmatics in the occident, he was neither a narrow-minded traditionalist nor an enemy of reason. A pious Augustinian Platonist, he described the various states leading up to the perfect contemplation of God. His thought moved in a world of allegory. See Mystics of Saint Victor; sacraments.

J. Kilgenstein, *Die Gotteslehre des Hugo v. St. Viktor* (Wurzburg, 1898); K. Th. A. Liebner, *Hugo v. St. Viktor* (Leipzig, 1832); H. Ostler, *Die Psychologie des Hugo v. St. Viktor* (Münster, 1906).

H.H.

Huguenots: It was in France between 1562 and 1598, a period of not fewer than eight civil wars, that the most significant chapter in political philosophy was written. The centralized system of French monarchy had proved to be subject to abuses so serious that they threatened to cost the crown the support of the higher middle classes upon which its power really depended. The theories opposing royal absolutism were first developed by Huguenot writers. They stood for decentralization and local autonomy. They were driven to oppose the king and to advocate deposition because of the persecution of their religion, and because of a fundamental conviction of the undesirability of the monarchial form of government. Cf. Camisards. See wars of religion.

J. W. Allen, *A History of Political Thought in the Sixteenth Century* (London, 1928); E. Armstrong, *The French Wars of Religion.* 2 ed. (Oxford, 1904); J. N. Figgis, *Studies of Political Thought from Gerson to Grotius* (Cambridge, 1923), 2 ed. H.H.

Huitzilopochtli: (Aztec) God of war, to whom was offered sacrifices of human hearts taken from

living bodies while placed on the sacrificial stone; god of the Eastern Paradise to which realm of delight fallen warriors were taken; a god sacramentally represented by a body of grain and bread and eaten; principal sanctuary was on top of the great pyramid in old Mexico City.
F.L.P.

human sacrifice: The ceremonial killing of a human being. The practice was worldwide among all peoples who had risen above the level of savagery. In most cases the victim was sacrificed for the welfare of the whole community but sometimes only individuals benefited. The rite was used for many purposes—to save crops from drought or too much rain, to stop epidemics, to secure victory, to get favorable winds, to heal the sick, as a firstfruits* offering, to provide a scapegoat*, to send a messenger to the gods or the dead, to guarantee a safe passage over water, to make foundations firm, to appease divine anger, to commune with a god by eating his human embodiment, to furnish servants and companions for the dead, to remove barrenness, to win great wealth. The mellowing of human manners led to the substitution of animals for human victims, redemption of the first born, and the use of effigies as companions of the dead. A.E.H.

humanism, classical: See Renaissance.

Humanism, the New: As used by Irving Babbitt, Paul Elmer More, and their followers, the term signifies a philosophic point of view stressing the human elements of experience in contradistinction to the animal. Assuming a dualism of man and nature, the New Humanists assert that the essential quality of human experience is ethical, that man's will is free, and that the ultimate freedom is to be found in "liberation from outer constraints and subjection to inner law." Although inclining to the Hellenic doctrine of reason rather than to distinctively Christian standards, some members of the school have attempted a synthesis with revealed religion.

See the symposium edited by Norman Foerster, *Humanism and America* (1930). L.W.C.

humanism, religious: Although humanists have appeared in many periods of the world's history, by religious humanism is generally meant a relatively recent movement, born doubtless of the modern scientific age, which has discarded all dependence upon anything outside of man himself for the attainment of the good life. Man is "on his own" in the universe which is essentially indifferent to him. Whatever satisfaction he is to enjoy he must achieve by his ability to control the physical world about him or through his manipulation of social forces which can thus be made to serve him. He is entirely this-worldly in his outlook. Science is the key to his hope of a better world. John H. Dietrich, a Unitarian minister, is frequently called the "father" of religious humanism, and most of the leaders of the movement have been furnished by the Unitarian* church. Indeed the humanist churches constitute for the most part the left wing of Unitarianism. The most representative statement of their position was the so-called Humanist Manifesto issued in May, 1933, which declares in part:—

> "Humanism asserts that the nature of the universe depicted by modern science makes unacceptable any supernatural or cosmic guarantees of human values . . . Religion must formulate its hopes and plans in the light of the scientific spirit and method.
>
> "Religion consists of those actions, purposes and experiences which are humanly significant. Nothing human is alien to the religious. It includes labor, art, science, philosophy, friendship, recreation—all that is in its degree expressive of satisfying human living. The distinction between the sacred and the secular can no longer be maintained.
>
> "The goal of humanism is a free and universal society in which people voluntarily and intelligently cooperate for the common good. Humanists demand a shared life in a shared world."

While religious humanism is generally nontheistic, there are many who call themselves theistic humanists or Christian humanists. They are at one with the more radical wing in their insistence upon human values and their denial of the *complete* impotence of man to work out his own salvation. Man cannot, they hold, achieve salvation without most vigorous self-effort, but he is not left wholly alone, for God works with him. Furthermore their outlook is not wholly this-worldly although they do not stress the future life. That, they are content to trust to a good and wise God. See Comte, A.; Foster, G. B.; positivism.

Representative writings of religious humanism include: Curtis Reese, *Humanist Religion* (1931); A. E. Haydon, *The Quest of the Ages* (1929); Charles F. Potter, *Humanism—A New Religion* (1930); R. W. Sellars, *Religion Coming of Age* (1928); J. C. F. Auer, *Humanism States its Case* (1933). The Movement publishes a monthly magazine *The Humanist.*
C.S.B.

humanitarianism: A term used technically to describe philanthropy as it broke away from the aegis of Christianity in the 17th and 18th centuries. Sometimes employed by liberals in contempt to indicate the attempt of the newly rich mercantilist class to salve their consciences by private doles. Sociologically, it can be viewed as private efforts in the commercial and urban community of the post-Reformation period to exercise the deeply imbedded pattern of mutual aid in a society in which the customary forms of mutual aid were either frustrated by the complexity of the problems of poverty or exploited.

Thorstein Veblen, *The Theory of the Leisure Class* (1879); Stuart A. Queen, *Social Work in the Light of History* (1922). F.J.B.

Hume, David: (1711-76) Scottish philosopher, probably greatest modern sceptic. Following the Occasionalists, Locke, Berkeley**, and ancient sceptics*, Hume dissolves experience into a shower of "impressions," fading off into mere "ideas", and without any unity or coherence except a mysterious "custom" or "association of ideas." Causation is regularity in the flow of impressions, which by habit we expect to continue. Knowing no objective principle of causation, we cannot infer a divine mind as cause of the world-order. Matter and mind alike fail to explain orderliness, since the impressions by which we know them are essentially separate, and how the mind controls even its own ideas, if it really does so, is a mystery. Hume's critique of theology depends also upon his assumption that though causality is inexplicable, it yet has absolute sway, forbidding all freedom of open alternatives. Hence a world-orderer, if there be such, must be responsible for all details of events—thus the problem of evil* appears insoluble. In the Dialogues, Cleanthes rejects, as "really atheistic", the purely absolute, timeless character imputed to God by "all the orthodox divines almost". Theism means that man is not wholly dissimilar to the supreme cause, and there can be no analogy between the human mind and a sheer absolute (see also Gerson, Levi ben). But no definite alternative is suggested, other than a crudely finite deity. (See finite God.)

Hume's fine treatment of ethics rests upon the idea of sympathetic or disinterested approval and disapproval. His view of religion stands or falls largely with the atomistic concept of experience, the assumption of determinism*, and the apparent assumption that there can be no higher synthesis of absolute and relative in the idea of God (see Perfect). Whitehead* and others have recently challenged all three assumptions. Kant's* famous answer to Hume effects some reform of the first. See cause.

D. Hume, *A Treatise of Human Nature* (1739-40); *Enquiry Concerning the Human Understanding* (1748); *Enquiry Concerning Morals* (1751); *Natural History of Religion* (1757); *Dialogues Concerning Natural Religion* (1779). Also N. K. Smith, *The Philosophy of David Hume* (1941). C.H.

humeral veil: (Lat. *humerus*, the shoulder) A cloth vestment about 2½′ x 8′ worn on the shoulders of the subdeacon in solemn Masses to hold the paten, from the Offertory to the Pater Noster, in imitation of the Levites of the O.T. It is also worn by the priest while giving benediction with the Most Blessed Sacrament and when carrying the same Holy Sacrament in procession. Lambing, *Sacramentals*, 291. B.S.

Humiliati: (It. The Humble Ones) A twelfth-century association of lay-penitents combining the prosecution of gospel ideals with the avowed application of Christian principles to economic practices. Although living in normal, family relationships, they frequently gathered in common assembly for mutual edification, social and spiritual. Denied, by the papacy, the full exercise of their renunciatory dedication, they led a checkered career of heresy and orthodox monastic* vocations. R.C.P.

humiliation of Christ: A Lutheran and Reformed doctrine, based on Philippians 2:5-9, denoting the limitations and sufferings submitted to by Christ in consequence of his humanity,—the supernatural conception, birth, circumcision, education, earthly life, passion, death, and burial; contrasted with his exaltation,—resurrection, ascension**, and seat at the right hand of God. See kenosis. F.G.E.

humility: In general usage an attitude of modest self-estimate characterized by a lowly and unpretending view of oneself, an absence of pride in one's achievements, and freedom from arrogance, presumption and conceit. It is stressed in Christianity as the initial grace of the Christian life. It indicates a sense of creatureliness, weakness and unworthiness before God, the Perfect Spirit, and so calls for constant dependence on His grace while it refers all personal gifts and virtues to Him as their true and only source. R.W.F.

Huntingdon's, Countess of, Connexion: A group of Calvinistic Methodists*, so called after Selina, Countess of Huntingdon (1707-1791), who had appointed Whitefield* and other Calvinistic Methodists as her chaplains, built chapels and a seminary, and supported and ruled the group until her death. In 1779 she was forced to separate from the Church of England and enroll as a dissenter*. A.K.R.

Hunzinger, August Wilhelm: (1871-1920) He taught in Leipzig and Erlangen. Then he was chief pastor in Hamburg. He was a leader in the effort to come to an understanding between conservative and critical theology.

Lutherstudien (Leipzig, 1906); *Der Glaube und das religionsgeschichtliche Christentum der Gegenwart* (Leipzig, 1907); *Zur apologetischen Aufgabe der evangelischen Kirche in der Gegenwart* (Leipzig, 1907); *Probleme und Aufgaben der gegenwärtigen systematischen Theologie* (Leipzig, 1909); *Theologie und Kirche* (Leipzig, 1912); *Das Wunder* (Leipzig, 1912); *Hauptfragen der Lebensgestaltung* (Leipzig, 1916); *Das Christentum im Weltanschauungskampf der Gegenwart* (3 ed., Leipzig, 1919). H.H.

huppah: Hebrew term for bridal chamber (Ps. 19:6; Joel 2:16). Originally the chamber in which the bride received the groom for the consummation of their marriage, it has come to be a portable canopy, consisting of a square covering of silk, satin or other cloth, stretched across four poles, which are either fixed in the ground or held by attendants, under which the wedding ceremony is solemnized according to traditional Jewish practice. (Cf. Isa. 4:5). S.S.C.

Hus, John: (1369-1415) The leader of the Czech Reform. Studied at the University of Prague, where he became acquainted with the philosophical writings of John Wyclif*. Later he studied his theological works, and gradually became the leader of the Czech Reform movement, since he was the preacher at Bethlehem Chapel, its chief center. He was a moderate and always critical Wyclifite, never sharing some of the most important tenets of Wyclif. He became involved in a conflict with Archbishop Zbynek over the papal schism, he adhering to Pope Alexander V, while Zbynek at first held to Pope

Gregory. Later, he lost the support of King Václav by disregarding the latter's prohibition of opposition to the sale of indulgences. In order to save Prague from an interdict, he left the city, and later voluntarily came to the Council of Constance*. But despite the imperial safe conduct, he was imprisoned and accused of the Wyclifiite heresy. Although the great majority of the charges against him were false, he was adjudged guilty of them. He was burned at the stake on July 6, 1415. See Hussitism; Moravian Church.

Matthew Spinka, *John Hus and the Czech Reform* (1941); Count Lützow, *Master John Hus* (London, 1900). M.S.

Husserl, Edmund: (1859-1938) Professor of philosophy at Göttingen and Freiburg. Founder of phenomenology*. In his *Philosophie der Arithmetik* (1891) he tried to base arithmetic on psychology. Later, in his influential *Logische Untersuchungen* (1900-01) he contended powerfully against all psychologisms. In this and his *Ideen,* etc. (1913) he attempts to establish a science of pure experience, based on intuition of essences, which shall refute naturalism by "bracketing" the factual and shall also overcome formalism and rationalism by showing that truth is based on ideal yet concrete *Wesenheiten.* See psychology, schools of.

Other Works: *Formale und Transcendentale Logik* (*Jahrbuch für Philosophie* etc. 1929); *Nachwort zu meinen Ideen* (*ibid.,* 1930); *Méditations cartésiennes* (1931). J.S.B.

Hussitism: The Czech Church Reform movement deriving from John Hus*. There were three main parties in Bohemia claiming spiritual descent from Hus: the most radical were the Taborites*, who went far beyond the teachings of Hus and regarded the Scriptures as their sole rule of faith and practice. Their armies, under John Zizka, proved at first victorious against all opposing forces, domestic and foreign, but were ultimately defeated, at the battle of Lipany (1435), by the combined forces of the Calixtines* and the Czech Catholics. The second group comprised the moderates, called the Calixtines or Utraquists, who by the Compacts* of Prague (1431), granted by the Council of Basel* were allowed certain reforms (especially the communion under both kinds) and were recognized as within the Roman Catholic Church. They perpetuated their separate organization until after the Battle of White Mountain (1620) when their privileges were abrogated along with those of all other Protestants. In a less direct way, the Unity of Brethren may also be included, although the spiritual father of this movement was Peter of Chelcice and the organizer was Brother Gregory.

Count Lützow, *The Hussite Wars* (London, 1909); J. Th. Müller, *Geschichte der böhmischen Brüder,* 2 vols. (Herrnhut, 1922-31). M.S.

Huterite (Bruederhof) communities: See communistic settlements, religious; Mennonites.

Huxley, Thomas Henry: (1825-1895) English biologist. Apart from his strictly technical studies, Huxley influenced 19th century thought by his brilliant exposition and defence of Darwinism. *Evidence as to Man's Place in Nature* (1863), *Lay Sermons, Addresses and Reviews* (1870), *Science and Morals* (1886), and *Evolution and Ethics* (1893) are representative titles. To describe his own theological position he coined the term agnosticism*. See evolution. L.W.C.

Hyacinthe, Fr.: See Loyson.

hybris: (Gr. *hybris*) Insolence or overweening pride, which brings down retribution (némesis) from the gods through blind infatuation (átē), which causes a man to commit some rash act leading to ruin. E.M.N.

Hyde, William Dewitt: (1858-1917) Graduated Harvard, 1879, Andover, 1882.

President and professor of Mental and Moral Philosophy, Bowdoin College, 1885-1917. President Hyde was a penetrative and persuasive teacher and writer on ethics and religion and was notably influential in these fields in the educational world.

Author: *Practical Ethics* (1892); *Practical Idealism* (1897); *Sin and its Forgiveness* (1909); *From Epicurus to Christ* (1904), republished as *The Five Great Philosophies of Life* (1911). J.W.B.

Hyde Lectureship on Foreign Missions, The: Established in 1867 by Henry Hazen Hyde of Boston at Andover Newton Theological School, Newton Centre, Mass. The capital sum is $10,000. Given at irregular intervals the lectures serve to bring to the seminary courses "on Christianity and its World Mission." Among those serving have been: John R. Mott; James L. Barton; Albert W. Palmer; and John A. Mackay.

(Data from the office of the President of the Theological School.) V.F.

Hyksos: An invading body of mixed peoples entering Egypt from Syria in the eighteenth century, B.C.; were expelled from the delta about 1580 B.C. by Ahmose I, founder of the Eighteenth Dynasty. F.L.P.

hylomorphism: See Aristotle; ontology.

hylozoism (Gr. *hulé,* wood or matter, and *zoé,* life) The theory that matter has an inner life of its own ("all things are full of gods," Thales). This view was accepted naively by the Milesians. There are traces of it in the Stoics*. It was later developed by the French materialists of the eighteenth century, who believed that nature could be explained on a completely mechanical basis. Whether as an immanent naturalistic teleology or as a mechanistic theory, it is of theological importance because it tends to make the hypothesis of God unnecessary, in spite of the Stoic identification of matter or the World Soul with God. J.E.N.

hymnals: See hymns.

hymnology: A hymn is a song of praise or prayer to God. Enjoined by the apostles, hymn singing became popular among early Christians. Though largely restricted to the clergy after 600, it led to the creation of vast treasures of hymnody both in the Greek and Latin churches. The Reformers reopened the floodgates of congregational song. Inspired by Luther, Germany achieved leadership in the composition of hymns and melodies. Wherever Calvinistic influence extended (as in England, Scotland, New England), rhymed versions of the psalms* were sung in place of hymns. Ken and Watts (around 1700) and Charles Wesley were the first in the long line of great hymnists in English speaking countries. But every Christian age and country has contributed to the imposing total of half a million hymns.

Article in Schaff-Herzog, *Encyclopedia of Religious Knowledge*. Vol. V. (1909); J. Julian, *Dictionary of Hymnology* (1882. New ed. 1907); Louis Benson, *The Hymnody of the Christian Church* (1927).

E.C.K.

hymns: (Gr. *humnos;* Lat., *hymnus*) Following the Last Supper* of Jesus, having sung praises to God (*humnesantes*) they went out to the Mount of Olives. (Mark 14:26.) From this occasion, which marks the origin of so many Christian traditions, to the present day, the hymn has been an exceedingly important vehicle for the expression and spread of Christian doctrine and devotion. The use of songs of praise is found in early pagan rites as well as in the psalmody of the early Hebrew synagogue. This practice was transferred quite naturally into the early Christian churches. Antiphonal psalmody was employed from the beginning in the Eastern Church.

The magnificent Latin hymnody was begun in the Western church in the period of St. Ambrose* who used the Syrian antiphonal hymn to combat the Arian heresy, much as it was used earlier in the East to combat gnosticism. Ambrosian hymns were the first true Western Christian poetry. They employed plainsong* melodies, but since the poetry was metrical, the music also became metrical without effort. The free rhythmed Gregorian chant* and the metrical hymn developed simultaneously.

A Spanish magistrate, Aurelius Prudentius Clemens, (348-413), wrote many Christian poems which were soon set to music. St. Benedict* about 530 provided in his monastic order that a hymn should be sung for each Office. The hymns of Venantius Fortunatus (530-609), bishop of Poitiers, mark the beginning of the medieval way of thought. They are rich in romantic symbolism, many written in honor of the Cross.

Used as part of the liturgy* there were communion hymns, processional hymns, and sequences. An Irishman, Sechnall, wrote a communion hymn as early as 690. A Carolingian poet, Theowulf, about 821 created a Palm Sunday processional hymn. The great hymn, *Pange lingua gloriosa,* of Fortunatus was also used for this purpose. In the 11th century the traditional sequence to the Alleluia* was replaced by the well-known *Veni sancte Spiritus,* sometimes attributed to Robert the Pious, king of France, who died in 1031. This was extended and developed into the Golden Sequence possibly done by Pope Innocent III but more likely by Stephen Langton, archbishop of Canterbury, 1207-1228. Out of the Easter sequence, *Victimae paschali,* by Wigo of Burgundy, died 1050, grew the medieval miracle and morality plays* and thence the modern drama. Musically there was derived from it the great Lutheran chorale*, *Christ lag in Todesbanden,* employed by Bach in a cantata of the same name. The greatest composer of sequences was conceded to be Adam, canon of St. Victor in Paris. Two other 13th century sequences have become great hymns: the *Dies irae* and the *Stabat mater.*

The essence of the hymn is its direct appeal to the spirit of the people. The declining use of Latin from the 14th century on led to a growing unfamiliarity with the meanings of hymns and to their decreasing usefulness. There was no decline in the production of hymns but a decided lack of quality aggravated by attempts to put the good medieval hymns into classical Latin, which only destroyed their original value. In 1629 Urban VIII had the Jesuits "correct" the hymns. These mutilations were retained as late as the Breviary of 1911.

Hymns in the vernacular appeared long before the reformation. Carols brought into sacred usage from folksong the refreshing dance rhythms which were no longer associated with pagan rites or immorality. Many carols used a mixture of Latin with the vernacular, such as *In dulci jubilo, Puer nobis,* and *O filii et filiae.* The tender spirit St. Francis in the 13th century, which brought a personal Christianity back to the people, gave rise to spontaneous religious song throughout Europe. From the *Laudi spirituali* in Italy came the hymns *Alta Trinita beata* and *Divinum mysterium;* from the Spanish *Cantus mariales* came *Tantum ergo,* used in a magnificent motet by Vittoria; among the French *Noëls* was Picardy; of the *Piae Cantiones* of Germany was *Es ist ein' Ros entsprungen,* set later by Praetorius; from the Bohemian Separatist group came the tune *Ravenshaw.*

The reformation added new impetus to vernacular hymnody. Luther* wrote, "It is my intention to make German Psalms for the people, spiritual songs whereby the word of God may be kept alive in them by singing." Luther himself, recognizing the value of congregational singing, wrote many chorales such as *Ein' feste Burg, Aus tiefer Noth schrei ich zu dir, Vater unser,* and *Vom Himmel hoch.* Heinrich Isaak adapted a popular folk tune to *O Welt, ich muss dich lassen.* The pietist* movement in the 18th century brought forth many more great chorales. The emphasis of Spener and Francke** upon emotional religion and individualism created an atmosphere in which great hymns arose. Paul Gerhardt, composer of the Passion Chorale, is second in importance in German hymnody only to Luther. Zinzendorf*, leader of a separatist movement, brought the German chorale to America where it was established in the Moravian* settlements in Pennsylvania and North Carolina. The loftiest result of pietism in music was the great opus of Johann Sebastian Bach (1685-1750) who made the chorale the center of his art. Not only did he write many original chorales but he used them in his passions, oratorios, cantatas, motets**, and chorale-preludes for organ.

The Huguenot movement was not popular in the French court. Clément Marot, who translated many Psalms into French, was forced to flee his position at the gay court of Francis I. At Geneva he met a follower of Calvin, Theodore Beza*, who completed the versification of the French Psalter. This was set to music by Louis Bourgeois, giving birth to *Old Hundredth, St. Michael,* and *Toulon.* Calvinism, however, imposed a serious restriction upon the growth of hymnody. The texts had to be drawn from the Bible.

In 1539 Miles Coverdale published an English translation of 36 German chorales in an unpopular hymnal, *Goostly Psalmes and Spiritualle Songs.* The early Anglican church prescribed the Calvinist ban upon non-Biblical texts. Thomas Sternhold made a poor English translation of 37 Psalms which pleased Edward VI. The strict rule regarding texts was relaxed under Elizabeth in 1559. *The Whole Booke of Psalmes* of 1562 was made up largely of the translations of Sternhold and Hopkins. In 1623 George Wither published *Hymns and Songs of the Church.* This included three tunes of Orlando Gibbons and was characterized by many good tunes but poor poetry.

The publication of new hymnals has increased in quantity from the 17th century to this. In 1701 Henry Playford published *The Divine Companion* which included hymns of Jeremiah Clark, called the first modern hymn-writer, George Herbert, Richard Crashaw, and William Croft, who contributed St. Anne and Hanover. This also included some translations of Breviary hymns. In 1708 the *Lyra Davidica* included translations from both Latin and German. The music was freer in style than the old Psalm tunes, illustrated by *Jesus Christ is Risen Today.*

The non-conformists contributed heavily to the great English production of hymns. They were much freer with subject matter than their predecessors. Isaac Watts (1674-1748) wrote over 400 hymns still sung, among them *When I Survey the Wondrous Cross* and *O God, Our Help in Ages Past.*

At Charles Town, S. C. in 1737 John Wesley* published *A Collection of Psalms and Hymns,* the first true Anglican hymnal, containing 70 tunes. This was proscribed by the church because it contained non-Biblical texts. After his return to England, Wesley wrote more hymns. At first closely associated with Moravian ideas, he later grew away from them because of their emphasis upon intimate personal emotions and the physical sufferings of Christ. This Moravian tendency in his brother prevented John from using some of Charles' most sentimental hymns. By his spiritual reserve John safeguarded the Wesleyan hymn from sentimental decay.

The melancholy poet, William Cowper (1731-1800), befriended a converted slaveship captain, John Newton, who was a clergyman at Olney. They published the famous Olney Hymns of excellent quality in 1779. As late as 1819 Thomas Cotterill, a vicar of Sheffield, was sued for introducing into his parish an unauthorized hymnal printed by his Moravian friend, James Montgomery, one of the best of the English hymn-poets.

Reginald Heber,* vicar of Hodnet, was exemplary of the new 19th century spirit of romanticism. Familiar with the Olney hymns, he produced many himself, making a collection which included works of most of his prominent predecessors both in English and in translations of Latin, German, and French sources. He was one of the first to unify his service by correlating hymns, scripture and sermon topically. His work, *Hymns written and adapted to the Weekly Church Service of the Year,* was published in 1827, (the year following his death in Calcutta where he spent the last three years of his life as bishop.)

The 19th century has seen several important movements in hymnology: the revival of the Latin hymn and the German chorale in translations, of the neglected carol, and of Gregorian chant. An English priest, John Mason Neale (1818-1866) made a great contribution to hymnology by his edition with Thomas Helmore of *The Hymnal Noted* in 1852 and 1854. This contained 105 Greek and Latin hymns translated and set to the original plainsong.

Many American and British denominations now have excellent recent hymnals.

W. Douglas, *Church Music in History and Practice* (1937); J. Julian, *Dictionary of Hymnology* (1915); G. Grove, *Dictionary of Music and Musicians* (1935), Article on Hymns; *Hymns Ancient and Modern, Historical Edition* (1909). E.H.B.

hymns, Hebrew and Jewish: The Psalms and other sacred songs of the Bible form the hymnal treasury of the Synagogue as well as the models for reconstructed liturgy, following the destruction of the Temple in 70 C.E. The post-Talmudic poems go under the name of *piyyut* (Gr. *poiesis,* poetry). The first of these creations were anonymous. From the 7th century come the distinguished names of Jose ben Jose, Yannai, and Eleazar Kalir. The *devotional* piyyut of Saadia Gaon (d. 942) and of the Spanish-Arabic school of the 10th-12th centuries, reaching its height in the works of Solomon ibn Gabirol, Moses and Abraham ibn Ezra, and Jehudah Halevi, is the lineal descendant of the Psalms. The *didactic* piyyut of Yannai and of Kalir and his followers of the Romano-German rites, like Meshulam ben Kalonymus, Kalonymus ben Jehudah, Gershom ben Jehudah, Shimeon ben Isaac, Joseph Tub Elem, etc., consists largely of versified Rabbinic homilies and even of laws and customs pertaining to various occasions of the year and events in the religious life.

Though produced by some of the foremost men of the Synagogue, the piyyut made its way into the liturgy under great protest, because 1) of its seeming disturbance of the religious spirit and unity of the established service, and 2) of its obscurities of style and cryptic language. Reform Judaism has objected to the piyyutim on theological grounds as well, and has retained only some of the more inspirational ones both in the original and in translations.

Reform Judaism introduced hymns in modern languages into the liturgy. The first collection of such hymns was issued by Israel Jacobson in 1810 (Cassel). The *Hamburg Hymnal* of 1845 enjoyed considerable popularity in Germany and affected the Jewish hymnals which appeared in the U. S. Of these the best known are Isaac S. Moses's *Sabbath School Hymnal* 14th ed. (1920), A. Z. Idelsohn's *Jewish Song Book* 2nd ed. (1929), and the *Union Hymnal,* published by the Central Conference of Amer. Rabbis, 3rd ed. (1932).

The fullest index of the sacred song of the Synagogue is I. Davidson's *Thesaurus of Mediaeval Hebrew Poetry,* 4 vols. (1924-33) (about 35,000 entries, many of them secular). A. Z. Idelsohn's *Thesaurus of Hebrew Oriental Melodies,* 10 vols. (1914-33), presents several thousand texts (generally first stanzas) and music of hymns and prayers sung in the synagogues and Jewish homes throughout the world. S.S.C.

hyperdulia: See dulia; latria; mariolatry.

hyperousios: See ousia.

hypnosis: See abnormal psychology; psychotherapy; suggestion.

hypocrisy: The act of simulating qualities of personality, moral character, religious convictions or other beliefs which are not actually present in the person or persons assuming that false appearance. While the term hypocrisy is applied in common usage to deliberate dissimulation or intentional insincerity, it may not properly be limited to conscious deception alone. The term may also have consistent, even if unwelcome, reference to man's unconscious distortion of the professed ideal, the unrecognized discrepancies or inconsistencies prevailing between that which man avows in theory and the quality of personality which man demonstrates in practice. H.W.J.

hypostasis: A Greek word of varying meaning: literally, "a support," used in early Christological discussions, first as a synonym for *ousia**, "substance," or "essence," latterly as a term for the divine substance in its personal modes. Thus, the members of the Trinity* came to be called *hypostases,* eternal distinctions within the divine unity. See Cappadocians, the Three. F.G.E.

hypostatical unity: A term employed to denote the union of divine and human natures in the one person (hypostasis) of Christ. It represents a formula worked out by the Council of Chalcedon (451) to reconcile the felt demand for unity in Christ's personality and also its humanity. It affirms that the human and divine natures, though distinct, are united inseparably in Christ. See Christology. Cf. hypostatical unity in impanation*. F.G.E.

hypothesis: Science has projected hypothesis into the spot-light of modern thought, but in fact the thought process, at any level, has employed it even long before its identification and recognition as hypothesis. The reason is that thinking itself is an abstractive process whose initial possibility necessitates assumption or hypothesis. Much the same as man's seeing instrument, the eye, sees other objects rather than itself and therefore man naturally slips into unconsciousness of his seeing organ, so in a sense hypothesis implements the origin and beginning of thoughts' processes in which thought tends to move on and likewise to become unconscious of the instrument of its initiation.

In more scientific terms, hypothesis may be said to stand as the initiator of a thought form destined, if it persists, to move on to the stage of theory and finally to that of fact. P.R.H.

hysteria: A functional disorder of unstable and neurotic persons that is usually classified under the psychoneuroses and held to be psychogenic in origin. Among its many symptoms are excessive impressionability, liability to emotional episodes, marked sensory, motor and psychic disturbances, and the unconscious simulation of all sorts of diseases. Among its principal causes are overstrain, emotional shock, faulty synthesis of personality and buried complexes. For two important theories about it consult the writings of P. Janet and S. Freud*. R.W.F.

I

I Am: A religious movement founded by Guy M. Ballard and his wife as a result of certain revelations received from the Ascended Master St. Germain in 1930 at Mt. Shasta in northern California, and subsequently. It attracted a large following during the late 1930's when it held great series of meetings in the larger cities of the United States. The founder died in 1939. Mrs. Ballard and son Donald were later indicted for using the mails to defraud, and an adverse judgment was rendered by the courts. No statistics as to the number of followers are available. Headquarters of the movement are in Los Angeles, California and Mrs. Ballard continues as its head.

The teaching of the movement may be stated briefly as follows.

The Mighty I am Presence, or God is the source of all life and power. There are certain Ascended Masters through whom knowledge of the I am is communicated. Jesus was one; St. Germain is the one through whom the revelation came to Ballard. Until his death he continued to receive communications from St. Germain which were published in *The Voice of the I Am.* Others bear names familiar to occultists. The Ballards styled themselves the accredited messengers. The power of the I Am Presence is always available, but can not be made effective until it is called for by humanity. This is accomplished through a decree. The decrees which, directed to the Ascended Masters release the forces necessary to produce the desired results, take the place of prayer in the I Am groups. Mass decree is the technique employed in group meetings. The entire congregation repeats the decrees, in unison, not in a voice of supplication but demand. These are furnished in the official book of decrees, which express the desire of the group. A great deal of use is made of light and color in the cult.

The teachings of I Am are clearly taken from various sources, particularly theosophy and its beliefs in Mahatmas**.

The chief textbooks of the movement are *Unveiled Mysteries* and *The Magic Presence* (1935) by the founder, under the pen name, Godfre Ray King; *The I AM Discourses* by St. Germain and the *I Am Adorations and Affirmations* by Chanera, all published by the St. Germain Press, Chicago.

C.S.B.

Ibas: (d. 457) Succeeded Rabbulas as Bishop of Edessa* in 435; later charged with Nestorian heresy because of his interest in and translation (into Syriac, the language of the Persian Church) of certain writings of Theodore of Mopsuestia*; deposed by the Council of Ephesus in 449; reinstated by the Council of Chalcedon in 451. His famous letter to the Persian bishop, Maris, was condemned (one of "The Three Chapters"*) by Justinian and by the Fifth Ecumenical Council (553). See Syrian churches.

E.T.R.

Iblis or Eblis: (Arabic *Iblis* from Greek *diabolos,* devil) The prince of fallen angels, who was turned into a devil for refusing to worship Adam at God's command. The Moslem equivalent for Satan*.

P.E.J.

Ibn-Gabriol, Soloman Ben Judah: (1021-1058) Jewish Spanish poet and philosopher, also known as Avicebron. Author of *Fons Vitae* (in Hebrew, *Mekor Chaim*), a philosophical discourse which helped revive the Neo-Platonic tradition in Christian Europe. *Fons Vitae* did not reveal the author's religion and he was long mistaken for a Christian scholastic. Gabriol's liturgical poems became the model for many Spanish Hebrew poets. His *Keter Malkut,* (Royal Crown), a philosophical ethical hymn reiterating the ideas expressed in *Fons Vitae,* was included in the synagogue ritual. Also written up under Avicebron; Gabirol.

B.Z.B.

Icarian settlements: See communistic settlements, secular.

I Ching: See Chinese Terminology.

icon: (From the Greek *eikon,* an "image" or "representation") It is used, especially in the eastern orthodox churches, of a painting, bas-relief, or mosaic of Christ, the Virgin Mary, or a saint. These images are venerated by the faithful. After a vigorous controversy over their use during the eighth and ninth centuries, their use was finally made legitimate, but the Nestorian* church opposes their use. See images.

C.T.C.

iconoclastic controversy: See images.

iconography: (Gr. *eikon,* a likeness, image, portrait) As an ecclesiastical term it refers to images, mosaics and paintings used as church decoration. F.T.P.

iconodulism: See images.

Id: See psychology, schools of.

ideal: (Lat. *idealis,* fr. Gr. *idea*) 1) A norm or standard of perfection (such as a Platonic Idea, a moral law, a principle of aesthetics, or the idea of God); a conception of what ought to be. An ideal as such is contrasted with a value. An ideal is not a value unless it is realized in actual experience. Hence the expression "objectivity of values" should be supplanted by "objectivity of ideals." 2) A plan of action; "a chosen end . . . for which other ends are sacrificed. 3) In Kant, "the Ideal of Pure Reason" is the idea of something absolutely necessary, determined throughout by mere idea, an inclusive concept (*Inbegriff*) of the whole of reality, not to be hypostatized as existing (see CPR, B, 594, 434-435, 602, 607, 610). 4) As an adjective: pertaining to ideas in any sense (Platonic or mental); often used in contrast to real. See value. E.S.B.

idealism, epistemological: Contrasted with epistemological realism and epistemological dualism. In general, the theory that the structure of knowledge is such that only consciousness or something inseparably related to consciousness is knowable. It assumes various forms. 1) Subjective idealism: The theory that only the ideas of a particular finite knower can be known by him; equivalent to solipsism*. Also, the theory that all knowable objects belong to one universal subject (Fichte). 2) Transcendental idealism: The Kantian theory that all knowledge refers to phenomena organized by the categories. 3) Absolutistic idealism: That type of epistemological monism for which ultimately all objects are identical with idea; and the ideal of knowledge is one all-inclusive system of ideas. 4) Platonic idealism: In so far as the Platonic Forms or Ideas are objects accessible only to thought and not to sense, Platonism* is a form of epistemological idealism; but because the Forms or Ideas are independent of the knowing mind, Platonism is also called realism. See epistemology.

W. H. Sheldon, *Strife of Systems and Productive Duality* (1918). E.S.B.

idealism, metaphysical: (Gr. idea, form or archetype) Any metaphysical system which holds that ideals belong to the objective structure of the universe and that mind (or something like mind) is the source and type of all real being. Antonyms: materialism, naturalism, realism.

Note: These historical antonyms are now being used in senses less antithetical to idealism than formerly. Dialectical materialism, for example, and Dewey's naturalism have much in common with Hegelianism*. The naturalism* of J. B. Pratt is personalism* of a kind, while that of H. N. Wieman is theistic (if impersonal). Vergilius Ferm has recently come out in defense of an "idealistic naturalism." (See bibliography: article: naturalism and theology. Also see "Varieties of Naturalism", Vergilius Ferm, *First Adventures in Philosophy* (1936), pp. 210 ff. and *passim.*) Much realism is akin to idealism at many points (cf. S. Alexander, R. W. Sellars, W. P. Montague). See B. Bosanquet, *The Meeting of Extremes in Contemporary Philosophy* (1921).

Historically there are four main types of idealism: 1) *The Platonic.* Plato is often called a realist on the ground that his Ideas are independent of mind, whether human or divine; but because he combines objectivity of ideal values with a personal theism, he is the great founder of idealism (perhaps anticipated by Anaxagoras). 2) *The Berkeleian.* Berkeley taught that all reality is of the nature of consciousness, consisting of ideas (passive and inert) and spirit (active). The *esse* of nature is not material, but perceptual; it consists only of ideas which the Divine Spirit gives to human spirits. 3) *The Hegelian.* The coherence of one absolute system, an individual whole, is the ground and explanation of everything. The *Idee,* as Hegel calls it, is an Absolute Spirit. 4) *The Lotzean.* For Lotze, selfhood or personality is the ultimate metaphysical fact. Everything that is is either a self or some aspect, process, part, or relation of a self or selves.— These four types (except perhaps Platonism) are also found in Indian, and to some extent in Chinese, thought.

The Platonic type may be called axiological; the Berkeleian, mentalistic or subjective; the Hegelian, organic, absolute, or objective; and the Lotzean, personalistic. These four types are not sharply distinguished from each other, and the chief systems of idealism combine traits from all four. Idealists like Bradley emphasize the Hegelian at the expense of the other three types; so, to some extent, do Bosanquet, Creighton, Barrett, and Robinson. In J. S. Bixler, the Platonic is dominant, although place is found for the others. All four types are merged and unified in the thought of idealists like W. R. Sorley, A. S. Pringle-Pattison, B. P. Bowne, J. Royce, M. W. Calkins, H. Münsterberg, W. E. Hocking, and J. S. Moore.

See Platonism, Hegelianism, Personalism, Berkeley, Lotze. See also ontology.

J. Royce, *The Spirit of Modern Philosophy* (1892); R. F. A. Hoernlé, *Idealism as a Philosophy* (1927); E. S. Brightman, *A Philosophy of Ideals* (1928); W. E. Hocking, *Types of Philosophy* (1929); A. C. Ewing, *Idealism: A Critical Survey* (1934); B. Blanshard, *The Nature of Thought* (1939). E.S.B.

idealism, practical: Devotion to ideals*, especially to social ideals. Independent of epistemological and metaphysical idealism, although most metaphysical idealists are also practical idealists (e.g., Plato and Hegel). E.S.B.

idealism, subjective: See Berkeley, George; epistemology; idealism, epistemological.

Idealistic School, Buddhist: See Buddhist Terminology.

idolatry: The worship of a physical object, usually an artifact, as god. It may refer to the worship of alien divinities, or to the adoration of what is seen and tangible as opposed to the invisible spiritual being, or to the excessive veneration of any human creation instead of the one true creator god. See sin. R.W.F.

idols and images: An idol is a representation of a deity in symbolic or human form, adored or worshiped as a tangible manifestation of the divine presence. Idols are images* but many images are not worshiped. Some are amulets effective through their own inherent qualities: others are fetishes made effective by an indwelling spirit. Pictured or sculptured images of saints, of events in the history of a religion, or in the life of the founder appearing in religious structures often serve the purposes of instruction or inspiration; they may or may not be worshiped. Images, but not idols, are such forms as the models of servants and companions buried with the dead in Egypt, China and Japan, or the portrait statue of the dead man indwelt by his *Ka** in the Egyptian tomb. Images of ancestors may be revered, or used as fetishes, or if the ancestors have attained divinity, worshiped as idols. On the border line between image and idol are the statues of the Jain Masters and of Confucius who were revered as great teachers rather than as gods.

Idols and images in human form are a late product of culture. The nature deities of early religions were tangible and visible realities and needed no symbolic representation. A material form was required to localize the presence of an invisible spirit. When the gods became spirits* their presence was associated first with tangible symbols—sun, moon, a lightning-shattered oak, a pillar of wood or stone, a phallus, a cairn, a mirror, a bird or an animal. The symbol usually had some relation to the activity or character of the god. Art worked first at the perfecting of the symbols and then turned to the representation of the gods in human form, retaining their symbols as attributes. Sometimes a ceremony was necessary to make the image come alive with the indwelling presence of the god. The effort to portray the powers of the various deities produced some fantastic idols in Hinduism and Buddhism.

The religions of Babylonia and Egypt* treated the idols as real embodiments of the gods. Hinduism and Buddhism** made large use of idols as aids to popular devotion although the intellectuals knew that no image, not even a mental image, could represent the divine reality. The religion of Israel* used images for many centuries until the struggle with neighboring cults led to a fanatical official rejection of them. Christianity created countless images but officially condemns idolatry. Since the destruction of the idols of Mecca by Mohammed*, Islam* has forbidden their use. Zoroastrianism* never represented deity in human form. See charms and amulets; fetishism. A.E.H.

Igigi: (Babylonian) Term for the gods of heaven, collectively; gods embodied in those stars which are above the horizon at any one time; gods embodied in stars that dip below the horizon are in the underworld and known collectively as *Anunnaki.* F.L.P.

Ignatius of Antioch: Traditional third bishop of Syrian Antioch (Eusebius, *H. E.* iii, 36, 2), believed to have been martyred at Rome during the reign of Trajan. During his trip from Antioch to Rome he wrote seven letters now included among the Apostolic Fathers, *viz.*, Ephesians, Magnesians, Trallians, Romans, Philadelphians, Smyrneans, and to Polycarp. In all of them two notes are dominant: 1. respect for the authority of the bishops of the several congregations; 2. a protest and warning against Docetism*, which denied reality to the sufferings of Jesus. The letter to the Romans is a passionate plea to the local Christians not to prevent (through mistaken kindness) his long anticipated martyrdom in the arena. In all of the letters the Christians addressed are urged to encourage Antioch to rally after her great loss. Two other versions—usually styled the "long recension" and the "Syriac abridgement"—are extant, but have little claim to originality. The authenticity of the traditional seven, although widely accepted, is not entirely free from difficulties. If genuine, the letters are important evidence as to the early rise of what may be called the "monarchical episcopate", and to the caution and restraint showed by Rome in the matter of martyring Christians. See clergy. The most convenient edition of the letters is K. Lake's *The Apostolic Fathers,* Vol. I (Loeb Classical Library, 1913). M.S.E.

ignorance: Partial or complete lack of knowledge. In law ignorance of the law does not, in general, excuse from responsibility for the consequences of one's acts. In ethics Socrates* held that virtue is knowledge and vice ignorance. This doctrine omits the role of will and habit in conduct. In matters moral and religious ignorance may be involuntary and unavoidable, or voluntary and removable. The former is called invincible ignorance and excuses from culpability in the Roman Catholic Church. The latter is called vincible ignorance and is sin. R.W.F.

ignorance, divine: See omniscience.

Ihmels, Ludwig Heinrich: (1858-1933) He was Lutheran professor of theology in Erlangen and Leipzig, and bishop of Saxony. Faith was for him not based upon dogma, but upon the revelation of God which consists in acts. Hence the certainty of the Christian is certainty of faith. Although he veered toward bible theology and Ritschlianism*, he nevertheless assigned to dogma and creed normative significance for theology.

Die Selbstständigkeit der Dogmatik gegenüber der Religionsphilosophie (Leipzig, 1900); *Die christliche Wahrheitsgewissheit, ihr letzter Grund und ihre Entstehung* (Leipzig, 1901); *Die Bedeutung des Autoritätsglaubens* (Leipzig, 1902); *Theonomie und Autonomie im Lichte der christlichen Ethik* (Leipzig, 1903); *Centralfragen der Dogmatik in der Gegenwart* (Leipzig, 1911); *Das Christentum Luthers in seiner Eigenart* (Leipzig, 1917). H.H.

I H S: There are the first three letters of the Greek word *Iesous,* when it is spelled in capital letters. Since H was later mistaken for a capital h, it was given the erroneous interpretation *Jesus Hominum Salvator,* "Jesus, the Savior of Men." In fact, it is simply an abbreviation of the name Jesus which served as a symbol for him. See fish as symbol; symbolism. Cf. labarum. C.T.C.

ijma: (Arabic *iima,* agreement) Agreement among the learned of Islam is the principle whereby religious beliefs become articles of faith. The plural *ijmaa* means the collective body of these decisions, making up the orthodox tradition. "My people shall never be unanimous in error", said Mohammed. P.E.J.

Ikhnaton: (Egyptian) King of Egypt, Amenhotep IV (c. 1375-1358 B.C.) who established the worship of Aton, the visible sun disc, as the religion of Egypt, displacing Amon, god of Thebes; took the name Ikhnaton ('spirit of Aton'); built temples, composed hymns, and established ceremonies for Aton; soon after his death Amon* worship was restored and the work of the reformer was destroyed. F.L.P.

illegitimacy: The act of giving birth to a child out of wedlock. Ordinarily the child conceived out of wedlock is the consequence of illicit sexual relations although in some cultures, sexual intercourse is looked upon as a normal part of courtship and conception is regarded as a guarantee of the potential fertility of the marriage*. Under these circumstances, the marriage is consummated and the position of the child is no different from those born in wedlock. More commonly, however, both the illegitimate child and its mother lose caste. In general within recent occidental culture the humanitarian movement has tended to mitigate the severity of treatment accorded both the illegitimate child and its mother as symbolized in the substitution of the terms, "illegitimate child" for bastard, "born out of wedlock" for illegitimacy, and "unmarried mother" for the illegitimate mother. Nevertheless in the United States it is a widespread practice for pregnant unmarried women to leave their local communities to give birth to their children in the privacy of a strange locale or in institutions which specialize in providing care for such persons. Not infrequently the child is then placed for adoption and reared by foster parents. Some states require that the father if known support his illegitimate child but he is not compelled to give it his name. The rural mores often sanction the compulsion of marriage between the two persons and these have become known colloquially as "shot-gun" marriages.

Kingsley Davis, "Illegitimacy and the Social Structure," *American Journal of Sociology,* vol. XLV (September, 1939), pp. 215-233; Percy G. Kammerer, *The Unmarried Mother* (1918); Ernest R. Mowrer, *Disorganization: Personal and Social* (1942); Ruth Reed, *The Illegitimate Family in New York City* (1934).
E.R.M.

Illuminati: A name applied to groups claiming to have special enlightenment, religious or intellectual. There are traces of Illuminati in Spain in the sixteenth century, and Ignatius Loyola was warned against association with them. There were groups in France that used the title, though often wholly distinct from one another. In Germany in the late eighteenth century, a society, half religious, half political, spread widely, but collapsed under persecution. G.R.C.

illusion: A sense perception which does not give the true character of the object or action perceived. Whether due to mistaken judgment about sense data or to erroneous perception is debatable. It is to be distinguished from hallucination in which the external sense stimulus is lacking. There are normal illusions of ordinary perception and pathological illusions that characterize insanity. Religious ascetics and mystics by virtue of their temperament or longing are believed to be easily subject to illusions. The term is sometimes applied to that non-literal ingredient of religious belief which consists of symbolical construction or imaginative interpretation placed upon a core of real fact or valid insights in order to communicate, vivify and drive home the essential truth of the belief. R.W.F.

image of God: According to Genesis 1:26. Adam was created "in the image of God." The reference here is evidently to spiritual resemblance alone, the gift of self-conscious reason, a faint adumbration of the supreme reason of God. This image does not belong only to man in his state of primeval innocence but is transmitted to Adam's descendants (*ibid.* 5:13). Whoever destroys a man does violence to God's image (*ibid.* 9.6).

Critical view: The term "image of God" calls up the highly controversial question of whether the Hebrews at any time worshiped an actual image of YHWH. Many scholars have held that the golden calf of Aaron and those set up by Jeroaboam, as well as the idol of Micah, Gideon's "ephod", etc., are all evidence of iconic worship of YHWH. But all this rejects the unanimous testimony of Israelite tradition. The written sources, plus the completely negative results of excavation indicate that the Mosaic religion was from the beginning aniconic and that material representations were foreign to its spirit from the beginning. L.F.—H.K.

images: The controversy which broke out in the Byzantine Empire* over the worship of images (or icons) is known as the Iconoclastic Controversy. It began in 725 with the prohibition of image worship by Emperor Leo III. The church both East and West opposed the edict, Pope Gregory II denouncing iconoclasm as a heresy (727); Patriarch Germanus of Constantinople was deprived of his see. The most important of the Eastern iconodules (image worshipers) was St. John of Damascus* who denied the Emperor's right to legislate in dogmatic matters. The struggle continued during the reign of Emp. Constantine V (741-775), but during the regency of Irene terminated with the victory for image worshipers. At the Seventh Ecumenical Council (787) it was decreed that images should be venerated but not adored.

But the struggle broke out anew in the reign of Emperor Leo V (813-20), who made the supreme effort to impose iconoclasm upon the church. The chief defender of iconodulism was Theodore of Studion* . However, this attempt failed again, this time in the regency of Theodora. She convoked a Council in 843 which restored the worship of images. Since that time it became the chief feature of the Orthodox type of piety. The event is celebrated to this day in The Festival of Orthodoxy. Cf. Caroline Books; icon; relic.

E. J. Martin, *A History of the Iconoclastic Controversy* (London, n.d.); A. A. Vasiliev, *History of the Byzantine Empire,* 2 vols. (1928). M.S.

images and idols: See idols and images.

imam or imaum: (Arabic *imam,* leader; from *amma,* to go before or precede) The officiating priest of a Moslem mosque. Also a title given to various Moslem leaders, such as the Caliph*, chiefs, the founders of the four orthodox sects, or a leading author on any subject. See Mohammedanism. P.E.J.

imitation in religion: (Lat. *imitatio*) The repetition of a behavior pattern observed in another person, or persons, in whom one is interested. Such interested perception tends automatically to issue in similar action unless inhibited by conflicting habit or critical judgment. Imitation is particularly characteristic of childhood, although not restricted to it. Together with suggestibility, it is the conservative or traditionalizing factor in community life. The individual tends, consciously or unconsciously, to copy the accepted behavior modes of his society and, in so doing, to acquire the associated attitudes and feelings. Learning by imitation is an important factor in character building and is an essential preliminary to the development of moral insight. In general, moral qualities and religious attitudes are most deeply rooted in persons in whom imitation of such qualities and attitudes began in early childhood. E.T.R.

Imitation of Christ: This is a classic of Christian devotional literature which has appeared in more than a thousand editions, has been translated into every common language, and apart from the Bible is the most widely read Christian book. The book is rich in counsel on the path of growth in the spiritual life*. It is unflinching in its insistence that *The Royal Road of the Holy Cross* can only be taken by those who are prepared to suffer with Christ, and that nothing short of the inevitable tribulation which a break with the lusts of this world will bring can serve to "scour off the rust of my defects." Although Thomas a Kempis (1380-1471) of Windesheim in Holland issued the book under his name in 1441, its authorship has long been in dispute. Albert Hyma (*Christian Renaissance,* 1925) maintains that a Kempis only assembled and worked over the writings of early members of the Brethren of the Common Life* such as Ketel, Zerbolt and Florentius Radwyn. Joseph Malaise (*The Following of Christ,* 1937) on the basis of the famous Lubeck mss., discovered in 1921; has presented the most convincing case for the *Imitation* being taken principally from the *Spiritual Diary of Gerard Groote,* the founder of the Brethren of the Common Life of which Thomas a Kempis was a member. See Groote. D.V.S.

immaculate conception: (Lat. *immaculata,* unspotted, sinless; and *conceptio,* conception) The doctrine that by Christ's merits and in view of the fact that she was to be his mother, the Blessed Virgin Mary* was from the moment of her conception in St. Anne's womb kept free from original sin. See Confessions, Formal of the Christian Church; Sixtus IV, Pope; Peter Aureoli; Pius IX. L.R.W.

immanence: (Lat. *in manere,* dwell in) In general philosophical usage the word refers to a) an activity when it produces its effect from within the patient, or b) an entity when its being *within* something else contributes to the existence of that thing. Immanence may be complete or partial, but the concept represents a protest against ultimate dualism or pluralism, and transitive causality.

In theology the term refers either to complete or to partial identification of God* with the world. The absolute immanence of God in the universe means pantheism*. The absolute independence of God from the world once created means deism*. The theistic tradition, mediating for metaphysical and moral reasons, posits a God immanent in the world but not exhausted in it (transcendent).

The manner of immanence has reflected both metaphysical differences and changes in scientific conceptions, ranging from resemblance, participation, and persuasion (Plato), to emanation, creation, degradation, evolution, organicity, and emergence. Some recent trends emphasize the importance of the world to God's development. See theism; transcendence. Cf. Fiske, John.

"Immanence" by A. C. McGiffert in J. Hastings, *Enc. of Rel. and Ethics.* P.A.B.

immediacy: (Lat. *in medius,* middle) Psychological and Epistemological.

Psychological immediacy is the condition in which the object of awareness is directly present to the mind. It contrasts with the reflective interpretation of the object, or knowledge-about.

Epistemological immediacy characterizes knowledge about reality (or the nature of the psychological object) gained without mediation, either as self-evident, or without resort to inference and interpretation.

An epistemological dualist, as opposed to the monist, holds that the psychological immediacy of the object does not involve epistemological immediacy, whether natural or mystical experience be in question. For example, God, or his agency, may be psychologically immediate without necessarily justifying the claim of the mystic that knowledge of God is epistemologically immediate. See datum; epistemology.

F. R. Tennant, *Philosophical Theology*, 2 vols. (1928, 1930); J. M. Moore, *Theories of Religious Experience* (1938). P.A.B.

immersion: Baptism* by complete submersion in water, as distinguished from affusion* (or aspersion) and infusion; the mode practised in the early church and certain modern religious bodies as the Eastern Orthodox, the Baptists, the Disciples of Christ**, and numerous sects. See trine immersion. W.M.B.

immortality, arguments for and against: As the term is employed in this article, immortality means the everlasting duration of the individual human personality. This definition admits a number of conceptions of personality, but is intended to imply some self-recognized continuity of purpose and memory from the present life into the future. See immortality, kinds of.

A. Some Popular but Uncritical Arguments.

1. *Consensus gentium.* The argument that immortality must be true because belief in it has always been universal among normal human beings is refuted by two considerations: a) that the belief has not been held by all normal men (unless an *ad hoc* definition of "normal" be adopted); and b) that even if belief had been so nearly universal until now as is claimed, that would not prove the belief true. The belief in an earth-centered physical universe would have been better supported by this argument in, let us say, the year 1000, than is belief in immortality now. But the geocentric theory was, nevertheless, false.

2. Origins of belief. It is often pointed out that in the individual child belief in a future life originates in teaching or "conditioning" by the home or church, both of which have often been subject to error. Similarly, it is said that primitive men first came to believe in the soul's survival of death by observing the apparent independence of the body shown by the soul in dreams. Now, it is argued, we have disclosed the real causes of the doctrine, in the individual and the race. Other evidences are in truth only rationalizations of a prior faith. Since the causes themselves are not adequate ground for the doctrine, it is therefore bared as a primitive and childish superstition. To such argument it may be replied that the doctrines of survival held by savages and children are as radically unlike the beliefs held by intelligent and mature men as astrology is unlike the astronomy which evolved from it, and equally irrelevant to the truth of the more mature views. Moreover, many a true conclusion has been drawn from false premises, as every logician knows.

3. Traditional associations of belief. Much contemporary doubt of immortality is affected by immoral and irrational ideas long associated with it, such as the notions of literal golden pavements in Heaven, and of infant damnation. Such associations have, obviously, no bearing on the truth of doctrines not including nor implying them.

4. Effect of desire on belief. Many persons who believe in immortality find their faith pleasant and comforting. It is therefore concluded by some uncritical minds that all so-called arguments for immortality must actually be instances of mere wishful thinking. But probably most men who expect to receive salary checks near the first of next month have good reasons for their expectation and the fact that they enjoy the prospect is quite irrelevant to the question of truth. Whether the reasons for belief in immortality are also good reasons must be determined by examining them, not by observing the emotions which accompany belief.

5. Supposed selfishness of belief. Some objectors think that belief in endless life is selfish. Probably some such belief is accompanied by selfish purposes. But surely belief in the immortality of others is not selfish. Moreover, it is hard to see why faith in a life after death is more selfish than belief in life after tonight's sleep. Whether either belief is selfish or not depends on the kind of life one purposes to live, not on its length.

6. Difficulties of describing a future life. More serious is the objection that no believer can accurately describe the life to come so that it can be presented in vivid detail to the imagination. Despite the sublime allegories of Bunyan, Dante, and the Apocalypse, the contention is doubtless true. Yet there are many of our present experiences which are fundamentally spiritual, as pure mathematics, prayer, moral aspiration, and the love of a kindred spirit. None of these can be presented to the sensory imagination, but all are real and rich in meaning. All may be conceived as continuing after death if consciousness persists. As for the means of communication beyond the grave, we cannot now predict them. But neither could a pre-existing human mind have predicted our present bodies nor their physical environment.

B. The Platonic Arguments. Famous in the history of theology but unimportant for present evaluation of the doctrine of immortality are the following arguments of Plato*:

1. When one kind of being generates its opposite, the former will in turn be generated by the latter. Therefore, as day generates night and night day, so life generates death but death will likewise generate life. Plato's principle is based on a few selected instances and does not hold true universally. E.g., fire "generates" cold ashes, but cold ashes do not generate fire.

2. The soul is by definition the life principle. A dead soul would, accordingly, be a contradiction in terms, like a cold fire. This is true. No such thing as a dead soul can exist. But it is not logically impossible that a soul may cease to be anything at all, or may become some being other than soul.

3. Since the soul knows the eternal Ideas, it shares their eternity to the extent of being everlasting in time, though not, like them, timeless. If one does not accept Plato's doctrine of Ideas, he will not be convinced, and even if he does believe in the eternal Ideas, he may insist that a

mere knowing of them no more implies a sharing in their immortality than does the participation in them exemplified in a destructible tree or stone.

4. The soul is simple and therefore not subject to dissolution. But it is questionable in exactly what sense the soul is simple. Moreover, some simple elements, such as sensations, do cease to be.

5. The soul is a self-mover. Since it provides its own motion and its motion is its very life and being, it will never die. But the most hardy exponent of free will today would scarcely go so far as to assert that the human soul has never received any impulsion from any other source whatsoever. If any impulsion has been received it may be that without the continuance, at intervals, of such impulsions, the soul will run down like an unwound clock. Moreover, this argument implies infinite pre-existence with all its difficulties. (See pre-existence.)

6. There is evidence in our present life that the human soul did not begin in time, but has always been in existence. If the soul did not begin it probably will not end. But the evidence for pre-existence is not convincing and there are serious objections. (See pre-existence.) However, when the critics argue further, that if the soul has begun in time it will also end they seem to be on uncertain ground. The series of positive integers has a beginning but no end. We have no way of knowing that every temporal series with a beginning has also an end.

C. Main Arguments Against Immortality.

1. Lack of sensory evidence. The souls of the dead are neither observed to depart from the bodies nor discovered by the senses to be in existence afterward. Since in a scientific age evidence of the senses must be demanded in support of every hypothesis, the lack of such evidence is, in many minds, a fatal blow to the doctrine of immortality. To this positivistic argument, two replies may conceivably be made. Both, in fact, have been set forth. First, it is insisted that the senses do bear witness to immortality as a fact. Orthodox Christians believe that Jesus was observed by the senses of the disciples, to be alive and active after his death. Even if this testimony were accepted by doubters, they might ask whether the survival of death by one professedly superhuman soul proved the immortality of other, merely human souls. But most doubters would question the historical evidence. The believer's reply to both questions would usually take the form of an appeal to the authority* of revelation. Whether such an appeal is valid is a problem to be examined later. But it is not an appeal to sensory evidence such as the positivist demands. Many persons would answer the positivist by adducing the evidence from psychic research*. But this evidence could at best prove only the survival of death, not an everlasting survival. Actually, while some well-attested psychic phenomena do give some evidence of ways of knowing unacceptable to traditional modern psychology, there seems to be little reason for supposing that these ways must involve the agency of departed human spirits. The second reply to the positivist is that many hypotheses not subject to sensory evidence are nevertheless well supported. Especially is this true of the present existence of human consciousness. If there were no evidence of any kind, it is admitted, belief would be indefensible, but the evidence need not be of a sensory character.

2. The psychophysiological objection. The most important evidence against immortality is the intimate relation between body and mind, which makes it difficult to believe that consciousness can endure after the death of the body. The conclusiveness of this argument depends on the belief that consciousness is a mere function of the brain, dependent upon the brain not only for its present mode of being and of communication with other minds, but also for its very existence. For this doctrine evidence is lacking. Many beings which, while in relation with others, are profoundly affected by them, are nevertheless capable of existing without them. Thus, a child's whole mind may be so completely controlled by a moving picture he is seeing that one might expect his consciousness to cease when the picture is at an end. But instead it is simply shifted to a new set of relations. If materialism is true, of course immortality is impossible. But so also is present consciousness and the meaningful quest of truth. If idealism is true, then the body itself is a system of experiences of minds and one might then reasonably expect it to be replaced at death, by other experiences. The true interpretation of the relation of body and mind cannot be established by scientific observation but is dependent upon one's whole world view.

D. Main Arguments For Immortality.

1. Arguments from intuition and revelation. Intuitions differ. Some persons profess to know intuitively that immortality is true, others with equal immediacy that it is false. Any adequate criteria for judging such intuitions would seem to depend upon further judgment as to the relation between various kinds of character and the fundamental meaning of the world. If one accepts theism then he may reasonably give considerable weight to the reported spiritual insights of saintly and intelligent men whom he has reason to think fitting vehicles of divine revelation. Without belief in God, such evidence will have little importance.

2. Pragmatic and moral arguments. It is often argued that the effects of faith in the future life are so salutary as to afford good evidence of the truth of this belief. To be sure, some effects have been bad, such as the cruelties of the Inquisition, the self-torture of Mohammedan fakirs, and such other-worldly preoccupation as to encourage toleration of human misery and injustice here. But these effects do not result from the more intelligent and ethical views. The latter views do, on the other hand, support such courage, hope, and comfort in peril and sorrow, and give such a sense of permanence and dignity to intellectual, aesthetic, educational, religious, and moral achievement as to be of incalculable pragmatic worth. But how do we know that a belief which

is so deeply and widely useful is also true. There seems to be ground for such faith only if truth about reality is inherently harmonious with our own highest aspirations, as it is if theism is true. Kant's moral argument for immortality as an ethical postulate depends on a similar belief in the relevance of duty to truth.

3. Rationality of the universe. All the achievements of modern science are founded on belief in the fundamental rationality of the world. Give up this postulate and all our vast system of inferences from present data to future and distant events falls like a house of cards. But if immortality is not true, then we are confronted with a strange irrationality. After an age-long evolution of ever more complex beings, there has been produced at last a creature whose worth is beyond question because he experiences his own worth and evaluates all things by ideals which enable him to unlock the secrets of nature itself. He cannot always live here. (See immortality, kinds of: Social Influence.) If this life is all there is for him then all of this long evolutionary process will finally come to naught, just when victory—the creation of something of value in and to itself—has been achieved. Is this what one would expect of a world so thoroughly rational as the world of modern thought and scientific achievement? It must be noted that this argument depends upon the conviction that the world is not only rational in its mechanical constancy but also in its fidelity to purpose. Many philosophers have believed that the mechanical constancy affirmed by scientific faith could not be explained without belief also in a fundamental purposive rationality, such as theism asserts. But again we find that without appeal to a theistic world-view, the evidence for immortality would be unconvincing. On the other hand, if theism is accepted, then not only this and some other evidences already cited give valid support to the doctrine of immortality, but there are also certain additional arguments which may now be briefly presented.

4. The Goodness of God.

a. If God is good, then He wills to conserve value, since even a minimum definition of goodness would imply at least that much. But if man is doomed to annihilation, then all the value achieved by men of all the ages will one day cease to be. If a good God would permit that it would be only because He was powerless to prevent it. The power He has displayed in the creation of man and the world would seem clearly adequate to prevent such a final catastrophe.

b. If this life is all, then many lives will end in peculiarly unjust conditions. The problem of injustice in the distribution of pains and pleasures in this life is, at best, a difficult one for the theist. But without the belief in immortality it will be completely insoluble. (For further discussion of the problem of just compensation for sin and virtue, see: rewards and punishments.)

c. Some persons enter upon this life with great promise of fine achievement. But environmental obstacles, disease, and accident seem, with terrible consistency to obstruct every aspiration, until death intervenes. Will a good God let such careers stop there? Or will He provide new media of work and growth?

d. The holiest of saints, the most learned of scientists, and the most gifted of artists are most keenly aware of the distance their finest efforts fall short of the goals set in their hearts. If theism is true, God has given to man an infinite task. If for this infinite task He has given only a finite time, then just when His most faithful children are seeking in deepest humility to obey His divine commission He sweeps them away into utter annihilation. To call such a being good would be a contradiction of terms.

Seldom has theism been held by enlightened thinkers without an accompanying belief in immortality. The above considerations indicate the reason. The two doctrines are so inextricably bound together by logical implication that either one without the other is precarious and incomplete. See annihilationism; immortality, conditional; immortality, kinds of; Ingersoll lectures; pre-existence; resurrection; rewards and punishments; soul, time; transmigration.

See W. F. Barrett, *Psychical Research* (1912); H. Bergson, *Matter and Memory* (1911); J. S. Bixler, *Immortality and the Present Mood* (1931); E. S. Brightman, *Immortality in Post-Kantian Idealism* (1925); J. W. Dunne, *The New Immortality* (1939); V. Ferm, *First Chapters in Religious Philosophy* (1937); G. Galloway, *The Idea of Immortality* (1919); H. Höffding, *Philosophy of Religion* (1906); W. James, *Human Immortality* (1897); R. Jones, *Spirit in Man* (1941); C. Lamont, *The Illusion of Immortality* (1935); W. P. Montague, *The Chances of Surviving Death* (1934); J. Royce, *The Conception of Immortality* (1900); R. A. Tsanoff, *The Problem of Immortality* (1924).

L.H.DE W.

immortality, conditional: Everlasting personal existence, conceived as a spiritual achievement or privilege of some human selves, rather than an inherent property or divinely given right of all.

The chief arguments urged in favor of this view are as follows: 1) Many passages of the Bible support it, e.g., Prov. 12:28; Matt. 10:28; John 3:16; 11:26; Rom. 2:7; I Tim. 6:16; I John 2:17. 2) Some of the Church Fathers stated the conditional view. Especially important are passages from Justin Martyr (*Trypho*, 4-6), Theophilus of Antioch (*Ad Autolycum,* ii, 37), Irenaeus (*Adversus Haereses,* 34), and Arnobius (*Disputationes Adversus Gentes*, ii, 14, 16, 62, etc.). 3) The annihilation of the wicked would be more in accord with the divine mercy and goodness than the everlasting punishment affirmed by traditional doctrines of Christianity and many other religions. 4) The most convincing philosophical arguments for immortality presuppose the intrinsic value of the human soul. There is, accordingly, little or no evidence for belief in the immortality of those souls which are not valuable to themselves nor to others. 5) Conditionalism would affirm a principle of the survival of the fittest in the spiritual realm coherent with the well-known biological law. 6) Immortality implies the soul's independence of the body. But souls which predominantly sensuous living has made dependent on the body would lack the moral autonomy and other resources of spiritual life to maintain any meaningful existence apart from the body.

The opponents of conditionalism reply: 1) The biblical passages cited by conditionalists depend, for such interpretation, on the understanding of such words as "death" to mean annihilation, and of "life" to mean continued existence. Actually, these words are often used figuratively to connote, respectively, spiritual disaster and blessedness. 2) Of the Church Fathers cited, only one, Arnobius, is clearly and consistently a conditionalist, while many patristic passages, even from the writings of men claimed as supporters of conditionalism, clearly affirm the everlasting punishment of the wicked. 3) To the other four arguments of the conditionalists, conservative opponents reply that justice requires eternal punishment, that the body is to be resurrected, and that it is not for men to deny the plain teachings of almost innumerable passages of scripture affirming everlasting punishment. To the third argument, many liberal opponents of conditionalism, on the other hand, reply that, while the doctrine of inescapable and everlasting punishment of the wicked is immoral, conditionalism is not the only, nor the best, alternative view. 4) Every human soul is intrinsically valuable. There may be disagreement concerning the question whether every biologically living human body, like that of the "zero" idiot, possesses a soul. But it is insisted that every self-conscious being capable of making choices affirms, by every act of will, even in murder or suicide, that there are ideals which to that soul are of intrinsic value. 5) Arguments from analogy are precarious, and there is no empirical ground for supposing the principle of survival of the fittest, which is true of biological species, to be true also of spiritual individuals. 6) Even the most sensuous soul has some ideal aspirations, or is capable of developing them under conditions more favorable than those which have degraded many lives from very infancy in our evil earthly society. A good God can be trusted to provide further opportunities for spiritual development, even of such degraded persons. 7) Furthermore, the belief in conditional immortality would set an infinite gulf between persons differing little in worth or spiritual attainment. For presumably some would be found barely worthy of immortality, others barely deficient. Between these classes would be a minute difference in merit. Yet their destinies would be separated by the infinity which divides a finite time from eternity. Such a disparity between difference in merit and difference in treatment would be grossly unjust.

The earliest recorded conditional view of a philosopher was that of Chrysippus, the Stoic (282-209 B.C.) Later Stoics were divided on the question. The Christian apologist, Arnobius (284-305), has been mentioned. His defense of the doctrine had little influence and conditionalism nearly disappeared from the literature of the Christian world for twelve centuries. It was revived by Fausto Sozzini (1539-1604), and vigorously defended by Hobbes (1588-1679), Locke (1632-1704), and Rousseau (1712-1778). The earliest systematic argument for conditionalism as a Christian doctrine was presented by H. Dodwell in 1706. The idea was revived in the nineteenth century by Richard Whately and Edward White, and then defended with especial thoroughness by E. Petavel. Since Petavel the belief in conditional immortality has been upheld by many thinkers, including, among its most recent defenders, J. Y. Simpson, W. E. Hocking, and E. S. Brightman. See immortality, arguments for and against; immortality, kinds of; pre-existence; rewards and punishments; soul.

See E. S. Brightman, *A Philosophy of Religion* (1940); W. E. Hocking, *Thoughts on Death and Life* (1937); J. H. Leckie, *The World to Come and Final Destiny* (1918); E. Petavel, *The Struggle for Eternal Life* (1875); S. D. F. Salmond, *Christian Doctrine of Immortality* (1897); J. Y. Simpson, *Man and the Attainment of Immortality* (1922).

L.H.DE W.

immortality, kinds of: A. Substitute Conceptions. Many persons who do not believe that the human personality or soul can survive death do, nevertheless, assert that they believe in immortality. The doctrines which they affirm and call by that name are of several kinds.

1. Social influence. The observation that an individual may influence others, and they yet others, does give to present choices an importance transcending the single life span. Ostwald, who says he "can think of no grander perspective of immortality than this," yet admits that the influence a man leaves behind loses "individuality and the possibility of being distinguished," and also points out that a universal catastrophe may finally extinguish the human race. Indeed, most astronomers would say that it is altogether irrational to expect an endless continuance of life on this planet. The relentless process of the fixation of our indispensable oxygen supply in solid forms goes on unceasingly and will eventually doom the race even if the earth escapes such spectacular catastrophes as are observed frequently to occur in other parts of the universe. If there is no other life than this earthly career, then even social influence is destined to end at last.

2. Biological continuity. The same objections apply equally against giving the name of immortality to the obvious biological continuity of the individual with his offspring.

3. Eternity of truth and value. J. S. Bixler says, "Perhaps immortality should stand not for an unending existence but for the realization in mortal life of that by which mortality is transcended. In the place of endless quantity we may have to put belief in a quality which temporal limits cannot confine." But it is not clear how anything more valuable than the abstract possibility of a quality can fail to be confined by the temporal limits of the beings in which it inheres.

4. Impersonal monism. Aristotle* affirmed the immortality of man's active intellect, by which he meant the system of intellectual ideals and implications which man shares with God. But

however important to ethics and logic is the idea of some such objective and absolute system, it is only by a strained figure of speech that its enduring truth can be called human immortality. No more should one confuse immortality with the continuance of the cosmic, purposeless Will, in the philosophy of Schopenhauer*, nor, on the other hand, with the absorption of the worker in his work. The latter is urged by Kirsopp Lake as the true immortality, and he insists concerning his own work, that after the annihilation of his individuality at death, "it will still be mine." What could be the meaning of "mine" when there is no "I" is a mystery. Obviously we are dealing here with rhetoric, not precise theology nor philosophy.

B. Conceptions of Personal Immortality.

1. Physical or quasi-physical survival. The Christian doctrine of the resurrection of the dead has never implied that the living body itself constituted the continuing individual. Rather, belief in the resurrection of the body has presupposed the immortality of the soul. Some other religions, however, have affirmed the continued existence of a soul which was itself a shadowy thing, like the body in form, but highly attenuated. (See resurrection.) But it may be safely assumed that those who hold such beliefs mean, however vaguely, to assert also the continuance of some awareness of personal identity.

2. Transmigration. One of the most widely held beliefs concerning immortality is the doctrine that at death the soul passes to another body, human or animal, the kind of body usually being thought dependent on the quality of the life just lived. While this ancient view still prevails in the Orient, it is generally regarded in the Occident as a fanciful superstition. Since its acceptance would imply that many or all persons now living had lived in other forms before this life, it is subject to the same objections as the belief in pre-existence*.

3. Spiritual monism. Another ancient view is the belief in the merging of the human soul into the life of an all-embracing Divine Spirit. This view is familiar to the philosophers of India. Probably the return of the individual soul to Brahmã was at first not meant to imply a complete loss of individuality. But there are many passages in the Upanishads and Vedanta** which do seem to assert that individuality, even now, is an illusion (māyā), and this view is dominant in Hindu thought, despite the arguments of opposing thinkers known in India as dualists. According to the prevailing monism, the real essence of the individual soul is Atman, and Atman is universal, being identical with Brahmā, the infinite, all-embracing absolute. Therefore, when the soul successfully concludes its pilgrimage and all māyā ceases, the individual, as such, is lost in the inconceivable vastness of Brahmā. The thought of Plotinus* is similar. The human soul, now enslaved by its preoccupation with evil matter, may free itself by asceticism and reverent contemplation of pure Intelligence. Even in this life the soul may experience an ecstatic union with the divine One, but permanent union awaits the discarding of the flesh in death. Both the rational demand for unity of conception and the mystical passion for drawing ever nearer to God have tended to develop such monistic conceptions. The former seems predominant in the thought of John Scotus Eriugena, Hegel, and Royce, and the latter in the teachings of Eckhart, St. Theresa, and Jacob Boehme**. The idea of reabsorption in God appears occasionally in modern Christian hymnology, as in the lines by George Matheson, "I give Thee back the life I owe, That in Thine ocean-depths its flow May richer, fuller be." Though in this particular instance the known beliefs of the poet support a monistic interpretation, the use of such expressions by theists often leaves doubt as to the precise meaning. The ethical influence of a spiritual monism will depend mainly upon the answer to the question whether the union with God will everlastingly affirm the value of all that is best in this life or whether it will forever negate it, so that our present highest good will have become evil, or at least of no account. Indian monists have often tended toward the latter, life-denying alternative; Christian mystics have differed, but in the last three centuries have usually been life-affirming, as are most of the occidental monistic philosophers.

4. Survival of a substrate soul. Many persons, untrained in philosophy or theology, think of immortality as indefinite survival of a soul, conceived as an unknown, immaterial being, subject neither to external nor introspective observation, which somehow has or produces the sensations and other elements of consciousness. It is as Locke's *tabula rasa* were to be, at death, divested of all which experience has written upon it and were to enter a new realm of experience where new content may be acquired. It is not strange that the idea of such a soul being immortal fails to arouse much interest. With no linkages of memory, purpose, nor even learned skills, there would seem little reason for identifying the future life of such an unknown thing with the present self. It is true that Roman Catholic theologians, and some Protestant theologians, believe in a substrate soul, as the subject or agent from which consciousness proceeds. But they believe also that consciousness, with meaningful memories and sense of identity, will continue to accompany this substrate in the life to come.

5. Immortality of the individual personal consciousness. In all of the conceptions of personal immortality, it seems to be tacitly assumed that after death I shall know that I am, in some form, living on. But what can be meant by calling the knower of that fact "I," if there is no consciousness of identity with my present self? And why should the "I" then observed to be still living be considered the same as the "I" now speculating about the future, unless there is continuity of memory and purpose to link that being with the present? Every argument for immortality which seems to have much weight is an argument for the continuance of that personal career of purpose begun, but unfinished, here below. The

teachings of the N.T. seem clearly to affirm such personal continuity, and so do nearly all Christian theologians, whether believing also in an underlying soul substance or not. Belief in the continuity of personal consciousness here and beyond the grave is also maintained by the Mohammedans, most modern Jews, the "dualistic" school of modern Hinduism, the personalistic philosophers, and many others. See immortality, arguments for and against; immortality, conditional; pre-existence; resurrection; rewards and punishments; soul; transmigration.

See J. Baillie, *And the Life Everlasting* (1933); the *Bhagavad-Gita;* J. G. Frazer, *The Belief in Immortality and the Worship of the Dead* (1922); K. Lake, *Immortality and the Modern Mind* (1922); W. Ostwald, *Individuality and Immortality* (1906); G. A. Reisner, *Egyptian Conceptions of Immortality* (1912); J. Royce, *The Conception of Immortality* (1900); and Vivekananda, *Jnana-Yoga* (1933).

L.H.DE W.

immortals, Taoist: See Chinese Terminology.

immunity: (Lat. *immunitas,* fr. *immunis,* free from a public obligation) Freedom from some burden or requirement. More specifically, a privileged exemption of a person or class from legal obligations or penalties to which others are subject. In most societies having clearly defined classes of religious leaders, such leaders enjoy immunities of various kinds. Among such privileges now extended to Christian clergymen and similar officials of all faiths, in America, are exemption from compulsory military service, from jury duty, and from payment of federal income tax on living quarters provided by the church or other religious organization served. The churches, also, are generally granted certain immunities, the chief being freedom from taxation of property used for services of worship. Such privileges vary greatly in different countries, and even among the states of the United States.

In general, immunities of religious bodies and their officers have been gradually reduced from feudal times to the present. The various remaining exemptions are criticized as undemocratic class privileges, as indirect but real means of supporting churches by public taxation in violation of liberal principles, as weakening the influence of the privileged clergymen with citizens not so privileged, and as degrading the ministry itself by encouraging those who engage in it to think of their office as a means of escape from responsibility rather than a call to heavier responsibility. On the other hand, immunities granted to the churches are defended on the ground that churches are rendering important public services, valuable to all but supported by all too few. Some legal privileges of clergymen are based on the claim of incompatibility between their religious offices and the services from which they are exempted, as military and jury services. Special tax exemptions are defended on the ground that clergymen are public servants whose income is at best disproportionately small when compared with the income of other men of comparable ability and education. See benefit of clergy.

See N. F. Brand, *The Pastor's Legal Adviser* (1942).

L.H.DE W.

imp: (Mid. Eng. *impa,* shoot, graft, scion) Little devil. A petty or inferior evil spirit; child of the devil is an imp of Satan.

F.L.P.

impanation: In the theology of the Eucharist*, the theory that asserts the perdurance under the sacramental species of the substance of the Body and Blood of Christ together with the substance of bread and wine, in a form of substantial, or hypostatic, union. By its emphasis on this latter point it differs from consubstantiation*, which asserts the simple coexistence of the two substances. The theory is first mentioned, and refuted as heretical, by Guitmond d'Aversa (d. *ca.* 1095); it was apparently held by certain unknown followers of Berengarius of Tours* (d. 1086). Some have maintained that Luther's doctrine on the Real Presence* was impanationist; more probably he held a form of consubstantiation, in dependence on Wyclif* and certain nominalist theories (*Smalkald Articles,* III, art. 6). But the theory of impanation was apparently held by certain Lutherans, whom Melanchthon* refuted. Cf. Lutheran Doctrine of the Lord's Supper.

J.C.M.

impediments, marital: See marital impediments.

implicit faith: In traditional Catholic theology, the term is employed to describe a faith which can exist in any man who assents to the two fundamental beliefs that a) God exists, and b) that he will reward those who seek to know him. Such implicit faith, acted upon, is sufficient to place its holder in the *way* of salvation, since it contains by implication the full Christian faith, although it cannot guarantee salvation. Cf. explicit faith.

W.N.P.

imprimatur: (Lat. it may be published) A bishop's approbation for a Catholic to publish certain types of books, esp. those in theology and philosophy. The words *Nihil obstat* are also used and mean that there is no reason why the book should not be published. See censorship of books.

L.R.W.

imputation: The doctrine that the guilt* of Adam's sin is attributed or transmitted to posterity; also the parallel doctrine that Christ's righteousness is laid to the account of Christian believers.

The Apostle Paul had taught that by Adam sin entered the world and death by sin, and so death passed to all men (Rom. 5:12). But through the free gift of God the righteousness of Christ also was transmitted to all men unto justification (Rom. 5:18). The doctrine remained somewhat vague and incidental, however, until lifted by Augustine* to the central position in a theological system. Undergirded by a Platonic realism, he made Adam the representative of the race and his transgression the generic sin of humanity. Hence, in Adam all sinned in a metaphysical rather than a metaphorical sense. His guilt is transferred to all men, formally, while materially his posterity received from him a corrupted nature (original sin). Calvin, while acknowledging the transference of guilt, stressed the material side—the punishment received through the corrupted nature,—sometimes called mediate imputation, as against the direct or immediate attribution of guilt for Adam's transgression. Protestantism emphasized the notion also that God imputes to the believer the merits of Christ, which makes it possible for Him to justify the believer. See justification; original sin. F.G.E.

inability, natural: The doctrine that, as a consequence of the Fall, man lacks the capacity to do the will of God. It was enunciated by Augustine* and defended by the Old School Calvinism*. F.G.E.

Inari: (Lit. probably from *ine,* "rice plant," and *naru,* "to grow," i.e., "growing rice") The name applied to a pantheon of food and fertility deities consisting of nine main personages, worshiped at the so-called Inari shrines of Japanese Shinto. D.C.H.

incantation: The practice, common among primitive peoples, of using verbal phrases or formulae in magical rites for coercing supernatural powers to act, bewitching persons, exorcising demons or curing disease. As a part of the ritual of magic the formulae are spoken, sung or chanted. R.W.F.

incarnations: Incarnation is the assumption by a deity temporarily or for a life span of a human or animal body. Rulers, saviors and religious leaders in many cultures received authority for office through direct contact with the gods. The relationship took many forms—inspiration, appearance of the god in a vision, lineal descent from the deity, possession by the Holy Spirit, endowment with divine illumination or incarnation. The "royal glory" of the Persian kings, the "divine light" of the Moslem Shi'ite Imams crowned these men with divine authority: the Imam of the Assassins, the Old Man of the Mountain, was revered as a divine incarnation. The Pharaohs of Egypt were divine because the sun god, Rē, took the form of the ruling monarch to impregnate the queen. Temporary incarnations of the gods were numerous in Greek religion. Zeus, Apollo and Poseidon appeared most frequently, and rarely for moral reasons. They came to punish insolence, to get revenge or to give divine parentage to heroes. The many amours of Zeus, in which he took animal or human form, were a scandal to the later intellectuals. These myths were made in the effort to unite the Aryan sky god, Zeus, with the many pre-Aryan fertility goddesses, the Earth Mothers.

The beneficent Vishnu is the hero of most of the incarnation stories in Hinduism. Episodes which originally belonged to other gods are now credited to him. He is incarnated whenever there is desperate need, when the world is sinking into decay, when iniquity flourishes and duty is neglected. At such times he comes to restore the teaching and to save. He has been incarnated as fish, tortoise, boar, man-lion, dwarf, Rāma with the axe, Rāma, Krishna, Buddha and in the decline of the present age will appear as Kalki. Many great saints in modern times have been honored as incarnations of him. In the beginning, Buddhism taught a way of salvation that asked no help from the gods but later developed the idea of the bodhisattva (see Buddhist terminology), a human being who had acquired supernatural power, wisdom and goodness in his climb toward buddhahood. These divine beings were incarnated in innumerable forms to help and save mankind. Whenever the truth is obscured, the law neglected and the world in distress one of these celestial bodhisattvas comes to the earth, as Gautama* did, to lead men to salvation. The future Buddha, Maitreya (see Buddhist terminology), is now waiting in the Tusita heaven for his hour of incarnation to strike. In Tibet, the Dalai Lāma and the Tashi Lāma are incarnations of the bodhisattva Avalokiteśvara and the buddha Amitābha respectively.

Early in the second century, the Christian savior was recognised as a god. Since Christianity was committed to monotheism he was asserted to be an incarnation of the divine essence.

Theories of divine incarnation arise for various reasons—to give great men status, to give god-value to a savior, to reconcile religions of separate origins or to bring divine help close to mankind in human form. A.E.H.

incense, significance of: A sacramental used in religious services; it is the granulated resin of certain tropical and eastern trees. It is burned in a covered vessel, the censer*, and used at Solemn Masses, benediction, vespers, funerals, and other services. In the blessing of the paschal candle five grains of incense represent the five wounds* of Our Risen Lord. The aromatic fragrance of burning incense signifies virtue; zeal is symbolized by the burning. The rising smoke is significant of prayer ascending to heaven.

Cf. *The Catholic Encyclopedia,* vol. viii, p. 716; *The New Catholic Dictionary,* p. 475. S.C.

incubi and succubi: Incubi, male demons* who copulated with women, and Succubi, female demons who had sexual intercourse with men, produced devil children according to mediaeval lore. Demon copulation was accomplished by three methods: 1) by a corpse activated by a demon, 2) by means of stolem semen, and 3) by diabolic illusion.

See *Demoniality, or, Incubi and Succubi,* (17th Century), Sinistrari, translated by the Rev. M. Summers (London, 1927). D.F.E.—J.T.M.

indefectibility: The quality of being exempt from liability to failure, decay, or imperfection. In theology it is used to describe the divine holiness, the divine grace, the Son, the heavenly state, and (in Roman Catholic literature) the Church. F.G.E.

independency: (Cong. polity) Originated by Robert Browne*. Browne taught that a church should consist of a company of true believers united by a public covenant with eachother and with God. Ecclesiastical authority consists only in Christ's supremacy over such local churches, their members interpreting the teachings of the Bible under the guidance of the Holy Spirit. Each church should choose its own officers, each member having equal rights with all the others. All churches are bound together only by the principle of mutual fellowship and cooperation. See Congregationalism; Separatists, Protestant.

W. Walker, *A History of the Congregational Churches in the U. S.* (1894); G. G. Atkins and F. L. Fagley, *History of American Congregationalism* (1942); Shaff-Herzog, *Encyclopedia of Religious Knowledge* (1908-1912) v. 2. F.T.P.

Independent Baptist Church of America: A group of 8 Scandinavian Baptist churches, holding the common Baptist doctrines, but stressing "the laying on of hands," pacifism, and the second coming of Christ. They have about 130 members. E.T.C.

Independent Puritans: See Puritanism.

indeterminism: See cause:

Index: See censorship of books.

India, missions to: Christianity came early to India. Tradition has it that the Apostle Thomas was the first to carry the gospel thither, but that cannot be proven. It is certain, however, that by the middle of the fourth century there was a Christian community in Malabar. They have been called Syrian Christians and are still there. The Nestorian* Christians seem quite certainly to have worked in India. John of Monte Corvino, pioneer Catholic missioner to China, spent some thirteen months in India on his way to China in 1292-93 and reported baptizing over a hundred Indians into the Christian faith.

The Portuguese explorer Vasco da Gama rounded the Cape of. Good Hope in 1498 and reached India. In 1500 a group of Portuguese monks were sent out for missionary service and soon had planted the Church in India. As early as 1543 Goa had been made a bishopric and by 1557 had been raised to an archbishopric. The great missionary Francis Xavier* was in India in 1542 for a time before continuing on to Japan. There were said to be as many as three hundred thousand Roman Catholic Christians as early as 1557. Today they number well over 3 million.

Protestant missions were carried on first by chaplains of the East Indian Trading Company but these were very few. The Danish government sent out two German missionaries in 1705, Bartholomew Ziegenbalg*, and Henry Pluetschau and later C. F. Schwartz, (1750). Pioneer British missionaries sent out by the churches were Wm. Carey*, Baptist, who did an enormous amount of translating the Bible into the native languages; and Alexander Duff, of the Established Church of Scotland who shaped the entire educational system of India.

American Protestant missions entered India in 1813, and have been very successful. Over half the entire Protestant Christian community is related to missions of American origin.

The entire Christian community of India numbers over 6,000,000, of which probably ninety per cent have come from the depressed classes. All types of missionary work are carried on, including educational, medical, industrial, as well as evangelistic.

In recent years with the rise of a capable and well trained leadership, the Indian churches are becoming more and more self-directing and self-propagating. There is a strong tendency toward union among the various denominational national groups, notably in South India and a somewhat less advanced movement represented in the United Church of North India. There is a National Christian Council which does much to promote a sense of solidarity among all Indian Christians and to coordinate their efforts to extend Christianity throughout the whole of India.

The Statistical Survey of the World Mission (International Missionary Council, N. Y. 1938) reveals a total of 1,042,416 communicants and 1,363,886 baptized non-communicants or a total of 2,406,302 baptized Protestant Christians, with an additional 260,697 persons under Christian instruction in India, (not including Burma). The national staff includes 2,440 ordained ministers, 9,854 unordained men and 5,129 women, a total of 17,323 native Indians engaged in Christian work. The foreign missionary staff numbered 5,112, of which 1,268 were ordained men, 372 not ordained men, 1,232 wives and 2,191 unmarried women and widows.

Protestant educational work is carried on in 13,274 elementary schools with 609,821 pupils; 302 high and middle schools with 67,229 students; and 158 special schools with 5,469 students. The national teaching staff is comprised of 21,996 men and 7,459 women. Their medical work is done in 283 hospitals with 18,283 beds and 525 dispensaries.

The Roman Catholic church at the same time reported 3,334,938 Catholics and 107,473 catechumens; 1,113 foreign priests, 2,583 native; 282 foreign brothers, 328 native; 1,842 foreign sisters, 5,762 native; 5,134 catechists and 9,365 other teachers. They report a total 328,624 students in 4,911 elementary schools; 116,854 in 782 secondary schools; and 2,623 in 46 seminaries. They have 43 hospitals and 264 dispensaries.

According to the Indian Census the reported Christian population, Protestant and Catholic in India in 1901 was 2,923,240; in 1911, 3,876,203; in 1921, 4,754,064 and in 1931, 6,297,000. The percentage of the total populations for the four decades was .99; 1.24; 1.51; and 1.79.

Julius Richter, *A History of Missions in India* (1908); *Interpretative Statistical Survey of the World Mission of the Christian Church.* Edited by Joseph E. Parker, International Missionary Council (1938). C.S.B.

India, religions of: India has been a prolific mother of religions and at the same time hospitable to religions which have come to her from outside her own borders. Hinduism* is of course the majority religion, but Hinduism is a broad term and gathers within its ample folds types of religious faith and practise which differ almost as day and night. The greater sects are Vishnuism (Vaisnavism*) and Shivism (Saivism*), but there are many others of greater or lesser importance, all recognized as phases of Hinduism. Three faiths which began as reform movements within Hinduism have come to be considered world religions, although only one of these has extended itself beyond the confines of Mother India. These are:

1. Jainism* whose traditional founder was Mahavira* in the sixth century B.C.

2. Buddhism*, founded by Gautama, the Buddha*, also in the 6th century B.C. Buddhism had almost disappeared from India by the year 1000 A.D. and is today found in considerable numbers only in the border states in the high Himalayas and in Burma which is hardly India proper.

3. Sikhism*, founded by Nanak* in the latter part of the 15th century A.D. largely as a result of Moslem influence on India.

Two other reform movements which arose in the 19th century, largely as a result of Christian influence, are enumerated as separate from Hinduism in the Indian census. They are:

1. The Arya Samaj*, founded by Dyananda Sarasvati in 1875.

2. The Brahma Samaj*, founded by Ram Mohan Roy* in 1828.

Numerous other movements which have arisen in the modern period which reflect in varying degree the impact of foreign cultures, especially Christianity, upon India. They are, however, not usually distinguished as other than modern forms of Hinduism.

In addition to all these the Indian census takes account of certain pocketed groups of aborigines which have not yet been assimilated to Hinduism. They figure in the census as tribal religions or "*animists*", though the term is but very loosely used.

Religions not native to India but at present found there in considerable strength are:

1. Islam, (see Mohammedanism) which came into India about 1000 A.D. and today claims approximately one-fifth of the total population. It has in the past played, and still plays, a highly significant role in the political life of India.

2. Christianity which came to India very early—tradition says it was first brought by St. Thomas one of the original twelve disciples of Jesus. Certainly the Syrian Christians of India have been there since the early Christian centuries. The earliest certain date is 343 A.D. The age of conquest and discovery in the 15th and 16th centuries brought Catholic Christianity to India in some strength, though the Catholic, John of Monte Corvino, had spent a year in India in the 13th century. Portuguese Catholics had made Goa a bishopric as early as 1543 and an archbishopric by 1557. The great Francis Xavier* visited the missions in India on his way to the farther East. Protestant missions began in the 17th century and from near the end of the 18th century increased rapidly. See India, missions to.

3. Zoroastrianism*—better known in India as the Parsi religion and its adherents as Parsis*. These followers of Zoroaster came to India in the 8th century A.D. seeking asylum from the invading Moslems. They constitute a small, closely-knit, self-contained community, concentrated chiefly in Western India, in and near Bombay.

Finally, there has been from very ancient times a small number of Jews in India, found mainly in the great cities.

The latest census of India gives the following enumeration of the adherents of each of the faiths mentioned:

Religion	*Number, 1931*	*% of Pop.*	*Number, 1921*	*% of Pop.*
Hindus	239,195,140	68.24	216,260,620	68.41
Moslems	77,677,545	22.16	68,735,233	21.74
Buddhists (12,348,037 in Burma)	12,786,806	3.6	11,571,268	36.6
Jains	1,252,105	.36	1,178,596	.37
Sikhs	4,355,771	1.24	3,238,803	1.02
Zoroastrians (Parsis)	109,752	.03	101,778	.03
Christians	6,296,763	1.79	4,754,064	1.51
Jews	24,141	.01	21,778	.007
Tribal	8,280,347	2.36	9,774,611	3.09
Arya-Samaj	468,000	.15	467,578	.15
Brahma-Samaj	5,378	....	6,388	.002

See Aryan religion; sacred literatures; temples, Indian.

J. B. Pratt, *India and Its Faiths* (1915); N. MacNicol, *Living Religions of India* (London, 1934). See also bibliographies under different religions. C.S.B.

Indian temples: See temples, Indian.

indifferentism: 1) A doctrine of Stoic* origin that certain things such as health, wealth, beauty, good birth and their opposites are beyond our power and neither help nor hinder moral conduct. Hence they are things indifferent. 2) In the medieval conflict between Realism and Nominalism** the mediating doctrine of Adelard of Bath* (12th century) to the effect that whether individuals remain individuals or become for us the species depends on whether we attend to their differences or non-differences (*indifferentia*). Thus everything depends on the point of view. 3) In the philosophy of right confessional indifferentism is the view that the religious opinions of a citizen fall outside the jurisdiction of the state, his rights being independent of his adherence to this or that confession. 4) In theology the doctrine that some differences of religious belief are not significant. R.W.F.

indigitamenta: (Lat. *indigitamenta*, from *indigito*, to call upon or invoke a deity) In Roman religion, priestly books, dating from very early times or modelled after those of early times, which recorded the names of the manifold numina of everyday life, along with set forms of prayer for their worship, prayers which lost their efficacy if altered in any way. E.M.N.

individual psychology: See psychology, schools of.

individualism: A movement of thought or that social policy which makes the desires, rights, initiative and well-being of individuals primary in religious, political, economic and social life. It holds that the measure of all institutions and social organization is their effects upon the interests, welfare and destiny of individuals. As a modern development it had its beginnings in the Renaissance and Reformation**. It became a prominent, widespread attitude with appropriate doctrines in the 18th and 19th centuries. It owes much to the Christian teaching of the supreme worth of the individual and to the Reformation doctrine of the priesthood of all believers. As a political philosophy it holds that the state exists for the individual, should trust individual initiative as the mainspring of conduct and should interfere as little as possible with its exercise. In political economy it stresses free enterprise, individual initiative, the *laissez faire* system of competition and is opposed to socialism. In ethics it is the doctrine that all values, rights and duties originate in individuals, that the interests of the individual should determine the supreme rule of conduct, and that the good of the community consists of the sum of the goods of the individuals who compose it. R.W.F.

individuation: A term indicating the philosophical problem about the grounds of numerical plurality within a class. The principle of individuation according to Saint Thomas Aquinas* (1225-6-1274) is matter, invested ("signata") with a certain extended quantity. For John Duns Scotus* (1270-1308) this principle, ultimately, is the individual substance itself. For Francis Suarez* (1548-1617) finiteness is the source of all multiplicity and individuality. S.C.T.

Indra: The Vedic god of war, of storm and fertility. Over 250 or about one-fourth of the hymns of the Rig-Veda are addressed to him. He represented only the more benevolent aspects of the storm, the destructive aspects being referred to Rudra*, possibly in part the precursor of the great Shiva* of later Hinduism. See virgin birth. C.S.B.

indulgence: The extra-sacramental remission by the Church of the temporal punishment due for sins whose guilt and eternal punishment have already been pardoned. According to Roman Catholic teaching sin involves guilt before God, eternal punishment at His hands, as well as temporal punishment (either on earth or in purgatory). The sacrament of Penance* removes the first two; the third can be commuted by indulgences. A full remission is called plenary and can be granted by the Pope alone. Partial remission—for a given period of time,—may be granted by a bishop or one authorized by him. The condition of their granting is contrition* and usually the performance of optional works of merit,—prayers, almsdeeds, visits to a church, etc.

It was the abuse of indulgences in the late medieval period which called forth Luther's* protest and inaugurated the Protestant Reformation*. While, strictly speaking, indulgences apply only to temporal punishment for sin, there was a widespread belief among common people unaware of the finer theological distinctions that indulgences removed guilt as well as punishment. Further, this remission could be obtained at that time for the payment of money, which, as Luther said, put a grievous instrument in the hand of avarice. In his famous *Theses* Luther contended, among other things, that the Church can only remit the ecclesiastical penalties it has imposed; it can remit neither guilt nor divine punishment, which are in the hands of God alone. See pardon; Theses, Ninety-Five, of Luther.

See the articles on "Indulgences" in *The Catholic Encyclopedia, The Encyclopedia Britannica,* Hastings' *Encyclopedia of Religion and Ethics,* and T. M. Lindsay, *A History of the Reformation* (reprint, 1922), I, 213 ff. F.G.E.

indult: A faculty or favor which the legislator benevolently grants for a time, either outside the law or contrary to it. It differs from a privilege in that it is not necessarily perpetual. See Catholic Societies. J.C.M.

infallibility: Broadly, exemption from error; the doctrine that an individual, institution, system of doctrine, or body of literature is inerrant.

Infallibility at the present time is most commonly associated with the claims of the Roman Catholic Church, and more especially the Pope* as its head, to be immune from error through divine assistance when enunciating a decision on questions of faith and morals. The Roman doctrine rests on a three-fold base: 1) God cannot err; any decree or utterance of His must be infallible; 2) God entrusted the keeping and teaching of his infallible truth to the Church (cf. Mt. 28:18-20, 16:18; Jn. 14, 15, 16; I Tim. 3:14-15; Acts 15:28 ff.); 3) since, however, such a prerogative left indiscriminately with the Church as a whole can have little practical benefit when decisions affecting the purity of the faith are to be made, a supreme and infallible authority must be exercised. This authority was lodged unequivocally with the Pope by the decree of the Vatican Council*, July 18, 1870. It affirmed that when the Bishop of Rome, touching questions of faith or morals, speaks *ex cathedra**—in his office as spiritual head of the universal Church with the intent to define a doctrine and bind all Christians—his decrees are divinely guaranteed against error and final. See Pius IX.

The Protestant Reformers held to the infallibility of the divine Word (1 above), but denied it had been entrusted to the Church (2). They contended that it is contained, or is present, in the Scripture and is to be apprehended by the faith of the believer. In time this doctrine was extended to mean that every letter of the Biblical text is inerrant. Thus, an infallible Book replaced an infallible Church. In recent Protestantism the idea of an infallible authority has tended to disappear. See Confessions, Formal of the Christian Church; Döllinger.

See the articles on "Infallibility" in *The Catholic Encyclopedia, The Encyclopedia Britannica,* and Hastings' *Encyclopedia of Religion and Ethics.* F.G.E.

infamy: Public disgrace or loss of good name because of notorious moral delinquency or conviction for certain crimes. May disqualify one for certain legal functions or social positions. R.W.F.

infant salvation: The doctrine that infants will be saved in the life to come, whether baptized or not. This view arose in Protestantism in reaction to the Augustinian view that unbaptized infants cannot be saved, though their place of abode—the *limbus infantum*—was not usually conceived as one of torture. Zwingli first denied the necessity of baptism for salvation. Calvin held to the salvation of elect infants. But the Arminians and most modern evangelicals include all infants among the elect. F.G.E.

infanticide: The practice of putting new-born infants to death or allowing them to die. The practice was usually conditioned by superstition. R.W.F.

infidelity: Unfaithfulness to the marriage* vows. With but few exceptions, sexual intercourse with another person other than the marriage partner is looked upon with condemnation in occidental countries at the present time. Thus all European countries and every state in the United States recognize infidelity as a cause for divorce* except South Carolina where divorce cannot be obtained except by legislative action. The terms, adultery and infidelity, are often used interchangeably and have the same meaning with reference to the marriage relationship.

Historical, primitive, and Oriental peoples, however, have not always regarded infidelity with the same distaste as that generally found in Euro-American cultures, particularly as regards the infidelity of the husband. In the Greek states adultery upon the part of the husband was not sufficient cause for divorce. The same was true among the Hebrews and still prevails today in some of the Latin-American countries. In fact until very recent times, sexual intercourse outside marriage upon the part of the husband was fairly generally condoned throughout occidental civilization.

While in most occidental cultures at the present time, infidelity upon the part of either party is recognized as a cause for divorce there still survives much of the old differential attitudes which characterized the past. Thus in contemporary United States, infidelity of the wife is generally regarded as more serious than that of the husband. This differential in attitudes is part of the double standard of morals which has long prevailed, although there are indications of its decline of recent years. Nevertheless, in divorce actions, where the wife has been found guilty of infidelity, her loss of status is greater than that which her husband would experience were he adjudged guilty of the same offense. The consequence is that infidelity or adultery has never been a particularly popular charge in divorce suits in those states in which other grounds are available.

Arthur W. Calhoun, *A Social History of the American Family,* (Cleveland, 1917-19); Willystine Goodsell, *A History of the Family as a Social and Educational Institution* (1927); Ernest R. Mowrer, *Family Disorganization* (rev. ed., 1939). E.R.M.

infinite: (Lat. *infinitus,* not bounded) In mathematics, a multitude so far as capable of one-to-one-correspondence ("equality") with some of its parts. An infinite number is not a member of the series, 1, 2, 3, etc., but is at least equal to the entire series itself. It may be greater, according to most mathematicians, who accept the theory of a hierarchy of infinites. However, it has been contended (by Felix Kaufmann) that the "higher infinites" are not legitimate conceptions; and "finitist" philosophers of mathematics maintain that mathematics has no need of infinity except in the sense of an unlimited possibility of addition. Thus infinity would not be a number, but merely the law that any number can be exceeded by other numbers.

It has been contended by many (e.g., Renouvier*, Parker) that an actually infinite plurality is impossible, that the concept is contradictory. It must be a whole some of whose parts are equal to it, although to be a part is by definition to be less than the whole. Again, the infinite must be an endless or never-completed series which nonetheless is complete. However, it can be argued that the contradictions are only apparent. The part is "equal" to the whole only in a technical sense, "one-to-one-correspondence", and the definition of part need not deny equality in this sense. The whole must by definition be the part and something else besides; this is true even of infinite wholes. The-odd-numbers-and-the-even-numbers are capable of one to one correspondence with the odd numbers alone; but they are nonetheless the odd numbers and other things besides. Again, one need not and mathematicians do not define an infinite series as one which cannot be completed, if by that is meant one whose members are not all there, or not all actual.

There is, however, at least one application of the idea of an actual infinite which leads to contradictions, the famous contradictions embodied in Zeno's paradoxes. It cannot be that a finite stretch of time contains an infinity of actual parts. If the parts have no temporal or spatial length, their sum can have none; if they have length, their sum will have infinite not finite length. Besides, it would be impossible to reach one part from another. A series which has not been entered and which cannot be begun, since it has no first member, cannot be entered and hence cannot be completed. Now the series: one minute past five, preceded by $\frac{1}{2}$ minute past five, preceded by $\frac{1}{4}$ minute past five, and so on, is a series which, at five o'clock, has not been entered, has no first member with which to begin, and which hence cannot be begun, and *a fortiori* cannot be completed. The solution of this difficulty is given by the "epochal theory of time" (Whitehead*), according to which the "and so on" above is subject to a limit beyond which time is not actually divided into real units or events. One may mathematically conceive divisions of time beyond the limit; but they represent only things which might happen, not things which in a given case do happen. In other words there is a least portion of time in which, after a given moment, anything actually happens. This is a generalization of the "specious present" of human consciousness described by James*. It implies that after five o'clock there is a first real division of time, 1/nth minute past five, with which one may begin in passing from five to a minute past five. Spatial subdivision is treated in the same way. The theory rests upon the recognition that potentiality is a real mode of being (see Time), that to be infinitely divisible is not the same as to be infinitely divided, and yet is something quite real.

The most plausible application of the idea of an actuality numerically infinite is that to the series of all past events. Here there is no problem of entering or beginning the series; for at no time was anyone or anything outside "all events" waiting to get into it. Kant's* attempt to prove a contradiction here presupposed that infinite must be defined as endless, a supposition which is mathematically untrue. The most one can say is that it is difficult to see how the idea of the infinite past can have any basis in direct experience or intuition. We cannot distinctly intuit or imagine each member of an infinite series. But perhaps we can indistinctly intuit the infinity of the past, for when we attempt to conceive the past as finite we seem to collide with the intuitive content of the idea of time, suggesting that we may not be utterly without the intuition of infinity. After all, very little of our awareness is wholly distinct.

In philosophy and theology, the term is often used in a non-quantitative sense, meaning absence of limitations or deficiencies, in some given, or in all, respects. Total absence of limitations, infinity in all respects, is a common conception or pseudo-conception of God. Its meaningfulness or consistency is doubtful. Its object must be that which lacks no positive being or value that could be present anywhere. But the question is whether what "lacks nothing in particular" could possess anything in particular. "Determination is negation", but indetermination is also negation, so how can a purely positive being be other than nonsense? To be this is not to be that, possibilities are often incompatible. From the realm of pure potentiality no one thing is missing more than another, because everything determinate and actual is missing, and what is there is precisely the impartially deficient mode of existence, potentiality. The doctrine that the deficiency can be, and in God is, impartially and exhaustively remedied has never been shown consistent with what we know of the meaning of potential and actual. Besides, there is the dilemma: either the finite, including man, makes no difference to the infinite being, and man's efforts are worthless; or the finite, in making differences to the infinite, somehow limits it (although perhaps not in all respects or aspects—see Transcendence). In other terms, if the impartial deficiency of pure potentiality is impartially and exhaustively overcome in God it is inconceivable why there should also be the partial and non-exhaustive realization of potencies in the creation. The wholly unlimited-and-the-limited cannot be more than the wholly unlimited by itself, or in any intelligible way distinguished from it. Nor is the problem solved by saying that the true infinite is what is limited only by itself. For it is by the creatures that God must in some fashion be limited, and in any case self-limitation is still in some sense limitation. The conclusion seems to be that the denial of limits requires itself to be limited, if it is to be consistent. See omnipotence; perfect; transcendence. D. H. Parker, ***Experience and Substance*** (1941). C.H.

infralapsarianism: (*infra,* after, *lapsus,* fall) The doctrine which holds that God's decrees of reprobation and election** came after the Fall of man, and were in order to redeem the purpose of creation. Held by Arminius and the more humanistic of the Dutch Calvinists. Defeated at the Synod of Dort*. Cf. supralapsarianism. E.P.B.

infusio gratiae: See infusion of grace.

infusion of grace: The Roman Catholic Church teaches that when grace, which is understood to be a divine *habitus* (a supernatural essence) is administered through the sacrament, it is "infused" in the human heart, thus restoring the gift of grace which God in creation had superadded to human nature but which through Adam's fall has been lost to all mankind. The Scriptural authority for this teaching is Rom. 5:5. W.P.

Ingersoll Lectureship: A lectureship at Harvard University established by the will of Miss Caroline Haskell Ingersoll in honor of her father, George Goldthwait Ingersoll providing for the annual delivery of a lecture at Harvard on "the Immortality of Man." The choice of the lecturer "is not to be limited to any one religious denomination, nor to any one profession, but may be that of either clergyman or layman." The first lecture was delivered in 1896 by George A. Gordon. Other distinguished lecturers on the foundation have included Wm. James, Josiah Royce, G. Lowes Dickinson, George H. Palmer, George Foot Moore, Kirsopp Lake, E. S. Brightman, Harry Emerson Fosdick. Until 1934 the lectures were printed separately in book form. Since then they have for the most part been published in the Harvard Divinity School Bulletin. A thorough analysis and criticism of the lectures up to 1935 is offered in "Premises of the Arguments Concerning Immortality in Thirty Ingersoll Lectures", an unpublished dissertation by L. Harold De Wolf, now in the Boston University Library. The Ingersoll Lecturer for 1941 was Alfred North Whitehead. J.S.B.

inheritance, social, group: See culture.

inhibition: 1) In psychology the checking or blocking of one neural or psychical process by another, usually explained as due to the conflict of competing or incompatible impulses, desires, habits or interests. It is a fundamental conception in psychology and a factor of great importance in the formation of habits and the integration of personality. 2) In ecclesiastical law it is a censure in the form of an official command to a clergyman or priest not to perform the functions of his office. R.W.F.

initiation rites: In early and simple cultures initiation is a maturity rite, introducing adolescent youth to adult responsibilities and privileges. Where the religious group does not include the whole society it is a ceremony admitting young people and adults to the benefits of religion, and by extension, the qualifying of selected persons for the official duties of the cult.

In its universal early use the rite marked the transition from childhood to maturity. When the infant was born, a public ritual of baptism* and naming recognised him as a member of the group with the right to enfoldment in tribal care. Initiation lifted him from this irresponsible status as a child and made him a fully qualified adult with social responsibilities as a brearer of the tribal heritage, a sharer in the duties of food-getting, family life, perpetuation of the ceremonies, maintaining of group loyalties and mores, and defense of his people in war. It was a second birth into a larger life.

The ceremonies of simple cultures usually emphasize the break with the past, test the physical and moral qualities of the initiate and, by emotional experiences, bind him in loyalty to the social structure of the tribe, its sacred traditions and its secret lore. Various means are used to mark the separation from the old way of life—relaxation of behavior restrictions, change of clothing, cutting the hair, a last meal on the mother's lap, bathing, baptism, sprinkling with water or some other fluid with cleansing power, separation from the women, a period of seclusion, the giving of a new name. Girls usually enter adult status by marriage marked by tatooing, or a new kind of dress or a new mode of wearing the hair. The testing of youth is often severe. It is intended to demonstrate courage in frightening situations and ability to endure pain without flinching. It serves also to impress upon the young people the superior status and authority of the older men. Scars and mutilations became signs of the initiated. The most important part of the ceremony is the instruction. In the early world the transmission from generation to generation of the law, the ceremonial techniques, the sacred literature and theology could only be done orally. In initiation the new generation viewed for the first time the sacred cult objects, received basic teaching in tribal wisdom, acquired a sense of unity with the ancestral past and was pledged to loyal support of the existing order. The total effect of the rite was to weld a chain of cultural continuity through the centuries.

In Hinduism* initiation was early associated with the beginning of education in the religious heritage. The rite removed the child from the śudra class with no Aryan privileges, gave him his second birth by investment with the sacred thread and handed him over to a teacher for twelve years of study in one of the sacred books. In the modern age of printed books the educational stress has fallen away and the ceremony becomes again simply a recognition of twice-born status. In Buddhism*, initiation is in two stages, the introduction of the novice to preliminary training, and the more elaborate ceremony of admission to the order of monks. The first initiation in Zoroastrianism* is a continuation of the ancient Aryan* rite. The child is bathed, puts on the sacred shirt and the sacred girdle, recites scripture texts and a summary confession of faith. The rite marks the beginning of education. The later priestly initiation is restricted to the families of priests and requires prolonged preparation and training. Initiation into the mystery religions of the old Mediterranean world involved a baptism for purification or forgiveness of sins and a viewing of the sacred symbols of the divine mythology. The intitiates were then eligible for participation in the communion meal which gave assurance of immortality. The bar-mitzvah* in Judaism and confirmation* or adult baptism in Christianity admitting to membership in the church retain some of the qualities of the early rites of initiation. See sacred literatures. A.E.H.

inner light: See Society of Friends.

inner mission: (German, *Innere Mission*) A movement in the evangelical church of Germany organized at the beginning of the 19th century to serve the neglected and unfortunate members of society. Deaconess* work, Sunday Schools, prison reform, orphanages, came from this movement. A large number of lay men and women as well as ministers have taken part in this work, aiding discharged prisoners and prostitutes, giving aid and protection to working girls, relieving the hardships of sailors, and caring for any in need. See Löhe, W. P.E.J.

innocence: The quality of stainless purity or freedom from sin, guilt or taint of evil, a condition which belonged to man before the fall according to Christian theology. It may refer to that childlikeness of spirit which Jesus required of members of His Kingdom and which Tertullian claimed was the characteristic grace of Christians, a childlikeness marked by the guilelessness, simplicity, gentleness, and humility begotten of confirmed, single-minded devotion to God. The term is also applied to children before the age of moral accountability. R.W.F.

Innocent III: Lothario Conti was born in 1160. His family on both sides were of the high Roman nobility. After finishing his early studies in Rome, he went to the University of Paris for his philosophy and theology, then to Bologna to study canon law. On completing his studies he returned to Rome and fulfilled several administrative positions at the papal court. He was made a cardinal deacon in 1190, and was elected Pope January 8, 1198,—the very day that his predecessor Celestine III died. Lothario took the name of Innocent on his elevation.

During his reign (Jan. 1198-July 1216) the papal theocracy reached its greatest development thanks to his great diplomatic skill and statesmanship. Basing his policy on canon law, the acts of his predecessors, and the ideas of his time, Innocent carried it to its logical conclusion. As vicar of Jesus Christ on earth he claimed and exercised an absolute and universal authority over the Church. Most political acts being moral acts, Innocent III, as guardian of the moral law, claimed and exercised the right to intervene in the most important political issues of his time. Thus he became political master of Italy, helped depose kings in Germany and England, and received as papal fiefs the kingdom of England, Portugal, Denmark, Aragon, etc. His policy was leading to a union of all the European states in one Christian commonwealth under papal leadership. The rise of nationalism was the principal reason for its failure to materialize. See Langton, Stephen.

J. Clayton, *Innocent III* (1941) J.A.C.

Innocent X, Pope: (1644-55) Giambattista Pamfili was born at Rome, May 6, 1574 and rose rapidly in Vatican diplomatic circles. In 1601 he became Consistorial Adviser; in 1604, Auditor of the Rota; in 1621 Nuncio (cf. "Papal Legates") to Naples, and later, Assistant to Cardinal Francesco Barberini, the Elder, in the papal legation to France and Spain. Appointed Titular Patriarch of Antioch, he was named Papal Nuncio to Madrid, 1621 and created Cardinal *in petto* (i.e., not published) Aug. 30, 1629. He took part in the deliberations of the Council of Trent*. Elected Pope on Sept. 15, 1644 as a compromise candidate of the French and Spanish factions, he favored rather the latter in their respective controversies. As pope, he assisted Venice in her struggles against the Turks. In his famous Bull, *Zelo domus Dei,* of Nov. 26, 1648 he approved of his Legate's, Fabio Chigi (later Pope Alexander VII rejection of those articles of the Westphalian Treaty (1648)* which involved the justification of usurpation and retention of usurped Catholic Church properties. On May 31, 1653 he condemned five propositions taken from the "*Augustinus*" of Jansenius, thus precipitating the later long-drawn out Jansenistic* controversies in France and Belgium. Like Pope Urban VIII, he declined to recognize King John IV Braganza of Portugal, when the latter country, following the insurrection of 1640, seceded from Spain. Accordingly, the pope contested John's usurped right of nominating bishops in the kingdom. It thus happened that towards the end of Innocent's pontificate there was only one legitimate bishop in all Portugal.

Cf. L. Pastor, *History of the Popes,* Vol. XXX (1940) where all the important sources will be found quoted; Ciampi, *Innocenzo X Pamfili e la sua corte* (Imola, 1878); Palatius, *Gesta Pontif. Roman.* IV (Venice, 1688), 571-94. R.M.H.

Innocents Day: A feast celebrated in honor of the male children slaughtered by order of Herod, who wished to kill the new-born Christ. These children died instead of Christ and are considered the first martyrs of the Church. In the Latin church the feast is kept on December 28. In the Greek church on December 29. It dates back to the fifth century. C.R.

Inquisition, The: The Inquisition, as a medieval ecclesiastical tribunal for the preservation of the Faith, and as distinct from similar imperial or royal decrees and courts to combat heresy, was instituted by Gregory IX (1227-41). It had essentially a three-fold purpose: 1) to inquire (*inquirere*: hence, Inquisition) into the spread of doctrines opposed to the Faith (heresies); 2) to call before its tribunals all Catholics suspected of heresy; and 3) to punish their infidelity, to convince them of error and to exhort them to repentance. To the medieval Christian the preservation of orthodoxy was self-evident and paramount. As conceived by the popes, the Inquisition was not an institution to force upon Jews, Saracens (Mohammedans) or Non-Catholics in general the tenets of Catholic doctrine. It was intended solely for the salvation, coercion and punishment of her own children. The use of torture, while rather abhorent to present-day mentality, was used only once on any given accused; furthermore, it was not distinctive of the Inquisition, but common to Roman and to all imperial or royal medieval tribunals of justice. In fact, religious intolerance, based albeit on sincere and deep-rooted convictions, was practiced also by certain XVI century Protestant reformers (cf. articles on Calvin, Servetus, Bullinger, Penal Laws) and by the American colonists. Instituted in the beginning to counteract the heresies of the Albigensians, the Waldensians and the Cathari**, the Inquisition was revived in the XVI century to safe-guard the faith of Catholics, especially in Italy, Spain and her dependencies. Sixtus IV objected to the harshness of the Spanish State Inquisition and Clement VIII published rules for humane treatment in all ecclesiastical tribunals. The Catholic Church refuses to be held responsible for excesses of the "secular arm". The Inquisitors—Local and General—were usually, although not exclusively, selected from among the members of the Franciscan and Dominican Orders, preferably the latter. Cf. Office, Sacred Congregation of the Holy.

Literature: An impartial complete history of the Inquisition still remains to be written. The standard English work on the I. by H. C. Lea, *A History of the Inquisition in the Middle Ages* (1887) 3 vols. is anti-Catholic. (cf. *Cath. Encyc.* VIII 38); a Catholic work is by J. Guiraud, *L'Inquisition Médiévale* (Paris, 3d, 1928). Other studies: Langlois, *L'Inquisition d'après les travaux récents* (Paris, 1902); Vacandard, *L'Inquisition. Etude historique et critique sur le pouvoir coercitif de l'Eglise* (Paris, 1907); Douais, *L'Inquisition. Ses origines. Sa procédure*

(Paris, 1906); William T. Walsh, *Characters of the Inquisition* (1941). R.M.H.

insanity: A broad term for mental disorder which unfits one to live a normal life. Strictly speaking it is a social and legal term for mental disease which disqualifies one for legal responsibility and civil duties and which requires institutional supervision for the patient. In general it means any form of *dementia,* i.e., deterioration or derangement of normal mental processes, and is distinguished from *amentia,* i.e., idiocy, imbecility, and feeblemindedness, which is due to inherent brain deficiency. Insanity may be organic (physiological) or functional (psychogenic) in origin. With the notable increase of insanity under our complex civilization the environmental social situation is more and more recognized as a contributory factor. Formerly insanity was regarded as due to demonic possession or a criminal nature and treated accordingly. Today it is recognized as mental disease and its scientific study and treatment is a social obligation assumed by the state. R.W.F.

inspiration: In religion as in art it is very generally believed that human actions of extraordinary insight, worth or power are due to inspiration, that is, to inflow of psychic force comparable to life-giving breath. The religious idea of inspiration is inseparably connected with the thought of personal divine power and of human dependence upon it. An antonym of inspiration is the term "religious genius" which represents the idea that extraordinary work is the product of the extraordinary man, acting more or less independently of God. The idea of inspiration in Christian theology may be traced, apart from its connection with such manifestations as those indicated in Acts 2 and in later church history, to Hebrew prophecy and to Greek philosophy. Plato's (e.g., in *Phaedrus* and *Timaeus*) and Philo's remarks on divination* have been used especially in the development of the more extreme theories of inspiration.

The most important theological problems of inspiration concern the subjects, the sources, the means and the criteria of true inspiration as distinguished from false, rather than the actuality of inspiration itself. The question of the proper subject of inspiration—whether a person, a community or a book may properly be said to be inspired—has been greatly confused in history by being involved in the problem of church authority. Thus the doctrine of the inspiration of Scriptures was largely developed to secure the church against the inroads of sectarianism with the latter's claims to the inspiration of special leaders or of individual members (e.g., Montanism, Anabaptism, the Society of Friends**). The doctrine that ecumenical councils or popes are inspired when speaking on matters of faith and morals has been developed partly in conflict with sectarianism, partly in opposition to the rigid, Scriptural "constitutionalism" of Protestantism. This confusion between the ideas of inspiration and of authority has led to the strange result that the great churches tend to regard Scriptures or these and the official pronouncements of the church as alone inspired while the more objective theology in these churches tends to agree that only a person or a community of persons may properly be said to be the subject of inspiration.

The problem of the source of inspiration was raised in Hebrew thought by the appearance of false prophecy, and by the consequent question for monotheism in what sense such inspiration came from God. In Christian theology the questions were to what extent the inspiring principle in the Godhead was distinct from the creating and redeeming principle, in what sense it proceeded from one or both of these.

The question about the means of inspiration has been dealt with indirectly and in confusion with the question of subject and criteria. The orthodox Protestant and Catholic churches have emphasized the importance of Scriptures, of church discipline and instruction as the ordinary means through which inspiration comes. Mystic and sectarian groups have shown a larger interest in other means—asceticism, the practice of silence, etc. In the Protestant doctrine of the "testimony of the Holy Spirit*" which must accompany the reading of the word if there is to be true inspiration and in Roman as well as Eastern Catholic acceptance of monasticism* the great churches have made some approach to the interests of the sects and mysticism*.

Among the criteria employed by religious thought to distinguish true from false inspiration the most important are: 1) the consistency of the product of inspiration not only in itself but also and primarily with accepted norms, i.e., with the moral laws, the "spirit of Jesus Christ," the Scriptures, the common understanding of the community (cf. I Cor. 12-14); 2) the truth of prediction (Dt. 18:22); this test, which has an analogy in modern science, has been used apologetically rather than critically, to validate the inspiration of Scriptures, as in the argument from prophecy*; 3) disinterestedness, that is the extent to which personal interests and opinions are absent or negated in the "inspired" utterance; in the extreme form, as represented by Philo, the idea is that the self retires wholly under true inspiration (*On Special Laws,* par. 65), but in Biblical thought the test was used less psychologically, more ethically (cf. Jer. 23, Ezekiel 13). 4) Intelligibility might be added as a fourth criterion of the validity of inspiration though not a test of its truth, since the unintelligible cannot be said to be true or false. See Bible; sacred literatures.

B. H. Streeter, ed., *The Spirit* (London, 1919); F. W. Camfield, *Revelation and the Holy Spirit* (London, 1933); W. Sanday, *Inspiration* (London, 1901); G. Hoelscher, *Die Profeten* (Leipzig, 1940); A. Guillaume, *Prophecy and Divination* (London, 1938). H.R.N.

installation: a) The ceremony by which a Canon* is invested with his office as one of the governing clergy of a Cathedral or Collegiate Church (R.C. or Anglican) by being formally put in possession of his official seat, or stall. E.R.H.

b) The ceremony of induction in non-episcopal churches of a minister into his new pastorate. V.F.

instinct: An inborn tendency or drive to act in a more or less definite way in response to special situations for the fulfilment of the vital needs of the organism. It usually has emotional concomitants, is more complex and less stereotyped than a reflex and while analogous to a habit it is not dependent upon previous learning or experience. Clear-cut cases are found among the insects. The question of the classification and even the existence of human instincts is in dispute. That there are important hereditary factors in human behavior is not doubted but that man has any such innate equipment of instinct-patterns as the lower animals possess is seriously questioned. The tendency among psychologists and especially sociologists is to be severely critical of the doctrine of human instincts. On the whole it has proved more enlightening to explain the complex behavior patterns of man in terms of an acquired organization of impulses which is the product of custom, habit and intelligence rather than in terms of congenital instincts. There is general agreement, however, that man has no specific moral or religious instincts. See psychology of religion, for list of instincts. R.W.F.

Institute for Religious Studies, The: The Institute for Religious Studies was established at the Jewish Theological Seminary of America to enable graduate ministers of various denominations to study the relationship between different faiths and the common religious background of the democratic tradition.

The Institute was established in 1939 by a grant from the Lucius N. Littauer Foundation. In 1942, the scope of the Institute was expanded to include study of the problems of religion and the world order, and group relations and group antagonisms. In 1943, the Board of Regents in the State of New York authorized the Seminary to confer upon graduates of the Institute the degrees of Master and Doctor of Comparative Religion, and Master and Doctor of Theology.

Among those who conducted courses at the Institute for Religious Studies during the academic year 1942-43 are: Professor F. Ernest Johnson, Professor Robert M. MacIver, Professor Hunter Guthrie, S. J., Professor William F. Albright, Professor George F. Thomas, and Doctor Ben Zion Bokser. L.F.

institutional church, the: An institutional church, at the time the name became current, was a church which had added to its traditional services of worship and pastoral oversight, a program of social activities carried on through the week. The name took its place in church literature with the organization of 'The Open and Institutional Church League", in 1894, an association of independent churches the manifesto of which announced their purpose to abolish "so far as possible distinctions between the religious and secular," and emphasized their lack of credal tests.

The League had but a short life and by no means included all institutional churches. Churches of practically all the greater denominations became "institutional" in equipment and practice, some such as the Wesleyan Missions in English cities developing social and cultural activities, without taking the name. The most notable of these was the West End Mission, London.

The institutional church's program for the most part was the result of shifts in population by which it found itself surrounded by transient, underprivileged and foreign born groups, where had been its stable and well-to-do constituency. The program sought to provide a social and cultural life for such underprivileged groups, for young people at work in the city and away from their own homes, for those whom the necessities of a livelihood prevented from attending the established schools, and for foreign born and others desiring adult education, particularly in language and domestic science. Included in the customary activities of the institutional church were kindergartens, clubs for young men and women, study classes, manual training for boys and girls, athletics, supervised games, nurseries, etc.

The name has now fallen into disuse, for which perhaps several causes can be assigned: The social program of the public schools, the Y.M.C.A. and the Y.W.C.A.** and the multiplication of social settlements, and the fact that many if not most Protestant churches maintain to some extent similar social and cultural activities. The most noted Institutional Church at the beginning of the century was St. George's, New York City, under the leadership of the Reverend Dr. William R. Rainsford. Others were the Ruggles Street Baptist Church, Boston, the Baptist Temple, Philadelphia, during the pastorate of Russell H. Conwell, the Plymouth Congregational Church, Indianapolis. Perhaps the best known today is the Morgan Memorial, Boston, from which developed, under the leadership of the Reverend Dr. E. E. Helms, the Goodwill Industries of America. See social work of the churches.

G. Hodges and J. Reichert, *The Administration of an Institutional Church* (1906); H. P. Douglass, *Protestant Cooperation in American Cities,* pub. by the Institute of Social and Religious Research (1930); H. P. Douglass and E. de S. Brunner, *The Protestant Church as a Social Institution* (1935); Leiffer, *City and Church in Transition* (1938). J.M.M.G.

institutions: See culture.

intelligence tests: See clinical psychology.

intemperance: Immoderate indulgence of any appetite; in the United States it refers particularly to the excessive use of intoxicants. See temperance movements. R.W.F.

intention, sacramental: In Roman Catholic sacramental doctrine, 1) the positive will, required in an adult, to receive a sacrament, and 2) the positive will of the minister in performing the visible rite "at least to do what the Church does" (Council of Trent, sess. 7, can. 11). The necessity of this latter intention for the validity of a sacrament is implicit in the doctrine that the sacraments were instituted by Christ as practical signs, whose sanctifying effect derives under given conditions from the position of the rite itself in the objective sacramental significance imparted to it by Christ (see opus operatum). In its sheerly material entity as a complex of words and actions the visible rite might signify a number of things; the minister, therefore, must determine it to its objective sacramental significance by willing to perform it formally as the rite which Christ instituted. To this end the minimum required is that he will to do what the Church does—the formula classic since William of Auxerre* (d. 1231)—or what the Gospel of Christ enjoins, what true Christians intend, or equivalent formulas. Given this sacramental intention, and the correct performance of the rite prescribed, the validity of the sacrament is not affected by the minister's own faith or probity, or lack of them; for, since only God through Christ sanctifies, the human agent of the sacraments acts in an essentially vicarious capacity (different from that of the minister of the word), and his instrumental alliance with the uniquely sanctifying power of Christ is accomplished by his intention, not by his faith or probity. This principle, implicit in the traditional practice of the Church (see Stephen I, Cyprian), was clarified notably by Augustine against the Donatists**. The necessity of this sacramental intention (not controverted in the early disputes on rebaptism) was denied by the Reformers (Calvin, *Acta syn. trid. cum antid.*, *Corpus Reform.*, XXXV, 946 ff.); in the inner logic of their system it was not necessary, since the visible rite itself, even though performed in jest by the minister, could still arouse the faith of the recipient, from which alone its efficacy derived. The question of the sacramental intention is important in connection with Anglican orders. J.C.M.

intercession: Theologically, a form of the prayer of petition: entreaty made to God for others. Examples are recorded in the O.T. (Ex. 32:11 ff.); the N.T. frequently records the intercessory prayer of Christ (Matt. 19:13; John 17:9-26; Luke 22:31; etc.), who enjoined it (Matt. 5:44; 6:7-13). The practice was familiar in the early Church (Acts 12:5), and is prominent in St. Paul (Rom. 15:30; I Tim. 2:1-2; etc.), who bases it on the doctrine of the Body of Christ. Its object is represented as the grace of salvation, together with favors of the temporal order inasmuch as they are related to it. In the second century the intercession of the martyrs*, while still living (through the *libellum pacis*) and after death, was acknowledged (cf. H. Delehaye, *Sanctus*, 1927). Thereafter all the Fathers attest the place in the Christian life of prayer held by belief in the intercession of the angels and saints in heaven. Vigilantius attacked the belief (or perhaps only its practical exaggerations), and was vehemently refuted by Jerome*. Simpler folk of unenlightened piety have, in fact, not always observed the proper bounds. But the belief itself has always supported an essential part of the popular and liturgical piety of the Roman Catholic Church; it is related to faith in the Communion of Saints*, the real solidarity and active, unbroken fellowship, through a share in the one Spirit of Christ, of the members of the Church in her different states, militant, suffering, and triumphant. The "Great Intercession" is a distinctive feature of all Oriental liturgies. The Protestant tradition admits in theory the intercession of Christians on earth for one another, but rejects all intercessory prayer in heaven, and correspondingly all invocation of the saints. Calvin was particularly emphatic on the point. The rejection is logically consistent with the Protestant concept of Christian unity. In the Communion Service of the first Book of Common Prayer (1549) the "Intercession" was retained, following the corresponding parts of the Roman canon (*Te igitur*, *Memento*, *Communicantes*), but all reference to the merits and intercessions of the saints was omitted. The revision of 1552 more radically omitted even the commemoration of the saints, and the prayer for the dead*; and it explicitly restricted the "Prayer for the Church" to the Church "militant here on earth" (words omitted in the American revision of 1928). In 1661 a short mention of the "departed" was added, in the form of a simple commemoration, which involves no idea of intercession, either for them or by them. Similarly, the collects never appeal to the intercession of the saints.

J.C.M.

Interchurch World Movement of North America: An interdenominational organization formed at the close of World War I, and comprising 59 societies representing the home and foreign missionary interests of the leading denominations, especially those active in the "Federal Council of Churches of Christ in America."* Its purpose was to perpetuate in the promotion of religious projects the increased interest in social and international problems and in interdenominational cooperation which the churches had experienced during the war. The first meeting was called by the Southern Presbyterian Church in New York, and formal organization was effected on December 17, 1918, under the chairmanship of John R. Mott, whose slogan, "the evangelization of the world in this generation," had captured the imagination of religious leaders a decade earlier. At a conference at Cleveland on April 30, 1919, the preliminary stages of organization were completed, and a program of action finally launched which included 1) a general survey of foreign and domestic missionary needs, 2) the formulation of a world-wide program adequate to meet the needs disclosed by the survey, covering the fields of evangelism and educational, social service, medical, industrial, and agricultural missions, 3) a unified budget estimating the cost of the program, 4) a plan of interdenominational comity assigning to each society its responsibility in the common effort, and 5) a united educational and financial drive to acquaint the home churches with the findings of the survey and to raise the funds required to execute its recommendations. The next year was devoted to carrying out the first four parts of the program. The educational and financial drive was begun in March, 1920. By July, 1920, the failure of the movement was conceded by its sponsors, the employed staff was dismissed, and the liquidation of the organization was begun. This was completed in 1922. Its research was continued on a small scale by the Institute of Social and Religious Research.

The most important permanent contribution of the Movement was its *Report on the Steel Strike of 1919*. This study exercised significant influence in arousing the public opinion which at last brought to an end the twelve hour day in the steel industry. The failure of the movement has often been attributed to the antagonism of powerful financial and industrial interests to the *Report*. This, however, was a minor factor. More important were the general social and political reaction at the close of the war, the worsening economic outlook, the lack of preparation of public opinion among the churches for the degree of cooperative action required by the movement, and the fear on the part of many denominational agencies that it would absorb or dominate their own work.

J. H. Oldham, "The Interchurch World Movements: Its Possibilities and Problems", *International Review of Missions*, vol. 9 (April, 1920), pp. 182-199; "Interchurch World Movement Number", *Missionary Review of the World*, Vol. 43 (March, 1920), pp. 161-238; "Embarrassment of the Interchurch Movement," *Literary Digest*, Vol. 65, (June 12, 1920), pp. 42-43; "Cooperation's Greatest Failure," *Literary Digest*, Vol. 80 (January 12, 1924) p. 33.

H.E.J.

interdenominational cooperation: See Federal Council of The Churches of Christ in America; Interchurch World Movement of North America; Sunday School movement in the United States.

Interdenominational Council of Religious Education: See Sunday School movement in the United States.

interdict: In canon law (*Codex Iuris Canonici**, 2268-77), an ecclesiastical punishment whereby the subjects of the Church, while remaining within her communion, are barred from certain sacred rites or functions—Mass, the sacraments, divine services. It may be either personal or local, general or particular. See ban. J.C.M.

interest: In psychology the attitude of the mind (and self) toward any object, activity or end of action which excites feeling, arouses concern, attracts and absorbs attention, and in general evokes spontaneous "whole-hearted" response. It is a mind-set characterized by a readiness to respond to, a propensity to attend to, and an inner urge to engage in further pursuit of such an object, activity or end of action. The term is also applied to the object of such an attitude or mind-set.

The roots of interest were formerly said to be the instincts. This explanation has proved to be too narrow and inaccurate. The desires, needs, habits and purposes of the self, all of which are socially conditioned and in large part socially defined, and all of which are too complex to be explained in terms of innate factors alone, are now held to be the main sources of interest.

R.W.F.

interim: A temporary agreement in religious matters between Catholics and Lutherans, made at the Diet of Augsburg, 1548, after Charles V* had crushed the Schmalcald League*. Though it compromised Reformation doctrines, it was to be binding on Lutherans until the next general council. Accepted by a few Lutheran princes, it was rejected by John of Saxony and most of the Lutheran cities, especially by Magdeburg. It was terminated in the Treaty of Passau, 1552, which followed Maurice of Saxony's victory over the emperor. E.C.K.

intermediate state: The state of the soul between death and final judgment. Zoroastrianism, late Hebrew religion, Stoicism, Christianity, and Mohammedanism** all have such a belief, as against Eastern religions generally. Frequently the belief is but slightly formulated even when, as in Mohammedanism, the doctrines of judgment, hell, and heaven are clear.

Contrary to Hellenistic views which developed the beliefs of the early Greeks into an intellectual immortality, Pharisee and apocalyptic* thought in Judaism expanded the prophetic this-worldliness with beliefs, usually pictorially described, that centre on the survival of the moral and religious elements of the whole personality. These included particular and general judgment, hell and heaven and an intermediate state and prayers for the dead.

In Christianity these beliefs were retained generally except by some medieval heretical sects and received fullest explication in medieval times as the doctrine of Purgatory*. The Reformers' protest against this is the basis for a general Protestant denial, until recently, of any intermediate state. T.J.B.

International Bible Students' Association: See Russell, Charles Taze; Russelism; Millenial Dawn; J. F. Rutherford.

International Church of the Foursquare Gospel: A religious sect of the fundamentalist type organized and controlled by Mrs. Aimee Semple McPherson (died, 1944). Its central church is the Angelus Temple at Los Angeles. From this center the movement has spread into about twenty states and to some Latin American countries, and it claims a total of 205 churches and 16,000 members.

The sect revolves about the personality of Aimee Semple McPherson. Born in Canada, first married to a travelling Baptist evangelist, she came to Los Angeles in 1918, "by divine call", where she founded the Echo Park Evangelistic Association and built Angelus Temple to large proportions. She was pastor of the Temple and president for life of the Foursquare sect, with power to appoint her successor, to name all trustees and directors and to hold veto power over their actions.

The Foursquare theology is thoroughly fundamentalist. The sect is adventist, charismatic, premillennarian, and pentecostal. Among the doctrines stressed in the declaration of faith (written by Mrs. McPherson) are verbal inspiration, literalism, spirit baptism and guidance, speaking in unknown tongues and interpreting the same, divine healing and miracles, the imminent second coming and millennial reign of Christ, and a literal heaven and hell. See pentecostal sects. E.T.C.

International Graded Sunday School Lesson: See Sunday School movement in the United States.

international law: See law.

International New Thought Alliance: See New Thought movement.

International Pentecostal Assemblies: See pentecostal sects.

International Sunday School Association: See Sunday School movement in the United States.

International Sunday School Convention: See Sunday School movement in the United States.

International Sunday School Council of Religious Education: See Sunday School movement in the United States.

International Uniform Sunday School Lesson: See Sunday School movement in the United States.

internuncio: (Lat. *inter*, between; *nuntius*, messenger) A papal diplomat having charge of the legation in a foreign country of secondary importance. He is either a titular archbishop or a domestic prelate, and has the same powers and privileges of a nuncio but without the latter's dignity. See legates and nuncios, papal. J.F.T.

interpolation: A word, phrase, sentence, or passage of greater length inserted by a copyist or editor of a writing, either unintentionally through a scribal error or intentionally to change or modify the meaning. The identification of these interpolations in the Bible and in other sources is a necessary part of critical study. Familiar examples: the addition to the Ten Commandments in the Samaritan Pentateuch*; the apocalypse in Isa. 24-27; the doxology to the Lord's Prayer (Matt. 6:13); the resurrection narrative in Mark 16:9-20; the *Pericope Adulterae* (Jn. 7:53-8:11); "He descended into Hell" in the Apostles' Creed; and the "*filioque*" clause in the Latin text of the Nicene Creed. M.R.

interpretation: See allegorical interpretation; anagogical interpretation; exegesis; literal interpretation; senses of Scripture; types.

interstice: (Lat. *interstitium*, an interval) The interval of time required by canon law* between the receptions of the various ranks of orders* in the Roman Catholic Church, e.g., between acolyte* (minor order) and subdiaconate (major order), one year; between subdiaconate and diaconate, and diaconate and priesthood, three months. J.F.T.

intichiuma: (Australian) A rite of natives of central Australia; ceremonies for the maintenance of the annual supply of food and drink, such as rain-making ceremonies and those in which the flesh of the kangaroo is ceremonially eaten. F.L.P.

introit: (Lat. *introitus*, entrance) The name in the Roman rite for the anthem sung as the priest approaches the altar at the beginning of Mass*. See plainsong; psalmody. E.R.H.

introspection: (Lat. *introspicere*, to look into) The observation of the presentations and processes of one's own consciousness; as such, the chief method, historically, of all philosophical analysis of mind and of spiritual autobiography; developed as a carefully controlled method by Titchener and his Structuralist* (existentialist) School, completely rejected by Watson and his behaviorist school, but now generally recognized as supplemental to behavioristic, psychoanalytic and other psychological methods. E.T.R.

intrusion: Thrusting a person into an ecclesiastical office illegally. The "non-intrusion controversy" which issued in the disruption of the Church of Scotland* in 1843 arose because ministers presented by patrons were thrust into parish churches by civil authority over the objection of congregations, in disregard of an act of the General Assembly. R.H.N.

intuitionism: See empirical theology; epistemology; immediacy; mysticism; religious datum; truth.

intuitionism, ethical: An intuition is a proposition that is self evident to an intelligent mind. While all ethical systems make some use of intuitions, the designation Intuitionism is commonly restricted to those relying almost wholly on intuitions, making little use of abstract reasoning and empirical observations. The Scottish Intuitionists (Thomas Reid, Dugald Stewart, Thomas Brown, et al.,) in opposition to their contemporary rivals, mostly Utilitarians* and Kantians, believed that a man's conscience, properly educated, enables him to know without much reflection what he ought to do. The term is now sometimes applied to Sir W. David Ross and others who affirm that "right" and "good", known intuitively, sometimes call for contrary actions between which choice has to be made. W.K.W.

investiture conflict: (1059-1122) Investiture was originally the bestowal of an ecclesiastical office by investing the recipient with the symbols (ring, staff, keys) of his authority. In this conflict the popes disputed the claim of the lay rulers to confer bishoprics, abbacies, and other ecclesiastical offices. Sovereigns had in early medieval times arrogated this right to themselves. Simony, an incontinent clergy, and the subordination of the spiritual to the temporal power resulted. From the reign of Nicholas II (1059-1061), the popes endeavored, for the sake of reform, to free the Church from this scourge and particularly from the tutelage of the Holy Roman Empire in Italy and in Germany. The struggle reached an acute stage in 1075 when St. Gregory VII* (Hildebrand) delivered an ultimatum to the emperor Henry IV. The latter resisted and was excommunicated. There followed the celebrated scene between the pope and the emperor at Canossa. Many have seen in it the humiliation of the civil power by the ambitious Church. Some are inclined to interpret it as a political triumph for Henry. The conflict continued under the successors of the pope and of the emperor and was settled by a compromise, the Concordat of Worms (1122)*, between Henry V and Callistus II. The civil authority was deprived of its unlimited power over the appointment of bishops, while the Church had to be satisfied with something less than the full exclusion of alien influence from canonical elections. In England Henry I had renounced investiture in 1107. In France a reform had been effected by 1080. Further action concerning lesser ecclesiastical offices was taken at the Lateran Council of 1179. See Lateran Councils.

E.A.R.

Invitatory: Psalm 95, "O come, let us sing unto the Lord", sung at the beginning of Matins* as a call to worship is the invitatory Psalm; the invitatories are phrases attached to it (Roman rite and newer Anglican Prayer Books) relating to the day or season being observed. E.R.H.

invocation: A term to describe the words employed to ask for the special presence of God at the opening of a religious service, or for some special purpose. Traditionally used, also, to describe the invocatory formula, "In the name of the Father and of the Son and of the Holy Ghost", with which sermons, acts of devotion, etc., are often begun in Catholic communions. In the Anglican liturgies, the word is used also to describe the "epiclesis"*, by which the Holy Spirit is "invoked" upon the elements of bread and wine. Cf. intercession. W.N.P.

Ionic style: See temples, Greek and Roman.

Ireland, Church of: That part of Irish Christianity which accepted the Reformation as introduced from England, and since 1560 has disputed with Roman Catholics the claim to continuity with the ancient and mediaeval Irish Church. Probably at all times about 10% of the population, it was at first largely Calvinist (see Irish Articles), and since 1800 has been the most strongly Evangelical Church of the Anglican Communion. After disestablishment in 1869 it revised its Prayer Book and Canons in an Evangelical and anti-ritualist direction, though reaffirming its claim to be the "Catholic and Apostolic Church of Ireland."

W. A. Phillips, ed., *History of the Church of Ireland*, 3 vols. (1933); J. T. Ball, *The Reformed Church of Ireland* (1886). E.R.H.

Irenæus: A second-century bishop of Lyons in Gaul and heresiologist*. He was born in Asia Minor (*ca.* 130 A.D.). Of his youth little is known save his own statement that he had as a boy seen and heard Polycarp. His mature life was spent in Gaul, first as a presbyter, then, following the death of Pothinus, as bishop of Lyons. His principle writing, *Against the Heresies*, (*ca.* 180 A.D.), was intended as an exposure and refutation of Gnosticism*. It was written in Greek, fragments of which are extant in the writings of Hippolytus, Eusebius, and Epiphanius; the whole being available in an early Latin translation. The writing was widely used in the early church and is still the fullest account of the Gnostic vagaries. Irenæus is properly regarded one of the most influential figures of the ante-Nicene church. The last three books of his *Against the Heresies* may be called the first systematic exposition of Christian belief. The date of his death is unknown. Mention of his martyrdom under Septimus Severus does not apparently antedate the fifth century. See clergy; recapitulation.

The standard edition of Irenæus is H. W. Harvey, *Sancti Irenaei episcopi Lugdunensis Libros quinque Adversus haereses*, 2 vols. (1857). M.S.E.

irenics: Irenical theology is the study of Christian doctrines with a view to conciliating differences which arise in religion and the church from one-sided theories. Its purpose is to promote the peace and harmony of the Christian Church. A.K.R.

Irish Articles: Adopted by the Convocation of the Church of Ireland* in 1615, revised the Thirty-Nine Articles* in a strongly Calvinist direction. Though disused in Ireland after the adoption of the Thirty-Nine Articles in 1634, they were used in part as a basis for the Westminster Confession*. E.R.H.

irregularity: In Roman Catholic and Anglican usage, the performance of a sacred act (e.g., the bestowal of Holy Orders*) with the essentials of validity but in violation of the rules involved; irregular orders cannot be repeated, but confer no right to exercise official functions in the Church unless the irregularity is rectified. E.R.H.

irresistible grace: See grace.

Irving, Edward: (1792-1834) Minister of the established Church of Scotland, known for his apocalyptic sermons and theology, which were instrumental in founding the Catholic Apostolic Church in London in 1832. A child prodigy, he entered the Church after graduation from the Uni. of Edinburgh and became an assistant to Thomas Chalmers. Removing to London his fiery sermons on prophecy and the millenial hope attracted great crowds. In 1830 he was excommunicated by the Presbyterian Synod of London for preaching the humanity of Jesus, and not long after going into forced retirement, died. His followers left the Church to form a new sect, which now has approximately 50,000 members in England and America. See Catholic Apostolic Church.

Mrs. M. Oliphant (Wilson), *Life of Edward Irving* (London, 1862); W. Wilks, *Edward Irving* (London, 1854); Samuel Taylor Coleridge, *Notes on English Divines* (London, 1853); Edward Miller, *History and Doctrine of Irvingism* (2 vols., London, 1878); Thomas Carlyle, *Miscellanies*, "Essay on Death of Irving," ed. Froude (1881). M.G.R.—W.W.S.

Irvingites: See Irving, Edward; Catholic Apostolic Church.

isagogics: That part of theology directly preliminary to actual exegesis*, and concerned with the literary history of the Bible. More generally known as Biblical Introduction* it deals with such subjects as authorship, date and place of writing, contents, style and peculiar difficulties of the different writings of Scripture. A.K.R.

Isaiah: The Book of Isaiah is composed of two halves that have been artificially combined: a book purporting to contain prophecies of Isaiah, an 8th century prophet (chs. 1-39), and a book of prophecies of a much later time (chs. 40-66).

1. Isaiah 1-39 may be divided into four main sections: 1-12, 13-27, 28-35, 36-39. The most valuable section is 1-12; it represents a combination of a number of separate collections—a) 1:1-31 belong to the closing days of Isaiah's career and look back on the war of 701 B.C. (Sennacherib). b) 2:1-4:6—early invective and predictions with some non-authentic hopeful additions 2:2-4 (Micah 4:1-4) and 4:2-6. c) 5:1-30—early invective. d) 6:1-9:6—sometimes called the "Isaiah Memoir," containing sections of first person narrative. e) 9:7-11:9—really the continuation of item c), with an appendix 11:10-12:5. The second main section, 13-27 is composed of a group of "burdens," 13-23 (i.e., oracles against particular nations of which few, if any, can be considered "authentic"), and of the "Isaiah-apocalypse," 24-27, a production of the late Persian or early Greek era. In 28-35 there are three groups of material: 28-32 we again have chiefly genuine utterances of Isaiah, belonging to his later days, with two appendices,—a "prophetic liturgy" (ch. 33) and a prophecy imitative of Deutero-Isaiah (34-35), both of much later vintage. Chapters 36-39, finally, are taken over from II Kings*. Isaiah is the most "classic" of the prophets in thought and diction.

2. "Deutero-Isaiah" is often used to describe Isaiah 40-66, but more particularly 40-55 (in which case 56-66 are called "Trito-Isaiah"). Chapters 40-55 are a collection of poems in a new rhapsodic style from the period of the exile. Modern "form-criticism"* provides an essential tool for the separation of the individual entities. The allusions to Cyrus as a rising figure and the imminent fall of Chaldaean Babylon suggest a date of 550-538 B.C. Torrey's attempt to preserve the unity of 40-66 by eliminating the Cyrus-Babylon passages and dating the whole work much later has not met with much favor. Of particular importance are the Servant songs, 42:1-4, 49:1-6, 50:4-9, 52:13-53-12. The problem of their authorship (composed by Deuter-Isaiah or by a follower?), and interpretation (the Servant a "collective" figure—the ideal Israel—or an individual—past (e.g., Jeremiah), present (the prophet himself), or future ("Messiah")—will probably never be solved. Entirely apart from any Messianic "predictions" contained in it, the book is full of profound insights and an important preparation for Christianity. "Trito-Isaiah" is the usual designation for 55-66. Some hold that they are the work of a single author. The most favored view today, however, is that 56-66 contain a number of poems of diverse origin. Of the units contained in it, chapters 60-62, 57:14-19, 66:6-16 seem to be by one hand—that of a pupil or imitator of Deutero-Isaiah, presumably writing about the time of Haggai and Zechariah**.

R. H. Pfeiffer, *Introduction to the Old Testament* (1941); J. A. Bewer; *Literature of the Old Testament* (rev. ed., 1933). E.G.K.

Isaiah, Ascension of: A 3-4 cent. A.D. compilation of several older works—a Jewish "Martyrdom of Isaiah" (1 cent. B.C.), interpolated with a fragment of a christian "Vision of Isaiah" 3:13-4:18 (100 A.D.) and augmented with a visionary ascension of Isaiah, 6-11 (2 cent. A.D.) E.G.K.

Ishtar: See Mesopotamian religion. Cf. Ashtoreth.

Ishvara: The personalized form of God as contrasted with the impersonal Brahman in Hinduism. Used chiefly by the theistic Hindu sects as the name of their Supreme God. C.S.B.

Isidore Mercator: See False Decretals.

Isidore of Seville: (c. 570-636) Succeeded his brother as Bishop of Seville 608; an extensive writer; his *Etymologies* and other text-books preserved learning, while his practical works are notable for sense if not for originality. E.R.H.

Isis: See Osiris; mother-goddesses; mystery religions.

Isis-Osiris: See mystery religions.

Islam: (Arabic, meaning submission to, or having peace with God) The religion of which Mohammed* was the prophet. As Mohammed preached submission to God he called his religion Islam. An adherent of Islam is called a Moslem* (Arabic, one who submits). See Mohammedanism. P.E.J.

Ismailis: A branch of the Shiite* sect in Islam, established by Adallah ibn Maymum in the 9th century. Members were initiated to its secret organization to prepare for the revelation of a concealed leader (*imam**) of the house of Ali. Groups are still found in Arabia, Egypt and India. See taqiyya. P.E.J.

Israel, religion and theology: Judaism regards all of its adherents as members of a religious order, a "kingdom of priests"; and it imposes on them a religious discipline, both moral and ceremonial, such as is prescribed in other religions, generally, only for members of special orders. This religious discipline is considered a means of communion with God. Thus the study of the Scriptures and their commentaries, and the observance of the Law*, are as much a part of Jewish worship as the recital of prayers or attendance at synagogue. Hence it comes about that much of the Jewish religion has to be practiced outside of the synagogue*. Judaism affects conduct not only in the religious school, but also in the marketplace, and above all in the home. This religious system, aside from its intrinsic appeal to the Jew who follows it, has an interest for the Christian and Mohammedan world, because of their close association with it in their origins; and its long history offers an excellent opportunity for the study of the development of religious thought generally.

The term "religion and theology of Israel" as used in this article, therefore covers the religion and theology which, inculcated in the Hebrew Scriptures, has survived in the form of Rabbinic Judaism* until our day. The whole constitutes a dynamic system, the origins of which we can trace back to Moses*, and the growth of which we can follow over the whole period of more than three thousand years from his time. The view, commonly held among some Bible critics a generation ago, that Moses himself was a mythical character, and that even if he existed, he was a "henotheist"* is today vanishing. An increasingly strong body of opinion even among higher critics holds that Moses was a monotheist.

The most obvious elements in the development of prophetic religion after Moses were its continuous battles against idolatry, and its increasing recognition of the importance and moral responsibility of the individual personality. With these there came a deepening of the understanding of life's moral issues, such as a recognition of the meaning of universal peace, and its indispensability to civilization.

The most impressive figure in the struggle against idol-worship was that of Elijah*, whose dramatic manner of winning the people of Israel away from the worship of the Phoenician Baal* to the worship of God, remained one of the most cherished memories of the Jewish tradition. The emphasis on the moral responsibility of the individual attained its highest expression in the teachings of the prophet, Ezekiel*, in the sixth century B.C.

The accentuation of the moral responsibility of the individual tended to raise the question of reward and punishment of individual persons, and with that of the problem of evil in the world. The problem is first suggested in the Pentateuch* itself (Genesis*, chap. 18), but is expressed with increasing clarity by Jeremiah* (seventh cent. B.C.) and by Habakkuk* (possibly a contemporary). The discussion reaches new levels in the portrayal of Israel as the "suffering servant of God" by the Second Isaiah* (in the sixth century B.C.), and in the argument about the theodicy* which constitutes the Book of Job* (probably composed in the fourth century B.C.).

The discussion entered a new phase with the emergence of the doctrine of the resurrection*, which appears in Israel clearly for the first time in Isaiah, 26.19, a section of the Book of Isaiah frequently assigned to the fourth or third centuries B.C.

The question of the belief in the resurrection, and its accompanying doctrine of personal immortality*, thus introduced, assumed continually greater importance in the Jewish consciousness. The Sadducean* sect, which denied the resurrection, came to be regarded as heretical by the Pharisees*, who ultimately constituted the majority of the Jews.

Together with the rise of the doctrine of the resurrection, there grew up a belief that the study of the Law and its elaboration led to personal salvation*. This doctrine, held in the first instance probably by the Hasideans* of the fourth and third centuries, and the Scribes* who led them, ultimately was accepted as basic by the Pharisaic sect. According to this doctrine, especial merit attached to the lay students who devoted themselves to the study of the Law, and to memorizing and transmitting the comments made upon it by their teachers. The whole body of traditions which grew up among these scribes became known as the "Oral Law" because it was handed down orally from master to pupil. The Pharisees accepted the authority of this Law, and the Sadducees, who also held that the Scriptures were of binding authority, did not admit that these oral traditions had any validity.

While the Pharisees insisted that personal salvation could be obtained by members of the Jewish faith only by the study and observance of the Law, in all its aspects, ceremonial as well as civil, they taught that all men could obtain salvation by the observance of seven basic moral principles. These were called the "Noachic Laws", because, according to Pharisaic doctrine, they applied to all the descendants of Noah, and according to one version were revealed to him. These laws are those forbidding idol-worship, blasphemy, murder, sexual irregularity, theft, and cruelty to animals, and establishing civil righteousness.

The Talmudic* writings are the products of the Pharisaic tradition; we have no ancient works stemming from the Sadducean tradition. Hence, Judaism as it has survived in the world is essentially ancient Pharisaism.

In the course of centuries, the Pharisaic Judaism has further been stimulated by its reaction to Greek philosophy (as in Philo* Judeus, Alexandria, first century of the Christian era), and also, in a less definite form, among the Rabbinical scholars of Palestine. In later times, scholars like Rab Saadia Gaon (882-942), Judah Ha-Levi (1085-1140), Ibn Gabirol (ca. 1021-ca. 1058), and Moses ben Maimon** (1135-1204) made efforts to interpret the traditional faith in terms of the later philosophical development, particularly as it became extant among the Arabs from the eighth to the twelfth centuries. The work of these philosophers, and some of their less well-known successors, like Hasdai Crescas (1340-1410), was of great significance not only for Judaism, but also for Christianity, which utilized their works for the clarification of its own philosophy.

The essential elements in the Jewish faith as it has emerged out of these developments are its insistence on the unity, the incorporeality, the timelessness and the immanence of God; on the authority of the Law, as interpreted in the Talmud writings, and later Rabbinic works; as well as the belief in the dignity and immortality of the individual human personality; and the belief in the ultimate redemption of mankind in the Messianic Age.

In the course of the 19th century, there developed first in Germany, and then also in the United States, a "Reform" movement in Judaism, the purpose of which is a re-statement of Judaism on the basis of modified system of observances. (See Judaism, Reform.) Among some extremist teachers, Reform Judaism tends to take the form almost of anti-nomianism*, while among more moderate teachers, it constitutes simply an effort to adjust Jewish traditional ceremonial discipline to the problems of a standardized, industrial age. To meet the challenge of Reform Judaism, there developed both in Germany and in America, a movement called "Conservative Judaism"*, which seeks to maintain the historic continuity of the Jewish tradition, and claims that all the social and theological problems of the modern day can be solved within the framework of that tradition, and the elasticity it allows to its interpreters. On the other hand, a third group, known as "Orthodox Jews"* deny that the traditional customs are in need of either adjustment or re-interpretation.

During the last decade of the 19th century, the traditional belief of Judaism that ultimately the center of its spiritual life would be restored to Palestine, as the Holy Land, led to the rise of the Zionist* movement which seeks to effect the re-establishment of Palestine as a homeland of the Jewish people. The rise of this movement led to the issuance of the Balfour Declaration by Great Britain in 1917, enunciating the promise that His Majesty's Government would favor the establishment of such a homeland for the Jews. The problems associated with this declaration, and its implementation, have been many and complicated; and they are still unsolved. The Zionist movement, while drawing numbers of adherents from Orthodox, Conservative, and Reform groups, also includes many who are not all affiliated with any of these groups.

These is no central Jewish body capable of giving final, authoritative interpretation to Judaism. Each learned teacher or rabbi* may turn to the Talmud and its related writings for his guidance. As a matter of practice, and by informal concensus, the leading teachers of each generation come to be recognized as such, but their authority extends only to those individuals and groups who consider them acceptable interpreters of the Law. See Jewish; Judaism; Semites, religion of. Also see cosmogonies.

W. F. Albright, *From the Stone Age to Christianity* (1940); *idem, Archaeology and the Religion of Israel* (1942); Salo W. Baron, *A Social and Religious History of the Jews* (1937); Elbogen, *Die Religionsanschauungen der Pharisaeer mit besonderer Beruecksichtigung der Begriffe Gott und Mensch* (Berlin, 1904); Louis Finkelstein, *The Pharisees, The Sociological Background of their Faith* (2nd ed., 1939); *idem, Beliefs and Practices of Judaism* (1941); Israel Friedlaender, *Past and Present,* A Collection of Jewish Essays (1919); Morris Joseph, *Judaism as Creed and Life,* (5th ed., London, 1925); Kaufmann Kohler, *Jewish Theology* (1918); G. F. Moore, *Judaism in the First Centuries of the Christian Era* (Cambridge, 1927); W. O. E. Oesterley and G. H. Box, *The Religion and Worship of the Synagogue* (London, 1907); W. O. E. Oesterley and T. H. Robinson, *Hebrew Religion* (1930); W. O. E. Oesterley, *Judaism and Christianity* (1937); Solomon Schechter, *Some Aspects of Rabbinic Theology* (1909); *idem, Studies in Judaism,* 3 vols. (1896-1924); J. Wellhausen, *Israelitische und juedische Geschichte* (8th ed., Berlin-Leipzig, 1921). L.F.

Israel: See Judaism (Introductory).

Israel ben Eliezer: See Chasidism.

Israfil or Israfel: The angel of music in Mohammedan mythology who is expected to sound the trumpet at the resurrection. P.E.J.

Itala: See versions of the Bible, ancient.

Italian pentecostal sects: There are two pentecostal sects among Italians in the United States, both growing out of a movement in Chicago about 1904. The Unorganized Italian Christian Churches of North America has 104 congregations and 9,500 members. Its headquarters are in Chicago. The Italian Pentecostal Assemblies of God, with headquarters in Newark, N. J., has 16 churches and 1,500 members. Both groups hold to the fundamentalist theology and stress the pentecostal gift of speaking in unknown tongues. See pentecostal sects. E.T.C.

itinerarium: A form of prayer used by monks and clerics before setting out on a journey, and is usually printed at the end of the Breviary. The use of such forms is probably to be traced to monastic observances. Among the Fathers of the Desert there were prescriptions on the conduct of monks before setting out on a journey. The rule of St. Benedict* gives two forms, one for those going on a short journey, and a second and more solemn form to be used by those about to go on a long journey. The Itinerarium of the present day is probably derived from the more solemn form used in medieval times. The usual form of the Itinerarium consists of the canticle "Benedictus," with an antiphon, certain versicles, and several collects. T.T.M.

ius divinum (*lex divina; lex aeterna*) In Scholastic, especially Thomist theory the immutable order of both nature and human society that derives immediately from God, as opposed to man-made, changeable *lex humana.* Within the comprehensive category of *ius divinum, ius naturale* constitutes that part that is known to man through reason, while *ius divinum positivium* would be unknown but for supernatural revelation.

See Canon Law; ius naturale; law. M.Rh.

ius naturale: See natural law; natural rights; ius divinum.

iustitia naturalis: (natural righteousness or perfection) By himself man was able to do good before he fell by reason of his natural righteousness or perfection by which the sensual was subject to his free will. See perfection, perfectionism. H.H.

iustitia originalis: (original or primitive righteousness or perfection) This is the righteousness or perfection given man at his creation. It is not a part of nature. It was given man before the Fall. The state of original righteousness is in Catholic thought a special supernatural gift, a *donum supernaturale*, which was added to the *pura naturalia,* that is the essential humanity which Adam had as man before he fell. The idea testifies to the fact that human sin cannot destroy the essential character of man to such a degree that it would cease being implied in, and furnishing a contrast to, what he has become. Catholic thought makes a complete distinction between natural law and original righteousness or perfection. See perfection, perfectionism. H.H.

Izanagi: Origin of word unknown. The name applied to the ancient Japanese sky father. D.C.H.

Izanami: Origin of word unknown. The name applied to the ancient Japanese earth mother. D.C.H.

J

J: Symbol used for one of the component narratives of certain O.T. books, derived from the initial letter of the divine name Jahveh (Jehovah*, Yahweh), which it employs before the time of Moses. It is found in Genesis-Judges, and possibly also in I, II Samuel*. J was written in Judah, probably in the tenth or ninth century B.C. While it has been subdivided by some scholars more minutely (J1, J2, L, S, etc.), it is possible to do justice to the facts by considering the J writer as both compiler and creative author. See Hexateuch.

See E. S. Brightman, *The Sources of the Hexateuch* (1918); O. Eissfeldt, *Hexateuch-Synopse* (1922).

J.P.H.

Jacobi, Friedrich Heinrich: (1743-1819) German philosopher of intuition. Himself a realist and an empiricist, Jacobi opposed Kant's* philosophy charging that it leads to solipsism*. Our consciousness of freedom, moreover, refutes the absolute determinism of Spinoza's* philosophy. The existence of God cannot be proven by some demonstrative or mediate method of rationalism or discovered outside of man in nature where mechanical causation is the rule. Our apprehension of God can come only through immediate perception, that is, through faith. In such an act of direct knowledge or intuition, the existence of God is revealed within us with the certainty of feeling. The understanding however must not attempt the impossible task of defining God's nature and attributes, which are beyond the grasp of human understanding.

Main works: *Ueber die Lehre des Spinoza* (1785); *David Hume über den Glauben* (1787); *Sendschreiben an Fichte* (1799).

H.W.J.

Jacobites: As the members of the Syrian National Church are generally known, represent the monophysite* members of the ancient patriarchate of Antioch who refused to accept the decisions of the Council of Chalcedon* of 451. The nickname is derived from Jacob Baradaeus (490-577), who organized their scattered forces during the reign of Justinian and Theodora. The latter was herself a Monophysite, and protected Jacob from the persecuting measures declared against her co-religionists by her husband, the Orthodox Justinian. When the Mohammedan Arabs conquered Syria, the Monophysite Jacobites were free to develop their own organization relatively unimpeded. At present they number about 200,000 members, ruled by the Patriarch of Antioch, whose seat is at Mardin in Iraq. See Antiochene (Syrian Rite); Syrian Churches.

J. B. Kidd, *The Churches of Eastern Christendom* (London, n.d.); Harry C. J. Luke, *Prophets, Priests and Patriarchs* (London, 1927).

M.S.

Jacopo da Voragine (or Varagine): (c. 1230-c. 1298) Popular preacher, Dominican, later Archbishop of Genoa. His *Legendae Sanctorum*, commonly called *Legenda Aurea*, a collection of legends* of the saints arranged according to their days in the calendar of the church, became one of the most popular books of the Middle Ages. After circulating in many manuscript copies for a century and a half, it was printed not only in the original Latin but in translations into five other languages within the first half century of printing. Caxton published it in 1483 as "The Golden Legend." The statement, by Sixtus of Siena, that Jacopo translated the whole Bible into Italian is generally disputed, but is defended by Richardson.

Potthast, *Bibliotheca his. med. aev.* (Berlin, 1896); E. C. Richardson, *Materials for a Life of Jacopo da Varagine* (1935); G. Ryan and H. Ripperger, *The Golden Legend of Jacopo da Voragine*, Translated and Adapted, 2 vols. (1941).

W.E.G.

Jagganath, Juggernaut: A variant name of Vishnu* the Preserver under which he is worshipped at Puri. The most notable feature of his worship is the car festival in which the great images of Jagganath, "Lord of the World" and his brother and sister, Balaram and Subadhra are hauled by thousands of pious worshipers from the temple a distance some four miles to the Garden House. The great car is 45 feet in height, 35 feet square and runs on 16 wheels seven feet in diameter.

C.S.B.

Jainism: One of the native religions of India. The 6th century saw two major reform movements in Hinduism*, both of which eventually came to be regarded as separate religions. These were Jainism and Buddhism*. Both were a reaction against current conceptions of divinity in the direction of non-theism; both were attempts to win salvation or *moksha*** without resorting to the help of gods, which, specifically denied by neither, were held to be unable to do anything for man. Jainism is slightly older than Buddhism, indeed, its beginnings may lie much farther back than the 6th century. Buddha* in his quest for salvation began by the way of asceticism which was central among the Jains. Traditionally however, it is considered that Vardhaman or Mahavira*, "Great Hero" as he is better known, was the founder of the organized movement historically known as Jainism. Born 599 B.C. and dying 527 B.C. he was thus an older contemporary of Gautama. According to the Jain scriptures he was the last of the twenty-four Tirthankaras, or Ford Finders, who had through asceticism attained release, and served to encourage man in his hard search for *moksha*.

Theoretically in Jainism, salvation is to be won through rigid self-effort, mainly through the observation of ascetic practise, though the Three Jewels, knowledge, faith and right conduct, are stressed as the way to final liberation. Jainism accepted with some modification the Hindu law of Karma and transmigration**. More than any other Hindu group they emphasize ahimsha* or non-injury. The temples are among the most striking and ornate of the numerous temples of India. The present Jain population of India according to the 1931 census was 1,252,105. This represents a slight increase over the 1921 census which revealed a Jain population of 1,178,596, but was nearly 200,000 less than the number in the census of 1891. See cycles of time; sacred literatures.

S. Stevenson, *The Heart of Jainism* (Oxford, 1915); J. B. Pratt, *India and Its Faiths* (1915); Nicol McNicol, *Living Religions of India* (London, 1934).

C.S.B.

James: (Gr. *Jacobus*) 1. Son of Zebedee, brother of John, and one of the twelve disciples; executed by Herod Agrippa 1 ca. 44 A.D. 2. The son of Alphaeus, also one of the twelve; possibly identical with James the son of Mary (Mark 16:1, etc.). In Mark 15:40 called "James the Younger." 3. The brother of the Lord and head of the early Christian community in Jerusalem; stoned to death in 62 A.D. 4. Father of a disciple of Jesus whom Luke (6:16) calls Judas.

S.M.G.

James, Letter of: James is an ancient sermon, dwelling upon the practical aspects of the Christian life, which it sets forth with great pungency and variety. The opposition it sets up between faith and works undoubtedly reflects acquaintance with Paul's collected letters, but is aimed not at Paul's doctrine of faith but at a current misconception of it. It is impossible to trace a course of thought through the little tract; it is less a chain of thought than a string of pearls. The ancient preacher seems to aim at having something for everybody in his audience, and so deals with every sort of human weakness. Illustrations, rhetorical questions, scorn and humor all play their vivid parts, recalling the diatribes of the Stoic street preachers, and the discourses of Epictetus. The writer was acquainted not only with the collected Pauline letters, but with Hebrews, I Peter, and probably Matthew and Luke**. The sermon was probably written early in the second century, and afterward published, addressed to Christians everywhere. The name James may have been suggested by the apparent opposition to Paul in 2:14-26, along with Paul's mention of James in Gal. 2:12 as the leader of the opposition in Jerusalem; in that case James the Lord's brother is meant.

J. H. Ropes, *The Epistle of St. James* (1916).

E.J.G.

James, William: (1842-1910) Psychologist, philosopher, expounder of religious theory, teacher at Harvard 1873-1907, one of the most original and influential figures in the American world of letters, son of Henry James the Swedenborgian theologian and brother of Henry James the novelist. James came to philosophy without B.A., M.A., or Ph.D. but as a man of the world who had read and travelled widely, and as an M.D. trained in the biological sciences. The results showed in the original and colorful qualities of his pragmatism and his radical empiricism. As a pragmatist he shifted attention from knower and known to organism and environment, interpreting knowledge as part of the larger practical situation where life adjusts itself to its world. Truth became thus not an antecedent reality, but what may or may not happen to ideas according as they work out satisfactorily. Logic became an instrument forged by life for the accomplishment of its demands. All intellectual operations derived their importance from their success in carrying out practical purposes.

Pragmatism* thus became a method for testing ideas. Radical empiricism began as a psychological theory and ended as an incomplete metaphysics which James left uncompleted at his death. As psychology it was the discovery of relations in transitive states of consciousness and therefore in the stream of experience itself, not supplied by an outside factor such as mind. As metaphysics it was an attempt to interpret reality as experience of the "strung-along variety", i.e., as having pluralistic and external relations and as being "what it is experienced as." Both pragmatism and radical empiricism had important results for religious theory. Pragmatism was, if anything, more successful as an interpretation of religious belief than of truth, since there is an obvious sense in which beliefs must be practical and must "outstrip the evidence" whereas the definition of truth in terms of results is open to question. The essays in *The Will to Believe* explain the part played by inner or emotional evidence and justify the appeal to purpose and will as an unavoidable element in determining one's world-view. *The Varieties of Religious Experience* describes the more passive, receptive attitude, where man is saved by a power outside himself, but the attempt to invoke radical empiricism to explain the nature of religious experience was somewhat obscured by its association with the "subconscious" and the phenomena of psychical research and hypnotism. (See subliminal self.) On the whole, James's greatest contribution to religion seems to rest on a) his pragmatic defence of emotional evidence, b) his pluralistic insistence that even for religion "all is not well' and God is limited, c) his empiricistic eagerness to take experience as it comes and in doing so to look for light in unexpected places. He bequeathed less a convincing definition of truth than a sense of the need of being ever on the alert for new truth; he will be remembered not for a stereotyped set of phrases but for his large-hearted generous attitude and for his remarkable ability to make the printed page reflect the color of living experience. In psychology, philosophy, and religion he did not so much offer a definition as determine a direction. His influence has grown since his death. See psychology, schools of.

Works: *The Principles of Psychology* (1890) 2 vols.; *The Will to Believe*, etc. (1897); *Human Immortality* (1898); *Talks on Psychology* (1899); *The Varieties of Religious Experience* (1902); *Pragmatism* (1907); *A Pluralistic Universe* (1909); *The Meaning of Truth* (1909); *Some Problems of Philosophy* (1911); *The Letters of William James* (1920). Cf. R. B. Perry: *The Thought and Character of William James* (1935), which contains not only an exhaustive analysis but many hitherto unpublished letters. J.S.B.

Jane Frances de Chantal (Jeanne Francoise Fremyot de Chantal), Saint: (1572-1641) A woman of rare spiritual qualities who as a widow, after raising her family, founded with the aid of her spiritual director, St. Francis de Sales*, the Congregation of the Visitation. See Visitation, Order of the. D.V.S.

Jansenism: A movement in the Roman Catholic Church named after Cornelius Jansen (Bishop of Ypres, 1636-8) whose posthumous *Augustinus* (1640) revived extreme Augustinian positions on predestination and grace. Jansenism was associated with rigorist ethics, especially in France, where Pascal's *Lettres provinciales* (1656-7) attacked the lax casuistry of some Jesuit* writers. In 1653 five Jansenist propositions were condemned by Pope Innocent X, but this merely provoked a controversy as to whether the propositions really appeared in the *Augustinus*, and whether the Pope's authority extended to matters of fact as well as of faith. A devotional work, the *Reflexions morales* of Quesnel*, became a means of Jansenist propaganda; in 1713 Clement XI condemned it in the bull *Unigenitus**, against which 20 French Bishops appealed to a General Council. But Jansenism had lost much of its religious force; on one side it fused with political Gallicanism*, on the other degenerated into the antics of the *Convulsionnaires*. In theology Jansenism merely led the Roman Catholic Church to reaffirm the Tridentine position on grace and free will; but its rigorism, though rejected as such, influenced the general development of moral theology.

A. Gazier, *Histoire générale du mouvement janseniste* (1922); L. von Pastor, *History of the Popes* (1938-1941) vols. 28-34. E.R.H.

Janson, Eric: See communistic settlements, religious, Bishop Hill colony.

Janus: (Lat. *Ianus*, from *ianua*, doorway) God of the doorway, a purely Roman divinity deriving from the ancient animism. Two-faced, he became the god of beginnings; hence January. His famous little bronze temple in the Roman Forum faced both east and west; it was open in time of war, closed in time of peace. In myth, he settled on the hill across the Tiber called from his name the Janiculum. E.M.N.

Japan, Christianity in: The story of Christianity in Japan is divided into two main periods: that of the Roman Catholic missions of the sixteenth and seventeenth centuries and that of the modern era which began with the arrival of the first Protestant missionaries in 1859. The former opened with the landing of Francis Xavier at Kagoshima on August 15, 1549, and in spite of temporary repressive measures under Toyotomi Hideyoshi in 1597, continued with a brilliant record until the second decade of the seventeenth century. Pagés, one of the modern Roman Catholic historians, estimates the number of Christian followers in 1605 at 750,000. This is probably an exaggeration. Bishop Cerqueira (1552-1614), who was in charge of the Jesuit mission to Japan at the time, states that the number of Christians under pastoral care in 1603 was 200,000. Many feudal lords and members of the nobility became followers of Christ. Nationalistic fears eventually led to violent anti-Christian reaction and persecution. By 1638 Christianity was supposedly completely blotted out. Actually it survived as a secret faith in various local areas until the change of governmental policy at the opening of the modern period made public profession of belief once more possible. The legal interdiction of Christianity was not removed until 1872.

The modern period has been characterized by exceeding diversity in propaganda agencies. Roman Catholic, Greek Orthodox, and a large representation of the Protestant denominations of Europe and America have sought to extend their communions to Japan. The first Protestant church was organized in Yokohama on March 10, 1872. In spite of the negative influence of anti-foreign reaction at the close of the nineteenth century and the disturbing effects of the "New Japanism" that developed with ever-rising tempo throughout the decade beginning with the opening of the Manchurian Affair in September, 1931, the general impact of the Christian movement on Japan, while not spectacular, has nevertheless had sufficient penetration to influence constructively many areas of the national life. Most of the movements for social melioration in modern Japan were cradled in the Christian church. On the other hand the rising national sentiment of the 1931-1941 period found an outlet in the Christian churches that widened constantly as the crisis of the Pacific war drew nearer.

Insofar as Protestant bodies are concerned, earlier diversity has been partially counterbalanced by a considerable degree of unification in general policies. This has been especially true since the formation of the National Christian Council of

Japan in 1922. The trend towards standardization was still further augmented by the adoption in the spring of 1940 of the Religious Organizations Law which placed all agencies of religious propaganda and education under a unified official control, and, in the summer of 1941, by the cooperation of forty denominations in the formation of a single Protestant Church ("The Church of Christ in Japan"—*Nippon Kirisuto Kyodan*). In this latter reorganization powerful totalitarian pressure from the state operated to accelerate preexisting tendencies toward closer coordination within the various churches themselves. Statistics covering the status of Protestant denominations at the close of 1940 showed 233,000 members of churches, 1,931 organized churches, and 951 self-supporting churches. For the same period the Roman Catholic Church reported 119,000 adherents, and the Greek Orthodox Church an additional 41,000. See Japanese religions; Shinto religion and theology.

Otis Cary, *A History of Christianity in Japan* (1909) 2 vols.; Hans Haas, *Geschichte des Christenthums in Japan* (1902-4) 2 Vols., Tokyo; *The Japan Christian Year Book* (Formerly *The Christian Movement in Its Relation to the New Life in Japan; The Christian Movement in Japan, Korea and Formosa; The Japan Mission Year Book*, Yokohama and Tokyo (1901—). D.C.H.

Japanese religions: The major religious movements of Japan are Shinto, Buddhism, Confucianism** and Christianity.

Shinto, or the Way of the Gods, has had an institutional existence of approximately two thousand years. Even prior to the introduction of Buddhism into Japan in the middle of the sixth century A.D., Shinto had incorporated elements of diverse origin. At an early period a primitive animism was apparently amalgamated with Mongolian Shamanism and an ancient cosmogony that shows affinities with the mythology of southeastern Asia and Indonesia. The early rituals (*norito*) reveal a complicated pantheon of nature deities worshiped as the protectors of family, clan and dynastic interests. Political centralization was eventually attained under the aegis of the sun goddess, Amaterasu-Omikami. This is the central element of the Japanese state religion today. The existing god-world is a composite of nature deities, interpreted as ancestors, and the spirits of rulers and heroes. As a state religion contemporary Shinto is primarily a cultus for unifying and deepening national sentiment. It is also institutionalized in the form of numerous popular sects that must be distinguished from the state system. (See article: "Shinto Religion and Theology.")

The traditional date of the introduction of Buddhism into Japan is 552 A.D. The Mahayana school has always had practically exclusive control. In spite of early opposition from Shinto, state protection soon favored Buddhism and, supported by the imperial prince, Shotoku Taishi (572-622 A.D.), it quickly attained the position of the most powerful religious and cultural influence in the land. The Nara Era (710-784 A.D.) showed rapid growth, with six sects coming into existence. Three of these, Hosso (635 A.D.), Kegon (739 A.D.), and Ritsu (754 A.D.), have survived to the present. The greatest of the modern sects are of later date. The important foundings are: Tendai (806 A.D.), Shingon (806 A.D.), Yuzu Nembutsu (1123 A.D.), Jodo (1174 A.D.), Zen (1191 A.D.), Shin (1224 A.D.), and Nichiren (1253 A.D.). The latest available statistics of Japanese Buddhism (1940) report: 42,250,000 adherents, 71,300 temples, 7,700 churches, 56,000 temple heads and 178,000 other priests. The figures cover the thirteen main sects and some fifty sub-sects. (See Buddhist Terminology.)

On the side of doctrine and ceremony Japanese Buddhism is almost infinitely complicated. At the one extreme, it is criticized by Japanese authorities for having retarded cultural progress by alliance with primitive Asiatic superstition and folkways, and by fostering pessimism and withdrawal from the world; at the opposite pole, Buddhist scholars pride themselves on the harmony of their doctrine with the most recent scientific thought, and their contribution to sound private and national morality. In the course of Japanese history Buddhist pantheism, ritual, ethics and architecture have profoundly influenced Shinto. This was especially true during the long period of the amalgamation of the two faiths between the ninth and the middle of the nineteenth centuries of the western era.

Confucianism found its way into Japan prior to the arrival of Buddhism, although the exact time of the introduction is unknown. The date of 405 A.D. is probable for the first importation of the Analects. Confucian influence reached its height in the Tokugawa Era (1603-1868 A.D.) and various schools flourished. The most important of these are the Shushi school which emphasized the ethics of a static social gradation as the manifestation of the immutable will of Heaven, and the Oyomei school which fostered tendencies towards a teaching and practice of human equality. The former has been by far the more potent in its effect on Japanese life. United with Zen Buddhism, the Shushi philosophy furnished the foundations of Bushido or the Way of the Warrior. Japanese national education and the ethics of the family system, as well as her political institutions, are even today built largely upon the teachings of Confucius. The Imperial Rescript on Education issued in 1890, a document which Japanese patriots exalt as the proclamation and inspiration of an independent nationalism over against the dangerous encroachments of Westernism, stands on an ethical foundation of almost pure Confucianism. See sacred literatures; temples, Far Eastern.

(For Christianity in Japan see article: "Japan, Christianity in.")

Masaharu Anesaki, *History of Japanese Religion with Special Reference to the Social and Moral Life of the Nation* (London, 1930); Masaharu Anesaki, *The Religious Life of the Japanese People: Its Present Status and Historical Background* (Tokyo, 1938); T. T. Brumbaugh, *Religious Values in Japanese Culture* (Tokyo, 1934); Wilhelm Gundert, *Japanische Religionsgeschichte; die Religionen der Japaner und Koreaner in geschichtlichem Abriss dargestellt* (Tokyo, 1935); Sir Charles Eliot, *Japanese Buddhism* (London, 1935); August Karl Reischauer, *Studies in Japanese Buddhism* (1925); Otto Rosenberg, *Introduction to the Study of Buddhism* (Tokyo, 1916); Otto Rosenberg, *Die Probleme des Buddhismus, Philosophie, Materialen zur Kunde* (Heidelberg, 1924); Arthur Lloyd, *The Creed of Half Japan*, (London, 1912); J. B. Pratt, *The Pilgrimage of Buddhism and a Buddhist Pilgrim* (1917); Robert Cornell Armstrong, *Light from the East: Studies in Japanese Confucianism* (Toronto, 1914); Inazo Nitobe, *Bushido, the Soul of Japan* (1905); Kaiten Nukariya, *The Religion of the Samurai* (London, 1913).

D.C.H.

JAPANESE TERMINOLOGY:

daibutsu: (Jap.) A large image of the Buddha, such as those found in Nara and Kamakura.

Dengyo Daishi: (Saicho, 767-822) Founder of the Tendai School in Japan. As a great scholar, he was sent by Imperial order to study Buddhism in China. After a sojourn of one year, he returned to spread the Tendai doctrine, Shingon mysticism, the Zen doctrine of meditation, and Vinaya practices.

Dogen: (1200-1253) Founder of the Soto Shu of Buddhism in Japan.

Eisai: (1141-1215) Founder of the Rinzai Shu of Buddhism in Japan.

Eison: (1201-1290) Founder of the New Disciplinary School of Buddhism in Japan.

Ekwan (Jap.), Hui-kuan (Chin.): A Korean priest, pupil of Chi-tsang, who introduced both the Satyasiddhi system and the Middle Doctrine of Buddhism into Japan in 625.

Honen: (1133-1212) Founder of the Jodo School of Buddhism in Japan.

Ingen: (1592-1673) Founder of the Obaku Shu of Buddhism in Japan.

Ippen: (1239-1289) Founder of the Ji Shu of Buddhism in Japan.

Koyasan: (Jap.) The Koya Mountain, center of the Shingon School in Japan.

nembutsu: (Jap.) "Thinking of Buddha", the name of the process of repeating Buddha's name and meditating on him.

Ryonin: (1071-1132) Founder of the Yuzunembutsu Sect of Buddhism in Japan.

Shinran: (1173-1262) Called *Shonin* or Saint. Disciple of Honen and founder of the Shin (Shu) of the Pure Land School in Japan; posthumous name, Kenshin Daishi, or "Seeing-truth Great-Master."

W.T.C.

The following terms are the Japanese equivalents for terms appearing under Buddhist Terminology: Amida: (Jap.) *idem*: Amita; bosatsu: (Jap.) *idem*: bodhisattva; Dai-nichi-nyorai: (Jap.) *idem*: Mahavairocana; Eno: (Jap.) *idem*: Huineng, see Meditation School; Hosso School: (Jap. Dharma Nature School) see Idealistic School, Buddhist; Jinshu: (Jap.) *idem*: Shen-hsiu see Meditation School; Jodo School: (Jap.) The Pure Land School founded by Honen; Jojitsu School: (Jap.) "Completion-of-Truth" School *idem*: Satyasiddhi School. Kegon School: (Jap. "Wreath" School) *idem*: Hua-yen School; koan: (Jap. public problem) see Meditation School; Kukai: (Jap.) name of Kobo Daishi; Kusha School: (Jap.) *idem*: Kosa School; Kwannon: (Jap.) *idem*: Avalokitesvara; Miroku: (Jap.) *idem*: Maitreya; Mondo: (Jap. question and answer) see Meditation School; Monju: (Jap.) *idem*: Manjusri; Ritsu School: (Jap.) *idem*: Disciplinary School; Sanron School: (Jap.) see Middle Doctrine School; satori: (Jap. enlightenment) see Meditation School; Shingon School: (Jap.) see Mystical School, Buddhist; Tomitsu: (Jap. Eastern Mystics) see Taimitsu and Mystical School, Buddhist.

The following Japanese terms will be found under Buddhist Terminology: Ji (Shu); Kobo Daishi; Nichiren; Obaku Shu; Rinzai Shu; Taimitsu; Tendai School; Yuzunembutsu Shu; Zen. Shu-shi: see Chinese Terminology.

W.T.C.

See under separate headings: Amaterasu-Omikami; Engi Shiki; gohei; Hachiman; harakiri; Inari; Izanagi; Izanami; jingu; jinja; kami; Kogoshui; Kojiki; Nihongi; norito; oharai; ohoharahi; Oyomei; samurai; seppuku; Shin Ritsu; Susano-o (no-Mikoto); Yamato-Damashii. Also see Buddhism; Japanese religions; Shinto religion and theology; temples, Far Eastern.

Jarrell Lectureship, The A. J.: Established by Charles C. Jarrell in 1916 at Emory University, Emory University, Georgia. The capital sum amounts now to about $5,000. It provides that "the lectures should be given by an outstanding or distinguished man or woman and should be in the field of practical Christianity or missionary theory and practice, or in the doctrines of the Holy Spirit, or in the field of higher ranges of Christian experience." A few outstanding lecturers and subjects are: Bishop Warren A. Candler, *The Christ and the Creed;* Halford E. Luccock, *Christianity and the Individual in a World of Enemies;* Henry Sloane Coffin, *Religion Yesterday and Today;* Bishop Paul B. Kern, *Methodism has a Message;* Bishop Arthur J. Moore, *Central Certainties;* and Bishop W. T. Watkins.

(Data from the office of the Dean of Candler School of Theology.)

V.F.

Jashar, Book of: See forgeries.

Jaspers, Karl: (1883-) Taught philosophy at Heidelberg 1916-38. Although he came to philosophy as a scientist and fresh from the study of psychopathology, Jaspers's main interest has been to work out the distinctive function of the one who philosophizes. His own philosophy is that of a subjective, introspective thinker who draws ideas out of his own intuitive insight and subjects them again and again to rigorous analysis and criticism. In his passion for sincerity he makes much of the limitations on all human thought and its necessary skepticism. Philosophy must pass first through

Welt-orientierung or scientific discovery, then *Existenz-erhellung*, personal illumination or discovery of individual freedom in time, and finally *Metaphysik* or awareness of dependence on transcendental being. In its "existential" and personal character Jaspers's thought has resemblances to that of Heidegger,* but where Heidegger is a realist influenced by scholasticism Jaspers tends toward idealism and shows the influence of Protestantism and Kant. See Spranger, Eduard.

Chief works: *Psychologie der Weltanschauungen* (1919); *Die geistige Situation der Zeit* (1931), Eng. tr. *Man in the Modern Age* (1933); *Philosophie,* 3 vols. (1932); *Vernunft und Existenz* (1935); *Nietzsche* (1936); *Existenzphilosophie* (1938).

J.S.B.

jealousy: A resentful emotion arising from suspicion of the faithfulness of husband, wife or friend, or from apprehension that a rival is supplanting one in some cherished relationship. It may engender emulation or malevolence, more often the latter. R.W.F.

Jehovah (Yahweh, Jahve): Jehovah was the personal name of the god of Israel, originally pronounced Yahweh (Jahve), (as is shown by Gr. transcriptions). When for the first time the vowels were inserted in the Heb. Bible in the 7th Cent. A.D., the vowels of the word "aDoNaY," "Lord," were written with the consonants YHWH to indicate that, for reasons of reverence, this word was to be substituted in reading aloud. The form "Jehovah" is a transliteration of the resulting hybrid, and first came into use in the 14th Cent. A.D. through the failure of Christian scholars to recognize the origin and purpose of the vocalization; it has now acquired by usage independent standing in Eng.

The name is found also in the shorter forms Yah (Exodus 15:2, etc.) and Yahu or Y^e^ho (as element in names, and in Assyrian inscriptions and Aramaic papyri); an original Yaw has been conjectured, and tentatively identified among the divine names of the Ras Shamra* documents from Northern Phoenicia (15th Cent. B.C.). That the name was pre-Mosaic is implied by its revelation as new to Moses (Exodus 3:13-15; 6:4); that it was originally non-Israelite is stated in Gen. 4:26, cf. Josh. 24:14. It is held by some that Moses learned to worship Yahweh through his marriage to the daughter of a Kenite priest in Midian (Exodus 3:1 ff., 18:8-12,24) (Kenite Theory). The longer form YHWH is attested externally as early as the 9th Cent. B.C. on the Moabite Stone.* Its etymology from the root "to be" proposed by the writer of Exod. 3:14 is a rough approximation, since the roots are not identical; but it is significant as giving to this Israelite form of the name a distinctive meaning consonant with prophetic teaching "He (who) is what he will (choose to) be," or—"He (who) causes to be what exists (or, what happens)." See cosmogonies; high place; tetragrammatom. R.B.Y.S.

Jehovah's Witnesses: See Russell, Charles Taze; Russelism; Millenial Dawn; Rutherford, J. F.

Jên: See Confucianism.

Jeremiah: The Book of Jeremiah, a prophet who lived in the days of the decline and fall of the Kingdom of Judah, may be divided roughly into three parts: 1-25—prophecies primarily against Judah; 26-45—chiefly narratives about Jeremiah; 46-51—prophecies against foreign nations. Chapter 52 is a historical appendix taken from II Kings 24:18f. The section 46-51 is of minor interest and only a nucleus can be by Jeremiah, though he did regard himself as "prophet to the nations" (1:5). The authentic oracles of Jeremiah which were contained in Baruch's original scroll (referred to in 36:32) are doubtless among the materials of 1—25. There was another source, however, which reported the speeches of Jeremiah in a free, prosaic form. The passages preserved from this source—7:1f.; 11:1f.; 18:1f.; 21:1f.; 25:1f.; 32:1f.; 34:1f.; 35:1f.; 44:1f.—all have the same superscription. A third group of materials—19:1f. and the bulk of 26-44 deals only briefly, but likewise in prose, with what Jeremiah said, for the interest is focussed on the external happenings. Chapters 30-31 form a special collection of sayings the Jeremianic origin of which is debatable. The genuine (poetic) oracles of the prophet contain a great deal of invective. Unique are the so-called confessions of Jeremiah (11:18-23, 12:1-6; 15:10-21, 17:12-18, 18:18-23, 20:7-18) in which the personal relation existing between a prophet and his God receives unusual light. See Lachish Ostraca; Lamentations.

J. Skinner, *Prophecy and Religion; Studies in the Life of Jeremiah* (Cambridge, 1922); R. H. Pfeiffer, *Introduction to the Old Testament* (1941).

E.G.K.

Jeremiah II, the Patriarch: (1536-1595) Was one of the great personalities of the Greek Orthodox Church in the 16th century. He is the author of the answers to the Augsburg Confession, which are the fundamental teachings of the Greek Church today. In reality he was a humanist, classical scholar and friend of the Lutheran Church. He was also the organizer of the Russian Church, spending more than five years in Russia. See Confessions, Formal of the Christian Church; Eastern Orthodox Churches. G.E.Z.

Jericho: Also called City of Palms, fortified city of the lower Jordan valley, Palestine, captured and destroyed by the Israelites (Jos. vi). Rebuilt by Hiel of Bethel (I Kgs xvi, 34) and enlarged by Herod the Great. Scene of several Gospel pericopes (Lke x, 30; Mk. x, 46; Lke xix, 1 ff.). See F. M. Abel, *Géographie de la Palestine,* vol. ii (1938), pp. 357-360; J. Garstang, *The Story of Jericho* (1940). S.L.T.

Jerome (ca. 347-420) Born at Stridon in Dalmatia. A visionary experience at Antioch in 374 determined him to devote himself to Biblical studies. He lived for a period in a monastic community in the Desert of Chalcis and then at Antioch and Constantinople. In 382 he went to Rome, but opposition to his monastic doctrines forced him to leave in 385. The following year he founded an establishment for monks and nuns at Bethlehem, where he spent the rest of his life. While at Rome, at the request of Pope Damasus, he revised the Latin NT by the use of Greek mss. This together with a new translation of the OT into Latin from the Hebrew, made at Bethlehem, became the official text of the Bible in the Western Church (the Vulgate*). Also the author of numerous Biblical commentaries and controversial works. See canon, Old and New Testament; intercession; versions of the Bible, ancient. S.M.G.

Jerome of Prague: A Czech Wyclifite. Studied at Prague with Hus then in 1398 went to Oxford; became acquainted with Wyclif's* writings. In 1407 returned to Prague as an outspoken Wyclifite. Travelled all over Europe. Came to the Council of Constance* to assist Hus, but was imprisoned. At first recanting, later he manfully repudiated his weakness. Was burned at the stake on May 30, 1416.

Count Lützow, *Master John Hus* (n.d.), 321 ff. M.S.

Jerusalem: The chief city of Palestine and for the greater portion of the last three thousand years the capital or seat of administration of the country. Jerusalem is first mentioned, under the name Ursalimmu, in the Amarna letters of the fourteenth century B.C. It was then an important city-state in southern Palestine. But it must have been founded at a much earlier date, although there is no justification whatever for the popular tradition that Jerusalem is the oldest city in the world. In the earliest historic times it was the home-city of the Jebusites, a subdivision of the pre-Israelite inhabitants of Palestine. Despite its reputed impregnability, it was captured by David at about 1000 B.C. He renamed it "City of David" and made it the capital of his kingdom. Some forty years later Solomon* erected the Temple there. After the division of the Kingdom Jerusalem, under its old name, continued as the capital of the Southern Kingdom. It was captured by the Babylonians in 586 B.C., by the Romans in 70 A.D. and by the Moslems in 636 A.D. Because of its persisting religious associations Jerusalem is regarded by both Jews and Christians as their holiest city, while the Moslems esteem it as second only to Mecca and Medina in sanctity. See Judas Maccabeus. J.M.

Jerusalem, Patriarchate of: The "mother of all churches," since here the earliest Christian communities were gathered. But despite its undoubted apostolic foundation, it was not granted the patriarchal rank until by the Council of Chalcedon* in 451, when Juvenal, by going over to the winning side, secured it, although even then it was the fifth in order. But upon his return, Patriarch Juvenal was repudiated by his people, and gained entry into the city only with the aid of the imperial army. The majority of the Christians of the newly created Patriarchate adopted Monophysitism,* and the Arab conquest of Palestine made the schism with the Chalcedonian church of the Empire permanent. At present, the Patriarchate is governed by a Greek hierarchy chosen exclusively from the Confraternity of the Holy Sepulchre. The native Christians resent this dominance by a handful of Greek monks, and it is likely that soon the control will pass to the natives.

Sir Anton Bertram and Harry C. J. Luke, *Report of the Commission appointed by the Government of Palestine to Inquire into the Affairs of the Orthodox Patriarchate of Jerusalem* (London, 1921). M.S.

Jerusalem, Synod of: Held in 1672, was summoned by Patriarch Dositheus (1669-1707), and its chief act was the declaration of the Orthodox faith in which the assertion that Cyril Lucaris, patriarch of Constantinople (d. 1638) had been the author of the Calvinistic "Confession" is derived. Furthermore, had he written it, it would still not be the Confession of the Orthodox Church, but merely his own personal view. The decrees of this synod are given in the form of a "Confession of Dositheus" in which the Calvinistic views of the "Confession" ascribed to Cyril are refuted.

Philip Schaff, *The Creeds of Christendom* (3 vols., New York, 1919), II, 401 ff. M.S.

Jesuits: (Society of Jesus) A Roman Catholic religious order, founded by St. Ignatius Loyola* and approved by Paul III in the bull *Regimini militantis ecclesiae* of September 27, 1540. When Loyola died in 1556 the order possessed one hundred and one houses and about a thousand members. It had spread to many parts of Europe, and foreign missions had been begun in the Portuguese Indian Empire and Japan under St. Francis Xavier,* and in South America and Africa. By 1550 Loyola had composed the Constitutions of the order, which aim at the advancement of the greater glory of God by the sanctification of the members and by work for the salvation of souls. *Ad majorem Dei Gloriam* (To the greater glory of God) is the motto of the order. The legislative power resides in the General Congegration, which usually meets only when a new General is to be chosen. The General has accordingly ordinary executive and judicial power and his tenure is for life. The members comprise priests, scholastics (candidates for the priesthood), and brothers. The Jesuits have no female branch and do not affiliate lay people. The spirit of the Society is that of the founder's *Spiritual Exercises.*

After 1556 the order increased rapidly in numbers and influence. In 1616 there were 13,112 members; in 1710, 19,978 and in 1749, 22,589. The order played an important rôle in the revival of Catholicism in Southern Europe in the sixteenth and seventeenth centuries. Leadership in the efforts made to bring the Protestants back to Rome was also partially in its hands. Many Jesuits were confessors to Catholic royalty. The Jesuit school of theology grew in influence with Vasquez,* Valencia, Lessius, Busenbaum and Suarez.* In philosophy the Jesuit school advanced a Christian Aristotelianism. Its dogmatic theology was tributary to fourteenth and fifteenth century Scholasticism and to the positive gains of the Renaissance as well as to Thomism. In moral theology the school was characterized by a moderate optimism in regard to man's moral capabilities. Jesuit foreign missions flourished especially in the Far East and in South America (Reductions*). In more than six hundred colleges the Society taught during the seventeenth and eighteenth centuries an élite of the Catholic youth of Europe. Sodalities* of the Blessed Virgin Mary were also sources of influence.

During the seventeenth century the opposition to the Society, which had never been wanting, grew in many places. In Europe the Jansenists* aimed at the destruction of the influence of Jesuit moralists in the Church. In the foreign missions the rise of Dutch and English sea power put an end to expansion, the fierce Japanese persecution all but wiped out one of the most promising missions, and controversies on missionary methods with other Catholic missionaries persisted. During the eighteenth century the Society was one of the leading defenders of Christian truth against the doctrines of the Enlightenment. In the second half of the century it fell a victim to the "enlightened" ministers of the Bourbon courts. Disbanded succesively in Portugal, France and Spain, the Society was suppressed throughout the world by a brief which had been extorted by the Bourbon courts from Clement XIV.* Catherine the Great of Russia refused to allow the brief to be published in her Polish dominions, and the Society survived there until its restoration. This survival was sanctioned by Pius VI as early as 1783.

Restored by Pius VII* in 1814, the Jesuit order again spread throughout the world despite continued attacks by various European governments. The Dutchman, John Philip Roothaan*, third General of the restored Society, was largely responsible for this rapid expansion. The revived Society has been distinguished by its work in education, spiritual retreats, and foreign missions. In 1939 it numbered 25,954 members in fifty provinces, of which seven were in the United States, seven vice-provinces, and forty-six missions throughout the world. See Ratio Studiorum; Chinese religions.

M. P. Harney, *The Jesuits in History* (1941); T. J. Campbell, *The Jesuits* (1921); J. Brucker, *La Compagnie de Jésus* (1919). E.A.R.

Jesus: See Christ.

Jesus, Lives of: See Lives of Jesus.

Jesus, our knowledge of: Our knowledge of Jesus is largely dependent upon the Gospels,* particularly the Synoptics;* but these, unfortunately, are hagiography* rather than biography. Moreover, they are scarcely by eye-witnesses, but instead are the deposit of anonymous units of gospel tradition, mostly oral, that originated and had their growth during the first generation of Christians. Overlaid as it is with accretions of Christology,* Mariology, miracles, etiological explanations of the Christian cultus, martyrology, anti-Semitism, accommodations to OT prophecies, conformations to OT proto-types, apocalyptic* expectations, and Hellenistic intrusions, the authentic tradition about Jesus is uncovered with the greatest of difficulty. To add to the difficulties, our sources of information are at times in irreconcilable conflict (cf. the resurrection* narratives), or frequently narrow down to a single, uncorroborated line of evidence (e.g., Mark,* a major source of the other Gospels, is for the most part unsupported by parallel independent evidence). However, through the rigorous application of historical methodology to the sources (as has been done by scholars like Guignebert, Case, Dibelius, and Riddle) the following summary is presented without further explanation and with a fair degree of assurance.

Jesus was born in Galilee, possibly in Nazareth, the son of a certain Joseph, a Jewish artisan, and his wife Mary. In addition there were several other sons and daughters. There is no indication that the life of this Jewish family differed materially from that of other Galilean families similarly situated. Jesus probably worked at his father's trade until that fateful day when he heard John the Baptist* proclaim his stirring message of repentance and the imminence of the Kingdom of God.* Along with many others he accepted John's baptism as a sign of repentance and probably became one of his followers. When John was imprisoned by Herod Antipas, probably because this puppet ruler feared his growing popularity, as Josephus* suggests, Jesus began his independent mission (lasting less than a year) which was largely if not entirely confined to the lost sheep of the house of Israel. Adopting the message of John as his own, he went throughout Galilee proclaiming the gospel of repentance, religious and ethical righteousness, and the immediate advent of the Kingdom. The Gospels represent Jesus as the Messiah,* but there is reason to believe that he thought of himself as a prophet, like the Baptizer, heralding the approach of the Kingdom and preparing people for its arrival. Christian tradition also depicts Jesus as consciously founding the Christian church, but more probably he had no thought of any break with Judaism.* Likewise, he is credited with the institution of the sacrament of the Eucharist, but the accounts of the last supper* may well be etiological in character. Further, the Gospels represent him as both an exorcist driving out demons* from the sick and as a worker of miracles, but there is no compelling reason to believe that he was either; moreover similar exorcisms* and miracles* were credited to many persons of antiquity.

In his teachings, in which he used methods and forms not unlike those of his Jewish contemporaries, Jesus was in substantial agreement with the Pharisees* on such basic subjects as: God; Satan; angels and demons; inspiration of the written Torah* (Scripture); the nature of the Kingdom of God; sin; repentance; forgiveness; resurrection of the dead; rewards and punishments; and ethical conduct. Moreover, he was loyal to the chief institutions of Judaism such as the temple, the synagogue, the Passover, and even the Sabbath.** There is no evidence that he abrogated the law of circumcision,* and little, save for a dubious passage, that he did away with the dietary laws—at least Paul* shows no knowledge of any cancellation of these laws by Jesus. Unlike the Pharisees, Jesus may have combined the apocalyptic hope with the Kingdom of God, but again the apocalypticism in the Gospels may be a later accretion. On the other hand, his laxity in certain observances; his neglect of regulations in the oral Torah (e.g., those specifying the precise manner in which the Sabbath should be observed); his association with sinners, the "lost," and the ritually unclean; and his urgent proclamation of the immediacy of the Kingdom may have brought him into conflict with some of the Pharisees.

Apparently Jesus, like John the Baptist, aroused the suspicions of Herod Antipas and left Galilee to escape John's fate. At length, accompanied by a group of loyal disciples, he went to Jerusalem, not to die but to proclaim the gospel of the Kingdom to the throng of worshipers there to celebrate the Passover. Although his entry into the city was probably unnoticed he soon attracted attention by his dramatic purging of the temple. This act, together with his teaching in the temple area, quite likely added to his popularity with the masses, but no doubt incurred the enmity of the Sadducean temple clique. Finally, Pontius Pilate, the Roman military governor, possibly fearing that this popular religious leader with his teaching about some kingdom other than Caesar's might become the center of a popular disturbance or revolt against Rome, arrested Jesus. Following a summary hearing, he was condemned and crucified as a criminal. With this tragic conclusion to his high hopes the story of Jesus ends. That which follows, including the resurrection appearances, the ascension,** the belief of his followers that he would soon return as an apocalyptic Messiah, and the concept that he was Savior* and Lord, belongs to the realm of Christology. Admittedly this outline is both sketchy and unsatisfactory, but in the light of our present knowledge it must suffice.

A. Schweitzer, *The Quest of the Historical Jesus* (tr. from the German, 1911); C. C. McCown, *The Search for the Real Jesus* (1940); D. W. Riddle, "Jesus in Modern Research," *Journal of Religion* XVII (1937), pp. 170-183; S. J. Case, *The Historicity of Jesus* (1912); M. Dibelius, *From Tradition to Gospel* (tr. from the German, 1935); D. W. Riddle, *The Gospels: Their Origin and Growth* (1939); H. B. Branscomb, *The Gospel of Mark* (The Moffatt N. T. Commentary, n.d.); C. G. Montefiore, *The Synoptic Gospels,* 2 vols. (2d. ed., 1927); B. T. D. Smith, *The Parables of the Synoptic Gospels* (1937); R. Bultmann, *Jesus and the Word* (tr. from the German, 1934); S. J. Case, *Jesus: A New Biography* (1927); M. Goguel, *The Life of Jesus* (tr. from the French, 1933); C. Guignebert *Jesus* (tr. from the French, 1935).

M.R.

Jesus Christ: The name Jesus (Yeshua, prb. an abbreviation of Yehoshua; same as Joshua) is the Greek equivalent of a common Jewish name in the first century; Christ is from the title Christos, meaning Anointed (the Greek translation of Aram. *Meshicha*—Heb. *Mashiakh*), which early became—even as early as the lifetime of St. Paul —more of a proper noun than a title.

Jesus Christ is the personal name of the Founder of the Christian religion. Several different approaches to his life and teaching are possible. A purely theological approach would begin with the idea of the Incarnation, according to which God, or rather the Son of God,* became incarnate, that is, took our flesh upon him and became man in Jesus of Nazareth. His life, therefore, was a succession of divine manifestations and his teaching had the oracular quality of the final proclamation of eternal truth. His purpose in coming into the world was to save the world from its sin and from death, the consequence of sin; in order fully to achieve this end, he founded the church to be the channel of divine grace and the repository and guardian of divine truth. This magnificent idea, which is the heart of the Catholic conception of Christianity, does not depend upon history or historical records for its support; it views the historical data mainly as confirming the appropriateness or congruity of the theological idea.

At the opposite extreme is the purely historical view, according to which Jesus was either a prophet or a *chasid* (i.e. a saint or holy man, who was also a healer and teacher) in Galilee early in the first century. He gathered about him a group of disciples, and the burden of his message was the coming Kingdom of God. He was put to death at Jerusalem by the Romans in the year 29 or 30. Convinced soon after his death that he had risen again from the dead as Messiah, his disciples began a movement within Judaism which resulted in the development of the Christian church. The records of Jesus' life are only the traditions preserved by his followers during this crucial period of strain and antagonism, resulting in the final expulsion of the Christians from the synagogues and the formation of the church as an independent religious organization. Meanwhile, Christianity had long-since crossed the borders of Judaism and was spreading in the Gentile world. Hence the traditions of the life and teaching of Jesus were influenced, in the second place, by conceptions and expectations inspired upon the Gentile mission field.

It is very important to grasp the full bearing of these divergent interpretations, and to understand the presuppositions from which they set out. Otherwise, modern NT research in this field may impress the reader as only a bewildering chaos of conflicting interpretations.

The sources for the life of Jesus are almost exclusively limited to the four gospels. Ancient Jewish and pagan authors alike disregarded it. The reference in Tacitus is undoubtedly authentic but tells us little. (On the gospels see art. "Gospel," also "Synoptic Gospels," and "Form Criticism"). The Fourth Gospel goes far towards justifying the theological view described above; although it contains an indubitable substratum of historical reminiscence, this has been largely overlaid by later theological interpretation and mystical exposition. The author aims to set forth the meaning Christ has come to have for him and the contemporary church, stating it in the dramatic form of a gospel. By contrast the synoptic gospels represent the tradition at a much earlier stage of development; but this does not mean that they contain no interpretation or exposition. Quite the contrary: interpretation was involved from the very beginning. Even in Mark, the earliest gospel, there is a theological element, reflecting, to some extent, the Pauline theology. The specific theories of the Gospel of Mark (such as the divine judgment upon the Jewish people which prevented them from recognizing and accepting Jesus as Christ, the similar blindness of the disciples, the parables as meant to conceal the truth from those outside, Jesus' secret Messiahship, his repeated announcement to his disciples that he was going to Jerusalem in order to die and rise again) have been followed by the later evangelists, though not without modification. It will not do simply to take Mark, the earliest gospel, and follow it uncritically. Every item in the evangelic tradition has to be examined and accepted or rejected upon its own merits.

The chronology of the life of Jesus is a very difficult subject, especially in view of the fact that neither Mark nor the oral tradition before him had any interest in chronology. The probability is that Jesus was born sometime before the death of Herod, that is, before 4 B.C.; and that he died in the year 29 or 30. His ministry was probably longer than a year, though we can hardly insist that it must have been four years in length. It is not certain that the Gospel of John presupposes a four-year or even a three-year ministry; furthermore, it may be that certain chapters in the Gospel of John are out of proper order and need to be rearranged. The oldest formulated tradition in the gospels is undoubtedly the Passion Narrative; and this narrative presupposes that Jesus was put to death just before the Feast of Passover. The oldest tradition represents Jesus as a native of Nazareth. The later legend of his birth in Bethlehem was doubtless inspired by the dogmatic interpretation of the Old Testament. As Son of David and Messiah, he must have been born in Bethlehem; but the older tradition (Mark 6:1) represents Nazareth as his *patris*—birth place and home town.

As a Galilean, Jesus grew up in a district somewhat remote from the religious capital of Judaism, with its temple services, priestly hierarchy, Sanhedrin, and scribal schools. Galilee at the opening years of the first century was far less influenced by scribism than it was, say in the middle of the second century, after the two destructions of Jerusalem and the establishment of the rabbinic schools in Tiberias, Sapphoris, and elsewhere. This does not mean that Galilee was totally uninfluenced by the scribal or Pharisaic type of Judaism, but only that it was still 'Galilee of the Gentiles.' Here Jews were brought into closer contact with Gentiles and the rigorous exclusiveness and separatism taught by the scribes were less practicable.

Jesus grew up among the poor. He was himself a 'carpenter,' i.e. he practiced the craft of the peasant builder, joiner, or carpenter, making wooden doors, plows, window frames, etc. No doubt it was his experience as a youth growing up among the people, the 'Am ha-Aretz' who could not devote all their time to observance of the law and who lived in a certain amount of unavoidable contact with Gentiles—this experience, coupled with a profound understanding of the religious message of the OT, the Bible of his people, helps to explain the form taken by his own teaching later on.

The sudden appearance of a prophet, John the son of Zacharias, was like a trumpet call to his generation. Among the many who responded to John's preaching was Jesus of Nazareth. He must indeed have been baptized (or baptized himself, as the custom was) at the bidding of John, for the Christian tradition would never have manufactured this incident. The story of his temptation which follows is replete with apocalyptic imagery and may be chiefly symbolical. It is the story of the ordeal of the Messiah, how, that is, Jesus *must* have faced the problems of his ministry. The presupposition of the story is Jesus' consciousness of his own Messiahship. This presupposition, natural enough in the early church, is widely questioned today. Undoubtedly Jesus was conscious of a divine call, at least as strong and clear as that of any of the OT prophets. Moreover, the characters portrayed in this role (the Messiah enduring his temptations and triumphing over the tempter) is the character of Jesus Christ as known and adored by his followers: he refuses to resort to miracle, sign, or prodigy, even for his own self-protection or for the advancement of his cause.

Although it is possible to combine the Fourth Gospel with the other three, by assuming a Judean ministry preceding the ministry in Galilee, the data are not specific enough to warrant such a combination. It is not at all improbable that Jesus' ministry included Judea as well as Galilee, but this must remain a probability rather than a certainty. As we see him pictured in the synoptic gospels, he is surrounded by great crowds of people who come to him for healing and in order to hear his Gospel of the Kingdom. As represented in Mark, an initial period of success is followed by one of failure and eventually Jesus leaves Galilee and moves to Jerusalem to die. But the tradition itself seems to protest against this Marcan "pragmatism": Jesus is still accompanied by loyal and enthusiastic supporters as he journeys southward and as he enters the city at the Triumphal Entry. The probability is that after a long-continued ministry among the people, running into many months, possibly extending over some years—at least two—Jesus was seized by the authorities when he went to Jerusalem for a Passover observance and was handed over to the Romans to be put to death as a dangerous agitator and insurrectionist (Luke 23:2, 5). The journeys of Jesus can no longer be traced on a map; but there is no doubt that there were many more such journeys than the old-fashioned maps ever depicted. He was a man of the people, at home among them, and he knew how to appeal to their better nature (Mark 3:31-35). It was among the poor that he expected to see the beginnings of the realized Kingdom of God (Luke 6:20-26). Although he did not begin by attacking the law or its interpretation by the scribes, he was fully aware of the inadequacy of the law, especially as expounded by the scribes and practiced by the Pharisees. His criticism, therefore, went farther than mere criticism of scribal interpretation. The law itself was subject to limitations and imperfections, from his point of view.

In view of the hopeless political outlook for Judaism, Jesus' teachings regarding non-resistance had an added urgency. It was the best common sense in the world for the Jews to renounce political ambition and especially their old apocalyptic dream of world domination. If only they had followed this counsel, their history might have been far different, from that day to this! But Jesus' teaching regarding non-resistance to evil (or rather of non-resentment and of cooperation with persecutors, in spite of their mistreatment) has a deeper religious basis than political common sense; for Jesus taught that God is the Father of all men and that they are brothers in the one great human family. Passages in the gospels which seem to point in the opposite direction are probably assignable, upon other grounds, to a strain of tradition affected by ultra-Judaistic groups in Jerusalem in the 40s and 50s. In the Kingdom of God, the character of those who are its members must correspond to the character of the King, that is, God (Matt. 5:43-48). Admission to the Kingdom is restricted to the humble, penitent, and child-like in heart. The proud, the violent, the self-assertive, and the self-righteous have no place in it. This was the gospel Jesus preached to the common people of Galilee, who heard him gladly.

He did not proclaim himself as Messiah nor did he undertake to gather a group of followers whom he could lead in a revolt against the Roman authority. It is clear from the tradition of the question about the tribute money (Mark 12:13-17), whatever its full meaning, that Jesus did not teach or encourage active resistance against the Romans.

As his influence grew and spread farther among the people, the authorities, both ecclesiastical and political, became suspicious; and when he went to Jerusalem for the Passover, he was seized, taken before the high priests for a secret examination, and in the morning was denounced before Pilate as a dangerous agitator and insurrectionist. The story of the last days of Jesus is of course told from the Christian point of view and was never looked upon as a documentary account of the proceedings. It is a question whether or not any of the disciples or other early Christians had personal recollection of what transpired in the high priests' court. What we are told in the Marcan Passion Narrative is probably either hearsay or inference. Hence, it is difficult to maintain the traditional view that Jesus claimed, in the presence of the high priest and his satellites, to be either the Messiah or the Son of Man* who was expected to come upon the clouds of heaven (Mark 14:61-62). At any rate, this was not the charge against him before Pilate. Before Pilate he was represented as claiming to be "King of the Jews," a title commonly assumed by revolutionists of that time, as we learn from Josephus.

Thus, in spite of his gospel of non-resistance, and the gentle manner of his dealing with others, Jesus was put to death upon a trumped-up charge. The only possible justification for the charge against him was the so-called cleansing of the temple, following the Triumphal Entry into Jerusalem, (Mark 11:1-19). But this was the act of a religious reformer and could only be represented as a threat of revolution by completely misinterpreting the incident.

According to the gospels, the life of Jesus did not come to an end with his crucifixion; the climax of the life of Christ was his triumph over death in his resurrection* and exaltation as heavenly Messiah. This conviction characterizes all later Christianity. The life of Jesus was no tragedy, and that character reflected in his teaching and in his personal life, which Christians recognize as the supreme revelation of God, is, we are convinced, destined to go on, "conquering and to conquer." It will, in fact, be the final test by which all mankind shall be judged (Matt. 25:31-46). This quality of life, this spirit, this mind, which is seen in Christ Jesus our Lord (Phil. 2:5), is the unique and distinctive thing about him and is the point at which a modern Christology must begin. For the primitive church it was not the historical Jesus but the spiritual Christ, the Lord of his community, the church, which was all important. This view pervades the whole NT, and is found even in the historical books. See Christology; Saviour.

See M. Goguel, *The Life of Jesus,* E. tr. (1933); S. J. Case, *Jesus, A New Biography* (1927); O. Holtzmann, *The Life of Jesus,* E. tr. (1904); J. Klausner, *Jesus of Nazareth* (1925); B. H. Branscomb, *Jesus and the Law of Moses* (1930); *The Teachings of Jesus* (1931); E. F. Scott, *The Ethical Teaching of Jesus* (1924); H. N. Wilder, *Eschatology and Ethics in the Teaching of Jesus* (1939); J. Knox, *The Man Christ Jesus* (1941); R. Bultmann, *Jesus and the Word,* E. tr. (1935); B. S. Easton, *What Jesus Taught* (1938); F. C. Grant, *The Gospel of the Kingdom* (1940). F.C.G.

Jesus, Society of: See Jesuits.

Jesus, the son of Sirach: Name of the author of a well known and oft cited Jewish aprocryphal work, commonly known as Ecclesiasticus, but not infrequently cited by the name of its author. It is similar in content and spirit to the biblical books, Proverbs and Ecclesiastes,** and like them belongs to the so-called Jewish Wisdom Literature.* The book was written originally in Hebrew about 180 B.C., and was translated into Greek by the grandson of the author. The entire work is preserved only in this Greek translation; but near the beginning of the present century quite extensive portions of the original Hebrew were discovered in the storechamber of an ancient synagogue in Egypt. See apocrypha, Old Testament. J.M.

Jewish: See Judaism.

Jewish Christianity: The original members of the church were Jews, and observed the Law in addition to faith in Christ. Paul, to whom faith alone was sufficient, found himself in opposition to this Jewish Christianity. In Palestine the Law was never abandoned, and there were many Jews of the Dispersion who continued to hold to it, and who occasionally made converts among the Gentiles.* No sharp line, however, can be drawn between Jewish and Gentile Christianity, except in the one matter of observance of the Law. See Ebionism; Judaizers; Nazarenes. E.F.S.

Jewish New Year: See New Year, Jewish.

Jewish philanthropy: See social work of the churches.

Jewish religious festivals: Because of Israel's long history and the successive stages of cultures through which it passed one expects a great deal of syncretism in observance. The Sabbath and New Moon are very ancient holydays and the former always occupied first place in the calendar. The Pilgrim festivals of Passover,* Weeks, and Tabernacles,* combine nature, historical, moral and religious features. The first will serve as illustration. In it are united the shepherd festival of sacrifice of part of the flock, the paschal lamb (in very ancient days we learn of a sheep-shearing celebration), the eating of the unleavened cakes in commemoration perhaps of the grain (barley) harvest and the redemption from Egypt and the moral lessons of the Providence of God in history and the great boon of freedom. Exodus 23 and Levit. 23 give a list of some of the feasts. Weeks commemorates the wheat harvest and the giving of the decalogue and Booths, the ingathering (Ex. 23:16; 34:22) at the end of the year of the produce and the fact that Israel once dwelt in tents. Out of the transitional period between the end of the old and the beginning of the new, emerged the actual New Year's* Day and the later very solemn day of Atonement.* This whole period is called the penitential season. The Feast of Dedication celebrates the Maccabean victory and the re-institution of the cult in and the cleansing of the Temple that the Syrians had defiled. The feast of Lots and the Fast of Esther which precedes it mark the deliverance from extermination of the Jews of Persia. The ninth day of Ab* recalled with mourning laments the destruction of the two great sanctuaries at Jerusalem.

List of Festivals

Sabbath—Seventh Day. Sundown to sundown.

Passover (Pesach)—Nisan 15-22. Four middle days semi-festive. Reform Jews observe first and seventh.

Weeks (Shabuot)—Swan 6-7. Reform Jews observe first day only.

Ninth of Ab (Tishab' Ab)—Ab 9. Not observed by Reform Jews.

New Year (Rosh ha-Shana)—Tishri 1-2. First day only by Reform Jews.

Atonement (Yom ha Kippurim)—Tishri 10.

Tabernacles (Sukkot)—Tishri 15-20. Middle days—semi-festive, first day and eighth day observed by Reform Jews instead of first and second and eighth and ninth. See following.

(Hoshana Rabbo)—Tishri 21. Great Hosanna—not observed by Reform Jews.

(Sh'mini Azeret)—Tishri 22. Solemn Assembly—Combined with next by Reform Jews.

(Simchat Torah)—Tishri 23. Rejoicing of Law—not observed by Reform Jews.

For Eight Days—Kislev 25. Dedication (semi-holyday).

(Ta'anit Esther, Purim)—Adar 14, 15. Fast of Esther (not observed by Reform Jews) and Feast of Lots (semi-holyday).

Minor Festivals: New Moon, Minor Day of Atonement (fast day before each new moon), Lag-Bo-omer, 15th day of Shebat and 15th day of Ab (Midwinter and Midsummer Days, the latter an Arbor Day) and others, including some celebrations purely local. None kept by Reform Jews.

Hayyim Schauss, *The Jewish Festivals* (1938).

F.A.L.

Jewish socialism: Among those who eminently contributed to the success of the modern Socialist movement, the Jews rank high. The perennial prophetic and rabbinic traditions of social justice, coupled with the various social disabilities they experienced, prompted many of them to join radical equalitarian movements. They supplied leaders to the socialist parties greatly beyond their numerical proportion. Overeager to accomplish the reign of justice, zealous in devotion to learning, extreme in logical clarity, possessing remarkable oratorical and dialectical aptitudes, organizing ability, compelling power of persuasion, delighting in sacrifice for realization of great ideas, love for the poor and weak, all these qualities combined tended to make the Jews understand the power of their ethnic tradition, and enabled them to become leaders of the unconscious strivings and aimless rebellion of the masses. Attachment to religion, family, and property tends to make the Jew conservative; but the prophets and Jesus are examples that stamp them as hereditary revolutionaries. The strong communal responsibility, permeating the ghetto, also stimulated opposition to anarchical liberalism.

During the last century there has been no social movement of any importance in which the Jews failed to play a not insignificant part, whether these movements were radical and antistate, or conservative, pro-government and nationalistic. Classic examples of the former were Marx and Lasalle; of the latter, Disraeli and F. J. Stahl, the latter being the greatest theorist of German Junkerdom. To what political party the Jew belongs depends largely on local situations of the different countries. Jews are absent from the ranks of the British communist and independent labor parties. A few joined the moderate wings of the Labor party. Due to their class position, they either belong to the Conservatives or Liberals. One may find them at the head of movements which marshal against one another the nationalities animated by a reciprocal hate. Daniel Main, Gambetta, E. Simson, Bamberger and Lasker are typical. They often constitute the advance guard of almost all of the strongly nationalist parties (German Bohemians, Italian irridentists, Polish and Hungarian nationalists).

Jewish leadership has assumed conspicuous importance in the labor movements of Germany, Austria, and Russia. In Germany Karl Marx* and Ferdinand Lasalle were foremost; in Austria Victor Adler, Max Adler, Adolf Braun, *etc.;* in Russia Leon Martov, Rosa Luxemburg, and Leon Trotzky. Marx, the founder of "scientific socialism," was mentally, no less than biologically, a true descendent of a long line of rabbis.

In all western countries, the Jewish socialist leaders were the spokesmen of the general, not the Jewish, proletariat. At times they merely rationalized the grievances of the persecuted, ethnic minority, into the protest of all oppressed classes. There was practically until the 1890's no Jewish working class west of Poland. In Russia the growing Jewish proletarian masses, suffering both as working men and as Jews, were even more inclined to join radical movements than their fellow-workers among the Christians. Their Jewish consciousness usually led them to organize separate Jewish socialist parties, which, in time, assumed a definitely nationalistic tinge.

Major contributions of the Jews to western socialism were the work of individuals rather than of the masses. Socialism did not become a major force in the Jewish world until the last half century. The constructive theoretical and practical contributions made by the Jews to European socialism enhanced its prestige. The myth that the Russian communist revolution is a Jewish attempt at world domination overlooks the numerous Jewish opponents of Bolshevism. The German and Rusisan socialists maintained a consistent attitude of combating anti-Semitism, which often raised its head in their own midst. The German Socialist Democratic party repeatedly condemned as reactionary all anti-Semitic tendencies. A similar stand was taken by the Russian communists. The Soviet government alone succeeded in suppressing all anti-Semitic outbreaks.

Lenin as far back as 1903-05 waged war against the major Jewish and non-Jewish socialist organizations. Even in 1917 the majority of Russian Jewish socialists were gathered under the flag of the *Bund,* the Poale Zion, Socialist Zionists, *etc.* All these organizations were soon outlawed as counter-revolutionary. Jewish radical communists were the chief opponents of nationalistic Zionism, denouncing the Palestine ideal as reactionary and bourgeois. Even before World War I socialist ideologies permeated the entire Zionist movement. In the special Zionist labor parties, the socialist idea, in combination with Zionism, achieved its greatest fruition. The Poale Zion took shape in 1900-05, made its greatest strides in the period of the 1905-06 Russian Revolution, when it encountered opposition by the newly organized Zionist socialist (SS) party, which had a pronounced territorial program. After World War I the Poale Zion hopelessly split into a multitude of intramural divisions. Notwithstanding the many warring camps the labor elements became decisive in the reconstruction of Palestine under the Mandate. See dialectic; socialism.

Main references: R. Michels, *Political Parties* (1915); A. Tartakower, *A History of the Jewish Labor Movement* (Yiddish) (Warsaw, 1929-31); H. Burgin, *The History of the Jewish Labor Movement in America, Russia and England* (Yiddish) (1915); W. Preuss, *Die jüdische Arbeiterbewegung in Palästina,* 2 vols. (Berlin, 1932-33); A. Yarmolonsky, *Jews and Other Minor Nationalities under the Soviets* (1928). H.H.

Jewish theology and religion: See Israel, religion and theology; Judaism.

Jewish theological schools: See theological schools, Jewish.

jihad or jehad: (Arabic *jihad,* struggle, contest) A religious war of Moslems against unbelievers, taught as a duty in the Koran* and traditions. Also a war or crusade for or against some doctrine or principle. P.E.J.

jingu: (Lit. "God Palace.") A Shinto shrine of special dignity. D.C.H.

jinja: (Lit. "God House.") A Shinto shrine. D.C.H.

jinn: (Arabic collective plural for demons, spirits, angels. Singular *jinni,* or in English *genie*) In Mohammedan demonology, an order of spirits lower than the angels with power to appear in human or animal forms, and to exercise supernatural influence. P.E.J.

jnana marga: The way of knowledge. One of the three major ways of attaining salvation in Hinduism. The kind of knowledge required for salvation differs in various branches of Hinduism. See salvation, Hindu. C.S.B.

Joachim of Fiore: (c. 1145-1202) Born at Celico (Calabria), brought up at court of Duke Roger of Apulia. On a pilgrimage to the Holy Land the death by plague of companions led to adopting the ascetic life as a Cistercian. Later he founded an abbey under still stricter rules (approved by Innocent III, 1204).

A commentator of Scripture and theologian of note, he is famous for *Concordia novi et veteris Testamenti, Expositio in Apocalypsin Psalterium decem chordarum, Concordia Evangeliorum contra Judaeos, De Articulis fidei, Confessio fidei, De Unitate Trinitatis.* Numerous spurious works have been attributed to him, owing to his extraordinary influence.

His major theme was that which came to be called "The Eternal Gospel". He dividad all history into three parts: 1) The Age of the Father (Law); 2) The Age of the Son (Gospel) which includes the history of the hierarchical church; and 3) The Age of the Holy Ghost in which monasticism will be universal, whose character will be contemplative, and in which there will be no need of the discipline of the church. This third age was popularly called The Eternal Gospel.

The Joachimites, his spiritual heirs, were particularly numerous among the Spiritual Franciscans* who held that the new age had begun with St. Francis. Among critics of Joachim's writings was Thomas Aquinas. In 1260 a Council at Arles condemned his writings. He is described as one of the blessed in Dante's Paradise, as "endowed with prophetic spirit" (Paradiso XII 140 f.).

H. C. Lea, *History of the Inquisition of the Middle Ages* (1888), vol. III, Ch. I.; *Catholic Encyclopedia*, "Joachim of Fiore." Q.B.

Joachimites: See Joachim of Fiore.

Joan of Arc: (1412-1431) Born in Domrémy, of farmer stock (her father was a leading man in the village), she grew up in a desperate time for France in its war with England whose ally was Burgundy. Apparently a normal, though grave, child, at thirteen she received voices and visions (St. Michael, St. Catherine, and St. Margaret) which by 1428 commanded her to deliver her country. Assuming male attire, she by persistence overcame the reluctance of army leaders and courtiers, and after being examined by theologians was commissioned by the king. Between April and July of 1429 she routed the English from Orléans, captured Troyes, and saw Charles VII crowned at Rheims (July 17). Her fortunes began to wane with her failure to relieve Paris, the continuous opposition at court, and finally with her capture (at Compiègne) by a Burgundian who sold her to the English. Pierre Cauchon, bishop of Beauvais (pro-Burgundian who had been expelled from captured Beauvais) instituted proceedings for heresy against her at Rouen; which was a subtler and for a time more effective way of discrediting Charles than killing Joan outright. The trial is infamous for treachery, bigotry, and cruelty, in which the University of Paris played a regrettable part. Joan's good sense and candor (on all but the visions) in her responses have added to her fame. The 70 propositions, condensed to 12, included condemnation of her male attire, of her voices and visions as "false and diabolical", and particularly her alleged responsibility to God alone and not the church. After a momentary and perhaps confused retraction Joan was tricked into relapsing into "heresy". She was burned at the stake May 30, 1431. In 1450 began attempts at *réhabilitation* which ended in 1456 in a complete reversal of the judgment of 1431. She was beatified in 1909 and canonized in 1920.

Jules Quicherat, *Procès de Condamnation et de réhabilitation de Jeanne d'Arc* (5 vols., Soc. de l'histoire de France, 1849); A. France, *Vie de Jeanne d'Arc* (1907); A. Lang, *The Maid of France* (1908); A. B. Paine, *Joan of Arc* (1927); G. B. Shaw, *St. Joan* (1924), a vital drama, with an understanding Preface. Q.B.

Job: Formerly considered a very ancient book because of its patriarchal background, it is now regarded as among the younger elements of the O.T. (probably fourth century B.C.). It belongs to the "wisdom literature"* but not as typically as Proverbs*. Edomite* or Arabian origin has been urged, but without sufficient reason. It reflects the crisis into which religiously oriented Hebrew wise men were thrown when their optimistic philosophy, which operated with a belief in the doctrine of divine retribution, was upset by the spectacle of undeserved suffering. The book develops this situation in such a way that the legendary hero, who is made to typify an afflicted wise man, maintains his belief in his righteousness and in his vindication by God, through chapter 19. The original intent of the climactic 19:25-27 is the hope of a vindication before death. At this point all viewpoints are exhausted and the rehabilitation of Job is really in order. A considerable literary problem is created by the third cycle of speeches which is not only incomplete but confused. Rearrangements are often attempted but are futile. Chapter 21, unlike chapters 3-19, portrays a sceptical Job who is made to reverse himself and praise the divine wisdom in chapter 28 and then, after a swan song and oath of clearance (30-31) basically parallel to the Job speeches of 3-19 in spirit, is unnecessarily reproved by a fresh contender Elihu (32-37), and finally by God Himself (38-39), who makes Job recant. There is thus a sharp cleavage between the earlier (3-19) and the succeeding portions of the book. Materials of a different provenance have apparently been joined to an "original" dialogue and then disrupted and repeatedly counteracted. Chapters 28, 32-37, 38-39 thus represent accretions (though many scholars who "restore" the third cycle of speeches attempt to hold chapter 38 f.). The prologue and epilogue are also composite. In 1-2:10 we have the torso of an older (8th century?) narrative about Job. In 2:11-13, abridged at the beginning, and 42:79, we have the real "framework narrative" of the original dialogue. Chapter 42:10-17 contains supplementary material partly redactional, partly independent tradition. In effect, the book overcomes the doctrine of retribution from which many of the Psalmists also suffer. Esthetically "Job" is the supreme production of Hebrew literary genius. Cf. Davidson, A. B.

Cf. E. G. Kraeling, *The Book of the Ways of God* (1939) for full bibliography; R. H. Pfeiffer, *Introduction to the Old Testament* (1941). E.G.K.

Jodl, Friedrich: (1848-1914) Was professor at the German university in Prague, Bohemia, then at the University of Vienna. Following the positivists Stuart Mill, Feuerbach and Comte, he projected a new religion of national culture. He upheld the humanistic formula: the idea in us and faith in the realization of the same by us.

Volkswirtschaftslehre und Ethik (Berlin, 1886); *Religion, Moral und Schule* (Berlin, 1892); *Wesen und Ziele der ethischen Bewegung in Deutschland.* 3 ed. (Frankfort a. M., 1909); *Geschichte der Ethik.* 3 rev. ed. (Stuttgart, 1920); *Wissenschaft und Religion* (Wien, 1909); *Der Monismus und die Kulturprobleme* (Leipzig, 1911). H.H.

Joel: A master poem, written in the third or fourth centuries B.C., telling of a devastating locust plague which had wasted Palestine. From 2:28 (3:1 in Hebrew) to the end are a series of appended supplements by other writers, mostly militant nationalists and eschatologists*. Interpolations by the Day of Yahweh* Editor within chs. 1-2 try to convert the plague description into a prophecy of God's judgment day. Joel simply recounted, with brilliant poetic imagery, the descent of the plague, ensuing devastation of fields, orchards, and vineyards, summoning of everyone to day of fasting and prayer, final departure of locusts, restored fertility, and then the great thanksgiving for deliverance. See *The Prophets and their Times* by J. M. P. Smith and W. A. Irwin (1941), pp. 280-85. R.E.W.

Jogues, St. Isaac: (1607-1646) French Jesuit, heroic missionary to the Hurons and Iroquois. Martyred by the latter at Auriesville, N. Y., on October 18, 1646. E.A.R.

Johanan ben Zakkai: Leading Tana*, or teacher, at the time of the destruction of the Temple* (70 C.E.). He was the youngest pupil of Hillel* and was characterized by the latter as the "father of wisdom." Johanan, sensing that Jerusalem would be destroyed, obtained permission from Vespasian to open an academy at Jabneh where he gathered most of the scholars of his day. In this manner he saved Judaism from disintegration. All the prominent teachers of the next generation were his pupils. E.B.—L.F.

Johannine problem: Primarily, the problem of identifying the author of the Fourth Gospel; in a larger sense it is the question whether or not a single author produced the Fourth Gospel, the three Johannine Epistles, and the Apocalypse of John; also whether or not this author can be identified with John the son of Zebedee. The general consensus of Protestant scholarship today is that the author of the Fourth Gospel can hardly be the son of Zebedee, although the tradition underlying the Gospel may in some way be connected with that apostle; the first epistle is probably by the author of the Gospel; Epistles II and III are probably by the 'Elder' John; the Apocalypse is an entirely different type of work by some early Christian apocalyptist who used some older Jewish and Christian material but can scarcely have been one of the apostles. Style, thought, diction, and theology of these various books provide the basis upon which the modern view of diverse authorship is supported. See John, Gospel of.

W. F. Howard, *The Fourth Gospel in Recent Criticism and Interpretation* (1931), supplemented by J. H. Scammon; "Studies in the Fourth Gospel, 1930-1941", in *Anglican Theological Review* 23.2 (April, 1941). F.C.G.

John: This was a common Jewish name, and was borne by three or perhaps four men who appear in the N. T.: 1) a kinsman of the high-priest, mentioned incidentally in Ac. 4:6; 2) John, surnamed Mark, the nephew (or cousin) of Barnabas, and author, in whole or in part, of the Gospel of Mark; 3) John the son of Zebedee, one of the four original disciples, later one of the three "pillars" of the church at Jerusalem, and the reputed author of the Fourth Gospel; 4) the seer of Revelation, who was possibly John the elder, a leader of the Asian church in the closing years of the first century. E.F.S.

John the Baptist: The Gospels all begin with an account of the ministry of John, and the circumstances of his birth are recounted by Luke in a long chapter, based, most probably, on documents preserved among John's followers. The N.T. record is supplemented by Josephus* (*Ant.* xxii), who is highly appreciative of John, although of Jesus he says nothing. John was the son of a priest, Zacharias, and was born, according to Lk., some months before Jesus. In his early manhood he retired into the wilderness beyond Jordan, where he lived a solitary, ascetic life. In the year 28 A.D. he came forward as a prophet, announcing the approach of the Kingdom of God, and calling on the people to repent. It is evident, from the fragments of his teaching preserved to us, that by repentance he meant little more than practical amendment, as contrasted with mere legal piety. To those who thus repented he offered his rite of baptism, which carried with it divine forgiveness, and ensured entrance into the Kingdom. From his practice of this rite he was known as the Baptiser,—a name by which he is designated by Josephus, as well as in the N.T. The whole nation acclaimed him as a new Prophet, and multitudes thronged to him in the wilderness to receive his baptism. Among them was Jesus. The arrest of John took place in the interval between the baptism of Jesus and the opening of his ministry. According to the Gospels John had excited the anger of Herod Antipas by denouncing his incestuous marriage. This may have been a contributory motive, but Josephus is no doubt right in his statement that Herod arrested him "lest his influence with the people might lead to a revolt". Josephus may also be trusted when he proceeds to tell that John was secretly put to death, by order of the king, in the fortress of Machaerus. The account of his murder at the royal banquet appears to be one of the popular legends which grew up around the Herodian family. John is represented in the Gospels as the conscious forerunner of Jesus, but it may be gathered, from notices in the Gospels themselves, that his interest in Jesus was only awakened when he heard during his imprisonment of the activities of the new Prophet. In so far as he foretold the Messiah it was only incidentally, when he described the Kingdom, in apocalyptic* fashion, as ushered in by a terrible Judge who would destroy the wicked. He prepared the way for Jesus by creating a religious revival which made the people responsive to Jesus' message. He also vitalised the apocalpytic hopes to which Jesus appealed, and connected them with ethical demands. Otherwise his work was of a different order from that of Jesus, and was by no means merged in it. During Jesus' ministry the disciples of John continued to be a distinct body, and gave rise to a sect which maintained itself alongside of the Christian church.

We hear of it in the second century as one of the recognized Jewish sects, and there is reason to believe that a controversy with it underlies the Fourth Gospel. It has been suggested that the Mandaean Community, which still survives, had its origin in the sect of John, but this is more than doubtful.

Foakes Jackson & Lake, *Beginnings of Christianity* (1920) Vol. I; D. Buzy, *Jean Baptiste* (1922).

E.F.S.

John Baptist de La Salle: See La Salle, St. John Baptist de.

John, Epistles of: The second and third of these Epistles are short personal notes, the first is of some length and of the highest religious value. They are all written in the style of the Fourth Gospel, and occasionally repeat its phrases and ideas. This similarity has sometimes been set down to imitation on the part of a later writer, but the 1st Epistle is so excellent and so original that this is hardly possible. It was occasioned by the secession from the church of some of its members who held views of a Docetic nature. They prided themselves on superior piety and intelligence, and those who remained had become doubtful of their own more conservative beliefs. John offers them three tests by which they may know whether the true Christian life is in them,—the tests of doctrine, of conduct and of love. In his application of these tests, and particularly of the last one, John penetrates more deeply perhaps than any other writer, into the inner meaning of the Christian religion. The 2nd and 3rd Epistles are concerned almost wholly with the question of visiting missionaries. They illustrate the transition from an itinerant to a local ministry, and for this reason have a great historical interest. On the date and authorship of the Epistles of John, see John, Gospel of.

A. E. Brooks, *The Epistles of John* (ICC, 1912); C. R. Dodd, *The Epistles of John* (In preparation).

E.F.S.

John, Gospel of: Since the latter part of the second century, and perhaps earlier, this Gospel has been one of the canonical four, although it is obviously different in character from the others. It aims not merely at recounting the history of Jesus but at disclosing its deeper significance, with the aid of conceptions derived, in large measure, from Alexandrian philosophy. These are briefly set forth in the Prologue (1:1-18); then follows the Gospel proper (1:19-20:31). The closing chapter (21) is of the nature of an appendix, and is the work of editors, who take care to distinguish themselves from the author. The Gospel appears to fall into three parts, in accordance with the idea that Christ drew to himself out of the world those whom God had chosen. (cf. 1:10, 11; 3:19-21; 11:52). In the first part (chs. 1-6) Jesus offers himself to men, and they waver in their judgment; in the second (7-12) his friends and his enemies draw gradually apart; in the third (13-20) he is fully accepted by "his own", and is crucified by the unbelieving world. Throughout the Gospel the history moves on two planes, the record of the earthly life suggesting what Jesus would be forever in the experience of his people. This double interest accounts for the apparent mingling of historical fact with free invention. John is by no means indifferent to facts. At some points, and most notably in his story of the Passion, he is more accurate than the Synoptists, and perhaps had before him a brief early document of great value. But he seeks to weave into the facts of history those spiritual facts which to his mind were equally real. Critical questions of great difficulty are involved in the study of this Gospel. The date of the Gospel of John and of the Epistles of John I, II, III is about 100 A.D.,—possibly several years earlier. The Gospel and the Epistles are almost certainly by the same author. Few scholars would now accept the traditional view that he was the Apostle John, and attempts have been made to identify him with one eminent teacher or another. He lived, however, in a period of which we have practically no record, and his name will probably never be recovered. See gospel and the gospels; Johannine problem; logos.

A. Loisy, *Le Quatrième Evangile* (1921); G. H. C. MacGregor, *The Gospel of John* (1929); H. L. Jackson, *The Problem of the Fourth Gospel* (1918); E. F. Scott, *The Purpose and Theology of the Fourth Gospel* (1906).

E.F.S.

John XXII: (Pope, 1316-1334): Aggressive Pontiff of the Avignon period best known for his long struggle with the Emperor Louis the Bavarian and his attack on the Franciscan* interpretation of poverty. He crushed the Spirituals and won the Order as a whole from the Minister General, Michael of Cesena*, who, with William of Ockham*, had supported Louis. Administratively, John remodeled the curia and greatly extended the financial exactions of the papacy. See Sabbatine privilege.

R.C.P.

John, sect of: See John the Baptist.

John of Antioch: See Chrysostom.

John of the Cross, Saint: (1542-91) Spanish Carmelite* mystic of the counter-reformation period and perhaps the greatest writer on mystical theology which the Roman Catholic Church has ever produced. He shared with Saint Teresa* of Avila the founding of the Discalced Carmelites and suffered even more than she in the persecution which that reform aroused. His *Dark Night of the Soul* and *Ascent of Mount Carmel* are among the great mystical treatises of all time.

New Edition of the *Works of St. John of the Cross* (London, 1934-5), edited by Allison Peers; Bede Frost, *St. John of the Cross* (1937).

D.V.S.

John of Damascus: Born of Arab stock about 700 A.D.; a strong defender of image* worship, which he held to be the logical expression of dogma; chiefly famous as the author of a large work entitled *The Fountain of Knowledge,* which is a systematisation of the whole doctrine of the Greek Fathers and the church councils up to his time. See perichoresis.

W. Smith, *A Dictionary of Christian Biography* (1877-87). E.F.S.

John Pupper of Goch: (c. 1410-1475) Superior of the Thabor Convent at Malines, adherent of the Brethren of the Common Life*, radical pre-reformer. Q.B.

John of Jandum: (c. 1300-1328) Early a teacher of arts at Paris, author of *De Laudibus Parisiis,* and collaborator with Marsilius of Padua* on *Defensor Pacis* for which both were condemned in 1327. His commentaries on Aristotle are strongly flavored with Averroism* and present a radical interpretation of the twofold-truth theory*.

C. W. Previté-Orton, *The Defensor Pacis* (Cambridge, 1928), xii f; P. Feret, *La faculté de thèologie de Paris,* III (1896). Q.B.

John (Quidort) of Paris: (d. 1306) Dominican teacher, author of *De potestate regia et papali* (1302) and of *De modo existendi corporis Christi in sacramento altaris* (1304). The former treatise advocates conciliar government; the latter was out of accord with orthodox medieval views of the Eucharist.

J. T. McNeill, "The Emergence of Conciliarism" in J. L. Cate, *Medieval and Historiographical Essays in Honor of J. W. Thompson* (1938). J.T.M.

John of Salisbury: (d. 1180) Bishop of Chartres. Friend and associate of Thomas a Becket. Chiefly remembered for his *Policraticus* (text edited by C. C. J. Webb, 1909). See two swords, the doctrine of. W.S.H.

Johnson, Gisle: (1822-1894) A Norwegian theologian who exercised wide influence through theological and church publications and through the establishment of the Inner Mission in Norway. Cf. neo-Lutheranism. C.J.B.

Jonah: Latest prophetic book of the O.T., written in the third century by an anonymous author, using a historical setting five hundred years earlier. It is religious fiction, with the key happenings historically impossible. In contrast with Jonah's anti-foreignness, the author pictures the supposed heathen as repentant and eager to embrace new religious conceptions. Contrasting with Jonah's God of the Hebrew people, the book shows a universal deity from whom Jonah could not escape by leaving Palestine. Jonah's vengeful deity, who destroys all non-Jews, is replaced by a God gracious, merciful, slow to anger, etc. This book is an allegory of the prophet nation which should have shared her religion with the world. In pre-exilic days she fled from duty and met apparent death in the storm of exile. The three days symbolize the three exiles. Then came the return and the renewed commission, but bigotry and legalism caused her last state to be worse than her first. This satire on prevalent beliefs is one of the greatest, yet one of the most misunderstood books in the Bible.

See J. M. P. Smith and W. A. Irwin, *The Prophets and Their Times* (1941), pp. 271-79. R.E.W.

Jones Lectureship, The Sam P.: Established in 1920 at Emory University, Georgia by the family of the Rev. Sam P. Jones with a capital sum of almost $3,000 these lectures (given from time to time) are designated to deal with the cause of evangelism. Drs. George R. Stuart, L. H. Hough, A. E. Day have appeared on this foundation.

(Data from the office of the Dean of Candler School of Theology.) V.F.

Joseph, Sisters of Saint: See Sisters of St. Joseph's Society for Foreign Missions.

Josephus, Flavius: Jewish historian and writer (37/38 to about 110) of priestly origin, well educated in Jewish lore and the Greek disciplines. During his youth he lived for three years as a rigid ascetic, later joining the Pharisees*. In 64 he went on a mission to Rome. At the outbreak of the war with Rome, he was assigned to unruly Galilee. He organized the province and raised an army. After some initial successes, he was defeated and escaped, later surrendered to the Romans under Vespasian. He is suspected of treachery.

According to his own account he predicted that the Roman general would be emperor and thus deeply impressed his captor. After Josephus' return from a campaign with Titus, against the Jews, wherein Josephus essayed the dual role of being loyal to his Roman masters and kind to his people, and with some success, he returned to Rome, where he was granted citizenship and a pension. He henceforth devoted himself to literature, writing perhaps in his native Aramaic dialect and with probably expert help to translate it into Greek. He produced the *Wars of the Jews, Antiquities of the Jews* and *Autobiography* not always reliable, and an apologetic work, the first of its kind, *Against Apion* in which he ably defended Jew and Judaism. He is often our sole source for a period or an event, hence, his importance. He tries to present himself and his conduct in the best possible light and attempts to show the world the greatness of the Jewish people and the exalted ethics of their religion. It was the Christian church that preserved his works because of an interpolated passage about Jesus found in them. (*Antiq.* XVIII, 3, 3).

F. Foakes Jackson, *Josephus and The Jews* (1930); Works of H. St. J. Thackery, Josephus in Loeb Classical Library (1926 ff.). F.A.L.

Joshua: A historical book of the O.T., included among the "Former Prophets"* in the Hebrew canon. It contains accounts of the invasion and conquest of Canaan by the Israelites (chapters 1-12), the allotment of territory to the various tribes (chapters 13-21), and the final acts and speeches of Joshua (chapters 22-24). The book derives its name from Moses' successor, Joshua, who is considered by Jewish tradition as the author (*Baba Bathra* 14b). This view cannot be correct, for the book has many marks of later date. In its present form it is in large part a product of the Deuteronomic school of historians (see D), who composed or re-wrote the history of the period on the basis of earlier traditional material. This material is usually assigned by critical scholars to J and E**, but this is not certain. In any case there is very little material which resembles J (mostly in chapters 15-17) and if E was used, it has been largely re-written. Most of the chapters dealing with the allotment of territory are usually attributed to P*, but they likewise may be Deuteronomic. The standard tradition of the conquest of Palestine is that it was made by a unified nation under Joshua's leadership, and was immediately and completely successful. There are traces, particularly in Joshua 15-17 and Judges* 1-2, of an earlier tradition which represented the conquest as having been made by tribes, as only partially successful, and as spread over a long period of time. This tradition is doubtless more authentic, and is supported by archaeological evidence. See Hexateuch.

M. Noth, *Das Buch Josua* (Handbuch zum Alten Testament I, 7) (1938); J. Garstang, *The Foundations of Bible History*: *Joshua, Judges* (1931).

J.P.H.

Jotunn: (Norse-Icelandic) Giant, earth monster; frost giant; cliff giant. Jotunheim, the home or world of the giants (Jotnar), is held to lie to the east of Norway; the giant is powerful, huge, and fairly intelligent; an earth god. Some giants had human and others non-human characteristics; known to marry gods (of the sky and air). There were giantesses, some of whom were held to be beautiful; but generally speaking, giants of either sex were not regarded as handsome. Many had personal names. Whether, as claimed by some scholars, the giants originated from the realm of the dead, it seems improbable that it is true for most of them. F.L.P.

Journalism, Catholic: See Catholic Journalism.

journalism, religious, in the U. S.: See religious journalism in the U. S.

Journals (General) of religion and theology:

Biblical Archaeologist, published quarterly by American Schools of Oriental Research to provide non-technical account of archaeological discoveries as they are related to the Bible. Editor, G. Ernest Wright; New Haven, 1938.

Bulletin of the American Schools of Oriental Research, published quarterly by the American Schools of Oriental Research. Editor, W. F. Albright; New Haven, 1919.

Christendom, published quarterly by the American Section of the World Conference on Faith and Order and the Universal Christian Council for Life and Work; an ecumenical review. Editor, Harlan Paul Douglas; New York City, 1935.

Christian Century, an undenominational weekly. Editor, Charles Clayton Morrison; 1902.

Christianity and Crisis, published bi-weekly, a journal of Christian opinion. Chairman of Editorial Board, Reinhold Niebuhr; New York City, 1941.

Christianity and Society, a quarterly devoted to

Church History, published quarterly by the American Society of Church History. Managing Editor, Matthew Spinka; Chicago, Illinois, 1932.

Church Management, published monthly. Editor, William H. Leach; Cleveland, Ohio, 1924.

The Crozer Quarterly, published by the Faculty of Crozer Theological Seminary. M. S. Enslin, Editor; 1923.

The Expositor and Homiletical Review, a Christianity and Social Reconstruction, published by the Fellowship of Socialist Christians. Editor, Reinhold Niebuhr; New York City, 1934. monthly journal of practical church methods, published by the F. M. Barton, Co., Cleveland, 1897.

Federal Council Bulletin, issued monthly by the Federal Council of Churches of Christ in America, a journal of inter-church cooperation. Editor, Roswell P. Barnes; New York City, 1918.

Harvard Theological Review, issued quarterly by the Faculty of Divinity in Harvard University. Embraces theology, ethics, history, and philosophy of religion and cognate subjects. Aims to enlarge knowledge and advance thought. 1908.

Information Service, published weekly by the Department of Research and Education of the Federal Council of Churches of Christ in America, New York, 1921.

International Journal of Religious Education, published monthly by the International Council of Religious Education. Editor, P. R. Hayward; Chicago, 1924.

Jewish Quarterly Review, published quarterly by the Dropsie College for Hebrew and Cognate Learning. Editors, Abraham A. Neuman and Solomon Zeitlin; Philadelphia, 1910. This supersedes *The Jewish Quarterly Review,* published in London, 1889-1908.

Journal of Bible and Religion, published quarterly by the National Association of Biblical Instructors to foster religion in education. Editor, Carl Everett Pennington; Somerville, New Jersey, 1933.

Journal of Biblical Literature, published quarterly by the Society of Biblical Literature and Exegesis. Editor, Robert N. Pfeiffer; Philadelphia, 1881.

The Journal of Liberal Religion, a quarterly published by the Unitarian Ministerial Association, The Universalist Ministerial Associaton, and The Meadville Theological School. Editor, James Luther Adams; Chicago, 1939.

Journal of Near Eastern Studies, a quarterly continuing the *American Journal of Semitic Languages and Literatures.* Editor, George A. Cameron; the journal of the Department of Oriental Languages and Literatures of the University of Chicago, 1942.

Journal of Religion, continuing the *Biblical World* and the *American Journal of Theology* (1897 to 1920), a quarterly issued by the Divinity Faculty and Conference of the University of Chicago, 1921.

The Moslem World, a quarterly review of current literature and thought among Mohammedans, published by the Hartford Seminary Foundation. Editors, Samuel M. Zwemer and Edwin E. Calverley; Hartford, Connecticut, 1893.

The Personalist, a quarterly journal of philosophy, religion and literature published by the School of Philosophy of the University of So. California. Editor, Ralph Tyler Flewelling; 1920.

The Protestant, (originally entitled *The Protestant Digest*) a bi-monthly journal of affirmation published by the Protestant Digest. Editor, Kenneth Leslie; New York, 1938.

Religion in Life, a Christian quarterly, published by the Abingdon-Cokesbury Press; Editor-in-chief, Nolan B. Harmon; New York, 1932.

Religion in the Making, published four times a year by the Florida School of Religion. Editor, Shirley Jackson Case; 1940.

Religious Education, a bi-monthly which seeks to present on an adequate, scientific plane those factors which make for improvement in religious and moral education; published by the Religious Education Association. Editor, Laird T. Hites; Chicago, 1907.

Review of Religion, published bi-monthly by the Columbia University Press. Editor, Horace L. Friess; New York City, 1936.

Social Action, a monthly magazine of fact, published by the Council for Social Action of the Congregational Christian Churches. Editor, Elizabeth G. Whiting; New York City, 1935.

A.C.M.

Jovinian: (ca. 390) A pre-Augustinian monk who conceived the communication of the spirit as an experience tied to the ecclesiastical acts of baptism and repentance. Not inferring the consequence of asceticism from pneumatism, he maintained the equal meritoriousness of the marital and celibate states and the moral equality of fasting and eating.

W. Haller, *Jovinianus* (Leipzig, 1897). H.H.

Jowett, Benjamin: (1817-1893) Distinguished English clergyman and educator, and Master of Balliol College in Oxford for many years, during most of which he was also regius professor of Greek. His translation of the Dialogues of Plato is the standard English text of the Platonic corpus. Jowett's influence as Master of Balliol was very wide, and gave rise to scores of characteristic legends and stories. Religiously, he was a broad churchman, whose essay on the Bible in *Essays and Peviews* caused much controversial discussion. W.N.P.

Jubilee, Year of: Following the analogy of the weekly seventh day of repose for man, the seventh year was to be a period of rest for the land. (Ex. 23:10, 11). A Sabbath of Sabbaths (49) of years was to precede the jubilee. During this fiftieth (in actual practice the preceding) year, 1) the land was to lie fallow; 2) it was to revert to original ownership; 3) Hebrew slaves were manumitted. Many students think that the jubilee legislation (Lev. 25:10 ff) is an ideal construction rather than provision for an actual situation. Later Jewish law adopted, developed and even rescinded some of the features of the Biblical legislation. F.A.L.

Jubilees, Book of: Apocalyptic book found in the O.T. pseudepigrapha*, known also under the Greek and Hebrew title of "The Little Genesis" as well as the Apocalypse of Moses. Was originally written in Hebrew and translated successively into Greek, Ethiopic, Latin and Syriac. It purports to be a revelation to Moses on Mt. Sinai by the Angel of the Presence of the history and religious laws and practices covered by the Bible, from Genesis I to Exodus XII, and emanated from an unknown sect at end of 3rd century. The whole is fitted into a chronology reckoned according to the years of the jubilee. The book is a highly interesting religious document with many mystic features, e.g., the pre-existence of the Torah* upon "heavenly tablets" before creation, the celebration in heaven of Pentecost, the date of the revelation of the Torah at Creation.

F.A.L.

Jud, Leo: See catechism; catechumenate.

Judah, the Patriarch, Rabbi: See mishnah.

Judaism: See Israel, religion and theology; Jewish.

Judaism: See Zionism.

Judaism: (Introductory) The term Judaism (Gr., *Ioudaismos*) was coined by Greek speaking Jews to designate their religious way of life in contrast with that of their neighbors, known as Hellenism. (2 Macc. 2.21; 8.1; 14.38; 4 Macc. 4.26) N.T. Greek uses the term in the sense of the Jewish religion (Gal. 1.13-14). Its Hebrew equivalent *Yahadut* dates from the Middle Ages (Rashi to Yebamot 23b; Esther Rabba 7 uses *Yehudut*).

While the term is late, the phenomenon to which it refers goes back to the beginnings of Jewish spiritual life. The distinction, which is commonly made, between the religion of Israel and Judaism, limiting the first to pre-exilic and the other to post-exilic developments, is purely artificial. They describe successive stages of the same religious process. The basic features of post-exilic* Judaism began long before the Exile. The worship of Yahweh* as Israel's covenant God and Savior, the revelation of His will to the prophets and its embodiment in the various codes that comprise the Torah*, and His demand of moral conduct from His worshipers are permanent elements of Judaism, which run unbroken from the days of Sinai to the present.

Judaism represents the religious experience of the Jewish people, that is their consciousness of the sacred as embodied in the Torah both Written and Oral, or Scripture and Tradition. The stages of its growth correspond to the stages of Jewish political, cultural and social evolution. Branching out of Semitic paganism (see Semites, religion of), the religion of the early tribes of Israel was shaped by Moses* at Sinai and Kadesh into the exclusive worship of Yahweh with a corresponding body of ritual and social legislation to meet the needs of the desert surroundings. In the agricultural economy of Canaan the nomadic religion acquired an elaborate sacrificial cult, festivals, sanctuaries, an organized priesthood, codes of law, etc. It was greatly enriched by the institution of kingship and by the unique body of prophets*, who advanced the monolatrous idea of Yahweh to the pure conception of ethical monotheism. The prophetic criticism of the cult and the subordination of ritual to righteousness affected priestly practice and resulted in the Deuteronomic Reformation, which centralized religious worship in Jerusalem and in the Zadokite* priesthood.

The Babylonian Exile marked the break up of the geographic unity of the Jews and the beginning of an ever widening diaspora. (See Babylonian Captivity.) The Davidic dynasty disappeared only to grow into an object of Messianic* hope. What was left of political independence took the form of a theocracy, headed by a high priest of the line of Zadok. The actual sovereignty passed into the hands of the Persians, Greeks and Romans. The spiritual life centered in the Second Temple and, to a lesser degree, in the new institution of the Synagogue. It was deepened and enriched by the Reformation of Ezra and Nehemiah and by the adoption of the Torah as the supreme source of authority of the Jewish people. This highly creative period was further distinguished by the virtual completion of the three-fold canon of Scripture, by the growth of the Apocrypha, and the beginnings of the Oral Law. It called forth the Samaritan secession, the heroic resistance on the part of the Jewish pietists of the tidal wave of Hellenism, and the rise of the Pharisees*, who challenged the Zadokite priesthood—who formed the nucleus of the politico-religious party of Sadducees*—by insisting that all Jews must constitute a kingdom of priests and a holy nation, and that the Torah is the common heritage of the entire congregation of Jacob. The messianic yearnings and eschatological hopes of the politically crushed people merged with the mystery cults of the neighboring peoples, and, centering in the person of Jesus, formed the world religion of Christianity.

The fall of the Jewish state and the destruction of the Second Temple* in 70 C.E. represents the great divide of Judaism as well as of Jewish history. Palestine was now completely in foreign hands, and the Jew was driven into *Galut*, exile, as a homeless wanderer among the nations. Out of the conflagration which destroyed his home and sanctuary the Jew carried away the Torah, which served him henceforth as the indestructible spiritual fatherland. Round it he built fences to safeguard it from hostile attacks. The synagogue* now rose in place of the Temple as the center of Jewish life. In it the ancient sacrificial worship was replaced by the service of prayer, study of Torah and charity. The leadership of the priests gave way to that of the rabbis*, whose main function consisted in interpreting the Torah and in applying it to everchanging conditions. In the schools and academies of Palestine and Babylonia they concentrated on the word of Scripture and developed the Haggadah (religious lore) and Halacha** (law) which endowed Judaism with new power. The rich products of their labors are embodied in the Mishnah* and in the Palestinian and Babylonian Gemaras* (See Talmud) and in the Midrashim.

About the time of the rise of Mohammedanism*—a religion derived in great part from Judaism—there began an intense activity on the part of the heads of the Babylonian academies, the Geonim, to make the newly completed Talmud the possession of all Jewry. Their zeal evoked the opposition of the Karaites* to the authority of both the Talmud and the Rabbis. Their call, "Back to Scripture" created a serious split in Judaism. Their challenge awakened the leaders of Rabbinic Judaism to the study of the text of the Bible, of Hebrew grammar and philology as well as to the systematic study of the Halacha, etc. The contact with Arabic culture stimulated further Jewish creativity in biblical exegesis, history, poetry, theology, philosophy and science.

Following the death of Maimonides* (1204), the codification of the Halacha, which reached its climax in his *Mishne Torah*, continued in Jacob b. Asher's *Tur* (14th cent.) and in Joseph Karo's *Shulhan Aruch* (16th cent.). However the dominant force of the period was the *Cabbala**. Developing in Talmudic and Geonic times, it made its appearance in the cryptic *Sefer Yezira* and reached its height in the *Zohar** (14th cent.). Its mysticism sought to offset the rationalism of the previous period and to correct the overemphasis on Talmudic legalism. The speculative Cabbala of Spanish Jewry was supplemented by the Practical Cabbala of Isaac Luria (16th cent.). Gathering up the occult sciences of angelology, demonology, astrology, etc., and combining them with neo-Platonic* conceptions, particularly with the doctrine of metempsychosis*, it created a strangely fantastic world, in which asceticism crushed the joy of living. The messianism of the Cabbala, which sought to offer anodyne to suffering Jewry, degenerated into vulgar imposture in the movements of Sabbatai Zevi and Jacob Frank. Its tragic aberrations were relieved by the deeply spiritual popular movement of Hasidism* (18th cent.).

The modern era began with the Enlightenment* in Germany under the leadership of Moses Mendelssohn*. This movement spread to Eastern Europe and renovated the cultural life of the Jewish people. The liberalism of the period expressed itself in the Emancipation of Western Jewry, in reaction to which Antisemitism* rose to ever greater power. It is the period of Jewish assimilation, on the one hand, and of secular nationalism and of Zionism*, on the other. It witnessed the renascence of Hebrew as a spoken language and the birth of modern Hebrew and Yiddish* literatures. Its outstanding spiritual expressions are the Science of Judaism (created by Krochmal, Rapoport, and Zunz) and of the Reform, Conservative** and Neo-Orthodox movements.

L. Baeck, *The Essence of Judaism* (Engl. tr., 1936); H. Cohen, *Die Religion der Vernunft* (1919); S. S. Cohon, *What We Jews Believe* (1931); M. Friedlander, *The Jewish Religion* (1891); M. Joseph,

Judaism as Creed and Life (4th ed., 1920); K. Kohler, *Jewish Theology* (1918); G. F. Moore, *Judaism*, 3 vols. (1927-30); C. G. Montefiore, *Outlines of Liberal Judaism* (1912); S. S. Schechter, *Some Aspects of Rabbinic Theology* (1909).

S.S.C.

Judaism, conservative: A designation of a school of thought or a cultural and religious trend within Judaism, rather than a party or sect. It had its modern origins in Germany in the middle of the nineteenth century. Its early exponents were Isaac Bernays (1792-1849), Zachariah Frankel (1801-1875), and the faculty and graduates of the Breslau Seminary founded in 1854. In the United States its leadership is centered around the Jewish Theological Seminary of America, founded in 1885, reorganized in 1902.

No lay or Rabbinical conference of conservatively minded Jews ever adopted a platform of principles or dogmas. There was, and is, however, a general agreement on objectives to be sought.

Conservative Judaism recognizes the authority of Jewish religious and ritual Law as it developed from the Bible through the Talmudic and later Rabbinic periods to modern times. That Law of necessity is subject to the universal principle of change and development. But the changes must accord with the inner logic and essential character of the Law. Opinions regarding that "inner logic and essential character" differ. But despite the differences, the conservative congregation will be readily recognized by its definite inclination to preserve the religious forms and traditions which give to Judaism its peculiar and distinctive manifestations.

The Hebrew language occupies a place of paramount importance in the outlook of conservative Judaism. Though prayers in the vernacular may be recited, Hebrew dominates the Synagogue service as well as the school curriculum. Moreover, its use as a vehicle for every form of modern literary expression is encouraged.

The hope for the restoration of a Jewish Commonwealth in Palestine, always an integral part of traditional Judaism, is cherished. That hope in no way conflicts with the legitimate demands of patriotic allegiance to democratically organized societies, and its realization is indispensable to a full and rich development of the Hebrew heritage in the modern world.

Emphasis upon a thorough and complete knowledge of the *whole* of the Jewish past, knowledge, based upon modern scientific methods of research and of study is another of the marked characteristics of Conservative Judaism. From its ranks, therefore, came many of the scholars, who during the past hundred years have recovered the history of the Jewish people and much of their vast literary and cultural achievement, out of the forgotten and dust-laden manuscripts of the libraries and private collections throughout the world.

Conservative Judaism neither eschews modern thought, nor accepts it as the final authority on matters of faith and tradition. It studies modern thought and accepts and incorporates it into the framework of Judaism when its truth has been proved beyond any reasonable doubt, and when its teachings and implications do not run counter to the ethical doctrines of Judaism, or to the laws of its being, as they have developed during forty centuries of varied experiences.

Solomon Schechter, *Seminary Address and Other Papers* (1915); Cyrus Adler, *Lectures, Selected Papers, Addresses* (1933), pp. 240-264; H. Graetz, *History of the Jews*, Jewish Pub. Society, Vol. V., Ch. XV, XVI, XVIII; Louis Finkelstein, "The Things That Unite Us", *Proceedings of Rabbinical Assembly of America* (1927).

S.G.

Judaism in China: See Chinese religions.

Judaism, Hellenistic: Hellenism, from *hellenizein*, used properly of a non-Greek speaking or imitating Greek; a term applied, especially since J. G. Droysen (1836), to the Grecizing influence of the Greek penetration of the Eastern Mediterranean, especially after the conquests of Alexander the Great. The process was carried on chiefly by the establishment of Greek cities, which then served as centers for the propagation of Greek culture. In Palestine traces of the new ideas have been discerned in some of the Wisdom books of the O.T. (e.g., Ecclesiastes)*; the Apocrypha naturally shows less doubtful influence (e.g., Wisdom of Solomon)* and the Books of the Maccabees* constitute the *locus classicus* for the struggle between traditionalists and innovators, religious as well as political. The struggle is taken cognizance of in rabbinic literature of all periods, and though this literature shows the influence of Greek language and ideas, the importations from the west cannot be said to have substantially affected the main stream of Jewish tradition. But in Alexandria, the focus of Hellenistic Judaism, the Greek current was so dominant as eventually to engulf the failing Jewish stream entirely. The tendency is apparent in Philo*, the great philosopher of Hellenistic Judaism, who, when Greek and Jewish ideas diverge, is apt by forced interpretation to assimilate the Jewish to the Greek. It is more apparent in the fact that Greek is the sole language of a considerable body of literature, produced to acquaint Jews themselves as well as the outer world with Jewish ideas and traditions. The chief monument is the Greek version of the Hebrew Bible known as the Septuagint*, a fanciful account of whose genesis is given in the Letter of Aristeas. Fragments of Jewish histories by Demetrius, Eupolemus, Artapanus, and others are preserved in Eusebius and Clement of Alexandria**. Philosophy is represented by Aristobulus as well as Philo; poetry by Ezekielos' drama on the exodus and by insertions in Phocylides and the Sybilline Oracles. Josephus'* work, though somewhat later and directed to a Roman audience, belongs to the same category. See Hellenism.

The standard work is still Emil Schürer, *Geschichte des jüdischen Volkes im Zeitalter Jesu Christi;* the English translation (1891) is of the first edition; subsequent German editions are superior. The literature is dealt with in Vol. III of Schürer, and perhaps more conveniently in Christ-Schmid-Stählin,

Geschichte der griechischen Litteratur (1920), II 1[6]. The texts are given in W. N. Stearns, *Fragments from Graeco-Jewish Writers* (1908). See also the relevant chapters and bibliographies in the *Cambridge Ancient History* (1928 and 1930), VII and VIII.

M.H.

Judaism, Lectureship on: Established and underwritten since 1936 by Jewish friends of Elyria, Ohio, this lectureship is given at the Graduate School of Theology, Oberlin, Ohio. It is concerned with Talmudic and post-Talmudic law, literature, philosophy and religion. The following have served as lecturers: Rabbi B. R. Brickner, Dr. Louis Finkelstein, Dr. Solomon Goldman, Rabbi S. B. Freehoff, Rabbi A. H. Silver and Prof. S. S. Cohon.

(Data from the office of the Dean of the Graduate School of Theology.) V.F.

Judaism, orthodox: The total Jewish tradition of living as determined by the basic Pentateuchal code of Moses*, amplified by three thousand years of Jewish life in Biblical and post-Biblical ages. The expansion of the written Mosaic law remained a living oral tradition until its primary codification in the Mishnah towards the end of the second century of the Christian era. This was later expanded in the Talmud, and in the Middle Ages classified in such orderly and authoritative codes as the Yad Ha-hazakah of Maimonides and the Shulhan Aruch of Joseph Caro*. Exigencies of life and the uprooting and dispersal of the Jews from Palestine necessarily brought into desuetude some elements of this system. But orthodox Judaism regarding the Mosaic code as divine revelation, gives theoretic allegiance even to those parts of it which can no longer be practically observed.

The necessity, and the acceptance of the principle of the constant interpretation of this law by qualified rabbis in every generation has kept orthodox Judaism fluid, and saved it from much of that rigidity which marked such an outgrowth as the unbending scripturalism of the Karaites*. The interpretation usually tends to alleviate the succinct Biblical law, which starkly applied might have been unbearably rigorous. Thus the numerous laws of the Sabbath, cardinal in orthodox Jewish life, make the traditional Jewish Sabbath a day of complete relaxation and refreshment of body, mind and spirit.

Because orthodox Judaism is based on authoritative written codes it has an essential unity all over the world. But local religious customs, many of which over the centuries have acquired the authority of law, give it considerable outward diversity.

The strength of orthodox Judaism lies in its intense and unbroken traditionalism. Clinging to Hebrew as a sacred tongue, the Hebrew Bible as its ultimate authority, the law of Moses, the admonitions of the prophets and the outpourings of the Psalmist for much of its liturgy, the religious obligation of constant study of the Biblical and rabbinic law by both old and young for its intellectual foundation, and the return to Palestine as integral in its Messianic hope, it has held unwaveringly to its course in the line marked out by Moses, the prophets and the rabbis. This, however, also constitutes a source of weakness because of the difficulty of maintaining an ancient Hebraic tradition outside of Palestine and outside of an essentially Jewish environment. In the Ghetto intensive Jewish living was comparatively easy. Outside the Ghetto, orthodoxy rapidly weakened under modern Western secularist influences, and sometimes through a reform movement seeking to adapt it to the standards of the environment.

The cardinal elements of orthodox Jewish faith are an uncompromising belief in the unity of God and an acceptance of His law as revealed to Moses. But the term orthodox, first used in the time of Napoleon, is a misnomer, because the main emphasis of traditional Judaism is not on creed but on the practise of the ceremonial, social, and ethical teachings of that law.

Orthodox Judaism has no world organization. It has local organizations such as the Union of Orthodox Jewish Congregations of America in the U. S. It has no authoritative ecclesiastical organization, since every duly ordained rabbi is theoretically of equal authority. Of world Jewry estimated at 15,700,000 souls, the great majority, outside of Soviet Russia, would be classified as affiliated with orthodox Judaism. See parochial schools.

Michael Friedlander, *The Jewish Religion* (1891); Isidore Epstein, *Judaism of Tradition* (1931); *The Jewish Library,* 4 series (1928, 1930, 1934), edited by Leo Jung.

D.S.P.

Judaism, rabbinic: See Akiba; Hillel; Midrash; Mishnah; rabbinism; Talmud.

Judaism, reform: Reform Judaism stems from the endeavor on the part of Jews in Western Europe to adjust themselves spiritually to the changed order introduced by the Enlightenment*, on the one hand, and by the political and social upheaval at the turn of the 18th century, on the other. The doctrine of the rights of man (see natural rights), culminating in the French Revolution, broke down the barriers wherewith both Church and State kept the Jews apart from their neighbors. In 1791 the National Assembly enfranchised all the Jews of France. Four years earlier the U.S.A. adopted its Constitution based on the principles of equality and of liberty of conscience. For the first time since their dispersion the Jews found themselves the equals of their fellowmen. The newly acquired status of the Jews in the U.S.A. and in France became the goal of their brethren in Germany and in other lands.

Political equality confronted the Jews with grave problems of adjustment. Some ultra-Orthodox Jews feared that under emancipation Jews might not remain loyal to rabbinical* law* and abandon the hope of deliverance and restoration in the Holy Land under the Messiah*. Extremists at the other end considered Judaism incompatible with the new freedom, and sought their salvation in total assimilation within Christian society. The leaders of Reform endeavored to avoid both extremes. Following the teaching of Moses Mendelssohn*, they resolved to enter the new European order as a religious people, i.e., to identify themselves with their neighbors in political, industrial, economic and cultural life, and to retain their separateness only in religion and in those social and cultural elements which pertain to religion.

This political and social change went hand in hand with the altered religious outlook under the influence of Deism, Kantian moralism and Hegelian rationalism**. The ferment of new ideas weakened the whole structure of Jewish belief and practice. To win back for Judaism those whose religious ardor had cooled became the primary object of Reform. At the first Reform Temple, built by Israel Jacobsohn at Seesen in 1810, and particularly at the Hamburg Temple (1818), which served as model for Reform synagogues in Germany and in other countries, stress was laid on the modernization of the service by revising the liturgy, introducing the vernacular in worship, instrumental music, family pews, confirmation of girls as well as of boys, etc. The external reforms were followed by the reinterpretation of the theological foundations of Judaism in the light of current philosophies and the historical sciences by Leopold Zunz (1794-1886), Samuel Holdheim (1806-1860), and Abraham Geiger (1810-1874). Through their disciples the movement spread to other lands and found a specially congenial home in democratic America, where, under the leadership of Isaac M. Wise (1819-1900), David Einhorn (1809-1879), Kaufmann Kohler (1843-1926), etc., Reform congregations were established in almost all cities of the land.

The Union of American Hebrew Congregations (org. 1873) numbers (1943) 308 congregations, consisting of 62,209 families. More than 450 rabbis belong to the Central Conference of American Rabbis (org. 1889). The movement is ministered to by the Hebrew Union College (org. by Isaac M. Wise, 1875) and by the Jewish Institute of Religion (org. by Stephen S. Wise, 1922).

As the product of the Enlightenment, Reform identified itself with the rational tradition in Judaism, and built its theology upon reason and upon the scientific interpretation of Scripture and the Oral Law. The dominant notes in its teaching have been the universal and the ethical without ignoring the particularistic and the ceremonial. In view of changing conditions in Jewish life today, the main task of Reform is no longer mere adjustment to the modern temper but rather the self-reaffirmation of Judaism as a religion in a world predominantly secularistic and nationalistic. Though absorbed in the struggle against the deadly forces of Anti-semitism* and in problems of relief and of aiding Palestinian fellow Jews to establish for themselves a secure home, Reform Judaism adheres to the wider view of its prophetic heritage and conceives its Messianic task to be "to co-operate with all men in the establishment of the kingdom of God*, of universal brotherhood, justice, truth and peace on earth".

Guiding Principles of Reform Judaism, Yearbook of Central Conference of American Rabbis (1937), Vol. 47, 94-114; *Union Prayerbook* (1940), Vol. 1, (1922), Vol. II; *Rabbi's Manual* (1928); Samuel S. Cohon (and Rall), *Christianity and Judaism Compare Notes* (1927); S. S. Cohon, *What We Jews Believe* (1931); K. Kohler, *Jewish Theology* (1918); C. G. Montefiore, *Outlines of Liberal Judaism* (1912); D. Philipson, *The Reform Movement in Judaism* (1931). S.S.C.

Judaism, Talmudic: See Talmud.

Judaizers: Those who inculcate Jewish doctrines and observances. Particularly is it applied to those Jewish Christians* who insisted that Gentiles* must observe their national rites, including circumcision*. The word is really derived from Paul's use of a verb, "to Judaize" (Gal. 2.14). The term appears again in the letters of Ignatius* (Mag. 8.1, Phil. 5) where the Bishop of Antioch opposes those who insist upon circumcision, sabbath observance, and the keeping of the Law. C.T.C.

Judas: (Iscariot) One of the inner circle of Jesus' followers, and His betrayer. According to John 12:6, also treasurer of the group. Iscariot probably means "man of Kerioth." S.M.G.

Judas Maccabeus: (the "hammerer") Third son of Mattathias the Hasmonean* priest of Modin, and his successor as leader in the holy war against Antiochus Epiphanes's* forceful hellenization of Judea. With his small and poorly equipped guerilla bands of patriots, this resourceful warrior overcame the well armed and disciplined hosts of Syria, and defeated Lysias the governor of Syria himself and Bacchides. After three years of struggle, Judas retook Jerusalem*, except the Citadel, cleansed the Temple* of heathen altars, and reconsecrated it to the God of Israel (25th of Kislev, 165 or 164), an event celebrated by the annual eight day celebration of *Hanukkah** (Dedication).

After two years of comparative quiet, Judas was forced to undertake campaigns against hostile neighbors in Transjordania and in Galilee. Taking advantage of the death of the king, he laid siege to the Citadel. Counterattacked by Lysias who had assumed the regency of Syria, Judas lifted the siege and met his opponent in battle. At Beth-Zacharias Judas was defeated (162 B.C.). He retreated to the Temple Mount, but could not hold out because of an acute food shortage. For political reasons Lysias dealt leniently with the Jews. He demolished the Temple fortification, but granted the Jews complete religious freedom, which was the goal of their fighting.

Following the murder of Lysias and his royal ward, the new king Demetrius I sent Bacchides back to Judea to remove Judas and to install Alcimus in the High Priesthood. The Hasidim* accepted Bacchides's promise to respect their religious freedom and withdrew from further fighting. The treacherous execution of sixty of their number confirmed Judas in his resolve to fight on until complete political as well as religious freedom would be secured. This time Nicanor was dispatched with a strong force to Judea (161 B.C.). At Capharsalama he suffered a crushing defeat, and in the next battle at Adasa he was slain. The day of Judas's greatest victory (13th of Adar) was observed as an annual festival.

Threatened by the continuous menace of Syria, Judas sent an embassy to Rome to secure its friendship. Before help could come from that quarter, Bacchides returned to Judea to avenge the defeat of Nicanor. He encamped at Berea. This time the courage of the Jewish soldiers sank. They turned and fled, leaving only eight hundred men with Judas. The lion hearted warrior battled desperately and performed wonders, but was overwhelmed and slain. (Nisan, 160 B.C.) Though defeated, his cause triumphed. His brothers Jonathan (161-142) and Simon (142-135) won through concessions from the rival claimants of the Syrian throne the independence for which Judas fought and died. See Maccabees; Maccabees, Books of; Jewish religious festivals.

1 and 2 Maccabees; Josephus, *Antiquities*, XII, 6-11; Art. in *Jewish Encyclopedia* (1903); Histories of the Jewish People. S.S.C.

Jude, Letter of: Written about A.D. 125, Jude is an encyclical to Christians everywhere, warning them against the groups of people of low morals and high pretensions that were infecting the churches. He probably has the Docetists* in mind. Nothing is known of the author; the only Jude, brother of James, in the N.T. was also the brother of Jesus, and would have been designated "the Lord's brother." If he is meant, the letter is pseudonymous, since the situation it reflects is later than the first century. It stands in two of our three earliest N.T. lists, Tertullian and the Muratorian.

J. B. Mayor, *The Epistle of St. Jude and the Second Epistle of St. Peter* (1907). E.J.G.

judge, ecclesiastical: (Lat. *judex ecclesiasticus*) A dignitary of the Roman Catholic Church with power to sit in judgment and pronounce sentence. His jurisdiction is either a) ordinary—that which is attached by law to an ecclesiastical office, or b) delegated—that which is committed to a cleric by competent ecclesiastical authority. The pope's jurisdiction is universal while that of each bishop is confined to his own diocese. In practice, the Sacred Roman Rota is the papal court of the first instance, appeal, or final appeal, except in those cases reserved by law to the pope himself. A diocesan judge, called the official, usually acts for the bishop. In some cases a collegiate tribunal of three or five judges is required. The judge alone exercises judicial power in all cases, whether civil or criminal, there being no jury system in church courts. J.F.T.

Judges: A historical book of the O.T., included among the "Former Prophets"* in the Hebrew canon. It contains three well-defined divisions: a brief survey of the occupation of Canaan by the Israelites (1:1-2:5); the history of the judges (2:6-16:31); and an appendix, comprising accounts of the Danite migration and of the war against Benjamin (chapters 17-21). The central and main portion of the book (2:6-16:31) is a product of the Deuteronomic school of historians (See D) who have used older material, possibly from J and E** narratives, and provided for the various judges a stereotyped framework of religious introductions and conclusions. They viewed the history of this period as a regular succession of cycles of apostasy by Israel, oppression by an enemy, outcry to Yahweh, and deliverance by a judge. To this Deuteronomic book were later added the introduction, 1:1-2:5, from old material which is paralleled in fragments of Joshua* (especially chapters 15-17) and the appendix, which contains old material with annotations. The story of Abimelech in chapter 9 and of the minor judges in 10:1-5, 12:8-15, which do not have Deuteronomic coloring, are probably also later additions. The Deuteronomic conception of the history of this period is artificial, but the book contains much valuable material. Of greatest importance is the Song of Deborah, chapter 5, a masterpiece of early Hebrew poetry which is nearly contemporaneous with the events it describes. The judges were military leaders and administrative chieftains who were probably local heroes of one of more tribes rather than rulers of the whole nation. Cf. Samson.

See G. F. Moore, *Judges* (International Critical Commentary, 1895); C. F. Burney, *The Book of Judges* (2nd ed., 1920). J.P.H.

judgment, final (or last): See final judgment.

Judith: Apocryphal book named after its heroine. Like Daniel and Esther** it celebrates the deliverance of the Jews from persecution and aims to endow them with courage. It is variously dated from Maccabean* times to the age of Hadrian. Composed in Hebrew, it has been preserved in Greek, Syriac and Latin versions. S.S.C.

Judson, Adoniram: (1788-1850) Pioneer foreign Baptist missionary. On way to Burma as appointee of American Board of Commissioners for Foreign Missions turned Baptist being immersed September 6, 1812. Translator of Bible into Burmese and author of Burmese dictionary (1849). Body buried at sea. C.H.M.

Julian the Apostate: (331-363) Successor to Constantius as Roman emperor, reigning from 361-363. Dismissed Christians from all official posts and enacted such repressive measure as forbidding them to teach the classics. He sought to reform paganism and to reestablish it in the Empire, but without results that survived his death. S.M.G.

Julian Calendar: See Gregorian Calendar.

Julian of Eclanum: Bishop of Eclanum in Apulia ca. 417, but exiled from Italy in 421. A Pelagian* who attacked Augustine and his teachings. particularly that of original sin*. S.M.G.

Jumpers, the: A derisive epithet applied to eighteenth century Welsh Calvinistic Methodists, whose worship was accompanied by ecstatic convulsions. F.G.E.

Jung, Carl G.: (1875-) Like Adler*, he is a distinguished pupil of Freud*, who founded his own "school" of psychoanalysis. A man of profound intellectual gifts and a comprehensive grasp of culture, his contribution of the famous introvert-extravert dichotomy of personalities is one of the earliest and undoubtedly the most influential from the point of view of the research on personality. He holds that the most basic distinction in personalities is that of orientation toward objective reality and toward subjective determinants. He also developed the discrete association test, an approach to the study of personality from the introspective side, by the verbal responses of the individual. He regards Freud's psychoanalytic method as the therapy of choice for many psycho-neuroses except in elderly people. In developing his own method of psychological healing, he insists in paying more attention to the primitive background of man's mind. For him the unconscious is essentially collective, racial, and perhaps universal. Unmasking, in particular, the different denizens in the unfamiliar realm of the unconscious, exploring the creative forces of the unconscious, he stresses that its unveiling should not be taken seriously until the second half of life. His psychoanalytic studies of mythology and religion are of great value. In most essentials his therapeutic principles and method of psychological healing are very different from Freud's. He interests himself, in particular, in the determination of the patient's personality type and in guiding him in his development of avocations. Special interest is shown in the more symbolic elements of the individual's phantasy life, and studying their similarities with those found in art, various religions, and mythologies. Much of his procedure appears to Freudians more as a stimulating academic tutorship than as an etiological therapy, providing the individual with a new philosophy with which to cloak his suffering rather than effecting a dynamic personality change for more mature development. Jung is by far the most sensitive of the founders of the psychoanalytic movement, to every echo in the secret recesses of the mind. Truly catholic in outlook and constructive in ideals, the truths of religion are as necessary as those of material science. Castigated as being a philosopher but no psychologist by the rival camps, he is unafraid to speak of the soul and the spiritual. He has been especially the source of inspiration for the English guild of pastoral psychologists, which is chiefly interested in promoting an understanding of psychotherapy among ministers of religion. See psychology, schools of.

His chief works are: *Dementia praecox* (1914); *Psychology of the Unconscious* (1916); *Studies in Word Association* (1918); *Psychological Types* (1923); *Modern Man in Search of a Soul* (1933); *Psychology of Religion* (1938); *The Integration of the Personality* (1939). H.H.

Jupiter: (Lat. *Iovis*—dies, day; *pater,* father) In Roman religion, originally the sky-spirit; then lord of heaven and earth. The thunder-bolt is his weapon. He became the people's protector in time of war; the god of justice and of oaths in time of peace. As Jupiter Optimus Maximus, he was later identified with the Greek Zeus*. His tree is the oak; his bird the eagle. E.M.N

jurisprudence: The term covers two essentially different types of science of law. As understood by lawyers, the science of law, on the European continent called "dogmatic jurisprudence", is the science of the rules of law. As a taxonomic science it sees its primary task in the clear formulation and the orderly arrangement of the rules of law, as they are found in statutes and judicial pronouncements. As a "Geisteswissenschaft"* it explores the meaning of these rules in order to develop for new and unforeseen situations such solutions as will be in accordance with the societal value judgments of which the existing rules of law are expressive.

In a different sense the word jurisprudence signifies a "Wirklichkeitswissenschaft", whose subject-matter is constituted by law as a real social phenomenon and which inquires into the role played by this phenomenon in social life. While the jurisprudence of the lawyers is concerned with one particular legal system, e.g., American law or French law, and with the present day, jurisprudence in the latter sense is concerned with the law of all times and climes. In England and the United States the term jurisprudence is often reserved to this latter science. Its various "schools" do not represent mutually exclusive philosophical systems but different branches of, or approaches to, the common subject-matter. *Historical jurisprudence* as History of Law is concerned with the development in time of the law of a country (e.g., W. S. Holdsworth's *History of English Law,* 1903-38) or system (e.g., the Common Law, the Civil Law or Mohammedan Law) or of a particular legal institution (e.g., contract, mortgage, divorce, etc.), or of law in the general course of human history. *Sociology of law* (N. S. Timasheff, Max Weber, A. Gurvitch, E. Ehrlich) is interested in determining law's role in human society, in finding correlations between law and other phenomena of social life and of nature (e.g., political power, forms of production, climate, race) and in discovering such statistical regularities ("social laws") as may exist in such correlations. *Comparative law* is sociology of law when directed toward the investigation of the social causes and effects of detailed legal institutions with special emphasis upon the differences existing between contemporary laws of different countries. *Ethnological jurisprudence* collects and interprets the pre-legal and legal institutions of primitive or backward peoples. Contemporary *American realism* (Llewellyn, U. Moore, J. Frank, Thurman Arnold) constitutes sociology of law carried on by a group of men trained in law rather than sociology, inspired by liberal political ideals, but inclined to underestimate the psychological reality of "rules" of law. So-called *sociological jurisprudence*, on the other hand (O. W. Holmes, B. Cardozo, R. Pound) is not sociology of law at all but that method of lawyers' practical jurisprudence that emphasizes the necessity for courts and lawyers to familiarize themselves with the facts of modern social, especially economic life, in order to arrive at adequate decisions. *Analytical jurisprudence* (J. Austin, Kocourek, H. Kelsen) is interested in clarifying the conceptual framework of a particular legal system or of legal thought in general. *Philosophy of law* finally seeks to comprehend the "essence" of law, to determine its metaphysical ends and to establish, by developing the notion of justice, the standards for the ethical evaluation of positive law. See law; natural rights.

R. Pound, "Jurisprudence", Vol. 8, *Enc. of Soc. Sci.*, p. 477 (with extensive bibliography); J. Hall, *Readings in Jurisprudence* (1938); W. Seagle, *The Quest for Law* (1941); H. Cairns, *Theory of Legal Science* (1941); R. Pound, *Contemporary Juristic Theory* (1940); H. E. Yntema, "Jurisprudence on Parade" (1941), Vol. 39, *Michigan Law Rev.*, p. 1154. M.Rh.

justice: 1) The standard of rights and duties applicable to all; 2) the cardinal virtue of those who conform to the standard. Conceptions of both standard and virtue vary as societies are low or high in culture, aristocratic or democratic. Justice is always a principle of "perfect obligation" with definite and universal connotation within a given society (e.g., with us, all must carry out contracts, pay taxes, refrain from crime) in contrast with benevolence or love, which is of "imperfect obligation" and individual conscience (e.g., whether and how much to contribute to a charity). With social progress, functions previously within the domain of imperfect obligation and individual conscience often become matters of prescribed justice: (e.g., compulsory contributions through taxes to the support of free elementary schools replace voluntary subscriptions, while the attendance of children becomes required and no longer is left to the option of parents).

In Plato's* Republic, justice is the inclusive virtue of the ideal state, in which all citizens are temperate and obedient, the military class in addition courageous, and the rulers wise. Every person performs the tasks for which he is best fitted. Justice for the individual means that his appetites are controlled by temperance, his emotions by courage, and his decisions by wisdom.

Aristotle*, in the Nicomachean Ethics, after observing that Justice had sometimes (as with Plato) been a designation for the whole of virtue, decides to limit his own discussion to the narrower and more specific definition of what is fair. He also distinguishes between Distributive Justice—the fair distribution of honors, wealth, and other goods in accordance with a rational principle—and Corrective Justice—the correction of violations of such just distribution (e.g., crimes, torts, breaches of contracts). Aristotle's usage has generally been preferred to Plato's.

In modern times, a typical individualistic definition of Justice is that of Herbert Spencer*: "every man is free to do that which he wills, provided he infringes not the equal freedom of any other man". This implies that the activities of government should be restricted to a minimum, and individuals allowed to benefit and suffer from the consequences of their own actions. Collectivists wish the state to promote the general good more actively, and to bring all persons upon an approximately equalitarian level, at least in the economic field. A mediating position proposes as its canon: "a just distribution of economic and other goods will render to the members of each class of society the facilities and rewards requisite to enable and to induce them to render the services which society has a right to expect of them". Capitalistic, communistic, and co-operative programs should be evaluated by this canon.

Conflicting interpretations of Corrective Justice were advanced during the last century, but the following points are now usually accepted. Although the essential motive leading to the apprehension and conviction of criminals is undoubtedly public moral indignation, yet no offender should be punished *merely* as an expression of retribution. Four other considerations should be taken into account: *moral education* of the public to the wrongfulness of the crime; *deterrence* of would be offenders by fear of like punishment; *prevention* (by execution, imprisonment, surveillance) of future misconduct by the criminal himself; if possible, *reformation* or rehabilitation of the criminal's character. Many believe that improved social conditions will prove in the long run more effective in diminishing crime than the efforts of Corrective Justice. See lex talionis; natural rights.

S. E. Mezes, *Ethics* (1901), Chap. on Justice; T. N. Carver, *Essays in Social Justice* (1915); J. H. Ryan, *Distributive Justice* (rev. ed., 1942). W.K.W.

justice, Divine: See sin; theodicy; wrath of God.

justice, Old Testament conception of: See righteousness, Old Testament conception of.

justification: By the teaching of the apostle Paul* the doctrine of justification has become central in all Christian thinking. When Paul speaks of 'justification by faith' he gives expression to the conviction that man cannot become acceptable in God's sight by fulfilling the law (of Moses), but that he can be saved only by trusting (believing) in the grace* of God revealed in Jesus Christ. To be "justified by God" means to be "righteous before God" (Rom. 2:13) and to be "regarded as righteous" by him (Rom. 9:19). But this acknowledgment of being righteous in the presence of God is due not to the fulfillment of religious and moral commandments (for such an accomplishment is impossible for man) but to the grace of God alone, who through Christ accepts even a sinner by forgiving him, thus making him his own. By faith man knows that he is God's.

Ancient Catholicism adhered to this Pauline teaching, but modified it by narrowing it down. It identified grace primarily with baptismal grace.

By reference to it, it declared the Christian to be free from obedience to the works of the law; but in anticipation of the divine judgment at the end of time, it expected him to do good works by which he could prove and maintain the salvation by grace. It introduced the teaching and practice whereby the Christian was to earn "merits" and "satisfactions"*. Thus Christianity was understood as a religion of grace as well as of good works. Absolute dependence upon God was combined with an insistence upon the moral freedom of man.

Only Augustine* returned to the original Pauline teaching on justification, but not without developing it further. Nor was his teaching such that thereby the established doctrines and practices were superseded. He started from the principle that the will is totally enslaved to sin and therefore incapable of accomplishing anything good. All salvation (attainment of goodness) is due to grace. As "prevenient grace" it creates a new heart in man by being infused in him as "charity" or "spirit". As "cooperating grace" it is present in all "works" of man, thus making it possible for him to become acceptable in God's sight. All this is understood as justification which is identical with the inspiration of the Holy Spirit (or of love) into the sinful heart of man. In full consistency with this view he advanced his doctrine of predestination.

Had Augustinianism been adopted without qualifications, the Roman Catholic Church would have been compelled radically to change its institutional practices. As a matter of fact, Augustine's predestinarianism* was not adopted in the interest of preserving room within the Christian life for free will and good works.

On this basis the medieval scholastics developed their doctrine of justification. They too endeavored to be loyal to the Pauline teaching that man lives by grace alone. But they made possible the practice of good works as an expression of man's moral will by strictly distinguishing the realm of grace from that of free will. With the help of Aristotelian philosophy they developed the theory of the "information" of the human soul with the "*habitus*" of divine grace: In order that God may dwell in man, the metaphysical center of the soul must be purified by an infusion of the supernatural "*habitus*" of grace (or love); thus man is rendered capable of performing good works and of earning merits. By this theory, which was classically developed by Thomas Aquinas, the freedom of the will could be acknowledged within the limits of the religion of grace.

Luther*, trained in Nominalism which had criticized the Thomistic doctrine to such an extent that it practically affirmed Pelagianism, overthrew the entire Roman Catholic tradition by a fresh interpretation of the Pauline doctrine of justification. He ceased to understand grace as an impersonal supernatural substance, bound to the sacraments, but interpreted it to mean God's personal relationship of mercy toward the sinner, assured to man in the Word. Confronted by the fatherly mercy of God revealed in Christ, man can do no other than in repentance to acknowledge his utter unworthiness and in faith to receive the assurance of the divine forgiveness. Thus he is justified and reborn. In the presence of God always a sinner, he lives by grace alone, so that he is forced to see himself as sinner and saint at the same time (*simul peccator ac iustus*).

Luther coupled this thinking, which represents the essential message of the Reformation*, with the doctrine of the "imputation" of the righteousness of Christ upon the undeserving sinner. By virtue of the forensic "imputation"* of the righteousness of Christ upon him, the sinner is "reputed" as righteous. Such became the teaching of Protestant Orthodoxy. It tended to regard justification as an extra-human event—in full contrast to Luther's original message according to which all human *experience* of God in Christ was viewed as a process of justification.

In the history of Protestantism, the doctrine of justification was developed either on the basis of the "Orthodox" teaching of the divine justifying decree (forensic justification) or as a reaction against it. In liberal Protestantism it lost all significance, partly in connection with the dissolution of the traditional Christology* and partly under the influence of the evolutionary interpretation of religious experience. However, under the impact of the recent revival of the Reformation faith, primarily in Lutheran circles, Luther's original teaching on justification is brought to the fore. See atonement in Christianity; common grace; regeneration; sanctification.

W.P.

Justin Martyr: (2nd cent.) Born ca. 100 A.D. of pagan parents at the Samaritan city of Flavia Neapolis (the ancient Shechem) and well educated in Greek philosophy. On his conversion to Christianity he travelled from place to place, like other professional philosophers, lecturing on the truth of Christian beliefs. Suffered a martyr's death in Rome sometime during the years 163-167. His "Apology," written at Rome ca. 150, is the earliest formal defense of Christianity that has survived. Justin refutes criminal charges brought against Christians, describes Christian worship, and develops a philosophy of the Christian religion. Also the author of a defense of Christianity against Judaism entitled "Dialogue with Trypho." See Apologists. S.M.G.

Justinian I: (483-565) Emperor at Constantinople, 527-565; reign was epoch in history of Byzantine* empire and Eastern Church. Brought temporary revival of area and prestige of old Roman empire. Instituted legal reforms and codified Roman law. Assumed control over the church and tried unsuccessfully to reconcile orthodox and Monophysite* views. See Constantinople, Councils of. K.H.C.

juvenile delinquency: A broad term that relates to the criminal or other anti-social acts of children which are sufficiently serious in their consequences for the community, or for the children themselves, as to bring them to the attention of the juvenile court. It should be noted that such a definition stops short of including acts of harmless mischief. Indeed, delinquency need not imply specific acts, such as are involved in the concept of adult crime, but is broad enough in its significance to include mere association with immoral or vicious persons; or, as one statute has it, the situation of a child who is "growing up in idleness and crime." In other words, such a conception takes cognizance of immoral or dangerous tendencies on the part of children and their need for protection from the same.

Furthermore, the legal conception of delinquency has reference to the age limit up to which the juvenile court has jurisdiction. According to state juvenile court laws this varies from 16 to 21 years, the prevailing age limit being 17 years. Above this limit, wherever it is placed, the definitely criminal acts of young persons make them liable to prosecution in the criminal courts. In them the procedure is vastly different from that of the juvenile courts. The former are concerned with specific illegal acts performed, and the identification of accused persons with them; the latter consider evidence relating to the character of children concerning whom a petition of delinquency has been filed, and to the reasons for their behavior. Delinquency involves, therefore, not only a different legal process, but also a fundamentally different type of inquiry, directed not toward conviction, but toward an understanding of the maladjustment of children. The explanation of their difficulties may involve constitutional defects, but perhaps to a larger degree unfavorable environmental influences in family or community life; or both types of circumstance may be present in a complex pattern of interaction.

From all this it appears that the term delinquency has a definitely sociological content, involving under the juvenile court a socialized procedure, looking toward a reorientation of badly adjusted children, and utilizing the facilities of medicine, psychiatry, social case work, or other techniques as may seem promising for the end in view. Finally, it may be observed that this concept of juvenile delinquency, and the institution of the juvenile court, have important implications for the socialization of our methods in dealing with adult crime. See juvenile protection; penology.

L. J. Carr, *Delinquency Control* (1941); W. Healy, *New Light on Delinquency and its Treatment* (1936); C. R. Shaw, *The Natural History of a Delinquent Career* (1931); S. and E. T. Glueck, *One Thousand Juvenile Delinquents* (1934). A.E.W.

juvenile protection: Pertaining to activities and agencies for the moral and physical protection of children. The greater complexity of our urban environment, the increasing moral hazards of childhood, and the lessening degree of family control have given rise to the necessity of extra-familial organization for the safeguarding of children from unwholesome influences, whether in the family or in the community at large. Agencies for this purpose were established in many states before 1900, and at present there are possibly over three-hundred such privately supported organizations in the United States, some of them being state-wide in their function. The earliest types were termed Societies for the Prevention of Cruelty to Children, but many of them now carry on under the name of Humane Societies which broadened their activities to care for children as well as animals. It is pertinent to observe that the latter had first place in public concern.

Some of these organizations play an important role in the prosecution under the statutes of cases of cruelty and neglect where children are involved. But besides these situations which relate to improper family care the agencies for juvenile protection are concerned with conditions in the community that are moral hazards for children. Such are to be found in dance halls, pool rooms, movies, night-clubs, and other places of recreation; and they are often associated with the unsavory environment of children in the street trades or other places of work. It is natural that these situations are found to be highly related to juvenile delinquency. Some of the organizations that we are discussing specialize in the protection of young girls in urban areas. Others work with unmarried mothers.

Meanwhile, the establishment of juvenile courts, policewomen's bureaus, boys' divisions of police departments, and the activities of the Federal Childen's Bureau indicate an increasing concern of publically constituted agencies for problems in this field. Moreover, the movement for juvenile protection has inspired new laws for the control and abatement of unwholesome conditions affecting children; and an increasing emphasis is being placed on preventive work. As yet the movement has only slightly affected conditions in the rural areas where there is undoubtedly much need. As for our cities the problems in this field would seem to indicate that child welfare has been an afterthought in our urban civilization. See juvenile delinquency.

S. and E. T. Glueck, *Preventing Crime* (1936); G. Abbott, *The Child and the State* (1938), 2 vols.; H. Folks, *The Care of Destitute, Neglected and Delinquent Children* (1902). A.E.W

K

ka: In early Egypt, the spirit guardian and companion which attends the human soul both while the soul is in the living flesh, and also in the after-life. See idols and images. F.L.P.

kaaba or caaba: (Arabic *kabah,* a square building from *kab,* cube) The small, nearly cubical stone building in the court of the Great Mosque at Mecca*, which contains the sacred black rock, thought by Moslems* to have been given by Gabriel to Abraham. It is the object of annual pilgrimage, and worship center to which Moslems turn in daily prayers. P.E.J.

Kabbalah: (Heb. *Kabel*—to receive, hence tradition) The esoteric mystic lore of Judaism based upon an occult interpretation of the Bible and handed down as secret doctrine to the initiated. The origin is obscure. Evidences of Kabbalistic themes both as speculative theosophy and practical thaumaturgy are found in Apocryphal and Apocalyptic literature and abundantly in Talmudic and Midrashic literature**. In the course of its long development, many streams from alien sources flowed into it—Gnosticism, Neo-Platonism, Neo-Pythagoreanism, possibly also Zoroastrianism and Suffism**. Its birthplace was Palestine, but it was in Babylonia, during the Geonic period (550-1000 A.D.) that it experienced its first substantial systematic development. At least two important Kabbalistic works were composed or edited here, the *"Sefer Yetzirah"* (The Book of Formation), on the creative powers of letters and numbers, a most widely studied and commented work, and the *"Shiur Komah"* (The Measure of the Height) an anthropomorphic work on the dimensions of the Deity.

From Babylonia the center of Kabbalah moved, in the ninth and tenth centuries, to Italy, Spain, the Provence and Germany. Among the forerunners of Kabbalah in Europe were Aaron ben Samuel, who brought it from Babylonia to Italy, Isaac the Blind and Azriel in the Provence, the Kalonymus family, who transplanted it from Italy to Germany, Judah the Pious and Eleazar of Worms, and, in Spain, Moses ben Nachman*. To this period belong the Kabbalistic classics "Masechet Atzilut" (A Treatise on Emanation) by Jacob Nazir (12 c); the "Sefer Ha-Bahir", (The Luminous Book—13 c); and the "Sefer Ha-Temunah", (The Book of the Image—13 c). The most significant book of this period, however, and the one which came to be regarded as the holiest of all Kabbalistic writings, and the very epitome of Jewish mysticism, was the Zohar*, made known to the public by Moses de Leon in 1300.

The next great period of Kabbalah was in the 16th century. Its principal center was in Palestine, more especially in the city of Safed. Next in importance was the center in Poland. The foremost Kabbalists of this period were Moses Cordovero (1522-1570), Isaac Luria (1533-1572), the father of modern "practical" Kabbalah, and his disciple, Chayim Vital (1543-1620) who committed the teachings of Luria to writing. Luria was the founder of a school of Kabbalistic speculation in which redemption and messianism figured prominently which greatly influenced the subsequent development of Kabbalah. The Lurianic Kabbalah was one of the spiritual sources of the popular mystic movement of Eastern Europe in the 18th and 19th centuries known as Chasidism*.

With the advent of the Zohar, the study of Kabbalah spread among the masses of the people. It ceased to be the secret doctrine of the few. Everybody studied it, even the young. Especially was this true of the Jews in Poland. Frequently leading Rabbinic authorities inveighed against this popular absorption in Kabbalistic studies which fed many superstitions and aberrations.

Kabbalism attracted the interest of Christian scholars in the Middle Ages. Prominent among them were Raymond Lully, Pico della Mirandola and John Reuchlin**—first as a reaction to medieval scholastic theology and then in the hope of finding substantiation for Christian doctrine in the mystic writings of the Jews.

The central themes of Kabbalah are the nature of the Deity—the "En Sof"—(The Limitless One) and the ways by which He has made Himself manifest—the "Ten Sefirot" (Emanations); the four Universes of Atzilah (Emanation), Beriah (Creation), Yetzirah (Formation), and Asia (Action); the Soul of man, its nature and consummation, the mysteries of the Divine Name, good and evil, man's place in the universe, heaven and hell, the order of the angels and demons, Israel, the Exile, redemption and the Messiah.

Kabbalah employed a characteristic exegetical technique which gave it great freedom and scope. It regarded not only every word of the Bible—written in Hebrew, the very language of God—but every letter, every vowel and all their possible permutations and combinations as holding profound mysteries. Thus the Bible was interpreted not only literally, allegorically, homiletically and anagogically, but also through the devices of Gematria (the interpretation of a word according to the numerical value of its letters), Notarikon (taking each letter of a word as the initial of some other word), Temurah (substituting one letter for another) and Tziruf or Chiluf (transposing the letters—anagram). Thus Kabbalah never felt the constraint of the "letter which killeth" and never came into conflict with the written Scriptures as Christian mystics frequently did. See Judaism (Introductory).

Adolf Franck, *The Kabbalah* (1926); Christian Ginsburg, *The Kabbalah* (1920); A. E. Waite, *The Holy Kabbalah* (1929); *Jew. Encycl.* (1901-05) s.v. "Cabala".

A.H.S.

kaddish: (Aramaic, holy) An ancient Jewish prayer for the hallowing of God's name and coming of His Kingdom. Its opening words parallel the first three phrases of the Lord's Prayer, pointing to a traditional prayer form from which both stem. This Aramaic doxology, originally closing a sermon, in the synagogue liturgy closes a section of the service. Since medieval times it has become the mourner's declaration of faith.

D.S.P.

Kaehler, Martin: Protestant theologian. Born 1835, Neuhausen, East Prussia, 1860 privatdozent in Halle, 1864 professor of Systematic Theology in Bonn, 1865-1912 in Halle. Under the early influences of R. Rothe, J. T. Beck** and neo-Lutheran pietism Kaehler developed a type of theology of great originality and depth. His aim was the combination of the cognitive and the experiential aspects of Biblical Christianity. His central idea was the indissoluble unity of the historical and the suprahistorical in the Biblical events. He did much to explode the "historical Jesus" of Protestant liberalism. According to Kaehler theology is primarily soteriology. His theological method is characterized by the triangular nature of its authorities: Bible, Church and personal experience in mutual interrelation. His theology is the mature re-integration of the theological developments of the nineteenth century, interpreted by a man of great intellectual force and spiritual warmth. The clumsiness and occasional obscurity of his literary style prevented his theology from becoming as popular as it deserved. He had no direct follower. But with ingenious certitude and vision he pointed to the problems which the theology of the twentieth century had to face. The theological development of Germany for the last thirty years reveals everywhere its indebtedness to Kaehler.

Principal works:

Die Wissenschaft von der christlichen Lehre (1883, 3rd ed. 1905); *Der sog. historische Jesus und der geschichtliche biblische Christus* (1892, 2nd ed. 1896); *Dogmatische Zeitfragen*, 3 vols. (1898-1913); *Das Kreuz Grund und Mass für die Christologie* (1911). For a list of his remarkable articles in Herzog's *Realencyclopädie*, 3rd ed. see vol. 22, p. xix. On Kaehler see: Ch. Boegner, *D. Martin Kaehler* (1912); O. Zänker, *Grundlinien der Theologie Martin Kaehlers* (1914); F. Kattenbusch, *Die deutsche Theologie seit Schleiermacher*, (2nd ed. 1934), p. 65ff.

O.A.P.

kafir or kaffir: (Arabic *kafir*, infidel, from *kafara*, to be skeptical) An epithet applied to all unbelievers by the Moslems. A non-Mohammedan or infidel. *Gabar** or *Gheber*, (Persian non-believer), is thought to be derived from *kafir*.

P.E.J.

Kaftan, Julius Wilhelm: (1848-1926) Professor of theology in universities in Germany, Kaftan's career like that of most of his theologian colleagues, was a song of ascent, going from strength to strength until arriving at Zion (Berlin University) in 1883. Kaftan was a leading member of the Religio-historical school.

Author: *The Essence* (Wesen) *of the Christian Religion* (1881); *The Truth* (Wahrheit) *of the Christian Religion* (1898); *Dogmatics* (1897); *The Philosophy of Protestantism* (1917); also volumes and addresses on Kant and his relation to Protestant theology.

Cf. *Die Religionswissenschaft in Selbstdarstellung*, edited by D. E. Stange (Leipzig, 1928).

J.W.B.

Kaftan, Theodor: (1847-1932) He was general church superintendent for Schleswig. As a Lutheran, he developed the modern theology of the old faith, a mild form of didactic method that placed the metaphysical back of the living faith, and sharply stressed the opposition to Troeltsch*.

Moderne Theologie des alten Glaubens (Schleswig, 1905); *Zur Verständigung über moderne Theologie des alten Glaubens* (Schleswig, 1909); *Ernst Troeltsch* (Schleswig, 1912).

H.H.

Kahnis, Karl Friedrich August: (1814-1888) He was professor in Breslau and Leipzig. He sought to surmount the opposition between the N.T. and the dogma of the Trinity by regarding the Son and the Spirit subordinistically as God in the word's second and third sense. He took a mediating rôle towards all dogmatic questions.

Lutherische Dogmatik, 3 vols. (Leipzig, 1861-68); *Der innere Gang des deutschen Protestantismus* (Leipzig, 1854); *Zeugnis von den Grundwahrheiten des Protestantismus gegen Hengstenberg* (Leipzig, 1862).

H.H.

kalam: (Arabic, meaning conversation) The fundamentals of religion as defended in public controversy within Islam and with members of other religious communities. Scholastic Moslem* theology.

P.E.J.

Kalevala: (Finn) National epic of Finland; a poem of fifty runes or divisions, each averaging nearly 500 lines; compiled from popular songs, by a Finnish patriot, and rated by some scholars as one of the few greatest epics of the world. Parts of the epic were composed by different unknown composers at different periods; along with the epic are lyric and folk poems. Songs of heroes reach back into pre-Christian Finland: some legendary poems are stories about Christ.

The epic was compiled by Elias Lonnrot, a Finn who visited districts of his land and brought the songs together. It was first published in 1835 and contained about 12,000 lines; a later edition, issued in 1849, is the epic as it stands today, and contains 22,793 lines.

The name, Kalevala, is derived from an ancestor of heroes, Kaleva, not mentioned in the epic. It means 'the land of the heroes', i.e., Finland. F.L.P.

Kali: Hindu goddess, the wife or Shakti of Shiva*. Represented as terrible in form, with a necklace of human heads, a girdle of several human arms, holding a bloody dripping sword in one of her many hands and sometimes standing with one foot on the prostrate body of her husband Shiva, she is nevertheless, known to many and lovingly worshiped as "the mother". She is one of the few Indian deities to whom animal sacrifice is still offered. To the more philosophical Hindus she is the personification of cosmic force which is by them thought to be feminine. She is said to be the creator of all things, even the gods, including Shiva himself. See Thags. C.S.B.

kalpa: A world period in Hinduism, the time between the creation of the world and its destruction. Some Indian schools of thought believe in an eternal succession of *kalpas,* e.g., Bhagavad-Gita IX, 7; VIII, 17-19, Svetāsvatara Up. III, 2, etc. C.S.B.

kami: (Japanese word translated variously by "deity," "deities," "god," 'goddess," etc.) In origin *kami* has a significance similar to that of *mana** or "occult power." D.C.H.

Kant, Immanuel: (1724-1804) Kant dealt with all branches of philosophy and some of science, but his chief aim was to harmonize cognitive and ethical interests. He said he had been forced to limit knowledge to make room for faith. But the faith was also limited, a "religion within the bounds of mere reason" (the title of one of his books). God was posited as cosmic judge and policeman to secure the happiness of the virtuous; immortality was an inconceivable timeless essence of the soul (as *noumenon* or thing in itself); freedom was not choice of open alternatives within time, but an unthinkable ability of the timeless self to have chosen an alternative temporal world. Yet faith, though beginning where knowledge ended, was neither irrational nor based upon mere intuition. It was based upon ethics, and Kant's ethics was the most rationalistic possible; for its principle was, act from precepts capable of rational generalization, valid, like truths of pure reason, for all thinking beings. Even the motive of ethical action is "respect" for rationality of will, not desire for happiness, whether our own or others'. A frequent misunderstanding takes this to mean we are to ignore probable consequences of our acts for human welfare. Kant says rather: man, by instinct, or without ethics, makes happiness a goal, and this goal can be rationalized or ethicized only by generalizing it to include the happiness of all. As ethical, we want to be rational in all things, therefore also in happiness-seeking. The whole of practical hedonism is included in Kant's system, save that certain *methods* of promoting the general happiness are vetoed as incapable of rationalization, even though their goal be rational. Thus if all men accepted the principle of lying in the general interest, this would destroy mutual trust, and the lies, not being believed, would serve no interest whatever. Yet, since life is based on probability, the chance that a man might be saying truth would perhaps give his words significance, even in the case supposed.

Kant's famous theory of knowledge is as follows. Experience, therefore positive knowledge, is temporal through and through. This temporal character supports *a priori* knowledge: the unity of time grounds causal connectedness; space, inseparable from time, grounds geometry; while we know *a priori* what time is, since it is the inherent pattern of our own intuitive perceptions, our innate way of seeing all things. Time and space must be viewed as dimensions, not of things, but only of our experience of things. For: if time and space were real apart from us, we could not know *a priori,* as, with respect to geometry, arithmetic, and such principles of science as causality, we must and do know it; further, time and space are self-contradictory ideas (involve antinomies*) when construed as real totalities; again, if the temporal side of things is real then the soul is not free, since time is causal through and through; finally, if time and space are ultimately real, then God, the ultimate being, must be temporal and spatial—for Kant, as for nearly all his predecessors, an absurdity. Upon these four arguments the system largely rests. Recent thought tends to undermine all of them. Many philosophers now hold that time* and space can be conceived as attributes of a real totality; that time is not causal in a strict or deterministic sense; and that God and the soul are in process (or process is in them)—see eternal, eternity. *A priori* knowledge might still, in Kantian fashion, be viewed as involving innate forms of possible experience given to us by intuition, but such forms, e.g., space (not, however, as Euclidian) and time, may be applicable to all things because they are dimensions not simply of human but even of divine experience (with which we are in intuitive contact), and because things as objects of divine experience and things as real are identical. (See omniscience). Post-Kantian Idealism (from Fichte to Royce or Bradley) reconstructs Kant in some such way, but confusedly or without freeing itself from unreconstructed (and inconsistent) elements. See autonomy; epistemology; heteronomy; infinite.

Immanuel Kant: *Critique of Pure Reason* (1781); *Fundamental Principles of the Metaphysic of Morality* (1785); *Critique of Practical Reason* (1788); *Critique of Judgment* (1790), Kant's views on aesthetics and teleology; *Religion Within the Bounds of Mere Reason* (1793-4). C.H.

Kaplan, Mordecai M.: (1881-) The leading mind among the exponents of modernistic Judaism, representing the crystallization of religio-culturism, known as Reconstructionism. The central threads of the texture of his thought are: Religion is the consciousness of group values. Universalistic aspirations of Judaism, Christianity and Islam are illusory. The vitalization of Jewish religion demands the intensification of Jewish national consciousness. Judaism is a civilization, not merely a religion. Religion is a healthy reaction to life. The residual element of belief which religion insists upon is that the universe is so constructed as to make sure that the ideals of humanity will ultimately be realized. Kaplan limits God to the actually observed striving of men. He believes the traditional principles of Judaism must be consciously reinterpreted, calling for a shift of the center of gravity from religion to nationalism.

Judaism as a Civilization (1934); *The Meaning of God in Modern Jewish Religion* (1937). H.H.

Karaites: A Jewish sect flourishing in the Near East, principally in Babylonia, from the 9th to the 12th centuries. The name *Karaites* means literally the "Readers of Scriptures", and they were so called because of their exclusive adherence to the Bible (O.T.) as a source of religious authority in Judaism, and the repudiation of the Talmud as a spurious invention of the rabbis. The movement was initiated by Anan ben David who had been shelved from succession to the political leadership of the Babylonian Jewish community. The inevitable necessity of implementing the Bible (O.T.) with details of procedure forced the Karaites, on the one hand, to permit the individual conscience freely to interpret the Bible (O.T.), with a resultant anarchy of religious observance; some of the Karaite communities even dividing on the fixation of the religious calendar. On the other hand, the repudiation of Talmudic developments of Biblical law forced the Karaites into a very severe religious discipline. Applying the Biblical enactments literally, they, for example forbade the use of fire on the Sabbath. Some 12,000 Karaites are still supposed to exist, most of them in Russian Crimea. Karaism was important in Judaism for stimulating among Jews a new emphasis upon the study of the Bible (O.T.) and a vigorous polemic in defense of the Talmud tradition. The best known representative of this anti-Karaite reaction was Saadi ben Joseph* (882-942), the brilliant Egyptian Jewish scholar and philosopher who subsequently became the head of the Rabbinic Academy in Sura, Babylonia.

B.Z.B.

karma: See Buddhist Terminology.

karma-marga: Term descriptive of "salvation by works" in Hinduism, i.e., salvation by what one does, not knowledge, or faith. The kind of "works" varies widely in different phases of Hinduism. In Vedic times it meant sacrifice, in Jainism it meant asceticism, at other times moral effort. C.S.B.

kathenotheism: A term invented by Max Müller* which literally denotes one-at-a-time theism. It symbolizes the Vedic monotheistic practice according to which the position of the gods is so arranged that each god is supreme in turn. H.H.

Kattenbusch, Ferdinand: (1851-1936) German Protestant theologian. He was born at Kettwig (Ruhr); in 1876 he became privatdozent at Goettingen. He was a disciple of Albrecht Ritschl*. From 1878-1904 he was professor of Church History in Giessen and from 1904-1923 at Halle. His main interest was in the history of Christian doctrine and "Konfessionskunde*". Editor of *Theologische Studien und Kritiken* 1910-1934.

Principal works: *Luthers Lehre vom unfreien Willen und von der Praedestination* (1875, 2nd ed. 1905); *Lehrbuch der vergleichenden Konfessionskunde*, vol. I (1892); *Die deutsche evangelische Theologie seit Schleiermacher* (1892, 6th ed. 1934); *Das Apostolische Symbol*, 2 vols. (1894-1900); *Deus absconditus bei Luther* (1920); *Der Quellort der Kirchenidee* (1921); *Die Doppelschichtigkeit in Luthers Kirchenbegriff* (1928). O.A.P.

Keble, John: (1792-1866) English clergyman, scholar, and poet. A leader in the Oxford Movement*, translator of Irenaeus and editor of Hooker, he became best known for his devotional verse, especially *The Christian Year* (1827), which attained great popularity. See Anglo-Catholics. L.W.C.

Keil, Wilhelm: Founder of communities at Bethel, Mo., and Aurora, Ore. See communistic settlements, religious.

Kelpius, Johann: See communistic settlements, religious.

Kempis, Thomas à: See Imitation of Christ; Groote.

kenosis: (From the Greek word *kenosis*, meaning "emptying") It is applied to the action of Christ on becoming man in Philippians 2.7, where the verb is used. The heavenly Christ gave up what he posssessed in contrast to grasping for something further as the first Adam had done (See also II Cor. 8.9). From this biblical use, the term came to be applied to the self-limitation of the divine attributes by the Son of God in the Incarnation*. The idea was given prominence by such nineteenth century theologians as Thomasius, Gess, and Frank** as they faced the problem of harmonizing the Christological statements of the orthodox creeds with the portrait of Jesus offered by the critical, historical study of the gospels. See humiliation of Christ. C.T.C.

Kepler, Johann: (1571-1630) He is the founder of exact modern science. His Neo-Pythagoreanism and Neo-Platonism enabled him to discover an illuminating proof of his Christian theology, clothed in animistic and allegorico-naturalistic statements. He conceived of God as the creator of the world in accordance with the Pythagorean principle of perfect numbers. The real world is the mathematical harmonies discoverable in phenomena. The mathematical harmonies in the mind of God are the genuine causes of things. Both speculatively and mathematically, Kepler thought the Copernican world scheme justified in the progressive achievements of mathematics and astronomy.

E. A. Burtt, *The Metaphysical Foundations of Modern Science* (1925). H.H.

Keshub Chunder Sen: (1838-1884) A distinguished leader of the Brahma-Samaj*. Disagreement with Devendra Nath Tagore led in 1866 to a division of the society into the Adi Brahma Samaj or Original Brahma Samaj which followed Tagore, and the Bharatvarshiya Brahma Samaj or the Brahma Samaj of India, the larger section, of which Keshub Chunder Sen was the leader. It was much more largely influenced by Christianity than the other which reacted in the direction of Hinduism. Sen attained enormous popularity and was heard by multitudes wherever he went. His movement was deeply affected when he permitted his thirteen year old daughter to marry the Hindu Raja of Cooch Behar. Having fought long against child marriage and the idolatrous Hindu rites, many even of his staunchest admirers were unable to accept his acquiesence in this marriage. A split took place in the Samaj and the Sadharan (inclusive) Brahma Samaj was formed. In 1880 Keshub founded the Navha Vidhan or Church of the New Dispensation in which he continued his ministry until his death in 1884. One Indian writer has said of him: "Keshub's chief service not only to Hinduism but to the world lies in the fact that he in his life and experience affiliated the mystic consciousness of the Hindu race to the Christ ideal".

M. C. Parekh, *Rajarshi Keshub Chunder Sen* (Rajkot, Kathiawad, India, 1926). C.S.B.

Kessler Lecture Foundation: A lectureship at Hamma Divinity School of Wittenberg College, Springfield, Ohio, established in 1921 by Mrs. Emma B. Kessler of Louisville, Ky., and providing an endowment of $10,000, the interest of which is to be used periodically for "a series of lectures dealing with subjects related to the practical work of the ministry". At first these lectures were held annually, but in recent years biennially. Among the lecturers have been: Dr. E. P. Pfatteicher, "Christian Social Science"; President F. H. Knubel, "The Ministry and the Church"; Prof. Otto Piper, "The Use of History and Doctrine in Preaching"; Dr. W. S. Sadler, "Pastoral Psychiatry"; Dr. Conrad Bergendoff, "The Divine Impulse in Preaching"; Dr. Bernhard M. Christensen, "The Impact of Preaching". Most of these lectures have been published. T.A.K.

Keswick Conference: An annual gathering of Evangelicals in the Church of England, held at Keswick in the Lake District during the summer. The conferences have been deeply influential in promoting the spiritual life of "low churchmen" in England, like Northfield meetings in America. W.N.P.

ketubah: (Heb., writ) Marriage contract, instituted by Simeon ben Shatah (1st cent., B.C.E.) for the protection of the wife in case of divorce or widowhood. Earlier references to deeds of marriage appear in the Assuan Papyri (5th cent.), and in Tobit 7:14 (also in the Code of Hammurabi). Serving as a mere memorandum of obligations assumed by the husband, without power of validating marriage, it is retained in Orthodox Jewish practice on traditional grounds. S.S.C.

keys, power of the: This refers to supremacy of jurisdiction in the Catholic Church as vested in the Holy Father. In conferring this power, Christ used the analogy of keys. Just as the one who possesses the keys of a house possesses complete authority over the house and its tenants, so also the Supreme Pontiff*, head of the house of God in this world, has the power or the keys or supreme dominion over the Church and its members. See Peter, St., First Bishop of Rome. W.H.

Keyserling, Hermann: (1880-) A free-lance writer on religious and philosophical topics who has had a considerable following in Germany. His *Schule der Weisheit* with semi-annual sessions at Darmstadt has attracted able lecturers. Keyserling teaches an intuitive approach to problems of truth and value with emphasis on the uniqueness of the individual and the need of differentiating between one's own abilities and those of other men. "He who always does what is in accord with his deepest nature necessarily does right." Keyserling has shown unusual ability to grasp the special features of a culture or a period and to describe them vividly.

Chief works in English: *Travel Diary of a Philosopher* (1925); *Book of Marriage* (1926); *Europe* (1928); *Creative Understanding* (1929); *Immortality* (1938). J.S.B.

khalif: See caliph.

Kharijites: (Arabic, *khawagri*, come-outers) An early Moslem* sect of Arabia. They were radical reformers who sought to establish a theocracy, urging that a faithful man of whatever tribe or nation might be called to the caliphate. They opposed the *Shi ites**, and eventually broke up into minor sects. P.E.J.

Khlysty: See Russian sectarianism.

Khnum: The ram god of Elephantine, Egypt. In early Egypt, the ram, along with other animals, rated as an actual god; each such animal god was associated with an Egyptian city. F.L.P.

kibla or kiblah: The direction of the *Kaaba** in Mecca, toward which Moslems face when in prayer. In a mosque* it is indicated by a niche in the wall called the *mihrab*. Mohammed is supposed to have started the custom at the beginning of his career by turning toward the sacred rock (*Kaaba*) to pray. P.E.J.

Kidd, Benjamin: (1858-1916) He maintained that just as in animal evolution every step costs an enormous price in the extermination of a great many lives, so any progress within mankind itself costs a great price. In order that a few individuals or groups could progress, a great many other individuals or groups have had to sacrifice themselves. Religion has also been a factor responsible for social progress. Human social evolution has not been due so much to egotistical reason as to ultra-rational faith. Religion is responsible for all the altruistic actions of men. The stronger religion is the more social the groups and the more chances they have to survive. Religion is responsible for man's non-revolt against progress and for his continuing to pay its terrible price.

B. Kidd, *Social Evolution* (1894). H.H.

kiddush: (literally sanctification) Prayer of the Sabbath* and festivals to usher in and sanctify the sacred day. According to the Talmud* (Berakot 33a) the ceremony of kiddush was instituted by the men of the Great Synagogue*. That it was firmly established during the first century of the Christian era, is evident from the various rules on the ceremony emanating from the schools of Hillel and Shammai.**

Cf. L. N. Dembitz in *Jewish Encyclopedia,* Vol. VII, pp. 483-484. B.C.

kiddush hashem and hillul hashem: The sanctification and desecration of God's name. Two terms denoting the positive and negative aspects of a concept which has always been an extremely important criterion of ethical behavior in Judaism.

The former refers to any act which reflects glory upon the name of God and finds its highest expression in martyrdom in the cause of religion. On the other hand, any act which discredits the name of God is hillul hashem and is to be avoided at all costs. E.B.—L.F.

Kierkegaard, Soeren: (1813-1855) Outstanding religious thinker and writer. Almost his whole life was spent in Copenhagen. Notwithstanding the remarkable literary qualities of his writings and the originality and freshness of his thought K. was hardly known outside Denmark during his lifetime and not taken seriously by his compatriots. His name became gradually familiar to theologians in the last third of the past century. But not until Karl Barth* had re-interpreted him in his *Epistle to the Romans* was his momentous significance fully realized.

In his nature a deep-seated melancholy—an heritage from his father—was coupled with an amazing gift of incisive analytical thinking and a very fertile imagination. Under the influence of melancholy scruples he broke his engagement with Christine Olsen in 1840, and this event, interpreted by K. both as necessity and as guilt, left its traces upon most of his writings. A polemic with a Copenhagen literary magazine, that had ridiculed him, as well as protracted literary attacks on what he thought was a godless church made his last years a period of great unhappiness to him.

Kierkegaard wanted to be an orthodox Lutheran Christian. Over against Hegel, Kierkegaard developed early the idea of existentiality (adopted recently by modern Existenz philosophy), meaning thereby an attitude towards life, in which a person commits himself totally to the claims of the Absolute without regard for the cost involved. This attitude is opposed to the 'spectator attitude' of science and speculative philosophy. With great emphasis K. pointed out that the hardships of such existential life were made tolerable only through the certainty of divine grace and forgiveness of sins. Next to St. Augustine and Pascal it is to his relentless selfscrutiny that we owe the most important contributions to the psychology of faith and Christian anthropology. Except for a number of "Devotional Discourses" Kierkegaard published his works pseudonymously or called himself merely the editor, thereby indicating that he had not succeeded himself in attaining to the ideal of true Christianity as portrayed in his books. While his thoughts do not lend themselves to systematization they begin to operate as a wholesome corrective both upon Protestant and Roman Catholic theology. See reason in religion. Cf. Unamuno, M.

Works: The Oxford University Press London, the Augsburg Publishing House, Minneapolis Minn., and the Princeton University Press, Princeton, N. J. share in the merits of having provided English translations of all of K.'s works. Among the translators Walter Lowrie excels in his literary qualities and his indefatigable zeal to introduce K. to the Anglo-Saxon world.

Philosophical Fragments (1936); *Purify Your Hearts* (London, 1937); another translation: *Purity of Heart Is To Will One Thing* (1938); *The Present Age* (London, 1940); *The Journals of S. Kierkegaard. A selection* (London, 1938); *Christian Discourses and The Lilies of the Field And the Birds In the Air, and three discourses at the communion on Fridays* (London, 1939); *The Point of View* (London, 1939); *Fear and Trembling* (London, 1939); *Stages on Life's Way* (1940); *Consider the Lilies* (London, 1940); *For Selfexamination* (1940, London, 1941); *Repetition* (1941); *The Sickness Unto Death* (1941); *Training in Christianity* (London, 1941); *Concluding Unscientific Postscript* (1941); *Thoughts on Crucial Situations in Human Life* (1941); On Kierkegaard: E. Geismar, *Soeren Kierkegaard,* 6 v. Danish and German. (Goettingen, 1926-29); W. Lowrie, *Kierkegaard* (London, 1938); E. L. Allen, *Kierkegaard, his life and thought* (London, 1935); John A. Bain, *Kierkegaard, his life and religious teaching* (London, 1935); Eduard Geismar, *Lectures on the religious thought of Kierkegaard* (1937); D. F. Swenson, *Something about Kierkegaard* (1941); G. Höfding, *Soeren Kierkegaard als Philosoph* (Stuttgart, 1902); M. Channing-Pearce, *The Terrible Crystal. Studies in Kierkegaard and Modern Christianity* (London, 1940). O.A.P.

Kilwardby, Robert: (unknown—1279) English Dominican of Augustinian tendencies, later Archbishop of Canterbury and Cardinal. Author of many Commentaries to the Aristotelian text and of a ranking treatise *On the Origin and Division of Philosophy.* His anti-Thomistic attitude led him to the condemnation of some of the doctrines of Saint Thomas Aquinas* in March 18, 1277. S.C.T.

kindness: That mode of affection and benevolence which is expressed in considerate, friendly, gracious and magnanimous behavior toward others. It is opposed to the spirit of callousness, harshness and ill-will. It seems to have its basis in the tender, social impulses of man and to be a natural expression of affection in the family and kinship group. With the growth of civilization it has come, by a process of ethical extension, to be regarded as a universal requirement in the treatment of all persons. The higher religions stress it as essential to the moral life. In Christianity it is held to be an expression of the loving character of God and a primary virtue for all men of good will. R.W.F.

King, Henry Churchill: (1858-1934) Graduated Oberlin College, 1879, Seminary, 1882; studied at Harvard and Berlin Universities. Professor of Philosophy, Oberlin College 1891-1897, Theology, Oberlin Seminary 1897-1925; President, Oberlin College, 1902-1927. His teaching and writing, based upon the philosophy of Lotze,* have done much to further Christian philosophy and theology and to promote "reverence for personality".

Author: *Reconstruction of Theology* (1901); *Theology and the Social Consciousness* (1902); *The Seeming Unreality of the Spiritual Life* (1908); *The Ethics of Jesus* (1910), and many other volumes.

J.W.B.

King James version: See Bible, English.

kingdom of God: (same as kingdom of heaven*) The term used in the NT, chiefly in the Synoptic Gospels, for the final realization and fulfillment of God's reign over the world. In its origin the term reflects the theocratic idea, deeply embedded in ancient Hebrew religious thought. "The Kingdom is the Lord's," and the earthly king is only the representative or 'Son' of God. Thus the ancient Hebrews shared the old Oriental idea of kingship, along with the neighboring peoples of the Near East. A more vigorous advocacy of the theocratic idea ("God alone is king") by the prophetic party resulted in conflict with the popular idea of the earthly king as head of the nation.

In the end the purely theocratic idea triumphed, with the result that Jewish apocalyptic conceived of the Kingdom as belonging to the Lord, without any independent Jewish king at the head of the nation. That is, world-sovereignty now belongs to God alone and he puts down and sets up earthly powers, even world empires, as he chooses (Daniel 7, esp. verse 27). Although in much of the literature of post-exilic Judaism the theocratic idea included a hierarchical organization, with a high priest at the head of the nation, the general tendency was to view all earthly figures as incidental or non-essential. That this idea was widely held is clear from the repeated protests of the Jews, chiefly of the Pharisees, against "the kingly and other forms of government," as we are told by Josephus.

Although in many of the apocalypses and also in the Old Testament itself an ideal figure is pictured as coming to hold the Last Judgment* or to destroy Israel's enemies, and to reign forever—or for a long time—over the restored nation, it is nevertheless true that there are prophetic and apocalyptic books which take no account of this ideal figure, the Anointed of the Lord, the Messiah.*

The profound religious significance of the whole idea of God's universal reign is clear from the prophets and from the Psalms (esp. Ps. 145). When God takes his great power and reigns over his world, then Israel will be exalted, sickness, suffering, and death will be done away, wars will be no more, peace and plenty will prevail, and "the earth will be full of the knowledge of the Lord, as the waters cover the sea" (Isaiah 11:9).

According to the Synoptic Gospels (Mark 1:15) Jesus began his ministry in Galilee by announcing that 'the Kingdom of God is at hand.' His ethics was ethics of the Kingdom, unfolding the kind of character God requires in those who belonged to his Kingdom (the Beatitudes, for example), his parables set forth various aspects of the coming of the Kingdom and of men's preparation for it by repentance and obedience to the will of God. Some scholars hold that Jesus believed the Kingdom had already begun ('Realized Eschatology'), others that it was still in the future, though not remote.

It was also clear that the Synoptic Gospels assume, following Mark, that Jesus was Messiah even during his earthly life, and did not have to wait for the resurrection to set him forth in his true nature—though only a few of his followers knew the secret. Perhaps the primitive idea was that he "became" Messiah at the resurrection; if so, that idea has been revised in the earliest gospel.

In the apostolic church, the Kingdom of God still means the future consummation of the divine reign; at the same time the church, the new community of the elect, the New or True Israel, shares in the good things of the age to come; its powers are already manifest in the mighty works not only of Jesus but of his disciples and of the Messianic community which represents the beginning of the New Age. It was an easy step from this view to the conception of the Kingdom as the empirical church, and we find late passages in the New Testament which reflect this high ecclesiastical view (e.g. Matt. 13:41). At the same time the ethical emphasis is made clear, especially by Paul (e.g. Rom. 14:17). It is clear that the New Testament conception, including the one set forth in Jesus' own teaching, transcends the limitations of nationality (e.g. Matt. 8:11), and also, at least in Paul, it transcends any possible realization in this world (I Cor. 15:50).

Thus the data are at hand within the NT itself for the later dogmatic and philosophical interpretations of the phrase. In general these have been as follows: 1) Retaining the purely eschatological* conception found in the Jewish apocalypses, and relying largely upon the supposed implications of the synonymous expression, Kingdom of Heaven, it has been maintained that the term means simply and exclusively the consummation, "when God shall be all in all," reigning triumphantly with his saints in Heaven, after this world has passed away. 2) An alternative view identifies the Kingdom of God with the divine or supernatural aspect of the existing church; that is, the Kingdom of God is really the Kingdom of Grace, engaged in constant warfare with the Kingdom of sin, Satan, and death, destined ultimately to be victorious and permanent (this is more or less the basic idea of St. Augustine's *City of God*). 3) Still another idea identifies the Kingdom of God completely with the empirical church, though for theology of this type the 'empirical' church is more than just the sum total of Christian communities in the world: it is the *Una Sancta* and is the organ and instrument of divine revelation and grace in this present world; eventually it is to take the place of this present world when the Church Militant will be merged with the Church Triumphant (this is more or less the idea underlying the theology of the Council of Trent*). 4) Still another interpretation is the one set forth by Albrecht Ritschl,* according to which the Kingdom of God represents the consummation of human history, an idea characteristic of 19th-century science and philosophy: it is "the one far-off divine event toward which the whole creation moves." At the same time there are expressions in the NT which seem to justify such a view (e.g. Col. 1:9-20).

5) Still another view popular in modern times interprets the Kingdom of God as a sublime social hope. It is the ancient Hebrew, Jewish, and early Christian way of setting forth the ideal of a world at peace and blessed with plenty. So far as the social hope remains religious, there are certainly elements in it which correspond to the primitive idea of the Kingdom of God—not only as reflected in the OT and in the Jewish apocalyptic literature, but also in the NT. For example, the reign of the saints upon earth (in Revelation 20:1-6) is a transitional period between this world and the next, and yet the reign takes place upon this present earth (see also Luke 22:28-30). However, nowhere in the NT or in biblical literature generally is the Kingdom of God viewed as a humanly-achieved new order of society. The roots of the conception are Semitic, not Greek; religious, not humanitarian or secular. From first to last the biblical idea emphasizes the fact that it is *God's* reign. The emphasis is upon the character of the King, not upon the extent or nature or even duration of the realm he controls, though these are assumed to be final and absolute.

Thus the doctrine of the Kingdom of God is one of fundamental, regulative importance for the NT and the early church. If we can trace the stages through which the idea passed in its biblical development, this is not to ignore but really to emphasize its far-reaching significance for Hebrew, Jewish, and (especially) for early Christian religious thought. See social gospel.

See J. Weiss, *Predigt Jesu vom Reiche Gottes,* 2nd ed. (1900); E. F. Scott, *The Kingdom of God in the New Testament* (1931); M. Goguel, *The Life of Jesus* (1933), E. tr.; R. Otto, *The Kingdom of God and the Son of Man* (1938), E. tr.; T. W. Manson, *The Teaching of Jesus* (1931); E. W. K. Mould, *The World-View of Jesus* (1941); C. H. Dodd, *The Parables of the Kingdom* (1935); F. C. Grant, *The Gospel of the Kingdom* (1940). F.C.G.

kingdom of heaven: Same as kingdom of God*; 'Heaven' was used by ancient Jews as a circumlocution for the divine name. F.C.G.

Kingo, Thomas Hansen: (1634-1703) Danish bishop, author of the official Danish Church Hymnal of 1699. A representative of orthodoxy of the baroque period, his best hymns treated of the themes of Lent and Easter. C.J.B.

kings, divine right of: Theory that kings have absolute authority because they hold their position directly from God and not from consent of their people. It owes something to ancient ideas of sacredness of monarchy and special honours given to emperor. In medieval period became associated with theories of imperial party in struggle against papal supremacy. With rise of nationalism and Protestantism there was exaltation of civil ruler in some quarters. In 17th century the theory centered in claims of Stuart kings in England. In recent centuries it has been expressed in extreme form in certain European autocratic monarchies. See emperor worship; divine right. K.H.C.

Kings, I and II: Historical books of the O.T., included among the "Former Prophets"* in the Hebrew canon, where they form a single volume. They recount the history of the Hebrew nation from the closing days of David* and accession of Solomon* (ca. 970 B.C.) to the release of King Jehoiachin from a Babylonian prison by Amel-Marduk (561 B.C.). The first edition of this work was written by a Deuteronomic historian ca. 600 B.C. (see D), and a later edition, with supplementary matter especially of North Israelite origin, was issued half a century later. References are made throughout the work to several sources employed in the writing: The Book of the Acts of Solomon (I 11:41), The Book of the Chronicles of the Kings of Israel (I 14:19), and a similar work on Judaean kings (I 14:29). These were probably biographies and histories based in part upon official annals. In addition, the editors apparently used temple chronicles and popular narratives concerning prophets, especially Elijah* and Elisha. While the Books of Kings are frequently our only or principal sources of information for long periods of Hebrew history, and while their information is largely authentic, they should not be considered as wholly objective history, either in intention or accomplishment. Being of Deuteronomic origin, they are largely commentary on and illustration in history of the great Deuteronomic doctrines of centralization of all sacrificial worship in the Jerusalem temple, and of divine retribution for human deeds.

See W. E. Barnes, *The First and Second Books of the Kings,* 2 vols. (The Cambridge Bible for Schools and Colleges), (2nd ed., 1928, 1932). J.P.H.

kismet: (Arabic, meaning fate*) A common ejaculation among Moslems, expressing their belief in a fate that rules the affairs of men. Not only a man's fortunes, but his deeds with their future consequences are pre-ordained and inevitable. P.E.J.

kiss of charity: A salutation as a token of Christian Brotherhood named from I Pet. 5:14 and otherwise known as the holy kiss (Rom. 16:16; I Cor. 16:20; I Th. 5:26) and later, among patristic writers, as the kiss of peace. A rite practiced widely and likely promiscuously among early

Christians, but now limited to the same sex and found only among certain religious groups like the Dunkers* and others. W.M.B.

Kittel, Rudolf: (1853-1929) Professor at various German universities, concluding his work at Leipzig; as translator and editor, he provided (in three editions) the critical edition of *Biblia Hebraica* used by practically all modern scholars; perhaps greatest authority on the history and religion of Israel. R.E.W.

Kleutgen, Joseph: (1811-1883) German Jesuit, philosopher and theologian. He was influential at the Vatican Council, and the revival of Scholastic philosophy in Roman Catholic schools was in part his work. E.A.R.

Kliefoth, Theodor: (1816-1895) He was pastor in Ludwigslust and held various executive and administrative church positions in the *Mecklenburg Landeskirche*. As a leading confessional Lutheran theologian he was interested more in the propagation of the old Protestant theology than in that of Luther's writings. He rejected Luther's subjectivistic extravaganzes. In his ecclesiology he accepted Catholic and Anglican elements and stressed eschatological implications. He also sought a new relation of faith towards history.

Einleitung in die Dogmengeschichte (Henstorff, 1839); *Acht Bücher von der Kirche* (Schwerin u. Rostock, 1854); *Christliche Eschatologie* (Leipzig, 1886).

H.H.

kneeling at communion: The medieval practice of kneeling to receive the sacrament was retained in the English Reformation but opposed by Knox, Hooper, and other Puritans. A declaration (later called the "Black Rubric") was inserted in the communion office in the second Prayer Book (1552) against any implication of transubstantiation* in the act of kneeling. See genuflexion.

M. M. Knappen, *Tudor Puritanism* (1939).

J.T.M.

Knights of Columbus, the: The name of a fraternal and beneficent society of Catholic laymen, founded at New Haven, Connecticut, in 1882. The original group consisted of two priests, Rev. M. J. McGinney and Rev. P. P. Lawlor; and eight laymen, James T. Mullen, Cornelius T. Driscoll, Dr. M. C. O'Connor, Daniel Colwell, William M. Geary, John T. Kerrigan, Bartholomew Healey, and Michael Curran. The purpose of the society, as originally founded, was to develop amongst its members a practical Catholicity which would manifest itself by aiding the cause of Catholic education and furthering Catholic charity, and at the same time, to serve as a means of aiding the families of its members through a system of insurance which would be held by each member; consequently, as originally founded the Knights of Columbus was an insurance organization with the added function of promoting the Catholic cause in every way possible. After the founding, subordinate councils spread rapidly throughout Connecticut, but it was not until 1885 that one was founded outside that state, when a council was set up in Westerley, R. I. The growth of the society was constant, and with the growth certain changes occurred. In 1893 it became apparent that the cause of the Knights would be greatly aided by accepting members who did not wish to share in the insurance privileges; as a result there have been two types of members since that time, the insurance and the associate. The legislating part of the governing body has gone through a number of evolutionary stages until today it consists of a National Council composed of the State Deputy and last Past State Deputy of each State Council, and one delegate from every thousand members of the insurance class. The membership, which is spread through every state of the Union, Canada, Newfoundland, the Philippines, Mexico, Cuba, Panama, etc., was greatest in the years just preceding World War I, reaching at that time about 1,000,000; but in the years following the War it declined. The work of the Knights has been of the most varied sort, but principally it has been centered in charity and education. The society has granted endowments to Catholic universities, and fostered sports and social enterprises besides.

M. F. Egan and J. B. Kennedy, *The Knights of Columbus in Peace and War* (1920), 2 vols.

T.T.M.

Knights Templar: The first and most notable of the military religious orders* of the Middle Ages. At the time of the Crusades* the spirit of the age gave rise to two types of religious orders, one was the order of ransom, the other was the military order to which the Templars belonged. The Templars were founded in 1118 by Hugue de Payens and Godeffroi de St. Omer under Baldwin II. The name of this congregation was derived from the fact that their first house was a part of Baldwin's palace lying next to the former mosque of al-Akra, the so-called "Temple of Solomon." The order adopted the rule of St. Benedict as reformed by the Cistercians,** and both the order and its adaptation of the rule were discussed and sanctioned by the Council of Troyes (1128). One of the most ardent supporters of this new group in that Council was St. Bernard of Clairvaux.* The members, who were admited either for life or for a term of years, were divided into knights or heavy cavalry, sergeants or light cavalry, farmers, who administered the temporals, and chaplains, who alone had sacerdotal power. Because they were subject only to their own Grand Master and to the pope, they soon gained the cordial dislike of the bishops and lesser clergy. But despite this fact the order grew rapidly since, besides the high favor it gained from the princes and popes, it united the two great tendencies of the Middle Ages: religious fervor and military prowess. The power of the Templars grew swiftly, not so much because of their large land holdings as because they became notable as international bankers, and their Temple at Paris became the center of the world's money market. The role of international financiers fell quite naturally to them since the Templars' strongholds were scattered throughout both the East and the West, and made exchange with the East a possibility; their military power and discipline ensured safe transmission of the treasures entrusted to them; and their reputation as monks guaranteed their integrity in handling the funds. Their reputation, rich in heroic legend, as brave and dauntless soldiers of the Cross was bought at the expense of tremendous losses of men in many and ruthless engagements with the enemies in the East. Because of their great wealth they attracted the attention of Philip the Fair of France who was hard pressed for funds, and wished to have this wealth at his disposal. By a charge of heresy and other insinuations, Philip was able eventually to bring the vacillating and weak Clement V to suppress the order by a decree of March 22, 1312, on the absurd grounds that blasphemy and desecration of holy things were prerequisites for entrance into the order. Upon the suppression of the order most of the Templars entered the ranks of their former rivals, the Hospitallers,* which order also took over most of the former wealth of the defunct Templars. The guilt or innocence of the Templars is still debated, but modern investigation points more and more to the fact that they were the victims of the rapacious Philip the Fair. See Vienne, Council of. T.T.M.

knots, religious use of: The significance attached to knots in religion is that of binding and holding or impeding and restricting. It may symbolize the binding character of marriage; the knots used by a Brahman in tying on his sacred girdle signify fidelity, finality. The phylacteries* of the Jews were bound on forehead and wrist as symbolic of binding character of the law. On the other hand, in India, Saxony and Lapland all knots in the house were untied at childbirth, lest anything impede the birth of the child. Ascetics in India and Syria avoid knots while on a pilgrimage. Primitive peoples cut or untie knots for release from illness, or a witch's spell, an oath or some taboo. See Frazer, *Golden Bough* (1911), Vol. 3, Tabu, pp. 293-313. M.L.C.

Knox, John: (1505? or 1513 or 1515-1572) The leading churchman in, though not the originator of, the Reformation in Scotland. He was born at Haddington, in East Lothian, and studied in the grammar school there before being admitted to the University of Glasgow. For some obscure reason, he seems to have left the latter institution without taking a degree. He probably became a priest about 1530, but little is known of this period of his life. He was associated with the Reformer, Wishart, and seems to have been influenced by the latter's martyrdom to take his place openly with the Protestant side. As a result, he found it wise to seek refuge in the castle at St. Andrews. When the French fleet seized the castle the next year, 1547, to avenge the death of Cardinal Beaton, Knox was taken prisoner to France, and there condemned to the galley slavery which kept him chained until early in 1549. He preached in England, until the death of Edward VI, where the Established Church, though episcopally governed, was strongly under Calvinistic influence. With the accession of Mary Tudor, he fled to the continent. Then began a period of wandering which included a brief visit to Geneva in 1555, and a short stay in Scotland late in 1555 and early in 1556. From the latter year until early in 1559, he was pastor of the English congregation in Geneva—a period when the fierce opposition to John Calvin had been overthrown, and the city had become very nearly a model of the Reformed ideal. Knox returned to Scotland in 1559; and when, the following year, the Scottish parliament adopted the Reformation, Knox was on hand to guide it and the newly organized Church, and to defend it against the destructive policies of Queen Mary. See Scotland, Church of; Scots Confession.

Works of John Knox, edited by D. Laing (Edinburgh, 1846-1864), 6 vols.; P. H. Brown, *John Knox, a Biography* (London, 1895), 2 vols. A.K.R.

kobold: (Ger.) Brownie, familiar spirit: underground spirit, as in mines, caverns; a figure in German mythology. F.L.P.

Kodesh Church Immanuel: A colored religious sect organized by Frank R. Killingsworth in Florida in 1929. The group claims to follow the Arminian theology and the Methodist ecclesiastical pattern. It believes in entire sanctification as a "second blessing," the second coming of Christ, and divine healing. It opposes the use of tobacco, extravagant dress, membership in lodges, indulgence in what it regards as worldly amusements. There are nine churches and 560 members. See holiness churches. E.T.C.

Kogoshui: "Gleanings from Ancient Stories." An account of early Japanese mythology and religion published probably in 806 A.D. D.C.H.

Koheleth: Meaning: the master of a school. Hebrew name for Ecclesiastes.* V.F.

koiné: (Gr. *Koiné,* common) A common Greek speech, gradually developing and replacing local dialects throughout the eastern Mediterranean from the time of Alexander. The Koiné is found in literary works (usually Atticizing) of the period, the Septuagint and NT writings, papyri,* inscriptions, and ostraca. It is simpler and less subtle than Attic, making rapid progress toward a purely analytic form of language. The period is roughly from 330 B.C. to 330 A.D. E.M.N.

Kojiki: "The Chronicle of Ancient Events." The oldest extant Japanese historical document compiled in 712 A.D. Begins with the myths of creation and ends with 628 A.D. Invaluable for the study of primitive Shinto. D.C.H.

kol nidre: (Lit. all vows) Prayer recited in the synagogue at the commencement of the evening service of the Day of Atonement.* The prayer was devised to ease the feelings of the devout who were conscience stricken on that solemn day at the very thought of the failure to fulfill all their religious vows.

Cf. Max Schlessinger, *Jewish Encyclopedia,* Vol. VII, pp. 539-542; I. Davidson, in *American Jewish Year Book* (1923), Vol. 25, pp. 180-194. B.C.

konfessionskunde: (Comparative Symbolics) The comparative treatment of the nature and peculiarities of the various Christian denominations. In the 16th and 17th centuries this study was largely identical with polemics* (M. Chemnitz,* Hospinianus, Bossuet*). Originally devoted merely to the study of the confessional standards of the churches and sects the field was extended by Marheinecke* (1810) to all the characteristic manifestations of the respective denominations, such as worship, constitution, geographical extension, statistics. The abundance of material available for such studies explains the paucity of works, in which Marheinecke's program is fully carried out. Only E. F. Karl Müller, Mulert and Neve offer a satisfactory comprehensive treatment of all denominations. In the majority of books the study is limited to one country (Brown, Carrol, Clark) or to one denomination (Kattenbusch, Loofs, Heiler).

The older type, that confines itself to the study of the doctrinal standards is represented by Oehler, Moehler, Schneckenburger, Winer (whose tabulation of doctrines was adopted by Grant, Rohnert, Guenther and Mouson), Chr. H. Schmidt, Schaff, Briggs, W. Walther. See Confessions, formal; symbolics.

Martin Chemnitius, *Examen Concilii Tridentini* (1565-1573), new ed. by Preuss (1861), reprint, 1915 (Lutheran view); Rudolf Hospinianus, *Concordia Discors* (1607) (the Lutheran *Concord* from the Reformed viewpoint); J. B. Bossuet, *Exposition de la doctrine de l'église catholique sur les matières de controverse* (1671); P. K. Marheinecke, *Christliche Konfessionskunde* (1810-1813); Herm. Mulert, *Konfessionskunde* (Giessen, 1927); J. L. Neve, *Churches and Sects of Christendom* (1940); W. A. Brown, *The Church in America* (a study of the present condition and the future prospects of American Protestantism, 1922); W. A. Brown, *The Church, Catholic and Protestant* (a study of differences that matter, 1935); H. K. Carroll, *The Religious Forces in the United States* (1893-1912); E. T. Clark, *The Small Sects in America* (1937); Ferdinand Kattenbusch, *Lehrbuch der vergleichenden konfessionskunde,* vol. I (Orthodox Eastern Church) (1892); Friedrich Loofs, *Symbolik oder christliche Konfessionskunde,* Vol. I (Oriental and Roman Catholic Churches) (1902); E. F. Karl Müller, *Symbolik* (1896); Friedrich Heiler, *Der Katholizismus. Seine Idee und seine Verwirklichung* (1923); Joh. Adam Möhler, *Symbolik oder Darstellung der dogmatischen Gegensätze der Katholiken und Protestanten nach ihren öffentlichen Bekenntnisschriften* (1832, 10th ed. 1921) (Roman Catholic), Engl. tr.; M. Schneckenburger, *Vergleichende Darstellung des lutherischen und reformierten Lehrbegriffes,* 2 vols. (1855); E. Sell, *Katholizismus und Protestantismus in Religion, Geschichte und Literatur* (1908); C. A. Briggs, *Theological Symbolics* (1914); Philip Schaff, *The Creeds of Christendom* (with a history and critical notes) 3 vols. (1877); *Corpus Confessionum. Die Bekenntnisse der Christenheit,* hersg. von Cajus Fabricius (1928), (projected as a comprehensive collection of all the characteristic manifestations of the churches united in the Faith and Order Movement); U. S. Bureau of Census: *Religious Bodies* (1936), 3 vols. (1941).

O.A.P.

Koran or Quran: (From the Arabic, *karaa,* to read; signifies, the reading) The sacred book of Islam, believed to be the eternal word of God, delivered by the angel Gabriel to the prophet Mohammed.* The term was at first applied to each revelation announced by the prophet, and eventually to the entire book of revelations, compiled after his death by his secretary Zaid Ibn Thabit at the direction of the Caliph Abu Bekr. The 114 *suras** (chapters), containing 77,639 words, are mechanically arranged by length, rather than logically or chronologically. The style is metrical; its strong cadences and cumulative repetitions are read aloud eloquently with great appeal to Moslem hearers. The content is unified; evidently the fervent expression of the mind of the prophet. It urges submission to the one God Allah,* and the true faith, shows the way of salvation through the prophets from Moses and Christ to the final prophet Mohammed. The day of judgment, rewards and punishments, laws, admonitions and warnings are illustrated by Arabian, Jewish and Christian stories though somewhat distorted by distance from those sources. The aim of the Koran is "guidance for the pious who believe in the mysteries of the faith, perform their prayers, give alms," and is accepted by them with profound reverence as above criticism. The Koran is in classical Arabic, and becomes the standard for literature, science, philosophy, morals as well as religion. Its influence on the history of the Moslem world can scarcely be exaggerated. See Mohammedanism; Ramadan. English translations by G. Sale (1734) and J. M. Rodwell (1861) are classic and available in later editions.

P.E.J.

kosher: This word, properly pronounced *kasher,* means "fit." In modern Hebrew and Yiddish, following the usage of Mishnaic Hebrew of the second century, it signifies primarily "fit to be eaten according to Jewish ritual." Jewish law prohibits the use of certain animals for food,* that those animals which may be eaten be slaughtered in accordance with a set ritual (intended to mitigate the animal's suffering); it also requires that meat and milk foods be separated, and that all meat be freed of its surface blood before being eaten. Food prepared in accordance with the prescribed rules, as set forth in the Talmud* and later works, is described as *kosher.* L.F.-H.K.

Köstlin, Julius: See neo-Lutheranism.

Krause, Karl Christian Friedrich: (1781-1832) He taught at the Universities of Jena, Dresden, Berlin and Gottingen. Most of his works have been published posthumously. The influence of his ideas was greatest in Spain and South America. He attempted to change the pantheism of identity into a panentheism.* He tried to reconcile the idea of God as known by faith and inner conscience with the idea of the world as known through the senses. He argued that God is not a personality, but an infinite, an all inclusive essence embracing the universe within itself. The divine is a divine organism. The process of development is through the formation of ever higher unities until the ultimate stage is reached in the identification of the world in God.

Die absolute Religionsphilosophie im Verhältnis zum gefühlsgläubigen Theismus und nach ihrer Vermittlung des Supernaturalismus und Rationalismus (Göttingen, 1834-1843), 2 vols. ed. by H. K. v.

Leonhardi; *Der im Lichte der Gotteserkenntnis als des höchsten Wissenschaftsprinzipes ableitende Teil der Philosophie* (Leipzig, 1889), ed by P. Hohlfeld und A. Wünsche; *Anschauungen und Entwürfe zur Höherbildung des Menschenlebens,* 3 vols. (Leipzig, 1890-1892), 4th vol. (Leipzig, 1902); *Zur Religionsphilosophie und spekulativen Theologie* (Leipzig, 1893); *Das Urbild der Menschheit* (Leipzig, 1903), 3 rev. ed. by P. Hohlfeld und A. Wünsche; A. Cless, *Das Ideal der Menschheit nach Krauses Urbild der Menschheit* (Stuttgart, 1881); B. Martin, *K. C. F. Krauses Leben, Lehre und Bedeutung* (Leipzig, 1885). H.H.

Krauth, Charles Porterfield: (1823-1883) Lutheran theologian, educator, champion of conservative Lutheranism in America. A leading figure in the revolt from a liberal type of Lutheranism (represented by his old teacher, S. S. Schmucker*), Krauth took an unequivocal stand in behalf of the old Lutheran symbols as normative for true Lutheranism. First professor of systematic divinity in the Lutheran Seminary at Mt. Airy, Philadelphia (established in opposition to that of Gettysburg) he set the stamp of his own theology upon a whole generation of Lutheran ministers. Many of his papers were collected in a *magnum opus* entitled *The Conservative Reformation and its Theology* (1871), a standard book of reference for a large section of the church. The General Council (org. 1867 in opposition to the more liberal General Synod) was a child after his own heart. He served the University of Pennsylvania as trustee, professor and vice-provost. As editor of conservative Lutheran journals he wielded tremendous influence. On matters of polity and liturgical practice as well as theology he was regarded as master. He took an active part on the American Revision Committee of the OT.

Adolph Spaeth, *Charles Porterfield Krauth* (2 vols. 1898-1909) contains a comprehensive bibliography; S. E. Ochsenford, *Documentary History of the General Council of the Ev. Lutheran Church in N. America* (1912). For the immediate background of the Krauthian development of American Lutheran theology, see Vergilius Ferm, *The Crisis in Am. Luth. Theology* (1927). V.F.

Krishna: One of the most widely worshiped deities of Hinduism, the greatest of the incarnations of Vishnu.* Represented variously in legend as warrior hero, cowherd, youthful prankster, lover par excellence, slayer of dragons, he becomes, in the Bhagavad Gita, very God, even Brahman. Here, as the supreme object of *bhakti,** it is through love, devotion and service to him that salvation is possible for all men regardless of caste. C.S.B.

kshatriya: The warrior, ruler class in ancient Indo-Aryan society. The name of the second of the three traditional, twice-born castes of India, Brahman, Kshatriya and Vaisya. C.S.B.

Kuan Ti, Kuan Kung: See Chinese Terminology.

Kübel, Robert Benjamin: (1838-1894) He was professor in Tübingen. Through him the Swabian realistic biblicism of Beck* was upheld with many moderations and in sharp antagonism against the other theological tendencies. *Christliches Lehrsystem* (Stuttgart, 1873); *Über den Unterschied der positiven und liberalen Richtung in der neueren Theologie* (Nördlingen, (1881). H.H.

Kuei, Kwei: See Chinese Terminology.

Kuenen, Abraham: (1838-1891) Dutch Christian OT scholar. Professor in the theological faculty of the University of Leyden.

Kuenen was one of the leaders of the modern school of OT critics. His chief work, a critical attempt to interpret the history of Hebrew religion from the premises of the new critical school, was his *Godsdienst van Israel* (1869-70, English translation *The Religion of Israel Till the Fall of the Jewish State*). In this work he elaborated on Graf's theory of the late origin of the priestly legislation of the OT. H.K.-L.F.

Ku-Klux Klan: The name of a secret organization made up of Southern whites, which arose during the years 1866-1867, to combat negro and carpet-bag rule in the ex-Confederate states. In 1871 Congress passed the Ku-Klux Act empowering the President to use Federal troops to suppress the organization, though without great success. With the restoration of white rule in the South the organization gradually disappeared. The memory of the Klan lived on in the South and its work was more or less idealized. In 1915 a new organization taking the name Ku-Klux Klan appeared in Georgia organized by Col. William J. Simmons. It amounted to little until the nineteen twenties when a nation-wide campaign for members under the direction of two professional publicity agents soon raised the membership to several millions. Its slogan was native, white, Protestant supremacy, and it denounced Aliens, Negroes and Catholics with equal vehemence. The symbol of the order was the Fiery Cross; the members wore hooded white robes and there was much marching, especially at night and fiery crosses were erected. It soon became a political power of temporary importance in Maine, Texas, Oklahoma, Louisiana and Indiana. As was inevitable the organization got into the hands of corrupt leaders, while its intolerance and terroristic methods aroused the disgust of the average citizen. By 1928 its influence had largely disappeared and many who had belonged returned, at least, to temporary sanity.

For the original Ku-Klux Klan: Lester and Wilson, *Ku-Klux Klan; Its Origin, Growth and Disbandment* (1905); The New Klan: J. M. Mecklin, *The Ku Klux Klan: a Study of the American Mind* (1924). W.W.S.

Külpe, Oswald: (1865-1915) He first was Wundt's* assistant at the psychological institute in Leipzig. He next taught in succession in Würzburg, Bonn and München. As the founder of the Würzburg school of experimental psychology, he initiated the experimental investigation of thought processes. He also continued Fechner's experimental study of aesthetics. He was a representative of a new critical and rational realism which aimed to conquer the neo-Kantian* anti-realistic tendencies. His polemics were never personal, but always matter of fact. He was opposed to contemporary naturalism. In opposition to Kant he regarded metaphysics as possible. Voluntarism and intellectualism he felt were inadequate. He regarded atheism theoretically irrefutable. He held a supplementation of our world view necessary from the religious and ethical standpoint. Theism, be held, the most suitable for our practical interests.

Outlines of Psychology (London, 1895); *Introduction to Philosophy* (London, 1897); *Philosophy of the Present in Germany* (London, 1913); *Einleitung in die Philosophie*, 9 ed. by A. Messer (Leipzig, 1919); *Die Philosophie der Gegenwart* (7 ed., Leipzig, 1920); *Die Realisierung*, vol. I (Leipzig, 1912), vols. II and III ed. by A. Messer (Leipzig, 1920). H.H.

Kulturkampf: (Ger. struggle for civilization) A term applied in the 1870's by the anti-Catholics in Germany to the struggle between the new Empire and Rome, incited by fears of increased Catholic power in Prussia (especially Jesuit) and directly occasioned by the violent liberal reaction to the decree of papal infallibility* of the Vatican Council* (1870). The State entered the conflict by expelling the Jesuits* from Germany and enacting the May Laws (1873-1875), designed to destroy Catholic political power within the country. The struggle was bitter and widespread and finally resolved only after the death of Pius IX (1878), when Bismarck turned to a program of conciliation with Rome, leading to the rescinding of the May Laws in 1886. E.T.R.

Kumarajiva: See Buddhist Terminology.

Kurtz, Benjamin: (1795-1865) Early associate and life-long friend of S. S. Schmucker* in establishing the Theological Seminary at Gettysburg and in the formative period of the General Synod of the Lutheran Church, editor of the *Lutheran Observer* from 1833 to 1861, vigorous spokesman for a liberal type of Lutheranism, defender and expositor of "American Lutheranism"* as well as the earlier movement known as "New Measures."* V.F.

Kuyper, Abraham: (1837-1920) Dutch Reformed theologian and statesman. He was born at Maasshuis, Holland. Originally under Scholten's liberal influence, he became converted to strict Calvinism. From 1863 he was pastor, and from 1880 professor of Systematic Theology at the Free University in Amsterdam where he died.

At about 1870 Kuyper became the leader of the orthodox Calvinists in Holland. He fought against liberalism in theology, church practice and politics and for the political and social ideals of Calvinism. He advocated the rights of church schools (partial success in 1889, full success in 1920) and the return of the established (Hervormd) Church to the status of the Snyod of Dort* (1619). When these attempts proved to be abortive he finally formed with his followers the Christian Reformed Church (Gereformeerd Kerk) in 1889. As a preparatory step the Free University in Amsterdam had been founded in 1880. Kuyper was not only a powerful preacher and writer and keen theologian, but also a great politician. He became the leader of the Christian Historical Party, that represented a conservative policy with a strongly social tendency. From 1902-1905 Kuyper was Dutch Prime Minister.

His theological method combines a highly developed intellectualism on a confessional and Biblical basis with an interest in the practical applicability of the Christian truth. His influence as a theologian extended far beyond Holland to the Reformed groups in Germany and U. S. A. See common grace.

Het werk van den Heiligen Geest (1888-1889) 3 vols. (Engl. tr. in 1 vol., 1900); *Encyclopaedie der heilige Godgeleerdheid* (1894), 3 vols., 2nd ed. (1908-1909), Eng. tr. (1898); *De engelen Gods* (1902); *De gemeene Gratie* (1902-1905), 3 vols.; *Dictaten Dogmatiek* (1910), 5 vols., 2nd ed. 6 vol. n.d.); *Calvinism* (Stone Lectures) (1898); *Pro rege*, or *Het koningschap van Christus* (1911-1912), 3 vols.; *His Decease*, meditations on the passion and death of our Lord (1928); *Asleep in Jesus* (1929); *In the shadow of death* (1929); *The Revelation of John* (1935). Biographies by: de Savornin Lohman (1889 and 1897); W. F. A Winkel (1919) and J. C. Bullmann (1928) (all in Dutch); Wilh. Kolfhaus (1925) 2nd ed. (German). On his theology see: B. O. Eerdmans, *De theologie vom Dr. A. Kuyper* (1909); *Kuyperbibliografie*, 2 vols., by J. C. Bullmann (1923-29). O.A.P.

Kwan-yin: See Buddhist Terminology.

kyrie eleison: (Gr. Lord, have mercy) The most common response to the petitions in the Greek and Syrian litanies.* It was taken over untranslated into the Latin rites, with the variant, *Christe eleison*, and is so used nine-fold in the Roman Mass* after the Introit*, probably the slight remnant of a vanished litany. P.V.N.

L

L: This stands for Lay Source, a supposed documentary strand of the O.T. running parallel to J, E, and P** from Creation to the death of David; proposed by Eissfeldt in 1922 but approved by few scholars; usually considered part of J. See J. Cf. Synoptic Gospels. R.E.W.

Labadists: A pietistic sect of the 17th and 18th centuries, founded by Jean de Labadie (1610-1674), a French ex-Jesuit. De Labadie left the Society of Jesus in 1639 and joined the Reformed Church at Montauban in 1650; subsequently he rejected the authority of his adopted church and founded a separate sect in Middleburg, Holland. Expelled from this city, he and his fifty-five followers migrated to Hereford, in Westphalia, 1670; again banished, the congregation settled at Altona where its founder died within two years. The peregrinations of the Labadists continued, including an attempted colonization of a New Bohemia on the Hudson River in the State of New York, but like the rest of their ventures it ended in failure. The high tide of their prosperity was reached in Wiewert, West Friesland, with about four hundred members, but this community, too, dispersed in 1732. Their doctrinal teaching stressed the importance of interior illumination by the Holy Spirit in understanding the Bible; only those reborn from sin are entitled to the sacraments, and hence they frowned on infant baptism, seldom celebrated the Lord's Supper, and declared marriage with an unregenerated person to be not binding. They held property in common in emulation of the primitive Church, supported themselves by manual labor, and held very lax views regarding the observance of the Sabbath. See communistic settlements, religious. J.F.T.

labarum: The standard of the Roman emperor Constantine*. Designed to commemorate the vision, supposed to have been seen by him before the Battle of the Mulvian Bridge, in which a Cross appeared to the emperor with the words "In hoc signo vinces." The labarum was a lance with a cross-bar, with crown and gems at the point, the letters IHS* (Greek letters beginning the name of Jesus), and a purple banner depending from the cross-beam. W.N.P.

Laberthonnière, Lucien: (1860-19?) French Catholic philosopher. In his *Essais de philosophie religieuse* (1903) and *Le Réalisme chrétien et l'Idéalisme grec* (1904) he opposed the scholastic conception of God as *actus purus,* and developed a doctrine of the "vital immanence" of God in the heart and conscience of mankind. This "immanentism" was condemned by Pius X* in the Encyclical *Pascendi* against modernism* (1907). W.M.H.

labor movements: Labor movements include all those efforts which the workers themselves, in their organized capacity, have made and are making to improve their conditions: unionism, labor politics, workers' education, and, in some measure, co-operation and socialism*. Under democratic institutions, such as have developed in Great Britain and the United States and to some extent elsewhere during the past century, labor has been able to exert pressure or leverage in at least three different ways: through its control of labor power and skill, through the direction of its purchasing power as a consumer, and through the ballot; and all of these have been used in differing degrees and combinations. As the most necessitous group, working people have always been most hospitable to new doctrines and plans for social reform, Christianity not excepted. But organized protest against unemployment, long hours, low wages, conditions dangerous to health and safety, inequality of wealth and opportunity, and class differences generally, has, for the most part, had to wait upon higher levels of intelligence and education, in America upon the partial assimilation of the immigrants, the rise of abler leadership, and a clearer recognition of the limitations of *laissez faire* individualism. So long as there remained a large geographic or economic frontier and a chance for the energetic individual or potential leader to allay his discontent by getting possession of land or entering business and himself becoming an employer, the labor movement languished and was at best sporadic in its manifestations.

Unionism, as the more moderate expression of labor unrest, had its beginnings in England far back in the early stages of modern capitalism*. Its ancestry is to be found in the organization of journeymen under the guild system when they found the masters too highhanded and too much inclined to disregard the customary rules of the trade. Until a recent period it has been chiefly confined to the relatively skilled crafts where there is some basis for cohesiveness and bargaining power in a common technique. The building trades (carpenters, bricklayers and masons, plumbers), the metal trades (blacksmiths, molders, machinists), the printers and allied trades, and the railroad engineers, firemen, and trainmen, have been typical of this somewhat aristocratic group. Most of them in the United States have been affiliated since 1886 with the American Federation of Labor, although the railway brotherhoods have eschewed even such entangling alliances. Effective organization among the semi-skilled and unskilled workers in the heavy and highly mechanized industries has been slower and more difficult. The Knights of Labor was able to sweep some of these into its heterogeneous ranks during the 1880's; and through able leadership and perhaps because of the physical stamina required in such occupations the coal miners in both Great Britain and the United States have been a power to reckon with for more than fifty years. But most of the inclusive unions now affiliated with the Congress for Industrial Organizations are products of the past decade. Structural differences between the two great federations are, to be sure, not absolute or clear-cut; but the unions which separated from the A. F. of L. after 1935 to form the C. I. O. were mainly industrial and set that pattern for later affiliates. The real business of unionism is done chiefly within each trade or industrial union and these federations (city, state, and federal) which attract so much attention in the press are useful mainly for propaganda, political activity, and the settlement of jurisdictional squabbles. This they could undoubtedly accomplish more effectively if the national bodies could sink personal animosities and combine under a single banner. Parallel with the trend toward federation and, more recently, toward industrial organization, has been a joining up of locals into nationals and even some intimations of international co-operation.

Like most other things, unionism has tended to thrive during periods of prosperity and high prices when it was easy to keep up dues and when employers were willing to make concessions. It has usually lost ground rather grievously during periods of depression. The decade since 1933, when the aggregate membership of all unions in the United States has reached the record figure of over 10,000,000, has been an exception chiefly because of the favorable attitude of the New Deal administration and the great progress in organizing mass-production industries.

Collective bargaining or the right to have a voice in the determination of wages, hours and other working conditions is the goal of the business type of labor union; and other tactics or methods, such as restrictions upon membership, opposition to technological changes, strikes and boycotts, and benefit features, are to be regarded as merely auxiliary. The most hopeful development of the past twenty years has been the rise of union-management co-operation, first in some railway shops and in some branches of the clothing industry, more recently in the hosiery, steel, electrical supply, and other industries. This promises to bring about a better understanding of the mutuality of interest between employers and employees and to dispel most of those unlovely characteristics and methods that were the result of suspicion and conflict.

The political activities of labor in both Great Britain and America have been directed primarily at facilitating unionism and collective bargaining: the removal of legal obstacles to organization and the safeguarding of unions and union leaders against the blacklist, "yellow-dog" contracts, labor spies, injunctions, and other disruptive tactics of employers. Only secondarily has the political weapon been used for supplementary purposes such as restriction of immigration, regulation of the hours of women and children and of other dependent or less well-organized groups, protecting wage-claims, etc. Minimum-wage legislation, at least in its earlier stages, and the whole program of security or social insurance legislation, including workmen's compensation for accidents, were evidently not originated by labor itself although it has given them its support. These were more largely of humanitarian origin and inspiration. In America labor's political influence has been mainly exerted through the nonpartisan methods of lobbying and the questioning of candidates for office put up by the old parties, whereas in Great Britain since about 1900 a separate labor party has evolved and has twice had control of the government. This difference has been partly due to the stronger hold which collectivist or socialist ideas and leadership have had in the British labor movement.

Both the co-operative movement and socialism or communism have appealed for support to wage-earning groups and, particularly during periods of depression and discontent, have found here a congenial soil. The Rochdale pioneers who set the pattern for consumers' co-operation* were a group of weavers who realized the advantages of small economies in buying, and the movement in Great Britain has always had its greatest strength in the large industrial centers like Manchester, Leeds, and Glasgow. In the United States co-operation has been more backward, partly because the chain stores forestalled it and partly because of the mobility and heterogeneity of our population. But it has had some success under the leadership of immigrant groups who have known its benefits abroad, and among the farmers. The Marxian* doctrines of exploitation, increasing misery, and the class struggle were certainly keyed to reach the proletariat*; but these are believed to have even less vogue than formerly in the English-speaking world. Socialistic sentiment in these countries is of the Fabian rather than the revolutionary type; and any progress which socialism is making as a possible solution for human ills is more largely from the viewpoint of the consumer than from that of the wage-earner.

J. R. Commons and Associates, *History of Labor in the United States* (vol. i-ii, 1918; vol. iii by D. D. Lescohier and Elizabeth Brandeis, 1935; vol.

iv by S. Perlman and P. Taft, 1935), 4 vols.; S. H. Slichter, *Union Policies and Industrial Management* (1941); Twentieth Century Fund, *How Collective Bargaining Works* (1942). W.B.C.

labyrinth: (Gr. *laburinthos,* a maze) A complicated building with winding passages. Many medieval churches had inlaid labyrinths in their pavements supposed to typify the difficulties of the Christian way through life; or, to have had some mystical meaning now lost. F.T.P.

Lachelier, Jules: (1834-1918) He made his influence orally felt by his teaching at the *Ecole Normale Superieure.* He was a leading pioneer of the spiritual metaphysical position in France. He called his philosophy spiritual realism. It is the true philosophy of nature. The world of free creative spontaneity of the spirit is not regarded as merely the complement of, or the reflex from, the world of mechanism and determinism. The new spiritualism of which Lachelier is one of the profoundest speculative minds, is not only acquainted with the place and results of the sciences, so unlike in this regard to the old spiritualism, but it also felt itself equal to a criticism of them. The sciences themselves are constructions of the synthetic creative activity of the human spirit. The real *a priori* lies in the absolute spontaneity of the spirit. Lachelier's spiritualism is independent of any religion. Duty is the fulfillment of our destiny, the suppression of all sensuous illusions, the realization that God in man is real and immortal. The religious life is the highest intellectual life.

Du fondement de l'induction (Paris, 1924); *Psychologie et de métaphysique* (Paris, 1924); G. Seailles, *La philosophie de Jules Lachelier* (Paris, 1920). H.H.

Lachish Ostraca: Discovered in Tell-el-Duweir (site of ancient Lachish, Palestine), from 1935 to 1938. About twenty letters written in the Old Hebrew Alphabet; several of them date from 589 B.C. and give valuable information upon the time of Jeremiah. See H. Torczyner, *The Lachish Letters* (1938). S.L.T.

Lacordaire, Jean-Baptiste Henri Dominique: (1802-1861) Renowned French pulpit orator. During his school-days he lost his faith, but in 1824 he was converted and abandoned his promising legal career to study for the priesthood. With Lamennais* he founded the political journal *L'Avenir.* In 1839 he entered the Dominican Order*, which he re-established in France, in 1843. With intervals in Rome, he occupied the pulpit of Notre Dame in Paris from 1835-1851. C.V.

Lactantius: (died ca. 330) Probably an Italian by birth, but educated as a rhetorician under Arnobius in North Africa. Appointed teacher of Latin eloquence by Diocletian in Nicomedia, where he was converted about 301 A.D. Became a leading adviser of Constantine*, who made him tutor of his son, Crispus. He was known as the Christian Cicero for his elegant style, in prose and poetry. His *Institutiones divinae* (seven books) was an exposition and defence of the Christian faith. He was a fanatical Chiliast*, and showed some Manichaean* tendencies of thought. A.K.R.

Lady-Chapel: A chapel dedicated in honor of the Virgin Mary. Usually but by no means invariably situated at the extreme eastern end of the church. B.S.E.

Lady-Day: March 25, on which, according to Church tradition, the Angel Gabriel appeared to St. Mary and announced to her that she was to be the Mother of God Incarnate. Also known as the Feast of the Annunciation*. The Biblical story is found in Luke 1:26-38. W.N.P.

Laestadians: A sectarian development within the Lutheran church in northern Sweden, Norway and Finland. Probably an outgrowth of the Herrnhuter (Moravian-Zinzendorfian**) movement. As early as 1734 the Herrnhuters sent missionaries to these bleak and forsaken regions. In 1825 a Lutheran pastor, Lars Levi Laestadius (1800-1861) of the State Church of Sweden, became pastor of the Karesuando parish and later moved to Pajala (1858). A few years after his arrival he had a thoroughgoing conversion experience, precipitated by a chance conversation with a humble shoemaker. Loathing his former life, he began preaching with holy zeal against the gross sins of his parishioners. His radical approach seemed to sow seeds for new and strange doctrines:

a. There is no direct approach to God. God must be approached through the congregation of Christians, or preferably through the medium of a single Christian layman. Sins must be confessed in painful detail to this layman, who in turn gives absolution.

b. The date of conversion, as well as the name of the spiritual "midwife" (lay confessor) must be known.

c. The "embrace" was a sign of fellowship and always followed the giving of absolution.

d. The devil entered heaven through the "door of baptism"; hence their opposition to baptism, especially that of infants.

e. Lay preachers were preferred to those of the established church, although the Sect retained membership in the established church.

f. Emphasis on "we" rather than "I".

g. Distinctive garb in terms of ascetic austerity.

There are traces of the movement in mid-western United States. The founder, the Rev. Lars Levi Laestadius, was a natural scientist of high standing, and had his studies published by the Swedish Academy of Science. Besides these scientific writings, he published theological treatises and a volume of sermons. The latter are being read at the services and prayer meetings held by his followers.

Nordisk Familjebok, vol. IX, p. 506. O.A.W.

Laetare Sunday: The name applied to the Fourth Sunday of Lent*, from the opening word

"Laetare" (Latin, rejoice) of the Introit of the Mass, to express the Church's joy over the coming baptism of candidates, which formerly took place on Easter Eve. When the old baptismal procedures passed into desuetude, new reasons for rejoicing were excogitated, such as the fact that Lent is then half over. Cf. golden rose. C.V.

Lagarde, Paul Anton de: (1827-1891) His original name was Bötticher. He taught at the University of Göttingen. He was an enthusiastic philologist and a foundation-laying Orientalist. His brilliant linguistic ability sharpened the weapons and the methodical conscience of historical theology. Although he exercised a most severe critique of contemporary culture, church and theology, he yet remained an enthusiastic theologian. Critical of the entire historically developed Christianity, he regarded Protestantism as a surpassed phenomenon. He almost hated Luther and St. Paul. Only a humble return to the Gospel, he thought, enabled him to establish a doctrine of faith. It was his belief that the state has to assist in bringing about the new national church for which his patriotic soul yearned.

Mittheilungen, von Paul Anton de Lagarde, 4 vols. (Göttingen, 1884-91); *Deutsche Schriften. Gesammtausgabe letzter Hand* (Göttingen, 1892); W. Hartmann, *Paul de Lagarde* (Halle, 1933); L. Schmid, *Paul de Lagardes Kritik an Kirchen, Theologie und Christentum* (Stuttgart, 1935); A. Rahlfs, *Lagardes wissenschaftliche Lebenswerk* (Berlin, 1928).

H.H.

Lagneau, Jules: (1851-1894) He taught philosophy at the Lycee Michelet. His thought was not only an important continuation of Kantianism in the domain of moral philosophy, but also of a moral rationalism. Man comes into direct contact with God in the moral act. God is the common principle of the speculative and practical order, of knowledge and action. To believe in God is to act morally.

Ecrits de Jules Lagneau (Paris, 1924); *L'existence de Dieu* (Paris, 1925). H.H.

Lainez, James: (1512-1565) Spanish theologian, influential at the Council of Trent* and the Colloquium of Poissy. Successor to St. Ignatius Loyola* as General of the Jesuits. E.A.R.

laity: (Ultimately from the Greek *laos,* people) Members of the Christian church who are not clergy. As the term, properly speaking, is not applied to unbaptized persons it denotes privilege as well as the absence of higher privilege.

B.S.E.

Lakshmi: Wife of the Hindu god Vishnu*, goddess of good fortune and prosperity. When Krishna appeared as incarnation of Vishnu, Lakshmi appeared as his favorite wife. When Rama became Vishnu's avatar, Lakshmi took the form of Sita. C.S.B.

Lāmaism: See Buddhist Terminology.

Lambeth Articles: Adopted Nov. 20, 1595, these articles state in nine points the predestinarian system then predominant in the Church of England*. They never had the force of law (P. Schaff, *Creeds of Christendom,* I, 658-662).

W.W.R.

Lambeth Conferences: Meetings of the Anglican episcopate held about every 10 years since 1867 (most recently in 1930) at the call of the Archbishop of Canterbury, and named from their usual place of meeting, the Archbishop's Palace at Lambeth; of importance as reflecting the mind of the Anglican Communion on theology and problems of the day.

W. R. Curtis, *The Lambeth Conferences* (1942).

E.R.H.

Lambeth Quadrilateral: Bases for reunion proposed by the Lambeth Conference* in 1888—the Bible, the Apostles' and Nicene Creeds, the two major Sacraments, and the Historic Episcopate.

E.R.H.

Lamennais, Hugues Félicitê Robert de: (1782-1854) Catholic apologist, later a rebel against the church. His *Essai sur l'indifférence en matière de religion* (1817) denounced the principle of private judgment as the source of the excesses of the French Revolution, and prescribed ecclesiastical authority and tradition as the cure of Europe's woes. By 1830, he was endeavoring to reconcile Catholicism with democracy, taking "God and Liberty" as the motto of his periodical, *L'Avenir.* The condemnation of *L'Avenir* by Gregory XVI drove Lamennais into open revolt and radical socialism. The *Paroles d'un croyant* (1834) which he issued in defiance of the church, are full of prophetic fire and literary power. Cf. Döllinger; Lacordaire. See traditionalism. W.M.H.

Lamentabili, the decree of 1907: See Pius X, Pope; modernism.

Lamentations: A book in the third division of the Hebrew O.T., "the writings"*, consisting of five poems (corresponding to our chapter divisions) written in the Kina or Lamentation metre, probably dating from the fifth century B.C. and composed for occasions commemorating the fall of Jerusalem. It is not clear whether they were written in Palestine or in Babylonia. The first four are "alphabetic acrostics"—a word beginning with the next letter of the Hebrew alphabet (22 letters) standing at the beginning of each unit of several lines or verses. The fifth poem has twenty-two (!) verses. Poems 1, 2 and 4 are in the vein of lamentations or dirges such as were sung at funerals. Jerusalem is figuratively considered the deceased. Poem 3 is in the style of an individual lamentation, with the unusual feature that a male (not female) figure personifies the people or city. Poem 5 is a collective lamentation. Kinship of diction with Isaiah* 40-66 appears in 1 and 3. Ascription of the poems to Jeremiah* by tradition is ancient; II Chronicles 35:25, however, hardly can have this collection in mind. The viewpoints do not coincide with Jeremiah's utterances, and 2:9, 4:17, 5:7 do not fit him.

R. H. Pfeiffer, *Introduction to the Old Testament* (1941); J. A. Bewer, *Literature of the Old Testament* (rev. ed., 1933). E.G.K.

Lanfranc: (d. 1089) Rising to prominence as a Pavian jurist, he achieved greater fame as prior and renovator of the monastery of Bec*. Here he emerged as a peerless teacher, and as the triumphant opponent of Berengar of Tours*. Subsequently abbot of St. Stephen in Caen, he was elected in 1070 to the archbishopric of Canterbury through which office he effected a disciplinary reorganization of ecclesiastical life in England. See William of Malmesbury. R.C.P.

Lang, Heinrich: (1826-1876) A radical reformed theologian who was pastor at Wartau, St. Gallen, Switzerland. He brought the ecclesiastical function more strongly to the fore than the historical function.

Versuch einer christlichen Dogmatik allen Christen dargeboten (Berlin, 1851); *Ein Gang durch die christliche Welt* (Berlin, 1859); *Martin Luther* (Berlin, 1870). H.H.

Lange, Frederick Albert: (1828-1875) As one of the most attractive of nineteenth century German thinkers, he denied the pretensions of a materialistic metaphysics on the ground that like metaphysics, it illegitimately extends the categories beyond experience, and on the ground that it must necessarily fail in its attempt to reduce mind to physical terms. Metaphysical and religious speculations have no theoretical but practical value in life. Materialism is only justified as a method and not as a world view. Ideals are the legitimate expressions of the moral, aesthetic and religious nature of man. Although errors arise when ideals are taken for actualities, they are to be judged only by their own standards.

History of Materialism (1925); J. M. Bösch, *Friedrich Albert Lange und sein "Standpunkt des Ideals."* (Frauenfeld, Switzerland, 1890); W. Genz, *Der Agnostizismus Herbert Spencers mit Rücksicht auf August Comte und Friedrich Albert Lange* (Greifswald, 1902); P. Grebe, *Die Arbeiterfrage bei Lange, Ketteler, Jörg, Schaffle. Aufgezeigt an ihrer Auseinandersetzung mit Lasalle* (Berlin, 1935). H.H.

Lange, Johann Peter: (1802-1884) He taught at the universities of Zürich and Bonn. He enriched biblicism through speculation, however, without the necessary discipline of thought.

Das Leben Jesu nach den Evangelien, 5 vols. (Heidelberg, 1844-47); *Christliche Dogmatik,* 3 vols. (Heidelberg, 1849-52, 2 ed., Heidelberg, 1870). H.H.

Langton, Stephen: Cardinal and Archbishop of Canterbury, 1207-1228; died in the latter year. He was a friend of Innocent III*, an influential statesman, and co-author of the Magna Charta*. He is responsible for the division of the Bible into chapters. (See chapters and verses) In 1222 he held a Provincial Synod at Osney, which was of enormous importance for the future of the Church in England. C.V.

Laodicea, Synod of: A local church council, held about A.D. 364, to deal mainly with questions of church organization. It fixed a Canon of Scripture which omitted the Book of Revelation*; tried to regulate the practice of penance*; and, probably with the practice of certain Gnostic sects in mind, it forbade the worship of angels* and the use of unauthorized hymns. A.K.R.

Lao-tse: See Chinese Terminology.

Lao Tzŭ: See Chinese Terminology.

lapidaries: Books describing the supernatural properties of jewels. Epiphanius* of Cyprus (d. 403) and Marbod of Rennes (d. 1123) are prominent authors of lapidaries.

J. Evans, *Magical Jewels of the Middle Ages and the Renaissance,* (1922); L. Thorndike, *History of Magic and Experimental Science* (1923-41), 6 vols. J.T.M.

lapsed: A term applied in the early Church to Christians who because of persecution fell away from Christian faith and practice. The numerous classes which have been distinguished among the lapsed may be principally grouped as follows: the *sacrificati,* who had sacrificed to the pagan gods; the *thurificati,* who had burned incense to the gods; the *libellatici,* who had won immunity by presenting papers secured by bribery or through other means containing the false or true declaration that they had performed the one or the other of the preceding idolatrous acts as required; the *traditores,* who under the persecution of Diocletian* gave up the sacred books or vessels of the Church. The question as to the leniency or severity to be shown to the lapsed who desired readmission to the Church led to bitter controversy and schisms, with the policy of readmission under a system of public confession and penance** finally prevailing. Cf. Novatian. H.W.J.

lares: See Roman religions.

LaSalle, St. John Baptist de: (1651-1719) French Roman Catholic priest, who founded at Rheims in 1684 the Institute of the Brothers of the Christian Schools. He has been called the Pestalozzi of France because of his educational reforms. See Christian Brothers. E.A.R.

last judgment: See final judgment.

Lateran Councils: There were five Ecumenical Councils* held at the Lateran Palace of the popes in Rome, so called because in ancient times the Laterani Family occupied the present site. The first of these General Councils was celebrated in 1123, under Callixtus II (1119-24) confirming the Treaty of Worms with King Henry V of Germany and putting an end to the Investiture* Controversies; the second, in 1139, under Innocent II (1130-43) excommunicating Roger of Sicily and the bishops appointed by the Anti-Pope*, Anaclete II; stabilizing the "privilegium canonis" in defense of clerics and re-approving the decree of Nicholas II regarding the election of popes; the third, in 1179 under Alexander

III* (1159-81) settling the controversies with Emperor Frederick I (Barbarossa) of Germany, and confirming the Peace of Venice; the fourth, in 1215, the most important of all five, under Innocent III* (1198-1216), stabilizing the use of the term "transubstantiation"* regarding the Eucharist* and enjoining under pain of excommunication the reception of Holy Communion at Easter time; and finally, the fifth, in 1512-17, under Julius II (1503-13) convoked to re-establish peace among the Christian princes, to promote the war against the Turks and to reform the Church "in its head and members".

The Acts of the various Councils were published by such well-known compilers as Mansi in his *Conciliorum nova et amplissima collectio* (Paris: 1901-24), and by Hefele, *Conciliengeschichte* (Freiburg in Br., 1886), (French transl. by Leclerq). Besides the Ecumenical Councils there were also many other councils celebrated at the Lateran but they were of local nature and are usually referred to as Synods.

Litt. G. D. Mansi, *Conciliorum Nova et Amplissima Collectio* (Venice, 1776) XXI, 278-304 (I); *ib.* 1776, XXI, 523-546 (II); *ib.* 1778, XXII, 203-468 (III); *ib.* 1778, XXII, 953-1086 (iv); Paris, 1902, XXXII, 649-1002 (V). C. J. von Hefele, *Conciliengeschichte* (Freib. in Br., 1855-90); French tr. by H. Leclercq, *Histoire des Concils* (Paris, 1907-18). P. Deslandres, *Les grands concils de Lateran* (Paris, 1913); L. Pastor, *History of the Popes* (London and St. Louis: Herder), Vol. VIII, (1923) IX; *Dict. de la Théol. Cath.* VIII, 2628-86; *Cath. Encyc.* IX, 16-19. R.M.H.

Latimer, Hugh: (c. 1490-1547) English reformer. His preaching, clearly implying Reformed doctrines, early made him a center of debate in Cambridge and London. Though he rose to be bishop of Worcester, his greatness lay in his power as a preacher. His sermons established Reformation principles in the hearts and minds of the people, and gave the movement its distinctive complexion. Martyred under Mary.

G.R.C.

Latin America, religion in: The Roman Catholic faith was introduced into Latin America at the time of the Spanish Conquest, which, in a sense, was a religious crusade. This was in the early part of the 16th century. Culturally and religiously, Latin America owes a debt to Spain and Portugal. The most notable work was the pioneer missionary activity of the religious orders. On the Spanish settlements the *encomienda* system had as its principal object the conversion of the Indians to the Catholic faith. Although masses of these were baptized they remained thoroughly pagan and even today their fundamental beliefs and practices are still pagan.

From the time of the Conquest and settlement of the New World the question of state and church relationship was of paramount importance and it continues to play an important part in the life of the Latin American republics. Ecclesiastical patronage was granted to the monarchs of Spain and Portugal. By this means and through the Inquisition* the mother countries sought to achieve political unity and a rigid control of cultural expression in colonial times.

Following political independence at the beginning of the 19th century the conflict between Church and State continued in all countries, over the questions of control of personnel, church property and education. Religious freedom became a prominent issue. Peru was the last country to give religious freedom (1915). During the last century party-politics had their basis largely in the religious questions and continue to do so today. The liberals, under different names, are generally anti-clerical though nominally Roman Catholics as individuals, while the conservatives stand for the prerogatives and power of the Church and are often drawn from the landowning aristocracy.

Today many of the educated classes, students, professionals and the like, are estranged from the Church. Formerly, some of them embraced agnosticism or atheism, but in recent years a deep spiritual unrest and a search for reality have been discernible. At the same time positivism*, spiritualism as well as oriental cults and philosophies have gained a considerable number of adherents, especially in Brazil and Chile.

The most significant religious movement of modern times is that of Protestantism, which, except for sporadic attempts in earlier centuries, was introduced effectively during the second half of the 19th century. This movement has emphasized the evangelical note and the ethical content of personal religion. British and North American missionary societies have made an outstanding contribution through their educational, medical and social institutions. In some cases these were begun at the invitation of liberal Latin American presidents. The American Bible Society and the British and Foreign Bible Society have distributed the Scriptures in all countries. (See Bible Societies). In recent years the Protestant Church has grown rapidly. From 1925 to 1938 the number of members trebled. The strongest churches are to be found in Brazil, Mexico and Argentina. In the last twenty years there has been a notable development in national leadership and indigenous churches.

A series of international conferences of Protestant forces have been held, beginning at Panama in 1916. At this conference the Committee on Cooperation in Latin America was created by representatives of the mission boards of most of the major Protestant denominations. This Committee, with headquarters at 156 Fifth Avenue, New York, seeks to coordinate the efforts of the different bodies, publishes the influential Spanish magazine *La Nueva Democracia,* promotes a literacy campaign throughout Latin America, using the Laubach method, and has a comprehensive program of Christian literature. Some of the larger mission boards working in Latin America include: The Board of Foreign Missions of the Presbyterian Church in the U. S. A., The Board of National Missions of the Presbyterian Church in the U. S. A., The Board of Missions and Church Extension of the Methodist Church; The American Baptist Home Mission Society; The National Council of the Protestant Episcopal Church; The

United Christian Missionary Society, (Indianapolis, Indiana).

At the present time the Roman Catholic Church is seeking to regain an ecclesiastical monopoly in Latin America through the exclusion of Protestant missionaries. Liberal groups in the Peruvian Congress and elsewhere have recently been vocal on this issue. The fear of communism and social upheaval has tended to strengthen the alliance between the conservative reactionary groups and the Roman Catholic hierarchy in many parts of Latin America.

Books on Religion in Latin America:
J. A. Mackay, *The Other Spanish Christ* (1933); J. L. Mecham, *The Church and State in Latin America* (1934); W. S. Rycroft, *On This Foundation, The Evangelical Witness in Latin America* (1942).

W.S.R.

Latin Christianity: Historical form of Christian beliefs and practices developed in the church of the Latin countries of Europe and overseas and other churches under pope at Rome. K.H.C.

Latin, ecclesiastical: See ecclesiastical Latin.

Latitudinarians: A body of Anglicans, sprung from the Low Church* party, who looked to Comprehension rather than toleration as the ideal for the Church of England*. Their aim was greater *Latitude*, alike from the narrowness of rigid Calvinism and rigid Catholicism of the Laudian* variety. The name was first attached to the Anglicans who conformed to the Cromwellian Church settlement, but the great age of Latitudinarians was from 1688, under the leadership of Archbishop Tillotson (1630-1694) under the influence of the writings of Chillingworth (1602-44) and the Platonism of Whichcote (d. 1683). Antagonism came not only from the Anglican side; Baxter referred to them as the "Cambridge Arminians." F.W.B.

latria: (Gr. the status of a servant) A term used, technically, to designate that supreme adoration rendered to Divinity, exclusively, as Sovereign Creator, sustainer, and last end of the creature. It is thus distinguished from *dulia**, which is the veneration due saints and angels, and *hyperdulia*, which is the special honor due Mary*. See Mariolatry. R.C.P.

Latter Day Saints: (general article on) A group of six religious sects, otherwise known as Mormons, first founded by Joseph Smith at Fayette, N. Y., in 1830. Smith claimed to have received a series of divine revelations instructing him about the second coming of Christ, the organization of a new church, and the whereabouts of certain golden plates bearing the message of a new dispensation. When he was twenty-one years old he secured these plates from which he and others translated the book of Mormon*, accepted by the believers as a divinely inspired revelation. According to this book America was settled by an ancient people dispersed from the east when human tongues were confused at the Tower of Babel and by Israelites who emigrated from Jerusalem six hundred years before Christ .

Smith and his friends gained some converts and established colonies in Ohio, Illinois, and Missouri, following a policy of segregating the converts from the "gentiles." They encountered opposition everywhere because of the extravagant claims of revelations from Christ, John the Baptist, and various apostles, and because of their advocacy of polygamy. In 1844 Smith was killed in a riot at Carthage, Ill. The remarkable Mormon leader, Brigham Young, led the main body to Utah in 1848, where they founded Salt Lake City and secured possession of large areas of territory. Young published his doctrine of "celestial marriage" (for eternity as well as time) and polygamy in 1852, and he and the Mormon leaders generally practiced plural marriage. This brought them into conflict with the laws of the United States and led practically to war between the Mormons and the authorities. Polygamy was publicly disavowed in 1890.

Mormon doctrine includes belief in the Bible and the main tenets of the Christian religion but it adds original elements of its own. Chief among these is the inspiration of the Book of Mormon, special divine revelations of various kinds, two orders of priesthood, the Aaronic and the Melchizedek, and the activities of various angels, especially the guiding spirit of the Mormons, Moroni. Its officers, headed by an all powerful president and two other "high priests," are apostles, patriarchs, seventies, elders, and bishops. Visions, prophecy, the gift of tongues, divine healing, and various other gifts are believed in. The second coming of Christ is imminent and he will set up his city of Zion in the United States, while the "ten tribes" will be restored and the Jews will return to Palestine.

The Mormons were reputed to have amassed vast wealth in Utah. Their noted temple (from which "gentiles" and lukewarm Mormons are excluded) and tabernacle at Salt Lake City are well known. They oppose the use of liquor, tobacco, tea, and coffee. They are energetic in proselyting and have sent missionaries into all parts of the world; many young Mormons serve a missionary apprenticeship before taking their places in the business world.

The total group of Mormons number about 775,000, mainly in Utah (340,000) and Idaho (100,000) and the western states. There are over 2,000 local churches. They are divided into six different denominations:

1. *The Church of Jesus Christ of Latter Day Saints* is the main, or Salt Lake City, group which has more than half the churches and 85% of the members.

2. *The Reorganized Church of Jesus Christ of Latter Day Saints* (567 churches and 94,000 members) claims to be the true Mormon Church founded by Joseph Smith*. It denied the claims of Brigham Young* and opposed polygamy. It was originally constituted by the few churches which survived after the main body went to Utah. The son of the original Joseph Smith was its head for many years, and a grandson is president at the present time. Headquarters are at Independence, Mo.

3. *Church of Christ* (*Temple Lot*) is a group of 16 churches and 700 members which originally moved from Illinois, where they remained when the main body went to Missouri, to Independence, Mo., in response to an alleged divine revelation in 1864. There they purchased the "temple lot," 2¾ acres of land said to have been selected in 1831 as the site of the temple in the "land of Zion." This lot has great significance in their eyes, since the temple which is to stand on it will be the center of the new world order to be ushered in when the New Jerusalem is built and Christ returns. In 1891 the Reorganized Church began legal proceeding to secure the lot and in 1895 the decision was rendered in its favor.

4. *Church of Jesus Christ* (*Bickertonites*). This group has 31 churches and 1600 members. It was founded by William Bickerton at Greenock, Pa., in 1862. This man claimed divine inspirations of various kinds and he gathered a group of believers who remained in the east after the departure of the main body, and who opposed Brigham Young, polygamy, baptism for the dead, and other Mormon ideas.

5. *Church of Jesus Christ* (*Cutlerites*). This little group of 30 Mormons has a church at Independence, Mo., and another at Cliterall, Minn. They claim to be the true church founded by Joseph Smith, all others having apostatised. The sect was founded by Alphens Cutler, one of Smith's elders, when he saw in the sky the sign of "two half-moons with their backs together." Cutler's successor tried to establish community of goods, and the principle that ownership should vest only in the church still prevails.

6. *Church of Jesus Christ* (*Strangites*). This sect of 4 churches and 120 members claims to be the original and only Mormon body. Its prophet and founder was James J. Strang who is said to have been designated by Joseph Smith as his successor. After the murder of Smith, Strang was "ordained by the hands of angels" and tried to assume leadership and started to build a "stake in Zion" at Voree, near Burlington, Wis. But he was rejected by the main body who "voted they wanted no more prophets of God to lead them." Strang continued his prophetic work, however, translated "by Urim and Thummim," from certain "plates of Laban" missed by Smith, a book called "Book of Law of the Lord," and was finally crowned king in 1850. He was assassinated in 1856. E.T.C.

Latter Day Saints: Or more correctly The Church of Jesus Christ (of Latter Day Saints was added for legal reasons), organized 6 April 1830 by Joseph Smith, Jr* ir Sebeca County, New York; later moved to Kirtland, Ohio, where temple was built; Independence, Missouri; Caldwell County, Missouri; Nauvoo, Illinois. After death of Joseph Smith Jr. by mob, 27 June 1844, most of the over 200,000 members were scattered. Some 20,000 followed Brigham Young to Utah; some others formed smaller groups and in 1852 reorganized, awaiting the coming of Joseph Smith III in 1860, together with the mother, brother, sisters and all descendants of Joseph Smith Jr. This group had headquarters at Plano, Illinois, then Lamoni, Iowa, and, since 1907, Independence, Missouri.

In doctrine, liberal with no set creed, but accepts principles of Apostles Creed, trinitarian; accepts the Bible as the fundamental work of Christianity; the Book of Mormon, as a record of the early inhabitants of America; present revelation, issued as Doctrine and Covenants; ordained priesthood with gradations of First Presidency; Apostles (12); Seventy (7 quorums); high priests, including High Council evangelists, bishops; also elders, priests, teachers and deacons; believes every one has right of approach to God, with spiritual gifts through confirmation, baptism by immersion, healing (James 5:15).

Also Christian economic order of Enoch to care for poor through donation of surplus with every man his home and stewardship.

Believe in endowment of the Spirit (Lk. 24:49, Acts 2:1-21), and that God is unchangeable.

Herman C. Smith, *History of the Church* (1896, 1897, 1900, 1903), Vols. 1-4; *Times and Seasons*, 1839-1846, Nauvoo; Elbert A. Smith, *Angel Message tracts;* Elbert A. Smith, *Faith of Our Fathers* (1940); Elbert A. Smith, *What Latter Day Saints Believe about God* (1937); Elbert A. Smith, *What Latter Day Saints Believe about Immortality* (1937). S.A.B.

Latter Day Saints—Reorganized: Has been held a continuation of the Original Latter Day Saints, alike in doctrine and practice. (Federal Reporter, 60-937; Court of Common Pleas, Lake County, Ohio, 1880, in re Kirtland Temple.) Headquarters—Independence, Missouri. President —Frederick M. Smith, grandson of Joseph Smith, Jr. S.A.B.

Latter Day Saints—Utah: Sometimes called Mormons, started with those who followed Brigham Young to Utah, there rebaptized and reconfirmed. On 29 August 1852 first published celestial marriage, popularly called polygamy, a practice previously started by Young and associate leaders and continued until Manifesto of 1890 and later proclamations of Presidency officially repudiated practice, but held as celestial marriage for life to come; ideal of God as once a man with celestial wives; Adam as God was once, taught by Young and others now rejected as only their personal, not official, teaching. To the three books named under Latter Day Saints, they add the Book of Abraham, in *The Pearl of Great Price* (1851). Build temples for ritual use with grips and pass words, baptism for dead ancestors. Headquarters—Salt Lake City. Heber J. Grant, President.

John A. Widstoe, *Rational Theology*, pp. 23, 24, 63, 148; Jas. E. Talmage, *The Articles of Faith*, pp. 435, 440, 457; B. H. Roberts, *Defense of the Faith and the Saints* (1907), p. 18 ff. S.A.B.

Latter, the, Prophets: See canon, Old and New Testament.

Laud, William: (1573-1645) Archbishop of Canterbury during the troubled days of the Stuart monarchy. Successively Bishop of London and Archbishop of Canterbury, Laud became first minister of the crown, standing with Charles I and Strafford against Puritanism and the commonwealth. He was a vigorous churchman, loyal to Catholic standards which he sought to impose by force. This caused disaster both in England and in Scotland, where his policy gave rise to the "Covenant." He was impeached, tried for treason, and executed by the Long Parliament, in 1640-44. His chief place in religious history is as a defender of the catholicity of the Church of England, and his *apologia* for that Church is his most important published work. W.N.P.

lauds: (Lt. *laudes*) The drawn service in the system of Hours*, usually, when sung in choir, following immediately upon Matins*. So called from the use of the *laudate* psalms (Ps. 148-50). See divine office. P.V.N.

Lavabo: (Lat. I will wash) The first word of verses 6-12 of Psalm XXV in the Vulgate, beginning, "Lavabo inter innocentes manus meas," said by the celebrant while washing and drying his fingers after the offertory of the Mass*; used as a name for the ceremony. The Lavabo originated in the practical necessity of cleansing the fingers after handling offerings of bread, fruit, etc., donated by the faithful. It now symbolizes that purity with which the sacred mysteries should be approached. J.F.T.

Lavater, Johann Caspar: (1741-1801) Protestant thinker. Born Zurich, Switzerland. Extensive journeys through Germany brought him into contact with most of the leading contemporaries. He became in 1769 pastor in Zurich where he died. The first Protestant theologian to conceive of the ministry primarily as cure of souls. Counselled many thousands in interviews and through an extensive correspondence. Christianity to him consisted mainly in personal relationships, "Virtuose der Freundschaft". His religion was open to philosophical arguments, but remained, nevertheless both Biblical and emotional. It contributed much to the defeat of the older type of rationalism and paved the way toward German idealism. The meticulous self-scrutiny of his *Secret Diary* inaugurated in Germany and Britain the fashion of writing "moral diaries".

Like Hamann* Lavater interpreted nature as the direct manifestation of the Divine Spirit. His works on physiognomics were an expression of this view. They were as successful as his religious writings.

Principal works: *Aussichten in die Ewigkeit* (1769-1773); *Physiognomische Fragmente* (1775-1778, Engl. tr. by H. Hunter, 1810 and Thos. Holcroft, 1808, illustrated by Wm. Blake and others); *Geheimes Tagebuch von einem Beobachter seiner selbst* (1772-1773, Engl. tr. 1795); *Jesus Messias*, or the Evangelists and Acts of the Apostles, 4 vol. *Gesammelte Werke* (1841-1844); Biographies by P. J. Heisch, 1842 (Eng); Fr. Munker, 1883, A. Vömel, 1927, and Chr. Janentzky, 1928 (all three in German); Ol. Guinandeau, 1924 (French). O.A.P.

law: In the juridical sense, the aggregate of those rules of conduct which the governing power of a community recognizes as those which it will enforce or sanction, and according to which it will regulate, limit, or protect the acts of its members. Theories as to the nature and origin of law vary with the different schools of jurisprudence. 1) To the *natural law school*, which grew out of the Stoic philosophy and Roman jurisprudence, law is the expression of right reason inhering in the nature of man and society which is ethically binding as a rule of civil conduct, and which it is the duty of society as politically organized to recognize and enforce; 2) to the *analytical school*, which was first definitely formulated by Thomas Hobbes* in his *Leviathan* (1651) but which became dominant among English-speaking peoples through the writings of John Austin (1790-1859), law is the command of the sovereign to his subjects to perform or abstain from performing definite acts, to the breach of which a definite penalty is attached; while 3) to the *historical* and *comparative schools*, originating with the historical and social sciences in the nineteenth century and popularized by the writings of Henry Sumner Maine (1822-88), law is a social product consisting of certain authoritative regulations of social relations which were slowly differentiated and developed out of the matrix of custom and distinguished from it by a) the nature of the authority or sanctions involved, (b) the procedure or mode of regulation, and (c) their social function or scope.

Many primitive peoples have not yet evolved law as distinct from custom in any meaningful sense of the term. Yet such societies are not on that account characterized by anarchy and ungoverned violence. On the contrary, in primitive society custom conditions, permeates, and controls every phase of man's social and personal behavior from birth to death. Agreement as to what is required and what is prohibited is so universal and conformity is so general that control is for the most part exercised by consensus rather than by constraint. Most of the violations which occur are dealt with by such informal and general or diffuse sanctions as disapprobation and ridicule. Some violations, however, involve religious sanctions, and are conceived of as producing in the offender a state of ceremonial uncleanness or pollution which endangers both himself and those in contact with him, and which can be removed only by the performance of prescribed religious rites.

Law, however, has developed out of certain customary methods of redress of public and private wrongs. Among most, if not quite all, peoples there exist powerful sanctions which are obviously communal in character. They are often visited upon the offender by means which express the moral indignation of the group in a manner quite similar to modern lynch law. They are especially concerned with maintaining certain customs which are felt as especially sacred and whose violation is therefore looked upon as a form of sacrilege which endangers the life of the group by rendering it ritualistically unclean and exposing it to the wrath of the gods. The offender is therefore stoned, burned, sacrificed to the gods, or outlawed from the group. Because uncleanness is looked upon as a form of physical pollution which can be communicated by contact, the entire family or blood group of the offender together with his property, is sometimes included in the penalty, as in the case of the punishment of Achan's theft (Joshua, ch. 7). Among the actions most commonly treated in this manner are witchcraft*, incest, and breaches of marriage customs, although any act may be included which is thought of as a serious violation of sacred prohibitions. Such sanctions provide the starting point for the evolution of primitive law.

Acts of private vengeance visited by the injured upon the guilty for violations of custom which are not felt to endanger the community as a whole constitute a second source of law. For private vengeance is casual and arbitrary at best, and the principle of solidarity and collective responsibility of the kindred which makes the blood* feud as interminable conflict between the families of the aggrieved and the aggressor, constitutes a perpetuate threat to social harmony. Hence custom, which at first sanctioned only the right of private vengeance, ultimately prescribes both its extent and duration. Thus arises the *lex talionis** which demands that there shall be an equivalence between the injury and the penalty, and that, when vengeance has once been exacted, further retaliation shall cease. But an offender may suffer in property as well as in person, and a further mitigation of the blood feud is the composition for offenses, or money payment in lieu of physical injury.

These methods for the redress of public and private wrongs are applicable only when rights are clear and violations apparent. They provide no means of settling controversies as to the existence of an injury and the actuality of alleged guilt. But every group has leaders whose authority is based on age, strength, courage, skill, intelligence, personality, or other valued qualities. These elders, headmen, or chiefs provide impartial arbiters to hear complaints and hand down decisions as to the character of the reparation due. But they did not dare to execute their own sentences for fear of involving themselves in the blood feud. Nor did they presume to determine cases in the light of their human wisdom alone. Hence they employed oaths* and ordeals by which the gods were called upon to render their judgments as to guilt or innocence.

Law, in the full juridical sense of the term, can hardly be said to exist until there emerges a central executive authority sufficiently powerful to enforce its decision without fear of blood vengeance. But even at this stage the administration of justice by a central power does not involve the right to make new laws by legislation and judicial action. Even at a relatively advanced stage of cultural development, kings who are justly described as autocrats are as much bound by custom as are their subjects. As an illuminating statement in King Alfred's Law expresses it, "I durst not set down much of my own."

Although true legislation, the power of creating new regulations by acts of political authority, which has become the chief source of law in modern complex societies, was attained by many advanced political societies of the Ancient World, not until the eighteenth century did the full potentialities of this power begin to be employed. Yet even today custom continues to be an important, though diminishing, source of law.

Law in modern society therefore has three sources. Legislative enactments constitute the *lex scripta,* or *statutory law.* Long prevailing customs, sanctioned by the consent of those who use them and recognized by the final courts of appeal, as reasonable, consistent, and established, constitute the *lex non-scripta,* or *common law.* The law established by judicial decision in adapting either statutory or common law to particular cases constitutes *case law.* If in the process of interpretation an absolutely new rule is added to the law, it is properly referred to as *judicial legislation.*

The scope of law has evolved *pari pasu* with its sanctions and procedures. Primitive society is marked by a strong predominance of the criminal over the civil law. This was due, as Maine has shown, not to the greater turbulence of primitive peoples, but to the fact that absence of contract, the regulation of personal relations by the status of individuals, the administration and inheritance of property according to custom, and the relative isolation and ethnocentrism of kinship and territorial groups, left little occasion for the development of other legal functions. But the evolution of social organization created new problems in social control and enlarged the scope of the law. The increasing interdependence of sovereign states has led to the compilation of *international law.* It consists of the system of rules which regulate the intercourse of states and determine their reciprocal rights and obligations. It is still almost wholly customary in character. It consists of acts and forbearances of states with respect to each other, and has no other sanctions than "a decent respect to the opinions of mankind." International courts and tribunals, like those of primitive society, must depend upon the willingness of the disputants to accept their decisions, and when this fails, the resort is to that modern form of organized vengeance and blood feud known as war. The body of law in force within the political jurisdiction of a state is called, not very appropriately, *municipal law. Substantive law* defines or creates the rights which the courts are called upon to administer in contradistinction to *adjective law,* which defines or creates the means and procedures of enforcing them. *Public law* consists of the legalization to which governmental power has become subjected in the process of its development. It includes 1) *constitutional law,* which defines the form of government and the relations of the different branches of government to each other, 2) *administrative law,* which prescribes the manner in which the powers of government shall be exercised within the constitution, and defines the rights and duties of governmental officials and the relations between government and private persons, and 3) *criminal law,* which deals with injuries to the government or to the public at large resulting from violations of law and prescribes penalties for the same. *Private,* or *civil law* defines the rights and privileges of persons, both natural and juridical, and deals with things as property or objects of private right. The term *political law* is used by some writers to refer to that part of jurisprudence* which relates to the organization and policy of states and their relations to each other and to their citizens and subjects. It includes international, constitutional, and administrative law, as here defined. See culture; primitive religion.

N. S. Timasheff, *An Introduction to the Sociology of Law* (1939); P. Vinogradoff, *Outlines of Historical Jurisprudence* (London, 1920-22); L. T. Hobhouse, *Morals in Evolution* (London, 1906).

H.E.J.

law: In its most general sense, especially as it was used by the Hebrews and in Greek philosophy, the word law signifies every observed regularity of nature as well as of human conduct, such regularity being thought of as taking place in obedience to divine command. Not until the eighteenth century is the meaning of law as an objectively observed regularity, i.e., a "law of nature" (see natural law) clearly and consistently distinguished from law as the idea of a norm or a system of norms of human conduct to which human beings owe obedience, but which a man is free to disobey provided he is willing to suffer the penalty. In the terminology prevailing among present-day lawyers the term law is confined to those rules of human conduct which are manipulated and enforced by the state or, at least to such bodies of norms as are applied and interpreted in the same method in which state enforced rules of human conduct are handled. If taken in this latter sense the term law is broad enough to cover the phenomena of International Law and Ecclesiastical Law which are not covered by the narrower meaning. The lawyer's definition emphasizes that feature which distinguishes "law" from such other bodies of norms of human conduct as those of social etiquette, religion and ethics. While the sanction of law is the infliction upon the violator of some detriment by a special functionary of politically organized society, the sanction of etiquette consists in ridicule, boycott or some other form of unfavorable reaction of society as an unorganized or, at least not politically organized, group. The sanction of the religious rule of conduct consists in the believer's notions of incurring the wrath of the deity in this or another world, and the ethical rule of conduct finds its sanction in the feeling of uneasiness, remorse or despondency which attends or follows upon the violation of the ethical imperative in the mind of the person endowed with ethical sensibility. While these various types of rules of human conduct are distinguished from each other in mature analysis, in so-called primitive law they form an indistinguished complex.

The ancient comprehensive meaning of the term law is also reflected in the terminology of Thomist philosophy, where eternal law, signifying "the plan of the Divine Wisdom as directing all actions and movements" is divided into the two categories of the physical law and the moral law. The former is obeyed perfectly and uniformly, the latter, however, but partially and imperfectly. Of the moral law, the following subdivisions are distinguished: *Natural Law* constitutes "the participation of the eternal law in the rational creature;" it is universal, perpetual, immutable, and easily known to any being endowed with reason. *Divine Law,* on the other hand, is inaccessible to human reason and has therefore been supernaturally revealed to man by God in his infinite goodness and mercy. Finally, *human positive law* is a rule of conduct, "mandatory in form and freely established and promulgated by human superiors for the common good." It is this latter category alone to which present-day lawyers apply the term law.

One of the outstanding characteristics of modern society is the monopolization of violence by the state. Self-help, feud and spontaneous violence are "out-lawed", except in the relations of states among each other where the outlawry of war has so far remained a pious wish. The application of violence as against individuals is not permitted to private persons but only to certain functionaries of politically organized society who, in contemporary America, are known under such names as sheriff, United States marshall, prison-warden, public executioner, policeman or constable. As a rule these "violence-officers" are not permitted to go into action except upon the express order of a member of another set of societal functionaries, the "determination officers," who are commonly known as courts or judges. These latter officers, in turn, are not allowed to order action against an individual by a violence officer unless they have found that such individual has behaved himself in a certain "illegal" way. If D does not pay the money he owes C, the latter is not allowed to resort to self-help but has to sue D before a court. If the latter after proper investigation finds that C's claim against D is justified under the law, it orders the sheriff to levy execution upon so much of D's assets as may be necessary to pay C's claim. The judgment of the court empowers the sheriff or his deputy to break all resistance D may offer, if necessary, by armed force. With all its might the state ranges itself behind its citizen whom it prevents from "taking the law into his own hands." Looked upon in such an analysis the law appears as that body of rules which tell the determination officers of the state under what circumstances they have to order the violence officers to apply violence against an individual.

The opinion held by contemporary American "realists" that law is not a body of rules but simply the sum total of the activities of the courts and other law people ("Law is nothing but what the judges do") overlooks the basic social need for certainty and predictability of official action. The Leviathan State would be unbearable if its functionaries were not bound to the observance of definite rules, which, of course, have no reality other than that of other contents of the human mind, but whose motivating force can hardly be denied by psychologists. The supreme functionaries of society cannot be curbed by "legal" sanctions in the narrow sense of the word. The guarantee that the judges of a supreme court or a chief executive will apply the law lies in the wisdom of political organization, for instance, the technique of separation of powers, in the restraining force of political prudence and public opinion, and ultimately in the motivating power of such bodies of meaning as ideas of morality and religion.

The content of the rules of law which, through the foreseen sanction of politically organized violence, are of motivating force to the individual members of society, are determined by numerous factors, which can be subsumed under the categories of 1) the ethical convictions and habits of the "elite", i.e., that group or those groups whose convictions, habits and tastes set the pattern for the society in question; 2) the traditions and techniques of the "law specialists", i.e., the judges and attorneys or, in certain countries, administrative officials of various kinds.

The effectiveness of the rules of law of a given society depends not only upon the efficiency of the enforcement machinery but upon the degree of correspondence of the rules of law with the religious beliefs, the ethical convictions and the traditions and habits of those to whom they are addressed. The strongest guarantee of the law consists, however, in the religious or ethical conviction, that law observance as such is pleasing to the Deity or constitutes an ethical imperative (Socrates!). Finally, law cannot dispense with the emotional appeal of myths, symbols and ceremonies. Definitions of law which exclude from this euphonious label politically enforced rules of human conduct which are not backed by the "ethical conviction of the people" or whose contents do not correspond to the ideals of the author of the definition may be means of propaganda against tyranny but are of little use in social science.

The systems of positive law being presently in force in the various countries of the earth are usually distinguished as belonging to either the group of the *Common Law* or to that of the *Civil Law.* The Common Law countries are those whose laws continue in an unbroken tradition those rules, techniques and legal usages which have been developed since the 11th century in the Royal courts of England. These countries are England itself, Ireland, the greater part of the British Dominions and colonies and the United States. The Civil Law grew up in the countries of continental Europe upon the basis of innumerable locally and socially different customs. Toward the second half of the Middle Ages the revived law of Imperial Rome exercised a powerful unifying and systematizing influence. Since the beginning of the 19th century the unifying trend has been counteracted by the growth of nationalism which resulted in the enactment of great national codifications. The codes of France and Germany became models for other countries so that the great family of so-called Romance laws (France, Belgium, Netherlands, Italy, Spain, Latin-American, and several Balkan countries) can now be distinguished from the German family of codes (Germany, territories formerly belonging to Austria-Hungary, Switzerland, Japan, China, etc.). French law has also been the model for the laws of the Canadian Province of Quebec and for the Civil Code of the State of Louisiana. Uncodified versions of Civil Law are in force in Scotland, in the Union of South Africa and certain smaller parts of the British Commonwealth of Nations. The Scandinavian countries, which were less affected by Roman law, have developed autonomous legal systems of their own, which have been considerably influenced, however, by the legal science of neighboring Germany. See jurisprudence; canon law; natural rights.

The literature on law is legion. William Seagle's *The Quest for Law* (1941) may serve as the best introduction and the most extensive collection of bibliographical data. Max Radin's *The Law and Mr. Smith* (1938) is another fine explanation for the uninitiated. See, also, the articles and bibliographies on Law in the *Encyclopedia of the Social Sciences,* especially those by A. B. Radcliffe-Brown (Primitive); L. Wenger(General View of Ancient); E. Seidl (Egyptian); P. Koschaker (Cuneiform); A. Gulak (Jewish); E. Weiss (Greek); A. A. Schiller (Hellenistic); E. von Kuenssberg (Germanic); S. Kutrzeba (Slavic); E. MacNeill (Celtic); J. Escarra (Chinese); M. Takikawa (Japanese); and S. Vesey-Fitzgerald (Hindu) in 9:202 et sq.; Schiller (Roman Law) 13:419; H. Hazeltine (Canon Law) 3:179; J. Declareuil (Civil Law) 3-502; R. Pound (Common Law) 4:50; and J. Schacht, (Islamic Law) 8:349; further articles on legal topics are indexed in vol. 15 at p. 553.

M.Rh.

law, canon: See canon law.

law, Hebrew: System of ritual practices and observances, and jurisprudence, believed by the Hebrews to have been divinely revealed to Moses on Sinai and incorporated in the Pentateuch*. As among all peoples of antiquity, ritual and law proper, i.e., jurisprudence were undifferentiated, and were regarded as having a common origin. In the course of time, Hebrew law underwent a long process of development. This is especially perceptible in the law of the Tannaitic period (the first two centuries of the Christian era) where we meet with many significant variations from and developments of Biblical Law. The main factors in the development of the Law were Interpretation, Enactment and Custom. When the Mishnah* was compiled by Rabbi Judah the Patriarch, it became the authentic guide to Jewish practice with regard to every matter affecting religion and law. The main task of the later scholars known as Amoraim* (who flourished between 200-500 of the Christian era) was to interpret the Mishnah and adjust it to contemporary living. In view of the fact that economic, social and political conditions of Palestine diverged in many respects from that of Babylonia, considerable differences in law and interpretation are to be found in the Palestinian and Babylonian Talmuds. During the Gaonic period (700-1040) it was the Babylonian Talmud which became the recognized authority for Jewish religious life and when the Palestinian Talmud presented a different interpretation, it was generally disregarded. With the dispersion of the Jews in North Africa and Europe, schools for the study of Jewish Law were founded in the new settlements. New living conditions precipitated new problems for the learned in the law, local variations in customs were inevitable in the course of time. From the eleventh century on we witness the growth of the Spanish, Franco-German, Italian, and later the Turkish schools of law differing in many important details with regard to liturgy, ritual and jurisprudence. However, throughout the Middle Ages and down to modern times, it is the Bible and the Talmud* which constitute the two main sources of Hebrew Law. See Hillel; Old Testament; tables of the law. Cf. Israel.

Cf. Louis Ginzberg, *Jewish Encyclopedia,* Vol. VII, pp. 635-647; A. Gulak, *Encyclopedia of Religion and Sciences,* Vol. V, pp. 219-224; S. R. Driver, *Hastings Dictionary of the Bible,* Vol. III, pp. 64-73; F. Perles, *Encyclopedia of Religion and Ethics,* Vol. VII, pp. 855-858. B.C.

Law, William: (1686-1761) English divine, moralist, and mystic. Born at King's Cliffe, Northhamptonshire, the son of a shopkeeper of good family, Law entered Emmanuel College, Cambridge, in 1705. In 1711 he was elected fellow of his college and ordained. Refusing in 1714 the double oath of allegiance to George I and abjuration of the Stuart Pretender, he lost his fellowship and every chance of preferment within the Church. Henceforth he supported himself as he could through tutoring and private chaplaincies and devoted himself in the utmost simplicity to the life of prayer, study, writing, and good works. His most influential works, *A Treatise of Christian Perfection* (1726) and *A Serious Call to a Devout and Holy Life* (1728), express the view of Christianity already put into practice by Law. Their influence on John Wesley* was marked and permanent, bearing fruit in his mature doctrine of Christian perfection. *The Case of Reason* (1732) was the first answer to Tindal's *Christianity as Old as Creation*—the foremost Deist* writing. About 1733 Law became acquainted with the writings of Jacob Boehme*. His writings after 1737 are mystical in the normative sense of the word and have earned him the title of "The English Mystic". See evangelicalism and evangelical revival; non-jurors.

Works (1892), 9 vols.; J. H. Overton, *William Law, Non-Juror and Mystic* (1881). C.W.L.

Laws of Manu: See manu; Vedas.

laws, natural: See law; natural law. Cf. American theology, early.

lay, layman: Strictly employed, these terms are to be understood through their opposition to the term *clericus,* and its derivatives, in such Churches as believe the clergy to be possessed of an indelible character, imparted through ordination. A layman is one who is not a cleric. However the terms are used more loosely to signify the non-ministerial status in Churches of any kind; and indeed they are often used to indicate simply the non-professional. A.K.R.

lay abbot: 1) A monastic abbot not in orders—possible even today in Eastern Church 2) commendatory—ecclesiastic or layman to whom Pope or King "commended" monastic endowments; custom widespread c. 1400-1800. E.R.H.

lay baptism: According to the Roman Catholic Church any lay person may validly baptize, and in case of emergency (i.e., when an unbaptized person is near death and no cleric can be obtained), is bound to do so. Anybody, whether man, woman, child, Catholic, Protestant or Jew, may baptize provided there is the intention to do what the Church intends when baptizing. Water is poured on the head of the subject while repeating the Scriptural formula, "I baptize thee in the name of the Father, and of the Son, and of the Holy Ghost." Though the sacrament may be validly administered by any layman, it is gravely illicit except in cases of emergency. J.F.T.

lay brother, lay sister: (Gr. *laikos, laos,* people) A member of a religious order who is neither in holy orders nor bound by the recitation of the Office in choir (cf. choir monk, nun), but whose occupation is concerned solely with the secular affairs of a monastery or convent. Such lay religious are clerics in the extended sense of the term and enjoy clerical immunities. The institution was unknown prior to the 10th century, when the ordination of monks was gaining ground and manual labor losing it. J.F.T.

lay clerk: A (strictly) self-contradictory term for a functionary connected with the choral part of the service in an English cathedral. The term "clerk" preserves the historical fact that the function used to be performed by an ordained official; the term "lay" indicates that it is now discharged by a lay person. A.K.R.

lay confession: Confession to a layman in the absence of a priest was common in the Middle Ages, either by extension of the practice of resorting to a monk for counsel (East) or by analogy with emergency baptism (West). E.R.H.

lay reader: Among Anglicans since Elizabethan times a layman authorized by the bishop to read services in church, especially when clergy are not available. Derived from neither but somewhat replacing both, the duties of the office are similar to those of readers in the ancient church, who however were in minor orders, and parish clerks, who however were usually paid parish assistants, sometimes sextons*. T.J.B.

lay religious teaching: See Sunday School movement in the United States.

lay tithes: 1) secular tithes paid to a secular landlord; 2) ecclesiastical tithes which, in the course of time, have, for one reason or another, been alienated from the Church to a lay proprietor. A.K.R.

laying on of hands: A method used by a qualified person to transmit blessing*, authority or grace to another. The hands were usually laid on the head. In the Christian church the rite has been used for exorcism* before baptism, to impart the Holy Spirit to the newly baptised, to transmit a special grace at ordination. In a less formal way it was used for healing, absolution and benediction**. The Prince of the Sanhedrin* or other members conferred authority upon a new member in this way. In Egypt and Babylonia the king and priests received authority for their offices by contact with the hands of the images of the gods. A variant appears in the ancient Hebrew ceremony in which the priest annually transferred the sins of the people to the scapegoat*. Underlying all such rites is the primitive idea of a mysterious potency which may be communicated by contagion. See confirmation. A.E.H.

Le Bon, Gustave: (1841-1931) He held that tenacious efficiency of beliefs is proof that man is not a logical creature. Man is likely to believe the most illogical and unreasonable things if these satisfy his emotions and feelings. Thus beliefs, not reason and logic, have been the real factors in life and history. Change in the beliefs of a people is followed by a great change in their whole social life.

G. Le Bon, *Psychology of Socialism* (1889). H.H.

League, German Catholic: Founded 1609 in Munich against the Protestant Union of 1608. By 1619 it included most of the Catholic estates of the empire under the leadership of Bavaria. It played an important part in the years preceding and immediately following the beginning of the Thirty Years' War*. It came to an end in the Peace of Prague, 1635. E.C.K.

League and Covenant, the Solemn: A covenant, based on the Scottish National Covenant of 1638, adopted by the English Parliament in 1644, to be imposed on all Englishmen over eighteen years of age. This amounted to an effort to make the Established Church in England* Presbyterian* in return for Scottish help in the struggle with Charles I. Cf. Covenanters.

See H. Gee and W. J. Hardy, *Documents Illustrative of English Church History* (1914), pp. 569-574. A.K.R.

leaven: Symbolic of unseen influences, for good or evil—the first (from the parable, Matthew 13:33) is common in literature, the second suggests an association of purity in faith and morals with the unleavened bread* of the Passover* (I Cor. 5:8) and unleavened altar-bread* E.R.H.

lectern: (From Lat., *legere*, to read) A reading desk of wood or metal, frequently employing the eagle symbol, upon which is placed the Bible read in public worship. P.V.N.

lection: A passage from Scripture, the writings of the Fathers, or the lives of the saints, read in the services of the Church, particularly in the Eucharist (Epistle, Gospel) and in Matins*. P.V.N.

lectionary: 1) A book containing the lections* read in the Eucharist (liturgical Epistles and Gospels) or in Matins. 2) A table of lessons appointed to be thus used. See pericope. P.V.N.

lector: Perhaps originally a charismatic* order allowed to read and expound the Scriptures—since the third century a minor order; in Anglican use (16th century and modern) a layman licensed to read part of the service. E.R.H.

Lectureships, Foundations and Institutes: See under separate headings: Adams; Alden-Tuthill; Avera; Ayer; Barrows; Beecher; Bohlen; Bross; Carew; Chancellor; Christian Biography; Clark; Cole; Colver; Crozer; Dudleian; Earl; Ely; Flowers; Fondren; Goldberg; Green; Haddon-Colt; Hale; Haskell (Oberlin); Haskell (U. of Chicago); Hazen; Hewitt; Holman; Hoyt; Hyde; Ingersoll; Institute for Religious Studies; Jarrell; Jones; Judaism, Lectureship on; Kessler; Lowell; McCauley; McNair; Mendenhall; Merrick; Moore; Morse; Noble; Paddock; Pollok; Porter; Quillian; Rauschenbusch; Richard; Robertson; Rockwell; Science, Philosophy and Religion, Conference on; Russell; Shaffer (Northwestern); Shaffer (Yale); Southworth; Sprunt; Stone; Students' Lectureship on Missions (Princeton); Swander; Taylor; Terry; Theology Lectures, the (U. of Va.); Thomas; West; Zimmerman.

Lee, Mother Ann: See communistic settlements, religious, Shaker communities.

legalism in religion and morality: The view that religion or morality consists in strict obedience to a prescribed code of laws. Often the term is used derogatively to signify a conformity which has missed the inner spirit or purpose of the laws and degenerated into a barren observance of externalities. Legalism stands opposed both to utilitarianism and to salvation by grace; it requires obedience to law without regard to consequences and rests the claim to redemption on good works. The scribes* of ancient Judaism and the Puritans* of the modern era are familiar examples. Both construed the Scriptures as a legal code. F.G.E.

legates and nuncios, papal: Both, Papal Legates and Papal Nuncios, are representatives of the Pope*. They differ in the degree of authority vested in them and according to the countries to which they are sent. A Legate, e.g., may be sent to another ruler or country merely in an honorary capacity, as e.g., to represent His Holiness at a King's Coronation or to preside in his name over a Eucharistic Congress. A *Legatus a Latere* is always a cardinal; he is sent by the Pope as another *ego* and enjoys as much power as is committed to him by the Pontiff, plenipotentiary (in a given case) or restricted, e.g., in signing contracts, concordats*, etc. (Canon 266 of the Code of Canon Law.) If the Legate represents not only the person of the Pope but also the Holy See which has diplomatic relations with that country, he is called a *Nuncio*. His position corresponds to that of an Ambassador; hence the terms Nunciature and Embassy are correlative. If the Legate represents diplomatically the Holy See in a country of second rank, so classified either by reason of its population or Catholic proportion, he is called an *Internuncio**. His rank would thus correspond to that of a Minister, diplomatically speaking. The principal ordinary duties of a Nuncio or Internuncio (besides extraordinary faculties) are to foster, according to stabilized norms, good relations between the Holy See and the government to which he is sent; to watch diligently over the status of the Church in that country and to report on the same to the Holy See. An *Apostolic Delegate* (Dex Legatus) represents the Holy See only in the last named sense and enjoys no diplomatic character, i.e., does not represent the Holy See with the government of the country to which he is sent. Hence despite the presence of an Apostolic Delegate, the Pope may discuss matters of mutual interest in any given country through another as his personal representative (e.g., Mr. Myron Taylor as personal *envoy* of President Roosevelt and any given Bishop or Archbishop as *personal* envoy of the Pope). An Apostolic Delegate, of course, may enjoy many *delegated* powers not ordinarily connected with his role or office, especially when relations with Rome become difficult as e.g., during a war. Unless otherwise specifically stated his duties do not expire with the death of the Pope; they do cease however, if the Legate or Delegate (Envoy) is sent only for a specific purpose that has been accomplished; or by recall from his mission, or by resignation, if accepted by the Pontiff. Legates may not interfere with the ordinary jurisdiction of bishops in their respective dioceses; they do however, enjoy precedence over all other prelates, even though they themselves be not consecrated bishops or (as is usual) archbishops, (excepting over cardinals). If the Legate be a consecrated bishop or archbishop he may, even without the permission of the Ordinary (excepting in the Cathedral) bless the faithful publicly, e.g., during processions, and perform all such pontifical functions (cf. Pontificals, Pontificalia) even with throne and canopy. If a bishop or archbishop enjoys the *title* of an Apostolic Legate by virtue of his see, he does not thereby obtain any special jurisdiction (Canons 1 c. No. 265-270). Such Legates, e.g., the Archbishops of Cologne, Rheims, Canterbury, etc., are known as *Legati Nati* (born Legates) in Canon Law*. All Legates, like Ambassadors, enjoy personal immunity. R.M.H.

legend: (Lat. *legere,* to read) A term denoting a popularly accepted narrative, or collection of narratives, of widely varying authenticity such as were current in the Middle Ages. Specifically, a medieval legend might concern itself with an edifying story of a saint's life; a collection of stories or readings in the saints, for instance, the famous *Golden Legend* of Jacobus de Voragine; a service book of readings or lessons combining excerpts from Scripture and saints' lore; or a bold traditional fabrication of religious data in response to popular needs. The uses of the legend in sermon, liturgy, religious drama, and private devotion were legion. See culture; folk lore; Holy Grail; Jacopo da Voragine. R.C.P.

Leibniz, Gottfried Wilhelm: (1646-1716) Mathematician, erudite man of affairs, and rationalistic philosopher. He believed that reality, in which *"causae efficientes pendent a finalibus,"* is a system of self-contained, unique centers of appetition and perception (monads). The quality of monads extends continuously from the obscure perception of the simple monad to the clearer perception of necessary truths envisioned by rational spirits. Each monad "mirrors" the universe from its viewpoint not because of mutual interaction, but because it was selected for its part by an omniscient, omnipotent, and provident God whose "fulgurations" brought into being this best world among possibilities. A finite world and moral freedom necessitate evil.

God, the source of the possible and the actual (compossible) world must exist, for nothing can contravene his possibility, while he alone could be the sufficient cause of the contingent world. In knowing God, faith and reason harmonize. See Enlightenment, the; monadism; panpsychism.

La Monadologie (1714); *Théodicée* (1710); *Principes de la Nature et Grace* (1714). P.A.B.

Leipzig, Interim of: A modification of the 26 articles of the Augsburg Interim* by Melanchthon* and his colleagues. Declared the law of the land at Leipzig in December, 1548, by Maurice of Saxony, it aroused intense opposition among strict Lutherans and led to the adiaphoristic controversy*. Cf. Majoristic controversy. E.C.K.

Lemme, Ludwig: (1847-1927) He was professor in Breslau, Bonn and Heidelberg. The impetus and clarity of theological group differences disappeared in his works.

Christliche Ethik (Gross-Lichterfelde-Berlin, 1905); *Theologische Enzyklopädie* (Berlin, 1909); *Christliche Glaubenslehre* (Berlin-Lichterfelde, 1918); *Christliche Apologetik* (Berlin, 1922). H.H.

Lempp, Otto: (1885-1914) Killed in World War I, he taught at the University of Kiel. With H. Süskind*, his fellow-Swabian, he was most strongly influenced by Troeltsch*.

Das Problem der Theodizee in der Philosophie und Literatur des 18 *Jahrhunderts* (Leipzig, 1910); *Tolstoi* (Tübingen, 1912); *Schiller* (Göttingen, 1915). H.H.

Lent: (Old Eng., *lencten,* spring) The penitential season of forty days from Ash Wednesday* to the eve of Easter*. In the official terminology of the Roman Catholic Church, *Quadragesima**, whence Fr. *carême*, etc., Ger., *Fastenzeit.* The pre-paschal fast was at first quite short, but was gradually extended backward to include Holy Week*, then a 'tithe' of the year, finally the period of forty days (Sundays of course excluded). The fast is otherwise reckoned in the Eastern Church. Anciently the Lenten season was a period of preparation for baptism at Easter, and of public penance* for those under discipline. The imposition of ashes is a survival of the later practice. See church year; church year cycle; Laetere Sunday; Shrovetide. P.V.N.

Leo the Great—Pope: (440-461) Leo I First Bishop of Rome to achieve general recognition of their claim to supremacy as successors of Peter. The Barbarian invasions contributed. Valentinian III, eastern Emperor, for political purposes, proclaimed his authority in the West.

Leo's definition of the person of Christ was adopted by the Council of Chalcedon (451)* and remains orthodox. R.E.E.H.

Leo IX: (Pope, 1049-1054) This reforming pope ascended the papal throne from the bishopric of Toul, from which he had been called by his cousin, the Emperor Henry III. Leo immediately embarked upon a program of reform which issued in a reorganized cardinalate, far-reaching appointments of such men as Hildebrand*, and a series of acts calculated to raise ecclesiastical morale and papal authority. See Cerularius, M; schism. R.C.P.

Leo X: (Pope, 1513-1521) Giovanni de 'Medici came to the papal throne with all the Renaissance* predilections of his famous family. His reign was marked, especially, by his struggle to advance the political fortunes of the papacy and those of his relatives with it, his Concordat* of 1516 with Francis I of France, and the beginning of the Protestant Revolt in Germany. With the challenge presented by this last, he was conspicuously unable to cope. See s.v. Defender of the Faith. R.C.P.

Leo XIII: (Pope 1878-1903) Vincenzo Gioacchino Pecci, b. March 2, 1810 at Carpineto, educated by the Jesuits* in Viterbo, at the Roman College and in the Academy for Nobles in Rome, was ordained priest and made a Domestic Prelate in 1831; Apostolic Delegate (cf. papal nuncio) to Benevento, where he combatted brigandry, in 1838; Apostolic Legate to Spoleto and Perugia in 1843 and Nuncio to Belgium in 1843 whence, for having sided with the bishops against the State in the question of Christian education, despite royal favor, he was recalled, 1846. It was here, as also as a result of his extensive travels to Cologne, Paris and London that he obtained that world-wide cultural and social viewpoint (*Weltanschauung*) that was later to characterize him as pope. Appointed by Gregory XVI Bishop of Perugia and created cardinal *in petto* (not published) he was unalterably opposed (since 1860) to the anti-clerical laws of the Italian government. Promulgated as cardinal by Pius IX* in 1853, he was called in 1877, after Antonelli's death, to act as Camerlengo of the Roman Curia. Elected pope in 1878 he sought incessantly to show through his many encyclicals* the perfect harmony of Christian principles with any justifiable form of government that stood for personal liberty; the justifiability of privately owned property and the rights of the working classes consistent with their natural and Christian dignity. (*Immortale Dei*, Nov. 1, 1885; *Libertas, praestantissimum*, June 29, 1888; *Graves de Communi*, Jan. 18, 1901 (Christian Democracy); *Rerum Novarum* May 15, 1891 (against Socialism and Liberalism), etc. His relations with the countries of Europe, excepting Italy (*"non expedit"*) were, despite his "captivity" in the Vatican, friendly and appreciated. As a missionary pope he did much to advance the cause of faith and religion in the Americas, China, Japan and Africa. He erected 48 missionary vicariates and 248 dioceses throughout the world. Personally highly educated, he took a great interest in the revival of Thomistic Scholasticism (see Neo-Scholasticism), Biblical Studies and higher education in general. He founded the Catholic Universities at Washington, D. C., at Fribourg in Switzerland and at Louvain, Belgium. His most ardent desire was to see the separated Slavic nations return to the fold of Rome. He fostered Catholic devotions. Although always physically weak, he was an intellectual giant in philosophical and theological knowledge; a classical Latinist and poet; a pioneer and leader in Christian politico-social sciences and an arbiter in national disputes that won for him and the papacy the admiration of the whole world. He died in 1903 and was laid to rest at St. John Lateran opposite the tomb of that other international pope of the Middle Ages, Innocent III*. See Americanism; Commission, the Biblical.

Litt. *Acta Leonis XIII* (Rome, 1881-1903), 22 vols. plus Index; *Acta Sanctae Sedis* (Rome, 1878 ff), Vol. XI, ff; *Allocutiones, Epistolae et Constitutiones—Leonis XIII* (Brügge, 1878-1900), 7 vols.; *Carmina, Inscriptiones, Numismata Leonis XIII*, publ. by J. Bach (1903), Engl. tr. by Henry (no date); *The Great Encyclicals of Leo XIII*, edit. by Father Wynn, S.J.; individual encyclicals translated into Engl. publ. by the Paulist Press, New York and by the NCWC of Washington, D. C. Biographies by B. O'Reilly (Paris, 1887); German tr. by V. Weinaud (1892); E. Keller (1882); J. McCarthy (London, 1896); Furey (1903); J. J. McGovern (1903). R.M.H.

LeRoy, Edouard: (1870-) French philosopher, Catholic modernist and follower of Bergson, first attained celebrity by his *Dogme et critique* (1906) which gave a pragmatic interpretation of Catholic dogmas. While this and his subsequent book, *Le Problème de Dieu* (1929), have been put on the Index*, M. LeRoy has remained a loyal Catholic layman, whose constant endeavor has been to reconcile Catholic faith with modern science by means of Bergsonian philosophy. Cf. his book on Bergson, *Une philosophie nouvelle* (1912). W.M.H.

Lessing, Gotthold Ephraim: (1729-1781) German dramatist, critic, librarian of the Wolfenbüttel* Library. The latter part of his life was devoted to freeing and broadening the conception of religion and defending the application of criticism to Christianity. In this cause he published *Zur Geschichte und Litteratur* (1774-1778) containing extracts from H. S. Reimarus'* caustic criticism of miracles. In the well-known drama *Nathan der Weise* (1779) Lessing pointed out the unity of aim in Mohammedanism, Judaism and Christianity, and in his great work *Die Erziehung des Menschengeschechts* (1780) (*The Education of the Human Race*) he portrayed life as the education of man through successive Divine revelations. These works have had a marked influence in promoting religious breadth and tolerance. See Lives of Jesus; Mendelssohn, Moses. J.W.B.

Lessius, Leonard: (1554-1623) Flemish Jesuit and theologian who played an important part in the disputes on grace in the Catholic Church at the beginning of the seventeenth century. Cf. Molinism. E.A.R.

Lesson Helps in Sunday School: See Sunday School movement in the United States.

Levellers, the: They formed the most important movement of popular political thought and of democratic radicalism during the 17th century English civil wars. In religion they favored religious toleration and were opposed to the establishment of either an episcopal or a presbyterian form of government. Though not of a very definite composition, the group formed for a brief time something like a political party, having a definite idea of the political aims of the English revolution, and a plan for re-settling the constitution on liberal lines. It failed in all of its purposes, but it represented with remarkable distinctness the modes of thought and argument which characterized revolutionary liberalism in the 18th and early 19th centuries. It drew the lines rather definitely between the liberalism of the less privileged economic classes and of the well-to-do. The name Leveller was meant to imply that the party sought to destroy differences in social position, of political rank, and even of property. The equality sought was equality before the law and equality of political rights for the small property owners. The Levellers were individualist rather than socialist in their radical democratic liberalism, and political rather than economic in their aims. See Diggers, the.

C. H. Firth, ed., *The Clarke Papers* (Camden, Eng., 1891-1901), 4 vols.; G. P. Gooch, *Political Thought in England from Bacon to Halifax* (London, 1914); Th. Pease, *The Leveller Movement* (Washington, 1916); G. P. Gooch, *English Democratic Ideas in the Seventeenth Century* (Cambridge, 1927); W. Haller, ed., *Tracts on Liberty in the Puritan Revolution, 1638-1647* (1934), 3 vols.

H.H.

levirate marriage: (Lat., *levir,* husband's brother) Deuteronomy 25.5-10 legislates that when a man dies without a male descendant, the widow* must not marry a stranger, but the surviving brother of the deceased must take her to wife; and the first son born of them succeeds to the name (and the property) of the deceased. This form of marriage, widely practiced among various nations, was connected in ancient Israel with the agrarian law which sought to preserve the integrity of the estate within each clan and family. (Cf. Num. 27.7-11) Taking over the land of the deceased, the brother inherits also the widow. The law also protected the childless widow by retaining her as part of her husband's family (Ruth 1.11; 3. 1ff.). The spiritual motive behind the law was to avert the extinction of the name of the deceased and possibly also to secure for him a son to perform the proper ancestral rites. Pre-Deuteronomic custom did not restrict the performance of this duty to the husband's brother, but permitted the nearest kinsman to discharge it (Gen. 38; Ruth 3-4). Both Tamar and Ruth* consider it to be their supreme obligation to supply their dead husbands with male progeny.

An aversion to the levirate marriage seems to have been attached throughout its history among the Jewish people. The Deuteronomic law (vss. 7-9) provides a substitute for it in the form of *Halizah* ("loosing the shoe") or release of the widow by the brother-in-law to marry whomever she pleases. The Code of Holiness* ignores both the levirate marriage and the Halizah, prohibiting, without exception, the marriage of a man and his brother's wife as incestuous (Lev. 18.16; 20.21). The Samaritans reconciled the discrepancy between the two codes by limiting the levirate marriage to instances where the woman was only betrothed but not yet married to the deceased brother. The Sadducees* appear to have shared this view. (Cf. Mat. 22.24ff.; Mk. 12.18 ff.; Lk. 20.27ff.) This, too, was the position of the Pharisaic school of Shammai and subsequently of some Karaites. The school of Hillel held that the law in the Holiness Code is suspended in the case of a childless widow. However, if the deceased left a child either male or female, the levirate law does not apply. According to Mt. 4.4 and Mk. 6.18 this was also the view of John the Baptist. The Rabbis in the Talmud and Codes differ as to whether levirate marriage or Halizah is preferable. Rabbi Gershom b. Jehudah of Mayence (c. 1000), by his interdict against polygamy, rendered levirate marriage impracticable. In consequence levirate marriage was completely replaced by Halizah in Ashkenazi Jewry. Inasmuch as the release becomes an empty ceremony where the levirate marriage is prohibited, Reform Judaism dropped the Halizah as requirement for childless widows for remarriage. See marriage; patriarchal system; widows, treatment of.

M. Burroughs, "Levirate Marriage in Israel," *Jour. Bibl. Liter.* (1940), 23-33; S. S. Cohon, "Marrying a Deceased Brother's Wife," *Yearbook Central Confer. Amer. Rabbis* (1925), 364-371; S. R. Driver, *Deuteronomy,* 280-285; M. Mielziner, *Jewish Law of Marriage and Divorce* (1884), 54-58; Strack-Billerbeck, *Kommentar zum n. Test.* to Matthew 22.24; J. Pederson, *Israel* (1926), 77-81.

S.S.C.

Leviticus: The third book of the Pentateuch*, which contains priestly legislation on the following subjects: sacrifices (1:1-6:7), priesthood (6:8-10:20; 21-22), purifications (11-15), sacred seasons (16, 23), meat-eating (17), marriage and chastity (18), sabbatical year and year of jubilee (25), vows and tithes (27), and various other matters. The book is wholly a product of the late priestly writer(s) designated by the symbol P*, incorporating an earlier work of the sixth century B.C., the Holiness Code* (most of chapters 17-26). In its present form Leviticus dates from cir. 500 B.C., and contains most of the P legislation as distinguished from P narrative. Except for orthodox Judaism*, the book as a whole has little more than antiquarian value today, but it does contain some high religious and ethical principles, especially in chapter 19. See A. Bertholet, *Leviticus* (Kurzer Hand-Commentar zum A.T., 1901). See Sifra. J.P.H.

Levy-Bruhl, Lucien: (1857-1939) Professor of sociology at the Sorbonne in Paris. As the most remarkable continuator of Comtian positivism*, minus its dogmatic religious and prophetic attitude, the main subject of his investigations dealt with the nature of primitive mentality of non-literate peoples. He showed by a commendable array of facts that the law of participation is the basic law of mystic mentality. He interpreted primitive mentality as pre-logical or mystical, not as anti-logical. He showed that the collective representations of primitive mentality are as a rule incomprehensible to civilized people. This is due to a greater socialization of primitive mentality.

Ethics and moral science (London, 1905); *Primitive mentality* (London, 1923); *How natives think* (1926); *Soul of the primitive* (1928); *Primitives and the supernatural* (1935). H.H.

lex divina; lex aeterna: See ius divinum.

lex evangelica: (evangelical law) It is the completion of the law of nature. H.H.

lex humana: See ius divinum.

lex naturalis: (natural law) Also called the *ius naturale* or the *ius divinum*. It designates the native direction towards the good in human reason, and embraces the immutable principles of reason for justice. It is the basis and norm for all positive law. It implies the universal ethical norms. H.H.

lex scripta: See law.

lex talionis: The law of retaliation or principle of equivalence which provided that the punishment should be the same in kind as the offense, "life for life, eye for eye, tooth for tooth," etc. (Exodus 21:23 ff.) Popularly conceived of as a primitive form of justice, it nevertheless marked an advance to a higher moral system, in which purely individual hostile acts of revenge against the transgressor were replaced by acts of socio-ethical retribution performed either by representatives of the group or by the offended individual himself under group sanctions, and in which the principle of proportion or adequacy was always the basis of retaliation. See blood revenge; law.

Rudolf Hirzel, "Die Talion," in *Philologus*, Supplementband XI (1907-1910), pp. 407-482; Ray Madding McConnell, *Criminal Responsibility and Social Constraint* (1912), pp. 22-59; Prosanto Kumar Sen, *From Punishment to Prevention* (London, 1932), pp. 15-20. H.E.J.

lexicography: The making of dictionaries especially of foreign languages, notably for the interpretation of the Hebrew O.T. and the Greek N.T. See exegesis. E.J.G.

Liber Pontificalis: (Book of the Popes) The work of a number of writers. Contains biographies of Popes* from Peter down to Stephen V (885-891). It was first given out by an unknown writer of the sixth century. Afterwards various writers added to it. Louis Duchesne's edition brings the lives up to 1431. Cf. the *Prologomena* of his work for details. C.R.

Liberal Catholic Church: A sect which has combined the esoteric ideas of theosophy* with Catholic sacramentarian notions into a ritual and created a creed of liberal thought. It claims to be a "Catholic Church" with valid orders in apostolic succession derived from the Old Catholic see of Utrecht. (See Old Catholics). One of the bishops created by the Jansenist church in Holland, James Ingall Wedgebody, was converted to or greatly influenced by the English theosophist, Charles W. Leadbeater, and consecrated Leadbeater as bishop of Australia. In 1917 Leadbeater came to America and consecrated Irving Steiger Cooper, who set up the Liberal Catholic Church in Los Angeles and became its bishop.

E. T. Clark, *The Small Sects in America* (1937); Piggott, *The Liberal Catholic Church*; Sheehan, *Teaching and Work of the Liberal Catholic Church*; Leadbeater, *The Christian Creed*. E.T.C.

liberal theology: The word "liberal" is defined by the Oxford Dictionary as "originally the distinctive epithet of those 'arts' or 'sciences' that were considered worthy of a free man, opposed to *servile* or *mechanical*." The implication is that liberalism is an educational and spiritual achievement and that it carries the dignities and responsibilities as well as the rights of freedom. In theology as in other fields the word is habitually associated with the attitudes that accompany thought and action untrammeled by prejudice or convention. Thus a liberal theologian is suspicious of authority and in revolt against it; he may or may not believe in revelation, but he tends to interpret it as continuous with and as furnishing data for rational and reflective methods of thought. He may accept the supernatural, but here again he tends to minimize its distinction from the content of ordinary experience and to find its difference from the natural in its ideal quality or the characteristics which give it value above what is usual. The liberal theologian is loyal to the religious institution but he tends, also, to consider it worthy of devotion not in itself but in so far as it becomes the bearer and representative of ideal truth. In theology as in politics the liberal is one who is favorably disposed to change, especially that which is in line with individualism and democracy.

Liberal theologians are thus bound by a common method rather than a definable common content. In his Baltimore sermon (1819) W. E. Channing* illustrated this method when he said: "Our leading principle in interpreting Scripture is this—that the Bible is a book written for men, in the language of men, and that its meaning is to be sought in the same manner as that of other books . . . We indeed grant that the use of reason in religion is accompanied with danger. But we ask any honest man to look back on the history of the church, and say, whether the renunciation of it be not still more dangerous." Liberalism became especially prominent in theology in the nineteenth and twentieth centuries as part of the general movement toward freedom of thought so that a list of liberals would include a large proportion of the outstanding theological thinkers of that period. It is a mistake, however, to think of it as limited to any one age. It springs from a way of thinking and feeling which is at least as old as the Greeks and the more humane Hebrew prophets and as new as the more recent developments in democratic theory. At present it is seriously challenged as too exclusively "rationalistic", as "blindly optimistic", and as promoting the attitude of spectator rather than participant. Its ability to meet the challenge would seem to depend upon humanity's confidence in its own capacity to assume the responsibilities of democracy and freedom. See modernist; reason in religion. Cf. fundamentalism. J.S.B.

libertarianism and necessitarianism: Respectively, belief in free-will, power in men of initial decision; denial of freedom since all action due to antecedent causes.

Science from Newton* on: unveiled necessity in nature (mechanistic naturalism); tendency ensued, helped by monistic inclination of thought, to bring ethics and psychology under same rule. 'The necessary character of our volitions fully established' (Haeckel). Resisting psychologists and moralists admitted determinism, but 'it is the self that determines' (self-determination). Present-day science wears another face; with discovery of quanta, 'physics no longer pledged to deterministic law' (Eddington). Libertarianism favored by revolt against the static in being and thought, under evolutionary and instrumentalist concepts.

Yet theoretical argument for necessity seems logically holeproof; can a mental state be other than conditioned? Against this is set 'the immediate affirmation of consciousness in the moment of deliberate action . . . I find it impossible not to think that I can now choose' (Sidgwick). There is wide acceptance of this; or since Kant, of freedom as involved in obligation; with acknowledgment that in anticipating the behavior of others our assumptions are commonly necessitarian.

The parallel issue in theology is the Pelagian-Augustinian**, some of whose elements re-appear in modern theology in Calvinism* and its contraries. Pelagius endowed man with freedom as alternate choice; Augustine viewed freedom as the establishment of the soul in goodness through indwelling grace*. Strict Calvinists feel that on any theory but theirs, there is a loophole for man becoming his own saviour; but many non-Calvinists (e.g., Evangelical Arminians*) would with equal zeal deny Pelagianism. Theology widely today seems moving toward an equilibrium of thought: God's sufficiency man's sole hope: man's answerability to God for his life and deeds. See cause; predestination.

H. V. Knox, *The Will to be Free: A critique of Deterministic Theory* (1928); N. Berdyaev, *Freedom and the Spirit* (1935); J. Maritain, *Freedom in the Modern World* (1936). J.L.

Libertines: 1) A 16th century pantheistic, antinomian sect in France and the Netherlands. Also known as the Spirituels, they denied the distinction between good and evil. 2) The political-religious party (also known as Perrinists, from their leader, Ami Perrin) which opposed Calvin's rigorous system in Geneva. They were overthrown in 1555. 3) According to Acts VI, 9, a group within the Jerusalem synagogue who opposed Stephen. They were probably descendants of Jewish freedmen who had been expelled from Rome by Tiberius. 4) In ethics: one who acts according to his lusts or impulses. E.C.K.

Libertines: A mixed group in Geneva which, from patriotic, antinomian, and other motives, resisted the discipline imposed by the Councils under Calvin's influence; also called Perrinists, after Ami Perrin, their leader from 1546. Their power, broken in 1553, was negligible by 1555. A.K.R.

libertines: A derogatory term in ethics applied to those who act without restraint, giving a free rein to their impulses and appetites. It may refer to irresponsible free-thinkers. R.W.F.

liberty: See religious liberty.

libido: See psychology, schools of.

licensed preacher: See licentiate. A.K.R.

licentiate: A person who has been authorized by competent authority, especially by a University or a Church court, to discharge the functions of a profession. In the Roman Catholic Church it signifies a friar who is authorized to hear confessions and grant absolution anywhere. In the Presbyterian Church, a licentiate is one whose right to preach has been recognized, but who has not yet been ordained and installed in a regular pastorate. A.K.R.

lie and lying: A statement made with intent to deceive and for the sake of some advantage to the deceiver. All lies are wrong according to ethical formalism because truth and truth-speaking are directly apprehended, either by intuition or reason, as having an intrinsic moral quality and as therefore unconditionally obligatory upon the moral conscience. Any deviation from the truth is wrong on these grounds. According to teleological ethical theory lies and lying are, as a rule, to be condemned because of their injurious consequences for the deceived and the deceiver. Truth-speaking is essential to human intercourse and social welfare, to personal integrity and trustworthiness. Without it human communication, social cooperation and mutual confidence would be impossible. Its value consists in its power to promote human welfare. On these grounds deception may be morally defensible in those rare cases where truth-speaking would definitely imperil life but where deception, e.g., the withholding of bad news from one critically ill, is judged likely to aid in saving it. See truth. R.W.F.

Liebner, Carl Theodor Albert: (1806-1871) He at first taught at the universities of Göttingen, Kiel and Leipzig. Then he was chief court chaplain in Dresden. He sought speculatively to attain the heights of a knowledge of God, the soul of which was an ethical mysticism. By the combination of the newer kenotism with the doctrine of the central man Christ, he built the bridge to a christocentric philosophy of history.

Die christliche Dogmatik aus dem christologischen Prinzip dargestellt (Göttingen, 1849). H.H.

Lieh Tzu: See Chinese Terminology.

Life and Advent Union: See Adventists.

light and darkness in religious symbolism: Light and darkness represent opposing principles of good and evil in religious symbolism*. The majority of religious myths posit darkness in the beginning of things. In advanced religions, light and darkness lose their physical aspects in an ethical and cosmological dualism. In Chinese religion, Yang* stands for heaven, light, truth, knowledge, order; Yin stands for earth, the lower nature, ignorance. Yang is male, Yin the female. They are two aspects of a total reality, but Heaven or Light is the higher or nobler order. Zoroastrianism* made this dualism purely ethical, one in which Light finally triumphed over darkness and evil was banished. In Buddhism*, the Buddha is associated with Light and Nirvana or pure knowledge; ignorance of the Buddha with darkness and the dull round of rebirth. In the N.T., the gospel is pictured as "the light," those without the gospel are in "darkness." A basic dualism is maintained in the conceptions of heaven and hell* in historical Christianity.

In primitive religions, light and darkness remain more as realities than symbols. Primitive peoples fear darkness; they seek to gain security by magical rites; they conceive evil spirits as enjoying darkness, fearing light. Strange phenomena-producing darkness, as an eclipse, are feared. Indeed primitive man was at a serious disadvantage in darkness compared with other animals. Religion sought through rites and mythologies to insure him against these uncertainties. Man's earliest accounts of creation, his explanations for the setting and rising of the sun, his awareness of the sun's rays, continually streaming on the earth, reveals an imagination and esthetic interest also. See article "Light and Darkness," Hastings *Encyclopedia of Religion and Ethics*, vol. 8 (1915). M.L.C.

Lightfoot, Joseph Barber: (1828-1889) Anglican theologian. He was born in Liverpool, entered Trinity College, Cambridge in 1847, and a disciple of Westcott. In 1857 he became tutor, 1861 Hulsean professor, Cambridge, and from 1875-1879 Lady Margaret Professor of Divinity, Cambridge. From 1870-1880 he was one of the revisors of the King James' Version. In 1879 he was made bishop of Durham. He died at Bournemouth.

Lightfoot was one of the outstanding N.T. scholars of the 19th century. His commentaries on the Pauline Epistles (Galatians 1865, Philippians 1868, Colossians and Philemon 1875) and his monumental edition of the *Apostolic Fathers* (5 vols. 1869-1885) are standard works in their field. On the basis of careful and extensive textual and grammatical studies he aimed at interpreting the authors out of the logic of their own thought (historical-grammatical method). He was a successful teacher, and through his numerous disciples influenced the study of exegesis in many theological schools. As minister and bishop he excelled himself no less in the clarity and depth of his sermons than in the active interest he took in church expansion work. Intimate friend of Westcott* (who succeeded him in Durham) and of Hort.

Works, not mentioned above: *Sermons* (1890-1891); *Biblical Essays* (1893); Biographies: by Hort in *Dictionary of National Biography* 33 (1893) pp. 232-240, and by H. W. Watkins (1894). O.A.P.

Liguori, St. Alphonsus: Italian bishop, born near Naples in 1696. After a short career as a lawyer, he was ordained priest in 1726 and founded in 1732 the Congregation of the Most Holy Redeemer (the Redemptorists*). In 1762 he was consecrated bishop of Sant' Agata dei Goti, resigning the see in 1775. The Roman Catholic saint of the century, he lived a life of great mortification, and is known especially for his writings on moral and ascetical theology, in which he gives proof of wise moderation and avoids with equal care rigor and laxity. He died in 1787. See equiprobabilism; probabilism. E.A.R.

limbo: (Lat. *limbus*, border, edge) The abode of those souls excluded from heaven through no fault of their own; so called because of the primitive belief that it was situated near the *borders* of hell. Roman Catholic theologians distinguish two kinds of limbo: 1) the limbo of the Fathers—a place and state of rest wherein the souls of the just who died before Christ's ascension were detained until he re-opened heaven to them, hitherto closed in consequence of Adam's fall; referred to as "Abraham's bosom" (Luke xvi, 22), "Paradise" (Luke xxiii, 43), and notably in Ephesians iv, 9, and I Peter iii, 18-20; 2) the limbo of children—Catholic faith holds that all children or adults who die without the baptism of water, blood, or desire and therefore in a state of original sin, are excluded from the vision of God in heaven (cf. beatific vision). The great majority of Catholic theologians—St. Augustine being a notable exception—teach that such children and unbaptized adults as are free from grievous actual sin eternally enjoy a state of perfect natural happiness, knowing and loving God by the use of their natural powers. This place and state is what is generally understood by the term limbo. J.F.T.

limitation: See self-limitation.

Lindberg, Conrad Emil: (1852-1930) Born in Sweden, Lindberg came to America in 1871 and in 1890 became professor of theology at Augustana Theological Seminary. Through four decades his teaching influenced the ministry of the Augustana Synod. His *Dogmatics* (Eng. tr. 1922) is a clear analysis of conservative Lutheran doctrine. C.J.B.

Ling Chos: (Tibet—*Chos,* stories; *ling,* country) Legends and tales of gods, demons, and giants; parts of an ancient pre-Buddhist religion, carried in the folklore of the peoples of Tibet. It is not entirely clear whether these religious elements derive from Indo-Europeans of Western Tibet, or the Indo-Chinese of Eastern Tibet. This ancient religion appears to have come down to the present day in the form of the Bon Chos. Tibetans call the old pre-Buddhist religion the Bon. (See Buddhist Terminology) In spite of the prevalence of basic Buddhist concepts in Tibet, many of the elements of the old Bon religion have survived within Buddhism*, as in the Ling Chos, particularly in those portions of Tibet not directly dominated by the Grand Lamas. F.L.P.

linga: The phallic* symbol under which Shiva* is almost universally worshipped in India. It represents fertility and generative power. C.S.B.

Lingayats: An Indian sub-sect of Shivism numbering about three million. Every member of the community wears a small silver box containing a stone phallic emblem, the symbol of his faith. The sect is chiefly non-Aryan, and in the beginning represented a revolt against the dominance of the Brahmans. Founded in the 12th century the movement was originally opposed to caste and child marriage and permitted the re-marriage of widows. C.S.B.

Linus: See Peter, St., First Bishop of Rome; Clement, St., Pope.

Lipsius, Richard Adelbert: (1830-1892) Professor of theology, in Kiel and Jena, Germany and in Wien, Austria. Religion was for him the solution of the riddle assigned to us by our empirical nature and our moral destiny. Dogmas of faith are descriptions of objective relations between God, man, and world. Revelation is the self-demonstration of God to man. It realizes itself in the orders of nature, of the moral world and of salvation, which are in the eternal world plan of God. Central to evangelical piety is immediate personal certainty of salvation.

Lehrbuch der evangelisch-protestantischen Dogmatik, 2 3e. (Braunschweig, 1879); *Dogmatische Beiträge* (Leipzig, 1878); *Philosophie und Religion* (Leipzig, 1885); E. Pfenningsdorf, *Vergleichungen der dogmatischen Systeme von R. R. Lipsius und A. Ritschl* (Gotha, 1896); K. Rule, *Erkenntnistheorie von R. A. Lipsius* (Gotha, 1894); A. Neumann, *Grundlagen und Grundzüge der Weltanschauung von R. A. Lipsius* (Jena, 1896). H.H.

liquors, use of: See temperance movement.

litany: (Gr. *litai,* Lat. *deprecatio litania*) Solemn intercessory prayers, often penitential, in which fixed responses are made by the people. Known in pagan and mystery religions*, in Christianity they appear in Antioch by the late 4th century and in Rome by the late 5th century. In the East they became and remain important elements of the Eucharist*. In the West they became separate services, used often in processions* as on Apr. 25, the Rogation Days*, and in times of peril. The Litany of the Saints, coming from the 5th century, appears in the Holy Saturday rite in the Roman Mass*. Other popular litanies appeared in medieval times, especially that of Loretto* and of the Holy Name. The Litany of the English Prayer Book is directed for use before the Sunday Eucharist or at other times. T.J.B.

literal interpretation: In contrast to the mystical, symbolic, typological, or allegorical types of interpretation, the literal interpretation of the Bible is according to the natural or usual construction of a passage, following the plain, ordinary, and apparent sense of the words. Greatly to be preferred to the allegorical* and other fanciful methods of interpretation, it tends to become mechanical unless applied with reference to the historical context. See exegesis. M.R.

literary criticism: See Biblical criticism.

liturgical churches: See liturgics.

liturgical movement: A revival in the Roman Catholic and Anglican Churches, dating roughly from 1920, and concerned with renewing the emphasis upon the worship of the Church as expressive both of its historic faith and of the implications of Christian "action" in personal and social life. The movement was inaugurated in Germany through the efforts of the Benedictine monks of the Abbey or Maria-Laach, under Abbott Ildefons Herwegen; others associated with the movement in Germany included Romano Guardini, whose book *The Spirit of the Liturgy* (1930—Engl. transl.) is a classic of the movement. The influence of the movement spread quickly to France, Belgium and England; and the Anglican Communion was soon affected, largely through A. G. Hebert's *Liturgy and Society* (1935). In America, the monks of the Benedictine Order (Roman Catholic), through a periodical "Orate Fratres", have popularized the ideas of the Liturgical Revival; an American Roman classic on the subject is G. Ellard's *Christian Life and Worship* (1939).

The movement is concerned to stress the centrality of eucharistic worship, as expressing the sacrifice of the whole Church, and through the Church of the whole created order, as being offered to God in union with Christ's self-sacrifice. Through this corporate offering of the Church, expression is also given to the Christian life as one of sacrifice to God; and the purpose of creation, which is to be used by God for his purposes, is declared. By carrying out the implications of this worship, Christian life is to be given significance as the manifesting through "the members of Christ" of the life of the Incarnate God who dwells in his Body the Church to restore man and human society to God and his purposes. W.N.P.

liturgics: The theological discipline which deals with Christian worship(cultus), the rites and ceremonies of the Church, its devotional and sacramental forms. The materials of liturgical science are: 1) liturgical texts and documents, including both the formularies used in the Church's worship and written directions for the due and proper execution of these formularies; 2) liturgical facts—the ceremonies accompanying the formularies of worship and sacraments, the things done as well as the words said. Its method is primarily historical; to discover the origins and trace the development of forms and ceremonies, to formulate the laws underlying their growth, to determine the persons and forces which have moulded this development, and to classify and inter-relate the several rites. On its historical side, liturgics makes use of the principles of historical and literary criticism.

Historical liturgics is of particular importance to those churches which have inherited forms and traditions of worship, those in which the cultus is basically a bequest from the past imposed by authority (the so-called liturgical churches). In the free or non-liturgical churches the historical side is of less moment and attention is directed largely to the practical: the construction and criticism of services in terms of reality, devotional value, or psychological effectiveness. Here, liturgics is perhaps less an historical science than an art—the art of worship. See hymns; liturgy; Löhe, W.; rubric; worship.

O. Hardman, *A History of Christian Worship* (London, 1937); E. Underhill, *Worship* (1937). P.V.N.

liturgy: In the Septuagint*, *leitourgia* (public work or duty) is used of the Temple ministry and services. Thence it passed into the N.T. (Lk. 1, 23, etc.) with a somewhat wider connotation. In Christian usage the term liturgy is employed: 1) Strictly, for the Eucharistic* service, the Church's public service *par excellence.* In the Eastern churches* its use is restricted to this meaning. The Divine Liturgy of the Orthodox is the equivalent of the Latin Mass. 2) More broadly, for any formal and stylized service, a rite. In this sense the term may include the Divine Office (Hours, Breviary), litanies**, and the forms used in administration of the sacraments and sacramentals. In this article we confine ourselves to the stricter and more technical meaning of the word (the Eucharist).

The historic liturgies emerge in the fourth and fifth centuries as the result of the crystalization and elaboration, with regional variations, of a primitive fluid rite such as that described by Justin Martyr (Apol. 65, 67, c. 160) and indicated by the *anaphora* in the *Apostolic Tradition* of Hippolytus (c. 220)**. While the structure of the Eucharistic liturgy was evidently determined much earlier, there is no evidence of fixed and binding forms prior to the fourth century, and improvisation continued much longer in the West, particularly in the regions of the Gallican rite*, and ceremonial elaboration by no means ceased with the fixing of the text.

The liturgies of the ancient Church are commonly classified under four basic types or families, two in the East (Greek) and two in the West (Latin).

1) Antiochene or Syrian. The so-called Clementine, in *Apost. Const.,* Bk. VIII, and the Liturgy of St. James (Jerusalem). From this is derived the Byzantine rite*, currently used in the Eastern Orthodox Church (the liturgies of St. Basil and St. John Chrysostom), the Armenian, and the orientalized East Syrian or Nestorian. The Antiochene rite proper is now used normally only by the Syrian Monophysites (Jacobites).

2) Alexandrian or Egyptian. The Liturgy of St. Mark. Surviving today among the Copts and Abyssinians.

3) Gallican, including the Celtic, Mozarabic (Spain) and the Romanized Ambrosian (Milan). The origin of the Gallican rite and its relationship to the Roman is still obscure. In the Carolingian period the Gallican was forced to yield to the Roman Mass, at the same time enriching the latter with colorful additions, but the Mozarabic* continues locally at Toledo.

4) Roman, originally terse and austere, limited to central and southern Italy (the old Roman rite), but from the eighth century enriched by borrowings from the Gallican, which it then supplanted north of the Alps.

These four families may be further reduced to two, since both of the Eastern types have common characteristics and the celebrant's prayers are not influenced by the Christian year (unvarying *anaphoras*), while both the Latin rites contain elements ("proper" collects and prefaces, etc.), changing from day to day. In the Gallican liturgies this element of seasonal variation was carried to an extreme.

Structurally, the liturgies fall into two parts:

1) The Liturgy of the Catechumens, didactic and exoteric, represents the Church's heritage from Judaism, the Christian appropriation of the synagogue services. It consists of lections* from the Scriptures, instruction, and psalmody*.

2) The Liturgy of the Faithful (offertory, consecration, communion), at which only the baptized

were allowed to be present. This is the Eucharist proper, the continuation of Christ's institution at the Last Supper, and probably also the *chaburah* fellowship of Christ and the Twelve. Opinion is sharply divided as to whether the Last Supper was a Passover meal, with the weight of the evidence against it. On Gentile soil the primitive Jewish-Christian forms of blessing (*Didache*, 9, 10) gave place to more elaborate consecration prayers (the *anaphoras**) of the third and fourth centuries, in which the offering of the eucharistic sacrifice is prominent (notably in the canon of the Roman Mass). But the Eastern rites still preserve the mystical-dramatic representation of Christ's redemptive work.

The ideal of the liturgy is corporate worship, the celebrant, deacon, lectors, cantors, choir, and people, all making their contribution to an artistic whole. Eastern Christendom has never departed from this ideal. In the medieval Western Church, on the other hand, altars and masses were multiplied, and the corporate character of worship was largely lost as the priest with server offered the sacrifice with special intention. Out of this practice (low or private masses) came the construction of Missals*, a type of liturgical book unknown in the early Church. The older Roman books, the Sacramentaries*, contain only the celebrant's part in the Eucharist and other sacraments. Cf. church year; hymns; mass, Roman Catholic; pontifical mass; Sarum Use; vestments.

Y. T. Brilioth, *Eucharistic Faith and Practice, Evangelical and Catholic* (Eng. transl. London, 1930); L. Duchesne, *Christian Worship: its origin and evolution* (5th ed., Eng. transl. London, 1927); A. Fortescue, *The Mass: a study of the Roman Liturgy* (London, 1914); D. G. Hislop, *Our Heritage in Public Worship* (1935); A. B. Macdonald, *Christian Worship in the Primitive Church* (Edinburgh, 1934); W. D. Maxwell, *An Outline of Christian Worship* (Oxford, 1936); J. H. Srawley, *The early History of the Liturgy* (Cambridge, 1913).

P.V.N.

Lives of Jesus: The gospels* were written as portrayals of the Christian message rather than as biographies of a hero. But when Tatian* (ca. 160) wove them together into his *Diatessaron*, he probably thought of it as a life of Jesus. Yet orthodox believers in the two natures of the God-man did not feel called upon to produce biographies of Jesus. Ludolf's* *Vita Christi* (d. 1377) does show, however, an example of the interest of medieval pietism. The Protestant Reformation produced no lives of Jesus.

It remained for rationalism to provide the stimulus. Lessing* published the first effort, a posthumous work by Reimarus*, *Concerning the Purpose of Jesus and his Disciples*. In contrast to the ruling supernaturalism, the aim was to give a purely rational explanation of the gospel miracles. Typical was that by H. E. Paulus (1828). Taking his clue from the idea of the Hegelian dialectic, David F. Strauss* then sought to interpret the life of Jesus from the standpoint of myth (1835); he thought that this was the synthesis between supernaturalism and rationalism. He did not believe that Jesus himself was a myth (as did later deniers of the historicity of Jesus, such as B. Bauer (1877) and A. Drews (1909), but he held that the gospels contained much mythical material. Yet men like Ewald and Neander** continued to defend stoutly the miraculous elements in the gospels.

Though Renan's* life of Jesus (1863) was a great popular success, it had no influence on research. That was dependent on the evaluation of the sources. Strauss and F. C. Baur* (1847) discounted the use of the Fourth Gospel. The demonstration of the priority of Mark by Weisse (1838) and Wilke (1838) made its way slowly at first because of the assumptions of the Tübingen school* that the Judaic Matthew must be the earliest gospel. T. Keim's massive life of Jesus (1867-72) was still written on that assumption. Yet, it really belongs with the liberal lives of Jesus which were developed under the stimulus of the Ritschlian* theology. These assumed the two-source hypothesis (that Mark and Q** were the basic documents of historical value) a theory which was firmly established by H. J. Holtzmann* (1863). Typical of the liberal lives of Jesus was the one by O. Holtzmann (1901). But the difficulties in finding a motivated life of Jesus on the basis of the Markan outline led to the skepticism of Wrede (1901) and the consequent eschatology of Schweitzer* (1901).

The latter position has been undermined by the more recent synoptic* criticism, though the importance of eschatology* for Jesus remains a permanent contribution. Wellhausen* showed that the original tradition consisted of small pericopes (1911). These were classified according to form by Dibelius (1919) and Bultmann** (1921) and others. The result is that N.T. scholarship now generally realizes that it is impossible to write a life of Jesus. No chronological framework for it exists, and the individual traditions inevitably bear the mark of the interests of the apostolic church.

Current lives of Jesus may be divided into three groups: (1) the Harmonistic lives, such as *The Days of his Flesh* by David Smith (1905); (2) Critical lives, such as those by S. J. Case (1927), M. Goguel (1933) and Chas. Guignebert (1935); (3) Studies of his teaching and career, recognizing that a "life" is impossible, such as Wernle (1918) and Dibelius (1939). The most recent survey of the lives of Jesus is that by C. C. McCown, *The Search for the Real Jesus* (1940). See Edersheim, A. C.T.C.

Living Christ: See Christ, the Living.

Livingstone, David: (1813-1873) Scottish missionary to Africa, pioneer explorer. He was born near Glasgow, worked in a cotton factory, studied theology and medicine, and sailed for Africa in 1840. There he explored the continent, healed, taught and set an unforgettable example of Christian courage and kindness until his death on his knees among his native friends. His work and writings led to the abolition of slave traffic, and the opening of the continent to the rest of the world. His explorations and scientific observations laid accurate foundations for African geography. P.E.J.

Lobstein, Paul: (1850-1922) An Alsatian theological savant who was professor at the University of Strassburg. Like Bouvier* he formulates extremely just criticisms against the traditional notion of God. He discusses in detail the theses that deny or impair the problem of the omnipotence of God. He dwells in particular upon the views of Wilfred Monod* regarding the impotence of God. He regards as indispensable the problem of divine personality and a revision of it as no less necessary. He thinks the psychological and historical methods as peculiarly applicable to the study of the problem of God. He realizes that the modern idea of personality is foreign to the biblical writings in their descriptions of the true God. Divine personality is a problem of religious knowledge. Lobstein's position here is that of the anthropomorphic symbolism as defined by Auguste Sabatier*. Liberating himself from the sterile intellectualism which weighs heavy upon traditional theology, he rejects the thesis of "the divine-human parallelism" defended by the neo-criticists and by G. Frommel*. Instead he upholds the indispensable union of psychology and history. His psychological analysis of personality remains singularly insufficient. He constantly depends upon the Bible to the exclusion of philosophic speculation. His study of the Christian doctrine of God is one of the most complete of French Protestantism.

Etudes sur la doctrine chrétienne de Dieu (Paris and Lausanne, 1907). H.H.

Loci Communes: A Latin title meaning "common topics" given by Melanchthon* to his treatise in dogmatics, the first Protestant work in systematic theology, published in 1521. The first edition adheres to Paul and Luther in presenting sin and grace, but the second edition, 1535, and the third, 1543, are synergistic*, recognizing three concurrent causes in man's conversion: the word of God, the Holy Spirit, and the human will. The title *Loci Communes* became a popular designation for doctrinal works among both Lutheran and Reformed theologians. T.A.K.

Loci Theologici: (Lat. "theological topics") A title used by early Lutheran dogmaticians for their doctrinal systems. The chief works bearing this title are those of Martin Chemnitz (1591) and Johann Gerhard (1610-1622). See Chemnitz; Gerhard. T.A.K.

Locke, John: (1632-1704) He regarded Christianity as the gospel of love. He would not demand of individuals an acceptance of the incomprehensible dogmas of the Trinity, Atonement and Eternal Punishment. He felt most drawn to those forms of Christianity which are least dogmatic and hierarchical. He laid chief stress upon the ethical side of religion, and demanded as few dogmas and ceremonies as possible. He denied anyone the right to force on others speculative opinions and definite forms of worship. He regarded revelation as an extension of natural religion founded in reason. Reason must control faith in revelation. As a dogmatic supernatural rationalist, he was in his personal life the distillation of the best qualities in Puritanism*. Although, he held, it is as certain that there is a God as it is that there are mathematical axioms, God's real essence is not known. Moreover, as we have no innate idea of God, a knowledge of Him may be attained by the right use of our abilities.

Locke's *Essay Concerning Human Understanding* (1690) is one of the most remarkable and pregnant works in the history of thought. He proposed a universal history of the mind, conceived on lines similar to Newton's physics, implying the psychological explanation of social processes without reference to the limitations by the evolution of institutions. He meant his attack on innate ideas to be a solvent for all kinds of prejudices in morality, religion and science; but as his greatest weakness as a philosopher was his inability to go back to first principles, he never perceived how far his empiricism, if logically developed, would carry him. After explaining the origin of ideas empirically, he denied the certainty of practically all empirical knowledge. In ethics and in the moral foundations of his political theory he retained the belief that a demonstrative science of morals analogous to geometry could be constructed.

As philosopher of parliamentary government, cautious exponent of a bloodless revolution, he was the most conservative of revolutionists. He championed the claims of Protestant dissent, the right of men of substance to rule, and was anxious to protect the interests of a middle class of traders and landowners against a king. Although he advocated toleration of non-conformists, he was uninterested in the wider issues of social justice. He never spoke for the disinherited. His celebrated theory of the mind as a *tabula rasa* is useful to one who wishes to insist on the doctrine of political equality, though it is difficult to reconcile with economic inequality. In his social philosophy, Locke was markedly tolerant and critical in defending religion and freedom, and yet was capable of being highly dogmatic in defending the rights of property. He held the view that certain forms of religion and irreligion are harmful to the state. Not sufficiently socialized in religious breadth and sympathy, he regarded Catholics, Jews and atheists as socially dangerous. Of what church a man is a member is no concern of the state. As a force propagating the ideals of liberal but not violent reform, Locke stands unexcelled. See Enlightenment, the.

R. I. Aaron, *John Locke* (London, 1937); E. Crous, *Die religionsphilosophischen Lehren Lockes und ihre Stellung zu dem Deismus seiner Zeit* (Halle a. S., 1910); W. Graham, *English Political Philosophy from Hobbes to Maine* (London, 1899); H. J. Laski, *Political Thought in England from Locke to Bentham* (London, 1920); H. McLachlan, *The Religious Opinions of Milton, Locke and Newton* (Manchester, Eng., 1941). H.H.

logia: Literally, announcements, oracles, sayings, —but in a somewhat elastic sense (see below).

Specifically, applied to groups of sayings of Jesus for the most part outside the gospel tradition. Thus the term was applied by Grenfell and Hunt to fragments of a collection of such sayings discovered by them at Oxyrhynchus in Egypt in 1897. It has been more commonly employed to designate a collection of sayings thought by older scholars to have been made by the apostle Matthew. The basis for this view is an enigmatic word of Papias*, preserved by Eusebius (*H. E.* iii, 39, 16): "Matthew collected the oracles (*ta logia*) in the Hebrew language, and each interpreted them as he was able."

Analysis of the three Synoptic gospels has convinced all investigators that Matthew and Luke are dependent upon Mark for most (if not all) of their narrative material. In addition to this so-called "triple tradition" Matthew and Luke have much material in common which is not found in Mark. If, as most critics assume, Matthew and Luke were produced independently of one another, the only probable explanation of this common material is a second source, commonly styled Q*, from which both independently drew. Since this "double tradition" is largely in the form of discourse, it has become the habit to refer to it as the "discourse source," and then to find an external guarantee for it in the word of Papias just quoted. Thus popularly the terms "the logia," "the Matthæan logia," "the logia referred to by Papias," or Q have been treated as equivalent titles and entirely unwarranted conclusions have been drawn.

To limit "logia" to a catena of sayings is (while popular) linguistically unwarranted. The Greek word can equally well be used of narrative stories or of a connected account containing both narrative and discourse. Sober exegesis of Papias' word would indicate that he is referring to our gospel of Matthew and not one of its sources; his five-volume work, from which this fragment comes and entitled *Exposition of the Lord's Oracles* (*logion*), may without undue violence be assumed to have been essentially a commentary upon our Matthew which Papias apparently prized highly and used as the standard for judging Mark. To continue to use logia as the equivalent of Q is misleading and deplorable.

B. W. Bacon, *Studies in Matthew* (1930).

M.S.E.

logos: The word logos is as old as the Greek language. It was introduced first by Heraclitus of Ephesus, 5th century B.C. into the circle of philosophic ideas as a principle of cosmic interpretation. Before Heraclitus, the nature of reality was thought to be mathematical (Pythagoras) and consequently static (Eleatics**). In Heraclitus' opinion the cosmos was in ceaseless change: "you could never step into the same river twice; for other and yet other waters flow on," (Diels, fr. 41-2). The cosmos is a concourse of becoming, with progressive and regressive sequences simultaneously: "fire lives the death of earth, and air lives the death of fire, (fr. 76). But "changing is rest" (fr. 84), if only stupid minds were able to grasp it. Because "the impression that any naif person gets who plants himself innocently in the flux of things, is that things are off balance," (W. James, *A Pluralistic Universe,* 88) "the philosopher . . . has to arise out of a sea of change and lay hold of true being" (Plato, *Republic,* 524 d). Philosophic wisdom, therefore, according to Heraclitus, apprehends that the total process of cosmic becoming is subjected to the regulative control of an agency to which he assigned the term logos. The logos technique accounted for the orderliness of nature. Change, if not chaos, must conform to fixed patterns. Therefore, order, law, measure, predictability, were formulations of cosmic transformations going on according to logos. "The permanence of all is preserved because all things observe their own 'measures.'" (C. Bailey *The Greek Atomists and Epicurus,* 21) "The fire is kindled in due measures and in due measures extinguished" (fr. 30). At least four fragments of Heraclitus employ logos as a principle of cosmic interpretation: "all things occur according to logos," (fr. 1), [fire] becomes liquid sea, and is measured by the same logos as it was before it became sea" (fr. 31), "logos is common-to-all" (fr. 2), "to the soul belongs the self-multiplying logos" (fr. 115). Finally, Heraclitus conceived of logos as intelligent, eternal and subjecting all change to an orderly law of change.

The term, logos, is found in both Plato and Aristotle, but in both it is vague and undeveloped. (S. D. F. Salmond, "Logos", *Enc. Brit.* (11th ed.) XIV, 803-4) Among Stoic thinkers there was injected into the logos idea theological connotations which it lacked in Heraclitus. The Stoics* were pantheists, identifying nature with God, both of which terms might serve as the context of logos. Philo* of Alexander, under the influence of Plato's demiurge, transformed the Hebrew idea of a creator God into the Platonic conception of an artisan God. Therefore, for Philo, logos is not identical with God, but something distinct and separate from Him, an instrument of creation.

Philo's conception is corrected according to the author of the Fourth Gospel*. Cannon Streeter remarks that in The Fourth Gospel Plato and Isaiah meet. (*The Four Gospels,* 367) It would be more correct to substitute Heraclitus for Plato. Heraclitus' conception of logos harmonizes with that of The Fourth Gospel. Heraclitus ascribed ultimate reality to logos. John identifies the logos with God. The Fourth Gospel claims that God and logos are two appellations for one, single divine reality and agency.

The presence of the logos idea within Christian thought signifies far more than customarily understood. Its context signals the confrontation of contrasting civilizations. Prior to The Fourth Gospel, the solution seemed to suppose either civilization could endure only by devastating the other. According to the synthesis of The Fourth Gospel, new in the Christian philosophy of history, the truth of both civilizations might endure within a new and higher synthesis wherein abiding values are merged and preserved. See Christology; spermatic word. P.R.H.

logos Christology: See Christology.

Löhe, Wilhelm: (1808-1872) Lutheran church leader. He was born in Fürth in Frankonia. As a theological student he became identified with the Lutheran revival. He is a representative of Lutheran confessionalism, with special emphasis on the centrality and dignity of the church as a historical body. Severe critic of the established church in Bavaria, he remained to the end in its service. Sacraments, liturgy and ecclesiastical organization no less than purity of doctrine were regarded as essentials of the true church. His constant emphasis on these points enabled Bavarian Lutheranism, and through it the German Lutheranism of the Middle West, to occupy leading positions in the Lutheran Church.

Löhe took a special interest in the religious and ecclesiastical needs of the German Lutheran immigrants, supported them spiritually and financially and organized them in the Missouri* Synod (1847, broke later away from L.), and the Iowa Synod (1854). In his parish Neudettelsau he founded a seminary for these churches and for Lutheran immigrants in Australia (*Neudettelsauer Missionsanstalt*). His disciples founded later on the Wartburg Seminary in Dubuque, Iowa. Löhe's personal influence survives to the present day in the educational and theological work of Prof. Martin Reu. Löhe's liturgy formed the basis of the 'Common Service of the American Lutheran Church'.

In his homeland Löhe's concept of Christian service, which he regarded as a concomitant of orthodoxy led to the formation of the Society for Inner Mission*, and to the founding of a home for deaconesses* (*Diakonissenanstalt*) in Neudettelsau (1854), and another home for male social workers in 1865. Grammar and High schools and the seminary together with homes for sick people formed a community of its own, which became a model church, famous for its reforms in architecture and liturgy. He was a strong and original personality. Great was his influence as preacher and in pastoral work. He encouraged private confession. In liturgical studies he was one of the outstanding authorities of all times. The 'Berneuchener Kreis' and the Lutheran liturgical movement are deeply indebted to him. See neo-Lutheranism.

Principal works: *Agende für christliche Gemeinden lutherischen Bekenntnisses* (1844, 3rd ed. 1884); *Drei Bücher von der Kirche* (1845, 3rd ed. 1883); *Evangelienpostille* (1848, 5th ed. 1886); *Kirche und Amt* (1851); *Epistelpostille* (1858, 3rd ed. 1897); Biography by Joh. Deinzer, 3 vols. (1873, 3rd ed. 1901). O.A.P.

Loisy, Alfred, Abbé: (1857-1940) Orientalist and Biblical critic, became the storm center of the Catholic Modernist* controversy after the publication of his *The Gospel and the Church* (1902), a reply to Harnack's *What is Christianity?* Thirty-eight of the sixty-five Modernistic propositions condemned in the Decree *Lamentabili* (1907) were concerned with Loisy's views on Biblical exegesis and Christian origins. Breaking with the Church after his condemnation, he taught many years at the *Collège de France* (1911-27). In 1917 he published a book (*La Religion*) in which he interpreted religion in purely sociological and humanistic terms, after the manner of Comte and Durkheim**. His Biblical studies run to many volumes, among which may be mentioned his books on the O.T. canon (1890), the N.T. canon (1891), the Synoptic Gospels (1893-94), the Religion of Israel (1901), the Fourth Gospel (1903), the Sermon on the Mount (1903), Mark (1912), Acts (1920), the Apocalypse (1923), and Luke (1924). Autobiography translated under the title, *My duel with the Vatican; the autobiography of a Catholic modernist* (1924).

An autobiographical essay with bibliography appears in *Religion in Transition* (London, 1937), edited by Vergilius Ferm, p. 126 ff. W.M.H.

Lokayatas: A materialistic school of philosophy in India founded by Charvaka. The adherents are known as Lokayatikas, or more frequently still as Charvakas. According to their belief matter is the only reality, mind is a function of the body. There is no soul but only intelligence, therefore with the dissolution of the material body the self returns to nothingness. On the ethical side the Charvakas esteem happiness the chief good, and this is to be found in the prudent enjoyment of sensual pleasures. They repudiate the basic beliefs of Hinduism in gods, Karma, and transmigration since these cannot be proven on the basis of sense-experience, the ultimate basis of all knowledge. Their school is no longer found as such in India today. C.S.B.

Loki: (Teut.) A Norse god of varying character: sometimes connected with the gods and sometimes with the giants; the name of an outstanding spirit of earth and underworld. In the ancient Scandinavian myth of the fall of the gods, he responded to the threat of a giant and lured Idunn, guardian of the apples of immortality, to a spot where the giant earth demon could seize her. He is represented as cunning, skillful, artistic; graceful and handsome in appearance, but lame; can assume human form. In later times he is centered in a nucleus of mythical ingredients in Christian stories about Satan*. F.L.P.

Lollards: (Literally: mumblers—of prayers and psalms) Originally applied to a Dutch group which arose at the time of an epidemic in 1350 to care for the sick and bury the dead, the name was transferred to the followers of Wycliffe* in England and Scotland. The Lollard movement was largely the result of the work of the "Poor Preachers," whom Wycliffe sent out among the common people to preach his peculiar doctrines. It grew until in the 1490's the Lollards felt strong enough to petition Parliament to aid in bringing about ecclesiastical reforms. But when Henry IV of Lancaster ascended the throne, they were persecuted and virtually wiped out under the statute *de haeretico comburendo* of 1401. Lollard sentiment survived in secret, however, and may have facilitated the introduction of the Reformation a century and a half later. See Bible, English.

J. Gairdner, *Lollardy and the Reformation in England,* 2 vols. (London, 1908).

E.C.K.

Lombard, Peter: See Peter Lombard.

longsuffering: The patient endurance of injuries and especially forebearance and loving toleration of enemies and offenders. The Greek original meant "long-tempered" as opposed to "short-tempered." In the Bible it is slowness to anger, stressed as an attribute of God and a Christian grace, a "fruit of the Spirit" in Gal. 5:22.

R.W.F.

Lord's Day: First used as a term for Sunday in Rev. 1.10 and then in Ignatius* (*Mag.* 9.1). The celebration by the Christians of the first day in the week is indicated by I Cor. 16.2 and Acts 20.7. The final form of the gospel tradition placed the resurrection of Jesus on the third day (Sunday) rather than "after three days". Though the seven day week corresponds to Jewish practice, they did not name the sabbath* for their God. In Egypt, months and days were named for gods. In Asia Minor, one day a month was consecrated to the emperor and called *sebaste.* But this was not weekly. Possibly the closest parallel is to be found in the reference by Justin to Saturday as dedicated to kronos in terms of *He kronike.* See Sabbath, Christian; Sunday.

S. V. McCasland, in *J. B. L.* 49, p. 65 ff; Paul Cotton, *From Sabbath to Sunday* (1933).

C.T.C.

Lord's Prayer: The name popularly given to the prayer found in Matt. 6:9-13 and, in a shorter form, in Luke 11:2-4. The doxology, appended to the prayer in liturgical use by Protestants, is missing from Luke entirely and from the earliest Gr. mss. of Matthew, as well as from the Vulgate*. Cf. kaddish. S.M.G.

Lord's Supper: The central rite of Christian worship, called variously the Eucharist (Greek, Thanksgiving), Holy Communion, Divine Mysteries (Eastern Orthodox), the Mass* (western Catholic usage). This service has developed historically out of the Last Supper of Jesus and his disciples before the Crucifixion, and has traditionally been related to the dominical words, "This is my body", "This is the new covenant in my blood", "Do this in remembrance of me", found in the several gospels and in I Corinthians. Two aspects have regularly been central in the Eucharist, with others finding varying emphasis: sacrifice and presence, as specially important, with memorial, thanksgiving in a restricted sense, Christian fellowship, etc., as secondary. Thanksgiving in the larger sense, however, has been a special characteristic of the rite, as based upon and representing a thanksgiving for "the benefits of Christ," and other "blessings of this life."

Various theories of the sacrifice have been held. Protestant theologians have tended to minimize this aspect, among Lutherans reaching an almost complete denial of the idea. Others would stress particularly the remembering of what Christ did, and would find a memorial of a past sacrifice on Calvary an important element in the Eucharist*. So with the followers of Zwingli. In the Catholic bodies, including Eastern Orthodox, Roman and Anglican, there has been insistence on a real sacrifice, but no agreement as to its precise nature. Anglican theology has emphasized "the continual remembrance of the sacrifice of the death of Christ", believed to be "represented" in the Eucharist; Roman theologians of recent date (esp. de la Taille, in *Mysterium Fidei*) (Eng. tr. 1941) have evolved a theory by which the Eucharist is a continual *offering* of the once-for-all *immolation* effected on Calvary, both elements of offering and immolation being essential to a true sacrifice. See liturgical movement.

The presence of Christ in the Lord's Supper has been explained by various theories, chief of which are transubstantiation, consubstantiation**, virtualism and receptionism. The first is the official Roman Catholic view, shared generally by the Eastern Orthodox (although they prefer such words as "trans-elementation" or "transmutation"); this teaches that the substances (the underlying reality as distinguished from all tangible, visible, sensible signs and appearances) of bread and wine are by consecration changed into the true body and blood of Christ, risen and glorified. The Lutheran notion of consubstantiation varies this view by insisting that to the substances of bread and wine, which remain, there are added the substances of the body and blood of Christ, truly present. (Cf. Lutheran Doctrine of the Lord's Supper). Virtualism, suggested before the Reformation by Berengar of Tours, and evidently the theory of Calvin and some other Reformers, holds that the elements remain unchanged, but through them the spiritual body and blood, and the benefits, of Christ are conveyed. Receptionism, also held by many Protestant theologians, finds a presence of Christ in the recipient, rather than in the elements of the Eucharist themselves. The Anglican Communion has never defined its theory; but in its insistence on "the real presence"* is closer to the Roman and Eastern views than to the others.

All responsible theologians, both Catholic and Protestant, hold to a truly spiritual conception of the Eucharist; as, e.g., in Aquinas's insistence on a presence "of the body of Christ", but not a "bodily presence." It is generally held that a true communion of the Christian with God in Christ is effected by the sacrament, which thereby conveys grace to the believer.

The Lord's Supper is observed with varying kinds of rites; in the Catholic communions with great solemnity and ceremonial enrichment; in the Protestant denominations more simply and, generally, rather less frequently. For further discussion, cf. D. Stone, *History of Doctrine of Holy Eucharist* (1909); and *Ministry and Sacraments* (1937) edited by Headlam and Dunkerly, in which all views of various groups are summarized. See agape; remanence; sacraments.

W.N.P.

Lord's Supper—early Christian practice and origin: No fact of the Gospel history is better attested than that Jesus, on the evening of his arrest, held a farewell Supper with his disciples. The incident is narrated in all three Synoptic Gospels, and also in I Cor. 11:23-26, where Paul explicitly says that he had received the account from the church before him. The Fourth Evangelist does not describe the Supper itself, but the central part of his Gospel is occupied with the teaching of Jesus before and after it. Of these various records the most authentic is probably the "short account" in Lk. 22:15-19,—omitting all that follows the word "body". MS evidence proves conclusively that this was how the passage originally ran in Luke, who apparently followed a primitive tradition. According to this narrative Jesus thought of the Supper as anticipating the feast of victory in the Kingdom of God*. He first took the cup, and bade all his disciples drink of it; then he broke a loaf of bread and distributed it, with the words "This is my body". The Synoptists assume that Jesus died on Passover day, and the Supper thus becomes the Passover meal, observed on the eve of the feast. John, however, is almost certainly right in dating the Crucifixion on the day before Passover*, and the Supper was therefore an ordinary meal, to which Jesus gave a sacred significance. Luke appears to suggest (22:15) that he had wished to survive until the Passover meal, but knew himself frustrated, and held this meal as a substitute. The main purpose of the Supper appears to have been to give a solemn pledge to the disciples that they would share in the victory which Jesus would achieve through his death. Much has been made of the particular elements which he took up and distributed, but apparently he made use of them because these ordinary constituents of a simple meal were all that he had before him. Emphasis is laid in all the accounts on the act of distribution, and it is probably here that we must look for the real significance of the Supper. It conveyed a promise in which all were to feel themselves included. The accounts all differ as to the formulae employed by Jesus, and agree only on the words "This is my body." The precise meaning of these words cannot be determined, but it seems best to connect them with the main idea of distribution. Jesus made each one of his disciples a participant in his own act of sacrifice. It is doubtful whether the Supper was meant to be repeated. A farewell, in the nature of things, is made once for all, and the words in which the disciples are bidden to perpetuate the ordinance were possibly added later. We can well understand, however, how the church adopted as a standing institution the act which conveyed a solemn pledge and promise. This was the more natural as it seems to have been Jesus' custom to close the day with a meal in company with his followers. After his death they continued the practice which recalled him to them more vividly than anything else, and now observed it with a special memory of his last Supper. We learn from Ac. 2:42 that the "breaking of bread" was a custom of the church from its earliest days. It was at first connected with the Agapê*, the common meal by which the believers signalized their brotherhood, but this combination of the ordinary meal with the sacred one was discontinued, owing, most likely, to such abuses as Paul condemns in I Cor. 11:20-22. In the time of Paul the Supper was second in importance to Baptism* but was fast acquiring a mystical significance, as is evident from the discussion in I Cor. 10:15-21. The influence of the Pagan cults may have had something to do with the conception of it as a literal communion with Christ. It was Paul himself who made it symbolical of the redemption effected by Christ's death. The earlier church had preserved Jesus' thought more faithfully, and had made it not so much a memorial feast as one of anticipation. Stress is laid in the opening chapters of Acts on the "gladness" which marked the primitive observance. See sacramental meal.

G. H. C. MacGregor, *Eucharistic Origins* (1929); A. B. Macdonald, *Christian Worship in the Primitive Church* (1938); W. Heitmüller, *Taufe und Abendmahl im Urchristentum* (1903; 1911).

E.F.S.

Lord's table: In I Cor. 10:21 used by metonymy for the Eucharist*; in Eastern Orthodox and Anglican liturgical books "Holy Table" is the official term for the altar (in Latin *mensa* is the top of the altar); in Protestant usage "Lord's Table" is an alternative term for the Lord's Supper* or the table used for it. See altar.

E.R.H.

Loreto, Holy House of: (It. *Santa Casa*) A small building, about thirty-one feet by thirteen feet, enshrined within the basilica at Loreto, near Ancona, Italy. Apart from unverifiable facts, a somewhat uncertain tradition claims the structure to be the house of the Holy Family at Nazareth, which was transported by angels to Illyria in 1291, and thence to Loreto in 1294. Despite the approval of the tradition by many popes and saints and the occurrence of miracles consequent upon devotion at the shrine, its historicity is held in severe doubt as a result of recent Catholic research, and is considered to rest on some unexplained misunderstanding.

J.F.T.

Lost Books of the Bible: A misnomer given some modern currency mainly through its use as a title for a 1926 reprint of William Hone's *Apocryphal New Testament,* first published in London in 1820 and actually containing the "Apostolic Fathers"*, a selection of N.T. apocrypha (Gospel of the Birth of Mary, Protevangelium of James, The Arabic Gospel of the Infancy, part of the Gospel of Thomas, The Epistles of Jesus Christ and Abgar, the spurious Epistle of Paul to the Laodiceans, the alleged correspondence of Paul and Seneca, a chapter of the Acts of Paul), and the Apostles Creed*. Later editions added the Gospel of Nicodemus (known also as the Acts of Pilate*). Also often included in this category were the medieval "Letters of Pilate and Herod" and sometimes the fragmentary second-century apocryphon, "Gospel of Peter*." The impropriety of the term is evident from the fact that most of these writings were never in the Bible nor had any serious chance for consideration as canonical. A few (I and II Clement, Letter of Barnabas, Shepherd of Hermas, Acts of Paul) were included in some ancient MSS but eventually rejected. The term is sometimes loosely and even more erroneously used of writings properly designated as spurious works or modern forgeries. See agrapha; apocrypha; canon; forgeries; pseudepigrapha. A.P.W.

lot: One of a set of objects used to secure a chance or decision in selecting officials designating preferment, dividing goods, etc. *Casting a lot*: drawing an object in a set to determine the share, the fortune, the condition or destiny of a person or thing. See sortes. F.L.P.

Lots, feast of: See Jewish religious festivals.

lottery: See gambling.

Lotze, Rudolf Hermann: (1817-1881) His creative scholarship in physiology, psychology, logic, and aesthetics form the background for an ethical idealism especially influential among Personalists*. Favoring universal mechanical causation in Nature, Lotze explained it as the "unalterable mode of action" fixed by a personal World-Ground as a prerequisite to human morality. God is the unconditioned transcendent Person, of whom all finite beings are parts without losing being-for-self (panpsychism*), and through whom alone they can enjoy reciprocal action.

Mikrokosmos (3 vols., 1856-64, Eng. tr., 1885); *Logik* (1874, Eng. tr., 1884); *Metaphysik* (1879, Eng. tr., 1884). P.A.B.

Lourdes: The name of a town in the department of Hautes Pyrenees in France. It was here between February 11 and July 16, 1858 that Our Lady appeared to a peasant girl, St. Bernadette Soubirous on eighteen different occasions. It is best known in our time as a place of pilgrimage for the sick because of the many proved and apparent miracles of healing. It is primarily, however, a pilgrimage of spiritual significance as is shown by the fact that although there are some 1,000,000 pilgrims visiting there each year, only about 15,000 are afflicted with some bodily ill. The feast of the Apparition of Our Lady at Lourdes is celebrated throughout the Western Church on February 11. T.T.M.

love: A complex psychical experience of strong attraction to, intense desire for, vivid appreciation of and joyous interest in another person, a group, cause or institution. In general it is characterized by tender affection, sympathetic understanding, admiration and loyalty with reference to its object.

There are many varieties and levels of love. Possessive or acquisitive love seeks the beloved object for the self's sake and may be gross or refined in its expression. Contemplative love admires, adores and enjoys its object as something intrinsically precious and worthy of appreciation for its own sake. Benevolent love seeks the good, increase and joy of its object. Sacrificial love counts nothing too precious, not even life itself, to be given for the sake of its object.

In Christian thought "God is love." An everlasting, all-comprehensive, benevolent and sacrificial love is held to be the very essence of God. This redeeming love was revealed in Christ who summed up the law and the prophets in the twofold commandment of love. He made the love of God the motive of obedience to His will. He made its correlative, love toward men, the basis of Christian ethics. Every commandment divinely intended to govern the relations of men was declared to be fulfilled in the law of love. Such love is set forth as both a gift of God and a task for men. The Kingdom of God* is the fellowship in which this spirit of love, born of God, animates all persons.

In Christianity Eros, the love born of natural desire or the yearnings of the soul, is held to be either transmuted or supplanted by agape*, that self-giving love whose source is God's sacrificial and redemptive love for all men. R.W.F.

love, Divine and Divine wrath: See wrath of God.

love feast: The *agape** or fellowship meal in which early Christians joined for brotherly love and commemoration of Christ's parting supper (Acts 2:42, 46; I Cor. 11:17-34; Jude 12). Paul describes such a meal as the special occasion for celebrating the Eucharist* as well (I Cor. 11:17-34). The fellowship meal was gradually separated from the Eucharist and dropped out of religious usage except as it was restored among the Moravian Brethren*, the early Methodists and other Pietistic* sects. It is still practised among the Mennonites and Dunkers** who hold a whole evening's ceremony consisting of feet-washing, the fellowship meal, and the Eucharist.

W.M.B.

lovingkindness, Old Testament conception of: This word is a mistranslation of the Hebrew word *hésed* (often translated also as "goodness", "kindness", "deal kindly"). The Hebrew term does not refer primarily to the love or the grace of God, but rather to the behavior which a covenant or blood relationship requires. In secular usage it refers to the obligations which community life, or any relationship by covenant, oath, or family tie, made necessary (cf. Gen. 24:49; I Sam. 15:6; 20:8). Since Israel believed itself to be bound in a special covenant relationship with God (see covenant), every member of the community must be loyal to the obligations of that covenant: that is, exercise *hésed*, and this involves obedience to the divine, ethical commandments which are the laws of the community, having a proper knowledge or fear (reverence) for God, being just, humble, and gracious (e.g., Micah 6:8; Hos. 2:19; 4:1; Prov. 3:3; etc.). On the other hand, God with whom the covenant has been made, will exercise or "show" *hésed* to His people: that is, will bring help and redemption to them, will be loyal to his promises, will be just, merciful, and righteous (e.g., Jer. 9:24; 16:5; Psa. 63:3; etc.). Thus "lovingkindness" or "kindness" are not proper translations of the Hebrew word. "Loyalty" or "faithfulness" are better terms, provided it is understood that loyalty to community obligations is meant (see further grace). G.E.W.

low church: The opposite of High Church* in its various senses; for positive associations see Evangelicals and Broad Churchmen. E.R.H.

low mass: See mass.

Low Sunday: Name for Sunday after Easter in English (the Latin is *Dominica in albis*, from white robes of neophytes)—origin uncertain, perhaps from *clausum paschae*. E.R.H.

Lowell Institute Lectures, The—Religious Series: John Lowell, Jr., a Boston merchant who died in 1836, left half of his estate, amounting to about $250,000, for the establishment of free public lectures in Boston, known as the Lowell Institute. The Institute is administered by a single trustee who has sole responsibility for selecting the lecturers and their subjects. Mr. Lowell directed that "each trustee shall appoint his successor, within a week after his accession to the office, in order that no failure of a regular nomination may take place. In selecting a successor the trustee shall always choose . . . some male descendant of my grandfather, John Lowell, provided there be one who is competent to hold the office of trustee, and of the name of Lowell." The first trustee was John Amory Lowell who developed the Institute most successfully in the more than forty years of his trusteeship. He was succeeded by Augustus Lowell who served until 1900, when A. Lawrence Lowell became trustee. At the death of Dr. Lowell in 1943, the trusteeship passed to Ralph Lowell. The management of the public relations of the Institute, arrangements with lecturers, distribution of tickets, etc., has been in the hands of a curator. The Institute has been fortunate in the character and ability of its curators, Dr. Jeffries Wyman (1839-42), Dr. Benjamin E. Cotting (1842-97), Prof. William Thompson Sedgwick (1897-1921), and Prof. William Henry Lawrence (1921-).

The Institute has offered lectures on a wide variety of topics. It was the express wish of John Lowell, Jr., that a course of lectures be delivered "on the historical and internal evidences in favor of Christianity" and the trustees have provided a course of religious lectures almost every year since 1839 when the public lectures began. The lecturers have represented many points of view and have been given complete freedom in the interpretation of religion.

Some outstanding lectures in the series are: *Evidences of Christianity*, by Mark Hopkins; *The Ascent of Man*, by Henry Drummond; *The Problem of Christianity*, by Josiah Royce; and *Religion in the Making*, by Alfred North Whitehead. J.E.N.

lower criticism: See Biblical criticism.

loyalty: The sentiment and practice of free, devoted allegiance to a person, group, institution or principle. It has been esteemed a cardinal virtue from its earliest tribal form through its articulate institutional embodiment in feudalism to its modern diversified expressions, notably in nationalism. While it involves obligation to what is held to be superior to the individual, as a person, group or principle by which one's conduct should be regulated, it is not mere law-abidingness. For it denotes service with one's entire heart and mind, "the team feeling," and self-identification with a whole. As such it is an important factor in self-realization and personal happiness. Many moral problems grow out of the modern conflict of loyalties. J. Royce* made "loyalty to loyalty" the central principle of his ethics. R.W.F.

Loyola: Saint Ignatius (Inigo Lopez de Loyola), founder of the Jesuits*, was born in 1491 in the Basque Province of Guipuscoa, Spain. Before his conversion in 1521, he had been a courtier and soldier. By 1523 his celebrated *Spiritual Exercises* were substantially complete. After studies at the University of Paris (1528-1535), Ignatius settled in Italy and soon became one of the most influential personalities in the Catholic Reformation. He founded the Society of Jesus in 1540, wrote its Constitutions, and governed it till his death at Rome on July 31, 1556. E.A.R.

Loyson, Fr. Hyacinthe (Charles): (1827-1912) French preacher, formerly a Carmelite, later reformer on Old Catholic lines (1869-1893); author of sermons and program of Catholic reform. E.R.H.

Lucian the Martyr (ca. 250-312) A presbyter of the church and head of a theological school at Antioch. Arius* and some of his associates were among his pupils. Revised the Septuagint* on the basis of the Hebrew text and published a recension of the Greek N.T. Suffered a martyr's death. See Antiochian school. S.M.G.

Lücke, Gottfried Christian Friedrich: (1791-1855) He taught at the universities of Bonn and Göttingen. He supplemented Schleiermacher's* hermeneutics in that he sought to give room to the contents of religious interest in the interpretation of scripture. He also was a pioneer in the awakening of church life.

Grundriss der neutestamentlichen Hermeneutik und ihrer Geschichte, 3 vols. (Göttingen, 1816); *Kommentar über die Schriften des Evangelisten Johannes* (Bonn, 1820-25, 3 ed., Bonn, 1840-56); *Versuch einer vollständigen Einleitung in die Offenbarung Johannis und die gesammte apokalyptische Literatur* (Bonn, 1832, 2 ed., Bonn, 1852). H.H.

Lucretius: (Titus Lucretius Carus) (ca. 99-55 B.C.) A Roman poet, author of *De Rerum Natura* (tr., W. H. D. Rouse, Loeb), a poetic essay on the atomic theory of Democritus and Epicurus*, written to explain the nature of the physical world so that men should cease to fear death and be free to find pleasure in life. He held that the soul is composed of very fine particles and is therefore mortal. He believed that the gods were eternal, but did not show how they fitted into his atomism. J.E.N.

Lüdemann, Hermann: (1842-1933) He taught at the University of Bern, Switzerland. He seriously struggled with Kant without being able to overcome his one-sided theory of knowledge. He constructed a world-transfigured metaphysics. He tried to work out the independence of religion in terms of a psychology that reminds us of Schleiermacher*. Christianity was for him the normative religion. In the inclusiveness and power of his thought his dogmatics kept the best idealistic inheritance vital.

Die Anthropologie des Apostels Paulus (Kiel, 1872); *Das Erkennen und die Werturteile* (Leipzig, 1910); *Christliche Dogmatik* (Bern, 1924-26). H.H.

Ludolf of Saxony: (d. 1377) A Carthusian* whose *Life of Christ* had an enormous vogue in the Middle Ages. Neither critical nor original, this work was more than a book of meditations conducing to the greater love of the Christ, human and divine. It stressed, even more, the pertinence and practicality of Christ and the Gospels to the everyday life of average men. In Ludolf's works are to be found both a beautiful, mystic insight and a prophetic challenge to renunciation and ecclesiastical reform. See Lives of Jesus.

S. J. Case, *Jesus Through the Centuries* (1932). R.C.P.

Luke, Gospel of: The first volume of Luke's two-volume work on Christian beginnings, which was written about A.D. 90, probably by Luke, the companion of Paul, in an effort to preserve the story of the rise of Christianity, which was already bidding fair to become a world religion. Luke was a Greek, and his work exhibits some of the Greek literary techniques of his day: he plans his book in two volumes, with a preface, dedication, and account of sources and purpose. He has a historical interest in ages and dates; about all we have on those subjects we owe to him. His fondness for poetry has preserved for us a series of early Christian hymns. He builds largely upon Mark*, but had two other written sources in common with Matthew*, as well as one or two of his own. He declares his purpose to be to verify the various sources known to him and unite them into one connected account. The Good Samaritan, the Prodigal Son, and the Pharisee and the Tax-collector are among the finest things we owe to Luke. The Gospel volume leaves the disciples waiting in Jerusalem for the spirit that is to come upon them precisely the point at which the second volume, the Acts*, takes up the narrative. See gospel and gospels; Synoptic Gospels.

Alfred Plummer, *The Gospel according to St. Luke* (4th ed., 1901). E.J.G.

lulab: (literally branch) The branch of the Palm tree used in connection with the ceremony of the Feast of Tabernacles*, ordained in Leviticus 23:40. To the lulab were attached three twigs of myrtle and two willow branches. Together with the etrog or citron, they were waved during the recitation of special passages from the Psalms.

Cf. I. M. Casanowicz, *Jewish Encyclopedia,* Vol. VIII, pp. 205-207. B.C.

Lullus, Ramon: (c. 1235-1316) A famed missionary leader of the Middle Ages who retired from luxury to a hermit* life in Majorca and, as a preparation for his work in the East, secured instruction in Arabic from a Moorish slave. In 1276 he established a Franciscan* college which, with linguistic studies, looked to service in African and Eastern missions. Soliciting ecclesiastical and political support for his project, East and West, he labored indefatigably as missionary, systematic theologian, and polemicist against the Saracen. He was instrumental in securing chairs of Oriental languages at Paris, Oxford, and Salamanca. Scholar, mystic, and zealous evangel for the faith, he died in 1316 from the effects of stoning by a North African mob. See Kabbalah.

W. T. A. Barber, *Raymond Lull* (London, 1903). R.C.P.

lumen naturæ: See under deism.

Lundensian theology: The name is sometimes applied to a school of theological thinking associated with the theological faculty at the Swedish university of Lund. Anders Nygren* is considered the leader, though his thinking developed under the influence of Einar Billing, Nathan Soderblom, and Gustav Aulen**, the latter being at one time a colleague in the department of systematic theology with Nygren. Aulen had already broken with Harnack's* interpretation of Christianity, when Nygren elaborated his thesis in *Eros and Agape,* (I, 1930; II, 1936). The essential nature of the Christian message is Love as Agape*, distinguished from all human forms of love as Eros. With this conception of divine love as wholly unmotivated by any quality in man, Nygren traced the varying course of Agape in Christian history. There results a new orientation of the relation of Christianity to philosophy and culture. His followers have applied the principle to the fields of eschatology, ethics (where especially the problem of the law is significant), and the history of doctrine. See neo-Lutheranism. C.J.B.

Lupercalia: (Lat. *Lupercālia,* from *lupus,* wolf; *arceo,* to ward off) An ancient Roman festival in honor of Lupercus (probably Faunus) on February 15, to secure the fertility of the fields, flocks, and people. Two youths ran a purificatory course around the Palatine with strips of goat's hide; these thongs were called *februa,* means of purification. Hence February, the month of purification. E.M.N.

Lurianic Kabbalah: See Kabbalah.

lust: (A. S. pleasure, longing; cf. lascivious) In general, any strong desire for anything, as for power; in particular, an inordinate craving for sexual pleasure. Called a capital sin because in desiring the end of lust, a person commits many other sins. L.R.W.

Lütgert, Wilhelm: (1867-1938) He taught in Greifswald, Halle and Berlin. His theological thought was characterized by a many-sidedness. In the field of systematic theology he fought for a realism of revelation against every spiritualistic idealism and naturalism. He especially aimed at the inclusion of nature into the doctrine of God and favored the restoration of the command of love in ethics.

Reich Gottes und Weltgeschichte (Gütersloh, 1928); *Der Erlösungsgedanke in der neueren Theologie* (Gütersloh, 1929); *Die Religion des deutschen Idealismus und ihr Ende,* 3 vols. (Gütersloh, 1923-25), 4th volume (Gütersloh, 1930); *A. Schlatter als Theolog innerhalb des Geisteslebens unserer Zeit* (Gütersloh, 1932); *Schöpfung und Offenbarung* (Gütersloh, 1934); *Die theologische Krise der Gegenwart und ihr geistesgeschichtlicher Ursprung* (Gütersloh, 1936). H.H.

Luthardt, Christoph Ernst: (1823-1902) He taught in Marburg and Leipzig. He was the most successful Lutheran apologist of the biblical world view against the attacks of modern natural science. See neo-Lutheranism.

Die Lehre vom freien Willen (Leipzig, 1863); *Über die Grundwahrheiten des Christentums* (Leipzig, 1864); *Über die Heilswahrheiten des Christentums* (Leipzig, 1867); *Über die Moral des Christentums* (Leipzig, 1872); *Die moderne Weltanschauung* (Leipzig, 1880); *Geschichte der christlichen Ethik,* 2 vols. (Leipzig, 1888); *Kompendium der theologischen Ethik* (Leipzig, 1896); *Kompendium der Dogmatik,* rev. ed. by R. Jelke (Leipzig, 1937). H.H.

Luther, Martin: He was born on November 10, 1483, in Eisleben as the second son of Hans Luther, a miner of peasant stock. He grew up at Mansfeld, where in the course of the years his father, by thrift and hard work, rose to a respected position in the community. After having spent his earliest school years in his home town, Luther was sent to the Latin Schools of Magdeburg (1497) and Eisenach (1498-1501). In April 1501, he matriculated in the University of Erfurt. In 1504, he obtained the B.A. degree and in April 1505 also the M.A. degree. Following the wishes of his father, who desired him to become a lawyer, he continued his studies in the juristic faculty. But on July 17, 1505, he abruptly ended these studies by entering the cloister of the Augustinian Friars of Erfurt. The reasons for this decision are not clear. Luther said later that he had become a monk "in order to get a merciful God," i.e., in order to effect such a relationship with God that he could be assured of God's love for him. He kept this purpose constantly before him, while he conformed conscientiously to the monastic discipline. Ordered to continue his studies in theology, he became a priest (April 4, 1507) and a theological teacher, gradually rising in academic rank. In 1508 he was temporarily transferred to the new University of Wittenberg, where his order had been put in charge of theological education and, in the summer of 1511, after a brief visit to Rome (1510) in connection with monastic affairs, settled there definitely. Having obtained the highest academic rank of the doctorate on October 19, 1512, he assumed the professorship in Biblical theology. He offered exegetical courses on the Psalms (1513-1515), the Epistle to the Romans (1515-1516), the Epistle to the Galatians (1516-1517), the Epistle to the Hebrews (1517-1518), and again on the Psalms (1518-1521).

In the meantime, he had religiously matured. He discovered (most probably in the period between November 1512 and July 1513) in connection with an exegetical pre-occupation with Rom. 1, 17, what he regarded as the true meaning of the Christian gospel, namely the disclosure of God's forgiving love in Christ which must be apprehended in faith and repentance. This new faith permeated his academic lectures. While it caused him to be critical of scholastic theology, it disturbed as yet neither his loyalty to the hierarchical-sacramental Roman Church nor his membership in a monastic order. He was firmly convinced that by preaching and teaching justification* by faith rather than justification by works (i.e., the accomplishment of religious moral perfection by the repentant trust in God's mercy rather than by the moral effort to conform to the divine standard of holiness), he articulated the true faith of the church.

It was this concern which caused him to publish (on October 31, 1517) 95 theses on Indulgences*. The papal practice of selling indulgences appeared to him as religiously harmful, because it tended to destroy the true spirit of repentance. His demand that the theology underlying the practice be clarified received a most unexpected response. "As if the angels were couriers," the theses were spread throughout Germany and hailed as an attack against the Roman Church. Luther suddenly ceased to be an obscure monk and professor and became a public figure. When the ecclesiastical authorities suspected him of heresy and opened a trial against him, he was compelled to defend himself and in doing so he revealed his theological attitudes. Confident that his understanding of the Christian gospel was Biblical, he refused to recant his views unless they were refuted by Biblical arguments. He gained followers among the clergy and the laity and his cause quickly became the focus of the demand for a reformation that had long been latent. Gradually he became conscious of the irreconcilability of his understanding of the gospel and that of the Roman Church. After his appearance before the papal legate Cajetanus in Augsburg (October 12-14, 1518), he appealed to a General Council and after a public debate with Professor Johannes Eck in Leipzig (July 4-14, 1519), he became convinced of the fact that the religious authority of the Papacy blocked the realization of the lordship of Christ in the hearts of Christians. In 1520 he published the pamphlets entitled "Manifesto to the German Nobility on the Improvement of the Christian Estate," "On the Babylonian Captivity of the Church," and "The

Freedom of a Christian Man." Suspecting the Papacy of being the Anti-Christ, he attacked the hierarchical organization and the sacramental practice of the Roman Church, demanded a reformation of the church according to the Bible and according to the spirit of personal freedom and responsibility. On December 10, 1520, he dramatically severed himself from obedience to the pope by publicly burning the papal bull that threatened him with excommunication unless he recanted. On January 3, 1521, the Curia answered by putting the papal ban upon him, an act which was confirmed by imperial authority at the diet of Worms (May 25, 1521), after Luther, appearing in person before the Emperor Charles V* and the German estates (on April 17 and 18, 1521), had refused to change his mind.

The reformation* was thus outlawed, but due to the political situation of Europe with which the Emperor and the Pope had to preoccupy themselves, it could not be stopped. Luther became its acknowledged leader. By nature conservative and inclined to be wary of an alliance between religion and politics, he assented only slowly to the political organization of the German Evangelicals. Yet only by this means, reformed Christian churches could come into being. But, nevertheless, until the end of his life, it remained Luther's belief "that the word must do it."

Having spent almost a year on the Wartburg, the castle of his protector Frederick the Wise, where he was believed to be safe from persecution, he returned to Wittenberg (March 1522). Having stopped there the outbreaks of an evangelical radicalism initiated by some of his colleagues and fellow monks, he resumed his academic lectures on the Bible. But his main work belonged to the extension and defense of the Reformation. The translation of the Bible, which during his exile on the Wartburg he had begun with a masterful and congenial rendering of the N.T. into German, kept him busy for more than twenty years. The rise of evangelical radicals and sectarians (he called them *Schwärmer*) compelled him to defend his work by stressing the objective and authoritative nature of the Biblical Word. A concern for the theocentric and Christocentric understanding of the Christian gospel caused him to set himself apart not only from the Humanists (in 1525 he refuted Erasmus* in his most systematic theological book "On the Bondage of the Will"), but also from Zwingli* and the Swiss Reformation (from 1525 till 1529 he was engaged in a literary debate with Zwingli on the meaning of the Lord's Supper). His refusal to sanction in the name of religion the social-economic demands of the disinherited peasants and his encouragement of princely authority to beat down the anarchistic revolution of the peasants (1525) cost him much popularity. (See peasants' war.) Henceforth he looked with suspicion upon the masses ("Master omnes") and reluctantly gave his consent to the formation of territorial state-churches (since 1526). His own chief contributions to their life were the catechisms (1529) in which he summed up his interpretation of the Christian faith in a manner that communicated the spirit of his Christian faith to many future generations. He participated in the making of creeds (Augsburg Confession*, 1530), by which the Lutherans distinguished themselves from Roman Catholics and from fellow-Protestants, but the ban of the Edict of Worms prevented him from sharing directly in the political activities by which, in the thirties and forties, the Reformation was protected and extended.

His last years were darkened by much sickness. However, the heavy burden of work and responsibility which he carried was lightened by the joy of being with his family (on June 13, 1525, he had married the former nun Katherine von Bora).

When on February 18, 1546, he died (in Eisleben, where he was born), he was sure that his work would live on. Two months later, the Lutherans were defeated in battle by Charles V and his Spanish armies, but even this catastrophe could not destroy the achievement of Luther of having won freedom for the Word of God*. See catechism; catechumenate; biblical history, Christian instruction in; festivals and holy days; hymns; justification; Theses, Ninety-five of Luther.

James Mackinnon, *Martin Luther and the Reformation,* 4 vols. (1925-30); Heinrich Boehmer, *Luther in the Light of Recent Research* (2nd ed., 1931).

W.P.

Luther League: See Young People's Societies, Christian.

Luther Renaissance: See neo-Lutheranism.

Lutheran Church in America: The Lutheran Church has been a factor in American life since the earliest colonial days. There were Lutherans in Florida in 1565 and on Hudson Bay in 1619. The first Lutheran congregations were organized by the Swedish and Finnish colonists who settled in Delaware in 1638. Their earliest pastors were R. Torkillus and J. Campanius. With the cessation of Swedish immigration, these churches became Anglican, and today such Lutheran landmarks as Gloria Dei Church in Philadelphia and Old Swedes' Church in Wilmington belong to the Episcopalians. In the Dutch colony of New Amsterdam the Lutherans had to struggle under laws permitting only the Reformed Church. Their first pastor, J. E. Gutwasser, was deported in 1659 after two years of secret ministry, and it was not until the English conquest of 1664 that congregational life became definitely established. The first German Lutheran service in America was conducted by a little group of Pietists* in Philadelphia in 1694. A decade later German Lutheran immigration to Pennsylvania began in earnest. Lutheranism was planted in the South with the arrival at Charleston, S. C., of a band of exiles from Salzburg in 1734. The oldest Lutheran congregation still in existence is St. John's in Charleston.

American Lutheranism entered upon an important new phase with the coming in 1742 of Henry Melchior Muhlenberg*, the Patriarch of the Lutheran Church in America, who envisioned a strong organized Church firmly planted in the life of the nation. He organized the scattered German congregations of eastern Pennsylvania into the first Lutheran synod in 1748, known now as the Ministerium of Pennsylvania of the United Lutheran Church. Various other synods were soon formed in the eastern and southern states. Muhlenberg's dream of an integrated evangelizing Church was not realized, however, for the distinguishing trait of American Lutheranism came to be the formation of numerous independent synods. There are still some small completely autonomous Lutheran synods, such as the Lutheran Brethren and the Eielsen Synod among the Norwegians, the Danish Lutheran Church, and three groups of Finnish Lutherans. Lutheran disunity has two main causes: 1) differences in doctrinal emphasis and 2) differences in language and national background. The seed sown by Muhlenberg had indeed come to fruition in 1821 in the Formation of the General Synod, but its leaders, especially the progressive S. S. Schmucker*, were accused of doctrinal laxity and of fraternizing with other denominations. Hence in 1861 the conservative elements withdrew to form the General Council. The southern synods, alienated from the North by the Civil War, formed their own United Synod in 1886. These three groups, however, all heirs of the Muhlenberg tradition, merged in 1918 to become the United Lutheran Church in America*. Decidedly more conservative in its doctrinal position than the old General Synod, this thoroughly Americanized body of 3,606 pastors and 1,714,945 members seeks to unite all Lutherans on the broad principles of the Augsburg Confession*.

Another spirit is represented by the Missouri Synod (see Missouri Lutherans), organized in 1847 by a new patriarch, K. F. W. Walther*, and exceeding even the Lutheran confessions in its meticulous insistence upon doctrinal correctness. To render it immune from surrounding influences the Missouri constitution originally demanded the exclusive use of the German language. Walther did much to restore emphasis upon central Lutheran principles, but his intolerance and penchant for controversy sowed disruption. The clear-cut conservative platform of Missouri, however, won many adherents, and the tremendous wave of nineteenth-century German immigration swelled their ranks. In 1872 the Missourians formed the second of the present general bodies of Lutherans by affiliating with four like-minded synods, the Joint Synod of Wisconsin, the Slovak Synod, the Norwegian Synod, and a Negro Mission, to constitute the Synodical Conference. Of its 4,922 pastors and 1,665,377 members, 4,110 pastors and 1,361,698 members belong to the Missouri Synod. Three independent conservative synods of German background, the Ohio, Iowa, and Buffalo synods, merged in 1930 to form the American Lutheran Church with 1,656 pastors and 571,545 members. This general body seeks to steer a middle course between the United Lutherans and Missouri.

With the opening of the flood-gates of Scandinavian immigration in the nineteenth century, the United States, especially the Middle West, received hundreds of thousands of sturdy pioneers with deeply entrenched and highly developed Lutheran traditions. These people had their own patriarchs organizing them into congregations and synods: the Norwegians Eielsen, the Swedes Hasselquist*, the Danes Clausen, the Finns Nikander. The largest of the Scandinavian synods are: the Norwegian Lutheran Church, formed by the merger of three synods in 1917 and having 1,473 pastors and 581,287 members; the Swedish Augustana Synod*, organized in 1860, now having 920 pastors and 356,584 members; the Lutheran Free Church (Norwegian) with 210 pastors and 49,506 members; the United Danish Church with 181 pastors and 35,845 members. These Scandinavian bodies, together with the American Lutheran Church, confederated in 1930 to form the American Lutheran Conference with a total of 4,440 pastors and 1,594,767 members. Both the American Lutheran Conference and the Synodical Conference differ from the United Lutheran Church in being only loose federations of autonomous synods.

In recent years the various Lutheran groups have drawn closer together. An important agency promoting mutual understanding and carrying out common tasks is the National Lutheran Council organized in 1918 for co-operative effort in the emergencies caused by the first World War. Representing all the important Lutheran bodies, with the exception of Missouri, it carries out co-ordinated projects of world service, social welfare, statistics, and publicity. The second World War, creating new crises in ministering to the armed forces and in maintaining mission fields, has produced new and unparalleled Lutheran co-operation. In 1941 the Lutheran bodies of America had a grand total of 13,565 pastors, 19,033 congregations, and 5,420,115 members, thus being the country's third largest Protestant denomination. See American theology, early; parochial schools.

J. L. Neve and W. D. Allbeck, *History of the Lutheran Church in America* (3d rev. ed., 1934); A. R. Wentz, *The Lutheran Church in American History* (2nd rev. ed., 1933); Vergilius Ferm, *The Crisis in American Lutheran Theology* (1927); Vergilius Ferm, editor, *What is Lutheranism?* (1930).

T.A.K.

Lutheran confessionalism: See neo-Lutheranism; Confessions, Formal of the Christian Church.

Lutheran doctrine of the Lord's Supper: The Lutherans have stressed the importance of the Lord's Supper* because of its intimate connection with the doctrine of grace*. "The chief things in the Sacrament", declares Luther's Catechism, "are the words 'given and shed for you for the remission of sins' ". The Sacrament*, therefore, is not a sacrifice, either propitiatory or eucharistic. It is not a rite by which we give something to God but a means of grace by which Christ in a peculiar and personal way gives Himself to us. As pledges of the assurance of forgiveness Christ offers His real body and blood, which the believer receives for the strengthening of faith and the unbeliever for condemnation. The emphasis on the real presence* of Christ results from taking the words of the institution in a literal sense. Luther interprets "This is my body" by the simile of the mother who points to a cradle, saying, "This is my child". Christ does not mean to say that the bread is His body any more than the mother implies that the cradle is her child. "In, with, and under" the elements of bread and wine the glorified spiritual body of Christ is present. Since in this glorified state the human nature of Christ has unrestricted use of the properties of the divine nature (communicatio idiomatum*), Christ can be bodily present everywhere (ubiquity*). This doctrine is neither transsubstantiation nor consubstantiation**. It lays primary stress neither on the faith nor on the love of the communicants but on the descending and pardoning love of Christ. The Sacrament also serves, however, as a memorial of Christ, a witness of faith, and a bond of Christian fellowship. Fidelity to the original institution led to the restoration of the cup to the laity. The doctrine is stated confessionally in Art. X, XXII, and XXIV of the Augsburg Confession* and its Apology, Luther's Catechisms, Art. VI of Schmalkald Articles, and Ch. VII of the Formula of Concord**. T.A.K.

Lutheran Free Church (Norwegian): See Lutheran Church in America.

Lutheranism in England: See England, Lutheranism in.

Lutheranism, neo: See neo-Lutheranism.

Lüttge, Willy: (1882-1928) He was professor in Berlin and Heidelberg. He concerned himself largely with questions of French Protestantism and its world view.

Die Rechtfertigungslehre Calvins (Berlin, 1909); *Religion und Dogma, ein Jahrhundert innerer Entwicklung im französischen Protestantismus* (Tübingen, 1913); *Christentum und Buddhismus* (Göttingen, 1916); "Der Pessimismus im Christentum" in *Festgabe für Julius Kaftan* (Tübingen, 1920); *Die Dialektik der Gottesidee in der Theologie der Gegenwart* (Tübingen, 1925); *Zur Krise des Christentums* (Gütersloh, 1926); *Religion und Kunst* (Gütersloh, 1929). H.H.

LXX: Abbrev. for Septuagint, designation of the O.T. in Gr. though properly applicable only to the Gr. Pentateuch. The name may be older than the legendary explanation of it given in the Letter of Aristeas (c. 100 B.C.), viz., that it was translated under extraordinary circumstances by 72 Jewish elders brought from Palestine for the purpose by Ptolemy II Philadelphus (285-246 B.C.). See Alexandrian Library; versions of the Bible, ancient. Cf. O. T. lit. R.B.Y.S.

Lyons, Councils of: Besides many provincial and diocesan synods, two general councils were held at Lyons: a) First Council of Lyons, the Thirteenth Ecumenical Council* of the Catholic Church (June to December 1245), issued no dogmatic constitutions but deposed Frederick II and voted levies for the relief of the Holy Land and the benefit of the Latin Empire of Constantinople. b) Second Council of Lyons (May to July 1274), the Fourteenth Ecumenical Council of the Catholic Church, had as its principal object the reestablishment of union between the East and the West. An ephemeral union was concluded, the "Filioque"* was solemnly defined, a profession of faith was prescribed for Michael Palaeologus, and among the reform decrees was an important one regulating papal elections. E.A.R.

Lyra, Nicolaus de: (1270-1340) French exegete; Franciscan; Sorbonne professor. His Biblical commentary, the Postillae, noted for its good presentation of the literal sense, was extensively used in the Middle Ages and by Luther. E.C.K.

M

ma'arib: (literally, who causes the evening to set) It is the evening prayer, the name being taken from the first benediction. According to a Talmudic* tradition, the Ma'arib prayer was instituted by the Patriarch Jacob. However in Talmudic times the evening prayer was regarded in some circles as optional.

J. D. Eisenstein, *Jewish Encyclopedia,* Vol. VII, pp. 233-234. B.C.

Maat: An ancient Egyptian goddess of justice, whose symbol is the ostrich feather. When the deceased is led before Osiris, king of the dead, and his court, the heart of the deceased is weighed in a balance against an ostrich feather, the symbol of Maat. F.L.P.

Maccabees: See Hasmoneans.

Maccabees, Books of: Three Jewish, historical or quasi-historical books, included in the Apocrypha of the OT,* and a fourth book, known as IV Maccabees, of philosophic and hortatory character, found in the Jewish pseudepigraphic* writings. Of these four books two, known as I and II Maccabees, deal with the struggle for religious freedom and political independence of the Jewish people, under the leadership of the five Hasmonean* brothers, against the Syrian Empire under Antiochus IV Epiphanes and his successors. III Maccabees, on the other hand, is actually a misnomer, for it deals only very remotely with this Jewish war, has but slight historical background and is in the main a legendary account of a miraculous deliverance of the Jews of Egypt from total destruction by Ptolemy Philopator. I Maccabees deals in objective and reliable historical manner with the military and political events from the accession of Antiochus Epiphanes* in 175 B.C. to the death of Simon the Hasmonean in 135 B.C. It was written in Hebrew about 100 B.C. II Maccabees is actually an epitome of an earlier history of the Maccabean war, covering only the period, 175-161 B.C., written by a Hellenistic Jew, Jason of Cyrene. Jason's history was probably written in the last quarter of the second century B.C., and II Maccabees about a half-century later. It was written in Greek. II Maccabees agrees in great measure with I Maccabees, but on the whole is less well organized and has less historical value. III Maccabees was also written in Greek, in Egypt, about 100 B.C. IV Maccabees was likewise written in Greek, for an Alexandrian Jewish audience, probably during the first half of the first century A.D. It makes frequent reference to heroic legends dealing with the Maccabean war; hence its name. See Judas Maccabeus.

R. H. Charles, *The Apocrypha and Pseudepigrapha of the Old Testament* (Oxford, 1913), I, 59-173; II, 653-685. J.M.

Macedonianism (Pneumatomachi): Name used after 380 to describe those of the Homoiousians* who regarded the Holy Spirit as a created being, subordinate to the Father and the Son (hence Pneumatomachi). Movement began in Alexandria, though name comes from Macedonius, Bishop of Constantinople, and was commonly applied to the sect after his deposition. K.H.C.

Machen, J. Gresham: (1881-1937) N.T. scholar, theologian, militant conservative leader. Graduated at Johns Hopkins University, 1901, and at Princeton Theological Seminary, 1905. After graduate study in Germany, he returned to Princeton Seminary in 1906 as Instructor in NT Greek. There he took sides with the group which opposed the policies of President Stevenson, holding, in common with that group, that the differences were basically doctrinal and were an aspect of the Liberal-Fundamentalist controversy which was then convulsing most of American Protestantism. When his group was defeated by the re-organization of Princeton Seminary in 1929, he, with three colleagues, withdrew and took an active part in the founding of Westminster Seminary, Philadelphia. In the controversies which later divided the latter group, leading to the formation of Faith Seminary, he stood for the Westminster Standards as opposed to Pre-millenialism* and Dispensationalism,* and for liberty as opposed to the "separated" life. As a result of his growing dissatisfaction with the policies of the Board of Foreign Missions of his Church (the Presbyterian Church in the U. S. A.), he was active in forming the Independent Board of Presbyterian Foreign Missions of which he became the first President. When ordered by his Church to withdraw from this Board, he refused, and, along with several other ministers, was suspended from its ministry. Accordingly a new Church was formed, in 1936, with Dr. Machen as Moderator of its first General Assembly. The new body first called itself The Presbyterian Church in America, but, when enjoined by the civil courts from the use of that title, it was renamed in 1939 The Orthodox Presbyterian Church. He died at Bismarck, N. D., January 1, 1937, while on a speaking tour in the interests of the new church. Cf. fundamentalism.

The Origin of Paul's Religion (1921); *Christianity and Liberalism* (1923); *The Meaning of Faith* (1925); *The Virgin Birth of Christ* (1930). See his essay in *Contemporary American Theology* (1932), Vol. I, edited by V. Ferm. A.K.R.

Machiavelli, Niccolo: (1469-1527) An Italian political philosopher who wished his country to become free, united, and great. He describes quite realistically the methods by which he thought that a prince untroubled by moral scruples might bring this about, using in his best known work, *The Prince* (c. 1513), Cesare Borgia as a model. W.K.W.

Mack, Alexander: (1679-1735) Born at Schriesheim, bred in the Reformed faith, and became a wealthy miller. Became a Separatist and was driven in poverty to Schwarzenau. Here, after serious study of Gottfried Arnold's works and the NT, he was the leading founder in 1708 of the German Baptist Brethren or Dunkers.* He defended their practices in *A Plain View of the Rites and Ordinances of the House of God.* In 1729 he came with a large body of them to Germantown, Pennsylvania, where he remained their leader until his death. W.M.B.

Macleod, Norman: (1812-1872) A clergyman who remained in the Established Church of Scotland* at the time of the Disruption (1843), through fear of democracy and revolution; but who strove as a preacher, an editor and a presbyter to alleviate the rigidity of his Church in thought and practice.

See D. Macleod, *Life of Norman Macleod* (1876). A.K.R.

Mādhyamaka: See Buddhist Terminology.

Madonna: (Lat. *mea domina,* my lady) A picture, statue, or other image of the mother of Christ, generally with the Child in her arms. The term is occasionally used in devotions to her. J.F.T.

Madsen, Peter: (1840-1911) A Danish theologian. Born at Binding near Holstebro. From 1875-1909 he was professor of Theology in the University of Kopenhagen and from 1909-1911 bishop of Seeland. He was an influential representative of orthodox Lutheranism in Denmark and the Scandinavian countries. Among his disciples is Alf. Theodor Joergensen in Kopenhagen. See neo-Lutheranism.

Principal works:
De Christnes aandelige praestedönne (1879, German tr. 1882); *Kenosis Laeren* (1898); *Ordinationens Betyding indenfor den lutherske Kirke-ofdeling* (1904); *Efeserbrevet* (1911, 2nd ed. 1926); *Kolosserbrevet og Brevet til Filemon* (1912); *Peters förste Brev* (1912). O.A.P.

maftir: The reader of the *haftarah** in the Synagogue* service. S.H.B.

Magdalen, Orders of St. Mary: Various religious communities of women, dating from the 11th century, dedicated to the reclamation of prostitutes and other unfortunates. At first comprised almost exclusively of penitent women, many communities eventually numbered only those of blameless reputation who tended degenerates, the sick, aged and infirm. Such institutions still exist, e.g., at Lauban, founded 1320, and Studenz. Their rule is generally based on that of St. Augustine or of St. Francis.* J.F.T.

Magdeburg Centuries: A collective historical work, the conception of which was the intellectual property of Matthias Flacius Illyricus (1520-1575), who was professor in Wittenberg and Jena. In dividing the material of the history of the church according to centuries the Magdeburg historians developed a system of heading in which everything was exactly classified. The work was the cry of a menaced and alarmed church, of protesting Protestantism, stressing the fact that the reformation was in agreement with the original apostolic church.

Ecclesia Historia, integram Ecclesiae Christi ideam . . . secundum singulas centurias perspicuo ordine complectens, 13 vols. (Basel, 1559-1574); J. S. Semler, *Centuriae Magdeburgenses,* 5 vols. (Nürnberg, 1757); W. Elert, *Morphologie des Luthertums,* 2 vols. (München, 1931). H.H.

magi: (Lat. for the Gr. *magoi*) In Matt. 2:1, Persian (or Babylonian) priests versed in astrology. In Acts 13:6, 8, the singular describes Bar-Jesus (Elymas) as a "magician" or "quack." See Zoroastrianism. S.M.G.

magic: Use of materials, rites and spells* believed to be automatically effective for the fulfilment of desires. The techniques fall roughly into three classes—the purely practical, a combination of practical and ceremonial and the purely ceremonial. When desires may be immediately satisfied by practical methods there is no need of ritual.* When there is a practical way but results are postponed or delayed ceremonies furnish psychical assurance of success as in the rites of agriculture, canoe-building, or hunting. When there is no practical method a purely ritual wish-fulfilment is attained by such forms as spell or prayer. A large proportion of these ceremonials are magic rites working by mechanical coercion of nature, spirits or gods. Some are persuasive appeals for help from personal divine beings. Both types are socially-approved religious techniques. The long debate among scholars over the relation between magic and religion was a futile discussion of an artificial problem created by arbitrarily defining religion on the pattern of Christianity with its peculiar emphasis on belief and its separation of the secular from the religious. All religions use magic. It played a dominant rôle in the religions of Babylonia, Egypt, Rome, Brahmanical Hinduism, and in the Tantric forms of both Hinduism and Buddhism.

Magic techniques range from such simple forms as the amulet* which automatically benefits its possessor, a wish embodied in emotion-charged words, a fetish working by the power of a captive spirit to such elaborate rites as the great Brahmanical sacrifices of India meticulously integrating spell, gesture and music with the acts of many priests and generating a power able to bind the gods as servants of the will of the sacrificer.

Magic is essentially wish-fulfilment. Desire flows out in word or gesture. The manifold rites take form from chance or mistaken relationships of things, taking a part of a person such as clothing, hair or name to represent him, false analogy, the release of emotion in action or words, the private or priestly control of a mysterious power. Magic used to satisfy private desires at the expense of the community is condemned but its use for such personal ends as protection of property or healing is socially approved. All desires are served by magic. The rites give assurance of success in love, labor or war, protection from dangers, cure of disease, safety from poison or the evil eye, guaranteed virility, fertility, good crops, wealth, happiness and power.

Only by their practical techniques have the peoples made their successful journey down the centuries. Magic has been a drag upon the development and introduction of practical control. On the other hand, in the absence of effective methods, it has provided cathartic, emotional release, a feeling of security and freedom from anxiety by furnishing imaginary cures for imaginary ills. See charms and amulets; exorcism; primitive religion; tabu. A.E.H.

magic: A practice based on the assumption that certain causes will produce certain effects not admitted by science. Like science, magic is based on logic, but the logic is fallacious. A large class of magical operations, known as "sympathetic" magic, depend upon the belief that certain relations between persons or things continue after the relations have ceased to exist. According to the logic of magic anything closely connected with one's person, such as hair, nails, clothing, or even name, may be used to the injury of the individual involved. Magic intended to produce evil effects is known as "black" magic and is contrasted with the use of the same methods to bring about good, and known as "white magic." Magic is responsible for the popular medical theory that "like cures like" (the bite of a dog can be cured by a hair of the animal that bit you), that warts can be removed by placing blood from the affected part on a piece of potato or bread and burying it or feeding it to a duck, that a person may be injured by melting or mutilating a wax image resembling the person to be affected, and that certain persons possess the power of injuring others by casting on them "the evil eye." Magic also plays a large part in the supposed effectiveness of many formulae, especially those used in divination* and in witchcraft. See witchcraft. Bibliography under folklore. T.P.C.

magic circle: A circle drawn around a person or object as protection from danger. The circle might be a simple line drawn on the ground, or marked by pebbles, fire, water or thorns. Sometimes a threefold circumambulation* was enough. Men who specialized in calling up spirits* for consultation stood inside a circle for safety. These circles were often made doubly secure by being inscribed with symbolic figures or divine names. A.E.H.

magister sacri palatii: (Lat. Master of the Sacred Palace) The Master of the Sacred Palace is the Roman Pontiff's personal theologian and canonist. St. Dominic* (1170-1221) was the first, and the office has always been held by a member of the Dominican Order.* The function tended to develop the Palace School*, which became the Roman Univ. in 1513. The holder of the office is a Palatine Prelate, the highest title in the pope's personal suite, though the post is no longer as important as formerly. J.F.T.

Magna Charta: (The Great Charter—originally so-called because of its length, in contrast with preceding charters.) A set of concessions extracted from King John of England in 1215 by a combination of feudal nobility, churchmen, and townspeople. Of the total of 61 original articles the majority were concerned with strengthening the position of the nobility as against the crown in the feudal system. The first article, however, enunciated the principle that elections of bishops and abbots should be free from royal influence and other articles dealt with the position of lesser figures in the feudal system and with the improvement of government in general. In later years—particularly in the seventeenth century—emphasis on these portions of the charter, fortified by a loose interpretation of the articles originally designed to benefit only the nobility, transformed the Charter into an arsenal of precedents for those working for political liberalism and ultimate democracy in England and the United States. See Langton, Stephen. M.M.K.

Magna Glossatura: See Peter Lombard.

magnificat: The hymn sung by the Blessed Virgin Mary (Luke 1:46-55), on the occasion of her visit to S. Elizabeth, before the birth of Jesus. The canticle has been incorporated in the Daily Office of the Church, and in Evening Prayer in the Anglican Communion. W.N.P.

Mahābhārata: The longer of the two great epics of India. It is the longest epic in the world containing 220,000 lines, over seven times the combined length of the Iliad and the Odyssey. It is not all strictly epic, but a combination of genuine epic and didactic material, the latter treating of politics, law, religion and other topics, and forming about three fourths of the whole. It is obviously the work of many hands, even the genuine epic portion. This was probably complete by about the beginning of the Christian era. The entire work as we have it was probably completed before 400 A.D.

The epic story is that of the struggle between the two branches of the house of Bhārata, the Kauravas, sons of the blind Dhrita-rashtra and the Pandavas, sons of his brother Pandu. During the exile of the Pandavas to the forest, friends come to comfort them and tell, among others, three famous stories that are greatly loved by Indians, Savitri and Satyavan, Nala and Damyanti and the story of Rāma* which later became India's other great epic. Probably the most notable part of the didactic epic is the Bhagavad Gīta* which has become India's best loved devotional book.

See E. W. Hopkins, *The Great Epic* (1902).
The entire epic was translated by Pratap Chundra Roy, 1883-1894. For partial translations see Romesh Dutt, *The Ramayana and Mahabharata* (London, 1929). Also Sir Edwin Arnold, *Indian Idylls* (1884). C.S.B.

Mahādeva: (Literally, great god) A variant name of the Hindu god Shiva*. Mahādevi is the wife of Shiva. C.S.B.

mahatma: (Literally, "great soul," *maha* and *atman*) A term of high respect as accorded by modern India to Mohandas K. Gandhi.*

In Theosophy* the term signifies a class of great ones, "elder brothers," "masters of wisdom and compassion," who, because of their sympathy for mankind, have renounced the privilege of continuing further in their spiritual evolution in order to help others less advanced than they themselves. They are supposed to be living in India and Tibet where Helen Blavatsky, foundress of Theosophy, had contact with them and received revelations from them. C.S.B.

Mahāvairocana: See Buddhist Terminology.

Mahāvīra: (Literally, great conqueror) It is the title given to Vardhamana generally held to be the founder of the Jain* faith. According to the Jains there have been 24 Jainas or conquerors who have become *Tirthankaras* or ford finders, of which Mahavira was the last. They are usually represented by images in Jain temples. They are not deities and can help no one, but having won through to salvation, others find help in their own efforts at salvation in contemplating them. Mahavira was an older contemporary of Gautama, the Buddha.* He placed no dependence for help on anything outside of himself; his movement was theoretically non-theistic. See virgin birth.

Mrs. Sinclair Stevenson, *The Heart of Jainism* (1915). C.S.B.

Mahāyāna: See Buddhist Terminology.

Mahdi: (Arabic, for the guided one) The future leader of Mohammedans expected to appear as a Messiah* to establish the better age to come. Other leaders (*imam*) have had their divine appointment in the past and present but the *Mahdi* will be the final leader, initiating the perfect rule of Allah on earth. The title has been assumed by several leaders of Moslem sects, but not all have accepted such leadership. See Admadiya; imam. P.E.J.

Mahzor: (Hebr. cycle) Jewish book of prayers and liturgic poems for the festivals. S.H.B.

Maimonides or Moses Ben Maimon: (1135-1204) Foremost Jewish Talmudist, philosopher and physician of the Middle Ages. Born in Cordova, Spain, he was forced in 1148 to leave his native city as a result of the Almohade invasion. In 1160, after years of wandering, he settled with his family in Fez, Morocco, whence they removed in 1165 to Fostat (Cairo), Egypt. After the death of his brother David, with whom he had participated in the jewelry trade, Moses Maimonides took up the practice of medicine. His fame as a healer caused him to be appointed as physician at the court of Saladin and his recognition as a rabbinical authority to be entrusted with the office of Nagid, *i.e.* official head of the Egyptian Jewish community. His most important works were the *Siraj*, a commentary on the Mishnah (1168), his comprehensive code of Jewish law entitled *Yad Hahazakah* (the Strong Hand) (1180) and his philosophical work "The Guide of the Perplexed," which attempted to harmonize rabbinic Judaism with Aristotelian philosophy (1190). Besides these he also wrote numerous responsa on Jewish legal questions and treatises on logic, astronomy and medicine. For a more complete enumeration of his writings, all of which, except for his code, were composed in Arabic see the *Jewish Encyclopedia*, Moses Ben Maimon. See Gerson, Levi ben; Israel, religion and theology; Judaism. S.R.

Maistre, Joseph de: (1754-1821) He was a leader of the French Catholic émigrés in their attack upon the philosophy of Voltaire and Rousseau, (*Considérations sur la France*, 1796). In his book *Du Pape* (1817) he exalts the papacy as the one absolute principle of social order in the world. In the *Soirées de St. Pétersbourg* (posthumous) he defends the social utility of war and capital punishment, and the superiority of intuition and tradition over reason. W.M.H.

Maitreya: See Buddhist Terminology.

Major (Mair), John: (1470-1550) A Scottish historian and scholastic theologian. Major taught at Paris, Glasgow and St. Andrews and wrote commentaries on the gospels and on theological and philosophical texts. His valuable *History of Greater Britain*, of which an English edition with apparatus was published by the Scottish History Society in 1892, exhibits his doctrine of limited monarchy. J.T.M.

Major Prophets: Traditional classification applying to Isaiah, Jeremiah, and Ezekiel;** based wholly on the supposed volume rather than the quality of their work; a grouping less significant since it is recognized there is no unity of authorship in any of these collections, that Ezekiel is low in quality, and that Isaiah is a complex of materials from a number of authors and periods. See Minor Prophets; prophets, prophecy, OT. R.E.W.

Majoristic controversy: A seventeenth century struggle which centered around the attitude of Georg Major (Protestant Reformer). In connection with the Leipsic Interim* (the statement of the Protestant position in the adiaphoristic controversy*), his orthodoxy regarding justification by faith was challenged. He was attacked by Amsdorf, and though at first the controversy was moderate, extreme views were advanced on both sides regarding the relation of good works to salvation. G.R.C.

majuscules: *idem* uncials*.

Malachi: An anonymous prophecy, "my messenger" (transliterated malachi) in 3:1 being mistaken as the author. This prophet was active about 460 B.C., in a time of religious slump and political humiliation due to failure of the Zerubbabel and Menahem messianic* movements. The book reflects popular hatred toward Edom, who had helped humiliate Judah. The last three verses are a supplement appended by a later editor to the completed OT. Most priestly of the prophets, the author addressed the whole book to the priests, stressing tithes, offerings, rituals, citing the high traditions of the early levitical priesthood, and upbraiding contemporary priests for their unworthiness. He told of the book of remembrance and the judgment day when God would come to refine and purge his nation. He opposed divorce, stated that other nations were more acceptable to God than Israel, and showed an international breadth of view not found since Amos.* Of post-exilic prophets, he was surpassed only by the author of Jonah.*

See *The Prophets and their Times* by J. M. P. Smith and W. A. Irwin (1941), pp. 266-70.

R.E.W.

Malebranche, Nicolas: (1638-1715) French metaphysician. See Occasionalism.

Malikites: Followers of Malik ibn Anas (713-795), Arabian jurist, widely revered as an authority on the *Koran,* and hadith** (tradition). His school of orthodox jurisprudence is still influential in Egypt and North Africa. P.E.J.

malleus maleficarum: Innocent VIII's bull, *Summis desiderantes,* (1484) gave papal support to the crusade of Henry Kramer and James Sprenger against witchcraft.* *Malleus maleficarum* (1489) was their treatise describing the manifestations of witchcraft and also prescribing appropriate answers for those who doubted the existence of devils and demons*.

See *Malleus Maleficarum,* translated with Introduction, by Rev. M. Summers (London, 1928).

D.F.E.-J.T.M.

Mamertine Prison: The medieval name (from the temple of Mars Ultor in the vicinity) of the double-chambered vault generally accepted as identical with "the prison . . . in the middle of the city, overlooking the forum," mentioned by Livy (I, 33). It now lies beneath the church of San Giuseppe dei Falegnami, via di Marforio, Rome.

J.F.T.

Mammon: (Lat. *mammona*: from Gr. *mamonas*: from Aramaic *mamona,* riches) Personified in the NT (Mt. 6:24, and Lk. 16:9-13) the term was taken by mediaeval writers to mean the devil of covetousness. From the 16th century it has been current in English as indicating the evil influence of wealth. P.E.J.

man: See Adam; anthropology; anthropology, theological; manu. The new man: See regeneration.

mana: (Melanesian) A power or influence that is inherent in, or pertains to, objects or forces in non-human nature, and to the 'dead'; a potency which spirits of nature and ghosts of the 'dead' have and can impart or convey; it may act from spirits through objects and forces. (For somewhat similar concept among Amerinds see orenda, manitou, wakanda.) See primitive religion. Cf. kami. F.L.P.

manaism: A word of doubtful utility; derived from Melanesian mana* which is not a power of universal character; is incapable of identifying a primitive religion in its wholeness aspect. F.L.P.

Manasseh: King of Judah, reigning 686-641 B.C.; most wicked of Hebrew monarchs; martyred the prophets and banished Yahwism; by reintroducing primitive faiths, idolatries, and human sacrifice, he inaugurated a renaissance of paganism in Jerusalem. See Tophet. R.E.W.

Manasses, Prayer of: A one-chapter book of the Apocrypha, based on the story of the repentance of Manasseh, King of Judah, after his imprisonment by the Assyrians (2 Chron. 33:11-13). In vv. 18, 19, we are told that the text of the original prayer is recorded in the unknown "Acts of the Kings of Israel" and "The History of the Seers."

Our apocryphal version is clearly a Jewish prayer of the devotional "hasid" style found in the later Psalms, though it is not certain that there is a Hebrew original. Jewish traditions do not know this prayer, though they have their own versions. See apocrypha, O.T. H.K.-L.F.

Mandel, Hermann: (1882-) He taught in Rostock and Kiel. Regarding Christianity as strictly supernatural, he turned his attention for apologetic purposes to the other religions and to natural morality. His theory of reconciliation combines modern historical and traditional traits.

Die Erkenntnis des Übersinnlichen (Leipzig, 1911); *System der Ethik als Grundlage der Religion* (Leipzig, 1912); *Der Wunderglaube* (Leipzig, 1913); *Christliche Versöhnungslehre* (Leipzig, 1916).

H.H.

Manegold of Lautenbach: (d. c. 1103) A German Augustinian monk who, on a contractual basis, supported Pope Gregory VII* in his struggle against the emperor, Henry IV.* He sought to justify the second excommunication of Henry as one who, having already broken his contract with his subjects, was, as a tyrant, subject to papal deposition. Manegold's theory, although obviously employed as a buttress to papal authority, had implicit in it, however, a defense of popular government. In this lies the historical significance of his work. R.C.P.

manes: In the early Roman republic, departed souls or "dead" which resided in the nether world; they were worshiped with offerings of food and drink at the graves or tombs. F.L.P.

Mani and Manicheism: During the past fifty years the materials for our knowledge of these great early rivals of Christ and Christianity have been greatly increased both in bulk and in quality. In this half century a large number of fragments of the original writings of Mani and his church have been recovered in at least three Iranian languages, in Uigur-Turkish, in Chinese, and in Coptic. The works of opponents in which Mani and the Manicheans are described and quoted have been enriched by at least one major Syriac source, Theodore bar Konai, and for the works of Augustine, the Acta Archelai, and the polemic of the Neoplatonist Alexander of Lycopolis we have new, more reliable editions. A comprehensive survey of all of the source material, new and old, published before 1918, may be found in Prosper Alfaric, *Les écritures manichéennes*, Paris, 1918-1919. This is supplemented to 1931 by A. V. W. Jackson in his *Researches in Manichaeism* (1931). The best comprehensive treatment in English, though naturally somewhat antiquated, is still F. C. Burkitt's *Religion of the Manichees* (Cambridge, 1925). The best treatment in any language is Hans Jakob Polotsky's article *Manichäismus* in Pauly-Wissowa's *Real-Encyclopädie der classischen Altertumswissenschaft*, Supplementband VI (Stuttgart, 1935), Columns 240-271; despite its late date, new publications make even this slightly out of date.

Mani, in the West named Manes or Manichaeus, was born in southern Babylonia in 215-216 A.D. His mother and perhaps his father, Patek, also, were related to the Parthian royal family of the Arsacids. His chief language was Aramaic; he knew enough Persian to compose one of his seven greater books in that language; he was apparently but little acquainted with Parthian. His father was a visionary and a member of an ascetic baptismal sect probably of simple gnostic tendencies. In his tenth year the Parthian royal house was overthrown by the Persian Sasanian dynasty. Whether or not precisely in his twelfth year, certainly at a very precocious age, he received his first revelation. Again we need not accept the second precise twelve of legend to say with fair certainty that he had completed his system, retained with little or no change thereafter, when he was still in his early twenties. In 240 or earlier his first missionary effort led him to northwestern India, perhaps following a Bardesanite trail. Late in 241 he came back to Persia for the coronation of the second Sasanian king of kings, Shapur I, at whose court he had reason to expect a favorable reception. Under Shapur, 241-272, and under his first successor, Hormizd-Ardashir, 272-273, Mani remained safe and in some measure favored by the court in Iran or on campaigns near the king in the Iranian armies' camp. Shapur, by his own inscriptions as published recently in Chicago, was and remained a professed Mazdayasnian or Zoroastrian. He does not appear ever to have become an avowed Manichaean, as two of his brothers seem to have done. But though he fostered and endowed Mazdaism,* for the first time in its history being organized as a state church, as he seems never to have done for Manicheism or any other religion, he in no way hindered, and by letters of recommendation to his subkings and governors even fostered, Manichaean missions. The curious statement about Shapur's collection of foreign literatures into a grand Avesta probably means simply that he took a kindly, paternalistic interest in all sorts of religious practices, beliefs, or missionizing in his empire, by Jews, Christians, Buddhists, Brahmins, as well as Manichaeans, allowing them considerable freedom of speech and movement and giving them police protection at court and throughout his realm. This is one of the elements of greatness in this first Shapur, never before fully recognized by historians under the influence of reports by his enemies; and this attitude was shared by the successor of his own choice, his son Hormizd-Ardashir, who was all too short-lived for the welfare and best interests of young Sasanian Iran. Complete dominance of the new state church and of its real founder and first great and fanatical leader, Kartīr, in imperial affairs begins only after Hormizd-Ardashir's early death in 273, under a far less favored, though probably elder son of Shapur I, Bahrām (in the Persian writing of his day, Varahrān) I, 273-276. Under him begins the persecution and the attempt to expel from the empire all foreign "devlish-Ahrimanic" religious belief and practice. This action is led by this same Kartīr, as he himself in a series of very extraordinary inscriptions tells us. Here for the first time, as the Arabs long ago correctly told us, the name Zandīks—false, heretical, mystical, allegorical, or typical interpreters of sacred texts, myths, and legends, Persian and others—is used of Mani's followers,—a smearing name, later in Moslem times becoming a name for heretics in general. Here for the first time Mani finds his movements restricted, then stopped by inquisitorial examination led by Kartīr, named Kerder in Parthian and Kardel in Coptic Manichaean sources, and presently so roughly handled that he died in prison in 276 A.D. He was not actually crucified, crucifixion being a mere general term for martyrdom in Manichaean diction. Contemporary sources know nothing of his having been flayed either alive or after his death, his skin stuffed with straw and exhibited to the populace, as was his head. All this is perhaps no more than the extreme expression of especially Christian hatred of a dangerous, attractive rival. His own church tells of him attended to the end by faithful women followers and his corpse, after death in prison, buried by his own people.

In the meantime his doctrine and church had prospered and spread westward through Egypt to North Africa, where it presently for a time attracted even so great a Christian theologian as Augustine,* and Rome; eastward (more precisely, northeastward), perhaps favored by one of Shapur's brothers during Mani's lifetime or shortly after, it reached the far-flung frontiers of Shapur's early Iranian empire, that is to say the boundaries of China. Later, like Nestorian* Christianity and Buddhism,* it penetrated deep into Chinese (see Chinese religions) and especially Turkish territory, where it became the official state religion and church of the Uigur Turks, sharing their fates, good and bad, until just about the end of both late in what is called the Middle Ages. What became of Mani's first foundation in India after his departure in 241 is thus far wholly unknown.

The complicated and comprehensive mythologizing worldview which constitutes the essence of the religion devised by Mani, and the ecclesiastical organization and practice that go with it, cannot here be described in detail; reference to Burkitt and especially Polotsky, with occasional additions especially by W. B. Henning and H. H. Schaeder, must suffice for this. Here a few fundamental facts only can and must be mentioned.

Mani and Manicheism is the ultimate and extreme apex reached by antique, dualistic gnosticism. He is, as the Arabs long have told us, the extremist successor more especially to two great gnostic or semignostic predecessors, the Pontian Marcion and the Syrian Bardesanes (Bardaisan), near enough to the latter, so that among other things the great, originally Bardesanite "Hymn of the Soul" and the Acts of Judas Thomas could be taken over with light retouching and small additions into the corpus of Manichaean sacred literature. But he and his followers hold him to be far more than that. His dualism is not merely Persian and an outgrowth of Zoroastrianism.* It outpasses by far any mild, refined, generally recognized form of Zoroastrianism, so that to Arabs and later Zoroastrians, *it,* and *not* Zoroastrian Mazdaism, is the real dualistic heresy. Beyond that he considers himself and is considered by his church to be the successor and consummator not only of Zoroaster and Buddha, and whatever great prophets may approach these in stature and significance, but most particularly also as the promised paraclete, who was to complete the work left unfinished by Jesus the Christ—Chrēstos. Mani distinctly prides himself on summing up within himself the essence of all such predecessors. He prides himself particularly on seeing to it in his lifetime that his gospel is preached in all sorts of terms and languages to suit the thought and feeling of all kinds of peoples which it might reach. To Christians he speaks in curiously deflected Christian terminology; to Greeks in mythologizing philosophical concepts, nailing the skins of primeval *gigantes* to the sky as constellations; to Persians he presents his great world drama in concepts drawn from all-pervading, primitive, and elemental Zervanism* rather than in terms of the new Zoroastrianism just being formulated and reformed by Kartīr in Mani's own day. He invents for the writing of Persian and Parthian in place of clumsy and complicated Pahlavi a new form of purely alphabetic writing, adopting and adapting for this purpose the Syriac-Aramaic alphabet, which with its language was his childhood heritage. For his *propaganda fidei* he further made effective use of poetry and song, of chastely fine calligraphy, illumination, graphic illustration, and in general fine bookmaking. His dramatic conception of the origin of evil in this present world and the process of salvation from it is seductively simple in its fundamental outlines and manifestly most acceptable to many men and women of his day. An aboriginal kingdom of darkness, evil, chaotic disorder, cupidity, and all manner of iniquity in mythologically primeval antiquity made an attack on an equally aboriginal kingdom of light, life, orderly peace and all manner of goodness. The attack succeeded in robbing a fairish portion of light, goodness, and beauty and in a cunning attempt to hold this loot by a self-perpetuating commingling of good and evil. The kingdom of light, incapable of unjust violence, devised a more subtly cunning method of using the ensuing mixed creation or universe for a process of gradual purificatory salvation to end in a complete restoration more stably and securely separating good and evil, light and darkness for all eternity to come. In the human world this process needed gnostic recognition for its furtherance, an elect group seeking perfection in quietistic asceticism, with a lay membership assisting and protecting them in their effort to slow down and bring to a stop the self-perpetuating commingling and to purify and refine out of it in their own persons uncontaminated light and goodness.

The adaptation of this fundamentally simple outline to a wide variety of antique mythological concepts and systems produced a complexity of dramatic action with allegory and actuality inextricably interpenetrating each other, which was clearly impressive to many sincerely searching and not too subtly sophisticated minds.

On the other hand the youthfully elementary and superficial comprehensiveness of Mani's system, ending early in unprogressively sterile fixity and rigidity, proved in the end unacceptable and intolerable to minds trained in methodical Greek and Latin thinking, the Neoplatonist Alexander of Lycopolis, Christian theologians like Augustine, Titus of Bostra, Theodore Bar Konai; to realistically imaginative Persians like the Zoroastrian Kartīr; to subtly earthy Chinese scholars; to scholastically developing Moslems. The faults and defects of Mani's worldview uncovered by such men as these are many; for us they with others are easy to discover. To these errors in large part may be due the widespread and almost universal, hostile opposition with which Manichaeism after a fair start met early, consistently, and continuously. Perhaps what has been said may in large measure account for the almost complete disappearance of the system and its continuity after brief initial success, in contrast with the persistence of systems and groups similar in kind and purpose. The brave sincerity and with it an element of greatness, not to say hugeness, in Mani's attempt to solve the riddle of this world remains as an abiding value in the story of this world of men and what they call thinking. M.SP.

manipule: (Lat., *manipulum,* handful) A decoration worn on the left arm as part of the eucharistic vestments* in the Western Church. E.R.H.

manitu, or manitou: (Algonquin) A force inherent in matter, felt as an expression of spirit; any sort of spirit, found mostly in non-human objects; medicine man or conjurer may have it. See orenda; wakanda. F.L.P.

Mañjusri: See Buddhist Terminology.

manners: See culture.

Manning, Henry Edward: (1808-1892) An English churchman who became a Roman Catholic Cardinal. A leader of the early Oxford Movement* in the Church of England, Manning was archdeacon of Chichester; he seceeded in 1851 to the Roman Church. After various offices, he became archbishop of Westminster in 1865, and later Cardinal. His works included a treatise on infallibility of the pope, and theological books on the Church. His associations with John Henry Newman* were bitter, during part of his career; and his life, written by Purcell (1896) occasioned acrimonious discussion in England. He was a strong supporter of the rights of labour, and played an important part in strikes in London during his term of office. W.N.P.

Manning, James: (1738-1791) Baptist clergyman and educator. Helped found Rhode Island College (Brown University). 1774, pleaded for civil and religious liberty before Continental Congress. Opposed to war, favored adoption of Constitution. C.H.M.

Mansel, Henry Longueville: (1820-1871) English metaphysician and churchman. Ordained priest, 1845; made Dean of St. Paul's, London, 1868. Influenced by the agnosticism of Sir William Hamilton,* Mansel affirmed the inability of man to know the necessarily-existent Absolute or God by a direct mystical apprehension, or to arrive at the Absolute or Infinite by means of the concepts of the human intellect without becoming involved in contradiction. Neither is finite and fallible man competent to render valid judgment upon the content or moral character of Christian revelation, the truth of which is guaranteed by the external supernatural evidences attending it.

Main works: *Prolegomena Logica* (1851); *The Limits of Religious Thought Examined* (Bampton Lectures, 1858); *Metaphysics* (1860); *Philosophy of the Conditioned* (1866); *Letters, Lectures and Reviews* (posthumous, 1873). H.W.J.

mantic: Of divination, in the archaic Greek period; suggests quality or ability of a person who practices seer-craft; of one who is credited with skill, often attributed to possession, in forecasting events by such omens as the actions of birds and animals. F.L.P.

mantra: A term applied in Vedic times to the hymns and prayers to the gods. It came also to mean a spell or charm and so had magical significance. The most popular mantra in Hinduism* is the Gayatri.* Mantras of different kinds are used in Hindu religious rites, varying all the way from those expressing the noblest type of religious aspiration to those of clearly magical character. See Aryan religion. C.S.B.

manu: (Literally, "man") The mythical first man. In this he shares honors with Yama in the Vedas.* In the Brahmanic flood story it is Manu who Noah-like is preserved from the great flood and becomes the father of all post-diluvian humanity. Both Manu and Yama were sons of **Vivasvant.**

The *Laws of Manu* is the greatest of ancient Hindu codes, the chief of the Dharmasastras. It is translated in *Sacred Books of the East,* Vol. 25. See food; sutras. C.S.B.

manuscripts of the Bible: MSS of the Bible are variously classified by material used, by script used, by language used, by the makeup of the book, etc.; needless to say these classifications overlap. The commonest materials are *Papyrus** (plural, *Papyri*), ancient paper; parchment or vellum, animal skins; and modern paper. Our oldest MSS are written on papyrus and come from Egypt. The oldest MSS are written in large, separate letters called uncials* or majuscules; in Greek MSS, from the 9th century on, they are written in a small, more-or-less cursive* script called minuscule. Each language has its own jargon for the varieties of its script. The MSS of the Hebrew OT are usually rolls; those of the NT (and the OT in its versions) are usually leaf-books, "codices." (See codex.)

MSS of the Bible are relatively numerous, giving a larger base for study than is available for any other ancient literature. Moreover, they are closer to their originals in date than is the case in other classics. The widest gap exists between Hebrew MSS and the author's copy; the oldest Hebrew MS of any extent comes from the 9th or 10th century. But MSS of the Greek NT reach as far back as the 2nd century. MSS of versions of the OT are as early as the 2nd century A.D., and those of the versions of the NT are not much later. See under codex.

General: Sir Frederic Kenyon, *Our Bible and the Ancient Manuscripts* (1940); I. M. Price, *The Ancestry of our English Bible: An Account of Manuscripts, Texts, and Versions of the Bible* (9th ed., 1934); E. C. Colwell, *The Study of the Bible* (1941).

Catalogues and Lists: C. D. Ginsburg, *Introduction to the Massoretico-Critical Edition of the Hebrew Bible* (London, Trinitarian Bible Society, 1897); C. R. Gregory, *Textkritik des Neuen Testaments* (Leipzig, Hinrich, 1900-1909); Alfred Rahlfs, *Verzeichnis der griechischen Handschriften des Alten Testaments* (Goettingen, 1914); H. A. A. Kennedy, "Latin Versions, the Old," in Hastings, *Dictionary of the Bible* (1900); Samuel Berger, *Histoire de la Vulgate pendant les premiers siècles du moyen age* (Paris, Hachette, 1893); Henri Quentin, *Memoire sur l'établissement du texte de la Vulgate* (Paris, Gabalda, 1922); H. Hyvernat, "Etude sur les versions coptes de la Bible," *Revue Biblique Internationale* (1896); F. Macler, *Le Texte Arménien de L'Evangile d'apres Matthieu et Marc* (Paris, Imprimerie Nationale, 1919); C. R. Gregory, *Die Griechische Handschriften des Neuen Testaments* (Leipzig: Hinrich, 1908). E.C.C.

Marburg, Colloquy of: A meeting in 1529 at Marburg of Protestant reformers in the interest of a reconciliation of Lutheran and Zwinglian views, particularly the question of the real presence in the Lord's Supper. The Marburg articles which were framed subsequently showed much agreement. The sacramental views of Luther and Zwingli** remained in open disagreement. See Philip of Hesse. V.F.

Marcellus of Ancyra: (d. c. 374) Defender of the Nicene faith, condemned and deposed by Eastern synods. In West his views came to be regarded as modification of orthodox position and were condemned. K.H.C.

Marcion, Marcionism: A highly significant second-century reformer, usually (but mistakenly) dismissed as an archheretic. Born in Pontus (*ca.* 100 A.D.), he went to Rome about the middle of the second century; soon his relations with that church too were strained. The rest of his life (about which little authentic is known, for the stories carried in the Fathers are palpably legendary) was spent in the attempt to purify Christianity from all contact with Judaism. His real cleavage with orthodoxy lay in his denial of unity to the First Principle. There were two gods, a just god depicted in the Jewish Scriptures (the *demiurge* or creator) and a good God revealed by Christ. The one demanded "an eye for an eye and a tooth for a tooth," the other "To him that smiteth on the one cheek offer also the other.' The former could say "I create evil." Since a good tree could not bring forth evil fruit, such a God could not himself be good. Hence the true word of Jesus, who came to reveal the good God who had remained undivulged from the beginning of time, was "I am not come to fulfil the law but to destroy it." Jesus, the revealer of the true God, was misunderstood by all and crucified. Only Paul properly understood him. He too fell prey to Jewish machinations. Marcion was then raised up to lift once again the torch of Paul and purge from Christianity all Jewish traces. Thus he rejected *in toto* the OT, until his time the sole inspired Christian Scripture, and in its place made the nucleus of a truly Christian Scripture the ten letters of Paul which he accepted as genuine. These he purged of the Jewish additions and accretions which had crept in after the apostle's death, and arranged them in the order of their apparent anti-Jewishness. In addition to this *apostolicon* he accepted the Gospel of Luke (but not Acts) in a probably somewhat altered form. These together with a writing of his own, the *Antitheses*, (in which he is said to have argued by a series of antithetical passages that not only was the OT contradicted by the Christian Scripture but was in contradiction to itself), thus formed the first "Christian" canon, for until his drastic step the specifically Christian writings, while coming into increasing use and favor, were not considered canonical nor put on an equality with the true Scriptures (the OT). Marcion's iconoclastic step forced the issue. Orthodoxy could not afford to ignore or deny the writings Marcion selected, nor could they appraise them less highly than had the archheretic. Precisely the writings which he had either denied or dismembered must become for an outraged orthodoxy weapons for both defense and offense. A single front was necessary; there had been too much individual action, too many individual opinions in the past. A common foe demanded a common and united answer. The faith once delivered was under attack; all must rally to its defense. Thus Marcion is to be seen as responsible for the emergence not alone of a Christian canon of Scripture but of a united (catholic) church.

The importance of his movement, which outlasted for centuries his death, is seen in the universal and savage attack it incurred. Tertullian of Carthage*, his particular enemy, devoted five flaming books to the refutation of his views, thereby immortalizing the notions he sought to destroy. Marcion and his followers are to be sharply differentiated from the run-of-the-mill second-century Gnostics; none of the mythical speculation, so prominent in the latter, was central in his thinking or in that of his earliest followers. Characterized by an austere, even ascetic, manner of life, as enthusiastic and sincere missionaries they sought to carry on their master's work. Their devotion compares favorably with that of their orthodox contemporaries by whom they were relentlessly, often savagely, opposed and later persecuted without retaliation. Many of them died as martyrs on the same funeral pyres with their orthodox opponents. See baptism for the dead.

The fullest and most adequate treatment of Marcion and his followers is A. Harnack's admirable monograph, *Marcion: das Evangelium vom fremden Gott* (1924). M.S.E.

Marcus Aurelius Antoninus: (121-180) Stoic* philosopher and Roman emperor. He was an adopted son of the Emperor Antoninus Pius. He early began the study of philosophy and later endowed chairs for the four schools of philosophy in Athens: the Academy, the Peripatetics, the Stoa, and the Garden. He developed the Stoic principles of the intrinsic value of the good will, independence of externals, conformity with nature as the expression of reason, and co-operation with other human beings. In spite of a fundamentally materialistic metaphysics, his view was essentially that of the fatherhood of God and the brotherhood of man. Nevertheless Marcus Aurelius lacked appreciation for Christianity and allowed Christians to be persecuted during his reign. Justin Martyr* addressed his *First Apology* to Antoninus Pius and his adopted sons, Marcus Aurelius and Lucius Commodus, but in vain. The *Meditations* of Marcus Aurelius are the classic expression of the Stoic philosophy.

See Sedgwick, *Marcus Aurelius* (1921). J.E.N.

Marduk: (Semitic) God of Babylon; a local Semitic god which absorbed the powers of Sumerian god of land and air, Enlil, and Ea, god of water and wisdom, to become head god of the Babylon pantheon; god of the Cosmogonic Epic, which gained power over other gods by destroying Tiamat,* and used her body to restrain the waters above and below the earth; determiner of destiny. See Mesopotamian religion. F.L.P.

Margaret of Navarre: (1492-1549) Sister of Francis I of France, was famous for the brilliant circle she gathered around herself. She was one of the leading patronesses in France of men of letters, and her court was the chief refuge of advocates of Reformed doctrines. G.R.C.

Marheineke, Philipp Konrad: (1780-1846) He taught at Heidelberg and Berlin. A many-sided and creative speculative theologian who was at first active as historian. His system of dogmatics had a profound influence upon his time. It was a popular presentation of ideas that were unusually similar to those of Daub*. He was unable to transcend the limits of speculative theology and to gain a free field for a faith-determined theology. See konfessionskunde.

System der christlichen Dogmatik (Berlin, 1847), ed. by St. Matthies u. W. Vatke; *Moral* (Berlin, 1847), ed. by St. Matthies u. W. Vatke; *Christliche Symbolik* (Berlin, 1848), ed. by St. Matthies u. W. Vatke; *Dogmengeschichte* (Berlin, 1849), ed. by St. Matthies u. W. Vatke. H.H.

Marian exiles: During the Marian reaction in England (1553-1558), some eight hundred English Protestants went into exile on the continent. When they returned on the accession of Elizabeth, they brought back the more advanced doctrines of the continental reformers.

See C. H. Garrett, *The Marian Exiles* (1938). W.S.H.

mariolatry: Idolatrous worship (latria*) of the Virgin Mary*, exceeding that veneration of the highest order (hyper-dulia*) which the Second Council of Nicea (787) following St. John Damascene*, affirms to be rightly hers because of her unique position as Mother of Christ. T.J.B.

mariology: The doctrines and opinions concerning St. Mary and her relation to the Person and work of Christ. See Virgin Mary. T.J.B.

marital impediments: Marriage*, according to the canon law*, is a permanent contractual relationship entered into for propagation and the nurture of Christian love and charity. Conditions, legally termed impediments, may preclude the conclusion of a valid contract by entailing absence of requisite physical, mental, moral, or spiritual qualifications. Impediments may be either *impedientia* or *dirimentia.* The former prevents marriage from taking place, while the latter operates to nullify a *de facto* union already concluded.

Some impediments preclude the free, mutual consent which is an indispensable prerequisite for marriage. One or both parties may lack the mental qualifications to conclude a binding contract because of immaturity, insanity, or intoxication. Naturally, no valid marriage can take place with the parties under duress.

A vow of celibacy or ordination to the four highest grades of the priesthood prevents marriage or necessitates separation. Disparity of cult arises if one party is unbaptized or baptized according to ritual not sanctioned by the church. Failure to conform to prescribed usages engenders the impediment of clandestinity. Adultery is an impediment since it violates the basically monogamous character of the marital union. Although impotence is an impediment, sterility cannot be taken as *prima facie* evidence of its existence.

Blood relationship within the fourth degree (consanguinity), as well as relationship by marriage (affinity) are impediments. Joint participation in the rituals of baptism or confirmation by the parties creates the marital impediment known as spiritual relationship, while marriage to a person who previously was betrothed to a relative may be prohibited by invocation of the impediment of "public honesty."

See consanguinity, marital impediment of.

A. Esmein, *Le mariage en droit canonique,* 2 vols. (Paris, 1891); M. Leitner, *Lehrbuch des katholischen Eherechts* (Paderborn, 1912); C. E. Smith, *Papal Enforcement of Some Medieval Marriage Laws* (1940). C.E.S.

Mark, Gospel of: The earliest of the written gospels was written in Rome, probably by Mark, in an effort to gather up and preserve those fragments of Peter's preaching which had told of his memories of Jesus. That is the tradition Papias* reports and no more probable explanation of its origin has been proposed. It consists principally of a series of incidents in which Jesus appears to do or say some extraordinary thing. There is little extended discourse; Jesus is presented rather as a doer, a man of action. Three times his life is endangered and he retreats before his foes, 3:7, 7:24, 8:27. Then at length he takes the offensive, and sets out for Jerusalem, 10:1 and 32, there to offer his message to the Jewish people gathered at their great feast. The story of their rejection of it and of his fate is a simple yet surpassing piece of heroic tragedy.

Mark was written about A.D. 70, and was soon imitated and expanded by other evangelists. It remained the pattern gospel all through the long gospel making movement, which saw the writing of a score of gospels. But no more dramatic or convincing account has ever been written of the heroic effort of Jesus to set up the Kingdom of God on earth. See Gospel and Gospels; logia; Synoptic Gospels.

B. W. Bacon, *The Gospel of Mark: its Composition and Date* (1925); E. P. Gould, *The Gospel according to St. Mark* (1913). A. Menzies, *The Earliest Gospel* (1901); B. H. Streeter, *The Four Gospels* (1925); C. G. Montefiore, *The Synoptic Gospels* (1927), vol. I, 2nd ed. E.J.G.

Marnix, Philip van: (1538-1598) Count of St. Aldegonde, poet, orator, satirist, and theologian who had studied under Calvin; a soldier and statesman, who was the closest friend and adviser of William the Silent, in the struggle for the independence of the Netherlands. A.K.R.

Maronites: A Syrian Uniate sect, inhabiting Lebanon for the greatest part, although some live in Palestine, Cyprus, and Egypt. They were organized into a separate community by monk Maro, who died in the fifth century. In 681 they separated themselves from the other Syrian Melchites. In 1182, having come into contact with the Crusaders, they accepted the supremacy of the Roman pope and have been in communion with him ever since. M.S.

Marprelate Tracts: These were bitter, taunting Puritan* polemics, published in 1588 and 1589 under the pseudonym Martin Marprelate. They were repudiated by the party leaders and met with general censure.

See William Pierce, *An Historical Introduction to the Marprelate Tracts* (1908). W.S.H.

Marquette, James: (1637-1675) French Jesuit, missionary among the American Indians of the Middle West. He founded an Algonkin mission at Sault Ste. Marie, one for the Hurons on Mackinac Island, and one for the Kaskaskia, an Illinois tribe. In 1673 he explored the Mississippi with Jolliet. Two years later he died at Ludington, Michigan. E.A.R.

Marranos: Were Spanish Jews who adopted Christianity under the stress of expulsions and riots. Jews, coerced by outward pressure to adopt *en masse* a foreign creed while secretly adhering to Judaism, are found in many historical periods and under various civilizations. They practice even today endogamous tendencies. Both as Jews and as Neo-Christians they held a prominent position in the economic life of the Iberian peninsula. From the beginning they were the victims of avarice and fanaticism. United in ethnic, social and religious bonds, facing constant common dangers, they entered into extensive cooperative relations. Not a few of them became leading anti-Jewish agitators. Syncretistic doctrinal formulations and rites assumed importance among them within two or three generations. They laid stress upon the apocryphal* books. Their influence was felt far beyond the confines of Spain and Portugal. The modern Judaism of America, England, France, Holland and Hamburg, Germany, owes its origin to no small extent to Marrano refugees. A Marrano was one of the main promoters of Columbus' expedition, another was the first Spaniard to tread American soil. These Neo-Christians shared in the upbuilding of modern capitalism; they made a great contribution to the rise of Christian Protestantism, and they played a prominent part in the international relations of the sixteenth and seventeenth centuries.

E. N. Adler, *Auto da Fé and Jew* (London, 1908); C. Roth, *A History of Marranos* (1932); L. Wolf, *The Marranos or Crypto-Jews of Portugal* (London, 1926); H. J. Zimmels, *Die Marranen in der rabbinischen Literatur* (Berlin, 1932). H.H.

marriage: Marriage is that type of sex relation which is approved as legitimate in a given society. What form of sex relation will obtain the social sanction depends on the ideologies, especially the religio-magical notions, the traditions, the economic and military organization and, possibly on other circumstances, prevailing in the society in question. Regularly no sex relation is granted that social recognition by which it is characterized as marriage unless it is meant to continue beyond sexual satisfaction, to provide the basis for the care of the offspring and to constitute the social-economic unit of a household. While polygymous and polyandrous forms of marriage are frequent among peoples of foreign civilizations, the actual existence of group marriage in the sense of sexual communism is denied by authoritative anthropological opinion. In Western civilization that form of marriage which, not without vicissitudes, has become the only permissible one to the exclusion of all others is the monogamous marriage in the sense of a union between one man and one woman involving a total communion of life between the partners and meant to persist for the entire duration of their joint lives.

Not only the general form of marriage but also its typical incidents are to a large extent socially determined by custom and the social norm systems of religion, ethics, etiquette and law. However, the limits within which the partners may work out their own individual patterns have expanded in recent times.

The marriage type sanctioned by the Christian religion is the monogamous marriage in the sense defined above, which early Christianity found firmly established in Hebrew as well as Hellenistic-Roman tradition. While early Christian and Patristic literature is indicative of an attitude in which celibacy is idealized and to which marriage appears as nothing but the *remedium concupiscentiae* and the minor evil in comparison with licentiousness, the Church at an early period came to elevate marriage to sublime dignity by endowing that human relation which involves man's most animalic function with the glory and mystery of a divine sacrament. (See sacraments) In this way marriage was not only firmly established as the basis of the family and, thereby, of all social life and organization, but also clearly marked as a spiritual union to be achieved in humble compliance with the moral and religious demands of the divine law. Individual happiness of the partners, although not recognized as the primary aim of marriage, was to be more profoundly achieved through the common strife for the establishment of a truly Christian home and family as part of the Divinely created cosmos. Indissolubility of the religious bond created through the sacrament was implied as self-evident in this Catholic notion of marriage. The fact that practice did not always come up to the standard should not detract from the appreciation of the beauty and life-strengthening force of this ideal. By attacking the sacramental character of marriage, the Reformers laid the foundation to the modern more individual notion of marriage and to a socially ambiguous attitude toward divorce. Both

Luther and Calvin admitted divorce, but not so much as a privilege of regaining one's freedom on the marriage-market as in the sense of a punishment for a party guilty of adultery or other grave marital misconduct; and all the Reformers continued to insist on the traditional Christian virtues. In England, where the Reformation started with Henry VIII's desire for a divorce from Catherine of Aragon, divorce was not recognized as a generally available remedy until 1857. Parliamentary divorce remained a rarely obtained privilege of the top-group in the hierarchy of wealth.

Legal regulations of marriage is necessary for those incidents with respect to which society cannot dispense with rules more clearly defined than the more general principles of religion or morality, or where authoritative determination is necessary in the interest of the community. The latter need exists especially with respect to the determination of the beginning and the termination of the marriage relation, whose existence or non-existence is determinative for such numerous and various problems as the existence of inheritance and dower rights, the legitimacy of the offspring, venue of the wife in civil law suits, liabilities of the parties to contract and tort creditors, the wife's domicil and so-called settlement, the children's and, frequently, the wife's nationality, the existence of community property rights, the extent of the parties' liability to income and other taxes, the existence of mutual rights of support, criminal liability for adultery and tort-liability for alienation of affections or criminal conversation (i.e., adultery), etc. Third parties must have a possibility of knowing whether two individuals are or are not married to each other and such possibility cannot be afforded by any type of regulation other than that of the law. Legal regulation is, furthermore, needed today for the enforcement of the social policies according to which certain marital unions are disapproved on ethical or medical grounds or upon grounds of racial policy; it is indispensible for the actualization of the principle which does not allow divorce except upon certain grave and narrowly defined reasons; for the enforcement of the mutual duties of support between husband and wife; and finally for the determination of conflicts about property rights that may arise between the spouses, or between one spouse and the kinship group of the other, or between the married couple and outside creditors. While most, but not all, of the property questions have long been taken care of by temporal authority, the more personal aspects of marriage were left to the jurisdiction of ecclesiastical courts until since the end of the religious wars, the co-existence in one state of several religious denominations, and, consequent thereto, the weakening of the influence of religion upon the masses, necessitated the replacement of ecclesiastical regulation of marriage by temporal legislation and jurisdiction. In the English colonies which were later to become the United States of America, jurisdiction of the ecclesiastical courts* of England was hardly recognized and temporal jurisdiction over marriage became firmly established. In the European continent, with the exception of Czarist Russia and the Balkan countries, marriage was secularized in the century following the French Revolution. In England the ecclesiastical courts were deprived of jurisdiction over matrimonial causes in 1857. In contrast to those numerous continental countries where a civil ceremony was made compulsory for the conclusion of marriage, in the United States and England, marriage before a minister of the Gospel is still optional with the parties. 19 of the United States have even preserved the anachronism of marriage without any initiating ceremony, so-called Common Law marriage.

The most conspicuous trend in the development of marriage in Western civilization is what may be called its individualization. Ever since the period of the Troubadours the ideal of marriage as a union based upon romantic love and entered for the purpose of achieving the parties' individual happiness through the fulfillment of such love has slowly and gradually replaced the older notion of marriage as an arrangement not so much between two individuals as between two families. The most radical actualization of this romantic notion of marriage has taken place in the United States, where the idea that marriage is primarily a means toward the achievement of individual happiness has resulted in the highest divorce rate on earth. Since 1932 about one out of every six marriages has ended in divorce. In 1935 divorce rates per 1000 population were as follows: United States, 1.710; Denmark, .809; Germany, .752; Japan .701; France, .501; Sweden, .434; Norway, .313; England, .100; Scotland, .101; Canada, .126.

The Soviet Union which, upon the basis of Marxist theories, started out upon its existence with a similar individualistic notion of marriage, has in recent years veered toward the more rigid conception of marriage constituting a service to the community which, if necessary, may be entitled to ask for the sacrifice of individual happiness to its higher aims.

The individualization of marriage has also found expression in the changed position of the wife. Older social and legal conceptions recognized that the basic social unit is not the individual but the family. In ancient Rome the law of the state in most respects did not deal with individuals at all but with households represented by their heads, the paterfamilias. In a similar way English Common Law only dealt with the husband-father in whose person the wife was regarded as legally merged. Such notions became intolerable with the social emancipation of women in the 19th century. However, instead of constituting the family as a unit with two equal managers the English and American Married Women's Acts brought about a situation in which husband and wife are regarded as almost complete strangers to each other as far as property relations are concerned. Only nine states in the Southwest and Far West, following continental European models, have adopted various systems of community property, under which marriage appears as constituting a sort of co-partnership between two equal partners.

Among some sociologists it has become fashionable to speak of a breakdown of marriage and the family. Undeniably the family has lost numerous of its former functions in consequence of the Industrial Revolution and the urbanization of large masses of the people. However, in spite of modern techniques of birth-control, monogamous marriage continues to constitute the only socially recognized type of sex relation and no other solution has so far been offered for the continuing needs of a companionship lasting from early love through the vicissitudes of life into the days of grey hair, of a relation founded upon absolute stability and mutual reliance, and of a home for parents and offspring that always constitutes a heaven of confidence and refuge in an unstable world. The family is still the basic social unit of consumption, to a large extent the unit of recreation and in important respect, even still a unit of production. In spite of rising divorce rates and falling birth rates, marriage continues for the majority of the people to be a union "in sickness and in health, for better or for worse, until death do us part." See child marriage; consanguinity; divorce; double standard of morals; endogamy; exogamy; family; infidelity; illegitimacy; levirate marriage; marital impediments; matriarchal system; motherhood; ne temere; patriarchal system; polyandry; polygamy; polygany; tempus clausum; woman, religious and ethical status of; widows, treatment of.

Federal Council of the Churches of Christ in America, Commission on the Church and Social Service, Committee on Marriage and the Home, Ideals of Love and Marriage (1932); Pius XI, *Encyclical on Christian Marriage (Casti Connubii)*, (1931); Bertrand Russell, *Marriage and Morals* (1929) (a radical attack upon traditional attitudes); Lowie, Art. "Marriage," vol. 10 *Enc. Soc. Sci.* p. 154 (with extensive bibliography); Library of Congress, Division of Bibliography, *Marriage and Divorce: A Selected Bibliography* (1940); K. Llewellyn, Behind the Law of Marriage and Divorce, *Columbia Law Rev.* (1932-33) Vol. 32., p. 1281 and Vol. 35 p. 249. M.Rh.

Mars: (Lat. *Mars,* the gleaming one) In the earliest times, an agricultural divinity (whence the month March), developing with the city-state into a god of war. The low land in the bend of the Tiber, where his altar stood, bore his name, the Campus Martius. He was identified with the Greek Ares. Hence the old translation, Mars Hill for Areopagus, in Acts xvii:22. E.M.N.

Marsh, James (1794-1847) James Marsh was born in Hartford, Vt., graduated from Dartmouth College, studied at Andover Seminary (where he devoted himself especially to the study of Plato, Kant and Coleridge). He was elected President of the University of Vermont in 1826, resigned in 1833 to take the chair of Philosophy in whose occupancy he exerted marked influence.

Marsh introduced the philosophy of Coleridge* in America by the publication of *Aids to Reflection,* with a Preliminary Essay (1829), a work which had a profound liberalizing and vitalizing effect upon religious thought through Bushnell* and others. He also published a translation of Herder's *The Spirit of Hebrew Poetry* (1833).

A Memoir of James Marsh by Joseph Torrey (1843, 2nd ed., 1845) contains "Remarks on Psychology," "Discourse on the Nature, Ground and Origin of Sin" and other of Marsh's productions.

Cf. John Dewey, "James Marsh and American Philosophy," *Journal of the History of Ideas,* Vol. II, No. 2. J.W.B.

Marshman, Joshua (1768-1837) For seven years refused membership in Baptist Church because of "head knowledge." Associate of Carey and Ward in the Serampore mission. 1813, drew up first organized plan for establishment of schools in India. C.H.M.

Marsilius of Padua: (Marsiglio Mainardino) Born 1275-80, died 1343. He studied and practiced medicine in Padua c. 1311, was rector of the University of Paris Dec. 1312-Mar. 1313, later Canon of the Cathedral of Padua. A protégé of John XXII*, he was converted to Ghibellinism*, and with John of Jandum* authored *Defensor Pacis,* published 1324. (Edited by C. W. Previté-Orton, Cambridge, 1928). Both condemned as heretics, they fled to court of Lewis IV, and helped Lewis put the principles of their book into practice in the short-lived "Roman Revolution".

Marsilius also wrote *Defensor Minor, Tractatus de iurisdictione imperatores in causis matrimonialibus* and *Tractatus de translatione imperii.* (Appendix *ad Fasciculum Rerum . . . ab Ortuino Gratio, T. secundus,* London MDCXC). Q.B.

Martensen, Hans Lassen: (1808-1884) Bishop, dogmatician, and moral philosopher of the Lutheran Church of Denmark. Professing to be a confessional Lutheran, Martensen was an original speculative thinker, combining influences from the idealism of Hegel, the theosophy of Franz von Baader, and the mysticism of Jakob Böhme. Over against Kierkegaard, he sought to harmonize Christianity with the human search for value.

Principal works: *Christian Dogmatics* (1849), and *Christian Ethics* (1878). See neo-Lutheranism T.A.K.

Martianus Capella: (flourished between 400 and 439) Martianus Capella of Carthage was not a Christian, yet his works exerted a tremendous influence upon the Middle Ages. In his *De Nuptiis Mercurii et Philologiae,* he first distinguished the "seven liberal arts" and gave us the earliest full compendium of the studies taught in his days. This book is acknowledged to be the first attempt to classify human intellectual enterprise and was often commented upon. Notker Labeo in the eleventh century translated it into German. S.C.T.

Martin, Gregory: See Bible, English.

Martin of Tours, St.: (c. 316-399) Simple, noble, and scrupulously just, he was born of pagan parents and was baptized at the age of twenty. Elected bishop of Tours, he destroyed pagan temples, uprooted superstitions, and fought against Arianism. Legend tells of a cloak he gave to a beggar, and of his subsequent vision from heaven. Founded the first monastery in Gaul. W.H.

Martineau, James: (1805-1900) Preacher and Prof. of Phil. at Manchester New College, timely and staunch defender of philosophy against a narrow, unempirical theology and a mechanistic interpretation of evolution. A strong exponent of moral experience as independent data for a complete philosophical view. His natural and ethical theism, inspired by religious experience, rationally depends on the Design which, immanent in Nature and especially reflected in man's conscience, indicates that the cosmic Will is intelligent, omnipotent, and moral. See Unitarianism.

Types of Ethical Theory (1889), 2 vols., 3rd ed.; *The Study of Religion* (1889), 2 vols., 2nd ed. P.A.B.

martyr: (Gr. *martus,*—Aedic dialect—martyr, a witness) 1) One who suffers persecution for his faith; martyrdom: to undergo torture or death for religious convictions. 2) The Martyrs, as such, are commonly understood to be the victims of the Roman persecutions during the first three centuries of the Church. Their relics* were the first to be venerated and churches were erected in their honor. 3) The martyrs in the primitive Church also connoted those who suffered in any way or were noteworthy confessors of their faith, irrespective of actual death. See intercession. J.F.T.

martyrology: An historical record listing the martyrs and/or saints, generally with a brief note on each, whose feasts or commemorations are celebrated in the Roman Catholic Church throughout the days of the liturgical year; it is read as a part of the choral office of Prime*. See Sylvester, I. J.F.T.

Maruts: Minor storm gods of Vedic Hinduism associated closely with Indra. They are the sons of Rudra and at times are called Rudras. C.S.B.

Marx, Karl: (1818-1883) M. proceeded from Hegel* whose metaphysics, however, he never really accepted, gradually transforming it into its very opposite. He believed himself to be the messenger of a new social Gospel* for the propagation of which he wrote all his books and pamphlets. He was accordingly not so much a philosopher but rather a political reformer. This fact is veiled by his peculiar theory derived from the Hegelian philosophy of history concerning the necessity of historical development. Like Hegel M. held that this development is ruled by a principle that can be known. But whereas the principle in Hegel's philosophy was spiritual, M. is of the opinion that material, i.e., the economic conditions regulate and determine the course of history. This is the position of the so-called "historical materialism".

The influence of M. and Marxism upon the political development of the 19th and 20th centuries is obvious, although the belief in the accuracy of his theory and of his predictions has decreased. See bourgeoisie; dialectic; Jewish socialism; proletariat; socialism.

Dissertation (1841); *Kritik der Hegelschen Rechts philosophie* (1843); *Das Kommunistische Manifest* (1847); *Das Kapital* (1867 ff); Karl Löwith, *Von Hegel bis Nietzsche* (1941); B. Croce, *Historical Materialism and the Economics of Karl Marx* (tr. by C. M. Meredith; introd. by A. D. Lindsay, 1922). R.K.

Mary, cult of: Technically St. Mary does not receive *latreia* (worship), which is due to God alone, but *hyperdulia* (adoration), the highest degree of *dulia* (veneration), which may be offered to the saints. Popularly this distinction has not always been observed. Beginning in the very earliest days of Christianity, deriving from the church's desire to safeguard the orthodox doctrine of the Deity of Jesus Christ and to maintain a human mediator before the Godhead, as well as from pagan goddess-worship, the adoration of Mary has grown with the passing years. The Middle Ages saw the development of the Rosary* and the Angelus*. In modern times Saturdays have been given to the recitation of the Little Office, the month of May is dedicated to Mary, and sodalities* of the Blessed Virgin have been established. In the early nineteenth century the devotion of the Miraculous Medal began and the decree of Pius IX* defining the dogma of the Immaculate Conception* (1854) and the apparitions at Lourdes* (1858) have caused the cult to increase immeasurably. Protestantism naturally rejects this practice. See mariology; mariolatry; Virgin Mary. A.C.

Mary, the Virgin: See mariolatry; Virgin Mary.

Mary's Day: See Sabbatine privilege.

Masorah: (Hebr.; deriv. uncertain, usually: tradition, from root m-s-r, to hand down) The work of so-called Masoretes, men who were piously intent upon preserving unchanged the text of the Hebrew Bible, and who, accordingly, provided it with vowel points and with copious annotations. These notes, written on the margins and at the end of MSS, are not critical or exegetical but merely describe what was, according to the masoretic tradition, the correct form of the text. For the most part they are enumerations of the occurrences of words or concern their proper orthography. The Masorah accumulated from c. 500 to c. 1100. S.H.B.

mass: (Lat. *missa*) The Christian eucharist; since the reformation referring only to the Roman Catholic service. The text is liturgical, the part which changes according to the season is called the Proper, the part which remains the same is called the Ordinary. The latter consists of kyrie, gloria, credo, sanctus et benedictus, and agnus dei**. Low mass is spoken, whereas High mass is sung throughout. It is known as solemn mass when officiating priest, deacon and subdeacon all take part. The music for the mass may be in any style of composition from the early Christian plainsong* to the many types of polyphony* to the present harmony*. Composers are known as early as Guillaume de Machaut in the polyphonic period of the 14th century. The following century saw the introduction into the mass of secular elements such as popular folk-tunes used polyphonically with the Gregorian* song, and various technical devices without religious or musical value merely for the sake of experimentation or amusement. The impurities were purged at the time of the Council of Trent*, 1545-1563, when the polyphony of Palestrina was held up as a model for sacred composition.

Masses of the Neapolitan operatic style of the 17th century followed a liturgical text but introduced a style of music as secular as the melodramatic opera of the period. Dominating the 18th century was the great *B Minor Mass* of Bach. Too long for liturgical use, at places with an untraditional text, the work, consisting of great choral fugues, elaborately ornamented arias, and orchestral accompaniment, is generally accepted as the greatest choral work ever written. The mass is here conceived as a great art-form, religious in its devout emotional concepts, like a great oratorio*. See liturgy; requiem.

E. K. Chambers, *The Medieval Stage* (1903); R. R. Terry, *The Music of the Roman Rite* (1931); G. Reese, *Music in the Middle Ages* (1940).

E.H.B.

mass, Anglican and Lutheran: The word "mass" as a name for the Eucharist was retained by Luther (cf. his liturgical experiments, *Formula Missae*, 1523, and *Deutsche Messe*, 1526), and in the first English Prayer Book, 1549. It has survived in Scandinavia, but with changes in usage; e.g., in Sweden the morning service, with or without Communion, is *Högmässa* (High Mass). In England the term dropped out of use, except as preserved in such terms as Christmas, Michaelmas, etc. Since the Oxford Movement* it has been revived among Anglo-Catholics*, and is used approximately as among Roman Catholics.

E.R.H.

mass, Roman Catholic: In the Roman Catholic Church, the Eucharistic Sacrifice of the New Law, instituted, together with the priesthood for its offering, by Christ at the Last Supper, as the representation and memorial of His death (Matt. 26:26-28; Mark 14:22-24; Luke 22:19-20; cf. I Cor. 11:23-26). The Mass is organically related to Catholic soteriology*, which teaches that Jesus Christ, the Word Incarnate, was essentially Priest, and that His death on the Cross was a genuine sacrifice, whereby mankind as a unit was objectively redeemed, since the sacrifice was offered by Christ as Head of humanity, in whom all men were objectively represented; that, consequently, His sacrifice was all-sufficing in its redemptive efficacy, but not sole-sufficing, since its efficacy needs to be communicated and applied, by means authoritatively determined by Christ Himself, chief among which is the Eucharistic Sacrifice, the center and source of Catholic personal and corporate life.

Its institution was a fulfillment of ancient prophecy (Mal. 1:11; cf. 3:3; Isai. 66:21). It was in harmony with the native exigence of man's dual nature for sacrifice, i.e., for the social and liturgical expression, by a pragmatic oblation of a sensible thing, of the unique interior sentiments of adoration, thanksgiving, and propitiation which man owes to God (St. Thomas, *Summa Theol.*, II-II, q. 85). It was especially congruous with the relation of solidarity that obtains between Christ and His Church: as He was essentially Priest, and as His supremely self-expressive act was a sacrifice, He willed that the Body of which He is Head should be essentially priestly by participation of His Priesthood, and that its central religious act, as a Body, should be a sacrifice, the memorial and mystical renewal of His own.

Against this background the Roman Catholic Church has always taught, first, that the Mass is not a simple rite of commemoration, purely psychological in its effects, but a true and proper sacrifice, offered by the sacerdotal Body of the Church as a unitary whole, but acting through an ordained priesthood; secondly, that the Mass is not an independent sacrifice, but is wholly relative to the one-offered and definitive sacrifice of Christ, with which it forms a unity: "there is one and the same victim, and He who offers now by the ministry of priests is identically He who then offered Himself on the Cross; only the manner of offering is different" (Council of Trent, sess. 7, chap. 2). Because it is a real sacrifice, the Mass has a real latreutic, eucharistic, and propitiatory value, available for the faithful, both living and dead. Because it is the same sacrifice as that of the Cross, whence all its value derives, the Mass does not derogate from the all-sufficiency of Christ's redemptive act. Moreover, this inner relation of unity between the Mass and the Cross explains the efficacy of the Mass *ex opere operato* (see opus operatum). The Mass has also a value *ex opere operantis,* which is proportioned to the sanctity of the Church, and to the devotion of the celebrant and the assistant faithful.

The essential rite of the Mass is that of the Supper—a mystical immolation, which is at the same time a real pragmatic oblation, of the Body and Blood of Christ to the Father, as a Victim for the world's sin. The immolation is mystical inasmuch as the separate consecration of bread and wine symbolizes the shedding of the Blood. The oblation is real inasmuch as the Body and Blood of Christ are really present under the sacramental species, and are therefore really presented to God in their symbolic state of death. The interior spiritual significance of the rite is the penitent and loving self-dedication of the Body of Christ as a unit, and in union with its Head, to the Father. By the Mass the Church actualizes in the present the oblation once made for it on the Cross, and imbibes the power of that oblation.

Pertaining to the integrity, if not to the essence, of the sacrifice is the Communion of the faithful, or at least of the priest. Thereby the Host*, offered by the Church to God, is given back, as it were, by Him to her members, effectively to communicate to them its own sanctity, and to be the efficacious sign of their unity as the one Body of Christ (cf. I Cor. 10:17).

After the example of Christ's own prayer of praise and thanksgiving (Mark 14:22), the Church from earliest times provided the sacrifice with a liturgical setting. At first, fluidity and improvisation, within the framework of the Supper rite, were permitted. Comparatively early, however, forms were fixed. Toward the end of the fourth century strong differentiation set in between Western and Eastern liturgy. In the East two mother-liturgies are distinguished, the Syrian and the Egyptian, whence have developed a rich variety of rites, among which today the Byzantine* is dominant. The West now almost universally follows the Roman rite; its development took place between the fourth and seventh centuries, and it has since been altered but slightly. It has four progressively simpler forms—Pontifical, Solemn, Sung, and Low Mass. In all rites the same two primitive divisions of the Mass are still discernible: 1) the Mass of the catechumens, a preparatory service of prayer and readings from Scripture; 2) the Mass of the faithful, in which the sacrifice itself is enacted amid a solemn setting of prayer, and is followed by the Communion, thanksgiving, and dismissal.

The Protestant tradition as a whole rejects the sacrificial character of the Eucharist, together with the Real Presence* and the ecclesiastical priesthood, its essential correlates. Orthodox Lutheranism and Calvinism regarded the Mass as subversive of the uniqueness of Christ's Priesthood and sacrifice, whose merits are applied by faith alone. Liberal Protestantism more radically excludes ritual sacrifice as a Christian act by its exclusive emphasis on the prophetic and exemplary character of Christ's redemptive function, to the exclusion of His priestly mediation, which is regarded as an ecclesiastical innovation, whose origins are variously explained. See eucharist; liturgy; Missal, Roman; pontifical mass.

Doctrine: H. J. Schroeder, *Canons and Decrees of the Council of Trent* (1941); F. Prat, *Theology of St. Paul* (1938), 2 vols.; M. Lepin, *L'Idée du sacrifice de la messe d'après les théologiens depuis l'origine jusqu'à nos jours* (1926); M. de la Taille, *Mysterium Fidei* (1924); *idem, Mystery of Faith and Human Opinion* (1930); E. C. Messenger, *The Reformation, the Mass, and the Priesthood* (1936), 2 vols.

Liturgy: L. Duchesne, *Christian Worship, Its Origin and Evolution* (1923); A. Fortescue, *The Mass, a Study of the Roman Liturgy* (1937); F. E. Brightman, *Liturgies Eastern and Western*, I (1895); J. M. Hannsens, *Institutiones Liturgicae* (1930), II, III: De Missa rituum orientalium.

Rubrics: J. O'Connell, *The Celebration of Mass* (1941), 3 vols. J.C.M.

Massoretic Hebrew text: See Masorah; versions of the Bible, ancient.

materia: This Latin word, coined evidently from *mater*, mother, clearly indicates the source of origin, that out of which something arises. It is a translation of the Greek *hyle*, a word which in the earliest Greek speculation was a living source out of which things arise. The English word "stuff" comes quite close to this ancient Greek meaning. Whether Plato's *chora* was abstract space or a stuff-like substratum, is not very easy to decide. Aristotle* differentiates first and second matter. First matter is universal potentiality to become actualized by the infiltration of forms. Second matter is something, an actualized potentiality, which is called matter, raw material, with reference to a new form, for instance the idea of a boat to be inserted in the second matter of lumber. See matter. S.C.T.

material cause: See cause.

materialism: See Charvakas; dialectic; Gassendi; historical materialism; Hobbes; Holbach; Lokayatas; ontology; socialism. See also s.v. naturalism.

Mathews, Shailer: (1863-1941) Prominent Baptist; dean of the Divinity School, University of Chicago, 1908-33; president, Federal Council of the Churches of Christ, 1912-16; president, Northern Baptist Convention, 1915; editor, *Biblical World*, 1913-20.

Mathews was one of the early and most influential exponents of the "social gospel"* which sought to give a social interpretation to Christianity, and of the modernist point of view which sought to bring religion and science together in the interest of constructing a tenable world-view. He also was active in the founding of the Religious Education Association, pioneered along new paths for theological education, and gave life-long service to the cause of Christian unity, both local and ecumenical, stressing the necessity for a practical rather than a theological approach for its ultimate realization. The catholicity of his interest is indicated by the fact that he taught successively rhetoric, history, political economy, N. T. interpretation, systematic theology, and historical and comparative theology.

His more important published works are: *The Social Teachings of Jesus* (1897); *A History of New Testament Times in Palestine* (1899); *The Messianic Hope in the New Testament* (1905); *The Church and the Changing Order* (1907); *The Social Gospel* (1909); *The Gospel and the Modern Man* (1909); *Scientific Management in the Churches* (1911); *The Individual and the Social Gospel* (1914); *The Spiritual Interpretation of History* (1916); *The Validity of American Ideals* (1922); *The Faith of Modernism* (1924); *Jesus on Social Institutions* (1928); *The Atonement and the Social Process* (1930); *The Growth of the Idea of God* (1931); *Immortality and the Cosmic Process* (1933); *Christianity and Social Process* (1934); *Creative Christianity* (1935); *New Faith for Old—An Autobiography* (1936); *The Church and the Christian* (1938); *Is God Emeritus?* (1940); "Theology as Group Belief" (autobiographical) in *Contemporary American Theology* (1933), vol. II, edited by Vergilius Ferm.

Mathews also edited: *Dictionary of Religion and Ethics*, with G. B. Smith (1921); *The Contributions of Science to Religion* (1924). W.S.H.

matins: (Lat. *ad matutinum*, at early morning) Original Latin name for Office said at dawn, later transferred to Night Office, previously called Vigils* or Nocturns*; also name of Anglican Morning Office (see Divine Office). E.R.H.

matriarchal system: A system of social organization in which women are dominant and men subordinate in contrast to the patriarchal system* in which the opposite relationship prevails. Historically, the patriarchal system has universally prevailed, but in pre-literate cultures some evidence has been found which gives credence to the possibility that a matriarchal system may have existed in some cultures or might have preceded the patriarchal system later found in others. Generally the theory of the matriarchate as a prior development to the patriarchal system is linked to the theory of the origin of the family out of promiscuity. According to this view, the earliest family* relationships were those between mother and child, the father being either unknown or at least recognizing no responsibility for the care of the child. Under these conditions the mother was the all-important member of the family group, descent being traced through her, and as she became older exercising control not only over her immediate offspring but their offspring as well so long as they remained a part of the family group. As marriage* became an established institution, common ancestry would serve to draw together larger groupings of individuals related by blood to the matriarch who would direct the affairs of the large family and eventually with other matriarchs the affairs of a tribe.

Nowhere is there conclusive evidence of the existence of a matriarchal system of society, although there have been preliterate peoples whose social organization has approached such a pattern. Chief among these were the five tribes of the Iroquois Confederacy in which the chiefs constituting the Council of the League were selected by the matrons of the maternal families represented. Not only did these matrons have the power of selecting the chiefs composing the Council, but they might also depose them if the chiefs failed to carry out the wishes of the maternal families. But even in the Iroquois Confederacy authority was divested in a Council of men, the matriarchal character of the Confederacy deriving from the fact that the matrons of the maternal families controlled the affairs of the Confederacy through their right to choose and depose the chieftains.

Robert Briffault, *The Mothers* (1931); Alexander Goldenweiser, *Early Civilization* (1922); Lewis H. Morgan, *Ancient Society* (1878); Edward Westermarck, *History of Human Marriage* (London, 1921).

E.R.M.

matter: (Lat. *materia**, *materies*, stuff, from *mater*, mother) In general, the substance of which anything consists (both *materia* and the Gr. *hulé* may mean wood or tree, the substance of much early construction). 1. In logic, the content of a proposition, as distinguished from its logical form. 2. In physics and materialistic* metaphysics, that which occupies space and moves in space; nonmental substance with attributes of extension and impenetrability. 3. In Aristotle, (indeterminate) potentiality, which, by being actualized, acquires form*. 4. In Kant, sensory content or quality, as distinguished from the forms of sensibility or categories of understanding.

See B. Russell, *Analysis of Matter* (1927).

E.S.B.

Matthew: (From an Aramaic word meaning "gift of God") One of the twelve. In the first Gospel described as "the publican" (10:3) and apparently confused with Levi (9:9, cf. Mark 2:14, Luke 5:27).

S.M.G.

Matthew, Gospel of: The Gospel in its ethical aspect, the richest presentation of Jesus as a teacher. Written perhaps ten years after Mark*, probably in Antioch, Matthew reproduces virtually everything in Mark except a small fraction, but casts Jesus' teaching into six sermons, the first of which, the Sermon on the Mount, ch. 5-7, remains the standard statement of Christian ethics. Matthew had other written sources for his gospel, especially for the teaching of Jesus. In the recent Fall of Jerusalem the evangelist saw the punishment of the Jews for their refusal of their Messiah*, which had led to the offering of the long promised salvation to all mankind. He seeks to show that the Jewish prophecies had been fulfilled in the work of Christ and the beginnings of the church, and so to establish the Jewish scriptures as a possession of the church. Church and synagogue were already in vigorous conflict, and Christian ethics are sharply defined against Jewish. The writer is, like Paul, Barnabas and Stephen, a Christian Jew of the Dispersion, but writes not for Jews but for the people of the Greek world. Renan called Matthew the most important book in the world. See Gospel and Gospels; logia; Synoptic Gospels.

B. W. Bacon, *Studies in Matthew* (1930). A. H. McNeile, *The Gospel according to St. Matthew* (1915).

E.J.G.

Matthew of Janov: (b. before 1355, d. 1393) An outstanding Czech reformer. After studying in Prague, he went to Paris (1373) where he received M.A. degree. Returning to Prague, he became a member of the reform movement. Having been forbidden to preach, he engaged in writing his greatest work, *Regulae veteris et novi testamenti*.

V. Kybal, *M. Matej z Janova* (Praha, 1905).

M.S.

Maundy Thursday: The Thursday before Easter, the traditional observance of which includes not only the commemoration of the Last Supper and part of the Passion, but the foot-washing ceremony (hence probably the name, from the command, mandatum, found in John 13), the blessing of holy oils, and the reconciliation of public penitents.

E.R.H.

Maurice, John Frederic Denison: (1805-1872) English clergyman, theologian, and social reformer. Leader of the Broad Church movement, although he viewed the name "Broad Church" with misgiving. (See Broad Churchmen) Maurice was ordained in the Church of England* in 1834. He was profoundly convinced of the truth of the Fatherhood of God. All men are divinely created in Christ and all men are therefore the children of God even though they do not all know or obey that truth. Because of the publication in 1853 of his *Theological Essays* Maurice lost his professorship in

Theology in King's College, London. He was a leader of the Christian Socialists and of the educational movements identified with the Working Men's College and Queen's College for Women. In 1866, he was appointed professor of moral philosophy at Cambridge. See social gospel.

Main works: *The Kingdom of Christ* (1842); *The Religions of the World* (1847); *Moral and Metaphysical Philosophy* (1848); *Theological Essays* (1853); *The Doctrine of Sacrifice* (1854); *The Conscience: Lectures on Casuistry* (1868).

H.W.J.

Maurists: Reformed Benedictine congregation of France, officially approved by Gregory XV, 1621; allowed to lapse, 1818. Not entirely free from Jansenist ideas, it was noted for strict liturgical observance and brilliant scholarly achievements. Luc d'Achéry, Denys de Sainte-Marthe, Martin Bouquet, Jean Mabillon, *et al.*, are Maurist names never to be forgotten in the realms of patrology, diplomatics, literary and ecclesiastical history.

A.C.

Maurus, Magnentius Rabanus: (784-856) Abbot of Fulda, 822-842; archbishop of Mainz, 847. Alcuin's student, Gottschalk's enemy, his encyclopedic learning (astronomy, grammar, Germanic philology, poetry) made him *Praeceptor Germaniae.* A.C.

Maximus the Confessor: (580-622) Easily the most eminent theologian of the seventh century. For this reason he is also known as Maximus the Theologian. He specialized in the doctrine of the Incarnation, warring in particular against Monothelitism*. W.H.

māyā: Best known as a Hindu philosophic term signifying in the Vedanta "illusion". There is but one real, Brahman-atman. The phenomenal world has no real existence. It is *māyā,* illusion which rises from *āvidya,* or ignorance. The illusion disappears with the knowledge of the alone reality of Brahman-atman. He who attains this knowledge attains *moksha,* or salvation*.

Māyā is also found in the Rig-Veda where it means occult, mysterious, or supernatural power. Also it sometimes means cunning. Indra triumphs over Vritra through Māyā.

Māyā is also the name of the mother of the Buddha. C.S.B.

Mazda: Name of two Iranian deities: 1) Before the sixth century B.C., in the Gathic period: Ahura (lord) Mazda (Wisdom) is a great, highly moralized and personified nature power; 2) Later, Mazda is a cosmic power, whose nature is akin to all human and non-human spiritual beings, and rules all. F.L.P.

Mazdaism: Iranian religion which evolved about the fifth century B.C., succeeding the prophetism (Zoroastrianism)* of an earlier period; a body of doctrines and practices centering about the chief cosmic deity, Mazda. See Parsiism and Parsees (the only significant fragment and development of Mazdaism extant today).

J. C. Archer, *Faiths Men Live By* (1934), Chap. 12 (on the faith and practice of the Parsee); M. N. Dhalla, *Zoroastrian Theology* (1914); A. V. W. Jackson, *Zoroastrian Studies* (1928). F.L.P.

Mazdak: A militant religious reformer of Persia, who, near the end of the fifth century A.D., led a socialistic reform movement against Mazdaism*. His heretical doctrines and practices, together with those of his followers, brought on bitter strife with the orthodox Mazdaens, which resulted in his own death, and almost complete extermination of his followers in the early part of the sixth century A.D. F.L.P.

Mazzella, Camillo: (1833-1900) Italian Jesuit and Cardinal. He was professor of theology in the United States at Georgetown University and Woodstock College (1867-1878), and at the Gregorian University in Rome. His theological works are esteemed in Catholic circles, and he had a part in the revival of Thomism* sponsored by Leo XIII*. E.A.R.

McCauley Memorial Lectureship, the Rev. Charles F.: Established in 1914 this course is given annually by a pastor on some practical subject relating to the ministry at the Theological Seminary of the Evangelical Reformed Church, Lancaster, Pennsylvania. Its capital sum is $1,000.

(Data furnished by the office of the President of the Seminary.) V.F.

McDougall, William: See psychology, schools of.

McGiffert, Arthur Cushman (1861-1933) Brilliant American church historian, author, and administrator. Studied at Marburg and Berlin, pupil of Harnack. His monograph on the *Apostles' Creed* advocated a theory generally held until 1919 and by some today. His reputation attained by critical translation and commentary upon *Church History of Eusebius,* 1890. Instructor and professor at Lane Theological Seminary, 1888-1893; Union Theological Seminary, New York, 1893-1926 (pres. 1917-1926). Ordained to Presbyterian Ministry 1888, became Congregationalist, 1899, in consequence of Briggs-Smith controversy and publication of *A History of Christianity in the Apostolic Age.* C.H.M.

McLaren, Alexander: (1826-1910) Noted Baptist preacher of Manchester, England. Ardent advocate of open membership. W.S.H.

McNair Lectures, the John Calvin: Established in 1908 at the University of North Carolina, Chapel Hill, with a capital sum of $16,000.00 by John Calvin McNair. Their purpose is "to show the mutual bearing of science and religion upon each other and to prove the existence (as far as may be) of God from nature." These lectures (three in a series) are given once or twice in a period of four years and published by the University. Among those appearing on this lectureship are: F. H. Smith; Presidents Patton, Jordan, Hadley, Vincent; John Dewey, Paul

Shorey, Arthur Compton, R. A. Millikan.
(The above data furnished by the Dean of Administration of the University.) V.F.

McTaggart, John Ellis: (1866-1925) An English philosopher noted for his interpretation of Hegel*, whom he claims to follow. Indebted to experience for the concept of being, McTaggart arrives by a process of *a priori* dialectic at a pluralistic idealism, according to which ultimate reality is not a single, central, timeless personal self but rather the complete system or society of eternal finite selves which are the differentiations of the Absolute. See neo-Hegelianism; pre-existence.

Main works: *Studies in the Hegelian Dialectic* (1896); *Studies in Hegelian Cosmology* (1901); *Some Dogmas of Religion* (1906); *A Commentary on Hegel's Logic* (1910); *The Nature of Existence* (1921). H.W.J.

mean, Aristotelian: Virtue as the stage of balance or moderation between the two vices of excess and defect. For example, courage as a virtue is the mean between rashness and cowardice. The mean is not a fixed point but depends on the person and the circumstances involved. It therefore requires good judgment or what Aristotle calls "insight" to determine the Golden Mean (as Horace later called it) in any particular case. J.E.N.

means: All New England Calvinists held that God was sovereign in man's regeneration. Old Calvinists* and later Taylorites (see Taylorism) held this sovereignty was preserved in "appointed means," i.e., that God's Spirit worked through the "means of grace" (Scripture reading, prayer, sermons, etc.), to renew the understanding which in turn inclined the heart or will from sin to holiness. Their opponents (Consistent Calvinists*, Tylerites) (see Tyler, Bennet) held that man was passive until the Spirit changed the heart, which in turn effected the "holy volition" or turning from sin to God which was conversion. See New England theology.

Moses Hemmenway, *Seven Sermons On the Obligation and Encouragement of the Unregenerate to Labour for the Meat which Endureth to Everlasting Life* (1767); Samuel Hopkins, *The True State and Character of the Unregenerate . . .* (1769); J. Haroutunian, *Piety Versus Moralism* (1932); S. E. Mead, *Nathaniel William Taylor* (1942). S.E.M.

Mecca: (Arabic *Makkah*) A city in central Arabia, the birthplace of Mohammed* and the chief sanctuary of Islam. As the object of annual pilgrimage, and the worship center to face in daily prayer it is the aspiration of every devoted Moslem. (See article on "Mecca" by D. S. Margoliouth in ERE, vol. viii, 511-514.) See Medina; Mohammedanism. P.E.J.

Mechitarists: An Armenian monastic order, following the Benedictine rule, founded by Abbot Mechitar in 1712; the Mechitarists, whose mother house is at Venice, have been of great service to Armenian scholarship and literature as well as to the Armenian Catholic (Uniat) Church. E.R.H.

medals, devotional: A flat metal (or plastic) disk, usually suspended about the neck, bearing a religious image of Christ, His mother, a saint, shrine, or mystery of religion, etc. The origin dates to the catacombs*, when they were apparently tolerated by the primitive Church to counteract the use of pagan *amuleti* (mentioned by Pliny). As mementoes they are mere signs of the prototypes to which due honor is accorded, and are blessed as such by clerics of the Roman Catholic Church; in themselves they have no merit, and to look upon them as talismans is rankest superstition. There are many kinds of medals, the most famous being that of St. Benedict, of the scapular, and the Miraculous Medal. The design of the last mentioned was said to have been revealed by the Mother of Christ in honor of her immaculate conception* in a vision granted to the Venerable Catherine Labouré in 1830; its name is due to the circumstances of its origin rather than to the miracles attributed to its pious use. J.F.T.

medicine men: Medicine men were the religious officials of the Indian tribes of America. They were specialists in the techniques of healing, sorcery and divination*, custodians of sacred objects and masters of ceremonial lore. Their functions varied greatly with the different tribes. In some cases they were shamans, mediators between man and the spirit world, who acquired their healing power and superior knowledge through their control over or possession by spirits. The shaman* was a spirit specialist and had little relation to the social phases of religion. Among the tribes of higher culture, the medicine man assumed more priestly functions. In addition to being a ritual and practical healer, he was a seer and confessor, educator, leader of "medicine" societies, master of tribal ceremonials and dances, and religious prophet. Both shaman and medicine man were trained for their work and usually selected from a special family. The shaman qualified by a predisposition to ecstatic, trance states. The medicine man was the product of elaborate training and initiation. See death and burial practices. A.E.H.

Medieval religious drama: See religious drama.

Medina: (Arabic for town, in contrast to the desert. Also known as *Yathrib*) The city to which Mohammed fled from Mecca*, where his rule was first accepted, and where he was finally buried. It was the political capital of Islam during the prophet's first three successors, and the seat of the first university. Visitation to Medina is considered a dutiful act, second only to the pilgrimage to Mecca. See hegira. P.E.J.

meditation: In religious usage the reverent, intense and sustained contemplation of God or of some religious theme or ideal. It is a strenuous spiritual exercise requiring composure of mind, internal quietude, abstraction from sense and persistent concentration of attention. Its aim is the strengthening and elevation of the moral life through communion with God. It is an important form of devotion in the higher religions and is especially emphasized and practiced by the great mystics. See mysticism. R.W.F.

Meditation School: See Buddhist Terminology.

meekness: That quality of spirit which is marked by peaceable temper, gentleness, self-respect without vanity, and patient submission to injury and offence without resentfulness or retaliation. It connotes not feebleness of will or easy compliance with wrong-doing, but rather that firm and constant mastery of oneself under provocation which springs from calm and trustful surrender to God's will and which accepts hard and perplexing experiences as a part of the discipline of the Christian life. It is a Christian virtue of primary importance. See humility. R.W.F.

meeting house style: See art, Christian, ecclesiastical.

Megillot: (Hebr. scrolls) The name given the five books Song of Songs, Ruth, Lamentations, Ecclesiastes, and Esther**, included in the Hebrew Bible among the Hagiographa* and read in the Synagogue on Passover, Pentecost, the Ninth of Ab, Tabernacles and Purim**, respectively.
S.H.B.

Meir: Second century rabbi who prepared a systematic edition of traditional Jewish law and doctrine, which paved the way for the final edition of the Mishnah.* B.Z.B.

Mekilta: (Aram. measures or rules of interpretation) 1) A Midrash of the school of Rabbi Ishmael (2nd cent.) on the legal portions of Ex. 12:1-23:19; 31:12-17; 35:1-3, consisting of nine tractates. Critical text and Eng. transl. J. Z. Lauterbach, 3 vols. (1933-35).

2) Mekilta of Rabbi Simeon ben Jochai, representing the school of R. Akiba, on Exodus, reconstructed by David Hoffmann, Frankfurt a.M. (1905). S.S.C.

Melanchthon, Philip: (1497-1560) German Reformer and theologian. His appointment as professor at Wittenberg marked the breach with the old scholastic methods and the triumph of the new spirit. He early recognized the spiritual depth of Luther's message, and it was his task to reduce it to systematic form. He played an important part in the various controversies and conferences of the period, and his conciliatory spirit made him a central figure in discussions among the Protestant leaders and between the Protestants and the Catholics. His theological position was also a mediating one, and he gradually modified the more extreme of Luther's statements. His clear thought and his polished style gave him a distinctive place as the spokesman of the Lutheran movement. See adiaphoristic controversy; Augsburg Confession; common grace; Loci Communes; Philippists; synergism. G.R.C.

Melchites: Originally those Christians of the patriarchates of Antioch, Jerusalem and Alexandria who accepted the dogmatic decisions of Chalcedon*. They comprised not only Greek and Hellenistic elements of the population but also, at least in Syria, important native groups. At present there are Catholic and Orthodox Melchites in Syria, and Orthodox Melchites in Egypt.
E.A.R.

meliorism: (Lat., *melior,* better, comparative of *bonum,* good) The doctrine that the world is such that it may be improved by human effort and by the advance of evolution. The term, coined by George Eliot, was popularized by Sully in his *Pessimism* (1877). Connected with theories of progress and humanism on the one hand, and with the doctrine of a finite God* on the other. See moral optimism; optimism; pessimism.
E.S.B.

Melito: Bishop of Sardis, in the Roman Province of Asia, in the second half of the 2nd century. A prolific writer (Eus. H. E. 4.26.2). One work ("On the Passion") has been recovered almost in its entirety in a papyrus ms. discovered in 1940. S.M.G.

Melkite churches: See Eastern Orthodox churches.

melody: A succession of tones with a rhythmic aspect. Plainsong* is pure melody embodying rhythmic pulsation without meter and without harmonic suggestion. Polyphony* is the combination of melodies which, because of the combination, must assume meter, and also secondarily form harmonies*. Homophony, or harmony, gives emphasis to one melody supported by a succession of chords which secondarily may or may not produce other melodies. E.H.B.

Melville, Andrew: (1545-1622) Distinguished Scottish scholar and defender of Presbyterianism*. After a brilliant period of study in Scotland, and a decade of study and teaching in France and Geneva, he returned to Scotland in 1575 and became successively Principal of Glasgow University and Principal of the new theological college at St. Andrews. He is better known however for his leadership in the fight against the royal efforts to establish Episcopalianism in Scotland, in which he took the extreme view that episcopacy was not merely inadvisable but positively unlawful. As a result, he was imprisoned, but spent the last eleven years of his life as a professor in Sedan, where he died in 1622. A.K.R.

memento: (Lat. remember) Two commemorative prayers, each beginning with the word *Memento,* in the sacrifice of the Mass*, one of the living, made at the beginning of the canon, and the other of the dead, occurring soon after the consecration. J.F.T.

memra: (Aram., word) A stereotype employed in the Targumim (Aramaic versions of the Bible) to avoid literal renditions that may disturb the religious sense of the readers. Wherever actions ascribed to God do not beseem His spiritual nature the Targumim use God's Memra (word), Yekara (glory) or Shekinta (Presence). Unlike the Logos in Philo and in John, these seemingly related terms never designated "a 'being' of any kind or in any sense, much less a personal being". (G. F. Moore, *Judaism,* I, 419). See shekinah.

S.S.C.

Men, the: The name popularly given to the leaders of certain fellowship meetings of an evangelistic character, which, led by laymen, characterized the religious life of the Scottish Highlands in the eighteenth century. The movement was highly emotional and fanatically orthodox.

A.K.R.

Menaion: See Menologion.

Mencius: See Chinese Terminology.

Mendelssohn, Moses: (1729-1786) Jewish philosopher, Bible translator and humanist who stands at the headwaters of the Enlightenment* and Emancipation period of German Jewry at the close of the 18th century, was born in Dessau, received a traditional Talmudic* training in his early youth, but later acquired also a wide general education in science, philosophy, languages and literature. He came to be regarded in his day as a leader of German and European philosophic thought. His *Phaedon* (1767) on the immortality of the soul was the most widely read book of its day and won for the author the title of the "German Socrates". Mendelssohn advocated the absolute freedom of belief and the separation of Church and State. He defined Judaism in his work *Jerusalem* (1783) and elsewhere not as a revealed religion in the sense of a creed or a set of dogmas which is indispensible to salvation, but rather as a revealed legislation entrusted to Israel and binding upon the Jewish people for all times. Thus, while insisting upon absolute conformity in practice, he allowed for freedom in doctrine.

Mendelssohn sought to bring his people closer to the culture and civilization of his day and out of the intellectual, economic and political confinement of the Ghetto*. He translated the Pentateuch* into German (1778-83) and printed it in Hebrew characters with a Hebrew commentary ("Biur", in which other scholars, too, collaborated) which among other services, helped his co-religionists to acquire the German language and thus opened for them a highway to the culture of the Western World. Together with a number of friends, he founded the Hebrew periodical "Ha-Meassef" ("The Collector", 1784) which served, for a time, as the mouthpiece of the Enlightenment movement among the Jews of Germany ("Haskalah", "Aufklaerung"). This movement aimed to modernize the social and intellectual life of the Jews, to spread culture and secular learning among them, to revamp the curriculum of Jewish education and to stimulate the scientific study of the Hebrew language and literature.

Mendelssohn was the friend of many of the great literary and philosophic figures of his day especially of the eminent German poet and champion of tolerance, Gotthold Ephraim Lessing*. The latter used Mendelssohn as his model for the hero of his play, *Nathan the Wise* (1779). See Judaism, reform.

H. Walter, *Moses Mendelssohn* (1930), H. Graetz, *History of the Jews,* Vol. V, (Eng. trans.) *Jew. Encycl.* (1901-05) s.v. Moses Mendelssohn. A.H.S.

Mendenhall Lectureship: Founded in 1913 at De Pauw University by the Rev. Marmaduke H. Mendenhall D.D., from whom a bequest of about $10,000 was received. Its purpose is to provide each year a series of lectures at the University on "the Divine Origin, Inspiration, and Authority of the Holy Scriptures". Among the lecturers have been E. H. Hughes, F. J. McConnell, W. H. P. Faunce, E. F. Tittle, J. R. Mott, C. R. Brown, A. C. Knudson, H. N. Wieman, Georgia Harkness, E. B. Marlatt, F. S. Hickman.

A.C.K.

Mendicant Orders: Religious fraternities pledged to renunciation of property, individually and in common, and subject, therefore, to the necessity of mendicancy or begging. Especially significant among such orders in the Middle Ages were the Franciscans, Dominicans, Augustinians, and Carmelites**. Each of these, in its own way, within the area of common mendicant experience, utilized begging as a means to greater ends. Thus among the Franciscans, alms-gathering became a proving ground for humility and poverty of spirit as well as a supplement to labor as a means of livelihood. That Francis* never meant begging to obviate the necessity of manual labor is incontestable. Labor coupled with mendicancy made possible the liberation of the Friars Minor* from economic preoccupation to versatile social service. The Dominicans, likewise, utilized mendicancy as an aid to renunciation. Founded in 1216 by St. Dominic, the Order of Preachers dedicated itself to the salvation of souls through a ministry of scholarly studies, preaching, and missionary labors. As an aid to that end the Preachers adopted poverty and begging. Less rigid in their interpretation of renunciation than the Minors, they adapted the mendicant life to their own working genius. The Hermits of St. Augustine like the Order of Carmelites brought together existing eremitical associations into mendicant brotherhoods. In all of these orders mendicancy was employed as a useful means to the ends of religious vocation. See monasticism; Trinitarians.

A. Jessopp, *The Coming of the Friars* (London, 1928). R.C.P.

mene, mene, tekel, upharsin: "The handwriting on the wall" at Belshazzar's feast, Dan. 5:5, 25-28; Aramaic, meaning "numbered, weighed, divided", interpreted by Daniel as a message of impending doom. R.B.Y.S.

Menegoz, Eugene: (1838-1921) French theologian, colleague of Sabatier*. Known for his "fideism"* and his views on miracles (*Publications diverses,* Vol. I, 1900). His nephew, Dr. Fernand Ménégoz, is the author of *Le Problème de la Prière* and other theological works. W.M.H.

Menno Simons: (1492-1559) Dutch Anabaptist from whom Mennonites* later took their name. Left priesthood of R. C. Church; became Anabaptist elder. His wisdom, moderation and spirituality steered movement away from fanaticism of extremists; gave it organization and direction. Writings gave statement of principal doctrines. Stress on N.T. Rejected state church, religious persecution, infant baptism, oaths, the taking of life. K.H.C.

Mennonites: American Mennonites are directly descended from three sects which originated in the European Reformation: the Swiss Brethren, Obenites, and Hutterites. Coming to America largely through immigration of members, each group continued to stress the particular beliefs of its European antecedent. All the Mennonites, however, adhered to antipedobaptist and antisacerdotal doctrines.

The larger groups of Mennonites in America are the Old Mennonites, General Conference Mennonites, Mennonite Brethren in Christ, Mennoniten Brüder Gemeinde, Reformed Mennonites, and Old Order Amish.

The Old Mennonites, tracing their beliefs to the Swiss Brethren, center in Lancaster County, Pennsylvania. Stressing strict discipline, baptism by immersion of believers only, and widespread home missions, the movement is lead by an unsalaried lay-clergy. Besides the usual ordinances, they practice foot-washing, the anointing of the sick, and the kiss of charity**. Their organ, the *Gospel Herald,* is issued at the publishing house in Scottdale, Pennsylvania. Goshen College in Goshen, Indiana, is the leading school. There are about 30,000 members, 8,000 of whom live in Lancaster County.

The General Conference Mennonites, a particularly progressive branch composed of German congregations West of the Mississippi, have dropped many of their former practices. Bethel College in Newton, Kansas, and Bluffton College in Bluffton, Ohio are their leading schools. The *Mennonite,* their journal, is published at the Mennonite Book Concern in Berne, Indiana. Present membership of this group exceeds 13,000.

The Mennonite Brethren in Christ, a very active group, has at present around 6,000 members. They baptize by immersion, have open communion, and practice foot-washing as an ordinance. Camp meetings of the Brethren are similar in character to those of some early American Methodists.

The Mennoniten Brüder Gemeinde is divided into two parts because of differing views on the subject of baptism. The larger branch (5,000 members) immerse the applicant for baptism forward, while the smaller (1,000 members) insist on backward immersion. The larger group publishes *Die Zionsbote* and supports Tabor College in Hillsboro, Kansas, as its school.

The Reformed Mennonites, also called Herrites, number 1700 members living mostly in Pennsylvania. Even in Mennonite circles, they are ultra-conservative.

The Old Order Amish, numbering over 4,500 members nationally, oppose all ritualism and closely follow N.T. precepts. Not allowing church buildings, as the first step in sacerdotalism, they meet in houses or barns. Services, conducted in German, take four hours. Their apparel and houses are very plain, and carpets, curtains, and pictures are forbidden, as is insurance. Largest settlements are found in Pennsylvania, Ohio, Indiana, and Ontario.

Besides the listed groups, several smaller bodies of Mennonites exist, such as the Huterites of South Dakota (see communistic settlements, religious), the Old Colony Churches of Saskatchewan, the Defenseless Mennonites, the Wisler Mennonites, and several others. Cf. Church of God as Organized By Christ; Dunkers; Menno Simons; River Brethren. See Confessions, Formal of the Christian Church; shunning.

F. Ellis and S. Evans, *History of Lancaster Co., Pa.* (n.d.). J. F. Funk, *The Mennonite Church and Her Accusers* (1878). *Melvin Gingerich, *Mennonites of Iowa* (1939). *H. Krehbiel, *Mennonite Church Statistics* (1911). *Schaff Herzog, *Encyl.* (1910), p. 200 ff. D. Musser, *Reformed Mennonite Church* (1878). A. H. Newman, *The Baptists, Amer. Ch. Hist. Ser.,* v. 2, (1894). Cornelius Ris, *Mennonite Articles of Faith* (1904). *C. H. Smith, *Mennonites in America* (1909; 2nd ed. 1941). C. H. Smith, *Menno Simons* (1936). Luella Smith, *The Mennonite Family in the Menn. Comm.* (1938). John C. Wenger, *Glimpses of Mennonite History* (1940). Joseph W. Yoder, *Rosanna of the Amish* (1940). (Imp. works starred). M.G.R.—W.W.S.

Menologion: The service-book of the Eastern Orthodox Church*. It frequently is used to designate the *Menaion,* a twelve-volume collection of liturgical services, a volume for each month. More commonly it designates a shorter work comprising historical sketches of the saints of the day, or the tables of scriptural lessons. Lastly, the term is applied to collections of lives of saints.

Maltzew, *Das Menologion* (Berlin, 1900), 2 vols. M.S.

menorah: The golden, seven-branched candelabrum in the tabernacle in the wilderness (Ex. 25.31-40; 37. 17-24) and in the Temple at Jerusalem (Zech. 4. 2-5, 10b-14). It stood at the far western end of the sanctuary, just in front of the holy of holies. In popular tradition the light of the Menorah symbolized the presence of God, the Shekinah*, within the Temple. Tradition told further that this light was never extinguished until the Shekinah voluntarily departed from the Temple, in anticipation of its impending destruction. In every synagogue, in imitation of the Temple, there are always one or two Menorahs upon the altar. Moreover, in Jewish thought and literature the flaming Menorah is a fitting and frequent symbol of the unquenchable and illuminating spirit of Judaism. J.M.

mental health: See mental hygiene; psychotherapy.

mental hygiene: Mental hygiene is that body of knowledge that is necessary to the maintenance of mental health. More broadly it includes also the promotion and good care and treatment for the mentally ill and mentally defective. The organized expression of mental hygiene dates from the publication by Clifford W. Beers of his experiences as a patient in a mental hospital in *A Mind That Found Itself* in 1908 (26th Printing, 1942). That same year the Connecticut Society for Mental Hygiene was founded and the following year the National Committee for Mental Hygiene.

From the beginning the movement has concerned itself with the improvement of conditions in mental hospitals. Surveys of hospitals and detention facilities (jails) have been conducted that have led to improved conditions. Commitment procedures and scientific processes have been studied in order, and those most in keeping with the needs of the patient have been promoted. The services of progressive states have been publicized in order that others might be impelled to make better provision. Surveys have been made in practically all states. In 1939 the United States Public Health Service assumed responsibility for making such studies and assisting states in improving hospital facilities.

From the beginning the mental hygiene movement has become more and more attentive to provision for early treatment and prevention. In view of the wider range of a preventive effort mental hygiene has drawn on many fields that have to do with relatively normal persons or those showing beginning disturbances of adjustment. It is recognized that the family doctor, minister, social worker, teacher, public health nurse and others not only see cases in their incipiency, but are in a position to deal with such cases early or to exercise preventive measures. It is recognized that prevention must come about through the refinement of the everyday services of these professions rather than through increase in the number of psychiatrists, although there is also a paucity of psychiatrists. It is significant that the Federal Council of the Churches of Christ in America* has provided clinical training in mental hospitals and clinics for men entering the ministry and that the other professional groups are more and more including mental hygiene in their professional curriculum. This same council has made a special study of the chaplaincy functions of mental hospitals.

It is evident then that mental hygiene cannot be formulated as a single program and made the responsibility of one professional group. It involves individualization of the client, pupil, communicant or patient in the work of the several respective professions, and the inclusion in professional training of the determinants of human behavior and the forces that may be appropriately used by each profession to promote mental health. Many university departments of psychiatry have developed a close working relation with departments of education, theology, social work, law and nursing. Special facilities have been set up at cross roads of life to assist those who are finding the complexities of life at these points overwhelming—the failing or bewildered college student, the ineffectual in industry, the inapt in the Army, the delinquent, the criminal, the broken family, the dependent child.

Many states have organized societies for mental hygiene. There are periodicals, *Mental Hygiene* and *Understanding the Child*, that serve as a medium of interchange between the various forces in the field, and a rich bibliography of books and pamphlets on the subject. Information on such matters is obtainable from The National Committee for Mental Hygiene, 1790 Broadway, New York, N. Y. See psychotherapy.

Albert Deutsch, *The Mentally Ill in America*: A History of their Care and Treatment from Colonial Times (1937).

G.S.S.

mental reservation: In casuistry the secret qualification of a statement, in the interests of justice or expediency, which alters materially its import to the hearer. The classical illustration is the man's reply to the murderers in search of a victim, "No one is concealed here," the man reserving to himself the clause, "of whom I can justly speak to men like yourselves." F.G.E.

mental science: See New Thought movement.

mentalism: See epistemology.

Mercersburg theology, the: A movement in philosophy and theology which took its rise, about 1836, in Marshall College and in the Theological Seminary of the German Reformed Church*, then located at Mercersburg, Pennsylvania. The leaders of this school of thought were Frederick A. Rauch, John W. Nevin, and Philip Schaff*, a gifted triumvirate of scholars. The three successive phases of the movement—philosophical, theological, and liturgical—were in close touch and in sympathy with the modern evangelical theology of Germany. It caused controversy and dissent, but it quickened the German Reformed Church to new activity, both in its thought and life. The issues that occasioned the Mercersburg Theology have been superseded, but its spirit and fruits have permanently enriched the denomination.

F. A. Rauch, *Psychology* (1846); J. W. Nevin, *The Anxious Bench* (1843); *The Mystical Presence* (1846). Philip Schaff, *The Principle of Protestantism* (1845); E. V. Gerhart, *Institutes of the Christian Religion* (1891), 2 vols.; *The Mercersburg Review*, vols. 1-12 (1849-60).

T.F.H.

Mercier, Désiré Joseph Cardinal: Archbishop of Malines, Belgium, b. at Braine-l'Allend, 1851, and d. in Brussels, 1926. Eight years after his ordination in 1874, Père Mercier occupied the chair of Thomist philosophy at the Univ. of Louvain; under him the Scholastic philosophy of St. Thomas Aquinas was brilliantly systematized to meet modern requirements. Consecrated Archbishop of Malines and created a cardinal by Pius X* in 1906, he shortly became the outstanding figure in Belgian public and intellectual life, as his *Pastoral Works*, lectures, conferences, and addresses as president of the Belgian Royal Academy testify. After the invasion of Belgium in 1914 he emerged as a world-famous and highly articulate symbol of his country's unvanquished spirit. In 1924 began the Malines Conversations, his renowned attempt at establishing grounds for a unification of the Roman Catholic and Anglican Churches. He died a few days after the last inconclusive Conversation in January, 1926. J.F.T.

Mercury: (Lat. *Mercurius,* from *merx,* trade) The old Roman god of traders and their wares, early identified with the Greek Hermes*, whose attributes, the broad hat and caduceus (herald's staff), he assumed, along with his functions of messenger to the gods and guide of the souls of the dead. E.M.N.

mercy: An attitude of compassion and active, gracious beneficence expressed in forgiving helpfulness toward a wrong-doer. While it is an attitude appropriate only to an ethical superior it does not denote condescension but a loving-kindness which would restore the offender to complete fellowship through forgiveness and the mitigation if not omission of deserved punishment. In the Bible the mercy of God is a free, unconstrained expression of His love and is without stint or prejudice, being open to all men, worthy and unworthy alike. Christian theology does not regard God's mercy as incompatible with His righteous judgment but looks upon both as a living expression of His love as revealed in Christ whose atoning death reconciles the divine demands of mercy and justice. In Christian ethics mercifulness in man is a part of the righteousness of the Kingdom and is called for as a grateful response to the mercy of God in which it finds its model and inspiration. The mercy of God is stressed also in Jewish and Mohammedan theology, both of which stem from Biblical teaching. R.W.F.

mercy, seven works of: See seven works of mercy.

Mercy, Sisters of: See Sisters of Mercy.

merit: A certain credit for righteous acts that may be used to compensate for the demerits of sin. The term is closely associated with that of good works, i.e., praiseworthy religious acts or conduct which are believed to deserve reward, to evoke divine approval and to entitle one to salvation.* The idea of merit is akin to the religious efficacy which primitive peoples attribute to the proper performance of rites. The higher religions, Buddhism, Zoroastrianism, Judaism, Mohammedanism, and some forms of Christianity, have doctrines of merit which emphasize in varying degrees the ethical nature of religion and the moral value of good works. In Roman Catholicism the doctrine has undergone a complex development. Various attempts have been made to correlate it with the doctrines of grace* and of faith. The doctrine finally took form in the teaching that the value of good works is due to the power of grace infused into them through the sacraments in which the communicant participates under the official sanction and control of the Roman Church. It was held, further, that good works are "meritorious . . . of eternal life" and that salvation is a reward for merit. Luther revolted against this position as absolutely opposed to the Christian gospel which teaches that salvation is by faith alone. Protestantism as a whole agrees with the position of Luther, is opposed to any conception of earning salvation by merit, and regards good works, not as a condition of righteousness, but as the inherent fruits of faith that works by love. See Thesaurus meritorum. Cf. penance. R.W.F.

Merrick Lectures, The: Established in 1884 by President Frederick Merrick (Ohio Wesleyan, 1860-1873) and given annually at Ohio Wesleyan University, Delaware, Ohio. The capital sum is $10,000. The lectureship provides for a course of at least five lectures upon experimental and practical religion, the founder "believing that the Christian religion tends above all else to the elevation of the human race" and emphasizing its importance in institutions of learning. Recent lecturers have included Canon Charles E. Raven, Dr. E. F. Tittle, Bishop Bromley Oxnam; in 1942 the lectures formed a part of the international conference on Bases of a Just and Durable Peace and in 1943 a part of the conference on Christian Bases of World Order.

(Data from the Office of the President of the College.) V.F.

Meru: A mountain according to Buddhist mythology, situated at the center of the earth which is regarded as a vast circular island. It is said to be 160,000 leagues high. C.S.B.

Mesopotamian religions: The religion of the Akkadian-speaking Babylonians and Assyrians of the second and first millennia goes back, essentially unchanged, to that of the Sumerians, inhabitants of Southern Mesopotamia in remote antiquity. The following sketch, though drawing on material from all periods, aims most particularly to depict the form which this religion took before the final disappearance of its originators, the Sumerians.

The Sumerian lived in a world created by gods and existing for their benefit. These gods, huge eternal beings, could move through the universe at will and were vastly more powerful than man. In all other respects, however, in form and in mentality, they were exactly like man and had his physical needs: food, clothing, housing, etc. These needs they satisfied by exploiting the natural resources of the country, in which they formed the upper social stratum, the landed aristocracy. Below them, as their family, followers and servants, ranked minor gods, and at the bottom of the social ladder, as serf, villein or sharecropper on their estates, stood man.

The relations of the individual Sumerian to the gods were of a different nature. They reflected essentially the different relations of an individual in the family, and of an individual in the community. He stood in an intimate child-parent relation to one or another deity, usually a minor figure of the pantheon, his personal god. This deity would help him to success in his personal activities and would in general act as his patron before the higher gods. With the higher gods, on the other hand, man came in contact, as an individual, mainly in case of severe personal crisis, and his contacts were those of a subject with his lord, not of a son with his father. If he were attacked by lawless elements, the evil demons of pain and disease, only a powerful god could help, and Marduk* and his father Enki (Ea*) were usually willing to assist him. Similarly if he himself by breaking some taboo had angered a god he would approach him to do penance before him or he would approach another high god to ask the latter's mediation.

In the course of time all individual suffering tended to be linked to sin. Breaking of taboos, it was thought, alienated the personal god and only thus the individual became a prey to evil forces. This raised the question of individual ethics and the gods, and the problem of the just sufferer emerged. The Babylonians answered it by denying the absoluteness of human values: what seems right to man may be evil in the eyes of the gods. Thus even the just can have no rights, must throw himself entirely upon divine mercy.

The gods would help the individual in sickness and calamity, but not in death. "When the gods created man they assigned death to him, life they kept in their own hands." When death came to the individual he went down to "the great dwelling," a shadowy, dust-filled place under the earth. His status here depended upon such things as the manner of his death and burial, how many children he left behind, and the sacrifices offered on his grave. There is no trace of any belief that evil was punished, virtue rewarded, after death.

Except for the cases quoted, man's relations with the high gods were essentially as a member of the community to which he belonged. These gods owned the Sumerian cities and ruled them through human stewards of their own choice. The steward, the so-called *ensi,* received his orders from the city god by way of dreams and omens and carried out the domestic and foreign policy of the city accordingly. The god's residence was the temple in which he lived surrounded by his divine family, followers and servants. Under the divine servants worked human house-servants, preparing and serving the god's meals, the regular offerings, and keeping the house in order. Here were also the administrators charged with running the temple and the huge estate. And on that estate a large part of the city's human population earned their bread as the god's villeins or sharecroppers.

The divine manor-lords of Sumer were organized in a state along primitive democratic lines. Supreme authority was vested in a general assembly which met each new year to make the decisions for the coming year. The decisions were written on the "tablet of fates" to be announced and carried out by the leaders of the assembly, An and Enlil. The assembly could delegate administrative functions to one of its members, who was given dictatorial powers as king of the gods. Simultaneously his steward on earth became overlord, king, of all the other cities in the country. Kingship was granted on a term and would be given now to one, now to another god, now held in abeyance.

The social aspect of the gods, though dominating the concept of divinity in historical times, does not exhaust it. Besides his functions as ruler and administrator of city and temple, each god had close and original connection with some phenomenon, some enduring element of man's physical and mental environment. A few of the most important deities may be listed as examples:

An (Akkadian Anum), "Heaven," is lord of the city Uruk, but also god of heaven. Enlil, "Lord Wind," lord of Nippur, is god of wind and storm. Enki (Akkadian Ea), "Lord Earth," lord of Eridu, is god of the earth and its sweet waters, also of profundity and wisdom. Ninhursag, "Lady Mountain," a mother goddess, is queen of Kesh and goddess of mountains. Utu (Akkadian Shamash), "Sun," owner of the cities Larsa and Sippar, is god of the sun and of justice. Nanna (Akkadian Sin), "Moon," ruler of Ur, is god of the moon. Inanna (Akkadian Eshtar, Ishtar), "The lady of heaven" whose cult-center is in Uruk, is goddess of the planet Venus and also goddess of war and of sexual love. Ningirsu, "Lord of the city Girsu"—worshiped in Nippur under the name Ninurta "Lord . . . "—is lord of Lagash, of which Girsu was a part, and also god of the thunder showers and floods of spring. Ishkur (Akkadian Adad) is lord of Muru and other cities and god of thunder and lightning. Marduk, "the hoe-spirit(?)," who as god of Babylon became the highest god of Babylonia in later times, seems originally to have been an agricultural god personifying the powers of the hoe. Dumuzi (Akkadian Tammuz), was god of the pasture. Nergal, lord of Kutha, whose original nature is not yet clear, and his spouse Ereshkigal, queen (of ?) the subsoil, were rulers of Hades.

There is ample evidence to indicate that this connection between god and phenomenon was once much closer. In prehistoric times, it would seem, the god was not merely an anthropomorphic being standing behind the phenomenon controlling it, but was actually the phenomenon itself, the specific powers which manifested themselves in it. Correspondingly we find traces of a different attitude toward them on the part of man, one which was not merely the passive obedience of the subject to his ruler but called for active intervention: man could in the cult enter into, clothe himself with, these powers, and thus by his own action bring the phenomenon to pass. This prehistoric attitude is alive in the great body of magical practices to which the Sumerians and Akkadians were addicted. More important, however, is the fact that it also underlies—perhaps even survives in—the great periodic cult festivals which formed the core and mainspring of the religious life in the agricultural and pastoral Sumerian community.

The divine marriage, one of the most widespread rites, may be exemplified by the ritual of the city Isin as celebrated there toward the close of the third millennium. In this city each new year the king took on the identity of the god Dumuzi, god of pastures and the new vegetation of spring, and as god he united sexually with the goddess Inanna, who was, we may assume, incarnated in some priestess. Thus, by a willed act of man, was achieved divine union and in it all-pervading, life-giving, recreative potency upon which depended not only "the life of all lands" but even the steady flow of days and the renewal of the moon each month through the coming new year.

Other highly important rites centered around the death and reappearance of vegetation in the spring. The best known are those belonging to the cult of Dumuzi and Inanna (Tammuz and Ishtar). Here again man acted in the cult to achieve his end: lamenting the god of vegetation who had died or disappeared, searching for him, and finally bringing him back.

Lastly there was the battle drama in which at the beginning of each new year the battle of the gods against the powers of chaos was refought, rewon, and the orderly world reconstituted. This battle is reflected in many myths, of which the best known is *enuma elish.* It deals with the victory of Marduk (originally Enlil) over Kingu and Tiamat, the forces of primeval chaos, and with his subsequent organization of the world. In the cult this battle was refought symbolically; the king, taking on the identity of Marduk, vanquished Kingu by burning a lamb in which that deity was realized. Whether also other forms in which humans taking the identity of gods acted out the battle mimetically occurred is as yet not certain. See temples, Mesopotamian.

Bruno Meissner, *Babylonien und Assyrien* (Heidelberg, 1925), Vol. II, pp. 1-197; Edouard Dhorme, *La Religion Assyro-Babylonienne,* Conférences données à l'Institut Catholique de Paris, par le P. Paul Dhorme (Paris, 1910); Charles Francois Jean, *La Religion Sumérienne d'après les documents antérieurs à la dynastie d'Isin* (-2186), (Paris, 1931); Svend Aage Frederik Dichman Pallis, *The Babylonian Akitu Festival* (Copenhagen, 1926). T.J.

Messalians: See Eu-chites.

Messiah (Heb.—*Mashiach;* Aramaic—*Meshicha,* hence the Grecized form "Messias" of the N.T.—anointed; Gr.—*Christos*) The word Messiah is not found in the O.T. as a proper name or as a technical term. There is no reference to "a Messiah" or to "the Messiah". As such it first appears in Apocalyptic literature* (Enoch 48.10; 52.4; Pss. Sol. 17.36; 18.6, 8; etc.) In the O.T. the term is applied to men, principally kings and high priests, whose consecration to their high office was symbolized by the ceremony of pouring oil on their heads. This rite gave them a unique, sacred and inviolable status and a certain divine afflatus. Sprinkling or smearing with oil sanctified also inanimate objects such as the altar, the ark, and the various paraphernalia of the Tabernacle* (Ex. 30.26; Lev. 8.10-11). (See anointing.)

Saul, David, Solomon, Jehu, and Jehoahaz are mentioned as having been anointed into kingship. Saul is designated "the Meshiach Yahweh"—the anointed of the Lord (I Sam. 24.6). In the Biblical writings of the Persian Period, when there were no longer kings over Israel, reference is made to the anointing of the high priests. (Ex. 29.7; Lev. 8.12). Prophets also are mentioned as having been anointed. (I K 19.16; Is. 61.1). In exilic and post-exilic times, the term came to have a wider use. Anyone designated by Yahweh for a special mission is said to have been anointed. Thus Deutero-Isaiah* speaks of Cyrus as "the anointed of the Lord" (Is. 45.1). One of the Psalms speaks of the patriarchs as "mine anointed" (Ps. 105.14). Because of their role in history as "a kingdom of priests and a holy nation" the Jewish people as a whole is frequently spoken of as God's anointed (Ps. 28.8; 84.10; 89.39; 52; Hab. 3.13: Ps. 2, probably also refers to the Jewish people as a whole).

In the centuries following the destruction of Judea (586 B.C.) the Jews entertained the hope of an early restoration of their independence and the re-establishment of the monarchy under a scion of the Davidic dynasty whose throne, according to the promise, would endure forever (II Sam. 7:16; Ps. 86.30). The prophets Haggai and Zechariah** saw in Zerubbabel the possible fulfillment of this hope. The future king of the restored monarchy would of course be the Meshiach Yahweh—"the anointed of the Lord".

The prophets of Israel, in their exalted conception of a united and spiritually regenerated humanity, early projected the vision of the coming of the Great Day of the Lord, when God's kingdom would be universally established, His name proclaimed everywhere and Jerusalem acknowledged as the spiritual center of the world. This hope carried with it as a natural corollary also the hope of the ingathering of the people of Israel from all the lands of their dispersion, and the restoration of the kingdom under a descendant of David who would be a just and ideal ruler. Thus the political hope of a restored Jewish kingdom headed by a "Meshiach Yahweh" came to be associated with the prophetic and apocalyptic vision of a Kingdom of God in the End of Days.

The figure of the future Davidic ruler however was not for a long time central or even prominent in the picture of the future society, nor for that matter, was it always present. Furthermore, these prophetic anticipations touching the "End of Days" as well as the political "messianic" expectations never assumed the character of dogma or of articles of faith.

After the fall of the Maccabean dynasty, and especially after the Romans imposed their yoke upon the country in the second half of the first century, B.C., the longing for the coming of a personal Messiah assumed greater and greater prominence in the minds of the people and the hope of a universal Kingdom of God became more and more centered in the coming of a uniquely endowed Messiah of the stock of David who would break the alien yoke, restore Israel to its former greatness and independence, and with his coming, the New Order, the golden age of the world would begin. A colorful and quite inconsistent variety of eschatological notions came to be interwoven with the personality, mission and times of this Messiah. The intense expectations of the people reached their climax as the age approached the year 5000 of the Creation Calendar when, according to the popular belief of the day, there would be inaugurated the millennium—the thousand years of universal righteousness, blessedness and peace, after which the world would return again to its primal chaos. See Mahdi; pseudo-messiahs; redemption.

Joseph Klausner, *The Messianic Idea in Israel* (1927), (Hebrew); Julius H. Greenstone, *The Messiah Idea in Jewish History* (1906); Adolf Posnanski, *Schiloh* (1904); Hugo Gressmann, *Der Messias* (1929); *Jew. Enc.* (1901-05) s.v. Messiah.

A.H.S.

messianic hope: Strictly the expectation of the coming and reign of the Messiah (lit., anointed), destined to deliver the Hebrew nation. In the O.T. the term Messiah is not a title limited to one specific figure destined to appear in the future for a specific purpose. Rather it is employed as an adjective modifying some noun expressed or understood. The normal phrase is "anointed *of the Lord*," and is used of various figures—kings, high priests, patriarchs, the nation as a whole, even Cyrus. As late as the days of Herod's temple, when the high priest was no longer actually anointed, he continued to bear the title "anointed high priest."

To continue to use the term "the Messianic hope" to describe the expectations of future blessedness to which all pious Jews in the days of Jesus were looking forward is doubly unfortunate. It suggests: 1) that there was but *one* such expectation, whereas the evidence makes certain that there were widely differing opinions, ranging all the way from a rigorous nationalism which awaited a political restoration of Israel with a scion of David once more seated on a temporal throne to the more vague and comfortable expectation that in the future all men everywhere would recognize Israel's God as supreme. 2) It shows into undue prominence the Messiah. Actually the expectation was for the age, not for the one who was to institute it. In large blocks of Hebrew thinking, notably the prophecy of the exile, there is no mention of such a figure. God alone is to be king. After the fall of Jerusalem (586 B.C.) the hope for the coming good time—the golden age—may well have gained a new lease of life. God could not so desert his people (see eschatology). Once the temple was rebuilt all would be well. The temple was rebuilt, but Israel's independence did not materialize. In those years of unrest and subjugation undoubtedly many viewed the golden age in terms of a restoration of the monarchy. But this nationalistic view was far from universal even then. Memories of the successors of David were far too vivid. And in subsequent years there were always many Jews—especially those in comfortable circumstances—who showed little enthusiasm for such a day to dawn. It smacked too much of revolution. Such apparently was the attitude of the Sadducees* in the days of Jesus. The experiences of the past century under the later Hasmonean* kings were still fresh. Alexander Jannæus had occupied the throne of David, but aside from breaking the heads of the heathen—one of the tasks of the coming ruler (Ps. 110)—his reign had done much to dampen enthusiasm for the "scion of David." When the golden age dawned, God, not any man, would be enthroned. In the second Christian century, decades after the destruction of Herod's temple, when it was rumored in Palestine that Jerusalem was to be turned into a pagan city, there was a distinct change of attitude; a devoted, if entirely mad, nationalism was for the moment revealed, and a Messianic aspirant, Bar Kokhba* ardently championed.

On the other hand, the nationalistic form of the hopes for the future, while far from being universally held, had never been banished. The Home Rule Party (styled by Josephus* the "fourth philosophy") continued to insist on political restoration and sought to foment rebellion against Rome, precisely as had their forbears against Persia. In addition to these variant opinions which may properly be styled Jewish was the whole apocalyptic fantasy of a cataclysmic end of the present evil age with a supernatural figure descending from heaven to institute a final judgment.* To what extent these originally alien ideas had been incorporated into Jewish thinking before the Christian era is uncertain. At any rate, it seems most unwise to lump together all the variant notes and emphases having to do with expectations for the future in the one fictitiously simple and misleading phrase "the Messianic hope." See also apocalypticism; eschatology; redemption; Son of man.

G. F. Moore, *Judaism*, 3 vols. (1927 and 1930); M. S. Enslin, *Christian Beginnings* (1938), pp. 138-143.

M.S.E.

metamorphosis: Shape-fitting or transformation on the part of various orders of being, animate and inanimate, believed to be due to witchcraft or magic.** Belief in it is common at low levels of culture.

R.W.F.

metaphysics: (Gr., *ta meta ta physika*—the things after the *Physics*—the name given by Andronicus of Rhodes, ca. 63 B.C., to Aristotle's *First Philosophy*, which he, as editor, placed after Aristotle's *Physics*. Lat., *metaphysica*, first used as one word by Boethius in 6th cent. and popularized in 13th cent. by Averroes and others.) In general, the philosophical theory of reality as distinguished from the normative sciences (theory of ideals) and epistemology* (theory of knowledge).

1. The first philosophy, or theology, of Aristotle; the science of being as being, the theory of first principles and causes, especially of the good (*Met.*, 982b, 9-10). 2. The rational science of

the supersensuous or supernatural (*transphysica,* Albertus Magnus, St. Thomas; the immaterial, Descartes). 3. The science of formal and final causes (Bacon). 4. "The science of all that is possible, so far as it is possible" (Wolff, who subdivided it into ontology, rational cosmology, rational psychology, rational theology; axiology* is a recent addition). 5. Knowledge of the transcendent, or of things in themselves (rejected by Kant as dogmatic; accepted by Schopenhauer). 6. Knowledge *a priori* of the principles of pure reason presented in systematic unity (Kant). 7. Systematic interpretation of experience and its implications, as a whole (Schopenhauer, Hegel); this is the predominant usage since Hegel, except among the neo-scholastics. Metaphysics is concrete and inclusive, as distinguished from the sciences which are necessarily abstract and exclusive. Hegel's "panlogism" or identification of logic with metaphysics (as "the science of things apprehended in thoughts") presupposes and includes the results of the *Phenomenology of Mind,* the exposition of "the concrete forms of consciousness" (*Enc.,* Sec. 24, 25). See Hegel; Hegelianism.

In the *Soviet Encyclopaedia,* metaphysics is defined as "a certain kind of ontology, namely, that kind which is committed to theological, mystical, or idealistic conceptions of a changeless, supernatural reality" (tr. Hollis).

In popular language the term "metaphysical" is used loosely to mean supersensuous, occult (Marlowe), obscure, mysterious, or (dubiously) theoretical.

See articles on metaphysics in the dictionaries of Baldwin, Lalande, Eisler, Runes, and Ferrater Mora; also Webster and Oxford. See ontology; reality. E.S.B.

metempsychosis: See transmigration.

Methodism: The religious movement, which traces its origin to John Wesley (1703-1791) and in a minor degree to his brother Charles (1707-1788) and George Whitefield (1714-1770). The name "Methodists", as John Wesley tells us, was first given "by way of reproach" to three or four young men at Oxford in 1729 or shortly thereafter because of "the exact regularity of their lives as well as studies". Several years later, in 1738, when the Wesley brothers, Whitefield, and other members of the so-called "Holy Club" had become popular preachers, the name was revived and applied to them all and to their followers.

The "conversion" of John Wesley* or the extraordinary religious experience, that he had on May 24, 1738, marked the beginning of Methodism as a distinct and aggressive evangelistic movement. At the outset there was no thought of separation from the established church. But the course of events gradually made this inevitable, despite Wesley's long struggle against it. The official separation took place in America in 1784 with the organization of the Methodist Episcopal Church. In England it was still opposed by many. But after Wesley's death in 1791 and the adoption of a compromise measure in 1795, known as the Plan of Pacification, the separatist movement rapidly gained ascendancy and became the accepted policy of the Societies.

Methodism during Wesley's life-time was dominated by his strong personality, his organizing genius, his amazing evangelistic activities, and his intellectual leadership. Field preaching, lay preaching, sustained and militant religious zeal, and strict discipline characterized the movement, and awakened much opposition and not a little persecution. After Wesley's death the same crusading type of evangelism persisted and won extraordinary successes throughout the Anglo-Saxon world. A world-wide missionary activity was gradually inaugurated, and significant contributions were made to public life and morals. In its organization Methodism developed along two different lines, episcopal and non-episcopal, but in both its non-sacerdotal character remained intact. A number of schisms arose, but of late there has been a marked tendency toward reunion. The most important reunions were that of British Methodism in 1932 and that of the Methodist Episcopal Church, the Methodist Episcopal Church, South, and the Methodist Protestant Church in America in 1939. It may also be noted that in 1925 the Methodist Church of Canada united with the Congregational Churches, the Presbyterian Church and the local Union Churches in Western Canada to form the United Church of Canada.*

In its polity American Methodism is for the most part episcopalian. But its episcopacy is an "office", not an "order." It has no connection with the apostolical succession of the sacerdotal churches. Its validity is based on its efficiency. This is also true of the Methodist ecclesiastical system as a whole. It claims no divine sanction other than that growing out of its utility. The system is complex. In the new united "Methodist Church", for instance, the governing bodies consist in an ascending scale of Quarterly Conferences in the local churches, District Conferences, Annual Conferences, Jurisdictional and on the foreign field Central Conferences, and a General Conference. In all of these Conferences laymen are represented. The Bishops are elected by the Jurisdictional and Central Conferences. Together they form the Council of Bishops, which meets at least once a year. In this Council the Bishops from the Central Conferences are limited in their voting privileges "to matters relating to their respective Central Conferences." The chief function of the Bishops, aside from supervising their "areas", is the annual appointment or reappointment of pastors to the churches. In making these appointments their authority is being increasingly limited by the wishes of the local churches. Between the Bishops and pastors are the "District Superintendents," who might be described as sub-bishops. These three orders of the Methodist ministry are closely coordinated and give a high degree of unity to the church organization and its activities.

It is characteristic of Methodism that it has throughout its entire history laid emphasis on life rather than on doctrine. "As to all opinions which do not strike at the root of Christianity", said Wesley, "we think and let think." The only thing on which he insisted as a condition of membership in the Methodist Societies was "faith working by love". To precisely formulated theological opinions both he and his preachers for the most part "sat loose". Such theological laxity, one might have expected, would lead to dissension and schism. But the very reverse was the result. Wesleyan Methodism has had no schisms due directly or chiefly to doctrinal differences. Its emphasis on life and religious experience has produced a larger degree of doctrinal uniformity and of freedom from theological strife than would probably have been possible if stricter doctrinal standards had been adopted. *The Welsh Calvinistic Methodists,** it is true, broke with Wesley in 1770 on theological grounds, but they owed their origin and development as a separate denomination to Calvinistic teachers, among them Whitefield*, and never accepted Wesley's leadership.

The history of Methodist theology may be divided into two periods of unequal length. The dividing line may be drawn through the last quarter of the past century. Up to that time Methodist theology was on the whole "realistic" in its philosophical background, and authoritarian and rationalistic in its method. Since then it has become increasingly idealistic in its underlying philosophy, and in its method empirical and rational.

The first period covered about one hundred and fifty years. During the earlier part of it considerable attention was given by Wesley and his preachers to certain doctrines such as those of predestination, free-will, and Christian perfection. But comparatively little was done in the way of systematic theological study. Not until 1834, ninety-five years after the beginning of organized Methodism, was the decision reached in England to establish a Methodist theological seminary; and not until 1839, seventy-three years after what is commonly regarded as the beginning of American Methodism, was a similar decision reached in America. The first comprehensive Methodist treatise on systematic theology was written in England by Richard Watson in 1823-29, and the second by William Burt Pope in 1875-1880. In America two treatises of a similar character appeared in this period, one by Miner Raymond in 1877-79, and the other by John Miley in 1892-94. These four men did creditable work in systematizing Methodist doctrine. But they were not creative thinkers, they introduced no new theological method, they were guided by no new organizing principle, they gave no new direction to theological thought. They reflected for the most part the authoritarian standpoint of the current traditional evangelicalism.

The transition from the first to the second period was in large measure due to the widespread acceptance of the conclusions of biblical criticism and the consequent abandonment of the doctrine of biblical infallibility. This change from "fundamentalism"* to "modernism" was effected in Methodism with much less strife than in most of the other Protestant churches. One reason for this was the influence of Borden P. Bowne* (1847-1910), the greatest thinker that Methodism has produced. He was a philosopher rather than a theologian. But his philosophy was one of the theological type. And it was in the religious field, and especially in American Methodism, that he exercised his greatest influence. The American Methodist theologians of the present century, such as H. C. Sheldon (1845-1928), O. A. Curtis (1850-1918), F. J. McConnell (1871-), H. F. Rall (1870-), Edwin Lewis (1881-), and A. C. Knudson (1873-) have been either directly or indirectly influenced by him. In his philosophy of personalism* Methodist philosophical theology has received its most fundamental and convincing expression, and with him a new era in the history of Methodist theology began,—an era in which theology has emancipated itself from the crude realism and authoritarianism of the past, and has grounded itself in the deepest insights of modern idealism.

In general it may be said that Methodist the ology has been a mediating theology. It has avoided extremes. It has been openminded to new truth, and yet has adhered firmly to the universal tenets of Christianity. It has laid no claim to uniqueness or novelty. And yet in both its "explicit" and "implicit" form it has had a definite structure of its own, and has exercized a pervasive influence on Christian life and thought.

The explicit theology of Methodism has centered in the idea of human freedom (D. D. Whedon, *The Freedom of the Will,* 1864). It was the pronounced belief in real freedom, the freedom of contrary choice, that underlay Wesley's life-long polemic against Calvinism and his doctrine of Christian perfection. These two outstanding characteristics of his teaching marked a significant departure from the Reformation type of theology. They introduced into Protestantism a more ethical view of "faith" and a more activistic and humanistic conception of the Christian life.

The "implicit" theology of Methodism is to be found in its emphasis on religious experience. According to Wesley the only genuine religion is experienced religion. This insight not only led to a large degree of liberality in doctrinal matters, it had in itself the germ of a new empirical type of theology. Conditions favorable to the development of this germ did not exist in early Methodism. But Wesley did much to prepare the way in the Anglo-Saxon world for the modern empirical theology associated with the names of Schleiermacher (1768-1834) and Ritschl (1822-1889).

The following statistical table gives the present approximate membership of the main divisions of world-wide Methodism, including its foreign missions and the United Church of Canada:

I. *The United States.*	
The Methodist Church	7,732,257
African Methodist Episcopal	650,000
African Methodist Episcopal Zion	414,244
Colored Methodist Episcopal	365,000
The Free Methodist	45,890
The Wesleyan Methodist	26,720
Other Smaller Methodist Churches	51,657
II. *United Church of Canada*	716,064
III. *British Empire*	
Great Britain	1,264,493
Australasia	189,437
New Zealand	24,813
South Africa	303,148
IV. *Mexico, Brazil, Korea, Japan*	86,169
	11,869,892

See assurance; evangelicalism and Evangelical Revival; holiness churches; United Meth. Church.

Wesley's *Journal* (stand. ed. by N. Curnock, 1909-16), *Letters* (stand. ed. by J. Telford, 1931), and *Sermons* (stand. ed. by E. H. Sugden, 1922); J. S. Simon, *John Wesley,* 5 vols.; F. J. McConnell, *John Wesley* (1939); G. C. Cell, *The Rediscovery of John Wesley* (1935); Abel Stevens, *History of Methodism* (1858) and *History of Methodist Episcopal Church* (1864); Luccock and Hutchinson, *The Story of Methodism* (1926); *Discipline of the Methodist Church* (1940). A.C.K.

Methodists, Calvinistic: See Calvinistic Methodists.

Methodius: (d. c. 311 A.D.) A bishop in Lycia, Asia Minor. Wrote in support of voluntary celibacy. Opposed Origen's* doctrines of eternal creation, of the body as a fetter of the soul, of pre-existence, and of the immateriality of the resurrection body. Martyred in the Diocletian persecution. A.K.R.

metropolitan: (Gr. *metropolis,* city) 1) In the Roman Catholic Church the title and rank added to that of an archbishop who presides over at least one suffragan (or supporting) see, other than his own, in a defined territory or province. A metropolitan must summon his suffragan bishops at least once every twenty years, and appeals from their courts are subject to his; but his right of interference in the dioceses of his suffragans is strictly limited by law.

2) In the Eastern churches, both Catholic and dissident, the title metropolitan, or metropolite, is distinct from that of archbishop, but tends to eclipse it entirely, notwithstanding the fact that there are numerous archbishops without provinces or metropolitical rights. See exarch; patriarch. J.F.T.

Metropolitan Church Association: A small sect, which is also known as the Burning Bush, having headquarters in Waukesha, Wis. It began in a revival in the Metropolitan Methodist Church in Chicago and became an independent sect in 1918. It is a holiness and "faith" group which specializes in evangelistic and missionary work. It has started work in several foreign countries. Its distinguishing mark is the "faith" principle. No worker receives a salary, solicits gifts, or owns property; money received is turned in to the general treasury and disbursed for the work of the association. It claims 14 churches (2 buildings) and 960 members. See Evangelistic Associations; holiness churches. E.T.C.

mezuzah: (Lit. door-post, Heb.) Name given to a piece of parchment inscribed with the passages Deut. 6, 4-9 and 11, 13-21 rolled up like a scroll and placed into a container fastened to the upper right-hand posts of the entrances of Jewish dwellings as a sign of faith in God. The biblical source of the rite is Deut. 6, 9 and 11, 20. S.R.

Micah: The authentic writings of Micah are confined to chs. 1-3 and a dozen scattered verses in chs. 6-7. The remainder of chs. 4-7 consists of appendixes by exilic optimists, post-exilic psalmists, and eschatologists*. In his six genuine prophetic poems, Micah attacked rulers, judges, priests, prophets, etc., for their corruption. Although Israel had been carried into exile twenty years earlier, Judah was becoming more corrupt instead of learning a lesson, and Assyria was encroaching farther to the west. By threat and exhortation, Micah tried to save his country from destruction as Amos and Hosea** had tried in the north. Micah was a resident, probably an artisan, of the village Mareshah on the Philistine border in southwest Judah. A proletarian prophet, Micah possibly had no contacts with his older contemporary, Isaiah*, who was of the aristocracy. Micah was the most notable of the prophets in denouncing wickedness in high places and in championing oppressed classes. He was most active around 711 B.C. and 701 B.C., the two national crises when Assyria invaded Palestine.

See *The Prophets and their Times* by J. M. P. Smith and W. A. Irwin (1941), pp. 122-30. R.E.W.

Michael of Cesena: (1270-1342) As Minister General of the Franciscans*, he led a growing party of opposition to Pope John XXII* who had in 1322-23 indicted the ideal of poverty as conceived of and practiced by the Order. Joined by a considerable party, including William of Ockham*, in his support of the Emperor Louis, he sought to unify divergent parties in his fraternity around the common repudiation of the pope, now declared heretical. But the Cesenists were repudiated by the Order at large, which accepted papal reconciliation at the Chapter General of 1329. Michael and his writings were condemned. R.C.P.

Michael Scot: (died shortly before 1235) Trained at Oxford and Paris, Michael Scot acquired his fame chiefly through his translations from the works of the Arabs. He latinized in Toledo the astronomical writings of Alpetragius (Abû Ishâk al-Bitrûschi), some of the commentaries of Averroes* to Aristotle and the *Abbreviationes* of Avicenna*. This latter work he dedicated to Emperor Frederick the Second who employed him as his court astrologist.

The leading scholastics of the Middle Ages considered Michael Scot as a heterodox philosopher and he was placed in the Inferno (XX, 115) by Dante. S.C.T.

Michaelmas: The festival of St. Michael the Archangel (*Dedicatio S. Michaelis Archangeli*), Sept. 29. In the Anglican calendar, St. Michael and All Angels. Cf. church year; church year cycle. P.V.N.

Midgard-serpent: (Teut.) Midgardsormr, in Norse mythology, a great snake-like monster which lies in the sea, coiled round the whole earth. It is one of the offspring of Loki*, the earth demon, and is opposed to the gods. When the world ends the great serpent will come out of the sea on to the land, breathing out poison and aid other monsters and giants in an attack upon the gods. Thor will battle with him and be killed by his poisonous breath. F.L.P.

midrash: From the Hebrew *dorash* which means probing. Rabbinic exposition of scripture aiming not alone at the simple elucidation of the Biblical text, but also at the discovery within Scripture of general norms which would have universal application. The inspiration for the Midrash was, on the one hand, the need for continued clarification of the Bible, and, on the other hand, the desire to order life in accordance with Biblical prescriptions. Since the changed circumstances prevailing in post-Biblical times had made the simple côde of the Bible insufficient in itself to direct life, the rabbis sought to probe more penetratingly into the Biblical text in order to discover implications, not always apparent on the surface, that might offer the required guidance. There are two types of Midrash: the *Midrash Halakah* which deals with the legal sections of the Bible and the *Midrash Hagadah* dealing with the non-legal. The *Midrash Halakah* is well illustrated in the interpretation of Deut. 24:6: "No man shall take the mill or the upper millstone as pledge; for he taketh a man's life to pledge." This law mentions specific utensils, but it was clearly designed to protect the poor debtor in the possession of domestic tools which were indispensable to him in the preparation of food. The rabbinic interpretation therefore generalized that it also was meant to apply to "all tools used in the preparation of food" (*Mishnah Baba Mezia* 9:13). The *Midrash Hagadah* is well illustrated in the rabbinical interpretation of Leviticus 19:18, which forbids taking "vengeance" or bearing a "grudge". The rabbinic interpretation distinguishes between the two. "Vengeance is where a person says to his fellow, 'Lend me your sickle,' and he refuses; and the next day the latter person says, 'Lend me your axe,' and he replies, 'I will not lend you anything, in the same way that you declined to lend me.' A grude is where a person says to his fellow, 'Lend me your axe,' and he refuses; and the next day the latter person says, 'Lend me your garment,' and he replies, 'Here it is! I am not like you who declined to lend me what I wanted'." (*Yoma* 23 a).

H. L. Strack, *Introduction to the Talmud and Midrash* (1931). B.Z.B.

Miéville, Henri: (1877-) A well-known Swiss thinker. The aim and main part of his recent work are religious in character. His is a very philosophical religion. Its great success is due to the intimate union of a very decided rationalism with a very genuine religious feeling, detached not only from all orthodoxy, but even from belief in a personal God. The work responded to the expectations of many Christians, spiritualistically inclined, who are troubled by the radical *fidéisme,* the extreme anti-intellectualism, of which Karl Barth* has been the eloquent propagandist. The argument against authority in matters of belief and dogmatic theology is striking. He points out with vigor whatever is anthropomorphic and immoral in the religious attitudes. His critique is nourished by a passion for goodness, truth, justice and beauty. Pure, ideal reason consists in an idea of totality, of harmony. God Himself combines in Himself synthesis and power of invention in a singularly complex unity which leaves nothing outside itself. He combines Himself with the efforts of men working to create a better order in the world, and to realize an ideal either by means of science or justice among peoples. God is at one and the same time living spiritual thought, nature, and absolute. He is above justice and reason, which are only limited and human attributes, but he is present in virtuous and intelligent acts.

Vers une philosophie de l'ésprit ou de totalité, reflexions et recherches (Lausanne and Paris, 1937). H.H.

Milic, John of Kromeriz: (d. 1374) A member of the Czech* reform movement. In 1363 he resigned all his benefices in protest against the corrupt papal methods of granting them, lived in poverty, and began preaching reform. Held that the Antichrist* was to appear in 1365-67, and identified Emperor Charles IV with him. Was imprisoned, but was allowed to appear before Pope Urban V (1367). In Rome he announced the appearance of the Antichrist, and wrote *Libellus de Antichristo.* In it, he demanded the calling of a general council, and a reform of the church. Appealed to the Pope just then returned to Rome to initiate the reform. Returned to Prague, gave himself to fervent work of preaching (as many as five times a day). He was accused of heresy, cited before the curia of Pope Gregory XI to Avignon, but died there before his case was settled.

Václav Novotny, *Nábozenské huuti ceské ve* 14. *a* 15. stol. (Prague, n. d.); F. Lützow, *The Life and Times of Master John Hus* (n. d.) M.S.

military religious orders: Associations of the Crusading* period in which the monastic* and the military life were joined for the prosecution of Christian objectives. Among such were the Knights Hospitallers* of St. John, the Templars, and the Teutonic Knights. The first of these, c. 1092, opened a pilgrim's hospital in Jerusalem, adopted a basically Augustinian* rule, and, in the centuries following, became an organization of power and influence whose wealth invited sure decay. The Poor Knights of the Temple, having joined to their knightly vows those of the monastic life as well, c. 1119, functioned as protectors of pilgrims and defenders of the Christian kingdom of Jerusalem, with quarters near the Temple site. Multiplying ecclesiastical privileges, an increasingly complicated officialdom, and mounting riches, elicited jealousies in many quarters and led ultimately to suppression at the hands of Pope Clement V in 1312. The Teutonic Knights*, with generally similar aims, had their origins in hospital work among poor and sick German pilgrims at Acre, c. 1189. As finally constituted, their order comprised German free knights, priest-brothers, and serving brethren committed to the service of the sick and the protection of the Holy Land. Thus, these orders evince a striking similarity in conception, function, and institutional history. See monasticism; Knights Templar.

F. C. Woodhouse, *The Military Religious Orders* (London, 1879); H. Prutz, *Die giestlichen Ritterorden* (Berlin, 1908); W. Moeller, *History of the Christian Church* (1910), vol. II. R.C.P.

milk and honey: A phrase used by several ancient culture peoples to indicate prosperity and abundance. As delicious foods, milk and honey came to be the symbols of plenty, then of happiness and well-being and finally of the material richness of the golden age to come. Use of these materials in religious rituals reflects sometimes the food* value, more often the symbolic meaning. The newly baptized person in the early Christian church tasted milk and honey, probably as a symbol of the blessedness of his new status.

A.E.H.

Mill, John Stuart: (1806-1873) British economist, logician, and moral philosopher. In economics he is in the main a defender of *laissez faire* capitalism, although he was aware of its abuses and at times made concessions to socialism. In logic an empiricist, he greatly improved the statement of the methods of induction. In ethics he modified the Utilitarianism of Bentham** (whom in most respects he ardently admired) to admit an internal sanction of conscience and qualitative differences in pleasures. His essay on *Liberty* is a classical defence of individual rights, and his *Representative Government* (1861) prophesies correctly both the benefits and dangers of increased democracy. Although in many respects a positivist, his posthumous essays show him to have been a theist, and one of the first advocates of the conception of God as limited in power. He was an enthusiastic supporter of the liberal political and social movements of his time. See happiness.

System of Logic, 2 vols. (1843); *Principles of Political Economy,* edited by W. J. Ashley (1923); *Utilitarianism* (1863); *Essays on Religion* (1874); Leslie Stephen, *The Utilitarians* (1900). W.K.W.

millenarianism: (Lat. *millenarius,* containing a thousand) Belief in the millenium or period of 1,000 years immediately following the bodily advent of Christ who with his saints will rule the world in person. Those who hold this view—commonly styled *pre*millennialists* in contrast to *post*millennialists*, who believe that Christ's return will be after the millennium—believe that the whole program read out of Revelation, especially chap. 20, will be literally fulfilled, though they commonly neglect the express statement (Rev. 20:5) that only those who have been "beheaded for the testimony of Jesus" are to live in this period.

In such apocalypses as IV Ezra and Revelation is to be seen an attempt to combine the specifically Jewish hopes for the future (see Messianic hope) with the views found in the apocalyptic* writings. Thus the earlier notion of an unending golden age is altered. In IV Ezra the Anointed (*i.e.*, the Davidic king of Israel) is to appear, destroy all opposition, and reign for 400 years. Then he will die. The Resurrection and Final Judgment* will follow and the New Age ("Age to Come") will dawn. Similarly in Revelation Christ will reign (with his martyred saints) 1,000 years. Then Satan will be loosed for one final onslaught, but will be destroyed by God and cast into the lake of fire. There will be a general resurrection of all believers, and a new heaven and earth will be created.

These pictures have been accepted literally by many Christians, and each generation has seen complicated calculations of the date of Christ's return. The lush details as to the delights of the future which abound in both the prophetic foretastes of the coming golden age and in the even less restrained apocalyptic pictures were eagerly appropriated and exaggerated. Irenæus* quotes the lost writing of Papias* (an enthusiastic chiliast*), in which Jesus is made to promise: "The days will come, in which vines shall grow, each having ten thousand branches, and in each branch ten thousand twigs, and in each twig ten thousand shoots, and in each one of the shoots ten thousand clusters, and in every one of the clusters ten thousand grapes, and every grape when pressed will give five and twenty *metretes* (200 gallons) of wine" (Irenæus, *Haer.* v, 33, 3).

Though in the latter half of the second century the earlier expectation that the return of Christ was imminent was becoming far less central than it had formerly been, the conviction that, though deferred, it would nonetheless occur continued, and is probably held even today by the mass of Christians. In the Greek church the chiliastic views tended more and more to be discredited. Anything that went beyond the admission of the visible advent of Christ and a literal hell for sinners came to be suspect as Jewish. In the Western church millenarianism continued to be at least tolerated, partly because it was an integral part of the tradition, partly because the Gnostics and Marcion** excluded it; but from the fourth century on it sank farther and farther below the surface. Augustine's insistence that the Church was the kingdom of Christ and that the millenial kingdom had thus actually started with the birth of Christ tended definitely to exclude the doctrine from Catholic theology. Nonetheless it continued beneath the surface and was a convenient weapon for opponents of the Church. In attacks on the papacy from the thirteenth to the fifteenth century and in the Anabaptists* and similar revolutionary movements of the fifteenth and sixteenth centuries the earlier millenarianism bloomed again in full vigor. It became a part of the baggage of the Reformation and has continued to the present day, a seemingly necessary consequence of verbal inspiration of the Scriptures*.

G. F. Moore, *Judaism,* 3 vols. (1927 and 1930).

M.S.E.

Millenial Dawn: A book by C. T. (Pastor) Russell* first published in 1881 at Allegheny, Pa. under the title, *Food for Thinking Christians.* Reissued in 1886 as *Millenial Dawn,* and carrying the sub-title, *Plan of the Ages,* it was later included in his six-volume series, *Studies in the Scriptures.* It reached a circulation of more than five and a half million copies.

Interpreting the Scriptures literally, Russell built up a system of prediction concerning Christ who he believed had already returned in 1874. The book presented a philosophy of history which held some dates as established, thus demonstrating revelation through an impinging of the divine in history. Using these dates as points of departure, he predicted the Millennium would occur "sometime before the end of A.D. 1914".

Russell held God had created man perfect and free, to learn by experiencing evil. The end of evil was physical death, from which man would be re-called at the resurrection. Man could be saved only by Christ, whose sinless birth and life had given him the "right to live". The result of the sin of Adam was the physical death of the race. The second death, from which there could be no redemption, would occur for willful disobedience during the Millennium which had already come. The second chance would divide forever the fate of all mankind. Russell demonstrated these beliefs with illustrations, using the Great Pyramid of Gizeth as his source.

M. C. Czatt, *International Bible Students and Jehovah's Witnesses* (1933); C. T. Russell, *Millenial Dawn* (1881); N. H. Barbour, and C. T. Russell, *Three Worlds, and the Harvest of this World* (1877); C. T. Russell, *Studies in the Scripture,* vol. I, II, (1886).

M.G.R.—W.W.S.

Miller, William: (1782-1849) and Millerism. William Miller an honest, earnest Baptist farmer-preacher began, in 1839, to stir the whole nation by fixing the date of the second coming of Christ at some time between March 21, 1843 and March 21, 1844. He had reached his conclusions by a long and careful study of the apocalyptical books of the Bible. The movement resulting influenced all the revivalistic churches in the nation though the excitement subsided after the passing of the latter date. Miller had discouraged his followers from withdrawing from the churches, but those continuing to hold that the final day was at hand gradually withdrew and in 1845 a loose organization was formed which took the name Adventists. These have since divided into several separate bodies. See Adventists.

W.W.S.

Milman, Henry Hart: (1791-1868) Ecclesiastical historian and poet. A priest of the Church of England, Milman was professor of poetry at Oxford from 1821 to 1831; he became Dean of St. Paul's in London in 1849. Apart from books of poetry, his writings include fifteen volumes of historical studies, on Judaism, early Christianity and Latin Christian churches.

W.N.P.

Milton, John: (1608-1674) English poet. Born in London, educated at St. Paul's School and Christ's College, Cambridge, he devoted the early years of his maturity to private study and to the writing of verse, both English and Latin, in a variety of Renaissance traditions. From 1641 to 1660 he was active in public affairs, serving as Secretary to the Council of State and producing a notable series of pamphlets on ecclesiastical, sociological, and political subjects. During his last years, spent in blindness and enforced retirement, he wrote his major epic, *Paradise Lost* (1667), a shorter epic, *Paradise Regained* (1671) and a drama, *Samson Agonistes* (1671), as well as a considerable body of prose. His principal theological work, *De Doctrina Christiana,* was probably completed about 1660 although possibly begun much earlier; it was not published until 1825.

Starting as an Anglican of moderate Puritan leanings, Milton became successively a Presbyterian and a radical Independent. His final position was Arian, Arminian, and in many other respects unorthodox. His so-called heresies, however, have been overemphasized by recent critics.

The Columbia Milton (18 vols., 1931-38) is the most inclusive edition, the only available source for much of the prose. David Masson's *Life of John Milton* (7 vols., 1859-94) is the standard biography. J. H. Hanford's *Milton Handbook* (3rd ed., 1939) is a compendium of modern scholarship and contains excellent bibliographical suggestions.

L.W.C.

mimbar: The pulpit* in a Moslem mosque.

P.E.J.

Miner, Alonzo Ames: Born Aug. 17, 1814; died June 14, 1895. Spent early years as teacher; later ordained to Universalist* ministry. Became noted champion of temperance, anti-slavery, and other reform movements. Was associated with Hosea Ballou* in Boston. Became President of Tufts College in 1862 and saved the institution in its days of crisis.

G. H. Emerson, *Life of Alonzo Ames Miner* (1896).

C.R.S.

Minerva: (Lat. *Minerva,* from *men-,* to remind) Probably an old Italian goddess of trade guilds, later identified with the Greek Athena, taking on martial characteristics. Vergil represents her as goddess of handicrafts and of war.

E.M.N.

minhah: (Heb., gift or offering) Afternoon service of the synagogue*, suggested by I Kings 18.29, and corresponds to the afternoon sacrifice at the

Temple* and particularly to the cereal portion of the daily offering. S.S.C.

Minims, or Minimi: (Lat. the least) The Minim Hermits of St. Francis of Paula, a mendicant order founded by that saint in 1453 for the purpose of giving retreats, missions, and assistance to the poor and neglected. Their name was intended to characterize an even greater humility than that of the Franciscan Friars *Minor**, after whom they were patterned. Once very widespread in Europe and foreign missions, they now number only about 500 religious in twenty-two monasteries. J.F.T.

ministry: See clergy; ordination; pastor; priesthood.

ministry, preparation for: See seminaries, major Roman Catholic; theological schools, Jewish; theological schools, Protestant, United States and Canada.

Minor Prophets: Traditional classification applying to the twelve smaller prophetic collections: Amos, Hosea, Micah, Zephaniah, Nahum, Habakkuk, Haggai, Zechariah, Obadiah, Malachi, Joel, and Jonah**; called the "Book of the Twelve" by Jewish writers because they were written on a single scroll. The term "minor" is based solely on the quantity rather than quality of each prophet's surviving work. Judged on a page-unit basis, many of these are not inferior to the supposed major prophets. See Major Prophets; prophets, prophecy (O.T.). R.E.W.

Minucius Felix, Marcus: First Latin Apologist*; known by his dialogue "Octavius", written perhaps shortly before 200 A.D. Tried to show the philosophic truth and moral attractiveness of Christianity. K.H.C.

minuscule: *idem* cursive*.

minyan: (Heb., count) The number of adult males required for Jewish public worship, fixed at ten. S.S.C.

miracle plays: See religious drama.

miracles: The term miracle is used in two senses: 1) referring to an event involving the upsetting of natural laws or the intrusion of the supernatural into the realm of the natural; 2) referring to an event which is incomprehensible. In the latter sense, what is miraculous for one age becomes commonplace for another. On purely philosophical grounds, it would be dogmatic to deny the possibility of miracles in the first sense of the term. However, on scientific grounds, where antecedent-consequent relations are sought to make for an understanding of the world of experience, an appeal to the miraculous as an intrusion into a supposedly orderly process is considered hazardous if not an outright denial of scientific method. In recent liberal Christian thought under the spell of scientific method, it has become considered highly dubious to place miracle (especially the "historic miracles") at the foundation of the Christian faith; miracles may, for the liberal Christian, be believed in but they are held to belong to the less essential. Conservatives, however, tend to hold to the pattern of the traditional mind which gravitated toward explaining certain events as evidences for the *special* infiltration of the divine into the natural course of events. V.F.

miracles in early Christian times: The Gospels, and the early Christian writings generally, tell of many incidents which seemed contrary to the order of nature and were set down to immediate divine action. These miracles were long regarded as the most impressive proofs that God was himself operative in the Christian mission; in modern times they have provided scepticism with its chief weapon. Miracles, it is argued, are incredible, and a history which is inseparably bound up with them cannot be true. The argument has now ceased to carry much weight in either direction. It is recognized that the ancient world ascribed to supernatural power everything that could not be explained by its rudimentary science. If the Christian writings are full of miracles, so are all the books of that time, and sober authors like Cicero and Tacitus do not hesitate to explain any strange phenomenon as a miracle. From the mere fact that an event in Christian history is described as miraculous we cannot infer that it did not happen. The fact itself may be indubitable although the explanation given to it in an unscientific age may be wrong. The Gospel miracles stand in a class by themselves. We have here to deal with a Personality which, on any view, was unique. It is impossible to say, from any comparison with ordinary men, what Jesus may or may not have done. No fact in his history is better attested than that he was regarded in his lifetime as a wonder-worker. It is evident, however, that the recorded miracles fall into several categories, each of which must be considered separately. In those instances where he appears as controlling the powers of nature a spiritual fact may be presented symbolically, or a coincidence viewed as a miracle, or an actual event exaggerated or fancifully explained. By far the greater number of the miracles are acts of healing, and especially of mental healing. There is no reason to doubt that Jesus had an extraordinary gift of calling spiritual forces into action, and influencing the body through the mind. It is significant that he required faith as the necessary condition for the exercise of his power. According to the Synoptic Gospels he did not rest his claim on the miracles. He pointed to them simply as evidences that the Kingdom of God was near, and declared that his followers, if they had sufficient faith, might themselves perform them. In the Fourth Gospel the miracles are singled out as the distinctive "signs" that Jesus participated in the divine nature. Throughout the early history of the church we continue to hear of miracles. It was believed that Jesus, on his departure, had bestowed the Spirit, through which his servants could act supernaturally. Many of their miracles are recounted in the book of Acts, where we may suspect the inroad of later legend, but Paul refers to "gifts of healing" and "miracles" as well-known manifestations of the Spirit (I Cor., 12:9, 10, 28, 29). They consisted, apparently of various forms of faith-healing, and depended on a magnetism with which particular men and women were endowed. Paul never claims that he himself possessed these powers, and distinctly says that they were of secondary religious value (I Cor. 12:28). At a later time the miracle-working gift was supposed to come through official ordination and directions are laid down in the Ep. of James for the performance of works of healing by church elders. Eventually the "exorcists"* were set apart as a special class in the ministry, and the office is still retained in the church of Rome.

J. Wendland, *Miracles and Christianity* (1911); D. S. Cairns, *The Faith that Rebels* (1929).

E.F.S.

miracles in non-Christian religions: In prescientific cultures it was taken for granted that a god, a spirit, a holy man, a magician or the possessor of a powerful spell could produce results in ways that today would be called miraculous. Yet none of the men whose names stand as symbols of the great religions—Zoroaster, Lao-tzu, Mahāvīra, Gautama Buddha, Confucius, Mohammed** made any use of miracles. Mohammed wondered at the blindness of his adversaries who asked for a sign. Gautama reproved his disciples for boasting to the followers of Mahāvīra of his marvelous powers. A member of the early Buddhist order who claimed to possess superhuman power was subject to discipline. Men spiritualized by asceticism, saints of superlative wisdom could of course perform miracles but, as the early texts say, miracles prove nothing by themselves. A skilled magician could match any marvel.

Yet the reverence of later generations and the growth of legends surround the lives of these great sages with an aura of miraculous events. Marvels cluster about them at conception, birth, temptation, when evil powers tried to destroy them, and at death and burial. Not only the sages themselves but also their followers who attained the status of saints worked miracles at will. They were performed to demonstrate power when challenged, to prove the authority of the prophet or his teaching, to convert unbelievers, or for such practical purposes as healing, escaping prison, providing food or speedy transportation. The saints of Hinduism and Buddhism were lavish with miracles. They could travel through the air, even to heaven, transport a company across a river without boats, bring rain, control storms and floods, heal the sick, remove barrenness, pass through the earth or a wall, assume any desired form, become invisible and invulnerable, provide illumination by burning a finger, remember past lives and foresee the future. At the birth of Buddha angelic music filled the air. The earth quaked, streams of water poured down for his bath, the four great kings of the quarters and a host of divine beings attended him. When he died flowers rained from heaven knee deep about the funeral procession and fire from heaven lit the pyre. Other religions were more restrained. Marvels accompanied the conception and birth of Zoroaster and he was miraculously rescued many times from the attempts of evil powers to destroy him. Miracles in the religion of Israel center chiefly around Moses, Elijah and his successor. Mohammed's ascent to heaven is the outstanding miracle of Moslem tradition. Some of the Moslem saints of India, however, rivaled the Hindu holy men as wonder workers. The Chinese immortals possessed supernatural power but their legends seem modest on the background of the miracle-starred lore of Chinese Buddhism. See virgin birth.

A.E.H.

Mirecourt, John of: (Fr. Jean de; Lat: Johannes de Mirecuria) A Cistercian monk of the 14th century, follower of John of Occam. With Nicholas of Autrecourt* he managed an energetic defense of the critical and skeptical tendencies of the school of Occam. In consequence, forty of the theses of his commentary on Peter Lombard's* *Liber Sententiarum* were condemned by the Univ. of Paris in 1347, two years after they were written for his baccalaureate in theology. A close relationship exists between his system of ontology, that of Augustine, and later, the Cartesian principle of the certitude of self. Mirecourt was strongly influenced by the theories of Thomas Bradwardine* and the ethical conception which maintains all human acts are derived from the omnipotent divine will or, more specifically, the permitting (concurrent) will of God. J.F.T.

Mirror of Princes: 1) Augustine's brief description of a Christian emperor, *City of God* V, 24. 2) One of the many books written for the guidance of rulers in the Middle Ages and the Renaissance. J.T.M.

miserere: The first word of Psalm 50 (Vulgate); hence the psalm itself. It is King David's act of contrition and plea for forgiveness after his sin of adultery with Bethsabee. S.C.

Mishnah: (Lit. teaching, from *shanah,* to repeat, to teach) Refers to the digest of laws made by Rabbi Judah the Patriarch (c. 135-220). The compiler made use of all the earlier collections of laws available to him. While the Mishnah was redacted in the beginning of the third century, it embodies many laws which antedate the Christian era. R. Judah's purpose in compiling the Mishnah was to halt the chaos and confusion brought about in Jewish life by the growth of rival collections of Jewish practice and ritual, none of which possessed more authority than the other, and to make his collection a code that it would be authoritative in all matters of ritual and law. R. Judah was eminently successful in his endeavor by reason of his great scholarship and the tremendous prestige he enjoyed as a spiritual leader of the Jews. The classification of the law in the Mishnah is most interesting. As is well known, the ritual and jurisprudence are not distinguished in the Bible, and we often find them side by side in the Scripture. In the Mishnah, the law is arranged into six orders and these in turn are subdivided into treatises. The first order, with the exception of the first treatise, deals with agricultural laws. The second order with the Sabbath and Festivals, the third with family law, the fourth with jurisprudence or civil and criminal law, the fifth with Temple laws and sacrifices, the sixth with laws of impurities. See Gemara; law, Hebrew; Talmud; Tanna; Tosefta. Cf. Meir.

Cf. J. Z, Lauterbach, *Jewish Encyclopedia,* vol. VIII, pp. 609-619; Boaz Cohen, *Mishnah and Tosefta* (1935). B.C.

Missa: (Lat., dismissal) The usual and official name for the Eucharistic liturgy in the Western Church, the Mass*. So called from the dismissal of the catechumens before the Offertory, and of the faithful (*Ite, missa est*) after communion. P.V.N.

Missal, Roman: (*Missale Romanum*) The official altar book of the Roman Catholic Church, issued in 1570 pursuant to a decree of the Council of Trent*, to supersede the various medieval 'uses' by a uniform rite. It contains, besides the Kalendar and elaborate rubrical directions: a) the Ordinary and Canon of the Mass*, b) the Proper of Seasons—the variable prayers, chants, and lections of the Christian year from Advent to Advent, c) the Proper of Saints, d) various supplementary material. See Pius V. P.V.N.

Mission Covenant Church of America: See Evangelical Mission Covenant Church of America.

missionary activities in China. See Chinese religions.

Missionary Bands of the World: A small holiness sect which grew out of a pentecostal group in the Free Methodist Church. It became independent in 1898 under the name of "Pentecost Bands of the World," taking the present name in 1925. It is Methodist in nature and general polity and is distinguished only by its stress on holiness. The sect had only 6 churches and about 200 members, but in 1933 it perfected a merger with a similar sect known as Church of God (Holiness) which reported 120 churches and 3,000 members. See Evangelistic Associations; holiness churches. E.T.C.

Missionary Church Association: A holiness fundamentalist, and premillennial sect with headquarters at Ft. Wayne, Ind. It has 47 churches and 3,600 members. It was organized in 1898 by bringing together various holiness groups which had broken away from their old denominational affiliations. It is distinguished from several other similar sects only by the extreme degree of its attachment to the fundamentalist theology and the second coming of Christ. It claims to be an interdenominational body, and send out its missionaries through the boards of other denominations, mainly the Christian and Missionary Alliance*. See holiness churches. E.T.C.

missionary movements, Christian: Christianity shares with Buddhism, Islam, Judaism and Zoroastrianism** the expansive purpose to save other peoples. The sense of world mission arises naturally from monotheistic universalism, as a commission from the one God to serve his children everywhere. No other trait is more characteristic of Christianity throughout its history than this missionary impulse. From the heritage of prophetic Judaism came a world vision and a mission to teach and bless all nations with the true faith.

Jesus sent forth disciples first to the house of Israel, and later to the whole world, "Go ye therefore and make disciples of all nations" (Mt. 28:19). Philip, Stephen, Barnabas, Paul and others carried the gospel around the Mediterranean from Asia Minor and Greece to Rome and Spain. Justin Martyr (c. 140 A.D.) claims there are no people of any race, "among whom prayers are not offered in the name of a crucified Jesus to the Father of all." (*Dial. c. Tryph.* 117) Harnack estimates that by the end of the third century Christians numbered nearly one-half of the population of the Roman Empire (*Mission and Expansion of Christianity,* vol. ii, 325).

The ancient period of Christian missions brought an amazing expansion. From the conversion of Constantine* in 325 A.D. it was not only the official religion but the fabric of civilization. Crossing the borders of the Empire Ulfilas* became apostle to the Goths about 325; Chrysostom founded in Constantinople a training school for Gothic evangelists in 404; Martin of Tours (ca. 316-400) evangelized central Gaul; Patrick* (389-461) established Christianity in Ireland as a center for missions from Switzerland to Iceland. Winfrid or Boniface (680-755) became the apostle to Germany while Ansgar* (801-865), Haakan and Fryggvason brought the message to the Scandinavians. From Constantinople missionaries won Russia and the Balkans to the eastern church. When Nestorius* and his followers were cast out in 431 they organized a powerful mission that moved from Baghdad and Babylon into China and India, surviving until the 14th century with considerable influence.

In mediaeval times Christian expansion was checked and pushed back by the Moslem* empire. The crusades* were not missionary in the true sense, but a mistaken effort to recapture the Holy Land by force of arms, which resulted in disaster and bitter rivalry. In 1245 Pope Innocent IV sent embassies to the Tartar courts, and the Polos came to China to establish relations with the Mongol leaders. Corvino, a Franciscan friar reached China in 1292 by the south sea route stopping at Madras on the way, winning royal converts.

When the new world was discovered and sea lanes opened, modern missions began. The Roman Catholic missions were immediately launched with vigor and success. Loyola founded the Society of Jesus* in 1534 sent Francis Xavier* in 1542 to India, Ceylon, Malacca and Japan. Other Jesuit missions came to Florida, Mexico, Peru, Canada, Chile, Paraguay, the Philippines, China and Tibet. Missionaries were also supported by the Augustinian, Dominican and Franciscan orders to the Americas, Africa, Asia and the islands.

The early Protestant churches were occupied at home, not yet ready for foreign missions, but settlers in the new world transplanted their faith wherever they came. In New England John Eliot translated the Bible for Indians (1661-1664), and the Quakers preached the gospel to Indians and Negroes. A bishop of London in 1701 secured a charter for a "society for the Propagation of the Gospel in Foreign Parts." In 1705 the King of Denmark sent a Christian mission to India, and by 1731 the Moravians were engaged in missionary work, sending John Wesley* to the Indians of Georgia, thus opening the way for Methodist missions. In 1793 William Carey* (Baptist) sailed for India and two years later the London Missionary Society was organized. In 1799 the Church of England established the Church Missionary Society for "missions to Africa and the East." In 1814 the Wesleyan Methodist Missionary Society was organized and in 1829 the Church of Scotland sent Alexander Duff, as an educational missionary. American missionary movements were also forming: American Board of Commissioners for Foreign Missions in 1806, the American Baptist Missionary Union in 1814, the Methodist Board of Foreign Missions in 1819, and the Presbyterian Board of Missions in 1837. The British and Foreign Bible Society* was formed in 1804 and the American Bible Society in 1816.

The high point in Christian missions was reached in 1928. In that year there were approximately 30,000 Protestant missionaries in foreign lands, and an equal number of Roman Catholic missionaries. During that year $60, 000,000 was devoted to foreign missions by Protestant churches and about half of that amount by Roman Catholics. (See K. S. Latourette, *Missions To-morrow* (1936), p. 12). The Student Volunteer Movement* since 1886 had enlisted thousands of young people in England, Canada and the United States for foreign missionary service. Medical and educational services have met human need in every land and demonstrated the practical value of Christianity to these peoples.

The unification of missionary enterprises was first effected in the allocation of fields to prevent duplication of work, cooperation in union schools and colleges, and joint consultation in national Christian councils. From the meeting of the World Missionary conference at Edinburgh in 1910 resulted the International Missionary Council, bringing together from various nations representatives of all missionary organizations. At the significant meeting of this Missionary Council at Jerusalem in 1928 where Orientals and Africans were well represented, thoughtful consideration was given to the Christian message, Christian education, relation of churches east and west, problems of race, industrialism and rural progress.

In 1932 the Laymen's Commission representing seven denominations in America published their foreign missions inquiry entitled *Re-thinking Missions* (ed. by W. E. Hocking, 1932) and seven supplementary volumes. Based upon intensive study of Christian missions in India, Burma, China and Japan of churches, education, literature, medical work, rural life, industrial developments, women's interests, administration and organization; recommendations were made to the missionary societies. Wide discussion and influences have followed the interpretations of emerging world culture, temporary and permanent functions of the Christian mission, the need to know, appreciate and associate with other religions.

The meeting of the International Missionary Council at Madras, India in 1938 brought together 470 delegates from seventy nations. In the face of mounting world conflicts, these delegates "call upon our fellow Christians throughout the world to join us in a new dedication. Surely God is summoning us in these times to let go our self-sufficiency, to frequent His altars, to learn of Him, and to make His ways known in all the relationships of life . . . Everywhere it involves self sacrificial service . . . till that love surround the earth, binding the nations, races and the classes into a community of sympathy for one another, undergirded by a deathless faith in Christ." *Madras Series* (1939), vol. vii, 170-171.

World War II is having a disastrous effect on Christian missions. The European conflict has orphaned many important missions of continental societies. The Japanese expansion has suppressed missionary activities and interned or driven out missionaries. Blockades and war requirements have blocked travel to and from fields of missionary labor. The future of the Christian world mission is at the moment unpredictable. Changes have come so suddenly and recently it is difficult to see what will develop next. However, it should be noted that heroic service of missionaries in such emergencies has won admiration and gratitude in China and elsewhere. The Christian life is deeply rooted in most of these countries, and there is reason to expect the indigenous Christian churches will carry on even though international connections may be severed. The ecumenical movement toward world unity among the churches and the sense of Christian brotherhood is standing well the stresses of global warfare. Much depends on the nature of the peace and the character of the post-war world. See China Inland mission; city missions; Grenfell; home missions; inner mission; Livingston, D.; Moffat, R.; Morrison, R. Also see anti-missionary movement in the U. S.; religious tract movement in the U. S.

Report of the World Missionary Conference, 9 vols. (1910); the *Complete Report of the Jerusalem Meeting of the International Missionary Council*, 8 vols. (1928); W. E. Hocking, ed., *Re-thinking Missions* and 7 fact-finding supplementary volumes (1932); *The Madras Series Presenting Papers Based on the Meeting of the International Missionary Council at Madras, India*, 7 vols. (1939); J. I. Parker, *Interpretative Statistical Survey of the World Mission of the Christian Church* (1938); *World Missionary Atlas* (2nd ed., 1925); *Little Atlas of Catholic Missions* (Rome, 1925); *The Encyclopedia of Missions*, ed. by H. O. Dwight, et al. (1904).

P.E.J.

missions in China and Japan: See Chinese religions; Japan, Christianity in.

missions to India: See India, missions to.

Missouri Lutherans: A body of conservative Lutherans organized under the leadership of K. F. W. Walther* in 1847 into "The Lutheran Synod of Missouri, Ohio, and Other States". It consisted originally of the congregations formed by the seven hundred pilgrims from Saxony who had settled in Perry County, Missouri, in 1839 and of the congregations in Ohio and Michigan served by missionaries sent by Pastor Wilhelm Löhe* of Neuendettelsau. Insisting upon strict adherence to confessional orthodoxy and developing effective methods of indoctrination, the Synod has enjoyed a rapid growth and now has 4,110 pastors, 4,114 congregations, and 1,361,698 members. Its theological school, the Concordia Seminary in St. Louis, with a faculty of 18 and a student body of 497 is among the largest of Protestant seminaries. Laying great emphasis upon the education of the young, the Synod has an extensive system of parochial schools* and junior colleges. Its eleven-year course of ministerial education is unique. Doctrinally, the Missourians hold the Bible to be an infallible and literally inspired revelation of absolute truth; demand acceptance of all the symbolical books of historic Lutheranism; use only purely Lutheran literature in church and school; oppose all forms of unionism and syncretism, such as prayer, worship or communion with other Christians, even with other Lutherans; condemn all synergism, i.e., man's co-operation in his salvation; consider the Pope as the Anti-Christ; denounce all lodges and secret societies. In polity, each congregation of the Synod is a sovereign unit, the Synod being only an advisory body whose resolutions are not binding unless accepted by the congregation as compatible with the Bible and suited to its own conditions. The doctrinal purity of the pastors is under close surveillance. The synod carries on an extensive evangelistic work, with thoroughly modern methods, one of its instruments being a radio station located on the campus of Concordia Seminary. See Lutheran Church in America; neo-Lutheranism.

Concordia Cyclopedia (1927), ed. L. Fuerbringer, et al. T.A.K.

miter or mitre: (Gr. *mitra*, a turban) A tall ornamental headdress worn by various church dignitaries, as popes, archbishops, bishops and abbots. It has evolved from a low soft cap, originally worn by the pope alone, into a high stiff hat consisting of two like parts, each stiffened by lining and rising to a peak. It is bound by a head-band at the bottom; two fringed lappets (infulae) hang down behind. Theoretically, it is always white, though there are three degrees of ornamentation, depending upon the dignity of the wearer and the occasion. In the rite of consecration it is considered symbolically as the helmet of salvation. J.F.T.

Mithraism: See mystery religions.

Mitnagdim: Opponents of the Chasidim*. A.H.S.

Mixcoatl, or Camaxtli: (Mexican) Ancient hunting god, war god, and thunder god; honored in an annual ceremonial hunt, and by the making of weapons; one of the gods which aid in the creation of the world; carries a bundle of arrows in his hand to signify his possession of the thunderbolts. F.L.P.

mizpah benediction: The name commonly given to the words of Laban at the treaty between him and Jacob (Gen. 31:49) "May Yahweh keep watch between me and thee when we are hidden (separated) from one another." Neither party is to pass the cairn or pillar, which had been set up, with hostile intent, and God (the third party of the covenant) is requested to enforce the agreement. The Hebrew world was one of covenant, and, lacking human sanctions by which agreements could be enforced, a deity or deities was or were made party to all agreements. The stabilizing element in Israelite society, therefore, was conceived to be the will of Yahweh, who was the source and protector of the social mores and the legal right (see further covenant and righteousness). G.E.W.

Mo Tzŭ: See Chinese Terminology.

Moabite stone: Stele of basalt, discovered in 1868, bearing an inscription of the ninth century B.C. relating the revolt of Mesha, king of Moab, against the Israelites (II Kgs. iii, 4 ff.). Written in the Moabite dialect with characters closely akin to the Old Hebrew alphabet. See alphabetic writing. S.L.T.

Moabites: Ancient people probably kindred to the Israelites, the Edomites*, and the Ammonites, and living at the East of the Dead Sea. Often mentioned in the O.T. See Chemosh; Moabite stone. S.L.T.

modalism: An ancient doctrine that the members of the Trinity* were not three distinct personalities but only successive modes in which the one God has manifested himself. The most famous representative of Modalism was Sabellius (fl. 230), an early Christian presbyter and theologian. See monarchianism; Sabellianism. F.G.E.

Moderates, The: A party, the best known representative of which was the eminent historian, Principal Robertson, which dominated the counsels of the Church of Scotland* for approximately a century following 1752. Its power began to wane about 1832. It stood consistently in favor of patronage*, based on the Patronage Act of 1712, and for recognizing the Civil Courts as the ultimate authority in ecclesiastical matters. At first stressing culture and morals rather than doctrine, it later became rigid in enforcing the doctrines of the Confession. A.K.R.

moderator: The official title, in Presbyterian churches, for the constitutionally designated presiding officer in a church court, e.g., a congregational meeting regularly called, a session, a presbytery, a synod or a General Assembly.

A.K.R.

modern religious drama: See religious drama.

modern style: See church building.

Modern Times community: See communistic settlements, secular.

modern translations of the Bible: See Bible, modern translations of the.

modernism: Modernism signifying in general anything new and in particular any new doctrine refers specifically today to that new trend of thought and doctrine in the religious world which, although not universally recognized as such, culminated as a synthesis at the beginning of the twentieth century. The development however, had been going on for years and was based in some form or other on all previous theological errors, hence stigmatized by Pope Pius X* in his encyclical "Pascendi" of Sept. 8, 1907 as the "synthesis of all heresies" and by Alfred Loisy*, one of its French adherents (whose books had been placed on the "Index"*, in 1903) as "the setting aside of every Catholic doctrine". The insidious feature about Modernism, this "neo-reformismus religiosus," as Pius X in his Allocution of April 17, 1907, styles it, was the fact that it used such acceptable theological terms as "faith", "revelation", "dogma", "conscience", "truth", "church", etc., in an entirely different sense from that traditionally understood or dogmatically defined. According to the Modernists "truth" is not stable, immutable and eternal, but something that may vary with the times, even with one's own interior experiences or reactions; hence, the possibility of a temporary objective progress of dogmas, during which transition period new doctrines may always be added and old ones, no longer adjudged conformable to the times, eliminated. "Revelation" is not a truth revealed, from without, by Almighty God either directly or through the medium of the prophets and especially through His Divine Son (cf. Heb. 1, 1-2), Jesus Christ, ascertainable and demonstrable by such unimpeachable documents as the Sacred Scriptures, but rather some indefinite, undefinable inner experience (Immanence Apologetics) that is to be distinguished both from philosophic proof and dogmatic pronouncement. Religion, thus, like truth has become not only personal but likewise individualistic to the exclusion of one general (catholic) religion for all. The need, therefore, of even the Bible is entirely secondary, because (according to them) it reveals only how God acted in others; hence there is no need of ecclesiastical authority or infallible interpretation, disciplinary regulations or external congregations. (The older non-confessional Germans expressed this idea in the phrase: "Religion ist Privatsache".) The Sacraments, according to the Modernists, are not external signs instituted by Christ to give grace but rather the outward expression of the soul's inward need of external symbolism. The dogmatic pronouncements of the Church are not the result of proven divine revelation but rather the manifestation of the soul's inner experiences set down in words and terms for the guidance of others having similar interior "experiences." This *"conscientia religiosa"* thus becomes through communication to others in the Church a "conscientia collectiva". Correspondingly, any or all authority in the Church is not that given by Christ to Peter and to his successors as Bishops of Rome; or to the other Apostles and their successors, the other bishops of the world, but rather that which grew out of the Christian communities founded by them. Wherefore dogmas are to be approved first by the faithful, and only then obeyed. To the Modernist the Christ of Faith is not the Christ of history; He is rather an evolution or figment of the hero-worshiping mind and soul. In fact, all ecclesiastical life—doctrinal, jurisdictional, juridical (not only through expansion, but in its essential concept)—is subject to evolution. Faith, dogma, cult and church develop in the laity which must offset the teachings of the clergy. Faith and science bear no relation to one another; hence may contradict each other, as though, to quote the Council of the Vatican*, God were not the Author of both. Certain, definite and individual historical personages, including Christ and especially the characters of the Old Testament, the same as concrete events in their lives, e.g., the Incarnation, the Resurrection, God's apparitions, etc. have been "transfigured" into "hero-worship" and into exaggerated, unrealistic myths. Miracles and prophesies as proofs of Divine Revelation find no place in a religion of pure Immanentism. Since only physical phenomena are the objects of science, everything else in Religion not subject to interior or exterior experience, (Agnosticism) has been added by Faith, which the Modernist choses to eliminate from his system of religion. As Faith and Science are to be entirely divorced from each other so also the Church and the State.

Perhaps no one Modernist taught the whole system as outlined, for it was nipped in the bud before it had time to crystalize and fully synchronize. In fact no two exponents fully agreed on anything. Pius X's condemantion caught them unawares. Everyone, nevertheless, of the above-named tenets was taught by one or the other Modernist.

The origin of Modernism is to be sought remotely in Pantheism and Gnosticism; proximately in the Subjective Philosophy of the XX century. Its two basic doctrines are Agnosticism and Immanentism. It leans on the teachings of such philosophers as Kant, Jacobi and Schleiermacher**, etc., who place the essence of religion in interior feeling and sentiment (Gefühlsreligion); or on James, Bergson** and Spitta who find the essence of religion in man's inner yearning for God. In Germany, the theory of "sentimental" or "interiorly experimental" religion found staunch adherents in A. Ritschl and A. Harnack**; in France, in A. Sabatier and E. Ménégoz (Fideismus)**. These philosophico-theological concepts of Faith, Truth and Revelation gradually worked their way also into Catholic circles, both clerical and lay. In France, they found both acceptance and propaganda by Edouard Le Roy and L. Laberthonière**; in England, by M. G. Tyrrell*, and in Italy by E. Buonaiuti, P. Murri and an anonymous author of *Programma dei modernisti* (Rome, 1907); in Germany, by Hugo Koch, Jos. Schnitzer and Jos. Wittig. In the United States foreign infiltration was hardly noticeable, although there were a few French and English teachers who sought to inoculate the American Seminaries with Modernistic theories. In one particular case the accusation was proven to have been entirely false. American Catholic theologians were too deeply rooted in the Rock of Peter to be shaken by the storm.

The Catholic Church, ever on the alert to challenge new doctrine not in conformity with the traditional teachings of antiquity, took swift action against the Modernistic movement. Many of the new tenets had already been pre-condemned by the Vatican Council in 1870. In chapters 2-4 the Council had clearly taught that faith in the Catholic sense rests on divine testimony or authority as revealed in the Scriptures and transmitted by tradition down the centuries, sustained by prophesies, miracles or other divine manifestations. A "coecus ductus", or blind leadership or impulse, resting on uncertain, individualistic and private feeling, sentiment or experience has no place in the Catholic concept of Faith. The Catholic Church demands infinitely more! Furthermore, in her Constitution "De Ecclesia Dei" the Council adamantly upheld the traditionally taught authority of the Church to defend the "depositum fidei" (the treasury of the Faith) and to spread the knowledge of the same only through her authorized teachers. Then as early as 1906 and 1907, after certain books had been placed on the "Index", individual Italian and French bishops took action against their respective priests who had become inoculate with Modernism. The first papal repercussion was the Decree "Lamentabili" of July 3, 1907 in which Piux X in the form of the Syllabus adopted by Piux IX, condemned 65 propositions and stigmatized them as: "Errores modernistarum de Ecclesia, Revelatione, Christo, Sacramentis". (See Syllabus of errors, papal.) This was followed on Sept. 8, 1907 by the Encyclical* "Pascendi" which contained a detailed characterization and criticism of Modernism. But the Encyclical went farther. It directed bishops to be vigilant regarding doctrinal tenets of their professors in philosophico-theological seminaries and concerning the books used and consulted by students. The Pope charged the bishops to establish vigilance committees to see that there be no further infiltration of false doctrines. He threatened the adherents of the latter with excommunication. On Sept. 1, 1910 Pius went even still farther and in his Motu-Proprio* "Sacrorum Antistitum" ordered every priest in the world to take the "Oath against Modernism"—a solemn profession of Faith and abjuration of all Modernistic errors, which are specifically enumerated. Those who refused to take the Oath were to be deposed and no longer permitted to function as pastors or teachers. (Decree of the Holy Office, Aug. 28, 1907). The Oath is still in vogue and demanded of all clerics before the reception of Major Orders; of professors at all Catholic philosophico-theological institutions of learning before accepting office as also at the beginning of each scholastic year; of all Pastors of souls, prelates (Bishops, Generals, Provincials) and of all Religious Superiors before canonical induction into office, or, as in the case of Bishops, before consecration or transferal to a new Diocese. This ruling was confirmed by a Decree of the Holy Office, March 22, 1918 and by the Constitution "Deus Scientiarum Dominus", of May 14, 1931, which required the Oath not only of all Catholic professors, lay and cleric, at Universities, but also of all candidates for academic degrees.

Modernism is practically a dead issue in the Catholic Church, whereas only a relatively small number of Protestant Divines still adhere strictly to its doctrines. The most of them cleve to the old doctrines and demand something more for their own convictions and from their followers than mere sentiment or personal interior experience as the basis of universal, absolute truth and the foundation of a religion that deals with eternal, unalterable values. See ecclesiastical commissions.

Lexikon f. Theologie u. Kirche VII, 249-253; *Cath. Encyc.* X, 415-421; *Dict. de la Theol. Cath.* X, 2009-47. For the recorded Acts of Pius X cf. *Acta Sanctae Sedis* and "Acta Apost. Sedis" of the corresponding years; also H. Denziger, *Enchiridion Symbolorum* pp. 564-586 (Freiburg in Br.: Herder, 1932); J. M. Sterret, *Modernism in Religion* (London, 1922); R. L. Moxon, *Modernism and Orthodoxy* (*ib.* 1924); J. Rickaby, *The Modernist* (*ib.* 1908); *The New Cath. Dictionary* (London and New York, 1929) p. 641; Seppelt-Löffler-Frommelt, *Short History of the Popes* (London and St. Louis: Herder, 1932) pp. 508-512 (a good explanation with citation of Papal Acts). R.M.H.

modernist: Broadly, one who makes the methods and results of modern thought and life the norms for judging the claims of religious tradition. Specifically, a modernist insists on applying the contemporary historio-critical method without favor to the sources, distinguishes the abiding experiences of religion reproducible today from the changing categories of Scripture and creed, and accepts the deliverances of tradition to the degree they are reconcilable with evolution, immanence, democracy and similar prevailing thought-forms of the modern world. See liberal theology; modernism. Cf. fundamentalism. F.G.E.

modes, ecclesiastical: (also medieval modes, church modes) Series of notes in scales with no definite pitch implied but with definite arrangements of whole and half-tone intervals between notes. The church modes grew out of the Greek system of modes. They were used as early as the second century. All Gregorian chant* and all polyphonic* music before 1600 was written in the modal system. In the final system of modes there were fourteen scales, the odd numbers being authentic where the extreme notes of the scale were the same as the final, and the even numbers being plagal where the final notes were the same as the corresponding authentic modes but the extreme notes were a fourth below the corresponding authentic modes. The dominant note of each mode was the reciting note. The dominant note was a fifth above the final of each authentic mode and a third above the final of each plagal mode, except when either dominant or final should fall on B in which case it was moved to C.

Mode I—Dorian
Extreme note D Final D Dominant A
Mode II—Hypodorian
Extreme note A Final D Dominant F
Mode III—Phrygian
Extreme note E Final E Dominant C
Mode IV—Hypophrygian
Extreme note B Final E Dominant A*
Mode V—Lydian
Extreme note F Final F Dominant C
Mode VI—Hypolydian
Extreme note C Final F Dominant A
Mode VII—Mixolydian
Extreme note G Final G Dominant D
Mode VIII—Hypomixolydian
Extreme note D Final G Dominant C
Mode IX—Aeolian
Extreme note A Final A Dominant E
Mode X—Hypoaeolian
Extreme note E Final A Dominant C
Mode XI—Ionian
Extreme note C Final C Dominant G
Mode XII—Hypoionian
Extreme note G Final C Dominant E
Mode XIII—Locrian (hypothetical)
Mode XIV—Hypolocrian (hypothetical)
* exception.

Many medievalists professed that each mode had its own ethos and was especially suitable to a particular use in time or place or mood, much like the Greek idea of ethos.

G. Grove, *Dictionary of Music and Musicians* (1935), article: modes, ecclesiastical; G. Reese, *Music in the Middle Ages* (1940); D. Ferguson, *A History of Musical Thought* (1935). E.H.B.

modus vivendi: See concordat.

Moffat, Robert: (1795-1883) Scottish missionary, born near Edinburgh, who set out for Africa in 1816. For more than twenty years he labored in South Africa, translated the N.T. and Psalms into the Bechuana tongue, and the whole of the Bible into Sechwana. He was a versatile builder, smith, farmer, linguist, author and teacher who converted his primitive followers into civilized Christians. David Livingstone* became his son-in-law. P.E.J.

Mohammed or Muhammad or Mahomet: (570-632 A.D.) The founder of the religion that bears his name (Mohammedanism*), was born into the powerful Kareish tribe at Mecca* in Arabia. At first he was called Ubu'l Kassim, later entitled Mohammed, meaning "the Praised One". His father died two months before his birth, and his mother when he was six years of age. He was reared first by a grandfather, and then by an uncle, as a boy joining the latter in caravan journeys. At the age of 25 he became the chief merchant and camel driver of a rich widow, Khadija, whom he married three years later. In business enterprises he visited Palestine and Syria, met Arabians, Jews and Christians, and conversed often with them of God. His reputation for honesty and justice was well established, and with four others he vowed to take the part of the oppressed.

With time to brood upon the larger issues of life, he sought a greater revelation of God. The popular belief in many gods and idol worship was abhorent to him. He decided there is only one God, Allah*, and salvation requires submission to him. With this conviction he committed himself to the service of the one true God, and received an urgent call to be his prophet. He recognized other prophets as Adam, Abraham, Moses and Jesus, and believed himself to be the final prophet to whom the complete revelation was given. A vision came to him and a voice saying, "*Iqra*" (recite), delivered a series of messages from God that became the *Koran**. His wife, Khadija, his nephew Ali, and the freedman adopted as his son Zaid, promptly accepted his revelations, which came over a period of twenty-three years.

In the first year of his mission he won only eight converts, who assembled in his home and prayed faithfully to Allah. After three years, with scarcely twenty followers, he publicly declared his purpose to overthrow the 360 idols and establish worship of Allah, the one God. Persecuted, boycotted and segregated, he appealed to the citizens of Yathrib (later called *al-Medina,* "the city", i.e., of the prophet), who agreed to receive him. His flight from Mecca to a mountain cave is known as the *hijra* or *hejira,* and initiated the era and calendar of Islam, July 16, 622 A.D.

At Medina by eloquent preaching he converted the whole city except the Jews, and became dictator upon a sixfold pledge: (1) we will not worship any but the one God; (2) we will not steal; (3) we will not commit adultery; (4) nor kill our children; (5) we will not slander in anywise; (6) nor will we disobey the prophet in anything that is right. He built a mosque for daily prayers and congregational worship, carried on a thorough program of military and religious education, attacked caravans from Mecca, and defeated Meccan armies in decisive battles.

When Mecca surrendered he became its dictator at the age of 60. His first act was to abolish the idols, a reform which has survived in Islam to this day. With military victory he changed from a prophet to a conquering ruler. He persecuted the Jews who refused to accept his religion, and reduced Christians to dependency. He sent embassies to the four great empires of Abysinia, Egypt, Greece and Persia, demanding allegiance to the faith, and when they refused he unified Arabia and invaded these empires. Two years later he died (632 A.D.) but his armies marched on in fanatical zeal until they conquered three continents.

As a prophet Mohammed saw a vision of one God and one brotherhood of the faith. He had the conviction and the courage to attack evil and proclaim his message. As a statesman he was vigorous, astute, determined and irresistible. He won and organized his followers by contagious purpose into a compact moral force. He was faithful to his family and friends until his first wife died, then provided himself with a harem, and attacked his enemies with fury and deception. The force of his personality continues to influence the millions of his devoted followers.

Sir William Muir, *The Life of Mahomet* (4 vols. London, 1858-1861, abridged in one vol. 1894); D. S. Margoliouth, *Mohammed and the Rise of Islam* (1905); Tor Andrae, *Mohammed the Man and His Faith* (1936); Essad Bey, *Mohammed* (tr. by H. L. Ripperger, 1936). P.E.J.

MOHAMMEDAN TERMINOLOGY: Abu Hanifa; Admadiya; Al-Kindi or Alchindus; Al-Gazzali or Al-Ghazali; Al-Farabi or Alfarabius; Allah; Avicenna or Ibn-Sina; Averrhoes or Averroes; Bahaism; bismillah; caliph or khalif; crescent; Druses; fakih; faker or faqir; Fatiha or Fatihah; fatwa or futwa; fiqh; Gabars or Ghebers; Gehenna; Hadith or hadis; hadj or hajj; Hallaj or al-Hallaj; hegira; Hanbal; Iblis or Eblis; ijma; imam or imaum; Islam; Ismailis; Israfil or Israfel; jihad or jehad; jinn; Kaaba or Caaba; kafir or kaffir; kalam; khalif; Kharijites; kibla or kiblah; kismet; Koran or Quran; Mahdi; Malikites; Mecca; Medina; mimbar; Moslem; mosque; mufti; mujtahid; mulla; Murjites; mutakallim or mutikallimum; Mutazilites; pir; qadi; Qadarites; Qarmatians; Quran; Ramadan; Sabaism; shaikh; Shi ites; Sufism; Sunna; Sunnites; suras; taqiyya; tauhid; ulama; Wahabites; welis or walis; zakat.

The above terms appear separately in this Encyclopedia. P.E.J.

Mohammedanism: The religion of the followers of Mohammed* (570-632 A.D.), who announced himself as the prophet of the one true God, Allah*. Numerous references to Hebrew and Christian traditions indicate unquestionably his indebtedness to these faiths. For a time he allied himself with the Jews and Christians, declaring the same God, honoring many of the same prophets, and facing Jerusalem in prayer. The primitive religion of Arabia and Zoroastrianism* were other sources providing content for the new faith taking form in the dynamic mind of Mohammed. Yet the prophet did not borrow slavishly from any source; and whatever passed through the crucible of his experience came forth transformed. Islam is less dependent upon Judaism than is Christianity. Before long Mohammed turned from Jerusalem to Mecca*, and the breach among these religions widened to a chasm.

The passionate zeal for the mission of Allah, which Mohammed found in revelations, was eloquently communicated to his family and friends, but resisted by the citizens of Mecca who thought him demented. Persecution drove him to flee and seek converts elsewhere. His first religious community was established at Medina*, and after bitter contests the city of Mecca was finally won. Ten years after his flight all Arabia was united in a powerful movement of radical reform. In less than 25 years his followers had taken Egypt, Palestine, Persia and Syria. In 75 years North Africa and Spain were embraced in the crescent*, and Islam remained for centuries the dominant empire of the Mediterranean world.

For 28 years after Mohammed's death the leadership was carried on successively by four of his closest comrades: Abu Bekhr, Omar, Othman and Ali. (See caliph). Thereafter permanent political divisions arose. 1) The Omayyad Caliphate (660-750 A.D.) at Damascus extended its sway over North Africa and Spain. 2) The Abbaside Caliphate (750-1258 A.D.) maintained its capital at Bagdad. 3) The Fatimite Caliphate (910-1171 A.D.) ruled Egypt and North Africa. 4) The Spanish Caliphate was established at Cordova (755-1236 A.D.); 5) the Moorish Caliphate at Granada (1238-1492 A.D.); 6) The Ottoman Turkish Caliphate came to power in 1299 and continued to 1924 A.D., when the Sultan at Constantinople was deposed by the National Assembly.

The two main sects of Islam split over the question of the successor to Mohammed. The *Sunnites** recognize the first four Caliphs as true successors of Mohammed, while the *Shi ites** uphold family succession, and regard Ali and his followers as the divinely ordained Caliphs. The Sunnites number 150,000,000 and as the majority body hold firmly to the orthodox traditions. They adhere strictly to the *Sunna** (Way) which has come down directly from the founder. The Shi ites represent the liberal branch of Islam, and continue to look for a future leader (*imam*). From this group arose the mystical devotion of *Sufism**, the messianic and missionary *Bahaist** and other movements.

The Moslem faith (*iman*) rests first of all in the basic conviction of one God and no other. Allah is addressed in prayer by 99 names, and his attributes include all-seeing, all-hearing, all-speaking, all-knowing, all-willing, all-powerful. He is loving, compassionate, forgiving yet stern in punishment and arbitrary in purpose. Associated with God are angels* who support his throne, guard hell, and serve as intermediaries. The four chief angels are Gabriel, who brings revelations; Michael, guardian of the Jews; Raphael (Azrael), the angel of death; and Uriel (Israfil) who is to sound the trumpet at the resurrection.* There are also good and evil spirits (*jinn** or *genii*).

Chief sources of revelation are sacred scriptures and prophets. Of 104 sacred books, only four are thought to have survived, The Pentateuch, the Psalms, the Gospel and the Koran**. The Koran is so final that no other book is needed. It is the created word of God, eternally preserved on tablets in heaven, revealed to Mohammed by

Gabriel. Many prophets are referred to and though the number is put as high as 300,000 the six chief prophets are Adam, Noah, Abraham, Moses, Jesus and Mohammed, each commissioned to proclaim a new dispensation. Mohammed, the last and greatest of the prophets is predicted by all of his predecessors.

The eschatology is an elaborate portrayal of the final judgment, heaven and hell. The souls of unbelievers will be tortured in hell until the resurrection at the end of the world, when the trumpet sounds and the graves will open. Good and evil deeds are weighed in the balance, and everyone must pass over hell on a bridge finer than a hair and shaper than a sword. As the righteous enter heaven they will be invited to feasting, music, fine garments, perfume, and large-eyed maidens.

The five duties (*din*) laid upon every Moslem are: 1) profession of faith, i.e., repeating the creed daily; 2) prayer five times every 24 hours facing Mecca; 3) almsgiving, or the payment of poor-rates; 4) fasting every day from dawn to dusk in the month of Ramadan; and 5) the pilgrimage to Mecca once in a life time.

Mohammedans number about 160,000,000 in Asia, 44,000,000 in Africa, 5,000,000 in Europe and 20,000 in North America, a total of approximately 209,020,000. The civil and criminal laws arise from the *Koran* and the *Sunna*. Circumcision is practiced, four wives are allowed, the husband may divorce a wife by declaration and refunding part of the dowry. Alcoholic liquors, pork and meat offered to idols, strangled or killed by a blow, are prohibited. The unity and traditionalism of Islam is deeply affected by the upheaval of modern civilization, but the loyalty of Moslems is not surpassed by adherents of any religion. See Alfarabi; sacred literatures; salvation.

A. S. Ameer, *The Spirit of Islam* (1922); T. W. Arnold, *The Legacy of Islam* (1931); R. Levy, *The Sociology of Islam* (2 vols. 1930-1933); D. B. MacDonald, *The Religious Attitude and Life in Islam* (1909); and *The Encyclopedia of Islam*. P.E.J.

Mohammedanism in China: See Chinese religions.

Mohenjo-daro: Site of an ancient city in the Indus Valley excavated and described by Sir John Marshall, revealing a highly developed culture in India as early as 3000 B.C., long before the invasion of the Aryans. Of the utmost importance in the study of the origins of Hinduism*.

Sir John Marshall, *Mohenjo-daro and the Indus Civilization* (London, 1931), 3 vols. C.S.B.

Mohism: See Chinese Terminology.

moira: See fate.

moksha: The general term meaning salvation in Hinduism. The specific content of the term varies according to the sect to which one belongs. See salvation, Hindu. C.S.B.

Molinism: One of the systems which tries to explain the action of divine grace on the human will. Luis de Molina (1535-1600), the Spanish Jesuit who first developed it, emphasizes the freedom of the will without detracting from the efficacy and priority of grace. Molinism as modified by Leonard Lessius* (1554-1623) is still taught in the theological schools of the Jesuits*. It occasioned a great theological struggle in the Roman Catholic Church in the seventeenth century. E.A.R.

Molinos, Michel: (1640-1692) Spanish priest who became popular director of conscience at Rome and chief exponent of Catholic Quietism*. His *Guide spirituelle* revealed in 1675 his theory of the union of purified souls with God in this life, thus nullifying the offices of the Church. His book was condemned and he was imprisoned by the Inquisition* until his death, the date of which is not certain. See Guyon, Madame. W.W.C.

Moloch or Molech: A pagan deity to whom children were sacrificed at Topheth in the Valley of Hinnom outside Jerusalem, mentioned in the Hebrew Bible in Lev. 18:21; 20:2-5; I Kings 11:7; II Kings 23:10; Jer. 32.35, in the Septuagint text of Amos 5:26, and in Acts 7:43. The form Molech is Hebrew, the Greek form being Moloch. The worship of this deity was apparently introduced by Ahaz, suppressed by Josiah, and possibly later revived. The common scholarly opinion has been that Moloch was a Canaanite fire-god *Melek* ("King") whose name was written by the Hebrews with the vowels of *bosheth* ("shame"). Recent studies have shown that there was an ancient Syro-Mesopotamian deity *Muluk* (or *Malik*), and that Punic *molok* meant "vow" or "pledge". It has therefore been conjectured that Moloch was an early Semitic deity who was the special patron of vows, to whom children were sacrificed as the most binding pledge of the sanctity of a vow (W. F. Albright). See Gehenna. J.P.H.

Molokans: See Russian sectarianism.

monadism or monadology: (Gr. *monas*, unit) The name referring to the pluralistic metaphysical theory which, denying quantitative monism, sponsors qualitative monism and finds in relatively (or completely) self-sufficient, animate entities autonomous and unique centers of action (monads).

Natural law and interaction among monads has received a different explanation ever since Bruno* first advanced this concept. In recent theory (cf. J. Ward, W. James, C. Hartshorne), the independence of monads has been used to explain natural evil, evolution, and to affirm some contingency at the heart of things. See Leibniz; panpsychism. P.A.B.

monarchianism: A doctrine current within the second and third-century Church stressing the unity (*monarchia*) of the divine nature as against the ultimately-prevailing tendency to affirm personal distinctions within the Godhead. It is customary to distinguish two broad types. The first, called dynamistic, was represented by the Alogi, Theodotus of Byzantium, Artemon, and Paul of Samosata*. They taught that Christ was a mere man who had been adopted or constituted the Son of God, rather than possessing a metaphysical equality with the Father. The second, called modalism, held that the persons of the Trinity* were but modes of the one God's manifestation. Noetus of Smyrna, Praxeas of Carthage, and Sabellius were among its adherents. See patripassianism; Sabellianism. F.G.E.

monarchomachs: The name was invented by William Barclay in his *De regno et regali potestate* (1600) to describe any writer who justified the right to resist. It did not imply an objection to monarchy as such. The monarchomachs were a group of Huguenot pamphleteers who developed arguments in opposition to absolute royal power. Their aim was constitutional monarchy, the king deriving his power from the people or community.

J. W. Allen, *A History of Political Thought in the Sixteenth Century* (London, 1928); J. N. Figgis, *Studies of Political Thought from Gerson to Grotius* (Cambridge, 1923), 2 ed.; R. Treumann, *Die Monarchomachen* (Leipzig, 1895). H.H.

monasticism: A concept used to denote a mode of life pertaining to people living in seclusion from the world, having religious vows, and following a fixed rule. The purpose is always the same: by withdrawing from the world the religious hopes to achieve a life whose ideal is different from and largely at variance with that followed by the majority of mankind, and the means used to gain this ideal are self-abnegation and an organized asceticism*. Monasticism is not something peculiar to Christianity for we find it being practiced in every religion that has reached a high ethical development and integration. Pre-Christian monasticism flourished amongst two groups of Jews, the Essenes and the Therapeutae**. The beginnings of Christian monasticism are found in Egypt of the third century A.D. where groups of hermits* bound themselves to a life of denial in certain things. Amongst these Egyptian cenobites* the most famous was St. Anthony*, and from him was derived that form of monastic life that prevailed in Egypt until the middle of the fifth century. However, this form of monasticism was more eremitical, and it was not until the time of St. Pachomius* (4th century) that true monasticism arose. About 315 Pachomius established the first Christian monastery at Tabennisi. Pachomius had introduced the idea of a "religious order" by giving laws that regulated the least detail of a monk's life, by having meals and prayers in common, and by making work a thing to be done for its own sake and not as a mere occupation, which it had been considered by the earlier hermits. The Pachomians spread rapidly through Egypt and Abyssinia until in 410 there were 7,000 Pachomian monks. This monachism began to wane about 500. In the Greek rite St. Basil* adapted the monastic ideal to the needs of the Eastern Church. (See Basilians) His variations of monasticism remained the standard among the Greeks and Eastern Slavs. Monasticism was brought to Rome by St. Athanasius* while visiting there in 340. The first permanent working adaptation of the ideal was effected by St. Benedict* who formed c. 500 the Benedictine* rule. Amongst the Benedictines the individual was enveloped in the corporate life of the community to which he bound himself. The great task of the day was the chanting of the Office; but amongst these monks work took a more important role than it had in Eastern monachism. Two innovations of Benedict were: 1) the ideal of law and order, i.e., the rule bound the abbot no less than the monk; 2) the idea of stability whereby a monk and the community were bound to each other for life. The only serious competitor in the West of the Benedictine rule was that of St. Columban* of Ireland; but in the 7th century the two rules met in the Columban abbeys of central Europe, and the rule of Benedict was adopted even by the Irish monks. With the wars against the Mohammedans arose two new types of religious orders: the orders of ransom and the military orders*; and the beginning of the 13th century saw the origin of the great mendicant orders*: the Franciscans, the Dominicans, the Carmelites and the Augustinian Hermits. The beginning of the 13th century was a period of flourishing monasticism for the friars were in the first fervor of their origin and the older orders of monks were reflecting the results of Hillebrand's reforms. But in the latter 13th century and the 14th century a period of decline set in which, with the exception of some reforms, continued until the Reformation. With the Reformation a new type of religious arose, the Regular Clerks*, of whom the most famous are the Jesuits*. From the time of the Reformation until the present the lot of religious orders has been a varied one, especially since suppression by ecclesiastical and secular power has been used frequently against them. Yet beginning with the last half of the 19th century they have shown a remarkable revival and vitality of growth coupled with a great increase in new types of communities, especially in religious institutes which have the common life and take simple vows of poverty, chastity, and obedience. Most of these are called institutes or congregations. See abbey; Acoemetae; Anchorite; Cassian; Cassiodorus; Hieronymites; Humiliati; novice; prior. T.T.M.

monergism: The doctrine of some Augustinians who affirmed that regeneration is the work of the Holy Spirit alone, the human will being passive and having no part. Cf. synergism. F.G.E.

monism, epistemological: See epistemology.

monism, metaphysical: See ontology.

Monod, Wilfred: (1867-) Professor of theology in the Faculty of Protestant Theology at Paris. Developing a modern gnosticism*, the impotency of God preoccupies him. He is of the opinion that there occurred a prehistoric moral and metaphysical fall. He distinguishes between a cosmogonic dynamism, a blind, instinctive, remarkable and demonic physical and vital impetus and a redemptive dynamism of the Logos. As the gnostics have been unjustly slandered and their dualism suppressed by the church, gnosticism did not have a chance to develop all its resources. The belief in the Demiurge*, the doctrine of the adversary, the view of "la quatrième idée" and the doctrine of trinity are the pivots of Monod's monumental system. His theology is partly a revival of Manichean* dualism. His dualism is not absolute, like that of the followers of Mani. The perpetuity and final victory of God and the good implies the ultimate redemption of the Demiurge of our world and the ultimate disappearance of demiurgic activity. Monod combines the Manichean tendencies with the theses of Giordano Bruno* and the angelology of St. Paul.

He admits that from the point of pure philosophy agnosticism is the only respectable and reasonable attitude towards the ontological problem of God. What he terms "la quatrième idée", is the hypothesis that the Father does not belong to the structure of the world. In order to believe in Him one must cease to seek Him in nature for nature remains an unknown X, sometimes divine, sometimes satanic. Thus God is different from the Father. He affirms God the Father but denies "God". The Father is neither in history nor in nature. Monod seeks to exculpate the true God from the responsibility of evil and suffering.

Aux croyants et aux athées (Paris, 1906); *Le problème du bien; Somme théologique; Journal d'un pasteur*, 3 vols. (Paris, 1935). H.H.

monophysitism: Purely dogmatically considered the concept signifies the doctrine that insists upon the unity of the divine and human in Christ in the realm of physical life. In principle, the logos becomes flesh; in reality, however, the flesh becomes transformed into divine nature. The Syrian Jacobites*, the Coptic, Abyssinian and Armenian churches were monophysitic. The party's decisive characteristic is in opposition to the orthodox two-nature doctrine of Christ's nature adopted by the Council of Chalcedon*. See Agnoetae; Christology; Dyophysites; Eutyches; henoticon; monotheletism; Three Chapter controversy; Theopaschites.

G. Krüger, *Monophysitische Streitigkeiten* (Jena, 1884); H. v. Schubert, *Geschichte der christlichen Kirche im Frühmittelalter* (Tubingen, 1921); C .W. F. Walch, *Entwurf einer vollständingen Histoire der Ketzereien, Spaltungen und Religions-streitigkesten, bis auf die Zeiten der Reformation* (Leipzig, 1762-1785) in eleven volumes. H.H.

monotheism: The belief that the cosmos is a unity, that only one God exists in the universe, and that he has created and orders all things. This belief was introduced in Israel first by Second Isaiah in the exile about 440 B.C. and became increasingly popular until fully established in the course of post-exilic days. Many Egyptian scholars assert (see works of J. H. Breasted) Pharaoh Ikhnaton (1375-1358 B.C.) was a monotheist and some scholars maintain this also of Moses. See S. Freud, *Moses and Monotheism* (1939); W. F. Albright, *From the Stone Age to Christianity* (1940) and *Archaeology and the Religion of Israel* (1942). The majority scholarly opinion is that both were still in the henotheistic stage. Although each worked relentlessly for the worship of the god he championed as the key to national unity, neither came to the point of denying the existence of other deities. The rival claims of primitive worshipers, each asserting that his particular god made sun, sky, land, sea, etc., should not be confused with monotheism, which is the product only of advanced philosophic speculation. See Amos; Elohim; henotheism; post-exilic; Isaiah (Second); shema; theism. R.E.W.

monotheletism: In its inception this Christological* doctrine held that the god-man acted as one, unitary energy. Later it asserted that Christ, as god-man, had one will. It was the monophysites who defended early a monergenetic and monotheletic Christology. The upholders of this doctrine were combated as heretics by the orthodox theologians. See Constantinople, Councils of; dyotheletism.

G. Owsepian, *Die Entstehungsgeschichte des Monotheletismus* (Leipzig, 1897); H. v. Schubert, *Geschichte der christlichen Kirche im Frümittelalter* (Tübingen, 1921). H.H.

monsignor: (Ital. my lord, but without any feudal connotation; plural, monsignori; abbreviation, Mgr., or Msgr.) A title pertaining, by virtue of their office, to all prelates* of the Roman Catholic Church in the West. In a narrower sense the title is used for the prelates of the Roman Court, active and honorary, such as papal or domestic prelate. In Europe it is more gracefully the common title of bishops, e.g., in France, *Monseigneur*. See clergy. J.F.T.

monstrance, or ostensorium: (Lat. *monstrare* or *ostendere*, to show) In the Roman Catholic Church a gold- or silver-plated vessel with a transparent section in which the Host* is carried in procession or exposed for adoration. Originally shaped like a tower, and later a Gothic chapel, the form now used is a band of precious metal about two inches deep encircling glass or crystals, front and back, between which (lunette) the Host is placed; this metal circlet, surrounded by metallic rays and surmounted by a cross, rests on a stem arising from a round and heavy base. J.F.T.

Montaigne, Michel Eyquem, Sieur de: French essayist, b. at the Château de Montaigne, Périgord, March 28, 1533 and there d. September 11, 1592. Wealthy, well-educated, and somewhat of a traveller, Montaigne dabbled in law and politics until the age of thirty-seven, when he retired to his château where, for ten years, he fashioned the first two books of his famous *Essays*. During his absence on a year and a half of travelling, he was made, like his father, the mayor of Bordeaux, which office he held for four years. In 1588 he published a new edition of his *Essays*, revised and augmented by a third book. Though sometimes a sharp satirist of the Roman Catholic Church, he never renounced her, sometimes praised her greatly, and died during the celebration of Mass in his sick-room. Although his works received a certain amount of ecclesiastical disapproval because of their Pyrrhonian skepticism and occasionally deliberate lasciviousness, they are classics of charming grace and lusty vitality, fascinating in their brilliant reflections of a worldly-wise student of human nature. J.F.T.

Montanism: A Christian sect of the second century A.D., named for Montanus of Ardabau in Phrygia. In 156 he proclaimed himself as the one through whom the dispensation of the Holy Spirit had begun. He was joined by the prophetesses Prisca and Maximilla in proclaiming the nearness of the end. The main body of the church rejected the validity of these prophets and division inevitably resulted. Many who opposed the increasing worldliness of the church were attracted to the Montanist movement, including Tertullian* the great African theologian who joined them in 207 A.D. The movement was an attempt to reassert a primitive point of view in the face of the growing Hellenization of the main body of the church. See baptism for the dead. C.T.C.

Montgomery, James: See hymns.

Moody, Dwight Lyman: (1837-1899) The outstanding American revivalist since the Civil War. Born in Northfield, Massachusetts, one of nine children he received little formal education. He went to work in Boston at seventeen, where, in a matter of fact way he decided to become a Christian, and from that moment his life was increasingly dedicated to advance the cause of personal religion. Coming to Chicago he became a shrewd shoe salesman, though he never permitted business to crowd out religion, and soon set about organizing a Sunday School class made up of street urchins. This grew into a Sunday School, then into a Church and finally into a Bible Institute. His evangelistic career began on the close of the Civil War and his two early campaigns in England (1867, 1870) gave him a reputation throughout the English speaking world. Returning to America he was continuously engaged until his death in holding great meetings throughout the United States and in Great Britain. Moody's success as an evangelist seems impossible to explain adequately. He has been characterized as "rough, honest, sincere, flat, without frills, old-fashioned, ungrammatical, always simple and grandly in earnest". The impression he always left was that there was truth behind him greater than he.

W. R. Moody, *D. L. Moody* (1930); Gamaliel Bradford, *D. L. Moody: A Worker in Souls* (1927).
W.W.S.

Moore Lectures, T. V.: The "T. V. Moore Lectures" were founded by a bequest of Thomas Verner Moore, formerly a professor in San Francisco Theological Seminary, San Anselmo, California. According to the terms of the gift the lectures shall be positive expositions or defenses of some aspect of Biblical study or of Christian truth, and shall be given only by men who are known as sincere believers in what is known historically as the evangelical Reformed Faith.

The endowment amounts to $17,000. The first series of lectures was given by Robert E. Speer. Other lecturers have been Hugh Thompson Kerr, Adolph Keller, and E. Stanley Jones. A.C.M.

moral a priori, or primacy of the practical reason: Kant, believing it "a fact of the practical reason" that man should do his duty and carry out the categorical imperative*, found implied three postulates: moral responsibility and the freedom of the will; an immortal life in which duty can be completed; God, who will recompense men according to their fulfillment of duty. In view of its capacity to affirm these postulates on subjects regarding which the purely theoretical reason can arrive at no conclusions, Kant recognizes a certain "primacy of the practical reason", sometimes called "the moral a priori". W.K.W.

moral argument for God: See God.

moral influence theory: See Abailard; atonement; satisfaction.

moral law: The ultimate principles that should govern human conduct. For Kant these are found in the categorical imperative*. See conscience; ethics; law. Cf. haustafel. W.K.W.

moral obligation: Moral obligation, or duty, is felt as a command to follow a prescribed course of action in preference to opposing inclinations. This feeling has been variously interpreted as: the dicta of conscience*; the voice of God; the authoritativeness of an ideal; the social pressure of one's group; the compulsive influence of moral tradition; the demand for integration in behalf of the whole self in overcoming refractory impulses; and so on. It has been attributed to intuition, reason, habit, experience, and divine revelation. W.K.W.

moral optimism: (religious meliorism) The attitude toward life which goes beyond meliorism* in asserting a divine factor which responds favorably to man's moral endeavor. This attitude is critically optimistic and goes beyond any heroic attitude, however good, which stops short of a belief in divine providence for man. As so defined, this view is held by D. C. Macintosh. See optimism. V.F.

moral progress: See progress:

moral realism: See realism, moral.

Moral Re-Armament: See Oxford Group.

moral sense: A capacity believed by Shaftesbury, Hutcheson, and other eighteenth century philosophers to develop in the mind as a result of the association of ideas. It affirms moral judgments intuitively, and affords pleasure of a somewhat aesthetic character in approval of right actions and displeasure in disapproval of wrong actions. See H. Bonar, *Moral Sense* (1930). W.K.W.

moral theology: A term regularly used to describe the study of the Christian life in relation to God's revealed will, and by extension the entire problem of human life in relation to God, morally speaking. This subject includes the principles of the divine will and that will relative to man (eternal law, natural law, positive law, etc.), a study of the nature and "end" of man in the light of the divine law; and a consideration of human behavior in relation to that law. The study of cases (casuistry), with various theories of their treatment, is also part of the general subject. W.N.P.

morality plays: See religious drama.

morals, double standard of: See double standard of morals.

Moravian Church, the: Its origin is traced to the evangelical movement in Bohemia led by John Hus*, who suffered martyrdom in 1415. Followers of the reformer effected an organization, 1457, called Unitas Fratrum* (Unity of Brethren). Four principles served as basis of their union (a) the Bible as the only source of Christian doctrine, (b) public worship to be conducted on the model of the Apostolic Church, (c) the Lord's Supper to be received in faith and defined in the language of Scripture, (d) true Christian life as essential evidence of saving faith. For their independent ministry the historic episcopate was secured through the Waldenses*, yet church polity inclined to the conferential pattern. Growth of the Church in Bohemia and Moravia was rapid. (See Bohemian (or Czech) Brethren.) By 1500, there were about 400 parishes and 200,000 members. Ecclesiastical resources were developed through elaboration of a confession of faith, translation of the Scriptures from the original tongues, schools, colleges, and theological seminaries, publication of catechisms and hymn-books. The Unitas Fratrum was the first church to put a hymnal* in the vernacular into the hands of the people, first edition 1501.

The history of the Unitas Fratrum, for two centuries, was largely one of cruel persecutions. Its organization was crushed during the Thirty Years' War*. With the death of Bishop John Amos Comenius*, famous educator, the first part of the history of the Unitas ends, but not before this man of vision had provided for possible resuscitation by perpetuating the episcopacy through regular consecration and by publication of his "Ratio Disciplinae", embodying the principles of the polity, the teaching, the work, and the discipline of the Unitas.

The second part opens, 1722, when a company of fugitives from Moravia (hence the modern name Moravian Church), who had preserved traditions of their fathers, found refuge in Saxony on the estate of Count Nicolaus Ludwig von Zinzendorf*, in the event their leader. Their settlement, Herrnhut, became the rallying center for like-minded compatriots, German pietists*, and others, so that renewal of the Church on the old principles was invigorated by an infusion of new life from the evangelical Church of Germany. The fame of Herrnhut, as presenting a union of spiritual life with good works and industrial activity, led to similar settlements elsewhere. Within two decades, centers were established in England and America. And a wonderful spiritual experience, 1727, inspired evangelizing zeal which led Moravians to embark on mission efforts in distant fields, thus inaugurating the modern Protestant missionary movement.

Present Condition and Characteristics.

(I). Enterprises. (a) Foreign missions in Labrador, Alaska, among the Indians of North America, in the West Indies, Nicaragua, Honduras, Demarara, Surinam, Africa (South Africa and East Central Africa), West Himalaya. (b) The "Diaspora Work", an extensive agency for promoting spiritual life within the National (Protestant) Churches, without drawing members into the Moravian Church, carried on in Germany, Denmark, Norway, Sweden, Switzerland, and Russia. (c) Boarding schools, colleges, theological seminaries. (d) Church evangelization in Bohemia and Moravia.

(II). Constitution and Government. The whole Moravian Church, home provinces and mission fields, is still an organic Unity, each portion maintaining its own characteristics. Constitution and government are essentially conferential. General Synods and Provincial Synods meet periodically, General and Provincial Boards discharge the administrative functions. Moravian orders of the ministry are bishops, presbyters, and deacons.

(III). Worship. This combines the liturgical element with large measure of freedom in order and forms of service. A litany is used at Sunday morning worship. Special liturgical services distinguish the festivals of the ecclesiastical year and certain "Memorial Days" in the history of the Moravian Church. The hymnology is rich and the music fully developed.

(IV). Doctrine. The Modern Moravian Church has not put forth a formal confession of faith, but the cardinal points of doctrine are found in its catechism, its Easter Morning Litany, and in its "Synodal Results". The Scriptures are held to be the only rule of faith and practice. In substantial agreement with other evangelical churches, the following truths are held to be essential, the doctrine of the total depravity of human nature, the love of God the Father, the real Godhead and the real humanity of Jesus Christ, our reconciliation to God and our justification by faith through the sacrifice of Jesus Christ, the Holy Ghost and His operations, good works as the fruit of the Spirit, the fellowship of believers, the second coming of the Lord, the resurrection of the dead unto life or unto condemnation, the Headship of Christ over the Church, which is His Body. See Spangenberg, A. G.

GENERAL STATISTICS (1942).

	Number of Congregations	Communicants	Total Membership
Continental Province (Europe)	25	8,022	9,909
Czechoslovakia Province	10	1,232	5,395
British Province	42	3,166	3,524
American Province, North	105	18,553	22,486
American Province, South	42	10,660	14,430
Totals of the Home Church	224	41,633	55,744
Foreign Missions	337	55,624	171,554
Affiliated Societies "Diaspora", Europe	42	———	30,000
Totals	603	97,257	257,298

E. deSchweinitz, *History of the Church Known as the Unitas Fratrum* (1885); J. Th. Mueller, *Geschichte der Boemischen Brueder*, 3 vols. (Herrnhut, 1922-1931); J. T. Hamilton, *History of the Moravian Church during the 18th and 19th Centuries* (1900). W.N.S.

More, Henry: (1614-1687) For this Cambridge Platonist God is infinitely extended throughout space and time and has at his disposal a subordinate spiritual being, the spirit of nature by which he can hold together in an orderly and purposive system a world which if left to mechanical forces would inevitably fly apart.

A Collection of Several Philosophical Writings (London, 1712), 4th ed.; *Opera omnia* (London, 1675-79), 4 vols. H.H.

More, Paul Elmer: (1864-1937) American critic and philosopher, leading exponent of the New Humanism*. Although he taught for brief periods at Harvard and Bryn Mawr, was for five years editor of *The Nation*, and later lectured occasionally at Princeton, he devoted himself mainly to writing.

His principal works include *Shelburne Essays* (11 vols., 1904-21), *Platonism* (1917), *The Religion of Plato* (1921), *Hellenistic Philosophies* (1923), *The Christ of the New Testament* (1924), *Christ the Word* (1927), *New Shelburne Essays* (3 vols., 1928-36), and *The Catholic Faith* (1931). L.W.C.

More, Sir Thomas: (1478-1535) His political satire, the *Utopia*, though modeled externally on Plato's *Republic*, really expressed its author's dislike of an acquisitive society, the economic business enterprise. His sharpest shafts of irony were reserved for the perfidy of diplomacy. The morality of an ideal community, as he saw it, was to produce good citizens and men of intellectual and moral freedom, to do away with idleness, to supply the physical needs of all without excessive labor, to abolish luxury and waste, to mitigate both poverty and wealth, and to minimize greed and extortion. His moral idea expressed the reasonableness and open-mindedness of humanism, the futility of a moral aspiration that cannot make its account with brute fact.

W. E. Campbell, *More's Utopia and his Social Teaching* (London, 1930); R. W. Chambers. "The Saga and the Myth of Sir Thomas More" *Proceedings of the British Academy* (London, 1927). H.H.

Morehouse, Henry L.: (1834-1917) For thirty-eight years prominent in Baptist Home Mission work. Supported founding of University of Chicago and selection of Harper as its first president. Established Ministers and Missionaries Benefit Board of the Northern Baptist Convention. C.H.M.

mores: See culture.

Morgan, Thomas: See deism.

Morgan, Thomas Jefferson: (1839-1902) Soldier, Baptist clergyman, educator, denominational leader. Favored just war. Commissioner of Indian Affairs under Harrison. Corresponding Secretary American Baptist Home Mission Society. C.H.M.

Mormon, Book of: Record of early inhabitants of America.

Joseph Smith, Jr.,* claimed angel visits in spring of 1820 and in September 1823, and that gold plates were given him September 22, 1827. The translation of these plates is the Book of Mormom, first published in March 1830, by E. B. Grandin, Palmyra, New York. (There have been over one hundred editions since then.) It relates to three migrations: a) circa 2200 B.C. from Tower of Babel. These were all killed. b) Descendants of Manasseh from Jerusalem circa 600 B.C. c) Colony from Jerusalem led by son of Zedekiah 588 B.C. The latter two immigrations combined, and later divided to form the Nephites and Lamanites. These were visited by Christ after his resurrection and for two hundred years lived in peace. Later, circa 400 A.D., war destroyed all but the Lamanites, who are the ancestors of the American Indians. S.A.B.

Mormons: See Latter Day Saints; Utah Mormon communism: See communistic settlements, religious.

Morrison, Robert: (1782-1834) The first Protestant missionary to China, born of Scottish parents at Buller's Green, Northumberland. He studied the Chinese language in England and was sent in 1807 by the London Missionary Society to Canton, where he became translator for the East India Company. He published a translation of the N.T. in 1814, and with Rev. William Milne a translation of the O.T. in 1818. He founded an Anglo-Chinese college in 1820, trained Chinese evangelists, and opened a dispensary. He constructed a Chinese grammar (1815) and a Chinese dictionary (6 vols. 1821.). He died in Canton, August 1, 1834. P.E.J.

Morse Lectureship, the: A lectureship established in 1865 by Professor Samuel F. B. Morse, the inventor of the telegraph. Its capital sum is $10,000; it is given at least once in two or three years at Union Theological Seminary, New York City. The donor expressed his desire that the lectures deal with the relation of the Bible to the sciences, "the vindication of the inspiration and authority of the Bible against attacks made on scientific grounds". Among the lecturers who have appeared on this foundation: J. H. Barrows, William Sanday, H. O. Taylor, J. H. Breasted, H. R. Marshall, G. F. Moore,

J. A. Thomson, J. E. Frame.
(Data furnished by the Office of the Registrar of Union Theological Seminary, N. Y.)
V.F.

mortal and venial sin: The major distinction in Catholic moral theology in regard to seriousness of sin*. Mortal sin is a deliberate sin in some weighty matter and thus an offence against God by which one cuts himself off from God or, in the scholastic phrase, deprives himself of sanctifying grace or, following I St. John v. 16, 17, brings on himself spiritual death. The act need not be with this deliberate intention, as in formal apostasy*, but only in fact, as in an act deliberately chosen that subverts right order in essential relations to God, fellowman, or self. Venial sin is that which is slight in matter or which is done without deliberation. See penance; retention of sins. T.J.B.

Moses: (Gr. form of Heb. *moshen*) The Egyptian name of the founder of the nation and religion of ancient Israel*, reputed author of the Pentateuch* and of the Oral Law of Judaism, and traditionally famous as the law-giver of Mount Sinai. Undoubtedly an historical person though no contemporary records of his life survive, except as incorporated in the Pentateuch from tradition transmitted orally for at least four centuries. The narratives of Exodus*, though in the form of a theological interpretation of Israel's constitutive period, and coloured with legend, embody the recollection of decisive events in which Moses was the leading figure; viz., a) the escape of the tribes from state-slavery in Egypt, culminating in an apparently miraculous deliverance from pursuit at a "sea of reeds" (traditionally, the Red Sea); and b) the creation of Israel as a people through a covenant mediated by Moses at Mount Sinai (Horeb) between Yahweh, whose presence was manifested by volcanic phenomena, and the escaped tribesmen. To the account of these events is prefixed the personal story of Moses, his Egyptian upbringing and Midian exile, his call to prophetic leadership and his return to demand, with the support of plagues sent by Yahweh, liberty for his people.

In spite of its theological setting, legendary elements and imaginary detail, there are good reasons to credit the substantial historicity of this account: the strength of the tradition, its congruity with the dating and circumstances of Egyptian history, Moses' Egyptian name and connections, and above all the distinctiveness of Israelite prophetic religion as reflecting the outstanding personality and work of a religious founder. Moses is remembered neither as a warrior nor as a law-giver in his own right, but as a prophet commissioned to speak for and to his people, to announce and interpret Yahweh's actions on the plane of history, to claim for Yahweh the exclusive allegiance of Israel, and to be a spokesman of Yahweh's will. The classical prophetic movement of the 8th and 7th centuries B.C. was consciously a renewal of Mosaic prophetism (see prophecy), and is inexplicable without it as an antecedent. To the moral stature and spiritual experience of Moses may be traced the thought of a God who is not localized, is without sex or consort and indeed is anthropopsychic rather than anthropomorphic and therefore cannot be represented by a god-image; who passionately demands the exclusive allegiance of his people, and whose presence is most distinctively felt in the demands of his ethical will for gratitude, loyalty and response to his righteous purpose and his mercy; whose power is manifest in abnormal physical and psychic phenomena, but also in the arena of events which condition man's moral choices; whose worship is the bond of society because it is fulfilled not only by cultic acts but by moral behaviour producing social cohesion and well-being. See decalogue; Israel, religion and theology; Old Testament; tables of the law. R.B.Y.S.

Moses, Apocalypse of: See Jubilees, Book of.

Moses, Assumption of: See Assumption of Moses.

Moses ben Nahman, known also as Bonastruc Da Porta: (1194-1270) Celebrated Spanish Jewish Talmudist, theologian and exegete. Born in Gerona, Spain, the Jewish community of which he later served as rabbi, he very early won fame as a Talmudic* scholar. The most popular of his writings was his semi-mystical and semi-rational commentary on the Pentateuch*. His success in defending Judaism against Christianity in a disputation held before King Jaime of Aragon in Barcelona in 1263 was responsible for his exile from his native land. In 1267 he migrated to Palestine where three years later he died. Cf. *Jewish Encyclopedia,* Moses ben Nahman. See Kabbalah. S.R.

Moses de Leon: See Zohar.

Mosheim, Johann Lorenz von: (1694-1755) German Lutheran theologian and Church historian, professor and chancellor at Helmstedt, later at Goettingen. Considered the outstanding scholar of the Lutheran Church of his day, Mosheim wrote on all branches of theology but he is best remembered for his historical writings, especially his *Institutes of Ecclesiastical History* (1726). He describes his theological position as "neither Pietist nor over-orthodox". T.A.K.

Moslem: (Arabic, *muslim,* active particple of *aslama* of which the noun is *islam,* meaning submission) One who professes the faith of Islam; a follower of Mohammed*. See Mohammedanism. P.E.J.

mosque: (French *mosquee* from Italian *moschea;* from Arabic, *masjid;* from *sajada,* to bow down, adore) A Mohammedan temple or place of worship. The *mosque* is also used to refer to the collective body of those who worship in *mosques.* P.E.J.

motet: A short, unaccompanied, polyphonic*, choral composition based upon a Latin text which is usually liturgical. Superseding the more restricted style of the conductus* the motet came into prominent usage at the opening of the 13th century and was applied to every choral part of the mass except the Credo. The lack of devotion shown in the use of secular texts in some of the parts in combination with the liturgical Latin in other parts was gradually eliminated by the 16th century when the motet reached its greatest development in compositions by Orlando di Lasso, Josquin des Prés, Giovanni Pierluigi da Palestrina, William Byrd and Orlando Gibbons. In the 16th century the motet ceased to be employed for the regular parts of the mass and was used in prescribed places much as the anthem* was used in Protestant services.

H. Leichtentritt, *Geschichte der Motette* (1908).

E.H.B.

mother of god: See Virgin Mary. See also mother goddesses.

mother-goddesses: Familiar figures in primitive nature cults where the maintenance of fertility is a central interest of religion. Each early civilization around the eastern end of the Mediterranean had its traditional mother-goddess, e.g., Isis* in Egypt, Ashtart (see Ashtoreth) in Phoenicia, Cybele in Phrygia and Demeter in Greece. In each case she was originally the patroness of productivity but in the course of time her life-giving power was transferred also to the souls of men. She insured a blessed immortality for the dead. This development was especially conspicuous in the case of Isis. There was a mother-goddess connected with all of the chief mystery religions* except Mithraism which was strictly a man's religion. The only mother-goddess to attain state recognition at Rome was Cybele from Phrygia. Tradition reported that the Romans, when hard pressed by Hannibal shortly before the year 200 B.C., officially introduced the worship of Cybele by importing a sacred meteoric stone from Pessinus in Phrygia and installing it with great solemnity in a shrine on the Palitine. Later a temple was reared upon the site where its remains may still be seen. She was known as "the mother of the gods" and in some respects was the prototype of the Christian Mary as "the mother of God." In general the function of a mother-goddess was to represent the deification of the female principle in the life of nature and mankind. See Gods; Roman religions. Cf. Kali; Mut.

G. Showerman, *The Great Mother of the Gods* (1910); H. A. Strong and J. Garstang, *The Syrian Goddess* (1913); L. R. Farnell, *Cults of the Greek States* (1907), vol. III; S. J. Case, *Evolution of Early Christianity* (1914), pp. 284-330.

S.J.C.

motherhood: Term applied to the experience of performing the function of caring for the needs of the young child by the mother. Usually includes the biological experience of giving birth to the child, the early satisfying of the organic needs of the infant, and its emotional development until maturity. Traditionally motherhood has been thought of as woman's primary role and the greatest honor accorded her has been for this function. Ancient cultures have glorified motherhood even though woman's status has been low, legally, socially, and religiously. With the emancipation of women leading to work outside the home, more careers open to them, motherhood in a more limited sense has come to be recognized in many groups, and a part of the traditional function has been transferred to others. Thus the role of the mother has undergone tremendous change. While her position in our culture is still exalted, other careers as well as that of motherhood have been opened to her. She is no longer expected to spend all of her time with her child; in fact modern psychology cautions against over-attachment, over-solicitude, and projection of her own ideas and aims upon the child. It is because of the early intimate association between the mother and child that the mother exerts a profound effect upon the personality pattern the child develops and his later social adjustment. See matriarchal system; woman, religious and ethical status of. H.R.M.

motive: Whatever consciously or unconsciously induces one to adopt a certain course of action. In ethics the term means a consciously desired end which prompts to decision and action. The Utilitarians* distinguished motive, as referring to the foreseen desired end, from intention, as referring to all the expected consequences of a decision. This is a distinction made for purposes of analysis and in view of the integral nature of the emotional and intellectual aspects of all action breaks down as a description of psychological fact. R.W.F.

motu proprio: (Lat. of his own accord) A term designating the manner of composition, issuance and interpretation of certain acts of the Roman Pontiff as embodied in a personal document (cf. rescript*). It signifies that the disciplinary decree in question has been issued on the Pontiff's own initiative after a diligent examination, and is an expression of the certain knowledge and positive wish of the occupant of the Apostolic See. This term is sometimes loosely used substantively to indicate the famous rescript, the Instruction on Sacred Music of Pius X* in 1903, which is only one of many such documents issued by the pope. See bull, papal. J.F.T.

Mozarabic liturgy: (Arabic *musta' rab*, meaning uncertain) The old Spanish liturgy, of the Gallican* type; preserved since 1500 by Cardinal Ximenes' Mozarabic Chapel at Toledo Cathedral. See liturgy. E.R.H.

mozetta: (Ital. *mozzo*, shortened) An abbreviated cape with a rudimentary hood of silk or wool, red, violet or black in color, reaching to the elbows, and with an open front that may be closed by a row of small buttons. It is a non-liturgical vestment, signifying jurisdiction, and is worn at functions whereat the prelate* is present officially but is not officiating. J.F.T.

Muenzer, Thomas: (1489-1525) Enthusiast, Anabaptist* preacher at Zwickau, Muhlhausen and elsewhere. A radical leader in the peasants' war*, he incited the peasants to violence and bloodshed, but was himself beheaded after his defeat at Frankenhausen in 1525. E.C.K.

mufti: (Arabic *mufti*, active participle of *afta*, to give a *fatwa** or legal decision) A Mohammedan priest or expounder of the law. Often an assessor to a court. In Turkey, it referred to the official head of the state religion and to deputies appointed by him. P.E.J.

Muhlenberg, Henry Melchior: (1711-1787) "Father of the Lutheran Church* in America". Ordained in Germany, former instructor in Halle and author of *Defence of Pietism* (1741), he was sent by Francke* to assume charge of the scattered Lutheran churches of eastern Pennsylvania and arrived in Philadelphia in 1742. With *Ecclesia Plantanda* (the Church must be planted) as his motto, he carried on an extensive missionary work from New York to Georgia, organizing congregations, training and ordaining pastors, and writing liturgies, hymnals, and church constitutions. In 1748 he founded the first Lutheran synod in America, now known as the Ministerium of Pennsylvania. Evangelist, scholar, and administrator, Muhlenberg combined fervency with tolerance and made a constructive adaptation of Lutheranism to American life. The United Lutheran Church today represents the fruit of his labors. Muhlenberg was also the founder of a distinguished family, the father of three illustrious sons: Peter (1746-1807), Revolutionary general and U. S. Senator; Frederick (1750-1801), speaker of the first and of the third Congress; and Gotthilf Henry Ernst (1753-1815), clergyman and botanist who discovered nearly 200 new species of American flora. Muhlenberg's *Journals* are being published in English translation, the first volume having appeared in 1942. T.A.K.

mujtahid: (Arabic, meaning one who exerts himself) A Moslem theologian. Among the Shi ites*, a religious teacher, who is an authority on matters of law or theology. P.E.J.

mukti: A variant term meaning salvation in Hinduism. See salvation, Hindu. C.S.B.

Mulert, Hermann: (1879-) Before he became professor at the University of Kiel, he successively taught at Leipzig, Halle and Berlin. He is particularly known by his various writings on Schleiermacher*. He also devoted his energies to the investigation of the creeds. Since 1932 he also is editor of *Die Christliche Welt.*

Schleiermachers geschichtsphilosophische Ansichten in ihrer Bedeutung für seine Theologie (Giessen, 1907); *Schleiermachers Sendschreiben an Lücke* (Giessen, 1908); *Weihnachtsfeier* (Leipzig, 1908); *Wahrhaftigkeit und Lehrverpflichtung* (Tübingen, 1911); *Der Christ und das Vaterland* (Leipzig, 1915); *Gebetserhörung, Freiheitsglaube, Gottesglaube* (Leipzig, 1921); editor of 2 ed. of *Wilhelm Diltheys "Leben Schleiermachers"* (Berlin, 1922); *Konfessionskunde* (Giessen, 1927, 2 ed., Berlin, 1937); *Evangelische Kirchen und theologische Fakultäten* (Tübingen, 1930); *Religion, Kirche, Theologie* (Giessen, 1931); *Schleiermacher und die Gegenwart* (Frankfurt a. M., 1934). H.H.

mulla: A learned teacher or expounder of laws and doctrines of Islam*. One trained in the mosque* schools who ranks as an official theologian. See ulama. P.E.J.

Müller, Friedrich Max: (1823-1900) Gifted orientalist of German origin, whose active life was spent in Oxford; distinguished exponent of comparative philology and of comparative religion; editor of *The Sacred Books of the East*, in fifty-one volumes (1875-). E.J.G.

Müller, George Friedrich: (1805-1898) German-born minister of Teignmouth, Devonshire, later the founder and superintendent of a large orphanage near Bristol, and author of many religious tracts and the widely popular book, *The Lord's Dealings with George Müller.* He taught that prayer should be relied upon to supply all temporal, as well as spiritual, needs, and accordingly, as a pastor, he refused a fixed salary. In old age he travelled and preached in many lands, including America. L.H.DEW.

Müller, Julius: (1801-1878) He taught at Marburg and Halle. He opposed the effacement of Christianity with speculative philosophy and pantheism. He greatly influenced both Neander and Tholuck** in their struggle against liberal theology, the enemies of Christianity, and confessionalism. He was in favor of the union of the confessional churches. Against the softening of the conception of sin on the part of the Enlightenment and idealism, he succeeded in reviving the full seriousness of sin. Müller's conception of sin, however, suffered from the same individualistic slant as that of the Enlightenment and idealism.

Christliche Lehre von der Sünde (Breslau, 1938-44), 2 vols.; *Die Union, ihr Wesen und ihr gottliches Recht* (Berlin, 1854). H.H.

Müller, Karl: (1852-1935) German Protestant theologian. He was born in Langenburg, Württemberg. In 1880 he became privatdozent in Berlin, in 1884 professor of Church History in Halle, in 1886 at Giessen, in 1891 at Breslau, and from 1903-1922 at Tübingen. Outstanding church historian, his aim was to discover the dynamic of the historical process and to describe its leading forces rather than to enumerate all the historical events irrespective of their historical significance.

Principal works:
Kirchengeschichte (1892-1919, 2nd ed. 1924-1929), 2 vols. in 3; *Der Kampf Ludwig des Bayern mit der römischen Kurie* (1879-1880), 2 vols.; *Luther und Karlstadt* (1907); *Kirche, Gemeinde und Obrigkeit nach Luther* (1910); *Beiträge zur Geschichte der Verfassung der alten Kirche* (1922); Autobiography in: *Aus der akademischen Arbeit* (*Vorträge und Aufsätze*) (1930). O.A.P.

Mullins, Edgar Y.: (1860-1928) Baptist clergyman, educator, author. Professor of Theology and President, Southern Baptist Theological Seminary, Louisville, 1879-1928. Author of *Axioms of Religion* (1908). C.H.M.

Munger, Theodore Thornton: (1830-1910) Graduated Yale, 1850, Andover, 1854; Pastor,

Congregational Church, North Adams, Mass., 1877-1883; United Church, New Haven, 1885-1910. Dr. Munger was notably influential in freeing religious thought and in relating the New Theology* to literature and to education.

Author: *The Freedom of Faith* (1883); *The Appeal to Life* (1887); articles in literary periodicals. Dr. Munger was notably influential in freeing religious thought and in relating the New Theology* to literature and to education.

Cf. *Theodore Thornton Munger* (1903), by Benjamin W. Bacon. J.W.B.

Muratorian canon: A list of the N.T. books that might be read in public worship in church. It is evidently a translation from a Greek original, and probably represents the usage of the church at Rome about A.D. 200; indeed it may be the work of Victor of Rome. It takes its name from the Italian scholar who found it in the Ambrosian Library at Milan and published it in 1740 as an example of barbarous Latin. E.J.G.

Murjites: (Arabic, meaning postponers) One of the early Moslem sects, which in opposition to the Kharijites*, declined to judge who was entitled to salvation as good Moslems. They were called "postponers," because they left to God to decide on the last day who was a true believer. P.E.J.

Murray, John: Born in Alton, England, Dec. 10, 1741. Died in Boston, Mass. Sept. 3, 1815. Rebelled against Calvinism; declared that all men will finally be saved. He came to America in 1770, preached up and down the New England coast, settled as pastor in Gloucester and Boston. Chaplain in the Revolutionary Army. Controversialist and author. Usually considered founder of the Universalist* movement in America.

Autobiography (1816); C. R. Skinner and A. S. Cole, *Hell's Ramparts Fell* (1941). C.R.S.

Muse: (Greek root *men-*, think, remember) A goddess, one of nine, all daughters of the ancient Zeus and Mnemosyme, and all inspirers: of music, poetry, dance, etc.; spirit which presides over the arts and sciences; a genius or spirit which dominates the poet or composer in his creative moments. F.L.P.

music: See agnus dei; alleluia; Ambrosian chant; anthem; benedictus; canon; cantata; canticles; chant; choir; chorale; conductus; credo; communion; diaphony; discant; dynamics; fugue; gloria; gloria in excelsis; gloria patri; gradual; Gradŭale; Gradual Psalms; Gregorian chant; Gregorian tones; harmony; hocket; hymns; hymns, Hebrew and Jewish; hymnology; introit; kyrie eleison; liturgics; liturgy; mass; melody; modes; motet; musicology; neumes; offertory; oratorio; organum; passion music; plainsong; polyphony; prose; psalmody; Psalms; Psalter; requiem; rhythm, musical; sanctus; schola cantorum; sequence; timbre; tonality; tract; trope. See also: bells; negro spirituals; piyyut.

musicology: Systematized knowledge about music resulting from the studies of scholars, philosophers or scientists. The field includes historical studies, theoretical systems, aesthetics, musical anthropology and ethnology, psychology, and acoustics.

G. Haydon, *Introduction to Musicology; a Survey of the Fields, Systematic and Historical, of Musical Knowledge and Research* (1941). E.H.B.

Muslim: See Mohammedanism.

Mut: The ancient mother-goddess of Thebes, Egypt, who represents the powers of the watery flood; the wife of the Nile; consort of Amon; her emblem of maternity is the vulture; protector of kings; queens represent her by wearing a vulture head-dress. F.L.P.

mutakallim or mutikallimum: (Arabic, meaning debaters) The scholastic theologians of Islam, who sought to confirm truth by reason. They were stigmatized "debaters" as those who foolishly argued about things God had put beyond reason, to be accepted as revelation. P.E.J.

Mutazilites: (Arabic, *mutazilah*, a body of seceders) A Shi ite* sect founded by Wasil ibn Ata in the 8th century. They admitted reason as a source of knowledge beside revelation. They accepted the *Koran* as a divine revelation, yet held everything in it must be interpreted to accord with reason. They called themselves "the Party of Equity and Unity" to emphasize the oneness and justice of God. P.E.J.

mutilation: The disfiguring, maiming, deforming or crippling of the body, a practice common among primitive peoples and one that survives in restricted form among civilized peoples. The motives for such mutilation are tribal custom, initiation ceremonial, indication of rank or prowess, adornment, punishment, health and religion. In religion mutilation is practiced as ascetic discipline and to signify submission to, propitiation of or special dedication to deity. For the various forms of mutilation see *Encyclopaedia Britannica*, Vol. 16, 14th ed. (1939). R.W.F.

mutual aid societies: See friendly societies.

Mysos, Demetrius: (1519-1570) A deacon who was sent to Württenberg by the Greek Patriarch (1557), in order to study the Protestant movement. He stayed with Ph. Melanchthon over a year studying the new religious movement. He cultivated a close friendship with Melanchthon and through him the Greek Orthodox Church had learned all about the Protestants. G.E.Z.

mystery plays: See religious drama.

mystery religions: A distinctive type of cult that had attained wide popularity in the Roman Empire contemporary with the rise of Christianity. The term is Greek in its origin and is now commonly employed to designate various religions that received initiates by secret rites the meaning of which might not be divulged to the public. And the possession of this secret knowledge was supposed to insure special blessings for the devotee both in the present and in the life beyond the grave. The Greek, the Phrygian, the Syrian, the Egyptian, and the Persian mysteries are most worthy of note.

1) The mysteries celebrated at Eleusis a few miles from Athens were the most famous among the Greeks. Originally these were agrarian rites honoring the mother-goddess* Demeter and her daughter Persephone. The teaching of the cult explained how Persephone while picking flowers in the field had been snatched away to the lower world by its ruler Hades. In her grief Demeter gave herself up to mourning and ceased her care for the maintenance of life in nature. When the earth produced no fruit starvation threatened mankind. But Zeus interfered to arrange that Persephone should be restored to her mother for eight of the twelve months of the year, and thus the mother went into mourning for only the four winter months. Thus it is apparent that the worship of Demeter was originally designed to insure divine help for the productivity of the soil. In the course of time, as cultural interests shifted to a more individualized type of social experience, the Eleusinian rites took on a more personal significance. They were thought to insure happiness in the world to come, to necessitate better morals in the life of the initiate, and to provide him with the true understanding of how life should be ordered in this world and the next.

Other Greek mysteries were celebrated at Andania in Messenia and on the island of Samothrace, but next to the Eleusinian cult the most popular was that of Dionysus whose mysteries were observed at different places by migratory groups of adherents. Originally these ceremonies were highly orgiastic in character. When the devotees imbibed the sacred wine, ate the raw flesh of the sacrificed animal, and drank its warm blood, they went into a frenzy of ecstasy inspired, as they believed, by the very presence of the deity within the worshiper. When the Dionysiac mysteries became more closely connected with the name of Orpheus they took on a more sober and speculative character. Members of the religious society were guaranteed a blessed immortality and furnished with passwords that would secure for them a happy entrance into Hades. See Greek religion.

2) The Phrygian mysteries centered around the mother-goddess Cybele, with whom the youthful male deity Attis had come to be associated at an early date. The doctrines of the cult clearly indicate that originally it was a spring festival celebrated in honor of the deity who was thought to awaken nature from the death of winter. Cybele was the wild nature-goddess who mourned the violent death of Attis until he arose to life again in the springtime. His triumph over death was the central theme of the ritual and the participant in the rites undoubtedly believed that his attachment to the victorious deity would insure a similar triumph for the devotee. This Cybele-Attis cult spread widely about the Mediterranean world reaching even to Rome where it was conspicuous in the first and second centuries of the Christian era.

3) In Syria a similar type of religious interest was fostered in the rites of different deities. In the Hellenistic* period Aphrodite and Adonis became the gods chiefly connected with the same sort of mysteries that had emanated from Phrygia. The goddess personified mother-life in nature and her male associate represented the dying and awakening vitality in vegetation. The death of Adonis was depicted in a mystic drama. Lamentation for his decease was followed by wild rejoicing over his return to life. The devotees expected to enjoy the gracious favor of the risen god throughout the remainder of the year and doubtless also in the hereafter.

4) The Egyptian mysteries of Isis-Osiris (Serapis) spread widely about the Graeco-Roman world. Isis was the mother-goddess who grieved for the violent death of her consort Osiris until she recovered his dismembered body, restored him to life and installed him as king in the nether world. Formerly as king of Egypt he had been engaged in bestowing the blessings of civilization upon mankind. Thus he was peculiarly fitted for entrance into the abode of the blest after death and to guide his worshipers to a similarly happy reward. Isis was honored by her followers as the queen of every land who had designed the arts of civilization, had taught men the mysteries of religion, and had ordained binding decrees in accordance with her divine knowledge. Men insured for themselves these blessings by a process of initiation requiring purificatory rites, preliminary fasting and devotion culminating in a mystical religious experience of attachment to, or union with, the deity. Ultimately one was sure of a blessed existence in the future life. See Egypt, religions of.

5) The last mystery religion to become popular in the Roman Empire was Persian Mithraism. Mithra was a hero-divinity who while upon earth had devoted himself to the service of mankind and, after a last supper celebrating the success of his redemptive labors, he ascended to heaven. Henceforth he continued to minister help to the faithful in their conflict with Satan* and his hosts. The process of initiation into full membership in the cult was elaborate. The candidate passed through seven grades which prefigured the passage of the soul after death through the seven heavens to the final abode of the blest. Each grade was entered by observing ablutions, sacred meals and other sacramental rites. Mithraism was the only mystery religion that restricted its membership to men and it prospered especially among the soldiers. During the second and third centuries it became Christianity's most popular rival, especially on the frontiers of the Roman world.

Ultimately Christianity supplanted the mystery religions by combining in itself many of the functions and values that the older mystery cults had sought to conserve, and by meeting more effectively the type of religious need that had been contributing to the popularity of the mysteries in Roman imperial times. In several respects Christianity and the mysteries occupied common ground:

1) Both in Christianity and in the mysteries membership rested upon the voluntary choice of the individual. Other religions conditioned membership upon locality of birth or racial inheritance; one's rights in the religion depended upon belonging in some clan, city, state or race. But in the fluid social conditions of Roman imperial times the individual was thrown more especially upon his own responsibility and he needed a religion capable of ministering to his personal necessities under all the varying conditions of life. The mysteries were of this type. Any person, irrespective of sex (except in Mithraism) or race or nationality, could gain equal favor with the gods of his voluntary choice. After Paul had won his battle with the Judaizers Christianity also met this current demand. When he made this move away from Jewish racialism in religion the Christian apostle was moving, either consciously or unconsciously, in the direction of the gentile mystery cults.

2) Both Christianity and the mysteries provided a lively emotional experience on entering the religion. The society of believers constituted a new fellowship of regenerated people who had submitted to specific ceremonies of initiation and had received a body of teaching the significance of which could be truly known only by those who had experienced the purificatory or sacramental rites necessary for membership in the cult.

3) In Christianity as in the mysteries the ultimate goal of the religious quest was for salvation to be obtained through the favor of a suffering but triumphant divinity to whom the believer became attached by means of a formal initiation into the new religious society. This divine help was thereafter available during the present life and in the world to come.

Following the lead of the apostle Paul, the Christian missionaries on gentile soil finally made of Christianity a more appealing religion than any of the older mystery cults. This was accomplished, not by any slavish process of imitation, but by a serious attempt to meet better the specific religious needs that the mysteries had awakened and nourished, and by phrasing religious assurances more convincingly in similar terminology. In this competition Christianity had certain great advantages. It was the most recent movement, and by its early break with Judaism it freed itself of hampering institutional techniques. At the same time it carried forward the rich moral heritage of Judaism. Also it discarded the multitude of different divinities in which the gentiles were losing faith and it eliminated confusion by substituting the supreme God of Judaism and the deified Christian Christ for the numerous gentile gods. And it was able to heighten the sense of reality for its heroic savior by stressing remembered facts about his earthly life supported by explicitly fulfilled predictions recorded in the ancient Hebrew scriptures. Thus the Christian mystery could claim to be older, deeper, more accurately reflective of the hidden purposes of God, more concretely historical in its manifestation, more rigid in its ethical demands, and more efficiently sacramental in its operations, than any of its older gentile rivals. But it owed no small measure of its success to the degree to which the mystery religions had prepared the soil for the Christian planting. See baptism, non-Christian; blood; gods; initiation rites; Gnosticism; regeneration; Roman religions; sacramental meal; theophagy.

Franz Cumont, *Oriental Religions in Roman Paganism* (1911); Samuel Angus, *The Mystery-Religions and Christianity* (1925); H. R. Willoughby, *Pagan Regeneration* (1929); A. Loisy, *Les Mystères paîen et le mystère chrétien* (Paris, 1919).

S.J.C.

Mystical School, Buddhist: See Buddhist Terminology.

mysticism: Mysticism may be defined as the intuitive and emotive apprehension of spiritual reality. Goethe* termed it "the dialectic of the feelings." Dean Inge described it as "the love of God." Its mission is to secure the vivid realization of eternal spiritual-personal values.

Mysticism infuses religion itself, as a sense of the sacred. It emerges in primitive religion* (where it is subject to many imaginative aberrations) as the apprehension of the *numinous*.* It is present and patent in varied forms in all advanced races and religions—in China as Taoism, in India as Bhaki and Yoga, in Persia as Sufism*, in Israel as Prophetism and in the Psaltery. It exists in various degrees, from what has been called "mild mysticism" ("Everyone is something of a mystic," said George Tyrrell,* while E. W. Hocking declared, "Everyman is an avowed or unavowed mystic.") to intense and absorbing forms of experience, mounting at times to ecstasy, and often accompanied by ascetic practises in living and devoted acts of service.[1]

Mysticism creates distinctive group as well as individual life, as the Friends of God, the Brethren of the Common Life, the Moravians and the Quakers** witness. In fact the life of the Christian Church itself, when it is true to its purpose has a mystical vein in it giving it warmth and devotion.

As a spiritual technique mysticism has developed what is known as the *Mystic Way* having three (sometimes four) stages: (1) awakening (2) purgation (3) illumination (4) unification.

In its wider manifestation the following types of normal mysticism may be distinguished, although they are often united in the same person or group: 1) Contemplative mysticism, generally with a monistic tendency, as in Plotinus, Augustine, Eckhart, the Christian Platonists, Emerson**; 2) Personal mysticism in which personal communion with God (or Christ) is dominant as in Jesus, Paul, Luther, Thomas à Kempis, Fra Angelico, George Fox, Fenelon,** Kagawa; 3) Nature mysticism in which Nature is invested with religious mystical meaning and feeling, as in St. Francis,* the chief of Nature mystics, Wordsworth and other nature poets, and in a number of nature writers, notably John Muir; and 4) Practical mysticism in which sacrificial service prompted by love is the ruling characteristic. Christian mysticism is predominantly Personal mysticism although it has also given large place to the Platonic contemplative type and especially to practical mysticism.

While the strongest impulse and ardor of Christian mysticism has been, and is, devoted to loving and exalting God (or Christ) and even to losing oneself in Him its effect has been to develop also individual personality and to produce characters of great strength and attractiveness, such as Paul, Augustine, St. Francis, St. Bernard, Eckhart, Boehme, St. Teresa, St. Elizabeth, St. Catherine of Genoa, Tauler, Luther, Pascal, Wesley, Zinzendorf, Jonathan Edwards, Schleiermacher**, Phillips Brooks.[2]

The mystics have always avowed (and truly) their experience to be inexpressible in its depth and joyousness, yet their spontaneous literary productions are among the chief treasures of literature, including the Psaltery, Second Isaiah, the Epistles of Paul, the "Confessions" of Augustine, the *Itinerarium Mentis Dei* of Bonaventura, Dante's "Divine Comedy," the *Theologia Germanica,* the *Imitation of Christ,* William Penn's *Fruits of Solitude,* Tauler's *Sermons,* Bunyan's *Pilgrim's Progress,* Milton's *Sonnet* on his Blindness, John Woolman's** *Journal,* George Herbert's *The Temple,* Whittier's Hymns, Thompson's "The Hound of Heaven" and a host of others. Next to the Psaltery the Christian Hymnal is the richest repository of the mystical spirit engaged in the act of devotion and praise.[3]

The lessons taught us by the mystics may be summarized as 1) to look for reality within, 2) to find meaning in mystery, 3) to discover the eternal in the temporal, 4) to realize the value of solitude, 5) to find joy in service, 6) to discern honor in humility, 7) to give supremacy to love.

A marked renascence of interest in mysticism sprang up in Britain and America soon after the opening of the present century—induced by Baron Friedrich von Hügel's* *The Mystical Element of Religion* (London, 2d e., 1923), 2 vols., Dean W. R. Inge's *Christian Mysticism* (third ed. 1913), William James' *The Varieties of Religious Experience* (1902), Rufus M. Jones' *Studies in Mystical Religion* (1909), *Some Exponents of Mystical Religion* (1930) and other volumes, Evelyn Underhill's* *Mysticism* (1913), *The Mystic Way,* etc.

Perhaps the most significant philosophical evaluation of mysticism that has yet been made is Henri Bergson's,* *The Two Sources of Religion and Morality* (translated by Audra and Brereton, 1935). See Dionysius the Areopagite; ecstasy; Eriugena; Hasidism; John of the Cross; Law, Wm; Neo Platonism; Quietism; Ruysbroeck; Suso; Tagore; unio mystica. Cf. Meditation School under Buddhist Terminology.

[1] One may be mystical without being, strictly speaking, a mystic.

[2] Most of these would be properly described as *mystical,* rather than mystics.

[3] Nowhere does mysticism find more complete expression than in music. Bach is one of the purest and most ardent of Christian mystics.

J.W.B.

mysticism, Jewish: See Chasidism; Hasidism; Kabbalah; Zohar.

mystics of Saint-Victor: General term for the school of mystic philosophy centered at the Abbey of Saint-Victor on the outskirts of Paris. The Royal Abbey and School of St. Victor was founded in 1108 by the renowned William of Champeaux,* later Bishop of Châlons. In a short time it became richly endowed; by 1260 it had nurtured several cardinals, many bishops and abbots, and had become a center of piety and learning to which scholars flocked from all over Europe; with the schools of Notre Dame and St. Genevieve it cradled the University of Paris. In time, the Abbey of St. Victor was known as the calix of the flower of mysticism which radiated throughout the Continent. Among its greatest teachers were Hugh of Blankenburg, better known as Hugh of St. Victor* (1096-1141), called the Augustine of his time, Peter Lombard* (c. 1100-1162), the "Master of Sentences," Adam, the greatest of medieval poets, and Richard,* the Scottish doctor of mystical theology. By the end of the 15th century the Abbey had fallen into disrepute, its canons enmeshed in the Jansenist* movement. The end finally came with the French Revolution; in 1800 the church and other buildings were sold, the famous library was dispersed, and a few years later everything had disappeared.

J.F.T.

myth: Most realities important to our living cannot be apprehended in the way required for our welfare unless we act in some appropriate manner. In case of water we must make contact with it and drink it. Inasmuch as true statements do not necessarily impel to the kind of action required, it is often necessary to supplement them with a story which will induce this needed behavior. For example, when one is thirsty for water or for God, he may be directed to the reality in question by true statements about it. On the other hand, a story may be told under such circumstances that one will be impelled to act in the manner required to find the living water or the living God. This latter is myth. It is said that American Indians were induced to meet the conditions for an abundant crop of corn by the fiction that a fish buried in the hill of corn gave its spirit to the budding grain. This fiction was a myth because it enabled them to deal effectively with the process of growth without understanding it. Indeed when fictions arouse and direct the attitudes and other behavior whereby important realities are most effectively appropriated, truth is hardly required.

The myth is generally believed to be a statement of fact by the people who use it. That belief is an error, but the error lies in taking the myth to be a truth. A myth is not a truth, but neither is it to be regarded, when recognized as a myth, to be false. Therefore, it is always a mistake to say that an effective myth is a kind of truth. Rather it is a stimulus to required behavior in dealing with some important reality. Effectiveness and not truth is the criterion to be applied to a myth. Truth may, of course, direct conduct beneficially, but when as assertion is justified on the ground of its edifying influence and not by rational, empirical evidence, it is a myth.

We appropriate the air and transform vital energy without our knowing the truths involved. Tradition, habit, and automatic reflexes, like breathing and heartbeat, do this for us. However, in case of other intimate, important and profound realities, the automatic reflexes are not sufficient and must be supplemented by myths. Further, when myths are insufficient, truth must be added. Truth is only sought and used as a last resort, and even then is never adequate to guide us but must be always supported by the automatic reactions and the myths.

When one single, coherent and inclusive tradition shapes the lives of all in the group, this tradition is like a channel guiding them to whatever reality is accessible by this route. In such case truth is not needed. All they need is some stimulus to drive them to follow the ways of the tradition. Myth serves this end. When, however, the guiding tradition breaks down, as all inclusive traditions are breaking today, the myth may lead to disaster. Truth must then intervene to take its place. Perhaps we shall always need myths, but control by myths must decline and control by truth must increase, as social complexity advances. See culture; symbolism.

Andrew Lang, *Myth, Ritual and Religion* (1901); G. F. Lipps, *Mythenbildung und Erkenntnis* (1907); Bronislaw Malinowski, *Myth in Primitive Psychology* (1926); A. N. Whitehead, *Symbolism, its Meaning and Effect* (1927).

H.N.W.

mythology (defined): Mythologies are the organized bodies of myths belonging to peoples having in common a tradition and inheritance. Mythology in a scientific sense is the exact study of the origin, history and nature of myths. It has been through the science of mythology that modern man has been able to survey, interpret and inter-relate the numerous mythologies. This science dates only from the end of the 18th century. Since De Brosses and Schelling, the interpretation of myth has advanced through the philological school of Max Mueller, the anthropological school of Mannhardt and Tylor, through Andrew Lang and Frazer to the modern psychologists, Jung, Freud. These men have uncovered a vast store of mankind's history, revealing inadvertantly both why he acted as he did and how he explains his own acts. Also hidden with them, innocent as a buried potsherd, are references to customs, folkways, geography and climate, indispensable value to the social historian.

All religions, both primitive and advanced, require myth. For the relating of the experience with the divine can be conveyed only in mythological conceptions. The creation myth in Babylonia tells the story of Marduk, his titanic struggle with the dragon Tiamat, as preparation for the creation of earth and man. In Hinduism, there is the story of Brahma, breathing in and out the life of the created universe. There are hero myths like that of Romulus and Remus; star myths to explain the constellations and star movements; the Egyptian sun myth, picturing Ra as crossing the firmament in a boat; myths of the underworld, such as that of Osiris, Orpheus, Charon, Izanagi; myths about the gods and a great flood, such as the Babylonian Ut-Napishtim, the Hebrew Noah; myths to explain festivals and customs, such as the flight from Egypt as an explanation of the Passover. Myths are designed to tell in story form the nature of an experience or awareness of God. Mythologies were the early teachers of mankind. See folklore; primitive religion.

M.L.C.

Bibl. mythology: Cyril Bailey, ed., *The Legacy of Rome* (Oxford, 1936); Sir Paul Harvey, *Oxford Companion to Classical Literature* (Oxford, 1937); R. W. Livingstone, ed., *The Legacy of Greece* (Oxford, 1937); H. J. Rose, *A Handbook of Greek Mythology* (1929).

E.M.N.

N

nabi, the: See soothsaying.

Nāgārjuna: See Buddhist Terminology.

Nahum: A collection of five poems on the fall of Nineveh (612 B.C.), written immediately before and after that event. A late acrostic psalm has been prefixed to the book. The first two poems (3:1-13) warn Nineveh of approaching doom. Nahum's poetic art climaxes in the third (1:11-2:10) which describes Babylonian mobilization, march northward, sack of Nineveh, slaughter, plunder, and desolation. The poems in 2:11-12 and 3:16-19 cast retrospect on this passing of empire. Nothing is known of Nahum. Perhaps he was an exile who witnessed these events. Instead of a prophet, he was a brilliant poet. The ethics, religion, and reforming genius of the prophets are missing. His was an outburst of indignation against Assyria, world tyrant for centuries and captivator of the ten tribes, with a song of rejoicing over her downfall. See *The Prophets and their Times* by J. M. P. Smith and W. A. Irwin (1941), pp. 149-55. R.E.W.

naiads: (Gr. *Naiades,* from *nao,* to flow; *ad-,* patronymic) Nymphs* of springs, rivers, and lakes. E.M.N.

name: (in primitive thought) A person's name is considered very important, and is often given him with ceremony. It is often that of a dead relative, and may be determined by some fixed rule, or by divination, dream, etc. Secondary names, indicating tribal and other relationships, may be added. Primitive people often seem to identify one's primary name with one's inmost self, and the pronunciation of this name is supposed most efficacious in magical rites. For this reason, it is often kept a secret and pronunciation of an individual's name, especially that of a chief or a god, is often tabu. The name may be changed in order to escape injury from the dead, or after the death of a child or any striking and important event. See baptism, non Christian. R.B.B.

Nanak: (1469-1538) Founder of the Sikh* faith in India. Born a Moslem in 1469 A.D. he was strongly influenced by Moslem ideas as was the poet Kabir an older contemporary. His faith combines both Hindu and Moslem elements. He was a Bhakta poet and sang innumerable songs of devotion to Hari (God). These, together with others from Kabir and some of the later Sikh gurus, constitute the Granth,* the sacred book of the Sikhs. C.S.B.

Nantes, Edict of: (1598) Issued by Henry IV* to define the position of the French Reformed Church. It granted freedom of conscience but in various ways limited the liberties of Protestants. Its revocation (1685) a disaster for French Protestants. See Camisards; Wars of religion. G.R.C.

Nārāyana: An epithet, applied to various Hindu gods, most frequently of all to Vishnu.* Shankara applies it to Brahman, but in modern India it is universally recognized as a name of Vishnu. C.S.B.

narthex: (Gr. *narthēx,* a portico) Any enclosed entrance or portico of a church. F.T.P.

Nashoba (Tenn.) community: See communistic settlements, secular.

Nasi: (Heb., prince) Political ruler of Judea (Ezra 1.8) and subsequently the president of the Sanhedrin.* S.S.C.

National Baptist Convention: See negro church, the.

National Baptist Evangelical Life and Soul Saving Assembly of the U. S. A.: A group of 28 churches (2,300 members) organized in 1920. There seem to be no distinctive doctrines or practices. The body specializes in personal evangelism. E.T.C.

National David Spiritual Temple of Christ Church Union: A sect founded by D. W. Short, a Baptist preacher, in Kansas City in 1932. There are eleven local churches and 1,900 members. The group refuses to be called a denomination and claims to represent the original church founded by Jesus Christ. In general it opposes all other churches as apostate and believes in healing, miracles, prophecy, sanctification, and speaking in unknown tongues. See pentecostal sects. E.T.C.

National Intercollegiate Christian Council: See student religious organizations.

National Lutheran Council: See Lutheran Church in America.

National Sunday School Convention: See Sunday School movement in the United States.

National socialism: See socialism.

Natorp, Paul: (1854-1924) Professor of philosophy at the University of Marburg. He was one of the chief philosophical representatives of the social movement of his day. He continued tendencies initiated by Pestalozzi. He was a thoroughgoing social ethicist. His ethic was an idealized democratic idealism. He defended a religion without God. He idealized human dignity. He understood by the religious, moral acts.

Religion innerhalb der Grenzen der Humanität (Tübingen, 1908) 2 ed.; *Allgemeine Psychologie nach kritischer Methode* (Tübingen, 1912) 2 ed.; *Sozialpädagogie* (Stuttgart, 1920) 4 ed.; *Die logischen Grundlagen der exacten Wissenschaften* (Leipzig, 1921) 2 ed.; *Platos Ideenlehre* (Leipzig, 1921) 2 ed.; *Sozialidealismus* (Berlin, 1922) 2 ed.; *Gesammelte Abhandlungen zur Sozialpädagogik* (Stuttgart, 1922), 3 vols., 2 rev. ed. H.H.

natura naturans, natura naturata: *Natura naturans* is God as the active power of nature; *natura naturata* is the world as the complex unity of individual things. The former is regarded as the creative force, the latter as the created substance. The terms were first used by Averroës, later by Nicholas of Cusa, Giordana Bruno and Spinoza.** J.E.N.

natural law: 1) In politics and jurisprudence, the doctrine that positive laws rightly rest upon a higher law attested by the common awareness of what is just, which is a natural endowment divinely set in man's nature, and indestructible. Christian thought took over the concept from antiquity and especially from Cicero. Phrases in Rom. 1:18-21 and 2:14-15 were generally interpreted by the fathers, scholastics and Reformers as affirming the doctrine, and the OT law was regarded as a codification of the *lex naturae.* Variations in the treatment of the topic are made with relation to the doctrine of sin and grace. (C. G. Haines, *The Revival of Natural Law,* 1930; O. Gierke, *Natural Law and the Theory of Society,* transl. E. Barker, 2 vols., 1934). 2) In physical science the body of generalizations reached by empirical study, or, in the plural, these generalizations themselves. See natural rights. J.T.M.

natural law: In scholastic theory that part of the divine law(ius divinum*) that is known to man through reason. The notion of an eternal Law of Nature as constituting the standard of evaluation of all man-made law was taken from Stoic philosophy. It has maintained a prominent place in political philosophy in post-medieval times. Conservative, liberal, revolutionary and collectivist schools of political thought have equally claimed for their respective basic postulates the transcendental validity of natural law and even the force of overruling positive law at variance with its maxims. The Natural Law of liberalism, which was developed by the philosophers and jurists of the Enlightenment and which is often referred to as Natural Law pure and simple, became of particular importance as constituting an effective check to monarchical absolutism, as providing the guiding principles of modern individualistic liberalism and democracy, including the doctrine of inalienable rights, and as furnishing since Grotius* the ideas guiding modern International Law. Cf. American theology, early.

A. Gurvitch, "Natural Law", vol. 11 *Enc. Soc. Sci.,* p. 284; C. Brinton, "Natural Rights", vol. 11 *Enc. Soc. Sci.,* p. 299; O. von Gierke, *Natural Law and the Theory of Society, 1500-1800* (tr. by E. Barker), 2 vols. (1934): F. Pollock, "History of the Law of Nature" in *Essays in the Law* (1922); C. G. Haines, *Revival of Natural Law Concepts* (1930); W. Seagle, *The Quest for Law* (1941), ch. 14. M.Rh.

natural rights: The capacity to get the protection of the state for some interest, privilege, or power, on one's own motion, is called a *legal* right. (Loosely, the interest or privilege protected may be called a right.) The capacity to get protection (not necessarily from the state) which one *ought* to have is called a *moral* right. The word "natural," here combined with "right," is one which historically has been used in ethics and politics to mean that an ethical or political principle was accepted universally as opposed to what had only local acceptance; or that it was rooted in the nature of things, in harmony with the course and purpose of nature and required by man's instinctive nature, as opposed to the customary, conventional, and merely traditional; or that it was self-evident; or that it was or would be practised in a state of nature as opposed to what occurs in civilization. Thus the conception of natural law* (in which the doctrine of natural rights may be said to have been implicit to some degree), as a fundamental law of reason, was distinguished from positive law as early as by Aristotle and the Stoics; in Roman law, as *ius naturale,* it was closely related to but not identical with *ius gentium.* Natural law consisted of generally accepted principles of equity, good faith, and moral principle: such as that no one should be allowed to profit by injuring others. At the beginning of the modern era it began to be asserted explicitly that there are natural *rights,* a claim which, in its fundamental defense of equality against privilege, was in part a result of Protestant ideas (cf. the Levellers and the Diggers). Hooker, Hobbes, Locke,** Halifax, and (in one part of his work) Rousseau* all held that in some sense man as man self-evidently has certain inalienable rights. This doctrine is embodied in the Virginian Declaration of Rights, the Declaration of Independence, the French Declaration of the Rights of Man, the preamble to the Constitution of 1793, etc. Such rights as the right to life, liberty of thought and private conduct, public meeting, contract, equality, property, pursuit of happiness, and government only by the consent of the governed are often mentioned. The Utilitarians* in practice accepted as an absolute right the greatest freedom compatible with the like freedom of others although in theory they accept utility as their only first principle. In more recent times this theory of natural rights has declined, partly because of general scepticism about supposed self-evident principles. Some writers would still use the term, partly to distinguish certain fundamental rights from those, e.g., which arise out of contract; that is, it may be said that protection of some privilege or power is a "natural right" if the realization of the ideal society requires that all persons receive such protection, at least where it does not conflict with the rights of others or interfere seriously with the general welfare. See American theology, early.

Ernest Barker, preface to Otto Gierke, *Natural Law and the Theory of Society* (1934); D. G. Ritchie, *Natural Rights* (1924); James Bryce, *Studies in History and Jurisprudence*, vol. II (1901); J. C. Gray, *Nature and Sources of the Law* (1921); T. H. Green, *Principles of Political Obligation* (1895); W. E. Hocking, *Present Status of the Philosophy of Law and Rights* (1926); A. O. Lovejoy and G. Boas, *Primitivism and Related Ideas in Antiquity* (1935); G. H. Sabine, *A History of Political Theory* (1937).

R.B.B.

natural theology: It is that knowledge of God obtained by observing the visible processes of nature. The inward frame of man responds to the external condition and circumstance of life, and his ability to observe the visible processes of nature is a means to discover what he is made for, and what duties bind him. The more man follows the tendency of nature toward a moral government the more joy he realizes, and the more he approaches a full harmony with the moral law. As he obeys the natural law the moral law becomes more categorical. Man is a law unto himself and he is obliged to obey this law from the simple fact that it is the law of his nature. Natural religion seeks no authority except natural theology.

W.G.H.

naturalism: *Methodological naturalism* is the name for that characteristic of scientific method which constructs its pattern of thought on the basis of natural causation as distinguished from a supernatural or occult explanation. Such a naturalism tends to be positivistic.

Metaphysical naturalism is a view of reality which holds that reality is nature; within the framework of nature is found the ultimate. For this view, the so-called "world-beyond" or supernatural is set within a wider interpretation of nature. The early Ionian thinkers were naturalists when they launched the view (the beginning of classical Western philosophy) that explanations are to be sought by looking for the original stuff of the world in the world rather than relying upon the traditions of their priests and extra-nature mythologies. Naturalists divide in their conception of nature. The old materialism of atoms-in-motion is a *materialistic naturalism.* Later materialistic naturalists, including contemporary, tended to make energy (conceived to be physical) the basis of their metaphysics. There are *dynamistic* as well as *neutralistic* naturalists. (See ontology). *Spiritualistic naturalists* hold nature to be fundamentally akin to spirit or the categories applicable to mind. Spinoza may be interpreted as a spiritualistic naturalist if his Substance is interpreted as God. An *agnostic naturalism* is the view which hesitates to commit itself to any ultimate explanation of the character of nature (e.g. Herbert Spencer's Unknowable). *Positivistic naturalism* is the view which holds that a philosophy of nature should be limited to human experience, and speculation beyond that experience avoided. (Auguste Comte* and John Dewey are examples).

In philosophical literature the tendency has been to equate naturalism with materialism. This spells much confusion. For a spiritualistic naturalist the immanence of the Divine is stressed (where the divine is affirmed) although some spiritualistic naturalists hold that the divine has transcendental characteristics as found in nature (see panentheism). Such a naturalism is not necessarily deterministic and mechanistic since nature may be held to reveal the broken relations of new beginnings as a characteristic of its processes.

V.F.

naturalism and theology: The most marked development in the newer naturalism is the growing recognition that there are many levels and orders in nature. Values, ideals, personality, community, the sense of beauty, tragedy, heroism, religion and God are as readily acknowledged and upheld by some forms of the newer naturalism as the quantum theory and the physics of relativity.

Naturalism was once identical with materialism and mechanism. It is not so any longer. Naturalism did once teach, and in some instances does still, that what physics says about nature is the basic truth about all reality, even as theology did once teach, and in some instances does still, that the Bible is verbally inspired. Students of naturalism continue to attribute to religious thought the beliefs which have been discarded by its advanced representatives, and students of religion still interpret naturalism in terms which have been cast off by its foremost exemplars.

Naturalism is based upon a certain method of inquiry. Its method accepts as data anything which can be experienced such as *a priori* propositions, "innate truths," authority, revelation, esoteric intuition. But these are data only and do not yield knowledge until they have been subjected to the method of inquiry by which knowledge is achieved. Knowledge is achieved by discovering how events (happenings) are related to one another, or how they might possibly be related. Therefore all the reality we can ever know must be reality made up of interconnected happenings and their possibilities. These happenings may be infinitely rich in the qualities of beauty, tragedy, pathos, heroism. Also every happening is made up of component happenings. But when happening or event is analyzed it is seen to be necessarily temporal and spatial, whatever else it may also be. Therefore naturalism holds that all actual reality is necessarily temporal and spatial. It does not deny the reality of ideal structures and possibilities which are not temporal and spatial, but these are not actual. They are only possible ways in which actual events *might* be distinguished and connected. Nature is precisely the totality of all that is temporal and spatial together with whatever possibilities this temporal and spatial process may carry. History, community, personality, God or any other actual reality is a structure of events distinguished and connected in the way that characterizes the particular reality under consideration. Some basic structure of events might, of course, be everlasting.

The doctrine of perspectives has greatly enriched the concept of nature. When the naive person speaks of nature he commonly means only one perspective, namely, his own. But nature includes an infinity of perspectives. None of these is self-sufficient by itself. The doctrine of perspectives can be easily illustrated. The penny in one perspective is a circle, in another a heavy line, and in still another an ellipse. But no one of these is self-sufficient since it requires all the others to make up the total penny. So our perspective of nature is not self-sufficient even though we cannot roll the universe around as we do the penny to get the other perspectives. If we live long enough we shall have another perspective.

The self-sufficiency of nature does not mean in the newer naturalism any self-sufficiency of that particular system which at any one time may be all that we happen just then to know. This system is not self-sufficient for two reasons: nature includes far more than our little system of knowledge at any one time can comprehend; nature will change so that what we know and what we do not know will both be different. This is the doctrine of the creativity of time which is one of the major teachings of the newer naturalism.

The self-sufficiency of nature in the sense stated is defended as follows: Anything whatsoever that we can ever experience must have the character and constitution which is necessary to experience. An analysis of experience reveals that it is impossible apart from time and space. In other words, experience is necessarily and essentially temporal and spatial. Therefore anything that we can ever experience must be some quality, form or movement pertaining to temporal and spatial reality. Since nature includes all temporal and spatial reality together with its possibilities, all that we can ever experience must be nature. This is the view of naturalism.

Vergilius Ferm, "Christianity—A Naturalistic Point of View", *Crozer Quarterly*, vol. XVII No. 3, July, 1940; B. E. Meland, *Modern Man's Worship* (1934); M. C. Otto, *The Human Enterprise* (1940); H. N. Wieman, *The Growth of Religion* (1938); F. J. E. Woodbridge, *An Essay on Nature* (1940); George Santayana, *The Realm of Spirit* (1940).

H.N.W.

nature worship: Expression of the feeling of dependence or gratitude toward helpful phases of the natural environment and of the feeling of fear of the dangerous elements. Almost all the gods of the early world were nature powers. Like other forms of life, man had to adjust his needs to the environment to secure the essential values of food,* shelter and safety. In that early adventure in living he found that nature in many of her forms and moods was kindly and helpful, in others hostile and destructive. He was grateful for fresh spring waters, fruit and nut bearing trees, the refreshing winds, cooling shade, the dawn which drove away the cold and dangers of the dark, the stimulating sun, the storm rain which revived the pasture lands and the crops after drought, the fertile, food-bearing earth. Many of these things lost their quality of mystery and were accepted without ceremony as parts of the commonplace world, but the great nature powers were beyond man's control and were so important for his wellbeing that he expressed his gratitude to them in elaborate cult and made appeals to them for ever larger benefits. These nature powers were the early gods. Against the dangerous powers man set up protective techniques. If he could win them to his service they too became gods, otherwise they were devils.* When the nature powers became spirits* and were humanized their nature origin was often obscured or forgotten. See Baalism; Gods. A.E.H.

Nauvoo (Ill.), communistic colony: See communistic settlements, religious, secular.

nave: (Lat. *navis,* a ship) The central or principal part of a three-aisled church, the upper portion of which, rising above the aisles, is called the clearstory.

F.T.P.

Nazarenes: Two Greek adjectives are translated by this word in the NT: *nazarenos* (Mk. 1.24, etc.) and *nazoraios* (Matt. 2.23, Acts 2.22, etc.). Though the former is clearly derived from Nazareth, there is no clear derivation for the latter. This is the term used for the Christians in Acts 24.5. It has been held that the *Nazoraioi* were a pre-Christian sect. (For refutation see G. F. Moore in *The Beginnings of Christianity,* Vol. I, by Foakes-Jackson and Lake). In the Apostolic Age, "Nazarenes" was probably the usual designation of Christians by Jews. In the fourth century it was used of Jewish-Christians* in Syria, either the same as Ebionites,* or similar to them.

C.T.C.

Nazarites or Nazirites: (Heb. *nāzar* to consecrate; cf. *nādar* to vow) An ascetic group in Judaism, who put themselves under a vow to abstain from wine, from cutting the hair, and from contact with anything unclean. Among the ancient Hebrews this vow would seem to have been binding throughout their lifetime (cf. Samson). Amos 2:12 suggests that they were regarded as an important group. The later legislation provided for a temporary vow—Josephus (*B. J.* ii, 15, 1) suggests that thirty days was the minimum period—but with an increased strictness. At the end of the period the hair was shaved and burnt as a sacrifice. The (later) Nazarite vow is given in Numb. 6:1-20. See article "Nazirite" in *Encyclopaedia Biblica,* cols. 3362 ff. See asceticism.

M.S.E.

Neale, John Mason: See hymns.

Neander, Johann August Wilhelm (1798-1850) As a converted Jew (his original name was David Mendel), he taught at the universities of Heidelberg and Berlin. Prepared by biographical and monographic studies, he wrote his main work in church history. The key to his church history was edification for the strengthening, purification and invigoration of the Christian life and community. His theology was borne by a piety which denied nothing of the religious awakening, of romantic idealism and supernaturalistic enlightenment. It was mildly pietistic, bible-believing and filled with profound love for Jesus Christ. Neander rejected the narrowness and brutality of ecclesiastical restoration. His historical studies have something of the lyrically monotonous. See Lives of Jesus.

Dr. August Neanders Werke (Gotha, 1862-67) 14 vols.; *History of the planting and training of the Christian church by the apostles* (Edinburgh, 1842) 2 vols.; *General history of the Christian religion and church* (Edinburgh, 1847-1855) 9 vols.; *Light in the Dark Places; or Memorials of Christian life in the Middle Ages* (1855); *Life of Jesus Christ in its historical connexion and historical development* (1848). H.H.

necessary being: (Lat., *necessitas*) That which cannot not-be; its essence is to be; that is, its existence is identical with its essence. Cf. contingent. See cause. L.R.W.

necessary cause: See cause.

necessitarianism: See s.v. libertarianism.

necrology: A list of the dead, often employed for purposes of prayer on All Soul's Day* or on some other occasion. W.N.P.

necromancy: Foretelling the future by communicating with the dead, strictly; but used loosely for all forms of divination.* Compare the story of Saul and the witch of Endor. P.G.M.

need-fire: A fire obtained in primitive manner by friction caused by turning a pole in or on another piece of wood, and supposed to have supernatural properties, particularly that of protecting or curing animals from pestilence. All other fires in the neighborhood must be extinguished while the need-fire is kindled, according to the superstition; the cattle then must be driven through it; and finally the family fires should be relit from a brand struck from the need-fire. The practice of using it was widespread among the peasants of Europe as late as the 19th century. See J. G. Frazer, *The Golden Bough,* Pt. VII, Vol. 1, (3d edn., 1935). R.B.B.

Neeser, Maurice: (1883-) He is professor of theology at the university of Neuchâtel, Switzerland. Inspired by Ritschl, Höffding, and above all by R. Eucken,** he distinguishes the aesthetic and the ethical type of religious thinker. In their absolute purity these reduced religion to nothing. Unrestricted immanence suppresses prayer, and absolute transcendence renders prayer impossible. There is something deceptive in the theological systems which pretend God in terms of human personality.

Le problème de Dieu (Neuchatel, 1915). H.H.

negro church, the: The Negro Church: It is the term given to distinguish the churches operated mainly for and by Negroes from those operated mainly for and by white people. It is one of the separate or segregated branches of the Christian church in America. According to the 1936 Government Census of Religious Bodies of the 256 denominations reporting, 59 reported Negro churches. Of the 59, the Census reveals that 33 were exclusively Negro in membership. The Baptists, the African Methodist Episcopal, The African Methodist Episcopal Zion, the Colored Methodist Episcopal, several Holiness* groups (see pentecostal sects) are illustrative of those religious bodies that are exclusively Negro in membership. The Negroes in the Methodist, Congregational, Episcopal, and Catholic churches are examples of Negro churches that are organically a part of white churches.

How the Negro Church Came to Be

"In accounting for the origin of the Negro church, three closely related factors must be taken into account: First, the Negro was hardly wanted in the white church. There, he was often segregated. The second largest Negro denomination, the African Methodist Episcopal Church, came into existence because in St. George's Church, Philadelphia, around the close of the eighteenth century, Negroes had been forced from their knees during prayer because they were not seated in the segregated places provided for them.

"The second reason for the existence of the Negro church grows out of and is a part of the first. A growing race consciousness stimulated the desire on the part of the Negroes to have their own churches. They wanted to preach, sing, direct the choir, and serve as chairmen of boards of deacons. Feeling that they would hardly have an equal chance to do these things in a church completely controlled by members of the dominant group, they set out to organize their own churches with the help and encouragement of the whites. Here in a church of their own they would be free to exercise their talents, display their pent up emotions, and prove their ability to organize in a way not permitted them in the white church.

"The third reason is inseparable from the second. The white church, and particularly the white minister, could not speak pointedly and effectively to the needs of the Negro. He spoke from the perspective of a free man who had never experienced what it really meant to be a slave and what it meant to be told by words and deeds that it was the will of God that he be a slave. When the white minister preached equality of the slave before God, he seldom meant that this equality should fulfill itself here and now.

"The Negro church, accordingly, sprang into existence partly because the Negro needed a church where a gospel could be preached which would speak to the needs of his soul; it was born out of the heartfelt needs of the Negro people. The writer makes bold to assert that, if there had been no segregation in white churches and if the Negro had been wholly welcomed in the white church, the needs of the race would have produced the Negro church. But if it had come wholly that way, it would have been a separate church, not a segregated church." Benjamin E. Mays, "The Negro Church in American Life," *Christendom,* Summer Number, 1940.

Number and Membership of Negro Churches

The Government Census of Religious Bodies shows that 38,303 Negro churches reported in 1936 (13,528 urban and 24,755 rural). These churches reported a membership of 5,660,618. Of this number, 2,958,630 were urban and 2,701,988 were rural members. In all probability there are approximately 42,000 or more Negro churches. These Negro churches in 1936 reported 390,454 Sunday School officers and teachers and an enrollment of 2,424,800 pupils in the Church school. In the same year these churches spent close to $28,000,000 on their programs.

The Seven Largest Negro Denominations: The Baptists* still lead in number of churches and in membership. The 1936 Religious Census reported 23,093 Negro Baptist churches with a membership of 3,782,464. More than 66 per cent of all Negro churches are Baptist. The second largest Negro denomination is the A.M.E. Church. The Religious Census of 1936 reported 4,578 A.M.E. churches with a membership of 493,357, approximately one half million members. The A.M.E.Z. Church comes third with a membership of 414,244. The fourth largest religious body among Negroes is the C.M.E. Church and it has 2,063 churches and 269,915 members. The 1936 Census of Religious Bodies reveals further that the number of Negroes in the Methodist Church constitute the fifth largest church group among Negroes. There are 1730 Negro churches with a membership of 193,761. The Negroes in the Roman Catholic Church are the sixth largest Negro church group. There are 178 Catholic churches for Negroes with a membership of 137,684. The Protestant Episcopal Church occupies the seventh place. There are 145 Negro Episcopal churches and the membership is 29,738. These seven denominations constitute more than 93 per cent of the total Negro membership in the 59 religious bodies reporting Negro members. In all these churches there are more than 25,000 Negro clergymen. Since space is at a premium in this encyclopedia, a statement of the number of churches and members in each of the other 52 denominations reporting Negro members is not possible.

Further Differentiation of Negro Denominations

The National Baptist Convention, Inc.: A statement by Doctor James M. Nabrit, Secretary of the convention follows: "The National Baptist Convention, Inc. is a religious organization with the largest constituency of any Negro religious body covering the entire United States. Primarily it is missionary in character doing both home and foreign mission work. Secondarily, it promotes ministerial and religious education, in cooperation with the denominational colleges in the several states and through the Seminary and Training School in Nashville, Tennessee. Finally, it develops business organizations through its publishing interests giving employment to its most competent writers and mechanics."

The National Baptist Convention of America: It should be noted here that the National Baptist Convention Incorporated and the National Baptist Convention of America were formerly one body. Dr. Henry Allen Boyd writing of this convention says: "The National Baptist Convention of America is a missionary Baptist convention, suporting the principles and the doctrines of the NT Church. It fosters Foreign Missions, Home Missions, Religious Education, Publishing and dissemination of religious helps and tracts. It has a benevolent Board, and is composed of the following boards: Foreign Mission, Home Mission, Educational, Publishing, B.Y.P.U., Evangelical, and Committe on Army and Navy Chaplains, with the Women's Auxiliary Board. It is a continuation of the expression of our foreparents in self-help religiously under chosen leadership, believing, as they did, so do we, in the virgin birth and that the administrator must be authorized, otherwise he cannot administer church ordinances." It is the second largest Negro church body in the United States.

The African Methodist Episcopal Church: This church began around the tenth decade of the eighteenth century. It had its beginning when an attempt was made to separate Negroes in St. George's Church in Philadelphia. Richard Allen, William White, and Absolom Jones led the movement when attempts were made to force them from their knees during prayer because they refused to sit in segregated seats planned for them in the gallery of St. George's. After the prayer was over they walked out of St. George's and organized a church of their own. They hired a storeroom and held worship. This was the beginning of the rise of the first church of the denomination which in April, 1816 became known as the African Methodist Episcopal Church. (Bishop Richard Allen, *The Life, Experience, And Gospel Labors,* pp. 1, 19, 20, 21, 22, 32.) Richard Allen was the first bishop elected April 10, 1816.

African Methodist Episcopal Zion Church: "A number of Negroes, most of whom were members of the John Street Methodist Episcopal church in New York City, took the first step toward separation from the connection in 1796. They had a "desire for a privilege of holding meetings of their own, where they might have an opportunity to exercise their spiritual gifts among themselves and thereby be more useful to one another. Such permission was obtained from Bishop Francis Asbury by a group of intelligent Negro Methodists. . . . "These workers continued in this situation until the year 1799 when with a further increase in the Negro membership of the Methodist Episcopal Church in New York City, they proposed to build a separate house of worship rather than merely hold separate meetings in the edifice belonging to the white Methodists." (C. G. Woodson) So in 1800 they erected a building at the corner of Church and Leonard Streets (New York) naming the edifice the African Methodist Episcopal Zion Church. They organized into a national body in 1821 with James Varick as first Bishop elected in 1822. (*Ibid*).

Colored Methodist Episcopal Church: The Methodist Episcopal Church, South, in conference in New Orleans in 1866 made provision for the organization of Negro members in a separate denomination if the Negroes so desired. It was further agreed that if the Negroes approved they could have a general conference like that of the Methodist Episcopal Church, South. Four years later in 1870 the Methodist Episcopal Church, South, met in Memphis. It was reported there that the Negroes had organized five annual conferences and had expressed desire to be a separate and distinct body. Resulting therefrom the first General Conference was held in Jackson, Tennessee, December 15, 1870. The first two bishops were W. H. Miles and R. H. Vanderhorst. (*Ibid*).

Richard Allen, *The Life, Experience and Gospel Labors;* Monroe Work, ed., *The Negro Year Book;* 1937-38 (Tuskegee Institute Press); "Understanding Our Neighbors" published by the Commission on Interracial Cooperation, Atlanta; James Weldon Johnson, *The Book of American Negro Poetry;* Carter G. Woodson, *The History of the Negro Church;* B. E. Mays, J. W. Nicholson, *The Negro's Church* (Institute of Social and Religious Research); Benjamin E. Mays, *The Negro's God; Census of Religious Bodies,* 1936; U. S. Dept. of Commerce, Bureau of Census, Volumes I, II, III: "The Negro Church in American Life:" *Christendom,* Summer Number, 1940 by Benjamin E. Mays. B.E.M.

negro's conception of God, the: Like the Jews in Biblical history, the Negro's ideas of God have grown out of his social situation. They are mainly the ideas of God found in the Old and New Testaments. But almost in every case they are ideas of God fashioned out of or influenced by the social situation in which the Negro finds himself. A study of the Negro's literature reveals that his "ideas of God are developed along three principal lines: 1) Ideas of God that are used to support or give adherence to traditional, compensatory patterns; 2) Ideas, whether traditional or otherwise, that are developed and interpreted to support a growing consciousness of social and psychological adjustment needed; 3) Ideas of God that show a tendency or threat to abandon the idea of God as "a useful instrument" in perfecting social change.

"The data show that however the ideas are used, they develop at the point of social crisis; at the point where justice is denied, hopes thwarted, and plans shattered, owing in part to the hampering proscriptions imposed upon the Negro by the dominant group. His ideas of God, so to speak, are chiseled out of the very fabric of the social struggle. Virtually all of them express the unfilled yearnings of the Negro group, whether they be worldly or other-worldly. They developed, as can be validated historically, along the line of the Negro's most urgent needs and desires. Prior to 1860, the Negro's ideas of God were developed around slavery. After the Civil War, they grew out of the wrongs of Reconstruction. Since 1914, they are inseparable from the social and economic restrictions which the Negro meets in the modern world.

"Unlike that of many people, the Negro's incredulity, frustration, agnosticism, and atheism do not develop as the results of the findings of modern science nor from the observation that nature is cruel and indifferent; but primarily because in the social situation, he finds himself hampered and restricted. The Negro is not interested in any fine theological or philosophical discussions about God. He is interested in a God who is able to help him bridge the chasm that exists between the actual and the ideal. The Negro's life has been too unstable, too precarious, too uncertain, and his needs have been too great for him to become sufficiently objective to theologize or philosophize about God."[1]

[1]Benjamin E. Mays, *The Negro's God,* (1938), pp. 245, 255. B.E.M.

negro education: There are 109 Negro colleges and junior colleges. Approximately 45,000 students are enrolled in these colleges in normal times. There are in addition close to 2,500 Negro students enrolled in colleges that are not strictly Negro. It is estimated that 5,000 are graduated a year in normal times with college degrees. More than two hundred Negroes have won the Ph.D. degree and an equal number have earned membership in the Phi Beta Kappa Society. B.E.M.

negro spiritual, the: The Negro Spiritual is one of the chief contributions the Negro has made to American culture. Though defined in various ways, in essence all definitions of the spiritual harmonize. Speaking of the spiritual, Kemper Harreld, Director of music at Morehouse and Spelman Colleges, has this to say: " 'The Spiritual' is generally understood to be any Afro-American religious folk song. There are however, some songs to be found among the "mountain whites" that are called spirituals—"Round About the Mountain."

"A more specific classification is sometimes needed:

Spiritual.—A song of prayer and contrition. "Swing Low Sweet Chariot." "Lord I Want to be A Christian in my Heart."

Jubilee.—A song of triumph. "Study War No More," "I'm Going Down to the River of Jordan," "Tell me How Did You Feel When You Come Out of The Wilderness."

Sorrow Song.—Can be sacred or secular. "I'm so Glad Trouble Don't Last Always," "Soon One Morning."

"There is also a sacred folk song that is difficult to classify between the spiritual and jubilee—"There is a Balm in Gilead." "

Frederick H. Hall of Montgomery State Teachers' College, Montgomery, Alabama, interprets the spirituals in the following manner: "The Spiritual had its beginning in the heart of the Negro as he labored in the fields of the South. These songs are outbursts of religious fervor and in many cases are influenced by conditions which surrounded the people in whose minds they were born.

"They are called Spirituals, Jubilees, Melodies, Folk Songs. Either name is correct. They are called Jubilees because of the ray of hope that is expressed in each. Regardless of how sad the song may be, or how miserable the conditions surrounding its birth, there is always found in it the hope of a great day of jubilee when all sadness will be turned into joy. They are called Spirituals because of the deep religious feeling they express. They are called Melodies because of the striking melody built upon a scale that was originated by the slaves. When a new song was born it usually began with a new melody hummed by one person. After the tune was caught, the whole group or congregation would join in, increasing the strength of the melody and adding harmony. These songs are called Folk Songs because they satisfy the well-known scientific definition of that term."[1]

Mays and Nicholson write of the Spiritual: "The creation of the spirituals was not an accident in Negro life. It was an imperative creation in order that the slave might adjust himself to the new conditions in the New World.

"These songs are the expressions of the restrictions and dominations which their creators experienced in the world about them. They represent the soul-life of the people. They embody the joy and sorrow, the hope and despair, the pathos and aspiration of the newly transplanted people; and through them the race was able to endure suffering and survive. Clearly, the Negro spirituals are not songs of hate; they are not songs of revenge. They are songs neither of war nor of conquest. They are songs of the soil and of the soul."[2]

[1]*Understanding Our Neighbors,* (Atlanta: Commission on Interracial Cooperation, Inc.), p. 16.
[2]Mays and Nicholson, *The Negro's Church,* (Institute of Social and Religious Research, 1938), p. 2.

B.E.M.

Nehemiah: Historical book of the O.T., which is contained in the third division of the Hebrew canon, the "Writings" or Hagiographa*. In Hebrew this book formed originally a single work with the Book of Ezra*. It is an account of the rebuilding of the wall of Jerusalem under the leadership of Nehemiah, promulgation of the Law by Ezra*, and subsequent reforms by Nehemiah. The book was written by the same author as I, II Chronicles* and the Book of Ezra, in the third or fourth century B.C. His principal source was the Memoirs of Nehemiah, comprising most of chaps. 1-7 and possibly also 12:27-43; 13:4-31, a highly authentic and valuable autobiography. Nehemiah was Persian governor of Judaea in 444-432 B.C., and a very efficient man of affairs who afforded much-needed leadership to the small Jewish community of Jerusalem in this period. His most important work was that of rebuilding the wall of Jerusalem, but he is said also to have promoted racial exclusiveness in marriage and stricter Sabbath-observance. See Esdras, Books of.

See L. W. Batten, *The Books of Ezra and Nehemiah* (International Critical Commentary), (1913).

J.P.H.

Nelson, Leonard: (1882-1927) As the leader and founder of the *Neufriessche Schule,* he was professor of philosophy at the University of Göttingen. In contrast to almost all neo-Kantians, he was like J. F. Fries* and E. F. Apelt for a psychological interpretation of Kant. His school has been severely criticized by representatives of the Marburger school, who interpret Kant from the point of transcendental philosophy.

Abhandlungen der Friesschen Schule. vols. 1-4 (Tübingen, 1904, 1908, 1911, 1914); *Vorlesungen über die Grundlagen der Ethik* (Leipzig, 1917); *Die Rechtswissenschaft ohne Recht* (Leipzig, 1917); *Democratie und Führerschaft* (Leipzig, 1920); *Die neue Reformation.* 2 vols. (Leipzig, 1918), 2 ed. (Leipzig 1922).

H.H.

Nemesis: Goddess, daughter of Night in the Greek mythology. Her function was the pursuit and punishment of the proud, the insolent, and criminals generally. Used in later literatures to express the inevitability of retribution, and even unjustifiable personal persecution.

P.G.M.

neo-Catholic: Term occasionally employed to describe the renascent Catholic movement in the Anglican Church (i.e., Anglo-Catholicism*), and the revival of interest in traditional Catholic ceremonial, doctrine and practice in other groups (as Lutheranism's St. James's Society). A common character of all these groups is their non-Roman nature, coupled with their insistence on "Catholic values".

W.N.P.

neo-Confucianism: See Confucianism.

neo-Friesian School: See Fries; Nelson, Leonard.

neo-Hegelianism: The philosophy of certain British (especially Scottish) and American idealists, influenced by Hegelianism*. Arose about the middle of the 19th century. Among British Neo-Hegelians are J. H. Stirling (whose *Secret of Hegel* was not very revealing), John and Edward Caird**, T. H. Green, F. H. Bradley**, B. Bosanquet, J. M. E. McTaggart* (*Commentary on Hegel's Logic, Studies in Hegelian Dialectic, Studies in Hegelian Cosmology*), and A. S. Pringle-Pattison* (*The Idea of God in Recent Philosophy*). In America, Neo-Hegelianism began with the St. Louis School (W. T. Harris, H. C. Brokmeyer); J. Dewey was influenced by it, but later departed from it; it was developed by J. Royce* (*The World and the Individual*) and M. W. Calkins (*Pesistent Problems of Philosophy*). The movement was conspicuous for its idealistic philosophy of religion, and its tendency to reconcile absolutism with personalism.

See G. W. Cunningham, *The Idealistic Argument in Recent British and American Philosophy* (1933); A. K. Rogers, *English and American Philosophy since 1800* (1922); and Muelder and Sears, *The Development of American Philosophy* (1940).

E.S.B.

neo-Kantianism: A German movement promoted first by Otto Liebmann and Albert Lange in the philosophical, and by Albert Ritschl* in the theological field about the middle of the 19th century and flourishing until about 1914. Neo K. had three different branches:

1) the so-called Marburg school, founded by Hermann Cohen* (successor of A. Lange in the chair of philosophy in the university of M.); his pupils are P. Natorp and E. Cassirer (now at Yale U.);

2) the so-called South-West Germany school represented by W. Windelband and H. Rickert, and their pupils, especially Emil Lask (died at the front in the first world war);

3) the Berlin school, founded by A. Riehl* whose only pupil is R. Hönigswald (now in this country).

The Marburg school can be characterized as the rationalistic, the Berlin school as the empiricist wing of Neo K.; the South-West-Germany school tried to reconcile the claims of reason and experience.

O. Liebmann, *Kant and his successors* (*K. und die Epigonen*, 1865); A. Lange, *History of Materialism* (1866). R.K.

neo-Lutheranism: During the 18th century the Lutheran churches had almost completely lost their specific character and emphasis, and had given way to rationalistic or pietistic interpretations of the Christian faith. In Germany the Romantic movement and the new historical sense led in the first third of the 19th century to a rediscovery of Luther's message. It resulted in a revival movement, which unlike pietism* laid the main emphasis on belief in justification* by faith, regular use of sacraments and regenerated community life, including church discipline (Klaus Harms* 1778-1855, Louis Harms 1808-1865, Volkening 1796-1877). The fresh interest in Luther led—after an interval of more than seventy years—to a new publication of his works *Erlanger Ausgabe* (1826 ff, 2nd ed. 1862-1885). This movement was followed by a renewal of Lutheran Confessionalism that fought against church union with the Presbyterians, and confessional indifference, and for the supreme authority of the confessional Lutheran standards in the organized life of the church (the poet K. F. Philipp Spitta 1801-1859, L. A. Petri 1803-1873, Hengstenberg* 1802-1869, Stahl 1802-1861, Luthardt* 1823-1902).

The interest then turned toward a historical study of the Lutheran confessions of faith (Fr. H. R. von Frank*, A. von Harless 1806-1879, Heinrich Schmid 1811-1885) and of the theology of Luther (Theodosius Harnack* 1817-1889, Julius Köstlin 1826-1902). Practical considerations led to a special study of Luther's idea of the church. Here two antagonistic groups came gradually into existence; those who under the influence of the earlier revival or of pietistic ideas laid the main emphasis on the congregation as the fellowship of the believers (Harless, Höfling 1802-1863, Carl Ferd. Walther 1811-1887), whereas the other group praised the dignity and upheld the authority of the organized church and its ministry (Löhe, Kliefoth** 1810-1895, Stahl, F. A. Philippi* 1809-1882, Vilmar 1800-1868). Historically this resurgence of Lutheranism strengthened the centripetal tendencies in continental Lutheranism. It preserved the churches in Europe from splitting up into sects and small groupings, and enabled them to eliminate the weeds of rationalism. But once this task had been accomplished, the movement became largely apologetic (Zöckler, Rich. Grützmacher*, Reinhold Seeberg*). Over against the barrenness and rigidity of a narrow Lutheran confessionalism the Erlangen School* (Thomasius, Hofmann, Harless, Frank**) insisted on the derived authority of the confessions and their Biblical foundation. Through their insistence on the primacy of Biblical exegesis these men enabled Lutheran theology to enrich the traditional beliefs by new thoughts on Christology, eschatology, sacraments and ethics. Between 1860 and 1870 the Lutheran movement had reached its climax. Even Ritschl*, in so many respects its antagonist, was deeply indebted to it. The subsequent generation lacked a vital interest in Luther, though in the historical field very valuable contributions were made, especially in the field of Luther biographies (Köstlin, Kolde, Berger, Kawerau, Rade). K. Knaake suggested the publication of a great critical edition of Luther's works, especially for the use of the scholar, and publication started in 1883 (*Weimarer Ausgabe*).

The twentieth century witnessed a fresh approach to Luther, in many respects similar to the earlier Luther revival (so-called Luther renaissance). Whereas the later 19th century assumed the identity of Luther's own thoughts with those of the Luther schoolmen, and thus interpreted Luther himself in terms of their theology, recent scholarship has noticed the influence of foreign ideas (especially Neo-scholasticism) upon the development of Lutheran theology in the second half of the 16th century. Thus the attempt is made to interpret Luther out of his own personal experience as contrasted both with piety and theology of the Middle Ages, and also of Protestant orthodoxy. Luther is no longer regarded primarily as a theological teacher, but rather as a religious genius and thinker in his own right (Karl Müller, Otto Scheel, Karl Holl, Carl Stange, Reinh. Seeberg, Aulén, Althaus**, Hirsch, Gogarten*, Elert and a whole pleiad of younger scholars).

The 19th century developments in Germany had their repercussions upon the Lutheran churches in the Scandinavian countries. In Sweden the contact with German Lutheranism called forth a type of High Church Movement in the 1850's, and a vital Lutheran theology in recent years (School of Lund). (See Lundensian theology). In Norway influences from the south resulted in a High Church Lutheran orthodoxy in theology and the conception of the ministry (Hersleb, Stevensen, W. A. Wexels), which opposed the prevailing pietism of the laity (Hauge*). But Gisle Johnson* succeeded in uniting the two movements into a living and active Lutheran national church. In the Danish church Mynster and Martensen* combined Lutheran confessionalism and High Church ideals with idealistic humanism over against Madsen's* orthodoxy. But their most powerful opponent was Sören Kierkegaard*, who interpreted Luther in the light of pietistic experiences. Kierkegaard's view in turn played a decisive role in Norwegian Lutheranism as well as in the German Luther Renaissance.

The Lutheran Churches in the U.S.A. faithfully reflect the European development. Their sole original contribution was the idea of the ministry held by C. F. Walther*, the leader of the Missouri Synod, which combines Löhe's emphasis on the local congregation with a very high conception of the authority and dignity of the ministry. See konfessionskünde.

The Church Histories by Karl Müller, Stephan-Leube, Gustav Krüger; the Histories of modern theology by Gustav Frank, F. Kattenbusch, F. H. R. von Frank.

Werner Elert, *Der Kampf um das Christentum seit Schleiermacher* (1921). O.A.P.

neo-orthodoxy: A term which designates that movement in contemporary Protestant theology which re-emphasizes the classic Protestant doctrines of God's transcendence, man's sin, and justification by faith, as over against the liberal conceptions of God's immanence, man's goodness and his gradual improvement. The roots of the movement go back to emphases in Paul, Augustine, the Protestant reformers, and Kierkegaard*. The leader of the movement in its beginnings was the Swiss pastor and theologian, Karl Barth*. Wide variations of view point among Barth's own followers and other representatives of the movement have appeared. Its influence has now been extended throughout Christendom. Few of its representatives apply the term "neo-orthodox" to themselves, though Edwin Lewis in America has done so.

Edwin Lewis, *The Faith We Declare* (1939), pp. 167 ff. D.D.W.

Neo Platonism: Neoplatonism is a blend of almost all the major lines of philosophical thought which preceded its epoch: one of the most remarkable attempts in history to weave all the strands of existing systems into a single web of thought. Its greatest interpreter was Plotinus who was born near Alexandria in 205 A.D. and died in Rome 270. He was initiated into philosophy by the self-taught Ammonius Saccas, who is the real founder of the movement.

Plotinus was a passionate disciple of Plato*, but he drew extensively upon Aristotle and the Stoics** for the material of his own intellectual structure. The work which the Arabic and Medieval Christian scholars entitled, "The Theology of Aristotle," was in reality a paraphrase of the philosophy of Plotinus. The influence of Plotinus and later Neoplatonists on Christian theology is of immense importance, especially on St. Augustine, Pseudo-Dionysius, John Scotus Erigena and St. Thomas Aquinas**, and, through successive revivals, on the later Christian thought of Europe.

At the center of all reality in the universe, in Plotinus' system of thought, set forth in his *Enneads*, is the Godhead, the One, the Absolute Good, the Source, which transcends thought and concrete being and utterance, an undivided and undifferentiated Unity. From this ultimate One, by an overflow from the superabundant Godhead, a succession of emanations* radiate out in stages of decreasing splendor and reality. First in Order is the *Nous**, Mind or Spirit, which radiates from the One as light emanates from a luminous body. This is the Over-Mind of the Universe, the World of Ideas, Patterns or Forms, of which all minds, and everything real and intelligible, partake. The Third Order of Plotinus' Trinity, and the second emanation, is the Over-Soul, which is the principle of life, of activity and process. It's the Life of all life and enfolds all souls. It floods out and makes the concrete world. Matter by itself is unreal. It is the limit or barrier against which the outflowing reality of soul is broken and splashes into multiplicity and differentiation. Soul* is amphibious and may live downward in the lower world or live upward in the World Yonder.

For Plotinus there is "a way down", by emanation, and "a way up", or return to Source. The Soul must first of all come to itself, withdraw from desires, objects of sense, and contemplate the true patterns of things, and rise to the height of thinking God's thoughts, and so attain the realm of Spirit—Nous. The last stage of the journey to the Fatherland, the Divine Center, or Source, can be reached only by a leap of ecstatic mystical experience, which Plotinus called "the flight of the alone to the Alone." He is the "father" of western mysticism which St. Augustine and "Dionysius"** brought into the Christian stream. Porphyry* (232-304) was his disciple and biographer. Other members of the School were Jamblicus, the Syrian (died 330) and, greatest of all after Plotinus, Proclus (411-485). See Platonism; Pletho.

The *Enneads* of Plotinus were translated in five volumes by Stephen Mackenna (London, 1917-1930); Proclus' *Elements of Theology* by E. R. Dodd (Oxford, 1933). Dean W. R. Inge, *The Philosophy of Plotinus* (London, 1918). R.M.J.

neo-Pythagoreanism: Although Pythagorean* philosophy was revived in Rome as early as Cicero, it did not acquire vogue until the time of Apollonius of Tyana (fl. 1st cent.). Its teachings contained elements from Plato, Aristotle, Stoics and Epicureans as well as from Pythagoras and the early Pythagoreans. According to Neo-Pythagoreanism a hierarchy of Gods existed. The supreme one should not be designated by a name but be apprehended only by reason. Numbers were still sacred, particularly the first ten, "one was God, reason, the principle of form and goodness, and two, the principle of inequality and change, of matter, evil, etc."

Ueberweg, *A History of Philosophy* I, 234.

P.R.H.

neo-realism: *Idem* New Realism*.

neo-Scholasticism: (Gr. *neos*, new; Lat. *scholasticus*, lecturer) A revival of Scholasticism* in the middle of the nineteenth century in Italy (Sanseverino, Cornoldi, Zigliara, Lorenzelli, Matussi); Germany (Kleutgen, Stockl, Grabmann, Schneid, Ehrle); France (Farges, Dormet de Vorges); and Belgium (Dupont, Lepidi). The movement sought to reassert basic philosophical principles and notions, carefully elaborated by Aristotle and the scholastics, which the prevailing positivism, materialism and scientism ignored. Leo XIII* recognized this trend in the encyclical "Aeterni Patris" August 4, 1879 and invited Catholic scholars to rediscover and represent the unchanging truths of the scholastic masters, enriching them with the well-founded truths of their successors in the philosophical tradition, eliminating excessive subtleties, and correcting the errors associated with their historical periods. This recommendation was implemented in 1891 by the foundation of the Institut Superieur de Philosophie at Louvain, Belgium under the direction of Désiré (later Cardinal) Mercier. Natural science, modern philosophy and psychology, and history were studied along with the original texts of St. Thomas and other medieval philosophers. The impetus furnished by the pope opened a vast movement of exhaustive historical (Grabmann, Ehrle, DeWulf, Mandonnet, Gilson, Van Steenberghen, Phelan) and critical (Nys, Noel, Maritain, Olgiatti) research to the enrichment of modern scholarship regardless of religious affiliation.

Cardinal Mercier and Professors of Louvain, *A Manual of Modern Scholastic Philosophy,* trans. by T. L. Parker (London, 1923-28); Cardinal Mercier, *Origins of Contemporary Psychology,* trans. W. H. Mitchell, M. A., (London, Manchester, 1918); Maurice de Wulf, *Scholasticism Old & New,* (Dublin, 1910); John S. Zybura, *Present-Day Thinkers and The New Scholasticism,* (1926); Joseph Louis Perrier, *Revival of Scholastic Philosophy in the 19th Century,* (1920); Louis J. A. Mercier, *Challenge of Humanism,* containing "Neo-scholasticism and the tradition of Dualism", (1933). J.J.F.

neo-Thomism: See Thomism.

nephesh: (Heb. *nephesh;* Arab. *nafs*) Hebrew: 1) Pre-Exilic Kingdom Period; the religious factor in man; the soul or shade understood to be in its nature different in kind from that of the natures of spirits, demons, gods, and spirit of Yahweh, all of which were spirits of non-human nature, and immortal; *nephesh* experiences death, is indestructible, eternal but not immortal. 2) After the 6th century B.C., the religious factor in man; the soul; understood to be *ruah* in its nature, the same nature as Yahweh; man's nature is now different from that of Yahweh in degree but not in kind: *Nephesh* identified with *ruah* in man. Arab. Evolution in meaning of *nafs* is similar to that of the Hebrew *nephesh* mentioned above, except that the great change in meaning occurred in the seventh century A.D. when Arabic primitivism was succeeded by Islam; after that time man is *ruh* nature. See ruah, ruh. F.L.P.

Neptune: (Lat., *Neptūnus,* cf. *nimbus,* rain) An old Italian water-deity, who under Greek influence assumed the attributes of Poseidon*. His festival is the Neptunalia (July 23). E.M.N.

nereids: (Gr. *Nēreides,* from *Nēreús,* son of Ocean and Tethys; *id-,* patronymic) Sea-nymphs, as opposed to naiads*, spring-nymphs. The most famous were Thetis, mother of Achilles, Amphitrite, wife of Poseidon, and Galatea. See nymphs. E.M.N.

Nergal: See Mesopotamian religions.

Nerthus: A Norse earth-goddess, sometimes identified with Frigga*, and idealized in Swinburne's famous poem *Hertha.* Also known as Huldra and Vrou-elde. The Milk Way was known as the street of Hertha. P.G.M.

Nestorianism: The doctrine of the Person of Christ set forth by Nestorius, Patriarch of Constantinople (428-31 A.D.) and the Antiochene School (See Antiochian School) represented by St. John Chrysostom and Theodore of Mopsuestia**. The School represents a rebellion against the hypostatic Christology* of Alexandria and the heresy of Apollinaris* by its own emphasis on the historic Jesus as well as the divine Son. The starting point of the controversy is to be found in their opposition to the attribute *Theotokos** applied to the Mother of Christ; in its place Nestorius suggested *Christotokos,* which offended contemporary piety. In place of *hypostatic union** of the divine and human natures, Nestorius suggested *prosopic union:* "The manhood is the face (*prosopon*) of the Godhead, and the Godhead is the face (*prosopon*) of the manhood." The doctrine was attacked by Cyril of Alexandria* who mistook *prosopon* as a philosophical term—either intentionally or ignorantly—and it was his caricature which was condemned at the Councils of Ephesus (431) and Chalcedon (451) See Christology.

J. F. Bethune-Baker, *Nestorius and his Teaching* (1909); F. Loofs, *Nestorius* (1914); R. V. Sellers, *Two Ancient Christologies* (1940). F. Nau has produced traditional evidence suggesting that Nestorius was not of Syrian but of Magian extraction. See canons of various churches. Cf. Syrian churches; Virgin Mary. F.W.B.

Nestorians: The followers of Nestorius, under Piroz, the Sasanid King (457-96), Barsauma assured the King that the doctrine of the Persian Christians differed from Constantinopolitan orthodoxy (at the time Monophysitism), and in 499 Nestorian doctrine became the orthodoxy of the Sasanid Church (Persia) under the Patriarch (*Catholicus*) of Babylon, who was duly invested by the Great King with the insignia and rank of a *wazir,* a custom continued under Muslim rule. Its centres of learning were Edessa (to 457) and then Nisibis. The Church accepted the Canons of Nicaea but not the Canons of Ephesus and Chalcedon**. In 553, the condemnation of The Three Chapters* at Constantinople aroused indignation and under the Catholicus Ishu-Yahb (582-96) the Nestorian Church reaffirmed the orthodoxy of Theodore of Mopsuestia*. The changes from Sasanid to Muslim and later Mongol rule had little effect on the life of the Nestorian Church, whose jurisdiction extended to its missions in China (See Chinese religions), India, Arabia Felix, Egypt (after 644) and into the heart of Central Asia. In the fifteenth century the patriarchate became hereditary. Under the Ottoman Turks the Nestorians became the victims of severe persecution and to the encroachment of the Church of Rome. In 1551 the Uniate Patriarchate of Babylon was established. The orthodox Nestorians joined the Allies against Turkey in 1914, but in the years following the Peace treaties of Sèvres (1920) and Lausanne (1923) their interests having been carelessly neglected by the diplomatists, they were almost exterminated. Their present Patriarch (1942) is Isa Mar Shimun XXI, who has been living in England and the U. S. A.

B. J. Kidd, *The Churches of Eastern Christendom* (1927); J. Labourt, *Le Christianisme dans l'Empire Perse* (1904); G. P. Badger, *Nestorians and their Rituals* (1862). F.W.B.

ne temere: The opening words of a decree issued on August 2, 1907 by the Sacred Congregation of the Council to clarify the Church's legislation on marriages*. The decree went into effect April 19, 1908. It set forth the proper conditions for betrothal and valid marriage. The chief article decreed that marriages of Catholics were thereafter null unless celebrated before a duly qualified priest and at least two witneses. The same law obliged when either party was a Catholic but did not bind those who were not and had not been Catholic. It also set forth other regulations concerning Catholic marriages. The chief points of this decree were embodied in the canons on marriage in the new Code of Canon Law*. T.T.M.

Neuchâtel, Independent Evangelical Church of: (organized 1873) has its origin in the preaching of Farel* in the canton of Neuchâtel. Churches were established independent of the State. They were governed by a body composed of the pastors, known as the "Company of Pastors" till the Revolution of 1848 when the "Company" was replaced by a synod of pastors and laymen. About 1865 the State seriously curtailed the freedom of the Synod, e.g., in appointments to the theological professorships. There were then forty churches. In 1873 twenty-one of these seceded from this state-controlled system to return to the old independence. The Independent Evangelical Church of Neuchâtel is controlled by a synod (all the pastors plus three laymen for each pastor). Pastors were paid from a central budget, not by parishes. About one-half of the congregations use church buildings owned by the State. Among the better known savants at its theological school was F. Godet*. See Godet's article in the *New Schaff-Herzog Encyclopedia of Religious Knowledge* (1910). Q.B.

neumes: (Gr. *neuma*, sign) A system of musical notation originating in Constantinople at the Church of Hagia Sophia in the seventh century. It was in common usage in both Byzantine and Latin churches by the ninth century. Neumes designate accentuation, changes in intensity and speed. Meter was not required since the words of Gregorian chant* follow prose rhythms and were sung as they would be spoken.

G. Grove, *Dictionary of Music and Musicians* (1935), Article on Notation; C. F. A. Williams, *The Story of Notation* (1903). E.H.B.

neutralism: See ontology.

New Apostolic Church, the: See Catholic Apostolic Church.

new birth: See conversion; regeneration; repentance.

New Church, the: See New Jerusalem, Church of the.

New Congregational Methodist Church: See holiness churches.

New England Primer: See catechumenate.

New England theology: Technically the "New England Theology" was the dominant theology of New England Congregationalism* during the last half of the Eighteenth and the first half of the Nineteenth Centuries. It may be dated quite specifically from Jonathan Edwards'* sermon on "Justification by Faith" in 1734. It lost its last authoritative defender and expounder when Edward Amasa Park* of Andover Theological Seminary was made emeritus in 1881. The system was, therefore, continuously taught, "improved" and preached for a century and a half and accepted, at least nominally, by New England orthodoxy. The preeminence of New England in American religious and educational life during most of that long period gave to its theological thought an unusual significance. It was from first to last geographically provincial, but it had an outstanding formative influence upon many movements in American christianity and was recognized in Great Britain.

The system was fundamentally Calvinistic in direct line of succession from the Continental Reformed churches and English Puritanism. The "Cambridge Synod" (Massachusetts Bay Colony) adopted the Westminister Confession* as authoritative for the Churches there represented in 1648. Ten years later (1658) English Independents supported by Oliver Cromwell* made their own "Declaration of the Faith and Order Owned and Practiced in the Congregational Churches in England." This is known from the place of meeting in London as the "Savoy Declaration."* It was rigidly Calvinistic and especially precise about "predestination."* Massachusetts made the "Savoy Declaration" official in 1680, Connecticut in 1708.

The New England Theology therefore inherited two Calvinistic formulae—one Puritan-Presbyterian, the other Independent-Congregational. The peculiar New England interest in theology was due in part to the isolation of the Colonies, their specific religio-political character, the predominance of the clergy in all their affairs and, beginning with Jonathan Edwards, a succession of speculatively-minded clergymen of unusual intellectual force.

More definitely the theology was the endeavor to find a working doctrinal basis—inside the pattern of inherited Calvinism—for the "revivalism" which began under the elder Edwards and prevailed in the orthodox churches for a hundred years. It was primarily a theology of the evangelical pulpit rather than the divinity school classrooms.

A resumé of it may be organized under two approaches, even the approximate indication of which is not possible here. First: the succession of the theological leaders: Joseph Bellamy (1719-1790) studied under Edwards and reflected his influence. Samuel Hopkins (1721-1803) organized his own theology into a "system." Nathaniel Emmons (1745-1840)** continued the succession. Nathaniel William Taylor (1786-1858) so modified the rigidities of the system as to make Horace Bushnell* and his successors possible. The succession ended, as said above, with E. A. Park of Andover. But there were also many thinkers and writers of less stellar magnitude.

The doctrines developed and debated were for the most part solutions of theological problems—human depravity; the function and responsibility of the will; the origin and nature of sin; the atonement, justification; the tests and nature of virtue; the rewards and punishments of the future life and, centrally and continuously, the sovereignty of God in the administration of all human affairs. There was always a background of controversy against rival systems; against "Arminianism" (the equivalent of later Liberalism); against Unitarianism, Universalism**; against the disestablishment of tax-supported churches; against the secularization of what began as a theocratic society.

A voluminous literature was created, in which even the specialists in the history of theology tend to lose themselves. In general there was a progressive modification of the extreme rigidities of inherited Calvinism. The movement founded three theological seminaries, Andover, Yale and the Hartford School, its powerfully motivated Foreign Missions and toward the end fostered agitations for various reforms in society. A new type and era of Congregational theology began with Horace Bushnell (1802-1876) and in general (again a loose but necessary phrase) the inherited theologies as closely articulated systems were dissolved in a new mind-order. See American theology, early; benevolence, disinterested; Calvinists; Hopkinsianism; means; New Haven theology; New School Presbyterian Church; New theology; Progressive orthodoxy.

Standard reference works are Williston Walker's *The Creeds and Platforms of Congregationalism* (1893). The biographies of the outstanding leaders specifically F. H. Foster, *A Genetic History of New England Theology* (1907), and G. N. Boardman, *New England Theology* (1899). G.G.A.

New England transcendentalism: See transcendentalism, New England.

New Harmony community: See communistic settlements, secular.

New Haven theology: New England Calvinism as "improved" by a group of Yale men and their friends to meet the changing currents of thought of the late eighteenth and early nineteenth centuries. The notable leaders of the movement were Timothy Dwight, Lyman Beecher, Chauncey A. Goodrich, Eleazer T. Fitch, and Nathaniel W. Taylor**. Taylor (1786-1858) made the most extensive statement of the system, which is therefore also known as "Taylorism"*.

Arminians, Deists, infidels and Unitarians in turn pressed upon Calvinists the inconsistency of determinism with man's responsibility. Edwards*, in his defense of Calvinism, upheld determinism and annihilated the Arminian notion of indeterminism as the basis for responsibility. But by drawing the distinction between "natural" and "moral" inability he was able to assert that man was responsible even though his will was determined, because he had freedom to do as he pleased and he pleased to sin. The New Haven men rejected Edwards' solution and held that the only possible basis for responsibility is the freedom to choose as well as to do. They defined all sin as the voluntary transgression of known law, and total depravity as the occasion but not the cause of sin. In spite of their protestations of loyalty to the essentials of Calvinism a large conservative group led by Bennet Tyler* rejected their leadership, separated from them, and founded Hartford Seminary in 1834. Cf. Calvinists, Old. See American theology, early.

Eleazer T. Fitch, *Two Discourses on the Nature of Sin* (1826); Nathaniel W. Taylor, *Concio ad Clerum* (1828); Zebulon Crocker, *The Catastrophe of the Presbyterian Church*.......(1838); F. H. Foster, *A Genetic History of the New England Theology* (1907); Sidney E. Mead, *Nathaniel W. Taylor, A Connecticut Liberal,* (1942). S.E.M.

New Humanists: See Humanism, the New.

New Jerusalem, Church of the: Followers of Swedenborg* organized the first congregation, or society, in London, 1788. The founding of the New Church is regarded by its members as dating back to the second coming of Christ, which took place when Swedenborg received the key to the interpretation of Scripture. His revelation of the spiritual meaning of Scripture became the doctrinal basis of the Church, whose former phases now gave way to the New Jerusalem. A General Conference met in 1789, organized in 1821 as the "General Conference of the ministers and other members of the new church signified by the New Jerusalem in the Apocalypse or Revelation of John." In 1926 this British Convention counted about 70 societies and 7,100 members. Since 1810 the Swedenborg Society had produced a great amount of literature, especially translations of Swedenborg's work into many languages. Missions of the New Church spread to Italy, Denmark, Austria, Russia, India, Africa, South America and other countries. The numbers were never large. In Swedenborg's home country, Sweden, there were in 1940, hardly 200 members.

The first New Church Society in the United States was organized at Baltimore in 1792. The "General Convention of the New Jerusalem in the United States" dates from 1817. Each local society has great freedom, but cooperates in an association, which in turn functions under the General Convention, meeting annually. The Convention provides for education and ordination of pastors, carries on missions, and orders the worship of the church. An American liturgy was adopted in 1876. Pastors serve local societies, while ministers may serve throughout the Convention. In 1890 the Pennsylvania Association, influenced by several leaders toward regarding the writings of Swedenborg as divinely inspired and insisting upon greater distinctiveness of life and work, withdrew from the Convention, and in 1897 adopted the name, "The General Church of the New Jerusalem." The bishop, cathedral, and school of the newer body is at Bryn Athyn, Pennsylvania. In 1930 the General Convention included 79 congregations and 5,363 members, served by 74 ministers. The General Church in the same year had 11 churches, 1,112 members, 25 ministers.

In general, the New Church follows the system of doctrine which Swedenborg found as the inner meaning of the Scripture. Confirmation, about the age of fourteen, admits to Junior membership, adult membership from about the age of twenty admits to the Communion Table. Baptism is retained as also modified forms of the marriage and burial service. The Liturgy (London, 1903) follows in the main the Anglican Book of Prayer, just as the polity of the church is a modified episcopate.

C. T. Odhner, *Annals of the New Church* (1904); R. Hindmarsh, *Rise and Progress of the New Jerusalem Church in England and other Parts* (London, 1861); C. F. Dole, *The New Church: What, How, Why?* (1906); Headquarters: General Convention of the New Jerusalem in the United States, Boston, Mass.; The General Church of the New Jerusalem, Bryn Athyn, Pa. C.J.B.

New Lights: The nick-name applied to the revivalists among New England Congregationalists during the Great Colonial Awakening*. In the great Western Revival, at the beginning of the nineteenth century, the name New Light was also applied to the revivalistic wing of the western Presbyterians, and later particularly to the followers of Barton W. Stone co-founder of the Church of the Disciples. W.W.S.

New Measures: The name given to the practices of certain American Lutherans of the earlier part of the 19th century emphasizing measures (regarded as questionable Lutheranism). Doctrinally lax, this group advocated experimental religion, conversion, revival meetings and even the "anxious bench". See Kurtz, Benjamin. V.F.

New Realism: See epistemology.

New School Presbyterian Church: The Presbyterian Church* in the U. S. A. underwent a schism in 1837. In 1838 one party, already known as the New School, being denied ecclesiastical recognition by the other, which controlled the General Assembly, formed its own organization. This claimed to continue the Presbyterian Church, as did also the other group or Old School*. The New School comprised about four-ninths of the church, mostly in the north and above all in New York. It contained many people of New England and Congregational antecedents. The two parties, which had been in controversy for several years before the separation, were generally progressive and conservative. The New School contended for liberal interpretation of the standards of the church in doctrine, recognizing some ideas of the New England theology* (see Auburn Declaration), and in polity, allowing the continuance of work in union with the Congregationalists*; it favored voluntary societies for missions and education rather than church boards, later modifying this position; it was prevailingly opposed to slavery, and hence at length in 1853 lost its presbyteries in border states. During the separation it embodied liberal Presbyterianism. The two Schools reunited in 1869, "each recognizing the other as a sound and orthodox body". See American theology, early. R.H.N.

New Side Presbyterians: The Great Awakening* occasioned a division among American Presbyterians*, as in other churches. The party called New Side favored the revival and practiced its methods. They considered spiritual experience more important as a qualification for the ministry than academic education. They were liberals regarding doctrinal standards and church discipline. They were largely, though not wholly, of New England antecedents. The controversy with the Old Side* caused the Synod, the general organization of colonial Presbyterianism to be divided in 1741. The New Side formed the Synod of New York (1745). This was by far the more active part of Presbyterianism during the separation. The two Sides reunited in 1758 as the Synod of New York and Philadelphia. R.H.N.

New Testament Books, the, in chronological order: See Books of the New Testament, dates of the.

New Testament, literature: The N.T. is the collection of Christian sacred books which was added to the Jewish Bible, the latter being known thereafter among Christians as the O.T. The word translated Testament (Greek, *Diathêkê*) might better be translated Covenant; the use of the term implies that the two collections contain the records or documents of the two Dispensations, one the Dispensation of the law given through Moses, the other the Dispensation of grace through Jesus Christ.

I. Canon: When the Christian books were gathered together and added to the Hebrew Bible, both had already been long in use in Christian services of worship. The O.T. was of course read in the Greek version, the Septuagint. The early Christian writings were likewise in Greek. It was by no arbitrary act or decision that the Christian sacred books were collected; instead it was a gradual process extending over three or four centuries. By the middle of the 2nd century the four gospels had been singled out and were viewed as inspired and authoritative. (The 'Four-Gospel Canon' was presupposed by Tatian's Diatessaron, c. 180 A.D., and Irenaeus assumed that there could be no more and no fewer gospels, since they corresponded with the four quarters of the heavens, the four beasts in Ezekiel's version, etc.). It has been thought that Marcion's N.T., containing the Gospel of Luke and the Pauline Epistles (omitting the Pastorals) had great influence, positively or negatively, in producing our New Testament; but this view is contested.

It is probable that the Epistles of Paul had been gathered together somewhat earlier, perhaps even before the end of the first century or early in the second. There is ample evidence to support the theory of Professor Goodspeed that the Pauline epistles were gathered together after the compilation and perhaps publication of Luke-Acts. Readers of this Lucan writing now became aware of the great importance of the Apostle Paul. His letters were in a somewhat fragmentary state of preservation. The Corinthian correspondence was incomplete and had to be pieced together; many scholars think that our 2nd Cor., e.g., is made up of at least two and possibly three letters or parts of letters. Romans is thought to contain miscellaneous fragments in chs. 12-16. The Epistle to the Ephesians may not be a letter by Paul but a kind of encyclical made up of Pauline quotations or paraphrases of his teaching, put together (as Goodspeed thinks) as the 'covering' letter or introduction to the Pauline corpus. The pastoral letters, (1st 2nd Timothy and Titus) are much later and probably come from the first half of the 2nd century. They presuppose conditions in the church which did not obtain in the lifetime of Paul.

Some of the later books of the N.T. like the Epistle to Hebrews, the Epistle of James, Jude, and 2nd Peter, and the 2nd and 3rd Epistles of John were admitted to the Canon only after long-continued debate. At the same time certain other books were acknowledged by some writers and were used in some parts of the church—books like the Shepherd of Hermas, the Epistle of Barnabas, 1st Clement, and the Apocalypse of Peter. This means that these books were used, here and there, both in public worship and in private study. One of the main tests for admission into the list of the sacred (i.e., 'canonical') books was apostolic authorship—or at least authorship by those close to the apostles and teaching their doctrine.

Eusebius of Caesarea, early in the fourth century, classified the Christian books as 1) canonical, 2) doubtful or disputed, 3) unauthentic and 4) heretical (*History of the Church*, 3.25).

Although a N.T. was in existence by the end of the 2nd century (Tertullian and Clement of Alexandria used the term), and although its chief components can be traced back to the 1st century, the canon was not completed until the 4th and 5th century. The books of the N. T. were first listed exactly as we have them today, in the Easter Epistle of Athanasius in the year 367. Athanasius' list was definitive for the East. It had great influence in the West though it was not finally adopted until the year 405, when Pope Innocent I sent a list of the canonical books to the Bishop Exsuperius of Toulouse.

II. Text: Although there have been many discoveries of early manuscripts*, chiefly in the papyrus collections from Egypt, we do not have a single autograph of a N.T. book, that is, the manuscript written by the author himself. This is not surprising, for the same is true of all ancient literary works. We have only copies of copies and we have no way of telling how many copies intervened between the autographs and the oldest surviving manuscripts. Hence, considerable variety was introduced into the text of the N.T. books at the very earliest stage of transmission. In general, our N.T. manuscripts seem to be descended from five or six leading textual 'families' in the 2nd century. These are probably to be associated with the great centers of Christian activity—Egypt (esp. Alexandria), Caesarea, Syria, Italy, North Africa, Gaul. The oldest versions (Old Latin and Old Syriac) also belong to this period and represent local types of text.

It is from these families or, rather, these leading local texts that our present manuscripts have descended, most of them, of course, bearing the marks of cross-influence of other types upon each other. The great Greek Uncials (e.g., Codex Sinaiticus, 4th century; Codex Alexandrinus, 5th century; Codex Vaticanus, 4th century; etc.), probably contained revised texts. The older theory of Westcott and Hort, viz., that Sinaiticus and Vaticanus are the best of all manuscripts and contain a 'neutral' text, has now been either greatly modified or abandoned by textual experts. They probably contain a text revised partly by consultation of good ancient manuscripts, partly by consideration of grammar and syntax.

The later manuscripts (Minuscules, that is, written in flowing script as contrasted with the Uncials, which were written in capital letters) date chiefly from the 9th to 16th centuries and contain a type of text which apparently resulted from conflation of variant readings. Thus the later text (Byzantine, or textus receptus) preserved quantities of divergent and sometimes incompatible readings. The task of textual criticism is to work back through this common or received text to the great 2nd century types and then, often by conjecture, to something approximating the autographs.

A distinction must be made between the text of the gospels which were as a rule copied as a whole and that of the Pauline Epistles, which also were copied as a body.

In addition to the early versions, Latin, Syriac, Coptic, there are many quotations of the N.T. in the writings of the early church fathers, e.g., Irenaeus, Clement of Alexandria, Origen, Tertullian, Hippolytus, Cyprian, and others. Of course the manuscript tradition of the writings of these fathers must itself be examined critically; for the copies of their writings which have come down to us have in many cases been influenced by the text of the N.T. current in the copyist's locality.

In spite of the thousands of variations found in the N.T. manuscripts, it is nevertheless true that very few of them would make any difference in the interpretation of the N.T. Most of these variations were the result of mistakes in copying; very few resulted from doctrinal differences or from propaganda. Where the latter is the case, there is little difficulty in recognizing the fact, and other manuscripts are at hand to check the aberration.

III. Growth of the N.T.: The earliest N.T. writings were undoubtedly the Epistles of Paul, probably in this order: 1-2 Thessalonians, Galatians, 1-2 Corinthians, Romans, Philippians, Colossians, Philemon. These letters come from the latter part of Paul's missionary career and the period of his imprisonment at Rome, that is, from 50 to 62 or 64 A.D., when Paul was martyred. The Gospel of Mark probably comes from about 68, and from the City of Rome, that is, after the martyrdom of Peter and Paul. The Gospel of Matthew is variously dated, a number of scholars assigning it to a date soon after A.D. 70, while others date it nearer the end of the century, and some even later still. Perhaps an exact date is impossible, since the book contains material new and old, and some additions were perhaps made to it even after it had left the author's hand. Luke-Acts is probably to be dated toward the end of the century. It is an apologetic work designed to prove that Christianity is not inimical to public order and to Roman authority; the most appropriate date is during the persecution under Domitian, probably about the year 95. To this same period belongs the Revelation of John which also, however, includes older material, some of it probably from the time of Nero, some from the time of Caligula, some perhaps even pre-Christian. The whole book presupposes persecution of the Christians by the champions of the emperor-cult.

Following the "publication" or circulation of Luke-Acts, the Pauline letters were gathered together and the Epistle to Ephesians was compiled to form an introduction to the collection. This means that Ephesians probably dates from the end of the century or soon after. The Pastoral Epistles (1-2 Timothy and Titus) are to be dated considerably later, either between 100 and 110 or possibly (with Goodspeed) around 150. Jude and 2d Peter are also late. Even conservative critics allow that the latter probably comes from the middle of the 2nd century.

It is extremely difficult to date the remaining N.T. literature. The Epistle to Hebrews presupposes some knowledge of the Pauline letters and probably comes from Rome. The title ("To Hebrews") is mistaken and is only an inference from its large amount of O.T. quotation. Perhaps a date soon before or after A.D. 95 is as close as we can come.

First Peter is also Pauline but in a different sense. Paul's theology is presupposed but is developed in a different direction than that followed by Hebrews; but its dependence upon Paul may be either upon Paul's collective letters or upon Paul's surviving influence in the Aegean mission field. It presupposes a persecution and it addresses Christians scattered over northern, western, central, and eastern Asia Minor—all but southern.

The Epistle of James was probably in its origin a homily, making use, as was natural, of a considerable amount of Jewish material. It is very difficult to say when it was probably written, or where. On the whole it seems not unlikely that it comes from Syria, perhaps Antioch, and probably early in the 2nd century.

The Gospel of John is undoubtedly the latest of the gospels and is really a reinterpretation of the gospel story with the purpose of setting forth the meaning of Christ in terms of popular Hellenistic religious philosophy. It assumes the doctrine of the Logos or Word of God and in fact substitutes this concept for the old concept of Messiah, as the key to the personality, the career, and the authority of Jesus. The author has placed upon the lips of Jesus a number of discourses and a whole body of doctrine which express the thought of the writer's time and place rather than the teaching of the historical Jesus. It is a sublime dramatization of a theological idea, rather than an historical record (see "Johannine Problem"). The date is probably early in the 2nd century, possibly between 115 and 125. Cognate with the Gospel of John is the 1st Epistle, probably by the same author. The other two epistles of John no doubt date from approximately the same period, but seem to come from another hand. B. W. Bacon and others have thought that the appendix to John (ch. 21) was added about the middle of the 2nd century. It is undoubtedly an appendix; but it is difficult to date.

Thus the N.T. literature grew, not as the result of certain great literary personalities producing the works of a 'school', but in order to meet the needs of the early church. The classic literature of Christianity is thus an 'occasional' literature—that is, designed to meet specific occasions and needs. In the case of the Pauline letters, this is perfectly obvious. It is true also of the gospels, which grew out of the old oral tradition of the church (see arts. "Gospel," "Synoptic Gospels," and "Form Criticism"). The Gospel of Mark was addressed to a martyr church and contained a selection of incidents from Jesus' life and sayings from his lips, designed 1) to encourage his followers faced with persecution, and 2) to prove that he had been Messiah even during his earthly life. The Gospel of Luke and the Book of Acts form one continuous apologetic work designed to show that Christianity was not an anarchistic movement, though it had been severely libeled by its enemies; instead, it deserved the same recognition and protection that the Roman authority accorded Judaism. The Gospel of Matthew is a didactic work arranged in five great sections, probably for convenience in teaching and in public reading and exposition. It presupposes a developed church which required rules for its regulation and it sets forth the teaching of Jesus in terms of the Christian Halakah or 'new law'. The Gospel of John is a polemical anti-Jewish, anti-Gnostic, reinterpretation of the whole gospel story, designed to show that Jesus was the Incarnate Logos, indeed, really God who had existed from the beginning, who "became" flesh, manifested his glory by many signs—chiefly the great seven described in chs. 2-12—and then, dying and rising again from the grave, returned to the Father. The theme of the Gospel of John is thus in essence the great epic of salvation.

The successive stages in the development of this religious literature correspond to stages in the development of early Christian theology. But it must not be supposed that these stages came in strict chronological succession. Instead, the N.T. presents us with a series of types of early Christian thought, probably six or seven in number, which reflect the spread of early Christianity into various areas of religious thought and feeling, of religious and moral outlook. See under specific N.T. books. Also see Books of the N.T., dates of the; canon, Old and New Testament; koiné; versions of the Bible, ancient.

I. See art, "New Testament Canon" (by K. Lake) in *Standard Bible Dictionary* (1936), 3rd ed.; E. J. Goodspeed, *The Formation of the New Testament* (1926); A. Harnack, *The Origin of the New Testament* (1925); E. C. Moore, *The New Testament in the Christian Church* (1904).

II. F. Kenyon, *The Story of the Bible* (1936); *The Text of the Greek Bible* (1937); *Our Bible and the Ancient Manuscripts* (1939); K. Lake, *The Text of the New Testament* (1928), 6th ed.

III. *Introductions to the New Testament*: E. J. Goodspeed (1937); E. F. Scott (1932); J. Moffatt (1912); A. H. McNeile (1927); K. and S. Lake (1937); M. Dibelius, *A Fresh Approach to the New Testament and Early Christian Literature* (1936); M. S. Enslin, *Christian Beginnings* (1938). F.C.G.

New Testament theology: This is a misleading term in so far as it suggests that the N.T. writers all teach the same doctrines, while differing in their modes of presentation. In the N.T. period the Christian mind worked freely. Every teacher made his own interpretation of the gospel, under the sole direction of the Spirit. The result was a number of theologies which need to be considered separately, and the effort to reduce them to a single type is futile. We have now learned to speak, not of a N.T. theology, but of the teaching of the primitive church, of the Pauline Epistles, of the Fourth Gospel, the Epistle to Hebrews, the book of Revelation**. Besides the main types of teaching others can be discerned, more or less distinctly, and each of them must be taken by itself. At the same time the general term is a convenient one, and cannot well be dispensed with. N.T. thought is radically different from that of the O.T. The books comprising the N.T. were all produced within a given period, and represent an attitude of mind which must not be confused with that of later times. As we speak of Greek philosophy or Elizabethan poetry, so we can apply the name "N.T. theology" to all the types of thought which emerged in the primitive church. The term is thus employed by modern writers (e.g., Holtzmann, Feine, Weinel) who deal with the general subject of early Christian thinking, as set forth in the various N.T. books. See separate N.T. books. E.F.S.

New theology, the:

I

A term used in America to designate the movement toward a liberalized, evangelical theology in the last two decades of the 19th century. The movement was influenced by the new humanitarian developmental views which found expression in Horace Bushnell*. It was sensitive to problems created for Christian thought by the development of modern sciences, particularly the evolutionary hypothesis and scientific biblical criticism. It incorporated the emphasis on religious experiences derived from Schleiermacher and his followers. The definitive characterization of New Theology was given by Professor Theodore T. Munger* in 1883 in his book, *The Freedom of Faith,* in which the first essay was entitled "The New Theology". Munger stressed the organic connection of the New Theology with historical Christian thought, its developmental conception of theology, its emphasis upon reason and intuition, its critical method of scriptural interpretation, its concern for the solidarity of humanity over against an excessive individualism, its broader and more scientific anthropology and its liberalized eschatology. Consult in addition to Munger's book, R. J. Campbell, *The New Theology* (1908) and F. H. Foster, *The Modern Movement in American Theology* (1939). D.D.W.

II

This term was quite generally used of the theological renascence in America represented by Horace Bushnell, Henry Ward Beecher, T. T. Munger, Washington Gladden, George Gordon**, Lyman Abbott, the Andover theologians, Newman Smyth, James M. Whiton, Henry C. King** and others, covering a period from about 1850 to 1920. Beecher once said that for many years he had been "hauling bricks for the New Theology." Gerald Birney Smith* wrote in *Religious Thought in the Last Quarter Century*: "There was much popular discussion in the last decade of the nineteenth century of the 'New Theology' which was being advocated by influential liberal preachers like Lyman Abbott, Washington Gladden and David Swing." (p. 95).

Regarding Bushnell as its leader, it may be said that the movement was chiefly indebted to Coleridge*; for Dr. Munger wrote that to Coleridge's *Aids to Reflection* (published in America by James Marsh in 1829) "it may almost be said that we are indebted for Bushnell." Its leading doctrinal emphases were: the Divine immanence, the centrality of Christ, continuous creation (evolution), rejection of verbal inspiration and materialistic ideas of future punishment, and, in general, acceptance of the conclusions of Modern Science with stress also upon Christian education vs. evangelism.

Although later in its rise than Unitarianism* and for the most part independent of it, it had much in common with the Unitarian movement, though less controversial and more constructive and "evangelical." Nor had it more than slight connection with Transcendentalism or with Universalism**.

George E. Ellis in the last chapter of his *Half Century of the Unitarian Controversy* wrote: "If the New Theology shall prove to be so much truer and better than Unitarianism as to obliterate the sect, whose visible increase it does withstand, we are ready to welcome it." (p. 402).

The only outstanding book bearing the title *The New Theology* was the controverted volume by R. J. Campbell, which however had little relation to the American movement bearing the name.

While the title "The New Theology" is colorless, and the movement long since gave place to others, there is much to be said for retaining the name as attached to it and indicating its nature when it arose and assigning it a definite place in the succession of theological movements and schools of theology in America. See Progressive Orthodoxy.

Cf. Horace Bushnell: *Christian Nurture* (1846), *Nature and the Supernatural* (1858); T. T. Munger: *The Freedom of Faith* (1883); George A. Gordon: *Religion and Miracle* (1909), *The New Epoch for Faith* (1901); *Progressive Orthodoxy* (1885) by members of the Faculty of Andover Seminary; Washington Gladden: *How much is Left of the Old Doctrines?* (1899), *Present-day Theology* (1913); Newman Smyth: *Old Faiths in New Light* (1879); Lyman Abbott: *The Theology of an Evolutionist* (1897). Cf. also J. W. Buckham: *Progressive Religious Thought in America* (1919); *Report of the Commission on Congregationalism and Theology*, International Congregational Council (1920). J.W.B.

New Thought movement: The constitution of the International New Thought Alliance adopted in 1916 states the purpose of the Alliance as follows: "To teach the infinitude of the Supreme One, the Divinity of Man and his Infinite possibilities through the creative power of constructive thinking and obedience to the voice of the Indwelling Presence which is our source of Inspiration, Power, Health and Prosperity".

The movement derives from the work of Phineas P. Quimby (1802-1866) of Portland, Maine, who practiced mental or spiritual healing for a quarter of a century prior to his death. Among those whom he healed was Mrs. Mary Baker Patterson, later and better known as Mary Baker Eddy. It is still a moot question as to how much Mrs. Eddy was indebted to him for the ideas and techniques which she later incorporated into Christian Science*. Certainly both she and another who had been brought back to health by Quimby, W. F. Evans, a former clergyman of the New Church (Swedenborgian), did much to spread the ideas of mental healing in the years which followed. Evans in his later work stressed the mental rather than the spiritual aspects of the healing and is more responsible for the "mental science" phase through which the movement passed than any other.

Quimby created no organization. Individuals whom he had benefited adopted his method and in turn passed it on to others, adding to or modifying it in the process. The result was that there developed many small groups under different names such as Divine Science, Unity**, Practical Christianity, Liveable Christianity, Home of truth, the Church of the higher life, etc. It was in the nineties that the term New Thought began to be used to characterize the general outlook of these groups, which had now come to embrace much more than the healing interest, particularly, inspiration, power, prosperity or plenty, and general well-being. National conventions were held annually from 1894 on.

In 1908 the name, The National New Thought Alliance, was adopted and in 1914 it became the International New Thought Alliance. New Thought groups are found in Europe, South America, Australia and Asia. Their literature has been translated into many languages and circulates widely even where there are no New Thought organizations. Among the more popular books are those of Ralph Waldo Trine, especially, *In Tune With the Infinite* and the works of Orison S. Marden. Typical of the magazine literature are *The Nautilus* and *Unity*. For the history of the movement see H. W. Dresser, *A History of the New Thought Movement* (1919). C.S.B.

New Year, Jewish: (Heb., *Rosh Hashanah*) The first day of the civil year and the first day of the seventh month of the ecclesiastical year (generally occurring in September), described as "a memorial proclaimed with the blast of the horn, a holy convocation", upon which no servile work is permitted. (Lev. 23.23-25; Num. 29.1-11) Invested by the Rabbis* with the character of a Day of Divine Judgment, it acquired great solemnity. The sounding of the ram's horn (*shofar**) during the morning service stirs the people to thoughts of repentance. The elaborate liturgy of the day dwells upon God's sovereignty, providence, revelation, and redemption. Orthodox Jews* observe two days of Rosh Hashanah. See Jewish religious festivals. S.S.C.

New Year's celebrations: 1) Judaism, in harmony with the Talmud* and probably with much earlier practice (as suggested by Nu. 29:1 & Neh. 8:1-10), observes the 1st of Tishri (falling in Sept. or early Oct.) as *Rosh Hashana* or New Year's. 2) The Christian Church has had no official New Year's Festival. Indeed, in the ancient world it regarded the Roman celebration of New Year's (Jan. 1 under the Julian Calendar) as viciously pagan (see e.g., Tertullian, *De Idol.*, xiv). To offset these festival debaucheries, to which its members were often attracted, the Church began, sometime after the 4th Cent. (when Dec. 25 was fixed as the birthday of Christ), to commemorate the day as that of the Lord's Circumcision* (i.e., 8th day after Christmas; Lk. 2:21). That this practice was well established by the 6th Cent. is clear from Canon 17 of the 2nd Council of Tours (567), which took for granted the designation of the first three days of Jan. as fast days "fixed by the Fathers to combat the heathen customs" and provided for a *Missa Circumcisionis*. By the Middle Ages, the secular celebrations associated with Jan. 1 continued (although March 25 had come to be regarded in Europe as the beginning of the year), indeed developed into the extravagant *Feast of Fools**. These excesses were finally suppressed by the Church. With the adoption of the Gregorian Calendar* (1582), Jan. 1 again became New Year's Day (not until 1700 in Germany and 1751 in England), although not recognized as such in the ecclesiastical calendar, remaining simply the Day of the Circumcision of Our Lord. Within Protestantism the Reformers were generally hostile toward any revival of New Year's celebrations, an attitude which became particularly strong among the Puritans. Gradually, however, popular interest in observing the occasion overcame Protestant scruples and it became widely celebrated, with many churches holding "watch nights" (a Methodist practice; see Wesley's *Journ.*, Dec. 31, 1761), singing the old year out and the new in, preaching New Year's sermons, extending greetings, etc. Cf. festivals and holy days, Christian; Jewish religious festivals. E.T.R.

Newcomer, Christian: (1749-1830) Leader of the westward expansion of the Church of the United Brethren in Christ*, crossed the Allegheny Mountains on horseback fifty times (1799-1829). Bishop, 1813-1830. His *Journal* (1795-1830) is an important historical document. W.E.R.

Newman, John Henry, Cardinal: (1801-1890) English theologian and man of letters. Newman's early career centered at Oxford, where in 1828, after being successively undergraduate, fellow, and tutor, he became vicar of St. Mary's, the University church. In 1833 he joined Keble* and others in the Oxford Movement*, advancing the cause both through his sermons and his contributions to *Tracts for the Times*. *Tract XC* (1841), on the compatibility of the Thirty-nine Articles with Catholicism, provoked such a violent reaction that he withdrew from the movement, gradually severed his Anglican connections, and four years afterwards entered the Roman Church. His later life was spent mainly at the Oratory of St. Philip Neri which he established near Birmingham. In 1879 he was created Cardinal.

Among Newman's voluminous writings the *Apologia pro Vita Sua* (1864), undertaken in reply to an accusation by Charles Kingsley, is his literary masterpiece. Other representative works are *The Arians of the Fourth Century* (1833), *Essay on the Development of Christian Doctrine* (1845), *Discourses on the Scope and Nature of University Education* (1852), and *A Grammar of Assent* (1870). Of his *Verses on Various Occasions* (1868) best known is the hymn "Lead, Kindly Light," written in 1833. See Anglo-Catholics; Tractarianism.

The standard biography is by Wilfred Ward (2 vols., 1912). Joseph J. Reilly's *Newman as a Man of Letters* (1927) is a good brief account. L.W.C.

Newton, Sir Isaac: (1642-1727) A sublime genius of physical science, who, peculiarly English, upheld the alliance between science and religion. He wrote as many theological treatises as scientific classics. A pronounced Arian flavor pervades his theological works. He held that indubitable evidences of intelligent purpose in the cosmic order attest the divine origin of the world. Nature was for Newton not its own self-sufficient end. Instead of making the world of nature independent of God for its continued existence, he assigned to God the duty of actively preventing the fixed stars from collapsing in the middle of space, and of providentially reforming the system of the world whenever its mechanism ran out of gear too far. The aesthetic and physical features of the universe are rooted in the continued exertions of the divine will which had chosen them as ends of his creative labor. See Copernican astronomy; Enlightenment, the.

The Mathematical Principles of Natural Philosophy (London, 1803), 3 vols.; *Opticks* (London, 1721), 3rd ed., corrected. H.H.

Nicene creed: See creeds of Christendom; Christology.

Nicene—Constantinopolitan Creed, the: See Constantinopolitan Creed.

Nichiren: See Buddhist Terminology.

Nicholas of Clémanges: (of Clamanges) (1360 (?)-1437) French conciliarist. Clémanges was a Paris scholar, with an interest in the classics. He became secretary to the Avignon pope Benedict XIII, but later supported the Council of Constance* and wrote (ca. 1320) *De corrupts ecclesiae statu.* See festivals and holy days, Christian.

A. Coville, *La traité de la ruine de l'Eglise de Nicolas de Clamanges* (1936). J.T.M.

Nicholas of Cusa: (1400-1464) A German cardinal and philosopher, finally also bishop of Brixen. His writings concern philosophy, theology, law and science. The title of his principal work, *De Docta Ignorantia* shows his views on the restricted powers of the human mind. C.R.

Nicholas, Saint, of Myra (or Bari): He was bishop of Myra, in Lycia, where he died in the fourth century as a confessor. His relics were transported in the eleventh century to Bari in southern Italy. His feast is almost universally observed on December 5, when he assumes the role of Santa Claus in some European countries. He is the patron saint of Russia and Greece, and of some localities and cities in Western Europe. M.S.

Nicholas I, Pope: (858-867) Saint Nicholas I, called "The Great", was a champion of the Holy See*, defended Christian unity in the affair of Photius*, and stood for the integrity of Christian marriage against Lothair, King of Lorraine, and Charles the Bold of Burgundy. Nicholas was a tireless worker, an impartial defender of justice, and a generous friend of the poor. C.V.

Nicodemus, Gospel of: Or Acts of Pilate* A fourth century work in two parts, 1. An account of the trial, passion and resurrection of Jesus, in which Pilate and Nicodemus are prominent; and 2, an account of the Descent into Hell, which was appended to Part 1 probably some time after 425. E.J.G.

Nicolaitans: 1) A party in Ephesus (Rev. 2.6), Pergamum (Rev. 2.15), and possibly more widely distributed in Asia Minor, described as hateful to the Holy Spirit but not otherwise specified. It probably had no historical connection with 2) the Gnostic sect of the same name which falsely traced its origin to Nicolaus the Deacon (Acts 6.5). It cultivated immorality as a method of asserting superiority to everything fleshly. For this reason it was regarded by Christians with such horror that, as late as the Middle Ages, the name Nicolaitanism was employed to designate practices among the clergy that were attributed to fleshly lusts. A.K.R.

Nietzsche, Friedrich Wilhelm: (1844-1900) "Prophet of a non-religious religion and an unphilosophical philosophy" (Wilamowitz-Moellendorf), sometime professor of classical philology at Basel, later a free-lance essayist whose works were hardly read during his lifetime but have been of great influence and have caused tremendous controversy since his death. Nietzsche rebelled against philosophical pretensions at arriving at "Truth" or knowledge of "Being", and adopted for himself, perhaps under the influence of Pascal, the aphoristic mode of writing, developing not so much a systematic philosophy as a series of brilliant thrusts at the accepted ideas of his time. Claiming that the individual should not passively accept but should impose his will on his environment, and should adopt a personal relation to his problems ("All truths are bloody truths"), he rebelled against Christianity for its stress on the weak virtues of pity and love, against nationalism, commercialism, democracy, the scientific spirit, and nineteenth century ideals in general. Influenced by Schopenhauer, but rebelling against him also, he developed the theory of the will to power as characteristic of all life and as providing for man the only acceptable basis for value. He thus argued for a "transvaluation of all (accepted) values" and for an "immoralism" which should teach men to be hard, live dangerously, adopt a "master-morality" which should justify the rights of the strong, and work to produce the "superman", since "man is something that is to be surpassed." Making one exception to his rule against metaphysical conceptions he maintained belief in "eternal recurrence", taking his own inconsistency here as evidence of the strife in all things.

Nietzsche maintained that "God is dead", killed by the uncompromising will of man himself to discover the facts. The result is tragedy and a new emphasis on suffering. Nietzsche agrees with Christianity that suffering must be given meaning but disagrees as to what the meaning is. The God on the Cross pronounces a curse on life and attempts to win salvation by appealing to what is higher than life. The god Dionysos cut to pieces is, on the other hand, a promise of life, since he is ever re-born out of his own destruction. Man must learn *amor fati*, love of the fate which eternally returns.

The eternal recurrence of contradictions in Nietzsche's own thought has led to the most diverse interpretations of his work. Christians have found in him a passionate plea for sincerity and an eloquent defence of the divine discontent. Anti-Christians have emphasized the need of taking literally his fulminations against the Christian virtues. In recent years the Nazis have claimed him because of his protest against pacificism and humanitarianism and his praise of authority and physical strength. They pass over in silence his revolt against nationalism and totalitarianism, his dislike of Germans and anti-Semites, and his plea for "good Europeans".

Works: *Werke* (19 vols. 1895-1913); *The Complete Works of F. Nietzsche* (18 vols. tr. O. Levy, 1909-13); also *The Philosophy of Nietzsche* (1937), 1 vol. Eng. tr. of the principal works with introd. by H. W. Wright. Of the scores of commentaries: K. Jaspers *Nietzsche, Einführung in das Verständnis seines Philosophierens,* (1936); W. M. Salter, *Nietzsche the Thinker* (1917); C. Brinton, *Nietzsche* (1941); G. A. Morgan, Jr. *What Nietzsche Means* (1941). J.S.B.

Nihil Obstat: See imprimatur.

nihilianism: (Lat. *nihil,* nothing) A view holding that the human nature of Christ had "no true subsistence"—that it was *nihil.* Mistakenly attributed to Peter Lombard*, it was condemned in 1179 by Pope Alexander III*. R.C.P.

Nihongi: "The Chronicles of Japan." Also known by the longer title of *Nihon Shoki.* Published in thirty books in 720 A.D. Tells the story of Old Japan from creation down to 697 A.D. D.C.H.

nimbus: In art, the halo of light and glory, usually of gold, surrounding the head of Christ, the Virgin Mary, or the Saints, as opposed to the aureola, which surrounds the whole body. Appeared in Christian art in the 5th century, but was known earlier in India and Egypt, and among the Greeks and Romans. See symbolism. R.B.B.

Ninurta: (Nin-ib) Babylonian-Assyrian god of war and storms, protector of the boundaries of fields, patron of physicians, son of Enlil* the god of Nippur. R.H.P.

nirvāṇa: See Buddhist Terminology.

Nitzsch, Carl Immanuel: (1787-1868) He was professor in Bonn and Berlin. Brought up in a Kantian purified supernaturalism, he overcame the latter through the influence of German idealism, above all through Schleiermacher*. In systematic theology his great service was mediation. In the development of practical theology he was a pioneer.

System der christlichen Lehre (Bonn, 1829); *Praktische Theologie* (Bonn, 1859), 2 ed. H.H.

Nitzsch, Friedrich: (1832-1898) He taught in Giessen and Kiel. He was less meritorious through his systematic theology than through the panorama and faithfulness with which he characterized the hitherto existing discussion of individual problems.

Grundriss der christlichen Dogmengeschichte (Berlin, 1870); *Lehrbuch der evangelischen Dogmatik* (Freiburg, 1889, 2 ed., Freiburg, 1896, 3 ed., ed. by H. Stephan, Leipzig, 1911). H.H.

Noachic laws: See Israel, religion and theology.

Noble Lectures, The William Belden: These lectures at Harvard University were established in 1898 by Nannie Yulee Noble with a gift of $20,000, the income of which was to be used for a lectureship in memory of her husband,

William Belden Noble. The deed of gift provides that there shall be at least six lectures annually and that they shall be published. The lecturers were originally appointed by a board of seven trustees but, in 1906, at the suggestion of the Founder, this function was transferred to the President and Fellows of the University. According to the deed, the purpose of the lectures was "to continue the mission of William Belden Noble, whose supreme desire it was to extend the influence of Jesus as the way, the truth, and the life; to make known the meaning of the words of Jesus, 'I am come that they might have life, and that they might have it more abundantly.' In accordance with the large interpretation of the influence of Jesus by the late Phillips Brooks . . . it is intended that the scope of the lectures shall be as wide as the highest interests of humanity . . . The lectures may include philosophy, literature, art, poetry, the natural sciences, political economy, sociology, ethics, history both civil and ecclesiastical, as well as theology, and the more direct interests of the religious life. Beyond a sympathy with the purpose of the lectures, as thus defined, no restriction is placed on the lecturer."

Among the Lectures published in this series are *The Field of Ethics*, by George Herbert Palmer; *Witnesses of the Light*, by Washington Gladden; *The Adventure of Life*, by Wilfred T. Grenfell; *The Spiritual Interpretation of History*, by Shailer Mathews; *Mysticism and Democracy in the English Commonwealth*, by Rufus M. Jones, and *The Church and its Teaching Today*, by William Temple.

J.E.N.

nocturn: Originally a monastic service sung or recited at night. Now one of the divisions (usually three) of the Roman Catholic Breviary* office called "Matins,"* designed so to be recited but almost invariably used the evening or afternoon before. B.S.E.

nolo episcopari: "I do not wish to be made Bishop", from a possible Latin verb *episcopare;* reluctance to accept episcopal office—sometimes actual, sometimes merely an ecclesiastical convention. E.R.H.

nominalism: (L. *nomen*, name fr. *noscere*, know; *nominalis*, titular) In logic and epistemology, the view that universals*, i.e., abstract ideas or concepts, are mere words or empty sounds, having no basis in reality or objective counterpart. It is more extreme in the direction of subjective idealism than conceptualism* and is opposed to and by moderate and extreme realism. It has been attributed to Antisthenes, Roscelin, Aureolus, Durandus, Hobbes, and Locke. The fictionism of Vaihinger is a modern version and the views of Mach likewise resemble nominalism.

Nominalism has much in common with sensism, phenomenism, empiricism, positivism, physicalism, operationalism, etc. However it is more than mere verbalism or psittacism.

See realism; Scholasticism; universals, battle over. D.C.O'G.

nominatio regia: Signifies royal designation of a person for ecclesiastical office. It is based on the right of patronage*, and generally pertains to the higher ranks (bishops, etc.). Institution must be made by the church. For controversies respecting *nominatio regia* see Concordat, esp. 1122, 1516, 1801. Q.B.

nonconformity: An early seventeenth century term descriptive of those Puritans who would neither subscribe nor separate. It included both the Episcopalian and Presbyterian groups of the Puritan party. Some historians have used the term for the Elizabethan Puritans, while others have utilized it as a broad term covering all dissent. After the Restoration, when the Nonconformists were put out of the established church and forced into dissent, the term did take on a broader meaning and was used as a descriptive label for all dissenting Protestant groups. See Dissenter; sect; Separatist. W.S.H.

non expedit: (Lat., it is not expedient) A decree from Rome in 1868 forbidding Italian Catholics to take part in certain elections. L.R.W.

non-jurors: Anglican Bishops and other clergy who refused to break former oaths to James II by swearing allegiance to William and Mary in 1689, and their followers—also later adherents of the sect, whose last Bishop died in 1805. Though few in number, the non-jurors carried much learning and piety out of the Church of England*, to its great loss. In theology their early emphasis on divine right was replaced by one on the spiritual freedom of the Church, growing out of their original refusal to recognize political depositions of Bishops*. In the early 18th cent. they did much for liturgical revival, especially in Scotland (where the Episcopalians generally were non-jurors till 1789). William Law*, controversialist and mystic was their greatest figure, though somewhat isolated among them. The memory of the non-jurors continued to be venerated among Anglo-Catholics*.

Thomas Lathbury, *A History of the Nonjurors* (1845); Henry Broxap, *The Later Nonjurors* (1924). E.R.H.

non-liturgical churches: See liturgics.

none: The office of the ninth hour—but in the Middle Ages often said by anticipation about 12 M., therefore called noon in English. See divine office. E.R.H.

norito: (Jap.) Shinto* prayers recited in Shinto ceremonies by Shinto priests and, in state ceremonies, by high government officials. Classical, stately, dignified, and unique in style and standardized in form, these prayers give thanks to Shinto deities and invoke their blessing. The recitation of *norito* is not only an expression of piety but also a ritual believed to have magical effect. Orthodox prayers are found in the *Engi Shiki** and other classics, and official prayers have been issued by the government in recent years. W.T.C.

Norm day or Norm year: See Westphalian Treaties.

norman: A type of architecture that existed in northern Europe and the British Isles during the latter part of the 11th and through much of the 12th centuries. It is allied closely to the Romanesque*, utilizes the wall-bearing form of construction, its walls are of considerable thickness, its arches usually round and in its later stages its arch rings were richly ornamented.

Many very small churches in the normal style still exist in England, and a number of larger examples as well. Some of the smaller churches seat but 100 or so people. Some have but a simple rectangular nave and a semi-circular apse, as at Nately Scures, 40 miles west of London. Others have a square chancel, separated from the nave by means of a low, massive chancel arch, as at Adel Church, near Leeds. Others have a rectangular chancel, a square central space and a rectangular nave, and with a central tower rising above the roof, as at Iffley, just south of Oxford. In these small churches, the side walls are usually three feet in thickness, and the main entrance is often in the south wall of the nave. The roofs are generally slightly more than 45 degrees in pitch, and supported by simple timber trusses. Windows are very small, and well above the floor level; although in many Norman churches, larger windows were inserted at a later date.

Norman work is often found in the great cathedrals*. At Exeter, the remarkable transeptal towers are Norman. Winchester's transepts are Norman, and much Norman work exists at St. Alban's, Peterboro, Ely and elsewhere. Many cathedrals and parish churches, originally in the Norman style, were enlarged or partially rebuilt in the Gothic style, but still retain portions of Norman work. In the large examples, clerestories are frequently present, supported by massive stone columns. See art, ecclesiastical, Christian; cathedrals; church building. F.R.W.

norns: The three "fates" of Norse mythology, Urd, Verdandi and Skuld. "Maidens, much knowing . . . laws they established, life allotted to the sons of men; destinies pronounced." B. Thorpe's *Völuspa.* P.G.M.

North African Church: (early centuries) A term usually restricted to Christianity in the Roman Provinces of North Africa stretching from Cyrenaica on the East to the Atlantic on the West. See Carthage, Synods of; Scillitan martyrs. S.M.G.

North American Phalanx: See communistic settlements, secular.

Norwegian Lutheran Church: See Lutheran Church in America; Sverdrup, G.

Notarikon: See Kabbalah.

Notre Dame (Fr. *notre dame,* our Lady) Notre Dame or "our Lady" is a title used in many places; e.g., for churches or cathedrals, such as Notre Dame in Paris, in Chartres, and so on, and for shrines such as Notre Dame du Chêne, and pilgrimages; and also in the U. S. for the University of Notre Dame, and the Sisters of Notre Dame, and the Schools Sisters of Notre Dame. L.R.W.

nous: (Greek) Only a mental attribute of a living person, until after the 6th century B.C., when it represents the religious factor in nature, common to all things human and non-human; the unifying factor, having no antithesis in its composition; the destiny-determining link in nature which made 'gods and men' akin. Nous is not the sole, but probably the most representative, word used by Greeks for this universal religious factor. In man it is the determining factor of the psyche, or is completely identified with the psyche. An early tendency to define the nature of the universal nous in antithetical terms led subsequently to a dualism in religious thinking from which historical Christianity, which took it over, never recovered. See Anaxagoras; Neo Platonism; psyche. F.L.P.

Novatian: A Roman Presbyter whose writings reveal considerable doctrinal and exegetical ability. His defence of the Trinity* against the Monarchians* is especially able, though it reveals subordinationist* tendencies. In opposition to the milder policies of Cornelius, bishop of Rome (A.D. 251-253), Novatian denied the right of the Church to restore the *lapsi* and advocated an extremely "purist" conception of church membership. He was chosen bishop by the dissenting party. The result was a schism which spread over most of the Roman empire and which continued to exist until the sixth century. Their strong support of the Nicene orthodoxy won for them friendly treatment from the Catholic Church, though towards the end of the 4th century they began to be treated as heretics. See lapsed. A.K.R.

novena: (Lat., ninth) A nine-days' devotion for some specific purpose or in honor of some saint. While such devotions are not part of the public cultus of the Roman Catholic Church, a number of novenas are authorized. Certain evangelical groups have (unofficially) made use of the term to some extent. P.V.N.

novice: (Lat. *novicius,* new) A person of either sex regularly admitted to a religious order*, usually after a period of preliminary testing, for a more extended probation of at least a year. Having been found free of legal impediments, the novice accepts a habit and gives himself to a formative religious discipline. Subject to arbitrary dismissal, and at the same time free to leave, during this period, he must, upon its completion, be professed, dismissed, or granted further trial. See monasticism. R.C.P.

Noyes, John Humphrey: See Oneida community, the.

number symbolism: See symbolism, Medieval number; neo-Pythagoreanism; Pythagoreanism. Cf. Kabbalah.

numbers, 666, 888: See s.v. beast.

Numbers: The fourth book of the Pentateuch*, which narrates the closing events in the sojourn of the Israelites at Sinai, including the taking of the census from which the book derives its name (1:1-10:10), their wandering for thirty-eight years and journey to the plains of Moab (10:11-22:1), and the events during their stay on the plains of Moab (22:2-36:13). The book is traditionally ascribed to Moses*, but is actually the work of J. E. and P**. The first section was written by P, and the remainder is a combination of the three sources. It is often difficult to disentangle J and E, but the JE material is not closely interwoven with P. P is concerned chiefly with the twofold census, the arrangement of the camp, and ritual laws, while JE consists largely of historical narrative and a few ancient poems. One of the original sources of the book is named in 21:14 as "The Book of the Wars of Yahweh." The authenticity of the basic narrative of JE is hardly to be doubted, but there are few extra-Biblical materials for verifying its details. Some of these details, however, are inherently improbable; for example, the figures given in the census imply a total population during the wilderness sojourn of two million persons or more, far more than the desert could have supported and inconsistent with other Biblical passages (e.g., Judges 5:8). See G. B. Gray, *Numbers* (International Critical Comm. 1912, 2nd ed; J. H. Greenstone, *Numbers* (The Holy Scriptures with Commentary, 1939).

J.P.H.

numen: In Roman religion* a divine power or spirit, anonymous as were most of the indigenous Roman deities, whose presence was felt, but of whose nature and personality they had but the vaguest conception. Cf. kami; mana; wakan.

P.G.M.

numinous: A word coined from the Latin "numen" by Rudolph Otto* to signify the *mysterium tremendum et fascinans* which is the unique object of religious apprehension, beyond reason, the good or the beautiful. The mysterious, awe-inspiring, terrible, holy, sacred quality that is of Deity. See his *Idea of the Holy* (rev. ed., 1925).

V.F.

nun: (Late Lat. *nonna,* an old woman) General designation for a member of a religious order of Catholic women. Canon Law* distinguishes between nuns properly so called, who belong to orders pronouncing solemn vows, and sisters*, who belong to congregations with simple vows. The various orders and congregations engage either in the active or the contemplative life, or in a combination of both. See under abbey.

C.V.

nunc dimittis: The Song of Simeon, Lk. 2, 29-32. The evangelical canticle assigned to Compline* in the Latin Church and used at Vespers among the Eastern Orthodox.

P.V.N.

nuncios: See legates and nuncios, papal.

Nuremberg, Religious Peace of: Made July, 1532, between the Emperor and the Protestants. In return for support in the war against the Turks, the estates were granted peace until the calling of a council or until the next diet.

E.C.K.

Nusku: The Assyrian parallel of the Babylonian god, Girru. A god of fire.

P.G.M.

Nut: Wife of Seb and mother of Isis, Osiris* and other Egyptian gods and goddesses. Usually represented on all fours as the sky, her arms and legs being the horizons, and the stars decorations on her body. Sometimes spelled Nout.

P.G.M.

Nygren, Anders Theodore Samuel: (1890-) Since 1924 Nygren has been professor of theology at the University of Lund. His and colleagues' works have been given name, Lundensian theology*. Nygren has sought to describe essential nature of Christian love, agape, as over against love in a human sense, and re-interpreted history of Christian doctrine to show adulteration of genuine Christian revelation.

C.J.B.

nymphs: (Gr. *Nymphai*) Lithe, graceful female sprites, sportive and gay, usually friendly, but occasionally destructive. They reside in various natural objects: the naiads* in springs, rivers, and lakes, the nereids* in the sea, the oceanids* in ocean, the oreads in the mountains, the dryads* and hamadryads in trees. Possessing certain divine gifts such as prophecy, they are long-lived, though not immortal. Only the dryads and hamadryads are distinctly short-lived, since they die with their trees.

E.M.N.

O

oath more judaico: Special oaths, accompanied by a variety of weird ceremonies, which were imposed on Jews by the courts in the Middle Ages, on the assumption that those outside the dominant faith required special intimidation to tell the truth. B.Z.B.

oaths: The scruple against oaths has been a characteristic of various mystical and perfectionist* groups, including the Anabaptists, Mennonites and Quakers**. Originally based on the Scriptural prohibitions of Matthew 5:34 and James 5:12, it is also prompted by the ideal of a single standard of honesty, which needs no outward sanction for truth-telling. See blessing and cursing; Roman religions. H.G.R.

Obadiah: Similar to Nahum and Habakkuk**, hardly worthy of the name "prophetic." Obadiah was primarily a poet, writing (in contrast with earlier opinion which placed him in the sixth century) shortly after 485 B.C. (Morgenstern) when Edom joined with other nations in unseating Menahem from his assumed throne and in despoiling Judah. Written on the eve of the Arab-Nabatean advance, which was to vanquish Edom, Obadiah cried for revenge on her for what she had done to Judah. See *The Prophets and their Times* by J. M. P. Smith and W. A. Irwin (1941), pp. 265-66. R.E.W.

obedience: The practical submission of one's will and the ordering of one's conduct with reference to what is held to be rightful authority. In ethics it is compliance with the moral law conceived as universally valid. In religion moral obedience to the will of deity may be regarded as the way of salvation or as evidence of piety. The will of God is held to be the absolute good to which one owes submission. In the Roman Catholic Church obedience is one of three monastic vows and requires conformity to the rule of the order and the will of its superior. R.W.F.

Oberammergau, The Passion Play of: See religious drama.

Oberlin, John Frederick (1740-1826) Alsatian pastor, educator, philanthropist, noted for his wise and effective system of Christian work in the Steinthal, an impoverished district in the Vosges Mountains. Here he lived most of his long life, building roads, improving agriculture, founding infant schools, and transforming the whole life of the region, materially and spiritually. Oberlin College in Ohio bears his name. He has influenced rural reconstruction movements in many distant lands, including Brazil and China. W.M.H.

Oberlin theology: A term applied to the theology that prevailed at Oberlin under the administrations of Charles G. Finney* and James H. Fairfield. Most characteristic teachings: duty of Christian perfection and "the simplicity of moral action"; i.e., a Christian's will was either utterly surrendered to God at a given moment, and hence perfectly holy, or else not so surrendered and hence perfectly unholy. The Oberlin theology may be regarded as a further development of **Taylorism***.

F. H. Foster, *A Genetic History of the New England Theology* (1907). W.M.H.

oblate: (Lat. *oblatus,* offered) A lay person who, though not monk or nun, joins in some rules and works of a religious order and shares in its benefits. See Catholic Societies. L.R.W.

obligation: A bond or necessity laid upon one to act in a certain way or to do a certain thing. The binding power may arise from the external compulsion of law and custom or it may come from internal moral constraint. In the latter case religion interprets the obligation as having its ultimate ~~ground in the moral goodness~~ and sovereignty of God as man's creator while acknowledging its immediate source in the moral nature of man. See natural rights. R.W.F.

Observants: Members of a reform movement within the R. C. Order of Friars Minor* (Franciscans). They advocated and practised a return to the original strictness of the rule of St. Francis. St. Bernardine of Siena (1380-1444 A.D.) was the most famous early member. The movement existed from the 13th to the end of the 19th century and during part of that time constituted a separate branch of the Franciscan* Order. In 1897 the Friars Minor were unified by order of the Pope into a single Order. V.J.B.

obsession: An idea or notion that persistently invades and engrosses the mind, is usually inaccessible to critical appraisal and tends to control thought, feeling and action. Formerly attributed to demonic possession or spiritualistic control; latterly traced to suggestion and subconscious drives. The group consciousness is regarded by some as liable to obsessional ideas. R.W.F.

occasionalism: A theory of causality to explain the interaction of mind and body, inexplicable (even by pineal gland) on dualistic Cartesian principles, by assuming that man's willing a certain act is the "occasional cause" for God to make a corresponding change in the physical world, and vice versa. The theory was developed by Arnold Geulincx*, who held that God is the sole cause both of perceptions in the mind and of bodily movements. Nicholas Malebranche taught that God produces in man a world of ideas which correspond to the corporeal world he has created and therefore we "behold all things in God." The view led to pantheism and determinism, although it was later adapted to theism by a personalist like Bowne*. See Cartesianism. J.E.N.

occultism: (Derived from "*occulo*" I conceal) A name given to a loosely organized group of rejected sciences—Astrology, Alchemy, Palmistry, and so on. Sundry writers have attempted to gather the *disjecta membra* of these human wanderings in blind alleys, to salvage what each considered worth saving, to build therefrom his own system. The word was favorably regarded by early Theosophists*. Cf. parapsychology.

A. W. Lair, *The Great Mystery* (1938). P.G.M.

Oceanids: (Gr . *Okeanides,* from *Okeanós,* Ocean; *id-*, patronymic) The 4000 daughters of Ocean and Tethys. In Homer, Ocean is the Great River which encircles the flat disc of earth, returning to itself; in Hesiod, he is personified as one of the Titans, father of the Oceanids. See nymphs. E.M.N.

Ockham, William of: (1280-1349) A fourteenth century Scholastic philosopher and polemical writer. Desiring to reform the method and content of Scholasticism*, he aimed at simplification and tended toward skepticism. He denied the existence of intentional species, the distinction between essence* and existence, and the Thomistic doctrine of active and passive intellect. In ethics he maintained that the distinction between right and wrong depends on God's free will. His theory on universals is a modified Nominalism*. Although rejecting the rational proofs for several truths which are basic to Catholic theology, he nevertheless adhered firmly to these truths from reasons of faith. See foreknowledge, Divine; law of parsimony; twofold-truth theory.

E. A. Moody, *The Logic of William of Ockham* (1936). C.V.

octave: The prolongation of a festival for eight days, brought into the Western church year* by analogy from Jewish festivals. E.R.H.

Odin or Odhin: (Teut.) One of the chief gods of early Sweden; middle member of the Norse triad with Thor and Freyr; an aristocratic court-god; wandering war-god to whom warriors appeal for help; as war-god he receives human sacrifices. Due to outside influences Odhin is represented as lord of the Hall of the Dead (Valhalla), the wise god of the court poets. Due to Christian influence he is also represented as the creator and director of the world, a sky-god, an all-father god. His omens are carried by wolves and ravens. He is pictured riding a gray horse, wearing a cloak, and carrying a spear. See Woden. F.L.P.

Oecolampadius, Johannes: (1482-1531) (Oecolampadius, Greek for candlestick, his name having been Heussgen—pronounced Hausschein) Born in Wurtemberg, he assisted Erasmus* in publishing his Greek N.T., was influenced first by Luther, then by Zwingli. He became the reformer of Basel. E.C.K.

Oesterreich, Traugott Konstantin: (1880-) He is professor of philosophy in Tübingen, Germany; and is the author of the fourth volume of the 12th ed. of Uberweg's *Geschichte der Philosophie* (Berlin, 1923). He upholds the indestructibility and identity of the ego. The essence of religion consists for him in specific states of exaltation in which man experiences values of a particular scale of quality. Expressing themselves in affective and conative relations, these experiences are a complete justification of religion, even if intellectual faith is in error. Oesterreich made penetrative analyses of obsession, vision, glossolalia and inspiration and their significance in the history of religion. He is the leading student of the religious significance of the parapsychological* data.

Die Phänomenologie des Ich in ihren Grundlagen (Leipzig, 1910); *Einführung in die Religionspsychologie als Grundlage f. Religionsgeschichte und Religionsphilosophie* (Berlin, 1917); *Grundbegriffe der Parapsychologie* (Pfullingen, 1921); *Occultism and modern science* (1927); *Possession, demoniacal and other.* (1930). H.H.

Oetinger, Friedrich Christoph: (1702-1782) A Swabian theologian whose biblical realism was an interweaving of spirit and nature, of consciousness and unconsciousness. As a pupil of J. A. Bengel* he burst the limits of the orthodox-pietistic attitude. Faithful to the biblical Lutheran belief, he strove towards a *philosophia sacra* in which Christ receives a cosmic-metaphysical significance.

Theologia ex idea vitae deducta (Frankfurt u. Leipzig, 1765); *Werke.* 11 vols. ed. by K. C. E. Ehmann (Stuttgart, 1858-63); K. A. Auberlen, *Über die Theosophie Oetingers* (Tübingen, 1847). H.H.

Oettingen, Alexander v.: (1827-1906) He was professor at the University of Dorpat (now Tartu, Estonia). He gave ethics a new turn by combining Schleiermacher's conception, the romantic conception of organism, the modern realism, the awakening of the social question and the experience of the rise of modern nationalism with the Christian conception. He gave his ethics empirical and statistical bases. His social ethics was an opposition against every spiritualistic personal ethic and against every materialistic social physics. It was Emil Brunner* who in our day revived Oettingen's importance.

Die christliche Sittenlehre (Erlangen, 1873), 2 vols.; *Die Moralstatistik in ihrer Bedeutung für eine Socialethik.* 3 ed. vol. II of his *Die christliche Sittenlehre.* (Erlangen, 1882). H.H.

offertory: Traditionally employed to describe the presentation of the bread and wine before their consecration, in the Eucharistic rite. In ancient days (cf. Hippolytus' *Apostolic Tradition,* c. 215), other articles were also presented at this time, and offered to God for blessing. Later, the term was restricted to the eucharistic elements. An appropriate selection from the Psalms is said or sung here (also called the Offertory). In Protestant denominations, the term has been taken to mean the presenting of alms, or the taking of a collection during a church service, and the choir anthem sung at this time. See plainsong; psalmody. W.N.P.

Office, Sacred Congregation of the Holy: An administrative branch of the Roman Catholic Church, erected in 1542 as a continuation and supersession of the Universal Roman Inquisition*. Its purpose is the protection of faith and morals, and to that end it passes judgment on heresies, dogmatic teachings on the sacraments and indulgences, impediments to marriage with non-Catholics, books considered pernicious or contrary to faith (Index*), etc. The pope is the prefect of this congregation, and its decisions are not considered infallible. J.F.T.

office of the dead: Service of psalms and lessons modelled on Vespers, Matins, and Lauds of the Divine Office*, used in commemoration of the dead or as part of funeral service; used in Roman rite since c. 800, and basis of Anglican Burial Office. See prayers for the dead. E.R.H.

oharai or ohoharahi: (Lit. "Great Expulsion") The Japanese purification ritual. D.C.H.

oils: The Bishop consecrates three holy oils on Holy Thursday. 1) Oil of Catechumens (O.C.), named derived from the use of oil in the baptism of Catechumens*. It is also used in the consecration of churches, blessing of altars, ordination of priests, and in the coronation of Catholic monarchs. 2) Chrism (S.C.), mixture of olive oil and balsam used at Baptism, Confirmation, Holy Orders; in the consecration of churches, altars, chalices, patens; in the blessing of bells and baptismal water. 3) Oil of the Sick (O.C.), olive oil used in Extreme Unction*. See anointing; chrism. B.R.

Olavus Petri: See Petri, Olavus.

old Calvinists: See Calvinists, old.

Old Catholics: A group of Churches professing loyalty to ancient Catholic principles, but repudiating such Tridentine* and later Roman decisions as do not conform thereto. Owing to difficulties caused by disputes between Jesuits and secular clergy (accused of Jansenism*), the Chapter of Utrecht has elected Archbishops independent of Rome since 1723. After 1870 German and Swiss Catholics who rejected the Vatican Council* formed Old Catholic Churches, obtaining episcopal succession from Holland. The Declaration of Utrecht, 1889, is the common doctrinal basis. There are probably about 20,000 Old Catholics in Holland, 50,000 in Switzerland, rather more in Germany (including German Austria and Czechoslovakia); some in Jugoslavia, and the Polish National Catholic Church in U. S. and Poland is affiliated—first Bishop consecrated at Utrecht, 1907. Certain unhappy consecrations have produced other self-styled Old Catholic Churches, repudiated by Utrecht. Within Old Catholic principles the Dutch tend to be conservative, Germans nationalist, Swiss liberal; Utrecht has followed the others in allowing marriage of clergy and adopting a vernacular liturgy (1909). There is a Seminary at Amersfoort, Netherlands, and a theological faculty at Bern. Interest in reunion on constitutional Catholic lines led to Bonn Conferences of 1874-5; the Old Catholics share in ecumenical movements, and intercommunion with Anglicans has been established on basis of mutual recognition (Bonn Agreement, 1931, since generally ratified). Cf. Döllinger; Liberal Catholic Church.

J. M. Neale, *History of the so-called Jansenist Church of Holland* (1858); B. A. VanKleef, "An Outline of the History of the Old Catholic Church," in Williams and Harris, *Northern Catholicism* (1933); *Internationale Kirchliche Zeitschrift,* (theological periodical), Bern. E.R.H.

Old Latin version: See versions of the Bible, ancient.

Old Lights: A nick-name applied to those who opposed revivalism among New England Congregationalists in the Colonial Awakening. W.W.S.

old Lutherans: See s.v. American Lutheranism.

old Mennonites: See Mennonites.

Old Order or Yorker Brethren: See River Brethren.

Old Roman Symbol: Early in the twentieth century, Professor A. C. McGiffert* of the Union Theological Seminary ably contended that the entire *Apostles' Creed* was pointed against the heretic Marcion*; identification of Creator-God with Father of Jesus; Jesus with son of Creator-God; genuine sonship not adopted at baptism; judge; resurrection of the flesh. In 1919 Karl Holl proposed a new interpretation of origin of *Apostles' Creed* which is now rather generally supported. See Apostles' Creed; creeds of Christendom. C.H.M.

Old School Presbyterian Church: See for origin: New School Presbyterian Church. The Old

School party, controlling the General Assembly at the division of the Presbyterian Church* in 1837, carried on the organization of the church, while the New School also continued the church from 1838. The Old School, comprising about five-ninths of the church, was located chiefly from Pennsylvania south and west. The Old School party, which had been in controversy with the New School before 1837, was conservative and the Old School Church was of this character. It maintained a strict interpretation of the standards of the church in doctrine and polity, against liberalizing tendencies of the New School; it favored church boards for missions and education. Because of its large southern element the Old School Church took no stand against slavery. During the separation it grew more than the New School, but in 1861 it lost its southern presbyteries, which withdrew to form the Presbyterian Church in the Confederate States of America. This in 1865 became the Presbyterian Church in the United States, still existing. The Old School and New School reunited in 1869, "each recognizing the other as a sound and orthodox body". See American theology, early.
R.H.N.

Old Side Presbyterians: American Presbyterians who doubted the value of the Great Awakening* and disapproved of the methods of its supporters, the New Side* men, particularly the practice of itinerating in other ministers' parishes, what they considered censorious and denunciatory preaching, and emotional outbreaks. They insisted on full academic education for the ministry, were conservative theologically and stood for strict ecclesiastical discipline. They were almost all Scotch-Irish. When the Synod was divided in 1741 the Old Side maintained its organization in the Synod of Philadelphia. The two Sides reunited in 1758 as the Synod of New York and Philadelphia.
R.H.N.

Old Syriac version: See versions of the Bible, ancient.

Old Testament, early Christian use of: In the time of Christ it was taken for granted by all pious Jews that the books of the O.T. contained the express revelation of God's will. All the N.T. writings are based on this assumption, and the O.T. is constantly quoted, and its word on every question is accepted as final. Paul is never satisfied unless he can adduce a text of scripture in support of any statement he makes. He believes that he himself possesses the Spirit; he is anxious, too, as a Hellenistic thinker, to find rational proof for what he believes. Yet he regards all other evidence as valid only when it is confirmed by the word of God himself as given in scripture. This is the attitude of all the N.T. writers, and finds expression in the formulae by which scriptural quotations are introduced: "It is written"; "The Holy Spirit says"; "The scripture says"; "God said through the prophet". Particular O.T. writers are rarely mentioned, and when they are named it is always understood that they were only the mouthpieces of the divine voice. This reliance on scripture might seem difficult to reconcile with the Christian belief that a new revelation, superseding all others, had been given through Christ. It was apparent, too, that the Christian position was often widely at variance with that of the O.T. There was the further objection that the O.T. books, written by different men over a long period of time, often contradicted each other, so that support for almost any view could be found somewhere in scripture. These difficulties, however, were overcome in various ways. 1) By subtle exegesis a new meaning was assigned to the biblical text. 2) The text was expounded allegorically, and so brought into harmony with Christian truth. 3) Scripture was answered by scripture. Among conflicting texts there was always one which came nearer than the others to the Christian position, and this one was chosen as revealing the true mind of God. Jesus himself adopted this method. He never challenged the authority of scripture, and his enemies pointed out, ever and again, that it was opposed to his teaching. On each of these occasions he quoted some verse which was in agreement with his own thought, and which cancelled the others. The later writers follow this method of Jesus, and are never hampered by scripture. They can invariably find some text which answers their purpose, and on the strength of this they can claim that scripture is on their side. Thus it is only in appearance that the N.T. teaching is based on the O.T. The real authority is the gospel as proclaimed by Jesus, and by this standard the word of scripture is itself tested. Most of the quotations are from the Psalms and the Prophets. All the O.T. books are formally acknowledged to be on the same level, and there are stray references to almost all of them; but the Christian mind fastened on those writings which are nearest in spirit to the gospel. It has been observed that the same texts appear repeatedly, sometimes in a cluster, and from this it has been inferred that the church used an abbreviated Bible, made up of O.T. passages which appeared to foreshadow the work of Christ. Quotations are made for the most part from the LXX version (see Septuagint), but sometimes the Hebrew Bible is used directly, particularly in the Synoptic Gospels and the book of Revelation. The O.T., in its Greek form, continued for more than a century to be the Bible of the church, and is quoted as freely by Gentile as by Jewish writers. It was only in the middle of the 2nd century that the need for a distinctively Christian scripture began to make itself felt. The movement in this direction came first from heretical teachers like Marcion*, who were shocked by the discrepancy between Christian beliefs and many statements in the O.T. When the N.T. came into being there was a danger for some time that the O.T. might be discarded. Its preservation was due, partly to the sound judgment of the church at large, and partly to the growing aversion to Gnosticism* and all the ideas connected with it.

R. Harris: *Testimonies* (1920); C. H. Toy, *Quotations in the N.T.* (1884).
E.F.S.

Old Testament Books, the, in chronological order: See Books of the Old Testament, the, in chronological order.

Old Testament, literature: The Christian name for the Jewish Scriptures, which constitute the first of the two parts of the Christian Bible. In its principal English versions it comprises the thirty-nine books of the Jewish Canon, which is written in Hebrew, with brief sections in Aramaic. The word "testament" (Lat. *vetus testamentum*) came into use through the ambiguous meaning of Gr. *diathēkē* (agreement, testament) by which Heb. *berith* (covenant) was translated in the Septuagint (LXX)* version. The Jewish Scriptures are first in 2 Cor. 3:14 called "the old covenant (or, testament)", i.e., through Moses* (cf. Exod. 34:27,28) in contrast to the new covenant through Christ (2 Cor. 3:6, cf. Mark 14:24, following Jer. 31:31). By the end of the 2nd century this had become the established Christian designation for the Jewish Scriptures (cf. Origen: *De Princip.* iv:i).

The O.T. comprises a variety of literature composed during the first millennium B.C., as preserved and edited in Judaism for religious purposes, and increasingly regarded (especially the Law, Prophets and Psalms) as authoritative for religion. The beginning of a canon or authoritative collection of sacred writings is seen in the reverential treatment accorded a book found in the temple in 621 B.C., apparently an earlier edition of Deuteronomy (2 Kings 22-23). This book was accepted as the written form of a prophetic utterance (in this case of Moses), and on the same principle the canon was expanded in subsequent centuries; all books included were ascribed to authors of a prophetic succession ending with the 5th century, though in fact many of them were composed or expanded later than this. The five books of Moses (Pentateuch, Torah), as successively enlarged from the book found in 621, were canonical scripture by the 4th century B.C.; as such they were translated into Gr. at Alexandria in the 3rd century (the LXX). The Torah has remained Jewish scripture par excellence. A second group of books, the Prophets*, attained final form and (in Palestine) canonicity of a second rank c. 200 B.C. In the LXX, however, these were not distinguished from a third group of more miscellaneous books, the Writings, which was gradually formed with the Psalms as a nucleus (cf. Luke 24:44), and the limits of which in the Heb. canon were determined by rabbinic decision c. 100 A.D. The Gr. version included other books (the Apocrypha), not found in the Heb. Bible, and since this was the first Christian Bible these are held as canonical by the R. C. Church (Council of Trent, 1546-), whereas Protestantism (following Jerome) has adhered to the Heb. canon.

The standard text of the O.T. is that edited by ben Asher in Palestine in the 10th century A.D., concluding the labours of Rabbinic scholars through 800 years to establish and safeguard a uniform text. The autographs had already long since disappeared, and Heb. MSS. now extant (except for a few fragments) are not older than the 10th century. Witnesses to earlier variations in the O.T. text are the ancient Versions, of which the LXX is the chief. This is the Greek O.T. derived by Christians from the Bible of the Alexandrian Jews which has not otherwise survived; it was translated from Heb. in the 3rd to 1st centuries B.C., and is found in MSS. of the 4th century A.D. and later. In the 3rd century Origen* collated the LXX with other Gr. versions, and brought the LXX into line with the existing Heb. text. Derived from the LXX are the Syriac translation of the Hexaplaric text, the Old Lat., Coptic, Ethiopic and other Versions. The Syriac Peshitta (2nd-3rd centuries) and the Lat. Vulgate of Jerome (390-405) were translated from Heb., (except for the Vulg. Psalter which is Jerome's revision of the Old Lat. from the Hexapla). The classical English version is the King James version of 1611, which climaxed the succession of translations by Tyndale (1530-31, partial), Coverdale (1535, from Vulg. and German), the "Matthew Bible" (1537), the "Great Bible" (1539), the Genevan Bible (1560) and the "Bishops' Bible" (1568). A Revised Version was published in England 1881-85 and in the U. S. A. in 1901; a further revision is now in progress.

Critical examination of the contents of the O.T. has demonstrated that the (late) Jewish traditions as to authorship are mistaken, that most of its books are composite and all bear the marks of editing in various periods. The order of the books is chronological neither in the Heb. canon nor in the LXX (followed by Eng. O.T., omitting Apocrypha), but is to some extent topical.

The Pentateuch is a corpus of religious and civil law ascribed to Moses in a narrative setting (Exodus from Egypt, Covenant at Sinai-Horeb, 40 years' wanderings), together with an introduction (Genesis) relating the origins of the earth, of mankind and of Israel. It has been edited from various materials, including continuous documents (J, E, D, P**), mainly of the 9th-4th centuries, but incorporating more ancient fragments of folk song, legends, and possibly reminiscences of Moses' teachings. The "Former Prophets", (Joshua-2 Kings), are a sequel to the Pentateuch narrating the history of Israel and Judah from the conquest of Canaan (13th century) to the fall of Jerusalem (586); they were edited chiefly in the 6th century, and (apart from Joshua) incorporate much authentic historical matter.

The "Latter Prophets" comprise a) the literary remains of the oracular prophets of the 8th-5th centuries (oracles, i.e., rhythmic utterances of the Word of Yahweh, together with memoirs and narratives), and b) derivative literary prophecy of the 6th-3rd centuries, partly in the form of supplements to a). The books of Isaiah 1-39, Amos, Hosea and Micah contain substantial remains from these prophets of the 8th century, as do Jeremiah, Zephaniah, Nahum and Habakkuk (?) from the 7th century (Jer. continues into the 6th century), Obadiah, Haggai and Zechariah 1-8 from the 6th century, and Malachi from the 5th century. Jonah is a 5th century prophetic parable. Isaiah 40-66 (with 35) includes the greatest of the written prophecies (6th or 5th centuries); Ezekiel includes remains of 6th century oral prophecy but in its present form is a 4th century literary work; Joel dates from the 4th century, Zechariah 9-14 from the 3rd or 2nd centuries.

The remaining books of the O.T. (the Writings) are: the Psalms, a much edited collection of liturgical and devotional poems ranging in origin from the 10th-2nd century; Proverbs, a collection of religio-ethical teachings in gnomic couplets and in longer poems, 6th-3rd centuries; Job, dramatic poem with prose prologue, 6th-3rd centuries (?); Song of Songs, love lyrics related to fertility cult, 4th-3rd centuries; Ruth, parabolic romance, based on fact, 4th century; Lamentations, small Psalter of dirges over Jerusalem, 6th-4th centuries; Ecclesiastes, the philosophy of a Jewish agnostic, 3rd-2nd centuries; Esther, a secular, nationalist romance, 2nd century; Daniel, cc. 1-6, edifying tales of faithful Jews, 3rd century, cc. 7-12, apocalyptic visions, 2nd century; Ezra-Nehemiah, a history of the post-exilic reconstitution of Judaism, by the author(s) of Chronicles, 4th-3rd centuries. Chronicles, an ecclesiastical, apologetic re-writing of pre-Exilic history, 4th-3rd centuries. See under specific books of O.T.; apocrypha, Old Testament; canon, Old and New Testament; manuscripts of the Bible; versions of the Bible, ancient. See also Books of the O.T., the, in chronological order.

O. Eissfeldt, *Einleitung in das Alte Testament* (1934); R. H. Pfeiffer, *Introduction to the Old Testament* (1941); *Abingdon Bible Commentary* (1929), edited by F. C. Eiselen, E. Lewis and D. G. Downey.

R.B.Y.S.

Olevianus: See Heidelberg Catechism; Ursinus.

Olivetans: An offshoot of the white monks of the Order of Saint Benedict, founded by Saint Bernard Ptolemei on his mountain-top estate, Mount Olivet, near Siena, and approved by John XXII in 1319. Though more rigorous at first than the Benedictines*, whose rule it copied, the order was graced with a flexible constitution which kept it in close harmony with the age, and accounted in part for its comparatively quick growth and widespread influence. The famous Benedictine reform, from which the present Cassinese Congregation resulted, is considered by many authorities to be attributable to the Olivetans. At present the monasteries and members of the order are small in number.

J.F.T.

Ollé-Laprune, Leon: (1830-1899) One of the greatest precursors of French modernism. Preoccupied with the problem of moral certainty, he combatted fideism* and intellectualism. His conception of original sin was opposed to that of Luther, Calvin and Jansenism. To him human reason and will were insufficient but not impotent. Catholicism was for him the only form of religion which corresponds with human life.

La philosophie et le temps présent (Paris, 1890); *Le prix de la vie* (Paris, 1893); *De la certitude morale* (Paris, 1898), 2 ed.; M. Blondel, *Ollé-Laprune* (Paris, 1932).

H.H.

Olney hymns: See hymns:

Olshausen, Justus: (1800-1882) Christian German orientalist. Professor of oriental languages at Kiel and Königsberg. His scientific activity was only partly devoted to O.T. criticism and theology. His commentary on the Psalms* (Leipzig, 1853) was epoch-making in its textual and historical criticism. His first work on the O.T. was a series of emendations, published in 1826. He was also a pioneer in the modern study of Hebrew grammar, forming a system opposed to that of Ewald*.

H.K.—L.F.

Olsson, Olof: (1841-1900) Born in Sweden, and ordained, 1863, after studies at Upsala, Olsson emigrated in 1869 and became the spiritual leader of the Swedish settlement at Lindsborg, Kansas. In 1876 he became professor at Augustana College and Theological Seminary at Rock Island, Illinois, and was president of this institution 1891-1900. He opposed the Socinian doctrine of the atonement as preached by Waldenstrom* in Sweden, and combined in his character a warm pietism with broad humanistic interests. At Lindsborg and Rock Island he was ahead of his time in the place he gave art and music in the liberal arts. His charitable nature found expression in movements leading to the Deaconess Institute at Omaha and the Augustana Hospital at Chicago.

C.J.B.

Oltramare, Paul: (1854-1930) A Swiss indologue and historian of religions. He assigned to the origin and value of religion an essentially positivist interpretation. Ignorance and impotence are the basis of all religions. With the progress of civilization, notably of science, industry and poetry, the *raison d'être* of religion diminishes increasingly. Spiritually man gains nothing by religion as he can achieve all that religion is able to give by other means. Revelations disclose nothing transcendental, only the desires, sentiments and illusions of their all too human intermediaries. The human soul does not yearn by nature for eternity, infinity, transcendence or the absolute. The immense services religion rendered to mankind do not necessarily prove its truths nor that it always is indispensable. As the spirit goes from conquest to conquest in the other domains, the church with its superannuated dogmas, its incomprehensible cult, and its absurd formulas, impoverishes the spirit. Oltramare proposes to substitute for religion biosophy, human wisdom, the science that shows men the way to the spiritualization of their existence.

La théosophie brahmanique (Paris, 1906); *Vivre. Essai de biosophie théorique et pratique* (Geneve, 1919); *La théosophie bouddhique* (Paris 1923); *La religion et la vie de l'ésprit* (Paris, 1925).

H.H.

Olympus: (Gr. *Olympos*) 1) A mountain in southern Thessaly, overlooking the Vale of Tempe.

The loftiest peak in Greece (9794 ft.), always cloud-capped, it was reputed to be the home of the gods. Whence the epithet of the Olympian Zeus. 2) Mysian Olympus, a peak in northwestern Asia Minor. E.M.N.

om: A mystical Indian symbol upon which devout Hindus of all schools meditate. Spelled also "aum" it serves to express the nature of Brahman or the world soul, represented in the three manifestations, Brahma, creator, Vishnu, preserver, and Shiva, destroyer. Properly used it is a powerful spell. It is usually pronounced at the beginning of the recitation of the *mantras**. C.S.B.

Oman, John Wood: (1860-1939) Professor of theology at Westminster College, Cambridge, 1907-1935. A leader in British liberal theological thought, he wrote several books urging that the conception of infallible revelation and the older ideas of faith, salvation, and grace are less consistent with the spirit of Christianity as a whole, and less compatible with morality than the thesis that religion is personal insight into sacred values, obligation, and the personal relation of the individual to God. In his most important work, *The Natural and the Supernatural,* he defends this personal insight as a veridical but specially religious form of knowing, contrasted with the abstract thought of science, closer to the experience of the poet or the child. He criticizes psychological theories of religion which "explain away"; he asserts rather that religious experience can be reasonably supposed to be a response or adjustment to the (in this case, supernatural) environment like any others of man's higher capacities. This insight, he holds, introduces man to absolute values, and to a fuller comprehension of the world as akin, and responsive, to human ideals and purposes. See religious datum.

The Natural and the Supernatural (1931); *Grace and Personality* (1917); *The Problem of Faith and Freedom* (1906); *Vision and Authority* (1929); and others. R.B.B.

omen: (Lat., *osmen;* possibly from *audire,* hear and-men) Occurrence or object supposed to portend or show the character of a future event. A wider usage among two-factor religions*; related to the subject of divination*: the endeavor to obtain information about things future or otherwise removed from ordinary perception, by consulting sources other than human. Omens are used a) in relation to a system built up, as is divination, from vaguely interpreted recurrences in nature; and b) apart from such systems.

What constitutes an omen, either good or bad, varies widely with peoples of the world. They derive from dreams, ghosts, man's bodily acts, ordeals, from behavior of animals, plants and other objects in the natural world. The use of omens survives to a considerable degree among peoples of complex religious systems. F.L.P.

omnipotence: (Lat., *omnis,* all; *potens,* powerful) Power over all things, the perfect form of power. It is sometimes viewed as a monopolistic concentration of power—the wielding, by one agent, of all the power there is or could be. This implies that all other beings are powerless. But if "being is power" (Plato), then power over being is power over power, and the ideal or perfect agent will enjoy the optimal concentration of efficacy which is compatible with there being other efficacious agents. This is the social view of being and power, according to which even the greatest possible or perfect power (see perfection) "influences", rather than coerces or fully determines, the partly self-determined actions of others. The non-social or monopolistic view seems to be involved when it is said that omnipotence conflicts with human freedom, or that the omnipotent must be able to prevent all evil, that is, render others powerless to produce it.

The social conception of divine power implies two things: 1) the reality of secondary causes, causes other than the supreme cause; 2) the ability of secondary causes to produce effects even upon the primary agent himself. 1) was denied by Occasionalism*, but asserted by Thomism and most theologians. 2) was until recently generally denied. God was said never to be passive or acted upon in any relation. But this meant that secondary causes produced no effects that were real as measured by the being of God, since their effects made no difference to him, and thus, since his omniscience* is the measure of reality, the effects could not be real after all. To avoid this and other paradoxes or contradictions there is today a strong tendency to combine 1) and 2), making influence between God and creatures a fully social relation.

It is often held that "omnipotence" cannot be used for the social view, since the term means "power to do all things"—absolute or unlimited power—whereas power which is shared is limited or relative. But if power is in principle shared, then the ideal power, though in a sense relative, need not be "limited" if this means, "less than the greatest possible." The greatest possible power cannot be absolute or monopolistic, if being is essentially social. The possibility of an absolute monopoly is too controversial to put into the definition of so universally used a term as omnipotence. Furthermore, ideally great social power may be truly absolute in goodness, the "unqualifiedly righteous" as well as the greatest possible power, relative only in the sense of involving some sort of partial dependence upon others for the effects it achieves (including effects upon its own being). One may question whether all-powerfulness, as a religious idea, ever has meant unqualified power to do all things, leaving nothing else for others to do. For instance, it has not meant power to commit sins or to repent of sins. There has always been a distinction between God's power and the power or powers that effect evil. Finally, to say, with the high religions, that God "loves" us, accords ill with denying that we make any difference to him by our actions, or effect in him any joy or sorrow which he would not as well have had without us. Just as the greatest possible power may be the same as the optimal form and degree of power, but not the same as a power-monopoly, so the greatest possible independence, or freedom from effects produced by others, may be the same as the optimal or best way and degree of suffering (or enjoying) such effects, but quite different from the zero degree. To be influenced, no matter how appropriately and excellently, by others, will seem a defect only to one who sees no meaning to "ideally appropriate reception of influences."

Omnipotence is influence (and susceptibility to influence) ideal in quality, degree, and scope, so that all beings are subject to its optimal (not absolute) control. This control is "irresistible" in the sense that no being can simply withdraw from its reach, and that nothing can prevent it from continuing its beneficent work everlastingly. Thus the idea of some skeptics that it is at least barely possible that all existence should cease, vanish into non-entity, is a denial of the omnipotence of God, who exists necessarily, and whose continued existence in some sphere of activity or universe cannot fail.

Since a social result is jointly produced by mutual influences, the best possible power will not be best in that no greater results than it achieves were possible, but in that such better results were possible, not because the supreme power might have been more supreme, but because the lesser powers might have been less inferior. Thus a best possible power in God need not imply a best possible world; for any possible world is in part self-determined, a world of partly self-made and self-making constituents. Further, if the very meaning of power is social interaction, then mechanical analogies should give way in theology to those drawn from the higher life of man. God does not, then, "make" the world as a carpenter makes a table, with the alleged difference that his material is "nothing" rather than wood; he leads the world as a father leads his children, the good father being he whose sensitiveness enables him also to be led by each child in proportion to the ability of each to contribute to life, including even, or especially, the life of the father. If this proportionality of passivity admits ideal perfection—and why should it not—then only God could possess such perfection. And proportional passivity, not the traditional impassivity, seems to describe God as the being imitation of whom constitutes the ideal for human striving. Mere independence of others seems not a valid ideal, but a caricature of the error of Stoicism.

See attributes of God; cause; God as personal; infinite; perfect; transcendence.

G. T. Fechner, *Zendavesta* (1851), Chapter 11; A. E. Garvie, *The Christian Faith* (1937); O. Pfleiderer, *Grundriss der Christlichen Glaubens- und Sittenlehre* (1888).

C.H.

omnipresence: Property (of deity) of being in all places and things. Sometimes said (as by Kant*) to be merely virtual, a presence as to power or control, not as to being; but others hold that space and time being essentially patterns of interaction, where a thing acts (and is acted upon) is where it actually is. So far as two things interact directly, without time lapse or mediation by other things, they are, on this view, in the same place. "My neighbor is he with whom I intimately interact." (Peirce*). Omnipresence is opposed, not only to total, but also to partial, absence, or localization—action upon this thing and not upon that (unless perhaps ineffective, negligible action).

Except God, entities are present only partially or locally, so that when it is said God is not really in space, it may be meant that he suffers no localization, no limitation upon his active relations with things.

Presence relatively without localization is a common phenomenon. The human mind seems to be in many parts of the brain at once, not in some one atom or point. This gives analogical basis for conceiving strict omnipresence. If all things are to God's mind as brain cells, that is, each directly contributing and receiving influences to and from his consciousness, then God is strictly everywhere, present but non-localized. Newton's* "Space is the sensorium of God" seems to point in this direction. Even Thomism* uses this analogy.

The reason more was not made of it is that God was supposed, by nearly all theologians until recently, to act but not to interact, to impart influences but receive none. On this, see G. W. Leibniz*, Correspondence with Clarke—*Opera philosophica* (ed. by Erdmann, 1840), 746 ff.

See infinity; omnipotence; transcendence.

C.H.

omniscience: (Lat., *omnis*, all; *scire*, know) Knowledge of all things, perfect knowledge. Traditionally, "all things" was taken to include future events as determinate in every detail, whereas many recent thinkers deny that there are any such entities as determinate future events and hold, with Gerson*, Socinus, *et. al.*, that God knows the future as it is, as more or less indeterminate. As the future becomes present, or the indeterminate determinate, there will be new facts for God to know. Thus "knowledge of all facts" does not necessarily imply in the knower, either foreknowledge* in the traditional sense or immutability; for the "all" may not be a sum eternally complete, but a growing totality which must be known temporally if at all.

An explanation of omniscience sometimes given is that the Cause of all, in knowing himself and his power, necessarily knows what he is able to produce, hence knows all things. But this would imply only that God knows all possible worlds as possible, and not that he knows just which world, of those he might produce, he actually does produce. If knowledge-of-the-world-as-actual is contained in God's self-knowledge, then the actuality of the world must be part of the divine being, and if this actuality is contingent, then there must be contingency in God. It seems, indeed, self-evident, that infallible knowledge-of-X must have X as part of its own being. Human knowledge seems often not to contain its objects, but human knowledge is in large part highly indirect, and for this very reason highly fallible.

Perfect immediate knowledge can hardly have the actuality of its objects simply outside itself. This does not imply "pantheism"* in the usual sense; for there may be two aspects of God, only one of which knows or contains contingent things (see pantheism, panentheism, transcendence).

The knower of all facts must know the facts of evil. Does this make evil a part of God? To know the quality of suffering, it seems that one must suffer. An idea of a feeling depends for its content entirely upon possession, at some time at least, of a feeling of the kind in question. It may seem that we can know as a fact that another is suffering without ourselves suffering at the time, but this knowledge is pale and abstract, and even it is dependent upon past suffering of our own. Traditional treatments of omniscience (as "impassive", wholly independent, etc.), seem to imply that God's knowing is akin to our most abstract and indirect awareness of things, a "knowledge about" not a "knowledge by acquaintance", remote not intimate, and by implication fallible and inadequate in the highest degree. And even so the implication remains that if God knows about suffering he must also in some measure be acquainted with it, that is, feel it. Thus the idea of a suffering God, who knows our sorrows by sharing them, is the only consistent, as it is the most religiously inspiring, conception of the Omniscient.

Though to be acquainted with suffering is to suffer, to be acquainted with sin is not to sin, for moral evil is not a quality but the absence of one. (See perfection.) It is the wilful failure to give adequate place in one's awareness (at the moment of choosing a course of action)to the interests of others. It is a kind of ignorance, though a voluntary and perhaps momentary one. To know ignorance it is not necessary to be ignorant, any more than to understand "not large" one must be small. If God sees the future (truly) as indeterminate, he can understand ignorance, for ignorance is an indeterminate awareness (or absence of determinate awareness) of what in itself is determinate, and thus ignorance is subjectively like knowledge of the future except that in true knowledge of the future the object is itself indeterminate and given as such. Thus ignorance is the double privation: absence of determinate awareness and absence of awareness that the object is similarly indeterminate. Hence God can know by acquaintance all the positive elements of ignorance and of sin without being ignorant or sinful. But there are no negative elements out of which the feeling of suffering can be constructed. Pain does not consist in the absence of pleasure. Thus the omniscient must suffer but he may and must be sinless.

A. E. Garvie, *Christian Faith* (1937) ; O. Pfleiderer, *Grundriss der Christlichen Glaubens- und Sittenlehre* (1888) ; O. Fock, *Der Socinianismus* (1847), pp. 437ff. C.H.

one-factor religions: A word coined by Fred L. Parrish to identify the great division of the historical religions of the world in which all religious ideas and practices of the faiths are based upon the assumption of the unity of nature: the interpretation that there is a common bond, natural and destiny-determining, linking the nature of man with natures of all non-human objects and powers and forces; the kind of religion represented by each religion in the great division; religion that assumes there is one common denominator through which world order operates and man makes his adjustments.

(About ninety per cent of the peoples of the world today belong to historical religions using the one-factor assumption, the one-factor assumption is basal to all the philosophical systems in world cultures.) See his *The Classifications of Religions* (1941). See classification of religions; religious 'powers'; two-factor religions. F.L.P.

Oneida community, the: A communistic society of religious Perfectionists* at Oneida, N. Y., 1848-1880. It was founded by John Humphrey Noyes, a graduate of Dartmouth and a student of law, who was deeply influenced by the New England revivalism of the early 1830s, and who entered training for the Congregationalist ministry, first at Andover and later at Yale. In 1834, as a result of a profound religious experience, he adopted Perfectionist views. The following year he returned to his boyhood home at Putney, Vt., where he organized the Putney Bible School, and began the development of the religious system which formed the basis of his communistic experiment. Noyes taught that the Second Coming of Christ had occurred with the Fall of Jerusalem in 70 A.D. and the events described in the twenty-fourth chapter of Matthew; that Christ now demands and expects of his followers perfection here on earth; that believers can and must live without sin as a result of their experience of fellowship with God; that selfishness is the root of all evil; and that the soul becomes free from sin only as selfishness is destroyed. These doctrines gradually led to the establishment of communism in property among the believers, and finally to a system of "complex marriage" in which any exclusive or monogamic relationship between the sexes was sternly disallowed as partaking of selfishness, and hence of sin. It was not, however, a system of promiscuity or license, and sex relations were carefully regulated by the community, which assumed responsibility for the support and education of the children. To this system in its entirety Noyes applied the term, *Bible Comunism.*

Internal dissension, court litigation, and public hostility forced the community to leave Putney and relocate at Oneida, N. Y. early in 1848. Here Noyes guided the community with great ability and business capacity, although Noyes himself attributed its success to the novel system of *mutual criticism*, under which each member sat silent while all the others disclosed his most intimate faults and attainments. These social pressures, tactfully guided and tempered by Noyes, served the ends of government and discipline within the group.

Beginning in 1849, branches were maintained at Putney and Campbridge, Vt., Wallingford,

Conn., and Brooklyn and Manlius, N. Y., but after 1855 all the interests of the community were concentrated at Oneida and Wallingford, and the membership limited to a more gradual increase. The success of the experiment dates from this concentration, and the next decade and a half was later looked back upon by the older members as their "happiest years." After a few years of struggle to live by agriculture, the community prospered through the addition of such industries as canning, lumbering, and the manufacture of steel traps, sewing and embroidery silk, and silverware.

The community carried on an extensive propaganda through periodicals, books, and pamphlets published by its own presses. This publicity aroused an intense hostility against the communists, especially among the churches, which was greatly intensified by their attempt, stimulated by the work of Francis Galton, to apply what scientific knowledge they possessed to the production of the best possible offspring by a system of selective mating within the community. Internal difficulties also developed with the rise of a new generation who lacked the religious fervor of the early founders and converts who had never ceased to consider themselves as revivalists and Perfectionists first, and social reformers secondarily. As a result of these influences, the system of "complex marriage" was abandoned in 1879, and a year later the community was reorganized as a joint stock company known as Oneida Community, Limited. It has gradually withdrawn from its varied industries, but has continued to prosper as manufacturers of Community Silver, for which it is internationally known. The present company declares that it "has no connection with the old beyond the personnel and traditions which it inherited from its forty years' experience as a community." See communistic settlements, religious.

Robert Allerton Parker, *An American Saint; John Humphrey Noyes and the Oneida Community* (1935); William Alfred Hinds, *American Communities and Collective Colonies* (1908); Pierrepont Noyes, *My Father's House: An Oneida Boyhood* (1937); John Humphrey Noyes, *History of American Socialisms* (1870).

H.E.J.

Onesimus: Runaway slave of Philemon*, who fell under Paul's influence probably at Rome, and became a Christian. Paul sent him back to his master at Laodicea, with a letter to Philemon urging the latter to accept him as a Christian brother, and let him return to Paul to help him in his religious work. Onesimus may be identical with Onesimus, bishop of Ephesus, who many years after befriended Ignatius of Antioch*.

E.J.G.

ontological argument: See God.

ontology: (Gr. *on*: being; *logos*: study of) The study of being or the fundamental stuff of existence. The problem of reality. A *metaphysical* inquiry. The following terms occur: In the question of reality, two considerations come to the fore: 1) the question of *quantity* or the number of realities; 2) the question of *quality*, the character of the fundamentally real. *Metaphysical monism* or *singularism* is the view that there is one reality; *metaphysical dualism* holds that there are two realities (generally mind and matter; or, God and the world-stuff); *metaphysical pluralism* asserts that there are many realities. As to the quality or character of the fundamentally real, the following positions may be taken: *Metaphysical idealism** or *spiritualism* asserts that reality is akin to mind or spirit. *Metaphysical materialism* holds that reality is fundamentally akin to the world of matter or that physical categories suffice to explain it. *Metaphysical neutralism* asserts that the fundamental is neither of the character of mind nor matter but neutral (entities, relations), static rather than dynamic. *Metaphysical dynamism* is the view that reality is sheer energy or process, neither mental nor physical, and dynamic. Other views relating to the character of reality are: *Hylomorphism* (Gr. *hule*: matter; *morphe*: form), a view held by Aristotle which asserts the close union of form and matter, God being the unmoved Mover, the incorporeal, indivisible, perfect, eternal, pure energy or form from which and to which things come and tend. *Positivism** in general asserts that the ontological inquiry is traditionally sterile and that the philosopher's quest may well end with the world of the here and now; our philosophy should be concerned with the making of successful practical adjustments. *Skepticism* is the avowal that our knowledge of the whole of reality is too fragmentary to make assertions thereof.

Each of these schools of metaphysical thought subdivides as to theory of the character of reality. Metaphysical idealists thus, are either *rationalistic* (emphasis upon mind as reason), *romanticists* (emphasis upon mind as feeling) *voluntarists* (mind as activity or will), *personalists** (mind as person or self) or *panpsychists** (all nature is soul-like). Thus, a metaphysical idealist may differ widely from another of the same school in theory. *Metaphysical materialists* may be *atomists* (the material atom being fundamental) or physical energists. Neutralists may differ as to whether reality is of the character of number (Pythagoreans) or "pure experience" (James) or compresent events (B. Russell). Dynamists may hold to the *elan vital* as fundamental (Bergson) or to activity-systems (Boodin). See metaphysics; naturalism.

For a survey of the ontological problem see V. Ferm *First Adventures in Philosophy* (1936), Chapters V-XIII.

V.F.

opera supererogationis: See supererogation, works of.

Ophites: (Gr., *ophianoi*, followers of the serpent) A Gnostic* sect originating in Syria which regarded the serpent as the symbol of the supreme emanation* of the Godhead.

S.M.G.

Optatus, Saint, bishop of Mileve: (4th century) A contemporary of Augustine and writer on the Donatist* schism. He defended the Catholic conception of the church independent of Augustinian ideas.

H.H.

optimism: (Lat., *optimum,* best, superlative of *bonum,* good) The view that the world, especially human life, is wholly good, or as good as possible (Plato, *Timaeus* 53B; Leibniz, *Théodicée,* 1710, attacked by Voltaire in *Candide,* 1757); or that the good will eventually triumph (eschatology); or that the whole is good even though parts are evil (absolute idealism). In some sense optimism or meliorism* characterizes religion and idealism. See meliorism; moral optimism; pessimism; value.

E.S.B.

opus operatum: The term appears for the first time in the *Gloss on the Sentences* attributed (falsely) to Peter of Poitiers, disciple of the Lombard. (See Peter Lombard) It seems to have been coined in the twelfth-century Porretan school to designate the sacramental rite itself in contradistinction from the *opus operans* (or *operantis*), which was originally the activity of the minister and was later widened to include the activity of the recipient. St. Thomas mentions the use of the antithesis "by some" (*In IV Sent.,* d. 1, q. 1, a. 5, qc. 1, sol.). Its common later use was sanctioned by the Council of Trent*, which adopted the phrase *ex opere operato** as apt to express the distinction between the traditional Catholic doctrine on the efficacy of the sacraments and that of the Reformers. The latter (cf. *Confessio Augustana,* art. 13; Melanchthon, *Apologia Altera,* Bretschneider and Bindsel, *Corpus Reform.,* XXVII, 570) equated the efficacy of the sacraments with that of the preaching of the word, limiting it to a purely psychological effect, the arousal of faith in the promise; properly, therefore, the content of the sacraments is not grace but the word of grace, and their efficacy lies not in their being performed but in their being believed. In the Catholic tradition the sacraments have a mode of efficacy distinctive of themselves, and produce an effect not simply on the consciousness, which alone is reached by the word, but on the very substance of the soul. Given the proper conditions in recipient and minister, they are instrumental in operating a union of the soul with God that takes place below any level to which introspection can reach. This effect is not caused by the conscious activity of the soul, which is natively powerless to effect its own supernatural union with God; it is directly the work of God, the sole cause of grace, done mediately through the sacramental sign itself, as validly demonstrated and administered—thus *ex opere operato.*

This doctrine rests on the fact that the sacraments* were instituted by Christ as means of sanctification in harmony with the incarnational character of God's redemptive counsels, wherein the visible (in the first instance, the humanity of Christ) is made the channel of God's invisible, creatively sanctifying action. It supposes, moreever, that the sacramental action is the action of Christ, vicariously performed through His Body, the Church, with which He is mystically one. In consequence, the sacraments "contain the grace which they signify" (Council of Trent, sess. 7, can. 6), as a practical sign contains its own significance. However, they actually confer it only "on those who put no obstacle" (*loc. cit.*), a formula which does not imply pure passivity (save in the baptism of infants), but vitally responsive religious activity, which varies according to the case; for instance, actually to receive the grace of baptism the adult must have faith, hope, the desire of arriving at the grace of God, penitence for sin, the will to obey the divine law. However, the negative formula, "non ponentibus obicem," points the fact that these dispositions simply condition, and do not cause, the efficacy of the sacrament, which in their presence has its effect *ex opere operato,* as the sanctifying instrument of the mystical Christ. In the controversy over the phrase *ex opere operato,* it is sometimes interpreted as implying "magic," of an immoral and mechanical concept of sanctification; Catholics assert this to be a radical misunderstanding of the theandric realism of their sacramental theology. Actually, the controversy has its roots in initially divergent doctrines on the whole God-relationship involved in the term grace.

J.C.M.

Opzoomer, Cornelius Willem: (1821-1892) He was professor of philosophy at Utrecht. At first he was a follower of Karl Christian Friedrich Krause. Then he represented a partially carried out empiricism akin to positivism. He was an emancipator of philosophy from the chains of classical philology and theology. On the basis of the doctrine of panentheism* he denied the supernatural. Christianity was for him one of the individual forms of religion and was not to be set up against the others as final. He contended at first that we must have theoretic knowledge of God, that we reach God by thinking. After he had embraced a peculiar empirical philosophy, he adopted religious feeling as one of the sources of knowledge. He held a special interference of the deity in prayer, inspiration and miracles as impossible as nature was the external form of appearance of the deity. There are no breaks in the fixed order of nature. In his view man had five sources of knowledge: sense perception, the feeling of pleasure and displeasure, aesthetic, ethical and religious feeling. The first three yield materialism, the first four positivism, the last a harmful mysticism, but the combination of all gives a sound knowledge of reality, a scientific and religious view of the world. Of the famous triad of beliefs God, freedom and immortality, Opzoomer regarded only the first as essential to religion. Insistence upon freedom is irreligious since the religious man desires only that God's will be done. Faith in immortality is not a religious but a scientific question. Evil was for him a necessary but temporary element in the evolution of the world. Evil exists only from man's point of view. Christianity was for Opzoomer the religion of loving trust in God as taught by Jesus. He used the N.T. as a source of historical knowledge. Protestant orthodoxy was not true Protestantism for him. Lessing, Herder, Goethe Schiller, Kant, Fichte and especially Schleiermacher** were for him the forerunners of the new reconciliation of faith and knowledge, the exponents of a new reconciliation of faith and knowledge, the pioneers of a new scholasticism.

De Leer van God bij Schelling, Hegel, en Krause. Een wijsgeerige Proeve. Eerste Stuk, Krause (Leiden, 1846); *De Weg der Wetenschap. Een Handboek der Logica* (Leiden and Amsterdam, 1851); *Wetenschap en Wijsbegeerte* (Amsterdam, 1857); *De Waarheid en hare Kenbronnen* (Amsterdam, 1859); *Het Wezen der Kennis. Een Leerboek der Logica* (Amsterdam, 1863); *De Godsdienst* (Amsterdam, 1863); *Losse Bladen.* 3 vols. (Haag, 1886 f.); T. Cannegieter, *De moderne Richting* (Baarn, 1908); A. M. Brouwer, *De moderne Richting* (Nijmegen, 1912); K. H. Roessingh, *De moderne Theologie in Nederland; hare Voorbereiding en eerste Periode* (Groningen, 1914); *Het Modernisme in Nederland* (Haarlem, 1922). H.H.

oracle: (Lat., *oraculum*, from *oro*, to pray) 1) The answer given by certain divinities to inquiries of pilgrims coming to their shrines. The methods of expressing the reply varied; e.g., the rustling of the oak leaves at Dodona, the cries of the priestess at Delphi, dreams at Epidaurus. In dealing with the future, replies were obscure and equivocal, capable of being interpreted in accordance with the event. 2) The shrine where oracles were given. The most famous were those of Zeus at Dodona in Epirus and of Apollo at Delphi. The Delphic Oracle came to be the most influential power in Greece, consulted by all states alike. There were no shrines in Italy comparable to the Greek ones, but the Sibyl's Cave at Cumae under the Temple of Apollo and the Temple of Fortuna at Praeneste are worthy of mention. See Sibylline oracles. E.M.N.

oral law: See Israel, religion and theology; law, Hebrew; Moses.

oratio: See collect.

Oratorians, or Oratory of St. Philip Neri: The Congregation of the Oratory was founded by St. Philip Neri at San Girolamo, a parish church in Rome, and canonically erected by Gregory XIII in 1575. It consists of independent communities of priests living under obedience to a rule but without vows. The central objective is the salvation of souls by means of prayer, preaching and the administration of the sacraments. The English Oratorians, living under the same rule, were founded by Cardinal (then Father) Newman* in 1847. The French Congregation of the Oratory, inaugurated by Cardinal (then Père) Peter de Bérulle in 1611, followed the general lines laid down by St. Philip Neri, but is a distinct organization under its own superior general. J.F.T.

oratorio: Originally musical services held in the Oratory founded by St. Philip Neri (d. 1595) at Rome; later applied to elaborate musical compositions on sacred themes employing orchestra, chorus, and solo voices—popularized in 18th cent. England by Handel (as a substitute for opera in Lent); his *Messiah* is the most popular and probably greatest oratorio. E.R.H.

ordeals: Methods for determining the guilt or innocence of suspected or accused persons by subjecting them to tests of a physically painful or dangerous nature. The tests were supposed to be under superhuman control although administered by human hands. Escape from injury was taken as evidence of miraculous divine intervention and proof of innocence. Ordeals have been employed among many peoples, primitive and civilized, as a part of judicial procedure. They persisted officially in Europe until the end of the Middle Ages and sporadically since then. See Hastings *Encyclopaedia of Religion and Ethics* for extensive discussion. R.W.F.

order of salvation: The logical order of the various acts by which the Holy Spirit originates, sustains and develops faith. The simplest division of this order includes Conversion, Justification and Sanctification. Some dogmaticians however further elaborate upon the distinctions within the Order of Salvation and include also under varying arrangements The Call, Illumination, Regeneration, Conversion, and Mystical Union. H.W.J.

orders, religious: See Augustinians; Benedictines; Capuchins; Carmelites; Dominicans; Franciscans. See also Catholic religious orders; Catholic societies; mendicant orders; monasticism. See holy orders.

ordinal: A liturgical text containing the forms used in ordination. (Usually incorporated in the *Pontifical* (R.C.) and in the Anglican Book of Common Prayer*. P.V.N.

ordination: The formal bestowal of ministerial office (see holy orders), supplementing the inward call (*vocatio*) of the Spirit with the authority of the Church publicly given by its agents competent to ordain (bishop, presbytery). Since the Reformation wide divergence has prevailed alike as to the form and theory of the ministry, the liturgical forms used in ordination, and the proper minister of ordination. In the Eastern and Roman Catholic Churches ordination (the sacrament of Order) is held to confer grace and indelible character, and therefore not to be repeated. Many Anglicans, and presumably the Prayer Book Ordinal, share this position. In churches of Catholic order ordination is set in the framework of the Eucharistic liturgy and restricted to bishops of historic succesion, as was the universal rule from the second to the 16th century.

The essential form of ordination consists of the laying on of hands* with prayer (major orders); admission to minor orders is by the giving of the appropriate symbol of office (out of which has developed the *porrectio instrumentorum*). This primitive simplicity has been retained by the Eastern Church, and to it the Reformed Churches have returned. In the Roman Catholic Church the ceremonial of ordination has been complicated by the fusion, in early medieval times, of old Roman and Gallican elements, so that the primitive form is somewhat obscured by later accretions (vesting, anointing, *porrectio*, imperative formulas, etc.). See clergy; initiation rites; ordinal; priest; reordination; sacraments; vocation.

A. C. Headlam and R. Dunkerley, editors. *The Ministry and the Sacraments* (1937); J. Hastings, *Encyclopedia of Religion and Ethics*. Art. "Ordination (Christian)", by A. J. MacLean. P.V.N.

Ordo Romanus: A text prescribing the ceremonies used in the Roman Church from the eighth to the fifteenth century. There are fifteen such *Ordines* extant. *Ordo Primus* describes the Pope's manner of celebrating public mass on greater days in the 8th century. P.V.N.

oreads: See nymphs.

orenda: (Iroquois) Inherent potency or energy which objects, in some characteristic manner, possess and exert. See manitou; wakanda. F.L.P.

organum (or diaphony) The earliest form of polyphonic* music. One voice part parallels the original unmeasured plainsong* at the interval of a fifth or a fourth with an octave added at times. The earliest record of "pure organum" comes from the end of the 9th century, from Hucbald, a monk of Flanders. The *Micrologus* of Guido d'Arezzo a century later describing "free organum" permitted the use of the occursus, a coming together of the parts at the cadence points. By 1100 John Cotton, an Englishman, in *Musica*, laid down rules for the "new organum" which, through the use of contrary rather than parallel motion of voices, established the independence of voice leading and the principles of polyphonic music.

H. E. Wooldridge, *Oxford History of Music*, Vol. I (1901). E.H.B.

Origen: (A.D. 185-251? or 254?) Christian scholar, teacher, and thinker—one of the greatest of all time. Educated in Alexandria under Clement and Ammonius Saccas (the teacher of Plotinus), he was head of the celebrated Catechetical School of his native city from 203 till 232. A little later he settled in Caesarea and opened a school. Here he died as a result of tortures endured in the Decian persecution.

Origen as a theologian sets out from the Rule of Faith but ends with a system which is a profound amalgamation of Christianity and Platonism. A third influence was the great Gnostic systems. His cosmology is inwardly a soteriology. Its determining end throughout is redemption, its presupposition an ante-mundane fall of finite spiritual beings or souls (called by Origen now rational essences, now intelligences, powers, and ideas). The agent of redemption as of all creation is the Divine Logos or Son of God, who is the perfect image or reflection of the eternal Father though a being distinct, derivative, and subordinate. The Logos is the educator, the inspirer, and, as incarnate, the redeemer of all fallen souls, though their free will remains a constant factor in the process of return to God. The historical impact of Origen was registered primarily through his Logos doctrine. On the one hand, he was the "grandfather" of Arianism and it is his widespread influence which explains the prolongation of the Arian conflict for sixty years. On the other hand, he taught the Church to think away time in conceiving of the generation of the Son and so paved the way for the idea of an eternal and immanent Trinity. See allegorical interpretation; pre-existence; restorationism; Rufinus Tyrranius; senses of Scripture; versions of the Bible, ancient.

Besides the *Hexapla*—one of the most monumental enterprises ever undertaken by a single scholar—and the Commentaries on *St. John* and on *St. Matthew*, the most important writings of Origen are *De Principiis, Contra Celsum*, and *De Oratione*. Of these *De Principiis*, the foremost treatise on systematic theology in the ancient Church, has survived in the main only in Rufinus' largely emended Latin translation. Koetschau's edition (E. T. based on it by Butterworth, 1936) of this work in the *Grieschischen Christlichen Schriftsteller* is indispensable. Othewise Migne and *The Ante-Nicene Fathers* suffice.

E. R. Redepenning, *Origenes, Eine Darstellung seines Lebens und seiner Lehre* (1841, 46) 2 vols.; J. Denis, *De la philosophie d'Origène* (1884); C. Bigg, *The Christian Platonists of Alexandria* (1886; 2nd ed., 1913); E. de Faye, *Origène: sa vie, son oeuvre, sa pensée* (1923-28) 3 vols.; *Origen and His Work* (E. T., 1929); C. W. Lowry, "Origen as Trinitarian" in *Jour. Th. Studies*, July 1936. Arts. on Origen by Westcott in *Dict. Chr. Biog.*, by Harnack in *Ency. Brit.* (11th ed.). C.W.L.

Origenistic Controversies: An outgrowth of the Arian* controversy, though grounded largely in personalities, occasioned by the frequent appeals of the Arians to the authority of Origen* (A.D. 185-254). It involved hostile bands of Egyptian monks; spread to Palestine about 394, where Jerome*, who had first supported Origen, was led to condemn his errors and thus became involved in bitter controversy with Rufinus*; and presently was carried to Constantinople where it was the occasion of the exile of Chrysostom*. A.K.R.

(Original) Church of God, the: A pentecostal sect with headquarters at Chattanooga, Tenn. It was organized in 1886 by R. J. Spurling. Its distinctive feature is speaking in unknown tongues. There are 58 churches and 2,200 members. See pentecostal sects. E.T.C.

original nature: See heredity.

For list of instincts see: psychology of religion.

original sin: The problem of the roots of sin in human life has pre-occupied religious thinkers and theologians throughout the ages. Christian theology has generally sought to derive sin* from man's abuse of the freedom with which he was created. But this explanation requires an answer to the question how it is possible for man to misuse his freedom so that as a sinner he will set himself against God. This answer is given in the doctrine of original sin (*peccatum originis*, sin of the origin). Its content is that the sin which caused Adam's* fall and expulsion from paradise is transmitted from generation to generation, so that all descendants of Adam must be regarded as being of a "perverted" or "depraved" nature.

The apostle Paul introduced this interpretation of the fall of Adam into Christian thinking. When he taught that as in Adam all men have sinned, so in Christ they are saved, he not only suggested an interpretation of the Genesis story of the fall of the first parents which no Jewish exegete had made before (as far as w know), but he also furnished Christian theology a major theme of thought. The ancient theologians (Irenaeus, Tertullian**) who first adopted this pattern of thought, never undertook to explain how the sin of Adam could be transmitted to all his descendants. They seem to have presupposed (as Paul himself probably did) a mystical identity or relationship between Adam and mankind. Only Augustine* fully developed the theory that Adam's sin is transmitted from parents to children throughout all generations through the sexual act which, by virtue of the lust that accompanies it, is inherently sinful. In this form the doctrine was adopted by medieval Roman Catholicism and later also by Orthodox Protestantism. In his own time, Augustine was opposed by Pelagius* who taught that sin originates in man's following the bad example of Adam and that it is continued in mankind by force of habit. His fundamental concern was to preserve the principle of human moral freedom over against Augustine's doctrine of man's total (moral) disability. Medieval Roman Catholic theology combined Pelagianism with Augustinianism insofar as it developed a doctrine of man which distinguished between the natural and supernatural aspects of human nature. Thus it could be asserted that Adam's fall entailed the loss of original righteousness insofar as the supernatural gift of divine grace was concerned, but not the destruction, only the staining of the natural endowment of man (particularly his rationality and therefore his freedom) by which he is distinguished from the beasts. The reformers rejected this doctrine of the dual character of human nature. They eliminated all traces of Pelagianism from their teaching and returned to a strict Augustinianism. They were concerned to emphasize the radical sinfulness of man over against the sovereignty of divine grace, believing (rightly) that their doctrine of salvation* by grace* alone required such teaching.

Modern Protestantism gradually rejected the theory of the origin of sin in Adam's fall and of the congenital depravity of human nature. Biblical criticism and the results of natural science have rendered it untenable. But the old doctrine of original sin nevertheless continues to be of importance in Protestant thinking, for it directs the attention of the modern Christian to two fundamental aspects of the Christian life, namely the recognition of the universality of sin and the acknowledgment of man's dependence upon divine grace. See depravity; fall of man; guilt; imputation; infant salvation; predestination; psychologists, English school of.

Lit: F. R. Tennant, *Sources of the Doctrines of the Fall and Original Sin.* 1903; Reinhold Niebuhr, *Nature and Destiny of Man.* 2 vols. 1941-43. W.P.

Ormazd: (Ahura Mazda) High god in the Zoroastrian religion. See Amesha Spentas; cosmogonies; Persia, religions of; Zoroastrianism. V.F.

orphanages: Children's institutions probably arose as a means of caring for large numbers of children made destitute by some catastrophe, such as famine, war or pestilence. Early Christian orphanages are mentioned by Julian (361-363 A.D.), but most institutions during the middle ages were hostels, in which children might be placed. This was also true of the English almshouse which came in with the Poor Law (1601). Religious motives, however, were responsible for establishing and maintaining most of these institutions on the Continent and in Great Britain. When the disadvantages of placing children in institutions with dependent, ill and delinquent adults became obvious, about the 18th century, separate orphanages for children were established. The first one in what is now the United States was established in New Orleans by the Ursalines in 1729 followin an Indian massacre; and the first public one in Charleston in 1787.

Orphanages became the most popular form of benevolence, and by 1930 there were over 1500 in the United States, but less than one-tenth under public auspices.

Criticism of institutional method of caring for children came to be voiced about the middle of the XIX Century, and there is coming to be general agreement that no child should be placed in an orphanage because of dependency, no matter how caused; that orphanages should be reserved for special services, such as diagnostic study of children about to be placed in foster homes or adopted, certain sick children, children presenting serious behavior problems and seriously defective children.

There is not uniformity of judgment regarding the institution's function in the treatment of delinquent* children. Some authorities stress the value of foster home placement; but for the most part, institutions are still used for their treatment; the sexes in separate locations; and attention directed toward re-education along physical, intellectual, emotional and vocational lines rather than punishment. Cf. widows, treatment of.

W. Healy, B. Bronner, and P. Murphy, *Reconstructing Behavior in Youth* (1929); R. W. Reeder, *How Two Hundred Children Live and Learn;* Homer Folks, *Care of Destitute, Neglected and Delinquent Children* (1911); H. W. Thurston, *The Dependent Child* (1930). F.J.B.

Orphics, the: See Greek religion; mystery religions; soul; transmigration.

Orthodox Churches, Eastern: See Eastern Orthodox Churches.

orthodox Judaism: See Judaism, orthodox.

Orthodox Presbyterian Church, The: See Machen, J. G.

orthodoxy: (Gr. *orthos,* right, straight; *doxa,* opinion) Correctness of religious belief, according to an authoritative standard; opposed to heterodoxy, or heresy**. The standard presupposed by orthodoxy may be, as with the Roman Catholic, dogma as defined by the Church in its creeds and by the deliverances of the Pope, or the official confessions, or, more generally, the teaching of Scripture, as with the Protestant. Orthodoxy, thus, is a relative term, varying with the norm. The Roman Catholic regards himself as orthodox in contrast with the Protestant, while the Trinitarian Protestant looks on himself as orthodox with respect to the Unitarian. Orthodoxy varies, too, with time; what is heterodox at one period may be orthodox in a later one. Christ was heterodox with respect to the Judaism of his day and yet was to become the founder of a new orthodoxy. It is to be noted that the standard by which orthodoxy is judged is established by social, or institutional, agreement. The deliverances of an individual's conscience or religious experience might be correct from the standpoint of truth but at odds with the accepted, authoritative view, and, hence, be heterodox. Orthodoxy is, thus, conformity to the official formulation of truth.

F.G.E.

orthodoxy, neo: See neo-orthodoxy.

Orthodoxy, Progressive: See Progressive Orthodoxy.

Osiander, Andreas: (1498-1552) German reformer. Pastor at Nuremberg, where he introduced the Reformation, 1522. Published Copernicus' "On the Motions of Heavenly Bodies," 1543. Pastor and professor at Koenigsberg, 1549. Here he aired his long-harbored views on justification, which led to the so-called Osiandrian controversy in the Lutheran church. Rejecting the forensic theory of justification*, Osiander held that God acts as physician rather than judge, "makes" rather than "declares" man just. He emphasized the part played by the divine nature of Christ and minimized the atonement. "The indwelling of Christ's divine nature is our righteousness." The controversy spread from the clergy among the people and lasted for many years after Osiander's death. It was finally settled in the Formula of Concord*. E.C.K.

Osiris: In the old Egyptian Kingdom: early Nile-god of Busiris in the delta; famous shrine up the river at Abydos. In the myth, Osiris is murdered by Set*: by piety his son Horus* brought together the dismembered body and restored life to Osiris. The means by which Osiris was restored must be equally potent for others. Life like that which was restored to Osiris becomes a possibility to men. Osiris lived and ruled the underworld. Later Osiris and the afterworld were transplanted to the sky where he sat on a throne. The King of Egypt is his son. Salvation through Osiris is achieved for the individual by the performance of rites, set up by priests, by which Osiris is held to have attained immortality.

In the later Middle Kingdom and Empire, moral conditions are involved for a future blessedness. There is now a formal judgment of the dead. Osiris is King of the Dead, and the dead are brought before him and tried. He is pictured seated on a throne with a sceptre and scourge in his hands.

In the annead of Heliopolis, Osiris is a member of the last generation in descent from Atum. In a myth, it is Isis and not Horus, who searches and finds the body of Osiris after he was slain by Set.

In the Roman Empire, Osiris is linked with Isis in the form of a mystery cult, of a god who died and became alive again. See Egypt, religions of; mystery religions. F.L.P.

ostensorium: See monstrance.

other-worldliness: See asceticism; conversion; monasticism.

Otterbein, Philip William: (1726-1813) A missionary to America from the Reformed Church in Germany, became a leader of the evangelical movement and, with Martin Boehm*, founded the Church of the United Brethren in Christ*. Bishop, 1800-1813. W.E.R.

Otto, Rudolf: (1869-1937) Protestant theologian and philosopher. Born Peine (Hanover), 1897 privatdozent Goettingen, 1904 professor Goettingen, 1914 professor Breslau, 1917-1937 professor of Systematic Theology Marburg. Applying philosophy and comparative religion to the study of theology O. attempted to establish a firm basis for the Biblical truth by pointing to its historical uniqueness, and thus to demonstrate the absoluteness of the Christian faith. His most remarkable achievement was his book on *The Idea of the Holy*. Therein he described the subject of religion as the Numinous*, which manifesting itself to man in a specific way could be apprehended only by means of man's religious faculty (Ahnung, divination). In this view he followed the philosopher Fries* (1773-1843), of whose works O. and his friends published a new edition. Like his brother he was a great student of Indian religion. He applied his philosophy of religion not only to the study of the N.T. and German mysticism, but also to the organization of the '*Religiöser Menschheitsbund*', an organization that was to unite adherents of all the world's faiths in the service of international understanding and collaboration. See phenomenology.

Naturalism and Religion (1907); *Das Heilige* (1917); Translated into all modern languages. Engl. tr. *The Idea of the Holy* (1923, rev. ed. 1929); *Religious Essays, a supplement to The Idea of the Holy* (London, 1931); *Mysticism, East and West* (1932); *The Kingdom of God and the Son of Man. A study in the history of religion* (1937); *Sünde und Urschuld und andere Aufsätze zur Theologie* (München, 1932).

Theodor Siegfried, *Grundfragen der Theologie bei Rudolf Otto* (*Marburger Studien*) (Gotha, 1931); J. M. Moore, *Theories of Religious Experience, with special reference to James, Otto and Bergson* (1938).

O.A.P.

ousia: A Greek word meaning "essence," or "substance," that Being which really is, that remains or abides in contrast to the fleeting, flowing particulars of the world phenomena,—as the genus abides in the members of the species. It figured in the Arian* controversy of the 4th century, which was over the relation of the divine *ousia* to the persons of the Trinity*. The orthodox party held that the Son was *homoousios**, "of the same substance," with the Father, while the Arians held variously to *homoiousios**, "of similar substance," and *heteroousios*, "of different substance." The Neo-platonists* said that God was *hyperousios*, beyond *ousia*, transcending the possibility of definition. F.G.E.

Overbeck, Franz Camillo: (1837-1905) Reared in France, Leningrad and Dresden, he taught at the universities of Jena and Basel. Of sharp critical mind, in intimate connection with the modern intellectual development through his friendship with Nietzsche, Treitschke and Rhode, he gradually grew cool towards religion and Christianity. His inward coolness towards religion, Christian belief and theological tradition enabled him to see many things clearly in the prevailing theology. As a historian of original Christianity, he took issue with the modernizing interpretations of the original historical sources and figures. He clearly recognized the eschatological attitude of primitive Christianity. He posed similar questions as did Kierkegaard about the possibility of Christianity in the modern world and the genuineness of every appeal of later generations to original Christianity and the N.T. Not his intellectual productivity—he wrote numerous studies on N.T. topics and the history of the ancient church—but his inner remoteness against religion and Christianity paralyzed his influence. Scientific theology was for him not a servant but a grave-digger of Christianity. He was led to a religious scepticism whose negative view of Christianity did not mentally disturb him in the least.

Über die Christlichkeit unserer heutigen Theologie (Leipzig, 1873); *Christentum und Kultur*, ed. by C. A. Bernoulli (Basel, 1919); R. Kiefer, *Die beiden Formen der Religion des Als-Ob* (Langensalza, 1932); W. Bigg, *Franz Overbeck* (München, 1931). H.H.

Owen, Robert: (Owenism) See communistic, settlements, secular.

Oxford, Franciscan School of: Brilliantly inaugurated by the lectures of the secular master, Robert Grosseteste*, its theological and philosophical studies flourished under Minors like Adam Marsh and Roger Bacon. R.C.P.

Oxford Group: A contemporary life-changer movement instituted by Frank Buchman, Lutheran minister, sometimes known as Buchmanism. Buchman is said to be the human founder and the Holy Spirit the real head. Buchman became disappointed with conventional religion and after heart-searching experience came to the conclusion that there was need to return to a kind of first-century Christian fellowship with more emphasis upon personal commitments than credal or theological loyalties. After a period of social service, Buchman, wide traveler, concentrated his efforts at Oxford University where conditions seemed ripe for just such an emphasis. The movement has spread into the far corners of the earth by the work of devoted crusaders, enlisting prominent men. There is no set organization; rather the movement claims to be an inner church in all churches for the deepening of the spiritual life. Meetings are held in the manner of house parties where divine guidance and testimony form the informal ritual. The human ego must surrender to the Christ "I". There is to be no compromise with the absolutes of honesty, purity, love and unselfishness. Surrender, restitution and sharing are implied in the changed life. The movement lacks a formal theology, which is considered a virtue. Its latest title: Moral Re-Armament.

A. J. Russell, *For Sinners Only* (1932). V.F.

Oxford movement: A movement within the Church of England, initiated at Oxford in 1833 under the leadership of John Henry Newman, John Keble, Edward B. Pusey** and others. In opposition to the prevailing latitudinarian and Erastian* tendencies of the day, these men insisted upon the historic significance of the Church as "more than a merely human institution" and as possessing "privileges, sacraments, a ministry, ordained by Christ." A revival of liturgical and ceremonial usages followed upon a reawakened sense of the values inherent in Catholic Christianity, and in its later phase the movement became identified with what was popularly known as "ritualism."* The emphasis of Newman and his associates, however, was primarily doctrinal. See Anglo-Catholics; Tractarianism.

See R. W. Church, *The Oxford Movement* (1891); S. L. Ollard, *A Short History of the Oxford Movement* (1915); W. G. Peck, *The Social Implications of the Oxford Movement* (1933). L.W.C.

Oyomei: (Jap.) *Idem* Wang Yang-ming*. W.T.C.

P

P: See Priestly Code; **Hexateuch.**

pa kua: See Chinese Terminology.

Pachomius, Saint: Founder of the cenobitical life, was born and died in Egypt where he introduced community life among the hermits who gathered around him. He was the founder of nine monasteries for men and two for women. His Order continued until the 11th century. His feast is celebrated on May 14. See Cenobite; monasticism. J.B.C.

pacifism, Christian: A word which the Oxford English Dictionary records as occuring for the first time in 1905 and denoting a doctrine or belief that international disputes can be settled "by peaceful means." But the term has come to mean, at least in religious writings, the doctrine that Christians can have no part in war. There are, of course, different interpretations of this general principle, most holding that police power within the state is not inconsistent with pacifism and some even conceding the necessity of an international police force. More commonly, however, the word *pacifism* is being reserved for what is known as the "absolutist" position, that a Christian can under no circumstances use armed force for the settling of international difficulties.

It is frequently said that the Early Church was pacifist, but this is a generalization which leads to an easy misunderstanding of the attitudes of the early Christians. The early Christians did not face the problem of war as we have it today, and there are no unquestioned statements concerning the Christian's participation in war before the middle of the second century. During the first three centuries there were several writers who took the position that a Christian can under no circumstances be a soldier. But these writers—the most often quoted was Tertullian*—also held that a Christian cannot hold civil office. After Constantine the Christians, who before his time were members of an organization not recognized by the state, had to decide whether the Christian could assume the burdens of civil and military office. The majority seem to have believed that, however dangerous such offices might be for the Christian, he should not shrink from them.

The Church has always condemned war, and no Christians have been more outspoken than some who have believed that under certain circumstances it is lawful for them to bear arms. During the Middle Ages efforts were made by the Church to mitigate the evils of war, and churchmen, both Catholic and Protestant, contributed to the creation of International Law. Notable among these were Vitoria and Suarez of the Catholics and Grotius, a Protestant. The pacifist tradition was kept alive by the monastic orders and by such minority groups as the Waldenses in the Middle Ages and the Quakers** in modern times.

In recent years a new type of Christian pacifism has arisen. Admitting the duty of the citizen to support the state, even in its police power, the modern pacifist denies only the right of the citizen himself to use force. Frequently, too, this is restricted to the use of force in international warfare. This view is sometimes said to have arisen partially, at least, out of the optimism which has been so characteristic of recent religion, especially in America. Following the first World War many seemed to believe that war could be avoided by a refusal on the part of Christians and others to take part. Unfortunately, there were too many exceptions made for this to become a successful program for avoiding war. Some were willing to admit the possible necessity of class warfare; others were willing to resort to economic sanctions against aggressor nations without seeming to understand that such sanctions are ineffectual unless backed up by force. The second World War has taken this question out of the realm of ecclesiastical debating societies and made it once more a problem of life and death for millions of Christians. Many, especially such groups as the Quakers and Mennonites,* have maintained the absolute-pacifist position concerning war; and the democracies, at least, have tried to protect the consciences of the objectors. But those who have been content to hold at one and the same time the necessity of a power state to promote the general welfare and the doctrine of absolute pacifism in international matters are compelled to rethink their positions. About all that can be said of discussions concerning pacifism growing out of the second World War is that the question is once more being set in the larger problem of the Christian's relation to the state.

James Moffatt, art. "War", *Dictionary of the Apostolic Church;* A. T. Cadoux, *Jesus and Civil*

Government (1923); C. J. Cadoux, *The Early Church and the World* (1925); G. H. C. Macgregor, *The New Testament Basis of Pacifism* (1936); Sherwood Eddy and Kirby Page, *The Abolition of War* (1924); Richard B. Gregg, *The Power of Non-Violence* (1934); Reinhold Niebuhr, "Why the Church is not Pacifist", *Christianity and Power Politics* (1940); Umphrey Lee, *The Historic Church and Modern Pacifism* (1943). U.L.

Paddock Lectures: Endowed at the General Theological Seminary, New York, by G. A. Jarvis in 1880 in honor of Bishop Paddock of Massachusetts, for the defence and confirmation of the faith and the historic order of the Church; lecturers have included W. R. Inge, W. Temple, J. N. Figgis, A. E. J. Rawlinson, A. J. Lilley, L. Hodgson, B. S. Easton, M. B. Stewart. E.R.H.

paedobaptism: See pedobaptism.

pagan: Derived from the Latin *paganus*, a "countryman." The term was first applied to those who clung to Greek and Roman faiths. Since Christianity first spread in the cities, this was true more of the rural than the urban population. It has also been held that the term was adopted because of the contrast between the regular soldier and the raw rustic. Pagans were civilians in contrast to the "soldiers of Christ."

The term "pagan" is now applied to one who does not belong to one of the great monotheistic faiths. In contrast to "heathen"* it implies a disinterested rather than a hostile point of view. C.T.C.

pageants: See religious drama.

pagoda: See temples, Far Eastern.

Paine, Thomas: (1737-1809) American pamphleteer of English birth, whose radical views on politics and religion found expression in *Common Sense* (1776), *The Crisis* (1776-83), *The Rights of Man* (1791-92), and *The Age of Reason* (1794-95). The last, a repudiation of the Bible and institutional Christianity, evoked violent controversy. Although he has been popularly regarded as an atheist, Paine's position was essentially deistic. L.W.C.

Palace school: Next to the monastical schools of a monastery, to the cathedral schools attached to the cathedral church at a bishop's seat, the episcopal schools, supported by some bishop, the capitular schools, maintained by the bishop's council the capitulum, the Middle Ages produced another type of school also: the palace school, *schola palatina*. This school usually was the foundation of the royal family itself or one of the great magnates of the country. Great fame was obtained by the palace school of Charlemagne at Aix-la-Chapelle (Aachen) in which children of the Frankish nobility received instruction. At this school Alcuin,* the famous monk from York, England, served as master of the school. See Theodulf of Orleans; Warnefrid, Paul. Cf. magister sacri palatii. S.C.T.

Palestrina: See s.v. mass; motet; requiem.

Paley, William: (1743-1805) A British moralist who made a most important contribution to ethical literature, namely, the statement of the doctrine of "theological Utilitarianism" in such clear, vigorous style and in such an unmistakable form. He respected the Scripture as a means of enforcing, by sufficient sanctions, known rules of morality evident through natural reason; and not as a means of bringing new principles to man's attention. In his *Natural Theology* (1802) he developed the famous analogy of the watchmaker (the design argument was common in the 18th century): God, the superhuman watchmaker has fashioned the machine of the world. Traces of an Intelligent Maker are in evidence in the structure of the world.

See God; Tucker, Abraham; Utilitarianism, theological.

His works include *Natural Theology; Evidences of Christianity* (1794); *Horae Paulinae; Moral and Political Philosophy* (1785); *Sermons on Several Subjects; Sermons on Public Occasions; Clergyman's Companion.* W.G.H.

palimpsest: A parchment manuscript from which the writing has faded or been erased, and on which some other text has been subsequently written. The Codex Ephraemi Rescriptus (at Paris) and the Old Syriac Gospels (at Mt. Sinai) are examples. See manuscripts of the Bible. E.J.G.

pall: (Lat., *pallium*, cover, cloak) A cloth, usually of linen and inclosing a cardboard, to cover the chalice during Mass; also a black cloth spread over the coffin in church at a funeral, or over the catafalque. L.R.W.

pallium: (Lat., cloak) In the Roman Catholic church a badge of jurisdiction conferred by the pope on archbishops, conventionalized into a circular band of white wool with pendants. B.S.E.

Palm Sunday: The Sunday before Easter. At Jerusalem in the fourth century Christians met on the Mount of Olives and, carrying palm branches, escorted the bishop into the city in commemoration of the event described in the Gospels (especially John 12:12ff). The practice of similar processions spread generally and gave the name to the Sunday. Cf. church year. B.S.E.

Palmer, Benjamin Morgan: (1818-1902) First Moderator, Presbyterian Church, U. S., 1861. Pastor, First Church, New Orleans, 1856 onward. Instrumental in establishing Southwestern, Presbyterian college, now at Memphis. Destroyed infamous Louisiana lottery. A.C.

Palmer, Christian David Friedrich: (1811-1875) He was professor in Tübingen. As a mediating theologian he did his best in developing the means of influence for the church.

Evangelische Homiletik (Stuttgart, 1842, 6 ed., Stuttgart, 1887); *Katechetik* (Stuttgart, 1844, 6 ed., Stuttgart, 1875); *Pädagogik* (Stuttgart, 1852, 5 ed., Stuttgart, 1882); *Hymnologie* (Stuttgart, 1865). H.H.

Palmer, George Herbert: (1842-1933) Harvard U. 1864, U. of Tübingen 1867-1869, Andover Seminary 1870. Tutor in Greek, Harvard U.

1870-1873; instructor, prof. philosophy 1873-1889; Alford Professor natural religion, moral philosophy and civil polity 1889-1913; overseer Harvard U. 1913-1919. An unsurpassed exemplar of the theory and practice of the art of teaching, disciplined and proficient in the field of philosophy and ethics, a resolute protagonist of Christian theism and a devoted member of the church of the Pilgrims, "Glorious old Palmer," as William James called him, exerted a wide and constructive influence in the sphere of religious thought in America.

Author: *The Odyssey: A Translation* (1891); *The Glory of the Imperfect* (1898); *The Field of Ethics* (1901); *The Nature of Goodness* (1904); *The Life and Works of George Herbert* (1906), 3 vols.; *The Life of Alice Freeman Palmer* (1908); *The Teacher* (1908); *The Problem of Freedom* (1911); *Intimations of Immortality in the Sonnets of Shakespeare* (Ingersoll Lecture) (1911); *Formative Types of English Poetry* (Earl Lectures) (1918); *Altruism* (1919); *The Autobiography of a Philosopher* (1903).

J.W.B.

panentheism: (Gr. *pan,* all; *en,* in; *theos,* god) The view that all things are within the being of God, who yet is not merely the whole of actual things. If God were merely the system of actual things, then, should a different system be possible, it would be possible that God should not exist, or should not be himself. Hence either God must be a purely contingent being, and anything might happen to him, including his destruction, or all things, just as they are, are necessary. On either construction God and other things are upon the same metaphysical level, whether of pure contingency or of pure necessity. Panentheism holds, on the contrary, that the self-identity of God is independent of the particular things which exist and the particular totality they form, and that consequently God may exist necessarily, although all other beings exist contingently. God exists, to be sure, in a different state for every difference in the existing whole, for he is that whole, but it is a different state of the same being, or of the whole as having a flexible selfhood, the individual essence of which is unaffected by the accidents of existence. This makes the inclusive whole analogous to a human personality, which contains many things not essential to its self-identity. A man is the sum of things which fall within his experience, but he is more than that sum, and many an item could have been missing (or have been replaced by another) without making his self-identity impossible. Panentheism claims to reconcile the legitimate motives of ordinary pantheism* (God is simply the *de facto*—or the eternal—whole of things) and the contrary extreme (things other than God are in no way parts of his being). Panentheism admits that there is in God something independent of particulars, but holds that this something is merely the "essence" of God whose entire nature includes also accidents, each of which is the integration of all the accidental being in a given state of the universe. Panentheism sees in God not just another example of whole or totality, unity in multiplicity, but the supreme and most excellent example, as He is the most excellent example of "goodness," "knowledge," and other conceptions. This supreme example as such deserves to be interpreted with care, and not (as commonly happens) according to casual associations, of such words as "all," "universe," "whole," "parts."

The earliest clear-cut panentheism (though without use of the term) seems to have been that of Fechner. The theological views of Montague and Whitehead are recent examples. See God as Personal; omniscience; pantheism; perfection; transcendence.

G. T. Fechner, *Zendavesta* (1851) Chapter 11; W. P. Montague, *The Ways of Things* (1940) Chapter 6; A. N. Whitehead, *Process and Reality* (1929), last chapter; V. Ferm's article, Panentheism, in the *Dictionary of Philosophy* (1941), ed. by D. Runes.

C.H.

panlogism: (Gr., *pan,* all; *logos,* word) Describes Hegel's* doctrine, "the real is the rational, the rational the real"; hence logic (theory of thinking) coincides with ontology (theory of being).

C.H.

panobjectivism: See epistemology.

panpsychism: (Gr., *pan,* all; *psyche,* soul) The view, closely related to ancient hylozoism, sponsored by such thinkers as Bruno, Leibniz, Fechner, Lotze Renouvier, W. K. Clifford, C. A. Strong, J. Ward, and C. Hartshorne, that all of reality is constituted by psychic unities so graded in perceptive quality and purposive organization as to explain inorganic, organic, and human phenomena. See Leibniz; monadology; ontology.

J. Ward, *The Realm of Ends* 3rd ed. (1920); C. Hartshorne: *Man's Vision of God* (1941).

P.A.B.

Pantaenus: The earliest of the masters of the Christian Catechetical School at Alexandria of whom we have any knowledge. Flourished ca. 200 A.D. The teacher of Clement of Alexandria.* Said by Eusebius to have made a missionary journey to India. See Alexandrian school. S.M.G.

pantheism: (Gr., *pan,* all; *theos,* god) The doctrine that the universe, the all of reality, is God. Unless further defined, the doctrine is exceedingly vague. What sort of unity and character has the cosmic whole which is equated with God? Is it a growing or a forever-fixed totality (see eternity)? Is it conscious? Do the parts possess freedom in relation to the whole, or the whole in relation to the parts? To which of the parts is the whole most analogous in character? Such questions are not answered by the mere identification of universe (in some sense) with God (in some sense). Confusion must result, therefore, from the employment of the term (without careful qualification) as synonym for an "impersonal" God, as though the universe as a whole could not possibly possess personality; or for the absence of freedom in man, as though a whole must coercively control its parts; or for sin and ignorance on God's part, as though properties of parts may automatically be ascribed to their wholes, so that, for example, a small part would mean a small whole! Such usages are attempts to smuggle highly controversial doctrines into the mere definition of a term in common use.

The phrase, "all is God," has two chief meanings, according as we construe the "all." 1) The totality of actual being, just as it stands, is simply God. In that case, God is completely bound by actuality, and actuality is completely bound by God. (See transcendence.) Neither God nor anything else has an identity distinguishable from that of other things, all is simply one and one is simply all. This view does indeed deny personality to God, and indeed it denies all definite character to anything; contradicting freedom, making it impossible to absolve God from responsibility for evil, at the same time making man as necessary to all the good in the world, and so by implication as much its creator, as God (there being no degrees of necessity). Spinoza's* philosophy is the classic example of this type of pantheism.

2) The totality of actual being and of potential being, this totality viewed as having a "flexible self-identity" independent of its actual parts, is God. On this view, actuality is not an eternally fixed sum but a variable, and God is the being who alone preserves his essential self-hood no matter what else may or may not be actual, or who has enjoyed and will enjoy "himself" at all times whatever. Not that God is in all respects the same no matter what his parts may be, but that he is in all cases the same individual, as a man (though here not in all circumstances) is the same person through the variety of his experiences. On this view there is an individual essence of God which is not identical with the whole of actuality, nor is any actual thing part of this essence; even though God as a whole, essence and accidents, is the same as actuality as a whole. (See transcendence.) This second form of pantheism is better called panentheism.* The first form might be called "traditional" pantheism, since it is usually, though perhaps not often clearly and unambiguously, intended by the term. See David of Dinant; immanence; omniscience; perfect; theism; Toland.

Wm. James, *A Pluralistic Universe* (1909); W. P. Montague, *The Ways of Things* (1940); B. Varisco, *Know Thyself* (1915). C.H.

Pao-p'o Tzŭ: See Chinese Terminology.

papacy: See pope.

papal bull: See bull, papal; encyclicals.

papal constitutions: See bulls and briefs; encyclicals.

papal legates: See legates and nuncios.

papal nuncio: See legates and nuncios, papal.

Papal States: The historical aspect of the Papal States is intimately connected with the moral and juridical rights of the popes,* as Bishops of Rome, to possess properties and lands lawfully acquired and to rule over the peoples inhabiting them as their temporal rulers and sovereign lords. That bishops in general, like other heads of organizations, ecclesiastical or political, needed funds to administer their dioceses properly, support the clergy, take care of the poor, etc., seems self-evident and is based on apostolic tradition. (Selection of Judas e.g. as treasurer of the Apostolic College; institution of the first seven deacons, etc.) Like other bishops, the popes of Rome also received properties and lands through pious donations, legacies, etc. from rich benefactors such as opulent private individuals, royal families, princes, (often in satisfaction for their sins), rulers and emperors, especially in Sicily and Dalmatia. All such lands became known in history, especially since the days of Pope Gregory I, the Great, (590-604)* as the *"Patrimonium Petri."* Eventually they embraced a stretch of land running crosswise across Italy from the Adriatic on the East to the Tyrrenian Sea on the West. Eventually also, as in feudal days, whole kingdoms became vassals of the Holy See with the Pope as Sovereign Lord, e.g. Naples, Apulia, Calabria, and even England and Ireland, etc. Chief among such donors to the Holy See were Constantine* (the "Constantinian Donation"* however as a document is an admittedly forged document of the early Middle Ages); Pepin, the Short ("Donation of Pepin") and Charlemagne.* The two last named Merivingian kings had responded to the appeals of the popes when they were molested by the Greeks (Exarchates of Ravenna as representatives of the Byzantine Emperors) and the Lombards. The pious kings not only came to the rescue of the popes but likewise gave them the lands which they conquered. With the founding of the Holy Roman German Empire* in 800 A.D. under Charlemagne* and Pope Leo III, the popes retained the right to their possessions and the German King as crowned Emperor was merely looked upon as the protector of the Papal States, as their illustrious predecessors had been who first protected the papal lands and then augmented them. Unfortunately later German Emperors had a wrong conception of their position; but this did not alter matters and the popes persistently protested against their usurpations and violations of trust. As temporal rulers the popes administered their lands through lay and clerical officials or through certain organizations which during the late Renaissance began to be known as "Roman Congregations" instituted as well for the spiritual care of the Church as for the temporal administration of the Papal States. The papacy reached the height of its glory as a political organization under Papal State Status and ecclesiastical prestige in virtue of the Primacy under Innocent III (1198-1216).* In virtue of the "Golden Bull" of 1213, Innocent was declared to be in possession of the Patrimonium Petri; of the March of Ancona; the Duchy of Spoleto; the bequest of Mathilda, countess of Tuscany; the exarchate of Ravenna and the Pentapolis (Rimini, Pesaro, Fano, Sinigalia and Ancona). Due to encroachments or threats of exploitation, especially by German emperors (Frederick I, Frederick II), French and Spanish rulers (Francis I; Philip IV; Charles V, etc.), and fears of Turkish invasions, during the Renaissance period especially, the popes were frequently, for the sake of self-protection and preservation of their rights and estates, obliged to enter into treaties with neighboring Italian Republics (Pisa, Genoa, Venice, Florence, etc.) or other European countries, sharing with them their gains and losses. To prevent or punish encroachments on the Papal States the popes, furthermore, often made use of ecclesiastical censures such as excommunications and interdicts, e.g. in regard to Venice by Pope Paul V. During the so-called Babylonian Captivity (1308-78) at Avignon* the authority over the Papal States was usurped at times by petty rebels (e.g. Cola di Riense, the "Roman Tribune" etc.). Only Cardinal Albornoz, by use of stringent measures was able to restore peace and bring order out of chaos. Despite the occasional tendency of the Papal States to break up into petty states and independent cities (e.g. Pesaro in charge of the Malatesta and Ferrara under the Este Family) Cesare Borgia, by the end of the XV century was able to unite once more the Church's lands. Julius II (1503-1513) completed the work begun by the Borgias. From 1500 onward the Papal States hardly changed their boundaries, excepting for the re-acquisition of Umbria, Pesaro and Ferrara, and the loss to the Farnese Family (due to nepotism of Paul III, 1545) of the valuable Parma and Piacenza territories. Although the sovereignty of the Papal States was repeatedly attacked and threatened, the worst defeat came at the hands of Napoleon I, who at one time (despite the Concordats of 1801 and 1806) annexed all the Papal States (including the Comtat Venaissin around Avignon) to his empire, only to see them restored practically in their entirety at the Congress of Vienna, 1815 through the dextrous manipulations of Cardinal Consalvi. Thereafter the Papal States enjoyed a new lease on life until 1860 when all of the States, excepting the Patrimony, joined in the rebellion for independence. In 1870 under the guise of national unity, which Pius IX* was willing to grant, plus Parliamentary representation under himself as traditional head, already in the very first years of his pontificate (1846-1878) the anti-clerical forces of Piedmont and Sardinia, aroused for decades by such leaders as Cavour and Mazzini and led by Garabaldi, broke through the walls of Rome, Sept. 20, 1870 and taking the city, declared Victor Emmanuel I the first King of United Italy. Pope Pius IX refused to recognize the usurpation and rejected the proferred indemnities and guarantees, as well for his own person as for the Church. From that time on the popes became the voluntary "prisoners of the Vatican." The same policy of aloofness which created the "Roman Question" was retained by Popes Leo XIII, Pius X and Benedict XV,** although during the latter's pontificate, especially after the First World War, a more friendly rapproachment was discernable. Pope Pius XI* finally solved the "Roman Question" when in the name of the Holy See Cardinal Pietro Gasparri, and Signor Benito Mussolini, as representative of the King and of the Italian Government, signed the Lateran Treaty Feb. 11, 1929, thus founding the Vatican City and placing it together with other papal property in and around the city of Rome (e.g. the Lateran Palace, Castel Gandolfo, summer home of the Popes on Lake Albano, etc.) under direct papal sovereignty and administration. With the subsequent signing of the Concordat between the Holy See and Italy, diplomatic relations were established for the first time. By the Lateran Treaty the Pope was made as independent as he ever was, but was now no longer encumbered by his predecessor's temporal cares, excepting in as far as they concern the 110 acres of Vatican City and adjoining properties.

Cath. Encyc. XIV, 257-268. R.M.H.

Papias of Hierapolis: Author of a five-volume *Exposition of the Lord's Oracles,* small fragments of which—notably concerning the Gospels of Matthew and Mark—are known by quotations from Eusebius (*H. E.* iii, 39). The exact nature of this lost work has been the subject of much controversy. Next to nothing of his life is known. According to Eusebius he was bishop of Hierapolis. Irenæus calls him a companion of Polycarp. The dates of his birth and death are not known. Perhaps the most probable date of his literary activity is *ca.* 150 A.D. The extant fragments of his writings, together with such early notices of his life and views as have survived, are conveniently assembled (in Greek and English translation) in J. H. Lightfoot, *The Apostolic Fathers* (1889, 1890), 5 vols., 2nd ed. See also logia. M.S.E.

papyrus, papyri: A water plant, most abundant in Egypt, where among other uses a writing material was very early developed out of the pith of its triangular stem. The green rind was cut away and the pith cut into thin slices, which were laid side by side to form a sheet ten or twelve inches square. Over this another layer of strips was laid at right angles, and the whole was dried and pressed together. Such sheets were then glued or pasted together into rolls, which in Egyptian mortuary texts were sometimes 150 feet long, but among the Greeks were usually not more than 25 to 30 feet. The Greeks called papyrus "biblos" and a roll of it a "biblion."* Only one side of the roll was ordinarily used, and that was smoothed with pumice. Papyrus was the regular material used in the publication of books in Greek antiquity. In the second century after Christ leaf books of papyrus began to come into use, especially for Christian texts, including the Greek version of the OT.

The discovery of great numbers of Greek papyrus documents of private life, from the fourth century before Christ to the seventh after Christ, in various places in Egypt, in the course of archeological excavations in the past fifty years, has revealed the fact that the NT was written in the familiar colloquial, not the literary, Greek of its day, and this has led to the large number of modern speech translations, which seek to translate the NT in the style in which it was written. See koiné; manuscripts of the Bible.

E.J.G.

parable: (From the Greek word *parabole,* "a placing beside," or a "comparison") This was commonly used in the LXX* to translate the Hebrew *maschal* (comparison). In the OT it is used of proverbial expressions (I Sam. 10.12) as well as illustrative stories (II Sam. II, 1f). The so-called "Parables of Enoch"* (40-71) get their name from the use of symbolic speech. Strictly speaking, a parable is an expansion of a simile as an allegory* is an expansion of a metaphor. It is not an illustration, but the lesson is to be transferred from one realm of experience to another.

See article by A. Jülicher in *Encyclopedia Biblica;* the best book on the parables of Jesus is that by B. T. D. Smith, *The Parables of the Synoptic Gospels* (1937). C.T.C.

Paracelsus: (1493-1541) Translated name from the German von Hohenheim (Aureolus Theophrastus). A native of Switzerland. One of the initiators of modern natural science. Outstanding physician who combines observation with theory. Chief work: *Opus Paramirum* (Mühlhausen, 1562). Although lost in astrological, alchemistic and theological speculations, his naturalistic approach to the "mysterium magnum" of the world makes him an influential figure in the history of thought. S.C.T.

paraclete: A term applied in the Fourth Gospel to the holy Spirit, though in the First Epistle of John it is also used of Christ himself. It means literally "called to one's side," for the purpose of assistance, and thus corresponds exactly to the Latin "advocatus." In the newer versions of the NT it is generally translated "Advocate," but this unduly narrows its meaning. It implies not merely intercessory help but help of every kind, and the old rendering "Comforter" is still the best one, when taken in its original sense of "strengthener." E.F.S.

paradise: (from Old Pers. *pairidaēza,* Gr. *paradeisos,* enclosure, park) The Garden of Eden of Gen. 2f. Then, figuratively, a state of bliss. So, Heaven,* the abode of righteous souls. S.H.B.

paralipomenon: Anything omitted or neglected; the plural, paraleipomena is the title given in the Greek version of the OT to the Books of Chronicles,* as containing matters not included in the Books of Kings. E.J.G.

parament: (Lat., *parare,* to prepare) Ornamental hangings, furniture, etc., as of a state apartment; rich and elegant robes worn by men of rank;—chiefly in the plural. (obsolete). The presence chamber of a monarch. F.T.P.

parapsychology: Being a recently emerged branch of psychology, it investigates the psychical and the psychophysical phenomena of mediums such as telepathy, visions and apparitions, monitions, premonitions, automatic writing and other forms of automatism, facts of psychometry, coincidental dreams, states of impersonation, clairvoyance and clairaudience, predictions, the physical phenomena of mediumship, such as materialization, telekinesis, rapping and other sounds. While the number of parapsychic phenomena scientifically established is still restricted, most investigators in the field consider the reality of all or most of the paranormal phenomena as possible of scientific verification. Fichte, Schelling, Baader, Hegel and other romantics shared the recognition of parapsychic manifestations. With the success of materialism and the scientific world view, the German and French parapsychical studies gradually fell into oblivion. Interest in occult phenomena was revived by representatives of the speculative theistic current in German philosophy. About the middle of the last century a new extra-scientific movement, spiritism, set in. The movement originated in America and was transplanted to Europe. It has been fashionable for mechanistic scientists to deny the reality of mediumistic phenomena.

It seems that parapsychic phenomena are almost completely neutral as far as religious meanings are concerned since they suggest to people with different cultural and personal backgrounds either divine or biological and completely impersonal dynamic forces. It is generally felt that the psychology of religion* and parapsychology are essentially separate and unrelated topics. One possible exception is James Leuba's *The Psychology of Mysticism* wherein he attributes mystical phenomena to sensory disorders. Religious interpretations of paranormal phenomena are, however, perfectly legitimate. But most religious experiences involve no paranormal phenomena. Some paranormal phenomena have religious significance to the individuals who experience them. The Proceedings of the London Society for Psychical Research* constitute by far the best source of scientific material in studying the relationship between religion and paranormal phenomena. See Oesterreich, T. K.

A. Beyer, *Religion and Suggestion* (Halle, 1922); W. J. Crawford, *The Reality of Psychic Phenomena,* (2 ed., London, 1919); *Experiments in Psychical Science* (London, 1919); *The Psychic Structures of the Goligher Circle* (London, 1920); Th. Flournoy, *Dès Indes a la Planète Mars* (Geneve, 1909); F. Grunewald, *Physikalisch-mediumistische Untersuchungen* (Pfullingen, 1920); Graf H. Keyserling, *Das Occulte* (Darmstadt, 1923); M. Kemmerich, *Prophezeiungen,* 3 ed., München, 1921); A. F. Ludwig, *Geschichte der metapsychischen occulten Forschungen von der Antike bis zur Gegenwart* (Pfullingen, 1922); T. K. Oesterreich, *Grundbegriffe der Parapsychologie* (Pfullingen, 1921); *Occultism and Modern Science* (London, 1923); J. B. Rhine, *New Frontiers of the Mind* (1937); Ch. Richet, *Traité de Metapsychique,* (2 ed., Paris, 1923); Baron v. Schrenck-Notzing, *Phenomena of Materialization* (1920); R. Tischner, *Telepathy und Hellsehen,* (2 ed., München, 1921). H.H.

pardon: In Catholic ecclesiastical use, an indulgence,* or the day or festival when this is granted. Otherwise equals forgiveness* (Gr., *aphesis,* most common NT word); three words in OT all rendered by both English words in A.V. (e.g. 'pardon' in Isa. 55:7 same in original as 'forgiveness' in Psa. 130:4).

P. Lehmann, *Forgiveness: Decisive Issue in Protestant Thought* (1940). J.L.

Pareto, Vilfredo: (1848-1923) With Ludwig Feuerbach and Sigmund Freud** Pareto shares in contributing to the conception of religion as wishful thinking. He was wholly destitute of sympathy for, or interest in religion, except in so far as he discovered religious phenomena to be social facts. They merely reflect for him the influence of group interests. Being a purely external critic of religion, his biting attack on all religion and metaphysics is unreasonable.

The Mind and Society (1935), vols. 4. H.H.

parish: Normally, the area or district within which a regularly installed pastor or priest rightfully exercises the pastoral office. A.K.R.

Parjanya: A minor Vedic deity of storm and fertility. Some scholars regarded him as one of the Adityas. In the hymn to Parjanya, Rig-Veda V. 83, he is addressed in terms almost identical with those addressed to Varuna. C.S.B.

Park, Edwards Amasa: (1808-1900) Theologian, was born in Providence, R. I. and was a son of Calvin and Abigail Ware Park. He graduated from Brown University in 1826 and from Andover Theological Seminary in 1831, after which he was pastor in Braintree, Mass. till 1835. After teaching for a year at Amherst he became in 1836, Professor of Sacred Rhetoric at Andover and in 1847 was transferred to the Abbott chair of Sacred Theology in which he remained for the rest of his active life.

Park was an exponent of the "New England Theology,"* a modified form of Calvinism* which he had formulated into a rigid system, which he persistently taught to the exclusion of all modern religious thought. He was the last teacher of Calvinism at Andover. He resigned his professorship in 1881, but spent the remainder of his life at Andover, laboring to perfect his system, which however, was never published.

He edited and translated *Selections from German Literature* (1839); he was co-editor and editor of the *Bibliotheca Sacra* (1844-1884); editor of the *Atonement,* by various authors (1859); co-editor of *The Sabbath Hymn Book* (1858); author, *Discources on Some Theological Doctrines* (1885). A *Memorial Collection* of his sermons was published posthumously in 1902. See Congregationalism; New England theology.

Dictionary of Am. Biography, v. 14, p. 204; *Congreg. Yr. Bk.,* 1901, p. 35. F.T.P.

Parker, Theodore: (1810-1860) American preacher and theologian, introduced German Biblical criticism and idealistic philosophy into Unitarian thought. Andrews Norton, a Unitarian of the Channing* school, described Parker's abandonment of supernaturalism for idealistic monism as "the latest form of infidelity"; but Parker's influence (along with Emerson's) dominated Unitarianism* in the next generation. W.M.H.

Parmenides (c. 470 B.C.) Ancient Greek philosopher, Eleatic,* classical exponent of extreme monism. Reality for him is Being (corporeal and material) filling all space, remaining constant in quantity, without beginning or end (early expression of the law of the conservation of mass). Creation is impossible since something cannot arise from nothing; change is impossible since whatever is cannot be different from what it is. Appearances are illusions (multiplicity, time, space, change). True being is thought, the one unchanging reality. His famous pupil, Zeno of Elea* developed an apologetic of this block-reality philosophy by his famous paradoxes. V.F.

parochial schools: A parochial school is here defined as a school, ordinarily at the elementary level, conducted by a religious group, for the purpose of general as well as religious education.* Roman Catholic parochial schools* are the most familiar, but several other religious bodies in the United States have, or have had, schools of this nature.

Prior to the American Revolution the Dutch, Moravians, Mennonites, German Lutheran, German Reformed, Quakers, Presbyterians, and Baptists held the conception that education was the responsibility of the church; and in the middle colonies parochial schools were the usual type.

With the gradual establishment of common schools there came also the secularization of public education. Many Protestant bodies debated whether to go with the tide as far as general education was concerned and rely on religious instruction in Sunday School and home, or to establish a system of parochial schools. The "Old School" Presbyterians* chose to experiment with the latter alternative; in 1846 the Assembly formally adopted a policy looking toward the establishment of a parochial school in every congregation, under the care of the Session, for all branches of elementary education, including religion. At least 264 Presbyterian parochial schools were established in 29 states, many being financially aided by the Presbyterian Board of Education. But the system never was popular; it met with numerous difficulties, especially since public systems of education were coming increasingly into favor; and it was formally abandoned as a denominational policy in 1870.

The Lutherans have concerned themselves with elementary education throughout their history in the United States. Their work in this respect falls into two periods. First: beginning in early Colonial days, in eastern colonies and states, several Synods pushed educational work which reached a peak about 1830; by that time some 400 schools had been established. In the second period, reaching to the present, school systems were established by the German Synods of Ohio, Missouri, Wisconsin, Iowa, Minnesota Michigan and Buffalo; by the Norwegian Synods; by the Augustana Swedish, and by Danish and Slovak Synods. By the end of the nineteenth century, Lutheran parochial schools exceeded 2500 in number. At present, Lutheran parochial schools are found principally in the Lutheran Synodical Conference, i.e., the Missouri, Joint Wisconsin, Norwegian and Slovak Synods and the Negro Missions. Chief among these is the system of parochial, or "Christian Day Schools," of the Missouri Synod; in 1942, with 3601 congregations, they report 1241 parochial schools, using 2248 teachers and enrolling 71,068 pupils.

Most of the teachers are men, called and installed in permanent positions. There is a carefully developed curriculum, with religion holding the leading place. (See Missouri Lutherans).

The Christian Reformed Church has a system of "Christian Schools." In this body much stress has been laid on the educational implications of the covenant of grace. They maintain 91 schools (1942), using 145 male teachers and 327 female, and enrolling 14,814 pupils.

The Church of Jesus Christ of Latter-Day Saints ("Mormons") have given much attention to developing a system of education in which the teaching of their faith might have its desired place, but accurately speaking they do not maintain parochial schools. In the present program "Institutes of Religion" are established in connection with colleges, 93 "Seminaries" are associated with Senior High Schools, and 385 "Junior Seminaries" are associated with Junior High Schools. These three types of institution, functioning chiefly in the Rocky Mountain states, offer courses in religion. In Juarez stake, (Mexico), the five elementary schools that are maintained might be called 'Parochial.'

The orthodox section of the Jewish group in the United States is said to have some 30 parochial schools in New York City, and a quite small number in other cities. These schools are called Yeshivah (Sing.) or Yeshivoth (Plu.). Some of them devote half the day to teaching Hebrew and religious subjects, the remainder to English and secular subjects. Others are private "progressive schools," interweaving Hebrew and religious subjects into the regular schedule. See catechumenate.

W. H. Beck, *Lutheran Elementary Schools in the United States,* (1939); *The Corner Stone of the Christian School* [Christian Reformed] (1934); E. P. Cubberley, *Public Education in the United States* (1919); *General Course of Study for Lutheran Elementary Schools* (1943); L. D. S. *Department of Education Bulletin* No. 1, 1937-38; L. J. Sherrill, *Presbyterian Parochial Schools 1846-1870* (1932).

L.J.S.

parochial schools, Catholic: This is the name usually given to the system of schools, primary and secondary, conducted under the auspices of Roman Catholic parochial or diocesan supervision. Although elementary Roman Catholic church-schools were founded in the regions of the present United States under the Spanish dominions as early as 1629, the special quality of parish support which we now associate with the parochial school system of the United States was found only in the English speaking settlements where Roman Catholics were a minority and were without state support. The usual history of the beginnings of the Catholic parochial schools, before the rise of large Catholic urban populations, consisted first of weekly religious instruction by the missionary and, then, when numbers permitted, of schools taught by Catholic laymen or laywomen; as soon as growth permitted the support of two or three teachers, religious sisterhoods or brotherhoods took over the teaching in the parochial establishments. In recent times in larger communities the formal parochial schools have frequently been begun with the foundation of the parish. The establishment of high schools frequently followed, chiefly in the larger centers of Catholic population and especially since 1900. Many private academies and colleges, under the direction of religious communities have supplemented the parochial arrangement, and in 1889 the Catholic University of America was founded at Washington, D. C. to unify and complete the system.

The provision of such religious instruction has always been a special interest of the Catholic hierarchy from colonial times. The First Provincial Council of Baltimore* in 1829 ordered the establishment of schools where religious instruction could be joined with instruction in "letters." Subsequent provincial councils of Baltimore reiterated this command and at the same time gave witness to a constant growth in the number of Catholic elementary schools where support could be obtained. The efforts to obtain state aid for the schools were unsuccessful and in some places, such as New York in 1842, caused outbreaks of anti-Catholicism. The First Plenary Council of Baltimore in 1852 begged the bishops to see that church schools be established and, if necessary, to use church funds for that purpose. The Second Plenary Council in 1866 added a plea to the parents to cooperate with the pastors in founding such schools. In 1875 the Sacred Congregation of the Propaganda in Rome, in a special "Instruction to the Bishops of the United States," classified the non-sectarian public schools as dangerous unless safeguards to the faith of the children were added, and urged the founding and fostering of Catholic schools. The Third Plenary Council of Baltimore in 1884, while admitting that many Catholic children must attend the public schools, ordered a school to be established within two years near each church unless the bishop allowed a postponement. The Council insisted on the obligation of Catholic parents to provide Catholic education for their children.

At the present time, while the parochial school is ordinarily under the supervision of the pastor the instruction is carried on by religious communities especially devoted to such work or by the clergy, assisted where circumstances require it by lay persons. The parish schools are in turn under the supervision of a diocesan superintendent or diocesan examiners appointed by the bishop. Some of these schools, especially high schools, are supported and directed by several parishes acting jointly or under the direct supervision of the bishop. Private academies and colleges are usually directed and owned by religious communities, although the seminaries devoted to the education of the secular clergy and some other diocesan institutions are directly under episcopal supervision. The Catholic University of America is a pontifical institution with the rector appointed by the Pope, but is under the general supervision of the hierarchy of the United States according to a definite constitution. The number of Roman Catholic parochial educational establishments in the United States according to the *Census of Re-*

ligious Bodies in 1936 was 6,825 with 65,001 officers and teachers and 2,095,254 scholars.

James A. Burns, *The Growth and Development of the Catholic School System in the United States* (1912); James A. Burns, *The Principles, Origin, and Establishment of the Catholic School System in the United States* (1908); *National Catholic Education Association Bulletin* (Washington, D. C. 1904 ff.). T.T.M.

parousia: The return of Christ in glory. The word means literally "presence" or "coming," and in Greek usage of the first century was often applied to a royal entry. This is the significance which it bears in the N.T. Christ, who on earth had appeared a man like others, will manifest himself hereafter in his true character of Messiah.* This will be, not his "Second Coming," but in the full sense his "Coming." See redemption. E.F.S.

parsimony, law of: A principle of scientific thinking and one which should be kept in mind in all thinking, viz., new phenomena should be explained in the simplest terms, by the already known in place of adding new terms or new concepts. William of Ockham* formulated this law: ***entia non sunt multiplicanda praeter necessitatem.*** The rule is sometimes called Ockham's razor, i.e., shaving down entities to the fewest in number and the simplest terms. V.F.

Parsism and Parsees: Parsism is also known as the religion of Zoroaster, whose original home was Pars or Persia. See India, religions of; Persia, religions of; Zoroastrianism. See also bibliography under Mazdaism. H.H.

Particular or Calvinistic Baptists: See Baptists.

Pārvatī: A Hindu goddess of the Shivite school, one of the consorts of Shiva;* a gentle, beautiful, attractive figure in contrast to Kali.* C.S.B.

Pascal, Blaise: (1623-1662) French mathematician and natural scientist, who turned to mysticism under the influence of the Jansenists of Port Royal. His *Pensées sur la religion*, a famous document of devotional literature, rejects rationalism and expresses the conviction that the heart or will is the means of discovering God. The *Pensées* were published in garbled form in 1670; a somewhat better edition appeared in 1776, edited by Condorcet, and a new edition from the original manuscript was brought out in 1844 by A. P. Faugère. Brunschvicg's is a standard modern edition.

His *Provinciales* (1657), written anonymously in defense of Antoine Arnauld of the Sorbonne against the Jesuits, were of high literary excellence. See mysticism; supernaturalism. Cf. probabilism. J.E.N.

Pascendi Dominici Gregis, Encyclical of Pope Pius X, Sept. 8, 1907: See modernism; Pius X, Pope.

The Encyclical will be found in *Acta Sanctae Sedis* (1907), vol. 40, 593-650. Cf. *Kirchl. Handlexikon* (München, 1912), II, 1345. R.M.H.

paschal candle: In the Roman Catholic liturgy a very large candle, lighted with solemn ceremonies the day before Easter and kept burning at service time until Ascension Day.* B.S.E.

paschal lamb: (Paschal is an adj. from the Gr. form *pascha* of the Hebr. *pesah*, passover.) In origin probably a pastoral sacrifice, then brought into connection with the Exodus—a lamb (or kid —Ex. 12.5), slaughtered, cooked and eaten, its blood sprinkled on the doorposts to ward off evil. Later applied symbolically to Jesus. See Passover. S.H.B.

paschal season: See church year cycle.

Passavant, William Alfred: (1821-1894) Pioneer in American home missions, of a wealthy, cultured family, originally Burgundians, who had settled near Pittsburgh Pa., he is known for his benevolence, editorial work and as the founder of orphanages in Zelienople and Rochester, Pa., and of hospitals at Pittsburgh, Chicago Milwaukee and Jacksonville, Ill. He studied philanthropic efforts in England and Germany and persuaded Pastor Fliedner of the Kaiserwerth Deaconess School to come to the U. S. A. with four deaconesses* in 1849. Passavant planned to establish schools for training institutional workers. He was instrumental in establishing the Lutheran orphanages in Germantown, Pa., Mt. Vernon, N. Y., and Boston, Mass., and the Emigrant House on State Street, New York City. A.S.

passion: (Lat., *passie*, from *pati*, to suffer) Term applied to the sufferings of Christ and his atoning death upon the cross; and by extension, to the sufferings of the martyrs.

Passion Sunday is the fifth Sunday in Lent,* and Passion Week the week preceding Holy Week. The period of two weeks from Passion Sunday to the eve of Easter is called Passiontide.

The long lections from the Gospels in Holy Week are technically termed Passions. P.V.N.

passion music: The solemn chanting of the story of the passion, begun by the eighth century, had by the twelfth been developed for the sacred ministers of the Mass* in the form and to the melodies now known. In Germany after the Reformation* the music* was separated from the liturgy:* in this form it reached its culmination in Bach's St. Matthew Passion. T.J.B.

A musical setting of the events of Holy Week. The passion grew from the medieval mystery play. The form was patterned after that of the motet or the oratorio. The most famous were those by Schütz, Handel, Bach, Haydn, and Beethoven, whose *Mount of Olives* is a passion. E.H.B.

passion offices: Commemorations of the passion of Christ in the Canonical Offices, first developed for the Passionist Fathers c. 1775 and now widely used on the Fridays in Lent and at other times. T.J.B.

passion plays: See religious drama.

Passionists: The common name for members of the Congregation of Barefooted Clerks of the Most Holy Cross and Passion of Our Lord Jesus

Christ. This institute was founded in Rome in 1720 by St. Paul of the Gross, known in the world as Paul Francis Danei, a native of Genoa. His brother John was closely associated with him in the first organization of the institute. Its rules were approved by Pope Benedict XIV on May 15, 1741. Its purpose is twofold: first, the sanctification of its members, and secondly, the sanctification of others. The idea of the founder was to unite in it the solitary life of the Carthusians* or Trappists with the active life of the Jesuits.* Its members are engaged in giving missions and retreats, doing parish work and carrying on foreign missionary work. The rule calls for recitation of the Office in choir, three fast days a week, and other austerities. They were introduced into England in 1841 and into the United States in 1852. Passionist nuns constitute a distinct group although founded under the direction of St. Paul of the Cross. They devote themselves to the contemplative life. There is also a second Order of Passionist nuns founded in England in 1850 which devote themselves to more active work.
T.T.M.

Passiontide: See church year cycle.

Passover: The name of a Hebrew festival—the translation of the Hebr. verb *pasah,* to skip or pass over, so named because of the tradition that the "destroyer" passed over the houses marked with the blood of the paschal lamb when he slew the first-born of Egypt (Ex. 12.21ff.). Pastoral in origin the festival may actually have been named for the "skipping" of lambs. But it came to be associated with the Exodus and in Canaan joined to itself the rites of an agricultural festival of Unleavened Bread.* It is still celebrated for 7 (8) days from the 14th of the first month (Nisan) as a memorial of the liberation of the Hebrews from Egyptian bondage. See Easter; Haggadah; Jewish religious festivals; sacramental meal; Seder.
S.H.B.

pastor: (Lat., shepherd) A Christian clergyman in charge of a congregation (Eph 4:11). The imagery is OT (Jer 2:8 RV, etc.) and perfectly natural in Christianity (John 21:15-17; compare John 10:7-16, etc.). See clergy.
B.S.E.

pastor aeternus: See pope; Vatican Council.

Pastoral Epistles: This inclusive title has been given, since the 18th century, to the three Epistles of First and Second Timothy and Titus**, which are closely related to one another, and are addressed, not to communities, but to individual church leaders. They deal, in the main, with subjects of a practical nature, church order and discipline, the selection of church officers, the character and duties of church members. Frequent mention is made of heresy, and one purpose of the Epistle, perhaps the chief one, is to safe-guard the church from the inroads of false teaching. The Epistles are written in the name of Paul, and are probably based on notes by him, which have been worked up into their present form by a later teacher.

W. Lock, *A Critical and Exegetical Commentary on the Pastoral Epistles* (ICC, 1924); E. F. Scott, *The Literature of the New Testament* (1932).
E.F.S.

pastoral theology: A systematic study of the work of the minister, as pastor, in the light of Christian principles, and of all relevant experience.
A.K.R.

Patarenes: A dualistic sect, originating in the Balkans, particularly in Bulgaria; in the twelfth century they became quite numerous in the Serbian territories now known as Bosnia-Herzegovina, where they became the predominant religious organization and where they survived till the Turkish conquest. This group is closely connected with the Bogomils* in Bulgaria. In northern Italy there appeared in the late twelfth and early thirteenth centuries a group of dualists known as Patarini; this name is commonly derived from Pattaria, a slum section of Milan. But on the theory that it represents a transplantation of the Patarenes from the Balkans, the name would more properly be traced to the latter group. In the thirteenth century, the name was applied indiscriminately to all such dualistic heretics as the Cathari, Albigenses, and even other, non-dualistic groups as the Waldenses.** Cf. Paulicians.

Matthew Spinka, *A History of Christianity in th Balkans* (1933).
M.S

paten: A plate, usually of precious metal, for the bread at the Communion service. See chalice.
B.S.E.

patience: That endurance of any evil, small or great, which is calm and self-controlled rather than dogged, peevish, defiant or cynical. It is a virtue in most religious ethics although it varies in accent from the passive, disciplined indifference of the East and the "apathy" of the Stoics* to its active Christian form of a glad perseverance in love and good works born of submission to the will of God and of trustful waiting in hope upon Him. Chrysostom called it the queen of the virtues.
R.W.F.

patriarch and patriarchate, ecclesiastical: High ranking ecclesiastical officer in R.C. and Eastern churches, superior in authority to the metropolitans or archbishops. Patriarchate is territory over which he has jurisdiction. Name was applied on analogy of Jewish usage but in a somewhat general way in early days of growth of episcopacy.* Church organization followed model of civil government of Roman Empire, and bishops* of more important areas became metropolitans* as they assumed control over a group of dioceses. Certain of these metropolitans asserted authority over other metropolitans. The first to gain superior recognition were Alexandria, Antioch and Rome and to them were added Constantinople and Jerusalem. By 5th cent. these stood at head of the most important ecclesiastical provinces and from 8th or 9th cent. "patriarch" was official title of a definite rank in the hierarchy. Patriarch of Constantinople became head of Eastern Church and still retains primacy of honour among all Eastern Orthodox churches* except Bulgaria. Each national section of the Eastern Orthodox Church has its own patriarch also. In addition the "heretical" Eastern churches and the Uniate churches* have their separate patriarchs. Rome as the only patriarchate in the west had predominant position. Bishop of Rome is both pope* and patriarch. See Holy Synod. K.H.C.

Patriarch, the: See Jeremiah II.

patriarchal system: While scattered traces of matriarchal* family organization appear in the OT, the patriarchal system prevailed in Israel from the very beginning of history. It forms the background of the traditions, institutions, and mode of thinking of Israel. The family unit was the *bet ab,* the father's house (Gen. 38.11; Judg. 6.15; 1 Sam. 18.18). The clan is an extension of the family, as the tribe is an extension of the clan (1 Sam. 9.20-21; Judg. 18.1, 11; Num. 1.20-43). The whole nation is descended through the heads of the tribes from the patriarchs. The Priestly* writer traces the history of the entire human race to a common father, Adam. Eve herself was fashioned out of a rib taken from Adam's body. In his geneologies this writer deals exclusively with the men. The seventy nations descended from the three sons of Noah (Gen. 2; 5; 10).

The Israelite family centers around the father. Marriage meant acquiring ownership of a wife. The husband is called *baal,* lord and master. He owned the wife as he owned his children and children's children and servants (Gen. 31.43; 46.26). His authority over them was at one time absolute (Gen. 22; 38.24; Judg. 11.39; etc.). In course of time his authority was checked somewhat. He could sell his daughter only while she was a minor (Ex. 21.7-11; Lev. 19.29; Num. 30.4-15). The relation between husband and wife was an intimate one. None the less he was the head and she was his helpmate (Gen. 2.18). She bore his name (Is. 4.1). Her foremost task was to bear him children and to help him establish a house (Gen. 30.23; 1 Sam. 1). (See levirate marriage). The marriage laws were determined from his standpoint (Lev. 18; Deut. 22.20-21). It is he that could dissolve the marriage, but not his wife. Polygamy naturally follows such marriage arrangements. The husband might add to his principal wife a number of secondary wives. In such case his children were differentiated by being designated by their maternal names. The family property, too, was bound up with the husband, the wife sharing in it by virtue of belonging to him. On his death, the inheritance went to his sons (Num. 27.8-11).

However, the mother was the equal of the father in the claim upon the respect of the children (Ex. 20.12; 21.15, 17; Lev. 19.3; 20.9; Deut. 21.18-21; 27.26; Ezek. 22.7; Prov. 20.20). In turn both parents were obligated to care for their children, to teach and to guide them (Prov. 1.1; Deut. 6.6-7).

M. Burrows, *Basis of Israelite Marriage* (1938); David Jacobson, *The Social Background of the O. T.* (1942); Johs Pederson, *Israel* (1926). S.S.C.

Patrick: (Lat., *Patricius*) Saint (389-461) Missionary to and patron saint of Ireland. He was born of Christian parents in Scotland, taken captive at the age of 16 by Irish marauders. After six years' bondage in Ireland he fled to a monastery, perhaps in Gaul, and prepared to return as a missionary to Ireland. In 432 he was consecrated bishop and proceeded to challenge the pagan faith and practices of Ireland. He built churches, established a monastery, trained clergy, organized Christian societies, introduced Latin, and brought Ireland in touch with Rome and European culture. P.E.J.

Patrimony of St. Peter: In early times the revenues and landed possesions of the Holy See* and called by Gregory the Great the property of the poor; also a term used sometimes up to 1870 for the States of the Church. See Papal States. L.R.W.

patripassianism: (Lat., *pater,* father; *patior,* suffer) A nickname applied by Cyprian* to the Modalistic Monarchian* Doctrine that the redemptive suffering of Christ was the suffering of God the Father, since Christ and the Father are the same Person. Noetus and Praxeas were prominent advocates of this doctrine which flourished during the second and third centuries. Cf. modalism; monarchianism; Sabellianism; Theopaschites. H.W.J.

patristics: The branch of historical theology dealing with the lives, writings, and doctrines of the Fathers. These are commonly divided somewhat arbitrarily by the Council of Nicæa (325 A.D.) into ante-Nicene and post-Nicene Fathers. With even less justification certain of the earlier noncanonical writings (I and II Clement, the epistles of Ignatius, the epistle and *Martyrdom* of Polycarp, the *Shepherd* of Hermas, and the *Epistle of Diognetus*) are styled Apostolic Fathers.* The writings of the early Fathers (*e.g.,* Justin, Aristides, Quadratus, Tatian) are often styled *apologies, i.e.,* defenses of Christianity against heathendom. In some quarters, notably Alexandria, the early Fathers (Pantænus, Clement, and Origen) strove, as had Philo before them for Judaism, to show that the best of pagan thought was in accordance with—had, in fact, been anticipated by—Christianity. Among the most influential figures of the rising orthodoxy at the end of the second and beginning of the third century were Clement and Origen, Tertullian, Cyprian, and Novatian, Irenæus and Hippolytus.** Leaders of thought among the post-Nicene Fathers included Arius, Athanasius, Hilary, Basil, Gregory of Nyssa, Cyril of Alexandria, Theodore of Mopsuestia, Jerome, and (perhaps the most influential of all) Augustine,** who laid the foundations upon which orthodox Christianity was long to stand. In the reconstruction of the text of the biblical writings quotations of the Scripture from the writings of the Fathers (*patristic citations*) are of great importance to the textual critic. Some of the Fathers have been admirably edited. Critical editions of the rest are greatly needed.

A. Harnack, *Geschichte der altchristlichen Litteratur* (1893-1904) 3 vols.; O. Bardenhewer, *Patrologie* (1910), 3rd ed.; *Geschichte der altchristlichen Literatur* (1913-1932), 5 vols.; E. J. Goodspeed, *A History of Early Christian Literature* (1942).

M.S.E.

patrology: That part of historical theology which deals with the lives, writings and teachings of the Fathers of the Christian Church. See **patristics.** H.W.J.

patron: See patronage.

patron saints: A saint chosen to be the guardian, special intercessor with God and protector of a place, person or association, according to the practice of the R.C. and Eastern churches. Developed in part from veneration* felt for early Christian martyrs and in some cases possession of their relics.* Churches, countries, towns, villages, professions, etc., as well as individuals are dedicated to a patron saint and are under his care. Many saints* are traditionally associated with a particular country or trade. There may be lesser patrons as well as a principal patron. St. Joseph is patron saint of the universal church. See wake. K.H.C.

patronage: Signifies the rights and obligations of a person(s) (clerical or lay) with respect to a benefice. In early medieval church history (both Greek and Latin) the patron often was a lord who at his own expense had built a church. The usual rights of patronage pertain to presentation,* honorary distinctions, and support of the patron's person when he is in need. The obligations involve duties of maintaining the benefice (rebuilding, etc.). Claims of patrons to control of appointments, interference in policy, and the like, have been modified in the course of history in accordance with varying traditions (e.g., R. Cath., Anglican). See also advowson; benefice; eigenkirche; simony. Q.B.

Paul, the Apostle: A first-century Jewish opponent of the followers of Jesus, commonly styled Saul of Tarsus, who following his conversion became an ardent and influential champion of the growing movement through his activity as a protagonist of the gentile mission and through his letters to his converts. The early years of his life are unknown. All that can be safely inferred from his letters is that he was a Jew of orthodox parentage; that he was strict to the point of fanaticism in his reverence for the Jewish law, in the interpretation of which he followed (as did all orthodox Jews) the Pharisees;* that he joined heartily in persecuting the early Christians. In the canonical Book of Acts* (the source of most biographical sketches of Paul, but of definitely secondary value for the historian) he is depicted as born in Tarsus, as possessing Roman citizenship, as a young man having studied in Jerusalem "at the feet of Gamaliel,"* an eminent Jewish teacher, and as being present at the stoning of Stephen. Nothing in his letters guarantees any of these data; the references to his pre-Christian activity in Jerusalem are distinctly suspect. During the fourth decade he suffered a right about-face, apparently in or near Damascus, becoming convinced that Jesus, far from being accursed of God as he had earlier apparently believed, had but done God's will, that he had risen from the dead and was now in heaven at God's right hand, and would soon come to judgment. From persecutor he became champion of the faith he had earlier sought to destroy. Following a period of work in Arabia (apparently hinted at in Gal. 1:17, but without details), he spent many years in Syria and Cilicia, eventually becoming prominent among the Christians in Syrian Antioch.* Then followed a decade or more of itinerant work in the hitherto untouched districts of Asia Minor and eastern Europe (Macedonia and Greece), in the course of which he wrote many letters to the churches which he had founded, some of which letters having been preserved came later to be regarded as sacred, eventually becoming part of the NT. He apparently planned to continue his missionary activities in the Roman West, after making a final visit to Jerusalem with a gift from his gentile churches to the Jewish Christians of that city. According to the narrative in Acts his plans miscarried; he was mobbed in Jerusalem, arrested, and after an imprisonment at Cæsarea was sent to Rome, where he drops from sight. The tradition of his martyrdom in Rome may well be correct; the traditional date for the execution (67 A.D.) is surely far too late, and rests upon the (probably) unjustified tradition of a temporary release, a short period of renewed missionary activity, and his subsequent re-arrest and condemnation.

Appraisals of Paul have been many and varied. To some he was the virtual founder of Christianity; to others a comparatively insignificant figure thrown into unwarranted prominence by the narratives in Acts. He has been represented as the greatest Christian theologian of all time, and as the muddleheaded and sinister figure who muddied the limpid waters of the preaching of Jesus. Probably both extremes are incorrect. He may well have been the most influential of the missionaries to the gentiles; he was surely neither the first nor the only one. The evidence would seem to indicate that others, for the most part to us unknown, were working in about the same general way as was he.

The debt of Christianity to Paul is threefold, and in each part it is concerned with human conduct. To the Jews, Paul insisted upon freedom from the law*—the law was not, could not be, the criterion of life: that was implicit and self-revealed in the mystic union of the believer with his crucified and risen Lord. In protest against the laxity in morals in the hellenistic world, he stressed the sturdy Jewish morality with its insistence on the purity of family life. For Paul morals and religion were to all intents indissoluble, if not actually identical. The proof that a man was "in Christ" was the quality of life he lived. The third, and perhaps the most lasting, note he struck was that of fellowship (*koinonia*), not alone with Christ but with the fellow believers. Thus he sought to weld his converts into an organic unity bound by the closest ties to a living source. This vertical bond to their common Lord must result in an equally real horizontal bond with their fellows. All Christians together—each one individually "in Christ"—comprised literally the body of Christ. Logically Paul's position was indefensible: By baptism the convert, the initiate, was plunged into mystic union with the risen Lord, by the impartation of whose spirit a new life began. He was so completely linked to Christ that he was no longer able to distinguish between his own desires and goals and those of his Lord. He had the mind of Christ, not because he thought *like* Christ but because Christ was actually thinking in him. Thus *faith* was not the intellectual assent to notions, however valuable they might be. To all intents it meant for Paul *new life*. The *faith* of the Christian was the new life he was living in Christ, the life Christ was living in him, the new life that was being lived by the newborn Christ-man. Yet Paul's letters make perfectly clear that a large part of his time was devoted to ethical admonitions to faltering Christians and a constant warning of the impending judgment. Logically, his admonitions and sharply defined rules of conduct—what was worthy, as he saw it, of one "in Christ"—were unnecessary. He who was in Christ would have supplied by the Spirit all necessary insights and help, would find himself borne along on the current streaming from Christ. The reason for the breakdown in logic is obvious. All about him Paul saw fellow Christians whose conduct he strongly disapproved. By precept and example he sought to encourage and strengthen those who, while in Christ, were but "babes in Christ"—instead of ostrichlike refusing to see the dangers to his theological opinion. (If no other evidence existed, this would be enough to prove Paul was not a theologian!) The breach in logic is obvious—was perfectly obvious to many of his gentile converts, as is evidenced by Galatians and the correspondence with Corinth—and is not to be rationalized away. Paul was not a theologian nor a logician but an eminently practical and forthright man who never seems to have shrunk from doing what he felt compelled under God to do by the fear or charge of being inconsistent. See Christology; justification; reason in religion; righteousness, N.T. conception of; soul. See also Pauline Epistles.

The Pauline literature is huge. Among others may be mentioned: Percy Gardner, *The Religious Experience of St. Paul* (1911); A. Deissmann, *The Religion of Jesus and the Faith of Paul* (1923); M. S. Enslin, *The Ethics of Paul* (1930); F. C. Porter, *The Mind of Christ in Paul* (1930); K. Lake, *Paul; his Heritage and Legacy* (1934); A. D. Nock, *St. Paul* (1938); D. W. Riddle, *Paul, Man of Conflict* (1940). M.S.E.

Paul of Samosata: Bishop of Antioch (260-272), the most famous expositor of dynamic monarchianism*. He taught that the power of the essentially impersonal Logos from above inspired the man Jesus, who had been born of the Virgin. Thus endowed by the Logos, Jesus was inseparably united to God in a perfect moral unity of will, but not in a unity of substance. Because of his merit Jesus was raised from the dead and exalted by the Father to a position of divinity. Paul of Samosata was excommunicated by the third of three synods meeting at Antioch from 264 to 269, but remained in his position until 272 when Aurelian conquered Zenobia. H.W.J.

Paulicians: The Paulicians were an Armenian Adoptionist* sect. Its origin is traditionally traced to a certain Bishop Paul of Samosata* in the third century, or a certain Constantine in the seventh century, although the adherents liked to derive the name from St. Paul. They were strongly iconoclastic, and opposed the cult of the Virgin and the saints. Some groups of them having been transplanted to Thrace by Emperor Constantine V, their influence (among other causes) gave rise to a native Bulgarian dualistic sect of Bogomils*. This latter movement received the name of Patarenes* in Bosnia-Herzegovina, and in ways no longer clear influenced the rise of the dualistic sects in southern France, such as the Cathari and the Albigenses**.

Matthew Spinka, *A History of Christianity in the Balkans* (1933); Karapet Ter-Mkrttschian, *Die Paulicianer in byzantinischen Kaiserreich* (Leipzig, 1893); F. C. Conybeare, *The Key of Truth* (Oxford, 1898). M.S.

Pauline Epistles: Thirteen so-called *epistles* (more properly *letters*) in the N.T. are commonly ascribed to Paul: Romans, I and II Corinthians, Galatians, Ephesians, Philippians, Colossians, I and II Thessalonians, I and II Timothy, Titus, and Philemon. Three of these—I and II Timothy and Titus—commonly styled the *Pastoral Epistles***, are widely (though not universally) regarded today as sub-Pauline, although, in the judgment of some critics, containing fragments of genuine Pauline material. The authenticity of three others—Ephesians, II Thessalonians, and Colossians—has frequently been challenged. Attempts at separation of the letters into two clear-cut groups—Earlier or Missionary *vs.* Later Epistles—and deductions as to fancied developments in Pauline thought have not infrequently been made but cannot be pronounced as of more than doubtful value. Four of the letters—Philippians, Colossians, Philemon, and (if genuine) Ephesians—appear to have been written while Paul was in prison, but opinions differ as to whether the imprisonment was in Ephesus, Cæsarea, or Rome. All of the genuine epistles would seem to fall within a brief span of years (50-55 A.D.; perhaps less probably 50-59 A.D.). Indications in the letters themselves suggest that these which have survived are but a fragmentary part of a larger correspondence and themselves show evidence of having been edited. For more detailed information as to the several letters and their purpose see articles Paul, Romans, Ephesians, etc. M.S.E.

Paulists, the: Members of the Missionary Society of St. Paul the Apostle, a community of priests founded in 1858 by Father Isaac Thomas Hecker in Rome and New York with the aid of Fathers Augustine F. Hewit, George Deshon, Francis A. Baker, and Clarence A. Walworth.

These men had been members of the Congregation of the Most Holy Redeemer and had been active in the American missions of the Congregation. When Father Hecker went to Rome to explain certain difficulties which had arisen concerning them, he was expelled from the community on August 29, 1857. Father Hecker,* with the support of many prominent American bishops appealed to the Pope, and he and the other priests were released from their vows. They then formed their own community with the approval of Archbishop John Hughes of New York. He assigned to them the mission and church which has since become their motherhouse in West 59th Street, New York. Their rule is based upon that of the Redemptorists*, although they do not take vows; their formula of profession, taken after their novitiate, calls for a declaration of their intention to obey the rules, to aspire after Christian perfection and to devote themselves to the Apostolic ministry. Besides their own personal sanctification the Paulists devote themselves particularly to the conversion of non-Catholics. They engage in lecturing, preaching, the printing and distribution of missionary literature and private conferences with prospective converts. They conduct some parishes, give missions and from 1925-1937 conducted their own radio station in New York. They publish the *Catholic World,* and conduct their own printing establishment for the publication of missionary magazines, pamphlets and books.

W. Elliott, *The Life of Father Hecker* (2nd ed., 1891); James M. Gillis, *The Paulists* (1932).

T.T.M.

pax: (Lat., peace, and so, kiss) The "holy kiss" (Rom. 16:16, etc.), became a general liturgical custom at the Eucharist. In the middle ages the "pax" was a small decorated tablet, kissed by the priest and then by the others in order.

B.S.E.

peal ringing: Peal ringing is an art practiced throughout the British Isles, in some of the colonies, and here and there in America. A peal is composed of eight, ten or twelve bells, although a few peals may be rung on as few as five or six bells. Such bells are always in the form of either a simple diatonic scale, or else a diatonic scale with two to four added notes above.

Bells for peal ringing are hung so as to be swung through a complete circle, with headstock, stay and slider arranged to prevent upsetting the bell. They are rung by means of wheels and ropes, the latter passing through the floor of the belfry and down into a ringers chamber below. There are as many ringers as there are bells, and they stand in a circle, facing toward the center.

Peal ringing, also called change ringing, is accomplished somewhat as follows: Usually the bells are played in rapid succession, in the form of a descending scale. Then, upon a signal from the leader, bells are made to change places with one-another, until finally a most intricate melody is rung. These melodies follow certain well-recognized methods, not easy to recognize by those unfamiliar with peal ringing. These melodies are constructed upon sound, scientific patterns, and require a considerable degree of skill on the part of the ringers. Some of the simplest methods require three hours and a half to complete. Others require more time. Among many famous peals that have been rung was a peal of 21,363 Stedman Caters, rung at Appleton, Berks., (tenor bell 14 cwt.), on April 22, 1922, which required twelve hours and twenty-five minutes. It was rung by the Oxford Diocesan Guild and Ancient Society of College Youths and the tempo of the peal was twenty-eight changes per minute.

On three bells, playing three successive notes of the diatonic scale, six changes may be rung. On four bells, 24 changes are possible. On five bells one may ring 120 changes. On eight bells (the usual number) 40,320 changes may be rung. On a peal of 12 bells, 479,001,600 changes may be rung, requiring 91 years, were they rung at the usual rate of two per second.

While peal ringing is practiced in comparatively few churches in America, and these largely in the New England states, yet poetry and literature contain frequent references to the art, and many familiar hymns refer to it. Without a little knowledge of the basic principles of ringing, many of these literary references are easily misinterpreted.

Many churches in America have a succession of eight or more bells, and often an attempt is made to ring changes on these either by means of hand levers or else by an Ellacombe wall rack. This is not true peal ringing, and must not be confused with the scientific method in which eight, ten or twelve men "ring the bells up" and then proceed with the intricate work of correct change ringing. See carillon.

F.R.W.

peasants' war, the: Armed rising in Germany, 1525. It took place at a period of great unrest, but was due rather to social forces of long standing than to the effect of the religious freedom proclaimed by the Reformation.* Feudalism* had destroyed the old peasantry. Virtual serfdom bound the rural worker to the land, and even the law was powerless to protect him from the burden of intolerable exactions.

The rising was the first clear effort to organize the whole peasantry of Germany, but there were various strands within the movement. The strongest centre was in Swabia, and here a clear programme was put forward as a basis for negotiation with the nobles. It took its inspiration from the Gospel, upheld the communal principle, and was primarily concerned with genuine agrarian grievances. Its twelve articles put forward in strong but moderate terms the peasants' demands. Though some nobles were willing to negotiate, others used discussions only as a screen for military preparation. Truchsess, the leader of the Swabian League (nobles), aimed at keeping the peasants divided and then utterly overthrowing them. Other strands in the peasants' movement were represented by the "Heilbroon plan" (a programme for radical political reconstruction as well as agrarian reform), while the extreme wing was Muenzer's* theocratic communism. In the actual struggle the peasants were quickly overthrown.

The significance of the peasants' war is threefold. 1) It is historically important because, though primarily an attempt to unify German peasantry, it brought into association the lower classes of town and country. 2) The social and economic results were appalling. The peasants were ruthlessly suppressed, and at the end their outlook was blacker than at the beginning. 3) Religious results. Luther's* relation to the rising was complicated both by his outlook and by the development of the rising. At the outset he hoped, by being honest with both sides, to initiate a reconciliation, but the outbreak of violence drove Luther into unbridled denunciation of the peasants. His horror of the rising combined with certain elements latent in his theology to confirm the erastianism* to which Lutheranism has always been liable. See Philip of Hesse.

Cambridge Modern History, ii; E. B. Bax, *The Peasants' War in Germany* (London, 1899); W. Stolze, *Der Deutsche Bauernkrieg* (Halle, 1907).

G.R.C.

Pécaut, Felix: (1827-1898) He was inspector general of primary instruction and co-founder of the Free Church in Neuchâtel, Switzerland. Opposed to compromise between orthodoxy and complete denial of the supernatural, he held that the logically clear and convincing problem of religion to be the complete humanisation of the Bible and the stripping off of the traditional magical disguise of the person of Christ, whose divinity Pecaut reduced to a mere moral sainthood. The name of Jesus was for him the symbol of popular idealism. Liberal Christianity was for him neither a congealed dogma nor a closed system but a grain capable of development.

Le christ et la conscience (Paris, 1859); *De l'avenir du théisme chretienne* (Paris, 1864); *De l'avenir du Protestantisme en France* (Paris, 1865); *Le christianisme libéral et le miracle* (Paris, 1869); *De l'argument de utilite liberal en matière de la religion* (Paris, 1870).

H.H.

Peck, John Mason: (1789-1858) Baptist pioneer preacher, missionary, author. Favored enforcement of Fugitive Slave Law. Promoted the founding of Shurtleff College.

C.H.M.

pedobaptism: See infant baptism.

Peirce, Charles Sanders: (1839-1914) American philosopher and scientist. Recognized by William James* as the originator of philosophical Pragmatism*, a theory of meaning which sees the import of concepts in their "conceivable practical bearings" (the emphasis is on "conceivable" a concept need not be actually useful to have meaning, provided one can imagine a use for it). Peirce also influenced James (and Royce*) through a daring cosmology, which regarded the laws of nature as merely the most stable habits of nature, not absolute or immutable, but evolving from an aboriginal chaos in the infinitely remote past toward perfect regularity in the infinitely remote future. Matter he held to be "mind hide-bound by habit," the portion of nature in which creative spontaneity is slight, hence largely without consciousness, though not without feeling. There is a continuum of all possible (though not of all actual) forms and qualities, so that differences commonly regarded as of kind (such as that between a color sensation and a sound sensation) are really differences of degree (theory of Synechism). The whole of evolution is a "divine poem". In a few passages of Peirce's writings it seems to be suggested that God is in some manner enriched by the world process, himself a temporal being, but in others God is referred to in traditional fashion as wholly independent of time and the world.

Primarily a logician, Peirce thoroughly revised many portions of logic and was one of the chief creators of symbolic logic. Among the matters best worked out in his fragmentary and often difficult writings are his frequency theory of probable reasoning, his theory of the categories (also called Phenomenology*), and his studies of the kinds and uses of signs.

The categories are First, Second, Third; or Feeling-quality, Reaction and Representation. A mere feeling, abstracted as much as possible from contrast and relation, is monadic or first; an experience of effort-resistance or passivity-activity, is dyadic or second; a sign, involving something meant, something by which it is meant, and a state of mind or mental habit for which the meaning obtains, is triadic or third. Signs or thirds themselves can be classified according to the same triadic system. Thus if a sign means primarily through its quality or internal character it is called an Icon (or resemblance); if through its reaction with something else, an Index; if through a mental habit, a symbol. An Icon tells us what something might be like; an Index that something exists; a Symbol that something is thought. In combination these elements yield propositions, arguments, and all the logical forms (never before so completely analyzed by one simple key idea).

Peirce published only articles in his lifetime. Six volumes of *Collected Papers,* edited by C. Hartshorne and P. Weiss, appeared in 1931-35. They contain all the philosophical articles published in Peirce's lifetime, and, in greater quantity, writings found among his remains. On Peirce's theological views see Hartshorne, "A Critique of Peirce's Idea of God," *Philos. Rev.,* L (1941), 516-23.

The best life of Peirce is by Weiss, in the *American Dictionary of Biography* (1928-36), ed. by A. Johnson and D. Malone.

Material on Theory of the Categories is chiefly in Vol. I, on Pragmatism in Vol. V, on Metaphysics and Philosophy of Religion in VI, and on Logic in II.

C.H.

Pelagianism: The body of teachings named after Pelagius*. Pelagianism denied original sin* and man's hereditary guilt. Physical death whether in the case of Adam or of his descendants is not the result of sin, but is necessarily involved in nature. Spiritual death is not the inherited consequence of Adam's sin, but comes to each individual will which misuses its power of free choice by choosing to sin. All men by virtue of their reason and free will have the power to avoid making this unrighteous choice. If in the exercise of his free and morally responsible will man so chooses, he may grasp the external aid of divine grace which is bestowed according to man's merit. Divine grace* is variously and ambiguously described as being the natural constitution of man, or as being God's Law which reveals the divine will, or again, as being the grace of Christ which works through His assurance of forgiveness* to those who are baptized and through the teachings of the Church. The unassisted human will however takes the determining initiative in the matter of salvation. After having been rejected by the North African Synods of Carthage* and of Mileve in 416, Pelagianism was officially condemned by the Third General Council of Ephesus* in 431. See Julian of Eclanum; libertarianism; Semi Pelagianism. H.W.J.

Pelagius: A monk of great learning and high moral character. He is said to have been of British birth. About the year 400 he went to Rome. There he was shocked by the lax morals of professing Christians and endeavored earnestly to raise the ethical standards by affirming the responsibility which men have before God for their actions. In 410 Pelagius with his follower Coelestius went to North Africa. Pelagius remained there but a short time, then going to Palestine. The teachings of Pelagius were zealously opposed by his contemporary Augustine*. The two North African Synods of Mileve and Carthage* condemned Pelagianism in the year 416. This condemnation was confirmed by Pope Innocent I, and later by Zosimus. Pelagius died about the year 420. See Pelagianism. H.W.J.

penal theory: See satisfaction.

penance: 1) The virtue of penitence, heartfelt sorrow for sin with the purpose of sinning no more. 2) In the early church, a canonical punishment for grave offenses (see longer article "penance"). 3) A prayer or work of reparation enjoined upon a penitent in the sacrament of penance, regarded as punitive (at least to the degree of indicating the penitent's willingness to receive punishment) and remedial. See penitential (manual). T.J.B.

penance: A sacrament of the Roman Catholic Church, consisting of contrition, confession*, and satisfaction on the part of the penitent, and absolution by the priest. It has to do only with baptized Christians who have sinned after baptism. The Eastern Orthodox Church* also regards penance as a sacrament; the Anglican Church* leaves its practice to the conscience of the individual.

Three stages may be distinguished in the development of penitential practices which culminated in the sacramental theory of penance. 1) In the early centuries, public penance was a means of discipline and probation whereby the Church sought to maintain its purity in a world of appalling moral laxity and to conserve its life in the face of severe and repeated persecution. Homicide, sexual impurity, and apostasy* were mortal sins* which necessarily excluded the sinner from the communion and fellowship of the Church; and he could be restored only by submission to a strict regimen of public penance for a set term of years, which might be shortened or lengthened at the discretion of the bishop. Persons were admitted to penance but once.

2) From the fifth century public penance fell into disuse, and there gradually developed a system of private penance and recurrent confession, which first grew up within the monasteries, but became finally established as the practice of the Church by a decree of the Fourth Council of the Lateran*, A.D. 1215: "Every *fidelis* of either sex shall after the attainment of years of discretion separately confess his sins with all fidelity to his own priest at least once in the year; and shall endeavor to fulfill the penance imposed upon him to the best of his ability, reverently receiving the sacrament of the Eucharist at least at Easter."

3) The first clear definition of penance as a sacrament was by Peter Lombard* (c. 1100-1160) who made it one of the list of seven sacraments which he devised. His doctrine on this point was accepted and elaborated by Thomas Aquinas, and became the faith of the Church by vote of the Council of Florence in 1439. The sacramental character of penance was reaffirmed, after the protest of the Reformers, at the Council of Trent*.

The sacramental system of penance had been the possession of the Church for three hundred years, when the Protestant Reformers denied it. Their attack was particularly upon the practice of absolution* by the priest, with the correlative theory of the power of the keys,* and upon the requirement of satisfaction. Even perfect contrition is viewed by the Roman Catholic as unavailing apart from the sacrament of penance, and attrition*, or imperfect contrition*, is held to be made sufficient by it; the priest thus becomes the indispensable means and administrator of forgiveness and salvation. The term satisfaction does not refer to the restitution or repair of wrong done (though the Church's insistence upon this principle was an important part of the service it rendered to the moral life); but it refers rather to the sinner's satisfaction of God's justice by working out the penalties assigned to him by the priest. The Canons of the Council of Trent draw a distinction between guilt and punishment, *culpa* and *poena*. The sinner's guilt is remitted by the words of absolution, and with it the eternal punishment which belongs to sin; but there is left a temporal punishment, of a degree and character suited to his guilt, which must in equity be endured, in order that the eternal justice of God may be satisfied. This distinction dates from the theologians of the twelfth century, Richard of St. Victor* being the one to fashion the form in which it became a permanent part of the Roman Catholic doctrine.

The distinction between *culpa* and *poena* is the root from which spring many of the errors and abuses which finally stirred Luther to protest—particularly the theory of *indulgences** and the practice of their sale. In opposition to the Roman Catholic system of penance, Luther asserted the doctrine of justification* by faith. Repentance, he held, is no sacramental transaction, requiring the intermediation of a priest and the satisfaction of God through works of penance. It involves contrition and faith—sorrow for sin and turning to God in trust and obedience. And good deeds are the fruit and consequence of repentance through faith, rather than the price with which men buy, or the merit wherewith they deserve, the salvation that comes from God. See commutation of penance; composition; forgiveness; lapsed; retention of sins; sacraments; satisfaction; sin; Thesaurus Meritorum.

J. Morin, *Commentarius Historicus de Disciplina in Administratione Sacramenti Poenitentiae* (Paris, 1651); Henry C. Lea, *History of Auricular Confession and Indulgences in the Latin Church* (1896); Oscar D. Watkins, *A History of Penance* (1920).
L.A.W.

Penates: Gods of the storeroom (*penus*) in Roman religion*, or as we should say, of the larder or pantry. Usually associated and invoked with the Lares (*familiares*), household spirits. Both groups were beneficent. The city of Rome, as the expanded household of the king also had its lares and penates. P.G.M.

Penington, Isaac: (1616-1679) Son of a distinguished Puritan father, Pennington led an unsettled religious life until adhering to Quakerism* in 1658, with his wife Mary. His spirituality and polished literary style, evidenced by previous writings, now made him an important Quaker spokesman. No Quaker writings exceed his *Letters* in spiritual maturity and depth.

Complete *Works of Isaac Penington* (1863); *Letters* (1859); For Life and Teachings: M. W. Hess, *The Name is Living* (1936). H.C.

penitence: Sorrow or repentance for sin as an offence against God, involving also a resolve to reform. These three factors are essential. 1) Regret for sin. 2) Acknowledgment of its offensiveness to God. 3) Determination af amendment. In Protestantism true penitence meets with complete forgiveness by God. In Roman Catholism the Church forgives. R.E.E.H.

penitential: (manual) One of various *libri penitentiales* (collections of penitential rules) according to which penances* suitable to sins* committed and confessed were imposed. Some of these rules were formulated by synods, some were suggested by Fathers of the Church. The most ancient of these books belonged to the Irish and British Churches of the sixth century. Subsequently they were known in France and Saxony. No such book was ever issued for the universal Church. With the collapse of the ancient penitential discipline these books fell into disuse. See confessional; seven deadly sins. C.V.

penitential orders: (Lat., *paenitens*, repentant) Those congregations or bodies of religious which stress the performance of works of penance*. Probably the most outstanding penitential Orders are the Carmelites and the Capuchins**.
W.H.

penitents, congregations of: Various confraternities* that flourished especially in Italy, Spain, and France from the 13th to the 16th century. Each confraternity had its own distinctive habit, worn during processions and ecclesiastical functions. Their rules prescribed works of mercy and penance, such as fasting, assisting prisoners, visiting the sick, burying the dead. C.V.

Penn, William: (1644-1718) Quaker* convert, leader, writer, and colonizer, one-time promoter and co-proprietor of New Jersey, founder and proprietor of Pennsylvania, 1681. An ardent advocate of civil and religious liberty in England, Penn sought to demonstrate his ideas in America. The charter, laws, and institutions of colonial New Jersey and Pennsylvania reflect his religious and political liberalism. See *Works* (1726).
T.E.D.

penology: That branch of criminological science which relates to the treatment of convicted offenders. Etymologically the term denotes punishment, and such a meaning would characterize most of those measures which have been undertaken against offenders, historically, and down to the present time. The severity of penalties have varied from capital punishment, under many different forms, to the infliction of bodily or mental suffering which stops short of death; and less severe measures as represented by fines, and, in modern times, by the use of incarceration or of probation under a suspended sentence. Banishment and transportation to penal colonies would need to be included in such a historical perspective, the one an ancient, and the other a relatively modern device. It would seem that the sadistic ingenuity of man had been thoroughly expended upon offenders against the customs or laws of society.

In modern times the merely punitive character of the treatment of criminals has been somewhat mollified due to a variety of considerations, such as the rise of humanitarian sentiments accompanying the revolutionary movements of the 18th century in Europe and America which were especially represented in the teachings of Beccaria (1738-1794). Another modifying element in modern penology came from the religious teachings of the Quakers*. Furthermore, the development of the social sciences during the 19th and 20th centuries has had its effect on penology, leading still further away from punitive sanctions, and toward an understanding of the criminal and his behavior as the basis of treatment. However, it can be said without question that there is a considerable lag between the methods of treatment that such an understanding might imply, and the punitive spirit which is still embodied in the law.

Meanwhile, it is important to emphasize that a radical change took place when toward the close of the 18th century in Europe and America incarceration in prisons became the chief means of punishment. Problems in penology, since that time, have largely centered in the prison system, with contending ideas as to what its purpose should be. Is it to punish or to reform the criminal? Or, is its main function the protection of society? Confusion of thought results from the fact that different answers are given to these questions, though among enlightened people one suspects that the merely punitive idea is giving way to the other two.

A still more recent alternative to incarceration in the treatment of offenders has come about through the system of supervised probation under a suspension of sentence. By this means a convicted person is permitted to live and work in the community under the supervision of a probation officer. If at the end of a certain period, one to five years, he has not violated the conditions of his probation he is completely released from custody; but, if he does break the probationary rules, he may then be made to serve a prison sentence for his offense. The aim of probation is not leniency, but rather to effect a more satisfactory readjustment of the offender than would be possible through a prison commitment. It is a type of treatment most suitable for first offenders, though not necessarily restricted to them, nor always desirable even for them. Whether such a milder form of treatment may be regarded as punishment, as the term penology implies, may be open to question, unless one holds that the irreducible element in punishment is the restriction of liberty on the part of the offender. The unmistakable trend in modern penology is in the direction of a more extended use of probation. Otherwise, the emphasis is upon the creation within our prisons of a regime conducive to the rehabilitation of such prisoners as may be amenable to an enlightened policy of treatment. For those who are not so, a rational procedure would be to keep them in permanent custody, not with the intent to punish, but solely as a measure for the protection of society. Provisions for this last step have yet to be embodied in law. See prison reform.

Harry Elmer Barnes and Negley K. Teeters, *New Horizons in Criminology* (1943); Arthur E. Wood and John Barker Waite, *Crime and Its Treatment* (1941); Edwin H. Sutherland, *Principles of Criminology* (1939); F. H. Wines, *Punishment and Reformation* (1895); John Lewis Gillin, *Criminology and Penology* (1926); Margaret Wilson, *The Crime of Punishment* (1931).

A.E.W.

Pentateuch: See Ezra; Hexateuch; Old Testament; Samaritan Pentateuch; Zohar.

Pentecost: (Literally "fifty days") The biblical festival which came exactly fifty days after the Passover* (Lev. 23. 15-21; Deut. 16. 9-12). It was originally a harvest festival of the Canaanites*, the pre-Israelite inhabitants of Palestine, and was borrowed from them by the Israelites, when they settled in that country. It was celebrated at the end of the seven weeks period of the grain-harvest, after the last sheaf had been gathered. In the earlier biblical writings it was called "Festival of the Harvest" (Ex. 23.16) or "Festival of First-fruits." Later it came to be known as *Shabuot*, "Festival of Weeks" (Deut. 16.10). In post-biblical Jewish literature it is said to commemorate the anniversary of the revelation of the Law at Mt. Sinai (Ex. 19).

J.M.

Pentecost, Christian: (Gr., *pentekoste*, "fiftieth (day)") In Acts 2:1 the Feast of Weeks* (which see). In Christian usage the seventh Sunday after Easter, commemorating the descent of the Holy Spirit. So observed from at least the early third century (Hippolytus*, *Apostolic Tradition*, ch. 29) and now a major feast in all liturgical churches. Known also as "Whitsunday"* (from "White Sunday," not "Whitsun Day"). Cf. church year.

B.S.E.

Pentecostal Assemblies of the World: See pentecostal sects.

Pentecostal Church of God in America: See pentecostal sects.

Pentecostal Church, Inc.: See pentecostal sects.

Pentecostal Fire-Baptized Holiness Church: See pentecostal sects.

Pentecostal Holiness Church: See pentecostal sects.

pentecostal sects: A group of ultra-perfectionist* sects* which magnify the "gift of tongues" (Acts 2:1-13), and insist on "speaking with other tongues* as the Spirit gives utterance" as the proof of the blessing of holiness. While espousing the customary doctrines of the "fundamentalist" type of theology, they lay stress on sanctification of the "second blessing" type, spirit guidance and "gifts," and premillenarianism. Not all holiness or perfectionist sects, however, are pentecostal in character. Their ever-present distinguishing mark is speaking with tongues. They are frequently dubbed "holy rollers," from the fact that extremely emotional devotees sometimes fall to the ground in trances or other experiences of an orgiastic nature.

The leading pentecostal sects in this country are: Catholic Apostolic Church (Irvingites)*; Church of God*; The (Original) Church of God*; (Tomlinson) Church of God*; Holiness Church*; Assemblies of God—General Council; Apostolic Faith Mission*; Pentecostal Holiness Church; Pentecostal Assemblies of the World; Pentecostal Assemblies of Jesus Christ; Pentecostal Church, Inc.; International Church of the Foursquare Gospel*; International Pentecostal Assemblies; Pentecostal Church of God of America; Pentecostal Fire-Baptized Holiness Church; Calvary Pentecostal Church; Church of God in Christ* (Pentecostal); New Apostolic Church*; Congregational Holiness Church*; General Council of the Italian Pentecostal Assemblies of God; Unorganized Italian Christian Churches of North America. (See Italian pentecostal sects.)

Many Negro sects are pentecostal in character and "tongue talking" and similar emotional automata are practiced among groups which have not definitely developed the theology of left-wing perfectionism. Among the Negro bodies which "speak in tongues" may be mentioned: Apostolic Overcoming Holy Church of God*; Church of the Living God*—Christian Workers for Fellowship; Church of the Living God—The Pillar and Ground of Truth; The House of Prayer*; Church of God in Christ*—Pentecostal; Fre

Church of God in Christ; Church of God-Holiness*; Church of Christ—Holiness*; Fire-Baptized Holiness Church of God of the Americas*; Christ's Sanctified Holy Church Colored*; House of the Lord*; National David Spiritual Temple of Christ Church Union*.

The pentecostal sects in the United States have approximately 5,650 local congregations and 350,000 members. The largest are the Assemblies of God, General Council* (2611 churches; 194,000 members), Church of God (1081 churches; 45,000 members); (Tomlinson) Church of God (441 churches; 18,000 members); Pentecostal Assembly of Jesus Christ (245 churches; 16,000 members); Pentecostal Holiness Church (375 churches; 13,000 members); Pentecostal Church, Inc. (168 churches; 10,000 members). Cf. holiness churches.

E. T. Clark, *The Small Sects in America* (1937); F. M. Davenport, *Primitive Traits in Religious Revivals* (1910); Cartwright, *Autobiography;* Frodsham, *With Signs Following, the Story of the Latter-Day Pentecostal Revival;* and the numerous tracts and publications issued by the Gospel Publishing House, Springfield, Mo., and the Church of God and (Tomlinson) Church of God, Cleveland, Tenn. E.T.C.

Peraldus (Guillaume Péraud): Author of a treatise on the education of a Prince. S.C.T.

perfect, perfection: (Lat., *per,* through; *facere,* do, make) Literally, finished, made thoroughly. Since God is generally viewed as not made at all, his "completeness" requires special analysis. Traditionally it is explained as the total absence of "defects," or the presence of all possible positive values. But many thinkers deny that all possible values are "compossible," capable of realization in one actuality. An alternative to the traditional view is that in God all actual values are present actually, and all possible ones are bound to be present if and when actualized. Thus God would pool the values of existence, the actual as actual, the potential as potential. Any possible being other than he must then in its value be but a fragment of his value, and thus he must surpass any even possible being other than himself. Yet he could also surpass himself; for, as hitherto potential values became actual, his own actual value would increase. So the perfect would be "the selfsurpassing being who surpasses all conceivable others than himself." This may be called "dynamic perfection," since it admits change in the perfect—though only change toward *more* value. Perfection is perfectibility (Tsanoff). The other, or static, form of perfection is, "the un-selfsurpassing being who surpasses all conceivable others." This has been the usual view, defended by the query, how can the perfect, that which lacks nothing, have any further value to acquire? But if the total absence of potentiality of further value, or the total realization of possible actuality in a "pure actuality", is itself not possible, then the "failure" to possess it is not a defect in the proper sense—the "it" being here meaningless, a mere absurdity.

Dynamic and static perfection contradict each other only if applied to the same being in the same respect, since there is no formal contradiction in the idea of a being dynamically perfect in respect *R* and statically perfect in respect *A*. Thus God may be selfsurpassingly happy or blissful, yet happier than all others than himself; but at the same time, un-selfsurpassingly good or benevolent, while more benevolent than all others. For, as the world which his goodness cherishes gains new values, his satisfaction in this world may increase. This assumes a genuine indeterminacy in the future as known by God (see foreknowledge); but the traditional view of omniscience as a seeing of the real as it is at all times, or from the standpoint of eternity, also involves an assumption, namely that there exists a final sum of reality, complete once for all, and capable of being known "in a single now." This assumption is now widely challenged.

The perfect as static-dynamic enjoys both self-identity and self-difference. As selfsurpassing, the perfect enjoys self-contrast; as un-selfsurpassing, he enjoys self-equality. If unity with difference is the obvious trait of concrete experience, from which mere unity or mere difference is abstracted, then static perfection must be abstract, and reflexive all-surpassing or dynamic perfection must be perfection in its concreteness. Abstractions naturally cannot surpass themselves; only concrete subjects or persons can do that. (See God as personal) The static perfection of God means that his abstract aspect surpasses all other abstractions; while his dynamic perfection means that he, as selfsurpassing, surpasses all other concrete beings or selfsurpassers. For example, only he grows without ever decaying, takes on new values without ever losing any—since his being pools all actuality, and since the past has the mode of actual, and only the future the mode of potential, reality. (See time).

Are there negative values in the perfect? Just as the total absence of potentiality may be impossible, so may the total absence of evil, suffering, for instance, be impossible. And if the perfect pools the actual, it must contain suffering. But whereas suffering is a positive quality, not the mere absence of one, moral evil, like ignorance, is a non-quality—namely a (wilful) not-taking-account of the interests of others. It is non-interest in interests. True, it is deliberate, but the evil is not in the deliberateness, but in the deliberate non-interest. The being which is perfect in knowledge (see omniscience) can no more be uninterested in, than it can be ignorant of, any real interest. The whole-value no more includes, as its own property, the absence of qualities in this or that part than a whole is small because its parts are so. Thus the traditional theory of the negativity of evil is applicable to evils of ignorance and neglect, but not to suffering; for it is precisely positive knowledge of and attention to the sufferings of others that compels, and indeed consists in, sympathetic suffering of our own.

As static, the perfect is immutable, independent, simple, unextended, absolute in knowledge, goodness, and power—nearly all the traditional attributes. As dynamic, the perfect is mutable (though only through additions to his reality); dependent (though only for the particular degree and kind of accidental values it attains, not for his existence or basic character as static-dynamic); he is complex (though incapable of dissolution into parts); he is identical with the whole of the real in space-time, ever gaining new objects to know and exert his goodness upon, and thereby reaching new satisfaction (tinged with suffering).

In sum, the perfect is superior to the non-perfect in all positive abilities, including the ability of self-enrichment through the enrichment of others, or the enrichment of others through self-enrichment. He surpasses the very essence of others, but only in accidents can he surpass himself. See infinite; omnipotence; omniscience; panentheism.

R. A. Tsanoff, *Religious Crossroads* (1942); E. S. Brightman, *The Problem of God* (1930); C. Hartshorne, *Man's Vision of God* (1941). C.H.

perfectio christiana: See perfectionism.

perfection, perfectionism: The attainment of perfection in God's sight is the content of all eschatological hope. This means that the human achievement of religious and moral perfection (sinlessness) belongs to the future rather than the present.

Generally speaking, such has been the teaching of the Christian religion. It has attributed perfection to God alone. Moreover, on the basis of the gospel of the divine forgiveness in Christ, it has also given to men the sure hope of reaching perfection. The Christian is told to believe that under divine grace he is on the road to perfection. In this sense, he is a pilgrim.

Perfectionism as the teaching that it is possible for man to attain and maintain religious and moral perfection has been comparatively rare in Christianity. It has been advocated particularly by mystics and moralists, who on account of an overemphasis either upon the experience of union with the divine or upon the possibilities of moral growth denied or qualified the teaching of the doctrines of sin and grace** and of justification and sanctification**.

Under the impact of their religious enthusiasm, some of the early Christians seem to have believed that they were able to keep themselves sinless. Origen* incorporated a perfectionist streak in his theology under the influence of Greek, especially neo-Platonic mysticism. Roman Catholic monasticism and mysticism were and are in part perfectionist. During the Reformation period, Anabaptist and Spiritualist sects and individuals opposed the Reformers' teaching on justification in the name of a religious perfectionism, the chief feature of which was the claim that the ethic of the Sermon on the Mount was an uneschatological ethic. Their direct and indirect descendants in Protestantism (particularly Mennonites and Quakers) have been and still are determined by a similar outlook. In the history of American Christianity, there have appeared numerous small perfectionist sects,* all of which were short-lived (e.g., the communities of Oneida*, N. Y., New Harmony, Ind., etc.). Today, perfectionism appears particularly among the so-called holiness* sects. In connection with pacifism*, it has become a partial attitude or conviction of many moralistically and mystically inclined liberal Protestants. W.P.

perfectionism: (Gates style) See Battle-Axe experiment.

perichoresis: (Literally, a surrounding, but used in a sense that involves permeation) A term used by John of Damascus, e.g., in *Exposition of the Orthodox Faith* IV, xviii (Migne, *Patrol Graec.* XCIV, 1183f.) to indicate the mutual inherence of the divine and human natures in Christ's person. In Greek theology, to which Lutheranism is here indebted (Cf. *Formula of Concord**, Article VIII), the *communicatio idiomatum** or sharing of properties is a development of this concept. J.T.M.

pericope: (Gr., *perikope*, something cut out, a section of a book) A portion of Scripture read at service time or used as a sermon text. Prescription of set sections for Sundays and feast days began probably in the early fifth century but the first known Roman list of such (Gospel) sections dates from the seventh century; at present at least the Roman Catholic, the Eastern, the Anglican and the Lutheran churches have official lectionaries*. The purpose of these lectionaries is partly to secure appropriate lessons for the various church seasons, partly to secure the orderly reading of representative Scriptural passages throughout the year. B.S.E.

perpetual adoration: (Lat., *perpetuum*, perduring, and *adorare*, to adore) Adoration of the Blessed Sacrament; literally perpetual, or interrupted after some days or at short intervals. L.R.W.

Perrinists: See Libertines.

persecution: In Christian history persecution has been directed against the church by hostile powers such as the Roman Empire and the modern totalitarian states, and by the church against dissenting groups and individuals.

The persecution of the church by the Roman Empire was motivated primarily by political and social considerations. Religiones were not persecuted as such, but only when considered subversive to public morality and order. Restrictions, however, were imposed on the dissemination of some foreign cults, and thus arose the distinction between *religiones licitae* and *illicitae*. Judaism was a permitted religion, but Christianity, when it emerged as a distinct cult, forfeited the immunity, and was persecuted as politically dangerous because of the Christian rejection of emperor worship*, as socially subversive because of Christian abstention from many walks of life and in general because Christian "atheism" with reference to the pagan gods would incur divine displeasure for the community. The charge of immorality was also levelled in a few instances, when Christians were accused of incest and cannibalism.

Christian persecution of dissenters was possible by force only after the state under Constantine came to be on the side of the church. The theory altered from that of the Roman Empire in that concern was no longer so much for tranquillity on earth as for salvation in heaven. The conditions of salvation were believed to be orthodox belief and membership in the visible church. The first instance of persecution on an extensive scale was that against the Donatists* of northern Africa in the early fifth century, who were both schismatics and disturbers of the peace. St. Augustine formulated the theory of Christian constraint. On two necessary counts he was already well convinced that the truth of the church's teaching can be known and that the points rejected by the heretics are important. On a third requisite point he was convinced by the actual success of coercion against the Donatists, namely that persecution is effective. Such constraint was harmonized with Christian love on the ground that force was designed to save alike the heretic and his victims from damnation. Heresy must be amputated like a diseased member to conserve the health of the body. Such statements were relatively innocuous in the mouth of St. Augustine because he did not personify the state nor admit the death penalty. But when these two further steps were taken the way was open for the Inquisition.

It was a long time in coming, however, for the western church was free from any important heretical movements from the barbarian invasions to the twelfth century, when after the first crusades dissenting movements began to swarm. Against them was established the Inquisition*. The Protestant Reformation brought little immediate change. The outstanding reformers like Luther, Calvin and Zwingli believed in the death penalty for heresy, or, as Luther preferred to say, for blasphemy. Though the legislation against heresy in the canon law was rejected by the reformers, the prescriptions of the revived code of Justinian took its place. But the Reformation, by breaking the unity of the medieval church, contributed unwittingly to the rise of religious liberty*.

E. G. Hardy, *Christianity and the Roman Government* (1894, reprint 1925); *Persecution and Liberty, Essays in honor of George Lincoln Burr,* 1931).

R.H.B.

Persephone: Daughter of Demeter, in Greek mythology. Abducted by Hades to become his wife and queen of the underworld, she was allowed to spend two-thirds of each year with her mother. This myth is believed to have been the core of the Eleusinian* mysteries. P.G.M.

perseverance of the saints: The last of the five points* of Calvinism*, as formulated by the Synod of Dort*, 1619, is thus named. The meaning is that those elected by God are sustained by Him in a state of grace*, despite weaknesses and falls, and thus assured of final salvation. The doctrine is stated in the Westminster Confession of Faith, chapter XVII. An old subject of controversy between Calvinists and Arminians (Methodists) was the possibility of falling from grace. See final perseverance. R.H.N.

Persia, religions of: The Aryan, Zoroastrian, and Shiite religions**. The religion of the ancient Iranians (Aryans), who invaded Iran about 2000 B.C., was that of their kinsmen, the Vedic Indians: they worshiped gods of nature or Daivas (Indra and the Nasatyas) and gods of human society or Asuras (Mithra and Varuna); they recognized the inflexible order of the world (*rita,* Iranian *asha*); they prepared the sacred drink *soma* (Iranian *haoma*); and they told the myths of the first man Yama (Iranian Yima) and of the killing of the dragon.

Zarathustra ("rich in camels"), or Zoroaster*, reformed this ancient Aryan religion. He was probably born in Media about 660 B.C. and was active in Bactria where, after many discouraging experiences, he converted king Vishtasp (Hystaspes). His teaching is best preserved in the five *Gathas**, the oldest hymns of the Avesta* (Yasna, chs. 28-53). In addition to the liturgical psalms of the Yasna, the Avesta includes the liturgies of the Vispered ("all lords"), the ritual prescriptions of the Vendidad* ("the law against the demons"), the 21 hymns in praise of angels (in part ancient Aryan deities) in the Yasht* ("worship by praise"), and the layman's prayer book called Khorda Avesta ("little Avesta"). Zoroaster did not entirely suppress the ancient Aryan mythology, but he emphasized, like Buddha* "good thoughts, words, and deeds." The world is the battlefield between the forces of good and evil. The ranks of the good are headed by Ahura Mazda* ("Lord Wisdom") or Ormuzd, the supreme god, and his seven Amesha Spenta ("blessing immortals"): Spenta Mainyu ("blessing spirit" or Holy Ghost), Vohu Mana ("good mind"), Asha ("truth," the cosmic order), Khshathra Vairya ("desirable royal rule"), Armaiti ("piety"), Haurvatat ("salvation"), Ameretat ("immortality"); two other angels are Sraosha ("obedience") and Ashi ("deserved good luck"). The army of good includes the diligent farmer and useful animals like the cock and the dog. The ranks of evil include demons who are the counterpart of the angels, particularly Druj ("deceit") and Aeshma ("wrath"); after Zoroaster Angra Manyu ("evil spirit"), or Ahriman*, was opposed to Ahura Mazda as the embodiment of evil. Plundering Bedouins, teachers of falsehood, sorcerers, snakes, wolves, ants, and the like, are fighters in the army of evil and darkness. The duties of Zoroaster's followers are the cultivation of the soil, the care of the flocks and herds, the persistent fight against the nomads, and the spread of the true doctrine. Their rewards are both terrestrial prosperity and heavenly bliss; but when an evil soul tries to cross after death, the Cinvat ("separation") Bridge, it precipitates into the House of Lies, to be tormented and be fed revolting food. At the end of time, after the final battle, there will be retribution "through the spirit and the fire": the truthful will receive eternal glory, the wicked will moan in darkness. In the late parts of the Avesta this teaching of Zoroaster was supplemented with survivals of Aryan mythology (in the Yashts), and more elaborate details about the liturgy and the eschatology (including the resurrection). Through the doctrine of Zurvan ("time" in the sense of fate) an attempt was made to solve the dualism between Ormuzd and Ahriman. Zoroastrianism survives today among about 10,000 Gabars in Persia and about 100,000 Parsis in Bombay and vicinity. After the Moslem conquest (637-650), the Persians adopted Islam* in its orthodox (Sunnite*) form, but after 1500 the Shiite* (from *Shi'ah,* party) movement, which regards Ali (d. 661) and his descendants as divinely inspired Imams, became the national religion of Persia. See mystery religions; Sufism; Zervanism.

A. V. W. Jackson, *Zoroaster the Prophet of Ancient Iran* (1899); J. H. Moulton, *Early Zoroastrianism* (1913); M. N. Dhalla, *Zoroastrian Theology* (1915); *History of Zoroastrianism* (1938); H. S. Nyberg, *Die Religionen des alten Iran* (Mitteil. d. Vorderasiat. Gesellsch. 43, Leipzig, 1938).

R.H.P.

personal, God as: See God as personal.

personal counseling: See counseling, personal.

personalism: (Lat., *persona,* a mask, an actor, his role, dignity; cf. Allport, *Personality,* 25-29) A philosophical system in which persons (or selves) are the sole (or dominant) metaphysical realities, as well as the only ultimate intrinsic values. Personalism means by person "an individual substance of a rational nature" (Boethius, 6th cent., although most modern personalists reject the old view of substance), rather than the psychophysical organism.

1) History. The term personalism was first used by Schleiermacher in his *Reden* (1799), as equivalent to theism*. It was first used philosophically in England by John Grote (1865). It seems to have been introduced into American terminology by Walt Whitman in his essay, "Personalism" (in the *Galaxy,* 1868); Bronson Alcott probably derived his use of the term from Whitman. Renouvier's *Le Personnalisme* (1903) led to its adoption in America by M. W. Calkins (1907) and B. P. Bowne (1908). W. Stern's critical personalism (1906) further popularized it. Some neo-scholastics (Maritain, Mounier) call themselves personalists. Modern personalism is especially influenced by Plato, Aristotle, Plotinus, St. Augustine, St. Thomas, Berkeley, Leibniz, Kant, Fichte, Hegel, Schleiermacher, Lotze, and Eucken**.

2) Types. Personalisms may be classified (following Knudson) as atheistic (M'Taggart), psychophysically neutral (Stern), relativistic (Renouvier), absolutistic (E. Caird, A. E. Taylor, J. Royce, M. W. Calkins) and theistic, which latter group may be subdivided into idealistic (Bowne, Howison, H. Rashdall, W. R. Sorley**, Knudson, Flewelling, Buckham, Brightman, D. Baumgardt, J. S. Moore), panpsychistic (J. Ward, C. Hartshorne, D. H. Parker, W. T. Stace), and dualistic (G. Harkness, Maritain, and perhaps P. Tillich and N. Berdyaev).

3) Main Ideas. Personalism proposes a psychology (self psychology, gestalt), a logic (synoptic method, coherence of total personality as criterion of truth), an epistemology (activity of mind in knowledge, dualism of idea and object), and a metaphysics (the universe a society of persons).

4) Theology. The predominant Christian theology is theistic personalism, despite the inroads of naturalistic, humanistic, and impersonalistic thought. Personalistic philosophy has exerted a fruitful influence on diverse theological movements, such as: neo-scholasticism (Gilson, Maritain), Christocentric thought sympathetic with neo-supernaturalism (E. Lewis, J. S. Moore, N. Ferré), and the ethical and social interpretation of Christianity (Scheler, H. E. Fosdick, F. J. McConnell). In the main, personalism has appeared in theology as a liberal, "modernistic" force, defending the concept of an omnipotent and absolute God (Bowne, Knudson, Rall, Buckham, Flewelling, Wilson, Youtz, Calkins, Sorley, Temple, Pratt), but more recently developing the idea of a God whose will is limited by factors not created by that will (Rashdall, Brightman, Tsanoff, Hartshorne, Parker, Stace, Harkness, Berdyaev, Bergson, Tillich, Bertocci). The nature of religious experience and the relations of Christianity to culture, society, and world religions have been investigated by Knudson and Hocking.

Personalists in general agree on the personality of God (M'Taggart excepted), teleology and freedomism vs. mechanistic interpretations, synoptic method as opposed to mere analysis, the objectivity of ideal values, and emphasis on ethical and social experience. Liberal personalists incline toward an ethical, personal, rational reinterpretation of Christian thought about the Trinity* (most personalists are modalists), the incarnation (rejecting the "two natures"), inspiration, revelation (denying the revelation of fixed dogmas), the sacraments (note Bowman, *A Sacramental Universe*), conversion (see Strickland, *Psychology of Religious Experience*), and salvation. Personalists tend toward semi-Pelagianism and toward Arminian rather than Calvinistic views. Liberal personalists oppose traditional authoritarianism, irrationalism, romanticism*, abstract impersonal Platonism and mediaeval realism, as well as Barthianism*. (Cf. reason in religion.) Kierkegaard*, like Nietzsche, is, however, irrationalistic and romantic but personalistic.

The Personalist (Los Angeles) and *Luminar* (Mexico City) are quarterly journals largely devoted to personalism and its relations to theology. Cf. Bois, Henri.

See B. P. Bowne, *Theism* (1902); A. C. Knudson, *The Philosophy of Personalism* (1927); Rall (ed.), *Religion and Public Affairs* (1937); E. S. Brightman, *A Philosophy of Religion* (1940): and C. Hartshorne, *The Vision of God* (1941).

E.S.B.

personalistic psychology: See psychology, schools of.

Peshitta: Standard Syriac version of Bible produced and authorized by Bishop Rabbula about 420 A.D. for use in churches of Syria and Mesopotamia; the O.T. was based on Old Syriac translation of Hebrew O.T. made in second or third century A.D., the Greek Septuagint*, and perhaps other sources; the N.T. was partly based on the Greek, partly a revision of the Old Syriac "Separated Gospels" translated from Greek about 200 A.D., and perhaps partly based on the still earlier Syriac Diatessaron* of Tatian*; valuable at places for determining original text of Bible. See s. v. Edessa; versions of the Bible, ancient. See works of F. C. Burkitt. R.E.W.

pessimism: (Lat., *pessimum,* worst, superlative of *malum,* bad). The view that the world, especially human life, is wholly bad, or at least as bad as possible. Introduced by Schopenhauer*; first used in English in this sense in 1878 (Oxford). For pessimism, evil is lasting, permanent, always victorious; good, transitory and doomed to defeat. Life is not worth living. F. C. S. Schiller in *Riddles of the Sphinx* states that pessimism may be based on frustration of the ideals of 1) happiness (Gautama Buddha*, Leopardi, Schopenhauer), 2) goodness (St. Paul's view of man apart from God), 3) beauty (aesthetic pessimism, the supersensitive Oscar Wilde), and 4) knowledge (skepticism, as Pyrrho, Sextus Empiricus, and irrationalism, as E. von Hartmann). To these may be added 5) culture (Spengler*). In addition to these theoretical pessimisms, there is psychological or pathological pessimism, an habitual mood of melancholy and despair. See evil; happiness; meliorism; optimism; value.

See articles "Optimism and Pessimism" in Baldwin; "Pessimism" in D. Runes, *Dictionary of Philosophy* (1942). E.S.B.

Petau, Denis: (Dionysius Petavius, 1583-1652) French Jesuit distinguished as an historian of dogma and chronologist. His theological works inaugurated a Roman Catholic theology less given to speculation and more to historical research. Because of his works on chronology, Petau is considered the founder with Scaliger of the science of ancient chronology. E.A.R.

Peter: A name conferred by Jesus himself on Simon, the disciple who stood closest to him throughout his ministry. In his house at Capernaum, Jesus made his home, and in almost all the incidents of the Gospel history he takes a prominent part. He was the one disciple who tried to defend Jesus when he was arrested, although during the trial his nerve broke down. It was Peter who had the first vision of the risen Lord, and the church at Jerusalem grew up under his leadership. At a later time he took second place to James, whose influence was perhaps responsible for his breach at Antioch with Paul, whose liberal position he had previously shared. According to tradition he finally made his way to Rome, and was put to death in the massacre on the Vatican hill in 64 A.D. Matthew, in his account of the Messianic declaration at Caesarea Philippi, inserts a passage in which Jesus acclaims Peter as the rock on which he will build his church. The passage itself is of doubtful authenticity, but it may be granted that without Peter the church could hardly have survived. By his faith and ardour, his kindly and broad-minded temper, and not least by his intellectual gifts (for Paul always speaks of him as his equal) he saved the church in its earliest and most difficult days. See chair of St. Peter; Peter, St., First Bishop of Rome; Roman Catholic Church. E.F.S.

Peter Aureoli, O.F.M.: Renowned French scholastic theologian and philosopher. The date of his birth is unknown; he died in 1322 at Avignon. He lectured at Bologna, Toulouse (where he vigorously defended the doctrine of Mary's Immaculate Conception*), and Paris. In the theory of cognition he favored a conceptualistic nominalism*. In 1321 he was appointed Archbishop of Aix, and was created cardinal. He is called the "Doctor Facundus" on account of his ready eloquence. C.V.

Peter of Chelcice: See Bohemian Brethren.

Peter Comestor: (died 1178) Chancellor in Paris and one of the first ones to write a commentary to the Four Books of the Sentences of Peter Lombard*. He is known as a writer in Homiletics and Biblical History. See biblical history in Christian instruction. S.C.T.

Peter Damian: Born at Ravenna in 1007, Peter passed through a childhood of hardship. Educated at Ravenna and at the University of Parma, he entered the hermitage of Fonte-Avellana around 1035. Friend of Gregory VII and other popes, he spent most of his life combatting evils among the clergy. He was named Cardinal-Bishop of Ostia by Stephen X in 1057. He died at Faenza in 1072. Though Peter was never formally canonized, his feast was extended to the whole Church by Leo XII in 1823, who also pronounced him a Doctor of the Church. P.S.M.

Peter de Bruys: (?-c. 1130) A zealous preacher of gospel poverty burned by a French mob (c. 1130) for his excessive attacks on the institutional church. See Petrobrusians. Cf. Henry of Lausanne.

Schaff-Herzog, *Religious Encyclopaedie* (1883) Vol. III, p. 1818. R.C.P.

Peter the Hermit: Peter was born at Amiens about 1050. Little is known of his earlier life into which legend has been woven. His rôle as instigator and preacher of the First Crusade has been exaggerated far beyond historical fact. He was but one of many preachers, and his preaching did not begin until after the Council of Clermont. As leader of a small band he went to the East, arriving in Constantinople in August, 1096. He was present at the siege of Antioch in January, 1098, and sometime after this he returned to the West. At Liége he founded the monastery of Neufmoutier, where he died in 1115. P.S.M.

Peter Lombard: Peter Lombard, as his name indicates, was born in the Italian province of Lombardy around the year 1100, and died as bishop of Paris in 1160. He studied first at Bologna, then went to Rheims, and from there to Paris, where he most probably arrived in 1139. His teaching in the cathedral school began soon thereafter, and between 1145-1152 he produced his greatest work, the *Libri IV Sententiarum.* Though this work was not characterized by originality, it was by far the most complete and systematic compendium of theology that had appeared. It soon became and long remained the theological textbook of the Middle Ages. More commentaries were written on it than on any other book, the Bible alone excepted. More important, Peter and his Sentencebooks inspired a school of speculative theologians at Paris, whose great works developed theological speculation, crowned by the *Summa Theologica** of St. Thomas Aquinas*. The Lombard also left two great biblical commentaries, one of the psalms, the other on the epistle to the Romans. Together these commentaries came to be designated as the *Magna Glossatura.* See mystics of Saint Victor; penance; Peter Comestor; satisfaction; Sentences. Cf. Gratian. P.S.M.

Peter Lombard's *Four Books of Sentences* displaced all other existing textbooks. The work is a compilation of the opinions of the Fathers, especially of Augustine, and of his contemporaries. He formally follows Abailard's* method of contrasting the patristic authorities, and in content he largely follows Hugo of St. Victor*. In refraining from the discussion of purely philosophical problems and from the application of philosophy to theology, he follows the example of both. He rejected Abailard's special views and Hugo's speculative elements. By the express recognition of the authorities he helped Abailard's method to victory. Although Hugh of St. Victor had already factually mentioned seven sacraments —baptism, confirmation, eucharist, last unction, marriage, ordination and repentance—it was Lombard who definitely effected their fixation in theological thought.

F. Protois, *Pierre Lombard* (Paris, 1881); J. N. Espenberger, *Die Philosophie des Petrus Lombardus* (Münster, 1901); M. Grabmann, *Geschichte der scholastischen Methode,* (Freiburg im Breisgau, 1911) Vol. II. H.H.

Peter, Acts of: A wholly apocryphal* work, giving a legendary account of Peter's last months in Rome and his martyrdom. Written in Greek in the early third century, it is known chiefly through an incomplete Latin version. See pseudepigrapha, N.T. English translation in M. R. James, *Apocryphal New Testament* (1924), pp. 300-336. B.S.E.

Peter, Apocalypse of: An early second century apocryphal* book, describing in some detail the rewards of the righteous and the pains of the wicked. The text, originally in Greek, has been preserved chiefly in Ethiopic. English translation in M. R. James, *Apocryphal New Testament* (1924), pp. 505-524. B.S.E.

Peter, First and Second Letters of: First Peter is an appeal from the church at Rome to all believers in the principal provinces of Asia Minor, to accept the test of persecution without hatred or bitterness for the emperor or the authorities. It seems to be a corrective for the vengeful spirit that found expression in the Revelation (18:6, 20). Christ's way of enduring persecution must be their pattern in the fiery trial that is now coming upon them. They must obey the authorities and respect the emperor. The Roman church had been called upon by the Letter to the Hebrews* to teach the other churches, 5:12, and responded not only with First Peter but with First Clement*, written to the church at Corinth at this very time. But to overtake the dangerous note in the Revelation it claims the authority of Peter, one of its great historic sponsors, who had suffered martyrdom in Rome, and whose tomb is guarded. It was written not far from A.D. 95, while the demand for emperor worship* still hung over the churches.

Second Peter was written not long after the middle of the second century, to recall the churches to a lively expectation of the Second Coming of Christ. The writer knows the Fourfold Gospel, and the collected letters of Paul, which ignorant unsteadfast people twist to their own ruin, a clear reference to the followers of Marcion*. He also knows I Peter, Hebrews and probably the Revelation; certainly Jude**, which he reproduces practically in full in his second chapter, giving that passionate invective a new object in those who deny the Second Coming. See pseudepigrapha, N.T.

F. J. A. Hort, *The First Epistle of St. Peter* (1898); J. B. Mayor, *The Epistle of St. Jude and the Second Epistle of St. Peter* (1907). E.J.G.

Peter, Gospel of: A Syrian docetic* work, written about 150. Only a fragment has survived, describing the Passion and Resurrection. English translation in M. R. James, *Apocryphal New Testament* (1924), pp. 90-94. See pseudepigrapha, N.T. B.S.E.

Peter, Preaching of: A second-century defence of Christianity, preserved only in short patristic* citations; English translation in M. R. James, *Apocryphal New Testament* (1924), pp. 16-19. But the first three extracts on p. 19 may come from a different work, *The Doctrine of Peter.* See canons of various churches. B.S.E.

Peter, St., First Bishop of Rome: (Catholic Conception) Since Christ established His Church as a perennial, living organization (cf. Math. 16, 18) there must be at all times someone to take His place as its official visible head. No perfect society can be conceived without members, a head, and a common purpose that unites all. Christ's first Vicar on earth as head of His Church was Peter. This is generally admitted, according to the well-known text: "Thou art Peter, and upon this rock I shall build my Church" (Matt. 16, 18-19). Since the Church was instituted as a living, perpetual organization ("the gates of Hell shall not prevail against her" Math. 16, 18) she was not to cease with the death of Peter. This seemed self-evident to the first Christians and thus, as Eusebius* (315) in his *History* (IV 1) narrates, they selected "Linus (67-79?) who was the first after Peter that obtained the Episcopate of the Church of the Romans". Then they selected Cletus (or Anacletus) and thereafter Clement (98-99?)*, etc., to take Peter's place as their head and bishop. (Cf. Vatican Council, Sess. 4, ch. 1, 2; *ib* Canon 1; also *ib.* ch. 4; H. Denziger-Umberg, *Enchiridion Symbolorum*, Freiburg in Br., 1932, pp. 501-8). Not only did the early Christians look upon every Bishop of Rome as successor to Peter, but likewise believed and professed that since his position was identical with that of Peter as primate of the Church universal, he was also endowed by the Saviour with the same prerogatives as was Peter (cf. Decree of the Council of Florence, 1439; cf. Denziger, 1 c. p. 253 No. 694); for, any and every head of any given organization enjoys the same rights, honors and privileges as his predecessor enjoyed, *in virtue of his office,* unless curtailed or enlarged by constitutional amendments made by duly qualified representatives of the whole body. Accordingly, the Apologists* and Fathers of the Church attribute to the successors of Peter, as visible head of the Church, who came to be known as popes* or Roman Pontiffs, the same attributes that Christ conferred on Peter, i.e.,: 1) unified and unqualified executive power, based on John 21, 15: "Feed my lambs, feed my sheep"; and on Math. 16, 18 "to thee I give the keys* of the kingdom of Heaven"; 2) universal legislative power; "Whatsoever thou shalt bind on earth, shall also be bound in Heaven; whatsoever that thou loose on earth shall also be loosed in Heaven" (Math. 16, 19); 3) supreme judicial power: "And if he (i.e., a brother who has sinned against another) refuse to hear them (i.e., two or three witnesses) appeal to the Church; but if he refuse to hear even the Church, let him be to thee as a heathen and the publican. Amen, I say to you whatsoever you bind", etc. (Math. 18, 17-18); 4) infallibility (not to be confounded with impeccability or prognostication, etc.,): "I have prayed for thee, Peter, that thy faith fail not" (Luke, 22, 32) and finally, 5) primacy over all other bishops in the Church: "And thou in turn confirm thy brethren" (*ib.*); "feed (not only) my lambs (i.e., the younger, the faithful of the flock, but also) feed my sheep" (John, 21, 15) i.e., the bishops or spiritual parents of the lambs (cf. I Cor. 4, 15; Philem. v. 10). That Christ refers here to a spiritual food, i.e., doctrine is evident from the whole context. After all St. Peter was not a shepherd by occupation, but a fisherman and even that trade Christ bade him relinquish for the spiritual catch of fish: "Henceforth thou shalt catch men" (Luke 5, 10). Peter's name invariably precedes the names of all the other Apostles (cf. Math. 10, 2; Mark. 3, 16; Luke 6, 13-14; Math. 17, 1), and yet he was not the first in point of time to have been called to the Apostolate by the Saviour. It is Peter who presides over the first Council of Jerusalem (Acts. XV). That the Bishops of Rome were also considered successors of Peter as head of the Church universal (not only of the See of Rome), is borne out by historical facts and references in both the Eastern and Western Churches to the complete satisfaction of Catholic Apologists, theologians and historians (cf. "Pope"). These latter hold also that the primacy of the Roman Pontiff both of honor and of jurisdiction over the Church Universal is entirely independent of the question of the historical proofs for the presence of Peter in Rome, although all hold that fact can be conclusively proven (cf. B. Conway, C.S.P. *Question Box* (1929), p. 143); that it is independent of the military power and expansion of the Roman Empire during the first three centuries which rather did everything to stay the progress of this Primacy rather than assist in its spread; and finally that it is entirely independent of Constantine's conversion (313) and the favors of subsequent Roman Christian Emperors, both before and after Charlemagne (800 A.D.). The position of the Roman Pontiffs, as successors of Peter, the first Bishop of Rome, rests primarily on biblical texts and traditional documents. It is for that reason both dogmatical and historical. All else is supplementary and corroborative. See clergy.

For the Catholic interpretation of the Biblical texts used cf. *A Commentary on the New Testament Prepared by the Catholic Biblical Association* (1942). R.M.H.

Peter, St., chair of: See chair of St. Peter.

Peter's pence: The name given to an annual tax, originally of a penny from each householder, levied in England by the papacy. W.S.H.

Petrarch: (1304-1374) Poet, scholar and rhetorician, who is regarded as the pioneer of the Renaissance* in Italy. A writer of Latin verse and prose and of Italian lyrics; a collector of mss.; an amateur diplomatist; a priest who remained orthodox in religion; and a close friend of Boccaccio*. S.M.G.

Petri, Laurentius: (1499-1573) A younger brother of Olavus Petri* became the first Lutheran archbishop of Sweden in 1531. His long episcopate marked the establishment of the evangelical church in Sweden, to which he gave the first legal constitution (ready, in main, in 1561, though first adopted in 1571). He gave his church leadership in resisting royal encroachment and maintaining independent status. The inner life of the church was enriched by his contributions in catechetical, homiletical, and devotional material, in Bible translation, hymn writing and liturgical formulations. The ecclesiastical structure of the Swedish Church in the Reformation period was due to his persistent and wise labors. C.J.B.

Petri, Olavus: (1493-1552) The spiritual leader of the Reformation in Sweden. Following training in Leipzig and Wittenberg, Olavus returned to Sweden and, with Laurentius Andrae* joined the king, Gustavus Vasa, in introducing reforms in Swedish Church and State. He was the ablest literary force of the Swedish Reformation, using his talents to produce devotional literature, Bible translation, apologetic treatises, a Swedish Mass, a Swedish Hymn Book, homiletical and historical works. Though aiding Gustavus in establishing a church independent of Rome, he withstood the royal attempts to dominate the Church. For generations to come the contributions of Olavus determined the spirit and character of the Lutheran Church in Sweden. C.J.B.

Petrobrusians: As followers of Peter de Bruys*, they reputedly disavowed church buildings, crosses, infant baptism, the Lord's Supper, prayers for the dead, ecclesiastical chants, and, indeed, all ceremonialism.

The Catholic Encyclopedia (1913), Vol. XI, p. 781. R.C.P.

Pfister, Oskar Robert: (1873-) He was pastor of one of the city churches in Zürich, Switzerland. He recommended as an enthusiastic follower of S. Freud* the method of psychoanalytical healing for dealing with the problems of pastoral care. As a leader in the psychoanalytic movement, he rejected Freud's view that all the higher developments of spiritual life, Christianity included, are so-called sublimations of repressed sexual complexes.

The Psychoanalytic Method (London, 1913); *Die Frömmigkeit des Grafen Zinzendorf* (Wien, 1925), 2 ed.; *Zur Psychologie des philosophischen Denkens* (Bern, 1923); *Analytische Seelsorge. Einführung in die praktische Psychoanalyse für Pfarrer und Laien.* (Göttingen, 1927). H.H.

Pfleiderer, Otto: (1839-1908) A German Protestant scholar and theologian. An adherent of the so-called Tübingen School*, an Hegelian in philosophy, Professor of Practical Theology at Jena from 1870, and of N.T. and Systematic Theology at Berlin from 1875. Most important writings: *Religionsphilosophie* (3rd ed. 1896) and *Das Urchristentum* 2nd ed. 1902). S.M.G.

phallic, phallicism, phallism: The worship of the generative or reproductive powers of nature symbolized by the sex organs, the phallus being the male organ of sex. Phallicism is found widely scattered over the whole earth among most primitive religions, and usually wherever there is a fertility cult*. The lingam*, emblem of the Hindu God Shiva*, found in temples dedicated to his worship is an example. Vestiges of phallicism are found in most of the more highly developed religions. See *E.R.E.*, Vol. 9, Article, *Phallism.* C.S.B.

Pharisees, the: The Pharisees (in Hebrew, *Perushim*, a word whose meaning is shrouded in uncertainty) emerged as a distinct group a short time after the Maccabean Revolt. Though the official adherents of this party were not many, they were the representatives, in actuality, of the religious beliefs, practices, and social outlook of the vast majority of the common people of their day. The Pharisaic leaders usually rose from the ranks of the masses and their long and bitter struggle against the Sadducees*, the representatives of the priestly aristocracy, was in essence an attempt to democratize the Jewish religion and remove it from the rigid control of the Temple priests. Thus, for example, a great many of the ceremonies introduced by the Pharisees in the home were originally part of the Temple ritual and limited to the confines of the Temple*. Similarly, in their theological doctrines, such as the belief in the future life and the existence of angels* (doctrines denied by the Sadducees) the Pharisees voiced the hopes of the oppressed masses.

The Pharisees, as a whole, possessed a high degree of ethical sensitivity. The N.T. characterizations of the Pharisees as "hypocrites" and "offspring of vipers" were directed against a minority of insincere, hypocritical members who were condemned by the recognized authorities of the group itself, and not, as is mistakenly assumed, against the Pharisaic group itself. See Hasideans; Israel, religion and theology; scribe.

Louis Finkelstein, *The Pharisees, The Social Background of their Faith* (2nd Rev. Ed. 1939); R. T. Herford, *Pharisaism, Its Aim and Method* (London, 1912); *What the World Owes to the Pharisees* (London, 1919); "The Significance of Pharisaism." in *Judaism and the Beginnings of Christianity* (London, 1924) pp. 125-166; *The Truth about the Pharisees* (1925); *The Pharisees* (London, 1924); H. Loewe, "Pharisaism." *in Judaism and Christianity*, I, edited by W. O. E. Oesterley (1937), pp. 3-58; "The Ideas of Pharisaism," *JQR*, N.S., VI. (1915-1916), pp. 415-422. E.B.—L.F.

phenomenalism: See epistemology.

phenomenology: Hegel uses the term to indicate the particular facts which express the progress of mind from the lower forms of experiencing to the highest stage of absolute thought. In current philosophical literature it is used chiefly to refer to the philosophy of Edmund Husserl* (1859-1938) and his associates. Literally it means "science of phenomena", where phenomenon is taken not in the Kantian but in the Greek sense of "that which displays itself". Influenced by Brentano's "intentional" theory of conscious states as always "of something" and by Dilthey's "correlativistic" view of subject and object as contributing mutually to a necessary relation, Husserl tried to apply Descartes's method of rigorous doubt in such a way as to eliminate all except the phenomenon as it must appear to pure consciousness. All relation to fact and the empirical world is "bracketed". In the phenomenological intuition we see the object as *eidos* or essence (*Wesen*), i.e., as it must be and cannot help being. In this way we begin where Kant left off and ask not how knowledge, but how logic itself is possible. We find that it is possible because we can intuit directly its relationships. Our task is that not of deducing the rational but describing the conceivable, or that which comes with *Evidenz* as incontrovertibly given.

After analyzing the essence as the *noëma* or objective pole of an intuition, the subjective pole of which is the *noësis,* Husserl went on in his later work to explain the nature of the transcendental consciousness which gives meaning to experience, and attempted to work out an *a priori* science of pure consciousness which should provide the groundwork for all science and knowledge. But his apparent withdrawal into idealism did not solve the problem as to the status of objects of intuition, or the relation of the empirical to the transcendental ego, or the extent to which what is "given" in intuition has already been "taken" by mind. Much debate has ensued.

In general, Husserl's followers have adopted his method of rigid analysis rather than his attempts at system building, important as he himself considered the latter, and have applied the method with significant results in different fields. Thus Max Scheler* (1874-1928) has used it in his analysis of values as essences and in his description of the experience of the holy, and Martin Heidegger* (1889-) has applied it to ontology, while Nicolai Hartmann* (1882-) has employed it in ethics. Moritz Geiger (1880-1937) applied phenomenology to aesthetics and Alexander Pfänder (1870-1941) rebelling, with Husserl, against psychologism, used Husserl's methods in his study of motivation. The Gestalt psychologists point to Husserl's article *Philosophie als strenge Wissenschaft* (1910) with its plea for a special psychological method as influencing their emphasis on configurations and on the intuitable nature of meanings. Rudolf Otto's (1869-1937) *Das Heilige* (1917) was accepted by Husserl as an application of phenomenology to religion. In the work of Karl Jaspers* (1883-) phenomenology fuses with the philosophy of *Existenz.* Cf. Peirce, C.

Cf. E. Husserl, *Logische Untersuchungen* (1900-01) 2 vols.; *Ideen zu einer reinen Phänomenologie und phänomenologischen Philosophie* (1913, Eng. tr. 1931); Max Scheler, *Der Formalismus in der Ethik* etc. (1926); M. Heidegger, *Sein und Zeit* (1926); N. Hartmann, *Ethik* (1926, Eng. tr. 1932) 3 vols.; M. Geiger, *Zum Problem der Stimmungseinfühlung* (*Zeitschrift für Aesthetik* etc. vol. VI); A. Pfänder, *Einführung in die Psychologie* (1920); M. Farber, *Phenomenology as a Method etc.* (1928), ed. *Philosophical Essays in Memory of Edmund Husserl* (1940); E. P. Welch, *The Philosophy of Edmund Husserl* (1941); D. Cairns, Art. *Phenomenology* in *Dictionary of Philosophy* (1942); S. Hook, "Husserl's Philosophical Idealism" *Journal of Philosophy* (1930). Also articles in *Jahrbuch für Philosophie und Phänomenologische Forschung* (1913-30) and *Philosophy and Phenomenological Research* (1940-)

J.S.B.

philanthropy: See practical religion.

Philemon, Letter to: A runaway slave, named Onesimus*, probably from Laodicea found his way into Paul's circle at Rome and became a Christian. Paul knew well enough that there could be no safety for him until he had made matters right with his master Philemon, so he sent the young man back to him with a short letter of explanation. Paul wishes Philemon to receive Onesimus not as a slave but as a Christian brother, and intimates a wish that Philemon would send Onesimus back to him, not to be his servant but to help him in his religious work. In the Roman empire a master could punish a runaway slave with the utmost cruelty, and Paul addresses his letter not only to Philemon but to Apphia (his wife?), Archippus (the minister of the local church?) and the church that meets in Philemon's house, thus making the whole local church aware of Onesimus' case and presumably of Philemon's action about it. Paul was sending Onesimus into the lion's mouth when he induced him to return to his master, and could hardly have done less than bring the social pressure of the local church to bear upon Philemon. This encourages the idea that Philemon is the Letter from Laodicea referred to in Col. 4:16, and explains why Paul should have wished this personal letter read to the neighboring church at Colossae. A prisoner far away at Rome, he could still throw the protection of these two churches of the Lycus valley about the defenceless slave Onesimus, when he made his appearance before his master Philemon. Probable date, 60 A.D.

John Knox, *Philemon among the Letters of Paul* (1935).

E.J.G.

Philip of Hesse: (1504-1567) Landgrave of Hesse, the most eminent of the Protestant princes at the time of the Reformation*. Having taken a leading part in the crushing of the Peasant* Revolution in 1525, Philip adopted the reformed faith and devoted himself to promoting unity among the Protestants and in securing military aid for them from abroad. Seeking to bring together the followers of Luther and of Zwingli he arranged the Marburg colloquy between the two leaders in 1529. The formation of the Schmalkald League* in 1530 was largely his work. In 1534 he won a brilliant victory over Emperor Charles V* at Laufen and restored Ulrich of Wuertemberg to his duchy. Philip's ambitious and successful course was halted by the disgrace attending his bigamy with Margaret von der Saale whom he married in 1540 with the consent of his legal wife Christine of Saxony. Philip had also wrung permission from the reformers on the condition that the second marriage be kept secret. It soon became known, however, alienating Philip from his confederates while strengthening the hand of his enemies. Surrendering to the Emperor in 1547, Philip was kept prisoner until 1552 when the defeat of the Hapsburgs at the hands of Philip's son-in-law Maurice of Saxony enabled him to return to Hesse. T.A.K.

Philippi, Friedrich Adolf: (1809-1882) He was professor in Dorpat (now Tartu, Estonia). As a converted Jew he applied Jewish legalism to the doctrines of the church. Showing an inquisitorial enthusiasm, he, with Kliefoth* and Diekhoff, made the Mecklenburg church one of the most intolerant churches in Germany. See neo-Lutheranism.

Kirchliche Glaubenslehre (Stuttgart, 1854-79) 6 vols.

H.H.

Philippians, Letter to the: Paul's most loyal friends, so far as we know, were the Philippians, who when they learned of his removal to Rome as a prisoner to await his trial, raised money for his needs and sent one of their number, Epaphroditus, to look after him. This is the situation reflected in 4:10-20, and the second half of our Philippians, 3:2—4:23, may be a letter sent them by Paul when he first received their gift. Epaphroditus became very sick in Rome, however, and when he was better, Paul sent him back to Philippi, with a letter explaining his return. This is the situation reflected in 2:19-30, so that the first half of our Philippians may be a letter put in the hand of Epaphroditus when Paul sent him home to Philippi. The outburst against the Judaizers, 3:2, is in strong contrast to the tranquil tone of 3:1, and favors this explanation of the letter as the putting together of two notes to Philippi, representing two stages in the matter of the Philippians' aid. If the letter is a unit, however, it is difficult to see why the "business" should not have been treated in one section, toward the end, which seems to have been Paul's way. The enforcement of humility by the example of Christ's humbling himself leads to a great Christological passage, 2:1-11. Paul's own disappointed hopes for a western mission have taught him the great lesson of thinking on what is true, worthy, right, pure, amiable, kindly, 4:8. The letter or letters, if it is two, must have been written early in Paul's stay in Rome, probably in A.D. 59 or 60.

J. B. Lightfoot, *St. Paul's Epistle to the Philippians* (4th ed., 1878). Marvin R. Vincent, *The Epistles to the Philippians and to Philemon* (1897).

E.J.G.

Philippists: Followers of Philip Melanchthon* who toned down Luther's doctrines of salvation by faith alone and of the Lord's supper, the latter to accommodate Calvinism. They accepted the Leipzig Interim* in 1548, were stoutly opposed by staunch Lutherans, and suppressed in 1574 by the Elector of Saxony. Cf. Formula of Concord.

E.C.K.

Philistines: Ancient people who gave to Palestine its name and are often mentioned in the O.T. By their attacks on the Israelites, they are partly responsible for the rise of the Israelite monarchy.

See R. A. S. Macalister, *The Philistines, their History and Civilization* (1914); O. Eissfeldt, *Philister und Phönizer* (1936).

S.L.T.

Philo Judaeus: (30 B.C.-50 A.D.) Being a pure combination of Hebraism and Hellenism, his extant writings form a fairly comprehensive theological system of the intellectual life of Diaspora Jewry in Hellenistic Egypt. His work is not systematic, being in the nature of a commentary on Holy Writ. As an apologist he tries to show that all wisdom of Hellas has its origin in the teachings of Moses. He explains God's relation to this imperfect world through the intervention of the *logos**. His negative theology is only a means of stressing the perfection of God. Not self-effacement, but ecstatic rapture, "enthusiasm" or "sober ebriety", will bridge the gap between man and God. By resorting to allegorical interpretation*, Philo transforms the historical personalities and events recorded in Scripture into personifications of abstract ideas and virtues. See Alexandrian school; Platonism.

W. Bossuet, *Die Religion des Spätjudentums im neutestamentlichen Zeitalter* (Leipzig, 1926), 3rd ed. by H. Gressmann; J. S. Boughton, *The Idea of Progress in Philo Judaeus* (1932); E. Brehier, *Les Idées philosophiques et religieuses de Philon d'Alexandrie* (Paris, 1925); F. Geiger, *Philon von Alexandreia also sozialer Denker* (Stuttgart, 1932); I. Heinemann, *Philos griechische und jüdische Bildung* (Breslau, 1932).

H.H.

philosophical theology: See theology.

philosophy: (*philos*: lover; *sophia*, wisdom) The following, taken together, may well serve to define the subject-matter of philosophy: Philosophy is the "attempt to think clearly and methodically about certain notions (concepts) which are always turning up in our thinking and which seem necessary to our thinking but which the special sciences do not tell us about." (William James). "Philosophy is an attempt to combine the common experiences of life on the one hand and the results of the special sciences on the other into a consistent and harmonious world-theory." (G. T. W. Patrick). "The philosopher", said Plato, "is the spectator of all time and of all existence." "Philosophy is the attempt to see life steadily and see it whole." (Matthew Arnold.)

Introductory texts: G. T. W. Patrick, *Introduction to Philosophy* (rev. ed., 1935); E. S. Brightman, *An Introduction to Philosophy* (1925); Vergilius Ferm, *First Adventures in Philosophy* (1936).

V.F.

philosophy of history: Herodotus is not only the "father of history", he is also the first philosopher of history. "The god likes to check exceeding things", he says. He wrote his book in order to prove the power and efficacy of Divine Providence. He does not, however, recognize any fundamental difference between nature and history. In that he is a genuine Greek. Greek thought is centered in the idea of the cosmos as the divine order; this order is eternal, it does not change. The strongest philosophic expression of this view is the Platonic conception of the realm of Ideals; in such a scheme no place exists for the ultimate meaning of an historical development, of the uniqueness and originality of the individual, of historical progress and eschatological visions. These aspects arose not before the Christian faith began to influence the thinking mind.

The first representatives of a philosophy of history proper were therefore Christian thinkers like Tertullian, Origen and Augustine**. Especially the last deserves the name of the first great thinker who gave an account of the meaning of history. Antiquity held that the cosmic forces produced cycles* of ever returning periods. This theory was seriously examined and rejected by Augustine (*De civitate dei* XII). The cosmos no longer is the ultimate reality, God is not like the gods subordinate to the cosmic order and to the all-powerful might of Fate*; He is the Creator of the world and His main purpose is the salvation of man. The appearance of Christ on earth is a unique event that makes history ultimately meaningful. History has a beginning in God, it has its center in Christ and its end in the final consummation and the Last Judgment*. It is not a process that repeats itself over and over again. Only by this Christian conception, a philosophy of history as distinguished from mere historical reports and from cosmological speculation becomes possible.

In modern times thought partly returned to the Greek cosmocentric point of view though in a fashion modified by the natural sciences. Instead of the religious philosophy of history a secular reflection emerged. Human life was regarded as akin to animal life, human development as akin to the biological evolution. The first thinker of rank in this respect is Giovanni Battista Vico (1668-1744). He described the development of nations as an analogue to that of the individual and tried to find out the law that controls both. This naturalistic, neo-pagan contemplation of man and human acts and accomplishments culminates in the 19th century in the materialistic conception of history proclaimed by Marx* and his followers and by the Darwinists.

In the classical period of German thought and poetry men like Lessing* and Herder, Kant and Fichte, Schelling and Hegel** created a philosophy of history that would combine both the Christian and the modern views by means of speculative ideas concerning the origin, the course and the end of human life. The greatest, but also the most severely criticized panorama of the entire world history in its concrete development was displayed by Hegel* who ventured to derive even details from his fundamental metaphysical principles in a dialectical fashion.

After the decay of this metaphysical period a new philosophic sciene of history was produced: the theory of historical knowledge. Especially in the last third of the 19th century a manifold of aspects in this field was discovered by thinkers like Gustav Droysen, *Grundriss der Historic*, engl. tr. *The Principles of History* (Bonn, 1893); Wilhelm Dilthey, *Einleitung in die Geisteswissenschaften* (1883); Georg Simmel, *Die Probleme der Geschichtsphilosophie* (1892); and Heinrich Rickert, *Die Grenzen der naturwissenschaftlichen Begriffsbildung* (1896-1902). See Heilsgeschichte; progress. R.K.

philosophy of religion: An inquiry into the general subject of religion from the philosophical point of view, *i.e.*, an inquiry employing the accepted tools of critical analysis and evaluation without a predisposition to defend or reject the claims of any particular religion. Among the specific questions considered are: the nature, function and value of religion; the validity of the claims of religious knowledge; the relation of religion and ethics; the character of ideal religion; the nature of evil; the problem of theodicy; revealed *versus* natural religion; the problem of the human spirit (soul) and its destiny; the relation of the human to the divine as to the freedom and responsibility of the individual and the character (if any) of a divine purpose; evaluation of the claims of prophecy, mystic intuitions, special revelations, inspired utterances; the value of prayers of petition; the human hope of immortality; evaluation of institutional forms of expressions, rituals, creeds, ceremonies, rites, missionary propaganda; the meaning of human existence; the character of value, its status in the world of reality; the existence and character of deity; the nature of belief and faith; etc.

The subject of the philosophy of religion is regarded in conservative circles not as a discipline given to free philosophical inquiry but as a particular religion's philosophy. In this form it is a more or less disguised apologetics or defense of an already accepted religious faith. While the data for this subject include the so-called classical religions, philosophy of religion, in the genuinely philosophical sense, takes for its material religious expressions of all types, whether classical or not, together with all the psychological material available on the nature of the human spirit and man's whole cultural development.

The philosopher of religion and the philosophical theologian in so far as they employ the spirit of free inquiry and philosophical method to matters pertaining to the question of God and related questions find their fields merging. Numbers of contemporary theologians are philosophers of religion and philosophers of religion theologians. In so far as the theologian may limit his inquiry to the problem of God and/or to a particular religion, his field becomes much more restricted than that of the philosopher of religion. See reason in religion; religion; theology.

W. E. Hocking, *The Meaning of God in Human Experience* (1912); J. Royce, *The Problem of Christianity* (1913), vols. I and II; G. Galloway, *The Philosophy of Religion* (1914); H. Höffding, *The Philosophy of Religion*, tr. from the German, 2nd ed. (1914); A. Sabatier, *Outlines of a Philosophy of Religion* (n. d.); S. Radhakrishnan, *The Reign of Religion in Contemporary Philosophy* (1920); W. R. Matthews, *Studies in Christian Philosophy* (1921); W. K. Wright, *A Student's Philosophy of Religion* (1922); D. C. Macintosh, *The Reasonableness of Christianity* (1925); F. R. Tennant, *Philosophical Theology*, in two volumes (1928, 1930); D. C. Macintosh, *The Pilgrimage of Faith* (1931); H. Bergson, *The Two Sources of Morality and Religion* (1932); *Contemporary American Theology*, vol. I (1932), vol. II (1933), ed. by Vergilius Ferm; H. N. Wieman and B. E. Meland, *American Philosophies of Religion* (1936); V. Ferm, *First Chapters in Religious Philosophy* (1937); E. S. Brightman, *A Philosophy of Religion* (1940); A. C. Garnett, *A Realistic Philosophy of Religion* (1942).
V.F.

Phoenicians: The word "Phoenician" is historically, geographically and culturally synonymous with "Canaanite*." The Phoenicians called themselves Canaanites down to the end of Phoenician cultural life in Syrai; and their Carthaginian descendants still did so in the fifth century A.D. Canaanite language and religion can be traced back to the beginning of the second millenium B.C., and there is no serious reason for denying that Canaanites had been living in Phoenicia and Palestine long before, in the Early Bronze Age.

Thanks to the great discovery of hundreds of Canaanite texts of circa 1400 B.C. at Ras Shamirah (ancient Ugarit*) in 1929-1939, we can show that the Phoenicians had just as sharply defined a religion as the Egyptians* and Sumero*-Accadians, though cruder in type.

The head of their pantheon was El and his consort was Ashirat. The great active god was Baal or Haadu (Hadad), the storm god and king of gods. His common later title is Baal Shamem (lord of heaven). The goddesses Astarte (Ashirat) and Anath were pictured as naked goddesses of fecundity, though also considered as virgins. See Baalism. H.K.—L.F.

Photius: (858-67; 877-86) Patriarch of Constantinople, was chosen for his office by Caesar Bardas, after the previous patriarch, Ignatius, had been deposed. Photius, the most learned man of the age, was a layman at the time of his appointment, and was consecrated uncanonically, within five days. He soon came into conflict with the masterful Pope Nicholas I*, who refused to acknowledge Photius as patriarch, for the latter had rejected the pope's request for the restoration of Illyricum and Calabria to papal jurisdiction. Consequently, Nicholas resolved to champion the cause of Ignatius. Acting on his claim to supreme jurisdiction, Nicholas excommunicated Photius and declared Ignatius restored (863). But Photius repudiated the papal claim to supremacy, and championed the theory that Rome's primacy is that of honor, not of jurisdiction. The ensuing struggle, augmented by the quarrel over Bulgaria, resulted in a schism.

When Emperor Basil I came to the throne (867), he deposed Photius, thus terminating the schism with Rome, and restored Ignatius. But after the latter's death (877), Photius once more took possession of the patriarchal throne, to be deposed the second time when Emperor Leo VI came to the throne in 886. He was sent into exile, where he died in 891.

W. Norden, *Der Papsttum und Byzanz* (Berlin, 1903); B. J. Kidd, *The Churches of Eastern Christendom* (London, n. d.). M.S.

phylacteries: (Gr. *phylakteria,* amulet; Heb. *tefillin,* sing. *tefillah,* some word as for prayer, i.e., object used in worship) Two small boxes of black leather, containing parchment slips on which are inscribed the four texts, which prescribe the use of "frontlets" (*tatafoth,* which the Targumim render with *tefillin*): Deut. 6.4-9; 11.13-21; Ex. 13.1-10; 13.11-16, and are bound on the forehead.and on the left arm by straps. The phylacteries may have replaced the practice of tatooing or the use of magic charms to protect against evil powers. Presented as "sign" and "memorial" of God's deliverance from bondage, they also aimed to direct the heart of the Jew to God and His commands. Worn by the Pharisees and the Rabbis** all day (cf. Matt. 23.5), they are limited in present Orthodox practice to morning worship by adult males on week days. See charms and amulets. S.S.C.

Phyrgian mysteries: See Mother Goddesses; mystery religions.

Physiologus: An allegorical treatise on real and imaginary animals to which fabulous qualities were ascribed. It originated in Alexandria, was widely translated in the West, and gave rise to an extensive series of "bestiaries."* J.T.M.

Pico della Mirandola, Giovanni, Count: (1463-1494) Renaissance* scholar, philosopher, Platonist*. Though devoutly Christian, he dreamed of a synthesis of Hebrew, Greek and Christian ideas. He studied Hebrew and Arabic as well as Greek, and knew Ficino's Latin translation of Plato, which was completed on the day when Pico first visited Ficino at Florence. Pico's strength was the breadth of his sympathy with man's quest for truth in all lands and ages. In this he followed Ficino who wrote that "a certain divine philosophy" was born among the Persians and Egyptians, nourished among the Thracians under Orpheus, came to youth in Pythagoras and to maturity with Plato, and reached the climax of its powers in Plotinus*. His weakness was an excessive addiction to the occult, hermetic and allegorical. His Hebrew studies led him to a preoccupation with the Kabbala*, and he dwelt less on the Dialogues of Plato than on the most fantastic writings of the late Neo-Platonists*. The brilliant precosity of his mind and the winsomeness of his personality have woven about his name a legendary charm disproportionate to the meagre value of his actual work. Pico was a friend and admirer of Savonarola*, but it was his nephew, Giovanni Francesco Pico della M., who was the biographer of Savonarola. Pico died in Florence at the age of 31.

Sir Thomas More, *Life* (1510). Prefatory essay by J. Rigg in edition of More's Life (1890); Walter Pater Chapter in *Studies in the History of the Renaissance* (1878); J. A. Symonds, *The Renaissance in Italy* (1885-1887), vols. I and V; J. B. Fletcher, *Literature of the Italian Renaissance* (1934); F. Schevill, *History of Florence* (1936). W.E.G.

Pierson, Allard: (1831-1896) He was for some time joint pastor with Albert Reville at the Walloon church in Rotterdam. As a result of his disbelief in supernatural religion he found his position as pastor of a church meaningless and unnatural. He first lectured on theology at the University of Heidelberg, then he lectured on aesthetics, the history of art and modern literature at the University of Amsterdam. A brilliant pupil of C. W. Opzoomer*, he was a sharp theological critic and humanist. He ended in total agnosticism. With A. D. Loman and W. C. van Manen he reached the radical view that probably both Jesus and Paul had never existed as persons. He was unable to reconcile religion and the newer results of natural science, religion and philosophy. He regarded Christianity as a free religious movement within Judaism, in which the conviction arose that the Messiah had appeared.

Bespiegling, Gezag, en Ervaring (Utrecht, 1855); *De Oorsprong der moderne Richting* (Haarlem, 1862); *Rigting en Leven,* 2 vols. (Haarlem, 1863); *De moderne Richting en de kristelijke Kerk* (Arnhem, 1866); *Gods Wondermacht en ons geestelijk Leven* (Arnhem, 1867); *Schoonheidszin en Levenswijsheid* (Arnhem, 1868); *De Bergrede en andere synoptische Fragmenten* (Amsterdam, 1878); A. Pierson and S. A. Naber, *Verisimilia* (Amsterdam and The Hague, 1886); A. Pierson, *Oudere Tijdgenooten* (Amsterdam, 1888); S. A. Naber, *Allard Pierson herdacht* (Haarlem, 1897); J. Herderschee, *De mod-*

ern-godsdienstige Richting in Nederland (Amsterdam, 1904) K. H. Roessingh, *Het Modernisme in Nederland* (Haarlem, 1922). H.H.

pietism: (Lat., *pietas,* piety) Historically, the movement originated by Philipp Jakob Spener* in Germany, seeking a return to vital evangelical Christianity as over against the intellectualism and formalism of seventeenth century Protestant orthodoxy. While the main stream of Lutheranism became channelized in rigid doctrinal and sacramentarian forms, and Calvinism settled into dogmatic legalism, the original emphasis of the Reformation upon heartfelt personal religion had been kept alive by such leaders as Johann Arndt, author of *True Christianity* (1606), and Theophilus Grossgebauer, author of *Alarm Cry* (1661). Pietism crystallized into a specific movement through the informal devotional meetings (conventicles, collegia pietatis) conducted by Spener in his home while serving as pastor in Frankfurt-am-Main. In his *Pia Desideria* (1675) Spener gave the movement a definite platform. The first of his recommendations, Bible study in conventicles, established the method for the spread of Pietism. It was from one of these groups, at Leipzig, that Spener obtained his principal associate, August Hermann Francke. From the University of Halle, founded by Spener, Francke*, and Christian Thomasius, pietism spread through Germany, Scandinavia, and Switzerland. The new spirituality which it engendered found expression in Francke's philanthropic institutions, the establishment of Protestant foreign missions (Ziegenbalg), the hymns of Paul Gerhardt, and the Moravian Church*, organized by Spener's godson Count von Zinzendorf*. Insisting upon individual regeneration, emotional warmth rather than correct doctrine, personal godliness and denial of the world, and universal spiritual priesthood, pietism effected a genuine and widespread spiritual revival, until its course was checked by the Enlightenment of the eighteenth century. In its decadent phase the movement led to the extremes of fanaticism, asceticism, and separation from the organized Church. The term "pietistic" thus came to have the derogatory connotation of religious affectation or a religiosity with more heat than light. The term has also been used to designate any form of personal, devotional, and mystical religion as distinguished from intellectual and formal types. See adiaphoristic controversy; assurance; Boehme, Jacob; hymns; sanctification; terminism.

A. Ritschl, *Geschichte des Pietismus* (1880-1886), 3 vols; W. Mahrholz, *Der deutsche Pietismus* (1921). T.A.K.

pietistic sects in America: A new religious emphasis was introduced into the American colonies with the coming of the Germans. Stressing Christianity as a life rather than a creed pietism gave chief place to the devotional side of religion. Mennonites, Dunkers, Schwenkfelders, and Moravians** constituted the principal bodies in the colonial period, though pietistic influence was strong among the German Reformed and German Lutheran bodies and also exercised a decided influence among the Dutch Reformed. Theodore J. Frelinghuysen (1691-1748) a pietist was the leader of an increasing revivalistic wing among the Dutch Reformed people and was one of the principal leaders in the great Middle Colony revival. Henry M. Mühlenberg*, the father of American Lutheranism, was also a pietist, having been sent to America through the influence of G. A. Francke* of the University of Halle, the center of pietistic emphasis in Germany. Through Mühlenberg's (1711-1787) influence other pietistic ministers came out from Halle to serve Lutheran churches in the colonies. Michael Schlatter (1716-1790) who may also be called the father of the German Reformed Church in America exercised a decided pietistic influence among the German Reformed people. Out of this pietistic strain in American Lutheranism and in the German Reformed church has come two independent revivalistic American churches, the United Brethren in Christ and the Evangelical Church. In its early years Methodism was influenced by pietism through John Wesley's contact with the Moravians. Cf. evangelicalism and evangelical revival.

W. W. Sweet, *Religion in Colonial America* (1942); A. W. Nagier, *Pietism and Methodism* (1918.) W.W.S.

Pilate, Acts of: (or Gospel of Nicodemus*) A Christian bit of pseudepigraphy* from about the middle of the 4th century, composed to assert the sole responsibility of the Jews for the death of Christ. Later an account of the Descent into Hell was added. S.M.G.

Pilgrim Fellowship: (Congregational) See Young People's Societies, Christian.

pilgrimage of grace: The name given to a revolt in the north of England during 1536 and 1537. It was the result of discontent engendered by the religious changes and by the economic dislocations attending the suppression of the monasteries.

See M. H. Dodds, *The Pilgrimage of Grace 1536-1537 and the Exeter Conspiracy 1538* (1915). W.S.H.

pilgrimage to Lourdes: See Lourdes.

Pillar of Fire: A holiness sect with headquarters at Zarephath, N. J. It was first organized as the Pentecostal Union in Colorado in 1901 and took its present name in 1917. Its founder is Mrs. Alma White, who is also the bishop of the sect. Mrs. White was the wife of a Methodist preacher. She came in touch with the "second blessing" theology and experience in Kentucky. Difficulties arose with the Methodist authorities when she began preaching and establishing missions, as a result of which Mrs. White branches out for herself. The theology of the sect is fundamentalist, premillennarian, literalist, and holiness. There are 46 churches and 4,000 members. See Evangelistic Associations; holiness churches. E.T.C.

pilpul: (derived from *pilpel,* to season, to spice, and figuratively, to debate) Dialectical method of studying the Talmud*. One of the outstanding characteristics of pilpul, is the harmonization of contradictions, and the establishment of unity in the Law.

Cf. J. Z. Lauterbach, *Jewish Encyclopedia* (1905), vol. X, pp. 39-43. B.C.

Pindar: Great lyric poet of Thebes (Greece). Born Cynoscephalae, near Thebes, 522 B.C. Died at Argos, c. 443 B.C. His works include hymns, songs, and panegyrics, both to gods and men. He celebrates the religious festivals, athletic games, the athlete's victory, the local hero, the illustrious dead, the men of noble birth. Men and gods, he held, have a common parentage but different destinies. Probably influenced by the Orphics which rose shortly before his day, he held that souls of men "come from the gods", and that human souls carry within themselves the power to free themselves, by their own efforts in a morally upright life, from the body or flesh which imprisons the soul. His influence was strongly felt in later classical thought in religion and philosophy. Historically, his religious ideas appear among the first of the Greeks to unify the spiritual order of the gods with the spiritual order of men.

F.L.P.

pious associations: See Catholic Societies.

pir: A religious guide in the mystical pursuit of Islam. The term is used especially in India to indicate a Moslem teacher in contrast to the Hindu *guru*. See shaikh. P.E.J.

Pitris: Literally the "Fathers", the ancestors to whom reverence is paid in two hymns in the tenth book of the Rig Veda, (15, 56). The custom has persisted until the present in popular Hinduism. Theoretically every devout Hindu home pays daily cult to the spirit of its ancestors. C.S.B.

Pius V, St., Pope: (1566-72) Michael Ghilieri (b. Jan. 17, 1504; d. May 1, 1672) entered at the age of fourteen the Dominican Order* in which later he distinguished himself as a preacher, professor and provincial. A friend as well as a near relative of Giampietro Caraffa (later Pope Paul IV) he received from him in 1556 the diocese of Nepi-Sutri, and in 1557 the purple (*Cardinalis Alexandrinus*). As General Inquisitor for the Roman Curia* in Milan and Lombardy he incorporated in his own person everything that the Catholic Reformation* exacted. Even as pope he continued the strict life he had led as a religious. One would not style him exactly a polished diplomat. This together with a certain lack of worldly experience placed him and the Church at times in precarious and delicate positions. But as a reformer in the church his memory will remain immortal. He doggedly pushed forward the reform in clergy and people as demanded by the Council of Trent*. In fact one might justly say that he not only pointed out the way in his own person but also influenced for all future times the papacy and the Roman Curia; the Catholic clergy and the Catholic people in the observance of the conciliar decrees. He likewise carried out the wishes of Trent in publishing the *Catechismus Romanus* (1566); the reformed Roman breviary (1568) and the Roman Missal (1570)**. He re-inculcated the Bull *"In coena Domini"* directed against secular princes for undue interference in matters purely ecclesiastical (1568); and reorganized the tribunal (*in foro interno*) of the Sacred *Penitentiaria* (1569) and other curial departments. One of the main external objectives of his pontificate was to break the Spanish politico-ecclesiastical pressure under Philip II; to fight new heresies and to keep the old faith intact, especially in Italy. (cf. "Bernardino Ochino", "Peter Valdes", etc.). On Oct. 1, 1567 he condemned 79 propositions of Michael Bajus, professor at Louvain. In virtue of the Bull *"Regnans in coelo"*, Feb. 28, 1570, he excommunicated Elizabeth of England and released her Catholic subjects from the oath of allegiance—the last time such an ecclesiastical penalty was invoked. But it signalized further persecutions of the Catholics of the realm, rather than desistance therefrom; neither did it hinder the eventual execution of Mary Queen of Scots. In the external regime of the Church, Pius, after the loss of Cyprus in 1571, was able to rally Spain and Venice to combine their forces with those of the Papal States* and obtain, under Don Juan of Austria, the brilliant naval victory of Lepanto, Oct. 7, 1572. Pius was beatified in 1672 and canonized in 1712, the last pope to date to be raised to the honors of the altar.

Litt. Official Acts in *Bullarium Diplomatum et Privilegiorum Summ. Roman. Pntif.* (Torino, 1860), Editio Taurinensis vol. VI; vol. VII (Naples, 1882); cf. L. Pastor, *History of the Popes* (1929), vols. XVII-XVIII; for Letters of a diplomatic nature cf. F. Gouban (Antwerp, 1640). Biographies by: F. van Ortroy, *Anal. Bolland.* vol. XXXIII, pp. 187-215; *Dict de la Théol. Cath* XII, col. 1647-53; *Lexikon f. Theologie u. Kirche* VIII, 304.

R.M.H.

Pius VI, Pope: (1775-99) Count Giovanni Angelico Braschi was born Dec. 17, 1717 at Cesena. Stationed since 1740 in Rome in the service of Cardinal Ruffo and Benedict XIV*, he became Papal Secretary and Canon of St. Peter's (1755); treasurer of the Roman Church under Clement XIII; Cardinal in 1773, and was elected pope on Feb. 15, 1775. The papacy at this time was in a precarious condition and the new pope was faced with an empirical age of doctrinal and political "enlightenment"; defense of episcopal prerogatives entirely independent of Rome; and royal absolutism. Through his fine sense of diplomacy Pius was able to brave the storm, gain many a point for the papacy and save the dignity of the Church, even in the face of apparent utter defeat. He had to combat Febronianism* in Germany (Congress of Ems, 1784-85)*; Josephinism in Austria, which a personal visit of the pope to Vienna in 1782 or even the Concordat of 1784 failed to remedy, and in Tuscany, where Joseph II's brother was ruler; also Gallicanism* in France. The schismatical Synod of Pistoia (1786) under Bishop Scipio Ricci forced the Pope to issue the Bull *"Auctorem Fidei"*, Aug. 28, 1794 condemning 85 Gallican and Jansenistical propositions. But the pope's greatest cross was the French Revolution and all that it implied for the

Church and the papacy. Avignon and Venaissin (cf. "Papal States") rebelled and were annexed to France, because Pius in his Brief of April 13, 1791 had condemned the "Civil Constitution" of the Clergy as schismatical and heretical and had enjoined the oath-bound clergy to repudiate it within 40 days. His alliance with the powers in 1792 who were opposed to the French Republic and the provocatory death in Rome of the Secretary of the French Legation at Naples, Basseville, induced Napoleon Bonaparte to occupy the Papal States* In the Treaty of Peace of Tolentino, Feb. 19, 1797 insult was added to injury by forcing the pope not only to give up Avignon, Venaissin, Ferrara, Bologna and the Romagna, but likewise to deliver to France 500 valuable manuscripts, 100 works of art and to pay a war indemnity of thirty million francs. (In 1796, on the occasion of the Truce of Bologna, twenty-one million had already been paid.) On Nov. 19, 1797 Ancona too was torn from the papal possessions. To fill to the very brim the chalice of the pope's woes, Joseph Bonaparte, the French Ambassador, induced Rome itself to rebel against the pope. After General Duphot had fallen during the revolution, French soldiers under Berthier entered the Eternal City, Feb. 10, 1798. On Feb. 15, the Roman Republic was proclaimed and during the night of Feb. 20th the pope, now in his 80th year, was dragged under military guard first to Siena and Florence; then in March, 1799 by way of Bologna and Modena to Parma and Torino; and finally, despite illness, over the Alps to Briancon, Grenoble and Valence where, succumbing to the inhuman hardships of so long drawn-out journey, the aged pope died in exile, Aug. 29, 1799. Buried at first at Valence, it was only in February, 1802 that his remains could be returned to Rome and interred (Feb. 17) at St. Peter's. In response to an appeal of the clergy of the United States, Pius VI, in virtue of a Papal Bull of 1789, erected the first Catholic diocese in the U. S. A., Baltimore, Md. with John Carroll as the first bishop.

. *Bullarii Romani Comtinuatio* ed. Barberi (Rome, 1842), vols. V-X; *Collectio Brevium Pii VI,* 2 vols. (Augsburg, 1796); *Acta Pii VI,* 2 vols. (Rome, 1871); Biographies by J. Bertrand, 2 vols. (Bar-le-Duc, 1897); Ferrari (Padua, 1802); J. Gendry, 2 vols. (Paris, 1907); L. Pastor, *Geschichte der Päpste* (Freiburg in Br., 1932). Eng. tr. not yet published. XVI, 3; F. Hayward, *Le dernier siècle de la Rome pontificale* (Paris, 1917), pp. 56-154; *Dict. de la Théol. Cath.,* XII, 1653-69; Sampson, "Pius VI and the French Revolution" in *Amer. Cath. Quarterly Review* (1906); *Cath. Encyc.,* XII, 132; Lillian Brown-Olf, *Their Name is Pius* (1941).

R.M.H.

Pius VII, Pope: (1800-23) Pope during the Napoleonic era, Pius VII, (born Luigi Barmola Charamonti, July 14, 1740 at Cesena) saw the Papal States* reduced to their lowest ebb, but also almost completely restored in the Congress of Vienna, 1815. At the age of 16 he entered the Benedictine Order*, became later, 1782 Bishop of Tivoli and in 1785 Bishop of Imola. Created cardinal (Feb. 14, 1785) by his predecessor, he was elected pope on March 14, 1800 at Venice. Venice was at that time under Austrian rule due to the fact that Pius VI* in exile (Nov. 13, 1798) had provided that on account of the French Revolution and the Napoleonic invasions of the Papal States, including Rome, the conclave be held in whichever city after his death, the largest number of cardinals chanced to be living. Crowned on Mar. 21, he was able to enter Rome, then under French domination, but enthusiastically welcomed by the people, July 3, 1800. Pius VII's greatest aide throughout practically the whole of his pontificate was the able Ercole Consalvi, Secretary of the Conclave, later chosen by Pius to be Cardinal-Secretary of State (Aug. 11, 1800). Two important problems immediately confronted the new pope: the return of normal conditions in the Papal States and, at the wish of the First Counsel, Napoleon, a rehabilitation of relations between Church and State in France, so flagrantly disturbed during the French Revolution. Negotiations threatened time and time again to be broken off indefinitely due to the violent opposition of the Constitutional Church of France, the unwarranted assumptions of the legitimist monarchists and the unreasonable demands of Napoleon himself. It was only when Consalvi personally went to Paris and made wide concessions that the Concordat* of 1801) which despite future alterations and even repudiation was to play for a whole century so important a rôle in later French politico-ecclesiastical relations) was signed (promulgated, April 18, 1802). At the same time, however, Napoleon published his hitherto secretly concocted 77 Organic Articles referring to the Catholic Church and 44 to the Protestant Churches, all infected with Gallicanism* and, in general, subjecting every public act of the Church to the previous approval of the government—in other words an enslavement of the Church by an inimical government. Despite the protest by the pope in 1803 and again in 1817, refusing to regard them as part of the Concordat, as also protested repeatedly by loyal French bishops, the Organic Articles (excepting Art. 24 referring to the subscribing to and teaching of the four Gallican Articles, adopted in 1682, by professors in ecclesiastical seminaries) remained nominally at least in force until 1905 when all diplomatic relations between the Church of Rome and France were severed. (cf. "Pius X") The Corsican violated with equal disregard of pledges and obligations the Concordat of 1803 regulating ecclesiastical conditions in the Italian (French controlled) Republic. When on May 18, 1804 Napoleon was pronounced hereditary emperor of the French, he invited Pius VII to Paris to perform the traditional unction and solemn coronation. Hoping to obtain perhaps concessions for the Papal States and a suspension of the Organic Articles, Pius rather reluctantly consented. Any illusions the pope might have entertained regarding the future Emperor's greater conciliatory attitude towards his person, the Church and the Papal States, must have been dispelled by the unceremonious reception accorded him, and by the self-coronation of the emperor at the Notre Dame Cathedral, leaving to the pope only the annointing. The sole favor received by Pius referred to

Religious Orders. On May 16, 1805 Pius in virtue of a previously pledged and signed agreement was able to return to Rome, although even then the Emperor would have preferred to retain him under guard somewhere in France. The emperor's hatred towards the pope mounted when the latter protested that he could not grant a divorce to Napoleon's brother, Jerome, from Miss Paterson of Baltimore; to crown his other brother, Joseph, King of Naples; or finally to become Napoleon's vassal in matters referring to the Emperor's enemies. On Feb. 2, 1808 Rome was invaded by the imperial troops and on May 17, 1809 the rest of the Papal States were incorporated into the French empire. When Pius retaliated with the Bull of excommunication (*Quum memoranda*) against the robbers and usurpers of the Papal States (the *Patrimonium Petri*) and all their abettors, even though the emperor's name was not mentioned, he was taken captive on the night of July 5-6, and together with Cardinal Pacca transferred by coach first to Grenoble, and later alone to Savona, where deprived of all his counsellors, he was treated most shamefully. To regulate ecclesiastical matters within the empire, with or without the consent of the pope, Napoleon convoked on June 17, 1811 a National Council that convened at Paris. Although not entirely submissive to his will, the Council did decide under pressure that if the pope refused to install the bishops selected by the emperor, this right should devolve upon the Metropolitans. An imperial commission succeeded in pressing from the weary and ailing pope his consent thereto. But Pius remained adamant in the question of the emperor's divorce from Josephine. Although seriously ill the pope was dragged (June, 1812) to Fountainbleu, where Napoleon importuned him to consent to 11 preliminary statutes of a new Concordat (Jan. 25, 1813) which the emperor then promulgated as the new Concordat of Fountainbleu. Tormented by qualms of conscience for his momentary weakness in signing an agreement that meant at least the indirect cession of the Papal States, Pius, advised and encouraged by Pacca and Consalvi, recalled his previous consent on March 23, 1813. The fall of Napoleon brought an end to all further pressure and humiliations on the weary exiled Roman Pontiff. On May 24, 1814 Pius once more entered the gates of Rome. Although once more forced by Murat to flee the Capital, March 22, 1815, Pius was finally able to return permanently on July 7. Consalvi's dextrous diplomacy was able to regain at the Congress of Vienna, 1814-15, with the consent of England and such statesmen as Wellington, Tallyrand and Metternich practically the complete return of the Papal States to the papacy. Only a small strip of land remained in the hands of Austria and this usurpation was protested. The intra- and inter-relations with the other powers were fixed by Consalvi and promulgated in the papal *motuproprio* of July 6, 1816. Certain modifications (reforms) already adopted during the French occupation were retained. Banditry however, continued, until finally on Sept. 17, 1821 Pius took strong measures by publishing his Bull against certain secret refractory agents known as the "Carbonari" (charcoal-burners). On Aug. 7, 1814 the Society of Jesus* was re-established; in 1817 concordats made with Bavaria and Sardinia; and in 1818 with Naples and Russia (referring especially to Catholic Poland). In 1808 the Pontiff erected for the growing Catholic Church in the U. S. A. the four new dioceses of Boston, New York, Philadelphia and Bardstown (later transferred to Louisville, Ky.) with Baltimore, now elevated to the rank of an Archdiocese, as the Metropolitan See. To these dioceses were added in 1820 Charleston and Richmond, and in 1821 Cincinnati. In 1817 Pius VII signed a new concordat with Louis XVIII, which provided for an additional number of dioceses and repealed the Organic Articles; but the French Chamber of Deputies refused to approve it, so that the Concordat of 1801 was again invoked. The erection of a few new French dioceses was the only appreciable effect obtained through the discussions. During the latter part of the reign of Pius VII the prestige of the papacy was enhanced by the presence in Rome of several European rulers. Under Pius' pontificate Rome became, despite the various changes of government, the favorite abode of sculptors and artists, including such renowned men as the Venetian, Canova; the Dane, Thorwaldsen; the Austrian, Führich; and the Germans, Overbeck, Pforr, Schadow and Cornelius. Pius VII re-opened the English, Scotch and German colleges in the Eternal City and established new chairs in the Roman College. The illustrious pope died Aug. 20, 1823. His faithful secretary, Consalvi, was destined to follow him into eternity in less than a year (Jan. 24, 1824).

For the Papal Bulls and official Acts of Pius VII cf. *Bullarii Romani continuatio,* edit. Barberi, vols. XI-XIV (Rome, 1846-53); C. D'Haussonville, *L'Eglise Rom. et le premier empire,* 5 vols. 3 (Paris, 1870, ff.); F. Hayward, *Le denier siécle de la Rome Pontificale* (Paris, 1927), vol. I, 55-238; G. Constant, *L'Eglise de France sous le consulat et l'empire* (Paris, 1928). Recent monograms and biographies by: Mary H. Allies (London, 1897); Lillian Brown-Olf, *Their Name is Pius* (1941); and J. Schmidlin, *Papsttum der neuesten Zeit* (1933), I. pp. 1-366; cf. *Dict. de la Thèol. Cath.* XII col. 1670-83; *Cath. Encyc.* XII 132-4; Wiseman, Card., *Recollections of the Last Four Popes* (1858); J. MacCaffrey, *History of the Catholic Church in the Nineteenth Century 2* (Dublin and St. Louis, 1910); Acton, in *The Cambridge Modern History* vol. X: "The Restoration" (1907); G. Head, Eng. tr. (London, 1850), Bartolomeo Card. Pacca, *Memorie Istoriche* (1830; 2d ed. 1843); Artaud de Montor, *Histoire du Rape Pie VII* 2 vols. *3* (Paris, 1839).
R.M.H.

Pius IX, Pope: (1846-78) Count Giovanni Maria Mastei-Ferretti, born May 13, 1792 at Sinigallia, received his early education at Volterra (1802-09) and later at Rome. In 1823 he was sent as Auditor to the Papal Legation in Chile, thus becoming the first (future) pope to labor on (south) American shores. Returning to Italy he was named Archbishop of Spoleto, May 21, 1827; Bishop of Imola, Feb. 17, 1832 and, after fruitful services in both dioceses, created cardinal, Dec. 14, 1840. After an unusually short conclave he was elected pope, June 16, 1846 and crowned on June 21. His pontificate is particularly noted: 1) for the loss of the Papal States* on Sept. 20, 1870, thus creating the "Roman Question" (cf. "Concordats"), despite the fact that in the beginning he was not adverse to a Parliamentary form of government; 2) for the Declaration of the Dogma of the Immaculate Conception*, Dec. 8, 1854, to date the last definition *"ex cathedra"** (cf. "Chair of St. Peter"); 3) for the celebration of the Vatican Council*, 1869-70 defining papal infallibility and re-affirming the primacy of the See of Rome; 4) for the Syllabus of Dec. 8, 1864 condemning 80 propositions of either theologically adjudged false or philosophically unsafe propositions; and 5) for the erection of many dioceses throughout the world, especially in the U. S. A., and the creation of many prefectures and vicariates in missionary countries. After having occupied the Chair of Peter longer than any of his predecessors (32 yrs.) he died at Rome, Feb. 7, 1878 and was buried, in accordance with his wish at San Lorenzo beyond the walls of Rome. See Kulturkampf; Syllabus of errors, papal.

Litt. *Acta Pii IX* (Rome, 1854-78); monograms and biographies by: J. M. Stepischnegg, 2 vols. (1879); A Pougeois (Paris, 1877-86), 6 vols.; E. Vercesi (1934), J. F. Maguire (London, 1878); W. Molitor, 4 (1875); M. F. Cusack (London, 1878); Th. O'Dwyer (London, 1879); Dr. Aen. M. Dawson, *Pius the Ninth and his Times* 1792-1878 (Canada, 1880); J. Gilmary Shea (1878); J. Mac Caffrey, *Hist. of the Cath. Church in the Nineteenth Century* (Dublin, 1909); L. Browne-Olf, *Their Name is Pius* (1941). R.M.H.

Pius X, Pope: (1903-1914) In marked contrast to the pontificate of his predecessor, Pope Leo XIII* but complementary to it, was the reign of Pius X. Giuseppe Melchiore Sarto was born June 2, 1835 at Riese in the Province of Treviso, northern Italy. Ordained priest in 1858 he was named chaplain in Tombolo, Pastor at Salzano, 1867; Canon of the Cathedral of Treviso, 1875; Bishop of Mantua, 1884; Patriarch of Venice and Cardinal, 1893; and in the conclave of Aug. 4, 1903, following the Austrian veto against Cardinal Rampollo, former Secretary of State under Leo XIII (instigated by Italy), he was elected pope. A simple devout soul, Pius was unalterably opposed to external pomp and ceremonial beyond what his dignity required. While criticized by some for his method of procedure, he had as pope only one purpose in view as announced in his first encyclical* of Oct. 10, 1903 and in his *motu proprio** of Mar. 19, 1904 "to renew all things in Christ." Among the outstanding solicitudes and reforms of his pontificate may be mentioned the preservation of the Faith against the initial inroads made by Modernism* against which he issued the decree "Lamentabili" and the Syllabus of Errors* (1907), accentuated by the encyclical *Pascendi* of Sept. 8, 1907 and the *Motuproprio* of Sept. 1, 1910 with corresponding explanations from the Sacred Congregation of the Consistorial dated Sept. 25, 1910 demanding that the oath against Modernism be taken by all ecclesiastical authorities (still in vogue); 2) the new codification of Canon Law* ordered on March 19, 1904 (*Arduum sane*) and virtually completed at the time of his death in 1914 (*Codex Juris Canonici**); 3) the reorganization of the Roman Curial Congregations, the first since the days of Sixtus V* (1587); 4) the creation of the periodical *Acta Apostolicae Sedis,* the official organ of the Holy See (first number: Jan. 1, 1909); 5) regulation regarding the ascetical and scientifical education of clerical students, especially in Italy (1907-08); concerning advanced studies in Biblical matters (Encyc. *Quoniam in re biblica*), March 27, 1906; and institution of the Biblical Institute at Rome (May 7, 1909); 5) reform of the Roman Breviary* through a re-arrangement of a complete weekly recitation of all of the Psalms; and the according of special privileges for the Sunday formulas of the Missal* (*Divino afflatu,* 1910); 6) prohibition of theatrical music during Divine Services and a re-accentuation of the Gregorian Chant*, but not exclusive of philharmonic motets (Dec. 20, 1905); and 7) reinculcation of regular explanation of the Word of God by the Clergy, especially in Italy (*Acerbo nimis* April 15, 1905); and 8) the early and frequent reception of Holy Communion (Dec. 20, 1905).

Pius sought to regulate as far as the existing disturbed conditions in Italy permitted the relations between Church and State, without however, actually permitting Catholics, generally and formally speaking, to take part in public political elections (1905). He abolished the hateful veto so frequently, and even in the conclave which elected him, exercised by Christian kings and princes, thus insuring for all future times complete freedom of papal election. The ecclesiastical hierarchy was expanded and augmented through the erection of Apostolical Delegations* (cf. "Papal Legates") in Mexico, 1904; in Australia, 1914; through the creation of new missionary vicariates in foreign fields and dioceses, especially in the U. S. A. Interest in the Oriental Churches was fostered not only through the permission to use the Ruthenian Rite* in North America (1910) but also in the erection of special Ruthenian dioceses in Canada and in the U. S. A.; through the celebration of the Jubilee of St. John Chrysostom in 1908; Armenian National Synod at Rome, 1911 (*Ex quo,* Dec. 26, 1910) and the Constitution, *Tradita,* Sept. 14, 1912. Diplomatic relations with France, which had already been strained during the last years of the pontificate of Leo XIII* were entirely broken off in 1905 through the repudiation of the Concordat of Pius VI* of 1801, with subsequent separation of Church and State. The pope also rejected the politico-social errors of the "Sillon" (1910), a French association of young Catholics independent of their bishops. In 1914 he condemned the *L'Action Francaise* due to its monarchistic tendencies. Diplomatic relations were also severed between Portugal and the Holy See (Encyc. *Jamdudum,* May 24, 1911); the same was true of Spain, at least temporarily (1910).

Kind but determined, intent on the inner supernatural elevation and purification of the Church rather than on her exterior glory before nations,

Piux X seems to have been destined by Providence to guide the Bark of Peter through the troublesome waters that agitated and rocked it during the first years of the XX century, prior to the First World War, which despite heroic efforts and personal appeal to the Emperor of Austria he was unable to prevent. Honored after death as much as he was revered in life, the process of his beatification was opened in 1923. He lies buried in the crypt of St. Peter's, where, in the basilica itself, a colossal statue by Astorri perpetuates his memory.

Acta Santae Sedis and *Acta Apostolicae Sedis* (1903-14) Seppelt-Löffler, *Papstgeschichte* (Munich, 1933) 494-521, Eng. tr. of an earlier edit. by Frommelt (1932); Eng. biographies by F. A. Forbes (London, 1919); Pieranini (London and Torino, 1928 and '29); A. Waal, Eng. tr. by Berg (1909); L. Brown-Olf, *Their Name was Pius* (1941). The Pope's encyclicals were published by Herder.

R.M.H.

Pius XI, Pope: (1922-39) Ambrosio Damiano Achille Ratti was born at Desio, near Milan, May 31, 1857; was ordained priest Dec. 20, 1879; obtained the doctorates of Philosophy, Theology and Canon Law at the Gregorian University, Rome; became professor at the Diocesan Seminary at Milan, 1882; librarian of the *Ambrosiana,* Milan, 1888, and Prefect of the same in 1907, during which tenure of office he edited many documents and studies pertaining to the Church of Milan (4 vols. Milan, 1890-99). Promoted to Pro-prefect of the Vatican Library in 1912 he collaborated with Francis Ehrle, S.J., whom he succeeded as Prefect in 1914. It was in this capacity that Msgr. Ratti represented the Vatican at the 700th centennary of the birth of Roger Bacon commemorated at Oxford. Benedict XV* made of the "diplomatist" a "diplomat" by sending him in 1918 to Poland as Apostolic Visitator and raised him to the rank of a Nuncio (cf. "Papal Legate"), Oct. 28, 1919, after that wartorn country, following the Treaty of Versailles, had received the status of an independent Republic. While functioning in this capacity he was named and consecrated Titular Archbishop of Lepanto. In 1920 the pope sent him as Commissary to watch over the important plebescites in Oberschlesien, East and West Prussia to determine the future German or Polish allegiance of those countries. In 1921 Ratti was appointed Archbishop of Milan and on Feb. 6, 1922 created cardinal. On the death of Benedict XV, he was elected pope on the seventh ballot, Feb. 6, 1922 and crowned on Feb. 11. The motto of the new pope "Peace of Christ in the Kingdom of Christ" became the program of his whole pontificate, viz., to instill peoples and nations with the spirit of Christ in their personal lives and in their relations to one another. Among the notable achievements of his busy pontificate (he was an indefatigable worker) should be accentuated: 1) his many encyclicals on timely topics that attracted the attention as well as the admiration of the Christian world, e.g., on the Christian Education of Youth; on Christian Marriage and Family Life (*Casti Connubii* condemning illicit birth control); on Christian Sociology, etc.; 2) the celebration of three Jubilees, 1925, '29 and '33, unparalleled in the history of the papacy; 3) his interest in Home and Foreign missions: insistance on the imparting of Christian Doctrine; Catholic Action or the Lay Apostolate; advocacy of a native clergy and the personal consecration of one Japanese and six Chinese Bishops in St. Peter's, Rome; 4) his love for the Oriental Church as manifested in the founding of a special commission for the Codification of Oriental Canon Law; the erection of the Russian, Ruthenian, Roumanian and Ethiopian Colleges; the solemn commemoration of the 1500th anniversary of the celebration of the Council of Ephesus* (431-1931); 5) the holding of the Mission and Press Exhibits at the Vatican and the founding of the Institute for Christian Archeology; the erection of the new Picture Gallery (Pinacotheca) to house the Vatican treasures of art; the building of the new Gregorian University and of the new seat of the Roman Congregations in Transtevere, Rome; 6) his promotion of higher studies through the famous encyclical *"Deus Scientiarum Dominus"* regulating university studies and the awarding of academic degrees in the Church; the founding of the Pontifical Academy of Sciences (cf. "Pontifical College"); the insistence on the reform of Church Music; 7) the solution of the Roman Question (cf. "Papal States" and "Pius IX") and the subsequent Lateran Treaty and Concordat with Italy (1929); 8) the defense of the Church and of her institutions against Atheistic Communism, Fascism and Naziism; 9) his great charity in finding homes for the poor refugees of Eastern Europe, including Russia, and in subsidizing the needy of Central Europe after the World War I; and finally 10) the Beatification and Canonization of many Servants of God including the English Martyrs, Sts. John Fisher and Thomas More, and the Canadian-American martyrs, Isaac Jogues and companions.

A highly educated and sympathetic soul, but at the same time a fearless and determined character (*Fides Intrepida,* according to the prophecy attributed to Bishop Malachy), Pius XI will live in history as one of the great popes of the Catholic Church. His life was blameless; his doctrines always abreast of the times; his viewpoints international and universal, and his philosophy of life dominated by one thought, the knowledge of the principles taught by Christ and the practice thereof by men and nations of all creeds, colors, races and professions.

Litt. For all official Acts: cf. *Acta Apostolicae Sedis* (Rome, 1922-39). Many of the Pope's encyclicals, transl. into English, were published by the NCWC of Washington, D. C.; by the Paulists Press and by the America Press, both of New York City. Cf. F. R. Hoare, *The Papacy and the Modern State* (London, 1940); George Seldes, *The Vatican, Yesterday, Today, Tomorrow* (N. Y. and London, 1934); *The Catholic Church in Contemporary Europe* (1919-31) edit. by Msgr. Peter Guilday (1932); Seppelt-Löffler, *Papstgeschichte* (Munich, 1933); English adaptation of an earlier edition by H. Frommelt, *History of the Popes* (St. Louis, 1932) 542-552.

Biographies by: C. Fumagalli (Rome, 1925); R. Fontenella (Paris, 1928); F. v. Lana 2 (1930); A. Ehrhard (Cologne, 1929); P. R. Veneziani (Rome, 1935); P. T. Lombardo (1925); W. L. Townsend (London, 1930); Hugh Walpole, *Roman Fountain* (1940); Philip Hughes (London, 1932); L. Brown-Olf, *Their Name is Pius* (1941); Benedict Williamson (London, 1931); Denis Gywnn (London, 1932). Special Studies: Lord Clonmore, *Pope Pius XI and World Peace* (London, 1938); William Teeling, *Pope Pius XI and World Affairs* (1937); Cuddihy and Schuster, *Pope Pius XI: Public American Opinion* (1939); Morgan, *An American Reporter at the Vatican* (1936). Cf. *The International Year Book* for the year 1939 (1940). For the Pope's own literary works cf. Achille Ratti, *Scritti Storici* (Florence, 1932) (also trans. into Eng.); N. Malvezzi, *Pio XI nei suoi scritti* (Milan, 1923); G. Galbiati, *Bio-Bibliografia di Achille Ratti* (Milan, 1923).

R.M.H.

Pius XII, Pope: (1939-) Born at Rome, March 2, 1876 of a (papal) noble family, Eugenio Pacelli was first destined by his father, a Vatican Lawyer, to the study of law, the same as his own brother, Francesco, who was later made a Papal Marquis for his services in helping to settle the Roman Question (cf. "Pius IX" and "Pius XI"), in 1929 as intermediary between Pope Pius XI and Benito Mussolini. Young Eugenio, however, preferred to study for the priesthood, entered the Capranica College and was ordained in 1899. He began his studies in diplomacy at the Pontifical Academy, where he later became professor of Canon Law*. Under the influence of (the later Cardinal) Pietro Gasparri, Msgr. Pacelli devoted his talents exclusively to the work of the Congregation of Extraordinary Ecclesiastical Affairs. In 1912 he became Under Secretary to Cardinal Merry del Val, then Secretary of State to Pope Pius X* and held this position until April 20, 1917, when he was named Nuncio (cf. "Papal Legates") to Munich and consecrated Titular Archbishop of Sardis, May 13, 1917. In the summer of 1917 he held, in the name of the Holy See, important conversations with the German Chancellor Bethmann-Holweg and, at military headquarters on the Western Front presented a personal letter from Pope Benedict XV* to the Kaiser urging him to endeavor to restore peace to the world. It was through Archbishop Pacelli that the pope in the following August (1917) made attempts to mediate between the Central Powers and the Allies. During the turbulent days after the war Pacelli remained in Munich and concluded negotiations for a Concordat with Bavaria. On June 22, 1920 he moved to Berlin as the first nuncio accredited to the German Republic and there on June 14, 1929, he won one of his greatest diplomatic victories by the arrangement of a successful concordat with the predominantly Protestant State of Prussia. On Dec. 16, 1929 he was created cardinal and recalled to Rome by Pius XI*. There, on Feb. 11, 1930, one year after the Lateran Treaty had been signed, he was appointed Papal Secretary of State to succeed Cardinal Gasparri. In this post as chief diplomat of the Church (he was also Camerlengo of the Sacred College of Cardinals) he shared with Pius XI the grave concern regarding the persecution of the Church in Russia, Mexico, Spain and Germany, despite in the latter case, the concordat of 1933, which Cardinal Pacelli himself had signed. On the death of Piux XI, Feb. 10, 1939 and in the conclave which followed, on March 2, 1939 he was chosen pope unanimously on the third ballot (61-1) and assumed the name of Pius XII. He was crowned on March 12, 1939 on the balcony of St. Peter's overlooking the piazza. On that occasion Joseph P. Kennedy, former United States Ambassador to England, represented President Roosevelt. The present pope is one of the most travelled of Catholic prelates. In 1911 he was a member of the Vatican delegation at the Coronation of George V in London; in 1934 he was Papal Legate to the International Eucharistic Congress at Buenos Aires; in 1935 he represented Pius XI at Lourdes, France; and in 1936 he visited the U. S. A., where he travelled extensively by rail and air, visiting many of the leading cities of the country. Throughout the World War II, Pius XII has been making constant efforts to effect conciliation, and alleviation of the sufferings attendant on the war. "Peace" (*Pax-Pacelli*) was the theme of practically everyone of his addresses during public audiences, allocutions, in consistories and radio addresses. Like Pius XI after the First World War he has been most charitable in trying to alleviate the sufferings of the Central and Eastern European peoples robbed of their homes and possessions through German invasion of their territories. One of the greatest consolations to the saddened heart of the Father of Christendom was the appointment by President Franklin D. Roosevelt of Myron C. Taylor as his personal ambassador to the Vatican where repeatedly he has both delivered and received messages of a highly important but confidential character. The present conflict has not only strained somewhat the relations between the Holy See and Italy but also, early in June 1940, caused the American College in Rome to be closed and the students to be sent back to American shores for the completion of their education. Many of them resumed their studies at the Catholic University of America at Washington, D. C. Fearlessly Pope Pius has not only exposed the persecution of the Church in Germany under Nazi regime but likewise in other countries: Poland, Alsace-Lorraine, Belgium, etc. On May 7, the Holy See signed a concordat with Portugal, one of the few countries in Europe to maintain peace. Despite the war, there were to date two canonizations of saints during his pontificate, Gemma Galgani and Mary of St. Euphrasia Pelletier, foundress of the universally known Sisters of the Good Shepherd who take care of wayward girls (May, 1940). Among the Beatifications was that of Bl. Rose-Philippina Duchesne, who established the Religious of the Sacred Heart in the U. S. A. in 1818. Among the important jubilees or commemorations of significant events was the fourth centenary of the canonical approval of the Jesuits*; the holding of the first Synod of the ecclesiastical jurisdiction of the Greek Rite in Italy, which began at the Greek Abbey of Grottaferrata, Oct. 13, 1940 to commemorate the Seventh Ecumenical Council held at Nice in 787; the 150th anniversary of the founding of the North American Hierarchy and the consecration of John Carroll as the first Bishop of Baltimore (cf. "Pius VI"); the Golden Jubilee of the founding of the Catholic University, Washington, D. C., etc. Deaths in the Sacred College of Cardinals have reduced their number, as of Oct. 24, 1942 to 49 of whom only twenty are foreigners. No new cardinals have been created since the Consistory of Dec. 13, 1937 under Pius XI. Among the missionary concerns of the Holy Father saddened by the ruin of so many chapels, churches and religious houses in mission fields was the consecration of twelve missionary bishops of various races, on the Feast of Christ, the King, October, 1939. Thirty nations now have diplomatic relations with the Holy See, the latest to send a representative being Uruguay, the first time since 1898.

For the official Acts of Pius XII to date cf. *Acta Apostolicae Sedis* (Rome, 1939, ff.). Cf. *The Americana Encycl. Annual* (1941), pp. 617-20; 723; *ib.* (1942) p. 629; *The New International Year Book* 1939 (1940), p. 681 ff.; (*ib.* 1941) Events of 1940, p. 661. R.M.H.

pixy, pisky: In English folklore, a fairy*; a possible origin or connection in Swedish *pysk*, a little demon or goblin*. F.L.P.

piyyut: (derived from the Greek *poietes*, poet) Hymns that were added to the older liturgy. The author of the piyyut was called payyetan. Some of the oldest payyetainim were Jose ben Jose, Yannai and Eldzar Kalir.

Cf. G. Deutsch, *Jewish Encyclopedia*, vol. X, pp. 65-68; I. Elbogen, *Der jüdische Gottesdienst in seiner geschichtlichen Entwicklung*, 2nd edition (Berlin, 1924), pp. 281 ff. B.C.

placet: (Lat., "it pleases"), or *Regium placet* (royal approval) The right claimed by the State to approve of Ecclesiastical enactments prior to their promulgation or execution. The practice made its appearance during the Western Schism* (1378-1417). In France it was applied by the Pragmatic Sanction* of 1438 as an instrument to regulate all acts and decrees emanating from Rome. Soon it spread to Spain and Portugal. In Germany it flourished especially during the periods of Josephinism and Febronianism. The Catholic Church has constantly and energetically opposed the *Placet* as an intolerable abuse against her liberty and rights. C.V.

plain chant: The ancient form of singing the church service, in unison and without meter. Known also as "Plain song"* or "Gregorian chant."* B.S.E.

plainsong: Monodic solo or unison chant, unaccompanied, unmetrical, modal. Gregorian chant* is plainsong, a prose text set in free rhythm making use of the ecclesiastical modes. Chants are either syllabic, in which one note serves each syllable, neumatic, in which some syllables have one note but most have groups of notes, or melismatic, in which several notes or groups of notes serve each syllable. See psalmody.

Rev. Dom. Johner, *A New School of Gregorian Chant* (1906). E.H.B.

Planck, Gottlieb Jakob: (1751-1833) He was professor at the University of Göttingen. Posing as a rational supernaturalist, he evaded theological quarrels. He was the founder of the comparative study of the confessions and of the history of Protestant theology. He delighted to unmask the history of the Christian church of its glorified reputation. He robbed history of its ideal meaning and had the mania of deducing the great historical events from accidental and insignificant causes. He ruthlessly criticized the bestialities and atrocities of church history. He debunked the great and famous men of the empirical church of their abiding value. Church and Christianity were not identical for him.

Geschichte der Entstehung, der Veränderungen und der Bildung unseres protestantischen Lehrbegriffs bis zur Konkordienformel (Leipzig, 1781-1800), 6 vols.; *Geschichte der protestantischen Theologie von der Konkordienformel bis in die Mitte des 18. Jahrhunderts* (Göttingen, 1831); *Geschichte der christlichkirchlichen Gesellschaftsverfassung* (Hanover, 1803-1809), 5 vols. H.H.

Plato: (c. 427-c. 347 B.C.) Son of Ariston and Perictione (a descendant of Solon's family), pupil of Socrates; one of the greatest philosophers and writers of all time. Born in Athens (or on Aegina). While accounts of his life are partly legendary (including the story that Apollo was his father), a highly probable outline can be established (largely following Ritter); there is a recent tendency among scholars to recognize some of Plato's "Epistles" as authentic sources for his life.

First period (427-407): through his ephebate. He received an excellent education, including music or poetry. As a boy he heard Gorgias and Protagoras, the sophists, and his first teacher was Cratylus the Heraclitean. Plato was impressed by the Peloponnesian War (431-404), which ruined the Athenian Empire.

Second period (407-399): as pupil of Socrates. During this time Plato learned the Socratic method, the dialectic, the irony, the doctrines that knowledge is virtue and virtue happiness. Xenophon until 401 was also in the Socratic group. Plato was present at the trial, but not at the death of Socrates (*Apol.* 34A, *Phaedo* 59B). The *Protagoras*, and perhaps the *Hippias Minor*, *Laches* and *Charmides*, may have been written before the death of Socrates in 399.

Third period (399-387): study and travel. From 399 to 395 Plato seems to have been at Megara with Euclides, and may have written the *Euthyphro*, the *Apology*, and the *Crito* at this time; and the *Hippias Major* (if genuine), the *Euthydemus*, the *Cratylus*, the *Meno*, and the *Menexenus* (387). In 389 he made his first journey to Sicily, where he met the elder Dionysius at Syracuse. Stories are told of his capture by pirates and his ransom by Anniceris on the return from Sicily. In 388 he purchased the Academy, a public park or grove, equipped as a gymnasium, and founded his school of philosophy there. He wrote the *Gorgias* (388 or 387) as a program of principles for his school.

Four period (387-367): constructive activity. Plato developed the Academy and engaged in his most brilliant literary activity, producing the *Symposium*, the *Phaedo*, the *Republic* (which was not all written at one time), the *Phaedrus* (379?), and the *Theaetetus* (369-368). In the *Parmenides* (367-366) Plato engaged in a closely reasoned dialectical self-criticism. In 367 he undertook his second journey to Sicily, meeting Dionysius II, with hopes of carrying out political reforms, but made an early and disappointed return.

Fifth period (367-347): the dialectical period. In 367, Plato's greatest pupil, Aristotle* entered the Academy. Aristotle said of his teacher: "Plato is my friend, but truth is a greater friend." About 364, Plato wrote the *Sophist;* after that, the *Statesman* (*Politicus*), the *Philebus*, the *Timaeus*, its sequel, the (unfinished) *Critias*, and the *Laws*. Plato made his third journey to Sicily (362-360). After his return, his friend Dion was murdered (352). Plato is said to have died while in the act of further literary composition.

See Platonism for bibliography. E.S.B.

Platonism: The philosophy of Plato*, and later systems influenced by him. It is based on the dialectic* of Socrates*, as a method of inquiry; its main tenet is that objects of thought (Ideas, forms, noumena) are eternally real, as opposed to the transitory and relatively unreal objects of sense perception (phenomena). Man can have knowledge (*epistēmē*) of Ideas, but only opinion (*doxa*) about phenomena. Mathematical objects and ideal values (such as justice, the Beautiful, the Good) are the highest realities, from which God and man alike derive the meaning and goal of their existence. The aim of life is the knowledge of truth and the control of individuals and society by reason, although Plato also manifested mystical traits. Platonism has exercised great influence on Christian thought.

The thought of Plato was presented chiefly in the original and brilliant literary form of Socratic dialogues, not in the lecture or textbook style of Aristotle. His mind was continually developing, and the results of many of the dialogues were vague and tentative. He did not present a complete or unified system, nor can one be reconstructed from the dialogues. Nevertheless, certain main ideas, summarized in the following, are characteristically Platonic.

I. *Socratic Elements in Plato's Thought.*

Note.—There is difference of opinion about the degree of originality to be assigned to Plato. All agree that the earliest dialogues are reports of the thought of Socrates*; most hold that from 387 (or earlier) on, the "Socrates" of the dialogues is to some extent a literary fiction, serving as spokesman for the thought of Plato. J. Burnet and A. E. Taylor, however, hold that most of the dialogues in which Socrates is spokesman are historically authentic. This article is based on the majority opinion. It is assumed that Plato agreed with the views of Socrates, whether historical or fictional, much as St. Paul agreed with Jesus and the tradition about him.

1. Criticism of the Sophists*. The Sophists, popular teachers of rhetoric and virtue, accepted pay for their instruction and held (Protagoras) that "man is the measure of all things." Socrates refused pay and taught that, not the individual, but the rational, universal man is the measure; as Plato said, therefore, "God is the measure" (*Laws*).

2. Method of dialectic.* This consisted of truth-seeking by question-asking; Socrates asked for a definition and then asked whether given instances fitted the definition; this led to search for a new definition.

3. Belief in universals. Particular facts are not knowledge; true science comes only from logical universals, correct definitions arrived at by dialectic.

4. Ethical emphasis. Socrates held that man's chief concern is knowledge of the good; knowledge is virtue for him, and virtue is happiness.*

5. Religious faith. Socrates, while not concerned about metaphysics, was a man of prayer, who believed in divine guidance (the *daimonion*); and in immortality (*Apology, Phaedo*).

II. *Plato's Main Ideas.*

Note.—While accepting the thought of Socrates, Plato went beyond him by moving from an almost exclusively ethical to a comprehensive interest, including all realms of experience and all values; by moving from a purely logical view of universals to to metaphysical view of them as eternal Ideas or Forms; and by a more developed psychology. He presented many of his highest thoughts in myths (cf. the parables of Jesus).

1. Psychology and ethics. The soul consists of reason and two "irrational" parts, spirit (man's active, conative nature) and appetite (sensuous desires). Reason is man's highest part; when properly developed, it produces wisdom. When wisdom controls the "irrational," spirit manifests courage, and appetite is controlled by temperance. The ethical ideal is realized by justice, that state of the soul in which each part functions under control of wisdom, "minding its own business" (cf. the charioteer in *Phaedr.* 246, 253-256). Piety is a part of justice (see Lodge, 531, n. 17).

2. Social philosophy. Plato's social philosophy is simply applied ethics. To each virtue, or part of the soul, there corresponds a social class (in the *Republic*): To wisdom, the philosopher-kings who are the chief guardians of the State (and live by communistic principles); to courage, the military class (auxiliary guardians); and to temperance, the class of workers (artisans, farmers). That state is just in which all classes do their work under the guidance of philosophical truth. This just state is an *aristocracy;* lower types are *timocracy, oligarchy, democracy* (which Plato strongly opposed), and *tyranny* (the worst of all).

3. Theory of knowledge. Plato was a rationalist*, holding that science (*epistēmē*) did not arise from sense perceptions, which yield only opinion (*doxa*). Universals (especially mathematical ones) are the objects of true knowledge; and their a priori character is symbolized by the doctrine of reminiscense—the theory that the universals were perceived in the soul's previous exis-

tence and are recalled by appropriate stimuli in this life.

4. The hierarchy of Ideas. The true universals (Ideas, forms) are objects of thought (*nooumena, noēta*), "colorless, nonspatial, intangible, truly existing essence" (*Phaedr.* 247), the eternal, objective source of truth and happiness for God and man alike. The highest Idea or Form is that of the Good; all others (such as justice, beauty, knowledge, etc.), are subordinated to it in what has been called the hierarchy of Ideas. This is the first classic formulation of the objectivity of values*, or ideals. The problem of the precise nature of the Forms, and their relation to the particulars of sense (participation, imitation, limitation), is perplexing both to Plato and to his students.

5. Philosophy of religion. Plato was deeply religious. His religion was both rational and mystical (influenced by the Orphic mysteries), ethical (hence his censure of the immoralities of the Homeric Olympian deities), and metaphysical. In religious devotion Plato is comparable to an Isaiah or a Jeremiah. The *Euthyphro,* a dialogue defending piety, composed shortly after 399, was the first book ever written on philosophy of religion. Plato's conception of God was that of ethical monotheism, although he often used the language of polytheism and expressed his thought in consciously inadequate myths. "We have never seen or rightly conceived a god" (*Phaedr.* 246, cf. 1 Jn. 4:12). The Platonic God is good (*Rep.* and *Laws* X), and the descriptions of the Idea of the Good have led some to identify it with God. The *Phaedrus* and *Timaeus,* however, plainly represent God as personal and the Good (the pattern) as external to God. God is the Father, Builder, Maker, Framer, or Artisan (*Demiourgos*) of the universe. He is not a Creator in the Jewish-Christian sense, but organizes a cosmos out of the chaotic matter (space-time) of the "receptacle," ordering it in the "best possible" way in accordance with the eternal pattern (*paradeigma*). Plato is therefore an exponent of the idea of a finite God*, and his view is a metaphysical dualism*, corresponding to his epistemological dualism of phenomena and noumena, illustrated in the famous myth of the Cave (*Rep.* Bk. VII). Thus Plato laid the foundation for the Christian realm of nature and realm of grace, and for Kant's idea of "man as a citizen of two worlds." Despite this dualism, Hegel rightly says that Plato teaches "how near to God and how truly one with him the human reason is."

III. *The Development of Platonism.*

1. The Old Academy (347-247), with Speusippus following after Plato, emphasized Pythagorean and ethical traits of Platonism. Aristotle* was, of course, the greatest of Platonists, although too independent to be head of the school.

2. The Middle Academy (247-129) became skeptical. Arcesilaus (315-241) advocated suspension of judgment; Carneades (213-129) taught that probability is the guide of life. Neither wrote books.

3. Neoplatonism* (250-529 A.D.) was founded by Ammonius Saccas (175-242) and brought to brilliant development by Plotinus (203-279). Emphasizing the mystical, dualistic, and pantheistic tendencies in Plato, Plotinus conceived the physical world as an emanation from deity (like a central sun), and regarded human individuality as the original sin, due to union of being with non-being (outer darkness). Man is redeemed when he finds mystical reunion with God. St. Augustine was for a time a Neoplatonist. The Academy was closed by Justinian (529 A.D.).

4. Alexandrian Platonism. Philo* of Alexandria* (20 B.C.-50 A.D.), a Jewish theologian, emphasized the similarities between Plato and Moses, which he ascribed to dependence on Moses as Plato's source. The New Testament and Neoplatonism were influenced by him. The Fathers, Clement (died 220 A.D.) and Origen** (c. 185-253), were chief among those called "Christian Platonists of Alexandria" (see Bigg's work of that title, 1913). (Boethius of Rome (c. 470-525) was famous for his definition of personality.)

5. Platonism in the Middle Ages. Until about 1200, the influence of Plato (chiefly through the *Timaeus* and the versions of Neoplatonism in Augustine and the Pseudo-Dionysius**) was predominant in Christian thought. John Scotus Eriugena (c. 800-877) held to a modified Neoplatonic pantheism. Anselm (1033-1109) and the School of Chartres** (12th cent.), owed much to Platonic thought. Neoplatonic mysticism influenced Christian mystics, notably Meister Eckhart* (c. 1260-c. 1327). The doctrine of mediaeval realism*, that universals (especially man, the church, the body of Christ), are real arose from Platonism, although there was a tendency to interpret the universals as thoughts of God.

6. Platonism in Italy. During the Renaissance* (late 15th cent.), Platonism experienced a revival, especially at Florence (Marsilius Ficinus, Pico della Mirandola**). See Pletho.

7. Cambridge Platonism*. Ralph Cudworth (1617-1688) and Henry More (1614-1687) used a modified Platonism to oppose atomistic and mechanistic philosophies. Berkeley* (1685-1753), in his *Siris,* although not of the Cambridge School, presented numerous Platonic ideas. "Many an empty head is shook at Plato and Aristotle," said he.

8. Recent philosophy. Plato continues to be the source of vigorous philosophical development. Platonic forms appear in the guise of the neutral entities of neo-realism (R. B. Perry), the essences of G. Santayana, and the eternal objects of Whitehead. W. R. Inge is the leading modern Neoplatonist. Modern estimates of Plato evidence his continued hold on men's minds. "All philosophic truth is Plato rightly divined; all philosophic error is Plato misunderstood" (Ferrier). "The safest general characterization of the European philosophical tradition is that it consists of a series of footnotes to Plato" (Whitehead). See Aristotle and Aristotelianism; immortality, arguments for and against; pre-existence; soul; universals, battle over.

The standard English translation of Plato is by Jowett (Oxford, Random House); the Greek text and more accurate translations appear in the Loeb Classical Library (Harvard University Press). See, in addition to the familiar works of Zeller, Gomperz, Wilamowitz-Moellendorf, and Lutoslawski; W. Pater, *Plato and Platonism* (1893); A. E. Taylor, *Plato* (1927); R. C. Lodge, *Plato's Theory of Ethics* (1928); P. E. More, *The Religion of Plato* (1928); J. Burnet, *Platonism* (1928); J. H. Muirhead, *The Platonic Tradition in Anglo-Saxon Philosophy* (1931); C. Ritter, *Essence of Plato's Philosophy* (1933); L. Robin, *Platon* (1935); F. M. Cornford, *Plato's Cosmology* (1937); R. Demos, *The Philosophy of Plato* (1939); F. Solmsen, *Plato's Theology* (1942). E.S.B.

Plenary Council: A council of the bishops and archbishops of a region, with a papal legate as chairman; power is had only over church government and discipline in the region. L.R.W.

plenitudo potestatis: (fullness of power) In the language of Leo I it was the unrestricted authority of the pope as against that of a metropolitan bishop. Medieval popes and their supporters often added to the expression *"in temporalibus et in spiritualibus"* in asserting absolute claims over church and secular power. This claim is controverted by Ockham, Marsiglio, the later Conciliarists and the Reformers.

O. Gierke, *Political Theories of the Middle Ages* (1900), trans. F. W. Maitland. J.T.M.

Pletho, George Gemisthus: (c. 1355-1450) A Byzantine who lived in Greece until in his eighties, then came to Florence for the Council (1439), and remained to lecture on Plato. He had founded a Neo-Platonic cult in which he interested Cosimo de' Medici and Cardinal Bessarion. It was chiefly through his influence that Plato was introduced to Renaissance Italy. His "Pletho" was an assumed name. W.E.G.

Plotinus: See Neo Platonism.

pluralism: See ontology.

Plymouth Brethren: A religious society founded in England in the early 19th century as a small opposition movement to the Anglican establishment. Particular protest was voiced against the close connection between church and state, the stereotyped forms of worship, and the church organizations which forced believers into many different groups. The first meetings were held in Dublin, Ireland, in 1827, and the first permanent organization was set up in 1829. The name Plymouth Brethren was taken from its prominent society at Plymouth. The most notable early leader, John Nelson Darby, established congregations over much of Europe, and made several visits to the American churches, after the movement came to America around 1850 through immigration.

Doctrinally the Brethren are non-credal, using the Scriptures as their only guide. They have strong millenial hopes, and stress the atonement of Christ for man and eternal punishment of the unregenerate. In organization, the Brethren hold that all are members of one great but invisible church, with Christ at its head, which was "begun at Pentecost and will be completed before the second Advent." Being loosely organized, they have divided on ecclesiastical grounds into six general bodies, all holding similar theological positions. The last available census listed 633 churches with 22,961 members, and property valued at over $1,186,000 for the six branches of the denomination in the U. S. A.

Bledsoe, art. in *Southern Review* (April, 1877); J. S. Teulon, *History and Doctrine of the Plymouth Brethren* (London, 1883); J. J. Herzog, *Les freres de Plymouth et J. Darby* (Lausanne, 1845); William B. Neatby, *History of the Plymouth Brethren* (London, 1901); Henry Pickering, *Chief Men Among the Brethren* (London, 1931). *Census of Religious Bodies,* "Plymouth Brethren", 1926 (1928). M.G.R.—W.W.S.

pneuma: See soul.

pneumatics: See Ambrosians.

Pneumatomachi: See Macedonianism.

poetry and theology: Poetry has made a unique, extremely valuable and far too little recognized contribution to Theology, vitalizing and enriching it intuitively, emotionally and imaginatively.

Most of the classic poems of universal literature are to a high degree theological in import, including Job, The Bhagavadgita**, the Greek tragedies, Second Isaiah, the Divina Commedia (see Dante), the Tempest, Paradise Lost, Paradise Regained (see Milton), Faust (see Goethe), In Memoriam (see Tennyson), and others and a multitude of the best beloved lyrics are not only religious but in their own way doctrinal, pregnant with ideas of God, Christ, Immortality, etc.

The influence of poetry in arousing, modifying and giving direction to religious thought is very great. In the rejection or modification of Calvinism*, for example, Robert Burns in Scotland and John G. Whittier* in America were quite as widely influential as the seated representatives of theology. In tempering and transforming the disturbing effects of evolutionary theory upon religious thought Tennyson and Browning** (and later Corruth in his widely read poem "A jelly fish and a saurian") have exerted a widely mediating and salutary influence.

The Fatherhood of God, the brotherhood of man, the love of God, the reality and consequences of sin, the character and teaching of Christ and the influences of the Spirit have been instilled into the mind and heart of the people by poetry in effective manner and full measure. Faith, hope and love have been given their vital worth and expressiveness by poetry, not only as graces but as ideals, in a way that has greatly illumined and reinforced Church theology and ethics.

Hymnody, as a form of poetry, constitutes what might almost be called a branch of theology, the more effectual in that it animates and beautifies ideas and motives through the instrumentality of imagination and musical harmony. See hymnology; hymns. J.W.B.

poetry, Hebrew: Hebrew poetry has certain earmarks differentiating it from prose. The most

obvious is the parallelism of lines. But there is also metre (really only rhythm) governing the length of lines. There are various theories of Hebrew metrics. The dominant one asserts that Heb. metre is "anapaestic" (ascending); the number of accented syllables is important, that of the unaccented possibly of no account. Thus a "3+3 metre" means that each of two parallel lines has three beats. Quite distinct is the Kina or Lamentation* metre, 3+2 beats. The existence of "strophe" is debatable. Refrain occurs, though rarely. (cp. Ps. 42-43, 46). Alphabetic Acrostics are poems in which each unit of one or more lines begins with the next letter of the alphabet. W. O. E. Oesterley and T. H. Robinson, *Introduction to the Books of the O.T.* (1934).
E.G.K.

poimenics: pastoral theology*. A.K.R.

polemics: Argument among professing Christians, in an effort to determine the true Christian view with regard to specific questions. A.K.R.

politia ordinata: (appointed or organized government) Although the Holy Spirit is operative in the church, it nevertheless is an appointed orderly government in which as in the secular state, it is necessary that there exists a gradation of rulers. The church therefore as a congregation of believers is also a political congregation. H.H.

political law: See law.

political science: See sociology.

polity: The provision made by a denomination for government and discipline. These differ widely. Perhaps the most radical distinction is between the "low" type, which thinks of the Church as constituted "from below", and the "high" type, which thinks of the Church as constituted "from above". The former, in its extreme form, regards all authority in the Church as residing in, and inalienable from, the individual member. The Church, which is identified with a single congregation, is constituted by a compact wherein a number of individual believers agree to common action for mutual spiritual benefit and service. Any officers chosen may act only in the name of the congregation, and not by right of authority delegated to them as inherent in their office. Any groups representing more than one congregation have only advisory authority over the participating congregations. The "high" type of polity attributes to the denomination as a whole, or to the Church Universal, an authority of its own (under God) which limits, or from which is derived, such authority as constituent groups, officers or individual members may possess or exercise. But "high" Churches still differ widely in polity. Some think of the Church as an indispensable mediator of saving grace from God to the believer, so that rights and authority move from God, through the Church, to the individual members; others think of grace as moving directly from God to the individual, who thus becomes a member in a body which is more than the sum of its members and which has an authority of its own over the individual members. The former is monarchical or aristocratic, while the latter is republican in its polity. The best example of a monarchical polity is that of the Roman Catholic Church, as conceived in accordance with the "ultramontane"* theory which now prevails in it. The Pope* is God's vice-gerent; all authority resides in him; the church is "the Pope's house". The Church of England*, as conceived by the "Anglo-Catholic* party" is the best-known example of an aristocratic polity. For them, supreme authority in the Church resides, under God, in the bishops*. Our best example of a republican polity is the Presbyterian*. It is "evangelical" because, like the congregational* type, it is based on the doctrine of the priesthood of all believers; but, unlike the congregational, it is "high" because it attributes to the body of believers an authority of its own, under God, which conditions the liberty of the individuals. It constitutionally delegates power to its elected officials. The four basic types of polity, then, are the congregational, the monarchical, the aristocratic and the republican; the actual polity of any denomination may, however, cut across these distinctions and may be still further modified by such factors as its attitude towards the civil authority. See Canon Law; clergy; deacon; ecclesiastical courts; hierarchy; presbyter; priest. Also see under various churches.
A.K.R.

Pollok Lectureship, The: Established in 1902 and 1912 by friends of Principal A. Pollok at Pine Hill Divinity Hall, Halifax, Nova Scotia. The capital sum is $4000. Lectures are presented about every three years dealing with the subject of homiletics. Among those who have appeared on this foundation are: Professors Denny of Glasgow, H. R. Mackintosh of Edinburgh, James Moffatt, Basil Matthews of London.

(Data from the Office of the Principal of Divinity Hall.) V.F.

polyandry: The marriage* of one woman to several men. This is a relatively rare form of marriage, the best known people practicing polyandry being the Todas of India prior to the period of British influence. Polyandry among the Todas was accompanied by female infanticide, a natural counterpart to a marriage system in which there is a plurality of husbands since universally the birth ratio between the sexes is essentially equal. Compare with polygamy. E.R.M.

Polycarp: Born about 69 A.D., died most probably in 159 A.D. He became bishop of Smyrna, and entertained Ignatius* on his way to martyrdom. His one surviving work is his letter to the Philippians, covering a collection of the Epistles of Ignatius. Shortly before his death he visited Rome, to support the Asian view of the celebration of Easter, and was received with veneration as the most eminent figure in the church. Returning to Smyrna he died at the stake during a popular outbreak against the Christians, and bore his martyrdom with unflinching courage.

J. B. Lightfoot, *The Apostolic Fathers* (1890); E. J. Goodspeed, *Early Christian Literature* (1942).

E.F.S.

polygamy: The marriage* of more than one woman to a man, of one woman to more than one man, or of several women to several men. In commonsense the word is misused since it generally refers to marriages in which a man has more than one wife, i.e., polygyny. Polygyny has been a widespread form of marriage among both historical and preliterate peoples. Compare with polyandry. E.R.M.

polyglot Bibles: Editions of the Bible in which the original text and several translations are placed in parallel columns. The first and most famous was the Hexapla of Origen*, which contained the O.T. in Hebrew, with a Greek transliteration and four Greek versions. The Complutensian Polyglot (1514-17) contained the N.T. in Greek and Latin, and the O.T. in Hebrew, Vulgate, Septuagint* (with a Latin translation) and Chaldaic. E.F.S.

polygyny: See polygamy.

polyphony: The combination of two or more melodies* simultaneously. The emphasis is horizontal in contrast to homophony which emphasizes the vertical combination of tones supporting a single melody. The history of music from the 9th century to the present is the history of polyphony. In the 17th century homophony challenged the supremacy of the polyphonic style. The greatest compositions of all times, vocal and instrumental, are those which maintain a balance between the polyphonic and homophonic principles. See canon; conductus; discant; fugue; modes; motet; organum. E.H.B.

polytheism: See theism.

Pomponazzi, Pietro: (1464-1525) Influential philosopher of the Italian Renaissance*. He held that the immortality of the soul, the possibility of miracles, and the freedom of the will could not be demonstrated philosophically, but admitted that these truths were established on the basis of faith. In general he upheld the "double verity", assigning philosophy to the speculative reason, and religion to the practical reason. In spite of his philosophical views, he insisted on his readiness to submit all his tenets to the judgment of the Church. C.V.

pontifical: The term "pontifical" (from the Latin: *pontifex*: *pons facere*, a bridge maker, intermediary between God and man) is applied to any number of objects or functions referring to a "pontifex" or bishop, and especially to the Roman Bishop as supreme head of the Catholic Church. In the pagan Roman Law the *pontifices* formed the supreme council of the emperor for the regulation of all religious matters and services. At the disestablishment of the old Roman religion and the introduction of Christianity, the Pope* as supreme head of the Church and Bishop of new Christian Rome assumed the title of *Pontifex Supremus* or *Maximus*. R.M.H.

pontifical college: In ancient Roman pagan parlance, the term signified the close advisers of the Pontifex Maximus in the administration and legislation concerning matters religious (College of the Pontifices). During the period immediately following the Protestant Reformation in the British Isles, the term signified any college or seminary even outside of Rome (hence the expression "Seminary Priests") founded by or placed directly under the jurisdiction of the Holy See, especially the Sacred Congregation of the Propaganda, for the education and training of Catholic missionaries intended specifically for England, Ireland, and Scotland, e.g., the missionary colleges at Douai, Valadolid, Lisbon, Paris, etc. Later the term was applied to all similar colleges or seminaries erected primarily for the education and training of foreign missionaries or intended for missions abroad, e.g., in South America, Asia, Africa, etc. Many of those in South America were in charge of Religious Orders*. Primary among all pontifical missionary colleges is the College of the Propaganda at Rome, known also from its founder, Urban VIII, *Collegium Urbanum* (Aug. 1, 1627), intended for the education of missionaries for all countries subject to the Sacred Congregation of the Propaganda. Since the publication of the decree *"Deus Scientiarum Dominus"* (May 24, 1931) the term has also come to apply to all those Catholic universities and colleges where academic degrees may be conferred presupposing of course a full observance of all the provisions required for such degrees as laid down by the decree, e.g., the Catholic University of America, Washington, D. C. If a College or seminary is empowered to give a degree only in one or other branch, e.g., in Sacred Theology it is classified as a *Pontifical Institute* or "Facultas Theologica Pontificia". From both are to be distinguished *Pontifical Academies,* which under the patronage of the Popes, are associations of learned men for the promotion of sciences or spread of religious devotions, etc. R.M.H.

pontifical mass: A pontifical mass is one celebrated by the Pope, a Bishop, or Prelate enjoying certain privileges of a bishop but not consecrated as such, e.g., a Protonotary* Apostolic or Monastic Abbot. The pontifical mass represents the oldest liturgical celebration and sacrifice of the Eucharist*. It was celebrated by the bishop, assisted by priests (who co-celebrated) and surrounded by the faithful. In distinction to this stood the Mass of the Catechumens, in which the bishop assisted, not at the altar but at the throne or faldstool. Among the distinctive features of a Pontifical Mass is, besides the vesting at the throne (if an Ordinary) or at the faldstool (if not the Diocesan Bishop, or if indeed an Ordinary, but celebrating in the presence of a Cardinal) the use of the *Pontificalia**; the kissing of the *Book of the Gospels* at the beginning of the Mass; chanting and recitation of the *Introit* and all succeeding prayers or lessons up to the *Credo* inclusive at the throne or faldstool; the washing of the hands *before* the *Offertory* (reminiscent of the old oblations of the faithful before the Offertory of the Mass); finally, the recitation of the *Last Gospel of St. John* (part of the first chapter of St. John) as the celebrant leaves the altar. During the celebration of a Pontifical High Mass today there are besides the minor clerics, also a *Presbyter Assistens,* two Deacons of Honor, a Deacon and Subdeacon of the Mass, and usually two Masters of Ceremonies. The ceremonies of the Pontifical Mass, as also of all other pontifical functions, are regulated by the *Ceremoniale Episcoporum.* See mass, Roman Catholic. R.M.H.

pontificalia: The word (cf. "pontifical") is used canonically and liturgically. According to Canon No. 337 of the new Code of Canon Law *Pontificalia* signify those episcopal functions at which in accordance with liturgical prescriptions the bishop must use mitre and crosier**, e.g., at a *Pontifical High Mass**, e.g., for the conferring of Major Orders; celebration of Solemn Vespers, etc. Liturgically speaking *pontificalia* signify all strictly episcopal rights and privileges, e.g., a) the right while performing or assisting at solemn functions to use such liturgical garments or paraphernalia when and as prescribed by the *Ceremoniale Episcoporum,* e.g., pontifical slippers, buskins or liturgical stockings, gloves, tunicella, dalmatic, mozetta, cappa magna and, formerly, the rationale breast-plate; furthermore such insignia as mitre, crozier, ring, pectoral cross and pallium* (if a Metropolitan Archbishop), and finally such sacred vessels or pieces of furniture as the bugia (candlestick and candle), Book of the Canon, throne or faldstool and canopy or baldachin over the throne; b) the right to perform such functions as reserved by the *Pontificale Romanum,* specifically to consecrated bishops, e.g., the conferring of Holy Orders, Major orders in particular; administration of the Sacrament of Confirmation; consecration of churches, etc.; and finally c) to function or assist at functions not restricted exactly to bishops, but accompanied nevertheless by special ceremonies as prescribed by the *Ceremoniale Episcoporum* when and if performed by them, e.g., the celebration of High Mass, ceremonies of Holy Week, exequies, etc. If the Ordinary of a Diocese is present, e.g., at the chanting of the *Libera* after a Solemn Requiem Mass he and he alone, besides the Celebrant, has the right to give the last absolution, even though he has not celebrated the Mass. Cardinals, however, do enjoy this privilege likewise and have the right of the pontificalia in all of the above named cases, excepting that they may not confer Major Orders unless they be also consecrated bishops. Abbots too, Prefects Apostolic and Protonotories* may use the *pontificalia,* but in a more restricted sense. Abbots may confer Minor Orders upon their own subjects and while doing so make use of the *pontificalia.* R.M.H.

pope: The word "Pope" is derived from the old ecclesiastical Latin "papa", from the Greek *papas,* meaning father; in classical Latin *pappas,* as used by Juvenal *Satires* VI, 633; hence the expression as applied to the Pope "Father of Christendom". Catholic theologians maintain, in accordance with the Constitution *Pastor Aeternus* of July 18, 1870 edited by the Council of the Vatican*, that all the prerogatives — Primacy, Infallibility, Universal Power, etc., accorded by Christ to St. Peter* ("Cath. Concept.")—are also the pope's in virtue of his being the successor of Peter as Bishop of Rome, Peter's See. Hence only he who rightfully and canonically succeeds to that See as Bishop is actually entitled to, and factually exercised down the centuries, the prerogatives of Peter (cf. "anti-pope"). In proof of this assertion Catholic historians point to the evidences of history. St. Cyprian*, e.g., in the middle of the III century (there is no doubt after that) claims that Cornelius succeeded to "the place of Fabian which is the place of Peter". (Ep. IV 8; cf. LIX, 14). Firmilian of Caesarea observes that Pope St. Stephen claimed the right to decide the controversy regarding the rebaptism of heretics in Northern Africa on the ground of his succession from Peter (Cyprian, Ep. LXXV 17). Tertullian*, writing about 220 A.D., when he had already lapsed into Montanism*, although disagreeing with the pope on the matter of absolution from sins against the flesh which he (Tert.) held to be irremissible, unwittingly calls him the "Bishop of Bishops" or "Episcopus Episcoporum" (*De Pudicitia* XXI) "who claims that he has the same power to forgive sins as Peter had". Tertullian, living at Rome would certainly have contested the claims of the pope had the papacy as such begun only in the III century. About the same time Hippolytus*, whom even Lightfoot* admits to have been the author of the first part of the famous "Liberian Catalog" of popes, reckons Peter in the list of Roman Pontiffs (*Clement of Rome,* I 259). A very ancient poem "*Adversus Marchionem*", written at the beginning of the III century, refers to Peter as having passed on to Linus "the chair" (*cathedra*: cf. "chair of St. Peter") on which he himself had sat" (Migne, PL II, 1077). In the second century we have the famous passage of Irenaeus* (d. 202) concerning the necessity of all churches, i.e., in this case, dioceses, being obliged to conform with and agree to Rome on account of its "superior primacy" ("*potiorem principalitatem*"). Irenaeus again speaks of Hyginius, "the ninth Bishop of Rome", thus employing an enumeration that necessarily included Peter as the first Bishop of that See. In the I century we have St. Clement, a disciple of the Apostles, who after Linus succeeded Peter as the fourth in the line of popes. In his famous Epistle to the Corinthians (cf. "Clement, St., Pope of Rome"), written in 95 or 96 A.D. he so evidently and authoritatively exhorts them in the Holy Ghost to receive the bishops who had been expelled through a turbulent faction, that Lightfoot (*Clement* I 70) calls it "the first step towards papal domination". St. Ignatius* of Antioch (about 107) in his opening letter to the Romans refers to their churches as "presiding over the brotherhood of love". But the most important testimony concerning both the primacy and the infallibility of the See of Peter is Irenaeus' celebrated passage (*Adversus Haereses* III 3, 2) telling the Gnostics that if they wish to know the truth all they need do is to look at the doctrines taught at Rome, because this is the Church founded by the glorious Apostles Peter and Paul, for which reason every other church must conform to it. The well-known decision of Pope St. Victor (189-98) in the question of the celebration of Easter in Asia Minor is an excellent example of the exercise of papal supremacy even and also in the Eastern Church in the II century. The primacy of the Roman Pontiffs, although long taught by the Catholic Church, was re-confirmed in 1870 by the Vatican Council in the famous Constitution of the IV Session under date of July 18, 1870, entitled *Pastor Aeternus*. As for the primacy, the above text of Irenaeus is important also for the infallibility of the Roman Pontiffs, based on Luke 22, 32 (cf. "St. Peter: Cath. Concept"). That this prerogative also was passed on to Peter's successors as heads of the Church was solemnly defined by the above quoted Constitution of the Vatican Council "Pastor Aeternus", which based itself "upon the decisions of numerous other Councils"—words taken from the Council of Florence*, (1439). Although there were a few Catholic Bishops opposed in debate to the definition of papal infallibility or at least to the advisability of defining it at that time, once the definition was declared they unanimously accepted it. The declaration was accompanied by an adequate definition that infallibility applied only when the Roman Pontiff spoke *ex cathedra* (cf. "chair of Peter") i.e., as supreme pastor and teacher of the whole church in a solemn pronouncement, thus excluding any private opinions which a pope may have as an individual. The extent of papal infallibility was not defined explicitly, but declared by the Council to be the same which the Divine Master desired His Church to possess. Hence whatever the extent of the infallibility of all the bishops of the world assembled under their common head, the pope, enjoy, that same infallibility the pope himself enjoys when he speaks *ex cathedra,* and this irrespective of the subsequent assent of the Church because the prerogative under the given conditions is personal, *vi officci.* Having once established the Pope's primacy and infallibility, his universal coercitive power *ex jure divino* logically follows (cf. Math. 16, 19); his immediate and ordinary jurisdiction over each and all the faithful taken singly or collectively; also the right to convoke, preside over and confirm Ecumenical Councils; his right of entertaining, as the supreme judge, appeals of all ecclesiastical causes, whether presented by an individual or by a canonically established diocesan or Roman court or tribunal. It thus follows that as supreme teacher, ruler and judge, the pope controls every department of the Church's life, whether immediately, as through the Roman Congregations (departments of State) and Tribunals; or mediately, through the appointment of bishops or promotion of archbishops, who while enjoying ecclesiastical jurisdiction (whether immediately from God, or mediately from the Pope, the Council of Trent* preferred not to decide) are nevertheless responsible to him as to the Supreme Pastor in their so-called quinquennial reports; subject to his rulings and amenable to his decisions in cases of appeal (*Causae Majores*)—and, in fact, even liable as to advancement and also to deposition or removal from office, even for disciplinary reasons or expediency. The pope, as Bishop of Rome, is also Patriarch of the West, Primate of Italy, Archbishop and Metropolitan of the Roman Province and Sovereign of the Vatican City. He is Prefect of the Holy Office (which decides in all matters pertaining to faith and morals); of the Consistorial (in charge of the appointment of bishops) and of the Oriental Congregation. He bears the titles of Pope, *Summus Pontifex, Pontifex Maximus, Servus Servorum Dei,* etc. Among his insignia and marks of honor is the use of the tiara* or triple crown signifying his supreme doctrinal, executive and judicial powers. The pope does not, like ordinary bishops, use the bent pastoral staff (sign of a restricted jurisdiction) but only the erect cross; wears the pallium* at all solemn ecclesiastical functions and consents to the kissing of his foot (or slipper), as the characteristic sign or reverence to the Vicar of Christ, a custom going back as far as the IX century. The Pope ranks as the first among the Christian princes and in Catholic Countries his ambassadors have precedence over all other members of the diplomatic corps. Although, especially during the Middle Ages often put into office through the influence of German emperors or powerful Roman families, the popes were elected, at first through the Roman Clergy and Roman people and, since the epoch-making decree of Nicholas II of 1059, by the cardinals of the Church. While elections were frequently delayed for months, even years, and often tampered with by ambassadoral interference and the use of the veto, the cardinals according to present day legislation as ratified by Pius X and Pius XI** meet in conclave at least 15 days (it may be extended to 20) after the death of a pope, and elect freely and accept unanimously the choice of the majority. A few days after his election the new pope is crowned with impressive ceremonies by the Cardinal of Ostia, whose historical privilege this is. The most important of the older chronological lists of popes are that of Irenaeus (d. 202), who writing between 175-190 A.D. enumerates the series from Peter to Eleutherius (*Adv. Hereses* III, 3, 3; Eusebius, *Hist. Eccles.* V 6); the "Liberian Catalog", so named from the pope whose name ends the list (Liberius: 352-366); and the "Liber Pontificalis"* (composed at the beginning of the V century) and, as regards the earlier popes, dependent on the "Liberian Catalog". A complete list of canonically elected or appointed popes can be found in any authorized Church History or ecclesiastical encyclopedia. (cf. *Cath. Encyc.* e.g., XII 272-4). See clergy; patriarch.

Roskovany, *Romanus Pontifex* (Neutra, 1867-79), 16 vols.; Duchesne, edit., *Liber Pontificalis* (Paris,

1892); H. Hurter, S. J., *Theologia Dogmaticae Compendium* (Innsbruck, 1903), vol. I; *Cath. Encyc.* XII 260-275; VII 790-800; *Lexikon. f. Theol. und Kirche* VII 927-42 (Freiburg in Br., 1935). R.M.H.

popes, captivity of: See Avignon.

popes or Roman pontiffs: Chronological List. Cf. Fernand Hayward, *History of the Popes* (1903); *The New Catholic Dictionary* (1929) p. 774. *The Catholic Directory* publ. each year By Kennedy, (N. Y.); *World Almanac* publ. each year by the New York World-Telegram, e.g., 1940 edition, p. 572; *Cath. Encyc.* XII 272-5. Any authorized Catholic Church History usually carries a list of popes at the end of the book or last volume. See end of article "pope". R.M.H.

Porphyry: (232 or 233—ca. 300 A.D.) Outstanding follower of Plotinus mainly in the ethical and religious doctrines of his master. His chief source of fame, however, comes from the treatise *Eisagoge* whereby he became one of the best known logicians throughout the ages. Also known for his polemic work against the Christians, the earliest attempt of biblical text-criticism. See s.v. Neo Platonism. S.C.T.

Porter Foundation, the Henry D.: The Henry D. Porter Foundation, in the amount of $3,500, was given to Pomona College, Claremont, California, in honor of the Reverend Henry D. Porter for many years a missionary in China. The income is used annually to bring to the college some prominent worker in the field of Christian Missions. The lecturer upon this foundation may share in the regular classroom work related to the history, geography, politics, or religion of the region from which he has come. A.C.M.

Poseidon: Brother of Zeus and god of the sea in Greek mythology. He appears in the Odyssey as the enemy of Odysseus and the source of that hero's misfortunes. P.G.M.

positio: 1) A course, or portion of food, served to monks. 2) In theology or philosophy, the thesis or view upheld in controverted questions. C.V.

positivism: The philosophy of Auguste Comte* and of thinkers influenced by Comte or by ideas similar to his. It starts, like Bacon's philosophy, with a rejection of final causes, and goes on to banish entirely the search for any causes, especially for a First Cause. It restricts knowledge to mathematics and to sciences derived from phenomena observable by the senses. This anti-theistic philosophy of science is accompanied by an anti-theistic "religion of humanity", combining a lofty altruistic ethics with a somewhat fantastic cultus.

Positivism exerted a wide influence in France (H. Taine, E. Renan, L. Weber, E. Durkheim, L. Lévy-Bruhl), Germany (E. Dühring, E. Laas, *Zeitschrift für positivistische Philosophie*), Austria (E. Mach), Switzerland (R. Avenarius), England (F. Harrison, J. H. Bridges, T. H. Huxley, W. K. Clifford, K. Pearson, *The Positivist Review*), and Italy (Ferrari, Villari, Marchesini, Fulci); a lesser influence in Hungary, Czechoslovakia (where Masaryk was inclined to positivism), Poland (J. Sniadicki), Russia (P. Lavrow—but positivism is heresy for Communists), and Rumania (B. Conta).

Comte's thought was introduced to the United States by a theistic critic of positivism, G. F. Holmes, in *The Methodist Quarterly Review* (1851), as is shown by R. L. Hawkins in *Auguste Comte and the United States* (1936). The chief positivist in the United States was P. Carus (Chicago), although positivistic ideas have had a rather wide influence through religious humanists* and certain writers on sociology and naturalism. J. Dewey's instrumentalism is colored by positivism.

During the nineteenth century positivism was the dominant philosophy in large sections of Latin America, representing, in part, a democratic reaction against scholasticism. Among the leading figures are: Enrique José Varona (1849-1933) of Cuba; Gabino Barreda (1818-1881) of Mexico; Eugenio María de Hostos (1839-1903) of Puerto Rico (whose interests were chiefly ethical, political, social, and educational, and whose works and bibliography were edited ably by his son, Adolfo de Hostos, in 1939-1940 under a governmental commission); González Prada (Peru); J. Alfredo Ferreira and José Ingenieros (1877-1925) of Argentina, the former being active in a specifically Comtean movement. It was in Brazil, however, that positivism had a more extensive influence than in any other part of the world. A positivistic motto, *Ordem e Progresso* (order and progress), appears on the flag of Brazil. Even earlier than the founding of the Republic (1889), a "church and positivistic apostolate," had been established in 1881 with a Temple of Humanity in Rio de Janeiro; it survives until the present time. One of its prominent leaders was R. Teixeira Mendes. Thought in Latin America has moved away from positivism in recent years under the influence of men like J. Vasconcelos, A Caso, and E. Nicol in Mexico; J. A. Fránquiz in Puerto Rico; and A. Korn, C. Alberini, and F. Romero in Argentina.

At present positivism is more influential as a philosophy of science (logical positivism) than as an organized religious movement, although its indirect influence is evident among humanists. See naturalism; ontology.

See E. Caird, *The Social Philosophy and Religion of Comte* (2nd ed., 1893); F. Harrison, *The Positive Evolution of Religion* (1913); J. Dewey, *Reconstruction in Philosophy* (1920); L. Zea, *El Positivismo en México* (1943). For bibliographies of positivism, see Rand in Baldwin's *Dictionary*, vol. III, Pt. II, pp. 634-638, and art. "Positivism", by Guido de Ruggiero in *Encyclopaedia of the Social Sciences*. The article is indebted to an unpublished paper by F. Romero, "Contemporary Tendencies in Hispano-American Thought" (1942). E.S.B.

post-exilic: In contrast with pre-exilic (before 586 B.C.) and exilic (586-538 B.C.), post-exilic designates the time between the first return and the Christian Era (538-1 B.C.); an obscure period with little historical writing except Ezra, Nehemiah, and Maccabees**; time of persecution of Jews, priestly dominance, legalism, and emerging scribalism. The religion of this period is spoken of as "Judaism" in contrast with "Hebrew Religion" or "Religion of Israel" in pre-exilic times. See exile; pre-exilic. R.E.W.

postillae: See Biblical history in Christian instruction.

postmillennialism or postmillenarianism: The belief that the thousand year reign of Christ on earth will come after the gospel has been spread and become effective throughout the world. The condition thus reached will last for a thousand years. In this period the Jews will be converted to Christianity. After a brief but terrible conflict between the Christian and evil forces Christ will appear and the general resurrection and the final judgment* will follow. The earth will then be destroyed by fire and a new heaven and a new earth will be revealed. See premillenarianism; millenarianism. S. J. Case, *The Millennial Hope* (1918). W.W.S.

post-Nicene Fathers: See patristics. Cf. Ante-Nicene Fathers.

postulant: (Lat., *postulans,* petitioner) Usually an applicant for admission to a religious order under preliminary probation. In the Episcopal Church a similar applicant for admission to ordination. B.S.E.

potentia: (L. *potens,* partic. of *posse,* to be able) Literally, power, ability, capacity. More adequately, the ability to change or a tendency toward actuality. Whereas possibility is the mere conceivability or non-repugnance of an idea, potency or potentiality is possibility plus, implying raw-material or sub-matter over and above the mere conceivability. Intrinsic possibility is but a thought, while potency is part of a thing and it exists in the real order. Aristotle escaped the extremes of Heraclitus and Parmenides by holding that all beings in the real order excepting the Pure Act (God) are compounded of potency and actuality. D.C.O'G.

poverty, evangelical: The voluntary surrender of outer possessions and inner possessiveness by those seeking gospel perfection through following Christ's counsels to renunciation. Some have espoused their ideal with religious vows. Others have served it without ecclesiastical authorization or in open criticism of the organized church. Poverty idealism throughout Christian history has been distinguished from both the nominal sacrifices of "average Christianity" and the involuntary indigence of humanity at large.

S. J. Turner, *The Vow of Poverty* (1929). R.C.P.

practical religion: See charity and almsgiving; charity organization; communistic settlements, religious; friendly societies; humanitarianism; institutional church, the; orphanages; social gospel; social work of the churches.

practical theology: In theological education, mostly American, a division of the curriculum. The expression is differently used in theological institutions and covers various subjects, among them preaching (homiletics), worship, pastoral care, church administration, church polity. See theology. R.H.N.

Praemunire, Statute of: The first Statute of Praemunire was enacted in 1353. It was designed to prevent appeals being made from the royal to papal courts. W.S.H.

pragmatic realism: See epistemology.

pragmatic sanction: (Lat., *sanctio pragmatica*) A late Roman term for a royal decree on public affairs; also applied to some mediaeval and modern French and Spanish royal edicts. See placet. L.R.W.

pragmatism: Called by Wm. James* "a new name for some old ways of thinking" pragmatism has become a blanket term covering theories of meaning, of truth, of being, of knowledge, and of intellectual method. Common to all is an emphasis on the evolutionary and changing character of reality, on the relevance of knowledge to practical situations, on the need of testing truth by its ability to "work", and on the instrumental nature of ideas. Thought is taken as a mode of conduct which arises in felt need and works purposefully to solve problematic situations in such a way as to produce future satisfactions, instead of "reflecting" or "copying" antecedent reality. Pragmatists thus minimize the distinction between thought and practice, claiming that thinking is a part of the continuous process of interaction characteristic of the real world and that to set it apart is bad or anti-social ethics as well as bad or inaccurate psychology and metaphysics.

Pragmatism is commonly supposed to have originated with a famous article by C. S. Peirce* in 1878 which defined the meaning of a concept in terms of its consequences. It was taken up by James who emphasized the notion of expectancy but modified Peirce's views by stressing the sensory and the particularistic aspects of the future experiences to which ideas point. Influenced by his biological studies and his belief in the primary role played by desire, purpose, and will in determining attention, and therefore what shall be "real" for the observing subject, James went on from the pragmatic method, or interpretation of ideas in terms of consequences, to a pragmatic definition of truth as an attribute of ideas. Truth "happens to ideas", ideas are "made true" by events, so that truth becomes, in some of James's more extreme writings, the process of verification by which ideas practically establish themselves. Throughout his work James was concerned to point out the ambiguity of ordinary definitions of truth in terms of "conformity" or "agreement". These terms, he argued, need explanation, and it is better to say that ideas are true when they lead to satisfactory adaptation to their objects or take account of them in a practical way. Mind "engenders truth upon reality." It acts not to copy its world but to complete it.

F. C. S. Schiller developed a "humanism" which had much in common with James's pragmatism and was welcomed by James as a substantially similar view, the chief difference being that where James stressed the claims of objective fact, its giveness, and the possibility of its presence in immediate perceptual awareness, Schiller was more inclined to say that *all* knowledge is provisional, that the object is what it is for the subject, and the individual with his beliefs is the more concrete object of study.

John Dewey was also welcomed as an ally by James, (although he uses the word "pragmatism" less than "instrumentalism" or "empiricism") and he has become the most influential thinker in the movement today. Dewey is more naturalistic and less individualistic than James and inclined to make much of the social categories of communication and participation. He is also preoccupied with the experimentalism of the scientific method and eager to see it become the dominant intellectual method in philosophy itself. Dewey's metaphysics is a reflection of his instrumental epistemology*, for which an idea is a means to controlled and enriched experience, since "knowledge *is* reality making a particular and specified sort of change in itself."

With its emphasis on ideas as working hypotheses pragmatism is still influential, especially in contemporary "operationalism" and the revival of an empirical positivism.* The vagueness of the movement and the name is shown in the fact that it has also had a direct effect on religious thought, chiefly through James's stress on the right of the individual, "other things being equal", to trust his emotions, including his hopes and spiritual ambitions. In recent years Dewey and the "Chicago School"* have affected methods and objects of religious education by interpreting religion as a life of practical devotion to social ideals rather than intellectual acceptance of a theological creed.

Cf. C. S. Peirce, "How to Make Our Ideas Clear" *Pop. Sci. Mo.* (1878) XII, 286; Wm. James, *The Will to Believe,* etc. (1897), *Pragmatism* (1907), *The Meaning of Truth* (1909), "Philosophical Conceptions and Practial Results" *U. of Cal. Chronicle* (1898), p. 4; F. C. S. Schiller, *Humanism* (1903), *Studies in Humanism* (1907), "Axioms as Postulates" in *Personal Idealism* (1902) ed. H. Sturt; J. Dewey, *The Influence of Darwin on Philosophy* (1910), *The Quest for Certainty* (1929), "What Does Pragmatism Mean by Practical?" *Journ. Phil.* (1908) V, 85; A. O. Lovejoy, "The Thirteen Pragmatisms" *Journ. Phil.* (1908) V. 5 and 29; J. B. Pratt, *What is Pragmatism?* (1915); J. Royce, "The Eternal and the Practical" *Philos. Rev.* XIII (1904), 129.

J.S.B.

Prajāpati: Literally, lord of creatures, appeared first in the Vedas as an epithet of Savitar and of Soma but in the late tenth book as an abstract god, the apotheosis of the creative activity of the universe. He becomes the chief deity in the later period of the Brahmanas. C.S.B.

prakriti: An Hindu term meaning primeval matter. In the Sankhya* system *prakriti* and *purusha* are the dual bases of all existence, material and spiritual. C.S.B.

prapatti-mārga: The Hindu way of salvation by complete and utter surrender to God. No effort on man's part is required aside from his surrender. Sometimes known as the "cat-way", referring to the way in which a kitten without effort on its own part is carried by the mother—in contrast to the "monkey-way" in which the little monkey must cling to the mother. C.S.B.

prayer: The act of prayer, whether with words or without, is the act of putting ourselves more completely into the power of God's working so that some good may be attained or some evil escaped. This essential act of prayer is not that of communicating our wants to God or of begging God, although the verbal forms of communication and petition may be the necessary devices by which the essential act is performed.

Prayer is here distinguished from worship. (See worship.) Prayer includes worship but has an added element which is petition. It is this element of petition which we here examine. Prayer is seeking some good, or escape from some evil, by appeal to God. We cannot understand its efficacy without some idea of that working reality of God which answers prayer. The understanding of prayer is the understanding of its answer, for prayer is meaningless unless it is answered.

The good which God creates most commonly requires the casting out of lesser goods which we with restricted vision uphold. This recreating of us operates by making us more actively and appreciatively aware of one another's interests. Innumerable obstructions and perversions hinder and retard this reciprocal apprehension of the hopes and fears, joys and sorrows, strivings and aversions which make up the lives of each and all. But in so far as the mind of each participates in the mind of all and the minds of all in the mind of each, we have the work of God in our midst. The Bible calls this love and identifies it with God. (I John 4:8) It is this creativity generating mutual awareness of one another's interests which answers prayer.

Most people agree that the words we use are not the prayer since we can use the words of prayer and not be really praying at all. Yet the same people often persist in thinking that prayer is a kind of language directed to God. Obviously it cannot be a language if it is not the use of words. Prayer is a certain attitude or predisposition of the personality by which we give ourselves more completely to the creativity of God. We use the language of prayer to acquire this predisposition, but the language is for ourselves, not for God. It is this predisposition which God demands, and not the words. Prayer, therefore, is not a language although we ordinarily must use the language to perform the act of prayer.

The act of prayer, when it is genuine, puts us under the control of that creativity which makes us more sensitive and responsive to the interests of people round about us and they reciprocally become more sensitive to our interests. This deepening and widening of community wherein we are more responsive to one another is what answers prayer. But this deepening and widening of community, this magnified inter-responsiveness and mutual awareness, is precisely the work of God in answer to the act of prayerful self-giving to God. Therefore when prayer is answered in this way, it is God that answers prayer. Study of the instances of answered prayer, when any line of a cause and effect can be traced, will reveal that this is the way prayer is answered, namely, by some wider and deeper inter-responsiveness of people to one another which God accomplishes in answer to that predisposition of personality which is the act of prayer.

By the act of prayer we so yield our established order of being to the creativity of God that our wants are: 1) so transformed that they can be fulfilled and then 2) are fulfilled to the extent that we participate in a community of persons made more responsive to one another by the work of God in answer to our prayer. Thus God answers prayer.

Friedrich Heiler, *Prayer, A Study in the History and Psychology of Religion* (1932); Baron Friedrich von Hugel, *The Life of Prayer* (1929); Pico Mario Puglisi, *Prayer* (1929); Evelyn Underhill, *Worship* (1937); H. N. and R. W. Wieman, *Normative Psychology of Religion* (1935); Robert Will, *Le Culte* (1924). H.N.W.

Prayer of Manasses: See Manasses, Prayer of.

prayers for the dead: Natural affection and community life that involves moral and spiritual welfare, coupled with a belief in survival, make prayers for the dead widespread. Out of Egypt the custom is first noticed in Judaism in 2nd century B.C. (2 Mac: 39-44), and has continued there to the present. It was apparently taken over by Christians, although little mention is found in early writers. The N.T. references (1 Cor. 15:29, 2 Tim. 1: 16-18, 4: 19) are obscure. The Catacomb* inscriptions, the Fathers, and liturgies make increasing references that show it a custom known by the 3rd or 4th century for both private and public prayer (cf. St. Augustine, *Conf.* ix). The early prayers were restrained in wording, although asking forgiveness. In the West, after St. Gregory's descriptions of visions of purgatory*, prayers more frequently asked release from suffering, and liturgical language still restrained took on a dolorous note. The western medieval doctrines of purgatory, especially in popular form, made for a greatly increased use of public and private prayers, especially the Office of the Dead* and requiem* masses. The attack of the Reformers* on indulgences* and votive masses* and the whole cultus of the dead led generally (despite Luther) to its disrepute and, following Calvin, most Protestants hold that the silence of the canonical scriptures weighs against the custom and that, because the souls of the righteous are in heaven awaiting the resurrection of their bodies, prayers for them are unavailing. The Anglican Church made varying reforms, never denying the practice and making provision for it in recent liturgical revisions. The Eastern Orthodox belief is that prayer especially the offering of the Eucharist aids the souls not yet ready for heaven. See Etruscan religion; intercession.

R. H. Charles, *Eschatology* (London, 1913); F. von Hügel, *Eternal Life* (Edinburgh, 1912); J. H. Newman, *Dream of Gerontius* (1866). T.J.B.

preaching: The proclamation of the gospel in sermon* form. The apostles, following Jesus' example and command, developed the missionary sermon, which became a feature of services in the early church. Influenced in form by the discourse of Graeco-Roman rhetoricians, it reached its height in the pulpit eloquence of Chrysostom and Augustine**. The trend toward liturgy crowded preaching into second place for centuries. Repopularized by the friars, it was reforged by Luther and Calvin** in the fires of the Reformation as a true sword of the spirit. Since then, whether wielded in time of peace or war, by pulpit orator of 17th century England or France, orthodox Lutheran, Wesleyan revivalist, modern gospel—or social gospel*—preacher, it has remained one of the church's mightiest weapons. See expository preaching; homiletics; homily; rhetorici.

Article in Schaff-Herzog, *Encyclopedia of Religious Knowledge* (1911) vol. IX; H. Hering, *Geschichte der Predigt* (1904); A. E. Garvie, *The Christian Preacher* (1920) (Survey with bibliography). E.C.K.

pre-Adamite: An inhabitant of the earth before Adam*; or, the belief in the existence of inhabitants before Adam. This term is associated especially with Isaac de la Peyrère (1594-1676), a French Calvinist who in 1655 published a book seeking to prove that Adam was the progenitor only of the Jews, the Gentiles being descended from previous inhabitants of the earth. According to his view, Gen. 1:26ff, describes the creation of the Gentiles' ancestors on the sixth day of creation, and Gen. 2:7 of Adam after the seventh day. He found support for this in the history of Cain and in Romans 5:12-14. He later renounced this theory and became a Catholic. The problem which pre-Adamitism sought to solve does not exist for critical O.T. scholars who do not consider the Genesis* account of creation as literal history. J.P.H.

prebend: (Lat., *praebeo*, grant) The stipend of a canon or member of Cathedral Chapter in England, or the land or tithe which provides for this stipend; hence, prebendary, for the holder of such a stipend. W.N.P.

precentor: A singer who directs the singing, especially in cathedrals the canon in charge of music. T.J.B.

precious blood: The Blood of Christ, shed on Golgotha for the redemption of mankind. Because it is essentially a part of our Lord's Humanity, it is honored and adored, and since 1849 a feast (July 1) is officially observed in its honor. L.R.W.

predestination: The doctrine of predestination is implied in the doctrine of salvation* by divine grace alone. If it is affirmed that man cannot save himself by reliance upon powers (also religious potentialities) inherent in him, but that he is redeemed only by the initiative of a gracious, merciful God, it must also be said that his eternal destiny is determined by God. The doctrine of predestination therefore stands in an immediate context with that of grace* and with that of original sin*. In the last resort, it is a soteriological and not metaphysical doctrine, for it is not designed to assert the truth that everything is predetermined by God (although it must be admitted that the doctrine of divine providence* has always stood in a close relation to the teaching on predestination); it is designed in order to give doctrinal expression to the religious conviction that man is altogether dependent upon God for his salvation. As a soteriological doctrine it was expounded and defended by Paul, Augustine, Luther, Calvin and their followers and spiritual descendants. In all these forms, it bore the imprint of the faith of the Hebrew prophets and their witness to the work of the living God as the only fountain of the spiritual life.

It was inevitable, however, that the predestinarian faith elicited metaphysical speculations about the work of an omnipotent* God of grace. Thus Paul developed a philosophy of history in connection with his consideration of the fate of the Jews in the light of divine predestination (Rom. 9-12). Augustine*, Luther, and particularly Calvin were led to assert a divine determinism as a consistent expression of their predestinarianism, although they always carefully distinguished it from fatalism*. Also the teaching that there is not only predestination to salvation but also one to damnation must be regarded as a metaphysical and logical outcome of soteriological predestinarianism. It was in part supported (as the theologies of Bucer and Calvin show) by the sociological observation that some people appear to be incapable of a positive response to the religious message of salvation.

The doctrine fell into discredit either when its assertion of the omni-potency of divine grace was denied (as it is in the case in Roman Catholicism which in the interest of preserving room for human religious freedom identifies predestination with divine foreknowledge) or when its metaphysical implications and consequences were rejected. Socinianism and Arminianism** criticized it on account of its moral insufficiency with regard to God as well as to man. Rationalistic criticisms of the doctrine were made particularly easy when the Calvinists* of the period of Protestant Orthodoxy argued about the question whether God had issued the predestinarian decree before or after the fall* of Adam (supra—and infralapsarianism**). All these discussions and criticisms were of a philosophical rather than a religious character. They did not really touch the central meaning of the doctrine, namely, that man is saved by divine grace alone. Also the discussion of the problem of the interconnection between divine predestination and the reality of evil is of a philosophical-speculative rather than of a religious-soteriological nature. See double predestination; election; fatalism; fate; foreknowledge; foreordination; libertarianism; reprobation; Semi-Pelagianism.

Karl Barth, *Kirchliche Dogmatik,* vol. II, 2 (1942). W.P.

predication: (Lat., *prae,* before, and *dicere,* to speak) In logic, the affirmation or denial of something of some subject. L.R.W.

pre-exilic: Period of Hebrew history before 586 B.C. (date when last Hebrew tribes were exiled to Babylon). Although it includes the Prehistoric, Patriarchal, Mosaic, and Judges periods, in practical usage the term pre-exilic usually refers to the period immediately before 586 B.C., i.e., the time of the Hebrew monarchies (1037-586 B.C.), the golden age of Hebrew prophecy, nationalism, and Solomon's Temple. See exile; post-exilic. R.E.W.

pre-existence: Existence of the human soul* before its incarnation in the body with which it is now united. More specifically, the existence of Christ before the Incarnation. The term is rarely used also of the existence of any being other than God before the creation of the world. The doctrine of the pre-existence of the soul is of ancient and obscure origin. It appears to have arisen independently in various lands. Often it is taught in conjunction with the doctrine of transmigration*, as among the Buddhists, Hindus, ancient Egyptians and Pythagoreans**, and in many primitive animistic religions. On the other hand, the soul may be thought of as having lived previously as an independent, unembodied spirit. Plato* taught the pre-existence of the soul as a strong evidence for post-existence or immortality. His main supporting argument was his doctrine that learning is actually reminiscence of earlier experience, when the soul, unfettered by the body, contemplated the eternal Ideas in their purity. Only so, he held, can we explain man's recognition of the validity of moral and intellectual ideals—as in mathematics—which are never objects of sense experience, but which are recalled to our minds, Plato believed, by associations with objects of sense perception. This doctrine has been revived in the present century by J. M. E. McTaggart*, and given added "proof" from the phenomena of "love at first sight," from individual differences in mental aptitude, and from McTaggart's metaphysical principles. Since the evidences adduced seem more plausibly explicable on other grounds, and since the facts of mental growth and the lack of memories are opposed, most occidental thinkers reject the idea of pre-existence as "strange and improbable" (Lotze*). Many Jews continue to hold the doctrine as revealed truth, since it appears frequently in the Talmud, but others critically reject it. Among Christians, both Manichaean and Platonic influences led to adoption of the belief in pre-existence by a number of thinkers, including Origen*, and it occasionally reappeared in Christian theology until the sixth century, when it was firmly suppressed.

See Plato, *Phaedo, Phaedrus,* and *Republic*; J. M. E. McTaggart, *Human Immortality and Pre-*

existence (1916); W. S. Bigelow, *Buddhism and Immortality* (1908); and G. F. Moore, *Metempsychosis* (1925). L.H.DEW.

prefect apostolic: (Lat., *praefectus,* one in charge) One in charge of a territory lacking a resident bishop; he directs mission work and has many of a bishop's powers. L.R.W.

prelate: (Lat., *praelatus; praeferre,* to prefer) Holder (e.g., a bishop or an abbot) of a prelature or church office with jurisdiction in external matters and with rights of precedence; or with the dignity but not the powers. L.R.W.

premillenarianism or premillennialism: The belief that the thousand year reign of Christ on earth will come at the beginning of the millennium rather than at its end. After the proclaiming of the gospel throughout the earth has proven to be of no avail and the world has become a hopeless wreck, then Christ will return and with his saints reign for a thousand years. The righteous will be raised and Satan bound and locked in the abyss. At the end of a thousand years Satan will be unbound and attempt to regain his power, but to no avail. Lost souls will then be raised, and they, together with Satan and his angels will be judged and hurled into a lake of fire where they are doomed to everlasting torment. The earth will then be cleansed by fire and become the eternal dwelling place of the redeemed. See millenarianism; postmillennialism. H. F. Rall, *Modern Premillennialism and the Christian Hope* (1920). W.W.S.

Premonstratensian Canons: Members of an order of canons regular founded by St. Norbert in 1119 in the valley of Premontre near Laon, France. St. Norbert adopted the habit and a modified rule of St. Benedict. The duties of the Canons included teaching, the care of souls, and preaching. The order spread throughout Europe, but its success was spectacular in Germany and other northern kingdoms. Their chief house in the United States is at St. Norbert's Priory, West de Pere, Wisconsin. T.T.M.

presbyter: A transliteration of Greek *presbuteros,* an adjective meaning "older" and noun meaning "elder"*. The Greek N.T. records *presbuteroi* (plural) in Christian organization, the word being translated "elders". Some of Paul's churches were governed by two groups of office-bearers, one of presbyters-elders, also called (Ac. 20:17, 28 ARV) bishops*, i.e., overseers; and another of deacons*. In the second century the threefold government of the local congregation by bishop, presbyters, deacons became practically universal in the catholic church. In the third century the clerical-lay distinction was established, so that the presbyterate became an order of the ministry. As the work of the bishops increased they assigned duties, including the administration of the sacraments and finally the care of churches, to their presbyters. Thus arose the state of things represented by the fact that "priest"* is a contraction of "presbyter". In episcopal polities now presbyter is the title of ministers next below bishops. In polities recognizing only one order the word is sometimes applied to ministers. See clergy; polity. R.H.N.

Presbyterian Church: A Church is presbyterian when it acknowledges in its polity no higher office than that of "presbyter"* or elder, and when its highest courts, therefore, are composed of presbyters. It is Protestant in the sense that it claims historical continuity with the Protestant Reformation, and adheres to the basic Reformation principles. It is catholic in the sense that it recognizes, and is proud to claim membership along with other non-Presbyterian bodies in one, universal Church, the body of which Christ is the Head, constituted by Him "from above". As evangelical, i.e., believing that the grace of God in salvation comes directly to the individual constituting him a priest unto God, it holds that the supreme authority in the Church, under God, resides in the body of the membership, and that the legitimate authority of its various courts is theirs by delegation from the membership. (See polity).

In addition to this common doctrine of the Church, and this common polity, Presbyterian Churches are united into a family by adherence to a common system of theology, usually designated as Calvinistic*. The importance which they attribute to this doctrinal allegiance is indicated by the number of great credal statements produced by this ecclesiastical family. They include the two Helvetic Confessions (1536 and 1566), the Heidelberg Catechism (1563), the Gallican Confession (1559), the Belgic Confession (1561), the Scotch Confessions (1560 and 1581), the Irish Articles (1615), the Canons of the Synod of Dort (1619), and the Westminster Doctrinal Standards (1647).**. Indeed Presbyterian Churches regard the common doctrinal allegiance as the basic aspect of their unity, the ecclesiology being a harmonious part of it, and the polity being derived from it or at least held as conformable to it. And so it might seem more appropriate to derive their name from their theology rather than, as in the name "Presbyterian", from their polity. Perhaps that is what is attempted in the name "Reformed", by which Churches of this family are commonly known on the continent of Europe. In practice, however, since their Calvinistic theology is also held by Congregationalists, by the Anglican Church in its Thirty-nine Articles, and by many Baptist bodies, the Presbyterian polity does serve as their most distinctive characteristic.

While it is claimed that the Calvinistic doctrine is the system taught in Holy Scripture, and that the Presbyterian polity is found (though perhaps not exclusively) in the New Testament, the historical origin of the Presbyterian Church, as a distinct member of the Church Universal, is traced to the work of John Calvin* in Geneva. There and then the system of theology, achieved through a significant clarification of Augustinianism*, which had been briefly but completely outlined in the first edition of Calvin's *Institutes,* was elaborated and established. There and then, also, the polity was expounded, and was put into practice as far as it could be within the limits of a single city. That is to say, since Geneva was thought of as constituting only one congregation, its government called for no court of wider scope than a Presbytery or Consistory. It was in France, where a formerly unorganized Protestantism quite suddenly took organized form in 1555, that the higher courts, first came into being. There the First National Synod (Paris, 1559) adopted a Constitution which, as subsequently modified, provided for a Consistory (or Session*) in each congregation, Colloques* (Presbyteries), Provincial Synods (our Synods), and a General Synod (our General Assembly). Thus the distinctive, Presbyterian system of government was complete.

This is the kind of Church which was adopted as the national Church of Scotland in 1560, and which, except for about a century of struggle with Episcopalianism, has been overwhelmingly dominant there ever since. The Scottish Presbyterian "members" number about 1,500,000, but there are numerous "adherents" in addition. In spite of a strong bid in the reign of Edward VI, which was cut short by the accession of Mary Tudor, and an even stronger bid in the first half of the English Revolution in the seventeenth century, Presbyterianism has never been strong in England. At present, the Presbyterian Church in England claims only about 190,000 members. Presbyterianism is the dominant form of Christianity in Northern Ireland*, whence it spread from Scotland during the first half of the seventeenth century. It now claims a membership of about 400,000. In spite of bitter opposition from Lutheranism, which was the dominant expression of Protestantism in Germany, Presbyterianism spread rapidly north and east into Germany after the middle of the sixteenth century, and was officially recognized as legal in the Treaty of Westphalia*, 1648. Its strength in Bohemia was an important element among the causes of the Thirty Years War* (1618-1648). In Prussia, through royal pressure, it was merged with the Lutheran Church, though a separate Lutheran Church survived the union. Presbyterianism was formally introduced into the Netherlands by the Synod of Antwerp in 1563, and it emerged as the dominant Protestant force during the struggle for independence from Spain.

It came to the American Colonies, mainly from Northern Ireland and Scotland, but also from the Netherlands and France. A total membership of about 3,000,000 is claimed by the nine bodies which are Presbyterian by name, though the addition of the membership of those Churches which are Presbyterian in fact but not in name would greatly increase this total. Various Presbyterian bodies, coming mainly from Scotland and from the Colonies to the South, were combined into one Presbyterian Church in Canada in 1875. By 1925, this was the second largest Protestant body in the Dominion. In that year, about seventy per cent of its membership entered, with the Congregationalists and the Methodists, into a United Church*, which is basically Presbyterian in polity, and which now claims a membership of about 2,000,000. The other thirty per cent continued as the Presbyterian Church of Canada, with a present membership of nearly 900,000. In Australia, the Presbyterians number about 700,000, and in New Zealand nearly 400,000.

All of these Presbyterian bodies, and others not mentioned, participated actively in the modern missionary movement; with the result that Presbyterians are represented, either as separate bodies or in fellowship with other denominations, in every land where Christianity is to be found.

See Alliance of Reformed Churches; Auburn Affirmation; Auburn Declaration; Cameronians; Covenanters; Cumberland Presb. Church; General Assembly; Knox, John; New School Presb. Church; New Side Presbyterians; Old School Presb. Church; Old Side Presbyterians; Reformed Presb. Church in N. A.; Scotland, Church of; United Presb. Church of 1847; United Presb. Church of N. A.; Wee Free Church; Westminster Assembly. Cf. Puritanism.

Charles Hodge, *The Constitutional History of the Presbyterian Church* (1851), 2 vols.; C. A. Briggs, *American Presbyterianism, its Origin and Early History* (1885); T. C. Johnson, *A History of the Presbyterian Church in the U. S.* American Church History Series, Vol. II (1894); D. H. Fleming, *The Scottish Reformation* (London, 1900). A.K.R.

presbytery: A body of presbyters*. The word occurs in I Tim. 4:14. Its principal modern use is in Presbyterian* polity*. Here the presbytery consists of the ministers of a region and elders* representing the churches, and exercises authority over churches and ministers, under the superior judicatories. In other Reformed polities "classis" and "colloquy"** are equivalent. In ecclesiastical architecture the presbytery is the part of the choir of a church where the high altar stands, which is reserved for seats for priests=presbyters. R.H.N.

presentation: A right of patronage* to nominate a cleric for a benefice. The patron may be either cleric or lay, and if the presentation is free from simony* the presented cleric has full right to institution. Presentation can be distinguished from election* and nomination*. See also eigenkirche. Q.B.

pretas: Literally the departed. They are the ghosts of the dead in India, spirits not yet at rest which haunt cemeteries and other places. C.S.B.

preterition: See double predestination.

prevenient grace: See grace.

pride: An attitude of lofty valuation of one's self, talents, attainments or possessions. At its best it has found ethical justification in that noble self-esteem exemplified in Aristotle's highminded man who is worthy of great things and holds himself worthy of them. But it tends toward an inordinate self-esteem marked by self-exaltation, independence of others, conceit of superiority and arrogance. In Christian ethics pride is one of the chief sins of the spirit. Dante gives it first place in his seven sins* following Thomas Aquinas for whom it was a mortal sin* of the most serious kind because at bottom it involves non-subjection to God. It is thus the central sin* for the Christian because it is essentially self-sufficiency.

R.W.F.

priest, priesthood, Christian: All Christians believe the priesthood of the Christian Church to be the priesthood of Jesus Christ (cf. *Hebrews*) exercised in and through the Church only by grace of God conferred in ordination*; but Christian churches differ in their beliefs how and by whom that priesthood is exercised in the Church, which reflect differences of historical judgment about the development of the ministry and differences in theological understanding of the nature of the work of Christ.

Congregationalist* polity (among both Congregationalists and Baptists*) holds the ministry an office conferred by each local congregation as a function of its life. Less individualist, Lutheran* polity holds the priesthood to be that "of all believers" but holds the *magisterium* to be conferred permanently to ordinands by congregations acting on behalf of all believers. Other churches are more concerned to preserve continuity as well as unity. Calvinist polity (in Presbyterian and Methodist** churches) thus holds the ministry of the Church to be continued by the presbyters* acting in their joint episcopal capacity. And the Roman Catholic, Anglican, and Eastern Orthodox Churches** hold the ministry to be conferred by episcopal ordination only (which is called "apostolic succession*").

Historically the ministry has developed into hierarchical* form in accordance with the two functions of administration of the sacraments and leadership in worship, and administration of discipline and jurisdiction. The latter is seen in the development of the monarchial episcopate by the 2nd century and in its universalization during the next three centuries when broader jurisdictional order was assigned to important sees in fashion parallel to the imperial administration. The former is seen in the development of the priesthood itself and of minor orders. The priesthood came to have regular administration of all the sacraments and priests became the normal celebrants of the Eucharist, while the diaconate and minor orders were developed for division of function in the local congregations and cities. The polity* of the Church in N.T. times is obscure historically; questions now under discussion include the Dominical institution of the ministry, mediate or immediate; the origin of the episcopate by elevation from the presbyterate or localization of the apostolate; the origin of the presbyterate in copy of the synagogal organization; the validity of the term priest for the Christian minister; the relation of the diaconate in Acts with that in 3rd century Rome. See clergy; deacon.

H. B. Swete, *Early History of the Church and Ministry* (London, 1928); J. B. Lightfoot, *Christian Ministry* (London, 1929); J. Moffatt, *Presbyterian Churches* (London, 1928); T. M. Lindsay, *The Church and Ministry in Early Centuries* (Glasgow, 1902); and J. Pohle and A. Preuss, *Sacraments* (1924).

T.J.B.

priesthood, Hebraic and Jewish: Biblical tradition sees the origin of Hebraic priesthood in the consecration at Sinai of Aaron and his sons as priests and the remainder of the tribe of Levi as priestly assistants. Actually, however, there were several stages in the development of the priesthood in Bible times: 1) a primitive stage in which priestly functions were performed by any Israelite, 2) the Deuteronomic stage in which all members of the tribe (or guild) of Levi served as priests, 3) a transitory stage, represented by Ezek. 40-48, in which Zadokite* (Jerusalem) priests were favored, and 4) a late post-exilic* stage, continuing into rabbinic times, in which the priesthood was monopolized by the supposed descendants of Aaron—other Levites occupying subordinate positions and ordinary Israelites excluded from priestly functions. It was in this last Biblical stage that the office of High Priest* had its origin. The priests had the right to tithes and portions of the offerings. They cared for the sanctuary and its utensils, presided at the altar and worship, consulted the oracle and rendered judgment, safeguarded the purity and holiness of the people and performed rites of atonement. In later Judaism the priest (*cohen*) retained the privilege of pronouncing the priestly blessing* and being called first to the reading of the Law.

S.H.B.

Priestleyanism: See Unitarianism.

Priestly Code: P, the symbol conveniently employed to designate the PRIESTLY CODE, the latest and most extensive of the four major literary and legislative strata of the Pentateuch*. It includes all of Ex. 25-31, 35-40; Lev. 1-16, Num. 1-10.28, as well as scattered sections, more or less extensive, of Gen., Ex. 1-24, Lev. 17-26, Num. 11-36 and a few passages in Deut. 31-34. A considerable section of Josh. must also be assigned to P. In significant contrast to the older literary strata of the Pentateuch and almost all the prophetic writings, P is animated very largely by that spirit of legalistic and ritualistic separatism and isolationism which evolved amid the Jewish exiles in Babylonia in the sixth and fifth centuries B.C. It is in the main the composition and reflects the theological and particularistic point of view of Zadokite* priests, who returned from Babylonia from 458 B.C. onwards. It was composed in Palestine, largely in the latter third of the fifth century B.C. and, speaking broadly, it records the ritual practice of the Jerusalem Temple from about 400 B.C. onwards. Fairly extensive secondary passages were interpolated from time to time until as late as approximately 250 B.C. It was late P writers and editors who first incorporated the somewhat older Holiness Code* (Lev. 17-26, in the main, dating from the last third of the sixth century B.C.) into their work, and then combined the older JE** and D* documents with their own work to form, first, the Hexateuch*, and then, with the omission, for theological reasons, of the Book of Joshua*, the present Pentateuch.

J. E. Carpenter and G. Harford, *The Composition of the Hexateuch* (London, 1902); R. H. Pfeiffer, *Introduction to the Old Testament* (1941).

J.M.

priests: See magic; medicine man; sacred literatures; shamanism; tabu.

primacy: See Peter, St., "Catholic Concept"; pope.

primate: An honorary title of certain archbishops, whose sees are or were the chief church centers in their respective countries. E.R.H.

prime: (Lat., *ad primam*) It was the office of the first hour of the day allegedly introduced at Jerusalem c. 400 to keep monks awake in morning. See divine office. E.R.H.

prime cause: See cause.

Primitive Adventist Christian Church: See Adventist sects.

Primitive Baptists: A group of ultra-conservative Baptist churches, found mainly in the South. They drew apart from other Baptists in connection with the controversy over missionary societies near the middle of the nineteenth century, the conservatives holding that such societies were unscriptural. These are the so-called "Hard Shell"* Baptists. They are strict Calvinists, believe in the total depravity of man and the "final perseverence" of the saints, practice immersion, "close communion," and feet washing, and oppose missionary and similar societies, Sunday schools, lodges, and the use of instrumental music in the churches. They do not encourage education for the ministry. There are 1726 churches and 69,000 members. There is also a group of Colored Primitive Baptists with 1,000 churches and 43,000 members. In the matter of missionary or aid societies and Sunday schools they appear to be somewhat more liberal than the white churches of the same general order. See anti-missionary movement in the U. S. E.T.C.

Primitive Methodists: A religious society begun in 1810 in Staffordshire, England, when Hugh Bourne and William Clowes seceded from the Methodist movement. While preserving the broad characteristics of Wesleyan Methodism, the Primitive Methodists laid greater emphasis on camp-meeting evangelism and field preaching (especially in the early days) and lay participation in the activity and government of the church. They united in 1932 with the Wesleyan Methodists and the United Methodist Church to form the Methodist Church. See Methodism. On the Primitive Methodist Church in the U. S. A. see holiness churches. F.G.E.

primitive religion: The "religious" phenomena among contemporary primitive peoples are so varied and so integral a part of the whole complex of life that it is difficult to define what may be properly called religious, and to mark it off from the non-religious. Nice definitions are, however, the less important, partly because the desideratum of science is an historical and psychological explanation of cultural complexes as a whole, and partly because it is now clear that the nature and value of present religious phenomena are independent of their cultural antecedents.

"Primitive religion" is a term which may be applied to any one, or complex, of several related phenomena, spread among primitive peoples, all of which are focussed upon the *supernatural,* and most of them on supernatural *power.* (a) Belief in spirits which, within the complex of attitudes and behavior derivative from it, has been called "animism" (Tylor), from the fact that persons and objects are believed animated by spirits. The spirits may or may not be the ghosts of departed ancestors. They sometimes inhabit objects (e.g., the moon, or a grove of trees) and persons which are striking or dangerous; or they may lead a disembodied existence which, however, is often sufficiently connected with the mundane to permit their control of sickness, death, and the well-being of individuals and the group in general. The primitive idea, although generally vague, is that a spirit is a subtle kind of corporeal being, which may have bodily needs, and at least in the case of the ghosts of the departed is often conceived to grow old and feeble, and finally to die. In some places specialists (shamans*) with proper gifts and information have trance communication with spirits for purposes of divination, healing, etc.; among the Crow Indians, however, visions are expected of all. An interesting feature of American religion is the development of the idea of a guardian spirit either of the individual or the tribe. Tylor took primitive religion to be primarily the supplication and propitiation of these spirits, and hence for him the problem of the origin of religion was simply that of an explanation of the belief in spirits; this he supplied by a theory of primitive inference from the difference between the living and the dead, and from adventures in dream and hallucination. His explanation of belief in spirits is still widely accepted. (b) "Pre-animistic" religious phenomena, sometimes called *animatism* (Marrett), centering around *mana** (Codrington: *The Melanesians*), i.e., *impersonal* supernatural power. Marrett emphasized this primitive notion of mana as a kind of potent fluid in important or dangerous persons or objects, partly because there are very primitive tribes which do not have the idea of spirits but which do have the idea of supernatural power, partly because it is apparently a simpler and more primitive idea, and partly because an explanation was needed for the fact that only certain spirits are worshiped, or only certain objects regarded as inhabited by spirits. Those spirits are worshiped, and those objects are regarded as the dwelling places of spirits, apparently, which are felt to have mana, and what has mana is whatever is extraordinary or remarkable, which evokes feelings of awe, admiration, or interest, i.e., what, as contrasted with the work-a-day, may therefore evoke a thrill: such as a successful fighter, a chief, a hurricane. Lowie remarks that in Polynesia "Mana was shown when a man undertook to do an unusual and almost impossible thing and yet succeeded . . . Conceived as somewhat in the nature of a supernatural fluid, it could be conducted into weapons by placing them in temples, where they might absorb the potency vested in the gods." (c) Belief in and worship of "high Gods". Andrew Lang (1898) questioned that the idea of a supreme deity and "maker" presupposed a developed idea of spirit and must be the culmination of an evolutionary process originating in more primitive ideas, and hence placed in doubt Tylor's theory of chronology and development. He called attention to evidence of belief in a supreme deity in many primitive societies, often alongside belief in spirits and relatively unconnected with this. Father W. Schmidt, relying on the methods of F. Graebner, has tried to prove that a fairly sophisticated approximation to monotheism can be proved to be chronologically prior to animism. Schmidt also went beyond Lang in claiming a definite cult for this God in the form of supplication and sacrifice, in very primitive peoples. It seems certain that many very primitive groups do believe in a supreme being, generally benevolent toward men, and "creative" in some crude sense. (d) Mythology. Primitive peoples have theories, often enormously complicated, about the origin and biography of important gods, the origin of the world and in particular of their own locale, the foibles of local spirits, the vicissitudes of ghosts after death, and so on. (e) Ritual, sacrifice, exorcism, prayer**. Corresponding to these different conceptions of the supernatural, various types of conduct are thought proper. Some (more evolutionary) writers believe that sacrifice and prayer developed out of spells and magic** when the idea of a spirit with a will of its own became developed; others held that some sort of sacrificial offering appeared very early in connection with belief in a "high-god", independently of desires to influence his will and rather as a result of a feeling of its suitability.

Two further phenomena, less directly continuous with developed religion, should be noted: (f) Magic.* Primitive peoples distinguish natural means of achieving results (e.g., cultivation of a garden) from supernatural ones, which may be called magical, although the line is sometimes hard to draw. Some writers think magic is distinguished from religion on account of the different attitude of will: in religion, one of submission and dependence; in the use of magic, one of desire to control. Nevertheless, both concern the supernatural, and both involve the emotion of awe or religious thrill. Some writers think that magic is essentially the art of controlling either mana or spirits. Frazer* developed the conception of sympathetic magic (operation, e.g., by imitating the desired effect, on something connected with the object to be "treated"), which he explained by appeal to the laws of association of ideas. Public rituals (e.g., to increase the catch of fish), the use of spells, rituals to prevent the penalty for infringing a tabu, trances and other forms of divination, and occasional use of supernatural methods for injuring others, are varying forms which primitive magic takes. (g) Tabus*, or restrictions on behavior or contact with certain objects, which are sanctioned by penalties supernaturally controlled. (E.g., the offender is expected to become ill.) Objects which have mana are often tabu, apparently because they are thought to be dangerous. (Cf. the stories of the Ark* of the Covenant.) Thus the person and name of the chief are often tabu, and his possessions are likely to be so. Certain foods are tabu for various groups, at least during certain periods (see totemism). Many kinds of behavior are tabu during festivals or when the community is about to undertake some important business. If breaking a tabu injures, endangers or outrages the community, it may have a natural penalty in addition to the supernatural one, at least in the form of criticism and disapproval.

Attention should be called to the theory of Durkheim, who has built his conception of religion very largely on totem phenomena in Australia. Durkheim* thinks that the real source and object of religious attitudes is society, whose influence on individuals he has emphasized in discussion of crowd situations generally. Society both dominates the individual and is the source of his strength; hence it is able to evoke attitudes of worship and respect. From the psychological point of view, society is the real god. Accordingly, the most distinctively religious behavior occurs in group activities, e.g., religious festivals. The true object of religion is too abstract for the primitive mind, so that it is represented symbolically by the totem animal; but the totem animal is not the object of worship, but only its symbol. See altar; ancestor worship; animals, worship of; blood; credulity, primitive; death and burial practices; family; fasting; feasting; fetishism; gods; harvest festivals; heart; human sacrifice; idols and images; initiation rites; law; progress; resurrection; rewards and punishments; soul; spirits; stones in religion; sun; cf. anthropology.

See Grant Allen, *Evolution of the Idea of God* (1897); Emile Durkheim, *Elementary Forms of the Religious Life* (1914); J. G. Frazer, *The Golden Bough* (1911); A. A. Goldenweiser, *Anthropology* (1937) and *History, Psychology, and Culture* (1933); A. L. Kroeber, *Anthropology* (1923); Andrew Lang, *The Making of Religion* (1898); R. H. Lowie, *Primitive Religion* (1924); B. Malinowski, "Magic, Science, and Religion" in *Science, Religion, and Reality* (1925) ed. Needham; R. R. Marrett, *The Threshold of Religion* (1914); Paul Radin, *Primitive Man as Philosopher* (1927), and *Monotheism among Primitive Peoples* (1924); Wilhelm Schmidt, *The Origin and Growth of Religion* (1931); E. B. Tylor, *Primitive Culture* (1871).

R.B.B.

primitive religious drama: See religious drama.

Pringle-Pattison, Andrew Seth: Originally Andrew Seth (1856-1931), Prof. of Logic and Metaphysics at Edinburgh, 1891-1919, acute critic of British Hegelianism and mechanistic evolutionary naturalism. He argued that the coherence criterion must be guided especially by the experience of value. Man, who is "organic to nature," reveals through his realistic intuitions of value, as well as by natural knowledge, the nature of things. Pringle-Pattison also labors to keep the independence of the individual self from being lost in the Absolute. See neo-Hegelianism.

The Idea of God in the Light of Recent Philosophy (1920); *The Idea of Immortality* (1922). P.A.B.

prior: (Lat., *prior*, elder) A monastic* superior differing in degree of importance and jurisdiction according to the Order or Congregation. Before the 13th century the superior corresponding to the term prior could be an abbot or another official, but since then it has been applied to the coadjutor of an abbot or the superior of an independent monastery which has no abbot.

Prioress (Lat., *priorissa*, fem. of prior) Superioress of a monastic community for women. Ordinarily her rights and duties correspond to those of a prior. See abbey. J.B.C.

Priscillianism: An ascetic doctrine with leanings towards Gnosticism and Manichaeism**. Priscillian, a Spanish theologian and mystic, was excommunicated by the Church in 380 and put to death by the emperor in 385. The doctrine persisted in Spain and Gaul into the 6th century. See Toledo, creed of. S.M.G.

prison reform: Relates to efforts toward the adoption of more rational and humane methods in the management of prisons. It may first be noted that the rise of the prison system, during the closing decades of the 18th century was a reform movement, for, in case of the great majority of offenders, it substituted incarceration in penal institutions for death or the infliction of some form of physical punishment such as whipping, the stocks, the pillory or other devices. Such a substitution has but shifted the area of interest in reform which is now concerned with the spirit and methods of penal administration.

We are here confronted with a long history of exploitation, public indifference and even brutality as affecting the treatment of imprisoned offenders. In general the concern of American prison reform has been with the following problems: a) the structure and size of prisons; b) prison labor; c) medical and psychiatric care; d) education; e) prison discipline; f) the individualization of treatment; g) release and after care of prisoners; h) the improvement of administrative personnel. Brief comment is made on developments within these fields.

In place of the monstrous Bastilles of the traditional type a few progressive states and the Federal government are developing differentiated systems of smaller prisons, adaptable to the needs of different classes of prisoners, and providing varying degrees of security. In regard to prison labor there has been a long struggle against exploitive systems, resulting in the adoption of the so-called state-use system whereby the products of prison labor are kept from the general market and sold only to other public institutions within the several states. This method is designed to remove entirely the element of private profit from the prison labor system. Ironically, however, it has increased the amount of idleness among prisoners, an evil commensurate with the traditional forms of exploitation. Progress is being made in many jurisdictions in the matter of improved facilities for the medical and psychiatric care of prisoners. Likewise, more attention is being given to the educational facilities and opportunities of prison inmates in the threefold aspects of academic and vocational education, and training for personal living. Moreover, purely arbitrary and mechanical systems of prison discipline are in some measure giving way to more enlightened methods in which a degree of recognition is given to prisoners' participation in the handling of some disciplinary problems. The better morale which this induces is enhanced by recreational programs in the planning and direction of which prisoners are being encouraged to participate.

These trends in modern prison reform all point to the substitution of individualized for mass treatment of offenders, culminating in some progressive institutions in the establishment of what is called classification. In accordance with this individual case records of prisoners are compiled, and effort is made to develop a suitable institutional program for each inmate, whose case is periodically reviewed by the members of the classification committee. Thus, the response of the inmate to the institutional program is noted, and decision is reached concerning the time when he may be safely released under parole. It follows that the parole system by which prisoners are supervised for a period after release from the institution is a necessary adjunct to the work of the prison itself; and much reform effort has been directed toward the improvement of this function. In short, the training of men in prisons, and their careful guidance for a period after their release on parole are dual aspects of the process of rehabilitation, which is the ultimate criterion of prison reform.

Implicit in all this discussion is the suggestion that the crowning objective of the movement for prison reform lies in the recruiting and training of personnel for the important work of prison administration. The removal of our prisons from the arena of political spoils has been achieved in some of the states and in the notable program of our Federal government for the penal institutions under its charge. To make prison administration a professional task for which men are trained and selected as they are for other professions is the foundation upon which must be laid all other plans for prison reform.

It must not be supposed that the progressive developments we have outlined characterize more than a substantial minority of our penal institutions. The majority of them still carry on under a burdensome heritage of outmoded architecture, overcrowding, political control and untrained personnel. Moreover, the improvements that have been made have affected but slightly conditions in the many thousand jails of the country that remain nothing short of a national disgrace. Penal institutions are an interrelated system, consisting of prisons, reformatories, jails, and other types. Reform must needs be all along the line. It is a task which requires the concentration upon it of all the moral forces of the nation in the coming decades. See penology.

Donold Clemmer, *The Prison Community* (1940); Sanford Bates, *Prisons and Beyond* (1936); Negley K. Teeters, *They Were in Prison* (1937); Frank Tannenbaum, *Crime and the Community* (1938); Orlando F. Lewis, *The Development of American Prisons and Prison Customs* (1922); Fred E. Haynes, *The American Prison System* (1939). A.E.W.

prithivi: Literally "earth". The ancient Vedic earth mother, celebrated alone in one Vedic hymn and in six in conjunction with the Sky-Father Dyaus* as Dyaus-Prithivi. C.S.B.

privation, divine: See Aristotle and Aristotelianism; omniscience.

privileges, ecclesiastical: Those granted in Canon Law* (canons 119-123) to all clergy and all religious in good standing; e.g., the privilege of ecclesiastical court. These cannot be waived. L.R.W.

probabiliorism: A system of teaching in Catholic moral theology which holds that it is wrong to act on an opinion favoring liberty as against law unless that opinion is the more probable. T.J.B.

probabilism: A system of teaching in Catholic moral theology since the 16th century, associated popularly with the Jesuits* although used generally by all Catholic moralists, which holds that in case of doubt about the lawfulness of a proposed action, the conscience may lawfully follow a solidly probable opinion, even though an opposite and more probable opinion favors the existence of a law that would forbid the proposed action. Laxity in application of this teaching provoked Pascal's* *Lettres Provinciales,* and led to its restatement by St. Alphonsus Liguori*, whose view is now generally followed. See equiprobabilism. T.J.B.

probation: See penology.

procession of the Holy Spirit: This differentiates the relation of the Spirit to God from that of the Son; the Son is begotten of, the Spirit proceeds from, the Father (John 15: 26). An issue that long exercised the Church was whether the Spirit proceeds also from the Son; the addition, at the council of Toledo in 589, of "filioque"* to the "who proceedeth from the Father" of the Nicene-Constantinopolitan Creed** has never been accepted by the Eastern Church.* The Western position claims N.T. justification (both the Father and Christ send the Spirit: John 14: 26; 15: 26; cf. Acts 2: 32, 33) and to favor the co-equality of Christ and God; though the question has receded in modern theology which uses other symbols than "filioque" of its Christological* differences.

H. B. Swete, *History of the Doctrine of the Procession of the Holy Spirit* (1876); E. F. Scott, *The Spirit in the New Testament* (1923). J.L.

processional: 1) A hymn sung in an ecclesiastical procession or by clergy and choir entering the church. 2) The liturgical book containing litanies, hymns, and anthems used in procession. P.V.N.

processions: To proceed from one shrine or church to another in solemn manner, singing hymns or psalms, is a Christian custom dating from at least the 4th century in Jerusalem. An original practical purpose is still apparent in the funeral procession to the church and to the graveyard, the marriage procession to the altar, in the Rogation* blessing of the fields, or in taking the Blessed Sacrament to the sick or in the Maundy Thursday* liturgy to an altar of repose. A mystical meaning is seen in the ancient processions of the Pope from the stational churches in Rome, or in processions before the high mass*, which indicate the inclusion of the whole congregation in the act of worship; and a mystical and dramatic meaning is seen in the Palm Sunday and Candlemas** processions. A precatory use is found in processions of the Host, as on Corpus Christi, and in litanies**. T.J.B.

Proclus: See s. v. Neo Platonism.

profession of faith: Usually employed in Protestant denominations to describe the act by which, at a public service, an intending member of the body indicates his belief in the creed of the group; and is, after this act, received into membership.

The term "Profession" is also used in Catholic circles to describe the formal ceremonial by which a novice becomes a member, either junior or fully professed, in a religious order. W.N.P.

progress: A term denoting the cumulative achievement in time of a desirable goal. In human affairs the term denotes the gradual realization of higher stages of culture.

The notion of progress, while not unrelated to other concepts, has received its full statement only in the modern period of Western thought. It arose in theories of the progress of human knowledge (Fontanelle), and was generalized by Abbe de St. Pierre, Condorcet, and others as a theory of the movement of all human life toward a more perfect state. Much of the thought of the nineteenth century developed on the basis of the fundamental assumption that human history "has moved, is moving, and will continue to move in a desirable direction" (Charles A. Beard).

The notion of progress cannot be equated with the notion of evolution* or with any particular theory of evolution. It is true, however, that in the nineteenth century Darwinian biology was taken by many as supporting the general theory of progress and the two concepts became constituent elements in the world view of the liberal movement in Christian theology. (See liberal theology). Christian theologians, however, were more cautious in dealing with the concept of progress than they have frequently been given credit for being. They distinguished between material progress and moral progress. They showed caution in treating the rate of progress and they suggested a distinction, which has become increasingly important in contemporary discussion, between the possibility and the inevitability of progress. Contemporary theology and philosophy are generally skeptical regarding universal and inevitable progress. Over the question whether there are at least some areas in human life in which a modified conception may still be held, there are varying view points.

J. B. Bury, *The Idea of Progress* (new ed., 1932), with Introduction by Charles A. Beard; E. L. Schaub, *Progressism: An Essay in Social Philosophy;* and the Oxford Conference publication, *The Kingdom of God and History* (1938). D.D.W.

progress: In the sense of a gradual advance in social life with respect to those qualities to which man can rationally attach value, is a relatively modern conception. To primitive man, existence is at best precarious and uncertain. His experience leads him to a belief, not in progress, but in luck. His best efforts are constantly overruled by the forces of a mysterious and baffling nature which he can neither comprehend nor control. The best he can hope for is to make these forces accessory to his efforts through the development and use of magic*. Nor were early civilizations more hospitable to the idea. Here its place was pre-empted by the widespread belief in a Golden Age*. In the classical cultures, some foretokens of the possibility of general social improvement through human effort did arise, but nothing corresponding to the modern conception of indefinite, if not infinite, progress. Thus Plato*, although he believed that the world had deteriorated from a more perfect state and was destined to pass through successive cycles of regeneration and relapse, also thought of man as capable, to a degree, of directing and controlling its course. The Epicureans* went further and developed a rudimentary theory of social evolution. The present state of civilization, they held, was not a relapse from the Golden Age, but a gradual achievement from a miserable and beast-like condition. But, although their Roman disciple, Lucretius*, used the word "progress," they did not think of the process as continuing into an indefinite future, and were often doubtful as to its value. On the whole, the outcome of both Greek and Roman thought was pessimistic. The universe and the social order within it were conceived as bound to an inexorable fate* which it would not only be impossible but impious to alter. This view paralyzed social effort, and left man only the possibility of an individualistic escape if perchance through the consolations of philosophy he might find for himself a tolerable life. And this Epicurean and Stoic* alike sought to do, each according to his own philosophical creed.

Diametrically opposed to this individualism and pessimism stand the Hebrew Prophets*. They scorned any solution of the problems of life that was not social in character. But they thought of themselves as restorers and conservators of Israel's ancient spiritual heritage. After the collapse of the Hebrew state their social message underwent a gradual transformation until it emerged at last as an ideal of a perfect state conceived of in ethical terms. But it differed from the idea of progress in at least three ways: It was to be achieved, not by human effort, but by the intervention of a Divine Deliverer; it was to be shared, not by the whole people, but by a Remnant, the Good Seed who had brought themselves into conformity to the will of Yahweh*; and it was thought of as the end of the world process, beyond which there lay no possibility of further achievement. As the great prophets passed and their work was taken up by the apocryphal and apocalyptic** writers, the idea degenerated in the hands of these lesser imitators. God was to bring all things to pass according to His own plan, in His own good time, and men had but to wait and hope. Such an idea, when consistently held, could neither inspire nor direct men in active effort for social reconstruction.

Whether or not Jesus repudiated this apocalyptic conception of an earthly state to be reserved for the elect of Israel, established by Divine intervention, and ruled by a Davidic Prince, and taught in its stead the Gospel of a Kingdom of God* to be realized inwardly in personal experience and outwardly in an ethical social order is at present a controversial question among New Testament scholars. At any rate, the early Church Fathers* shared the prevailing pessimism of their times. Despairing of the world, they sought the realization of their ideal either in an earthly millennial kingdom or in a life beyond the grave; but in any event, the blessed estate was reserved for the elect few. Man was created perfect, corrupted by the Fall*, and saved by Grace. The earth was the stage for the playing of a heavenly drama, history was its enactment, and men the puppets of the play. The play was in its last act, and the end was soon. It might, thought some, be possible to ameliorate somewhat the conditions of these last days, even to increase knowledge, or at least knowledge of the Divine Revelation, but the chief end of human effort was to make one's calling and election sure, that he might reign with the redeemed saints in an earthly millennium, or in a celestial city of God eternal in the heavens. "For here we have no abiding city." Early and medieval Christianity did, however, thoroughly condition men's minds to the idea of an ultimate happy destiny for mankind, and thus laid the foundation for the development of the modern conception of progress. It also accustomed them to think in terms of a universal human brotherhood, an idea which, assimilated to the Greco-Roman ideal of world unity, furnished the basis for the medieval doctrine of a world-wide spiritual and political community. Here is probably the most fundamental element in the theory of progress, for it is becoming increasingly clear that a world-wide integration of human interest and purpose is an essential condition of the perpetuation of civilization itself.

The conditions necessary to the development of the idea of progress began to appear only with the Renaissance*, and culminated toward the end of the 19th century. They may be summarized as the accumulation of recorded history, the growth of the humanitarian spirit, and the new confidence in human reason achieved through the accomplishments of scientific method and invention in the explanation and control of nature. The tragic course of events during and following the First World War have again been unfavorable to the doctrine of progress, and an increasing number of writers have arisen to challenge the idea. Some, like Oswald Spengler in his *Decline of the West,* are returning to the Greek notion of cycles* of change, while others, like P. A. Sorokin in his *Social Mobility* and other works, are interpreting social change as a trendless flux.

Much confusion in the discussion of this problem is due to a failure to distinguish between progress as a philosophical conception and progress as an historical fact. It is a fact that social life has advanced with respect to at least some of those qualities to which man can rationally attach value. Knowledge of nature and the mastery of physical forces have developed with few if any serious losses since earliest times, and with a greatly accelerated pace during the past century. Although progress in native intelligence and in the normal and spiritual aspects of life is more difficult to establish, there can be little doubt of rationally demonstrable improvement in mankind as a whole in these respects also since the appearance of the first fossil races recognizable as human. Philosophically, however, certain writers, like J. B. Bury, in his *Idea of Progress,* have held that the concept is logically inconsistent, in that it implies perpetual change, and at the same time implies a final goal beyond which further change is retrogression, for progress seems to be meaningless unless there is an ultimate objective. Thus, Comte's* objective as the final positive stage of knowledge which society was then entering, Hegel's* objective as the freedom already realized in the Prussian state, or Marx's* classless society which would bring to an end the process of class struggle through which history proceeds, all explain the past by a process which at some time ceases to explain the future.

But criticism of the idea of progress on account of its inconsistency in positing a final goal reveals a curious misconception as to the nature of the problem. It admits the possibility of progress with respect to the means whereby ends are achieved, but it denies its possibility as regards the ends themselves. The problem of progress is concerned with the extent to which man is able rationally and volitionally to determine his own destiny, while the demand for a fixed goal implies that he is moving automatically, irresistibly, inevitably toward an end which he can not miss, which his intelligence may hasten or his stupidity delay, but which in any event his errors can not ultimately defeat. Such criticisms illustrate how slow are men's minds to grasp the full meaning of the concept of progress. For centuries the prevailing theory of man's destiny has been that it does not lie within himself, but with his stars. He is the sport of chance, the victim of Fate, the pawn of Providence*, or the darling child of evolution*, the beneficiary, willy-nilly, of forces that guarantee him the attainment of an earthly paradise at the end of a cosmic joy-ride. Theories of progress which posit an ultimate goal, though modern in their phrasing, do not differ essentially from the views of antiquity and medievalism. The problem of progress is, to what extent are man's times in his own hands? To what extent can he profit by what experience has taught him of success or failure in modifying his methods and changing his goals? To demand a fixed goal by which progress can be measured reduces to the absurdity of demanding that man's control over his own destiny be measured by a standard which places his destiny beyond his own control.

Progress in the field of science, where all authorities admit that the clearest evidence for its reality exists, does not consist in setting up a definite content of science as a goal to be attained, for to do so would presuppose foreknowledge of facts and laws not yet discovered. Nor does it consist in the quantity of concepts and laws, for many of the most marked advances of science have resulted in reducing their multiplicity to more fundamental discoveries. The progress of science is not a matter of quantitative measurement, but of logical judgment; that is, it is a matter of its growth in validity, of the increasing adequacy and universality with which its concepts and laws symbolize objects and their relationships, of the consistency, unity, and absence of contradiction in the theoretical formulation of its principles as a body of logical propositions, and, therefore, of its dependableness in providing intelligible explanation and effective control over the phenomena with which it deals. Progress in science does not consist in a finality of content, but in adequacy of method to purge and enrich its content, less by increasing its discoveries quantitatively than by improving them qualitatively in order that they may better satisfy the logical criterion of validity as the universal of knowledge.

Nor is it otherwise in other fields of human interest and endeavor. Moral progress, like scientific progress, does not consist in the development of a final body of truth nor the increase in the number of generally accepted concepts and principles, but in qualitative changes in the concrete content of moral values which satisfy more adequately the logical requirements of validity; that is, in the development of a conception of the good life in terms, not of what men subjectively and individually desire, but in terms of what is rationally and objectively desirable, and an objective ordering of the chaos and confusion of personal aims and ends into a common purpose directed toward the common good. So conceived, the achievement of progress is a joint enterprise of ethics*, science, and practical endeavor. As L. T. Hobhouse expressed it, it involves 1) an inquiry into the nature of values*, the problem of ethics, 2) an inquiry into the actual relations of human beings, the problem of social science, and 3) the development and utilization of means of applying our knowledge of facts in the service of values, the problem of social improvement.

L. T. Hobhouse, *Social Evolution and Political Theory* (1911); H. E. Jensen, "A Forecast of Progress," in W. P. King (ed.), *Social Progress and Christian Ideals* (1931). H.E.J.

Progressive Orthodoxy: The title of the papers, later published in book form under the same title, which the new faculty at Andover Theological Seminary published in the early years of the *Andover Review*—about 1884-5. This term, they felt, described their own theological position, which at that time they regarded as both within the framework of Calvinistic orthodoxy and also moving toward necessary modifications. Within a very few years they dropped this term as a descriptive title for their position as they moved farther from their Calvinist base line.

See New England theology; New theology.

D. D. Williams, *The Andover Liberals* (1941). D.D.W.

prohibition: See temperance movement.

prohibitions: See tabu.

proletariat: A socialist term used to indicate a growing and more or less permanent and class-conscious wage-earning group. Under a money economy this group is assumed to have a considerable degree of freedom and mobility but its economic dependence upon capital and the capitalists is held to make its position relatively hopeless. Hence it offers a good soil for revolutionary proposals and is expected, when the time is ripe, to rise up in its despair, overthrow the capitalist* system, and introduce the collective commonwealth.

The wage-earning group has been recruited from the remnants and surpluses of previous labor systems, such as the family or clan system, slavery and serfdom; and the handicraft or guild system; but in most cases its position, however low, may be held to have been improved instead of being made more miserable, as the Marxian* assumption implies. Wage-payment existed even in ancient times and is mentioned in several Bible passages. In Great Britain a labor supply to man the factory system in the eighteenth century was drawn, often with the domestic system as a half-way house, from a class of handicraftsmen and apprentices who had been left stranded in the decline of the guilds, from a landless agricultural group usually with a high birth rate, and in some measure from immigration, especially from Ireland. Much the same has been true in other industrial countries. In the United States we depended principally, down to about 1850, on the sons and daughters of native farmers, but thereafter more and more upon immigrants, first from northern and western Europe, later from Italy, Austria-Hungary, Greece, and Russia. Many of these people were landless farmers or farm laborers before they came. In 1910 more than half of the employees in several of our large industries, such as coal-mining, iron and steel, textiles, and the garment trades were foreign-born. Today it is more largely the second and third generations from these strains.

Whether the wage-earning status, either on higher or lower levels, is to be regarded as relatively permanent for the individual and for his children after him, is a complicated matter, depending in part upon the ability or kind of stuff with which different people are endowed, upon the extent to which the size of the business unit and the amount of capital required (often several thousand dollars per laborer) limits entrance to a trade, upon the degree to which our supposedly democratic educational system and other legal and social arrangements afford complete equality of opportunity, and upon the chances for advancement on the basis of merit in the business world itself. See labor movements.

H. W. Laidler, *A History of Socialist Thought* (1927), ch. xiv; W. B. Catlin, *The Labor Problem in the United States and Great Britain* (1935) 2nd ed., ch. ii-iii, x; P. Sorokin, *Social Mobility* (1927), esp. pp. 438 ff., 457 ff. W.B.C.

propaedeutics: The preliminary or preparatory instruction connected with any art or study. Used by Schaff, *Theological Propaedeutic* (1893), to designate an introduction to the entire field of theology in which the various departments of theology were outlined, and their respective natures, aims, limits, organic connections, and values were defined. A.K.R.

Propaganda, Congregation of: The body or congregation *de Propaganda Fidei* founded in 1622 by Gregory XV to look after ecclesiastical matters in missionary countries; i.e., wherever the Church is yet imperfectly established. L.R.W.

prophets: See Major Prophets; Minor Prophets.

Prophets, "the Former": See canon, Old and New Testament; Old Testament.

Prophets, "the Latter": See canon, Old and New Testament; Old Testament.

prophets, prophecy: (Old Testament) A succession of Hebrew men of religion who claimed to be inspired by their God and to speak in his name, and whose claim is confirmed by the spiritual vitality and permanent worth of their work and message. The essence of spiritual religion was clarified in the course of their struggle against Nature (Baal) worship*, its social and cultural forms and its ethic. The prophets were not forecasters or philosophers, but mystics, preachers, moralists, poets and men of action who felt themselves to be mouthpieces of Yahweh (cf. Exod. 4:14-16; 7:1) and instruments of Yahweh's creative purpose in man's historic life.

The classical prophets of the 8th and 7th cents. B.C. mark the emergence of a new, unique quality in a movement with a long history and lowly beginnings. Among their antecedents were the priestly diviners, augurs, and seers who undertook to ascertain the divine will and to forecast the future through instruments of divination, dreams and induced ecstasy (I Sam. 30:7 ff.; Deut. 13:1; 2 Kings 3:15). The first prophets so-called were dervish ecstatics, like "the prophets of Baal" (I Kings. 18:25-29) and other contemporary groups whose psychopathic acts and cries were attributed to divine possession (I Sam. 10: 5, 6). These eventually became institutionalized communities of "sons of the prophets" (2 Kings 1-6), among whom individuals of exceptional insight and integrity stood out as immediate forerunners of the classical prophets (I Kings 18:1 ff.; 22:5-28). The professional prophets continued into the classical period when they were denounced as "false prophets" who speak without authentic inspiration what men wish to hear (Micah 3:5; Jer. 28; 29:8 ff.). Divination and related practices are rejected as alien to true prophecy after the fashion of Moses (Deut. 18:9-22). The predictive element in prophecy is incidental, not primary; it extends the margin of the moral and religious present into a future which is its immediate consequence, and is morally conditioned (Isa. 1:19, 20).

The primary literary record of prophecy consists of oracles written down after oral utterance; these, as subsequently collected and edited along with narratives of the prophet concerned, and sometimes incorporating his memoirs (e.g., of Jeremiah) form the substantial nuclei of most of the prophetic books. Again, there is later written prophecy, mostly anonymous and undated, added as supplements to the prophetic collections; in 2 Isaiah (cc. 35, 40 ff.) this rises to great heights. There are also three types of material relating the antecedents of 8th Cent. Prophecy, viz., in the Pentateuch, the picture of Moses as prophet; in Judges, Samuel and Kings, narratives in which individual prophets appear; and the narrative sections (partly legendary) in 1 and 2 Kings which relate the actions (rather than the words) of Elijah and Elisha.

Hebrew prophecy can best be understood from the records of its greatest representatives, Amos, Hosea, Isaiah and Micah of the 8th Cent., and Jeremiah of the 7th and 6th Cents. The prophet is a man called and commissioned through an ecstatic experience (Amos 7:15; Isaiah 6:1 ff.; Jeremiah 1:4 ff.), and henceforth possessed by a knowledge of Yahweh's will which demands articulation from time to time in a "word" from Yahweh related to a particular situation. The oracle is a new kind of ecstatic speech (in contrast to the meaningless babblings of the old ecstatics); it is intelligible, searching, morally profound, revealing behind phenomena the true spiritual situation and the immediate demand of Yahweh's holy will. The God whose mouthpiece the prophet is manifests himself as a passionate, righteous will to whose unique sovereignty man must conform in the sphere of his ethical, historic life, or suffer. Sin is rediscovered as a dreadful reality, rooted in the failure to recognize the true nature of God and of the Divine covenant which is the bond of human community. The "Day of Yahweh"* is the imminent moment of his characteristic action of judgment, righteousness and mercy in the light of man's moral and spiritual state. The divine will is the final determinant of human history where man makes his moral decisions.

The prophets were deeply concerned with the social order because of their belief that it was Yahweh's purpose to create a people through a social covenant* embodying the ethical imperatives of his nature. The actual society they knew was an uneasy accommodation of Israelite tradition to Canaanite* mores and institutions, which were based on nature worship and derived from the pagan view that security and satisfaction are to be sought through power and material possessions. They rejected the form and purposes of constituted society as they denounced its particular denials and frustrations of Yahweh's justice and right; and at the same time they exposed the falsity of the Canaanized religious cult by which it was sanctioned, and in which Yahweh's name was honored while his nature was outraged. The cult was in all but name the worship of other gods because it sanctioned a way of life abominable to Yahweh.

The prophets taught men to know and reverence God as he really is, a living personal Being of unique ethical character; not a static or abstract "Being" but a "Doer", Lord of nature and history, whose good purpose for humanity leads to his concern for man's character and behaviour, and to his participation in man's historic experience. To serve such a God means to discern and honour his presence by living in social relationships which are right in his sight, and so to give to him the obedience in life's actual decisions, of which formal worship is the symbol. Religion is the response through loyalty, obedience and trust to the ethical reality of God. It is the building of life upon the genuine conviction that the Supreme Power in the beginning, now and in the end, is a God who seeks to realize his goodness in the life-experience of individuals and of a people. See Major Prophets; Minor Prophets; progress; word of God. See under separate books of the O.T. Also, see Old Testament literature.

B. Duhm, *Israels Propheten* (1922) 2nd ed.; J. M. P. Smith, *The Prophets and their Times* (1941) 2nd ed. edited by Irwin; W. C. Graham, *The Prophets and Israel's Culture* (1935); A. Lods (tr. Hooke), *The Prophets and the Rise of Judaism* (1937). R.B.Y.S.

propitiation: (Gr., *hilaskomai,* to propitiate, render favorable to one alienated; to make propitiation for (Heb. 2: 17); *hilasmos* (1 John 2: 2; 4: 10), *hilasterios* (Rom. 3: 25), propitiation, atoning sacrifice* (mercy-seat, the gold covering of the Ark* of the Covenant in the Holy of Holies* on which was sprinkled the blood of the victim on the day of atonement*, in Heb. 9: 5).

General sense of mankind has been that wrong cannot be done with impunity; redress is necessary; forgiveness* not just gratuitous or without cost or condition. Sin* against God especially an affront for which there must be amends. In the Jewish system, moral or ceremonial offence excluding from the favor of God expiated by the sin-offering. For Christians expiation, propitiation, made once for all by Christ; the Cross*, Christianity's sin-offering (Heb. 9: 24-28). Its effect is continuous ('there is no more offering for sin': Heb. 10: 18); on condition of repentance* man by it can evermore be restored to divine favor ('by one offering He hath perfected for ever them that are sanctified' v. 14). The Cross is the perfection not alone of the sacrifice where the victim is offered by another; but of that higher vicarious propitiatory in which the victim offers himself. It must be remembered that, while the figure of propitiation is valuable as indicating benefits to men of Chr'st's sacrifice, it is not complete; God, in view of man's sin, does not just wait to be placated; He is Himself the source of the benefits; the sacrifice is His gift to win a rebellious world back to its allegiance. See atonement.

V. Taylor, *Jesus and His Sacrifice* (1937); A. B. Macaulay, *The Death of Jesus* (1938). J.L.

prose: See sequence.

proselyte: (*Ger* in Hebrew) Meaning a stranger and denoting a convert to Judaism. The "righteous proselyte" became part of the Jewish people, and his initiation included the baptismal bath as well as, in the case of a male, circumcision. The "Proselyte of the Gate" did not affiliate with the Jewish people but he accepted the universal element of the Jewish religion as summarized in "seven Noahitic laws", which stressed the promotion of justice, and the prohibition of idolatry, cruelty to animals, theft, murder and blasphemy. Perhaps the best known modern Proselyte to Judaism is Aimé Palliere, a student of a Catholic Theological Seminary, and a candidate for the priesthood in France, who recently embraced Judaism. He subsequently wrote the story of his conversion in *The Unknown Sanctuary* (1930) 3rd ed. B.Z.B.

pro-slavery doctrine: The most effective Biblical and theological defense of slavery* was that advanced by James H. Thornwell* in the *Southern Presbyterian Review,* July 1850. He held that the Holy Scriptures unequivocally authorize the relation of master and slave; that masters and slave alike, when believers, are brethren, each having duties toward the other grounded upon their relation to God. In a perfect world there would be no slavery, just as there would be no poverty or disease. Both have come as a result of man's sin. Both slavery, poverty and disease are a part of the curse which sin has introduced into the world. But slavery is not a sin any more than poverty is a sin; both however are great evils. After death, master and slave would have equal status, provided both had lived as God had ordained,—the slave as an obedient servant; the master as just in the fulfillment of his obligations. W.W.S.

prosopic union: See Nestorianism.

Protestant seminaries: See theological schools, Protestant, United States and Canada.

Protestant social work: See social work of the churches.

Protestantism: At present a neutral, collective, covering term for all Christian groups immediately or remotely related to the Reformation*. The word derives from the "protestation" made at the meeting of the *Reichstag* at Speyer, 1529, by the minority of evangelical estates. Historically and sociologically, Protestantism was merely the religious phase of the transition to the modern age as democracy, capitalism, and public education were the political, economic, and cultural aspects of that transition.

What Protestantism unknowingly accomplished was the weakening of the medieval church system by the destruction of its supernatural postulates. When the complete deification of the church as an institution was abandoned, the supernatural hierarchy, creeds and Bible came tumbling down like a row of dominoes and what is now lamented as "secularization" began to spread over all Western culture. The price of puncturing the authority of the Holy Father included, before accounts were fully settled, the adoption of the historical approach to the Bible, the discovery of the Jesus of history, the re-examination of the God idea, the definite assignment of the church to sociological classification, and its surrender to the modern state.

The earlier Protestant types were Lutheranism, Anabaptism, Calvinism and Anglicanism** with democratic Christianity appearing toward the close of the sixteenth century. In addition to the larger denominations, Protestantism has meant narrow biblicism and apocalypticism**. Whether American cults should be classified as Protestant is still violently debated. Unity in Protestantism stems from opposition to Roman Catholicism, the insistence upon the Bible as primary, the emphasis upon the congregation as religious cell, and the universal priesthood of all believers. Protestantism by raising the historical question of the origin and content of the Bible and emphasizing the right of private judgment has made doctrinal unity and conformity impossible. Cf. American theology, early; on Protestant Canon see apocrypha, Old Testament.

A. C. McGiffert, *Protestant Thought Before Kant* (1911); C. H. Moehlman, *Protestantism's Challenge* (1939); Wilhelm Pauck, "Nature of Protestantism," *Church History,* March, 1937; Ernst Troeltsch, *Protestantism and Progress* (1912). C.H.M.

Protestantism in China: See Chinese religions.

Protestantism in India and Japan: See India, missions to; India, religions of; Japan, Christianity in.

prothonotary: In the Roman Catholic church, in the Middle Ages, a very high official of the papal chancery; since 1838 the number of this group has been fixed at seven members, not counting the honorary *protonotarii.* M.S.

protopope: The highest rank which a priest of the Eastern Orthodox or the Uniate churches** may attain. Since the hierarchs are chosen exclusively from among the monks, the hierarchical rank may never be attained by the married priest, unless he become a widower and assume the monastic habit. The rank of protopope corresponds in general to the archpriest or dean of the Western churches. M.S.

Proverbs: Representative book of Oriental "wisdom" literature* in Hebrew adaptation. This type of literature giving practical counsel tinged with hedonistic philosophy of life was much cultivated in Egypt. Present book a compilation of seven collections: I) 1:1-9:18, the youngest (4th-3rd century B.C.); II) 10:1-22:16, perhaps pre-exilic* but with younger accretions; III) 22:17-24:22, pre-exilic: directly dependent on an Egyptian wisdom-book of 1,000 B.C. (*Amenemope*); IV) 24:23-34, a brief collection with a title of its own, but no clues as to date; V) 25-29, origin at time of Hezekiah may be correct; VI) chapter 30, Words of Agur of Massa (Arabian tribe, Gen. 25:14), showing dependence on Book of Job*; VII) chapter 31, Words of Lemuel, King of Massa (v. 10-31 ascribed to Solomon* in Septuagint which arranges some materials differently). Not impossible that some sayings of Solomon or of his time (I Kings 5:9f.-10:1f.) may have been preserved amid younger materials. The "wisdom" attitude, on the whole, is secular, though the attempt is made to harness it to religion by the principle that "the fear of the Lord is the beginning of wisdom" (ch. 1:7). Cf. R. H. Pfeiffer, *Introduction to the Old Testament* (1941). J. A. Bewer, *Literature of the Old Testament* (rev. ed., 1933). On Amenemope, see W. O. E. Oesterly, *The Wisdom of Egypt and the Old Testament* (1927). E.G.K.

providence: The doctrine of providence is a phase of Christian theism*. It is to be distinguished from Deism* on the one hand, and impersonalistic conceptions of God, on the other. Thus it holds that God, the Author of the world, is ever active within it, with power to direct or overrule events. He employs this power not arbitrarily, nor from necessity as a Force or Principle of nature. But His activity is of conscious intent and always with a view to ends, which He foresees and wills. An aspect of providence is divine Guidance; God's assistance to individuals in the ordering of their lives. Providence as distinct from Guidance is seen in the divine direction, not so much of individuals, as of outward events that affect their life and welfare. Yet providence means that human history and nature alike are the sphere of divine determining action. As men of their will and purpose produce change in the inner and outer conditions of others' lives, so God from His profounder initiative and to His infinite sweep of command can effectually will and do, always in harmony with His own character and conformably to the sure good and faith of those who know their dependence upon Him. Providence is specially meaningful as moral providence: God's provision for man's growth in righteousness and constant help in his endeavour to fulfil God's righteous demands. Cf. predestination.

H. H. Farmer, *The World and God* (1935); K. Barth, *God in Action* (1936). J.L.

provincial: In the monastic organization, the provincial is the ecclesiastic who presides over a province; a province is an area, which may include one or more countries, comprising several departments, each of which includes a number of cloisters. At the head of any one monastic order may be the general; and the provincials rank next below him. A.K.R.

Provisors, Statute of: The first Statute of Provisors was enacted in 1351. Its purpose was to prevent the filling of ecclesiastical benefices in England by means of papal provisions. W.S.H.

provost: (Lat., *praepositus,* one placed before) In ecclesiastical usage the term is applied to 1) the chief dignitary of a cathedral or collegiate chapter in England, Scotland, Poland, Austria, etc.; sometimes he is second in dignity to a dean or prior** whose duties approximate his own; 2) a Protestant clergyman who has charge of the principal church in a district of Germany; 3) provost general, the superior of certain Roman Catholic religious orders and congregations, e.g., the Passionists, Discalced Carmelites, Fathers of Charity, Barnabites, etc.

In civil usage the term is applied to 1) the head of a faculty at Oxford or Cambridge Univ., the principal of the Univ. of Dublin, or the head of the Univ. of Penna. and a few American colleges; 2) the mayor of a Scottish city; 3) the keeper of a prison; 4) the judge of certain royal and feudal courts in France. J.F.T.

prudence: (Lat., *prudentia*) The control of conduct in the light of consequences; practical wisdom; foresight. "Skill in the choice of means to one's own greatest well-being" (Kant). Cf. hedonism; Plato; St. Thomas. J.E.N.

Przywara, Erich: (1889-) Born in Kattowitz, Germany; student in Jesuit schools; professor of theology in the University of München and associated with various Catholic publications. His work in the philosophy of religion is notable both as an indication of the role of Catholic thinkers in the general cultural movement and for its own intrinsic value as a speculative achievement. His fundamental concept which serves as the center of reference is the doctrine of the analogy of being (*analogia entis*). He sees the task facing Catholic philosophers of religion in the embracing in one comprehensive system the metaphysical foundation developed by the Scholastics and the modern scientific and psychological superstructure. His doctrine of the analogy of being is for him the basic ideological law of all sound philosophy. The ontological relation between creator and creature is for him the best formulation of his central doctrine. For him immanence and transcendence must enter into polar relation or unity of contraries, that is *analogia entis,* if they are to pretend to be transcriptions of reality. His investigations in the history of philosophy and his analyses of contemporary tendencies led him at every turn to his central notion of polarity as the basic law of reality and the metaphysical foundation of an adequate philosophy of religion. In the development of his central principle he took St. Augustine and St. Thomas Aquinas as his guides.

Religionsbegründung (Freiburg im Breisgau, 1923); *Gottgeheimnis der Welt* (München, 1923); *Ringen der Gegenwart* (Augsburg, 1929) 2 vols.; *Das Geheimnis Kierkegaards* (München, 1929); *Kant Heute* (München, 1930); *A Newman Synthesis* (1931); *Analogia Entis* (München, 1932); *Polarity* (1935).

H.H.

psalmody: The liturgical use of the Psalter, particularly in the Divine Office (Hours)**. In the Breviary* the psalms of the Psalter are distributed among the hours (variable in Matins and Vespers) in such wise as to be sung or read through in the course of a week. In practice, however, this use of the Psalter is impeded by the intrusion of saints' days (the *Sanctorale*) with recurring proper psalms.

In the Anglican Prayer Book the Psalter is divided into sixty portions for use morning and evening through a month. P.V.N.

The practice of singing Psalms in the Christian Church, begun in the earliest times and probably adapted from a similar Hebrew practice. The precursor of the chorale* and the hymn*, and indirectly, of the motet, the anthem, and the cantata**. Antiphonal psalmody is an alternation of two choirs. Responsorial psalmody is an alternation of choir and soloist. Direct psalmody uses no alternation. See plainsong.

G. Reese, *Music in the Middle Ages* (1940).

E.H.B.

Psalms: The Psalter has been called the hymnal of the Second Temple. While it contains some pre-exilic* poems, most of the psalms are post-exilic*. Ascription of Psalms to David in the titles is due to pious imagination of late editors. The phraseology even of late psalms, however, often shows traditional affinity with old North Canaanite poetry (Ras Shamra)*. The Psalter is divided into five books—the echo of praise elicited in the heart of the Jew by the five books of his law: I, 1-41; II, 42-72; III, 73-89; IV, 90-106; V, 107-150. This arrangement succeeded earlier ones; thus 42-83 must once have formed a collection that underwent "Elohistic"* revision, the holy name "Jahweh" being replaced by "God" (cf. the duplicates 14 and 53, 40:14-18 and 70). The recent study of the Psalms has been dominated by Gunkel's "form-criticism"*. He tried to establish the "life situations" out of which such productions arose. Comparative study of Oriental, notably Babylonian, psalmody lent much help. There were three primary occasions for such poetic effort—when it was desired to praise, to give thanks, and to lament; out of these situations arose the Hymns, the Songs of Thanksgiving, and the Lamentations. The second and third groups may be either "collective" (i.e., the utterance of a group) or "individual." A number of minor categories stem forth from these. Thus a song in praise of a king is really related to a hymn, and a penitential psalm is only a species of lamentation. There has been some disruption of original patterns in our Psalter. Some poems of a "mixed" nature take on the character of "liturgies". In others the stereotyped forms have been softened because the individual has begun to assert himself and utter his feelings. Ideas not germane to the old cultic situations, such as the "prophetic" or "wisdom" elements, have also crept in. See Olshausen; seven penitential psalms.

James Fleming, *Thirty Psalmists* (1938); R. H. Pfeiffer, *Introduction to the Old Testament* (1941); E. O. W. Oesterley, *A Fresh Approach to the Psalms* (1937).

E.G.K.

Psalms of Solomon, the: A Jewish pseudepigraphic* work, consisting of eighteen poetic compositions, patterned after the biblical psalms, written in Hebrew, in Palestine, about the middle of the first century B.C., and, in general, voicing Pharisaic thought and doctrine. Tradition has mistakenly regarded Solomon* as the author.

J.M.

Psalter: (Lat., *psalterium,* fr. Gk., *psaltērion*) The Book of Psalms, particularly as arranged for use in the Divine Office*, as in the Breviary or the Book of Common Prayer**. P.V.N.

pseudepigrapha: Etymologically, collection of writings fictitiously claiming the authorship of great men of the past. Practically, the non-canonical and non-apocryphal Jewish books written between 200 B.C. and 200 A.D. and dealing mostly with apocalyptic* matter. They include The Book of Jubilees*, c. 135-105 B.C.; The Letter of Aristeas, c. 130-70 B.C.; The Books of Adam and Eve, uncertain date, probably A.D.; The Martyrdom of Isaiah, 1-50 A.D.; The Book (or Books) of Enoch and fragments, the more important of which are The Parables of Enoch (chapters xxxvii-lxxi), c. 94-64 B.C., and The Secrets of Enoch, 1-50 A.D.; The Testaments of the Twelve Patriarchs, c. 109-107 B.C.; The Sibylline Oracles, uncertain dates (second century B.C.; first century A.D.); The Assumption of Moses*, 7-30 A.D.; The Syriac Apocalypse of Baruch or Second Baruch, uncertain date; The Greek Apocalypse of Baruch or Third Baruch, uncertain date; The Fourth Book of Ezra or Second Esdras, first century A.D.; The Psalms of Solomon, uncertain dates, before 70 A.D.; sometimes included are also The Fourth Book of Maccabees, The Story of Akhikar, and Pirke Abhoth or Sayings of the Fathers. See R. H. Charles, *The Apocrypha and Pseudepigrapha of the Old Testament* (1913) vol. ii. See apocrypha; apocalyptic literature; canons of various churches; eschatology; kingdom of God. S.L.T.

pseudepigrapha, New Testament: (From the Greek *pseudepigraphos,* meaning "false or spurious writings") More often called The Apocryphal New Testament, gospels and acts written under the name of apostles. None of our canonical books of this type makes any claim to authorship, though II Peter* might be included under pseudepigrapha. Not all of the apocryphal* gospels are pseudonymous but we might include the Gospel of Peter* and the Gnostic Gospel of Thomas*. The Acts of Paul, of John, and of Peter* belonged to a popular type of religious fiction. (The fullest edition in M. R. James, *The Apocryphal New Testament* (1924); the books are fully described in E. J. Goodspeed, *A History of Early Christian Literature* (1942), Ch. 3-5). The Apostolic Fathers* (as Clement) and the Apologists (as Justin) do not belong in this category. See apocrypha in the N.T. church; canons of various churches; Pilate, Acts of. C.T.C.

pseudepigraphy: The ascription of a writing to some other hand than its real author's. The practice of ascribing all Hebrew laws to Moses, all Psalms to David and all Proverbs to Solomon is a sweeping gesture of pseudepigraphy. The ascription of Hebrews to Paul, as in the King James and English Revised versions, although it is silent as to its writer, is an individual instance. E.J.G.

Pseudo-Dionysius: See Dionysius, the Aeropagite; Neo Platonism; Platonism, "Platonism in the Middle Ages".

pseudo-Isidorian decretals: See canon law; clergy; decretals; False Decretals; Hincmar.

pseudo-Messiahs: The hope for the coming of the Messiah* was continuous among the Jewish people from the time of the loss of their national independence. Critical events in the history of the world, which affected the Jewish community, invariably stimulated messianic anticipations and frequently projected messianic pretenders. The Maccabean wars, the struggle with Rome, the fall of the Temple, the Bar Kochba* uprising, the Perso-Roman wars, the fall of Rome, the rise of Islam, the Crusades, the coming of the Tartars, the expulsions, the Ottoman conquests, the religious wars of the sixteenth and the seventeenth centuries, the Cossack rebellion of 1648, and many other momentous occurrences intensified, each in its time, the messianic hope among the people and precipitated adventist speculations and movements in Israel.

Calculations based upon the Book of Daniel* which seemed to hold the key to the mysteries of "the end of days", as well as other Biblical passages, frequently set the time for these messianic movements.

Prior to the first century B.C., the messianic interest was not great, but the first century, especially the generation before the destruction of the Temple, witnessed a remarkable outburst of messianic emotionalism due, principally, to the popular chronology of the day which indicated that the age* was on the threshold of the Millennium—the year 5000 in the Creation Calendar. Josephus mentions a "false prophet", Theudas, in the procuratorship of Cuspius Fadus (44 C.E.) who was put to death. Numerous false messiahs appeared under the procuratorship of Felix (52-60 C.E.). Mention is also made by Josephus* of an Egyptian prophet, undoubtedly an Egyptian Jew, whose short messianic career brought sharp reprisals upon the Jews (also mentioned in Acts 21.38). The century following the destruction witnessed intense messianic hopes and produced the revolutionary leader, Bar Kochba*, whom many acclaimed as the Messiah. Following the frustration of the messianic hopes in the second century, it was not until the fifth century that another strong resurgence of such hopes occurred. A pseudo-messiah by the name of Moses appeared in Crete. The rise of Islam in the seventh century and the crumbling of the Persian and Byzantine empires again set aflame messianic hopes among the people. This period gives us at least three pseudo-messiahs. Abu Isa al Ispahani in Persia (8c), Serene about the year 720 C.E. and Yudghan of Hamadan, surnamed al-Rai. In the 9th century, there also appeared Eldad Ha-Dani, who though not claiming to be the Messiah, brought reports of the lost Ten Tribes whose restoration was an essential feature of the Messianic saga.

During the period of the Crusades, numerous pseudo-messiahs appeared. In 1121, there appeared a Karaite pseudo-messiah in northern Palestine. In Chazariah, Solomon ben Doudji announced himself as the forerunner of the Messiah, and his son, Menahem, as the Messiah. Maimonides mentions the appearance of false messiahs in Yemen in 1172, in Fez in 1127, in Spain in 1117, and in France in 1087. The most spectacular messiah of this period is David Alroy who appeared among the Babylonian Jews in 1147.

In 1284, in Sicily, Abraham Abulafia announced himself as the Messiah. Two of his disciples, one Samuel called the prophet, in the City of Ayllon, in the Spanish province of Segovia, and the other Abraham, in Avila, in Old Castile continued Abulafia's messianic prophecies and pretensions.

Soon after the terrible persecutions of the Jews in Spain (1391), the Spanish Kabbalist, Moses Botarel, proclaimed himself Messiah in Cisneros (1393). The expulsion of the Jews from Spain in 1492 and the catastrophies which followed brought to the fore a number of pseudo-messiahs. Asher Lämmlein, a German Jew, in 1503, David Reubeni (c. 1490-d. after 1535), who was received by Pope Clement VII, and who aroused great messianic fervor among the people; and Solomon Molko (c. 1500-1532), a Portuguese Marrano who was burned at the stake in Mantua. The foremost messianic pretender of them all, and one who stirred the Jewish world profoundly, was Shabbetai Zebi* (1621-c. 1676) of Smyrna whose advent focused in the miracle years 1648 and 1666. A sect of his followers known as Dönmeh has survived to this day.

After the disastrous Shabbetian movement, there set in a recession in pseudo-messiahs. Official Judaism came to frown upon messianic speculations. A few false messiahs, however, did make their appearance. Prominent among them were Jacob Frank (1726-1791), founder of the Frankists. Of lesser moment were Chaim Malach,

Mordecai Mochiach of Eisenstadt, Judah Chasid and Löbele Prossnitz, all of the 18th century.

A. H. Silver, *Messianic Speculations in Israel* (1927); Julius H. Greenstone, *The Messiah Idea in Jewish History* (1906). A.H.S.

pseudonymity: The literary practice of writing in another's name, as in the Book of Enoch, in Daniel, ch. 7-12, and in Ecclesiastes, which without naming Solomon** speaks in his person. Ephesians, based on all the genuine Pauline letters, probably as an introduction to them when first collected and published, I and II Peter, I and II Timothy and Titus** are N.T. examples. The Gospel of Peter and the Revelation of Peter are also pseudonymous. E.J.G.

psyche: (Greek). 1) Before about the Sixth Century B.C. the religious factor in man; the soul understood to be, in its nature, different in kind from that of non-human powers of nature, such as gods, demons, etc. It is indestructible and eternal, but not immortal: unlike the spirit powers, it experiences death. 2) Later, the religious factor in man, understood to share the same kind of nature as that of a cosmic Zeus, and divinities; the psyche is closely identified with nous, or as nous in man. See nous; soul. F.L.P.

psychiatry: See psychotherapy.

psychical research, societies for: Though the phenomena of apparent telepathy*, clairvoyance, premonitions, etc., have attracted attention since before the dawn of history, organized research into the basis of such occurrences did not begin until past the middle of the nineteenth century. A group of scholars in England established in 1882 a Society for Psychical Research, Henry Sidgwick being its first president, Eleanor Mildred Sidgwick being an active investigator, and Frederic W. H. Myers playing an important role in the gathering of data and the systematization of results.

The Society has published since that date *Proceedings* and a *Journal*. Studies of telepathy have been reported throughout the history of the Society, while from time to time the chief research has been concerned with the phenomena of mediumship, involving the analysis of messages purporting to come from the deceased, and as reported, containing large quantities of material not known to the medium or sitter. Such studies of mediumship were largely in the hands of Dr. Richard Hodgson during the closing years of the nineteenth century and until his death in 1905. Similar investigations have been carried on throughout the present century, notably by Dr. James Hervey Hyslop, Sir Oliver Lodge, Hon. Gerald Balfour, Mrs. W. H. Salter and Rev. C. Drayton Thomas. Since 1920 there has also been much research in clairvoyance and precognition. The alleged physical phenomena of psychical research, though studied now and then, have been subordinated to the mental phenomena.

In 1885 an American Society for Psychical Research was founded, William James* playing an important part. In 1890 this became a branch of the parent society in London. Dr. Hodgson died in 1905 and the American Branch of the English Society was dissolved. The year before this, in 1904, Dr. James Hervey Hyslop founded the American Institute for Scientific Research, the chief concern of which was the study of psychical phenomena, Dr. Hyslop himself doing extensive studies of mediumship until his death in 1920. The name of the corporation was changed in 1922 to the American Society for Psychical Research, Inc. The Society publishes a quarterly *Journal*, and *Proceedings* without a fixed date.

1942—President of the Society for Psychical Research, London—Dr. R. H. Thouless

1942-43—President of the American Society for Psychical Research, Inc.—Dr. George H. Hyslop

From 1925 until his death in 1934 the Boston Society for Psychic Research carried on extensive investigations under the directorship of Dr. Walter Franklin Prince. In 1941 the Boston Society amalgamated with the American Society for Psychical Research, Inc.

There is in France the *Institut Metapsychique International*, founded in 1920. There are similar societies in almost all countries. See parapsychology.

F. W. H. Myers, *Human Personality and Its Survival of Bodily Death* (1903, reprinted in 1939); W. F. (Sir) Barrett, *Psychical Research* (1911); G. N. M. Tyrrell, *Science and Psychical Phenomena* (1939); Pratt, Rhine, Smith and Stuart, with Greenwood, *Extra-Sensory Perception After Sixty Years* (1940). G.M.

psychoanalysis: See Freud; psychology, schools of; psychotherapy.

psychologism: Often defined by the phrase "Idealism as opposed to sensationalism." Used in general to refer to the effort to limit problems of knowledge, value, and being to the data studied by psychology, as, e.g., in the work of J. H. Leuba. The term is used frequently in recent German literature, sometimes to refer to subjectivism, such as that of Franz Brentano*, and, by contrast, the revolt against that feature of Brentano's work by Edmund Husserl.* Ordinarily used to stigmatize the exaggeration of psychology by one's opponent.

Cf. Karl Heim, *Psychologismus oder Anti-Psychologismus* (1910). J.S.B.

psychologists, English school of: A group of clergymen, psychologists, psychotherapists, neurologists and physicians in England and Scotland who, during World War I, almost succeeded in forming a special school of religious and moral psychology based upon a revised Freudianism* with a direct application to morals, Christianity and the shocks of war. The outstanding book of this group was J. A. Hadfield, *Psychology and Morals* (1923). Other writers were: T. W. Pym, C. E. Hudson, E. J. Bicknell, R. S. Moxon, R. H. Thouless, W. M. Mackay, E. R. Micklem, F. R. Barry, William Brown. This unorganized group ("the New Psychology") made much of man's fundamental drives (instincts, instinctive emotions) as the raw material of human behavior and the maladjustment of these nonmoral drives to his social order. Intelligent sublimation and the techniques thereof formed much of the basis of their constructive practical psychology. Original sin* was made distinct from actual sin, the latter being the refusal to moralize inherited drives. Moral disease (organic and functional nervous disorders) is to be distinguished from sin. Sin and guilt, horribly confused terms in theological theory, receive their proper distinctions in moral theory based upon the genetic approach. Later books developed a special interest in a type of psychology aimed to be practical for the use of ministers in the work of the parish and general counselling. See clinical psychology; psychotherapy.

T. W. Pym, *Psychology and the Christian Life* (1922); F. R. Barry, *Christianity and Psychology* (n. d.); C. E. Hudson, *Recent Psychology and the Christian Life* (1923); R. H. Thouless, *An Introduction to the Psychology of Religion* (1923); E. R. Micklem, *Miracles and the New Psychology* (1922). Also see W. M. Horton, *A Psychological Approach to Theology* (1931); V. Ferm, *First Chapters in Religious Philosophy* (1937), p. 159 ff. V.F.

psychology, abnormal: See abnormal psychology.

psychology, clinical: See clinical psychology.

psychology of religion, the: The psychology of religion, originating during the last two decades of the nineteenth century, is the result of the determination to study the facts of religion (a) objectively and factually; (b) critically and scientifically; (c) universally,—not religion just, but the religions,—of persons and peoples; and (d) appreciatively, that is, to apply the factual and experimental findings to the nature and setting in human experience of the *meanings* and *values* of religion which are among the reals by and for which we live.

This new department of study and research has borne rich fruitage in articles and volumes by Coe, Leuba, Pratt, Ames, Thouless, James, Clark, Conklin, Ferm, Josey, Hocking, Seldie, Jones, Inge, Dunlap, Stratton, and many others among the best trained psychologists.

What are the "problems" of the psychology of religion? How are they attacked and with what results? A brief catalogue of a few of them may be the clearest and most concise way of "defining" the nature and temper of this field of thoughtful concern.

The first five of them may, at first flush, feel like more of the metaphysics, or theology, or philosophy, from which the *psychology* of religion, which ventures to be "scientific," has broken away. Empiricism, however, must keep clear its orientations. "Science" that has become self-sufficient,—is it not like the spoiled child severing the apron strings that have bound it to its mother?

1. *Man Viewing the Majesty of the Universe and His Place Therein.* Psychology interweaving with all the other sciences tries to gain perspective. Where are we and what are we,—this *genus homo,*—in the total scheme of things?

We are residents of a big,—or little,—planet, the Earth, which, with eight other planets, is held captive in its repetitious circuit around the sun. We designate the time required for the journey, "a year." "Our" sun, so bright and hot because it is so near,—only 93,000,000 miles,—seen from afar, would look like a star. In fact, it *is* a star,—one of billions of others, that playing their game together, form our "stellar system" or "star cluster." Then, beyond our stellar system there are at least a hundred million other such systems, separated from each other, on the average, by a distance of two million light years. And light travels pretty fast,—186,000 miles per second. In total picture, we live in an observed and computed universe at least a thousand million "light *years*" across.

What is man that he should parade his little conceits? They and the petty deities he has forsooth created to gratify his trivial desires might well sublimate themselves into simplicity and adoration, so that he could respond heartfully to Walt Whitman: "And I say to any man or woman, let your soul stand cool and composed before a million universes."

2. *Man as a Psychic Entity.* No longer is it needful to affirm that man is *basically* a *body* which possesses attributes of mentality. Physics, chemistry, physiology and other sciences, working together, have arrived at an *"energy concept of matter."* Every atom of the stuff of which sticks and stones and stars and the flesh and bone of our bodies is composed is a dramatic center of pulsing energies, not necessarily different in kind from those energies that would grasp the sticks, hurl the stones, admire the stars and manipulate the body. Materialism in the old-fashioned sense has hardly a devotee amongst those of academic distinction. Perceptions and ideas, as also their objects, are abstractions *from* realities and it will remain a fascinating problem in each and every case the extent to which they are abstractions *of* elements in relatively abiding reals. The escape from rude factualities may lead even to an enrichment of meanings and values. Thus the joys of Christmas time may be enriched for the child and the spirit of worship enhanced for the grown-up when Santa Claus for the one and absentee deities for the other are treated *symbolically.* Both may be fitting events on the highway leading to the temples of Beauty and Devotion. It may not be straining a point or belaboring a truth to assume that we are spirit and live in and by and for a world of meaning and values, whose real reality is indubitable.

3. *Man as Resident of a Planet that is Pregnant with LIFE.* In the earliest stages of earth history, as soon as temperature, terrain and assemblages of biochemical elements were congenial,—there arose, spontaneously, the *living* cells. These cells could divide,—and thus multiply. Many of them colonized,—by twos, and fours and more, into simple organisms. Life, pulsing, pushing, moving on, hit upon many devices for release. One of the most fortuitous of these was

the discovery of masculinity and femininity. Through the union of basically similar but complementary pairs of cells,—ova and spermatozoa—, it was possible to shake out or shell out, in a big way, eccentricities, or variants, upon which "selection" could operate while watching the "fittest" creatures survive.

Life pressing on! An organism with myriads of cells in cooperation, and becoming highly integrated. A dozen or so special senses sensitive to needed adjustments within and without the body. A central nervous system for coordinating all of them in the interests of fuller life. Awareness and self-direction ripening into choice and thoughtfulness. Anticipations developing into idealisms.

There were always devices for the *deepening* of life and of lives, and binding them into the totality of Life. One of the mightiest of these is the law of *recapitulation**. Each individual must start, in the egg or womb, as a single cell and repeat in its individual career the myriads of centuries of earth history. The species is thus deepened and enriched and all species share something of the common life of the plant kingdom and of the entire animal kingdom.

4. *The Perfection of Childhood.* Development and evolution can, with the aid of selection, become anticipatory. The child, at birth and after, bears so many indications of its superiority, when viewed comparatively in the human scale of perfections, that one stands in admiration and wonder in its presence. Among these marks are: largeness of head as compared with size of body; hairlessness; shortness of jaw; fewness of teeth; texture of skin; fineness of feature; grace of movement; quality of voice; sensitiveness of social responses; fullness and roundness of mental and somatic integrations; radiance of facial expressiveness. A sort of "Heaven lies about him" and is incarnate within him.

He usually stumbles out of this Heaven of perfection into a rude world of specificities and jobs; and duties; and social and institutional compulsions; and teachers trained in quantity production of definite knowledges and skills.

He *may* enter, in the teens or later—the chances are against it—another Paradise of the dramatic, higher cultures of the race, incarnate.

Is it not possible, through right culture and training, to build the racial highway, straight and sure, from the Paradise of Childhood into the land of the All-pervading Beauty and the Righteousness of an adult world?

Should humanity not worship constantly at the sacred shrines, not of *a* child, but of *the* child!

5. *Religion as a Symphony of Urges, or Drives, or Instincts or Native Tendencies, and of their Affective Qualities.* We do, in a way, during foetal life and after, clamber up the biological tree. We travel the racial highway. Not only do we share basic structures and metabolisms of the various creatures all the way from the inception of life to the present, but are inheritors of the tones and overtones, the motifs and melodies of feeling and valuation that express themselves, on occasion, in every organism. We hunt names for these mechanisms or devices. In the caption just above we have been content to sling four names at them, knowing that not one of them is satisfactory.

As we start the list of "instincts" or "urges" or "native tendencies," with their feelingful qualities, we are coming into immediacy with the red blood of human experiences,—the pure gold of valuation, which it is the function of religion to try to release, to idealize and to glorify. Among these are: self-preservation, "the first law of life"; fear, leading to caution, and if all goes well, may be "the beginning of wisdom"; mating, that guarantees the continuity of life and does ripen into ideal Love, "the fulfillment of the law"; anger, the raw stuff out of which resentment at injustice is made, and culminating sometimes in "righteous indignation" and "holy wars"; hunger, when disciplined and rightly used, may be an element in righteousness; sociality, that may bind the many into a blessed fellowship; ownership, with its scores of fruitages, good and bad, when discreetly seasoned may lead to "treasures in Heaven"; enjoyment of simple Beauty, blossoming into appreciation, admiration and adoration; the Ego, maturing into the joys of high leadership; the sense of melody and harmony interfusing and glorifying all of life's relationships.

It would be possible to extend greatly the catalogue of basic urges and drives and their ramifications which it is the function of education, art and religion to cultivate and glorify. William James* was inclined to think it possible to list profitably a score or perhaps a half hundred of them.

The game of rightly interpreting the basic drives has perhaps been delayed slightly by persons with a desire for simplification. All persons with a monistic propensity can speak and write truly, if not adequately, for the reason that *all* the urges or drives interfuse to such an extent that a strain or coloring from a favorite "instinct" *is* found in *every* impulse and response.

We venture to return to the analogy of the *Symphony* of urges and of valuations. Each person carries in his thought and heart those themes and motifs that make now and progressively for the fullest and most satisfying living. Each, in a small or great way, is an orchestral conductor, in home or playground or church or school or business house or laboratory or congress, in some phase of the music of humanity that gives fresh release to Life.

6. *Periodicities in Religious Development.* The fact that religious maturing is eventful rather than evenly continuous is indicated by many researches. There are, for example, the studies by Starbuck, Coe and others on the age of conversion*. The instances appear sparsely at ages 8 to 10. The curve of frequency rises at 11 and 12, declines for both sexes at 13, swings upward sharply at 15 to 17, near the period of pubescence, declines abruptly into the early twenties, after a

definite bit of an increment at 18-19, and pretty much disappears after that age. As evidence that these eccentricities are not accidental is the fact that the pattern of the age curve of frequencies was very similar for each of the eleven quite diverse groups that together built up the picture for the 1250 cases that were studied in that particular research. The sex-theorists can, of course, extract quite a blessing out of the coincidence of pubescence and the main peak of the conversion curves. They will have some difficulties with the phenomena of "sanctification" (Starbuck, *Psychology of Religion,* Chap. XXIX), the story of many converts who, after a lapse of a decade or so (only one of the cases studied was short of 10 yards), with ups and downs and difficulties, move on into "a second experience" in which "the service of God is a constant delight," "far exceeding in depth and fullness the first blessing." (Page 384).

It is rather characteristic of religious geniuses to be disrespectful of conventional types of religiosity and of modal curves of frequency. Mrs. Jonathan Edwards entered suddenly her deep and lasting religious career at the age of eight. Tolstoi's most dramatic revolution of values was in his middle years and he was in the midst of a still more challenging soul-reach as his career was coming to a close.

7. *The Center of Gravity of the Religious Personality.* The religious attitudes, convictions and behaviors that count for most in the personal life and in the human drama have their sources, for most part, in the intimate, inner *feelings of meaning and worth and values* rather than in rational constructs and conceptualized forms and patterns of thinking,—just as is true in friendships, in love relations, artistic participations—and in scientific achievements and discoveries. We suffer from our sentiments of rationality. We think that we think. By actual testing there is little ground for the conviction.

Only latterly (one or two or three decades), have students of structures and functions of the organism begun to appreciate fully the fact that we have two nervous systems: the *central* nervous system with its cerebral cortex, cerebellum, spinal cord, spinal ganglia and efferent nerves in control of the striped or striated musculature; and another nervous system, the *autonomic,* or sympathetic, consisting of the hypothalamus, basal ganglia, and substations in the vital organs of the body, busy with the control of the smooth muscle tissue that regulates circulation, digestion, reproduction, metabolisms, secretions and the activities of a dozen sets of glands, and is in control of the vital functions. The autonomic is older biologically and doubtless more basic in feeling out the intricacies of right adjustments and adaptations.

The heart, consisting of both striated and smooth muscle tissue, stands between the central nervous system and the autonomic as the sensitized determiner of needs and aspirations.

Those who edited the Bible appealed to the things of the heart more than 60 times, always with warmth. The word "belief" occurs less than half as frequently, and often unsympathetically. "The devils also believed."

8. *Lower-Sense Imagery in Religious Meanings and Values.* Since sight and hearing present to the mind *definable* data that are readily perceived and shared, the custom arose of designating them the "higher" senses, leaving the other eight (or more), taste, touch, smell, temperature, pain, equilibrium, kinaesthetic and organic—as the "lower." There has been a lag in appreciating generally the fact that in capturing specific *meanings* and *values* in appreciated experiences and then in words, the lower do not suffer in the comparison. That fact led the graduate pupils of the writer of these lines to attempt to rate the work-value or worth or meaning-significance of all the words or phrases in favorite selections of literature, like the 23rd Psalm or the "Blow, blow" of Shakespeare. The report on sample instances is in Volume I of *The Journal of Religion.* In total picture, the kinaesthetic and organic imagery values essentially match those of sight and hearing, with the other six falling much lower, but always significant. We proposed to make a new designation and classification, calling the two,—the visual and auditional,—the "defining sensory processes" and the other eight the "intimate sensory processes." In religious observances not one of the ten types of imagery has been slighted. In literature the success of the artist seems to correlate positively with his ability to thrum the subtler end of the imagery scale.

9. *The Imagination, the Light and the Life of the Mind.* It is the imagination rather than ideation and reason that releases values. It is delicate, with wings like those of a fairy. It emancipates the mind from the thraldom of things. It gives orientation, perspective, knowledge, wisdom.

10. *Intelligence, Thought, Reason, as the Stabilizers of Life.* It is ours to know that, within limits, truth is inviolable. Two and two make four. The law of falling bodies works. To be a vertebrate with a straight spine and not molluscan. To find in the shifting sands of time a hut and dwell therein. To find a friend, forever and a day. To walk straight with steady step towards the greater Temple of Wisdom and Beauty and Righteousness.

See psychologists, English school of.

E. S. Ames, *The Psychology of Religious Experience* (1910); W. E. Bingham, "A Study of the Relations which the Galvanic Skin Response and Sensory Reference Bear to Judgments of the Meaningfulness, Significance and Importance of 72 Words" in *Journal of Psychology* (1943), 16, 21-34; George A. Coe, *Motives of Men* (1928); Elmer T. Clark, *The Psychology of Religious Awakening* (1929); E. S. Conklin, *Psychology of Religious Adjustment* (1929); G. B. Cutten, *Instincts and Religion* (1940); John Dewey, *A Common Faith* (1934); Knight Dunlap, *Mysticism, Freudianism and Scientific Psychology* (1930); J. M. Evvard, "Is the Appetite of Swine a Reliable Indication of Physiological Needs?" *Proceedings of the Iowa Academy of Sciences,* vol. XXII (1915); V. T. A. Ferm, *Religion in Transition* (London, 1937); Ruth Griffiths, *A Study of Imagination in Early Childhood* (London, 1935); P. R. Hightower, "Biblical Information in Relation to Character and Conduct." *University of Iowa Studies in Character,* vol. III, No. 2; W. R. Inge, *God and the Astron-*

omers (1933); W. E. Hocking, *Living Religions and a World Faith* (1940); William James, *Varieties of Religious Experience* (reprint, 1938); W. L. Jones, *Psychological Study of Religious Conversion* (1937); C. C. Josey, *The Psychology of Religion* (1927); Richard Kroner, *The Religious Function of Imagination* (1941); B. C. Leeming, *Imagination, Mind's Dominant Power* (1926); James H. Leuba, *A Psychological Study of Religion* (1912); E. M. Ligon, *Their Future is Now* (1940); E. L. Mudge, "The Lower-Sense Complexes Conditioning the God-Experience." Summarized in following citation: E. D. Starbuck, "The Intimate Senses as Sources of Wisdom", *Journal of Religion*, vol. I, pp. 129-145 (1921); J. B. Pratt, *The Religious Consciousness* (reprint, 1930); *Research Publications*, vol. XX. The Hypothalamus and Central Levels of Autonomic Function (1940); *Research Publications*, vol. XXI. The Diseases of the Basal Ganglia (1942); A. A. Roback, *Psychology of Character* (London, 1927); W. B. Selbie, *The Psychology of Religion* (1929); Edwin D. Starbuck, "The Intimate Senses as Sources of Wisdom", *Journal of Religion*, vol. I, pp. 129-145 (1921); *The Psychology of Religion* (1899); K. R. Stolz, *Psychology of Religious Living* (1937); G. M. Stratton, *Psychology of the Religious Life* (2nd ed.); L. P. Thorpe, *Psychological Foundations of Personality* (1938); R. H. Thouless, *Introduction to the Psychology of Religion* (1936); John B. Watson, *Kinaesthetic and Organic Sensations: Their Role in the Reactions of the White Mice to the Maze* (1907); Henry N. Wieman, *Normative Psychology of Religion* (1935). E.D.S.

psychology, schools of: Groups into which psychologists may be classified on the basis of their leanings toward one or another general conception of psychology. Members of a school agree in general, though not necessarily in detail, on such topics as the definition of the subject matter, approved and preferred methods of research, significant problems, general organization and interpretation of the body of factual material. A system of psychology usually consists of the organized tenets of a school, but may represent the views of only one person. At present schools are not organized groups and systems are regarded as working hypotheses. Many psychologists neither adhere to a school nor subscribe to a system.

Schools have centered about the following points of view.

Rational psychology: A speculative treatment of the soul as contrasted with empirical and experimental psychology. Typical problems concern the unity, immortality, and powers of the soul. It characterizes scholastic thought and parts of Aristotle's psychology.

Faculty psychology: A system which, classifying mental performances into groups, explains them by mental powers or faculties assumed to correspond to those groups,—e.g., a faculty of reason explains judgment and inference. It is characteristic of scholastic thought. A typical representative is Christian Wolff (1679-1754)*.

Associationism: The theory that all mental formations are reducible to elements (simple ideas, sensations) variously and lawfully associated. Laws of association (similarity and contiguity) were first stated by Aristotle, but associationism as a comprehensive system was the work chiefly of a succession of British writers of the seventeenth, eighteenth and nineteenth centuries: Hobbes, Locke, Berkeley, Hume, Hartley, J. Mill, J. S. Mill, and Bain. Associationism is noteworthy as an empirical psychology which preceded experimental psychology.

Herbartianism: A system proposed by J. F. Herbart (1776-1841)* who, unlike the associationists, emphasized the dynamic relations among ideas. Ideas, inhibiting and otherwise influencing each other, strive singly and in groups to rise to consciousness and repel competing ideas. The apperceiving mass, the ideas already present in the mind, determine to what extent and in what manner new ideas are received and incorporated into knowledge. The conception of the apperceiving mass was influential for a time in educational theory and practice. Herbart believed mental processes capable of quantitative, but not experimental treatment. He opposed faculty psychology.

Wundtian psychology: The system formulated by Wilhelm Wundt (1832-1920)* founder of the first psychological laboratory (Leipzig, 1879). Consciousness is accepted as the subject matter of psychology, experimentally controlled introspection as its distinctive method. Consciousness is conceived as analyzable into elementary processes (sensation, affection, image) which, combined in various ways (fusion, assimilation, complication, etc.), give the more complex forms of consciousness. The system is sometimes called *Existentialism* to characterize its subject matter as sensibly experienced, sometimes *Content Psychology* in contrast with *Act Psychology*, and sometimes (in America) *Structuralism* in contrast with *Functionalism*. Its chief representative in America was E. B. Titchener (1867-1927).

Act psychology: A system formulated by Wundt's contemporary, Franz Brentano (1838-1917)* who recognized in the subject matter of psychology mental acts in addition to contents—e.g., the act of sensing red, as well as the sensational content red. His distinctive method is phenomenological observation as contrasted with experiment and experimentally controlled introspection. The system is called empirical in traditional contrast with Wundt's experimental psychology. Among its adherents were Lipps, Stumpf, Witasek, Husserl, Messer, and Kulpe, each of whom introduced modifications.

Functionalism: A point of view widely and informally adopted which, as represented by John Dewey (1859-) and J. R. Angell (1869-) became the rallying point of an American school opposing the Wundtian tradition. It was greatly influenced by William James (1842-1910)* himself not identified with any school. Functionalists study psychological processes not primarily as conscious contents, but as activities having utility in the organism's adjustments to its environment. Bodily activities,—e.g., motor learning and other adjustments—are included in the subject matter of psychology. Introspection, though not rejected, is not regarded as central; objective methods are emphasized. In America Ladd, Baldwin, and Carr, in Europe Höffding, Ward and Stout were among those who adopted a functionalistic standpoint.

Behaviorism: A system advanced in America by J. B. Watson (1878-) who wholly rejecting consciousness and introspection as unsuitable to scientific treatment, regards psychology as the study of behavior by objective methods exclusively. Watson treats psychological events—i.e., behavior—as reducible to the action of stimulus-response mechanisms variously combined and conditioned. The role of conditioning (learning) is emphasized, that of heredity minimized. Instincts are denied. Many variants of behaviorism have arisen, among them E. C. Tolman's (1886-) *Purposive Behaviorism* which studies behavior not as a composition of minute or 'molecular' stimulus-response mechanisms, but as 'molar' wholes or behavior acts from which immanent determinants such as purposes and cognitions are inferred, not introspectively observed.

Gestalt psychology: A theory advanced by M. Wertheimer (1880-), W. Kohler (1887-) and K. Koffka (1886-1941) who deny that psychological processes, whether behavioral or conscious, are explicable as elements in association. The central concept is the gestalt or organized whole, which if analyzed loses its distinctive properties. The gestalt-principle, originally utilized in explaining perceptual phenomena, has been extended throughout psychology, and by Kohler into biology and physics. Gestalten differ from the form-qualities recognized by certain act psychologists in that form qualities are conceived as based on fundaments which are themselves elements. Kurt Lewin's *Topological and Vectorial Psychology*, a variant of Gestalt Psychology, emphasizes problems of action and motivation utilizing topology for mathematical representation of its concepts. Gestaltists utilize both objective and introspective (phenomenological) methods, characteristically arranging conditions which permit experimentation on wholes and their properties.

Hormic psychology: The theory of William McDougall (1871-1938) that human behavior, essentially purposive, is basically determined by inherited psycho-physical dispositions called instincts. Seven primary instincts (pugnacity, flight, curiosity, repulsion, self-assertion, self-abasement, the parental instinct) each paired with a primary emotion, are the prime movers of human activity, including the intellectual, and are the major determinants of social customs and institutions.

Psychologies deriving from psychoanalysis: Psychoanalysis, developed by Sigmund Freud (1856-1939)* was designed to relieve neurotic patients by bringing to consciousness their unconscious motivation. Freud originally conceived the human personality as organized about two poles, a superficial conscious self (ego) in conflict with a vast, powerful unconscious (libido) the seat of primitive urges, mainly sexual. These, repressed but active, achieve indirect expression, circumventing or overcoming the ego's resistances through numerous devices. Conflicts in infancy and childhood largely determine the adult personality pattern. Freud's later works picture a more complexly organized personality centered about an unconscious Id, a perceptive Ego, and the Superego or conscience, the individual's unconscious morality. Many variants of Freud's system have arisen. C. G. Jung's (1875-)* *Analytic Psychology* differs from Freud's teachings in placing less emphasis on sex, and more on present conflict as compared with infantile and childhood experiences. A. Adler's (1870-1937)* *Individual Psychology* traces personality disturbances to feelings of inferiority which may express themselves in various forms of overcompensation.

Personalistic psychologies: Systems that regard the proper subject matter of psychology as the whole, concrete, individual person. W. Stern (1871-1938) defines his immediate subject matter as experience 'in its matrix, the unitary goal-seeking person'. G. W. Allport (1897-) emphasizing the uniqueness of the individual personality, seeks general laws which account for uniqueness. The *Verstehungspsychologie*, of W. Dilthey (1833-1911)* a student of biography and E. Spranger (1882-)* aims at a description of the total personality based on an understanding which transcends scientific explanation. See psychologists, English school of.

R. S. Woodworth, *Contemporary Schools of Psychology* (1931); E. Heidbreder, *Seven Psychologies* (1933); E. G. Boring, *History of Experimental Psychology* (1929, 3rd printing, 1935); G. Murphy, *A Historical Introduction to Modern Psychology* (1929, 2nd ed. 1932); G. S. Brett, *A History of Psychology*, vol. I (1912); vol. II (1921); vol. III (1921); C. Murchison (ed.), *Psychologies of 1925* (1925); *Psychologies of 1930* (1930); F. S. Keller, *The Definition of Psychology* (1937).

EDN.H.

psychology, systems of: See psychology, schools of.

psychopathology: See abnormal psychology.

psychotherapy: (Gr. *psyche*—mind; *therapeia*, cure) The attempt to heal or cure by means of personal conferences with the patient. As distinguished from psychiatry it is not limited to the more severe disorders, and where psychiatry includes all that has to do with the more serious disorders of the personality, psychotherapy is limited to the realm of psychic influence. The term is strictly a medical one. Among religious workers the common equivalent is "personal counseling."

Two major types of psychotherapy may be distinguished: those which rely primarily upon suggestion, and those which seek to discover and correct the fundamental maladjustments and to enable the patient to achieve some degree of autonomy and maturity.

The first of these may be designated as "faith-healing." It is the type which has prevailed among religious workers. It takes the patient as he is, making little or no attempt to discover the roots of his difficulty, and directs his attention to comforting and constructive thoughts through prayer, devotional books and friendly advice. It would do the church serious injustice not to recognize that much good sense has been brought to bear by individual workers and that rather generally a great deal of stress has been placed upon facing the facts, squaring accounts and correcting misunderstandings. It remains true however that among religious workers anything in the nature of a co-operative attempt to organize and test their insights and techniques of treatment has been practically absent. In such forms as Christian Science* suggestion is even carried to the point of denying the reality of evil and pain and asserting the absolute omnipotence of Mind and Love and Truth. The results secured at religious revivals in the years gone by have been due very largely to the influence of suggestion, so also the cures effected at such shrines as Lourdes and Ste. Anne de Beaupré.

Among medical men faith-healing has been represented in its more dramatic form by the use of hypnosis. Among the great pioneers in the therapeutic use of hypnosis was the French physician, Charcot, the teacher of Freud* and of Janet. Of recent years the use of deep hypnosis has been limited. The tendency among those who use hypnosis at all is merely to give suggestions while the patient is in a relaxed condition, or under light hypnosis. It is also used sparingly for exploratory purposes. The disfavor into which hypnotic therapy has now fallen is due to the view that results secured with its help, while often striking, are not permanent. They are suggestions imposed from without and tend therefore to weaken the patient's will.

An interesting method which lies half way between the faith-healing type and the exploratory type is that of moral re-education as practiced by the Swiss physician, Dr. Dubois at the beginning of the present century. In this country the re-education plan has been associated chiefly with the name of Dr. Riggs of Stockbridge, Mass.

The form of psychotherapy now most in the public eye is psychoanalysis. This in its aims is the antithesis of faith-healing. It has often been compared by its proponents to surgery, and major surgery at that. It is the attempt to lay bare and bring into clear consciousness the disowned instinctual desires which, it assumes, have become detached from the conscious self and are responsible for the neurotic symptoms. Its aim is to make over the harsh conscience and the rigid standards which constitute one of the factors in the inner conflict.

Great stress was at the beginning laid upon "catharsis." Cure was effected, so it was thought, by getting the poisons out of the system and bringing the difficulty into clear awareness. It is now recognized that socialization is the important factor. Cure is only effected in so far as the sufferer tells his real difficulties to some one whom he trusts, some one who stands for him as the prototype of the father and the representative of authority, and who is yet able to hear the worst without condemning him. He thus gets rid of the "sense of guilt" which is the primary evil in all mental illness.

Psycho-analysis has had a profound influence not only in the field of psychiatry but also in psychiatry and sociology* and that influence has extended into literature and into popular thought. It has not been without its effects upon religious thinking, especially in the field of the psychology of religion*.

Psychoanalysis is represented today by a number of variant schools. In addition to orthodox psychoanalysis as taught and practiced by Sigmund Freud, the great Viennese physician, we have the followers of Jung, of Adler** and of Rank, all of them heretical students of Freud.

Mention should be made of "psychobiology", a school of psychiatry developed in this country under the leadership of Adolf Meyer. This school explains mental illness in terms of the total organism reacting to a difficult environmental situation and it seeks to effect cure by making all necessary inner and outer adjustments.

See mental hygiene; psychologists, English school of.

S. Freud, *General Introduction to Psychoanalysis* (1920); also *An Autobiographical Study* (1927); C. G. Jung, *Two Essays on Analytical Psychology* (1928); Otto Rank, *Will Therapy* (1936); Pierre Janet, *Principles of Psychotherapy* (1924); Paul Dubois, *The Psychic Treatment of Nervous Disorders* (1909).

A.T.B.

Ptah: The Egyptian creator; worshiped at Memphis as far back as Manetho's first dynasty. His statue is in the form of a mummy, but he was not primarily a god of the underworld. P.G.M.

Ptolemaic astronomy: For fourteen centuries the leading theory of the movements of heavenly bodies, until Copernicus, Kepler, and Newton** constructed a superior one. Claudius Ptolemaeus (fl. in Alexandria, 127-151) held that each of the bodies, other than the earth, in the solar system moved in a small circle or "epicycle" whose center moved in a large circle around the earth. The theory was fitted to the new facts which became known during the Middle Ages by complicated additions of epicycles—or epi-epicycles. Thus the axioms, the earth does not move, and the heavenly motions are circular (this being the most perfect form of curve), could nominally be retained. Ptolemy had the merit of attempting to find mathematical order in nature, and thus he carried out the first part of the Whiteheadian injunction, "Seek simplicity, and then mistrust it;" the Arabians accumulated facts which showed that the simplicity was deceptive; and Copernicus achieved a new simplicity which, having been distrusted by Kepler, gave way to still a newer and subtler one —and so on.

C. Ptolemaeus, *Syntaxis* (Heiberg's ed. of the astronomical works of Ptolemy, 1899-1907); A. Berry, *Short History of Astronomy* (1898); Sir Wm. Smith's *Dictionary of Gk. and Rom. Biog.* (1849).

C.H.

public honesty, marital impediment of: See marital impediments.

public law: See law.

publican: A tax farmer. In the ancient world taxes were collected not by state officials but by private individuals employed for the purpose, who profited by any excess they could extract from the people. That a publican could be honest was regarded as impossible. B.S.E.

publication, early Christian: The multiplication of copies of works of literature for sale was a familiar feature of life in the Graeco-Roman world in the first century. They were not of course printed, but they were published and sold through numerous book sellers, in all the great cities of the empire. Martial, a contemporary of Luke, gives us vivid pictures of authors, publishers and bookstores in Rome. The great libraries, especially that of Alexandria*, numbered their books, that is, papyrus rolls, by the hundreds of thousands. Every large house in those times had its library, and in one of these, destroyed in the eruption of Vesuvius in A.D. 79, were found the remains of eight hundred books.

Christianity very soon began to express itself in writing, in Greek, at first in the letters of Paul, not meant for publication and for a generation left unpublished. The Gospel of Mark* was the first Christian book of which we have any knowledge, and it was soon followed by the Gospel of Matthew*, a carefully organized and edited expansion of it. A decade later, Luke's* work on Christian Beginnings in two volumes, with a prefaoe and dedication, and some account of its sources and the occasion of its composition, carried Christian publication a definite stage further. It was probably its picture of Paul, the most vivid and graphic ever produced, that stimulated some Pauline Christian to search out and collect such letters of Paul as could be found, and publish them, prefacing them with a general letter to all believers, which has come down to us as Ephesians*. The Pauline letters* would form two ordinary Greek rolls, as Luke's work had done. It was reflected almost immediately in the letter corpus that begins the book of Revelation*, a book addressed to the churches of Asia, and carefully safeguarded against alteration by the most solemn warnings, 22:18, 19. The writer evidently expected the book to be copied and circulated. I Peter*, an encyclical from the Roman church to the Christians of all Asia Minor, followed almost immediately, aiming to correct some attitudes taken in the Revelation not only in Asia but all through the adjacent provinces which the Revelation would naturally reach. Its address "to those who are scattered as foreigners over Pontus, Galatia, Cappadocia, Asia, and Bithynia" obviously implies publication; how else could they be reached? Hebrews and I Clement** are other examples of Christian literary activity and publication from this fruitful time. All these books after Luke-Acts, show the stimulating influence of the collected Pauline letters upon Christian publication.

Early in the second century the Gospel of John* presented the Christian gospel in a form more acceptable to Greek minds, and showed the influence of Paul's letters and of the earlier gospels. Half dialogue in form, it was unmistakably meant for publication and was very soon republished together with the earlier local gospels in a great quartette, the twenty-first chapter being added. This second great collection of Christian writings, reflected in the Gospel of Peter, Papias, the British Museum Gospel, the Letter of the Apostles, Justin, and II Peter**, was a great achievement of publication, and may have necessitated the adoption of the leaf book in place of the ancient and usual roll form; certainly the leaf book was in use among Christian publishers by the middle of the second century (the Rylands John fragment) and was preferred by Christians from that time on, though pagan publishers came to it more slowly.

The fourfold gospel was not only the climax of Christian publication, but has never been surpassed, and still remains the most popular and influential published unit in the world. Just as the N.T. is the cutting edge of the Bible, the Four Gospels are the cutting edge of the N.T. A score of private gospels followed, and Christian publication was on its fruitful way. Letters, revelations, acts (Christian novels), apologies, dialogues, hymns, homilies, memoirs, polemics, fill the second century. Christianity swiftly adopted virtually all the contemporary techniques of Greek literature and developed others of its own. Its swift and complete adoption of the art of publication was not the least of the factors in its extraordinary progress.

See E. J. Goodspeed, *Christianity Goes to Press* (1940); *A History of Early Christian Literature* (1942). E.J.G.

pūjā: Worship, cult, in India. Puja is performed daily in every devout Hindu home sometimes by a priest, most frequently by the householder, but in the temples it is the Brahmin* priests who perform it. It takes many different forms according to the sect of the worshiper and the occasion. C.S.B.

Pullus, Robert: (died 1150) Although not an original mind, he was particularly instrumental in the development of the doctrine of repentance.* He stressed the significance of the inner processes preceding full contrition and made liberation from sin dependent upon a sacramental process.

Migne 186: *Sententiarum libri octo;* P. Schmoll, *Die Busslehre der Frühscholastik* (München, 1909). H.H.

pulpit: (Lat., *pulpitum,* staging or platform) An elevated preaching stand, usually on the Gospel side of the chancel*. In Protestant churches, till recent times, usually in the center of the chancel. In these churches often a desk on a platform, from which the service is conducted and the sermon preached. See mimbar. F.T.P.

punishment: See rewards and punishments; penology.

Purānas: A collection of 18 books of religious poems which constitute the real scriptures of Hindu popular religion. They are the sources of popular belief concerning the origin of things, the world, time, the gods, the Vedas. They contain some ancient material, but in their present form come from probably later than the fourth century of the Christian era. They are the bases of sectarian teaching, each of them being made use of by some one or more of the sects as its book of origins, thus the Vishnu Purāna is a Vishnavite document.

J. N. Farquhar, *Outline of the Religious Literature of India* (1920). C.S.B.

Pure Land School: See Buddhist Terminology.

purgation: See purification.

Purgatorial Societies: Confraternities* of the Church having for their main purpose to assist in every possible way the poor souls in purgatory*. The historical origin of these societies can be found in the prayers for the dead* in the most ancient liturgy of the Church; their radical cause is Christian charity for one's neighbor which extends even beyond the grave; and their basis is found in the doctrine concerning purgatory, the condition of the poor souls after death, the communion of saints, and the satisfactory value of good works. The best known of these societies in modern times is the Archconfraternity of Prayer for the Poor Souls of Purgatory which was founded by the Brief of May 25, 1898 of Pope Leo XIII*. T.T.M.

purgatory: In Catholic teaching, purgatory is a condition of temporal punishment after death for venial sins* and as satisfaction for sins. Definitions of faith at the Councils of Florence and Trent*, received by the Roman Catholic Church, say that there is a purgatory and that the offerings of prayer and especially of the Mass* aid souls there. Aquinas and Bonaventure**, following S. Gregory, hold the punishment to be both absence from God and burning by fire (*poena damni* and *poena sensus*), although the description was not upheld at Florence against the Greeks. Temporal periods are of a duration different from earthly time; thus, the times mentioned in indulgences* are the heavenly equivalent of what would have been a suitable earthly penance (cf. penance) that was commuted into prayer. The protest of Luther and others against materialistic forms of this teaching has resulted in little teaching on the intermediate state* in Protestantism, and in the cautions of Trent against speculative curiosities.

The Orthodox Church, although it does not use the word, and the Anglican Church, which has recently paid more attention to the belief, both hold doctrines that involve the purification of souls in their progress to final bliss and the efficacy of prayers for the departed. See prayers for the dead; Sabbatine privilege. T.J.B.

purification (Lat., *purificatio*) In general, beginning at the primitive level, any process designed to remove the uncleanness resulting from the violation of a tabu* or from the failure properly to care for such critical events as death, child birth, puberty, marriage, or illness. The demand for such ceremonial cleansing of the affected person or persons rises out of the solidarity of the group and is rooted in the belief that individual impurity may have dreadful and far-reaching social consequences, such as, bad luck, crop failure, widespread death or illness. The forms of purification vary greatly in different societies but commonly involve some medium of cleansing, such as water, blood, change of garments, etc., and some ceremonial rite. At the higher religious levels, the term purification is used to denote any of various disciplines or rituals for the moral or spiritual cleansing of the inner life from sin. See blood; death and burial practices; Lupercalia. E.T.R.

Purim: The name (explained in Esth. 9.24 f. as "lots") of a Jewish festival celebrated on Adar 14-15 traditionally as a memorial of the escape of the Jews of Persia from the machinations of Haman. The ritual of the festival includes the reading of the scroll of Esther*. S.H.B.

Puritan ethics: Essentially a religion of action, rather than of contemplation, Puritanism* stressed the virtues of sobriety, honesty, and thrift. An outstanding element was moral fervor, which is shown in Edward Dering's rebuking Queen Elizabeth and in William Prynne's attacks on bishops and theatres, and which gave to Puritanism a dogged strength and vigor. Otherworldly as it was, its emphasis upon the practical virtues, according to such writers as Max Weber, fostered the rise of capitalism*, although later writers, such as R. H. Tawney, declare this view is an over-simplification. Richard's Baxter's* *A Christian Directory* contains the best summary of Puritan ethics.

N. M. Knappen, *Tudor Puritanism* (1939); William Haller, *The Rise of Puritanism* (1938). E.W.K.

Puritanism: The doctrine of the Puritans, a sect originally so-called because 1) they wished to purify English protestantism by removing all traces of Roman Catholic forms and ceremonies. Puritan thinking was largely dependent upon Continental Protestant predecessors. It emphasized 2) the Bible instead of tradition or reason as the chief source of authority. Though its early leaders were influenced by Lutheran ideas these were thrown off by 1550 and eventually 3) Puritan theology became almost purely Calvinist. Puritanism also represented 4) a protest against the Erastianism* of the established church and an unwillingness to see the reform program limited by royal opposition or indifference. In this form it can be traced back as far as the time of Tyndale*, who in 1524 went to Germany, in defiance of a royal statute, to translate the Bible into English. To the extent that it championed the rights of the church as against the secular authority state and believed in the doctrine of the two swords* Puritanism was in substantial agreement with the medieval Catholic tradition, and from the same source it drew its well-known 5) emphasis on strict morality. The Puritan protest against the theatre, card-playing, and dancing may be traced back to medieval monasticism, and Puritan Sabbatarianism has a similar medieval origin.

The first generation of Puritan leaders espoused no particular form of 6) church government, and throughout the history of the movement some Puritans continued to accept the established church with its episcopalianism. After the Anglican bishops under Elizabeth began to enforce the conservative vestiarian rules of the establishment, however, the majority of the Puritans became critical of government by bishops and began to champion presbyterianism*. Since presbyterianism involved regional and national assemblies which could not operate effectively without a change of national policy, in the 1580's a minority of the Puritans who had abandoned episcopalianism* began to agitate for reform "without tarrying for any" and so came to advocate independency or congregationalism. This permitted of a fully reformed church establishment as soon as a small group of Puritans could be gathered together. Since these extremists thus organized their own bodies and left the established they were also known as Separatists*, though at a later time some Independents recognized the Anglican communion as genuinely Christian and thus came to be known as non-Separatist Independents. John Smith*, leader of a Separatist congregation which went to Holland in 1608, there adopted the practice of adult baptism. Some of his followers returned to England and organized the first Baptist church there. Perhaps because the Baptists* were distinctly a minority sect they were pioneers in developing the idea of genuine religious toleration and the complete separation of church and state.

The Puritan movement naturally allied itself with the opposition to the Stuart kings and with the meeting of the Long Parliament (1640) and the outbreak of the Civil War (1642) it became a powerful political force. After a period of enforced cooperation the cleavage between Presbyterian and Independent Puritans became pronounced. From 1643 to 1648 the Presbyterians predominated and during this period the Westminster Assembly held its sessions and produced the Confession of Faith and the Larger and Shorter Catechisms**. Cromwell* was an Independent, however, and after his rise to power Presbyterianism, though tolerated, was forced to yield precedence to its younger rival. After the Restoration of the Stuarts and the adoption of the so-called Clarendon code both types of Puritanism became illegal and thereafter Puritanism was generally known as Dissent and Puritans as Dissenters* because of their refusal to conform to the rites of the officially established church.

New England was largely settled by Independent Puritans. Those who came to Plymouth Bay in 1620 were moderate Separatists, sometimes called semi-Separatists, while Massachusetts Bay and Connecticut—the major New England colonies—were founded by non-Separatists. In the settlement of Rhode Island, however, the Baptists played a prominent part. See American theology, early; Bible, English; Puritan ethics; Sabbatarianism, Puritan. Cf. covenant (or federal) theology; Marprelate Tracts.

M. M. Knappen, *Tudor Puritanism* (1939); William Haller, *The Rise of Puritanism* (1938); Perry Miller, *The New England Mind* (1939). M.M.K.

purohita: The domestic priest of a king or noble in Vedic times. Often served as adviser not alone on spiritual matters, but on temporal affairs as well. In later times only the *purohita* could officiate at a sacrifice for the king. C.S.B.

purpose, divine: See analogy; cause; God; teleology; teleological argument for God.

purposive behaviorism: See psychology, schools of.

purusha: Rig Veda X, 90, the hymn to Purusha is said to be the "starting point of the pantheistic philosophy of India". Purusha, or Cosmic Man, sacrificed by the gods becomes the origin of all things. Thus all that is constitutes a unity. There is but one basic world-ground. This tendency ultimately triumphed over the trend toward monotheism represented in Prajāpati*. In the Sankhya* system *purusha* means the individual soul, an infinite number of which exist entirely distinct from matter, *prakriti** and act upon it. C.S.B.

Pūsan, Pūshan: One of the lesser sun gods of Vedic Hinduism, probably introduced by some pastoral tribe. His car is drawn by goats. He is a shepherd and the protector of flocks. Also he is the lord of paths or the pathfinder. His aid is sought in the search for lost objects. C.S.B.

Pusey, Edward Bouverie: (1800-1882) Professor of Hebrew at Oxford from 1828 and a leader in the Oxford Movement* from 1836; his prominence as Anglo-Catholic* scholar and controversialist led to the popular terms Puseyite and Puseyism. E.R.H.

Pyrrhonism: Extreme skepticism*. Named from Pyrrho of Elis (fl. 300 B.C.), who believed that one should refrain from all dogmatic assertions since perceptions often mislead and much may be said for each side in any argument. No value judgments are necessary. Hence, suspension of judgment (*epoche*) is indicated on every matter of belief; apathy or peace of mind (*ataraxia*) was the goal of life for him, as for certain Stoics. J.E.N.

Pythagoreanism: Reputed founder, Pythagoras of Samos, c. 6th century B.C., headed a school and brotherhood in Southern Italy, both vegetarian and esoteric. Traveled widely, collected learning and was revered by disciples who tended to immortalize him. From him comes the famous dictum *ipse dixit.*

Pythagoreanism held that the soul* was timeless, changeless, self-existing and at intervals found itself imprisoned within successive bodies without being any part of them. Through life and death it retained full memory of experiences of earthly incarnations. If he did not think of it in a tripartite relation as some claim, soul was quite certainly regarded as a double principle—hot and cold. Also, this school of thought advocated the eternal repetition of everything, and there is a report that the cycle was ended somtimes by fire and sometimes by water. Another basic principle of Pythagoreanism was that numbers are things. That is to say that the nature of reality is number. This, of course, should not be understood to mean Arabic or Roman numbers, but gnomic or forms. The tetraktys of the dekad seems to have been the integral notion of the Pythagorean theory of number. The tetraktys was considered sacred and divine, the influence of which idea has come down to us in manifold forms of numerology. Pythagoreans were supposed to have prayed to the holy tetraktys, possibly representative of the four elements, earth, air, fire and water. The principle of number was applied to music. By experimenting with an instrument with a string and moveable bridge, Pythagoras discovered the relationship of the tones in the tetrachord to certain definite proportions, thus laying the numerical foundations of musical harmony, which continued as a subject of study in Oxford University down into the 18th century. In medicine also the number principle was employed. The body, like the string of a musical instrument, is tuned to a certain pitch and proper atunement is health.

Pythagoras' conception of number, form, was influential on Plato's thinking. It was more abstract than Milesian thought, more imaginative than that of the Eleatics and more distinct than that held by the Heraclitans**. See neo-Pythagoreanism; transmigration. P.R.H.

pyx: (Gr. *puxis,* a box) The box or case or tabernacle in which the Host* is reserved. F.T.P.

Q

Q: Abbreviation for Quelle, "source"; symbol used for a supposed source of the Synoptic Gospels*, postulated by many scholars to explain the presence in Matthew and Luke of *common* material not contained in Mark. Some would assign to it the *peculiar* material of Matthew and Luke as well. It is an adjunct of the two-document hypothesis, which formerly explained the resemblances of Matthew and Luke by the use of Mark and the Logia of Matthew; but now explains them by the use of Mark and Q. See logia. E.J.G.

Qadarites: (From Arabic *qadar,* power) The Moslem name for those who believe that man has freedom and power to act independently, not subject in all things to the absolute predestination of God. This view was also held by the *Mutazilites**. P.E.J.

qadi: A Moslem official appointed to decide religious duties and interpret laws such as inheritance and marriage. P.E.J.

Qarmatians: See Ismailis. P.E.J.

Quadragesima: (Lat., *fortieth.* Cf. Fr. *carême*) The official Roman Catholic term for the Lenten season of forty days from Ash Wednesday* to the eve of Easter. See church year cycle; Lent. P.V.N.

Quadratus: A Christian apologist* of the early 2nd century whose "Apology," now lost, was presented to Hadrian at Athens in A.D. 125 or 129. S.M.G.

Quakers: According to the Journal of George Fox* (Cent. Ed., I: 4) it "was Justice Gervase Bennett of Derby that first called us Quakers because we bid him tremble at the word of God, and this was in the year 1650." The name, first used in scorn, at once became popular. The proper name of Quakers is the Religious Society of Friends. See Society of Friends. Also see Lee, Mother Ann. W.W.C.

Quartodecimans: (Lat., adherents of the fourteenth) A name given by the later Church to Christians in the 2nd century, chiefly in Asia Minor, who held that Easter* should be observed on the day of the Jewish Passover* celebration, the 14th day of the moon following the vernal equinox, whatever day of the week that might be. S.M.G.

Quesnel, Pasquier : (1634-1719) French religious writer, b. Paris; d. Amsterdam. After joining the Congregation of the Oratory*, his writings fell under the condemnation of Clement XI because of their strong impregnation with the doctrines of Baius and the Jansenists**. Expelled from the Congregation of the Oratory in 1864, Quesnel published numerous works in Belgium under assumed names. Arrested in 1703, he fled to Holland where he continued his work. He sought and received reconciliation with the Roman Catholic Church before his death. See Unigenitus (Bull of 1713). J.F.T.

Quetzalcoatl: (Aztec) Wind god; creator of men; god of the waning moon; 'feathered snake' god; counterpart of the god Tezcatlipoca*. F.L.P.

Quicun(m)que: (Athanasian Creed*) A creed which contains in short definite affirmations and negations the Catholic teaching on the Trinity and the Incarnation. Erroneously attributed to St. Athanasius* of Alexandria, the creed was composed at a later period and originally in Latin. Various authors have been suggested. It was first cited by Caesarius of Arles*. See creeds of Christendom. E.A.R.

quidditas: Scholastic term, synonymous with the word "essence". Quidditas is derived from the Latin form of the Aristotelian definition of essence: *"To ti en einai"*, *"quod quid est"*. Quiddity is that by which a thing is what it is, both logically and ontologically. In the first case, quiddity gives us the logical definition of a thing; in the second, its physical essence. S.C.T.

Quietism: A 17th century group of mystics which held to a pessimistic doctrine of human nature and the correlative doctrine of the need for and the fact of divine initiative in man's salvation. God may act on man only as he surrenders himself utterly. Pure faith is beyond ideas and beliefs; pure love is without a love of any particular thing but a love for love's sake. Absolute calm unmixed with self ambition is the true receptive mind for divine grace. Rufus Jones calls this movement "the most acute stage of European mysticism." Among the conspicuous representatives were: Molinos, Michel; Guyon, Madame; Fénelon; and Bourignon, Mme. Antoinette**. V.F.

Quillian Lectureship, The: Established at Emory University, Georgia, in 1897 by the Rev. W. F. Quillian. The capital sum is about $7,500. The lecturers are free to choose their topics "within the range of apologetical, doctrinal, exegetical, pastoral, or historical theological subjects." The course is given annually. A few of the lecturers: Bishop Charles B. Galloway, Dr. H. F. Rall, Dr. Ralph W. Sockman, Dr. Edwin Lewis and Dr. Y. C. Yang.

(Data from the office of the Dean of Candler School of Theology.) V.F.

Quimby, Phineas P.: See New Thought movement. Also see Christian Science.

Quinisext Council: See Constantinople, Councils of.

Quinquagesima: The first Sunday before Lent or the seventh before Easter. See church-year cycle. E.R.H.

Quran: See Koran. P.E.J.

Qutb: (Arabic) In Islam, leading saint; prominent spiritual being with a special abode or abodes and special activities among men on earth; has ability, under Allah, to do unusual things. F.L.P.

R

R: See redaction.

rabbi: The Hebrew for master which became a title of ordination for authoritative teachers of Judaism in the period after the destruction of the Temple in 70 C.E. B.Z.B.

rabbinism: (Rabbinic Judaism) (Hebrew *rab,* or *rabbi* -master) The religious discipline by which the teachers of post-Biblical (O.T.) Judaism implemented Biblical (O.T.) religion to the needs of their day. Cf. Akiba; Hillel; midrash; Mishnah; Talmud. B.Z.B.

racial psychology: See anthropology; culture epochs.

Radbertus, Paschasius: (?-died after 856) Abbot of Corbie, 842-852. The most learned Frankish theologian of the century. His famous work, *De corpore et sanguine Domini,* the first devoted exclusively to that subject, clarified the doctrine of transubstantiation* as a miracle produced by the words of consecration. His formulation eventually became the dogma of the church, though meeting with the instant protest of contemporaries, Rabanus Maurus, John Scotus Eriugena, and especially a fellow monk, Ratramnus**. A.C.

ragnarok: (Teut.) In the Teutonic cosmogony, the end of the present condition of the world, marked by a struggle between the gods and the giants, and the overthrow of evil; to be followed by a new age of righteousness in a new earth. F.L.P.

Raikes Sunday School in America: See Sunday School movement in the United States.

Rainy, Robert: (1826-1906) Ordained minister in the Free Church of Scotland, 1851; became Professor of Church History in the New College, Edinburgh, 1863, and Principal in 1874. He was the outstanding churchman in his denomination, swaying its General Assemblies by his superb oratory, and leading it by word and pen towards greater openness of mind and to union with the United Presbyterian Church*. His best known books were *The Delivery and Development of Christian Doctrine* (1874) and *The Ancient Catholic Church* (1902). See Carnegie Simpson, *The Life of Rainy.* A.K.R.

rākshas: Demons in Hinduism*. In Rigveda VII, 104, Indra is besought to destroy the rakshas or demons "that flourish in the dark". It is Ravana the Raksha who in the Ramayana* abducts Sita and carries her away to his capital. C.S.B.

Ram Mohan Roy: (1772-1833) Best known as the founder of the Brahma Samaj* Ram Mohan Roy is frequently called the father of New India, and is sometimes credited with being the founder of the study of comparative religions. Certain it is that he was one of the earliest students of comparative religion having studied Islam, Hinduism, and Christianity, all in the original languages. He was greatly influenced by Islam toward monotheism, and became a staunch theist. His first book, written in Persian was definitely deistic in tone. He thought that he found a basis for his theism in the Upanishads which he translated from the Sanskrit and published. Studying the Bible he was greatly attracted by Jesus. He wrote in 1817 that he had "found the doctrines of Christ more conducive to moral principles, and more adapted for the use of rational beings than any other which have come to my knowledge." He recommended a book which he published, *The Precepts of Jesus* as "the guide to peace and happiness". He undertook to translate the gospels into Bengali, but this apparently was not completed. He aided in the establishing of a Unitarian mission in Calcutta, and at one time declared his own religious position to be that of Unitarian Christianity. In the Brahma Samaj which he founded in 1828 he made central the non-idolatrous worship of one god, but drew most of the liturgy from Hindu sources. An innovation was the introduction of congregational worship. The moral reforms which he, and later the Brahma Samaj, undertook derived largely from the Christian ethic.

Ram Mohan Roy played a prominent part in the introduction of western education into India and was one of the first distinguished Indians to visit England. He died there in 1833.

Sophia Dobs Collett, *Life and Letters of Rajah Rammohun Roy* (1914); Manilal C. Parekh, *Rajarshi Ram Mohan Roy* (Rajkot, Kathiawad, India, 1927). C.S.B.

Rāma, Ram: Hero of the Indian epic, the Rāmayana*. He became one of the chief avatars of Vishnu* and next to Krishna is the most popularly worshiped deity of the Vishnuite* sect. Like Krishna* he is a gracious savior deity to those who in loving trust (bhakti) yield themselves to him. See salvation, Hindu. C.S.B.

Ramadan: The ninth month of the year in the Moslem lunar calendar, during which the faithful keep a strict fast in the daylight hours. Only the sick and soldiers are exempt. By this observance the first revelation of the Koran* is commemorated. It has value only to those who perform it willingly, seeking reward from God alone. See fasting. P.E.J.

Rāmakrishna: (1836-1886) A remarkable Indian mystic, who in the latter half of the 19th century attracted many disciples from all ranks of Hindu society and became the founder of the Ramakrishna mission, or as known in the west the Vedanta* Society. He is regarded as an incarnation of divinity and worshiped by his followers. He was a Hindu, but eclectic in his thought. He experimented with various faiths including Islam and Christianity and professed to arrive by all of them at *Samadhi**, the goal of God-consciousness. As a result, he taught as do his followers that all paths lead to God. It was Vivekānanda*, a brilliant, highly educated, high caste follower who was the organizer of the movement and founder of the Vedanta societies in the western world.

The Memoirs of Ramakrishna (Calcutta, 1939, Revision of the older *Gospel of Ramakrishna*, N. Y., 1907); Max Muller, *Ramakrishna, His Life and Sayings* (1898); Romain Rolland, *Prophets of the New India* (1930). C.S.B.

Rāmānanda: (b. 1299) Originally a Vishnuite of the same school of Ramanuja* with whose philosophy he was in agreement, he founded a new sect now called the Ramanandis, and indirectly exercised a profound influence over the whole subsequent religious life of Northern India. Both Kabir and Nanak, and much later the poet Tulasi Dasa, were deeply influenced by his spirit and teaching. His major emphases were upon bhakti or devotion to God (Rama*) and the brotherhood of the servants of God without respect to caste. C.S.B.

Ramanuja: (b. 1027 A.D.) Author, like Shankara*, of a commentary on the Vedanta-Sutras, he takes sharp issue with the unqualified monism of Shankara. The phenomenal world and individual souls so far from being illusory, he contends, constitute the body of Brahman*. Within the impersonal divine unity he makes place for the Supreme personal spirit and thus provides a philosophical and theological basis for the theistic worship of Vishnu* and his incarnations. Salvation, or emancipation from rebirth, is achieved through love and devotion to the Lord, and does not consist in the complete loss of individuality, but in a continued existence of eternal bliss in the presence of the Lord (Vishnu) when the bonds of rebirth are broken. C.S.B.

Rāmāyana: The shorter of the two great epics of India. It tells the story of prince Rama* who, because of the intrigue of the jealous mother of a rival half-brother was exiled for fourteen years in the forest. Here Sita, his ever faithful wife was abducted by a wicked demon and carried away to Ceylon. Unable himself to find her he was aided in his search by his friend Hanuman, the monkey, who was successful in his search and after an epic struggle restored her to her husband. To prove her faithfulness she submitted to an ordeal, but refusing his later demand for a second test she disappeared into the earth in a furrow. Reputedly the epic is the work of the poet Valmiki, but to critical scholarship it shows the marks of multiple authorship. It has exerted an enormous influence on Indian life. Rama, Sita and Hanuman have long since become deified, Rama being one of the chief avatars of Vishnu* is an exceedingly popular object of devotion and worship.

Translated in part by Romesh Dutt, *The Rāmāyana and Mahābharata* (London, 1926). The entire poem is translated by Ralph T. H. Griffith, *The Rāmāyana of Valmiki* (London, 1870-1874), 5 volumes. C.S.B.

Ramman: See Adad.

ransom theory: See atonement in Christianity; redemption; satisfaction.

Ranters, the: A nickname given to a rather chaotic and ill-defined seventeenth-century movement, antinomian*, spiritualistic, and individualistic, which sought to reproduce in England the principles and practices (especially the psychic phenomena) of the primitive church. F.G.E.

Rappites: (Harmonists) See communistic settlements, religious.

Ras Shamra: See Ugaritic tablets.

Rashdall, Hastings: (1858-1924) British philosopher and theologian, best known for his *Theory of Good and Evil* (1907), in which in a position he named "Ideal Utilitarianism", he reconciled features taken from the Idealism of T. H. Green* with others taken from the Utilitarianism* of Henry Sidgwick*; e.g., he affirmed with the former the intrinsic value of character as an end in itself, and with the latter the evaluation of actions by their consequences. In metaphysics Rashdall was a Personal Idealist, and in theology he believed in a limited God. W.K.W.

Rashi: Abbreviation of Rabbi Solomon Itzhaki (1040-1105), of Troyes, France, leading rabbinic* commentator of the Bible and most of the tractatates of the Babylonian Talmud*. S.S.C.

Rashnu: The Zoroastrian* spirit of truth (hence his title Razista, "truest"), who with Mithra and Sraosha* judges the departed; he weighs their deeds in the balance; he is invoked at the performance of an ordeal; criminals cannot escape him; Yasht* 12 is in his honor. R.H.P.

Ratio Studiorum: (*Ratio atque Institutio Studiorum Societatis Iesu*, 1599) The educational code of the early Jesuits*. Based on a half century of experience, it also reflects some of the ideals and practices of the Dutch humanistic schools and of the University of Paris, and remained in force until 1773. E.A.R.

rational psychology: See psychology, schools of.

rationalism: (Lat., *ratio*, reason) The doctrine of the supremacy of reason.

In philosophy, it means 1) the deductive (Cartesian, mathematical) method of drawing logical inferences from elementary concepts (intuitions, axioms, innate or apriori truths), as opposed to the empirical method; or 2) the doctrine (opposed to sensationalism) that reason is a higher source of knowledge, independent of sense (when Locke* said that "there is nothing in the intellect that was not first in sense," Leibniz* added "except the intellect itself); or 3) the appeal to coherent thought (as opposed to irrationalism) as criterion of truth. Rationalism in all three senses has often been friendly to a spiritual and religious view of life; for example, Descartes, Leibniz, Hegel**.

In theology, it means the theory that reason is the judge of all supposed revelations. It subordinates "dogmatic theology to the dictates of reason and conscience" (Lecky, *History of Rationalism*, I, 16). It assumes two forms, the first primarily anti-authoritarian, and often called liberalism or modernism (see liberal theology); the second, primarily anti-supernaturalistic, and tending toward humanism, free-thinking, and agnosticism. Failure to specify the exact meaning intended has led to many misunderstandings. See reason in religion. E.S.B.

rationalism, ethical: 1) Moral principles can be apprehended by intuition and rational deduction, without need of empirical confirmation, or appeal to theological authority. In this sense, Spinoza, Kant, and Hegel are rationalists. 2) All systems, whether emphasizing reason or experience, which regard ethics as a science in its own right, independent of revelation and theology. In this sense, most non-Catholic moral philosophers since Shaftesbury have been rationalists. Catholic writers believe that a large portion of morality can thus be treated and so come under Moral Philosophy, but that this subject must be subordinated to Moral Theology. W.K.W.

Ratramnus: (fl. ca. 850) Gottschalk's* friend. Charles the Bald, to whom Radbertus* dedicated his work, requested Ratramnus' opinion. Rejecting Radbertus' literalistic interpretation, Ratramnus explained the Eucharist as a mystery, with a great difference between Christ's body and the Host, which was a figure of believers as well as of Christ. A.C.

Rauh, Frederic: (1861-1909) He was the most interesting representative of moral philosophy and psychology in France during the last quarter of the 19th century. Having radically broken with the metaphysical and religious enthusiasm of his earlier years, the experimental science of the laboratory was for him the model of the moralist. He defended with great energy the rights of the individual against society, the rights of personal character and of the creator of morality.

Essai sur le fondement métaphysique de la morale (Paris, 1890); *De la méthode dans la psychologie de sentiments* (Paris, 1899); *Psychologie appliquée a la morale et l'éducation* (Paris, 1900); *De l'experience morale* (Paris, 1903). H.H.

Rauschenbusch, Walter: (1861-1918) Studied in Germany, at University of Rochester and Rochester Theological Seminary. Pastor Second German Baptist Church, New York City, 1886-1897. Editor *Jugend Herold*, 1892-1896. Translator of Gospel Hymns into German. Author of *Leben Jesu* (1895) and three other books in German. Taught at German Baptist Theological Seminary, 1897-1902. Professor Church History at Rochester Theological Seminary, 1903-1918. Lecturer on various American foundations. Author of *Christianity and the Social Crisis* (1907); *Christianizing the Social Order* (1912); and a *Theology for the Social Gospel* (1917). See social gospel. C.H.M.

Rauschenbusch Memorial Lectureship, The: Founded in memory of Walter Rauschenbusch* in 1929 through an initial gift of $10,000 by Mrs. Edmund Lyon of Rochester, N. Y. and subsequent gifts by Alumni and friends of the Colgate-Rochester Divinity School. The general field of the lectureship is Christianity in its social expression and application. Four lectures are given each year under the auspices of the Colgate-Rochester Divinity School and are subsequently published in enlarged form. The Revd. Justin Wroe Nixon of the Brick Presbyterian Church, Rochester, N. Y. inaugurated the series in 1931, speaking upon, *The Moral Crisis in Christianity*. C.H.M.

Rauwenhoff, Ludwig Wilhelm Ernst: (1828-1889) Professor at the University of Leyden. The supersensible is not a subject of science; but faith in it is a postulate of the practical law in us. Religion does not consist in the mere conviction of the existence of a higher power, but is the consciousness of a personal relation to this power. The essence of religion is the feeling of respect or esteem. The religious ideas about God are inventions or fabrications of creative phantasy.

Religionsphilosophie (Braunschweig, 1894) 2nd ed.; O. Pfleiderer, "Die religionsphilosophische Weltanschauung von Rauwenhoff und Martineau", *Jahrbücher f. protestantische Theologie* (Braunschweig, 1890) vol. XVI; R. Schultze, *Kritik der Religionstheorie Rauwenhoffs* (Erlangen, 1898). H.H.

Re: (Egyptian) Sun god in the religion of the priests of Heliopolis; in the Empire, there was a fusion of Re with Amon, god of Thebes, as Amon-Re, a more powerful Amon which led Egyptians against the foreigners. F.L.P.

real presence: The doctrine that Jesus Christ is truly present in the Holy Eucharist*, under the sacramental species of bread and wine. The view is held with certain differences by Eastern Orthodox, Roman Catholic, Anglican and Lutheran communions.

The Eastern Churches do not closely define the mode of the presence, but speak of it as real, and secured by "metabolism" of some type. In the Roman Church, the doctrine of transubstantiation* is held; in Lutheran circles, consubstantiation* is held (see Lutheran doctrine of the Lord's Supper). The Anglican Church like the Eastern does not define the method of presence, but asserts it to be "spiritual" but real.

In classical Catholic theology, the term is used with two significations: *praesentia realis* and *praesentia rei.* The former indicates a true or genuine presence of Jesus Christ, body and soul, God and man, in the elements; the latter, that the presence is *of the thing* (namely, the body and blood of Christ), thereby distinguishing the Eucharistic sacrament from other sacraments which possess matter, form, intention, minister and benefit, but not the *res sacramenti* (which is the body and blood of Christ).

In recent years, Anglican theologians particularly have endeavoured to re-state the doctrine of the real presence; typical examples are W. Spens and A. E. Taylor in *The Eucharist* (London, 1930); and O. C. Quick, *The Christian Sacraments* (London, 1934). See impanation; Lord's supper; remanence. Cf. Corpus Christi. W.N.P.

realism: (Lat., *res,* thing; *realis,* real) 1) In epistemology*, the theory that the objects of knowledge exist outside the mind and independently of it. Realism is thus opposed to and by modern, subjective idealism, solipsism, etc. However the ultra-realism or *extreme realism* of Plato* and his followers is similar to objective idealism or absolutism. For such ultra-realists, universals, i.e., abstract ideas or concepts have an existence outside the mind, as universals. (See universals, battle over.) The first definition above describes the position of Aristotle, Aquinas and perhaps the majority of the philosophers. It is sometimes designated *moderate realism.*

A distinction is made between direct or presentative realism and indirect or representative realism. According to the latter, the mind knows objective reality or things only through the intermediacy or agency of some representation, picture or symbol. This view requires the invocation of the principle of causality to escape subjectivism or idealism.

Two American schools of realism appeared in the twentieth century with the labels Neo-realism* and Critical Realism*.

2) In social philosophy, realism signifies a practical point of view in contradistinction to a visionary, utopian outlook.

Realism is frequently though not necessarily associated with a materialistic metaphysic and with a scientific or empiricistic attitude. See nominalism; conceptualism. D.C.O'G.

realism, epistemological: See epistemology.

realism, moral: The view that at least the highest moral standards, ideals, or values, like love and justice, are objectively valid and independent of human knowledge or realization, though man has an affinity for them. The moral standard is nowhere to be found in natural processes and cannot be derived by empirical generalization from human experience. Such realism is the nerve of the moral argument for God as found in thinkers like J. Martineau, A. S. Pringle-Pattison, H. Rashdall, A. E. Taylor, and W. R. Sorley.**

Moral realism in essence simply asserts a transcendental realm of values complementary to and worthy of existential realization. The exact status of the real (e.g., subsistence, or existence in God) is an additional problem. Moral realism is usually accompanied by epistemological realism which claims direct, unmediated knowledge of moral values independent of the knower. See God (moral argument). P.A.B.

reality: (Med. Lat., *realitas,* thinghood, from Lat. *res,* thing) 1) Thinghood; the essence of a thing or an existent, as such. 2) Empirical reality; any item or organization of experience; usually referred to organized sense experience (it is a Kantian category), but often applied to other experiences, such as the moral and religious. 3) Metaphysical (or ontological) reality: the permanent, ultimate, objective source of experience, whether conceived as first cause (scholasticism), or productive activity (Berkeley, Leibniz, Lotze, Bowne, Bergson); or any set of entities and principles which explain the ongoing of the universe (Whitehead). 4) As viewed by Hegel* and many other idealists, reality is the total object to which thought refers; in this sense, reality is what we think about when we think adequately (coherently). E.S.B.

reason in religion: There have been three main views among Christians regarding the relations of reason and religion. 1) They are in complete harmony, their content is identical. Reason sets forth logically what religion feels and practices; Justin Martyr, John Scotus Eriugena, and Hegel** defend this position from different points of view. 2) They are consistent, but religion (faith, Biblical revelation) transcends reason without contradicting it. This is the view of St. Thomas Aquinas, John Locke**, and most moderate conservatives. 3) They are, at least partially, in conflict. The so-called doctrine of the double truth* (the acceptance of which by anyone is questioned by Gilson) arises from this conflict. Those who hold this view declare that every proposition of reason and of faith must be accepted as true, each in its own realm, regardless of contradictions between them. Tertullian (*credo quia absurdum,* I believe because it is absurd), Averroës, Duns Scotus, William of Occam (what is philosophically true may be theologically false), Martin Luther, and Thomas Hobbes**, all inclined to this view. It was often sustained sincerely in order to exalt the transcendent otherness of God (*totaliter aliter,* totally other); sometimes cynically, as by P.

Bayle*, who, tongue in cheek, wrote in his *Dictionary* that the more irrational the truths of faith, the more meritorious it is to believe them.

The conflict between reason and religion, fateful as its consequences have been, is far from being settled. In the gospels there is hardly any trace of it. Jesus make his appeal to experience, both inner (the Beatitudes) and outer ("by their fruits"), and also to reason in the sense of logical thought ("Why even of yourselves judge ye not what is right?" Lk. 12:57). Nowhere does he suggest that his gospel conflicts with reason. Paul*, after his great psalm on love (I Cor. 13), writes a psalm on reason (I Cor. 14): "I will pray with the spirit, and I will pray with the understanding also . . . I had rather speak five words with my understanding . . . than ten thousand words in an unknown tongue." When in Col. 2:8 Paul coupled philosophy with vain deceit, he does not repudiate reason but simply attacks the esoteric "philosophy" of the Essenes*. Nevertheless, this passage, with I Cor. 1:22-23, encouraged Tertullian and others to stigmatize all philosophy as a source of heresy, although the Alexandrians (Clement, Origen**) viewed Greek philosophy as a preparation for the gospel. St. Thomas accepted Aristotle as "the philosopher" and supplemented reason (Aristotle) with revelation (Scripture), which added to reason without contradicting it.

During the Enlightenment*, abstract reason crowded out revelation and vital religion, until the revivals of J. Wesley and J. Edwards**. In the nineteenth century, Hegel held that religion and philosophy set forth the same truth from different points of view. Kierkegaard* protested against reason and systematization in religion in favor of the subjective, the individual, and the "existential." The rise of romanticism, Nietzsche's irrationalism, and recent neosupernaturalism among men like Karl Barth, Emil Brunner**, and Reinhold Niebuhr, have challenged the rights of reason in religion. The cause of reason has been defended in various ways by philosophers of religion and theologians like H. Rashdall, W. R. Sorley, A. S. Pringle-Pattison, and F. R. Tennant** in Great Britain, and by W. E. Hocking, A. C. Knudson, J. S. Bixler, W. M. Urban, H. N. Wieman, E. W. Lyman, John Bennett, and others in America. The philosophy of instrumentalism (John Dewey) rejects both the claims of revelation and the usual conception of reason.

Grounds for disparagement of reason in religion are: 1) the need for simplicity and universal appeal (to "the serving-maids of Ephesus," Harnack*), as against the technical and aristocratic nature of philosophy; 2) the need for fixed authority in the church for disciplinary purposes; 3) the need for Christian unity as against the diversity of philosophies; 4) the claims of divine revelation as against the supposed pride of reason (R. Niebuhr); 5) the impossibility of attaining complete rationality (rational investigation an "infinite task", Kant); 6) the conviction that mystery and irrationality (the "numinous,"* R. Otto*) are marks of the divine.

In support of the place of reason in religion are the following considerations: 1) God is truth, and reason is unbiassed search for truth; 2) truth cannot be self-contradictory or incoherent; 3) there is no way to test rival revelation-claims, within or without the Bible, other than appeal to reason; 4) blind, unreasoning faith is a violation of the integrity of personality; 5) reason and faith need each other ("there is no knowledge without faith nor faith without knowledge," Clem. Alex., *Strom.*, II, 373); 6) reason is a humble search for truth, not proud self-assertion; 7) reason always deals with experienced revelations of reality which reason alone could not create; 8) the inexhaustibility of the task of reason is in harmony with faith in immortality and with the kinship of the soul with God; 9) it is not reasonable for God or man to expect any individual to penetrate further into philosophy than he is able—but reason should be followed to the extent of one's ability; 10) without some true ideas, there can be neither ethics nor religion.

See faith; liberal theology; philosophy of religion; rationalism; revelation.

See E. Gilson, *Reason and Revelation in the Middle Ages* (1938); J. S. Bixler, *Religion for Free Minds* (1939); H. R. Mackintosh, *Types of Modern Theology* (1937); A. C. Knudson, *The Validity of Religious Experience* (1937); E. S. Brightman, *A Philosophy of Religion* (1940). Art., "Philosophy" in Smith's *Dictionary of the Bible.* E.S.B.

recapitulation: 1) (In theology) The doctrine of Irenaeus*, a second-century churchman, that Christ went through (recapitulated) the successive stages of human life, from infancy onwards, becoming what we are "that He might make us completely what He is."

2) (In education) The theory that the individual human organism repeats in its own growth the successive stages of the race's development. See culture epochs; psychology of religion. F.G.E.

receptionism: See Lord's supper.

Rechabites: An ascetic group in Judaism, traditionally regarded as descendants of Jonadab, son of Rechab; they abstained from the use of wine, from building or living in permanent houses, and from cultivating the ground—apparently as a protest against the settled life of Israel after the conquest of Canaan. They are described in Jer. 35: 1-19. See asceticism; temperance movement. M.S.E.

recluse: A popular term for one withdrawing from the world, especially for the purpose of more complete, religious dedication. It is correctly used in the technical sense when applied to hermits*, particularly monks and nuns who are privileged by their bishops to undertake permanent seclusion in their cells. See anchorite; asceticism; monasticism. R.C.P.

reconciliation: (*katallasso*, to reconcile, Rom. 5: 10; I Cor. 7: 11; 2 Cor. 5: 18, 19, 20; *katallage*, reconciliation, Rom. 5: 11; 11: 15; 2 Cor. 5: 18, 19) Reconciliation in its general meaning is the effecting or restoration of unity or harmony where harmony ought to be, but where estrangement or conflict is the present fact. The connection in Christian theology is with the inner estrangement depicted in Rom. 7: 14-25, or the separation of men from God on account of sin. Reconciliation is the abolishing of this separation. A major issue is that of the relation of reconciliation to the work of Christ. It can be held that as man by his sinful disobedience severed himself from God, so Christ by His sinless life and perfect obedience unto death healed the breach or paved the way for man's restoration. Or it is nearer to the Church's general belief to say that on the Cross Christ met the full onset of God's reaction against sin and broke the entail of sin in the life of man. For those who accept the deliverance thus wrought, the barrier between man and God is removed. The question comes whether reconciliation is from man's side only; our fathers used to sing, My God is reconciled. The more modern view is thought to have sanction in Paul's words in 2 Cor. 5: 19; the reconciling work of Christ was equally the work of God. Yet the revival by Aulen and others of the Patristic or "Classical" doctrine of the Atonement*, and deeper reflection on what sin means to God and His judgment upon it, are today making us ask again if it is not necessary for the full meaning of Redemption* that God be both Reconciler and Reconciled. Reconciliation is variously related to Forgiveness and Regeneration**, perhaps it is conceived most simply as the relationship to God with resultant inner peace which these others create and establish. Many theologians distinguish Reconciliation from Redemption, as the condition we may enter upon here from that the fulness of which we can only hope for and await while in the present life. See salvation; wrath of God.

J. Denney, *The Christian Doctrine of Reconciliation* (1917); G. Aulen, *Christus Victor* (1937); Vincent Taylor, *Forgiveness and Reconciliation* (1941).

J.L.

reconciliation: (cancellation of interdict, etc.) 1) An episcopal act by which the ecclesiastical censure of interdict** is removed from one or more members of the Roman Catholic Church, permitting them to participate in certain liturgical functions, and to receive or administer certain of the sacraments previously denied them because of violations of church law.

2) Reconciliation of penitents: A Roman Catholic practice in usage up to the thirteenth century by which public sinners who had been expelled from the church on Ash Wednesday were reinstated on Maundy Thursday.

3) Reconciliation of a church: The blessing by which a Roman Catholic church that has undergone violation (e.g., impious or sordid uses, homicide in the body of the building) is restored as a sanctified place of worship. If the church was consecrated it must be reconciled by a bishop or his deputy; if blessed only, by a priest. J.F.T.

rector: The incumbent of the benefice of the parish, possessing all the original rights and endowments; he is, as the parson (*persona ecclesiae*), a 'corporation sole' inasmuch as he represents in his own person the invisible Church in the parish. The vicar* is, theoretically his deputy and *locum tenens*. The origin of the distinction goes back to the time when monasteries took over the tithes of the parish and put in a monk as vicarius. At the Reformation, monastic lands given to laymen carried with them the rector's rights, hence the 'lay rector' of a parish governed by a vicar.

F.W.B.

recusant: One who from his allegiance to the Pope refuses (Lat. *recusat*) to submit to the Act of Uniformity* (under Edward VI and Elizabeth) and to take the oath of allegiance to the monarch as supreme head (or governor) of the Church of England; or to attend the services at his parish church. F.W.B.

Red Cross: A national and international social service agency originally organized to care for the sick and wounded in the armies in time of war. But as the military forces developed adequate medical corps and the character of warfare changed, the Red Cross extended its activities to assistance to the families of soldiers at home, to services for prisoners of war, to the establishment of bureaus of information, and to relief to bombed out and evacuated populations. Since 1919 it has shown a world-wide tendency to regard the alleviation of human suffering, especially when it assumes a wide-spread, sudden, epidemic, or catastrophic form as within its field. It has thus become the most extensive and popular of all voluntary social service agencies. In 1940 there were 63 officially recognized national societies with over 20,000,000 members. In Mohammedan lands, Turkey, Egypt, and parts of Russia the Red Crescent has been substituted for the Red Cross, while in Persia it operates under the symbol of the Red Lion and Sun.

Meager medical and sanitary services had long been provided by the military authorities but for the most part these provisions were regarded as a part of the military establishment and the legitimate target of the enemy. Public opinion had been awakened to these conditions by the work of Florence Nightingale (1820-1910) in the Crimean War in 1854, and Clara Barton (1821-1912) in the American Civil War, but the movement took organized form as the result of the agitation bebun by the Swiss philanthropist, Jean Henri Dunant.

Dunant had been present at the battle of Solferino on June 24, 1859, and had witnessed the unnecessary suffering due to the inability of the regular surgical staff to care for the thousands of wounded upon the field. Three years later he published a widely read book, *Un souvenir de Solferino* in which he proposed the organization of societies in each country which should train nurses and collect supplies in times of peace which might supplement the regular military medical corps in case of war. A conference of representatives of 16 European states, held at Geneva in

1863, led in the following year to the convocation by the Swiss government of a diplomatic conference which signed the Geneva Convention by which the participating states agreed to sanction the formation of relief societies, to recognize the neutrality of wounded men and of all personnel and equipment employed in their relief, and to respect the red cross on a white ground as the emblem officially designating such services. The Hague conferences in 1899 and 1907 extended to naval warfare the Geneva Convention of 1864 and the revised convention of 1906.

The organization of the international movement is highly decentralized. The International Red Cross Committee, a self-perpetuating group of 25 members, all Swiss citizens, assisted by a secretarial and special delegations, sits at Geneva, but has no governing functions. Its objects are to extend the Red Cross movement, to act as guardian of its basic principles, to maintain contact between the national societies and to assist them in coordinating their activities, to secure the observance by all nations of the Geneva Convention, and to denounce such violations as may occur; and in time of war, to create international agencies for the assistance of prisoners and other war victims, to visit prisoners' camps, and to better their situation by the use of all available influence.

Each national society is completely autonomous. It must, however, have a central committee which represents it in all international relations, and it must have been recognized as an auxiliary to the army medical services by a government adhering to the Geneva Convention. Membership must be open to all nationals irrespective of sex, religion, or political opinion. It must serve the entire national area and embrace all appropriate aspects of the medical military services. Funds for their support are in most countries derived from membership fees supplemented by special drives for private subscriptions in times of emergency.

After World War I a need was felt for a representative and effective medium through which to develop and intensify the humanitarian activities of the Red Cross in peace time. The result was the organization of the League of Red Cross Societies in 1919. It is administered by an international secretariat under the supervision of the chairman of a board of governors composed of one representative of each member society. In addition to the general branches of the office of the secretary-general, it comprises technical divisions on disaster relief, health (with special emphasis on educational and preventive activities), nursing, Junior Red Cross, and emigration.

The Junior Red Cross is a relatively new department of work. It was the outgrowth of the participation of children in work for wounded soldiers during World War I, which was later developed on a gigantic scale by the American Red Cross after the United States became a belligerent power. Its unique possibilities for self-education of children in health and civic ideals was recognized by educators. After preliminary experimentation, it was adopted as an integral part of the League's program in 1922, when its purposes were defined as "to inculcate in children the ideal of peace and the practice of service, especially in relation to the care of their own health and that of others, the understanding and acceptance of civic responsibility, and the cultivation and maintenance of a spirit of friendly helpfulness towards other children in all countries." Most of the national societies now have regular provisions for children's membership.

America, preoccupied with the Civil War and Reconstruction and impeded by official apathy, did not adhere to the Geneva Convention until 1882, becoming the thirty-second nation to ratify. In 1905 the Red Cross was organized as a quasi-governmental body, with the President of the United States as president and the War Department as auditor. The government of the agency was vested in a central committee of 18 members, six of whom are appointed by the President. Its greatest period of expansion came during 1914-18, when nearly $400,000,000 were expended in various war activities. At the close of the war it continued its relief work in destitute countries abroad, and provided for disabled veterans and ex-servicemen and enlarged the scope of its civilian services at home. It now provides for the following divisions of service: Civilian Relief, Disaster Relief, First Aid and Life Saving, Home and Farm Accident Prevention, Home Hygiene and Care of the Sick, Junior Red Cross, Nursing, Nutrition, Public Health Nursing, Volunteer, and War.

James Magill, *The Red Cross: the Idea and Its Development* (London, 1926); Martin Gumpert, *Dunant: The Story of the Red Cross* (1938); W. E. Barton, *The Life of Clara Barton* (1922).

H.E.J.

redaction: O.T. books show a great deal of editorial activity, called redaction (esp. in the case of the fusion of the originally separate pentateuchal sources). The Redactor (often abbreviated to R) is a hypothetical but necessary factor of O.T. criticism. Most of the redactional activity took place in post exilic* times. E.G.K.

redemption: (Gr., *agorazō; lutroō*: to redeem) Redemption as a religious principle belongs to religion in its highest forms. Religions have been classified as religions of nature, religions of law, religions of redemption. Religions of the third category as against the second regard man as needing something more than to be enlightened as to the divine requirement by some law or code; he is already enmeshed in evil or spiritual ruin and needs to be extricated or delivered. Buddhism* is a religion of redemption. It sees man tied to the wheel of karma* and sequent re-births, a condition that through his insatiable cravings can only mean recurrent evil and misery. The cause of the cycle of re-births is the good or evil activity which, occurring in one existence, can have its merited requital only in another. Redemption or salvation* lies in subjugating the desire that leads to this activity. It is from personal existence and its pain that the Buddhist is redeemed.

The religion of redemption *par excellence* is Christianity*. Its ideal of redemption is not that of Buddhism, but bears the marks of Christianity's Hebraic origin and background. There is much about redeeming in the O.T.: the word is used of money payments for the recovery of property (Lev. 25: 25ff); for the redemption of the firstborn (Num. 3: 44-51); for the release of persons from slavery (Ex. 21: 7, 8; Lev. 25: 47ff). The idea of buying back with money passes into the general meaning of to reclaim or save from evil or calamity, whatever means be used. Redemption is especially associated with great national deliverances, such as from Egypt (Deut. 7: 8); and from Babylon (Isa. 62: 12; 63: 4). God is the 'Redeemer' of His people, especially in Second Isaiah (e.g., 41: 14). The idea of redemption from sin occurs specifically in Ps. 130; 8. The word 'redeemer' (*goel*) has the force of vindicator in some passages, notably Job. 19: 25.

In the N.T., redemption (*lutrosis, apolutrosis;* derivatives of *agorazō* also used) fills a large place; the teaching concerning it is a rich, deep vein of N.T. truth. It sums up God's work in Christ in behalf of men. The figure of buying back re-appears, Christ's life being the ransom price (*lutron*: Mk. 10: 45); His blood that with which we have been bought (1 Pet. 1: 18, 19; cf. I Cor. 6: 20); the believer's final portion a "purchased possession" (Eph. 1: 14). But the idea broadens again to that of full deliverance as a gift of grace*. Redemption is especially through Christ's sacrificial* death, as above and further in Heb. 9: 15; Eph.: 1: 7; Rom. 3: 24, 25). It is redemption from sin emphatically and is associated with forgiveness* (Eph. 1: 7; Col. 1: 14; Tit. 2: 14). But there is a wider connotation recalling Israel's Messianic* redemption which would be communal and bring emancipation from evil in all forms (Lk. 1: 68ff; 2: 38). So the Church looks for the 'Day of Redemption' (Eph. 4: 30), when God will gather His redeemed people (Lk. 21: 28) and His whole creation will be purged and healed (Rom. 8: 19-23; Rev. 21: 1-4; 22: 1-3); to the Parousia* and final consummation when God, having vanquished all His and man's enemies, will rèsume full dominion and be all in all (I Cor. 15: 24-28).

The doctrine of redemption is a prime ingredient in the theology of the Church. It is found at all periods both in its cruder and profounder forms; the former when the 'ransom' is taken literally and the question becomes, To whom was the price paid? Patristic theology regarded it as paid to the devil who held man captive; later 'commercial' and other views saw it as compensatory payment to God whom man's sin had robbed of His just due. But with such notions there has always gone higher teaching; all theories, commercial, satisfaction, governmental et al, have enshrined some truth which, rather than their crudities, explains their hold on the Church. This truth—the true meaning of redemption—is that Christianity is not a legal cult or a goal set before man with promise of highest rewards to him who achieves it. Rather it reveals man's good as something beyond his power to attain; but secured for him, purchased at uttermost cost, and now freely offered. Man is not called to earn salvation by arduous duty; all things are his through what God has done and given. It is for man in penitence to turn to God and receive His gift; then follows duty, service to God and man, not as condition of the gift, but as glad response for God's bestowal of it.

The N.T. redemption is the hope of the world. It is the assurance* that God decrees the total destruction of evil and man's freedom from it, not least in those forms of tyranny and injustice, inner and outer spiritual bondage, against which man today rebels. It is an assurance most precious as man discovers how little he can do of himself; and it cannot fail for those who in faith and life are joined to the purpose of God. See atonement; satisfaction.

A. G. Hogg, *Redemption from this World* (1922); A. C. Knudson, *The Doctrine of Redemption* (1933); H. W. Robinson, *Redemption and Revelation* (1942); R. Niebuhr, *The Nature and Destiny of Man*, II: *Human Destiny* (1943). J.L.

Redemptoristines: A Roman Catholic Congregation of contemplative nuns founded in 1731 with the aid of St. Alphonsus Liguori*. It had in 1936 about 800 members in twenty-seven convents. E.A.R.

Redemptorists: The Roman Catholic Congregation of the Most Holy Redeemer was founded in 1732 by St. Alphonsus Liguori* at Scala near Amalfi in Italy. Its primary object is the sanctification of its members by the imitation of Jesus Christ. The secondary purpose is the preaching of the word of God to the people, and especially to the poor and abandoned. The Congregation has spread throughout the world and numbered 6,663 members in 1936. E.A.R.

reductions: (In Spanish *reducciónes*, after 1654 *doctrinas*) Theocratic, communal mission villages of converted Indians under the direction of missionaries in the Spanish American colonies. The suppression of the Society of Jesus* (1773) and the development of the South American states led to their destruction. E.A.R.

Reform Judaism: See Judaism, Reform.

Reformation: The movement which was initiated by Martin Luther* in 1517 and resulted in the rise and establishment of Protestant churches apart from Roman Catholicism is generally called the Reformation. The term "reformation" was frequently used in the later Middle Ages by individuals and groups who demanded a reform of the church "in head and members" as a protest against the secularization of Christianity and the abuses of power and privilege which had grown general especially among the clergy, from the popes down to the common priests. The "Reformation" allied itself with these tendencies of reform, but it did not spring from them.

The *origins* of the Reformation lie primarily in the religion of Luther. In the course of his inner development he was led to rediscover the N.T. faith of salvation* by grace*. Henceforth, the meaning of the Christian gospel was for him identical with the teaching implied in the Pauline teaching of the justification* by faith and not by works. He was convinced that his religion was in agreement with the teaching of the Bible which he read in the light of Paulinism and that it was confirmed by the central doctrines of the Fathers, especially Augustine*, and by the writings of some medieval thinkers, particularly Bernard of Clairvaux* and the German mystics such as Tauler* and the author of the "German Theology". His thinking was determined by the monastic discipline which he received among the Augustinian Friars, the Occamist theology which he learned among them, and his appointment to the chair of Biblical Theology at the University of Wittenberg. When he posted 95 theses against the prevailing practice of selling indulgences on the door of the castle church of Wittenberg on October 31, 1517, he did not intend to inaugurate a reformation, but merely to effect a clarification of the church's teaching. However, the theses were received with unexpected acclaim because they were read as an expression of a fresh Christian voice speaking for the renewal of Christianity. When spokesmen of the Roman church accused Luther of heresy and when the papal Curia opened an ecclesiastical trial against him, he refused to recant his convictions. Believing that they rested on the authority of the Word of God*, he defended himself in writings which, as the years went on, became more and more saturated with criticisms of the Roman church as they had been voiced in the past and as they were current among the people of his own time. Then it became evident that Luther's creative religious genius was to be the exponent and perfecter of the long latent desire for a reformation of the church. Supported by an ever increasing following recruited from the ranks of princes and patricians; noblemen, towns-people and peasants; churchmen and monks; humanistic scholars and patriots, he brought to a fruition their hopes for a break-up of the power which Roman Catholic institutionalism held over them. Thus Luther's cause became that of a popular movement which spread rapidly throughout Germany and soon all over Europe.

While he never surrendered the conviction that he had been divinely called to make room in the world for the saving gospel of Christ and refused to become a political and social reformer, he was regarded by the Germans as a national hero and as such a leader of a movement much broader than that of a merely religious and ecclesiastical reform. He and his followers availed themselves of the new means of communication which the recent invention of the printing press had made possible. Their books and pamphlets spread rapidly all over the European world. They used the historical criticism and understanding of Christian history and institutions which the scholars of Humanism*, especially Erasmus* of Rotterdam, had accomplished. They availed themselves of the teachings of the so-called pre-reformers, particularly of Huss, Wyclif and the Brethren of the Common Life**. They adopted as their own many of the attacks against the papacy and the higher clergy, against the political and social-economic practices of the Roman church that had been the subject of many complaints (*gravamina*), particularly on the part of the German nation. In part consciously but mostly unconsciously they employed for themselves the sentiments of a growing nationalism and the spirit of a new civilization which, since the beginnings of the Renaissance*, had made themselves felt all over the European world. They themselves tremendously furthered these new cultural trends when, under the leadership of Luther, they rejected the medieval principle of the domination of the state by the church, declared asceticism and the distinction between the "religious" and the "secular" as invalid, and broke up the separation between the clergy and laity by claiming the universal priesthood of all believers. In accordance with these convictions, they accepted the protection which princes and magistrates extended to them. They even made the political leaders responsible for the reformation itself, declaring that upon the refusal of the regular bishops to effect a change they had to act as "emergency-bishops" and that as divinely instituted authorities they had to maintain law and order as the basis of the Christian life.

The *development* of the Reformation was decisively determined by political conditions as they prevailed not only in Germany, but also in Europe as a whole. Germany was divided in numerous large and small territories, which since the days of the Hohenstaufen had no longer been unified under a strong central imperial authority. When several of these territories under the leadership of the Elector of Saxony, Luther's prince, and the Margrave of Hesse effected an evangelical reformation of their churches, thereby establishing territorial churches the possibility for which had been formed in the 14th and 15th centuries by virtue of the decline of papal authority, no higher political or ecclesiastical power proved able to prevent such a development. Nor was it possible to prevent the politically autonomous cities, especially of Southern Germany, from effecting an ecclesiastical reformation.

The Emperor Charles V*, who had been elected in 1519, was a declared enemy of the Reformation. But as the head of the House of Habsburg, he was ruler not only of Germany but also of Spain and her newly won American colonies, of the Netherlands and Burgundy. He had claims upon Northern and Southern Italy—and by the marriage policy of his house, he was drawn into the affairs of practically every European state. Shortly after his assumption of the German throne, he was drawn into a war with his arch-enemy and rival, Francis I of France, about the issue of the control of Italy. The war kept him occupied almost throughout his reign. When the defense of Italy against France did not keep him busy, the affairs of his Spanish Kingdom and the necessity of protecting Europe from the rapidly rising power of the Turks demanded his attention. He was not only absent from Germany for long periods of time, but by his political entanglements he was unable to effect an execution of the Edict of Worms*, by which in 1520 he had outlawed the movement of Luther. He could thus not prevent the establishment of the Reformation churches in German territories. Nor could he hinder the expansion of the Reformation into Switzerland, East Prussia, Denmark, Sweden, England, all of whom separated from Rome in the twenties and thirties, or stop its appeal to Europeans everywhere. When, after many time-saving compromises with the German Reformation, he was finally, in 1546, ready to launch a war of annihilation against the "heretics", he succeeded in defeating them (1547) but was unable to crush them or to reap the fruits of his victory. He left the settlement of the religious controversy to his successor, his brother Ferdinand, in whose favor he abdicated as Emperor in order to retire to Spain. The peace of Augsburg* (1555) recognized the established evangelical territorial churches.

On account of the fact that the immediate object of Charles' dynastic imperialism was the control of Northern Italy, the popes were politically suspicious of him. Occasionally, they even favored his enemies, hoping thereby to protect the autonomy of the papal state as well as to preserve a balance of power within the European system of states. By these policies which prevented Charles from taking decisive steps against the Protestants* (this name was given to the German Lutherans at the diet of Spires* in 1529 after they had issued a "Protestation" in reaction against a vote of the diet's majority which had repealed the limited provisional liberties granted them in 1526) the popes themselves made the expansion of the Reformation possible and became its indirect allies.

The *effects* of the Reformation were determinative of the future of all Western civilization. The movement which Luther had begun destroyed the universalism of the control of the Roman church over all spheres of life. This breakup of the unity of Christendom inaugurated a new cultural period. One is therefore justified to mark the beginning of modern civilization with the Protestant Reformation. While the reformers themselves continued to adhere to the medieval sociological principle of the *corpus Christianum,* according to which all life was to be regulated by the spirit of the Christian religion, their teaching on the distinction of the Church and the State and their frank anti-ascetic recognition of secular life as the place where every Christian is to realize the will of God laid the groundwork for the development of an autonomous secular civilization.

It was also significant for the future that the new churches of the Reformation were unable to achieve doctrinal or ecclesiastical unity. The Reformation produced not only several national and territorial churches, but also several types of Protestant Christianity. Lutheranism, Zwinglianism, Calvinism, Anglicanism, Socinianism, Anabaptist** and Spiritualist Christianity represent the various types of Christianity which were the immediate result of Luther's attack against Roman Catholic sacramentalism and hierarchalism. See Augsburg Confession; Reformed Churches; religious liberty; Theses, Ninety-Five, of Luther.

Preserved Smith, *The Age of the Reformation* (1920); T. M. Lindsay, *The Reformation* (1917), 2 vols. W.P.

Reformation, Catholic: See Catholic Reformation, The.

Reformed Church in the United States, the: Formerly called the German Reformed Church, adopted the official title, The Reformed Church in the United States in 1869; in 1942, at the General Synod, in Lancaster, Pennsylvania, a merger became effective between the Reformed Church in the United States and the Evangelical Synod of North America, officially named, The Evangelical and Reformed Church.

The Reformed Church in the United States, as one branch of this merger, represents a national type of the Church founded by Huldreich Zwingli and John Calvin** in Switzerland, during the Reformation* in the 16th century. It dates its origin in America from the first quarter of the 18th century (ca. 1725), when German, Swiss, French, and Dutch emigrants settled along the Atlantic seaboard, and organized scattered congregations.

Fostered and supported by the Reformed Church of Holland, this American branch of the Reformed Church organized an ecclesiastical body known as the Coetus. In 1793, it declared its independence of the mother-church in Holland, and established the Synod of the Reformed Church in the United States.

At the time of its merger with the Evangelical Synod of North America, the Reformed Church in the United States had a membership of about 350,000, with 1757 congregations and 1317 ministers, raising, annually, over five millions for congregational and benevolent purposes. Its organization consisted of 58 Classes, 7 Synods, and a General Synod, meeting triennially. It had established 5 Boards, and maintained flourishing missions and educational institutions in Japan and China. It had founded and fostered 3 theological seminaries, 11 colleges and academies, besides various hospitals and homes for orphans and old folks. The doctrinal standard of the Reformed Church in the United States, until its recent merger, was the Heidelberg Catechism*, and in its polity it adhered to the Presbyterian System established by John Calvin.

J. H. Dubbs, *American Church History* Series, vol. 8 (1895); idem, *The Reformed Church in Pennsylvania* (1902); T. Appel, *The Beginnings of the Theological Seminary* (1886); William J. Hinke, *Minutes and Letters of the Coetus of Pennsylvania 1734-1792,* Reformed Church Publication Board (Philadelphia, 1903); *Life and Letters of the Reverend John Philip Boehm* (1916). T.F.H.

Reformed Churches: The Reformed Church represents one of the two major branches of the Reformation*. It arose in Switzerland, simultaneously with the movement in Germany headed by Martin Luther*. Its founders were Huldreich Zwingli (1484-1531), and John Calvin** (1509-1564). In 1529, at the famous colloquy held at Marburg, Zwingli and Luther met, and, finally, failed to agree on the doctrine of Sacraments.

The Reformed Church owes its distinctive genius, both in theology and polity, mainly to Calvin*. Under his leadership, Geneva became an asylum for persecuted refugees from other lands, and his epochal treatise, "The Institutes of the Christian Religion", was widely accepted and adopted as the authoritative doctrinal confession of faith.

From its cradle in Switzerland, the Reformed Church spread far and wide into the countries of Europe, and, beyond the seas into other continents. Generally, it retained the simple name "Reformed," and then added to that old appellation by its founders the name of the country in which it was being established. Thus came into existence the Reformed Church in Holland, in Germany, in France, in Hungary, etc. In Scotland, under the leadership of John Knox*, the Reformed Church was named "The Presbyterian Church," after its form of government.

Through immigration, these various national types of the Reformed Church were transplanted during the colonial era to our soil, where each branch maintained its separate existence. The Dutch Reformed Church was established in New Amsterdam (New York) by settlers from Holland. Immigrants from Germany and Switzerland founded German Reformed Churches in the eastern Atlantic Region, and absorbed many French Huguenots of the Reformed Faith. The Presbyterian Church, originating in Scotland, founded and formed several separate branches throughout the United States of America.

These American branches of the Reformed Church bore the imprint of the theological and administrative genius of John Calvin. In their theology and polity, they remained Calvinistic Churches, as contrasted with denominational bodies that adhered to Arminian* types of theology and to congregational or episcopal systems of polity. But under new cultural and political conditions, the Reformed Churches on American soil were bound to create variations of their common prototype, and produce a distinctively American Christianity that is lending its sanction and support to the ecumenical movement.

The Reformed Churches belong to The Alliance of the Reformed Churches* throughout the World holding the Presbyterian System. This body, formed in London in 1875, exercises no legislative authority over its constituent groups, but it is the rallying point of all the Reformed and Presbyterian Churches. The Alliance, as a delegate body, meets quadrennially, and alternately in England and in America. During the interim, it functions through its Executive Commission, divided into an Eastern Section in Great Britain, and a Western Section located in America. These two sections meet biennially. The Alliance represents about thirty million souls, holding a common system of doctrine, and adhering to a common polity. It forms a closely integrated and influential family of Churches throughout the entire world. See classis; colloquy; common grace; consistory; elder; Confessions, Formal of the Christian Church; Gallican Confession; Heidelberg Catechism; Helvetic Confessions; Mercersburg theology; Schweitzer, Alexander; Tetrapolitan Confession.

On *Reformed Churches,* as one of the two main branches of the Reformation, consult standard Church Histories; especially the histories of the Reformation. On individual or national types of the family of Reformed Churches, consult particular references. On the Alliance of the Reformed Churches, consult the Quarterly Register of the Alliance, 1886 to date, published in Edinburgh, 44 Queen Street, and the *Proceedings* of the meetings of the Alliance, edited by W. H. Hamilton, Edinburgh, 44 Queen Street.

T.F.H.

Reformed Episcopal Church: A denomination formed in 1873, when a group of clergy and laymen withdrew from the Protestant Episcopal Church because of dissatisfaction with "ritualistic"* and Catholic tendencies. In theology, the denomination claims to follow the Book of Common Prayer*, but takes a rather Calvinistic interpretation of that book; it is opposed to sacerdotalism and prelacy, and refuses its bishops a separate house in its governing body. A theological seminary was maintained for some years in Philadelphia. Recently relations with Protestant bodies have become much closer than previously. There are about 80 parishes, with some 25,000 members.

See *Book of Common Prayer of the Reformed Episcopal Church,* for statement of theological position. For account of origin of the denomination, see W. W. Manross, *History of the Episcopal Church* (1938).

W.N.P.

Reformed Mennonites: See Mennonites.

Reformed Methodist Church: See holiness churches. Also see anti-missionary movement in the U. S.

Reformed New Congregational Methodist Church: See holiness churches.

Reformed Presbyterian Church in North America, and Reformed Presbyterian Church of North America: Covenanters* from Scotland and the north of Ireland, members of the connection which organized in Scotland in 1743 as the Reformed Presbytery, formed the Reformed Presbytery of America in 1774 near Harrisburg, Pennsylvania. In 1782 this joined with two Associate presbyteries to form the Associate Reformed* Synod. But dissenters caused the constitution of the Reformed Presbytery of North America in 1798. This grew, especially in western Pennsylvania, to be a synod in 1809 and a general synod in 1823. The Reformed Presbyterians in the 1810's required members to free slaves, thus being in advance of most churches. In 1833 they divided over the question of whether the prohibition of voting and holding civil office because the Federal Constitution does not recognize God and the supremacy of Christ should continue to be the church's witness. The result was the Reformed Presbyterian Church in North America, General Synod, which rejected "political dissent" and the Reformed Presbyterian Church of North America, Old School. These churches are better known as "Covenanter" than by their official titles. They have not their earlier strength, the former having in 1943 about 1,600 communicants, the latter about 6,000. R.H.N.

Reformed Presbyterians: See Cameronians.

refuge: See asylum.

regale: (Lat., *jus regale*, royal prerogative) A term denoting the sovereign rights of a king. Specifically it refers to a right, assumed by medieval and later kings, of appropriating the revenues of vacant sees or imperial abbeys during the time of vacancy. The right was often extended to cover the period of a full year following the death of a bishop or abbot, and to include the collation of all dependent benefices* vacated during the time of the vacancy in the diocese, excepting those involving the care of souls. The law of regale did not apply to all dioceses or abbeys and was not assumed by kings alone, but in France by certain powerful nobles as well. Its origins can be traced to the system of patronage* but more particularly to the feudal conception that the estates held by the bishops and abbots were royal properties granted as fiefs by the crown. It was often the cause of conflict between kings and popes particularly in the 12th and 13th centuries. F.W.N.

regeneration: Being re-born. Greek, *gennao*, to beget, with *anothen*, again or from above, in John 3: 4, 7; *anagennao*, to beget again, in I Pet. 1: 3, 23; cf. 2: 2. Paul has kindred ideas: new creation (2 Cor. 5: 17; Gal. 6: 15); renewal of nature or mind (Rom. 12: 2; 2 Cor. 3: 18; 4: 16; Eph. 4: 23); the new man (Eph. 4: 22-24; Col. 3: 9, 10). Of the same order is the doctrine of resurrection* life: believers have passed from death to life (John 5: 24; 11: 25, 26); have died and risen with Christ (Rom. 6: 3-6; I Cor. 15: 20-23; Col. 3: 1); are new-begotten by the resurrection (I Pet. 1: 3).

Regeneration is complementary to justification*; there is no establishing of the believer in a right relation unaccompanied by divine work within. Justifying faith is itself such work and opens the inner life to the agency of the Spirit. Pauline and Johannine ideas of renewal of nature are thought by some to reflect Greek dualism (transformation is from flesh to spirit: Rom. 8: 9, Gal. 5: 16-26; John 3: 6, 7); but the spiritual factor that forbids regarding salvation* as merely external lies equally against viewing it as quasi-physical. "God is conceived, not only as revealing His will, but as imparting the life which makes conformity to that will possible. This consciousness of new power and ideals—fruit and evidence of God's activity in the soul of man—finds expression in the doctrine of regeneration" (W. Adams Brown).

A theological issue is the connection of regeneration with baptism*. The belief that in baptism sin is washed away and the new nature born (baptismal regeneration) is traceable at least to the second century (cf. 'laver of regeneration': Tit. 3: 5). The influence of the mysteries (see mystery religions) on Christian Sacramentalism* still divides scholarly opinion; it has, perhaps, been over-stressed to the obscuring of apparent N.T. support of baptismal regeneration (Rom. 6: 3, 4; Gal. 3: 27; Col. 2: 12; John 3: 5). In these and other texts, baptism does seem the medium of special participation in the death, burial and resurrection of Christ; just as by it the Spirit is bestowed, as not by John's baptism (Mtt. 3: 11; Mk. 1: 8; Lk. 3: 16; John 1: 26; Acts 19: 2-6). But on baptism, doctrines of regeneration differ; they unite on the fundamental that, whatever the means, the Agent of regeneration is the Holy Spirit*. The doctrine is the testimony to the work of the Spirit and the assurance that through Him men do know renewal of life and divine peace and power. See conversion.

W. James, *The Varieties of Religious Experience* (1902); H. Begbie, *Twice-Born Men: A Clinic in Regeneration* (1909); W. L. Jones, *A Psychological Study of Religious Conversion* (1937). J.L.

Regensburg, Conference of: Hard pressed politically in 1540, Charles V* was desirous of pacifying Germany and attempted to iron out religious differences in a series of conferences, of which that at Regensburg was last. Interlocutors on the one side were Butzer, Pistorius, and Melanchthon*, on the other, Gropper, Pflug, and Eck.* Up for discussion was the so-called Regensburg Book, 23 ambiguously worded articles, previously prepared. Though several compromises were effected at the beginning, the conference ended in failure. Both parties were suspicious of the Emperor, but he in the meanwhile had made a few advantageous political alliances with Protestants at the diet, which sat simultaneously with the conference at Regensburg. E.C.K.

registers, parochial: Written records of baptisms, marriages, and deaths, became customary about 1550 (required by Council of Trent*, and about the same time in England and Protestant countries); in the absence of complete civil records, they often serve historical and statistical purposes as well as ecclesiastical. E.R.H.

regula fidei: See rule of faith.

Regular Baptists: A group of conservative Baptist churches which claim to represent the original strain of English Baptists before differences developed over the Arminian and Calvinist theologies. Most of them are in the South. Each association has its own confession of faith, and there are differences among them, but in general they are Calvinistic. They practice "close communion*," excluding outsiders from the communion, and feet washing. There are 266 churches and approximately 17,000 members. E.T.C.

regular clergy: The professed members of the Roman Catholic clergy* who live under the rule (*regula,* hence *regulares*) of one of the religious Orders or Congregations of the Church. Though the "rules" of the various religious groups are of varying degrees of strictness and complexity, the taking of the vows of poverty, obedience and chastity is a common feature. In contrast to the "Seculars", the regular clergy devote themselves primarily to religious work other than the care of parishes (contemplation, special preaching, missions, teaching and the care of the poor and sick). See Jesuits; monasticism; secular clergy.

V.J.B.

Rehmcke, Johannes: (1848-1930) As a pupil of A. E. Biedermann*, the Swiss liberal theologian, he first taught religion and philosophy at the gymnasium of St. Gall, Switzerland. He next taught philosophy in succession at the universities of Berlin and Greifswald. Dissatisfied with the fundamental philosophical problems, he sought to redeem philosophy by a theory of knowledge. He developed the view that knowledge was a relationless having. He rejected thinking as activity and regarded will not a fundamental element of consciousness. His philosophy has been unjustly grouped with the immanentist philosophy of Avenarius and Schuppe. He rejected phenomenalism and theoretical idealism for their overt or concealed materialism, as they reduce the world to appearance. He strove to surmount the antithesis of materialism-idealism. To surpass idealism meant the destruction of materialism in its ultimate secret recess. He was primarily concerned in gaining clarity about the essence of consciousness or spirit.

God was for him the all-comprehensive psychic and spiritual individuality, the subject of the whole of the given. Opposed to pantheism, God was the real as such, but there is also something real outside of God. As God and man influence each other, divine and human communion is real. Only that philosophy which in its epistemology determines the spirit or consciousness as something ontological and that explains its essence as something explicable is fit as a basis of theology. Philosophy with its concept of God must place theology upon the sure ground of being. Rehmcke exerted a special influence upon theology through his pupil Friedrich Karl Schumann (1886-) who is professor of theology at the University of Halle and who published *Religion und Wirklichkeit* (Leipzig, 1913).

Die Welt als Wahrnehmung und Begriff (Berlin, 1880); *Philosophie als Grundwissenschaft* (Frankfurt a. M., 1910); *Das Bewusstsein* (Heidelberg, 1910); *Die Lehre vom Gemüt* (2nd ed., Leipzig, 1911); *Die Willensfreiheit* (Leipzig, 1911); *Grundriss der Geschichte der Philosophie* (3rd ed., Leipzig, 1912); *Die Seele des Menschen* (5th ed., Leipzig, 1920); *Logik oder Philosophie als Wissenschaft* (2nd ed., Leipzig, 1923); *Grundlegung der Ethik als Wissenschaft* (Leipzig, 1925); *Anmerkungen zur Grundwissenschaft* (2nd ed., Leipzig, 1925); *Lehrbuch der Allgemeinen Psychologie* (3rd ed., Leipzig, 1926); *Gesammelte philosophische Aufsätze* (ed. by K. Gassen (Erfurt, 1928); S. Hochfeld, *Johannes Rehmcke* (München, 1923); H. Sacher, *Vergleich zwischen Rehmckes und Drieschs Philosophie* (Dresden, 1933); J. E. Heyde, *Johannes Rehmcke und unsere Zeit* (Berlin, 1935).

H.H.

Reimarus, Hermann Samuel: (1694-1768) Professor of Hebrew and Oriental languages a the Gymnasium in Hamburg (1727-1768). In ad dition to his edition of *Dio Cassius* (1750-1752) he published several philosophical works. His most important work, *Apologie oder Schutzschrift für die vernünftigen Verehrer Gottes,* published posthumously and anonymously by Lessing* (1774-1778) under the title *Wolfenbüttel Fragments*,* reveals a vigorous and independent thinker, far superior to most of the English deists* with whom he has often been compared. See Lives of Jesus.

M.S.E.

reincarnation: See Hinduism; transmigration.

Reischle, Max Wilhelm Theodor: (1858-1905) He was professor at the universities of Giessen, Göttingen and Halle. His chief contribution was in the profound Ritschlian transformation of German theology prior to 1914.

Ein Wort zur Kontroverse über die Mystik in der Theologie (Freiburg, 1886); *Christentum und Entwicklungsgedanke* (Leipzig, 1898); *Werturteile und Glaubensurteile* (Halle, 1900); *Christliche Glaubenslehre* (Halle, 1902); *Theologie und Religionsgeschichte* (Tübingen, 1904); *Aufsätze und Vorträge,* ed. by Th. Häring and Friedrich Loofs (Tübingen, 1906).

H.H.

relationships, spiritual: A kinship arising between the principals in the administration of baptism and confirmation. Since baptism is considered a spiritual rebirth, those who concur in it are considered spiritual (god-) parents of the baptized person. In the Roman Catholic Church it is an impediment to marriage between a) the minister and the baptized, b) the sponsors and the baptized. The spiritual relationship contracted in confirmation is not a marriage impediment.*

J.F.T.

relativism, ethical: The view that since moral values vary between individuals and groups according to cultural condiitons and other circumstances, there are no absolute criteria that ought to hold universally. Edward Westermarck, *Origin and Development of the Moral Ideals* (1906), *Ethical Relativity* (1932), defends this standpoint, although he affirms an evolution of the altruistic sentiment. John Dewey and his school are accused by their critics of being ethical relativists; however, they seem to believe in the absolute value of democracy, and in the complete co-ordination of all elements in any given moral situation.

W.K.W.

relic: (Lat., *reliquiae,* remains) An object venerated because of its association with a martyr or saint**. Relics are of three classes: first, the body of a saint or any part thereof; second, any part of his clothing; third, any thing intimately connected with him, e.g., a prayerbook. In the Roman Catholic Church a document, certifying to its authenticity, accompanies every important relic, but this does not guarantee the genuineness of a single specific relic. Such a document only implies that the relic is not manifestly spurious and that there is no compelling evidence known to the competent authenticator—a cardinal, bishop, or other dignitary to whom the faculty of authenticating relics has been granted by the papacy—which militates against its lawful veneration. This veneration is held to be legitimate but not compulsory. An authenticated relic is required to be placed within the altar-stone of every altar for the licit celebration of Mass*. Purchase, sale, or simulation of relics is unlawful, and those who knowingly sell or display false relics for veneration incur excommunication* *ipso facto*. The primary purpose of the veneration of relics is to increase the sanctity of the faithful by encouraging imitation of the heroic virtues of God's most faithful servants. This honor is purely relative, insofar as it is basically rendered to the saint or martyr with whom the relics are associated; in nowise is it to be confused with the worship rendered to God. The veneration of relics was admitted by the Iconoclasts (heretics of VIII and IX centuries) and was not repudiated by the Protestants at first. See charms and amulets; images. Cf. saints, veneration of. J.F.T.

Relief Act of 1791: This Act for Catholic Relief (31 George III, c. 32), passed by the English Parliament, was the second of four major measures which eliminated some of the disabilities under which the Roman Catholics labored in England since the time of Queen Elizabeth. Like the first Act of 1778, it imposed an oath on all Catholics but the consequences were much more favorable: those who took the oath were freed from persecution for celebrating or hearing Mass, for being in the clerical state, or for otherwise exercising their religion; Catholic schools were legalized; the legal and military professions were open to Catholics, but they could not be officers, judges, or king's counsel. Further emancipation was delayed, despite the support of Pitt and Fox, by the obduracy of George III and dissension among the Catholics themselves. J.F.T.

Relief Church: A small denomination of little more than a hundred congregations, which separated from the Church of Scotland*, in 1762, on the question of patronage*, under the leadership of Thomas Gillespie. Desiring to serve as a "relief" to all who felt the establishment undesirable, it maintained a spirit of charity towards all. In May, 1847, it united with the Secession Church to form the United Presbyterian Church*. A.K.R.

relief organization: See charity organization.

religion, comparative: See comparative religion.

religion, philosophy of: See philosophy of religion.

religion, practical: See practical religion.

religion, primitive: See primitive religion.

religion, the problem of definition: The term religion belongs to that large class of popular words which seems acceptable as common coin of communicative exchange but which on closer examination fails to carry the imprint of exact meaning. A valid definition must avoid 1) the first major mistake of vagueness if it is to be useful as a definition. 2) It is common practice to turn to etymology when one defines. In many cases this is helpful; but in this case of little use. The appeal to the Latin source *religare* (meaning "being bound") or *relegere* (meaning "gather together") may, by the process of ingenious Origenistic allegory, throw light upon the word in some homiletical sense; but it suffers as a second major mistake of inadequacy. A worship at the shrine of origins is precarious. 3) A third mistake is the indiscriminate use of the word where the same word carries different meanings. For example, to say that a person is religious may mean that he performs a religious act without *being religious* or that he *is religious* without performing an act considered as religious. An object may be a religious object but not *in the same sense* as a person who is said *to be religious*. One word thus covers two different meanings. 4) Classical definitions fall into a fourth general mistake, viz., the psychological error of defining in terms of one phase of mental life. For example, to say that one is religious when one *believes in* or *affirms* a god is to commit the error of confining the meaning to *intellectual* activity; to say that one is religious when one *feels* (e.g., the feeling of absolute dependence—Schleiermacher) is to confine the meaning to emotional experience; to say that one is religious when one *performs* or *behaves* in a given way may well confine the meaning to *activity*. Man is ever more than a *mere* thinking, feeling and active creature. He is a *whole* person with intermingled inner and outer responses and activities. Classical definitions have tended to follow the error of the old faculty psychology. 5) A fifth mistake has been to relegate the term to an indefinable instinct, experience or *a priori* (specific or otherwise) and thus invite the charge of violating a fundamental principle of careful thinking, viz., the law of parsimony.* If the religious response merits, by definition, a place in the mysteries of some special and hidden recess of the mind,—what prevents the addition of countless other special subterranean compartments of mind, e.g., a philosophical instinct, a musical *a priori* or a tennis experience? 6) A sixth major mistake is to define too narrowly: religion is going to church or being a Christian. Such a definition outlaws those who well may be religious, who never have had such social expressions as well as those outside the one faith. 7) A seventh mistake is to make the meaning so broad as to lose all significance. To say that religion is wonder or love is a case in point. May one not wonder or love and not be religious? 8) An eighth mistake is to confuse the term with ethics. The difficulty here is that one may be ethical and not necessarily be religious. One may be non-moral (e.g., Otto's conception of the essential religious spirit as *numinous**) or even immoral and still be religious. Religious people have often committed immoral acts as page upon page of human history reveal.

9) A common error (the ninth) is the normative, viz., of defining the *ought* rather than the *is*. What a religion ought to be and what it is are two separate inquiries. 10) A tenth mistake is to define the term in connection with a god concept. Two considerations appear here: how are those persons to be classified who behave in ways very much like conventional religious theists but who do not believe in god (in any conventional sense)? The term God indeed may need definition! Furthermore, a person may well assert his belief in a deity without his being religious. A definition may well need to include extreme humanists, extreme mystics, extreme pantheists, devotees of nature, Utopian enthusiasts, agnostics and avowed atheists (whose atheism* may well mean non-theism).

In the light of the above, although it is precarious to offer a constructive statement, a sincere attempt is here offered which, it is believed, does no violence to the above mistakes and sets forth a valid *descriptive* series of definitions. One is faced with the dilemma, on the one hand, of not defining, possessing a vague concept or holding inadequate or mistaken notions, and, on the other, of setting forth a position at the risk of severe criticism. The following statements seem wholly justifiable: "*To be religious* is to effect in some way and in some measure a vital adjustment (however tentative and incomplete) to whatever is reacted to or regarded implicitly or explicitly as worthy of serious and ulterior concern." Again, "*a religion* is a set of meanings and behaviors having reference to individuals who are or were or could *be religious*." "Again, *religion* is a generic term referring to all conceivable religions, formal or informal."

An elaboration of the problem of definition as above set forth is found in this writer's *First Chapters in Religious Philosophy* (1937), Part I, "What is Religion?" A list of definitions is found in James H. Leuba, Appendix to *A Psychological Study of Religion* (1912). See the discussion in E. S. Brightman, *A Philosophy of Religion* (1940).

V.F.

religion, psychology of: See psychology of religion.

religion, reason in: See reason in religion.

religion, sociology of: See sociology of religion.

religions, historical: Divisions and classes: See one-factor religions, and two-factor religions. Criterion of classification: See religious factor. 'Powers' in historical religions: See religious 'powers'.

F.L.P.

religious authority: See authority.

religious census: See federal census of religious bodies.

religious certainty: See certainty, religious.

religious communistic settlements: See communistic settlements, religious.

religious datum: The unique, irreducible object of conscious experience, whose quality is said to reveal God's being and nature at least partially, involving as it does the direct presence of the divine being as the *basis for* inference and reason. Those who assert such a datum* claim that its essential quality is non-sensory, and non-natural, though accompanied by emotional, sensory and ideational responses. The datum is also said to be non-rational, ineffable, and primordial. The knowledge it provides is said to be prior to and more ultimate than mediate or conceptual moral knowledge. The faculty of knowledge seems on the whole to be a cognitive "feeling" of objective presence (W. James, Schleiermacher, and R. Otto**). The object of the numinous "creature-feeling" is, for Otto, *mysterium tremendum, et fascinans*, or it may be a sense of absolute, sacred value (J. Oman* and D. C. Macintosh).

F. R. Tennant* has been one of the strongest critics of the view that there is a unique religious *datum* analogous to the sensory given. He suggests that psychological immediacy* is confused with epistemological immediacy in analyzing the numinous object, which, far from being determinate or having a specific *quale* is more like a "vague generic idea" and "indeterminate enough to enter equally well into a multitude of diverse theologies and religions." (See *Philosophical Theology*, vol. 1, p. 309). See empirical theology.

D. C. Macintosh, *The Problem of Religious Knowledge* (1940); R. Otto, *The Idea of the Holy* (tr., 1923); John Oman, *The Natural and the Supernatural* (1931).

P.A.B.

religious drama: The word 'drama' comes directly from the Greek and means 'deed' or 'action.' Strictly speaking, religious drama might be defined as religion shown in deeds as distinguished from abstractions. Thus, "The Word became flesh and dwelt among us" is a graphic way of saying that God dramatized his word for us in the life of Jesus. That is still Christianity's supreme drama. The term 'religious drama' has always had something of this connotation. In practice, however, the more conventional use of the word 'drama' has designated a story acted out upon a stage by a group of players in such a way as to arouse emotion in an audience. Such a drama becomes religious when it has a religious effect; that is, when it sends the audience away exalted in spirit and with a deepened sense of fellowship with God and man. This is admittedly a modern definition, growing out of the experience of twentieth century churches which have been using drama in their services of worship and religious education. Back of it lies a long history which can be only briefly summarized here.

1) Primitive Religious Drama. In practically every culture of the world, religion and drama were closely associated in their beginnings. Primitive man dramatized his prayers to his gods—danced and sang before his altars to let the gods know his need of rain for his crops or food for his children. As he climbed higher in the scale of civilization he used drama to honor the gods

and to thank them for their blessings, and to ask for more.

2) Greek Religious Drama. Among the Greeks of the fifth century B.C. drama emerged from this embryonic phase and within the short space of a single century, under the genius of Aeschylus, Sophocles and Euripides, developed into a major art with a clearly defined form. The great tragedies (Agamemnon, Antigone, Oedipus, etc.), of these poets were all written to be acted in the most sacred spot in Athens—the Temple of Dionysus, god of fertility—and at the most sacred season of the year—Spring, or the resurrection of Nature. Not only the poets, but the actors and directors, were considered ministers of religion during the drama festivals. The organized religion sponsored the plays, and the State financed them. Audiences reached twenty thousand or more. The plays sought to interpret life, not to escape from it. They dealt with the livest religious and social issues of the day with such timeless insight and depth of spirituality that they have survived twenty-four centuries and are probably still unsurpassed in beauty and dramatic power.

3) Medieval Religious Drama. When Rome conquered Greece the drama quickly declined. Rome was interested more in drama of escape than of interpretation. Under Roman influence the drama not only lost its religious significance but became bloody and obscene. When the Christian Church came into power, one of its first official acts was to put its foot on the Roman theater and crush it. For nearly a thousand years it remained crushed—with only minor and vestigial survivals—until it had a rebirth in the ninth and tenth centuries in Europe and especially in England. It was the church that revived it—not on the grand scale of Ancient Greece, but as a practical method of telling the Gospel story to the illiterate masses. The first experiments were simple indeed: lowering the cross on Good Friday while the choir sang Misereres, then raising it again on Easter morning while the choir sang Alleluias; or a visit by the three Marys to the tomb, and their discovery that their Lord had risen. These first experiments, coming as embellishments of the service of the mass itself, were performed by clerics, and restricted to the chancel. They were called *Passion Plays* or *Chancel Plays.* Next came *Saints' Plays,* developing out of the processions in honor of the saints. These were held in the nave of the church where both clerics and laymen re-enacted incidents, usually miracles, from the lives of the saints. One of the Passion Plays and Saints' Plays grew, in time, the *Mystery* or *Miracle Plays,* dramatizing the whole series of events of sacred history from the creation of the world to the final judgment. (At first, 'Mystery' seems to have designated a cycle of plays on the life and passion of Christ, while 'Miracle' was used for the longer cycles—twenty to fifty-two plays—that included Old Testament, New Testament, and saints' lives as well. But ultimately the terms 'mystery' and 'miracle' came to be used interchangeably.) These Miracle Plays were performed by guilds of laymen on double or triple decked platforms just outside the doors of the great cathedrals. The various guilds enacted the episodes most closely associated with their own craft; thus, the shipwrights' guild came to be responsible for the story of the building of the ark, the goldsmiths for the story of the Magi, etc. As the popularity of these cycles of religious dramas increased someone thought of the idea of putting wheels under the platform and rolling it out from the church yard to the street corner or the marketplace. This led to the plays being called *pageants.* ('Pageant' is a French word meaning 'rolling platform.') From this time on the Miracle Plays gradually lost their religious quality, becoming more and more secular with increasing elements of comedy and buffoonery until, in 1603, the ecclesiastical authorities forbade them in the churches. By this time the secular theater had developed from them. A few years more, and the Reformation swept away the last remnants of religious drama. However, meanwhile an offshoot of the earlier church plays took the form of *Moralities,* didactic allegories in dramatic form in which the various virtues and vices were personified. Best known of these was *Everyman,* translated from the Dutch into English about 1500, picturing the relative abiding values of certain virtues in the face of death.

4) The Passion Play of Oberammergau. This is not to be confused either with the medieval mysteries or with modern religious dramas. It is in a class by itself. It had its origin in 1633 when the citizens of Oberammergau (in the Bavarian Alps, sixty-four miles southwest of Munich) made a vow to perform such a play in gratitude for their deliverance from a plague. Since then this drama of the Passion of Christ has been performed as a religious service by the villagers every tenth year. It has developed in scope and effectiveness through the centuries until it is now a dramatic work staged in a large open-air theater and requiring nine hours for production. Each episode in the Passion story is prefaced by an appropriate tableau from the Old Testament. Music to accompany the production was added in 1814 by Rochus Dedler, a local schoolmaster. Some seven hundred persons—about half the village population—are required for the production. These devout people, who earn their living for the most part by carving rosaries, crucifixes, scenes from the lives of the saints, and children's toys, perform with great reverence. The parts for the major characters have become hereditary in certain families, who regard the characterizations as acts of devotion.

5) Modern Religious Drama. About the beginning of the twentieth century, religious drama again came into use, particularly in America and England. As in Medieval times, it began as a teaching device. Church schools presented crudely written pageants, making graphic certain great religious ideas. These were followed by dramatized Bible stories in the effort to help young people recover the life-experience of Bible characters. From Bible plays the liturgical churches went on to a revival of the Medieval miracle plays

adapted for modern use, while non-liturgical churches, for the most part, went directly to modern formal dramas, centering around present-day characters in the midst of spiritual struggles. Surveys have revealed that many thousands of churches now use drama, either ancient or modern, formal or informal, not only as a teaching instrument to show religion in terms of deeds, but as a means of inspiring congregations, purging their emotions, and deepening their sense of fellowship with God and man.

Eastman and Wilson, *Drama in the Church* (1942); N. B. Miller, *The Living Drama* (1924); A. E. Haigh, *The Tragic Drama of the Greeks* (1896); Gilbert Murray, *Ten Greek Plays* (1929); K. L. Bates, *The English Religious Drama* (1926); P. E. Osgood, *Old-time Church Drama Adapted* (1928); E. W. Bates, *The Church Play and Its Production* (1938).

F.E.

religious education: The term "religious education" stands for two processes which are necessarily related, but may be distinguished. One is the process of education, when this is undergirded and inspired by religious faith; the other is the gaining of personal religious faith, when this is nurtured, informed and sustained by educational methods. The first is the function of the school, the college, the university, and the community; the second is the function of the church, the Sunday school, and other religious associations. Both are functions of the family and the home.

Historically, the relation of religion and education has been intimate. Jesus Christ chose the methods of the teacher rather than those of propaganda, politics, or violence. Candidates for membership in the early church were carefully instructed as catechumens. Preaching was not merely to proclaim the gospel, but for instruction in the Christian faith and for the edification of believers and the building up of the church. Christians kept alive the light of learning in the Middle Ages; and the Christian church was largely responsible for the founding of the schools and universities of Europe. The Protestant Reformation, wth its emphasis upon the authority of the Word of God as recorded in the Scriptures and upon the right and responsibility of the individual to read and understand and accept this Word for himself, gave great impetus to the educational interest inherent in the Christian faith.

The beginnings of public education in America are directly attributable to the spirit of the Protestant Reformation. Throughout our early history the public schools, as well as private and parochial schools, gave full place to religious faith.

In the nineteenth century, a gradual secularization of education began to take place. This was not purposed, but incidental; it was not founded in principle, but occasioned by circumstances. It was largely due to the sectarianism of religious organizations. Not infidels or atheists or free thinkers have done most to take religion out of the public schools, but people who spoke in the name of religion. Whenever a group, or even an individual, has chosen to object to some religious element in the program or curriculum of the public schools, that element has forthwith been eliminated, and no other religious element has taken its place. The movement has been almost wholly negative; there has been no coming together of the different religious groups for a positive reconsideration of its total trend and inevitable results. Adherents of all faiths in America have been more concerned that the public schools should not contain any element to which they could object, than they have been to conserve in these schools the great principles of morals and religion upon which they agree. Protestant, Catholic, and Jew have shared in this movement. All must shoulder some of the responsibility for the situation into which we have drifted.

In the twentieth century, there has been a disposition to accept the exclusion of religion from the public schools as a matter of course, something closed and done, inevitable and irrevocable. Discussion of the problem has usually been more concerned with a rationalization of the present situation than with its serious reconsideration. This somewhat surprising readiness to be content with the omission from public education of religious elements has been due, not so much to the sectarianism of religion, though that has remained, as to other factors which bear more directly and purposively upon the secularization of public education. Among these may be named: 1) the general secularization of life and cheapening of human interests which have characterized the twentieth century thus far; 2) the prevalence in theology until very recently of a one-sided emphasis upon the immanence of God to the neglect or denial of His transcendence; 3) the popular vogue of pragmatism, instrumentalism and experimentalism—to use the successive names which the movement has borne—and the tremendous influence of this pragmatic point of view in education; 4) the resulting confusion with respect to the aims of education, and the disregard of problems of ultimate value or relation to God.

Yet America has a common religious faith—common not in the sense that everybody shares it, for there are some among us who deny or ignore God; but in the sense that it is common to the three great religious groups—Protestant, Catholic, and Jewish—to which the great majority of American citizens profess to belong. These citizens—Protestant, Catholic, and Jew—worship the one God, Creator of all things and Father of men. They believe that His will has been revealed in the life and literature of the Hebrew people, as this is recorded in the Bible, and that it is discernible in nature about us and in conscience within. They acknowledge the principles of human duty set forth in the Ten Commandments, in the teachings of the Hebrew prophets, in the Golden Rule, and in the law of love to God and to fellow-men.

The religious faith of America has inspired our history as a people and is embodied in our most characteristic institutions. There is nothing in the status of the public school as an institution of the state to render it godless. There is nothing in the principle of religious freedom or the separation of church and state to hinder the school's acknowledgment of the power and goodness of God. The common religious faith of the American people, as distinguished from the sectarian forms in which it is organized, may rightfully be assumed and find appropriate expression in the life and work of the public schools.

A significant change is taking place in the attitude of progressive educators toward what in the first hey-day of the movement was given the bad name "indoctrination." Their view then was that at all points where decision may be involved and attitudes are being formed, the teacher must not intrude and the school must be neutral. For the teacher or even the parent to share his faith with the children and to hope to win them to a like faith, was regarded as an unwarranted imposition, a sin against the child's individuality. This view is now sharply criticized, and most educational leaders oppose what they now call "the myth of neutrality" in education.

The Sunday school movement came to America in the early years of the nineteenth century, and has grown until one-half of the Sunday school enrollment of the world is in the United States and Canada. The International Council of Religious Education is the cooperative agency of forty-four Protestant denominations, and under its leadership great advances have been made in curriculum-making, teacher-training, and the organization and administration of the religious educational work of the churches.

In the field of religion, as in education generally, the movement now is away from exclusive pre-occupation with educational method, and toward new interest in the content of teaching. Psychology is an indispensable aide to education, but it cannot determine the ends or final values of life, or spin out of itself the web of knowledge. It cannot take the place of history or literature or the physical sciences or ethics or philosophy or theology or the Word of God. The experimental method is fruitful, not when it is used without presupposition or content, but when it is applied to new material in the full light of what we already know and believe. Genuinely creative teaching takes place, not in the absence of transmission of a heritage, but where transmission is so adequate that it serves as a base for further action and inquiry.

The new community of old and young in interests, in dangers, in sacrifices, and in service, makes obsolete and worse than useless many of our old neat schemes of classification and partition. Young and old are being educated together by the impact of life. The community itself is educating the young as really as do the schools. The better education of adults is now seen to be of vital importance to the education of the young. More things can be done and learned by old and young together than we had formerly thought. Stanley Hall's idea that children should be taught what their elders do not believe, in the interest of their recapitulation of race experiences, has disappeared; and with it should go into oblivion the new psychological dogma that children are incapable of learning anything articulate about God. We must share with our children, honestly, freely, intelligently, what we ourselves know and believe, in matters of religious faith and moral principle, as well as of loyalty to our country.

There is a new emphasis upon commitment. The world is no place, in these days of sore trial, for half-way, hesitant, tentative people who do not know what they believe or in whom they trust or to what they are loyal. We may well hope that "the myth of neutrality" is gone from education forever. Certainly Christian education fails if it does not beget faith in God in response to His supreme revelation of Himself in Jesus Christ—the faith that saves from futility and sin, and issues in Christian character and service. See Bible Societies; Biblical history in Christian instruction; catechetics; catechism; catechumenate; parochial schools; parochial schools, Catholic; Sunday school movement in U. S. A.; Young People's Societies, Christian. See also anti-Sunday School movement in the U. S.

W. C. Bower, *Christ and Christian Education* (1943); G. A. Coe, *What is Christian Education?* (1929); John Dewey, *A Common Faith* (1934); H. S. Elliott, *Can Religious Education be Christian?* (1940); C. M. Hill, ed., *Educational Progress and School Administration* (1936), chaps. 19, 20, 21; W. E. Hocking, *Human Nature and Its Remaking* (1918); International Council of Religious Education, *Christian Education Today* (1940); M. L. Jacks, *God and Education* (1939); Jerusalem Conference, I. M. C., vol. II, *Religious Education* (1928); Mary A. Jones, *The Faith of Our Children* (1943); J. H. Newlon, *Education for Democracy in Our Time* (1939); Oxford Conference, *The Christian Understanding of Man* (1938); Oxford Conference, *Church, Community and State in Relation to Education* (1938); W. E. Powell, *Education for Life with God* (1934); P. H. Vieth, *Objectives of Religious Education* (1930); L. A. Weigle, *Jesus and the Educational Method* (1939). L.A.W.

religious experience: See s.v. empirical theology; mysticism; Schleiermacher.

religious factor: The destiny-determining property of objects, forces, 'powers', etc., which comprise the world of human experience; any kind of power in the world when construed as operating in a capacity affecting the life's span, course of life, fortune, or destiny of man and other 'objects' in nature; a natural, universal, determining, and operative power or influence, which, in its differentiation in man, is identified wth the soul, or the destiny-determining property or power of the soul; the criterion by which historical religions as historical wholes may be classified without impairing their wholeness. See one factor religions; two factor religions. F.L.P.

religious humanism: See humanism, religious.

religious journalism in the United States: Applied to religious press activity the term "journalism" loses its popularly restricted association with newspaper production and takes on its broader professional significance of reference to all manner of publications "issued at stated or regular intervals". The history of religious journalism, therefore, extends beyond the realm of the religious newspaper to include that heterogeneous body of publications collectively designated "religious periodicals". Although "religious newspaper" and "periodical" thus become but types of "religious journal", the need for distinction between the two is not obviated. Essential differences exist in format, periodicity and content.

Differentiation is simplified if the sharpest distinction is drawn in the area of format. This is done by nodding assent to the widely accepted definition of the "proper newspaper" as being a folded sheet of folio size without stapling, stitching or cover. Applied literally to the output of the religious press, this makes all journals of folio size religious newspapers, all of smaller size religious periodicals.

This sharp distinction of format, although not universally accepted, has decided advantages in designation of periodicity and content. Strict association of the religious newspaper with the folio sheet automatically bestows upon it the additional characteristics of 1) Publication at the highest frequency common to the field of religious journalism—the weekly interval (semi-weekly and daily religious papers having always been oddities). 2) Content consisting of a minimum of essay matter and a maximum of current summary. Similarly strict association of the religious periodical with the smaller than folio size automatically bequeaths upon it the additional characteristics of 1. Publication, in the main, less often than at the weekly interval (though by definition never less frequently than at the semi-annual interval). 3) Content consisting of maximum of essay matter and a minimum of current summary.

A further word concerning periodicity and content will add definiteness to the distinctions drawn. At the outset largely a depository of cumbersome essay matter published at infrequent intervals, the religious journal progresed rapidly to a point where it became a weekly vehicle of lighter reading matter, especially of religious news. Waiving strict chronology, this evolutionary development may be said to have been by way of four stages designable as those of 1. Review 2. Magazine 3. News-Magazine 4. Newspaper. The first three stages represent the evolutionary growth of the "periodical" or non-folio format, while the last is obviously the province of the folio religious sheet. The "religious review" being restricted to scholarly theological articles and criticisms of recent books has been most exclusively essay in content. Its other characteristics have been publication in octavo form and at quarterly intervals. The "religious magazine" has been less a repository of critical articles and reviews, more a "storehouse" of lighter types of essay matter such as brief extracts from authors, biographical sketches, moral stories, anecdotes, poetry, etc., but to the exclusion of notices of current religious events. Its other characteristics have been publication in octavo or smaller form and at monthly or bi-monthly intervals. The "news-magazine" was the natural transition medium from religious magazine to religious newspaper and has remained to this day a hybrid product, hardly to be placed in either category. Though admitting a certain amount of essay matter of the magazine type, it has tended to allot a third or half of its space to current "religious news" consisting of reports of missionary activity, the proceedings of religious societies, accounts of revivals, correspondence, lists of new religious publications, notices of ordinations and installations, church dedications, obituary, etc. But for the general practice of excluding secular summary and advertisements, there is many times no distinction to be made between "news-magazine" and "newspaper". Similarity to the newspaper extends itself into the areas of format and periodicity. Though not a folio, the "news-magazine" has tended to larger size, appearing as often in quarto as octavo form. Though not exclusively a weekly, it has tended in that direction, being more likely to appear as such than at less frequent intervals. Turning from this last of the periodical types to the weekly folio religious newspaper, its content proportions may be estimated as one fourth light religious essay matter, one-half religious news as designated above, and one-fourth secular summary and advertisements.

Terminology explained, the sketching of the rise of religious journalism in the United States becomes a relatively simple task. Three periods of development stand out.

I. *Establishment*, 1743-1830. The first exclusively religious journal in America was the weekly *Christian History*, Boston, 1743-1745, an octavo news-magazine devoted to the promotion of the Great Revival. Its short life indicates its precocious nature. Half a century was yet to elapse before religious journalism was to experience even initial success. From 1745 to 1772 three religious papers were attempted at New York, two magazines in the environs of Philadelphia, but one of the five outlasting its first year. Thereupon, the exigencies of war enforced a total blackout until 1789. Then came the phenomenal burst of activity that established religious journalism as a national institution by 1830. From 1789 through 1830 over 500 religious journals were founded of which 175 survived to enjoy simultaneous publication in the latter year. Life expectancy so increased that approximately a fourth of the journals founded were now assured an existence ranging from ten to over one hundred years. Centers of publication were to be found as far westward as the Mississippi, as far south as Georgia and Alabama. Circulation figures of 5,000 to 10,000 were common, while the Methodist *Christian Advocate's* subscription list of 25,000 in 1829 was hailed as the world's largest, *London Times* not excepted. With respect to journalistic type, the newspaper and news-magazine quite surpassed magazine and review in popularity. Functional characteristics also became evident. As so capably suggested by Jensen, these were 1. Socialization and 2. Propaganda. Widely separated groups of common belief along the coast and on the frontier were bound together into a working social unit through this medium of communication. At the same time, new converts were constantly sought by the spreading of journalistic propaganda in parts both near and far. Already by 1830 upwards of sixty religious groups were availing themselves of these functional advantages, being essentially 1. Denominational bodies 2. Schismatical sects, and 3. Special Interest groups such as Missionary, Sunday School, Tract, Peace, Temperance, etc., societies. Each group had its official organ and frequently a number of non-official ones. Unquestionably, religious journalism had established itself in America by 1830.

II. *Marked Growth,* 1830-1880. The next half century was to be the golden age. The yearly output of religious journals increased steadily until by 1880 the number was upwards of 550. Average length of life increased apace. Centers of publication pressed steadily westward to the Pacific Coast. Circulation figures rose until it has been estimated that three copies of religious journals were being issued per inhabitant. The religious newspaper became by far the favored journalistic type. Numerous cult, slavery and sectional religious journals cropped up to increase greatly the diversity of interests represented. Scarcely any religious group claiming adherents beyond the local scene was without some type of journalistic voice.

III. *Difficulties and Adjustments,* 1880, to date. Although the number of religious journals published yearly has increased steadily since 1880 until today some 1,200 are being issued, the period has been characterized by two restricting factors. 1. Waning denomination interest. 2. Increasing financial distress. The first was a natural aftermath of the Civil War which served as a ghastly reminder of the results of untempered inter-group strife. Circulation figures of religious journals of restricted interest began to drop; those of broader interest to rise. Whereas the religious *Independent* founded in 1848 was a pioneer, by the close of the nineteenth century its cause was being bolstered by such influential organs as the *Christian Union, Christian Herald* and *Christian Century.* The trend has continued into the twentieth century in the founding of numerous non-sectarian journals designed to instruct in specialized fields such as the *Journal of Religion* for scholars, *Church Management* for ministers, the *International Journal of Religious Education* for teachers, etc. Financial difficulties have accelerated the trend. Sensitiveness to the type of advertising suitable for inclusion has in itself steadily decreased extra-circulation income since 1880. The falling circulation of the average denominational journal has aggravated the situation by causing advertisers to withdraw copy to concentrate it in papers of wider circulation. The result has been fewer copies of religious journals published per inhabitant, but an increase in quality of religious journalism. Items of purely regional interest are now placed in the "church page" of the local secular paper. Matters of broader and more lasting significance are saved for the official group journals which are now tending to be of news-magazine and review type and more appreciative of opposition views.

IV. *Coming Recognition of Value of Religious Journal as Historical Source.* Combined knowledge of types and production should at once create an awareness of the unparalleled value of the religious journal as a source of historical information. Three invaluable qualities characterize the content of its pages to a greater degree than other sources: 1. Contemporaneity; 2. Continuity; 3. Variety.

By virtue of its frequency of publication the religious journal assumes the role of "on-the-spot" reporter, impulsive and opinionative to be sure, because of the haste of composition, but on account of its prejudices and exaggerations all the more faithful a reflector of the mood of the day. Continuity of record is also a quality derived from frequency of publication. Following the content of the religious journal month by month or week by week or at other intervals as the case may be over a period of years, one witnesses a moving picture of "religion in the making" as contrasted to random snapshots derived from miscellaneous pamphlets, manuscripts and books. Add the quality of variety of content extending from learned theological essays to local bits of personal interest and the worth of the religious journal appears in full perspective. Until now largely overlooked as a historical source, its pages contain a mine of information for the re-evaluation of American religious history. The new data disclosed in the article on the "anti-missionary movement"* is but a sample of discoveries awaiting use of this fertile source. See Catholic Journalism; religious tract movement in the U. S.

A history of religious journalism in the United States has not yet been published. The following will provide leads for those primarily interested in the interpretative aspects of the subject: W. C. Bower, *Church at Work in the Modern Field* (1935), pp. 236-64; C. L. Cannon, *Journalism: A Bibliography* (1924), pp. 273-276; H. E. Jensen, "The Rise of Religious Journalism in the United States to 1845" (Doctoral Dissertation, University of Chicago, 1920); F. L. Mott, *History of American Magazines* (1938). Those interested in religious journals for historical purposes should proceed as follows. Consultation of G. P. Albaugh, *An Annotated Bibliography of Religious Periodicals and Newspapers in What is now the United States, 1730-1830* (1943) will reveal titles and locations of all religious journals known to have been published through 1830. Subsequent to 1830, examination of the following sources arranged chronologically will reveal significant titles and denominational affiliations: Jensen, *supra,* for years 1831-1845; I. Garwood, *American Periodicals From 1850-1860* (1931); G. P. Rowell, *American Newspaper Directory* (1869 ff.); N. W. Ayer and Sons, *American Newspaper Annual and Directory* (1880 to date: title varies slightly); S. N. D. North, *History and Present Condition of the Newspaper and Periodical Press* (Tenth Census Report, 1884); Batten and Co., *Directory of the Religious Press* (1897); A. W. Faxon, *Checklist of American and English Periodicals* (1908 to date); H. O. Severance, *A Guide to Current Periodicals and Serials of the United States and Canada* (five editions, 1906-1931); J. H. Meier, *Catholic Press Directory* (1928 and 1932); *Yearbook of the American Churches* (biennially 1933-1941 +). Titles ascertained from these sources, the library locations of many can be found by consultation of the *Union List of Serials in the Libraries of United States and Canada* (1943). Correspondence with religious libraries and state historical societies will produce other locations.

G.P.A.

religious journals: See Journals of religion and theology. Also: Catholic Journalism.

religious liberty: The struggle for religious liberty in Christendom may conveniently be reckoned as commencing with the Protestant Reformation,* despite the many ideas favoring liberty which emerged in the late Middle Ages, when mysticism portrayed religion as too inward to be cut by the sword of the magistrate and humanism fought for freedom of historical investigation. Yet the Protestant Reformation, though intensifying religious fanaticism, at the same time wrecked the unity of the medieval ecclesiastical structure and thus opened a chapter which could end only in mutual extermination or religious liberty. Many factors, some religious and some secular, made for the second alternative. The three presuppositions requisite for religious persecution*, namely that the truth can be known, that the point denied by the heretic is important and that coercion is effective were all subjected to attack by men who were concerned for religion itself. At the same time attention was diverted from religion by a growing secularism in economics, politics and general outlook.

Modern states have dealt with the problem of diverse religions in three ways: territorialism, comprehension and complete toleration. The first two were tried when the sects were intolerant of each other. The third requires a tolerant temper.

Territorialism* permits only one religion in one territory, but permits subjects to emigrate, so that in the case of neighboring states with differing religions the problem is solved by an exchange of populations. This system is called *cuius regio eius religio* (Whose region his religion), and was adopted at the Peace of Augsburg in 1555, the Peace of Westphalia** in 1648 and by the American Constitution in 1787, for although no religion was established by our national government, each state was left free to establish whatever religion it might choose, and state churches actually survived in the United States throughout the first third of the nineteenth century.

The second system of comprehension establishes one religion in a given area and, in order to win the allegiance of the entire populace without emigration, makes the doctrinal and other demands very few. Such latitudinarianism characterized the Anglican settlement.

The third system of complete religious liberty has been called the *pax dissidentium,* where divergent groups agree to live together with no weakening of affirmation and no intimidating of persons. The first experiment along this line was made in Poland in 1783. The next great attempt was made by Oliver Cromwell.* In both of these instances the groups agreeing to respect each other were limited. Cromwell excluded Catholics and Socinians. This system without restriction has come to prevail in the United States, and, despite the establishment, in England also. Prevailingly, too, religious liberty had been achieved on the continent prior to the flare up of persecution by totalitarian states.

The best factual survey of the whole field is that of Francescò Ruffini, *Religious Liberty* (1912); for England a great wealth of material has been gathered by Wilbur K. Jordan, *The Development of Religious Toleration in England* (1932-40) 4 vols.; a briefer treatment of the theory is given by Thomas Lyon, *The Theory of Religious Liberty in England, 1603-39* (1937); for the United States there is but one general work, that of Sanford H. Cobb, *The Rise of Religious Liberty in America* (1902); a full outline of the whole subject with bibliography is given by Roland H. Banton, "The Struggle for Religious Liberty," *Church History* X (1941), pp. 95-124.

R.H.B.

religious magazines in U. S.: See religious journalism in the U. S.; religious journals.

religious newspapers in U. S.: See religious journalism in the U. S.

religious orders: See orders, religious.

religious organizations: See anti-national religious organization agitation in the U. S.

religious periodicals in U. S.: See religious journalism in the U. S.; religious journals.

religious 'powers': (historically considered) In two-factor religions* the following terms or words most properly apply:

god, goddess; (more or less personalized and moralized non-human nature forces or powers)

shade, hero, ghost, 'dead', soul of the underworld, living soul (human religious forces or 'powers').

In one-factor religions* the following terms or words apply:

deity, divinity, saint, angel, devil, ancestors, worthies, human soul (living or deceased). Deity stands at the top or center of a vast hierarchy of 'powers' which extends out or down to human souls and beyond; in religions where there is no Deity, the general pattern of entities is in all other respects quite similar to those with a Deity. The general ideology of 'government', inclusive of man and his environment, holds all religious entities in a frame of reference of some kind, intelligible to the adherents, whether they be primitives or members of a complex human society. See classification of religions.

F.L.P.

religious press in the U. S.: See religious journalism in the U. S.

religious societies: See evangelicalism and evangelical revival; Wesley, Charles and John.

Religious Society of Friends: See Quakers.

religious tract movement in the United States: Basically, an organized Protestant attempt to reach the unchurched by means of gratuitous or pittance distribution of low-cost evangelistic leaflets or "tracts" within destitute areas. With the passing of the years, however, increasing attention has been given to the distribution of other types of low-cost evangelistic literature than "tracts".

The founding of the Methodist Book Concern at Philadelphia in 1789 marks the planting of the tract idea in America. Jointly a means of eliminating the middlemen's profit in publication and of authorizing large editions to meet the needs of all representatives of the denomination, this Concern produced religious literature so cheaply and on so large a scale as to make wholesale distribution for the first time practicable in the new country. The Methodist circuit rider with bulging pouch of low-cost evangelistic literature became a familiar figure in unchurched areas. At the most he asked only a pittance for his wares. Frequently, aided by financial grants of interested friends, he distributed copies gratuitously. The results in terms of conversions were impressive.

Conditions at the opening of the nineteenth century were ripe for growth of the idea. Ignorance and indifference to religion among the indigent poor in the populated areas along the seacoast had for some time been a concern. Religious destitution along the rapidly expanding frontier was a newer, but equally provocative source of anxiety. An alarming dearth of ministers to supply a corrective in either instance made the situation acute. English Deism and French Illuminatism were spreading unchallenged in destitute areas. Free-lance evangelists were arousing the people to emotional excesses, creating numerous sectarian apostacies. Religion was obviously in a state of confusion. Unless some means could be found to bridge the yawning gap between need and lagging leadership, it would remain in such a state for some time to come.

Quite logically the Methodist precedent of promoting religion in destitute areas through the printed word was seized upon as general remedy. One after another local religious group of varied description organized for the express purpose of printing or purchasing and distributing low-cost religious literature. Whereas the Methodists made considerable use of books, these newly formed groups favored the unbound leaflet of "tract", thereby coming to be called "tract societies". Organization was simple. One became a member by contributing a sum suited to his means. In return he received a certain number of cheap tracts of his choice. These were then distributed, usually gratuitously, in destitute areas. Over 450 local societies so organized are known to have been founded 1800-1825, mostly in the East. None distributed less than a few thousand tracts; one, the New England Tract Society of Boston, over 4,000,000.

The year 1825 brought an important change in emphasis. Through the formation of the American Tract Society, in New York, the various local groups were knit together into a working national unit, greatly increasing their effectiveness. Sponsored by an interdenominational board of directors, the Society besought all regional organizations interested in propagation of the "essential truths" of the faith to become auxiliaries in a master attempt at evangelization through the printed page. The plan was essentially a division of labor. The Society with its unexcelled stereotyping equipment would concentrate upon the mass production of approved tracts to make them available at a fraction of previous cost. Auxiliaries relieved of printing and purchasing problems would spend full time in distribution. Response was immediate. Evangelical groups with few exceptions fell in with the plan. Only minority groups objecting to the "essential truths" withheld support—such as the Unitarians, Universalists, etc., and, of course, the Catholics. Denominational publication societies for the most part turned their attention to specific interests, leaving the production of tracts for general evangelization purposes largely to the interdenominational American Tract Society which has to date printed over 525,000,000 copies of tracts, several thousand distinct tracts being involved.

Simultaneous with national organizations periodical publication was undertaken. The American Tract Society has successively sponsored in the English language the: *American Tract Magazine* (N. Y., 1825-42); *American Messenger* (N. Y., 1843-1923); and *Truth* (N. Y., 1941 to date). Auxiliary societies have upon occasion become active in this area. The Evangelical Tract Society at Newburgh, N. Y., issued the *Christian Witness* (1822-1826). The New York State Tract Society supported the *New York Tract Magazine* (1824-1827). The *Pennsylvania and Delaware Tract Magazine* (Phila., 1828-1831) represented the societies of the respective states. During Civil War years the branch society at Boston was particularly active, supporting in turn the: *Christian Banner and Tract Journal* (Boston and N. Y., 1859-72); *Child at Home* (Boston, 1860-73); *Freedman's Journal* (Boston, 1864-69?); and *Freedman* (Boston, 1865-1866). Future research will undoubtedly reveal other titles. Meantime, the "American" Society's singular achievement of circulating since 1825 over 336,000,000 periodical issues speaks in itself of the influence exerted.

A further undertaking termed the "Volume Enterprise" was entered upon in 1828. At that time, in consultation with auxiliaries, the American Tract Society projected publication of a series of fifteen books, quality reflected by the inclusion of such works as Bunyan's *Pilgrim's Progress*, Baxter's *Saints Everlasting Rest* and Dodderidge's, *Rise and Progress of Religion in the Soul.* Solid worth, attractive make-up and low cost worked together to make the project a marked success. Ministers and Christian workers in their enthusiastic distribution quickly exhausted the initial supply and entered a plea for larger editions and a wider selection of titles. The evangelical slogan came to be "at least one such volume in every home in the Union". Formidable as the undertaking was, it did not miss its mark far. Other series of books followed, including a library for children. Some 36,000,000 volumes have been published to date, representing several hundred distinct works.

The institution of "colporteur service" about 1840 added appreciably to the success of the movement. Home missionaries of humble gift but deep devotion, colporteurs have carried the Christian message in evangelical leaflet and volume to the neglected extremes of the country, viz., the congested districts of the city and the lonely frontier farm. At one time more than five hundred such workers were employed by central society and auxiliaries with instructions to sell or give away literature as seemed best to the furtherance of evangelistic effort.

Several more specialized features of the movement remain to be mentioned. Since the Mexican War (1846-48) the "American" Society has served as coordinator in a persistent tract ministry to the soldier and sailor. Chaplains have been supplied with an enormous amount of literature, much of it free. To be closely associated with this ministry is the Society's seventy-year-old custom of presenting Scriptures to West Point graduates. Of different aspect, but quite as established as a custom, is organized work among immigrants. Through library and workers based on Ellis Island the Society has long met the immigrant with citizenship manual in one hand, gospel leaflet in the other. This has required the printing of literature in many foreign languages. So it has been that nearly a fifth of all publications printed by the Society—some 150,000,000 copies including tracts, periodicals and volumes—have been issued in foreign language. Only a portion have been distributed on the Island proper. The rest have followed the immigrant inland.

Were it possible to add figures respecting independent tract activity carried on by non-cooperating groups within the evangelical fold, by non-evangelical connections like the Unitarians and by the Catholics, the powerful influence wielded by quantity distribution of low-cost religious literature would become even more impressive. The citation of such figures, however, lies within the province of denominational history, having no relevance to the "Tract Movement" proper which has been cooperative and non-controversial in spirit. See anti-Tract movement in the U. S.

For comprehensive treatment to 1825 see M. V. Mussina, "The Backgrounds and Origins of the American Religious Tract Movement" (Unpublished Doctoral Dissertation, Drew University, 1936). For data since 1825 see E. N. Hardy, *Century of Revivals* (forthcoming 1943) which is a history of the operations of the American Tract Society (N. Y.). The pamphlet *A Brief History of the American Tract Society, Boston* (1855, by said Society) is an informing sketch of the activities of the important branch society at Boston which began in 1814 as the New England Tract Society, changed its name to American Tract Society in 1823 and has retained such since despite appropriation of the name by the central society at New York in 1825. For further reliable information, original sources must be consulted. Best-balanced of these are the various periodicals mentioned *supra*. For summary listings of titles and volumes published, circulation statistics and other concise data the *Annual Report* of the American Tract Society (1825 to date) is superior. The Society has carefully preserved copies of its various publications along with other material relevant to the Tract Movement and is eager to grant the research student access to its collection. Dr. H. R. Monro, present president, has furnished the basic information for this article, and Dr. W. H. Matthews, secretary, has offered valuable assistance. G.P.A.

remanence: (Lat., *remanere,* to remain) A term denoting a view of the Lord's Supper which upholds the belief that the material elements of bread and wine remain (*remanent*) in the sacrament after consecration coexistent with the body and blood of Christ, in contradistinction to the Roman Catholic view of transubstantiation in which, at the time of consecration, only the external form (accidents) of the bread and wine is believed to remain while the substance of both elements is changed into the true body and blood of Christ. The doctrine is most closely associated with the teaching of John Wyclif* on the Lord's Supper (Cf. his *De Eucharistia*). Cf. consubstantiation; impanation; Lutheran doctrine of the Lord's supper; transubstantiation. F.W.N.

Remonstrants, the: The forty-five ministers, defenders of Arminian* views, who signed the Remonstrance in 1610 were called the Remonstrants. In 1619, at the Synod of Dort*, the Remonstrants were deposed from their ministry. Later, they were sentenced to banishment. In 1630, they were granted complete freedom to live and work anywhere in Holland. See five points of Arminianism. W.E.R.

Renaissance: A wave of intellectual and esthetic awakening and of secular culture which may be thought of as originating in Italy in the fourteenth century and having its Italian culmination at the end of the fifteenth and early in the sixteenth, and rising and falling at correspondingly later dates in France, Germany, the Low Countries, England and Spain. The word means "re-birth." The figure of a re-birth is ancient and common, especially in connection with religion. In its secular application, the phrase, "Roma renascitur," was used in the ninth century in connection with the Carlovingian schools. In the fifteenth century the great Florentine Platonist, Ficino*, declared, "Plato renascitur." Macchiavelli* spoke (1527) of "Roma renata." In his *Lives of the Painters* (1550), Vasari mentioned "la rinascita di questi arti"—meaning the fine arts. In French (about 1700) there is reference to "la renaissance de lettres . . . des arts." The use of the term, "La Renaissance" to designate a particular period is first found in French early in the nineteenth century, and about 1840 the French word began to be adopted in English with the same meaning. Matthew Arnold (1869) substituted the form derived directly from the Latin, "Renascence," but this never gained wide currency.

The most brilliant definitions of the renaissance have generally been interpretations or evaluative judgments rather than factual descriptions. Michelet: "The discovery of the world and of man." Walter Pater: "A general excitement and enlightening of the human mind." Symonds: "The attainment of self-conscious freedom to the human spirit." On the other hand, modern Roman Catholic writers and neo-medievalists generally, since they find the climax of culture in the thirteenth century solidarity of European thought and society under ecclesiastical authority at its apogee, view the Renaissance as no "re-birth" at all but a period of disintegration and decadence, much as a French monarchist with a firm attachment to Bourbon ideals would view the French Revolution.

Whether for better or for worse, the Renaissance certainly had the character of a revolution. Its keynote was a secular humanism implying recognition of human and mundane values as having validity unconditioned by theological considerations or ecclesiastical approval. Ignoring, without troubling to dispute, the Augustinian view of man as a victim of original sin and as wholly dependent upon a hierarchically controlled church for the means of grace by which he might enjoy status in the present world and the hope of future felicity, the men of the Renaissance found that the natural man, in his own right and by his own powers, has resources of knowledge and satisfying experience. For this conscious and unashamed delight in life, they found their models and their "Scriptures" in the literature of classical antiquity. The "revival of learning," generally associated and sometimes erroneously identified with Renaissance humanism, was therefore more than a series of antiquarian discoveries and linguistic exercises. It was the apparatus by which men could be put into possession of patterns of life and thought which had prevailed before humanity had lost the title-deeds to joy and freedom. This secular humanistic delight in the life that now is and the classicism which gave it an honored tradition and an intellectual formulation were the primary characteristics of the Renaissance.

Secondary characteristics which naturally followed from these included: a general exaltation of the ideal of liberty; a high degree of individualism both in thought and in the conduct of life; a free exercise of criticism in regard to accepted ideas and existing institutions; a development of the spirit of experiment and exploration; the stimulation of creativity; love of sensuous beauty for its own sake and for the joy it gives; a realistic attitude toward human and natural phenomena; sensuality, in those who found the pagan freedom going to their heads and for whom the restraints of the Christian code of morals ceased to be (or had never been) effective; and, especially for men of exceptional powers, the ideal of versatility as more admirable than concentrated attention to a single field of endeavor.

While the rise of the Renaissance in Italy has been dated, roughly, in the mid-fourteenth century —say, with Petrarch and Boccaccio**—it must be noted that its roots run farther back. The rise of the vernacular literatures, especially in the twelfth and thirteenth centuries, the widening of horizons due to the Crusades*, the economic changes which these stimulated, and the indirect influence of Arabian and Jewish scholarship—all tended to disturb that "integrated society" which was the ideal, if never the perfect achievement, of the high Middle Ages. The forces of revolt and dissent were, indeed, at work long before the forces of institutional solidarity and integration had reached their peak.

It is unnecessary here to trace the historical events in which the spirit of the Renaissance found expression. Its immediate effects on the Roman Catholic Church were: a) some loss of prestige and control over the masses, and especially over the intellectuals, even where its authority was not directly challenged; b) the corruption of much of the personnel of the hierarchy, who adopted the pagan morals and sensuality of the Renaissance without adopting its liberating intellectual processes (since free-living was easier and, with their resources of wealth and luxury, more tempting than free-thinking); c) the development of techniques of thought and criticism which, in the hands of serious reformers, became effective instruments for combatting not only the abuses of the church but the whole theory and structure of its claim to world-dominion; d) the Counter-reformation*, which was not only a housecleaning to get rid of the abuses which had marred the church, and a marshalling of its forces to repell the inroads of Protestantism, but also a Counter-Renaissance. The Protestant Reformation*, both Lutheran and Calvinistic, was also, to a very considerable extent, a reaction against the central concepts of the Renaissance, though it made effective use, especially in its early phases, of impulses and resources which the Renaissance had supplied. The more direct heritage of Renaissance thought—or of the individualistic, empirical and rationalistic methods which it employed—are found in the developments of modern science, in the application of scientific and critical methods to the study of religion, in philosophies of Locke, Hume and the Enlightenment**, and in all phases of liberalism. Cf. Pico della Mirandola; Pletho; Pomponazzi; progress; universals, battle over; Vittorino da Feltre.

J. A. Symonds, *The Renaissance in Italy* (London, 1886); E. M. Hulme, *The Renaissance, The Protestant Reformation and the Catholic Reformation.* (1914); J. B. Fletcher, *Literature of the Italian Renaissance* (1934). W.E.G.

Renaissance style: See art, Christian, ecclesiastical.

Renan, Joseph Ernest: (1823-92) French orientalist, historian, theologian and philosopher. For a time Professor of Hebrew in Collège de France. Was sent to Phoenicia by the government in 1860, where he laid the basis for the *Corpus Inscriptionum Semiticarum,* 1881-1892. Jumped to fame in 1863 through his *Vie de Jésus,* later expanded to an eight volume *Histoire des Origines du Christianisme* (1886). Also wrote 5 volumes on *Histoire du peuple d'Israel* (1887-1891) and many works in the field of philosophy. See Lives of Jesus. C.T.C.

Rendtorff, Franz: (1860-1937) German Protestant theologian. He was born in Gütergotz near Potsdam. From 1902-1910 he was professor of Practical Theology, Kiel and from 1910-1930 in Leipzig. His main academic interest was in the historical roots of Protestant public worship and of religious education. As president of the *Gus-*

tav-Adolf-Verein, an organization for the support of Protestant minorities in Roman Catholic countries, he took a very active part in the efforts to strengthen their national selfconsciousness as Germans.

Principal books:

Die Taufe im Urchristentum (1905); *Das Problem der Konfirmation und der Religionsunterricht in der Volksschule* (1910); *Die Geschichte des chirstlichen Gottesdienstes unter dem Gesichtspunkte der liturgischen Erbfolge* (1914). O.A.P.

Renouvier, Charles: (1818-1903) French philosopher; held that reality consists of phenomena, experiences of subjects. Influenced by Kant and Leibniz**, he rejected the thing-in-itself of the first and the causal determinism of both earlier thinkers. Probably the first modern to do justice to the aspect of contingency in experience (followed in this by Wm. James*), and one of the first to break with the absolutistic conception of God, who was, he held, perfect in goodness and intelligence, but not in every respect unlimited. A radical finitist, he affirmed a first moment of time—an actually infinite series being logically impossible. See finite God; infinite.

C. Renouvier, *Essais de critique générale* (1851-64); *Le Personnalisme* (1903); *Uchronie* (European history as it might have happened, had human freedom chosen another alternative) (1857). C.H.

reordination: a) Catholic theology excludes reordination as Bishop, priest, or deacon; but ordination* may be repeated if previous orders are not recognized or (conditionally) if previous ordination is doubtful; b) some Protestant views (especially early American Congregationalist) considered ordination as admission to a particular pastoral charge, and therefore repeated the ceremony on occasion. E.R.H.

Reorganized Church of Jesus Christ: See Latter Day Saints.

repentance: (Gr. *metanoia*) Literally, change of mind. Turning from courses or ends hitherto preferred, to seek other ends or try other ways. So in O.T., God is represented as repenting, changing His intention (Amos 7: 1-6), or undoing His own work through disappointment with the result (Gen. 6: 5, 6). More generally, repentance is on man's part Godward; it is turning from the evil life of disobedience to God to the path His will ordains. So Jesus (Mt. 4: 17; Mk. 1: 14, 15) calls men to repent, to change their mind, purpose and expectation concerning God. In evangelical Christianity, following Apostolic and Pauline teaching, repentance is not merely an act but a full experience, including abhorrence of the sin from which one turns and a constant disposition toward complete amendment of life (2 Cor. 7: 9, 10; Acts 26: 20). The depth of the experience is sometimes seen in portrayals where the word 'repentance' is not used; as when Paul speaks of the believer as being buried with Christ and raised to total newness of life (Rom. 6: 3-5; Col. 2: 12). In John, the word 'repent' does not occur; but there is the same idea of change or renewal under the figure of the New Birth, which parallels repentance as the condition of entrance to the Kingdom (cf. Mk. 1: 15 and John 3: 3). Repentance is not produced by man's unaided resolve, but is God's gift or 'operation' (Col. 2: 12; cf. Acts 3: 26). Repentance as act, turning, has its completion in Faith*, its fruit or reward in Forgiveness* (Acts, 2: 38; 3: 19; 26: 18), or in Repentance as experience as indicated above. See conviction of sin; Pullus, Robert; salvation; terminism.

C. Ryder Smith, *The Bible Doctrine of Salvation* (1941); L. Arpee, *The Atonement in Experience* (1932); V. Taylor, *Forgiveness and Reconciliation* (1941). J.L.

rephaim: Race of legendary giants mentioned in the O.T. (Gen. xiv, 5; xv, 20; Deut. iii, 11; II Sam. xxi. 16-22, etc.). S.L.T.

reprobation: Final apostasy* from God. A part of the doctrine of election* whose *classicus locus* is Calvin, *Institutes,* III. xxi ("God determined . . . every individual; . . . eternal life foreordained for some, eternal damnation for others"). Outstanding precursors of Calvin*: Paul (Rom. 1: 28; 9: 18) and Augustine. Premise of reprobation: Divine Sovereignty and Foreknowledge*; that God's will prevails, He foreknows all and purposes as He foreknows, applicable to fact of the unsaved. Many hold premise without the consequence; 'reprobation not necessary inference of doctrine of election' (Denney).

S. A. McDowall, *Is Sin Our Fault?* (1932), Westminster Books; C. H. Valentine, *Moral Freedom and the Christian Faith* (1932). J.L.

requiem: A mass* for the dead sung at funerals and on All Souls' Day*. The sections differ from the regular form of the mass, the joyful gloria and the credo** being omitted and other sections added. The usual arrangement is introit, kyrie, gradual and tract, sequence, offertory, sanctus et benedictus, agnus Dei, and communio**. Outstanding composers are Palestrina, Vittoria, Cherubini, Fauré, and Dvorák. The German Requiem of Brahms may not be properly called a requiem for it is a setting of seven unliturgical texts from the German Bible. See prayers for the dead. E.H.B.

requiescat: The first word of the Latin formula *requiescat in pace,* "May he (or she) rest in peace"; generalized to cover any prayer for the repose of the dead. See prayers for the dead. B.S.E.

reredos: (Rear—Fr. *dos,* back, from Lat., *dorsum*) The screen back of an altar*, often rich with ornament and religious symbolism. F.T.P.

rescript: In Roman law, an answer on a question of law given by the Emperor in writing, either by a *subscriptio* on the original petition or by an independent *epistola,* at the request of a petitioner. Strictly speaking, it was personal in character and was not intended to constitute a precedent. In canon law* (*Codex Iuris Canonici,* 36-62), a reply in writing, given by the Holy

See* or an Ordinary, concerning matters relating to judicial controversies (*r. justitiae*) or granting favors (*r. gratiae*). Rescripts may be in the form of Bulls, Briefs**, Apostolic Letters, or (most commonly) simple rescripts. Like a particular precept, a rescript affects only the person or persons for whom given. Cf. bull, papal; motu proprio. J.C.M.

reservation of the sacrament: In the Roman Catholic and the Eastern churches, after administration of the Holy Communion a portion of the consecrated species is reserved to communicate those unable to be present, especially the sick and, above all, those at the point of death. The custom has been revived in many Anglican churches but is virtually absent from Protestantism. B.S.E.

response: The liturgical answer of the people to a declaration or invitation uttered by the officiant at a service. A fixed group of such declarations with the responses is a "Responsary" (Lat., *responsorium*), often very elaborate in form. B.S.E.

restitution: Ordinary meaning, return of what has been misappropriated to rightful possessor, or reparation for injury done. This is a Christian obligation, prerequisite of acceptable approach to God (Math. 5: 23, 24). Special theological meaning: restoration (Gr., *apokatastasis*: Acts 3: 21), through God's triumph over all that has marred His work, of man's life and the entire creation to His original design. J.L.

restorationism: The belief that God's purpose, interpreted as the ultimate restoration of all things including therefore the final salvation of all men, cannot be forever frustrated but must be completely accomplished. This belief which was advocated by Origen* and which has appeared in subsequent Christian thought, is definitely affirmed by the Universalists*. However the doctrine of restorationism is regarded as heretical by the R. C. Church and by the Protestant Churches generally. The advocates of this belief protest against any tendency in religious thought to isolate God's act of judging from His eternal nature as Sovereign Love. Since God's holiness is the holiness of Sovereign Love the reality of that divine holiness* is redemptive and sanctifying rather than punitive in its ultimate effect upon sinners. This doctrine does not deny that so long as the rebellious soul remains impenitent it will experience the fierce intensity of God's reaction against evil as a punishment or torment. Nevertheless, the doctrine of restorationism affirms that it would be an unworthy representation of God, who would have all men to be saved, to hold that He is not able to accomplish that which he purposes. It must be believed therefore that the infinitely resourceful and Sovereign Love of God will overcome all evil with the Divine Goodness so that all beings will finally live a blessed life with God "that God may be all in all." (I Cor. 15:28). H.W.J.

resurrection: (Lat., *re-*, again; *surgere*, rise) Restoration of the dead to life; especially the reanimation of the bodies of the dead. The historic Christian doctrine is based on the accounts of the resurrection of Jesus* and other passages of the N.T., and was affirmed by the Fourth Lateran Council (1215), which stated that all men, saved and reprobate alike, "will rise again with their own bodies which they now bear about with them." (See resurrection of the dead—for Jewish and Christian views.) A vague notion that the dead body will rise is widely prevalent among primitive animists. This must be the explanation of many wide-spread burial customs, such as the burial of tools and food with the dead. The antiquity of such customs is well attested by paleolithic remains. However, primitive men do not distinguish sharply between material and spiritual realities, nor, as a rule, define their views consistently. It is therefore impossible to determine, even in some existing tribes, whether it is believed that the body will rise again, or, rather, that a quasi-material soul, of similar form, leaves the body and engages in activities analogous to those of the present life. Likewise, the Greek and Roman doctrine of the soul's sojourn in Hades* was of a finely attenuated, yet material being, recognizably similar to the earthly body, and deeply affected by the treatment accorded the body, yet not identical with it. Zoroastrianism* presents a doctrine of the life hereafter which is much more vividly materialistic in conception, but even Zoroastrians do not clearly affirm the resurrection of the body. The clearest assertion of belief in bodily resurrection, outside of Jewish and Christian thought is to be found in the Mohammedan *Koran**, which is, of course, deeply influenced by the Christian teaching. According to the *Koran*, God will call the angels* to bring out the dead and raise them up as living bodies of flesh. They will occur the judgment. Thereafter the elect will live in sensuous enjoyment of abounding food, dazzling gems, and "large-eyed damsels," while the wicked will be cast into everlasting and equally physical torment. Some Mohammedans have interpreted such descriptions as figurative representations of spiritual pleasure and pain, but these interpretations have been vigorously rejected by the orthodox. See descent into hades; final judgment; immortality, kinds of; primitive religion; soul.

See J. Hastings, *Encyclopedia of Religion and Ethics*, "State of the Dead." L.H.DEW.

resurrection of Jesus: Of this event there are seven, or perhaps eight, different accounts in the N.T. (Mt. 28, Mk. 16, Jn. 20, Jn. 21, I Cor. 15: 3-8, Ac. 1: 2, 3, Lk. 24: 13-32) and allusions to it are constant. This abundance of evidence is, however, a source of difficulty, since the accounts are often in conflict with one another. Undoubtedly the primary one is that of Paul in I Cor. 15. It is the earliest in date, and Paul expressly states that he repeats the testimony of all the Apostles. At several points he is in agreement with the Gospel narratives. 1) Christ arose on the third day. 2) He appeared first to

Peter (cf. Lk. 24:34). 3) From the mention of James and the "500 at once" it may be inferred that most or all of the visions took place in Galilee. But in Paul's account there are significant differences. 1) The whole stress is laid on the visions, and no mention is made of the empty tomb. 2) The visions continued through a considerable period, as we also learn from the notice in Ac: 1:3. 3) The appearance to Paul himself is placed on the same footing as the earlier ones. What Paul saw on the way to Damascus was Christ in his glorified body, and it would follow that the visions of Peter and the others were of the same character. Of the Gospel accounts that of Mark is the earliest, and is much simpler than those in the other Gospels, although it centers like them on the empty tomb. From a comparison of the various narratives it may be gathered that a tendency was at work to make a mysterious event ever more mysterious. It may be gathered, too, that the story of the tomb was originally a confirmation of the visions. The disciples had seen the Lord in Galilee; returning to Jerusalem they met the women, who reported that they had found the tomb empty. This in itself was obviously no evidence that the Lord had risen, but in course of time the whole emphasis came to be laid on it.

There can be no question that the faith in the resurrection was grounded on some fact. In the narrative of Paul we have evidence which came directly from eye-witnesses, who were fully convinced that they had seen the risen Lord. To explain the nature of their experience will always be impossible, and it must have been inexplicable to themselves. They were in a mood of ecstasy, in which they were conscious only of the momentary impression. Attempts were made later to reflect on it, and to these we owe the narrative in the Gospels; but Paul wisely confines himself to the bare fact, "the Lord was seen". The difficulties which have always been felt are much more concerned with the mode of the resurrection than with the fact,—that the disciples were in some way brought into living contact with Christ after his death. Modern psychology has sought, in its own manner, to explain their experience, or explain it away; but the theories offered deal only with the mechanism and not with the fact. To say that the resurrection visions were subjective means nothing, for a knowledge given subjectively may still be real. The problem is insoluble, not because of the inadequacy of our information, but because of our ignorance of the unseen world and its relations to this one.

M. Goguel, *La foi a la résurrection* (1933); K. Lake, *The Resurrection of Jesus* (1907); C. Bowen, *The Resurrection of Jesus* (1911). E.F.S.

resurrection of the dead: A term which is often loosely employed to denote the future life. It applies, however, not to immortality in the large sense, but to that conception of it which was peculiar to the Hebrew mind. For Greek thought the body was nothing but a prison in which the higher rational principle was confined, and from which it must be released before it could attain to its true being. For the Hebrews the body was essential to full life. The soul in itself had no force or substance, and must be reunited with the body if the actual man was to exist after death. In the O.T. this idea of resurrection is never definitely set forth, though in several passages it is at least suggested. According to Daniel (12:2, 13) those who have remained faithful through persecution will be raised up hereafter. Job declares his conviction (19:25) that although he dies and is buried he will appear in his flesh before God, who will vindicate him. For the most part, however, the O.T. accepts the primitive view that after death the soul* survives only as a ghost in Sheol*, the world of shadows underneath the earth. The idea of immortality* is by no means absent from the O.T., but it expresses itself in the purely religious faith that fellowship with God must needs be for ever. This belief finds its grandest utterance in Ps. 73:23ff, but underlies all the religion of the Psalms and Prophets. The doctrine of resurrection first becomes prominent in the apocalyptic* books, which take their departure from the O.T. idea of the "day of Jahveh", when the new age will be ushered in by a general Judgment. On this day, according to the apocalyptists, the dead of past ages will be raised up to receive sentence of acquittal or of condemnation. Much of the detail in this conception can be traced to Persian sources. In some of the books it is assumed that all men will be restored to their bodies and judged; in others, God will concern himself only with Israel. Some of the writers think only of a "resurrection of the just", the mass of men will pass out of being, or remain forever as ghosts in Sheol. In the time of Christ the belief in a resurrection had become general, but was not obligatory. It was rejected by the Sadducees as a later accretion which had no place in genuine O.T. teaching. There was doubt also as to whether all men would be raised up or only the righteous. Jesus himself takes the fact of a future life for granted, and no doubt relates it to the Jewish conception of a resurrection. But he nowhere lays any stress of the reunion of soul and body. What he believes in is simply an eternal life, assured to those who by faith and obedience have part in the Kingdom of God. The one passage in which he deals explicitly with the subject is in his answer to the question of the Sadducees*, (Mk. 12: 18ff.) where he bases the fact of immortality on the eternity of God. In this passage, and elsewhere in his teaching, Jesus disclaims all knowledge of the nature of the resurrection and the life which follows it. Such details as may be found in his parables (e.g., the Rich Man and Lazarus, the Last Judgment*) are mere imagery, taken over from popular belief. In later N.T. thought the idea of resurrection assumes a new importance in view of the assurance that Christ himself had risen. Paul devotes his longest chapter (I Cor. 15) to a refutation of the doctrine, held apparently by Greek Christians at Corinth, that the soul, in the future life, is no longer clothed with a body. At the same time he admits that the immortal body is not the earthly one restored, but a new body, woven of heavenly substance. His chief interest is to maintain the continuance of personal identity, and he cannot conceive of it without some kind of body. In I Cor. 15 he holds to the apocalyptic idea of a general resurrection, but in 2 Cor. 5: 1-8 he thinks of each believer as passing immediately after death into the new "tabernacle" awaiting him in Heaven. The Fourth Evangelist formally accepts the belief in a rising again at the last day (Jn. 6: 30) but in his own thinking he has broken with apocalyptic ideas. The resurrection, as he conceives it, takes place here and now in the act of faith in Christ (Jn. 11: 25, 26). In the period following the N.T. the doctrine of a resurrection of the body became a fixed element of the creed, and was often construed in the crudest and most literal way. At the same time the hope of immortality was independent of it. Christians have always believed, however inconsistently, that in death they are released from this bodily life, and enter at once into another. See Israel, religion and theology.

M. Goguel, *La foi a la résurrection* (1933); W. Morgan, *Religion and Theology of Paul* (1917); J. Baillie, *And the Life Everlasting* (1933). E.F.S.

retention of sins: In the Sacrament of Penance* as existent in the Roman Catholic Church, the exercise in a negative sense of the power of the keys* (John 20:23; Matt. 16:19; 18:18). In popular language the act of retaining sins is called the "denial of absolution*." In itself, however, it is not a simply refusal to absolve, as one might refuse to baptize, but a positive juridical act, which effects in the subject of the Church an obligation again to submit his case to her sacramental judgment, in consequence of the fact that his guilt has been authoritatively affirmed to be as yet unforgiven by her. This obligation remains even though the guilt of the retained sin may be subsequently forgiven in virtue of an act of perfect contrition*. The existence of the power of retention is intrinsically related to the doctrine that Christ instituted the Sacrament of Penance in the form of a judicial procedure, and as an obligatory means for the remission of post-baptismal mortal sin* (Council of Trent, sess. 14). The priest may legitimately use the power only when he is certain from positive evidence that the subject is indisposed for absolution, which would therefore be of no avail to him, in defect of true sorrow for his sins or of a sincere present will to forsake them. See sacraments. J.C.M.

retreat: A period of withdrawal for special devotions, usually by a group led by a conductor. B.S.E.

Reuchlin, Johann von: (1455-1522) German humanist and student of Hebrew and Cabala*. He became involved in a dispute with a Dominican Friar, Pfefferkorn, who had inspired an imperial edict, issued in 1509, to destroy the Talmud* and other Hebrew writings. Through Reuchlin's efforts the edict was finally rescinded. Reuchlin's writings include the first Hebrew grammar and dictionary written by a Christian.

L. Geiger, *Johann Reuchlin, sein Leben und seine Werke* (Leipzig, 1871). B.Z.B.

Reuss, Eduard G. E.: (1804-91) French Protestant theologian who taught at the University of Strasbourg from 1834-88. A leader in the development of the application of historical method to scripture, mediating German scholarship to French protestantism. In addition to his biblical studies he collaborated in a complete edition of the works of Calvin. Among his writings were *Histoire de la théologie chrétienne au siècle apostolique* (1852) and *La Bible, traduction nouvelle avec introductions et commentaires* (16 bde. 1874-81). C.T.C.

Reuter, Hermann: (1817-1889) Professor in Breslau, Greifswald and Göttingen, he was the most notable representative of the monographic study of church history.

Alexander III. und die Kirche seiner Zeit, vol. I (Leipzig, 1845), vols. II and III (Leipzig, 1860-64); *Geschichte der religiösen Aufklärung im Mittelalter* (Berlin, 1875-77); *Augustin* (Gotha, 1887). H.H.

revelation: The general notion which the word and its equivalents (Gr., *apokalypsis,* Lat., *revelatio,* Ger., *Offenbarung*) represent is that of the uncovering of the previously hidden. It receives its special meanings in Jewish and Christian theology from its use in connection with ideas of a personal or, at least, dynamic Godhead, with specific historical events and persons, and with the sacred writings. Thus the term is significantly used in three types of statements: 1) those which assert that God as personal makes his reality, nature and presence known to men by his own action; 2) those which affirm that such self-manifestations of God or disclosures of his plan or demands have been made in certain events, such as the history of the Hebrews, the birth, life, death and resurrection of Jesus Christ; 3) those which assert that the Scriptures or some part of them publish the content of the divine will or the knowledge necessary to salvation. In statements of the first type revelation is contrasted with discovery in which the human mind takes the initiative and employs previously held categories for the understanding of the divine. In such statements attention is directed to divine initiative as characteristic of present-day as well as of past experience of God or of faith in him. In the second type of statement revelation is contrasted with non-historical, conceptual thought and attention is directed to the concreteness, the "once-for-all", unrepetitive character of divine self-manifestation. The third type of statement sets up a claim for the authority of Scriptures which must, however, be validated by reference to inspiration*. While the three types of statements—that God manifests himself, making his goodness and power known by his own action, that he does so through certain events and their recollection, that the Bible contains his statements about truth and right—are not exclusive of each other neither do they necessarily imply each other and great variations occur in the theology of revelation according to the point of departure which is taken. Recent theological discussion, in distinction from the empiricism which began with man's search for God and from popular orthodoxy which at all times begins with the claim to Biblical authority, has tended to emphasize revelation in the first and second senses, dealing with Scriptures as record and means of revelation rather than revelation proper. Its problems are mainly those of the relation of personal faith to historical events.

Apart from this question the major problems theology has sought to solve with the aid of revelation concepts are those of the relative values of divine and human action in the achievement or gift of faith in God, and of the relation of general moral and metaphysical principles to historically conditioned faith. These and some subordinate problems have been dealt with traditionally, not without confusion of issues, in efforts to answer the question about the relative functions of reason and revelation. Gilson's classification of the four main positions taken in Christian thought in answering this question seems definitive. They are: 1) "Tertullianism" which contends for the complete self-sufficiency of revelation, decrying reason as a means to true faith or knowledge; 2) "Averroism", which regards revelation as a psychologically and sociologically desirable but logically unnecessary republication of the "truths of reason"; 3) "Thomism", which values reason as preparatory to the reception of revelation; 4) "Augustinianism" which regards reason as dependent on faith, true faith and hence true reasoning as dependent on revelation. While these positions are all represented in modern theology more precise definition of meanings and of issues as well as the prevalence of the historical and sociological approach to both philosophy and Scriptures have led to a restatement of the problems of revelation and to efforts at more comprehensive solutions. See sacred literatures; Word of God.

K. Barth, *Kirchliche Dogmatik,* Vol. I, *Die Lehre vom Wort Gottes,* Pt. I (Munich, 1932); Pt. II (Zollikon, 1938); E. Brunner, *Philosophy of Religion* (London, 1937); E. Gilson, *Reason and Revelation in the Middle Ages* (1938); J. Baillie, (ed.) *Revelation* (London, 1937); H. R. Niebuhr, *The Meaning of Revelation* (1940); A. E. Taylor, *The Faith of a Moralist,* Vol. II (London, 1930).

H.R.N.

Revelation of John: The Roman demand of emperor worship* as a token of loyalty to the empire, in the latter part of the reign of Domitian* threatened the church with destruction and must have tempted many to compromise. The Revelacion is written to the seven churches of the Roman province of Asia, to warn them against such a step and to revive their faith in the final triumph of the Kingdom of God. Strongly influenced by the recently published collection of Paul's letters, it opens with a similar corpus of letters to seven churches, preceded by a general letter to all seven. They must be victorious over the temptation that threatens them. Then in three great visions, John*, the prophet of Ephesus declares the certainty of the future triumph of Christ over the empire, and portrays the heavenly city that is to be the home of the redeemed. The book is strongly colored by the vocabulary and imagery of Jewish apocalyptic*, but it is also influenced by Greek drama, dawning Christian liturgy, and the collected Pauline letters. It predicts the fall of the persecuting empire and the destruction of Rome, which John with the other apocalyptists of his day viewed as a modern Babylon. In perhaps the darkest hour of early Christian history, the Revelation proclaimed the Christian's indomitable faith in God and in the triumph of his cause. Probable date c. 93 A.D. See beast; canons of various churches; final judgment.

S. J. Case, *The Revelation of John* (1919); R. H. Charles, *The Revelation of St. John* (1920), 2 vols.

E.J.G.

reverend: The accepted title in English for any clergyman; it should be preceded by the definite article and should never be used with the surname alone. For the higher clergy according to English usage a dean is entitled "Very Reverend," a bishop "Right Reverend," an archbishop "Most Reverend." But in very recent Roman Catholic practice bishops and archbishops alike are styled "Most Reverend," while priests granted the rank of "Monsignor"* are addressed as "Right Reverend." The title "Father" historically applied only to members of religious orders ("choir fathers" as distinguished from "lay brothers"); its use in English for any Roman Catholic priest appears to have originated in Ireland, a practice followed in America. In England, however, the usage did not appear until about 1865 and is said to be decreasing today. For Anglican clergy the title "Father" is a matter of individual preference.

B.S.E.

revers: (Lat., *reversus,* return) This word, referring originally in German usage to any written acknowledgment of obligation, came to be used by the Lutherans to signify a solemn written acceptance of doctrine and polity on the part of pastors, candidates for ordination, and congregations. The requirement of signing a revers in the presence of witnesses was prevalent in Germany during the eighteenth century and was imported thence to America. T.A.K.

Revised versions: (1881 and 1901) See Bible, English.

revivals: See Awakening, the Great; evangelicalism and evangelical revival; Finney, C. G.; holiness churches; Moody, D. L.; New Measures; pietism; pietistic sects in America.

rewards and punishments: Pleasant and painful experiences distributed according to merit. More specifically, such experiences in a life after death.

Among most primitive peoples there is a prevalent belief in the soul's survival of death, but the conception of it is often too vague to permit any clear idea of rewards or punishments. Even when vivid and detailed descriptions of the future life are given, the dead are pictured as continuing according to their status in this world, though the entire realm of the dead is usually regarded as inferior to the land of the living. The doctrines of the ancient Babylonians also were of this type. Greek mythology presented a similar view, but the Orphic and Pythagorean mysteries introduced notions of a last judgment, and this notion appears in Plato's *Phaedrus, Republic*, and *Gorgias*. The Egyptians taught, two thousand years before Plato's time, that all men would be judged by Osiris, the ones who were found worthy being resurrected to enter upon an everlasting life of blessedness similar to earth's more prosperous and happy hours. Those failing to pass the test were to remain in the dark, subterranean region of the hopeless dead, or, according to other accounts, to be vengefully tortured by burning, drowning, or dissection. According to the Hindu *Rigveda*, the warrior-dead, sages, priests, and wealthy patrons of the priesthood would enjoy the bliss of heaven, where music, flowers, and many other pleasures of mind and body abound. For the wicked a terrible dark abyss was waiting. The fate of others was not made clear. Later Hindu* teachings have differed. (See transmigration and immortality, kinds of: Spiritual Monism.) Buddhist* teaching provides an enormous variety of destinies, all dependent upon moral and religious merit, but, according to Mahayana doctrine, affected also by the saving power of the Bodhisattvas. There are eight or more hot hells, sixteen or more minor hells, and, according to some writers, eight cold hells. A vast period of torture in a specific one of the hells is the prescribed punishment to be suffered for each of many designated sins. There are also six sensual heavens, thirteen or more heavens of form (Rupaloka), and four where the bounds of human understanding are completely transcended. At death, a human being may be born into one of the hells or heavens or reborn in some human or animal form of this world. (See transmigration.) Zoroastrian* teachings depict a judgment at the Chinvad Bridge, from which the evil fall into hell, but over which the righteous pass to enter the appropriate one of the seven heavens. In hell there is the most precise fitting of punishments to the wrongs committed, but all are terrible to contemplate. The Mohammedan *Koran** describes physical torments and both physical and spiritual delights which are to follow the resurrection, all according to the merit of the individual, especially his religious fidelity or infidelity. (See resurrection.) The ancient Hebrews thought of divine retribution as falling on the nation as a whole, in this world, long before there emerged a belief in the future judgment of individuals for reward or punishment. But by the beginning of the Christian era there was a highly developed individual, as well as national, eschatology among the Jews. See death and burial practices; eschatology; final judgment; heaven and hell; immortality, conditional; immortality, arguments for and against; immortality, kinds of; penology.

See K. Kohler, *Heaven and Hell in Comparative Religion* (1923); J. Hastings (ed.), *Encyclopedia of Religion and Ethics* (1921), "State of the Dead."

L.H.DEW.

Rheims New Testament: See Bible, English. Cf. Douai Bible.

rhetorici: Known as sophists in Plato's time, who used rhetoric for display of virtuosity and glory of the speaker. Plato's ultimate objection to them is moral. Aristotle* insists that rhetoricians use their art to "energize knowledge" and must never divorce speech from significant subject matter. Classical oratory marks three stages of deliberative, forensic, and occasional, and tends with the last to jejuneness. Christian preaching* initiates a return to the Platonic and Aristotelian moral emphasis. St. Augustine's* *De Doctrina Christiana*, Book IV is the classic of Christian rhetoric. Using Cicero's canons of "instruct, win, move" and "subdued, moderate, and grand style", Augustine illustrates them with materials from Scripture and patristics*. Rhetoric has become homiletics*.

C. B. Baldwin, *Ancient Rhetoric and Poetic* (1924); *Medieval Rhetoric and Poetic* (1928); Sister Thérèse Sullivan, *De Doctrina Christiana Liber IV, A Commentary, with a Revised Text, Introduction and Translation*, The Catholic University of American Patristic Series, vol. XXIII (1930).

Q.B.

rhythm, musical: A pulsating, flowing, ordered movement of tones. Metrical rhythm is a regular occurrence of accented and unaccented beats in a time pattern. Free rhythm is an irregular occurrence of strong and weak beats such as one finds in plainsong*. E.H.B.

Ricci, Matteo: (1552-1610) Italian Jesuit and pioneer Christian missionary to China in modern times. Through his scientific attainments, especially in mathematics, and his skill in making maps, clocks, and other instruments, he won the respect of the Chinese. After a thorough study of their language, literature, and customs, Ricci adopted toward the culture of the Chinese a favorable attitude which caused protracted controversy after his death. E.A.R.

Rice, Luther: (1783-1836) Pioneer Baptist missionary and educational organizer (Columbian College, Washington). Responsible for Triennial Convention, 1814. "Coming of Luther Rice, the most important event in Baptist history in nineteenth century." C.H.M.

Richard Lectureship in the Christian Religion, The James W.: Established in 1920 by Miss Este Coffinberry at the University of Virginia, Charlottesville, Virginia. The capital sum is now about $24,000. The purpose of the lectureship is the "advancement and application of the principles of the Gospels." The lectures have been given biennially since 1931. The following is the list of lectures and subjects: W. F. Albright, "Archaeology of Palestine and the Bible" (1931); J. Moffatt, "The Epi-Christian Age" (1933); W. E. Hocking, "The Idea of God and the Unity of the World" (1935); E. H. Gilson, "Reason and Revelation in the Middle Ages" (1937); E. J. Goodspeed, "Christianity Goes to Press" (1939); and R. L. Calhoun, "The Law of God and the Will of Man" (1941).

(Data furnished by the Office of the President of the University.) V.F.

Richard of St. Victor: (?-1173) Eminent Scottish monk and theologian. A follower of the mystic, Hugo, he viewed profane knowledge as worthless unless linked in some way with divine knowledge. Well known for his mystical theology and for his works on the Trinity. See mystics of Saint-Victor. See s.v. penance.

Rickel, Dionysius: See Carthusians.

Ridley, Nicholas: (1500-1555) English Protestant martyr. Bishop of Rochester and later of London. Influential under Edward VI, he died at the stake with Latimer* at Oxford under Queen Mary. E.C.K.

Riehl, Alois: Representative of the Neo-Kantian* school in Germany during the last third of the 19th century. He stressed the empirical element in Kant's theory of knowledge and held that this theory was the legitimate heir and successor of English thought from Locke to Hume.
The Philosophical Criticism (1876 ff.). R.K.

right: In ethical theory the term may refer to the moral law or standard of conduct, however its source and nature are conceived; or it may refer to action or choice which conforms to that law or standard. These are its substantive and adjectival uses respectively. Duty is always a correlative of Right inasmuch as the moral law always involves the obligation of obedience. Right is the basic conception in those ethical theories which regard morality as conformity to some standard. Good is the basic conception in those which regard morality as the pursuit of some end. The relation of the right to the good is variously conceived by the different schools of ethical theory.

In social ethics a right is a justifiable moral claim upon others that implies a duty or duties on the part of others. A legal right is a claim that is recognized and supported by law. A political right is a capacity or function granted to a citizen and guaranteed by the State. A natural right is a claim or liberty that belongs to man as man. It is one that is not derived primarily from the state or positive law but is conceived as having its source in the law of nature and therefore as something more basic and inviolable than a right granted and guaranteed by positive law. See natural rights. R.W.F.

right of asylum: See asylum.

Rig-Veda: The chief of the four Vedas of ancient India, the others being the Sama-Veda, the Yajur-Veda, and the Atharva-Veda. Consists of hymns and prayers of the Ancient Aryans, many of them doubtless old before the migrants reached India. They were used in the worship of the various Vedic gods. There are ten books, obviously of composite authorship, produced over a long period of time. The tenth book gives evidence of relatively later composition, but probably was completed before 800 B.C. Held in Hinduism to be *sruti,* i.e., the very inspired word of God. C.S.B.

righteous anger: See wrath of God.

righteousness, New Testament conception of: Apart from the particular connotation of the term given to it by St. Paul*, righteousness in the N.T. means that behaviour upon the part of man that is well-pleasing to God and in obedience to His will. It has a forensic content in the thought of St. Paul. Paul started with the familiar Pharisaic idea that God would accept only the righteous man at the day of judgment. He denied that man could obtain righteousness by striving to fulfil the regulations of the *Torah**. He can be "declared just" only by the "righteousness of God," which he appropriates by an attitude of humble and thankful receptivity that Paul calls "faith." The believer is not "justified" by any personal achievement but only because he is allowed by an act of grace* to share in the righteousness of God. At the same time he participates in the gift of the Spirit, which makes him righteous in fact as well as by imputation. The righteousness of God enables him to be declared just before the bar of judgment and at the same time provides him with a new dynamic by which his life is henceforth governed. S.M.G.

righteousness, Old Testament conception of: The conception of justice and righteousness in the O.T. is contained in the Hebrew words 1) *ṣedek* and its cognates (most frequently translated "righteousness"), 2) *mishpaṭ* (usually translated "judgment", or occasionally "justice"), and 3) *yashar* (primarily meaning "to be straight", "upright").

Righteousness in the O.T. is no abstract or formal principle, but has its basis in the conception of the community as grounded in a covenant relation between God and man, and man and man (see covenant). It is primarily an inward quality, the presupposition of right action, which makes healthful, wholesome, and harmonious personal and community life possible. It outwardly manifests itself in that which permits the maintenance of the covenant, while unrighteousness, sin, is a breach of the community obligations (see lovingkindness).

The immediate background of the terms *ṣedek* and *mishpaṭ* seems to have been in legal practice. *Sedek* is primarily the "right" to which one is legally entitled. God is righteous, therefore, because he helps his people to their "right": that is, he "saves" them (cf. Isa. 45:21; Zech. 9:9, etc.). *Mishpaṭ* refers primarily to the custom or law regulating the office or position of each member of the covenant (thus the king's *mishpaṭ,* I Sam. 8:9; the first-born's *mishpaṭ,* Deut. 21:17, etc.). Since such customs or laws are frequently established by kings or law courts, the word may refer also to a statute or judicial decision (thus the AV and RV translation "judgment").

In religious usage the terms are charged with ethical and theological meaning. Thus to the prophets the "right" and *mishpat* of man are moral: hating evil and loving good (Amos 5:15; Micah 3:2); and this in turn is identified with the will of God, for it is what God requires of man (Micah 6:8, etc.). God, therefore, is the source of righteousness. The content of the term might vary with different times and minds. Yet, fundamentally, the conception was not that of a formal, ethical postulate, or ideal based on a categorical imperative, but that of a definite quality of personality, standing over all norms and laws as well as in them. Violating God's righteousness means breaking up the divine world order or covenant community; yet the positive, personal quality involved created the possibility of healing or reconstructing the broken bond.

The O.T. idea of righteousness, therefore, remained a living, religious conception, rooted in the belief in God, the Creator and Ruler, whose will and revelation was the source of ethics. It is to be seen in the movement between two parties in the realm of volition: man is righteous when, and only when, he is obedient to the will of God (i.e., keeping the law, being just to the poor and sojourner, having proper reverence for God, etc.), and God is righteous because he is ever faithful to the promises made to his covenanted people. G.E.W.

rishi: An inspired seer, sage or poet. The most famous *rishis* are those to whom the sacred Vedas* were revealed. There are priestly *rishis,* and divine or *deva rishis.* In more recent Hinduism* they are sometimes great ascetics or *yogins.* C.S.B.

rita: The concept of Order, cosmic and ethical, found in Vedic Hinduism and almost certainly reaching back into ancient Indo-European culture. From rita comes the word "right". Varuna is *par excellence* the guardian of rita in the Rig-Veda. C.S.B.

Ritschl, Albrecht: (1822-1889) Leading German theologian, latter half of nineteenth century. Born in Berlin (1822), son of a preacher who became a bishop, he studied theology in Bonn (1839-1841) and Halle (1841-1843). His doctoral dissertation was "An exposition of Augustine's doctrine of the creation of the world, sin, and grace." He became *Privatdozent* in Bonn in 1846, where he taught until 1864. The remainder of his life was spent as professor of theology in Göttingen (1864-1889). Early in his career, somewhat under the influence of Hegel and Baur, he wrote *Das Evangelium Marcions und das kanonische Evangelium des Lucas* (1846). *Die Entstehung der altkatholischen Kirche* (2nd. ed., 1857) marked his break with the Hegelian school. His greatest work, *Die christliche Lehre von der Rechtfertigung und Versöhnung* (1st ed., 1870-1874, 2nd ed., 1882, 3rd ed., 1888), presented his characteristic views. His *Geschichte des Pietismus* (1880-1886), 3 vols., expressed hostility to mysticism.

See Otto Ritschl, *Albrecht Ritschls Leben* (1892-1896), 2 vols. E.S.B.

Ritschl, Otto Karl Albrecht: (1860-) He taught at the universities of Kiel and Bonn. As son of A. Ritschl he realized on a grand scale the further comprehension of the conception of the history of dogmas. He is one of the investigators who developed the history of dogma to the discipline in which historical theology improved its methodology most independently and attained its most mature results.

Schleiermachers Stellung zum Christentum in seinen Reden über die Religion (Gotha, 1888); *Uber Werturteile* (Freiburg, 1895); *A. Ritschls Leben,* 2 vols. (Freiburg, 1892-1896); *System und systematische Methode in der Geschichte des wissenschaftlichen Sprachgebrauchs und der philosophischen Methode* (Bonn, 1906); *Dogmentgeschichte des Protestantismus,* 4 vols. (Leipzig, 1908-27). H.H.

Ritschlianism: The ideas of A. Ritschl* and of theologians influenced by him. From about 1875 to the World War of 1914, Ritschlianism was the dominant influence in German and Anglo-American liberal Protestant theology. Building on Luther (faith), Kant (primacy of the practical reason, man a citizen of two worlds), Hegel (historical and social emphasis), Schleiermacher (whose feeling of dependence he criticized in favor of an asertion of personality against nature), and Lotze (personalistic theism, value judgments), Ritschl emphasized the following ideas:

1) The Kingdom of God and Redemption are the two foci of Christianity. Jesus Christ is founder of the Kingdom.

2) The Community is the religious unit. Despite this strongly social and institutional emphasis, Ritschl rejected the authority of dogmatic tradition on ethical, social and rational grounds.

3) Value judgments are the source of religious knowledge. Ritschl's theory of faith-knowledge based on value judgments (a kind of religious quasi-pragmatism) is commonly, but falsely, said to have been derived from J. Kaftan. W. Herrmann declares that it was suggested by Lotze, whose *Mikrokosmus* Ritschl read in 1864 and with whom he was associated at Göttingen. Much of the modern philosophical interest in value* and axiology* is thus derived from Lotze and Ritschl.

4) Religious experience is more fundamental than doctrine (religious empiricism). Ritschl, however, stressed the historical, ethical, and social aspects of Christian experience to the disparagement of the mystical (see his *Geschichte des Pietismus*). The "social gospel," at least in part influenced by Ritschl, has shared his suspicion of mysticism with its subjectivism and indivdualism.

5) Theology should not be based on metaphysics. By this Ritschl meant to make clear his belief that religion is not derived from any knowledge of nature (but rather from value judgments), nor from theoretical reason (but from the moral); and also his opinion that the Pure Form of Aris-

totle and the Absolute of Hegel are too remote to serve as objects of religious worship. In his earlier writing he was so strongly anti-metaphysical as to incline toward positivism*. Later he made clear his hitherto latent theistic metaphysics, grounded in value-theory, and akin to Lotze's personalism*.

In 1875 W. Herrmann* came under Ritschl's influence. In 1876 A. Harnack* became a Ritschlian; in the same year Schürer founded the *Theologische Literatur-Zeitung,* which was to be a great Ritschlian organ. The *Christliche Welt* (1887-1941) continued the Ritschlian school, of which men like J. Kaftan, F. A. Loofs, M. Rade, and J. Weiss were prominent representatives. Ritschl influenced British theology without gaining close adherents; in America, there have been several Ritschlians, notably G. B. Smith* of Chicago.

C. Fabricius, *Die Entwicklung in Albrecht Ritschls Theologie* (1909); A. E. Garvie, *The Ritschlian Theology* (1899, 1902); A. T. Swing, *The Theology of Albrecht Ritschl* (1901); R. Mackintosh, *Albrecht Ritschl and his School* (1915); E. S. Brightman, "Ritschl's Criterion of Religious Truth," in *Am. Jour. Theol.,* 21 (1917), 212-224); Garvie, Art. "Ritschlianism," in *ERE* (1919); S. L. Akers, *Some British Reactions to Ritschlianism* (1934). E.S.B.

ritual: (Lat., *ritualis,* fr. *ritus,* rite) A prescribed form of activity, determined by considerations of tradition and symbolism*. Originally the word designated such activity when governed by religious purpose, and it is still most often, though not always, used in that restricted sense.

At an early age most children show a liking for ceremonial behavior, and often they protest against deviations, however minute, in the forms of familial observances. The less the activity is controlled by practical considerations of efficiency and the more it calls imagination into play, the more children tend to insist on such exact uniformity. Probably from similar causes, all communities, primitive or civilized, deeply religious or avowedly anti-religious, have rituals which serve as bonds of social unity and symbolic reminders of common ideals.

In religion, ritual has the value of increasing the worshiper's sense of the ancient origins, dignity, and mysterious suggestiveness of the beliefs and aspirations expressed, as well as serving to foster institutional unity and loyalty. It is also fraught with peril, however, as the history of the most diverse religions indicates. When ritualistic precision is emphasized, as it must be if elaborate rituals are to be made effective, thought of the ritual often tends to crowd out thought of God and of the needs and ideals which originally provided the very purpose of the observance. Then, too, ritualistic activity may satisfy the religious aspirations of the worshiper, so that he is not driven by his sense of the divine to such good works as would more significantly advance the Kingdom of Righteousness. The frequent conflicts between the ancient Hebrew priests and prophets, and the remarkable moral leadership of the modern nonritualistic Quakers, afford significant evidence. On the other hand, those who favor ritual argue that ritualistic forms have been authoritatively commanded, that the more ritualistic institutions have shown the greater stability, that the discarding of old forms is usually followed by the eventual adoption of new, less significant ones, and that even the prophetic exhortations of nonritualistic reformers would have little effect were they not able to appeal to sentiments firmly established by centuries of ritualistic practice. See culture; liturgy; magic; ritualism; Roman religions. L.H.DEW.

ritualism: (Lat., *ritus*) Should properly mean interest in or study of sacred rites, but is commonly used for attachment to the accompanying ceremonies. In England the term was applied in a hostile sense to those Anglo-Catholics* who after 1845 revived mediaeval vestments* and ceremonies, on the legal basis of the Ornaments Rubric, which directs the use of the ornaments of the 2nd year of Edward VI (1548-9). What mattered more for the ritualists was the exhibition of the continuity of the Church and the dignity of the Eucharist; a determined effort was made to suppress them in a series of court decisions, followed by the Public Worship Regulation Act (1874). This collapsed owing to the refusal of the clergy involved to recognize the authority of civil courts in church matters. In the disestablished Anglican Churches anti-ritualist legislation was attempted, which failed in the United States (1871-4), but succeeded in Ireland (1871-7). In 1890 Archbishop Benson in the case of the Bishop of Lincoln declared several of the contested ceremonies lawful, after which decision of church authority the agitation died down. Much of what was once "ritualistic" is now customary in Protestant as well as Anglican churches, though the principles involved continue to be disputed.

C. P. S. Clarke, *The Oxford Movement and After* (1932); G. W. E. Russell, *Saint Alban the Martyr* (Holborn, 1915). E.R.H.

River Brethren: A group of three conservative sects similar to the Dunkers* and Mennonites* which originated in a revival among the German people in Lancaster County, Penna., about 1770. One of the first group was in the southern part of the country "down by the river" and baptized in the river, hence the name. They practice trine forward immersion, anoint the sick with oil, dress in the plainest manner, wash feet, cover the heads of the women with a veil or cloth, have few or no salaried ministers, and forbid organs in worship, fairs, lightning rods, life insurance, lodges, worldly amusements, participation in war, and indulgence in tobacco or liquor.

The misunderstandings which split the River Brethren into three sects concerned the washing of feet and the sacramental meal. The "one made" school held that both washing and drying of feet should be performed by the same person, while the "two made" insisted on different individuals for the two acts. There was a controversy as to whether the bread and wine should be on the table with the general communion meal or brought forward after the meal. One group organized to secure legal recognition of the pacifist position. There are no important differences between them, although the Old Order or Yorker Brethren (1843) are more conservative; these have no church buildings but worship in barns. The sects are:

Group	Churches	Members
Brethren in Christ (f. 1862)	90	5,500
Older Order or Yorker Brethren	7	300
United Zion's Children (Brinsers, f. 1853)	24	1,250

E.T.C.

Robert of Melun: (died 1167) A sentence writer of the school of St. Victor*, surpassing his master Hugh in rigor and precision of presentation of ideas.

M. Grabmann, *Geschichte der scholastischen Methode* (Freiburg im Breisgau, 1911), vol. II.

H.H.

Robertson, Frederick William: (1816-1853) Famous English preacher of the nineteenth century. Best known as "Robertson of Brighton", because of his pastoral connection with that city, he exercised a wide influence through his sermons on "The Kingdom of God." With Maurice*, he is often said to have been one of the most influential men in returning the English Church to realistic preaching about the Church in the world.

W.N.P.

Robertson Memorial Lectureship, The James: Established in 1913 by the Presbyterian Church in Canada with a capital sum of $20,000, these lectures are given annually at the eight theological colleges of the United Church. The lectures deal with the following topics: the obligation and principles of missions and the history of missions in the Canadian Church, both home and abroad; the lives of great missionary pioneers; the Christianization of the Indian tribes and the evangelization of foreigners in Canada; district history of the several branches now making up the Presbyterian Church in Canada and the history of the influence of Presbyterianism on the educational, political or social life of Canada and cognate subjects. One of the lectures is designated to deal with some phase of Dr. Robertson's life or of the field of labor in which he served. James Robertson was for 25 years—1880-1905—superintendent of Presbyterian Home Missions in Western Canada. The following have appeared as lecturers: J. A. Falconer, J. McLean, J. U. Tanner, J. A. Cormie, J. M. Shaver, G. A. Wilson, W. H. Sedgewick and J. Endicott.

(Data from the Office of the Secretary of the Board of Home Missions, The United Church of Canada.)

V.F.

Robinson, Ezekiel Gilman: (1815-1894) Baptist educator. Professor or president of Rochester Theological Seminary, 1853-1872. President Brown University, 1872-1889. Translator of Neander's *Planting and Training of the Christian Church* (1865).

C.H.M.

Robinson, John: (c. 1576-1625) Pastor of the Pilgrim Fathers, was probably born in Gainsborough, England. He was educated at Corpus Christi College, Cambridge, took orders in the Church of England, had a parish near Norwich and was suspended for non-conformity about 1603. He emigrated to Amsterdam with the church at Scrooby in 1608. He was chosen pastor and removed to Leyden in 1609. He organized the movement to emigrate in 1617, but remained in Holland with the older and more infirm members. He died in Leyden in March, 1625. His most important works are: *A Justification for separation from the Church of England* (1610); *Of Religious Communion* (1614); *Essays and Observations Divine and Moral* (1625). See Congregationalism; Separatists, Protestant.

W. Walker, *A History of the Congregational Churches in the U. S.* (1894); G. G. Atkins & F. L. Fagley, *History of American Congregationalism* (1942); Schaff-Herzog, *Encyclopedia of Religious Knowledge,* vol. 10, p. 60.

F.T.P.

rochet: A vestment, usually of linen, similar to a surplice*, but with close-fitting sleeves. It is not strictly a liturgical vestment. Worn only by prelates or those having a special privilege.

C.R.

Rockwell Lectureship, The: Provided on a year-to-year basis by Mr. James W. Rockwell of Houston and given at The Rice Institute, Houston, Texas each year on religious subjects. This lectureship was inaugurated in 1938 and the following have served: Sir Robert Falconer, Dr. H. E. Kirk, Dean R. Pound, Dr. J. R. Sizoo, Dr. W. E. Hocking and Dean R. R. Wicks.

(Data furnished by the office of the president of the Institute.)

V.F.

Rogation Days: (Lat., *rogatio,* petition) The three days before Ascension Day, observed as days of prayer, especially for agriculture—custom organized by Bishop Mamertus of Vienne c. 470, general in Middle Ages, survived Reformation in England.

E.R.H.

Rogation Sunday: In modern Anglican usage, the Sunday before the Rogation Days.

E.R.H.

Rohmer, Friedrich: (1814-1856) As a thinker he sought to balance theism with pantheism. The world consists of a God and creatures of God. The universe, as a macrocosmic nature, is the body of God. Space and time are component parts of God, who is eternal becoming. Every man is a different person because he is a peculiar idea of God. At death the body with its soul enters into the macrocosmic matter, whence they arose. Rohmer was greatly admired by the noted Swiss political scientist, J. C. Bluntschli.

Kritik des Gottesbegriffes in den gegenwärtigen Weltansichten (Nördlingen, 1856); *Gott und seine Schöpfung* (Nördlingen, 1857); *Der natürliche Weg des Menschen zu Gott* (Nördlingen, 1858); H. Staeps, *Ueber Friedrich Rohmers "Wissenschaft von Gott"* (Erlangen, 1897).

H.H.

Roman Catechism, the: See Confessions, Formal of the Christian Church; Pius V.

Roman Catholic: See Catholic.

Roman Catholic burial practice: See burial practice, Roman Catholic.

Roman Catholic Catechisms: See catechism; Confessions, Formal, of the Christian church.

Roman Catholic Church: *Origin*: Roman Catholic historical thought considers legitimate the development of the world-Church, as it emerges into secular history at about 180, from Jesus and His Apostles as portrayed in the N.T. Peter, leader of the Apostles, had fixed his see at Rome, and the primacy which Jesus had given him (Matthew 16: 16-20; John 21: 15-23) passed to his successors in that see. Paul had broken the grip of Judaism, and John by his doctrine of the Logos had pointed out the way theology was to take. Eventual Hellenization and Romanization of the Gospel are admitted, but without conceding that Christianity was denatured in the process.

Although the ancient Catholic Church did not know a centralization at all comparable to that of later centuries, the preëminence of the Bishop of Rome is expressed in the writings of Clemens Romanus, Ignatius of Antioch, Tertullian and Irenaeus** as well as in the controversy on the celebration of Easter* under Victor I (189-198). After the persecutions the centrifugal tendencies of the great ecclesiastical capitals, the caesaropapism of the Eastern emperors, and the lack of a common language tended to weaken the external cohesion of the Church although the Roman primacy was maintained. In the West the Vandal persecution of the African Church and the transfer of the capital from Milan to Ravenna put an end to centrifugal movements, while the conversion of Anglo-Saxons by missionaries sent by Gregory the Great (590-604) and the work of Boniface* in Germany and Frankland contributed greatly to Western unity. But relations between the West and the East, where the theory of the five patriarchates was popular, grew rarer as the centuries passed. The rise of Islam by breaking Mediterranean unity accentuated the opposition to Rome which the rise of Constantinople had created. Since the Monophysite* heresy had almost completely destroyed the influence of orthodox Christianity in Syria and Egypt and since the patriarchate of Jerusalem was hampered by Mohammedan rule, Constantinople was left as Rome's rival in the East. It is the contention of Roman Catholics that, however much the Greeks may have thought themselves justified in the rupture with Rome which was consummated in 1054, they were objectively unjustified, and so remained separate from the Church Catholic, which persisted in the West.

Owing particularly to the crippling influence of the civil power, the Church in the West had at the beginning of the eleventh century long been in need of reform. The Byzantine emperors during the sixth, seventh and early eighth centuries had claimed the right of ratifying papal elections. The Franks also exercised a similar power. But neither of these temporal overlords was near enough to Rome to dominate it. The case was different when during the feudal anarchy the house of Theophylactus and the Crescentii secured a hold on the papacy. This hold was broken by the German emperors for their own profit. It was against this oppression that the popes struggled in the conflict over investiture*. St. Gregory VII (1073-1085)* and his immediate successors freed the Church from the domination of civil rulers. They also originated the Crusades*, and it can be said that the specifically mediaeval papacy dates from this time.

During the twelfth century the centralization of the Church, which made the popes master of the whole ecclesiastical organism, was pushed steadily forward, culminating in the reigns of Alexander III (1159-1181) and Innocent III (1198-1216)**. At the same time the supremacy of the Church in practically all fields of culture was established. This is not to be attributed to Roman thirst for power but rather to the fact that the Latin-Christian element in mediaeval civilization represented by the Church, possessed a *de facto* superiority over the younger Germanic element, represented by the Empire. Ecclesiastical supremacy even in non-religious spheres was a condition for the flowering of the Middle Ages, although it did not express the permanent relationship between the two elements.

Papal supremacy outside the religious sphere did not last. Gradually the differentiation between Germanic and Romance Europe increased. France attained to great power and the struggle between Philip the Fair and Boniface VIII (1294-1303)*, which ended with the humiliation of Boniface and the Avignon* papacy, marked the end of the specifically mediaeval papacy. The European nations emerged and, despite the idea of Christendom's universality, maintained themselves. The Great Western Schism and the Conciliar Movement** show that an analogous tendency existed in the Church. Meanwhile the revival of classical culture led to a resurgence of ancient absolutism and ancient philosophical outlook. The humanists created historical science, and later in their hands natural science took on a new form. The Protestant revolt of the sixteenth century was tributary to these changing currents. Catholics maintain that the existence of abuses and survivals in the Catholic Church did not warrant an overthrow of the Church's constitution. In spite of the good faith of many, the rejection of Rome by so much of Northern Europe was unjustified, and by it Protestant Europe cut itself off from the unity of the Church Catholic, which survived in Roman Catholicism.

The modern period of the Catholic Church begins with the Catholic Reformation*, the greatest revival the Church has known. The Council of Trent* answered the Protestant reformers and inaugurated a Catholic reform. Catholic missionaries carried the Gospel to the ends of the earth while Catholic thinkers produced an unrivalled theology. The period of the Enlightenment* marked a sharp decline and this was hastened by Jansenism* and disputes on moral questions within the Church. But the nineteenth century saw another resurgence and the consecration of the papal religious monarchy by the Infallibility Decree of the Vatican Council (1869-1870)*.

Theology: Roman Catholic theology builds not only on the Sacred Scriptures and the decisions of the teaching Church but also on the great theologians of the past, on the Fathers of the East as well as of the West, on thirteenth century Scholasticism and on the theologians of the sixteenth and seventeenth centuries. It recognizes the debt of patristic thought to the Platonism of the time, of mediaeval thought to mediaeval Aristotelianism, and of sixteenth and seventeenth century theologians to the Renaissance.* Moreover the teaching Church is ever the final authority and the thought of no period is absolutized. Even the Fathers must be shown to have taught a doctrine unanimously in order to compel assent. The criticism of the Scholastic synthesis which appeared in the fourteenth and fifteenth centuries has not been forgotten. The seventeenth century saw the rise of historical theology among Catholics. The great extension of historical studies in the last century has been parallelled by an increase of historicization in Catholic theological schools. But this movement has been accompanied by an even more powerful revival of Scholasticism, particularly of Thomism**, which has served as a corrective. Biblical theology is likewise beginning to enjoy a renascence.

Polity: According to Roman Catholic teaching the Church is by the will of Christ not only a supernatural but also an independent society. Christ gave the power of teaching, sanctifying and ruling not to the community but to the Apostles. This power passed to the bishops, successors of the Apostles. The Roman Pontiff has supreme and full jurisdiction over the universal Church in all that pertains to discipline and government of the Church as well as in matters of faith and morals. This power is episcopal, ordinary and immediate. There can be no General Council unless convoked by the Roman Pontiff. The bishops are placed by divine law over the individual churches, which they govern with ordinary authority under the authority of the Roman Pontiff. The Cardinals are the principal counselors and assistants of the Pontiff in the ruling of the Church. Church polity is determined in detail in the *Codex juris canonici* (1917)*.

Creeds: The principal creeds of the Roman Catholic Church are the Apostles', the Nicene, the *Quicumque*, the Creed of Toledo (675)**, the Creed of Leo IX (1053), the profession of faith prescribed for the Waldenses (1208), the chapter *Firmiter* of the IV Lateran Council (1215), (See Lateran Councils), the profession of faith prescribed for Michael Palaeologus (1274), the decree for the Greeks (1439), the decree for the Jacobites (1442), the Tridentine profession of faith (1564)**, the profession of faith prescribed for the Greeks by Gregory XIII (1575)*, the profession of faith prescribed for the Orientals (Maronites*), by Benedict XIV* (1743). (See creeds of Christendom; ecumenical councils.) To these should be added the solemn definitions of the popes and of ecumenical councils. The councils recognized as ecumenical in whole or in part by the Roman Church are twenty: Nicaea (325), Constantinople (381), Ephesus (431), Chalcedon (451), Constantinople (553), Constantinople (680-681), Nicaea (787), Constantinople (869-870), Lateran (1123), Lateran (1139), Lateran (1179), Lateran (1215), Lyons (1245), Lyons (1274)**, Vienne (1311-1312)*, Constance (1414-1418), Florence (1438-1445), Lateran (1512-1517), Trent (1545-1563), and Vatican (1869-1870). Among the solemn definitions of the popes the condemnation of the Jansenists (1653) by Innocent X* and the anti-Modernist oath (1910) of Pius X* are of special importance.

Divisions: The pope* is Bishop of Rome, vicar of Jesus Christ, successor of St. Peter, supreme pontiff of the universal Church, patriarch of the West, primate of Italy and archbishop and metropolitan of the Roman province. The College of Cardinals*, which is the senate of the Church and numbers about seventy members, consists of cardinal-bishops, cardinal-priests and cardinal-deacons. The six cardinal-bishops are occupants of the suburbicarian sees. Historically the fifty cardinal-priests were the parish priests of Rome, but actually many of them are chosen from among the bishops and archbishops of the Catholic world. The fourteen cardinal-deacons are priests and members of the papal curia.

The Church embraces the Western Church and Eastern Churches. In addition to the pope there were in 1940 in the Western Church four major patriarchs, viz., the Latin patriarchs of Constantinople, Alexandria, Antioch and Jerusalem of whom only the last named had jurisdiction; and four minor patriarchates: Venice, Lisbon, East Indies and West Indies.

In the Western Church a country normally comprises one or several ecclesiastical provinces. An ecclesiastical province consists of an archdiocese and usually one or more dioceses. An archbishop or metropolitan is head of an archdiocese, and besides ordinary jurisdiction in his own territory has certain limited powers over the bishops of his province, called his suffragans.

In the United States, excluding Alaska and other possessions, there were at the beginning of 1942 twenty archdioceses and ninety-three dioceses in addition to two dioceses for Oriental Catholics, the Military Ordinariate, and an *abbatia nullius*, Belmont Abbey; the archbishops of Boston and Philadelphia were cardinals.

The Eastern Churches in union with Rome in 1932 (*Statistica con cenni storici della gerarchia e dei fedeli di rito orientale*) numbered seventeen. Nine of them use the Byzantine rite* or variants of it. They are the Albanian, the Bulgarian, the Greek, the Italio-Albanian, the Yugoslavian, the Melchite, the Rumanian, the Ruthenian and the Hungarian Churches. The Melchites* have a patriarch. Three Churches use the Antiochene rite* or derivatives. They are the Syrian, the Maronite and the Malankarese Churches. The Syrian patriarch, Cardinal Tappouni, resides in Beirut. The

Maronites likewise have a patriarch. Two Churches follow the Alexandrian rite*: the Coptic and the Ethiopian. The Copts have a patriarch. Two Churches follow the Chaldean rite*: the Chaldean and the Malabarese. The Chaldeans have a patriarch. The Armenians also have a patriarch.

Statistics: Roman Catholics number 382,190,000 or 18.71% of mankind. Europe has 211,734,-000; Asia 19,450,000; the Americas 141,528,000; Africa 7,595,000; Australia and Oceania 1,883,-000. [H. A. Krose in *Lexikon für Theologie und Kirche*, VIII, 791 (1936)] 8,200,000 belong to the Eastern Churches in union with Rome. (D. Attwater, *The Catholic Eastern Churches*, 1935). On Roman Catholic canon, see apocrypha, Old Testament.

The Catholic Encyclopedia (1907-1914), 16 vols; *Dictionnaire de théologie catholique* (1903-1939), 14 vols., not complete; *Dictionnaire apologétique de la foi catholique* (1911-1929), 4 vols.; *Lexikon für Theologie und Kirche* (1930-1938), 10 vols.

E.A.R.

Roman Catholic journalism: See Catholic journalism.

Roman Catholic, major seminaries: See seminaries, major Roman Catholic.

Roman Catholic parochial schools: See parochial schools, Catholic.

Roman Catholic religious orders, abbreviations of names of: See Catholic religious orders, abbreviations of names of.

Roman Catholic societies: See Catholic societies.

Roman Curia: See Curia Romana. Cf. Pius V; Pius X; Sixtus V.

Roman mass: See mass, Roman Catholic.

Roman Missal: See Missal, Roman.

Roman pontiffs: See popes.

Roman Question, the: See Papal States; Pius IX; Pius XI.

Roman religions: The word religion itself (Lat. *religio*, etym. obscure) probably originally meant for the Roman the sense of awe felt in the abode of a *numen**, or spirit, which was therefore a holy place. The primitive religion of the Romans was animistic, recognizing the existence of spirits (*numina*) dwelling in natural objects, such as trees, springs, rivers, sky, which could be propitiated by offerings, presented with due ritual. Likewise there were spirits in the house and on the farm. Each Roman home had its own Lares (spirits of the fields) and Penates* (spirits of the pantry). As the city-state developed, the old *numina* took on new functions: e.g., Jupiter, god of the open sky, became the god of justice; Mars, protector of the fields, became the god of war, protecting the state. Under Etruscan* and Greek influence came the anthropomorphic conception of the gods. The old Roman city-gods were transformed and new ones added, such as Minerva, Hercules, Castor, and Pollux. Jupiter, Minerva, and Juno, the Etruscan triad, were established in their temple on the Capitol. The old gods were in many cases identified with Greek gods, endowed with their attributes and even their myths, Jupiter with Zeus, Mars with Ares, etc. The introduction of the cult of Apollo brought the Sibylline* Books to Rome, thus paving the way for other Greek divinities. By the Second Punic War (201 B.C.) the amalgamation was practically complete. Roman religion was highly ritualistic, putting great stress upon the minutiae of ritual*; any departure from the set form might vitiate the whole rite. The bargaining nature of Roman religion is seen in the frequent use of the *votum* (vow), a solemn promise to make a specific sacrifice or offering if a specified success were gained or peril averted. Hence Roman religion became largely a formal thing. As time went on and the civil wars came, the shrines of the old gods were deserted, their rites neglected. Emerging as princeps, Augustus did what he could to restore the old religion, but against it two forces had long been operating, Greek philosophy among the educated classes and the Eastern mystery religions* among the common people.

The embassy of Greek philosophers in 155 B.C. seems to have created much interest in philosophy in Rome, and a few years later the Stoic Panaetius of Rhodes joined the Scipionic circle. Stoicism*, with its noble emphasis upon endurance and its developing realization of the brotherhood of man, found a ready welcome in Rome. It reaches its climax in the writings of the slave Epictetus and the emperor Marcus Aurelius**. The coldly intellectual Epicureanism, though eloquently set forth by Lucretius**, made little headway, except in its later degraded form of personal indulgence, which can hardly be classed as religion.

The mystery religions of the east were a much more potent force, with their appeal to the emotions rather than to the intellect. Through initiatory rites they brought the promise of happiness after the troubles of this world, and for the present they gave the comforting sense of personal relationship with the Divine. In an effort to end the Second Punic War, the Romans imported the cult of the Magna Mater, Cybele, from Pessinus in Asia Minor. Shortly after, the orgiastic worship of Dionysus spread over Italy, to be suppressed temporarily in 186 B.C. With the Mithradatic Wars came Mā, sanguinary goddess of Comana in Cappadocia. Later, contact with Egypt brought Isis and Osiris, most popular of them all among the common people of Rome. Under the Empire, the army was the great disseminating agency. The soldiers worshiped not only the old Roman gods but also the local deities. The popularity of the Persian Mithras, the Syrian Heliopolitanus, and the Anatolian Sabazius is easily understood; gods of strife and conquest, they promised the soldier present power and victory, and eternal happiness beyond the grave.

The imperial cult of Rome and Augustus, developing during the principate of Augustus outside of Italy, was symbolic of the unity of the Empire and of the loyalty of the provincials. It was a political gesture with little religious significance. The deification of the Emperors doubtless was suggested by eastern customs, but found ready acceptance among the people of imperial Rome.

The need for reconciling the various religious and philosophical cults led to Plotinus' Neo-Platonism*, in which monotheism is the central theme. But Christianity was already at work, with a solution diametrically the opposite; it would brook no compromise with other faiths; it would not bow to a deified Emperor. And in the end it triumphed. Constantine recognized it as a state religion in 313 A.D. Neither the old Roman religion nor the eastern cults disappeared at once, but they had lost the initiative. Curiously enough, the last great fight of Christianity was against the *pagani* (country people) still clinging to their ancestral *numina*. See emperor worship; mother goddesses; temples, Greek and Roman. Cf. Greek religion.

Franz Altheim, *A History of Roman Religion*, trans. by Harold Mattingly (1937); Cyril Bailey, *Phases in the Religion of Ancient Rome* (1932); William Warde Fowler, *The Religious Experience of the Roman People* (London, 1911); Terrot R. Glover, *The Conflict of Religions in the Early Roman Empire* (11th ed., London, 1927). E.M.N.

Roman rite: See liturgy; mass, Roman Catholic.

Roman Symbol, Old: See Old Roman Symbol.

Romanesque style: See art, ecclesiastical, Christian; church building.

Romans, Letter to the: What has long been called Paul's third missionary journey culminated at Corinth, where Paul had hoped to turn westward to visit Rome and then proceed to a missionary campaign in Spain. But the collection for the Christian poor of Jerusalem had to be carried to Jerusalem, and this Paul felt obliged to do in person. He therefore wrote a letter to Rome, telling of his plan of visiting them and why it had now to be deferred. He took the opportunity to set forth to them his great idea of righteousness through faith, instead of through law, chs. 1-5, following it with an account of the effects of this experience upon the believer, chs. 6-8. He followed this with an appendix on the failure of the Jews to accept their Messiah and his gospel, chs. 9-11. Chs. 12:1-15:13 present a practical summary of the Christian's duties in the world, the state and the church. Ch. 16 is a letter of introduction for a Christian woman named Phoebe, who was leaving Cenchreae, one of the ports of Corinth, either for Rome or Ephesus. Romans is the most systematic presentation of Paul's view of faith that we possess; elsewhere it is incidentally presented; here it is the main theme. Ch. 14 is a great plea for Christian tolerance. The letter shows Paul in his greatest stature, seeking with the collection to bind Greek and Jew together in the Christian fellowship; a great missionary statesman, reaching out to Rome with this great letter, while he himself turns back to Jerusalem, to make sure Jewish Christianity understands and accepts the gift of their Greek brethren. The letter was written probably in A.D. 56 or 57.

W. Sanday and A. C. Headlam, *St. Paul's Epistle to the Romans* (1895; 11th ed. 1906). E.J.G.

romanticism: A term used, often without precise signification, to designate (1) an attitude of mind and (2) an historical movement. The romantic attitude may be distinguished from the classical and the realistic by its emphasis upon imagination rather than reason or a sense of literal fact. It is individualistic, introspective, tending to give personal sentiments and intuitions precedence over objective standards. Historically this attitude became dominant in the late 18th and early 19th centuries, manifesting itself in parallel political, religious, philosophical, and literary movements. Despite the diversity of tendencies comprehended, there is a common denominator in the reaction against established traditions and the search for more liberal grounds of thought and action. L.W.C.

rood: (A.S. *rod*, a cross) A cross or crucifix**. Used especially of the cross on the screen at the entrance of the chancel*or choir. F.T.P.

rood screen: A device used in many ancient and Mediaeval church buildings* in order to mark the transition from the nave to the chancel. In some churches a chancel arch served this purpose, but where this arch was lacking, as in many churches in the southwestern part of England, a rood screen was used.

A rood screen is composed of a paneled parapet below, vertical mullions, groining, a richly carved cornice and often a rood loft. At the head of the center passage aisle was a wide opening, fitted with double doors of open construction. There were similar openings at each side aisle. The framing of such screens generally was of fairly heavy oak timbers, with rich mouldings and leaf ornament carved out of the solid, or sometimes, in later years, merely attached to the timbers. The groinings formed a rich canopy on both sides of the screen. The cornice, which projected two feet or so on either side of the screen, was enriched with two, three or more bands of extremely rich carving in the form of conventionalized leaves, the grape, the hawthorn and even sea weeds forming the motif. Between the vertical mullions was open tracery, usually rich and intricate in design. The rood loft overhead was a platform five feet or so in width, and extending from wall to wall of the church. It had richly paneled parapets on either side, and narrow circular stairways led up to it. Its use is not fully known today, but it is supposed that the Epistle and Gospel may have been read from this rood loft, and that it may have been used by the singers. In Exeter and Lincoln cathedrals, and elsewhere, large organs still stand on the rood loft, and these extend forward and to the rear and rest on ornate brackets.

A large number of rood screens still exist, particularly in England. Perhaps 140 screens, or portions of screens still exist in Devon alone. Somerset has a number of rich screens, but in Cornwall and Wales not many remain. Scores of screens disappeared within comparatively recent times, during periods when a bare church interior was the fashion. Many old screens which had become damaged or mutilated have been restored by such men as the late Mr. Harry Hems, and especially by Herbert Read, Esq. In England a number of new screens, following closely the best early 15th century models, have been erected in recent years, and some of these are fully equal in design and honesty of craftsmanship with Mediaeval work. A few simple screens exist in America, such as Calvary in Pittsburgh, St. Mark's at Mt. Kisco, N. Y., at Great Neck, L. I., and until recently in Worcester, Mass.

A full account of rood screens and their construction is found in F. B. Bond and B. Camm, *Rood Screens and Rood Lofts* (London, 1909).

F.R.W.

Roothaan, John Philip: (1785-1853) Dutch priest, General (1829-1853) of the restored Society of Jesus*, which again spread through the world under his wise government. E.A.R.

rosary: A form of prayer consisting of 15 decades of Hail Marys*, each decade preceded by an Our Father and followed by a Gloria. While reciting the prayers on beads, the joyful or sorrowful or glorious mysteries of Christ's life make up the meditation. Five decades are usually said at a time.

Also any chaplet* composed of beads and on which prayers are recited.

Cf. *Catholic Encyclopedia,* vol. XIII, p. 184.

S.C.

Roscelin of Compiègne: (ca. 1050-ca. 1120) A monk who in his prime was the most influential propounder of nominalism* and demolisher of realism*. Insisting emphatically on the reality of the individual, he repudiated the charge of tritheism* imputed to him. His views are known only through the accounts of others. See Scholasticism; William of Champeaux.

M. Grabmann, *Geschichte der scholastischen Methode* (Freiburg im Breisgau, 1909), vol. I; F. J. Picavet, *Roscelin philosophe et theologien* (Paris, 1896). H.H.

Rosenius, Carl Olof: (1816-1868) Rosenius studied for the ministry but was never ordained. As lay preacher in Stockholm associated at first with George Scott of the Methodist congregation, he became the central figure in revival movements in the Church, preaching after 1857 in the Bethlehem Church. His greatest influence lay in devotional writings which, through the periodical *Pietisten,* reached multitudes in the Scandinavian countries and Swedish immigrants in America. He sought to contain a revived Christianity within the established church. C.J.B.

Rosetta Stone: See hieroglyphic writing.

Rosicrucians: The history of the movement, which is found in Europe, England, Scotland, South Africa, Australia, New Zealand, South America, India and elsewhere, is obscure, possibly due to the fact that it discloses its secrets only to the initiated and these seem to have kept the secrets well. It is said to have been founded by Christian Rosencranz about 1420, though by some authorities he is considered as but a legendary figure. He is supposed to have gotten his wisdom and philosophy from ancient sources in various places he visited, Palestine, Damascus, Egypt and Spain.

The movement attracted those of kabbalistic* tendencies, and concerned itself with astrology, alchemy, and to some extent with the principles of Free Masonry.*

One branch of the movement in America, The Rosicrucian Fellowship, with headquarters at Oceanside, California, describes the Rosicrucian Philosophy as "a mystical philosophy, founded upon Christian principles and based upon the reality of Christ and the work he came to earth to do". It believes in a sixth sense latent in man which, when developed, enables one to investigate the realm of the super-physical where dwell the dead. They do not, however, approve of spiritualistic methods of making contact with the dead. They make much use of astrology, and believe in the principle of re-birth. C.S.B.

Rothe, Richard: (1799-1867) He taught at the Wittenberg Theological Seminary and at the universities of Heidelberg and Bonn. Working with speculative ideas as a historian, he preferred to search for the traces of divine Providence in seemingly profane connections. His church history was in fact a history of culture of Christian mankind. His theology was an ingenious work of art of biblical realism and philosophical idealism, theosophical mysticism and modern ideas. Protestantism was for him the gradual transition of Christianity from the ecclesiastical form into the ethical-humane form, both in dogma and cult. Its task was to help to emancipate Christianity from the church, from its institutional impulse.

Die Anfänge der christlichen Kirche und ihrer Verfassung (Wittenberg, 1837); *Theologische Ethik,* 3 vols. (Wittenberg, 1845-48), 2nd ed. 5 vols. (Wittenberg, 1869-71); *Die Dogmatik* (Heidelberg, 1870); *Kirchengeschichte* (Heidelberg, 1875); *Geschichte der Predigt* (Bremen, 1881). H.H.

Rousseau, Jean Jacques: (1712-1778) By his search for liberty and equality he laid the basis for a new tyranny. He presents an astounding theory of religion and of the position of the church in the scheme of temporal government in his famous *Social Contract.* Contrary to his views on religious teaching contained in his educational utopia, *Emile,* and to his sympathetic and instinctive piety magnificently portrayed in his *La Nouvelle Héloise,* in which he returned to the very basis of Protestantism, of individual faith and of personal intimation of divine goodness, in his *Social Contract,* religion is outward, secular and rigidly organized. He returns to an inflexible authoritarian view of religion. Religion exists for state purposes. A secular religion is devised for the advantage of the government. He sketches the minimal and necessary dogmas of a state religion as being the belief in the existence of a powerful and rational God, the belief in a life of rewards and punishments to come, the belief in the sacred character of the social contract and the laws made thereunder. He distinguishes between religion *per se* and the political implications of religion. Belief should be free, but in so far as it involves political behavior, it has to be controlled. He outlines in detail the punishment for heretics and unbelievers for their failure to believe in the doctrines of his secular church.

J. Morley, *Rousseau* (London, 1883), 2nd ed. 2 vols.; B. Bosanquet, *The Philosophical Theory of the State* (London, 1899); E. Faguet, *La politique comparée de Montesquieu, Rousseau et Voltaire* (Paris, 1902); C. E. Vaughan, *The Political Writings of Jean Jacques Rousseau* (Cambridge, 1915), 2 vols.; I. Babbit, *Rousseau and Romanticism* (Boston, 1919); A. Schinz, *La pensee de Jean Jacques Rousseau* (Paris, 1929); E. H. Wright, *The Meaning of Rousseau* (Oxford, 1929); F. J. C. Hearnshaw, ed., *The Social and Political Ideas of some Great French Thinkers of the Age of Reason* (London, 1930); C. W. Hendel, *Jean Jacques Rousseau, Moralist* (London, 1934), 2 vols. H.H.

Royce, Josiah: (1855-1916) The most prominent American representative of absolute idealism. The heart of his idealistic argument is found in chapter XI of his earliest book, *The Religious Aspect of Philosophy* where he claims that both error and truth are possible only if an idea can aim at its special object and that an Absolute Mind is needed to bring the aiming relation about. In his *magnum opus, The World and the Individual* Royce goes on to argue that since realism, mysticism, and "critical rationalism" are all defective, idealism must be accepted. The world is mind, which means that it is a community of selves included in a larger Self. From the beginning Royce stressed the element of will and, partly under the influence of James, continued to formulate his idealism in such a way as to give it a voluntaristic and empirical flavor. Ideas are wills and purposes; reality must be what fulfills them; to be is to be the fulfilment of a purpose. But he remains an absolutist by insisting that the conditions of truth are absolute in the sense that the attempt to get rid of them implies their presence. Royce had great influence during his lifetime, less after his death. Prominent among those who drew from him are Miss Mary W. Calkins and W. E. Hocking. He taught philosophy at Harvard from 1882 to 1916. See idealism, metaphysical; neo-Hegelianism.

Works: *The Religious Aspect of Philosophy* (1885); *The Spirit of Modern Philosophy* (1892); *The Conception of God* (1897); *Studies of Good and Evil* (1898); *The Conception of Immortality* (1899); *The World and the Individual* (1900, 1901), 2 vols.; *Outlines of Psychology* (1902); *The Philosophy of Loyalty* (1908); *Wm. James and Other Essays* (1911); *The Sources of Religious Insight* (1912); *The Problem of Christianity* (1913), 2 vols.; *Lectures on Modern Idealism* (1919); *Fugitive Essays* (1925). J.S.B.

ruah: (Heb., *ruah;* Arab., *ruh*) Hebrew: 1) Pre Exilic Kingdom Period: the religious factor in non-human natural forces; spirits and gods, including Yahweh, are ruah in nature, and unlike man who is nephesh, a different kind of religious factor; 2) After the Exile: a universal religious factor, common to the natures of all things human and non-human; religious factor shared by Yahweh and man. Arab: *ruh.* From the Seventh Century A.D. onward the religious factor common to all things; shared by Allah and all spiritual agents or powers, including man. (See nephesh, nafs). *Ruh* remains to this day the potent concept among Moslems; but due to cross fertilization of Hebraic with Hellenic cultures, ruah has been displaced from its old basal position by Hellenic concepts, both for Christians and Jews. F.L.P.

rubric: (Lat., *rubrica*—red earth) Directions in a liturgical* book concerning rite or ceremony, or collectively all such regulations, so called because formerly printed in red, now usually in italics. T.J.B.

Rückert, Leopold Immanuel: (1797-1871) He taught at the University of Jena. He wrote several commentaries on the Epistles of St. Paul. He was strongly ethically oriented in his works against his external theological enemies.

Christliche Philosophie oder Philosophische Geschichte und Bibel nach ihren wahren Beziehungen zueinander, 2 vols. (Leipzig, 1825); *Das Abendmahl, sein Wesen und seine Geschichte in der alten Kirche* (Leipzig, 1856); *Der Rationalismus* (Leipzig, 1859). H.H.

Rudra: A storm god of Vedic Hinduism* but of relatively minor importance, celebrated in but three entire hymns in the Rig Veda*. In contrast to Indra* who is beneficent, Rudra represents the destructive maleficent aspects of the storm. It was long thought that the great god Shiva*, the destroyer of the Hindu Trimurti* had his origin in Rudra. See art. Shiva. At any rate they must early have been identified. C.S.B.

Rufinus Tyrranius: (ca. 345-410; also called Rufinus of Aquileia) Born at Concordia in Italy and died in Sicily. Spent much of his life in a monastery near Jerusalem where he translated many of Origen's* works into Latin. A friend of Jerome but later estranged by the Origenist controversy. S.M.G.

rule of faith: (*Regula Fidei*) This is a standard or norm for testing Divine Truths. The true Rule of Faith is the ecclesiastical magisterium, that is, the teaching Church. Its living voice can pronounce infallible judgment on Divine Truths. The Church exercises Her office as Teacher when the bishops of the world convene in a General Council under the supervision of the Supreme Pontiff; when a bishop issues a pastoral letter to the people of his diocese; when any priest explains the word of God to the faithful; and even when the child is taught his catechism or instructed by his parents.

See Herve, *Manuale Theologiae Dogmaticae* (Paris, 1929), vol. I, n. 568; S. J. Hunter, *Outlines of Dogmatic Theology* (1894), vol. I, nn. 78, 87, 89,

290; Wilhelm and Scannell, *A Manual of Catholic Theology* (London, 1908), vol. I, n. 85. W.H.

Rumanian Church: See Eastern Orthodox Churches.

Russell, Charles Taze: (Pastor) (1852-1916) Born of Scotch-Irish descent in Allegheny, Pa., on Feb. 16, 1852, where he received his education in the common schools. A Congregationalist, he revolted against the doctrine of eternal punishment. In a pamphlet, *Object and Manner of our Lord's Return,* he held that an invisible second coming of Christ had occurred in the Autumn of 1874. Since 1874 is the Millenial Age, or "Day of Jehovah", marked by an international revolution of the working classes, bringing the world to chaos. After this would occur the resurrection of the dead, a last judgment taking 1000 years, and the final establishment of the Messianic Kingdom on earth.

His following rapidly increased. By 1878, his periodical *The Watch Tower,* had a circulation of 45,000 copies monthly, and, through the influence of his organization, the International Bible Students Association, his six-volume *Studies in the Scriptures* sold millions of copies. The Jehovah's Witnesses, as they are commonly known, numbered 1200 congregations by 1909. Unfavorable publicity concerning his private life, and his "miracle wheat sales" in 1911, in addition to the general disillusionment after 1914, tended to weaken the society. Russell died on October 31, 1916. See Millenial Dawn; Russellism.

M. S. Czatt, *International Bible Students, Jehovah's Witnesses* (1933); Charles T. Cook, *All about One Russell* (n. date); J. F. Rutherford, *A Great Battle in the Ecclesiastical Heavens* (1915); *Watch Tower,* June 1, 1916, Dec. 1, 1916; C. T. Russell, *Plan of the Ages* (1924 ed. pref.); *New York Times,* Nov. 1, 1916; *New York Herald-Tribune,* Nov. 1, 1916; *Brooklyn Daily Eagle,* Sept. 23 and Oct. 19, 1911.
M.G.R.—W.W.S.

Russell Lectureship, The: Founded in 1918 by Mrs. Susan M. Russell of Syracuse in honor of her husband, Archimedes Russell, architect and citizen of Syracuse, and presented as a foundation to the Auburn Theological Seminary, formerly at Auburn, New York and now associated with Union Theological Seminary, New York City. The principal amounts to $10,000. Lecturers and subjects are selected by the faculty. Among the more than twenty distinguished lecturers are: Hugh R. Mackintosh, David S. Cairns, James Moffatt, Kirtley Mather, Ernest F. Tittle, John T. McNeill and John S. Whale.

(Data furnished by W. S. Davison, Executive Director of Auburn Theological Seminary.)
V.F.

Russellism: The religious movement which grew out of the teachings of Charles T. Russell (1852-1916)*. Known first as Russellites, the movement later took the name "International Bible Students Ass'n", better known as "Jehovah's Witnesses." Using a literal interpretation of the Scriptures, the members believe that Christ returned invisibly in 1874. All but the "little flock" who are living a spiritual life with Jesus, have been put beyond the reach of divine Justice by Christ's atonement, and are now sleeping until the second resurrection. Return to physical life will give man a second probationary period. His actions, decided by his own free will, will determine his fate. Those willfully rebellious will be cut off after 100 years through death by electric shock. Those making wrong choices will not survive the Millennium. Thus by the end of the thousand-year period, the earth will be cleared of wickedness and will ever contine an Eden for the "little flock."

The Association stresses systematic sale of literature, nearly all of which is produced by its leaders, and uses such modern techniques as radio speaking, recordings for door-step sales, and sales supervisors, to propagate its ideas. In 1932, the depression peak, the Witnesses distributed 14,405,072 books and booklets.

Because of their aggressive methods and their refusal to take part in temporal affairs, the Jehovah's Witnesses have been subjected to frequent arrests and court actions. This litigation has covered selling without licenses, refusal to recognize draft summons, refusal to permit vaccination, and failure to salute the flag. Actual statistics are difficult to obtain, the only report, listing approximately ninety thousand members, was made in the *Watch Tower* in 1925-27.

See Millenial Dawn; Charles T. Russell; J. F. Rutherford. See anti-missionary movement in the U. S.

Milton S. Czatt, *The International Bible Students: Jehovah's Witnesses* (1933); C. T. Russell, *Millenial Dawn* (1881); C. T. Russell, *Studies in the Scripture* (1886).
M.G.R.—W.W.S.

Russian Churches, the: See Eastern Orthodox Churches; Holy Synod; Russian sectarianism.

Russian sectarianism: Beside the Russian Orthodox and the Old Ritualist, the Russian Christian churches comprise numerous groups of sectarians. Of the modern groups, Khlysty are the oldest. They originated some time in the seventeenth century, and the chief characteristic tenet of the group is the continuous incarnation of Christ in the line of Khlyst leaders. Hence the name, which is a corruption of "Christs." The movement developed antinomian, orgiastic tendencies.

As an ascetic reaction from these immoral elements there arose, in the sixties of the eighteenth century, a sect which saw in procreation the root of all evil, and therefore practiced emasculation (hence their name, Skoptsy or Eunochs). Contemporaneously with them arose a group which assumed the name of Dukhobortsy, the Spirit-Wrestlers. Their doctrine had certain mystical, Quaker characteristics, and they stressed "spiritual understanding." The teachings of the Ukrainian philosopher and mystic, Gregory S. Skovoroda, greatly influenced this group. In the second half of the nineteenth century they adopted Tolstoyan* doctrines, pacifism*, and many migrated to Canada.

But the uncontrolled mysticism of the Dukhobors produced dissatisfaction among some of their members. Even the son-in-law of the leader, Simeon Ukleyin, revolted, and elevated the Scriptures to the place of the norm of life and teaching. Thus arose the evangelical sect of the Molokans (Milk Drinkers), who however, prefer to call themselves Spiritual Christians.

There were many other minor sects of native Russian origin, such as the Beguni (Runners), the New Israel, and others. But besides these, some sects were of foreign origin. Among these the Stundists and the Baptists are the most important. The latter arose in the middle of the nineteenth century among the German peasants of Bessarabia and southern Russia. They were pietistic in character. In the seventies, they were strongly influenced by a Baptist missionary, Popov, so that in the end they adopted the tenet of believers' baptism. Thus the movement became Stundobaptist. In the nineties, this group united with a Baptist group organized in the north of Russia. Since then, it is among the largest of the sectarians.

Frederick C. Conybeare, *Russian Dissenters* (1921); Matthew Spinka, "Molokane, the Russian 'Spiritual Christians'" in *The Congregational Quarterly* (London, 1929), p. 10 ff.; Z. F. C. Wright, *Slava Bohu, The Story of the Dukhobors* (1940). M.S.

Ruth: A book of the O.T. which has become classic as a Hebrew idyl or short story. While included among the historical books and placed after Judges* in English Bibles, following the Septuagint and Vulgate, it is found in the Hebrew canon in the division called "Writings" or Hagiographa*, and is one of the five *Megilloth** ("Scrolls") in that division. In Jewish usage the Book of Ruth is read at the Feast of Weeks* (Pentecost). It tells the story of the fidelity of the Moabitess Ruth to her Hebrew mother-in-law and her subsequent marriage to Boaz, whereby she became great-grandmother of King David. The book has usually been interpreted by modern scholars as a work of the Persian period designed to protest against the strict views in this age (e.g., of Ezra and Nehemiah**) regarding intermarriage with foreigners. This date has recently been doubted; the language of the book and its socio-legal background (if real rather than purely fictional) suggest a late pre-exilic date. It is possible that it was intended as a protest against the antipathy expressed in Deuteronomy* towards Moabites* and other foreigners (see Deut. 23: 3ff.). The view advanced by Staples and Haller that the story is based upon an ancient myth of the Bethelehem fertility cult is far-fetched. See levirate marriage.

See M. Haller and K. Galling, *Die fünf Megilloth (Handbuch z. Alten Testament)*, (1940); M. Burrows, "The Marriage of Boaz and Ruth," *Journal of Biblical Literature* LIX (1940), pp. 445-454. J.P.H.

Ruthenian Rite: The Byzantine Rite* as used in the Galician Church in union with Rome (since 1595)—the variations are minor, partly local customs, partly Latin influences. E.R.H.

Ruthenians: A Slavic people who live for the most part in the Ukraine, Southeastern Poland, Czecho-Slovakia, and Roumania; also called Little Russians and Ukrainians. E.A.R.

Rutherford, J. F.: (Judge) 1869-1942) Successor to Charles T. Russell* as leader of the International Bible Students' Association, was born in Booneville, Missouri. After an academy education, he read law, and later was made Special Judge in the 14th Judicial District of Missouri. Following the death of Pastor Russell*, he was made president of the I. B. S. A. (Jehovah's Witnesses). His aggressiveness and managerial ability centralized the organization, and turned the emphasis from Russell's books to new ones which he wrote. New methods, such as radio preaching and recorded doorstep salestalks were introduced in the book-selling activities of the Witnesses.

M. S. Czatt, *International Bible Students: Jehovah's Witnesses* (1933). M.G.R.—W.W.S.

Ruysbroeck, John: (1293-1381) A Flemish mystic who after a career as a parish priest in Brussels, at the age of 50, accompanied by several companions, retired to a hermitage in the forest of Soignes and there founded a religious community His *Adornment of the Spiritual Marriage* (London, 1916), edited by Evelyn Underhill, is a classic of mysticism*. D.V.S.

S

S: Symbol used by R. H. Pfeiffer for one of the component narratives of the Book of Genesis*. The symbol is derived from South or Seir,—that is, Edom, which Pfeiffer considers as the place of its origin, probably in the tenth century B.C. It consists of the account of the origin and early history of mankind in Gen. 1-11 which is not P*, and the account of the origin of the peoples in Southern Palestine and Transjordania, concluding with a summary history of Edom before David (parts of Gen. 14-38).

See R. H. Pfeiffer, *Introduction to the Old Testament* (1941), pp. 159-167. J.P.H.

Saadia ben Joseph: Saadia ben Joseph (usually referred to as Saada Gaon), born in Fayyum, Upper Egypt, in 882, was one of the most brilliant Jewish personalities of the Middle Ages. He was the first who, having mastered Arabic literature and thought as well as the Bible and Talmud*, attempted to synthesize the two cultures. The great philosophical work "Emunot Ve Deot" (Faith and Reason) which resulted from this attempt has become one of the classics of Jewish religious philosophy. Saadia also translated the Bible into Arabic in order to bring its treasures to the attention of Arabic speaking Jews and Mohammedans. Aside from these two great contributions to Judaism, Saadia's versatile genius made itself felt in the fields of Rabbinic law, astronomy, liturgy, grammar, lexicography, and apologetics. Indeed, in the words of Abraham ibn Ezra, he was "the foremost authority in every field." See Israel, religion and theology.

E.B.—L.F.

Sabaism: The beliefs of a semi-Christian sect of Babylonia, mentioned in the *Koran* (2:59; 5:73; 22:17), as *Sabeites.* They are also called *Sabians* or *Mandeans,* and survive as a small sect of 2000, holding John the Baptist as the true prophet, observing baptism, a eucharistic meal, and several feasts. Their teachings reveal a syncretism of many faiths. P.E.J.

Sabatier, Auguste: (1839-1901) French theologian, dean of the Protestant theological faculty at Paris. Best known for his theory of religious knowledge, "critical symbolism," according to which theological dogmas are transient symbolic expressions of abiding religious experiences. This theory, borrowed in part from Schleiermacher and Ritschl**, was so powerfully stated in Sabatier's *Philosophy of Religion* (1901) and *Religions of Authority and the Religion of the Spirit* (1903) that it dominated Liberal Protestant and Catholic Modernist thought for over a generation. Auguste Sabatier must not be confused with his younger relative Paul Sabatier (1858-1928), author of the *Life of St. Francis of Assisi* (1894) and many other Franciscan studies. W.M.H.

Sabatier, Paul: See Sabatier, Auguste.

Sabbatarianism: The identification of the Lord's Day with the Jewish Sabbath* and the consequent application of the fourth commandment to its observance. It was a medieval doctrine, rejected by the reformers, but revived by English Puritans during the reign of Queen Elizabeth and officially adopted by the Westminster Assembly. W.S.H.

Sabbatarianism, Puritan: The Puritan* idea of Sunday as a day of sermons, meditation, and sobriety was founded 1) ideologically upon the Mosaic code governing the observance of the Sabbath* and 2) historically upon a reaction against the lax ideas of the pre-reformation era. A factor in the seventeenth century was the hostility of Puritan clergy to the Book of Sports, which was issued by James I (1618) ostensibly to check the anti-sabbatarianism of recusants in Lancashire, but which led to the identification of prelacy and anti-sabbatarianism by the Puritans. The repressive legislation of 1640-1660 banned both manual labor and games on Sunday*.

W. B. Whitaker, *Sunday in Tudor and Stuart Times* (London, 1933). E.W.K.

sabbath: The seventh day of the week which was ordained as a day of rest (Sabbath in Hebrew) to commemorate creation and Israel's redemption from Egypt (Exodus 20:8, 11; Deut. 5:15). The link of the sabbath with the deliverance from Egypt emphasizes its humanitarian character as a day of universal release from physical labor, even for the slave and the animal.

The sabbath was to be observed, according to Jewish tradition, by abstaining from physical labor and, positively, by cultivating the spiritual life through worship, study, and reading of the religious classics. Of course, when the necessities of preserving life were involved, all observance of the sabbath was to be suspended, for the Sabbath was made for man and not man for the Sabbath (Talmud, Yoma, 85b). The synagogue developed its most important worship service on the sabbath. This consists of the service Friday at sundown and Saturday morning, when the weekly Scriptural lesson is read to the congregation. In modern times many synagogues, particularly, in America, have instituted a late Friday evening service, to accommodate those who return at a late hour from business.

Morris Joseph, *Judaism as Creed and Life* (1919), pp. 200-212; H. Schauss, *The Jewish Festivals* (1938), pp. 3-37. B.Z.B.

sabbath, Christian: (Hebr. *shabbath*) The Sabbath, as a Jewish institution (the seventh day of the week, prescribed in the Decalogue* as a day of rest), though observed by Jewish-Christians in the early Church, was not recognized by Gentile* Christianity. The holy day for Christians was the first day of the week (Sunday*) and called the Lord's Day, commemorating his resurrection. Nevertheless, in actual practice, the Lord's Day* came early to assume certain characteristics of the Jewish Sabbath. Not only did it become a day of worship, but, by decree of Constantine in 321, Sunday was set aside as a legal day of rest from general labor. The idea that Sunday is indeed the Christian Sabbath, carrying with it the obligation imposed by the Decalogue, was developed chiefly in Seventeenth Century English Protestantism, from which it has come into popular Protestant acceptance in both Britain (particularly Scotland) and America. E.T.R.

sabbatical year: Every seventh year when the Bible (O.T.) (Lev. 25:1-25, Deut. 15:2) ordained that loans be cancelled, pledged property restored, and land remain fallow, with all uncultivated growth left to the poor and the stranger. The cancellation of debts was subsequently circumvented through a legal reform instituted by the famous Pharisee, Hillel*. B.Z.B.

Sabbatine privilege: A belief among members of the R. C. Church that Mary, the Mother of Christ, will secure the release from purgatory of the souls of those who have been especially devoted to her. The name came from the fact that Saturday (the Sabbath) is considered Mary's Day. A 14th century document, attributed to Pope John XXII*, declared that the Blessed Virgin would rescue from purgatory*, on the Saturday following their death, the souls of those who had satisfied certain devotional conditions. Though scholars regard this document as apocryphal, the belief in the extraordinary intercessive powers of Mary is universally held by Catholics. V.J.B.

Sabellianism: A theory of the Godhead named after its first advocate, Sabellius, a third-century churchman, who affirmed that there is but one divine essence which became operative in three temporally successive manifestations: as Creator and Lawgiver in the Father, as Redeemer in the Son, and as Life-Giver in the Holy Ghost. See modalism; monarchianism; patripassianism; Trinity. F.G.E.

sacerdotalism: Strictly, a religious system in which a priesthood occupies an essential place as mediator between men and God; the spirit, methods, or character of such a system. Often used in a hostile sense to denote the exaltation of a priestly class at the expense of the laity and spiritual values. F.G.E.

Sack, Karl Heinrich: (1789-1875) He taught first in the University of Bonn. He later was consistorial councilor in Magdeburg. He sought to realize Schleiermacher's demand for a philosophical theology. In the attempt he changed its type from the formal to the inner content.

Die christliche Apologetik (Hamburg, 1829, 2nd ed., Hamburg, 1841); *Die christliche Polemik* (Hamburg, 1838). H.H.

sacra romana rota: See ecclesiastical courts.

sacramental intention: See intention, sacramental.

sacramental meal: A familiar feature of many ancient religions. The idea attaching to the religious feast was either that of table fellowship with the deity or else an actual absorption of the god by the worshiper as he partook of the sacred food in which the deity was thought to be present. The principal religious meal in Judaism was the Passover* feast celebrated in the springtime to commemorate the deliverance of the Hebrews from bondage in Egypt. At the opening of the Christian era this feast had taken on chiefly a memorial and grateful significance in appreciation of the new covenant that had been established between the Hebrews and their God. Thus it furnished the prototype for Christianity's distinctive religious meal, the Lord's Supper, or Eucharist** as it was called from the prayer of thanksgiving (*eucharistia*) offered at the celebration. The earliest literary attestation to the Lord's Supper (I Cor. 11:23-26) shows it to have been a memorial of Jesus' death by which a new covenant had been established, and also an anticipatory act looking toward the return of Jesus. But in this same connection Paul introduces a third idea implying that the Lord's Supper meant actual participation of the body and blood of Christ as sacramental food. The table of the Lord* is compared to the table of demons who were "eaten" by their communicants and Christians who thus partake of demons must not assume that Christ will share the same human dwelling (I Cor. 10:14-22; 11:27). In the Gospel of John the sacramental significance of the Christian religious meal is explicitly indicated (6:52-58). By a gradual process of development the meal came to be a strictly sacramental act, *ex opere operato**, in Roman Catholicism, while the Protestant communions vacillate between a rigid sacramentalism and an edifying memorial or dedicatory significance. See agape; food; love feast; mystery religions; theophagy.

M. Goguel, *L'Eucharistie des Origines a Justin Martyr* (1910); W. M. Groton, *The Christian Eucharist and the Pagan Cults* (1914); G. H. C. MacGregor, *Eucharistic Origins* (1928). S.J.C.

sacramentalism: Broadly, the doctrine and use of sacraments; narrowly, the ascribing of inherent saving power to sacraments, or their power to impart grace even, if need be, without the operation of active faith. F.G.E.

sacramentarian: Originally, a Zwinglian or Calvinist who held the sacraments* to be merely visible symbols and denied the Lutheran doctrine of consubstantiation* (cf. Lutheran doctrine of the Lord's Supper), as well as Roman Catholic transubstantiation*. By a curious inversion the term has come in recent years to mean a sacramentalist, one who holds to the saving efficacy of the sacraments. F.G.E.

sacramentary: A book containing many prayers, such as those used by priest or bishop at certain parts of the Mass* and at ordinations. L.R.W.

sacraments: The essential background for consideration of sacraments includes the truth that man is a mind-body or sense-spirit organism, and that the world is a two-level reality in which matter and purpose are related and interpenetrating. The realm of space-time, therefore, is regarded by Christian theologians as expressing God's will and assisting man to cooperate therewith; while man himself, as also a two-level being, is touched by God and helped by him, primarily, through material and visible "signs" or means. Against this background is set the fact of the Incarnation, in which Reality (ultimate being, or God) penetrates and employs human nature to express himself to men and to aid them. Jesus Christ, so understood, is also believed by Christian theologians to have ordained either by implicit word or deed, or explicitly during his earthly life, certain continuing means by which he may still energize through the church in the world.

Various theories have been entertained as to the dominical institution of the sacraments. Of the seven traditionally called sacraments, Baptism and the Lord's Supper** are more directly dominical; the others have often been said to be "mediately", implicitly, or *in genere* instituted by Christ: these others include confirmation, marriage, penance, holy orders, and unction**. The number of sacraments had been established as seven, by medieval tradition; although Protestant theologians generally took only "the sacraments of the gospel" and retained the major two.

The normal definition of a sacrament is found in Hugh of S. Victor*: *sacramentum est corporale vel materiale elementum foris sensibiliter propositum, ex similitudine repraesentans, et ex institutione significans, et ex sanctificatione continens, aliquam invisibilem et spiritualem gratiam.* The Anglican Catechism, which more briefly speaks of "an outward and visible sign of an inward and spiritual grace given unto us, ordained by Christ himself; as a means whereby we receive this grace, and a pledge to assure us thereof", expresses the same ideas. Roughly these include: a sign, grace, dominical establishment in some form, and efficacy for the recipient. In traditional Catholic theology, from which various Protestant theologians have departed in one respect or another, a sacrament has its efficacy through the divine will, the part of the recipient being to accept with faith and in penitence for sin the benefits which are given. Those sacraments are valid in which the proper form (words said) and matter (physical or material sign employed) are found, and the intention is to perform the Church's rites. Hence, in regular Catholic theology, a sacrament is performed *ex opere operato**, which signifies not mechanical operation but the divine reliability in carrying out the purpose of a sacrament despite the possible "unworthiness of the minister."

In each sacrament there are certain constant elements, including the matter and form, regularly known as *sacramentum;* the grace or benefit of the sacrament, objectively given but subjectively apprehended by faith, called the *virtus;* the minister, who acts always as the Church's functional organ in celebrating the sacrament; and, in the case of the Eucharist, the *res sacramenti,* or thing of the sacrament, the body and blood of Christ.

The several rites traditionally listed as sacraments are analyzed below under those elements: *Baptism*—water is the matter; a formula stating the baptism in the triune name is the form; the minister is normally a priest, although in emergency a layman may act; the benefit is the washing away of "original sin" (concupiscence is not removed), and incorporation into the Church. Catholic theologians insist upon "baptismal regeneration"*, with "character" given by the act; Protestants have normally held to a more "declaratory" conception of the sacrament.

Confirmation—the completion of baptism by "ordination" to full lay responsibility; the matter is laying-on of hands, chrism**, or both; the form is some reference to conferring of the Holy Spirit; the minister is normally a bishop, although (in Eastern Orthodox Churches) a priest may act as deputy; the benefit is empowering by the Holy Spirit for lay responsibility, for one who is baptized.

*Penance**—by confession of sins in the presence of a priest, and the statement by the priest of God's forgiveness, absolution is conveyed in God's name by the Church; the matter is some outward act to express reconciliation with the Church after worthy confession (in contrition and faith) by the penitent; the form includes some words of absolution*; the minister is always a priest; the benefit, conferred upon a baptized person, is remission of sins after baptism and welcome into the Church's fellowship which has in part been broken by sin.

*Holy Eucharist**—the matter is bread and wine; the form is a consecrating prayer including "words of institution" set in a formula of thanksgiving to God for the work of Christ; the benefit is "strengthening and refreshing" of soul, and union with God by assimilation of Christ as present in both humanity and deity; the minister is a priest; the recipient is a baptized, and normally (in Catholic communions) a confirmed person; the *res sacramenti* is the true but spiritual body and blood of Christ present. For further discussion of varying theologies of the Eucharist, cf. *Lord's Supper.*

Holy Orders—the conferring of power and privilege to a ministry, by a rite whose material means is imposition of hands, whose form is some ordination formula defining the intention; the minister, normally a bishop (one ordained to ordain); the recipient a baptized man; and the benefit the grace for ministering. For varying views of the ministry, cf. articles on that subject.

Holy Matrimony—an outward rite by which a life-long monogamous union is entered upon by a man and woman; the Church's function is to bless this marriage. The matter is a lawful contract of marriage; the form is the words used to indicate this contract; the minister is the two parties who marry (in the west, although in the east the priest is the minister); the benefit is grace to fulfil marriage's purposes (union and mutual help, procreation of children, preservation of chastity, etc.); the recipients are baptized persons not barred by impediments* to marriage*.

*Unction**—anointing of a sick (or in Roman practice, a dying) person, to confer grace in serious illness. The matter is anointing with oil; the form, a prayer for grace; the minister a priest; the recipient, a baptized person who is ill; the benefit, grace to assist in bodily illness, and remission of sins in special cases, but not supplanting normal penance.

The outline given above is on the basis of normal western Catholic theology; departures from this are made by various theologians, and Reformation and Protestant theology disregards all but Baptism and the Lord's Supper. For discussion of these views, cf. articles on the particular faith of the several denominations. See grace; intention, sacramental; opus operatum; Peter Lombard.

A. L. Lilley, *Sacraments* (1929); Pohle-Preuss, *Dogmatic Theology* (1911-1917); F. J. Hall, *Dogmatic Theology* (1909-1920) or Hall (and Hallock), *Outlines of Dogmatic Theology* (1933). For historical development, Pourrat, *Theology of the Sacraments* (1910); Lowther-Clarke and Harris (eds.), *Liturgy and Worship* (1932). W.N.P.

Sacred Heart of Jesus: The name of many religious congregations, and also the object of many devotions, each of them being but a special form of devotion to Jesus. L.R.W.

sacred literatures: Since prehistoric time the peoples of the earth have transmitted from generation to generation the growing heritage of wisdom learned by hard experience in their struggle for the material and social goods of life. The custodians of the lore were the old men, the priests and seers. The wisdom consisted of the legends of the past, heroic tales, origin myths, ceremonials, spells and incantations, hymns to the gods, moral codes and practical techniques. This heritage was taught to the young only after solemn initiation*. It was the sacred treasure-store of tribal wisdom. As the tradition grew it required a specialized class to keep it in memory and transmit it orally. Even after the coming of writing, the Hindus for many centuries preferred to preserve their sacred learning by oral transmission. Early or late, however, all peoples of high culture recorded the sacred lore in a book, the book par excellence, nucleus and fountain-head of their religious literatures.

The sacred heritage is always deeply revered. Initiation ceremonies at adolescence* in preliterate cultures and for novices in preparation for the priesthood at all times are intended to instill an awed reverence for the ancient lore. Attitudes toward Scriptures vary from a deep respect for the treasured wisdom of the past to bibliolatry*. The sacred books have been treated as divine revelation*, as teaching that saves, as a heritage of social wisdom or as records of the divine age which justify a racial hope. Direct divine revelation has been claimed for the Zoroastrian, Jewish-Christian and Moslem Scriptures. The Hindu sacred books are also revelation, embodying the truth "seen" in ancient time by the *rishis** and handed down word by word, syllable by syllable through a long line of teachers. The divine light which inspired the teachings of the Sikh *gurus** remains enshrined in their idolized holy bible. The Buddhist and Jain Scriptures record the gospels of the great teachers who pointed the way to salvation. The idea of divine revelation would be meaningless for them since these great sages were teachers of both gods and men. China's sacred books embody a heritage of social and philosophic wisdom and make no claim to divine inspiration*. The Japanese books are presented as history reaching back to the age of the gods. Their divine authority supports the philosophy of the throne, race and empire.

Sacred literatures are usually divided into two classes, (1) the canon of revealed truth or the teachings of the masters and their immediate disciples and (2) the tradition, commentaries and development of the teaching by later thinkers, which has a lesser degree of sanctity.

The writings that have come down to us from Egypt and Babylonia are heavily weighted with ritual magic. They consist of variants of old myths, spells and incantations, prayers, hymns to the gods, ritual on behalf of the dead, festival songs, lamentations, moral tales and proverbial wisdom.

The earliest sacred books of India were the *Rik, Yajur,* and *Sāma Vedas,* "the Triple Veda". The ten books of the *Rigveda* contain more than a thousand hymns used in connection with the sacrifices. The *Sāmaveda* is a collection of the many melodies to which the hymns were chanted. The *Yajurveda* consists of sacrificial formulae with instructions as to how the words and gestures fall into their proper places in the rhythm of the sacrifice. Each of these *Vedas* had its own class of priestly specialists. A fourth *Veda,* the *Atharva,* was added later. Into it are gathered 730 magic spells for the fulfilment of all kinds of desires. To each of the four *Vedas* were added *Brāhmaṇas, Araṇyakas* and *Upanishads.* The *Brāhmaṇas* are massive texts for the specialists in the sacrificial techniques giving directions and explanations of the ceremonies mixed with theorizing, speculation and philosophizing on their significance. The *Araṇyakas,* called the Forest Books because they were taught in the secrecy of the forest, are fanciful and mystical meditations on the meaning of the ritual lore. The *Upanishads* are philosophic texts in which the idea of a spiritual absolute comes to full flower and realization of the unity of the soul and this timeless being is proclaimed as the way of salvation. All the foregoing works are *śruti* (*sṛti*), sacred in the highest sense. They embody the revelation "seen" by the *rishis.*

Tradition, *smṛti,* begins with the three *Kalpa-sūtras,* the *Śrauta, Gṛhya* and *Dharma,* attached to each of the *Vedas* and considered compulsory sacred learning. The *Śrauta-sūtras* are very condensed handbooks for specialized priests giving instructions in the conduct of the sacrifices. The *Gṛhya-sūtras,* "House Books", deal with the rites for the crisis points of life from birth to death and the family sacrifices. The *Dharma-sūtras* are law books, laying down the rules of conduct for the four stages of life, the duties of the king and the codes of the four main classes of society.

For the last two thousand years the real bible of popular Hinduism has been the two great epics, the *Mahābhārata* and the *Ramayana,* and the *Purāṇas.* The epics were originally heroic ballads later transformed by priests into poems preaching salvation by faith through the earthly incarnation of the high god. In their early form the *Purāṇas* dealt with origins, cosmogony and genealogies; but they also became sectarian works celebrating the saving power of the popular gods, especially *Viṣṇu* and *Śiva.* The later *Tantric* literature is the religious expression of the resurgent pre-Aryan culture centering in the mother goddesses. In addition to philosophic teaching, instruction in conduct and ceremonials, the *Tantras* are much concerned with magic techniques and yoga.

The Jain canon of scriptures, the *Āgamas,* was fixed, according to tradition, in 300 B.C. After a final revision it was put into written form about 454 A.D. It consists of eleven *Aṅgas* (the twelfth is lost), twelve *Upāṅgas,* ten *Paiṇṇas,* six *Chheda-sūtras* and four *Mula-sutras.* The various sections are not restricted to specific topics. The worldview, doctrine of salvation, monastic rules and discipline, the moral code and the rules for ascetics are presented in the *Aṅgas.* Most of these themes recur in the *Mula-sutras.* The *Chheda-sutras* emphasize especially the monastic rules. In addition to doctrine and discipline, the *Upāṅgas* and *Paiṇṇas* teach astronomy, astrology, physiology and geography.

Like all the other sacred books of India, the Buddhist teachings were transmitted orally for many centuries and reduced to writing only toward the close of the first century B.C. The canon of early Buddhism in its final revision of 247 B.C. is made up of three baskets, *Tipiṭaka* (Sk. *Tripiṭaka*). The sermon basket, *Sutta-piṭaka,* in five divisions, includes many hundreds of longer and shorter discourses on the doctrine, in which Gotama or his immediate disciples expound the teaching. The *Vinaya-Piṭaka* expounds and explains the discipline for monks. The *Abidhamma-piṭaka,* a later addition, is composed of discussions of doctrinal, philosophical and psychological themes. With the development of different schools of thought, the contents of this section of the scriptures varied according to the peculiar emphases of the sects.

As the early *Hīnayāna* Buddhism gradually changed to the *Mahāyāna,* a new sacred literature appeared to embody the new gospel. Three lives of Buddha mark the progressive transition from the early to the later interpretation of the Master —the *Mahā-vastu,* the *Buddha-charita* and the *Lalita Vistara.* Of the many *sūtras* of *Mahāyāna* Buddhism the most important are the *Saddharma-puṇḍarika,* "the Lotus of the Good Law", in which the Buddha preaches the gospel surrounded by an innumerable host of super-human beings, the *Prajnaparamita,* philosophic texts, expounding the doctrine of the void, the *Daśabhūmīsvara,* explaining the ten stages on the way to Buddahood, the *Samādhi-rāja,* on the stages of meditation leading to highest enlightenment, the *Kāraṇḍavyūha,* glorifying Avalokiteśvara the bodhisattva of providence and mercy, the *Gandavyūha,* celebrating Manjusrī, bodhisattva of wisdom, the *Laṅkāvatāra,* an exposition of the teaching with an eye on rival Hindu schools, the *Suvarṇaprabhāsa,* on philosophy and ritual, the *Sukhāvatīvyūha,* praise of Amitābha, Buddha of saving grace, and the glories of his Western Paradise. The *Tathāgata guhyaka* is a Buddhist *Tantra,* very similar to the Tantric texts of Hinduism.

The sacred book of the Sikhs, the *Ādī-Granth,* is a collection of the writings of the first five *gurus* beginning with Nanak (b. 1469). It includes hymns, prayers, theology and religious teaching. Since the close of the 17th century the book has taken the place of the living *gurus* and receives divine honors.

The sacred literature of Zoroastrianism fared badly during its first thousand years. The canon, fixed in the 4th century A.D. is only a fragmentary reconstruction of the original Avesta. It includes the *Yasna,* records relating to morality, theology and ceremony (the *Gāthās,* attributed to Zoroaster himself, belong in this section), the *Vīsparad,* invocations, the *Yashts,* hymns of praise of the divine company surrounding Ahura Mazda, *Nyaishes* and *Gāhs,* litanies, and the *Vendīdād,* a priestly code giving detailed instruction regarding purification, punishments and techniques of expiation. Religious texts of later origin, with the sacredness of tradition, are the *Dīnkart,* legendary materials and philosophic thinking of an age a thousand years later than the prophet, the *Būndahishn* and the *Arda Viraf Nameh,* dealing with eschatology, cosmogony and cosmology, *Śāyast lā-Śāyast,* on the proper and improper, *Dātistān-i-Dinik,* religious opinions, and *Shikand Gūmānīk*

Vigar, "the Doubt-dispelling 'Explanation' ", a product of the age of rivalry between Zoroastrianism and Islam and Christianity.

The Chinese sacred books draw their authority from the wisdom of the great sages and the treasure-trove of social experience associated with their names. As the basis of the education and training of officials they have had a far-reaching influence in the shaping of Chinese culture, especially during the last two thousand years. The texts fall into two groups, the Five Classics and the Four Books. The Classics include the *Shu-Ching*, the book of history; the *Shih-Ching*, a book of 305 odes, some of them poetry collected from the various states and some odes used on ceremonial occasions; the *I Ching*, or Book of Changes, developed from the ancient technique of divination into moral and political essays; the *Li Chi*, a compendium of ceremonial usages and rules of propriety; the *Ch'un Ch'iu*, annals of the state of Lu from 722-484 B.C. The Four Books are the *Lun-Yü*, Analects, conversations of Confucius and his disciples; the *Ta Hsüeh*, the Great Learning (its teaching is intended to lead one "to exemplify illustrious virtue, to love the people and to rest in the highest good"); the *Chung Yung*, the Doctrine of the Mean, expounding the virtues of the superior man, the five relationships of a harmonious society and the relation of human nature to the cosmic order. These last two texts are included in the *Li Chi*. Last of the Four Books is a collection of the political, moral and philosophical discussions of Mencius.

The classic of the early Taoïst school in China is the *Tao Te Ching*, a collection of aphorisms on the nature of the Tao, the cosmic ultimate and *Te*, its manifestation through human nature.

The revelations given by Allah to Mohammed during the years of his service as warrior in Mecca and Apostle of God at Medīna were collected after his death into the 114 *Sūrahs* of the *Koran*. Mohammed thought his messages came through the angel Gabriel from the same divine book from which Jews and Christians before him received their revelations. Moslem dogma claims that the book is uncreated and has existed eternally with God. After the death of the prophet, it became the primary authority for the law codes which developed in the various areas of the Moslem world. Both education and worship depend for their materials upon the *Koran**.

The *Kojiki* (712 A.D.) and the *Nihongi* (720 A.D.) are the two chief texts of the sacred literature of Japanese Shinto. Both of them are chronicles of ancient times. They deal with the origins of the islands and of the gods, myths of the divine age, the establishment of the imperial dynasty by the Sun Goddess, Amaterasu, and histories of the emperors. A third book, the *Kujiki*, was lost by fire but its material is probably embodied in the *Nihongi*. A tenth century work, the *Engishiki*, describes the official Shinto ceremonies and includes a collection of *Norito*, ritual spells. Japanese ideas of a divine emperor, of their peculiar advantages and obligations as a people and of their national destiny are rooted in the teaching of the *Kojiki* and *Nihongi*. See Bible; Egypt, religions of; Judaism; New Testament; Old Testament; Zohar. See also various religions and books mentioned in this article.

The Sacred Books of the East, ed. by F. Max Müller, 50 vols. (1879-1910); *The Bible of the World*, ed. by R. O. Ballou (1939); M. Winternitz, *A History of Indian Literature*, trans. Mrs. S. Ketkar & H. Kohn (1927-33); *The Hymns of the Rigveda*, trans. R. T. H. Griffith, 3rd ed. (1920-26); *Mahābhārata*, trans. M. N. Dutt (1895-1905); *Rāmāyana*, trans. M. N. Dutt (1891-93); A. Guérinot, *La Religion Djaina*, pt. 1, chap. 9 (1926); *Sacred Books of the Buddhists*, trans. by various Oriental scholars (1895-); *The Adi Granth or Holy Scriptures of the Sikhs*, trans. Ernest Trumpp (1877); H. A. Giles, *A History of Chinese Literature* (1901); J. Legge, *The Chinese Classics* (1861-72); *The Koran*, trans. J. M. Rodwell (1909); "Kojiki", trans. B. H. Chamberlain, *Transactions of the Asiatic Society of Japan*, Suppl. to vol. 10; *Nihongi*, trans. W. G. Aston (1924).

A.E.H.

sacred thread: A thread worn from the time of initiation by members of the three higher or *twice-born* castes in India. C.S.B.

sacred vessels: Utensils used in Temple* service. In the Jerusalem Temple there was a special Vessel Chamber into which priests entered only after sanctifying themselves, by ceremoniously washing their hands and feet. For the Temple sacrifices, the vessels used included: dishes, baskets, pitchers, ladles, spoons, basins and covers. In the incense service there were various snuff dishes, tongs and candlesticks. In all, the Temple had 93 vessels which were made of silver, gold, copper and brass. The sacred vessels of the modern synagogue* include: the "eternal light", candelabra, a wine goblet, an incense box and various adornments on the Pentateuchal* scroll. B.Z.B.

sacredness: That quality which belongs to persons or things by virtue of their being dedicated to deity or consecrated to religious uses. Contrasted with profane. According to E. Durkheim* whatever society sanctifies is sacred. According to R. Otto* the sacred or holy is the unique and distinctive nature of deity and the experience of it is *sui generis*, the original and irreducible root of religion. R.W.F.

sacrifice, Christian: (For background, see sacrifice, Hebrew and Jewish) Sacrifice may have originated in common feasting and other sharing of group life. With monarchic government, bringing cattle and fruits to the king to enable his hospitality may have incited like offerings to God—meal-and drink-offerings. The ethicizing of God's requirements gave disobedience the character of sin; hence sin- or guilt-offering; sacrifice becomes piacular, expiatory. But perfecting of conception of God's holiness makes such recompense unavailing; what is demanded is beyond man. Whence the thought of divine remedy for sin; sacrifice, expiation, no longer man's offering but provision of redemptive* grace*: God's Righteous Servant is led to the slaughter, justifies many by bearing their iniquities (Isa. 53: 7, 11).

Christian sacrifice embodies all values of this great tradition; that of Christ is the perfect sin-offering, providing full atonement* (Heb. 9: 24—10: 18). Jesus views His own sacrifice under highest of O.T. prototypes: the divine Servant in whom God's gracious energies flow redemptively to man (Lk. 4: 17ff; Mtt. 12: 14-21; Mk. 10: 42-45).

The sufficiency of Christ's sacrifice is the Church's common faith. Catholics so confess as well as Evangelicals; their claim that 'the Sacrament of the Eucharist* is a propitiatory and impetratory sacrifice' (Thorndike) is on the ground, not of need of other sacrifice, but that Christ's own is, by Himself within the veil, continually offered (Heb. 9: 24; 10: 19-21). This to Protestants is medieval accretion to Sacrament (9th century to Innocent III); Christ's expiation is once for all; there needs no more sin-offering but only thank-offering for reconciliation Christ has effected. As the early fathers: 'our sacrifice is the offering of prayer and praise and a humble heart'. Yet essentially, for Catholics and Protestants, there is One Sacrifice. All look finally to Christ's self-offering wherein God laid the entail of sin and opened from the heart of the human jungle the way to Himself; all own the call, not to repeat the Sacrifice, but to sacrificial devotion to Him whose it was, to them for whom it was, in grateful remembrance thereof. See mass, Roman Catholic; propitiation; redemption.

F. C. N. Hicks, ***The Fullness of Sacrifice*** (1930); V. Taylor, *Jesus and His Sacrifice* (1937). J.L.

sacrifice, eucharistic: See mass, Roman Catholic.

sacrifice, Hebrew and Jewish: The principle medium of worship of the Deity, both in the ancient religion of Israel and in the earliest stages of evolving Judaism. The principles and rules of this sacrifice are formulated in detail in the books of Leviticus, Numbers and Deuteronomy**. Primarily sacrifices seem to represent either the food* given to the Deity or a gift tendered to Him. Ancient Israelite sacrifices fell into two broad classifications, a) the covenant-sacrifice, wherein the sacrifice constituted a sacrament or sacred meal, at which the Deity was regarded as host and the sacrificer and his family and friends as guests, the latter consuming the major portion of the sacrifice, but leaving the choice portions for the Deity, and thus, through this process of eating together, establishing a covenant* and bond of relationship between Deity and worshipers; and b) the taboo-sacrifice, which assumed basically that all the products of nature, such as grain, fruits, domestic animals and even human beings, were created by the Deity, and so in principle belonged to Him. Therefore a taboo was inherent in them and forbade their use for the ordinary purposes of daily existence, until they were redeemed. The underlying principle of redemption was that the sacrifice to the Deity of a part of the object removed the taboo, redeemed the remainder and rendered it fit for profane use. This taboo-sacrifice consisted usually of the first, and presumably the best, part of the tabooed object; i.e., first-fruit* and firstling sacrifices. In contradistinction to the covenant-sacrifice, under no condition might the sacrificer partake of or derive benefit from his taboo-sacrifice. This had either to be burned completely upon the altar, or else a small, symbolic portion thereof was burned, and the remainder was given to the priests or to the poor, regarded as the clients of the Deity.

Sacrifices consisted of only domestic animals, grain and the first-fruits of trees, vineyards and gardens. Under no condition might wild animals be sacrificed. In addition to offering the entire animal, or at least a portion thereof, to the Deity, the blood had either to be sprinkled upon the altar or else be allowed to soak into the ground. Accordingly sacrifices could be offered only at a sanctuary. Originally every domestic animal slain for food as well as for specific worship was regarded as a sacrifice, of which the prescribed portions had to be given to the Deity. The Deuteronomic Reformation, in 621 B.C., legislated that sacrifices might be offered at only the one, single sanctuary in the entire land, the Temple at Jerusalem (Deut. 12); with this, of necessity, it abolished the ancient practice and permitted the slaughter of animals for food purposes alone; but it reaffirmed the principle that the blood might never be eaten.

In the post-exilic* period (i.e., after 539 B.C.) Jewish sacrificial practice was systematized. The ancient covenant-sacrifice was now designated as the "peace-offering", while the taboo-sacrifice was divided into several classifications, the "burnt-offering"*, the "meal-offering", the "sin-offering", with its subordinate classification, the "guilt-offering", both working atonement for sins. The destruction of the Temple at Jerusalem by the Romans in 70 A.D. brought the entire Jewish sacrificial system to a sudden and permanent end. According to the dictum of the Rabbis of that period, prayer and service in the synagogue superseded sacrifice as the basic medium of divine worship.

See altar; blood; feasting; holocaust.

W. Robertson Smith, *The Religion of the Semites* (London, 1927), 3rd ed.; G. B. Gray, *Sacrifice in the Old Testament* (Oxford, 1925). J.M.

sacrifice, human: See human sacrifice.

sacrifice in primitive religion: See primitive religion.

sacrilege: The desecration or profanation of sacred things. Sacrilege was a violation of tabu, the primitive defense against it, and was believed to be fraught with mystic danger. The O.T. contains many examples of the offense and its punishment. See Judges vii. 20-25 for the graphic story of Achan. In classical Greek and Roman usage the term referred to theft of property dedicated to sacred uses but it has been stretched far beyond these limits. In English law it is breaking into a place of worship with intent to steal therefrom. The term has gradually lost its magical import and punishment for the offense has been greatly mitigated. R.W.F.

sacristan: (Fr. from Latin *sacer*) A church officer, sometimes in orders, who cares for sacred vessels, vestments*, etc. Formerly, a sexton*. T.J.B.

sacristy: (Latin, *sacer*, sacred) A room in a church near the high altar, used as a vestry, the storage of vestments and where much of the business of the church is transacted. F.T.P.

Sadducees, the: The Sadducees—the name of the party that opposed the teachings and doctrines of the Pharisees* during the latter half of the Second Commonwealth.

The name "Sadducee" may best be taken to mean anyone who is a sympathizer with the Zadokites, the priestly descendants of Zadok, the high priest in the days of David and Solomon. The party was composed largely of the wealthier elements of the population—the powerful priests, the prosperous merchants and the worldly aristocracy—and represented a more conservative point of view. The major difference between them and the Pharisees lay in their attitudes toward the Oral Law. The Sadducees refused to accept any of the oral traditions with which the Pharisees supplemented the Written Law. The Sadducees denied the idea of the resurrection of the body. Aside from these broad disputes, there were a great many legal ritualistic details, especially those connected with the Temple*, upon which these two parties differed.

For a bibliography, see Pharisees, the. E.B.—L.F.

sadhana: In Tantric Buddhism* it means a ceremony by the performance of which the worshiper renders visible any god he desires and is enabled to get control of the deity. It is also used in Hinduism to denote the means through which the Hindu mystic attains to *samadhi**. C.S.B.

Saint Simon, Claude Henri de Rouvroy, Comte de: (1760-1825) As a social reformer he made central the seminal ideas of the increasing use of positive science, free from a purely conjectural basis, as a foundation for a new and better social order. In achieving the new order the external form of government was to him a matter of indifference. The insight into the harmony of interests was his life-long guiding principle as a social reformer. There must be a new Christianity concerned not as of old with preparation for a future life, but with the physical and moral betterment of the humbler classes in this life. Though he had lost his fortune, he continued to have faith in the advent of a better social order. He advocated a new science of society to do away with the inequalities in the distribution of property, power and happiness. He suggested in an undeveloped form most of the ideas of August Comte*. His numerous disciples extended and transformed his social views to extravagant dimensions, changing them from a movement into a social cult of degenerate form. See communistic settlements, secular; social gospel.

Oeuvres de Saint Simon (Paris, 1865-1877), vols. 46; G. Brunet, *Le mysticisme de Saint-Simon* (Paris, 1925); E. M. Butler, *The Saint-Simonian religion in Germany; a study of the Young German movement* (Cambridge, 1926); S. Charléty, *Histoire du saint-simonisme* (1825-1864) (Paris, 1931); H. Shine, *Carlyle and the Saint-Simonians, the concept of historical periodicity* (1941). H.H.

saints, canonization of: See canonization.

saints, communion of: See communion of saints.

saints' plays: See religious drama.

saints, veneration: The honor or homage, called "dulia", paid by the Christian to saints because of their worthiness, an honor expressed in his imitating them and asking their intercession before God. See beatification; canonization; festivals and holy days; patron saints. Cf. Mary, cult of. L.R.W.

Saivism, Shivism, Shivaism: One of the two major theistic sects of Hinduism which centers its worship about the great personal god, Shiva, or his wives. Like Vishnuism* it attracts people of all kinds. Within it may be found the most elevated and sophisticated beliefs and practices as well as some that are naive, and even debasing. Various sub-sects emphasize each some special aspect of the god, thus to some he is the supreme ascetic, to others it is his destructive and creative power that is important, to others still he is the ultimate reality behind all that exists. He is the object of contemplation of the philosopher but also the object of bhakti or devotion to countless worshipers. The Shaktas (See Shaktism) worship his *shakti*, Kali or Durga, while many worship him in his elephant headed son Ganesha and other local deities. See Hinduism. C.S.B.

salamander: (Greek, *salamandra*) An amphibian once believed by many people to be able to live unharmed in fire; an elemental spirit living in fire, according to the theory of Paracelsus; a nymph in water, sylph in air, and gnome in earth. F.L.P.

Salmeron, Alphonsus: (1515-1585) Spanish Jesuit, theologian and exegete. He was influential at the Council of Trent*, and published commentaries on the Gospels, Acts of the Apostles, and the Epistles of St. Paul. E.A.R.

salvation: The term used in Christianity to express the supreme benefit which is afforded mankind through the life and death of Jesus Christ the savior, sent of God expressly to redeem man and restore the broken fellowship which evil had wrought between God and man. The word was used in the O.T., though not with identical meaning. There is an equivalent term used in Hinduism, *moksha* or release. Other religions lack a specific word, but each one does hold out a supreme good to men who fulfill the conditions, just as Christianity does. It might therefore be convenient for the purposes of comparative religion to define salvation as the goal of religion, that highest good which any faith offers to its followers.

Just as within Christianity all do not conceive of salvation in the same way, so in other faiths the ideal and the method of its attainment may vary considerably. Some general types of idea may be noted. Thus, salvation may be this-worldly or other-worldly; it may be individual or social; it may be attained once and for all, or it may be conceived of as a process of growth; it may be dominantly an escape, salvation from something, sin, fear, danger, death, or it may be conceived of as chiefly positive, saved to or for something; it may be conditioned or it may be absolute and eternal. Salvation may be won by self-effort or by the aid of a savior. It may be attained through *works*, something one does, asceticism, performance of ceremonies, moral effort, self surrender; it may be won through *faith* in a savior, sometimes vicariously, or it may be won through some kind of saving *knowledge*. A brief characterization of the ideal and method in the great living religions follows. Obviously in so brief a sketch, only *dominant* concepts can be indicated.

Buddhism: Primitive Buddhism (Hinayana) held out as the ideal the attainment of Nirvana, or the cessation of the round of rebirth, a state of "passionless peace", possibly even annihilation. It was to be attained strictly by self-effort, the belief in the four Noble Truths and the following of the Eight-fold Path. Mahayana or Northern Buddhism conceived the ideal as that of attaining Buddhahood. This could be done by passing through ten stages in the latter of which the aspirant after Buddhahood, a Boddhisattva, became himself a cosmic helper, or savior to others. Popular northern sects hold out salvation in the western Paradise to those who exercise faith, devotion, love, toward some one of the great savior Buddhas, of whom Amitabha Omito-fu in China, Amida in Japan, is chief. (See Buddhist Terminology.)

Chinese religions: Confucianism has been dominantly this-worldly in character, and reliance has been mainly upon the performance of *works*, defined chiefly in terms of moral effort. Taoism as a religion has been distinctly more other-worldly, borrowing heavily from Buddhism's heavens and hells, and appealing to the gods for help. In its philosophical form salvation was to be won chiefly through non-action. (See Chinese Terminology.)

Christianity: Salvation within Christianity is variously conceived. All groups agree that in some manner it is mediated to man through Jesus, though Jesus' part in the process differs widely according to the group. In the Unitarian type of Christianity, and in Liberal Christianity generally, the work of Christ is that of reconciling man to God, and salvation is achieved through the faithful embodiment in life and character of the spirit and ideals of Jesus. In Conservative Christianity, including both Protestants and Catholics of all varieties, salvation is vicariously won for humanity by the suffering, death, and resurrection of Jesus. In the beginning man had been sinless but Adam's fall brought upon humanity an entail of guilt which must be removed in some way before God could forgive man and restore him to the fellowship which had been broken by sin. In some manner, variously conceived by different groups, the suffering and death of Christ were the sufficient means of offsetting man's guilt, so that if appropriated by faith or through the sacraments or by some other method, man could feel himself forgiven and restored to divine sonship. The Roman Catholic has held that only through the sacraments can the grace of Christ be made available to man and the sacraments are alone to be administered by the church which Christ founded. This seemed to Martin Luther to be a reassertion of the ancient Hebrew emphasis upon salvation by works or the fulfillment of the law. He reacted strongly against this to the Pauline basis of salvation by faith, and most of Protestantism has maintained this faith emphasis.

The ideal has been for the most part, other-worldly in character, though always with some regard for the present life. Roman Catholicism introduced into the thought an intermediate stage of purgatory* through which all save the most worthy must pass before the attainment of full salvation. From the time of Augustine, there has existed the belief among some churches that salvation is only for the elect; that God chooses whom he will for salvation. Within Protestantism, Calvinism has upheld this view. Liberal Christianity whether Socinian, Pelagian or the Unitarian type as well as the Liberal Protestant type has generally emphasized the this-worldly aspects of salvation, though at the same time looking toward a full realization of the good life in a life to come. Universalism, a comparatively modern movement within Christianity, has stressed the belief in the ultimate salvation of all men, thus denying a widespread orthodox insistence upon the everlasting punishment of the wicked.

In general, the emphasis has been upon individual salvation, but in recent times there has appeared a strongly social emphasis. Not only individual men but society itself must be redeemed. See assurance of salvation; atonement; conversion; Gnosticism; mystery religions; order of salvation; redemption; regeneration; soteriology; terminism.

*Hinduism**: The salvation ideal and method in Hinduism varies from period to period. In Vedic Hinduism the ideal was distinctly this-worldly and was mainly concerned with an abundant physical and social life, though there was the beginning of an interest in an other-worldly existence. The method of attainment of salvation was chiefly through sacrifice. Most of the hymns of the Rig-Veda which accompanied the sacrifice are expressive of the desire for a full and abundant physical life. The ideal in the Brahmanic period becomes increasingly other-worldly in character, and the concepts of Karma and reincarnation begin to emerge.

Moksha is attained primarily still, through the faithful performance of the cult, which has now grown enormously complex and exacting.

In Philosophic Hinduism the ideal has become distinctly that of escape from the round of rebirth. Inasmuch as this ultimate release removed one from the earthly plane it is other-worldly, or at least, not this-worldly in character. The means to salvation is predominantly that of knowledge. Distinct Indian schools define the necessary knowledge in different ways; for the Vedanta in its final development it was knowledge of the alone reality of Brahman-Atman and the identification of the self with God. For the Sankhya school, it was the knowledge of the complete separateness of matter and spirit, and other schools had slightly differing views. The method of attaining knowledge was through meditation or Yoga. It was possible only through abandonment of the normal, work-a-day life of the world.

Devotional Hinduism, or Theistic Hinduism conceived of salvation as the attainment of Heaven or as eternal existence in the presence of god, and so is also other-worldly. A great variety of heavens and hells are thought of through which one may pass before attaining the highest heaven. This ideal is generally considered by the Philosophic Hindus as only a lesser and incomplete salvation, but for the followers of the great theistic cults, it furnished an adequate ideal. The goal was to be attained mainly through *bhakti-marga**, i.e., faith, devotion, love, or service to one of the great personal deities, Vishnu, Krishna, Rama, Shiva, Kali or others depending on the particular sect to which one belonged.

*Sikh**: The Sikh ideal of salvation is essentially that of the devotional sects and the method is Bhakti-Marga.

*Jain**: The Jain religion founded by Mahavira in the 6th century B.C. as a protestant movement in Hinduism, holds as its ideal escape from rebirth, just as most of the Hindus do. It is therefore other-worldly, or at least not this-worldly in character. Its hells and heavens are likewise impermanent. Unlike most schools of Hinduism and like Buddhism, the attainment of salvation is wholly by self-effort, for the gods, if any exist, can afford no help to man. The method of salvation is that of Karma-Marga, or works. Emphasis is placed upon the three jewels, right faith, right knowledge, right conduct, but it is upon ascetic practices and the observance of non-injury or *ahimsha* that greatest stress is placed.

*Jewish**: The earliest Hebrew concept of salvation was distinctly this-worldly and social in nature. The development of a concept of the afterlife as anything beyond a colorless, rather unpleasant continued existence came quite late in Hebrew history. Nor did the individual ideal emerge until near the time of the exile. Later Judaism became other-worldly and continued so until now, though the preeminent emphasis, particularly of the reformed groups, is distinctly this-worldly in character. Salvation was and is still thought to be possible through obedience to the will of God. The emphasis has been chiefly upon doing rather than belief or faith. Sometimes ritual works assume central importance but, particularly in prophetic religion, the demands have been primarily ethical. A trace of the idea of a treasury of merit whereby one is helped by the merit of his ancestors occurs at some periods, but in the main, man has had to win salvation through his own effort and his trust in the goodness and power of God.

*Moslem**: The Moslem ideal has from the first been other-worldly and the emphasis seems to be strongly upon the idea of escape from the judgment of Allah. The method of salvation is predominantly that of doing, that is, works; the performance of the five or six obligations that rest upon all Moslems, repeating the creed, repeating the five daily prayers, fasting, alms giving, making the holy pilgrimage, and heeding the call to the holy war, though the two latter seem not to be universally demanded. Belief is also requisite, that is, belief in the oneness of God, that Mohammed is his prophet, the belief in the Holy Book, the Koran, the belief in judgment and in angels. All this is however complicated by the fact that ultimate salvation depends upon election to salvation by Allah himself. Only those whom he elects, whatever they may do or believe, are finally saved. In the Shiah sect there are some indications of a salvation by faith concept.

*Zoroastrianism**: Zoroastrianism was from the first other-worldly in character, though the other-worldly element became much more marked in its later development. God is righteous and condemns evil men to destruction but the good to eternal life. The method of salvation seems clearly to be that of works. The emphasis is upon good thoughts, good words, good deeds, and man largely earns what he gets in an after life by his thoughts, words and deeds. Later Zoroastrianism has an elaborate eschatology in which a savior, Saoshyant, appears as a help toward salvation.

GENERAL: Charles S. Braden, *Man's Quest for Salvation* (1941). J. W. Parker, *The Idea of Salvation in the World's Religions* (London, 1935). HINDUISM: Rudolph Otto, *India's Religion of Grace* (London, 1930); Sidney Cave, *Redemption, Hindu and Christian* (London, 1919). CHRISTIANITY AND JUDAISM: George B. Stevens, *The Christian Doctrine of Salvation* (1917); George W. Richards, *Christian Ways of Salvation* (1923); Albert C. Knudson, *The Doctrine of Redemption* (1933); George Cross, *Christian Salvation, A Modern Interpretation of Salvation* (1923); Charles S. Braden, *Varieties of American Religion* (1936); John C. Bennett, *Social Salvation* (1935).
C.S.B.

Salvation Army: An international religious and philanthropic organization founded by William Booth (1829-1912), an English evangelist who began his religious career in boyhood as a local preacher of the Wesleyan Methodists at Nottingham, England. In 1849 he came to London, where his sensational methods of slum street corner preaching often provoked disorder. The criticism of his co-religionists caused his severance from the Wesleyans and led to his ordination as a minister of the Methodist New Connection. He left that body in 1861 to engage in "travelling evangelization" in Cornwall, Cardiff, and Walsall. In 1865 he returned to London and founded a body successively known as the East London Revival Society, the East London Christian Mission, and the Christian Mission. He continued to develop his characteristic methods of evangelism 1) by outdoor meetings and processions, 2) by the use of music, especially brass bands, tambourines and cymbals to attract crowds from beyond the range of the human voice, 3) by meetings and personal contacts in private homes, prisons, public houses, theatres, factories, and other unusual places, 4) by adapting popular song tunes to religious themes, 5) by abandoning the formal sermon and cultivating an informal and colloquial type of preaching, and 6) by making of every convert a witness for Christ by both private life and public testimony.

This militant evangelism culminated in the adoption of the title "Salvation Army" and the re-organization of the movement along quasi-military lines between 1878 and 1880. Its "Orders and Regulations" were patterned after those of the British Army, its workers assumed military titles, its trainees became "cadets", its local units were designated as "corps", their headquarters or places of worship as "citadels" or "outposts", and their evangelistic undertakings as "campaigns".

The Army is divided into "Territories", each under a "Commissioner". The territories usually conform to national boundaries, although the United States comprises four and Canada two such units. These "Territories" are usually further sub-divided into "Provinces" and "Divisions".

At first bitterly opposed by both conventional churchmen and their secular opponents, notably T. H. Huxley, the Army finally acquired enormous popularity. No small credit for this gain in prestige is due to Booth's wife, Catherine Mumford Booth (1829-1890), a woman of charm and ability, who won the sympathy of many of the upper classes for the new movement. The Prince of Wales became its most prominent patron, and at his instance Booth was officially invited to his coronation as Edward VII in 1902. To "Mother Catherine" is also due the development of the "Female Ministry", and the establishment of the principle that women have absolute parity with men in privilege, position, and dignity within the Army.

In the meantime, the movement had become international in scope. It was extended to the United States in 1880, to Australia in 1881, then to the European continent and finally to most Christian lands and many mission fields.

Booth early realized that the physical and social environment of the submerged masses, especially in the great cities, made it difficult for them to appreciate the Army's message. He accordingly embarked upon social work to clear the way for evangelism. These services ranged from night shelters and free breakfasts to the selection and training of prospective emigrants and their settlement overseas. Booth's experiences in this field led to the publication in 1890 of his *In Darkest England, and the Way Out,* in which he proposed the concentration of the nation's philanthropic funds upon the slums, hitherto largely left to the care of the local parish churches, and suggested a list of practical expedients to this end. The Army now maintains an extensive system of summer camps, nurseries, children's and old people's homes, hostels, settlements, men's social service centers, employment offices and missing persons bureaus, provides Thanksgiving and Christmas dinners, and carries on Americanization, family service, transient and emergency relief, and other case work services for individuals and families.

Theologically the Army is conservative and fundamentalist. Its preaching stresses the reality of sin, a future life of rewards and punishments, the necessity of the work of redemption, the individual's need of conversion, preceded by penitence, and followed by growth in holiness. Officers wear a regulation uniform as a symbol of their consecration and separation from the world.

In government, the Salvation Army is highly centralized and autocratic, unquestioning obedience being required of all ranks. It is directed from "International Headquarters" in London, under the control of a "General", who issues all orders and regulations, assisted by a "Chief of Staff", a "Foreign Secretary", a "Chancellor", and other officials who also possess large powers. By a deed poll of 1878, each General was empowered to appoint his successor under seal, but the name of the person designated was not divulged until the time for succession. A second deed poll executed in 1904 provided for the removal of a General and the election of his successor by a High Council in the event of mental incapacity or other unfitness. The announcement of Booth's death in 1912 was accompanied by the statement that his eldest son, William Bramwell Booth (1856-1929), had become the new General. Bramwell Booth had become his father's "Chief of Staff" in 1878, at the age of twenty-two, and had long been the organizing genius of the movement. He continued to direct its affairs until he was removed by the High Council in February, 1929, on the ground of senility, and for the first time the self-perpetuating leadership was broken, though not without a bitter fight within the Army. The Generalship has since been elective.

But the autocracy had not been heretofore unquestioned, even within the Booth family itself. William Booth's second son, Ballington (1859-1940), and his wife had come to America in 1886 in full charge of the Army. But ten years later they resigned because of differences with the founder, and established a rival organization, the Volunteers of America*. Leadership of the American Salvation Army then passed to William Booth's son-in-law, Commander Frederic de L. Booth-Tucker (1853-1929), who was in turn succeeded by Booth's daughter, Evangeline (1865-). On her retirement in 1939, she was succeeded by the present Commander, Edward J. Parker.

During the First World War, the Salvation Army gained wide-spread recognition for its work for the armed forces, especially in the Allied countries. In the United States, Commander Evangeline Booth placed the entire resources of her organization at the disposal of the Government. Extensive welfare work was carried on for the families of service men at home and Salvationist men and women ministered to the comfort of soldiers right up to the front line trenches. With the outbreak of the Second World War, the Army suffered eclipse in Axis countries and in territories subject to their jurisdiction, the Italian government having banned the Salvation Army uniform and forbidden both outdoor and indoor meetings. Direct communications between International Headquarters in London and the Army in Axis territory ceased, but private sources indicated that a greatly curtailed program was still in existence. Among the United Nations, however, the Salvation Army found new opportunities for service. It became one of the six United Service Organizations in the United States to provide recreational, spiritual, and welfare services to members of the armed forces outside of military reservations, and to workers in war production centers. The war also imposed heavy demands upon the family welfare, juvenile delinquency, and unmarried mother services of the Army. Cf. Church Army.

Bramwell Booth, *These Fifty Years* (London); St. John Ervine, *God's Soldier: General William Booth* (1935). H.E.J.

samādhi: The final stage reached by the Indian mystic, a superconscious state in which all distinction between subject and object is lost and the One Self is realized. A foretaste of the final state of emancipation or *moksha**. C.S.B.

Samaria: City built by Omri, king of Israel, during the ninth century B.C. (I. Kgs. xvi, 24), destroyed by the Assyrians in 722 B.C. Rebuilt several times, especially by Herod the Great who named it Sebaste.

See G. A. Reisner, *Harvard Excavations at Samaria* (1924) 2 vols.; J. W. Jack, *Samaria in Ahab's time* (1929); F. M. Abel, *Géographie de la Palestine* (1938), vol. II, pp. 443-446. S.L.T.

Samaritan Pentateuch: The version of the first five books of the Bible current among the Samaritans, and employed by them in religious exercises since the Samaritan Schism, shortly after 432 B.C., when the Samaritans separated themselves from the Jewish people and established themselves as an independent religious community. It too is written in Hebrew, and only in scroll form; but unlike the Jewish Torah scrolls, it employs only the ancient Hebrew system of writing. It differs in approximately six thousand passages from the traditional version of the Pentateuch*. Occasionally these divergent readings make possible a restoration of the original text. J.M.

Sama-Veda: Literally the "chant" Veda, or Veda of music. One of the four Vedas of early Hinduism. There is little original material in it, all but 75 of the 1225 stanzas being taken from the Rig-Veda*. It was used by the Udgatri, the priest who sang the strophes at the Soma sacrifice. C.S.B.

Samhain: (Celt) New Year's harvest festival on October 31, or November 1 and lasting about a week. Celebration includes the three days before and three days after the day. The feast was linked not only with the departure of the sun and summer, but also with rites that concerned the use of weapons, and the worship of ghosts of the dead. F.L.P.

Samhita: The name of the text of the Vedas fixed about 600 B.C. according to the rules of *sandhi* which control the classical Sanskrit. The word which means "collection" is often used to describe the Vedas. Thus, Dasgupta writes of the four *Samhitas,* meaning the four Vedas. C.S.B.

samsara: The Hindu wheel of life. The endless round of birth and rebirth, or transmigration*, the cessation of which for the Hindu meant *moksha* or salvation. C.S.B.

Samson: Hero of the ancient Hebrew story cycle found in Judges* 14-16 preceded by an introductory chapter 13 dealing with his parents and birth. Some scholars doubt his historicity and explain him as a solar mythological hero (Samson, Heb. Sun-man). In any case the question is of little importance since Samson is not the initiator or furtherer of any movement political or religious in Israel which would give him special historical significance. The real value of the story lies in its genuine local setting. It seems, unlike other hero-tales of the O.T. to emanate not from prophetic literary circles, but from popular traditions of country folk. H.K.—L.F.

Samuel, I and II: Historical books of the O.T., included among the "Former Prophets"* in the Hebrew canon. In the Hebrew text they originally formed a single book. The division was first made in the Septuagint*, in which the two rolls are called The First and Second Books of the Kingdoms. They cover the history of Israel for approximately a century, during the lives of Samuel and Saul and almost the whole of the life of David. Because of the presence of duplicate, or even triplicate, narratives of the same events, and pronounced differences in literary style and religious points of view, it is certain that these books contain at least two sources. They may be continuations of the J and E** narratives of the hexateuch*, but this view has not been proved in detail. The early source was apparently written in the reign of Solomon*, and represented the establishment of the Israelite kingdom as having Yahweh's approval; it is a highly authentic and objective narrative in classical Hebrew prose. Its account of the life and reign of David* is especially valuable. The later source (or sources) represented the establishment of the kingdom as apostasy from Yahweh, magnifies Samuel, and is generally homiletical in tone. It was written before Deuteronomy*, but its exact date is difficult to establish. The Books of Samuel received only slight editing by the Deuteronomists (See D) and later writers.

See H. P. Smith, *The Books of Samuel* (International Critical Commentary, 1899); O. Eissfeldt, *Die Komposition der Samuelisbücher* (1931). J.P.H.

samurai: (From *samurau* meaning "to guard") The name applied to members of the Japanese warrior caste in feudal times. D.C.H.

sanctification: This term generally refers to the process or experience by which a person (in primitive religions also things) are rendered holy.

Theologically, the term means the divine process by which the Christian life of faith and love is fulfilled. According to a very old tradition, the Holy Spirit is the source and agent of sanctification. This means that whosoever has the Holy Spirit* (or is "in Christ") is truly in God, sharing in his life of love as one who is redeemed and as such wholly acceptable in God's sight.

In Roman Catholic thought, sanctification is conceived of as taking place by the infusion of justifying sacramental grace. The doctrine of sanctification became of particular importance in Protestantism. Under the leadership of Luther, the reformers distinguished justification* from sanctification in such a way that sanctification was understood as the process begun and assured of fulfillment by the divine justification. (A Christian, taught Luther, is one who under the Holy Spirit is continually becoming a Christian). Under the influence of the exclusively forensic interpretation of justification by the later Protestants, sanctification became more and more separated from justification (as was also repentance, which in the original Reformation teaching was, like sanctification, an essential part of the experience or act of justification). The effects of such teaching was that the Orthodox Protestants overemphasized justification neglecting the concern for the renewal of life expressed in the doctrine of sanctification; that the Pietists*, reacting against the one-sidedness of the Orthodox, so stressed sanctification that they failed fully to recognize justification as its ground; and that the Rationalists, unable to agree either with the Orthodox or the Pietists, rejected both doctrines altogether. A re-construction of them in terms of Christian experience was begun by Schleiermacher and Ritschl**. Under the impact of the recent rediscovery of the faith of the Reformation, this re-construction is now in full swing. See perfection; psychology of religion; seven gifts of the Holy Spirit. W.P.

sanctity: Holiness of life, saintliness. The religious ideal for the individual—in all religions that call for transformation of life. Conceived mystically, as ever closer union with God; or more ethically, as the attainment of the true disposition and character—in Christianity, the Christlike spirit. May pertain to institutions, as being hallowed, worthy of reverence (e.g., the 'sanctities of the home'). See perfection; sanctification.

R. N. Flew, *The Idea of Perfection in Christian Theology* (1934). J.L.

sanctorum communis: See communion of saints.

sanctuary: (Lat., *sanctus*, holy) The most sacred part of a religious building. The place of the altar* in a Christian church. See chancel. F.T.P.

Sanctus: (Lat., *holy*) The last part of the preface, just before the Canon, of the Mass*; the words, beginning *"Sanctus, sanctus, sanctus,"* are from Isaiah, vi, 3, and were in use as early as Clement of Rome (d. 104). L.R.W.

Sanday, William: (1843-1920) N.T. scholar, Professor of Divinity and Canon of Christ Church Oxford from 1895. With A. C. Headlam, he wrote the I. C. C. on Romans (1895); also *Outlines of the Life of Christ* (1905). In many ways his most important work lay in mediating continental research to English scholarship, as in *The Criticism of the Fourth Gospel* (1906) and *The Life of Christ in Recent Research* (1907). C.T.C.

Sandemanians: See Glassites.

sanhedrin: The supreme judicial body in the Jewish state from some time in the third century B.C., or even earlier, and until its destruction by the Romans in 70 A.D. Actually there seem to have been two Sanhedrins, one dealing with the administration of justice in civil and political matters, and presided over by the high-priest; the other concerned only with religious matters. Each Sanhedrin seems to have consisted of from seventy to seventy-two members. Both Sanhedrins sat in the Temple at Jerusalem, but in different chambers. It is the first Sanhedrin to which frequent reference is made in the Gospels. See Gamaliel I; laying on of hands; Nasi. J.M.

Sankhya: One of the six traditional systems of Indian philosophy, probably the oldest. It was founded by Kapila who lived somewhat earlier than Gautama Buddha*. He repudiated the monism of the Upanishads* represented in the Brahman concept and specifically denied the existence of God. The system is dualistic. It conceives of two utterly distinct substances, uncreated and existing eternally, prakriti, matter and purusha, soul. Matter is real, not illusion, and not one but an infinite number of souls exist. The soul itself is without qualities or parts. It can only be described negatively. By their mere presence and through no conscious will of their own the souls excite matter "as a magnet acts on iron" disturbing the perfect equilibrium which exists between the three constituent *gunas** and so the evolution of the physical universe is begun. At the end of a world period there is a return to the original state of balance. The cyclic evolution and devolution of the universe is eternal.

The Sānkhya is a profoundly pessimistic system. All existence is suffering. Escape from existence is therefore sought. How is it achieved? The soul and matter are completely separate and distinct, but through lack of discrimination arises the pain of existence. The remedy can therefore be only in "discriminating knowledge", by which their utter difference is discerned. Salvation must therefore be by knowledge. Through it comes emancipation. Once emancipated, the soul abides, says Oldenberg, "eternally released from the delusion and suffering of this world, as a seer who no longer sees anything, a glass in which nothing is any longer reflected, as pure untroubled light by which nothing is illuminated". (Quoted by R. Garbe, *Encyclopedia of Religion and Ethics*, Vol., 11, p. 192a). See cosmogonies.

S. Das Gupta, *History of Indian Philosophy* (1922, 32, 41), 3 vols.; S. Radhakrishnan, *Indian Philosophy* (London, 1923, 1927). C.S.B.

Sankhya Yoga: See Yoga—as a philosophy. C.S.B.

sannyāsī: One who has entered upon the fourth of the stages of life through which high caste Hindus were traditionally supposed to pass, student, householder, forest dweller, and homeless mendicant. Holy man,—ascetic, one who has dedicated himself completely to the quest for *moksha**. C.S.B.

Santayana, George: (1863-) Litterateur, and Prof. of Phil. at Harvard, 1889-1912. For this critical realist and materialist, the universe consists, at one extreme, of Matter, the ultimate, independent and changing causal agency, purposeless though indefinitely fertile in potentiality. At the other extreme is the realm of Essence, consisting of timeless qualities and relations which are open to "spirit" and bear only relevant witness to physical events. The conscious spirit, an emanation from the bodily psyche, thus guides the body, but it has no causal power. It finds freest expression in the detached contemplation of essence. Religion is a constructive work of imagination: "Religions are the great fairy-tales of the conscience," and as such a joy to an unmoralizing spirit.

The Sense of Beauty (1896); *The Life of Reason* (2nd ed., 1922); *Scepticism and Animal Faith* (1923); *The Realm of Essences* (1927); *The Realm of Matter* (1930). P.A.B.

saoshyant: A Zoroastrian term variously used to denote priest or apostle (usually plural); holy men who will at the millenium aid in the renovation of the world; or, particularly in later Zoroastrianism, the last of the miraculously born sons of Zoroaster who will preside over the general resurrection at the end of the age. See salvation—Zoroastrianism. C.S.B.

Sarasvati: Hindu goddess of learning and wife of Brahma*.

Also it is the name of an order of Hindu ascetics to which the founder of the Arya Samaj* once belonged, and from which he took the name by which he is best known, Dyananda Sarasvati. C.S.B.

Sartorius, Ernest Wilhelm Christian: (1797-1859) He was professor in Marburg and general church superintendent of Prussia. He was a most extreme representative of supernaturalism. As revelation was for him a historical fact, its validity and truth were to be proved by historical means. He was a pioneer of theological repristination.

Die lutherische Lehre vom Unvermoegen des freien Willens zur hoeheren Sittlichkeit, in Briefen, nebst einem Anhange gegen Herr D. Schleiermachers Abhandlung ueber die Lehre von der Erwählung (Gottingen, 1821); *Beiträge zur Vertheidigung der evangelischen Rechtgläubigkeit*, 2 vols. (Heidelberg, 1825-26); *Die Lehre von Christi Person und Werk in populären Vorlesungen* (Hamburg, 1831, 7th ed., Hamburg, 1860). H.H.

Sarum Use: Utilized by St. Osmond (d. 1099) in his new diocese of Salisbury (Lat., *Sarum*), this Use became, by mid-thirteenth century, the prevalent English liturgy*. Embodying local variations within the basic Western Rite, it constituted a unified service of dignity and beauty. Probably comprising a Breviary, Missal, and Manual, the Sarum Use provided the basis for the later Book of Common Prayer*. R.C.P.

Satan: Mentioned in the O.T. only three times, in Zech. 3. 1-2; Job 1-2; and I Chron. 21.1. All three passages are post-exilic*, i.e., later than 539 B.C., and evidence the influence of the Zoroastrian* doctrine of dualism upon the evolving Judaism of this period. In pre-exilic* Jewish thought the figure of Satan was entirely unknown. The absolute monotheism of normative Judaism affirmed that there was only one divine power, one God, and, in purposed refutation of the dominant Persian dualism of the day, that He was the creator of both light and darkness, the source of evil as well as good (Isa. 45. 6-7). But to the popular Jewish mind of that day dualism seemed to solve conveniently one of the baffling problems of existence, the problem of good and evil, and so, contrary to the tenets of official Judaism, evolved the figure of Satan, patterned obviously after the Zoroastrian power of evil, Ahriman. Actually Satan never had any place in the theology of normative Judaism. The name, *Satan,* in Hebrew means "adversary; accuser"; and just this role Satan plays in the O.T. and in subsequent Jewish apocalyptic literature*. He is the adversary of God and man. He seeks to frustrate God's purposes of good and to entice men to defy God and do evil. Then he accuses them before God and brings about their punishment and destruction. However in Jewish thought and legend Satan was never more than a figure of secondary rank and power, always subordinate to God and subject to discipline by Him. Only in Christianity, as it emerged from Judaism, did Satan come to be regarded as a divine being, altogether independent of and hostile to God, the malevolent worker of evil in the world, and thus to be identified with the Devil. See Beelzebub; devil; Iblis. Cf. demons; rakshas. J.M.

In the Apocrypha, Satan is represented as the author of all evil (Wisdom II, 24) and as the seducer of Eve who was hurled from heaven because of his iniquity (Slavonic Bk. of Enoch xxix). The names, Satanel (*ibid*, XXXI, 3), Mastema (Jubilees, XVII, 18), Asmodeus (Tobit), and Samael are used as equivalents of "Satan".

In the N.T., Satan and his kingdom are regarded as encompassing the entire world, and of factors of all the events of daily life. Satan is the author of all evil (Luke X, 19) who beguiled Eve (II Cor. XI, 3) and who brought death into the world (Heb. II, 13) being ever the tempter (I Cor. VII, 5). Satan is God's enemy whom he fights and casts from heaven, but not permanently, for after one thousand years, Satan must be fought again (Rev.). Besides the name, "Satan," he is also referred to as "devil,"* (Matt. IV), "adversary" (I Peter), "enemy" (Matt. xiii 39), "accuser" (Rev. xii, 10), "old serpent" (*ibid*, xx, 2), "great dragon" (*ibid*, xii, 9), "Beelzebub"* (Matt. x, 25) and "Belial."* See descent into hades. H.K.—L.F.

sati: See suttee.

satisfaction: (Lat., *satisfactio*, fr. *satisfacere*, to satisfy) The essential idea in the various uses of the term within the Christian Church has been the rendering to God of a sufficient compensation, or reparation, for sin* as the antecedent condition for forgiveness*. Until the Middle Ages the term had to do solely with repentance. In this sense it was introduced, in the late 2nd Cent., by Tertullian*, who took it from Roman law (see his *De poenitentia*): God, who as Judge demands justice of his rational creatures, accepts repentance* as satisfaction for sin (i.e., as the price for granting pardon), which, in the case of sin following baptism, must include *exomologesis* (i.e., public acts of humiliation). By the Middle Ages repentance, or penance*, had become a sacrament involving three parts (contrition, confession and works of penance) with the term satisfaction referring both to the entire penance and, more specifically, to the third part or works (i.e., almsdeeds, fasting and prayer). Peter Lombard*, in his *Liber Sententiarum*, fixed this useage for Catholic theology and Aquinas elaborated it (*Summa Theolog.*, III, Suppl., qq. 12-15). To the Protestant Reformers, the notion of God's being satisfied by works of repentance was abhorrent, Luther saying that "it is only by the faith of a contrite heart that He is satisfied" (*Babylon. Captiv.*) and Calvin calling the whole useage "sophistry" and "falsehood" (*Institutes*, III, iv. 25). Against these criticisms the Catholic view was reaffirmed, in 1551, in the Decree on Penance (chp. viii) of the Council of Trent*, with the explanation that such penitential satisfaction is "through Jesus Christ" who "satisfied for our sins." In the Church of England, Hooker sought to conform to this Catholic practice of making penitential works of satisfaction subsidiary to the primary satisfaction rendered by Christ (*Laws of Eccl. Polity*, VI, v, 1-6).

The fundamental use of the term, since the Middle Ages, has been soteriological. N.T. writers had variously agreed that the passion and death of Christ had accomplished our redemption* but provided no unified or consistent explanation of its ground or efficacy. It was Anselm* (11th Cent.) who, in rejecting the ransom theory of Christ's atonement* (*Cur Deus Homo*, I, vii; II, xix), applied the idea of satisfaction to the soteriological problem (hence satisfaction theory). Agreeing in general with Tertullian's view that Divine Justice requires satisfaction (reparation) for sin, Anselm denied that repentance (or works) *per se* could render the necessary satisfaction (*ib.*, I, xx); indeed nothing that man could do could repay the debt to God's honor which man had robbed by sinning (I, xi), because man owes every good work to God anyway, apart from sin; because man has lost all ability to repay through the Fall*; and because Divine Justice required either eternal punishment for man's sin (I, xi) or an infinite satisfaction of the Divine Honor (II, vi); hence the necessity of the voluntary death of a God-man. God thus revealed both his justice, in requiring satisfaction (in lieu of punishment), and his love, in providing redemption. Direct forgiveness of sins, without such satisfaction, would have been to let sin go unpunished; to remove the difference between the guilty and the not guilty; and therefore to violate the Divine Justice (I, xii & xxiv). Anselm's theory, as amplified by Aquinas (*Summa Theolog.*, III, qq. 46-50), became normative for Catholic theology and the presupposition of the later Protestant formulations. In the penal theory of the Reformers, Christ's death is still understood as the satisfaction rendered for sin (both original and actual), but whereas Anselm had made sin a violation of the Divine Honor and had distinguished between satisfaction and punishment, the Reformers treated sin as a violation of the Divine Justice and satisfaction as consisting in the actual punishment accepted by Christ (see e.g., Calvin's *Institutes* II, xii-xvii). Grotius*, in the so-called governmental theory, similarly assumed the necessity of an "antecedent satisfaction" as the condition for the remission of sins, but defined it as the punishment accepted by Christ, not in the interest of retributive justice, but for the purpose of providing a "distinguished example" of the punishment which sin deserves and therefore acting as a deterrent to further sin in the interests of the common good (*Satisfaction of Christ*, esp. II-VI). Motivating all these substitutionary theories is the desire to conserve the N.T. view that Christ died for us, to discover an adequate theoretical explanation of his death (and in such a way as to conserve both the love and justice of God), and to impel non-believers to faith in Christ through fear of the consequences of the Divine Wrath. It was this appeal to fear and the too rigid restriction of the love of God by his justice, together with major interest in the life, as well as the death, of Christ, that led Abailard* (12th Cent.), and much liberal thought since, to find the significance of Christ's redemptive work in the influence of his love and example (moral influence theory).

In addition to the primary works referred to, the following studies may be mentioned: F. Godet and others, *The Atonement in Modern Religious Thought* (1901); G. B. Stevens, *The Christian Doctrine of Salvation* (1905); J. K. Mozley, *The Doctrine of the Atonement* (1915); H. Rashdall, *The Idea of Atonement in Christian Theology* (1919); A. C. Knudson, *The Doctrine of Redemption* (1933), chap. vii; Shailer Mathews, *The Atonement and the Social Process* (1930); Emil Brunner, *The Mediator*, Engl. trans. (1934), chaps. xvii-xxi. E.T.R.

Satyasiddhi School: See Buddhist Terminology.

satyr: One of a class of classical Greek woodland deities in human form with a horse's ears and tail; or, as with the Romans, represented with goat's ears, tail, legs, and budding horns; a lustful or beastly-minded man. F.L.P.

Saussaye, Daniel Chantepie de la, the elder: (1818-1874) He was professor at the University of Groningen. He (with J. H. Gunning) was the spiritual progenitor of the *ethische richting*. Starting from religious experience, not from external authority, they were strongly influenced by Schleiermacher, Ritschl, Herrmann and less strongly by Vinet**. Although orthodox in theology, they were both examples of intimate personal piety that bequeathed to their pupils the task of realizing a reconciliation between culture and faith. They both opposed the church legalistic attempt to meet the negative criticism of modern theology. They sought to surmount its negation through preaching, prayer and study, and tried to make clear the significance of Christian truth in the Calvinistic-Reformed sense for the inner man. They termed this the ethical significance of faith, a term which caused much confusion and which really signified nothing moral. On the contrary, they aimed to combat moralism, intellectualism and mysticism, which in reality were derived from the ethos, the deepest essence of man. Faith was the trustful surrender to the person of Christ, who for them was the norm of the good which was discoverable in all parties and groups, even in the moderns. They called their theology ethical-irenic.

La crise religieuse en Hollande (Leyde, 1860); J. H. Gunning, *Het protestantisch Nederland onzer dagen* (Groningen, 1889); A. M. Brouwer, *Daniel Chantepie de la Saussaye* (Groningen, 1905); J. J. P. Valeton, *De Ethische Richting* (Baarn, 1909); O. Noordmans, *Ontwikkeling en Toekomst van de Ethische Theologie. In Geestelijke Perspektieven* (Amsterdam, 1930). H.H.

Saussaye, Pierre Daniel Chantepie de la, the younger: (1848-1920) He first was pastor of the Reformed church; then taught in succession at the universities of Amsterdam and Leyden. He was a leader of the left wing of the ethical group whose spiritual progenitors were his father and J. H. Gunning. Through him, H. Th. Obbink and G. van de Leeuw, the *ethische richting* rendered meritorious service to the history and science of religion. His ideas were akin to those of the religious-historical school with its longing of a universal-human religiosity in which Christ occupies an important but no longer a decisive position.

Lehrbuch der Religionsgeschichte, 2 vols. (Tübingen, 1887-89); *Manual of the Science of Religion* (London, 1891); *Religion of the Teutons* (1902); J. J. P. Valeton, *De Ethische Richting* (Baarn, 1909); G. van der Leeuw, *Ethisch: modern of orthodox* (Utrecht, 1924); J. Lindeboom, *Geschiedenis van het vrijzinnig Protestantisme*, 2 vols. (Huis ter Heide, 1927, Assen, 1933). H.H.

saving faith: In opposition to the Catholic emphasis on faith as being primarily intellectual submission to doctrines whose truth is guaranteed by the infallible authority of the Church, love being the animating principle of faith and the Church being the object to which the *fiducia* in faith has reference, Protestant theologians have affirmed that there can only be saving faith when *notitia* (knowledge of the Word of God) and *assensus* (acknowledgment that the Word of God is true) are followed by *fiducia* which is personal trust in the saving and unmerited grace of God in Christ. See assurance of salvation. H.W.J.

Saviour: In its origin this was a pagan term applied to various divinities and occasionally to deified men. Certain kings of Syria and Egypt were invested with the title of "Soter" as part of their proper names. It was perhaps because of its pagan associations that the term was at first avoided by Christians. In the N.T. it occurs rarely, and always with a general sense, as a variant of the more usual expression "he who has saved us". It was not until well on in the 2nd century that "the Saviour" came to be one of the acknowledged names of Christ. From that time on, however, it tended to displace the earlier names of Messiah and Lord, and has continued ever since to be the distinctive title. The adoption of the name has been adduced by some modern scholars as one of the proofs that Christianity borrowed from the mystery cults, and transferred to Jesus the honours hitherto attached to Attis and Serapis. This appears to be contrary to the facts. So long as there was danger of a confusion between Jesus and the gods of the cults the name "Saviour" was not applied to him in any specific sense. It only became usual when Christianity had fully established its claim to be a new and separate religion. The name was adopted for no other reason than that it was inevitable. From the outset it had been the cardinal Christian belief that Christ had brought salvation, and the belief could not but embody itself, sooner or later, in the one word that definitely expressed it. Attempts have been made to trace back the name to some particular theology, but this also is unnecessary. It is indeed significant that the name came into general use during the conflict with Gnosticism* and emphasized the conception of Christ as the sole agent of salvation. This, however, was not a dogma but the fundamental faith of the church. Here we may find the ultimate reason why Christ is known pre-eminently as "the Saviour". While they hold many different theories as to the nature of his salvation, all Christians are agreed on the fact that he has saved. A title is chosen for him which is independent of sect or creed.

W. Bousset, *Kyrios Christos* (1914); A. Harnack, *History of Dogma* (1886 ff.), vols. I and II.
E.F.S.

Savitri: 1) A variant spelling of Savitar, the Vedic sun god. 2) The heroine of the poem *Savitri and Satyavan,* or *Love Conquers Death,* told to the Pandava brothers while exiled in the forest—one of the episodes of the great Hindu epic, the Mahabharata. 3) It is also used to designate the "most sacred of prayers, the Savitri." 4) Also it is the name of one of the less important Upanishads. C.S.B.

Savonarola, Jerome: (1452-1498) Dominican monk. Italy's greatest preacher. In fiery, popular sermons he castigated the morals of his time and uttered prophecies, one of which, the invasion of Charles VIII of France, made such an impression when fulfilled that he was able to set up a theocratic government in Florence and bring about a spectacular reform in outward morals. A reaction set in. He was excommunicated by the pope, captured by a fanatical mob and condemned to be burned at the stake. Savonarola's ideals were those of monkish asceticism. He did not depart from Catholic dogma, except to deny the pope's infallibility. E.C.K.

Savoy Declaration: A statement agreed upon by Congregationalist leaders at a meeting in the Savoy palace, London, in October 1658. It contains an explanatory preface, and a series of revisions of and additions to the Westminster Confession. These changes were adopted by American Congregationalism*. P. Schaff, *Creeds of Christendom,* III (1919). See New England theology.
J.T.M.

Saybrook Platform, The: Adopted by Connecticut Congregationalists* in 1708. It contained the *Savoy Confession,* an English Congregational revision of the Westminster Confession; the *Heads of Agreement**, an English Presbyterian-Congregational document, and *Fifteen Articles* for the administration of Church discipline. The latter provided for county associations, called *Consociations,* which were to have oversight of individual congregations. From that time forward Connecticut Congregationalism tended, in its polity, in the direction of Presbyterianism, so that by the end of the colonial period the names Congregational and Presbyterian were used interchangeably. W.W.S.

scala sancta: (Lat., *scala,* stairs; *sanctus,* holy) Holy Stairs consist of twenty-eight marble steps near the Lateran at Rome. According to tradition these stairs led once to the pretorium of Pilate at Jerusalem, and are the ones up which Christ was led during His Passion. The stairs were brought from Jerusalem to Rome about 326 by St. Helena, the mother of Constantine.

Beringer, *Der Ablaesse* I, 501. B.S.

scandal: In biblical usage a stumbling block that gives offense to the religious feelings or is the occasion of lapse of faith or of religious disobedience in others. In modern usage an offense or outrage against the moral feelings of a community. It often denotes detraction or defamation of character due to common talk, evil report or malicious gossip. R.W.F.

scapegoat: One of the two goats which played the central role in the complex ritual of the annual Day of Atonement* (Lev. 16. 8ff.). Upon it the sins of the entire Jewish people, accumulated during the year just ended, were loaded by the high-priest with symbolic ceremony. It was then led forth into the wilderness, bearing the sins of the people with it. There it was pushed over a steep and high cliff, not far from Jerusalem, and killed. Its death in this strange manner was thought to work atonement for the people and to bring remission of their sins. Because of this unique role, the term, scapegoat, has come to designate any person or people, who is made to suffer, and especially to perish, innocently and unjustly for, and usually through the conscious purpose of, another, more guilty person, who, in turn, escapes the consequences of his evil deeds. See human scarifice; laying on of hands.
J.M.

scapular: (Lat., *scapula,* shoulder) A part of the religious garb of monastic orders, so called because it covers the shoulders, extending almost to the feet in front and in back. The smaller scapular is worn by members of third orders living in the world. See Tertiaries. W.H.

scepticism: See skepticism.

Schaeder, Erich: (1861-1936) He was professor in Königsberg, Göttingen, Kiel and Breslau. Rejecting the apologetic wooing of the modern, he developed a biblical theology that seeks advance solely in the deeper disclosure of biblical truth. He saw the harm of almost all conservative, as well as critical theology, in its anthropocentric attitude, which he tried to destroy. In showing a negative attitude towards German idealism he fought the historicism of the religious-historical theology and the tyranny of the Lutheran and pietistic soteriological viewpoints in faith and theology.

Theozentrische Theologie, vol. I (Leipzig, 1825), vol. II (Leipzig, 1928); *Das Geistes problem der Theologie* (Leipzig, 1924). H.H.

Schaff, Philip: (1819-1893) Biblical scholar, writer, historian, professor and active leader in many lines of church life and thought. A Swiss, trained in Germany, his main contribution was made in the U. S. A. See Mercersburg theology.
K.H.C.

Schartau, Henric: (1757-1825) Early impressed by the intellectual clarity of orthodoxy, and interested in the analysis of religious experience, Schartau was affected by Moravian pietism, but later opposed its subjectivism and sentimentality. He stressed the *ordo salutis,* the place of the ministry, and the idea of the call. He wielded a powerful influence through correspondence with spiritual inquirers, a rigid homiletical method, and a deep sense of seriousness, which for a century has characterized West Sweden. His ministry was spent in Lund. Of materials published since his death, the correspondence is remarkable for its psychological study of Christian faith and experience.

Predikningar öfver kyrkoarets gamla högmessotexter (12th ed., 1917); *Undervisning i Christendomskunskapen* (13th ed., 1900); H. Hägglund. *Henric Schartau* (1924); A. Lindeblad, *Henric Schartau's lefnad och lära* (2nd ed., 1864, reprinted, 1917).

C.J.B.

Scheel, Otto: (1876-19) German Protestant theologian. He was born in Tondern, Sleswig. In 1900 he was privatdozent Kiel; from 1906-1924 professor of Church History Tübingen; from 1924-1933 professor of German History, Kiel. Scheel was influential through his studies in the history of the Reformation, and particularly in the early phase of Luther's development, where he successfully combined the psychological and the theological approach. He was Co-editor of *Die Religion in Geschichte und Gegenwart* (1st ed.). An active politician, he especially worked for the rights of the German minorities abroad.

Die Kirche im Urchristentum (1912); *Martin Luther,* 2 vols. (1915-1917, 3rd ed., 1921-1930).

O.A.P.

Scheibe, Max: (1870-) He taught at the University of Halle. Since 1902 he is pastor of the evangelical-reformed community in Leipzig. Being more of a follower of his teacher R. A. Lipsius*, he postulates religious ideas on a basis of need and value.

Die Bedeutung der Werturteile für das religiöse Erkennen (Halle, 1893); *Calvins Prädestinationslehre* (Halle, 1897).

H.H.

Scheler, Max Ferdinand: (1874-1928) Influenced by Brentano, Eucken, and Husserl**, Scheler applied the phenomenological method especially to the living data of instinct and emotion. In his first (Protestant) period his most systematic work, *Der Formalismus in der Ethik und die materiale Wertethik* (1913-16) was a defence of the objectivity of value by the use of what he called "ethical absolutism" and "material apriorism" or theory of the *a priori* nature of content as well as form. In his Catholic period *Von Ewigem im Menschen* (1921) analyzed the religious experience as an act of love. Later, outside of the church, Scheler emphasized the distinction between *Leben* and *Geist.* Denying life, man, with phenomenological insight, sensitizes himself to spiritual possibilities. Scheler's *Wesen und Formen der Sympathie* (1926) is often quoted by sociologists. Brief, but important, is *Die Stellung des Menschen im Kosmos* (1928). Nicolai Hartmann* has been influenced by his value theory.

J.S.B.

Schelling, Friedrich Wilhelm Joseph: (1775-1854) His persistent openmindedness for the problematic of realities enabled Schelling to push ahead again and again to new thought positions. His eternal beginning and productive scepticism made him a leader of a new philosophical movement within the ranks of idealism. Having revealed the problematic of idealism, his final philosophy centers in the relation of idealism to Christianity. Christianity and idealism are irreconcilable on idealistic grounds. Schelling rejects the pantheism of idealism, its utopianism, its system of necessity and apriorism which suppress the personality and liberty of both God and man, its being merely a science of ideas, not a metaphysic that solves and answers the great problems of man's existence. In his final philosophy Schelling seeks to formulate a speculative theism in which the problems of divine and human sovereign liberty, and the creative personality of God become central in an anti-idealistic philosophy. The reality of the concrete world with all its incompletenesses; the reality of religion; the reality of mythology; the reality of Christianity the acts of the content of which are the acts of God; the reality of the ultimate world and the reality of immortality are so many boundaries of an *a priori* rational science, whereas a positive philosophy, as the philosophy of the living God and his creative acts, is a synthesis of faith and knowledge. The elder Schelling offers a union of theology and philosophy in his explanation of a Christian philosophy of existence. Through his emphasis on man's central categories of his personality: decision and responsibility, he came close to Kierkegaard's* Christian philosophy of existence. By intention Schelling's final philosophy touched the fringes of an existential philosophy; in reality, however, he, like Hegel, put his philosophy at the end of a historical process by which an absolute standpoint in which the contradictions of existence have vanished, is achieved.

H. Dreyer, *Der Begriff Geist in der deutschen Philosophie von Kant bis Hegel* (Berlin, 1908); P. Genths, *Die Identitätsphilosophie Schellings in ihrem Verhältnis zur Religion* (Würzburg, 1926); Th. Hoppe, *Die Philosophie Schellings in ihrem Verhältnis zum Christentum* (Rostock, 1875); O. Platinius, *Schellings Fortführung der Lehre Kants vom Bösen* (Hilchenbach, 1928); P. Tillich, *Die religionsgeschichtliche Konstruktion in Schellings positiver Philosophie, ihre Voraussetzungen und Prinzipien* (Halle, 1910); *Mystik und Schuldbewusstsein in Schellings philosophischer Entwicklung* (Gütersloh, 1912); A. Weber, *Examen critique de la philosophie religieuse de Schelling* (Strassburg, 1860).

H.H.

Schenkel, Daniel: (1813-1885) He taught at the University of Heidelberg. As a systematic theologian he was strongly ethically oriented in his apologetic and polemical works.

Das Wesen des Protestantismus, 3 vols. (Schaffhausen, 1846-51); *Die christliche Dogmatik vom Standpunkt des Gewissens,* 2 vols. (Wiesbaden, 1858); *Charakterbild Jesu* (Wiesbaden, 1864, 4th ed., Wiesbaden, 1873) *Die Grundlehren des Christentums aus dem Bewusstsein des Glaubens dargestellt* (Leipzig, 1877).

H.H.

Schérer, Edmond: (1815-1889) He was for a time professor of exegesis at the University of Geneva, Switzerland. The religious need and inspiration were for him purely inward facts. As theology was for him an empty speculation, positive religion gets its support by the history and psychology of the religious genius. He conceived sin as a necessary part of the divine plan of education. Whatever is not pure morality and pure feeling is subject to criticism.

Dogmatique de l'église chrétienne (Paris, 1843); *Esquisse d'une théorie de l'église chretienne* (Paris, 1845); *La critique et la foi* (Paris, 1850), 2 vols.; *Mélanges de critique religieuse* (Paris, 1853).

H.H.

schism: A word which in its N.T. usage signified a rent, a division, or a dissension, acquired in the Roman Catholic Church in course of time a definite technical meaning, that of non-subjection to the authority of the papacy. Accordingly, a church may theoretically be wholly orthodox and yet schismatic, or it may be heretical as well as schismatic. But since the article of papal supremacy is of dogmatic character, its rejection necessarily involves the schismatic in heresy. As such, it is *ipso facto* punishable by excommunication. (See heresy; sect.)

The "Great Schism" of 1054 produced a separation between the four Eastern and the Roman patriarchates which exists to this day. Pope Leo IX* (1049-54), inspired by the ideals of the Cluniac* Reform and under provocation from the aggressive Patriarch of Constantinople, Michael Cerularius* (1043-58), demanded that the latter acknowledge the supreme jurisdiction of the Holy See in the church universal. When after Leo's death Cerularius refused even to acknowledge his legates legal authority to negotiate in the matter, they placed the bull of excommunication on the high altar of St. Sophia. But it would be a mistake to think that the immediate occasion of the "Great Schism" was its actual cause: the causes were centuries old, and comprised deep-seated political, cultural, as well as religious differences. Cerularius, despite his aggressive manner, defended the historic attitude of the Eastern patriarchates in the matter of papal supremacy: they always conceded the primacy of honor of the Roman among the existing five patriarchates, but repudiated its claim to the primacy of jurisdiction. In other words, they held that the Roman patriarchates is *primus inter pares*. See Byzantine empire; creeds of Christendom; placet.

Louis Brehier, *Le schisme oriental du XIe siècle* (Paris, 1899).

M.S.

Schlatter, Adolf: Protestant theologian. Born 1852 in St. Gallen, Switzerland, 1880 privatdozent in Bern, 1888. Professor of N.T. in Greifswald, 1893 in Berlin, 1898-1932 in Tuebingen. Died 1938. The leading representative of Biblical realism in modern Protestant theology. He applied his vast knowledge of early Judaism to the study of the N.T. By pointing energetically to the Hebrew-Aramaic background of Jesus and the Primitive Church he opened new ways to the study both of the N.T. age and of N.T. theology. As an exegete of great originality he wrote commentaries on all the N.T. books. His exegesis is characterized by unbiased search for the historical truth, common sense, a realistic view of the nature of man and simple piety. Protagonist of a modern theology of faith as opposed both to apologetics and to all ancient and modern compromises of theology with philosophy. In his own presentation, dogmatics is stripped of all accretions that are un-Biblical or have no significance for actual faith. Open to the truth in science and philosophy Schlatter was, nevertheless, anxious to preserve the originality and uniqueness of the Gospel message. Before the First World War his influence on contemporary theology was relatively small, owing to the almost offensive independence of his mind, but at present a number of leading students of theology is greatly indebted to him, and his amazing scholarship as well as the power and depth of his exegesis are generally recognized. Gerh. Kittel's *Wörterbuch zum Neuen Testament,* for instance, would not have been possible without the stimulus given by Schlatter to the study of the history of Biblical ideas.

Principal works (an English translation of which is long overdue):

Der Glaube im Neuen Testament (1885, 4th ed., 1927); *Erläuterungen zum Neuen Testament* (1887-1904, 6th ed., 1936), 3 vols.; *Geschichte Israels von Alex. d. Gr. bis Hadrian* (1901, 3rd, ed., 1925); *Die Theologie des Neuen Testaments* (1909-1910, 2nd ed., 1921-22), 2 vols.; *Das christliche Dogma* (1911, 2nd ed., 1923). Founder and co-editor of: *Beiträge zur Förderung christlicher Theologie.* See also: Wilh Lütgert, *Adolf Schlatter als Theologie* (1932).

O.A.P.

Schleiermacher, Friedrich Daniel Ernst: (1768-1834) Protestant theologian, philosopher, and translator of Plato's works, was minister of the Reformed Church, professor at the University of Halle (1804-1806) and of Berlin (1810-1834). He wrote and lectured on a wide variety of subjects, including logic, epistemology, metaphysics, ethics, aesthetics, the history of philosophy, theology, church history, the N.T., and psychology. His most substantial contribution lay in the fields of (a) theory of knowledge, through his influencing German philosophers in the direction of a critical empirical realism, (b) Plato scholarship, and (c) systematic theology, where his idea of an "empirical theology" has exercized a very wide influence. This work in theology constitutes his real claim to a place in the history of thought. Although influenced by Kant and Fichte**, he was never a subjective idealist*. In his earlier period (c. 1800) he identified God and the world, taken as a whole, somewhat like Spinoza*. He believed that the universe as a whole, as it stands, is harmonious and perfect. He did not believe in personal immortality. He might be called an idealist in the sense that he believed that dialectical thought will disclose, and hence shows a kinship with, natural processes. Religion, which is a natural activity of man, is at its best a synthetic grasp (intuition) of this system and the relating of events to it, and an emotional response to these insights, which side of religion he particularly emphasized and valued. In his later period (c. 1820), he laid more stress on the distinction between the world and God, whom he now regarded as the "ground" of the agreement between nature and rational processes, the role of which in knowledge (and their connection with the given element in sense experience) he made the subject of a good deal of sound analysis. It is doubtful whether he meant by "ground of the world" an entity different from and sustaining the world; his writings suggest more the relation between genus and species, and he says that the world is necessary to God's being. His "theism" was at least very close to his earlier "pantheism". Religion he regarded as a natural, even necessary, aspect of the developed human personality, essentially feeling (probably better, *attitude*) which is sympathy or love for the universe, often called a feeling of absolute dependence on God. Sometimes he seems to regard this feeling as partially cognitive awareness of divine reality. Theological doctrines are expressions of this experience, or descriptions of its relations (e.g., to Christ as the cause of Christian religious fulfilment). Thus doctrine is dependent on religious experience, not experience on belief in dogma. This view he thought made theology a special science, in that it has its own data for elaboration, and need not be merely philosophy or an explication of what is implicit in the Bible. This general view enabled him to defend the religious attitude while dispensing with the features of orthodoxy most objectionable to modern science and philosophy. He emphasized that religious experience is an unique and autonomous mental activity, which deserves examination separate from, e.g., the psychology of cognition or volition. See empirical theology.

Writings and commentaries: Collected works, 31 volumes, Reimer, Berlin, mostly still in print. Critical editions of the *Reden über Religion* (by G. C. B. Pünjer, 1879), the *Monologen* (Schiele and H. Mulert, 1911), the *Ethik* (O. Braun, 1927), the *Dialektik* (I. Halpern, 1903), the *Aesthetik* (R. Odebrecht, 1931). English translations of the *Reden* (J. Oman, 1892), *Monologen* (H. Friess, 1926, under the title of *Soliloquies*), the *Weihnachtsfeier* (W. Hastie, 1890), the *Kurze Darstellung des theologischen Studiums* (W. Farrer, 1850), *Der Christliche Glaube* (H. R. Mackintosh and J. S. Stewart, 1928, paraphrased in G. Cross, *The Theology of Schleiermacher,* 1911). Four volumes of letters (*Aus Schleiermachers Leben in Briefen,* edited by W. Dilthey, 1858-63), the first two translated by F. Rowan (1860). W. Bender, *Schleiermachers Theologie* (1876); R. B. Brandt, *The Philosophy of Schleiermacher* (1941); W. Dilthey, *Leben Schleiermachers* (1870 and 1922); R. Haym, *Die Romantische Schule* (1870); R. Munro, *Schleiermacher: Personal and Speculative* (1903); W. B. Selbie, *Schleiermacher* (1913); H. Süskind, *Der Einfluss Schellings auf die Entwicklung von Schleiermachers System* (1909), and *Christentum und Geschichte bei Schleiermacher* (1911); Franz Vorländer, *Schleiermachers Sittenlehre* (1851); Georg Wehrung, *Der geschichtsphilosophische Standpunkt Schleiermachers,* etc. (1907); *Die Dialektik Schleiermachers* (1920); *Schleiermacher in der Zeit seines Werdens* (1927); Bruno Weiss, *Untersuchungen über Schleiermachers Dialektik* (1878); Georg Weissenborn, *Vorlesungen über Schleiermachers Dialektik* (1847).

R.B.B.

Schmalkald Articles: A Lutheran confessional document, written by Luther himself in 1537 in response to a request from Elector John Frederick of Saxony for a summary of all his teaching. In it the mature reformer states concisely the sovereignty of God, the mediatorial work of Christ, justification by faith, and the evangelical view of the church and the ministry. This position is contrasted sharply with Rome, whose mass, penance, saints, relics, etc., are denounced, and whose head, the Pope, is attacked as the Antichrist. The Elector's purpose of laying Luther's articles before a convention of all the Protestant powers at Schmalkald was never realized, but the document gained prestige and was included in the Book of Concord* as an official creed together with an anti-papal appendix by Melanchthon* dating back to the time of the original articles. To this statement of faith, in which Luther shows characteristic depth and vigor, the reformer himself attached great importance. Unlike most confessions, it is a spontaneous outpouring of faith rather than a formal series of articles and did not come by its present title until 1553. See Lutheranism.

T.A.K.

Schmalkald League: A coalition of German Protestant powers, five principalities and eleven cities, formed in 1531 for mutual protection against the Emperor Charles V*. Other German potentates and Denmark joined later. The League did more than promote the Protestant interests. It became an important factor in European politics and its co-operation was sought by France and England against the Hapsburgs. The League was dissolved in 1547 when the Schmalkald War of 1546-47 ended in the defeat of the Protestants at Muehlberg and resulted in captivity for both Philip of Hesse* and John Frederick, the Elector of Saxony, the leaders of the League. T.A.K.

Schmucker, Samuel Simon: (1799-1873) Leading figure in the American Lutheran Church of the early and middle period of the 19th century on the side of liberal Lutheranism and of interdenominational fellowship. American born, raised in the atmosphere of a German pietistic home, touched by the prevailing Puritanism of current American Protestantism, educated under private tutors and at the University of Pennsylvania (grad. 1819) and at Princeton Seminary, early in contact with broad organizational interests of his clergyman father, S carried on a manysided interest into his professional career. He helped to forward the first united Lutheran church in America (the General Synod), to establish the Lutheran Theological Seminary at Gettysburg (its first theological professor), founded the classical school which later became Pennsylvania College (now Gettysburg). He framed model constitutions for synods and congregations; published the first English Lutheran work on systematic theology in America (*Elements of Popular Theology,* 1834); prepared hymnbooks and liturgical forms; edited, with free interpretations Luther's catechism. In 1838 he published his *Appeal to the American Churches* (a fellowship plan antedating the present Federal Council) and took active part in the organization in 1846 of the Evangelical Alliance. His influence suffered a tragic eclipse following the influx of German and Scandinavian immigrants with their strongly conservative confessional bias. Prophetic of an American Lutheran theology set free from Lutheran scholasticism his full stature remains still officially unrecognized within his denomination. For his part in the Definite Platform Controversy see "American Lutheranism." For a bibliography see Vergilius Ferm, *The Crisis in American Lutheran Theology* (1927). V.F.

Schöberlein, Ludwig Friedrich: (1813-1881) He taught in Heidelberg and Göttingen. He developed a Lutheran orthodoxy, widened and softened through mysticism and theosophy.

Die Grundlehre des Heils, entwickelt aus dem Prinzip der Liebe (Stuttgart, 1848); *Prinzip und System der Dogmatik, Einleitung in die christliche Glaubenslehre* (Heidelberg, 1881). H.H.

schola cantorum: A school for singers of the Papal choir, said to have been established by Pope Gregory the Great*, 590-604. It served to standardize the Gregorian chant* throughout the Western church. A course of study required nine years. Teachers were sent out to establish schools in England, at Metz in Germany, and at St. Gall in Switzerland. E.H.B.

Scholasticism: (Lat., *scholasticus,* lecturer; Gr., *scholē,* school) Historically, it denotes the teachings of the ecclesiastical schools founded by Charlemagne* to reestablish the Christian learning eclipsed by the Frankish invasion of Gaul. By extension, it connotes the long period of Western learning, especially philosophical and theological, originating in the ninth century and terminating in the fifteenth century. Two notable features of this learning are its intimate association with Catholic theology and its rigorous logical formalism. Its progressive elaboration covers four distinct periods.

I. Early Scholasticism (IXth-XIIth century). Principally concerned with the systematic treatment of Catholic dogma and the exposition of the arts which such treatment presupposed. Alcuin of Tours* (730-804) introduced the study of the liberal arts dividing them into the *trivium* (grammar, rhetoric, and dialectic) and the *quadrivium* (arithmetic, geometry, astronomy and music). The translation into Latin of the works of the pseudo-Denys, the Areopagite, (see Dionysius, the Areopagite) by John Scotus Eriugena (833-880)* gave to Scholasticism a permanent neo-Platonic character with its hierarchized grades of being emanating from and forever returning to God. The problem of universals* resulting from Roscelin's* (1050-1120) identification of ideas with their verbal signs (nominalism*) found its ablest exponent in Peter Abailard* (1079-1142). Against the exaggerated realism of his neo-Platonic contemporaries, Abailard held with Aristotle that our ideas do not exist as such outside of the mind. Against the nominalists, he maintained that they have a material basis in extra-mental realities from which they are extracted by intellectual abstraction. Anselm* of Canterbury (1033-1109) foreshadowed the formal distinction of philosophy and theology in his attempts to prove the existence of God by reason alone. The whole period is one of agitation and discovery—focused in dogma and the dialectical instruments of its elaboration and systematization. Works of St. Augustine*, the neo-Platonists, and the logic of Aristotle* furnished the materials for these developments.

II. The XIIIth century—The Golden Age of Scholasticism. The translation of hitherto unknown works of Aristotle; the rise of the universities (Paris, Oxford, Bologna); and the foundation of the mendicant orders—especially the Franciscan and Dominican**, together furnished the conditions which produced the most fruitful period of Scholasticism. At Paris, the eager study and enthusiastic acceptance or rejection of Aristotle's works both in the original and in the interpretations of the Arabian commentator, Averroes* (1126-1198), issued in violent controversies and the formation of three outstanding schools of thought.

The traditionalists under Bonaventura*, while conveniently adopting some of the basic Aristotelian notions, rejected his teaching as incompatible with Christian dogma and revelation. A unique wisdom achieved through the efforts of faith guided by reason is the end of all human inquiry. Though distinct in method and formal object from theology, philosophy is incomplete and even deceptive when not guided by and directed to theology as Aristotle's teaching on the eternity of matter clearly demonstrated. Not only in things perceived through the senses, but in the soul and God perceived through the divine illumination of the active intelligence does man achieve true understanding. Knowledge for its own sake is a chimera; only as leading to the possession in love of the Absolute Good is it fructified. In man, as in God, the will is superior to the intelligence. For polemical purposes this school called themselves Augustinians.

The Latin Averroists under Siger of Brabant* (1235?-1281-1284) found in Aristotle as interpreted by Averroes, the definitive statement and solution of all speculative problems. Where Aristotle and revelation conflicted, a dual standard of truth, reason and revelation was recognized. The admitted primacy of revelation over reason did not prevent the acceptance of the conclusions of both in their proper order of nature and supernature. The eternity of the world, moral naturalism and the unity of the human intellect negating personal immortality, freedom and responsibility were the principal doctrines of this school.

The Christian Aristotelians under St. Thomas Aquinas* (1224-1274) integrated Aristotelian philosophy into the scholastic tradition by appropriately reinterpreting such principles as issued in the Averroistic extremes. Against both the Augustinians and the Latin Averroists, their most potent weapon was the stagirite's texts. Reason alone can neither prove nor disprove creation in time. Corporeal substances are thrice composed (essence and existence, substance and accident, matter and form) to account for their becoming within the fixed limits of their nature and their transformation into one another. Human intelligence is extrinsically dependent on matter for its natural object, material being, but is intrinsically independent of matter in its operations. The existence and nature of God as creator and end of all things, from which he is essentially distinct, can be demonstrated inductively by reason alone. Philosophy and theology are in method and object formally distinct. Both issue in valid conclusions which are in no wise contradictory.

The characteristic difference of these schools of thought did not exclude a fundamental agreement on the distinction between faith and reason, the essential distinction between God and creatures, and the dependence of creatures in their being and in their action upon the divinity. The genius of Aquinas and Bonaventura produced vast treatises (*Summa Theologiae, Summa Theologica**) synthesizing and elaborating the whole philosophical heritage from antiquity to their time, including the important works of the Arabs and Jews Avicenna (980-1037), Avicebron (1045-1070), Maimonides (1135-1204)**.

III. Later Scholasticism (XIVth-XVth centuries). Characterized by excessive formalism in method and remoteness from living problems, whence the decay of the doctrine. This decay resulted from internal and external causes. The roundness and completeness of the XIII century synthesis appeared to leave small place to further developments. Lesser minds turned to dogmatizing the masters, and quibbled over unimportant matters. Words displaced ideas and argument discussion. Partisanship sponsored artificial differences. Externally, the growing tension between secular and spiritual powers, and the eventual triumph of experimental science effectively completed the internal decay and scholasticism generally was interred in seminary manuals. The outstanding figure of this period was William of Ockham (1270-1347)*. See Scotists; Thomism; universals, battle over.

IV. Modern Scholasticism (XIXth century to the present). See neo-Scholasticism.

S. Thomas Aquinas, English Editions: *Selected Writings*, Rev. Martin D'Arcy, S. J. (1939); *Aquinas Ethicus* or Moral Teachings of S. Thomas (London, 1896); *On Being and Essence* (Toronto, Canada, S. Michaels College, 1934); *On the Governance of Rulers*, trans. by Gerald B. Phelan (Toronto, Can., S. Michaels College, 1935); *Summa Contra Gentiles*, trans. by English Dominican Fathers (London, 1923-29); *Summa Theologica*, trans. by English Dominican Fathers (London, 1920-32); *Summa Theologica*, published by Benziger Brothers (1912-25).

S. Bonaventura, *De reductione artium ad theologiam*: Commentary, Introduction and translation by Sister Emma Theresa (S. Bonaventure College, 1940); *Philosophy of S. Bonaventure*, Etienne Gilson, trans. by Dom Illtyd Trethowan and F. J. Sheed (1938); *S. Thomas and the Problem of the Soul in the 13th Century*, Anton Charles Pegis (Toronto, Canada, S. Michael's College, 1934); "S. Bonaventure, the Seraphic Doctor," Ludger Wegemer, O. F. M., "The Doctrine of S. Bonaventure Concerning our Knowledge of God," Vincent Mayer, O. M. C., in *Franciscan Studies*, No. 2, July, 1924.

Duns Scotus, *Duns Scotus*, C. R. S. Harris (Oxford, 1927); *Origin and Development of the Franciscan School*: Duns Scotus and S. Thomas, Bernard Vogt, O. F. M. (1925).

William Ockham, *De Sacramentis Altaris*, edited by T. Bruce Birch, Latin text and English translation (1930); *Logic of William Ockham*, Ernst A. Moody (1935); *Ockham Studies and Selections*, by Stephen Chak Tournay (1938). J.J.F.

Scholz, Heinrich: (1884-) First professor of theology in Breslau, now professor of philosophy in Kiel, Germany. He distinguishes between ponderable, experienceable religion and imponderable, dead religion. Religion is for him an acosmic, unearthly experience of the presence of God. The truth of religion consists in the truth of existential judgments. In religious experience we not only have a subjective value-exaltation of man, but a genuine experience of an objective potency. Though there are no demonstrative proofs of immortality, we have argumentative proofs.

Der Unsterblichkeitsgedanke als philosophisches Problem, 2nd ed. (Berlin, 1922); *Die Religionsphilosophie des Als-Ob* (Leipzig, 1921); *Die Religionsphilosophie*, 2nd rev. ed., (Berlin, 1923). H.H.

schools: See Chartres, the school of; Palace school; parochial schools; parochial schools, Catholic; religious education; seminaries; Sunday schools; theological schools.

Schopenhauer, Arthur: (1778-1860) Represents a powerful reaction against German idealism, intellectualism and spiritualism. He held that the true nature of the world consists in an unspiritual will to live, a dark urge or impulse. The intellect transforms this intrinsic substance of all things into a world of ideas and concepts. It is the task and the function of philosophy and religion to deliver man from the bondage of the universal power of the world will. The supreme moral principle is compassion, because it overcomes the separation of the individuals and leads them back to the original unity from which they originate. Sch. was one of the best German writers amongst the philosophers in the 19th century. He exercised his greatest influence in the second half of this century. See pessimism.

The World as Will and Idea (1819); Kuno Fischer, *Schopenhauer* (2nd ed., 1898); Georg Simmel, *Schopenhauer and Nietzsche*. R.K.

Schroeckh, Johann Matthias: (1733-1808) At first he was professor of philosophy in Leipzig. Later he taught poetic art in Wittenberg. Writing the most exhaustive church history, its main disadvantages were tiresome repetitions, a too great epic breadth, an excessive verbosity and an undue emphasis of the biographical. Compared with Semler* he was a wholly uncritical mind, in attitude little aggressive and polemical. His chief merit was the radical break with the centurial division of church history.

Christliche Kirchengeschichte, 35 vols. (Leipzig, 1768-1803). H.H.

Schürer, Emil: (1844-1910) A famous Protestant theologian who taught at the leading universities of Germany. He wrote the famous classic *Geschichte des Jüdischen Volkes in Zeitalter Jesu Christi* (1898-1901; 4th ed. 1901-1909). This has been translated into English in six volumes as *A History of the Jewish People in the Time of*

Jesus Christ by J. Macpherson (Division I) and S. Taylor and P. Christie (Division II, Edinburgh 1885-1900). Schürer represents an older and more critical view of the Pharisees* which has latterly been corrected by the works of T. Herford and George F. Moore. B.Z.B.

Schwabach Articles: A historically important confessional document consisting of 17 articles drawn up in 1529 by Melanchthon and Luther for Elector John of Saxony. These articles are the first attempt to create a common confession for Protestantism in Germany and seek to define a basis upon which Saxony, Brandenburg, and the south German cities could unite for political action. Doctrinally they lay special stress on Luther's conception of the Eucharist as over against that of Zwingli*. The articles are the principal written source of the first part of the Augsburg Confession*.

For an English translation see H. E. Jacobs, *Book of Concord,* II (1883). T.A.K.

Schweigger, Solomon: (1551-1622) Succeeded Gerlach* as a Champlain of the German Embassy in Constantinople. He continued the work of his predecessors with more zeal, love and interest. He worked with all his energy for the union of the two churches (Greek Orthodox and the Lutheran). He also made many journeys in the Near East collecting valuable information for the Greek Orthodox Church. G.E.Z.

Schweitzer, Albert: (1875-) As music critic, author of the standard life of Bach, editor (with C. M. Widor) of Bach's organ works, and concert organist whose interpretations of Bach are now recorded, Schweitzer has contributed to the understanding of Bach, particularly with reference to the "objectivity" he requires and the *tempi* his works demand. As theologian and student of N.T. literature Schweitzer has laid special emphasis on the apocalyptic element in the teaching of Jesus. As philosopher he has stressed "reverence for life", finding, in contrast to many "vitalists", that it leads not to will to power but will to love. As medical missionary in Lambarene, equatorial Africa, he has demonstrated not only his remarkable versatility but a practical synthesis of *Leben* and *Geist,*—his thought centering in "life", his practical life receiving its direction from the spiritual ideals of justice and fellow-feeling. See Lives of Jesus.

Chief Works in English: *J. S. Bach* (2 vols., 1911); *Paul and his Interpreters* (1912); *Civilization and Ethics* (1923); *Quest of the Historical Jesus* (1926); *Mysticism of Paul* (1931); *Out of my Life and Thought* (autobiog.) (1933); *Indian Thought and its Development* (1936). J.S.B.

Schweitzer, Alexander: (1808-1888) Prominent Swiss Reformed theologian, student and follower of Schleiermacher*. As professor in the University of Zurich, and as vicar of the cathedral for over thirty years, he was one of the leading expounders and defenders of the Reformed* type of theology.

Five volumes of sermons, 1834-1862; *autobiography,* edited by P. Schweizer (Zurich, 1889). T.F.H.

Schwenkfeldian doctrine: That advanced by Casper Schwenkfeld von Ossig (1490-1562), an early supporter of the German reformation. He held that the Scriptures do not contain everything necessary for salvation, but there must be added the *Living Word.* The Scriptures, therefore, did not occupy the exalted place as in Luther's thought, nor did he hold that the Sacraments were the vehicles of grace. Accordingly Luther condemned his teaching and considered him a dangerous heretic. W.W.S.

Science, Philosophy and Religion, The Conference on: The Conference on Science, Philosophy and Religion in Their Relation to the Democratic Way of Life, Inc. was organized in 1939 to bring together leaders in various disciplines in order to obtain greater clarity regarding the intellectual and spiritual foundations of democracy. The annual meetings of the Conference held in September, 1940, at the Jewish Theological Seminary of America, in September, 1941, and August, 1942, at Columbia University, have developed a new technique looking toward integration of the experience and learning of the various participants. The papers prepared for each of the meetings have been published in a symposium. A fourth Conference was held in September, 1943 to discuss the relationship of different fields of learning and experience to the creation and maintenance of world peace.

In April, 1943, there were 163 members. The Board of Directors includes: William F. Albright, Van Wyck Brooks, Lyman Bryson, Henry S. Dennison, Louis Finkelstein, Lawrence K. Frank, Theodore M. Greene, Caryl P. Haskins, Robert J. Havighurst, Charles W. Hendel, F. Ernest Johnson, Harold D. Lasswell, David E. Lilienthal, Alain L. Locke, Robert M. MacIver, John U. Nef, Harry A. Overstreet, Anton C. Pegis, Gerald B. Phelan, Harlow Shapley, George F. Thomas, Harold C. Urey, Gerald G. Walsh, S. J., Luther A. Weigle.

scientific method in theology: See empirical theology.

Scillitan martyrs: Group of 7 men and 5 women of North African Church* put to death in 180 A.D. for adherence to Christianity. K.H.C.

Scotists: Followers of John Duns Scotus*. Most Scotists have been of the Franciscan* Order, as was the Subtle Doctor himself. They are noted for keen and independent criticism of other scholastics, especially the Thomists*, and for their devotion to the doctrine of free will, the principle of formal distinction, and the dogma of the immaculate conception*. Despite many sharp attacks from prominent churchmen, no Scotist proposition has ever been the subject of papal censure and Scotist literature in general has received official commendation. Among leading early Scotists were Francis Mayron (d. 1327) and Pope Alexander V. (d. 1410). In the twentieth century

Scotism has been defended especially zealously by Deodot-Marie de Basley. See congruism.

See E. Longpré, *La Philosophie du B. Duns Scot.* (Paris, 1924). L.H.DEW.

Scotland, Church of: That one of the Presbyterian Churches* in Scotland which has consistently valued, and, throughout most of its existence, maintained an official state connection. It was constituted by action of the Scotch Estates, and the consequent meeting of the First General Assembly, in 1560; and was finally secured against successful attack from Roman Catholic quarters before the death of John Knox*. Almost immediately it had to defend itself against an effort, furthered by the royal power, to impose episcopal forms of government and of worship upon it. The struggle lasted about a century, but ended with the victory of Presbyterianism in 1688. Since then its only challenge has come in the form of schisms, based on opposition to the principle, or to some outcome of, the state connection. They began with the setting up of the Associate Presbytery in 1733, under Ebenezer Erskine*. The last and greatest of them was the Disruption of 1843. Since the middle of the nineteenth century the tendency within Scottish Presbyterism has been towards union; and this culminated in the uniting of the Church of Scotland and the United Free Church* in 1929. The united body retained the name, "The Church of Scotland", and it preserved the state connection, though in a form which provides for the spiritual freedom of the Church. Its present membership, not including "adherents", is about 1,300,000. See action sermon; Cameronians; catechism; Free Church of Scotland.

K. Hewatt, *Makers of the Scottish Church at the Reformation* (Edinburgh, 1920). A.K.R.

Scotland, Free Church of: See Free Church of Scotland.

Scotland, United Free Church of: See United Free Church of Scotland.

Scots Confession, The: A Calvinistic, strongly anti-Roman Catholic Confession, drawn up by John Knox* and five other ministers and adopted by the Scottish Estates in 1560. It served as the credal basis of Scottish Presbyterianism* until it was replaced by the Westminster Confession*.

See P. Schaff, *Creeds of Christendom* (1877), III, pp. 437-479. A.K.R.

scribe: The term scribe is the translation of the Hebrew *sopher,* and is used to describe the lay Jewish scholars of the four or five pre-Christian centuries in Palestine. Presumably these scholars were called scribes because, following the analogy of Babylonian custom, the Palestinian scribe was generally also the trained scholar. In an edict issued by Antiochus III, in the year 198 B.C., on his conquest of Palestine, he provides special immunities for the "scribes of the Temple." In various Rabbinic passages Moses* is described as a "scribe", and he may therefore be regarded, from the point of view of the Rabbinic tradition, as the founder of this calling. Ezra* bears the title "a ready scribe in the law of Moses" (Ezra 7.6) and it has been suggested that he was historically the first of the scribes. In the N.T., the term "scribe" is frequently associated with that of Pharisees*, presumably because the scribes were, as lay scholars, the leaders of the Pharisees. L.F.

scriptorium: (Lat., *scribere,* to write) A room in a monastic building devoted to the writing or copying of manuscripts. F.T.P.

Scripture: (Lat., *scriptura,* writing) In general, the religious literature of any people that is regarded by it as sacred and authoritative. In particular, the Old and New Testaments**. See sacred literatures; senses of Scripture. S.M.G.

scruple: Conscientious hesitation, doubt or misgiving about the fitness, moral or religious propriety of a course of action. R.W.F.

scrutiny: (Lat., *scrutinium* from *scrutari* to search, examine) 1. An examination of those who were about to receive baptism, regarding their faith and dispositions.

2. Examination of a candidate about to be promoted to Orders.

3. Form of ecclesiastical election and is made either by written ballot or by pronouncing the chosen name before legitimate scrutators alone. The former is the usual form of electing the Pope. Since 1139 the election is by the Cardinals alone; two-thirds majority being needed. To preserve secrecy the ballots must be burned after being counted. See conclave. B.S.

seal, sacramental: Commonly called "character". A spiritual sign, indelibly impressed on the soul by the sacraments of Baptism, Confirmation, and Holy Orders. By this seal Christians are deputed to certain offices and discerned from those not so deputed. This seal remains on the soul even in the life after death, adding to the glory of the good who go to heaven and to the shame of the wicked who go to hell.

Herve, III, 439 ss. B.S.

seal of confession: The most strict obligation of keeping entirely secret everything said by the penitent in confession for the purpose of obtaining absolution. Without the free consent of the penitent, the priest who heard the penitent's confession may not in any way use this information, not even to save himself from the threat of death.

Genicot II, 379. B.S.

Seamen's movement in the United States: A form of missionary enterprise which has from the time of its inception in the early nineteenth century stood as one of the finer examples of applied or "social" Christianity.

The years 1812 to 1826 were formative. During this period some eight local societies designed primarily to promote the spiritual welfare of seamen were established in coastal cities extending from Portland, Me., to New Orleans. The distribution of religious tracts among sailors and the holding of services on shore or anchored ships were especially emphasized. With view to exciting the general public to action the *American Sailor's Magazine* (N. Y., 1824-1825) and the *Mariner's Magazine* (N. Y., 1825-1826) were circulated.

The latter magazine under the energetic editorship of Rev. John Truair ushered the movement into its second phase. His stirring "Call from the Ocean; or an Appeal to the Christian in Behalf of Seamen" issued in 1826 led immediately to organization on a national scale. The various local societies pooled their resources to form in 1828 the American Seamen's Friend Society of New York, the announced purpose of which was: ". . . to improve the social and moral condition of Seamen, by uniting efforts of the wise and good in their behalf; by promoting in every port, Boarding Houses of good character, Savings Banks, Register Offices, Libraries, Reading Rooms and Schools; and also the ministrations of the Gospel, and other religious blessings".

Subsequent history has been essentially the translation of visions into realities. The registered private boarding house of 1828 has grown to be such a magnificent institution as the million dollar Seamen's House of present-day New York which serves at once as hotel, recreation, educational and religious center. The crude Savings Bank of 1829 founded to educate the sailor not to squander his money in disreputable dives has grown into a ten-story New York establishment with branches. Concern for the sailor's reading interests has quickly passed from the stage of shore library at home to concerted effort to place a loan library on every ship leaving port to the care of reading rooms in foreign ports, thereby affording opportunity for self-schooling both on land and sea. More specifically viewed as "ministrations of the gospel" have been the conducting of religious meetings for men at home bases, the sending of chaplains abroad to perform services in foreign ports, the distribution of Bibles and tracts, the publication of à *Seaman's Manual of Worship* (three basic editions 1830, 1887, 1927), the monthly issuance of the *Sailor's Magazine* (N. Y., 1828-1933) incorporating devotional helps and religious news, the annual presentation of good books or the Bible to Midshipmen graduating from the Naval Academy, together with a goodly number of other worthy projects. Throughout, the religious emphasis has been evangelical, but non-denominational. Societies in local ports have been under no compulsion to affiliate with the central society in New York but in most cases have willingly cooperated.

The *Mariner's Magazine* and the *Sailor's Magazine* (*supra*) provide a continuous history of the varied aspects, 1825-1933. The *Annual Report* of the American Seamen's Friend Society, 1833 to date will add official data. G. S. Webster, *The Seamen's Friend* (1932), is a centennial history of said society. G.P.A.

Sebastian, Saint: Christian martyr at Rome during Diocletian* persecution. Tradition says he was a soldier and that he was shot to death with arrows. Popular subject in religious art. K.H.C.

second birth: See baptism, non Christian; initiation rites; new birth; psychology of religion; regeneration; transmigration.

second blessing: See holiness churches; pentecostal sects.

Second Great Awakening: See American theology, early; Dwight, Timothy.

secondary cause: See cause.

secret societies in China: See Chinese religions.

Secrétan, Charles: (1815-1895) A French Swiss, who was professor of philosophy at the University of Lausanne. He understood the Christian dogmas as being purely ethical and wished them to be translated into a language that did not contradict the critical scientific spirit. Christ was for him only divine in his holiness. Justifying his faith in a revelation, he minimized the miraculous. For him Christ was the ultimate answer of the political and social question.

La philosophie de la liberté (Paris, 1849), 2 vols.; *La raison et le christianisme* (Lausanne, 1863); *La civilisation et la croyance* (Paris, 1887); *Le principe de la morale*, 2nd ed. (Paris, 1893). H.H.

sect: (Lat., *secta*, fr., *sequi*, to follow) In classical Latin, any group or movement (philosophical, medical, political or religious) claiming special leadership or teaching. In religion the term has indicated such a group or following *within* an organized religion (e.g., Pharisees, Sadducees, etc., in Judaism). In Catholic usage, essentially synonymous with heresy*, i.e., a religious body which has set itself up independently of the divinely established Church. For the several established churches of Protestantism, any nonconformist* or dissenting group. Used roughly by other Protestant churches with reference to smaller, more recently organized Christian bodies. In all these uses within the Christian religion, the term has been derogatory and therefore unacceptable to the groups to which it has been applied, such groups regarding themselves as true churches. The term has now received fairly sharp sociological definition, thanks to E. Troeltsch [*The Social Teaching of the Christ. Churches* (1931), Engl. tr.;] H. Richard Niebuhr [*The Social Sources of Denominationalism* (1929)] and Liston Pope [*Mill-hands and Preachers* (1942)]. So defined, a sect is a schismatic* group springing from, and developing in opposition to, an organized church and becoming independent of it. Finding its authority in what it regards as a truer understanding of the Scriptures or of primitive Christianity, it sustains a critical attitude toward the parent institution and, indeed, toward the patterns of contemporary culture in general; and seeks in its detachment a more positive realization of the Christian life. Developing sects find their fertile soil among the socially and economically insecure and tend to lose their sectarian features as the social and economic status of their membership improves. See Adventist sects; communistic settlements, religious; Confessions, Formal of the Christian Church; holiness churches; pentecostal sects; Russian sectarianism. E.T.R.

secular clergy: Men who have received Holy Orders in the R. C. Church and who live, not under the rule of a religious congregation but "in the world" (*in saecula*), devoting themselves chiefly to parochial work. Seculars do not take solemn vows of poverty and obedience but they do live in chastity. Since they are most essential to the ministry of the Church, they take ecclesiastical precedence over regulars. See regular clergy. V.J.B.

secularism: Specifically a variety of utilitarian social ethic (named and formulated by G. J. Holyoake, 1817-1906) which seeks human improvement without reference to religion and exclusively by means of human reason, science and social organization. In general that movement of protest against the dominance and control of human life by ecclesiastical bodies or by religious faith and dogma which had its new birth at the Renaissance*. It has developed into a positive and widely adopted outlook which aims to direct all activities and institutions by a non-religious concern for the goods of the present life and for social well-being. It is applied derogatively by religionists to that emancipation of all departments of life, science, philosophy, art, economics and politics, from central religious control which results in the fissiparous pursuit of specialized interests without any sense of the unity of life and which has initiated a crisis in the religious and cultural life of modern man. R.W.F.

secularization: (med; Ref.) The taking over of church property by the state for secular purposes; sometimes for selfish and unworthy ends, sometimes devoted to charitable and educational purposes. After the 4th century church had steadily accumulated property and by Middle Ages was large landowner in many countries. This was temptation to civil rulers with empty treasuries and as early as Charles Martel (8th cent.) confiscations were made. Became an issue in conflict between empire and papacy. Process of secularization was accelerated in areas that became Protestant at time of the Reformation, e.g., in Germany and Sweden and in the suppression of monasteries in England. K.H.C.

seder: (Heb., order) The order of the home service on the first and second nights of the Passover*. The ritual for the occasion is known as the *Seder Haggadah,* Order of the Narrative of the Passover, or *Haggadah**. S.S.C.

seduction: Enticement to wrong doing by false promises, specious arts of deceitful charms. Specifically in law the enticement of a woman to illicit sex relations by allurement or promise of marriage. R.W.F.

see: (Lat., *sedes*, seat) A particular bishopric, with its rights, traditions, and administration; Holy See or Apostolic See, the See of Rome. E.R.H.

Seeberg, Reinhold: (1859-1935) German Protestant theologian. Born at Pörrafer, Latvia. In 1884 he was privatdozent at Dorpat, in 1889 professor of Systematic Theology in Erlangen, and from 1898-1928 at Berlin where he died. He was the leading representative of the "Modern Positive School", which, with a strongly apologetic leaning, interpreted orthodox Lutheranism in terms of Hegel's and Fichte's** ethical idealism. For a long time he was president of the "Evangelisch-Sozialer Kongress". Conservative in politics he had a noticeable influence upon the rising nationalism of the post-1918 generation. His lasting significance is to be found mainly in his works on the history of the dogma. See neo-Lutheranism.

Principal works:
Lehrbuch der Dogmengeschichte, 4 vols. (1895-1920, the volume on Luther is a standard work); *Die Theologie des Joh. Duns Scotus: eine dogmengeschichtliche Untersuchung* (1900); *Die Grundwahrheiten der christlichen Religion* (1906, Engl. tr. 1908); *Aus Religion und Geschichte* (essays) (1908-1909), 2 vols.; *Offenbarung und Inspiration* (1909, Engl. tr. 1909); *System der Ethik* (1911, 2nd ed., 1920); *Christliche Dogmatik* (1924 ff.), 2 vols.; Autobiography in: *Die Religions-wissenschaft in Selbstdarstellungen* (1925), vol. I. O.A.P.

Seekers: In a religious sense commonly applied to the large number of persons in seventeenth century England not attached to any organized church, but seeking an expression of personal religion which should satisfy their needs. William Penn described them as having left "all visible churches and societies", and says they "wandered up and down as sheep without a shepherd, and as doves without their mates; seeking their beloved but could not find Him (as their souls desired to know Him) whom their souls loved above their chiefest joy." It was from the Seekers in the northern shires that the Society of Friends* recruited many of its early members.

W. C. Braithwaite, *The Beginnings of Quakerism* (1923), chaps. iii-iv; R. M. Jones, *Spiritual Reformers of the 16th and 17th Centuries* (1928). W.W.C.

seelsorge: See cure of souls.

selah: An obscure Heb. word occurring 71 times in the Psalter and 3 times in the psalm in Habakkuk 3; transliterated in the Eng. versions. Apparently from the stem s-l-l "to lift up" (sc., the voice), a directional rubric marking a liturgical response or refrain. R.B.Y.S.

Selected Scripture Lessons: See Sunday School movement in the United States.

self-defense: The act of defending one's person, property or reputation against destructive attacks. In law it is, under certain circumstances, recognized as a right which constitutes a valid plea against the charge of murder. Ethically the taking of another's life in self-defense may be justified on the ground that the aggressor is making war upon society in a situation where the normal protective machinery of the law cannot work until it is too late. The individual who acts in self-defense is thus willing the will and the good of society. But the exercise of self-defense poses many problems for the moral judgment. There are those who deny the right to employ violence in self-defense on religious or ethical grounds. R.W.F.

self-denial: The subordination or renunciation of one's own appetites, possessions, pleasures or purposes for the sake of realizing some higher end or larger good. It is ethically justifiable and praiseworthy in the promotion of any greater good though to be condemned as pernicious when practiced as an end in itself. While it is fundamental in asceticism, monasticism and Puritanism, in which it has found both high and aberrant expressions, it is an essential condition of daily life, personal development and communal existence, for these all require choices among alternatives, concentration of purpose, subordination of interests and division of labor if there is to be growth, achievement and interdependent living. In Christianity self-denial (taking up one's cross) is enjoined as necessary for discipleship. It involves renunciation of one's sinful self and positive, complete surrender to God's will. Here self-sacrifice is regarded as an act both of the human will and of divine working and is the highest expression of Christian love. R.W.F.

self-limitation: See finite God; infinite; omnipotence.

self-preservation: Biologically it is the instinctive endeavor of every organism to maintain its existence. This instinctive tendency has been made the imputed basis of a political doctrine that there is a natural right to life, even the right to defend one's life against the state that unjustly threatens its existence and well-being. In ethics it may refer 1) to the particular duty of preserving one's physical life in so far as this is in accord with the highest good or 2) to the view that the preservation of the individual in the struggle for existence is the supreme rule of conduct. The ideal here is the strong man for whom might is right. R.W.F.

self-realization: The moral ideal of a teleological, perfectionist theory of ethics which conceives the ethical goal as the fullest development of personality, i.e., as the comprehensive, lasting and harmonious realization of the potentialities of the person. Self-realization is a dynamic process of the actualization and organization of personal capacities; it involves not only the integration of the various levels of personal being but also the integration of the individual with society; and inasmuch as such self-realization is conducive to happiness it may be said to embrace eudaemonism*. Notable recent exponents of this theory are T. H. Green, F. H. Bradley, J. Seth and J. H. Muirhead. R.W.F.

selfishness: That excessive or exclusive self-love which consists in the determination of one's ambitions, choices and interests solely with reference to one's own advantage. Some ethicists, as T. Hobbes, hold that self-love is both the psychological motive and the ultimate ethical end of all action. Because of its personal and social consequences, selfishness is ethically condemned. There is a legitimate moral self-love, however, approved in both Christian and secular ethics. R.W.F.

Semi-Arianism: Broadly, the doctrines and party in the fourth-century Church which affirmed that the Son is in essence like (*homoiousios*), not identical with (*homoousios*), the Father. It was a mediating position between the Arians*, who had held essentially that the Son is different from the Father (*heteroousios*) and the Nicene Council, which had proclaimed their identity. See homoios; homoiousios; homoousios. Cf. Antioch, Synod of; Hilary of Poitiers. F.G.E.

Semi-Pelagianism: Unfortunately, it has been customary to characterize under the term "semi-pelagianism" a series of theologians in the fifth century A.D., who rejected with full conviction the Pelagian doctrine*, and were unable to accept entirely the Augustinian doctrine of grace. While much of Augustine impressed them, the whole appeared to them as containing too many innovations. They preferred the older view to Augustine's bold and extreme speculations about the absolute lack of freedom of the will to do good, the irresistible power of grace and predestination**.

P. Sublet, *Le sémipélagianisme* (Namur, 1897); F. Wörter, *Zur Dogmengeschichte des Semipelagianismus* (Paderborn, 1899). H.H.

seminaries: See seminaries, major Roman Catholic; theological schools, Jewish; theological schools, Protestant, United States and Canada.

seminaries, major Roman Catholic: Roman Catholic seminaries are of two kinds, major seminaries and preparatory or minor seminaries. The preparatory seminaries receive aspirants to the priesthood at 12 to 14 years of age; the course embraces the "traditional classical studies" which have long been included in the training of priests, and is roughly equivalent to a four-year high school course followed by the first two years of college. In 1940 there were 83 of these schools in the United States. In the major seminaries the young men receive their immediate preparation for ordination. The Third Plenary Council of Baltimore fixed the curriculum of diocesan seminaries to "embrace not fewer than six years," two of these years being spent in the study of philosophy and four in theology. In 1940 there were 98 major seminaries in the United States. They are divided, according to control, into two classes, the episcopal for the training of secular or diocesan clergy, and the religious for the training of the clergy of the various orders or societies.

MAJOR SEMINARIES

Alabama: St. Bernard Abbey, St. Bernard, Ala., Benedictine Fathers.

Arkansas: New Subiaco Abbey and Seminary, Subiaco, Ark., Benedictine Fathers; St. John's Home Missions Sem., Little Rock, Ark., Secular Clergy.

California: Dominguez Seminary, Compton, Calif., Claretian Missionary Fathers; Franciscan Theological Sem., Old Mission, Santa Barbara, Calif., Franciscan Fathers; St. Patrick's Seminary, Menlo Park, Calif., Society of St. Sulpice.

Colorado: The St. Thomas Theological Seminary, Denver, Colo., Vincentian Fathers.

Connecticut: St. Mary's Seminary, Ferndale, Norwalk, Conn., Holy Ghost Fathers.

District of Columbia: Atonement Seminary of the Holy Ghost, Brookland, D. C., Franciscan Fathers of the Atonement; Dominican House of Studies, Washington, D. C., Dominican Fathers; Holy Cross College, Washington, D. C., Congregation of the Holy Cross; The Marist College, Brookland, D. C., Society of Mary; Oblate Scholasticate, Washington. D. C., Oblates of Mary Immaculate; St. Joseph's Seminary, Brookland, D. C., St. Joseph's Society of the Sacred Heart; St. Paul's College, Brookland, D. C., Congregation of St. Paul; Theological College of the Catholic University, Washington, D. C., Society of St. Sulpice.

Illinois: College of St. Thomas Aquinas, River Forest, Ill., Dominican Fathers; Marian Hills Seminary, Hinsdale, Ill., Marian Fathers; Mater Dolorosa Seminary, Hillside, Ill., Servite Fathers; St. Bede Seminary, Peru, Ill., Benedictine Fathers; St. Joseph's Seminary, Teutopolis, Ill., Order of Friars Minor; St. Mary of the Lake Seminary, Mundelein, Ill., Secular Clergy and Society of Jesus; St. Mary's Mission House, Techny, Ill., Society of the Divine Word; St. Mary's Seminary, Lemont, Ill., Slovene Fathers; St. Procopius Seminary, Lisle, Ill., Benedictine Fathers.

Indiana: Moreau Seminary, Notre Dame, Ind., Congregation of Holy Cross; Holy Family Theological Seminary, Oldenburg, Ind., Franciscan Fathers; St. Meinrad Seminary, St. Meinrad, Ind., Benedictine Fathers; West Baden College, West Baden Springs, Ind., Society of Jesus.

Kansas: St. Augustine Mission Seminary, Kansas City, Kans., Augustinian Recollects; St. Benedict's Seminary, Atchison, Kans., Benedictine Fathers; St. Fidelis Seminary, Victoria, Kans., Capuchin Order; St. Mary's College, St. Mary's, Kans., Society of Jesus.

Kentucky: Sacred Heart Retreat, Louisville, Ky., Passionist Fathers.

Louisiana: Notre Dame Seminary, New Orleans, La., Marist Fathers.

Maryland: Mt. St. Mary's Seminary, Emmitsburg, Md., Diocesan Clergy; St. Joseph Passionist Monastery, Baltimore, Md., Passionist Fathers; St. Mary's Seminary, Baltimore, Md., Sulpician Fathers; Woodstock College, Woodstock, Md., Society of Jesus.

Massachusetts: Oblate Fathers College, South Natick, Mass., Oblates of Mary Immaculate; St. Gabriel's Monastery, Brighton, Mass., Passionist Fathers; St. John's Boston Ecclesiastical, Brighton, Mass., Secular Clergy; Weston College, Weston, Mass., Society of Jesus.

Michigan: St. Paul's Monastery, Brightmoor, Mich., Passionist Fathers; SS Cyril and Methodius Seminary, Orchard Lake, Mich., Secular Clergy.

Minnesota: St. John's Seminary, Collegeville, Minn., Benedictine Fathers; St. Paul Seminary, St. Paul, Minn., Diocesan Clergy.

Mississippi: St. Augustine's Seminary, Bay St. Louis, Miss., Society of the Divine Word.

Missouri: Kendrick (St. Louis Roman Catholic Theological) Seminary, St. Louis, Mo., Vincentian Fathers; St. Mary's Seminary, Perryville, Mo., Vincentian Fathers.

Nebraska: Immaculate Conception Seminary, Hastings, Nebr., Crosier Fathers; St. Columban's Seminary, St. Columbans, Nebr., Society of St. Columban.

New Jersey: Don Bosco College, Newton, N. J., Salesian Society; Immaculate Conception Seminary, Ramsey, N. J., Diocesan Clergy; St. Mary's Monastery, Morristown, N. J., Benedictine Fathers; St. Michael's Passionist Seminary, Union City, N. J., Passionist Fathers.

New Mexico: Seminario Pontifico Central Mexicano de Nuestra Senora de Guadelupe, Montezuma, N. M., Society of Jesus.

New York: Immaculate Conception Monastery, Jamaica, N. Y., Passionist Fathers; Immaculate Conception Seminary, Huntington, N. Y., Secular Clergy; Maryknoll Seminary, Maryknoll P. O., N. Y., Catholic Foreign Mission Society of America; Mount St. Alphonsus Seminary, Esopus, N. Y., Redemptorist Fathers; Oblate House of Philosophy, Newburgh, N. Y., Oblates of Mary Immaculates; Seminary of Our Lady of Angels, Niagara University P. O., N. Y., Vincentian Fathers; Seminary of Our Lady of Salette, Altamont, N. Y., Missionaries of Our Lady of La Salette; St. Anthony on Hudson, Rensellaer, N. Y., Order of Friars Minor Conventual; St. Bernard's Seminary, Rochester, N. Y., Secular Clergy; St. Bonaventure's Seminary, St. Bonaventure, N. Y., Friars Minor; St. Joseph's Seminary, Yonkers, N. Y., Secular Clergy; St. Mary's Monastery, Dunkirk, N. Y., Passionist Fathers; St. Stephen's House of Studies, Croghan, N. Y., Franciscan Fathers.

Ohio: Dominican House of Studies, Somerset, O., Dominican Fathers; Mount St. Mary of the West, Norwood, O., Secular Clergy; Our Lady of the Angels Seminary, Cleveland, O., Franciscan Fathers; Our Lady of Carey Seminary, Carey, O., Friars Minor Conventual; Our Lady of the Lake Seminary, Cleveland, O., Secular Clergy; Pontifical College Josephinum, Worthington, O., Secular Clergy; Sacred Heart Seminary, Shelby, O., Missionaries of the Sacred Heart; St. Charles Seminary, Carthagena, O., Society of Precious Blood; St. Joseph's Seminary, Cleveland, O., Fathers of the Blessed Sacrament.

Oregon: Mt. Angel Seminary, St. Benedict, Oreg., Benedictine Fathers.

Pennsylvania: St. Ann's Monastery, Scranton, Pa., Passionist Fathers; St. Charles Seminary, Overbrook, Philadelphia, Pa., Secular Clergy; St. Francis Seminary, Lorette, Pa., Third Order Regular of St. Francis of Penance; St. Mary's Hall, Augustinian Scholasticate, Villanova, Pa., Augustinian Fathers; St. Vincent Seminary, Latrobe, Pa., Benedictine Fathers.

Texas: De Mazenrod Scholasticate, Rt. 10, San Antonio, Tex., Oblates of Mary Immaculate; St. John's Seminary, San Antonio, Tex., Diocesan Clergy; St. Mary's Seminary, La Porte, Tex., Diocesan Clergy; Scotus College, Hebbronville, Tex., Franciscan Fathers.

Washington: Mt. St. Michael's Scholasticate, Hillyard Station, Spokane, Wash., Society of Jesus; St. Edward's Seminary, Seattle, Wash., Sulpician Fathers.

Wisconsin: Immaculate Conception Seminary, Oconomowoc, Wis., Redemptorist Fathers; St. Anthony's Monastery, Marathon, Wis., Capuchin Fathers; St. Francis College, Burlington, Wis., Franciscan Fathers; St. Francis Seminary, St. Francis, Wis., Diocesan Clergy; St. Mary of the Angels Theological Seminary, Green Bay, Wis., Franciscan Fathers; St. Norbert Seminary, West de Pere, Wis., Premonstratensian Canons.

L.J.S.

Semites, religion of: The term "Semites" (first used, by A. L. Schlözer in 1781) was derived from Gen. 10:22, where the sons of Shem are: Elam, Asshur, Arphaxad (i.e., Hebrews and Arabs), Lud (i.e., Lydia), and Aram. The Semites are a group of nations who lived in Western Asia south of the Taurus and Armenia, and west of Iran. They constitute a linguistic unit (like the Indo-Europeans) but by no means a racial unit. The Semitic languages are classified as follows: I) East-Semitic (Akkadian, Babylonian, Assyrian). II) North-Semitic: a) Aramaic group (Eastern: Syriac, Mandaean, the language of the Babylonian Talmud; Western: Aramaic inscriptions, Biblical Aramaic, Palestinian Jewish and Christian Aramaic, Palmyrene, Nabataean); b) Canaanitic or Amoritic group (Phoenician, Ugaritic* (Ras Shamra), Hebrew, Moabitic; also Punic (Carthage)). III) South-Semitic: a) Arabic (Northern: inscriptions, classical Arabic, modern dialects; Southern: Minaean and Sabaean inscriptions; also Ethiopic). It is generally thought that the Arabian peninsula was the original homeland of the Semites, although Babylonia, North Africa, and Amurru (in the Lebanon region) have also been suggested. It is generally supposed that the Semites poured out of Arabia in great waves about 3000 (Amorites), 2500 (Akkadians), 2000 (Canaanite-Phoenicians), 1500 (Arameans and Hebrews), 500 B.C. (Nabataeans), as the Arabian Moslem set forth after the death of Mohammed in 632. Even if such was the case, with the exception of the Bedouin Arabs, none of the "Semitic" nations (Babylonian, Assyrians, Syrians, Phoenicians, Canaanites, Israelites, Moabites, Ammonites, Edomites, etc.,) in historic times exhibits the anthropological characteristics of a supposed "Semitic" racial group; only their languages are closely related. The religions of these nations, like their cultures, vary profoundly and should be studied individually. Since the three great monotheistic religions of salvation (Judaism, Christianity, and Islam) arose on Semitic soil out of the religion of the primitive Semites (directly out of the prophetic reformation of the religion of Israel), it may be said with E. Renan that "the tent of the Semitic patriarch was the starting point of mankind's religious progress."

It has been said that the earliest Semitic religion was monotheism (E. Renan, M. J. Lagrange), totemism (W. Robertson Smith), ancestor worship (Herbert Spencer), or polydaemonism (J. Wellhausen); the original significance of animal sacrifice would correspond to one of these theories. Although traces of all these notions about the gods may be detected in the polytheistic systems of Semitic nations in historic times, polydaemonism seems to have prevailed among the early Semites. They regarded stones, trees, springs, mountains, and other natural objects as the domiciles of spirits (*numina loci*), each of which was generically called an *il* (Arabic *ilah*, Hebrew *el*) and resembled the jinn of later Arabs. A few among them, like the el of a spring who saved Hagar and Ishmael from death in the desert (Gen. 16:13-14) and the el of a stone who made Jakob rich (Gen. 31:13; 35:7, 15), through such outstanding acts acquired a personality and a history, were given a personal name (El Roi and El Bethel ["the el of the domicile of the el"], respectively), and received regular worship: thus they emerged from the anonymous class of the els and became gods. Some of the gods remained attached to their domicile, which became the goal of pilgrimages (Arabic *khaj*, Hebrew *khag* [festival]), and were worshiped by passing tribes; others were adopted by certain tribes as their gods, and thus moved about with their tribe. Eventually El (or Ilah) was used as a proper name for a particular god, so among the Phoenicians (in the Ras Shamra poems, El, "the father of years," is the supreme god; Philo of Byblos identifies him with Kronos), among the Arameans (Panammu's inscription on a statue of Hadad, found at Zenjirli), among the Arabs (Allah [i.e., al-Ilah, the God] was becoming the supreme god even before Mohammed), and in the Book of Job (El is the one true God). The strong sense of tribal solidarity among the nomadic Semites (manifested in blood revenge, circumcision [an ancient initiation rite], and particularly in war) was based, at least in principle, on ties of blood. Accordingly, the tribal god was regarded as the father (or some other relation) of the tribe. Just as blood sealed the covenant between two parties in Arabia (Herodotus III:8), so Yahweh became the god of Abraham by walking between the two bleeding halves of sacrificial victims (Gen. 15:9-12, 17-18). The earliest sanctuaries were natural objects (springs, trees, mountains, stones) inhabited by a god. The rites of worship (purifications in approaching a sacred spot, sacrifices, offerings, prayers), the pilgrimages, and the celebration of the festivals (with dancing and feasting), did not at first require a regular priesthood; the earliest Semitic priests were probably diviners. The integrity of the clan was secured by the iron rule of ancestral customs, in which no distinction was made between social, legal, ethical, and religious obligations or tabus. Out of such crude beginnings arose the polytheism of the civilized Semitic kingdoms, and later the great monotheistic religions. See altar; blood.

W. W. Baudissin, *Studien zur semitischen Religionsgeschichte* (Leipzig, 1876 and 1878), 2 vols.; J. Wellhausen, *Reste arabischen Heidentums* (Berlin, 1887, 2nd ed., 1897); F. Baethgen, *Beiträge zur semitischen Religionsgeschichte* (Berlin, 1888); W. Robertson Smith, *Lectures on the Religion of the Semites* (London, 1889, 3rd ed. (by S. A. Cook), 1927); S. I. Curtiss, *Primitive Semitic Religion today* (London, 1902); M. J. Lagrange, *Etudes sur les religions sémitiques* (Paris, 1902, 2nd ed., 1905); A. Lods, *Israel* (1932); G. A. Barton, *Semitic and Hamitic Origins* (1934); E. Dhorme, *La religion des Hébreux nomades* (Bruxelles, 1937); F. V. Winnett, "Primitive Arabian and Semitic Religion" in *Review of Religion*, 4 [1939], 282-285.

R.H.P.

Semler, Johann Salomo: (1725-91) Church historian and biblical critic; Professor of Theology in Halle from 1757. In his more than 170 writings he developed the scientific treatment of theology in contrast to pietistic edification. His investigation of the canon challenged the ruling ideas of biblical inspiration, and his rational and historical approach challenged the finality of dogma.

C.T.C.

Seneca: (c. 4 B.C.-A.D. 65) One of the chief representatives of Roman Stoicism*. Born at Corduba, Spain; early entered public life in Rome from which he was banished in 41 A.D.; recalled, eight years later, as tutor to the young Nero; honored for a period as a trusted imperial minister; forced finally to retire and to take his own life. Like Epictetus and Marcus Aurelius**, not philosophically original, but a devoted teacher of Stoic ethical and religious ideas. Wrote extensively on various subjects, but most influentially on practical moral questions. His essays and letters have had wide reading within the Christian Church.

E.T.R.

senses of Scripture: Origen* developed the theory that Scripture has a three-fold sense, literal, moral and spiritual. Later his "spiritual" sense was divided into "allegorical" and "anagogical,"** and these principles of hermeneutics* governed Biblical exegesis* until the time of the Reformation. The Reformers were hard-headed literalists. Luther declared: "The literal sense of Scripture alone is the whole essence of faith and of Christian theology." S.M.G.

Sentences: The title of Peter Lombard's* (died 1160) famous book *Libri Quattuor Sententiarum.* This most commented upon book of the Middle Ages is a compilation of statements taken from the works of the Church Fathers, especially from those of Saint Augustine, arranged according to the four topics On God, On the Creatures, On the Incarnation and the virtues and on the Seven Sacraments. The innumerable commentaries written to this book and its central position in the curriculum of theological studies is the best illustration of the spirit of submission to authorities so characteristic for the Middle Ages. S.C.T.

sentimentalism: The view that human nature is inherently good and therefore amenable to the power of sympathy. Such a view is implicit in much of the literature of the 18th century, sentimental drama and fiction being then well defined types. Mackenzie's *Man of Feeling* (1771) is an extreme example of a class which includes such familiar works as Richardson's *Pamela* (1740) and Goldsmith's *Vicar of Wakefield* (1766). L.W.C.

Separate Baptists: A group of Baptist churches which "separated" from the regular group in the "New Light" controversy in connection with the work of Whitefield* and the Tennants in the middle of the eighteenth century. Most of the separating churches rejoined the regular group, but one body in North Carolina developed considerable strength and the movement spread through other states. In theology they are mildly Arminian, and differ little from the larger Baptist groups. They practice immersion and feet washing. There are 69 churches and about 5,000 members. E.T.C.

separatists, German communities: See communistic settlements, religious.

Separatists, Protestant: A term used to designate the English Independents or Congregationalists* who wished to separate from the established church. This involved the loss of government financial support as well as freedom from state control, and it approximates the position later realized by all churches in the United States. Independent is a more inclusive term covering all those who desired each church to be legally independent with no ecclesiastical authority higher than that of the local institution. Consequently the Separatists must be distinguished from the Non-Separatist Independents who wished to remain within the established church and in time achieve a state-supported and state-established Independency. It was a group of Separatists who settled Plymouth Colony, while Non-Separatist Independents were responsible for the establishment of Massachusetts Bay Colony. See Brewster, William; independency.

Perry Miller, *Orthodoxy in Massachusetts* (1933). W.S.H.

Sephardim: (Sepharad, Obadiah 20, traditionally translated as Spain) Jews who lived in the Iberian Peninsula until approximately the end of the fifteenth century, and their descendants. D.S.P.

seppuku: (Lit., "cut abdomen") Japanese suicide by disembowelment. D.C.H.

Septuagesima: The third Sunday before Lent or the ninth before Easter. See church year cycle. E.R.H.

Septuagint: See Alexandrian Library; LXX; Old Testament; targum; versions of the Bible, ancient.

sequence: (Lat., *sequentia*) A rhythmical hymn, usually in honor of some feast or saint—often used in the Middle Ages following (hence the name) the Gradual* between Epistle and Gospel. E.R.H.

sequence: (or prose) A particular type of trope* which closes the Alleluia*. The long melisma on the final vowel of the Alleluia was divided into phrases for ease in breathing. To assist in remembering the elaborate series of notes each musical phrase was given words in syllable style. The origin of the sequence has been falsely attributed to Notker Balbulus, a 9th century monk of St. Gall, who called his sequences hymns.

G. Reese, *Music in the Middle Ages* (1940). E.H.B.

Seraphim: (Hebrew *Saraph*) Winged guardians of God's throne (Isa. 6, 2.6)—associated with Cherubim* in Book of Enoch XX, 7; LXI.10; LXXI. 7; — originally identified with "fiery serpent" of Deut. 8, 15 and "winged Saraph" of Isaiah 14, 29; 30, 6. N.G.

Serapion: A bishop of the Church in Egypt in the 4th century, a friend of Athanasius, and a defender of the Nicene Faith at the Council of Sardica in 343. S.M.G.

Serapis: See mystery religions.

Serbian Orthodox Church: See Eastern Orthodox Churches.

sermon: (from Lat., *sermo,* talk) A religious discourse delivered in connection with Christian worship; in origin the name marks it as more informal than an oration, though formal rhetoric has often found a place in sermon composition. See homily; preaching. E.R.H.

(Servatus) Lupus of Ferrières: (ca. 805—ca. 862) Abbot. Friendly to both Gottschalk and Rabanus Maurus**, he was a humanistic scholar, more concerned with philology, Boethian prosody, textual criticism, pure Latinity, and collecting

manuscripts than the contemporary theological controversies. He carried on vast correspondence regarding learned interests and was employed by many writers to improve their literary style.
A.C.

Servetus, Michael: (1511-1553) Born in Spain and trained in law, Servetus came to public attention through his studies in medicine and theology. In the former he is credited with the first modern understanding of the pulmonary circulation of the blood. In the latter he became a strong and argumentative anti-Trinitarian. He wrote *De Trinitatis Erroribus,* 1531, and *Christianismi Restitutio,* 1553, sharply attacking the doctrines of the Trinity, the Two-Nature Christ, and Infant Baptism. Condemned by the Roman ecclesiastical authorities of Lyons, he escaped and came to Geneva where Calvin* was slowly gaining control. There condemned as a heretic, he was burned at the stake by order of the City of Geneva on October 27, 1553.
E.P.B.

Servites: A mendicant order founded near Florence in Italy in the thirteenth century and soon spreading over Europe and into the Orient and in the nineteenth century to England and America. See Annunciation, Orders of. Cf. Seven Sorrows of our Lady.
L.R.W.

session: The court in a particular Presbyterian congregation to which is delegated responsibility and powers of general oversight (including supervision of other local courts, such as the board of trustees and the board of deacons), but having special oversight over the spiritual welfare of the congregation. Representatives of sessions constitute the membership of higher courts, such as Presbyteries, Synods, and the General Assembly. The session is made up of the pastor (or pastors) and the active ruling elders.
A.K.R.

Set: (Egyptian) God of kings of Upper Egypt; god of darkness, and enemy of Horus*, the sun or sky god of Lower Egypt; in myth of Osiris*; Set accomplishes the murder of his brother, Osiris, by forcing his body in a chest and throwing the chest into the Nile: came to be regarded as an enemy of Egypt; a temple to him erected by the Hyksos*.
F.L.P.

seven deadly sins: Various lists of capital, principal or deadly sins appear in patristic literature. John Cassian* described eight: gluttony, fornication, avarice, anger, dejection (*tristitia*), sloth (*accedia*), vainglory and pride. Gregory the Great's* list of seven is in a different order: Pride (the source of the others), envy, anger, dejection, avarice, gluttony and lust. Both classifications were widely repeated: that of Gregory came to prevail. Each of these capital sins was attended by a number of minor sins. The *Penitentials** and other ascetic books of guidance prescribe treatments for the deadly sins; and the seven penitential psalms* were severally matched against them.
J.T.M.

seven gifts of the Holy Spirit: In scholastic theology the sanctifying gifts of the Holy Spirit are wisdom, understanding, counsel, fortitude, knowledge, piety and the fear of the Lord. Cf. Is. 11:2. These are distinct from the charismatic gifts indicated in the N.T., from the "fruits of the spirit" of which the classical list is in Gal. 5:22-23, and from the seven virtues*.
J.T.M.

seven penitential psalms: Psalms 6, 32, 38, 51, 102, 130, 143 (numbers as in Protestant versions) were so distinguished by St. Augustine, it is said, on his deathbed. They were chanted as penitential exercises, and were sometimes set to counteract respectively the seven deadly sins*. To pride was assigned Ps. 32; to wrath, Ps. 6; to envy, Ps. 130; to avarice, Ps. 102; to gluttony, Ps. 38; to sloth, Ps. 143; to lust, Ps. 51.

C. L. Marson, *The Psalms at Work* (1895), 2nd ed.
J.T.M.

Seven Sorrows of Our Lady: A devotion promoted by the Order of Servants of Mary (Servites*) and celebrated in two feasts—one in Lent dating from the late Middle Ages, the other on September 15 from 1686. See Stabat Mater.
E.R.H.

seven virtues: The four "cardinal virtues,"* prudence, temperance, fortitude and justice, were distinguished by Plato and the Stoics**. To these were added by Christian writers the three "theological virtues," faith, hope and love. Ambrose gives a Christian interpretation of the cardinal virtues: thus he makes kindness and altruism essential to justice; patience to fortitude. The virtues are variously listed by ecclesiastical writers, often without reference to the number seven. Aristotle's conception of virtues as habits enters into the scholastic teaching. Virtues are distinct from duties.

O. Schilling, *Lehrbuch des Moraltheologie* (1927), vol. I.
J.T.M.

seven works of mercy, spiritual and corporal: In scholastic theology (Aquinas, *Summa* II, ii, 32) the seven spiritual works of mercy are: to teach the ignorant, to counsel the doubtful, to console the sad, to reprove the sinner, to forgive the offender, to bear with the oppressive and troublesome (*onerosos et graves*), and to pray for all. The corporal works of mercy are: to feed the hungry, to give drink to the thirsty, to clothe the naked, to shelter the homeless, to visit the sick and prisoners, to ransom captives and to bury the dead. Cf. Matt. 25:35-44. The works of mercy are not counsels of perfection but required by natural law. They are variously catalogued, explained and illustrated in many popular handbooks of medieval piety.

A. Koch, and A. Preuss, *Moral Theology* (1924), vol. IV, 2nd ed.
J.T.M.

Seventh Day Adventist denomination: See Adventists.

Seventh Day Baptists: Baptists who observe the Jewish Sabbath* rather than the first day of the week. The group represents a survival of the Fifth Monarchy* movement in England and adopted their particular emphasis in reaction against the identification of the Lord's Day with the Jewish Sabbath by the Westminster Assembly. Cf. Sabbatarianism. See Baptists. W.S.H.

There are now about 66 churches and 6,700 members. E.T.C.

Seventh Day Baptists: (German, 1728) A group of three small Baptist churches in Pennsylvania (137 members), survivors of the work of John Conrad Beissel, who in 1732 organized the famous Ephrata Society* as a monastic society on the basis of celibacy and community of goods. The community still survives, but the original principles have long since disappeared. These churches have affinities with the Dunkers*. They observe the seventh day as the Sabbath, bless infants, teach non-resistance, wash feet, anoint the sick, and baptize by trine forward immersion.

E.T.C.

Severus, Sulpicius: (ca. 360-425) A Latin Church historian. Author of "The Chronicle," a history of the world to A.D. 400, and a "Life of St. Martin." S.M.G.

Sexagesima: The second Sunday before Lent or the eighth before Easter. See church year cycle.

E.R.H.

sext: The office of the sixth hour. See divine office. E.R.H.

sexton: (Middle English from Lat. *sacer*) A church officer who cares for the fabric of a church, rings the bells, digs graves, etc. T.J.B.

Seydel, Rudolf: (1835-1892) Was professor of philosophy in Leipzig. He preferred to labor in the history of religion and write about the problem and essence of religion. His speculations remind one of Schelling*, whose intellectual intuition he accepted for the apprehension of the absolute.

Das Evangelium von Jesu in seinen Verhältnissen zur Buddha Sage und Buddhalehre mit fortlaufender Rücksicht auf andere Religionskreise untersucht (Leipzig, 1882); *Die Buddhalegende und das Leben Jesu* (Leipzig, 1884); *Religion und Wissenschaft* (Breslau, 1887); *Religionsphilosophie im Umriss*, ed. by P. W. Schmiedel (Freiburg and Leipzig, 1893); H. Lischewski, *Über R. Seydels Religionsphilosophie* (Erlangen, 1902). H.H.

Shabbethai Zvi Ben Mordecai: Born 1626 at Smyrna, died 1676 in Albania. Jewish mystic and ascetic who lost all mental balance and proclaimed himself a Messiah. The times were indeed ripe for such a claimant. Between 1648 and 1658 at least 100,000 Jews had been massacred in Eastern Europe; and everywhere men awaited the divine emissary who would vindicate Israel. Shabbethai journeyed throughout the Orient and won large numbers of followers, among them the very influential and wealthy Raphael Joseph Chelebi, treasurer of the Court of the Cairo governor, the Amsterdam rabbis Isaac Aboab and Raphael Moses d'Aguilar, and two fellow-students of Spinoza*, Moses Zacuto and Isaac Noar. He proclaimed himself the Messiah in Gaza in 1666 with due solemnity; and large sections of Jewry hailed him as their deliverer. Shabbethai came to Constantinople with the mission of conquering the Sultan by a miracle but he was imprisoned on landing. His followers continued to believe in him and prayed for his release. The sudden appearance of another pseudo-prophet from Galicia who predicted the coming of a different Messiah discredited Shabbethai; and in the end, to save his life, he embraced Mohammedanism. A great dissolutionment followed among those who had believed in him, Shabbethai, meanwhile, trying to retain his hold by playing a double role as a Mohammedan and a Jew. Turkish officials finally grew tired of his plots and banished him to Dulcingo, Albania, where he died. See pseudo-Messiahs.

J. Kastein, *Messiah of Ismir* (1931). B.Z.B.

Shaffer Foundation, The John C.: Established at Northwestern University, Evanston, Ill. and designed "to promote the appreciation of the life, character, teachings and influence of Jesus."

Lecturers to date have been: Bishop Francis J. McConnell, Professor John Adams Scott, Dr. S. Parkes Cadman, Dr. Charles Reynolds Brown, Dr. Ernest F. Tittle, Dr. Albert E. Day, Dr. Paul A. Wolfe, Dr. W. W. Whitehouse and Bishop George Craig Stewart. Publications include: *We Would Know Jesus* (1936) by John Adams Scott; *The Life of Jesus Christ in His Church* (1941) by Bishop George Craig Stewart; *Christ of God* (1929) by S. Parkes Cadman. C.S.B.

Shaffer Lectures: A lectureship at the Yale University Divinity School, established May 16, 1929, in memory of Kent Shaffer, Ph.B., 1907. The lectures are concerned with some phase of the life, character, and teachings of Jesus. Among the courses have been those by Benjamin W. Bacon, Jesus The Son of God, 1930; Toyohiko Kagawa, The Rediscovery of Christ's Life, 1932; Richard Roberts, That Strange Man on His Cross, 1934; C. Harold Dodd, Parables of the Kingdom, 1935; Ralph W. Sockman, Paradoxes of Jesus, 1936; Martin Dibelius, The Sermon on the Mount, 1937; James Moffatt, Jesus Christ the Same, 1940; William Paton, The Gospel and World Issues, 1942. L.A.W.

Shaik 'Adi: See devil worshipers.

shaikh: A leader in the mystical orders of Islam. The election of such a leader by his own group is democratic and enhances his influence with his followers. He instructs and develops loyalty and upholds moral standards. P.E.J.

Shaker communities: See communistic settlements, religious.

Shaktaism: See shakti.

shakti, Shaktism, Saktism: The Sanskrit term *shakti* means energy, power or force. Shaktism then is the worship of power or force in the universe conceived of as a goddess. Every god is thought of as having his shakti and in Shaktism she is worshiped rather than her consort. The major Shakta sects worship the shakti of Shiva as Kali or Durga. The Tantras* are their scriptures. The worship of the lefthand shaktas is held in secret and is orgiastic in character. C.S.B.

shamanism: Narrowly, a phase of the religion of Tunguese people: faith and practices centering in the shaman (priest or medicine-man*), involving priestly, prophetic, and medical functions. Broadly, similar features in the religions of other peoples, such as found among American Indians. Faith and practice based upon the theory of possession, in which a spirit from outside the individual takes possession of the individual and operates through the possessed one. F.L.P.

Shamash: Ancient Semitic Babylonian sun god; god of divination; Assyrian all-seeing god of right and justice, friendly to hunters, herdsmen, and travelers; judge of the innocent and guilty. F.L.P.

Shammai: See Bet Hillel and Bet Shammai.

Shang-ti: See Chinese Terminology.

Shankara, Shankaracharya: An Indian philosopher born late in the eighth century. He is best known for his doctrine of absolute or unqualified monism, or absolute nonduality, which, briefly stated, is that Brahman* alone is real, the phenomenal world is unreal, or mere illusion. Individual souls have no reality apart from Brahman, though caught by *maya** or illusion they as well as the world around them seem to have a kind of reality. This is due to ignorance of the alone reality of Brahman. This being so, salvation or *moksha* comes in the knowledge of the identity of the individual soul with the world soul, Brahman. Little is known certainly concerning Shankara's life, but he is said to have travelled widely throughout India, refuting other interpretations of the Vedanta* and establishing his own. He wrote commentaries on the Brahma-Sutras, on ten of the principal Upanishads*, on the Bhagavad-gita* and other important works. C.S.B.

Shedd, William Greenough Thayer: (1820-1894) A Calvinist theologian who, after professorial appointments in the University of Vermont, and in Auburn and Andover Seminaries, was successively Professor of Biblical Literature (1863-74) and Professor of Doctrinal Theology (1874-90) in the Union Theological Seminary, New York City.

His best known books were *A History of Christian Doctrine* (1865), 2 vols.; *Dogmatic Theology* (1889-94), 3 vols.; *Orthodoxy and Heterodoxy* (1893); and *Calvinism Pure and Mixed* (1893). A.K.R.

shekinah: (Heb., dwelling, presence) Literally, divine presence. As in the Targumim so in Rabbinic writings, its usage is prompted by 1) motives of reverence and 2) need of preserving the sense of Divine nearness. Generally representing the idea of immanence, where it is employed as a mere metonymy for God, it denotes transcendence. The danger of anthropomorphism, which it sought to avert, was increased by its usage, taking on occasionally the character of a quasi-independent being. However, care was taken not to permit it to figure as an intermediary. See memra. S.S.C.

shema: (Heb. hear) The watchword of Jewish monotheism, taking its name from the first word of Deut. 6:4, "Hear, O Israel, the Lord our God, the Lord is One." It consists of three sections: a) Deut. 6:4-9; b) Deut. 11:13-21; c) Num. 15:37-41. (Cf. Matt. 19. 16ff.). Its use in Jewish worship is preceded and followed by benedictions. S.S.C.

Shemoneh Esreh: (Lit. eighteen) The name given to the collection of benedictions (originally 18; now 19) which forms the main section of the morning, afternoon and evening prayers. (On festivals and the Sabbath*, the thirteen middle benedictions which are of a petitionary nature are not recited; yet the name Shemoneh Esreh was retained). This section is also known as Tefillaḥ, the prayer *par excellence* and Amidah (standing) referring to the position of the worshiper during its recitation. E.B.—L.F.

Shên: See Chinese Terminology.

sheol: (Heb. etymology uncertain) Literally, pit, grave, and nether-world. A dark and dreary subterranean abode of the dead, where the shades are given over to deep sleep, forgetfulness, silence, and destruction. While generally evoking a sense of horror and dismay, some sufferers welcomed it as a place of rest and social equality (Job 3:17-19). The practice of necromancy assumed that a degree of consciousness continued in Sheol, and could be temporarily aroused. Sheol is pictured as a gaping monster and as "the appointed house of all living", whence none return (Isa. 5.14; Job 10:21; 30:23; 7:10). The growing belief in God's sovereignty in death as in life, transformed Sheol into the scene of punishment of the wicked. In post-Canonical Jewish literature Sheol merged with Gehinom (Gr. Geena, based on Jer. 7:31-32; Isa. 66:24). The Septuagint renders Sheol with *Haides*, and the Authorized version occasionally with *Hell** (e.g., Deut. 32:22; Ps. 9:17; 18:5; Isa. 14:9). See eschatology. S.S.C.

Shepherd of Hermas: See Hermas, Shepherd of.

Shih Ching: See Chinese Terminology.

Shi ites: (Arabic, meaning sectarians) One of the two leading divisions of Islam, the other and larger being the *Sunnites**. The *Shi ites* represent the Persian branch of Islam, and resent the passing of the Caliphate to other lands. They regard Ali and his followers as divinely ordained caliphs*, and continue to look for the true leader (*imam* or *mahdi***). They hold many festivals cherish saints, produce more dervishes. Sufism and Bahaism** arose from them. See Ismailis; Kharijites; Mohammedanism; mujtahid; Mutazilites; Persia, religions of. P.E.J.

Shin Ritsu: See Buddhist Terminology: Disciplinary School.

Shinto religion and theology: Shintō, or Shindō, is the Sino-Japanese reading of two ideograms that are rendered into pure Japanese by the term, *Kami-no-Michi,* meaning "The Way of the *Kami,*" or "The Way of the Gods." Shintō thus signifies the characteristic cult practices and beliefs, relating for the most part to the worship of the indigeneous Japanese deities, whereby the Japanese people have celebrated, dramatized, interpreted, and supported the chief values of their group life.

The term Shintō in its proper historical usage does not carry us back to the earliest manifestations of the Japanese national religion. The word does not appear in the literature until the latter part of the sixth century of the Western Era. In its more remote stages Shintō as a system appears to have been nameless. The designation came into existence after the introduction of Buddhism into Japan and was evidently created in order to distinguish the original Japanese cultus from the Way of the Buddha.

Modern Shintō has two main branches. The one has special relations with the official organization of the national life. The other is dependent entirely on the voluntary support of adherents for institutional maintenance and propaganda. The former is generally called State (*Kokka*) Shintō, sometimes Shrine (*Jinja*) Shintō because of having its ritualistic center in the shrines or *jinja;* the latter is designated Sectarian (*Shūha*) Shintō. Both branches have received influences from the parent stream of the ancient cultus, the former more directly and, on the whole, in more unmixed character than the latter. Modern exponents of the state system generally insist that the ceremonies and beliefs connected with the shrines represent the true and uncontaminated line of pure Shintō, while the sectarian form has been more or less modified by foreign infiltrations and the contributions of founders and other teachers. On the other hand, adherents of the sects have occasionally declared that they alone preserve the true and original Shintō and that the state cultus may not inexactly be regarded as another sect, officially sponsored and claiming nation-wide allegiance.

The Shintō of the people exists in the form of thirteen officially recognized sects and numerous sub-sects. The thirteen sects are: Shintō Honkyoku ("Main Bureau Shintō," sometimes also called Shintō Kyō or "Shintō Teaching"), Shinri Kyō ("Divine Reason Teaching"), Taisha Kyō ("Great Shrine Teaching," after the great shrine of the sect at Izumo), Shūsei Ha ("Society for Improvement and Consolidation"), Taisei Kyō ("Great Accomplishment Teaching"), Jikkō Kyō ("Practical Conduct Teaching"), Fusō Kyō (from Fusō, a poetical name for Japan), Mitake Kyō ("Great Mountain Teaching," after the sacred peak of Ontake), Shinshū Kyō ("Divine Learning Teaching"), Misogi Kyō ("Purification Teaching"), Kurozumi Kyō (after the name of the founder, Kurozumi Munetāda), Konkō Kyō ("The Teaching of the Glory of the Unifying God"), and Tenri Kyō ("Heavenly Reason Teaching"). The statistical totals for all sects combined show 18,000,000 adherents, 121,000 priests and teachers, and 16,000 churches.

The Shintō of the state does not publish statistics of adherents. Theoretically all Japanese subjects are included. State Shintō maintains 110,500 shrines, large and small, and 15,800 priests. Features that distinguish Sectarian Shintō from State Shintō should be carefully noted, since the two are often confused. Sectarian Shintō is for the most part the result of the labors of historical founders, organizers, and teachers who have systematized special forms of doctrine and ritual and propagated these for the purpose of creating followings and thereby benefiting the individual and the community. This statement is not exclusively true, since at least three of the thirteen sects declare that they are without personal founders and that they merely expound the orthodox Shintō inheritance. Most of the sects represent movements that came into existence in the Meiji Era (1868-1912), in certain cases, however, the foundations date from earlier periods of Japanese history.

The state cultus opened its modern career in 1868 when the classical revival that had made vigorous progress in the latter part of the Tokugawa Era (1603-1868) came to fruition in the establishment of "Pure Shintō" as the state religion. A definition of relations with popular Shintō movements soon became imperative and, beginning with the opening of the Meiji Era and culminating in the eighties of the last century, the government took steps to make clearly drawn administrative distinctions between the rapidly growing sects and the official system centering in the shrines. Regulations were set up under which all the recognized institutions of the state were to reserve to themselves the title of *Jinja* or *Jinsha* ("God House"), while, in contradistinction, the institutions of the sects were to be called *Kyōkai* ("Churches") and classified as ordinary religion along with Buddhism and Christianity. Since the promulgation of the written constitution in 1889, guaranteeing liberty of religious faith to all subjects, governmental officials, supported by various scholars and writers, have been careful to propagate the idea that State Shintō is not a religion, notwithstanding the fact that another group, including Japanese Shintoists of the first rank, has been equally emphatic in insisting that State Shintō is *de facto,* if not *de jure,* a genuine religion. The main cause of difference of opinion at this point lies in the relative weight given to governmental expediency in the matter of classification. The purpose of the authorities in this is to set up an administrative control which makes it impossible for a subject to repudiate State Shintō on religious grounds.

The sects, like all recognized religious bodies, have their own independent organizations, and possess legal properties that are almost exclusively distinct from those of the shrines. In general they are not permitted to make use of the latter as meeting places for sectarian purposes. The state shrines receive supervision and a measure of support from village, district, municipal, prefectural, or national governments, depending on the rank of the shrine concerned. Other and more extensive sources of income for the shrines are revenues from shrine properties, voluntary offerings and subscriptions, earnings from the sale of charms and talismans, and fees for divination and exorcism. The sects carry on voluntary, non-official religious propaganda, employ their own priests and teachers, in addition to a large number of unpaid instructors of various sorts, and maintain churches, schools, kindergartens, social welfare activities, and different kinds of organizations for young people and adults, as well as extensive agencies for literary propaganda.

Over against this, State Shintō finds its major function in the celebration of rites and ceremonies considered appropriate to the deepening of national sentiment. As the central element of these ceremonies, the priests read ritualistic prayers (*norito**) before the deities of the shrines, in which supplication is made for good crops, peaceful homes, prosperous occupations, success in war, stability of government, security in the food supply, and long and majestic reign on the part of the emperor. The deities or *kami* honored in the official cultus are of multiform origin. They include numerous primitive nature forces, interpreted as "ancestors," the spirits of a limited number of emperors, and the spirits of heroes who have given their lives in the service of nation and throne. Taking the sects as a whole, it may be said that they have included in their god-world the entire pantheon of State Shintō and have added certain deifications of their own, notably the spirits of founders. The most noteworthy theological movement in contemporary Shintō, manifested especially in the sects but also appearing in the state religion, is a trend towards integration in terms of either a unitary pantheistic background of all existence or a fundamental monotheism. Both Buddhist and Christian influences are manifest here. The various deities of Shintō polytheism are interpreted as attributes of a monistic absolute that is spiritual in essence.

Finally, the Shintō of the state is managed by a special Bureau of Shrines in the Department of Home Affairs; Sectarian Shintō, along with all other recognized religions, is controlled by a Bureau of Religions in the Department of Education. The new Religious Organizations Law which went into effect April 1, 1940, embodies a recognition of this distinction. Sectarian Shintō is included within the scope of the new enactments, State Shintō is excluded on the grounds that it is not legally classified as a religion. See Japanese religions; Japanese Terminology; sacred literatures; temples, Far Eastern. See Susano-o.

W. G. Aston, *Shinto, the Way of the Gods* (London, 1905); Tasuku Harada, *The Faith of Japan* (1914); D. C. Holtom, *The Political Philosophy of Modern Shinto* (Tokyo, 1922); D. C. Holtom, *The Japanese Enthronement Ceremonies* (Tokyo, 1928); D. C. Holtom, *The National Faith of Japan* (London, 1938); Genchi Kato, *A Study of Shinto, the Religion of the Japanese Nation* (Tokyo, 1926); Georg Schurhammer, *Shin-To, der Weg der Götter in Japan* (Bonn, 1923); A. C. Underwood, *Shintoism, the Indigenous Religion of Japan* (London, 1934).

D.C.H.

Shiva, Siva, Civa: A great Hindu God, the central object of worship of the Shivaite (Saiva*) sect of Hinduism. In the Hindu *trimurti** he is the destroyer while Brahma* is Creator and Vishnu*, Preserver. His universal symbol is the *linga**, emblem of the creative energy of the universe. Also Nandi the bull is frequently associated with his worship. He is represented in the more philosophical aspect of his cult as the great ascetic seated eternally in contemplation. In another aspect it is in his dance that the activity of the universe is expressed.

Since the active energy of the universe is regarded as feminine many of his worshipers worship his *Shakti** or consort under various names, Kali*, Durga, Deva, Parvati, Uma**.

He was long thought to have evolved from the ancient Vedic* deity Rudra* who was the destructive storm god, and certainly he bears a like character. Comparatively recent archaeological finds in the Indus valley have convinced many scholars that Shiva was known to the pre-Aryan Indus people. If this be true, then it would appear that with the coming of the Aryans he was temporarily submerged, or at least that he was not Aryanized to the point of being mentioned in the Vedic literature. But as the process of racial and cultural amalgamation with the native races went on there came a resurgence of the ancient deity, until he became the supreme God of a large section of the Indian people. Cf Māhadeva. C.S.B.

shofar: Hebrew name for horn or ram or other clean animal, used in Bible times by the side of the trumpet in processions and in orchestral accompaniment; also to sound the alarm of war, and in the ritual of the New Moon, of solemn feasts and fasts, and particularly on the Day of Atonement* of the Jubilee year. The New Moon of the seventh month (Tishri), being the New Year, was termed "a memorial of blowing" and a "day of blowing" the shofar. It still holds the central place in the Synagogue liturgy of the New Year, calling the worshipers to repentance and reminding them, by means of accompanying Scriptural verses, of God's kingship, Revelation at Sinai, and future Messianic redemption. It is also blown at the end of the Day of Atonement. In Orthodox synagogues it is sounded during the morning service of the entire month of Elul in anticipation of the New Year. See New Year, Jewish. S.S.C.

shohet: (Hebr., butcher) One who slaughters animals for food in a manner prescribed by Jewish dietary laws. S.H.B.

shrāddha: Hindu ancestral rite performed by relatives at the death of an individual and periodically thereafter for a time, by which, it is thought, a new body is provided for the ancestral spirit and it is aided in its progress from lower worlds to higher and back to earth. Beginning probably as a simple ceremony of feeding the dead, it has become a highly complex rite in its modern form. Though celebrated differently at different levels of Hinduism, its practice in some form is well-nigh universal in India. C.S.B.

Shrovetide: (From *shrive*—to hear the confession of) Monday and Tuesday immediately before Ash Wednesday*; carnival; period of festivity before Lent*. B.R.

Shu Ching: See Chinese Terminology.

shunning, doctrine of: A practice among the Mennonites* of completely shutting out from all intercourse with the faithful of those who have been excommunicated from the congregation. This meant that the faithful were neither to eat, drink, visit, buy or sell with any excommunicated person. W.W.S.

Sibylline oracles: Oracles* or prophecies issuing from a sibyl, a woman who, in ancient times, acted at various places as a medium or mouthpiece of some god; a collection or collections of prophecies, advice, information, attributed to a sibyl or sibyls. In the days of the old Roman republic, Sibylline Books were often consulted by the magistrates for guidance in state affairs. See pseudepigrapha; Roman religions. F.L.P.

Siddur: (Hebr. arrangement [of prayers]) Jewish book of common prayer arranged for worship throughout the year. S.H.B.

Sidgwick, Henry: (1838-1900) British philosopher, political scientist, and economist, advanced improved versions of the classical British political economy, and fairly liberal individualistic political philosophy. His *Methods of Ethics* (6th ed. 1901), which ran through many editions and still has influence upon moral philosophers, advocates a modified form of Utilitarianism, with concessions to Intuitionism**. He was active in securing the admission of women students to the University of Cambridge, and in promoting investigations in Psychical Research*. W.K.W.

Sifra: Abbreviated from the Aramaic Sifra de-be-Rab, "the book of the school". An anonymous Rabbinic commentary to Leviticus* composed in early Talmudic times. The primary interest of the book is the application of the general principles in the Levitical legislation to new cases. B.Z.B.

Siger of Brabant: (died ca. 1282) Being completely earnest with Aristotle's philosophy, he understood him according to the interpretation of Arabic Neo-Platonism, especially of Averroes. See Scholasticism.

Cl. Bäumker, *Die Impossibilia des Siger von Brabant* (Münster, 1888); P. Mandonnet, *Siger de Brabant, et l'averroisme latin au XIII siècle* (Fribourg, Suisse, 1899). H.H.

sign of the cross: An ancient devotional practice, in which the cross* is traced over the forehead, breast, and from shoulder to shoulder, as a token of the faith of the believer. It is employed at blessings, absolutions, etc., and may also be used over objects (set apart for holy use) as well as over persons. W.N.P.

Sikh, Sikhism: A faith that arose in India as a result of the coming of Islam. It is a good illustration of the tendency to syncretism which inevitably appears when two faiths come into contact. The founder of the movement was Nanak (1469-1538)*, a follower of the poet Kabir. Born a Hindu, near Lahore which was predominantly Moslem, he reacted strongly against current Hindu teachings and practices. He repudiated caste; he could not accept the authority of the Brahman priesthood, and found little satisfaction in the study of the Hindu scriptures. After a period of wandering as an ascetic he attained release and began to teach the way he had found to others. He was a poet and sang innumerable songs, many of which, together with many from Kabir and others, form the Granth*, the sacred book of the Sikhs.

Both Kabir and Nanak taught that the way of salvation was through *bhakti** the way of faith or devotion. Both were of the Vishnu* sect. They taught the oneness of God, to whom they gave various names, Ram, Brahma, Govind, Hari. The latter, another name of Vishnu, was the preferred name in Nanak's songs. They carried over the Hindu belief in rebirth from which release was sought. Release meant the mergence of the individual soul in God. There are passages in the Granth that indicate a belief that salvation is, as in Islam, only for the elect. On the other hand there are numerous passages which seem to assume that salvation is open to all.

After the death of Nanak, the founder and Guru*, successive Gurus modified the faith at various points. The fifth Guru, Arjun compiled the Granth. The Sikh community became increasingly militant and ultimately became a nation. They were finally crushed by the Moslem emperors, but they have remained a warlike people until now. They are considered the finest soldiers which India produces. The tenth Guru declared that thenceforth, the Granth should be their Guru. The great temple at Amritsar is the center of the faith. It has with the passing centuries seen the return of some Hindu ideas and practices, but it still maintains its separate identity and claims to be a religion apart from Hinduism, one of the living religions of the world. The last census (1931) gave the number of Sikhs at 4,335,771. See sacred literatures.

See M. A. Macauliffe, *The Sikh Religion* (1909), 6 vols.; Ernest Trumpp, *Adi-Granth* (London, 1877). A translation of the sacred book. C.S.B.

Siloam inscription: Inscription in Old Hebrew characters found on the rock-wall of a water tunnel dug under the reign of Hezekiah from Gihon to the Pool of Siloam in ancient Jerusalem (II Chr. xxxii, 4, 30). See alphabetic writing. S.L.T.

Simmel, Georg: (1858-1918) Professor at the Universities of Berlin and Strassburg. Noted for his extensive sociological and social-psychological investigations, for his transfer of the predominant psychological interpretation of the *a priori* into the historical field, a religious mystic vein permeated his metaphysical discussions. The negative theology of mysticism appeared to him as freer and deeper as all earlier and later religious philosophy. Though he rejected the substantiality of the soul, it appeared to him not impossible that life is not the sole form of existence.

Einleitung in die Moralwissenschaft (Stuttgart, 1911), 3rd ed.; *Die Probleme der Geschichtsphilosophie* (Leipzig, 1921), 4th ed.; *Die Religion* (Frankfurt, 1912), 2nd ed.; *Philosophische Kultur. Gesammelte Essays* (Leipzig, 1919), 2nd rev. ed.; M. Adler, *Georg Simmels Bedeutung f. die Geistesgeschichte* (Wien, 1919); W. Knevels, *Simmels Religionstheorie* (Leipzig, 1926); A. Mamelet, *La philosophie de Georg Simmel* (Paris, 1914); N. J. Spykman, *The Social Theory of Georg Simmel* (1925).

H.H.

Simon Magus: The magician of Samaria who offered money to the Apostles for the gift of the Holy Spirit (Ac. 8:9-24). According to church tradition he was the originator of the Gnostic* heresy. E.F.S.

Simon, Richard: (1638-1712) A French Roman Catholic scholar. A pioneer in textual studies of the Old and New Testaments and a translator of the Bible from the Vulgate*. S.M.G.

Simon, Saint: See Saint Simon.

Simon Stylites, St.: See anchoret.

Simons, Menno: See Menno Simons.

simony: The purchase or sale of a church office by money payments or other unworthy benefits. The term arises from the story of Simon Magus (Acts 8:18-24). R.E.E.H.

sin: Sin as distinguished from crime (violation of the civil law) and vice (immorality resulting from the disregard of the social and ethical standards of society) is an act or attitude by which the reality of God is denied or violated. The conception of sin is therefore meaningful only in the context of religion. The history of religion shows that at all times sin and sins were understood to be offenses against the divine holiness. Among primitive people the notion of *tabu** was closely related to that of sin. Also in the Christian religion, the conception of sin is determined by the knowledge of God. The apostle Paul furnished a definition of it, which is profoundly religious and in harmony with the fundamental character of Christianity. It has been reaffirmed whenever the Christian faith renewed itself by a return to its deepest spiritual resources. He wrote that "what does not come from faith is sin." This interpretation guided men like Augustine, Luther, Kierkegaard** in their important reaffirmation of the Christian faith.

The most adequate definitions of sin as developed by Christian theology (in harmony with its identification with unfaith) were those in which it is interpreted as *superbia* (pride) and *concupiscentia* (concupiscence*, meaning selfish desire and, in the narrower sense, sensuous lust). Sin as pride is in the last resort the refusal on man's part to acknowledge God as God. It is imbued with the attitude of *hybris* by which man tries to deify, absolutize himself as if he could be self-sufficient. Sin as concupiscence is every expression of egotism and selfishness in which an utter disregard of both God's sovereignty and love is shown.

The details of the Christian doctrine of sin were developed not only in accordance with these conceptions, but also in connection with standards that evolved within the life of the church. These standards were determined both by intra-ecclesiastical practices and by the relations of the church with the world. As the church formed for itself definite religious and moral norms in Scripture, creeds and ecclesiastical statutes of all sorts, violations of these norms came to be regarded as sins. Furthermore, with the church's assumption of responsibility for the character of civilization, there arose necessarily definitions of sin that were determined by the social milieu in which the church lived. Detailed definitions of sin have therefore varied in accordance with the nature of church-groups of different times and places.

In the very beginnings of Christianity it was held possible for a person who had been baptized in the name of Christ to be sinless. But this high standard which reflects the religious enthusiasm of the early Christians could not actually be maintained. One introduced therefore the distinction between mortal* (unforgivable) and venial (forgivable) sins. Mortal sins, by the commission of which a person exposed himself to excommunication* from the Christian community for having defied and offended the majesty of God, were idolatry, murder, and adultery. It is important to note that among these idolatry was regarded as the worst of all sins. Hence it was the last of the mortal sins that were finally declared as forgivable upon proper penance.

To this day Roman Catholicism makes the distinction between mortal and venial sins. Mortal sin is regarded as that transgression of God's law which causes the sinner to lose the effect of grace*, thus rendering him subject to eternal punishment in hell. A venial sin is a violation of God's law which does not alienate the sinner from God, entailing no loss of grace, but requiring submission to penitential discipline. A mortal sinner can acquire forgiveness only by fulfilling the requirements of the sacrament of penance* through which grace is restored in him.

The Reformers rejected the Roman Catholic teaching. In terms of Pauline faith, they defined sin as any act or attitude by which man estranges himself from God. In later Protestantism this high religious standard was replaced by norms which reflected the moral-social mores of the individual churches and groups. Not without the direct influence of the Reformers, especially Calvin, the injunctions of the Bible, of the O.T. as well as the New, read in the light of contemporary social ideals and practices, came to be regarded as normative of the Christian life, so that by them one could define sin and sins. Modern Protestantism and its theology broke with these traditions and introduced a definition of sin that was determined by the insights of the natural and social sciences in the moral development of mankind and of human groups and individuals. In certain groups of Protestant Liberals, the term sin came to be regarded as practically meaningless. Recently, however, Protestant thought has re-discovered the Biblical, particularly Pauline, teaching of sin. See conviction of sin; evil; guilt; original sin; seven deadly sins; retention of sins; wrath of God. Cf. ethics; satisfaction; temptation.

Julius Muller, *The Christian Doctrine of Sin* (1868), 2 vols.; Reinhold Niebuhr, *The Nature and Destiny of Man* (1941-43), 2 vols. W.P.

Sin, Nannar: (Semitic Babylonian) Moon-god of the early Akkadians and later Semites*; 'The bright one'; his cult appears to have originated in Ur and to have migrated early to Harran, later to Assyria; father of the circling hosts of heaven; overseer of the world at night.

His cult appeared early in Palestine and Sinai. Some influences from this cult survived in the Hebrew feasts of new moons and trumpets; and in the fixation of their lunar calendar.

Sin's symbol is a crescent, or crescent and disk. He is represented as an old man with beard and cap on which were horns of the moon. The horn came to be regarded as his crown, and a symbol of his power. Assyrian kings wore a horned crown as a symbol of their kinship to deity. F.L.P.

sinecure: Properly an ecclesiastical benefice without parochial "cure of souls"* (e.g., in cathedral or university), but often used in common sense for one with no duties; scarcely found today except as honorary. E.R.H.

sins, retention of: See retention of sins.

Sirach, wisdom of Jesus, son of: See Jesus, son of Sirach.

sisterhood: Sisters and nuns collectively; women bound by vows, usually living in communities, following a common rule of life and striving for perfection. In the different communities there are slight variations regarding rules, constitutions, garbs and the like. Contemplative communities have no contact with the world and aim at personal perfection through a close union with God in prayer. Partly contemplative and partly active communities devote themselves to religious and charitable works, such as educating youth, caring for the sick, the aged, wayward, orphans, and the mentally deficient. Some communities take solemn vows, others simple vows; congregations are under pontifical authority; diocesan communities are under the bishop. B.R.

sisters: See s.v. nun.

Sisters, Black: See Black Fathers and Black Sisters.

Sisters of Charity: The name popularly attributed to the nuns belonging to the Sisters of Charity of St. Vincent de Paul*. The order was founded in 1633 and is devoted to corporal and spiritual works of mercy. Although it first arose as a group of young women who cared for the sick, it was founded as an order of religious by St. Vincent de Paul, Venerable Louise de Merilla, and Mlle. le Gras. The first house in the United States was founded by Mother Elizabeth Seton in 1809 at Emmitsburg, Maryland. In the United States there are also several diocesan communities which follow a modified rule of the Sisters of Charity of St. Vincent de Paul. T.T.M.

Sisters of the Good Shepherd: See Pius XII.

Sisters of Mercy: A congregation of women founded in Dublin, 1827, by Catherine McAuley, for the practice of all the works of mercy, spiritual and corporal, e.g., visitation of the sick and imprisoned, management of hospitals, orphanages, homes for the destitute and the aged, etc. They have more than one hundred establishments in Great Britain, and number above 9,000 members in the U. S. J.F.T.

Sisters of St. Joseph's Society for Foreign Missions: A small religious community of women of the Third Order Regular of St. Francis*. Founded by Cardinal Vaughan and Mother Mary Francis Ingham in 1883 to cooperate with the Mill Hill Fathers. J.F.T.

Six Articles, 1539: See Act of Six Articles.

Sixtus IV, Pope: (1471-84) Born in 1414 at Celle near Savona, Francesco delle Rovere became early in life a Conventual Franciscan, of which Order he became in 1464 General. Created Cardinal in 1467 by Paul II he was elected pope on Sept. 9, 1471 and was immediately acclaimed for his patronage of the arts and sciences. Despite the low state of revenues in the Papal States, he enlarged and made accessible to the public the Vatican Library; beautified Rome; built the *Ponte Sisto* across the Tiber; brought good water into the city of Rome and erected many churches and hospitals (*Santo Spirito* still extant and functioning). His name will ever remain associated with the world-wide known Sistine Chapel, embellished by the famous frescos of the immortal Michelangelo and other artists. He fostered and promoted the devotion to the (later defined dogma of the) Immaculate Conception (cf. "Pius IX"); favored Religious Communities (*Mare Magnum*) and celebrated the Jubilee of 1475. He continued the policy of Paul II regarding the freedom of the Church in France. His efforts to create interest in a new Crusade against the Turks met with apparent apathy, and had to be relinquished; neither was he successful in effecting a reunion of the Russian Church with Rome or of reaping the fruits of the Pazzi conspiracy led by his nephew Girolomo Riario against Lorenzo da Medici. He disapproved of the excesses of the Spanish Inquisition*; vigorously opposed the Waldenses* and annulled the decrees of the Council of Constance* that had not been expressly confirmed by any of his predecessors. He quelled the attempts of Zomometic to convoke an anti-papal General Council at Bâle in 1482. Although addicted to Nepotism his own life was otherwise blameless. His theological works appeared during his life-time at Rome, 1470-72.

Litt.: For his letters written as General of the Franciscan Order and as Cardinal cf. *Archiv. Franc. Histor.* (1936), pp. 198-234 and 477-91. Platina's Life of Sixtus IV was published by L. A. Muratori in his *Rerum Italicarum Scriptores* (Milan, 1723-51), vol. XXXIII; L. Pastor, *The History of the Popes,* vols. III and IV (1923); Gregorovius, *Rome in the Middle Ages* (London, 1902). R.M.H.

Sixtus V, Pope: (1585-90) Born of a poor family, Dec. 12, 1521 at Grottamare, near Montalto, Felice Peretti was received as a boy of nine years by the Friars Minor Conventuals by whom he was educated. He later joined their Order; was ordained priest, 1547, and eventually became a famous Lenten preacher. He functioned as Superior successively at Siena, Naples and Venice; became in 1560 Consultor of the Inquisition at Rome and professor at the Roman University. Appointed Vicar General over his Order, he was named by Pius V* Bishop of S. Agata; confessor to the pope and created cardinal in 1570. In 1571-77 he served as Bishop of Fermo and on April 24, 1585 was elected pope. Sixtus V is looked upon as one of the great Roman Pontiffs. He was a commanding and imposing figure; was indefatigable in work and of inflexible will power. Mercilessly and without regard for consequences he extirpated banditry in the Eternal City and in the Papal States*; set in order the crippled finances of the papacy, and through a canonical visitation of churches and monasteries enforced in their minutest details the regulations and prescriptions of the Council of Trent* (cf. Catholic Reformation) for the reform of clergy and religious. Bishops were ordered to come to Rome at stated times to give an account of their respective dioceses (*visitatio ad limina*). In virtue of the Bull, *Postquam verus,* Dec. 3, 1586 he fixed the number of cardinals at 70, four of whom at least were to be Religious; and by the Bull *Immensa Aeterni* of Jan. 22, 1588 created 15 Roman Congregations (Departments), all properly circumscribed, of which six were intended for the temporal administration and juridical tribunals of the Papal States; the remaining, for the spiritual care of the Church at large. In the question of the succession of Henry IV of Navarre to the throne of France, Sixtus remained neutral and refused to be cajoled by Philip II and the Guises in a move that would destroy the balance of power in Europe by crippling France. He was, however, willing to assist Philip in his war against England, hoping thereby to regain that country for Catholicism; but the defeat of the Armada (1588) put an end to the aspirations of both pope and king. In 1587 Sixtus installed a special printing press in the Vatican for the publication of the Septuagint* text of the Old Testament; but he was less fortunate in the editing of a corrected edition of the Latin Vulgate*, all his personal work, which he published in virtue of the Bull *Aeternus Ille* as the authentic text of Holy Writ prescribed by the Council of Trent and ordered the same to be adopted by all as the exclusive version. Due to remonstrations and difficulties the sale of copies was checked and the Bull recalled shortly after the pope's death (Aug. 27, 1590). Sixtus was a generous patron of the arts, sciences and architecture, in all three of which the religious motif always predominated. Under Sixtus V, Rome became the city of the Baroque style. He provided good drinking water (*Aqua Felice*) for Rome; connected the principal churches of the city by wide avenues; placed in St. Peter's Square (as in three other piazzas) a huge Egyptian obelisk; constructed the new Vatican Library; erected the pope's quarters in the Vatican and caused the cupola over St. Peter's Basilica to be completed by Michelangelo.

Litt.: *Bullarium Diplomatum et Privilegiorum Summ. Roman. Pontiff.* Editio Taurinensis (Naples, 1882), vol. IX; L. Pastor, *History of the Popes,* vol. XXI (1932); Biographies by Tempesti, Casimir, O. M. Conv., *Storia della Vita e delle Gesta di Sisto Quinto* (Rome; Minaldi, 1866), 2 vols.; L. Wadding, *Annales Minorum* (Florence, 1934), vol. XXII; Count Ugo Balzani, "Rome under Sixtus V" in *Cambridge Modern History* (1934), vol. III, ch. 13, p. 422 ff.; *Cath. Encyc.* XIV, 33. R.M.H.

Skaneateles (N. Y.) community: See communistic settlements, secular.

Skarga, Peter: (1536-1612) Polish Jesuit. A pulpit orator and apologist, he contributed to the restoration of Catholicism in Poland and to the Union of the Ruthenians* with Rome (1596). E.A.R.

skepticism: (Gr., *skeptein,* to reflect or consider) Antonym, dogmatism*. 1) The view that no knowledge (or no certain knowledge) is possible; based on deceptiveness of the senses, fallacies in reasoning, incompleteness of evidence, etc. 2) The view that some particular type of knowledge is inherently impossible; e.g., metaphysical knowledge of things in themselves as distinguished from experience (Kant*), or of the objects of religious belief such as God and immortality (cf. H. Spencer*, "the Unknowable"). 3) The method of complete doubt at the outset of investigation; e.g., Descartes'* methodological skepticism, and F. H. Bradley's* view that skepticism means "to become aware of and to doubt all preconceptions." See agnosticism; Carneades; Pyrrhonism. E.S.B.

skills: See culture.

Skoptsy: See Russian sectarianism.

slander: The malicious utterance or communication of a false report or misrepresentation of another which is expressed in his absence and which tends to injure his reputation. Essentially it consists of calling good evil. "The devil"* in the NT is preeminently a "slanderer." Slander is condemned by most if not all moral and religious codes. R.W.F.

slang: See culture.

slavery: A social and industrial system in which the person and labor of one individual may be disposed of as the property of another. The exclusive right of the owner in his slave as property is generally limited by law or custom, but such restrictions are mitigations of slavery, not a part of its essential nature. Slavery has often been confused with 1) the subjection of wives and children in preliteration societies, 2) the subordination of the members to the head of a despotic state, or 3) the status of subjugated tribes, provinces or classes in a highly stratified society. Slavery, however, differs from the first situation in that it is an institution which extends beyond the limits of the family; from the second, in that it implies the existence of a society which recognizes the status of slave in contradiction to the status of freeman; and from the third in that slavery implies the individual, not the collective, subjugation of men and extends to the whole personality of the slave. It is also distinguished from serfdom by the fact that in the latter case the master has no property right in the person of the serf, nor can he dispose of all his labor, but only of a specified portion of it. As Nieboer says: "The slave-owner may do with his slave whatever he is not by special laws forbidden to do; the master of the serf may require from his man such services or tributes only as the law allows him to require."

The earliest slaves were captives in war, since primitive custom everywhere forbids the enslavement of fellow-tribesmen. Only after the institution of extra-tribal slavery has become established is it extended to members of the kinship group, chiefly as a consequence of debt or as a punishment for crime.

Slavery does not exist among peoples in the lowest stages of culture. Hobhouse has shown that it is unknown among the lower hunting tribes, and infrequent among higher hunters. Such peoples are relatively peaceful, and lack the economic and moral development necessary to the growth of slavery as an institution. Slaves are useful to their masters only when agricultural and industrial techniques have become sufficiently productive to enable the worker to produce a surplus above the necessities of his own existence. This condition does not generally prevail, and slavery is not extensively practiced, before the higher stages of agriculture have been reached.

The early Christian church inherited the traditions of slavery from both the Hebrew and the classical civilizations. Christians lived in anticipation of the speedy return of their Lord. Earthly concerns were of secondary importance, and while the Church Fathers generally showed pity for the slave, they did not condemn the institution, but asserted the equality of master and slave before God. St. Augustine's time slavery had come to be thought of as a result of sin, and to grapple with sin a more important task than to grapple with its consequent. The net result seems to have been that while the Church made slavery milder, it also perpetuated it by its emphasis on the rights of masters.

After the fall of the Western Roman Empire, the ranks of the slaves were recruited from freemen who sought protection or escape from deprivation, and from captives taken in war by Clovis, Charlemagne, Henry the Fowler, and others. With the gradual amelioration of the condition of the slave and the depression of the lot of the free laborer, the status of both merged into serfdom. The transition in process is reflected in a seventh century decree that slaves of the Church shall work three days a week for themselves and shall spend three days at labor on the desmesne. By the tenth century the change was completed in Southern France, and in the North two centuries later. During the twelfth century the Emperors began to grant to imperial towns the privilege of liberating serfs and slaves seeking refuge within them, and by 1300 domestic slavery was extinct. The Domesday Book records 25,000 slaves in England in 1086, but the institution was already merging into villeinage, and but few vestiges survived into the fourteenth century.

The Mediterranean lands present a different situation. Domestic slavery ceased in Bologna in 1283, in Castile before 1300, and in several other Spanish and Italian states before the close of the Middle Ages, but conflict of Christian with Turk and Moor perpetuated the trade in war captives, so that with the exploration of Africa and the settlement of America the adventurers and exploiters found ready to hand a decaying institution which they were able to revive and expand on the largest and most inhumane scale known to history.

Negro slavery was first introduced into Europe and America by the Portuguese. Slave raids upon Africa increased in frequency after the Middle of the fifteenth century, but began in earnest in 1511 when Ferdinand the Catholic granted permission for their importation into Hispaniola. Six years later Charles V urged their substitution for Indians in his New World possessions on account of their greater efficiency, and granted permission to a Flemish trader to transport 4000 Africans a year to the West Indies. The French, Dutch, and Spaniards rapidly expanded the traffic, but Queen Elizabeth bitterly reproached the illicit participation of Sir John Hawkins and her English subjects in the enterprise.

British participation was first officially sanctioned by a charter of Charles I to the African Company in 1631. The royal scruples once overcome, the trade grew apace. By the Asiento contract of 1713, England engaged to furnish Spain 4800 slaves a year for 30 years, each monarch to receive 25 percent of the profits. When the agreement was terminated by George II in 1750, the English were exporting annually 20,000 Negroes from Africa. By this time opposition to the trade was arising from under the leadership of the Quakers, soon to be supported by the bishops of the Established Church, the rising power of Methodism, and the religious and intellectual classes of England generally. It culminated in the Bill for the abolition of the Slave Trade in 1807. Final termination of the trade, to become effective after a term of years, was agreed to by the European Powers at the Congress of Vienna, the last nation to act being Portugal in 1836.

England was also the first of the Great Powers to abolish slavery in her overseas possessions. By an Act of Parliament of 1833, the 770,280 slaves throughout the Empire became free on August 1, 1834, and the owners granted 20 million pounds sterling in compensation. Slavery was abolished in the French colonies in 1848, and in the Dutch West Indies in 1863. The Spanish government abolished it for Porto Rico in 1873 and for Cuba in 1886. The Brazilian government took similar action in 1888. In the United States of America slavery was more easily abolished in the North, where the slaves were few in number, and where their ownership was confined to a few wealthy owners who could afford to liberate them, or who could find a profitable market for them in the South. But in the Southern States it became an integral part of the socio-economic system after the rise of the cotton industry. As popular sentiment against the slave system became irrepressible in other sections of the country, even Southerners who were aware of its economic fallacies were faced with a dilemma. Since the slaves constituted a majority of the population in two states, South Carolina and Mississippi, and a considerable minority in the rest, such Southerners feared the result if they were to be given full citizen status. On the other hand, the creation of a permanent class with limited citizenship rights also presented difficulties, and their colonization in Africa, where the Republic of Liberia had been created for that purpose in 1822, would not only create insuperable difficulties of transportation under conditions then prevailing, but would completely disrupt the economic system of the slave states through the dislocation of their labor supply. Economic factors, however, would doubtless have gradually modified and eliminated slavery in a few decades had not the Proclamation of Emancipation ended it as a war measure, and the full citizenship status of the freedman, in legal theory if not in practice, been guaranteed by the Fourteenth (1868) and Fifteenth (1870) Amendments.

Slavery survived longest in the Portuguese possessions and in Africa, where it still survives as a quasi-legal institution as well as in Arabia, the frontiers of India and Burma, and in China. Harris has recently estimated that 5,000,000 persons still linger in slavery or in a status closely analogous thereto.

As Dunoyer has observed, the economic regime of every sedentary society has been founded on the slavery of at least a portion of the industrial and agricultural classes. It has undoubtedly played an important, though often exaggerated, role in human progress through disciplining man to the monotony of regular toil, and still more as a stimulus to the division of labor and the creation of a leisure class, but it has also retarded ethical advance through fostering contempt for manual labor, through its degradation of the human personality to the level of property, and to the inevitable abuses of power inherent in the master-slave relationship. See pro-slavery doctrine.

John Hobbis Harris, *A Century of Emancipation* (London, 1933); Henry Charles Lea, *Studies in Church History* (1869); Herman Jeremias Nieboer, *Slavery as an Industrial System* (2nd ed., The Hague, 1910).

H.E.J.

Smith, Gerald Birney: (1868-1929) Graduated, Brown University, Union Seminary; studied in Berlin, Marburg and Paris. Professor of Theology, University of Chicago 1900-1929. Dr. Smith was one of the leaders of Chicago University Divinity School Faculty in modernizing and socializing Theology. See s.v. Ritschlianism.

Author: *Practical Theology* 1903); *Social Idealism and the Changing Theology* (1913); *Principles of Christian Living* (1942), 2nd ed. Editor: *American Journal of Theology, Journal of Religion, A Guide to the Study of the Christian Religion* (1916); co-editor, *A Dictionary of Religion and Ethics* (1921).

J.W.B.

Smith, Henry Preserved: (1847-1927) Author of biblical commentaries, O.T. history, *Heretic's Defense* (1926), autobiographical. Dismissed from Lane Theological Seminary in 1893 (where he had been professor of Old Testament since 1874) for defending historical criticism of the Bible, he became a Congregationalist and taught in succession at Amherst and Meadville becoming librarian at the Union Theological Seminary, New York, in 1913, and professor of Semitic Languages four years later.

C.H.M.

Smith, John: (d. 1612) The founder of the first English Congregation (1606), Smith sought in Holland religious liberty for his flock and himself. Later he adopted antipaedobaptist views, and through Mennonite* influence was won over to Arminianism*. See s.v. Puritanism.

Walter A. Burgess, *John Smith the Se-Baptist, Thomas Helwys, and the First Baptist Church in England* (London, 1911).

E.W.K.

Smith, Joseph, Jr.: Born Sharon, Vermont, 23 Dec. 1805; organized Latter Day Saint Church* 6 April 1830; claimed angel showed him plates, 23 September 1823, and he received 1827, translated and published as Book of Mormon 1830; revelations published in Doctrine and Covenants 1835 (Book of Commandments 1833); prepared MS of Bible corrected by inspiration, preserved by his wife and published 1867; killed by mob, Carthage, Illinois, 27 June 1844.

S.A.B.

Smith, William Robertson: (1846-1894) Scottish Biblical critic, philologist, and encyclopedist, born at Keig, Aberdeenshire. He was professor of Oriental languages and Old Testament exegesis in the Free Church College, Aberdeen, 1870-1881, being removed from his chair after a heresy trial which resulted in acquittal but a vote of want of confidence. He was soon appointed an editor of the ninth edition of the *Encyclopaedia Britannica*, in 1883 was made professor of Arabic at Cambridge University, and in 1886 librarian of that university. He was a leader in the introduction to the English-speaking world of scientific Biblical criticism and of comparative method in the study of Semitic religions. J.P.H.

smriti: Revelation of a lower grade than *sruti* in Hinduism. Smriti is regarded as sacred literature, but not on the same level as *sruti**. The *sutra* literature (See Manu, Laws of) for example is *smriti*, so also the Epics and Puranas.* C.S.B.

Smyth, Egbert Coffin: (1829-1904) Graduated Bowdoin College, 1848; Bangor Theological Seminary, 1854; Professor of Natural Religion and Revelation, Bowdoin College 1856-1863; Ecclesiastical History, Andover Theological Seminary, 1863-1904, president of the Faculty, leading founder and editor of *The Andover Review*, 1884-1894.

Charged, together with other members of the Faculty, with departure from the Creed of Andover Seminary by the Board of Visitors in 1887, Smyth appealed to the Supreme Court of Massachusetts, and was acquitted in 1901.

Author of editorials and articles in *The Andover Review*, co-author, *Progressive Orthodoxy* (1885); author, *The Andover Defence* (1891), defining the principles for the interpretation of Creeds. See biographical sketch in J. W. Buckham's *Progressive Religious Trought in America* (1919). See Andover Controversy, The.

J.W.B.

Smyth, Newman: (1843-1925) Graduate of Bowdoin College, 1863; served with the 16th Maine Volunteers, 1864; graduated, Andover Theological Seminary, 1867.

Pastor of the historic First Congregational Church, New Haven, Conn., 1882-1907.

One of the leaders of the New Theology* in New England.

His books represent the following advance movements:

(1) Emphasis on the return to Intuition and Progress in Theology: *The Religious Feeling* (1877); *Old Faiths in New Light* (1879); (2) The religious interpretation of Science: *The Place of Death in Evolution* (1897); *Through Science to Faith* (1902); *Constructive Natural Theology* (1913); (3) Church Unity: *Passing Protestantism* and *Coming Catholicism* (1908); (4) Emphasis upon Personality: *The Meaning of Personal Life* (1916). Biographical sketch in J. W. Buckham, *Progressive Religious Thought in America* (1919). J.W.B.

social action: See social work of the churches.

social anthropology: See anthropology.

social ethics: The study of the functioning of social institutions in so far as such functioning is regarded as morally good or bad, right or wrong. In its concern for the finding and correlation of facts, it is scientific; in its concern for critical evaluation of the norms appealed to within the social process, it is philosophical; in its concern for particular methods of social improvement, it is practical. Social ethics therefore brings together into one discipline the fields of the social sciences and of theoretical and applied ethics*. Although the term itself is of recent origin, the criticism of existing social institutions or of institutional practices is as old, within western culture, as the 8th and 7th Century Hebrew Prophets. More explicitly, its foundations as a theoretical science were laid in Plato's *Republic* and *The Laws* and in Aristotle's *Politics*. In the modern period it has had a utopian phase, represented by such works as More's *Utopia* (1516), Bacon's *New Atlantis* (1627), and Saint-Simon's *The New Christianity* (1825), and its present, increasingly solid, scientific phase, rooting in the work of Karl Marx (*Das Kapital*, 1867). Social ethics is distinguished from Christian Ethics* in its concern with social institutions and conditions *qua* social, rather than with both social and personal morality, and in its approach to these as secular rather than religious problems. Among the important controversial issues in the field today are the following: 1) whether the institution (social environment*) or individual character (heredity* plus personal choices) is the primary determinant in social behavior; 2) whether norms of social morality can, in some sense, be defined objectively and universally, or whether they are exclusively relative to the cultural context in which they emerge; 3) whether such norms, however defined, can be used, through the educational process, in the realization of gradual and deliberate social evolution or whether significant change must necessarily come violently as antagonistic social forces move toward resolution; and 4) whether structural change in institutions can of itself socialize human motivation. Cf. haustafel.

F. G. Peabody, *The Approach to the Social Question* (1909); L. T. Hobhouse, *The Elements of Social Justice* (1922); R. Niebuhr, *Moral Man and Immoral Society* (1932); J. H. Tufts, *America's Social Morality* (1933); P. A. Sorokin, *Man and Society in Calamity* (1942). E.T.R.

social gospel: This term appears in the late nineteenth century being popularized by the Christian Commonwealth Community as the title of its monthly magazine, 1897-1900. But the ancestry of this trend of sincere Christians to make Christian faith and love dynamic in contemporary life and especially in promoting the welfare of workers is reaction to the individualization of the gospel accompanying the rise of the modern age.

Ecclesiastical control of the economic and social life began to decline with the coming of Protestantism*, democracy, economic liberalism and public education. By mid-seventeenth century the church was sanctioning the taking of interest and religious toleration and liberty were depriving the churches of earlier exercised social applications of Christian ethics. In Geneva and Massachusetts Calvinism* introduced bibliocracies. Elsewhere it denoted the acceptance of status as willed by God. Long ago it should have been observed that just as the churches lose their socio-economic jurisdiction, the word "gospel" takes on a strange novel meaning. As early as 1652, "gospel" signifies something serving as "guide to human action". Jonathan Edwards* a century later divorces religion from society. This desocialization of Christianity by 1790 turned "gospel" into a "doctrine preached with fervor as a means of social and political action". Thereupon Thomas Carlyle* could refer to a "gospel of economy" and Frederick Denison Maurice* plead for a kingdom of God within a dead church and Charles Kingsley* emphasize freedom, equality and brotherliness as demands of the gospel.

After 1848 in consequence of the February Revolution, Maurice, Kingsley, and Ludlow headed a movement known as *Christian Socialists**, while Saint Simon* twenty-five years earlier defined the core of the gospel to be brotherliness. Meanwhile Marx* had launched his theory of society upon boisterous waves. In 1849, Christians in Germany became interested in socialism*, called attention to the guilt of the churches regarding social issues and demanded Christian love and responsibility in expiation. Some four or five competing social interpretations can be traced in Germany.

Between 1731 and 1830 the only interest in articles in American religious journals concerned with peace, slavery, prison reform, improvement of the lot of seamen, temperance and such like is "the rescue of the individual by an emotional religious experience rather than any definite application of the teachings of Jesus to the social order". Then Channing, Bushnell, and Parker** discuss social problems vehemently and the Brook Farm Association, 1841, organizes to "apply principles of justice and love to our social organization in accordance with the laws of Divine Providence". Stephen Colwell and Edward Chapman follow with Gladden, Herron, Henderson, Mathews*, Batten, Rauschenbusch* and a host of others keeping them company.

The fatal error of Rauschenbusch and his group was to identify Jesus' view of the kingdom of God* with the twentieth century evolutionary hypothesis. Jesus' thought of the kingdom as "principally in the future and wholly in the realm of miracle." In seven items, Rauschenbusch differed from Marx: 1) Positive religious faith; 2) Value of the church; 3) Necessity of regeneration; 4) Reality of spiritual forces; 5) Moral responsibility of the individual; 6) Sanctity of the family; 7) Insistence upon prohibition. After accepting evolution and science, this group refused to be scientific in its view of the kingdom of God and thus lost the war to fundamentalism* and economic reaction. See also Christian Social Union; communistic settlements.

Abraham Cronbach, *The Bible and Our Social Outlook* (1941); C. H. Hopkins, *Rise of the Social Gospel in American Protestantism,* 1865-1915 (1940); C. E. Hudson, and M. B. Reckitt, *The Church and the World,* II, III (1940); F. E. Johnson, *The Social Gospel Re-examined* (1940); M. C. Latta, "*Background* for the Social Gospel in American Protestantism," *Church History* (1936), p. 256 ff.; Ola E. Winslow, *Jonathan Edwards,* 1703-1758 (1940).

C.H.M.

social work of the churches: A term designating the agencies and techniques through which the social motive finds expression in religious groups, including the maintenance of hospitals, homes, and settlements, case work with families and individuals, group work, social education, and social action. The social work of Catholic, Protestant (for the modern development of theoretical basis in Protestantism, see article on the *Social Gospel*), and Jewish communions is based upon the social and ethical teachings of the Old and New Testaments and on the communal traditions of early Christianity. Within Christianity, however, this early communal emphasis was soon obscured as the church became absorbed in defining its doctrine and perfecting its organization. Also, the ascetic* spirit within Christianity, the popular views of poverty as a divinely established condition to be relieved rather than removed and of almsgiving as a penance of value to the donor in the next world rather than to the recipient in this, tended to place the emphasis in practical Christianity upon individual redemption rather than upon the redemption of the social order. Nevertheless, the rise of monasteries and hospitals as institutions for the poor, sick, infirm, aged, and orphans, the emphasis on the ransoming of captives, the ecclesiastical attempts to preserve peace and to regulate industry and commerce in the interest of justice and human welfare, and the rise of parish charity and spontaneous individual almsgiving, bear testimony to the widespread concern of the medieval church with human suffering.

However, with the decay of feudalism*, the confiscation of the monasteries and other sources of Catholic charity, and the rise of modern capitalism, industrialism, and urbanization, distress was greatly augmented. The haphazard efforts of parochial and individual charity were no longer adequate, and relief became increasingly a function of the municipalities and later of the national states. During this period the Catholic Church laid the foundations for its modern charitable and institutional enterprises, while the Protestant Reformation and the outbreak of new sects with their interest in the restoration of the primitive church in faith and practice, often including its communistic features, contributed to the development of the social conception of Christianity. During the seventeenth century and later the Quakers* especially became apostles of love and justice among men, crusaders against slavery and war, and on behalf of prison reform, popular education, and the social care of the insane and the defective.

The rise of modern secular social work in England and America since the middle of last century, with its emphasis upon investigation, attention to causes, individualized treatment, self-help, record-keeping, and cooperation of agencies, owes much to the religious motivation of many of its founders. It has also reacted upon the social work of religious groups in certain fundamental ways common to them all. In the first place, they have all adapted the new principles and techniques to their traditional types of service. This is seen in the enlarged scope of hospital services, in the gradual substitution of home care of children and the aged for the earlier institutional types, in the adoption of case work techniques in dealing with individuals and families and in the willingness to surrender the functions of purely material relief to governmental agencies. Second, all groups have modernized and enlarged the scope of their services by establishing new agencies under religious auspices paralleling those in the secular field. Here may be mentioned the special schools of social and religious work set up within the Catholic and the Protestant denominational colleges and universities and the recently closed Jewish Graduate School of Social Work in New York. The National Conference of Catholic Charities, the National Conference of Jewish Social Welfare, and the Church Conference of Social Work, recently organized by the Federal Council of Churches*, parallel the secular National Conference of Social Work. Third, all have adapted educational, recreational and other group work programs to the needs of their own constituencies which in the more highly developed parish houses approximate the settlement programs in scope and personnel. Fourth, all have engaged in experimentation with new forms of social service, such as psychiatric clinics, family consultation, and in some cases birth control, which they have often relinquished to secular agencies when firmly established. Finally, all have developed programs of "social action," a series of social pronouncements and reform measures directed toward changes in the economic and social *status quo* from which many individual social problems arise. The most important of these is the "Social Ideals of the Churches," first formulated by the Methodist Episcopal Church in 1908 and adopted by the First Quadrennial Meeting of the Federal Council of Churches in Philadelphia in the same year. It consists of a declaration of principles with reference to child welfare, labor legislation, the minimum wage, collective bargaining, old age security, social justice, and the application of Christian ethics to the acquisition and use of property. It has frequently been revised and expanded. Similar pronouncements have been made by all the leading denominations. The Bishops' Program for Social Reconstruction, formulated at the National Catholic Welfare Council in 1919, and the Social Justice Program, drawn up by the Central Conference of American Rabbis in 1920, with their more recent emendations, serve a similar function for these groups. Most Protestant denominations have social service commissions under various names which are active in promoting such reforms. The common interests in this field of the 24 Protestant denominations constituting the Federal Council of Churches is expressed through its Commission on Religion and Health, the departments of Race Relations, International Justice and Good Will, Research and Education, and especially through its department of the Church and Social Service. Certain departments of the International Council of Religious Education, especially those dealing with youth and adults, are also active in this field. Similar functions are performed among the Jews by the Social Justice Commission, and among the Catholics by the Social Action Department of the National Catholic Welfare Council.

Despite these similarities, Catholic, Protestant, and Jewish groups have developed clearly differentiated patterns of social work in accordance with their distinctive religious attitudes and forms of organization. *The Catholic pattern* remains supernatural in outlook. Social work is conceived of as motivated by a love of God above all creatures, and by a love of others for the sake of God. It is thus an essentially religious function, and is organized as an integral part of the work of parish and diocese, with a complete range of services paralleling those of the secular community. Central diocesan organizations, usually called "Catholic Charities," have been formed in 79 dioceses. They serve as the organ through which the bishop directs the social service agencies and charitable institutions under his jurisdiction. Volunteer lay organizations, some of them national and international in scope and often employing professionally trained workers, have also been established. The more important are the Society of St. Vincent de Paul, among men, and among the women, the Ladies of Charity, the Ladies Auxiliary, the Catholic Women's League, and the National Council of Catholic Women. The Catholic Daughters of America, the Knights of Columbus*, the Catholic Order of Foresters, the Christ Child Society, and other organizations, also undertake some social service. The Catholic Youth Organization conducts religious, social, recreational, and culture activities for young people in certain centers, generally under diocesan auspices.

The Jewish pattern is communal rather than specifically religious in character. Although most Jewish communal organizations are of twentieth century origin, they represent the adaptation to current conditions of the Scriptural and Talmudic traditions of communal responsibility of all classes of the needy. This communal pattern was developed through centuries of persecution, and was firmly established in Jewish life and thought on their arrival in America in large numbers from Eastern Europe after 1881. Its perpetuation and development has been facilitated in America by the fact that of the 5,000,000 Jews in the United States, 70 per cent live in the 11 largest cities, with nearly 40 per cent in Greater New York alone. In these cities Jewish philanthropy is comprehensive and highly differentiated, with specialized agencies on every recognized field, while the small communities are served by a single communal agency covering the entire field. All the larger communities are organized in federations of Jewish welfare work. More recently, Jewish social and fraternal as well as welfare activities have been further coordinated by the organization of community councils which provide a medium for joint consideration of communal problems and an instrumentality for joint action with regard to all aspects of Jewish life. Jewish agencies find it necesary to provide relief for large numbers of aged immigrants whose citizenship status excludes them from public relief, and to maintain certain institutions, hospitals and homes for children and the aged, in which a Jewish environment is considered essential. Because of the Talmudic doctrine of self-help as the highest form of charity and because of the large role of small business enterprise in Jewish economy, a distinctive feature of Jewish social work is the Hebrew Free Loan Society, which makes small loans on endorsed notes without interest to meet emergencies and to finance self-employment ventures. Refugee service has recently assumed large proportions. Since the accession of the Nazi regime in Europe some 200,000 Jews have arrived in the United States, usually without funds because of the confiscation of their property. In 1941, $4,500,000 was expended for this purpose. Another important task is the relief and rehabilitation of dislocated Jewish populations overseas through the United Palestine appeal, which purchases land in Palestine and aids in its colonization, and through the Jewish Joint Distribution Committee, which assists Jews overseas, especially in Eastern and Central European countries.

The Protestant pattern is the most heterogeneous of all. Protestant denominations have continued their traditional institutional services such as hospitals, orphanages*, and homes for the aged, but the fact that these denominations generally regard themselves as voluntary associations rather than as organizations representing the entire community has led them to find in community-wide secular organizations the natural channels for the expression of the Christian social motive. Protestantism has diffused its leadership widely through these agencies and contributed its means to their support rather than duplicate their efforts in a parallel set of agencies under denominational auspices. Moreover, the fact that the major denominations share a common religious mood which is more fundamental than their differences has made it comparatively easy for them to support joint socio-religious enterprises such as the Young Men's and Young Women's Christian Associations** and the Church Federation Movement. In the past persons of Catholic or Jewish affiliation who have been in need of special services, such as persons discharged from hospitals or released from prison, juvenile* delinquents, and the like, have been promptly assisted by the appropriate agency, but Protestants, owing to the lack of denominational organization, have been less fortunate. This need is now being supplied in many urban centers under federated auspices by interdenominational case work organizations or by referral to other social agencies.

On a national scale, the Home Missions Council has been an active force for social betterment, especially in rural areas. Other joint social work agencies developed since the outbreak of the war, many of them administered or fostered by the Federal Council of Churches, include the Christian Commission for Camp and Defense Communities, the Commission on Aliens and Prisoners of War in America, the Committee on Foreign Relief Appeals, the Church Committee for China Relief, the American Committee for Christian Refugees, and the War Prisoners Aid of the Y.M.C.A. The Federal Council's Commission on Army and Naval Chaplains, which assists in the selection of chaplains, has assumed new functions as the chaplains have undertaken social case work functions in relation to personal and family problems.

Much local Protestant effort has been of a pioneering character in areas of special need. The institutional church*, with its elaborate program of social services on a community rather than a parish basis, was formerly a popular form of religious enterprise, but as secular social work has covered urban areas more adequately, they have declined in popularity. A similar pioneering effort is the National Association of Good Will Industries, originally developed under Methodist auspices, but now interdenominational and nonsectarian, which in 1942 provided social services and economic self-support for the handicapped in 82 local centers.

The most recent development in the Protestant field is the incorporation of social work principles and techniques into the regular training of pastors, missionaries, and other church workers. At least eight seminaries now provide clinical training, the students serving as internes in general and mental hospitals and family case working agencies. A unique contribution is being made by the Council for Clinical Training, conducted by the Federal Council of Churches. In 1941 it maintained centers in five federal penal and correctional institutions and provided at least three months training to 65 students. See charity and almsgiving; charity organization; communistic settlements, religious; friendly societies; social gospel.

F. E. Johnson, *The Social Work of the Churches*, The Federal Council of Churches (1930); M. T. Boylan, *Social Welfare in the Catholic Church* (1941); E. Fritsch, *An Historical Survey of Jewish Philanthropy* (1924); M. J. Karpf, *Jewish Community Organization in the United States* (1938); R. Niebuhr, *The Contribution of Religion to Social Work* (1932).

H.E.J.

socialism: I. Socialism means community of ownership, as opposed to private property. It signifies different things in different contexts. The rulers of Plato's republic, the early Christians, the monasteries to this day, practice socialism as an ascetic way to their emancipation from distracting worldly interests and to their concentration on their spiritual responsibility. Modern socialism claims to organize the world for economic prosperity and makes of this claim a philosophy.

II. Socialism is opposed to, but also derived from, liberal capitalism. Liberalism is deistic or materialistic. It says that God or nature have so created man as to make him naturally contribute to universal harmony. Politically this means a rational, individualistic, bourgeois society: man can only be made free, and he also must be made free, if this is the condition of universal harmony. Economically,, the free play of forces is supposed to work harmoniously by way of the price mechanism; upward and downward movements of price, expressive of growing or declining demand for the product, attract or determine profit-seeking producers and thus adjust supply to demand. But further implications were neglected by the liberal doctrine. Unregulated freedom makes the (financially) strong the lord of the weak by ruining the small shops and forcing their owners into "proletarian"* dependent industrial work in the superior large enterprises. At the same time, the growth of the latter, while increasing the productivity of the system, diminishes its adaptability and flexibility (fixed capital) and thus produces or intensifies the economic crisis and its accompaniment, unemployment.

Socialism is primarily the critique of these defects of liberalism. Since they appear as results of a historical development, socialism becomes a doctrine of historical change through an autonomous economic change (economic interpretation of history). According to Marxism (see Marx, Karl), the most elaborate form of socialism, history is dialectic; it leads from any organization of society through the conflict with its victims to the next higher and more comprehensive stage, in a self-determining progressive movement. When all men will be on the same footing of liberty, as equals, in the most comprehensive organization of the classless society, the dialectic of history reaches its end. Capitalism* is the second-to-the-last stage, a system of collective, dependent, propertyless work for the profit of private owners, often interrupted by unemployment. The solution of the class struggle in capitalism is the "social revolution", which organizes this collective system of production as the collective property of the workers and unifies its operation under a comprehensive crisis-proof plan. This is the logical—dialectically logical—consequence of the contradictory system of capitalism, which combines personal liberty with dependent work and collective production with private appropriation of the product.

The workers' state, shaped to achieve that final reorganization, is democratic as the rule of the huge majority, but dictatorial towards the former exploiters and their intellectual and armed lackeys, whose counter-revolutionary aspirations it suppresses. The state will finally "wither away" for lack of a function as soon as all have been reeducated by dictatorial pressure for a free cooperative association—the goal of history.

III. The political problems of socialism rise from its anticipation of a development to a unified proletarian system by way of the universal spread of large-scale mechanical production. This is only partly confirmed by the facts. Labor-saving devices—supplemented by cheap electrical power and co-operatively-owned machines—restore the efficiency of individual farming in the most progressive countries of agriculture. In industry, labor-saving machines dissociate the growth of production and output from any growth of labor proper but require increasing numbers of engineers and accountants, as well as middlemen for the distribution of the growing output,—the new middle classes gain in numbers and functions. The result is a growing diversity in late capitalist society, although all its members suffer from the crisis and inequality has become excessive, as predicted by Marx.

In this situation, socialists decided either to postpone their uniform proletarian program until history would produce its precondition, or to impose it forcibly on a largely non-proletarian society, by way of a minority dictatorship. The former was the way of the German socialists—their inaction in a disintegrating bourgeois system paved the way to the action of the National Socialists. The latter is the way of Russian communists—their action betrayed democracy and contributed the model of their dictatorship towards the growth of fascism. The political problem of socialism is, then, the conflict between its totalitarian proletarian claim and its democratic ideal, which requires diversity and decentralization as the condition of liberty. The French socialist Proudhon (1808-1865) has opposed the idea of a balanced pluralistic constitution to the Marxian dictatorship of the proletariat.

IV. Philosophically, socialism is, first of all, the punishment inflicted on liberal society for its claim to automatic human perfection. This is the starting point of religious socialism—the divine wrath uses the proletarian sufferers as a scourge on a complacent and overbearing bourgeois* world and reveals through their protest the social and economic disintegration of a supposedly harmonious system. But only British socialism drew the positive conclusion to preach socialism as a Christian commandment rather than to teach it as social science. Continental and American socialism is heir to the tradition of materialism and atheism. It relies on the growth of automatic perfection, not indeed by virtue of the given natural faculties of man, but as a product of causally inevitable economic changes. The result is parallel to that of the liberal utopia, a self-contained world of man, individualistic here, collectivist there, and redeemed from evil, once and for all, by the economic process, much as this requires men conscious of their opportunity. This is an overtly anti-Christian doctrine. This can be seen from the theory of the final stage of the development, where the evil has been overcome and the state, the guardian against evil, withers away for lack of a function; but it can also be seen from the preceding, dialectically opposite stage, the proletarian dictatorship, where the dictatorial class or its heads act as the infallible trustees of salvation, immune to the temptation of unchecked power and inspired only by the spirit of their mission. This supposedly scientific, but unverifiable theory rationalizes the unlimited power of a certain group of men as the guarantee of the salvation of mankind; it justifies their every act of violence or trickery as securing that objective. It has become a pseudo-religious dogma, the center and meaning of life for many millions, and has superseded the Christian dogma, which they reject because of its dogmatic, unverifiable nature.

And yet the Christian heritage is unmistakable in communism. All forms of socialism are inspired by the Christian ideas of justice, liberty, and peace. Communism is a Christian heresy. Its heretical character, its reliance on the redeeming force of man, or of certain men, is responsible for the absurdity of its logic and the atrocity of its politics.

But its objective—contrary to any fascist objective, where liberty and peace are ridiculed and justice is only another name for racial supremacy—makes communism a part of the Christian world and permits the hope that some re-Christianization will be forced on the official doctrine by the profoundly Christian Russian peasants, from below, and by the alliance with the West, from without. See anarchism; dialectic; Jewish socialism; labor movements.

Karl Marx and Friedrich Engels, *The Communist Manifesto* (first published in 1849); Friedrich Engels, *The Development of Socialism from Utopia to Science* (first published in 1882); N. Lenin, *State and Revolution* (first published in 1917); Reinhold Niebuhr, *Moral Man and Immoral Society* (1933); Eduard Heimann, *Communism, Fascism, Or Democracy?* (1938).

E.H.

Society of Friends (Quakers): Quakerism* evolved in the later stages of the Protestant Reformation in England, precipitated by the ministry and personality of George Fox*. His preaching in 1647 and following made converts among Seekers*, Independents, Baptists, and other sectarians, who loosely united as "Children of the Light," "Friends," or "Friends in the Truth." Fox and his converts soon spread the new faith through the British Isles, to the Continent, and to America (1656). Persecution fortified them in their zeal to publish the "Truth" of the "Light of Christ that lighteth the heart of every man." Hangings in Boston and imprisonment in Cromwellian and Restoration England failed to discourage them. Missionaries travelled widely, and settlers migrated to the New World until, when Fox himself visited America in 1671-73 he found Friends in Barbados, and from the Carolinas to New England. Rhode Island was their greatest mainland stronghold, until in 1681 Pennsylvania was granted by Charles II to the distinguished Quaker convert, William Penn*.

Fox's death in 1691 marked the end of the pioneer phase of Quakerism. He witnessed its growth to forty or fifty thousand adherents in Britain and some thirty thousand abroad. He helped perfect an organization of monthly, quarterly, and yearly meetings, with the monthly meeting serving as the local congregational group, the quarterly meeting drawing a number of these units together, and the yearly meeting, semi-representative, semi-popular, exercising final authority in the region under its jurisdiction. Friends eschewed a formal creed, but their code of morals was very strict. Quaker humanitarianism, springing from the doctrine of the Inner Light, began to flower, as Friends pioneered in eighteenth-century social reform. Quaker theology, at least as interpreted by Robert Barclay* in his *Apology* (1678), was English liberal Protestantism, modified by the emphasis on direct revelation, a lay ministry, and the "spiritualization" of the sacraments.

The eighteenth century was marked by a growing quietism in Quaker religious thought and practice. No longer persecuted, Friends lived as a people apart, refining their discipline in matters of conduct and dress, and extending their humanitarianism which had already renounced war, to Indian relations and Negro slavery. From this age of quietism they were shaken by the new philosophy of the Revolutionary period, by the great westward migrations in the United States after the War, and by the evangelical movement, English and American. The migrations carried Quakerism over the mountains to the Ohio Valley, to Canada, and eventually to the plains states and the Pacific Coast. Liberal, unitarian ideas clashed with a growing evangelicalism to produce a great Separation in America in 1827-28. English Quaker leaders, themselves increasingly evangelical, sided with the "Orthodox" party, although some felt that the theology of the "Hicksites" (so-named because one of their leaders was Elias Hicks, a prominent Long Island minister) more closely approximated that of the "first publishers of Truth."

Further separations followed among the Orthodox. A small, conservative New England group, led by John Wilbur (1845), kept more closely to the mystical faith and quietistic practices of earlier days. Others embraced the evangelical theology whole-heartedly, and gradually took on the color of the evangelical churches around them. Hymn singing, paid pastors, and programmed meetings became common among "Friends Churches." Only their peace testimony and their refusal to celebrate the sacraments in the physical form distinguished them from other evangelical Protestants. The Orthodox Philadelphia Yearly Meeting, however, where the first great separation had begun, avoided further schisms by ceasing to correspond with other American Yearly Meetings, and refusing to join their evangelical Five Years Meeting (1887). The Hicksite Yearly Meetings united loosely in a biennial General Conference (1902).

Evangelicalism* brought revivalism, missionary and reform activity to Friends, as it did to all Protestants. Humanitarianism, mystical as well as evangelical in origin, continued to distinguish Friends of all branches. Education, prison reform, temperance, Indian aid, and antislavery were Quaker favorites, although Friends could be found in all kinds of philanthropic organizations from "soup societies" to Bible associations. Officially they shrank from the use of force which they feared some of these reforms, notably abolition, might provoke. But they stood firmly on the ethical principles involved, and some Friends shared in the activities of the Underground Railroad and the radical antislavery groups.

The twentieth century has seen an extension of the opportunities for humanitarian and religious service, and a corresponding growth toward unity among Friends everywhere. The high tide of evangelicalism has receded, and, among "conservative" Friends, the outward distinctions of speech and dress have given way. The first World War saw the organization of an American Friends Service Committee, with representatives from all branches in this country. English and American Friends likewise drew more closely together in service and religious fellowship. An All-Friends Conference in London in 1920 was followed by a World Conference in 1937 at Swarthmore and Haverford Colleges, near Philadelphia. Out of this has come a World Committee for Consultation which brings together the approximately 163,135 Friends now in the world. Their subdivisions were in 1940: Great Britain and Ireland, 22,124; North America, 116,090; Latin America, 7,172; Europe, 627; Asia, 2,338; Africa, 14,429; Australia and New Zealand, 932. Of these some were obviously mission groups; others varied in theology and practice. In the United States, rural meetings, both evangelical and conservative, seemed to be on the decline, while united meetings, or independent meetings, free of any connections with older branches but strongly convinced of the validity of the early Quaker approach to God and man, were springing up in cities and educational centers. A Wider Quaker Fellowship even enabled members of other churches to join with Friends in the task of bringing together man and God and man and man. See Gurney; oaths; Pennington; Woolman.

See E. Russell, *History of Quakerism* (1942).

T.E.D.

Society of Jesus: See Jesuits.

Society for the Propagation of the Gospel in Foreign Parts (S.P.G.): Founded in 1701, the oldest missionary society of the Church of England*. E.R.H.

Society for Psychical Research (S.P.R.): See psychical research, societies for.

Society of true inspiration: Amarites. See communistic settlements, religious.

Socinianism: The name (derived from its most influential thinker, Faustus Socinus, 1539-1604) applied to an anti-trinitarian movement developed in Poland in the 16th and 17th centuries, and eventually in England and America transformed into Unitarianism*; in Poland erroneously called Arianism. S. originated about the middle of the 16th century among Humanists in Italy who on scriptural or rational grounds objected to the Catholic doctrines about God and Christ. Forced to flee the Inquisition* they first sought refuge in Switzerland (Gribaldi, Biandrata, Alciati, Gentile, Ochino, Laelius Socinus), where they were much influenced by Servetus's criticisms of the Trinity. Those who survived persecution here took shelter in tolerant Poland. Their views of doctrinal reform found wide acceptance in the Retormed Church of Poland (1565). They had a fellowship, whence they organized as the Minor Reformed Church of Poland (1556). They had a centre at Raków (Racovia) with a notable college and an active press, and they sent books and emissaries hence through western Europe.

Socinus coming to them in 1579 soon gained leadership, brought about agreement on vexed doctrinal and social questions, and left them a body of doctrine in the *Racovian Catechism* (1605) compiled by his disciples, which was widely circulated for a hundred years, and had no little influence on doctrinal thinking among Protestants. It based its teachings strictly on Scripture, and adhered to the Apostles' rather than the Nicene and Athanasian Creeds. The Socinians maintained rigid moral standards, aiming to revive the simple ways of the primitive Christian communities. They taught non-resistance, steadfastly refused to take part in war, and would not hold serfs. Though widely influential, they were the smallest of the Protestant confessions in Poland, and had perhaps not more than 200 congregations all told, a few in large towns but mostly in the rural villages of the gentry. Unlike the other sects, they welcomed on terms of Christian equality peasants and artizans no less than gentry. Their polity was similar to that of the Reformed, with synods in which the laity took large part, supervision by district Elders, and a general Superintendent over all.

The movement spread steadily for two generations despite bitter opposition and exclusion from fellowship with the other confessions; but the Catholic reaction, led by the Jesuits*, brought about steadily increasing persecution. In 1638 their centre at Raków was broken up by act of the Diet, their school abolished, their press destroyed, and their leaders proscribed. Suppression became steadily harsher until 1658 when the whole sect was banished on pain of death. Many had no choice but to conform to the Catholic Church; but a few score of noble families sacrificing all went into exile: some to Transylvania, where they maintained a congregation in fellowship with the Unitarians until late in the 18th century; some into East Prussia, where the last Socinian church in history expired early in the 19th century; and a notable group to Holland, where they made no attempt at separate organization, being hospitably received among Collegiants, Mennonites and Remonstrants. These exercized considerable influence in liberalizing Dutch thought and were influenced by it in turn; but by the middle of the 18th century they had lost their separate identity and become absorbed in the general religious life of the country, though their influence was long felt in the growth of rationalistic views. Through their contact in Holland with Dissenters from England or liberal Anglicans, their views were transplanted into England, where they presently became the most important single source of Unitarianism. See atonement in Christianity.

See F. Trechsel, *Protestantische Antitrinitarier vor Faustus Socin* (1839-'44); F. S. Bock, *Historia Antitrinitariorum* (1774-'84); Otto Fock, *Socinianismus* (1847); E. M. Wilbur, *History of the Socinian-Unitarian Movement* (in press); Stanislas Kot, *Social and Political Ideals of the Polish Brethren* (in press).

E.M.W.

sociology: (Lat., *socius*, companion; Gr., *logos*, science) The generic and comparative study of all the interactions and interrelationships which exist among human beings, or, as C. A. Ellwood expresses it, "The science of the origin, development, structure, and functioning of social groups." The word was first used by Auguste Comte* in 1838 to designate a division of his *Cours de philosophie positive*, and Comte is generally acknowledged as the founder of the science. But sociology did not originate with Comte as an offspring without a genealogy. If all theories which deal with the general nature of human association and the reciprocal relationships of men to one another are sociological, then sociology is implicit in the folklore* of primitive peoples, and reached a high development in Plato (427-347 B.C.) and Aristotle (384-322 B.C.), which has not again approached until the *Summa Theologiae* of Thomas Aquinas (1225?-1275). But science is distinguished by its method rather than by its content, and it was Comte who prepared the way for a new conception of social phenomena and a new method of treating them. He was the first to combine 1) a clear distinction between society and its specifically delimited political and economic forms as an independent focus of theoretical interest with 2) an observational method competent to deal with social relationships in their completeness and 3) relatively free from *a priori* theological, metaphysical, and normative limitations. But it was the publication of Herbert Spencer's* *Study of Sociology* in 1873 which established the subject in general favor, and prepared the ground for the popular reception accorded in the next fifteen years to four great attempts at a systematic exposition of the field, in Spencer's *Descriptive Sociology* (1874-81) and *Principles of Sociology* (1877-86), Albert Schäffle's *Bau und Leben des socialen Körpers* (1875-78), Lester F. Ward's *Dynamic Sociology* (1883) and Guillaume de Greef's *Introduction à la Sociologie* (1886-89).

During this formative period the field of sociology was defined and clarified, first, as a general science of social relationships studying the characteristics common to all social phenomena as distinguished from the special social sciences, economics, political science, education, jurisprudence, etc., which treat of the internal structure and specific functions of specialized social groups and processes, industry, the state, the school, law, etc. Economics, for example, treats of cooperation and competition in the wealth-producing, distributing, and consuming activities, while sociology studies cooperation and competition as general processes of interaction among human beings in all group relationships. Political science is interested in social control as exercised by the state, while sociology considers the control function as it operates in all social behavior. Both economics and political science study industry and the state as specialized institutions, while sociology studies the basic characteristics of social institutions as such. Second, sociology emerged before specialized social sciences dealing with many social institutions and group relationships, like the family, the church, and recreation, had developed. Sociology has investigated these intensively in order to complete its detailed knowledge of many types of specialized social phenomena. Third, since social phenomena are obviously conditioned by the kind of biological organisms human beings are, and the kind of geographical environment they have, sociology has also found it necessary to study the relationships and correlations between the social and such non-social phenomena as the biological, the geographical and the individual-psychological.

During the past half century, sociologists have been concerned less with comprehensive systems of social theory like those of Comte and Spencer and more with detailed research upon the types of problems indicated above. This has resulted in a number of different schools of sociology, the geographical, the biological, the psychological, the economic and other variants, owing to the undue emphasis upon one or another of the factors which constitute or affect society as a complex whole. The most fundamental cleavage, however, is the methodological one, which gives rise to two schools, the "natural science" and the "autonomous," based on a difference of view as to the nature of social facts and the proper methods of their scientific study. The former school, taking its cue from the physical sciences, holds that social facts are facts of external observation. Consequently, sociology is a science of overt behavior, and the inner life of thought and feeling, if it is considered at all, is treated as inferences drawn from the data of external observation, precisely as are the physicist's inferences as to the internal structure of the atom. From this standpoint, all scientific knowledge is quantitative knowledge, the only valid scientific problems are those which admit of quantification, and the only valid research techniques are those of counting and measuring, together with the mathematical analysis of the values so ascertained. The opposing school, on the other hand, insists that social facts possess a dual character. They must be understood, not only as observed data, but also as felt experiences. The personal and dramatic qualities which social relationships have for those who participate in them are as essential to their scientific description and interpretation as are their external manifestations in overt behavior. Since all social facts involve these subjective aspects which have no analogues in the subject matter of the sciences of external nature, it must become an autonomous science in the sense that it is not limited by the methodological assumptions of those sciences in the formulation of its problems and the development of its research techniques. It must make whatever assumptions, formulate whatever postulates, develop whatever conceptual systems, and adopt whatever research techniques, its data may require. The sociologist may and should learn much from his studies in the methodology of the physical and biological sciences, he may and should adapt their methods of quantification and experiment wherever they are applicable, but he must not be limited by them. In proportion as his data are different, he must be left free to adopt a different methodology, leaving to philosophy the task of criticism and synthesis of the methods and the results of all the sciences into an organic unity of all knowledge. See anthropology.

C. A. Ellwood, *Methods in Sociology* (1933); L. L. Bernard, *The Fields and Methods of Sociology* (1934); P. A. Sorokin, *Socio-cultural Causality, Space, and Time* (1943).

H.E.J.

sociology of religion, the: The sociology of religion involves two aspects. From the sociological side it refers to the group life of man as manifested in the interactions and relationships that occur in human society; from the standpoint of religion it refers to man's beliefs in a deity or deities superior to men and upon whom they are considered to be dependent, and to the behavior that ensues from such beliefs.

Thus, the sociology of religion is definable as a study of the processes and results of human association as affecting, and affected by, man's religious beliefs.

Such a definition in itself serves to account in large measure for the numerous and widely divergent religions that exist in the world, for—like industrial, political, or other cultural phenomena—the content and manner of any faith will reflect the life and times and environment of a society and its reaction to them, and of its members to each other. Thus, sociology within this field explains that particular religions will be backward or advánced according to the corresponding cultural level of the people: local and primitive deities will be believed in where cultures are local or primitive; universal and intelligent deities will be believed in by those who have a world-wide and highly educated outlook. A warlike people will have warlike gods, whereas peace-loving and humanitarian civilizations will conceive of their's in terms of benevolence, and concerned with human well-being. The old-time divinities of storm-driven Scandinavia were like their own thunder and lightning; whereas acceptance of the philosophy of ancient Greece led to the conception by the early Church of a single triune Being which combined the characteristics of the mystic Logos with those of a heavenly Father, and an earthly Son.

In similar fashion the sociological approach makes clear that specific doctrines are an outgrowth of the settings in which they originate. Thus, a long-subject people like the ancient Hebrews, centered their faith about a Messiah* who would bring temporal deliverance on earth; and the early Christians, persecuted for their beliefs, were inspired by the idea of an escape from earth to heavenly mansions. Ancient pastoral folk thought of Elysian Fields after death, whereas the American Indian looked forward to happy hunting grounds. Nor does it stop there; for sociology makes clear how, as a result of the cultural lag that frequently accompanies tradition, beliefs which originated in an earlier day tend to persist even when out of harmony with the findings of modern research.

On the other hand, the sociology of religion undertakes to account for the remarkable effects of religious beliefs on human relations past and present: the centuries-long conflict between church and state, the earnest effort to work toward a "Christian" society, the impact of various faiths in creating, maintaining, or modifying social institutions (family, school, government, and others), all stand forth as cause-and-effect sociological sequences, emerging from the interaction of men with men, as conditioned by environment.

Just as there is only one Chemistry, the identical principles of which are applied to separate fields, (e.g., bio-chemistry, chemistry of agriculture), so there is only one sociology, variously applied (e.g., sociology of art, of education, of religion). Occasionally in the last-named it is confused with a statement of religious teachings. This is an error to be guarded against, for sociology, like any other science, deals with principles, based upon adequate data, logically interpreted; and as science, by definition it can deal only with factually-based evidence and not with value judgments nor metaphysics *per se*. Its principles, however, may become guides to the validity of ideals which religion teaches.

Wm. Cecil Dampier, *A History of Science, and its Relations with Philosophy and Religion* (1943); C. A. Ellwood, *The Reconstruction of Religion* (1922); Earle Edward Eubank, "Fields and Problems of the Sociology of Religion," chap. 12 of *Fields and Methods of Sociology* (1934), L. L. Bernard, editor; C. Luther Fry, "Changes in Religious Organizations," chap. 20 of *Recent Social Trends* (1933), vol. II, Pres. Hoover's Research Committee Report. W. F. Ogburn & H. W. Odum, Directors; James M. Hastings, *Encyclopedia of Religion and Ethics;* E. W. Hopkins, *Origin and Evolution of Religion* (1923); Wm. James, *Varieties of Religious Experience* (1902); Arthur L. Swift, *New Frontiers of Religion* (1938); J. A. Thomson, *What is Man?* (1924).

E.E.E.

Socrates: (c. 380-444) Historian of the early church. Advocate in Constantinople. His history covers period c. 305-439, dealing chiefly with the theological controversies. Is not a critical history in the modern sense but is of interest and value for description of contemporary scene.

K.H.C.

Socrates: Greek thinker (469-399 B.C.), the son of an Athenian stone-cutter and a mid-wife. Much of his life was spent in the discussion of lofty problems of philosophical and religious import. As recorded by Xenophon and Plato*, these discussions were marked by keen wit and high ideals. Socrates was convinced that he was negatively guided in his pursuit of wisdom by a familiar spirit (*daemon*). (See daimon.) The story of his execution at the direction of the Athenian court (Plato, *Apology, Crito* and *Phaedo;* Xenophon, *Memorabilia*) is a touching account of the last hours of a great man. Though the Socratic method* is probably his greatest contribution, certain positive views are traditionally attributed to him. The contention that "virtue is knowledge" (*Protagoras* and *Meno* of Plato) indicates his high regard for practical wisdom. Socrates was not wanting in respect for the State gods of Athens but there is evidence that he placed a Supreme God on a different level from that of the minor divinities and that he was a believer in a form of personal immortality*. Possibly Plato's account of piety (*Euthyphro,* 5 E) stems from Socrates. In Platonism, Cynicism and Stoicism, Cyrenaicism and Epicureanism**, and among some Renaiscence* moralists (Erasmus*), the influence of Socratic ethics is important.

E. Zeller, *Socrates and the Socratic Schools,* trans. by Reichel (London, 1885).

V.J.B.

Socratic method: The style of discussion used by Socrates* in his frequent talks with the Sophists* and the young men of Athens. The significant characteristics of this method are: 1) a profession of ignorance on the part of the questioner (learned ignorance); 2) the pointed use of series of questions leading to the discovery of a universal definition; 3) the contention that the rôle of the teacher is not to confer knowledge but to draw it from the learner (mid-wife analogy); 4) the admission of the superior wisdom of others leading to a demonstration of their basic ignorance (Socratic Irony). Good examples of the use of this method are found in Plato's* *Meno* and *Protagoras*. V.J.B.

sodalities: Pious unions of the faithful erected for the carrying on of some particular work of piety or charity. They differ from other pious unions in that they constitute an organic body or moral person, and from confraternities* which are devoted chiefly to public worship. The most important pious organization called a sodality in the United States is the Sodality of the Blessed Virgin Mary, founded in 1563 and erected into an archsodality in 1584. The confraternities of the Holy Rosary and of the Scapular of Our Lady of Mt. Carmel, which are not ordinarily called sodalities in the United States, also have large memberships in this country. See Catholic Societies. T.T.M.

Söderblom, Lars Olof Jonathan (Nathan): (1866-1931) Son of a pastor, Söderblom studied theology at Upsala, ordained 1893. Pastor of the Swedish church at Paris, 1894. Interested in the social aspects of the church, also studied at Sorbonne in the field of history of religions, especially attracted to Auguste Sabatier*. Doctor of theology at Sorbonne, 1901, and called to professorship at Upsala, Söderblom exerted a tremendous influence on the younger student generation. Himself a brilliant and gifted personality with interest in music, art, literature, he advocated freedom of research in the Church, but also with deep respect for tradition he labored on winning all classes for the church, whose spiritual home the Church should be, as spiritual power more than organization. Following a brief professorship at Leipzig, 1912-14, Söderblom became archbishop in 1914. Throughout the war he sought to maintain fellowship between churches of various warring countries, and afterwards became a leader in the ecumenical movement, arranging the Stockholm Conference of 1925, and heading the Life and Work movement, though also active in Faith and Order. His leadership and genius for friendship made Sweden a center of interchurch interest. In the field of scholarship his main contributions lay in studies in Mazdaism*, *La vie future d'apres le mazdeisme* (1901), in philosophy of religion, *Uppenbarelsereligion* (1903), *Das Werden des Gottesglauben* (1913), *The Living God* (Gifford Lectures, 1930), and in Luther studies, *Humor och melancholi* (1917). His devotional writings and sermons were widely read, and his leadership at home and abroad made him one of Protestantism's outstanding figures of the century. C.J.B.

Sohm, Rudolf: (1841-1917) German jurist and canonist. Born in Rostock, Mecklemburg. In 1866 he became privatdozent at Goettingen, from 1872-1887 he was professor at Strasburg, and from 1887-1917 at Leipzig. His main fields of interest were History of Germanic Law and History of Ecclesiastical Law. He combined the historical and systematic approach with great logical power, and by his ingenuous interpretation of its historical development laid the foundation for modern Protestant church law in Germany. He held that any legal order was incompatible with the nature of the Gospel, and thus regarded the coming into existence of the church of the second century as the most fatal deviation from the original ideas of Jesus. His views had a considerable influence upon Harnack's* interpretation of the ancient church. Active Lutheran; friend, and for some time collaborator of Fr. Naumann.

Principal works:
Kirchenrecht, vol. I (1892), vol. II (posthumous, 1922); *Wesen und Ursprung des Katholizismus* (1909, 3rd ed., 1912); *Die altdeutsche Reichs-und Gerichtsverfassung* (1871). See also: Otto Barion, *Rud. Sohm und die Grundlegung des Kirchenrechts* (1931). O.A.P.

Sol Invictus: Name applied by the Romans to a sun-god or divinity imported from the Near East to Rome, along with other foreign gods, in the years following disasters to Romans during the Second Punic War; identified with Mithras, a high divinity derived from religion of the Persians; as Mithras, Sol Invictus had a festival which led to the Christmas celebration of the Christians, on December 25; a syncretic god of the Roman imperial state cult. For a time in the late Roman Empire certain equations were drawn between Sol Invictus (Mithras) high divinity in relation with Mazda*, and Christ, high divinity in relation with God (Zeus*). See mystery religions. F.L.P.

sola gratia: See grace.

Solemn League and Covenant: See League and Covenant, the Solemn.

solemn mass: See mass.

solifidianism: (Lat., *solus,* alone; *fides,* faith) A term applied, sometimes with disparagement, to the doctrine of justification by faith* alone, apart from good works. See Romans 3:28. H.W.J.

solipsism: See epistemology.

Sollen und Sein: "What ought to be and what is", a contrast referring to the cardinal opposition in the philosophy of Kant* between the realm of moral obligations and that of natural existence. R.K.

Solomon: Greatest king of Hebrew Monarchy, ruling 977-937 B.C.; organized elaborate government; introduced horses, chariots, and other military innovations; with help of Phoenician* artisans built palace, temple, Millo, store and chariot cities, and Red Sea fleet which made three-year trips to S. Arabia, W. Africa, and possibly India; mined in Sinai and constructed copper refinery on Gulf of Akabah; transformed small country into world empire by marriage alliances; poet, musician, and naturalist. After his death this empire collapsed as the ten tribes broke away to escape work conscription, regimentation, and taxation for the vast public works. See I Kings 1-12. See altar; Chemosh; Song of Solomon; Wisdom literature. R.E.W.

Solomon, Odes of: A curious pseudonymous collection of 42 hymns, probably written in Greek in N. Syria between 75 and 150 A.D.; although ascribed to Solomon, they are in no way connected with him; perhaps a collection of baptismal hymns used for initiations into one of the mystery cults; a Christian work but containing many non-Christian elements, especially Gnostic, Jewish, and Oriental; the hymns are highly poetic and reflect deep spiritual experience, great devotion, and joyousness in religion; remarkable recent addition to early Christian literature.

J. R. Harris *The Odes and Psalms of Solomon* (1909 and 1911). R.E.W.

Solomon, the Psalms of: See Psalms of Solomon, the.

Solomon, Song of: See Song of Solomon.

Solomon, the Wisdom of: See Wisdom of Solomon, the.

Soma: Originally, probably a plant from which the soma juice, the favorite libation to the Vedic gods was extracted. Soma becomes also one of the principal gods of Vedic Hinduism* to whom the entire ninth book of the Rig-Veda* is dedicated. See Aryan religion. C.S.B.

somatology: See anthropology.

Son of God: Hebrew religion was strictly monotheistic, and the term "Son of God", as found in the O.T., must not be understood in any literal sense. It has its origin in the Semitic idiom which expresses any intimate relation as one of sonship. As royal ministers are sons of the king, so the angels are sons of God, and this name is likewise given to judges and sovereigns, ruling in God's name. Israel as God's people, is personified as his son. The name is nowhere applied definitely to the Messiah*, except in certain passages in the Psalms, where the interpretation is doubtful. In apocalyptic literature the name is used with a Messianic reference in only one or two instances. The N.T. writers repeatedly describe Jesus, in his Messianic character, as Son of God. Their idea is still, fundamentally, the Semitic one of close relation, but it merges in the further idea that Christ in some way participates in the divine nature. The author of Hebrews (1:5ff.) thinks of him as an angel, whom God had exalted above all others, investing him with his own majesty and calling him by the name of Son. The Nativity stories in Matthew and Luke might seem to suggest a literal sonship, but the thought is rather that Christ had entered the world like Adam by an immediate divine creation. Paul assumes that God himself is manifested in Christ, and this is affirmed still more explicitly by the Fourth Evangelist, who sees in Christ the incarnation of the Logos* which had dwelt from all eternity within the being of God. This advance on the older conception of Messianic Sonship was due not so much to a speculative as to a religious need. If Christ were to bring men into fellowship with God he must be intrinsically divine, not merely a heavenly being, however exalted. The later Christology* takes its rise from the Logos conception of Sonship, as set forth in the Fourth Gospel. It was soon recognized that in his metaphysical account of the nature of Christ the evangelist had left many vital questions unanswered. Did the Logos share in all the attributes of God? Was he originated by God, or co-eternal with him? Did Christ have two personalities, a human and a divine, and if so, what was the relation between them? The discussion of such questions occupied the Greek theologians throughout the second and third centuries and came to a head in the Arian controversy, which ostensibly was settled by the Nicene creed. At this point, however, it began again under new forms, and has never come to any real conclusion. No metaphysical definition of the nature of Christ will ever be possible. This is realized by the Fourth Evangelist himself, who falls back in the end on ethical categories. The Father loves the Son. Christ is perfectly at one with the will of God and is thereby his Son. See Son of man.

C. A. Briggs, *The Messiah of the Gospels* (1897); H. J. Holtzmann, *N. T. Theologie* (1897). E.F.S.

Son of man: A title ascribed to Jesus in the gospels and signifying his destined role in the conduct of the Final Judgment*. Popularly the phrase is used as an equivalent of Messiah*, a practice to be deplored since their origin and connotations are totally distinct. The confusion may well be seen as a consequence of the developing Christology*, in the course of which both titles were ascribed to Jesus; thus in seeming conformity to the principle of good mathematics, "things equal to the same thing are equal to each other."

The use of the phrase as the designation of the coming final judge is probably due to Dan. 7:3. In the apocalyptic* imagery of this book the heathen nations are represented pictorially by awesome beasts; in contrast to them stands "one like unto a son of man," who represents Israel, the kingdom of the Most High. The phrase son of man (Aram. *bar nasha;* Heb. *ben adam*) properly means simply man (Lat. *homo;* Gr. *anthropos*). Gradually the colorless phrase seems to have become the technical designation in apocalyptic circles of the supernatural figure destined to preside over the Final Judgment.

That Jesus made use of this phrase in this technical sense is highly probable, although it has been frequently denied. That he meant thereby to designate himself, while popularly held, is far less certain. Before the gospels were written his followers had come to believe that when he had referred to the advent of the son of man he had been speaking obliquely of himself. Not infrequently the later gospels (Matt. and Luke), sharing this view, substitute the phrase son of man for Mk's original "I" (Matt. 16:13; cf. Mk. 8:27). In at least two passages (Mk. 2:10 f.; 2:27 f.) the phrase "son of man" is almost certainly to be seen as a mistranslation of the Aramaic and should be rendered "man."

The popular notion that "son of man" indicates Jesus' humanity as "son of God" does his divinity is quite indefensible. The term, when used as a title, as already indicated, properly means a supernatural figure charged with the superlatively great task of destroying evil and acting as a truly cosmic figure.

F. Jackson and K. Lake, *The Beginnings of Christianity* (1920), vol. I; M. S. Enslin, *Christian Beginnings* (1938). M.S.E.

Song of Solomon: This book became canonical owing to the suppositions that it was by Solomon* and that it sang of the love of God for His people Israel in accordance with Hosea's* symbolism. Both suppositions were false. It sings of the love of man and woman in a manner illustrated by numerous Oriental songs, ancient (notably Egyptian parallels—recently much new material!—) and modern (Palestinian-Arab). The custom of treating bride and groom as king and queen at Arab marriage festivities in certain localities has been invoked to explain the allusions to Solomon and Shulamith (supposedly the Shunammite of I Kings 1-2; cf. Hebrew "Shunem," today "Solem"). On the other hand the "brother and sister" terminology for the lovers is illuminated by the Egyptian love songs. Whether the Song is a collection of separate poems or forms a poetic cycle accompanying some sort of dramatic action is controversial. While the book may have a nucleus of early material (cf. allusion to Israelite capital Tirza, I Kings 16:23), other indications (loan words) suggest origin in the late Persian or early Greek period.

R. H. Pfeiffer, *Introduction to the Old Testament* (1941); J. A. Bewer, *Literature of the Old Testament* (rev. ed., 1933). E.G.K.

Song of the Three Children: See Three Children, Song of the.

soothsaying: Action or profession of one who is accepted as competent to foretell events; interpretation of dreams, visions, omens, portents by certain priests assumed to be under the immediate influence of the gods so as to possess power to predict events or perform other unusual feats. In Babylonia, soothsaying was closely related to astrology, and hepatoscopy* which dealt much with externals and had fixed rules.

Among the Ancient Arabs: Persons with familiar spirits possess powers of prediction through the revelation from the spirit. Among the Hebrews: the *nabi* is a type of soothsaying. The Nabi ('Speaker') is not a poet, nor philosopher, nor priest, nor judge, but the mouthpiece, herald or messenger of the deity or spirit; the one who speaks for another; the interpreter of the oracles. The nabi type of soothsaying, unlike that of ancient Babylonia, was less concerned with the external, and with set rules; it developed into profound moral and social attitudes and insights which under the great prophets of Israel, deeply affected the outlook and conduct of a whole people. See divination. F.L.P.

Sophists: Popular teachers of philosophy and rhetoric, the Chautauqua lecturers of their day, who travelled about the country attempting to spread culture and dialectical skill and accepting pay from their pupils. They did not hold to a common body of doctrine. Some, like Prodicus and Protagoras, were defenders of sound traditional morality. Some, like the Thrasymachus of *Rep.* I, were ruthlessly selfish and immoral. Some, like Gorgias, avowed complete skepticism. The most famous formula of Protagoras, "Man is the measure of all things," has been taken by some (perhaps unfairly) to express a complete relativism. Plato* represents Socrates* as attacking the Sophists. See Socratic method. J.E.N.

Sorley, William Ritchie: (1885-1935) Knighbridge Prof. of Moral Philosophy at Cambridge, philosophical historian, critic of naturalistic ethics, and strong exponent of the moral argument for God. Insisting that true philosophical synopsis must give an adequate account of the irreducible "ought" in seeking the clue to existence, Sorley finds objectively valid values revealed in human moral experience. The coherent interpretation of these in relation to natural existence, and the human realization of values, leads reasonably to a personal God in whom these values have their being as ends of existence. See conservation of value; empirical theology.

A History of English Philosophy (1920); *Moral Values and the Idea of God* (3rd ed., 1930). P.A.B.

sortes: "Lots*," or devices for appeal to chance in divination*. In a special sense books laid open to disclose an oracle where the eye alighted. The *sortes virgilianae* had their counterpart in *sortes apostolorum* and *sortes sanctorum* which contained scriptural materials. Their use was frequently condemned in the Middle Ages. J.T.M.

soteriology: (Gr. *soteria,* deliverance; *logy*) A term of 19th Cent. origin, used particularly in Protestant writing, to designate the traditional branch of Christian theology devoted to the doctrine of salvation*. At first the distinction was frequently made between objective soteriology (the redemptive work of Christ as once-and-for-all accomplished) and subjective soteriology (the administration of that redemption by the Holy Spirit*). The term is now used more commonly to designate simply the doctrine of the saving work of Christ as distinguished from the doctrine of his person (Christology*). See mass, Roman Catholic. E.T.R.

Soto, Domingo de: (1494-1560) Representative of the Dominican order at the Council of Trent* and adviser to Charles V on colonial policy, he developed both the essential principles of morality on which policy towards the natives should be based and a doctrine of international relations not unlike that of Vittoria*.

J. W. Allen, *A History of Political Thought in the Sixteenth Century* (London, 1928). H.H.

soul: The primitive notion of the soul was that of an unsubstantial human image or shadow held to be the cause of life and possessing an independent personal consciousness and volition, manifesting power over man's existence, appearing as a phantasm in his conscious and semi-conscious experience and capable of independent flights and infusions into both animate and inanimate nature. Considerations which, it is believed, played into the early conception of the ghost-soul are: extraordinary experiences such as dreams, visions, memory-images; the contrast of living bodies as over against the dead; the experienced power of will; the tendency to conceive of certain qualities of life (necessary attributes of successful adaptation) in terms of actual entities or quasi-substances; the mystery of existence; and the like. Great variations of form attend the primitive notions: the soul is the shadow, the breath, the permeating power, the flowing blood, the hovering presence of the departed in the grave or in natural phenomena and in the locus of some far-distant scene.

The tendency to separate the soul from the body is not surprising in view of the following factors: language tends to substantialize and even personify adjectival qualities; man naturally tends to deplore the transitory and seek something permanent and stable; the prominence of certain qualities above others; the tendency to focus attention upon some whole as distinguished from its changing characteristics. Thus the concept of soul-as-substance has played a normal, natural and almost major rôle in the development of the notion.

The primitive Hebrew conception follows the pattern of the primitive ghost-soul. The earlier view as found in the O.T. suggests the soul to be the seat of feeling and desire and secondarily that of intelligence. At death, the soul leaves the body, lingering at the place of burial, visiting familiar scenes and then (the development of later thought) travelling on to the gloomy and empty existence of Sheol*, the dark and desolate underworld. (Is. 14:9-17) The view that man consists of soul and body is known as dichotomy. The later view in the O.T. distinguishes the spirit from the soul and (with body) man thus becomes a trichotomy. The spirit survives; the soul becomes the vital principle making for mental life, perishing with the body. Spirit returns to Spirit and personal existence is submerged. The two views became rivals; but the trichotomous view failed to win general popularity.

The Platonic-Aristotelian tradition exerted an enormous influence in the history of Western thought. Particularly evident is this in the doctrine of the soul.

Plato's* doctrine of the soul has rootage in a long history: the ghost-soul in the pre-Homeric period; the soul in Olympian religion (the Homeric epic) was conceived to be a shadowy image inhabiting the body and departing by way of the mouth or open wound of the dying, descending into Hades* devoid of powers; the soul in the mystery-religions of the 7th and 6th centuries B.C. took on the leading rôle in schemes of personal redemption and mystic union with the gods. Prominent among the religious cults was the Orphic (6th century B.C.) which set forth a theology and soteriology teaching the doctrine of its distinct nature as over against the body and giving to Plato the characteristic ideas of pre-existence, the imprisonment in the body and deliverance. Purification rites were also set forth by the Pythagoreans* and other pre-Platonic philosophers. For Plato the soul is intelligence, immortal, self-moving, the divine in man which apprehends eternal truth and is independent of the fluctuations of the senses. By achieving the purest thoughts the soul truly comes to its own for its homeland lies in the pure world of ideal patterns.

For Aristotle* the soul is a vital principle pervading the world of life and mind. All material things are besouled. It is the formal, the efficient and the final cause. The world is not a split dichotomy of soul and body; the two intermingle. This is his characteristic doctrine. The soul cannot, he thought, be separated from the body; and yet, he added, there may be some parts thereof which are separable! Only creative reason alone, this class of soul, highest of functions, is capable of existing as the eternal from the perishable. Whether this is personal is, of course, open to question.

It is well-known that the religious-philosophical cults in the Graeco-Roman world which was the immediate background and foreground of early Christianity gave more emphasis to the practical than to the theoretical interests. Stoicism* had taught the doctrine of the logos*, the world-reason, the soul being an offshoot of fine material substance like warm air. The Stoics introduced the word *pneuma*, a kind of pervasive spirit or principle possessing a meaning more than soul (*psyche**). A trichotomy was thus re-introduced into the stream of thought. Convergence of the Hebrew and Greek currents of ideas began to crystalize in the third century B.C. particularly among the Jews of Alexandria in Egypt. Philo*, a contemporary of Jesus, a liberal theologian and the forerunner of the Platonic mystic Plotinus* (204-269) combined Platonism, Stoicism and the Pentateuch adopting the view of pre-existence of souls and holding to the logos as the intermediary between a transcendent God and an alien world, speaking of the sojourn in human flesh as an unfortunate descent of the soul. He took over the Stoic *pneuma* and identified it with the breath of the Hebrew God and the reason of Plato and of Aristotle in a kind of trichotomous doctrine. The author of the Fourth Gospel with boldness identified Jesus as this intermediary logos, as is well known.

The N.T. nowhere gives a clear statement of theoretical human psychology. Passages in the Pauline writings teach a dichotomy; others a trichotomy (e.g., I. Thess. 5:23. Cf. also Hebrews 4:12). In the Gospels *psyche* and *pneuma* are used synonymously, the former emphasizing the idea of individual personality. As to its origin, the soul appears as a concreation with the body. "The present body", writes F. C. Porter (work cited below), "which does not rise, Paul calls not physical or material but psychical, a body fitted for the human soul. Soul, *psyche,* the word of honour in Plato's hope, is lowered in Paul, and made inseparable from the physical, to which in Plato it is absolutely contrasted; and the word spirit, *pneuma,* which to the Greeks was more material and less personal than *psyche,* and contained less promise and potency of immortality for man, is exalted and becomes the essential nature of the risen Christ and so of risen Christians; it becomes also . . . the expression for that present experience of the indwelling Christ. . . . It would seem that to Paul the word "body" means individual personality, and is essential in his thought to the distinction and the permanence of the separate self."

Early Christian thought continued to mix Hebraic and Greek ideas of the soul in various forms and degrees. (Cf. the synthetic philosophical theology of Clement of Alexandria and the systematic theology of Origen who wedded tradition and speculation into a vast structure.) Influenced by Neo-Platonism* (which had taught the attributeless One issuing in a *Nous** or Pure Intelligence which, in turn, produces a World-Soul from which, in turn, emanates individual immaterial souls whose essence is the spark of Divinity and whose purification consists in contemplation upon divine origins), St. Augustine* set the standards for later Christian orthodoxy when he taught the divine origin and unique character of the human soul and its immortal destiny and its created beginning. St. Augustine became overshadowed by Aquinas* in later Catholic thought and the Platonic and Neo-Platonic conceptions gave way to the Aristotelian. Aquinas held to Aristotle's naturalism, viz., that the soul is the form of the body; but he rejected the doctrine of Aristotle which held that the active reason is separable. For Aquinas, the soul was a whole, a unity. The soul is an immaterial substance (Platonism) but intimately connected with nature and is the form of the body (Aristotelianism). The world, however, is good because it is God's world created by him and man's destiny is not that of a withdrawal from the world (Neo-Platonism) but the fulfillment of his function in the world. There is for Aquinas a hierarchy of souls, reaching from the lowest (those souls bound up with matter without the capacity to dominate), passing through degrees (plants, animals) and reaching the higher stages in the intellect of man. This higher quality assures its superiority and independence and its character of separability and immortality. The hierarchy continues in forms higher than man, beyond angels to the form of forms, God. Man's soul has qualities in common with the lower forms although it is higher; but his soul is lower as regards the world of spirits. Man's soul does not pre-exist. His soul has both a natural and supernatural setting. To explain its high possibilities, it becomes necessary to introduce the concept of special creation. The ultimate state for man is the re-union of body and soul (resurrection*).

In spite of the influence in Catholic thought of the Aristotelian naturalism (the close union of soul and body) the soul came to be regarded more and more as a separate entity. Christianity became dramatized by the church as a redemptive religion in which the soul sought release from mundane connections and its salvation out of the world sought. Stress upon other-worldness and the promise of a haven of release and rest marked the soul as wholly unique and its nurture as the paramount end of life's adventure. Soul, again, becomes a substance *sui generis.* In Catholicism there remains the alternating stress upon the Aristotelian and Platonic emphases, although Aquinas remains the norm for its theology.

In modern thought it was Descartes* who proclaimed the philosophical divorce between soul and body, each, henceforth, to go, in thought, its way as a separate entity although having strange commerce with each other during the brief span of life. Both Catholic and Protestant orthodox circles have found the Platonic conception to their liking as witness the hymns, poetry and the ritualistic dramatizations of the soul's journey and destiny. Modern psychological thought, however, finds the Aristotelian naturalism much more compatible with the scientific approach in the current emphasis upon man as a *psychophysical* organism in a world which calls for adaptation. Man is not a trichotomous nor a dichotomous being but a unitary organism whose destiny beyond this world, it is held, remains an open question. Modern psychology has, for the most part, lost the soul and substituted terms less encumbered by traditional theologies and metaphysics. The soul now becomes the self or the person or one's spirit or the id or the psycho-physical or a mere SR (stimulus-response), depending upon the particular brand of psychological theory. See death and burial practices; eschatology; immortality; pre-existence; primitive religion; spirits; transmigration. See also psychology, schools of.

For a survey of the development of ancient and medieval ideas on the soul see V. Ferm, *First Chapters in Religious Philosophy* (1937), chap. VIII. For a survey of "Recent Theories of Soul-Mind" see the same author's *First Adventures in Philosophy* (1936), chap. XVIII. Consult: E. B. Tylor, *Primitive Culture* (3rd ed., 1889), vol. I; Wm. McDougall, *Body and Mind* (5th ed., 1920); F. C. Porter, "Paul's Belief in After Death" in E. H. Sneath, ed., *Religion and the Future Life* (1922); art. "Soul" in *A Dictionary of Christ and the Gospels* (1917), ed. by J. Hastings; C. W. Morris, *Six Theories of Mind* (1932); G. S. Brett, *A History of Psychology, Ancient and Patristic* (1912); P. Coffey, *Ontology, or the Theory of Being* (1929).

V.F.

Southworth Lectureship on Congregationalism, The: Established in 1866 by Edward Southworth of West Springfield and Wells Southworth of New Haven, Conn., at Andover Newton Theological School, Newton Centre, Mass. This lectureship (capital sum, $7,000) was founded "to interpret the Congregational polity in its relation to the Christian Church." Lectures are presented at irregular intervals. Lecturers have included the Rev. Newman Smyth, Dr. H. J. Cadbury and Prof. R. M. Jones.

(Data from the Office of the President of the Theological School.) V.F.

Sower, Christopher: (1693-1758) American printer and publisher born near Marburg, Germany, educated at Halle and Marburg universities, migrated to Pennsylvania in 1724 with his wife and only son Christopher (1721-1784). After a period of farming and medical practice, he established a press in Germantown where in 1743 he produced the first German Bible printed in America. His son, who became an elder or bishop of the Dunkers*, joined him in the business. They published almanacs, school books, a newspaper, hymn books, Bible lesson cards, later editions of the Bible, and other incidental works. During the Revolution the second Sower was persecuted as a pacifist and much of his business was ended. The name has, however, been connected with Philadelphia publishing ever since. W.M.B.

Sozomen: (c. 400-443) Church historian. Native of Palestine. Advocate in Constantinople. His history deals with period c. 323-439 and is largely based on work of his contemporary Socrates*, but is of less value. Good use is also made of other sources. Monasticism* is given large place. K.H.C.

Spangenberg, August Gottlieb: (1704-1792) Bishop of the Moravian Church, studied at Jena and lectured there on philosophical subjects. After brief service as adjunct of the theological faculty at Halle, he joined the Moravian Church*, 1733. He is known as capable organizer of Moravian enterprises in England and the West Indies; his best work as administrator was achieved in Pennsylvania and North Carolina. From 1762 onward he participated in framing the new constitution of the Church of whose governing Board he was chief member. Among his literary works are *Idea Fidei Fratrum* (1782) a compendium of Christian faith of the Moravians, and *Leben des Herrn Nicolaus Ludwig Grafen und Herrn von Zinzendorf** (1775). Spangenberg was also a writer of hymns.

J. Risler, *Leben August Gottlieb Spangenberg's* (Barby, 1794); G. Reichel, *August Gottlieb Spangenberg* (Tuebingen, 1906). W.N.S.

speaking in unknown tongues: See charismata; pentecostal sects; tongues, gift of.

Spegel, Haquin: (1645-1714) Bishop in Skara, 1685, in Linköping, 1691, and archbishop of Upsala, 1711. One of Sweden's greatest ecclesiastical leaders, Spegel was influential in the codification of the Church Law, 1686, especially in its provisions for education, in the new Catechism of 1689, and the revision of the Bible translation. He was one of Sweden's foremost hymn-writers, assisting Jesper Swedberg* in the new hymn-book of 1695, published the first church-history in Sweden (1707-08), and contributed to Swedish philology and literature through his *God's Work and Rest*, an epic, biblical poem, and his *Glossarium Sveogothicum*. C.J.B.

spell: Spoken words, written words, or symbols used for the purpose of working changes in the nature of behavior of objects; an attraction or a fascination exercised by a person or place or thing, upon other persons, etc.; a trait that is common to the religious customs and practices of all peoples. See death and burial practices; magic; om; primitive religion. F.L.P.

Spencer, Herbert: (1820-1903) English philosopher. Trained in engineering; one of the first to make bold use of the idea of evolution, applying it to all the fields of inquiry. He enjoyed a great vogue, but his ideas were comprehensive rather than exact: his claim to deduce evolution from the conservation of energy is a curiosity of intellectual history. Proclaiming Mansell's* doctrine of the inconceivability of God's nature, he tried to reconcile science and religion in the one proposition that the ultimate is unknowable. Evolution was from simple homogeneity to complex heterogeneity. Spencer in part anticipated, in part echoed, Darwin*. See sociology.

H. Spencer, *System of Synthetic Philosophy* (*First Principles of Biology, Psychology, Sociology, Ethics*) (1862-92); *On Moral and Physical Education* (1861); etc. C.H.

Spener, Philipp Jakob: (1635-1705) German Lutheran theologian and "father of Pietism".* A scholar of broad learning and a principal founder of the University of Halle (1694), Spener was pre-eminently a practical churchman, holding influential pastoral positions at Frankfurt-am-Main, Dresden, and Berlin. Influenced by devotional reading of the Scriptures and the writings of Luther, Arndt, Baxter, and Grossgebauer, as well as by emphasis on practical religion acquired through theological study at Strassburg and Geneva, Spener began to hold informal religious meetings (*collegia pietatis*) in his home to counteract the sterile intellectualism of the prevailing orthodoxy. The pietistic movement thus engendered received its manifesto in Spener's most influential work, *Pia Desideria* or Earnest Desires for a Reform of the Evangelical Church (1675). His six "desideria" were: Bible study in informal groups; the restoration of the spiritual priesthood of all believers; practical Christianity in daily life; love instead of argument in dealing with dissenters and unbelievers; reform of theological education in the direction of vital personal religion; deeper spirituality in preaching, with a return to apostolic simplicity and sincerity. Although he drew abuse from the orthodox theologians, Spener cannot be held personally responsible for the ascetic and separatistic tendencies in later Pietism. T.A.K.

Spengler, Oswald: (1880-1936) Rebelling, with Nietzsche*, against optimism and rationalism, Spengler taught that the intellect killed its objects, turning them into fixed, mummified caricatures of living things. Cultures grow and decay like organisms and must be experienced or "seen into" with "deep, wordless understanding". Since 1800 the world has been in a period of decadence. Men should accept this and cultivate the scientific and political interests which decay has brought without attempting the impossible task of seeking the real behind the changing and the relative. Spengler calls himself a "representative of historical-psychological skepticism." His *Der Untergang des Abendlandes* had a profound influence in Germany. The English translation (1926) and his *Man and Technics* (1932) have affected American thought. J.S.B.

Spenta Mainyu: The Holy Ghost in Zoroastrianism*, sometimes identified with Ahura Mazda* (Yasna* 30 and 45); the name means, "blessing spirit." He is the good cosmic spirit fighting against the evil spirit, and the mediator between the supreme god and man. R.H.P.

spermatic word: A Stoic* term for Primary Being understood as the creative or generative force in the universe in which the seed or germ of all things is contained. See logos. S.M.G.

Speyers, Diets of: See Spires, Diets of.

Spinoza, Benedict: (1632-1677) "God-intoxicated" to some, "atheist" to others; a monist, affirming there is but one substance or reality. Substance, "God or nature," is "absolutely infinite," perfect. So-called substances are merely "modes" of Substance. Neither they nor Substance act freely in the sense of having alternatives for action. Substance can only act out its nature; freedom is self-determination. We can be free by seeing ourselves as part of God's self-determined being. "Intellectual love of God" is salvation, which, through Bible and churches, even common men can obtain. Spinoza was one of the first to apply scientific scholarship to the Bible (in his *Tractatus*). Atheistic or not, his views are deductions from Substance, defined as independent existence, (existence *in se*) and God, defined as *absolutely* independent, self-active being. (See omnipotence.) The purely self-active can be only active toward us, while we remain passive toward it; hence, since substantiality means self-activity, in relation to God we are insubstantial. So God loves only himself, not us. Spinoza forced into his system many precious ethical insights. He wrote chiefly in Latin, otherwise in Dutch. See Enlightenment, the; pantheism.

B. Spinoza, *Tract. Theol. Politicus* (1670); *Ethics, demonstrated in geometrical order* (1677); etc. C.H.

spire: (A.S. *spīr*) The upper or tapering part of a tower or steeple. F.T.P.

Spires, Diets of: Spires was the scene of four diets during the Reformation* period. In 1526 Charles V* was anxious to enforce the Edict of Worms* but the political situation in Europe forced him to concur in the resolution of the diet: "Each one is to rule and act as he hopes to answer to God and his Imperial Majesty." This decision opened the door for the spread of Lutheranism and divided Germany religiously. In 1529 Charles V felt he was powerful enough to crush Lutheranism. In the diet of this year he accordingly cancelled the resolutions of 1526 and commanded strict enforcement of the Edict of Worms by the Estates. On April 19 the Lutherans protested in these words: "In matters concerning God's honor and the salvation of souls each one must for himself stand before God and give account." From this protest at Spires all Protestants take their name.

In two other diets at Spires Charles V was once more obliged to make concessions to get Lutheran help against the Turk (1542) and against France (1544). His victory over the latter enabled him to turn against the Lutherans and crush them at Muehlberg in 1547. E.C.K.

spirit: See ruah; soul; spiritual life, the.

Spirit, Holy: See Holy Spirit.

spirits: Beings of the invisible environment active for good or ill in human affairs. Gods* may be spirits and spirits may grow into gods but usually their powers rank them below the gods and above mankind.

The idea of a human soul* separable from the body was the model for the conception of a nonhuman spirit. This idea was probably the most fruitful of all the blundering adventures in the interpretation of the world achieved by primitive man. It split the universe in two, making possible the dualisms of spiritual-material, soul-body, this world-other world. It transformed the real gods of nature of early religions into spiritual beings and released them for limitless growth in the unseen realm. It made possible all the varied forms of belief in afterlife existence and, in ages of frustration, furnished a safe haven for values unattainable on earth.

The spirit population of the earth has always been greater than the human. Not only in religions of pre-literate peoples but also in those of Egypt, Babylonia, Iran, Greece, Rome, India, China, Japan, in Buddhism, Judaism, Christianity and Islam hosts of spirits worked with and against man. Their activity was seen in all startling or super-usual happenings. The good spirits could fulfil human desires, bring luck, fertility and protect from dangers. Sometimes a spirit could be persuaded to take up its abode in a material object and be a constant companion as the beneficent power of a fetish. The evil spirits, demons*, were blamed for the dangerous and destructive moods of nature, for sickness, pestilence, death, possession, nightmare. Sometimes it is difficult to differentiate the activity of spirits from that of ghosts* who linger about their old homes. Ancestral souls care for the welfare of their families like good spirits. Souls of the unhappy dead such as women who died in childbirth, unmarried persons, the unburied, murdered or forgotten dead act with all the malignancy of demons.

In the higher religions spirits are usually specialized and named according to their activity for weal or woe. Sometimes a name applied to a class of spirits merges the vague multitude into one who becomes a god or a powerful devil*. Since they are not human, spirits may take any imaginable form. India* has many picturesque types. There is a wide difference between the magnificent archangels and arch fiends of Zoroastrianism* and the tricky little household spirits, between the regal Iblis of Islam* and a fever demon.

Spirits are sometimes classified according to their dwelling place in sky, air, earth, underworld, water, forests or mountains. Good spirits were treated as lesser gods. Demons had to be held in check by powerful charms. Tantric Buddhism* had spells for the control of more than sixty thousand different kinds of them. See angels; exorcism; fetishism; jinn; primitive religion; totemism. Cf. Chinese religions. A.E.H.

spirits, discernment of: See discernment of spirits.

spiritual, the negro: See negro spiritual, the.

spiritual direction: Guidance given by a competent person to one in search of perfection and holiness. The wisdom of centuries of Christian ascetics and saints is applied to the needs of the individual soul. Much of this is done in the confessional*. See cure of souls. C.R.

spiritual life, the: Life that is either (humanly) controlled by spirit, or (divinely) directed by and toward the Holy Spirit*, or both.

The concept of spirit has had a checkered history. Common to all stages is the idea of power (usually with emotional intensity) and of value (there are good and evil spirits, but no neutral ones). It has often been associated with abnormal phenomena, such as speaking with tongues* and "holy rolling," and with literalistic beliefs, frequently chiliastic, as in Montanism* and later sects and cults. The spiritual life has therefore come to be identified with fanaticism and emotional excesses, devoid of rational or moral control, and has therefore fallen into disrepute in some quarters.

Among more thoughtful believers, however, spirit has meant that in man which is most akin to God, man's experience of the highest values of goodness, truth, beauty, and holiness. Thus every person is to some extent potential spirit. In particular, the spiritual life is the development of a conscious relation to the divine Spirit (the Holy Spirit), in prayer, fellowship, service, and growth.

That the spiritual life is supersensuous is emphasized by Platonists*; that it is a transforming power, a work of divine grace*, is St. Paul's contribution; that it leads to union with God is the insight of mysticism* of the East and the West; that it is a rational and social power building institutions is shown by Hegel*; that it is nobly superior to the "pettily human" is Eucken's* thought. In the Orient the spiritual life has for centuries been cultivated as Yoga* (union with God).

One of the chief traits of the spiritual life is its relative freedom from determination by economic, racial, and physical conditions, combined with devotion to the task of changing those conditions when they can be changed, and of rising above them when they cannot. This freedom is not absolute, and Marx is partially justified in holding that the "realm of freedom" cannot be fully realized in an unjust social order. Religious faith brings spiritual life to its highest fruition when human spirituality is regarded as conscious co-operation with the eternal Spirit of God, and therefore as grounded in an eternal power that cannot be defeated.

See Hegel, *Philosophy of Mind* (1817, trans. 1894); R. Eucken, *The Unity of the Spiritual Life* (1888); B. H. Streeter, *The Spirit* (1919); G. Santayana, *The Realm of Spirit* (1940); E. S. Brightman, *The Spiritual Life* (1942). E.S.B.

spiritual relationships: See relationships, spiritual.

Spiritualism: 1) a theory of reality. See ontology. 2) A religious-philosophical cult which is given to the study of psychic phenomena and which holds that these are to be explained in terms of discarnate spirits who have a lively interest in the living. Spiritualism was formally inaugurated in 1848, "mid-wifed" by the fantastic exhibitions of the Fox sisters. The origin of the movement is plural. Man's insatiable curiosity about post-mortem existence makes any form of spiritualism a natural religion. In general, spiritualists hold to unending development and progress of each one in a glorious hereafter; a cosmos that is friendly; affectionate converse between earth dwellers and their beloved in Summerland; seeks spiritual guidance from spirits who once were here; salvation for all; spiritual democracy; man is to enjoy freedom, love, joy and not to degenerate into the morose attitudes implied in conventional soteriological ideas. Spiritualists lack a holy book; their churches are congregational in polity. The N.S.A. was organized in 1893 with headquarters in Washington. The Morris Pratt Institute at Whitewater, Wis. is the first spiritualist seminary. Lily Dale, N. Y. is the most famous of the spiritualist camps and a mecca for its devotees and the curious. Since 1879 meetings have been held there continuously. Cf. psychical research, societies for.

George Lawton, *The Drama of Life after Death* (A study of the Spiritualist Religion) (1932). V.F.

Spittler, Ludwig Timotheus, Freiherr von: (1752-1810) Created a baron in 1806, he was made minister of state and curator of the University of Tübingen by the Duke of Würtemberg. He was considered as one of the best historians in his time. He developed the peculiarities of the histories during the Enlightenment* period once more with rigorous exactness. His aim was to write the most terse history of the church. It is almost an epigrammatic narrative. The ability for compactness and conciseness is still more prominent in his works on secular history. He was a convinced pupil of Voltaire*. Of all the pragmatic historians he was the most faithful to the heritage of Semler*. The writing of church history received through him a really political, mundane and modern character.

Grundriss der Geschichte der christlichen Kirche (3rd ed., Gottingen, 1791); *Sämmtliche Werke,* 15 vols. (Stuttgart und Tübingen, 1827-37). H.H.

sponsor: (Lat. *spondeo,* promise) A godfather* or godmother, one who undertakes profession of faith* on behalf of a child at baptism* and is responsible for its religious education. Anglicans require three godparents, Roman Catholics one, requiring another at confirmation*. T.J.B.

Spranger, Eduard: (1882-) with Karl Jaspers* he is the chief living exponent of the school of *Verstehende Psychologie,* the originator of which was Wilhelm Dilthey*, the philosopher. The school has concerned itself exclusively with the various dynamic functions that represent the apex of development in the mature personality. The method of the school consists in the postulate of ideal types, representing ultimate and absolutely coherent patterns of value, unifying any personality capable of following one of them consistently. The various authors of the school admit that no individual is perfectly self-consistent. The different ideal types, Spranger's being the best known, are merely "schemata of comprehensibility" to aid in understanding people. The value directions of the mature personality are for Spranger the religious, the esthetic, the theoretical, the economic, the social, and the political. His classification offers a starting point for empirical investigation of the complex philosophies of life that serve to confer unity upon the mature personality. His six ideal types of personality are merely theoretical guides in psychological understanding. The unity of a man's life is understood through its approximating reference to an ideal scale of over-individual values. The individual is viewed as striving to fit himself into the objective spirit which is itself embodying these values. See psychology, schools of.

Types of Men (Halle a. d. Saale, 1928); G. W. Allport and P. E. Vernon, *A Study of Values* (1931); E. Bosshart, *Die systematischen Grundlagen der Pädagogik Eduard Sprangers; mit einer monographischen Bibliographie Eduard Spranger* (Leipzig, 1935); A. A. Roback, *The Psychology of Character* (1927); G. Murphy, *Historical Introduction to Modern Psychology* (1930). H.H.

Sprecher, Samuel: (1810-1906) A pupil and brother-in-law of S. S. Schmucker*, professor of theology and president of Wittenberg Lutheran Seminary (founded in 1845 at Springfield, Ohio), prominent leader in the affairs of the General Synod of the Lutheran Church. He advocated a frank statement of "American Lutheranism"* leading his district synod in 1855 in the formal adoption of the Definite Synodical Platform, an American version of the Augsburg Confession offered as an antidote to the growing Lutheran conservatism of that time. He later affirmed a more favorable attitude toward the old Lutheran symbols. V.F.

sprinkling: See affusion.

sprite: (A Middle English-1200 to 1500 A.D.-word for spirit) An elf*; a fairy*. F.L.P.

Sprunt Lectureship, The James: Established by Mr. James Sprunt of Wilmington, N. C., at Union Theological Seminary, Richmond, Virginia for the purposes of enabling the Seminary to secure each year the services of scholars as special lecturers on subjects connected with various aspects of Christian thought and work and the creation of permanent Christian literature. The foundation was created in 1911 with a capital sum of $30,000 and increased in 1919 to $50,000. Among the volumes published in connection with this lectureship are: *The Bearing of Recent Discovery on the Trustworthiness of the New Testament* by Sir William M. Ramsay (1913-1914); *Christian Psychology* by Prof. James Stalker (1913-1914); *The Origin of Paul's Religion* by Dr. J. Gresham Machen (1920-1921); *In His Image* by Hon. William Jennings Bryan (1921-1922); *The Mystery of Preaching* by Dr. James Black (1923-1924); *Fundamental Christianity* by Dr. Francis L. Patton (1924-1925); *Jesus and the Educational Method* by Dean Luther A. Weigle (1924-1925); *The Unfinished Task of Foreign Missions* by Dr. Robert E. Speer (1925-1926); *The Christian Apprehension of God* by Dr. H. R. Mackintosh (1927-1928); *The Garment of the Living God* by Prof. J. Y. Simpson (1933-1934); *The Church of Christ and the Problems of the Day* by Prof. Karl Heim (1934-1935); *The Philosophy of Christian Education* by Prof. H. H. Horne (1936-1937); *A Preface to Theology* by Dr. John A. Mackay (1939-1940). (Data furnished by the Seminary.) V.F.

Spurgeon, Charles Haddon: (1834-1892) English Baptist, one of the most popular preachers of the nineteenth century. He was something of a fanatic and withdrew from the Baptist Union at 1887. W.S.H.

Sraosha: Zoroastrian divine being, forming a triad together with Mithra and Rashnu* (Yasht* 10: 41, 100). His name means "obedience," and he is first mentioned in the Gathas*; Yasna 57 and Yasht 11 are dedicated to him. He protects the faithful and fights the demons. R.H.P.

sruti: (shruti) There are two kinds of sacred writings recognized in Hinduism, *sruti,* the very highest type of revelation, the very word of God, and *smriti,** revelation of a lower order. Vedic literature is regarded as *sruti.* Sometimes also the Bhagavad-Gita is so regarded. C.S.B.

Stabat Mater: 13th century hymn on the Blessed Virgin at the cross, ascribed to the Franciscan Jacopone da Todi (d. 1305); used liturgically on the Feast of the Seven Sorrows* of Our Lady, it remains primarily a popular hymn, both in its original form and in Anglican and Protestant adaptations. E.R.H.

stalls: (Gr. *stellein,* to set or place) Seats for clergy and choristers on the north and south sides of the choir or chancel* in a church. Often elaborately carved. F.T.P.

Stange, Carl: (1870-) He taught in Königsberg, Greifswald and Göttingen. He attempts to bring philosophy and theology, philosophy of religion and systematic theology into a more intimate apologetically valuable relation. His main achievements are directed towards a new Lutheran theology prepared by competent studies on Luther as well as by ethical and dogmatic studies.

Die christliche Ethik in ihrem Verhältnis zur modernen Ethik (Göttingen, 1892); *Das Dogma und seine Beurteilung in der neueren Dogmengeschichte* (Berlin, 1898); *Christentum und moderne Weltanschauung* (Leipzig, 1913); *Die Wahrheit des Christusglaubens* (Leipzig, 1915); *Die Religion als Erfahrung* (Gütersloh, 1919); *Der Untergang des Abendlandes von O. Spengler* (Gütersloh, 1922); *Grundriss der Religionsphilosophie* (Leipzig, 1922); *Christliche und philosophische Weltanschauung* (Gütersloh, 1923) *Dogmatik* (Gütersloh, 1927); *Studien zur Theologie Luthers* (Leipzig, 1928). H.H.

Stanley, Arthur Penrhyn: (1815-1881) English clergyman, professor at Oxford and Dean of Westminster from 1863. His friendship with Queen Victoria gave him a wide influence; he was a broad churchman, championing Colenso and writing vigorously for latitudinarian* principles. His best-known work is a study of the eastern churches. W.N.P.

station: In Methodist polity a conference appointment consisting of a single church, in distinction from a circuit of churches. F.G.E.

stations of the cross: Also called the Way of the Cross*. A Catholic devotion in honor of Christ's journey from the house of Pilate to Calvary. Beginning around the year 1350, the devotion consists of meditation before 14 crosses and pictures depicting the sufferings of Christ. The Stations are attached to the walls of the church, requiring a special blessing before an indulgence can be gained.

The 14 stations are as follows: Jesus is condemned to death; Jesus is laden with the Cross; Jesus falls under the Cross; Jesus meets His holy Mother; Simon of Cyrene helps Jesus to carry His Cross; Veronica presents her veil to Jesus; Jesus falls the second time; Jesus comforts the women of Jerusalem; Jesus falls the third time; Jesus is stripped of His garments; Jesus is nailed to the Cross; Jesus dies upon the Cross; Jesus is taken down from the Cross and placed in Mary's arms; Jesus is laid in the sepulchre.

Cf. *Catholic Encyclopedia,* vol. XV, p. 569; *The New Catholic Dictionary,* p. 1015. S.C.

Staupitz, Johann von: (? -1524) Vicar-general of the Augustinian monastic order in Germany at the beginning of the Reformation. In the Erfurt convent of the order he met distressed young Martin Luther and comforted him by directing his thoughts to the grace of God in Christ. An influential friend and counselor of the future reformer, Staupitz encouraged him to study for a doctorate in theology, and in 1512 gave over to him his own chair of the Bible in the University of Wittenberg where he had been professor and dean of the theological faculty. In spite of his strong leanings toward the evangelical faith and his warm personal friendship for Luther, Staupitz remained a faithful Roman Catholic. During the heresy proceedings against Stephan Agricola, a follower of Luther, in 1523, Staupitz condemned Lutheranism as a heresy. From 1520 until his death he was the abbot of the Benedictine convent in Salzburg. T.A.K.

Steffensen, Karl: (1816-1888) He taught at the University of Basel, where he exercised a strongly prophetic influence as a teacher. He possessed a most intense metaphysical feeling for the secret of the world and life. He had a style of beauty and pregnancy. He opposed naturalism and positivism. Notwithstanding the idealistic tendency of his metaphysics, he abhorred all false idealizations of history. The contemporary optimistic theism was for him a poetic falsification. Evil and good were for him the ultimate grounds of the world. As a member of the contemporary speculative theism, he was both profound and independent.

Karl Steffensen. Gesammelte Vorträge und Aufsätze mit einigen Erinnerungsblätter von Freunden und Schülern (Basel, 1890); *Zur Philosophie der Geschichte,* edited by R. Eucken (Basel, 1894). H.H.

Steinbart, Gotthilf Samuel: (1783-1809) He was professor in Frankfurt a. O. As the soul of neology, pioneer in laying the foundations of rationalism, his chief work was characterized by the apologetic aim, the popular philosophical attitude, the reduction of the content of faith to a doctrine of happiness. Under renunciation of radical criticism of the world and of eschatology, his religious view measured everything according to the feeling of happiness, and Jesus was given only the role of a pioneer towards happiness.

System der reinen Philosophie oder Glueckseligkeitslehre des Christenthums, für die Bedürfnisse seiner aufgeklärten Landsleute und anderer, die nach Wahrheit fragen, eingerichtet. (Zuellichau, 1778, 4th ed., Zuellichau, 1794). H.H.

Steiner, Rudolf: (1861-1925) Born in Krajewitz, Hungary, he was the spiritual head and founder of the anthroposophical movement, an offshoot of the theosophical* movement. A manysidedly gifted personality, he was the author of eurhythmics, a new art of dancing and his own architecture of the temple at Dornach, Switzerland. The theosophical movement obtained through him a still more intellectual character. He contended that the ascent to higher supernormal levels of cognition was only possible by a growing liberation of the chains of egoism. Steiner devised special exercises in meditation in order to reach higher levels of knowledge. He combined the idea of rebirth with his doctrine of higher capacities of knowledge; which are dormant in all men. In his later years he devoted himself to social problems and medicine.

Das Christentum als mystische Tatsache (Berlin, 1910); *Wie erlangt man Erkenntnisse höherer Welten* (Berlin, 1919); *Die Geheimniswissenschaften im Umriss* (Leipzig, 1920); F. Rittelmeyer, ed. *Vom Lebenswerk Rudolf Steiners* (München, 1921); A. Sichler, *Die Theosophie in psychologischer Beleuchtung* (München, 1921); H. Leisegang, *Die Grundlagen der Anthroposophie* (Hamburg, 1922); A. Mager, *Moderne Theosophie, eine Wertprüfung der Lehre Steiners* (München, 1922). H.H.

Steinmann, Theophil: (1868-) He was professor in Gnadenfrei and in Herrnhut, Germany. He cultivated the relations of faith with the contemporary world view, of theology with the general intellectual life, and above all with philosophy.

Der religiöse Unsterblichkeitsglaube (Leipzig, 1908); *Die Geheimreligion der Gebildeten* (Göttingen, 1913). H.H.

Stephan, Horst: (1873-) He taught first in Marburg and Halle. Now he is professor in Leipzig. Starting from historical studies about Schleiermacher, Hamann, Herder and New Protestantism, he tried to represent the Christian faith from its center and to make it fertile within the range of modern thought.

Der Pietismus als Träger des Fortschrittes in Kirche, Theologie und allgemeiner Geistesbildung (Tübingen, 1908); *Die heutigen Auffassungen vom Neuprotestantismus* (Giessen, 1911); *Glaubenslehre. Der evangelische Glaube und seine Weltanschauung* (Giessen, 1928), 2nd ed.; in cooperation with H. Leube *Die Neuzeit*, 4th volume of G. Krüger's *Handbuch der Kirchengeschichte* (Tübingen, 1931), 2nd ed.; *Geschichte der evangelischen Theologie seit dem deutschen Idealismus* (Berlin, 1938). H.H.

Stephen: One of seven Greek-speaking Jews in the Church at Jerusalem who were set apart, according to Acts 6:1 ff., to look after secular matters. Later brought before the Sanhedrin* for criticizing Judaism and stoned to death by mob action after having delivered a long speech. S.M.G.

Stevens, George Barker: (1854-1906) Graduated Rochester University, 1877, Yale Divinity School, 1880, studied theology at Berlin and Leipzig Universities, 1885-1886.

Professor of N.T., Yale Divinity School, 1886-1906. An esteemed teacher and contributor to N.T. theology.

Author: *The Teaching of Jesus* (1901); *The Theology of the New Testament* (International Theological Library, 1902); *The Christian Doctrine of Salvation* (1905); articles in theological journals. J.W.B.

Stevens, William Arnold: (1839-1910) Studied at Leipzig and Berlin. Professor N.T., Rochester Theological Seminary, 1877-1910. Author *Select Orations of Lysias* (1876) and commentaries on N.T. Formulated principles of the functional significance of the N.T. participle. C.H.M.

stigmata: (pl. of Gr. *stigma*, mark) Physical wounds like those of the crucified Jesus, reputedly imprinted on persons, like St. Francis*, vouchsafed a peculiar intimacy of renunciatory suffering with their Lord. R.C.P.

stigmatization: The production of stigmata or marks on the body which are believed to have religious meaning and to be due to supernatural infliction. Among Christians stigmata have taken the form of wounds resembling those of the crucified Jesus. St. Francis of Assisi* had such wounds in his hands, feet and sides according to his contemporary biographers. Stigmata are now held to be due to strong religious emotion and to be connected with some form of hysteria.* R.W.F.

Stöcker, Adolf: (1835-1909) German Lutheran minister and political organizer. He served as court preacher at Berlin (1874-1890), a conservative member of the Reichstag, and founder of the Christian Socialist Workers' Party (1877). He was a paternalistic monarchist, a bitter opponent of the Social Democratic Party, and a virulent antisemitist. L.H.DEW.

Stoddard, Solomon: (1643-1729) Congregational clergyman, was graduated from Harvard University in 1662. In 1667 he went as chaplain to the Congregationalists in the Barbados, returning to Boston in 1669. When about to embark for England he was asked to preach in the church in Northampton, Massachusetts. Found satisfactory he was given a call and was ordained there on Sept. 11, 1672. In that pulpit he remained until his death, being assisted after 1727 by his grandson, Jonathan Edwards*. Stoddard took a prominent part in the religious and political movements of his day, and for fifty years was the most influential man in western Massachusetts. He stood out against the principles of the prevailing Congregationalism* and advocated a national church organized along Presbyterian lines. He early accepted the Half-Way Covenant* proposed by the Synod of 1662, which permitted the children of those who had been baptized in infancy and who would "own the covenant," to have their children baptized. These grandchildren, however, were not admitted to the Lord's supper or given voting privileges in the church.

Around 1677 Stoddard introduced the practice, called *Stoddardeanism*, which erased the line between "half-way" and full church members, and permitted all to full church privileges, even when they could not relate a specific experience of regenerating grace. Baptism and the Lord's supper, he argued, "were not designed merely to increase faith in those who already had it—since no one could tell who did—but to be 'converting' ordinances for all men." Stoddard's practice was stoutly opposed, especially by the Mathers of Boston, but in time it came to prevail in western Massachusetts.

W. Walker, *Creeds and Platforms of Congregationalism* (1893); W. B. Sprague, *Annals of the American Pulpit*, I (1857); "Stoddardeanism," *New Englander*, July, 1846; Perry Miller, "Solomon Stoddard," *Harvard Theol. Review*, XXXIV (1941). S.E.M.

Stoicism: It is the generative reason, the Divine Word, or Reason, that is the seed, or vital principle, whence all things come, and in virtue of which they live. All things come from fiery breath and return to it. The whole universe is one polity in virtue of the spirit that is its origin and its life of the common end to which it tends, of the absolute and universal scope of law it obeys —mind, matter, God, man, form one community. All men are of one blood, of one family, all and each are sacred to one another. Harmony with nature and oneself is the ideal life. (See happiness) Preeminently a rule of life and religion, it sought to teach self-sufficiency by a rigorous training of the will, a sense of duty reenforced by a religious teaching not unlike Calvinism, a strong belief in the overruling power of Divine Providence, making men feel their own life as a calling and as a duty assigned by God. Although the Stoics defended popular religion, they objected to the superstitions and anthropomorphical elements in it, and offered an allegorical interpretation of it. Stoicism had a profound humanitarian effect upon the development of Western jurisprudence. See Cleanthus; Epictetus; fate; logos; Marcus Aurelius; Roman religions; spermatic word; Seneca; Zeno of Citium. Cf. Cynics.

E. V. Arnold, *Roman Stoicism* (Cambridge, 1911); E. Caird, *Evolution of Theology in the Greek Philosophers* (Glasgow, 1904), vol. 2; R. D. Hicks, *Stoic and Epicurean* (London, 1910); R. M. Wenley, *Stoicism and its Influence* (1927); E. Zeller, *Stoics, Epicureans and Sceptics* (London, 1880). H.H.

Stolberg, Friedrich Leopold, Graf zu: (1750-1819) Danish ambassador in Berlin and appointed president of the government in Eutin, Holstein, by the Prince-Bishop of Lübeck, he embraced Roman Catholicism. He wrote the first distinctly romantic history of the church. His contemporaries welcomed the striking religious note of his work. He chiefly aimed at the recruiting of misled youth for the Catholic church. The work was largely preoccupied with the religion of Jesus Christ.

Geschichte der Religion Jesu Christi, 53 vols. (Hamburg, Mainz, 1806-1864). H.H.

stole: A scarf-shaped vestment, often of valuable material, worn by priest and deacons when administering sacraments or performing other sacred rites. See vestments. E.R.H.

Stone Lectureship: The Levi P. Stone Foundation was established at Princeton Theological Seminary in 1871. Five lectures on the Foundation have been given annually since 1879. In 1883 the income of the fund was permanently designated by Mr. Stone for lectures "upon some topic kindred to theological studies, provided always that the lectures shall not controvene the system of doctrine taught in the standards of the Presbyterian Church."

Noteworthy lectures were:

R. S. Storrs, "Bernard of Clairvaux, the times, the man, and his work" (1878-79); Robert Flint, Croall Lecture for 1887-88: "Agnosticism" (1880-81); Mark Hopkins "The scriptural idea of man" (1882-83); H. J. Van Dyke, "The church, her ministry and sacraments" (1889-90); R. E. Thompson, "De civitate Dei. The divine order of human society" (1890-91); M. W. Jacobus, "A problem in New Testament criticism" (1897-98); Abraham Kuyper, "Calvinism" (1898-99); W. J. Beecher, "The prophets and the promise" (1902-03); James Orr, "God's image in man, and its defacement in the light of modern denials" (1903-04); D. H. Fleming, "The reformation in Scotland" (1907-08); Herman Bavinck, "The philosophy of revelation" (1908-09); L. F. Benson, "The English hymn" (1909-10); A. T. Robertson, "The Pharisees and Jesus" (1915-16); K. D. Macmillan, "Protestantism in Germany" (1916-17); H. E. Dosker, "The Dutch Anabaptists" (1918-19); W. L. Phelps, "Reading the Bible" (1918-19); L. F. Benson, "The hymnody of the Christian church" (1925-26); Adolf Keller, "Religion and revolution" (1933-34); C. G. Osgood, "Poetry as a means of Grace" (1939-40). For a complete list, see the Biographical Catalogue of Princeton Theological Seminary (1933), page xxvii. J.A.M.

stones in religion: Stones occur as amulets and charms*, as centers for magical rites, as altars for sacrifice, as boundary stones, as phallic* symbols, even as gods themselves or their places of abode. The shape, size or appearance of stones gave primitive people cause to wonder and served to make unusual stones the objects of devotion. Among advanced religions, the Black Stone of Mecca, the Ka'bah, is still kissed by thousands of Moslem pilgrims. In India, the lingam as symbol of the god, is worshipped by the act of pouring water or placing flowers thereon. Red powder is also sprinkled on it, doubtless in imitation of a blood sacrifice. In Buddhism, rocks bearing the imprint of Gotama's foot or hand were worshipped. The stupa or relic shrine was chiefly a great heap of stones and rubble. Boundary stones are frequently objects of veneration in India.

Stones played a prominent role in the tribal religion of the OT. Jacob called the stone on which he slept and dreamt, God's house, "Bethel," and anointed it (Gen. 28:18). He set up and consecrated a stone pillar and heap on several occasions. Rocks served as altars* (Judg. 6:20; 13:19). No religion has been without its sacred stones. No people have lacked the imagination to see in them the form or spirit of something divine and living.

See art. "Stones" in Hastings *Encyclopedia of Religion and Ethics.* M.L.C.

Strauss, David Friedrich: (1808-1874) German theologian and man of letters. A disciple of both Hegel and F. C. Baur**, while a *repetent* or tutor in philosophy at Tübingen the young Strauss decided that the gospels did not constitute the fundamental *Begriff* (idea) of religion, but rather they represented the temporary *Vorstellung* (concept) of thought to which faith was not bound. This led to his radical and bitterly criticized *Leben Jesu* (1835) which established his reputation but wrecked his academic career overnight. Although he accepted the historicity of Jesus, he refused to accept the authority of the gospels, denied that they were reliable accounts, and stated that many of their narratives concerning Jesus, including his birth and childhood, his last days and resurrection, and his miraculous deeds, were "myths," patterned to a great extent on O.T.

proto-types and prophecies. This work, despite its limitations, marks the beginnings of the modern study of the life of Jesus. (See Lives of Jesus.) Among the more important of his later contributions are the following: *Christliche Glaubenslehre* (1840-41), in which he posited the opposition of faith and knowledge and denied personal immortality; *Das Leben Jesu für das deutsche Volk* (1864), a popularization of his earlier life, *Christus des Glaubens und der Jesus der Geschichte* (1865), a critique of Schleiermacher's posthumously published lectures on the life of Jesus; and *Der alte und der neue Glaube* (1872), an attempt to harmonize idealism with the materialism of natural science and Darwinianism which produced almost as great a reaction as his *Leben Jesu.* Cf. Ullmann, Karl. M.R.

Streeter, Burnett Hillman: (1874-1937) English theologian and N.T. scholar. Canon of Hereford (1915-34); Provost of Queen's College, Oxford (1933-37). A university teacher for 38 years and one of the intellectual leaders in the Anglican Church, Streeter is best known for his studies of the Gospels. In his *magnum opus, The Four Gospels: A Study of Origins* (1924) he developed his multiple source (four document) hypothesis of Synoptic* relationships and origins, including his Proto-Luke theory which, perhaps, has been unduly acclaimed. In a later work stemming from his N.T. studies, *The Primitive Church: Studied with Special Reference to the Origins of the Christian Ministry* (1929), he reaches the conclusion that no one order prevailed in the primitive church, and expressed the hope that this result of historical investigation might remove one of the barriers to Christian reunion. As a Christian apologist Streeter wrote several books and edited and contributed to others in which he attempted to show that there was no necessary conflict between science and religion. This thesis is fully developed in *Reality: A New Correlation of Science and Religion* (1926), in which his theory of knowledge, bi-representation, is presented. Among his other writings are: *The Message of Sadhu Sundar Singh* (1921), in collaboration with A. J. Appasamy; *The Buddha and the Christ* (1933); and *The God who Speaks* (1936). He also edited and contributed to the following: *Foundations* (1912); *Concerning Prayer* (1916); *Immortality* (1917); *The Spirit* (1919); and *Adventure* (1928). M.R.

Strong, Augustus Hopkins: (1836-1921) Baptist educator and theologian. President Rochester Theological Seminary, 1872-1912. Author of *Systematic Theology,* final edition, 3 vols., 1907-1909. *Tour of Missions* (1918), provoked fundamentalist controversy. His proposals for a greater Baptist University in New York City stimulated movement resulting in University of Chicago. C.H.M.

structuralism (structural psychology): See psychology, schools of.

Stuart, Janet Erskine: (1857-1914) English nun and superior-general of the Society of the Sacred Heart. Her writings on educational subjects, her ascetical teaching and gift of understanding have made her a force in the Catholic world. E.A.R.

student religious organizations: Christian student societies are as old as the universities. They antedate all other voluntary student organizations. Some of the most creative movements in the history of the Chrisian church had their beginnings in these societies. There are records of societies in American colleges as early as 1706.

Societies at Harvard in 1721 and 1723 met "twice a week for the worship of God" and for discourses "of 20 minutes" by "one of the Society on any subject he pleases"—the students "taking turns in leadership." In 1742 at Yale a number of students "associated themselves with one another for mutual conversation and assistance in spiritual things."

For seventy-five years the Moral Society of Yale (1797) exerted a powerful influence on the moral and religious life of the college. The Society of Brethren (Haystack group) that formed around Samuel Mills at Williams College in 1806 and its successor at Andover Seminary (1810) stirred up students in other colleges who formed student missionary societies, and awakened the church of New England to its foreign missionary responsibility leading to the formation of the first missionary sending society—the American Board of Commissioners for Foreign Missions.

From 1810 to 1858 as new colleges were founded on the frontier, religious societies spontaneously developed. These societies seem to be as indigenous to colleges as professors and class rooms. Generally they were called Societies of Inquiry or Societies of Religious or Missionary Inquiry. While there was no intercollegiate or world student organization, yet these associations were united in fact and spirit by a network of correspondence involving societies in Great Britain and Europe as well as the United States. They have always been, as they are today, ecumenic in spirit, *practising Christian fellowship* across all the lines that divide men— racial, geographical and ecclesiastical. Perhaps here lies one of their greatest gifts to the church. "Thanks be to God" wrote British students to American in 1822, "for the grand union of believers in Christ. No distance of place, difference of color nor adversity of circumstance can prevent its exercise."

It is against this background of indigenous, ecumenic, intercollegiate and international Christian student societies that the history of all student religious organizations in American colleges must be written.

Student Y.M.C.A. 1858—

For more than three-quarters of a century the Student Y.M.C.A. has been a major channel for voluntary student religious activity. On October 12, 1858, students at the University of Virginia, dissatisfied with their scattered religious activities, banded together to form the first Student Y.M.C.A. It combined the discussional, theological, ethical and missionary interests of earlier student religious societies into one comprehensive campus-centered Christian Association. The inclusiveness and practicality of this Association commended itself to students and faculty alike with the result that in two decades Y.M.C.A.'s developed spontaneously in from 70 to 100 colleges, generally replacing older societies of inquiry.

At Louisville, Kentucky, in 1877 representatives of these student Y.M.C.A.'s created the Intercollegiate Y.M.C.A. as a part of the general Y.M.C.A. movement, calling Luther D. Wishard of Princeton to be the first national student Y.M.C.A. secretary. In the next decade Associations were formed in more than 250 colleges.

In answer to a call by the Student Y.M.C.A. and Dwight L. Moody* 250 students from 90 colleges in 26 states came together in 1886 at Mt. Hermon, Massachusetts, for the first summer conference for students, beginning a way of doing religious work with students that has since spread around the world and that established the pattern for the summer conferences and training institutes for young people promoted by the denominations in recent years. Out of the Missionary awakening in the Mt. Hermon conference came the forces which led in 1888 to the creation of the Student Volunteer Movement*.

In 1888 John R. Mott accepted "for one year only" the national secretaryship of the Student Y.M.C.A., thus beginning a Christian lay ministry among students which for five decades influenced the religious life of universities in every corner of the world.

Full-time student secretaries were introduced by the Y.M.C.A.'s at Yale and Toronto in 1886. Today, in fully 125 larger colleges and universities in the United States, Advisory Boards of Student Y.M.C.A.'s exist for the employment of secretaries, most of whom now have taken graduate work in theology for advanced degrees—M.A., B.D. and Ph.D. Buildings as social and religious centers were also introduced in the late 80's and have spread to most larger colleges. These Associations have not only developed a wide range of social and religious activities and extensive service programs for the campus and community, but they have pioneered thinking and action among students and faculty in the areas of social concerns and in interracial understanding.

The movement's national headquarters are at 347 Madison Ave., New York. Its policies are determined in an annual meeting by the National Council of Student Christian Associations, made up of 100 students, secretaries, and professors elected by the white and Negro colleges of the country to represent them. This Council elects a National Student Committee and Executive Committee subject to the approval of the National Council of the Y.M.C.A. to administer the work between meetings. There are regional offices, councils and secretaries in each section of the country. In 1943 more than 100,000 students are banded together in the work of 600 local student Y.M.C.A.'s. The movement has been fortunate in its succession of national executives, Luther D. Wishard (1877-1888), John R. Mott (1888-1915), David R. Porter (1915-1934), Arthur Roland Elliott (1934-1943), and R. H. Edwin Espy (1943-).

World's Student Christian Federation, 1895-

Ardently desiring to achieve a union of Christian students of all lands, John R. Mott and Luther D. Wishard, representing Christian students of U.S.A. and Canada and the beginning Student Christian Movements in foreign mission lands, joined British, German and Scandinavian leaders of Student Christian Movements in the ancient castle of Vadstena on the shores of Lake Vettern in Sweden in August, 1895, to form the World's Student Christian Federation, which the late Bishop Charles H. Brent once described as "the greatest movement of the Spirit of God in modern times." The Federation has no individual membership but is a union of autonomous national student Christian movements—only one movement in a country being recognized for membership. In the United States, in 1943, denominational groups as well as the Y.M.C.A., Y.W.C.A. and S.V.M. may unite with the Federation through the Provisional Council of the W.S.C.F. Regular or affiliated movements are found in more than 40 nations and its General Committee meetings once in three years bring together students and professors from every race and nation and communion of the Christian Church.

It organized and directed in World War No. 1 and in the reconstruction period following—as it is also doing in World War No. 2—an extensive program of relief for dislocated student groups, student refugees and prisoners of war in Asia and Europe, and in many open and hidden ways kept lines for spiritual communication open between students in enemy countries.

The World headquarters is at 13 Rue Calvin, Geneva, Switzerland. Since 1935 Robert Mackie of the British Movement has been its secretary. Its magazine published quarterly is *The Student World.* Its work and world conferences held since 1900 have established the pattern for the ecumenical World council of Churches and most of the leaders for movements of the Church have come from its ranks. The present general secretary of the World Council of Churches, Dr. W. A. Visser t'Hooft is the former general secretary of the W.S.C.F.

Student Y.W.C.A.
(*see Y. W.C.A.*) 1873-

The first student Y.M.C.A.'s in coeducational colleges had women as well as men members. The first separate Student Y.W.C.A. was formed at Illinois State Normal School in 1872 although prior to this date there were in most of the early women's colleges and coeducational institutions young ladies' religious and moral societies. Between 1880 and 1885 many separate women's Associations were formed and in August, 1886, at Lake Geneva, Wisconsin, 19 women students met as representatives of 80 Associations to form the

National Y.W.C.A. Miss Nettie Dunn of Hillsdale College was called to be its national secretary.

In 1894 it became a charter member of the World's Y.W.C.A. and in 1906 under the leadership of Miss Grace Dodge it united with the Women's Christian Association to form the National Board of the Y.W.C.A. Like the Student Y.M.C.A. it developed local and national secretaryships, summer student conferences, and in addition to the social and religious pioneering that characterized the student Y.M.C.A. it has always performed two functions unique to it as a women's movement. It has been a center for women's student life on most campuses, offering many opportunities for growth and leadership not otherwise available for women students to the same degree as for men students; it has also achieved great solidarity with the general Y.M.C.A. movement in its struggle for better conditions for women and children in the nation's life and for more of interracial equality.

The national headquarters are at 600 Lexington Avenue, New York. It bands together fully 100,000 women students in more than 600 colleges and universities. Miss Eleanor French (1943) is Executive Secretary. It has regional councils and secretaries and its national policies are made by the National Student Council of the Y.W.C.A., subject to the approval of the National Board of the Y.W.C.A.

National Intercollegiate Christian Council

Since 1920, locally and nationally, the Student Y.W.C.A. and Y.M.C.A.'s have been increasing their areas of cooperative work—locally through councils and in many cases united Student Christian Associations, and nationally through the National Intercollegiate Christian Council. Its membership is made up of the National Student Councils of the Y.M.C.A. and Y.W.C.A. It is not an overhead organization but a council through which the two Associations can think and work together without breaking their connections with the parent Y.M.C.A. and Y.W.C.A. organizations. It meets annually for national policy making and entrusts the carrying out of these to an administrative Committee and various program commissions which meet frequently during the year. The executive secretaryship of N.I.C.C. alternates each year between the two movements. Summer student conferences in all parts of the country are now on a joint basis. The N.I.C.C. has led the two movements on many social issues, its Christian message and churchmanship policies, and in the adoption of advanced interracial policies and practices. In many cases locally or regionally a man or a woman is employed jointly by the Associations to give leadership on behalf of both movements.

Church Student Movements (1900-)

The Church has always ministered to the religious needs of students through the parish church and religiously founded colleges. Specialized ministries to the religious needs of students and the encouragement of denominational student organizations are, however, quite recent. They are the result of the rapid growth of public higher education. By 1910 it was apparent to educational leaders of the Protestant denominations and of the Roman Catholic Church that in any given state there were already more of the churches' students in the state universities than there were in the colleges of the denomination. This led to local experimentation with church student programs and to decisions by the larger denominations to provide special pastoral, program and teaching leadership for students in state universities. University pastors were employed by national and state agencies of the denomination in cooperation with the parish church and attached to the local churches in the state university centers as full-time student workers. Gradually about the campuses of larger state universities fine student houses ("a home away from home") have been built as centers for student religious program and activity. The term *foundation* was first used by the Methodists at the University of Illinois when in 1913 they incorporated their student program under the leadership of Rev. (now Bishop) James C. Baker as the Wesley Foundation of the University of Illinois. In 1916 the term Wesley Foundation was officially adopted for its student program in state universities by the General Conference of the Methodist Episcopal Church. Other denominations later adopted similar terms, the Presbyterians (Westminster Foundation), Congregationalists (Pilgrim Foundation), Baptists (Roger Williams Clubs), and Episcopalians (Canterbury Clubs). All of this work has been established by national leadership of the denominations and has been subsidized by grants from national and state denominational educational agencies.

The gradual adoption of the society idea for the denominational student program underscores a fact of immense importance. The denominations in the first two decades of this century followed their students in state universities with university pastors who were to give pastoral leadership. It was in the main *a work of the denominations for their students.* In the past two decades it has become a work *of* as well as *for* students based on the principles pioneered by earlier student societies and especially by the S.C.A.. The local denominational student societies today are generally as clearly student led and in spirit as ecumenic as are the Student Christian Associations and they too are expressions of the student religious society tradition.

The Lutheran and Episcopal policy has been to strengthen the parish church as the center for its ministry to students with a lesser emphasis on special student workers. However among Lutheran students there has grown up the Lutheran Student Association of America with clubs in most colleges where there are Lutheran students. The Southern Baptists have followed the Student Movement pattern, organizing locally Baptist Student Unions and promoting statewide and Southwide student conferences that attract large numbers of students. Their summer student conference at Ridgecrest, N. C. is the largest annual gathering of students in the United States. Since the reunion of the Methodist Church, the term Methodist Student Movement has been used to describe both the Wesley Foundations in state institutions and the Methodist fellowships in Methodist colleges.

The national administration of the denominational programs centers in the university departments of the Boards of Education of the various denominations. Through the University Commission of the Council of Church Boards of Education—national plans are made for strengthening denominational work and for interdenominational student activity. Much cooperative work is done among the denominations and with the Christian Associations through local campus religious councils, through joint regional movements like the New England S.C.M. and through national agencies like the War Emergency Council for Student Christian work. In a number of larger universities, denominations and Christian Associations pool their leadership and financial resources for the strengthening both of local church's ministry to students and interdenominational work.

College Catholic Clubs

In 1880 Catholic students at the University of Wisconsin met in the home of Mrs. John Melvin to form the Melvin Catholic Club. This was one of the earliest of the college Catholic clubs. Others were formed in this decade at Yale, Harvard and Michigan. Today they are found in more than 500 colleges and universities. The first of these to be named Newman Club in honor of Cardinal Newman*—a name now widely used—was at the University of Pennsylvania in 1894. Pope Leo XIII* urged the erection of chapels at institutions like Oxford as a means of safeguarding the faith of Catholic students. In 1905 Pope Pius X* issued his encyclical *Acerbo Nimis* commanded "the establishment of schools of religion for teaching the truths of our faith and the precepts of Christian morality" to youths attending "such public institutions wherein no mention is made of religion." This pronouncement greatly accelerated the formation of College Catholic Clubs. The movement has had the warm support of the American hierarchy and the reasons given for encouraging the formation of clubs, the erection of student chapels and the support of chaplains have been almost identical with those of the Protestant denominations for the support of their student religious organizations. The Federation of College Catholic Clubs was formed in 1915 at the home of Mrs. John Phillips in New York City and its first conference was held in 1916. The Federation has aroused the interest of the hierarchy and the laity in the student problem, has raised funds for Newman Halls, secured the appointment of chaplains and drawn together in the program of Catholic action large numbers from the more than 85,000 Catholic students in some 600 non-Catholic colleges. The Federation is international and collaborates with *Pax Romana*, a world-wide organization of Catholic students similar to the World's Student Christian Federation. The Federation recognizes first the authority of each bishop, and, as a Federation working with clubs in the U. S., has been placed as a separate division in the Educational Department of the National Catholic Welfare Conference with headquarters in Washington, D. C.

B'nai B'rith Hillel Foundation

While Jewish cultural and religious societies have had a place in the universities for many years—notably such societies as the Intercollegiate Menorah Society and Avukah—yet it was not until 1923 that a special religious and social program was developed among Jewish students comparable in any way to the denominational university pastorate. This new Jewish youth movement—the Hillel Foundation—is sponsored by B'nai B'rith, a national order nearly a century old. The movement is the product of the vision and perseverance of a young rabbi, the late Benjamin Frankel, who had been serving as a biweekly student rabbi at Champaign, where the University of Illinois is located. Upon his ordination in 1923 he determined to remain in Champaign and organize a student center for the growing body of Jewish students. He had the support of the Champaign Jewish community and of a group of earnest and public-spirited men in Chicago. Largely through their assistance the first year of the Hillel Foundation was successfully completed. In the next year, the project, with all of its potentialities, was offered to the Executive Committee of B'nai-B'rith, which undertook sponsorship for the movement. This decision was approved at the international convention of the Order, in 1925, and a great Jewish student movement was launched.

The Hillel Foundations consciously followed the patterns developed by the Christian Associations and the denominations, making of the local organization "a democratic institution governed by a student council elected by the Jewish student body." They steadily seek to increase the areas of cooperation and work with Christian student groups to increase interfaith understanding.

At two points a Hillel Foundation differs from other denominational foundations:

1. It is not under the control of the synagogues locally or nationally. In this respect it is an extra-church agency like the Y.M.C.A. and Y.W.C.A.

2. Its religious and social aims are inextricably interwoven with the necessity for preserving Jewish integrity, training students in neglected elements of Jewish culture, surrounding the Jewish college student with a Jewish atmosphere, social, educational and religious. "Except for this distinctive Jewish cultural note, the report of a Hillel Foundation would read very much like that of a Wesley, Westminster, or Pilgrim Foundation."

Hillel Foundations, like those of the Christian denominations, have been organized in the larger state and independent universities where the need has seemed greatest and where there has been the greatest concentration of Jewish students. By 1930 there were foundations in 12 universities; in 1943 there are foundations in more than 80 universities, a number that is being rapidly increased because of the war emergency.

Dr. Abram L. Sachar, Director of the Foundation at the University of Illinois, is the National Director of the B'nai B'rith Hillel Foundation with office at Champaign, Illinois. C.P.S.

Student Volunteer Movement for Foreign Missions: An agency for promoting missionary interest among college students and recruiting candidates for service under the various mission Boards of North America.

This Movement originated in the first Y.M.C.A. conference for college students, convened by D. L. Moody* and held at Mt. Hermon, Mass. in July 1886. Despite the absence of official plans for missionary promotion, Robert Wilder from Princeton awakened much interest among the 251 delegates. One hundred of them signed a statement already used at Princeton, "We are willing and desirous, if God permit, to become foreign missionaries". In 1886-87 Wilder and John Forman, both India born and from Princeton, visited 162 colleges and theological seminaries and enrolled over 2000 Student Volunteers. Robert Speer was the travelling secretary in 1889-90 and enrolled 1100 in 110 schools. By 1891 the total was 6200.

Formal organization was effected in 1888 and the Movement, though autonomous, became the missionary department of the student Christian Associations and the recruiting agency for the mission Boards of the churches. In 1900 the Movement was incorporated and the headquarters were set up in New York. From 1888 to 1920 the chairman of the executive committee was John R. Mott who was one of the "Mt. Hermon Hundred" and an influential leader in the student Y.M.C.A. He did much to unify the various phases of the student Christian movement and to relate them to the growing missionary program of the churches.

The program of the Movement included campus visits by travelling secretaries and the promotion of voluntary mission study classes which in 1919 enrolled 47,681 college students. Most noted were the Quadrennial Conventions which began in 1891 and became widely noted for their size and enthusiasm as well as for their slogan, "The evangelization of the world in this generation". The eighth was held in 1920 and drew 6890 people from 949 schools. Each student generation was thus faced with a missionary appeal by such noted leaders as John R. Mott, Robert E. Speer, G. Sherwood Eddy, Robert P. Wilder and others.

Between 1886 and 1936 the Movement enrolled just under 50,000 Student Volunteers, of which number over 13,000 sailed to the foreign mission fields. These Volunteers constituted about half of the total number of missionaries sent out. Gifts for missions were stimulated so that in 1918-19 over $303,000 were contributed by student religious organizations.* By 1920 the Movement was the recognized recruiting agency for the mission Boards and its ideology and objectives served as a unifying center for all branches of the student Christian movement.

The last two decades have been marked by confusion and decline in both the general student Christian movement and in the missionary program of the churches. Accordingly the work and influence of the Movement have greatly decreased. By 1940 only a small staff remained and both the objectives and relationships of the Movement had become less clear.

John R. Mott, *Five Decades and a Forward View* (1939); Clarence P. Shedd, *Two Centuries of Student Christian Movements* (1934); Robert P. Wilder, *The Great Commission* (1936); William M. Beahm, *Factors in the Development of the Student Volunteer Movement for Foreign Missions*, unpublished dissertation at University of Chicago (1941). W.M.B.

Students' Lectureship on Missions: The Students' Lectures on Missions were endowed in 1893 by the students of Princeton Theological Seminary with the generous assistance of James Shepard Dennis. A course of five lectures on foreign missions has been given annually. Among the lecturers there have been many famous missionaries, as: Robert Eliot Speer, John R. Mott, Charles Roger Watson, Wilfred T. Grenfell, Sir Andrew Fraser, Charles E. Scott, Samuel M. Zwemer, J. C. R. Ewing, Webster E. Browning, Charles Allen Clark, Augustus K. Reischauer, John Van Ess, Albert B. Dodd, John A. Mackay, Nicol Macnicol, Kenneth Scott Latourette, William Paton.

For a complete list of lectures consult the Biographical Catalogue of the Seminary (1933) page XXX. J.A.M.

Stundists: See Russian sectarianism.

Stundobaptists: See Russian sectarianism.

Stylites: See anchoret.

Suarez, Francisco: (1548-1617) Spanish Jesuit* theologian, known as Doctor Eximius. As a religious he was firmly devoted to prayer and mortification, a tireless worker, humble and modest. As a theologian he taught in the ranking educational centers of his day, at Avila, Segovia, Valladolid, Rome, Alcala, Salamanca, and Coimbra. He also taught philosophy at Avila and Segovia. His voluminous writings testify to their author's marvellous grasp of the field, his depth of thought and clarity of expression. They have merited many Scholastic commentaries. W.H.

subdeacon: One who has received the lowest of the three Major Orders, which culminate in the priesthood. He assists the deacon at the altar, sings the epistle during a Solemn High Mass, and washes the sacred linens used at Mass*. W.H.

subjective idealism: See idealism, subjective.

sublapsarianism: (*sub*, under; *lapsus*, fall) The doctrine which holds that God did not decree the Fall* of man, but foresaw it, thus holding the decrees of reprobation and election** to be *sub*ordinate to the fact of the Fall.

Held by some of the orthodox Dutch Calvinists. Neither rejected nor affirmed, as such, at the Synod of Dort*, but congenial to the orthodox. See predestination. Cf. infralapsarianism; supralapsarianism. E.P.B.

subliminal self: (Lat., *sub; limen,* under the threshold) A term used in the 1890's by F. W. H. Myers, and subsequently made popular in religious psychology (now much less commonly used), to designate what was believed to be the larger portion of the self lying below the level (threshold) of consciousness yet constantly influencing thought and behavior. The unconscious factors or processes comprehended under the term are now widely recognized: the influence of racial history, infantile and childhood conditionings (habits acquired through suggestion and imitation*, and complexes of ideas and emotions accumulated around traumatic experiences), dream mechanisms, short-cut problem-solving, dissociation, etc. The interpretation of such factors and processes, however, is not uniform, some psychologists regarding them as purely physiological mechanisms, others as predominantly psychological or mental (Freud*, for example, speaks of "unconscious psychic states"). William James* used the concept of the subliminal or subconscious self to suggest the area of human experience in which contact with the Divine Life may occur (*Varieties,* 511 ff.). See mysticism. E.T.R.

subordinationism: (fr. Lat. *subordinare,* to subordinate) A modern term referring in general to any interpretation of the Doctrine of the Trinity* which treats the Second or Third Persons as metaphysically inferior to the First, but applied in particular to those early views of the relation between the Son and the Father (and incidentally to the relation of the Holy Spirit* with the Son and the Father) which anticipated, but fell short of, the Nicene formulation of consubstantiality (homoousia*) and the subsequently definitive *Symbolum Quicunque** (Athanasian Creed). E.T.R.

subsistence: (Lat. *subsistere,* fr. *sub,* under; *sistere,* cause to stand) In most current usage, the kind of being attributable to relations between terms, or to any possible object of thought, whether or not the object exists, and whether or not it is an object of actual thought. In scholasticism, an individualizing mode of a substance. L.H.DeW.

substance: (Lat. *substantia,* fr. *sub,* under; *stare,* to stand) The real being which possesses attributes, endures through change, and underlies external appearances. The essence of an existent. Philosophers differ concerning the questions whether substance is one (Spinoza) or many (Leibniz), knowable (Aristotle) or unknowable (Hume), material (Democritus) or mental (Lotze), etc. L.H.DeW.

substance, Aristotelian: See Aristotle and Aristotelianism.

substitutionary theories: See redemption; satisfaction.

sudra: The lowest of the four traditional *varnas* or castes in India. The three upper castes are called the twice born. The Sudra, formed, according to Rig-Veda* X, from the feet of the Purusha*, performs the humble, menial tasks in Indian society. Still below the sudra is the outcaste or untouchable, though the line of demarcation is not sharply drawn between them and the Sudras. C.S.B.

suffering: See atonement; evil; passion; perfect.

sufficient cause: See cause.

suffragan: A diocesan bishop is suffragan to his archbishop—by analogy an auxiliary bishop* is so called in mediaeval English and modern Anglican usage. E.R.H.

Sufism: A system of Mohammedan mysticism, arising chiefly in Persia. The Arabic *sufi,* means wool, and refers to the woolen garments worn by such ascetics from the 2nd century. In common with Hinduism and Christianity it offers steps toward union with God, as repentance, abstinence, renunciation, poverty, patience, trust. Love is the key to the *Sufi* ethics. The most brilliant poetry of Persia* is *Sufi.* Recent revivals appear in Egypt and Turkey. See Alfarabi; dervish; Mohammedanism; tauhid. P.E.J.

suggestion: (Lat., *suggestio*) The process by which an individual tends uncritically to accept, as true or normative, ideas and attitudes to which he is exposed. The tendency to such credulous response is the psychological law directly exploited by much commercial advertising and political propaganda. More important, it is a chief factor in the individual's conformity to the mores and prevailing attitudes of the group or groups to which he belongs, and no where more obviously than in the life of the cultus. Suggestibility tends to diminish with increase in critical intelligence. E.T.R.

suicide: Self-destruction by the intentional taking of one's life. Although now held to be reprehensible legally, morally and religiously in the West, various positions have been taken toward it historically from approval and even recommendation of it under certain circumstances (as in Stoicism* and Japan) to positive condemnation. On the whole the Christian church has condemned it unqualifiedly as an offense against God's will, grace and judgment. The recent trend is to attribute it to insanity or to personal disorganization viewed as a function of social disorganization. See harakiri; seppuku.

For historical survey see Hasting's *Encyclopaedia of Religion and Ethics.* For contemporary interpretation see *Encyclopaedia Britannica and* R. S. Cavan: *Suicide* (1928). R.W.F.

Sulpicians: Members of the Congregation of St. Sulpice, founded in 1642 by M. Olier, a French priest. The Congregation takes its name from its

first establishment. The life work of the Sulpicians is to prepare young men for the priesthood.
W.H.

Sumerians, religion of: See Mesopotamian religions.

Summa Theologica: The *summa theologica* is a "compendium containing brief, systematic, comprehensive and well thought out exposition of the principal truths of Christian doctrine." It developed out of the sentencebooks, which began to be compiled in the late patristic and early mediaeval period, and which at first were impersonal collection of excerpts (*sententiae*) from the writings of the Fathers of the Church. In systematic presentation these works continued to develop, while they gradually became more personal, especially from the early twelfth century on. By the late twelfth century, therefore, the character of the sentencebooks had greatly changed, and to denote this change the title *summa theologica* began to appear around the turn of the thirteenth century. The best known of sentencebooks is the *Libri IV Sententiarum* composed by Peter Lombard* between 1145-1152; the greatest *summa* is the *Summa Theologica,* written by St. Thomas Aquinas* between 1267-1273. This latter work is divided into three parts, of which the first two are each in turn divided into two parts. In general, part one treats of God, part two of man and his relations to God, part three of Christ in his Incarnation and in his continuation through the Church and her sacraments. St. Thomas completed this work only as far as part three, question ninety, article four. The scholastic method of handling theological questions, so well exemplified in St. Thomas' *Summa,* developed during the hundred years or so immediately preceding its writing, and has its origin principally in the *Sic et non* of Peter Abailard* and in the logical works of Aristotle*, all of which became available in translation to scholars in the West only in the twelfth century. See Sentences. P.S.M.

summum bonum: (Lat., the highest good) The highest ideal of conduct. The good is the object of desire, "that at which all things aim" (Aristotle, *Nic. Eth.,* I, 1, i); it is substantially identical in meaning with value*. Greek ethics, dominated by the idea of the highest good, was teleological, in contrast with the formalism of Kantian ethics. The central problem of Greek ethics was the definition of the *summum bonum.* Although Plato (Socrates)** identified the good with pleasure in the *Protagoras* and then repudiated this identification in the *Gorgias,* he hesitated to commit himself to any definition of the Idea of the Good (*Rep.* 506DE). Aristotle described it as happiness. (See eudaemonism.) The hedonists (see Cyrenaics, Epicureanism) found it to be pleasure, either physical or mental. The Cynics* declared that the *summum bonum* is knowledge, while the Stoics*, nearer to Kant, found it solely in a good will (independent of "externals"). For the Neo-Platonists*, as for many Christian mystics, the *summum bonum* was the union of the soul with God. See axiology.

See article, "*Summum Bonum*" by P. Shorey in Hastings, *Encyclopedia of Religion and Ethics.*
E.S.B.

sun, sun worship: Sun myths are found in the mythologies of all races. The sun has been one of the most persistent and ancient objects of interest of the human race. Sun symbols occur in Neolithic deposits around the globe. Max Mueller ascribed to sun worship the earliest form of religion. But it cannot be assumed that sun myths and symbols are always evidence of sun worship. The elaborate calendars of ancient peoples and the simple calculations of the most primitive tribes on the course of the sun, reveal other interests associated with the sun. The observed relation of the sun to food production gave the shaman his clue to weather prediction and crop protection. In more advanced civilizations, such as the Babylonian and Mayan, the study of the sun's movements, correlated with that of moon and stars, led to the science of astronomy and aided the development of mathematics.

Sun worship reached its highest development in Egypt, Mexico and Japan. It was only in Mexico that this development was accompanied by a high degree of perfection of astronomical and mathematical sciences. In Egypt, the pyramids were probably associated with sun-worship as shown by their orientation. The sun god Ra persists through Egyptian ancient history. In the 13th century B. C. Ikhnaton* established a monotheistic religion of high ethical character, centering about the sun god Aton, represented by a disk with rays extended as beneficent hands. Solar worship spread to Greece and into Western Europe. In Mexico, the Mayans pictured the sun god as a jaguar. Human sacrifice came to be associated with the cult. Their priests worked out an exhaustive calendar and mathematical tables. Among other American Indians there was the sun dance of the Plain Indians, the vision experience of the Crow in Montana (see Lowie, *Primitive Religion*) and the ceremonial offering of sacred meal to the dawn by the Pueblo in Arizona. In Japan, the royal house is believed to stem from the Sun goddess Amaterasu* and to have maintained an unbroken line for 26 centuries. Her earliest mythologies, centering about this solar cult, are associated with the struggle for food against a harsh climate.

In all solar cults, the sun represents healing, fruitful qualities. And in the ethical religions, as that of Aton, the Sun was a harsh judge of men's deeds as well as a benevolent sovereign.
M.L.C.

Sunday: Prior to the late sixteenth century Christianity did not identify Sabbath and Lord's Day. Luther, Zwingli, Calvin and other early Protestant reformers taught that the Sabbath was abrogated in Christianity. Calvin thought it an insult to the Jews to change their day. It was English Puritanism* which first identified Sunday with Sabbath and the Westminster Confession of Faith* popularized the innovation in 1647. New England Congregationalism* introduced this new theology to America and all American Calvinistic groups promoted it. Opposition to First Day Sabbath in colonial days was led by the Rogerenes and Seventh Day Baptists who were joined by the Seventh Day Adventists** in the mid-nineteenth century. The invention of the automobile and the building of good roads are destroying both Seventh and First Day Sabbaths. See Lord's Day; Sabbatarianism, Puritan; sabbath, Christian.

C.H.M.

Sunday School Council of the Evangelical Denominations: See Sunday School movement in the United States.

Sunday School movement in the United States: Essentially an evangelical Protestant endeavor to provide religious education in schools held on Sunday, promotional and instructional aspects of growth designable by periods, as follows:

I. *Sporadic Beginnings*, 1674-1815: *Catechetical-Centered Instruction of Children.* First practical application of the Sunday School idea in America is credited to Roxbury, Massachusetts, where in 1674 children are claimed to have been gathered for Sunday religious instruction, details uncertain. Thereafter until 1816 followed a comparatively ineffectual struggle to achieve more than fitful local expression. For over a century progress was virtually negligible, only a few accounts of activity of Roxbury type slipping into historical record, notice so limited in most instances as to leave authenticity of report open to question. It was not until Robert Raikes popularized the Sunday School in England in the 1780's and news of his success crossed the Atlantic that anythink like a Sunday School "movement" took shape in America.

The basic features of the Raikes' scheme appealed to the current evangelical temper. Being a philanthropic plan for ameliorating the condition of poor and neglected children, it naturally fell in line with mounting evangelical missionary spirit. Considerably more significant, however, was the thoroughly lay character of the project. Lay promoted, lay supported and lay taught, increasingly on the voluntary principle, the Raikes' school offered the ordinary religious individual a means of practical service unlike any he had had before. No longer need his revival-engendered evangelical zeal remain pent-up for lack of concrete expression.

Thus there cropped up, 1785-1815, a fair number of Sunday Schools based on the new English model. First recorded of these was a home-conducted project of William Elliott, a Methodist layman who aimed to better the condition of the white children, servants and slaves working on his Virginia (Accomack County) estate. By 1790 enthusiasm had spread sufficiently in the South to prompt the Charleston (S.C.) Methodist Conference to urge the establishment of "Sunday Schools" for "poor children, white and black", such to be held "in or near the place of public worship" under the leadership of "persons" appointed by church officials. Poor attendance, however, soon induced the Conference to abandon official appointments and return the cause to its initial base of voluntary lay initiative. Meantime, the movement was spreading northward, devoid of fast denominational ties, to experience better reception. By 1791 Philadelphia, New York and Boston had each initiated a project in Sunday instruction of needy children. Occasionally satellite adventures developed, typified in the East by the Pawtucket (R. I.) Sunday School for cotton mill youth, in the West by the Pittsburgh effort to provide Sunday instruction for frontier children.

Still the movement remained essentially a series of uncoordinated local efforts. Only activity in Philadelphia appears to have enjoyed a degree of extended influence. There, in 1790 under the leadership of the Reverend William White, a group of citizens of varied faith united to form the "First Day or Sunday School Society" for the purpose of systematic promotion of the Raikes-type school. Rooms were secured in various parts of the city, teachers employed and classes begun. During the first ten years some 2,000 underprivileged children were so served with religious instruction. Thereafter success was less marked. Finally, on account of encroachments upon the curriculum of the newly founded Pennsylvania school system of which it had been largely the inspiration and to difficulties of the war years, the society closed its schools in 1814 and turned its attention to less conspicuous promotion of the voluntary lay-taught school.

The instructional aspects of the period prior to introduction of the Raikes-type school are obscure. Thereafter a general plan of operation becomes apparent. Children between the ages of six and twelve or fourteen were chief objects of attention; pre-school, adolescent and adult ages practically ignored. School sessions of five to eight hours on a single Sunday were not unusual, time being equally divided before and after morning worship service. Lengthy session was dictated by course of study. Inasmuch as the children taught were highly underprivileged, pupil illiteracy was so universal as to require elementary instruction in reading, writing, spelling, etc. before much progress could be made in religious improvement. Thus the early Sunday School dispensed both rudimentary and religious education, a dual service that required keeping scholars the greater part of the day. Religious emphasis was maintained throughout by employment of Cathechism* and Bible as basic texts, a conscious yet forced limitation of teaching materials, since other text-books would not have been available in quantity even if desired. Choice of catechism varied with sponsoring group, all historic Protestant catechisms as well as the private adaptations of Watts, Rayner and Packard seeing use. The Bible played a secondary role, being used chiefly as a reader, passages chosen with view to illustrating catechetical teaching.

The ultimate aim of instruction in this period appears that of righting the child with God by exposing him to and urging his acceptance of "correct doctrine". It was a material-centered program, theology and preparation for the other world in the foreground, children in the background. Gradation of materials to suit the age of child non-existent in the modern sense although the catechisms of Watts and the Methodist Church made a special effort to word complex doctrines more simply for the younger ages. Memoriter catechetical method of teaching requiring pupils to memorize answers to questions asked by preceptor added appreciably to the educational ordeal. The introduction of the reward ticket (*ca* 1811) to liven enthusiasm indicates rather clearly that the process was an ordeal.

II. *Promotion by Union, heydey* 1816-1858: *Transition to Bible-Centered Curriculum and Halting Advance toward Standardization of Materials and Method.* With the close of the War of 1812 the stage was set for a Sunday School boom. Restored transatlantic communication brought fresh suggestions of way and means of promotion from England. Renewed interest in education and religion created a favorable atmosphere for their application. Welling national spirit encouraged application on a nation-wide scale.

The forward surge began in New York City in 1816 with the joint founding of the "Female Society for Promotion of Sabbath Schools" and the "New York Sunday School Union Society", the former to promote work among women and girls of the city, the latter among boys. Though thoroughly lay organizations, by the end of their first year they had together under their care 44 schools, 5,200 scholars and several hundred teachers, a number of denominations being represented in the endeavor.

The founding of the Sunday and Adult School Union in Philadelphia in 1817 proved to be even more eventful. Announcing the nation as its mission field, this Union steadily forged ahead to gain unquestioned precedence. By 1824 there were in its connection 723 schools, 7,300 teachers and 49,619 scholars representing seventeen states, the District of Columbia and various Protestant faiths. In addition, major responsibility for publishing Sunday School literature had been assumed.

Clearly bested as promotional agencies the New York societies magnanimously chose to become auxiliaries to the Philadelphia Union and urged other local societies not yet affiliated to do the same. The Union responded by changing its charter and name to suit the situation, becoming on May 25, 1824 the American Sunday School Union pledged to 1) Secure unity of effort. 2) Circulate appropriate literature in every part of the land. 3) Plant a Sunday School wherever there was a population.

For approximately forty years the "American" Union held its position as central agency of Sunday School progress in America; but it was an up-hill, down-hill existence. The first ten years were mostly up. Within eighteen months nearly 400 local and regional unions representing 22 of the 24 states lined up with the main effort, whereupon the Union settled back to consolidate gains rather than stress further auxiliary expansion. By 1830 the results of organizational effort were obvious. Now the Union had in its connection 6,000 schools, 60,000 teachers and 400,000 scholars. In addition it had issued since 1824 some 6,000,000 Sunday School works: this exclusive of the establishment of three periodicals, one for infants, one for children, one for teachers. Contemporaneous with this report came the launching of the gigantic "Mississippi Valley Enterprise" designed to place within two years a Sunday School in every community west of the Alleghanies. Success achieved to the extent of 3,000 new schools founded and another 1,000 revived, a "Southern Enterprise" was projected on a similar scale in 1833. At this point spectacular advance ceased. Opposition forces that had been biding their time leaped to life to bring the new project to an untimely end. Thenceforth the principle of centralized control by Union received repeated rebuff; within thirty years was pushed aside.

The factors undermining Union leadership were general and ecclesiastical. Of general nature were various objections to the plan and purpose of the Sunday School itself, such as that it usurped the role of the parent; overlapped the program of the public school; imposed on the leisure of the child; profaned the Sabbath, etc. As a pioneering organization the Union tread a much rockier path in these areas than did its successors. More specifically ecclesiastical in nature as well as more telling in consequence were the numerous denominational attacks upon the "Union" principle of control. One after another, beginning 1826 with the Episcopalians, the major denominations flouted Union effort by founding Sunday School societies of their own, determined thereby to make the Sunday School a church auxiliary for inculcating peculiar doctrinal tenets. Even non-evangelicals, not heretofore inclined to Sunday School activity, founded religious education projects of their own, Unitarians leading the way in 1830. Only the more radical anti-missionary groups (see anti-missionary movement) resisted to any degree the urge to denominational promotion, a matter of little comfort in face of their blatant accusation that the Union was a "priestly" design to effect merger of Church and State. By 1859 it was clear that the days of centralized promotion by Union were over. Its literature had been successfully challenged by the output of partisan presses; its treasury was drained; most of its auxiliaries were dissolved. Graciously it acknowledged its loss of prestige and gave way to "National" Convention, bequeathing the latter supervisory welfare of some 3,000,000 scholars. The Union has, however, carried on in subsidiary capacity to date, having to its credit the impressive average of nearly four Sunday Schools founded daily during the entire period of its existence.

Chief instructional aspects 1816-1859 were: 1) Firm establishment of the principle of "voluntary", i.e., unpaid, lay teaching. 2) Forsaking of sole ministry to the underprivileged to conduct work among all classes of society. 3) Extension of age range upwards to include adults (*ca* 1815) and downward to include infants (*ca* 1827). 4) Curricular change reducing Sunday School from a more or less all-day session of elementary instruction centered about catechism to a relatively brief period of Biblical exercise.

Curricular change merits special notice. Improvement of public school facilities progressively reduced the need for instructing the poor in the rudiments of reading, writing and spelling. Expansion among educated classes pushed this practice still further into the background. Soon day school subjects were dropped completely, reduced scope of curriculum leading to shortened instruction period, approximating that customary today.

Of the exclusively religious developments in the area of curriculum, several bear mention. First came an English-inspired turn away from catechism toward unrestricted memorization of Biblical material. Taking hold in a modest way about 1815, by 1825 the latter practice became the vogue, making the Sunday School little more than a place for recitation before the teacher of random passages of Scripture memorized during the week. Rewards were dispensed on the basis of the quantity of material so mastered, some of the more enthusiastic pupils memorizing whole books of the Bible.

About 1825 this memorization process was significantly modified by the introduction of "Selected Scripture Lessons". Whereas haphazard pupil choice of memory verses had come to be the rule, premium placed on quantitative recitation rather than quality of material chosen, now teacher or organization "selected" definite portions of Scripture for memorization each Sunday of the year, seldom more than ten to twenty verses in length, and required all who would receive credit for instruction to comply with these "limited" selections. Thus orderly and qualitative Biblical instruction pressed to the fore. The privately published lesson lists of Goodrich (1820), Fowle (1823), Parmele (1823) and Tomlinson and Seaton (1824) paved the way for the advance. The American Sunday School Union's "Selected Lessons", first appearing in 1825 reaped the harvest. So popularly were these received throughout the country that standardization of Sunday School curriculum came near to being an established fact.

Almost immediately various types of "Lesson Helps" appeared to further enhance the effectiveness of instruction. Hereby the untrained lay teacher was provided with a means of interpreting Selected Lessons to the pupil. The "Union Bible Dictionary" was a preliminary gesture in this area, providing meanings of names, descriptions of places, explanations of customs, etc. Sunday School periodicals provided additional suggestions. Most significant of all, however, was the "Question Book Annual". First Judson (1826), then Fisk (1828), then the "American" Union (1828) published books of questions designed to test the pupil's mastery of the content of the Selected Lessons for the current year. The "Union Questions" quickly gained the day, making for another conspicuous advance toward the standardization of curriculum of materials.

Thence ensued the so-called "Babel Era" of Sunday School instruction. Private and denominational agencies becoming alarmed at Union monopoly of Sunday School literature, flooded the market with alternative materials. As early as 1831 the Moravian "Verse-a-Day Plan" received widespread publicity, calling for memorization of an assigned verse each day and the basing of the Sunday-Lesson on the seven verses learned during the week. Thereupon followed a confusion of Scripture Selections, Question Books and periodicals bent on teaching doctrines of specific groups. Some organizations even reverted to the old basis of catechetical instruction. It appeared as though Union efforts to introduce orderliness into Sunday School curricula were to go for naught.

Yet the libertinism of the period was not without its positive side. If nothing else, it gave impetus to a crude move toward gradation of lesson materials. Some private lesson writers, in addition to making the usual superficial adaptations of materials for Infants and Adults, went so far as to prepare four grades of instructional helps for the ages 6 to 12. Older adolescents, however, continued to be herded with adults.

III. *Promotion by Convention, haydey 1859-1905: Practical Achievement of Standardized Bible Study.* The meeting of the "National" Sunday School Convention at Philadelphia in 1859 heralded a new era in the life of the American Sunday School. This was not because the Convention idea was particularly new. Local Sunday School gatherings of Convention sort had been common since about 1820. Even two National Conventions had been held by the "American Union" in 1832 and 1833 in connection with a Sunday School survey. The significant thing about the 1859 Convention at Philadelphia was that it was the first of "National" scope to take serious thought for its succession. Before adjournment, a non-partisan lay committee was appointed to call another Convention, which gathering was in turn to make similar provision for its continuation, and so each succeeding one in turn. Thus central leadership other than that of the American Sunday School Union emerged.

Although the outbreak of the Civil War postponed the meeting of the next National Convention, planned for 1861, until 1869 the response to the new leadership was at this time most reassuring, 526 workers from 28 states attending. The next session held at Indianapolis in 1872 brought an enthusiastic expansionist motion that Canada be invited to participate fully in the scheme. Canadians responding favorably, the Baltimore gathering of 1875 appropriately became the First "International" Sunday School Convention. Ever since International gatherings of Sunday School workers of the United States and Canada have been held regularly, up to 1914 at triennial intervals, after that quadrennially. So far as the exercise of central leadership of the

Sunday School Movement on this continent goes, however, the International Convention was forced to step aside in 1905 to make way for newer developments (*infra*). Poor attendance did not figure into the superseding process, inasmuch as the International Convention of 1905 had an attendance just short of 2,000. Moreover, the Convention idea was at that very time assuming even greater expression in another form. In 1889 a World Sunday School Convention had been formed as a separate organization for promoting International cooperation on a larger scale. Still meeting as regularly as conditions of war and peace allow, it has so far met twelve times, last gathering being held at Oslo, Norway, in 1936, 3,000 delegates from 60 nations attending. Quite obviously the Convention spirit is still very much alive in Sunday School circles. It is only as main channel of Sunday School development that it has been superseded.

The half century of Conventional ascendancy was due largely to two factors. First of these was the extremely democratic theory of organization upon which the Convention system was conceived. Each Convention was cautiously considered a separate enterprise, a new election of officers being held before adjournment to allow unseating of any undesired leadership. As for powers of jurisdiction, the officers elected were to confine their attention to the immediate problems involved in calling the next Convention. During the interim between gatherings local and denominational leaders were to carry on without interference. This arrangement placated the chief fear that had brought Union efforts to grief, *viz.*, that of a permanent board of managers which might become so powerful jurisdictionally as to dictate universal policy over minority opposition. Consequently evangelical groups of nearly all descriptions reunited for promotional purposes. Hereupon the second factor began to exert its influence. Attendance at a large National or International Convention returned the Sunday School worker to his church with widened perspective, enthusiasm and knowledge which appreciably enhanced his effectiveness as a leader. Attendant looked forward eagerly to the next Convention; those whom he had led to the new inspiration he would bring back.

Educationally speaking, the rise of the Convention to power signified revival of the "American Union's" dream of standardized Sunday School curriculum, so effectively stopped on the threshhold of realization by the wilful confusion of the "Babel Era".

The priming factor in this educational development was the adoption of the Normal Class method of training Sunday School teachers. Undoubtedly influenced by the Normal School movement in public education, the Rev. John Vincent both conceived the idea of and successfully held a local Sunday School Normal Class at Joliet, Illinois. The founding of the first regular Sunday School Teacher's Institute followed at Galena, Illinois, in 1861. Rapidly the practice spread to other parts of the country, achieving perhaps its most memorable expression in the establishment of the Chatauqua Sunday School Assembly for Teachers in 1874, perhaps its most spectacular success by way of influencing theological seminaries to offer courses in the field of religious education beginning 1906.

This emphasis on teacher-training inevitably meant change in the area of curriculum. Teachers trained in methods of lesson presentation at an Institute or Assembly revolted against their traditional role as listening post in memoriter and catechetical exercise. Theirs was the urge to exercise the true teaching mission of interpreting lesson to scholar. Unitedly they began to clamor for less confusion, more planning in the issuance of lesson lists and helps that they might be able to exercise newly felt mission to best advantage.

Curricular adjustment came by way of adoption of a Uniform Bible Lesson system which called for the study of the same text by all ages, children and adults, on a given Sunday. The Reverend J. H. Vincent laid the foundation for the development, first by founding in 1865 at Chicago a *Sunday School Teacher's Quarterly* whereby new lesson plans could easily be circulated over a large area, secondly by beginning publication in this quarterly in 1866 a course of "uniform" lessons entitled "A Two Years' Course With Jesus". So the periodical lesson help for teachers and the first significant course of uniform lessons were born simultaneously. Vincent, relinquishing his editorial duties in 1867, was succeeded by the Rev. Edward Eggleston who sought to promote the uniform policy on a thoroughly national scale by changing the name of the "Quarterly" to *National Sunday School Teacher* and by publishing therein beginning 1868 a *National Series* of lessons. Similar attempts followed. Soon Convention officials fell wholeheartedly behind the movement, adopting as their objectives for Sunday School lessons: 1) One Lesson for all ages. 2) One lesson for all schools. 3) Expositions of the lesson in all religious and secular papers that could be induced to cooperate. Accordingly an International Lesson Committee was appointed by the 1872 Convention. In 1873 the familiar *International Uniform Bible Lessons* made their official appearance. Adoption within evangelical circles was practically immediate. Publication has continued to date in five to eight-year lesson cycles within which Old and New Testament materials have been used in variant plan. The overthrow of Convention leadership in 1905, however, was tantamount to official repudiation of the Uniform Lesson System, so that its popularity has since been steadily on the wane, though its circulation is by no means inconsiderable even now.

As the International Uniform Lesson appeared without commentary, the matter of producing adequate lesson helps became urgent. Private and denominational publishers soon placed upon the market a goodly variety of such helps. Perhaps as widely used as any of these were the *Eclectic Library* (1872-1879); its successor, the *Lesson Commentary* (Vincent and Hurlburt, editors, 1880-1900) and *Select Notes on the International Sun-*

day School Lessons (F. N. Peloubet, editor, 1875). Quite clearly such helps reflected a move away from the older mechanical means of instilling Scriptural precept by memoriter and catechetical method, a move in the direction of focussing pupil attention upon the deeper meaning of the Scripture selection by way of explanations and illustrations designed to excite imagination and kindle emotions.

Yet despite improved teaching helps, the fundamental nature of the Sunday School program remained unchanged. It was still material centered as contrasted to child-centered in emphasis. Impartation of a specific body of knowledge continued to be the chief educational objective. It could scarcely be otherwise so long as the idea of a Uniform Lesson for all ages remained in command. Adaptation to specific age needs was necessarily limited to the process of diluting or stepping up of lesson commentary as the immediate situation demanded. So, in a way, the Uniform Lesson was a backward step. It definitely throttled the move toward gradation of lesson materials which had begun to take form late in the "Babel Era". On the other hand, its part in bringing order out of instructional chaos is not to be underestimated. The growing teaching consciousness which prompted this return to orderliness was in itself insurance that the ultimate outcome would be adaptation of lesson material to meet the scholar at his specific age level.

IV. *From Convention to Council,* 1905 *to date*: *Re-evaluation of Objectives Leading to Closely Graded Church School Curriculum.* Although the central guiding body of the American Sunday School Movement has borne varying names since displacement of Convention leadership, general development are such as to advise singular treatment of events transpiring from that time to this. Throughout this latest period of Sunday School growth two inter-related trends stand out: 1) A gradual shift of key leadership positions from voluntary lay to professional religious hands. 2) Correspondingly an increasing application of the best of educational techniques resulting in finer and finer adaptations of methods and practice.

The gathering force of these interrelated trends were directly responsible for the rise of the International Sunday School Association to the place of central leadership in 1905. Unswerving attachment of lay Convention leaders to the International Uniform Lesson had for some time proved irksome to professional religious educators. Democratic as the organization of this central guiding body was in theory, in practice its powerful lay executives seemed consistently able to rally sufficient backing to defeat any proposed changes in the Uniform system. Finally professional advocates of lesson reform were driven to separate action. In 1884 a group of specialists bent on securing graded lessons for younger ages organized a National Primary Union which functioned separately from the Convention Executive, but none the less demanded the right of a special session at Convention meetings. In 1892 the graded *Blakeslee Lessons* appeared as formidable rivals to the Uniform lessons. Contemporaneously Northern Baptist educators were preparing a Primary, Junior and Advanced lesson course independent of Uniform selections. In succession, the Field Workers Association (1892), the Sunday School Editorial Association (1901), the Religious Education Association (1903) and other lesser known bodies were established for the purpose of promoting advances as best they could independent of Convention ties. Significant Schools of Sunday School Method were also founded throughout the 1890's, such as those at Northfield (Mass.), Winona Lake (Ind.) and Asbury Park (N.J.). Schools of Demonstration in which methods were applied in actual situations followed (1899 ff), such as those of the Hyde Park Baptist and Congregational churches of Chicago, under the leadership of faculty members of the University of Chicago, and the Union School of Religion in connection with Columbia University. The pressure of profession organization and research could no longer be successfully resisted. About 1900 the Convention Lesson Committee agreed to make concessions with respect to lesson adjustments; first for younger children, then for college students, then for adults. Simultaneously traditional control by Convention at large gave way in practice to central control by an Executive Committee compromised of representatives of the leading Sunday School forces that had pressured alteration in the Uniform system. Now in effect Sunday School policy was being formulated by a permanent board of officials over which Convention meetings had but nominal control. Accordingly, it was considered appropriate in 1905 to change the name of the central guiding body to International Sunday School Association.

Association leadership proved to be of brief duration. Most unfortunately the decision was made in 1907 to reinforce functional Executive permanence with Incorporation proceedings. Denominational revolt flared anew. The implications of control by a legally incorporated Board of Managers were no more acceptable now than in the early days of the American Sunday School Union. By 1910 the "Sunday School Council of Evangelical Denominations", consisting of employed officers of the Sunday School boards and agencies of nineteen denominations, had been formed purposely to combat the Associational principle of leadership and was operating effectively. For a decade territorially-minded Association officials tried to stand off denominationally-conscious Council. Strife at last ended in 1922 in the compromise formation of the International Sunday School Council of Religious Education which in 1924 became simply the International Council of Religious Education. Within the new Council set-up executive and committees were constituted on a bi-cameral basis whereby "territorial" and "denominational" interests received equal representation. In like democratic spirit legislative power of the Convention was restored with respect to fundamental issues. Such permanent organization as existed between Conventions was to be by way of "Professional Advisory Sections" for children, young people, adults, field workers, editors, etc. So, under the professional leadership of the International Council, the Sunday School Movement has continued to exhibit a united front to the present day.

Amidst this recent organizational upheaval, its provoking feature, the move for child-centered graded curriculum, was taking strides apace. Coincidental with Associational rise, the International "Closely Graded" Lessons appeared in their initial form in 1909. Similarly with the rise of opposition to Associational leadership, a succession of rival graded lessons made their appearance: *The Lutheran Graded Series* (of gradual making since 1895); the Chicago *Constructive Studies in Religion* (1910, being a belated printing, W. R. Harper's Hyde Park School of Demonstration); Scribner's *Completely Graded Series* (1911, a revision of the old Blakeslee Lessons); the *Christian Nurture Series* (1912 ff., Protestant Episcopal), the *Westminster Series of Departmental Graded Lessons* (1915 ff., Presbyterian). The Unitarian-sponsored *Beacon Course in Religious Education* (1912 ff) also deserves mention as indication that non-evangelicals were also feeling the influence of the atmosphere. With the restoration of organizational unity under the International Council no specific effort was made to curb the trend toward multiplication of curriculum materials. Rather, through its "Professional Advisory Sections", the Council confined its attention to supplying specific groups with knowledge of basic educational principles upon which they could formulate lessons suited to their own cherished beliefs. Consequently few distinct religious groups are to be found today without their own graded lessons standardized in keeping with the Council's departmental scheme for the various ages, *viz.*: Nursery (1-3), Beginners (4-5), Primary (6-8), Junior (9-11), Junior High School Age (12-14), Senior High School Age (15-17), Young People (18-*ca.* 25), Young Adults (*ca.* 25-*ca.* 35), Adults (*ca.* 35). Within each department the various ages are also treated separately. Cradle Roll and Home Department are frequently added to the scheme of grading, the former to display interest in the babe-in-arms; the latter to provide for religious needs of the shut-in.

Far more important than these outward evidences of curriculum advance in direction of the pupil-centered curriculum is the changing philosophy of religious education that underlies them. The ideal of imparting a specific body of Biblical knowledge has been superseded by a desire to arouse commitments, loyalties and enthusiasms that will translate themselves into actual religious living on the part of the child or adult; or, in other words, to build religious "character". Religious education and character education have become in a very real sense synonymous terms. Accordingly every educational device useful in soliciting actual religious response from the pupil has come to be considered appropriate as lesson material. Hence the inclusion of much extra-Biblical matter in the way of inspirational biography, studies of social problems, etc.; also, an emphasis on pupil activities designed to mould character through the medium of creative experience.

To be considered as counterpart of this developing philosophy of religious education is the growing conviction that the terms Sunday School and Church must cease to be considered as separate entities. Rather they are to be considered one and the same. The Church, instead of having such a school in its connection is to be considered "in all its parts and functions itself a school". Sunday School, morning worship, the sermon, Young People's Groups, Adult Fellowships, Mission Bands, Week-Day Religious Instruction and Vacation Schools are but variant aspects of one unitive Church School of Christian living.

V. *Non-Evangelical Sunday School Activity.* Although the organized Sunday School Movement has been an evangelical affair, the non-evangelical religious bodies in the United States have not been inactive in the field as occasional reference to Unitarian activity has already indicated. The latest religious census figures (1926) gives the total number of Sunday School Scholars in the United States as over 21,000,000. Of this number, some 1,000,000 are to be found in Catholic Churches, another 500,000 or so scattered among Christian Science, Jewish, Mormon, Spiritualist, Unitarian and other such groups. Obviously, however, the percentage of enrollment within these groups is very small when compared with the whole. If allowance is made for the extremely different set-up of the Catholic catechetical classes conducted by priests on Sunday, the scope of the actual "school" idea outside evangelical circles appears even more limited. See anti-Sunday school movement in the U. S.; Biblical history, instruction in; catechumenate; parochial schools; religious education; Young Peoples' Societies.

The following four sources will provide at once excellent general coverage and exhaustive research references to *ca.* 1930: T. Nelson and Sons, *Encyclopedia of Sunday Schools and Religious Education,* Vols. I-III (1915); E. M. Fergusson, *Historic Chapters in Christian Education in America* (1935); F. G. Lankard, *A History of the American Sunday School Curriculum* (1927); E. W. Rice: *The Sunday School Movement, 1780-1917* (1917). For developments since 1930, consult the official publications of the Religious Education Association as listed in the *Union List of Serials.* For a general statement of the place of the Sunday School in non-evangelical bodies see P. Monroe, *A Cyclopedia of Education,* (1919), Vol. V. p. 453; for more detail, consult histories of the specific groups concerned. The latest religious census figures on the Sunday School are to be found in most convenient form in the *Statistical Abstract of the United States,* U. S. Dept. of Commerce, Bureau of Census, (1938).

G.P.A.

Sunna: (Arabic, *sunnah,* usage, tradition) The religious tradition in Islam, held with the *Koran* to be of divine authority. The term was applied first to the sayings and doings of Mohammed, then to collections of moral and legal traditions supplementing the Koran*. See Hadith; Mohammedanism.

P.E.J.

Sunnites: One of two main divisions in the Moslem world, the other being the *Shi ites**. The

Sunnites comprise 150,000,000 Moslems and represent the largest body of the faithful. They are the orthodox party, accepting as authoritative traditions (*sunna**) of Mohammed rejected by others. They acknowledge the first four caliphs* to be true successors of Mohammed. Most of the Moslems in Turkey, Arabia and Africa are *Sunnites.* See Abu Hanifa; Mohammedanism; Persia, religions of. P.E.J.

sūnya, sūnyatā: See Buddhist Terminology.

superintendent: See clergy.

supernatural in primitive religion: See primitive religion; virgin birth.

supernaturalism: Name of a school in modern Protestant theology. Strictly speaking this designation is a misnomer, because by definition God, who is the subject of all theology, is above nature. The term obtained its specific significance, however, as a result of the conflict of traditional with 'natural' theology in the age of rationalism. Against the attacks that Socinians, Deists and Neologists made on orthodox theology some of their opponents pointed out 1) that the central beliefs of the Christian faith, though being reasonable, are not attainable through mere reasoning, yet that their truthfulness is confirmed, nevertheless, by prophecies and miracles, and 2) that the Bible is the divinely inspired and infallible source, from which knowledge of the saving truth as well as of the confirmatory facts can and must be derived. Pascal* was the first clearly to develop that line of apologetics. For its insistence on supernatural events this school was later on called supernaturalism.

While prior to the rationalistic criticisms the supreme authority of the Bible had been taken for granted everywhere within the Protestant churches it became then necessary for those, who accepted its authority, to demonstrate the legitimacy of this claim. The conflict between supernaturalism and rationalism is not primarily concerned with epistemology, but rather results from divergencies in ontology. Rationalists believe in the essential oneness of all reality, whereas the supernaturalists hold that the nature of God is fundamentally different from that of this created world, so that any divine operation in this world must appear as something extraordinary.

In the 18th century outstanding representatives of supernaturalism on the Continent were J. A. Bengel (1687-1752)* and the school of Swabian Pietism, J. C. Lavater (1741-1801) and J. G. Hamann (1730-1788)**. The Moravians* brought the new views to England and America, and they obtained popularity there through the Evangelicals, Wesley and Whitefield.** But on the whole the reaction against rationalism developed on independent lines in the Anglo-Saxon world. William Law, Paley, Bishop Butler and Jonathan Edwards** defended the cause of supernatural religion by adopting the method of the rationalists and pointing to the inadequate or faulty use of reason made by them.

The second phase of supernaturalism began, when the idea of 'natural religion' succumbed under the attacks of Kant's and Hegel's philosophies and Schleiermacher's theology. For their analysis of human consciousness created a new confidence in human reason and called forth a new rationalism. Thus it tended at the same time to debilitate the authority of the Bible. Critical study of the Bible, vigorously started in the second half of the eighteenth century, worked in the same direction. These developments demanded new efforts and methods on the part of the supernaturalists. Epistemologically they pointed to the existence of a specific religious faculty in the human mind (Fries*), ontologically they stressed the absolute transcendence of the divine being (Kierkegaard, R. Otto**), theologically they emphasized the personal character of God and his dealing with men, over against the impersonal nature of the Divine in modern idealism and positivism (W. Herrmann*, James Orr, Lofthouse, H. R. Mackintosh). Exegetically this school was aided by men of great erudition (Franz Delitzsch, Zahn, B. F. Westcott, J. B. Lightfoot, Ad. Schlatter**) and of profound insight (Godet*, Dean Alford, Hermann Cremer*). Renewed study of the reformers (Th. Harnack, Holl, B. B. Warfield**, Westphal) opened new avenues for the presentation of supernaturalistic theology. In the nineteenth and twentieth centuries supernaturalism developed on four different lines which represent different ways of looking at God's work in this world and interpreting it in harmony with historical Christianity: 1) Biblicism (J. T. Beck, Schlatter, C. F. Chr. von Hofmann** and the school of Erlangen*, Martin Kaehler*, the Evangelicals in England and America, R. W. Dale*, A. B. Bruce); 2) Confessionalism (Vilmar, Abr. Kuyper*, Princeton Theology, Karl Barth*, P. Althaus*); 3) Sacramentalism, especially in the Anglican Church (Pusey, Cardinal Newman**); and 4) Apocalyptic and premillennian* theology. This list is far from being exhaustive. Belief in the sufficiency of reason and in the authority of the Bible will blend so completely in many a theologian's mind that it is impossible to say to which of the contending parties he belongs. Cf. rationalism; natural theology; naturalism; naturalism and theology.

Art. Rationalism and Supernaturalism by O. Kirn and C. A. Beckwith in Schaff-Herzog's *Encyclopedia,* vol. IX, pp. 393-402; John Hunt, *Religious Thought in England* (London, 1873), vol. III; John Hunt, *Religious Thought in England in the 19th Century* (London, 1896); F. Kattenbusch, *Die deutsche evangelische Theologie seit Schleiermacher* (6th ed., Giessen, 1931); Jacques Maritain, *The Degrees of Knowledge* (1938); Niels Ferré, *Swedish Contributions to Modern Theology* (1939); Gustav Frank, *Geschichte des protestantischen Theologie* (Leipzig, 1875), vol. III; G. P. Fisher, *History of Christian Doctrine* (2nd ed., Edinburgh, 1908). O.A.P.

super-personal: This is a term applied to God to indicate that the essential characteristics of personality involve such limitations that God can not work under them and still be God. The scope and diversity of his activities and the intimacy with which he deals with each individual person are such as to render the concept of personality inapplicable. The fact that we have no pronoun other than he and she to refer to the super-personal is a limitation of our language and signifies nothing about the nature of God. Also distinction must be made between the symbolic terms of personality used in worship and attempts to use personal terms to state accurately the nature of God. Only in the latter case is the concept of personality questionable. The word "impersonal" has been used to designate the idea of the super-personal, but this expression totally falsifies the idea. Cf. God as personal. H.N.W.

superstition: A word commonly derived from *supersto* in its meaning to stand over, menace, hence implying religious dread; could more intelligibly come from its other meaning, to stand over, remain over, survive. So understood, the application of the term to practices still preserved while their significant connections have perished, is apt. Superstitions may thus be understood as survivals of extinct, defeated religions, and in fact the common use of the term to condemn bears witness in its animus to a not utterly extinct rivalry. See Chinese religions; folklore.

J. Michelet, *Satanism and Witchcraft* (1939). P.G.M.

Supper, the Last: See Lord's Supper.

supralapsarianism: (*supra,* before; *lapsus,* fall) The doctrine which holds that God's decrees of reprobation and election** were before the actual Fall* of man, and were part of the original purposes of God. The general position of the orthodox Dutch Calvinists. Confirmed at the Synod of Dort.* See predestination. Cf. infralapsarianism; sublapsarianism. E.P.B.

Supremacy, Acts of: A short Act of 1534 declared Henry VIII* "only supreme head in earth of the Church of England." This was an extreme form of the mediaeval imperialist theory; it was applied by the exercise of ecclesiastical jurisdiction in the King's name under Henry VIII and Edward VI. Repealed under Queen Mary, 1554, it was not revived under Elizabeth. But a new act of 1559 declared the Queen "supreme governor" of the realm in all matters, authorized to visit and correct the Church. This phrase, perhaps deliberately chosen as one open to varying interpretations, does not challenge the spiritual position of the Church as crassly as the other; but in practice the Act of Supremacy subjected the administrative system of the Church of England* first to royal control, and since 1689 to dependence on parliamentary legislation. Civil lawyers are likely to interpret it as making the Church of Engand a purely national institution, while ecclesiastics may regard its acceptance as a kind of Concordat* between the nation and the English part of the Catholic Church. E.R.H.

suras: (Arabic, *surah,* a step, a degree) The chapters or sections of the *Koran**, sacred book of Islam. There are 114 *suras* arranged evidently from the longest to the shortest without logical or chronological order, by Zaid the secretary of Mohammed* after the prophet's death. P.E.J.

surplice: (Late Lat., *super* and *pellis,* fur) A loose white vestment* of linen or cotton with wide sleeves, derived from the alb* for use over coats. Worn by the clergy in the Roman Catholic, Anglican and Moravian churches and by choristers. Its use in England was made a matter of controversy by the Puritans*. See rochet. T.J.B.

Sūrya: One of the minor sun gods in Vedic Hinduism, usually associated with the round red orb of the sun. He is regarded variously as the child of Ushas (dawn), and as her husband. A dozen hymns of the. Rig-Veda* are addressed to him. C.S.B.

Susannah, History of: Apocryphal addition to Daniel*. The Septuagint and Vulgate place it at the end of the book, and Theodotian at the beginning. The devout wife of Joakim resists the advances of two elders who acted as judges and was falsely accused by them. As the condemned woman was being led to her execution, Daniel came to her aid. By his wise cross-examination of the accusers he established her innocence. Thereupon the congregation condemned the accusers to death in accordance with Deut. 19:19. The story was probably written by a Palestinian Jew during the early part of the first century B.C. in Hebrew or Aramaic, illustrating the Pharisaic insistence on strict examination of witnesses and severe punishment of malicious witnesses. (Makkot 5b) See apocrypha, Old Testament. S.S.C.

Susano-o- (no-Mikoto): (Jap.) Literally "Impetuous Male (the August One," Susano-o is, according to Shinto* mythology, the brother of Amaterasu o Mikaki* the Sun Goddess. While the Sun Goddess reigned over the Plain of High Heaven and the Moon God ruled over the night, he was master of the sea and the domain of hidden things. His violent character so frightened his sister that she hid in a cave and thus brought darkness to the universe. Enticed by a multitude of deities with a mirror and a set of jewels, she emerged and again illumined the world. The council of deities banished Susano-o from the High Plain to the earth. He descended to Izumo, subdued rebels, and secured a sword from the Eight-Headed Serpent, which sword he presented to the Sun Goddess. Eventually he became not only the ruling deity of Izumo, but also the Storm God for all Japan and the agent of mysterious things and evil doings. Both he and his sword, which is believed to be the very one jealously guarded as a national treasure, have been an encouragement of the militant spirit in Shinto. Because of these reasons, Susano-o is a very important deity in Japan today. W.T.C.

Süskind, Hermann: (1879-1914) He taught in Tübingen. Killed in World War I, he was one of those most strongly influenced by Troeltsch*. He sought to understand Schleiermacher* from the angle of philosophy.

Der Einfluss Schellings auf die Entwicklung von Schleiermachers System (Tübingen, 1909); *Christentum und Geschichte bei Schleiermacher* (Tübingen, 1911). H.H.

Suso, Henry: (ca. 1295-1366) A south German Dominican mystic whose *Autobiography* and *Book of Heavenly Wisdom* interpret the mystical approach of Meister Eckhart* in terms of the intensely passionate love lyric of an age of chivalry. See Friends of God. D.V.S.

sutras: A late stage of Vedic literature designed to present in extremely concise form the requirements of Vedic religion*. Some of them are so brief and aphoristic that they cannot be understood by the uninitiated without the aid of commentaries. They are of four kinds: 1) *Srauta,* or priestly sutras, 2) *Grihya* sutras which deal with the domestic rites, 3) *Dharma* sutras, which deal with social duties, and 4) Sutras which deal with grammar, philosophy, astronomy, magic, etc. The Laws of Manu* is a late form of one of the most important Dharma Sutras. See Forty-two Chapter Sutra (under Buddhist Terminology). C.S.B.

suttee, sāti: The practice of widow-burning in India. It was outlawed by the authorities early in the nineteenth century. Ram Mohan Roy* was one of those who vigorously opposed the institution. C.S.B.

Sverdrup, George: (Dec. 16, 1848-May 3, 1907) Lutheran theologian and church leader. He was born in Balestrand, Norway, son of a Lutheran pastor and politician. He studied theology in Christiania, Norway, and in Germany, Oriental studies in Paris. His friend and later colleague Oftedal brought him in 1874 as professor of O.T. and Dogmatics to the Augsburg Seminary, Minneapolis, Minn., whose president he was from 1877-1907.

Under the influence of Hauge* he worked very actively among the Norwegian immigrants in the Middle West. He was anxious to activate the laity in church life, and following Grundtvig's* ideas, to transform the congregation into a cultural and educational unit. His sincerity, the strength of his religious convictions, his fearless presentation of his views and his independent mind made him a great church leader, but also a fierce and redoubtable polemicist. As a protest against the formation of the United Lutheran Church Sverdrup and his friends founded the Norwegian Lutheran Free Church in 1897 upon a congregationalist basis (since 1917 united with the other branches in the Lutheran Norwegian Church).

Principal works (all in Norwegian): *Sammelte Skrifter i Udvalg* (a collection of articles and essays), 6 vols., ed. by A. Helland (1909-1912); *Aand og Liv* (sermons), ed. by Oftedal, 2 vols.; Biography in A. Hauck's *Realenzyklopaedie,* 3rd ed., vol. XXIV, pp. 537-575. See also *American Lutheran Biography,* pp. 789-791. O.A.P.

Swain, Richard La Rue: (1860-) Author of the stimulating and widely read volume *What and Where is God* (1920). J.W.B.

Swander Lectureship, The: Founded by the Rev. John I. Swander and his wife in 1901 this lectureship is given annually at the Theological Seminary of the Evangelical and Reformed Church, Lancaster, Pennsylvania. Its capital sum is $10,000 and the lectures, four or more, are designated to promulgate "sound Christological science", the lecture topics being mutually agreed upon. The latest course was given by Dr. E. S. Brightman.

(Information from the office of the President of the Seminary.) V.F.

swastika: A very ancient and widespread ornamental form or symbol, found both in the Eastern and Western hemispheres. It is usually regarded as a symbol of the sun. In India it is a symbol of good luck. It may be either right hand (male) 卍, or left hand (female) 卐. The former is most widely used in India. In Germany where it is the emblem of the Nazi state the latter is used.

Thomas Wilson, "The Swastika, the Earliest Known Symbol and its Migration," *U. S. National Museum, Annual Report, 1894* (1895); Leon de Millone, Le Swastika in *Annales du Musees Guimet,* vol. 31 (Paris, 1909); G. Bellew, "Aryan Peoples and the Swastika," *Blackwoods Magazine,* vol. 247, pp. 653-658, May, 1940. C.S.B.

Swedberg, Jesper: (1653-1735) Professor at Upsala and bishop of Skara. Swedberg was sympathetic toward Pietism's stress on a faith which showed itself in a godly life. Himself of a warm, child-like, nature, he was interested in the doctrines of *unio mystica* and of angels, believing in their presence and activity. He published a Hymnbook with many of his own hymns, but failed to have it officially received. He was friendly towards the Church of England, especially with Bishop Robinson of London. As bishop of Skara he supervised the Swedish Church in London, and Lisbon, and befriended greatly the Swedish Church on the Delaware. His literary activity included devotional, homiletical, catechetical, philological works; also a record of the Swedish Church on Delaware, in *America Illuminata.* C.J.B.

Swedenborg, Emanuel: (1688-1772) Son of Jesper Swedberg. Swedenborg's student days included impressions from Rudbeck at Upsala, Newton, Boyle, Halley, Locke, in England, Polhem in Sweden, the Cartesian philosophy and the Cambridge Neo-platonists.

The *Principia* (1734) explained the universe in mechanistic terms. A mystical view pervaded the *Oeconomia regni animalis* (1736); the world was now less a machine, more an organism. The *anima* receives illumination from the central source of life and light when the *mens* controlls man's physical nature. Between the physical and spiritual world there is a close correspondence, each natural phenomenon shadowing a spiritual reality. In the *Clavis hieroglyphica arcanorum* this idea was extended to the mystical correspondence between words and their inner meaning—a basis for his later spiritual interpretation of Scripture, which was the means whereby the divine was communicated to the mind of man.

In Amsterdam, 1736, Swedenborg had an experience of photism; in Amsterdam, 1744, and in London, 1745, he experienced visions which he interpreted as revelations of the Creator-Redeemer. Henceforth he proclaimed a truth received by didirect vision, though the biblical imagery of *De Cultu et Amore Dei* (1745) concealed much the same cosmology and psychology as the earlier works. Even his visions were more a confirmation than a source of his speculations.

The theology of Swedenborg is systematically presented in *Vera Christiana religio* (1771). The orthodox doctrines of the Trinity and the Atonement were repudiated. Redemption consists of the Incarnate God overcoming the increasing powers of hell. Man's freedom enables him to choose and follow the good. On death he enters the realm of the spirits when he either ascends to the heavenly sphere, becoming an angel, or descends to hell, becoming an evil spirit. Following a spiritual mode of interpreting Scripture, which he held to be inspired, Swedenborg considered the Judgment to have come in 1757 and Christ's Second Coming as a victory over rebellious spirits. The heavenly world corresponds to the human, and even marriage finds transcendent meaning in heavenly marriage of kindred souls, (*Arcana Coelestia, Apocalypsis, De Ultimo Judico, De Amore Conjugiali*). The orthodox churches must give way to the New Church (which dates from the completion of *Vera Christiana religio,* 1770) when men will be correctly instructed in the truth of God. See New Jerusalem, Church of.

R. L. Tafel, *Documents concerning the Life and Character of Swedenborg* (1875-77), 3 vols.; *Works,* Swedenborg Society (London, 1916); B. Worcester, *Life and Mission of Emanuel Swedenborg* (1883); S. Warren, *Compendium of the Theological Writings of Emanuel Swedenborg* (1885); M. Lamm, *Emanuel Swedenborg* (1915).

C.J.B.

Swedish Ev. Mission Covenant Church: See Evangelical Mission Covenant Church of America.

syllabus of errors, papal: A collection of errors. There are two such collections of errors, one issued in 1864 by Pius IX*, the other in 1907 by Pius X*. The Syllabus of Pius IX contains 80 condemned theses. All of these are succinct expressions of important errors of the times which had previously been condemned by the Pope. It aroused great opposition among the Church's enemies. The Syllabus of Pius X is the decree *Lamentabili sane exitu.* It condemns in a list of 65 theses the main errors of Modernism*. One of its effects was an increase of exegetical work among Catholic scholars to offset the false scriptural interpretations of Loisy* and other Modernists. For a complete list of the condemned propositions of both Syllabi see Denziger's *Enchiridion Symbolorum,* nn. 1701 ff. and 2001 ff.

C.R.

Sylvania Phalanx: See communistic settlements, secular.

Sylvester, I, St., Pope: (314-335) As Bishop of Rome, during the age when Constantine* was changing the pagan Roman State into a Christian government, with religious worship a matter of conscientious conviction to all, Pope Sylvester I and his predecessor, Miltiades (311-314) are the two hinges of Christian antiquity on which the door which closes the age of the persecutions and opens the period of religious freedom revolves. His friendly associations with Constantine alone would explain the rising power of the papacy which needed not the medieval fictitious "Constantine Donation"* to accentuate its historical existence. Of doctrinal importance are the decrees of the Council of Arles, 314*, regarding the Donatists*, sent to Sylvester for approval; also the celebration, during his pontificate, of the first Ecumenical Council of Nicea, 325, which condemned Arius*, who had denied the divinity of Jesus Christ and His equality (consubstantiality: homoousios*) with God the Father. It was Sylvester who, according to certain early MSS, presided over the deliberations and confirmed its Acts not in person indeed, but through his Legates* Hosius*, Bishop of Cordova and two Roman priests. According to the *Liber Pontificalis** Sylvester consecrated the Basilica of St. Peter, erected by Constantine; also the Lateran, former imperial palace, now converted into the Cathedral of Rome; St. Paul's, Beyond the Walls; and the basilica of the Sesorian Palace (*Santa Croce*). The so-called *Constitutum Sylvestri* or *Canon Sylvestri* is a VI cent. spurious fabrication. During his pontificate it is highly probable that the first Martyrology* was compiled; also the establishment of a Roman School for ecclesiastical chant. His feast is celebrated on Dec. 31; by the Greeks and Syrians, on Jan. 2.

Litt.: *Liber Pontificalis* (ed., Duchesne: Paris, 1886-92), vol. I, pp. 170-201; Bollandists, *Bibliotheca hagiographica* (Brussels, 1898-1901), vol. II, pp. 1119-21; *Id., Bibl. Hag. Graeca* (*Ib.* 1909), p. 230 ff.; I. von Döllenger, *Papstfabeln, 2* (Munich, 1890), p. 61 ff.; Jaffé, *Regesta Romanor. Pontificum, 2,* vol. I, pp. 28-30; Marucchi, *La Basilica Papale del cimitero de Priscilla* (Rome, 1908).

R.M.H.

Sylvester II, Pope: See Gerbert of Aurillac.

symbol and symbolism: Religious symbols direct attention, awaken response and guide behavior in dealing with realities too complex, intimate or otherwise inaccessible to precise designation. However, the term symbol has become highly ambiguous in recent learned discussion. In symbolic logic, for example, it means the most precise kind of designative sign that can be used. This is very different from the symbolism in religious usage of the Cross, the Church spire, and ritual. To distinguish the religious symbol from these other kinds we must analyze the nature and use of signs.

A sign represents some structure of existence and possibility. The honk of a horn may represent a possible sequence that will injure me if I do not get out of the way of the oncoming automobile.

The cry "Auto coming" is a sign for the same thing under proper circumstances. Every statement made by words is a sign.

In order to have signs and meanings we must have structures, which is to say, distinctions and connections, whereby events can be so demarcated and related that when a few happen these few can represent all the others, including possibilities. In this way I can through representation by a few events deal emotionally, theoretically and practically with all the other events and possibilities which pertain to that total structure in which the signs are minor components. All meanings are, then, structures whereby events are (or might be) so demarcated and related that a few of them, called the signs, can represent all the others.

Our physiological reactions, however, are so much more complex, subtle and changing than our intelligible structures of well-defined meaning that we are always dealing physiologically with realities which exceed the scope of those demarcations and relations which our signs represent. The statement "I love you", when spoken sincerely in love, is not only a sentence pointing out the individual loved and stating the fact that one loves. Nor is it merely an expression of the emotion of the lover. It also refers to all that is so connected and associated as to make up the total personality loved, much of which the lover cannot clearly and fully specify. A symbol of this sort adumbrates, while other signs specify and designate. So it is in religion that a symbol is a sign which awakens and directs our response to that matrix and context which overflows and encompasses the limited structures which are precisely designated by our linguistic signs. The Cross is a symbol of this sort. Some doctrines of the faith, at least as used by many religious folk, are symbols and myths (see myth) rather than statements of truth in the sense of representing some specifiable structure of events.

Ernst Cassirer, *Der Begriff der Symbolischen Form in Aufbau der Geistes Wissenschaften* (1923); C. W. Morris, *Foundations of the Theory of Signs* (1938); Ogden and Richards, *The Meaning of Meaning* (1923); W. M. Urban, *Language and Reality* (1939); A. N. Whitehead, *Symbolism, Its Meaning and Effect* (1927). H.N.W.

symbolics: The essential things of religion are unseen and eternal (2 Cor. 4: 18); but they can be mediated to our finite and imaginative apprehension under symbols* of word and form. Symbolics may be the study of religious symbols. But the reference is commonly specific, to doctrinal or creedal symbols. Creeds and Confessions** are symbols of the Christian Faith, as held in the various ages and communions; 'Symbol' used of Apostles' Creed as early as third century. Symbolics divided thus: Fundamental, study of Symbols belonging to the whole Church (Apostles', Nicene, Athanasian Creeds**); Particular, study of Symbols of particular Churches (Augsburg Confession, Helvetic Confessions, Thirty-nine Articles**, etc.). Creeds and Confessions retain their character as Symbols of Faith, their place in the structure and inheritance of Church or Churches, however religious thinking and expression may change or the Churches unite their testimony. These developments may yield other attempts to define Christian principles, and so other data for Symbolics. See konfessionskunde.

C. A. Briggs, *Theological Symbolics* (1914).

J.L.

symbolism: Representation of one entity or idea in terms of another, usually the translation of an abstraction into concrete form. Sometimes used for mystification as in the O.T. prophetic books, sometimes for the purpose of confining knowledge of sacred mysteries to the elect as in gnostic theologies. The early Christian Fathers, esp. Augustine, followed the rabbinical practice of interpreting scriptural naratives as elaborate symbolical representations of spiritual truths. See idols and images; myth. V.F.H.

symbolism: A symbol is a sign or an identifying mark. In the days of persecution certain pictures and abbreviations were used in order to conceal some truth from the enemy. Thus the three Greek letters IHC became the abbreviation for IHCOYC, or *Jesus;* and XPI for XPICTOC, or *Christ.* The Latin cross, of course, signified the Crucifixion, and later came to denote Christianity. The assurance of eternal life was signified by the circle, the Trinity by an equilateral triangle, and regeneration by an octagon.

In later years, when Christians were permitted to build houses of worship, and when the arts of wood-carving and stained glass were developed, our Lord was often pictured together with the four evangelists, or again He was shown on the cross, with His mother on one side and St. John on the other. Certain signs were evolved, so as to distinguish them one from another, for some of the early converts could not read, and names would prove of no value to them. Thus it became customary to identify our Lord by means of a nimbus*, or circle about His head, and from this circle emanated four rays, forming a cross. His mother was given a nimbus with stars adorning its border, and she was usually garbed in light blue. St. John was shown with an eagle at his feet. Each of the other apostles was given a mark of identification. St. Peter usually carried two keys in his hand, St. Andrew leaned upon a cross saltire and St. Paul was given a sword and a book.

These symbols usually recalled some well-known fact in the life of the apostle or the O.T. worthy. Isaiah was given a saw, the supposed instrument of his martyrdom, Moses his two tablets of stone, Noah held in his hands a small model of the ark, and St. Stephen was shown with stones lying at his feet.

Although the number of symbols multiplied so that today they fill a fairly thick book, yet their use in ancient and mediaeval art is by no means as lavish as is generally supposed. It would seem that the ancients rarely used symbolism merely as decoration, but employed it only when necessary.

During the second and third decade of the present century there was a profuse, and frequently needless use of symbols. Instead of using, for example, the symbols of the apostles in order to distinguish them one from another, these symbols were painted and carved at random, often where there were neither painted nor carved figures to identify. Frequently such symbols were used inappropriately, as for example when the symbols of our Lord's Passion were displayed on the sides of a font. A fanciful symbolism of numbers was carried to ridiculous extremes, and three steps at the church entrance were said to signify the Trinity, four posts under the gallery the four evangelists and six panels in the altar the six days of creation.

It is well to know symbolism so that one may identify the figures in ancient and modern stained glass and carving, but to use it in the thoughtless, lavish way in which it is used in this country is to rob it of any meaning that it may have had. Those who would know the meaning of the thousands of symbols of ecclesiastical art* would do well to consult E. Geldart's *Manual of Church Decoration and Symbolism* (London, 1897). See I H S. F.R.W.

symbolism, Medieval number: Method by which the medieval mind assured itself of cosmic order. Convinced that "God has arranged all things in number..." (*Wisdom* XI, 20), theologians found symbolic relationships in scriptural numbers and other observed or created numerical groupings. On the basis of Pythagorean and gnostic theories, each number* was assigned a root meaning and diversified representations. Some root meanings were: 1 = Unity of God and Spirit; 2 = Diversity of Earth and Matter; 3 = Trinity, extension of Godhead; 4 = Extension of Duality, Earth; 5 = Flesh (senses); 6 = Earthly Perfection (days of Creation); 7 = 3 + 4, Universe of Spirit and Matter; 8 = Immortality; 9 = Extension of Trinity, Angelic Number; 10 = Extension of Unity, Perfect Completeness.

Isidore of Seville, *Liber numerorum*; Hrabanus Maurus, *De numero;* Petrus Bungus, *Mysticae numerorum significationis liber*; Vincent F. Hopper, *Medieval Number Symbolism* (1938). V.F.H.

symbols, particular Christian: (Gr., *symbolon,* a sign) Christian symbols are outward and visible signs of divinity, doctrines, spiritual ideas, sacred seasons, characters in Christian history, etc. Among the earliest symbols of God are the hand and the all-seeing eye. Among the numerous symbols of Christ are the fish*, the letters of whose Greek name are the initials of the Greek words, "Jesus Christ Son of God, Savior," the vesica, a closely related symbol, the candle, the crown and the lamb. The Holy Spirit is represented by the dove and by various forms of the candlestick. The Trinity is symbolized by the triangle in various forms, the trefoil, the shamrock and similar devices. Various monograms such as X P and I H S* stand for Christ, while the cross* in numerous forms stands for his suffering and redemptive love. The star stands for the Epiphany* and many other Christian ideas. The symbols for Christian doctrines are numerous; e.g., the ox for patience and sacrifice, the anchor for hope, the peacock for the resurrection and the butterfly for immortality. The Evangelists, the Apostles and the Virgin have their appropriate symbols and every feature of the church edifice has its especial symbolic significance.

F. R. Webber, *Church Symbolism* (1927); T. A. Stafford, *Christian Symbolism in the Evangelical Churches* (1942); V. O. Vogt, *Religion and Art* (1921). F.T.P.

symbols, particular, in early Christian times: The primitive church possessed symbolic rites in Baptism and the Lord's Supper**. It made use of symbolic gestures, as in the laying on of hands.* It had symbolic forms of speech, e.g., "maranatha" (the Lord cometh) which served as a watchword by which Christians recognized each other. But there is no mention in the N.T. of visible objects connected with worship or with dress and behaviour. Christianity distinguished itself from pagan religion by avoiding these outward signs, which savoured of idolatry. In the second century, however, the symbol of the Cross* became customary, and Tertullian says that it was used by Christians to bless almost all their actions. Strangely enough it is not found in the Catacombs*, where Christian ideas are conveyed not so much by symbols as by types (e.g., the Good Shepherd, the Orante, the Ark of Noah* &c). Almost the only real symbol is the fish*, the Greek word for which contains the initials of the name and titles of Christ. A symbol of the same kind is the labarum*, the monogram of Christ which Constantine adopted as the Roman standard, and which was doubtless of early origin.

F. R. Webber, *Church Symbolism* (1938); R. A. Lanciani, *Pagan and Christian Rome* (1896). E.F.S.

Symeon Metaphrastes: (To be most probably identified with Symeon Magister the Logothete) Flourished in the second half of the tenth century. His fame rests on his compilation of the legends of saints in the Byzantine *Menologion.* He was canonized by the Eastern Orthodox Church*. Later additions to his authentic collection have been likewise ascribed to him. He wrote other less known works.

K. Krumbacher, *Geschichte der byzantinischen Litteratur* (Munich, 1897), 2nd ed., pp. 200-3. M.S.

sympathy: The emotional and imaginative experience of entering into and sharing the mind, particularly the thought and sentiment, of some one else. As a "feeling with" others it is experienced at non-reflective levels and makes for social solidarity. At higher levels it involves mental assimilation, communion and personal insight. It has its basis in original nature, may be developed and extended through social experience and is the main root of altruism. As a virtue it is made primary in Buddhism, is stressed in Christianity, was exalted by Schopenhauer and repudiated by Nietzsche.** It is a personal and culture force of great significance. R.W.F.

synagogue: (From the Greek "assembly" or "place of assembly") Used to designate the religious community of the Jews or, more often, the house of their worship. The origin of the synagogue is still a matter of conjecture. Some scholars trace it back to pre-exilic* times, others date it as late as the Seleucidan or Maccabean era. Sacral and secular origins have alike been suggested, some seeing in the synagogue a continuation of the ancient local sanctuaries, others assuming that it evolved from communal assemblies in post-exilic Palestine. Plausible seems the view, backed by Jewish tradition, which seeks the early formation of the synagogue among the captives of the Babylonian exile who unable on foreign soil to continue with sacrificial ritual, developed a more spiritual form of worship. Prayer and study took the place of offerings, and the synagogue became a substitute for the destroyed temple.

Whatever the time and circumstances under which it originated, the synagogue marks a departure in the history of religion. Without a visible symbol of the deity to lend sacredness to an especial place, without propitiation by sacrifice or a privileged clergy to mediate or intercede for the common man, the public worship of the synagogue, spiritual and democratic throughout, permitted anyone anywhere to commune with God. The new institution had a great historic influence, within and without Judaism. In all the ages, and in all the lands of dispersion, the synagogue became the focus of the religious, social and intellectual life of the Jews, serving not only as place of public worship, but also usually as elementary school, law-court, communal center and even hostelry for strangers. The synagogue also, and not the temple, supplied the mould and model for the worship of both Christianity and Islam. Its historic effect earned the synagogue the praise of being "la création la plus originale et la plus féconde du peuple juif" (E. Renan).

The earliest synagogues, thus far unearthed in Palestine, date as late as the first century C.E. Older are the remains in Egypt and Greece which point respectively to the third and second pre-Christian century. Recent excavations, both in Palestine and adjacent lands, yielded evidence of a lost pictorial art of the ancient synagogue (notably the cycle of biblical frescoes in the synagogue of Dura-Europos, built in 244 C.E.). The new finds seem to bear also on the old question of the origin of early Christian art. See Bet Hamidrash; Ezra; Great Synagogue, the.

S. Krauss, *Synagogale Altertuemer* (Berlin-Vienna, 1922); E. L. Sukenik, *Ancient Synagogues in Palestine and Greece* (Schweich Lectures) (London, 1934). S.S.

synaxis: (Gr., assembly) A gathering (early Church) for public worship, whether eucharistic (liturgical) or non-eucharistic. P.V.N.

syncretism: In the field of religion it is the term descriptive of the mingling of faiths which come in contact one with another. It may take place consciously as in the case of some modern religions which are products of the deliberate weaving together of various strands of religious thought to form a new religion. More frequently it is a quite unconscious process of give and take such as inevitably occurs where differing faiths meet. See W. E. Hocking, *Living Religion and a World Faith* (1940). Examples are the flowing together of Hebrew and Greek thought in early Christianity; the fusion of certain Moslem and Hindu ideas in the Sikh* faith, etc. C.S.B.

syncretistic controversy: A seventeenth century debate centering around the extent to which harmony and reconciliation were possible between different religious groups. It brought into conflict those who stressed respectively the exclusive and the inclusive aspects of truth. The immediate issue was the relation between Lutheran and Reformed Churches**. Calixtus* was prominently involved in the controversy. G.R.C.

synderesis: (late Gr. *synteresis,* spark of conscience) See conscience. H.H.

synergism: Represents the modification, in a slightly semi-pelagian direction, of the strict Augustinianism which marked early Lutheranism. Its leading representative was Melanchthon*, and the chief issue was the nature and status of fallen man, especially in relation to conversion. See grace. Cf. Loci Communes; monergism.

G.R.C.

synod: An authoritative ecclesiastical assembly. In the ancient church the word at first was equivalent to "council". This came to be used for ecumenical conventions and "synod" was applied to those representing particular territories or jurisdictions or communions. In modern churches the word has different technical meanings. In Presbyterian polity* the synod is the judicatory intermediate between the presbytery and the supreme body, the General Assembly* or in some cases General Synod. In the various groups of American Lutheranism the synod is the controlling organization, e.g., Missouri Synod. In the Eastern Orthodox Church of Russia the supreme governing body is the Holy Synod. In churches having diocesan bishops there are diocesan synods.

R.H.N.

Synodical Conference, the (Lutheran): See Lutheran Church in America.

Synoptic Gospels: The Gospels of Matthew, Mark, and Luke** called 'synoptic' either because they present a common view or because they may be viewed side by side. The reason for this common view, it is now recognized, is the use made by Matthew and Luke of the earlier Gospel of Mark. (See article "Harmony of the Gospels"). Matthew rearranges the material in Mark in order to fit it into his five main divisions (chs. 3-7, 8-10, 11-13, 14-18, 19-25). Luke, on the other hand, retains the order of Mark but omits a long section (most of chs. 6-8) and makes two long insertions into Mark. Much of the material found in these long insertions is spread widely over the Gospel of Matthew. In brief, Mark's narrative was not viewed by the later evangelists as infallibly accurate; Matthew could adapt the Marcan material to his arrangement of material by subject, while Luke either inserted other material into Mark or (as the late Canon Streeter* held) inserted Mark, in seven sections, into his earlier collection of discourse material and anecdotes. (The so-called "Proto-Luke Hypothesis").

The priority of Mark is recognized by practically all N.T. scholars except those influenced by the ancient ecclesiastical theory that Matthew wrote first and then Mark abridged Matthew. Upon this theory of the priority of Mark have been based a number of extravagant views which would make Mark practically infallible, in order and chronology and in interpretation.

By 1900 the majority of Protestant critics had come to recognize not only the priority of Mark but also the existence of another source, chiefly consisting of sayings of Jesus, used by Matthew and Luke in addition to their use of Mark, (the so-called "Two Document Hypothesis"). Much attention has been given to the reconstruction of this Sayings Source ("Q"* for *Quelle,* which means "source"), one of the most widely followed still being that of Harnack*.

At the present time various modifications of the two-source theory (or "Two Document Hypothesis") are maintained. One is the "Four Document Hypothesis" of Canon Streeter, Vincent Taylor, and others. In addition to Mark and "Q", each of the later synoptists had a document peculiar to himself: the special document or source of Matthew is designated "M", while that of Luke is designated "L". Another theory, which really goes back to an earlier date than Streeter's hypothesis, recognizes not only four sources but several. This "Multiple Source Hypothesis" was first advanced by Professor Burton* of Chicago and has been widely held in this country. There are probably sources underlying even the Gospel of Mark —some of them undoubtedly written sources, as Professor Branscomb holds.

This Multiple Source Hypothesis fits the requirements of Form Criticism*: the earliest sources are fragmentary crystallizations of the oral tradition. No doubt these fragments grew into larger 'blocks' and eventually into collected 'sources' like "Q" and "M", but oral tradition did not cease to exist when sources were compiled; nor were the sources looked upon as definitive and infallible. Each one still "interpreted [or translated] as he was able", as Papias observed in the second century.

Thus the Synoptic Gospels contain our earliest sources for the life and teaching of Jesus. Mark was probably written in Rome in the year 68. Luke, the first volume of a work on Christian origins (Luke-Acts), was probably written late in the reign of Domitian, perhaps about 95 A.D., but where we do not know. It was somewhere in the Graeco-Roman world and presumably outside Palestine. Matthew is variously dated from 85-110, or even a little later. It presumably comes from Antioch or its hinterland. Of course, the tradition contained in the Gospels is much older than the writing of the Gospels, and the authenticity of a passage or a saying is not determined by the date of the Gospel in which it appears. See gospel.

See also B. H. Streeter, *The Four Gospels* (1924); A. von Harnack, *The Sayings of Jesus* [trans. 1908]; E. D. Burton, *A Short Introduction to the Gospels* (1904) [rev. by H. R. Willoughby, 1926]; F. V. Filson, *Origins of the Gospels* (1938); D. W. Riddle, *The Gospels, Their Origin and Growth* (1939); F. C. Grant, *The Growth of the Gospels* (1933).

F.C.G.

synteresis: A moral sense, classed by Aquinas as a habit, common to all men; a residuum or remnant of man's unfallen nature. Jerome explains it as a spark (scintilla) of conscience which man retained at the Fall.

A. Koch and A. Preuss, *Moral Theology* (1925), vol. I, 3rd ed.

J.T.M.

Syrian churches: A group of Churches, located in the nearer East, including those border provinces within and beyond the boundary which separated the Roman Empire from Persian territory; so-called because the basic language was Syriac. The leading city was Edessa*. Under the leadership of St. James of Nisibis and his disciple, Ephraim Syrus, both of whom attended the Council of Nicea*, these churches accepted the Nicene orthodoxy. Rabbulas, Bishop of Edessa (412-435 A.D.) also tried to hold them to orthodoxy in face of the Nestorian* heresy; but his successor Ibas (435-457)* welcomed Nestorianism and established a famous Nestorian School at Edessa. Subsequently those of the Syrian churches within the Empire became Monophysite* while the others were Nestorian. These churches are also important for various texts of the N.T. including the Peshitta and the Diatessaron of Tatian**. See canons of various churches; versions of the Bible, ancient. A.K.R.

Syrian National Church: See Jacobites.

Syro-Hexaplar version: See versions of the Bible, ancient.

systematic theology (history of, etc.): Theology* is literally discourse about God; as the term is used, belief concerning God and other beliefs cognate to it. Systematic theology concerns these beliefs in ordered elucidation and in their relation to contemporary thought and life—'contemporary' in each age, the task of theology falling to be done continually as the intellectual outlook and even the meanings of words undergo change. Thus there is a history of Systematic Theology.

The sources of Christian theology are the Scriptures and Christian testimony through the centuries. The seminal minds in theology are the writers of the N.T.; these are not systematic theologians, though Paul, particularly in 'Romans', the writers of 'John' and 'Hebrews' do interpret formally the meaning of Christ, salvation, etc., in view of current conceptions and needs. But essentially theirs is the creativity of preachers of the Word.

The post-Apostolic age was not fruitful theologically; the Apostolic witness was received but imperfectly grasped. Theology began when pagan assaults and heresies forced a double strategy in the truth's defence; the one evoked apologetic*, the other theology strictly so named. Irenaeus* (c. 125-202: *Adversus Haereses*); Tertullian* (c. 150-220: *De Praescriptione Haereticorum*), the father of Latin Theology, wrote theology in combating heresy; Origen* (185-253) fought on both fronts, confuting heathen assailants (*Contra Celsum*) and producing in *De Principiis* what is regarded as the earliest systematic doctrinal treatise. A little later the Arian* Christological* heresy found more than its theological match in Athanasius* (298-373: *De Incarnatione*); who, with the School of Antioch* where theology was less speculative and more historico-exegetical, the Cappadocians* and others did much to win for theology its royal place in Greek Christianity; to John of Damascus* (8th century) and beyond it was never without outstanding names.

Theology in the West found equally stout champions; some of them, Augustine, Anselm, Aquinas**, among the greatest figures in the annals of the Church. These men were the philosophers of their age as well as the theologians; the Bible was still the foundation of theology but philosophy had a large hand in shaping its problems. The concepts of Plato (Neo-Platonism) and Aristotle** lay side by side with Scriptural beliefs and metaphors in a massive concord of Reason and Faith.

With the Reformation came recoil from rational dilution of theology and fresh zeal for its Biblical originals. Luther and Calvin** were superb theological minds; Calvin's *Institutes* achieved *system* on the new principles that vied with Aquinas' *Summa Theologica* of the former type. But theology was now due for a long eclipse. This was because, with the Renaissance* and break-up of medievalism, science and philosophy sloughed the imprimatur of the Church; by converse, theology receded from the intellectual forefront, becoming overshadowed even in her own field by philosophy and psychology of religion**, as philosophy and the sciences increased and their method pervaded the world of knowledge.

The nineteenth century saw theology's self-recovery as an independent discipline. Schleiermacher and Ritschl** wrought the change, although their psychologic and evaluative approach makes their constructions quite inept to more radical proponents of the integrity of theology of our own time. These are in the wake of Kierkegaard* who saw Time and Eternity, Reason and Faith as discontinuous; so for Barth* and others, the Truth or Word of God* is not homogeneous with other truth, even as God is not the idealization of man. Hence the theology of the Word, living and having its being not in man's wisdom but in what God has revealed. Here in the re-capture of its mission of confession and exposition of Truth committed to it lies, it is believed, the restoration of theology as a living spiritual force; while its effort toward ever deeper understanding of the Revealed· Word and its meanings *hic et nunc*, provides scope for a vigorous and creative intellectual life. See dogmatic theology.

C. A. Briggs, *History of the Study of Theology*, 2 vols. (1916); K. Barth, *The Word of God and the Word of Man*, trans. Horton (1928); K. E. Kirk and others, *The Study of Theology* (1939).

J.L.

T

tabernacle: (Heb., *mishkan,* dwelling place, i.e., of Yahweh*. Ex. 25.8) The portable tent sanctuary used by the Israelites during their desert wanderings and early life in Canaan until it was replaced by the permanent sanctuary at Jerusalem*. While the detailed instructions to Moses* of its measurements and specifications (Ex. 25-27) and the minute account of their execution (Ex. 36.8-38.31) are presented by the Priestly writer as a contemporary report, critical study shows that the description of the tabernacle is a post-exilic* idealization of the Temple* of Jerusalem. In the mind of the author the requirement of a single sanctuary for Israel dates from the days of Moses. Following the covenant at Sinai, God revealed to him the pattern of its construction, which the inspired artists Bezalel and Oholiab used in creating the Tabernacle out of the materials voluntarily offered by the people. (Ex. 31. 1-11; 35-36.7). As the place where God met with the representative of the people, it was known also as the Tent of Meeting. (Ex. 29.42-45).
S.S.C.

Tabernacles or Feast of Booths: (Heb., *sukkot*) Annual autumnal harvest festival, observed from the 15th till the 22nd of Tishri. Beginning as a purely agricultural "feast of ingathering", it was invested with sanctity by the priestly legislation. The first day constitutes a "a holy convocation", upon which all servile work must cease. It was observed by erecting booths from palm branches, boughs of willows, etc., as memorials of the booths in which the Israelites lived after their deliverance from Egypt. (Lev. 23. 33-43; Num. 29. 12-38; cf. Neh. 8. 15 ff.). The agricultural nature of the feast is evident also from its water-drawing ceremonies. (Cf. Mishnah* Sukkah) In post-biblical times the seventh day acquired a special character as *Hoshana Rabbah**. The eighth day (22nd of Tishri)—*Shemini Azeret*—is treated as a separate "day of solemn rest". An added day originated in Babylonia in post-Talmudic times, which is designated *Simhat Torah,* Rejoicing in the Law*, upon which the annual cycle of Pentateuchal reading is finished and resumed again. See Jewish religious festivals; lulab.
S.S.C.

table of the Lord: See Lord's table; sacramental meal.

tables of the Law: According to Ex. 24.12 Moses* ascended the mountain and received from God "the tables of stone, and the Torah* (Law) and commandment". Subsequently they are spoken of as "written with the finger of God" (Ex. 31.18; 32.15-16). On the way down the mountain, as Moses beheld the people dancing around the golden calf, he dropped and shattered the tablets. (Ex. 32.19). Commanded to prepare exact copies of the tablets, he spent forty days and nights on the mountain and "wrote upon the tables the words of the covenant, the ten words". (Ex. 34.1-4, 27-28). As he descended with them his face shone with a divine splendor. He placed these "tables of the testimony" in the ark*.

Rabbinical* opinion differed regarding the arrangement of the Decalogue* on the tables. Some thought that it was inscribed on each table, while others held that five commandments were written on one and the remaining five on the other. (Canticles Rabba 5.4) The latter view is followed in the synagogue* presentations of the tables of the Law*.
S.S.C.

Taborites: The Taborites were the leftist party among the Hussites*, and were so named after the fortified city of Tabor in southern Bohemia which they had built. Their radicalism took the form of strict biblicism, although they repudiated extreme chiliastic* groups which originated among them and which developed various antinomian practices and held that the Lord's Supper is a mere memorial, repudiating both transubstantiation* and every other form of the real presence* theory. The ecclesiastical leader of the Taborites was Bishop Nicholas of Pelhrimov, while the chief military commander of their armies was John Zizka.

Joseph H. Müller, *Geschichte der böhmischen Brüder* (Herrnhut, 1922).
M.S.

tabu: A prohibition of acts and contacts immediately dangerous to the doer and through him to his group. The word comes from the Pacific area where tabu (tapu, kapu) was expanded into a technique of social control. When the scientists began the study of religions the term was used generally to indicate the caution signs set up by groups to guard against things and actions inherently dangerous. The attitudes involved in the tabu belong to the earliest phases of culture when man was making his first faltering steps toward group security in a world little understood and filled with potential menace. The approved pattern of behavior in relation to environment and of individual to individual in the group was established by long experience in the satisfaction of basic desires. Within this tested pattern the individual was safe. When the approved mode of behavior was violated there was a feeling of apprehension, of danger. Moreover, there were many things and events that had a mysterious quality in regard to which the only established pattern of behavior was one of caution, a warning against contact. Violation of the group code or contact with these sources of infection was an immediate threat to the safety of the individual. He acquired a contagion which might prove fatal to him and might spread to the whole group in contact with him. Punishment came automatically from the dangerous situation itself. It was not a human sanction nor the action of a god or supernatural being. These latter sanctions were later developments. The concern of the group at first was not in punishment but in purification* of the individual to make him once more safe for social relations.

The tabu caution against contact applied almost universally to death and blood. The contagion of a corpse often required the destruction or abandonment of objects in contact with it, even the dwelling, and always the purification of mourners before normal living could be resumed. Blood of menstruation or childbirth was dangerous, demanding isolation and rites of purification. Warriors returning from battle were also tabu. Offenders against the sex code or murderers carried a contagion that might even endanger the food supply. Like the warrior, a stranger was tabu until he was made safe by ceremony. Rulers, chiefs, priests and magicians were sometimes hedged about with a mysterious potency that made them dangerous for ordinary mortals to touch. The danger might even extend to their regalia, clothing, food*, land or name. The sanctity of objects of religious cult and associated with the gods marks them off in the same way. Property was protected by infecting it with danger to the transgressor by means of a curse or spell*. Prohibition in some cultures of the use of certain foods by women and the uninitiated and of touching the new crops until they were released for general use by a first fruits* ceremony seems to be an extension of the original meaning of tabu.

The danger involved in the tabu situation sometimes results in the death of the offender. If not, the group may protect itself against his contagion by banishment, by his public confession, or by some form of cleansing ceremony. When divine or legal sanction assumes control of behavior the primitive, automatic sanction of tabu is weakened, absorbed or ignored. See primitive religion.

A.E.H.

Tagore, Sir Rabindranath: (1861-) Indian poet and educator who by his personality and teaching, his mystical poems, *Gitanjali*, his essay *Sadhana*, The Realization of Life, and other writings interpreted the religious faith and philosophy of India in such a way as to win the sympathetic understanding of the West.

See his *The Religion of Man* (1931). J.W.B.

T'ai Chi: See Chinese Terminology.

talisman: (Arabic) An amulet*; an object which owes its efficacy to a property transmitted from without, such as a tooth, claw, or horn of an animal; supposed to aid the possessor in warding off evil and bringing good fortune. F.L.P.

tallit: Prayer shawl worn by Jews at morning worship. It is woven of wool or silk, with fringe attached to the four corners as ordained in Numbers 15: 37-39. B.Z.B.

Talmud: (derived from the Hebrew *lomed* which means study) The Talmud is an encyclopaedia of Jewish tradition supplementing the Bible (O.T.) and summarizing more than seven centuries of cultural growth. Its origins go back to the close of the Biblical (O.T.) canon and it did not reach its final stage of development till the end of the 5th century. It is primarily concerned with law, but it also includes many copious discussions in the fields of religion, ethics, social institutions, history, folklore and science.

The makers of the Talmud accepted the Torah* as the revealed will of God; its mandates were, therefore, abidingly valid and were not to be altered by the will of man. But the dynamic of a changing world had created new facts in Jewish political and social life, new developments in culture, in religious doctrines and ethical ideas. Thus the Bible (O.T.) (Deut. 24:1) recognizes the possibility of dissolving the marriage ties, but does not specify under what circumstances or by what procedure this was to take place. The Bible (O.T.) visualizes all religious life as centering around the central sanctuary in Jerusalem, with the sacrificial cult as the principal medium of worship. When the Jerusalem Temple ceased to be, a new ordering of Jewish religious life obviously became necessary. Similarly, true to its largely rural background, the Bible (O.T.) offers us no body of precedents or principles governing the regulation of trade, labor and industry. The Talmud is the record of new enactments, procedures and interpretations by which the basic religious ideology of the Bible (O.T.) was implemented so as to function in a changed Jewish society.

Historically, Talmudic literature developed in two layers. The oldest, the Mishnah (derived from the Hebrew *repeat* or *study*), is the product of the scholarly edition of Rabbi Judah the Prince and his disciples who were active in 3rd century Palestine. It is written in a clear and lucid Hebrew and is divided into six principal sections which are subdivided into an aggregate of sixty-three tractates; these being again divided into chapters and paragraphs.

The six main sections to the Mishnah* are called "Sedarim", *orders*, derived from the fact that each section represents an orderly arrangement of opinions and laws on its particular subject. The six Sedarim are Zeraim, Moed, Nashim, Nezikim, Kodashim, Taharot. *Zeraim* or seeds, deals with agriculture; appended to it is the all important tractate *Berakot* which deals with prayer. *Moed* meaning festivals, deals with the Sabbath, holidays, fasts and feasts of the Jewish calendar. *Nashim* which means women, discusses marriage, divorces and other phases of family life. *Nezikim* or injuries, deals with civil and criminal law. *Kodashim*, holy things, discusses the sacrificial cult and other details of the Temple service. The last section *Taharot*, cleanliness, deals with all questions of ritual purity.

Because of its very brevity, the statements in the Mishnah required constant amplification and interpretation. And Jewish society continued to change, requiring constantly newer techniques for ordering life along the ideals of the religious tradition. A second layer was consequently developed in the literature of the Talmud to supplement the Mishnah. This second layer is known as *Gemara**.

Derived from the Aramaic *gemar* and meaning study or teaching, the Gemara exists in two versions, both in the Aramaic vernaculars current respectively among the Jews of Palestine and Babylonia. For in post-Mishnaic times, the Jewish community in Babylonia had overtaken Palestine as a center of Jewish learning, and the Babylonian schools developed a parallel supplement to the Mishnah, which indeed proved even more influential than the Palestinian supplement. Frequently the same teachers are represented in both Gemaras, for there was a constant interchange of visits among the Palestinian and Babylonian rabbis and the academies in each country were fully informed on the work being done by their sister academies in the other country. Not all tractates of the Mishnah are supplemented by the Gemara; only those that were of interest to the teachers that created the Gemara. The Palestinian Gemara, frequently called Yerushalmi or Jerusalem Gemara, supplements thirty-nine tractates; the Babylonian only thirty-six and a half. In compass, however, the latter is three times as large as the former, the Babylonian Gemara being more elaborate and more copious in its expositions. The Mishnah and Gemarah taken together comprise the Talmud.

The Talmud and various related literary creations of the same period has frequently been called the Oral Torah, because for centuries it was expounded and transmitted orally. Individual students probably employed notes to aid their memories, but none of these compilations were officially edited until a considerably later date. The Palestinian Talmud was concluded some time in the 5th century as a result of the general decline of the Jewish community in Palestine, marked by the abolition of the last vestige of Jewish autonomy, the patriarchate, in 425 C.E. The Babylonian Talmud was concluded toward the end of the same century, for in Babylonia, too, Jewish life was declining, following the persecutions of Jews under the Sassanian Kings, Jezdegerd II (438-457) and Perez (459-484). The final canonization of the supplementary Torah in the crystallized texts of the Talmud brought to a close one of the most creative epochs in the history of Jewish tradition. See Israel, religion and theology; law, Hebrew; Moses ben Naham; pilpul; Rashi; Saadia ben Joseph; Tanna.

The Talmud has been translated into English by a group of scholars under the chairmanship of Rabbi I. Epstein and is being published by the Soncino Press, London, England. A good anthology of significant Talmudic statements on every phase of religion and life is A. Cohen's *Everyman's Talmud* (London, 1934). An accurate and exhaustive survey of the world outlook of Talmudic Judaism is G. F. Moore's *Judaism in the First Centuries of the Christion Era*, 2 vols. (Cambridge, 1927). B.Z.B.

tamid: See s.v. holocaust.

Tammuz: See Mesopotamian religions.

Tanna: (Aramaic, meaning teacher; plural, *tannaim*) One of the Jewish scholars of the first two centuries, whose teachings are contained in the *Mishna**, (the rabbinical laws) and in the *Baraita**, (additional teachings outside the *Mishna.*) Cf. Akiba. P.E.J.

Tantras: Relatively late sacred writings of Hinduism*, dating in their present form from the seventh or eighth centuries of the Christian era or even later. Only a few of them have been translated. They are used particularly by the Shivaite sects, especially the Shaktas* who worship the female principle of the universe, usually represented in Kali*, wife of Shiva. They contain, a great deal of the mystical and magical; discuss a wide variety of subjects such as medicine, science, religion; enjoin the use of *mantras**, mystic diagrams, and strange symbolism; and serve as the source of the rituals used in tantric worship. The practices of the left-hand *saktis* are abhorrent to the moral sense of most Hindus today. See sacred literatures. C.S.B.

Taoism: See Chinese Terminology.

tapas: The first meaning of the word is heat. It comes to mean fervour or heat of devotion and finally penance, self-mortification, austerity, asceticism. C.S.B.

taqiyya: A principle by which Moslems in a hostile country are permitted to conform to the alien religious practices for the sake of their own security. It seems to have originated with the *Ismailis**. P.E.J.

targum: The Hebrew term for translation and usually referred to the specific translations of the Bible (O.T.) The most important of these was the Greek translation known as the Septuagint* or the Targum of the Seventy, so called because it was executed by a commission of seventy scholars. Another Greek translation was executed in the 2nd century by the Greek proselyte, Aquila, from

Pontus. He became so famous for his translation that he was also credited in later time with the popular Aramaic translation which was used as an official text in Babylonia and subsequently also in Palestine, to accompany the reading of the weekly Scriptural lessons in the synagogues. The technical name of this translation is *Targum Onkelos*, but it is also referred to by the more general designation, Targum. B.Z.B.

Tartarus: See heaven and hell.

Tatian: A Christian writer in the middle part of the 2nd century. An Assyrian by birth, he became at Rome a follower of Justin Martyr*, and wrote an apologetic work, *An Address to the Greeks,* which still survives. Towards the end of his life he joined the heretical sect of the Encratites*. He is most celebrated for his Diatessaron* a harmony of the Gospels which for a time displaced the Gospels themselves. See Lives of Jesus; Syrian churches; versions of the Bible, ancient.

E. J. Goodspeed, *Early Christian Literature* (1942); H. M. Gwatkin, *Early Church History* (1916). E.F.S.

tauhid: The unity of God in Moslem theology. Among pantheistic *Sufis** the term came to mean the unity of the soul with God, but this was not accepted by the orthodox. P.E.J.

Tauler, John: (ca. 1300-1361) A Dominican mystic of the school of Meister Eckhart* and a preacher of great power whose life was chiefly associated with the city of Strasbourg. He was a member of the loosely organized mystical band known as The Friends of God*. His *Sermons* have lived on in many translations.

R. M. Jones, *The Flowering of Mysticism* (1938). D.V.S.

taurobolium: Early Roman empire; a rite used in the mystery of Attis* to assure immortal life; the sacrifice of a bull upon a covering over a pit, in which rite the worshiper, in the pit, is baptized by the bull's blood streaming through openings in the platform overhead. F.L.P.

Tausen, Hans: (1494-1562) Tausen, an early Danish convert to Lutheranism, after 1526, as chaplain of Frederick I, was an influential preacher in Copenhagen, advocating Reformation doctrines against Romanists, especially Paul Helgeson. After victory of Lutherans in Denmark, 1536, Tausen became a leader in the reconstruction of the church, aiding in translation of Bible, devotional writings, composition of hymnbook, and ecclesiastical reorganizations. C.J.B.

Taverner, Richard: See Bible, English.

Taylor, Alfred Edward: (1869-) Erudite philosophical scholar, authority on Platonic and ancient thought, Prof. of Moral Phil. in Edinburgh since 1924. He roots his theism not so much in the cosmological and teleological arguments, which merely suggest an intelligent, immutable Will, but in the objective deliverances of moral insight and revelatory religious experience. An idealistic absolutist when he wrote *Elements of Metaphysics* in 1903, his two volumes, *Faith of a Moralist* (1930), reveal a theist with Anglo-Catholic leanings. See also *Plato, The Man and His Work* (1927). P.A.B.

Taylor, Jeremy: (1613-1667) English theologian and prose writer, called by Emerson "the Shakespeare of divines." Among his principal works are *A Discourse of the Liberty of Prophesying* (1647), *The Rule and Exercises of Holy Living* (1650), *The Rule and Exercises of Holy Dying* (1651), and *The Golden Grove* (1655). L.W.C.

Taylor, Nathaniel: (1786-1858) American theologian, abandoned Jonathan Edwards'* theory of "moral inability" and asserted that man "not only can if he will, he can if he won't." Far from being providentially decreed, sin enters the world because "such is the nature of *free agency* that God could not wholly prevent its perversion." See American theology, early; New Haven theology; Taylorism. W.M.H.

Taylor, Nathaniel W. Lectures: A lectureship at the Yale University Divinity School, established March 14, 1902, in memory of the Reverend Nathaniel W. Taylor, B.A. 1807, who was Professor of Systematic Theology and Chairman of the Faculty, 1822-1858. The lectures are upon some topic in the field of theology. Among the courses have been those by George W. Knox, The Direct and Fundamental Proofs of the Christian Religion, 1903; William N. Clarke, The Use of the Scriptures in Theology, 1905; Henry C. King, The Seeming Unreality of the Spiritual Life, 1907; George A. Gordon, Religion and Miracle, 1909; William E. Hocking, Human Nature and its Remaking, 1916; Walter Rauschenbusch, A Theology for the Social Gospel, 1917; Douglas C. Macintosh, The Reasonableness of Christianity, 1925; Hugh R. Mackintosh, Types of Nineteenth Century Theology, 1928; Frank C. Porter, The Mind of Christ in Paul, 1929; Robert L. Calhoun, God and the Common Life, 1934; John Baillie, Our Knowledge of God, 1936; H. Richard Niebuhr, The Meaning of Revelation, 1940. L.A.W.

Taylorism: Name given to Nathaniel Taylor's* modified Edwardean theology, which so stressed the freedom of the will as to limit God's sovereignty. Viewed by its antagonists as a fatal concession to Arminianism*. See Edwards, Jonathan; means; New Haven theology; Oberlin theology.

F. H. Foster, *A Genetic History of the New England Theology* (1907). W.M.H.

Te Deum: A hymn, probably by Bishop Niceta of Remesiana (4th cent.), in praise of God and Christ, to which supplicatory versicles have been added—used on special occasions of rejoicing and at Matins* on festivals. E.R.H.

technology: See culture.

Tefillah: See Shemoneh Esreh.

Teichmüller, Gustav: (1832-1888) Was professor at Dorpat, now Tartu, Estonia. He wrote a number of works dealing with the history of ancient philosophy. He coined the concept of a semiotic knowledge, the use of linguistic signs for feelings which themselves are not knowledge but which can be made available for knowledge. Religion symbolizes for Teichmüller the synthetic function of intellect, feeling and action. Energetically defending personal immortality, he polemicized against positivism and Darwinism.

Ueber die Unsterblichkeit der Seele (Leipzig, 1874); *Darwinismus und Philosophie* (Dorpat, 1877); *Ueber das Wesen der Liebe* (Leipzig, 1879); *Die wirkliche und die scheinbare Welt* (Breslau, 1882); *Religionsphilosophie* (Breslau, 1886). H.H.

teleological argument for God: This argument takes the fundamental form: The order pervading the inorganic, organic, and human realm is indicative of an intended plan in an intelligent and good Purposer. This argument complements the causal reasoning in the cosmological argument* in calling attention to the adaptive interrelation of the various parts or aspects of the universe to each other in a way conducive to the production and conservation of human values.

Introduced by Plato (*Laws*), the particular form of the argument has been moulded by the knowledge and concept of the natural world affecting the thinkers who advanced it. Thus, as long as organisms were thought to have originated in their present forms, with ready-made specialization of organ to function and of part to whole (as one part of a clock is to the other parts), one could expect the teleological views of a Paley or Butler** in the 18th century. But their pre-Darwinian appeal to special, external design was denied in favor of an immanent purposive operation when it was shown that the present forms of organism were evolutionary modifications from one source.

Meanwhile, the change from Newtonian absolutes to the modern field-theories of physics discouraged mechanical conceptions of natural entities in favor of organism (e.g., Whitehead*). Finally, the fact that the preparation of the physical universe for life definitely exceeded the expectations of chance, along with the theory of "emergent evolution," increased the suspicion that the order of nature was an order of purposive development.

Throughout the history of the argument is the insistence that such order as there is in the organic and inorganic world is a surd mystery in the mechanical view of the world. However, a synoptic view of the world, including the values human beings realize and serve, weighs the balance in favor of the teleological hypothesis.

Thus the argument has moved design within from without, and emphasized not specific adjustment of various parts, interesting though that be, but the interrelation of the ultimate collocations of the universe. This "wider" teleological argument, as presented by one of its best adherents (F. R. Tennant*), rests on the suggestiveness of the coherent adaptation between a) nature and human cognitive powers, b) the inorganic and life, and between organic parts to preserve whole organisms, and c) human values and the rest of the human world. See God.

L. Henderson, *The Fitness of the Environment* (1924), *The Order of Nature* (1925); F. R. Tennant, *Philosophical Theology* vol. 2 (1930); H. Bergson, *Creative Evolution*, Eng. tr. (1911). P.A.B.

teleology: (Gr. *telos*, end) A term used to identify the branch of philosophy which has to do with ends or final causes. The whole is considered as ideally prior to the parts and constitutes the explanation of their mechanical processes. The whole is an unchangeable form, and controls all movement, giving all movement purpose and goal, with all processes subordinate to a purpose. The idea of teleology is older than the word. The concept was evident in the organic view of nature which was developed in ancient Greek philosophy against the mechanical view. Anaxagoras* was the first of the ancient philosophers to use the argument. Christian Wolff* was the first to use the term. The argument is prominent in the teachings of Thomas Aquinas, (1224-1274), Joseph Butler (1692-1752)*, Immanuel Kant (1724-1804), Abraham Tucker (1705-1774)*. See cause; Fiske, John; God; teleological argument for God. W.G.H.

telepathy: The direct communication of mind with mind without the use of sense perception. J. B. Rhine of Duke University claims to have found experimental evidence in support of the view that there are certain supernormal faculties. This claim has been the subject of considerable controversy. See abnormal psychology; parapsychology; psychical research, societies for.

See J. B. Rhine, *Extra-Sensory Perception* (1934). A.T.B.

Tell El-Amarna Tablets: More than three hundred sun-baked tablets and fragments discovered at Tell-el-Amarna, Egypt, from 1887 to 1933. Most of them are diplomatic letters written in Akkadian and received by the Egyptian kings Amenophis III (1411-1375 B.C.) and Amenophis IV or Ikhnaton (1375-1358 B.C.) from their Syrian and Palestinian vassals. Important source of information on the Near-Eastern civilization in the second millenium B.C.

See S. A. B. Mercer, *The Tel-el-Armana Tablets*, 2 vols. (1939). S.L.T.

Tell-el-Duweir: See Lachish Ostraca.

Teller, Wilhelm Abraham: (1734-1804) He was first professor in Helmstedt, then provost and superior consistorial councillor in Berlin. He applied the idea of progress to Christianity; subjected the content of the N.T. to the viewpoint of historical conditionality. His aim was a modest practical rational change of the Christian faith. As a neologist he claimed to surmount orthodoxy and pietism, to revive the unity of Christianity with the temporal movement, giving reason a wider room and opening the path for rational and historical criticism.

Lehrbuch des christlichen Glaubens (Helmstedt und Halle, 1764); *Wörterbuch des Neuen Testaments zur Erklärung der christlichen Lehre* (Berlin, 1772); *Die Religion der Vollkommeneren* (Berlin, 1792).

H.H.

temperance movement: A series of interrelated efforts to limit or prohibit the use, sale, or manufacture of alcoholic beverages. Its objectives and methods have undergone extensive modification and expansion in the course of their historical development. Such efforts are almost as old and as universal in human society as the use of intoxicating beverages. In Chinese tradition, one of their emperors ordered all vineyards destroyed as early as the eleventh century, B.C. Temperance was encouraged by the priests of ancient Persia and India and by the O.T. Scriptures; total abstinence was taught by certain Hebrew sects such as the Rechabites*, as well as by Buddhists and Moslems; and the Mogul emperors tried to prohibit the liquor traffic in India. Among the Carthaginians intoxicants were prohibited to magistrates and on military campaigns; among the Romans various emperors sought to curb drinking; and in Mexico the Aztecs made drunkenness among the young a capital offense, and permitted the free use of alcohol only to the aged and on holidays.

During the Middle Ages, the manufacture of wines and beers was so restricted by social conditions as not to permit of much abuse, but with the spread of distillation after the thirteenth century over-indulgence in hard liquors became common, especially in Northern Europe. The insobriety of the masses aroused the opposition of the ruling, military, and employing classes, and more determined restrictive measures were adopted, especially with the rise of the factory system.

In the American colonies many local restrictive and regulatory measures were adopted during the seventeenth and eighteenth centuries, and the churches endeavored to encourage moderation by moral suasion, and by resolutions against the distillation of ardent spirits. Dr. Benjamin Rush is generally accredited with laying the foundations of the modern temperance movement with the publication of his *Inquiry into the Effects of Ardent Spirits upon the Human Body and Mind* in 1785. The first organized temperance society on record in America was created by 200 farmers in Litchfield County, Conn., who in 1789 pledged themselves not to use any distilled liquors during the ensuing farming season; but the first society of more than local and temporary influence was formed at Moreau, N. Y., by a young physician, Dr. Billy J. Clark, in cooperation with the Congregational minister, the Rev. Lebbeus Armstrong, and with Dr. Rush as an honorary member. Dr. Rush also appeared before various ecclesiastical bodies to urge the necessity of inaugurating a plan to arouse public opinion on the liquor issue. His activities resulted in the appointment of temperance committees by the leading denominations to devise ways and means, and inspired the efforts of an influential group of clergymen, notably Lyman Beecher*, Jedediah Morse, and Jeremiah Evarts. Beecher's sermons at East Hampton, L. I., and Litchfield, Conn., eventuated in the organization of the Connecticut Society for the Reformation of Morals in 1813, and in the same year the Massachusetts Society for the Suppression of Intemperance, founded in Boston by Morse and Evarts, spread the movement throughout New England and New York.

With the organization of the American Temperance Society, later known as the American Society for the Promotion of Temperance, and still later as the American Temperance Union, in Boston on February 13, 1826, the movement assumed the proportions of a national crusade. Agents were employed to organize and affiliate local, county, and state auxiliaries with the national body. Within a decade over 8,000 such groups had been formed comprising more than 1,500,000 members, and with a periodical press of 11 weekly and two monthly journals to serve as a medium of communication and propaganda.

The earlier temperance reformers were chiefly concerned with the abuse of distilled liquors. They thought little of total abstinence, or of extending the ban to light wine and beer. But with a new generation new issues arose. Proposals came before the convention of the American Temperance Union at Saratoga, N. Y., in 1836 1) to denounce the anti-slavery reformers within the movement and to appease the Southern societies, 2) to abandon the exclusive reliance upon moral suasion and to turn to legislative coercion, and 3) to bring all alcoholic beverages, fermented as well as distilled, under the ban of total abstinence. A decision on the first two issues was avoided, but the total abstinence plank was adopted two years later, by a narrow margin, and the movement declined owing to the defection of a minority who could not be persuaded that temperance required total abstinence.

But the next decade witnessed the rise of more nation-wide temperance organizations than any similar period in American history. Most of these took the form of secret societies or lodges with dues-paying members, each of whom took the total abstinence pledge or initiation. The movement now took on a contagious emotionalism, exemplified in the Washingtonian Movement and in the oratory of John B. Gough (1817-86) for over forty years the most popular lecturer on the temperance issue in America. This phase culminated with the arrival in the United States of Father Theobald Mathew, of Cork, Ireland, "the greatest of all temperance missionaries," who in his American tour of 27 months, is reported to have traveled more than 27,000 miles, and to have administered the total abstinence pledge to more than 500,000 Catholics.

Public opinion was now prepared for the second phase of the temperance movement, that of state and national prohibition, which advanced over the country in three waves. 1) The first wave lasted from 1846 to 1855, when thirteen states and territories enacted statutory prohibition. But attention was diverted from the liquor issue by the problems of the Civil War, Reconstruction, and the Westward Expansion, and these laws were soon repealed. Only five of them survived the conflict, and only two remained in effect in 1880. During this period the temperance movements which had sprung up in the different countries became increasingly conscious of each other, and organizations of international scope began to appear. The Independent Order of Good Templars, formed in Utica, N. Y., in 1851, spread to Canada, England, Scandinavia, Australasia, South Africa, and South America before the century closed. The National Woman's Christian Temperance Union, founded at Cleveland, Ohio, in 1874, gave rise to the World Christian Woman's Temperance Union, with national organizations in fifty countries. A conference of leaders in the national movements in London in 1909 resulted in the International Prohibition Confederation, and the World League Against Alcoholism was formed at the close of World War I a decade later. 2) The initiation of the second wave began with the enactment of constitutional prohibition in Kansas in 1880. Before the close of the decade six states had written prohibition into their basic law, and a seventh had re-enacted statutory prohibition. Again there was a recession, and by 1907 all but three of these enactments had been rescinded. 3) The third wave began in that year. Heretofore the prohibition had been confined to the East and Middle West, but now the movement shifted southward. Within five years seven states, all Southern, had joined Kansas, Maine, and North Dakota in the dry column, and by 1919 thirty-nine states had enacted such legislation.

In addition, a considerable proportion of the rural and suburban territory in wet states was dry by local option. This privilege of the people of a precinct, ward, municipality, township, or country to decide by petition or by popular vote whether or not the liquor traffic should be licensed in their locality had first been accorded by Indiana in 1832. The Anti-Saloon League had actively fostered such legislation after its organization in 1893, and by 1919 over nine-tenths of the land area and two-thirds of the population of the United States were in dry territory.

Although proposals to amend the Federal Constitution to provide for national prohibition had been introduced into Congress as early as 1876, not until 1913 did the dry forces, led by the Anti-Saloon League, actively press the measure, and in December of 1917 it had received the necessary two-thirds majority in both Houses. Within fourteen months it had been ratified by three-fourths of the states, and it was proclaimed effective as of January 17, 1920, one year after ratification.

In the meantime, the Food Control Act of August, 1917, had forbidden the use of any form of foodstuffs in the distillation of spirits for the duration of the War, and complete War Time Prohibition, approved in September, 1918, became effective on July 1, 1919, and remained in effect until superceded by the legislation enacted under the Eighteenth Amendment.

The Amendment had prohibited the importation, manufacture, transportation, or sale of "intoxicating beverages", but had not further defined the term. The Volstead Act, which gave effect to the Amendment, defined intoxicating beverages as those containing one-half of one percent or more of alcohol. This extreme definition was challenged in the Courts and finally sustained, but it later contributed to the breakdown of the measure.

Organized opposition to the Eighteenth Amendment began immediately, supported by large industrial interests which wished to shift taxation to the liquor industry, by other groups who held the matter a proper field for local and state rather than federal action, and by the urban wing of the Democratic Party, which had always been hostile to the measure. Proponents of the Amendment declared that it had reduced industrial accidents, improved the public health, increased savings accounts, diverted enormous purchasing power from alcoholic beverages to other purposes, and released productive resources for employment in more constructive ways. Opponents argued that the banishment of the saloon was a gain, but that it had been replaced by "speak easies," night clubs, rum running, racketeering, corruption in enforcement units, and general disrespect for law.

The legislative revolt against the measure began with New York, which repealed its State Enforcement Act in 1923, followed by Montana in 1926 and Wisconsin in 1929, but it was not until the economic collapse of the early 1930's that the full extent of the change in public opinion was revealed. Finally, the Democratic platform of 1932 declared for repeal, and the appropriate resolution was passed by Congress in February, 1933. The states acted in record time, and on December 5, 1933, the Twenty-First Amendment passed the control of the liquor traffic back to the states.

But the temperance movement continues. It is again placing heavier stress on education and moral suasion, and is insisting on more effective supervision over the conditions of sale while endeavoring to recreate popular sentiment in favor of more effective legislative control.

Ernest H. Cherrington, *The Evolution of Prohibition in the United States of America* (1920); Charles Merz, *The Dry Decade* (1931); August F. Fehlandt, *A Century of Drink Reform in the United States* (1904).

H.E.J.

Templar, Knights: See Knights Templar.

temple: Although the term is variously employed in popular speech, strictly speaking any place or edifice dedicated to the worship of deity, or regarded as the dwelling place of deity is a temple. The earliest temples may have been caves such as those found on the island of Malta, or in Egypt or in India. Very simple and little adorned in primitive times, the temples in most religions became, in time, elaborate structures upon which were lavished the wealth and the best creative skill of the architects and artists of the respective cultures which produced them. Naturally temples differ greatly from culture to culture, each expressing something of the genius of its own culture, as the great temples of Karnak and Luxor in

Egypt, the Parthenon in Greece, the temple at Jerusalem, the cathedrals of medieval Europe, the elaborate temples of Hinduism and Jainism and Buddhism in India and the far east and the simple, rude shrine of the Sun Goddess at Ise in Japan.

Common to most of them is a central place of exceptional holiness, the very dwelling place of deity, the altar*, a rich symbolism expressive of the faiths and hopes of the people, and some attempt to convey, whether through the dim light, the architectural pattern, the artistic decorations, or otherwise the sense of mystery and awe which resides at the heart of most religious worship.

Generally, worship in the temples is rather individual than corporate. In the synagogue* and the mosque* and the church the worship is usually congregational, though in the Catholic churches this is not always true. Great churches and synagogues are frequently called temples, and the term has been borrowed by secular organizations such as the Masonic order and other fraternal organizations as the designation of the edifices in which they meet and carry out their peculiar rituals. See church building. C.S.B.

temples, Egyptian: Known as the "god's dwelling" or "house," the latter term often including the temple estate as well as the building proper. All temples were built and endowed by royal decree in the name of the reigning monarch, never by private gift. Many, like the great temple of Amon* at Karnak, amassed vast wealth and exercised great influence in local and national affairs.

The primitive temple was a single-roomed structure of matting, wattle or mud-brick, without windows, housing the image of the god or the animal worshiped. It might be surrounded by a fence, while before it stood two poles attached near the top to the front of the building. Of temples, other than those connected with royal tombs, we have practically no remains before the XVIII dynasty (16th cent. B.C.) By that time the temple had become a large stone structure of which the primitive shrine, developed into a dimly-lighted room formed the nucleus, the "great place" or "seat", where dwelt the cult image and where the regular daily services were performed. It was surrounded by a complex of rooms and passages, and was preceded by one or more columned or hypostyle halls used for ceremonies in which the image of the god was carried in procession by priests, open courts where non-priestly worshipers might enter, and pylons. The approach to the shrine extended directly from the main pylon entrance along the central axis of the building, the floor-level of which rose from front to rear while the roof became correspondingly lower. Entrance to each section of the building was closed by massive wooden doors overlaid with gold or copper decorated with figures of the deity. The columned halls were sometimes lighted by windows in a clerestory above the central axis, though the interior became progressively darker towards the rear of the building.

The fence which had enclosed the primitive shrine was replaced by massive mud-brick walls like fortifications, within and without which were numerous subsidiary temples and shrines, offices, workshops, storehouses and quarters for the temple staff. Adjacent to each temple was a pool or lake used in ceremonies connected with the sun-cult. Before the entrance stood one or more pairs of obelisks and against each pylon tower and extending above it were from one to four flagstaffs with colored streamers near the top. The approach to the pylon, flanked by recumbent sphinxes, led from a landing stage by a canal along with the god's river barge, used in certain feasts, could be brought near the entrance. The temple was equipped with vessels of gold, silver, faience and other material, altars and offering tables, small silver images of the king in various attitudes of the cult, and other rich furnishings. About the building stood stone statues of the gods, the king and individuals who apparently secured this privilege by royal favor. The walls of the building were covered with reliefs, showing the king performing the acts of the cult or engaged in warlike activities, the latter appearing on those parts of the temple more remote from the central shrine. Reliefs, inscriptions, columns, cornices, and statues were painted in detail with strong colors. Trees and gardens were planted about the building.

The Old and Middle Kingdom temples connected with the royal tombs differ radically from the Empire temples just described, as do those of Hatshepsut at Deir-el-Bahari and of Seti I at Abydos. However, the other temples in the necropolis at Thebes follow in general the pattern given above but in them much greater emphasis is laid on provision for the cult of the king as distinct from that of the god than in the normal temple. The Ptolemaic and Roman temples not connected with royal tombs, contain the essential elements of the earlier buildings but present certain variations of their own. The temple of the Aton at Amarna is unique in its structure.

A. Erman-H. Ranke, *Aegypten* (1923), pp. 319-330; M. A. Murry, *Egyptian Temples* (no date); A. M. Blackman, *Luxor and its Temples* (1923); U. Hoelscher, *The Excavation of Medinet Habu* (1934), vol. I. H.H.N.

temples, Far Eastern: The Far East is profusely adorned with temples. They are found in every village and town, in many crossroads, and in practically every scenic spot. At their best they are the highest achievement of Far Eastern architecture. The "wonder" of Far Eastern architecture is, of course, the Temple of Heaven.

I) The Temple of Heaven. The Temple of Heaven is part of the Altar of Heaven. There are nine altars in and around Peiping: the Altar of Heaven in the south, the Altar of Earth in the north, the Altar of the Sun in the east, and the Altar of the Moon in the west, and five others. The largest and the most important is the Altar of Heaven. It is an enclosure of 737 acres surrounded by a red wall of over three miles long. Inside this enclosure there are cypress groves, wide avenues, majestic gateways, the Altar proper, minor altars, the Temple, halls for the emperor's fasting and for the rehearsal of ceremonies, treasure house, slaughter house, brewery, kitchens, storage, bell towers, wells, etc. The whole structure was built in 1420 and enlarged and beautified in 1754. Some of the buildings were used by the government of the Republic for schools, hospital, etc., and part of the compound was turned into an agricultural experimental station.

The Altar proper is a raised platform of three white marble terraces with elaborately carved railings and balustrades. Measurements are based on odd numbers, especially the number 9 which is symbolic of infinity. The diameter of the lower terrace is 21 (3x7) *chang* (A *chang* is 11 ft. 9 in.); that of the middle terrace, 15 (3x5) *chang;* and that of the upper terrace, 9 (1x9) *chang.*

From this Altar a broad walk raised 8 ft. above ground leads to a circular building facing south, popularly called the Temple of Heaven. This edifice is 9.9 *chang* high, supported by 24 huge columns outside and four inside. It stands on a stone platform of three terraces surrounded by carved stone railings. It has two projecting eaves and a most gracefully curved roof, giving the impression of three stories, although there is only one story inside. The lower eave of blue tiles has a diameter of 25 *chang;* the second one of yellow tiles has a diameter of 22.26 *chang;* and the roof of green tiles has a diameter of 21.5 *chang* and is crowned with a "button" of gold color. The number of tiles and steps of the terraces is based on the number 9. Under the roof and above the entrance there is a tablet reading "The Temple for the Prayer of Agricultural Prosperity."

Inside this Temple there is neither any image nor tablet, but an altar in the center with a nine-dragon screen. Here on every winter solstice the emperor used to make sacrifice to Heaven on behalf of his people and to pray for a good year. Ceremonies of grand sacrifices were performed in both Spring and Autumn.

II) Temples of Confucius. Similar grand sacrifices, led by high government officials, were performed in Confucian temples. The principal temple of Confucius* is the one in the native place of the Sage, Ch'üfu in Shantung province, where the first Confucian temple was built as early as 442 A.D. Imposing lines of cypress and stone memorial arches lead to the Gate of Grand Perfection. Entering the enclosure by a side gate and proceeding northward, one finds a rock-like trunk of a juniper which tradition holds to have been planted by the Sage himself. Further north is a small pavilion on the site where Confucius taught his pupils. Still further north is the temple proper, the Temple of Grand Perfection built in 1724. It is an edifice 70 ft. high and 134 ft. long raised on a platform with a finely carved stone railing. The ten stone columns in its front, exquisitely carved all around with dragon design, are gems of Chinese sculpture.

In the center of the temple is the altar dedicated to the Sage, whose image in sitting position is behind a "Tablet of the Perfect Sage and Foremost Teacher Confucius." Four side altars are dedicated to Confucius' "Four Equals": pupil Yen Hui (521-481 B.C.) and grandson Tzŭ Ssŭ (483-402 B.C.) on the east and pupil Tsêng Tzŭ (505-436 B.C.) and follower Mencius (371-289 B.C.) on the west. Behind these are the altars of the Twelve Virtuous Men, all pupils of Confucius. North of this temple is a temple for the Sage's wife, who is represented by a tablet. Further north is the Temple of the life of Confucius where some 200 stone tablets depict the life of the Sage. It is here that one finds the stone carving of the famous portrait of Confucius painted by the greatest of Chinese painters, Wu Tao-tzŭ (d. 792). South of the Confucian Temple, on the southern part of the compound, are gateways and buildings, including a two-storied treasury of books and art objects.

Outside and to the east of this compound are houses and family temples of the direct descendent of Confucius and a well from which tradition believes Confucius' family drew its water. Further northeast stands a special temple of Yen Hui. Some two miles to the north is the Confucian Grove in which is located the Confucian Grave. The stone tablet in front of the grave measures some 15 ft. Leading to the grave is the Temple of Sacrifice, the original of which was built in 155 A.D. Its approach is lined with stone figures of men and animals 13 ft. high.

Almost all counties in China and Korea and some places in Japan have a Confucian temple, variously called *wên miao, K'ung miao,* and *hsüeh kung.* None, however, approaches this principal temple in dimension or in grandeur. Usually a Confucian temple consists of three courts in a central axis. The temple proper is in the north of the second court. The third court is sometimes to the east of the second. The south gate was made only when a native obtained the highest degree (*chuang yüan*) in civil service examination, and then it was used only by the emperor and the *chuang yüans.*

III) Ancestral halls. Like Confucian temples, ancestral halls (called *tz'ŭ*) in both China and Korea usually face south and are in the style of dwellings, schools, and palaces. In simple form, this style involves one brick building with a straight and unglazed roof. In elaborate form, this style becomes the "palace style" which usually involves one or more buildings in a central axis, often with subsidiary buildings on both sides and sometimes with gardens around. Each building has one, two, or three halls intervened with open courts and side corridors. In general they have brick walls, gently curved roofs and eaves of glazed tiles and elaborately decorated with dragon designs as well as human and animal figures, and beautiful columns, beams, and ceilings intricately carved or painted.

The central altar in each building faces the main entrance in the south. There are often secondary altars on both sides. In front of the altar stands a long table on which are placed an incense burner, a pair of candle sticks, and a pair of flower stands. Behind this table are lines of tablets of ancestors covering the whole wall. To the right of the main entrance of the first hall there is usually a small altar dedicated to the Guardian Deity of the Gate or the God of Ground or both. In front of the hall are high wooden posts supported by stone tablets indicating degrees obtained by members of the clan in competitive civil examinations. Services are held in these halls on memorial days and grand sacrifices are in some places conducted every Spring and Autumn. These halls are also used for schools, community meetings, exhibitions, etc.

IV) Temples of deities of the masses. The description of ancestral halls applies to the temples of deities worshiped by the masses in China. These temples, called *miao* (or *tz'ŭ* in the cases of illustrious historical persons) are labelled by Western writers as Confucian or Taoist without justification (see Chinese Religions). Unlike ancestral halls, these temples usually contain images instead of tablets, have one or more resident priests, are frequented by superstitious women, are not well kept, and, in many cases, are used for commercial and other secular purposes. Small shrines are barely spacious enough to house an altar with an image or a tablet.

V) Taoist temples. The description of ancestral halls also applies to Taoist temples, called *kuan* and, in the cases of large ones, *kung*. The larger the Taoist temple, the more closely it approaches Buddhist temples in both exterior and interior arrangement as well as in decoration.

VI) Buddhist temples. Buddhist temples are called *ssŭ* in Chinese and *ji* in Japanese. In both China and Korea the general style is the "palace style," which is the style for all Far Eastern temples except the Temple of Heaven and Shinto shrines. Like Confucian temples, ancestral halls, or Taoist temples, Buddhist temples usually consist of a group of brick buildings, facing south. Entering the main gate, ascending terraces, and passing by a brick screen, one comes to an open court which is often paved and decorated with walks and lotus ponds in artistic patterns. Facing the screen is the main building the portal of which is guarded by two huge and fierce looking Guardians. Inside the hall are the Four Heavenly Guardians, two on each side, and a few feet to the north, in the center, is the sanctuary of Maitreya (see Buddhist Terminology) the Welcoming Buddha whose smile greets the worshiper as he enters the hall. Going north and passing an open court, one comes to the sanctuary of the patron deity. Immediately behind him and separated by a wall is Wei-t'o, the guardian of the sanctuary and the upholder of the Law. He faces the Buddha in the hall across an open court, so that law is always tempered with compassion. The open court is often paved with stone slabs, adorned with small pagodas, stone protecting lions, stone tablets, lotus ponds, bronze incense burner, a small drum tower and a bell tower. The hall of the Buddha is called the Precious Hall of the Great Hero. It is supported by huge vermilion pillars on a raised platform, covered with single or double projecting roofs of green tiles. The main altar is located north of the center of the hall, with one or three images of the Buddha (see Buddhist Terminology: Triad), each on its own platform. In front of each platform is a long table covered with incense burners, candle sticks, flower stands, musical instruments, and offerings of all sorts. Large bells and red lacquered wooden boxes are placed on stands by the altars, and silk draperies, elaborately designed lamps, and other articles hang down from the ceiling. Along the two side walls of the hall are altars for groups of *arhats* (see Buddhist Terminology) or Heavenly Beings or the various transformations of the Buddha. Often there are two side shrines against the rear wall of the hall for such deities as Wên-shu, P'u-hsien, Yao-shih-fu, and Ti-tsang. Sometimes these deities and the *arhats* have their own halls. At the back of the altar of the Buddha is the altar of Kwan-yin* and attendants, all facing north, and at the corner behind the Buddha's altar is a small shrine dedicated to Kuan Ti* or Ti-tsang.

In addition to this main hall, there are in many cases Halls of the Ten Thousand Buddhas, Meditation Hall, Hall of Wisdom, Hall of the Patriarch, etc., further to the north. Also, further north, but more often on both sides of the main hall, there are usually abbot's hall, reception halls, study halls, halls for other purposes, dormitories, refectory, kitchens, storages, bath hall, etc. Larger monasteries have an infirmary, rooms for solitary confinement, a library on the second floor, a printing press, animal pens, a crematorium, vegetable gardens, and other units. Most temples have artistic gardens. All have a bell tower and a pagoda (the pre-Buddhist mound for the remains of the dead known as the *stupa* took the form of a pagoda which is dedicated to housing supposed bones or ashes, scriptures, and other sacred relics of the Buddha).

The pagoda ranges from several feet to 360 ft., is usually octagonal, has many stories with projecting eaves of various colors. Pagodas for an *arhat* has four stories; for a *bodhisattva* (see Buddhist Terminology), seven stories; and for a Buddha, at least eight and usually 13 stories. There is, however, only one story inside the pagoda. In some cases there is a winding staircase up to a certain level. On top of the pagoda is a chain of nine wheels or circles.

Buddhist temples in the Far East, especially in Japan, are gems of architecture and attract both Buddhists and non-Buddhists alike. Buddhist temples in Korea are similar to those in China. In Japan, however, they are made of wood with sliding doors. They do not follow a general pattern in arrangement nor do they usually face south, as styles varied from period to period. Many, however, follow the general scheme adopted in China. In any case, the compound usually consists of a number of buildings, courts, and gardens, all surrounded by a wall with monumental gateways. The single or double roofs of the buildings are generally high and look heavy, but are gracefully sweeping. In the approach to the main building there is sometimes a Shinto gateway, the *torii*. Outside the gate of the building there is usually an altar of an *arhat*. In many cases, the portal is guarded by the two Guardians, as in Chinese temples. Within the gateway there is often a Shinto shrine. The inside of the temple is remarkably clean and spacious, the whole attention being directed towards the central altar. On this altar there is a large image of the Buddha, other smaller images and tablets, and often a Shinto mirror. There are side altars for Kwannon, Monju, (see Japanese Terminology), Jizō, etc., as well as altars for the founder of the sect, patriarchs, and ancestral tablets. Besides, there are small altars for Buddhist and Shinto deities and nobility.

The courtyard of a Japanese Buddhist temple is usually more artistic than that in Chinese or Korean temples. It is decorated with pine trees, fountains, stone lanterns, museums, etc. Here festivals are held, old people enjoy their leisure, and children have their fun. The pagoda in Japanese temples (*sotōba*) is usually of three or five stories, which are shaped from bottom to top like a cube, a sphere, a cone, a crescent, and a ball, symbolic of earth, water, fire, wind, and ether respectively. It is generally only a few feet high.

VII) Shinto shrines. Shinto* temples, which number about 150,000 in Japan, are found all over the country, in almost every village and town, and wherever the Japanese migrate. More important ones are located in scenic spots amidst a magnificent grove. The approach is inevitably marked by a *torii* (the meaning of which is uncertain), a gateway made of wood, and sometimes of stone, with two horizontal and projecting beams supported by two round columns. The square enclosure is surrounded by a wooden fence or wall, sometimes by trees and even stones, and marked off by a sanctified rope of straw, from which pieces of paper are hung to keep evil spirits away. Inside the compound there is a small wooden or bamboo pole in which is inserted a piece of paper or cloth so cut that the parts hang down over both sides of the pole. There are a sanctified well or rock for the use of the deity and a fountain for the purification of worshipers. The building is square and is of unpainted wood, never of stone, with a thatched or bark roof, in the style of a dwelling house. Over the angle and each end of the roof there are beams projecting in an oblique cross. Although there is no decorative effect, the simplicity and dignity of the building against the background of green trees are very impressive. Inside the shrine there are a hall for worshipers and a sanctuary facing the entrance and accessible only to priests. In this sanctuary a box is enshrined which contains a mirror, a stone, a sword, or in some cases some other relic, wrapped in silk and never to be seen by a human eye. Under the influence of Buddhism since the Nara period (645-783), some shrines have eaves, tile and curved roofs, vermilion pillars, colonnades and two-storied gates instead of a simple fence, two or more buildings including reception halls and art treasury, a stage for religious dance, etc. The Daijingu Shrine at Ise, dedicated to Amaterasu* the Sun Goddess, is the national shrine, the most sacred place in all Japan. W.T.C.

temples, Greek and Roman: Temple (Lat., *templum*, Gr., *temnō*, to cut) meant originally a rectangular space of earth or sky, marked off by a priest, to be used in making sacrifices or taking auguries; then, a shrine built on consecrated ground. Hence our English temple.

Greek Temples

The earliest Greek temple, dating from perhaps the ninth century B.C., was a simple one-room structure (Gr. *nāos*), the dwelling-place of the god and his image. Later, this nāos was divided into aisles by rows of columns on either side. An open porch (*pronāos*), supported by columns, was placed in front of it, and a corresponding vestibule (*opisthodomos*) behind it. Colonnades were added, sometimes only in front (a prostyle temple); sometimes both in front and behind (amphiprostyle); more often in later temples on all four sides (peripteral). The whole temple was built on a platform (stylobate, or podium), approached by steps, usually three. Its orientation was normaly east.

Two styles of Greek temple developed almost simultaneously on opposite sides of the Aegean, the Doric among the Dorians of Greece and the West, the Ionic among the Ionians of Asia Minor. The Doric, with simple sturdy lines, gives an impression of weight and dignity; the more slender Ionic embodies buoyancy and grace. The Doric frieze reflects its earlier wooden construction in the triglyphs, the old beam ends, and the metopes, the spaces between; the Ionic frieze presents a flat, uninterrupted surface. The Doric metopes, the Ionic frieze, and the triangular space below the gable (pediment) at either end of the temple were adorned by artists with appropriate sculptured figures. Polychrome paint, of which only traces remain, added richness and depth to the whole.

The Acropolis of fifth century Athens provides the finest expression of both orders, of the Doric in the stately Parthenon, of the Ionic in the exquisite Erechtheum. The Propylaea, monumental gateway to the Acropolis, significantly combines the two.

A third order, the Corinthian, variant of the Ionic adding the acanthus leaf motif, appeared in the late fifth century. The most conspicuous example is the colossal temple of the Olympian Zeus in Athens, completed in the time of the Roman Emperor Hadrian (135 A.D.).

Roman Temples

The earliest Roman temple followed the Etrusco-Italian plan with its nearly square triple cella (*nāos*), which provided separate rooms for the Etruscan triad, Jupiter, Minerva, and Juno. The high podium, with steps only in front, remained a characteristic feature of Roman temple architecture. The Greek temple with fixed orientation was accessible from all sides. The practical Romans, orienting their temples as the specific site dictated, stressed the frontal view. They deepened the pronāos, enlarged the cella, and more often than not omitted the opisthodomos. Even in the peripteral, the colonnade usually stopped at the extended rear wall of the cella. In the purely Roman pseudo-peripteral, the cella occupied the full width of the podium, and engaged columns along the sides gave the illusion of a peripteral temple.

The ornate Corinthian order was a Roman favorite; from it arose the still more ornate Composite. The finest existing example of the Corinthian order comes from the Augustan Age, the Maison Carrée at Nîmes, France; the earliest datable example of the Composite is found in the Colosseum at Rome (80 A.D.).

A second type of temple, the small round temple, is of every ancient origin. Several are known, e.g., the temple of Vesta at Tivoli. The most impressive example is the massive Pantheon, rebuilt by Hadrian, combining the use of the arch, vault, and dome.

Neither in Greece nor in Rome was the temple itself a place of assembly for worshipers. It is interesting to reflect that the prototype of the Christian church is found not in the temples but in the basilicas of Rome.

William J. Anderson and R. Phené Spiers, *The Architecture of Ancient Greece* (rev. by William Bell Dinsmoor, 1927); same author, *The Architecture of Ancient Rome* (rev. by Thomas Ashby, 1927); Walter Hege and Gerhart Rodenwaldt, *The Acropolis* (Oxford, 1930); D. S. Robertson, *A Handbook of Greek and Roman Architecture* (Cambridge, 1929).

E.M.N.

temples, Hebrew: Several places of worship were used by the Hebrews in the course of the centuries (Ark* of the Covenant, sanctuaries of Bethel, Shechem, Shiloh, etc.), but the more important ones are those of Jerusalem*: I. First Temple, erected by Solomon* (976-936 B.C.), described in I Kgs. v-vii; destroyed by the Babylonians in 586 B.C. II. Second Temple, built by Zerubbabel in 521 B.C. (?). III. Third Temple, begun by Herod the Great in 19 B.C., completed in 64 A.D., and destroyed by the Romans in 70 A.D. Also description of an Ideal Temple in Ezekiel xl-xliii, at the time of the Babylonian Exile. See Babylonian captivity. Cf. sacred vessels; tabernacle.

See H. Vincent, *Jérusalem, recherches de topographie, d'archéologie et d'histoire*, 2 vols. (1912-1914); K. Möhlenbrink, *Der Tempel Solomons* (1932); G. E. Wright, Solomon's Temple resurrected, in *The Biblical Archeologist*, vol. IV, No. 2 (May, 1941), pp. 17-31.

S.L.T.

temples, Indian: Early Vedic Hinduism* built no temples. If any were built before the rise of Buddhism* they have completely disappeared. Now Mother India is a land of temples. There are said to be 1500 in the sacred city, Benares, alone. They vary in size from modest village temples to vast structures that compare with the most imposing cathedrals of Europe. The central feature of all Hindu temples is a cell or room in which the image of the god to whom the temple is dedicated is found. This is usually very simple in construction, but everything else about the temple is subordinate to it. A temple of Shiva* will contain the linga*, the sacred symbol of the god, usually a conical stone upon which sacred leaves or flowers are placed and holy water from the Ganges is sprinkled. In a temple to Vishnu* will be found an image of Vishnu and/or his *avataras**, and offerings of food are made to the accompaniment of music, chanting, and incense.

Beside the central shrine there may be a few or many courts and other buildings, housing the priests and the women attendants. Ornamentation varies in different sections of India, many of them lavish beyond description, some having literally thousands of statues and carvings. The Jain* temples are perhaps the most lavishly decorated.

C.S.B.

temples, Mesopotamian: *General character.* The Mesopotamian temple was in all historical periods conceived as the house of the god to whom it was dedicated. Here the god lived and worked and from here he supervised—like any human manorial lord—the large temple estate from which he derived his livelihood (For this aspect of the temple see Mesopotamian religions).

The concept of the temple as a god's dwelling did not prevent it from acquiring numinous qualities and from being itself personalized to a certain extent. Ningirsu's temple in Lagash greets its owner, when it espies him from afar, with a roar that makes the heavens tremble; its terrifying nimbus reaches to the sky and awe of it inspires all lands. In ritual laments designed to placate an angry god his temple often has a voice, and the brickwork of a temple may intercede for a petitioner with the god. Similarly temples often appear in the personal names of Ancient Mesopotamia as active divine powers granting offspring, giving protection, and hearing petitions just as would a deity.

Prehistoric periods. The character of divine dwelling, which pertains to the Mesopotamian temple in historical times, fits in with and explains also the evidence which we have for the temples of the prehistoric periods. The prehistoric temple plan which developed from Al Ubaid times through the Uruk, Proto-literate, and Early Dynastic periods contains as its basic feature a long rectangular room, the cella. In the earlier of these periods entrance to the cella was frequently through a door in one of the end walls ("Langhaustempel"), but by and by it became customary to have the door in the side wall, still, however, near the corner ("Herdhaustempel"). The room usually has a hearth in the middle and, beginning with the Uruk period, a dais against the end wall farthest from the door; later parallels indicate that this dais was the place of the cult image. As pointed out by Andrae this plan has features typical of a primitive dwelling-house suited to an adverse climate: a hearth in the middle of the room to heat and light it as evenly as possible, and the best seat (that of the master of the house) placed in a commanding position against the end wall where it is also farthest away from the cold draft coming in through the door. We should therefore, in all probability, view this basic unit of the Mesopotamian temple plan as an all purpose living room in a primitive house, as yet little specialized. Here the god sat throughout the day receiving visitors, issuing orders, listening to petitions and settling disputes. Here too, at mealtime, he presided over the family banquet, and here he most likely spent the night.

Some amount of specialization must be assumed, however, already in the oldest periods; for although the central unit will on occasion constitute the whole temple, it usually formed merely a core around which smaller subsidiary rooms grouped themselves. Our oldest plans (Al Ubaid, Uruk, and Proto-literate periods) all show a row of such subsidiary rooms along either side wall. The functions which these rooms served are for the major part obscure but a few stand out clearly. When the entrance shifted from the end wall to the side wall it came to lead through one of these subsidiary rooms, which thus took on the character of a vestibule. The side room directly opposite this vestibule, on the other side of the central room, shows on many plans a stairwell, presumably accommodating stairs leading to the roof. Lastly, a side room communicating with the cella through a door near the dais served, as may be concluded from remnants of ovens sometimes found there, as the god's kitchen where his food was prepared.

The building material used for Mesopotamian temples was the native unbaked brick, and the walls show, as far back as the late Al Ubaid period, the decoration with vertical T-shaped grooves which is so characteristic of sacred architecture in Mesopotamia in later times. Our first example of another feature well known in historical times, the *ziqqurrat,* dates from the Uruk period. The *ziqqurrat* is an artificial mound of clay or unbaked bricks and serves as substructure for the temple. Originally of rounded outlines it was later stylized as a stepped pyramid. It never became an obligatory feature of the Mesopotamian temple and its ultimate significance still eludes us. Efforts to establish significant differences of plan and function between temples on the ground ("Tieftempel") and temples on the *ziqqurrat* ("Hochtempel") have not proved successful.

Historical periods. The Early Dynastic period saw the beginning of several developments which were instrumental in shaping the later Mesopotamian temple plan. The temple is still the house of the god, but the emphasis seems subtly shifted from dwelling to office, from home life to administration. A court, focus of the administrative activities of the temple, makes its appearance and takes a prominent position in the heart of the plan. The old deep living room cella where the visitor shared in the home life of the god is replaced by a shallow audience or reception room where one may see the god on business.

On the basis of the actual development as it can be followed in the plans of the Sin temple in Khafaje, Frankfort has plausibly suggested that the temple court in general originated by a walling in of the open space before the temple, which by and by had become an integral part of its life. Through subsequent building of subsidiary structures along the inside of this wall a central court came into being. In its most imposing form this new feature meets us in the temple ovals excavated by Delougaz in Khafaje and in Al Ubaid. The temple itself lies on a raised artificial mound in one end of the oval and is reached by a flight of stairs. The oval, a substantial wall of mud bricks, is built up along the inside with rooms leaving an open square in the middle, the court. In succeeding periods the oval tended to square off more and more. It is preserved in final form in the temple complex in Ishchali (Old-Babylonian period) which contains—squared—all the essentials of the arrangement of the Khafaje oval: surrounding wall with subsidiary rooms along the inside leaving a square court in the middle; from here steps lead up to the temple itself which lies on a raised platform at the end farthest from the entrance. A similar complex, but with both court and temple on the same level, is exemplified by the Ningal temple in Ur (Cassite period).

Another significant development led—after the Early Dynastic period, and in Babylonia only—to changes in the plan of the cella and of the temple itself. The new plan shows an open rectangular court surrounded by rooms on all sides. The entrance gate is in the middle of one end wall of the complex; across the court, in the same axis as the main gate, lies the cella, sometimes preceded by an antecella. The cella is a rectangular room with the door in the middle of the side wall toward the court; the dais with the cult image stands in a shallow niche in the middle of the other side wall, directly opposite the door ("Breitraum").

The origin of this new plan is not yet clear. The writer is inclined to view it as resulting from an enlargement of the old deep cella to proportions beyond the point where it could be conveniently roofed. The end of the cella in which the dais stood could still be spanned and became the new cella. This end had already been partly separated from the rest of the room in Early Dynastic times by brick pillars and sometimes by square pilasters in the side wall. The remainder of the room was left unroofed as an open court with the old rows of subsidiary rooms around it. The entrance stayed in many cases in the side wall of the complex ("bent axis approach") but a new door in the end wall of the complex facing the new cella was added to the plan and finally won out as the main entrance.

In Assyria, on the other hand, the old plan survived in essentials down to the second millennium B.C. It was superseded, not by the plan which had developed in Babylonia, but by a slightly modified form of the old plan in which proportions and arrangement of the cella remained intact except that the entrance was shifted from the side wall to the end wall opposite which stood dais and cult image ("Langraumtempel").

W. Andrae, *Gas Gotteshaus und die Urformen des Bauens* (Berlin, 1930); Th. A. Busink, *Sumerische en Babylonische tempelbouw* (Batavia, 1940); H. Frankfort's chapter "Conclusions" in P. Delougaz and S. Lloyd, *Pre-Sargonic Temples in the Diyala*

Region (1942); G. Martiny, *Die Gegensätze im babylonischen und assyrischen Tempelbau* (Leipzig, 1936). T.J.

temporal power: Any authority of the Church over earthly goods, as that exercised formerly over the Papal States* and now over the Vatican City. L.R.W.

temporality of God: The view that time* is an irreducible aspect of God's experience—a reaction from the rationalistic view that additive change cannot be attributed to God or to the universe as a whole. The claim that the time-process brought no enrichment to a world essentially and eternally rational was said to be intolerable for moral, aesthetic, and religious reasons. "It was better to admit the world to be not at present entirely rational, and retain some hope of its amendment, than to conceive of it as perfectly rational—and utterly hopeless." See A. Lovejoy, *The Great Chain of Being* (1936), p. 245.

But non-temporalism was also hard to reconcile with speculative and scientific descriptions of the world's basic development. On metaphysical grounds such contentions, as Leibniz', that time cannot exist independent of events (cf. H. Bergson's *durée réelle*) led to taking time seriously as applied to the divine experience. The temporality of God is also more consonant with finitistic* views of God designed to account for evil especially. See God. P.A.B.

temptation: Usual meaning, solicitation to evil-doing; ascribed to outside spiritual or diabolic agency, in many religions. So Jesus was tempted: Mt. 4: 1 ff. Many now hold that we have more to fear from our own evil impulse than from any satanic tempter (James 1: 14). In O.T., Satan*, perhaps the personification of a divine function, was at first (Job 1 and 2) God's vigilance officer who tested men and reported on their sincerity. Under dualistic ideas, the tester, natural adversary to the insincere, became the tempter (cf. 2 Sam. 24: 1 and 1 Chron. 21: 1), the enemy of God and man. In N.T., temptation (*pierasmos*) includes trial, tribulation, especially as presaging the End (Lk. 22: 28, 9 and in the Lord's Prayer). See sin.

K. E. Kirk, *Conscience and its Problems* (1933); S. A. McDowall, *Is Sin our Fault?* (1932); R. E. D. Clark, *Conscious and Unconscious Sin* (1934). J.L.

tempus clausum: (Lat., literally "Closed Time") The period from the First Sunday of Advent to Christmas inclusive, and from Ash Wednesday to Easter Sunday inclusive, during which the solemn celebration of marriage, that is, matrimony contracted at Mass* with solemn benediction imparted by the priest, is prohibited in the Catholic Church. However, with the permission of the Bishop, granted only for a grave reason, solemn nuptials may be celebrated during this time. Marriage* without such solemnities may, of course, be contracted by Catholics at any period of the year. C.V.

temŭrah: See Kabbalah.

Ten Articles, The: (1536) Were issued by Henry VIII* to define what is necessary to be believed for salvation and the ceremonies, rites and usages to be retained. They represent a compromise between the Old Learning and the New. The grounds of Faith are limited to the Bible, the three Creeds, the Four General Councils and the traditions not contrary to Scripture. The sacraments of baptism, penance and the altar are retained; justification is included without particular designation; veneration of images, honour and prayers to saints and the doctrine of purgatory are also retained. They were supplanted the following year by "the Bishop's Book" (*The Institution of a Christian Man*). F.W.B.

ten stages: See Buddhist Terminology: stages, ten.

tenebrae: (Lat., darkness) The public chanting of Matins and Lauds for Holy Thursday, Good Friday and Holy Saturday. A candle is extinguished as each of fourteen psalms is completed, and the last candle, the fifteenth, is placed behind the altar; hence the name "tenebrae" or darkness. L.R.W.

Tennant, Frederick Robert: (1866-) Lecturer in theology and philosophy of religion at Cambridge, 1907-1938, Dr. Tennant stresses a broad empirical approach to theological and philosophical problems. Accordingly, his theism is sustained by the facts of experience and science, including values, and not by appeal to supposedly independent and unique religious or moral data. His "wider" teleological argument* uses the regularity and interdependence of nature, knowledge, and value as the most probable indication that a good Person created and directs the ultimate collocations of reality. See empirical theology; religious datum.

The Concept of Sin (1912); *Miracle and Its Philosophical Presuppositions* (1925); *Philosophical Theology*, 2 vols. (1928, 1930). P.A.B.

Tennyson, Alfred: (1809-1892) English poet. Less original and profound than many of his contemporaries, Tennyson is probably the most representative literary man of his age. He was inclusive in his choice of materials, and he sensed perfectly the typical thoughts and aspirations of the middle-class Victorian. For this reason the whole body of his work is significant, quite apart from any question of intrinsic merit. Particularly important is *In Memoriam* (1850), which presented a widely accepted solution to the conflicts of science and religion.

The standard edition of the *Poems* (9 vols., 1898-99) contains Tennyson's own annotations. L.W.C.

teraphim: (Heb. deriv. uncertain; only plural) A seemingly opprobrious term applied in the Bible to images (I Sam. 19: 13, 16) or household gods (Gen. 31: 19, 34 f.) sometimes used in divination (Ezek. 21: 26). S.H.B.

terce: (Lat., *ad tertiam*) The office of the third hour of the day. See divine office. E.R.H.

Teresa, Saint: (1515-1582) Of old Spanish nobility, de Cepoda family. Influenced by S. Augustine's Confessions and by Jesuit priests, she entered Carmelite* convent, 1535. Known for her visions and reform efforts, she saw her vocation to found a very ascetic sisterhood to be known as *Descalzos* (Barefoots). Division of Carmelite order followed opposition. Teresa then established and supervised sixteen convents, fourteen monasteries. Her writings, *Life by Herself, The Way of Perfection,* which is a guidebook for nuns, and many extant letters show her to be a good psychologist and mystic. Canonized, 1622. See John of the Cross. A.S.

terminism: *idem* nominalism. See s.v. universals, battle over.

terminism: (fr. Lat., *terminus,* limit) The view that God's offer of saving grace has a terminus or limit for each individual beyond which repentance* is futile and salvation* impossible, formulated as a doctrine chiefly among English Friends and German Pietists* in the late 17th and early 18th centuries, and motivated by the desire to hasten the experience of repentance and conversion. Prominent among the terminists were J. G. Böse and A. Rechenberg. E.T.R.

territorialism: A theory of church government which came in with the Reformation* but was formulated in the late 17th century. It ascribed to a temporal ruler, by virtue of his office, the right to govern the church within his realm, both in external and internal affairs—though not to impose his own faith on his subjects. See s.v. religious liberty. E.C.K.

Terry Lectures: A lectureship at Yale University established November 1, 1905, by gift from Dwight H. Terry, for lectures on religion in the light of science and philosophy. Among the courses have been those by J. Arthur Thomson, Concerning Evolution, 1924; Robert A. Millikan, Evolution in Science and Religion, 1927; Arthur H. Compton, The Freedom of Man, 1932; John Dewey, A Common Faith, 1934; John Macmurray, The Structure of Religious Experience, 1936. L.A.W.

Tertiaries: (Lat., *tertiarius,* having a third part) Those who belong to the "Third Order"* of certain religious institutes. These institutes embrace a "first order" or those male religious living in a monastery; a "second order," or those female religious living in convents; and a "third order," or those lay people living in the world. Tertiaries however may also live in a community. By becoming members of the "third order," tertiaries can avail themselves of many privileges otherwise denied to those outside the cloister. See Catholic Societies. W.H.

Tertullian: A native of the Roman Province of Africa, of pagan parentage, born c. 160 A.D., converted probably in mature manhood, widely read in law, literature and philosophy. He appears, in his Christian writings, as the prosecutor of paganism. His strong ascetic leanings led him later to embrace Montanism*. He probably remained a layman throughout his life. His main surviving works are (Souter's dating, following d'Alès) *Ad Martyras, Ad Nationes, Apologeticus,* (197); *De Testimonio Animae, De Spectaculis, De Praescriptione Haereticorum* (c. 200); *De Oratione, Baptismo, Patientia, Paenitentia, Cultu Feminarum, Adv. Judaeos* (200-206); *Adv. Marcionem, Valentinianos, Marcioneus* (207-210); *De Corona, Idolatria, Ad Scapulam* (211-212); then his *Montanist Works* (213-222). Some of his works—the *Apologeticus* (probably) and the *de Spectaculis* (certainly) were issued in Greek. The date and manner of his death are unknown. The most vigorous of the early Christian apologists*, he has never been canonized. See reason in religion; revelation; satisfaction; traducianism. Cf. Marcion. F.W.B.

Test Act, the: (1673) Prescribed the reception of the sacrament of Holy Communion according to the rites of the Church of England, and a declaration renouncing belief in the doctrine of transubstantiation* as a preliminary test and condition to the enjoyment of a temporal office or trust in England. It is a revival of the corresponding clauses of Elizabeth's Act of Supremacy*. Its object was to exclude from public office Roman Catholics who had received indulgences from Charles II. James, Duke of York (later James II), convert to the Church of Rome, resigned his position of Lord High Admiral in consequence. F.W.B.

testament: For meaning of term see Bible; Old Testament; New Testament.

tetragrammatom: The four letters of the ineffable name of God, YHWH. This name is never pronounced save with the vowels of Adonai or Elohim**. Cf. Zohar; Jehovah. A.H.S.

Tetrapolitan Confession: This confession of four imperial cities is the oldest theological symbol of the Reformed Church* in Germany. Prepared by Bucer*, in 1530, during the sessions of the Diet of Augsburg, it sought to present a doctrinal compromise between Lutheran and Reformed sacramental theories. It was an early, but futile, attempt at a Protestant-Evangelical union symbol.
Philip Schaff, *The Creeds of Christendom* (1877), vol. I. T.F.H.

Tetzel, Johann: (ca. 1450-1519) Dominican friar whose high-pressure methods of hawking indulgences* called forth Luther's protest and thus led directly to the Reformation*. See Theses, Ninety-Five, of Luther. E.C.K.

Teutonic order (Knights): German religious military order. Originated during third Crusade* (c. 1190) as hospital brotherhood. Adopted semi-monastic life. Undertook military service. Discipline was strict, the life was simple and the organization efficient. Important later in Prussia and as Baltic power. Finally reverted to original duty of caring for the sick. See military religious orders. K.H.C.

textual criticism: See Biblical criticism. Cf. manuscripts of the Bible; translations of the Bible.

Tezcatlipoca: (Aztec) Warrior god; observer and punisher of evil doers; god of the waxing moon who wanders about at night; a counterpart of the god Quetzalcoatl*. F.L.P.

Thags, Thugs: A secret organization which existed for several centuries in India, dedicated to robbery and murder by strangulation. It was put down by the British authorities in the first half of the nineteenth century. They had in all they did the sanction of religion, believing that their patron goddess, Kali*, wife of Shiva, required this service of them. Every act of brigandage was preceded by worship, and a share of the ill-gotten gains was presented to the goddess in one of her temples. C.S.B.

Thanksgiving: As a special day of prayer and thanksgiving it was first instituted by Governor Bradford of the Plymouth colony in 1621 after the first successful harvest. After 1630 it became an annual observance after each harvest, and other New England Colonies soon took up the practice. New York was the first state to inaugurate an annual Thanksgiving Day (1830) and other northern states gradually followed. Virginia was the first southern state (1855) to observe a Thanksgiving Day. Abraham Lincoln in 1864 began the practice of issuing a proclamation calling upon the nation to give thanks to Almighty God, fixing the fourth Thursday of November as the day. Later this was changed to the last Thursday in November. President Franklin D. Roosevelt in 1939 set a new precedent by placing Thanksgiving on the third Thursday of November, though many Governors of states refused to follow his suggestion.

Robert H. Schauffler, *Thanksgiving: Its origin, celebration and Significance,* etc. (1925).

W.W.S.

theater: See religious drama.

Theatines: Members of a religious Order of men in the R. C. Church. Founded in 1524, it derived its name from the Italian city of Chieti (Theate) of which one of its founders, G. P. Carafa (afterwards Pope Paul IV), was Bishop. The original purpose of the group was to perfect the lives of the clergy and laity but its members have been prominent in missionary activities, in preaching, and in hospital work. The rule is quite strict. There are also two groups of nuns following a modified Theatine rule. V.J.B.

theft: The act of obtaining the property of another wrongfully. The term is often used broadly to cover larceny, swindling, embezzlement and fraud. Theft has been ethically condemned and is legally punishable—within the limits and under the circumstances determined by the mores—among all peoples. It was a legitimate means of livelihood in the Hindu robber caste and at a certain period of Jewish history was not regarded as a crime when practiced upon Samaritans or thieves. R.W.F.

theism: (Gr., *theos,* god) The terms *theist* and *theism,* following their slightly earlier etymological equivalents *deist* and *deism**, are altogether modern, first occurring (according to the *Oxford Engl. Dict.*) in the 17th Cent., and first used in contrast to the already established terms *atheist* and *atheism** (Plato had used *atheos* and *atheotes*), as, e.g., in Cudworth's *The True Intellectual System of the Universe* (London, 1678; see preface). During the 18th cent. *theism* and *deism* were used interchangeably (indeed as late as 1827, the 2nd Ed. of Sam. Johnson's *Dictionary* makes them synonymous) to indicate a philosophical as opposed to a dogmatic belief in God (natural theology as contrasted with revealed), with *deism,* however, as the dominant and more controversial term. Although Shaftesbury, as early as 1709, had written (through Palemon): "I consider still that, in strictness, the root of all is Theism; and that to be a settled Christian, it is necessary to be first of all *a good* Theist" (The Moralists, Pt. I, Sect. 2), it was not until the 19th century that theism came commonly to be recognized as the normative philosophical expression of the Christian religion, and, at the same time, critically to be distinguished from deism and pantheism* as its logical extremes.

Theism is distinguishable from monotheism* (belief in one God) only in that it is chiefly a philosophical term and connotes something more than mere contrast with polytheism (belief in a plurality of gods). Its essential idea is that of a unitary, personal Being as the creative source or ground of the physical world, man and value, at once transcendent to nature (i.e., distinct from it and never exhausted by it) and immanent in it (i.e., natural processes involving the continuing divine activity). Theism is thus contrasted with deism, which implies the total transcendence* of God to nature, and with pantheism, which by identifying God with nature becomes a doctrine of exclusive immanence*. It assumes that God is both knowable, to some degree at least, and dynamically available in human experience. It may be idealistic (viewing the physical world in terms of mind-activity and therefore denying to it any metaphysical independence) or realistic (interpreting the physical world as in some sense metaphysically real). Although a modern term, it is manifestly applicable, in varying degrees, to many ancient and medieval, as well as modern, philosophies, e.g., those of Plato, Aristotle, Plotinus, Anselm, Albert, Aquinas, Descartes, Locke, Leibniz, Kant, Lotze**, etc. A recent use of the term in combination with naturalism*, viz., *theistic naturalism* (see e.g., *The Growth of Religion* by H. N. Wieman and W. M. Horton, 1938) makes God an aspect of, or a principle within, the process of nature; with natural process as the ultimate category, however, such a view is to be sharply distinguished from theism in the strict sense. See God.

Out of a vast literature the following may be mentioned: R. Flint, *Theism* (1877); B. P. Bowne, *Theism* (1902); J. Ward, *The Realm of Ends* (1911, 3rd ed. 1920); A. Seth Pringle Pattison, *The Idea of God* (1916, 2nd ed. 1920); G. D. Hicks, *The Philosophical Bases of Theism* (1937); J. Laird, *Theism and Cosmology* (1942). E.T.R.

Themis: (Gr. *Thémis,* from *tithēmi,* to place, put) 1) Law, not as fixed by statute, but as established by custom. 2) Themis, personified, is the goddess of law and order. Aeschylus represents her as Gaia (Earth), the mother of Prometheus (Forethought). E.M.N.

Themistians: See Agnoetae.

theocracy: (Gr. *theos,* God; *kratein,* to rule) The rule of God in human organization. Historically, the rule of a State or Church by the representatives of God, usually a priesthood, but possible, as with Calvinism*, the people. Both the idea and the resultant organization are properly called "theocracy". See kingdom of God. E.P.B.

theodicy: See evil; omniscience; omnipotence; perfect.

Theodore of Mopsuestia: (ca. 350-428 A.D.) Born probably in Antioch, and educated there as the friend and fellow-student of John Chrysostom*. He became a presbyter in Antioch, but in A.D. 393 became Bishop of Mopsuestia in Cilicia. He was one of the more orthodox members of the Antiochian school*. See Zervanism. A.K.R.

Theodore of Studion: (759-826) Became the hegumenos of the Studion monastery in Constantinople in 799. He gained fame for his adaptation of the Rules of St. Basil*, and his version has become the prevailing monastic rule throughout the Orthodox East. He was the chief defender of the image* worship during the reign of Emp. Leo V, denying the Emperor's right to interfere in dogmatic matters. Exiled, he was allowed to return in the next reign, but was not able to secure victory for the iconduIic* cause. See Basilians.

Alice Gardner, *Theodore of Studion* (London, 1905). M.S.

Theodore of Tarsus: (602-690) Educated Athens. Consecrated Archbishop of Canterbury (668). Organized and disciplined the English Church compelling full submission to Canterbury. Wrote a Penitential, regulating morals and religion. R.E.E.H.

Theodoret: (ca. 386-457) Born and educated in Antioch; became Bishop of Cyrus in Syria about 420; an exegete who used the gramatico-historical method of his teacher, Theodore of Antioch, while avoiding the latter's rationalism; a historian who continued the work of Eusebius*. He took a prominent part in the Christological controversies, defending a modified Nestorianism but attacking the Monophysitism of Eutyches**. See Antiochian School; Three Chapter controversy. A.K.R.

Theodosius, the Great: See Constantinople, Councils of.

Theodulf of Orleans: (c. 750-827) The versatile Bishop of Orleans whose influence is shown by his promotion of monastic, clerical, educational, and judicial reform. Capable *missus dominicus* of Charlemagne. Poet of the Palace School*. F.W.N.

Theologia Germanica: Late fourteenth century anon. didactic writing: series of talks to young religious by a priest-teacher in the House of the Order of Teutonic Knights, Frankfurt, Main. The writing treats briefly of God's truth in the individual soul, of growth toward perfection, of Jesus' example in suffering, of "The middle way" between the active and contemplative self. The ideas resemble teachings of Friends of God*, active in the Rhine valley and are classed as practical mysticism. First published in part (cvii-xxvi) in 1516, and complete in 1518, by Martin Luther who added the title. Twenty different editions in German, and many in French and Latin were printed in the sixteenth century. Placed on R. C. Index 1621.

Franz Pfeiffer, *Theologia deutsch* (4th ed., Gutersloh, 1900) for parallel original and modern German texts; Susanna Winkworth's edition in English (1854) pref. by Charles Kingsley; Maria David-Windstosser, *Etude sur la "Theologie Germanique"* (Paris, 1911). Excellent bibliography. A.S.

theological anthropology: See anthropology, theological.

theological education: See theological schools, Jewish; seminaries, major Roman Catholic; theological schools, Protestant, U. S. and Canada. See also anti-theological education agitation in the U. S.

theological encyclopaedia: The study of theology falls into a number of departments, each of which must be considered separately. All of them, however, are inter-related, and may be presented in such a manner as to indicate their mutual dependence. This survey of theological knowledge with regard to the whole field as well as to each part of it is denoted by the term "Encyclopaedia". The technical term has now fallen into disuse, but conveys an idea which can never be safely neglected. E.F.S.

theological journals: See Journals of religion and theology.

theological schools, Jewish: The major theological seminaries as listed in the *American Jewish Year Book* (1942-3) are: Reform: Hebrew Union College (1875), Cincinnati, Ohio; Jewish Institute of Religion (1922), New York City. Conservative: Jewish Theological Seminary of America (1886; re-organized, 1902), New York City. Orthodox: Hebrew Theological College (1922), Chicago; Ner Israel, Rabbinical College of America (1933), Baltimore, Md.; Rabbi Isaac Elchanan Theological Seminary and Yeshiva College (1896; re-organized, 1928), New York City. F.A.L.

theological schools, Protestant, United States and Canada: *United States.* Several types of educational preparation for the ministry have existed in the United States. While each of these served the needs of its own day, each also eventually proved insufficient and helped to pave the way for its successor. In rough chronological order of origin the types are these:

1. European universities. The Protestant ministers who migrated to the colonies before about 1700 were, predominantly, men educated in European universities; Anglicans and Puritans chiefly at Oxford and Cambridge, and the Dutch at Leyden and Utrecht. Ministers thus trained continued to come in later years, and the Lutherans relied on European-trained ministers until about the end of the eighteenth century. But with the rise of a 'native ministry' there was need for American educational institutions.

2. American colleges. The next step was the creation of American colleges patterned after European examples, the influence of Emmanuel College, Cambridge, being especially strong. Harvard (1636), William and Mary (1693), Yale (1701), and Princeton (1701), were founded with the preparation of ministers as a large part of the purpose, as was true of many later colleges. Theological materials were included in the college curriculum; e.g., the curriculum for A.B. contained Hebrew and Greek, Bible, and dogmatic theology. But the A.B. graduate was considered to be "raw and unfurnished" for the work of the ministry; often the candidate for ordination remained in residence after graduation, studying divinity for two or three years more, and perhaps proceeding to A.M.

3. Chairs of Divinity in colleges marked a step toward specialization in theological education in America. The Hollis Professorship of Divinity at Harvard (1721) whose first incumbent was the Rev. Edward Wigglesworth; the Yale Professorship of Divinity (1756) with the Rev. Naphtali Daggett as first incumbent; and the College of New Jersey (Princeton) Professorship of Divinity and Moral Philosophy with the Rev. John Blair, established a pattern of theological work leading to A.B. and A.M. which still persists in many colleges, although other degrees have frequently been substituted.

4. Private instruction. Distance and difficulties of travel, expenses of a regular college course, revival movements which engendered criticism of existing scholastic training for ministers, and doctrinal controversies which produced dissatisfaction with some of the college teaching, conspired to encourage candidates to seek private theological instruction from a suitable minister. Several instances of Congregational ministers privately instructed in America are known for the seventeenth century. In the eighteenth century, especially in the latter half, this type of instruction played a major role in American theological education; Shewmaker estimates that at least 150 ministers engaged in such teaching among the Congregationalists, Dutch Reformed, and Presbyterians. Besides these, many Lutheran ministers gave private instruction. In many cases a minister taught only a few students, but some individuals prepared numerous candidates, as Nathaniel Emmons of Wrentham, Mass., who is said to have trained 87 men. Teaching of this kind is not to be confused with that of private academies for general education, which of course were common. But some ministers attempted to meet the need for both general and theological education, thus establishing institutions which flourished briefly as academies for all of a minister's education. Examples are the famous "Log College" of the Tennents at Neshaminy, Pa.; and the academies of the Blairs at Faggs Manor, Pa., of Robert Smith at Pequa, Pa., of John McMillan at Chartiers, Pa., William Graham at Timber Ridge, Va., Samuel Doak at Bethel, Tenn., and David Caldwell at Buffalo and Allamance, N. C. The "Shepherd's Tent," established by the Rev. Timothy Allen at New London, Conn., in 1742, was an outgrowth of the revivalist movement; outlawed in Connecticut, the school was removed to Rhode Island. Many eminent divines were prepared by private instruction, and there was value in the apprentice feature often accompanying private education. But as a whole the result of the method was a lowering of standards for the ministry. Private instruction tended to sever theological education from the college setting and to turn it in the direction of schools created exclusively for the preparation of ministers. Two trends can be discerned in the private instruction of the eighteenth century: that which had the purpose of maintaining denominational conceptions in theology and worship; and that which was chiefly concerned with a particular experiential form of piety. The first led to the denominational seminaries; the second is related at least indirectly to the Bible Schools.

5. Theological seminaries. Private instruction merged so gradually into the formal theological seminary as to make it almost impossible to say where one ends and the other begins. The connecting thread is the appointment of an individual to be the official teacher of theology for a given religious group. Some such men left no permanent institutions, while others, receiving financial support from the church, established schools.

Beginning about 1754 the Dutch Reformed attempted to establish a chair of divinity either in Kings College (now Columbia University), or in the College of New Jersey (Princeton), or in Queens College (Rutgers). Failing in each of these attempts, they determined to establish a professorship under their own ecclesiastical control and having no connection with any college. On October 8, 1784 they appointed the Rev. John Henry Livingston, one of the pastors of the Collegiate Reformed Dutch Church of New York City, as Professor of Sacred Theology, and the Rev. Hermanus Meyer of Pompton Plains, New Jersey, as Instructor in Sacred Languages. This action is usually reckoned as the establishing of the first Protestant theological seminary in the United States. Livingston began his teaching in 1785, in New York, while continuing as a pastor. In 1810 he removed to New Brunswick, N. J., where he became President of Queens and Professor of Theology. The theological school and the college were intimately related, but the theological school has a continuous existence from 1784 and is now the New Brunswick Theological Seminary.

In 1794 the Associate Presbytery of Pennsylvania appointed the Rev. John Anderson as its professor. Continuing as pastor at Service, Pa., he built a log house for his school and immediately began instruction in theology and other subjects, with a small number of students. The school is known as Service Seminary. In 1821 it was transferred to Canonsburg, Pa.; and thence to Xenia, O., in 1855. By the union of 1858 it became a seminary of the United Presbyterian Church of North America. In 1920 Xenia Seminary was removed to St. Louis, and in 1930 merged with the Pittsburgh Seminary to become the present Pittsburgh-Xenia Theological Seminary.

About 1797 the work of the Hartwick Foundation was begun among the Lutherans. From about the middle of the eighteenth century the Lutherans had desired a theological school of their own; but, aside from European-trained ministers, had been obliged to rely on private instruction. The Rev. John Christopher Hartwick left his estate for the establishing of an institution of learning. The representatives of the estate resolved in 1797 to establish a 'theological and missionary seminary,' and teaching was begun; in 1815 the seminary was located at Hartwick, N. Y., and was chartered in 1816. It was Lutheran in teaching and in the personnel of the trustees, but was not an official seminary of the church. A school opened at Gettysburg, Pa., September 5, 1826, was the first official theological seminary of the Lutheran Church, and continues as the Lutheran Theological Seminary of Gettysburg.

Anti-Trinitarian views were gaining strength in New England when the Rev. Henry Ware, a Unitarian, was elected to the Hollis Professorship in Harvard, in 1805. Resentment over 'the defection of Harvard' being strong among the orthodox Congregationalists, Andover Theological Seminary was opened in 1808, representing the views of the 'moderate Calvinists,' and the 'consistent Calvinists' or Hopkinsians.** The pioneer Baptist school for the theological instruction of college graduates was Newton Theological Institution, established in 1825 at Newton Centre, Mass. In 1931 these institutions merged, forming the present Andover Newton Theological School at Newton Centre, Mass.

Among the Presbyterians, after the Log College at Neshaminy (ca. 1726-1746) had disappeared and the schism between the New Side and the Old Side** had been healed by the reunion of 1758, the Professorship of Theology at the College of New Jersey, together with private instruction and various schools, served the needs of theological education until early in the nineteenth century. Sweet observes that the Presbyterians established "an even hundred schools" between 1726 and the end of the century, and "all were primarily ministerial training schools," (*Religion in Colonial America*, p. 269), yet none fully met the need as the Presbyterians saw it. In 1811 the General Assembly adopted "The Plan of a Theological Seminary," which was established at Princeton, and began its work in 1812 with one professor, the Rev. Archibald Alexander, and three pupils. The School continues as Princeton Theological Seminary. The Assembly left Synods free to establish theological schools on what was called "the principle of locality," and several other Presbyterian seminaries were founded by the end of the 1820's.

In the Protestant Episcopal Church, opinion was divided over the question whether theological education should be carried on in diocesan seminaries or whether one seminary should be established for the whole church, but in 1817 the General Convention established the General Theological Seminary, in which instruction was begun in 1819.

The first of the Baptist seminaries was the Hamilton Literary and Theological Institution, organized in 1820 at Hamilton, N. Y., by the Education Society of the State of New York. It became Colgate Theological Seminary, and is in the ancestry of the present Colgate-Rochester Divinity School.

The German Reformed Church founded a seminary in 1825 in connection with Dickinson College at Carlisle, Pa.; in 1829 the school was independently established at York, Pa. In 1871 the seminary was removed to Lancaster, Pa., where it continues as the Theological Seminary of the Reformed Church in the United States, serving the now merged Evangelical and Reformed Church.

The Methodists, perhaps less from conviction against theological education than from realistic acceptance of pioneer conditions, were late in their development of seminaries. The first is said to have been the theological department of an academy at Newbury, Vermont, which began instruction in 1841. That school is in the line forming the present School of Theology of Boston University. But the Methodists have shown great ingenuity in developing methods of 'education on the job' for their ministers.

Such events as have been sketched are signs of a conviction coming to be generally held among Protestants in the United States early in the nineteenth century, viz., that each denomination could best discharge its responsibility for the education of ministers by founding one or more seminaries under some form of direct denominational control. Given this conviction, when the nation expanded in population and territory and when denominational differences played so large a part as they have done in the United States, it was inevitable that seminaries should multiply. The following Table (from E. G. Dexter, *A History of Education in the United States*, p. 312), serves to show both the rate and the geographical distribution of the growth.

Theological Schools

Year	N. Atlantic	S. Atlantic	S. Central	N. Central	Western	Total
1890-1902	3	3	6	9	2	23
1880-1889	2	4	2	7	—	15
1870-1879	1	1	4	7	2	15
1860-1869	11	4	2	9	1	27
1850-1859	9	—	4	7	—	20
1840-1849	4	—	—	4	—	8
1830-1839	4	2	1	4	—	11
1820-1829	7	2	—	1	—	10
Totals	41	16	19	48	5	129

Not all denominations, however, shared the conviction that seminaries provided the best way to prepare ministers. The Disciples of Christ, e.g., traditionally had a definite conviction against seminaries. Their colleges, however, gave large attention to Bible study as the principal elements in the training of ministers. In the first ninety years of their history the Disciples founded 54 colleges, each having a chair or department of Bible. The College of the Bible, founded at Lexington, Ky., in 1865, set a different pattern—a school definitely for ministers, but placed in connection with 'a scientific and literary institution.' Five other Bible Colleges of similar type have been established, purposely avoiding use of the term 'theological school.'

It is impossible in limited space to trace further the development of individual schools or even of denominational policies. Many histories of particular institutions are available, and denominational histories usually give attention to ministerial education.

For approximately a century theological seminaries pursued their way in relative isolation from one another, isolated also to a large degree from other types of educational institutions. Taking the period as a whole (say from 1800 to 1918), certain facts stand out. (a) Religious liberty was furthered by the seminary plan of theological education. Religious bodies large or small were free to establish and maintain schools, with no external pressure, where any interpretation of religion could be taught to ministers in the making. By the same token the way was left equally open to set up schools representing 'dissenting' or 'heretical' points of view. The results are far-reaching, since both the right to maintain and the right to remake religious convictions were preserved at one of the fountain sources, viz., the education of ministers. But this aspect of religious liberty was kept at a heavy cost; for (b) a serious decline in educational standards for the American ministry accompanied the rise of theological seminaries. This phenomenon itself is too complicated to admit any single explanation, but apparently it does bear some relation to the existence of schools for ministerial education which were responsible to the religious body for doctrine, but were not responsible to any group for the maintenance of educational standards. It became easy to admit students without college preparation. Between 1785 and 1835 there was a sharp drop in the number of college graduates among Congregational clergymen in New England. In the years 1881-1885, in all seminaries reporting, only 23.6 per cent of the graduates held college degrees. The admission of a large percentage of men without college preparation dragged down the level of teaching. Libraries commonly were poor. As a whole scholarship in seminaries was at a low ebb.

The year 1918 marks a turn toward cooperative measures which have not taken away the autonomy of individual schools, but which have cross-fertilized theological education and have had the direct result of raising educational standards. In that year problems incident to World War I led to the gathering of a representative group of theological educators at Cambridge, Mass., out of which grew The Conference of Theological Seminaries and Colleges in the United States and Canada, meeting biennially until 1936. In 1922-23 a survey of theological education was conducted and reported in *Theological Education in America*, by R. L. Kelly, (New York, 1924). The Conference, in collaboration with the Institute of Social and Religious Research, soon sponsored a much more thorough survey which was reported in *The Education of American Ministers*, by Mark A. May, William Adams Brown, and others (4 vols., 1934). In 1936 the Conference became The American Association of Theological Schools, with a membership at that time of 64 institutions in the United States and Canada. The Association adopted standards for accrediting, appointed a Commission on Accrediting, and authorized the Commission to "institute and maintain a list of Accredited Theological Seminaries and Theological Colleges," the latter being the common term in Canada.

The standards place theological education at the graduate level, separating it from undergraduate instruction; requiring an A.B. or its equivalent for admission to candidacy for the B.D.; calling for a three-year course leading to the B.D.; requiring a faculty of at least four full-time professors; with other sections relating to library, equipment, finances, etc.

Inspections with a view to being accredited are made only upon invitation by an institution. In 1938 the Commission reported its first list of accredited schools; 45 in number; the report for 1942 contains 57 institutions. The 1938 report, summarizing the accredited institutions, showed an enrolment of 5102 students, 577 faculty members, a plant value for 37 schools totaling $29,438,634, and income-producing investments for 35 schools totaling $57,546,825.

Theological education in the United States is now so complex that only by a careful definition of terms can one say how many theological schools are in existence. For example: (1) The Roman Catholics in 1940 reported 98 "major seminaries" which provide "courses in the Sacred Sciences as prescribed by Canon Law and give young men immediate preparation for ordination," enrolling 5237 students. (2) The Roman Catholics in the same year report 83 "minor" or preparatory seminaries, usually covering four years of high school work and two years of college classical work, admitting students as early as 12 or 14; some but not all of these schools are given over exclusively to training candidates for religious orders or societies, or secular priests, or both. They report 9692 students, only 1788 of these being lay students. (3) There are, in 1943, 57 accredited Protestant theological schools in the United States and Canada, four of these being in Canada and the remaining 53 in the United States. (4) There are some 57 other theological schools in the United States, the basis of whose work approximates that of the accredited schools, but which vary from the 'standard' in one or more particulars such as size of faculty, standards of admission or graduation, etc. (5) There are at least 32 colleges in the United States, not included in the above classes, which include the preparation of ministers as part of their function. Typically they maintain a Department of Theology, or a School of Theology, and confer such degrees as Th.B., or in some instances a B.D. (6) There are 9 junior colleges which also include the preparation of ministers as part of their function and, similarly, maintain a Department of Theology. (7) There are 31 other theological schools or departments of theology, reported to be in existence; but the nature of their work is too uncertain to justify listing them in other classifications. (8) Besides all these, there are at least 17 Bible Schools which often, and perhaps normally, serve as places of preparation for ministers. Addition of these figures gives a total of 181 Roman Catholic institutions, and 199 for Protestants. The latter total has not varied greatly since about 1930, for the Survey of Theological Education reported 198 institutions in the United States existing primarily for theological education, 157 being primarily for white students and 41 for Negro students. But not all theological schools are stable institutions; e.g., 23 schools reported to exist in 1936 cannot be found in current lists.

At present the trend in the United States seems to be toward raising of standards, and either mergers or various forms of affiliation which reduce the number of small isolated schools. At the same time the appearance of new schools does not thus far suggest actual diminution of the total number of schools devoted to theological education.

Canada. The earliest settlers in what is now Canada were predominantly French and Roman Catholic. The early Protestant clergymen came from England, Scotland, and the United States. But the Protestants were numerically a minor part of the total population until about the time of the American Revolution, with the result that provisions for the education of a native Protestant ministry came later than in the United States.

The story of theological education in Canada is, to a large degree, a reflection of the struggle for religious equality in respect of educational advantages. One of the results was the creation of numerous small colleges, with denominational affiliation, which had the education of ministers as a prominent purpose. Many of these have, in later years, devoted themselves almost entirely to theological education.

The Church of England was made the established church of Nova Scotia in 1758. King's College, under Anglican control, was founded at Windsor, N. S., by the provincial legislature in 1789. Strict Anglican tests were imposed on professors and students, and dissenters were excluded. Thomas McCulloch, a Presbyterian minister, founded a 'log college' at Pictou early in the nineteenth century, to secure educational rights for Presbyterians, and to prepare ministers. The case of Pictou Academy became a storm center, dividing Anglicans and dissenters, forcing the issue of educational rights for the latter. Dalhousie College, founded in 1818, was "intended for those who are excluded from Windsor College [King's]." In 1838 Acadia College was founded by the Baptists at Wolfville. Pictou Academy is perpetuated in Pine Hill Divinity Hall, while Acadia College became Acadia University in 1891 and has a faculty of theology. In the twentieth century the Carnegie Corporation attempted to have all the colleges of Nova Scotia move to Halifax and join with Dalhousie University, each constituent maintaining its identity and funds, but giving up its examining and degree-granting power except in Divinity, thus forming a great university center with affiliated theological colleges. Only the University of King's College, successor to King's College, agreed; it now is a theological college associated with Dalhousie University.

When Upper Canada, now Ontario, became a separate province in 1791, the Constitutional Act of that year set aside one-seventh of the lands of the province as "clergy Reserves" to endow "a Protestant Clergy." This was interpreted by many to mean the Church of England, and Bishop Strachan gained a large measure of control over education in the province. In 1827 he secured a charter for King's College, Toronto, which was to be under Anglican control, its professors to be Anglican and its divinity degrees confined to those who subscribed to Anglican tests. Efforts were made to permit professorships of divinity in King's College to be established by any denominations of Christians desiring to do so, but the plan came to nothing. The Methodists opened Upper Canada Academy at Cobourg in 1836, which became Victoria College in 1841. The Kirk Presbyterians obtained a charter for Queen's College at Kingston in 1841, and the Free Presbyterians founded Knox College in 1844. King's College in 1849 was changed to become the University of Toronto and the Divinity Faculty was abolished, whereupon the Anglicans established Trinity College in 1851. The Act of 1853 made it possible for denominational colleges to affiliate with the University of Toronto. The Federation Act of 1887 brought into federation with the University of Toronto the theological colleges of Knox (Presbyterian), Wycliffe (Anglican), Victoria (Methodist), now Emmanuel College in Victoria University, of the United Church, and St. Michael's (Roman Catholic). Trinity College federated with the University in 1904. "The essence of the scheme [of federation] is a group of Arts or Divinity Colleges gathered about a central University, supported and controlled by the State, the University conducting examinations, conferring degrees except in Divinity, and giving the instruction in those branches of learning which are costly to conduct, or are taken by only a few students, or are professional in character."

At Montreal four Protestant theological colleges were affiliated with McGill University; the number now stands at three: Diocesan Theological College (Anglican), Presbyterian Theological College, and United Theological College (United Church).

The constitutions of the four western universities were modelled largely after Toronto, and the affiliation of theological colleges with the universities is thus familiar through western Canada. The University of Manitoba has five affiliated theological colleges: St. Boniface College at St. Boniface, and St. Paul's College, Roman Catholic; St. John's College (Anglican); Manitoba College and Wesley College (United Church); the latter four being at Winnipeg. The University of Alberta has two: St. Stephens (United Church), and St. Aidan's (Anglican), St. Andrew's (Anglican), and the Lutheran Seminary; and at Regina, St. Chad's. The University of British Columbia has two: Union College of British Columbia (United Church), and the Anglican Theological College of British Columbia.

A canon of the General Synod of the Church of England in Canada provides that degrees in divinity are to be conferred after examination by a Joint Board consisting of the Archbishop of Rupert's Land as chairman and representatives of the church universities and theological colleges, viz., the Universities of King's, Bishop's, and Trinity Colleges, and Montreal Diocesan, Wycliffe, Huron, St. John's, Emmanuel at Saskatoon, St. Chad's, and Anglican Theological College of B. C.

Thus Canada has made a signal achievement in the clustering of theological schools in university centers, and in establishing an affiliation of the theological colleges with the universities. The process seems to have been more completely worked out in the western than in the eastern provinces. But at present there are few isolated 'theological seminaries' in Canada. Affiliation with the universities has preserved denominational autonomy, but has also kept theological education in a university setting.

UNITED STATES. *Centennial of the Theological Seminary of the Reformed Church in America, 1784-1884* (1885). E. G. Dexter, *A History of Education in the United States* (1922). F. G. Gotwald, "Theological education in the Lutheran Church prior to the founding of Wittenberg College and Seminary in 1845," *Lutheran Quarterly*, XLVI (pp. 82-100), Jan., 1916. J. Johnson, "Early theological education west of the Alleghanies," *Papers of the American Society of Church History*, Second Series, vol. V, pp. 119-130 (1917). J. McNaugher, *Theological Education in the United Presbyterian Church and its Ancestries* (1931). R. B. Montgomery, *The Education of Ministers of Disciples of Christ* (1931). S. E. Morison, *Three Centuries of Harvard*, 1636-1936 (1942). W. O. Shewmaker, "The training of the Protestant ministry in the United States of America, before the establishment of theological seminaries," *Papers of the American Society of Church History*, Second Ser., vol. VI, pp. 71-191 (1921). S. Simpson, "Early ministerial training in America," *Papers of the Am. Soc. of Ch. Hist.*, Second Ser., vol. II, pp. 117-121 (1910). "Theological seminaries" [articles on history of individual schools], *New Schaff-Herzog Encyclopedia of Religious Knowledge*, vol. XI, pp. 343-394 (1911). Numerous histories of particular institutions, denominational histories, biographies, etc.

CANADA. N. Burwash, *The History of Victoria College* (1907). W. Gregg, *History of the Presbyterian Church in Canada* (1885). W. McCulloch, *The Life of Thomas McCulloch, D.D.* (n. p., n. d.). J. T. McNeill, *The Presbyterian Church in Canada, 1875-1925* (1925) E. H. Oliver, *The Winning of the Frontier* (1930). J. E. Sanderson, *The First Century of Methodism in Canada*, vol. I (1908). A. Shortt and A. G. Doughty, *Canada and its Provinces*, vol. XI (1914). *The University of Toronto and its Colleges*, 1827- 1906 (1906). *Universities Yearbook*, 1936 (London, 1936).

Both U. S. and Canada. R. L. Kelly, *Theological Education in America* (1924). M. A. May and others, *The Education of American Ministers*, 4 vols. (1934). Bulletins of the American Association of Theological Schools, especially Bulletin 12, June sp, 1938, "First Report of the Commission on Accrediting."

LIST OF THEOLOGICAL SCHOOLS, UNITED STATES AND CANADA

The following list contains: (1) The theological schools which are members of the American Association of Theological Schools, indicated by *; (2) The theological schools which are accredited by the A.A.T.S., indicated by **; all these are also members of the A.A.T.S.; and (3) Certain others.

UNITED STATES

California: **Berkeley Baptist Divinity School, Berkeley, Calif., No. Baptist, 1904; *Church Divinity School of the Pacific, Berkeley, Calif., Prot. Episcopal, 1893; **Pacific School of Religion, Berkeley, Calif., Cong.-Chrn., 1866; *Pacific Unitarian, School for the Ministry, Berkeley, Calif., Unitarian, 1904; **San Francisco Theological Seminary, San Anselmo, Calif., Presb. U. S. A., 1871; *University of Southern Calif., School of Religion, Los Angeles, Calif., Methodist, 1880.

Colorado: **Iliff School of Theology, Denver, Colo., Methodist, 1892.

Connecticut: *Berkeley Divinity School, New Haven, Conn., Prot. Episcopal, 1854; **Hartford Theological Seminary, Hartford, Conn., Cong.-Chrn., 1834; **Yale University, Divinity School, New Haven, Conn., Cong.-Chrn., (1701); 1822.

District of Columbia: **Howard University, School of Religion, Washington, D. C., Non-denom., 1871.

Georgia: **Candler School of Theology, Emory Univ., Emory University, Ga., Methodist, (1836); 1914; **Columbia Theological Seminary, Decatur, Ga., Presb. U. S., 1828; **Gammon Theological Seminary, Atlanta, Ga., Methodist, 1883.

Illinois: **Augustana Theological Seminary, Rock Island, Ill., Augustana Lutheran, 1860; **Bethany Biblical Seminary, Chicago, Ill., Ch. of the Brethren, 1905; *Chicago Lutheran Seminary, Maywood, Ill., United Lutheran, 1891; **Chicago Theological Seminary, Chicago, Ill., Cong. Chrn., 1855; Concordia Theological Seminary, Springfield, Ill., Mo. Lutheran, 1846; **Evangelical Theological Seminary, Naperville, Ill., Evangelical Ch., 1873; **Garrett Biblical Institute, Evanston, Ill., Methodist, 1855; **McCormick Theological Seminary, Chicago, Ill., Presb. U. S. A., 1829; **Meadville Theological School, Chicago, Ill., Unitarian, 1844; *Northern Baptist Theological Seminary, Chicago, Ill., No. Baptist, 1913; **Seabury Western Theological Seminary, Evanston, Ill., Prot. Episcopal, 1858; **University of Chicago, Divinity School, Chicago, Ill., No. Baptist, 1866.

Indiana: Anderson College Theological Seminary, Anderson, Ind., Ch. of God, 1917; *Butler University, College of Religion, Indianapolis, Ind., Disciples, 1925.

Iowa: Drake University, Bible College, Des Moines, Iowa, Disciples, 1881; *University of Dubuque, Theological School, Dubuque, Iowa, Presb. U. S. A., 1852; Wartburg Theological Seminary, Dubuque, Iowa, Amer. Lutheran, 1853.

Kansas: *Central Baptist Theological Seminary, Kansas City, Kans., No. Baptist, 1901.

Kentucky: *Asbury Theological Seminary, Wilmore, Ky., Non-denom., 1923; **College of the Bible, Lexington, Ky., Disciples, 1865; **Louisville Presbyterian Seminary, Louisville, Ky., Presb. U. S. & U. S. A., 1853; **Southern Baptist Theological Seminary, Louisville, Ky., So. Baptist, 1859.

Louisiana: *Baptist Bible Institute, New Orleans, La., So. Baptist, 1918.

Maine: *Bangor Theological Seminary, Bangor, Me., Cong.-Chrn., 1814.

Maryland: **Westminster Theological Seminary, Westminster, Md., Methodist, 1882.

Massachusetts: **Andover Newton Theological School, Newton Centre, Mass., Cong.-Chrn.; No. Bapt., 1808; **Boston University, School of Theology, Boston, Mass., Methodist, 1841; *Divinity School of Gordon College of Theology and Missions, Boston, Mass., Non-denom., 1889; **Episcopal Theological School, Cambridge, Mass., Prot. Episcopal, 1867; **Harvard University, Divinity School, Cambridge, Mass., Non-denom., (1636); 1816; *New Church Theological School, Cambridge, Mass., Gen. Conv. New Jerus., 1866; *Tufts College, School of Religion, Medford, Mass., Universalist, 1851.

Michigan: *Calvin Theological Seminary, Grand Rapids, Mich., Chrn. Reformed, 1876; **Western Theological Seminary, Holland, Mich., Ref. Ch. in Amer., 1866.

Minnesota: Augsburg Theological Seminary, Minneapolis, Minn., Lutheran Free Ch., 1869; Luther Theological Seminary, St. Paul, Minn., Norwegian Lutheran, 1876; *Northwestern Lutheran Theological Seminary, Minneapolis, Minn., United Lutheran, 1921.

Missouri: Concordia Theological Seminary, St. Louis, Mo., Mo. Lutheran, 1839; **Eden Theological Seminary, Webster Groves, Mo., Evang. & Ref., 1850.

Nebraska: *Presbyterian Theological Seminary, Omaha, Nebr., Presb. U. S. A., 1891; Trinity Theological Seminary, Blair, Nebr., United Danish Ev. Lutheran, 1894.

New Jersey: *Bloomfield Seminary, Bloomfield, N. J., Presb. U. S. A., 1868; **Drew Theological Seminary, Madison, N. J., Methodist, 1867; **New Brunswick Theological Seminary, New Brunswick, N. J., Ref. Ch. in Amer., 1784; **Princeton Theological Seminary, Princeton, N. J., Presb. U. S. A, 1812.

New York: *Alfred University, School of Theology, Alfred, N. Y., Seventh Day Bapt., 1861; *Biblical Seminary in New York, New York, N. Y., Non-denom., 1900; **Colgate-Rochester Divinity School, Rochester, N. Y., No. Bapt., 1820; **General Theological Seminary, New York, N. Y., Prot. Episcopal, 1817; Hartwick Seminary, New York, N. Y., United Lutheran, 1797; St. Lawrence Univ., Theological School, Canton, N. Y., Universalist, 1858; **Union Theological Seminary, New York, N. Y., Non-denom., 1836.

North Carolina: **Duke University, Divinity School, Durham, N. C., Methodist, 1926; *Johnson C. Smith Univ., School of Theology, Charlotte, N. C., Presb. U. S. A., 1867.

Ohio: Ashland Theological Seminary, Ashland, O., Brethren Ch., 1878; **Bonebrake Theological Seminary, Graduate School of Theology, Dayton, O., United Brethren, 1871; *Divinity School of Kenyon College (Bexley Hall), Gambier, O., Prot. Episcopal, 1824; **Hamma Divinity School, Springfield, O., United Lutheran, 1845; Evangelical Lutheran Seminary, of Capital University, Columbus, O., Amer. Lutheran, 1830; **Oberlin Graduate School of Theology, Oberlin, O., Cong.-Chrn., 1833.

Oklahoma: *College of the Bible, Phillips University, Enid, Okla., Disciples, 1906.

Pennsylvania: **Crozer Theological Seminary, Chester, Pa., No. Bapt., 1868; *Divinity School of the Protestant Episcopal Church in Philadelphia, Philadelphia, Pa., Prot. Episcopal, 1857; *Eastern Baptist Theological Seminary, Philadelphia, Pa., No. Bapt., 1925; **Evangelical School of Theology, Reading, Pa., Evangelical, 1905; Lincoln University, Theological Seminary, Lincoln University, Pa., Presb. U. S. A., 1856; **Lutheran Theological Seminary, Gettysburg, Pa., United Lutheran, 1826; **Lutheran Theological Seminary, Mt. Airy, Pa., United Lutheran, 1864; *Moravian College and Theological Seminary, Bethlehem, Pa., Moravian, 1807; **Pittsburgh-Xenia Theological Seminary, Pittsburgh, Pa., United Presb., 1794; Reformed Presbyterian Theological Seminary, Pittsburgh, Pa., Reformed Presb., 1810; **Temple University, School of Theology, Philadelphia, Pa., Non-denom., 1884; **Theological Seminary of the Reformed Church in the United States, Lancaster, Pa., Evang. & Reformed, 1825; Theological Seminary of the Reformed Episcopal Church, Philadelphia, Pa., Reformed Episcopal, 1886; **Western Theological Seminary, Pittsburgh, Pa., Presb. U. S. A., 1825; Westminster Theological Seminary, Philadelphia, Pa., Orthodox Presb., 1929.

Puerto Rico: *Evangelical Seminary of Puerto Rico, Rio Piedras, P. R., Presb. U. S. A., 1919.

South Carolina: Erskine College Theological Seminary, Due West, S. C., Assoc. Ref. Presb., 1839; *Lutheran Theological Seminary, Columbia, S. C., United Lutheran, 1830.

Tennessee: *Cumberland Presbyterian Theological Seminary, McKenzie, Tenn., Cumberland Presb., 1914; University of the South, Theological School, Sewanee, Tenn., Prot. Episcopal, 1878; **Vanderbilt University, School of Religion, Nashville, Tenn., Non-denom., 1875.

Texas: **Austin Theological Seminary, Austin, Texas, Presb. U. S., 1902; **Brite College of the Bible, Ft. Worth, Texas., Disciples, 1914; Dallas Theological Seminary and Graduate School of Theology, Dallas, Texas, Non-denom., 1924; **Southern Methodist University, School of Theology, Dallas, Texas, Methodist, 1915; *Southwestern Baptist Theological Seminary, Seminary Hill, Texas, So. Bapt., 1907.

Virginia: **Union Theological Seminary, Richmond, Va., Presb. U. S., 1812; **Protestant Episcopal Seminary in Virginia, Alexandria, Va., Prot. Episcopal, 1823.

Wisconsin: *Mission House, Plymouth, Wisc., Evang. & Reformed, 1859; Nashotah House, Nashotah, Wisc., Prot. Episcopal, 1842; Theological Seminary of the Joint Evangelical Synod of Wisconsin and Other States, Thiensville, Wisc., Evang. Lutheran Joint Syn. of Wisc. &c., 1865.

CANADA

Alberta: St. Aidan's College, Edmonton, Alberta, Anglican; St. Stephen's College, Edmonton, Alberta, United Church, 1903.

British Columbia: Anglican Theological College of British Col., Vancouver, B. C., Anglican, 1912; *Union Theological College, Vancouver, B. C., United Church, 1927.

Manitoba: Manitoba College, Winnipeg, Man., United Church, 1871; *St. John's College, Winnipeg, Man., Anglican, 1820; Wesley College, Winnipeg, Man., United Church, 1877.

Nova Scotia: *Pine Hill Divinity School, Halifax, N. S., United Church, 1926; Acadia University, Faculty of Theology, Wolfville, N. S., Baptist, 1838; University of King's College, Halifax, N. S., Anglican, 1789.

Ontario: **Emmanuel College in Victoria University, Toronto, Ont., United Church, 1836; Evangelical Lutheran Seminary of Canada, Waterloo, Ont., Evang. Lutheran, 1911; Huron College, London, Ont., Anglican, 1863; *Knox College, Toronto, Ont., Presbyterian, 1844; *McMaster University, Faculty of Theology, Hamilton, Ont., Baptist, 1887; **Queen's Theological College, Kingston, Ont., United Church, 1842; Toronto Baptist Seminary, Toronto, Ont., Baptist, 1927; Toronto Bible College, Toronto, Ont., Non-denom., 1894; **University of Trinity College, Toronto, Ont., Anglican, 1851; Wycliffe College, Toronto, Ont., Anglican, 1877.

Quebec: *Diocesan Theological College, Montreal, Que., Anglican, 1873; **Presbyterian Theological College, Montreal, Que., Presbyterian, 1864; United Theological College, Montreal, Que., United Church, 1864; University of Bishop's College, Lennoxville, Que., Anglican, 1843.

Saskatchewan: Emmanuel College, Saskatoon, Sask., Anglican, 1879; Lutheran Seminary, Saskatoon, Sask., United Lutheran, 1918; St. Andrew's College, Saskatoon, Sask., Anglican, 1912; St. Chad's College, Regina, Sask., Anglican, 1907. L.J.S.

theological schools, Roman Catholic: See seminaries, major Roman Catholic.

Theological Society, American: A society composed of theologians and philosophers meeting annually in New York for the discussion of theological problems. The Society was organized at Union Theological Seminary in New York, April 8, 1912. This meeting was the outgrowth of a conversation between D. C. Macintosh (Yale) and E. W. Lyman (Bangor) who had chanced to meet in Heidelberg in July, 1911. W. A. Brown (Union) had been approached and had heartily endorsed the proposal, inviting several other scholars to meet in his home in February, 1912, for the discussion of details. At the April, 1912, meeting a constitution was adopted, and officers elected, with fifteen charter members: W. A. Brown, E. S. Drown, G. Cross, A. M. Dulles, D. Evans, M. G. Evans, R. C. Knox, E. W. Lyman, A. C. McGiffert, D. C. Macintosh, S. B. Meeser, D. S. Miller, H. S. Nash, F. C. Porter, and E. Sneath. The formal purpose of the Society, as expressed in the constitution, was: "to promote the interests of present-day constructive theology, by the holding of meetings for the discussion of theological problems and for the furthering of acquaintance and fellowship among those working in this field, and by arranging for coöperation in theological investigation." During the early years two meetings each year were held; since 1918 this has been changed to an annual meeting in the spring. The original intent of a small membership limited to experts residing in the general vicinity of New York has been observed. The present membership is sixty. In recent years a daughter society has been established in the Midwest. M.S.E.

theology: (Gr., *theos*, god; *logos*, study) The discipline which concerns God (or the Divine Reality) and God's relation to the world. In the widest and most inclusive sense theology is a branch of philosophy or that field of philosophical inquiry which concerns God and related questions. So conceived, the discipline may well be called philosophical theology. In this sense theology need have no relation to any religion. Many writers, however, view theology as associated with religion and define it as the intellectual expression of religion. Such a conception is less adequate since a theologian may well carry on his work of investigation in the spirit of free inquiry without being religious or having any commitment to any given religion. For clear thinking, it seems best to employ the generic term theology (somewhat as defined above in the opening sentence) and add a qualifying adjective to denote the particular area of interest and approach: e.g., philosophical, primitive, medieval, modern, contemporary, Jewish, Mohammedan, Christian, Catholic, Liberal, Reformed, Lutheran, or even by further restricted qualifications, as e.g., apologetic, revealed, polemic, rational, systematic, ecclesiastical, historical, scientific.

It has become the tendency, however, for many theologians to use the term without any qualifying adjective to designate their particular faith or commitment. Thus, since in Western Christian thought God predominantly has been conceived to be a personal being who has revealed himself in a definite course in history, in human form, by a supernatural direction in sacred writings and through a social organism (the church), many theologians employ the term exclusively to designate the ideology of a particular religion. This has been true both in Catholic and Protestant thought. Theology then becomes distinct from philosophy as revelation is said to be distinct from speculation. A few examples: "Theology is the science of religion." "Theology is related to philosophy as revelation is to reason." "Theology starts from revelation and the consciousness of God; philosophy starts from reason and self-consciousness." "Theology is in possession of the truth; philosophy is in quest of the truth." (Philip Schaff in the work cited below.) Unhappily, because of this restricted conception of theology—which has enjoyed a traditional usage of long standing—philosophers (particularly the more recent philosophers of religion) have come to consider any alleged affiliation with theologians as a mark of intellectual degeneration. The theologian and the philosopher although interested in a common field of inquiry look upon one another with suspicion: the philosopher to the theologian becomes a secular play-boy in holy matters while the theologian to the philosopher becomes an arrogant dogmatist. Broadly conceived, however, both the philosopher and the theologian may well be the same person in a field of free inquiry concerning the existence and character of the Divine Reality (however conceived) and the world of experience and nature as these relate to what is considered divine. In these latter days we are coming to see more clearly that revelation and inquiry need no longer be viewed as incompatibles, rightly understood.

Protestant theologians have, up until quite recent times, divided their theological field into many patches, each theologian cultivating his particular patch under the more or less avowed direction of the dogmatic (systematic) theology of his church. Such traditional and particular theological disciplines were: propaedeutic; theology and religion; exegetical (biblical) subdivided into: biblical philology, biblical archaeology, isagogics, criticism, canonics, hermeneutics and biblical theology; historical (ecclesiastical) subdivided into biblical history, church history, patristics; systematic (philosophical) subdivided into apologetics, biblical theology, dogmatics, symbolics, polemics, irenics, ethics, statistics and such particular inquiries as e.g., Christology, soteriology, etc.; practical subdivided into the ministry, ecclesiology, polity, liturgics, homiletics, catechetics, poimenics and evangelistics**. Recent tendencies in the division of the theological field have aimed at simplification of division under more comprehensive groupings and in the case of some liberal theological curricula unhappily less unified by a constructive and comprehensive system. Some such generic divisions are: history and philosophy of religion; O.T. (literature and theology); N.T. (literature and theology); church history; systematic theology with emphasis upon one particular religion; historical theology of a particular religion; homiletics and public speaking; religious education and practical theology; church administration; foreign missions; individual and social ethics; music and art. See religion, the problem of definition; God; theism. See under specific headings, e.g., systematic theology.

Philip Schaff, *Theological Propaedeutic* (1892); John Baillie, *The Interpretation of Religion* (1928), chaps. I-IV; Vergilius Ferm, ed., *Contemporary American Theology*, vol. I (1932), Vol. II (1933).

V.F.

theology: See American theology, early; Chicago school; dogmatic theology; empirical theology; Lundensian theology; Mercersburg theology; natural theology; New theology; New England theology; New Haven theology; New Testament theology; Oberlin theology; practical theology; symbolics; systematic theology. Also Biblical theology.

Theology Lectures, The: Given annually at the University of Virginia; established in 1934, with the object of compensating for the lack of formal theological instruction in contemporary secular education by providing an undenominational scholarly discussion of theological subjects before University students.

(Data from the office of the Secretary of the University.)

V.F.

Theopaschites: (from the Greek *Theos*, God, and *pascho*, I suffer) A name given to the Monophysites*, because, holding as they did that there was only one nature in Christ, they embodied that belief in a liturgical formula, "God has been crucified". The school arose in opposition to the Christological* decisions of the Council of Chalcedon*, A.D. 451. Cf. patripassianism.

A.K.R.

theophagy: (Gr., *theos*, god; *phagein*, to eat) Eating the god. The practice can be traced back to the eating of the sacred animal to secure *mana*, or the god in the form of an animal. The later widespread custom of eating the god sacramentally as in the mystery religions* has been carried over into Christian practice. See sacramental meal.

Preserved Smith, *A Short History of Christian Theophagy* (1922); H. R. Willoughby, *Pagan Regeneration* (1929).

V.F.

theophany: An intimate manifestation of God to a human being at a definite time and place; often very physical as in the Iliad and Genesis; more spiritual in later classic form such as Moses at burning bush, Moses on Sinai, Elijah on Horeb, Jesus at Transfiguration, etc.; more spectacular and personal than mere revelation.

R.E.W.

Theophilanthropy, Society of: Deistic* group originating in Paris in 1796 during the Directory period of the French Revolution when atheism was rampant. Creed consisted of three articles, God, virtue, immortality of the soul. Worship and practice were very simple. Died out after 1802.

K.H.C.

Theophilus, The Battle-Axe: See Battle-Axe experiment.

Theophronians: See Agnoetae.

theopneustia: A term employed by some German theologians and taken from 2 Tim. 3,16 (*theopneustos*) to mean the mysterious power of the Divine Spirit which inspired the writers of the Christian scriptures. The title of a volume by L. Gaussen which is a conservative apologetic for the Divine truth of the Christian scriptures. See inspiration.

V.F.

theosophy: A term which, in general, refers to a system of thought claiming to be divine wisdom. More particularly, the term is associated with the Theosophical Society founded in 1875 by the Russian Madame Blavatsky. Leadership in America has for many years fallen to Mrs. Besant who describes the thought as the *Ancient Wisdom*. Reality is held to be One, the source of all existence containing within a cyclic process of emanation and evolving ascension. Man's salvation consists in his achievement by discipline, resignation and purgation of ascending planes toward the astral way by the help of the secret divine wisdom. The symbol of reality is the wheel. Theosophy represents the grafting of Eastern thought upon Western. Cf. I Am; Liberal Catholic Church; mahatma; R. Steiner; Vedanta. See communistic settlements, religious.

G. G. Atkins, *Modern Religious Cults and Movements* (1923); C. Ferguson, *The Confusion of Tongues* (1928). V.F.

theotokos: See Virgin Mary.

Therapeutæ: A group of ascetics having their centre near Alexandria in Egypt about the time of the Christian beginnings, and described by Philo of Alexandria* in an essay *Concerning the Contemplative Life.* This group, composed (unlike the Essenes*) of both men and women, is said by Philo to have devoted their time to contemplation, "studying . . . the laws and sacred oracles of God enunciated by the holy prophets, and hymns, and psalms, and all kinds of other things by reason of which knowledge and piety are increased and brought to perfection." They lived in separate huts or cells, assembling only on the Sabbath and the *Pannuchis* ("all night festival") which occurred every fiftieth day. Their origin and fate are alike unknown. The only reference to them is in the above-mentioned treatise of Philo. See asceticism. M.S.E.

Thesaurus Meritorum: The Roman Catholic Church claims to be in the possession of a treasury of spiritual merits, accumulated partly from the satisfaction* of Christ for the sins of the world, an act redundant because of its infinite value, and partly from the superabundant satisfactions of the Saints for their own sins. It is from this treasury of overflowing merits that the Catholic Church grants indulgences*, that is, the remission of temporal punishments which men, even after the absolution* of their sins, otherwise would had to incur. S.C.T.

Theses, Ninety-Five of Harms: For the Reformation festival of 1817, Claus Harms*, pastor at Kiel, published Luther's 95 theses together with 95 of his own against rationalism and the proposed union between the Lutheran and Reformed churches. His theses caused a tremendous sensation and elicited some 200 replies. E.C.K.

Theses, Ninety-Five, of Luther: A series of propositions drawn up by Martin Luther* asking for a theological debate on the question of indulgences*. October 31, 1517, the day when Luther nailed these theses to the door of the castle church at Wittenberg, is generally considered to mark the beginning of the Reformation*. Occasioned by the indiscriminate manner in which Tetzel*, a Dominican friar, sold indulgences, Luther's theses were not designed for general circulation nor to constitute an attack on the Church or the papacy. Luther claimed, indeed, to express the true mind of the Pope over against Tetzel. Germs of the evangelical position, however, are evident throughout, e,g., the first thesis: "the whole life of believers should be penitence"; the sixth: "The Pope has no power to remit any guilt, except by declaring . . . it to have been remitted by God;" the thirty-sixth: "Every Christian who feels true compunction . . . has remission of pain and guilt, even without letters of pardon"; the sixty-second: "The true treasure of the Church is the Holy Gospel . . . of the grace of God". Heroic resolve to accept battle is revealed in the ninety-fourth: "Christians should strive to follow Christ their head through pains, deaths, and hells". Having unconsciously exposed vulnerability of the whole medieval Church, Luther's theses stirred up an unexpected commotion which eventuated in the Reformation. T.A.K.

Thesmophoria: (Gr., *Thesmophória,* from *thesmóphoros,* law-giving) A festival celebrated in Athens and elsewhere in Greece in October, honoring Demeter* under her ancient name, the law-giver. A festival for women only, it sought to insure fertility for farm and folk alike. There was a strange chthonian ritual with a symbolic visit to Hades, to induce fertility. E.M.N.

Thessalonians, First and Second Letters to the: The earliest of the letters of Paul that have come down to us are those written at Corinth, to the church at Thessalonica, in the midst of the second missionary journey. Paul had been obliged to leave Thessalonica before his work there was completed, or even well established. In his anxiety over the fate of the churches he had founded at Thessalonica and Philippi, he had sent Silvanus and Timothy back from Athens to find out what had become of them and to do what they could for them. Paul waited anxiously for the news they would bring, and was greatly relieved to learn that the Thessalonians had stood firm in their new faith. First Thessalonians is the expression of his relief over Timothy's report and of his great interest in them. It was written in A.D. 50. The closing chapters give a picture of Christian problems and hopes. One problem was the idleness of some who thought the Day of the Lord had come, and so gave up their daily work, and became a charge upon their brethren. This became a scandal in the church and the community, and Paul wrote his second letter to correct it. He appeals to the Antichrist doctrine, and points out that as the Antichrist* has not appeared, the Day of the Lord has not come. The second letter was also written from Corinth, probably only a few months after the first. Aspersions have been cast upon the genuineness of II Thessalonians, but the letter is historically more difficult to explain as spurious than it is as genuine.

Ernst von Dobschutz, *Die Thessalonicher-Briefe* (1909); James E. Frame, *Epistles of St. Paul to the Thessalonians* (1912); George Milligan, *St. Paul's Epistles to the Thessalonians* (1908). E.J.G.

Thieme, Karl: (1862-1932) He was professor in Leipzig. He exercised a sharp criticism on the revivals of the old Christology and the doctrine of the Trinity, and achieved great merits through the working out of certain concrete details in Luther's theology.

Die sittliche Triebkraft des Glaubens (Leipzig, 1895); *Die christliche Demut* (Giessen, 1906); *Jesus und seine Predigt* (Giessen, 1908); *Von der Gottheit Christi* (Giessen, 1911); *Die Augsburger Konfession und Luthers Katechismen* (Giessen, 1830). H.H.

Thierry of Chartres: (died ca. 1150) Famous teacher at Paris and at Chartres, whose *Heptateuchon,* a handbook of the seven liberal arts, is one of the chief sources of our knowledge regarding studies in the first half of the twelfth century. Thierry freely utilizes the first translations from arabic sources in the field of medicine, astronomy and mathematics. His theology is characterized by a peculiar Christian neo-Pythagoreanism.* S.C.T.

Third Order: An association of lay persons called tertiaries*, established by some monastic groups, such as Augustinians or Dominicans, and allowed on stated conditions to share in the works of the monastic body. See Catholic Societies. L.R.W.

Thirteen Articles: Framed by English and German theologians in 1538 on the basis of the Augsburg Confession*; never published, but a source for the Forty-Two Articles*. E.R.H.

Thirty-nine Articles: The basic doctrinal formula of the Anglican Church. These articles were a revision of the Forty-two Articles* which had been framed under the leadership of Thomas Cranmer during the reign of Edward VI. Although they were first approved in 1563, they did not gain general acceptance until 1571.

See E. T. Green, *The Thirty-nine Articles* (1896). W.S.H.

Thirty Years' War: Series of wars fought mainly in Germany but involving most of Europe. Causes: 1) Conflict between Protestants and R. Cs. as aftermath of Reformation. Peace of Augsburg had left number of matters unsettled. R. Cs. were growing in strength through success of Counter-Reformation* and activity of Jesuits. 2) National and political rivalries; suspicion of imperial designs, opposition of France to Hapsburgs, tangled web of international diplomacy involving Spain, France, England, the Low Countries, Denmark, Sweden. Political and religious motives thus closely interwoven. Religious lines not always sharply drawn, e.g., French support of Protestant armies. Terrible devastation was wrought by the bitterness of the conflict and the plundering of the armies.

Began as religious and national revolt in Bohemia. Was suppressed but wider area was already involved. Protestants rallied under Christian IV of Denmark but were defeated and Peace of Lübeck followed. Edict of Restitution, ordering restoration of R. C. property secularized since 1552 brought renewal of war. Gustavus Adolphus of Sweden intervened to uphold Protestantism and to protect and extend Swedish interests. He defeated imperial armies under Tilly at Breitenfeld and Wallenstein at Lützen. His death in battle was severe blow to Protestants. Their defeat at Nördlingen brought temporary Peace of Prag (1635) on basis of status quo of 1627. Political motives overweighed the religious in later stages of the war. Finally the Peace of Westphalia* (1648) brought only minor political adjustments. Main religious change was recognition of Calvinism as well as Romanism and Lutheranism. See League, German Catholic. K.H.C.

Tholuck, August: (1799-1877) He was professor in Berlin and Halle. His most influential works were exegetical works. His far-reaching and profound influence resulted more from his powerful sermons and his devout pastoral care of the students rather than from his theological achievement. He sought to revive something of the central Pauline doctrine and make Luther again vital. Theologically he remained in the scheme of a pietistically and idealistically deepened supernaturalism. In Tholuck the theology of the awakening failed to achieve a systematic reflection upon its enthusiastic faith and Christianity.

Lehre von der Sünde und vom Erlöser, oder die wahre Weihe des Zweiflers (Gotha, 1923); 9th ed. (Gotha, 1871); *Glaubwürdigkeit der evangelischen Geschichte* (Hamburg, 1837); *Der Geist der lutherischen Theologen Wittenbergs im 17. Jahrhundert* (Hamburg u. Gotha, 1852); *Das kirchliche Leben des 17. Jahrhunderts* (Berlin, 1861); *Geschichte des Rationalismus* (Berlin, 1865). H.H.

Thomas, St.: (From the Aramaic word for "twin," which in Gr. is *didymus* [Joh. 11:16, etc.]) Surname (or nickname) of one of the twelve. According to a lost *Acts of Thomas,* known to Origen, first missionary to Parthia. According to the extant *Acts of Thomas,* missionary to India. See Thomas Christians. S.M.G.

Thomas, Acts of: 13 purported "acts" of St. Thomas, who is said to have been sold as a slave into India by Jesus, together with an account of his martyrdom. An early 3rd century document with Gnostic interests. See apocrypha in the N.T. church; pseudepigrapha, N.T. S.M.G.

Thomas of Becket: See Becket, Thomas à.

Thomas, Gospel of: A Gnostic Gospel from the middle of the 2nd century, often condemned as heretical by early Christian writers. Preserved in abbreviated form in three Gr. mss. and in several translations. See pseudepigrapha, N.T. S.M.G.

Thomas à Kempis: See Kempis, Thomas à.

Thomas, The Hiram W., Lectures: Established in 1916 at the University of Chicago by Mrs. Vandalia Varnum Thomas as a memorial to Dr. Hiram W. Thomas, distinguished clergyman, to be given by men "of the larger faith" who are to interpret the growing thought of the world in religion and life. The six lecturers have been: M. I. Pupin, R. A. Millikan, W. L. Sperry, W. E. Hocking, I. F. Lewis, G. Vlastos. Endowment, $2,214.00.

(Data from the offices of the Dean of the Divinity School and the Secretary of the University.) V.F.

Thomas Christians, the: There is a Church in South India known as the Syrian Church of Malabar. It holds the tradition that the apostle organized the Church and suffered a martyr's death in A.D. 58. Cosmos, a Greek traveller of the 6th Century, wrote of this Church. In May 1613 the Church divided, the Uniat Section remaining loyal to Rome, and the Jacobite* Section looking to the Patriarch of Antioch. Despite schisms this Church is experiencing a new growth.

See J. N. Farquhar's articles in the *Bulletin of the John Rylands Library*, vols. 10-11 (Manchester, 1926); A. Fortesque, *The Lesser Eastern Churches* (London, 1913). D.F.E.—J.T.M.

Thomas Matthew Bible: See Bible, English.

Thomasius, Gottfried: (1802-1875) He was professor at the University of Erlangen. As a Lutheran he developed a biblical interpretation of the old Protestant doctrine of *kenosis**. For him it was an act of the divine *logos*. He also gave Kliefoth's* theory of the four circles of dogma (the theological, the christological, the anthropological and the soteriological) its classical development in his history of dogma. See neo-Lutheranism.

Christi Person und Werk (Erlangen, 1852-61); *Die christliche Dogmengeschichte*, 2 vols. (Erlangen, 1876). H.H.

Thomism: (From Thomas Aquinas, its founder) Historically, this term denotes the philosophico-theological synthesis embodied in the mature works (*Summa Contra Gentiles, Summa Theologica**) of the thirteenth century Dominican monk and master in the faculty of arts at Paris. Though essentially theological in method and object, these works contain an implicit Christian Aristotelianism characterized by moderate realism and pluralism—a Weltanschauung platonic in structure but Christian in spirit.

In contemporary philosophy it denotes that branch of Neo-Scholasticism which considers present day problems in the philosophy of science, knowledge theory, social and political philosophy in the light of principles elaborated by St. Thomas. Outstanding exponents of modern Thomism (sometimes called neo-Thomism) are Jacques Maritain, Mortimer Adler, Leon Noel, Etienne Gilson, Peter Hoenen, Martin D'Arcy). See Scholasticism; neo-Scholasticism; St. Thomas Aquinas. J.J.F.

Thor: (Teut.) Thunder-god of Norway and Iceland who breaks up the winter ice and snow and restores fertility; a god of fertility and agriculture. The oak is his tree. He is the god of the sailor, the guardian of ships, and his effigy on the ship brings good luck. Winter sacrifices to him bring back the return of spring and fruitfulness. As a god of fertility his worship continued in Europe into the eighteenth century; his day (Thursday), set aside for him, is a good day for weddings. He came to be pictured wearing red hair, a long beard, and carried a hammer. Thunder is represented as the sound from his playing nine-pins with the other gods. F.L.P.

Thorn, Conference of: Called by King Ladislaus IV of Poland in 1645 to prevent religious strife among Catholics, Lutherans and Reformed within his borders, this conference was conducted by foreign champions of each faith but accomplished nothing after three months of acrimonious bickerings except to worsen the lot of the Evangelicals in Poland and to embitter both Lutherans and Reformed against each other in Germany. E.C.K.

Thornwell, James Henley: (1812-1862) Theologian, Columbia (S. C.) Theological Seminary, 1855 onward. Moving spirit in organizing Presbyterian Church, U. S., 1861. Prodigious scholarship gained him Bancroft's commendation, "most learned of the learned." A.C.

Thoth: (Egyptian) Ibis god of ancient Egypt; god of wisdom, inventor of writing, patron of literature; moon god and chief minister of Re*, the sun god; in the myth of Osiris*, he separates the fighters, Horus and Set**, heals their wounds; he frees Osiris of grave accusations brought by Set. F.L.P.

Three Chapter controversy: An incident in the later stages of the Christological* controversies. In A.D. 544 the Emperor Justinian*, orthodox but theologically innocent, was persuaded by his crafty consort, Theodora, to issue an edict approving the "Three Chapters" (or formulated statements), in which the alleged errors of Theodoret* were drawn up along with those of the Nestorians*. This edict was violently resisted in the West, and thus broke out the Three Chapter Controversy, which was not brought to a close until the time of Gregory the Great*. The real centre of the controversy was Monophysitism*. See Constantinople, Councils of; Ibas; Theodore of Mopsuestia. A.K.R.

Three Children, Song of the: Fragment preserved in the Apocrypha*; a forty verse antiphonal psalm sung supposedly by Hananiah, Mishael, and Azariah when saved from the fiery furnace; an interpolation (written between 150 and 50 B.C.) which, with an independently interpolated "Prayer of Azariah" (28 verses) which precedes it, forms the "First Addition" to the canonical book of Daniel, inserted after Daniel 3:23 in Theodotion, Septuagint, Vulgate, and some versions dependent upon the Septuagint; absent in the Hebrew and Aramaic. See Apocrypha, Old Testament. See R. H. Charles, *Apocrypha* (1913). R.E.W.

thrice born: See conversion.

Thurneysen: Eduard: Protestant theologian. Born 1888 Wallenstatt, Switzerland. 1913 pastor in Leutwil, since 1927 preacher at the "Muenster" in Basel, 1927 privatdozent, 1939 professor of Practical Theology in Basel. Friend of Karl Barth* of old standing, and one of the originators of Dialectical* Theology. Indebted to the influence of Blumhardt Junior and Kutter. His literary activity is devoted to the practical-ecclesiastical rather than the purely theoretical problems of theology. Was co-editor of *Zwischen den Zeiten,* the magazine of the Barthian group.

Principal works:
Chr. Blumhardt (1926); *Dostojewski,* 2nd ed. (1930); *Das Wort Gottes und die Kirche* (1927); *Die Bergpredigt* (1936); *Die Verkündigung des Wortes Gottes in unserer Zeit* (1941). Volumes of sermons published jointly by Th. and K. Barth: *Suchet Gott sowerdet ihr leben* (1917, 2nd ed. 1929), Engl. tr.: *God's Search for Man* (1935); *Komm Schöpfer Geist* (1924, 2nd ed. 1929), Engl. tr.: *Come Holy Spirit* (1933); *Die grosse Barmherzigkeit* (1935). O.A.P.

Tiamat: (Semitic-Babylonian) Primeval waters; undifferentiated matter out of which gods and men, heaven and earth, sprang. In the Creation myth the primeval mother (Tiamat) linked with a primeval father (Apsu) as parents of the gods; at a later stage, Tiamat is overcome by Marduk* who cuts up her body: Marduk as god of life or light, and Tiamat the personification of the power of darkness and chaos. Tiamat is represented as chaotic waters, as a raging serpent, and as a monster dragon. Tiamat may personify the destructive flood waters of the Tigris and Euphrates; or personify the salt waters of the Gulf at the mouths of the rivers. The most advanced notion of Tiamat appears in the preface of the Cosmogonic Epic in which two waters, Apsu and Tiamat, by interaction brought the universe into existence. See cosmogonies. F.L.P.

tiara: The crown worn by the Pope* as a symbol of his sovereignty. The crown is round and cylindrical, having three tiers, representing his threefold power as Father of princes. Ruler of the world, and Vicar of Jesus Christ.
Cf. *Catholic Encyclopedia,* vol. XIV. S.C.

T'ien: See Chinese Terminology.

T'ien-t'ai School: See Buddhist Terminology.

timbre: The quality of a tone by which we distinguish one instrument or voice from another. This is determined by the shape of the sound wave. E.H.B.

time: (A.S. *tima,* akin to A.S. *tid*—origin of tide —and Dan. time, hour) As quantity, the "measure of change" (Aristotle); more generally, the system of relationships which change involves, such as before, after, and contemporary. Before and after are usually left undefined. However, Augustine* attempted to define them as follows: the past (or what is before the present event) is the remembered as such; the future, the anticipated as such. This makes time essentially psychological. Augustine inferred from this theory that time does not apply to God, but he seems not to have reflected sufficiently upon the fact that creaturely memory and anticipation seem far from coextensive with past and future, and that most of the past might be defined as that which we fail to remember (unless in deep subconsciousness). Only with a perfect memory could past and remembered be identical, and who unless God could enjoy such a memory?

The psychological theory explains the difference between before and after through the difference between memory and anticipation. The explanation can be carried further. Bergson, Whitehead**, and others hold that memory is awareness of the determinate and actual, while anticipation is awareness of the more or less indeterminate and potential. "Time is a species of objective modality." (Peirce*.) It is the way in which the actual or determined is related to the potential or indeterminate-determinable. "Time is creation or nothing." (Bergson.) Events become, but there is no corresponding unbecoming of events. A happening, once it has occurred, evermore or "immortally" has occurred (Whitehead). This modal or creation theory of time, when combined, as it has often been, with the psychological theory, implies that past events are somehow, by someone, remembered forever; but that future events are anticipated (even by Omniscience*) only as more or less indefinite possibilities, this being what they really are so long as future. (See Gerson, Levi ben.) The modal theory explains time's "arrow" (Eddington) or directional character, since it makes the basic temporal relations asymmetrical or irreversible. If *B* remembers *A* while *A* has no memory (conscious or unconscious feeling whose object is determinate) of *B,* then *A*'s actuality will be involved in *B*'s as its past, but *B's* actuality will not be involved in *A*'s. Thus the modal theory may also be called the "snowball" theory (Bergson).

Relations of contemporary things are defined by their symmetry or mutuality of involvement, either as mutually involving or mutually not involving each other. The latter or negative view is held by Whitehead and by relativity physics, according to which contemporaries are without effect on each other. Perhaps, however, there is such effect, but it is too slight or unsystematic to be verified in human perception and inference.

Ancient thought failed to state clearly either the psychological or the modal theory of time, and saw in change a puzzling and melancholy mixture of being and not-being. It was not observed that past events, at least, need not be classified as non-entities. Change, to have positive meaning, must involve creation of the previously unreal, but it need not involve destruction of any previous reality. Addition, though without subtraction, of reality is real change and sufficient for the reality of time. And though for human consciousness the past is for the most part no longer possessed, the psychological theory of time need not measure change by human psychology. The cosmos or God need not be so forgetful as man, whose mind is precisely not cosmic or divine. Thus the non-psychological or supposedly objective theory of time, in its usual form, has been perhaps unwittingly subjective in a peculiarly narrow sense, in that human forgetting was taken a proof of the unreality or cosmic forgottenness of past events.

Some objectivists (as Santayana) as well as some idealists suppose that future, past, and present events are all real in the same sense. But then time, or the order of change, is really the order of an unchanging totality, "all events", each of which, in its place in the totality, or in "eternity"* simply is, rather than becomes. This is the attempt to reduce becoming to mere being, to deny all difference in principle between memory and anticipation or between actuality and potency. It is a "spatialization" of time (Bergson) which explains it away.

The reality of time has been questioned on the ground that it involves contradictions. For example, it is held both necessary and impossible to conceive a first event of time. Some answer that a first event is conceivable, others that an actually infinite* past involves no strict inconceivability, although a kind of unimaginability. Again, it has been argued (by Bradley and McTaggart**) that, since an event which is before another event retains this position when both are in the past and already enjoyed it when both were in the future, the happening of the event changes nothing in its relationships and hence effects nothing and is unreal. The assumption is that future events are real and have real relations. The creation* theory denies this, holding that there are no determinate future events, and that what are called such are dates on the calendar*, or rather, items in the abstract schema which distinguishes the future as relatively indeterminate from the pure indeterminacy of possibility in general. An event comes into being as involving (remembering) earlier events, and thus as related to them, but such relations do not in their full determinateness exist in advance. Time is not a mere relation of becomings but a becoming of relations. The determinate present is related to the determinate past, not vice versa. We have to do with George Washington as an individual; he had not and (unless in heaven) still has not to do with us as individuals but only as the vague class, "my (Washington's) posterity." Washington is past to us not because we do not have his full actuality as content of our present awareness, but because, so far as we are aware of him, it is as having nothing to do with us while we do have to do with him. Were we to retain him in our awareness ever so perfectly, he would still be past to this awareness so long as his non-relationship to it was given. What is past is not what is unreal now but what, as real now, does not contain in its nature the relationships in which it stands. These belong to the present as such, which alone stands in no relations except those which it intrinsically involves.

The denial that the past is real now implies that statements ascribing determinate characters to past events cannot be true, for truth is correspondence to the real. The inactuality of the future means that statements ascribing wholly determinate characters to it are all false. (See Gerson, Levi ben.)

Even so destructive an agency as war does not remove from actuality any events actually elapsed or any experiences actually experienced, but only cuts off the hope of certain additional experiences which otherwise might have been enjoyed. The vast scope of human forgetting, by a natural anthropomorphism*, tends to make us feel that the values of the present, as apparently not containing those of the past, plus the values of the near future, make up almost the sum of values to be taken into account. This anxious absorption in the present and near future may be the real "defect" of "temporal" existence of which Berdyaev* and so many have complained, but it is a defect of human temporality not of temporality as such. To dismiss time as of merely creaturely concern without exploring the possibility of a super-creaturely form of time is as illegitimate as to deny personality to God merely because creaturely personality, like creaturely anything, is imperfect. (See analogy; God as personal).

If all experience is indestructible, then, as is often said, we are immortal not just in the future but in our present being. Our present self-realization contributes to the real not some deposit or mere effect, it contributes itself. If there be a divine form of temporality, such that God is able to receive new content, then our "service" to him is to become, and help our fellows to become, as precious additions to the divine being as possible. A purely timeless God could receive no additions and could not in any way be served or advantaged. The history of theology must have been vastly different than it has been had the modal-psychological theory of time been clearly thought of two thousand or even five hundred years before Bergson.

See cycles of time; Zurvan.

Augustine, *Confessions*; A. N. Whitehead, *Adventures of Ideas* (1933); DeWitt H. Parker, *Experience and Substance* (1941); C. D. Broad, *Mind and its Place in Nature* (1925). (The last gives a criticism of the type of theory set forth above.)

C.H.

Timothy, First and Second Letters to: Of these two Epistles the Second is probably the earlier, and is certainly the finer and more valuable. It purports to be written by Paul on the eve of his martyrdom at Rome to his assistant Timothy at Ephesus, and offers him counsels and warnings to aid him in the future conduct of the Christian mission. Second Timothy, is not so much a letter as a manual of church order, although it also contains passages of great importance for Christian ethic and theology.

I and II Timothy (along with Titus), in their present form, may be dated about 120 A.D.

See Pastoral Epistles.

W. Lock, *A Critical and Exegetical Commentary on the Pastoral Epistles* (ICC, 1924); E. F. Scott, *The Literature of the New Testament* (1932).

E.F.S.

Tindal, Matthew: See deism; Enlightenment, the.

Tischendorf, Lobegott Friedrich Constantin von: (1815-1874) Distinguished German discoverer of N.T. manuscripts, most notably the Codex Sinaiticus;* and editor of the Greek text of the O.T., the N.T., and the N.T. Apocrypha. His 8th large critical edition of the Greek N.T. (1869-72), though too much influenced by the Codex Sinaiticus, is still indispensable, for its immense apparatus of variant readings. E.J.G.

tithes: A tithe is a tenth part, specifically, in the Bible, a tenth part of ones produce set aside for a religious purpose. At different times it was 1) brought by the worshiper to the sanctuary and there consumed by him, 2) delivered as a charity to the needy, and 3) paid as dues to the priests and Levites. S.H.B.

Titius, Arthur: (1864-1936) He was professor in Kiel, Göttingen and Berlin. Greatly interested in social questions, he took pains to study the philosophical basis of the natural sciences and to achieve the correct relationship to the natural sciences, which he brilliantly mastered in all fields, and which he opened for theology.

Religion und Naturwissenschaft (Tübingen u. Leipzig, 1904); *Recht und Schranken des Evolutionismus in der Ethik* (Berlin, 1910); "Psychiatrie und Ethik" in *Studien z. systematischen Theologie. Theodor von Haering zum 70. Geburtstag . . . dargebracht.* (Tübingen, 1918). H.H.

Titus, Epistle to: A letter which purports to be written by Paul to Titus, whom he had left behind him in Crete, to follow up a mission which he had himself begun. Along with counsels of a more general nature for the right ordering of a Christian community, the Epistle pays special attention to heresy, which in Crete had become a growing evil. The Pauline authorship of Titus is more than doubtful, since there is no place in the known career of Paul for a sojourn in Crete. He can only have written the letter if he was set free from his Roman imprisonment and resumed his missionary work on new ground. The Epistle (along with I and II Timothy), in its present form, may be dated about 120 A.D. See Pastoral Epistles.

W. Lock, *A Critical and Exegetical Commentary on the Pastoral Epistles* (ICC, 1924); E. F. Scott, *The Literature of the New Testament* (1932). E.F.S.

Tobit: An Apocryphal book, probably composed originally in Aramaic cir. 200 B.C. by a pious Egyptian Jew, and the name of its central figure. See apocrypha, Old Testament. S.H.B.

tokens: Small metal disks, often oval in shape, that were distributed by the elders in the Scottish church to those of the members who were qualified to participate in the Communion service. They were returned by the members at the service and thus enabled the session to check on attendance. A.K.R.

Toland, John: (1670-1722) For him there is nothing in Christian doctrine either against or above reason. Reason alone convinces men of the inspiration of the Scriptures. Neither the account of creation nor miracles are contrary to reason. Toland justifies a nature religion, which he terms pantheism*, a term first coined by him. See deism; Enlightenment, the.

G. Berthold, *John Toland und der Monismus der Gegenwart* (Heidelberg, 1876); G. V. Lechler, *Geschichte des englischen Deismus* (Stuttgart und Tübingen, 1841); J. M. Robertson, *Short History of Free Thought*, 2 vols. (London, 1899); A. Seeber, *John Toland als politischer Schriftsteller* (Schramberg (Württemberg), 1933). H.H.

Toledo, Creed of: A creed elaborated in one of the eighteen councils of Toledo (400-702), especially the creed of the Eleventh Council (675) which was directed against Priscillianism*. E.A.R.

toleration: See religious liberty.

Toleration, Act of: (1689) Originally limited to Trinitarian Protestants, but significant as marking the end of the effort to maintain complete religious uniformity in England. E.R.H.

Tolstadius, Erik: (1693-1759) An early leader in Swedish pietism. His Stockholm church became a spiritual center in the capitol, his preaching and counselling attracting eager followers. Though influenced by Dippel, Tolstadius maintained an independent attitude towards more radical pietism, and gave no support to the Zinzendorf* movement. C.J.B.

Tolstoy, Leo: (1828-1910) Russian social reformer and prolific writer. He is known for his Christian anarchistic ideas and his life of renunciation. See anarchism. V.F.

(Tomlinson) Church of God: A pentecostal holiness sect with headquarters at Cleveland, Tenn. Its early history corresponds with that of the Church of God* but a division occurred in 1922 and the group adhering to the principles of the general overseer, A. J. Tomlinson, added his name to the title to distinguish the group. The census reports 441 churches and 18,000 members. See pentecostal sects. E.T.C.

tonality: The sense of key. The relationship of tones both melodically and harmonically to a central fixed tone. Whereas the modes* had tonal centers, the relationships of other tones to them were melodic and not harmonic. When the harmonic relationship became apparent in the 17th century, tonality assumed its complete modern meaning.

J. Yasser, *Theory of Evolving Tonality* (1932). E.H.B.

tongues, gifts of: According to Luke (Ac. 2: 4 ff.,) this gift consisted in a power to speak in foreign languages, previously unknown. Paul, however, discusses the subject at length in I Cor. 12 and 14, and makes it clear that the language spoken was a succession of unmeaning sounds, improvised in a state of ecstasy*. These sounds were often so varied that they gave the impression of a regular language, which would be intelligible to some race which used it. The phenomenon is one that has often manifested itself in religious revivals, and the listeners have been convinced that they heard articulate speech. Luke, apparently, thought of the tongues in this manner. Paul, who himself possessed the gift in a pre-eminent degree, is aware that the sounds convey nothing to human ears, but still believes that they represent a heavenly language,—the tongues of angels (I Cor. 13:1) which the Spirit would naturally employ. Modern psychology would say that the ecstatic, seeking an outlet for emotions for which he could find no words, falls back on a language intelligible only to himself. See charismata; pentecostal sects.

G. B. Cutten, *Speaking With Tongues* (1927).

E.F.S.

tonsure: (Lat., *tonsura,* a shearing) A ceremony initiating one into the clerical state, which consists in cutting the subject's hair. The custom dates from the earliest years of Christianity, and signifies renunciation of the world. It confers no power. W.H.

Tophet (or Topheth): Altar of human sacrifice, outside Jerusalem in Valley of Hinnom, where children were laid in the red hot arms of Molech; most famous and most abominable of the idolatries practiced there; popularized, and possibly introduced, by King Manasseh; destroyed by Josiah (620 B.C.) but apparently rebuilt; vigorously condemned by Jeremiah; symbol of paganism; since Milton, a synonym for Hell. See Manasseh.

R.E.W.

topological psychology: See psychology, schools of.

Torah: A Hebrew word, the basic meaning of which seems to have been "casting (of the sacred lot)" in oracular divination. As the religion of Israel and subsequent Judaism evolved, the word acquired a steadily expanding connotation; oracle, the content of divine revelation, a single divinely revealed law, then the entire body of divinely revealed law, and, finally, the total content of God's unending revelation to and through Israel. This last is its specific meaning in its broadest sense, as it is employed in modern Jewish literature. In a narrower sense, Torah designates the first five books of the Bible, the so-called Pentateuch* or five Books of Moses, in which, according to orthodox Jewish doctrine, all the laws revealed by God to Moses* are contained. Torah designates likewise the scroll, upon which these five books are written, always by the hand of a trained scribe, at least one copy of which is deposited in the ark* in every Jewish synagogue, and from which sections are read in regular order at the religious services throughout the Jewish calendar.

See O.T.; tables of the law; law, Hebrew. Cf. Jubilees, Book of; Talmud. J.M.

Torgau Articles: A statement of the reasons for the abolition of ecclesiastical abuses, drawn up at the request of Elector John of Saxony in March, 1530, by Melanchthon* in collaboration with Luther, Jonas, and Bugenhagen. This document, discovered in the Weimar archives in 1830, is important only as a source of the Augsburg Confession*, in the second part of which its content is substantially reproduced. It is printed in English translation in H. E. Jacobs, *Book of Concord,* II (1883). T.A.K.

Torrey, Joseph: (1797-1866) Graduated Dartmouth College 1816, Andover 1819. Professor of Intellectual and Moral Philosophy, University of Vermont; President of the University 1862-1866; continued the philosophy of James Marsh*.

Author: *A Theory of Art;* translator of Neander's *General History of the Christian Religion and Church* (1847-1854), 5 vols.; (republished in London and Edinburgh).

Henry A. P. Torrey (a nephew of Joseph Torrey), professor of Philosophy in the University of Vermont 1868-1902, also represented the Marsh, or "Burlington" school of philosophy and was a teacher of rare insight. He was author of *Selections from the Works of Descartes* (1892) and of a series of articles on "The Theodicèe of Leibnitz" (*Andover Review,* Vol. IV). J.W.B.

Tosefta: The word *Tosefta,* (literally, "additions") is used primarily to describe a Rabbinic work, apparently compiled in the third century, but containing traditions much older, and put into writing much later. This work contains material which supplements the Mishna* or authoritative code of Jewish law established by Rabbi Judah I the Patriarch and his colleagues early in the third century. Inevitably, the scholars who formulated the Mishna were compelled to exclude from it a mass of material which was relevant and important. This was studied and memorized by special students, and part of it was collected by scholars of the day as Tosefta. Other parts are included in other Rabbinic works, such as the Mekilta, the Sifra, the Sifre, etc. The word, *Tosefta* is also used sometimes to denote additions to other works than the Mishna, but in this sense it is rare.

L.F.

total depravity: See depravity.

totemism: (Ojibwa, *ototeman,* brother-sister kinship) Belief in totems and totemistic relationships; extends usually to limits of the tribe; a system of distinguishing families, by which privileges and obligations of individuals concerning marriage, protection, food supply, etc., are fixed; originally applied to the American Indians, later to counterpart systems all over the world, and particularly among certain contemporary primitives. See animals, worship of; fasting; food; primitive religion; spirits. F.L.P.

Tower of Babel: (A word related to the Hebrew "Balal" to confound) Name of a tower . . . built by the peoples of Shinar (Babylonia) as recounted in Genesis 11 . . . in an attempt to reach heaven . . . therefore God "confounded" them so that each spoke a different language and scattered them over the face of the earth.

N.G.

tract: The only division of the chant* that represents direct psalmody in the mass. Originally for a soloist, the melody is ornate and florid. See plainsong; psalmody. E.H.B.

tract movement: See religious tract movement.

tract periodicals: See religious tract movement.

tract, religious, movement in the U. S.: See religious tract movement in the U. S.

Tractarianism: A name given to the principles set forth in *Tracts for the Times* (1833-41), a series of ninety pamphlets issued by the early leaders of the Oxford Movement*. See Anglo-Catholics. L.W.C.

tradition: See culture; folklore.

tradition, Roman Catholic: The sum of revealed truths pertaining to faith and morals, not consigned to Scripture, but transmitted by God by word of mouth to the Church. (Denziger n. 783) In the strict theological sense Tradition is a source of revelation having equal authority with Sacred Scripture. Its complexus of truths has come from God through the words of Christ or through the Apostles inspired by the Holy Spirit. Its content is all that revealed truth which has not been written down in Scripture. An infallible teaching body, the Church, defines through the Pope and in general councils and in its universal ordinary doctrine which truths are contained in Tradition. The chief source is the unanimous declarations of early Christian writers. C.R.

traditionalism: (Lat., *traditio,* fr. *tradere,* to give up, transmit)

1) Specifically, a 19th Cent. philosophical point of view developed within the Catholic Church (but soon repudiated by it) under the literary leadership of F. R. de Lamennais*, and subsequently centering at Louvain, according to which, because of the untrustworthiness of individual reason, faith in revelation mediated through the traditions of mankind is the only channel of truth.

2) In general the appeal to, or apotheosis of, tradition as normative and authoritative above modern discovery and criticism; chiefly, therefore, a liberal term of reproach. The R. C. Church makes much of tradition but would repudiate the charge of traditionalism on the ground that the Church itself is the locus of authority*, with reason as confirmatory and independently valid for fundamental metaphysical truths. Anglo-Catholicism has formulated the norm of Christian truth in terms of tradition, i.e., the witness of the undivided Church (before the Schism of 1054), but counts itself as entirely open to new scientific knowledge and insight, hence refusing to accept the negative connotation of traditionalism. See *Northern Catholicism* (London, 1933), ed. by N. P. Williams and Chas. Harris. Protestant Fundamentalism and Jewish Orthodoxy** are commonly accepted as traditionalist. E.T.R.

traducianism: The view that the soul of a child is generated from the souls of its parents. The view first appears in the thought of Tertullian*. V.F.

Traherne, Thomas: (1636?-1674) English poet and prose writer. Living the life of an obscure Anglican clergyman, Traherne was known two hundred years after his death only for a few unimportant essays. His *Poems* were first published in 1903, his prose *Centuries of Meditations* in 1908. The former compare favorably with the work of Herbert and Vaughan**; the latter, revealing the author even more clearly as a man of original mind and deep spiritual insight, are a valuable addition to the literature of devotion. L.W.C.

transcendence: (Lat., *trans,* across; *scandare,* to climb) Used especially for the superiority and independence of deity, and in contrast to immanence*. But the two may be so defined as to be capable of inhering in the same being. God* may be both "in" and "beyond" the world. If he is merely beyond, then he is not in; if merely in, then not beyond; but remove the merely, and he may be both. Sheer transcendence, God merely outside the world, suggests that the world is equally outside God, sheer separation being a mutual relation. Transcendence would thus not be unique to deity. But non-exclusive transcendence, God both in and beyond things, may be non-mutual and unique; for things may be in God yet not beyond him. If so, he is whole and they are parts (see panentheism); and if the things are contingent, God will have accidents. But he may also have an essence which is purely necessary, and this may be "in" the world while the world is not in it. (What is as a whole accidental may yet involve a necessary part or factor; but the necessary factor can contain no accident.) A necessary essence may be beyond the world, in the sense of being independent of just what world exists. God as both essence and accidents contains the world, but even in his accidental aspect is beyond it in being a whole greater than the parts through an over-all integrity or "whole-quality" (Wertheimer) that expresses, not just the world, but himself as possessing the world. Thus the transcendence of the divine essence is abstract (see perfection), the world being external to it; the transcendence of God's total being, essence and accidents, is concrete, the world and all reality being internal to it. The one is mere Cause, abstracting from all effects; the other is Cause-with-effects.

The denial of abstract or essential transcendence is what many mean by "pantheism". Such denial destroys freedom and self-identity in God; for he then has no essential nature independent of the world, just as it is, and either all difference between what is and what might be disappears, since all is necessary, or else all is contingent, and God may become utterly undivine at any moment (where nothing is necessary, anything may happen).

The denial of concrete transcendence might be called deism* (but most traditional "theism" would have to be so classified). This denial destroys the inclusiveness of God. God-and-the-world becomes a whole which is more than God —for how, on the assumption, can it be less, or merely equal to him? Concrete transcendence banishes the paradox by identifying "God and the world" with "God in his total being", in which total being the world is included as content of the divine knowledge and love. The insistence of religion upon the superiority of God is not more marked than its teaching that we are within, not outside, his "love and care." If it be said that this does not mean, within his reality, it must be replied that then either God's love and care are not parts of his reality, or else their direct objects are entirely external to the love and care which embraces them. It hardly seems that the infallible adequacy of God's awareness to its objects is compatible with such externality.

Transcendence and immanence have abstract and concrete aspects thanks to which the seeming mutual opposition between the two disappears in a complementary contrast. Not only is God both in and beyond the world, but the world is both outside of and within God; for it is not involved in his necessary essence, but is in his total being as also accidental. The world is not beyond God; for where it is, there is he; whereas he is where the world is not, for example, actually in some other, say, earlier world, and potentially in some other possible world.

See infinite; omnipresence; pantheism; theism.

R. A. Tsanoff, *Religious Crossroads* (1942); A. N. Whitehead, *Process and Reality* (1929), last chapter; G. T. Fechner, *Zendavesta* (1851), chap. 11.

C.H.

transcendentalism, New England: A name applied to the doctrines of a philosophic and literary group centering in Concord, Massachusetts (c. 1836-60), of which Emerson*, Thoreau, Alcott, and Margaret Fuller were representative members. Although its strongest impulse came from Kantian idealism, it was broadly eclectic, owing much to Platonic and Oriental influences as well as to the Unitarian reaction against Calvinism. Reliance on intuition and an extreme optimism regarding human nature were characteristic tenets.

See H. C. Goddard, *Studies in New England Transcendentalism* (1908).

L.W.C.

transept: (Lat., *trans septum,* enclosure) The transverse part of a church, usually at the entrance of the choir* and projecting beyond the sides of the building.

F.T.P.

transfiguration: The incident described in Mark 9:2-8 and Synoptic parallels. As Mark narrates it, the story describes a divine confirmation of Jesus' Messiahship, despite the fact that He has to suffer. In vs. 9 Mark adds that the disciples were charged to keep what they had seen a secret until after the resurrection. Perhaps the story originally belonged to the cycle of resurrection* narratives and has been moved forward by Mark to become an incident in the earthly life of Jesus. Mark wishes to assert that three intimate followers, even during Jesus' lifetime, knew Him as the glorified Son of God, a fact that was hidden from others until after the resurrection.

S.M.G.

translatio imperii: The medieval theory that the power of the ancient empire was authoritatively transferred to the medieval empire. The papal claim was that this was effected by action of the papacy in the latter's exercise of its divinely bestowed authority in things temporal.

A. Dempf, *Sacrum Imperium, Geschicts-und Staatsphilosophie des Mittelalters* (1929).

J.T.M.

translations of the Bible: See Bible, English; modern translations; versions of the Bible, ancient; targum.

transmigration: Rebirth of a soul* at death in another body. There is a tendency to use the word reincarnation for rebirth in another body of the same species, especially the human. Transmigration has the broader meaning of passage back and forth across the boundaries of all forms —plant, animal, human, demonic and divine. The origin of the idea is obscure. Early and pre-literate cultures had such concepts as of the multiple souls of a man residing in animals, the appearance of the dead to survivers in animal form at the grave or near their old home, the return of an ancestor in a new-born child. Yet belief in transmigration does not seem to have grown from such seed ideas. Since it flourished chiefly in late and higher cultures, it may have emerged as a satisfying way of binding the idea of personal survival of death to moral responsibility.

Transmigration is a fundamental idea in Hindu* thought. The *Vedas* know nothing of it, but the creators of the *Brāhmanas* began to be troubled by the idea of repeated deaths. Coupled with *Karma**, the inexorable law which made each birth depend upon previous deeds, it set the problem for all religious philosophies for twenty-five centuries—how to escape the wheel of eternally recurring birth and death. The stream of lives is beginningless and rolls on forever unless broken by an effective method of salvation. The *Charvakas** alone of all India's thinkers refused to accept the idea. The Buddhists* denied the existence of a soul but did not question transmigration. They explained that the *skandhas* of a dying being created an "intermediary being" which entered the womb to create the *skandhas* of the new being.

The Orphics and Pythagoreans** taught transmigration. Plato and Platonism were attracted by the belief but it was not essential to their philosophies. In Greece the imprisoning of souls in bodies had a retributive purpose. In India good and evil deeds alike bound the soul on the wheel. Since release was the ultimate goal, it was no gain to merit rebirth as a god. The *Zohar** tried to weave the idea of transmigration into Judaism but beyond the Kabbala* had no lasting effect upon Jewish thought.

Man's hope of building an ever-perfecting culture on the earth makes reincarnation more attractive than immortality* as a theory of future life for some minds. See samsara.

A.E.H.

transubstantiation: (Lat., *trans,* across or over and *substantia,* substance) The word officially used since the Council of Trent* to express the changing of the substance of bread and of wine into the substance of the Body and the Blood of Christ, the accidents of bread and of wine remaining. See Lateran Councils; Radbertus. Cf. remanence.

L.R.W.

Trappists: Popular name for the Cistercian Reform of de Rance, inaugurated in the Abbey of

La Trappe in the seventeenth century. When the primitive rigor of the Cistercians* had waxed cold, the blame could be laid at the feet of inconstant abbots, the contemporary political scene, and human weakness. Reforms had taken place in France, Spain, Germany, Italy, and Portugal, but these were always very limited in scope. The reform inaugurated by de Rance however attained eminent stature. From the Abbey's location at La Trappe the Reformed Cistercians became known as Trappists. W.H.

Traub, Friedrich: (1860-) He taught at the University of Tübingen. As a neo-Kantian*, he was a devoted Ritschlian* who did much for the spread and development of the Ritschlian movement.

Theologie und Philosophie (Tübingen, 1910); *Glaube und Geschichte* (Gotha, 1926). H.H.

treason: A breach of allegiance to or attack upon the safety of the government or head of the state to which one owes loyalty. It is a high crime in all nations and is usually punishable by the severest measures. R.W.F.

treasury of merits: The merits of Christ and the saints. See Thesaurus Meritorum. L.R.W.

trees, sacred: The O.T. story of man begins with a garden and two sacred trees (Gen. 2:9). Abraham frequented the Oaks of Mamre (Gen. 13:18; 14:13). The burning bush was the place of Moses'* sense of God's presence. Deborah held court under her palm tree (Judges 4:5). The struggle of the Hebrews against the old Canaanitish religion was against their groves, high hills which concealed their venerated places.

Religion abounds with an amazing variety of practices in the treatment of sacred trees. In the earliest savage cults, a belief in tree spirits is found. Mythologies are replete with tree cults, and the sculpture and the decorative arts of ancient cultures carry the theme of the life-giving fertility of the tree. For the tree symbolizes both living vitality and the fellowship with nature for the worshiper. Buddha's* conversion under the Bohdi tree provided a link thereafter between the Buddha's followers and the living Bo tree. Throughout Europe, once covered with great forests, tribes had their sacred trees. When a daring Irish monk brought Christianity to the Saxons in the 8th century, his first act was to cut down their sacred tree. The oak tree was especially sacred among the Greeks, the Celts and Germans.

Sacred trees may be the abode of deities or may be the divine beings themselves. Thus, they are treated as human beings, appealed to by voice and offering, threatened if not fruitful, married to other trees, treated with great respect as taboo. The social value of tree cults was to increase respect for trees, insure their preservation. Among some tribes no tree was cut down without offering a prayer to the tree spirit. The deer parks in Japan around her shrines represent a deep veneration for trees, which has been socially beneficial to the nation in preservation of forests and of the beauty of their valleys. See yggd-rasil. M.L.C.

Trench, Richard Chevenix: (1807-1886) Anglican Archbishop of Dublin. Apart from several collections of poems, he is best known for studies in N.T. and etymological questions both Greek and English. An Irishman by birth, most of his ministry was passed in that country. W.N.P.

Trent, Council of: According to Roman Catholics the nineteenth ecumenical council of the Catholic Church, it formulated the Church's reply to the Protestant Reformation. With interruptions of about three and ten years it lasted from December 13, 1545 to December 4, 1563.

Luther had appealed to a general council, stipulating that it should be held north of the Alps. The popes were afraid of an assembly so far from Rome. Trent, an imperial German city but located south of the Brenner Pass, was suggested as a compromise. Protestants were, however, represented at the Council only briefly. Italy, Spain, France and Germany sent the largest delegations. Only during intervals of peace in the war between Spain and France could the Council meet.

The papal bulls summoning the Council fix as its principal aims the elimination of religious disunity caused by the Protestant secession and the reformation of morals. In its dogmatic decisions the Council refrained from deciding points controverted in Catholic schools and limited itself to rejecting specifically Protestant tenets. Dogmatic tradition as well as Holy Scripture was declared a source of faith and the Vulgate was held authentic in matters of doctrine. The doctrine of original sin was defined. Justification by faith alone and the intrinsic corruption of fallen man were rejected. Finally, many Protestant doctrines on the Sacraments* were anathematized. The principal disciplinary decrees of the Council concerned the obligation of residence of bishops and priests, the training of priests, the reform of religious orders and the reform of Church finance. In general these decrees were characterized by prudence rather than by rigor. Although not accepted by all Catholic rulers, the decisions of the Council played an important rôle in the revival of Catholicism in the sixteenth century. See canons of various churches; Catholic Reformation; Confessions, Formal of the Christian Church; versions of the Bible, ancient: Latin Vulgate.

Sources of the Council are in course of publication in *Concilium Tridentinum,* 12 volumes incomplete (1901-1938); cf. P. Richard, *Concile de Trente* (1930-1931) and A. Michel, *Les Décrets du Concile de Trente* (1938), both in Hefele-Leclercq, *Histoire des Conciles* (1907-1938). E.A.R.

triad, Babylonian (An, Enlil, Enki): See Mesopotamian religions.

triad, Buddhist: See Buddhist Terminology.

triad, Christian: See Trinity.

triad, Hindu, the: See s.v. Vishnu; Trimūrti.

triad, Norse: See s.v. Odin or Odhin.

Triad Society: See Chinese religions.

triad, Taoist: See San-ch'ing under Chinese Terminology.

triad, Zoroastrian: See s.v. Sraosha.

triads: (Gr. *trias, triados,* a group of three) Groups or unions of three Gods. There is a tendency in religious history for the gods to be grouped in threes, except when opposed by a contradictory principle, such as that of one sole God, as in Judaism, Christianity and Mohammedanism. Even in Christianity, the Trinity* of the Father, Son and Holy Ghost reflects the underlying tendency. In India, the great Triad include Brahma, the Creator, Vishnu, the Preserver and Shiva**, the Destroyer. These represent the cycle of existence, just as the Babylonian triad of Anu, Enlil and Ea represent the materials of existence, air, water, earth. While no satisfactory explanation for the formulation of triads has been given, it need not be regarded as mysterious. There seems to be a similar tendency toward conceiving of one god, two gods, four gods. In Christian history, the Virgin was gradually added to the Trinity in popular religion and in art. In China, it was the balance of heaven and earth, yang and yin*, darkness and light, which needed to be maintained. Or it was the rhythm of the four seasons, the four cardinal directions, for which their pantheon was arranged. M.L.C.

tribal God: A deity who is worshiped by and considered as the patron of a particular tribe, especially among nomadic peoples. Some of the tribes who made up the Hebrew nation originally worshiped such deities. It is possible that Jahveh* was originally the god of one or more of the Hebrew tribes. See gods. J.P.H.

tribal personality: See corporate personality.

trichotomy: See soul.

Tridentine Profession of Faith: The profession of faith, prescribed by Pius IV in 1564 to meet the requirements of the Council of Trent*, is a full and definite statement of the Catholic faith on those points particularly which were assailed in the sixteenth century. See Confessions, Formal of the Christian Church. E.A.R.

triduum: (Latin *tres,* three; *dies* day) A period of three days chosen for special prayer or devotion for the preparation or celebration of a feast. S.C.

Trimurti: The Hindu triad of gods, Brahma, the creator, Vishnu, the preserver, and Shiva** the destroyer. C.S.B.

trine immersion: A mode of baptism* wherein the candidate is immersed three times successively in the name of the Father and of the Son and of the Holy Spirit. It is based on the formula of Mt. 28:19 and early Patristic writings, practised widely in the Eastern Church and by several groups in the West such as the Dunkers*, and is recognized universally as a valid form. See baptism, non Christian. W.M.B.

Trinitarians: The Order of the Holy Trinity, founded in 1198 during the crusading* period to secure the release of Christian captives taken by the infidels. Originally regularized as canons according to St. Augustine, the religious have, since their seventeenth-century recognition as mendicant* friars, distinguished themselves by diversified, social contributions. R.C.P.

Trinity: The doctrine, accepted as a dogma by all Catholic and Eastern Orthodox Christians and by the principal Protestant Churches, that God is one in being (or substance), power, and majesty, but subsists eternally in three co-equal, perfect persons or hypostases, to which are appropriated respectively the individual names Father, Son or Word (*Logos*), and Holy Spirit. This doctrine received full expression for the first time as the result of the work of the Cappadocian Fathers so-called (see Cappadocians, the three), Basil, Gregory of Nyssa, and Gregory Nazianzus**. It was given formal statement in the synodical letter of a council held in Constantinople* A.D. 382—preserved by Theodoret*, *Historia Ecclesiastica,* v. 9 (Eng. tr., *Nicene and Post-Nicene Fathers,* Series II, Vol. XIV). The Constantinopolitan formulation may be taken as the definitive theological statement of the doctrine. The religious formula of the Trinity—that God is to be believed in and worshiped as both one and three—is implicit in the N.T. adherence, on the one hand, to Hebraic Monotheism (the *shema** of Israel) and, on the other, to the distinct religious significance of Jesus Christ "The Lord", "The Only—begotten Son", and of the Spirit, "another Comforter." Recognizing, as modern scholarship does, the reality of development and of organic process in Christian doctrine and the presence of this factor in the N.T. period as well as later, it is in the highest degree remarkable that a work as early as *the Gospel according to St. Matthew* should associate with Baptism an explicit Trinitarian formula. This fact proved determinative for the structure of the Creed of Nicea A.D. 325 and the Creed commonly called the Apostles'*. It informed the theological work of the Ante-Nicene Fathers, of whom the most important in the development of the doctrine of the Trinity are Ignatius, Irenaeus, Tertullian, and Origen**. Tertullian first used the Western formula *una substantia, tres personae.* To the acute heresiarch Sabellius* is to be credited the elimination for the first time of every vestige of subordination in thinking of the three persons, while to Apollinarius (heretical only on the person of Christ) and to St. Athanasius** the Cappadocians mainly owed their conversion from Semi-Arianism (*homoiousion to patri*) to the Nicene position.

In the West from the time of St. Augustine* (fl. A.D. 400) a distinctive approach to the ideas alike of Deity in general and of the Trinity prevailed. God was conceived of in personal and concrete terms. Psychological categories were brought into the service of theology. This is the background of the Augustinian construction of the persons of the Trinity as inner relations or aspects of the one Divine being, the living and personal God. These relations are however self-subsistent and equal respectively to the Divine essence in its fulness, since in God there is nothing partitive but only perfect simplicity. Thus for St. Augustine the Word or Son is eternally generated as the object of thought in the Divine mind, while the Holy Spirit proceeds eternally as love by the act of the Divine will. This treatment is normative for Scholasticism*. St. Thomas in his "Treatise on the Trinity" in the *Summa Theologica** does little more than expand it and give it a systematic exposition.

The two principal developments of Trinitarian thought in modern times are to be found in the philosophical system of Hegel* and in the attempt to think of God as in Himself a Divine Society. The first is a variant of the psychological approach in the form which its analysis of Divine being takes. It differs sharply from the Augustinian-scholastic theory in making the evolutionary advance of nature and progression of history organic to the dialectical process in which the Divine self-consciousness is itself constituted and eternally realized. The second modern development, which may be called the social interpretation of the Trinity, is not strictly new. Adumbrations of it can be found in the great Gnostic heresiarch Valentinus* (Hippolytus, *Ref.*, VI. 24), in St. Augustine's analysis of the sentence, "God is Love" (*De Trin.*, vi. 7, viii. 14, ix. 2), in Richard of St. Victor* (fl. A.D. 1160), and in the learned Bishop Bull (*Works*, II, p. 9). Yet in the characteristic recent elaborations of such an idea, in which *persona* is deliberately equated with personality or ego (C. F. D'Arcy, F. J. Hall) and God is declared to be in His innermost being an Eternal Society or Family (Fairbairn, Illingworth, Geo. A. Gordon), it cannot be doubted that we have to do with a socially conditioned facet of modernism. It can hardly be doubted further that this general development goes beyond traditional Catholic doctrine. With Tennant* it must be admitted that experience yields no analogy which quite fits the Catholic and Reformation doctrine of relations which are yet substantive "persons." It is perhaps at this point that the Cappadocians, with their attempt to hold one being (*ousia*) from the standpoint of internal analysis but three objective hypostases or individual subsistences or modes of existence, have a permanent contribution. See creeds of Christendom; filioque; procession of the Holy Spirit; subordinationism; tritheism. See also Greek terms.

Select Bibliography—Historical: F. C. Baur, *Die Christliche Lehre von der Dreieinigkeit*, 3 vols. (Tübingen, 1841-3); J. A. Dorner, *Hist. Doct. Person of Christ*, Engl. tr., 5 vols. (1872); A. von Harnack, *Hist. Dogma*, Engl. tr., 7 vols. (1894-9); F. Loofs, *Leitfaden*, 4th ed. (1906); J. LeBreton, *Histoire du Dogme de la Trinité* (Tomes I and II, 1910, 1928); *Essays Trinity and Incarnation*, ed. A. E. J. Rawlinson (1928); G. L. Prestige, *God in Patristic Thought* (1936). General: C. Gore, *Incarnation of Son of God* (1891) and later works; A. M. Fairbairn, *Place of Christ . . .* (1893); J. R. Illingworth, *Personality Hum. and Div.* (1894) and later works; G. A. Gordon, *Ult. Conceptions of Faith* (1903); F. J. Hall, *The Trinity* (1910); C. C. J. Webb, *God & Personality* (1919); W. Temple, *Christ the Truth* (1924); A. E. Garvie, *Christian Doct. Godhead* (1925); H. Rashdall, *God and Man* (1930); F. R. Tennant, *Phil. Theol.*, II (1930); N. Micklem, *What is the Faith?* (1936). C.W.L.

Trinity Sunday and Season: The Feast of the Trinity*, observed on the Sunday after Pentecost* in various places from the 10th cent., was extended to the whole Latin Church in the 14th (in the Eastern Orthodox Church the Trinity is specially honored at Pentecost). In various north-European uses (continued in Anglican and Lutheran Prayer Books) it replaced Whitsunday* as the Sunday after which Sundays were numbered till Advent*. See church year cycle. E.R.H.

trisagion: (Gr., *treis*, three; *hagios*, holy) 1) The antiphonal chant of the angels in the inaugural vision of Isaiah (6:3), invoking God as thrice holy. It forms the basis of the Kedushah (Sanctification) in the morning and afternoon liturgy of the Synagogue. It is used in the Eastern and Western Churches, and is known also as Sanctus, Ter Sanctus, Cantus or Hymnus Seraphicus or Cherubicus and Hymnus Gloriae. 2) It designates specifically the short hymn of the Greek Christian liturgies: "Holy God, Holy and Mighty, Holy and Immortal, have mercy upon us", dating from the reign of Theodosius II (408-50) or from the fourth cent. It appears also in the Roman Missal for Good Friday. S.S.C.

tritheism (Gr., *tri*, three; *theos*, god) Literally, the view that there are three gods, often attributed to Christianity by those who have not understood the Doctrine of the Trinity*, but probably never intentionally held by a Christian theologian. The charge of tritheism has occasionally been made within the Church against extreme interpretations of the Trinitarian doctrine, e.g., in the 6th Cent., the view of John Philopon that the three hypostases must mean three substances, and in the 11th Cent., the view of Roscelin* that the three persons of the Trinity are only nominally one. E.T.R.

Trithemius, John: (of Trittenheim 1462-1516) Abbot at Sponheim (near Trier). Humanist. Student of theology, history, occultism. As historian he invented sources, is unreliable except for his own time. E.C.K.

Trito-Isaiah: See Isaiah.

Triton: (Gr., *Trītōn*) In Greek mythology, a merman, son of Poseidon* and Amphitrite, whose trumpet is the conch. Fish-shaped, he may be compared with certain Oriental gods, e.g., Dagon* of the O.T. (I Sam. 5:3, 4). E.M.N.

trivium: The lower disciplines in medieval universities, i.e., grammar, logic and rhetoric. See Scholasticism. P.G.M.

Troeltsch, Ernst: (1865-1923) Professor of theology at Heidelberg and of philosophy at Berlin, Troeltsch devoted his main efforts to the solution of the problems raised for both theology and philosophy by the development of historical science and the rise of historical relativism. Noting the strong interdependence of religion and social culture (as in *The Social Teachings of the Christian Churches*), he was unable to regard either as wholly a function of the other, though Christianity could not claim validity beyond its sphere in Western civilization. The independent core of religion he designated, in the thought-form of his neo-Kantian* philosophy, as a religious *a priori*. The problem of social history seemed to him soluble only in the form of culminating yet passing "syntheses of culture" which were less the product of historical determinism, as with Spengler*, than of human freedom. Troeltsch is the leading theologian of the religio-historical school and a chief representative of non-sceptical relativism in philosophy of history.

E. Troeltsch, *Gesammelte Schriften*, 4 vols. (Tuebingen, 1912-1925); *The Social Teachings of the Christian Churches*, 2 vols. (Trans. by Olive Wyon. London, 1931); *Absolutheit des Christentums* (2d ed. Tuebingen, 1912); *Christian Thought* (London, 1923); *Glaubenslehre* (Munich, 1925); H. R. Mackintosh, *Types of Modern Theology* (1937); R. S. Sleigh, *The Sufficiency of Christianity* (London, 1923). H.R.N.

troll: (Teut.) An earth demon, or giant; a personified non-human nature power in the religion of the early Germanic and Scandinavian peoples; later, a friendly but a mischievous dwarf.

F.L.P.

trope: The addition of words, a syllable to each note, to the elaborate melismas of the Gregorian chant*. The additions never formed a part of the official liturgy. They were introduced into the chant from the 9th to the 12th centuries.

E.H.B.

truce of God, the: Medieval Church institution which forbade private war on Friday, Saturday and Sunday of every week on pain of excommunication* or interdict*. This institution—to be distinguished from the Peace of God—later included other periods in the calendar, such as parts of the Lent and the periods extended up to Whitsuntide and to St. John's Day, June 24. Private war was also forbidden from the Day of the Ascension of the Virgin, August 15 to Saint Martin's Day, November 11. S.C.T.

truth: The problem of truth involves two inquiries: its nature and criteria. Two types of criteria of truth are: the non-philosophical and the philosophical. By the first is meant those judgments claimed to be true by assertion: **e.g.**, appeal to some authority; social agreement (*consensus gentium*); appeal to feeling; appeal to intuition; appeal to self-evident or axiomatic principles. The criticisms of these several appeals are fundamentally alike: all are either dogmatic (non-philosophical) or inconsistent. If one asserts something about which there is no further appeal one is dogmatic; if one appeals to reason to sustain any one or all of the above criteria, one is inconsistent—for, then one has set up another criterion (reason) to sustain the appeal. Philosophically, the above criteria lie outside the pale of argument. A further common criticism is that authorities, feelings, intuitions conflict in the testimony of men; self-evident truths are not always so self-evident; the agreement of the majority turns out often to be false.

The philosophical criteria of truth fall into three types: 1) The coherence theory asserts that to be true which fits into a harmony. Truth cannot fundamentally be inconsistent. A systematic liar will eventually fail to harmonize a system of lies. To deny coherence is to appeal philosophically to another system of coherence (system of denials). 2) The correspondence theory asserts that that idea is true which conforms with an actual situation. My judgment of a fact or reality is a true judgment if it agrees with what is presented. The problem raised here is the question of knowledge: how am I to know that ideas correspond to the extra-mental? The holders of this view must sustain their appeal by a well-worked out epistemological theory if they are to escape the charge of dogmatism. John Locke* is representative of this view and he failed to dodge the critic's charge of dogmatism. 3) The pragmatic theory in general is that a truth is a judgment which works. There are pragmatists and pragmatists. To say that an idea works may mean: it satisfies; it works for most people; it is a name for successful adaptation (John Dewey); it is experimentally justified (the laboratory technician). Criticisms of this theory are: May there be a truth which lies beyond the demonstration of workability? May not a lie work? Is not satisfaction even to a large number as precarious as *consensus gentium?* Is truth only an abstraction of that which works truly?

It is possible that all of the philosophical criteria must be applied in judgments; perhaps they are not so much antithetical as complementary. As to the nature of truth, philosophers disagree in accordance with their epistemology and metaphysics. For an objective idealist, truth is inherent in objective reality if truth is taken to mean a systematic whole of the Universal Idea or God; for a pragmatist truth may not exist ontologically but be a concept relative to a particular judgment. The pragmatist has been criticized by his application of a defensible *test* of truth beyond legitimate application to the *nature* of truth.

The criteria of religious truth follow the same pattern: non-philosophical and philosophical with the virtues and vices named above. See pragmatism; myth; twofold-truth theory. Cf. epistemology; reason in religion.

W. P. Montague, *The Ways of Knowing* (1925); G. T. W. Patrick, *An Introduction to Philosophy* (1924); E. S. Brightman, *An Introduction to Philosophy* (1925); V. Ferm, *First Adventures in Philosophy* (1936). V.F.

Tuatha de Danaan: (Celtic, collective name; 'the folk of the goddess Danu' or 'folk of the god whose mother is called Danu'). Gods in early Ireland; gods living in underground. In the mythical tales of Medieval Chroniclers these gods were one of several groups which successively colonized Ireland; each group was affiliated with the Hebrew patriarchs; once lords of the country, they were finally overthrown by the Milesians, ancestors of the Irish. The surviving members of the Tuatha de Danaan retired to the hills, lived underground and became a race of wizards, or fairies: in their natures they are still gods or divinities. After Ireland became Christian they were thought to be harmful to agriculture.

F.L.P.

Tübingen School: Designation of a group of theologians who under the leadership of F(erdinand) C(hristian) Baur (professor of theology at Tübingen, 1826-1860) sought to explain the evolution of Christianity in terms of a rigidly maintained Hegelian* philosophy of history. Compromise and the reconciliation of opposites—the universal law of progress—Baur found unmistakably present in the life and thought of the apostolic age and its resultant writings. In its earliest stage Christianity was a form of Judaism: Jesus was the Messiah of the Jews, not the founder of a world religion. Such was the view of the Jewish Christian wing under the leadership of Peter and James. In contradistinction to this view (*thesis*) Paul maintained that Jesus was the Messiah of the whole world, and Christianity was wholly distinct from Judaism and thus unrestricted by the Mosaic law (*antithesis*). Out of this clash, which convulsed the church throughout the first century, arose the later reconcilement and more or less colorless "union Christianity" of the second century (*synthesis*). Upon this Procrustean bed all the writings of early Christianity were forced to lie. Only those writings which revealed the intensity of this struggle were apostolic. Of the so-called Pauline letters only four—Romans, I and II Corinthians, and Galatians (especially the latter two)—could be adjudged from the pen of Paul. The other epistles and Acts, being more or less conciliatory, were, of course, postapostolic. In the gospels they fancied they found the same situation. Matthew was the product of the earliest (Jewish) position and was thus the most trustworthy, only imperfectly so, since it was the result of several reconstructions of the original material. Luke represented the Pauline opposition—this gospel was the best representative (after the *Hauptbriefe*) of the Pauline *antithesis*. Mark was the unionistic epitomist. As for John—and the same is true of the Johannine letters—since the whole controversy is already far below the horizon, it was to be seen as the product of the later second century, when harmony had been gained, and was therefore worthless as an historical document. Great weight was laid on the so-called *Clementine* Homilies* and *Recognitions*. In these writings Baur and his pedisequi thought they discerned Paul (thinly disguised as Simon Magus) in constant conflict with his archopponent Peter. Since they found a similar hostility to Paul in Revelation, that writing was regarded as primitive, the earliest and most Jewish of all the N.T. In spite of its overemphasis, its hobby-riding, and its all too evident critical weaknesses—especially in synoptic criticism—this school of thought made an invaluable contribution. It has properly been styled "a fruitful failure."

In addition to Baur, as members of this important and distinctive school of criticism should be included Schwegler, Zeller, Volkmar, Hilgenfeld, Lipsius*, Hausrath*, Weizsäcker*, Pfleiderer*, and Schmiedel. For an excellent and fair discussion see the anonymous article, translated under the title, "the Tübingen Historical School," *Bibliotheca Sacra,* Vol. XIX (1862), pp. 75-105. See Lives of Jesus.

M.S.E.

Tucker, Abraham: (1705-1774) A British moralist and the original exponent of Utilitarianism.* Author of *The Light of Nature Pursued* in which he "pursued the scheme of Reason, by the Light of Nature". He exerted a major influence on the subsequent trend of philosophy especially on Paley*, who first formulated a theory of Utilitarianism. He accepted the universe as a constitution, composed of individual facts through which man must plow slowly and inductively. Author of *Man In Quest of Himself.*

W.G.H.

Tucker, William Jewett: (1839-1926) Born in Griswold, Conn., July 13, 1839; graduated, Dartmouth College, 1861, Andover Theological Seminary 1866; Pastor, Franklin St. Church, Manchester, N. H., 1867-1875 and Madison Square Presbyterian Church, New York, 1875-1879; Bartlett Professor of Sacred Rhetoric, Andover Theological Seminary, 1880-1893; co-editor *The Andover Review;* President Dartmouth College, 1893-1909.

Dr. Tucker was founder of the Andover House (later South End House) Boston, 1891 (one of the earliest social settlements in America), and was one of the foremost in arousing interest in Christian social ethics in the churches, also teaching a course on this subject in Andover Seminary. As preacher, teacher and college president he won the admiration and fealty of youth and was potent in vitalizing Christian thought and life.

Author: *From Liberty to Unity* (1892); *The Making and Unmaking of the Preacher* (1899) (Lyman Beecher Lectures); *Public-Mindedness* (1910); *Personal Power* (1910); *The Function of the Church in Modern Society* (1911); *My Generation, an Autobiographical Interpretation* (1920). Tributes to Dr. Tucker by President Ernest W. Hopkins and by Robert F. Leavens, appeared in *The Dartmouth Alumni Magazine,* April, 1939. Cf. J. W. Buckham, *Progressive Religious Thought in America* (1919).

J.W.B.

Tung Chung-shu: See Confucianism.

Tung Shan Shê: See Chinese religions (Secret Societies).

tunic: The vestment which the bishop places on the sub-deacon at ordination, similar to a dalmatic* also a short vestment worn by a bishop under the dalmatic.

Cf. Addis and Arnold, *A Catholic Dictionary,* p. 821.

S.C.

Tunkers: See Dunkers.

tutelary god: A religious entity or 'power' serving as a guardian or protector of an individual, family, clan, tribe, city, or nation. Among one-factor religions* as in Christianity and Buddhism, a patron saint*, or guardian angel*, or minor divinity which has its duties and jurisdiction fixed and conditioned by a spirit or spirits of higher or highest authority in the spiritual government by which the universe is operated; derived from historical and mythological persons, separately, or in combination of characters.

Among the two-factor religions*, guardian spirits whose duties and authority are not unified or systematized with the others in a single 'order' of religious power; such tutelary gods are derived from powers of deceased persons, animals, plants, and other objects. F.L.P.

tutiorism: A system of teaching in Catholic moral theology, but not favoured by it, which holds that in cases of doubt as to the lawfulness of an action, it is better to be on the safe side, i.e., one must favour a law as against liberty and, when laws conflict, one must favour that law opposed to natural inclinations. T.J.B.

Twenty-Five Articles, the: A rescension of the Thirty-Nine Articles* of the Anglican Church given by John Wesley to the American Methodists and adopted by the Baltimore Conference in 1784 as an informal basis of belief. It omits or modifies Articles of the older creed not applicable to American polity, or out of harmony with distinctive Wesleyan emphasis. F.G.E.

two-document hypothesis: See Q; Synoptic Gospels.

two-factor religions: A word coined by Fred L. Parrish to identify the great division of the historical religions of the world in which all religious ideas and practices of the faiths are based upon the assumption that the religious factor* native to man and the religious factor native to non-human nature 'powers', are different kinds of factors, mutually exclusive; the kind of religion represented by each religion in the great division; historical religions which assume that there is no religious factor of unity, but on the contrary, two impinging 'worlds': 1) of the human here and hereafter, and 2) of the 'immortal' spirits, gods and demons of non-human derivation.

(About ten per cent of the peoples of the world today belong to historical religions using this two-factor assumption; the two-factor assumption is used so rigidly that separate bodies of ideas and practices obtain among all primitives for making religious adjustments with the two different groups of religious powers.) See his *The Classification of Religions* (1941). See religious 'powers'; one-factor religions; classification of religions. F.L.P.

twofold truth theory: According to this view "something may be true theologically which is not true philosophically, and *vice versa.*" (Windelband, *History of Philosophy,* 1919, pp. 320 ff.) Throughout the Middle Ages many had thought and acted in accordance with it, but William Ockham* provided it with an acute epistemological analysis. (Cf. R. McKeon, *Selections from Medieval Philosophers,* II, 351-421) Ockham's statement was a moderate one compared with that of later Averroists*, or of Marsilius of Padua*, Pierre Bayle* and numerous moderns. The idea was of influence in the development of mysticism, political history, theology (cf. Luther's concept of justification), and was of great importance in secularizing science. See common grace; John of Jandum; Pomponazzi; reason in religion; truth. Cf. Satyasiddhi School under Buddhist Terminology. Q.B.

Two-Seed-in-the-Spirit Predestinarian Baptists: A group of 16 conservative Baptist churches having 200 members in Tennessee, Kentucky, and Alabama. They have the same origin and general principles as the Primitive Baptists* and have been known as "Hard Shell"* Baptists. Their distinctive "Two-Seed-in-the-Spirit" doctrine is an involved theory. In the "earthly generation of mankind" there are two "seeds," a good seed from God and a bad seed from the devil, and each unchangeably produces good and bad, saved and lost, people. "Close communion" and feet washing are practiced, and paid ministers and "church activities" are opposed; evangelistic work is unnecessary, since "Christ came to save sinners" and "finished his work." See Baptists. See also anti-missionary movement in the U. S. E.T.C.

two swords, the doctrine of: The mediaeval theory of the division of powers between church and state, based on S. Luke xxii: 38. While earlier theorists declared that the two powers, secular and ecclesiastical, held their authority directly from God, twelfth century theologians, such as St. Bernard and John of Salisbury*, maintained that the prince, as agent of the "Sacerdotium," received his power from the church. E.W.K.

tychism: (Gr., *tuche,* fortune*, chance) A term employed by Charles Peirce*, meaning chance or the unpredictability of events. V.F.

Tyconius: (4th century) A Donatist who rejected the rebaptism of those who were baptized into the Catholic church; who maintained that unholy men are permitted to live in the holy church, that the administration of the sacraments by unholy priests can be efficacious, that the Catholic church is anti-Christian and that the coming of the last days was to proceed from the Donatist* church.

F. C. Burkitt, "The Book of Rules of Tyconius," *Texts and Studies,* III, 1 (Cambridge, Eng., 1894); T. Hahn, *Tyconius Studien* (Leipzig, 1900).

H.H.

Tyler, Bennet: (July 10, 1783-May 14, 1858) Congregational clergyman, theologian, educator. When fifteen years of age an accident incapacitated him for manual work, so his family, although very poor, raised the money to send him to Yale College which he entered in 1800 as a classmate of Nathaniel W. Taylor* who later became his great theological opponent. Graduating in 1804 he taught and studied theology, and was ordained over the church at South Britain, where he remained for fourteen years. In 1822 he became president of Dartmouth College, leaving in 1828 to take the pastorate of the Second Church of Portland, Maine. Alarmed by the liberal tendency emanating from Yale College, and especially aroused by the publication of Taylor's *Concio ad Clerum* in September, 1828, Tyler returned to Connecticut to lead the conservative revolt against the New Haven Theology. When the East Windsor Seminary (later Hartford) was founded in 1834 Tyler became its first president and professor of theology, and retained that position until he resigned in July, 1857. He remained throughout his life an ardent and consistent opponent of all the liberal movements within the Calvinistic orthodoxy of his day. See New Haven theology; means.

See the *Memoir* by Nahum Gale, vol. I of Tyler's *Lectures on Theology* (1859); F. B. Dexter, *Biographical Sketches of the Graduates of Yale College*, V (1911); C. M. Geer, *Hartford Theological Seminary* (1934).

S.E.M.

Tyndale, William: (1495?-1536) In exile from his native England, Tyndale translated from their original languages the N.T. (1526), the Pentateuch (1530), and the Book of Jonah (1531), as well as other portions of the O.T. He was burnt at the stake for heresy in Vilvorde, Belgium. His translations were used in the Great (Cranmer's) Bible of 1538, and subsequently in the Authorized and Revised Versions. See Bible, English.

Works (3 vols., Parker Society, Cambridge, 1848-1850). See J. F. Mozley, *William Tyndale* (1937).

E.W.K.

types: Typology is a technique, closely related to allegory*, by which persons or events in the O.T. are interpreted as adumbrating Jesus Christ or some doctrine or practice of the Christian Church. St. Paul and the author of the *Epistle to the Hebrews* made use of O.T. "types," and in a number of instances Jesus is represented by the Gospels as having so expounded O.T. Scripture. The method flourished as an exegetical* device until the rise in modern times of historical criticism.

S.M.G.

typology: See types.

tyrannicide: Literally, the killing of a tyrant. The theoretical justification of this act was the subject of considerable theological discussion during the medieval and reformation periods.

W.S.H.

Tyrrell, George: (1861-1909) Liberal R. C. in England. Leaving the Anglican Church, he was received into the R. C. Church in 1879, and entered the Society of Jesus* in 1880. Because of his views denying the inerrancy of R. C. theology and affirming the mutability of the visible Church organism, Tyrrell was expelled from the Society in 1906. As a result of his criticism of the encyclical "Pascendi"*, Tyrrell incurred virtual excommunication in 1907. See Modernism. Among his more importing writings are:

A Much-Abused Letter (1907); *Medievalism* (1908); *Christianity at the Crossroads* (1909).

H.W.J.

Tzadikim: See Chasidism.

tziruf: (chiluf) See Kabbalah.

Tzschirner, Heinrich Gottlieb: (1778-1828) He was professor in Wittenberg and in Leipzig. As a representative of supernatural rationalism or rational supernaturalism, he was open towards other theological movements. He also achieved a certain understanding of Schleiermacher. His influence was notable in spite of his early death.

Christliche Kirchengeschichte seit der Reformation. A continuation of J. M. Schroeckh's* great work, 10 vols. (Leipzig, 1804-12); *Vorlesungen über die christliche Glaubenslehre* (Leipzig, 1829).

H.H.

U

ubiquity: (Lat., *ubique,* everywhere) A term used in the doctrinal discussions of the sixteenth century to explain the Lutheran view of the real or bodily presence of Christ in the Lord's Supper. In answer to their opponents' argument that the human nature of Christ (real body and blood) could not be present because it could not be in more than one place at the same time, the Lutherans contended: by virtue of its union with His divine nature, Christ's human nature *acquires* the property of being present simultaneously wherever He wills. In this sense of relative omnipresence ubiquity is taught by Luther* and by the Formula of Concord* (Art. VII). See communicatio idiomatum; Lutheran doctrine of the Lord's Supper. T.A.K.

Ugaritic tablets: Hundreds of clay tablets discovered in Ras Shamra, northern coast of Syria, from 1929 to 1939. Most of them are inscribed in an alphabetic writing of cuneiform* appearance which was deciphered without the help of a bilingual inscription. Written in Ugaritic dialect, akin to Canaanite, Phoenician** and Hebrew, they offer fragments of epic, liturgical, and mythological literatures and date from about 1400 B.C. Extremely valuable for the study of the Semitic languages and of the O.T.

See bibliography in C. F. A. Schaeffer, *Ugaritica* (1939); C. H. Gordon, *Ugaritic Grammar* (1940). S.L.T.

ulama: (Arabic, meaning the wise or learned men; plural of *alim,* wise, learned) Learned scholars in Moslem tradition and canon law. A college or body composed of *imams, muftis***, and *cadis* (priests, expounders and judges.) See mulla. P.E.J.

Ulfilas: (c. 311-383) The apostle of Christianity to the Gothic people. He was born among the Goths in the region of the Danube, and was sent at an early age to Constantinople, where he became an Arian Christian. At the age of 30 he was sent as missionary bishop for forty years' leadership among the Goths. When his success drew the persecution of a pagan chief, he led his followers across the Danube and established a Christian community. His Gothic translation of the Scriptures raised the dialect to a literary language. See Arianism. P.E.J.

Ullmann, Karl: (1796-1865) He taught at the universities of Halle and Heidelberg. He was largely polemically active in the struggle against Friedrich Strauss and L. Feuerbach**.

Historisch oder Mythisch? (Hamburg, 1838); *Das Wesen des Christentums* (Hamburg, 1845, 5th ed., Gotha, 1865). H.H.

Ulrici, Hermann: (1806-1884) Was professor in Halle and a strong critic of Hegel*. His doctrine of God is a mediation between deism and pantheism. The world not only endures through God, but also in Him. God is the necessary presupposition of scientific ontology and cosmology. Liberty and reason have their origin in God. The human spirit discriminates the divine not only by logical but also by ethical categories.

Glauben und Wissen, Speculation und exacte Wissenschaft (Leipzig, 1858); *Gott und die Natur* (Leipzig, 1861); *Gott und der Mensch* (Leipzig, 1866); J. E. Schweicker, *Ulricis Gotteslehre* (Würzburg, 1905). H.H.

ultramontanism: (Lat., *ultra montes,* beyond the mountains) A name used in regard to certain features of organization in the Roman Catholic Church whereby it is unified under the control of the Pope. The term has been used since mediaeval times, because in relation to most European peoples the Pope lives beyond the mountains, i.e., the Alps. Sympathetically employed, as it was in the beginning and is still by some Catholic writers, ultramontanism simply denominates the centralized, unified, hierarchical order which is a notable feature of Roman Catholicism. In a critical and pejorative sense, which is more frequent in modern times, the term is used to describe what is regarded as an extreme form of over-centralization, particularly in political organization of the R. C. Church, which does not give sufficient voice to the non-Italian members who may not have the same cultural and national interests. Contrasted with movements to found "national" branches of the Church, as in Gallicanism*.

U. Benigni, "Ultramontanism," in *Cath. Encyclopedia,* XV, 125. V.J.B.

Umā: A Hindu goddess, one of many of the consorts of Shiva, gentle, kindly and winsome in character, in contrast to Kali*. C.S.B.

Unam Sanctam, The: The Bull "Unam Sanctam", published Nov. 18, 1302 by Boniface VIII* against Philip IV, the Fair, of France was the protest of the pope to the king for having violated the rights of the Church (the *privilegium fori*), abused the *jus regaliae* (royal acquisition of the revenues of purposely unfilled episcopal sees) and for having imprisoned the Papal Legate. It is a solemn defense of the rights of the Church against molestations by the Crown and a vindication of the superiority of the spiritual power (or sword) over the temporal. R.M.H.

Unamuno, Miguel de: (1864-1936) The outstanding Spanish thinker and writer since Cervantes, and one of the greatest of modern men of letters. Born in Bilbao in the Basque provinces, Unamuno was educated in Madrid and spent most of his life as a professor, and a period as Rector, in the University of Salamanca. While the most universally read literary man of his time, Unamuno never lived outside Spain, except during a period of exile in France in 1925-30. Essayist, poet, novelist, dramatist, philosopher, and mystic, his best known works are: *Vida de Don Quixote y Sancho* (1905), English translation by H. P. Earle (1927); *Del Sentimento Tragico de la Vida* (1912), English translation by Crawford Flitch (1921); *Essays* (7 volumes published by the Residence de Estudients de Madrid 1916-18); *L'Agonie de Christianisme,* published in Paris in 1925, English translation by P. Loving (1928).

Unamuno was profoundly influenced by Kierkegaard*, about whom he wrote in 1907, before the Danish writer had become known outside his own country. By stressing the concrete "man of flesh and bone" over against the so-called rational man, and exalting the significance of struggle, decision, and vocation in life, Unamuno became a precursor of the existential* movement in thought. He is, moreover, the greatest interpreter of the Spanish spirit. While being ecclesiastically neither Roman Catholic nor Protestant, Unamuno was a devoted Christian. J.A.M.

uncials: Large or capital letters such as were used in antiquity in book hands, in books prepared for sale. The name may be due to the habit of some Roman publishers of using twelve letters to the line (as the Romans counted twelve ounces to the pound and twelve inches to the foot). Manuscripts written in book hands are called uncials. Biblical uncials range in date from the second century before Christ (the Rylands Deuteronomy) to the tenth century after Christ. See manuscripts of the Bible. E.J.G.

unction: See anointing; extreme unction; oils; sacraments.

Underhill, Evelyn (Mrs. Stuart Moore): (1875-1941) Author of important studies in religious mysticism. Her best known work *Mysticism* (first edition, 1911; 13th edition, 1940) first appeared when she was much influenced by H. Bergson*. The frame of her interpretation of mysticism was considerably altered in the following thirty years as she was drawn to von Hügel, Whitehead** and more recently to Maritain and this is reflected in the later editions of *Mysticism.* As a religious poet, her *Immanence* takes its place with the poems of Crashaw, Herbert, and Donne among the finest of English mystical verse. Late in her life, her admirable historical studies of the mystics gave way to her own free interpretation of the spiritual life in *Concerning the Inner Life,* and *The Golden Sequence.* An Anglican of Catholic sympathies, her appraisal of *Worship* (1936) showed a penetrating grasp of liturgical worship but little sympathetic understanding of free Protestant worship. D.V.S.

Uniate Churches: Comprise such communions which, although originally deriving from the Eastern Orthodox (or separated) churches*, and commonly still retaining the Byzantine rite* and usages (such as the married priesthood), yet have accepted the supremacy of the papacy; they accept the doctrines of the Roman Catholic Church.

Adrian Fortescue, *The Uniate Eastern Churches* (1903). M.S.

Unigenitus (Bull of 1713): (Lat., *unus,* one; *genitus,* begotten) This document is so called from the Latin *Unigenitus Dei Filius,* "The Only-Begotten Son of God", which are the opening words of the text. The bull was issued by Pope Clement XI, Sept. 8, 1713, against the Jansenistic* doctrines of Pasquier Quesnel*. C.V.

unio mystica: (Lat. mystical union) The joining of the soul of man to God in an essentially indescribable experience, transcending all ordinary conditions of human consciousness. Such a state, cognitive or affective, may occur as a natural phenomenon, or may require supernatural intervention. Beginning with biblical references (the soul as the bride of Christ in the Song of Songs, the experiences of Jacob, St. Paul's third heaven), Christian writers (St. Augustine, St. Bernard of Clairvaux, the Victorines, St. Bonaventure, Meister Eckhart, St. John of the Cross, St. Theresa, B. Ramon Lull, J. Boehme**) have developed mystical exercises and terminology related philosophically to the spiritualism of Plato and Plotinus. It is quite possible that some form of mystical experience is found among the religions of India, in Mohammedanism, and in the Russian Orthodox Church. Henri Bergson* stimulated interest in the condition as a source of religious motivation in his: *Deux Sources de la morale et de la religion* (Paris, 1932). See mysticism. V.J.B.

Unitarianism: The doctrinal system characterized chiefly by belief in the unipersonality of God and the normal humanity of Jesus, as contrasted with the Trinity* and the eternal deity of Christ.

1. In *Transylvania* Unitarianism, splitting off from the Reformed Church, first took form in 1568 (almost simultaneously with Socinianism* in Poland, though independently of it). Having won the adherence of the ruling Prince and of many of the nobility the Unitarian Church was given legal standing as one of the four "received religions," spread rapidly, and became firmly rooted. A change of government was soon fol-

lowed by a period of two centuries and a half of persistent oppression by Calvinists and Catholics in turn, which together with frequent wars greatly weakened the church; but its members held on heroically, and since the middle of the 19th century have generally enjoyed peace and friendly relations with the other confessions.

After the downfall of Socinianism in Poland the Unitarians of Transylvania led an isolated existence, unaware of kindred movements elsewhere until 1821, when they learned of the Unitarian movements then taking form in England and America, with which they have ever since maintained fraternal relations.

Their constituency is mostly of Szekler and Magyar free farmers. Their faith is a simple, undogmatic Christian theism, tending to be more conservative than that of Unitarians elsewhere, with little stress upon dogma and strong emphasis on practical religion. They are known for their high standards in morals and education. Their polity is in the main like that of the Reformed Church, is closely knit, and administered by a General Consistory, district Deans, and a Bishop and a lay Curator over all. The church suffered heavily in World War I, but has a constituency of about 70,000, in about 100 regular congregations, including a few in Hungary proper. The larger congregations have parish schools, and there are two higher academies, besides a college and a theological school at Kolozsvár.

See S. Székely, *History of the Unitarian Faith* (1839); F. Kanyaró, *Unitarians in Hungary* (1891) (both in Hungarian); E. M. Wilbur, *Our Unitarian Heritage* (1925).

2. In *England* sporadic instances of Unitarianism occurred all through the 16th century, and half a score were put to death, and many imprisoned, for "Arianism."* In the 17th century Socinian influences coming from Holland or even from Poland became widespread in the Church of England, despite the laws; but no organization existed. At length the Trinitarian Controversy at the end of the 17th century and the Arian Controversy at the beginning of the 18th century in the Church of England, made such telling attacks on the Athanasian doctrine that those that could not accept it were nevertheless allowed to remain in the Church unmolested.

While Anglicans were thus discussing the Trinity, Dissenters* were occupied with the deity of Christ, and verging toward Arianism. This raised the question whether ministers should be compelled to subscribe the Westminster Confession*. Non-subscription won, and being left free from doctrinal restraint the Presbyterian churches rapidly grew liberal, and in two generations had practically all become Unitarian in belief. A similar change took place in the Welsh and Irish churches.

Doctrinal unrest meanwhile persisted among the Anglican clergy and led to an appeal to Parliament for relief from subscription to the Articles and liturgy: it was rejected by a large majority. A single one of the petitioners (followed later by a few others) then withdrew from the Church. Theophilus Lindsey gave up his living and going to London opened in 1774 the first Unitarian chapel in England, which attracted numerous adherents and survives to this day. A more influential leader was the Unitarian Dissenter, Joseph Priestly, who as minister of large congregations at Leeds and Birmingham championed aggressive Unitarianism with great effect, and much promoted it by his controversial writings. He gave latent and timid Unitarians the courage of their convictions in promoting their cause. After he had removed to America in 1794, his successor Thomas Belsham effectively rallied and organized the forces until in 1825 the British and Foreign Unitarian Association was formed, and systematic extension work was promoted.

In the 19th century the English Unitarians long had to struggle for the removal of civil disabilities, and for possession of their old church properties, but steadily gained strength and coherence. Under the leadership of James Martineau* their thought was transformed from a cold doctrinal liberalism to a warm spiritual faith, and doctrinal peculiarities were left in the background. Their members have had marked prominence in proportion to their numbers in liberal politics, social reform, philanthropy, education and literature. Their polity is congregational, their worship often mildly liturgical. They number about 350 congregations in the British Isles and about a score more in the colonies; and they have three theological colleges.

See Henry Gow, *The Unitarians* (1928); S. H. Mellone, *Liberty and Religion* (1925).

3. Unitarianism in *America* did not derive from the similar movement in England, but arose independently of it and contemporaneously with it. With two or three exceptions it developed out of Massachusetts Congregationalism, whose original strict Calvinism began before the middle of the 18th century to be outgrown, somewhat influenced by the English liberals, both Anglican and Presbyterian. It tended toward Arian views, and was quite averse to the bald Unitarianism of Priestley and his school, with which orthodoxy strove to identify it. It laid little stress on creeds, ignored objectionable doctrines, and aimed simply to promote positive Christianity. By the end of the 18th century all the Boston ministers but one, and more than half of those in eastern Massachusetts, had thus quietly abandoned the Trinitarian position. When the orthodox attacked them for this, Channing* became their spokesman in a famous sermon on Unitarian Christianity at Baltimore in 1819, which gave them a platform to rally round; and when the orthodox denied them Christian fellowship they were forced in 1825 to organize the American Unitarian Association to promote their cause. More than a third of the old churches had become Unitarian.

The new denomination grew slowly, being averse to sectarianism or to controversy, but was bitterly attacked by the orthodox for thirty years. Aside from rejection of the Trinity, its doctrine was not defined, and difference as to various minor points long hindered effective growth, so that it was not until the organization of the National Conference in 1865 that the church was thoroughly organized for action. There was still unhappy division between conservatives and radicals, but harmony was finally achieved, preserving complete spiritual freedom without resort to the restraint of a creed. The later history of the movement has been uneventful. Attention has been centered far less on doctrinal questions than on the application of Christianity to personal and social life, political reform, philanthropy and education. Though there is general voluntary acceptance of liberal Christian doctrine, the emphasis has so far shifted from a doctrinal centre that modern Unitarianism is now characterized not so much by its beliefs as by its insistence upon the fundamental principles of entire *freedom* in belief, the full use of *reason* in religion, and generous *tolerance* of differences of view.

The Unitarian polity is pure Congregationalism; and church extension is managed by the American Unitarian Association in regional departments. Active congregations number about 360, and the total consistency is estimated at about 145,000. There are three schools for the training of ministers. See anti-missionary movement in the U. S.; Confessions, Formal of the Christian Church; Parker. Cf. humanism, religious; liberal theology.

See George Willis Cooke, *Unitarianism in America* (1902); E. M. Wilbur, *Our Unitarian Heritage* (1925). E.M.W.

Unitas Fratrum: See Moravian Church, the; Unity of (Bohemian) Brethren.

United American Free Will Baptist Church (Colored): A sect of "general" or Arminian Baptists among the colored people of the South. They are closely related to the white Free Will Baptists*. They have 226 churches with nearly 20,000 members. E.T.C.

United Baptists: A group of conservative Baptist churches having the same general origin and characteristics as the Regular Baptists*. Nearly all of them are in the South, more than half of the congregations and members being in Kentucky. They are generally Arminian in theology and practice "close communion" and feet washing. There are 277 churches and 27,000 members. E.T.C.

United Brethren in Christ: Influenced by the pietistic* movement, some of the German speaking people of the middle colonies experienced "spiritual quickening" in the eighteenth century. Many became preachers of "experimental religion". After more than thirty years as leaders in this work, Philip William Otterbein* (1726-1813), of the German Reformed Church, and Martin Boehm* (1725-1812), of the Mennonites, became co-founders of a new denomination. At the first legislative conference held near Frederick, Maryland, in 1800, it was determined that the name should be "The United Brethren in Christ," that conferences should be held annually and that Otterbein and Boehm should be the first bishops of the church. Christian Newcomer* (1749-1830) became the leader of the early period of expansion westward.

The General Conference is the supreme legislative body of the church. It has met quadrennially since 1817. It elects bishops for four-year terms. Pastors are appointed according to the itinerant plan.

The theology is Arminian*. Baptism and the Lord's Supper are recognized as sacraments but the mode of baptism and the manner of observing the supper are left to be determined by the individual. The church has been a pioneer in social advance. Anti-slavery legislation was passed in 1821, temperance, in 1841.

The headquarters are in Dayton, Ohio. The Bonebrake Theological Seminary is in Dayton, Ohio. The colleges are Otterbein, in Westerville, Ohio; Lebanon Valley, in Annville, Pennsylvania; Indiana Central, in Indianapolis, Indiana; York in York, Nebraska; and Shenandoah, in Dayton, Virginia.

The membership is 441,970. In the continental United States, there are 2790 organized churches with 1858 ordained ministers. Cf. Evangelical Church, the.

A. W. Drury, *United Brethren Church History* (1930); *Discipline of the Church of the United Brethren in Christ* (1941); S. S. Hough, *Christian Newcomer, His Life, Journal and Achievements* (1941). W.E.R.

United Christian Youth Movement: See Young People's Societies, Christian.

United Church of Canada, the: This body was formed in 1925 by the Union of the Methodist Church, the Presbyterian Church, and the Congregational Churches of Canada (and Newfoundland). The movement for union had grown out of a common desire at the beginning of the century to avoid unseemly rivalry and the waste of men and money in mission work on the rapidly expanding northern and western frontiers. The union idea had also gathered some momentum from the numerous unions effected in the half-century preceding by the two main families, Methodist and Presbyterian; these unions had proved to be highly beneficial. But the union of 1925 was not complete. While a few individual Methodists stood aside, and a small number of Congregational Churches, no less than a third of the Presbyterian body declined to enter the United Church.

In 1925 there were approximately 600,000 communicant members in the United Church; in 1941 there were 715,651. At the latter date the Church had 3,469 ministers (about 2,750 in active service) and 7,109 preaching places. There are nearly 1,800,000 persons under pastoral oversight. These figures indicate that it is largely a church of the frontier, of country villages and the open country, and of the thinly settled expanses of the north and west. Half of the preaching places are in Home Mission territory. The people of the older parts are called to liberal giving if those in the newer parts are not to be deprived of the comfort and strength of religion.

The load was heavy from 1929 to 1939, and it is heavy still (1943).

The Church maintains Foreign Missions in India, China, Japan, Trinidad and Portuguese West Africa. The Church has three arts colleges (Sackville, N. B., Toronto, Winnipeg), and eight theological schools (Halifax, Montreal, Kingston, Toronto, Winnipeg, Saskatoon, Edmonton, Vancouver). Very few are admitted to the ministry with less than a B.A. and three years of theology.

Before 1925 Methodist and Presbyterian organizations were very much alike; amalgamation was not difficult. A General Council, with legislative, administrative, and judicial powers, meets biennially. There are 11 Conferences (Synods), each Conference meeting annually, and 115 Presbyteries (Districts), each Presbytery meeting from 2 to 10 times a year. The Conference ordains and appoints ministers to their charges (usually the congregation has already called them); the Presbytery inducts (installs) them.

The faith of the Church is embodied in 20 *articles* of doctrine (part of the Basis of Union). It was discussed fully in T. B. Kilpatrick's *Our Common Faith,* and it has been recently declared in a somewhat less formal 2000-word *Statement of Faith,* (1940). The worship of the Church is regulated by a *Book of Common Order* (1932) and a Hymnary (1930). The law and organization of the Church is set forth in a *Manual* of Government (revised every two years). See theological schools, Protestant, U. S. and Canada.

Some account of the beginnings may be found in E. L. Morrows's *Church Union in Canada* (1925) and C. E. Silcox's *Church Union in Canada* (1933); and of developments since in the *Year Book* and the (biennial) *Proceedings of the General Council.* The offices of the Church are at 299 Queen Street West, Toronto.

R.D.

United Danish Church (Lutheran): See Lutheran Church in America.

United Evangelical Church: See s.v. Evangelical Church, the; Ev. Congregational Church.

United Free Church of Scotland: This was formed in 1900 by the Free Church of Scotland* and the United Presbyterian Church*. A small minority continuing the Free Church obtained a court judgment for all its property, but Parliament gave the United Free Church an equitable share. Efforts for union with the Church of Scotland*, begun in 1909, interrupted by war, then resumed, were furthered in 1921 by an act of Parliament recognizing the spiritual freedom of the established church. The union was accomplished in 1929 under the name of the Church of Scotland. See Wee Free Church.

J. R. Fleming, *The Church in Scotland, 1843-1929* (2 vols., Edinburgh, 1927, 1932); J. Buchan and G. A. Smith, *The Kirk in Scotland, 1560-1929.*

R.H.N.

United Lutheran Church in America: The largest integrated body of Lutherans in the United States and Canada, formed in 1918 by the merging of the General Synod (organized 1821), the General Council (organized 1867), and the United Synod in the South (organized 1886). Following in the tradition of its eighteenth-century patriarch, H. M. Muhlenberg*, this Church has led other Lutherans in its adaptation of Lutheranism to American thought and life and in its tolerant spirit toward other denominations. In its doctrinal basis, however, it is conservative, holding "the canonical Scriptures of the Old and New Testaments as the inspired word of God", accepting the three ecumenical creeds, regarding the unaltered Augsburg Confession "as a correct exhibition of the faith", and recognizing the other confessions of the Book of Concord* "as in harmony of one and the same pure Scriptural faith". Larger powers are exercised by the general organization than in any other body of American Lutherans, although the constituent "synods alone have the power of discipline" and control the theological seminaries. The United Lutheran Church is composed of 32 synods, having 3606 ordained pastors, 4065 congregations, and 1,714,945 members. It has 15 colleges, 12 theological seminaries, 20 children's homes, 19 homes for the aged, 9 hospices, 13 hospitals, 30 inner mission agencies, 2 deaconess motherhouses. It supports 70 ordained missionaries serving a baptized membership of 212,530 in mission fields in all continents. The legislative powers are vested in a biennial convention of delegates from the synods. The headquarters of the Church are in New York City, and the first President, Dr. F. H. Knubel, is still in office (1944). Among the objects of the Church, as defined in its constitution, is "to cultivate co-operation among all Lutherans" and it has taken a leading part in promoting a world-wide unity of the Church. See Lutheran Church in America.

T.A.K.

United Methodist Church, The: A church formed in England in 1907 by the union of the Methodist New Connexion, the Bible Christians, and the United Methodist Free Churches, all of whom had seceded at various times from the Wesleyan Methodist Church. It joined in 1932 with the parent church and the Primitive Methodists to form the Methodist Church. See Methodism.

F.G.K.

United Presbyterian Church of 1847: Two secessions from the Church of Scotland* protesting against disregard of the right of congregations to call ministers (1733, 1761) grew to the Associate or "Secession" Synod (1745) and the Relief Synod (1763). In 1847 the United Secession Synod, which had developed out of the Associate body, joined with the Relief Synod to form the United Presbyterian Church. Holding the doctrinal basis common to Scottish Presbyterians, this church maintained "voluntaryism", disapproval of church establishment. It was notable for its preaching and its foreign missionary enterprise. In 1900 it united with the Free Church of Scotland* to form the United Free Church*, having then 195,596 members. See Relief Church.

J. R. Fleming, *The Church in Scotland, 1843-1929* (2 vols., Edinburgh, 1927, 1932); D. Woodside, *The Soul of a Scottish Church* (1917).

R.H.N.

United Presbyterian Church of North America: The Associate Reformed Church was formed in America in 1782 by presbyteries whose antecedents were in the Associate Synod, which originated in a secession from the Church of Scotland* in 1733, and a Reformed presbytery whose antecedents were in the Reformed Presbyterian (Covenanter*) Church of Scotland, organized in 1743. In 1858 the General Synod of the Associate Reformed Church and the Associate Synod, descending from dissenters from the 1782 union, in a joint meeting in Pittsburgh constituted the United Presbyterian Church of North America. The Westminster Confession of Faith* was adopted and also a "Judicial Testimony" protesting against slavery, secret societies, open communion and the singing of "devotional compositions" other than the Psalms. The United Presbyterian Church has spread widely in the United States, chiefly among people of Scotch-Irish descent, but more than half of its membership is in Pennsylvania and Ohio. It is conspicuous for foreign missionary interest and the generous giving of its people. In practice it has modified its position regarding secret societies, communion and the use of hymns. The church has five colleges and two theological seminaries. In 1919 it adopted a new creed, the "Confessional Statement". In 1941 it had 853 churches and 187,470 members.

J. B. Scouller, *History of the United Presbyterian Church of North America* (1894), *American Church History Series*, XI; W. E. McCulloch, *The United Presbyterian Church and Its Work in America* (1925).

R.H.N.

United Society of Believers in Christ's Second Coming: See communistic settlements, religious, Shaker communities.

United Zion's Children: See River Brethren.

Unity: The Unity School of Christianity in Kansas City, Missouri was founded by Charles and Myrtle Fillmore in 1889. It is related to the general movement known as New Thought* in that the ends and values sought after are essentially the same. But it is much closer to traditional Christianity than New Thought generally. Indeed it seems to be a rather conservative form of Protestant Christianity which puts its major emphasis on the characteristic New Thought ends, namely health, well-being, and prosperity.

The Unity School reports over five hundred centers and more than two million members who follow its courses of readings and studies. The Movement publishes six magazines, numerous books, and tracts without number.

Widely used books by Charles Fillmore the founder are *Christian Healing; The Twelve Powers of Man; Prosperity.*

C.S.B.

Unity of Brethren: See Bohemian (or Czech) Brethren; Hussitism.

Universalism: The basic doctrine of Universalism centers about the belief that all men will finally be saved. This doctrine is of ancient origin and has existed among many of the schools of Christianity. There are Biblical passages in both the Old and New Testaments which are interpreted as furnishing Scriptural authority for the belief. Such men as Clemens, Alexandrinus, Origen, Diodorus, Theodore of Mopsuestia and others laid the foundations for the system. They taught that punishment was remedial, that the nature of God was love, and that the Divine mercy could not be satisfied with partial salvation or everlasting punishment.

The doctrine became heretical about the sixth century and was largely neglected during the Middle Ages. It was revived during the latter part of the 18th century, and became wide-spread during the 19th and 20th centuries.

The modern movement of Universalism originated in England, being a logical development of anti-Calvinistic teaching. It carried the Wesleyan system of free grace* to the point where the grace of God would be accepted by all. John Relly of London taught Universalism in his sermons and in a pamphlet, "Union" which was widely read. John Murray, who had been a member of a Calvinistic church, then a Wesleyan, accepted the doctrine and brought it to America in 1770.

Universalism was taught in the colonies by several groups, such as mystics and anabaptists*, as well as by some individual leaders among the Congregationalists, Episcopalians, etc., and by independents. Universalist churches were organized up and down the New England coast, people coming out from orthodox churches to make up the congregations.

Hosea Ballou* early gave to the world a systematic account of Universalism in his *Treatise of the Atonement* (1805) in which he outlined the doctrine of Unitarianism* as the basis for his Universalism.

No exact form of creed is required of believers, freedom of interpretation being guaranteed; but statements of faith have been adopted, such as the "Winchester Confession," the "Worcester Declaration," and the "Washington Statement."

The system of government of the churches is congregational. The local parish is largely autonomous. It can call its own minister and make its own decisions. There are, however, several organizations with which the local parish is affiliated. First, the Universalist Church of America is the parent body, meeting in biennial sessions in various cities. It has a President, a General Superintendent, Treasurer, Trustees, etc. It is a delegate body and determines general policies. The national office is at 16 Beacon Street, Boston. There are also national associations of women, youth, Sunday schools, etc., which usually meet with the General Convention and have offices at the Boston headquarters. Several academies and schools were founded between 1830 and 1880.

There are State Conventions, each with Superintendent, etc., which assist local parishes in solving their problems. There are also a few "associations" which include all the churches in a particular restricted area. See Ballou, Hosea

(2nd); Confessions, Formal of the Christian Church; Miner, A. A.; Murray, John; restorationism. Also see anti-missionary movement in the U. S.

Statistics of the Church are as follows:
Number of churches 488.
Number of members 48,923.
Number of constituency 78,883.
Official journal: *The Christian Leader*, a bi-weekly.

Hosea Ballou, *The Ancient History of Universalism* (2nd ed., 1829); Richard Eddy, *Universalism in America* (1884).
C.R.S.

universals, battle over: The question of the nature of universals has been disputed throughout ancient and mediaeval philosophy but with less emphasis in modern philosophy. It has important ramifications in theology. Generally, it is agreed that the human mind has the capacity to take a group of somewhat similar individuals and represent them under one general thought, or at least under one name. Such a unity in a manifold is called a universal. As to the precise nature of these universals, three chief positions have been found in the history of thought: (1) *extreme realism** maintains that universals are existing things or essences (or in modern terminology, objective values) apart from their ideas in finite minds and from their realization in the individuals pertaining to their class; (2) *nominalism** or *terminism* holds that universals not only have no reality in themselves, there is no real resemblance among the individual members of their class and there is no objective basis for the concepts by which they are thought in the minds of men; (3) *moderate realism* maintains a position somewhere between the foregoing: there are no real and actual universals in themselves but there are actual universal ideas in the intellects of men and these concepts have an objective basis in the real similarities of individuals of real classes of things. It should be noted that many variations of these three positions are possible and have occurred historically. Plato* is the classic example of an extreme realist: his Ideas or Intelligible Forms are perfect archetypes metaphysically and logically prior to the "many" individuals participating in them. Thus, there is one perfect "treeness", or pattern of tree, and all individual trees share in some way in its nature. The Neo-Platonists* (Plotinus, Porphyry) introduced the variation which would make these Ideas thoughts in the Divine Mind. In this they were followed by the Christian Fathers (Augustine, John Damascene). John Scottus Eriugena** (9th c.), Remigius of Auxerre (9th c.), Wm. of Champeaux* (11th c.), the School of Chartres* (12th c.) and J. Duns Scotus* (13th-14th c.) supported various degrees of extreme realism during the middle ages. With the revival of Platonism in the Renaissance* (Marsiglio Ficino*, the Mirandolas, Nicholas of Cusa*, the Cambridge Platonists*) this form of realism appears again in the 15th and 16th centuries. Nominalism is found in an embryonic state in the sensistic theories of knowledge of the Stoics and Epicureans**, possibly in some of the logical treatises of Aristotle*, but it reached its peak in the 11th c., in the dialectics of Peter Abailard, and again appears with Wm. of Ockham and J. Buridan** in the 14th c. Many professors of theology in the 14th and 15th c. were nominalistic. Moderate Realism is best represented in ancient thought by the metaphysics of Aristotle. Avicenna (11th c.), Averroes (12th c.), and St. Thomas Aquinas (13th c.)** are outstanding exponents of this view. It has remained the generally accepted teaching in Catholic philosophy. Until the contemporary period, modern thought has been largely nominalistic, but its pre-occupation with problems of knowledge has made classification from this point of view very difficult. Hegel*, for instance, seems to have tended toward extreme realism, not because of his idealism (for idealists can be and frequently are nominalists) but because of his emphasis on the concrete universal and lack of regard for the individual. In the twentieth century there have been noteworthy approaches to some form of realism. This is true of Santayana's* theory of essences, of Whitehead's* metaphysics, and of many contemporary axiologists who think of values* in the objective sense.

One's position in regard to the nature of universals affects one's theology in many points, but two chief items may be mentioned. In the doctrine of the Divine Trinity*, the extreme realist may tend to emphasize the distinction of the Divine Persons. From Boethius* (5th c.) onward the theological definition of person is modified by the amount of reality which is granted to substance. The same may be said about Divine relations. Nominalists, on the other hand, incline to a minimization of such distinctions. The other great point of contact is found in the doctrine of the Eucharist. There, it is evident that realism suggests a realistic, "fundamentalist" interpretation, and nominalism usually brings about a symbolical view of transubstantiation*. See Scholasticism.

The literature of the problem of universals is very extensive. Consult M. De Wulf, *History of Medieval Philosophy*, transl. by Messenger (3rd Eng. ed., 1935), 2 vols., and F. Ueberweg, *Grundriss der Geschichte der Philosophie*, V Bande (Berlin, 1924-1928) for bibliography.
V.J.B.

unleavened bread: The bread eaten by Jews on the Passover* holiday to commemorate the exodus from Egypt, when the Israelites in their haste could not let their dough rise and baked the bread in the unleavened state. B.Z.B.

Unmoved Mover: See Aristotle and Aristotelianism.

Upanishads: The basic philosophic texts of Hinduism*, upon which all the orthodox schools of Hindu philosophy are supposed to rest. They are writings which record the speculations of the Hindu sages upon the nature of the world and of ultimate reality and how man may find salvation.* There are thirteen principal Upanishads, most of which are early, but there are many others from later periods of Indian history. The thirteen best known are Brihad Āranyaka, Chāndogya,

Aitareya, Kena, Mundaka, Isā, Taittirīya, Svetāsvatara, Prasna, Maitrayana, Katha, Kaushītaki and Māndūkya.

S. Radhakrishnan, *Indian Philosophy* (London, 1923), vol. I; R. E. Hume, *Thirteen Principal Upanishads* (1921). C.S.B.

Upright, the: See forgeries.

urim and thummim: The Urim and Thummim were objects attached to the breastplate of the High Priest* (Ex. 28:30) and used by him to ascertain the will of God on questions of national importance. (Num. 27:21). The exact nature of these objects is unknown for they disappeared at a very early date (Ezra, 2:63). See divination. E.B.—L.F.

Ursinus, Zacharias: (1534-1583) One of the two authors of the Heidelberg Catechism*, published in 1562, under the direction of Elector Frederick III of the Palatinate, surnamed The Pious. This influential symbol of the Reformed faith owes its mild Calvinism mainly to the erudition of the scholarly Ursinus, a member of the faculty of the University of Heidelberg, while its fervent piety and simplicity of language reflect the genius of Olevianus, its co-author, who was a popular preacher in Heidelberg.

K. Sudhoff, *Olevianus und Ursinus* (Elberfeld, 1857). T.F.H.

Ursula, Saint: A virgin martyred at Cologne sometime before the fourth century. Details of her life and martyrdom are lost to us, and their place has been taken by several legendary accounts. None of these have convincing authority. C.V.

Ursulines: A Catholic order of religious women, founded by St. Angela de Merici in Brescia, Italy in 1535, for educating young women. The first female teaching order, it soon opened convents in Germany and France. American foundations were begun in Quebec (1639) and New Orleans (1727). C.V.

Ushabti: Ancient Egyptian glazed figurine* in the shape of a mummy, placed in the tomb and expected to cultivate the fields for the deceased in the next world. R.H.P.

Ushas, Usas: Vedic goddess of the dawn, the only goddess of importance in the Vedic pantheon. She is celebrated in 21 hymns in the Rig-Veda. She is beautiful, gracious, and distinctly feminine in character. Sometimes regarded as mother, at other times as husband of the sun god Surya. C.S.B.

Ussher, James: (1581-1656) From 1625 the Archbishop of Armagh and primate of Ireland, returning to England for literary work in 1640. He was one of the most learned Reformed theologians of his time and propounded the chronology which was later inserted in the margin of the King James Version of the Bible, according to which the Creation was assigned to 4004 B.C. C.T.C.

utilitarianism: Utilitarianism or universalistic hedonism*, affirms as moral standard the extension of the most possible pleasure and least pain among all sentient beings. Pleasure and happiness are used as practically synonymous terms. Jeremy Bentham*, James Mill, and John Stuart Mill* were leaders of the movement, also then known as Philosophical Radicalism, during the first part of the nineteenth century. They believed psychological hedonism* to be self evident, and endeavored to show that if individuals intelligently seek what will bring most pleasure to themselves (egoistic hedonism) they will be led through the operation of various sanctions to promote the general happiness*. They actively supported the social and political reforms of the time. During the latter part of the 19th century Henry Sidgwick* was the ablest interpreter of theoretical Utilitarianism, while Herbert Spencer* and Leslie Stephen gave Utilitarianism an evolutionary application. All the Utilitarians thus far mentioned defended individualism, believing that every man is best judge of what will bring most pleasure to himself, and so ought to be allowed freedom of initiative, except when his conduct will be detrimental to others. James MacKaye, however, in the 20th century in *Americanized Socialism* (1918) gave Utilitarianism a socialistic slant, claiming that collectivistic measures will best promote universal happiness. Hastings Rashdall* regarded his own view in ethics as "Ideal Utilitarianism". Cf. Tucker, Abraham.

E. A. Albee, *History of English Utilitarianism* (1902); Leslie Stephen, *The Utilitarians* (1900), 3 vols.; Elie Halevy, *The Growth of Philosophical Radicalism* (Eng. transl., 1928). W.K.W.

utilitarianism, theological: Utilitarianism is a theory of ethics that considers moral obligation and moral judgment in the light of their capacity to produce happiness for everybody. *Theological* utilitarianism regards the common good as the will of God. See Paley, Wm. W.G.H.

Utnapishtim or Per-napishtim (Haupt): The Babylonian Noah. The story is told of his rôle in the Deluge* in Tablet XI of the Gilgamesh* narrative. Translated with critical notes and commentary by Paul Haupt in E. Schrader: *Die Keilinschriften und das Alte Testament* 3rd ed. (Berlin, 1908). P.G.M.

Utopia: See communistic settlements; More, Thomas.

Utraquists: *Idem,* Calixtenes. See Bohemian Brethren; Hussitism.

V

Vāc: Vedic goddess of speech, in India.

C.S.B.

Vacherot, Etienne: (1809-1897) A director of the *Ecole Normale Superieure.* He was a convinced naturalist who did not despise metaphysical inquiry. An irreconcilable and unsatisfactory dualism in which the real and the ideal are set against one another is typical in his thought. The world for him is unity, eternal and infinite, but lacking perfection. The ideal, perfection, is incompatible with reality. Thus the real is not at all ideal, and the ideal has no reality. God is for humanity the category of the ideal. For Vacherot the concept of God arises in human consciousness from a combination of the ideas of the infinite and of perfection.

La métaphysique et la science (Paris, 1858), 3 vols.; *La religion* (Paris, 1868); *Le nouveau spiritualisme* (Paris, 1884).

H.H.

Vaicesika, Vaiseshika: One of the six traditional schools of Indian philosophy, which sets forth an atomic theory. See Hinduism. C.S.B.

Vaihinger, Hans: (1852-1933) He was professor of philosophy at the University of Halle, Germany. His main work *The Philosophy of "As-if"* is a system of theoretical, practical and religious fictions of mankind upon the basis of an idealistic positivism. For him religious ideas were beautiful myths and useful fictions, even though knowledge as such has no real truth value. His "as-if" point of view triumphed particularly in religious philosophy. Acknowledging the aesthetic and ethical value of religious fictions, his philosophical viewpoint was a solution and liberation for those who inwardly and outwardly felt pressed by the inert formulas of orthodoxy.

The Philosophy of "As-if" (London, 1924); F. Lindstaedt, *Grundwissenschaftliche Kritik der Hauptbegriffe von Vaihingers Philosophie des Als-Ob* (Greifswald, 1914); H. Hegenwald, *Gegenwartsphilosophie und christliche Religion* (Leipzig, 1913); J. Spickerbaum, *Das Vaihingersche Als-Ob und die Methode der Formsprache in Religion und Theologie* (Munchen, 1922).

H.H.

Vaisnavism: See Vishnu; Vishnuism.

vaisya: The third of the four traditional castes of India, the lowest of the twice-born. Supposed to include the merchant-farmer class of society. Formed according to the myth (Rig Veda X, 90, 12) from the thighs of purusha* or cosmic man.

C.S.B.

Valentine Day, St.: The early martyrologies mention three Saint Valentines on February 14th. Many believe that the one especially honored is Valentine, the holy priest of Rome who ministered to the martyrs in the persecution of Claudius and who was himself beheaded by him on February 14th, about the year 270.

That Saint Valentine is the patron of lovers is easily understood since on his feast, about the middle of the month, birds begin to mate. And lovers chose the day as their festival and began to call one another "valentine." Legend attributes to him the power of healing lovers' quarrels.

Another explanation states that the pagan youths had a lewd superstitious custom of drawing the names of girls in honor of the goddess Februata Juno, whose festival was celebrated on the middle of the month. Several pastors substituted the names of saints in the lists for this day.

Cf. Butler, *Lives of the Saints; Catholic Encyclopedia,* vol. XV, p. 254.

S.C.

Valentinian decree: See clergy.

Valentinus: Gnostic* teacher in Rome, c. 135-165. One of ablest minds of his age. Valentinian gnosticism has threefold division of personality instead of the more usual two.

K.H.C.

value: (Lat., *valere,* to be strong or well) Whatever is desired, liked, esteemed or approved. Synonym: good. Antonyms: evil*, disvalue. Values are to be distinguished from ideals. A value is the actual experiencing of what is liked; an ideal is the definition or concept of what is (or ought to be) experienced as a value. Valuation is the ascription of value (likability) to an experience. Evaluation is judging a value by an ideal of what ought to be (a standard, a norm). Psychologically, value has been viewed as pleasure (hedonism: Epicurus,** Meinong), fulfillment of purpose, desire or interest (voluntarism: Aristotle, Spinoza**, Ehrenfels, Perry), rational will (formalism: Stoics, Kant, Royce**), integration of personality (idealism, perfectionism, synopsis: Plato, Hegel, T. H. Green**, Bosanquet).

Values are either intrinsic or instrumental. Intrinsic values are prized as ends; they are enjoyed for their own sake, independently of what they may lead to. Instrumental values are means to or causes of intrinsic values. All intrinsic values are also instrumental, although sometimes instrumental to evil, as well as to good. Most instrumental values may also be valued intrinsically. Thus the distinction is relative, not absolute; it is largely a difference in point of view. However, everything external to a mind is purely instrumental, for intrinsic value exists only as an actual personal consciousness of liking or interest, a personal enjoyment. Hence, all natural things, processes and events, and all economic goods and processes, in so far as they are not within the experience of a mind, are purely instrumental values.

The intrinsic values may be classified, in order of increasing value (breadth, inclusiveness, coherence): bodily (the joys of health and bodily activity—not the physical existence of the body), recreational (play, humor, amusement), work (usefulness, productive employment), associational (co-operation or sharing with individuals or groups), character (a rational will, loyal to what is believed best), aesthetic (beautiful, sublime, tragic, comic, etc.), intellectual (thinking, truth-seeking, truth-finding), religious (the holy, experiences of worship, co-operation with the divine, etc.). The intrinsic values are interdependent; they "interpenetrate" (Everett) or coalesce. Hence the ideal of intrinsic value is a personal-social life in which the unique contribution of each value is realized in harmonious interrelation with all the other values.

Experience moves from empirical values as given (value-claims, apparent values) to "true" or "ideal" values (a coherent and critical organization of value experience).

All philosophers hold to the subjectivity of value in the sense that value is primarily personal experience. Idealists and many realists (Platonic, scholastic, religious) hold also to the objectivity of value, or, better, of the ideals to which true values should conform. The objective ideals are cosmic norms (Platonic Ideas) or purposes. See axiology; conservation of value; ethics; perfect; summum bonum.

See: C. von Ehrenfels, *System der Werttheorie* (1902); W. M. Urban, *Valuation* (1909); B. Bosanquet, *The Principle of Individuality and Value* (1912); W. G. Everett, *Moral Values* (1918); E. S. Brightman, *Religious Values* (1925); R. B. Perry, *A General Theory of Value* (1926); J. Laird, *The Idea of Value* (1929); J. Hessen, *Wertphilosophie* (1937); J. Dewey, *Theory of Valuation* (*Int. Enc. of Unified Science*, II, 1939); art. "Valor" in J. Ferrater Mora, *Diccionario de la Filosofia* (1941).

E.S.B.

vampire: A ghost who sucks the blood of the living. A normal person might become a vampire unwillingly if a cat should chance to jump over his corpse before it was buried. The superstition seems to have originated in central Europe in the middle ages. The word itself is probably Slavic.

P.G.M.

Vanir: Norse mythol; name of a group of gods, including Njord, Frey, Freyja, and possibly others who dwell in Vanaheim. Deities of wealth, fruitfulness, commerce, they were supposed to have quarrelled with the other gods led by Odin*, a myth possibly reflecting the opposition of rival cults.

R.B.B.

Varuna: Sky god of Vedic Hinduism. He was the guarantor of *rita**, the God of law and order in the world. His most notable feature was his concern for the moral law. He was all-seeing; could discern even the inner heart of man; he was the punisher of sin; but was also gracious to forgive. Noblest of all the Vedic divinities, possessing all the qualities that might have led to his supremacy as an ethical, monotheistic deity, Varuna's power and influence waned until he became a relatively unimportant Lord of the waters. Ahura Mazda* in Persia stems from the same original Aryan divinity. See Aryan religion.

C.S.B.

Vāsudeva: A variant name of Vishnu and of Krishna**.

C.S.B.

Vatican: The official residence of the Pope* in Vatican City. It comprises the papal apartments, the apartments of prelates, officials, and staff, apartments of state, numerous chapels, the famous Vatican Library, archives of the Catholic Church, five museums of antiquities, two art galleries, a polyglot printing press, and an astronomical observatory. See Papal States.

C.V.

Vatican Council: The Twentieth Ecumenical* Council of the Catholic Church. Pius IX* announced in 1867 his intention of convoking a general council, the first since Trent. When a report circulated that a definition of papal infallibility* was expected of the Council, an anti-infallibility campaign was started under the leadership of Döllinger*, a leading German historian. About seven hundred bishops were present at the opening on December 8, 1869. The dogmatic constitution "Dei filius" on creation, revelation, faith, and the relationship of faith and reason was promulgated on April 24, 1870. The debate on papal prerogatives was lively and lasted from May to July. A large majority held that a definition of infallibility was in order. A notable minority, consisting principally of German, Austro-Hungarian, French and North American bishops opposed such a step. The members of this minority with but few exceptions were not opposed to the doctrine but considered its definition inopportune. The majority prevailed and the dogmatic constitution "Pastor aeternus" was promulgated on July 18, 1870. In it in addition to papal infallibility, the doctrine of the primacy was formulated. With the outbreak of the Franco-Prussian War the membership of the Council dwindled and on October 20, 1870 the meetings were suspended after only a fraction of the program had been completed. The infallibility decree occasioned the schism of the Old Catholics*. See canons of various churches; pope.

C. Butler, *The Vatican Council* (1930), 2 vols.

E.A.R.

Vatke, Wilhelm: (1806-1882) Professor of theology at the University of Berlin. As a liberal theologian he developed the tools in the methodical improvement of historical criticism. He had to struggle for a long time against the opposition of orthodox theology, especially of E. W. Hengstenberg's*. He not only took sympathetic cognizance of natural science, but also exhaustively treated the psychological appearance of religion in human self consciousness.

Die Religion des Alten Testaments (Berlin, 1835); *Die menschliche Freiheit in ihrem Verhältnis zur Sünde und zur göttlichen Gnade* (Berlin, 1841); G. S. Preiss, *Historische kritische Einleitung ins alte Testament* (Bonn, 1886); *Religionsphilosophie oder allgemeine philosophische Theologie nach Vorlesungen* (Bonn, 1888); S. H. Benecke, *Wilhelm Vatke in seinem Leben und seinen Schriften* (Bonn, 1883).

H.H.

Vaughan, Henry: (1622-1695) English poet, noteworthy for a collection of religious poems, *Silex Scintillans* (1650-55), written largely under the influence of George Herbert*. L.W.C.

Vāyu (Vata): There are two Vedic words for wind, Vāyu and Vāta, and both are used also for the wind god in Vedic Hinduism. Vayu is said to be used more commonly as the god name, though in the Rig-Veda there is but one entire hymn to Vāyu and two to Vāta. C.S.B.

Vazquez, Gabriel: (1549-1604) Spanish Jesuit and theologian, whose works are distinguished for their critical acumen, historical information, and boldness of view. E.A.R.

vectorial psychology: See psychology, schools of.

Vedānta: The best known and most popular formulation of Indian philosophy. One of the traditional six philosophic schools. As expounded by Shankara*, (circa 800 A.D.) in his commentary on the Vedānta Sutras, there is but one real, Brahman. The phenomenal world is illusion. It has only seeming reality, as have also the apparent individual selves of the world. There is truly but one self, Brahman-Ātman. Ignorance of the oneness of the self with Brahman* is the cause of samsara* or rebirth which is also only illusory. Knowledge then of the identity of the soul with Brahman is the key to salvation.* Who knows, "that, soul art thou," is emancipated from the wheel of existence. He has attained *moksha**.

Shankara, it is true, recognized a lower as well as a higher knowledge. On the lower plane, Brahman becomes the personal Brahma and by the techniques of sacrifice and worship union with Brahma may be achieved. But it is only a temporary salvation. Final emancipation comes only by the knowledge of identity with Brahman.

As interpreted by Rāmānuja* about 1100 A.D. also in a commentary on the Vedanta Sutras it becomes a qualified monism, *Visishtadvaita.* The phenomenal world and individual souls have real existence, though apart from Brahman they could not do so. They are the body of Brahman. Ramanuja believed in the continuing existence of emancipated souls, and salvation or *moksha* was attained through *bhakti** or the way of faith and love toward God.

S. Radhakrishnan, *Indian Philosophy* (London, 1923, 1927), 2 vols.; Also S. DasGupta, *History of Indian Philosophy* (Cambridge, 1922, 1932), vols. I and II; Paul Deussen, *The Vedanta* (1912).

C.S.B.

Vedas: Ancient scriptures of India held to be *sruti** or the very revealed word of divinity. They go back to the early centuries of Aryan migration into India, some of the hymns doubtless having been in use before the arrival in India. There are four Vedas, the basic Rig-Veda* upon which the remaining three depend to a considerable degree; the Sama-Veda* or Chant-Veda; the Yajur-Veda* and the late Atharva-Veda*. Theoretically the later Hindu sacred writings serve but to elucidate further the teachings of the Vedas. Actually they are but little used by modern Hindus save the Arya-Samajists who represent a "back to the Vedas movement". Dyananda Sarasvati*, the founder, evolved an interpretation of the sacred texts which finds in them the all sufficient source of all that is of value in his version of Hinduism* which is essentially monotheistic.

So sacred were the Vedas at the time the Laws of Manu* took form that no low caste man might hear or recite them under penalty of having molten metal poured into his ears or his tongue cut out. C.S.B.

Vedic religion: See Hinduism.

Vendidad: A priestly code in the Avesta*, prescribing certain purifications, penances, and expiations. Beginning with the creation, the golden age, and the flood, it deals with agriculture, burial, civil and penal law, purifications after contact with a corpse and other impurities, commendation of the dog and of the cock, etc. R.H.P.

veneration of relics: See images; relic.

veneration of saints: See saints, veneration of; ancestor worship; hero worship; icon; patron saints.

vengeance: See asylum; blood revenge; law.

venial sin: See mortal and venial sin; sin.

Venus: An Italic goddess of gardens, who was identified with the Greek Aphrodite, goddess of love and beauty. Almost all the myths about Venus consequently belong to Aphrodite, whose character was much less simple. P.G.M.

Veronica, Saint: (Incorrectly derived from *verum ikon*, true image) A legendary woman, who gradually became associated with a famous picture of Christ that belongs to the twelfth century. Both Veronica and the picture were woven into the story of Christ's passion. Traces of the legend mount to the fourth century, but without connection with the passion. The association with the passion comes only in the late Middle Ages. C.V.

verse division of the Bible: While the Vulgate was divided into chapters early in the thirteenth century by Stephen Langton*, the further division of the chapters into verses was begun by Robert Estienne (Stephanus, the Latin form of his name, used in publication), the French printer, in his fourth edition (very rare) of the Greek N.T., 1551, in which he broke the text into 7959 verse paragraphs. This was followed by William Whittingham at Geneva in his revision of the N.T. in 1557, and in the Geneva Bible of 1560 was extended to the O.T. and the Apocrypha. See chapters and verses of the Bible. E.J.G.

versions of the Bible, ancient: The translations of the Bible into other languages provide valuable help to the student who seeks the exact form of the original wording of the scriptures. In the case of the O.T., early versions compensate somewhat for the lack of early Hebrew manuscripts*. In the N.T., the ancient translations increase our knowledge of its transmission by indicating the geographical location of particular forms of the text. These versions came into being spontaneously, to serve missionary needs or the devotional life of those who did not know the original language of the scriptures. The earliest and freest translations were in time replaced by "official" church versions.

I. Versions of the Old Testament. The important ancient translations of the O.T. in their approximate chronological order follow.

1. The Septuagint (Greek) is the most important of all versions of the O.T. Made in Alexandria by various translators who worked from about the 3rd to the first century B.C., its parts vary widely in linguistic level and degree of literalness. Origen's edition (The Hexapla*) led to the corruption of the Greek by the Hebrew. The common symbol for this version is LXX*; more than 2000 of its manuscripts (from the 2nd to the 16th century) have been catalogued.

2. The Old Latin, so-called to distinguish it from the later Latin vulgate, was in existence at the end of the 2nd century A.D. This version is relatively unimportant in the O.T. since it is a translation from the LXX and exists only in fragmentary manuscripts.

3. The Peshitta* (Syriac) was the standard O.T. of Syrian Christians; it probably is as old as the 2nd century and was made from the Hebrew. However it was later revised by the Septuagint text, which diminishes its usefulness somewhat.

4. The Syro-Hexaplar (Syriac) was translated from Origen's edition of the LXX in 617 A.D. by Bishop Paul of Tella, who preserved the critical notations of Origen's Greek text. By this means, scholars are able to remove much of the corruption of post-Origen Septuagint manuscripts. This version, therefore, is of great value in the study of the Septuagint.

5. Four Coptic (Egyptian) versions of the O.T. exist. The oldest of these, the Sahidic or Thebaic, was made in Southern Egypt from the LXX in the 2nd century. It aids in attaining a form of the Greek text older than Origen. The Bohairic or Memphitic was made in Northern Egypt at least a century or two later. We have but a few fragments of the Fayumic and Akhmimic versions of the O.T.

6. The Latin Vulgate was made by Jerome* toward the end of the 4th century. Jerome made three translations of the Psalter, each one closer to the Hebrew; but it was the second, not the third of these, that won its way into the official vulgate. Throughout the area of the Protestant O.T. Jerome translated from the Hebrew, and wished to omit the apocryphal* books entirely, but he did translate two of them (Judith and Tobit**), and the others were added later. This Latin Vulgate became the commonly accepted Bible of the West through the Middle Ages; it exists in as many as 8000 manuscripts. In general Jerome's version is a witness to the Massoretic Hebrew text (see Masorah), and gains in value from its position as the earliest extensive witness to this form of the text.

7. Minor versions of the O.T.: Under this heading may be grouped the Greek versions other than the LXX, and the Gothic, Ethiopic, and Armenian. Greek versions were made about the 2nd century A.D. by Aquila, Symmachus, and Theodotion; the first being closest to the Hebrew, and all being included in Origen's Hexapla. Only fragments remain. The Ethiopic, Gothic, and Armenian were made from the LXX about the 4th century A.D. and are extant today.

II. Versions of the New Testament.

1. The Old Latin version of the N.T. originated by the end of the 2nd century, probably in Africa, and exists in at least two forms, which are usually called the African and the European Latin. The "Itala" of older studies was shown by Burkitt to be Jerome's Vulgate. The Old Latin is of primary importance in the study of the text of the N.T. The "African" was used by Cyprian*.

2. The Diatessaron* was a harmony of the gospels made by Tatian* about 160 A.D. The recent discovery of one page of it in a Greek manuscript of the 3rd century in Syria strengthens the hypothesis that it was made in Greek and translated into Syriac. Aside from this leaf it is known in an Armenian version of St. Ephrem's commentary and less accurately in an Arabic translation recently edited by Marmardji.

3. The Old Syriac, so-called to distinguish it from the Peshitta, exists in two manuscripts in variant forms. These codices, the Sinaitic and the Curetonian Syriac MSS, belong in the front rank of textual witnesses. The text they represent is probably no later than 200 A.D. and can be assigned to Syria with certainty.

4. Five Egyptian (Coptic) versions of the N.T. are known today. The oldest of these is the

Sahidic from Southern Egypt. It may be as early as the 2nd century A.D. The Bohairic version from Northern Egypt was evidently the dominant version of the later period since it has the richest manuscript attestation. Known only in part are the Fayumic, Akhmimic, and Middle Egyptian versions; some of these may be older than the Bohairic or as old as the Sahidic; the Akhmimic, for example, exists in two fourth century manuscripts. The Bohairic is well and favorably known for its support of Hort's Neutral Text; all the other versions listed this far have strong non-Neutral elements.

5. The Armenian version was made at least by 400 A.D. from a source whose text was close to that of MSS Theta, 565, and 700. The Old Georgian version was made from the Armenian and shares its quality, a quality which Streeter called Caesarean.

6. The Latin Vulgate was a revision of the Old Latin made by Jerome after 380 A.D. In the gospels, Jerome seems to have used a Greek manuscript of the type of Sinaiticus; in Acts, one similar to Alexandrinus. (See Codex Sinaiticus; Codex Alexandrinus.) The text of Jerome's revision is the official text of the Roman Church since the action of the Council of Trent* in 1546.

7. Minor Versions of the N.T.: The Gothic, Ethiopic, and Syriac Peshitta versions are definitely secondary in origin and importance. Originating in the 4th to the 5th centuries, they are close to that form of the Greek text which Hort called Syrian. Of the minor Syriac versions, the Harklean made in 616 A.D. is an important non-Neutral witness, and the Palestinian lectionary of the 13th century contains a small percentage of early readings. See translations of the Bible.

A. General: K. Lake, *The Text of the New Testament* (6th ed., rev. by Silva New, London, Rivingtons, 1928); L. Vaganay, *An Introduction to the Textual Criticism of the New Testament* (trans. by B. V. Miller, London, 1937); I. M. Price, *The Ancestry of our English Bible* (9th ed., 1934); F. G. Kenyon, *Our Bible And the Ancient Manuscripts* (4th ed., 1940); H. W. Robinson, *The Bible in its Ancient and English Versions* (Oxford, 1940); C. R. Gregory, *Textkritik des Neuen Testamentes,* vol. II (Leipzig, 1902).

B. By versions. (1) The Septuagint: A. Rahlfs, *Septuaginta* (Stuttgart, Privilegierte Württemburgische Bibelanstalt, 1935); A. E. Brooke and N. McLean, *The Old Testament in Greek according to the Text of Codex Vaticanus* (Cambridge, 1906-); see the various *Septuaginta Studien* of the Göttingen Septuaginta Unternehmung. (2) Old Latin: Adolf Jülicher, *Itala, Das Neue Testament in Altlateinischer Ueberlieferung, Vol. I, Matthäus Evangelium, Vol II, Marcus Evangelium* (Berlin, 1938, 1940). (3) Latin Vulgate: A. Gasquet, *Biblia Sacra iuxta Latinam Vulgatum Versionem* (Rome: Vatican, 1926-); J. Wordsworth and H. I. White, *Nouum Testamentum Domini nostri Iesu Christi latine, secundum editionem Sancti Hieronymi ad codicum manuscriptorum fidem recensuit* (Oxford, 1889-). (4) Syriac Diatessaron: M. J. Lagrange, *Introduction a l'étude du Nouveau Testament: Manuel de critique textuelle du Nouveau Testament II. Critique rationelle* (Paris, 1935), pp. 184-202; O. P. Marmardji, *Diatessaron de Tatien* (Beirut, Imprimerie Catholique, 1935). (5) The Old Syriac: F. C. Burkitt, *Evangelion da-Mepharreshe* (Cambridge, 1904). (6) The Egyptian (Coptic) versions: Sahidic—G. Horner, *The Coptic Version of the New Testament in the Southern Dialect* (Oxford, 1911-1924); H. Thompson, *The Coptic Version of the Acts of the Apostles and the Pauline Epistles in the Sahidic Dialect* (Cambridge, 1932). Bohairic—G. Horner, *The Coptic Version of the New Testament in the Northern Dialect otherwise called Memphitic and Bohairic* (Oxford, 1895-1905). General articles and other dialects—A. Vaschalde, "Ce qui a été publie des Versions coptes de la Bible," *Revue Biblique* (1919-1922); *Le Muséon* (1930-1933); Jean Simon in *Le Muséon* (1941); H. Thompson, *The Gospel of St. John according to the Earliest Coptic Ms.* (London, 1924). (7) and (8) Armenian and Old Gregorian: S. Lyonnet in M. J. Lagrange, *Critique Textuelle* (Paris, 1935). (9) Syriac Peshitta: Pusey-Gwilliam, *Tetra-euangelium Sanctum uxta simplicem syrorum versionem* (Oxford, 1901); *The New Testament in Syriac* (London, 1905-1920). (10) The Syro-Hexaplar: A. M. Ceriani, *Codex syro-hexaplaris ambrosianus photolithographice editus* (Milan: Ambrosian Library, 1874). (11) Gothic: W. Streitberg, *Die Gotische Bibel* (2nd ed., Heidelberg, Winter, 1919); C. W. S. Friedrichsen, *The Gothic Version of the Gospels* (Oxford, 1926). (12) Ethiopic: see C. R. Gregory's *Textkritik.*

E.C.C.

verstehungspsychologie: See psychology, schools of.

vespers: The early evening hour of the Divine Office*. See evensong. E.R.H.

Vesta: Chief of the Roman household divinities, perhaps originally the hearth-life, *ignis in foco.* The significance of the hearth for warmth and food is central. The hearth-fire of the king's house later became the "Temple" of Vesta, and after the kings were banished, the place of his daughters, guardians of the fire, was taken by Vestal Virgins, officially appointed by the state. Cf. Hestia. P.G.M.

Vestal Virgins: Guardians of the perpetual fire in the Atrium of Vesta. At first four in number, but later six. Their service lasted for thirty years (ca. 6-36) during which time they were forbidden to marry. They had many royal prerogatives, for example, lictors preceded them on the streets and even the highest magistrates made way; they had reserved seats at public games; and if a criminal on the way to execution encountered a Vestal, he was automatically pardoned and set free.

P.G.M.

Vestiarian controversy: A controversy over clerical dress in sixteenth century England. The initial phase occurred in 1550 when John Hooper objected to the requirement in the new ordinal prepared by Cranmer that candidates for ordination appear in white vestments. The controversy was revived in 1564 when Elizabeth sought to enforce uniformity of clerical dress. W.S.H.

vestments: Christian vestments are a particular example of a widespread custom of retaining in ceremonial use (civic or religious) styles of clothing otherwise discarded. They have developed further in church use, and serve to emphasize the office rather than the man, to express the dignity of worship, and to preserve historic continuity. The chief vestments come from the Roman daily dress of the 1st century—a tunic and cloak—which after the disuse of the toga was worn on official occasions as well. Since the adoption of trousers about the 7th century these garments survive as alb* and chasuble (late Latin *casula,* little house). Napkins carried first for use, then for ornament, became the stole and maniple**. In the East the chasuble is open in front, and often worn without alb outside of the Eucharist. In the West it is open at the side (in modern usage often much curtailed), and is the primary eucharistic vestment. For other services vestments derived from the alb are worn—surplice*, cotta, or rochet. The monastic habit was similarly formalized from workman's dress; from monastic sources comes the cope, an ornamented cloak worn for various solemn functions. In the later Middle Ages hoods or capes worn over the surplice for convenience developed into insignia—hence the tippet and hood of Anglican clergy, the chimere of Anglican and mozetta or mantellettum of Roman Bishops. Most Protestants abandoned vestments, though Scandinavian and some other Lutherans retained the alb and chasuble. But the gown commonly worn by the professional classes in the 16th century became in effect a vestment; about 1900 the frock coat started on a similar development, but the gown or some of the older vestments are now often used. In England vestments were retained in principle at the Reformation; but in practice all except the surplice and cope were disused until the 19th century. See ritualism.

J. Braun S. J., *Die liturgische Gewandung* (1907); P. Dearmer, *The Ornaments of the Ministers* (1908).

E.R.H.

vestry: 1) A room attached to a church in which the vestments, altar ornaments, sacramental vessels and parish register are kept; it is the place of vesting (*vestiarium*) the clergy; 2) It is also used as the place of meeting of the parish council, also called the *Vestry.* The powers of the Vestry are the control of parish funds, authorization of changes in or repair of the fabric of the church, election of certain officers (including the vestry clerk). Vestries in England also retained certain civil powers, e.g., control of poor law arrangements, from the reign of Elizabeth down to the beginning of the nineteenth century.

F.W.B.

viaticum: The Holy Communion administered to a person at the point of death; not to be confused with the sacrament of Extreme Unction*.

A.C.

vicar: In English Ecclesiastical law*, the priest of a parish the tithes of which are owned by the bishop*, a spiritual corporation or a layman; any incumbent of a benefice* who is not a rector*. In America in the Episcopal Church, the priest in charge of a chapel within a parish, or in charge of a parish of which the bishop is the rector.

T.J.B.

vicar apostolic: Formerly a bishop* who was delegated by the Pope to have certain jurisdictional authority outside his diocese. Now in the Roman Catholic Church 1) a prelate* commissioned to administer vacant sees or to discharge the functions of a disabled diocesan, or 2) in certain missionary countries a titular bishop delegated by the Pope for the government of the Church there.

T.J.B.

Vicar of Christ: The Pope*; a title that refers to the doctrine that the Pope is representative of Christ as head of the church on earth.

T.J.B.

vicar-general: In the Church of England* a layman, chancelor to the Archbishop of Canterbury or York, who acts as his deputy in certain legal matters such as, institution to benefices*, provincial appointments to the episcopate, and marriages. In the Roman Catholic Church* the deputy of a bishop in jurisdictional matters; the name after Trent for the archdeacon*.

T.J.B.

vicarious suffering: See atonement in Christianity; sacrifice; salvation.

Victor, Saint, mystics of: See mystics of Saint Victor.

vidhi: A rule or formula, sacred precept or scripture.

P.G.M.

Vienne, Council of: The Fifteenth Ecumenical* Council of the Catholic Church (1311-1312) was called by Clement V to treat of the suppression of the Knights Templar*, a crusade, the reform of morals, and the defense of ecclesiastical liberty. The acts of the council have disappeared almost entirely. It refused to condemn the Templars unheard, voted money for a crusade, condemned the errors of Peter John Olivi, and issued reform decrees.

E.A.R.

vigil: (Lat., *vigilia,* night watch) Originally the night office of festivals (see matins); later the penitential observance of the day before certain festivals.

E.R.H.

Vinaya School: See Buddhist Terminology.

Vincent de Paul, St.: (1581-1660) French priest, founder of the Congregation of Priests of the Mission (Vincentians or Lazarists), of the Sisters of Charity*, and of the Ladies of Charity. In the revival of Catholicism in seventeenth century France, there is no brighter name than that of this poor shepherd boy who became the father of the poor, a restorer of the clergy, and the great saint of "le grand siècle." See foundling asylums.

E.A.R.

Vincent, J. H.: See Sunday School movement in the United States.

Vincent of Lerins: A "religious" of the early Church (died cir. 440), best known for his *Commonitorium,* in which Christian faith is discussed and tests are suggested for orthodox belief. Succinctly summed up in the phrase, *quod ubique, quod semper, quod ab omnibus,* the Vincentian canon has been widely employed in historic Christianity. Another phrase from Vincent, *non nova sed nove,* has also been used extensively to describe the relation of Christian faith to newer forms of expression.

W.N.P.

Vinet, Alexandre: (1797-1847) Swiss theologian, built his theology on a Kantian faith in the autonomy of the individual conscience, from which he deduced the necessity of complete religious liberty, separation of church and state, and the duty of testing all traditional doctrines by direct personal experience. See Frommel. W.M.H.

virgin birth: There are many instances of unusual, miraculous and supernatural conceptions in the history of religions. Emphasis upon the virginity of the mother is relatively rare. In simple cultures conception might occur through contact with the elements or objects of mysterious potency such as amulets, fetishes or images**. Stories of divine parentage gave added prestige or authority to many men in the lands bordering on the Mediterranean in ancient times. The rulers of Egypt were sons of the high god, Rē. Zeus and Apollo fathered some of the most illustrious men of Greece and Rome including Plato, Alexander, Apollonius of Tyana and Augustus. In these cases the virginity of the mother was not important. Supernatural intervention attended the conceptions of Isaac, Samson and John the Baptist in the Biblical story. The materials for the body and spirit of Zoroaster were brought from heaven by the Amesha Spentas*, made into the sacred liquor, haoma*, mixed with the milk of unimpregnated cows and fed to the parents of the prophet. The embryo of Mahāvira*, founder of Jainism, took form in the womb of a Brāhman lady. The god Indra* transferred it to a mother of more aristrocratic and wealthier lineage. Gotama Buddha* surveyed the world from the Tusita heaven and chose the woman for his final rebirth. These conceptions were miraculous or at least unusual, but all of the mothers were married.

Romulus was certainly virgin born since he was the child of a Vestal* priestess and the god Mars. The Zoroastrian* prophets who appear at the close of each millennium of the last age of the world are conceived by virgins impregnated by the seed of Zoroaster while bathing in an Iranian lake. The account of the conception of Jesus in Luke's Gospel follows the pattern of supernatural intervention as in the conception of Isaac or John the Baptist. Matthew's account, however, stresses the virginity of Mary* although the claim to virgin birth ruins the genealogical argument of the gospels by which Jesus has status as Messiah* by descent from David through Joseph. The doctrine of Virgin Birth was universally accepted by the middle of the second century. It was necessary to insist upon it then since only the union of the divine and human essences in him could make Jesus an adequate savior. A.E.H.

Virgin Mary: The place of Mary, the mother of Jesus, in Christian thought and devotion is based on the meaning of her unique position as the human mother of Incarnate God, rather than upon the N.T., or upon apocryphal gospels (e.g., Proto-evangelion of St. James), or upon patristic opinions (e.g., the comparisons with Eve in Justin Martyr and St. Irenaeus**), for these are considerations of that meaning. The references in the N.T. to the Blessed Virgin Mary are few and their information slight. Except in the Infancy Narratives in St. Luke which speak of her acceptance of her vocation as Mother of Christ, she is present in the background of events.

With the development of the cultus of the saints*, devotion to her held a first place that was enhanced by the decision of the Council of Ephesus* (431) which centered its attention on the question raised by the Nestorians*, the unity of the Person of our Lord, in connection with their term, *Christotokos*. The decision in favour of St. Cyril's* term, *Theotokos* (literally, God-bearer, and thus less liable to misunderstanding than *Mater Dei* or Mother of God), was based on affirmation of the reality underlying the *communicatio idiomatum**. This understanding of her honour was assured by the decision of II Nicea against excess (See Mariolatry). By the 7th century feast days in her honour in the calendar included her Nativity, the Purification, the Annunciation*, and the Falling Asleep. In the East her cultus has always been close to the Liturgy*, while in the West after 1000 there came a certain separation of her cultus from devotion to Christ (in votive masses*, the Little Office, the Angelus*, the Rosary* and the Salve Regina). In doctrine St. Mary is regarded as typifying the response of humanity to Deity as in the Church and the Christian soul. She is regarded as the first of the saints who in her life was preeminent in purity and obedience and who now, because she already enjoys the Beatific Vision*, is preeminent in prayer. Pious opinions have stated this in terms of her sinlessness, her perpetual virginity, her mediatorship and her bodily assumption—the first three of these being matters of faith for Roman Catholics. Definition of the sinlessness led to the medieval controversy in which the Scotists* upheld the Immaculate Conception* as against the Thomists*, the view that by the anticipated merits of Christ Mary was preserved from, rather than freed from, original sin*, a position made matter of faith by Papal bull of 1854. See Mary, cult of; Sabbatine privilege. T.J.B.

virtualism: See Lord's Supper.

virtues, seven: See seven virtues.

Vishnu: A relatively minor sun god in the Vedas, one of the Adityas**, Vishnu became the supreme god of the great Vishnuite or Vaisnava* sect of Hinduism*. He is the Preserver in the Hindu Triad in which Brahma* is Creator, and Shiva*, Destroyer.

Traditionally Vishnu is held to have appeared in many different incarnations*, including some in animal or half animal form, as the fish, and tortoise, the boar, the man-lion. The greater incarnations or avatars are Krishna, Rama, Buddha**, representing an attempt to assimilate Buddhism to Vishnuism; and Kalki is yet to come. See Lakshmi; Narayana. C.S.B.

Vishnuism, Vaisnavism: One of the two major theistic sects of Hinduism*, which center about the worship of the great personal god Vishnu* or some one or more of his incarnations, of whom Krishna and Rama** are the most important. Its beginnings are to be found well back in the pre-Christian era. The Bhagavad-Gita* is perhaps its noblest literary expression. Its fuller development came under Ramanuja* and Ramananda* leaders of the two principal subdivisions of the sect. Other subdivisions are the Madhvas, dating from the 13th century, the Vallabha-Charyas, and the Chaitanyas from the 16th century. In general the Vishnu worship is of the *bhakti** type, and some subsects have carried it to an extreme which has offended the moral sensibilities of most cultured Indians. In its more advanced forms it is essentially monotheistic in belief and practice. C.S.B.

visions: Visual imagery which impresses its beholder with its meaningful and objective character yet which is without the appropriate sense stimulus or physical presence. In psychological structure and origin visions are not unlike dreams and are not necessarily pathological. They may be normal dreams or vivid memories or vigorous imaginings.

In religion the term refers to a not uncommon experience of persons under the influence of intense religious emotion or of mystics* and those of mystical temperament. Religious visions have historically been believed to be supernatural in origin and revelatory in significance. They are characteristic phenomena of religious ecstacy* though not esteemed its most important feature. Their content is derived from the current religious beliefs and expectations of the subject and his culture. They are now held to be induced by concentrated emotional attention upon religious objects or themes. Psychologists classify and interpret them as visual automatisms and hallucinatory phenomena. In later Israel the visions of the true prophets were distinguished from those of false prophets by their ethical content and their worth for practical life. This continues to be the important test of their value. They may also have diagnostic value for psychologists and psychiatrists in their study of personality disorders. R.W.F.

Visitation: A name given to the visit of Mary, the mother of Jesus, to Elizabeth, the mother of John the Baptist, before the birth of their respective children as narrated in Luke 1:39-56. Also the name of a Feast adopted by the Franciscans* in the 13th century and extended to the Church at large in the 14th century. Assigned to July 2nd. S.M.G.

Visitation, Order of the: An order of religious women, known as the Visitation nuns, founded in 1610 by St. Francis de Sales, Bishop of Geneva, and St. Jane Francis de Chantal**. This order, which stresses the unaustere, common life of prayer and poverty, spread rapidly through Europe. It now conducts residential schools for girls, including a number in the United States. C.V.

visitation of the sick: A regular ministry of the clergy in the Christian Church from the earliest times to aid the sufferer in the sanctification of his illness. Ancient offices for annointing* and visitation required several of the clergy and choir. Modern offices in the Roman Catholic, the Anglican, and the Eastern Churches are for the priest alone. They comprise Unction, Confession, Communion**, and prayers for the sick and dying. There is now in all churches a greater attention to pastoral as well as liturgical* ministrations to the sick. See sacraments. T.J.B.

Vittoria, Francisco de: (1480-1546) Chief Spanish Dominican ethico-political theorist of the Counter-Reformation*. As God is the ultimate source of political authority, it is the duty of government to use its power for the welfare of the governed. His doctrine of international law is the most original part of his thought. He argued that there was an international community, including Christian and non-Christian nations, which had equality as members thereof. International law rests ultimately on an agreement of the majority of nations. He held that lack of an acceptable authority to adjudicate a dispute between states and the existence of a legitimate ground for war did not justify the actual making of war. He insisted that the government of colonial empire has the moral responsibility of giving the natives nothing less than human treatment.

J. B. Scott, *The Spanish Origin of International Law, Francisco de Vittoria and his Law of Nations* (London, 1934); H. F. Wright, ed., *Francisco de Vittoria* (1932). H.H.

Vittorino da Feltre: (1378-1446) The greatest teacher of the Italian Renaissance*, with a disinterested love of learning, virtue and youth, and combining classic culture with Christian piety. His school at Mantua, which grew out of his post as tutor for the Gonzaga family, employed methods later developed by Pestalozzi.

Orelli, *Vittorino da Feltre* (Zurich, 1812); Rosmini, *Vita de Vittorino* (Bassano, 1801); J. A. Symonds, *Revival of Learning* (1877), pp. 289-299; W. H. Woodward, *Vittorino and other Humanist Educators* (Cambridge, 1905). W.E.G.

Vivekānanda, Swami: (1862-1902) The name assumed by a young high-caste Bengali, Narendra Nath Datta, a follower of Ramakrishna* and organizer of the Ramakrishna Movement in India, when, after his master's death, he became a sannyasi. He represented Hinduism* at the Parliament of Religions at the Chicago World's Fair in 1893, and founded the Vedanta Society in America. He was a great mystic as well as teacher and organizer.

Sister Nivedita, *The Master as I Knew Him*; Romain Rolland, *Prophets of the New India* (1930). C.S.B.

vocation: This word is employed in two senses, both of them with their roots in the N.T. 1) The Christian calling. It is assumed in the O.T. that a great leader or prophet is directly called by

God, either in his lifetime (e.g. David, Isaiah) or even before his birth (e.g., Jeremiah). This idea was taken up and expanded by Christian teachers, who held that men became disciples in response to a special call by God. The Gospel was offered to all, but only those could accept it whom God had singled out from the mass of men and "called to be saints". Paul and the Fourth Evangelist ground their certainty of salvation in this assurance* that God has called his servants before they entered the world (see predestination). 2) The word is also applied to the activity or the condition of life which a man finds allotted to him, and in this sense has passed into our common language. Paul thinks of slaves and free men as "called" to the status they occupy. He can say "Let every man abide in the same calling to which he is called". (I Cor. 7:20) It is implied that men should regard their everyday tasks and duties as divinely appointed to them, and it was this new estimate of labour which brought about a social transformation.

W. Morgan, *Religion and Theology of Paul* (1917). E.F.S.

vogue: See culture.

Volkelt, Johannes: (1848-1930) Of eminent importance in the field of aesthetics, he was professor of philosophy at the University of Leipzig. He not only held a critical metaphysics possible, but he favored an unlimited realism. He regarded the religious attitude an intuitive, immediate subjective experience with reference to a transempirical reality. It is in essence an immediate subjective certainty, of being in unity with the absolute, God. He felt that the life of religion could be saved by an inductive and hypothetical metaphysics.

Die Quellen der menschlichen Gewissheit (München, 1900); *System der Aesthetik*, 3 vols. (München, 1905, 1910, 1914); *Was ist Religion?* (Leipzig, 1913); *Die Gefühlsgewissheit* (München, 1922); Fr. Lipsius, "Volkelt als Religionsphilosoph" in *Volkelt Festschrift* (München, 1918). H.H.

Voltaire, Francois Marie Arouet de: (1694-1778) French popularizer of Newton's physics and Locke's* philosophy, no one labored so tirelessly as he for freedom of discussion and publication. His onslaught on persecuting Christianity was probably the greatest contribution to freedom of speech ever made. The novelty of his ideas of religion and tolerance consisted not in any quality intrinsic to them. He believed in the need for God as a club over the heads of the masses. Closely akin to Puritanism* in his views on moral virtues, he was not a supporter of the harsh life without graces. He also advocated a secular and uniform religion, though he was less concerned with its precise content. See Enlightenment, the.

K. Martin, *French Liberal Thought in the Eighteenth Century* (Boston, 1929); F. J. C. Hearnshaw, ed., *The Social and Political Ideas of some Great French Thinkers of the Age of Reason* (London, 1930); H. N. Brailsford, *Voltaire* (London, 1935); N. L. Torrey, *The Spirit of Voltaire* (1938). H.H.

Volume enterprise: See religious tract movement.

Volunteer Movement for Foreign Missions, Student: See Student Volunteer Movement for Foreign Missions.

Volunteers of America: A religious and philanthropic organization founded in 1896 by Ballington Booth (1859-1940). It was the outgrowth of a dispute over organizational policies between Ballington Booth, then Commander of the Salvation Army in America*, and his father, William Booth, founder and "General" of the Army. It is similar to the Salvation Army in doctrine, methods, and activities, but it is more democratic in government and less extensive in scope, having but 104 stations or mission posts, as compared with 1,566 for the parent body. Mrs. Maud Charlesworth Booth, widow of the founder, continues as Commander-in-Chief of the Volunteers. H.E.J.

votive mass: A Mass* which does not correspond to the Office of the day. As a rule the Mass complements the Office, that is, it agrees with the feast of the breviary. Such a Mass may be celebrated for some grave reason, for any reasonable cause, or at any time permitted by liturgical law. See forty hours' devotion. W.H.

votive offering: (Lat., *vovere*, to promise to God) A general name given to those things promised or dedicated to God or a saint and in consequence looked upon as set apart by this act of consecration. Votive offerings are divided into 1) things vowed to God or the saints in some trouble or crisis of life, and 2) things presented in gratitude for a recovery or deliverance without having been previously promised. B.S.

votive office: A liturgical prayer not entered in the general calendar but adopted with a view to satisfying a special devotion. Such offices were called votive (*vovere*, wish) because their recitation remained optional since it was the object of a privilege. All votive offices were abolished Nov. 1, 1911 by the apostolic constitution of Pope Pius X. B.S.

vows: See oaths; Greek religion; Roman religions.

Vulgate, the Latin: See canon, Old and New Testament; Jerome; Sixtus V; versions of the Bible, ancient.

W

wafer: See altar bread.

wagering: See gambling.

Wahabites: A reforming sect of Islam, founded by Mohammed ibn Abd al' Wahab in the 18th century. The aim is to restore the pure religion of the *Koran**, strict monotheism and a literal interpretation of the scripture. Elaborate worship or dress, pilgrimages to tombs of saints, or prayers to saints were condemned as idolatry. The movement had considerable political power throughout Asia, and still has religious influence. Their intolerance has separated them from other Moslems*. P.E.J.

wakan, or wakanda: (Sioux) A life-power permeating all natural objects and forces; a natural but unusual power inherent in objects affecting all phases of man's life. See manitu; orenda. F.L.P.

wake: (fr. A.S. *wacan,* to wake) 1) The keeping of a watch or vigil at the side of a dead body until the time of burial. Chiefly an Irish custom, sometimes observed with great solemnity, but more commonly with considerable festivity. 2) An annual local parish festival formerly observed in the Church of England in connection with the feast of a patron saint* or with the dedication of a church. Originally a religious observance lasting through the night but becoming (at least by the 16th cent.) a holiday occasion for village games, dancing and drinking, often riotous in its excesses. See death and burial practices. E.T.R.

Waldenström, Paul Peter: (1838-1917) Swedish churchman, D.D. (Yale), Ph.D. (Uppsala), linguist, author, teacher, preacher, and formidable controversialist. Deeply influenced by the revivals, he became the outstanding leader of the dissenting movements. In 1872, he attacked the doctrine of the atonement* as taught by the state church. "God is love," he said, "and does not need to be reconciled, but a reconciliation which takes away the sin of the world is needed, and has been given in Christ." Independent as a member of the Riksdag, conservative as a leader of the Mission Covenant* organized in 1878, he continually pointed to the text of the Bible asking the question, "Where is it written?" E.G.H.

Waldo, Peter and Waldenses: Experiencing a conversion in 1170, Waldo gave up all his landed property to his spouse after a pilgrimage to Palestine, where he had been directed in Matthew 19: 21. The rest of his property he distributed to the poor, and devoted himself to the study of Scripture. Having taken a formal vow of poverty, he gathered about him a group of followers, begging their way and preaching a message of self-abnegation. He died 1217 A.D. His followers were known as Poor Men of Lyon. They travelled in strict observance of Christ's direction to the seventy (Luke 10:1-4). Their appeal for papal recognition denied and put under ban at the Council of Verona (1184), they were driven out of Lyon and found their way with their message into southern Europe. Renunciation of private property, an ascetic life, separation of husbands from their wives, and three days' fast in the week were the conditions for membership into their communion. They repudiated indulgences, purgatory and masses for the dead. They denied the efficacy of the sacraments administered by unworthy priests. A literal appreciation of the teachings of Christ as contained in the gospels was their chief theme. They had no fixed and articulate theology.

Known among its own membership as Vaudois, the Waldensian church is a Protestant community, Calvinistic in principle, before the Reformation. They were a community of hardy mountaineers and simple folk. The question of their historical origin is highly controversial. They repudiate the view that they were simply the followers of Peter Waldo of Lyon. They deny that they first appeared as a sect of heretics, breaking off from the historic church. They lay claim to apostolic origin, having preserved the purity of faith through the centuries. They also claim to owe their existence to a schismatic bishop during the episcopate of Sylvester in the fourth century, who broke off with Rome because it placed the church under imperial rule. Still another claim is that the communion owes its origin to Claude, bishop of Turin in the eighth century, who revived the Augustinian doctrine of predestination, and who ignored Augustine's teaching according to which the church was the appointed medium of communication between God and man. The alleged connection between the Waldenses, inhabiting the southern and Italian valleys of the Alps, and the

Cathari* or Albigenses*, neighbors of the Waldenses, living in the northern and French side of the Alps, has been refuted. It is not certain what factors were responsible for the gradual disappearance of the Cathari and the survival and slow progress of the Waldensian movement. It is probable that the Cathari were absorbed by it. One thing is certain that the Waldenses are not a direct offshoot of the Cathari movement.

The Waldensian church grew in reality out of a fusion of the work of Peter Waldo and the Poor Men of Lyon with movements originated by Arnold of Brescia, Peter de Bruys* and Henry of Cluny. It came to contain elements in the teaching of these four men, and matured into a distinctly organized church. Waldo's movement was the most vigorous of them all. The ideas of Protestantism were in the air. Its spirit was alive when Waldo and his Poor Men came to embrace them and blend them with their own version of the teaching of Jesus. What attracted so powerfully wide circles of the population to these schismatic movements were not their "doctrines", but the ethical seriousness and the consequence with which they carried out the moral demands of the gospel. Enthusiastic about the imitation of Christ, their strict biblicism became a blazing criticism of the church against the hierarchical lust of power, lust of money, wealth, pomp and worldly pleasures. As preachers of apostolic poverty, they rejected Rome and its papal claims. Although they aimed to become inwardly independent of the church that had degenerated into a rival world power, they strove principally for the personal experience of peace and perfection.

J. J. v. Döllinger, *Beiträge zur Sektengeschichte des Mittelalters* (München, 1890), 2 vols.; T. Gay, *Histoire des Vaudois, refaite d'après les plus récentes recherches* (Gay, 1912); H. Lea, *History of the Inquisition of the Middle Ages* (1901-1906); K. F. Müller, *Die Waldenser und ihre einzelnen Gruppen* (Gotha, 1886). H.H.

Walkyries: Daughters of Odin* virgin warriors, who took part in battles with men, and carried away the souls of dying heroes to Valhalla; also Valkyries, Walküre. P.G.M.

Wallin, Johan Olof: (1779-1839) Sweden's greatest hymn-writer, Wallin earlier was interested in other forms of poetry, but after 1811 gave himself to revision of the hymnbook of the Swedish Church (issued 1819), of which he gradually became the prime author. His hymns reveal his humanistic, philanthropic nature, as well as a lyric, biblical quality. He held many ecclesiastical offices, and was elected archbishop in 1837.

C.J.B.

Walter of Mortagne: Bishop and theologian, born at Mortagne, Flanders, first decade of the twelfth century. From 1136 to 1144 he taught at Ste. Geneviève, Paris. On the question of universals he was an indifferentist, thereby opposing both William of Champeaux and Abailard**. He died in 1174, as Bishop of Laon. C.V.

Walter of St. Victor: (lived in the twelfth century) As a coarse polemicist, he condemned all natural knowledge, and particularly contemptuous of dialectic and speculative learning. H.H.

Walther, Karl Ferdinand Wilhelm: (1811-1887) Organizer and first president of the Lutheran Missouri Synod and outstanding exponent of conservative and confessional Lutheranism* in America. A young pastor steeped in the theology of the Reformation and rebelling against the prevalent rationalism, he arrived in Perry County, Missouri, in 1839 in the company of seven hundred devout Saxon pilgrims led by Martin Stephan. In 1841 he became pastor at St. Louis, and in 1846 he founded the Missouri Synod, bringing together Lutherans in various parts of the country under a democratic constitution which he had drafted. From 1850 until his death he was professor of theology at Concordia Theological Seminary in St. Louis. Of his many writings on doctrinal, ecclesiastical, and pastoral themes, the following are outstanding: *Kirche und Amt* (1852), *Die Rechte Gestalt einer vom Staate unabhängigen evangelisch-lutherischen Ortsgemeinde* (1863), *Postil on the Gospels* (1871), and *The Proper Distinction Between the Law and the Gospel* (1897, Eng. ed., 1929). He also edited J. W. Baier's *Compendium of Theology* in three volumes (1879). Walther exerted further influence through two journals which he founded and edited, *Der Lutheraner* and *Lehre und Wehre.* An uncompromising and indefatigable defender of confessional orthodoxy, colloquially called "the Lutheran Pope", he debated vehemently on such topics as the nature of the Church, the Anti-Christ, conversion, and predestination. He left the impress of his powerful personality on his followers and made his influence felt throughout the Church at large. See Missouri Lutherans; neo Lutheranism. T.A.K.

Wang Yang-ming: See Chinese Terminology.

Ward, James: (1843-1925) Professor of Mental Philosophy at Cambridge, creative psychologist and influential panpsychist. For him the phenomena of physical law, biological evolution, the conservation of values, and the human experience of objective value are inexplicable by metaphysical pluralism, or mechanistic naturalism. The world is ultimately a realm of ends. It is constituted by the interaction of purposive psychic entities, which, created and sustained by a cosmic Person, differ progressively in the quality of their conative and cognitive power.

Naturalism and Agnosticism (1915), 4th ed.; *Psychological Principles* (1920), 2nd ed.; *The Realm of Ends or Pluralism and Theism* (1920), 3rd ed.

P.A.B.

Warfield, Benjamin Breckinridge: (1851-1921) Presbyterian theologian. Born near Lexington, Ky. Graduate of the College of N. J. (Princeton) 1871, of Princeton Theological Seminary 1876. Graduate studies in Leipzig. After a short pastorate he became in 1878 instructor and from 1879-1887 professor of N.T. Exegesis in Western Theological Seminary, Pittsburg, Pa. From 1887-1921 he was professor of Systematic

Theology in Princeton Theological Seminary. He was chief editor of the Presbyterian and Reformed *Review*, 1890-1903, then for many years editor of the *Princeton Theological Review*. In the succession of Charles Hodge* and together with Abr. Kuyper* in Holland he was for many decades the protagonist of confessional Presbyterianism. Aided by an indefatigable study of N.T. criticism and interpretation, patristics, church history and Reformed theology, and familiar with all that was being written in foreign languages, he expounded in innumerable articles the truths of the Bible and, based upon the Bible, those of the Westminster Confession.* In his writings he was polemical and critical rather than constructive, interested in the particular doctrines rather than in their systematic connection, because he took the plenary inspiration of the Bible and the truthfulness of the great Presbyterian tenets as his imperturbable starting point.

Principal works: *Introduction to the Textual Criticism of the New Testament* (1886); *The Gospel of the Incarnation* (1893); *The Lord of Glory* (1907); *The Plan of Salvation* (1915). His numerous articles and reviews were collected and in topical arrangement published in ten volumes (1927-1932). Among them are: *Revelation and Inspiration* (1927); *Studies in Tertullian and Augustine* (1930); *Calvin and Calvinism* (1931); *The Westminster Assembly and Its Work* (1931); *Perfectionism* (1931-1932), 2 vols. Bibliography by John R. Mackay in *The Expositor* (London, 1922); see also the *Memorial Address* by F. L. Patton (1921); Biography in *Dictionary of American Biography*, vol. XIX, p,. 453 f. O.A.P.

Warnefrid, Paul (Paul the Deacon): (c. 725-c. 799) Monk, historian, poet, member of the palace school* of Charlemagne. Most noted for his history of the Lombards. F.W.N.

Wars of religion: Huguenots*, 1562- . Cruel persecutions prompted the Huguenots of France to take up arms to achieve religious liberty in 1562. Eight separate wars were fought with the Catholic party in the next three decades. The most notorious event in this struggle was the Massacre of St. Bartholomew*, August 24, 1572, in which 30,000 Huguenots lost their lives. Chief leaders on the Catholic side were Catherine de' Medici* and the Guises; on the Protestant side, Coligny, Conde, and Henry of Navarre—later Henry IV*, who guaranteed Huguenots a measure of freedom in the Edict of Nantes*, 1598. But persecution and civil strife began anew after his death and culminated in the Revocation of the Edict of Nantes in 1689, through which several hundred thousand Huguenots, the most skilled artisans and the best intellects of France, were forced into exile. Religious toleration for Protestants was not attained until 1787. E.C.K.

washing: (ritual, in O.T.) Washing of the person and of the clothes is frequently specified in the Levitical legislation as part of the requirements for removing a ritual taboo (uncleanness), e.g., Levit. 14:9; 16:24, 28. Washing of the hands also was a symbolic protestation of innocence, cf. Deut. 21:6; Psalm 26:6. See feet washing. R.B.Y.S.

water: See holy water; baptism; baptism, non Christian rites.

Watts, Isaac: See hymns.

Weber, Hans Emil: (1882-) He first taught in Bonn. Now he is at Münster. His greatest contribution is the conquest of the immanentistic world view by a better, faith-determining application of the critical method, and the facing of the difficulties resulting from the lay orthodoxy strengthened by the communal movement.

Die philosophische Scholastik des deutschen Protestantismus (Leipzig, 1907); *Der Einfluss der protestantischen Schulphilosophie auf die orthodox-lutherische Dogmatik* (Leipzig, 1908); *Das Problem der Heilsgeschichte nach Römer 9-11* (Leipzig, 1911); *Die Vollendung des neutestamentlichen Glaubenszeugnisses durch Johannes* (Leipzig, 1912); *Glaube und Mystik* (Gütersloh, 1927); *Eschatologie im Neuen Testament* (Gütersloh, 1930); *Reformation, Orthodoxie und Rationalismus* (Gütersloh, 1937); *Das Geisteserbe der Gegenwart und die Theologie* (Leipzig, 1925). H.H.

Weber, Max: (1865-1920) One of the most outstanding German economists and sociologists. His three volumes devoted to the sociology* of religion represent one of the most valuable contributions in this field. The principal topic of the work is an analysis of the relationship between religion and economic phenomena based upon an immense amount of factual material. He studied the economic ethics of Confucianism, Taoism, Hinduism, Buddhism, Christianity, Islam and Judaism on the life of the peoples who adhere to these religions. He also studied particularly the relationship between Western capitalism and Protestantism. A modern capitalistic organization is made possible by a definite psychology, conduct and corresponding social conditions. Weber maintains that modern Western capitalism* was originated by the Protestant religion and its economic ethics. The spirit of modern capitalism is that of Protestantism, of its rules of conduct and practical ethics.

M. Weber, *Gesammelte Aufsätze zur Religionssoziologie* (Tübingen, 1920), 3 vols.; *Wirtschaftsgeschichte* (München, 1924); R. H. Tawney, *Religion and the Rise of Capitalism* (1926) is a recapitulation of Weber's theory. H.H.

Wee Free Church: In 1901 the Free Church of Scotland* and the United Presbyterian Church* formed the United Free Church of Scotland*. 25 ministers and 63 congregations of the Free Church, mostly Gaelic-speaking, abstained from the union and maintained that they were the legal Free Church, because this church had departed from its principles by joining with the United Presbyterian Church and also by adopting in 1892 an interpretation of the Confession of Faith. On the allegation of a breach of trust thus committed suit was brought by the dissenters for all the property of the Free Church. Defeated in the Scottish courts, they won in the House of Lords and all the property was adjudged theirs. This decision was practically overruled by an act of Parliament, which yet gave the successful litigants more than their numbers entitled them to. With this support the present Free Church of Scotland began. It has grown somewhat; in 1929 it had 8,500 communicants. It has a theological college at Aberdeen. R.H.N.

Weeks, festival of: See Jewish religious festivals.

Wegscheider, Julius August Ludwig: (1771-1849) He taught at the University of Halle. His main work dominated the last generation of rationalism. He exerted a great personal influence through his long teaching career. He decided with brief authoritative sentences the correctness of theological doctrine. Despite the gigantic ballast of learned annotations, he refrained from investigating the *ratio* and its relation to religion and Christian faith. His standard was the naive feeling of certainty of the human understanding. Jesus was for him neither God nor the supernaturally direct revelation of God. But He was for him the most excellent and first originator of human salvation.

Ethices Stoicorum recentiorum fundamenta cum ethicis principiis quae critica rationes practicae secundum Kantium exhibt, comparata (Hamburg, 1797); *Über die von der neuesten Philosophie geforderte Trennung der Moral von der Religion* (Hamburg, 1804); *Institutiones Theologiae Christianae Dogmaticae. Scholis suis scripsit addita singulorum dogmatum historia et censura* (4th ed., Halle, 1815, 8th ed., Leipzig, 1844). H.H.

Weigel, Valentin: (1533-1588) German mystic. Influenced by Sebastian Franck, Paracelsus, Neoplatonism, and the "Friends of God"**, he developed a philosophy of monistic subjective idealism in which all truth was traced to a divine "inner light" in man. A successful Lutheran pastor, Weigel reconciled his ideas with the accepted dogmas by placing an allegorical interpretation upon the latter. The real import of his teaching did not appear until the posthumous publication of his writings, the chief of which is *Dialogus de Christianismo* (1616). Weigel's influence was felt by such important thinkers as Böhme, Leibniz, and Arndt. T.A.K.

Weisenburg Catechism: See catechism.

Weiss, Johannes: (1863-1914) German theologian and professor of N.T. in Göttingen, Marburg, and Heidelberg. Of the many important volumes which Weiss produced, none was more significant than the little monograph, *Die Predigt Jesu vom Reiche Gottes* (1892) which may properly be regarded as the manifesto of thoroughgoing eschatology* (though the more vociferous Schweitzer* is usually regarded as the father of the movement) as the key to an understanding of the mission of Jesus and of the resulting early Christianity. Among other volumes of lasting worth are his *Commentary on First Corinthians* (Meyer series, 9th ed., 1910) and *Das Urchristentum* (1917) which latter, still unfinished at time of his death, was subsequently completed and published by Rudolph Knopf. A list of his other writings is contained in the preface to the English translation of the last work, *The History of Primitive Christianity*, edited by F. C. Grant (1937). M.S.E.

Weisse, Christian Hermann: (1801-1866) As professor of philosophy in Leipzig, he elaborated an ethical theism in close relation with Christian dogma, the later Schelling and Jacob Boehme**. The concept of liberty was central for him. God is bound to the logical and mathematical laws of existence, but He is free within the same.

Die Idee der Gottheit (Dresden, 1833); *Reden über die Zukunft der evangelischen Kirche* (Leipzig, 1849); *Über die Christologie Luthers* (Leipzig, 1852); *Philosophische Dogmatik oder Philosophie des Christenthums* (Leipzig, 1855-62), 3 vols.; *Psychologie und Unsterblichkeitslehre*, ed. by R. Seydel (Leipzig, 1869). H.H.

Weizsäcker, Karl Heinrich von: (1822-99) Mediating theologian, professor of Church History at Tübingen from 1861. Best known today for his modern translation of the N.T. (1875) and his book on *Das Apostolische Zeitalter* (1886) which was translated into English. A distinguished preacher to the community as well as scholar. See Tübingen school. C.T.C.

welis or walis: Moslem saints who are thought to have miraculous powers. Worship is not due them, but as holy ones who intercede with God for men, they are often appealed to for aid. P.E.J.

Wellhausen, Julius: (1844-1918) German Protestant Orientalist and leader of a school of Higher Criticism of the Bible. Devoted himself to disentangling the historical process that produced the religion and literature of Israel and to establishing the correct order of the documents composing the Hexateuch*. He is linked with Graf's hypothesis of the lateness of the Priestly Code*. He also made notable contributions to Islamic and N.T. studies. See Lives of Jesus. S.S.C.

Welsh Calvinistic Methodists: See Calvinistic Methodists; Methodism.

Wendt, Hans Hinrich: (1853-1928) He taught in Kiel, Heidelberg and Jena. He was one of the furtherers of Ritschlianism who considered questions of world view. He also created an entirely different type of dogmatics than Ritschl had in mind.

Die christliche Lehre von der menschlichen Vollkommenheit (Göttingen, 1882); *Die Lehre Jesu* (Göttingen, 1886-90, 2nd ed., Göttingen, 1901); *System der christlichen Lehre* (Göttingen, 1906-7, 2nd ed., Göttingen, 1920); *Erklärung der Augsburger Konfession* (Göttingen, 1927). H.H.

werewolf: In north European folklore, a man (or woman) who could at times turn into a wolf, to satisfy an appetite for human flesh. Late Anglo-Saxon *wer*: man and wulf. P.G.M.

wergild: In Teutonic law, the price to be paid by one guilty of manslaughter to the relatives of the victim. It was a valuable means of ending blood feuds, a step beyond lex talionis*. Similar laws have been worked out among many other primitive peoples. P.G.M.

Wernle, Paul: (1872-) He is professor at the University of Basel, Switzerland. Himself a notable religious-historical investigator, he opposes at important points the investigations of Troeltsch, Bousset** and Heitmüller. He also has written from the scientific point of view one of the best introductions to theological study.

Einführung in das theologische Studium (Tübingen, 1921), 3rd ed.; *Die Anfänge unserer Religion* (Tübingen, 1904), 2nd ed.; *Der schweizerische Protestantismus im 18. Jahrhundert* (Tübingen, 1923-25), 3 vols. H.H.

Wesel, Johann: (1419 or 20- 1498) "Light of the World", educated by the Brethren of the Common Life* at Zwolle, knew Greek and Hebrew, and studied theology at Paris. Head of a nunnery at Groningen, he spent much time in the Monastery of Mount St. Agnes (Agnietenberg), near Zwolle. Knew Hegius, Agricola, von Langen. Criticized by Gansfort* for "scholastic subtlety" and "inconsiderateness . . . with the unlearned." Q.B.

Wesley, Charles: (1707-1788) and **John:** (1703-1791) Founders with George Whitefield* of the Evangelical Revival and (through the "United Societies" organized by them) of Methodism as a distinct branch of the Christian Church. Among Christian evangelists, missionaries, organizers, and preachers of all time, John Wesley stands in the front rank. A graduate of Oxford (Christ Church) and Fellow of Lincoln College, he was a thorough scholar, an expert linguist and grammarian, and a poet and hymn writer of exceptional ability. It is Charles Wesley however who was the poet of the Evangelical Revival and of world Methodism. He wrote in all more than 6000 hymns, at least ten of which are among the great hymns of the Christian Church. His only rival among modern hymnodists is Isaac Watts*, and Canon Overton has held him to be, quantity and quality alike considered, "the great hymn writer of all ages".

The Wesleys were the fifteenth and eighteenth children respectively of Samuel and Susannah (Annesley) Wesley. Both parents were children of distinguished non-conformists* and entered the Church of England* by deliberate choice, Samuel being disinherited in consequence. The story of their life for 38 years at Epworth Rectory, Lincolnshire, is an epic. It is above all a story of "plain living and high thinking". The influence of Susannah upon her sons, whose education and spiritual nurture from the cradle was her especial care, is particularly notable. It was at Oxford in 1727 or 1728 that Charles began the Evangelical Revival by going to the weekly Sacrament and persuading two or three fellow-students to do the same. This was the beginning of the "Holy Club", also called "a new set of Methodists", of which John on his return to Oxford in 1729 assumed the leadership. In October 1735 the two brothers set sail for Georgia. On shipboard and later they saw much of the Moravians*. Through the latter John after the disillusionment of his career as a Parish Priest and Missionary in Georgia discovered Luther and was led to a personal experience of salvation through faith alone. Charles had a similar experience and both began to preach a Gospel of power. Joining forces with Whitefield early in the following year (1739), they began the powerful movement known as the Evangelical Revival. Henceforth their lives were bound up with its progress, John taking the more active and executive role and hardly living save for his preaching, direction of societies, and literary and educational projects. He was accustomed to travel five thousand miles a year on horseback and to preach an average of fifteen sermons a week. Both brothers married, Charles in 1749, John in 1751. The marriage of the latter to a widow, Mrs. Vazeille, was in every way unfortunate. Charles was a stiffer, though not an essentially stronger, churchman than John, and opposed the ordinations for America in 1784 by the latter, who that same year had given the Societies a legal constitution. Their separation from the English Church was inevitable, though John Wesley counseled against it with strong words until his death in 1791, three years after that of his brother. Both are among the Saints of the Universal Christian Calendar.

See Articles of Religion; assurance; evangelicalism and evangelical revival; hymns; Methodism.

Select Bibliography.—Charles Wesley: *Journal* and *Letters*, ed. Thos. Jackson (1849); *Early Journal* (1910); *Poetical Works of John and Charles Wesley* (1868), 13 vols.; *Lives* by Thomas Jackson (1841), John Telford (1886), and F. L. Wiseman (1933). John Wesley: *Collected Works* (1872); *Journal*, Standard ed., N. Curnock (1909-16), 8 vols.; *Standard Sermons*, ed. E. H. Sugden (1921); *Lives* by Robert Southey (1820), Luke Tyerman (1870), 2 vols., J. H. Overton (1891), J. S. Simon (1927), F. J. McConnell (1939). See also G. C. Cell, *Rediscovery of John Wesley* (1933); Umphrey Lee, *John Wesley and Modern Religion* (1936); Maximim Piette, *John Wesley in the Evolution of Protestantism* (Eng. tr., 1937). C.W.L.

Wesleyan Methodist Connection: See holiness churches.

West Memorial Lectures on Immortality, Human Conduct and Human Destiny, The Raymond F.: Established in 1910 at Stanford University, Palo Alto, California by Mr. and Mrs. Frederick W. West. This lectureship (capital sum, $10,000) calls for a guest lecturer "of the highest personal character and of superior intellectual endowment." The lectures are, on the present plan, delivered in alternate years in a series of at least three.

Among the lecturers the following have served: Charles E. Jefferson, Hastings Rashdall, John Dewey, Henry O. Taylor, Irving Babbitt, Julian S. Huxley, Carl L. Becker, J. R. Angell and R. M. Jones.

(Data from the Office of the Secretary of the University.) V.F.

Westcott and Hort: Cambridge scholars who while still young men planned a critical text of the Greek N.T., which they published in 1881, after twenty-eight years of work. In the course of their work they developed the principles of textual criticism*, and the history of the text to a degree unequalled before or since. E.J.G.

Westminster Assembly: The Long Parliament (1640) gave the Puritans* opportunity to achieve their aim of "a further . . . reformation" of the Church of England.* To this end Parliament called "an Assembly of . . . divines", with certain of the two houses, to meet on July 1, 1643 in Westminster Abbey. It was instructed to prepare plans for a reformation of the church which would bring it into nearer accord with the Church of Scotland* and the continental Reformed churches, for Parliamentary action. The Westminster Assembly thus was not an independent council but an advisory body to Parliament. It consisted of 121 clergymen of England and Wales, many of whom were eminent as theologians or Biblical scholars or preachers, with 10 Lords and 20 Commoners. Almost all were Puritans and of these the great majority were Presbyterians.* There were small groups of Independents (Congregationalists) and Erastians.** A few Episcopalians were appointed but bore little part. After the Solemn League and Covenant* was taken by Parliament and by the Assembly at its order, in September, 1643, as the condition of Scottish help to the Parliamentary army, 6 Scottish commissioners entered the Assembly and were influential.

The Assembly's principal documents were: 1. A form of church government, on which rested the abortive establishment by Parliament of Presbyterianism in the Church of England, in 1646 and 1648; 2. A directory for church discipline, approved by Parliament with a reservation; 3. A directory for ordination, approved; 4. The Directory for Worship, to replace the Book of Common Prayer, approved; 5. The Confession of Faith (see Westminster Confession of Faith) to replace the 39 Articles, submitted in December, 1646, which received partial Parliamentary approval in 1648; 6. The Larger Catechism* and 7. The Shorter Catechism, composed in 1647, the latter being approved. In 1648 and to its last session in February, 1649 the Assembly occupied itself chiefly with examining ministers for appointment to livings in the Church of England. The authority of the Assembly's documents as a constitution for the church was annulled at the Restoration (1660). They have had great influence otherwise, especially in the Presbyterian churches.

W. Beveridge, *A Short History of the West. Ass.* (Edinburgh, 1904); S. W. Carruthers, *The Everyday Work of the West. Ass.* (1943); A. F. Mitchell, *The West. Ass.* (1897); W. A. Shaw, *History of the English Church, 1640-1660,* vol. I (London, 1900).

R.H.N.

Westminster Catechism: See catechism; catechumenate.

Westminster Confession of Faith: In 1645 the House of Commons asked the Westminster Assembly* to present to it a confession of faith for the Church of England*. The Assembly, which already on its own motion had this under consideration by committee, from July, 1645, worked as a whole on the Confession, with interruptions, completing it in December, 1646. Its composition was marked by large unanimity reflecting the theological agreement of the members. The Confession is a summary of Christian doctrine in 33 chapters, occupying about 35 ordinary octavo pages. The work of Puritan divines with cooperating Scottish commissioners, it embodies British Calvinistic theology, on the whole of the more moderate type respecting predestination*. With this it combines emphasis on the federal theology* or doctrine of the covenants, highly esteemed by Puritans and Scots. Its structure was based largely on the Irish Articles of Archbishop Ussher* of 1615. Published in 1647, the Confession received partial Parliamentary approval in 1648, but its life as a creed of the Church of England was brief. It was adopted in 1647 by the General Assembly of the Church of Scotland*, wherein it still has authority. The Savoy Declaration* of 1658 of the English Congregationalists and the London Confession of 1677 of the English Baptists in great part incorporated it. The Confession was the doctrinal standard of New England Congregationalists to the end of the 18th century. It is now authoritative in most of the Presbyterian churches* of the world, in some with interpretations and revisions. No Protestant doctrinal formulation has had or has higher position. See Confessions, Formal of the Christian Church; Irish Articles.

P. Schaff, *Creeds of Christendom,* vol. I, historical and critical, vol. III, text of Confession (1877); A. F. Mitchell, *West. Assembly* (1897); E. D. Morris, *Theology of the West. Symbols* (1900); B. B. Warfield, *The West. Assembly and Its Work* (1931).

R.H.N.

Weston, Henry Griggs: (1820-1909) Baptist preacher and educator. Editor of *Baptist Quarterly,* 1869-1877. President of Crozer Theological Seminary, 1868-1909. C.H.M.

Westphalian Treaties: (1648) The Westphalian Treaties followed the Thirty Years' War* (1618-48). The one concluded at Münster between the emperor and the French; the other at Osnabrück, between the imperials and the Swedes may be considered from either a political or religious viewpoint. Both were dextrously manipulated by Richelieu in the interest of France. Politically and nationally speaking, the Thirty Years' War and the subsequent Peace Treaties meant a hitherto unheard of loss and humiliation for Germany; a lasting weakening of both the united German States and of the imperial authority in the Reich, which only Bismark was later somewhat able to remedy. Denmark and Spain too were debilitated (Treaty of the Pyrenees); Sweden became a power of great strategic importance while France from now on headed towards the absolutistic age of Louis XIV. Moreover, not only Germany, but all Central Europe became a loose association of many substantially independent States. The medieval centralized Europe of one Religion, with pope and emperor representing respectively the spiritual and the temporal power was definitely dead and the modern system of equally autonomous territories took its place. Henceforth also, the idea that religious differences should and could be settled by force of arms gradually passed out of the minds of men and rulers. Religiously, Protestantism gained a stronger, politically recognized, foothold in Europe, whereas Catholicism lost an inestimable number of churches, properties and revenues. The Lorraine dioceses of Metz, Toul and Verdun remained in the possession of France. Sweden obtained besides the German territory of Pomerania, also the ecclesiastical revenues and benefices of Bremen and Verden. In compensation for these losses Germany was to receive the secularized ecclesiastical territories of Brandenburg and Mecklenburg. The Religious Peace of Augsburg (1555)* was re-confirmed, with the proviso, however, that Calvinism* was to be permitted publicly to function. The retention of ecclesiastical properties and the holding of religious services were to be adjudged as of Jan. 1, 1624, the mean or compromise year between 1618 and 1630, and to be known as the "Norm Day" or "Norm Year" according to which all disputes were to be settled. Both ecclesiastical and secular estates were to enjoy the "jus reformandi", i.e., the right to introduce Protestantism into those places that could not be regulated by the "Norm Year". Other minority dissenters were to be permitted to worship at home according to the dictates of their conscience and to frequent their own churches outside of their native or adopted territory, if they so desired. Emperor Frederick III (1637-57) refused to accept the "Norm Year" for Austria, which generally speaking up to that time had not been affected substantially by either Protestantism or the Thirty Years' War. The principle "cujus regio, illius religio" was amended in such a way as not to apply in future to the people or lands of a prince who changed his religious convictions or affiliations. Practically, this was a renunciation of the "reservatum ecclesiasticum". In the future all religious questions were to be discussed and settled in the Reichstag by the *Corpus Catholicorum* and the *Corpus Evangelicorum* not indeed by a majority vote but by an amicable settlement known as *"Itio in partes."* Pope Innocent X*, represented at the Treaty of Münster by his Legate*, Fabio Chigi (the later Pope Alexander VII), while approving of the provisions of the Treaties ending the Thirty Years' War, for which all Europe longed, refused to recognize in virtue of the Brief *Zelus domus Dei*, Nov. 26, 1648, the articles referring to the retention of confiscated church properties and revenues once belonging *bona fide* to the Catholic Church.

Litt. *Cath. Encyc.* XIV, 656-7; XV 601-5; *Lexikon f. Theologie u. Kirche* X, 842-3; L. Pastor, *History of the Popes*, Herder (1940), vol. XXX, ch. III. R.M.H.

wheel of life: See karma; samsara; theosophy; transmigration; Vedanta.

White Friars: See Carmelites.

White Lotus Society: See Chinese religions.

Whitefield, George: (1714-70) English religious leader, co-founder with John and Charles Wesley* of the Evangelical Revival, one of the great preachers in point of power and effectiveness of all time. Born in Gloucester at the Bell Inn, at fifteen he was taken from the school of St. Mary de Crypt, where he had shown promise in elocution and play-acting, to assist his widowed mother in the public-house. In 1733 he entered Pembroke College, Oxford, as a servitor, taking a degree in 1736. Here he came under the influence of Charles and later John Wesley and became one of the Oxford "Methodists". Ordained deacon in 1736 he began independently his remarkable career as a preacher and evangelist. On his return from America late in the year 1738 he joined forces with the Wesleys who had begun to lead a revival. In 1740 the difference between him and John Wesley over election, final perseverance, and sanctification led to an open rupture. Though speedily reconciled, the two henceforth went largely separate ways. Whitefield's Calvinism, which was uncompromising, had three roots: personal experience; contact with Calvinist Divinity through reading and association with Calvinists in England, Scotland, and America; and the Articles of Religion*. In a letter to John Wesley he says, "I never read anything that Calvin wrote: my doctrines I had from Christ and his Apostles." His influence upon Evangelicalism within the Church of England (see Evangelicals, Anglican), which tended spontaneously toward Calvinism, was in consequence greater than that of the Wesleys. After 1748 Whitefield enjoyed the friendship and influential patronage of Selina, Countess of Huntingdon.* His real life remained in his evangelical tours, during one of which, on his seventh visit to America, he died, worn out with ceaseless ardors and toils. He was buried, where he died, in Newburyport, Massachusetts.

See evangelicalism and evangelical revival.

Select Bibliography.—His *Works* were collected in 1771-2 in seven volumes. *Memoirs*, 1834 (by John Gillies—revised) and *Sermons* in one vol. *Lives* by J. P. Gledstone (1871), Luke Tyerman (1876-7), 2 vols., A. D. Belden (1930). C.W.L.

Whitehead, Alfred North: (b. 1861) British-American philosopher. Taught mathematics and theoretical physics at Cambridge, 1911-14, and at University College, London, 1914-24. Professor of philosophy at Harvard University from 1924 until retirement in 1938, during which time his chief philosophical works appeared (earlier writings being either mathematical or near the boundary between mathematics [or physics] and philosophy). Whitehead's system has been called "the most large-minded synthesis since Hegel" (Lovejoy). It includes a conception of cosmic evolution recalling views of Bergson, Peirce, Alexander**, or Lloyd Morgan; a Platonic doctrine of forms or "eternal objects;" a theology which, like much recent Protestant thought, conceives God as receiving enrichment from the world process and so in some sense temporal. But the central and most original feature is the theory of "societies of occasions." The unit of reality is neither mere being nor mere becoming, but the "experient occasion", as a social union of a number of such occasions, and having aspects both of being and of becoming. Occasions immediately "prehend" or feel other occasions, and this prehension is sympathetic, a "feeling of feeling." There is no hard core of dead matter, such as could neither have feelings itself nor furnish content to the sympathetic feelings of others. A man, for example, feels his own just past feelings in immediate memory, but he also feels feelings just previously felt by his bodily cells or other entities in his body. All such entities are constituted by streams of experience on some level, however primitive. Each such stream (or "society with personal order") is made *one* by its feeling of feelings in its own past. But also, by feeling of feeling it is united to other streams. Self-identity and unity with others do not differ absolutely. Egoism and altruism have the same root in the immediate sympathy of the occasion for other occasions. Time and space are only the relational structures into which the "of" is articulated in the becoming of feelings of feelings. The past consists of occasions prehended in a given occasion *a*, but not prehending it; the future, of occasions not prehended in *a*, but such that, if they occur, they are bound to prehend *a*. The non-immanence of future occasions in the present gives freedom or indetermination. Strictly, no future events exist, but only certain potentialities from which events can be created. This holds even for God, who knows events as fully determinate only as the events occur, and who himself is in process (or process is in him) of a uniquely perfect kind by which he inherits all the richness of past events. Thus in God our experiences, though they "perish, yet live forevermore." God is perfect in his power of synthesizing events into the most meaningful whole they are capable of forming, but just what events shall occur as material for this synthesis depends partly upon the inherent freedom or self-determination which is the essence of every event-unit of reality. God can set limits to the discords or conflicts resulting from the plurality of freedoms, and in this way he is the "ground of order" or "harmony" in the world. But he cannot destroy freedom, and he does not wish to diminish it below the point at which decreased risk of conflict would mean an equally increased risk of the opposite evil, namely "tedium", loss of "zest" in the occasions. God has two natures, 1) the Primordial, which is "infinite," "unconditioned", "unchanged", and the home of the eternal forms, objects of his "conceptual feelings"—in so far, like the God of Thomist and other traditional theologies—but is *not* "eminent in actuality", rather by itself is "abstract," "deficient in actuality"; 2) the Consequent Nature which is finite, "conditioned by the creative advance of the world," and thus "fluent", "in a sense temporal," "concrete," "conscious". It is by the consequent nature that there is a "reaction of the world upon God." Thus God illustrates the chief categories of the system, in that his actuality, like all actuality, is essentially a sympathetic union of experiences responsive to the feelings of others and literally prehending them; and in that he consists neither of mere being nor of mere becoming, but of a) indeterminate but determinable future potentialities, b) the process of creative advance from determinable to determinate occasions, and c) the treasury of past becomings, past events, as "living forevermore," "immortal" in their indestructible being. The units of change do not change, events do not alter, they only become, but having become they belong always thereafter to the wealth of reality, which is enriched, never diminished, with temporal passage. The final tragedy is not loss of what has been actual, but rather the occurrence of suffering as actual, and also the non-occurrence of what might have been actual had the various freedoms been more fortunately exercised. Such tragedy is inherited by the consequent nature of God to whom it is "profane" to attribute "arbitrary power [see omnipotence] or mere happiness." Rather God is the "fellowsufferer who understands", whose joy has an "heroic" tinge, since it involves sharing in our sorrows. See infinite; time.

Principal works: *A Treatise on Universal Algebra* (1898); (with Bertrand Russell) *Principia Mathematica* (1910-1913); *Religion in the Making* (1926); *Process and Reality* (1929); *The Aims of Education* (1929); *Adventures of Ideas* (1933); *Modes of Thought* (1938). *The Philosophy of Alfred North Whitehead* (1941), ed. by P. A. Schilpp, contains Whitehead's Ingersoll Lecture on Immortality and Lecture on the Good, also essays by various authors on Whitehead's philosophy, including "Whitehead's Philosophy of Religion" by J. S. Bixler and "Whitehead's Idea of God" by C. Hartshorne. Probably for most readers *Adventures of Ideas* (especially parts Three and Four) is the best account of the Whiteheadian philosophy, though for the theology the final chapter of *Process and Reality* is essential. C.H.

Whiton, James Morris: (1833-1920) A.B. Yale 1853, Ph.D. 1861. Teacher, pastor, professor of ethics, Meadville Theological School 1893-1894; on staff, New York *Outlook*, 1896-1920.

Whiton was one of the active protagonists of the New Theology*.

Author of books on education and theology, including *Gloria Patri*, or *Talks on the Trinity* (1892); *Miracles and Supernatural Religion* (1903); *Interludes in a Time of Change* (1909).

J.W.B.

Whitsitt, William Heth: (1841-1911) Baptist minister and church historian. Served in Confederate Army. Article in Johnson's *Encyclopedia*, 1896, on Baptists precipitated the controversy over the introduction of immersion in 1642 and his resignation from presidency of Southern Baptist Theological Seminary followed in 1899.

C.H.M.

Whitsunday: The name of the feast of Pentecost* in the Church of England. The word apparently occurs first in the Ancrewn Riwle in the thirteenth century. A corruption of White Sunday, but authorities differ as to why the day was so called. See church year cycle. Cf. Trinity Sunday and Season.

W. M. Campion, *The Prayer Book Interleaved* (1872).

P.G.M.

Whittier, John Greenleaf: (1807-1892) Poet, abolitionist, and influential member of the Society of Friends* (Quakers). Author of "Snow-Bound," "Our Master," "The Eternal Goodness," etc. He often expressed in poetry his opposition to religious ritual including the communion service; a part of one such poem, "The Brewing of Soma," has been taken out of context and is now widely used in Protestant churches as a communion hymn, "Dear Lord and Father of Mankind." The authorized biography by S. T. Pickard is still standard (revised ed., 1907) but Albert Mordell's *Quaker Militant* (1933) is fuller for the anti-slavery activities. T. F. Currier's *Whittier Bibliography* (1937) is exhaustive. E.D.SN.

Wichern, Johann Hinrich: (1808-1881) He was the father of the *Innere Mission*—the national mission in Germany. He was its leading and foundation-laying mind, the aims of which have remained determinative. In practical life he was the director of the *Rauhen Haus* in Hamburg.

Gesammelte Schriften (Hamburg, 1901-1908), 6 vols.; vols. 1-2, 4-6, ed. by J. Wichern; vol. 3, ed. by F. Mahling; M. Gerhardt, *Johann Hinrich Wichern* (Hamburg, 1927-28), 2 vols. H.H.

Wiclif: See Wycliffe.

widows, treatment of: Culture* sets the general framework of behavior toward the widow and there has been considerable variation in the treatment accorded them among different peoples of the world throughout history. From the first, the Christian Church supported dependent widows and orphans*. Widows were given higher status than women in general in that women could publicly work in the Church only as widows. Among the ancient Hebrews there existed the custom of *levirate** whereby the brother of a man who died childless was expected to marry his widow and carry on the family name. Thus the widow in this culture was looked upon as property to be handed over to the next of kin. In ancient China, while it was considered a disgrace for the widow to remarry, there was this same cleavage to the husband's family*. If the widow returned to her own parents, she lost all her rights in her husband's property, including what she brought with her. She usually remained with the husband's parents, if they were living, as their daughter. Perhaps the most degraded position to which widows have been subjected was in India prior to British control. There it was a comparatively frequent practice for the widow to commit suicide by throwing herself upon the funeral pyre of her husband.

In the American colonies widows were held in high regard, a number of distinguished gentlemen having had love affairs with them. They had the life use of property left to them by their deceased husbands. In our own culture the attitude toward the widow has been inconsistent. She has been thought of at once as glamorous, yet dangerous, shrewd and mercenary, using her experience to secure a husband to support her. On the other hand the widow has often been considered timid, unsophisticated, the easy victim of those persons who would defraud her. This anomalous position of the widow in American culture persists although with some relaxation particularly in urban areas. Cf. suttee. H.R.M.

Wilberforce, William: (1759-1833) English statesman and philanthropist, born at Hull, educated at St. John's College, Cambridge, who devoted his entire public life to parliamentary reforms. He opposed the war against America in 1775, and the war against France in 1792. His greatest achievement after twenty years of constant endeavor was to secure the passage of a bill to abolish the slave trade. He wrote on religious themes and helped to found the Bible Society*. P.E.J.

Wilburites: See Society of Friends.

Wilfrid: (c. 634-709) Bishop of York, leading English churchman, monastic and missionary; champion of learning and culture. Life of vicissitudes and travels. Set precedent of making appeals to Rome. At Synod of Whitby was influential in securing victory of Roman forms over the Celtic. See Anglo-Saxons and the Introduction to Christianity. K.H.C.

William de la Mare: (died 1298) Oxford Franciscan and author of the best Bible *Correctorium* of the 13th century. With his pamphlet against Saint Thomas Aquinas, entitled *Correctorium fratris Thomas,* the Franciscan order took an open stand against the Angelic Doctor. S.C.T.

William of Auvergne: (died 1249) Predominantly Augustinian in theological method, his systematic monographs were of great significance for the development of scholasticism. He laid particular stress upon the independence of religious certainty and upon the idea that the unity of God already involves a triad.

M. Baumgartner, *Die Erkenntnislehre des Wilhelms v. Auvergne* (Münster, 1900); St. Schindele, *Beiträge zur Metaphysik des Wilhelm von Auvergne* (München, 1900); J. M. N. Valois, *Guillaume d'Auvergne* (Paris, 1880). H.H.

William of Auxerre: (died ca. 1231) He shared with his contemporaries the growing influence of peripatetic philosophy in epistemology, and the exclusion of Aristotelian influence upon religious questions. Cf. intention, sacramental.

Summa aurea (Paris, 1500 A.D.). H.H.

William of Champeaux: (ca. 1070-1121) A student of Roscelin*, the father of verbalism or vocalism, whose doctrines, however, he strenuously opposed with his realistic interpretation of the problem of the universals*. Abailard*, who is the chief source to learn William's doctrines, heard his lectures in the Cathedral School in Paris. William of Champeaux was a life-long friend of Saint Bernard* of Clairveaux, whose mysticism he shared. At the time of his death, we find him as bishop of Châlons-sur-Marne. S.C.T.

William of Conches: (1080-1145) A writer of varied interests whose books comprise astronomical, physiological, psychological and physical subjects. Most outstanding was he in the field of grammar. His philosophical treatises show the influence of Democritus, Seneca and Cicero. In his scientific views William presents a remarkable independence from the church fathers. S.C.T.

William of Malmesbury: (died ca. 1143) Author of the *De gestis pontificorum Anglorum* to be found in the *Patrologia Latina.* This work is an important source to learn about historic personages such as Lanfranc*, Archbishop of Canterbury (d. 1089), John Scotus Eriugena* (ca. 800-ca. 880) and many others. S.C.T.

William of St. Thierry: (1119-1148 or 1153) Author of many exegetic and mystic writings of psychological penetration such as *Libri duo de natura corporis et animae.* An intimate friend of Saint Bernard* of Clairveaux, he led a campaign against Peter Abailard* with his *Disputatio adversus Abaelardum.* S.C.T.

Williams, Sir George: (1821-1905) Born October 11, 1821. The youngest of eight sons of Amos and Elizabeth Williams of Ashway Farm, Didverton, in the County of Somerset, England. English Grammar School education. Apprenticed in a "draper's" shop in Bridgewater (1836)—"a careless, godless swearing young fellow." Following meeting in Zion Chapel (Congregational) returned to his shop bedroom to "yield himself wholly to God"—the beginning of a life-long lay Christian ministry. Entered employ of Hitchcock, Rogers & Co., leading London drapery establishment. Moved by the wretched living and working conditions of London clerks and the church's neglect of youth, he with eleven other young men met frequently for prayer in an upper bedroom in the shop. On June 6, 1844 this fellowship became the Young Men's Christian Association*, an organization designed "to bring religion into the sphere of the daily occupation." He lived to see this "wide-spreading league of Christian youth" encircle the globe and to be knighted for its achievement by Queen Victoria at its Jubilee celebration in London, 1894. A great ecumenic lay Christian leader and a pioneer in social betterment (Early Closing Movement) he died at the age of 84, mourned by leaders of youth around the world. He was buried in the crypt of St. Paul's Cathedral. C.P.S.

Williams, Roger: (c. 1604-1684) Banished by Massachusetts Bay in 1635, he became a founder of Rhode Island. A Calvinist, he argued for religious liberty on the basis of predestination. An unimmersed Baptist for a few weeks, 1639, he was separated from membership in all churches, 1639-1684. Contrary to usual assumptions, he did not advocate unlimited religious liberty, holding that "there could be no government in the world without the sword." C.H.M.

Windelband, Wilhelm: (1848-1915) He taught at the universities of Strasburg and Heidelberg. He was a member of the Baden or Southwestern German school of philosophy. His general aim was to emancipate the cultural sciences from the course of the method of natural science. Religion transcends for him the empirically given. The holy or the divine is the normal consciousness of the true, the beautiful and the good experienced as transcendent reality.

History of Modern Philosophy, translated by J. H. Tufts (1893); *Geschichte und Naturwissenschaft* (Freiburg, 1894); "Das Heilige", chapter II in *Praeludien* (Tübingen, 1902); *Lehrbuch der Geschichte der Philosophie,* 13. ed., edited by H. Heimsoeth (Freiburg, 1935). H.H.

Winer, Johann Georg Benedikt: (1789-1858) A German Protestant theologian who taught at Leipzig and Erlangen. Chiefly noted for a Grammar of N.T. idioms (1st ed., 1822). S.M.G.

Wisdom of Jesus, the Son of Sirach: See Jesus, the Son of Sirach.

Wisdom of Solomon, The: An important Jewish apocryphal book, and so included in the Catholic version of the Bible. It belongs to the so-called Wisdom Literature*. It is of composite authorship, and was probably written in Greek, in Alexandria, in the last half-century B.C. Its first section (1.1-6. 8) treats of righteousness and sin, reward and punishment, divine justice and immortality. The second section (6.9-10.21) extols Wisdom as the supreme guiding force in life and history. The third section (11.1-19.22) is a panegyric of the Jewish people. Tradition has mistakenly attributed this book, like Proverbs and Ecclesiastes**, to Solomon*. See apocrypha, Old Testament. J.M.

Wisdom literature: Unlike the Torah and the Prophets**, the biblical books of wisdom were the products neither of authoritative guardians of the cult nor of spokesmen of God, but of keen observers of human nature and patient teachers of the art of living. Their favorite medium of instruction was the *mashal* or proverb, the terse enunciation of truth that is self-evident and self-illustrative. Their teaching covered the whole range of human life and was expressed in a tone that is sober and realistic, sometimes spiced with humor and sarcasm.

Much of the wisdom of the Bible is of great antiquity. Tradition speaks of wisdom as the universal possession of the Children of the East, of Egypt and of the South. Much of it was ascribed to Solomon*. (I Kings 5.9-14) The oldest collection of Hebrew wisdom is the book of Proverbs*. Parts of its nucleus of Aphorisms (chs. 10-24) may possibly hark back to Solomon. The latest part of the book (chs. 1-9) came from the late Persian, if not from the Greek period, and displays a high conception of wisdom as the well-encompassing intelligence of God, the first of His works and His helper in creation, the foundation of the world and the guide of man.

The highest point of Hebrew wisdom was reached in the sublime drama of Job*, which

Heine characterized as "the Song of Songs of scepticism". In its wrestling with the mysteries of life and providence, doubt rises to the vindication of conscience and of the transcendent nature and justice of God. In Ecclesiastes* wisdom takes on a gloomy coloring. The reality of God and the moral government of the world still form the starting point of the sage's reflection, but he gazes with weary and disillusioned eyes on a world that is grey and chilly and on the pageant of human effort that is all "emptiness and striving after the wind".

Sapiential material is found also in the books of the Prophets and Psalms**, in the apocryphal Letter of Aristeas (No. 187-300), Ahikar, Testament of Twelve Patriarchs, (see pseudepigrapha) Four Maccabees*, and especially in the books of Sirach and Wisdom of Solomon**. The same type of teaching continues in Rabbinic* literature (Cf. *Pirke Abot*) and in the N.T. (Sermon on the Mount, James, etc.).

Beside commentaries on the books mentioned in the article, see T. K. Cheyne, *Job and Solomon* (1887); W. T. Davison, *The Wisdom Literature of the O. T.* (1894); J. F. Genung, *Hebrew Literature of Wisdom* (1906); D. B. MacDonald, *The Hebrew Philosophical Genius* (1936); C. H. Toy, art. "Wisdom Literature," *Enc. Biblica* (1903), IV.

S.S.C.

Wise, John: See American theology, early.

Wiseman, Nicholas Patrick Stephen: Cardinal and first Archbishop of Westminster. He was born at Seville in 1802, died in London in 1865. After receiving the doctorate in divinity he became professor at the Sapienza, Rome. From 1828 to 1840 he was rector of the English College in Rome. He was co-founder of the *Dublin Review*. In 1850 he was created cardinal and appointed first Archbishop of Westminster. His remaining years were spent in lecturing, writing, and promoting Catholic social reform. C.V.

witchcraft: Witchcraft in general consists in the use of magic* to injure the bodies or goods of others. Though witches may practice "white" magic, their activities are generally believed to be malevolent and the witches themselves to derive their powers from devils or other evil spirits. By reason of their magic powers witches are reputed to be able to produce or cure disease, to induce love or aversion, to "conjure" others, to give life to inanimate objects, to bring about storms and sell winds, and to fly through the air. They are often associated with toads or black cats, which are supposed to embody their "familiar" demons. Though the practice of witchcraft has existed all over the world from ancient times, the most extensive witchcraft persecution in the modern world began in Europe about the close of the Middle Ages and lasted until the eighteenth century. During the late seventeenth century it found echoes in the well-known trials in Salem, Massachusetts, and elsewhere in the American colonies.

See bibliography under folklore. See malleus maleficarum. T.P.C.

witchcraft: (AS. *wiccecraeft,* fr. masc. *wicce,* fem. *wicca,* wizard, witch, and *craeft,* power, art) Supposed practice of malevolent sorcery, especially by women in league with evil spirits.

Among uncivilized peoples magic arts have a recognized place prescribed by socially approved priests or medicine men*. But even in such communities there are often unofficial sorcerers who claim superhuman powers of calling up spirits of the dead, predicting the future, causing or curing disease, and otherwise affecting the tides of fortune. Often such persons are hated by the official practitioners of magic* and become social outcasts, sought after by those who wish superhuman aid in secret, antisocial enterprises. These furtive contrivers of occult arts are the typical witches of our most ancient literature. Even when employed by kings they are regarded as beyond the pale of approved religion or morality (as in I Sam. 28), and usually there are strict laws against their activities.

In classical Greece and Rome witchcraft was outlawed and severe penalties were prescribed, but the laws were seldom enforced. During the first twelve centuries of the Christian era, ecclesiastical authorities generally doubted the reality of witchcraft or belittled its importance. But the schoolmen of the thirteenth and fourteenth centuries, with their insistence on literal acceptance of the Bible, their professed elaborate knowledge of the supernatural world, and their ardent warfare against heresy, returned the belief in witchcraft to respectability and called on church and state to enforce the command, "Thou shalt not suffer a witch to live" (Exod. 22:18). The Inquisition* blamed witchcraft for the swelling tide of heresy, and in the fifteenth and sixteenth centuries, church, state, and mob vied with one another in the ardor of their persecutions of alleged witches. In 1437 and 1445, Pope Eugene IV issued bulls commanding punishment of witches who caused bad weather, and in 1484 the bull *Summis Desiderantes*, by Pope Innocent VIII, started a wave of torture and execution in which many scores of thousands were killed. Similar bulls were issued by Julius II and Adrian VI. Nor did the Reformation put an end to the terror. Luther joined in the denunciation of witches and there were many executions in protestant Scotland in the seventeenth century. One of the latest witch-hunting epidemics occurred at Salem, Massachusetts, in 1692, when in six months twenty persons were executed for witchcraft. Even in the twentieth century many ignorant persons believe in the reality of witchcraft, and some conservative theologians, especially Roman Catholic, defend its "abstract possibility." See, e.g., H. Thurston's article, "Witchcraft," in *The Catholic Encyclopedia* (1912). Yet probably most of the latter would agree with Thurston in denouncing the persecutions and in asserting that "in 99 cases out of 100 the allegations rest upon nothing better than pure delusion."

To most intelligent persons witchcraft is now of interest only for historical or psychological reasons. Psychologists regard the epidemics of witch-hunting, and the many voluntary confessions of black magic during such episodes, as examples of individual and social psychopathology, especially hysteria and paranoia. These epidemics serve as terrible warnings of the results which may be produced by attempts to suppress mental disease with cruelty. To liberal theologians they typify also the peril of setting religious dogma beyond the province of rational and moral examination.

See A. D. White, *A History of the Warfare of Science with Theology* (1896); W. S. Nevins, *Witchcraft in Salem Village in 1692* (1916).

L.H.DEW.

Wittenberg, Concord of: An agreement between Lutheran and Reformed theologians on the controverted doctrine of the sacraments reached as the result of a conference at Wittenberg, Germany, in 1536. The Reformed (Swiss and Upper German followers of Zwingli) agreed to Luther's view of the eucharist that "with the bread and wine the body and blood of Christ are truly and substantially present". They agreed also that "through baptism there comes to infants the forgiveness of original sin". The Concord was signed by Luther, Melanchthon, and Bugenhagen for the Lutherans and by Bucer (the convener), Capito, and Aulbert for the Reformed. The Concord raised high hopes for Protestant union but it never received general official recognition and resulted only in polite correspondence and a temporary truce. T.A.K.

wizard: Commonly regarded as a male witch, but more properly a magician or sorcerer.

P.G.M.

Wizenmann, Thomas: (1759-1787) He was vicar at Essingen, Württemberg, Germany, for three years. Then he accepted a tutorship with a wealthy family. He overworked himself and ruined his health. He succumbed to tuberculosis. As a very spiritual-minded Swabian theologian and philosopher, he was not only able to continue but also to advance beyond the ideas of Zinzendorf, Oetinger** and Collenbusch. Still more pronouncedly soteriological in thought than they, he struggled also much more seriously with the philosophy of his own day, and established a promising connection with the idealism of Hamann*.

Die Resultate der Jacobsichen und Mendelsohnschen Philosophie (Leipzig, 1786); *Die Geschichte Jesu nach dem Matthäus als Selbstbeweis ihrer Zuverlässigkeit betrachtet* . . . (Leipzig, 1789); *Göttliche Entwicklung des Satans durch das Menschengeschlecht* (Dessau, 1792); A.v.d. Goltz, *Wizenmann, der Freund Jacobis* (Gotha, 1859). H.H.

Wobbermin, Georg: (1869-) He has been teaching at the universities of Marburg, Breslau, Heidelberg and Göttingen. He gives a most comprehensively methodical reflection on and exhibition of systematic theology. As adherent of the neo-idealistic movement, he seeks to realize for his time the best inheritance of Schleiermacher* by means of the religious-historical and religious-psychological stimulations in close association with the inheritance of Ritschl*. In careful delimitation of *a priori* rationalism, neo-Friesianism* and mere empirical religious psychology, he established his transcendental-psychological method which unites the fundamental tendencies of Schleiermacher and William James in mutual correction.

Theologie und Metaphysik (Berlin, 1901); *Der christliche Gottesglaube in seinem Verhältnis zur gegenwärtigen Philosophie und Naturwissenschaft* (Leipzig, 1911), 2nd ed.; *Systematische Theologie nach religion-psychologischer Methode* (Leipzig, 1924), 3 vols., 2nd ed.; *Schleiermacher und Ritschl in ihrer Bedeutung für die heutige Lage und Aufgabe* (Tübingen, 1927); *Richtlinien evangelischer Theologie zur Überwindung der gegenwärtigen Krisis* (Göttingen, 1929); *Christian Belief in God* (1918); *Nature of Religion* (1933). H.H.

Woden, Wuotan: (Teut.) Wind-, storm-, and war-god of early Germany. As a wind-god he may bring good or evil to the crops and cattle; as a storm-god he leads assaulting hosts of men to cattle. As a war-god he early received human sacrifices and horse sacrifices; in later times the sacrifice was beer. He is also a god of trees and a god of fertility. In later times his day (Wednesday) is considered the best for planting and sowing. Like Odin* he is pictured riding a gray horse, wearing a cloak and hat and carries a spear. Corn left in the fields by the farmers is for Woden's horse. F.L.P.

Wolfenbüttel Fragments: Lengthy extracts from the most important work of H. S. Reimarus*, published in seven installments by Lessing* (1774-78) while librarian at Wolfenbüttel, Brunswick. The last extract to be published, "The Aims of Jesus and his Disciples," is a brilliant anticipation of thoroughgoing eschatology, stressed twelve decades later by Johannes Weiss and Albert Schweitzer**. The publication of these Fragments aroused a storm of protest and debate. The original manuscript is in the municipal library at Hamburg.

M.S.E.

Wolff, Christian: (1679-1754) The first German to establish a "school" of philosophy. He adopted the theories of Leibniz, combined them with ideas taken from Aristotle, and modified them to organize his comprehensive system. He set rationalism and empiricism against each other to advance the theory that they are essentially the same. Every object has a rational and an empirical character which agree in results. Reason is deduced from the contradiction. Wolff unified German thought and developed a philosophical vocabulary that is still in use. See psychology, schools of. W.G.H.

Wolsey, Thomas: (1471-1530) Born at Ipswich; educated at Magdalen College, Oxford, B.A. 1486, ("Boy Bachelor"); turned to Divinity (B.D. 1510), Thomist rather than Renaissance point of view. 1506, chaplain to Henry VII; Dean of Lincoln 1509; 1511, Privy Councillor; Bishop of Lincoln 1514, and Archbishop of York; 1515, Lord Chancellor and Cardinal; 1518, joint *legatus a latere;* 1529 Bishop of Winchester (*in commendam*); twice expected election to the Papacy. His main spheres of distinction lay in the field of diplomacy and in law. He attempted, and for a time succeeded, in effecting the "Reception" of Roman Law and Jurisprudence in English Courts. His downfall was caused when he failed to secure the nullification (miscalled 'divorce') of Henry VIII's* marriage to Catherine of Aragon. He died in disgrace at Leicester Abbey on his way from York to London to answer a charge of high treason. F.W.B.

woman, religious and ethical status of: Generally used to describe the religious, ethical and moral conceptions of women held by the dominant influential group in any society. These conceptions which go to define woman's status are usually first held by a person of great influence of the opposite sex, often a religious or political leader, and then gradually inculcated into the culture of the group. Thus woman's status today is not alone the result of conceptions held in present-day society, but a reflection of attitudes toward woman's conduct throughout history. Woman's religious, economic, ethical, and social status are all interwoven in cultural history and show her advance from subjection to men to somewhat equality with them.

Traditional attitudes toward women in our society are derived largely from the early Christian teachings of the Church Fathers. It was the Apostle Paul who expressed the earliest authoritative opinion of Christianity in regard to the status of women. Women he thought inferior. They must, he said, keep silence in the churches and "adorn themselves in modest apparel, with shamefacedness and sobriety." Women were all tainted with the sin of Eve and therefore needed discipline. The charitable work of the church was entrusted to none but women over sixty. Woman was dangerous to men; sex and sex desires sinful according to the Church Fathers. It was woman who had brought sin into the world. Marriage* although never explicitly condemned was placed third and lowest in the scale of Christian purity. Highest was absolute virginity; next, celibacy that is voluntarily adopted after marriage or after the death of husband or wife. Thus the view of woman as a thing both inferior and evil found expression very early in the history of the Church and while not accepted explicitly by all groups did find expression in the course of the Middle Ages in the idea of the subjection of women. On the other hand, it was medieval theory which developed a counter doctrine of the superiority of women. This was in the form of the adoration toward the Virgin* in heaven and the lady upon earth and it was this doctrine which handed down to the modern world the ideal of chivalry. Thus the cult of the lady was the mundane counterpart of the cult of the Virgin. The romantic worship of a woman as well as the worship of God was the necessary quality of a perfect knight. But chivalry* like asceticism* was practiced by only a limited group and yet it does show the inconsistencies existent about women, teaching simultaneously her superiority and inferiority.

Although a number of important factors have led to the emancipation of women in our Western society, many vestiges of these two earlier doctrines still exist in relation to the ethical status of women today and in the mores governing her conduct. The Industrial Revolution gave woman an opportunity to earn money outside the home and become economically independent of man to some extent. The extension of equal suffrage to woman gave to her to a large degree political equality. With these symbols of feminine emancipation and emerging equality with men came imitation of much of men's behavior and attitudes, such as speech, dress, smoking and drinking habits. Yet women have remained in the paradoxical position of being both dependent and independent, of resenting their feminine rôle whenever it does not carry with it complete equality with men, yet exaggerating their femininity in order to receive equal or special privileges. They appeal, in other words, to man's chivalrous rôle which symbolizes woman's inferiority and inequality of the past. Woman is still thought of at once as the temptress and siren and the embodiment of all that is kind, pure and virgin. She is recognized as man's intellectual, political, and social equal; yet sex differences still govern her ethical status in that she is bound by ethical restrictions unknown to men as well as being more restricted in her conduct by many of the mores common to both men and women. See double standard of morals; family; motherhood; widows, treatment of.

Willystine Goodsell, *The Family as a Social and Educational Institution* (1927); Una Bernard Sait, *New Horizons for the Family* (1938); Bernhard Stern, *The Family Past and Present* (1938); Kimball Young, *Personality and Problems of Adjustment* (1940). H.R.M.

Woolman, John: (1720-1772) Quaker, mystic, social reformer. Woolman's quest for pure religion, which made him an American Quaker* "saint," and caused him to attack the evils of slavery, war, poverty, and greed, is recounted in his famous *Journal*. T.E.D.

Woolston, Thomas: (1669-1731) See deism.

Word of God: In the O.T. we read over and over again of the coming of God's word to a prophet*. It was the spoken word of God. Also it was the expression of his power by which he created the world (Gen. 1.3). This word was found in the Torah* or Law, and it abides forever (Is. 40.8). In the later Jewish literature there was a tendency to personalize the concept, but it never became a separate hypostasis.

In early Christianity, the word of God was found not in Torah but in the message about Christ (Acts 10.36, etc.). I Pet. 1.23 speaks of Christians being begotten by the word, and Heb. 4.12 vividly personifies the penetration of the word, but it is still the message about Christ. Rev. 19.11 calls Christ the word of God and I John 1.1 refers to him as the "word of life." The prologue to the gospel of John*, however, goes beyond any of these. (1:1-18) Here we have a hymn to Christ as the word of God. Though it was interpreted by the later Greek church in terms of Stoic and Philonic** philosophy, it is more probable that the evangelist used the term in contrast to Jewish Toraology, and with some influence from Hellenistic redeemer concepts.

Since the Bible* contains the written word of God the terms have been for many Christians identical. That has been especially true of those who hold to its plenary inspiration*. Especially in Lutheran theology has the concept of the "word of God" been emphasized. Most Lutheran theologians, however, would employ the term for the biblical message about Christ rather than for the literal text of the Bible itself. It is God's saving deed, which creates faith in the hearts of those who are saved. See logos; Mohammedanism. Cf. sruti. C.T.C.

Wordsworth, William: (1770-1850) English poet. An active boyhood in the Lake District, four years at Cambridge, and one turbulent year in France during the first stages of the Revolution furnished the background for Wordsworth's poetic career; the rest of his life was uneventful. The inner record of those years, which saw the development of his transcendental philosophy, are recorded in his greatest work, *The Prelude* (completed 1805, published 1850). Later he harmonized his views with the historic doctrines of Christianity, writing the result into the *Ecclesiastical Sonnets* (1822). Of the shorter poems, *Tintern Abbey* (1798), *Intimations of Immortality* (1807), and the *Ode to Duty* (1807) are among the most significant.

The best edition of *The Prelude* is by E. de Selincourt (1926), and there is a good one-volume edition of the *Poetical Works* by T. Hutchinson (1933). The standard biography is G. M. Harper's *William Wordsworth, His Life, Works, and Influence* (2 vols., 1916). L.W.C.

World Sunday School Convention: See Sunday School movement in the United States.

World's Student Christian Federation: See student religious organizations.

Worms, Concordat of: An agreement between Emperor Henry V and Pope Calixtus II (23 Sept. 1122) concluding the investiture* controversy in Germany which had troubled the German ecclesiastical scene for nearly a century and had developed into an open conflict between Henry IV and Gregory VII**. By the terms of this agreement, which was one of the earliest concordats, Henry V relinquished investiture by ring and staff and permitted the free election of bishops; Calixtus on his part agreed that all elections should be held in the presence of the emperor who would have the right to invest the elected ecclesiastic with the temporal prerogatives of the office. See concordat. F.W.N.

Worms, Diet of: (1521) A convention of the estates of the German Empire convoked by Emperor Charles V* and held in the town of Worms to hear the case of Martin Luther* who had already been excommunicated by the Pope. Asked to retract his writings against the papacy, Luther declared: "Unless I shall be convinced by the testimonies of the Scriptures or by clear reason . . . I neither can nor will make any retraction, since it is neither safe nor honorable to act against conscience". Referred to the authority of the Church, particularly to the Council of Constance* with which he was at variance, Luther insisted, "The Church universal is the number of the elect". According to tradition, Luther concluded his self-defence with the words, "Here I stand. I cannot do otherwise. God help me. Amen". Luther's courage won him admirers, but the Diet adopted an edict declaring him an outlaw. On the following day Elector Frederick of Saxony took him into protective custody and concealed him in the castle of, Wartburg. Luther's appearance at Worms is a dramatic landmark in the struggle for free conscience. See Worms, Edict of. T.A.K.

Worms, Edict of: Was issued by the famous Diet of Worms*, 1521, in condemnation of Luther's position. It was notable for its comprehensiveness in denouncing Luther's views, the severity of its penalties, and for its practical ineffectiveness. It also attempted to subject the press to a rigid ecclesiastical censorship. See Reformation; Spires, Diet of. G.R.C.

worship: Worship is renewed self-commitment to God. (See God; prayer; Living Christ.) It is the practice of whatsoever rites, ceremonies or other means may serve to put the individual more completely under the control of God's creativity by releasing him from those enthrallments and constraints that resist this divine working. No one is entirely free of the bonds which limit the power of God in the life of man. But these conscious and unconscious resistances may be indefinitely reduced and some of them cast off quite completely by methods of worship. However, new resistances are always developing and so worship is required as a regular or recurrent practice.

While the forms of worship may be practiced by any one at any time, genuine worship is impossible until certain preconditions are met. These prerequisites are four.

The first requirement opening the way to genuine worship is the awakening of the sense of need for the true and living God. This is perhaps the most difficult condition of all to meet. Men very commonly have the sense of need but what they think they need is that which they have learned to cherish as the basis of their personal stability. No human being begins by finding this support and basis in the living God. Each child begins by finding it in the home. Finding personal stability in the home is not the same as finding it in God however much God may be in the home. After leaving the home, the child may seek the security and goods of life in some other established order, or in self-confidence, or in moral idealism, or in stoical resignation, or in clever adaptation, or in some illusion. But none of these are identical with the creativity of God, however much some of them may be the gifts of God. Not until these give way beneath the individual and he discovers the inadequacy of them all, will he turn from the gifts to the giver and find the ultimate source of personal integrity. No one can truly worship until he awakens to this deepest need of human life.

The second requirement is that he have some contact with people who do truly worship and who seek to commit themselves to the reality of God. Our appreciative awareness of realities most pervasive and most difficult to apprehend must be aroused and directed by participation in the appreciative activities of others.

The third requirement is that he develop some evaluative sense of the inadequacy of all other ways of living and some recognition of the superiority of life that is free of every other ultimate bond save that of God's creativity.

The fourth requirement is decision, made with utmost sincerity, and ever again renewed, that he will cast off every constraint that opposes the work of God in his life.

After these prerequisites have been met, the methods of worship are the following.

1) Association with others who are truly and faithfully worshiping. This social influence is a powerful agent in delivering the individual from the obstructions in his mind and personality which prevent the creativity of God from possessing him.

2) Confession and repentance of sin. This means to search out and apprehend in their specific character so far as possible what these obstructions may be in one's living which resist the work of God. It also means to recognize that one's deepest sins are never conscious.

3) Repeated act of self-commitment to God. This must be practiced again and again. It means to resolve with one's whole self that one will meet every possible condition required to give God free way in one's life.

4) Facing the worst. This means to search out imaginatively the very worst that is likely to happen and learn to face it with the freedom and security of deeper self-commitment to God's creativity.

5) Aspiration after the best that one knows. One's vision of the best is renewed and clarified in worship.

6) Praise and thanksgiving, practiced not because God wants to be praised, but because this is the way that one exposes himself most fully and expansively to the presence and power of God.

Confession and repentance of sin on the one hand, praise and thanksgiving on the other, are perhaps the two most important parts of worship. The one cuts out obstructions in the personality, the other opens out the shut-in personality. Both clear the way for God's creativity to gain supreme control over the life of man. This supreme control and the goodness of life that issues from it are the aims of worship. See liturgics; liturgy.

B. E. Meland, *Modern Man's Worship* (1936); William L. Sperry, *Reality in Worship* (1925); Evelyn Underhill, *Worship* (1937); H. N. Wieman, *Methods of Private Religious Living* (1929); Robert Will, *Le Culte, Etude d'Histoire et de Philosophie religieuses* (1924). H.N.W.

worship of ancestors: See ancestor worship.

wounds, the five sacred: The wounds in the hands and feet made by the nails in crucifying Jesus Christ, and the gash in His side made by the spear of the Roman soldier as the Savior hung dead on the cross. Devotion to the five sacred wounds was widely spread during the Middle Ages. In many dioceses and religious orders the Feast of the Five Wounds is celebrated on the fourth Friday of Lent. Cf. incense. C.V.

wrath of God: Symbolical and inadequate language, necessarily anthropomorphic in character, used in an attempt to indicate the qualitative intensity of the reaction of God in the fundamental character of His Being as Eternal and Sovereign Holy Love against all that is not in harmony with His will. The doctrine of divine wrath, when interpreted as though that wrath existed or could exist in isolation from Sovereign Love (I Jn. 4: 7-19), has been presented in poetry and painting as well as in some theological statements in a form which constitutes a caricature of the character of God as He is revealed in "Christ who is the image of God" (2 Cor. 4:4; cf. Heb. 1:3; Jn. 14:9). It is helpful to approach any consideration of the wrath of God by noting N.T. references to anger in connection with the life of Christ. Although warning against sinful anger such as is involved in any uncontrolled and carnal indulgence of selfish and vehement fits of temper (cf. Eph. 4:31; Col. 3:8), a type of wrath or anger which despite its readiness to pose as "righteous" (cf. Ja. 1:19-20; Tit. 1:7) must be branded as a vice (cf. Eph. 4:26) the N.T. nevertheless recognizes, both directly and by implication, that in the life of Christ instances of holy anger do occur, and that such righteous anger is to be regarded as, and actually is, a virtue. For examples of such sacred anger read Mt. 23:13-33; Mk. 3:5; 10:13, 14; 11:15-17; cf. Mt. 16:23; 18:6. It follows therefore that righteous anger against evil cannot be ruled out as a mode of the essential character of love which is in Christ (cf. Lk. 13:34; 19:41), and therefore, according to the Christian faith, in God. The Christian view affirms that since the Being of God as Sovereign Love is eternally holy God confronts evil* with severity, condemnation and opposing power, the wrath of God being in truth the wrath of His Sovereign Love, whose purpose in the manifestation of wrath, since God cannot deny Himself, can never be other than the overcoming of evil by His own Goodness and the establishment of the rule of His Sovereign Love. The wrath of God as described in the Scriptures is not only to be thought of as a reality but also as the present judgment of evil and the divine opposition to it.

Men have long experienced both the necessity and the difficulty of attempting to interpret the holiness and the love of God in such a way that what is regarded as the immanent tension between them does not become an irreconcilable contradiction or a religiously-unendurable type of antinomy between the holiness involved in Sovereign Love and the Sovereign Love affirmed to be holy. It is urged that if the divine love could abrogate its own holy wrath against evil (Rom. 1:18) it would not be Holy Love. Dispossessed of holiness, God could neither be nor supply the moral imperative and dynamic for man's ethical needs. Even in the case of man it is pointed out that the absence of a righteous anger or wrath against evil indicates the absence of vital love for the good. Again, it is maintained that if the holiness of God be interpreted in a manner which denies the conviction of faith that God's holiness is the holiness of His Sovereign Love, the result is a religiously-untenable doctrine in which God, dispossessed of His essential character of love, could Himself experience no triumphant constraint to seek and to save that which is lost. Such a God would be religiously valueless. In opposition to any exaltation of love to the exclusion of holiness, or to any emphasis on holiness at the cost of love, as if either could be ontologically abstracted from the other, Christian faith, while admitting that holiness and love may be distinguished for the purposes of human thought and necessary discussion, affirms nevertheless their existential identity in God. God as Sovereign Love cannot defeat Himself by being untrue to the character of His own Being which involves the divine fidelity to the objects of His own Love. Nor can the Sovereign Love which is eternally holy cease to confront evil with condemnation. Nevertheless if the fundamental character of Sovereign Love is truly sovereign it must be the Lord of all even within the Being of God Himself, "for God is love." Though Sovereign Holy Love may be concealed by its own mode of wrath which appears as though it were the contradiction of God's fundamental character of Love, the deepest Christian faith triumphantly affirms that the Reality of that wrath, experienced by man in terms of warning, chastising, cleansing or in any other way, is in truth the Reality of the Sovereign Love accomplishing its own redemptive and sanctifying purposes. Christian faith could not endure any doctrinal formulation in which the Unity of the Being of God would be defeated by the alleged antinomy of two eternal "sovereignties" within God, i.e., Sovereign Love and "sovereign" wrath. For while the character of Holiness is eternal in the eternally Sovereign Love, the wrath of that Holy Love must pass away from God's relationship to the penitent man who is reconciled to God through Christ. Ignoring neither the Sovereignty nor the Holy severity of Love the N.T. describes Sovereign Love as proving its sovereignty by "taking the form of a servant" (Phil. 2:7) and obeying the stern constraint of that Holy Love by "becoming obedient even unto . . . the death of the cross." (Phil. 2:8) The sacrificial love of Christ, manifested in giving Himself "for all" (2 Cor. 5:14) as the Victim who takes the sin of the world upon Himself and into Himself being "made to be sin on our behalf" (2 Cor. 5: 21), is acknowledged by Christian faith as the triumphant deed of God Himself who was in Christ reconciling the world unto Himself, "that in the ages to come he might show the exceeding riches of his grace in kindness toward us in Christ Jesus" (Eph. 2:7). For the Christian believer, God's work of reconciliation* through Christ is at once the supreme revelation of Sovereign Holy Love and an ultimate "mystery of the faith" (I Tim. 3:9): God is Himself reconciled to the world by His own work of reconciling the world unto Himself. H.W.J.

Wren, Sir Christopher: See art, ecclesiastical, Christian; church building.

Writings, the: See hagiographa; Old Testament.

Wu Shan Shê: See Chinese religions (under Secret Societies).

wu wei: See Chinese Terminology.

Wundt, Wilhelm Max: (1832-1920) He first taught physiology in Heidelberg. Next he taught philosophy in Zürich. Last he was professor of philosophy at the University of Leipzig. He was the founder of the institute for experimental psychology*. He owed his international reputation to his achievements in psychology. In scope of interests and knowledge he resembled Leibniz, but not in logical precision of his thought. He was equally conversant in the natural sciences and the cultural sciences. He developed a philosophical system that sought to arrive at a non-contradictory world view in which the totality of reality finds its place. His was a spiritualistic idealism, and idealistic monism. The fundamental characteristic of the psychical was for him a creative synthesis, voluntaristically colored. He was opposed to a substantialist view of the soul. He postulated the law of the increase of psychic energy because the law of the conservation of energy was ill adapted to explain the evolution of the mind. He not only pioneered in experimental psychology and physiological psychology, but also in folk psychology—the study of social groups and problems of the psychology of language, religion, art, and morality. He constructed his ethics from the standpoint of ethical personality based on the needs of society.

Lectures on Human and Animal Psychology (London, 1894, 2nd ed., London, 1896, 3rd ed., London, 1901); *Ethics*, 3 vols. (London, 1897-1901); *Ethik* (4th ed., Stuttgart, 1912); *Principles of Morality and Departments of Moral Life* (London, 1901); *Principles of Physiological Psychology* (London, 1904); *Völkerpsychologie*, 10 vols. (3rd ed., Leipzig, 1900-1920); *Logik*, 3 vols. (3rd ed., Stuttgart, 1906-1908); *System der Philosophie*, 2 vols. (3rd ed., Leipzig, 1907, 4th ed., Leipzig, 1919); *The Elements of Folkpsychology* (London, 1916); R. Eisler, *Wilhelm Wundts Philosophie und Psychologie* (Leipzig, 1902); E. König, *Wilhelm Wundt, seine Philosophie and Psychologie* (3rd ed., Stuttgart, 1909); A. M. Selitrennikow, *Die ethischen und religiösen Anschauungen W. Wundts* (Charkow, 1910); K. Thieme, *Zu Wundts Religionspsychologie* (Leipzig, 1910); F. Emmel, *Wundts Stellung zum religiösen Problem* (Würzburg, 1911); W. Nef, *Die Philosophie Wilhelm Wundts* (Leipzig, 1923); P. Petersen, *Wilhelm Wundt und seine Zeit* (Stuttgart, 1925); P. S. Hess, *Das Religiöse Bedürfnis Eine kritische Studie anhand der Religionstheorie Wilhelm Wundts* (St. Gall, 1935). H.H.

Wundtian psychology: See psychology, schools of.

Wycliffe (or Wyclif) John: (ca. 1320-1384) English preacher, reformer and Biblical translator.

Having initially studied nominalism, he found his way to St. Augustine and to the Bible. He accepted the metaphysical realism of the older scholastics because both Augustine and the Bible represented it. He felt that since Augustine and his pupils correctly understood the Scripture, they also rightly taught what was correct in philosophy. As a realist he critically examined the elements of his age. In social and political questions he advocated the overthrow of the old order in the name of a legal biblicism. His conjoined Augustinianism and biblicism became a strong, effective weapon in the realization of his reform-criticism of the church and its doctrine. Like his great contemporaries he exhibited a renewed interest in the *City of God* by Augustine, whose predestinarian grace enabled him to establish a new idealistic conception of the church, and to exercise a penetrative critique of sacramental doctrine. His biblicism made him a pitiless critic of the contemporary church. The great Hussitic movement was nothing but a practical realization of his revolutionary, biblically inspired, reform ideas. Cf. Bible, English; catechism; catechumenate; canons of various churches; Grosseteste, R.; Lollards; remanence.

R. Buddensieg, *J. Wiclif* (Halle, 1885); H. Fürstenau, *J. Wiclif's Lehre von der Einteilung der Kirche und von der Stellung der weltlichen Gewalt* (Berlin, 1900); D. Heine, *Wiclif's Lehre vom Güterbesitz* (Gütersloh, 1903); G. Lechler, *J. Wiclif und die Vorgeschichte d. Reformation* (Leipzig, 1873), 2 vols.; B. Manning, "Wyclif," *Cambridge Mediaeval History* (1932), vol. VII. H.H.

X Y Z

Xaverian Brothers: A Roman Catholic Congregation of Lay Brothers, founded at Bruges, Belgium, by Theodore James Rijken in 1839, principally for the education of poor boys. In 1929 the Congregation possessed some fifty houses and numbered about 440 members. E.A.R.

Xavier, St. Francis: Born in Spanish Navarre in 1506, he became one of the first Jesuits*, and sailed in 1541 to blaze a trail for the Faith in the huge Portuguese Indian Empire. He was the first to preach Christ to the Japanese, and was trying to enter China when he died in 1552. E.A.R.

Xenophanes: (c. 569-480 B.C.) Xenophanes of Colophon, Asia Minor, reputed founder of Eleatic* school, reformer in practical and intellectual affairs. Opposed anthropomorphistic conception of the gods, introduced monism: "God is one, supreme among gods and men, and not like mortals in body and mind (thoughts).[1] According to Xenophanes "Die Gottheit ist ganz Auge, ganz Geist, ganz Ohr," "The whole of God sees, the whole thinks, the whole hears."[2]

[1] H. Diels, *Die Fragmente der Vorsokratiker,* 11 B, 23;
[2] *Ibid.,* 11B, 24. P.R.H.

Ximénes, De Cisneros, Francisco: Famous Spanish statesman and prelate. He was born at Torrelaguna in 1436, and died at Roa in 1517. In 1484 he became a Franciscan, and in 1495 was appointed archbishop of Toledo and chancellor of Castile. The University of Alcalá was founded by him. He was created cardinal and designated Grand Inquisitor in 1507. Under his leadership the Moors were defeated at Oran in 1509. In 1516 he was appointed regent of the Kingdom. C.V.

X P I: See symbolism.

Yahadut: See Judaism (Introductory).

Yahweh: See Jehovah. Also see cosmogonies; tetragrammatom.

Yajur-Veda: One of the four Vedas of early Hinduism, representing a later stage of religion than the Rig-Veda.* It contains a good deal of material taken from the Rig-Veda, but used in a different connection. It is highly ritualistic in character. The most characteristic features are the *yajus* or prose formulas which give the name to the book. C.S.B.

Yama: In the Vedas Yama and Yami are twin brother and sister who are the parents of the human race. A variant tradition makes Manu the first parent. Yama is the first to find a pathway from Earth to Heaven and becomes king of the blessed dead, though later he is also ruler of hell. He is most frequently known as the god of the dead. C.S.B.

Yamato-Damashii: (Lit., "The Soul of Japan." *Yamato,* an ancient name for the region about Nara and later for Japan as a whole). The Japanese national spirit. D.C.H.

Yang and Yin: See Yin yang.

yantras: Mystic diagrams usually drawn on copper or other metal tablets which are believed to possess occult powers. Used in connection with an appropriate *mantra** their power is irresistible. C.S.B.

Yashts: Avestan* hymns of praise in honor of Zoroastrian* divine beings, some of whom (notably Anahita*, the star Tishtrya, Mithra) are ancient Iranian deities, and of angels (fravashis*); although later than Zoroaster, they represent in part an earlier religious stage. R.H.P.

Yasna: Zoroastrian* liturgies in the Avesta*. They include invocations to Ahura-Mazda* and other gods, liturgies for the preparation of the sacred drink (*haoma**), commentaries on the prayers, and the five Gathas* (in chs. 28-34, 43-51, 53) containing the teaching of Zoroaster. R.H.P.

Yazatas: The Avestan* term for the minor deities of Zoroastrianism* (literally "worthy of praise;" *ized* in modern Persian). They are subordinated to Ahura Mazda* and his angels. Although not mentioned in the Gathas*, they are praised in the Yashts*. R.H.P.

Yellow Hat Lāmaism: See Lāmaism.

Yellow Springs (Ohio) community: See communistic settlements, secular.

Yezidi: See devil worshippers.

yggdrasil: The world tree in Norse mythology, rooted in Niflheim, Midgard and Asgard. Its topmost bough overshadowed the hall of Odin.* Its leaves are always green. The Norns*, or Fates dwell at its foot, by the Urdar fountain. It is to be destroyed by fire in the twilight of the gods.
P.G.M.

Yi Ching: See Chinese Terminology.

Yiddish: The vernacular of about two-thirds of Ashkenazi Jewry (i.e., ten or eleven million), derived from Middle High German, and fused with Hebrew-Aramaic expressions and survivals of Old French, and with elements of Polish, Russian, English, etc. It is believed to have originated as a separate dialect about a thousand years ago in the Rhine provinces, whence it was transplanted by waves of migration to Poland, Lithuania, Austria, Bohemia, Hungary, etc. As a literary medium it was first used for devotional purposes, for translations of Bible, prayers, homilies, and ritual customs, and subsequently for entertainment, such as translations of popular romances and tales, and of original poems, stories, dramas, etc.

Because of its use of Hebrew characters, Yiddish was designated *Ivre-Taitsch* (Hebrew-German). It was also referred to as *Taitsch, Juedish-Teutsch,* and *Jiddisch.* The Mendelssohnian Enlightenment (18th cent.), striving to adjust the Jews to European culture, stigmatized Yiddish as *Jargon,* a name, which, though carried into general use, is currently avoided as discrediting. Though a mixed language, it has acquired a character of its own, expressive of the inner needs of the Jewish people.

The Enlightenment movement among East European Jews in the 19th cent. as well as the nationalist and socialist movements utilized Yiddish for educational purposes. Through the skill with which they carried on their work, and through the labors of a number of gifted poets, novelists, and dramatists in Europe and in America, Yiddish —during the past half century—developed an extensive literature of high quality.

S. Birnbaum, *Grammatik der jiddischen Sprache* (1915-16); A. Roback, *The Story of Yiddish Literature* (1940); M. Waxman, *A Hist. of Jew. Liter.*, vol. II, ch. xii; vol. IV, chs. vi-vii; xii; Weinrich, art. "Yiddish," *Allgemeine Enzyklopedie, Yidden,* II, 23-90; L. Wiener, *Hist. of Yiddish Liter. in the 19th Cent.* (1899).
S.S.C.

Yima: The Indo-Iranian counterpart of the Vedic Yama*.
C.S.B.

Yin yang: See Chinese Terminology.

Y. M. C. A., Student: See student religious organizations.

Yoga: Literally the word means in Sanskrit "to yoke". Today it is used in two senses in India: 1) to denote a technique or system of discipline by means of which a yogin attains to moksha* or salvation, 2) to denote a system of philosophy, one of the six major schools that have developed in India.

As a philosophic school it takes its rise from the Yoga-Sutras of Patanjali, who borrowed heavily from the atheistic Sankya* system particularly the dualistic doctrine of the prakriti and purusha**, and the belief that *moksha* lay in the knowledge of the utter separateness of matter and spirit. To this he added, however, belief in Ishvara*, a personal god, thus making his system, known indeed as Sankhya-Yoga, theistic.

The Sankhya had asserted the necessity of attaining knowledge, but had not elaborated specific techniques for so doing. This the Sānkhya-Yoga does in great detail. The Yoga-Sūtras furnish minute directions as to the steps necessary to reach the desired goal. There are eight stages, the first two being negative and positive ethical preparation, *yamas* and *niyamas;* then comes physical preparation, the *asanas* or postures of which there are many, and *pranayama* or breathing exercises (eight kinds); then follow exercises in concentration, the withdrawal of the senses *pratyahara;* concentration, *dharana;* contemplation, *dhyāna,* and finally *Samādhi,* first conscious, and at last super-conscious, in which all sense of subject and object is completely lost, and matter and spirit stand wholly apart. Complete deliverance is not, however, attained until after death.

On reaching the more advanced stages of Yoga the yogins are believed to attain to miraculous powers. Marvelous stories are told of their prowess in the literature of India and in the writings of some westerners as Yeats-Brown, *Lives of a Bengal Lancer,* and Paul Brunton, *A Search in Secret India.*

Various kinds of Yoga are distinguished: *hatha-yoga,* or bodily yoga which includes the earlier stages enumerated above as a preparation for concentration, but is also much used as a therapeutic technique for healing various bodily ills; *bhakti-yoga* attains the desired goal of union with god through devotion: *raja-yoga* is the yoga of concentration; and *jnana-yoga* is the highest type which attains through knowledge to the desired goal. See Hinduism.

F. H. Woods, *The Yoga System of Patanjali* (1914); K. T. Behanan, *Yoga, a Scientific Evaluation* (1937).
C.S.B.

Yogācāra: See Buddhist Terminology.

yogī, yogin: A Hindu term for one who practices the yoga* discipline in order to attain salvation. Popularly used for any Hindu ascetic.
C.S.B.

Yom Kippur: See Atonement, Day of.

Yorker Brethren: See River Brethren.

Young, Brigham: (1801-1877) Born in Vermont; carpenter, joiner, painter, glazier; left the Methodist Episcopal church for Latter Day Saints, 1832; Apostle, 1835; President of the Twelve Apostles, 1840; after death of Joseph Smith Jr., assumed leadership and led a group to Utah. (See Latter Day Saints—Utah). He made public polygamy in August 1852; started Salt Lake Temple 1853; built temple at St. George, Utah. Led settlement and development of Utah and was first territorial governor.
S.A.B.

Young Men's Christian Association, The: The Young Men's Christian Association was organized on June 6, 1844, by George Williams* and twelve young men in London. The original purpose, "the improvement of the spiritual condition of the young men engaged in the drapery and other trades," was soon broadened until the American movement adopted the symbol of the triangle for spirit, mind and body to reach the whole man, and later the young men and boys of the whole world. Robert McBurney was the pioneer city secretary in New York who conceived and constructed the first of a thousand model buildings in America alone, now valued at over $250,000,000.

Under Richard C. Morse and later John R. Mott as General Secretary of the International Committee for the United States and Canada, specialized work was rapidly developed for city young men and for students in some eight hundred colleges; in the physical, educational, and religious activities; for men in the Railroad, Industrial, Army and Navy, County, and Colored work, and other departments. (See Y.M.C.A., Student.)

The foreign outreach of the North American Associations began in 1889 and thirty-two countries were eventually entered by some six hundred secretaries in its World Service to develop indigenous, self-directing, self-supporting, self-propagating institutions which would in time leaven the masses in their own lands. There are now some two million members in sixty countries endeavoring to offer a concrete program that is at once practical and spiritual, for individual character building and national regeneration. In countries like Poland, where 99 per cent of racial Poles are Roman Catholics, the movement is conducted within a Catholic framework entirely by Polish Catholic laymen. Among the Greeks or Russians, the Association is loyal to the Orthodox Church. In Protestant countries, it is managed by members of the evangelical Protestant churches, but it is an ecumenical movement loyal to all Christian churches.

The World Alliance of the Associations is under the World's Committee situated at Geneva, Switzerland. As the Association has just completed its first century, 1844-1944, it now enters upon a new century generally agreed upon certain basic elements in the YMCA philosophy as conditions and principles which must be realised for its future success: 1. It must be loyal to its dominant spiritual purpose as a Young Men's *Christian* Association; 2. This purpose must permeate with spiritual passion the whole breadth of its manifold work; 3. A bold and comprehensive program must be built upon the needs of each local and national community; 4. The Association must concentrate upon its field of the young men and boys of the nation and the world; 5. It must aim at sound but bold financing without debts or deficits; 6. It must be loyal to its tradition of lay leadership, as laymen sacrificially give their life, time and money to the work; 7. It must have adequate buildings and yet a community-wide program beyond all its buildings; 8. It must avoid selfish isolationism as a mere competing social and religious organization, but must cooperate loyally with the church, the home, the school, and all other social and religious agencies; 9. It must in its World Service outlook take account of all the four hundred million young men and boys of the world as its parish; 10. It must ever remember its objectives to build a new man and a new society, by a whole program of a whole gospel, for the whole man, the whole country, and the whole world.

Sherwood Eddy, *A Century with Youth*: One Hundred Years of the Y (1944).

S.E.

Young People's Societies, Christian: By "young people's society" is meant a local church organization of youth in the age range of 12 to 24, to provide a program of worship, commitment, testimony, Bible study, recreation, Christian service, and related activities, with or without adult sponsorship, but always more or less self-motivated and directed. It is the happy meeting point of a natural desire on the part of young people for an "endeavor" of their own, and of adult leaders' concern with the development and conservation of the religious interests of youth.

Societies of young people for one or more of the above purposes were not unknown in Europe and America in the seventeenth, eighteenth and nineteenth centuries. Some were for prayer and devotion, some singing societies, some temperance, some missionary, and some very nearly like the more modern young peoples' society. Young people were, of course, also included in the Sunday schools. However, the active beginning of the wave of interest in young people's organizations in the church may be dated with the formation of the first Christian Endeavor Society in the Williston Congregational Church of Portland, Maine, on February 2, 1881 by Dr. Francis E. Clark. The Christian Endeavor society idea took hold on the imagination of people, and the movement spread so rapidly that in six years over seven thousand societies were reported, with a membership of nearly half a million, in the churches of many denominations, on several continents.

Christian Endeavor became a national and later an international movement, non-denominational in character, and made a bid to become the inclusive organization for youth of all evangelical churches, thus in spirit anticipating the ecumenical movements of today. But, whether due to weaknesses in the non-denominational idea or in the program of Christian Endeavor, or to the desire of denominations for holding and guiding their own youth, or both, it was not long until many of the denominations had set in motion youth movements of their own, notable among them the Epworth League of the Methodist churches organized in 1889, the Baptist Young People's Union organized in 1891, the Luther League of the Lutheran Church organized in 1895. Some denominations used the Christian Endeavor as their own youth organization, and local units of Christian Endeavor continued to exist in some churches of denominations which sponsored their own youth organization.

Though differing widely in purpose, structure and program, youth organizations in general hold these features in common: They include members of both sexes (there are some marked exceptions to this general rule), limit their membership to persons in the age-range of young people, engage these young people in active participation in program and work, have a strong religious emphasis with an accent on service, foster and maintain a bond of fellowship. They seek to win young people to Christ, build them up in Christian living, and train them for Christian service.

The very success of youth organizations has been one of their weaknesses. They have tended to be "another" organization in the church, often more in the church so far as place of meeting is concerned than of the church in organization and responsibility. In 1914 Walter S. Athearn published a memorable book, *The Church School*, in which he pointed out the way in which the church has been atomized into many subsidiary organizations and programs, with its attendant evils, so that the church itself has often been lost in the many lesser loyalties. This led to his plea for unification of all educational organization and program into a church school, which is still in process of being worked out. This emphasis on unification has developed to where it is now unity in the whole church program which is sought, so that there might be "a church and only a church", yet with desirable differentiation so as to provide for individual and group differences. In this process youth organizations are playing an important part.

The recent endeavor of every denomination as well as of interdenominational agencies has been to devise a plan for youth work which will at one and the same time provide youth with an organization of their very own, while yet keeping them consciously an integral part of the church as a whole. Within the youth division itself this endeavor to provide for unification and integration has led to the formation of youth organizations which are inclusive of all the youth of the church, and make provision for all the activities and experiences which should normally be provided by the church for young people. This is leading to the disappearance of the organized Sunday school class, the organized Sunday school department, the distinctive "society" organization, the club for through-the-week activity, in favor of a single, inclusive youth organization of the church. As a transition stage, these separate organizations may be continued, but some plan for correlation is provided so that essential unification may result. Out of this has come the Youth Fellowship of the Methodist Church, the Pilgrim Fellowship of the Congregational Church, the Youth Fellowship of the Evangelical Reformed Church, the Baptist Youth Fellowship, and similar inclusive organizations for most of the denominations. Program differentiations are resulting from this unified approach to youth work, looking in the direction of a more intensive worship and study program for Sunday morning, a discussion-forum type of program for Sunday evening, with provision for fellowship, service and recreational activities tied in to meet the needs of the whole youth group rather than as a necessary adjunct of each separate meeting.

This unified approach to the youth of the church lays a new burden on curriculum makers, that of providing the materials for a unified program. Steps in this direction have been under way for several years, and are coming to fullest fruition in the curriculum plans being developed jointly by the denominations through the International Council of Religious Education.

Christian youth in North America today are brought into fellowship through the United Christian Youth Movement, a cooperative program of national denominational and state and national interdenominational youth agencies, including in their constituency approximately 10,000,000 Protestant young people. This Movement, operating through delegated representatives, including adult leaders of the cooperating agencies as well as young people who are members of the Christian Youth Conference of North America, the Christian Youth Council of North America, and the annual regional planning conferences for youth, seeks to unite Christian youth in conviction, purpose, long-range objectives, and projects by means of which these convictions may find expression and these objectives be achieved. See Student Volunteer movement.

F. O. Erb, *The Development of the Young People's Movement* (1917); H. T. Stock, *Church Work With Young People* (1929); N. C. Harner, *Youth Work in the Church* (1942); I. K. Beckes, *Young Leaders in Action* (1941); M. M. Chambers, *Youth Serving Organizations,* American Council on Education (1937).

P.H.V.

Young Womens Christian Association: The Young Womens Christian Association is an international Christian woman movement. The first Y.W.C.A. was organized in London in 1855, growing out of the simple desire to meet the needs of women and girls. In the United States, Association work for young women was begun in New York City in 1858, having as part of its first program housing and the holding of religious meetings. The present national organization, the Young Womens Christian Associations of the United States of America, was formed in 1906 by the coming together of two earlier national organizations. The executive body of this national organization is the National Board, with headquarters at 600 Lexington Avenue, New York, N. Y. President, Mrs. Henry A. Ingraham; General Secretary, Mrs. Harrison S. Elliott.

The purpose of the Young Womens Christian Associations of the U.S.A. as stated in the national constitution is as follows:

"The immediate purpose of this organization shall be to unite in one body the Young Women's Christian Associations of the United States; to establish, develop and unify such Associations; to participate in the work of the World's Young Women's Christian Association; to advance the physical, social, intellectual, moral and spiritual interests of young women. The ultimate purpose of all its efforts shall be to seek to bring young women to such a knowledge of Jesus Christ as Saviour and Lord as shall mean for the individual young woman fullness of life and development of character, and shall make the organization as a whole an effective agency in the bringing in of the Kingdom of God among young women."

From its earliest beginnings the Y.W.C.A. has always tested its work by its two major objectives, that of a Christian organization and a primary interest and responsibility in all that concerns women. It has considered increasingly important and necessary the inclusion within its interests, program, activities and its policy groups, of women from a wide range of social, educational and economic background and experience. In 1942 nearly 3,000,000 women and girls shared in the life of the Association, including business and professional women and girls, industrial girls, students, younger girls, home and farm women, Negro women and girls and girls of foreign birth or foreign speaking.

A major characteristic of the Y.W.C.A. is that of diversity; its programs vary from the simplest kind of service in terms of providing housing and food to the most carefully developed group work along accepted modern lines. The central emphasis of the Association in all its program is on the development of the religious life of the individual and the building of a society in which Christian ideals of living may be realized as fully as possible. Through a wide variety of cooperative relationships, locally, nationally and internationally, with social agencies, with churches and religious organizations, with schools and educational agencies and with women's organizations, the Y.W.C.A. brings to these groups its major emphases of Christian purpose and the interests of women.

There are in the United States at the present time 417 community Y.W.C.A.'s, 580 Associations of students in colleges and universities, 67 branches for Negro women and girls, 74 groups of American Indians, 13 International Institutes and 409 Registered Y.W.C.A.'s in rural centers. The present membership of the Association is about 500,000. See Y.W.C.A., Student. M.S.S.

Youth Fellowship, Methodist and Reformed: See Young People's Societies, Christian.

Yule: (M.E. *yol,* fr. A.S. *gēol*) The traditional English (esp. northern dialects) and Scottish term (occurring in many forms) for the Christmas* season and the festivities associated with it.

E.T.R.

Y. W. C. A., Student: See student religious organizations.

Zaddick, Joseph Ibn: (1080-1147) Appointed judge of the Jewish community at Cordova, Spain, he was both a Talmudic scholar and a poet. His fame rests on his philosophical work the *Microcosm,* written in Arabic, known only in Hebrew translation of unknown authorship. Though he wrote a general compendium of mathematical and philosophical science for beginners, his central theme was to justify Judaism before his own people and especially before the Jewish-Arabic intelligentsia. The trend of thought in his work *Microcosm* (Heb. *Olam Katon*) is Neo-Platonic, combining Aristotelian physics with Platonic metaphysics, ethics and psychology. As his Aristotelianism is probably derived from secondary sources, many of the Stagirite's ideas are misunderstood, giving rise to an increased sort of turgid Aristotelianism. Starting his metaphysics with proofs of the world's creation, of God's unity and his attributes, he tones down the extremes of Neo-Platonism*, seeking a level in which Aristotelianism and Platonism meet by compromising. His *Microcosm* was the first summary view of science, philosophy and theology in Jewish literature. He makes man's knowledge of himself central in his philosophy. Uncritical towards the various schools of philosophic thought, particularly of Plato and Aristotle—typical of the Middle Ages—he developed a harmonistic attitude in the presence of conflicting authorities. He argues that in the literal and positive sense no attributes can be applied to God. All of God's attributes are figurative expressions. God's essence cannot be known at all. We arrive at divine attributes by transferring them from God's effects in nature to his own essence.

M. Doctor, *Die Philosophie des Joseph ibn Zaddik, nach ihren Quellen, insbesondere nach ihren Beziehungen zu den Lauteren Brüdern und zu Gabirol untersucht* (Münster, 1895); L. Weinsberg, *Der Mikrokosmos, ein angeblich im 12. Jahrhundert von dem Cordubenser Joseph ibn Zaddik verfasstes philosophisches System, nach seiner Echtheit untersucht* (Breslau, 1888); I. Husik, *A History of Mediaeval Jewish Philosophy* (1941).

H.H.

Zadokites: See s.v. Sadducees.

Zahn, Theodor von: (1838-1933) German Protestant theologian. Born, Moers, Rhineland; in 1868 privatdozent Goettingen, 1877 professor of N.T. Exegesis, Kiel, 1888 at Leipzig, and from 1892-1909 at Erlangen. One of the leaders of conservative N.T. scholarship in the 19th century, of a most comprehensive erudition, aided by a solid knowledge of the ancient languages and gifted with keen exegetical insight, but sometimes straining the documents beyond the legitimate limits. By means of original research Zahn succeeded in many cases in re-establishing the traditional views concerning the genuineness of the N.T. books, the historicity of the records and the reliability of the ancient Christian tradition. His studies in the history of the N.T. canon are inexhaustible mines of information, and they advanced the study of that subject immeasurably. In exegesis he followed his teacher J. Chr. K. von Hofman* to a certain extent, without adopting, however, all of the latter's theological views.

Principal works:

Forschungen zur Geschichte des Neutestamentlichen Kanons, 11 vols. (1881-1916); *Geschichte des Neutestamentlichen Kanons,* 2 vols. (1888-1892) Engl. tr.; *Einleitung in das Neue Testament,* 2 vols. (1897-1899, 3rd ed., 1905-1907, Engl. tr. in 3 vols., 1909, 2nd ed. 1917); Editor of: *Kommentar zum Neuen*

Testament (1903, ff.). He wrote the volumes on the Gospels, Acts, Romans, Galatians, Revelation; Editor (together with v. Gebhardt and Harnack) of: *Patrum apostolicorum opera,* 3 vols. (1875-78) ; ***Bread and Salt from the Word of God*** (in sixteen sermons, 1905) ; Autobiography in: *Die Religionswissenschaft der Gegenwart in Selbstdarstellungen,* vol. I (1925). O.A.P.

zakat: The Moslem tax for the benefit of the poor. The giving of alms is one of the five duties of Islam. Alms were at first voluntary charity, but eventually became a system of taxation, not only for the poor but for the building of mosques and other community projects. They are now usually left to the conscience of the individual. P.E.J.

Zandīks: See Mani and Manicheism.

Zarathushtra: See Persia, religions of; Zoroastrianism.

Zealots: (Hebrew, *Kanna'im*) Name of a party opposing the attempt to bring Judea under the dominion of Rome . . . especially from the time of Herod (37 B.C.-4 A.D.) until the fall of Jerusalem . . . (70 A.D.) . . . some authorities trace them to a religious sect of the Maccabean period. . . . They were particularly active at the taking of the census by Quirinus, governor of Syria, in 6 A. D. . . . they were most influential in Galilee. . . . It was only after its capture in 67 A.D. that they fled to Jerusalem and took a definite part in the defense of the city. They were fanatic patriots who would brook no compromise with Rome, and zealots for the particularistic fulfillment of religious laws. N.G.

Zechariah: Companion book to Haggai*, Zechariah's four prophecies are confined to chs. 1-8 consisting of an introductory oracle on avoiding the mistakes of the ancestors, an eight-fold vision on impending international events, plans for coronation of Zerubbabel, and a long exhortation sermon on ethical living. Chapters 9-14 consist of later supplements, mostly eschatological* or nationalist in nature. Zechariah carried on Haggai's work, after the latter presumably died or returned to Babylon, delivering prophecies between 520 and 516 B.C. when the temple was completed by Zerubbabel. He used the obscure vision to conceal his seditions from the Persian government. Zechariah glowed with optimism, anticipating world revolution in which the Hebrew nation would be restored to power and all peoples would embrace the Jewish religion. Zechariah was a priest, but with some of the ethical emphasis of the pre-exilic prophets. See *The Prophets and their Times* by J. M. P. Smith and W. A. Irwin (1941), pp. 248-57, 285-89. R.E.W.

Zen: See Buddhist Terminology.

Zend-Avesta: See Avesta.

Zeno of Citium: (ca. 342-260 B.C.) Founder of the Stoic* school at Athens. A student of Crates, the Cynic. He had a pragmatic interest in science for the sake of life. Believing in suicide (like many Stoics), he took his own life. His writings are lost. J.E.N.

Zeno of Elea: (b. 490-85 B.C.) The Eleatic* and the father of dialectic* (mental experimentation), conceived of reality (mathematically) as constituted of discrete, non-extended points obtainable from repeated division of extension. This permitted the conception of an infinite* number of non-extended points within a finite distance and provided the assumption for his tantalizing paradoxes. See Parmenides. P.R.H.

Zeno of Verona: Patron saint* of Verona. Historicity of the tradition that he was bishop there, possibly in 4th century, and authority of the Tractates, is fairly well established. K.H.C.

Zephaniah: First of the seventh century prophets, successfully breaking the seventy year silence during which all aspiring prophets were martyred, he revived the teachings of Amos, Hosea, Isaiah, and Micah**. He denounced the national degeneracy fostered by Manasseh and Amon**, opposed the renaissance of heathenism, and inspired the Deuteronomic* reform, possibly assisting in writing that book. Influenced most by Micah, Zephaniah was a proletarian among the royal family. He envisioned all persons of class and wealth eliminated from Judah, with the remnant of the godly poor as the nucleus of the new Jerusalem. Chapter 2, together with the eschatological and "day of the Lord" passages in chs. 1 and 3, are probably secondary interpolations. Zephaniah usually is appraised on the basis of these spectacular supplements rather than his real writings. His two notable addresses (chs. 1 and 3) probably were delivered in Jerusalem 332-330 B.C., and martyrdom may have followed. See *The Prophets and their Times* by J. M. P. Smith and W. A. Irwin (1941), pp. 131-39. R.E.W.

Zervan Akarana: "Eternal (or uncreated) time," mentioned in the Vendidad*; Zervan (time) in a later Zoroastrian* doctrine (first mentioned by Eudemos of Rhodes, a pupil of Aristotle) was either the primaeval deity, or fate, or one of two original gods. See Zurvan. R.H.P.

Zervanism: (Zervān, "Time," Gr. *kronos,* cf. *chronos*) As Kronos is the father of Zeus, so in an old Zoroastrian myth Zervan is the father of Ahuramazdah*—but also of Ahuramazdah's twin, the evil Ahriman* (cf. Zoroaster's *Gāthā, Yasna* 30, 3-6). Until recently this belief was considered a late aberration from pure Zoroastrianism. The researches of Benveniste and especially those of Nyberg have shown that: 1) it is older than the introduction of the reformed Iranian calendar early in the time of Xerxes; 2) it is in the primitive and somber form known in Western Asia especially from information traceable to Theodore of Mopsuestia*, very probably the Magian form of ancient Median religion before the time when the Magi* adopted Zoroastrianism; 3) before the rise of the Magi in the West it was known east of the Caspian in some form to Zoroaster himself (note the Gathic verses referred to above); 4) opposed to the spirit of Zoroastrianism both in its oldest form and in later developments and frequently condemned by various types of Zoroastrian orthodoxy, it nevertheless left its mark on Zoroastrianism from earliest times onward, the greatest bulk of it which entered Zoroastrianism coming with the conversion of the Magi before the time of Xerxes and Darius; 5) a rather crude and primitive form of it appears as an accepted form of Zoroastrianism to the Armenian Christian Eznik and probably to Theodore of Mopsuestia as late as the fifth century A.D., a similar form being known in a similar way to Mani in the third century (cf. Manicheism); 6) in formulating a reformed Zoroastrian orthodoxy for the Sasanian state-church Kartīr (c. 250-290 A.D.) clearly omits and probably opposes the crude forms of Zervanism, as do later Zoroastrian theologians after him, though some of these give it surprisingly broad scope in their system. In spite of Mani's* use of the myth and in general of a strongly Zervanic type of Zoroastrianism in the formulation of his religion for Persians* the Manicheans, too, found themselves obliged to combat crude Zervanism far to the eastward, as their famous Confessional or Khuāstuānift, even in its Turkish form, shows. For further information one may see in English Emile Benveniste: *The Persian Religion* (Paris, 1929), pp. 76 ff., and later, more elaborate, and better, H. S. Nyberg: *Die Religionen des Alten Iran* (Leipzig, 1938), 380 ff. and *passim*. M. Sp.

Zeus: See Aryan religion; Greek religion. Cf. Jupiter.

Ziegenbalg, Bartholomaus: (1683-1719) One of the two first Protestant missionaries to India—Heinrich Plütschau was the other. Although themselves German, they were sent as "royal Danish missionaries" at the direction of king Frederick IV of Denmark, in 1706. He did important literary work in the Tamil language, including a translation of the entire N.T. and part of the O.T. C.S.B.

Ziegler, Theobald: (1846-1918) Professor of philosophy in Strasburg. He wrote a great many works on education. He demanded a reconstruction of society. The ethical free from all the supernatural was the product of societal evolution. It was society that evaluates the ethical acts, not the individual. He thought it highly questionable if the Christian world view was able to survive in view of the modern world view.

In Sachen des Straussschen Buches: *Der alte und der neue Glaube* (Schaffhausen, 1874); *Geschichte der Ethik* (Strasburg, 1886), 2 vols.; *Grundlinien eines Systems der Ethik* (Strasburg, 1890); *Religion und Religionen* (Strasburg, 1893); *Individualismus und Sozialismus* (Dresden, 1899); *Die geistigen und sozialen Strömungen des neunzehnten Jahrhunderts* (Berlin, 1900), 2nd ed. H.H.

Zimmerman Lectureship: In 1929 Dr. and Mrs. Jeremiah Zimmerman of Syracuse presented the Lutheran Theological Seminary at Gettysburg the sum of $5,000 to endow a lectureship on effective preaching. A series of five lectures during Gettysburg Seminary Week is held each year on this foundation. Lecturers have included preachers of national reputation.

(Data from the office of the President of the Gettysburg Lutheran Theological Seminary.)

V.F.

Zinzendorf, Nicolaus Ludwig, Count of Zinzendorf und Pottendorf: (1700-1760) German pietist, religious reformer, founder of Moravianism. He was born in Dresden, of parents affiliated with the Pietist* movement. Spener* the founder of Pietism was his godfather. Of remarkable religious precocity, Zinzendorf at ten was put under the severe discipline of Francke's* *Paedagogium* at Halle and at sixteen was sent to the University of Wittenberg, where the theological climate was anti-Pietist and orthodox. The two influences by action and mutual reaction stamped Zinzendorf permanently. His theological position was closer to that of Luther than was Spener's, his emphasis being on simple, heartfelt trust in God through Christ rather than on conscious conversion or ardent endeavor after personal holiness. He continued however, the initial impulse of Pietism in so far as it was a protest against high and dry orthodoxy and a seeking for heart religion. It was through Moravian missionaries, disciples of Zinzendorf, that John Wesley* was led both to the discovery of the doctrine of justification by faith alone and to the experience of having "his heart strangely warmed". He and the Count broke sharply however and decisively on the issue of sanctification.

Zinzendorf's activity as a reformer began modestly. His idea at first was to create a Christian band or association the members of which by preaching, writing, traveling, and works of charity would seek to awaken living religion within the Lutheran Church. It was only with the arrival and organization as a social and religious community of Bohemian refugees, to whom the Count had given asylum at Herrnhut on his Berthelsdorf estate, that the opportunity arose of founding and directing a movement on international scale. In Germany it remained for long within the Lutheran Church. For foreign missionary purposes Zinzendorf permitted the independent perpetuation of the ancient Moravian ministry and in this way the Moravian Church (or Brethren) as a distinct Christian Church came into being. The importance of Moravianism in the modern missionary movement can hardly be exaggerated.

See Bohemian Brethren; evangelicalism and evangelical revival; hymns; Moravian Church; pietism.

Sixteen Discourses (Eng. tr. 1740); *Hymns* (Eng. tr. 1749); *Lives* by A. G. Spangenberg (1772-5; Eng. tr. 1838); F. Bovet (1860; Eng. tr. 1896); W. Walker in *Greatest Men of the Christian Church* (1908). Cf. John Wesley, *Journal*; J. T. Hamilton, *A History of the Moravian Church* (1900); and L. Hennig, *Kirche und Offenbarung bei Zinzendorf* (Zurich, 1939). C.W.L.

Zionism: The movement for the return of the Jews to the Promised Land, i.e., Palestine. Jewish tradition regarded the dispersion of the Jews as a temporary incident. Israel was punished for its sins, and the Jews were driven into exile. But Jews believed that there would come a time when God would forgive them and bring them back to the Promised Land. The Return was associated with the prophetic doctrine of the Messiah* and the Messianic days. The Messiah would "gather the children of Israel around him and march to Jerusalem; and then after overcoming the hostile powers establish the Temple and set up his own dominion." (*Jewish Encyclopedia*, Messiah, Vol. VIII, page 511b).

Modern Zionism aims to utilize political conditions and methods to establish a publicly and legally assured home in Palestine for all Jews in need of a homeland, or who wish to link their destiny with that of their own people in a free land in which they would settle as a matter of right and not on sufferance. The Zionist movement was initiated and its ideology formulated in a book called *A Jewish State,* written in 1896 by Theodor Herzl, a Viennese journalist and playwright. The term Zionism was used to distinguish the followers of Herzl from the Chovevei Zionists (Lovers of Zion) who, since 1880, had carried on an agitation for the founding of Jewish agricultural colonies in Palestine with a view to the ultimate reestablishment of a free Jewish community. The ideas of the Chovevei Zionists were based on the doctrine of *Geulath Haaretz,* the Redemption of the Land, as prescribed in Talmudic teachings. Heinrich Graetz, the author of *The History of the Jews,* wrote an essay in 1863 in which he endeavored to show that the Jewish nation was its own Messiah and should bring about its own redemption and rejuvenescence without waiting for the coming of the Redeemer. The growth of the sentiment to return to Palestine was due to the recrudescence of nationalistic sentiment throughout the world, which was accompanied by a parallel development of anti-Semitism. Rabbi Kalisher held that the salvation promised by the prophets could come only gradually and through self-help on the part of Jews. The thought of self-liberation was contained, in its most vivid form, in a brochure written in 1881 by Leo Pinsker, a Russian Jew. The Chovevei Zionists were inspired by these writings, organized groups in many Russian cities, and carried on a program of colonization and settlement in Palestine over a period of two decades.

Theodor Herzl formulated the thought behind these groping steps for a return to Palestine in his booklet, which he followed up with the preliminary steps for the organization of a public movement to incorporate his ideas. This was the Zionist Congress, the first session of which was held in 1897. The means suggested were to be "The Society of Jews" and "The Jewish Company", the first to serve as the legal representative of the movement, the second as the economic instrument for the building of the Homeland. The Society was to approach the powers with a demand for sovereignty over some part of the world surface, large enough to serve the needs of the Jewish people. Palestine was then only vaguely indicated. There was to be a complete break with the principle of gradual infiltration of the Jews, as practiced by the Chovevei Zionists. The Jewish Company, which subsequently became the Jewish Colonial Trust, was to be the executive instrument for migration and settlement.

Herzl's ideas were opposed by the Hebrew philosopher Asher Ginsberg, known as Achad Ha'Am, who placed the emphasis on the spiritual aspects of Jewish life and the need for a spiritual regeneration. He believed in the establishment of a national spiritual or cultural center to act as a centrifugal force against the disintegrating tendencies within Jewish life. A renaissance of the spirit must come gradually through a process of education and development. Only when the spirit of the people had acquired a center, and had become centralized, would it become possible to establish the material counterpart of a rejuvenated Jewish people.

The Herzlian Zionists rejected the emphasis placed upon the spiritual Return by the followers of Achad Ha'Am. Nevertheless, in the development of the Zionist movement considerable attention was given to culture and spirit advocated by the followers of Achad Ha'Am. Great impetus was given to the revival of the Hebrew language and literature. There developed a devotion to the traditional ideals of the Jewish people from a national view-point. The practical work begun in Palestine inevitably adopted forms which had their origin in Jewish tradition. Although greatly influenced by the teachings of Achad Ha'Am, the Zionist movement continues in the spirit of Herzl. It was in accordance with the foundations laid by Herzl that Dr. Chaim Weizmann pursued the lead in the direction of engaging the interest of England. The Balfour Declaration was issued by the English Government in 1917; it incorporated the purposes of the Basle Program formulated by Herzl. Subsequently, the Balfour Declaration was made part of the Palestine Mandate issued by the League of Nations to the English Government.

The term used in the Basle Program in 1897 was "a publicly assured and legally secured home for the Jewish people in Palestine." The Palestine Mandate uses the formula of a Jewish Home. In 1942, the formula of a Jewish Home was merged in the idea of Palestine as a Jewish Commonwealth. Under the pressure of anti-Semitism* disseminated throughout the world by the Hitler Nazis, the Jewish settlement in Palestine grew in a most remarkable way. In 1917 the Jewish population was considered to be approximately 65,000. In 1941 it was estimated that the Jews had increased to over 500,000. They had settled in many agricultural colonies and developed many industries. They had conquered by peaceful methods many of the historical places in Palestine formerly occupied by Jews. They had acquired about a million dunams of land owned and settled by Jews. They had built the all-Jewish city of Tel-Aviv with a population of over 125,000. The ancient city of Jerusalem, formerly contained within the historic walls, spread out and a new Holy City was built and occupied by thousands of Jews. The Hebrew University, which opened its doors to Jews and Arabs alike, was founded on Mount Scopus, overlooking the city of Jerusalem, and a network of schools and high schools, carried on in the Hebraic spirit, was established. The peaceful efforts of the Jews to establish themselves in the Holy Land were interrupted from time to time by clashes instigated by the Arabs of Palestine, who were constantly being appeased by the Mandatory Power. During the second World War, recognizing that the totalitarian states were the enemies of the Jewish people, the Jews of Palestine in large numbers offered their military service to the English, but the Arabs were found to be largely envenomed by the Nazi spirit and refused to align themselves with the English cause. The Jews of Palestine had developed industrial and commercial resources which were placed in the service of the English cause, and they contributed substantial reinforcement of the Allied armies in the Near East. During the second World War, the Jews were preparing to register their demand for the recognition of Palestine as a Jewish Commonwealth or State. See Israel, religion and theology.

Achad Haam, *Selected Essays* (1912); Theodor Herzl, *A Jewish State* (1896); Theodor Herzl, *Altneuland* (1902); *Pinsker's Auto-Emancipation* (1882). L.L.

Zoar, separatist society of: See communistic settlements, religious.

Zöckler, Otto: (1833-1906) He taught in Giessen and Greifswald. Conversant with the facts of the natural sciences, he wrote informative apologetic-historical studies with a theosophical woof. He was influential more through polyhistory than through the power of creative method.

Theologia naturalis. Entwurf einer systematischen Naturtheologie vom offenbarungsgläubigen Standpunkte aus (Frankfurt a. M. und Erlangen, 1860); *Geschichte der Beziehungen zwischen Theologie und Naturwissenschaft, mit besonderer Rücksicht auf die Schöpfungsgeschichte*, 2 vols. (Gütersloh, 1877-79); *Gottes Zeugen im Reich der Natur. Biographien und Bekenntnisse grosser Naturforscher aus alter und neuer Zeit* (Gütersloh, 1881); *Handbuch der theologischen Wissenschaften in enzyklopädischer Darstellung, mit besonderer Rücksicht auf die Entwicklungsgeschichte der einzelnen Disziplinen*, 3 vols. (Nördlingen, 1883-84), 4 vols., 3rd ed. (Nördlingen, 1889-90). H.H.

Zohar: (Splendor, Brightness—derived from Daniel 12.3) A Jewish mystical work of diverse origin which became the classic text of Kabbalah* and the Bible of medieval mysticism. The Zohar is in the form of a commentary on the Pentateuch*, written in Aramaic and in Hebrew, which purports to be the record of the revelations made to Rabbi Simeon ben Yochai (2nd C. A.D.) while hiding in a cave for thirteen years, and by him transmitted to his disciples. This pseudepigrapha* was compiled by Moses de Leon, of Granada, Spain (1250-1305) and made public in 1300.

The body of the Zohar is interspersed and supplemented with special tracts and dissertations which together form an unsystematic and frequently contradictory compendium of Jewish mystic lore on the nature of God, His attributes and dimensions, the mysteries of the Tetra-grammaton*, the evolution of the cosmos, the nature of the human soul, heaven and hell, angelology, magic and astrology, besides expositions on many ethical themes, on prayer and the recondite meanings of the commandments and ceremonies.

Next to the Bible, the Zohar came to be regarded in the centuries following its publication as the holiest book in Judaism and profoundly influenced the theology, liturgy, poetry and the messianic hopes of the people. The Zohar also influenced Christian thought in the 16th and 17th centuries, and a considerable number of eminent Christian scholars were attracted to it, translated portions of it, wrote commentaries upon it and used it for purposes of Christian apologetics. See transmigration. A.H.S.

Zoroaster: See Persia, religions of; Zoroastrianism.

Zoroastrianism: A religion developed in eastern Iran as a result of the work of Zoroaster (Zarathushtra) c. 1000 B.C. The prophet protested against a new teaching with extravagant emphasis upon sacrifice and the slaughter of cattle which he felt was undermining the ancient lore and endangering the material and social values of the agricultural, cattle-raising community. He condemned the priestly cults, repudiated his rivals' gods as demons and exalted the heaven god, Ahura Mazda*, the "Wise Lord" as the single divine power, embodying cosmic and social order, the celestial champion of the ideal. Two ways of life were in conflict, the good against the evil, and all beings, earthly and spiritual were involved in the struggle. Zoroaster challenged men to choose the good or the evil side in the battle. Allegiance was manifested by good thoughts, good words, good deeds or their opposites. To those who chose to fight on the side of Ahura Mazda and the good there was promised a share in the glorious future when the final victory over evil shall be won.

After Zoroaster's death the religion spread westward to make missionary conquest of all the Aryan states of Iran. The high monotheism and severe moral idealism which the prophet made central in his teaching were diluted by the inclusion of elements from the religions of the western districts. Ahura Mazda was again surrounded by a court of old Aryan* gods whom Zoroaster had denied. The priests of Media, the Magi*, adopted the religion and introduced their ceremonies, magic rites of purification, astrology and the practice of exposure of the dead. The Persian rulers gave the religion the prestige of their power. In later centuries the Magian priests spread its influence to Mesopotamia, Egypt and Asia Minor.

The central emphasis of Zoroastrianism is on practical moral living. It has never sanctioned asceticism or world-flight. The good life is ethical life, loyally dedicated to the realization of the good society in a world finally freed from all evil. Two eternal spiritual beings are engaged in a cosmic battle to decide the issue between good and evil. The leader of the hosts of light is the high god, Ahura Mazda (Ormazd). Opposed to him is Angra Mainya (Ahriman), the spirit of darkness. All living things are involved on the good or bad side of this battle array, from celestial spirits and demons to men, animals, insects and planets. Closest to Ahura Mazda are the six Amesha Spentas*, the holy immortal ones. Originally they were the mental, material and moral values of Zoroaster's ideal community; then they became divine attributes. Later they were personified as angelic companions around his throne and became his executives presiding over various divisions of the earthly scene. Six arch-demons surround Angra Mainyu. The Good God is not omnipotent and needs the help of his creatures if the ideal world is to be won. Consequently there can be no free grace, no easy forgiveness of sin. Every evil deed is a betrayal of the cause and must be made up for by a surplus of good deeds. Ahura Mazda is altogether good and the creator only of good things. He is therefore not responsible for the evil of the world, all of which is created by Angra Mainyu. At death each man is judged by the weighing of his good and evil deeds and goes to heaven or hell according to the fateful decision of the scale. An intermediary place of both pain and pleasure is provided for those whose deeds balance. At the close of the world struggle, when Ahura Mazda has at last triumphed, these temporary regions of the dead will end. All souls will be purified by fire. A new heaven and a new earth will come into existence and the eternal kingdom of righteousness, happiness and peace will be established upon earth as Ahura Mazda intended it in the beginning before Angra Mainyu intruded upon God's good creation with his evil works. Angra Mainyu will then be banished to the realm of eternal darkness from which he came.

During five centuries following the conquest of Persia by Alexander in 330 B.C. Zoroastrianism languished. It was kept alive by the priests and revived under the Sassanian rulers of the third century A.D. The scriptures, destroyed by Alexander, were partially restored. Unfortunately the sections best remembered were the ritual and ceremonial books. The Moslem conquest in the 7th century almost crushed the religion. A mass migration to India* preserved it in a more hospitable land. Under scholarly leadership the Indian Parsis* are developing a critically renovated, historically oriented, modernized form of the old faith. See Chinese religions; cycles of time; Gabars; Mazdaism; Persia, religions of; sacred literatures; salvation; saoshyant; Zervanism.

M. N. Dhalla, *Zoroastrian Theology* (1914); M. N. Dhalla, *History of Zoroastrianism* (1938); L. H. Gray, *The Foundations of the Iranian Religion* (1929); A. V. W. Jackson, *Zoroaster, the Prophet of Ancient Iran* (1899); J. H. Moulton, *Early Zoroastrianism* (1913); J. C. Pavry, *The Zoroastrian Doctrine of a Future Life* (1926); H. S. Nyberg, "Die Religionen des Alten Iran," German trans. H. H. Schraeder *Mitteilungen der vorderasiatisch-aegyptischen Gesellschaft* (1938). A.E.H.

zuccheto: (It., *zucca*, head) A small round skull cap worn by the members of the hierarchy of the Church. The Pope's zucchetto is white, a cardinal's red, a bishop's purple. S.C.

Zürich, Concensus of: The document which created unity among the Swiss Protestants. Drafted by Calvin*, with the aid of Bullinger* of Zürich, it is Calvinistic in theology but Zwinglian* in language. It was accepted by the various Swiss centres, and by ending dogmatic disputes, united Swiss Protestants under one creed. G.R.C.

Zurvan: See Persia, religions of; Zervan Akarana.

Zwingli, H. (1484-1531) and Zwinglianism: Swiss reformer, was born or free peasant stock. He was educated in Swiss schools and universities, and had some experience of monastery life. His father did not intend him for the cloister, and sent him to the university of Vienna. Presently we find him teaching classics at Basel. Huldreich Zwingli was already in training and outlook a humanist. Here he contrasts sharply with Luther*, who never wholly escaped from the influence of scholasticism. Zwingli early appreciated the need of a purer theology and of closer study of the Scriptures. He was also prepared for bold criticism of Roman Catholic sacraments, vows, indulgences, etc.

When 22, he was ordained and became parish priest of Glarus. His ten years here laid the foundation of his subsequent work. He began the study of Greek, improved his Hebrew and read the Fathers. From this period dates his opposition to the use of the Swiss as mercenaries abroad, while his criticism of French alliances was so outspoken that he had to leave Glarus. For the next three years he was priest at Einsiedeln, and considered this as the period when he attained to evangelical truth. He studied the Greek Testament and began to base his preaching on "the Gospel". He found in the Bible a sufficient revelation of God, and was willing to abandon the philosophy and theology of the later Roman Church. In the early Fathers he saw useful but not infallible exponents of the Bible. It is important to notice his definite recognition of the theological importance of Scripture. At this point he furnished a lead to the other Reformed churches*. During this period, his opposition to the papacy was sharpening, but he still hoped for reform from within the church. It was chiefly with the grievances created by papal politics that he was now concerned, but since the Swiss were very necessary to the pope's plans, Zwingli was leniently treated.

In 1518 he was elected people's priest of the minster at Zürich. Early the next year he began a series of sermons on the N.T. which mark the beginning of the Reformation* in Zürich. He used scripture to attack the abuses of the Roman church—e.g., fasting and celibacy. When the pope asked Zürich to abandon him, he proposed a disputation and produced his famous sixty-seven theses. The Council upheld him, and its decision gave a legal sanction to the Reformation in Zürich.

The Reformation became of immediate political importance in Switzerland. The Forest cantons